S. Pub.109-12

2005-2006

OFFICIAL CONGRESSIONAL DIRECTORY
109TH CONGRESS

CONVENED JANUARY 4, 2005

JOINT COMMITTEE ON PRINTING
UNITED STATES CONGRESS

UNITED STATES GOVERNMENT PRINTING OFFICE
WASHINGTON, DC

Front Cover

On April 27, 1789, Congress agreed that the inauguration of President George Washington should take place on the outdoor balcony of Federal Hall in New York City, so that the largest possible audience could observe this most important national ceremony. On January 20, 2005, the tradition continued with the 109th Congress hosting the 55th Presidential Inauguration, on the west front of the United States Capitol, as seen on the front cover.

U.S. GOVERNMENT OFFICIAL EDITION NOTICE

Use of ISBN Prefix

This is the Official U.S. Government edition of this publication and is herein identified to certify its authenticity. Use of the 0-16 ISBN prefix is for U.S. Government Printing Office Official Editions only. The Superintendent of Documents of the U.S. Government Printing Office requests that any reprinted edition clearly be labeled as a copy of the authentic work with a new ISBN.

For sale by the Superintendent of Documents, U.S. Government Printing Office
Internet: bookstore.gpo.gov Phone: toll free (866) 512-1800; DC area (202) 512-1800
Fax: (202) 512-2250 Mail: Stop SSOP, Washington, DC 20402-0001

Paper Cover   ISBN-0-16-072467-8
Casebound   ISBN-0-16-072466-X

NOTES

Closing date for compilation of the Congressional Directory was July 11, 2005.

[Republicans in roman, Democrats in *italic*.]

The following changes have occurred in the membership of the 109th Congress since the election of November 5, 2004:

Name	Resigned or [Died]	Successor	Elected or [Appointed]	Sworn in
REPRESENTATIVE				
Robert T. Matsui, 5th CA [1]..	[Jan. 1, 2005]	*Doris O. Matsui*	Mar. 8, 2005	Mar. 10, 2005
Rob Portman, 2d OH [2]	Apr. 29, 2005	....	....	

[1] Representative *Robert T. Matsui* died after the *sine die* adjournment of the 108th Congress as a representative-elect of the 109th Congress.
[2] Representative Portman resigned to become U.S. Trade Representative.

The following changes occurred in the membership of the 108th Congress after the election of November 5, 2002:

Name	Resigned or [Died]	Successor	Elected or [Appointed]	Sworn in
REPRESENTATIVES				
Ed Case, 2d HI [1]	....	....	Jan. 4, 2003	Jan. 7, 2003
Larry Combest, 19th TX	May 31, 2003 ...	Randy Neugebauer	June 3, 2003	June 5, 2003
Ernie Fletcher, 6th KY	Dec. 8, 2003	*Ben Chandler*	Feb. 17, 2004 ...	Feb. 24, 2004
Ralph M. Hall, 4th TX [2]	....	....	....	
William J. Janklow, At-Large SD.	Jan. 20, 2004	*Stephanie Herseth*	June 1, 2004	June 3, 2004
Frank W. Ballance, Jr., 1st NC.	June 11, 2004 ...	*G.K. Butterfield*	July 20, 2004 ...	July 21, 2004
Rodney Alexander, 5th LA [3]	....	....	....	
Doug Bereuter, 1st NE	Aug. 31, 2004 ...	....	....	
Porter J. Goss, 14th FL [4]	Sept. 23, 2004 ...	....	....	
Robert T. Matsui, 5th CA ...	[Jan. 1, 2005]	....	....	

[1] This special election was held to fill this seat for the 108th Congress. A separate special election, also won by *Ed Case*, had been held on November 30, 2002, to fill the seat for the remainder of the 107th Congress after the death of Representative *Patsy Mink* on September 28, 2002; however, representative-elect *Case* was never sworn in during the 107th Congress.
[2] Changed party affiliation from Democrat to Republican on January 5, 2004.
[3] Changed party affiliation from Democrat to Republican on August 6, 2004.
[4] Representative Goss resigned to become the Director of the Central Intelligence Agency.

FOREWORD

The Congressional Directory is one of the oldest working handbooks within the United States government. While there were unofficial directories for Congress in one form or another beginning with the 1st Congress in 1789, the Congressional Directory published in 1847 for the 30th Congress is considered by scholars and historians to be the first official edition because it was the first to be ordered and paid for by Congress. With the addition of biographical sketches of legislators in 1867, the Congressional Directory attained its modern format.

The Congressional Directory is published by the United States Senate in partnership with the Government Printing Office, at the direction of the Joint Committee on Printing under the authority of Title 44, Section 721 of the U.S. Code.

JOINT COMMITTEE ON PRINTING

Trent Lott, Senator from Mississippi, *Chairman.*

Robert W. Ney, Representative from Ohio, *Vice Chairman.*

Senate	House
Thad Cochran, of Mississippi.	John T. Doolittle, of California.
Saxby Chambliss, of Georgia.	Thomas M. Reynolds, of New York.
Daniel K. Inouye, of Hawaii.	*Juanita Millender-McDonald,* of
Mark Dayton, of Minnesota.	California.
	Robert A. Brady, of Pennsylvania.

The 2005–2006 Congressional Directory was compiled by the Government Printing Office, under the direction of the Joint Committee on Printing by:

Project Manager.—Kim Dutch.

Deputy Project Manager.—Nicole Timmons.

Editors: Joanne Hayes; Amy Welch.

Typographers: Kathie Connor; Don Davis.

Special Assistance.—Peter Byrd, Senate Sergeant at Arms staff.

State District Maps.—Election Data Services, Inc.

Representatives' Zip Codes.—House Office of Mailing Services / U.S. Postal Service.

For sale by the Superintendent of Documents, U.S. Government Printing Office
Internet: bookstore.gpo.gov Phone: toll free (866) 512–1800; DC area (202) 512–1800
Fax: (202) 512–2250 Mail: Stop SSOP, Washington, DC 20402–0001

Paper Cover	ISBN–0–16–072467–8
Casebound	ISBN–0–16–072466–X

CONTENTS

Name Index on page 1089

Contents

ix

Contents

Contents

xiii

Contents

Contents

xvii

Contents

Contents

109th Congress*

THE VICE PRESIDENT

RICHARD B. CHENEY, Republican, of Wyoming, born on January 30, 1941, in Lincoln, NE; education: B.A., and M.A., degrees from the University of Wyoming; public service: served on the Cost of Living Council and Office of Economic Opportunity in the Nixon Administration; served as Assistant to the President and White House Chief of Staff for President Gerald R. Ford; elected to the U.S. House of Representatives in 1978, and reelected 5 times, through 1988; in the House he served as Chairman of the House Republican Conference and House Minority Whip; in 1989 he was nominated to be Secretary of Defense by President George H.W. Bush, and was confirmed by the U.S. Senate; he served from 1989 to 1993; on July 3, 1991, President Bush awarded Secretary Cheney the Presidential Medal of Freedom; after leaving the Department of Defense, he joined the Halliburton Company serving as Chairman of the Board and Chief Executive Officer; religion: Methodist; family: married to Lynne Cheney, 1964; two daughters; elected Vice President of the United States on November 7, 2000; took the oath of office on January 20, 2001; reelected November 2, 2004.

The Ceremonial Office of the Vice President is S–212 in the Capitol. The Vice President has offices in the Dirksen Senate Office Building, the Eisenhower Executive Office Building (EEOB) and the White House (West Wing).

Chief of Staff.—Lewis Libby, EEOB, Room 276, 456–9000.
Deputy Chief of Staff.—Dean McGrath, EEOB, Room 276, 456–9000.
Counsel to the Vice President.—David Addington, EEOB, Room 268, 456–9089.
Assistant to the Vice President and Deputy Chief of Staff for Operations.—Claire O'Donnell, EEOB, Room 269, 456–6770.
Principal Deputy Assistant to the Vice President for National Security Affairs.—Toria Nuland, EEOB, Room 298, 456–9501.
Assistant to the Vice President for Legislative Affairs.—Brenda Becker, EEOB, Room 285, 456–6774.
Assistant to the Vice President for Domestic Policy.—Kevin O'Donovan, EEOB, Room 288, 456–2728.
Executive Assistant to the Vice President.—Debra Heiden, West Wing, 456–7549.
Assistant to the Vice President and Chief of Staff to Mrs. Cheney.—Stephanie Lundberg, EEOB, Room 200, 456–7458.
Deputy Assistant to the Vice President and Director of Scheduling.—Elizabeth Kleppe, EEOB, Room 279, 456–6773.
Director of Correspondence.—Cecelia Boyer, EEOB, Room 265, 456–9002.

---

*Biographies are based on information furnished or authorized by the respective Senators and Representatives.

ALABAMA

(Population 2000, 4,447,100)

SENATORS

RICHARD C. SHELBY, Republican, of Tuscaloosa, AL; born in Birmingham, AL, May 6, 1934; education: attended the public schools; A.B., University of Alabama, 1957; LL.B., University of Alabama School of Law, 1963; professional: attorney; admitted to the Alabama bar in 1961 and commenced practice in Tuscaloosa; member, Alabama State Senate, 1970–78; law clerk, Supreme Court of Alabama, 1961–62; city prosecutor, Tuscaloosa, 1963–71; U.S. Commissioner, Northern District of Alabama, 1966–70; special assistant Attorney General, State of Alabama, 1968–70; chairman, legislative council of the Alabama Legislature, 1977–78; former president, Tuscaloosa County Mental Health Association; member of Alabama Code Revision Committee, 1971–75; member: Phi Alpha Delta legal fraternity, Tuscaloosa County; Alabama and American bar associations; First Presbyterian Church of Tuscaloosa; Exchange Club; American Judicature Society; Alabama Law Institute; married: the former Annette Nevin in 1960; children: Richard C., Jr. and Claude Nevin; committees: Appropriations; Banking, Housing, and Urban Affairs; Special Committee on Aging; elected to the 96th Congress on November 7, 1978; reelected to the three succeeding Congresses; elected to the U.S. Senate on November 4, 1986; reelected to each succeeding Senate term.

Office Listings

http://shelby.senate.gov

110 Hart Senate Office Building, Washington, DC 20510	(202) 224–5744
Administrative Assistant.—Louis Tucker.	FAX: 224–3416
Personal Secretary / Appointments.—Anne Caldwell.	
Press Secretary.—Virginia Davis.	
P.O. Box 2570, Tuscaloosa, AL 35403	(205) 759–5047
Federal Building, Room 321, 1800 5th Avenue North, Birmingham, AL 35203	(205) 731–1384
308 U.S. Court House, 113 St. Joseph Street, Mobile, AL 36602	(251) 694–4164
One Church Street, Room C–561, Montgomery, AL 36104	(334) 223–7303
Huntsville International Airport, 1000 Glenn Hearn Boulevard, Box 20127, Huntsville, AL 35824	(256) 772–0460

* * *

JEFF SESSIONS, Republican, of Mobile, AL; born in Hybart, AL, December 24, 1946; education: graduated Wilcox County High School, Camden, AL; B.A., Huntingdon College, Montgomery, AL, 1969; J.D., University of Alabama, Tuscaloosa, 1973; professional: U.S. Army Reserves, captain, 1973–86; attorney; admitted to the Alabama bar in 1973 and commenced practice for Guin, Bouldin and Porch in Russellville, 1973–75; Assistant U.S. Attorney, South District of Alabama, 1975–77; attorney for Stockman & Bedsole, 1977–81; U.S. Attorney, South District of Alabama, 1981–93; attorney for Stockman, Bedsole and Sessions, 1993–94; Attorney General, State of Alabama, 1994–96; member: Huntingdon College Board of Trustees; Samford University, Board of Overseers; delegate, General Conference, United Methodist Church; Montgomery Lions Club; Mobile United Methodist Inner City Mission; American Bar Association; Ashland Place United Methodist Church; married: the former Mary Blackshear, 1969; children: Ruth, Mary Abigail and Samuel; committees: Armed Services; Budget; Health, Education, Labor, and Pensions; Judiciary; Joint Economic Committee; elected to the U.S. Senate on November 5, 1996; reelected to each succeeding Senate term.

Office Listings

http://sessions.senate.gov

335 Russell Senate Office Building, Washington, DC 20510	(202) 224–4124
Chief of Staff.—Rick Dearborn.	FAX: 224–3149
Scheduler.—Stormie Janzen.	
Executive Assistant.—Peggi Hanrahan.	
Press Secretary.—Mike Brumas.	
341 Vance Federal Bldg., 1800 Fifth Avenue North, Birmingham, AL 35203	(205) 731–1500
Field Representative.—Shannon McClure.	
Colonial Bank Cntr., Suite 2300-A, 41 W. I–65 Service Rd. N., Mobile, AL 36608	(251) 414–3083
Field Representative.—Valerie Day.	
200 Clinton Avenue, NW, Suite 802, Huntsville, AL 35801	(256) 533–0979
Field Representative.—Lisa Ramsey.	
7550 Halcyon Summit Drive, Suite 150, Montgomery, AL 36117	(334) 244–7017
State Director.—Chuck Spurlock.	

REPRESENTATIVES

FIRST DISTRICT

JO BONNER, Republican, of Mobile, AL; born in Selma, AL, November 19, 1959; education: B.A., in Journalism, University of Alabama, 1982; organizations: Rotary Club; Mobile Area Chamber of Commerce; University of Alabama Alumni Association; Leadership Mobile; Junior League of Mobile; International Committee for the Mobile Tricentennial; professional: congressional aide to Representative Sonny Callahan, serving as Press Secretary, 1985–1989; and Chief of Staff, 1989–2002; married: Janee; children: Jennifer Lee and Josiah Robins, III; committees: Agriculture; Budget; Science; elected to the 108th Congress on November 5, 2002; reelected to each succeeding Congress.

Office Listings
http://bonner.house.gov

315 Cannon House Office Building, Washington, DC 20515	(202) 225–4931
Chief of Staff.—Alan Spencer.	FAX: 225–0562
Legislative Director.—Kelle Strickland.	
Scheduler.—Marcy Pack.	
1141 Montlimar Drive, Suite 3010, Mobile, AL 36609	(251) 690–2811
	(800) 288–8721
1302 North McKenzie Street, Foley, AL 36535	(251) 943–2073

Counties: BALDWIN, CLARKE (part), ESCAMBIA, MOBILE, MONROE, WASHINGTON. Population (2000), 635,300.

ZIP Codes: 36420, 36425–27, 36432, 36436, 36439, 36441, 36444–46, 36451, 36456–58, 36460–62, 36470–71, 36475, 36480–83, 36502–05, 36507, 36509, 36511–13, 36515, 36518, 36521–30, 36532–33, 36535–36, 36538–39, 36541–45, 36547–51, 36553, 36555–56, 36558–62, 36564, 36567–69, 36571–72, 36575–85, 36587, 36590, 36601–13, 36615–19, 36621–22, 36628, 36633, 36640, 36652, 36660, 36663, 36670–71, 36685, 36688–89, 36691, 36693, 36695, 36720–23, 36726, 36728, 36741, 36751, 36762, 36768–69, 36784

* * *

SECOND DISTRICT

TERRY EVERETT, Republican, of Enterprise, AL; born in Dothan, AL, February 15, 1937; education: attended Enterprise State Junior College; professional: journalist; newspaper publisher; Premium Home Builders; Everett Land Development Company; Union Springs Newspapers, Inc.; owner and operator, Hickory Ridge Farms; Alabama Press Association; chairman of the board, Union Springs Newspapers, Inc.; married: Barbara Pitts Everett; committees: Agriculture; Armed Services; Veterans' Affairs; Permanent Select Committee on Intelligence; elected on November 3, 1992 to the 103rd Congress; reelected to each succeeding Congress.

Office Listings
http://www.house.gov/everett

2312 Rayburn House Office Building, Washington, DC 20515	(202) 225–2901
Chief of Staff.—Wade Heck.	FAX: 225–8913
Legislative Director.—Forrest Allen.	
Press Secretary.—Mike Lewis.	
Scheduler.—Susan Swift.	
3500 Eastern Boulevard, No. 250, Montgomery, AL 36116	(334) 277–9113
256 Honeysuckle Road, Suite #15, Dothan, AL 36305	(334) 794–9680
101 North Main Street, Opp, AL 36467	(334) 493–9253

Counties: AUTAUGA, BARBOUR, BULLOCK, BUTLER, COFFEE, CONECUH, COVINGTON, CRENSHAW, DALE, ELMORE, GENEVA, HENRY, HOUSTON, LOWNDES, MONTGOMERY (part), PIKE. Population (2000), 635,300.

ZIP Codes: 35010, 36003, 36005–06, 36008–10, 36015–17, 36020, 36022, 36024–43, 36046–49, 36051–54, 36061–62, 36064–69, 36071–72, 36078–82, 36089, 36091–93, 36101–18, 36120–21, 36123–25, 36130, 36132, 36135, 36140–42, 36177, 36191, 36301–05, 36310–14, 36316–23, 36330–31, 36340, 36343–46, 36349–53, 36360–62, 36370–71, 36373–76, 36401, 36420, 36426, 36429, 36432, 36442, 36449, 36453–56, 36467, 36471, 36473–77, 36483, 36502, 36524, 36703, 36749, 36752, 36758, 36761, 36775, 36785

* * *

THIRD DISTRICT

MIKE ROGERS, Republican, of Saks, AL; born in Hammond, IN, July 16, 1958; education: B.A., Jacksonville State University, 1981; M.P.A., Jacksonville State University, 1984; J.D., Birmingham School of Law, 1991; professional: attorney; awards: Anniston Star Citizen of the

Year, 1998; public service: Calhoun County Commissioner, 1987–1991; Alabama House of Representatives, 1994–2002; family: married to Beth; children: Emily, Evan, and Elliot; committees: Agriculture; Armed Services; Homeland Security; subcommittees: Conservation, Credit, Rural Development and Research; Economic Security, Infrastructure Protection and Cybersecurity; Emergency Preparedness, Science and Technology; Livestock and Horticulture; chairman, Management, Integration and Oversight; Readiness; Specialty Crops and Foreign Agriculture Products; Strategic Forces; elected to the 108th Congress on November 5, 2002; reelected to each succeeding Congress.

Office Listings
http://www.house.gov/mike-rogers

514 Cannon House Office Building, Washington, DC 20515	(202) 225–3261
Chief of Staff.—Rob Jesmer.	FAX: 226–8485
Press Secretary.—Marshall Macomber.	
Office Manager.—Debby McBride.	
1129 Noble Street, 104 Federal Building, Anniston, AL 36201	(256) 236–5655
1819 Pepperell Parkway, #202, Opelika, AL 36801	(334) 745–6221
7550 Halcyon Summit Drive, Montgomery, AL 36117	(334) 277–4210

Counties: CALHOUN, CHAMBERS, CHEROKEE, CLAY, CLEBURNE, COOSA (part), LEE, MACON, MONTGOMERY (part), RANDOLPH, RUSSELL, TALLADEGA, TALLAPOOSA. Population (2000), 635,300.

ZIP Codes: 35010, 35014, 35032, 35044, 35069, 35078, 35080–82, 35088–89, 35096, 35105, 35136, 35160, 35183, 35674, 35973, 35982–83, 36002, 36013, 36023, 36026, 36031, 36036, 36039, 36043, 36046–47, 36052, 36057–58, 36064–65, 36069–70, 36075, 36088, 36101–21, 36123–25, 36201, 36215, 36252–63, 36265–76, 36278–80, 36766, 36801, 36825, 36830, 36850, 36853–55, 36858–65, 36867, 36871–79, 36959

* * *

FOURTH DISTRICT

ROBERT B. ADERHOLT, Republican, of Haleyville, AL; born in Haleyville, July 22, 1965; education: graduate, Birmingham Southern University; J.D., Cumberland School of Law, Samford University; professional: attorney; assistant legal advisor to Governor Fob James, 1995–96; Haleyville municipal judge, 1992–96; George Bush delegate, Republican National Convention, 1992; Republican nominee for the 17th District, Alabama House of Representatives, 1990; married: Caroline McDonald; children: Mary Elliott, Robert Hayes; committees: Appropriations; elected to the 105th Congress; reelected to each succeeding Congress.

Office Listings

1433 Longworth House Office Building, Washington, DC 20515	(202) 225–4876
Chief of Staff.—Hood Harris.	FAX: 225–5587
Legislative Director.—Mark Dawson.	
Communications Director.—Wade Newton.	
Scheduler/Office Manager.—Tiffany Noel.	
247 Carl Elliott Building, 1710 Alabama Avenue, Room 247, Jasper, AL 35501	(205) 221–2310
District Director.—Bill Harris.	
205 Fourth Avenue, NE., Suite 104, Cullman, AL 35055	(256) 734–6043
Director of Constituent Services.—Jennifer Butler.	
107 Federal Building, 600 Broad Street, Gadsden, AL 35901	(256) 546–0201
Field Representative.—Jason Harper.	
Morgan County Courthouse, P.O. Box 668, Decatur, AL 35602	(256) 350–4093

Counties: BLOUNT, CULLMAN, DEKALB, ETOWAH, FAYETTE, FRANKLIN, LAMAR, MARION, MARSHALL, MORGAN (part), PICKENS (part), ST. CLAIR (part), WALKER, WINSTON. Population (2000), 635,300.

ZIP Codes: 35006, 35013, 35016, 35019, 35031, 35033, 35038, 35049, 35053, 35055–58, 35062–63, 35070, 35077, 35079, 35083, 35087, 35097–98, 35121, 35126, 35130–31, 35133, 35146, 35148, 35172, 35175, 35179–80, 35205–07, 35212–13, 35215, 35441, 35447, 35461, 35466, 35481, 35501–04, 35540–46, 35548–55, 35559–60, 35563–65, 35570–82, 35584–87, 35592–94, 35601, 35603, 35619, 35621–22, 35640, 35651, 35653–54, 35670, 35672–73, 35747, 35754–55, 35760, 35765, 35769, 35771, 35775–76, 35901–07, 35950–54, 35956–57, 35959–64, 35966–68, 35971–76, 35978–81, 35983–84, 35986–90, 36064, 36117, 36271–72, 36275

* * *

FIFTH DISTRICT

ROBERT E. (BUD) CRAMER, JR., Democrat, of Huntsville, AL; born in Huntsville, August 22, 1947; education: graduated, Huntsville High School, 1965; B.A., University of Alabama, Tuscaloosa, 1969, ROTC; J.D., University of Alabama School of Law, Tuscaloosa, 1972;

professional: U.S. Army, 1972; captain, U.S. Army Reserves, 1976–78; attorney; instructor, University of Alabama School of Law, Tuscaloosa; director of clinical studies program, 1972–73; assistant district attorney, Madison County, AL, 1973–75; private law practice, Huntsville, AL, 1975–80; district attorney, Madison County, 1981–90; member: Alabama District Attorneys Association; National District Attorneys Association; founder, National Children's Advocacy Center, Huntsville; National Center for Missing and Exploited Children Advisory Council; American Bar Association, 1975–present; State of Alabama Bar Association, 1972–present; American Bar Association's National Legal Resource Center for Child Advocacy and Protection; awards and honors: received certificate of appreciation, presented by President Ronald Reagan, for outstanding dedication and commitment in promoting safety and well-being of children from the President's Child Safety Partnership, 1987; 1986 recipient of the Vincent De Francis Award, presented by the American Humane Association; selected as National Public Citizen of the Year, 1984; Alabama District Attorneys Investigators Association, "District Attorney of the Year, 1986''; Methodist; widower; one daughter: Hollan C. Gaines; committees: Appropriations; Permanent Select Committee on Intelligence; elected to the 102nd Congress, November 6, 1990; reelected to each succeeding Congress.

Office Listings
http://www.house.gov/cramer

2368 Rayburn House Office Building, Washington, DC 20515	(202) 225–4801
Administrative Assistant.—Carter Wells.	
Legislative Director.—Jenny Di James.	
Scheduler.—Alex Igou.	
401 Dallas Street, Huntsville, AL 35801	(256) 551–0190
District Coordinator.—Jim McCamy.	
Morgan County Courthouse, Box 668, Decatur, AL 35602	(256) 355–9400
1011 George Wallace Boulevard, Tuscumbia, AL 35674	(256) 381–3450

Counties: COLBERT, JACKSON, LAUDERDALE, LAWRENCE, LIMESTONE, MADISON, MORGAN (part). Population (2000), 635,300.

ZIP Codes: 35016, 35205–06, 35209–10, 35212, 35215, 35540, 35582, 35601–03, 35609–20, 35630–34, 35640, 35643, 35645–54, 35660–62, 35671–74, 35677, 35699, 35739–42, 35744–46, 35748–52, 35755–69, 35771–74, 35776, 35801–16, 35824, 35893–96, 35898–99, 35958, 35966, 35978–79, 36104

* * *

SIXTH DISTRICT

SPENCER BACHUS, Republican, of Vestavia Hills, AL; born in Birmingham, AL, December 28, 1947; education: B.A., Auburn University, 1969; J.D., University of Alabama, 1972; professional: law firm, Bachus, Dempsey, Carson, and Steed, senior partner; member: Hunter Street Baptist Church; Alabama State Representative and Senator; school board; Republican Party Chair; children: Warren, Stuart, Elliott, Candace, and Lisa; committees: Financial Services; Judiciary; Transportation and Infrastructure; elected to the 103rd Congress, November 3, 1992; reelected to each succeeding Congress.

Office Listings
http://www.house.gov/bachus

442 Cannon House Office Building, Washington, DC 20515	(202) 225–4921
Chief of Staff.—Larry Lavender.	
Press Secretary.—Jason Goggins.	
Legislative Director.—Jason Reese.	
1900 International Park Drive, Suite 107, Birmingham, AL 35243	(205) 969–2296
Northport Civic Center, P.O. Box 569, 3500 McFarland Boulevard, Northport, AL 35476	(205) 333–9894
703 Second Avenue, North, P.O. Box 502, Clanton, AL 35046	(205) 280–0704

Counties: BIBB, CHILTON, COOSA (part), JEFFERSON (part), SHELBY, ST. CLAIR (part), TUSCALOOSA (part). CITIES AND TOWNSHIPS: Adamsville, Alabaster, Argo, Brookside, Brookwood, Calera, Cardiff, Clanton, Columbiana, County Line, Fultondale, Gardendale, Graysville, Harpersville, Helena, Homewood, Hoover, Hueytown, Irondale, Jemison, Kimberly, Leeds, Maytown, Montevallo, Morris, Mountain Brook, Mulga, North Johns, Northport, Pelham, Pell City, Pleasant Grove, Ragland, Sumiton, Sylvan Springs, Thorsby, Trafford, Trussville, Vestavia Hills, Vincent, Warrior, West Jefferson, Wilsonville, Wilton, and portions of Bessemer, Birmingham, Tarrant, Tuscaloosa, and West Blocton. Population (2000), 635,300.

ZIP Codes: 35004–07, 35015, 35022–23, 35035, 35040, 35043, 35046, 35048, 35051–52, 35054, 35060, 35062–63, 35068, 35071, 35073–74, 35078–80, 35085, 35091, 35094, 35096, 35111–12, 35114–20, 35123–28, 35130–31, 35133, 35135, 35137, 35139, 35142–44, 35146–48, 35151, 35171–73, 35175–76, 35178, 35180–88, 35201–03, 35205–07, 35209–10, 35212–17, 35219, 35222–26, 35230, 35233, 35235–37, 35240, 35242–46, 35249, 35253–55, 35259–61, 35266,

35277–83, 35285, 35287–99, 35402–03, 35406–07, 35444, 35446, 35452, 35456–58, 35466, 35468, 35473, 35475–76, 35480, 35482, 35490, 35546, 35579, 35953, 35987, 36006, 36051, 36064, 36091, 36750, 36758, 36790, 36792–93

* * *

SEVENTH DISTRICT

ARTUR DAVIS, Democrat, of Birmingham, AL; born in Montgomery, AL, October 9, 1967; education: Harvard University, graduated *magna cum laude;* Harvard Law School, graduated *cum laude;* professional: attorney; public service: interned with U.S. Senator Howell Heflin (D–AL); interned with the Southern Poverty Law Center; clerked for Federal Judge Myron Thompson; served as an Assistant U.S. Attorney for four years; community serv-ice: volunteer work for the Birmingham Public School System; served as a legal and political commentator for Birmingham's Fox 6 News; religion: Baptist; committees: Budget; Finan-cial Services; elected to the 108th Congress on November 5, 2002; reelected to each succeeding Congress.

Office Listings

http://www.house.gov/arturdavis

208 Cannon House Office Building, Washington, DC 20515	(202) 225–2665
Chief of Staff.—Dana Gresham.	FAX: 226–9567
Deputy Chief of Staff / Communications Director.—Corey Ealons.	
Legislative Director.—Amy Chevalier Efantis.	
2 20th Street North, Suite 1130, Birmingham, AL 35203	(205) 254–1960
908 Alabama Avenue, Federal Building, Suite 112, Selma, AL 36701	(334) 877–4414
102 East Washington Street, Suite F, Demopolis, AL 36732	(334) 287–0860
205 North Washington Street, UWA Station 40, Suites 236–237, Livingston, AL 35470	(205) 652–5834
1118 Greensboro Avenue, Suite 336, Tuscaloosa, AL 35401	(205) 752–5380

Counties: CHOCTAW, CLARKE (part), DALLAS, GREENE, HALE, JEFFERSON (part), MARENGO, PERRY, PICKENS (part), SUMTER, TUSCALOOSA (part), WILCOX. Population (2000), 635,300.

ZIP Codes: 35005–06, 35020–23, 35034, 35036, 35041–42, 35061, 35064, 35068, 35071, 35073–74, 35079, 35111, 35117, 35126–27, 35173, 35175, 35184, 35188, 35203–15, 35217–18, 35221–22, 35224, 35228–29, 35233–35, 35238, 35243, 35401, 35404–06, 35440–44, 35446–49, 35452–53, 35456, 35459–60, 35462–64, 35466, 35469–71, 35473–78, 35480–81, 35485–87, 35490–91, 35546, 35601, 35603, 35640, 35754, 36030, 36032, 36040, 36064, 36105, 36435–36, 36451, 36482, 36524, 36540, 36545, 36558, 36701–03, 36720, 36722–23, 36726–28, 36732, 36736, 36738, 36740–42, 36744–45, 36748–54, 36756, 36758–59, 36761–69, 36773, 36775–76, 36782–86, 36790, 36792–93, 36901, 36904, 36906–08, 36910, 36912–13, 36915–16, 36919, 36921–22, 36925

ALASKA

(Population 2000, 626,932)

SENATORS

TED STEVENS, Republican, of Girdwood, AK; born in Indianapolis, IN, November 18, 1923; education: graduated, UCLA, 1947; Harvard Law School, 1950; military service: served as a first lieutenant (pilot), 1943–46; 14th Air Force in China, 1944–45; professional: practiced law in Washington, DC, and Fairbanks, AK, 1950–53; U.S. Attorney, Fairbanks, AK, 1953–56; legislative counsel, U.S. Department of the Interior, 1956–57; assistant to the Secretary of the Interior (Fred Seaton), 1958–59; appointed solicitor of the Department of the Interior by President Eisenhower, 1960; opened law office, Anchorage, AK, 1961; Alaska House of Representatives, 1964–68; assistant Republican leader, 1977–85; member: Rotary, American Legion, Veterans of Foreign Wars, Igloo No. 4 Pioneers of Alaska; American, Federal, California, Alaska, and District of Columbia bar associations; married: Catherine Chandler of Anchorage, AK; one daughter; five children with first wife, Ann Cherrington (deceased, 1978); committees: Appropriations; chairman, Commerce, Science, and Transportation; Homeland Security and Governmental Affairs; Rules and Administration; Joint Committee on the Library of Congress; Senate President Pro Tempore; appointed by the governor December 24, 1968 to fill a vacancy; elected November 3, 1970 for a term ending January 2, 1973; reelected to each succeeding Senate term.

Office Listings
http://stevens.senate.gov

522 Hart Senate Office Building, Washington, DC 20510	(202) 224–3004
Chief of Staff.—George Lowe.	
Legislative Director.—Karina Waller.	
Administrative Director.—John Hozey.	
Scheduling Director.—DeLynn Henry.	
222 West Seventh Avenue, No. 2, Anchorage, AK 99513	(907) 271–5915
Federal Building, Room 206, Box 4, 101 12th Avenue, Fairbanks, AK 99701	(907) 456–0261
Federal Building, Room 971, Box 20149, Juneau, AK 99802	(907) 586–7400
130 Trading Bay Road, Suite 350, Kenai, AK 99611	(907) 283–5808
540 Water Street, Suite 101, Ketchikan, AK 99901	(907) 225–6880

* * *

LISA MURKOWSKI, Republican, of Anchorage, AK; born in Ketchikan, AK, May 22, 1957; education: Willamette University, 1975–77; Georgetown University, 1978–80, B.A., Economics; Willamette College of Law, 1982–85, J.D.; professional: attorney; private law practice; Alaska and Anchorage Bar Associations: First Bank Board of Directors; organizations: Catholic Social Services; YWCA; Alaskans for Drug-Free Youth; Alaska Federation of Republican Women; Arctic Power; public service: Anchorage Equal Rights Commission; Anchorage District Court Attorney, 1987–89; Task Force on the Homeless, 1990–91; Alaska State Representative, 1998–2002; family: married to Verne Martell; children: Nicholas and Matthew; committees: Energy and Natural Resources; Environment and Public Works; Foreign Relations; Indian Affairs; appointed to the U.S. Senate on December 20, 2002; elected to the 109th Senate.

Office Listings
http://murkowski.senate.gov

709 Hart Senate Office Building, Washington, DC 20510	(202) 224–6665
Chief of Staff.—Tom Daffron.	FAX: 224–5301
Legislative Director.—Isaac Edwards.	
Scheduler.—Kristen Nothdurft.	
510 L Street, #550, Anchorage, AK 99501	(907) 271–3735
101 12th Avenue, Room 216, Fairbanks, AK 99701	(907) 456–0233
709 W. 9th, Room 971, Juneau, AK 99802	(907) 586–7400

REPRESENTATIVE

AT LARGE

DON YOUNG, Republican, of Fort Yukon, AK; born in Meridian, CA, June 9, 1933; education: A.A., Yuba Junior College; B.A., Chico State College, Chico, CA; Honorary Doctorate of Laws, University of Alaska, Fairbanks; State House of Representatives, 1966–70; U.S. Army, 41st Tank Battalion, 1955–57; elected member of the State Senate, 1970–73; served on the Fort Yukon City Council for six years, serving four years as mayor; educator for nine years; river boat captain; member: National Education Association, Elks, Lions, Jaycees; married: Lula Fredson of Fort Yukon; children: Joni and Dawn; committees: Homeland Security; Resources; chairman, Transportation and Infrastructure; elected to the 93rd Congress in a special election, March 6, 1973, to fill the vacancy created by the death of Congressman Nick Begich; reelected to each succeeding Congress.

Office Listings

http://www.house.gov/donyoung

2111 Rayburn House Office Building, Washington, DC 20515	(202) 225–5765
Administrative Assistant.—Michael Anderson.	FAX: 225–0425
Press Secretary.—Grant Thompson.	
Executive Assistant / Office Manager.—Sara Parsons.	
510 L Street, Suite 580, Anchorage, AK 99501	(907) 271–5978
101 12th Avenue, Box 10, Fairbanks, AK 99701	(907) 456–0210
971 Federal Building, Box 21247, Juneau, AK 99802	(907) 586–7400
540 Water Street, Ketchikan, AK 99901	(907) 225–6880
130 Trading Bay Road, Suite 350, Kenai, AK 99611	(907) 283–5808
851 East Westpoint Drive, #307, Wasilla, AK 99654	(907) 376–7665

Population (2000), 626,932.

ZIP Codes: 99501–24, 99540, 99546–59, 99561, 99563–69, 99571–81, 99583–91, 99599, 99602–15, 99619–22, 99624–41, 99643–45, 99647–72, 99674–95, 99697, 99701–12, 99714, 99716, 99720–27, 99729–30, 99732–34, 99736–86, 99788–89, 99791, 99801–03, 99811, 99820–21, 99824–27, 99829–30, 99832–33, 99835–36, 99840–41, 99850, 99901, 99903, 99918–19, 99921–23, 99925–29, 99950

ARIZONA

(Population 2000, 5,140,683)

SENATORS

JOHN McCAIN, Republican, of Phoenix, AZ; born in the Panama Canal Zone, August 29, 1936; education: graduated Episcopal High School, Alexandria, VA, 1954; graduated, U.S. Naval Academy, Annapolis, MD, 1958; National War College, Washington, DC, 1973; retired captain (pilot), U.S. Navy, 1958–81; military awards: Silver Star, Bronze Star, Legion of Merit, Purple Heart, and Distinguished Flying Cross; chair, International Republican Institute; married to the former Cindy Hensley; seven children: Doug, Andy, Sidney, Meghan, Jack, Jim, and Bridget; committees: Armed Services; Commerce, Science and Transportation; chairman, Indian Affairs; elected to the 98th Congress in November, 1982; reelected to the 99th Congress in November, 1984; elected to the U.S. Senate in November, 1986; reelected to each succeeding Senate term.

Office Listings

http://mccain.senate.gov

241 Russell Senate Office Building, Washington, DC 20510	(202) 224–2235
Administrative Assistant.—Mark Salter.	TDD: 224–7132
Legislative Director.—Christine Dodd.	
Communications Director.—Marshall Wittmann.	
Scheduler.—Ellen Cahill.	
5353 N. 16th Street, Suite 105, Phoenix, AZ 85016	(602) 952–2410
	TDD: 952–0170
4703 S. Lakeshore Drive, Suite 1, Tempe, AZ 85282	(480) 897–6289
407 West Congress Street, Suite 301, Tucson, AZ 85701	(602) 670–6334

* * *

JON KYL, Republican, of Phoenix, AZ; born in Oakland, NE, April 25, 1942; education: graduated Bloomfield High School, Bloomfield, IA, 1960; B.A., University of Arizona, Tucson, 1964 (Phi Beta Kappa, Phi Kappa Phi); LL.B., University of Arizona, 1966; professional: editor-in-chief, *Arizona Law Review*; attorney, admitted to the Arizona State bar, 1966; former partner in Phoenix law firm of Jennings, Strouss and Salmon, 1966–86; chairman, Phoenix Chamber of Commerce (1984–85); married: the former Caryll Louise Collins; children: Kristine and John; committees: Finance; Judiciary; chairman, Republican Policy Committee; elected to the 100th Congress on November 4, 1986; reelected to each succeeding Congress; elected to the U.S. Senate in November, 1994; reelected to each succeeding Senate term.

Office Listings

http://kyl.senate.gov

730 Hart Senate Office Building, Washington, DC 20515	(202) 224–4521
Chief of Staff.—Tim Glazewski.	FAX: 224–2207
Legislative Director.—Elizabeth Maier.	
Office Director.—Sherry Reichel.	
Scheduler.—Jill Cernock.	
Suite 120, 2200 East Camelback Road, Phoenix, AZ 85016	(602) 840–1891
Suite 220, 7315 North Oracle, Tucson, AZ 85704	(520) 575–8633

REPRESENTATIVES

FIRST DISTRICT

RICK RENZI, Republican, of Flagstaff, AZ; born in Sierra Vista, AZ, June 11, 1958; education: B.S., Northern Arizona University, 1980; J.D., Catholic University, 2002; professional: businessman; founded Renzi and Co., an insurance company designed to help non-profit organizations; while working on his law degree, he served as a legal extern for members of Arizona's congressional delegation; researched legal issues on religious freedoms, Federal land policies, and private property rights; married: Roberta; twelve children; committees: Financial Services; Resources; Permanent Select Committee on Intelligence; subcommittees: Capital Markets, Insurance, and Government-Sponsored Enterprises; Financial Institutions and Consumer Credit; Forests and Forest Health; Housing and Community Oportunity; Intelligence Policy; Oversight; Terrorism, Human Intelligence, Analysis and Counterintelligence; elected to the 108th Congress on November 5, 2002; reelected to each succeeding Congress.

Office Listings
http://www.house.gov/renzi

418 Cannon House Office Building, Washington, DC 20515	(202) 225–2315
Chief of Staff.—Karen Lynch.	FAX: 226–9739
Legislative Director.—Alix Crockett.	
Office Manager.—Teri Grier.	
Communications Director.—Joseph Brenckle.	
P.O. Box 11186, Casa Grande, AZ 85203	(520) 876–0929
Congressional Liaison.—Teresa Martinez.	
123 North San Francisco Street, Suite 105, Flagstaff, AZ 86001	(866) 537–2800
District Director.—Joanne Keene.	
107 North Cortez, Suite 208, Prescott, AZ 86301	(928) 708–9120
Congressional Liaison.—Don Packard.	
1420 First Avenue, Suite 100, Safford, AZ 85546	(928) 428–8194
Congressional Liaison.—Keith Alexander.	
10 West Tonto, EPA Building, P.O. Box 0, San Carlos, AZ 85550	(928) 475–3733
Congressional Liaison.—Keith Alexander.	
1151 East Duce of Clubs, Suite A, Show Low, AZ 95901	(928) 537–2800
Congressional Liaison.—Jack Latham.	
201 East Walnut, Apache Veteran's Center, Whiteriver, AZ 85941	(928) 521–2810
Congressional Liaison.—Walter Phelps.	
Highway 254 and Route 12, DNA Legal Services Building, P.O. Box 4673,	
Window Rock, AZ 86515	(928) 853–3750
Congressional Liaison.—Walter Phelps.	

Counties: APACHE, COCONINO, GILA, GRAHAM, GREENLEE, NAVAJO (part), PINAL (part), YAVAPAI. CITIES AND TOWNSHIPS: Flagstaff, Prescott, Payson, Show Low, and Casa Grande. Population (2000), 641,329.

ZIP Codes: 85218, 85221–23, 85228, 85230–32, 85235, 85237, 85241, 85245, 85247, 85272–73, 85291–92, 85324, 85332, 85362, 85501–02, 85530–36, 85539–48, 85550–54, 85618, 85623, 85631, 85653, 85901–02, 85911–12, 85920, 85922–42, 86001–04, 86011, 86015–18, 86020, 86022–25, 86028–29, 86031–33, 86035–36, 86038, 86040, 86044–47, 86052–54, 86301–05, 86312–14, 86320–27, 86329–43, 86351, 86503, 86505, 86514–15, 86520, 86535, 86538, 86540, 86544–45, 86547, 86549, 86556

* * *

SECOND DISTRICT

TRENT FRANKS, Republican, of Phoenix, AZ; born in Uravan, CO, June 19, 1957; education: attended Ottawa University; graduate of the Center for Constitutional Studies; professional: small business owner; oil field and drilling engineer; Executive Director, Arizona Family Research Institute; conservative writer, and former radio commentator, with Family Life Radio and NBC affiliate KTKP 1280 AM; public service: Arizona House of Representatives, 1985–87; appointed in 1987 to head the Arizona Governor's Office for Children; awards: True Blue award, Family Research Council; Spirit of Enterprise award, U.S. Chamber of Commerce; Taxpayer Hero, Council for Citizens Against Government Waste; Friend of Education award, Education Freedom Coalition; religion: Baptist; member, North Phoenix Baptist Church; married: Josephine; committees: Armed Services; Judiciary; subcommittees: vice-chair, Constitution; elected to the 108th Congress on November 5, 2002; reelected to each succeeding Congress.

Office Listings
http://www.house.gov/franks

1237 Longworth House Office Building, Washington, DC 20515	(202) 225–4576
Chief of Staff.—Tom Stallings.	FAX: 225–6328
Legislative Director.—Doyle Scott.	
Scheduler.—Lisa Teschler.	
Press Secretary.—Ross Groen.	
7121 W. Bell Road, Suite 200, Glendale, AZ 85308	(623) 776–7911

Counties: COCONINO (part), LAPAZ (part), MARICOPA (part), MOHAVE, NAVAJO (part), YAVAPAI (part). Population (2000), 641,329.

ZIP Codes: 85029, 85037, 85051, 85098, 85301–10, 85312, 85318, 85320, 85326, 85335, 85338, 85340, 85342, 85345, 85351, 85355, 85358, 85360–61, 85363, 85372–76, 85378–83, 85385, 85387, 85390, 86021, 86030, 86034, 86039, 86042–43, 86401–06, 86411–13, 86426–27, 86429–46

THIRD DISTRICT

JOHN B. SHADEGG, Republican, of Phoenix, AZ; born in Phoenix, October 22, 1949; education: graduated Camelback High School; B.A., University of Arizona, Tucson, 1972; J.D., University of Arizona, 1975; professional: Air National Guard, 1969–75; admitted to the Arizona bar, 1976; law offices of John Shadegg; special counsel, Arizona House Republican Caucus, 1991–92; special assistant attorney general, 1983–90; advisor, U.S. Sentencing Commission; founding director/executive committee member, Goldwater Institute for Public Policy; member/former president, Crime Victim Foundation; chairman, Arizona Juvenile Justice Advisory Council; advisory board, Salvation Army; vestry, Christ Church of the Ascension Episcopal, 1989–91; member, Law Society, ASU College of Law; chairman, Arizona Republican Caucus, 1985–87; chairman, Proposition 108—Two-Thirds Tax Limitation Initiative, 1992; member, Fiscal Accountability and Reform Efforts (FARE) Committee, 1991–92; counsel, Arizonans for Wildlife Conservation (no on Proposition 200), 1992; Victims Bill of Rights Task Force, 1989–90; member, Growing Smarter Committee, (yes on Proposition 303), 1998; married: Shirley; children: Courtney and Stephen; assistant whip; committees: Energy and Commerce; chairman, Republican Policy Committee; Republican Steering Committee; Republican Study Committee; subcommittees: Energy and Air Quality; Environment and Hazardous Materials; Health; elected to the 104th Congress; reelected to each succeeding Congress.

Office Listings

http://johnshadegg.house.gov

306 Cannon House Office Building, Washington, DC 20515 .... (202) 225–3361
   Chief of Staff.—Elise Finley.   FAX: 225–3462
   Legislative Director.—Eric Schlecht.
   Scheduler.—Kristin Nelthorpe.
   Press Secretary.—Michael Steel.
301 East Bethany Home Road, Suite C–178, Phoenix, AZ 85012 .... (602) 263–5300
   District Chief of Staff.—Sean Noble.

Counties: MARICOPA (part). CITIES AND TOWNSHIPS: Carefree, Cave Creek, Paradise Valley, and Phoenix (part). Population (2000), 641,329.

ZIP Codes: 85012–24, 85027–29, 85032, 85046, 85050–51, 85053–54, 85060, 85071, 85075, 85078–80, 85082, 85098–99, 85250–51, 85253–54, 85262, 85308, 85310, 85327, 85331, 85377

* * *

FOURTH DISTRICT

ED PASTOR, Democrat, of Phoenix, AZ; born in Claypool, AZ, June 28, 1943; education: attended public schools in Miami, AZ; graduate of Arizona State University; B.A., chemistry, 1966; J.D., Arizona University, 1974; professional: member, Governor Raul Castro's staff; taught chemistry, North High School; former deputy director of Guadalupe Organization, Inc.; elected supervisor, board of supervisors, Maricopa County; served board of directors for the National Association of Counties; vice chairman, Employment Steering Committee; president, Arizona County Supervisors Association; member, executive committee of the Arizona Association of Counties; resigned, May, 1991; board of directors, Neighborhood Housing Services of America; National Association of Latino Elected Officials; served as director at large, ASU Alumni Association; founding board member, ASU Los Diablos Alumni Association; served on board of directors of the National Council of La Raza; Arizona Joint Partnership Training Council; National Conference of Christians and Jews; Friendly House; Chicanos Por La Causa; Phoenix Economic Growth Corporation; Sun Angel Foundation; vice president, Valley of the Sun United Way; advisory member, Boys Club of Metropolitan Phoenix; married: Verma; two daughters: Yvonne and Laura; appointed a Chief Deputy Minority Whip; committees: Appropriations; subcommittees: Energy and Water Development, and Related Agencies; Transportation, Treasury, HUD, the Judiciary, District of Columbia, and Independent Agencies; elected by special election on September 24, 1991, to fill the vacancy caused by the resignation of Morris K. Udall; elected in November, 1992, to the 103rd Congress; reelected to each succeeding Congress.

Office Listings

http://www.house.gov/pastor

2465 Rayburn House Office Building, Washington, DC 20515 .... (202) 225–4065
   Executive Assistant.—Laura Campos.
411 N. Central Avenue, Suite 150, Phoenix, AZ 85004 .... (602) 256–0551
   District Director.—Ron Piceno.

Counties: MARICOPA (part). Population (2000), 641,329.

* * *

FIFTH DISTRICT

J.D. HAYWORTH, Republican, of Scottsdale, AZ; born in High Point, NC, July 12, 1958; education: graduated, High Point Central High School, 1976; B.A., speech communications and political science, *cum laude*, North Carolina State University, Raleigh, 1980; broadcaster; public relations consultant; insurance agent; member: Rotary Club of Phoenix (Paul Harris Fellow); Boy Scouts of America (Eagle Scout); married Mary Denise Yancey Hayworth, 1989; three children: Nicole, Hannah, and John Micah; committees: Resources; Ways and Means; elected to the 104th Congress; reelected to each succeeding Congress.

Office Listings
http://www.house.gov/hayworth

2434 Rayburn House Office Building, Washington, DC 20515 .... (202) 225–2190
  Administrative Assistant.—Joe Eule.   FAX: 225–3263
  Executive Assistant.—Tricia Evans.
  Legislative Assistants: Katharine Mottley, Erik Rasmussen, Ryan Serote, Todd
    Sommers.
  Press Secretary.—Larry VanHoose.
14300 North Northside Boulevard, Suite 101, Scottsdale, AZ 85260 .... (480) 926–4151

Counties: MARICOPA (part). CITIES AND TOWNSHIPS: Chandler, Fountain Hills, Mesa, Phoenix, Rio Verde, Scottsdale, Tempe. Ahwatukee, the Salt River Pima Indian Reservation, and the Fort McDowell Yavapai Apache Indian Reservation. Population (2000), 641,329.

* * *

SIXTH DISTRICT

JEFF FLAKE, Republican, of Mesa, AZ; born in Snowflake, AZ, December 31, 1962; education: Brigham Young University; B.A., International Relations; M.A., Political Science; religion: Mormon; served a mission in South Africa and Zimbabwe; professional: businessman: Shipley, Smoak & Henry (public affairs firm); Executive Director, Foundation for Democracy; Executive Director, Goldwater Institute; married: Cheryl; children: Ryan, Alexis, Austin, Tanner, and Dallin; committees: International Relations; Judiciary; Resources; subcommittees: Africa, Global Human Rights and International Operations; Crime, Terrorism, and Homeland Security; Forests and Forest Health; Immigration, Border Security, and Claims; Oversight and Investigations; elected to the 107th Congress on November 7, 2000; reelected to each succeeding Congress.

Office Listings
http://www.house.gov/flake

424 Cannon House Office Building, Washington, DC 20515 .... (202) 225–2635
  Chief of Staff.—Margaret Edmunds.   FAX: 226–4386
  Scheduler.—Noelle Lecheminant.
  Press Secretary.—Matthew Specht.
1640 South Stapley, Suite 215, Mesa, AZ 85204 .... (480) 833–0092

Counties: MARICOPA (part), PINAL (part). CITIES AND TOWNSHIPS: Apache Junction, Chandler, Gilbert, Mesa, and Queen Creek. Population (2000), 641,329.

* * *

SEVENTH DISTRICT

RAÚL M. GRIJALVA, Democrat, of Tulsa, AZ; born in Tucson, AZ, February 19, 1948; education: Sunnyside High School, Tucson, AZ; B.A., University of Arizona; professional: former Assistant Dean for Hispanic Student Affairs, University of Arizona; former Director of the El Pueblo Neighborhood Center; public service: Tucson Unified School District Governing Board, 1974–1986; Pima County Board of Supervisors, 1989–2002; family: married to Ramona; three daughters; committees: Education and the Workforce; Resources; Small Business; elected to the 108th Congress on November 5, 2002; reelected to each succeeding Congress.

Office Listings

http://www.house.gov/grijalva

1440 Longworth House Office Building, Washington, DC 20515	(202) 225–2435
Chief of Staff.—Glenn Miller.	FAX: 225–1541
Legislative Director.—Chris Kaumo.	
Press Liaison / Scheduler.—Amy Emerick.	
810 East 22nd Street, Suite 102, Tucson, AZ 85713	(520) 622–6788
1455 South 4th Avenue, Suite 4, Yuma, AZ 85364	(928) 343–7933

Counties: LA PAZ (part), MARICOPA (part), PIMA (part), PINAL (part), SANTA CRUZ (part), YUMA. Population (2000), 641,329.

ZIP Codes: 85033, 85035, 85037, 85043, 85221–22, 85226, 85228, 85232, 85239, 85242, 85248–49, 85273, 85321–23, 85325–26, 85328–29, 85333–34, 85336–37, 85339–41, 85343–44, 85346–50, 85352–54, 85356–57, 85359, 85364–67, 85369, 85371, 85601, 85621, 85628, 85631, 85633–34, 85639–40, 85648, 85653, 85662, 85701–03, 85705–06, 85711, 85713–14, 85716–17, 85719, 85721–26, 85733–36, 85743, 85745–46, 85754

* * *

EIGHTH DISTRICT

JIM KOLBE, Republican, of Tucson, AZ; born in Evanston, IL, June 28, 1942; education: graduated, U.S. Capitol Page School, Washington, DC, 1960; B.A., political science, Northwestern University, Evanston, IL, 1965; M.B.A., Stanford University, CA, 1967; study abroad program, International School of America, 1962–63; served in Vietnam, U.S. Navy, lieutenant, 1967–69; lieutenant commander, U.S. Naval Reserves (inactive); professional: vice president, Wood Canyon Corporation, Sonoita, AZ; consultant, real estate development and political affairs; Arizona State Senator, 1977–82; special assistant to Governor Ogilvie of Illinois, 1972–73; board of directors, Tucson Community Food Bank; committees: Appropriations; elected to the 99th Congress on November 6, 1984; reelected to each succeeding Congress.

Office Listings

http://www.house.gov/kolbe

237 Cannon House Office Building, Washington, DC 20515	(202) 225–2542
Chief of Staff.—Kevin Messner.	FAX: 225–0378
Office Manager/Scheduler.—Patrick Baugh.	
Suite 112, 1661 North Swan, Tucson, AZ 85712	(520) 881–3588
District Director.—Patricia Klein.	
Suite B–160, 77 Calle Portal, Sierra Vista, AZ 85635	(520) 459–3115

Counties: COCHISE, PIMA (part), PINAL (part), SANTA CRUZ (part). Population (2000), 641,329.

ZIP Codes: 85602–03, 85605–11, 85613–17, 85619–20, 85622, 85624–27, 85629–30, 85632, 85635–38, 85641, 85643–46, 85650, 85652–55, 85670, 85704–16, 85718–19, 85728, 85730–32, 85736–45, 85747–52

ARKANSAS

(Population 2000, 2,673,400)

SENATORS

BLANCHE L. LINCOLN, Democrat, of Helena, AR; born in Helena, September 30, 1960; education: graduate of Helena Central High School; daughter of the late Jordan Bennett Lambert, Jr., and Martha Kelly Lambert; B.S., in biology, at Randolph Macon Woman's College, Lynchburg, VA, 1982; also attended the University of Arkansas, Fayetteville; member, Chi Omega sorority; American Red Cross volunteer; married to Dr. Stephen R. Lincoln; mother of twin boys, Bennett and Reece; committees: Agriculture, Nutrition, and Forestry; Finance; Special Committee on Aging; subcommittees: ranking member, Forestry, Conservation and Rural Revitalization; elected to the U.S. House of Representatives for the 103rd and 104th Congresses; elected to the U.S. Senate on November 3, 1998; reelected to each succeeding Senate term.

Office Listings
http://lincoln.senate.gov

355 Dirksen Senate Office Building, Washington, DC 20510	(202) 224–4843
Chief of Staff.—Kelly Bingel.	FAX: 228–1371
Legislative Director.—Jim Stowers.	
Press Secretary.—Betty Dudik.	
Scheduler.—Stephen Hourahan.	
912 West Fourth Street, Little Rock, AR 72201	(501) 375–2993
6700 McKennon Boulevard, Suite 122, Fort Smith, AR 72903	(479) 782–9215
Federal Building, Suite 315, 615 South Main, Jonesboro, AR 72401	(870) 910–6896
Drew County Courthouse, 210 South Main Street, Monticello, AR 71655	(870) 367–6925
Miller County Courthouse, 400 Laurel Street, #101, Texarkana, AR 71854	(870) 774–3106

* * *

MARK PRYOR, Democrat, of Little Rock, AR; born in Fayetteville, AR, January 10, 1963; education: B.A., University of Arkansas, 1985; J.D., University of Arkansas, 1988; professional: attorney; Wright, Lindsey & Jennings (law firm); public service: elected, Arkansas House of Representatives, 1990; elected, Arkansas Attorney General, 1998; family: married to Jill; children: Adams and Porter; his father, David Pryor, was a former Governor and U.S. Senator from Arkansas; committees: Commerce, Science, and Transportation; Homeland Security and Governmental Affairs; Small Business and Entrepreneurship; Select Committee on Ethics; elected to the U.S. Senate on November 5, 2002.

Office Listings
http://pryor.senate.gov

257 Dirksen Senate Office Building, Washington, DC 20510	(202) 224–2353
Chief of Staff.—Bob Russell.	FAX: 228–0908
Legislative Director.—Walter Pryor.	
Communications Director.—Rodell Mollineau.	
Office Manager.—Kathryn Melcher.	
500 Clinton Avenue, Suite 401, Little Rock, AR 72201	(501) 324–6336

REPRESENTATIVES

FIRST DISTRICT

MARION BERRY, Democrat, of Gillett, AR; born in Stuttgart, AR, August 27, 1942; education: graduated, DeWitt High School; B.S., pharmacy, University of Arkansas, 1965; professional: Gillett, Arkansas city council, 1976–80; Arkansas Soil and Water Conservation Commission, 1964–86; White House Domestic Policy Council, 1993–96; special assistant to President William Clinton for Agricultural Trade and Food Assistance, 1993; member, Domestic Policy Council, The White House, 1993–96; member, Arkansas Soil and Water Conservation Commission, 1986–94, serving as chairman in 1992; Gillett City Councilman, 1976–80; married: the former Carolyn Lowe in 1962; children: Ann Coggin and Mitchell; co-chairman, Democratic Blue Dog Coalition's Health Care Task Force; co-chair, House Affordable Medicines Task Force; Congressional Methamphetamine Caucus; Congressional Missing and Exploited Children's Caucus; Congressional Rural Caucus; Congressional Silk Road Caucus;

co-chair, Congressional Soybean Caucus; Congressional Steel Caucus; House Renewable Energy and Energy Efficiency Caucus; New Democrat Coalition; Rural Health Care Coalition; Brain Injury Caucus; Rural Working Group; committees: Appropriations; subcommittees: Energy and Water Development and Related Agencies; Homeland Security; elected to the 105th Congress; reelected to each succeeding Congress.

Office Listings

http://www.house.gov/berry

2305 Rayburn House Office Building, Washington, DC 20515	(202) 225–4076
Chief of Staff.—Thad Huguley.	FAX: 225–5602
Press Secretary.—Andrew Nannis.	
Legislative Director.—Chad Causey.	
116 North First Street, Suite C–1, Cabot, AR 72023	(501) 843–3043
108 East Huntington Avenue, Jonesboro, AR 72401	(800) 866–2701
1 East 7th Street, Suite 200, Mountain Home, AR 72653	(870) 425–3511

Counties: ARKANSAS, BAXTER, CLAY, CLEBURNE, CRAIGHEAD, CRITTENDEN, CROSS, FULTON, GREENE, INDEPENDENCE, IZARD, JACKSON, LAWRENCE, LEE, LONOKE, MISSISSIPPI, MONROE, PHILLIPS, POINSETT, PRAIRIE, RANDOLPH, ST. FRANCIS, SEARCY, SHARP, STONE, WOODRUFF. Population (2000), 668,360.

ZIP Codes: 72003, 72005–07, 72014, 72017, 72020–21, 72023–24, 72026, 72029, 72031, 72036–38, 72040–44, 72046, 72048, 72051, 72055, 72059–60, 72064, 72067, 72069, 72072–76, 72083, 72086, 72101–02, 72108, 72112, 72121, 72123, 72130–31, 72134, 72137, 72139–40, 72142–43, 72153, 72160, 72165–66, 72169–70, 72175–76, 72179, 72189, 72301, 72303, 72310–13, 72315–16, 72319–22, 72324–33, 72335–36, 72338–42, 72346–48, 72350–55, 72358–60, 72364–70, 72372–74, 72376–77, 72383–84, 72386–87, 72389–92, 72394–96, 72401–04, 72410–17, 72419, 72421–22, 72424–45, 72447, 72449–51, 72453–62, 72464–67, 72469–76, 72478–79, 72482, 72505, 72503, 72512–13, 72515, 72517, 72519–34, 72536–40, 72542–46, 72550, 72553–56, 72560–62, 72564–69, 72571–73, 72575–79, 72581, 72583–85, 72587, 72610, 72613, 72617, 72623, 72626, 72629, 72631, 72633, 72635–36, 72639, 72642, 72645, 72650–51, 72653–54, 72658, 72663, 72669, 72675, 72679–80, 72685–86

* * *

SECOND DISTRICT

VIC SNYDER, Democrat, of Little Rock, AR; born in Medford, OR, September 27, 1947; education: graduated from Medford High School, 1965; corporal, U.S. Marine Corps, 1967–69, including one year in Vietnam with Headquarters Company, First Marine Division; B.A., chemistry, 1975, Willamette University, Salem, OR; M.D., 1979, University of Oregon Health Sciences Center, Portland; family practice residency, 1979–82, University of Arkansas for Medical Sciences; family practice physician in central Arkansas, 1982–present; medical missions to Cambodian refugee camps in Thailand, El Salvadoran refugee camps in Honduras, a West African mission hospital in Sierra Leone, and an Ethiopian refugee camp in Sudan; J.D., 1988, University of Arkansas at Little Rock School of Law; Arkansas State Senator, 1991–96; committees: Armed Services; Veterans' Affairs; elected to the 105th Congress; reelected to each succeeding Congress.

Office Listings

http://www.house.gov/snyder

1330 Longworth House Office Building, Washington, DC 20515	(202) 225–2506
Staff Director.—Ed Fry.	FAX: 225–5903
Press Secretary/District Scheduler.—Jennifer Oglesby.	
Legislative Director.—Mike Casey.	
3118 Federal Building, 700 West Capitol Avenue, Little Rock, AR 72201	(501) 324–5941
District Director.—Amanda Nixon White.	

Counties: CONWAY, FAULKNER, PERRY, PULASKI, SALINE, VAN BUREN, WHITE, YELL. Population (2000), 668,176.

ZIP Codes: 71772, 71909, 72001–02, 72010–13, 72015–18, 72020, 72022–23, 72025, 72027–28, 72030–35, 72039, 72045–47, 72052–53, 72057–61, 72063, 72065–68, 72070, 72076, 72078–82, 72085, 72087–89, 72099, 72102–04, 72106–08, 72110–11, 72113–22, 72124–27, 72131, 72135–37, 72139, 72141–43, 72145, 72149, 72153, 72156–57, 72164, 72167, 72173, 72178, 72180–81, 72183, 72190, 72199, 72201–07, 72209–12, 72214–17, 72219, 72221–23, 72225, 72227, 72231, 72260, 72295, 72419, 72568, 72629, 72645, 72679, 72823–24, 72827–29, 72833–34, 72838, 72841–42, 72853, 72857, 72860, 72943

* * *

THIRD DISTRICT

JOHN BOOZMAN, Republican, of Rogers, AR; born in Shreveport, LA, December 10, 1950; education: Northside High School, Fort Smith, AR; University of Arkansas, completing his pre-optometry requirements; graduated, Southern College of Optometry, 1977; professional:

optometrist; entered private practice as a co-founder of the Boozman-Hof Eye Clinic; community service: volunteer optometrist at the Arkansas School for the Blind, and at area clinics; public service: Rogers School Board, serving two terms; member: state and local cattlemen's associations; Benton County Fair Board; Fellowship of Christian Athletes; Arkansas Athletes Outreach Board; religion: Baptist; married: the former Cathy Marley; three daughters; committees: International Relations; Transportation and Infrastructure; Veterans' Affairs; subcommittees: Africa; Aviation; chair, Economic Opportunity; Highway Transit; Middle East; Oversight; Water Resources; elected to the 107th Congress, by special election, on November 20, 2001; reelected to each succeeding Congress.

Office Listings

http://www.house.gov/boozman

1519 Longworth House Office Building, Washington, DC 20515	(202) 225–4301
Deputy Chief of Staff.—Matthew Sagely.	FAX: 225–5713
Press Secretary.—Patrick Creamer.	
Scheduler.—Jennifer Brady.	
4943 Old Greenwood, Suite 1, Fort Smith, AR 72903	(479) 782–7787
303 N. Main, Suite 102, Harrison, AR 72601	(870) 741–6900
207 West Center Street, Fayetteville, AR 72701	(479) 442–5258
Deputy Chief of Staff.—Stacey McClure.	

Counties: BENTON, BOONE, CARROLL, CRAWFORD, FRANKLIN, JOHNSON, MADISON, MARION, NEWTON, POPE, SEBASTIAN, WASHINGTON. Population (2000), 668,479.

ZIP Codes: 71937, 71944–45, 71953, 71972–73, 72063, 72080, 72601–02, 72611, 72613, 72615–16, 72619, 72624, 72628, 72630–34, 72638–41, 72644–45, 72648, 72653, 72655, 72660–63, 72666, 72668, 72670, 72672, 72675, 72677, 72679, 72682–83, 72685–87, 72701–04, 72711–12, 72714–19, 72721–22, 72727–30, 72732–42, 72744–45, 72747, 72749, 72751–53, 72756–58, 72760–62, 72764–66, 72768–70, 72773–74, 72776, 72801–02, 72811–12, 72820–21, 72823, 72830, 72832, 72837–43, 72845–47, 72852, 72854, 72856–58, 72860, 72901–06, 72908, 72913–14, 72916–19, 72921, 72923, 72927–28, 72930, 72932–38, 72940–41, 72944–49, 72951–52, 72955–57, 72959

* * *

FOURTH DISTRICT

MIKE ROSS, Democrat, of Prescott, AR; born in Texarkana, AR, August 2, 1961; education: Hope High School; B.A., University of Arkansas at Little Rock, 1987; professional: small businessman; owner of Ross Pharmacy, Inc., in Prescott, AR; public service: Chief of Staff to Arkansas Lt. Governor Winston Bryant, 1985–89; three term State Senator, 1991–2000; organizations: Executive Director, Arkansas Youth Suicide Prevention Commission, 1985–89; First United Methodist Church in Prescott, AR; awards: National Association of Social Workers Public Citizen of the Year, 1999; Arkansas State Police Association Distinguished Service Award; Arkansas Kids Count Coalition Achievement Award; married: Holly; children: Alex and Sydney Beth; committees: Energy and Commerce; elected to the 107th Congress on November 7, 2000; reelected to each succeeding Congress.

Office Listings

http://www.house.gov/ross

314 Cannon House Office Building, Washington, DC 20515	(202) 225–3772
Chief of Staff.—Cori Smith.	FAX: 225–1314
Legislative Director.—Monique Frazier.	
Communications Director.—Adrienne Elrod.	
District Director.—Chris Masingill.	
221 West Main Street, Prescott, AR 71857	(870) 887–6787
2300 West 29th, Suite 1A, Pine Bluff, AR 71603	(870) 536–3376
300 Exchange Street, Suite A, Hot Springs, AR 71901	(501) 520–5892
Union County Courthouse, Suite 406, 101 North Washington Street, El Dorado, AR 71730	(870) 881–0681

Counties: ASHLEY, BRADLEY, CALHOUN, CHICOT, CLARK, CLEVELAND, COLUMBIA, DALLAS, DESHA, DREW, GARLAND, GRANT, HEMPSTEAD, HOT SPRING, HOWARD, JEFFERSON, LAFAYETTE, LINCOLN, LITTLE RIVER, LOGAN, MILLER, MONTGOMERY, NEVADA, OUACHITA, PIKE, POLK, SCOTT, SEVIER, UNION. Population (2000), 668,385.

ZIP Codes: 71601–03, 71611–13, 71630–31, 71635, 71638–40, 71642–44, 71646–47, 71651–63, 71665–67, 71670–71, 71674–78, 71701, 71711, 71720–22, 71724–26, 71728, 71730–31, 71740, 71742–45, 71747–54, 71758–59, 71762–66, 71768, 71770, 71772, 71801–02, 71820, 71822–23, 71825–28, 71831–42, 71844–47, 71851–55, 71857–62, 71864–66, 71901–03, 71909–10, 71913–14, 71920–23, 71929, 71932–33, 71935, 71937, 71940–45,

71949–50, 71952–53, 71956–62, 71964–65, 71968–73, 71998–99, 72004, 72015, 72046, 72055, 72057, 72065; 72072–73, 72079, 72084, 72087, 72104–05, 72128–29, 72132–33, 72150, 72152, 72160, 72167–68, 72175, 72182, 72379, 72826–27, 72833–35, 72838, 72841–42, 72851, 72855, 72863, 72865, 72924, 72926–28, 72933, 72943–44, 72949–51; 72958

CALIFORNIA

(Population 2000, 33,871,648)

SENATORS

DIANNE FEINSTEIN, Democrat, of San Francisco, CA; born in San Francisco, June 22, 1933; education: B.A., Stanford University, 1955; elected to San Francisco Board of Supervisors, 1970–78; president of Board of Supervisors: 1970–71, 1974–75, 1978; mayor of San Francisco, 1978–88; candidate for governor of California, 1990. Recipient: Distinguished ·Woman Award, *San Francisco Examiner;* Achievement Award, Business and Professional Women's Club, 1970; Golden Gate University, California, LL.D. (hon.), 1979; SCOPUS Award for Outstanding Public Service, American Friends of the Hebrew University of Jerusalem; University of Santa Clara, D.P.S. (hon.); University of Manila, D.P.A. (hon.), 1981; Antioch University, LL.D. (hon.), 1983; Los Angeles Anti-Defamation League of B'nai B'rith's Distinguished Service Award, 1984; French Legion d'Honneur from President Mitterand, 1984; Mills College, LL.D. (hon.), 1985; U.S. Army's Commander's Award for Public Service, 1986; Brotherhood/Sisterhood Award, National Conference of Christians and Jews, 1986; Paulist Fathers Award, 1987; Episcopal Church Award for Service, 1987; U.S. Navy Distinguished Civilian Award, 1987; Silver Spur Award for Outstanding Public Service, San Francisco Planning and Urban Renewal Association, 1987; All Pro Management Team Award for No. 1 Mayor, *City and State* Magazine, 1987; Community Service Award Honoree for Public Service, 1987; American Jewish Congress, 1987; President's Award, St. Ignatius High School, San Francisco, 1988; Coro Investment in Leadership Award, 1988; President's Medal, University of California at San Francisco, 1988; University of San Francisco, D.H.L. (hon.), 1988. Member: Coro Foundation, Fellowship, 1955–56; California Women's Board of Terms and Parole, 1960–66, executive committee; U.S. Conference of Mayors, 1983–88; Mayor's Commission on Crime, San Francisco; Bank of California, director, 1988–89; San Francisco Education Fund's Permanent Fund, 1988–89; Japan Society of Northern California, 1988–89; Inter-American Dialogue, 1988–present; Trilateral Commission, 1988; Biderberg Foreign Policy Conference, Baden, Germany, 1991; married: Dr. Bertram Feinstein (dec.); married on January 20, 1980, to Richard C. Blum; children: one child; three stepchildren; religion: Jewish; committees: Appropriations; Energy and Natural Resources; Judiciary; Rules and Administration; Select Committee on Intelligence; elected to the U.S. Senate, by special election, on November 3, 1992, to fill the vacancy caused by the resignation of Senator Pete Wilson; reelected to each succeeding Senate term.

Office Listings

http://feinstein.senate.gov

331 Hart Senate Office Building, Washington, DC 20510	(202) 224–3841
Chief of Staff.—Mark Kadesh.	
Legislative Director.—Peter Cleveland.	
Director of Communications.—Howard Gantman.	
750 B Street, Suite 1030, San Diego, CA 92101	(619) 231–9712
Federal Office Building, Suite 2446, 1130 O Street, Fresno, CA 93721	(559) 485–7430
One Post Street, Suite 2450, San Francisco, CA 94104	(415) 393–0707
11111 San Monica Boulevard, Suite 915, Los Angles, CA 90025	(310) 914–7300

* * *

BARBARA BOXER, Democrat, of Greenbrae, CA; born in Brooklyn, NY, November 11, 1940; education: B.A., economics, Brooklyn College, 1962; professional: stockbroker and economic researcher with securities firms on Wall Street, 1962–65; journalist and associate editor, *Pacific Sun* newspaper, 1972–74; congressional aide, Fifth Congressional District, California, 1974–76; elected Marin County Board of Supervisors, 1976–82; first woman president, Marin County Board of Supervisors; Edgar Wayburn award, Sierra Club, 1997; Policy Leadership award, Family Violence Prevention Fund, 2000; Circle of Courage award, Afghan Women Association International and the Women's Intercultural Network, 2003; Children's Champion award, California Head Start Association, 2003; married: Stewart Boxer, 1962; children: Doug and Nicole; elected November 2, 1982 to 98th Congress; reelected to the 99th–102nd Congresses; committees: Commerce, Science, and Transportation; Environment and Public Works; Foreign Relations; subcommittees: Aviation; Communications; Competition, Foreign Commerce, and Infrastructure; Surface Transportation and Merchant Marine; International Operations and Terrorism; Near Eastern and South Asian Affairs; Western Hemisphere, Peace Corps, and Narcotics Affairs; Superfund and Waste Management; Transportation and Infrastructure; elected to the U.S. Senate on November 3, 1992; reelected to each succeeding Senate term.

Office Listings
http://boxer.senate.gov

112 Hart Senate Office Building, Washington, DC 20510	(202) 224–3553

Chief of Staff.—Karen Olick.
Legislative Director.—Matthew Baumgart.
Communications Director.—David Sandretti.

1700 Montgomery Street, Suite 240, San Francisco, CA 94111	(415) 403–0100
312 North Spring Street, Suite 1748, Los Angeles, CA 90012	(213) 894–5000
501 I Street, Suite 7–600, Sacramento, CA 95814	(916) 448–2787
201North E Street, Suite 210, San Bernardino, CA 92401	(909) 888–8525
600 B Street, Suite 2240, San Diego, CA 92101	(619) 239–3884
1130 O Street, Suite 2450, Fresno, CA 93721	(209) 497–5109

REPRESENTATIVES

FIRST DISTRICT

MIKE THOMPSON, Democrat, of Napa Valley, CA; born in St. Helena, CA, January 24, 1951; education: graduated, St. Helena High School, St. Helena, CA; U.S. Army, 1969–72; Purple Heart; B.A., Chico State University, 1982; M.A., Chico State University, 1996; teacher at San Francisco State University, and Chico State University; elected to the California State Senate, 2nd District, 1990–98; chairman of the Budget Committee; married to Janet; two children: Christopher and Jon; committees: Ways and Means; elected to the 106th Congress; reelected to each succeeding Congress.

Office Listings
http://mikethompson.house.gov   http://www.house.gov/writerep

231 Cannon House Office Building, Washington, DC 20515	(202) 225–3311
Legislative Director.—Jonathan Birdsong.	FAX: 225–4335
1040 Main Street, Suite 101, Napa, CA 94559	(707) 226–9898

Chief of Staff/Press Secretary.—Ed Matovcik.

317 Third Street, Suite 1, Eureka, CA 95501	(707) 269–9595
Post Office Box 2208, Fort Bragg, CA 95437	(707) 962–0933
712 Main Street, Suite 1, Woodland, CA 95695	(530) 662–5272

Counties: DEL NORTE COUNTY. CITIES AND TOWNSHIPS: Crescent City, Fortdeck, Gasquet, Klamath, Prison, Smith River. HUMBOLDT COUNTY. CITIES AND TOWNSHIPS: Alderpoint, Areata, Bayside, Blocksburg, Blue Lake, Burcka, Carlotta, Eureka, Ferndale, Fortuna, Garberville, Hoopa, Hydseville, Kneeland, Korbel, Loleta, McKinlayville, Myers Flat, Orick, Petrolia, Redcrest, Redway, Rio Del, Scotia, Trinidad, Whitehorn, Willow Creek. LAKE COUNTY. CITIES AND TOWNSHIPS: Clearlake, Clearlake Oaks, Clearlake Park, Cobb, Glenhaven, Kelseyville, Lakeport, Lower Lake, Lucerne, Middletown, Nice, Upper Lake. MENDOCINO COUNTY. CITIES AND TOWNSHIPS: Albion, Boonville, Calpella, Compiche, Covelo, Elk, Finley, Fort Bragg, Gualala, Hopland, Laytonville, Little River, Manchester, Mendocino, Philo, Piercy, Point Arena, Potter Valley, Redwood Valley, Talmage, Ukiah, Willits, Yorkville. NAPA COUNTY. CITIES AND TOWNSHIPS: American Canyon, Angwin, Aetna Springs, Calistoga, Deer Park, Oakville, Pope Valley, Rutherford, St. Helena. SONOMA COUNTY (part). CITIES AND TOWNSHIPS: Alexander Valley, Cloverdale, Geyserville, Healdsburg, Mark West, Santa Rosa, Sonoma, Windsor. YOLO COUNTY (part). CITIES AND TOWNSHIPS: Davis, West Sacramento, Winters, and Woodland. Population (2000), 639,087.

ZIP Codes: 94503, 94508, 94515, 94558–59, 94562, 94567, 94573–74, 94576, 94581, 94589–90, 94599, 95403–04, 95409–10, 95415–18, 95420, 95422–29, 95432–33, 95435, 95437, 95441–43, 95445, 95448–49, 95451–54, 95456–61, 95463–64, 95466, 95468–70, 95476, 95481–82, 95485, 95487–88, 95490, 95492–94, 95501–03, 95511, 95514, 95518–19, 95521, 95524–26, 95528, 95531–32, 95534, 95536–38, 95540, 95542–43, 95545–51, 95553–56, 95558–60, 95562, 95564–65, 95567, 95569–71, 95573, 95585, 95587, 95589, 95605, 95612, 95615–16, 95618, 95691, 95694–95, 95776, 95798–99, 95899

* * *

SECOND DISTRICT

WALLY HERGER, Republican, of Marysville, CA; born in Sutter County, CA, May 20, 1945; education: graduated East Nicolaus High School; attended California State University, Sacramento, CA; professional: cattle rancher; small businessman; East Nicolaus High School Board of Trustees, 1977–80; California State Assemblyman, 1980–86; member: National Federation of Independent Business; Sutter County Taxpayers Association; Yuba-Sutter Farm Bureau; California Cattlemen's Association; California Chamber of Commerce; Big Brothers/Big Sisters Board of Directors; South Yuba Rotary Club; married: the former Pamela Sargent; children: eight; committees: Ways and Means; subcommittees: chairman, Human Resources; Trade; elected to the 100th Congress, November 4, 1986; reelected to each succeeding Congress.

Office Listings

2268 Rayburn House Office Building, Washington, DC 20515 .... (202) 225-3076
  Administrative Assistant.—John P. Magill.
  Legislative Director.—Derek Harley.
  Press Secretary.—Daniel MacLean.
  Executive Assistant / Scheduler.—Laura Cannon.
Suite 104, 55 Independence Circle, Chico, CA 95973 .... (530) 893-8363
  District Director.—Fran Peace.
410 Hemsted Drive, Suite 115, Redding, CA 96002 .... (530) 223-5898

Counties: BUTTE (part), COLUSA, GLENN, SHASTA, SISKIYOU, SUTTER, TEHAMA, TRINITY, YOLO (part), YUBA. Population (2000), 639,087.

ZIP Codes: 95526–27, 95552, 95563, 95568, 95595, 95606–07, 95627, 95637, 95645, 95653, 95659, 95668, 95674, 95676, 95679, 95692, 95697–98, 95837, 95901, 95903, 95912–14, 95917–20, 95922, 95925–29, 95932, 95935–39, 95941–43, 95947–48, 95950–51, 95953–55, 95957–58, 95960–63, 95967, 95969–74, 95976–79, 95981–82, 95987–88, 95991–93, 96001–03, 96007–08, 96010–11, 96013–14, 96016–17, 96019, 96021–25, 96027–29, 96031–35, 96037–41, 96044, 96046–52, 96055–59, 96061–65, 96067, 96069–71, 96073–76, 96078–80, 96084–97, 96099, 96101, 96103–04, 96114, 96118, 96122, 96124, 96134, 96137, 96161

* * *

THIRD DISTRICT

DAN LUNGREN, Republican, of Gold River, CA; born in Long Beach, CA, September 22, 1946; education: St. Anthony's High School, Long Beach, CA, 1964; B.A., English, University of Notre Dame, 1968 (with honors); attended University of Southern California Law Center, 1968–69; J.D., Georgetown University Law Center, 1971; professional: attorney, associate and partner, Ball, Hunt, Brown & Baerwitz (law firm), 1973–78; U.S. House of Representatives, 1979–89; elected California Attorney General, 1990, served two terms; Republican nominee for Governor of California, 1998; radio talk show host; consultant; private law practice, 1999–2004; religion: Catholic; married: the former Barbara (Bobbi) Knolls, 1969; children: Jeff, Kelly, and Kathleen; committees: Budget; Homeland Security; Judiciary; subcommittees: Crime, Terrorism, and Homeland Security; chair, Economic Security, Infrastructure Protection, and Cybersecurity; Immigration, Border Security, and Claims; Intelligence, Information Sharing, and Terrorism Risk Assessment; Prevention of Nuclear and Biological Attack; elected to the 109th Congress on November 2, 2004.

Office Listings

http://www.house.gov/lungren

2448 Rayburn House Office Building, Washington, DC 20515 .... (202) 225-5716
  Chief of Staff.—Victor Arnold-Bik.   FAX: 226-1298
  Communications Director.—Brian Seitchik.
  Scheduler.—Caley White.
11246 Gold Express Drive, Suite 101, Gold River, CA 95670 .... (916) 859-9906

Counties: ALPINE, AMADOR, CALAVERAS, SACRAMENTO (part), SOLANO (part). CITIES AND TOWNSHIPS: Amador, Arden-Arcade, Carmichael, Citrus Heights, Elk Grove, Fair Oaks, Folsom, Foothill Farms, Galt, Gold River, Ione, Jackson, Laguna, Laguna West, LaRiviera, North Highland, Rancho Cordova, Rancho Murieta, Rio Linda, Rio Vista, Roseville, Sacramento, Vineyard, and Wilton. Population (2000), 639,088.

ZIP Codes: 94571, 94585, 95221–26, 95228–30, 95232–33, 95236, 95245–52, 95254–55, 95257, 95601, 95608, 95610–11, 95615, 95620–21, 95624, 95626, 95628–30, 95632, 95638–40, 95642, 95646, 95652, 95654–55, 95660, 95662, 95665–66, 95668–71, 95673, 95675, 95683, 95685, 95688–90, 95693–94, 95699, 95742, 95758–59, 95763, 95821, 95825–30, 95832, 95835–37, 95841–43, 95864, 96021–22, 96029, 96035, 96055, 96061, 96080, 96120

* * *

FOURTH DISTRICT

JOHN T. DOOLITTLE, Republican, of Rocklin, CA; born in Glendale, CA, October 30, 1950; education: graduated Cupertino High School, Cupertino, CA, 1968; University of California at Santa Cruz, 1972; University of the Pacific, McGeorge School of Law, 1978; professional: lawyer; member: California bar; elected to the California State Senate, 1980; reelected 1984 and 1988; served as chairman of the Senate Republican Caucus, May 1987–April 1990; married: the former Julia Harlow, 1979; children: John, Jr. and Courtney Doolittle; committees: Appropriations; House Administration; Joint Committee on Printing; subcommittees: Agriculture, Rural Development, Food and Drug Administration, and Related Agencies; vice-chair, Energy and Water Development, and Related Agencies; Interior, Environment, and Related Agencies; elected to the 102nd Congress, November 6, 1990; reelected to each succeeding Congress.

Office Listings
http://www.house.gov/doolittle

2410 Rayburn House Office Building, Washington, DC 20515 .... (202) 225–2511
Chief of Staff.—David Lopez.   FAX: 225–5444
Executive Assistant.—Alisha Perkins.
Legislative Director.—Jason Larrabee.
4230 Douglas Boulevard, Suite 200, Granite Bay, CA 95746 .... (916) 786–5560
District Director / Deputy Chief of Staff.—Richard Robinson.

Counties: BUTTE (part), EL DORADO, LASSEN, MODOC, NEVADA, PLACER, PLUMAS, SACRAMENTO (part), SIERRA. Population (2000), 639,088.

ZIP Codes: 95602–04, 95609, 95613–14, 95617, 95619, 95623, 95626, 95628–31, 95633–36, 95648, 95650–51, 95656, 95658, 95661–64, 95667–68, 95672, 95677–78, 95681–82, 95684, 95701, 95703, 95709, 95712–15, 95717, 95720–22, 95724, 95726, 95728, 95735–36, 95741, 95746–47, 95762, 95765, 95816, 95910, 95915–16, 95922–24, 95930, 95934, 95940–41, 95944–47, 95949, 95956, 95959–60, 95965–66, 95968, 95971, 95975, 95977, 95980, 95983–84, 95986, 96006, 96009, 96015, 96020, 96054, 96056, 96068, 96101, 96103–30, 96132–33, 96135–37, 96140–43, 96145–46, 96148, 96150–52, 96154–56, 96158, 96160–62

* * *

FIFTH DISTRICT

DORIS OKADA MATSUI, Democrat, of Sacramento, CA; born in Posten, AZ, September 25, 1944; education: B.A., University of California, Berkeley, CA, 1966; professional: staff, White House, 1992–98; private advocate; organizations: Meridian International Center Board of Trustees; Woodrow Wilson Center Board of Trustees; California Institute Board of Directors; married: Robert Matsui, 1966; children: Brian Robert; committees: Rules; elected by special election on March 8, 2005 to the 109th Congress, to fill the vacancy caused by the death of her husband, Representative Robert Matsui.

Office Listings
http://www.house.gov/matsui

2310 Rayburn House Office Building, Washington, DC 20515 .... (202) 225–7163
Chief of Staff.—Joe Trahern.   FAX: 225–0566
Executive Assistant.—Shirley Queja.
Legislative Director.—Shari Taylor Davenport.
Press Secretary.—Rob Leondard.
501 I Street, 12–600, Sacramento, CA 95814 .... (916) 498–5600
District Director.—Anne Sanger.

County: SACRAMENTO COUNTY (part). CITY: Sacramento. Population (2000), 639,088.

ZIP Codes: 94204–09, 94211, 94229–30, 94232, 94234–37, 94239–40, 94244, 94246–49, 94252, 94254, 94256–59, 94261–63, 94267–69, 94271, 94273–74, 94277–80, 94282, 94284–91, 94293–99, 95660, 95670, 95758, 95812–20, 95822–29, 95831–35, 95838, 95840–43, 95851–53, 95860, 95864–67, 95887, 95894

* * *

SIXTH DISTRICT

LYNN C. WOOLSEY, Democrat, of Petaluma, CA; born in Seattle, WA, November 3, 1937; education: graduated from Lincoln High School, Seattle; B.S., University of San Francisco, 1981; president and founder, Woolsey Personnel Service, 1980–92; human resources manager, Harris Digital Telephone Systems, 1969–80; elected member, Petaluma City Council, 1984–92; vice mayor, 1989 and 1992; member: Sonoma County National Women's Political Caucus, chair; Sonoma County Commission on the Status of Women, chair; Business and Professional Women; National Organization for Women; Sierra Club; Sonoma County Hazardous Materials Management Commission, chair; Association of Bay Area Governments, Regional Hazardous Materials Representative; CAL Energy Commission, advisory committee; Education Task Force of the California Delegation Bipartisan Caucus, co-chair; the Renewable Energy Caucus; the Congressional Human Rights Caucus; the Missing and Exploited Children's Caucus (founding member); the Congressional Task Force on Health and Tobacco; the Internet Caucus; the Congressional Task Force on International HIV/AIDS; the Congressional Friends of Animals; and the Livable Communities Task Force; chair of the Children's Task Force; co-chair of the Democratic Caucus Task Force on Welfare Reform; co-chair of the Progressive Caucus; member of the House Democratic leadership as an Assistant Whip; committees: Education and the Workforce; Science; subcommittees: ranking member, Education Reform; Energy; four children: Joseph Critchett, Michael Woolsey, Ed Critchett, and Amy Critchett; two grandchildren; elected on November 3, 1992 to the 103rd Congress; reelected to each succeeding Congress.

Office Listings
http://www.house.gov/woolsey

2263 Rayburn House Office Building, Washington, DC 20515 .... (202) 225–5161
    Chief of Staff.—Nora Matus.
    Press Secretary.—Susannah Cernojevich.
1101 College Avenue, Suite 200, Santa Rosa, CA 95404 .... (707) 542–7182
    District Director.—Wendy Friefeld.
1050 Northgate Drive, Suite 140, San Rafael, CA 94903 .... (415) 507–9554

Counties: MARIN, SONOMA (part). CITIES AND TOWNSHIPS: Santa Rosa, Sebastapol, Cotati, Petaluma, and Sonoma to Golden Gate Bridge. Population (2000), 639,087.

ZIP Codes: 94901, 94903–04, 94912–15, 94920, 94922–31, 94933, 94937–42, 94945–57, 94960, 94963–66, 94970–79, 94998–99, 95401–07, 95409, 95412, 95419, 95421, 95430–31, 95436, 95439, 95441–42, 95444, 95446, 95448, 95450, 95452, 95462, 95465, 95471–73, 95476, 95480, 95486, 95492, 95497

* * *

SEVENTH DISTRICT

GEORGE MILLER, Democrat, of Martinez, CA; born in Richmond, CA, May 17, 1945; education: attended Martinez public schools; Diablo Valley College; graduated, 1968, San Francisco State College; J.D., 1972, University of California at Davis School of Law; member: California State bar; Davis Law School Alumni Association; served five years as legislative aide to Senate majority leader, California State Legislature; past chairman and member of Contra Costa County Democratic Central Committee; past president of Martinez Democratic Club; married: the former Cynthia Caccavo; children: George and Stephen; four grandchildren; committees: ranking member, Education and the Workforce; Resources; elected to the 94th Congress, November 5, 1974; reelected to each succeeding Congress.

Office Listings
http://www.house.gov/georgemiller   george.miller@mail.house.gov

2205 Rayburn House Office Building, Washington, DC 20515 .... (202) 225–2095
    Chief of Staff/Press Secretary.—Daniel Weiss.
    Personal Secretary.—Sylvia Arthur.
1333 Willow Pass Road, Suite 203, Concord, CA 94520 .... (925) 602–1880
    District Director.—Barbara Johnson.
Room 281, 3220 Blume Drive, Richmond, CA 94806 .... (510) 262–6500
    Field Representative.—Latressa Alford.
375 G Street, Suite 1, Vallejo, CA 94592 .... (707) 645–1888
    Field Representative.—Kathy Hoffman.

Counties: CONTRA COSTA (part), SOLANO (part). CITIES AND TOWNSHIPS: Benicia, Clayton, Concord, Crockett, El Sobrante, Green Valley, Hercules, Martinez, Pinole, Pittsburg, Port Costa, Richmond, Rodeo, San Pablo, Sulsun Valley, Vacaville, and Vallejo. Population (2000), 639,088.

ZIP Codes: 94503, 94510, 94517, 94519–25, 94527, 94529, 94533–34, 94547, 94553, 94564–65, 94569, 94572, 94585, 94589–92, 94801–08, 94820, 94875, 95687–88, 95696

* * *

EIGHTH DISTRICT

NANCY PELOSI, Democrat, of San Francisco, CA; born in Baltimore, MD, March 26, 1940; daughter of the late Representative Thomas D'Alesandro, Jr., of MD; education: graduated, Institute of Notre Dame High School, 1958; B.A., Trinity College, Washington, DC (major, political science; minor, history), 1962; northern chair, California Democratic Party, 1977–81; state chair, California Democratic Party, 1981–83; chair, 1984 Democratic National Convention Host Committee; finance chair, Democratic Senatorial Campaign Committee, 1985–86; member: Democratic National Committee; California Democratic Party Executive Committee; San Francisco Library Commission; Board of Trustees, LSB Leakey Foundation; married: Paul F. Pelosi, 1963; children: Nancy Corinne, Christine, Jacqueline, Paul, Jr., and Alexandra; committees: Permanent Select Committee on Intelligence; elected by special election, June 2, 1987, to the 100th Congress to fill the vacancy caused by the death of Sala Burton; elected Minority Leader for the 108th Congress; reelected to each succeeding Congress.

Office Listings

http://www.house.gov/pelosi   sf.nancy@mail.house.gov

2371 Rayburn House Office Building, Washington, DC 20515 .... (202) 225–4965
    Chief of Staff.—Terri McCullough.   FAX: 225–8259
    Office Manager.—Paula Short.
Room 14370, 450 Golden Gate Avenue, San Francisco, CA 94102 .... (415) 556–4862
    District Director.—Catherine Dodd.

County: SAN FRANCISCO COUNTY (part). CITY: San Francisco. Population (2000), 639,088.

ZIP Codes: 94101–12, 94114–15, 94117–26, 94128–47, 94150–52, 94155–56, 94158–66, 94168, 94170, 94172, 94175, 94177, 94188, 94199

* * *

NINTH DISTRICT

BARBARA LEE, Democrat, of Oakland, CA; born in El Paso, TX, July 16, 1946; education: graduated, San Fernando High School; B.A., Mills College, 1973; MSW, University of California, Berkeley, 1975; congressional aide and public servant; senior advisor and chief of staff to Congressman Ronald V. Dellums in Washington, DC, and Oakland, CA, 1975–87; California State Assembly, 1990–96; California State Senate, 1996–98; Assembly committees: Housing and Land Use; Appropriations; Business and Professions; Industrial Relations; Judiciary; Revenue and Taxation; board member, California State Coastal Conservancy, District Export Council, and California Defense Conversion Council; committees: Financial Services; International Relations; elected to the 105th Congress on April 7, 1998, by special election, to fill the remaining term of retiring Representative Ronald V. Dellums; reelected to each succeeding Congress.

Office Listings

http://www.house.gov/lee

1724 Longworth House Office Building, Washington, DC 20515 .... (202) 225–2661
    Administrative Assistant.—Julie Nickson.   FAX: 225–9817
    Scheduler.—Tatyana Kalinga.
    Communications Director.—Nathan Britton.
    Legislative Director.—Ven Neralla.
1301 Clay Street, Suite 1000–N, Oakland, CA 94612 .... (510) 763–0370
    District Director.—Jeffrey Thomas.

Counties: ALAMEDA COUNTY. CITIES: Alameda, Albany, Berkeley, Emeryville, Kensington, Piedmont. OAKLAND COUNTY (part). Population (2000), 639,088.

ZIP Codes: 94541–42, 94546, 94552, 94577–80, 94588, 94601–13, 94615, 94617–26, 94643, 94649, 94659–62, 94666, 94701–10, 94712, 94720

* * *

TENTH DISTRICT

ELLEN O. TAUSCHER, Democrat, of Alamo, CA; born in East Newark, NJ, November 15, 1951; education: graduated, Harrison High School, Harrison, NJ, 1969; B.S., early childhood education, Seton Hall University, NJ; founder and CEO, The Registry Companies, first national child care provider pre-employment screening service, 1992–present; one of the first women to hold a seat on the New York Stock Exchange (1977–79); Wall Street trader and investment banker, 1979–88; author of *The Child Care Source Book*; created the Tauscher Foundation, which has provided $150,000 to California and Texas elementary schools for purchase of computer equipment; member: NARAL, CARAL, Planned Parenthood, Seton Hall University Board of Regents; endorsed by Emily's List; co-chair, Dianne Feinstein's 1992, and 1994, U.S. Senatorial campaigns; married William Y. Tauscher in 1989; one child: Katherine; committees: Armed Services; Transportation and Infrastructure; elected to the 105th Congress; reelected to each succeeding Congress.

Office Listings

http://www.house.gov/tauscher

1034 Longworth House Office Building, Washington, DC 20515 .... (202) 225–1880
Chief of Staff.—Peter Muller.   FAX: 225–5914
Legislative Director.—Simon Limage.
2121 North California Boulevard, Suite 555, Walnut Creek, CA 94596 .... (925) 932–8899
District Director.—Jennifer Barton.
2000 Cadenasso Drive, Suite A, Fairfield, CA 94533 .... (707) 428–7792
420 West Third Street, Antioch, CA 94509 .... (925) 757–7187

Counties: CONTRA COSTA (part), ALAMEDA (part), SACRAMENTO (part), SOLANO (part). CITIES AND TOWNSHIPS: Alamo, Antioch, Blackhawk, Bethel Island, Brentwood, Byron, Clayton, Concord, Danville, Diablo, Dublin, Fairfield, Lafayette, Livermore, Moraga, Oakley, Orinda, Pleasant Hill, and Walnut Creek. Population (2000), 639,088.

ZIP Codes: 94507, 94509–12, 94516, 94518, 94520–21, 94523, 94530–31, 94533–35, 94548–51, 94556, 94561, 94563, 94570–71, 94575, 94585, 94588, 94595–98, 94706–08, 94803, 95377, 95391, 95620, 95625, 95641, 95680, 95690

* * *

ELEVENTH DISTRICT

RICHARD W. POMBO, Republican, of Tracy, CA; born in Tracy, January 8, 1961; education: attended California State University at Pomona; rancher; Tracy, CA, City Councilman, 1990–91; cofounder, San Joaquin County Citizens Land Alliance; member, Tracy Rotary Club; married to Annette Pombo since 1983; children: Richard Jr., Rena, and Rachel; committees: Agriculture; chairman, Resources; subcommittees: Department Operations, Oversight, Nutrition, and Forestry; Livestock and Horticulture; elected on November 3, 1992, to the 103rd Congress; reelected to each succeeding Congress.

Office Listings

http://www.house.gov/pombo

2411 Rayburn House Office Building, Washington, DC 20515 .... (202) 225–1947
Chief of Staff.—Jessica Carter.   FAX: 226–0861
Communications Director.—Nicole Philbin.
Legislative Director.—Marla Sousa.
Scheduler.—Jon Haubert.
2495 West March Lane, Suite 104, Stockton, CA 95207 .... (209) 951–3091
District Director.—Nicole Goehring.
3000 Executive Parkway, Suite 104, San Ramon, CA 94583 .... (925) 866–7040
Bay Area Director.—Cindy Chin.

Counties: ALAMEDA (part), CONTRA COSTA (part), SAN JOAQUIN (part), SANTA CLARA (part). CITIES AND TOWNSHIPS: Blackhawk, Brentwood, Byron, Clements, Danville, Diablo, Discovery Bay, Dublin, Escalon, Farmington, Linden, Lockeford, Lodi, Manteca, Morada, Morgan Hill, Pleasanton, Ripon, San Ramon, Stockton, Sunol, Tracy, and Woodbridge. Population (2000), 639,088.

ZIP Codes: 94506–07, 94509, 94513–14, 94526, 94528, 94539, 94550, 94566, 94568, 94583, 94586, 94588, 95020, 95023, 95037–38, 95046, 95127, 95132, 95135, 95138, 95140, 95204, 95207, 95209–12, 95215, 95219–20, 95227, 95230, 95234, 95236–37, 95240–42, 95253, 95258, 95267, 95297, 95304, 95320, 95336–37, 95361, 95366, 95376–77, 95391, 95686

* * *

TWELFTH DISTRICT

TOM LANTOS, Democrat, of San Mateo, CA; born in Budapest, February 1, 1928; during World War II active in anti-Nazi underground; came to the United States in 1947 on academic scholarship; education: B.A., University of Washington, 1949; M.A., University of Washington, 1950; Ph.D., University of California, 1953, Phi Beta Kappa; professor of economics; consultant, TV news analyst and commentator; member, Millbrae Board of Education, 1950–66; administrative assistant, economic and foreign policy adviser, U.S. Senate; married: Annette Tillemann; two married daughters: Annette Tillemann-Dick and Katrina Swett; 17 grandchildren; committees: Government Reform; ranking member, International Relations; co-chairman, Congressional Human Rights Caucus; member, U.S. Holocaust Memorial Council; elected to the 97th Congress on November 4, 1980; reelected to each succeeding Congress.

Office Listings
http://www.house.gov/lantos

2413 Rayburn House Office Building, Washington, DC 20515 .... (202) 225–3531
Administrative Assistant.—Robert R. King.
Legislative Director.—Ron Grimes.
Suite 410, 400 South El Camino Real, San Mateo, CA 94402 .... (650) 342–0300
District Representative.—Evelyn Szelenyi.

Counties: SAN MATEO COUNTY (part). CITIES: Brisbane, Burlingame, Colma, Daly City, Foster City, Hillsborough, Millbrae, Montara, Moss Beach, Pacifica, Redwood City, San Bruno, San Carlos, San Mateo, South San Francisco. SAN FRANCISCO COUNTY (part). CITIES: San Francisco. Population (2000), 639,088.

ZIP Codes: 94005, 94010–11, 94013–17, 94021, 94030, 94037–38, 94044, 94061–63, 94065–66, 94070, 94080, 94083, 94099, 94112, 94116–17, 94122, 94127–28, 94131–32, 94143, 94401–09, 94497

* * *

THIRTEENTH DISTRICT

FORTNEY PETE STARK, Democrat, of Fremont, CA; born in Milwaukee, WI, November 11, 1931; education: graduated from Wauwatosa, WI, High School, 1949; Massachusetts Institute of Technology, B.S., 1953; University of California, Berkeley, M.B.A., 1960; East Bay Skills Center, Oakland, G.E.D. (honorary), 1972; served in U.S. Air Force, 1955–57, first lieutenant; banker, founder, and president, Security National Bank, Walnut Creek, CA, 1963–72; trustee, California Democratic Council; chairman, board of trustees, Starr King School of Ministry, Berkeley; trustee, Graduate Theological Union, Berkeley; sponsor, Northern California American Civil Liberties Union; board member: Housing Development Corporation and Council for Civic Unity; director, Common Cause, 1971–72; children: Jeffrey Peter, Beatrice Stark Winslow, Thekla Stark Wainwright, Sarah Stark Ramirez, Fortney Stark III, Hannah and Andrew; married: Deborah Roderick; committees: Ways and Means (senior member); Joint Committee on Taxation; elected to the 93rd Congress, November 7, 1972; reelected to each succeeding Congress.

Office Listings

239 Cannon House Office Building, Washington, DC 20515 .... (202) 225–5065
Administrative Assistant.—Debbie Curtis. FAX: 226–3805
Personal Assistant.—Deborah Chusmir.
39300 Civic Center Drive, Fremont, CA 94538 .... (510) 494–1388
District Administrator.—Jo Cazenave.

Counties: ALAMEDA COUNTY (part). CITIES AND TOWNSHIPS: Alameda, Castro Valley, Fremont, Hayward, Milpitas, Newark, Oakland, San Leandro, San Lorenzo, Sunnyvale, Sunol, and Union City. Population (2000), 639,088.

ZIP Codes: 94501–02, 94536–46, 94552, 94555, 94557, 94560, 94566, 94577–80, 94586–88, 94603, 94605, 94621, 94622

* * *

FOURTEENTH DISTRICT

ANNA G. ESHOO, Democrat, of Atherton, CA; born in New Britain, CT, December 13, 1942; education: attended Canada College; San Mateo supervisor, 1983–92; served on the House Committees on Science, Space, and Technology, and Merchant Marine and Fisheries; Democratic Regional Whip since 1993; selected to co-chair the House Medical Technology Caucus, 1994; committees: Energy and Commerce; House Permanent Select Committee on Intelligence; subcommittees: Telecommunications and the Internet; Health; elected on November 3, 1992, to the 103rd Congress; reelected to each succeeding Congress.

Office Listings
http://www-eshoo.house.gov

205 Cannon House Office Building, Washington, DC 20515 .... (202) 225–8104
Chief of Staff.—Jason Mahler. FAX: 225–8890
Executive Assistant.—Dana Sandman.
Legislative Director.—Steven Keenan.
698 Emerson Street, Palo Alto, CA 94301 .... (650) 323–2984
Chief of Staff.—Karen Chapman.

Counties: SAN MATEO (part), SANTA CLARA (part), SANTA CRUZ (part). CITIES AND TOWNSHIPS: Amesti, Aptos, Atherton, Belmont, Ben Lomond, Bonny Doon, Boulder Creek, Brookdale, Corralitos, Davenport, East Palo Alto, Felton, Half

Moon Bay, Interlaken, La Honda, Los Altos, Los Altos Hills, Menlo Park, Monte Sereno, Mountain View, Palo Alto, Portola Valley, Redwood City, San Carlos, Scotts Valley, Stanford, Sunnyvale, and Woodside. Population (2000), 639,088.

ZIP Codes: 94002, 94018–28, 94035, 94039–43, 94060–64, 94074, 94085–89, 94301–06, 94309, 95003, 95005–08, 95014, 95017–18, 95030, 95033, 95041, 95051, 95060, 95065–67, 95070–71, 95073, 95076, 95130

* * *

FIFTEENTH DISTRICT

MICHAEL M. HONDA, Democrat, of San Jose, CA; born in Walnut Creek, CA, June 27, 1941; education: San Jose State University, received degrees in Biological Sciences and Spanish, and a Masters Degree in Education; awards: California Federation of Teachers Legislator of the Year; Outreach Paratransit Services Humanitarian Award; AEA Legislator of the Year; Service Employees International Union Home Care Champion Award; Asian Law Alliance Community Impact Award; AFL–CIO Distinguished Friend of Labor Award; public service: Peace Corps; San Jose Planning Commission; San Jose Unified School Board; Santa Clara County Board of Supervisors; California State Assemblyman; married: Jeanne; children: Mark and Michelle; committees: Science; Transportation and Infrastructure; subcommittees: Aviation; Coast Guard and Maritime Transportation; ranking member, Energy; Highways, Transit, and Pipelines; Space; elected to the 107th Congress on November 7, 2000; reelected to each succeeding Congress.

Office Listings
http://www.house.gov/honda

1713 Longworth House Office Building, Washington, DC 20515	(202) 225–2631
Chief of Staff.—Jennifer Van der Heide Escobar.	FAX: 225–2699
Legislative Director.—Chris Mitchell.	
Senior Legislative Counsel.—Bob Sakaniwa.	
Communications Director / Counsel.—Jay Staunton.	
1999 South Bascom Avenue, Suite 815, Campbell, CA 95008	(408) 558–8085
District Director.—Meri Maben.	

Counties: SANTA CLARA COUNTY (part). CITIES AND TOWNSHIPS: Campbell, Cambrian Park, Cupertino, Fruitdale, Gilroy, Lexington Hill, Los Gatos, Milpitas, San Jose, and Santa Clara. Population (2000), 639,088.

ZIP Codes: 94024, 94087, 95002, 95008–09, 95011, 95014–15, 95020–21, 95026, 95030–33, 95035–37, 95044, 95050–56, 95070, 95101, 95112, 95117–18, 95120, 95123–34, 95150, 95153–55, 95157, 95160–61, 95170

* * *

SIXTEENTH DISTRICT

ZOE LOFGREN, Democrat, of San Jose, CA; born in San Mateo, CA, December 21, 1947; education: graduated Gunn High School, 1966; B.A., Stanford University, Stanford, CA, 1970; J.D., Santa Clara Law School, Santa Clara, CA, 1975; admitted to the California bar, 1975; District of Columbia bar, 1981; Supreme Court, 1986; member: board of trustees, San Jose Evergreen Community College District, 1979–81; board of supervisors, Santa Clara County, CA, 1981–94; married: John Marshall Collins, 1978; children: Sheila and John; committees: Homeland Security; House Administration; Judiciary; Joint Committee on the Library of Congress; subcommittees: Courts, the Internet, and Intellectual Property; Economic Security, Infrastructure Protection, and Cybersecurity; Immigration, Border Security, and Claims; ranking member, Intelligence, Information Sharing, and Terrorism Risk Assessment; Management, Integration, and Oversight; elected to the 104th Congress; reelected to each succeeding Congress.

Office Listings
http://www.house.gov/lofgren

102 Cannon House Office Building, Washington, DC 20515	(202) 225–3072
Chief of Staff.—David Thomas.	FAX: 225–3336
Communications Director.—Steve Adamske.	
Executive Assistant / Scheduler.—Bridget Fallon.	
635 North First Street, Suite B, San Jose, CA 95112	(408) 271–8700
Chief of Staff.—Sandra Soto.	

Counties: SANTA CLARA COUNTY (part). CITIES AND TOWNSHIPS: San Jose, San Martin, and unincorporated portions of southern Santa Clara County. Population (2000), 639,088.

ZIP Codes: 95008, 95013, 95020, 95035, 95037, 95042, 95046, 95103, 95106, 95108–13, 95115–16, 95118–28, 95131–36, 95138–40, 95148, 95151–52, 95156, 95158–59, 95164, 95172–73, 95190–94, 95196

SEVENTEENTH DISTRICT

SAM FARR, Democrat, of Carmel, CA; born in San Francisco, CA, July 4, 1941; education: attended Carmel, CA, public schools; B.S., biology, Willamette University, Salem, OR; studied at the Monterey Institute of International Studies; served in the Peace Corps for two years in Colombia, South America; worked as a consultant and employee of the California Assembly; elected to the California Assembly, 1980–93; member: Committees on Education, Insurance, and Natural Resources; married to Shary Baldwin; one daughter: Jessica; committee: Appropriations; subcommittees: Agriculture, Rural Development, Food and Drug Administration, and Related Agencies; Military Quality of Life and Veterans' Affairs, and Related Agencies; elected on June 8, 1993, by special election, to fill the vacancy caused by the resignation of Representative Leon Panetta; reelected to each succeeding Congress.

Office Listings
http://www.farr.house.gov

1221 Longworth House Office Building, Washington, DC 20515	(202) 225–2861
Administrative Assistant.—Rochelle Dornatt.	
Legislative Director.—Debbie Merrill.	
Press Secretary.—Jessica Schafer.	
701 Ocean Avenue, Santa Cruz, CA 95060	(831) 429–1976
100 West Alisal Street, Salinas, CA 93901	(831) 424–2229

Counties: MONTEREY, SAN BENITO, SANTA CRUZ (southern half). Population (2000), 639,088.

ZIP Codes: 93426, 93450–51, 93901–02, 93905–08, 93912, 93915, 93920–28, 93930, 93932–33, 93940, 93942–44, 93950, 93953–55, 93960, 93962, 95001, 95003–04, 95010, 95012, 95019, 95023–24, 95039, 95043, 95045, 95060–65, 95073, 95075–77

* * *

EIGHTEENTH DISTRICT

DENNIS A. CARDOZA, Democrat, of Atwater, CA; born in Merced, CA, March 31, 1959; education: B.A., University of Maryland, 1982; professional: businessman; public service: Atwater City Council, 1984–1987; California State Assembly, 1996–2002; awards: California State Sheriff's Association Legislator of the Year; Small Business Roundtable Legislator of the Year; Small Business Association Legislator of the Year; and University of California Legislator of the Year, for his work on behalf of U.C. Merced; religion: Catholic; family: married to Kathleen McLoughlin; children: Joey, Brittany, and Elaina; committees: Agriculture; International Relations; Resources; elected to the 108th Congress on November 5, 2002; reelected to each succeeding Congress.

Office Listings
http://www.house.gov/cardoza

503 Cannon House Office Building, Washington, DC 20515	(202) 225–6131
Deputy Chief of Staff.—Jennifer Walsh.	FAX: 225–0819
Senior Policy Advisor.—Robin Adam.	
Legislative Director.—Gary Palmquist.	
415 West 18th Street, Merced, CA 95340	(209) 383–4455
Chief of Staff.—Mark Garrett.	

Counties: FRESNO (part), MADERA (part), MERCED, SAN JOAQUIN (part), STANISLAUS (part). CITIES AND TOWNSHIPS: Atwater, Ceres, Dos Palos, Gustine, Lathrop, Livingston, Los Banos, Modesto, Newman, Patterson, and Stockton. Population (2000), 639,088.

ZIP Codes: 93606, 93610, 93620, 93622, 93630, 93635, 93637, 93661, 93665, 93706, 93722, 95201–08, 95210, 95213, 95215, 95231, 95269, 95296, 95301, 95303–04, 95307, 95312–13, 95315, 95317, 95319, 95322, 95324, 95326, 95330, 95333–34, 95336–37, 95340–41, 95344, 95348, 95350–54, 95357–58, 95360, 95363, 95365, 95369, 95374, 95380, 95385, 95387–88, 95397

* * *

NINETEENTH DISTRICT

GEORGE RADANOVICH, Republican, of Mariposa, CA; born, June 20, 1955; education: graduated, Mariposa County High School; B.A., California State Polytechnic University, 1978; assistant manager, Yosemite Bank, 1980–83; opened Mariposa County's first winery, 1986;

charter member and president of the Mariposa Wine Grape Growers Association; founder, Mariposa Creek Parkway, 1985; treasurer, Mariposa Historical Society, 1982–83; member: Wine Institute; California Farm Bureau; California Association of Wine Grape Growers; Chambers of Commerce; California Ag Leadership, class XXI; chairman: Mariposa County Board of Supervisors; Mariposa County Planning Commission; executive director of the California State Mining and Mineral Museum Association; former chairman, Western Caucus, 106th Congress; founding member of the Wine Caucus; committees: Energy and Commerce; Resources; subcommittees: Commerce, Trade, and Consumer Protection; Energy and Air Quality; Telecommunications and the Internet; National Parks, Recreation and Public Lands; Water and Power; elected to the 104th Congress; reelected to each succeeding Congress.

Office Listings

http://www.radanovich.house.gov

438 Cannon House Office Building, Washington, DC 20515 .... (202) 225–4540
Chief of Staff.—Ted Maness.   FAX: 225–3402
Scheduler.—Connie Dwyer.
2350 West Shaw, Suite 137, Fresno, CA 93711 .... (559) 449–2490
District Director.—Darren Rose.

Counties: FRESNO (part), MADERA (part), MARIPOSA (part), STANISLAUS (part), TUOLUMNE. CITIES AND TOWNSHIPS: Ahwahnee, Auberry, Bass Lake, Big Oak Flat, Cathey's Valley, Ceres, Chinese Camp, Chowchilla, Coarsegold, Columbia, Coleville, Coulterville, Crows Landing, Dardanelle, Denair, El Portal, Farmington, Firebaugh, Fish Camp, Fresno, Groveland, Hickman, Hornitos, Hughson, Kerman, Keyes, La Grange, Long Barn, Madera, Mariposa, Mendota, Midpines, Mi Wuk Village, Moccasin, Modesto, North Fork, Oakdale, Oakhurst, O'Neals, Pinecrest, Raymond, Riverbank, Salida, San Joaquin, Snelling, Sonora, Soulsbyville, Standard, Strawberry, Tranquillity, Tuolumne, Turlock, Twain Harte, Vernalis, Waterford, Wishon, and Yosemite National Park. Population (2000), 639,088.

ZIP Codes: 93601–02, 93604, 93610–11, 93614, 93622–23, 93626, 93630, 93637–40, 93643–45, 93650, 93653, 93660, 93668–69, 93704–06, 93710–11, 93720, 93722, 93726, 93728–29, 93741, 93755, 93765, 93780, 93784, 93790–94, 95230, 95305–07, 95309–11, 95313–14, 95316, 95318, 95321, 95323, 95325–29, 95335, 95338, 95345–47, 95350–51, 95355–57, 95360–61, 95364, 95367–68, 95370, 95372–73, 95375, 95379–80, 95382–83, 95386, 95389

* * *

TWENTIETH DISTRICT

JIM COSTA, Democrat, of Fresno, CA; born in Fresno, April 13, 1952; education: BA., California State University, Fresno, CA, 1974; professional: Chief Executive Officer Costa Group, 2002–present; employee, Costa Brothers Dairy, 1959–74; Senator California State Senate, 1994–2002; assembly member, California State Assembly, 1978–94; administrative assistant, California Assemblyman Richard Lehman, 1976–78; special assistant, Congressman John Krebs, 1975–76; member of the California State Assembly, 1978–94; member of the California State Senate, 1994–02; private advocate; member Fact Steering Committee Fresno County Farm Board; religion: Catholic; committees: Agriculture; Resources; Science; elected to the 109th Congress on November 2, 2004.

Office Listings

http://www.house.gov/costa

1004 Longworth House Office Building, Washington, DC 20515 .... (202) 225–3341
Chief of Staff.—Scott Nishioki.   FAX: 225–9308
Scheduler.—Kerri Hatfield.
2300 Tulare Street, #315, Fresno, CA 93721 .... (559) 495–1620
District Director.—Jack Hall.

Counties: FRESNO (part), KERN (part), KINGS. Population (2000), 639,088.

ZIP Codes: 93202–04, 93206, 93210, 93212, 93215–16, 93220, 93230, 93232, 93234, 93239, 93241–42, 93245–46, 93249–50, 93263, 93266, 93280, 93282, 93301, 93305, 93307, 93383, 93387, 93518, 93607–09, 93616, 93620, 93622, 93624–25, 93627, 93631, 93640, 93648, 93652, 93656–57, 93660, 93662, 93668, 93701–09, 93712, 93714–18, 93721–22, 93724–25, 93727–28, 93744–45, 93750, 93760–62, 93764, 93771–79, 93786, 93844, 93888

* * *

TWENTY-FIRST DISTRICT

DEVIN NUNES, Republican, of Pixley, CA; born in Tulare County, CA, October 1, 1973; education: A.A., College of the Sequoias; B.S., Agricultural Business, and a Masters Degree in Agriculture, from California Polytechnic State University, San Luis Obispo; graduate, California Agriculture Leadership Fellowship Program; professional: farmer and businessman;

elected, College of the Sequoias Board of Trustees, 1996; reelected, 2000; appointed by President George W. Bush to serve as California State Director of the U.S. Department of Agriculture Rural Development Office, 2001; religion: Catholic; married: the former Elizabeth Tamariz, 2003; committees: Agriculture; Resources; Veterans' Affairs; subcommittees: Department Operations, Oversight, Nutrition and Forestry; Economic Opportunity; Health; Livestock and Horticulture; chairman, Parks; Water and Power; elected to the 108th Congress on November 5, 2002; reelected to each succeeding Congress.

Office Listings
http://www.nunes.house.gov

1017 Longworth House Office Building, Washington, DC 20515	(202) 225–2523
Chief of Staff.—Johnny Amaral.	FAX: 225–3404
Legislative Director.—Damon Nelson.	
Executive Assistant.—Jennifer Buckley.	
113 North Church Street, Suite 208, Visalia, CA 93291	(559) 733–3861
264 Clovis Avenue, Suite 206, Clovis, CA 93612	(559) 323–5235

Counties: TULARE, FRESNO (part). Population (2000), 639,088.

ZIP Codes: 93201, 93207–08, 93212, 93215, 93218–19, 93221, 93223, 93227, 93235, 93237, 93242, 93244, 93247, 93256–58, 93260–62, 93265, 93267, 93270–72, 93274–75, 93277–79, 93286, 93290–92, 93602–03, 93605, 93609, 93611–13, 93615–16, 93618, 93621, 93625–26, 93628, 93631, 93633–34, 93641–42, 93646–49, 93651, 93654, 93656–57, 93662, 93664, 93666–67, 93670, 93673, 93675, 93703, 93710, 93720, 93726–27, 93740, 93747

* * *

TWENTY-SECOND DISTRICT

WILLIAM M. THOMAS, Republican, of Bakersfield, CA; born in Wallace, ID, December 6, 1941; education: graduated, Garden Grove High School, 1959; A.A., Santa Ana Community College, 1961; B.A., San Francisco State University, 1963; M.A., San Francisco State University, 1965; professor, Bakersfield Community College, 1965–74; served in California State Assembly, 1974–78; member: Agriculture; Revenue and Taxation; and Rules committees; selected by the American Council of Young Political Leaders as a delegate to the Soviet Union, 1977; committees: chairman, Ways and Means; chairman, Joint Committee on Taxation; married to the former Sharon Lynn Hamilton, 1968; two children: Christopher and Amelia; elected to the 96th Congress on November 7, 1978; reelected to each succeeding Congress.

Office Listings
http://www.house.gov/billthomas

2208 Rayburn House Office Building, Washington, DC 20515	(202) 225–2915
Chief of Staff.—James Min.	
Scheduler.—Renee Edelen.	
4100 Empire Drive, Suite 150, Bakersfield, CA 93309	(661) 327–3611
5805 Capistrano Avenue, Suite C, Atascadero, CA 93422	(805) 461–1034

Counties: KERN COUNTY (part). CITIES AND TOWNSHIPS: Arvin, Bakersfield, Bodfish, Boron, Caliente, California City, Cantil, China Lake, Edison, Edwards, Fellows, Frazier Park, Glennville, Havilah, Inyokern, Keene, Kernville, Lake Isabella, Lebec, Maricopa, McKittrick, Mojave, Monolith, North Edwards, Onyx, Randsberg, Ridgecrest, Rosamond, Taft, Tehachapi, Tupman, Weldon, Willow Springs, Wofford Heights, Woody. SAN LUIS OBISPO COUNTY (part). CITIES AND TOWNSHIPS: Arroyo Grande, Paso Robles, San Miguel, Atascadero, Shandon, Templeton, San Luis Obispo, Nipomo. LOS ANGELES COUNTY (part). CITIES AND TOWNSHIPS: Lancaster. Population (2000) 639,088.

ZIP Codes: 91390, 92832, 92834, 93203, 93205–06, 93215, 93222, 93224–26, 93238, 93240–41, 93243, 93249–52, 93255, 93263, 93268, 93276, 93283, 93285, 93287, 93301–09, 93311–14, 93380, 93384–86, 93388–90, 93401–02, 93405, 93407, 93409–10, 93420, 93422–23, 93426, 93428, 93430, 93432, 93442, 93444, 93446–47, 93451, 93453–54, 93461, 93465, 93501–02, 93504–05, 93516, 93518–19, 93522–24, 93527–28, 93531–32, 93534–36, 93539, 93554–56, 93558, 93560–61, 93581, 93584, 93596

* * *

TWENTY-THIRD DISTRICT

LOIS CAPPS, Democrat, of Santa Barbara, CA; born in Ladysmith, WI, January 10, 1938; education: graduated Flathead County High School, Kalispell, MT, 1955; B.S. in Nursing, Pacific Lutheran University, 1959; M.A. in Religion, Yale University, 1964; M.A. in Education, University of California at Santa Barbara, 1990; professional: head nurse, Yale New Haven

Hospital; staff nurse, Visiting Nurses Association, Hamden, CT; elementary district nurse, Santa Barbara School District; director, Teenage Pregnancy and Parenting Project, Santa Barbara County; director, Santa Barbara School District Parent and Child Education Center; instructor of early childhood education, Santa Barbara City College; board member: American Red Cross, American Heart Association, Family Service Agency, Santa Barbara Women's Political Committee; married: Walter Capps, 1960; children: Lisa, Todd, and Laura; committees: Budget; Energy and Commerce; elected by special election on March 10, 1998, to the 105th Congress, to fill the vacancy caused by the death of her husband Rep. Walter Capps; reelected to each succeeding Congress.

Office Listings

http://www.house.gov/capps

1707 Longworth House Office Building, Washington, DC 20515 .... (202) 225–3601
    Chief of Staff.—Jeremy Rabinovitz.   FAX: 225–5632
    Legislative Director.—Randolph Harrison.
    Press Secretary.—Shannon Lohrmann.
    Executive Assistant.—Erin Shaughnessy.
1411 Marsh Street, Suite 205, San Luis Obispo, CA 93401 .... (805) 546–8348
    District Representatives: Betsy Umhofer, Greg Haas.
1216 State Street, Suite 403, Santa Barbara, CA 93101 .... (805) 730–1710
    District Director.—Sharon Siegel.
141 South A Street, Suite 204, Oxnard, CA 93030 .... (805) 385–3440
    District Representative.—Vanessa Hernandez.

Counties: SAN LUIS OBISPO COUNTY (part). CITIES AND TOWNSHIPS: Baywood-Los Osos, Cambria, Cayucos, Grover Beach, Morro Bay, Nipomo, Oceano, Pismo Beach, San Luis Obispo. SANTA BARBARA COUNTY (part). CITIES AND TOWNSHIPS: Carpinteria, Goleta, Guadalupe, Isla Vista, Mission Canyon, Montecito, Santa Barbara, Santa Maria, Summerland, Toro Canyon. VENTURA COUNTY (part). CITIES AND TOWNSHIPS: Channel Island, El Rio, Oxnard, Port Hueneme, and San Buenaventura. Population (2000), 639,088.

ZIP Codes: 92832, 93001, 93003, 93013–14, 93030–36, 93041, 93043–44, 93067, 93101–03, 93105–11, 93116–18, 93120–21, 93130, 93140, 93150, 93160, 93190, 93199, 93401–03, 93405–06, 93408, 93412, 93420–21, 93424, 93428, 93430, 93433–35, 93442–45, 93448–49, 93452, 93454–56, 93458, 93483

* * *

TWENTY-FOURTH DISTRICT

ELTON GALLEGLY, Republican, of Simi Valley, CA; born in Huntington Park, CA, March 7, 1944; education: graduated Huntington Park High School, 1962; attended Los Angeles State College; businessman; member, Simi Valley City Council, 1979; mayor, city of Simi Valley, 1980–86; Congressional Aerospace Caucus; Congressional Autism Caucus; Congressional Automotive Caucus; Congressional Fire Services Caucus; chairman, Task Force on Urban Search and Rescue; Congressional Caucus to Fight and Control Methamphetamine; Congressional Friends of Animals; Congressional Human Rights Caucus; Congressional Task Force on Alzheimer's Disease; Congressional Task Force on Tobacco and Health; Congressional Wine Caucus; Diabetes Caucus; Fairness Caucus; House Renewable Energy and Energy Efficiency Caucus; Older Americans Caucus; Congressional Taiwan Caucus; Western Caucus; former vice-chairman and chairman, Ventura County Association of Governments; former member, board of directors, Moorpark College Foundation; delegate to 1988 Republican National Convention; married: the former Janice L. Shrader, 1974; children: Shawn G., Shawn P., Kevin, and Shannon; committees: International Relations; Judiciary; Resources; Permanent Select Committee on Intelligence; subcommittees: Courts, the Internet and Intellectual Property; chair, Europe and Emerging Threats; Immigration, Border Security and Claims; National Parks, Recreation and Public Lands; Technical and Tactical Intelligence; Terrorism, Human Intelligence Analysis, and Counterintelligence; elected to the 100th Congress on November 4, 1986; reelected to each succeeding Congress.

Office Listings

2427 Rayburn House Office Building, Washington, DC 20515 .... (202) 225–5811
    Chief of Staff.—Patrick Murphy.
    Executive Assistant.—Pamela Roller.
    Press Secretary.—Tom Pfeifer.
2829 Townsgate Road, Suite 315, Thousand Oaks, CA 91361 .... (805) 497–2224
    District Chief of Staff.—Brian Miller.   (800) 423–0023

Counties: VENTURA COUNTY (part). CITIES AND TOWNSHIPS: Bell Canyon, Camarillo, Fillmore, Moorpark, Newbury Park, Oak Park, Oak View, Ojai, Piru, Santa Paula, Simi Valley, Somis, Thousand Oaks, Ventura, Westlake Village. SANTA BARBARA COUNTY (part). CITIES AND TOWNSHIPS: Buellton, Lompoc, Los Alamos, Los Olivos, Orcutt, Santa Barbara, Santa Ynez, and Solvang. Population (2000), 639,088.

ZIP Codes: 91301, 91304, 91307, 91311, 91319–20, 91358–62, 91377, 91406, 91413, 93001, 93003–07, 93009–13, 93015–16, 93020–24, 93030, 93033, 93036, 93040–42, 93060–66, 93094, 93099, 93105, 93111, 93117, 93225, 93252, 93254, 93427, 93429, 93436–38, 93440–41, 93454–55, 93457–58, 93460, 93463–64

* * *

TWENTY-FIFTH DISTRICT

HOWARD P. (BUCK) McKEON, Republican, of Santa Clarita, CA; born in Los Angeles, CA, September 9, 1938; education: graduated, Verdugo Hills High School, Tujunga, CA; B.S., Brigham Young University; owner, Howard and Phil's Western Wear; mayor and city councilman, Santa Clarita, 1987–92; member: board of directors, Canyon Country Chamber of Commerce; California Republican State Central Committee; advisory council, Boy Scouts of America; president and trustee, William S. Hart School District, 1979–87; chairman and director, Henry Mayo Newhall Memorial Hospital, 1983–87; chairman and founding director, Valencia National Bank, 1987–92; honorary chairman, Red Cross Community Support Campaign, 1992; honorary chairman, Leukemia Society Celebrity Program, 1990 and 1994; president, Republican Freshman Class of the 103rd Congress; married: to the former Patricia Kunz, 1962; children: Tamara, Howard D., John Matthew, Kimberly, David Owen, and Tricia; committees: Armed Services; Education and the Workforce; subcommittees: Employee-Employer Relations; Military Readiness; Tactical Air and Land; 21st Century Competitiveness; elected on November 3, 1992, to the 103rd Congress; reelected to each succeeding Congress.

Office Listings

http://www.house.gov/mckeon

2351 Rayburn House Office Building, Washington, DC 20515	(202) 225–1956
Chief of Staff.—Bob Cochran.	FAX: 226–0683
Executive Assistant / Appointments.—Michelle A. Baker.	
District Director.—Scott Wilk.	
26650 The Old Road, Suite 203, Santa Clarita, CA 91355	(661) 254–2111
1008 West Avenue, M–14, Suite E1, Palmdale, CA 93551	(661) 274–9688

Counties: INYO, LOS ANGELES (part), MONO, SAN BERNARDINO (part). CITIES AND TOWNSHIPS: Acton, Adelanto, Baker, Barstow, Benton, Big Pine, Bishop, Bridgeport, Castaic, Canyon Country, Coleville, Death Valley, Edwards, Ft. Irwin, Helendale, Hesperia, Hinkley, Independence, Inyokern, June Lake, Keeler, La Crescenta, Lancaster, Littlerock, Little Lake, Little Vinning, Llano, Lone Pine, Mammoth Lakes, Newberry Springs, Newhall, Nipton, Olancha, Oro Grande, Palmdale, Pearblossom, Phelan, Pinon Hills, Ridgecrest, Santa Clarita, Shoshone, Stevenson Ranch, Sunland, Sylmar, Tecopa, Topaz, Trona, Tujunga, Valencia, Valyermo, Victorville, and Yermo. Population (2000), 639,087.

ZIP Codes: 91042, 91214, 91310, 91321–22, 91350–51, 91354–55, 91380–81, 91383–87, 91390, 92301, 92309–12, 92328, 92342, 92345, 92347, 92364–65, 92368, 92371–72, 92384, 92389, 92392–94, 92398, 92832, 93510, 93512–17, 93524, 93526–27, 93529–30, 93534–35, 93541–46, 93549–53, 93560, 93562, 93586, 93590–92, 93599, 96107, 96133

* * *

TWENTY-SIXTH DISTRICT

DAVID DREIER, Republican, of San Dimas, CA; born in Kansas City, MO, July 5, 1952; education: Claremont McKenna College, B.A. (cum laude), political science, 1975; Claremont Graduate School, M.A., American Government, 1976; Winston S. Churchill Fellow; Phi Sigma Alpha; professional: director, corporate relations, Claremont McKenna College, 1975–78; member: board of governors, James Madison Society; Republican State Central Committee of California; Los Angeles Town Hall; named Outstanding Young Man of America and Outstanding Young Californian, 1976 and 1978; director, marketing and government affairs, Industrial Hydrocarbons, 1979–80; vice president, Dreier Development, 1985–present; author of congressional reform package incorporated into the House Rules; committees: chairman, Rules; elected to the 97th Congress on November 4, 1980; reelected to each succeeding Congress.

Office Listings

http://www.house.gov/dreier

233 Cannon House Office Building, Washington, DC 20515	(202) 225–2305
Chief of Staff.—Bradley W. Smith.	FAX: 225–7018
Administrative Assistant.—Ryan Maxson.	
Legislative Director.—Alisa Do.	
2220 East Route 66, Suite 225, Glendora, CA 91740	(626) 852–2626

Counties: LOS ANGELES (part). CITIES: Altadena, Arcadia, Bradbury, Claremont, Covina, El Monte, Glendora, La Canada Flintridge, La Crescenta, La Verne, Monrovia, Montrose, Pasadena, San Antonio Heights, San Dimas, San Gabriel,

San Marino, Sierra Madre, Walnut. SAN BERNARDINO (part). CITIES: Montclair, Rancho Cucamonga, Upland, and Wrightwood. Population (2000), 639,088.

ZIP Codes: 91001, 91006–07, 91010–12, 91016–17, 91020–21, 91023–25, 91066, 91077, 91104, 91107–08, 91118, 91131, 91185, 91187, 91191, 91214, 91390, 91410, 91701, 91711, 91730, 91737, 91739–41, 91750, 91759, 91763, 91773, 91775, 91784, 91786, 91789, 92329, 92336, 92345, 92358, 92371–72, 92397, 92407

* * *

TWENTY-SEVENTH DISTRICT

BRAD SHERMAN, Democrat, of Sherman Oaks, CA; born in Los Angeles, CA, October 24, 1954; education: B.A., *summa cum laude,* UCLA, 1974; J.D., *magna cum laude,* Harvard Law School, 1979; professional: admitted to the California bar in 1979 and began practice in Los Angeles; attorney, CPA, certified tax law specialist; elected to the California State Board of Equalization, 1990, serving as chairman, 1991–95; committees: Financial Services; International Relations; Science; subcommittees: ranking member, International Terrorism and Non-proliferation; Africa, Global Human Rights and International Operations; Space; Energy; Capital Markets' Insurance and Government-Sponsored Enterprises; International Domestic and International Monetary Policy, Trade and Technology; elected to the 105th Congress; reelected to each succeeding Congress.

Office Listings

1030 Longworth House Office Building, Washington, DC 20515	(202) 225–5911
Chief of Staff.—Andrew S. Wright.	FAX: 225–5879
Legislative Director.—Ryan Donovan.	
Communications Director.—Sharon Singh.	
Legislative Correspondent.—Marc Korman.	
5000 Van Nuys Boulevard, Suite 420, Sherman Oaks, CA 91403	(818) 501–9200
District Director.—Erin Prangley.	

Counties: LOS ANGELES COUNTY (part). Population (2000), 639,088.

ZIP Codes: 91040–41, 91043, 91303–06, 91309, 91311–12, 91316, 91324–30, 91335, 91337, 91342–46, 91352, 91356–57, 91364, 91367, 91371, 91394–96, 91401, 91403, 91405–06, 91409, 91411, 91416, 91423, 91426, 91436, 91470, 91482, 91495–96, 91504–07, 91510, 91601, 91605–06

* * *

TWENTY-EIGHTH DISTRICT

HOWARD L. BERMAN, Democrat, of Van Nuys, CA; born in Los Angeles, CA, April 15, 1941; education: B.A., international relations, UCLA, 1962; LL.B., UCLA School of Law, 1965; California Assembly Fellowship Program, 1965–70; Vista volunteer, 1966–67; admitted to the California bar, 1966; practiced law until election to California Assembly in 1972; named assembly majority leader in first term; served as chair of the Assembly Democratic Caucus and policy research management committee; member: regional board of the Anti-Defamation League; past president, California Federation of Young Democrats; married: Janis; children: Brinley and Lindsey; committees: International Relations; Judiciary; subcommittees: ranking member, Courts, the Internet, and Intellectual Property; elected to the 98th Congress on November 2, 1982; reelected to each succeeding Congress.

Office Listings

http://www.house.gov/berman

2221 Rayburn House Office Building, Washington, DC 20515	(202) 225–4695
Chief of Staff.—Gene Smith.	
Legislative Director.—Doug Campbell.	
Executive Assistant/Appointments.—Nancy Milburn.	
14546 Hamlin Street, Suite 202, Van Nuys, CA 91411	(818) 994–7200
District Director.—Bob Blumenfield.	

Counties: LOS ANGELES COUNTY (part). Portions of the city of Los Angeles, including all or part of the communities of Arleta, Encino, North Hollywood, North Hills, Pacoima, Panorama City, San Fernando, Sherman Oaks, Studio City, Valley Village, and Van Nuys. Population (2000), 639,087.

ZIP Codes: 90028, 90046, 90049, 90068, 91316, 91331, 91333–34, 91340–43, 91345, 91352–53, 91356, 91388, 91392–93, 91401–08, 91411–12, 91423, 91436, 91497, 91499, 91505, 91601–12, 91614–18

TWENTY-NINTH DISTRICT

ADAM B. SCHIFF, Democrat, of Burbank, CA; born in Framingham, MA, June 20, 1960; education: B.A., Stanford University, 1982; J.D., Harvard University, 1985; professional: Attorney; U.S. Attorney's Office, served as a criminal prosecutor; chosen by the Dept. of Justice to assist the Czechoslovakian government in reforming their criminal justice system; public service: elected to the California State Senate, 1996; involved in numerous community service activities; awards: Dept. of Justice Special Achievement Award; Council of State Governments Toll Fellowship; California League of High Schools Legislator of the Year; family: married: Eve; children: Alexa and Elijah; committees: International Relations; Judiciary; elected to the 107th Congress on November 7, 2000; reelected to each succeeding Congress.

Office Listings

http://www.house.gov/schiff

326 Cannon House Office Building, Washington, DC 20515 .... (202) 225–4176
Chief of Staff.—Gail Ravnitzky.   FAX: 225–5828
Press Secretary.—Rebecca Kutler.
Executive Assistant.—Christopher Hoven.
35 South Raymond Avenue, Suite 205, Pasadena, CA 91105 .... (626) 304–2727
District Director.—Ann Peifer.

Counties: LOS ANGELES COUNTY (part). CITIES: Alhambra, Altadena, Burbank, Glendale, Griffith Park, Monterey Park, Pasadena, San Gabriel, South Pasadena, and Temple City. Population (2000), 639,088.

ZIP Codes: 90004–06, 90010, 90020, 90026–27, 90029, 90035–36, 90038–39, 90046, 90048, 90064, 90068, 91001, 91003, 91007, 91011, 91030–31, 91046, 91101–10, 91114–17, 91121, 91123–26, 91129, 91175, 91182, 91184, 91186, 91188–89, 91201–10, 91214, 91221–22, 91224–26, 91501–06, 91508, 91521–23, 91775–76, 91780, 91801, 91803–04

* * *

THIRTIETH DISTRICT

HENRY A. WAXMAN, Democrat, of Los Angeles, CA; born in Los Angeles, September 12, 1939; education: B.A., political science, UCLA, 1961; J.D., School of Law; admitted to the California State bar, 1965; served three terms as California State Assemblyman; former chairman, California Assembly Health Committee; Select Committee on Medical Malpractice; and Committee on Elections and Reapportionment; president, California Federation of Young Democrats, 1965–67; member: Guardians of the Jewish Home for the Aged; American Jewish Congress; Sierra Club; married: the former Janet Kessler, 1971; children: Carol Lynn and Michael David; committees: Energy and Commerce; ranking member, Government Reform; elected to the 94th Congress on November 5, 1974; reelected to each succeeding Congress.

Office Listings

http://www.house.gov/waxman

2204 Rayburn House Office Building, Washington, DC 20515 .... (202) 225–3976
Chief of Staff.—Philip M. Schiliro.   FAX: 225–4099
Administrative Assistant.—Patricia Delgado.
Personal Secretary / Office Manager.—Amanda Molson.
8436 West Third Street, Suite 600, Los Angeles, CA 90048 .... (323) 651–1040
District Director.—Lisa Pinto.

Counties: LOS ANGELES COUNTY (part). CITIES AND TOWNSHIPS: Agoura Hills, Bel-Air, Beverly Hills, Brentwood, Calabasas, Canoga Park, Century City, Chatsworth, Hidden Hills, Malibu, Northridge, Pacific Palisades, Pico-Robertson, Santa Monica, Tarzana, Topanga, West Hills, West Hollywood, Westlake Village, West Los Angeles, Westwood, and Woodland Hills. Population (2000), 639,088.

ZIP Codes: 90024–25, 90027–29, 90032, 90034–36, 90038–39, 90046, 90048–49, 90057, 90063–64, 90067–69, 90072–73, 90075–77, 90095, 90209–13, 90263–65, 90272, 90290–91, 90401–11, 91301–04, 91307–08, 91311, 91313, 91324, 91356, 91361–65, 91367, 91372, 91376, 91399

* * *

THIRTY-FIRST DISTRICT

XAVIER BECERRA, Democrat, of Los Angeles, CA; born in Sacramento, CA, January 26, 1958; education: graduated, McClatchy High School, Sacramento, 1976; B.A., Stanford University, 1980; J.D., Stanford Law School, 1984; admitted to California bar, 1985; attended

Universidad de Salamanca, 1978–79; staff attorney, "Reggie Fellow," Legal Assistance Corporation of Central Massachusetts, 1984–85; administrative assistant for State Senator Art Torres, California State Legislature, 1986; Deputy Attorney General, Office of the Attorney General, State of California, 1987–90; Assemblyman, California State Legislature, 1990–92; member: Mexican American State Legislators Policy Institute; Mexican American Bar Association; chairperson: Hispanic Employee Advisory Committee to the State Attorney General, 1989; honorary member: Association of California State Attorneys and Administrative Law Judges; former member: steering committee, Greater Eastside Voter Registration Project; Construction and General Laborers Union, Local 185 (Sacramento); Pitzer College Board of Trustees; National Association of Latino's Electoral and Appointed Official Board of Directors; married to Dr. Carolina Reyes; children: Clarisa, Olivia, Natalia; committee: Ways and Means; subcommittees: Human Resources; Social Security; elected on November 3, 1992, to the 103rd Congress; reelected to each succeeding Congress.

Office Listings
http://www.house.gov/becerra

1119 Longworth House Office Building, Washington, DC 20515	(202) 225–6235
Chief of Staff.—Debra Dixon.	FAX: 225–2202
1910 Sunset Boulevard, Suite 560, Los Angeles, CA 90026	(213) 483–1425
District Director.—Laura Arciniega.	

Counties: LOS ANGELES COUNTY (part). CITIES: Los Angeles. Population (2000), 639,088.

ZIP Codes: 90004–07, 90011–12, 90015, 90018, 90020–22, 90026, 90028–29, 90031–32, 90037–39, 90041–42, 90048, 90057–58, 90065, 90072

* * *

THIRTY-SECOND DISTRICT

HILDA L. SOLIS, Democrat, of El Monte, CA; born in Los Angeles, CA, October 20, 1957; education: B.A., California Polytechnic University, Pomona; M.S., University of Southern California; professional: White House Office of Hispanic Affairs during the Carter Administration; management analyst, U.S. Office of Management and Budget; Rio Hondo Community College Board of Trustees; Los Angeles County Insurance Commission; public service: California State Assembly, 1992–94; California State Senate, 1994–2000; first Latina to serve in the State Senate; recognized and honored by numerous community and civic organizations; co-chair, Congressional Caucus on Women's Issues; member, Congressional Hispanic Caucus; committees: Energy and Commerce; subcommittees: ranking member, Environment and Hazardous Materials; Energy and Air Quality; elected to the 107th Congress on November 7, 2000; reelected to each succeeding Congress.

Office Listings
http://www.house.gov/solis

1725 Longworth House Office Building, Washington, DC 20515	(202) 225–5464
Chief of Staff.—Don Lyster.	FAX: 225–5467
Legislative Director.—Jennifer Grodsky.	
Scheduler.—Juan López.	
4401 Santa Anita Avenue, Suite 211, El Monte, CA 91731	(626) 448–1271
4716 Cesar Chavez Avenue, Building A, East Los Angeles, CA 90022	(323) 307–9904
Deputy District Director.—Benita Duran.	

Counties: LOS ANGELES COUNTY (part). CITIES: Azusa, Baldwin Park, Covina, Duarte, El Monte, South El Monte, Irwindale, Monterey Park, Rosemead, San Gabriel, South San Gabriel, and portions of East Los Angeles, Citrus CDP, Glendora, Industry City, Los Angeles, Temple City, Vincent CDP, and West Covina. Population (2000), 639,087.

ZIP Codes: 90022, 90032, 90034–36, 90044–45, 90047–48, 90063–64, 90066–67, 90089, 91009–10, 91016, 91702, 91706, 91722–24, 91731–33, 91740, 91754–55, 91770, 91790–93

* * *

THIRTY-THIRD DISTRICT

DIANE E. WATSON, Democrat, of Los Angeles, CA; born in Los Angeles, November 12, 1933; education: Bachelor of Arts Degree in Education from the University of California, Los Angeles; Master of Science Degree in School Psychology from California State University, Los Angeles; attended the John F. Kennedy School of Government at Harvard University and earned a Ph.D. in Educational Administration from the Claremont Graduate University; professional: served as an elementary school teacher, acting principal, assistant superintendent of child welfare and attendance, and school psychologist; served on the faculty at both California State University, Los Angeles, and Long Beach; Health Occupations Specialist, California Department of Education; awards: named Legislator of the Year by numerous California universities, associations, and organizations; public service: Los Angeles Unified School District Board Member; served in the California State Senate for 20 years; served as U.S. Ambassador to Micronesia, 1999–2001; committees: Government Reform; International Relations; subcommittees: Africa, Global Human Rights and International Operations; Asia and the Pacific; Criminal Justice, Drug Policy, and Human Resources; ranking member, Energy and Resources; elected to the 107th Congress, by special election, on June 5, 2001; reelected to each succeeding Congress.

Office Listings

125 Cannon House Office Building, Washington, DC 20515 .... (202) 225–7084
    Chief of Staff.—Jim B. Clarke.   FAX: 225–2422
    Legislative Director.—Gregory Adams.
    Scheduler / Special Assistant.—Barbara Hamlett.
    Communications Director.—Bert Hammond.
4322 Wilshire Boulevard, Suite 302, Los Angeles, CA 90010 .... (323) 965–1422
    District Director.—Paullette Starks.

Counties: LOS ANGELES COUNTY (part). CITIES: Culver City, Los Angeles City, communities of Ladera Heights and View Park-Windsor Hills. Population (2000), 639,088.

ZIP Codes: 90004–08, 90010–11, 90016, 90018–20, 90022, 90026–29, 90033–39, 90043–45, 90047–48, 90053, 90056–58, 90062–64, 90066, 90068, 90070, 90078, 90083, 90093, 90099, 90103, 90230–33, 90291–92, 90302

* * *

THIRTY-FOURTH DISTRICT

LUCILLE ROYBAL-ALLARD, Democrat, of Los Angeles, CA; born in Los Angeles, June 12, 1941; education: B.A., California State University, Los Angeles, 1965; served in the California State Assembly, 1987–92; married: Edward T. Allard III; two children: Lisa Marie and Ricardo; two stepchildren: Angela and Guy Mark; the first woman to serve as the chair of the California Democratic Congressional Delegation in the 105th Congress; in the 106th Congress, she became the first woman to chair the Congressional Hispanic Caucus, and the first Latina in history to be appointed to the House Appropriations Committee; committees: Appropriations; Standards of Official Conduct; subcommittees: Homeland Security; Labor, Health and Human Services, Education and Related Agencies; the first Mexican-American woman elected to Congress on November 3, 1992 to the 103rd Congress; reelected to each succeeding Congress.

Office Listings

http://www.house.gov/roybal-allard

2330 Rayburn House Office Building, Washington, DC 20515 .... (202) 225–1766
    Chief of Staff.—Ellen Riddleberger.   FAX: 226–0350
    Associate Staff for Appropriations.—Don DeArmon.
    Executive Assistant.—Lisa Pablo.
255 East Temple Street, Suite 1860, Los Angeles, CA 90012–3334 .... (213) 628–9230
    District Director.—Ana Figueroa-Davis.

Counties: LOS ANGELES COUNTY (part). CITIES: Bell, Belflower, Bell Gardens, Boyle Heights, Chinatown, Commerce, Cudahy, Downey, Downtown Los Angeles, East Los Angeles, Florence, Huntington Park, Little Tokyo, Maywood, Pico Union, South Park, Vernon, and Westlake. Population (2000), 639,088.

ZIP Codes: 90001, 90011–15, 90017, 90021–23, 90026, 90033, 90040, 90057–58, 90063, 90071, 90081, 90086–87, 90091, 90201, 90239, 90241–42, 90255, 90270, 90280, 90703, 90706, 90712–13, 90723

* * *

THIRTY-FIFTH DISTRICT

MAXINE WATERS, Democrat, of Los Angeles, CA; born in St. Louis, MO, August 15, 1938; education: B.A., California State University; honorary degrees: Harris-Stowe State College, St. Louis, MO, and Central State University, Wilberforce, OH, Spelman College, Atlanta, GA, North Carolina A&T State University, Howard University, Central State University, Bishop

College, Morgan State University; elected to California State Assembly, 1976; reelected every two years thereafter; member: Assembly Democratic Caucus, Board of TransAfrica Foundation, National Women's Political Caucus; chairperson, Ways and Means Subcommittee on State Administration; chair, Joint Committee on Public Pension Fund Investments; married to Sidney Williams, former U.S. Ambassador to the Commonwealth of the Bahamas; two children: Karen and Edward; founding member, National Commission for Economic Conversion and Disarmament; member of the board, Center for National Policy; Clara Elizabeth Jackson Carter Foundation (Spelman College); Minority AIDS Project; Chief Deputy Minority Whip; committees: chair, Democratic Caucus Special Committee on Election Reform; Financial Services, Judiciary; elected to the 102nd Congress on November 6, 1990; reelected to each succeeding Congress.

Office Listings

2344 Rayburn House Office Building, Washington, DC 20515 .... (202) 225–2201
  Executive Assistant / Scheduler.—Joyce Freeland.
  Legislative Director.—Gary Goldberg.
10124 South Broadway, Los Angeles, CA 90003 .... (323) 757–8900
  District Director.—Mike Murase.

Counties: LOS ANGELES COUNTY (part). CITIES: Gardena, Hawthorne, Inglewood, Lawndale, Los Angeles, Playa Del Ray, and Torrance. Population (2000), 639,088.

ZIP Codes: 90001–03, 90007, 90009, 90037, 90044–45, 90047, 90052, 90056, 90059, 90061, 90066, 90082, 90094, 90189, 90247–51, 90260–61, 90293, 90301–13, 90397–98, 90504, 90506

* * *

THIRTY-SIXTH DISTRICT

JANE HARMAN, Democrat, of Venice, CA; born in New York, NY, June 28, 1945; education: University High School, Los Angeles, CA, 1962; B.A., Smith College, Northampton, MA, 1966; J.D., Harvard University Law School, Cambridge, MA, 1969; professional: attorney; admitted to the District of Columbia Bar, 1969; counsel for Jones, Day, Reavis and Pogue (law firm); Director and General Counsel for Harman International Industries; Special Counsel, Department of Defense, 1979; Regents' Professor at UCLA, 1999; organizations: L.A. County High Technology Committee; South Bay Alliance for Choice; Center for National Policy; International Human Rights Law Group; member of the Visiting Committee of the John F. Kennedy School of Government, Harvard University; National Commission on Terrorism; family: married to Sidney Harman, 1980; children: Brian Lakes Frank, Hilary Lakes Frank, Daniel Geier Harman, and Justine Leigh Harman; elected to the 103rd, 104th, and 105th Congresses; candidate for Governor of California, 1998; committees: Homeland Security; ranking member, Permanent Select Committee on Intelligence; elected to the 107th Congress on November 7, 2000; reelected to each succeeding Congress.

Office Listings
http://www.house.gov/harman

2400 Rayburn House Office Building, Washington, DC 20515 .... (202) 225–8220
  Chief of Staff.—John Hess.   FAX: 226–7290
  Legislative Director.—Eric Edwards.
  Scheduler.—Jessie Grant.
2321 East Rosecrans Boulevard, Suite 3270, El Segundo, CA 90245 .... (310) 643–3636
544 North Avalon Boulevard, Suite 307, Wilmington, CA 90744 .... (310) 549–8282

Counties: LOS ANGELES COUNTY (part). CITIES: El Segundo, Harbor City, Hermosa Beach, Lawndale, Lennox, Los Angeles, Manhattan Beach, Marina Del Rey, Playa Del Rey, Redondo Beach, San Pedro, Torrance, Venice, Westchester, West Carson, and Wilmington. Population (2000), 639,087.

ZIP Codes: 90009, 90025, 90034, 90039, 90045, 90064, 90066, 90080, 90245, 90248, 90254, 90266–67, 90277–78, 90291–92, 90294–96, 90304, 90404–05, 90501–10, 90710, 90717, 90731–34, 90744, 90748

* * *

THIRTY-SEVENTH DISTRICT

JUANITA MILLENDER-McDONALD, Democrat, of Carson, CA; born in Birmingham, AL, September 7, 1938; education: graduated from University of Redlands, CA; graduate work at California State University–Long Beach and University of Southern California; professional:

teacher, director of gender equity programs; coordinator of Career Education, Los Angeles Unified School District; member, California State Assembly, 1992–96, serving as California's representative, Education Commission of the States (executive committee), and vice chair, Commerce Committee, National Conference of State Legislatures; first woman chair, Assembly Revenue and Taxation Committee, 1995–96; first woman chair, Assembly Insurance Committee, 1994; first woman vice chair, Assembly Governmental Organization Committee, 1993; mayor pro tempore, Carson City Council, 1991–92; member, Carson City Council, 1990; life member, NAACP; member, Alpha Kappa Alpha Sorority; board of directors, Southern California SCLC; board of trustees, Second Baptist Church; serves on the National Commission on Teaching and America's Future; married since 1955 to James McDonald, Jr.; children: Valerie, Angela, Sherryll, and Keith; committees: ranking member, House Administration; Small Business; Transportation and Infrastructure; Joint Committee on the Library of Congress; ranking member, Joint Committee on Printing; elected to the 104th Congress in a special election; reelected to each succeeding Congress.

Office Listings

http://www.house.gov/millender-mcdonald

2445 Rayburn House Office Building, Washington, DC 20515	(202) 225–7924
Chief of Staff.—Shirley Cooks.	FAX: 225–7926
Legislative Director.—John Young.	
Press Secretary.—Craig Rassmussen.	
970 West 190th Street, East Tower, Suite 900, Torrance, CA 90502	(310) 538–1190

Counties: LOS ANGELES COUNTY (part). CITIES: Carson, Compton, and Long Beach. Population (2000), 639,088.

ZIP Codes: 90002–03, 90044, 90059, 90061, 90220–24, 90247, 90501–02, 90713, 90723, 90745–47, 90749, 90755, 90801–10, 90813–15, 90822, 90842, 90844–48, 90888, 90899

* * *

THIRTY-EIGHTH DISTRICT

GRACE F. NAPOLITANO, Democrat, of Los Angeles, CA; born in Brownsville, TX, December 4, 1936; maiden name: Flores; education: Brownsville High School, Brownsville, TX; Cerritos College; Southmost College; professional: Transportation Coordinator, Ford Motor Company; elected to Norwalk, CA, City Council, 1986; became mayor of Norwalk, CA, 1989; elected to the California Assembly, 58th District, 1992–98; married: Frank Napolitano; children: Yolanda Dyer, Fred Musquiz, Edward Musquiz, Michael Musquiz, and Cynthia Dowling; organizations: Norwalk Lions Club; Veterans of Foreign Wars (auxiliary); American Legion (auxiliary); Soroptimist International; past director, Cerritos College Foundation; director, Community Family Guidance Center; League of United Latin American Citizens; director, Los Angeles County Sanitation District; director, Los Angeles County Vector Control (Southeast District); director, Southeast Los Angeles Private Industry Council; director, Los Angeles County Sheriff's Authority; National Women's Political Caucus; past national board secretary, United States-Mexico Sister Cities Association; chair, Hispanic Caucus; co-chair, Mental Health Caucus; committees: International Relations; Resources; subcommittees: Energy and Mineral Resources; Europe and Emerging Threats; Water and Power; Western Hemisphere; elected to the 106th Congress; reelected to each succeeding Congress.

Office Listings

http://www.house.gov/napolitano

1609 Longworth House Office Building, Washington, DC 20515	(202) 225–5256
Chief of Staff.—Kate Krause.	FAX: 225–0027
Legislative Director.—Daniel Chao.	
Press Secretary.—Joel Eskovitz.	
Scheduler.—Jennifer Silva.	
11627 East Telegraph Road, Suite 100, Santa Fe Springs, CA 90670	(562) 801–2134
District Director.—Raymond Cordova.	

Counties: LOS ANGELES COUNTY (part). Population (2000), 639,088.

ZIP Codes: 90601, 90605–06, 90640, 90650–52, 90659–62, 90665, 90670, 90703, 90731, 90806, 91715–16, 91744–47, 91766–70, 91789–90, 91792, 91795

THIRTY-NINTH DISTRICT

LINDA T. SÁNCHEZ, Democrat, of Lakewood, CA; born in Orange, CA, January 28, 1969; education: B.A., University of California, Berkeley; J.D., U.C.L.A. Law School; passed bar exam in 1995; professional: attorney; she has practiced in the areas of appellate, civil rights, and employment law; International Brotherhood of Electrical Workers Local 441; National Electrical Contractors Association; and Orange County Central Labor Council Executive Secretary, AFL–CIO; organizations: National Women's Political Caucus; Women in Leadership; religion: Catholic; committees: Government Reform; Judiciary; Small Business; elected to the 108th Congress on November 5, 2002; reelected to each succeeding Congress.

Office Listings
http://www.house.gov/lindasanchez

1007 Longworth House Office Building, Washington, DC 20515 .... (202) 225–6676
Chief of Staff.—Janice Morris. FAX: 226–1012
Legislative Director.—Virginia Mosqueda.
Deputy Chief of Staff / Communications Director.—Betsy Arnold.
Scheduler.—Ruth Carnegie.
4007 Paramount Boulevard, Suite 106, Lakewood, CA 90712 .... (562) 429–8499
District Director.—Bill Grady.

Counties: LOS ANGELES COUNTY (part). Population (2000), 639,088.

ZIP Codes: 90001–02, 90059, 90255, 90262, 90280, 90601–06, 90608–10, 90637–39, 90670, 90701–03, 90706, 90711–16, 90723, 90805, 90807–08

* * *

FORTIETH DISTRICT

EDWARD R. ROYCE, Republican, of Fullerton, CA; born in Los Angeles, CA, October 12, 1951; education: B.A., California State University, Fullerton, 1977; professional: small business owner; controller; corporate tax manager; California State Senate, 1982–92; member: Fullerton Chamber of Commerce; board member, Literacy Volunteers of America; California Interscholastic Athletic Foundation board of advisers; married: Marie Therese Porter, 1985; committees: Financial Services; International Relations; subcommittees: vice-chairman, Africa, Global Human Rights and International Operations; Capital Markets, Insurance and Government Sponsored Enterprises; Financial Institutions and Consumer Credit; chairman, International Terrorism and Non-Proliferation; Oversight and Investigations; elected on November 3, 1992 to the 103rd Congress; reelected to each succeeding Congress.

Office Listings
http://www.royce.house.gov

2202 Rayburn House Office Building, Washington, DC 20515 .... (202) 225–4111
Chief of Staff / Legislative Director.—Amy Porter. FAX: 226–0335
Press Secretary.—Julianne Smith.
305 North Harbor Boulevard, Suite 300, Fullerton, CA 92832 .... (714) 992–8081
District Director.—Sara Carmack.

Counties: ORANGE COUNTY. The north and west part including the cities of Anaheim, Buena Park, Cypress, Fullerton, Garden Grove, La Palma, Los Alamitos, Orange, Placentia, Rossmoor, Stanton, Villa Park, and Westminster. Population (2000), 639,088.

ZIP Codes: 90620–24, 90630–31, 90638, 90680, 90720–21, 90740, 90808, 92647, 92683–84, 92705–06, 92801–02, 92804–07, 92821, 92831–38, 92840–41, 92844–46, 92856–57, 92859, 92861, 92863, 92865–71

* * *

FORTY-FIRST DISTRICT

JERRY LEWIS, Republican, of Redlands, CA; born in Seattle, WA, October 21, 1934; education: graduated, San Bernardino High School, 1952; B.A., UCLA, 1956; graduate intern in public affairs, Coro Foundation; life underwriter; former member, San Bernardino School Board; served in California State Assembly, 1968–78; insurance executive, 1959–78; married to Arlene Willis; seven children; committees: chairman, Appropriations; elected to the 96th Congress, November 7, 1978; reelected to each succeeding Congress.

Office Listings

http://www.house.gov/jerrylewis

2112 Rayburn House Office Building, Washington, DC 20515	(202) 225–5861
Administrative Assistant.—Arlene Willis.	FAX: 225–6498
Associate Staff / Appropriations Committee.—Carl Kime.	
Deputy Chief of Staff / Communications Director.—Jim Specht.	
1150 Brookside Avenue, No. J5, Redlands, CA 92373	(909) 862–6030
District Representative.—Corrine Spears.	

Counties: RIVERSIDE (part), SAN BERNARDINO (part). CITIES AND TOWNSHIPS: Adelanto, Amboy, Angelus Oaks, Apple Valley, Argus, Arrowbear Lake, Banning, Beaumont, Big Bear City, Big Bear Lake, Blue Jay, Bryn Mawr, Big River, Cabazon, Cadiz, Calimesa, Cedar Glen, Cedar Pines Park, Cherry Valley, Cima, Colton, Crestline, Crest Park, Daggett, Desert Hot Springs, Earp, East Highlands, Essex, Fawnskin, Forest Falls, Grand Terrace, Green Valley Lake, Havasu Lake, Hesperia, Highland, Joshua Tree, Kelso, Lake Arrowhead, Landers, Loma Linda, Lucerne Valley, Ludlow, Mentone, Morongo Valley, Mountain Pass, Needles, Newberry Springs, Nipton, Oro Grande, Parker Dam, Redlands, Rim Forest, Running Springs, San Bernardino, San Jacinto, Sky Forest, Spring Valley Lake, Sugarloaf, Twentynine Palms, Twin Peaks, Valle Vista, Vidal, Yucaipa, and Yucca Valley. Population (2000), 639,088.

ZIP Codes: 92220, 92223, 92230, 92240–42, 92252, 92256, 92258, 92267–68, 92277–78, 92280, 92282, 92284–86, 92304–05, 92307–08, 92311, 92313–15, 92317–18, 92320–27, 92332–33, 92338–42, 92345–46, 92350, 92352, 92354, 92356–57, 92359, 92363–66, 92368–69, 92371, 92373–75, 92378, 92382, 92385–86, 92391–92, 92399, 92404–05, 92407–08, 92410, 92424, 92427, 92544, 92555, 92557, 92581–83

* * *

FORTY-SECOND DISTRICT

GARY G. MILLER, Republican, of Diamond Bar, CA; born in Huntsville, AR, October 16, 1948; education: Loma Vista Elementary School, Whittier, CA; California High School, Whittier, CA; Lowell High School, LaHabra, CA; Mount San Antonio College, Walnut, CA; military service: private, U.S. Army, 1967; professional: developer; owner, G. Miller Development Company; public service: Diamond Bar, CA, City Council, 1989–95; Mayor, 1992; California State Assembly, 1995–98; married: Cathy Miller; children: Brian, Elizabeth, Loren, and Matthew; committees: Financial Services; Transportation and Infrastructure; elected to the 106th Congress; reelected to each succeeding Congress.

Office Listings

http://www.house.gov/garymiller

1037 Longworth House Office Building, Washington, DC 20515	(202) 225–3201
Chief of Staff.—John Rothrock.	FAX: 226–6962
Legislative Director.—Lesli McCollum.	
Executive Director.—Kevin McKee.	
1800 East Lambert Road, Suite 150, Brea, CA 92821	(714) 257–1142
District Director.—Steven Thornton.	

Counties: LOS ANGELES (part), ORANGE (part), and SAN BERNARDINO (part). CITIES AND TOWNSHIPS: Anaheim, Brea, Chino, Chino Hills, Diamond Bar, La Habra, La Habra Heights, Las Flores, Mission Viejo, Placentia, Rancho Santa Margarita, Rowland Heights, Yorba Linda and Whittier. Population (2000), 639,088.

ZIP Codes: 90601–05, 90607, 90631–33, 91708–10, 91729, 91743, 91748, 91758, 91765, 92676, 92679, 92688, 92691–92, 92807–08, 92821–23, 92833, 92885–87

* * *

FORTY-THIRD DISTRICT

JOE BACA, Democrat, of San Bernardino County, CA; born in Belen, NM, January 23, 1947; education: graduated from California State University, Los Angeles, with a bachelor's degree in Sociology; professional: GTE Corp. (community relations); Interstate World Travel (owner); military service: Army; public service: elected to the California State Assembly, 1992, and served as Assistant Speaker Pro Tempore, and the Speaker's Federal Government Liaison, 1997–1998; elected to the California State Senate, 1998; awards: American Legion California Legislator of the Year; VFW Outstanding Legislator; League of Women Voters Citizen of Distinction; San Bernardino Kiwanis Club Kiwanian of the Year; Boy Scouts of America Distinguished Citizen; 2004 National Farmers Union Presidential Award; U.S. Department of Agriculture Coalition of Minority Employees Award of Excellence; Democratic Caucus Task Force on Homeland Security; vice chair, Democratic Caucus Task Force on Immigration; first vice chair, Congressional Hispanic Caucus; co-chair, Congressional Sex and Violence in the

Media Caucus; House Army Caucus; Congressional Diabetes Caucus; Cancer Caucus; Military/Veterans Caucus and U.S.-Mexico Caucus; married: Barbara; four children: Joe Jr., Jeremy, Natalie, and Jennifer; committees: Agriculture; Financial Services; subcommittees: Capital Markets, Insurance, and Government Sponsored Enterprises; Departmental Operations, Oversight, Nutrition and Forestry; Financial Institutions and Consumer Credit; Water and Power; elected to the 106th Congress on November 16, 1999, by special election; reelected to each succeeding Congress.

Office Listings

328 Cannon House Office Building, Washington, DC 20515	(202) 225–6161
Chief of Staff.—Linda Macias.	FAX: 225–8671
Executive Assistant.—Erica Woodward.	
Press Secretary.—Joanne Peters.	
201 North E Street, Suite 102, San Bernardino, CA 92401	(909) 885–2222
District Director.—Mike Trujillo.	

Counties: SAN BERNARDINO COUNTY (part). CITIES: Colton, Fontana, Ontario, Redlands, Rialto, and San Bernardino. Population (2000), 639,087.

ZIP Codes: 91758, 91761–62, 91764, 92316, 92324, 92334–37, 92346, 92376–77, 92401–08, 92410–13, 92415, 92418, 92423

* * *

FORTY-FOURTH DISTRICT

KEN CALVERT, Republican, of Corona, CA; born in Corona, June 8, 1953; education: Chaffey College (CA), A.A., 1973; San Diego State University, B.A. in economics, 1975; professional: congressional aide to Rep. Victor V. Veysey, CA; general manager, Jolly Fox Restaurant, Corona, 1975–79; Marcus W. Meairs Co., Corona, 1979–81; president and general manager, Ken Calvert Real Properties, 1981–92; County Youth Chairman, Rep. Veysey's District, 1970, then 43rd District, 1972; Corona/Norco Youth Chairman for Nixon, 1968 and 1972; Reagan-Bush campaign worker, 1980; co-chair, Wilson for Senate Campaign, 1982; Riverside Republican Party, chairman, 1984–88; co-chairman, George Deukmejian election, 1978, 1982 and 1986; co-chairman, George Bush election, 1988; co-chairman, Pete Wilson Senate elections, 1982 and 1988; co-chairman, Pete Wilson for Governor election, 1990; member: Riverside County Republican Winners Circle, charter member; Corona/Norco Republican Assembly, former vice president; Lincoln Club of Riverside County, chairman and charter member, 1986–90; Corona Rotary Club, president, 1991; Corona Elks; Navy League of Corona/Norco; Corona Chamber of Commerce, past president, 1990; Norco Chamber of Commerce; County of Riverside Asset Leasing, past chairman; Corona/Norco Board of Realtors; Monday Morning Group; Corona Group, past chairman; Economic Development Partnership, executive board; Corona Community Hospital Corporate 200 Club; Silver Eagles (March AFB Support Group), charter member; Corona Airport Advisory Commission; Generic Drug Equity Caucus, co-chair; Caucus to Fight and Control Methamphetamine, co-chair; Manufactured Housing Caucus, co-chair; Defense Study Group; Hellenic Caucus; Fire Caucus; National Guard & Reserve Caucus; Human Rights Caucus; Baltic Caucus; Travel and Tourism Caucus; Coalition for Autism Research and Education; Diabetes Caucus; Missing and Exploited Children's Caucus; Zero Capital Gains Tax Caucus; Medical Technology Caucus; Law Enforcement Caucus; Correctional Officers Caucus; Western Caucus; Sportsman's Caucus; Native American Caucus; Coastal Caucus; committees: Armed Services; Resources; Science; subcommittees: chairman, Water and Power; elected on November 3, 1992 to the 103rd Congress; reelected to each succeeding Congress.

Office Listings

http://www.house.gov/calvert

2201 Rayburn House Office Building, Washington, DC 20515	(202) 225–1986
Chief of Staff.—Dave Ramey.	FAX: 225–2004
Legislative Director.—Maria Bowie.	
Press Secretary.—Bob Carretta.	
District Manager.—Linda Fisher.	
3400 Central Avenue, Suite 200, Riverside, CA 92506	(951) 784–4300

Counties: ORANGE COUNTY (part). CITIES AND TOWNSHIPS: Coto d' Casa, Ledera Ranch, Margarita, Rancho Santa, San Clemente, San Juan Capistrano. RIVERSIDE COUNTY (part). CITIES AND TOWNSHIPS: Corona, March AFB, Mira Loma, Norco, Perris, and Riverside. Population (2000), 639,088.

ZIP Codes: 92501–09, 92513–18, 92521–22, 92532, 92557, 92570, 92596, 92672–75, 92679, 92694, 92860, 92879–83

FORTY-FIFTH DISTRICT

MARY BONO, Republican, of Palm Springs, CA; born in Cleveland, OH, October 24, 1961; daughter of Clay Whitaker, retired physician and surgeon, and Karen, retired chemist; Bachelor of Fine Arts in Art History, University of Southern California, 1984; Woman of the Year, 1993, San Gorgonio Chapter of the Girl Scouts of America for her assistance to victims of a tragic Girl Scout bus crash in Palm Springs; board member: Palm Springs International Film Festival; first lady of Palm Springs and active in a wide range of community charities and service organizations; leadership role in support of the D.A.R.E. program, Olive Crest Home for Abused Children, Tiempos de Los Ninos; certified personal fitness instructor in martial arts (Karate, Tae Kwan Do); accomplished gymnast with Gymnastics Olympica; appointed chair, Congressional Salton Sea Task Force; married Sonny Bono, 1986; two children: Chesare Elan and Chianna Maria; committees: Energy and Commerce; subcommittees: Commerce, Trade and Consumer Protection; Energy and Air Quality; Environment and Hazardous Materials; Health; elected by special election on April 7, 1998 to the 105th Congress, to fill the vacancy caused by the death of her husband Rep. Sonny Bono; reelected to each succeeding Congress.

Office Listings
http://www.house.gov/bono

405 Cannon House Office Building, Washington, DC 20515	(202) 225–5330
Chief of Staff.—Frank Cullen.	FAX: 225–2961
Legislative Director.—Linda Valter.	
Communications Director.—Kimberly Pencille.	
Scheduler / Executive Assistant.—Katie Angliss.	
707 East Tahquitz Canyon Way, Suite 9, Palm Springs, CA 92262	(760) 320–1076
District Director.—Marc Troast.	
1600 E. Florida Avenue, Suite 301, Hemet, CA 92544	(951) 658–2312

Counties: RIVERSIDE COUNTY (part). CITIES AND TOWNSHIPS: Bermuda Dunes, Blythe, Cathedral City, Coachella, East Blythe, East Hemet, Hemet, Idyllwild-Pine, Indian Wells, Indio, La Quinta, Mecca, Moreno Valley, Murrieta, Palm Desert, Palm Springs, Rancho Mirage, Thousand Palms, and Winchester. Population (2000), 639,088.

ZIP Codes: 92201, 92203, 92210–11, 92220, 92225–26, 92234–36, 92239–41, 92253–55, 92260–64, 92270, 92274, 92276, 92282, 92536, 92539, 92543–46, 92548–49, 92551–57, 92561–64, 92567, 92571, 92584–86, 92590–92, 92595–96

* * *

FORTY-SIXTH DISTRICT

DANA ROHRABACHER, Republican, of Huntington Beach, CA; born in Coronado, CA, June 21, 1947; education: graduated Palos Verdes High School, CA, 1965; attended Los Angeles Harbor College, Wilmington, CA, 1965–67; B.A., Long Beach State College, CA, 1969; M.A., University of Southern California, Los Angeles, 1975; writer/journalist; speechwriter and special assistant to the President, The White House, Washington, D.C., 1981–88; assistant press secretary, Reagan/Bush Committee, 1980; reporter, City News Service/Radio News West, and editorial writer, *Orange County Register*, 1972–80; committees: International Relations; Science; subcommittees: Asia and the Pacific; chairman, Oversight and Investigations; Research; Space and Aeronautics; elected on November 8, 1988, to the 101st Congress; reelected to each succeeding Congress.

Office Listings
http://www.house.gov/rohrabacher

2338 Rayburn House Office Building, Washington, DC 20515	(202) 225–2415
Chief of Staff/Legislative Director.—Richard T. (Rick) Dykema.	FAX: 225–0145
Communications Director.—Rebecca Rudman.	
101 Main Street, Suite 380, Huntington Beach, CA 92648	(714) 960–6483
District Director.—Kathleen M. Hollingsworth.	

Counties: ORANGE COUNTY (part). Communities of Fountain Valley, Huntington Beach, Costa Mesa, Westminster, Seal Beach, Santa Ana, Midway City, Garden Grove, Newport Beach, Sunset Beach, Surfside. LOS ANGELES COUNTY (part). COMMUNITIES OF: Avalon, Long Beach, Palos Verdes, Palos Verdes Estates, Rancho Palos Verdes, Rolling Hills, Rolling Hills Estates, and San Pedro. Population (2000), 639,088.

ZIP Codes: 90274–75, 90704, 90731–32, 90740, 90742–44, 90802–04, 90808, 90813–15, 90822, 90831–35, 90840, 90853, 92626–28, 92646–49, 92655, 92683, 92702, 92708, 92711–12, 92725, 92735, 92799, 92841, 92843–44

42 *Congressional Directory* CALIFORNIA

FORTY-SEVENTH DISTRICT

LORETTA SANCHEZ, Democrat, of Anaheim, CA; born in Lynwood, CA, January 7, 1960; education: graduate of Chapman University; M.B.A., American University; specializes in assisting public agencies with finance matters; member, Blue Dog Coalition; Law Enforcement Caucus; Congressional Women's, and Hispanic Caucuses; married: Steven Brixey; committees: Armed Services; Homeland Security; Joint Economic Committee; elected to the 105th Congress; reelected to each succeeding Congress.

Office Listings
http://www.house.gov/sanchez

1230 Longworth House Office Building, Washington, DC 20515 .... (202) 225-2965
Chief of Staff.—Lee Godown. FAX: 225-5859
Office Director.—Carrie Brooks.
Legislative Director.—Edward Steiner.
Legislative Assistants: Chris Beck, Ann Norris.
12397 Lewis Street, Suite 101, Garden Grove, CA 92840 .... (714) 621-0102
District Director.—Raul Luna.

Counties: ORANGE COUNTY (part). CITIES: Anaheim (west and north-south of the Anaheim Stadium-Disneyland corridor), Fullerton, Garden Grove, Orange, and Santa Ana. Population (2000), 639,087.

ZIP Codes: 90680, 92609, 92616, 92619, 92623, 92650, 92652, 92654, 92658, 92679, 92697–98, 92701–04, 92706–07, 92735, 92781, 92801–02, 92804–05, 92812, 92815–17, 92825, 92832–33, 92840–41, 92843–44, 92850, 92868

* * *

FORTY-EIGHTH DISTRICT

CHRISTOPHER COX, Republican, of Newport Beach, CA; born in St. Paul, Ramsey County, MN, October 16, 1952; education: graduated, St. Thomas Academy, St. Paul, 1970; B.A., University of Southern California, Los Angeles, 1973; J.D., Harvard Law School, Cambridge, MA, 1977; M.B.A., Harvard Business School, Boston, MA, 1977; attorney; admitted to the California bar in 1978 and commenced practice in Los Angeles; law clerk, U.S. Court of Appeals, San Francisco, CA, and Honolulu, HI, 1977–78; associate, Latham and Watkins, Newport Beach, CA, 1978–84; cofounder, Context Corporation, St. Paul, MN, 1984–86; partner, Latham and Watkins, Newport Beach, CA, 1984–86; senior associate counsel to the President, The White House, 1986–88; member: Republican Associates, California Republican Assembly, and Rotary Club of Orange County; married: Rebecca Gernhardt Cox; children: Charles, Kathryn and Kevin; committees: chairman, Homeland Security; elected November 8, 1988, to the 101st Congress; reelected to each succeeding Congress.

Office Listings
http://cox.house.gov   christoper.cox@mail.house.gov

2402 Rayburn House Office Building, Washington, DC 20515 .... (202) 225-5611
Chief of Staff.—Peter Uhlmann. FAX: 225-9177
Scheduler.—Mary Christ.
Office Manager.—Kelly Blundt.
Senior Legislative Assistant.—William Schulz.
One Newport Place, Suite 420, Newport Beach, CA 92660 .... (949) 756-2244
District Representative.—Steven DiGerLando.

Counties: ORANGE COUNTY (part). CITIES: Aliso Viejo, Corona del Mar, Dana Point, Foothill Ranch, Irvine, Laguna Beach, Laguna Hills, Laguna Niguel, Laguna Woods, Lake Forest, Newport Beach, Orange, San Juan Capistrano, Santa Ana, and Tustin. Population (2000), 639,089.

ZIP Codes: 92602–04, 92606–07, 92610, 92612, 92614, 92618, 92620, 92624–25, 92629–30, 92651, 92653, 92656–57, 92660–63, 92674–75, 92677–79, 92690, 92693, 92705, 92780, 92782

* * *

FORTY-NINTH DISTRICT

DARRELL E. ISSA, Republican, of Vista, CA; born in Cleveland, OH, November 1, 1953; education: Siena Heights College; military service: U.S. Army; attended college on an ROTC scholarship; professional: Businessman; founder and CEO of Directed Electronics, Inc.; past Chairman, Consumer Electronics Association; Board of Directors, Electronics Industry

Association; awards: public service: Co-Chairman of the campaign to pass the California Civil Rights Initiative (Proposition 209); Chairman of the Volunteer Committee for the 1996 Republican National Convention; Chairman of the San Diego County Lincoln Club; candidate for the U.S. Senate in 1998; architect of 2003 California recall campaign of former Governor Gray Davis; married: Kathy; children: William; committees: Government Reform; International Relations; Judiciary; elected to the 107th Congress on November 7, 2000; reelected to each succeeding Congress.

Office Listings

http://www.house.gov/issa

211 Cannon House Office Building, Washington, DC 20515 .... (202) 225–3906
    Chief of Staff.—Dale Neugebauer.   FAX: 225–3303
    Legislative Director.—Paige Anderson.
    Press Secretary.—Frederick Hill.
    Scheduler.—Suzy Augustyn.
1800 Thibodo Road, #310, Vista, CA 92081 .... (760) 599–5000

Counties: RIVERSIDE (part), SAN DIEGO (part). Population (2000), 639,087

ZIP Codes: 92003, 92025–28, 92036, 92049, 92051–52, 92054–61, 92065–66, 92068–70, 92081–86, 92088, 92128, 92530, 92532, 92548, 92562–63, 92567, 92570–72, 92584–87, 92589–93, 92595–96, 92599

* * *

FIFTIETH DISTRICT

RANDY (DUKE) CUNNINGHAM, Republican, of Del Mar, CA; born in Los Angeles, CA, December 8, 1941; education: graduated, Shelbina High School, Shelbina, MO; University of Missouri, B.S. in education, 1964, and M.S. in education, 1965; M.B.A., National University, San Diego, CA; dean, School of Aviation and Flight Training, and businessman; coached swim teams at Hinsdale and at the University of Missouri, training 36 All Americans, two Olympic gold and silver medalists; member: Naval Aviation Hall of Fame, 1986–present; Golden Eagles, 1985–present; Miramar Aviation Hall of Fame, 1974–present; American Fighter Aces Association, 1972–present; author of "Fox Two," on his experiences as a naval aviator, and produced "Top Gun—The Story Behind the Story" video about his career as a fighter pilot instructor at Miramar NAS; joined the Navy at the age of 25 and became one of the most highly decorated fighter pilots in the Vietnam War; retired in 1987 with the rank of commander; married: the former Nancy Jones; children: Randall Todd, April, and Carrie; committees: Appropriations; Permanent Select Committee on Intelligence; subcommittees: Defense; Labor, Health and Human Services, Education, and Related Agencies; District of Columbia; elected to the 102nd Congress on November 6, 1990; reelected to each succeeding Congress.

Office Listings

http://www.house.gov/cunningham

2350 Rayburn House Office Building, Washington, DC 20515 .... (202) 225–5452
    Chief of Staff.—Dave Heil.   FAX: 225–2558
    Legislative Director.—Nancy Lifset.
    Executive Assistant.—Susan B. Woodworth.
    Press Secretary.—Harmony Allen.
613 West Valley Parkway, Suite 320, Escondido, CA 92025 .... (760) 737–8438
    District Director.—Nathan Fletcher.

Counties: SAN DIEGO COUNTY (part). Population (2000), 639,087.

ZIP Codes: 92007–09, 92013–14, 92018, 92023–27, 92029–30, 92033, 92037, 92046, 92067, 92069, 92075, 92078–79, 92081–84, 92091, 92096, 92109–11, 92117, 92121–22, 92126–30, 92145, 92172, 92177, 92191, 92196, 92198

* * *

FIFTY-FIRST DISTRICT

BOB FILNER, Democrat, of San Diego, CA; born in Pittsburgh, PA, September 4, 1942; education: B.A., Cornell University, Ithaca, NY, 1963; M.A., University of Delaware, 1969; Ph.D., Cornell University, 1973; professor, San Diego State University, 1970–92; San Diego Board of Education, 1979–83 (president, 1982); San Diego City Council, 1987–92 (deputy mayor, 1990); member: Sierra Club, NAACP, Navy League, Gray Panthers, Economic Conversion Council, Common Cause, ACLU, ADL, NWPC, MAPA; married in 1985 to Jane Merrill Filner; children: Erin and Adam; committees: Transportation and Infrastructure; Veterans' Affairs; subcommittees: Aviation; ranking member, Coast Guard and Maritime Transportation; Health; Railroads; elected on November 3, 1992 to the 103rd Congress; reelected to each succeeding Congress.

Office Listings
http://www.house.gov/filner

2428 Rayburn House Office Building, Washington, DC 20515	(202) 225–8045
Chief of Staff.—Tony Buckles.	FAX: 225–9073
Executive Assistant.—Kim Messineo.	
Legislative Director.—Thaddeus Hoffmeister.	
Senior Legislative Assistant.—Sharon Schultze.	
333 F Street, Suite A, Chula Vista, CA 91910	(619) 422–5963
1101 Airport Road, Suite D, Imperial, CA 92251	(760) 355–8800

Counties: SAN DIEGO COUNTY (part), IMPERIAL COUNTY. CITIES: Brawley, Calexico, Calipatria, Chula Vista, El Centro, Holtville, Imperial, National City, San Diego, San Ysidro, and Westmorland. Population (2000), 639,087.

ZIP Codes: 91902, 91905–06, 91908–15, 91917, 91921, 91934, 91945, 91947, 91950, 91963, 91977, 91980, 92102, 92105, 92113–15, 92136, 92139, 92143, 92149, 92153–54, 92173, 92179, 92222, 92227, 92231–33, 92243–44, 92249–51, 92257, 92259, 92266, 92273–75, 92281, 92283

* * *

FIFTY-SECOND DISTRICT

DUNCAN HUNTER, Republican, of Alpine, CA; born in Riverside, CA, May 31, 1948; education: graduated, Rubidoux High School, 1966; J.D., Western State University, 1976; first lieutenant, U.S. Army Airborne, 1969–71; professional: trial lawyer; admitted to the California bar, 1976; commenced practice in San Diego; member: Baptist Church, Navy League; married: the former Lynne Layh, 1973; children: Duncan Duane and Robert Samuel; committees: chairman, Armed Services; elected to the 97th Congress, November 4, 1980; reelected to each succeeding Congress.

Office Listings
http://www.house.gov/hunter

2265 Rayburn House Office Building, Washington, DC 20515	(202) 225–5672
Administrative Assistant.—Victoria Middleton.	FAX: 225–0235
Office Manager / Appointment Secretary.—Valerie Snesko.	
Press Secretary.—Michael Harrison.	
366 South Pierce Street, El Cajon, CA 92020	(619) 579–3001

Counties: SAN DIEGO COUNTY (part). CITIES AND TOWNSHIPS: Alpine, Barona I.R., Borrego Springs, Boulder Park, Boulevard, Campo, Descanso, Dulzura, El Cajon, Guatay, Indian Res., Jacumba, Jamul, Lakeside, La Mesa, Lemon Grove, Mount Laguna, Pine Valley, Potrero, Poway, Ramona, San Diego, Santee, Spring Valley, Tecate, and Palo Verde. Population (2000), 639,087.

ZIP Codes: 91901, 91903, 91905–06, 91915–17, 91931, 91935, 91941–45, 91948, 91962, 91976–79, 92004, 92019–22, 92025, 92036, 92040, 92064–66, 92071–72, 92074, 92090, 92108, 92111, 92115, 92119–20, 92123–24, 92126, 92128–29, 92131, 92142, 92145, 92150, 92158–60, 92190, 92193–94, 92199

* * *

FIFTY-THIRD DISTRICT

SUSAN A. DAVIS, Democrat, of San Diego, CA; born in Cambridge, MA, April 13, 1944; education: B.S., University of California at Berkeley; M.A., University of North Carolina; public service: served three terms in the California State Assembly; served nine years on the San Diego City School Board; former President of the League of Women Voters of San Diego; awards: California School Boards Association Legislator of the Year; League of Middle Schools Legislator of the Year; family: married to Steve; children: Jeffrey and Benjamin; grandson: Henry; granddaughter: Jane; committees: Armed Services; Education and the Workforce; elected to the 107th Congress on November 7, 2000; reelected to each succeeding Congress.

Office Listings
http://www.house.gov/susandavis

1224 Longworth House Office Building, Washington DC 20515	(202) 225–2040
Chief of Staff.—Lisa Sherman.	FAX: 225–2948
Press Secretary.—Aaron Hunter.	
Scheduler.—Cynthia Patton.	

4305 University Avenue, Suite 515, San Diego, CA 92105 .... (619) 280–5353
District Director.—Todd Gloria.

Counties: SAN DIEGO COUNTY (part). Population (2000), 639,087.

ZIP Codes: 91932–33, 91945–46, 91977, 92037–39, 92092–93, 92101–18, 92120–23, 92132–38, 92140, 92147, 92152, 92155, 92161, 92163–71, 92175–76, 92178, 92182, 92184, 92186–87, 92192, 92195

COLORADO

(Population 2000, 4,301,261)

SENATORS

WAYNE ALLARD, Republican, of Loveland, CO; born in Fort Collins, CO, December 2, 1943; education: graduated, Fort Collins High School, 1963; preveterinary studies, Colorado State University, 1964; Doctor of Veterinary Medicine, Colorado State University, 1968; received veterinarian license in Colorado; Chief Health Officer, Loveland, CO, 1970–78; Larimer County Board of Health, 1978–82; Colorado State Senate, 1982–90; chair, Health and Human Services Committee and majority caucus; member: American Veterinary Medical Association, National Federation of Independent Business, Chamber of Commerce, Loveland Rotary, American Animal Hospital Association, American Board of Veterinary Practitioners, Companion Animal; married: the former Joan Elizabeth Malcolm; children: Christi and Cheryl; Deputy Majority Whip; in February 2001, appointed by Senate Majority Leader Trent Lott to serve on the High Tech Task Force and the National Security Working Group; chairman, Senate Renewable Energy and Energy Efficiency Caucus, and the Veterinary Caucus; elected to the 102nd Congress, November 6, 1990; reelected to each succeeding Congress; committees: Appropriations; Banking, Housing, and Urban Affairs; Budget; subcommittees: chairman, Housing and Transportation; chairman, Strategic Forces; Emerging Threats and Capabilities; Financial Institutions; Fisheries, Wildlife and Water; Readiness and Management Support; Securities and Investment; Superfund and Waste Management; elected to the U.S. Senate on November 6, 1996; reelected to each succeeding Senate term.

Office Listings

http://allard.senate.gov

521 Dirksen Senate Office Building, Washington, DC 20510	(202) 224–5941
Chief of Staff.—Sean Conway.	FAX: 224–6471
Scheduler.—Ali Monroe.	
Press Secretary.—Angela deRocha.	
7340 East Caley, Suite 215, Englewood, CO 80111	(303) 220–7414
5401 Stone Creek Circle, Suite 203, Loveland, CO 80538	(970) 461–3530
111 S. Tejon Street, Suite 300, Colorado Springs, CO 80903	(719) 634–6071
411 Thatcher Building, Fifth and Main Streets, Pueblo, CO 81003	(719) 545–9751
215 Federal Building, 400 Rood Avenue, Grand Junction, CO 81501	(970) 245–9553
954 East Second Avenue, #107, Durango, CO 81301	(970) 375–6311

* * *

KEN SALAZAR, Democrat, of Denver, CO; born in Alamosa, CO, March 2, 1955; education: B.A., Colorado College, Political Science, 1977; J.D., University of Michigan School of Law, 1981; professional: attorney; Sherman & Howard (law firm), 1981–1986; Parcel, Mauro, Hultin & Spaanstra (law firm), 1994–1998; public service: chief legal counsel to Colorado Governor Roy Romer, 1986–1990; executive director, Colorado Department of Natural Resources, 1990–1994; Colorado Attorney General, 1999–2004; married: Hope; children: Melinda and Andrea; committees: Agriculture, Nutrition, and Forestry; Energy and Natural Resources; Veterans' Affairs; elected to the U.S. Senate on November 2, 2004.

Office Listings

http://salazar.senate.gov

702 Hart Senate Office Building, Washington, DC 20510	(202) 224–5852
Chief of Staff.—Ken Lane.	FAX: 228–5036
Deputy Chief of Staff.—Alan Gilbert.	
Press Secretary.—Cody Wertz.	
Executive Assistant.—Joan Padilla.	
2300 15th Street, 4th Floor, Denver, CO 80202	(303) 455–4600
State Director.—Jim Carpenter.	

REPRESENTATIVES

FIRST DISTRICT

DIANA DeGETTE, Democrat, of Denver, CO; born in Tachikowa, Japan, July 29, 1957; education: B.A., political science, *magna cum laude*, The Colorado College, 1979; J.D., New York University School of Law, 1982 (Root Tilden Scholar); professional: attorney with

McDermott, Hansen, and Reilly; Colorado Deputy State Public Defender, Appellate Division, 1982–84; Colorado House of Representatives, 1992–96; board of directors, Planned Parenthood, Rocky Mountain Chapter; member and formerly on board of governors, Colorado Bar Association; member, Colorado Women's Bar Association; past memberships: board of trustees, The Colorado College; Denver Women's Commission; board of directors, Colorado Trial Lawyers Association; former editor, *Trial Talk* magazine; listed in 1994–96 edition of *Who's Who in America*; committees: Energy and Commerce; elected to the 105th Congress; reelected to each succeeding Congress.

Office Listings

1527 Longworth House Office Building, Washington, DC 20515 .... (202) 225–4431
    Chief of Staff.—Lisa B. Cohen.   FAX: 225–5657
    Appointment Secretary.—Michael Carey.
    Press Secretary.—Josh Freed.
600 Grant Street, Suite 202, Denver, CO 80203 .... (303) 844–4988
    District Administrator.—Greg Diamond.

Counties: ADAMS (part), ARAPAHOE (part), DENVER, JEFFERSON (part). Population (2000), 614,465.

ZIP Codes: 80110–11, 80113, 80121, 80123, 80127, 80150–51, 80155, 80201–12, 80214–24, 80226–32, 80235–39, 80243–44, 80246–52, 80255–57, 80259, 80261–62, 80264–66, 80270–71, 80273–75, 80279, 80281, 80285, 80290–95, 80299

* * *

SECOND DISTRICT

MARK UDALL, Democrat, of Boulder, CO; born in Tucson, AR, July 18, 1950; son of Morris "Mo" Udall, U.S. Representative, 1961–91, and candidate for President of the United States, 1976; education: B.A., Williams College, 1972; professional: course director, educator, and executive director, Outward Bound, 1985–95; Colorado State House of Representatives, District 13, 1997–98; married: Maggie Fox; two children; committees: Armed Services; Resources; Science; elected to the 106th Congress; reelected to each succeeding Congress.

Office Listings

http://www.house.gov/markudall

115 Cannon House Office Building, Washington, DC 20515 .... (202) 225–2161
    Chief of Staff.—Alan Salazar.   FAX: 226–7840
    Legislative Director/Senior Legislative Counsel.—Stan Sloss.
    Press Secretary/Legislative Assistant.—Lawrence Pacheco.
    Scheduler.—Lisa Carpenter.
8601 Turnpike Drive, Suite 206, Westminster, CO 80031 .... (303) 650–7820
291 Main Street, P.O. Box 325, Minturn, CO 81645 .... (970) 827–4154

Counties: ADAMS (part), BOULDER (part), BROOMFIELD, CLEAR CREEK, EAGLE, GILPIN, GRAND, JEFFERSON (part), SUMMIT, WELD (part). Population (2000), 614,465.

ZIP Codes: 80003, 80005, 80007, 80020–21, 80025–28, 80030–31, 80035–36, 80038, 80212, 80221, 80229, 80233–34, 80241, 80260, 80263, 80301–10, 80314, 80321–23, 80328–29, 80403, 80422–24, 80426–28, 80435–36, 80438–39, 80442–44, 80446–47, 80451–52, 80455, 80459, 80463, 80466, 80468, 80471, 80474, 80476–78, 80481–82, 80497–98, 80503–04, 80510, 80514, 80516, 80520, 80530, 80540, 80544, 80602, 80614, 80640, 81620–21, 81623, 81631–32, 81637, 81645, 81649, 81655, 81657–58

* * *

THIRD DISTRICT

JOHN SALAZAR, Democrat, of Manassas, CO; born in Alamosa, CO, July 21, 1953; education: B.S., Adams State College, Alamosa, CO, 1981; graduated from the Colorado Agricultural Leadership Forum, 1992; professional: served in the U.S. Army, 1973–1976; farmer; rancher; business owner; public service: Governor's Economic Development Advisory Board; the state Agricultural Commission; board of directors of the Rio Grande Water Conservation District; board of directors of the Colorado Agricultural Leadership Forum; Colorado Agricultural Commission, 1999–2002; Colorado state House of Representatives, 2003–2004; married: Mary Lou Salazar; children: Jesus, Esteban, and Miguel; committees: Agriculture; Transportation and Infrastructure; elected to the 109th Congress on November 2, 2004.

Office Listings
http://www.house.gov/salazar

1531 Longworth House Office Building, Washington, DC 20515 .... (202) 225–4761
Chief of Staff.—Ronnie Carleton.   FAX: 226–9669
Legislative Director.—Laura Marquez.
Special Assistant.—Brian Ross.
134 West B Street, Pueblo, CO 81003 .... (719) 543–8200
225 North 5th Street, Suite 702, Grand Junction, CO 81501 .... (970) 245–7107

Counties: ALAMOSA, ARCHULETA, CONEJOS, COSTILLA, CUSTER, DELTA, DOLORES, GARFIELD, GUNNISON, HINSDALE, HUERFANO, JACKSON, LA PLATA, LAS ANIMAS, MESA, MINERAL, MOFFAT, MONTEZUMA, MONTROSE, OTERO (part), OURAY, PITKIN, PUEBLO, RIO BLANCO, RIO GRANDE, ROUTT, SAGUACHE, SAN JUAN, SAN MIGUEL. Population (2000), 614,467.

ZIP Codes: 80423–24, 80428, 80430, 80434–35, 80443, 80446–47, 80456, 80459, 80463, 80467, 80469, 80473, 80479–80, 80483, 80487–88, 80498, 81001–12, 81019–20, 81022–25, 81027, 81029, 81033, 81039–41, 81043–44, 81046, 81049–50, 81054–55, 81058–59, 81062, 81064, 81067, 81069, 81077, 81081–82, 81089, 81091, 81101–02, 81120–38, 81140–41, 81143–44, 81146–49, 81151–55, 81157, 81201, 81210–12, 81215, 81220–26, 81228, 81230–33, 81235–37, 81239–41, 81243, 81248, 81251–53, 81301–03, 81320–21, 81323–32, 81334–35, 81401–02, 81410–11, 81413–16, 81418–20, 81422–35, 81501–06, 81520–27, 81601–02, 81610–12, 81615, 81621, 81623–26, 81630, 81633, 81635–36, 81638–43, 81646–48, 81650, 81652–56

* * *

FOURTH DISTRICT

MARILYN N. MUSGRAVE, Republican, of Fort Morgan, CO; born, January 27, 1949; raised in Weld County, CO; education: graduated, Eaton High School, and Colorado State University; professional: school teacher; businesswoman (agricultural business); public service: Fort Morgan School Board; State House of Representatives, and State Senate; elected State Senate Republican Caucus Chairman; religion: First Assembly of God Church; married: Steve Musgrave; four children; committees: Agriculture; Education and the Workforce; Resources; Small Business; subcommittees: Education Reform; Employer-Employee Relations; Fisheries and Oceans; General Farm Commodities and Risk Management; National Parks; Rural Enterprises, Agriculture, and Technology; chair, Workforce, Empowerment, and Government Programs; elected to the 108th Congress on November 5, 2002; reelected to each succeeding Congress.

Office Listings
http://www.house.gov/musgrave

1507 Longworth House Office Building, Washington, DC 20515 .... (202) 225–4676
Chief of Staff.—Guy Short.   FAX: 225–5870
Senior Legislative Analyst.—Nina Schmidgall.
Press Secretary.—Aaron Johnson.
Office Manager / Executive Assistant.—Jessica Rager.
5401 Stone Creek Circle, #204, Loveland, CO 80538 .... (970) 663–3536
705 South Division Avenue, Sterling, CO 80751 .... (970) 522–1788
109½ South 3rd Street, Sterling, CO 81054 .... (970) 522–1788

Counties: BACA, BOULDER (part), CHEYENNE, CROWLEY, KENT, KIOWA, KIT CARSON, LARIMER, LINCOLN, LOGAN, MORGAN, PHILLIPS, PROWERS, OTERO (part), SEDGEWICK, WASHINGTON, WELD (part), YUMA. Population (2000), 614,466.

ZIP Codes: 80501–04, 80510–13, 80515, 80517, 80521–28, 80530, 80532–43, 80545–47, 80549–51, 80553, 80603, 80610–12, 80615, 80620–24, 80631–34, 80638–39, 80642–46, 80648–54, 80701, 80705, 80720–23, 80726–29, 80731–37, 80740–47, 80749–51, 80754–55, 80757–59, 80801–02, 80804–05, 80807, 80810, 80812, 80815, 80818, 80821–26, 80828, 80830, 80832–34, 80836, 80861–62, 81021, 81024, 81027, 81029–30, 81033–34, 81036, 81038, 81041, 81043–47, 81049–50, 81052, 81054, 81057, 81059, 81062–64, 81071, 81073, 81076, 81084, 81087, 81090, 81092

* * *

FIFTH DISTRICT

JOEL HEFLEY, Republican, of Colorado Springs, CO; born in Ardmore, OK, April 18, 1935; education: graduated, Classen High School, Oklahoma City, OK, 1953; B.A., Oklahoma Baptist University, Shawnee, 1957; M.A., Oklahoma State University, Stillwater, 1962; Gates Fellow, Harvard University, Cambridge, MA, 1984; management consultant; executive director, Community Planning and Research Council, 1966–86; Colorado State House of Representatives, 1977–78; Colorado State Senate, 1979–86; assistant minority whip, 1989–94; married: the former Lynn Christian, 1961; children: Janna, Lori, and Juli; committees: Armed Services; elected to the 100th Congress on November 4, 1986; reelected to each succeeding Congress.

Office Listings

2372 Rayburn House Office Building, Washington, DC 20515 .... (202) 225–4422
    Scheduler.—Erin Sanford.   FAX: 225–1942
104 South Cascade Avenue, Suite 105, Colorado Springs, CO 80903 .... (719) 520–0055
    Chief of Staff.—Loren Whittlemore.

Counties: CHAFFEE, EL PASO, FREMONT, LAKE, PARK (part), TELLER. Population (2000), 614,467.

ZIP Codes: 80104, 80106, 80132–33, 80135, 80420, 80432, 80438, 80440, 80443, 80448–49, 80456, 80461, 80475, 80808–
    09, 80813–14, 80816–17, 80819–20, 80827, 80829–33, 80835, 80840–41, 80860, 80863–64, 80866, 80901, 80903–
    22, 80925–26, 80928–37, 80940–47, 80949–50, 80960, 80962, 80970, 80977, 80995, 80997, 81008, 81154, 81201,
    81211–12, 81221, 81223, 81226–28, 81233, 81236, 81240–42, 81244, 81251, 81253

* * *

SIXTH DISTRICT

THOMAS G. TANCREDO, Republican, of Littleton, CO; born in North Denver, CO, December 20, 1945; education: graduated, Holy Family High School, 1964; B.A., University of North Colorado, 1968; elected to the Colorado State Legislature in 1976, and served until 1982; appointed, Secretary of Education's Regional Representative, served from 1982 to 1992, during the Reagan and Bush administrations; in 1993, accepted presidency of the Independence Institute, a public policy research organization in Golden, CO; Christian; married: Jackie; children: Ray and Randy; committees: International Relations; Resources; elected to the 106th Congress; reelected to each succeeding Congress.

Office Listings

http://www.house.gov/tancredo   tom.tancredo@mail.house.gov

1130 Longworth House Office Building, Washington, DC 20515 .... (202) 225–7882
    Chief of Staff.—Jacque Ponder.   FAX: 226–4623
    Legislative Director.—Mac Zimmerman.
    Scheduler.—Rachel Hayes.
6099 S. Quebec Street, #200, Centennial, CO 80111 .... (720) 283–9772
1800 West Littleton Boulevard, Littleton, CO 80120 .... (720) 283–7575
240 Wilcox Street, Suite 111, Castle Rock, CO 80104 .... (303) 688–3430

Counties: ARAPAHOE (part), DOUGLAS, ELBERT, JEFFERSON (part), PARK (part). Population (2000), 614,466.

ZIP Codes: 80013–16, 80018, 80046, 80101–09, 80111–12, 80116–18, 80120–31, 80134–38, 80160–63, 80165–66, 80225,
    80231, 80235–36, 80247, 80401, 80403, 80421, 80425, 80433, 80437, 80439, 80453–54, 80457, 80465, 80470, 80808,
    80828, 80830–33, 80835

* * *

SEVENTH DISTRICT

BOB BEAUPREZ, Republican, of Arvada, CO; born in Lafayette, CO, September 22, 1948; education: graduated, University of Colorado, 1970, with a B.S. degree in Education; professional: dairy farmer; Chairman and CEO, Heritage Bank; community service: Colorado Republican Party; serving as a Precinct Committeeman, Chairman of a Congressional District, County Chairman, and State Chairman (1999–2002); married: Claudia; four children; committees: Ways and Means; subcommittees: Human Resources; Oversight; elected to the 108th Congress on November 5, 2002; reelected to each succeeding Congress.

Office Listings

http://www.house.gov/beauprez

504 Cannon House Office Building, Washington, DC 20515 .... (202) 225–2645
    Chief of Staff.—Sean Murphy.   FAX: 225–5278
    Legislative Director.—Marc Scheessele.
    Scheduler.—Jean Carbutt.
4251 Kipling Street, Suite 370, Wheat Ridge, CO 80033 .... (303) 940–5821

Counties: ADAMS (part), ARAPAHOE (part), JEFFERSON (part). CITIES AND TOWNSHIPS: Arvada, Aurora, Bennett, Brighton,
    Commerce City, Edgewater, Golden, Lakewood, and Wheat Ridge. Population (2000), 614,465.

ZIP Codes: 80001–07, 80010–14, 80017–19, 80021–22, 80030, 80033–34, 80040–42, 80044–45, 80047, 80102–03, 80105,
    80123, 80127, 80136–37, 80212, 80214–16, 80221, 80226–35, 80241, 80247, 80401–03, 80419, 80465, 80601–03,
    80640, 80642–43, 80654

CONNECTICUT

(Population 2000, 3,405,565)

SENATORS

CHRISTOPHER J. DODD, Democrat, of East Haddam, CT; born in Willimantic, CT, May 27, 1944; son of Thomas J. and Grace Murphy Dodd; education: graduated, Georgetown Preparatory School, 1962; B.A., English Literature, Providence College, 1966; J.D., University of Louisville School of Law, 1972; admitted to Connecticut bar, 1973; served in U.S. Army Reserves, 1969–75; Peace Corps volunteer, Dominican Republic, 1966–68; married to Jackie Clegg; one child, Grace; founded the Senate Children's Caucus; House committees: served on the Rules Committee, Judiciary Committee, and Science and Technology Committee; appointed to the Select Committee on the Outer Continental Shelf and the Select Committee on Assassinations; committees: Banking, Health, Education, Labor, and Pensions; Foreign Relations; Housing and Urban Affairs; ranking member, Rules and Administration; Joint Committee on the Library of Congress; appointed to the Commission on Security and Cooperation in Europe; elected to the 94th Congress, November 5, 1974; reelected to the 95th and 96th Congresses; elected to the U.S. Senate, November 4, 1980; reelected to each succeeding Senate term.

Office Listings

http://dodd.senate.gov

448 Russell Senate Office Building, Washington, DC 20510	(202) 224–2823
Chief of Staff.—Sheryl Cohen.	
Legislative Director.—Shawn Maher.	
Putnam Park, 100 Great Meadow Road, Wethersfield, CT 06109	(860) 258–6940
State Director.—Ed Mann.	

* * *

JOSEPH I. LIEBERMAN, Democrat, of New Haven, CT; born in Stamford, CT, February 24, 1942; education: attended Stamford public schools; B.A., Yale University, 1964; law degree, Yale Law School, 1967; Connecticut State Senate, 1970–80; majority leader, 1974–80; honorary degrees: Yeshiva University, University of Hartford; Connecticut's 21st attorney general, 1983; reelected in 1986; author of "The Power-Broker" (Houghton Mifflin Company, 1966), a biography of late Democratic Party chairman John M. Bailey; "The Scorpion and the Tarantula" (Houghton Mifflin Company, 1970), a study of early efforts to control nuclear proliferation; "The Legacy" (Spoonwood Press, 1981), a history of Connecticut politics from 1930–80; "Child Support in America" (Yale University Press, 1986); "In Praise of Public Life" (Simon and Schuster, 2000); and "An Amazing Adventure" (Simon and Schuster, 2003); married: Hadassah Lieberman; children: Matthew, Rebecca, Ethan, and Hana; member, Democratic Leadership Council; Democratic candidate for Vice President, 2000; committees: Armed Services; Environment and Public Works; ranking member, Homeland Security and Government Affairs; Small Business and Entrepreneurship; elected on November 8, 1988, to the U.S. Senate; reelected to each succeeding Senate term.

Office Listings

http://lieberman.senate.gov

706 Hart Senate Office Building, Washington, DC 20510	(202) 224–4041
Administrative Assistant.—Clarine Nardi Riddle.	FAX: 224–9750
Executive Assistant.—Melissa Winter.	
Legislative Director.—William B. Bonvillian.	
One Constitution Plaza, 7th Floor, Hartford, CT 06103	(860) 549–8463
State Director.—Sherry Brown.	

REPRESENTATIVES

FIRST DISTRICT

JOHN B. LARSON, Democrat, of East Hartford, CT; born in Hartford, July 22, 1948; education: Mayberry Elementary School, East Hartford, CT; East Hartford High School; B.A., Central Connecticut State University; Senior Fellow, Yale University, Bush Center for Child Development and Social Policy; professional: high school teacher, 1972–77; insurance broker, 1978–98; president, Larson and Lyork; public service: Connecticut State Senate, 12 years,

President Pro Tempore, 8 years; married: Leslie Larson; children: Carolyn, Laura, and Raymond; committees: Ways and Means; subcommittees: Select Revenue Measures; Trade; elected to the 106th Congress; reelected to each succeeding Congress.

Office Listings

http://www.house.gov/larson

1005 Longworth House Office Building, Washington, DC 20515 .... (202) 225–2265
Legislative Director.—Jonathan Renfrew.   FAX: 225–1031
Press Secretary.—Michael Timothy Kirk.
Scheduler.—Evelene Corrigan.
221 Main Street, Hartford, CT 06106–1864 .... (860) 278–8888
Chief of Staff.—Elliot Ginsberg.

Counties: HARTFORD (part), LITCHFIELD (part), MIDDLESEX (part). Population (2000), 681,113.

ZIP Codes: 06002, 06006, 06010–11, 06016, 06021, 06023, 06025–28, 06033, 06035, 06037, 06040–41, 06045, 06057, 06060–61, 06063–65, 06067, 06073–74, 06088, 06090–91, 06094–96, 06098, 06101–12, 06114–15, 06117–20, 06123, 06126–29, 06131–34, 06137–38, 06140–47, 06150–56, 06160–61, 06176, 06180, 06183, 06199, 06416, 06422, 06444, 06457, 06467, 06479–80, 06489, 06759, 06790

* * *

SECOND DISTRICT

ROB SIMMONS, Republican, of Stonington, CT; born in New York, NY, February 11, 1943; education: B.A., Haverford College, 1965; Harvard University, 1979; military service: U.S. Army, 1965–69; U.S. Army Reserve; professional: CIA, 1969–79; staff of Senator John H. Chafee (R–RI), 1979–81; staff director of the Senate Select Committee on Intelligence, 1981–85; public service: Connecticut State Representative, 1991–2000; organizations: Stonington Police Commission, 1987–88; Stonington Community Center, 1986–88; Stonington Republican Town Committee, 1986–present; American Legion Post 58; religion: Episcopal; married: Heidi Paffard; children: Jane and Robert; committees: Armed Services; Homeland Security; Transportation and Infrastructure; elected to the 107th Congress on November 7, 2000; reelected to each succeeding Congress.

Office Listings

http://www.house.gov/simmons

215 Cannon House Office Building, Washington, DC 20515 .... (202) 225–2076
Chief of Staff / Press Secretary.—Todd Mitchell.   FAX: 225–4977
Legislative Director.—Lise Lynam.
37 Pearl Street, Enfield, CT 06082 .... (860) 741–4053
2 Courthouse Square, Norwich, CT 06360 .... (860) 886–0139

Counties: HARTFORD (part), MIDDLESEX (part), NEW LONDON, TOLLAND, WINDHAM. Population (2000), 681,113.

ZIP Codes: 06029, 06033, 06040, 06043, 06066, 06071–73, 06075–78, 06080, 06082–84, 06093, 06226, 06230–35, 06237–39, 06241–51, 06254–56, 06258–60, 06262–69, 06277–82, 06320, 06330–40, 06349–51, 06353–55, 06357, 06359–60, 06365, 06370–80, 06382–85, 06387–89, 06409, 06412–15, 06417, 06419–20, 06422–24, 06426, 06438–39, 06441–43, 06447, 06456–57, 06459, 06469, 06474–75, 06498

* * *

THIRD DISTRICT

ROSA L. DeLAURO, Democrat, of New Haven, CT; born in New Haven, March 2, 1943; education: graduated, Laurelton Hall High School; attended London School of Economics, Queen Mary College, London, 1962–63; B.A., *cum laude*, history and political science, Marymount College, NY, 1964; M.A., international politics, Columbia University, NY, 1966; professional: executive assistant to Mayor Frank Logue, city of New Haven, 1976–77; executive assistant/development administrator, city of New Haven, 1977–78; chief of staff, Senator Christopher Dodd, 1980–87; executive director, Countdown '87, 1987–88; executive director, Emily's List, 1989–90; married: Stanley Greenberg; children: Anna, Kathryn, and Jonathan; committees: Appropriations; Budget; co-chair, Democratic Steering and Policy Committee; subcommittees: ranking member, Agriculture, Rural Development, Food and Drug Administration, and Related Agencies; Labor, Health and Human Services, Education, and Related Agencies; elected to the 102nd Congress on November 6, 1990; reelected to each succeeding Congress.

Office Listings

2262 Rayburn House Office Building, Washington, DC 20515 .... (202) 225-3661
    Chief of Staff.—Ashley Turton.
    Legislative Director.—Rebecca Salay.
    Executive Assistant.—Nancy Mulry.
59 Elm Street, New Haven, CT 06510 .... (203) 562-3718
    District Director.—Jennifer Lamb.

Counties: FAIRFIELD (part), MIDDLESEX (part), NEW HAVEN (part). CITIES AND TOWNSHIPS: Ansonia, Beacon Falls, Bethany, Branford, Derby, Durham, East Haven, Guilford, Hamden, Middlefield, Middletown, Milford, Naugatuck, New Haven, North Branford, North Haven, Orange, Prospect, Seymour, Shelton, Stratford, Wallingford, Waterbury, West Haven, and Woodbridge. Population (2000), 681,113.

ZIP Codes: 06401, 06403, 06405, 06410, 06418, 06422, 06437, 06450, 06455, 06457, 06460, 06471-73, 06477, 06481, 06483-84, 06492-94, 06501-21, 06524-25, 06530-38, 06540, 06607, 06614-15, 06706, 06708, 06712, 06762, 06770

* * *

FOURTH DISTRICT

CHRISTOPHER SHAYS, Republican, of Bridgeport, CT; born in Stamford, CT, October 18, 1945; education: graduated, Darien High School, Darien, CT, 1964; B.A., Principia College, Elsah, IL, 1968; M.B.A., New York University Graduate School of Business, 1974; M.P.A., New York University Graduate School of Public Administration, 1978; member, Peace Corps, Fiji Islands, 1968–70; professional: business consultant; college instructor, realtor; executive aide, Trumbull First Selectman, 1971–72; Connecticut House of Representatives, 1974–87; married: Betsi Shays, 1968; children: Jeramy; committees: Financial Services; Government Reform; Homeland Security; elected by special election, August 18, 1987, to the 100th Congress to fill the vacancy caused by the death of Stewart B. McKinney; reelected to each succeeding Congress.

Office Listings

http://www.house.gov/shays   rep.shays@mail.house.gov

1126 Longworth House Office Building, Washington, DC 20515 .... (202) 225-5541
    Chief of Staff.—Betsy Wright Hawkings.   FAX: 225-9629
    Legislative Director.—Matt Meyer.
    Executive Assistant.—Diana White.
888 Washington Boulevard, Stamford, CT 06901–2927 .... (203) 357-8277
10 Middle Street, Bridgeport, CT 06604–4223 .... (203) 579-5870
    District Director.—Paul Pimentel.

Counties: FAIRFIELD (part), NEW HAVEN (part). CITIES AND TOWNSHIPS: Bridgeport, Darien, Easton, Fairfield, Greenwich, Monroe, New Canaan, Norwalk, Oxford, Redding, Ridgefield, Shelton, Stamford, Trumbull Weston, Westport, and Wilton. Population (2000), 681,113.

ZIP Codes: 06468, 06478, 06483-84, 06491, 06601-02, 06604-08, 06610-12, 06673, 06699, 06807, 06820, 06824-25, 06828-31, 06836, 06838, 06840, 06850-58, 06860, 06870, 06875-81, 06883, 06888-90, 06896-97, 06901-07, 06910-14, 06920-22, 06925-28

* * *

FIFTH DISTRICT

NANCY L. JOHNSON, Republican, of New Britain, CT; born in Chicago, IL, January 5, 1935; daughter of Gertrude Smith (deceased), and Noble W. Lee (deceased); education: attended University of Chicago Laboratory School, 1951; University of Chicago, 1953; B.A., Radcliffe College, *cum laude,* Cambridge, MA, 1957; attended University of London (English Speaking Union Scholarship), 1958; Connecticut State Senate, 1977–82; member, board of directors, United Way of New Britain; president, Sheldon Community Guidance Clinic; Unitarian Universalists Society of New Britain; founding president, Friends of New Britain Public Library; member: board of directors, New Britain Bank and Trust; New Britain Museum of American Art; adjunct professor (political science), Central Connecticut State College; married: Dr. Theodore Herbert Johnson, 1958; children: Lindsey, Althea, and Caroline; committees: Ways and Means; subcommittees: chair, Health; Human Resources; elected on November 2, 1982, to the 98th Congress; reelected to each succeeding Congress.

Office Listings

2409 Rayburn House Office Building, Washington, DC 20515 .... (202) 225–4476
    Chief of Staff.—Dave Karvelas.   FAX: 225–4488
    Press Secretary.—Brian Schuebert.
    Scheduler.—Katie Godburn.
1 Grove Street, New Britain, CT 06053 .... (860) 223–8412
    District Director.—Ken Hiscoe.
100 Grand Street, Waterbury, CT 06702 .... (203) 573–1418
198 Main Street, Suite 1, Danbury, CT 06810 .... (203) 790–6856
22 West Main Street, Meriden, CT 06451 .... (203) 630–1903

Counties: FAIRFIELD (part), HARTFORD (part), LITCHFIELD, NEW HAVEN (part). CITIES: Danbury, Meriden, New Britain, Torrington, and Waterbury. Population (2000), 681,113.

ZIP Codes: 06001, 06013, 06018–20, 06022, 06024, 06030–32, 06034, 06039, 06050–53, 06058–59, 06062, 06068–70, 06079, 06081, 06085, 06087, 06089, 06092, 06107, 06404, 06408, 06410–11, 06440, 06450–51, 06454, 06470, 06482, 06487–88, 06701–06, 06708, 06710, 06716, 06720–26, 06749–59, 06762–63, 06776–79, 06781–87, 06790–91, 06793–96, 06798, 06801, 06804, 06810–14, 06816–17

DELAWARE

(Population 2000, 783,600)

SENATORS

JOSEPH R. BIDEN, JR., Democrat, of Wilmington, DE; born in Scranton, PA, November 20, 1942; education: St. Helena's School, Wilmington, DE; Archmere Academy, Claymont, DE; A.B., history and political science, University of Delaware; J.D., Syracuse University College of Law; married: Jill Tracy Biden; children: Joseph R. Biden III, Robert Hunter Biden, and Ashley Blazer Biden; admitted to the bar, December 1968, Wilmington, DE; engaged in private practice until 1972; served on New Castle County Council, 1970–72; committees: ranking member, Foreign Relations; Judiciary; elected to the U.S. Senate on November 7, 1972; reelected to each succeeding Senate term.

Office Listings

http://biden.senate.gov   senator@biden.senate.gov

201 Russell Senate Office Building, Washington, DC 20510	(202) 224–5042
Chief of Staff.—Danny O'Brien.	FAX: 224–0139
Legislative Director.—Jane Woodfin.	TDD: 224–4048
Communications Director.—Norm Kurz.	
Office Manager.—Bill Clapp.	
1105 North Market Street, Suite 2000, Wilmington, DE 19801–1233	(302) 573–6345
State Director.—John DiEleuterio.	
24 NW Front Street, Windsor Building, Suite 101, Milford, DE 19963	(302) 424–8090

* * *

THOMAS R. CARPER, Democrat, of Wilmington, DE; born in Beckley, WV, January 23, 1947; education: B.A., Ohio State University, 1968; M.B.A., University of Delaware, 1975; military service: U.S. Navy, served during Vietnam War; public service: Delaware State Treasurer, 1977–1983; U.S. House of Representatives, 1983–1993; Governor of Delaware, 1993–2001; organizations: National Governors' Association; American Legacy Foundation; Jobs for America's Graduates; religion: Presbyterian; family: married to the former Martha Ann Stacy; children: Ben and Christopher; committees: Banking, Housing, and Urban Affairs; Environment and Public Works; Homeland Security and Governmental Affairs; Special Committee on Aging; subcommittees: ranking member, Clean Air, Climate Change and Nuclear Safety; ranking member, Federal Financial Management, Government Information and International Security; elected to the U.S. Senate on November 7, 2000.

Office Listings

http://carper.senate.gov

513 Hart Senate Office Building, Washington, DC 20510	(202) 224–2441
Chief of Staff.—Jonathon Jones.	FAX: 228–2190
Legislative Director.—Sheila Murphy.	
Office Manager.—Judy Rainey.	
Communications Director.—Bill Ghent.	
2215 Federal Building, 300 South New Street, Dover, DE 19904	(302) 674–3308
State Director.—Brian Bushweller.	
3021 Federal Building, 844 King Street, Wilmington, DE 19801	(302) 573–6291

REPRESENTATIVE

AT LARGE

MICHAEL N. CASTLE, Republican, of Wilmington, DE; born in Wilmington, July 2, 1939; education: graduate of Tower Hill School, 1957; B.S., economics, Hamilton College, Clinton, NY, 1961; J.D., Georgetown University Law School, 1964; attorney; admitted to the District of Columbia and Delaware bars, 1964; commenced practice in Wilmington; Delaware House of Representatives, 1966–67; Delaware Senate, 1968–76; Lieutenant Governor of Delaware, 1981–85; Governor, 1985–92; awarded honorary degrees: Wesley College, 1986; Widener College, 1986; Delaware State University, 1986; Hamilton College, 1991; Jefferson Medical College, Philadelphia, PA, 1992; active in the National Governors Association, serving three years as chairman of the Human Resources Committee; co-vice chairman for NGA's Task Force on Health Care with President Clinton; past president of the Council of State Governments; past chairman of the Southern Governors Association; chaired the Republican Governors Association, 1988; American Diabetes Association's C. Everett Koop Award for Health Promotion and Awareness, 1992; member: Delaware Bar Association, American Bar Association; former member: National Governors Association, Republican Governors Association, National Assessment Governing Board, Council of State Governors, Southern Governors Association; honorary board of directors, Delaware Greenways; task forces: co-chairman, Congressional Task Force to the National Campaign to Reduce Teen Pregnancy; House Social Security Task Force; House Tobacco Task Force; married: Jane DiSabatino, 1992; committees: Education and the Workforce; Financial Services; subcommittees: Capital Markets, Insurance and Government Sponsored Enterprises; Domestic and International Monetary Policy, Trade, and Technology; chairman, Education Reform; Financial Institutions and Consumer Credit; 21st Century Competitiveness; elected to the 103rd Congress on November 3, 1992; reelected to each succeeding Congress.

Office Listings
http://www.house.gov/castle

1233 Longworth House Office Building, Washington, DC 20515 .... (202) 225–4165
    Chief of Staff.—Mike Quaranta.   FAX: 225–2291
    Deputy Chief of Staff/Press Secretary.—Elizabeth Brealey Wenk.
    Legislative Director.—Kate Dickens.
    Scheduler.—Amy Greenan.
201 North Walnut Street, Suite 107, Wilmington, DE 19801 .... (302) 428–1902
    Office Director.—Jeff Dayton.   FAX: 428–1905
J. Allen Frear Federal Building, 300 South New Street, Dover, DE 19904 .... (302) 736–1666

Counties: KENT, NEW CASTLE, SUSSEX. CITIES AND TOWNSHIPS: Brookside, Camden, Claymont, Delaware City, Dover, Edgemoor, Elsmere, Georgetown, Harrington, Highland, Acres, Kent Acres, Laurel, Lewes, Middletown, Milford, Millsboro, New Castle, Newark, Pike Creek, Rising Sun-Lebanon, Rodney Village, Seaford, Smyrna, Stanton, Talleyville, Wilmington, Wilmington Minor, and Woodside East. Population (2000), 783,600.

ZIP Codes: 19701–03, 19706–18, 19720–21, 19725–26, 19730–36, 19801–10, 19850, 19880, 19884–87, 19890–99, 19901–06, 19930–31, 19933–34, 19936, 19938–41, 19943–47, 19950–56, 19958, 19960–64, 19966–71, 19973, 19975, 19977, 19979–80

FLORIDA

(Population 2000, 15,982,378)

SENATORS

BILL NELSON, Democrat, of Orlando, FL, born in Miami, FL, September 29, 1942; education: Melbourne High School, 1960; B.A., Yale University, 1965; J.D. University of Virginia School of Law, 1968; professional: attorney; admitted to the Florida Bar, 1968; captain, U.S. Army Reserve, 1965–1971; active duty, 1968–1970; public service: Florida State House of Representatives, 1973–1979; U.S. House of Representatives, 1979–1991; Florida Treasurer, Insurance Commissioner, and State Fire Marshal, 1995–2001; Astronaut: payload specialist on the space shuttle *Columbia*, January, 1986; married: the former Grace Cavert; children: Bill Jr. and Nan Ellen; committees: Armed Services; Budget; Commerce, Science, and Transportation; Foreign Relations; Special Committee on Aging; elected to the U.S. Senate on November 7, 2000.

Office Listings

http://billnelson.senate.gov

716 Hart Senate Office Building, Washington, DC 20510	(202) 224–5274
Chief of Staff.—Pete Mitchell.	FAX: 228–2183
Deputy Chief of Staff, Communications.—Dan McLaughlin.	
Deputy Chief of Staff, Administration.—Brenda Strickland.	
Legislative Director.—Dan Shapiro.	
U.S. Courthouse Annex, 111 North Adams Street, Tallahassee, FL 32301	(850) 942–6415
State Director.—Pete Mitchell.	
801 North Florida Avenue, 4th Floor, Tampa, FL 33602	(813) 225–7040
2925 Salzedo Street, Coral Gables, FL 33134	(305) 536–5999
3416 University Drive, Ft. Lauderdale, FL 33328	(954) 693–4851
500 Australian Avenue, Suite 125, West Palm Beach, FL 33401	(561) 514–0189
225 East Robinson Street, Suite 410, Orlando, FL 32801	(407) 872–7161
1301 Riverplace Boulevard, Suite 2281, Jacksonville, FL 32207	(904) 346–4500
2000 Main Street, Suite 801, Ft. Myers, FL 33901	(239) 334–7760

* * *

MELQUIADES (MEL) R. MARTINEZ, Republican, of Orlando, FL; born in Sagua La Grande, Cuba, October 23, 1946; immigrated to the United States in 1962; lived with foster families until reunited with his family in Orlando, FL, in 1966; education: B.A., Florida State University, 1969; J.D., Florida State University School of Law, 1973; professional: admitted to Florida Bar, 1973; U.S. District Court for Middle District of FL, 1973; U.S. Supreme Court, 1979; U.S. District Court for Southern District of FL, 1986; attorney and partner, Martinez, Dalton, Dellecker and Wilson, Orlando, FL, 1973–85 and Martinez, Dalton, Dellecker, Wilson and King, 1985–98; Florida co-chair, Presidential campaigns of Robert J. Dole, 1996 and George W. Bush, 2000; delegate to Republican National Convention, 2000; Orange County Chairman; secretary, Department of Housing and Urban Development, 2001–04; married: Kitty; children: Lauren Shea, John, Andrew; committees: Banking, Housing and Urban Affairs; Energy and National Resources; Foreign Relations; Special Committee on Aging; elected to the U.S. Senate on November 2, 2004.

Office Listings

http://martinez.senate.gov

317 Hart Senate Office Building, Washington, DC 20510	(202) 224–3041
Chief of Staff.—John Little.	FAX: 228–5171
Legislative Director.—Tripp Baird.	
315 East Robinson Street, Landmark Center 1, Suite 475, Orlando, FL 32801	(407) 254–2573

REPRESENTATIVES

FIRST DISTRICT

JEFF MILLER, Republican, of Chumuckla, FL; born in St. Petersburg, FL, June 27, 1959; education: B.S., University of Florida, 1984; professional: real estate broker; public service: Executive Assistant to the Commissioner of Agriculture, 1984–88; Environmental Land Management Study Commission, 1992; Santa Rosa County Planning Board Vice Chairman, 1996–98; elected to the Florida House of Representatives in 1998; reelected in 2000; served as House Majority Whip: organizations: Kiwanis Club of Milton; Florida Historical Society; Santa Rosa County United Way; Milton Pregnancy Resource Center Advisory Board; Gulf Coast Council of Boy Scouts; Florida FFA Foundation; religion: Methodist; married: Vicki Griswold; children: Scott and Clint; committees: Armed Services; Veterans' Affairs; subcommittees: chairman, Disability Assistance and Memorial Affairs; Readiness; Terrorism, Unconventional Threats and Capabilities; elected to the 107th Congress, by special election, on October 16, 2001; reelected to each succeeding Congress.

Office Listings

324 Cannon House Office Building, Washington, DC 20515 .... (202) 225–4136
    Chief of Staff.—Dan McFaul.
    Legislative Director.—Helen Walker.
    Scheduler.—Kelly Adamson.
    Legislative Counsel.—Elby Godwin.
4300 Bayou Boulevard, Suite 17–C, Pensacola, FL 32503 .... (850) 479–1183
    District Director.—Kris Tande.
348 SW Miracle Strip Parkway, Unit 21, Ft. Walton Beach, FL 32548 .... (850) 664–1266
    Okaloosa County Director.—Lois Hoyt.

Counties: ESCAMBIA, HOLMES, OKALOOSA (part), SANTA ROSA, WALTON (part), WASHINGTON. CITIES AND TOWNSHIPS: Bonifay, Carryville, Crestview, DeFuniak Springs, Destin, Fountain, Freeport, Ft. Walton Beach, Gulf Breeze, Jay, Laurel Hill, Lynn Haven, Milton, Noma, Pace, Paxton, Pensacola, Sunnyside, Westville, and Youngstown. Population (2000), 639,295.

ZIP Codes: 32501–09, 32511–14, 32516, 32520–24, 32526, 32530–31, 32533–42, 32544, 32547–49, 32559–72, 32577–79, 32580, 32583, 32588, 32591, 32598

* * *

SECOND DISTRICT

ALLEN BOYD, Democrat, of Monticello, FL; born in Valdosta, GA, June 6, 1945; education: graduated, Jefferson County High School, Monticello, 1963; B.S., Florida State University, 1969; professional: partner and general manager, F.A. Boyd and Sons, Inc., family farm corporation; first lieutenant, U.S. Army 101st Airborne Division, Vietnam, 1969–71, receiving the CIB and other decorations; Florida House of Representatives, 1989–96; elected majority whip; chaired Governmental Operations Committee (1992–94) and House Democratic Conservative Caucus (Blue Dogs); member: Peanut Producers Association; Farm Bureau; Cattlemen's Association; local historical association; Chamber of Commerce; and Kiwanis; board member, National Cotton Council; member, First United Methodist Church; married: the former Stephannie Ann Roush, 1970; children: Fred Allen Boyd III (d), Suzanne, John, and David; committees: Appropriations; subcommittees: Agriculture, Rural Development, Food and Drug Administration, and Related Agencies; Military Quality of Life and Veterans' Affairs, and Related Agencies; elected to the 105th Congress; reelected to each succeeding Congress.

Office Listings
http:/www.house.gov/boyd

1227 Longworth House Office Building, Washington, DC 20515 .... (202) 225–5235
    Administrative Assistant.—Libby Greer.   FAX: 225–5615
    Legislative Director.—Jason Quaranto.
    Legislative Assistants: Megan Murphy, Craig Stevens, Matt Sulkala.
    Executive Assistant/Scheduler.—Robin Nichols.
1650 Summit Lake Drive, Suite 103, Tallahassee, FL 32317 .... (850) 561–3979
    District Director.—Jerry Smithwick.
30 W. Government Street, Panama City, FL 32401 .... (850) 785–0812
    District Representative.—Bobby Pickles.

Counties: BAY, CALHOUN, DIXIE, FRANKLIN, GADSDEN, GULF, JACKSON, JEFFERSON (part), LAFEYETTE, LEON (part), LIBERTY, SUWANNE, TAYLOR, WALKULLA, WALTON (part). Population (2000), 639,295.

ZIP Codes: 32008, 32013, 32024, 32038, 32055, 32060, 32062, 32064, 32066, 32071, 32094, 32096, 32126, 32140, 32170, 32175, 32267, 32301–18, 32320–24, 32326–34, 32336, 32343–44, 32346–48, 32351–53, 32355–62, 32395, 32399, 32401–13, 32417, 32420–21, 32423–24, 32426, 32428, 32430–32, 32437–38, 32440, 32442–49, 32454, 32456–57, 32459–61, 32465–66, 32541, 32550, 32578, 32628, 32648, 32680, 32692

THIRD DISTRICT

CORRINE BROWN, Democrat, of Jacksonville, FL; born in Jacksonville, November 11, 1946; education: B.S., Florida A&M University, 1969; master's degree, Florida A&M University, 1971; education specialist degree, University of Florida; honorary doctor of law, Edward Waters College; faculty member: Florida Community College in Jacksonville; University of Florida; and Edward Waters College; served in the Florida House of Representatives for 10 years; first woman elected chairperson of the Duval County Legislative Delegation; served as a consultant to the Governor's Committee on Aging; committees: Transportation and Infrastructure; Veterans' Affairs; member: Congressional Black Caucus; Women's Caucus; and Progressive Caucus; one child: Shantrel; elected on November 3, 1992, to the 103rd Congress; reelected to each succeeding Congress.

Office Listings

http://www.house.gov/corrinebrown

2444 Rayburn House Office Building, Washington, DC 20515	(202) 225–0123
Chief of Staff.—E. Ronnie Simmons.	FAX: 225–2256
Executive Assistant/Scheduler.—Darla E. Smallwood.	
Legislative Director.—Nick Martinelli.	
Senior Legislative Assistant.—Lee Footer.	
101 East Union Street, Suite 202, Jacksonville, FL 32202	(904) 354–1652
219 Lime Avenue, Orlando, FL 32802	(407) 872–0656

Counties: ALACHUA (part), CLAY (part), DUVAL (part), LAKE (part), MARION (part), ORANGE (part), PUTNAM (part), SEMINOLE (part), VOLUSIA (part). Population (2000), 639,295.

ZIP Codes: 32003, 32007, 32043, 32066, 32073, 32102, 32105, 32112–13, 32130–31, 32134, 32138, 32140, 32147–49, 32160, 32177, 32179–80, 32182, 32185, 32190, 32201–11, 32215–16, 32218–19, 32231–32, 32234, 32236, 32238–39, 32244, 32247, 32254, 32277, 32601–04, 32627, 32631, 32640–41, 32653–54, 32662, 32666–67, 32681, 32702–03, 32712–13, 32720–24, 32736, 32751, 32757, 32763, 32767–68, 32771–73, 32776, 32789, 32798, 32801, 32804–05, 32808–11, 32818–19, 32835, 32839, 32855, 32858, 32861, 32868, 33142, 33160–61, 33179, 34488, 34761

* * *

FOURTH DISTRICT

ANDER CRENSHAW, Republican, of Jacksonville, FL; born in Jacksonville, September 1, 1944; education: B.A., University of Georgia, 1966; J.D., University of Florida, 1969; professional: investment banker; religion: Episcopal; public service: former member of the Florida House of Representatives and the Florida State Senate; served as President of the Florida State Senate; married: Kitty; children: Sarah and Alex; committees: Appropriations; Budget; subcommittees: Foreign Operations, Export Financing, and Related Programs; Homeland Security; Military Quality of Life and Veterans' Affairs, and Related Agencies; elected to the 107th Congress on November 7, 2000; reelected to each succeeding Congress.

Office Listings

http://www.house.gov/crenshaw

127 Cannon House Office Building, Washington, DC 20515	(202) 225–2501
Chief of Staff.—John Ariale.	FAX: 225–2504
Legislative Director.—Erica Striebel.	
Communications Director.—Ken Lundberg.	
1061 Riverside Avenue, Suite 100, Jacksonville, FL 32204	(904) 598–0481
District Director.—Jacqueline Smith.	
212 North Marion Avenue, Suite 209, Lake City, FL 32055	(386) 365–3316

Counties: BAKER, COLUMBIA, DUVAL (part), HAMILTON, JEFFERSON (part), LEON (part), MADISON, NASSAU, UNION. CITIES AND TOWNSHIPS: Greenville, Hilliard, Jacksonville, Jacksonville Beach, Jasper, Jennings, Lake Butler, Lake City, Lee, Macclenny, Madison, Monticello, Nassau Village-Ratliff, Palm Valley, Tallahassee, White Springs, and Yulee. Population (2000), 639,295.

ZIP Codes: 32009, 32011, 32024–26, 32034–35, 32038, 32040–41, 32046, 32052–56, 32058–59, 32061, 32063, 32072, 32083, 32087, 32094, 32096–97, 32204–05, 32207, 32210–12, 32214, 32216–18, 32223–29, 32233–35, 32237, 32240–41, 32244–46, 32250, 32255–58, 32266, 32277, 32301, 32311, 32317, 32331, 32336–37, 32340–41, 32344–45, 32350, 32643, 32697, 33142

FIFTH DISTRICT

GINNY BROWN-WAITE, Republican, of Brooksville, FL; born in Albany, NY, October 5, 1943; education: B.S., State University of New York, 1976; Russell Sage College, 1984; Labor Studies Program Certification, Cornell University; professional: served as a Legislative Director in the New York State Senate for almost 18 years; public service: Hernando County, FL, Commissioner; Florida State Senate, 1992–2002; served as Senate Majority Whip, and President Pro Tempore; recipient of numerous awards for community service; married: Harvey; children: three daughters; committees: Financial Services; Government Reform; Veterans' Affairs; elected to the 108th Congress on November 5, 2002; reelected to each succeeding Congress.

Office Listings

http://www.house.gov/brown-waite

414 Cannon House Office Building, Washington, DC 20515	(202) 225–1002
Chief of Staff.—Pete Meachum.	FAX: 226–6559
Scheduler.—Jennifer Fay.	
Senior Legislative Assistant.—Amie Woeber.	
Press Secretary.—Charlie Keller.	
20 North Main Street, Room 200, Brooksville, FL 34601	(352) 799–8354
38008 Meridian Avenue, Suite A, Dade City, FL 33525	(352) 567–6707

Counties: CITRUS, HERNANDO, LAKE (part), LEVY (part), MARION (part), PASCO (part), POLK (part), SUMTER. CITIES AND TOWNSHIPS: Brooksville, Dade City, and Clermont. Population (2000), 639,295.

ZIP Codes: 32159, 32162, 32621, 32625–26, 32635, 32639, 32644, 32658, 32668, 32683, 32696, 32778, 32825, 33513–14, 33521, 33523–26, 33537–38, 33540–44, 33548–49, 33556, 33558–59, 33574, 33576, 33585, 33593, 33597, 33809–10, 33849, 33868, 34218, 34220, 34423, 34428–34, 34436, 34442, 34445–53, 34460–61, 34464–65, 34481–82, 34484, 34487, 34498, 34601–11, 34613–14, 34636, 34639, 34653–55, 34661, 34667, 34669, 34711–13, 34731, 34736–37, 34748, 34753, 34755, 34762, 34785, 34787–89, 34797

* * *

SIXTH DISTRICT

CLIFF STEARNS, Republican, of Ocala, FL; born in Washington, DC, April 16, 1941; education: graduated, Woodrow Wilson High, Washington, DC, 1959; B.S., electrical engineering, George Washington University, Washington, DC, 1963; Air Force ROTC Distinguished Military Graduate; graduate work, University of California, Los Angeles, 1965; served, U.S. Air Force (captain), 1963–67; businessman; past president: Silver Springs Kiwanis; member: Marion County/Ocala Energy Task Force, Tourist Development Council, Ocala Board of Realtors, American Hotel/Motel Association in Florida, American Hotel/Motel Association of the United States, Grace Presbyterian Church; board of directors, Boys Club of Ocala; trustee: Munroe Regional Hospital; married: the former Joan Moore; children: Douglas, Bundy, and Scott; committees: Energy and Commerce; Veterans' Affairs; subcommittees: chairman, Commerce, Trade and Consumer Protection; vice-chairman, Health; Oversight and Investigations; vice-chairman, Telecommunications and the Internet; elected November 8, 1988, to the 101st Congress; reelected to each succeeding Congress.

Office Listings

http://www.house.gov/stearns

2370 Rayburn House Office Building, Washington, DC 20515	(202) 225–5744
Chief of Staff.—Jack Seum.	FAX: 225–3973
Legislative Director.—Lauren Semeniuk.	
Scheduler/Office Manager.—Joan Smutko.	
115 Southeast 25th Avenue, Ocala, FL 34471	(352) 351–8777
District Manager.—Judy Moore.	
5700 S.W. 34th Street, #425, Gainesville, FL 32608	(352) 337–0003
1726 Kinglsey Avenue S.E., Suite 8, Orange Park, FL 32073	(904) 269–3203

Counties: ALACHUA (part), BRADFORD, CLAY (part), DUVAL (part), GILCHREST, LAKE (part), LEVY (part), MARION (part). CITIES AND TOWNSHIPS: Ocala, Gainesville, Leesburg, Orange Park, Middleburg, and Jacksonville. Population (2000), 639,295.

ZIP Codes: 32003, 32006, 32008, 32030, 32042–44, 32050, 32054, 32058, 32065, 32067–68, 32073, 32079, 32083, 32091, 32099, 32111, 32113, 32133, 32140, 32158–59, 32162, 32179, 32183, 32195, 32205, 32210, 32215, 32219–22, 32234, 32244, 32254, 32276, 32601, 32603, 32605–12, 32614–16, 32618–19, 32621–22, 32631, 32633–34, 32643, 32653, 32655–56, 32658, 32663–64, 32666–69, 32681, 32686, 32693–94, 32696, 33142, 33160–61, 34420–21, 34432, 34436, 34470–76, 34478, 34480–83, 34491–92, 34731, 34748–49

SEVENTH DISTRICT

JOHN L. MICA, Republican, of Winter Park, FL; born in Binghamton, NY, January 27, 1943; education: graduated, Miami-Edison High School, Miami, FL; B.A., University of Florida, 1967; professional: president, MK Development; managing general partner, Cellular Communications; former government affairs consultant, Mica, Dudinsky and Associates; executive director, Local Government Study Commissions, Palm Beach County, 1970–72; executive director, Orange County Local Government Study Commission, 1972–74; Florida State House of Representatives, 1976–80; administrative assistant, U.S. Senator Paula Hawkins, 1980–85; Florida State Good Government Award, 1973; one of five Florida Jaycees Outstanding Young Men of America, 1978; member: Kiwanis, U.S. Capitol Preservation Commission, Tiger Bay Club, co-chairman, Speaker's Task Force for a Drug Free America, Florida Blue Key; U.S. Capitol Preservation Commission; brother of former Congressman Daniel A. Mica; married: the former Patricia Szymanek, 1972; children: D'Anne Leigh and John Clark; committees: Government Reform; House Administration; Transportation and Infrastructure; subcommittees: chairman, Aviation; elected on November 3, 1992 to the 103rd Congress; reelected to each succeeding Congress.

Office Listings

http://www.house.gov/mica

2313 Rayburn House Office Building, Washington, DC 20515	(202) 225–4035
Chief of Staff.—Russell L. Roberts.	FAX: 226–0821
Executive Assistant / Scheduler.—Lawrence Lyman.	
Legislative Director / Press Secretary.—Gary Burns.	
668 N. Orlando Avenue, Suite 208, Maitland, FL 32751	(407) 657–8080
840 Deltona Boulevard, Suite G, Deltona, FL 32725	(386) 860–1499
770 W. Granada Boulevard, Suite 315, Ormond Beach, FL 32174	(386) 676–7750
3000 N. Ponce de Leon Boulevard, Suite 1, St. Augustine, FL 32084	(904) 810–5048
613 St. Johns Avenue, Suite 107, Palatka, FL 32177	(386) 328–1622
1 Florida Park Drive South, Suite 100, Palm Coast, FL 32137	(386) 246–6042

Counties: ORANGE COUNTY (part). CITIES AND TOWNSHIPS: Maitland, Winter Park. SEMINOLE COUNTY. CITIES AND TOWNSHIPS: Altamonte Springs, Casselberry, Heathrow, Lake Mary, Longwood, Sanford, Winter Springs. VOLUSIA COUNTY (part). CITIES AND TOWNSHIPS: Daytona Beach, Debary, Deland, Deltona, Holly Hill, Lake Helen, Orange City, Ormond Beach, Pierson. FLAGLER COUNTY. CITIES AND TOWNSHIPS: Beverly Beach, Bunnell, Flagler Beach, Marineland, Palm Coast. ST. JOHNS COUNTY. CITIES AND TOWNSHIPS: Hastings, Ponte Vedra Beach, St. Augustine, St. Augustine Beach. PUTNAM COUNTY (part). CITIES AND TOWNSHIPS: Crescent City, Palatka, Pomona Park, and Welaka. Population, (2000), 639,295.

ZIP Codes: 32004, 32033, 32080, 32082, 32084–86, 32092, 32095, 32110, 32112, 32114–22, 32125, 32130–31, 32135–37, 32139, 32142, 32145, 32151, 32157, 32164, 32173–78, 32180–81, 32187, 32189, 32193, 32198, 32259–60, 32701, 32706–08, 32713–15, 32718, 32720, 32724–25, 32728, 32730, 32738, 32744, 32746–47, 32750–53, 32763–64, 32771, 32773–74, 32779, 32789, 32791–92, 32795, 32799

* * *

EIGHTH DISTRICT

RIC KELLER, Republican, of Orlando, FL; born in Johnson City, TN, September 5, 1964; education: Boone High School, 1982; B.S., East Tennessee State University, 1986; J.D., Vanderbilt University, 1992; professional: attorney; partner in the law firm of Rumberger, Kirk & Caldwell; community service: Chairman of the Board of Directors of the Orlando/Orange County COMPACT Program; co-author of two amendments to Florida's Constitution (the Everglades Polluter Pays amendment, and the Everglades Trust Fund amendment); religion: United Methodist; divorced; children: Nick and Christy; committees: Education and the Workforce; Judiciary; Small Business; elected to the 107th Congress on November 7, 2000; reelected to each succeeding Congress.

Office Listings

http://www.house.gov/keller

419 Cannon House Office Building, Washington, DC 20515	(202) 225–2176
Chief of Staff.—Bryan Malenius.	FAX: 225–0999
Legislative Director.—Mike Shutley.	
Scheduler.—Stefanie Higgins.	
605 East Robinson Street, Suite 650, Orlando, FL 32801	(407) 872–1962
District Director.—Cheryl Mills.	

Counties: ORANGE (part), OSCEOLA (part), MARION (part), LAKE (part). CITIES AND TOWNSHIPS: Astatula, Azalea, Bay Hill, Bay Lake, Belle Isle, Belleview, Celebration, Conway, Doctor Phillips, Edgewood, Eustis, Fairview Shores, Howeyin-the-Hills, Holden Heights, Leesburg, Meadow Wood, Mid Florida Lakes, Montverde, Oakland, Ocala Part, Ocoee, Orlando, Silver Springs Shores, Sky Lakes, Tavares, Umatilla, Union Park, Williamsburg, Windermere, Winter Garden, and Winter Park. Population (2000), 639,295.

ZIP Codes: 32113, 32179, 32192, 32617, 32702–03, 32710, 32726–27, 32735–36, 32756–57, 32777–78, 32784, 32789, 32792, 32801–07, 32809–12, 32814, 32817–19, 32821–22, 32824–25, 32827, 32829–30, 32835–37, 32839, 32853–54, 32856–57, 32859–60, 32862, 32867, 32869, 32872, 32877, 32885–87, 32890–91, 32893, 32896–98, 33030, 33032–33, 33161, 33186, 34470–72, 34475, 34479–80, 34488–89, 34705, 34711, 34729, 34734, 34740, 34746–47, 34756, 34760–61, 34777–78, 34786–88

* * *

NINTH DISTRICT

MICHAEL BILIRAKIS, Republican, of Tarpon Springs, FL; born in Tarpon Springs, July 16, 1930; raised in western Pennsylvania; education: B.S. in engineering, University of Pittsburgh, 1955–59; accounting, George Washington University, Washington, DC, 1959–60; J.D., University of Florida, Gainesville, 1961–63; U.S. Air Force, 1951–55; attorney and small businessman, petroleum engineer, aerospace contract administrator, geophysical engineer (offshore oil exploration), steelworker, and judge of various courts for eight years; honors in college include Phi Alpha Delta Annual Award for Outstanding Law Graduate and president of the student body of School of Engineering and Mines; honors after college, civil activities, and organizations include Citizen of the Year Award for Greater Tarpon Springs, 1972–73; founder and charter president of Tarpon Springs Volunteer Ambulance Service; past president and four-year director of Greater Tarpon Springs Chamber of Commerce; past president, Rotary Club of Tarpon Springs; board of governors, Pinellas Suncoast Chamber of Commerce; board of development, Anclote Manor Psychiatric Hospital, AHEPA; elected commander, Post 173 American Legion, Holiday, FL (1977–79, two terms); 33rd degree Mason and Shriner; member: West Pasco Bar Association, American Judicature Society, Florida and American bar associations, University of Florida Law Center Association, Gator Booster, American Legion, and Veterans of Foreign Wars; holds college level doctorate teaching certificate; member: Juvenile Diabetes Association, Elks, Eastern Star and White Shrine of Jerusalem, Royaler of Jesters of Egypt Temple Shrine District, Air Force Association; former member: Clearwater Bar Association, National Contract Management Association, American Society of Mining, Metallurgical and Petroleum Engineers, and Creative Education Foundation; married: the former Evelyn Miaoulis, 1959; children: Manuel and Gus; committees: vice-chair, Energy and Commerce; vice-chair, Veterans' Affairs; subcommittees: Energy and Air Quality; Health; Telecommunications and the Internet; chair, Oversight and Investigations; elected to the 98th Congress, November 2, 1982; reelected to each succeeding Congress.

Office Listings

http://www.house.gov/bilirakis

2408 Rayburn House Office Building, Washington, DC 20515	(202) 225–5755
Administrative Assistant.—Rebecca Hyder.	FAX: 225–4085
Communications Director / Legislative Assistant.—Christy Stefadouros.	
Deputy Administrative Assistant / Scheduler.—Douglas Menorca.	
35111 US Highway 19 North, Suite 301, Palm Harbor, FL 34684	(727) 773–2871
Director of District Operations.—Sonja Stefanadis.	
10330 North Dale Mabry, Suite 205, Tampa, FL 33618	(813) 960–8173

Counties: HILLSBOROUGH (part), PASCO (part), PINELLAS (part). CITIES AND TOWNSHIPS: Bearss, Bloomingdale, Brandon, Carrollwood Village, Citrus Park, Clearwater, Countryside, Crystal Springs, Dale Mabry, Eastlake Woodlands, Elfers, Fishhawk, Holiday, Hudson, Hunters Green, Lutz, New Port Richey, Odessa, Oldsmar, Palm Harbor, Plant City, Safety Harbor, Seffner, Seven Springs, Tarpon Springs, Temple Terrace, Thonotosassa, Trinity, Valrico, and Veterans Village. Population (2000), 639,296.

ZIP Codes: 33511, 33527, 33530, 33539–40, 33542, 33547–49, 33556, 33558–59, 33563, 33565–67, 33569, 33583–84, 33587, 33592, 33594–95, 33598, 33612–13, 33617–18, 33624–26, 33637, 33647, 33688, 33755–59, 33761, 33763–66, 33769, 33810, 34652–56, 34667–69, 34673–74, 34677, 34679–80, 34683–85, 34688–91, 34695

* * *

TENTH DISTRICT

C.W. BILL YOUNG, Republican, of Indian Shores, FL; born in Harmarville, PA, December 16, 1930; elected Florida's only Republican State Senator in 1960; reelected 1964, 1966, 1967 (special election), and 1968, serving as minority leader from 1963 to 1970; national committeeman, Florida Young Republicans, 1957–59; state chairman, Florida Young Republicans, 1959–61; member, Florida Constitution Revision Commission, 1965–67; married: Beverly;

children: three sons; committees: Appropriations; subcommittees: chairman, Defense; Military Quality of Life and Veterans Affairs, and Related Agencies; elected to the 92nd Congress, November 3, 1970; reelected to each succeeding Congress.

Office Listings

2407 Rayburn House Office Building, Washington, DC 20515 .... (202) 225–5961
  Chief of Staff.—Harry Glenn.   FAX: 225–9764
  Legislative Director.—Brad Stine.
360 Central Avenue, Suite 1480, St. Petersburg, FL 33701 .... (727) 893–3191
  Administrative Assistant.—George N. Cretekos.
801 West Bay Drive, Suite 606, Largo, FL 33770 .... (727) 581–0980

Counties: PINELLAS COUNTY (part). Population (2000), 639,295.

ZIP Codes: 33701–16, 33729, 33731–32, 33734, 33736–38, 33740–44, 33755–56, 33760–65, 33767, 33770–82, 33784–86, 34660, 34681–84, 34697–98

* * *

ELEVENTH DISTRICT

JIM DAVIS, Democrat, of Tampa, FL; born in Tampa, October 11, 1957; education: B.A., Washington and Lee University, 1979; J.D., University of Florida Law School, 1982; professional: admitted to the Florida bar in 1982 and began practice with Carlton Fields law firm in Tampa; partner, Bush, Ross, Gardner, Warren and Rudy law firm, 1988–96; member, Florida House of Representatives, 1988–96, serving as majority leader from 1994 to 1996; member of the Tampa, Brandon and Riverview chambers of commerce and Old Seminole Heights Preservation Committee; married: Peggy Bessent Davis since 1986; children: Peter and William; committees: Energy and Commerce; subcommittees: Commerce, Trade, and Consumer Protection; Energy and Air Quality; Health; elected to the 105th Congress, and selected Democratic freshman class president; reelected to each succeeding Congress.

Office Listings
http://www.house.gov/jimdavis

409 Cannon House Office Building, Washington, DC 20515 .... (202) 225–3376
  Chief of Staff.—Karl Koch.   FAX: 225–5652
  Deputy Chief of Staff / Legislative Director.—Tricia Barrentine.
  Scheduler/Executive Assistant.—Joan Rodriguez Vogel.
  Press Secretary.—Diane Pratt-Heavner.
3315 Henderson Boulevard, No. 100, Tampa, FL 33609 .... (813) 354–9217
  District Director.—John Kynes.
  Florida Toll Free 1 (888) 266–0205
1186 62nd Avenue, South, St. Petersburg, FL 33705 .... (727) 867–5301
  Field Representative.—Nikki Gaskin-Capehart.

Counties: HILLSBOROUGH (part), MANATEE, PINELLAS. CITIES: Apollo Beach, Bradenton, Carrollwood, Carrollwood Village, Citrus Park, Ellenton, Gibsonton, Gulfport, Lutz, Northdale, Oldsmar, Palmetto, Riverview, Ruskin, St. Petersburg, Tampa, Temple Terrace, and Town 'N' Country, Ybor City. Population (2000), 639,295.

ZIP Codes: 33534, 33549, 33559, 33569–70, 33572, 33586, 33601–19, 33621–26, 33629–31, 33634–35, 33637, 33647, 33650–51, 33655, 33663–64, 33672–75, 33677, 33679–82, 33684–87, 33690, 33694, 33697, 33701, 33705, 33707, 33710–13, 33730, 33733, 33747, 33784, 34205, 34208, 34221–22, 34677

* * *

TWELFTH DISTRICT

ADAM H. PUTNAM, Republican, of Bartow, FL; born in Bartow, FL, July 31, 1974; education: Bartow High School; University of Florida, B.S., Food and Resource Economics; professional: farmer; rancher; awards: Outstanding Male Graduate of the University of Florida; Who's Who in American Politics; organizations: Florida 4–H Foundation; Sheriff's Youth Villa Board of Associates; Chamber of Commerce; Polk County Farm Bureau; married: Melissa; public service: Florida House of Representatives, 1996–2000; committees: Budget; Rules; elected to the 107th Congress on November 7, 2000; reelected to each succeeding Congress.

109th Congress

Office Listings
http://www.house.gov/putnam

1213 Longworth House Office Building, Washington, DC 20515 .... (202) 225–1252
Chief of Staff.—John Hambel.   FAX: 226–0585
Executive Assistant.—Chanel Dedes.
Legislative Director.—Karen Williams.
Director of Communications.—Shawn Dhar.
650 East Davidson Street, Bartow, FL 33830 .... (863) 534–3530
District Director.—Matthew Joyner.

Counties: HILLSBOROUGH (part), OSCEOLA (part), POLK (part). CITIES AND TOWNSHIPS: Apollo Beach, Auburndale, Babson Park, Bartow, Brandon, Davenport, Dundee, Eagle Lake, Fort Meade, Frostproof, Gibsonton, Haines City, Highland City, Hillcrest Heights, Indian Lake Estates, Lakeland, Lake Alfred, Lake Hamilton, Lake Wales, Mulberry, Plant City, Poinciana, Polk City, Riverview, Ruskin, Seffner, Sun City Center, Tampa, Temple Terrace, Thonotosassa, Wimauma, and Winter Haven. Population (2000), 639,296.

ZIP Codes: 33030, 33033, 33170, 33183, 33186, 33503, 33508–11, 33527, 33534, 33547, 33550, 33563–64, 33566–73, 33575, 33584, 33592, 33594, 33598, 33610, 33617, 33619, 33637, 33689, 33801–07, 33809–11, 33813, 33815, 33820, 33823, 33825, 33827, 33830–31, 33834–41, 33843–47, 33850–51, 33853–56, 33859–60, 33863, 33867–68, 33877, 33880–85, 33888, 33896–98, 34758–59

* * *

THIRTEENTH DISTRICT

KATHERINE HARRIS, Republican, of Sarasota, FL; born in Key West, FL, April 5, 1957; education: bachelor's degree, Agnes Scott College, in history; master's degree, Harvard University, in international trade and negotiations; professional: IBM marketing executive, and vice president of a commercial real estate firm; public service: Florida State Senate, 1994–1998; Florida Secretary of State, 1999–2002; awards: Florida Arts Advocacy Award; Florida Economic Development Council Legislator of the Year; Milton N. Fisher Award for International Trade Advocacy; Florida United Business Association Outstanding Legislator Award; Sarasota Humanitarian of the Year Award; married: Anders Ebbeson; one child, Louise; committees: Financial Services; Homeland Security; International Relations; elected to the 108th Congress on November 5, 2002; reelected to each succeeding Congress.

Office Listings
http://www.house.gov/harris

116 Cannon House Office Building, Washington, DC 20515 .... (202) 225–5015
Chief of Staff.—Chris Battle.   FAX: 226–0828
Deputy Chief of Staff.—Peggy Evans.
Scheduler.—Mona Tate Yost.
1991 Main Street, Suite 181, Sarasota, FL 34236 .... (941) 951–6643
District Director.—Sally Tibbets.
1112 Manatee Avenue West, Suite 902, Bradenton, FL 34205 .... (941) 747–9081

Counties: CHARLOTTE (part), DESOTO, HARDEE, MANATEE (part), SARASOTA. Population (2000), 639,295.

ZIP Codes: 33138, 33160–61, 33598, 33834, 33865, 33873, 33890, 33946–47, 34201–12, 34215–19, 34221–24, 34228–43, 34250–51, 34260, 34264–70, 34272, 34274–78, 34280–82, 34284–89, 34292–93, 34295

* * *

FOURTEENTH DISTRICT

CONNIE MACK, Republican, of Fort Myers, FL; born in Fort Myers, August 12, 1967; education: B.S., University of Florida, Gainesville, FL, 1993; professional: marketing executive; member, Florida state House of Representatives, 2000–2003; son of U.S. Senator Connie Mack III, step-great-grandson of Senator Tom Connally, great-grandson of Senator Morris Sheppard, and great-great-grandson of Congressman John Levi Sheppard; married: Ann; children: Addison and Connie; committees: Budget; International Relations; Transportation and Infrastructure; elected to the 109th Congress on November 2, 2004.

Office Listings
http://www.house.gov/mack

317 Cannon House Office Building, Washington, DC 20515 .... (202) 225–2536
  Chief of Staff.—Jeff Cohen. FAX: 226–0439
  Legislative Director.—Francis Gibbs.
  Executive Assistant.—Betsy Kampas.
2000 Main Street, Suite 303, Fort Myers, FL 33901 .... (239) 332–4677
3301 Tamiami Trail E, Bldg. F, First Floor, Naples, FL 34112 .... (239) 774–8035

Counties: CHARLOTTE (part), COLLIER (part), LEE. Population (2000), 639,295.

ZIP Codes: 33030, 33033, 33160, 33186, 33189, 33901–22, 33924, 33927–28, 33931–32, 33936, 33945–46, 33948, 33953–57, 33965, 33970–72, 33981, 33990–91, 33993–94, 34101–10, 34112–14, 34116, 34119, 34133–36, 34140, 34142, 34145–46, 34224

* * *

FIFTEENTH DISTRICT

DAVE WELDON, Republican, of India Lantic, FL; born in Long Island, NY, August 31, 1953; education: graduated Farmingdale High School, Farmingdale, NY, 1971; B.S., biochemistry, State University of New York, Stony Brook, 1978; M.D., State University of New York, Buffalo, 1981; U.S. Army Major, 1981–87; physician, internal medicine; member: American College of Physicians, Florida Medical Association, Brevard County Medical Society, Retired Officers Association, Good Samaritan Club, Brevard Veterans Council, Vietnam Veterans of Brevard, American Legion; founder, Space Coast Family Forum; married: Nancy Weldon, 1979; children: Katherine and David; committees: Appropriations; subcommittees: Labor, Health and Human Services, Education and Related Agencies; Science, The Departments of State, Justice, and Commerce, and Related Agencies; elected to the 104th Congress; reelected to each succeeding Congress.

Office Listings
http://www.house.gov/weldon

2347 Rayburn House Office Building, Washington, DC 20515 .... (202) 225–3671
  Chief of Staff.—Dana Gartzke. FAX: 225–3516
  Deputy Chief of Staff.—Stuart Burns.
  Scheduler / Office Manager.—Cathy Graham.
  Legislative Director.—Paul Webster.
Building C, 2725 Judge Fran Jamieson Way, Melbourne, FL 32940 .... (321) 632–1776
  District Director.—J.B. Kump.
2000 16th Avenue, Indian River County Courthouse, Room 157, Vero Beach,
  FL 32960 .... (772) 778–3534

Counties: BREVARD (part), INDIAN RIVER, OSCEOLA (part), POLK (part). Population (2000), 639,295.

ZIP Codes: 32815, 32899, 32901–12, 32919–20, 32922–26, 32931–32, 32934–37, 32940–41, 32948–53, 32955–58, 32960–71, 32976, 32978, 33837, 33848, 33858, 33868, 33896–98, 34739, 34741–47, 34758–59, 34769–73, 34972

* * *

SIXTEENTH DISTRICT

MARK FOLEY, Republican, of West Palm Beach, FL; born in Newton, MA, September 8, 1954; education: graduated Lake Worth High School, Lake Worth, FL; attended Palm Beach Community College, Lake Worth; president, Foley Smith and Associates, Inc., real estate company; Florida House of Representatives, 1990–92; Florida Senate (Agriculture Committee chairman), 1992–94; Lake Worth city commissioner, 1977; Lake Worth vice mayor, 1983–84; deputy whip; chairman, Entertainment Task Force; co-chair of Missing and Exploited Children's Caucus; Travel and Tourism Caucus; Congressional Real Estate Caucus; committees: Ways and Means; elected to the 104th Congress; reelected to each succeeding Congress.

Office Listings
http://www.house.gov/foley

104 Cannon House Office Building, Washington, DC 20515 .... (202) 225–5792
  Deputy Chief of Staff.—Elizabeth Nicolson. FAX: 225–3132
  Director of Operations.—Dean Lester.
  Legislative Director.—Bradley Schrieber.
  Communications Director.—Jason Kello.

4440 PGB Boulevard, Suite 406, Palm Beach Gardens, FL 33410 .... (561) 627–6192
    Chief of Staff.—Don Kiselewski.
County Annex Building, 250 Northwest Country Club Drive, Port St. Lucie, FL
    34986 .... (772) 878–3181
    District Manager.—Ann Decker.
18500 Murdock Circle, Suite 536, Port Charlotte, FL 33948 .... (941) 627–9100
    District Manager.—Dick Keen.

Counties: CHARLOTTE (part), GLADES, HENDRY (part), HIGHLANDS, MARTIN (part), OKEECHOBEE, PALM BEACH (part), ST. LUCIE (part). Population (2000), 639,295.

ZIP Codes: 33138, 33160–61, 33170, 33186, 33410–12, 33414, 33418, 33421, 33440, 33455, 33458, 33467, 33469–71, 33475, 33477–78, 33825–26, 33852, 33857, 33862, 33870–72, 33875–76, 33917, 33920, 33930, 33935, 33938, 33944, 33948–55, 33960, 33972, 33975, 33980, 33982–83, 34142, 34945–47, 34949–53, 34956–58, 34972–74, 34981–88, 34990–92, 34994–97

* * *

SEVENTEENTH DISTRICT

KENDRICK B. MEEK, Democrat, of Miami, FL; born in Miami, September 6, 1966; education: B.S., Florida A&M University, 1989; organizations: NAACP; 100 Black Men of America, Inc.; Greater Miami Service Corps; Omega Psi Phi Fraternity; awards: Mothers Against Drunk Driving Outstanding Service Award; Ebony Magazine's 50 Leaders of Tomorrow; Adams-Powell Civil Rights Award; public service: Florida House of Representatives, 1994–1998; Florida State Senate, 1998–2002; married: Leslie Dixon; children: Lauren and Kendrick B., Jr.; son of former Florida U.S. Representative Carrie P. Meek; committees: Armed Services; Homeland Security; subcommittees: Intelligence, Information Sharing and Terrorism Risk Assessment; ranking member, Management, Integration, and Oversight; Tactical Air and Land Forces; Readiness; elected to the 108th Congress on November 5, 2002; reelected to each succeeding Congress.

Office Listings

http://www.house.gov/kenmeek

1039 Longworth House Office Building, Washington, DC 20515 .... (202) 225–4506
    Chief of Staff.—John Schelble.   FAX: 226–0777
    Senior Advisor.—Tasha Cole.
    Legislative Director.—Clarence Williams.
    Scheduler.—Lisa Kohnke.
111 N.W. 183rd Street, Suite 315, Miami Gardens, FL 33169 .... (305) 690–5905
    District Office Director.—Anthony Williams.

Counties: DADE (part), BROWARD (part). Population (2000), 639,296.

ZIP Codes: 33008–09, 33013, 33020–25, 33054–56, 33081, 33083, 33090, 33092, 33101, 33110, 33127, 33136–38, 33142, 33147, 33150–51, 33156, 33160–62, 33164, 33167–69, 33179–81, 33197, 33238, 33242, 33247, 33256, 33261

* * *

EIGHTEENTH DISTRICT

ILEANA ROS-LEHTINEN, Republican, of Miami, FL; born in Havana, Cuba, July 15, 1952; education: B.A., English, Florida International University; M.S., educational leadership, Florida International University; Ed.D, University of Miami, 2004; certified Florida school teacher; founder and former owner, Eastern Academy; elected to Florida House of Representatives, 1982; elected to Florida State Senate, 1986; former president, Bilingual Private School Association; regular contributor to leading Spanish-language newspaper; during House tenure, married then-State Representative Dexter Lehtinen; children: Amanda Michelle and Patricia Marie; committees: Budget; Government Reform; International Relations; subcommittees: National Security, Emerging Threats, and International Relations; chair, The Middle East and Central Asia; elected on August 29, 1989 to the 101st Congress; reelected to each succeeding Congress.

Office Listings

2160 Rayburn House Office Building, Washington, DC 20515 .... (202) 225–3931
    Chief of Staff.—Arthur Estopinan.   FAX: 225–5620
    Deputy Administrative Assistant.—Christine del Portillo.
    Legislative Director.—Fred Ratliff.
    Press Secretary.—Alex Cruz.
Suite 100, 9210 Sunset Drive, Miami, FL 33173 .... (305) 275–1800

Counties: DADE (part), MONROE (part). CITIES AND TOWNSHIPS: Coral Gables, Florida City, Homestead, Key Biscayne, Miami, Miami Beach, South Miami, and West Miami. Population (2000), 639,295.

ZIP Codes: 33001, 33030, 33032–34, 33036–37, 33039–45, 33050–52, 33070, 33109, 33111–12, 33114, 33119, 33121, 33124–36, 33139–46, 33149, 33154–59, 33165, 33170, 33174, 33176, 33186, 33189–90, 33195, 33197, 33199, 33231, 33233–34, 33239, 33243, 33245, 33255, 33257, 33265, 33296, 33299

* * *

NINETEENTH DISTRICT

ROBERT WEXLER, Democrat, of Boca Raton, FL; born in Queens, NY, January 2, 1961; education: graduate of Hollywood Hills High School; University of Florida, 1982; George Washington University Law School, 1985; admitted to the Florida bar in 1985; attorney; Florida State Senator, 1990–96; member: Palm Beach Planning and Zoning Commission, 1989–90, Palm Beach County Democratic Executive Committee, 1989–92, Palm Beach County Affordable Housing Committee, 1990–91, Florida Bar Association, South Palm Beach County Jewish Federation, Palm Beach County Anti-Defamation League; married to the former Laurie Cohen; three children; committees: International Relations; Judiciary; subcommittees: Asia and the Pacific; Courts, the Internet, and Intellectual Property; ranking member, Europe; elected to the 105th Congress; reelected to each succeeding Congress.

Office Listings

213 Cannon House Office Building, Washington, DC 20515	(202) 225–3001
Chief of Staff.—Eric Johnson.	FAX: 225–5974
Press Secretary.—Lale Mamaux.	
2500 North Military Trail, Suite 100, Boca Raton, FL 33431	(561) 988–6302
District Director.—Wendy Lipsich.	
5790 Margate Boulevard, Margate, FL 33063	(954) 972–6454

Counties: BROWARD (part), PALM BEACH (part). CITIES AND TOWNSHIPS: Boca Raton, Boynton Beach, Coconut Creek, Coral Springs, Deerfield Beach, Delray Beach, Lauderhill, Lake Worth, Margate, North Lauderdale, Parkland, Pompano Beach, Sunrise and Tamarac. Population (2000) 639,295.

ZIP Codes: 33063–66, 33068–69, 33071, 33073, 33075–77, 33093, 33140, 33155, 33309, 33321, 33401, 33406, 33409, 33411, 33413–15, 33417, 33422, 33426, 33428, 33431, 33433–34, 33436–37, 33441–42, 33445–46, 33448, 33454, 33461–63, 33466–67, 33474, 33481–82, 33484, 33486–88, 33496–99

* * *

TWENTIETH DISTRICT

DEBBIE WASSERMAN SCHULTZ, Democrat, of Weston, FL; born in Forest Hills, Queens County, NY, September 27, 1966; education: B.A., University of Florida, Gainesville, FL, 1988; M.A., University of Florida, FL, 1990; professional: Public Policy Curriculum Specialist, Nova Southeastern University; Adjunct Instructor, Political Science, Broward Community College; aide to United States Representative Peter Deutsch, 1989–92; member, Florida State House of Representatives, 1992–2000; member, Florida State Senate, 2000–04; organizations: Board of Trustees, Westside Regional Medical Center; Outstanding Freshman Legislator, Florida Women's Political Caucus; Secretary; Board of Directors, American Jewish Congress; Member, Broward National Organization for Women; Board of Directors, National Safety Council, South Florida Chapter; religion: Jewish; married: Steve; children: Rebecca, Jake, Shelby; Senior Democratic Whip; committees: Financial Services; elected to the 109th Congress on November 2, 2004.

Office Listings
http://www.house.gov/wasserman-schultz

118 Cannon House Office Building, Washington, DC 20515	(202) 225–7931
Chief of Staff.—Tracie Pough.	FAX: 226–2052
Communications Director.—Jonathon Beeton.	
Senior Legislative Assistant.—Emily Coyle.	
Scheduler/Office Manager.—Evonne Marché.	
10100 Pines Boulevard, Pembroke Pines, FL 33026	(954) 437–3936
19200 West Country Club Drive, Third Floor, Aventura, FL 33180	(305) 936–5724

Counties: BROWARD COUNTY (PART). CITIES: Dania Beach, Davie, Lazy Lake, Plantation, Wilton Manors, Weston. DADE COUNTY (part). CITIES: Bay Harbor Island, North Bay Village, and Sunny Isles. MIAMI-DADE COUNTY (part). CITIES: Davie, Fort Lauderdale, Hollywood, Miami Beach, North Miami, Sunrise. Population (2000), 639,295.

ZIP Codes: 33004, 33009, 33019–21, 33024, 33026, 33030, 33033, 33084, 33137, 33139–41, 33147, 33154, 33156, 33160–61, 33170, 33180–81, 33301, 33304–05, 33309, 33311–15, 33317–19, 33321–32, 33334, 33336, 33338, 33345, 33351, 33355, 33394

* * *

TWENTY-FIRST DISTRICT

LINCOLN DIAZ-BALART, Republican, of Miami, FL; born in Havana, Cuba, August 13, 1954; education: graduated, American School of Madrid, Spain, 1972; B.A., New College of the University of South Florida, Sarasota, 1976; J.D., Case Western Reserve University Law School, 1979; professional: attorney; admitted to the Florida bar, 1979; partner, Fowler, White, Burnett, Hurley, Banick and Strickroot, P.A., Miami; Florida State House, 1986–89; Florida State Senate, 1989–92; founding member, Miami-Westchester Lions Club; member, Organization for Retarded Citizens; married the former Cristina Fernandez, 1976; two children: Lincoln Gabriel and Daniel; Majority Assistant Whip; Congressional Human Rights Caucus; committees: vice-chair, Rules; House Republican Policy Committee; subcommittees: chair, Legislative and Budget Process; elected on November 3, 1992 to the 103rd Congress; reelected to each succeeding Congress.

Office Listings

http://diaz-balart.house.gov

2244 Rayburn House Office Building, Washington, DC 20515 .... (202) 225–4211
    Chief of Staff.—Ana M. Carbonell.
    Administrative Assistant.—Stephen Cote.
    Legislative Director.—Towner French.
    Deputy Press Secretary.—Daniell Holland.
8525 NW 53 Terrace, Suite 102, Miami, FL 33166 .... (305) 470–8555
    District Director.—Ana M. Carbonell.

Counties: BROWARD COUNTY (part), DADE COUNTY (part). CITIES AND TOWNSHIPS: Central Kendall, Doral, Fontainebleau, Hialeah, Miami Lakes, Miami Springs, Miramar, Pembroke Pines, Richmond Heights, Sweetwater, Virginia Gardens, and Westchester. Population (2000), 639,295.

ZIP Codes: 33002, 33010–17, 33027–29, 33054–55, 33082, 33102, 33107, 33116, 33122, 33126, 33143, 33148, 33152, 33155–58, 33165–66, 33172–74, 33176, 33178, 33186, 33188, 33266, 33283

* * *

TWENTY-SECOND DISTRICT

E. CLAY SHAW, JR., Republican, of Fort Lauderdale, FL; born in Miami, FL, April 19, 1939; education: graduated, Miami Edison Senior High School, 1957; B.S., Stetson University, Deland, FL, 1961; M.B.A., University of Alabama, 1963; J.D., Stetson University College of Law, 1966; professional: former certified public accountant; lawyer; admitted to the Florida State bar in 1966 and commenced practice in Fort Lauderdale; admitted to practice before the federal court in the Southern District of Florida and the U.S. Supreme Court; assistant city attorney, Fort Lauderdale, 1968; chief city prosecutor, 1968–69; assistant municipal judge, 1969–71; city commissioner, 1971–72; vice mayor, 1973–75; mayor, 1975–80; member: executive committee, U.S. Conference of Mayors; executive committee, Republican National Committee; president, National Conference of Republican Mayors; U.S. special ambassador, Papua, New Guinea (President Ford); director, Fort Lauderdale Chamber of Commerce; vice chairman, Sun Belt Mayor's Task Force; Broward County Charter Commission; national vice chairman, Mayors for Reagan, 1980; chairman, Florida Congressional Delegation; member, St. Anthony's Church; married: the former Emilie Costar, 1960; children: Mimi Shaw Carter, Jennifer Shaw Wilder, E. Clay Shaw III, and John Charles Shaw; committees: Ways and Means; Joint Committee on Taxation; subcommittees: Oversight; Social Security; chairman, Trade; elected to the 97th Congress, November 4, 1980; reelected to each succeeding Congress.

Office Listings

http://www.house.gov/shaw

1236 Longworth House Office Building, Washington, DC 20515 .... (202) 225–3026
    Chief of Staff.—Eric Eikenberg.   FAX: 225–8398
    Press Secretary.—Gail Gitcho.
1512 East Broward Boulevard, Fort Lauderdale, FL 33301 .... (954) 522–1800
    District Director.—Joel Gustafson.
222 Lakeview Avenue, Suite 225, West Palm Beach, FL 33401 .... (561) 832–3007

Counties: BROWARD (part), PALM BEACH (part). CITIES: Aventura, Bal Harbour, Bay Harbor Islands, Biscayne Park, Boca Raton, Boynton Beach, Bring Breezes, Cloud Lake, Dania, Deerfield Beach, Delray Beach, Fort Lauderdale, Glen Ridge, Golden Beach, Gulf Stream, Hallandale, Highland Beach, Hillsboro Beach, Hollywood, Hypoluxo, Indian Creek, Juno Beach, Lake Park, Lake Worth, Lantana, Lauderdale by the Sea, Lazy Lake, Lighthouse Point, Manalapan, North Bay Village, North Palm Beach, Oakland Park, Ocean Ridge, Palm Beach, Palm Beach Gardens, Palm Beach Shores, Pembroke Park, Pompano Beach, Rivera Beach, Sea Ranch Lakes, South Palm Beach, Surfside, West Palm Beach, and Wilton Manors. Population (2000), 639,295.

ZIP Codes: 33004, 33009, 33015, 33033, 33060–62, 33064–65, 33067, 33071–74, 33076, 33097, 33128, 33153, 33155–56, 33161, 33163, 33165, 33179, 33186, 33189, 33280, 33301, 33303–09, 33312, 33314–17, 33324, 33328, 33334–35, 33339, 33346, 33348, 33401, 33403–08, 33410–12, 33415, 33418–20, 33424, 33426–27, 33429, 33431–36, 33441–45, 33458, 33460–64, 33468, 33477–78, 33480, 33483, 33486–87

* * *

TWENTY-THIRD DISTRICT

ALCEE L. HASTINGS, Democrat, of Miramar, FL; born in Altamonte Springs, FL, September 5, 1936; education: graduated, Crooms Academy, Sanford, FL, 1954; B.A., Fisk University, Nashville, TN, 1958; Howard University, Washington, DC; J.D., Florida A&M University, Tallahassee, 1963; attorney; admitted to the Florida bar, 1963; circuit judge, U.S. District Court for the Southern District of Florida; member: African Methodist Episcopal Church, NAACP, Miami-Dade Chamber of Commerce, Family Christian Association, ACLU, Southern Poverty Law Center, National Organization for Women, Planned Parenthood, Women and Children First, Inc., Sierra Club, Cousteau Society, Broward County Democratic Executive Committee, Dade County Democratic Executive Committee, Lauderhill Democratic Club, Hollywood Hills Democratic Club, Pembroke Pines Democratic Club, Urban League, National Bar Association, Florida Chapter of the National Bar Association, T.J. Reddick Bar Association, National Conference of Black Lawyers, Simon Wiesenthal Center, The Furtivist Society; Progressive Black Police Officers Club, International Black Firefighters Association; Helsinki Commission; three children: Alcee Lamar II, Chelsea, and Leigh; committees: Rules; House Permanent Select Committee on Intelligence; elected on November 3, 1992, to the 103rd Congress; reelected to each succeeding Congress.

Office Listings

http://www.house.gov/alceehastings

2353 Rayburn House Office Building, Washington, DC 20515	(202) 225–1313
Chief of Staff.—Fred Turner.	
2701 West Oakland Park Boulevard, Suite 200, Ft. Lauderdale, FL 33311	(954) 733–2800
Chief of Staff.—Arthur W. Kennedy.	
5725 Corporate Way, Suite 208, West Palm Beach, FL 33407	(561) 684–0565

Counties: BROWARD (part), HENDRY (part), MARTIN (part), PALM BEACH (part), ST. LUCIE (part). Population (2000), 639,295.

ZIP Codes: 33025, 33027–28, 33033, 33060, 33064, 33066, 33068–69, 33142, 33155–56, 33158, 33160–61, 33179, 33269, 33301–02, 33304–05, 33309–13, 33315, 33317, 33319–22, 33330–32, 33334, 33340, 33349, 33351, 33359, 33401–09, 33411, 33413–17, 33425, 33430, 33435, 33437–41, 33444–45, 33447, 33459–62, 33465, 33467, 33470, 33476, 33483, 33493, 34945–48, 34950–51, 34954, 34956, 34972, 34974, 34979, 34981, 34986–87

* * *

TWENTY-FOURTH DISTRICT

TOM FEENEY, Republican, of Oviedo, FL; born in Abington, PA, May 21, 1958; education: B.A., Pennsylvania State University, 1980; J.D., University of Pittsburgh, 1983; professional: attorney; business interests: Real Estate; religion: Presbyterian; organizations: Cornerstone, Inc., Distribution Center Board of Directors; City of Light Business Leadership Council; Mosley's High-Tech Tutoring Board of Directors; East Orange, Southwest Volusia, Sanford, and Oviedo Chambers of Commerce; James Madison Institute Board of Directors; OIA Kidsway, Inc., Board of Directors; Orange and Seminole County Republican Executive Committees; The Empowerment Network; American Legislative Exchange Council National Education Task Force; public service: Florida House of Representatives, 1990–1994, and 1996–2002; Republican nominee for Lieutenant Governor, 1994; Florida Speaker of the House of Representatives, 2000–2002; family: married to Ellen Stewart; children: Tommy and Sean; committees: Financial Services; Judiciary; Science; elected to the 108th Congress on November 5, 2002; reelected to each succeeding Congress.

Office Listings
http://www.house.gov/feeney

323 Cannon House Office Building, Washington, DC 20515	(202) 225–2706
Chief of Staff.—Jason Roe.	FAX: 226–6299
Legislative Director.—Ryan Visco.	
Executive Assistant.—Audra Ozols.	
12424 Research Parkway, Suite 135, Orlando, FL 32826	(407) 208–1106
1000 City Center Circle, Second Floor, Port Orange, FL 32129	(386) 756–9798
400 South Street, Suite 413, Titusville, FL 32780	(321) 264–6113

Counties: BREVARD (part), ORANGE (part), SEMINOLE (part), VOLUSIA (part). Population (2000), 639,295.

ZIP Codes: 32114, 32118–19, 32123–24, 32127–29, 32132, 32141, 32168–70, 32701, 32703–04, 32707–09, 32712, 32714, 32716, 32719, 32732–33, 32738–39, 32751, 32754, 32757, 32759, 32762, 32764–66, 32775, 32779–83, 32789–90, 32792–94, 32796, 32798, 32810, 32816–17, 32820, 32824–29, 32831–33, 32878, 32922, 32926–27, 32953–54, 32959, 33313, 33319, 33337, 33388

* * *

TWENTY-FIFTH DISTRICT

MARIO DIAZ-BALART, Republican, of Miami, FL; born in Ft. Lauderdale, FL, September 25, 1961; education: University of South Florida; professional: President, Gordon Diaz-Balart and Partners (public relations and marketing business); religion: Catholic; public service: Administrative Assistant to the Mayor of Miami, 1985–1988; Florida House of Representatives, 1988–1992, and 2000–2002; Florida State Senate, 1992–2000; committees: Budget; Transportation and Infrastructure; elected to the 108th Congress on November 5, 2002; reelected to each succeeding Congress.

Office Listings
http://www.house.gov/mariodiaz-balart

313 Cannon House Office Building, Washington, DC 20515	(202) 225–2778
Chief of Staff.—Omar Franco.	FAX: 226–0346
Legislative Director.—Charles Cooper.	
12851 SW 42nd Street, Suite 131, Miami, FL 33175	(305) 225–6866
District Director.—Miguel Otero.	
4715 Golden Gate Parkway, Suite 1, Naples, FL 34116	(239) 348–1620
District Representative.—Stephen Hart.	

Counties: COLLIER (part), DADE (part). Population (2000), 639,295.

ZIP Codes: 33015–16, 33018, 33030–35, 33157, 33166, 33170, 33175–78, 33182–87, 33189–90, 33193–94, 33196, 34113–14, 34116–17, 34120, 34137–39, 34141–43

GEORGIA

(Population 2000, 8,186,453)

SENATORS

SAXBY CHAMBLISS, Republican, of Moultrie, GA; born in Warrenton, NC, November 10, 1943; education: graduated, C.E. Byrd High School, Shreveport, LA, 1962; B.A., University of Georgia, 1966; J.D., University of Tennessee College of Law, 1968; professional: served on the state bar of Georgia's Disciplinary Review Panel, 1969; member: Moultrie-Colquitt County Economic Development Authority; Colquitt County Economic Development Corporation; married: the former Julianne Frohbert, 1966; children: Lia Chambliss Baker, and C. Saxby (Bo), Jr.; committees: chair, Agriculture, Nutrition, and Forestry; Armed Services; Rules and Administration; Select Committee on Intelligence; Joint Committee on Printing; elected to the 104th Congress; reelected to each succeeding Congress; elected to the U.S. Senate on November 5, 2002.

Office Listings

http://chambliss.senate.gov

416 Russell Senate Office Building, Washington, DC 20510	(202) 224–3521	
Chief of Staff.—Krister Holladay.	FAX: 224–0103	
Office Manager.—Kate Vickers.		
Executive Assistant.—Teresa Ervin.		
100 Galleria, Suite 1340, Atlanta, GA 30339	(770) 763–9090	
State Director.—Greg Wright.		
950 Plantation Centre, Macon, GA 31210	(478) 476–0788	
Field Representative.—Bill Stembridge.		
419–A South Main Street, Moultrie, GA 31768	(229) 985–2112	
Field Representative.—Debbie Cannon.		
2 East Bryan Street, Suite 620, Savannah, GA 31401	(912) 232–3657	
Field Representative.—Eric Betts.		
1058 Claussen Road, Suite 105, Augusta, GA 30907	(706) 738–0302	
Field Representative.—Jim Hussey.		

* * *

JOHNNY ISAKSON, Republican, of Marietta GA; born in Fulton County, GA, December 28, 1944; education: University of Georgia; professional: real estate executive; president, Northside Realty; public service: Georgia State House of Representatives, 1976–90; Georgia State Senate, 1992–96; appointed chairman of the Georgia Board of Election, 1996; awards: Republican National Committee "Best Legislator in America," 1989; organizations: chairman of the board, Georgian Club; trustee, Kennesaw State University; board of directors, Metro Atlanta and Georgia Chambers of Commerce; past president, Cobb Chamber of Commerce; executive committee, National Association of Realtors; president, Realty Alliance; advisory board, Federal National Mortgage Association; married: Dianne; children: John, Kevin, and Julie; religion: Methodist; election to the 106th Congress on February 23, 1999, by special election; reelected to each succeeding Congress; committees: Environment and Public Works; Health, Education, Labor, and Pensions; Small Business and Entrepreneurship; Veterans' Affairs; elected to the U.S. Senate on November 2, 2004.

Office Listings

http://isakson.senate.gov

120 Russell Senate Office Building, Washington, DC 20510	(202) 224–3643	
Chief of Staff.—Heath Garrett.	FAX: 228–0724	
Deputy Chief of Staff.—Chris Carr.		
Communications Director.—Joan Kirchner.		
Scheduler.—Tempe Landrum.		
100 Colony Square, 1175 Peachtree Street, NE., Suite 300, Atlanta, GA 30361	(404) 347–2202	

REPRESENTATIVES

FIRST DISTRICT

JACK KINGSTON, Republican, of Savannah, GA; born in Bryan, TX, April, 24, 1955; education: Michigan State University, 1973–74; University of Georgia, 1974–78; insurance salesman; vice president, Palmer and Cay/Carswell; Georgia State Legislature, 1984–92;

member: Savannah Health Mission, Isle of Hope Community Association, Christ Church; married: Elizabeth Morris Kingston, 1979; children: Betsy, John, Ann, and Jim; vice chairman, Republican Conference; committees: Appropriations; subcommittees: Agriculture, Rural Development, Food and Drug Administration, and Related Agencies; Defense; elected on November 3, 1992 to the 103rd Congress; reelected to each succeeding Congress.

Office Listings
http://www.house.gov/kingston

2242 Rayburn House Office Building, Washington, DC 20515	(202) 225–5831
Chief of Staff.—Bill Johnson.	FAX: 226–2269
Legislative Director.—Heather McNatt.	
Legislative Assistant.—Emily Howard.	
Communications Director.—Jennifer Hing.	
One Diamond Causeway, Suite 7, Savannah, GA 31406	(912) 352–0101
P.O. Box 40, Baxley, GA 31515	(912) 367–7403
Brunswick Federal Building, 805 Gloucester Street, Room 304, Brunswick, GA 31520	(912) 265–9010
P.O. Box 9348, Warner Robins, GA 31095	(478) 923–8987

Counties: APPLING, ATKINSON, BACON, BEN HILL, BERRIER, BRANTLEY, BRYAN (part), CAMDEN, CHARLTON, CHATHAM (part), CLINCH, COFFEE, COLQUITT (part), COOK, ECHOLS, GLYNN, HOUSTON (part), IRWIN, JEFF DAVIS, LANIER, LIBERTY, LONG, LOWNDES (part), MCINTOSH, PIERCE, PULASKI (part), WARE, WAYNE, WILCOX (part). Population (2000), 629,761.

ZIP Codes: 30426–27, 31001, 31005, 31008, 31015, 31028, 31030, 31036, 31047, 31069, 31071–72, 31079, 31088, 31091–93, 31098, 31301, 31304–05, 31309–10, 31313–16, 31319–20, 31323, 31327–28, 31331, 31333, 31406, 31409–11, 31416, 31419, 31422, 31501–03, 31510, 31512–13, 31515–16, 31518–25, 31527, 31532–35, 31537, 31539, 31542–43, 31545–48, 31550–58, 31560–69, 31598–99, 31602, 31604–05, 31620, 31622–24, 31627, 31630–32, 31634–37, 31639, 31641–42, 31645, 31647–50, 31699, 31722, 31733, 31749–50, 31760, 31768–69, 31773–74, 31778, 31783, 31788, 31790, 31794, 31798

* * *

SECOND DISTRICT

SANFORD D. BISHOP, JR., Democrat, of Albany, GA; born in Mobile, AL, February 4, 1947; education: attended Mobile County public schools; B.A., Morehouse College, 1968; J.D., Emory University, 1971; professional: attorney; admitted to the Georgia and Alabama bars; Georgia House of Representatives, 1977–91; Georgia Senate, 1991–93; former member: Executive Board, Boy Scouts of America; YMCA; Sigma Pi Phi Fraternity; Kappa Alpha Psi Fraternity; 32nd Degree Mason, Shriner; member: Mt. Zion Baptist Church, Albany, GA; committee: Appropriations; elected to the 103rd Congress; reelected to each succeeding Congress.

Office Listings
http://www.house.gov/bishop

2429 Rayburn House Office Building, Washington, DC 20515	(202) 225–3631
Chief of Staff.—Phyllis Hallmon.	FAX: 225–2203
Legislative Director.—Roger Manno.	
Communications Director.—Jennifer Hoelzer.	
Administrative Assistant / Scheduler.—Martina Morgan.	
Albany Towers, 235 W. Roosevelt Avenue, Suite 114, Albany, GA 31701	(229) 439–8067
District Director.—Kenneth Cutts.	
101 S. Main Street, Dawson, GA 31742	(229) 995–3991
Field Representative.—Elaine Gillespie.	
401 North Patterson Street, Room 255, Federal Building, Valdosta, GA 31601	(229) 247–9705
Field Representative.—Michael Bryant.	
18 Ninth Street, Suite 201, Columbus, GA 31901	(706) 320–9477
Field Representatives: Elaine Gillespie, Wallace Sholar.	

Counties: BAKER, BROOKS, CALHOUN, CHATTAHOOCHEE, CLAY, COLQUITT (part), CRISP, DECATUR, DOUGHERTY, EARLY, GRADY, LEE, LOWNDES (part), MILLER, MITCHELL, MUSCOGEE (part), QUITMAN, RANDOLPH, SEMINOLE, STEWART, SUMTER, TERRELL, THOMAS, TIFT, TURNER, WEBSTER, WORTH. Population (2000), 629,735.

ZIP Codes: 30150, 30290, 31010, 31015, 31039, 31068–69, 31072, 31092, 31201, 31204, 31211, 31217, 31328, 31601–03, 31605–06, 31625–26, 31629, 31636–38, 31641, 31643, 31698, 31701–12, 31714, 31716, 31719–22, 31727, 31730, 31733, 31735, 31738–39, 31743–44, 31747, 31749, 31753, 31756–58, 31763–65, 31768, 31771–72, 31775–76, 31778–84, 31787–96, 31799, 31803, 31805, 31814–15, 31821, 31824–25, 31832, 31901–07, 31914, 31995, 31997–99, 39813, 39815, 39817–19, 39823–29, 39832, 39834, 39836–37, 39840–42, 39845–46, 39851–52, 39854, 39859, 39861–62, 39866–67, 39870, 39877, 39885–86, 39897

THIRD DISTRICT

JIM MARSHALL, Democrat, of Macon, GA; born in Ithaca, NY, March 31, 1948; education: graduated from high school in Mobile, AL, in 1966; received a National Merit Scholarship to attend Princeton University, and graduated in 1972; military service: U.S. Army; infantry combat in Vietnam; served as an Airborne-Ranger reconnaissance platoon sergeant; decorated for heroism; received Purple Heart and two Bronze Stars; professional: graduated from Boston University Law School, 1977; joined the Mercer University Law School faculty in 1979; public service: participates in numerous community service activities; elected Mayor of Macon, GA, in 1995; married: Camille; children: Mary and Robert; committees: Agriculture; Armed Services; elected to the 108th Congress on November 5, 2002; reelected to each succeeding Congress.

Office Listings

http://jimmarshall.house.gov

515 Cannon House Office Building, Washington, DC 20515	(202) 225–6531
Chief of Staff.—John Kirincich.	FAX: 225–3013
Legislative Director.—Bradley Edgell.	
Communications Director.—Doug Moore.	
682 Cherry Street, Suite 300, Macon, GA 31201	(478) 464–0255
503 Bellevue Avenue, Suite C, Dublin, GA 31021	(478) 296–2023

Counties: BALDWIN, BIBB (part), BLECKLEY, CANDLER, CRAWFORD, DODGE, DOOLY, EMANUEL, EVANS, HANCOCK, HOUSTON (part), JOHNSON, JONES (part), LAURENS, MACON, MARION, MONROE, MONTGOMERY, PEACH, PULASKI (part), SCHLEY, TATTNALL, TAYLOR, TELFAIR, TOOMBS, TREUTLEN, TWIGGS, WASHINGTON, WHEELER, WILCOX (part), WILKINSON. Population (2000), 629,748.

ZIP Codes: 30204, 30233, 30401, 30410–14, 30417, 30420–21, 30423, 30425, 30427–29, 30436, 30438–39, 30441, 30445, 30447–48, 30450–54, 30457, 30464, 30470–71, 30473–75, 30477, 30499, 30678, 30820, 31001–03, 31006–09, 31011–23, 31025, 31027–42, 31044–46, 31049–52, 31054–55, 31057–63, 31065–72, 31075–78, 31081–84, 31086–99, 31201–13, 31216–17, 31220, 31294–97, 31328, 31544, 31549, 31601–02, 31632, 31711, 31735, 31801, 31803, 31806, 31812, 31824

* * *

FOURTH DISTRICT

CYNTHIA McKINNEY, Democrat, of Lithonia, GA; born in Atlanta, GA, March 17, 1955; education: graduated, St. Joseph High School, Atlanta; B.A., International Relations, University of Southern California; M.A., Fletcher School of Law and Diplomacy, Tufts University; currently working on a Ph.D. program at the University of California, Berkeley; Georgia State House of Representatives, 1988–92; U.S. House of Representatives, 1993–2003; member, NAACP; one child: Coy; committees: Armed Services; Budget; subcommittees: Military Personnel; Terrorism, Unconventional Threats and Capabilities; elected to the 109th Congress on November 2, 2004.

Office Listings

http://www.house.gov/mckinney

320 Cannon House Office Building, Washington, DC 20515	(202) 225–1605
Staff Assistant.—Adrienne Cole.	FAX: 226–0691
Special Assistants: Jabriel Ballentine, Hugh Esco, Kelly O'Meara, Afra Yehwalashet.	
2050 Lawrenceville Highway, Suite D–46, Decatur, GA 30033	(404) 633–0927
3523 Buford Highway, NE., Suite 201, Atlanta, GA 30329	(404) 320–2001

Counties: DEKALB (part), GWINNETT (part). CITIES: Avondale Estates, Chamblee, Clarkston, Decatur, Doraville, Dunwoody, Lithonia, and Stone Mountain. Population (2000), 629,690.

ZIP Codes: 30002–03, 30012, 30021, 30030–38, 30058, 30071–72, 30074, 30079, 30083–88, 30091–92, 30094, 30306–07, 30316, 30319, 30322, 30324, 30329, 30338, 30340–41, 30345–47, 30350, 30356, 30359–60, 30362, 30366, 30376, 31107, 31119, 31141, 31145, 39901

* * *

FIFTH DISTRICT

JOHN LEWIS, Democrat, of Atlanta, GA; born in Pike County, AL, February 21, 1940; education: graduated Pike County Training School, Brundidge, AL, 1957; B.A., American Baptist Theological Seminary, Nashville, TN, 1961; B.A., Fisk University, Nashville, TN, 1963; civil rights leader; Atlanta City Council, 1982–86; member: Martin Luther King Center for Social

Change, African American Institute, Robert F. Kennedy Memorial; married the former Lillian Miles in 1968; one child, John Miles Lewis; appointed senior chief deputy Democratic whip for the 109th Congress; committees: Ways and Means; subcommittees: Health; Oversight; elected to the 100th Congress on November 4, 1986; reelected to each succeeding Congress.

Office Listings

http://www.house.gov/johnlewis

343 Cannon House Office Building, Washington, DC 20515	(202) 225–3801
Chief of Staff.—Michael Collins.	FAX: 225–0351
Officer Manager / Scheduler.—Jacob Gillison.	
Director of Communications.—Brenda Jones.	
Legislative Director.—Michaeleen Crowell.	
Suite 1920, 100 Peachtree Street NW., Atlanta, GA 30303	(404) 659–0116
District Director.—Love Williams.	

Counties: CLAYTON (part), COBB (part), DEKALB (part), FULTON (part). Population (2000), 629,727.

ZIP Codes: 30067, 30075–76, 30080, 30082, 30126, 30213, 30272, 30296, 30301–21, 30324–34, 30336–37, 30339, 30342–44, 30346, 30348–50, 30354–55, 30357–58, 30361, 30364, 30368–71, 30374–75, 30377–79, 30384, 30392, 30394, 30904, 30909, 31032, 31106, 31126, 31131–32, 31156, 31192–93, 31328

* * *

SIXTH DISTRICT

TOM PRICE, Republican, of Roswell, GA; born in Lansing, MI, October 8, 1954; education: B.A., University of Michigan, 1976; M.D., University of Michigan, 1979; professional: physician; member of the Georgia state senate, 1997–2004; member: Cobb Chamber of Commerce; Civil Air Patrol; Advisory Board, Georgia Partnership for Excellence in Education; religion: Presbyterian; married: Elizabeth; one child, Robert; committees: Education and the Workforce; Financial Services; elected to the 109th Congress on November 2, 2004.

Office Listings

http://www.house.gov/tomprice

506 Cannon House Office Building, Washington, DC 20515	(202) 225–4501
Chief of Staff.—Matt McGinley.	FAX: 225–4656
District Director.—Jared Thomas.	
3730 Roswell Road, Suite 50, Marietta, GA 30062	(770) 565–4990

Counties: CHEROKEE (part), COBB (part), FULTON (part). CITIES AND TOWNSHIPS: Dunwoody, Marietta, Roswell, Sandy Springs, and Smyrna. Population (2000), 629,725.

ZIP Codes: 30004–07, 30009–10, 30022–24, 30041, 30060, 30062, 30064–68, 30075–77, 30092, 30096–97, 30101–02, 30106, 30115, 30127, 30141, 30144, 30152, 30156, 30160, 30168, 30188–89, 30327–28, 30339, 30342, 30350, 31032, 31146, 31150, 31156, 31602, 31632

* * *

SEVENTH DISTRICT

JOHN LINDER, Republican, of Duluth, GA; born in Deer River, MN, September 9, 1942; education: graduate, Deer River High School, 1957; B.S., 1963, and D.D.S., 1967, University of Minnesota; captain, U.S. Air Force, 1967–69; former dentist; president, Linder Financial Corporation; Georgia State Representative, 1975–80, 1983–90; member: Georgia GOP, Rotary Club, American Legion; married: Lynne Peterson Linder, 1963; children: Matt and Kristine; committees: Homeland Security; Ways and Means; Joint Committee on Printing; elected on November 3, 1992, to the 103rd Congress; reelected to each succeeding Congress.

Office Listings

http://www.house.gov/linder

1026 Longworth House Office Building, Washington, DC 20515	(202) 225–4272
Chief of Staff.—Rob Woodall.	FAX: 225–4696
Legislative Director.—Don Green.	
Administrative Assistant.—Bill Evans.	
Deputy Chief of Staff.—Joy Burch.	
District Offices	(770) 232–3005

Counties: BARTOW (part), CHEROKEE (part), FORSYTH (part), GWINNETT (part), PAULDING (part). Population (2000), 629,725.

ZIP Codes: 30004–05, 30012, 30017, 30019, 30024, 30039–47, 30049, 30052, 30071, 30078, 30087, 30092, 30095–97, 30101–03, 30107, 30114–15, 30120–21, 30123, 30127, 30132, 30134, 30137, 30141–43, 30145–46, 30153, 30157, 30168–69, 30178–80, 30183–84, 30188–89, 30515, 30518–19, 31139

* * *

EIGHTH DISTRICT

LYNN A. WESTMORELAND, Republican, of Sharpsburg, GA; born in Atlanta, GA, April 2, 1950; education: graduated from Therrell High School, Atlanta, GA; attended Georgia State University, Atlanta, GA, 1969–71; member of the Georgia State University, 1993–2004; professional: real estate developer; public service: Minority Leader, Georgia State House, 2000–04; Representative, Georgia State House, 1992–2004; religion: Baptist; organizations: Fayette Board of Realtors; Fayette County Safe Kids Council; Georgia Homebuilders; National Board of Realtors; National Rifle Association; married: Joan; children: Heather, Marcy, and Trae; committees: Government Reform; Small Business; Transportation and Infrastructure; subcommittees: vice-chair, Railroads; elected to the 109th Congress on November 2, 2004.

Office Listings

http://www.house.gov/westmoreland

1118 Longworth House Office Building, Washington, DC 20515	(202) 225–5901
Chief of Staff.—Chip Lake.	FAX: 225–2515
Deputy Chief of Staff/Communications Director.—Brian Robinson.	
Legislative Director.—Joe Lillis.	
Office Manager.—Alice James.	
2753 East Highway 34, Suite 3, Newnan, GA 30265	(770) 683–2033

Counties: BIBB COUNTY (part). CITIES AND TOWNSHIPS: Macon, Payne. BUTTS COUNTY (part). CITIES AND TOWNSHIPS: Flovilla, Jackson, Jenkinsburg. CARROLL COUNTY (part). CITIES AND TOWNSHIPS: Bowdon, Carrollton, Mount Zion, Roopville, Temple, Villa Rica, Whitesburg. COWETA COUNTY (part). CITIES AND TOWNSHIPS: Grantville, Haralson, Lone Oak (also Meriwether), Luthersville, Moreland, Newnan, Palmetto, Senoia, Sharpsburg, Turin. DOUGLAS COUNTY (part). CITIES AND TOWNSHIPS: Austell, Douglasville, Lithia Springs, Winston. FAYETTE COUNTY. CITIES AND TOWNSHIPS: Brooks, Fayetteville, Peachtree City, Tyrone, Woolsey. HARRIS COUNTY (part). CITIES AND TOWNSHIPS: Cataula, Ellerslie, Fortson, Hamilton, Midland, Pine Mountain, Pine Mountain Valley, Shiloh, Waverly Hall, West Point. HENRY COUNTY (part). CITIES AND TOWNSHIPS: Hampton, Locust Grove, McDonough, Stockbridge. JASPER COUNTY (part). CITIES AND TOWNSHIPS: Monticello, Shady Dale. JONES COUNTY (part). CITIES AND TOWNSHIPS: Gray, Haddcock. LAMAR COUNTY. CITIES AND TOWNSHIPS: Aldora, Barnesville, Milner. MUSCOGEE COUNTY (part). CITIES AND TOWNSHIPS: Bibb City, Columbus. NEWTON COUNTY (part). CITIES AND TOWNSHIPS: Covington, Mansfield, Newborn, Oxford, Porterdale. PIKE COUNTY. CITIES AND TOWNSHIPS: Concord, Meansville, Molena, Williamson, Zebulon. ROCKDALE COUNTY (part). CITIES AND TOWNSHIPS: Conyers. SPALDING COUNTY (part). CITIES AND TOWNSHIPS: Griffin, Orchard Hill, Sunny Side. TROUP COUNTY (part). CITIES AND TOWNSHIPS: Hogansville, LaGrange. UPSON COUNTY (part). CITIES AND TOWNSHIPS: Thomaston, and Yatesville. Population (2000), 629,700.

ZIP Codes: 30013–14, 30016, 30055–56, 30094, 30108, 30110, 30116–17, 30122, 30133–35, 30154, 30170, 30179–80, 30185, 30187, 30204–06, 30213–17, 30220, 30223–24, 30228–30, 30233–34, 30236, 30238, 30240–41, 30248, 30252–53, 30256–59, 30263–66, 30268–69, 30271, 30273, 30275–77, 30281, 30284–86, 30289–90, 30292, 30295, 30904, 31002, 31004, 31016, 31024, 31029, 31032, 31038, 31046, 31064, 31066, 31085, 31097, 31204, 31210–11, 31220–21, 31602, 31632, 31801, 31804, 31807–08, 31811, 31820, 31822–23, 31826, 31829–31, 31833, 31904, 31907–09, 31993

* * *

NINTH DISTRICT

CHARLIE NORWOOD, Republican, of Evans, GA; born in Valdosta, GA, July 27, 1941; education: graduated, Baylor Military High School, Chattanooga, TN, 1959; B.S., Georgia Southern University, Statesboro, 1964; D.D.S., Georgetown University Dental School, Washington, DC, 1967; served as captain, U.S. Army, 1967–69, including tour of duty in Vietnam with the 173rd Airborne Brigade; awarded the Combat Medic Badge and two Bronze Stars; dentistry practice, Augusta, GA, 1969; elected president of the Georgia Dental Association, 1983; member, Trinity-on-the-Hill United Methodist Church, Augusta, GA; started several small businesses over the years, including Northwood Tree Nursery in Evans, GA, and Park Avenue Fabrics in Augusta, GA; married: Gloria Norwood, 1962; children: Charles and Carlton; two grandchildren; committees: Education and the Workforce; Energy and Commerce; subcommittees: chairman, Workforce Protections; vice chairman, Health; Energy and Air Quality; Select Education; elected on November 8, 1994, to the 104th Congress; reelected to each succeeding Congress.

Office Listings

2452 Rayburn House Office Building, Washington, DC 20515 .... (202) 225–4101
Chief of Staff.—John Walker.
Deputy Chief of Staff.—Rodney Whitlock.
Communications Director.—John Stone.
1054 Claussen Road, Suite 316, Augusta, GA 30907 .... (706) 733–7066
District Director.—Michael Shaffer.
315 West Savannah Street, Toccoa, GA 30577 .... (706) 886–2776
District Director.—Wanda Tate.

Counties: BANKS, BARROW, COLUMBIA, ELBERT, FRANKLIN, GREENE, HABERSHAM, HART, JACKSON, LINCOLN, LUMPKIN, MADISON, MCDUFFIE, MORGAN, NEWTON (part), OCONEE, OGLETHORPE (part), PUTNAM, RABUN, RICHMOND (part), STEPHENS, TOWNS, UNION, WALTON (part), WHITE, WILKES. Population (2000), 629,762.

ZIP Codes: 30011, 30014, 30016, 30018, 30025, 30052, 30054–56, 30510–12, 30514, 30516–17, 30520–23, 30525, 30528–31, 30533, 30535, 30537–38, 30544–49, 30552–53, 30557–58, 30562–63, 30565, 30567–68, 30571–73, 30575–77, 30580–82, 30596–99, 30607, 30619–25, 30627–30, 30633–35, 30638–39, 30641–43, 30645–48, 30650, 30655–56, 30660, 30662–63, 30665–69, 30671, 30673, 30677–78, 30680, 30683, 30802, 30806, 30808–09, 30813–14, 30817–18, 30824, 30904–05, 30907, 30909, 30917, 31024, 31026, 31033, 31038, 31061, 31064, 31907

* * *

TENTH DISTRICT

NATHAN DEAL, Republican, of Clermont, GA; born in Millen, GA, August 25, 1942; education: graduated, Washington County High School, Sandersville, 1960; B.A., Mercer University, Macon, GA, 1964; J.D., Mercer University, Walter F. George School of Law, Macon, GA, 1966; admitted to the Georgia bar, 1966; captain, U.S. Army, 1966–68; Georgia State Senate, 1981–92; president pro tempore, 1991–92; married: the former Emilie Sandra Dunagan, 1966; children: Jason, Mary Emily, Carrie, and Katie; committees: Energy and Commerce; subcommittees: Commerce, Trade, and Consumer Protection; Environment and Hazardous Materials; chair, Health; elected on November 3, 1992, to the 103rd Congress; reelected to each succeeding Congress.

Office Listings

http://www.house.gov/deal

2133 Rayburn House Office Building, Washington, DC 20515 .... (202) 225–5211
Chief of Staff.—Chris Riley.
Press Secretaries: Chris Riley, Todd Smith.
108 W. Lafayette Square, Suite 102, Lafayette, GA 30728 .... (706) 638–7042
P.O. Box 1015, Gainesville, GA 30503 .... (770) 535–2592
Suite 108, 415 East Walnut Avenue, Dalton, GA 30721 .... (706) 226–5320

Counties: CATOOSA, DADE, DAWSON, FANNIN, FORSYTH (part), GILMER, GORDON, GWINNETT (part), HALL, MURRAY, PICKENS, ROCKDALE (part), WALKER, WALTON (part), and WHITFIELD. CITIES AND TOWNSHIPS: Auburn, Blue Ridge, Braselton, Buford, Calhoun, Chatsworth, Chickamauga, Clermont, Cohutta, Conyers, Cumming, Dacula, Dalton, Dawsonville, East Ellijay, Ellijay, Eton, Fairmount, Flowery Branch, Fort Oglethorpe, Gainesville, Gillsville, Grayson, Jasper, LaFayette, Lawrenceville, Loganville, Lookout Mountain, Lula, McCaysville, Morgantown, Nelson, Oakwood, Plainville, Ranger, Rest Haven, Resaca, Ringgold, Rossville, Snellville, Talking Rock, Trenton, Tunnel Hill, and Varnell. Population (2000), 629,702.

ZIP Codes: 30011–13, 30017, 30019, 30028, 30039–41, 30045, 30052, 30078, 30103, 30107, 30139, 30143, 30148, 30151, 30171, 30175, 30177, 30501–04, 30506–07, 30510, 30512–13, 30517–19, 30522, 30527, 30534, 30539–43, 30548, 30554–55, 30559–60, 30564, 30566, 30572, 30575, 30701, 30703, 30705, 30707–08, 30710–11, 30719–22, 30724–26, 30728, 30731–36, 30738–42, 30746–47, 30750–53, 30755–57, 30811, 31002

* * *

ELEVENTH DISTRICT

PHIL GINGREY, Republican, of Marietta, GA; born in Augusta, GA, July 10, 1942; education: B.S., Georgia Tech, 1965; M.D., Medical College of Georgia, 1969; professional: Physician; set up a pro-life OB-GYN practice; organizations: Cobb County Medical Society; Medical Association of Georgia; American Medical Association; Georgia OB-GYN Society; public service: Marietta School Board, 1993–1997; Georgia State Senate, 1999–2002; married: Billie Ayers; children: Billy, Gannon, Phyllis, and Laura; committees: Rules; House Policy Committee; elected to the 108th Congress on November 5, 2002; reelected to each succeeding Congress.

Office Listings
http://www.house.gov/gingrey

119 Cannon House Office Building, Washington, DC 20515	....	(202) 225–2931
Chief of Staff.—Mitch Hunter.		FAX: 225–2944
Legislative Director.—Rob Herriott.		
Executive Assistant / Office Manager.—Catherine Gabrysh.		
219 Roswell Street, Marietta, GA 30060	....	(770) 429–1776
600 East 1st Street, Suite 301, Rome, GA 30161	....	(706) 290–1776

Counties: BARTOW (part), CARROLL (part), CHATTOOGA, COBB (part), COWETA (part), DOUGLAS (part), FLOYD, HARALSON, HARRIS (part), HEARD, MERIWETHER, MUSCOGEE (part), PAULDING (part), POLK, TALBOT, TROUP (part), UPSON (part). Population (2000) 629,730.

ZIP Codes: 30008, 30060–64, 30066–67, 30069, 30080–82, 30090, 30103–06, 30108–13, 30116–22, 30124–27, 30129, 30134–35, 30137–40, 30145, 30147, 30149–50, 30153, 30161–65, 30168, 30170–73, 30176, 30178–80, 30182–84, 30217–20, 30222, 30230, 30240–41, 30251, 30259, 30261, 30263, 30276, 30286, 30293, 30548, 30701, 30730–31, 30733, 30747, 30753, 31016, 31058, 31072, 31079, 31097, 31801, 31810, 31812, 31816, 31822, 31826–27, 31830–31, 31833, 31836, 31904, 31906–07, 31917

* * *

TWELFTH DISTRICT

JOHN BARROW, Democrat, of Athens, GA; born in Athens, October 31, 1955; education: graduated from Clarke Central High School, Athens-Clarke County, GA, 1973; B.A., University of Georgia, Athens, GA, 1976; J.D., Harvard University, Cambridge, MA, 1979; professional: law clerk for Judge, Savannah, GA; law clerk for Judge, Fiftieth Circuit Court of Appeals; founding member, Wilburn, Lewis, Barrow and Stotz, PC.; county commissioner; lawyer, private practice; Athens-Clarke, GA, city-county commissioner, 1990–2004; volunteer, Athens-Clarke Heritage Foundation; volunteer, Parkview Playschool; charter member, Second Consolidated City-County Government; religion: First Baptist Church of Athens; married: Victoria Pentlarge; children: James and Ruth; committees: Agriculture; Education and the Workforce; Small Business; subcommittees: General Farm Commodities and Risk Management; Livestock and Horticulture; ranking member, Rural Enterprises, Agriculture, and Technology; Specialty Crops and Foreign Agriculture Programs; 21st Century Competitiveness; Workforce, Empowerment, and Government Programs; Workforce Protections; elected to the 109th Congress on November 2, 2004.

Office Listings
http://www.house.gov/barrow

226 Cannon House Office Building, Washington, DC 20515	....	(202) 225–2823
Chief of Staff.—Roman Levit.		FAX: 225–3377
Staff Assistant.—Omonigho Ufomata.		
Senior Legislative Assistant.—Aaron Schmidt.		
Scheduler.—Ashley Jones.		
320 East Clayton Street, Suite 500, Athens, GA 30601	....	(706) 613–3232

Counties: BRYAN (part), BULLOCH, BURKE, CHATHAM (part), CLARKE, EFFINGHAM, GLASCOCK, JEFFERSON, JENKINS, OGLETHORPE (part), RICHMOND (part), SCREVEN, TALIAFERRO, WARREN. CITIES AND TOWNSHIPS: Augusta, Athens, Savannah, and Statesboro. Population (2000) 629,735.

ZIP Codes: 30413, 30415, 30417, 30424–26, 30434, 30439, 30441–42, 30446, 30449–50, 30452, 30455–56, 30458–61, 30467, 30471, 30477, 30601–09, 30612, 30619, 30631, 30660, 30664, 30667, 30669, 30678, 30683, 30803, 30805, 30807–08, 30810, 30812–13, 30815–16, 30818–24, 30828, 30830, 30833, 30901, 30903–04, 30906–07, 30909, 30911–14, 30916, 30919, 30999, 31045, 31206, 31302–03, 31307–08, 31312, 31314, 31318, 31321–22, 31324, 31326, 31329, 31401–08, 31412, 31414–15, 31418–22

* * *

THIRTEENTH DISTRICT

DAVID SCOTT, Democrat, of Atlanta, GA; born in Aynor, SC, June 27, 1945; education: Florida A&M University, graduated with honors, 1967; University of Pennsylvania Wharton School of Finance, MBA degree, graduated with honors, 1969; professional: businessman; owner and CEO, Dayn-Mark Advertising; public service: Georgia House of Representatives, 1974–82; Georgia State Senate, 1982–2002; married: Alfredia Aaron, 1969; children: Dayna and Marcye; committees: Agriculture; Financial Services; elected to the 108th Congress on November 5, 2002; reelected to each succeeding Congress.

Office Listings

http://davidscott.house.gov

417 Cannon House Office Building, Washington, DC 20515 .... (202) 225–2939
    Chief of Staff.—Rob Griner.   FAX: 225–4628
    Executive Assistant / Office Manager.—Angie Borja.
    Legislative Director.—Donni Turner.
173 North Main Street, Jonesboro, GA 30236 .... (770) 210–5073
127 Main Street, Lilburn, GA 30047 .... (770) 381–0135

Counties: BUTTS (part), CLAYTON (part), DEKALB (part), FAYETTE (part), FULTON (part), GWINNETT (part), HENRY (part), NEWTON (part), ROCKDALE (part), SPAULDING (part), WALTON (part). Population (2000) 629,732.

ZIP Codes: 30012–16, 30025–26, 30029, 30034, 30038–39, 30044–45, 30047–48, 30054, 30058, 30070–71, 30084, 30087, 30093–94, 30096–99, 30212–16, 30223–24, 30228, 30233–34, 30236–38, 30248, 30250, 30252–53, 30260, 30268, 30273–74, 30281, 30287–88, 30291, 30294, 30296–98, 30315–16, 30331, 30337, 30340, 30349, 30353–54, 30368, 30380, 30385–90, 30396, 30398–99, 30655–56

HAWAII

(Population 2000, 1,211,537)

SENATORS

DANIEL K. INOUYE, Democrat, of Honolulu, HI; born in Honolulu, September 7, 1924; education: A.B., government and economics, University of Hawaii, 1950; J.D., George Washington University Law School, 1952; majority leader, Territorial House of Representatives, 1954–58; Territorial Senate, 1958–59; enlisted as private, 442nd Infantry Regimental Combat Team, 1943; battlefield commission, second lieutenant, 1944; served in France and Italy; retired captain, U.S. Army; Methodist; married: the former Margaret Shinobu Awamura of Honolulu; one son, Daniel Ken Inouye, Jr.; committees: Appropriations; co-chair, Commerce, Science and Transportation; Indian Affairs; Rules and Administration; Joint Committee on Printing; subcommittees: ranking member, Defense; elected on July 28, 1959, to the 86th Congress; reelected to the 87th Congress; elected to the U.S. Senate on November 6, 1962; reelected to each succeeding Senate term.

Office Listings

http://inouye.senate.gov

722 Hart Senate Office Building, Washington, DC 20510	(202) 224–3934
Administrative Assistant.—Patrick H. DeLeon.	TDD: 224–1233
Office Manager.—Beverly MacDonald.	
Personal Secretary.—Jessica Lee.	
Legislative Director.—Marie Blanco.	
Suite 7–212, 300 Ala Moana Boulevard, Honolulu, HI 96850	(808) 541–2542
Hilo Auxiliary Office, 101 Aupuni Street, No. 205, Hilo, HI 96720	(808) 935–0844

* * *

DANIEL K. AKAKA, Democrat, of Honolulu, HI; born in Honolulu, September 11, 1924; education: graduated, Kamehameha High School, 1942; University of Hawaii, 1948–66, bachelor of education, professional certificate, master of education; served in the U.S. Army, 1945–47; teacher, 1953–60; vice principal, 1960; principal, 1963–71; program specialist, 1968–71; director, 1971–74; director and special assistant in human resources, 1975–76; member, Kawaiahao Church; board of directors, Hanahauoli School; Act 4 Educational Advisory Commission; Library Advisory Council; Na Hookama O Pauahi Scholarship Committee, Kamehameha Schools; commissioner, Manpower and Full Employment Commission; Minister of Music, Kawaiahao Church; married: the former Mary Mildred Chong; children: Millannie, Daniel, Jr., Gerard, Alan, and Nicholas; elected to the 95th Congress in November, 1976; reelected to each succeeding Congress; committees: Armed Services; Energy and Natural Resources; Homeland Security and Governmental Affairs; Indian Affairs; ranking member, Veterans' Affairs; Select Committee on Ethics; appointed to the U.S. Senate in April, 1990, to fill the vacancy caused by the death of Senator Spark Matsunaga; elected to complete the unexpired term in November, 1990; reelected to each succeeding Senate term.

Office Listings

http://akaka.senate.gov

141 Hart Senate Office Building, Washington, DC 20510	(202) 224–6361
Administrative Assistant.—James Sakai.	FAX: 224–2126
Legislative Director.—Melissa U. Hampe.	
Fiscal Office Secretary.—Patricia L. Hill.	
Prince Kuhio Federal Building, 300 Ala Moana Boulevard, Room 3–106, P.O. Box 50144, Honolulu, HI 96850	(808) 522–8970
Chief of Staff.—Joan Ohashi Akai.	
101 Aupuni Street, Suite 213, Hilo, HI 96720	(808) 935–1114

REPRESENTATIVES

FIRST DISTRICT

NEIL ABERCROMBIE, Democrat, of Honolulu, HI; born in Buffalo, NY, June 26, 1938; education: graduated from Williamsville High School, Williamsville, NY; B.A., Union College, 1959; Ph.D., University of Hawaii, 1974; professional: candidate for election to the U.S. Senate, 1970; Hawaii House of Representatives, 1974–78; Hawaii State Senate, 1978–86; elected to the

U.S. House of Representatives on September 20, 1986, to fill the vacancy caused by the resignation of Cecil Heftel; Honolulu City Council, 1988–90; married: Nancie Caraway; committees: Armed Services; Resources; elected to the 102nd Congress, November 6, 1990; reelected to each succeeding Congress.

Office Listings

http://www.house.gov/abercrombie

1502 Longworth House Office Building, Washington, DC 20515 .... (202) 225–2726
    Legislative Director.—Tom Wanley.
    Chief Counsel and Communications Director.—Mike Slackman.
Room 4–104, 300 Ala Moana Boulevard, Honolulu, HI 96850 .... (808) 541–2570
    Chief of Staff.—Amy Asselbaye.

Counties: HONOLULU COUNTY (part). CITIES AND TOWNSHIPS: Aiea Pearl City, Ewa Beach, Honolulu, Mililani, and Waipahu. Population (2000), 606,718.

ZIP Codes: 96701, 96706, 96782, 96789, 96797, 96801–28, 96830, 96835–44, 96846–50, 96853, 96858–61

* * *

SECOND DISTRICT

ED CASE, Democrat, of Honolulu, HI; born in Hilo, HI, September 27, 1952; education: Hawai'i Preparatory Academy, 1970; B.A., Williams College, 1975; J.D., University of California/Hastings College of Law, 1981; professional: attorney; Law Clerk, Hawai'i Supreme Court Chief Justice William Richardson, 1981–82; Carlsmith Ball (law firm), 1983–2002; partner, 1989–2002; managing partner 1992–94; public service: Legislative Assistant, U.S. Representative/Senator Spark Matsunaga, 1975–78; Manoa Neighborhood Board, 1985–89; Hawai'i State House of Representatives, 1994–2002; Majority Leader, 1999–2000; Candidate, Governor of Hawai'i, 2002; family: married to the former Audrey Nakamura; children: David, Megan, James, and David; committees: Agriculture; Budget; Small Business; subcommittees: Conservation, Credit, Rural Development, and Research; ranking member, Livestock and Horticulture; Regulatory Reform and Oversight; Rural Enterprises, Agriculture, and Technology; Tax, Finance, and Exports; elected to the 107th Congress, by special election, on November 30, 2002; reelected to the 108th Congress, by special election, on January 4, 2003; elected to the 109th Congress on November 2, 2004.

Office Listings

http://www.house.gov/case   ed.case@mail.house.gov

115 Cannon House Office Building, Washington, DC 20515 .... (202) 225–4906
    Chief of Staff.—Esther Kia'aina.   FAX: 225–4987
    Deputy Chief of Staff.—Pamela Hayashi Okimoto.
    Legislative Director.—Anne Stewart.
Room 5104, Prince Kuhio Federal Building, PO Box 50124, Honolulu, HI 96850 .. (808) 541–1986
    State Director.—Jimmy Nakatani.

Counties: HAWAI'I COUNTY. CITIES: Hawi, Hilo, Honoka'a, Kailua-Kona, Na'alehu, Kealakekua, Pahoa, Ocean View, Volcano, Waimea, Waikoloa. MAUI COUNTY. CITIES: Hana, Kahului, Kaunakakai, Lahaina, Lana'i City, Makawao, Wailuku. KALAWAO COUNTY. CITY: Kalaupapa. HONOLULU COUNTY (part). CITIES: Hale'iwa, Honolulu, Kailua, Kane'ohe, Kapolei, La'ie, Makakilo, Nanakuli, Wahiawa, Waialua, Wai'anae, Waimanalo. KAUA'I COUNTY. CITIES: Hanalei, Hanapepe, Kalaheo, Kapa'a, Kekaha, Kilauea, Koloa, Lihue, Waimea. NORTHWESTERN HAWAIIAN ISLANDS. ISLANDS OF: Becker, French Frigate Shoals, Gardener Pinnacles, Hermes and Kure Atolls, Laysan, Lisianski, Maro Reef, Nihoa, and Pearl. Population (2000), 604,819.

ZIP Codes: 96703–05, 96707–10, 96712–22, 96725–34, 96737–57, 96759–74, 96776–81, 96783–86, 96788–93, 96795–97, 96854, 96857, 96862–63

Congressional Directory

IDAHO

(Population 2000, 1,293,953)

SENATORS

LARRY E. CRAIG, Republican, of Payette, ID; born in Council, ID, July 20, 1945; education: attended Midvale public schools; graduated, University of Idaho; student body president, University of Idaho, 1968–69; USANG 1970–72; graduate work in economics and the politics of developing nations, George Washington University, 1970; Idaho State president and national vice president, Future Farmers of America, 1966–67; Idaho State Senate (three terms); chairman, Senate Commerce and Labor Committee; member: National Foundation for Defense Analysis; Idaho State Republican Executive Committee, 1976–78; president, Young Republican League of Idaho, 1976–77; chairman, Republican Central Committee, Washington County, 1971–72; board of directors, National Rifle Association; policy chairman, Republican Study Committee, 1990; farmer-rancher, Midvale area, for 10 years; married to the former Suzanne Thompson; three children: Mike, Shae, and Jay; Senate co-chairman, Congressional Coalition on Adoption; co-founder and co-chair, Senate Private Property Rights Caucus; co-chairman, Congressional Leaders United for a Balanced Budget (CLUBB); committees: Appropriations; Energy and Natural Resources; chairman, Veterans' Affairs; Special Committee on Aging; elected to the 97th Congress on November 4, 1980; reelected to each succeeding Congress; elected to the U.S. Senate on November 6, 1990; reelected to each succeeding Senate term.

Office Listings

http://craig.senate.gov

520 Hart Senate Office Building, Washington, DC 20510	(202) 224–2752	
Chief of Staff.—Michael O. Ware.	FAX: 228–1067	
Executive Assistant/Scheduler.—Katie Palmer.		
Legislative Director/Counsel.—Brooke M. Roberts.		
Press Secretary.—Dan Whiting.		
225 North Ninth Street, Suite 530, Boise, ID 83702	(208) 342–7985	
610 Hubbard, Suite 121, Coeur d'Alene, ID 83814	(208) 667–6130	
313 D Street, Suite 106, Lewiston, ID 83501	(208) 743–0792	
801 E. Sherman Street, Room 193, Pocatello, ID 83201	(208) 236–6817	
560 Filer Avenue, Suite A, Twin Falls, ID 83301	(208) 734–6780	
490 Memorial Drive, Suite 101, Idaho Falls, ID 83402	(208) 523–5541	

* * *

MICHAEL D. CRAPO, Republican, of Idaho Falls, ID; born in Idaho Falls, May 20, 1951; education: graduated, Idaho Falls High School, 1969; B.A., Brigham Young University, Provo, UT, 1973; J.D., Harvard University Law School, Cambridge, MA, 1977; professional: attorney; admitted to the California bar, 1977; admitted to the Idaho bar, 1979; law clerk, Hon. James M. Carter, Judge of the U.S. Court of Appeals for the Ninth Circuit, San Diego, CA, 1977–78; associate attorney, Gibson, Dunn, and Crutcher, San Diego, 1978–79; attorney, Holden, Kidwell, Hahn and Crapo, 1979–92; partner, 1983–92; Idaho State Senate, 1984–92, assistant majority leader, 1987–89, president pro tempore, 1989–92; member: American Bar Association, Boy Scouts of America, Idaho Falls Rotary Club, 1984–88; married: the former Susan Diane Hasleton, 1974; children: Michelle, Brian, Stephanie, Lara, and Paul; co-chair, Western Water Caucus; co-chair, Sportsman Caucus; co-chair, COPD Caucus; committees: Agriculture, Nutrition, and Forestry; Banking, Housing, and Urban Affairs; Budget; Finance; Indian Affairs; elected on November 3, 1992, to the 103rd Congress; reelected to each succeeding Congress; elected to the U.S. Senate on November 3, 1998; Deputy Republican Whip; reelected to each succeeding Senate term.

Office Listings

http://crapo.senate.gov

239 Dirksen Senate Office Building, Washington, DC 20510	(202) 224–6142
Chief of Staff.—John Hoehne.	
Administrative Assistant.—Peter Fischer.	
Communications Director.—Susan Wheeler.	
Legislative Director.—Ken Flanz.	
251 E Front Street, Suite 205, Boise, ID 83702	(208) 334–1776
Chief of Staff.—John Hoehne.	
610 Hubbard Street, Suite 209, Coeur d'Alene, ID 83814	(208) 664–5490
Director.—Stefany Bales.	

313 D Street, Suite 105, Lewiston, ID 83501 .... (208) 743–1492
   Director.—Mitch Silvers.
275 South 5th Avenue, Suite 225, Pocatello, ID 83201 .... (208) 236–6775
   Director.—John Atkins.
524 E. Cleveland, Suite 220, Caldwell, ID 83605 .... (208) 455–0360
   Director.—Jake Ball.
490 Memorial Drive, Suite 102, Idaho Falls, ID 83402 .... (208) 522–9779
   Director.—Leslie Huddleston.
202 Falls Avenue, Suite 2, Twin Falls, ID 83301 .... (208) 734–2515
   Director.—Heather Tiel.

REPRESENTATIVES

FIRST DISTRICT

C.L. (BUTCH) OTTER, Republican, of Star, ID; born in Caldwell, ID, May 3, 1942; education: College of Idaho, B.A., Political Science; Mindanao State University in the Philippines, Honorary Doctorate; professional: businessman; J.R. Simplot Co.; Kyn Ten Oil Drilling Co.; organizations: Idaho International Trade Council; Elks Club; Ducks Unlimited; National Rifle Association; Idaho Agricultural Leadership Council; public service: Idaho Army National Guard, 1968–73; Idaho House of Representatives, 1972–76; Lt. Governor of Idaho, 1987–2000; committees: Energy and Commerce; subcommittees: Commerce, Trade, and Consumer Protection; Energy and Air Quality; Environment and Hazardous Materials; elected to the 107th Congress; reelected to each succeeding Congress.

Office Listings
http://www.house.gov/otter

1711 Longworth House Office Building, Washington, DC 20515 .... (202) 225–6611
   Chief of Staff.—Jeff Malmen.   FAX: 225–3029
   Communications Director.—Mark Warbis.
   Deputy Chief of Staff/Legislative Director.—Jani Revier.
802 W. Bannock Street, Suite 101, Boise, ID 83702 .... (208) 336–9831
   District Director.—Tana Cory.
610 W. Hubbard, Suite 206, Coeur d'Alene, ID 83814 .... (208) 667–0127
111 Main Street, Suite 170, Lewiston, ID 83501 .... (208) 298–0030

Counties: ADA (part), ADAMS, BENEWAH, BOISE, BONNER, BOUNDARY, CANYON, CLEARWATER, GEM, IDAHO, KOOTENAI, LATAH, LEWIS, NEZ PERCE, OWYHEE, PAYETTE, SHOSHONE, VALLEY, WASHINGTON. Population (2000), 648,774.

ZIP Codes: 83501, 83520, 83522–26, 83530–31, 83533, 83535–37, 83539–49, 83552–55, 83602, 83604–07, 83610–12, 83615–17, 83619, 83622, 83624, 83626–32, 83634–39, 83641–45, 83647, 83650–57, 83660–61, 83666, 83669–72, 83676–77, 83680, 83686–87, 83702, 83704–06, 83708–09, 83711, 83713–14, 83716, 83719, 83799, 83801–06, 83808–16, 83821–27, 83830, 83832–37, 83839–58, 83860–61, 83864–74, 83876–77

* * *

SECOND DISTRICT

MICHAEL K. SIMPSON, Republican, of Blackfoot, ID; born in Burley, ID, September 8, 1950; education: graduated, Blackfoot High School, 1968; Utah State University, 1972; Washington University School of Dental Medicine, 1977; professional: dentist, private practice; Blackfoot, ID, City Council, 1981–85; Idaho State Legislature, 1985–98; Idaho Speaker of the House 1992–98; married: Kathy Simpson; committees: Appropriations; Budget; elected to the 106th Congress; reelected to each succeeding Congress.

Office Listings
http://www.house.gov/simpson   mike.simpson@mail.house.gov

1339 Longworth House Office Building, Washington, DC 20515 .... (202) 225–5531
   Chief of Staff.—Lindsay Slater.   FAX: 225–8216
   Scheduler.—Megan Milam.
   Legislative Director.—John Revier.
   Press Secretary.—Nikki Watts.
802 West Bannock, Suite 600, Boise, ID 83702 .... (208) 334–1953
1201 Falls Avenue East, #25, Twin Falls, ID 83301 .... (208) 734–7219
490 Memorial Drive, Suite 103, Idaho Falls, ID 83402 .... (208) 523–6701
801 E. Sherman, Suite 194, Pocatello, ID 83201 .... (208) 478–4160

Counties: ADA (part), BANNOCK, BEAR LAKE, BINGHAM, BLAINE, BONNEVILLE, BUTTE, CAMAS, CARIBOU, CASSIA, CLARK, CUSTER, ELMORE, FRANKLIN, FREMONT, GOODING, JEFFERSON, JEROME, LEMHI, LINCOLN, MADISON, MINIDOKA, ONEIDA, POWER, TETON, TWIN FALLS. Population (2000), 645,179.

ZIP Codes: 83201–06, 83209–15, 83217–18, 83220–21, 83223, 83226–30, 83232–39, 83241, 83243–46, 83250–56, 83261–63, 83271–72, 83274, 83276–78, 83281, 83283, 83285–87, 83301–03, 83311–14, 83316, 83318, 83320–25, 83327–28, 83330, 83332–38, 83340–44, 83346–50, 83352–55, 83401–06, 83415, 83420–25, 83427–29, 83431, 83433–36, 83438, 83440–46, 83448–52, 83454–55, 83460, 83462–69, 83601–02, 83604, 83623–24, 83627, 83633–34, 83647–48, 83701–09, 83712, 83714–17, 83720–33, 83735, 83744, 83756

ILLINOIS

(Population, 2000 12,419,293)

SENATORS

RICHARD J. DURBIN, Democrat, of Springfield, IL; born in East St. Louis, IL, November 21, 1944; son of William and Ann Durbin; education: graduated, Assumption High School, East St. Louis; B.S., foreign service and economics, Georgetown University, Washington, DC, 1966; J.D., Georgetown University Law Center, 1969; professional: attorney, admitted to the Illinois bar in 1969; began practice in Springfield; legal counsel to Lieutenant Governor Paul Simon, 1969–72; legal counsel to Illinois Senate Judiciary Committee, 1972–82; parliamentarian, Illinois Senate, 1969–82; president, New Members Democratic Caucus, 98th Congress; associate professor of medical humanities, Southern Illinois University School of Medicine; married: the former Loretta Schaefer, 1967; children: Christine, Paul, and Jennifer; committees: Appropriations; Judiciary; Rules and Administration; Select Committee on Intelligence; appointed as Assistant Democratic Leader in 2001; elected to the 98th Congress, November 2, 1982; reelected to each succeeding Congress; elected to the U.S. Senate on November 5, 1996; reelected to each succeeding Senate term.

Office Listings

http://durbin.senate.gov

332 Dirksen Senate Office Building, Washington, DC 20510		(202) 224–2152
Chief of Staff.—Ed Greelegs.		FAX: 228–0400
Staff Director.—Patrick Souders.		TTY: 224–8180
Legislative Director.—Tom Faletti.		FAX: 228–1611
Director of Scheduling.—Andrea Del'Aguila.		
230 South Dearborn, Kluczynski Building 38th Floor, Chicago, IL 60604		(312) 353–4952
Chief of Staff.—Mike Daly.		
525 South Eighth Street, Springfield, IL 62703		(217) 492–4062
Director.—Bill Houlihan.		
701 N. Court Street, Marion, IL 62959		(618) 998–8812

* * *

BARACK OBAMA, Democrat, of Chicago, IL; born in Hawaii, August 4, 1961; education: B.A., Political Science, Columbia University, 1983; J.D., Harvard Law School, *magna cum laude,* 1991; professional: attorney; civil rights lawyer; University of Chicago Law School lecturer in constitutional law; public service: Illinois State Senator, 1997–2004; religion: Church of Christ; organizations: chairman, Chicago Annenberg Challenge; Cook County Bar Association; Community Law Project; Joyce Foundation; Center for Neighborhood Technology; married: Michelle; children: Malia and Sasha; committees: Environment and Public Works; Foreign Relations; Veterans' Affairs; subcommittees: African Affairs; Clean Air, Climate Change, and Nuclear Safety; East Asian and Pacific Affairs; Fisheries, Wildlife, and Water; International Economic Policy, Export and Trade Promotion; Near Eastern and South Asian Affairs; elected to the U.S. Senate on November 2, 2004.

Office Listings

http://obama.senate.gov

713 Hart Senate Office Building, Washington, DC 20510		(202) 224–2854
Chief of Staff.—Peter Rouse.		FAX: 228–5417
Legislative Director.—Chris Lu.		
Communications Director.—Robert Gibbs.		
Scheduler.—Alyssa Mastromonaco.		
230 South Dearborn Street, #3900, Chicago, IL 60604		(312) 886–3506
670 East Adams, #1520, Springfield, IL 62701		(217) 492–5089
701 North Court Street, Marion, IL 62959		(618) 997–2402

REPRESENTATIVES

FIRST DISTRICT

BOBBY L. RUSH, Democrat, of Chicago, IL; born in Georgia, November 23, 1946; education: B.A., with honors, Roosevelt University, Chicago; M.A., University of Illinois, Chicago; professional: served in U.S. Army, 1963–68; Democratic Ward Committeeman, second ward, Chicago, 1984, 1988; Democratic State Central Committeeman, First Congressional District, 1990; deputy chairman, Illinois Democratic Party, 1990; Department of Commerce and Community Affairs Illinois Enterprise Zone Award; Operation PUSH Outstanding Young Man Award; Henry Booth House Outstanding Community Service Award; South End Jaycees Outstanding Business and Professional Achievement Award; Chicago Black United Communities Distinguished Political Leadership Award; cofounder, Illinois Black Panther Party; co-chair, Congressional Biotechnology Caucus; Regional and Assistant Democratic Whip; married: Carolyn; five children; committees: Energy and Commerce; elected on November 3, 1992, to the 103rd Congress; reelected to each succeeding Congress.

Office Listings
http://www.house.gov/rush

2416 Rayburn House Office Building, Washington, DC 20515 .... (202) 225–4372
   Chief of Staff.—Kimberly Parker.   FAX: 226–0333
   Legislative Director.—Yardly Pollas-Kimble.
   Executive Assistant/Scheduler.—Lenette Myers.
   Communications Director.—Tasha Harris.
700–706 East 79th Street, Chicago, IL 60619 .... (773) 224–6500
   District Director.—Rev. Stanley Watkins.
3235 West 147th Street, Midlothian, IL 60445 .... (708) 385–9550
   Suburban Director.—Younus Suleman.

Counties: COOK COUNTY (part). CITIES AND TOWNSHIPS: Alsip, Blue Island, Chicago, Country Club Hills, Evergreen Park, Homewood, Midlothian, Oak Forest, Orland Hills, Orland Park, Palos Heights, Posen, Robbins, and Tinley Park. Population (2000), 653,647.

ZIP Codes: 60406, 60445, 60452, 60456, 60462–63, 60469, 60472, 60477–78, 60482, 60615–16, 60619–21, 60636–37, 60643, 60652–53, 60803, 60805

* * *

SECOND DISTRICT

JESSE L. JACKSON, JR., Democrat, of Chicago, IL; born in Greenville, SC, March 11, 1965; education: B.S., business management, *magna cum laude,* North Carolina A&T State University, 1987; M.A., Chicago Theological Seminary, 1989; J.D., University of Illinois College of Law, 1993; member, Congressional Black Caucus, Congressional Progressive Caucus; elected Secretary of the Democratic National Committee's Black Caucus; national field director, National Rainbow Coalition, 1993–95; member, Rainbow/Push Action Network; married: the former Sandra Lee Stevens; committees: Appropriations; elected to the 104th Congress (special election); reelected to each succeeding Congress.

Office Listings
http://www.house.gov/jackson

2419 Rayburn House Office Building, Washington, DC 20515 .... (202) 225–0773
   Chief of Staff.—Kenneth Edmonds.   FAX: 225–0899
   Legislative Director.—Charles Dujon.
   Legislative Assistant.—Sandi Pessin.
   Executive Assistant/Scheduler.—DeBorah Posey.
17926 South Halsted, Homewood, IL 60430 .... (708) 798–6000
   District Director.—Rick Bryant.
2120 East 71st Street, Chicago, IL 60649 .... (773) 241–6500

Counties: COOK (part), WILL (part). CITIES AND TOWNSHIPS: Blue Island, Burnham, Calumet City, Calumet Park, Chicago, Chicago Heights, Country Club Hills Crestwood, Dixmoor, Dolton, East Hazel Crest, Flossmoor, Ford Heights, Glenwood, Harvey, Hazel Crest, Homewood, Lansing, Lynwood, Markham, Matteson, Midlothian, Monee, Oak Forest, Olympia Fields, Park Forest, Phoenix, Posen, Richton Park, Riverdale, Robbins, Sauk Village, South Chicago Heights, South Holland, Steger, Tinley Park, Thornton, and University Park. Population (2000), 653,647.

ZIP Codes: 60406, 60409, 60411–12, 60417, 60419, 60422–23, 60425–26, 60429–30, 60438, 60443, 60445, 60449, 60452, 60461, 60466, 60471, 60473, 60475–78, 60615, 60617, 60620, 60628, 60633, 60636–37, 60643, 60649, 60827

* * *

THIRD DISTRICT

DANIEL W. LIPINSKI, Democrat, of Chicago, IL; born in Chicago, July 15, 1966; son of former Congressman William Lipinski, 1983–2004; education: B.S., Mechanical Engineering, Northwestern University, *magna cum laude,* 1988; M.S., Engineering-Economic Systems,

Stanford University, 1989; Ph.D., Political Science, Duke University, 1998; professional: professor, James Madison University Washington Program, Washington, DC, 2000; professor, University of Notre Dame, South Bend, IN, 2000–01; professor, University of Tennessee, Knoxville, TN, 2001–04; aide to United States Representative George Sangmeister, 1993–94; aide to United States Representative Jerry Costello, 1995–96; aide to United States Representative Rod Blagojevich, 1999–2000; married: Judy; committees: Science; Small Business; elected to the 109th Congress on November 2, 2004.

Office Listings

http://www.house.gov/lipinski

1217 Longworth House Office Building, Washington, DC 20515	(202) 225–5701
Administrative Assistant.—Jennifer Sypolt.	FAX: 225–1012
Legislative Director.—John Rattliff.	
Senior Legislative Assistant.—Ashley Musselman.	
6245 South Archer Avenue, Chicago, IL 60638	(312) 886–0481
Chief of Staff.—Jerry Hurckes.	
19 West Hillgrove Avenue, LaGrange, IL 60525	(708) 352–0524

Counties: COOK COUNTY (part). CITIES AND TOWNSHIPS: Alsip, Argo, Bedford Park, Berwyn, Bridgeview, Burr Ridge, Chicago, Chicago Ridge, Cicero, Countryside, Hickory Hills, Hinsdale, Hometown, Hodgkins, Indian Head Park, Justice Burbank, LaGrange, Lyons, McCook, North Riverside, Oak Lawn, Oak Park, Palos Hills, Palos Park, Proviso, Riverside, Stickney, Summit Brookfield, Western Springs, Willow Springs, and Worth. Population (2000), 653,647

ZIP Codes: 60126, 60130, 60154, 60162, 60402, 60415, 60426, 60430, 60453–59, 60463–65, 60477, 60480, 60482, 60499, 60501, 60513, 60521, 60525–27, 60534, 60546, 60558, 60570, 60608–09, 60616, 60620, 60623, 60629, 60632, 60636, 60638, 60643, 60652, 60655, 60803–05

* * *

FOURTH DISTRICT

LUIS V. GUTIERREZ, Democrat, of Chicago, IL; born in Chicago, December 10, 1953; education: B.A., Northeastern Illinois University, 1974; professional: Chicago Alderman; social worker, State of Illinois; teacher; married: 1977 to Soraida Arocho; children: Omaira and Jessica; committees: Financial Services; Veterans' Affairs; subcommittees: ranking member, Oversight and Investigations; elected on November 3, 1992, to the 103rd Congress; reelected to each succeeding Congress.

Office Listings

2367 Rayburn House Office Building, Washington, DC 20515	(202) 225–8203
Chief of Staff.—Jennice Fuentes.	FAX: 225–7810
Deputy Chief of Staff.—Enrique Fernandez.	
Legislative Director.—Susan Collins.	
Press Secretary.—Scott Frotman.	
3455 West North Avenue, Chicago, IL 60647	(773) 384–1655
1310 West 18th Street, Chicago, IL 60608	(312) 666–3882

Counties: COOK COUNTY (part). CITIES: Berkeley, Brookfield, Chicago, Ciero, Elmwood Park, Forest Park, Hillside, Maywood, Melrose Park, Northlake, Oak Park, Stickney, Stone Park, and Westchester. Population (2000), 653,647.

ZIP Codes: 60130, 60141, 60153–55, 60160, 60162–65, 60304–05, 60402, 60443, 60446, 60473, 60513, 60526, 60542, 60546, 60608–09, 60612, 60614, 60616, 60618, 60622–23, 60625, 60629, 60632, 60639, 60641, 60644, 60647, 60651, 60707, 60804

* * *

FIFTH DISTRICT

RAHM EMANUEL, Democrat, of Chicago, IL; born in Chicago, November 29, 1959; education: B.A., Liberal Arts, Sarah Lawrence College, 1981; M.A., Speech and Communication, Northwestern University, 1985; professional: Illinois Public Action (consumer rights organization); managing director, Dresdner Kleinwort Wasserstein (global investment bank); Democratic Party activities: worked on Paul Simon's successful U.S. Senate campaign, 1984; national campaign director, Democratic Congressional Campaign Committee, 1988; senior advisor and chief fundraiser for Richard M. Daley's successful Mayoral campaign, 1989; Assistant to the President under President Bill Clinton, 1993–2000; married: Amy; children: Zachariah, Ilana, and Leah; committees: Ways and Means; subcommittees: Health; Human Resources; elected to the 108th Congress on November 8, 2002; reelected to each succeeding Congress.

Office Listings
http://www.house.gov/emanuel

1319 Longworth House Office Building, Washington, DC 20515 .... (202) 225–4061
Chief of Staff.—Elizabeth Sears Smith.   FAX: 225–5603
Communications Director.—Cecelia Prewett.
Executive Assistant / Scheduler.—Koren Bell.
Legislative Director.—Pete Spiro.
3742 West Irving Park Road, Chicago, IL 60618 .... (773) 267–5926

Counties: COOK COUNTY (part). Population (2000), 653,647.

ZIP Codes: 60018, 60106, 60131, 60153, 60160–61, 60164–65, 60171, 60176, 60504, 60525, 60613–14, 60618, 60625, 60630–31, 60634, 60639–41, 60646, 60656–57, 60659–60, 60677, 60706–07, 60712, 60714

* * *

SIXTH DISTRICT

HENRY J. HYDE, Republican, of Wood Dale, IL; born in Chicago, IL, April 18, 1924; education: graduated St. George High School, Evanston, IL, 1942; B.S.S., Georgetown University, 1947; J.D., Loyola University School of Law, Chicago, 1949; professional: ensign, U.S. Navy, 1944–46; commander, U.S. Naval Reserves (retired); admitted to the Illinois bar, January 9, 1950; State Representative in Illinois General Assembly, 1967–74; majority leader, Illinois House of Representatives, 1971–72; married: the late Jeanne Simpson, 1947; children: Henry Jr., Robert, Anthony, Laura; committees: chair, International Relations; Judiciary; elected to the 94th Congress, November 5, 1974; reelected to each succeeding Congress.

Office Listings
http://www.house.gov/hyde

2110 Rayburn House Office Building, Washington, DC 20515 .... (202) 225–4561
Administrative Assistant.—Judy Wolverton.
Suite 200, 50 East Oak Street, Addison, IL 60101 .... (630) 832–5950
Executive Assistants: Patrick Durante, Alice Horstman.

Counties: COOK (part), DUPAGE (part). CITIES AND TOWNSHIPS: Addison, Arlington Heights, Bensenville, Bloomingdale, Carol Stream, Des Plaines, Elk Grove, Elk Grove Village, Elmhurst, Glen Ellyn, Glendale Heights, Hanover Park Streamwood, Itasca, Leyden Proviso, Lombard, Maine, Milton, Oak Brook, Oak Brook Terrace, Roselle, Villa Park, Wayne, Westchester, Westmont, Wheaton, Winfield, and York. Population (2000), 615,419.

ZIP Codes: 60005, 60007–09, 60016–18, 60056, 60067, 60101, 60103, 60105–08, 60116–17, 60120, 60125–26, 60128, 60131–33, 60137–39, 60143, 60148, 60157, 60172–73, 60176, 60181, 60185, 60187–95, 60197, 60199, 60399, 60515, 60523, 60532, 60559, 60563, 60666, 60688, 60701

* * *

SEVENTH DISTRICT

DANNY K. DAVIS, Democrat, of Chicago, IL; born in Parkdale, AR, September 6, 1941; education: B.A., Arkansas A.M. & N. College, 1961; M.A., Chicago State University; Ph.D., Union Institute, Cincinnati, OH; educator and health planner-administrator; board of directors, National Housing Partnership; Cook County Board of Commissioners, 1990–96; former alderman of the Chicago City Council's 29th ward, receiving the Independent Voters of Illinois "Best Alderman Award" for 1980–81, 1981–82, and 1989–90; co-chair, Clinton-Gore-Braun '92; founder and past president, Westside Association for Community Action; past president, National Association of Community Health Centers; 1987 recipient of the Leon M. Despres Award; married to Vera G. Davis; two sons: Jonathan and Stacey; committees: Education and the Workforce; Government Reform; Small Business; elected to the 105th Congress; reelected to each succeeding Congress.

Office Listings
http://www.house.gov/dannydavis

1526 Longworth House Office Building, Washington, DC 20515 .... (202) 225–5006
Chief of Staff.—Richard Boykin.   FAX: 225–5641
Legislative Director.—Caleb Gilchrist.
Director of Issues and Communications.—Ira Cohen.

3333 West Arthington Street, Suite 130, Chicago, IL 60624 .... (773) 533–7520
1030 South 17th Avenue, Maywood, IL 60153 .... (708) 345–6857

Counties: COOK COUNTY (part). CITIES AND TOWNSHIPS: Bellwood, Berkley, Broadview, Chicago, Forest Park, Hillside, Maywood, Oak Park, River Forest, and Westchester. Population (2000), 653,647.

ZIP Codes: 60104, 60130, 60141, 60153–55, 60160, 60162–63, 60301–05, 60546, 60601–12, 60614–16, 60621–24, 60636–37, 60639, 60644, 60651, 60653–54, 60661, 60663–65, 60667–75, 60678–81, 60683–88, 60690–91, 60693–97, 60707, 60804

* * *

EIGHTH DISTRICT

MELISSA L. BEAN, Democrat, of Chicago, IL; born in Chicago, January 22, 1962; education: graduated, Maine East High School, Park Ridge, IL, 1980; A.A., Oakton Community College, Des Plaines, IL, 1982; B.A., Roosevelt University, Chicago, IL, 2002; professional: president, sales; Resources Incorporated, 1995–present; vice president, sales, Data flex Corporation, 1994–95; area manager, UDS/Motorola, 1989–91; branch manager, MTI Systems Incorporated/Arrow Electronics, 1985–89; district sales manager, DJC Corporation 1982–1985; member of the Business Woman; Palatine Chamber of Commerce; Barrington area Professional Women; National Association of Women Business Owners; president of Deer Lake Homeowners Association; boards of Barrington Children's Choir and the Lines Elementary parentteacher organization; religion: Serbian Orthodox; married: Alan; children: Victoria, Michelle; committees: Financial Services; Small Business; subcommittees: Capital Markets, Insurance and Government-Sponsored Enterprises; Domestic and International Monetary Policy, Trade and Technology; Tax, Finance, and Exports; Workforce, Empowerment, and Government Programs; elected to the 109th Congress on November 2, 2004.

Office Listings

http://www.house.gov/bean

512 Cannon House Office Building, Washington, DC 20515 .... (202) 225–3711
  Chief of Staff.—John Michael Gonzalez.   FAX: 225–7830
  Legislative Director.—Elizabeth Hart.
1430 North Meatham Road, Schaumburg, IL 60173 .... (847) 519–3434
  District Director.—Brett Smiley.

Counties: COOK COUNTY (part). TOWNSHIPS: Barrington, Hanover, Palatine, and Schaumburg. LAKE COUNTY (part). TOWNSHIPS: Antioch, Avon, Bentor, Cuba, Ela, Fremont, Grant, Lake Villa, Libertyville, Newport, Warren, Wauconda, and Zion. McHENRY COUNTY (part). CITIES: Burton, Dorr, Greenwood, Hebron, McHenry, Nunda, and Richmond. Population (2000), 653,647.

ZIP Codes: 60002, 60004–05, 60007–08, 60010–14, 60020–21, 60030–31, 60033–34, 60038, 60041–42, 60046–51, 60060–61, 60067, 60071–75, 60081, 60083–85, 60087, 60095–99, 60103, 60107, 60120, 60133, 60159, 60168, 60172–73, 60179, 60192–96

* * *

NINTH DISTRICT

JANICE D. SCHAKOWSKY, Democrat, of Evanston, IL; born in Chicago, IL, May 26, 1944; education: B.A., University of Illinois, 1965; consumer advocate; program director, Illinois Public Action; executive director, Illinois State Council of Senior Citizens, 1985–90; State Representative, 18th District, Illinois General Assembly, 1991–99; served on Labor and Commerce, Human Service Appropriations, Health Care, and Electric Deregulation Committees; religion: Jewish; married: Robert Creamer; children: Ian, Mary, and Lauren; committees: Energy and Commerce; subcommittees: ranking member, Commerce, Trade, and Consumer Protection; Environment and Hazardous Materials; Oversight and Investigations; elected to the 106th Congress; reelected to each succeeding Congress.

Office Listings

http://www.house.gov/schakowsky

1027 Longworth House Office Building, Washington, DC 20515 .... (202) 225–2111
  Chief of Staff.—Cathy Hurwit.   FAX: 226–6890
  Legislative Director.—Jon Samuels.
  Appointments Secretary.—Kim Muzeroll.

5533 Broadway, Chicago, IL 60640 .... (773) 506–7100
District Director.—Leslie Combs.

Counties: COOK COUNTY (part). CITIES: Chicago, Evanston, Glenview, Golf, Lincolnwood, Morton Grove, Niles, and Skokie. Population (2000), 653,647.

ZIP Codes: 60016, 60018–19, 60025, 60029, 60053, 60056, 60068, 60076–77, 60091, 60176, 60201–04, 60208, 60611, 60613, 60626, 60630–31, 60640, 60645–46, 60656–57, 60659–60, 60706, 60712, 60714

* * *

TENTH DISTRICT

MARK STEVEN KIRK, Republican, of Highland Park, IL; born in Champaign, IL, September 15, 1959; education: New Trier East High School, Winnetka, IL, 1977; B.A., Cornell University, 1981; J.D., Georgetown University, 1992; professional: attorney; military service: Lt. Commander, U.S. Navy Reserve; Administrative Assistant to Rep. John Porter (R–IL), 1984–90; World Bank, served as an International Finance Corp. officer; Dept. of State, served as Special Assistant to the Assistant Secretary for Inter-American Affairs; Baker & McKenzie (law firm); House Committee on International Relations, served as Counsel; married: Kimberly Vertolli; committees: Appropriations; subcommittees: Foreign Operations, Export Financing, and Related Programs; Military Quality of Life and Veterans' Affairs, and Related Agencies; Science, The Departments State, Justice, and Commerce, and Related Agencies; elected to the 107th Congress on November 7, 2000; reelected to each succeeding Congress.

Office Listings
http://www.house.gov/kirk

1717 Longworth House Office Building, Washington, DC 20515 .... (202) 225–4835
Chief of Staff.—Liesl Hickey.   FAX: 225–0837
Legislative Director.—Jeannette Windon.
102 Wilmot Road, Suite 200, Deerfield, IL 60015 .... (847) 940–0202
Press Secretary.—Matt Towson.

Counties: COOK (part), LAKE (part). Population (2000), 653,647.

ZIP Codes: 60004–06, 60008, 60010, 60015–16, 60022, 60025–26, 60030–31, 60035, 60037, 60040, 60043–45, 60047–48, 60056, 60060–62, 60064–65, 60067, 60069–70, 60074, 60078–79, 60082–83, 60085–93, 60173, 60195, 60201

* * *

ELEVENTH DISTRICT

JERRY WELLER, Republican, of Morris, IL; born in Streator, IL, July 7, 1957; education: graduated, Dwight High School, 1975; B.A., agriculture, University of Illinois, 1979; aide to Congressman Tom Corcoran, 1980–81; aide to John R. Block (U.S. Secretary of Agriculture), 1981–85; former State Representative, 1988–94; National Republican Legislative Association Legislator of the Year; listed in the 1990 *Almanac of Illinois Politics*; committees: International Relations; Ways and Means; subcommittees: Asia and the Pacific; Oversight; Western Hemisphere; Select Revenue Measures; assistant majority whip; House Republican Steering Committee; elected to the 104th Congress; reelected to each succeeding Congress.

Office Listings
http://www.house.gov/weller

108 Cannon House Office Building, Washington, DC 20515 .... (202) 225–3635
Chief of Staff.—Jeanette Forcash.   FAX: 225–3521
Executive Assistant.—Danielle Hernandez.
Deputy Chief of Staff/Legislative Director.—Alan Tennille.
Press Secretary.—Telly Lovelace.
2701 Black Road, Suite 201, Joliet, IL 60435 .... (815) 740–2028
District Manager.—Reed Wilson.

Counties: BUREAU (part), GRUNDY, KANKAKEE, LA SALLE, LIVINGSTON (part), MCLEAN (part), WILL (part), and WOODFORD (part). Population (2000), 653,658.

ZIP Codes: 60401, 60407–11, 60416–17, 60420–21, 60423–24, 60430–37, 60442, 60444–45, 60447–51, 60466, 60468, 60470, 60474–75, 60477, 60479, 60481, 60504, 60518, 60531, 60541, 60544, 60548–49, 60551–52, 60557, 60625,

60640, 60646, 60660, 60901–02, 60910, 60912–15, 60917, 60919, 60922, 60935, 60940–41, 60944, 60950, 60954, 60961, 60964, 61238, 61240–41, 61254, 61262, 61273, 61301, 61312, 61314–17, 61320–23, 61325–26, 61328–30, 61332, 61334, 61337–38, 61341–42, 61344–45, 61348–50, 61354, 61356, 61358–62, 61364, 61368, 61370–74, 61376–77, 61379, 61701–02, 61704, 61725, 61732, 61736, 61744–45, 61748, 61752, 61754, 61760–61, 61772, 61774, 61790

* * *

TWELFTH DISTRICT

JERRY F. COSTELLO, Democrat, of Belleville, IL; born in East St. Louis, IL, September 25, 1949; education: graduated, Assumption High, East St. Louis, 1968; A.A., Belleville Area College, IL, 1970; B.A., Maryville College of the Sacred Heart, St. Louis, MO, 1973; professional: law enforcement official, 1970–80; elected chairman of the county board, St. Clair County, 1980–88; member: East-West Gateway Coordinating Council, Metro Counties of Illinois, Southwestern Illinois Leadership Council, Southwestern Illinois Small Business Finance Alliance, Light Rail Transit Committee; chairman, St. Clair Heart Fund drive, and United Way drive, 1985; co-chairman of the St. Clair County March of Dimes, 1988; married: the former Georgia Jean Cockrum, 1968; children: Jerry II, Gina Keen, and John; committees: Science; Transportation and Infrastructure; elected by special election to the 100th Congress on August 9, 1988, to fill the vacancy caused by the death of Charles Melvin Price; reelected to each succeeding Congress.

Office Listings

http://www.house.gov/costello

2269 Rayburn House Office Building, Washington, DC 20515	(202) 225–5661
Administrative Assistant.—David Gillies.	FAX: 225–0285
1363 Niedringhaus Avenue, Granite City, IL 62040	(618) 451–7065
8787 State Street, Suite 210, East Saint Louis, IL 62203	(618) 397–8833
155 Lincoln Place Court, Belleville, IL 62221	(618) 233–8026
201 East Nolen Street, West Frankfort, IL 62896	(618) 937–6402
250 West Cherry Street, Carbondale, IL 62901	(618) 529–3791
1330 Swanwick Street, Chester, IL 62233	(618) 826–3043

Counties: ALEXANDER, FRANKLIN, JACKSON, MADISON (part), MONROE, PERRY, PULASKI, RANDOLPH, ST. CLAIR, UNION, WILLIAMSON (part). Population (2000), 653,647.

ZIP Codes: 62002, 62010, 62018, 62024–25, 62035, 62040, 62048, 62059–60, 62071, 62084, 62087, 62090, 62095, 62201–08, 62217, 62220–26, 62232–34, 62236–44, 62246, 62248, 62254–61, 62263–65, 62268–69, 62272, 62274, 62277–80, 62282, 62284–86, 62288–89, 62292–95, 62297–98, 62812, 62819, 62822, 62831–32, 62836, 62840, 62846, 62859–60, 62865, 62883–84, 62888, 62890, 62896–97, 62901–03, 62905–07, 62912, 62914–18, 62920, 62922–24, 62926–27, 62932–33, 62939–42, 62948–52, 62956–59, 62961–64, 62966, 62969–71, 62973–76, 62983, 62987–88, 62990, 62992–94, 62996–99

* * *

THIRTEENTH DISTRICT

JUDY BIGGERT, Republican, of Hinsdale, IL; born in Chicago, IL, August 15, 1937; education: graduated from New Trier High School, 1955; B.A., Stanford University, 1959; J.D., Northwestern University School of Law, 1963; professional: attorney, 1975–99; Illinois House of Representatives (81st District), 1993–98; Assistant House Republican Leader, 1995–99; has served on numerous local civic and community organizations and groups; religion: Episcopalian; married: Rody P. Biggert; children: Courtney, Alison, Rody, and Adrienne; committees: Education and the Workforce; Financial Services; Science; Standards of Official Conduct; subcommittees: Capital Markets, Insurance and Government-Sponsored Enterprises; vice-chair, Domestic and International Monetary Policy, Trade, and Technology; Education Reform; chair, Energy; Environment, Technology, and Standards; Financial Institutions and Consumer Credit; vice-chair, Workforce Protections; elected to the 106th Congress; reelected to each succeeding Congress.

Office Listings

1317 Longworth House Office Building, Washington, DC 20515	(202) 225–3515
Chief of Staff.—Kathy Lydon.	FAX: 225–9420
Press Secretary.—Melissa Guido.	
Legislative Director.—Paul Doucette.	
Scheduler.—Dean Franks.	
6262 South Route 83, Suite 305, Willowbrook, IL 60527	(630) 655–2052

Counties: COOK (part), DUPAGE (part), WILL (part). Population (2000), 653,647.

ZIP Codes: 60181, 60432, 60435, 60439–41, 60446, 60448, 60462–65, 60467, 60477, 60490–91, 60504, 60514–17, 60519, 60521–23, 60527, 60532, 60540, 60543–44, 60555, 60559, 60561, 60563–67, 60597, 60599

FOURTEENTH DISTRICT

J. DENNIS HASTERT, Republican, of Yorkville, IL; born in Aurora, IL, January 2, 1942; education: graduated, Oswego High School, 1960; B.A., Wheaton College, IL, 1964; M.S., Northern Illinois University, DeKalb, 1967; teacher/coach, Yorkville High School; partner, family restaurant business; member, Illinois General Assembly House of Representatives, 1980–86; Republican spokesman for the Appropriations II Committee; chairman, Joint Committee on Public Utility Regulation; member, Legislative Audit Commission; named one of Illinois' 20 top legislators in 1985 by *Chicago Sun-Times*; member, Yorkville Lions Club; board of directors, Aurora Family Support Center; married the former Jean Kahl in 1973; two children: Joshua and Ethan; elected Speaker of the House for the 106th Congress; reelected Speaker for the 107th, 108th, and 109th Congresses; committees: Permanent Select Committee on Intelligence; elected to the 100th Congress on November 4, 1986; reelected to each succeeding Congress.

Office Listings

http://www.house.gov/hastert

235 Cannon House Office Building, Washington, DC 20515 .... (202) 225–2976
    Chief of Staff.—Scott Palmer.   FAX: 225–0697
    Scheduler.—Helen Morrell.
    Legislative Director.—Anthony Reed.
27 North River Street, Batavia, IL 60510 .... (630) 406–1114
    Office Manager.—Lisa Post.
119 West First Street, Dixon, IL 61021 .... (815) 288–0680

Counties: BUREAU (part), DEKALB (part), DUPAGE (part), HENRY (part), KANE, KENDALL, LEE, WHITESIDE (part). CITIES AND TOWNSHIPS: Amboy, Ashton, Aurora, Barrington Hills, Bartlett, Batavia, Big Rock, Bristol, Burlington, Carol Stream, Carpentersville, Clare, Compton, Cornell, Cortland, DeKalb, Dixon, Dundee, East and West, Earlville, Elburn, Elgin, Esmond, Forreston, Franklin Grove, Geneva, Genoa, Gilberts, Hampshire, Harmon, Hinckley, Kaneville, Kingston, Kirkland, Lee, Leland, Malta, Maple Park, Mendota, Millbrook, Millington, Minooka, Montgomery, Mooseheart, Nelson, Newark, North Aurora, Oswego, Paw Paw, Plano, Plato Center, St. Charles, Sandwich, Shabbona, Sleepy Hollow, Somonauk, South Elgin, Steward, Sublette, Sugar Grove, Sycamore, Virgil, Warrenville, Wasco, Waterman, Wayne, West Brooklyn, West Chicago, Wheaton, Winfield, and Yorkville. Population (2000), 653,647.

ZIP Codes: 60010, 60102–03, 60109–10, 60112, 60115, 60118–23, 60134, 60136, 60140, 60142, 60144, 60147, 60150–52, 60170, 60174–75, 60177–78, 60183–87, 60190, 60431, 60447, 60450, 60504–06, 60510–12, 60518, 60520, 60530–31, 60536–39, 60541–45, 60548, 60550, 60552–56, 60560, 60563, 60568, 60640, 60660, 61006, 61021, 61031, 61042, 61057–58, 61068, 61071, 61081, 61234–35, 61238, 61240–41, 61243, 61250, 61254, 61258, 61270, 61273–74, 61277, 61283, 61310, 61318, 61324, 61330–31, 61342, 61344, 61346, 61349, 61353, 61367, 61376, 61378, 61434, 61443

* * *

FIFTEENTH DISTRICT

TIMOTHY V. JOHNSON, Republican, of Sidney, IL; born in Champaign, IL, July 23, 1946; education: B.A., University of Illinois, Phi Beta Kappa; J.D., University of Illinois College of Law, graduated with high honors; professional: attorney; public service: Urbana, IL, City Council, 1971–75; Illinois House of Representatives, 1976–2000; Deputy Majority Leader; Champaign County, IL, Republican Party Chairman, 1990–96; committees: Agriculture; Science; Transportation and Infrastructure; elected to the 107th Congress on November 7, 2000; reelected to each succeeding Congress.

Office Listings

http://www.house.gov/timjohnson

1229 Longworth House Office Building, Washington, DC 20515 .... (202) 225–2371
    Chief of Staff.—Jerome T. Clarke.   FAX: 226–0791
    Legislative Director.—Stephen Borg.
2004 Fox Drive, Champaign, IL 61820 .... (217) 403–4690

Counties: CHAMPAIGN, CLARK, COLES, CRAWFORD, CUMBERLAND, DEWITT, DOUGLAS, EDGAR, EDWARDS (part), FORD, GALLATIN (part), IROQUOIS, LAWRENCE (part), LIVINGSTON (part), MACON (part), MCLEAN (part), MOULTRIE, PIATT, SALINE (part), VERMILION, WABASH (part), WHITE (part). CITIES AND TOWNSHIPS: Bloomington-Normal, Champaign-Urbana, Charleston-Mattoon, Danville, Decatur, Mount Carmel, and Pontiac. Population (2000), 653,647.

ZIP Codes: 60420, 60423, 60437, 60449, 60460, 60518, 60531, 60551–52, 60901–02, 60911–14, 60917–22, 60924, 60926–34, 60936, 60938–42, 60945–46, 60948–49, 60951–53, 60955–57, 60959–64, 60966–70, 60973–74, 61252, 61270, 61311, 61313, 61319, 61321, 61333, 61364, 61401, 61434, 61448–49, 61530, 61701–02, 61704, 61709–10, 61720, 61722, 61724, 61726–28, 61730–31, 61735, 61737, 61739–41, 61743, 61748–50, 61752–53, 61758, 61761, 61764, 61769–70, 61772–73, 61775–78, 61791, 61799, 61801–03, 61810–18, 61820–22, 61824–26, 61830–34, 61839–59, 61862–66, 61870–78, 61880, 61882–84, 61910–14, 61917, 61919–20, 61924–25, 61928–33, 61936–38, 61940–44, 61949, 61951, 61953, 61955–56, 62401, 62410, 62413, 62420–21, 62423, 62427–28, 62432–33, 62435–36, 62439–42, 62445, 62447, 62449, 62451, 62454, 62460, 62462, 62466–69, 62474, 62477–78, 62481, 62521–22, 62526, 62532, 62544, 62549–50, 62701–03, 62821, 62827, 62844, 62863, 62867, 62869, 62871, 62930, 62934, 62946, 62984

SIXTEENTH DISTRICT

DONALD A. MANZULLO, Republican, of Egan, IL; born in Rockford, IL, March 24, 1944; education: B.A., American University, Washington, DC, 1987; J.D., Marquette University Law School, Milwaukee, WI, 1970; president, Ogle County Bar Association, 1971, 1973; advisor, Oregon Ambulance Corporation; founder, Oregon Youth, Inc.; admitted to Illinois bar, 1970; member: State of Illinois and City of Oregon chambers of commerce, Friends of Severson Dells, Natural Land Institute, Ogle County Historic Society, Northern Illinois Alliance for the Arts, Aircraft Owners and Pilots Association, Ogle County Pilots Association, Kiwanis International, Illinois Farm Bureau, Ogle County Farm Bureau, National Federation of Independent Business, Citizens Against Government Waste; married: Freda Teslik, 1982; children: Niel, Noel, and Katherine; committees: Financial Services; chairman, Small Business; elected on November 3, 1992, to the 103rd Congress; reelected to each succeeding Congress.

Office Listings

2228 Rayburn House Office Building, Washington, DC 20515	(202) 225–5676
Chief of Staff.—Adam Magary.	
415 South Mulford Road, Rockford, IL 61108	(815) 394–1231
Director of Communications.—Rich Carter.	
5186 Northwest Highway, Suite 130, Crystal Lake, IL 60014	(815) 356–9800
Caseworker.—Bridget McNally.	

Counties: BOONE, CARROLL, DEKALB (part), JO DAVIESS, MCHENRY (part), OGLE, STEPHENSON, WHITESIDE (part), WINNEBAGO. Population (2000), 653,647.

ZIP Codes: 60001, 60010, 60012–14, 60021, 60033–34, 60039, 60042, 60050–51, 60098, 60102, 60111, 60113, 60115, 60129, 60135, 60140, 60142, 60145–46, 60150, 60152, 60156, 60178, 60180, 60530, 61001, 61006–08, 61010–16, 61018–21, 61024–25, 61027–28, 61030–32, 61036, 61038–39, 61041, 61043–44, 61046–54, 61059–65, 61067–68, 61070–75, 61077–81, 61084–85, 61087–89, 61091, 61101–12, 61114–15, 61125–26, 61130–32, 61230, 61250–52, 61261, 61266, 61270, 61285

* * *

SEVENTEENTH DISTRICT

LANE EVANS, Democrat, of Rock Island, IL; born in Rock Island, August 4, 1951; education: graduated, Alleman High School, Rock Island, 1969; B.A., Augustana College, Rock Island, 1974; J.D., Georgetown University Law Center, Washington, DC, 1978; admitted to Illinois bar in 1978 and commenced practice in Rock Island; served in U.S. Marine Corps, 1969–71; attorney for the Western Illinois Legal Foundation, 1978–79; national staff, Kennedy for President campaign, 1980; entered private practice as a partner in Community Legal Clinic, 1982; legal representative for ACLU, APRI, and LULAC, 1979; awards: Vietnam Veterans of America "National Legislator of the Year" (1985), President's Award for Outstanding Achievement, 1990; committees: Armed Services; ranking member, Veterans' Affairs; elected on November 2, 1982, to the 98th Congress; reelected to each succeeding Congress.

Office Listings

2211 Rayburn House Office Building, Washington, DC 20515	(202) 225–5905
Administrative Assistant.—Dennis King.	FAX: 225–5396
Office Manager.—Eda Robinson.	
Press Secretary.—Steve Vetzner.	
1535 47th Avenue, Room 5, Moline, IL 61265	(309) 793–5760
District Representative.—Phil Hare.	
261 North Broad, Suite 5, Galesburg, IL 61401	(309) 342–4411
236 North Water, Suite 765, Decatur, IL 62523	(217) 422–9150

Counties: ADAMS (part), CALHOUN, CHRISTIAN (part), FAYETTE (part), FULTON, GREENE (part), HANCOCK, HENDERSON, HENRY (part), JERSEY (part), KNOX (part), MACON (part), MACOUPIN, MADISON (part), MCDONOUGH, MERCER, MONTGOMERY (part), PIKE (part), ROCK ISLAND, SANGAMON (part), SHELBY (part), WARREN, WHITESIDE (part). Population (2000), 653,647.

ZIP Codes: 61037, 61071, 61081, 61201, 61204, 61230–33, 61236–37, 61239–42, 61244, 61251, 61256–57, 61259–65, 61272, 61275–76, 61278–79, 61281–82, 61284, 61299, 61318, 61342, 61364, 61401–02, 61410–20, 61422–23, 61425, 61427, 61430–43, 61447–48, 61450, 61452–55, 61458–60, 61462, 61465–78, 61480, 61482, 61484, 61486, 61488–90, 61501, 61519–20, 61524, 61531, 61533, 61542–44, 61553, 61560, 61563, 61569, 61572, 61611, 61701, 61761, 62001–02, 62006, 62009, 62011–14, 62017, 62019, 62021, 62023, 62027, 62031–33, 62036–37, 62044–45, 62047, 62049–53, 62056, 62058, 62063, 62065, 62069–70, 62077–79, 62082, 62085–86, 62088–89, 62091–94, 62097–98, 62262, 62301, 62305–06, 62311, 62313, 62316, 62320–21, 62326, 62329–30, 62334, 62336, 62338, 62341, 62343, 62345, 62348, 62351, 62354–56, 62358, 62360–61, 62366–67, 62370, 62373–74, 62376, 62379–80, 62431, 62513–15, 62520, 62523, 62525–26, 62537, 62539, 62544, 62549–51, 62557, 62560–61, 62572, 62615, 62624, 62626, 62629–30, 62640, 62644, 62649, 62661, 62667, 62670, 62672, 62674, 62683, 62685, 62690, 62692, 62701–05, 62707–08, 62713, 62781, 62794, 62796

EIGHTEENTH DISTRICT

RAY LaHOOD, Republican, of Peoria, IL; born in Peoria, December 6, 1945; education: graduate of Spalding High School; Canton Junior College, Canton, IL; B.S., education and sociology, Bradley University, Peoria, IL, 1971; previous memberships: Academy of Our Lady/ Spalding Board of Education (president), Notre Dame High School Board (president), Peoria Area Retarded Citizens Board of Directors, Bradley University National Alumni Board (president) and Peoria Area Chamber of Commerce Board; junior high school teacher, director of Rock Island County Youth Services Bureau, chief planner for Bi-State Metropolitan Planning Commission, administrative assistant to Congressman Tom Railsback and chief of staff for Congressman Bob Michel; member, Illinois House of Representatives, 1982; Peoria Economic Development Council Board of Directors, Heartland Water Resources Council, Children's Hospital of Illinois Advisory Board, Peoria Rotary Club, Junior League Community Advisory Committee, United Way Pillars Society and Holy Family Church; married: Kathy Dunk LaHood, 1967; children: Darin, Amy, Sam, and Sara; committees: Appropriations; House Permanent Select Committee on Intelligence; elected on November 8, 1994, to the 104th Congress; reelected to each succeeding Congress.

Office Listings

http://www.house.gov/lahood

1424 Longworth House Office Building, Washington, DC 20515	(202) 225–6201
Chief of Staff.—Diane Liesman.	FAX: 225–9249
Deputy Chief of Staff.—Joan DeBoer.	
100 Monroe Street NE, Room 100, Peoria, IL 61602	(309) 671–7027
District Chief of Staff.—Brad McMillan.	
209 West State Street, Jacksonville, IL 62650	(217) 245–1431
Office Manager.—Barb Baker.	
3050 Montvale Drive, Suite D, Springfield, IL 62704	(217) 793–0808
Office Manager.—Donna Miller.	

Counties: ADAMS (part), BROWN, BUREAU (part), CASS, KNOX (part), LOGAN, MACON (part), MARSHALL, MASON, MCLEAN, MENARD, MORGAN, PEORIA, PIKE (part), PUTNAM, SANGAMON (part), SCHUYLER, SCOTT, STARK, TAZEWELL, WOODFORD (part). Population (2000), 653,647.

ZIP Codes: 61314, 61320–21, 61326–27, 61330, 61334–36, 61340, 61345, 61349, 61362–63, 61369–70, 61375, 61377, 61401, 61410, 61414, 61421, 61424, 61426, 61428, 61434, 61436, 61440, 61443, 61448–49, 61451–52, 61455, 61458, 61467, 61472, 61479, 61483–85, 61488–89, 61491, 61501, 61516–17, 61523, 61525–26, 61528–37, 61539–42, 61545–48, 61550, 61552, 61554–55, 61558–62, 61564–65, 61567–72, 61601–07, 61610–12, 61614–16, 61625, 61628–30, 61632–41, 61643–44, 61650–56, 61704, 61721, 61723, 61729, 61733–34, 61738, 61742, 61747, 61749, 61751, 61755–56, 61759–61, 61771, 61774, 61778, 61830, 62305, 62311–12, 62314, 62319–20, 62323–25, 62338–40, 62344, 62346–47, 62349, 62352–53, 62357, 62359–60, 62362–63, 62365, 62367, 62375, 62378, 62501, 62512, 62515, 62518–22, 62524, 62526, 62535, 62539, 62541, 62543, 62548, 62551, 62554, 62561, 62573, 62601, 62610–13, 62615, 62617–18, 62621–22, 62624–25, 62627–29, 62631, 62633–35, 62638–39, 62642–44, 62650–51, 62655–56, 62660–68, 62670–71, 62673, 62675, 62677, 62681–82, 62684, 62688, 62690–95, 62701–07, 62713, 62715, 62719, 62721–22, 62726, 62736, 62739, 62746, 62756–57, 62761, 62765, 62767, 62769, 62776–77, 62781, 62786, 62791, 62796

* * *

NINETEENTH DISTRICT

JOHN SHIMKUS, Republican, of Collinsville, IL; born in Collinsville, February 21, 1958; education: graduated from Collinsville High School; B.S., West Point Military Academy, West Point, NY, 1980; teaching certificate, Christ College, Irvine, CA, 1990; MBA, Southern Illinois University, Edwardsville, 1997; U.S. Army Reserves, 1980–85; government and history teacher, Collinsville High School; Collinsville township trustee, 1989; Madison county treasurer, 1990–96; married: the former Karen Muth, 1987; children: David, Daniel, and Joshua; committees: Energy and Commerce; subcommittees: Energy and Air Quality; Health; Telecommunications and the Internet; elected to the 105th Congress; reelected to each succeeding Congress.

Office Listings

http://www.house.gov/shimkus

513 Cannon House Office Building, Washington, DC 20515	(202) 225–5271
Chief of Staff.—Craig Roberts.	FAX: 225–5880
Legislative Director.—Ray Fitzgerald.	
3130 Chatham Road, Suite C, Springfield, IL 62704	(217) 492–5090
District Director.—Deb Detmeys.	
508 West Main, Collinsville, IL 62234	(618) 344–3065
221 East Broadway, Suite 102, Centralia, IL 62801	(618) 532–9676
120 South Fair, Olney, IL 62450	(618) 392–7737
110 East Locust Street, Room 12, Harrisburg, IL 62946	(618) 252–8271

Counties: BOND, CHRISTIAN (part), CLAY, CLINTON, EDWARDS (part), EFFINGHAM, FAYETTE (part), GALLATIN (part), GREENE (part), HAMILTON, HARDIN, JASPER, JEFFERSON, JERSEY (part), JOHNSON, LAWRENCE (part), MADISON (part), MARION, MASSAC, MONTGOMERY (part), POPE, RICHLAND, SALINE (part), SANGAMON (part), SHELBY (part), WABASH (part), WASHINGTON, WAYNE, WHITE (part), WILLIAMSON (part). Population (2000), 653,647.

ZIP Codes: 61957, 62001–02, 62010, 62012, 62015–17, 62019, 62021–22, 62024–26, 62028, 62030, 62034–35, 62040, 62044, 62046, 62049, 62051–52, 62054, 62056, 62061–62, 62067, 62074–76, 62080–81, 62083, 62086, 62088, 62094, 62097, 62214–16, 62218–19, 62230–31, 62234, 62237, 62245–47, 62249–50, 62252–55, 62257–58, 62262–63, 62265–66, 62268–69, 62271, 62273, 62275, 62281, 62284, 62293–94, 62338, 62401, 62410–11, 62413–14, 62417–28, 62431–36, 62438–52, 62454, 62458–69, 62471, 62473–81, 62510, 62513, 62515, 62517, 62520–22, 62526, 62530–31, 62533–34, 62536, 62538–40, 62545–48, 62550, 62553, 62555–58, 62560, 62563, 62565, 62567–68, 62570–72, 62615, 62629, 62689–90, 62703–04, 62707, 62716, 62723, 62762–64, 62766, 62791, 62801, 62803, 62805–12, 62814–25, 62827–31, 62833–44, 62846, 62848–72, 62874–87, 62889–99, 62908–10, 62912, 62917, 62919, 62921–23, 62926, 62928, 62930–31, 62934–35, 62938–39, 62941, 62943, 62946–47, 62953–56, 62959–60, 62965, 62967, 62972, 62977, 62979, 62982–85, 62987, 62991, 62995

INDIANA

(Population 2000, 6,080,485)

SENATORS

RICHARD G. LUGAR, Republican, of Indianapolis, IN; born in Indianapolis, April 4, 1932; education: graduated, Shortridge High School, 1950; B.A., Denison University, Granville, OH; Rhodes Scholar, B.A., M.A., Pembroke College, Oxford, England, 1956; served in the U.S. Navy, 1957–60; businessman; treasurer, Lugar Stock Farms, Inc., a livestock and grain operation; vice president and treasurer, 1960–67, Thomas L. Green and Co., manufacturers of food production machinery; member, Indianapolis Board of School Commissioners, 1964–67; mayor of Indianapolis, 1968–75; member, advisory board, U.S. Conference of Mayors, 1969–75; National League of Cities, advisory council, 1972–75, president, 1971; Advisory Commission on Intergovernmental Relations, 1969–75, vice chairman, 1971–75; board of trustees, Denison University and the University at Indianapolis; advisory board, Indiana University-Purdue University at Indianapolis; visiting professor of political science, director of public affairs, Indiana Central University; 31 honorary doctorates; recipient of Fiorello LaGuardia Award, 1975; GOP National Convention Keynote Speaker, 1972; SFRC chairman, 1985–86; NRSC chairman, 1983–84; member, St. Luke's Methodist Church; married the former Charlene Smeltzer, 1956; four children; committees: Agriculture, Nutrition and Forestry; chairman, Foreign Relations; elected to the U.S. Senate on November 2, 1976; reelected to each succeeding Senate term.

Office Listings

http://lugar.senate.gov

306 Hart Senate Office Building, Washington, DC 20510	(202) 224–4814
Administrative Assistant.—Martin W. Morris.	
Legislative Director.—Chris Geeslin.	
Press Secretary.—Andy Fisher.	
Scheduler.—Justin Ailes.	
10 West Market Street, Room 1180, Indianapolis, IN 46204	(317) 226–5555
Federal Building, Room 122, 101 NW Martin Luther King Boulevard, Evansville, IN 47708	(812) 465–6313
Federal Building, Room 3158, 1300 South Harrison Street, Fort Wayne, IN 46802	(260) 422–1505
175 West Lincolnway, Suite G–1, Valparaiso, IN 46383	(219) 548–8035
Federal Center, Room 103, 1201 East 10th Street, Jeffersonville, IN 47132	(812) 288–3377

* * *

EVAN BAYH, Democrat, of Indianapolis, IN, born in Terre Haute, IN, December 26, 1955; education: graduated St. Albans School, Washington, DC, 1974; received a B.A. with honors in business economics from Indiana University, 1978; J.D. from University of Virginia Law School, 1982; professional: admitted to the District of Columbia and Indiana bars, 1984; law clerk for the Southern District of Indiana court, 1982–83; attorney with Hogan and Hartson, Washington, 1983–84; attorney for Bayh, Tabbert and Capehart, Washington, 1985; attorney for Bingham Summers, Welsh and Spilman, Indianapolis, 1986; elected as Secretary of State of Indiana, 1986–89; elected Governor of Indiana, 1988; reelected 1992; chairman of the Democratic Governors' Association, 1994; chairman of the National Education Goals Panel, 1995; chairman of the Education Commission of the States, 1995; Above and Beyond Award from Indiana Black Expo, 1995; Breaking the Glass Ceiling Award Women Executives in State Government, 1996; keynote speaker at the National Democratic Convention, 1996; member of the executive committee on the National Governors' Association, 1996; Red Poling Chair, business economics at Indiana University, 1997; twin sons, Birch Evans IV, and Nicholas Harrison; married: Susan Breshears, April 13, 1985; committees: Armed Services; Banking, Housing and Urban Affairs; Small Business and Entrepreneurship; Special Committee on Aging; Select Committee on Intelligence; chairman, Democratic Leadership Council; elected to the U.S. Senate on November 3, 1998; reelected to each succeeding Senate term.

Office Listings

http://bayh.senate.gov

463 Russell Senate Office Building, Washington, DC 20510	(202) 224–5623
Chief of Staff.—Tom Sugar.	FAX: 228–1377
Executive Assistant.—Brianne Lute.	
Legislative Director.—Charlie Salem.	
Scheduler.—Sarah Rozensky.	
130 South Main Street, Suite 110, South Bend, IN 46601	(574) 236–8302
1650 Market Tower, 10 W. Market Street, Indianapolis, IN 46204	(317) 554–0750

10 Martin Luther King, Jr. Boulevard, Evansville, IN 47708 .... (812) 465–6500
1300 South Harrison Street, Ft. Wayne, IN 46802 .... (219) 426–3151
1201 East 10th Street, Suite 106, Jeffersonville, IN 47130 .... (812) 218–2317
Hammond Courthouse, Suite 3200, 5400 Federal Plaza, Hammond, IL 46320 .... (219) 852–2763

REPRESENTATIVES

FIRST DISTRICT

PETER J. VISCLOSKY, Democrat, of Merrillville, IN; born in Gary, IN, August 13, 1949; education: graduated, Andrean High School, Merrillville, 1967; B.S., accounting, Indiana University Northwest, Gary, 1970; J.D., University of Notre Dame Law School, Notre Dame, IN, 1973; LL.M., international and comparative law, Georgetown University Law Center, Washington, DC, 1982; professional: attorney; admitted to the Indiana State bar, 1974, the District of Columbia Bar, 1978, and the U.S. Supreme Court Bar, 1980; associate staff, U.S. House of Representatives, Committee on Appropriations, 1977–80, Committee on the Budget, 1980–82; practicing attorney, Merrillville law firm, 1983–84; two children: John Daniel and Timothy Patrick; committees: Appropriations; subcommittees: Defense; ranking member, Energy and Water Development, and Related Agencies; elected to the 99th Congress on November 6, 1984; reelected to each succeeding Congress.

Office Listings

http://www.house.gov/visclosky

2256 Rayburn House Office Building, Washington, DC 20515 .... (202) 225–2461
    Administrative Assistant.—Charles Brimmer.   FAX: 225–2493
    Appropriations Director.—Peder Maarbjerg.
    Executive Assistant/Scheduler.—Korry Baack.
    Press Assistant.—Justin Kitsch.
701 East 83rd Avenue, #9, Merrillville, IN 46410 .... (219) 795–1844
    District Director.—Mark Lopez.   (888) 423–7383

Counties: BENTON, JASPER, LAKE, NEWTON, PORTER (part). Population (2000), 675,767.

ZIP Codes: 46301–04, 46307–08, 46310–12, 46319–25, 46327, 46341–42, 46345, 46347–49, 46355–56, 46360, 46366, 46368, 46372–73, 46375–77, 46379–85, 46390, 46392–94, 46401–11, 47917, 47921–22, 47942–44, 47948, 47951, 47963–64, 47970–71, 47977–78, 47984, 47986, 47995

* * *

SECOND DISTRICT

CHRIS CHOCOLA, Republican, of Bristol, IN; born in Jackson, MI, February 24, 1962; education: graduated, *summa cum laude,* from Hillsdale College, 1984, with a double major in Business Administration and Political Economy; J.D., *magna cum laude,* Thomas Cooley Law School, 1988; professional: businessman; Chief Executive Officer, CTB International Corp.; community organizations: Rotary International; Oaklawn Psychiatric Center; South Bend Center for the Homeless; family: married to Sarah; children: Caroline and Colin; committees: Ways and Means; elected to the 108th Congress on November 5, 2002; reelected to each succeeding Congress.

Office Listings

http://chocola.house.gov

510 Cannon House Office Building, Washington, DC 20515 .... (202) 225–3915
    Chief of Staff.—Brooks Kochvar.   FAX: 225–6798
    Legislative Director.—Rob Vernon.
    Scheduler.—Katie Pike.
    Press Secretary.—Maureen Carter.
100 East Wayne Street, Suite 330, South Bend, IN 46601 .... (574) 251–0596
444 Mall Road, Logansport, IN 46947 .... (574) 753–4700
801 Michigan Avenue, LaPorte, IN 46300 .... (219) 326–6216

Counties: CARROLL, CASS, ELKHART (part), FULTON, LAPORTE, MARSHALL, PORTER (part), PULASKI, ST. JOSEPH, STARKE, WHITE (part). CITIES: Elkhart, Kokomo, LaPorte, Logansport, Monticello, Mishawaka, Plymouth, Rochester, South Bend, and Westville. Population (2000), 675,767.

ZIP Codes: 46041, 46051, 46056, 46065, 46143, 46301, 46304, 46340–42, 46345–46, 46348, 46350, 46352, 46360–61, 46365–66, 46371, 46374, 46382–83, 46390–91, 46501, 46504, 46506, 46511, 46513–17, 46524, 46526, 46528, 46530–

32, 46534, 46536–37, 46539, 46544–46, 46550, 46552, 46554, 46556, 46561, 46563, 46570, 46572, 46574, 46595, 46601, 46604, 46613–17, 46619–20, 46624, 46626, 46628–29, 46634–35, 46637, 46660, 46680, 46699, 46901–02, 46910, 46912–13, 46915–17, 46920, 46922–23, 46926, 46929, 46931–32, 46939, 46942, 46945, 46947, 46950–51, 46960–61, 46967–68, 46970, 46975, 46977–79, 46982, 46985, 46988, 46994, 46996, 46998, 47920, 47923, 47925–26, 47946, 47950, 47957, 47959, 47960, 47997

* * *

THIRD DISTRICT

MARK E. SOUDER, Republican, of Fort Wayne, IN; born in Grabill, IN, July 18, 1950; education: graduated from Leo High School, 1968; B.S., Indiana University, Fort Wayne, 1972; M.B.A., University of Notre Dame Graduate School of Business, 1974; professional: partner, Historic Souder's of Grabill; majority owner of Souder's General Store; vice president, Our Country Home, fixture manufacturing business; attends Emmanuel Community Church; served as economic development liaison for then-Representative Dan Coats (IN–4th District); appointed Republican staff director of the House Select Committee on Children, Youth and Families, 1984; legislative director and deputy chief of staff for former Senator Coats; member: Grabill Chamber of Commerce, former head of Congressional Action Committee of Ft. Wayne Chamber of Commerce; married: the former Diane Zimmer, 1974; children: Brooke, Nathan, and Zachary; committees: Education and the Workforce; Government Reform; Homeland Security; elected to the 104th Congress; reelected to each succeeding Congress.

Office Listings
http://www.house.gov/souder

1227 Longworth House Office Building, Washington, DC 20515	(202) 225–4436
Chief of Staff.—Renee Howell.	FAX: 225–3479
Scheduler.—Dawn Gerson.	
1300 South Harrison, Room 3105, Fort Wayne, IN 46802	(260) 424–3041
District Director.—Mark Wickersham.	
102 West Lincoln Avenue, 1st Source Building, Suite 250, Goshen, IN 46526	(574) 533–5802
700 Park Avenue, The Boathouse, Suite D, Winona Lake, IN 46590	(574) 269–1940

Counties: ALLEN (part), DEKALB, ELKHART (part), KOSCIUSKO, LAGRANGE, NOBLE, STEUBEN, WHITLEY. Population (2000), 675,617.

ZIP Codes: 46502, 46504, 46506–08, 46510, 46516, 46524, 46526–28, 46538–40, 46542–43, 46550, 46553, 46555, 46562, 46565–67, 46571, 46573, 46580–82, 46590, 46701, 46703–06, 46710, 46721, 46723, 46725, 46730, 46732, 46737–38, 46741–43, 46746–48, 46750, 46755, 46760–61, 46763–65, 46767, 46771, 46773–74, 46776–77, 46779, 46783–89, 46793–99, 46801–09, 46814–16, 46818–19, 46825, 46835, 46845, 46850–69, 46885, 46895–99, 46910, 46962, 46975, 46982

* * *

FOURTH DISTRICT

STEVE BUYER, Republican, of Monticello, IN; born in Rensselaer, IN, November 26, 1958; education: graduated from North White High School in 1976; B.S., business administration, The Citadel, 1980; J.D., Valparaiso University School of Law, 1984; admitted to the Virginia and Indiana bars; professional: U.S. Army Judge Advocate General Corps, 1984–87, assigned Deputy to the Attorney General of Indiana, 1987–88; family law practice, 1988–92; U.S. Army Reserves, 1980–present; major; legal counsel for the 22nd Theatre Army in Operations Desert Shield and Desert Storm; married: to the former Joni Lynn Geyer; children: Colleen and Ryan; co-chairman, National Guard and Reserve Components Caucus; committees: Energy and Commerce; chairman, Veterans' Affairs; subcommittees: Health; Assistant Whip; elected to the 103rd Congress, November 3, 1992; reelected to each succeeding Congress.

Office Listings
http://www.house.gov/buyer

2230 Rayburn House Office Building, Washington, DC 20515	(202) 225–5037
Chief of Staff.—Mike Copher.	
Executive Assistant.—Sarah Mulligan.	
Legislative Director.—Myrna Dugan.	
Press Secretary.—Laura Zuckerman.	
148 North Perry Road, Plainfield, IN 46168	(317) 838–0404
District Director.—Jim Huston.	
100 S. Main Street, Monticello, IN 47960	(574) 583–9819
1801 I Street, Bedford, IN 47421	(812) 277–9590

Counties: BOONE, CLINTON, FOUNTAIN (part), HENDRICKS, JOHNSON (part), LAWRENCE (part), MARION (part), MONROE (part), MONTGOMERY, MORGAN, TIPPECANOE, WHITE (part). Population (2000), 675,617.

ZIP Codes: 46035, 46039, 46041, 46049–50, 46052, 46057–58, 46060, 46065, 46067, 46069, 46071, 46075, 46077, 46102–03, 46106, 46111–13, 46118, 46120–23, 46125, 46131, 46142–43, 46147, 46149, 46151, 46157–58, 46160, 46165–68, 46172, 46175, 46180–81, 46183–84, 46214, 46221, 46224, 46231, 46234, 46241, 46254, 46268, 46278, 46920, 46923, 46979, 47108, 47260, 47264, 47403–04, 47420–21, 47429–30, 47433, 47436–37, 47446, 47451, 47456, 47460, 47462–64, 47467, 47470, 47901–07, 47909, 47916, 47918, 47920, 47923–24, 47929–30, 47932–41, 47944, 47949, 47952, 47954–55, 47958–60, 47962, 47965, 47967–68, 47970–71, 47978, 47980–81, 47983, 47987–90, 47992, 47994–96

* * *

FIFTH DISTRICT

DAN BURTON, Republican, of Indianapolis, IN; born in Indianapolis, June 21, 1938; education: graduated, Shortridge High School, 1956; Indiana University, 1956–57, Cincinnati Bible Seminary, 1958–60; served in the U.S. Army, 1957–58; U.S. Army Reserves, 1958–64; businessman, insurance and real estate firm owner since 1968; served, Indiana House of Representatives, 1967–68 and 1977–80; Indiana State Senate, 1969–70 and 1981–82; president: Volunteers of America, Indiana Christian Benevolent Association, Committee for Constitutional Government, and Family Support Center; member, Jaycees; 33rd degree Mason, Scottish rite division; married the former Barbara Jean Logan, 1959; three children: Kelly, Danielle Lee, and Danny Lee II; committees: Government Reform; International Relations; Veterans' Affairs; subcommittees: vice chairman, Asia and the Pacific; Criminal Justice, Drug Policy, and Human Resources; National Security, Emerging Threats, and International Relations; chairman, Western Hemisphere; elected on November 2, 1982, to the 98th Congress; reelected to each succeeding Congress.

Office Listings

http://www.house.gov/burton

2185 Rayburn House Office Building, Washington, DC 20515	(202) 225–2276
Chief of Staff.—Mark Walker.	FAX: 225–0016
Scheduler / Office Manager.—Diane Menorca.	
Press Secretary.—Nick Mutton.	
8900 Keystone at the Crossing, Suite 1050, Indianapolis, IN 46240	(317) 848–0201
District Director.—Rick Wilson.	
209 South Washington Street, Marion, IN 46952	(765) 662–6770

Counties: GRANT, HAMILTON, HANCOCK, HOWARD (part), HUNTINGTON, JOHNSON (part), MARION (part), MIAMI, SHELBY, TIPTON, WABASH. Population (2000), 675,794.

ZIP Codes: 46030–34, 46036, 46038, 46040, 46045, 46047, 46049, 46055, 46060–61, 46064, 46068–70, 46072, 46074, 46076–77, 46082, 46110, 46115, 46117, 46124, 46126, 46129–31, 46140, 46143, 46148, 46150, 46154, 46161–63, 46176, 46182, 46184, 46186, 46217, 46220, 46226–27, 46229, 46236–37, 46239–40, 46250, 46256, 46259–60, 46280, 46290, 46307, 46347, 46355, 46379–80, 46702, 46713–14, 46725, 46750, 46766, 46770, 46783, 46787, 46792, 46901–04, 46910–11, 46914, 46919, 46921, 46926, 46928–30, 46932–33, 46936–38, 46940–41, 46943, 46946, 46951–53, 46957–59, 46962, 46965, 46970–71, 46974–75, 46979–80, 46982, 46984, 46986–87, 46989–92, 46995, 47234, 47246, 47272, 47342, 47384

* * *

SIXTH DISTRICT

MIKE PENCE, Republican, of Columbus, IN; born in Columbus, June 7, 1959; education: Hanover College, 1981; J.D., Indiana University School of Law, 1986; professional: former Republican nominee for the U.S. House of Representatives in the 2nd District in 1988 and 1990; President, Indiana Policy Review Foundation, 1991–93; radio broadcaster: the Mike Pence Show, syndicated statewide in Indiana; married: Karen; children: Michael, Charlotte, and Audrey; committees: Agriculture; International Relations; Judiciary; elected to the 107th Congress on November 7, 2000; reelected to each succeeding Congress.

Office Listings

http://mikepence.house.gov

426 Cannon House Office Building, Washington, DC 20515	(202) 225–3021
Chief of Staff.—Bill Smith.	FAX: 225–3382
Legislative Director.—Ryan Fisher.	
Press Secretary.—Matt Lloyd.	
1134 Meridian Street, Anderson, IN 46016	(765) 640–2919
District Director.—Lani Czarniecki.	

Counties: ALLEN (part), ADAMS, BARTHOLOMEW (part), BLACKFORD, DEARBORN (part), DECATUR, DELAWARE, FAYETTE, FRANKLIN, HENRY, JAY, JOHNSON (part), MADISON, RANDOLPH, RUSH, SHELBY (part), UNION, WAYNE, WELLS. Population (2000), 675,669.

ZIP Codes: 46001, 46011–18, 46036, 46040, 46044, 46048, 46051, 46056, 46063–64, 46070, 46104, 46110, 46115, 46124, 46126–27, 46131, 46133, 46140, 46142, 46144, 46146, 46148, 46150–51, 46155–56, 46160–62, 46164, 46173, 46176, 46181–82, 46186, 46711, 46714, 46731, 46733, 46740, 46745, 46750, 46759, 46766, 46769–70, 46772–73, 46777–78, 46780–83, 46791–92, 46797–98, 46809, 46816, 46819, 46928, 46952–53, 46989, 46991, 47003, 47006, 47010, 47012, 47016, 47022, 47024–25, 47030, 47035–37, 47060, 47201, 47203, 47225–26, 47234, 47240, 47244, 47246, 47261, 47263, 47265, 47272, 47280, 47283, 47302–08, 47320, 47322, 47324–27, 47330–31, 47334–42, 47344–46, 47348, 47351–62, 47366–71, 47373–75, 47380–88, 47390, 47392–94, 47396, 47448

* * *

SEVENTH DISTRICT

JULIA CARSON, Democrat, of Indianapolis, IN; born in Louisville, KY, July 8, 1938; education: graduated, Crispus Attucks High School, Indianapolis, IN, 1955; attended: Martin University, Indianapolis, IN; Indiana University-Purdue University at Indianapolis; professional: manager and businesswoman; Indiana House of Representatives, 1972–76; Indiana State Senate, 1976–90; as Indianapolis center township trustee, 1990–96, she targeted fraud and waste to eliminate the city's $20-million debt; twice named Woman of the Year by the *Indianapolis Star*; children: two; committees: Financial Services; Transportation and Infrastructure; subcommittees: Financial Institutions and Consumer Credit; Housing and Community Opportunity; Highways, Transit, and Pipelines; Railroads; elected on November 5, 1996, to the 105th Congress; reelected to each succeeding Congress.

Office Listings

http://www.juliacarson.house.gov

1535 Longworth House Office Building, Washington, DC 20515	(202) 225–4011
Deputy Chief of Staff.—Deron Roberson.	FAX: 225–5633
Legislative Director.—Marti Thomas.	
Legislative Assistants: Mia Clarkson, Michael Snavely, Michael Wallace.	
Executive Assistant.—Aarti Nayak.	
300 East Fall Creek Parkway, Suite 300, Indianapolis, IN 46205	(317) 283–6516
Chief of Staff.—S. Sargent (Sarge) Visher.	

Counties: MARION COUNTY. City of Indianapolis, township of Center, parts of the townships of Decatur, Lawrence, Perry, Pike, Warren, Washington, and Wayne, included are the cities of Beech Grove and Lawrence. Population (2000), 675,456.

ZIP Codes: 46107, 46160, 46201–09, 46211, 46214, 46216–22, 46224–31, 46234–35, 46237, 46239–42, 46244, 46247, 46249, 46251, 46253–55, 46260, 46266, 46268, 46274–75, 46277–78, 46282–83, 46285, 46291, 46295–96, 46298

* * *

EIGHTH DISTRICT

JOHN N. HOSTETTLER, Republican, of Blairsville, IN; born in Evansville, IN, June 19, 1961; education: graduated from North Posey High School, Poseyville, IN, 1979; B.S.M.E., Rose-Hulman Polytechnic University, 1983; professional: performance engineer, Southern Indiana Gas and Electric; religion: Baptist; married: the former Elizabeth Hamman, 1983; children: Matthew, Amanda, Jaclyn and Jared; committees: Armed Services; Judiciary; subcommittees: The Constitution; chairman, Immigration, Border Security, and Claims; Projection Forces; Readiness; elected to the 104th Congress; reelected to each succeeding Congress.

Office Listings

http://www.house.gov/hostettler

1214 Longworth House Office Building, Washington, DC 20515	(202) 225–4636
Chief of Staff.—Carl Little.	FAX: 225–3284
Press Secretary.—Michael Jahr.	
Federal Building, Room 124, 101 NW Martin Luther King, Jr. Boulevard, Evansville, IN 47708	(812) 465–6484
Toll Free (Indiana only)	(800) 321–9830
328 North Second Street, Suite 304, Vincennes, IN 47591	(812) 882–0632
District Director.—Carl Little.	

Counties: CLAY, DAVIESS, FOUNTAIN (part), GIBSON, GREENE, KNOX, MARTIN, OWEN, PARKE, PIKE, POSEY, PUTNAM, SULLIVAN, VANDERBURGH, VERMILLION, VIGO, WARREN, WARRICK. Population (2000), 675,564.

ZIP Codes: 46105, 46120–21, 46128, 46135, 46165–66, 46170–72, 46175, 47403–04, 47424, 47427, 47429, 47431–33, 47438–39, 47441, 47443, 47445–46, 47449, 47453, 47455–57, 47459–60, 47462, 47465, 47469–71, 47501, 47512, 47516, 47519, 47522–24, 47527–29, 47535, 47537, 47541–42, 47553, 47557–58, 47561–62, 47564, 47567–68, 47573, 47578, 47581, 47584–85, 47590–91, 47596–98, 47601, 47610–14, 47616, 47618–20, 47629–31, 47633, 47637–40, 47647–49, 47654, 47660, 47665–66, 47670, 47683, 47701–06, 47708, 47710–16, 47719–22, 47724–25, 47727–28, 47730–37, 47739–41, 47744, 47747, 47750, 47801–05, 47807–09, 47811–12, 47830–34, 47836–38, 47840–42, 47845–66, 47868–72, 47874–76, 47878–82, 47884–85, 47917–18, 47921, 47928, 47932, 47952, 47966, 47969–70, 47974–75, 47982, 47987, 47989, 47991–93

* * *

NINTH DISTRICT

MICHAEL E. SODREL, Republican, of New Albany, IN; born in New Albany, December 17, 1945; education: attended Indiana University; professional: United States Army National Guard, 1966–1973; Founder/Owner, Free Enterprise System; Owner, Sodrel Logistics; Owner, Sodrel Truck Lines; organizations: American Legion; Boys and Girls Club; National Federation of Independent Business; chair, Rotary Club; Southern Indiana Chamber of Commerce; religion: Southeast Christian Church; married: Marquita (Keta) Dean; children: Noah and Keesha; committees: Science; Small Business; Transportation and Infrastructure; elected to the 109th Congress on November 2, 2004.

Office Listings

http://www.house.gov/sodrel

1508 Longworth House Office Building, Washington, DC 20515	(202) 225–5315
Chief of Staff/Senior Legislative Council.—Tom Washburne.	FAX: 226–6866
Scheduler.—Kristen Sabella.	
Director of Communications.—Cam Savage.	
279 Quartermaster Drive, Jeffersonville, IN 47130	(812) 288–3999
812 South Walnut Street, Bloomington, IN 47401	(812) 330–1543

Counties: BARTHOLOMEW (part), BROWN, CLARK, CRAWFORD, DEARBORN (part), DUBOIS, FLOYD, HARRISON, JACKSON, JEFFERSON, MONROE (part), OHIO, ORANGE, PERRY, RIPLEY, SCOTT, SPENCER, SWITZERLAND, WASHINGTON. Population (2000), 675,599.

ZIP Codes: 46151, 46160, 46164, 46181, 47001, 47006, 47011, 47017–23, 47025, 47031–34, 47037–43, 47102, 47104, 47106–08, 47110–12, 47114–20, 47122–26, 47129–47, 47150–51, 47160–67, 47170, 47172, 47174, 47177, 47199, 47201–03, 47220, 47223–24, 47227–32, 47235–36, 47240, 47243–45, 47247, 47249–50, 47260, 47264–65, 47270, 47273–74, 47281–83, 47401–08, 47426, 47432, 47434–36, 47448, 47452, 47454, 47458, 47462, 47468–69, 47513–15, 47520–21, 47523, 47525, 47527, 47531–32, 47536–37, 47541–42, 47545–47, 47549–52, 47556, 47564, 47574–77, 47579–81, 47586, 47588, 47590, 47601, 47611, 47615, 47617, 47634–35, 47637

IOWA

(Population 2000, 2,926,324)

SENATORS

CHARLES E. GRASSLEY, Republican, of Cedar Falls, IA; born in New Hartford, IA, September 17, 1933; education: graduated, New Hartford Community High School, 1951; B.A., University of Northern Iowa, 1955; M.A., University of Northern Iowa, 1956; doctoral studies, University of Iowa, 1957–58; professional: farmer; member, Iowa State Legislature, 1959–74; Farm Bureau, State and County Historical Society, Masons, Baptist Church, and International Association of Machinists, 1962–71; married: the former Barbara Ann Speicher, 1954; children: Lee, Wendy, Robin Lynn, Michele Marie, and Jay Charles; co-chairman, International Narcotics Control Caucus; elected to the 94th Congress, November 5, 1974; reelected to the 95th and 96th Congresses; committees: Agriculture, Nutrition, and Forestry; Budget; chairman, Finance; Judiciary; Joint Committee on Taxation; elected to the U.S. Senate, November 4, 1980; reelected to each succeeding Senate term.

Office Listings
http://grassley.senate.gov

135 Hart Senate Office Building, Washington, DC 20510	(202) 224–3744
Chief of Staff.—Ken Cunningham.	FAX: 224–6020
Director of Communications.—Jill Kozeny.	
Legislative Director.—Kolan Davis.	
721 Federal Building, 210 Walnut Street, Des Moines, IA 50309	(515) 288–1145
State Administrator.—Robert Renaud.	
206 Federal Building, 101 First Street SE, Cedar Rapids, IA 52401	(319) 363–6832
120 Federal Courthouse Building, 320 Sixth Street, Sioux City, IA 51101	(712) 233–1860
210 Waterloo Building, 531 Commercial Street, Waterloo, IA 50701	(319) 232–6657
131 West 3rd Street, Suite 180, Davenport, IA 52801	(319) 322–4331
307 Federal Building, 8 South Sixth Street, Council Bluffs, IA 51501	(712) 322–7103

* * *

TOM HARKIN, Democrat, of Cumming, IA; born in Cumming, November 19, 1939; education: graduated from Dowling Catholic High School, Des Moines, IA; B.S., Iowa State University, Ames, 1962; LL.B., Catholic University of America, Washington, DC, 1972; U.S. Navy, 1962–67; military service: LCDR, U.S. Naval Reserves; admitted to the bar, 1972, Des Moines, IA; married: the former Ruth Raduenz, 1968; children: Amy and Jenny; committees: Agriculture, Nutrition, and Forestry; Appropriations; Health, Education, Labor, and Pensions; Small Business and Entrepreneurship; elected to the 94th Congress on November 5, 1974; reelected to four succeeding Congresses; elected to the U.S. Senate on November 6, 1984; reelected to each succeeding Senate term.

Office Listings
http://harkin.senate.gov

731 Hart Senate Office Building, Washington, DC 20510	(202) 224–3254
Chief of Staff.—Brian Ahlberg.	TDD: 224–4633
Press Secretary.—Allison Dobson.	
Federal Building, Room 733, 210 Walnut Street, Des Moines, IA 50309	(515) 284–4574
150 First Avenue NE, Suite 370, Cedar Rapids, IA 52401	(319) 365–4504
1606 Brady Street, Suite 323, Davenport, IA 52801	(563) 322–1338
Federal Building, Room 110, 320 Sixth Street, Sioux City, IA 51101	(712) 252–1550
Federal Building, Room 315, 350 West Sixth Street, Dubuque, IA 52001	(563) 582–2130

REPRESENTATIVES

FIRST DISTRICT

JIM NUSSLE, Republican, of Manchester, IA; born in Des Moines, IA, June 27, 1960; education: graduated, Carl Sandburg High School, 1978; attended Ronshoved Hojskole, Denmark, 1978–79; Luther College, Decorah, IA, 1983; Drake University Law School, Des Moines, IA, 1985; admitted to the bar, January 1986; Delaware County Attorney, 1986–90; family: married to Karen; children: Sarah and Mark; committees: chairman, Budget; Ways and Means; subcommittee: Trade; elected to the 102nd Congress; reelected to each succeeding Congress.

Office Listings
http://www.house.gov/nussle

303 Cannon House Office Building, Washington, DC 20515 .... (202) 225–2911
    Chief of Staff.—Tom Wolfe.
3641 Kimball Avenue, Waterloo, IA 50702 .... (319) 235–1109
2255 John F. Kennedy Road, Dubuque, IA 52002 .... (563) 557–7740
209 West 4th Street, Davenport, IA 52801 .... (563) 326–1841
712 West Main Street, Manchester, IA 52057 .... (563) 927–5141
    District Director.—Shane Johnson.

Counties: BLACK HAWK, BREMER, BUCHANAN, BUTLER, CLAYTON, CLINTON, DELAWARE, DUBUQUE, FAYETTE, JACKSON, JONES, SCOTT. Population (2000), 585,302.

ZIP Codes: 50601–02, 50604–08, 50611, 50613–14, 50619, 50622–23, 50625–26, 50629, 50631, 50634, 50636, 50641, 50643–44, 50647–51, 50654–55, 50660, 50662, 50664–68, 50670–71, 50674, 50676–77, 50681–82, 50701–04, 50706–07, 50799, 52001–04, 52030–33, 52035–50, 52052–54, 52056–57, 52060, 52064–66, 52068–79, 52099, 52135, 52141–42, 52147, 52156–59, 52164, 52166, 52169, 52171, 52175, 52205, 52207, 52210, 52212, 52223, 52226, 52237, 52252, 52254, 52305, 52309–10, 52312, 52320–21, 52323, 52326, 52329–30, 52362, 52701, 52722, 52726–33, 52736, 52742, 52745–48, 52750–51, 52753, 52756–58, 52765, 52767–68, 52771, 52773–74, 52777, 52801–09

* * *

SECOND DISTRICT

JAMES A. LEACH, Republican, of Davenport, IA; born in Davenport, October 15, 1942; education: graduated, Davenport High School, 1960; B.A., Princeton University, 1964; M.A., School of Advanced International Studies, Johns Hopkins University, 1966; further graduate studies at the London School of Economics, 1966–68; staff member of U.S. Congressman Donald Rumsfeld, 1965–66; foreign service officer assigned to the Department of State, 1968–69; administrative assistant to the director of the Office of Economic Opportunity, 1969–70; foreign service officer assigned to the Arms Control and Disarmament Agency, 1970–73; member: U.S. delegation to the Geneva Disarmament Conference, 1971–72; U.S. delegation to the United Nations General Assembly, 1972; U.S. delegation to the United Nations Conference on Natural Resources, 1975; U.S. Advisory Commission on International Educational and Cultural Affairs, 1975–76; Federal Home Loan Bank Board of Des Moines, 1975–76; president, Flamegas Companies, Inc., family business, 1973–76; organizations: Bettendorf Chamber of Commerce; National Federation of Independent Business; Davenport Elks; Moose; and Rotary; religion: Episcopal Church; family: married to the former Elisabeth Foxley; two children: Gallagher and Jenny; committees: Financial Services; International Relations; elected to the 95th Congress on November 2, 1976; reelected to each succeeding Congress.

Office Listings
http://www.house.gov/leach

2186 Rayburn House Office Building, Washington, DC 20515 .... (202) 225–6576
    Administrative Assistant.—Greg Wierzynski.   FAX: 226–1278
    Legislative Director.—Mary Andrus.
    Office Manager.—Sheila Delunery.
214 Jefferson Street, Burlington, IA 52601 .... (319) 754–1106
129 12th Street, SE., Cedar Rapids, IA 52403 .... (319) 363–4773
125 South Dubuque Street, Iowa City, IA 52240 .... (319) 351–0789
105 East 3rd Street, Room 201, Ottumwa, IA 52501 .... (641) 684–4024

Counties: APPANOOSE, CEDAR, DAVIS, DES MOINES, HENRY, JEFFERSON, JOHNSON, LEE, LINN, LOUISA, MUSCATINE, VAN BUREN, WAPELLO, WASHINGTON, WAYNE. Population (2000), 585,241.

ZIP Codes: 50008, 50052, 50060, 50123, 50147, 50165, 50238, 52201–02, 52213–14, 52216, 52218–19, 52227–28, 52233, 52235, 52240–48, 52253, 52255, 52302, 52305–06, 52314, 52317, 52319–20, 52322–24, 52327–28, 52333, 52336–38, 52340–41, 52344, 52350, 52352–53, 52356, 52358–59, 52401–11, 52497–99, 52501, 52530–31, 52533, 52535–38, 52540, 52542, 52544, 52548–49, 52551, 52553–57, 52560, 52565–67, 52570–74, 52580–81, 52583–84, 52588, 52590, 52593–94, 52601, 52619–21, 52623–27, 52630–32, 52635, 52637–42, 52644–56, 52658–60, 52720–21, 52731, 52737–39, 52747, 52749, 52752, 52754–55, 52759–61, 52766, 52769, 52772, 52776, 52778

* * *

THIRD DISTRICT

LEONARD L. BOSWELL, Democrat, of Des Moines, IA; born in Harrison County, MO, January 10, 1934; education: graduated from Lamoni High School, 1952; B.A., Graceland College, Lamoni, IA, 1969; military service: lieutenant colonel, U.S. Army, 1956–76; awards: two

Distinguished Flying Crosses, two Bronze Stars, Soldier's Medal; Iowa State Senate, 1984–96; Iowa State Senate President, 1992–96; lay minister, RLDS Church; member: American Legion, Disabled American Veterans of Foreign Wars, Iowa Farm Bureau, Iowa Cattlemen's Association, Graceland College Board of Trustees; Farmer's Co-op Grain and Seed Board of Directors, 1979–93 (president for 13 years); married Darlene (Dody) Votava Boswell, 1955; three children: Cindy, Diana and Joe; The Coalition (Blue Dogs); co-chair and member emeritus, Mississippi River Caucus; co-chair, Methamphetamine Caucus; committees: Agriculture; Transportation and Infrastructure; Permanent Select Committee on Intelligence; subcommittees: Aviation; General Farm Commodities and Risk Management; Livestock and Horticulture; Human Intelligence, Analysis and Counterintelligence; Railroads; elected to the 105th Congress; reelected to each succeeding Congress.

Office Listings
http://www.house.gov/boswell

1427 Longworth House Office Building, Washington, DC 20515 .... (202) 225–3806
Chief of Staff.—E.H. (Ned) Michalek.   FAX: 225–5608
Legislative Director / Communications Director.—Eric Witte.
Executive Assistant.—Sandy Carter.
300 East Locust Street, Suite 320, Des Moines, IA 50309 .... (515) 282–1909
District Director.—Sally Bowzer.

Counties: BENTON, GRUNDY, IOWA, JASPER, KEOKUK, LUCAS, MAHASKA, MARION, MONROE, POLK, POWESHIEK, TAMA. Population (2000), 585,305.

ZIP Codes: 50007, 50009, 50015, 50021, 50027–28, 50032, 50035, 50044, 50047, 50049, 50054, 50057, 50061–62, 50068, 50073, 50104, 50109, 50111–12, 50116, 50119, 50127, 50131, 50135–39, 50143, 50148, 50150–51, 50153, 50156–58, 50163, 50168–71, 50173, 50206–08, 50214, 50219, 50222, 50225–26, 50228, 50232, 50237–38, 50240, 50242–43, 50251–52, 50255–58, 50265–66, 50268, 50272, 50301–23, 50325, 50327–36, 50338–40, 50347, 50350, 50359–64, 50367–69, 50380–81, 50391–96, 50398, 50601, 50604, 50609, 50612–13, 50621, 50624, 50627, 50632, 50635, 50638, 50642–43, 50651–52, 50657, 50660, 50665, 50669, 50672–73, 50675, 50680, 50936, 50940, 50947, 50950, 50980–81, 52203–04, 52206, 52208–09, 52211, 52213, 52215, 52217, 52220–22, 52224–25, 52228–29, 52231–32, 52236, 52248–49, 52251, 52257, 52301, 52307–08, 52313, 52315–16, 52318, 52322, 52324–25, 52332, 52334–35, 52339, 52342, 52345–49, 52351, 52354–55, 52361, 52404, 52531, 52534, 52543, 52550, 52552, 52561–63, 52568–69, 52576–77, 52585–86, 52591, 52595

* * *

FOURTH DISTRICT

TOM LATHAM, Republican, of Alexander, IA; born in Hampton, IA, July 14, 1948; education: attended Alexander Community School; graduated Cal (Latimer) Community College, 1966; attended Wartburg College, 1966–67; Iowa State University, 1976–70; agriculture business major; professional: marketing representative, independent insurance agent, bank teller and bookkeeper; member and past president, Nazareth Lutheran Church; past chairman, Franklin County Extension Council; secretary, Republican Party of Iowa; 5th District representative, Republican State Central Committee; co-chairman, Franklin County Republican Central Committee; Iowa delegation whip; member: 1992 Republican National Convention, Iowa Farm Bureau Federation, Iowa Soybean Association, American Seed Trade Association, Iowa Corn Growers Association, Iowa Seed Association, Agribusiness Association of Iowa, I.S.U. Extension Citizens Advisory Council; married: Mary Katherine (Kathy), 1975; children: Justin, Jennifer, and Jill; committees: Appropriations; subcommittees: Agriculture, Rural Development, Food and Drug Administration, and Related Agencies; Energy and Water Development, and Related Agencies; Homeland Security; elected to the 104th Congress; reelected to each succeeding Congress.

Office Listings
http://www.house.gov/latham

440 Cannon House Office Building, Washington, DC 20515 .... (202) 225–5476
Chief of Staff.—Michael R. Gruber.   FAX: 225–3301
Press Secretary.—James D. Carstensen.
Legislative Director.—Kevin Berents.
Scheduler.—Jennifer Crall.
1421 South Bell Avenue, Ames, IA 50010 .... (515) 232–2885
District Director.—Clarke Scanlon.
812 Highway 18 East, P.O. Box 532, Clear Lake, IA 50428 .... (641) 357–5225
Regional Representative.—Lois Clark.
1426 Central Avenue, Suite A, Fort Dodge, IA 50501 .... (515) 573–2738
Staff Assistant.—Jim Oberhelman.

Counties: ALLAMAKEE, BOONE, CALHOUN, CERRO GORDO, CHICKASAW, DALLAS, EMMET, FLOYD, FRANKLIN, GREENE, HAMILTON, HANCOCK, HARDIN, HOWARD, HUMBOLDT, KOSSUTH, MADISON, MARSHALL, MITCHELL, PALO ALTO, POCAHONTAS, STORY, WARREN, WEBSTER, WINNEBAGO, WINNESHIEK, WORTH, WRIGHT. Population (2000), 585,305.

ZIP Codes: 50001, 50003, 50005–06, 50010–14, 50028, 50031, 50033–34, 50036–41, 50046–47, 50050–51, 50055–56, 50058–59, 50061, 50063–64, 50066, 50069–72, 50075, 50078, 50101–02, 50105–07, 50109, 50118, 50120, 50122, 50124–26, 50129–30, 50132, 50134, 50139, 50141–42, 50145–46, 50148–49, 50151–52, 50154–56, 50158, 50160–62, 50166–67, 50201, 50206, 50210–13, 50217–18, 50220, 50222–23, 50225, 50227, 50229–31, 50233–36, 50239–41, 50244, 50246–49, 50252, 50257–59, 50261, 50263, 50266, 50269, 50271, 50273, 50276, 50278, 50320, 50323, 50325, 50401–02, 50420–21, 50423–24, 50426–28, 50430–36, 50438–41, 50444, 50446–61, 50464–73, 50475–84, 50501, 50510–11, 50514–33, 50536, 50538–46, 50548, 50551–52, 50554, 50556–63, 50566, 50568–71, 50573–75, 50577–79, 50581–83, 50586, 50590–91, 50593–95, 50597–99, 50601, 50603, 50605, 50609, 50616, 50619–21, 50625, 50627–28, 50630, 50632–33, 50635–36, 50645, 50653, 50658–59, 50661, 50672, 50674, 50680, 51334, 51342, 51344, 51358, 51364–65, 51433, 51443, 51449, 51453, 51462, 51510, 52101, 52132–34, 52136, 52140, 52144, 52146, 52149, 52151, 52154–56, 52159–63, 52165, 52168, 52170–72

* * *

FIFTH DISTRICT

STEVE KING, Republican, of Odebolt, IA; born in Storm Lake, IA, May 28, 1949; education: graduated, Denison Community High School; attended Northwest Missouri State University; professional: agri-businessman; owner and operator of King Construction Company; public service: Iowa State Senate, 1996–2002; religion: Catholic; family: married to Marilyn; children: David, Michael, and Jeff; committees: Agriculture; Judiciary; Small Business; elected to the 108th Congress on November 5, 2002; reelected to each succeeding Congress.

Office Listings
http://www.house.gov/steveking

1432 Longworth House Office Building, Washington, DC 20515	(202) 225–4426
Chief of Staff.—Chuck Laudner.	FAX: 225–3193
Deputy Chief of Staff.—Brenna Findley.	
Legislative Director.—Paula Steiner.	
Scheduler.—Melissa Obermoller.	
607 Lake Avenue, Storm Lake, IA 50588	(712) 732–4197
526 Nebraska Street, Sioux City, IA 51101	(712) 224–4692
40 Pearl Street, Council Bluffs, IA 51503	(712) 325–1404
P.O. Box 650, Spencer, IA 51301	(712) 580–7754
P.O. Box 601, Creston, IA 50801	(641) 782–2495

Counties: ADAIR, ADAMS, AUDUBON, BUENA VISTA, CARROLL, CASS, CHEROKEE, CLARKE, CLAY, CRAWFORD, DECATUR, DICKINSON, FREMONT, GUTHRIE, HARRISON, IDA, LYON, MILLS, MONONA, MONTGOMERY, O'BRIEN, OSCEOLA, PAGE, PLYMOUTH, POTTAWATTAMIE, RINGGOLD, SAC, SHELBY, SIOUX, TAYLOR, UNION, WOODBURY. Population (2000), 584,967.

ZIP Codes: 50002, 50020, 50022, 50025–26, 50029, 50042, 50048, 50058, 50065, 50067, 50070, 50074, 50076, 50103, 50108, 50110, 50115, 50117, 50119, 50123, 50128, 50133, 50140, 50144, 50146, 50149, 50151, 50155, 50164, 50174, 50210, 50213, 50216, 50222, 50233, 50250, 50254, 50257, 50262, 50264, 50273–77, 50510, 50535, 50565, 50567–68, 50576, 50583, 50585, 50588, 50592, 50801, 50830–31, 50833, 50835–37, 50839–43, 50845–49, 50851, 50853–54, 50857–64, 51001–12, 51014–16, 51018–20, 51022–31, 51033–41, 51044–56, 51058–63, 51101–06, 51108–09, 51111, 51201, 51230–32, 51234–35, 51237–50, 51301, 51331, 51333, 51338, 51340–41, 51343, 51345–47, 51350–51, 51354–55, 51357, 51360, 51363–64, 51366, 51401, 51430–33, 51436, 51439–52, 51454–55, 51458–61, 51463, 51465–67, 51501–03, 51510, 51520–21, 51523, 51525–37, 51540–46, 51548–49, 51551–66, 51570–73, 51575–79, 51591, 51593, 51601–03, 51630–32, 51636–40, 51645–54, 51656

KANSAS

(Population 2000, 2,688,418)

SENATORS

SAM BROWNBACK, Republican, of Topeka, KS; born in Garnett, KS, September 12, 1956; education: graduated from Prairie View High School, 1974; B.S., with honors, Kansas State University, Manhattan, KS, 1978; J.D., University of Kansas, Lawrence, 1982; professional: Kansas Bar; attorney, broadcaster, teacher; U.S. House of Representatives, 1994–96; State Secretary of Agriculture, 1986–93; White House Fellow, Office of the U.S. Trade Representative, 1990–91; member: Topeka Fellowship Council, Kansas Bar Association, Kansas State University and Kansas University alumni associations; married: the former Mary Stauffer, 1982; children: Abby, Andy, Liz, Mark and Jenna; committees: Appropriations; Judiciary; Joint Economic Committee; chairman, U.S. Helsinki Commission; elected to the U.S. Senate in November, 1996, to fill the remainder of the vacancy caused by the resignation of Senator Bob Dole; reelected to each succeeding Senate term.

Office Listings
http://brownback.senate.gov

303 Hart Senate Office Building, Washington, DC 20510	(202) 224–6521
Chief of Staff.—Rob Wasinger.	FAX: 228–1265
Scheduler.—Sally Berwick.	
Communications Director.—Brian Hart.	
612 South Kansas, Topeka, KS 66603	(785) 233–2503
Kansas Scheduler.—Denise Coatney.	
1001–C North Broadway, Pittsburg, KS 66762	(316) 231–6040
Grant Director.—Anne Emerson.	
245 N. Waco, Suite 240, Wichita, KS 67202	(620) 264–8066
State Director.—Chuck Alderson.	
11111 West 95th, Suite 245, Overland Park, KS 66214	(913) 492–6378
Deputy Chief of Staff.—George Stafford.	
811 N. Main, Suite A, Garden City, KS 67846	(620) 275–1124
Regional Director.—Dennis Mesa.	

* * *

PAT ROBERTS, Republican, of Dodge City, KS; born in Topeka, KS, April 20, 1936; education: graduated, Holton High School, Holton, KS, 1954; B.S., journalism, Kansas State University, Manhattan, KS, 1958; professional: captain, U.S. Marine Corps, 1958–62; editor and reporter, Arizona newspapers, 1962–67; aide to Senator Frank Carlson, 1967–68; aide to Representative Keith Sebelius, 1969–80; U.S. House of Representatives, 1980–96; founding member: bipartisan Caucus on Unfunded Mandates, House Rural Health Care Coalition; shepherded the 1996 Freedom to Farm Act through the House and Senate; awards: honorary American Farmer, Future Farmers of America; 1993 Wheat Man of the Year, Kansas Association of Wheat Growers; Golden Carrot Award, Public Voice; Golden Bulldog Award, Watchdogs of the Treasury; numerous Guardian of Small Business awards, National Federation of Independent Business; 1995 Dwight D. Eisenhower Medal, Eisenhower Exchange Fellowship; 2001 U.S. Marine Corps Semper Fidelis Award; married: the former Franki Fann, 1969; children: David, Ashleigh, and Anne-Wesley; committees: Agriculture, Nutrition, and Forestry; Armed Services; Health, Education, Labor and Pensions; Select Committee on Ethics; chairman, Select Committee on Intelligence; elected to the U.S. Senate in November, 1996; reelected to each succeeding Senate term.

Office Listings
http://roberts.senate.gov

109 Hart Senate Office Building, Washington, DC 20510	(202) 224–4774
Chief of Staff.—Jackie Cottrell.	FAX: 224–3514
Legislative Director.—Keith Yehle.	
Scheduler.—Maggie Ward.	
100 Military Plaza, P.O. Box 550, Dodge City, KS 67801	(620) 227–2244
District Director.—Debbie Pugh.	
155 North Market Street, Suite 120, Wichita, KS 67202	(316) 263–0416
District Director.—Karin Wisdom.	
Frank Carlson Federal Building, 444 SE Quincy, Room 392, Topeka, KS 66683	(785) 295–2745
District Director.—Gilda Lintz.	
11900 College Boulevard, Suite 203, Overland Park, KS 66210	(913) 451–9343
State Director.—Chad Tenpenny.	

REPRESENTATIVES

FIRST DISTRICT

JERRY MORAN, Republican, of Hays, KS; born in Great Bend, KS, May 29, 1954; education: B.S., economics, 1976, and J.D., 1981, University of Kansas; M.B.A. candidate, Fort Hays State University; partner, Jeter and Moran, Attorneys at Law, Hays, KS; former bank officer and university instructor; represented 37th District in Kansas Senate, 1989–97, serving as vice president in 1993–95 and majority leader in 1995–97; Special Assistant Attorney General, State of Kansas, 1982–85; Deputy Attorney, Rooks County, 1987–95; governor, board of governors, University of Kansas School of Law, 1990 (vice president, 1993–94; president, 1994–95); member: board of directors, Kansas Chamber of Commerce and Industry, 1996–97; Hays Chamber of Commerce; Northwest Kansas and Ellis County bar associations; Phi Alpha Delta legal fraternity; Rotary Club; Lions International; board of trustees, Fort Hays State University Endowment Association; founding co-chair, Congressional Rural Caucus; co-chair, Dwight D. Eisenhower Memorial Commission; married: Robba Moran; children: Kelsey and Alex; committees: Agriculture; Transportation and Infrastructure; Veterans' Affairs; subcommittees: chairman, General Farm Commodities and Risk Management; elected to the 105th Congress; reelected to each succeeding Congress.

Office Listings

http://www.house.gov/moranks01

2443 Rayburn House Office Building, Washington, DC 20515	(202) 225–2715
Chief of Staff.—Travis Murphy.	FAX: 225–5124
Legislative Director.—Jennie Guttery.	
Press Secretary.—Ryan Wright.	
Office Manager—Crystal Emel.	
1200 Main Street, Suite 402, P.O. Box 249, Hays KS 67601–0249	(785) 628–6401
District Representative.—Daron Jamison.	
1 North Main, Suite 525, Hutchinson, KS 67504–1128	(620) 665–6138
District Director.—Kirk Johnson.	

Counties: BARBER, BARTON, CHASE, CHEYENNE, CLARK, CLAY, CLOUD, COMANCHE, DECATUR, DICKINSON, EDWARDS, ELLIS, ELLSWORTH, FINNEY, FORD, GEARY (part), GOVE, GRAHAM, GRANT, GRAY, GREELEY, GREENWOOD (part), HAMILTON, HASKELL, HODGEMAN, JEWELL, KEARNY, KIOWA, LANE, LINCOLN, LOGAN, LYON, MCPHERSON, MARION (part), MARSHALL, MEADE, MITCHELL, MORRIS, MORTON, NEMAHA (part), NESS, NORTON, OSBORNE, OTTAWA, PAWNEE, PHILLIPS, PRATT, RAWLINS, RENO, REPUBLIC, RICE, ROOKS, RUSH, RUSSELL, SALINE, SCOTT, SEWARD, SHERIDAN, SHERMAN, SMITH, STAFFORD, STANTON, STEVENS, THOMAS, TREGO, WABAUNSEE, WALLACE, WASHINGTON, WICHITA. Population (2000), 672,105.

ZIP Codes: 66401, 66403–04, 66406–08, 66411–13, 66423, 66427, 66431, 66438, 66441, 66501–02, 66507–08, 66514, 66518, 66523, 66526, 66534, 66536, 66538, 66541, 66544, 66547–48, 66610, 66614–15, 66801, 66830, 66833–35, 66838, 66840, 66843, 66845–46, 66849–51, 66853–54, 66858–62, 66864–66, 66868–70, 66872–73, 66901, 66930, 66932–33, 66935–46, 66948–49, 66951–53, 66955–56, 66958–64, 66966–68, 66970, 67009, 67020–21, 67028–29, 67035, 67053–54, 67057, 67059, 67061–63, 67065–66, 67068, 67070, 67073, 67104, 67107–09, 67112, 67114, 67124, 67127, 67134, 67138, 67143, 67151, 67155, 67335, 67401–02, 67410, 67416–18, 67420, 67422–23, 67425, 67427–28, 67430–32, 67436–39, 67441–52, 67454–60, 67464, 67466–68, 67473–76, 67478, 67480–85, 67487, 67490–92, 67501–02, 67504–05, 67510–16, 67518–26, 67529–30, 67543–48, 67550, 67552–54, 67556–57, 67559–61, 67563–68, 67570, 67572–76, 67578–79, 67581, 67583–85, 67601, 67621–23, 67625–29, 67631–32, 67634–35, 67637–40, 67642–51, 67653–61, 67663–65, 67667, 67669, 67671–75, 67701, 67730–41, 67743–45, 67748–49, 67751–53, 67756–58, 67761–62, 67764, 67801, 67831, 67834–42, 67844, 67846, 67849–51, 67853–55, 67857, 67859–65, 67867, 67869–71, 67876–80, 67882, 67901, 67905, 67950–54

* * *

SECOND DISTRICT

JIM RYUN, Republican, of Lawrence, KS; born in Wichita, KS, April 29, 1947; education: graduated, Wichita East High School, 1965; B.S., photojournalism, University of Kansas; professional: product development consultant, president of Jim Ryun Sports, Inc., professional photographer, and author of two books; represented the U.S. in three consecutive Olympics (1964, 1968, 1972): silver medal in the 1500-meter race, 1968, and World Record Holder in the 880-yard, one-mile, and 1500-meter races; awards: Sports Illustrated Sportsman of the Year, 1966; AAU Sullivan Award; Jaycees of America Top Ten Young Men of the United States, 1968; married: Anne Snider Ryun, 1969; children: Heather, Ned, Drew, and Catharine; committees: Armed Services; Budget; Financial Services; elected to the 105th Congress; reelected to each succeeding Congress.

Office Listings
http://www.house.gov/ryun

1110 Longworth House Office Building, Washington, DC 20515 .... (202) 225–6601
    Chief of Staff.—Mark Kelly.   FAX: 225–7986
    Press Secretary.—Nick Reid.
    Deputy Chief of Staff.—Jay Rinehart.
800 SW Jackson Street, Suite 100, Topeka, KS 66612 .... (785) 232–4500
    District Director.—Michelle Butler.
The Stilwell Hotel, 701 North Broadway, Pittsburg, KS 66762 .... (620) 232–6100
    Regional Representative.—Jim Allen.

Counties: ALLEN, ANDERSON, ATCHISON, BOURBON, BROWN, CHEROKEE, COFFEY, CRAWFORD, DONIPHAN, DOUGLAS (part), FRANKLIN, GEARY, JACKSON, JEFFERSON, LABETTE, LEAVENWORTH, LINN, MIAMI, NEMAHA (part), NEOSHO, OSAGE, POTTAWATOMIE, RILEY, SHAWNEE, WILSON, WOODSON. Population (2000), 672,102.

ZIP Codes: 66002, 66006–08, 66010, 66012–17, 66020–21, 66023–27, 66032–33, 66035–36, 66039–50, 66052–54, 66056, 66058, 66060, 66064, 66066–67, 66070–73, 66075–80, 66083, 66086–88, 66090–91, 66093–95, 66097, 66109, 66112, 66401–04, 66407, 66409, 66413–20, 66422, 66424–29, 66431–32, 66434, 66436, 66439–40, 66442, 66449, 66451, 66502–03, 66505–06, 66509–10, 66512, 66515–17, 66520–24, 66527–28, 66531–40, 66542–44, 66546–50, 66552, 66554, 66601, 66603–12, 66614–22, 66624–26, 66628–29, 66636–37, 66642, 66647, 66652–53, 66667, 66675, 66683, 66692, 66699, 66701, 66710–14, 66716–17, 66720, 66724–25, 66728, 66732–36, 66738–43, 66746, 66748–49, 66751, 66753–63, 66767, 66769–73, 66775–83, 66834, 66839, 66849, 66852, 66854, 66856–57, 66864, 66868, 66870–71, 66933, 67047, 67330, 67332, 67335–37, 67341–42, 67351, 67354, 67356–57

* * *

THIRD DISTRICT

DENNIS MOORE, Democrat, of Lenexa, KS; born in Anthony, KS, November 8, 1945; education: Jefferson Elementary School, and Charles Curtis Intermediate School, Wichita, KS; B.A., University of Kansas, 1967; J.D., Washburn University of Law, 1970; professional: attorney; admitted to Kansas Bar, 1970, first practiced in Topeka, KS; Assistant Attorney General of Kansas, 1971–73; Johnson County District Attorney, 1977–89; Johnson County Community College Board of Trustees, 1993–99; member, American Legion; married: Stephene Moore; seven children: Todd, Scott, Andrew, Felicia Barge, Valerie Swearingen, Nathan Hansen, and Adam Hansen; military: U.S. Army, 2nd Lieutenant, 1970; U.S. Army Reserves, Captain, 1970–73; committees: Budget; Financial Services; subcommittees: Capital Markets, Insurance and Government Sponsored Enterprises; Financial Institutions and Consumer Credit; Oversight and Investigations; elected to the 106th Congress; reelected to each succeeding Congress.

Office Listings
http://www.house.gov/moore

1727 Longworth House Office Building, Washington, DC 20515 .... (202) 225–2865
    Chief of Staff.—Howard Bauleke.   FAX: 225–2807
    Scheduler.—Andrew Shaw.
    Communications Director.—Christie Appelhanz.
8417 Santa Fe Drive, Room 101, Overland Park, KS 66212 .... (913) 383–2013
    District Director.—Julie Merz.
500 State Avenue, Room 176, Kansas City, KS 66101 .... (913) 621–0832
647 Massachusetts Street, #212, Lawrence, KS 66044 .... (785) 842–9313
    Constituent Services Director.—Becky Fast.

Counties: DOUGLAS (part), JOHNSON, WYANDOTTE. Population (2000), 672,124.

ZIP Codes: 66006–07, 66012–13, 66018–19, 66026, 66030–31, 66035–36, 66044–47, 66049–51, 66053, 66061–64, 66071, 66077, 66083, 66085, 66092, 66101–06, 66109–13, 66115, 66117–19, 66160, 66201–27, 66250–51, 66276, 66282–83, 66285–86

* * *

FOURTH DISTRICT

TODD TIAHRT, Republican, of Goddard, KS; born in Vermillion, SD, June 15, 1951; education: attended South Dakota School of Mines and Technology; B.A., Evangel College, Springfield, MO, 1975; M.B.A., Southwest Missouri State, 1989; professional: proposal manager, The Boeing Company; married: the former Vicki Holland, 1976; children: Jessica, John, and Luke; committees: Appropriations; Permanent Select Committee on Intelligence; elected to the 104th Congress; reelected to each succeeding Congress.

Office Listings

http://www.house.gov/tiahrt

2441 Rayburn House Office Building, Washington, DC 20515 .... (202) 225–6216
    Administrative Assistant.—Jeff Kahrs.   FAX: 225–3489
    Legislative Director.—Amy Claire Brusch.
    Scheduler.—Melissa James.
    Communications Director.—Chuck Knapp.
155 North Market Street, Suite 400, Wichita, KS 67202 .... (316) 262–8992
    District Director.—Robert Noland.

Counties: BUTLER, CHAUTAUQUA, COWLEY, ELK, GRENWOOD (part), HARPER, HARVEY, KINGMAN, MONTGOMERY, SEDGWICK, SUMNER. Population (2000), 672,101.

ZIP Codes: 66840, 66842, 66853, 66863, 66866, 66870, 67001–05, 67008–10, 67012–13, 67016–20, 67022–26, 67030–31, 67035–39, 67041–42, 67045, 67047, 67049–52, 67055–56, 67058, 67060–62, 67067–68, 67070, 67072, 67074, 67101, 67103, 67105–08, 67110–12, 67114, 67117–20, 67122–23, 67131–33, 67135, 67137–38, 67140, 67142, 67144, 67146–47, 67149–52, 67154, 67156, 67159, 67201–21, 67226, 67230, 67235, 67260, 67275–78, 67301, 67333–35, 67337, 67340, 67344–47, 67349, 67351–53, 67355, 67360–61, 67363–64, 67522, 67543

KENTUCKY

(Population 2000, 4,041,769)

SENATORS

MITCH McCONNELL, Republican, of Louisville, KY; born in Colbert County, AL, February 20, 1942; education: graduated Manual High School, Louisville, 1960, president of the student body; B.A. with honors, University of Louisville, 1964, president of the student council, president of the student body of the College of Arts and Sciences; J.D., University of Kentucky Law School, 1967, president of student bar association, outstanding oral advocate; professional: attorney, admitted to the Kentucky bar, 1967; chief legislative assistant to U.S. Senator Marlow Cook, 1968–70; Deputy Assistant U.S. Attorney General, 1974–75; Judge/Executive of Jefferson County, KY, 1978–84; chairman, National Republican Senatorial Committee, 1997–2000; chairman, Joint Congressional Committee on Inaugural Ceremonies, 1999–2001; Senate Majority Whip, 2002–present; married to Elaine Chao on February 6, 1993; children: Elly, Claire, and Porter; committees: Agriculture, Nutrition, and Forestry; Appropriations; Rules and Administration; subcommittees: chairman, Foreign Operations; elected to the U.S. Senate on November 6, 1984; reelected to each succeeding Senate term.

Office Listings
http://mcconnell.senate.gov

361A Russell Senate Office Building, Washington, DC 20510	(202) 224–2541
Chief of Staff.—William H. Piper.	FAX: 224–2499
Scheduler.—Karen Willard.	
Press Secretary.—Robert Steurer.	
601 West Broadway, Suite 630, Louisville, KY 40202	(502) 582–6304
State Director.—Larry Cox.	
1885 Dixie Highway, Suite 345, Fort Wright, KY 41011	(606) 578–0188
300 South Main Street, Suite 310, London, KY 40740	(606) 864–2026
Professional Arts Building, Suite 100, 2320 Broadway, Paducah, KY 42001	(502) 442–4554
771 Corporate Drive, Suite 530, Lexington, KY 40507	(606) 224–8286
Federal Building, Room 102, 241 Main Street, Bowling Green, KY 42101	(502) 781–1673

* * *

JIM BUNNING, Republican, of Southgate, KY; born in Southgate, October 23, 1931; education: graduated, St. Xavier High School, Cincinnati, OH, 1949; B.S., Xavier University, Cincinnati, OH, 1953; professional: baseball player, Hall of Fame; investment broker and agent; president, Jim Bunning Agency, Inc.; member of Kentucky State Senate (minority floor leader), 1979–83; member: Ft. Thomas City Council, 1977–79; appointed member, Ohio, Kentucky, and Indiana Regional Council of Governments, Cincinnati, OH; National Committeeman, Republican National Committee, 1983–92; appointed member, President's National Advisory Board on International Education Programs, 1984–88; member: board of directors of Kentucky Special Olympics, Ft. Thomas (KY) Lions Club, Brighton Street Center Community Action Group; married: the former Mary Catherine Theis, 1952; children: Barbara, Jim, Joan, Cathy, Bill, Bridgett, Mark, David and Amy; elected to the 100th Congress, November 4, 1986; reelected to each succeeding Congress; committees: Banking, Housing, and Urban Affairs; Budget; Energy and Natural Resources; Finance; elected to the U.S. Senate in November, 1998; reelected to each succeeding Senate term.

Office Listings
http://bunning.senate.gov

316 Hart Senate Office Building, Washington, DC 20515	(202) 224–4343
Personnel Assistant/Scheduler.—Amy Davis.	FAX: 228–1373
Chief of Staff.—Jon Deuser.	
Legislative Director.—Kim Taylor.	
Press Secretary.—Michael Reynard.	
1717 Dixie Highway, Suite 220, Fort Wright, KY 41011	(859) 341–2602
State Director.—Debbie McKinney.	
The Federal Building, 423 Frederica Street, Room 305, Owensboro, KY 42301	(270) 689–9085
717 Corporate Drive, Lexington, KY 40503	(606) 219–2239
1100 South Main Street, Suite 12, Hopkinsville, KY 42240	(270) 885–1212

REPRESENTATIVES

FIRST DISTRICT

ED WHITFIELD, Republican, of Hopkinsville, KY; born in Hopkinsville, May 25, 1943; education: graduated, Madisonville High School, Madisonville, KY; B.S., University of Kentucky, Lexington, 1965; J.D., University of Kentucky, 1969; attended American University's Wesley Theological Seminary, Washington, DC; military service: first lieutenant, U.S. Army Reserves, 1967–73; professional: attorney, private practice, 1970–79; vice president, CSX Corporation, 1979–90; admitted to bar: Kentucky, 1970, and Florida, 1993; began practice in 1970 in Hopkinsville, KY; member, Kentucky House, 1973, one term; married: Constance Harriman Whitfield; children: Kate; committees: Energy and Commerce; subcommittees: Energy and Air Quality; chair, Oversight and Investigations; Telecommunications and the Internet; elected to the 104th Congress; reelected to each succeeding Congress.

Office Listings

301 Cannon House Office Building, Washington, DC 20515 .... (202) 225–3115
    Chief of Staff.—Karen Long.   FAX: 225–3547
    Scheduler/Office Manager.—Emily Chandler.
    Legislative Director.—John Halliwell.
1403 South Main Street, Hopkinsville, KY 42240 .... (270) 885–8079
    District Director.—Michael Pape.
200 North Main, Suite F, Tompkinsville, KY 42167 .... (270) 487–9509
    Field Representative.—Sandy Simpson.
222 First Street, Suite 206A, Henderson, KY 42420 .... (270) 826–4180
    Field Representative.—Ed West.
100 Fountain Avenue, Room 104, Paducah, KY 42001 .... (270) 442–6901
    Field Representative.—David Mast.

Counties: ADAIR, ALLEN, BALLARD, BUTLER, CALDWELL, CALLOWAY, CARLISLE, CASEY, CHRISTIAN, CLINTON, CRITTENDEN, CUMBERLAND, FULTON, GRAVES, HENDERSON, HICKMAN, HOPKINS, LINCOLN (part), LIVINGSTON, LOGAN, LYON, MARSHALL, MCCRACKEN, MCLEAN, METCALF, MONROE, MUHLENBERG, OHIO (part), RUSSELL, SIMPSON, TODD, TRIGG, UNION, WEBSTER. Population (2000), 673,629.

ZIP Codes: 40009, 40328, 40437, 40442, 40448, 40464, 40484, 40489, 42001–03, 42020–25, 42027–29, 42031–33, 42035–41, 42044–45, 42047–51, 42053–56, 42058, 42060–61, 42063–64, 42066, 42069–71, 42076, 42078–79, 42081–88, 42101, 42104, 42120, 42122–24, 42129, 42133–35, 42140–41, 42150–51, 42153–54, 42164, 42166–67, 42170, 42201–04, 42206, 42209–211, 42214–17, 42219–21, 42223, 42232, 42234, 42236, 42240–41, 42251–52, 42254, 42256, 42261–62, 42265–67, 42273–74, 42276, 42280, 42283, 42286–88, 42301, 42320–28, 42330, 42332–34, 42337, 42339, 42344–45, 42347, 42349–50, 42352, 42354, 42356, 42367–69, 42371–72, 42374–76, 42402–04, 42406, 42408–11, 42413, 42419–20, 42431, 42436–37, 42440–42, 42444–45, 42450–53, 42455–64, 42516, 42528, 42539, 42541, 42544, 42565–67, 42602–03, 42629, 42642, 42711, 42715, 42717, 42720–21, 42728, 42731, 42733, 42735, 42740–43, 42746, 42749, 42753, 42759, 42786

* * *

SECOND DISTRICT

RON LEWIS, Republican, of Cecilia, KY; born in South Shore, KY, September 14, 1946; education: graduated, McKell High School, 1964; B.A., University of Kentucky, 1969; M.A., higher education, Morehead State University, 1981; U.S. Navy Officer Candidate School, 1972; laborer, Morehead State, Armco Steel Corporation; Kentucky Highway Department, Eastern State Hospital; sales for Ashland Oil; teacher, Watterson College, 1980; minister, White Mills Baptist Church; member, Elizabethtown Chamber of Commerce; past president, Hardin and Larue County jail ministry; member, Serverus Valley Ministerial Association; honored for his voting record by League of Private Property Rights, Council for Citizens Against Government Waste, National Federation of Independent Business; married: the former Kayi Gambill, 1966; children: Ronald Brent and Allison Faye; committees: Ways and Means; subcommittees: Human Resources; Select Revenue Measures; Social Security; elected to the 104th Congress; reelected to each succeeding Congress.

Office Listings

http://www.house.gov/ronlewis

2418 Rayburn House Office Building, Washington, DC 20515 .... (202) 225–3501
    Chief of Staff.—Daniel London.
    Legislative Director.—Eric Bergren.
    Press Secretary.—Mike Dodge.
    Scheduler.—Lindy Salem.
1690 Ring Road, Suite 260, Elizabethtown, KY 42701 .... (270) 765–4360
    District Administrator.—Keith Rogers.

Warren Co. Justice Ctr, 1001 Center St., Suite 300, Bowling Green, KY 42101 ..... (270) 842–9896
1100 Walnut Street, Suite P15 B, Owensboro, KY 42301 .... (270) 688–8858

Counties: BARREN, BRECKINRIDGE, BULLITT, DAVIESS, EDMONSON, GRAYSON, GREEN, HANCOCK, HARDIN, HART, JEFFERSON (part), LARUE, MARION, MEADE, NELSON, OHIO (part), SHELBY, SPENCER, TAYLOR, WARREN, WASHINGTON. Population (2000), 673,244.

ZIP Codes: 40003–04, 40008–09, 40012–13, 40018–20, 40022–23, 40033, 40037, 40040, 40046–49, 40051–52, 40057, 40060–63, 40065–69, 40071, 40076, 40078, 40104, 40107–11, 40115, 40117–19, 40121, 40129, 40140, 40142–46, 40150, 40152–53, 40155, 40157, 40159–62, 40164–65, 40170–71, 40175–78, 40219, 40229, 40245, 40272, 40291, 40299, 40328, 40330, 40342, 40448, 40468, 40601, 42101–04, 42122–23, 42127–31, 42133, 42141–42, 42152, 42156–57, 42159–60, 42163, 42166, 42170–71, 42201, 42206–07, 42210, 42251, 42257, 42259, 42270, 42274–75, 42283, 42285, 42301–04, 42320, 42327, 42333–34, 42338, 42343, 42347–49, 42351–52, 42355–56, 42361, 42364, 42366, 42368, 42370, 42375–78, 42701–02, 42712–13, 42716, 42718–19, 42721–22, 42724, 42726, 42728–29, 42732–33, 42740, 42743, 42746, 42748–49, 42754–55, 42757–58, 42762, 42764–65, 42776, 42782–84, 42788

* * *

THIRD DISTRICT

ANNE M. NORTHUP, Republican, of Louisville, KY; born in Louisville, January 22, 1948; education: graduated from Sacred Heart Academy, Louisville, 1966; graduated from St. Mary's College, Notre Dame, IN, 1970; Kentucky State Legislature, 1987–96; legislative appointments: member, U.S. Helsinki Commission, 2003; Speaker's Prescription Drug Action Team, 2002; Free Trade Working Group, 2000; World Trade Organization Congressional Advisory Group, 1999; Chairwoman of Speaker's Task Force on Education, 1998; Speaker's Drug Free Task Force, 1998; Education Caucus; Founder and co-chair of the House Reading Caucus; Congressional Coalition on Adoption; Education Caucus; Republican Israel Caucus; Missing and Exploited Children Caucus; Congressional Friends of Animals; African Trade and Investment Caucus; Medical Malpractice Crisis Task Force; awards: Legislator of the Year for the Association of the Equipment Distributors; Chamber of Commerce Spirit of Enterprise Award; Watchdogs of the Treasury Bulldog Award; Citizens for a Sound Economy Jefferson Award; Legislative Achievement in Economic Development; Southern Economic Development Council the NFIB Guardian of Small Business Award; Literacy Leadership Award, Kentucky Reading Association; Community Service Recognition Award, Louisville Defender Newspaper; Legislator of the Year—NOISE (National Organization to Insure a Sound-controlled Environment; Silver Anchor Award—Friends of the Waterfront; Community Healthcare Champion Award, National Association of Community Health Centers; Friend of the Farm Bureau; BIPAC Adam Smith Award, 2003; member, Holy Spirit Catholic Church; Greater Louisville, Inc.; Rotary Club of Louisville; Leadership Louisville; Metropolitan Republican Women's Club; National Order of Women Legislators; Ladies Auxiliary to the VFW; married: Robert Wood Northup, 1969; children: David, Katie, Joshua, Kevin, Erin, Mark; committees: Appropriations; elected to the 105th Congress; reelected to each succeeding Congress.

Office Listings
http://www.house.gov/northup

2459 Rayburn House Office Building, Washington, DC 20515 .... (202) 225–5401
   Chief of Staff.—Terry Carmack.   FAX: 225–5776
   Legislative Director.—Clinton Blair.
   Press Secretary.—Annie Reed.
   Scheduler.—Beth Strategier.
600 Martin Luther King, Jr. Place, Suite 216, Louisville, KY 40202 .... (502) 582–5129
   District Director.—Sherri Craig.

Counties: JEFFERSON COUNTY. Population (2000), 674,032.

ZIP Codes: 40018, 40023, 40025, 40027, 40041, 40059, 40109, 40118, 40201–25, 40228–29, 40231–33, 40241–43, 40245, 40250–53, 40255–59, 40261, 40266, 40268–70, 40272, 40280–83, 40285, 40287, 40289–99

* * *

FOURTH DISTRICT

GEOFFREY C. DAVIS, Republican, of Hebron, KY; born, October 26, 1958; education: attended public schools, West Pittsburgh, PA; B.S., U.S. Military Academy, West Point, NY, 1981; professional: U.S. Army, 1976–87; Assault Helicopter Flight Commander, 82nd Airborne Division; Army Ranger and Senior Parachutist; manufacturing consultant; founder, Republic Consulting, formerly known as Capstone, Incorporated, 1992–present; organizations: 82nd Airborne Association; American Legion volunteer chaplain; National Rifle Association; Northern Kentucky Chamber of Commerce; married: Pat; six children; committees: Armed Services; Financial Services; subcommittees: Capitol Markets, Insurance, and Government-Sponsored Enterprises; Housing and Community Opportunity; Oversight and Investigations; Strategic Forces; Terrorism, Unconventional Threats and Capabilities; elected to the 109th Congress on November 2, 2004.

Office Listings

http://www.house.gov/geoffdavis

1541 Longworth House Office Building, Washington, DC 20515	(202) 225–3465
Chief of Staff/Legislative Director.—Justin Brasell.	FAX: 225–0003
Scheduler/Office Manager.—Roberta Quis.	
Communications Director.—Jessica Towhey.	
277 Buttermilk Pike, Fort Mitchell, KY 41017	(859) 426–0080
1405 Greenup Avenue, Suite 236, Ashland, KY 41101	(606) 324–9898

Counties: BATH (part), BOONE, BOYD, BRACKEN, CAMPBELL, CARROLL, CARTER, ELLIOTT, FLEMING, GALLATIN, GRANT, GREENUP, HARRISON, HENRY, KENTON, LEWIS, MASON, NICHOLAS, OLDHAM, OWEN, PENDLETON, ROBERTSON, SCOTT (part), TRIMBLE. Population (2000), 673,588.

ZIP Codes: 40006–07, 40010–11, 40014, 40019, 40026, 40031–32, 40036, 40045, 40050, 40055–59, 40066, 40068, 40070, 40075, 40077, 40241, 40245, 40311, 40324, 40329, 40334, 40346, 40350–51, 40353, 40355, 40358–61, 40363, 40366, 40370–71, 40374, 40379, 40601, 41001–08, 41010–12, 41014–19, 41022, 41030–31, 41033–35, 41037, 41039–46, 41048–49, 41051–56, 41059, 41061–65, 41071–76, 41080–81, 41083, 41085–86, 41091–98, 41101–02, 41105, 41114, 41121, 41128–29, 41132, 41135, 41137, 41139, 41141–44, 41146, 41149, 41156, 41159, 41164, 41166, 41168–69, 41171, 41173–75, 41179–81, 41183, 41189, 41472, 42254, 45275, 45277, 45298, 45944, 45999

* * *

FIFTH DISTRICT

HAROLD ROGERS, Republican, of Somerset, KY; born in Barrier, KY, December 31, 1937; education: graduated, Wayne County High School, 1955; attended Western Kentucky University, 1956–57; A.B., University of Kentucky, 1962; LL.B., University of Kentucky Law School, 1964; professional: lawyer, admitted to the Kentucky State bar, 1964; commenced practice in Somerset; member, North Carolina and Kentucky National Guard, 1957–64; associate, Smith and Blackburn, 1964–67; private practice, 1967–69; Commonwealth Attorney, Pulaski and Rockcastle Counties, KY, 1969–80; delegate, Republican National Convention, 1972, 1976, 1980, 1984, and 1988; Republican nominee for Lieutenant Governor, KY, 1979; past president, Kentucky Commonwealth Attorneys Association; member and past president, Somerset-Pulaski County Chamber of Commerce and Pulaski County Industrial Foundation; founder, Southern Kentucky Economic Development Council, 1986; member, Chowder and Marching Society, 1981–present; married the former Shirley McDowell, 1957; three children: Anthony, Allison, and John Marshall; committees: Appropriations; Republican Steering Committee member; subcommittees: Homeland Security; Transportation, Treasury, HUD, The Judiciary, District of Columbia, and Independent Agencies; elected to the 97th Congress, November 4, 1980; reelected to each succeeding Congress.

Office Listings

http://www.house.gov/rogers

2406 Rayburn House Office Building, Washington, DC 20515	(202) 225–4601
Administrative Assistant.—Will Smith.	FAX: 225–0940
Office Manager.—Julia Casey.	
Communications Director.—Leslie Cupp.	
551 Clifty Street, Somerset, KY 42501	(606) 679–8346
District Administrator.—Robert L. Mitchell.	
601 Main Street, Hazard, KY 41701	(606) 439–0794
100 Resource Drive, Suite A, Prestonsburg, KY 41653	(606) 886–0844

Counties: BATH (part), BELL, BREATHITT, CLAY, FLOYD, HARLAN, JACKSON, JOHNSON, KNOTT, KNOX, LAUREL, LAWRENCE, LEE, LESLIE, LETCHER, MAGOFFIN, MARTIN, MCCREARY, MENIFEE, MORGAN, OWSLEY, PERRY, PIKE, PULASKI, ROCKCASTLE, ROWAN, WAYNE, WHITLEY, WOLFE. Population (2000), 673,670.

ZIP Codes: 40313, 40316–17, 40319, 40322, 40329, 40336–37, 40346, 40351, 40358, 40360, 40371, 40387, 40402–03, 40409, 40419, 40421, 40434, 40445, 40447, 40456, 40460, 40467, 40481, 40486, 40488, 40492, 40701–02, 40724, 40729–30, 40734, 40737, 40740–45, 40751, 40754–55, 40759, 40763, 40769, 40771, 40801, 40803, 40806–08, 40810, 40813, 40815–16, 40818–20, 40823–24, 40826–31, 40840, 40843–45, 40847, 40849, 40854–56, 40858, 40862–63, 40865, 40868, 40870, 40873–74, 40902–03, 40906, 40913–15, 40921, 40923, 40927, 40930, 40932, 40935, 40939–41, 40943–44, 40946, 40949, 40951, 40953, 40955, 40958, 40962, 40964–65, 40972, 40977, 40979, 40981–83, 40988, 40995, 40997, 40999, 41124, 41129, 41132, 41159–60, 41164, 41168, 41180, 41201, 41203–04, 41214, 41216, 41219, 41222, 41224, 41226, 41230–32, 41234, 41238, 41240, 41250, 41254–57, 41260, 41262–65, 41267–68, 41271, 41274, 41301,

41307, 41310–11, 41313–14, 41317, 41332–33, 41338–39, 41342, 41344, 41347–48, 41351–52, 41360, 41362, 41364–68, 41385–86, 41390, 41397, 41408, 41410, 41413, 41419, 41421–22, 41425–26, 41433, 41451, 41459, 41464–65, 41472, 41477, 41501–03, 41512–14, 41517, 41519–20, 41522, 41524, 41526–28, 41531, 41534–35, 41537–40, 41542–44, 41546–49, 41553–55, 41557–64, 41566–68, 41571–72, 41601–07, 41612, 41615–16, 41619, 41621–22, 41630–32, 41635–36, 41640, 41642–43, 41645, 41647, 41649–51, 41653, 41655, 41659–60, 41663, 41666–67, 41669, 41701–02, 41712–14, 41719, 41721–23, 41725, 41727, 41729, 41731, 41735–36, 41739–40, 41743, 41745–47, 41749, 41751, 41754, 41759–60, 41762–64, 41766, 41772–78, 41804, 41810, 41812, 41815, 41817, 41819, 41821–22, 41824–26, 41828, 41831–40, 41843–45, 41847–49, 41855, 41858–59, 41861–62, 42501–03, 42518–19, 42533, 42544, 42553, 42558, 42564, 42567, 42603, 42631, 42633–35, 42638, 42642, 42647, 42649, 42653

* * *

SIXTH DISTRICT

BEN CHANDLER, Democrat, of Woodford County, KY; born in Versailles, KY, September 12, 1959; education: B.A., History, University of Kentucky; J.D., University of Kentucky College of Law; public service: elected Kentucky State Auditor, 1991; elected Kentucky Attorney General, 1995; reelected in 1999; Democratic nominee for Governor, 2003; religion: member of Pisgah Presbyterian Church; family: married to Jennifer; children: Lucie, Albert IV, and Branham; committees: Agriculture; International Relations; Transportation and Infrastructure; elected to the 108th Congress, by special election, on February 17, 2004; reelected to the 109th Congress on November 2, 2004.

Office Listings

1504 Longworth House Office Building, Washington, DC 20515 .... (202) 225–4706
    Chief of Staff.—Dennis Fleming, Jr.   FAX: 225–2122
    Legislative Director.—Clinton Dockery.
    Communications Director.—Lillian Pace.
1021 Majestic Street, Suite 280, Lexington, KY 40503 .... (859) 219–1366

Counties: ANDERSON, BOURBON, BOYLE, CLARK, ESTILL, FAYETTE, FRANKLIN, GARRARD, JESSAMINE, LINCOLN (part), MADISON, MERCER, MONTGOMERY, POWELL, SCOTT (part), WOODFORD. Population (2000), 673,626.

ZIP Codes: 40003, 40046, 40076, 40078, 40310–12, 40320, 40324, 40328, 40330, 40334, 40336–37, 40339–40, 40342, 40346–48, 40353, 40355–57, 40361–62, 40370, 40372, 40374, 40376, 40379–80, 40383–86, 40390–92, 40403–05, 40409–10, 40419, 40422–23, 40437, 40440, 40444–47, 40452, 40461, 40464, 40468, 40472–73, 40475–76, 40484, 40489, 40495, 40502–17, 40522–24, 40526, 40533, 40536, 40544, 40546, 40550, 40555, 40574–83, 40588, 40591, 40598, 40601–04, 40618–22, 41031, 41901–06, 42567

LOUISIANA

(Population 2000, 4,468,976)

SENATORS

MARY L. LANDRIEU, Democrat, of New Orleans, LA; born in Alexandria, VA, November 23, 1955; education: B.A., Louisiana State University, 1977; real estate broker, specializing in townhouse development; represented New Orleans House District 90 in Louisiana Legislature, 1979–87; State Treasurer, 1987–95; vice chair, Louisiana Council on Child Abuse; member, Business and Professional Women; majority council member, Emily's List; past national president, Women's Legislative Network; past vice president, Women Executives in State Government; delegate to every Democratic National Convention since 1980; married: E. Frank Snellings; children: Connor, and Mary Shannon; committees: Appropriations; Energy and Natural Resources; Small Business and Entrepreneurship; Congressional Coalition on Adoption; elected to the U.S. Senate on November 5, 1996; reelected to each succeeding Senate term.

Office Listings
http://landrieu.senate.gov

724 Hart Senate Office Building, Washington, DC 20510	(202) 224–5824
Chief of Staff.—Norma Jane Sabiston.	FAX: 224–9735
Scheduler.—Amy Cenicola.	
Executive Assistant.—Gina Ormand.	
Legislative Director.—Jason Matthews.	
Hale Boggs Federal Building, Room 1005, 500 Poydras Street, New Orleans, LA 70130	(504) 589–2427
U.S. Courthouse, 300 Fannin Street, Room 2240, Shreveport, LA 71101–3086	(318) 676–3085
U.S. Federal Court House, 707 Florida Street, Room 326, Baton Rouge, LA 70801 ..	(225) 389–0395
Hibernia Tower, One Lakeshore Drive, Suite 1260, Lake Charles, LA 70629	(337) 436–6650

* * *

DAVID VITTER, Republican, of Metairie, LA; born in Metairie, May 3, 1961; education: Harvard University; Oxford University Rhodes Scholar; Tulane University School of Law; professional: attorney; adjunct law professor, Tulane and Loyola Universities; religion: Catholic; public service: Louisiana House of Representatives, 1992–1999; U.S. House of Representatives, 1999–2005; awards: Alliance for Good Government "Legislator of the Year"; Victims and Citizens Against Crime "Outstanding Legislator" and "Lifetime Achievement Award"; married: Wendy Baldwin Vitter; children: Sophie, Lise, Airey, and Jack; committees: Commerce, Science and Transportation; Environment and Public Works; Small Business and Entrepreneurship; elected to the U.S. Senate on November 2, 2004.

Office Listings
http://vitter.senate.gov

516 Hart Senate Office Building, Washington, DC 20510	(202) 224–4623
Chief of Staff.—Kyle Ruckert.	FAX: 228–5061
Deputy Chief of Staff.—tonya Newman.	
Legislative Director.—Evelyn Fortier.	
Communications Director.—Mac Abrams.	
2800 Veterans Boulevard, Suite 201, Metairie, LA 70002	(504) 589–2753
858 Convention Street, Baton Rouge, LA 70801	(225) 383–0331
1217 N. 19th Street, Monroe, LA 71201	(318) 325–8120

REPRESENTATIVES

FIRST DISTRICT

BOBBY JINDAL, Republican, of Baton Rouge, LA; born in Baton Rouge, June 10, 1971; education: B.S., Brown University, with honors, 1991; M. Litt, Oxford University, 1994; professional: secretary, Louisiana Department of Health and Hospitals, 1996–1998; appointed executive director of the National Bipartisan Commission on the Future of Medicare, 1998; president, University of Louisiana system, 1999; appointed Assistant Secretary for Planning and Evaluation, Department of Health and Human Services by President George W. Bush on March 7, 2001; consultant for McKinsey & Company; religion: Catholic; married: the former Supriya Jolly; children: Selia Elizabeth and Shaan Robert; committees: Education and the Workforce; Homeland Security; Resources; elected to the 109th Congress on November 2, 2004.

Office Listings

http://www.house.gov/jindal

1205 Longworth House Office Building, Washington, DC 20515	(202) 225–3015
Chief of Staff.—Timmy Teepell.	FAX: 226–0386
Office Manager.—Allee Bautsch.	
Press Secretary.—Chris Paolino.	
3525 North Causeway Blvd., Suite 1020, Metairie, LA 70002	(504) 837–1259
District Director.—Luke Letlow.	

Parishes: JEFFERSON (part), ORLEANS (part), ST. CHARLES (part), ST. TAMMANY, TANGIPAHOA, WASHINGTON. Population (2000), 638,355.

ZIP Codes: 70001–06, 70009–11, 70033, 70047, 70053, 70055–56, 70058, 70060, 70062, 70064–65, 70072, 70087, 70094, 70115, 70118–19, 70121–24, 70160, 70181, 70183–84, 70401–04, 70420, 70422, 70426–27, 70429, 70431, 70433–38, 70442–48, 70450–52, 70454–67, 70469–71

* * *

SECOND DISTRICT

WILLIAM J. JEFFERSON, Democrat, of New Orleans, LA; born in Lake Providence, LA, March 14, 1947; education: graduated, G.W. Griffin High School, Lake Providence, LA, 1965; B.A., Political Science and English, Southern University and A&M College, Baton Rouge, LA, 1969; J.D., Harvard Law School, Cambridge, MA, 1972; LL.M., Georgetown University, 1996; professional: admitted to the bar, New Orleans, LA, 1972; attorney, Jefferson, Bryan, Jupiter, Lewis and Blanson, New Orleans, LA; first lieutenant, U.S. Army, J.A.G. Corps, 1975; member, board of trustees, Greater St. Stephen's Baptist Church; Urban League of Greater New Orleans; Southern University Foundation Board; Louisiana State Senate, March, 1980 to January, 1991; family: married: the former Andrea Green in 1970; children: Jamila, Jalila, Jelani, Nailah, and Akilah; committees: Budget; Ways and Means; subcommittees: Trade; elected to the 102nd Congress; reelected to each succeeding Congress.

Office Listings

2113 Rayburn House Office Building, Washington, DC 20515	(202) 225–6636
Chief of Staff.—Nicole Venable.	
Deputy Chief of Staff.—Roberta Hopkins.	
Communications Director.—Melanie Roussell.	
1012 Hale Boggs Federal Building, 500 Poydras Street, New Orleans, LA 70130 ..	(504) 589–2274
District Office Manager.—Stephanie Butler.	
200 Derbigny Street, Suite 3200, Gretna, LA 70053	(504) 368–7019
Congressional Aide.—Ericka Edwards.	

Parishes: JEFFERSON (part), ORLEANS (part). Population (2000), 638,562.

ZIP Codes: 70001, 70003, 70053–54, 70056, 70058, 70062–63, 70065, 70067, 70072–73, 70094, 70096, 70112–19, 70121–31, 70139–43, 70145–46, 70148–54, 70156–67, 70170, 70172, 70174–79, 70182, 70185–87, 70189–90, 70195

* * *

THIRD DISTRICT

CHARLIE MELANCON, Democrat, of Lafayette, LA; born in Napoleonville, LA, October 3, 1947; education: B.S., University of Southwestern Louisiana, Lafayette, LA, 1971; professional: businessman; chairman, Louisiana State University Agricultural Development Council; member, Louisiana State House of Representatives, 1987–1993; awards: named Outstanding Legislator by the Louisiana Municipal Association; received the Distinguished Service Award from the Louisiana Restaurant Association; member: UL–Lafayette Alumni Association; Ducks Unlimited; Kappa Sigma Alumni Association; married: Peachy; children: Charles Joseph, Claire; committees: Agriculture; Resources; Science; elected to the 109th Congress on November 2, 2004.

Office Listings

http://www.house.gov/melancon

404 Cannon House Office Building, Washington, DC 20515	(202) 225–4031
Chief of Staff.—Casey O'Shea.	FAX: 226–3944
Legislative Director.—Jacob Roche.	
Scheduler.—Jody Comeaux.	

828 S. Irma Boulevard, 212A, Gonzales, LA 70737 .... (225) 621–8490
    District Director.—Barney Arceneaux.
423 Lafayette Street, Suite 107, Houma, LA 70360 .... (985) 876–3033
210 East Main Street, New Iberia, LA 70560 .... (337) 367–8231
8201 West Judge Perez Drive, Chalmette, LA 70043 .... (504) 271–1707

Parishes: ASCENSION (part), ASSUMPTION, IBERIA, JEFFERSON (part), LAFOURCHE, PLAQUEMINES, ST. BERNARD, ST. CHARLES (part), ST. JAMES, ST. JOHN THE BAPTIST, ST. MARTIN, ST. MARY, TERREBONNE. Population (2000), 638,322.

ZIP Codes: 70030–32, 70036–41, 70043–44, 70047, 70049–52, 70056–58, 70067–72, 70075–76, 70078–87, 70090–92, 70301–02, 70310, 70339–46, 70353–54, 70356–61, 70363–64, 70371–75, 70377, 70380–81, 70390–95, 70397, 70512–14, 70517–19, 70521–23, 70528, 70538, 70540, 70544, 70552, 70560, 70562–63, 70569, 70582, 70592, 70723, 70725, 70734, 70737, 70743, 70763, 70778, 70792

* * *

FOURTH DISTRICT

JIM McCRERY, Republican, of Shreveport, LA; born in Shreveport, September 18, 1949; education: graduated Leesville High, Louisiana, 1967; B.A., Louisiana Tech University, Ruston, 1971; J.D., Louisiana State University, Baton Rouge, 1975; attorney; admitted to the Louisiana bar in 1975 and commenced practice in Leesville, LA; Jackson, Smith, and Ford (Leesville), 1975–78; assistant city attorney, Shreveport, 1979–80; district manager, U.S. Representative Buddy Roemer, 1981–82; legislative director, U.S. Representative Buddy Roemer, 1982–84; board of directors, Louisiana Association of Business and Industry, 1986–87; chairman, Regulatory Affairs Committee, Louisiana Forestry Association, 1987; regional manager for Government Affairs, Georgia-Pacific Corporation, 1984–88; committee: Ways and Means; subcommittee: chairman, Social Security; elected by special election to the 100th Congress, April 16, 1988, to fill the vacancy caused by the resignation of Charles E. (Buddy) Roemer; reelected to each succeeding Congress.

Office Listings

http://www.house.gov/mccrery

2104 Rayburn House Office Building, Washington, DC 20515 .... (202) 225–2777
    Chief of Staff.—Bob Brooks.   FAX: 225–8039
6425 Youree Drive, Suite 350, Shreveport, LA 71105 .... (318) 798–2254
    District Manager.—Linda Wright.
Southgate Plaza Shopping Center, 1606 South Fifth Street, Leesville, LA 71446 .... (337) 238–0778

Parishes: ALLEN (part), BEAUREGARD, BIENVILLE, BOSSIER, CADDO, CLAIBORNE, DESOTO, GRANT, NATCHITOCHES, RED RIVER, SABINE, VERNON, WEBSTER. Population (2000), 638,466.

ZIP Codes: 70633–34, 70637–39, 70644, 70648, 70651–57, 70659–60, 70662, 71001–04, 71006–09, 71016, 71018–19, 71021, 71023–25, 71027–34, 71036–40, 71043–52, 71055, 71058, 71060–61, 71063–73, 71075, 71078–80, 71082, 71101–13, 71115, 71118–20, 71129–30, 71133–38, 71148–49, 71151–54, 71156, 71161–66, 71171–72, 71222, 71235, 71251, 71256, 71268, 71275, 71360, 71403–04, 71406–07, 71411, 71414, 71416–17, 71419, 71423, 71426–29, 71432, 71434, 71438–39, 71443, 71446–47, 71449–50, 71452, 71454–63, 71467–69, 71474–75, 71486, 71496–97

* * *

FIFTH DISTRICT

RODNEY ALEXANDER, Republican, of Quitman, LA; born in Bienville, LA, December 5, 1946; education: attended Louisiana Tech University; professional: businessman, with a background in the insurance and construction industries; organizations: member, Louisiana Farm Bureau and the National Rifle Association; public service: Jackson Parish Police Jury, 1970–1985; served as President during the last seven years of his tenure; Louisiana House of Representatives, 1987–2002; religion: Baptist; married: Nancy; three children; committees: Appropriations; subcommittees: Agriculture, Rural Development, Food and Drug Administration, and Related Agencies; Science, The Departments of State, Justice, and Commerce, and Related Agencies; elected to the 108th Congress on December 7, 2002; reelected to each succeeding Congress.

Office Listings

http://www.house.gov/alexander

316 Cannon House Office Building, Washington, DC 20515 .... (202) 225–8490
    Chief of Staff.—Royal Alexander.   FAX: 225–5639
    Press Secretary.—Adam Terry.

1900 Stubbs Avenue, Suite B, Monroe, LA 71201 .... (318) 322–3500
1412 Centre Court, Suite 402, Alexandria, LA 71301 .... (318) 445–0818

Parishes: ALLEN (part), AVOYELLES, CALDWELL, CATAHOULA, CONCORDIA, EVANGELINE (part), EAST CARROLL, FRANKLIN, IBERVILLE (part), JACKSON, LASALLE, LINCOLN, MADISON, MOREHOUSE, OUACHITA, POINT COUPEE (part), RAPIDES, RICHLAND, TENSAS, UNION, WEST CARROLL, WIN. Population (2000), 638,517.

ZIP Codes: 70532, 70554, 70576, 70585–86, 70655–57, 70759–60, 70764–65, 70772, 70781, 70783, 71001, 71031, 71201–03, 71207–13, 71218–23, 71225–27, 71229–30, 71232–35, 71237–38, 71240–43, 71245, 71247, 71249–51, 71253–54, 71256, 71259–61, 71263–64, 71266, 71268–70, 71272–73, 71275–77, 71279–82, 71284, 71286, 71291–92, 71294–95, 71301–03, 71306–07, 71309, 71315–16, 71320, 71322–31, 71333–34, 71336, 71339–43, 71346, 71348, 71350–51, 71354–57, 71360–63, 71365–69, 71371, 71373, 71375, 71377–78, 71401, 71404–05, 71407, 71409–10, 71415, 71417–18, 71422–25, 71427, 71430–33, 71435, 71438, 71440–41, 71447–48, 71454–55, 71457, 71463, 71465–67, 71471–73, 71477, 71479–80, 71483, 71485

* * *

SIXTH DISTRICT

RICHARD H. BAKER, Republican, of Baton Rouge, LA; born in New Orleans, LA, May 22, 1948; education: graduated, University High School; Louisiana State University, Baton Rouge; professional: real estate broker; Louisiana House of Representatives, 1972–86; chairman, Committee on Transportation, Highways, and Public Works, 1980–86; member: Southern Legislative Conference, ALEC, Central Area Homebuilders, East Baton Rouge Airport Commission, Baton Rouge Lodge No. 372 Central Region Planning Commission; married: the former Kay Carpenter in 1969; children: Brandon and Julie; committees: Financial Services; Transportation and Infrastructure; Veteran's Affairs; subcommittees: Aviation; chairman, Capital Markets, Insurance and Government-Sponsored Enterprises; Economic Opportunity; Financial Institutions and Consumer Credit; Health; Highways, Transit and Pipelines; Housing and Community Opportunity; Water Resources and Environment; elected to the 100th Congress on November 4, 1986; reelected to each succeeding Congress.

Office Listings

341 Cannon House Office Building, Washington, DC 20515 .... (202) 225–3901
    Administrative Assistant.—Paul Sawyer.   FAX: 225–7313
    Office Manager / Executive Assistant.—Lynn Kirk.
5555 Hilton Avenue, Suite 100, Baton Rouge, LA 70808 .... (225) 929–7711
    Chief of Staff.—Christina Kyle Casteel.

Parishes: ASCENSION (part), EAST BATON ROUGE, EAST FELICIANA, IBERVILLE (part), LIVINGSTON, POINTE COUPEE (part), ST. HELENA, WEST BATON ROUGE (part), WEST FELICIANA. CITIES: Addis, Albany, Angola, Baker, Batchelor, Baton Rouge, Bayou Goula, Blanks, Brittany, Brusly, Bueche, Carville, Clinton, Denham Springs, Duplessis, Erwinville, Ethel, Fordoche, French Settlement, Geismar, Glynn, Gonzales, Greenburg, Greenwell Springs, Grosse Tete, Hardwood, Holden, Innis, Jackson, Jarreau, Labarre, Lakeland, Lettsworth, Livingston, Livonia, Lottie, Maringouin, Maurepas, Morganza, New Roads, Norwood, Oscar, Pine Grove, Plaquemine, Port Allen, Prairieville, Pride, Rosedale, Rougon, Slaughter, Sorrento, Springfield, St. Amant, St. Francisville, St. Gabriel, Sunshine, Torbert, Tunica, Ventress, Wakefield, Walker, Watson, Weyanoke, White Castle, Wilson, and Zachary. Population (2000), 638,324.

ZIP Codes: 70403, 70422, 70436, 70441, 70443–44, 70449, 70453, 70462, 70466, 70586, 70704, 70706–07, 70710–12, 70714–15, 70718–19, 70721–22, 70726–30, 70732–34, 70736–40, 70744, 70747–49, 70752–57, 70759–62, 70764, 70767, 70769–70, 70772–78, 70780, 70782–89, 70791, 70801–23, 70826, 70831, 70833, 70835–37, 70874, 70879, 70883–84, 70892–96, 70898

* * *

SEVENTH DISTRICT

CHARLES W. BOUSTANY, JR., Republican, of Lafayette, LA; born in New Orleans, LA, February 21, 1956; education: graduated Cathedral Carmel High School, Lafayette, LA, B.S., University of Southwestern Louisiana, Lafayette, LA, 1978; M.D., Louisiana State University School of Medicine, New Orleans, LA, 1982; professional: surgeon; public service: served on the Louisiana Organ Procurement Agency Tissue Advisory Board; board of directors for the Greater Lafayette Chamber of Commerce, 2001; Chamber of Commerce as Vice President for Government Affairs, 2002; president of the Lafayette Parish Medical Society; chaired the American Heart Association's Gala; Healthcare Division of the UL-Lafayette Centennial Fundraiser, which provided $75 million of university endowed chairs, professorships and scholarships; member of Leadership Lafayette Class IIIXX, 2002; member, Lafayette Parish Republican Executive Committee, 1996–2001; vice-chairman of the Bush/Cheney Victory 2000 Campaign for Lafayette Parish; board of directors for Lafayette General Medical Center; married: the former Bridget Edwards; children: Erik and Ashley; committees: Agriculture; Education and the

Workforce; Transportation and Infrastructure; Republican Policy Committee; elected to the 109th Congress on December 4, 2004.

Office Listings
http://www.house.gov/boustany

1117 Longworth House Office Building, Washington, DC 20515	(202) 225–2031
Chief of Staff.—Jeff Dobrozsi.	FAX: 225–5724
Legislative Director.—Anne Bradbury.	
Scheduler.—Michell Wizov.	
800 Lafayette Street, Suite 1400, Lafayette, LA 70501	(337) 235–6322

Parishes: ACADIA, CALCASIEU, CAMERON, EVANGELINE, JEFFERSON DAVIS, LAFAYETTE, ST. LANDRY, VERMILION. Population (2000), 638,430.

ZIP Codes: 70501–12, 70515–18, 70520, 70524–29, 70531–35, 70537, 70541–43, 70546, 70548–51, 70554–56, 70558–59, 70570–71, 70575, 70577–78, 70580–81, 70583–84, 70586, 70589, 70591–92, 70596, 70598, 70601–02, 70605–07, 70609, 70611–12, 70615–16, 70630–33, 70640, 70643, 70645–48, 70650, 70655, 70658, 70661, 70663–65, 70668–69, 70750, 71322, 71345, 71353, 71356, 71358, 71362

MAINE

(Population, 2000 1,274,923)

SENATORS

OLYMPIA J. SNOWE, Republican, of Auburn, ME; born in Augusta, ME, February 21, 1947; education: graduated from Edward Little High School, Auburn, ME, 1965; B.A., University of Maine, Orono, 1969; member, Holy Trinity Greek Orthodox Church of Lewiston-Auburn; active member of civic and community organizations; elected to the Maine House of Representatives, 1973, to the seat vacated by the death of her first husband, the late Peter Snowe; reelected for a full two-year term in 1974; elected to the Maine Senate, 1976; chaired the Joint Standing Committee on Health and Institutional Services; elected to the 96th Congress on November 7, 1978—the youngest Republican woman, and first Greek-American woman elected; reelected to the 97th through 103rd Congresses; past member: House Budget Committee; House Foreign Affairs Committee; leading member of the former House Select Committee on Aging, ranking Republican on its Subcommittee on Human Services; Senate committees: Commerce, Science and Transportation; Finance; chair, Small Business and Entrepreneurship; Select Committee on Intelligence; subcommittees: Health Care; International Trade; Taxation and IRS Oversight; Aviation; Communications; chair, Oceans, Fisheries and Coast Guard; Surface Transportation and Merchant Marine; past member: Budget; Armed Services; Foreign Relations; married to former Maine Governor John R. McKernan, Jr.; elected to the U.S. Senate on November 8, 1994; reelected to each succeeding Senate term.

Office Listings

http://snowe.senate.gov

154 Russell Senate Office Building, Washington, DC 20510	(202) 224–5344
Chief of Staff.—John Richter.	
Executive Assistant.—Lindsey Ledwin.	
Communications Director.—Antonia Ferrier.	
2 Great Falls Plaza, Suite 7B, Auburn, ME 04210	(207) 786–2451
Regional Representative.—Diane Jackson.	
40 Western Avenue, Suite 408C, Augusta, ME 04330	(207) 622–8292
Regional Representative.—Deb McNeil.	
One Cumberland Place, Suite 306, Bangor, ME 04401	(207) 945–0432
State Director.—Gail Kelly.	
231 Main Street, P.O. Box 215, Biddeford, ME 04005	(207) 282–4144
Regional Representative.—Peter Morin.	
3 Canal Plaza, Suite 601, P.O. Box 188, Portland, ME 04112	(207) 874–0883
Regional Representative.—Cheryl Leeman.	
169 Academy Street, Suite 3, Presque Isle, ME 04769	(207) 764–5124
Regional Representative.—Sharon Campbell.	

* * *

SUSAN COLLINS, Republican, of Bangor, ME; born in Caribou, ME, December 7, 1952; education: graduated, Caribou High School, 1971; B.A., *magna cum laude*, Phi Beta Kappa, St. Lawrence University, Canton, NY; Outstanding Alumni Award, St. Lawrence University, 1992; staff director, Senate Subcommittee on the Oversight of Government Management, 1981–87; for 12 years, principal advisor on business issues to former Senator William S. Cohen; Commissioner of Professional and Financial Regulation for Maine Governor John R. McKernan, Jr., 1987; New England administrator, Small Business Administration, 1992–93; appointed Deputy Treasurer of Massachusetts, 1993; executive director, Husson College Center for Family Business, 1994–96; committees: Armed Services; chair, Homeland Security and Governmental Affairs; Special Committee on Aging; elected to the U.S. Senate on November 5, 1996; reelected to each succeeding Senate term.

Office Listings

http://collins.senate.gov

461 Dirksen Senate Office Building, Washington, DC 20510	(202) 224–2523
Chief of Staff.—Steven Abbott.	FAX: 224–2693
Communications Director.—Jen Burita.	
Legislative Director.—Jim Dohoney.	
P.O. Box 655, 202 Harlow Street, Room 204, Bangor, ME 04402	(207) 945–0417
State Representative.—Judy Cuddy.	
40 Western Avenue, Room 507, Augusta, ME 04330	(207) 622–8414
State Representative.—William Card.	

160 Main Street, Biddeford, ME 04005 .... (207) 283–1101
   State Representative.—William Vail.
11 Lisbon Street, Lewiston, ME 04240 .... (207) 784–6969
   State Director.—Sarah McCarthy.
25 Sweden Street, Suite A, Caribou, ME 04736 .... (207) 493–5873
   State Representative.—Philip Bosse.
One City Center, Suite 100, Portland, ME 04101 .... (207) 780–3575

REPRESENTATIVES

FIRST DISTRICT

THOMAS H. ALLEN, Democrat, of Portland, ME; born in Portland, April 16, 1945; education: graduated, Deering High School, Portland; Bowdoin College, Phi Beta Kappa; Oxford University, Rhodes scholar; Harvard University, J.D.; Bowdin College Board of Trustees; board of directors of Shalom House and the United Way of Greater Portland; president, Portland Stage Company; Executive and Legislative Policy committees; Maine Municipal Association; chair, Governor's Task Force on Foster Care; Portland City Council and Mayor; married: Diana Allen; children: Gwen and Kate; committees: Budget; Energy and Commerce; elected to the 105th Congress; reelected to each succeeding Congress.

Office Listings
http://tomallen.house.gov

1127 Longworth House Office Building, Washington, DC 20515 .... (202) 225–6116
   Chief of Staff.—Jacqueline Potter.   FAX: 225–5590
   Executive Assistant.—Jolene Chonko.
   Legislative Director.—Todd Stein.
   Legislative Assistants: James Bradley, Matt Coffron, Susan Lexer, Matt
     Nelson, Kate Turner, Allison Vogt.
57 Exchange Street, Suite 302, Portland, ME 04101 .... (207) 774–5019
   Office Manager / Scheduler.—Stephanie Betzold.

Counties: CUMBERLAND, KENNEBEC (part), KNOX, LINCOLN, SAGADAHOC, YORK. Population (2000), 637,461.

ZIP Codes: 03901–11, 04001–11, 04013–15, 04017, 04019–21, 04024, 04027–30, 04032–34, 04038–40, 04042–43, 04046–50, 04053–57, 04061–64, 04066, 04069–79, 04082–87, 04090–98, 04101–10, 04112, 04116, 04122–24, 04259–60, 04265, 04284, 04287, 04330, 04332–33, 04336, 04338, 04341–55, 04357–60, 04363–64, 04530, 04535–39, 04541, 04543–44, 04547–48, 04551, 04553–56, 04558, 04562–65, 04567–68, 04570–76, 04578–79, 04841, 04843, 04846–56, 04858–65, 04901, 04910, 04917–18, 04922, 04926–27, 04935, 04937, 04941, 04949, 04952, 04962–63, 04973, 04987–89, 04992

* * *

SECOND DISTRICT

MICHAEL H. MICHAUD, Democrat, of East Millinocket, ME; born on January 18, 1955; education: graduate, Harvard University John F. Kennedy School of Government Program for Senior Executives in State and Local Government; professional: mill worker; community service: actively involved in a variety of local, regional, and statewide civic and economic development organizations; public service: Maine House of Representatives, 1980–1994; Maine State Senate, 1994–2002; religion: Catholic; committees: Small Business; Transportation and Infrastructure; Veterans' Affairs; elected to the 108th Congress on November 5, 2002; reelected to each succeeding Congress.

Office Listings
http://www.house.gov/michaud

437 Cannon House Office Building, Washington, DC 20515 .... (202) 225–6306
   Chief of Staff.—Peter Chandler.   FAX: 225–2943
   Legislative Director.—Matt Robison.
   Scheduler.—Diane Smith.
23 Water Street, Bangor, ME 04401 .... (207) 942–6935
179 Lisbon Street, Ground Floor, Lewiston, ME 04240 .... (207) 782–3704
445 Main Street, Presque Isle, ME 04769 .... (207) 764–1036
16 Common Street, Waterville, ME 04901 .... (207) 873–5713

Counties: ANDROSCOGGIN, AROOSTOOK, FRANKLIN, HANCOCK, KENNEBEC (part), OXFORD, PENOBSCOT, PISCATAQUIS, SOMERSET, WALDO, WASHINGTON. Population (2000), 637,461.

ZIP Codes: 04010, 04016, 04022, 04037, 04041, 04051, 04068, 04088, 04210–12, 04216–17, 04219–28, 04230–31, 04234, 04236–41, 04243, 04250, 04252–58, 04261–63, 04266–68, 04270–71, 04274–76, 04278, 04280–83, 04285–86, 04288–92, 04294, 04354, 04401–02, 04406, 04408, 04410–24, 04426–31, 04434–35, 04438, 04441–44, 04448–51, 04453–57, 04459–64, 04467–69, 04471–76, 04478–79, 04481, 04485, 04487–93, 04495–97, 04549, 04605–07, 04609, 04611–17, 04619, 04622–31, 04634–35, 04637, 04640, 04642–46, 04648–50, 04652–58, 04660, 04662, 04664, 04666–69, 04671–77, 04679–81, 04683–86, 04691, 04693–94, 04730, 04732–47, 04750–51, 04756–66, 04768–70, 04772–77, 04779–81, 04783, 04785–88, 04848–51, 04857, 04903, 04911–12, 04915, 04920–25, 04928–30, 04932–33, 04936–45, 04947, 04949–58, 04961, 04964–67, 04969–76, 04978–79, 04981–88, 04992

MARYLAND

(Population 2000, 5,296,486)

SENATORS

PAUL S. SARBANES, Democrat, of Baltimore, MD; born in Salisbury, MD, February 3, 1933; son of Spyros and Matina Sarbanes; education: graduated, Wicomico Senior High School, 1950; A.B., Princeton University, 1954, *magna cum laude* and Phi Beta Kappa; Rhodes scholar, Balliol College, Oxford, England, 1954–57, first-class B.A. honours in School of Philosophy, Politics and Economics; LL.B., *cum laude,* Harvard Law School, 1960; admitted to practice by Maryland Court of Appeals, 1960; law clerk to Judge Morris A. Soper, U.S. Court of Appeals for the Fourth Circuit, 1960–61; associate in Baltimore law firms Piper and Marbury, 1961–62, and Venable, Baetjer and Howard, 1965–70; administrative assistant to Walter W. Heller, chairman of the Council of Economic Advisers, 1962–63; executive director, Charter Revision Commission of Baltimore City, 1963–64; elected to the Maryland House of Delegates in November 1966, serving from 1967–71; member, Greek Orthodox Cathedral of the Annunciation, Baltimore, MD; married: Christine Dunbar of Brighton, England; three children and six grandchildren; committees: ranking member, Banking, Housing, and Urban Affairs; Budget; Foreign Relations; Joint Economic Committee; elected to 92nd Congress on November 3, 1970; reelected to 93rd and 94th Congresses; elected to the U.S. Senate on November 2, 1976; reelected to each succeeding Senate term.

Office Listings

http://sarbanes.senate.gov

309 Hart Senate Office Building, Washington, DC 20510	(202) 224–4524
Chief of Staff.—Julie Kehrli.	FAX: 224–1651
Legislative Director.—John Davidson.	TDD: 224–3452
Appointment Secretary.—Elise Gillette.	
Press Secretary.—Jesse Jacobs.	
100 South Charles Street, Tower I, Suite 1710, Baltimore, MD 21201	(410) 962–4436
1110 Bonifant Street, Suite 450, Silver Spring, MD 20910	(301) 589–0797
113 Baltimore Street, Suite 201, Cumberland, MD 21502	(301) 724–0695
110 W. Church Street, Suite D, Salisbury, MD 21801	(410) 860–2131
2505 Westview Place, P.O. Box 119, Bryans Road, MD 20616	(301) 283–0947

* * *

BARBARA A. MIKULSKI, Democrat, of Baltimore, MD; born in Baltimore, July 20, 1936; education: B.A., Mount St. Agnes College, 1958; M.S.W., University of Maryland School of Social Work, 1965; former social worker for Catholic Charities and city of Baltimore; served as an adjunct professor, Department of Sociology, Loyola College; elected to the Baltimore City Council, 1971; Democratic nominee for the U.S. Senate in 1974, winning 43 percent of vote; elected to the U.S. House of Representatives in November, 1976; first woman appointed to the Energy and Commerce Committee; also served on the Merchant Marine and Fisheries Committee; became the first woman representing the Democratic Party to be elected to a Senate seat not previously held by her husband, and the first Democratic woman ever to serve in both houses of Congress; Secretary, Democratic Conference; first woman to be elected to a leadership post; committees: Appropriations; Health, Education, Labor, and Pensions; Select Committee on Intelligence; subcommittees: ranking member, Aging; Commerce, Justice, Science, and Related Agencies; Defense; Homeland Security; Interior and Related Agencies; State, Foreign Operations and Related Programs; Transportation, Treasury, the Judiciary, HUD, and Related Agencies; elected to the U.S. Senate in November, 1986, with 61 percent of the vote; reelected in November, 1992, with 71 percent of the vote; reelected in November, 1998, with 71 percent of the vote; reelected to each succeeding Senate term.

Office Listings

http://mikulski.senate.gov

503 Hart Senate Office Building, Washington, DC 20510	(202) 224–4654
Chief of Staff.—Julie Frifield.	
Legislative Director.—Dennis Kelleher.	
1629 Thames Street, Suite 400, Baltimore, MD 2123	(410) 962–4510
State Director.—Betty Deacon.	
32 West Street, Suite 202, Annapolis, MD 21401	(410) 263–1805
6404 Ivy Lane, Suite 406, Greenbelt, MD 20770	(301) 345–5517
94 West Washington Street, Hagerstown, MD 21740	(301) 797–2826
1201 Pemberton Drive, Suite 1E, Building B, Salisbury, MD 21801	(410) 546–7711

REPRESENTATIVES

FIRST DISTRICT

WAYNE T. GILCHREST, Republican, of Kennedyville, MD; born in Rahway, NJ, April 15, 1946; education: graduated from Rahway High School, 1964; attended Wesley College, Dover, DE; B.A. in History, Delaware State College, Dover, 1973; graduate studies, Loyola University, Baltimore, MD, 1984–present; military service: served in the U.S. Marine Corps, 1964–68; awarded the Purple Heart, Bronze Star, Navy Commendation Medal, Navy Unit Citation, and others; professional: government and history teacher, Kent County High School, 1973–present; member: Kent County Teachers Association, American Legion, Veterans of Foreign Wars, Order of the Purple Heart; religion: Kennedyville Methodist Church; married: the former Barbara Rawley; children: Kevin, Joel, and Katie; committees: Resources; Science; Transportation and Infrastructure; subcommittees: Coast Guard and Maritime Transportation; Environment, Technology and Standards; chairman, Fisheries Conservation, Wildlife, and Oceans; Forests and Forest Health; Water Resources and Environment; elected to the 102nd Congress; reelected to each succeeding Congress.

Office Listings

2245 Rayburn House Office Building, Washington, DC 20515 .... (202) 225–5311
  Chief of Staff.—Tony Caligiuri.   FAX: 225–0254
  Office Manager / Scheduler.—Kathy Hicks.
  Legislative Director.—Dave Solan.
  Press Secretary / District Director.—Cathy Bassett.
315 High Street, Suite 105, Chestertown, MD 21620 .... (410) 778–9407
  District Office Manager.—Karen Willis.
One Plaza East, Salisbury, MD 21801 .... (410) 749–3184
  District Office Manager.—Monica Bell.
112 W. Pennsylvania Avenue, Suite 102, Bel Air, MD 21014 .... (410) 838–2517
  District Office Manager.—Virginia Sanders.

Counties: ANNE ARUNDEL (part), BALTIMORE (part), CAROLINE, CECIL, DORCHESTER, HARFORD (part), KENT, QUEEN ANNE'S, SOMERSET, TALBOT, WICOMICO, WORCESTER. Population (2000), 662,062.

ZIP Codes: 21001, 21009, 21012–15, 21018, 21023, 21028, 21030–32, 21034, 21047, 21050–51, 21054, 21057, 21078, 21082, 21084–85, 21087, 21092–93, 21108, 21111, 21113, 21122, 21128, 21131, 21136, 21144, 21146, 21156, 21162, 21206, 21225–26, 21234, 21236, 21240, 21286, 21401–05, 21411–12, 21601, 21606–07, 21609–10, 21612–13, 21617, 21619–20, 21622–29, 21631–32, 21634–36, 21638–41, 21643–45, 21647–73, 21675–79, 21681–85, 21687, 21690, 21801–04, 21810–11, 21813–14, 21817, 21821–22, 21824, 21826, 21829–30, 21835–38, 21840–43, 21849–53, 21856–57, 21861–67, 21869, 21871–72, 21874–75, 21890, 21901–04, 21911–22, 21930

* * *

SECOND DISTRICT

C.A. DUTCH RUPPERSBERGER, Democrat, of Cockeysville, MD; born in Baltimore, MD, January 31, 1946; education: Baltimore City College; University of Maryland, College Park; J.D., University of Baltimore Law School, 1970; professional: attorney; partner, Ruppersberger, Clark, and Mister (law firm); public service: Baltimore County Assistant State's Attorney; Baltimore County Council; Baltimore County Executive, 1994–2002; married: the former Kay Murphy; children: Cory and Jill; committees: Government Reform; Permanent Select Committee on Intelligence; elected to the 108th Congress on November 5, 2002; reelected to each succeeding Congress.

Office Listings

http://dutch.house.gov

1630 Longworth House Office Building, Washington, DC 20515 .... (202) 225–3061
  Deputy Chief of Staff for Legislation.—Walter Gonzales.   FAX: 225–3094
  Deputy Chief of Staff for Communications.—Heather Molino.
  Scheduler.—Brenda Connolly.
The Atrium, 375 West Padonia Road, Suite 200, Timonium, MD 21093 .... (410) 628–2701
  Deputy Chief of Staff.—Tara Oursler.

Counties: ANNE ARUNDEL (part), BALTIMORE CITY (part), BALTIMORE COUNTY (part), HARFORD (part). Population (2000), 662,060.

ZIP Codes: 20755, 21001, 21005, 21009–10, 21017, 21022, 21027, 21030–31, 21034, 21040, 21047, 21050–52, 21056–57, 21060–62, 21065, 21071, 21076–78, 21085, 21087, 21090, 21093–94, 21104, 21111, 21113, 21117, 21122–23, 21130, 21133, 21136, 21144, 21162–63, 21204, 21206, 21208, 21212–14, 21219–22, 21224–27, 21230, 21234, 21236–37, 21239, 21244, 21252, 21284–86

THIRD DISTRICT

BENJAMIN L. CARDIN, Democrat, of Baltimore, MD; born in Baltimore, October 5, 1943; education: attended Baltimore public schools; graduated Baltimore City College, 1961; B.A., University of Pittsburgh, PA, 1964, *cum laude*; J.D., University of Maryland, Baltimore, 1967, (first in class); professional: attorney; admitted to Maryland bar November 1967 and began practice in Baltimore; member of the Maryland House of Delegates, 1967–86; Speaker of House of Delegates, 1979–86; chairman, Ways and Means Committee, 1974–79; vice chairman, Ways and Means Committee, 1971–73; member, Presidential Advisory Committee on Federalism; chairman, State Federal Assembly, National Council of State Legislators, 1980–81; member, National Council of State Legislators, executive committee; member, Council of State Governments, executive committee, 1979–86; co-chairman, Legislative Policy Committee, Maryland General Assembly, 1979–86; trustee, Baltimore Museum of Art; member, Baltimore Jewish Community Relations Council; trustee, Baltimore Council on Foreign Affairs; member, Associated Jewish Charities Welfare Fund; member, board of visitors of the University of Maryland School of Law; trustee, Goucher College; former chairman, Maryland Legal Services Corporation; MACO Legislator of the Year Award, 1984; ranking member, Commission on Security and Cooperation in Europe; married: the former Myrna Edelman, 1964; committees: Ways and Means; subcommittees: ranking member, Trade; Social Security; elected to the 100th Congress, November 4, 1986; reelected to each succeeding Congress.

Office Listings
http://www.cardin.house.gov

2207 Rayburn House Office Building, Washington, DC 20515	(202) 225–4016
Chief of Staff.—Christopher Lynch.	FAX: 225–9219
Office Manager.—Amy Daiger.	
600 Wyndhurst Avenue, Suite 230, Baltimore, MD 21210	(410) 433–8886
District Director.—Bailey Fine.	
Press Secretary.—Susan Sullam.	

Counties: ANNE ARUNDEL (part), BALTIMORE (part), HOWARD (part), BALTIMORE CITY (part). TOWNS: Arbutus, Crofton, Ellicott City, Elkridge, Glen Burnie, Halethrope, Lansdowne, Linthicum, Maryland City, Odenton, Owings Mills, Parkville, Pikesville, Reisterstown, Russett City, Severn, and Towson. Population (2000), 662,062.

ZIP Codes: 20701, 20723–24, 20755, 20759, 20794, 21022, 21029, 21032, 21035, 21037, 21043–46, 21054–55, 21060–61, 21071, 21075–77, 21090, 21093, 21098, 21108, 21113–14, 21117, 21122, 21136, 21139, 21144, 21146, 21150, 21153, 21201–02, 21204–06, 21208–15, 21218, 21222–25, 21227–31, 21234, 21236–37, 21239, 21281–82, 21285–86, 21401–05, 21411–12

* * *

FOURTH DISTRICT

ALBERT RUSSELL WYNN, Democrat, of Largo, MD; born in Philadelphia, PA, September 10, 1951; education: graduated DuVal High School, Lanham, 1969; B.S., University of Pittsburgh, PA, 1973; attended Howard University Graduate School of Political Science, 1974; J.D., Georgetown University Law School, Washington, DC, 1977; professional: attorney; admitted to the Maryland bar, 1979; Maryland House of Delegates, 1983–86; Maryland State Senate, 1987–92; executive director, Prince George's County Consumer Protection Commission, 1979–82; member: Kappa Alpha Psi Fraternity; J. Franklyn Bourne Bar Association; board of directors, Consumer Credit Counseling Service; Prince George's County Economic Development Corporation; Ploughman and Fisherman; committees: Energy and Commerce; elected to the 103rd Congress, November 3, 1992; reelected to each succeeding Congress.

Office Listings
http://www.wynn.house.gov

434 Cannon House Office Building, Washington, DC 20515	(202) 225–8699
Chief of Staff.—Curt Clifton.	FAX: 225–8714
Legislative Director.—Alon Kupferman.	
Press Secretary.—Amaya Smith.	
9200 Basil Court, Suite 221, Largo, MD 20774	(301) 773–4094
18401 Woodfield Road, Suite D, Gaithersburg, MD 20879	(301) 987–2054

Counties: MONTGOMERY (part), PRINCE GEORGE'S (part). CITIES AND TOWNSHIPS: Bladensburg, Brentwood, Brookeville, Capitol Heights, Cheverly, Colmar Manor, Cottage City, District Heights, Edmonston, Fairmount Heights, Glenarden, Landover Hills, Largo, Laytonsville, Morningside, Mount Rainier, New Carrollton, North Brentwood, Olney, Riverdale, Rockville, Seat Pleasant, University Park, and Upper Marlboro. Population (2000), 662,062.

ZIP Codes: 20703, 20706–07, 20710, 20720–21, 20731, 20735, 20737, 20743–48, 20750, 20752–53, 20757, 20762, 20769, 20772, 20774–75, 20777, 20781–85, 20788, 20790–92, 20797, 20799, 20830, 20832–33, 20841, 20853, 20855, 20860–62, 20866, 20868, 20871–72, 20874, 20876–77, 20879, 20882, 20886, 20901, 20903–06, 20910–12, 21771, 21797

* * *

FIFTH DISTRICT

STENY H. HOYER, Democrat, of Mechanicsville, MD; born in New York, NY, June 14, 1939; education: graduated Suitland High School; B.S., University of Maryland, 1963; J.D., Georgetown University Law Center, 1966; Honorary Doctor of Public Service, University of Maryland, 1988; admitted to the Maryland Bar Association, 1966; professional: practicing attorney, 1966–90; Maryland State Senate, 1967–79; vice chairman, Prince George's County, MD, Senate delegation, 1967–69; chairman, Prince George's County, MD, Senate delegation, 1969–75; president, Maryland State Senate, 1975–79; member, State Board for Higher Education, 1978–81; married: Judith Pickett, deceased, February 6, 1997; children: Susan, Stefany, and Anne; committees: Appropriations; subcommittees: Labor, Health and Human Services, Education, and Related Agencies; Democratic Steering Committee; Democratic Whip; elected to the 97th Congress on May 19, 1981, by special election; reelected to each succeeding Congress.

Office Listings

http://www.hoyer.house.gov

1705 Longworth House Office Building, Washington, DC 20515	(202) 225–4131

Chief of Staff.—Cory Alexander.
Legislative Director.—Geoff Plague.

U.S. Federal Courthouse, Suite 310, 6500 Cherrywood Lane, Greenbelt, MD 20770	(301) 474–0119
401 Post Office Road, Suite 202, Waldorf, MD 20602	(301) 843–1577

Counties: ANNE ARUNDEL (part), CALVERT, CHARLES, PRINCE GEORGE'S (part), ST. MARY'S. Population (2000), 662,060.

ZIP Codes: 20601–04, 20606–13, 20615–30, 20632, 20634–37, 20639–40, 20643, 20645–46, 20650, 20653, 20656–62, 20664, 20667, 20670, 20674–78, 20680, 20682, 20684–90, 20692–93, 20695, 20697, 20704–09, 20711, 20714–21, 20725–26, 20732–33, 20735–38, 20740–42, 20744, 20748–49, 20751, 20754, 20758, 20764–65, 20768–74, 20776, 20778–79, 20781–84, 20904, 21035, 21037, 21054, 21106, 21113, 21140

* * *

SIXTH DISTRICT

ROSCOE G. BARTLETT, Republican, of Frederick, MD; born in Moreland, KY, June 3, 1926; education: B.A., Columbia Union College, 1947; M.A., 1948, and Ph.D., University of Maryland, 1952; still an active farmer, prior to his election to Congress, he had retired after owning and operating a small business for ten years; awarded 20 patents for inventions during his scientific career as a professor and research engineer; held positions at Loma Linda University, the Navy's School of Aviation Medicine, John Hopkins Applied Physics Laboratory, and at IBM; married to Ellen; 10 children; committees: Armed Services; Science; vice chairman, Small Business; subcommittees: Energy; Space and Aeronautics; chairman, Projection Forces; Regulatory Reform and Oversight; Terrorism, Unconventional Threats and Capabilities; elected to the 103rd Congress; reelected to each succeeding Congress.

Office Listings

http://www.bartlett.house.gov

2412 Rayburn House Office Building, Washington, DC 20515	(202) 225–2721
	FAX: 225–2193

Chief of Staff.—Bud Otis.
Legislative Director.—John Biddison.
Office Manager / Scheduler.—Barb Calligan.

11377 Robinwood Drive, Hagerstown, MD 21742	(301) 797–6043
7360 Guilford Drive, Suite 101, Frederick, MD 21704	(301) 694–3030
15 Main Street, Suite 110, Westminster, MD 21157	(410) 857–1115
1 Frederick Street, Cumberland, MD 21502	(301) 724–3105

Counties: ALLEGANY, CARROLL, FREDERICK, GARRETT, BALTIMORE (part), HARFORD (part), WASHINGTON. CITIES AND TOWNSHIPS: Baltimore, Boonsboro, Cumberland, Emmitsburg, Frederick, Frostburg, Funkstown, Hagerstown, Hancock, Middletown, Mount Airy, Oakland, Reisterstown, Sharpsburg, Smithburg, Thurmont, Timonium, Walkersville, Westminster, Williamsport, Woodsboro. Also includes Antietam National Battlefield and Camp David. Population (2000), 662,060.

ZIP Codes: 20842, 20871–72, 20876, 20882, 21014, 21020, 21029–30, 21034, 21036, 21041–43, 21047–48, 21050, 21053, 21074–75, 21084, 21088, 21102, 21104–05, 21111, 21120, 21131–32, 21136, 21152, 21154–55, 21157–58,

21160–61, 21163, 21501–05, 21520–24, 21528–32, 21536, 21538–43, 21545, 21550, 21555–57, 21560–62, 21701–05, 21709–11, 21713–23, 21727, 21733–34, 21740–42, 21746–50, 21754–59, 21762, 21766–67, 21769–71, 21773–84, 21787–88, 21790–91, 21793, 21795, 21797–98

* * *

SEVENTH DISTRICT

ELIJAH E. CUMMINGS, Democrat, of Baltimore, MD; born in Baltimore, January 18, 1951; education: graduated, Baltimore City College High School, 1969; B.S., political science, Phi Beta Kappa, Howard University, Washington, DC, 1973; J.D., University of Maryland Law School, 1976; professional: attorney; admitted to the Maryland bar in 1976; delegate, Maryland State Legislature, 1982–96; chairman, Maryland Legislative Black Caucus, 1984; speaker pro tempore, Maryland General Assembly, 1995–96; vice chairman, Constitutional and Administrative Law Committee; vice chairman, Economic Matters Committee; president, sophomore class, student government treasurer and student government president at Howard University; member: Governor's Commission on Black Males; New Psalmist Baptist Church, Baltimore, MD; active in civic affairs, and recipient of numerous community awards; co-chair of the House AIDS Working Group; Task Force on Health Care Reform; one child: Jennifer; committees: Government Reform; Transportation and Infrastructure; Joint Economic Committee; subcommittees: ranking member, Criminal Justice, Drug Policy and Human Resources; Highways, Transit and Pipelines; Railroads; elected to the 104th Congress by special election in April, 1996; reelected to each succeeding Congress.

Office Listings

http://www.house.gov/cummings

2235 Rayburn House Office Building, Washington, DC 20515	(202) 225–4741
Chief of Staff.—Vernon Simms.	FAX: 225–3178
Legislative Director.—Kimberly Ross.	
Legislative Assistant.—Lucinda Lessley.	
1010 Park Avenue, Suite 105, Baltimore, MD 21201	(410) 685–9199
754 Frederick Road, Catonsville, MD 21228	(410) 719–8777

Counties: BALTIMORE (part), HOWARD (part), BALTIMORE CITY (part). Population (2000), 662,060.

ZIP Codes: 20701, 20723, 20759, 20763, 20777, 20794, 20833, 21029, 21036, 21042–45, 21075, 21104, 21117, 21133, 21163, 21201–03, 21205–18, 21223–24, 21227–31, 21233, 21235, 21239, 21241, 21244, 21250–51, 21263–65, 21268, 21270, 21273–75, 21278–80, 21283, 21287–90, 21297–98, 21723, 21737–38, 21765, 21771, 21784, 21794, 21797

* * *

EIGHTH DISTRICT

CHRIS VAN HOLLEN, Democrat, of Kensington, MD; born in Karachi, Pakistan, January 10, 1959; education: B.A., Swarthmore College, 1982; Masters in Public Policy, Harvard University, 1985; J.D., Georgetown University, 1990; professional: attorney; legislative assistant to former Maryland U.S. Senator Charles McC. Mathias; staff member, U.S. Senate Committee on Foreign Relations; senior legislative advisor to former Maryland Governor William Donald Schaefer; public service: elected, Maryland House of Delegates, 1990; elected, Maryland State Senate, 1994; married: Katherine; children: Anna, Nicholas, and Alexander; committees: Education and the Workforce; Government Reform; Judiciary; elected to the 108th Congress on November 5, 2002; reelected to each succeeding Congress.

Office Listings

http://www.house.gov/vanhollen

1419 Longworth House Office Building, Washington, DC 20515	(202) 225–5341
Chief of Staff.—Karen Robb.	FAX: 225–0375
Legislative Director.—Phil Alperson.	
Press Secretary.—Marilyn Campbell.	
51 Monroe Street, Suite 507, Rockville, MD 20850	(301) 424–3501
District Director.—Joan Kleinman.	

Counties: MONTGOMERY (part), PRINCE GEORGES (part). Population (2000), 662,060.

ZIP Codes: 20712, 20722, 20782–83, 20787, 20810–18, 20824–25, 20827, 20837–39, 20841–42, 20847–55, 20857, 20859, 20871, 20874–80, 20883–86, 20889, 20891–92, 20894–99, 20901–08, 20910, 20912–16, 20918, 20997

MASSACHUSETTS

(Population 2000, 6,349,097)

SENATORS

EDWARD M. KENNEDY, Democrat, of Barnstable, MA; born in Boston, MA, February 22, 1932; son of Joseph P. and Rose F. Kennedy; education: graduated, Milton Academy, 1950; A.B., Harvard College, 1956; professional: International Law School, The Hague, the Netherlands, 1958; LL.B., University of Virginia Law School, 1959; enlisted in the U.S. Army as a private and served in France and Germany, 1951–53; married: Victoria Reggie Kennedy; children: Kara, Edward M., Jr., Patrick J., Curran, and Caroline; committees: Armed Services; ranking member, Health, Education, Labor and Pensions; Judiciary; Joint Economic Committee; elected to the U.S. Senate on November 7, 1962, to fill the unexpired term of his brother John F. Kennedy; reelected to each succeeding Senate term.

Office Listings

http://kennedy.senate.gov

315 Russell Senate Office Building, Washington, DC 20510	(202) 224–4543
Chief of Staff.—Danica Petroshius.	FAX: 224–2417
Legislative Director.—Carey Parker.	TDD: 224–1819
Administrative Manager.—Ngozi Pole.	
2400 John F. Kennedy Federal Building, Boston, MA 02203	(617) 565–3170
State Administrative Director.—Barbara Souliotis.	

* * *

JOHN F. KERRY, Democrat, of Boston, MA; born in Denver, CO, December 11, 1943; education: graduated, St. Paul's School, Concord, NH, 1962; B.A., Yale University, New Haven, CT, 1966; J.D., Boston College Law School, Boston, MA, 1976; served, U.S. Navy, discharged with rank of lieutenant; decorations: Silver Star, Bronze Star with Combat "V", three Purple Hearts, various theatre campaign decorations; attorney, admitted to Massachusetts bar, 1976; appointed first assistant district attorney, Middlesex County, 1977; elected lieutenant governor, Massachusetts, 1982; married to Teresa Heinz; appointed to Democratic Leadership for 104th and 105th Congresses; committees: Commerce, Science, and Transportation; Finance; Foreign Relations; ranking member, Small Business and Entrepreneurship; elected to the U.S. Senate on November 6, 1984; reelected to each succeeding Senate term.

Office Listings

http://kerry.senate.gov

304 Russell Senate Office Building, Washington, DC 20510	(202) 224–2742
Administrative Assistant.—David McKean.	FAX: 224–8525
Legislative Director.—George Abar.	
Personal Secretary.—Patricia Ferrone.	
One Bowdoin Square, 10th Floor, Boston, MA 02114	(617) 565–8519
Suite 311, 222 Milliken Place, Fall River, MA 02722	(508) 677–0522
One Financial Plaza, Springfield, MA 01103	(413) 747–3942

REPRESENTATIVES

FIRST DISTRICT

JOHN W. OLVER, Democrat, of Amherst, MA; born in Honesdale, PA, September 3, 1936; education: B.S., Rensselaer Polytechnic Institute, 1955; M.A., Tufts University, 1956; taught for two years at Franklin Technical Institute, Boston, MA; Ph.D., Massachusetts Institute of Technology, 1961; professional: chemistry professor, University of Massachusetts-Amherst; Massachusetts House, 1968–72; Massachusetts Senate, 1972–91; became first Democrat since the Spanish-American War to represent the First Congressional District, 1991; elected by special election on June 4, 1991, to fill the vacancy caused by the death of Silvio Conte; married: Rose Olver; children: Martha; committees: Appropriations; subcommittees: Interior, Environment, and Related Agencies; ranking member, Transportation, Treasury, HUD, The Judiciary, District of Columbia, and Independent Agencies; elected on June 4, 1991, by special election, to the 102nd Congress; reelected to each succeeding Congress.

Office Listings

http://www.house.gov/olver

1111 Longworth House Office Building, Washington, DC 20515	(202) 225–5335
Chief of Staff.—Hunter Ridgway.	
Press Secretary / Scheduler.—Nicole Letourneau.	
Legislative Director.—Abbie Meador.	
463 Main Street, Fitchburg, MA 01420	(978) 342–8722
Office Manager.—Peggy Kane.	
57 Suffolk Street, Suite 310, Holyoke, MA 01040	(413) 532–7010
District Director.—Jon Niedzielski.	
78 Center Street, Pittsfield, MA 01201	(413) 442–0946
Office Manager.—Cindy Clark.	

Counties: BERKSHIRE, FRANKLIN, HAMPDEN (part), HAMPSHIRE (part), MIDDLESEX (part), WORCESTER (part). Population (2000), 634,479.

ZIP Codes: 01002–05, 01007–08, 01011–12, 01026–27, 01029, 01031–34, 01037–41, 01050, 01054, 01059, 01066, 01068–75, 01077, 01080–82, 01084–86, 01088–90, 01093–94, 01096–98, 01102, 01107, 01201–03, 01220, 01222–27, 01229–30, 01235–38, 01240, 01242–45, 01247, 01252–60, 01262–64, 01266–67, 01270, 01301–02, 01330–31, 01337–44, 01346–47, 01349–51, 01355, 01360, 01364, 01366–68, 01370, 01373, 01375–76, 01378–80, 01420, 01430–31, 01436, 01438, 01440–41, 01452–53, 01462–63, 01468–69, 01473–75, 01477, 01531, 01564, 01585

* * *

SECOND DISTRICT

RICHARD E. NEAL, Democrat, of Springfield, MA; born in Springfield, February 14, 1949; education: graduated, Springfield Technical High School, 1968; B.A., American International College, Springfield, 1972; M.A., University of Hartford Barney School of Business and Public Administration, CT, 1976; instructor and lecturer; assistant to mayor of Springfield, 1973–78; Springfield City Council, 1978–84; mayor, city of Springfield, 1983–89; member: Massachusetts Mayors Association; Adult Education Council; American International College Alumni Association; Boys Club Alumni Association; Emily Bill Athletic Association; Cancer Crusade; John Boyle O'Reilly Club; United States Conference of Mayors; Valley Press Club; Solid Waste Advisory Committee for the State of Massachusetts; Committee on Leadership and Government; Mass Jobs Council; trustee: Springfield Libraries and Museums Association, Springfield Red Cross, Springfield YMCA; married to Maureen; four children: Rory Christopher, Brendan Conway, Maura Katherine, and Sean Richard; committees: Budget; Ways and Means; subcommittees: Social Security; elected on November 8, 1988, to the 101st Congress; reelected to each succeeding Congress.

Office Listings

http://www.house.gov/neal

2266 Rayburn House Office Building, Washington, DC 20515	(202) 225–5601
Administrative Assistant.—Ann Jablon.	FAX: 225–8112
Executive Assistant.—Sarah Bontempo.	
Press Secretary.—Bill Tranghese.	
Federal Building, Room 309, 1550 Main Street, Springfield, MA 01103	(413) 785–0325
District Manager.—James Leydon.	
4 Congress Street, Milford, MA 01757	(508) 634–8198
Office Manager.—Virginia Purcell.	

Counties: HAMPDEN (part), HAMPSHIRE (part), NORFOLK (part), WORCESTER (part). Population (2000), 634,444.

ZIP Codes: 01001, 01009–10, 01013–14, 01020–22, 01027–28, 01030, 01035–36, 01053, 01056–57, 01060–63, 01069, 01075, 01079–81, 01083, 01092, 01095, 01101–09, 01111, 01115–16, 01118–19, 01128–29, 01133, 01138–39, 01144, 01151–52, 01199, 01504, 01506–09, 01515–16, 01518–19, 01521, 01524–27, 01529, 01534–38, 01540, 01542, 01550, 01560, 01562, 01566, 01568–71, 01585–86, 01588, 01590, 01607, 01611, 01747, 01756–57

* * *

THIRD DISTRICT

JAMES P. McGOVERN, Democrat, of Worcester, MA; born in Worcester, November 20, 1959; education: B.A., M.P.A., American University; legislative director and senior aide to Congressman Joe Moakley (D–South Boston); led the 1989 investigation into the murders of six Jesuit priests and two lay women in El Salvador; managed George McGovern's (D–SD) 1984 presidential campaign in Massachusetts and delivered his nomination speech at the Democratic National Convention; board of directors, Jesuit International Volunteers; former volunteer, Mt.

Carmel House, an emergency shelter for battered and abused women; married: Lisa Murray McGovern; committees: Rules; subcommittees: Technology and the House; elected to the 105th Congress; reelected to each succeeding Congress.

Office Listings
http://www.house.gov/mcgovern

430 Cannon House Office Building, Washington, DC 20515 .... (202) 225–6101
    Chief of Staff.—Christopher Philbin.   FAX: 225–5759
    Legislative Director.—Cindy Buhl.
    Press Secretary.—Michael Mershon.
34 Mechanic Street, Worcester, MA 01608 .... (508) 831–7356
    District Director.—Matthew Pacheco.
1 Park Street, Attleboro, MA 02703 .... (508) 431–8025
    District Representative.—Shirley Coelho.
218 South Main Street, Room 204, Fall River, MA 02721 .... (508) 677–0140
    District Representative.—Patrick Norton.
255 Main Street, Room 104, Marlborough, MA 01752 .... (508) 460–9292
    District Representative.—Sean Navin.

Counties: BRISTOL (part), MIDDLESEX (part), NORFOLK (part), WORCESTER (part). CITIES AND TOWNSHIPS: Ashland, Attleborough, Auburn, Boylston, Clinton, Fall River, Franklin, Holden, Holliston, Hopkinton, Marlborough, Medway, North Attleborough, Northborough, Paxton, Plainville, Princeton, Rehoboth, Rutland, Seekonk, Shrewsbury, Somerset, Southborough, Swansea, West Boylston, Westborough, Worcester, and Wrentham. Population (2000), 634,585.

ZIP Codes: 01501, 01505, 01510, 01517, 01520, 01522, 01527, 01532, 01541, 01543, 01545–46, 01580–83, 01601–15, 01653–55, 01721, 01745–46, 01748–49, 01752, 01772, 01784, 02038, 02053, 02070, 02093, 02703, 02720–21, 02723–26, 02760–63, 02769, 02771, 02777

* * *

FOURTH DISTRICT

BARNEY FRANK, Democrat, of Newton, MA; born in Bayonne, NJ, March 31, 1940; education: graduated, Bayonne High School, 1957; B.A., Harvard College, 1962; graduate student in political science, Harvard University, 1962–67; teaching fellow in government, Harvard College, 1963–66; J.D., Harvard University, 1977; admitted to the Massachusetts bar, 1979; executive assistant to Mayor Kevin White of Boston, 1968–71; administrative assistant to U.S. Congressman Michael F. Harrington, 1971–72; member, Massachusetts Legislature, 1973–80; partner: Sergio Pombo; Senior Whip; co-chair, Democratic Parliamentary Group; committees: ranking member, Financial Services; elected to the 97th Congress, November 4, 1980; reelected to each succeeding Congress.

Office Listings
http://www.house.gov/frank

2252 Rayburn House Office Building, Washington, DC 20515 .... (202) 225–5931
    Chief of Staff.—Peter Kovar.   FAX: 225–0182
    Deputy Chief of Staff / Scheduler.—Maria Giesta.
    Assistant to the Chief of Staff.—Julie McQuade.
29 Crafts Street, Suite 375, Newton, MA 02458 .... (617) 332–3920
    District Director.—Dorothy Reichard.
558 Pleasant Street, Room 309, New Bedford, MA 02740 .... (508) 999–6462
    Office Manager.—Elsie Souza.
The Jones Building, Suite 310, 29 Broadway, Taunton, MA 02780 .... (508) 822–4796
    Office Manager.—Garth Patterson.

Counties: BRISTOL (part), MIDDLESEX (part), NORFOLK (part), PLYMOUTH (part). CITIES AND TOWNSHIPS: Acushnet, Berkley, Brookline, Dartmouth, Dighton, Dover, Fairhaven, Fall River, Foxboro, Freetown, Halifax, Lakeville, Mansfield, Marion, Mattapoisett, Middleborough, Millis, New Bedford, Newton, Norfolk, Norton, Raynham, Rochester, Sharon, Sherborn, Taunton, Wareham, Wellesley, and Westport. Population (2000), 634,624.

ZIP Codes: 02021, 02030, 02032, 02035, 02048, 02053–54, 02056, 02067, 02130, 02135, 02215, 02330, 02333, 02338, 02344, 02346–47, 02349, 02360, 02367, 02445–47, 02456–62, 02464–68, 02472, 02476, 02481–82, 02492–93, 02495, 02532, 02538, 02558, 02571, 02576, 02702, 02712, 02714–15, 02717–23, 02738–48, 02764, 02766–70, 02779–80, 02783, 02790–91

* * *

FIFTH DISTRICT

MARTIN T. MEEHAN, Democrat, of Lowell, MA; born in Lowell, December 30, 1956; education: graduated from Lowell High School, 1974; B.A., University of Lowell, 1978; M.P.A., Suffolk University, Boston, MA, 1981; J.D., Suffolk University Law School, 1986;

attorney; admitted to the Massachusetts bar, 1986; First Assistant District Attorney for Middlesex County; Deputy Secretary of State; married Ellen Murphy, July 1996; committees: Armed Services; Judiciary; elected on November 3, 1992, to the 103rd Congress; reelected to each succeeding Congress.

Office Listings

http://www.house.gov/meehan

2229 Rayburn House Office Building, Washington, DC 20515	(202) 225–3411
Chief of Staff.—Lori Loureiro.	FAX: 226–0771
Press Secretary.—Matt Vogel.	
11 Kearney Square, Lowell, MA 01852	(978) 459–0101
305 Essex Street, 4th Floor, Lawrence, MA 01840	(978) 681–6200
Haverhill City Hall, 2nd Floor, Room 201A, 4 Summer Street, Haverhill, MA 01830	(978) 521–1845

Counties: ESSEX (part), MIDDLESEX (part), WORCESTER (part). CITIES AND TOWNSHIPS: Acton, Andover, Ayer, Berlin, Bolton, Boxborough, Carlisle, Chelmsford, Concord, Dillerjca, Drocut, Dunstable, Groton, Harvard, Haverhill, Hudson, Lawrence, Lancaster, Littleton, Lowell, Maynard, Methuen, Shirley, Stow, Sudbury, Tewksbury, Tyngsborough, Wayland, and Westford. Population (2000), 635,326.

ZIP Codes: 01432, 01450–51, 01453, 01460, 01464, 01467, 01470–72, 01503, 01523, 01561, 01718–20, 01740–42, 01749, 01754, 01775–76, 01778, 01810, 01812, 01821–22, 01824, 01826–27, 01830, 01832, 01835, 01840–44, 01850–54, 01862–63, 01865–66, 01876, 01879, 01886, 01899, 02493, 05501, 05544

* * *

SIXTH DISTRICT

JOHN F. TIERNEY, Democrat, of Salem, MA; born in Salem, September 18, 1951; education: graduated, Salem High School; B.A., political science, Salem State College, 1973; J.D., Suffolk University, 1976; professional: attorney, admitted to the Massachusetts bar in 1976; sole practitioner, 1976–80; partner, Tierney, Kalis and Lucas, 1981–96; member: Salem Chamber of Commerce, 1976–96 (president, 1995); trustee, Salem State College, 1992–97; married: Patrice M., 1997; committees: Education and the Workforce; Permanent Select Committee on Intelligence; subcommittees: Employer-Employee Relations; 21st Century Competitiveness; elected to the 105th Congress; reelected to each succeeding Congress.

Office Listings

http://www.house.gov/tierney

120 Cannon House Office Building, Washington, DC 20515	(202) 225–8020
Legislative Director.—Kevin McDermott.	FAX: 225–5915
Executive Assistant.—Bambi Yingst.	
17 Peabody Square, Peabody, MA 01960	(978) 531–1669
District Director.—Gary Barrett.	
Room 410, Lynn City Hall, Lynn, MA 01902	(781) 595–7375

Counties: ESSEX, MIDDLESEX. CITIES AND TOWNSHIPS: Amesbury, Bedford, Beverly, Boxford, Burlington, Danvers, Essex, Georgetown, Gloucester, Groveland, Hamilton, Ipswich, Lynn, Lynnfield, Manchester by the Sea, Marblehead, Merrimac, Middletown, Nahant, Newbury, Newburyport, North Andover, North Reading, Peabody, Reading, Rockport, Rowley, Salem, Salisbury, Saugus, Swampscott, Topsfield, Wenham, West Newbury, Wakefield, and Wilmington. Population (2000), 636,554.

ZIP Codes: 01730–31, 01801, 01803, 01805, 01810, 01821, 01833–34, 01845, 01860, 01864, 01867, 01880, 01885, 01887, 01889, 01901–08, 01910, 01913, 01915, 01921–23, 01929–31, 01936–38, 01940, 01944–45, 01949–52, 01960–61, 01965–66, 01969–71, 01982–85

* * *

SEVENTH DISTRICT

EDWARD J. MARKEY, Democrat, of Malden, MA; born in Malden, July 11, 1946; education: graduated, Malden Catholic High School, 1964; B.A., Boston College, 1968; J.D., Boston College Law School, 1972; professional: lawyer; served in the U.S. Army Reserves, 1968–73; member, Massachusetts House of Representatives, 1973–76; committees: Energy and Commerce; Homeland Security; Resources; elected to the 94th Congress, November 2, 1976, to fill the vacancy caused by the death of Representative Torbert H. Macdonald; at the same time elected to the 95th Congress; reelected to each succeeding Congress.

Office Listings

http://www.house.gov/markey

2108 Rayburn House Office Building, Washington, DC 20515 .... (202) 225–2836
Chief of Staff.—David Moulton.
Executive Assistant.—Nancy Morrissey.
Legislative Director.—Jeff Duncan.
5 High Street, Suite 101, Medford, MA 02155 .... (781) 396–2900
188 Concord Street, Suite 102, Framingham, MA 01701 .... (508) 875–2900

Counties: MIDDLESEX (part), SUFFOLK (part). CITIES AND TOWNSHIPS: Arlington, Belmont, Everett, Framingham, Lexington, Lincoln, Malden, Medford, Melrose, Natick, Revere, Stoneham, Waltham, Watertown, Wayland, Weston, Winchester, Winthrop, and Woburn. Population (2000), 634,287.

ZIP Codes: 01701–02, 01760, 01773, 01778, 01801, 01890, 02148–49, 02151–52, 02155, 02176, 02180, 02420–21, 02451–54, 02472, 02474–76, 02478, 02493

* * *

EIGHTH DISTRICT

MICHAEL E. CAPUANO, Democrat, of Somerville, MA; born in Somerville, January 1, 1952; education: graduated, Somerville High School, 1969; B.A., Dartmouth College, 1973; J.D., Boston College Law School, 1977; professional: admitted to the Massachusetts Bar, 1977; Alderman in Somerville, MA, 1977–79; Alderman-at-Large, 1985–89; elected Mayor for five terms, 1990 to January, 1999, when he resigned to be sworn in as a U.S. Representative; Democratic Regional Whip; married: Barbara Teebagy of Somerville, MA, in 1974; children: Michael and Joseph; committees: Financial Services; Transportation and Infrastructure; subcommittees: Aviation; Capital Markets, Insurance and Government-Sponsored Enterprises; Highways, Transit and Pipelines; Housing and Community Opportunity; elected to the 106th Congress; reelected to each succeeding Congress.

Office Listings

http://www.house.gov/capuano

1530 Longworth House Office Building, Washington, DC 20515 .... (202) 225–5111
Chief of Staff.—Robert Primus.   FAX: 225–9322
Legislative Director.—Jon Skarin.
Office Manager / Scheduler.—Mary Doherty.
Senior Legislative Assistant.—Christopher Huckleberry.
110 First Street, Cambridge, MA 02141 .... (617) 621–6208
District Director.—Michael J. Gorman.

Counties: MIDDLESEX (part), SUFFOLK (part). CITIES AND TOWNSHIPS: Boston, Cambridge, Chelsea, and Somerville. Population (2000), 634,835.

ZIP Codes: 02108–11, 02113–22, 02124–26, 02128–31, 02133–36, 02138–45, 02150–51, 02155, 02163, 02199, 02215–17, 02228, 02238–39, 02295, 02297, 02446, 02458, 02467, 02472, 02478

* * *

NINTH DISTRICT

STEPHEN F. LYNCH, Democrat, of South Boston, MA; born in South Boston, March 31, 1955; education: South Boston High School, 1973; B.S., Wentworth Institute of Technology; J.D., Boston College Law School; Master in Public Administration, JFK School of Government, Harvard University; professional: attorney; former President of Ironworkers Local #7; organizations: South Boston Boys and Girls Club; Boston Children's Museum; Colonel Daniel Marr Boys and Girls Club; Chinatown Trust Fund; South Boston Harbor Academy Charter School; Friends for Children; public service: elected to the Massachusetts House of Representatives in 1994, and the State Senate in 1996; family: married to Margaret; one child: Victoria; committees: Financial Services; Government Reform; elected to the 107th Congress, by special election, on October 16, 2001; reelected to each succeeding Congress.

Office Listings

319 Cannon House Office Building, Washington, DC 20515 .... (202) 225–8273
Chief of Staff.—Kevin Ryan.   FAX: 225–3984
Legislative Director.—Caroline Powers.
Legislative Counsel.—Kerry Lawrence.
Executive Assistant.—Greta Hebert.

88 Black Falcon Avenue, Suite 340, Boston, MA 02210 .... (617) 428–2000
    District Director.—Stacey Monahan.
166 Main Street, Brockton, MA 02401 .... (508) 586–5555

Counties: BRISTOL (part), NORFOLK (part), PLYMOUTH (part), SUFFOLK (part). Population (2000), 634,062.

ZIP Codes: 02021, 02026–27, 02032, 02052, 02062, 02071–72, 02081, 02090, 02101–10, 02112, 02114, 02116, 02122, 02124–27, 02130–32, 02136–37, 02151, 02169–71, 02184–87, 02196, 02201–12, 02222, 02241, 02266, 02283–84, 02293, 02297, 02301–05, 02322, 02324–25, 02333–34, 02337, 02341, 02343, 02350, 02356–57, 02368, 02375, 02379, 02382, 02467, 02481, 02492, 02494

* * *

TENTH DISTRICT

WILLIAM D. DELAHUNT, Democrat, of Quincy, MA; born in Boston, MA, July 18, 1941; education: B.A., political science, Middlebury College, VT; M.A., J.D., Boston College Law School, 1967; U.S. Coast Guard Reserves, 1963–71; professional: admitted to the Massachusetts Bar in 1967 and began practice in Boston; assistant majority leader, Massachusetts House of Representatives, 1973–75; Norfolk County District Attorney, 1975–96; president, Massachusetts District Attorneys Association, 1985; member, Council of Young American Political Leaders fact-finding mission to Poland, 1979; named citizen of the Year by South Shore Coalition for Human Rights, 1983; delegate, Human Rights Project fact-finding mission to Cuba, 1988; member, Anti-Defamation League of B'nai B'rith fact-finding mission to Israel, 1990; chairman, Development Committee, South Shore Association for Retarded Citizens; Democratic State Committeeman, Norfolk District; advisory board member, Jane Doe Safety Fund; honoree of the Boston Area Rape Crisis Center for contribution to preventing sexual assault, 1993; New England Region honoree, Anti-Defamation League, 1994; Massachusetts Bar Association Public Service Award, 1994; member, Board of Directors, RYKA Rose Foundation; co-chair, Coast Guard Caucus; Older Americans Caucus; Democratic Task Force on Crime; Law Enforcement Caucus; Congressional Human Rights Caucus; two daughters: Kirsten and Kara; committees: International Relations; Judiciary; Democratic Steering Committee; elected to the 105th Congress; reelected to each succeeding Congress.

Office Listings

http://www.house.gov/delahunt

2454 Rayburn House Office Building, Washington, DC 20515 .... (202) 225–3111
    Chief of Staff.—Steve Schwadron.   FAX: 225–5658
146 Main Street, Hyannis, MA 02601 .... (508) 771–0666
    Regional Representative.—Mark Forest.
1250 Hancock Street, Suite 802N, Quincy, MA 02169 .... (617) 770–3700
    Regional Representative.—Corinne Young.

Counties: BARNSTABLE, DUKES, NANTUCKET, NORFOLK (part), PLYMOUTH (part). Population (2000), 635,901.

ZIP Codes: 02018, 02020, 02025, 02035, 02040–41, 02043–45, 02047, 02050–51, 02055, 02059–61, 02065–66, 02169–71, 02184, 02186, 02188–91, 02269, 02327, 02330–32, 02339–41, 02345, 02351, 02355, 02358–62, 02364, 02366–67, 02370, 02381, 02532, 02534–37, 02539–43, 02552–54, 02556–57, 02559, 02561–65, 02568, 02573–75, 02584, 02601, 02630–35, 02637–39, 02641–53, 02655, 02657, 02659–64, 02666–73, 02675, 02713

MICHIGAN

(Population 2000, 9,938,444)

SENATORS

CARL M. LEVIN, Democrat, of Detroit, MI; born in Detroit, June 28, 1934; education: graduated, Central High School, Detroit, 1952; Swarthmore College, Swarthmore, PA, 1956; Harvard Law School, Boston, MA, 1959; professional: lawyer; Grossman, Hyman and Grossman, Detroit, 1959–64; assistant attorney general and general counsel for Michigan Civil Rights Commission, 1964–67; chief appellate defender for city of Detroit, 1968–69; counsel, Schlussel, Lifton, Simon, Rands and Kaufman, 1971–73; counsel, Jaffe, Snider, Raitt, Garratt and Heuer, 1978–79; admitted to the Michigan bar in 1959; member, City Council of Detroit, 1969–77; president, City Council of Detroit, 1974–77; member: Congregation T'Chiyah; American, Michigan and Detroit bar associations; former instructor at Wayne State University and the University of Detroit; married: the former Barbara Halpern, 1961; children: Kate, Laura, and Erica; committees: Armed Services; Homeland Security and Governmental Affairs; Small Business and Entrepreneurship; Select Committee on Intelligence; Permanent Subcommittee on Investigations; elected to the U.S. Senate on November 7, 1978; reelected to each succeeding Senate term.

Office Listings

http://levin.senate.gov

269 Russell Senate Office Building, Washington, DC 20510	(202) 224–6221
Administrative Assistant.—David Lyles.	
Legislative Director.—Rich Arenberg.	
Executive Secretary.—Susan Cameron.	
Press Secretary.—Tara Andringa.	
477 Michigan Avenue, McNamara Building, Room 1860, Detroit, MI 48226	(313) 226–6020
Federal Building, Room 720, 110 Michigan Street, NW, Grand Rapids, MI 49503..	(616) 456–2531
1810 Michigan National Tower, 124 West Allegan Street, Suite 1810, Lansing, MI 48933	(517) 377–1508
524 Ludington Street, Suite LL103, Escanaba, MI 49829	(906) 789–0052
515 North Washington, Suite 402, Saginaw, MI 48607	(989) 754–2494
30500 VanDyke, Suite 206, Warren, MI 48093	(810) 573–9145
107 Cass Street, Suite E, Traverse City, MI 49684	(616) 947–9569

* * *

DEBBIE STABENOW, Democrat, of Lansing, MI; born in Gladwin, MI, April 29, 1950; education: Clare High School; B.A., Michigan State University, 1972; M.S.W., Michigan State University, 1975; public service: Ingham County, MI, Commissioner, 1975–1978, chairperson for two years; Michigan State House of Representatives, 1979–1990; Michigan State Senate, 1991–1994; religion: Methodist; married to Thomas Athans; children: Todd and Michelle; committees: Agriculture, Nutrition, and Forestry; Banking, Housing, and Urban Affairs; Budget; elected to the U.S. House of Representatives in 1996 and 1998; elected to the U.S. Senate on November 7, 2000.

Office Listings

http://stabenow.senate.gov

133 Hart Senate Office Building, Washington, DC 20510	(202) 224–4822
Chief of Staff.—Sander Lurie.	FAX: 228–0325
Legislative Director.—Noushin Jahanian.	
Deputy Chief of Staff for Communications.—Karen Finney.	
Scheduler.—Sally Cluthe.	
221 West Lake Lansing Road, Suite 100, East Lansing, MI 48823	(517) 203–1760
Marquette Building, 243 West Congress, Suite 550, Detroit, MI 48226	(313) 961–4330
2503 South Linden Road, Flint, MI 48532	(810) 720–4172
3335 South Airport Road West, Suite 6B, Traverse City, MI 49684	(231) 929–1031
3230 Broadmoor Street, Suite B, Grand Rapids, MI 49512	(616) 975–0052
1901 West Ridge, Suite 7, Marquette, MI 49855	(906) 228–8756

REPRESENTATIVES

FIRST DISTRICT

BART STUPAK, Democrat, of Menominee, MI; born in Milwaukee, WI, February 29, 1952; education: graduated, Gladstone High School, Gladstone, MI, 1970; B.S., Saginaw Valley State College, 1977; J.D., Thomas Cooley Law School, 1981; professional: attorney; admitted to the

Michigan bar, 1981; Michigan State House of Representatives, 1989–90; member: Elks Club; State Employees Retirement Association; Sons of the American Legion; Wildlife Unlimited; National Rifle Association; Knights of Columbus; national committeeman, Boy Scouts of America; married: the former Laurie Ann Olsen; children: Ken and Bart, Jr. (deceased); committees: Energy and Commerce; elected on November 3, 1992, to the 103rd Congress; reelected to each succeeding Congress.

Office Listings

http://www.house.gov/stupak

2352 Rayburn House Office Building, Washington, DC 20515	(202) 225–4735
Chief of Staff.—Scott Schloegel.	FAX: 225–4744
Press Secretary.—Adrianne Marsh.	
District Administrator.—Tom Baldini.	
512 East Houghton Avenue, West Branch, MI 48661	(989) 345–2258
902 Ludington Street, Escanaba, MI 49829	(906) 786–4504
1229 West Washington, Marquette, MI 49855	(906) 228–3700
111 East Chisholm, Alpena, MI 49707	(989) 356–0690
2 South 6th Street, Suite 3, Crystal Falls, MI 49920	(906) 875–3751
616 Sheldon Avenue, Room 213, Houghton, MI 49931	(906) 482–1371
200 Division Street, Petoskey, MI 49770	(231) 348–0657

Counties: ALCONA, ALGER, ALPENA, ANTRIM, ARENAC, BARAGA, BAY (part), CHARLEVOIX, CHEBOYGAN, CHIPPEWA, CRAWFORD, DELTA, DICKINSON, EMMET, GOGEBIC, HOUGHTON, IRON, KEWEENAW, LUCE, MACKINAC, MARQUETTE, MENOMINEE, MONTMORENCY, OGEMAW, ONTONAGON, OSCODA, OTSEGO, PRESQUE ISLE, SCHOOLCRAFT. Population (2000), 662,563.

ZIP Codes: 48610–13, 48618–19, 48621, 48623–24, 48628, 48631, 48634–36, 48642, 48647, 48650, 48652–54, 48658–59, 48661, 48703, 48705–06, 48721, 48728, 48730, 48737–40, 48742–43, 48745, 48748–50, 48756, 48761–66, 48770, 49611–12, 49615, 49622, 49627, 49629, 49648, 49659, 49676, 49701, 49705–07, 49709–13, 49715–30, 49733–40, 49743–49, 49751–53, 49755–57, 49759–62, 49764–66, 49768–70, 49774–77, 49779–85, 49788, 49790–93, 49795–97, 49799, 49801–02, 49805–08, 49812, 49814–22, 49825–27, 49829, 49831, 49833–41, 49845, 49847–49, 49852–55, 49858, 49861–64, 49866, 49868, 49870–74, 49876–81, 49883–87, 49891–96, 49901–03, 49905, 49908, 49910–13, 49915–22, 49925, 49927, 49929–31, 49934–35, 49938, 49945–48, 49950, 49952–53, 49955, 49958–65, 49967–71

* * *

SECOND DISTRICT

PETER HOEKSTRA, Republican, of Holland, MI; born in Groningen, the Netherlands, October 30, 1953; education: graduated, Holland Christian High School; B.A., Hope College, Holland, 1975; M.B.A., University of Michigan, 1977; professional: vice president for product management, Herman Miller, Inc.; married: the former Diane Johnson; children: Erin, Allison, and Bryan; committees: Transportation and Infrastructure; chair, Permanent Select Committee on Intelligence; elected on November 3, 1992, to the 103rd Congress; reelected to each succeeding Congress.

Office Listings

http://hoekstra.house.gov

2234 Rayburn House Office Building, Washington, DC 20515	(202) 225–4401
Chief of Staff.—Amy Plaster.	FAX: 226–0779
Legislative Director.—Justin Wormmeester.	
Scheduler/Executive Assistant.—Leah Scott.	
District Director of Policy.—Jon DeWitte.	
184 South River, Holland, MI 49423	(616) 395–0030
900 Third Street, Suite 203, Muskegon, MI 49440	(231) 722–8386
210½ North Mitchell Street, Cadillac, MI 49601	(231) 775–0050

Counties: ALLEGAN (part), BENZIE, KENT (part), LAKE, MANISTEE, MASON, MUSKEGON, NEWAYGO, OCEANA, OTTAWA, WEXFORD. Population (2000), 662,563.

ZIP Codes: 49010, 49078, 49080, 49303–04, 49307, 49309, 49312, 49314–15, 49318–19, 49321, 49323, 49327–30, 49333, 49336–38, 49343, 49345–46, 49348–49, 49401–06, 49408–13, 49415, 49417–31, 49434–37, 49440–46, 49448–49, 49451–61, 49463–64, 49544, 49601, 49613–14, 49616–20, 49623, 49625–26, 49628, 49630, 49633–35, 49638, 49640, 49642–45, 49649–50, 49655–56, 49660, 49663, 49668, 49675, 49677, 49683, 49688–89

* * *

THIRD DISTRICT

VERNON J. EHLERS, Republican, of Grand Rapids, MI; born in Pipestone, MN, February 6, 1934; educated at home by his parents; attended Calvin College; undergraduate degree in physics and Ph.D. in nuclear physics, University of California at Berkeley; taught and did research at Berkeley for 6 years; returned to Calvin College; taught physics and became chairman, Physics Department; served on various boards and commissions; member, Michigan House and Senate; first research physicist in Congress; while on Science Committee in 1997–98, was selected to rewrite the nation's science policy; introduced National Science Education Acts aimed at reforming K–12 science, mathematics, engineering, and technology education; as member of House Administration Committee, guided the program to revamp the House computer system, connect it to the Internet, and allow all citizens to access House documents; member and former elder, Eastern Avenue Christian Reformed Church, Grand Rapids, MI; married: the former Johanna Meulink; four adult children: Heidi, Brian, Marla, and Todd; three grandchildren; one great-grandchild; committees: Education and the Workforce; House Administration; Science; Transportation and Infrastructure; Joint Committee on the Library of Congress; subcommittees: chairman, Environment, Technology, and Standards; elected to the 103rd Congress, by special election, on December 7, 1993; reelected to each succeeding Congress.

Office Listings
http://www.house.gov/ehlers

1714 Longworth House Office Building, Washington, DC 20515 .... (202) 225–3831
Chief of Staff.—Bill McBride.
Legislative Director.—Matt Reiffer.
Executive Assistant/Scheduler.—Loraine Kehl.
Press Secretary.—Jon Brandt.
110 Michigan Street, NW, Suite 166, Grand Rapids, MI 49503 .... (616) 451–8383
Community Services Director.—Rick Treur.

Counties: BARRY, IONIA, KENT (part). CITIES: Belding, Cedar Springs, East Grand Rapids, Grand Rapids, Grandville, Hastings, Ionia, Kentwood, Lowell, Portland, Rockford, Walker, and Wyoming. Population (2000), 662,563.

ZIP Codes: 48809, 48815, 48834, 48837–38, 48845–46, 48849, 48851, 48860–61, 48865, 48870–71, 48873, 48875, 48881, 48887, 48890, 48897, 49017, 49021, 49035, 49046, 49050, 49058, 49060, 49073, 49080, 49083, 49301–02, 49306, 49315–17, 49319, 49321, 49325–26, 49331, 49333, 49341, 49343–45, 49347–48, 49351, 49355–57, 49418, 49468, 49501–10, 49512, 49514–16, 49518, 49523, 49525, 49530, 49544, 49546, 49548, 49550, 49555, 49560, 49588, 49599

* * *

FOURTH DISTRICT

DAVE CAMP, Republican, of Midland, MI; born in Midland, July 9, 1953; education: graduated, H.H. Dow High School, Midland, 1971; B.A., Albion College, Albion, MI, 1975, *magna cum laude*; J.D., University of San Diego, 1978; attorney, member of State Bar of Michigan, State Bar of California, District of Columbia bar; U.S. Supreme Court; U.S. District Court, Eastern District of Michigan and Southern District of California; Midland County Bar Association; law practice, Midland, 1979–91; Special Assistant Attorney General, 1980–84; administrative assistant to Congressman Bill Schuette, Michigan's 10th Congressional District, 1985–87; State Representative, Michigan's 102nd district, 1989–91; chairman, Corrections Day Advisory Group; assistant majority whip; National Republican Congressional Committee; Executive Committee; Rural Health Care Coalition; 1998 Adoption Hall of Fame Inductee; American Farm Bureau Federation 1998 Golden Plow award recipient; married: attorney Nancy Keil of Midland, 1994; three children; committees: Ways and Means; subcommittees: Health; Human Resources; chairman, Select Revenue Measures; elected to Congress on November 6, 1990; reelected to each succeeding Congress.

Office Listings
http://www.house.gov/camp

137 Cannon House Office Building, Washington, DC 20515 .... (202) 225–3561
Chief of Staff.—Jim Brandell.   FAX: 225–9679
Communications Director.—Sage Eastman.
Legislative Director.—Joanna Foust.
Scheduler.—Sarah Ahlgren.
135 Ashman Street, Midland, MI, 48640 .... (989) 631–2552
121 East Front Street, Suite 202, Traverse City, MI 49684 .... (231) 929–4711

Counties: CLARE COUNTY. CITIES: Clare, Farwell, Harrison, Lake, Lake George. CLINTON COUNTY. CITY: Carland. GRAND TRAVERSE COUNTY. CITIES: Acme, Fife Lake, Grawn, Interlochen, Kingsley, Mayfield, Old Mission, Traverse City, Williamsburg. GRATIOT COUNTY. CITIES: Alma, Ashley, Bannister, Breckenridge, Elm Hall, Elwell, Ithaca, Middleton, North Star, Perrinton, Pompeii, Riverdale, Sumner, St. Louis, Wheeler. ISABELLA COUNTY. CITIES: Blanchard, Millbrook, Mt. Pleasant, Rosebush, Shepherd, Weidman, Winn. KALKASKA COUNTY. CITIES: Kalkaska, Rapid City, South Boardman. LEELANAU COUNTY. CITIES: Cedar, Empire, Glen Arbor, Lake Leelanau, Leland, Maple City, Northport, Omena, Suttons Bay. MECOSTA COUNTY. CITIES: Barryton, Big Rapids, Canadian Lakes, Chippewa Lakes, Mecosta, Morley, Paris, Remus, Stanwood. MIDLAND COUNTY. CITIES: Coleman, Edenville, Hope, Laporte, Midland, North Bradley, Poseyville,

Sanford. MISSAUKEE COUNTY. CITIES: Falmouth, Lake City, McBain, Merritt, Moorestown. MONTCALM COUNTY. CITIES: Alger, Butternut, Carson City, Cedar Lake, Coral, Crystal, Edmore, Entrican, Fenwick, Gowen, Greenville, Howard City, Lakeview, Langston, Maple Hill, McBride, Pierson, Sand Lake, Sheridan, Sidney, Six Lakes, Stanton, Trufant, Vestaburg, Vickeryville. OSCEOLA COUNTY. CITIES: Evart, Hersey, LeRoy, Marion, Reed City, Sears, Tustin. ROSCOMMON COUNTY. CITIES: Higgins Lake, Houghton Lake, Houghton Lake Heights, Prudenville, Roscommon, St. Helen. SAGINAW COUNTY (part). CITIES: Birch Run, Brant, Bridgeport, Burt, Carrolton, Chesaning, Fosters, Freeland, Fremont, Hemlock, Merrill, Oakley, Richland, Saginaw, Shields, Spalding, St. Charles, University Center. SHIAWASSEE COUNTY (part). CITIES: Bancroft, Caledonia, Chapin, Corunna, Henderson, Laingsburg, Morrice, New Haven, New Lothrup, Owosso, Perry, Shaftsburg, Venice, and Vernon. Population (2000), 662,563.

ZIP Codes: 48415, 48417, 48429, 48433, 48436, 48449, 48457, 48460, 48476, 48601–04, 48608–09, 48614–18, 48620, 48622–30, 48632–33, 48637, 48640–42, 48649, 48651–53, 48655–57, 48662, 48667, 48670, 48674, 48686, 48706, 48722, 48724, 48801–02, 48804, 48806–07, 48809, 48811–12, 48817–18, 48829–32, 48834, 48837–38, 48841, 48845, 48847, 48850, 48852–53, 48856, 48858–59, 48862, 48866–67, 48874–75, 48877–80, 48883–86, 48888–89, 48891, 48893, 48896, 49305, 49307, 49310, 49320, 49322–23, 49326, 49328–29, 49332, 49336–40, 49342–43, 49346–47, 49601, 49610, 49612, 49620–21, 49630–33, 49636–37, 49639–40, 49643, 49646, 49649, 49651, 49653–55, 49657, 49659, 49663–67, 49670, 49673–74, 49676–77, 49679–80, 49682–86, 49688, 49690, 49696, 49738

* * *

FIFTH DISTRICT

DALE E. KILDEE, Democrat, of Flint, MI; born in Flint, September 16, 1929; education: graduated, St. Mary High School, 1947; B.A., Sacred Heart Seminary, Detroit, 1952; M.A., University of Michigan, Ann Arbor, 1961; graduate studies in history and political science, University of Peshawar, Pakistan, under Rotary Foundation Fellowship; professional: teacher, University of Detroit High School, 1954–56; Flint Central High School, 1956–64; served as State Representative, 1965–74; State Senator, 1975–77; member: Optimists, Urban League, Knights of Columbus, Phi Delta Kappa national honorary fraternity, American Federation of Teachers; life member, National Association for the Advancement of Colored People; married: the former Gayle Heyn, 1965; children: David, Laura, and Paul; committees: Education and the Workforce; Resources; elected to the 95th Congress, November 2, 1976; reelected to each succeeding Congress.

Office Listings

2107 Rayburn House Office Building, Washington, DC 20515	(202) 225–3611
Administrative Assistant.—Christopher J. Mansour.	FAX: 225–6393
Legislative Director.—Callig Coffman.	
Personal Secretary.—Greta Moore.	
432 North Saginaw, Suite 410, Flint, MI 48502	(810) 239–1437
District Director, all Districts.—Tiffany Anderson-Flynn.	(800) 662–2685
515 North Washington Avenue, Suite 401, Saginaw, MI 48607	(989) 755–8904
916 Washington Avenue, Suite 205, Bay City, MI 48708	(989) 891–0990

Counties: BAY (part), GENESEE, SAGINAW (part), TUSCOLA. Population (2000), 662,563.

ZIP Codes: 48411, 48415, 48417–18, 48420–21, 48423, 48426, 48429–30, 48433, 48435–39, 48449, 48451, 48453, 48457–58, 48460, 48462–64, 48473, 48501–07, 48509, 48519, 48529, 48531–32, 48550–57, 48601–07, 48623, 48631, 48663, 48701, 48706–08, 48710, 48722–23, 48726–27, 48729, 48732–36, 48741, 48744, 48746–47, 48757–60, 48767–69, 48787

* * *

SIXTH DISTRICT

FRED UPTON, Republican, of St. Joseph, MI; born in St. Joseph, April 23, 1953; education: graduated, Shattuck School, Fairbault, MN, 1971; B.A., journalism, University of Michigan, Ann Arbor, 1975; professional: field manager, Dave Stockman Campaign, 1976; staff member, Congressman Dave Stockman, 1976–80; legislative assistant, Office of Management and Budget, 1981–83; deputy director of Legislative Affairs, 1983–84; director of Legislative Affairs, 1984–85; member: First Congregational Church, Emil Verbin Society; married: the former Amey Rulon-Miller; committees: Energy and Commerce; subcommittees: Commerce, Trade, and Consumer Protection; Health; chair, Telecommunications and the Internet; elected to the 100th Congress on November 4, 1986; reelected to each succeeding Congress.

Office Listings

2183 Rayburn House Office Building, Washington, DC 20515	(202) 225–3761
Administrative Assistant.—Joan Hillebrands.	FAX: 225–4986
Executive Assistant.—Ryan Hollowell.	
800 Centre, Suite 106, 800 Ship Street, St. Joseph, MI 49085	(269) 982–1986
157 South Kalamazoo Mall, Suite 180, Kalamazoo, MI 49006	(269) 385–0039

Counties: ALLEGAN (part), BERRIEN, CALHOUN (part), CASS, KALAMAZOO, ST. JOSEPH, VAN BUREN. CITIES AND TOWNSHIPS: Allegan, Augusta, Bangor, Baroda, Benton Harbor, Berrien Springs, Berrien Center, Bloomingdale, Breedsville, Bridgman, Buchanan, Burr Oak, Cassopolis, Centreville, Climax, Coloma, Colon, Comstock, Constantine, Covert, Decatur, Delton, Dowagiac, Eau Claire, Edwardsburg, Fulton, Galesburg, Galien, Gobles, Grand Junction, Hagar Shores, Harbert, Hartford, Hickory Corners, Jones, Kalamazoo, Kendall, Lacota, Lakeside, Lawrence, Lawton, Leonidas, Marcellus, Mattawan, Mendon, Nazareth, New Troy, New Buffalo, Niles, Nottawa, Oshtemo, Otsego, Paw Paw, Plainwell, Portage, Pullman, Richland, Riverside, Sawyer, Schoolcraft, Scotts, Sodus, South Haven, St. Joseph, Stevensville, Sturgis, Three Oaks, Three Rivers, Union Pier, Union, Vandalia, Vicksburg, Watervliet, and White Pigeon. Population (2000), 662,563.

ZIP Codes: 48867, 49001–15, 49017, 49019, 49022–24, 49026–27, 49030–32, 49034, 49038–43, 49045, 49047–48, 49051–53, 49055–57, 49060–67, 49070–72, 49074–75, 49077–81, 49083–85, 49087–88, 49090–91, 49093, 49095, 49097–99, 49101–04, 49106–07, 49111–13, 49115–17, 49119–21, 49125–30, 49311, 49315–16, 49323, 49328, 49333, 49335, 49344, 49348, 49408, 49416, 49450

* * *

SEVENTH DISTRICT

JOHN J.H. (JOE) SCHWARZ, Republican, of Battle Creek, MI; born in Battle Creek, November 15, 1937; education: graduated from Battle Creek Central High School; B.A., University of Michigan, 1959; M.D., Wayne State University, Detroit MI, 1964; professional: United States Navy, 1965–1967; served in the Central Intelligence Agency, 1968–1970; Battle Creek City Commissioner, 1979–1985; mayor of Battle Creek, 1985–1987; member of the Michigan state Senate, 1987–2002; organizations: President-Elect, University of Michigan Alumni Association, 2003–2004; Trustee, Olivet College, 1991–2004; Trustee, Library of Michigan, 1994–2003; Director/Treasurer, American Legacy Foundation, 1999–2002; American Medical Association; The Society of Medical Association; The Society of Medical Consultants to the Armed Forces; religion: Roman Catholic; family: one child, Brennan Louise; committees: Agriculture; Armed Services; Science; subcommittees: Conservation, Credit, Rural Development and Research; Energy; Environment, Technology, and Standards; Readiness; Specialty Crops and Foreign Agriculture Programs; Strategic Forces; elected to the 109th Congress on November 2, 2004.

Office Listings

http://www.house.gov/schwarz

128 Cannon House Office Building, Washington, DC 20515	(202) 225–6276	
Chief of Staff.—Matt Marsden.	FAX: 225–6281	
Legislative Director.—Charles Yessaian.		
Legislative Assistants: Meghan Kolassa, Louie Meizlish, Jared Page, Mark Ratner.		
Special Assistant.—Rob Blackwell.		
6604 W. Saginaw Highway, Lansing, MI 48917	(517) 323–6600	
District Representative.—Paul Egnatuk.		
142 N. Mechanic Street, Jackson, MI 49201	(517) 783–4486	
District Representative.—Rob Glazier.		
249 W. Michigan Avenue, Battle Creek, MI 49017	(269) 965–9066	
District Representative.—Danielle Moreland.		

Counties: BRANCH, CALHOUN (part), EATON, HILLSDALE, JACKSON, LENAWEE, WASHTENAW (part). Population (2000), 662,563.

ZIP Codes: 48103, 48105, 48115, 48118, 48130, 48158, 48160, 48167, 48170, 48175–76, 48178, 48189, 48601, 48813, 48821, 48827, 48837, 48849, 48861, 48876, 48890, 48906, 48908, 48911, 48917, 49011, 49014–18, 49020–21, 49028–30, 49033, 49036, 49040, 49051–52, 49058, 49068–69, 49073, 49076, 49082, 49089, 49092, 49094, 49096, 49201–04, 49220–21, 49224, 49227–30, 49232–42, 49245–59, 49261–69, 49271–72, 49274–77, 49279, 49281–89

* * *

EIGHTH DISTRICT

MIKE ROGERS, Republican, of Brighton, MI; born in Livingston County, MI, June 2, 1963; education: B.S., Adrian College, also attended the University of Michigan as an Army ROTC member; military service: U.S. Army; 1st Lieutenant, served in a rapid deployment unit as a Company Commander; professional: FBI Special Agent, assigned to public corruption and organized crime units; businessman; co-founder of E.B.I. Builders, Inc.; organizations: American Heart Association; Women's Resource Center; Brighton Rotary Club; Society of Former Special Agents of the FBI; religion: Methodist; married: Diane; children: Erin and Jonathan; committees: Energy and Commerce; Permanent Select Committee on Intelligence; elected to the 107th Congress on November 7, 2000; reelected to each succeeding Congress.

Office Listings
http://www.house.gov/mikerogers

133 Cannon House Office Building, Washington, DC 20515 .... (202) 225–4872
    Chief of Staff.—Matt Strawn.   FAX: 225–5820
    Legislative Director.—Heather Keiser.
    Press Secretary.—Sylvia Warner.
1327 East Michigan Avenue, Lansing, MI 48912 .... (517) 702–8000

Counties: CLINTON, INGHAM, LIVINGSTON, OAKLAND (part), SHIAWASSE (part). Population (2000), 662,563.

ZIP Codes: 48114, 48116, 48137, 48139, 48143, 48169, 48178, 48189, 48329, 48346–48, 48350, 48353, 48356–57, 48359–62, 48366–67, 48370–71, 48380, 48386, 48414, 48418, 48428–30, 48436, 48438–39, 48442, 48451, 48455, 48462, 48504, 48507, 48805, 48807–08, 48816–17, 48819–27, 48831, 48833, 48835–37, 48840, 48842–45, 48848, 48854–55, 48857, 48863–64, 48866–67, 48872–73, 48875, 48879, 48882, 48892, 48894–95, 48901, 48906, 48909–13, 48915–19, 48921–22, 48924, 48929–30, 48933, 48937, 48950–51, 48956, 48980, 49078, 49080, 49251, 49264, 49285

* * *

NINTH DISTRICT

JOE KNOLLENBERG, Republican, of Bloomfield Hills, MI; born in Mattoon, IL, November 28, 1933; education: B.S., Eastern Illinois University; professional: operated family insurance agency; Troy Chamber of Commerce, past vice chairman; Birmingham Cable TV Community Advisory Board, past member; St. Bede's Parish Council, past president and board member; Evergreen School PTA, past president; Bloomfield Glens Homeowners Association, past president; Cranbrook Homeowners Association, past president; Southfield Ad Hoc Park and Recreational Development Committee, past coordinator; Southfield Mayor's Wage and Salary Committee, past member; married to the former Sandra Moco; two sons, Martin and Stephen; elected to the Freshman Class Leadership, liaison to the National Republican Congressional Committee; committees: Appropriations; subcommittees: chairman, Transportation, Treasury, HUD, The Judiciary, District of Columbia, and Independent Agencies; Foreign Operations, Export Financing, and Related Programs; elected on November 3, 1992, to the 103rd Congress; reelected to each succeeding Congress.

Office Listings
http://www.house.gov/knollenberg

2349 Rayburn House Office Building, Washington, DC 20515 .... (202) 225–5802
    Chief of Staff.—Jeff Onizuk.   FAX: 226–2356
    Legislative Director.—Craig Albright.
    Press Secretary.—Christopher Close.
30833 Northwestern Highway, Suite 100, Farmington Hills, MI 48334 .... (248) 851–1366

Counties: OAKLAND (part). CITIES AND TOWNSHIPS: Auburn Hills, Berkley, Beverly Hills, Bingham Farms, Birmingham, Birmingham Farms, Bloomfield Hills, Bloomfield, Clawson, Farmington, Farmington Hills, Franklin, Keego Harbo, Lake Angelus, Oakland, Orchard Lake Village, Orion, Pontiac, Rochester, Rochester Hills, Royal Oak, Sylvan Lake, Troy, Waterford, and West Bloomfield. Population (2000), 662,563.

ZIP Codes: 48007, 48009, 48012, 48017, 48025, 48067–68, 48072–73, 48083–85, 48098–99, 48167, 48301–04, 48306–09, 48320–36, 48340–43, 48346, 48359–60, 48362–63, 48367, 48370, 48382, 48387, 48390, 48398

* * *

TENTH DISTRICT

CANDICE S. MILLER, Republican, of Harrison Township, MI; born in St. Clair Shores, MI, May 7, 1954; education: attended Macomb Community College and Northwood University; public service: Harrison Township Board of Trustees, 1979; Harrison Township Supervisor, 1980–1992; Macomb County Treasurer, 1992–1994; Michigan Secretary of State, 1994–2002; professional: worked in a family-owned marina business before she became involved in public service; religion: Presbyterian; married: Macomb County Circuit Court Judge Donald Miller; children: Wendy; committees: Armed Services; Government Reform; House Administration; Joint Committee on the Library of Congress; elected to the 108th Congress on November 5, 2002; reelected to each succeeding Congress.

Office Listings
http://www.house.gov/candicemiller

228 Cannon House Office Building, Washington, DC 20515 .... (202) 225–2106
    Chief of Staff.—Jamie Roe.   FAX: 226–1169
    Legislative Director.—Sean Moran.
    Legislative Assistant.—Kimberly R. Bird.
48653 Van Dyke Avenue, Shelby Township, MI 48317 .... (586) 997–5010

Counties: HURON, LAPEER, MACOMB (part), SAINT CLAIR, SANILAC. Population (2000), 662,562.

ZIP Codes: 48001–06, 48014, 48022–23, 48027–28, 48032, 48039–42, 48044–45, 48047–51, 48054, 48059–65, 48074, 48079, 48094–97, 48306, 48310–18, 48371, 48401, 48410, 48412–13, 48416, 48419, 48421–23, 48426–28, 48432, 48434–35, 48438, 48440–41, 48444–46, 48450, 48453–56, 48461–72, 48475, 48720, 48725–27, 48729, 48731, 48735, 48741, 48744, 48754–55, 48759–60, 48767

* * *

ELEVENTH DISTRICT

THADDEUS G. McCOTTER, Republican, of Livonia, MI; born in Detroit, MI, August 22, 1965; education: B.A., University of Detroit, 1987; J.D., University of Detroit Law School, 1990; professional: attorney; public service: elected to the Schoolcraft Community College Trustees, 1989; elected to the Wayne County Commission, 1992; elected to the Michigan State Senate, 1998; awards: Michigan Jaycees Outstanding Michigander, 2001; Police Officers Association of Michigan Legislator of the Year, 2002; religion: Catholic; married: Rita; children: George, Timothy, and Emilia; committees: Budget; International Relations; Small Business; Joint Economic Committee; elected to the 108th Congress on November 5, 2002; reelected to each succeeding Congress.

Office Listings
http://www.house.gov/mccotter

1632 Longworth House Office Building, Washington, DC 20515 .... (202) 225–8171
    Chief of Staff.—Martin Van Valkenburg.   FAX: 225–2667
    Legislative Director.—Patrick Rothwell.
17197 N. Laurel Park Drive, Suite 161, Livonia, MI 48152 .... (734) 632–0314

Counties: WAYNE COUNTY. CITIES: Livonia, Canton Township, Plymouth City, Plymouth Township, Northville City, Northville Township, Belleville, Van Buren Township, Wayne, Westland, Garden City, Redford Township, Dearborn Heights. OAKLAND COUNTY. CITIES: Novi, South Lyon, Lyon Township, Milford, Wixom, Walled Lake, Commerce Township, White Lake, Highland, and Waterford. Population (2000), 662,563.

ZIP Codes: 48111–12, 48127, 48135–36, 48141, 48150–54, 48165, 48167, 48170, 48174, 48178, 48184–88, 48239–40, 48327, 48329, 48346, 48356–57, 48374–77, 48380–83, 48386–87, 48390–91, 48393

* * *

TWELFTH DISTRICT

SANDER M. LEVIN, Democrat, of Royal Oak, MI; born in Detroit, MI, September 6, 1931; education: graduated, Central High School, Detroit, 1949; B.A., University of Chicago, 1952; M.A., Columbia University, New York, NY, 1954; LL.B., Harvard University, Cambridge, MA, 1957; professional: attorney, admitted to the Michigan bar in 1958 and commenced practice in Detroit, MI; member: Oakland Board of Supervisors, 1961–64; Michigan Senate, 1965–70; Democratic floor leader in State Senate; served on the Advisory Committee on the Education of Handicapped Children in the Department of Health, Education, and Welfare, 1965–68; chairman, Michigan Democratic Party, 1968–69; Democratic candidate for governor, 1970 and 1974; fellow, Kennedy School of Government, Institute of Politics, Harvard University, 1975; assistant administrator, Agency for International Development, 1977–81; married: the former Victoria Schlafer, 1957; children: Jennifer, Andrew, Madeleine, and Matthew; committees: Ways and Means; elected on November 2, 1982, to the 98th Congress; reelected to each succeeding Congress.

Office Listings
http://www.house.gov/levin

2300 Rayburn Office House Building, Washington, DC 20515 .... (202) 225–4961
    Administrative Assistant.—Hilarie Chambers.
    Scheduler.—Monica Chrzaszcz.

27085 Gratiot Avenue, Roseville, MI 48066 .... (586) 498–7122
District Administrator.—Judy Hartwell.

Counties: MACOMB (part), OAKLAND (part). CITIES: Center Line, Clinton Township, Eastpointe, Ferndale, Fraser, Hazel Park, Huntington Woods, Lake Township, Lathrup Village, Madison Heights, Mt. Clemens, Oak Park, Pleasant Ridge, Roseville, Royal Oak, Royal Oak Township, Southfield, St. Clair Shores, Sterling Heights, and Warren. Population (2000), 662,563.

ZIP Codes: 48015, 48021, 48025–26, 48030, 48034–38, 48043, 48046, 48066–67, 48069–71, 48075–76, 48080–82, 48086, 48088–93, 48220, 48236–37, 48310, 48312, 48397

* * *

THIRTEENTH DISTRICT

CAROLYN C. KILPATRICK, Democrat, of Detroit, MI; born in Detroit, June 25, 1945; education: attended Ferris State University; graduate, Western Michigan University, 1972; M.S., Education Administration, University of Michigan, 1977; teacher; served in Michigan House of Representatives, 1979–96; member, Detroit Substance Abuse Advisory Council; former chair, Michigan Legislative Black Caucus; participated in first-of-its-kind African Trade Mission; delegate, U.N. International Women's Conference; led Michigan Department of Agriculture delegation to the International Agriculture Show, Nairobi, Kenya; awards: Anthony Wayne Award for leadership, Wayne State University; Burton-Abercrombie Award, 13th Congressional District; Distinguished Legislator Award, University of Michigan; named Woman of the Year by Gentlemen of Wall Street, Inc.; listed in *Who's Who in Black America* and *Who's Who in American Politics*; U.S. Air Force Academy Board; 2nd vice-chair, Congressional Black Caucus; Women of Achievement and Courage Award; two children: Kwame and Ayanna; committee: Appropriations; elected to the 105th Congress; reelected to each succeeding Congress.

Office Listings

http://www.house.gov/kilpatrick

1610 Longworth House Office Building, Washington, DC 20515 .... (202) 225–2261
Chief of Staff.—Kimberly Rudolph.   FAX: 225–5730
Executive Assistant.—Gerri Houston.
Legislative Director.—Gene Fisher.
Press Secretary.—Denise Mixon.
1274 Library Street, Suite 1B, Detroit, MI 48226 .... (313) 965–9004

Counties: WAYNE COUNTY (part). Population (2000), 628,363.

ZIP Codes: 48146, 48178, 48192, 48195, 48201–18, 48220, 48222, 48224–26, 48229–34, 48236, 48238, 48242–44, 48255, 48260, 48264–69, 48272, 48275, 48277–79

* * *

FOURTEENTH DISTRICT

JOHN CONYERS, JR., Democrat, of Detroit, MI; born in Detroit, May 16, 1929; son of John and Lucille Conyers; education: graduated from Wayne State University (B.A., 1957); graduated from Wayne State Law School (LL.B., June 1958); served as officer in the U.S. Army Corps of Engineers, one year in Korea; awarded combat and merit citations; married to Monica Esters-Conyers; engaged in many civil rights and labor activities; legislative assistant to Congressman John D. Dingell, December 1958 to May 1961; appointed Referee for the Workmen's Compensation Department, State of Michigan, by Governor John B. Swainson in October 1961; former vice chairman of Americans for Democratic Action; vice chairman of the National Advisory Council of the ACLU; member: Kappa Alpha Psi; Wolverine Bar; NAACP; Tuskegee Airmen, Inc.; organizations: Congressional Black Caucus; Congressional Urban Caucus; Progressive Caucus; committees: ranking member, Judiciary; elected to the 89th Congress on November 3, 1964; reelected to each succeeding Congress.

Office Listings

http://www.house.gov/conyers   john.conyers@mail.house.gov

2426 Rayburn House Office Building, Washington, DC 20515 .... (202) 225–5126
Legislative Director.—Cynthia Martin.   FAX: 225–0072
Federal Courthouse, Suite 669, 231 West Lafayette, Detroit, MI 48226 .... (313) 961–5670

Counties: WAYNE COUNTY (part). CITIES AND TOWNSHIPS: Allen Park, Detroit, Dearborn, Gibraltar, Grosse Ile, Hamtramack, Highland Park, Melvindale, Riverview, Southgate, and Trenton. Population (2000), 662,563.

ZIP Codes: 48101–02, 48120–22, 48124, 48126–27, 48138, 48173, 48180, 48183, 48192, 48195, 48203–04, 48206, 48210–12, 48219, 48221, 48223, 48227–28, 48235, 48238–40

* * *

FIFTEENTH DISTRICT

JOHN D. DINGELL, Democrat, of Dearborn, MI; born in Colorado Springs, CO, July 8, 1926; education: B.S., Georgetown University, 1949; J.D., Georgetown University Law School, 1952; professional: World War II veteran; assistant Wayne County prosecutor, 1953–55; member: Migratory Bird Conservation Commission; married: the former Deborah Insley; committees: ranking member, Energy and Commerce; elected to the 84th Congress in a special election to fill the vacant seat of his late father, the Honorable John D. Dingell, December 13, 1955; reelected to the 85th and each succeeding Congress.

Office Listings
http://www.house.gov/dingell

2328 Rayburn House Office Building, Washington, DC 20515	(202) 225–4071
Chief of Staff.—Rick Kessler.	
Press Secretary.—Adam Benson.	
19855 West Outer Drive, Suite 103–E, Dearborn, MI 48124	(313) 278–2936
District Administrator.—Terry Spryszak.	
23 East Front Street, Suite 103, Monroe, MI 48161	(734) 243–1849
5 South Washington Street, Ypsilanti, MI 48197	(734) 481–1100

Counties: WAYNE COUNTY (part). CITIES AND TOWNSHIPS: Brownstown Township, Dearborn, Dearborn Heights, Flat Rock, Gibraltar, Rockwood, Romulus, Taylor, Woodhaven. MONROE COUNTY. CITIES AND TOWNSHIPS: Azalia, Carleton, Dundee, Erie, Ida, Lambertville, LaSalle, Luna Pier, Maybee, Milan, Monroe, Newport, Ottawa Lake, Petersburg, Samaria, S. Rockwood, Temperance. WASHTENAW COUNTY (part). CITIES AND TOWNSHIPS: Ann Arbor, Pittsfield Township, York Township, Superior Township, Ypsilanti, and Ypsilanti Township. Population (2000), 662,563.

ZIP Codes: 48103–11, 48113, 48117, 48123–28, 48131, 48133–34, 48140–41, 48144–45, 48157, 48159–62, 48164, 48166, 48170, 48173–74, 48176–77, 48179–80, 48182–84, 48186, 48190–92, 48197–98, 48228, 48239, 49228–29, 49238, 49267, 49270, 49276

MINNESOTA

(Population 2000, 4,919,479)

SENATORS

MARK DAYTON, Democrat, of Minneapolis, MN; born in Minneapolis, January 26, 1947; education: B.A., Yale University, 1969; professional: worked as a teacher in the New York, NY, public school system, 1969–71; also worked as a counselor and administrator for a Boston, MA, social services agency, 1971–75; religion: Presbyterian; public service: legislative assistant to Senator Walter Mondale, 1975–76; assistant to Minnesota Governor Rudy Perpich, 1977–78; Minnesota Commissioner of Energy and Economic Development, 1983–86; Minnesota State Auditor, 1991–95; committees: Agriculture, Nutrition, and Forestry; Armed Services; Homeland Security and Governmental Affairs; Rules and Administration; Joint Committee on Printing; elected to the U.S. Senate on November 7, 2000.

Office Listings
http://dayton.senate.gov

123 Russell Senate Office Building, Washington, DC 20510	(202) 224–3244
Chief of Staff.—Jack Danielson.	FAX: 228–2186
Office Manager.—Kristen Gentile.	
Legislative Director.—Chani Wiggins.	
Scheduler.—Britta Gustafson.	
Federal Building, Suite 298, Fort Snelling, MN 55111	(612) 727–5220
Chief of Staff.—Sharon Ruhland.	
401 DeMers Avenue, East Grand Forks, MN 56721	(218) 773–1110
P.O. Box 608, Renville, MN 56284	(320) 905–3007
222 Main Street, Suite 200, P.O. Box 937, Biwabik, MN 55708	(218) 865–4480

* * *

NORM COLEMAN, Republican, of St. Paul, MN; born in Brooklyn, NY, August 17, 1949; education: B.A., Hofstra University; J.D., University of Iowa; professional: attorney; public service: served for 17 years in the Minnesota Attorney General's office, holding the positions of Chief Prosecutor and Solicitor General of Minnesota; Mayor of St. Paul, MN, 1993–2001; Republican candidate for Governor of Minnesota, 1998; married: Laurie; children: Jacob and Sarah; committees: Agriculture, Nutrition, and Forestry; Foreign Relations; Homeland Security and Governmental Affairs; Small Business and Entrepreneurship; subcommittees: chair, Permanent Subcommittee on Investigations; elected to the U.S. Senate on November 5, 2002.

Office Listings
http://coleman.senate.gov

320 Hart Senate Office Building, Washington, DC 20510	(202) 224–5641
Chief of Staff.—Erich Mische.	FAX: 224–1152
Legislative Director.—Jeff Harrison.	
Administrative Director.—Lucia Lebens.	
Communications Director.—Tom Steward.	
2550 University Avenue West, Suite 100N, St. Paul, MN 55114	(651) 645–0323
State Director.—Bill Heupenbecker.	
12 Civic Center Plaza, Suite 2167, Mankato, MN 56001	(507) 625–6800

REPRESENTATIVES

FIRST DISTRICT

GIL GUTKNECHT, Republican, of Rochester, MN; born in Cedar Falls, IA, March 20, 1951; education: graduated, Cedar Falls High School; B.A., University of Northern Iowa; professional: real estate broker and auctioneer; served as State Representative, 1982–94, floor leader, House Republican Caucus; married: Mary Catherine Gutknecht, 1972; children: Margie, Paul, and Emily; committees: Agriculture; Government Reform; Science; subcommittees: chair, Department Operations, Oversight, Dairy, Nutrition and Forestry; elected to the 104th Congress; reelected to each succeeding Congress.

Office Listings
http://www.house.gov/gutknecht

425 Cannon House Office Building, Washington, DC 20515 ....   (202) 225–2472
   Chief of Staff.—Stephanie Brand.
   Legislative Director.—Ryan McLaughlin.
   Executive Assistant.—April Dabney.
   Legislative Assistants: Chris Grieco, Eric Keber, Julie Philp.
1530 Greenview Drive, SW., Suite 108, Rochester, MN 55902 ....   (507) 252–9841

Counties: BLUE EARTH COUNTY. CITIES: Amboy, Eagle Lake, Garden City, Good Thunder, Lake Crystal, Madison Lake, Mankato, Mapleton, Pemberton, St. Clair, Vernon Center. BROWN COUNTY. CITIES: Comfrey, Hanska, New Ulm, Sleepy Eye, Springfield. COTTONWOOD COUNTY. CITIES: Mountain Lake, Storedon, Westbrook. DODGE COUNTY. CITIES: Claremont, Dodge Center, Hayfield, Kasson, Mantorville, West Concord, Windom. FARIBAULT COUNTY. CITIES: Blue Earth, Bricelyn, Delavan, Easton, Elmore, Frost, Huntley, Kiester, Minnesota Lake, Walters, Wells, Winnebago. FILLMORE COUNTY. CITIES: Canton, Chatfield, Fountain, Harmony, Lanesboro, Mabel, Ostrander, Peterson, Preston, Rushford, Spring Valley, Whalan, Wykoff. FREEBORN COUNTY. CITIES: Albert Lea, Alden, Clarks Grove, Conger, Emmons, Freeborn, Geneva, Glenville, Hartland, Hayward, Hollandale, London, Manchester, Myrtle, Oakland, Twin Lakes. HOUSTON COUNTY. CITIES: Brownsville, Caledonia, Eitzen, Hokah, Houston, La Crescent, Spring Grove. JACKSON COUNTY. CITIES: Heron, Jackson, Lake Field. MARTIN COUNTY. CITY: Fairmont. MOWER COUNTY. CITIES: Adams, Austin, Brownsdale, Dexter, Elkton, Grand Meadow, Lansing, LeRoy, Lyle, Rose Creek, Sargeant, Taopi, Waltham. MURRAY COUNTY. CITIES: Fulda, Slayton. NICOLLET COUNTY. CITIES: North Mankato, St. Peter. NOBLES COUNTY. CITIES: Adrian, Worthington. OLMSTED COUNTY. CITIES: Byron, Dover, Eyota, Oronoco, Rochester, Stewartville, Viola. PIPESTONE COUNTY. CITIES: Edgerton, Jasper, Pipestone Ruthton. ROCK COUNTY. CITY: Lurverne. STEELE COUNTY. CITIES: Blooming Prairie, Ellendale, Hope, Medford, Meriden, Owatonna. WABASHA COUNTY. CITIES: Elgin, Hammond, Kellogg, Lake City, Mazeppa, Milleville, Plainview, Reads Landing, Theilman, Wabasha. WASECA COUNTY. CITIES: Janesville, New Richland, Otisco, Waldorf, Waseca. WATONWAN COUNTY. CITIES: Madelia, St. James. WINONA COUNTY. CITIES: Altura, Dakota, Goodview, Homer, Lewiston, Minnesota City, Rollingstone, St. Charles, Stockton, Utica, and Winona. Population (2000), 614,935.

ZIP Codes: 55021, 55027, 55041, 55049, 55052; 55060, 55901–06, 55909–10, 55912, 55917–27, 55929, 55931–36, 55939–47, 55949–57, 55959–65, 55967–77, 55979, 55981–83, 55985, 55987–88, 55990–92, 56001–03, 56006–07, 56009–11, 56013–14, 56016, 56019–21, 56023–29, 56031; 56033–34, 56036–37, 56039, 56041–43, 56045–48, 56050–51, 56054–55, 56058, 56060, 56062–63, 56065, 56068, 56072–74, 56078, 56080–83, 56085, 56087–91, 56093, 56096–98, 56101, 56110–11, 56114–23, 56125, 56127–29, 56131, 56134, 56136–41, 56143–47, 56149–53, 56155–56, 56158–62, 56164–68, 56170–74, 56176–77, 56180–81, 56183, 56185–87, 56266

* * *

SECOND DISTRICT

JOHN KLINE, Republican, of Lakeville, MN; born in Allentown, PA, September 6, 1947; education: B.A., Rice University, 1969; M.P.A., Shippensburg University, 1988; military service: U.S. Marine Corps, 1969–1994; retired at the rank of Colonel; organizations: Boy Scouts of America; Marine Corps League; Veterans of Foreign Wars; Marine Corps Association; American Legion; Retired Officers Association; past president, Marine Corps Coordinating Council of Minnesota; religion: Methodist; family: married to Vicky; children: Kathy and Dan; committees: Armed Services; Education and the Workforce; elected to the 108th Congress on November 5, 2002; reelected to each succeeding Congress.

Office Listings
http://www.house.gov/kline

1429 Longworth House Office Building, Washington, DC 20515 ....   (202) 225–2271
   Chief of Staff.—Steven Sutton.   FAX: 225–2595
   Legislative Director.—Jean Hinz.
   Executive Assistant.—Brooke Dorobiala.
   Press Secretary.—Angelyn Shapiro.
101 West Burnsville Parkway, Suite 201, Burnsville, MN 55337 ....   (952) 808–1213

Counties: CARVER COUNTY. CITIES: Chanhassen, Chaska, Waconia, Victoria. DAKOTA COUNTY (part). CITIES: Apple Valley, Burnsville, Eagan, Farmington, Hastings, Inver Grove Heights. GOODHUE COUNTY. CITIES: Cannon Falls, Pine Island, Red Wing, Zumbrota. LE SUEUR COUNTY. CITIES: Le Sueur, Le Center, Montgomery. RICE COUNTY. CITIES: Faribault, Northfield. SCOTT COUNTY. CITIES: Shakopee, Savage, Prior Lake, New Prague, Jordan, Belle Plaine. WASHINGTON COUNTY (part). CITIES: Woodbury, and Cottage Grove. Population (2000), 614,934.

ZIP Codes: 55001, 55009–10, 55016, 55018–20, 55021, 55024, 55026–27, 55031, 55033, 55041, 55044, 55046, 55049, 55052–54, 55057, 55065–66, 55068, 55076–77, 55085, 55087–89, 55103, 55118, 55121–25, 55129, 55306, 55313, 55315, 55317–18, 55322, 55328, 55330–31, 55336–37, 55339, 55350, 55352, 55360, 55367–68, 55371–75, 55378–79, 55382–83, 55386–88, 55393–94, 55397, 55399, 55550–54, 55556–60, 55562, 55564–68, 55573, 55575, 55580–91, 55594, 55946, 55951, 55953, 55956, 55963, 55983, 55985, 55992, 56011, 56014, 56017, 56022–26, 56028, 56030–32, 56035, 56037, 56039, 56042, 56044, 56046–47, 56050, 56052, 56056–58, 56063, 56065, 56068–69, 56071, 56096

THIRD DISTRICT

JIM RAMSTAD, Republican, of Minnetonka, MN; born in Jamestown, ND, May 6, 1946; education: University of Minnesota, B.A., Phi Beta Kappa, 1968; George Washington University, J.D. with honors, 1973; military service: first lieutenant, U.S. Army Reserve, 1968–74; elected to the Minnesota Senate, 1980; reelected 1982, 1986; assistant minority leader; attorney; adjunct professor; Representative of the Year by the National Association of Police Organizations, 1997, 2000; Legislator of the Year by the National Association of Alcoholism and Drug Addiction Counselors, 1998; Legislator of the Year by the National Mental Health Association, 1999; Fulbright Distinguished Public Service award; co-chair, Medical Technology Caucus; co-chair, Law Enforcement Caucus; co-chair, Addiction, Treatment and Recovery Caucus; committee: Ways and Means; subcommittee: chair, Oversight; elected to the 102nd Congress, November 6, 1990; reelected to each succeeding Congress.

Office Listings

103 Cannon House Office Building, Washington, DC 20515 .... (202) 225–2871
    Administrative Assistant.—Dean Peterson.
    Legislative Director.—Karin Hope.
    Executive Assistant/Scheduler.—Valerie Nelson.
1809 Plymouth Road South, Suite 300, Minnetonka, MN 55305 .... (952) 738–8200
    District Director.—Lance Olson.

Counties: ANOKA (part), HENNEPIN (part). CITIES AND TOWNSHIPS: Bloomington, Brooklyn Center, Brooklyn Park, Champlin, Coon Rapids, Corcoran, Dayton, Deephaven, Eden Prarie, Edina, Excelsior, Greenwood, Hassan, Hopkins, Independence, Long Lake, Loretto, Maple Grove, Maple Plain, Medicine Lake, Medina, Minnetonka Beach, Minnetonka, Minnetrista, Mound, Orono, Osseo, Plymouth, Rogers, Saint Bonifacius, Shorewood, Spring Park, Tonka Bay, Wayzata, and Woodland. Population (2000), 614,935.

ZIP Codes: 55304–05, 55311, 55316, 55323, 55327, 55331, 55340–41, 55343–48, 55356–57, 55359, 55361, 55364, 55369, 55373–75, 55378, 55384, 55387–88, 55391–92, 55410, 55416, 55420, 55422–26, 55428–31, 55433, 55435–39, 55441–48, 55569–72, 55574, 55576–79, 55592–93, 55595–99

* * *

FOURTH DISTRICT

BETTY McCOLLUM, Democrat, of North St. Paul, MN; born in Minneapolis, MN, July 12, 1954; education: A.A., Inver Hills Community College; B.S., College of St. Catherine; professional: teacher and sales manager; single; children: Sean and Katie; public service: North St. Paul City Council, 1986–1992; Minnesota House of Representatives, 1992–2000; organizations: Girl Scouts of America; VFW Ladies' Auxiliary; and American Legion Ladies' Auxiliary; elected Midwest Regional Whip 2002; appointments: Democratic Steering and Policy Committee; National Council on the Arts; Regional Whip; committees: Education and the Workforce; International Relations; elected to the 107th Congress on November 7, 2000; reelected to each succeeding Congress.

Office Listings

http://www.house.gov/mccollum

1029 Longworth House Office Building, Washington, DC 20515 .... (202) 225–6631
    Chief of Staff.—Bill Harper.   FAX: 225–1968
    Legislative Director.—Stacy Stordahl.
    Office Director.—Shelly Schafer.
165 Western Avenue North, Suite 17, St. Paul, MN 55102 .... (651) 224–9191
    Communications/District Director.—Joshua Straka.

Counties: DAKOTA (part), RAMSEY, WASHINGTON (part). Population (2000), 614,935.

ZIP Codes: 55016, 55042, 55055, 55071, 55075–77, 55090, 55101–10, 55112–20, 55125–29, 55133, 55144, 55146, 55150, 55155, 55161, 55164–66, 55168–70, 55172, 55175, 55177, 55182, 55187–88, 55190–91, 55199, 55421, 55432, 55449

* * *

FIFTH DISTRICT

MARTIN OLAV SABO, Democrat-Farmer-Labor, of Minneapolis, MN; born in Crosby, ND, February 28, 1938; education: graduated Alkabo High School, ND, 1955; B.A., Augsburg College, Minneapolis, MN, 1959; graduate studies, University of Minnesota, 1960;

served in the Minnesota House of Representatives, 1961–78; served as House Democrat-Farmer-Labor minority leader, 1969–73; Speaker of the House, 1973–78; presidential appointee to the National Advisory Commission on Intergovernmental Relations; president, National Conference of State Legislatures; president, National Legislative Conference; chairman, Intergovernmental Relations Committee of the National Conference of State Legislatures; Nuclear Test Ban Leadership Award, 1992; Arms Control Leadership Award, 1988; Endowment for Leadership in Community and Public Service, established in his name, 1994; Distinguished Service Award from the Committee on Education Funding, 1994; inducted into the Scandinavian American Hall of Fame, October 12, 1994; honorary lifetime member, Hospital and Nursing Home Employees Union, Local No. 113, SEIU AFL–CIO; Minneapolis Jaycees Man of the Year Award, 1973–74; Augsburg College Distinguished Alumnus Citation; Lloyd M. Short Merit Award of the Minnesota Chapter of the American Society for Public Administration; chair, House Budget committee, 1993–1994; married: the former Sylvia Lee, 1963; children: Karin and Julie; 6 grandchildren; committees: Appropriations; subcommittees: Defense; ranking member, Homeland Security; elected to the 96th Congress, November 7, 1978; reelected to each succeeding Congress.

Office Listings
http://sabo.house.gov

2336 Rayburn House Office Building, Washington, DC 20515 .... (202) 225–4755
Chief of Staff.—Michael Erlandson.   FAX: 225–4886
Press Secretary.—Jenifer McCormick.
Office Manager.—Bonnie Gottwald.
Marquette Plaza, 250 Marquette Avenue, Suite 225, Minneapolis, MN 55401 .... (612) 664–8000

Counties: ANOKA (part), HENNEPIN (part), RAMSEY (part). CITIES: Columbia Heights, Crystal, Ft. Snelling, Fridley, Golden Valley, Hilltop, Hopkins, Minneapolis, New Hope, Richfield, Robbinsdale, St. Anthony, St. Louis Park, and Spring Lake Park, Population (2000), 614,935.

ZIP Codes: 55111–12, 55305, 55343, 55401–30, 55432–33, 55440–41, 55450, 55454–55, 55458–60, 55470, 55472, 55474, 55479–80, 55483–88

* * *

SIXTH DISTRICT

MARK R. KENNEDY, Republican, of Watertown, MN; born in Benson, MN, April 11, 1957; education: B.A., St. John's University; M.B.A., University of Michigan; professional: businessman; certified public accountant, Arthur Andersen; executive positions with Department 56, Shopko Stores, and Pillsbury; organizations: Minnesota Rough Riders Issues Forum; Center of the American Experiment; Lions Club; married: Debbie; children: Charles, Emily, Sarah, and Peter; committees: Financial Services; Transportation and Infrastructure; elected to the 107th Congress on November 7, 2000; reelected to each succeeding Congress.

Office Listings
http://markkennedy.house.gov

1415 Longworth House Office Building, Washington, DC 20515 .... (202) 225–2331
Chief of Staff.—Pat Shortridge.   FAX: 225–6475
Executive Assistant.—Elisa Thiede.
Legislative Director.—Edward Skala.
District Director.—Mark Matuska.
1111 Highway 25 North, Suite 204, Buffalo, MN 55313 .... (763) 684–1600
22 Wilson Avenue, NE., Suite 104, P.O. Box 6010, St. Cloud, MN 56302 .... (320) 259–0992
14660 Fitzgerald Avenue, North, Suite 100, Hugo, MN 55038 .... (651) 653–5933

Counties: ANOKA (part), BENTON, SHERBURNE, STEARNS (part), WASHINGTON (part), WRIGHT. CITIES: Andover, Anoka, Blaine, Elk River, Forest Lake, Lino Lakes, St. Cloud, Stillwater, Ramsey, and Woodbury. Population (2000), 614,935.

ZIP Codes: 55001, 55003, 55005–06, 55011, 55014, 55025, 55031, 55038, 55042–43, 55047, 55070, 55073, 55079, 55082–83, 55092, 55110, 55112, 55115, 55125, 55128–29, 55301–04, 55308–09, 55313, 55319–21, 55328–30, 55341, 55349, 55353, 55358–59, 55362–63, 55365, 55371, 55373–74, 55376, 55380–82, 55388–90, 55395, 55398, 55412–13, 55417–18, 55429–30, 55432, 55434, 55448–49, 56301, 56303–04, 56307, 56310, 56314, 56320, 56329–31, 56340, 56352, 56357, 56362, 56367–68, 56373–75, 56377, 56379, 56387–88, 56393, 56395–99

SEVENTH DISTRICT

COLLIN C. PETERSON, Democrat, of Detroit Lakes, MN; born in Fargo, ND, June 29, 1944; education: graduated from Glyndon (MN) High School, 1962; B.A., Moorhead State University, 1966: (business administration and accounting); U.S. Army National Guard, 1963–69; CPA, owner and partner; Minnesota State Senator, 1976–86; member: AOPA, Safari Club, Ducks Unlimited, American Legion, Sea Plane Pilots Association, Pheasants Forever, Benevolent Protective Order of Elks, Cormorant Lakes Sportsmen Club; three children: Sean, Jason, and Elliott; committees: ranking member, Agriculture; elected to the 102nd Congress, November 6, 1990; reelected to each succeeding Congress.

Office Listings
http://collinpeterson.house.gov

2159 Rayburn House Office Building, Washington, DC 20515 .... (202) 225–2165
    Assistants: Liz Bolstad, Mark Brownell, Jim Creevy, Robin Goracke, Chris
    Iacaruso, Cherie Slayton.
Lake Avenue Plaza Building, Suite 107, 714 Lake Avenue, Detroit Lakes, MN
    56501 .... (218) 847–5056
Minnesota Wheat Growers Building, 2603 Wheat Drive, Red Lake, MN 56750 ..... (218) 253–4356
320 Southwest Fourth Street, Centre Point Mall, Willmar, MN 56201 .... (320) 235–1061

Counties: BECKER, BELTRAMI (part), BIG STONE, CHIPPEWA, CLAY, CLEARWATER, DOUGLAS, GRANT, KANDIYOHI, KITTSON, LAC QUI PARLE, LAKE OF THE WOODS, LINCOLN, LYON, MAHNOMEN, MARSHALL, MCLEOD, MEEKER, NORMAN, OTTER TAIL, PENNINGTON, POLK, POPE, RED LAKE, REDWOOD, RENVILLE, ROSEAU, SIBLEY, STEARNS (part), STEVENS, SWIFT, TODD, TRAVERSE, WILKIN, YELLOW MEDICINE. Population (2000) 614,935.

ZIP Codes: 55307, 55310, 55312, 55314, 55321, 55324–25, 55329, 55332–36, 55338–39, 55342, 55350, 55353–55, 55366, 55368, 55370, 55381–82, 55385, 55389, 55395–96, 55409, 55970, 56011, 56044, 56054, 56058, 56083, 56085, 56087, 56113, 56115, 56129, 56132, 56136, 56142, 56149, 56152, 56157, 56164, 56166, 56169–70, 56175, 56178, 56180, 56201, 56207–12, 56214–16, 56218–32, 56235–37, 56239–41, 56243–45, 56248–49, 56251–53, 56255–58, 56260, 56262–67, 56270–71, 56273–74, 56276–85, 56287–89, 56291–97, 56301–04, 56307–12, 56314–16, 56318–21, 56323–24, 56326–27, 56329, 56331–32, 56334, 56336, 56339–40, 56343, 56345, 56347, 56349, 56352, 56354–55, 56360–62, 56368, 56372–74, 56377–79, 56381–82, 56385, 56387, 56393, 56395–99, 56433–34, 56436–38, 56440, 56443, 56446, 56453, 56458, 56461, 56464, 56466–67, 56470, 56475, 56477–79, 56481–82, 56501–02, 56510–11, 56514–25, 56527–29, 56531, 56533–38, 56540–54, 56556–57, 56560–63, 56565–81, 56583–94, 56601, 56619, 56621, 56623, 56633–34, 56644, 56646–47, 56650–52, 56661, 56663, 56666–67, 56670–71, 56673, 56676, 56678, 56682–87, 56701, 56710–11, 56713–16, 56720–29, 56731–38, 56740–42, 56744, 56748, 56750–51, 56754–63

* * *

EIGHTH DISTRICT

JAMES L. OBERSTAR, Democrat, of Chisholm, MN; born in Chisholm, September 10, 1934; education: graduated, Chisholm High School, 1952; B.A., *summa cum laude*, French and political science, College of St. Thomas, St. Paul, MN, 1956; M.A., European area studies, College of Europe, Bruges, Belgium, 1957; Laval University, Canada; Georgetown University, former teacher of English, French, and Creole; served as administrative assistant to the late Congressman John A. Blatnik, 1963–74; administrator of the House Public Works Committee, 1971–74; co-chair, Congressional Travel and Tourism Caucus; Democratic Study Group; Great Lakes Task Force; National Water Alliance; Northeast Midwest Congressional Coalition; Steel Caucus; Conference of Great Lakes Congressmen (chairman); married: Jean Kurth, 1993; children: Thomas Edward, Katherine Noelle, Anne-Therese, Monica Rose, Charlie, and Lindy; committee: ranking member, Transportation and Infrastructure; elected to the 94th Congress, November 5, 1974; reelected to each succeeding Congress.

Office Listings
http://www.house.gov/oberstar

2365 Rayburn House Office Building, Washington, DC 20515 .... (202) 225–6211
    Administrative Assistant.—William Richard.
    Office Manager.—Marianne Buckley.
    Legislative Director.—Chip Gardiner.
    Communications Director.—Mary Kerr.
231 Federal Building, Duluth, MN 55802 .... (218) 727–7474
    District Manager.—Jackie Morris.
Chisholm City Hall, 316 West Lake Street, Chisholm, MN 55719 .... (218) 254–5761
    District Representative.—Peter Makowski.
Brainerd City Hall, 501 Laurel Street, Brainerd, MN 56401 .... (218) 828–4400
    District Representative.—Ken Hasskamp.
38625 14th Avenue, Suite 300B, North Branch, MN 55056 .... (651) 277–1234
    District Representative.—Alana Petersen.

Counties: AITKIN, BELTRAMI (part), CARLTON, CASS, CHISAGO, COOK, CROW WING, HUBBARD, ISANTI, ITASCA, KANABEC, KOOCHICHING, LAKE, MILLE LACS, MORRISON, PINE, ST. LOUIS, WADENA. CITIES: Brainerd, Chisholm, Cloquet, Duluth, Grand Rapids, Hibbing, International Falls, and Little Falls. Population (2000), 614,935.

ZIP Codes: 55002, 55005–08, 55012–13, 55017, 55025, 55029–30, 55032, 55036–37, 55040, 55045, 55051, 55056, 55063, 55067, 55069–70, 55072–74, 55078–80, 55084, 55092, 55330–31, 55362, 55371, 55377, 55398, 55408, 55601–07, 55609, 55612–16, 55701–13, 55716–26, 55730–36, 55738, 55741–42, 55744–46, 55748–53, 55756–58, 55760, 55763–69, 55771–72, 55775, 55777, 55779–87, 55790–93, 55795–98, 55801–08, 55810–12, 55814–16, 56028, 56058, 56304, 56307, 56309–11, 56313–15, 56317–19, 56323, 56325–33, 56335–36, 56338–45, 56347, 56350, 56353–61, 56363–64, 56367–69, 56371, 56373, 56376–77, 56381–82, 56384, 56386, 56389, 56401, 56425, 56430–31, 56433–35, 56437, 56441–44, 56446–50, 56452–53, 56455–56, 56458–59, 56461, 56464–70, 56472–75, 56477, 56479, 56481–82, 56484, 56601, 56623, 56626–31, 56633, 56636–37, 56639, 56641, 56647, 56649, 56653–55, 56657–63, 56668–69, 56672, 56678–81, 56683, 56688

MISSISSIPPI

(Population 2000, 2,844,658)

SENATORS

THAD COCHRAN, Republican, of Jackson, MS; born in Pontotoc, MS, December 7, 1937; education: B.A., University of Mississippi, 1959; J.D., University of Mississippi Law School, 1965; received a Rotary Foundation Fellowship and studied international law and jurisprudence at Trinity College, University of Dublin, Ireland, 1963–64; military service: served in U.S. Navy, 1959–61; professional: admitted to Mississippi bar in 1965; board of directors, Jackson Rotary Club, 1970–71; Outstanding Young Man of the Year Award, Junior Chamber of Commerce in Mississippi, 1971; president, young lawyers section of Mississippi State bar, 1972–73; married: the former Rose Clayton of New Albany, MS, 1964; two children and two grandsons; elected to the 93rd Congress, November 7, 1972; reelected to 94th and 95th Congresses; chairman of the Senate Republican Conference, 1990–96; committees: chairman, Appropriations; Agriculture, Nutrition, and Forestry; Rules and Administration; Joint Committee on the Library of Congress; Joint Committee on Printing; co-chairman, National Security Working Group; elected to the U.S. Senate, November 7, 1978, for the six-year term beginning January 3, 1979; subsequently appointed by the governor, December 27, 1978, to fill the vacancy caused by the resignation of Senator James O. Eastland; reelected to each succeeding Senate term.

Office Listings
http://cochran.senate.gov

113 Dirksen Senate Office Building, Washington, DC 20510	(202) 224–5054
Chief of Staff.—Mark E. Keenum.	
Legislative Director.—Blake Thompson.	
Office Manager.—Mary-Cates Permenter.	
Scheduler.—Doris Wagley.	
188 East Capitol Street, Suite 614, Jackson, MS 39201	(601) 965–4459
P.O. Box 1434, Oxford, MS 38655	(662) 236–1018
14094 Customs Boulevard, Suite 201, Gulfport, MS 39503	(228) 867–9710

* * *

TRENT LOTT, Republican, of Pascagoula, MS; born in Grenada, MS, October 9, 1941; son of Chester P. and Iona (Watson) Lott; education: University of Mississippi, B.P.A., 1963, J.D., 1967; served as field representative for the University of Mississippi, 1963–65; acting Law Alumni Secretary of the Ole Miss Alumni Association, 1966–67; practiced law in Pascagoula in 1967 with Bryan and Gordon law firm; administrative assistant to Congressman William M. Colmer, 1968–72; member: Sigma Nu social fraternity, Phi Alpha Delta legal fraternity, Jackson County Bar Association, American Bar Association, the Masons, First Baptist Church of Pascagoula; married Patricia E. Thompson of Pascagoula, 1964; two children: Chester T., Jr. and Tyler Elizabeth; elected to the 93rd Congress, November 7, 1972; reelected to each succeeding Congress; elected to the U.S. Senate on November 8, 1988; Republican Whip, 1995–1996; Senate Republican Leader, 1996–2003; committees: Commerce, Science, and Transportation; Finance; chairman, Rules and Administration; Select Committee on Intelligence; chairman, Joint Congressional Committee on Inaugural Ceremonies; Joint Committee on the Library of Congress; chairman, Joint Committee on Printing; Joint Committee on Taxation; subcommittee: Surface Transportation and Merchant Marine; reelected to each succeeding Senate term.

Office Listings
http://lott.senate.gov

487 Russell Senate Office Building, Washington, DC 20510	(202) 224–6253
Chief of Staff.—William Gottshall.	FAX: 224–2262
Scheduler.—Hardy Lott.	
Press Secretary.—Lee Youngblood.	
Legislative Director.—Jim Sartucci.	
245 East Capitol Street, Suite 226, Jackson, MS 39201	(601) 965–4644
3100 South Pascagoula Street, Pascagoula, MS 39567	(228) 762–5400
2012 15th Street, Suite 451, Gulfport, MS 39501	(228) 863–1988
911 Jackson Avenue, Suite 127, Oxford, MS 38655	(662) 234–3774

REPRESENTATIVES

FIRST DISTRICT

ROGER F. WICKER, Republican, of Tupelo, MS; born in Pontotoc, MS, July 5, 1951; education: graduated, Pontotoc High School; University of Mississippi: B.A., 1973, J.D., 1975; president, Associated Student Body, 1972–73; Mississippi Law Journal, 1973–75; Air Force ROTC; U.S. Air Force, 1976–80; lieutenant colonel, U.S. Air Force Reserve, 1980–2004; U.S. House of Representatives Rules Committee staff for Representative Trent Lott, 1980–82; private law practice, 1982–94; Lee County Public Defender, 1984–87; Tupelo City Judge pro tempore, 1986–87; Mississippi State Senate, 1988–94, chairman: Elections Committee (1992), Public Health and Welfare Committee (1993–94); member: Lions Club; University of Mississippi Hall of Fame; Sigma Nu Fraternity; Omicron Delta Kappa; Phi Delta Phi; religion: Southern Baptist, deacon, adult choir, First Baptist Church, Tupelo, MS; married: Gayle Long Wicker; children: Margaret, Caroline and McDaniel; committees: Appropriations; Budget; deputy majority whip; Republican Policy Committee; elected to the 104th Congress, November 8, 1994; president, Republican freshman class, 1995; reelected to each succeeding Congress.

Office Listings
http://www.house.gov/wicker

2455 Rayburn House Office Building, Washington, DC 20515	(202) 225–4306
Chief of Staff.—John Keast.	
500 West Main Street, Suite 210, P.O. Box 1482, Tupelo, MS 38802	(662) 844–5437
Administrative Assistant/Press Secretary.—Kyle Steward.	
8700 Northwest Drive, Suite 102, P.O. Box 70, Southaven, MS 38671	(662) 342–3942
1360 Sunset Drive, Suite 2, Grenada, MS 38901	(662) 294–1321
523 Main Street, Columbus, MS 39701	(662) 327–0748

Counties: ALCORN, BENTON, CALHOUN, CHICKASAW, CHOCTAW, CLAY, DESOTO, GRENADA, ITTAWAMBA, LAFAYETTE, LEE, LOWNDES, MARSHALL, MONROE, PANOLA, PONTOTOC, PRENTISS, TATE, TIPPAH, TISHOMINGO, UNION, WEBSTER (part), WINSTON (part), YALOBUSHA. Population (2000), 711,160.

ZIP Codes: 38601–03, 38606, 38610–11, 38618–21, 38625, 38627, 38629, 38632–35, 38637–38, 38641–42, 38647, 38649–52, 38654–55, 38658–59, 38661, 38663, 38665–66, 38668, 38670–74, 38677, 38679–80, 38683, 38685–86, 38801–04, 38820–21, 38824–29, 38833–35, 38838–39, 38841, 38843–44, 38846–52, 38854–60, 38862–66, 38868–71, 38873–80, 38901–02, 38913–16, 38920, 38922, 38925–27, 38929, 38940, 38948–49, 38951, 38953, 38955, 38960–61, 38965, 39108, 39339, 39701–05, 39710, 39730, 39735–37, 39740–41, 39743–46, 39750–56, 39759, 39766–67, 39769, 39771–73, 39776

* * *

SECOND DISTRICT

BENNIE G. THOMPSON, Democrat, of Bolton, MS; born in Bolton, January 28, 1948; education: graduated, Hinds County Agriculture High School; B.A., Tougaloo College, 1968; M.S., Jackson State University, 1972; teacher; Bolton Board of Aldermen, 1969–73; mayor of Bolton, 1973–79; Hinds County Board of Supervisors, 1980–93; married to the former London Johnson, Ph.D.; one daughter: BendaLonne; Congressional Black Caucus; Sunbelt Caucus; Rural Caucus; Progressive Caucus; Housing Assistance Council; NAACP 100 Black Men of Jackson, MS; Southern Regional Council; Kappa Alpha Psi Fraternity; committees: ranking member, Homeland Security; elected to the 103rd Congress in a special election; reelected to each succeeding Congress.

Office Listings
http://www.house.gov/thompson   thompsonms2nd@mail.house.gov

2432 Rayburn House Office Building, Washington, DC 20515	(202) 225–5876
Administrative Assistant.—Marsha G. McCraven.	FAX: 225–5898
Communications Director.—Lanier Avant.	
Office Manager.—Tara Smith.	
107 West Madison Street, P.O. Box 610, Bolton, MS 39041–0610	(601) 866–9003
District Director.—Charlie Horhn.	
3607 Medgar Evers Boulevard, Jackson, MS 39213	(601) 982–8582
263 East Main Street, Marks, MS 38646	(662) 326–9003
Mound Bayou City Hall, Room 134, 106 West Green Street, Mound Bayou, MS 38762	(662) 741–9003
509 Highway 82 West, Greenwood, MS 38930	(662) 455–9003
910 Courthouse Lane, Greenville, MS 38701	(662) 335–9003

Counties: ATTALA, BOLIVAR, CARROLL, CLAIBORNE, COAHOMA, COPIAH, HINDS (part), HOLMES, HUMPHREYS, ISSAQUENA, JEFFERSON, LEAKE (part), LEFLORE, MADISON (part), MONTGOMERY, QUITMAN, SHARKEY, SUNFLOWER, TALLAHATCHIE, TUNICA, WARREN, WASHINGTON, YAZOO. Population (2000), 711,164.

ZIP Codes: 38606, 38609, 38614, 38617, 38621–23, 38626, 38628, 38630–31, 38639, 38643–46, 38664–65, 38669–70, 38676, 38701–04, 38720–23, 38725–26, 38730–33, 38736–40, 38744–46, 38748–49, 38751, 38753–54, 38756, 38758–62, 38764–65, 38767–69, 38771–74, 38776, 38778, 38780–82, 38901, 38912, 38917, 38920–21, 38923–25, 38927–28, 38930, 38935, 38940–41, 38943–48, 38950, 38952–54, 38957–59, 38961–64, 38966–67, 39038–41, 39045–46, 39051, 39054, 39056, 39058–61, 39063, 39066–67, 39069, 39071–72, 39077–79, 39083, 39086, 39088, 39090, 39095–97, 39107–08, 39110, 39113, 39115, 39120, 39144, 39146, 39150, 39154, 39156–57, 39159–60, 39162–63, 39166, 39169–71, 39173–77, 39179–83, 39191–92, 39194, 39201–07, 39209–10, 39212–13, 39215–17, 39225, 39235, 39269, 39271–72, 39282–84, 39286, 39289, 39296, 39653, 39661, 39668, 39745, 39747, 39767

* * *

THIRD DISTRICT

CHARLES W. (CHIP) PICKERING, Jr., Republican, of Laurel, MS; born in Laurel, August 10, 1963; education: B.A., Business Administration, University of Mississippi, 1986; M.B.A., Baylor University; professional: farmer; legislative aide to Senate Majority Leader Trent Lott, 1992–96; Bush administration appointee, U.S. Department of Agriculture, 1989–91; Southern Baptist missionary to Budapest, Hungary, 1986–87; Congressional Wireless Caucus; married: the former Leisha Jane Prather; children: Will, Ross, Jackson, Asher, and Harper; assistant whip at large; committees: Energy and Commerce; subcommittees: Energy and Air Quality; Health; Oversight and Investigations; Telecommunications and the Internet; elected to the 105th Congress; reelected to each succeeding Congress.

Office Listings

http://www.house.gov/pickering

229 Cannon House Office Building, Washington, DC 20515	(202) 225–5031
Chief of Staff.—Susan Butler.	FAX: 225–5797
Press Secretary.—Brian Perry.	
Legislative Director.—Mike Hurst.	
Scheduler.—Marcy Scoggins.	
110–D Airport Road, Pearl, MS 39208	(601) 932–2410
District Director.—Stanley Shows.	
823 22nd Avenue, Meridian, MS 39301	(601) 693–6681
Staff Assistants: Lynne Compton, Carol Mabry.	
1 Research Boulevard, Suite 206, Starkville, MS 39759	(662) 324–0007
District Representative.—Henry Moseley.	
230 South Whitworth Street, Brookhaven, MS 39601	(601) 823–3400
Staff Assistant.—Mary Martha Dixon.	
308 Franklin Street, Natchez, MS 39120	(601) 442–2515

Counties: ADAMS, AMITE, COVINGTON, FRANKLIN, HINDS (part), JASPER (part), JEFF DAVIS, JONES (part), KEMPER, LAUDERDALE, LAWRENCE, LEAKE (part), LINCOLN, MADISON (part), MARION (part), NESHOBA, NEWTON, NOXUBEE, OKTIBBEHA, PIKE, RANKIN, SCOTT, SIMPSON, SMITH, WALTHALL, WEBSTER (part), WILKINSON, WINSTON. Population (2000), 711,164.

ZIP Codes: 39041–44, 39046–47, 39051, 39057, 39062, 39069, 39071, 39073–74, 39078, 39080, 39082–83, 39087, 39090, 39092, 39094, 39098, 39108–12, 39114, 39116–17, 39119–22, 39130, 39140, 39145, 39148–49, 39151–53, 39157–58, 39161, 39165, 39167–68, 39189–91, 39193, 39202, 39206, 39208–09, 39211, 39213, 39216, 39218, 39232, 39236, 39288, 39298, 39301–05, 39307, 39309, 39320, 39323, 39325–28, 39332, 39335–39, 39341–42, 39345–46, 39350, 39352, 39354, 39358–59, 39361, 39364–65, 39402, 39421–22, 39427–29, 39439, 39443, 39460, 39474, 39478–80, 39482–83, 39601–03, 39629–33, 39635, 39638, 39641, 39643, 39645, 39647–49, 39652–54, 39656–57, 39661–69, 39701, 39735, 39739, 39743, 39750, 39755, 39759–60, 39762, 39769

* * *

FOURTH DISTRICT

GENE TAYLOR, Democrat, of Bay St. Louis, MS; born in New Orleans, LA, September 17, 1953; education: graduated from De LaSalle High School, New Orleans, LA, 1971; B.A., Tulane University, New Orleans, LA, 1974; graduate studies in business and economics, University of Southern Mississippi, August 1978–April 1980; U.S. Coast Guard Reserves, 1971–84, first class petty officer, search and rescue boat skipper; sales representative, Stone Container Corporation, 1977–89; city councilman, Bay St. Louis, 1981–83; State Senator, 1983–89; member: American Legion; Rotary; Boys and Girls Club of the Gulf Coast; married the former Margaret Gordon, 1978; children: Sarah, Emily, Gary; committees: Armed Services; Transportation and Infrastructure; elected to the 101st Congress, by special election, on October 17, 1989, to fill the vacancy caused by the death of Larkin Smith; reelected to each succeeding Congress.

Office Listings
http://www.house.gov/genetaylor

2311 Rayburn House Office Building, Washington, DC 20515 .... (202) 225–5772
   Chief of Staff.—Stephen Peranich.   FAX: 225–7074
   Legislative Director.—Stacy Ballow.
   Executive Assistant.—Courtney Littig.
2424 Fourteenth Street, Gulfport, MS 39501 .... (228) 864–7670
   District Manager.—Beau Gex.
215 Federal Building, 701 Main Street, Hattiesburg, MS 39401 .... (601) 582–3246
1314 Government Street, Ocean Springs, MS 39564 .... (228) 872–7950
527 Central Avenue, Laurel, MS 39440 .... (601) 425–3905

Counties: CLARKE, FORREST, GEORGE, GREENE, HANCOCK, HARRISON, JACKSON, JASPER (part), JONES, LAMAR, MARION (part), PEARL RIVER, PERRY, STONE, WAYNE. CITIES AND TOWNSHIPS: Biloxi, Gulfport, Hattiesburg, Laurel, and Pascagoula. Population (2000), 711,170.

ZIP Codes: 39301, 39307, 39322, 39324, 39330, 39332, 39347–48, 39355–56, 39360, 39362–63, 39366–67, 39401–04, 39406, 39422–23, 39425–26, 39429, 39436–37, 39439–43, 39451–52, 39455–57, 39459, 39461–66, 39470, 39475–78, 39480–82, 39501–03, 39505–07, 39520–22, 39525, 39529–35, 39540, 39552–53, 39555–56, 39558, 39560–69, 39571–74, 39576–77, 39581, 39595

MISSOURI

(Population 2000, 5,595,211)

SENATORS

CHRISTOPHER S. (KIT) BOND, Republican, of Mexico, MO; born in St. Louis, MO, March 6, 1939; education: B.A., *cum laude*, Woodrow Wilson School of Public and International Affairs of Princeton University, 1960; J.D., valedictorian, University of Virginia, 1963; held a clerkship with the U.S. Court of Appeals for the Fifth Circuit, 1964; practiced law in Washington, DC, and returned to Missouri, 1967; assistant attorney general of Missouri, 1969; state auditor, 1970; Governor of Missouri, 1973–77, 1981–85; married: the former Linda Holwick; children: Samuel Reid Bond; committees: Appropriations; Environment and Public Works; Small Business and Entrepreneurship; Select Committee on Intelligence; elected to the U.S. Senate on November 4, 1986; reelected to each succeeding Senate term.

Office Listings

http://bond.senate.gov

274 Russell Senate Office Building, Washington, DC 20510	(202) 224–5721
Chief of Staff.—Julie Dammann.	FAX: 224–8149
Legislative Director.—Brian Klippenstein.	
Legal Counsel.—Jack Bartling.	
Scheduling Secretary.—Kathleen Youngblood.	
911 Main Street, Suite 2224, Kansas City, MO 64105	(816) 417–7141
7700 Bonhomme, Suite 615, Clayton, MO 63105	(314) 725–4484
1700 S. Campbell, Suite E, Springfield, MO 65807	(417) 864–8258
Federal Building, Room 140, 339 Broadway, Cape Girardeau, MO 63701	(573) 334–7044
308 East High, Suite 202, Jefferson City, MO 65101	(314) 634–2488

* * *

JAMES M. TALENT, Republican, of Chesterfield, MO; born in St. Louis, MO, October 18, 1956; education: graduated from Kirkwood High School, 1973; B.A., Washington University, St. Louis, 1978; J.D., University of Chicago Law School, 1981; Attorney; admitted to the Missouri bar, 1981; clerk for Judge Richard Posner, U.S. Court of Appeals, 7th Circuit; associate of Moller, Talent, Kuelthau, and Welch; counsel of Lashly and Baer; Missouri State House of Representatives, 1985–92, elected minority leader, 1989–92; member: West County Chamber of Commerce; Chesterfield Chamber of Commerce; Twin Oaks Presbyterian Church; married the former Brenda Lyons, 1984; three children: Michael, Kate, and Chrissy; elected on November 3, 1992, to the 103rd Congress; not a candidate for reelection to the House in 2000; committees: Agriculture, Nutrition, and Forestry; Armed Services; Energy and Natural Resources; Special Committee on Aging; elected to the U.S. Senate on November 4, 2002 by special election to the term ending January 3, 2007, a seat previously held by appointed Senator Jean Carnahan and took office on November 25, 2002.

Office Listings

http://talent.senate.gov

493 Russell Senate Office Building, Washington, DC 20510	(202) 224–6154
Chief of Staff.—Mark N. Strand.	FAX: 228–1518
Legislative Director.—Brett Thompson.	
Legislative Counsel.—Faith Cristol.	
Communications Director.—Rich Chrismer.	
122 East High Street, Second Floor, Jefferson City, MO 65101	(573) 636–1070
State Director.—Gregg Keller.	
3 City Place Drive, Suite 1020, St. Louis, MO 63141	(314) 432–5211
H&H Building, 400 Broadway, Suite 520, Cape Girardeau, MO 63701	(573) 651–0964
1721 W. Elfindal, Suite 301, Springfield, MO 65807	(417) 831–2735
Federal Office Building, 400 East 9th Street, Suite 40 Plaza Level, Kansas City, MO 64106	(816) 421–1639

REPRESENTATIVES

FIRST DISTRICT

WM. LACY CLAY, Democrat, of St. Louis, MO; born in St. Louis, July 27, 1956; education: Springbrook High School, Silver Spring, MD, 1974; B.S., University of Maryland, 1983, with a degree in government and politics, and a certificate in paralegal studies; public service: Missouri House of Representatives, 1983–91; Missouri State Senate, 1991–2000; nonprofit organizations: St. Louis Gateway Classic Sports Foundation; Mary Ryder Homes; William L. Clay Scholarship and Research Fund; married: Ivie Lewellen Clay; children: Carol, and William III; committees: Financial Services; Government Reform; elected to the 107th Congress on November 7, 2000; reelected to each succeeding Congress.

Office Listings
http://www.house.gov/clay

131 Cannon House Office Building, Washington, DC 20515 .... (202) 225–2406
    District Director.—Darryl Piggee.   FAX: 225–1725
    Legislative Director.—Michele Bogdanovich.
    Press Secretary.—Ishmael-Lateef Ahmed.
625 North Euclid Avenue, Suite 326, St. Louis, MO 63108 .... (314) 367–1970
8525 Page Boulevard, St. Louis, MO 63114 .... (314) 890–0349

Counties: ST. LOUIS (part). Population (2000), 621,690.

ZIP Codes: 63031–34, 63042–44, 63074, 63101–08, 63110, 63112–15, 63117, 63119–22, 63124, 63130–38, 63141, 63145–47, 63150, 63155–56, 63160, 63164, 63166–67, 63169, 63171, 63177–80, 63182, 63188, 63190, 63195–99

* * *

SECOND DISTRICT

W. TODD AKIN, Republican, of St. Louis, MO; born in New York, NY, July 5, 1947; education: B.S., WPI, 1971; military service: Officer, U.S. Army Engineers; professional: engineer and businessman; IBM; Laclede Steel; taught International Marketing, undergraduate level; public service: appointed to the Bicentennial Commission of the U.S. Constitution, 1987; Missouri House of Representatives, 1988–2000; organizations: Boy Scouts of America; Missouri Right to Life; Mission Gate Prison Ministry; family: married to Lulli; children: Wynn, Perry, Micah, Ezra, Hannah and Abigail; committees: Armed Services; Science; Small Business; elected to the 107th Congress on November 7, 2000; reelected to each succeeding Congress.

Office Listings
http://www.house.gov/akin

117 Cannon House Office Building, Washington, DC 20515 .... (202) 225–2561
    Chief of Staff.—Rob Schwarzwalder.   FAX: 225–2563
    Scheduler.—Tressa Merola.
301 Sovereign Court, Suite 201, St. Louis, MO 63011 .... (314) 590–0029
    District Director.—Patrick Werner.

Counties: LINCOLN, ST. CHARLES (part), ST. LOUIS (part). Population (2000), 621,690.

ZIP Codes: 63001, 63005–06, 63011, 63017, 63021–22, 63024–26, 63038, 63040, 63043, 63049, 63069, 63088, 63099, 63110, 63114, 63117, 63119, 63122–29, 63131, 63134, 63141, 63144–46, 63301–04, 63333–34, 63338, 63343–44, 63346–49, 63359, 63362, 63366–67, 63369–70, 63373, 63376–77, 63379, 63381, 63383, 63385–87, 63389–90

* * *

THIRD DISTRICT

RUSS CARNAHAN, Democrat, born in Columbia MO, July 10, 1958; education: B.S., Public Administration, University of Missouri-Columbia, 1979; J.D., University of Missouri-Columbia School of Law, 1983; professional: Missouri State Representative, 2001–04; BJC Healthcare, 1995–2004; private law practice; organizations: United Way of Greater St. Louis; Louis Regional Commerce and Growth Association; FOCUS Leadership St. Louis, Class of 1997–98; State Historical Society of Missouri; Landmarks Association of St. Louis; Compton Heights Neighborhood Association; Missouri Bar Association; Bar Association of Metropolitan St. Louis; Boy Scouts, Eagle Scout recipient; Friends of Tower Grove Park, Missouri Botanical Gardens and DeMenil Mansion; awards: St. Louis Regional Chamber of Commerce and Growth Association Lewis and Clark Statesman Award; St. Louis Business Journal 2002 Legislative Award and the Missouri Bar 2002 Legislative Award; married: Debra Carnahan; children: Austin and Andrew; committees: Science; Transportation and Infrastructure; elected to the 109th Congress on November 2, 2004.

Office Listings
http://russcarnahan.house.gov

1232 Longworth House Office Building, Washington, DC 20515 .... (202) 225-2671
Administrative Director.—Allen Todd. FAX: 225-7452
Legislative Director.—Cary Gibson.
Communications Director.—Heather Lasher Todd.
8764 Manchester Road, Suite 203, St. Louis, MO 63144 .... (314) 962-1523

Counties: JEFFERSON, SAINTE GENEVIEVE, ST. LOUIS, ST. LOUIS CITY. CITIES: St. Louis. Population (2000), 621,690.

ZIP Codes: 63010, 63012, 63015-16, 63019-20, 63023, 63025-26, 63028, 63030, 63036, 63041, 63047-53, 63057, 63060, 63065-66, 63069-72, 63087, 63102, 63104-05, 63109-11, 63116-19, 63122-30, 63132, 63139, 63143-44, 63151, 63157-58, 63163, 63627-28, 63640, 63645, 63661, 63670, 63673

* * *

FOURTH DISTRICT

IKE SKELTON, Democrat, of Lexington, MO; born in Lexington, December 20, 1931; education: graduated, Lexington High School, 1949; attended Wentworth Military Academy, Lexington; graduated, University of Missouri: A.B., 1953, LL.B., 1956; attended University of Edinburgh (Scotland), 1953; lawyer; admitted to the Missouri bar in 1956 and commenced practice in Lexington; elected, State Senate, 1970; reelected, 1974; prosecuting attorney, Lafayette County, 1957-60; special assistant attorney general, 1961-63; member: Phi Beta Kappa honor society, Missouri Bar Association, Lions, Elks, Masons, Boy Scouts, First Christian Church; married the former Susan B. Anding, 1961; three children: Ike, James, and Page; committees: Armed Services; elected to the 95th Congress on November 2, 1976; reelected to each succeeding Congress.

Office Listings
http://www.house.gov/skelton

2206 Rayburn House Office Building, Washington, DC 20515 .... (202) 225-2876
Chief of Staff.—Robert Hagedorn.
Administrative Assistant.—Whitney Frost.
Legislative Director.—Dana O'Brien.
Press Secretary.—Lara Battles.
514-B North West 7 Highway, Blue Springs, MO 64014 .... (816) 228-4242
Chief of Staff.—Robert Hagedorn.
908 Thompson Boulevard, Sedalia, MO 65301 .... (660) 826-2675
1401 Southwest Boulevard, Jefferson City, MO 65109 .... (573) 635-3499
219 North Adams, Lebanon, MO 65536 .... (417) 532-7964

Counties: BARTON, BATES, BENTON, CAMDEN (part), CASS (part), CEDAR, COLE, DADE, DALLAS, HENRY, HICKORY, JACKSON (part), JOHNSON, LACLEDE, LAFAYETTE, MONITEAU, MORGAN, PETTIS, POLK (part), PULASKI, RAY, SALINE, ST. CLAIR, VERNON, WEBSTER. Population (2000), 621,690.

ZIP Codes: 64001, 64011, 64013-14, 64016-17, 64019-22, 64024, 64029, 64034-37, 64040, 64058, 64061-62, 64067, 64071, 64074-77, 64080, 64082, 64084-86, 64088, 64090, 64093, 64096-97, 64624, 64637, 64668, 64670-71, 64701, 64720, 64722-26, 64728, 64730, 64733, 64735, 64738-48, 64750, 64752, 64755-56, 64759, 64761-63, 64765, 64767, 64769-72, 64776, 64778-81, 64783-84, 64788, 64790, 64832, 64855, 65011, 65018, 65020, 65023, 65025-26, 65032, 65034, 65037-38, 65040, 65042, 65046, 65049-50, 65052-53, 65055, 65065, 65072, 65074, 65076, 65078-79, 65081, 65084, 65101-11, 65287, 65301-02, 65305, 65320-21, 65323-27, 65329-30, 65332-40, 65344-45, 65347-51, 65354-55, 65360, 65452, 65457, 65459, 65461, 65463, 65470, 65473, 65534, 65536, 65543, 65550, 65552, 65556-67, 65572, 65583-84, 65590-91, 65601, 65603-04, 65607, 65632, 65634-36, 65640, 65644, 65646, 65648-50, 65652, 65661-62, 65668, 65674, 65682, 65685, 65706, 65713, 65722, 65724, 65727, 65732, 65735, 65742, 65746, 65752, 65757, 65764, 65767, 65774, 65779, 65783, 65785-87

* * *

FIFTH DISTRICT

EMANUEL CLEAVER II, Democrat, of Kansas City, MO; born in Waxahachie, TX, October 27, 1944; education: MDiv, Saint Paul School of Theology, MO, 1974; B.S., Prairie View A&M University, TX, 1972; professional: Senior Pastor, St. James United Methodist Church; host, Under the Clock, KCUR radio, 1999-2004; founder, Harmony in a World of Difference, 1991; founder, Southern Christian Leadership Conference, Kansas City Chapter; public service: Mayor of Kansas City, MO 1991-1999; member, President-elect Bill Clinton's Transitional Team, 1992; City Councilman, Kansas City, MO, 5th District, 1979-1991; married: Dianne; four children; two grandchildren; committees: Financial Services; elected to the 109th Congress on November 2, 2004.

Office Listings
http://www.house.gov/cleaver

1641 Longworth House Office Building, Washington, DC 20515 .... (202) 225–4535
   Chief of Staff.—Susan McAvoy.   FAX: 225–4403
   Scheduler.—Joyce Elkins.
400 East 9th Street, Suite 9350, Kansas City, MO 64106 .... (816) 842–4545
   District Director.—Geoff Jolley.

Counties: CASS COUNTY (part), JACKSON COUNTY (part). CITIES AND TOWNSHIPS: Belton, Grandview, Greenwood, Independence, Kansas City, Lee's Summit, Peculiar, Raymore, Raytown, and Sugar Creek. Population (2000), 621,691.

ZIP Codes: 64012, 64014–15, 64029–30, 64034, 64050–58, 64061, 64063–65, 64070, 64075, 64078, 64080–83, 64086, 64101–02, 64105–06, 64108–14, 64120–21, 64123–34, 64136–39, 64141, 64145–49, 64170–71, 64179–80, 64184–85, 64187–88, 64191–94, 64196–99, 64701, 64734, 64944, 64999

* * *

SIXTH DISTRICT

SAM GRAVES, Republican, of Tarkio, MO; born in Fairfax, MO, November 7, 1963; education: B.S., University of Missouri-Columbia, 1986; professional: farmer; organizations: Missouri Farm Bureau; Northwest Missouri State University Agriculture Advisory Committee; University Extension Council; Rotary Club; awards: Associated Industries Voice of Missouri Business Award; Tom Henderson Award; Tarkio Community Betterment Award; Missouri Physical Therapy Association Award; Outstanding Young Farmer Award, 1997; Hero of the Taxpayer Award; NFIB Guardian of Small Business Award; public service: elected to the Missouri House of Representatives, 1992; and the Missouri State Senate, 1994; religion: Baptist; married: Lesley; children: Megan, Emily, and Sam III; committees: Agriculture; Small Business; Transportation and Infrastructure; elected to the 107th Congress on November 7, 2000; reelected to each succeeding Congress.

Office Listings
http://www.house.gov/graves

1513 Longworth House Office Building, Washington, DC 20515 .... (202) 225–7041
   Chief of Staff.—Jeff Roe.   FAX: 225–8221
   Press Secretary.—Jason Klindt.
201 S. Eighth Street, Room 330, St. Joseph, MO 64501 .... (816) 233–9818
113 Blue Jay Drive, Suite 100, Liberty, MO 64068 .... (816) 792–3976

Counties: ANDREW, ATCHISON, BUCHANAN, CALDWELL, CARROLL, CHARITON, CLAY, CLINTON, COOPER, DAVIESS, DEKALB, GENTRY, GRUNDY, HARRISON, HOLT, HOWARD, JACKSON (part), LINN, LIVINGSTON, MERCER, NODAWAY, PLATTE, PUTNAM, SCHUYLER, SULLIVAN, WORTH. Population (2000), 621,690.

ZIP Codes: 63535–36, 63541, 63544–46, 63548, 63551, 63556–57, 63560–61, 63565–67, 64013–16, 64018, 64024, 64028–29, 64048, 64056–58, 64060, 64062, 64064, 64066, 64072–75, 64077, 64079, 64085–88, 64092, 64098, 64116–19, 64144, 64150–58, 64161, 64163–68, 64188, 64190, 64193, 64195, 64243, 64401–02, 64420–24, 64426–34, 64436–49, 64451, 64453–59, 64461, 64463, 64465–71, 64473–77, 64479–94, 64496–99, 64501–08, 64601, 64620, 64622–25, 64628, 64630–33, 64635–61, 64664, 64667–68, 64670–74, 64676, 64679, 64681–83, 64686, 64688–89, 65018, 65025, 65046, 65068, 65081, 65230, 65233, 65236–37, 65246, 65248, 65250, 65254, 65256–57, 65261, 65274, 65276, 65279, 65281, 65286–87, 65301, 65322, 65347–48, 65354

* * *

SEVENTH DISTRICT

ROY BLUNT, Republican, of Branson, MO; born in Niangua, MO, January 10, 1950; member, the Travel-Tourism Caucus; before election to Congress, president of Southwest Baptist University; author; two-term Missouri Secretary of State; Greene County, Missouri Clerk and chief election officer; past chair: Missouri Housing Development Commission, Governor's Council on Literacy; past co-chairman, Missouri Opportunity 2000 Commission; past member, Project Democracy Commission for Voter Participation in the United States; board member, American Council of Young Political Leaders; served as first chairman of the Missouri Prison Fellowship; named one of the Ten Outstanding Young Americans, 1986; children: Matt, Governor of the state of Missouri and Naval reserve officer; Amy, a lawyer in the Kansas City area; and Andy, an attorney in Jefferson City; Majority Whip; committees: Energy and Commerce; Republican Leadership Steering Committee; elected to the 105th Congress; reelected to each succeeding Congress.

Office Listings

http://www.majoritywhip.gov   http://blunt.house.gov

H–329, U.S. Capitol Building (Office of the Majority Whip), Washington, DC
20515 .... (202) 225–0197
    Chief of Staff.—Brian Gaston.
    Communications Director.—Burson Taylor.
    Director of Scheduling.—Richard Eddings.
217 Cannon House Office Building, Washington, DC 20515 .... (202) 225–6536
    Chief of Staff.—Amy Field.   FAX: 225–5604
    Legislative Director.—Jennifer Douris.
    Legislative Correspondents: Joelle Cannon, Jim Fotenos.
2740–B East Sunshine, Springfield, MO 65804 .... (417) 889–1800
    Chief of Staff.—Amy Field.
Northpark Mall, 101 Range Line Road, Box 20, Joplin, MO 64801 .... (417) 781–1041
    District Director.—Sharon Nahon.

Counties: BARRY, CHRISTIAN, GREENE, JASPER, LAWRENCE, MCDONALD, NEWTON, POLK (part), STONE, TANEY (part). Population (2000), 621,690.

ZIP Codes: 64748, 64755–56, 64766, 64769, 64801–04, 64830–36, 64840–44, 64847–50, 64853–59, 64861–70, 64873–74, 65603–05, 65608–20, 65622–27, 65629–31, 65633, 65635, 65637–38, 65640–41, 65645–50, 65652–58, 65661, 65663–64, 65666, 65669, 65672–76, 65680–82, 65686, 65702, 65705, 65707–08, 65710, 65712, 65714–15, 65720–21, 65723, 65725–30, 65733–34, 65737–42, 65744–45, 65747, 65752–57, 65759–62, 65765–73, 65781, 65784–85, 65801–10, 65814, 65817, 65890, 65898–99

* * *

EIGHTH DISTRICT

JO ANN EMERSON, Republican, of Cape Girardeau, MO; born in Washington, DC, September 16, 1950; education: B.A., political science, Ohio Wesleyan University, Delaware, OH, 1972; Senior Vice President of Public Affairs, American Insurance Association; director, State Relations and Grassroots Programs, National Restaurant Association; deputy communications director, National Republican Congressional Committee; member: board of directors, Bread for the World; co-chair, board of directors, Congressional Hunger Caucus; PEO Women's Service Group, Cape Girardeau, MO; Copper Dome Society, Southeast Missouri State University; advisory committee, Children's Inn, National Institutes of Health; advisory board, Arneson Institute for Practical Politics and Public Affairs, Ohio Weslyan University; married: Ron Gladney, 2000; children: Victoria and Katharine; six stepchildren: Elizabeth, Abigail, Victoria, Stephanie, Alison, Jessica, and Sam; committees: Appropriations; subcommittees: Agriculture, Rural Development, Food and Drug Administration, and Related Agencies; Energy and Water Development, and Related Agencies; Homeland Security; elected on November 5, 1996, by special election, to the 104th Congress: reelected to each succeeding Congress.

Office Listings

http://www.house.gov/emerson

2440 Rayburn House Office Building, Washington, DC 20515 .... (202) 225–4404
    Deputy Chief of Staff.—Grant Erdel.   FAX: 226–0326
    Communications Director.—Jeffrey Connor.
    Executive Assistant / Scheduler.—Atalie Ebersole.
339 Broadway, Cape Girardeau, MO 63701 .... (573) 335–0101
    Chief of Staff.—Lloyd Smith.
612 Pine Street, Rolla, MO 65401 .... (573) 364–2455
22 East Columbia, Farmington, MO 63640 .... (573) 756–9755

Counties: BOLLINGER, BUTLER, CAPE GIRARDEAU, CARTER, CRAWFORD, DENT, DOUGLAS, DUNKLIN, HOWELL, IRON, MADISON, MISSISSIPPI, NEW MADRID, OREGON, OZARK, PEMISCOT, PERRY, PHELPS, REYNOLDS, RIPLEY, ST. FRANCOIS, SCOTT, SHANNON, STODDARD, TANEY (part), TEXAS, WASHINGTON, WAYNE, WRIGHT. Population (2000), 621,690.

ZIP Codes: 63028, 63030, 63036, 63071, 63080, 63087, 63601, 63620–26, 63628–33, 63636–38, 63640, 63648, 63650–51, 63653–56, 63660, 63662–66, 63674–75, 63701–03, 63730, 63732, 63735–40, 63742–48, 63750–52, 63755, 63758, 63760, 63763–64, 63766–67, 63769–72, 63774–76, 63779–85, 63787, 63801, 63820–30, 63833–34, 63837, 63839–41, 63845–53, 63855, 63857, 63860, 63862–63, 63866–70, 63873–82, 63901–02, 63931–45, 63950–57, 63960–67, 65401–02, 65409, 65436, 65438–41, 65444, 65446, 65449, 65453, 65456, 65459, 65461–62, 65464, 65466, 65468, 65479, 65483–84, 65501, 65529, 65532, 65541–42, 65546, 65548, 65550, 65552, 65555, 65557, 65564–66, 65570–71, 65586, 65588–89, 65606, 65608–09, 65614, 65616, 65618, 65620, 65626–27, 65629, 65637–38, 65652–53, 65655, 65660, 65662, 65666–67, 65676, 65679–80, 65688–90, 65692, 65701–02, 65704, 65711, 65713, 65715, 65717, 65720, 65729, 65731, 65733, 65740–41, 65744, 65746, 65753, 65755, 65759–62, 65766, 65768, 65773, 65775, 65777–78, 65784, 65788–91, 65793

NINTH DISTRICT

KENNY C. HULSHOF, Republican, of Columbia, MO; born in Sikeston, MO, May 22, 1958; education: graduated from Thomas W. Kelly High School, Benton, MO; agriculture economics degree, University of Missouri School of Agriculture, 1980; J.D., University of Mississippi Law School, 1983; attorney, admitted to Missouri and Mississippi bars in 1983; Assistant Public Defender, 32nd judicial circuit, 1983–86; Assistant Prosecuting Attorney, Cape Girardeau, MO, 1986–89; Assistant Attorney General, State of Missouri, 1989–96; member: Newman Center Catholic Church, Boone County Farm Bureau, Farm House Foundation, Ducks Unlimited; married: Renee Howell Hulshof, 1994; committees: Budget; Ways and Means; elected to the 105th Congress; reelected to each succeeding Congress.

Office Listings

http://www.house.gov/hulshof

412 Cannon House Office Building, Washington, DC 20515	(202) 225–2956
Chief of Staff.—Manning Feraci.	FAX: 225–5712
Executive Assistant/Scheduler.—Eileen Gardner.	
33 Broadway, Suite 280, Columbia, MO 65203	(573) 449–5111
201 N. 3rd Street, Hannibal, MO 63401	(573) 221–1200
516 Jefferson Street, Washington, MO 63090	(636) 239–4001

Counties: ADAIR, AUDRAIN, BOONE, CALLAWAY, CAMDEN (part), CLARK, CRAWFORD, FRANKLIN, GASCONADE, KNOX, LEWIS, MACON, MARIES, MARION, MILLER, MONROE, MONTGOMERY, OSAGE, PIKE, RALLS, RANDOLPH, ST. CHARLES (part), SCOTLAND, SHELBY, WARREN. Population (2000), 621,690.

ZIP Codes: 63005, 63013–15, 63037, 63039, 63041, 63055–56, 63060, 63068–69, 63072–73, 63077, 63079–80, 63084, 63089–91, 63303–04, 63330, 63332–34, 63336, 63339, 63341–42, 63344–45, 63348–53, 63357, 63359, 63361, 63363, 63365–67, 63376, 63378, 63381–85, 63388, 63390, 63401, 63430–43, 63445–48, 63450–54, 63456–69, 63471–74, 63501, 63530–34, 63536–40, 63543–44, 63546–47, 63549, 63552, 63555, 63557–59, 63563, 64631, 64658, 64856, 65001, 65010, 65013–14, 65016–17, 65024, 65026, 65031–32, 65035–36, 65039–41, 65043, 65047–49, 65051, 65054, 65058–59, 65061–67, 65069, 65072, 65074–77, 65080, 65082–83, 65085, 65101, 65201–03, 65205, 65211–12, 65215–18, 65230–32, 65239–40, 65243–44, 65247, 65251, 65255–60, 65262–65, 65270, 65275, 65278–85, 65299, 65337, 65441, 65443, 65446, 65449, 65452–53, 65456, 65459, 65486, 65535, 65559–60, 65565, 65580, 65582, 65586, 65591

MONTANA

(Population 2000, 902,195)

SENATORS

MAX BAUCUS, Democrat, of Helena, MT; born in Helena, December 11, 1941; education: graduated, Helena High School, 1959; B.A. in economics, Stanford University, 1964; LL.B., Stanford University Law School, 1967; attorney, Civil Aeronautics Board, 1967–71; attorney, George and Baucus law firm, Missoula, MT; married to the former Wanda Minge; one child, Zeno; member, Montana and District of Columbia bar associations; served in Montana House of Representatives, 1973–74; elected to the 94th Congress, November 5, 1974; reelected to the 95th Congress; committees: Agriculture, Nutrition, and Forestry; Environment and Public Works; ranking member, Finance; Joint Committee on Taxation; elected to the U.S. Senate, November 7, 1978, for the six-year term beginning January 3, 1979; subsequently appointed on December 15, 1978, to fill the vacancy caused by the resignation of Senator Paul Hatfield; reelected to each succeeding Senate term.

Office Listings

http://baucus.senate.gov

511 Hart Senate Office Building, Washington, DC 20510	(202) 224–2651
Chief of Staff.—Jim Messina.	
Legislative Director.—Sara Roberts.	
Press Secretary.—Barrett Kaiser.	
DC Scheduler.—Farrar Johnston.	
222 North 32nd Street, Suite 100, Billings, MT 59101	(406) 657–6790
32 East Babcock, Room 114, Bozeman, MT 59715	(406) 586–6104
125 West Granite, Butte, MT 59701	(406) 782–8700
113 3rd Street North, Great Falls, MT 59401	(406) 761–1574
30 West 14th Street, Helena, MT 59601	(406) 449–5480
75 Claremont, Suite I, Kalispell, MT 59901	(406) 756–1150
1821 South Avenue West, Suite 203, Missoula, MT 59801	(406) 329–3123
State Chief of Staff.—Jim Foley.	(800) 332–6106

* * *

CONRAD BURNS, Republican, of Billings, MT; born in Gallatin, MO, January 25, 1935; education: graduated, Gallatin High School, 1952; attended University of Missouri, Columbia, 1953–54; served, U.S. Marine Corps, corporal, 1955–57; farm broadcaster and auctioneer; county commissioner, Yellowstone County, 1986; member: Rotary, American Legion, National Association of Farm Broadcasters, American Association of Farm Broadcasters, Atonement Lutheran Church; married to the former Phyllis Kuhlmann; two children: Keely and Garrett; committees: Appropriations; Commerce, Science, and Transportation; Energy and Natural Resources; Small Business and Entrepreneurship; Special Committee on Aging; elected to the U.S. Senate on November 8, 1988; reelected to each succeeding Senate term.

Office Listings

http://burns.senate.gov

187 Dirksen Senate Office Building, Washington, DC 20510	(202) 224–2644
Chief of Staff.—Clark Johnson.	
Legislative Director.—Ric Molen.	
Executive Assistant/Scheduler.—Angela Schulze.	
Administrative Director.—Margo Rushing.	
208 North Montana Avenue, Suite 202–A, Helena, MT 59601	(406) 449–5401
222 North 32nd Street, Suite 400, Billings, MT 59101	(406) 252–0550
321 First Avenue North, Great Falls, MT 59401	(406) 452–9585
116 West Front Street, Missoula, MT 59802	(406) 728–3003
324 West Towne, Glendive, MT 59330	(406) 365–2391
211 Haggerty Lane, Bozeman, MT 59715	(406) 586–4450
125 West Granite, Suite 211, Butte, MT 59701	(406) 723–3277
1845 Highway 93 South, Suite 210, Kalispell, MT 59901	(406) 257–3360

REPRESENTATIVE

AT LARGE

DENNIS R. REHBERG, Republican, of Billings, MT; born in Billings, October 5, 1955; education: B.A., Washington State University, 1977; professional: rancher; manages the Rehberg

Ranch; public service: interned in the Montana State Senate, 1977–79; legislative assistant to Rep. Ron Marlenee (R–MT), 1979–82; elected to the Montana House of Representatives, 1984; appointed Lt. Governor of Montana in 1991; elected Lt. Governor in 1992; Chairman, Drought Advisory Committee; Worker's Compensation Task Force; and the Montana Rural Development Council; Republican nominee for the U.S. Senate, 1996; married: Janice; children: A.J., Katie, and Elsie; committees: Appropriations; elected to the 107th Congress on November 7, 2000; reelected to each succeeding Congress.

Office Listings
http://www.house.gov/rehberg

516 Cannon House Office Building, Washington, DC 20515 .... (202) 225–3211
   Chief of Staff.—Erik Iverson.   FAX: 225–5687
   Communications Director.—Brad Keena.
1201 Grand Avenue, Suite 1, Billings, MT 59102 .... (406) 256–1019
   District Director.—Randy Vogel.

Counties: BEAVERHEAD, BIG HORN, BLAINE, BROADWATER, CARBON, CARTER, CASCADE, CHOUTEAU, CUSTER, DANIELS, DAWSON, DEER LODGE, FALLON, FERGUS, FLATHEAD, GALLATIN, GARFIELD, GLACIER, GOLDEN VALLEY, GRANITE, HILL, JEFFERSON, JUDITH BASIN, LAKE, LEWIS AND CLARK, LIBERTY, LINCOLN, MADISON, McCONE, MEAGHER, MINERAL, MISSOULA, MUSSELLSHELL PARK, PETROLEUM, PHILLIPS, PONDERA, POWDER RIVER, POWELL, PRAIRIE, RAVALLI, RICHLAND, ROOSEVELT, ROSEBUD, SANDERS, SHERIDAN, SILVER BOW, STILLWATER, SWEET GRASS, TETON, TOOLE, TREASURE, VALLEY, WHEATLAND, WIBAUX, YELLOWSTONE. Population (2000), 902,195.

ZIP Codes: 59001–04, 59006–08, 59010–16, 59018–20, 59022, 59024–39, 59041, 59043–44, 59046–47, 59050, 59052–55, 59057–59, 59061–72, 59074–79, 59081–89, 59101–08, 59201, 59211–15, 59217–19, 59221–23, 59225–26, 59230–31, 59240–44, 59247–48, 59250, 59252–63, 59270, 59273–76, 59301, 59311–19, 59322–24, 59326–27, 59330, 59332–33, 59336–39, 59341, 59343–45, 59347, 59349, 59351, 59353–54, 59401–06, 59410–12, 59414, 59416–22, 59424–25, 59427, 59430, 59432–36, 59440–48, 59450–54, 59456–57, 59460–69, 59471–72, 59474, 59477, 59479–80, 59482–87, 59489, 59501, 59520–32, 59535, 59537–38, 59540, 59542, 59544–47, 59601–02, 59604, 59620, 59623–24, 59626, 59631–36, 59638–45, 59647–48, 59701–03, 59710–11, 59713–22, 59724–25, 59727–33, 59735–36, 59739–41, 59743, 59745–52, 59754–56, 59758–62, 59771–73, 59801–04, 59806–08, 59812, 59820–21, 59823–35, 59837, 59840–48, 59851, 59853–56, 59858–60, 59863–68, 59870–75, 59901, 59903–04, 59910–23, 59925–37

NEBRASKA

(Population 2000, 1,711,263)

SENATORS

CHUCK HAGEL, Republican, of Omaha, NE; born in North Platte, NE, October 4, 1946; education: graduated, St. Bonaventure High School, Columbus, NE, 1964; Brown Institute for Radio and Television, Minneapolis, MN; University of Nebraska, Omaha; military service: served with U.S. Army in Vietnam, 1968, receiving two Purple Hearts, other decorations; professional: president, McCarthy and Company, Omaha, NE; president and CEO, Private Sector Council (PSC), Washington, DC; deputy director and CEO, Economic Summit of Industrialized Nations (G–7 Summit), 1990; president and CEO, World USO; cofounder, director, and executive vice president, VANGUARD Cellular Systems, Inc.; cofounder and chairman of VANGUARD subsidiary, Communications Corporation International, Ltd.; president, Collins, Hagel and Clarke, Inc.; former deputy administrator, Veterans' Administration; former administrative assistant to Congressman John Y. McCollister (R–NE); former newscaster and talk show host, Omaha radio stations KBON and KLNG; member: American Legion; Veterans of Foreign Wars; Disabled American Veterans; Military Order of the Purple Heart; Business-Government Relations Council, Washington, DC; Council for Excellence in Government; University of Nebraska Chancellors Club; board of directors, Omaha Chamber of Commerce; board of trustees: Bellevue University, Hastings College, Heartland Chapter of the American Red Cross; chairman: Building Campaign, Great Plains Chapter of Paralyzed Veterans of America; 10th Anniversary Vietnam Veterans' Memorial; board of directors and national advisory committee, Friends of the Vietnam Veterans' Memorial; board of directors, Arlington National Cemetery Historical Society; chairman of the board, No Greater Love, Inc.; awards: first-ever World USO Leadership Award; International Men of Achievement; Outstanding Young Men of America; Distinguished Alumni Award, University of Nebraska, Omaha, 1988; Freedom Foundation (Omaha Chapter) 1993 Recognition Award; married: the former Lilibet Ziller, 1985; children: Allyn and Ziller; committees: Banking, Housing and Urban Affairs; Foreign Relations; Rules and Administration; Select Committee on Intelligence; subcommittees: chair, Securities and Investment; chair, International Economic Policy, Export and Trade Promotion; elected to the U.S. Senate on November 5, 1996; reelected to each succeeding Senate term.

Office Listings
http://hagel.senate.gov

248 Russell Senate Office Building, Washington, DC 20510	(202) 224–4224
Legislative Director.—Jill Konz.	FAX: 224–5213
Office Manager.—Marilouis Hudgins.	
Communications Director.—Michael Buttry.	
11301 Davenport Street, Suite 2, Omaha, NE 68154	(402) 758–8981
State Director.—Bill Protexter.	
294 Federal Building, 100 Centennial Mall North, Lincoln, NE 68508	(402) 476–1400
Constituent Services Director.—Dorothy Anderson.	
4111 Fourth Avenue, Suite 26, Kearney, NE 68845	(308) 236–7473
Constituent Services Representative.—Julie Brooker.	
115 Railway Street, C102, Scottsbluff, NE 69361	(308) 632–6032
State Agriculture Director.—Mary B. Crawford.	

* * *

E. BENJAMIN NELSON, Democrat, of Omaha, NE; born in McCook, NE, May 17, 1941; education: University of Nebraska at Lincoln; received a bachelor's degree in 1963, a master's degree in 1965, and a law degree in 1970; professional: attorney; Director, Nebraska Department of Insurance; President and CEO of the Central National Insurance Group; Executive Vice President and Chief of Staff of the National Association of Insurance Commissioners; Kennedy, Holland, DeLacy, and Svoboda (law firm); awards: Thomas Jefferson Freedom Award; George W. Norris Award; National Eagle Scout Association Distinguished Eagle Award; family: married to Diane; four children; Governor of Nebraska, 1991–1999; committees: Agriculture, Nutrition, and Forestry; Armed Services; Commerce, Science, and Transportation; Rules and Administration; elected to the U.S. Senate on November 7, 2000.

Office Listings
http://bennelson.senate.gov

720 Hart Senate Office Building, Washington, DC 20510	(202) 224–6551
Chief of Staff.—Tim Becker.	FAX: 228–0012
Communications Director.—David DiMartino.	

Federal Building, Room 287, Centennial Mall North, Lincoln, NE 68508 .... (402) 441–4600
    State Director.—W. Don Nelson.
7602 Pacific Street, Suite 205, Omaha, NE 68154 .... (402) 391–3411
P.O. Box 1891, Scottsbluff, NE 69361 .... (308) 631–7614
P.O. Box 1033, Chadron, NE 69337 .... (308) 430–0587

REPRESENTATIVES

FIRST DISTRICT

JEFF FORTENBERRY, Republican, of Lincoln, NE; born in Baton Rouge, LA, December 27, 1960; education: B.A., Louisiana State University, 1978; M.P.P., Georgetown University, Washington, DC, 1986; M. Div., Franciscan University, Steubenville, Ohio, 1996; professional: Lincoln City Council, 1997–2001; publishing executive; worked as economist; managed a public relations firm; congressional aide for the Senate Subcommittee on Intergovernmental Relations; family: married to Celeste Gregory; children: four; committees: Agriculture; International Relations; Small Business; elected to the 109th Congress on November 2, 2004.

Office Listings
http://www.house.gov/fortenberry

1517 Longworth House Office Building, Washington, DC 20515 .... (202) 225–4806
    Chief of Staff.—Ben Sasse.   FAX: 225–5686
    Legislative Director.—Ginger Langemeier.
    Legislative Assistant.—Alan Feyerherm.
    Scheduler.—Tyler Grassmeyer.
301 South 13th Street, Suite 100, Lincoln, NE 68508 .... (402) 438–1598
629 North Broad Street, P.O. Box 377, Fremont, NE 68025 .... (402) 727–0888

Counties: BURT, BUTLER, CASS, CEDAR (part), COLFAX, CUMING, DAKOTA, DIXON, DODGE, GAGE, JOHNSON, LANCASTER, MADISON, NEMAHA, OTOE, PAWNEE, RICHARDSON, SARPY (part), THURSTON, WASHINGTON, WAYNE. Population (2000), 570,421.

ZIP Codes: 68001–04, 68007–09, 68014–20, 68023, 68025–26, 68028–31, 68033–34, 68036–42, 68044–48, 68050, 68055, 68057–59, 68061–68, 68070–73, 68112, 68122–23, 68133, 68136, 68138, 68142, 68144, 68152, 68301, 68304–05, 68307, 68309–10, 68313–14, 68316–21, 68323–24, 68328–33, 68336–37, 68339, 68341–49, 68351, 68355, 68357–60, 68364, 68366–68, 68371–72, 68376, 68378, 68380–82, 68401–05, 68407, 68409–10, 68413–15, 68417–24, 68428, 68430–31, 68433–34, 68437–39, 68441–43, 68445–48, 68450, 68452–58, 68460–67, 68501–10, 68512, 68514, 68516, 68520–24, 68526, 68528–29, 68532, 68542, 68583, 68588, 68601, 68621, 68624, 68626, 68629, 68631–33, 68635, 68641–44, 68648–49, 68658–59, 68661–62, 68666–67, 68669, 68701–02, 68710, 68715–17, 68723–24, 68727–28, 68731–33, 68739–41, 68743, 68745, 68747–49, 68751–52, 68757–58, 68767–68, 68770–71, 68776, 68779, 68781, 68784–85, 68787–88, 68790–92

* * *

SECOND DISTRICT

LEE TERRY, Republican, of Omaha, NE; born in Omaha, January 29, 1962; education: B.A., University of Nebraska, 1984; J.D., Creighton Law School, 1987; attorney; elected to the Omaha, NE, City Council, 1990–98; served as vice president and president, and on the audit, legislative, and cable television committees; religion: Methodist; married: Robyn; children: Nolan, Ryan, and Jack; committees: Energy and Commerce; elected to the 106th Congress; reelected to each succeeding Congress.

Office Listings
http://www.house.gov/terry

1524 Longworth House Office Building, Washington, DC 20515 .... (202) 225–4155
    Chief of Staff.—Eric Hultman.   FAX: 226–5452
    Legislative Director.—Jamie Karl.
    Appointment Secretary.—Lindsey Witt.
    Press Secretary.—Jen Rae Hein.
11640 Arbor Street, Suite 100, Omaha, NE 68144 .... (402) 397–9944
    District Director.—Molly Koozer-Lloyd.

Counties: DOUGLAS, SARPY (part). CITIES: Bellevue, Bennington, Boys Town, Elkhorn, Gretna, La Vista, Omaha, Offutt AFB, Papillion, Plattsmouth, Ralston, Springfield, Valley, and Waterloo. Population (2000), 570,421.

ZIP Codes: 68005, 68007, 68010, 68022, 68028, 68046, 68056, 68064, 68069, 68101–14, 68116–20, 68122–24, 68127–28, 68130–39, 68142, 68144–45, 68147, 68152, 68154–55, 68157, 68164, 68172, 68175–76, 68178–83, 68197–98

THIRD DISTRICT

TOM OSBORNE, Republican, of Lemoyne, NE; born in Hastings, NE, February 23, 1937; education: B.A., History, Hastings College; M.A., Educational Psychology, University of Nebraska; Ph.D., Educational Psychology, University of Nebraska; professional: Educator; Head Football Coach at the University of Nebraska, 1973–1998; won three National Championships, 1994, 1995, and 1997; author of several books; married: Nancy; three children; community service: developed and underwrote the Team Mates Mentoring Program for at-risk students; committees: Agriculture; Education and the Workforce; Transportation and Infrastructure; elected to the 107th Congress on November 7, 2000; reelected to each succeeding Congress.

Office Listings

http://www.house.gov/osborne

507 Cannon House Office Building, Washington, DC 20515 .... (202) 225–6435
Deputy Chief of Staff.—Christina Muedeking.
Legislative Director.—Erin Duncan.
Press Secretary.—Erin Hegge.
Scheduler.—Daffnei O'Bryan.
819 Diers Avenue, Suite 3, Grand Island, NE 68803 .... (308) 381–5555
Chief of Staff.—Bruce Rieker.
21 E. 20th Street, Scottsbluff, NE 69361 .... (308) 632–3333
Rural Initiatives Director.—Scot Blehm.

Counties: ADAMS, ANTELOPE, ARTHUR, BANNER, BLAINE, BOONE, BOX BUTTE, BOYD, BROWN, BUFFALO, CEDAR (part), CHASE, CHERRY, CHEYENNE, CLAY, CUSTER, DAWES, DAWSON, DEUEL, DUNDY, FILLMORE, FRANKLIN, FRONTIER, FURNAS, GARDEN, GARFIELD, GOSPER, GRANT, GREELEY, HALL, HAMILTON, HARLAN, HAYES, HITCHCOCK, HOLT, HOOKER, HOWARD, JEFFERSON, KEARNEY, KEITH, KEYA PAHA, KIMBALL, KNOX, LINCOLN, LOGAN, LOUP, MCPHERSON, MERRICK, MORRILL, NANCE, NUCKOLLS, PERKINS, PHELPS, PIERCE, PLATTE, POLK, RED WILLOW, ROCK, SALINE, SCOTTS BLUFF, SHERIDAN, SHERMAN, SIOUX, THAYER, THOMAS, VALLEY, WEBSTER, WHEELER, YORK. Population (2000), 570,421.

ZIP Codes: 68303, 68310, 68313, 68315–16, 68319, 68322, 68325–27, 68333, 68335, 68338–43, 68350–52, 68354, 68359, 68361–62, 68365, 68367, 68370–71, 68375, 68377, 68401, 68405–06, 68416, 68423–24, 68429, 68436, 68440, 68444–45, 68452–53, 68460, 68464–65, 68467, 68601–02, 68620–23, 68627–28, 68631, 68634, 68636–38, 68640, 68642–44, 68647, 68651–55, 68658, 68660, 68662–66, 68701, 68711, 68713–14, 68717–20, 68722–27, 68729–30, 68734–36, 68738–39, 68742, 68746–48, 68752–53, 68755–56, 68758–61, 68763–67, 68769, 68771, 68773–74, 68777–78, 68780–81, 68783, 68786, 68789, 68792, 68801–03, 68810, 68812–18, 68820–28, 68831–38, 68840–50, 68852–56, 68858–66, 68869–76, 68878–79, 68881–83, 68901–02, 68920, 68922–30, 68932–50, 68952, 68954–61, 68964, 68966–67, 68969–82, 69001, 69020–30, 69032–34, 69036–46, 69101, 69103, 69120–23, 69125, 69127–35, 69138, 69140–57, 69160–63, 69165–71, 69190, 69201, 69210–12, 69214, 69216–21, 69301, 69331, 69333–37, 69339–41, 69343, 69345–48, 69350–58, 69360–61, 69363, 69365–67

NEVADA

(Population 2000, 1,998,257)

SENATORS

HARRY REID, Democrat, of Searchlight, NV; born in Searchlight, December 2, 1939; education: graduated, Basic High School, Henderson, NV, 1957; associate degree in science, Southern Utah State College, 1959; B.S., Utah State University, Phi Kappa Phi, 1961; J.D., George Washington School of Law, Washington, DC, 1964; admitted to the Nevada State bar in 1963, a year before graduating from law school; while attending law school, worked as a U.S. Capitol police officer; city attorney, Henderson, 1964–66; member and chairman, South Nevada Memorial Hospital Board of Trustees, 1967–69; elected: Nevada State Assembly, 1969–70; Lieutenant Governor, State of Nevada, 1970–74; served, executive committee, National Conference of Lieutenant Governors; chairman, Nevada Gaming Commission, 1977–81; member: Nevada State, Clark County and American bar associations; married the former Landra Gould in 1959; five children: Lana, Rory, Leif, Josh, and Key; committees: Appropriations; Assistant Democratic Leader, 1998–2004; elected Democratic leader for the 109th Congress; elected to the 98th Congress on November 2, 1982, and reelected to the 99th Congress; elected to the U.S. Senate on November 4, 1986; reelected to each succeeding Senate term.

Office Listings

http://reid.senate.gov

528 Hart Senate Office Building, Washington, DC 20510	....	(202) 224–3542
Chief of Staff.—Susan McCue.		FAX: 224–7327
Deputy Chiefs of Staff: David McCullum, Gary Myrick.		
Executive Assistant.—Janice Shelton.		
Legislative Director.—Kai Anderson.		
600 East Williams Street, Room 302, Carson City, NV 89701	....	(775) 882–7343
Office Director.—Yolanda Garcia.		
333 Las Vegas Boulevard South, Suite 8016, Las Vegas, NV 89101	....	(702) 388–5020
Office Director.—Rebecca Lambe.		
400 S. Virginia Street, Suite 902, Reno, NV 89501	....	(775) 686–5750
District Manager.—Mary Conelly.		

* * *

JOHN ENSIGN, Republican, of Las Vegas, NV; born in Roseville, CA, March 25, 1958; education: E.W. Clark High School, Las Vegas, NV, 1976; B.S., University of Nevada at Las Vegas, 1976–79; Oregon State University, 1981; Colorado State University, 1985; professional: veterinarian; organizations: Las Vegas Southwest Rotary; Las Vegas Chamber of Commerce; Sigma Chi (fraternal organization); Meadows Christian Fellowship; married: Darlene Ensign, 1987; children: Trevor, Siena, and Michael; committees: Armed Services; Budget; Commerce, Science, and Transportation; Health, Education, Labor, and Pensions; Veterans' Affairs; elected to the U.S. House of Representatives in 1994; reelected in 1996; elected to the U.S. Senate on November 7, 2000.

Office Listings

http://ensign.senate.gov

364 Russell Senate Office Building, Washington, DC 20510	....	(202) 224–6244
Chief of Staff.—Scott Bensing.		FAX: 228–2193
Scheduler.—Jim Shepard.		
Legislative Director.—Pam Thiessen.		
Communications Director.—Jack Finn.		
333 Las Vegas Boulevard South, Suite 8203, Las Vegas, NV 89101	....	(702) 388–6605
State Director.—Sonja Joya.		
600 East William Street, Suite 304, Carson City, NV 89701	....	(775) 885–9111
Rural Coordinator.—Kevin Kirkeby.		
400 S. Virginia Street, Suite 738, Reno, NV 89501	....	(775) 686–5770
Northern Nevada Director.—Verita Black Prothro.		

REPRESENTATIVES

FIRST DISTRICT

SHELLEY BERKLEY, Democrat, of Las Vegas, NV; born in New York, NY, January 20, 1951; education: graduate of Clark County, NV, public school system; B.A., University of Nevada at Las Vegas, 1972; J.D., University of San Diego School of Law, 1976; professional:

attorney; Nevada State Assembly, 1982–84; former deputy director of the Nevada State Commerce Department; hotel executive; vice-chair, Nevada University and Community College System Board of Regents, 1990–98; has served on numerous civic, business, and professional organizations; married: Larry Lehrner; children: Max and Sam; committees: International Relations; Transportation and Infrastructure; Veterans' Affairs; elected to the 106h Congress; reelected to each succeeding Congress.

Office Listings
http://www.house.gov/berkley

439 Cannon House Office Building, Washington, DC 20515 .... (202) 225–5965
    Chief of Staff.—Richard Urey.   FAX: 225–3119
    Legislative Director.—Heather Urban.
    Communications Director.—David Cherry.
    Scheduler.—Joanne Jensen.
2340 Paseo Del Prado, Suite D–106, Las Vegas, NV 89102 .... (702) 220–9823
    District Director.—Tod Story.

Counties: CLARK COUNTY (part). CITIES: Las Vegas, and North Las Vegas. Population (2000), 666,088.

ZIP Codes: 89030–33, 89036, 89084, 89086, 89101–04, 89106–10, 89114–17, 89119, 89121–22, 89125–35, 89137, 89142–46, 89149–56, 89160, 89170, 89177, 89185, 89193

* * *

SECOND DISTRICT

JIM GIBBONS, Republican, of Reno, NV; born in Sparks, NV, December 16, 1944; education: B.S., geology, and M.S., mining geology, University of Nevada at Reno; J.D., Southwestern University; admitted to the Nevada bar in 1982 and began practice in Reno; military service: colonel, U.S. Air Force, 1967–71; vice commander of the Nevada Air Guard since 1975; professional: pilot, Delta Airlines; mining geologist; mining and water rights attorney; Nevada State Assemblyman, 1989–93; member: advisory board, Committee to Aid Abused Women; Nevada Landman's Association; American Association of Petroleum Landsmen; Nevada Bar Association; National Conference Board; University of Nevada Alumni Association; Reno Board of Realtors; board of directors, Nevada Council on Economic Education; Nevada Development Authority; married: Theresa D. Snelling in 1986; children: Christopher, Jennifer, and Jimmy; committees: Armed Services; Homeland Security; Resources; elected to the 105th Congress; reelected to each succeeding Congress.

Office Listings

100 Cannon House Office Building, Washington, DC 20515 .... (202) 225–6155
    Chief of Staff / Press Secretary.—Amy Spanbauer.   FAX: 225–5679
    Legislative Director.—Cory Kennedy.
    Legislative Assistants: Tray Abney, Don Bevis, Mackenzie Coon, Emy
      Lesofski.
400 South Virginia Street, Suite 502, Reno, NV 89501 .... (775) 686–5760
    District Director.—Dianne Cornwall.
600 Las Vegas Blvd. South, Suite 680, Las Vegas, NV 89101 .... (702) 255–1651
    Constituent Representative.—Judith Ray.
491 Fourth Street, Elko, NV 89801 .... (775) 777–7920
    Constituent Representative.—Betty Jo Vonderheide.

Counties: CARSON CITY, CHURCHILL, CLARK (part), DOUGLAS, ELKO, ESMERALDA, EUREKA, HUMBOLDT, LANDER, LINCOLN, LYON, MINERAL, NYE, PERSHING, STOREY, WASHOE, WHITE PINE. Population (2000), 666,087.

ZIP Codes: 89001, 89003, 89008, 89010, 89013, 89017, 89019–24, 89026–27, 89030–31, 89041–43, 89045, 89047–49, 89052, 89060–61, 89115, 89124, 89137, 89139, 89141, 89156, 89191, 89301, 89310–11, 89314–19, 89402–15, 89418–36, 89438–40, 89442, 89444–52, 89460, 89496, 89501–07, 89509–13, 89515, 89520–21, 89523, 89533, 89557, 89570, 89701–06, 89711–14, 89721, 89801–03, 89815, 89820–26, 89828, 89830–32, 89834–35, 89883

* * *

THIRD DISTRICT

JON C. PORTER, Republican, of Boulder City, NV; born in Fort Dodge, IA, May 16, 1955; education: attended Briar Cliff College in Sioux City, IA; professional: insurance business; worked with the Farmers Insurance Group; public service: former Mayor (1987–1991), and City

Councilman (1983–1993), in Boulder City; elected to the Nevada State Senate, 1994; awards: Nevada League of Cities' Elected Official of the Year; Clark County School District's Crystal Apple Award; religion: Catholic; married: Laurie; children: J. Chris and Nicole; committees: Education and the Workforce; Government Reform; Transportation and Infrastructure; elected to the 108th Congress on November 5, 2002; reelected to each succeeding Congress.

Office Listings

http://www.house.gov/porter

218 Cannon House Office Building, Washington, DC 20515 .... (202) 225–3252
    Chief of Staff.—Windsor Freemyer.   FAX: 225–2185
    Legislative Director.—Trevor Kolego.
    Administrative Assistant.—Stacey Parker.
    Press Secretary.—Adam Mayberry.
2501 North Green Valley Parkway, Suite 112D, Henderson, NV 89014 .... (702) 387–4941
    District Director.—Kay Finfrock.

Counties: CLARK COUNTY (part). Population (2000), 666,082.

ZIP Codes: 89004–05, 89007, 89009, 89011–12, 89014–16, 89018, 89025, 89028–30, 89039–40, 89046, 89052–53, 89070, 89074, 89077, 89101–4, 89108–11, 89113, 89117–24, 89128–29, 89134–36, 89138–39, 89141–42, 89146–49, 89156, 89159, 89162–63, 89170, 89173, 89177, 89180, 89185, 89191, 89193, 89195, 89199

NEW HAMPSHIRE

(Population 2000, 1,235,786)

SENATORS

JUDD GREGG, Republican, of Rye, NH; born in Nashua, NH, February 14, 1947; education: graduated Phillips Exeter Academy, 1965; A.B., Columbia University, New York City, 1969; J.D., 1972, and LL.M., 1975, Boston University; attorney, admitted to the New Hampshire bar, 1972; commenced practice in Nashua, NH; practiced law, 1975–80; member, Governor's Executive Council, 1978–80; married to the former Kathleen MacLellan, 1973; three children: Molly, Sarah, and Joshua; committees: Appropriations; chairman, Budget; Health, Education, Labor, and Pensions; elected to the 97th Congress, November 4, 1980, and reelected to the 98th–100th Congresses; elected Governor of New Hampshire, 1988–92; elected to the U.S. Senate on November 3, 1992; reelected to each succeeding Senate term.

Office Listings
http://gregg.senate.gov

393 Russell Senate Office Building, Washington, DC 20510	(202) 224–3324
Chief of Staff.—Joel Maiola.	
Administrative Assistant.—Vasiliki Christopoulos.	
Communications Director.—Erin Rath.	
125 North Main Street, Concord, NH 03301	(603) 225–7115
41 Hooksett Road, Unit #2, Manchester, NH 03104	(603) 622–7979
16 Pease Boulevard, Portsmouth, NH 03801	(603) 431–2171
60 Pleasant Street, Berlin, NH 03570	(603) 752–2604

* * *

JOHN E. SUNUNU, Republican, of Bedford, NH; born in Boston, MA, September 10, 1964; education: graduated, Salem High School, Salem, NH, 1982; B.S., mechanical engineering, Massachusetts Institute of Technology, 1986; M.S., mechanical engineering, Massachusetts Institute of Technology, 1987; M.B.A., Harvard University Business School, Boston, MA, 1991; Chief Financial Officer and Director of Operations, Teletrol Systems, Inc.; married to Catherine Halloran Sununu, 1988; three children: John Hayes, Grace, and Charlotte; elected to the 105th Congress; reelected to each succeeding Congress; committees: Banking, Housing and Urban Affairs; Commerce, Science, and Transportation; Foreign Relations; Joint Economic Committee; elected to the U.S. Senate on November 5, 2002.

Office Listings
http://sununu.senate.gov

111 Russell Senate Office Building, Washington, DC 20510	(202) 224–2841
Chief of Staff.—Paul Collins.	FAX: 228–4131
Legislative Director.—Jamie Burnett.	
Communications Director.—Barbara Riley.	
One New Hampshire Avenue, Suite 120, Portsmouth, NH 03801	(603) 430–9560
1589 Elm Street, Suite 3, Manchester, NH 03101	(603) 647–7500

REPRESENTATIVES

FIRST DISTRICT

JEB BRADLEY, Republican, of Wolfeboro, NH; born, October 20, 1952; education: Governor Dummer Academy (prep school), Byfield, MA; Tufts University, Medford, MA; professional: businessman; owner of a health food store and a paint contracting business; also developed commercial and residential real estate; public service: served on the local planning board and budget committee; New Hampshire State Representative, 1990–2002; family: married to Barbara; children: Jan, Ramona, Urs, and Sebastian; committees: Armed Services; Budget; Small Business; Veterans' Affairs; elected to the 108th Congress on November 5, 2002; reelected to each succeeding Congress.

Office Listings

http://www.house.gov/bradley

1218 Longworth House Office Building, Washington, DC 20515 .... (202) 225–5456
Chief of Staff.—Debra Vanderbeek.   FAX: 225–5822
Legislative Director.—Michael Liles.
Press Secretary.—Stephanie DuBois.
1095 Elm Street, Manchester, NH 03101 .... (603) 641–9536
104 Washington Street, Dover, NH 03820 .... (603) 743–4813

Counties: BELKNAP (part), CARROLL, HILLSBOROUGH (part), ROCKINGHAM, STAFFORD. CITIES: Bedford, Conway, Derry, Dover, Exeter, Goffstown, Laconia, Londonderry, Manchester, Merrimack, Portsmouth, and Rochester. Population (2000), 617,575.

ZIP Codes: 03032, 03034, 03036–38, 03040–42, 03044–45, 03053–54, 03077, 03101–06, 03108–11, 03218, 03220, 03225–27, 03237, 03246–47, 03249, 03253–54, 03256, 03259, 03261, 03263, 03269, 03290–91, 03298–99, 03307, 03801–05, 03809–10, 03812–22, 03824–27, 03830, 03832–33, 03835–60, 03862, 03864–75, 03878, 03882–87, 03890, 03894, 03896–97

* * *

SECOND DISTRICT

CHARLES F. BASS, Republican, of Peterborough, NH; born in Boston, MA, January 8, 1952; education: graduated, Holderness School, Plymouth, NH, 1970; B.A., Dartmouth College, NH, 1974; vice president, High Standard Inc., Dublin, NH; chairman, Columbia Architectural Products, Beltsville, MD; New Hampshire State Representative, 1982–88; vice chairman, Judiciary Committee; New Hampshire State Senate 1988–92; chairman, Public Affairs and Ethics committees; co-chairman, Economic Development Committee; member: Monadnock Rotary Club (president, 1992–93); Amoskeag Veterans; Altermont Lodge, FA&M; trusteeships: New Hampshire Higher Education Assistance Foundation, Monadnock Conservancy, New Hampshire Humanities Council; married: Lisa Levesque Bass, 1989; children: Lucy and Jonathan; committees: Energy and Commerce; elected to the 104th Congress; reelected to each succeeding Congress.

Office Listings

http://www.house.gov/bass   cbass@mail.house.gov

2421 Rayburn House Office Building, Washington, DC 20515 .... (202) 225–5206
Chief of Staff.—Darwin Cusack.
Legislative Director.—Tad Furtado.
Press Secretary.—Margo Shideler.
142 North Main Street, Concord, NH 03301 .... (603) 226–0249
170 Main Street, Nashua, NH 03062 .... (603) 889–8772
76 Main Street, Suite 2C, Littleton, NH 03561 .... (603) 444–1271
1 West Street, Suite 208, Keene, NH 03431 .... (603) 358–4094

Counties: BELKNAP (part), CHESHIRE, COOS, GRAFTON, HILLSBOROUGH (part), MERRIMACK (part), ROCKINGHAM (part), SULLIVAN. Population (2000), 618,211.

ZIP Codes: 03031, 03033, 03037, 03043, 03045–49, 03051–52, 03055, 03057, 03060–64, 03070–71, 03073, 03076, 03079, 03082, 03084, 03086–87, 03215–17, 03220–24, 03226, 03229–31, 03233–35, 03238, 03240–45, 03251–52, 03255, 03257–58, 03260–64, 03266, 03268–69, 03272–76, 03278–82, 03284, 03287, 03289, 03293, 03301–05, 03307, 03431, 03435, 03440–52, 03455–58, 03461–62, 03464–70, 03561, 03570, 03574–76, 03579–85, 03587–90, 03592–93, 03595, 03597–98, 03601–05, 03607–09, 03740–41, 03743, 03745–46, 03748–56, 03765–66, 03768–71, 03773–74, 03777, 03779–82, 03784–85, 03811

NEW JERSEY

(Population 2000 8,414,350)

SENATORS

JON S. CORZINE, Democrat, of Hoboken, NJ; born in Willey's Station, IL, January 1, 1947; education: B.A., University of Illinois, 1969 (Phi Beta Kappa); M.B.A., University of Chicago, 1973; military service: U.S. Marine Corps Reserve, 1969–1975; professional: businessman; Chairman and CEO of Goldman Sachs (investment bank); organizations: co-chairman, YMCA Second Century Campaign; director, Family Services of Summit; chairman, New Jersey Performing Arts Center Council of Trustees; Progressive Policy Institute; awards: Time Magazine's Top 50 Technology Executives, 1997; chair, President's Commission to Study Capital Budgeting, 1997–1999; family: three children; committees: Banking, Housing, and Urban Affairs; Budget; Energy and Natural Resources; Select Committee on Intelligence; elected to the U.S. Senate on November 7, 2000.

Office Listings

http://corzine.senate.gov

502 Hart Senate Office Building, Washington, DC 20510	(202) 224–4744
Chief of Staff.—Heather Howard.	FAX: 228–2197
Press Secretary.—David Wald.	
Office Manager.—Margaret Van Tassell.	
1 Gateway Center, 11th Floor, Newark, NJ 07102	(973) 645–3030
208 Whitehorse Pike, Suite 18, Barrington, NJ 08007–1322	(856) 757–5353

* * *

FRANK LAUTENBERG, Democrat, of Cliffside Park, NJ; born in Paterson, NJ, January 23, 1924; education: Nutley High School, Nutley, NJ, 1941; B.S., Economics, Columbia University School of Business, New York, NY, 1949; professional: U.S. Army Signal Corps, 1942–46; data processing firm founder, and CEO, 1952–82; commissioner, Port Authority of New York and New Jersey, 1978–82; commissioner, New Jersey Economic Development Authority; member: U.S. Holocaust Memorial Council; Advisory Council of the Graduate School of Business, Columbia University; four children: Ellen, Nan, Lisa and Joshua; elected to the U.S. Senate on November 2, 1982; appointed by the Governor on December 27, 1982, to complete the unexpired term of Senator Nicholas F. Brady; reelected in 1988 and 1994; not a candidate for reelection in 2000; replaced Senator Robert Torricelli as the Democratic candidate for the U.S. Senate in October 2002; committees: Commerce, Science, and Transportation; Environment and Public Works; Homeland Security and Governmental Affairs; elected to the U.S. Senate on November 5, 2002.

Office Listings

http://lautenberg.senate.gov

324 Hart Senate Office Building, Washington, DC 20510	(202) 224–3224
Chief of Staff.—Tim Yehl.	FAX: 228–4054
Chief Counsel.—Dan Katz.	
Legislative Director.—Gray Maxwell.	
Communications Director.—Alex Formuzis.	
1 Gateway Center, Suite 102, Newark, NJ 07102	(973) 639–8700

REPRESENTATIVES

FIRST DISTRICT

ROBERT E. ANDREWS, Democrat, of Haddon Heights, NJ; born in Camden, NJ, August 4, 1957; education: graduated, Triton High School, Runnemede, NJ, 1975; B.S., political science, Bucknell University, *summa cum laude*, Phi Beta Kappa, Lewisburg, PA, 1979; J.D., *magna cum laude*, Cornell Law School, Cornell Law Review, Ithaca, NY, 1982; Camden County Freeholder, 1986–90; Camden County Freeholder Director, 1988–90; married: Camille Spinello; children: Jacquelyn and Josi; committees: Armed Services; Education and the Workforce; subcommittees: Education Reform; ranking member, Employer/Employee Relations; Military Personnel; Terrorism, Unconventional Threats and Capabilities; elected by special election on November 6, 1990, to the 101st Congress, to fill the vacancy caused by the resignation of James Florio; elected at the same time to the 102nd Congress; reelected to each succeeding Congress.

Office Listings

http://www.house.gov/andrews

2439 Rayburn House Office Building, Washington, DC 20515 .... (202) 225–6501
Legislative Director.—Robert Knotts.   FAX: 225–6583
506A White Horse Pike, Haddon Heights, NJ 08035 .... (856) 546–5100
District Director.—Amanda Caruso.

Counties: BURLINGTON COUNTY. CITIES AND TOWNSHIPS: Maple Shade, Palmyra, Riverton. CAMDEN COUNTY. CITIES AND TOWNSHIPS: Audubon, Audubon Park, Barrington, Bellmawr, Berlin, Berlin Township, Brooklawn, Camden, Chesilhurst, Clementon, Collingswood, Gibbsboro, Gloucester City, Gloucester Township, Haddon Heights, Haddon Township, Hi-Nella, Laurel Springs, Lawnside, Lindenwold, Magnolia, Mt. Ephraim, Oaklyn, Pennsauken, Pine Hill, Pine Valley, Runnemede, Somerdale, Stratford, Tavistock, Voorhees, Winslow, Woodlynne. GLOUCESTER COUNTY. CITIES AND TOWN-SHIPS: Deptford, E. Greenwich, Greenwich, Logan Township, Mantua, Monroe, National Park, Paulsboro, Washington Township, and Wenonah. Population (2000), 647,258.

ZIP Codes: 08002–04, 08007, 08009, 08012, 08014, 08018, 08020–21, 08026–33, 08035, 08037, 08043, 08045, 08049, 08051–52, 08056, 08059, 08061–63, 08065–66, 08071, 08076–80, 08081, 08083–86, 08089–91, 08093–97, 08099, 08101–10

* * *

SECOND DISTRICT

FRANK A. LoBIONDO, Republican; born in Bridgeton, NJ, May 12, 1946; education: graduated, St. Joseph's University, Philadelphia, PA, 1968; professional: operations manager, LoBiondo Brothers Motor Express, 1968–94; Cumberland County Freeholder, 1985–87; New Jersey General Assembly, 1988–94; currently serves as Member of Congress (1995–present); committees: Transportation and Infrastructure; subcommittees: Aviation; chairman, Coast Guard and Maritime Transportation; awards and honors: honorary Coast Guard Chief Petty Officer; Board of Directors, Young Mens Christian Association; Honorary Rotarian; Taxpayer Hero award; Watchdog of the Treasury award; "Super Friend of Seniors" award; two-time winner of the "Friend of the National Parks" award; March of Dimes FDR award for community service; 2001 President's award, Literacy Volunteers of America, NJ, Inc.; committees: Armed Services; Transportation and Infrastructure; elected to the 104th Congress; reelected to each succeeding Congress.

Office Listings

http://www.house.gov/lobiondo

225 Cannon House Office Building, Washington, DC 20515 .... (202) 225–6572
Chief of Staff.—Mary Annie Harper.   FAX: 225–3318
Executive Assistant.—Heather Fallon.
5914 Main Street, Mays Landing, NJ 08330 .... (609) 625–5008
District Director.—Linda Hinckley.

Counties: BURLINGTON (part). CITIES AND TOWNSHIPS: Shamong, Washington, Waterford. CAMDEN COUNTY (part). ATLANTIC COUNTY. CITIES AND TOWNSHIPS: Absecon, Atlantic City, Brigantine, Buena, Cardiff, Collings Lake, Cologne, Corbin City, Dorothy, Egg Harbor, Estell Manor, Galloway, Hammonton, Landisville, Leeds Point, Linwood, Longport, Margate, Mays Landing, Milmay, Minotola, Mizpah, Newtonville, Northfield, Oceanville, Pleasantville, Pomona, Port Republic, Richland, Somers Point, Ventnor. CAPE MAY COUNTY. CITIES AND TOWNSHIPS: Avalon, Bargaintown, Beesley's, Belleplain, Burleigh, Cape May, Cape May C.H., Cape May Point, Cold Springs, Del Haven, Dennisville, Dias Creek, Eldora, Erma, Fishing Creek, Goshen, Green Creek, Greenfield, Marmora, Ocean City, Ocean View, Rio Grande, Sea Isle, South Dennis, South Seaville, Stone Harbor, Strathmere, Tuckahoe, Villas, Whitesboro, Wildwood, Woodbine. CUMBERLAND COUNTY. CITIES AND TOWNSHIPS: Bridgeton, Cedarville, Centerton, Deerfield, Delmont, Dividing Creek, Dorchester, Elwood, Fairton, Fortescue, Greenwich, Heislerville, Hopewell, Leesburg, Mauricetown, Millville, Newport, Port Elizabeth, Port Norris, Rosenhayn, Shiloh, Vineland. GLOUCESTER COUNTY (part). CITIES AND TOWNSHIPS: Clayton, Ewan, Franklinville, Glassboro, Harrisonville, Malaga, Mantua, Mickleton, Mullica Hill, Newfield, Pitman, Richwood, Sewell, Swedesboro, Williamstown, Woodbury. SALEM COUNTY. CITIES AND TOWNSHIPS: Alloway, Carney's Point, Daretown, Deepwater, Elmer, Elsinboro, Hancocks Bridge, Monroeville, Norma, Pedricktown, Penns Grove, Pennsville, Quinton, Salem, and Woodstown. Population (2000), 647,258.

ZIP Codes: 08001, 08004, 08009, 08019–20, 08023, 08025, 08028, 08037–39, 08051, 08056, 08061–62, 08067, 08069–72, 08074, 08079–80, 08085, 08088–89, 08094, 08098, 08201–05, 08210, 08212–15, 08217–21, 08223, 08225–26, 08230–32, 08234, 08240–48, 08250–52, 08260, 08270, 08302, 08310–24, 08326–30, 08332, 08340–50, 08352–53, 08360–62, 08401–04, 08406

* * *

THIRD DISTRICT

JIM SAXTON, Republican, of Mt. Holly, NJ; born in Nicholson, PA, January 22, 1943; education: graduated, Lackawanna Trail High School, Factoryville, PA, 1961; B.A., Education, East Stroudsburg State College, PA, 1965; graduate courses in elementary education, Temple University, Philadelphia, PA, 1968; professional: public school teacher, 1965–68; realtor, owner of Jim Saxton Realty Company, 1968–85; New Jersey General Assembly, 1976–82; State Senate, 1982–84; chairman, State Republican Platform Committee, 1983; former member: Chamber of Commerce, Association of the U.S. Air Force, Leadership Foundation of New Jersey, Boy Scouts of America, Rotary International; former chairman: American Cancer Committee; children: Jennifer and Martin; committees: Armed Services; Resources; chair, Joint Economic Committee; elected to the 98th Congress, by special election, on November 6, 1984; reelected to each succeeding Congress.

Office Listings

2217 Rayburn House Office Building, Washington, DC 20515	(202) 225–4765
Chief of Staff.—Elise Kenderian Aronson.	FAX: 225–0778
Executive Assistant.—Derek Walker.	
100 High Street, Mount Holly, NJ 08060	(609) 261–5800
District Representative / Business Manager.—Sandra Condit.	
1 Maine Avenue, Cherry Hill, NJ 08002	(856) 428–0520
247 Main Street, Toms River, NJ 08753	(732) 914–2020

Counties: BURLINGTON (part), CAMDEN (part), OCEAN (part). Population (2000), 647,257.

ZIP Codes: 08002–06, 08008–11, 08015–16, 08019, 08034, 08036, 08043, 08046, 08048, 08050, 08053–55, 08057, 08060, 08064–65, 08068, 08073, 08075, 08077, 08087–88, 08092, 08109, 08215, 08224, 08352, 08501, 08511, 08562, 08618, 08640–41, 08690, 08721–23, 08731–32, 08734–35, 08739–41, 08751–59

* * *

FOURTH DISTRICT

CHRISTOPHER H. SMITH, Republican, of Robbinsville, NJ; born in Rahway, NJ, March 4, 1953; B.A., Trenton State College, 1975; attended Worcester College, England, 1974; businessman; executive director, New Jersey Right to Life Committee, Inc., 1976–78; married to the former Marie Hahn, 1976; children: Melissa Elyse, Christopher, and Michael; religion: Catholic; co-chairman, Commission on Security and Cooperation in Europe; co-chairman, Congressional Pro-Life Caucus; committees: vice-chairman, International Relations; subcommittees: chairman, Africa, Global Human Rights and International Operations; elected to the 97th Congress, November 4, 1980; reelected to each succeeding Congress.

Office Listings

http://www.house.gov/chrissmith

2373 Rayburn House Office Building, Washington, DC 20515	(202) 225–3765
Chief of Staff.—Mary Noonan.	FAX: 225–7768
Office Manager.—Katie Doherty.	
1540 Kuser Road, Suite A9, Hamilton, NJ 08619	(609) 585–7878
Regional Director.—Joyce Golden.	
108 Lacey Road, Whiting, NJ 08759	(732) 350–2300
Regional Director.—Loretta Charbonneau.	

Counties: BURLINGTON COUNTY. MUNICIPALITIES: Bordentown City, Bordentown Township, Burlington City, Burlington Township, Chesterfield, Fieldsboro, Florence, Mansfield, Springfield. MERCER COUNTY. MUNICIPALITIES: East Windsor, Hamilton, Highstown, Trenton, Washington Township. MONMOUTH COUNTY. MUNICIPALITIES: Allentown, Brielle, Colts Neck, Farmingdale, Freehold, Freehold Borough, Howell, Manasquan, Millstone Township, Roosevelt, Sea Girt, Spring Lake Heights, Upper Freehold, Wall. OCEAN COUNTY. MUNICIPALITIES: Bay Head, Brick, Jackson, Lakehurst, Lakewood, Manchester, Mantoloking, Plumstead, Pt. Pleasant, and Pt. Pleasant Beach. Population (2000), 647,258.

ZIP Codes: 07710, 07715, 07719, 07722, 07726–28, 07731, 07753, 07762, 08010, 08016, 08022, 08041–42, 08060, 08068, 08075, 08501, 08505, 08510, 08512, 08514–15, 08518, 08520, 08526–27, 08533, 08535, 08554–55, 08561, 08601–07, 08609–11, 08619–20, 08625, 08629, 08638, 08645–48, 08650, 08666, 08690–91, 08695, 08701, 08720, 08723–24, 08730, 08733, 08736, 08738, 08742, 08750, 08753, 08757, 08759

* * *

FIFTH DISTRICT

SCOTT GARRETT, Republican, of Wantage Township, NJ; born in Englewood, NJ, July 7, 1959; education: High Point Regional High School, 1977; B.A., Montclair State University, 1981; J.D., Rutgers University Law School, 1984; professional: attorney; counsel attorney with law firm of Sellar Richardson; organizations: Big Brothers, Big Sisters; Sussex County Chamber of Commerce; Sussex County Board of Agriculture; public service: New Jersey State Assemblyman, 1990–2002; family: married to Mary Ellen; children: Jennifer and Brittany; committees: Budget; Financial Services; elected to the 108th Congress on November 5, 2002; reelected to each succeeding Congress.

Office Listings

http://www.house.gov/garrett

1318 Longworth House Office Building, Washington, DC 20515	(202) 225–4465
Chief of Staff.—Evan Kozlow.	FAX: 225–9048
Legislative Director.—Jay Fahrer.	
Press Secretary.—Phillip Brown.	
210 Route 4 East, Suite 206, Paramus, NJ 07652	(201) 712–0330
93 Main Street, Newton, NJ 07860	(973) 300–2000

Counties: BERGEN (part), PASSAIC (part), SUSSEX, WARREN. Population (2000), 647,257.

ZIP Codes: 07401, 07403, 07416–23, 07428, 07430, 07432, 07435–36, 07438–39, 07446, 07450–52, 07456, 07458, 07460–63, 07465, 07480–81, 07495, 07498, 07620–21, 07624, 07626–28, 07630, 07640–42, 07645–49, 07652–53, 07656, 07661–62, 07670, 07675–77, 07820–23, 07825–27, 07829, 07831–33, 07838–40, 07844, 07846, 07848, 07851, 07855, 07860, 07863, 07865, 07871, 07875, 07877, 07879–82, 07890, 08802, 08804, 08808, 08865–86

* * *

SIXTH DISTRICT

FRANK PALLONE, JR., Democrat, of Long Branch, NJ; born in Long Branch, October 30, 1951; education: B.A., Middlebury College, Middlebury, VT, 1973; M.A., Fletcher School of Law and Diplomacy, 1974; J.D., Rutgers University School of Law, 1978; member of the bar: Florida, New York, Pennsylvania, and New Jersey; attorney, Marine Advisory Service; assistant professor, Cook College, Rutgers University Sea Grant Extension Program; counsel, Monmouth County, NJ, Protective Services for the Elderly; instructor, Monmouth College; Long Branch City Council, 1982–88; New Jersey State Senate, 1983–88; married the former Sarah Hospodor, 1992; committees: Energy and Commerce; Resources; elected to the 100th Congress, by special election, on November 8, 1988, to fill the vacancy caused by the death of James J. Howard; reelected to each succeeding Congress.

Office Listings

420 Cannon House Office Building, Washington, DC 20515	(202) 225–4671
Chief of Staff.—Jeff Carroll.	FAX: 225–9665
Legislative Director.—Kathy Kulkarni.	
Communications Director.—Andrew Souvall.	
District Director.—Shawn Brennan.	
504 Broadway, Long Branch, NJ 07740	(732) 571–1140
67/69 Church Street, Kilmer Square, New Brunswick, NJ	(732) 249–8892
Suite 104, I.E.I. Airport Plaza, Highway 36, Hazlet, NJ	(732) 264–9104

Counties: MONMOUTH COUNTY. CITIES AND TOWNSHIPS: Aberdeen, Allenhurst, Asbury Park, Atlantic Highlands, Avon-by-the-Sea, Belmar, Bradley Beach, Deal, Hazlet, Highlands, Interlaken, Keansburg, Keyport, Loch Arbour, Long Branch, Manalapan, Marlboro, Matawan, Middletown, Monmouth Beach, Neptune City, Neptune Twp., Ocean, Red Bank, Sea Birght, South Belmar, Union Beach, West Long Branch. MIDDLESEX COUNTY. CITIES AND TOWNSHIPS: Dunellen, Edison, Highland Park, Metuchen, Middlesex, New Brunswick, Old Bridge, Piscataway, Sayerville, South Amboy. SOMERSET COUNTY. CITIES: Franklin. UNION COUNTY. CITIES: Plainfield. Population (2000), 647,257.

ZIP Codes: 07060–63, 07080, 07701–02, 07704, 07709–12, 07715–21, 07723–24, 07726, 07730, 07732, 07734–35, 07737, 07740, 07746–48, 07750–56, 07758, 07760, 07764, 08812, 08816–18, 08820, 08830–31, 08837, 08840, 08846, 08854–55, 08857, 08859, 08871–73, 08877–79, 08899, 08901, 08903–04, 08906, 08922, 08933, 08988–89

* * *

SEVENTH DISTRICT

MIKE FERGUSON, Republican, of Warren, NJ; born in Ridgewood, NJ, July 2, 1970; education: Delbarton School, Morristown, NJ; B.A., University of Notre Dame; M.P.P., George-town University; professional: educator and small businessman; Executive Director, Better Schools Foundation; Executive Director, Catholic Campaign of America; Director, Save Our Schoolchildren; President, Strategic Education Initiatives, Inc.; organizations: National Federation of Independent Business; Knights of Columbus; Epilepsy Foundation of New Jersey; Sierra Club; Friendly Sons of St. Patrick; National Italian American Association; religion: Roman Catholic; family: married to Maureen; four children; committees: Energy and Commerce; elected to the 107th Congress on November 7, 2000; reelected to each succeeding Congress.

Office Listings
http://www.house.gov/ferguson

214 Cannon House Office Building, Washington, DC 20515 .... (202) 225-5361
Chief of Staff.—Chris Jones. FAX: 225-9460
Legislative Director.—Greg Orlando.
Scheduler.—Erin Connolly.
Press Secretary.—Abby Bird.
45 Mountain Boulevard, Building D, Suite 1, Warren, NJ 07059 .... (908) 757-7835
District Director.—Marcus Rayner.

Counties: MIDDLESEX COUNTY. MUNICIPALITIES: Edison, South Plainfield, Woodbridge. UNION COUNTY. MUNICIPALITIES: Berkeley Heights, Clark, Cranford, Fanwood, Garwood, Kenilworth, Linden, Mountainside, New Providence, Roselle Park, Scotch Plains, Springfield, Summit, Union, Westfield, Winfield. HUNTERDON COUNTY. MUNICIPALITIES: Alexandria, Bethlehem, Bloomsbury, Califon, Clinton Township, Clinton, Flemington, Glen Gardner, Hampton, High Bridge, Holland, Lebanon, Lebanon Township, Milford, Oldwick, Raritan, Readington, Tewksbury, Union. SOMERSET COUNTY. MUNICIPALI-TIES: Bedminster, Bernardsville, Bound Brook, Branchburg, Bridgewater, Far Hills, Green Brook, Hillsborough, Manville, Montgomery Township, Millstone, North Plainfield, Peapack-Gladstone, Rocky Hill, South Bound Brook, Warren, and Watchung. Population (2000), 647,257.

ZIP Codes: 07001, 07008, 07016, 07023, 07027, 07033, 07036, 07040, 07059-60, 07062-64, 07066-67, 07069, 07076, 07080-81, 07083, 07090-92, 07095, 07204, 07830, 07901-02, 07921-22, 07924, 07931, 07934, 07974, 07977-79, 08502, 08504, 08540, 08551, 08553, 08558, 08801-02, 08804-05, 08807, 08809, 08812, 08820-22, 08825-27, 08829-30, 08832-37, 08840, 08844, 08848, 08853, 08858, 08863, 08867, 08870, 08876, 08880, 08885, 08887-89

* * *

EIGHTH DISTRICT

BILL PASCRELL, JR., Democrat, of Paterson, NJ; born in Paterson, January 27, 1937; education: B.A., journalism, and M.A., philosophy, Fordham University; veteran, U.S. Army and Army Reserves; educator; New Jersey General Assembly, 1988–96: elected Minority Leader Pro Tempore; mayor of Paterson, 1990–96; named Mayor of the Year by bipartisan NJ Conference of Mayors, 1996; started Paterson's first Economic Development Corporation; married to the former Elsie Marie Botto; three children: William III, Glenn, and David; committees: Homeland Security; Transportation and Infrastructure; subcommittees: Aviation; Economic Security, Infrastructure Protection, and Cyber Security; Emergency Preparedness, Science, and Technology; Highways, Transit and Pipelines; Management, Integration, and Oversight; Water Resources and Environment; elected to the 105th Congress; reelected to each succeeding Congress.

Office Listings
http://www.pascrell.house.gov

2464 Rayburn House Office Building, Washington, DC 20515 .... (202) 225-5751
Office Manager.—Selvin J. White, Jr. FAX: 225-5782
Legislative Director.—Ben Rich.
200 Federal Plaza, Suite 500, Paterson, NJ 07505 .... (201) 523-5152
Chief of Staff.—Ed Farmer.

Counties: ESSEX COUNTY. CITIES: Belleville, Bloomfield, Cedar Grove. Glen Ridge, Livingston, Montclair, Nutley, South Orange, Verona, West Orange. PASSAIC COUNTY. CITIES: Clifton, Haledon, Little Falls, North Haledon, Passaic, Paterson, Pompton Lakes, Prospect Park, Totowa, Wayne, and West Paterson. Population (2000), 647,258

ZIP Codes: 07003-04, 07009, 07011-15, 07028, 07039, 07042-44, 07052, 07055, 07079, 07107, 07109-10, 07424, 07442, 07470, 07474, 07477, 07501-14, 07522, 07524, 07533, 07538, 07543-44

* * *

NINTH DISTRICT

STEVEN R. ROTHMAN, Democrat, of Fair Lawn, NJ; born in Englewood, NJ, October 14, 1952; education: graduate, Tenafly High School, 1970; B.A., Syracuse University, Syracuse, NY, 1974; LL.B., Washington University School of Law, St. Louis, MO, 1977; attorney; two-term mayor of Englewood, NJ, spearheaded business growth and installed a fiscally conservative management team, transforming Englewood's bond rating from one of the worst to the best in Bergen County; Judge, Bergen County Surrogate Court, 1993–96; founding member, New Democratic Coalition; authored the Secure Our Schools Act; two children; committees: Appropriations; subcommittees: Foreign Operations, Export Financing and Related Programs; Transportation, Treasury, HUD, The Judiciary, District of Columbia, and Independent Agencies; elected to the 105th Congress; reelected to each succeeding Congress.

Office Listings
http://www.house.gov/rothman

2303 Rayburn House Office Building, Washington, DC 20515 .... (202) 225–5061
    Chief of Staff.—Bob Decheine.   FAX: 225–5851
    Executive Assistant / Scheduler.—Mary Flanagan.
    Legislative Director.—Kelly Dougherty.
25 Main Street, Court Plaza, Hackensack, NJ 07601–7089 .... (201) 646–0808
    District Director.—Michael Soliman.
130 Central Avenue, Jersey City, NJ 07306–2118 .... (201) 798–1366
    Office Director.—Al Zampella.

Counties: BERGEN COUNTY. CITIES AND TOWNS: Bogota, Carlstadt, Cliffside Park, East Rutherford, Edgewater, Elmwood Park, Englewood, Englewood Cliffs, Fair Lawn, Fairview, Fort Lee, Garfield, Hackensack, Hasbrouck Heights, Leonia, Little Ferry, Lodi, Lyndhurst, Maywood, Moonachie, New Milford, North Arlington, Palisades Park, Ridgefield, Ridgefield Park, Rutherford, Saddle Brook, South Hackensack, Teaneck, Teterboro, Wallington, Wood Ridge. HUDSON COUNTY. CITIES AND TOWNS: Kearny (ward 1: districts 1, 2, and 6; ward 3; and ward 4: districts 5–7), Secaucus, North Bergen, Jersey City. PASSAIC COUNTY (part). BOROUGH: Hawthorne. Population (2000), 647,258.

ZIP Codes: 07010, 07020, 07022, 07024, 07026, 07031–32, 07042, 07047, 07057, 07070–75, 07094, 07096–97, 07099, 07306–08, 07407, 07410, 07601–08, 07631–32, 07643–44, 07646, 07650, 07657, 07660, 07663, 07666, 07670

* * *

TENTH DISTRICT

DONALD M. PAYNE, Democrat, of Newark, NJ; born in Newark, July 16, 1934; education: graduated, Barringer High School, Newark, 1952; B.A., Seton Hall University, South Orange, NJ, 1957; businessman; elected to the Essex County Board of Chosen Freeholders, 1972–78; elected to the Newark Municipal Council, 1982–88; president, YMCA of the USA, 1970–73; member: NAACP, Council on Foreign Relations, Bethlehem Baptist Church; former chairman, Congressional Black Caucus; serves on the advisory council of the U.S. Committee for UNICEF; Advisory Commission on Intergovernmental Relations; board of directors: Congressional Black Caucus Foundation, National Endowment for Democracy; widower; three children; committees: Education and the Workforce; International Relations; Democratic Steering Committee; subcommittees: ranking member, Africa; Employer-Employee Relations; 21st Century Competitiveness; Western Hemisphere; elected on November 8, 1988, to the 101st Congress; reelected to each succeeding Congress.

Office Listings

2209 Rayburn House Office Building, Washington, DC 20515 .... (202) 225–3436
    Chief of Staff.—Maxine James.   FAX: 225–4160
    Legislative Director / Press Secretary.—Kerry McKenney.
50 Walnut Street, Room 1016, Newark, NJ 07102 .... (973) 645–3213
333 North Broad Street, Elizabeth, NJ 07202 .... (908) 629–0222
253 Martin Luther King Drive, Jersey City, NJ 07305 .... (201) 369–0392

Counties: ESSEX, HUDSON, SHORT HILLS, UNION. CITIES AND TOWNSHIPS: Bayonne, East Orange, Elizabeth, Hillside, Irvington, Jersey City, Linden, Maplewood Millburn, Montclair, Newark, Orange, Rahway, Roselle, South Orange, Union, and West Orange. Population (2000), 647,258.

ZIP Codes: 07002, 07017–19, 07028, 07036, 07040–42, 07044, 07050–52, 07065, 07078–79, 07083, 07088, 07101–03, 07105–08, 07111–12, 07114–75, 07184, 07188–89, 07191–95, 07197–99, 07201–03, 07205–08, 07304–05

* * *

ELEVENTH DISTRICT

RODNEY P. FRELINGHUYSEN, Republican, of Morristown, NJ; born in New York, NY, April 29, 1946; education: graduated Hobart College, NY, 1969; attended graduate school in Connecticut; named Legislator of the Year by the Veterans of Foreign Wars, the New Jersey Association of Mental Health Agencies, and the New Jersey Association of Retarded Citizens; honored by numerous organizations; served in the New Jersey General Assembly, 1983–94; chairman, Assembly Appropriations Committee, 1988–89 and 1992–94; member: Morris County Board of Chosen Freeholders, 1974–83 (director, 1980); served on: Welfare and Mental Health boards; Human Services and Private Industry councils; served, U.S. Army, 93rd Engineer Battalion; honorably discharged, 1971; member: American Legion, and Veterans of Foreign Wars; Morris County state and federal aid coordinator and administrative assistant, 1972;

married: Virginia Frelinghuysen; children: Louisine and Sarah; committees: Appropriations; subcommittees: Energy and Water Development and Related Agencies; Defense; elected to the 104th Congress in November, 1994; reelected to each succeeding Congress.

Office Listings
http://www.house.gov/frelinghuysen

2442 Rayburn House Office Building, Washington, DC 20515 .... (202) 225–5034
Chief of Staff.—Nancy Fox.
Press Secretary.—Steve O'Halloran.
Legislative Director.—Steve Wilson.
Scheduler.—Meredith Kenny.
30 Schuyler Place, 2nd Floor, Morristown, NJ 07960 .... (973) 984–0711

Counties: ESSEX COUNTY. CITIES AND TOWNSHIPS: Caldwell, Essex Fells, Fairfield Township, Livingston, Millburn, North Caldwell, Roseland, West Caldwell. MORRIS COUNTY. CITIES AND TOWNSHIPS: Bernardsville, municipalities of Boonton Town, Boonton Township, Brookside, Budd Lake, Butler, Califon, Cedar Knolls, Chatham Borough, Chatham Township, Chester Borough, Chester Township, Convent Station, Denville, Dover Town, East Hanover, Flanders, Florham Park, Gillette, Green Pond, Green Village, Hanover, Harding, Hibernia, Ironia, Jefferson, Kenvill, Kinnelon, Lake Hiawatha, Lake Hopatcong, Landing, Ledgewood, Lincoln Park, Long Valley, Madison, Mendham Borough, Mendham Township, Millington, Mine Hill, Montville, Morris Plains, Morris Township, Morristown, Mount Arlington, Mountain Lakes, Mount Olive, Mount Tabor, Netcong, Newfoundland, New Vernon, Oak Ridge, Parsippany-Troy Hills, Passaic Township, Pequannock, Picatinny, Pine Brook, Randolph, Riverdale, Rockaway Borough, Rockaway Township, Roxbury, Schooley's Mountain, Stanhope, Stirling, Succasunna, Towaco, Victory Gardens, Washington Township, Wharton, and Whippany. PASSAIC COUNTY. CITIES: Bloomingdale. SOMERSET COUNTY. CITIES AND TOWNSHIPS: Bernards Township, Bridgewater, Raritan Borough, and Somerville. SUSSEX COUNTY. CITIES AND TOWNSHIPS: Byram, Hopatcong, Sparta, and Stanhope. Population (2000), 647,258.

ZIP Codes: 07004–07, 07021, 07034–35, 07039, 07041, 07045–46, 07054, 07058, 07068, 07078, 07082, 07405, 07438, 07440, 07444, 07457, 07801–03, 07806, 07821, 07828, 07830, 07834, 07836–37, 07840, 07842–43, 07845, 07847, 07849–50, 07852–53, 07856–57, 07866, 07869–71, 07874, 07876, 07878, 07885, 07920, 07926–28, 07930, 07932–36, 07938–40, 07945–46, 07950, 07960–63, 07970, 07976, 07980–81, 07983, 07999, 08807, 08869, 08876, 08896

* * *

TWELFTH DISTRICT

RUSH D. HOLT, Democrat, of Hopewell Township, NJ; born in Weston, WV, October 15, 1948; son of the youngest person ever to be elected to the U.S. Senate; education: B.A., Carleton College, 1970; M.S. and Ph.D., physics, New York University, 1981; physicist; New York City Environmental Protection Administration, 1972–74; teaching fellow, New York University, 1974–80; Congressional Science Fellow, U.S. House of Representatives, Office of Representative Bob Edgar, 1982–83; professor, Swarthmore College, 1980–88; acting chief, Nuclear & Scientific Division, Office of Strategic Forces, U.S. Department of State, 1987–89; assistant director, Princeton Plasma Physics Laboratory, Princeton, NJ, 1989–97; Protestant; married: Margaret Lancefield; children: Michael, Dejan, and Rachel; committees: Education and the Workforce; Permanent Select Committee on Intelligence; elected to the 106th Congress; reelected to each succeeding Congress.

Office Listings
http://holt.house.gov

1019 Longworth House Office Building, Washington, DC 20515 .... (202) 225–5801
Chief of Staff.—Jim Papa.   FAX: 225–6025
Legislative Director.—Bill Goold.
Press Secretary.—Patrick Eddington.
Executive Assistant.—Lesley Muldoon.
50 Washington Road, West Windsor, NJ 08550 .... (609) 750–9365

Counties: HUNTERDON COUNTY. CITIES AND TOWNSHIPS: Delaware, East Amwell, Franklin, Frenchtown, Kingwood, Lambertville, Stockton, West Amwell. MERCER COUNTY. CITIES AND TOWNSHIPS: Ewing, Hopewell Borough, Hopewell Township, Lawrence, Pennington, Princeton Borough, Princeton Township, West Windsor. MIDDLESEX COUNTY. CITIES AND TOWNSHIPS: Cranbury, East Brunswick, Helmetta, Jamesburg, Monroe, North Brunswick, Old Bridge, Plainsboro Township, South River, Spotswood, South Brunswick. MONMOUTH COUNTY. CITIES AND TOWNSHIPS: Eatontown, Englishtown, Fair Haven, Freehold Township, Holmdel, Little Silver, Manalapan, Marlboro, Middletown, Oceanport, Rumson, Shrewsbury Borough, Shrewsbury Township, Tinton Falls. SOMERSET COUNTY. CITIES AND TOWNSHIPS: Franklin Township. Population (2000), 647,258.

ZIP Codes: 07701–04, 07712, 07724, 07726, 07728, 07733, 07738–39, 07746, 07748, 07751, 07753, 07757, 07760, 07763, 07765, 07777, 07799, 08512, 08525, 08528, 08530, 08534, 08536, 08540–44, 08550–51, 08556–57, 08559–60, 08570, 08608–09, 08611, 08618–19, 08628, 08638, 08648, 08690, 08801, 08803, 08809–10, 08816, 08822–25, 08828, 08831, 08844, 08850, 08852, 08857, 08859, 08867–68, 08873, 08875, 08882, 08884, 08890, 08901–02, 08905, 08922

THIRTEENTH DISTRICT

ROBERT MENENDEZ, Democrat, of Hoboken, NJ; born in New York City, NY, January 1, 1954; education: graduated, Union Hill High School, 1972; B.A., St. Peter's College, Jersey City, NJ, 1976; J.D., Rutgers Law School, Newark, NJ, 1979; professional: attorney; admitted to the New Jersey bar, 1980; elected to the Union City Board of Education, 1974–78; mayor of Union City, 1986–92; New Jersey Assembly, 1987–91; New Jersey State Senate, 1991–92; chairman, New Jersey Hispanic Leadership Program; Vice Chair, Democratic Caucus, 1998–2002; member, New Jersey Hispanic Elected Officials Organization; New Jersey Mayors Coalition; president and co-founder, Alliance Civic Association; elected Chairman, Democratic Caucus, 2002; children: Alicia and Robert; committees: International Relations; Transportation and Infrastructure; elected on November 3, 1992, to the 103rd Congress; reelected to each succeeding Congress.

Office Listings

http://www.house.gov/menendez

2238 Rayburn House Office Building, Washington, DC 20515	(202) 225–7919
Chief of Staff.—E. Ivan Zapien.	FAX: 226–0792
Office Manager / Scheduler.—Judi Wolford.	
Legislative Director.—Chris Schloesser.	
Communications Director.—Matthew Miller.	
911 Bergen Avenue, Jersey City, NJ 07306	(201) 222–2828
654 Avenue C, Bayonne, NJ 07002	(201) 823–2900
263 Hobart Street, Perth Amboy, NJ 08861	(732) 324–6212
3109 Bergenline Avenue, Union City, NJ 07087	(201) 558–0800

Counties: ESSEX (part), HUDSON (part), MIDDLESEX (part), UNION (part). CITIES AND TOWNSHIPS: Bayonne, Carteret, East Newark, Elizabeth, Guttenberg, Harrison Township, Hoboken, Jersey City, Kearny, Linden, Newark, North Bergen, Port Reading, Perth Amboy, Sewaren, Union City, Weehawken, West New York, and Woodbridge. Population (2000), 647,258.

ZIP Codes: 07002–03, 07008, 07029–30, 07036, 07047, 07064, 07077, 07086–87, 07093, 07095, 07102–05, 07107, 07114, 07201–02, 07206, 07302–11, 08861–62

NEW MEXICO

(Population 2000, 1,819,046)

SENATORS

PETE V. DOMENICI, Republican, of Albuquerque, NM; born in Albuquerque, May 7, 1932; education: graduate of St. Mary's High School, 1954; University of New Mexico, B.S., 1966; Denver University, LL.D., 1958; professional: admitted to New Mexico bar, 1958; elected to Albuquerque City Commission, 1966; chairman (ex officio mayor), 1967; married: Nancy Burk, 1958; children: Lisa, Peter, Nella, Clare, David, Nanette, Helen, and Paula; committees: Appropriations; Budget; chairman, Energy and Natural Resources; Homeland Security and Governmental Affairs; Indian Affairs; elected to the U.S. Senate on November 7, 1972; reelected to each succeeding Senate term.

Office Listings
http://domenici.senate.gov

328 Hart Senate Office Building, Washington, DC 20510	(202) 224–6621
Chief of Staff.—Steve Bell.	
Administrative/Systems Director.—Lynden Armstrong.	
Legislative Director.—Edward Hild.	
Press Secretary.—Chris Gallegos.	
201 3rd Street NW, Suite 710, Albuquerque, NM 87102	(505) 346–6791
Federal Building, Loretto Town Centre, 505 South Main, Suite 118, Las Cruces, NM 88005	(505) 526–5475
Room 302, 120 South Federal Place, Santa Fe, NM 87501	(505) 988–6511
Federal Building, 227 Roswell, NM 88201	(505) 623–6170

* * *

JEFF BINGAMAN, Democrat, of Santa Fe, NM; born in El Paso, TX, October 3, 1943; raised in Silver City, NM; graduate of Western High (now Silver High), 1961; B.A., government, Harvard University, 1965; J.D., Stanford Law School, 1968; U.S. Army Reserves, 1968–74; Assistant New Mexico Attorney General, 1969, as counsel to the State constitutional convention; private practice, 1970–78; New Mexico Attorney General, 1979–82; member: Methodist Church; married: the former Anne Kovacovich; one son, John; committees: ranking member, Energy and Natural Resources; Finance; Health, Education, Labor, and Pensions; Joint Economic Committee; elected to the U.S. Senate on November 2, 1982; reelected to each succeeding Senate term.

Office Listings
http://bingaman.senate.gov

703 Hart Senate Office Building, Washington, DC 20510	(202) 224–5521
Administrative Assistant.—Stephen Ward.	TDD: 224–1792
Legislative Director.—Trudy Vincent.	
Press Secretary.—Jude McCartin.	
Personal Assistant.—Virginia White.	
Loretto Town Centre, Suite 148, 505 South Main, Las Cruces, NM 88001	(505) 523–6561
625 Silver Avenue SW, Suite 130, Albuquerque, NM 87102	(505) 346–6601
105 West Third Street, Suite 409, Roswell, NM 88201	(505) 622–7113
119 East Marcy, Suite 101, Santa Fe, NM 87501	(505) 988–6647
118 Bridge Street, Suite 3, Las Vegas, NM 87701	(505) 454–8824

REPRESENTATIVES

FIRST DISTRICT

HEATHER WILSON, Republican, of Albuquerque, NM; born in Keene, NH, December 30, 1960; George S. Emerson Elementary School, Fitzwilliam, NH; Keene High School, NH; B.S., United States Air Force Academy; Rhodes Scholar, Oxford University, England; Masters and Doctoral degrees in Philosophy (international relations); United States Air Force, Captain, 1978–89; President, Keystone International, Inc., 1991–95; New Mexico Sec. Of Children, Youth, and Families; 1995–98; married: Jay R. Hone, 1991; children: Scott, Joshua, and Caitlin Hone; committees: Energy and Commerce; Permanent Select Committee on Intelligence; subcommittees: Energy and Air Quality; Environment and Hazardous Materials; Health; Strategic Forces; Readiness; Telecommunications and the Internet; elected to the 105th Congress on June 23, 1998, by special election; reelected to each succeeding Congress.

Office Listings
http://www.house.gov/wilson

318 Cannon House Office Building, Washington, DC 20515 .... (202) 225–6316
  Chief of Staff.—Bryce Dustman.   FAX: 225–4975
  Legislative Director.—Erik Einertson.
  Executive Assistant.—Barbara Cohen.
20 First Plaza, NW., Suite 603, Albuquerque, NM 87102 .... (505) 346–6781
  Scheduler.—Darlene Garcia.

Counties: BERNALILLO (part), SANDOVAL (part), SANTA FE (part), TORRANCE, VALENCIA (part). CITIES AND TOWNSHIPS: Albuquerque, Belen, Estancia, Los Lunas, Moriarty, Mountainair, and Rio Rancho. Population (2000), 606,391.

ZIP Codes: 87001–02, 87004, 87008–09, 87015–16, 87031–32, 87035–36, 87042–43, 87047–48, 87059–61, 87063, 87068, 87070, 87101–25, 87131, 87151, 87153–54, 87158, 87176, 87181, 87184–85, 87187, 87190–99, 88301, 88321

* * *

SECOND DISTRICT

STEVAN PEARCE, Republican, of Hobbs, NM; born in Lamesa, TX, August 24, 1947; education: B.B.A., New Mexico State University; M.B.A., Eastern New Mexico University; professional: businessman; owner, Trinity Industries; military service: U.S. Air Force pilot, 1970–76; attained the rank of Captain; awarded the Distinguished Flying Cross; public service: New Mexico House of Representatives, 1996–2000; religion: Baptist; married: Cynthia; children: Lori; committees: Financial Services; Homeland Security; Resources; elected to the 108th Congress on November 5, 2002; reelected to each succeeding Congress.

Office Listings
http://www.house.gov/pearce

1607 Longworth House Office Building, Washington, DC 20515 .... (202) 225–2365
  Chief of Staff.—Jim Richards.   FAX: 225–9599
  Press Secretary.—Jim Burns.
  Scheduler.—Peggy Mallow.
1717 West 2nd Street, Suite 100, Roswell, NM 88201 .... (505) 622–0055
400 North Telshor, Suite E, Las Cruces, NM 88011 .... (505) 522–2219
1923 North Dal Paso, Hobbs, NM 88240 .... (505) 392–8325
  District Director.—Bob Carter.
111 School of Mines Road, Socorro, NM 87801 .... (505) 838–7516

Counties: BERNALILLO (part), CATRON, CHAVES, CIBOLA, DEBACA, DONA ANA, EDDY, GRANT, GUADALUPE, HIDALGO, LEA, LINCOLN, LUNA, MCKINLEY (part), OTERO, SIERRA, SOCORRO, VALENCIA (part). Population (2000), 606,406.

ZIP Codes: 87002, 87005–07, 87011, 87014, 87020–23, 87026, 87028, 87031, 87034, 87038, 87040, 87045, 87049, 87051, 87062, 87068, 87105, 87121, 87315, 87321, 87327, 87357, 87711, 87724, 87801, 87820–21, 87823–25, 87827–32, 87901, 87930–31, 87933, 87935–37, 87939–43, 88001–09, 88011–12, 88020–21, 88023–34, 88036, 88038–49, 88051–56, 88058, 88061–63, 88065, 88072, 88081, 88114, 88116, 88119, 88134, 88136, 88201–03, 88210–11, 88220–21, 88230–32, 88240–42, 88244, 88250, 88252–56, 88260, 88262–65, 88267–68, 88301, 88310–12, 88314, 88316–18, 88323–25, 88330, 88336–55, 88417, 88431, 88435

* * *

THIRD DISTRICT

TOM UDALL, Democrat, of Santa Fe, NM; born in Tucson, AZ, May 18, 1948; son of U.S. Representative (1955–61), and Secretary of the Interior (1961–1969), Stewart Udall; education: McLean, VA, High School; B.A., Prescott College, 1970; Cambridge (England) University, 1975; J.D., University of New Mexico, 1977; professional: law clerk for Chief Justice Oliver Seth of the Tenth Circuit Court of Appeals, Santa Fe, NM; assistant U.S. Attorney, 1977–81; private attorney, 1981; chief counsel, New Mexico Health and Environment Department, 1983–84; New Mexico Attorney General, 1990–98; married: Jill Z. Cooper; one child; committees: Resources; Small Business; Veterans' Affairs; elected to the 106th Congress; reelected to each succeeding Congress.

Office Listings
http://www.house.gov/tomudall

1414 Longworth House Office Building, Washington, DC 20515 .... (202) 225–6190
Chief of Staff.—Tom Nagle.   FAX: 226–1331
Legislative Director.—Mike Collins.
Press Secretary.—Glen Loveland.
Appointment Secretary.—Donda Morgan.
811 St. Michaels Drive, Suite 104, Santa Fe, NM 87505 .... (505) 984–8950
District Director.—Michele Jacquez-Ortiz.
321 N. Connelly Street, P.O. Box 868, Clovis, NM 88102–0868 .... (505) 763–7616
800 Municipal Drive, Farmington, NM 87401 .... (505) 324–1005
Constituent Services Representative.—Pete Valencia.
110 W. Aztec, Gallup, NM 87301 .... (505) 863–0582
1700 N. Grand Avenue, P.O. Box 160, Las Vegas, NM 87701 .... (505) 454–4080
Field Representative / Veterans Liaison.—Thomas Garcia.
3900 Southern Boulevard, SE, Room 105–A, Rio Rancho, NM 87124 .... (505) 994–0499
Field Representative.—Sarah Cobb.

Counties: BERNALILLO (part), COLFAX, CURRY, HARDING, LOS ALAMOS, MCKINLEY (part), MORA, QUAY, RIO ARRIBA, ROOSEVELT, SANDOVAL (part), SAN JUAN, SAN MIGUEL, SANTA FE (part), TAOS, UNION. Population (2000), 606,249.

ZIP Codes: 87001, 87004, 87010, 87012–13, 87015, 87017–18, 87024–25, 87027, 87029, 87037, 87041, 87044–48, 87052–53, 87056, 87064, 87072, 87083, 87114, 87120, 87123–24, 87144, 87174, 87301–02, 87305, 87310–13, 87316–17, 87319–23, 87325–26, 87328, 87347, 87364–65, 87375, 87401–02, 87410, 87412–13, 87415–21, 87455, 87461, 87499, 87501–25, 87527–33, 87535, 87537–40, 87543–45, 87548–49, 87551–54, 87556–58, 87560, 87562, 87564–67, 87569, 87571, 87573–83, 87592, 87594, 87701, 87710, 87712–15, 87718, 87722–23, 87728–36, 87740, 87742–43, 87745–47, 87749–50, 87752–53, 88101–03, 88112–13, 88115–16, 88118, 88120–26, 88130, 88132–35, 88401, 88410–11, 88414–16, 88418–19, 88421–22, 88424, 88426–27, 88430, 88433–34, 88436–37, 88439

NEW YORK

(Population 2000, 18,976,457)

SENATORS

CHARLES E. SCHUMER, Democrat, of Brooklyn and Queens, NY; born in Brooklyn, November 23, 1950; education: graduated valedictorian, Madison High School; Harvard University, *magna cum laude*, 1971; J.D. with honors, Harvard Law School, 1974; professional: admitted to the New York State bar in 1975; elected to the New York State Assembly, 1974; served on Judiciary, Health, Education, and Cities committees; chairman, subcommittee on City Management and Governance, 1977; chairman, Committee on Oversight and Investigation, 1979; reelected to each succeeding legislative session until December 1980; married: Iris Weinshall, 1980; children: Jessica Emily and Alison Emma; elected to the 97th Congress on November 4, 1980; reelected to each succeeding Congress; committees: Banking, Housing, and Urban Affairs; Finance; Judiciary; Rules and Administration; Joint Committee on the Library of Congress; subcommittees: ranking member, Administrative Oversight and the Courts; Antitrust, Competition Policy and Consumer Rights; Crime and Drugs; ranking member, Economic Policy; Housing and Transportation; International Trade; Immigration, Border Security and Citizenship; Securities and Investment; Taxation and IRS Oversight; elected to the U.S. Senate on November 3, 1998; reelected to each succeeding Senate term.

Office Listings

http://schumer.senate.gov

313 Hart Senate Office Building, Washington, DC 20510	(202) 224–6542
Chief of Staff.—David Hantman.	FAX: 228–3027
Communications Director.—Israel Klein.	
Executive Assistant.—Vincent Indelicato.	
757 Third Avenue, Suite 1702, New York, NY 10017	(212) 486–4430
Leo O'Brien Building, Room 420, Albany, NY 12207	(518) 431–4070
111 West Huron, Room 620, Buffalo, NY 14202	(716) 846–4111
100 State Street, Room 3040, Rochester, NY 14614	(585) 263–5866
100 South Clinton, Room 841, Syracuse, NY 13261–7318	(315) 423–5471
Federal Office Building, 15 Henry Street, #B6, Binghamton, NY 13901	(607) 772–8109
Two Greenway Plaza, 145 Pine Lawn Road and 300 N, Melville, NY 11747	(631) 753–0978
P.O. Box A, Red Hook, NY 12571	(845) 758–9741

* * *

HILLARY RODHAM CLINTON, Democrat, of Chappaqua, NY; born in Chicago, IL, October 26, 1947; education: B.A., Wellesley College, 1969; J.D., Yale University, 1973; professional: attorney; Children's Defense Fund; U.S. House of Representatives' Judiciary Committee; University of Arkansas at Fayetteville; and private legal practice; family: married to former Arkansas Governor and President William Jefferson Clinton, 1975; one daughter: Chelsea, 1980; First Lady of Arkansas, 1979–1981, and 1983–1993; First Lady of the United States, 1993–2001; author: *It Takes a Village and Other Lessons Children Teach Us; Dear Socks, Dear Buddy: Kids' Letters to the First Pets; An Invitation to the White House*; religion: Methodist; recipient of numerous awards; committees: Armed Services; Environment and Public Works; Health, Education, Labor, and Pensions; Special Committee on Aging; elected to the U.S. Senate on November 7, 2000.

Office Listings

http://clinton.senate.gov

476 Russell Senate Office Building, Washington, DC 20510	(202) 224–4451
Chief of Staff.—Tamera Luzzatto.	FAX: 228–0282
Press Secretary.—Philippe Reines.	
Communications Director.—Lorrie McHugh.	
Scheduler.—Lona Valmoro.	
Federal Office Building, 1 Clinton Square, Room 821, Albany, NY 12207	(518) 431–0120
Guaranty Building, 28 Church Street, Suite 208, Buffalo, NY 14202	(716) 854–9725
Federal Office Building, 100 State Street, Room 3280, Rochester, NY 14614	(585) 263–6250
Federal Office Building, 100 South Clinton Street, P.O. Box 7378, Syracuse, NY 13261	(315) 448–0470
P.O. Box 273, Lowville, NY 13367	(315) 376–6118
P.O. Box 617, Hartsdale, NY 10530	(914) 725–9294
Three Greenway Plaza, 155 Pinclawn Road, Suite 250 North, Melville, NY 11747	(631) 249–2825

REPRESENTATIVES

FIRST DISTRICT

TIMOTHY H. BISHOP, Democrat, of Southampton, NY; born in Southampton, June 1, 1950; education: Southampton High School, 1968; A.B., in History, from Holy Cross College; M.P.A., Long Island University, 1981; professional: educator; Provost of Southampton College, 1986–2002; community service: Southampton Rotary Club Scholarship Committee; Southampton Town Board of Ethics; Eastern Long Island Coastal Conservation Alliance; Bridgehampton Childcare and Recreation Center; religion: Catholic; married: Kathryn; children: Molly and Meghan; committees: Education and the Workforce; Transportation and Infrastructure; elected to the 108th Congress on November 5, 2002; reelected to each succeeding Congress.

Office Listings
http:/www.house.gov/timbishop

1133 Longworth House Office Building, Washington, DC 20515	(202) 225–3826
Chief of Staff.—Sean Sweeney.	FAX: 225–3143
Legislative Director.—Aprill Springfield.	
Communications Director/Legislative Assistant.—Brian Farber.	
3680 Route 112, Suite C, Coram, NY 11727	(631) 696–6500

Counties: SUFFOLK COUNTY (part). CITIES: Brookhaven, Smithtown, Southampton, and Montauk. Population (2000), 654,360.

ZIP Codes: 00501, 00544, 11713, 11715, 11719–20, 11727, 11733, 11738, 11741–42, 11745, 11754–55, 11763–64, 11766–68, 11772, 11776–80, 11784, 11786–90, 11792, 11794, 11901, 11930–35, 11937, 11939–42, 11944, 11946–65, 11967–73, 11975–78, 11980

* * *

SECOND DISTRICT

STEVE ISRAEL, Democrat, of Huntington, NY; born in Brooklyn, NY, May 30, 1958; education: B.A., George Washington University, 1982; professional: public relations and marketing executive; public service: Legislative Assistant for Rep. Richard Ottinger (D–NY), 1980–83; Suffolk County Executive for Intergovernmental Relations, 1988–91; elected to the Huntington Town Board, 1993; reelected two times; organizations: Institute on the Holocaust; Touro Law Center; Nature Conservancy; Audubon Society; awards: Child Care Council of Suffolk Leadership Award; Anti-Defamation League and Sons of Italy Purple Aster Award; committees: Armed Services; Financial Services; elected to the 107th Congress on November 7, 2000; reelected to each succeeding Congress.

Office Listings
http://www.house.gov/israel

432 Cannon House Office Building, Washington, DC 20515	(202) 225–3335
Chief of Staff.—Jack Pratt.	FAX: 225–4669
Communications Director.—Ryan Rudominer.	
Legislative Director.—Heather McHugh.	
150 Motor Parkway, Suite 108, Hauppauge, NY 11788	(631) 951–2210
District Director.—Holli Dunayer.	(516) 505–1448

Counties: NASSAU COUNTY (part), SUFFOLK COUNTY (part). CITIES: Asharoken, Bay Shore, Bayport, Bohemia, Brentwood, Brightwaters, Centerport, Central Islip, Cold Springs Harbor, Commack, Copiague, Deer Park, Dix Hills, East Farmingdale, East Northport, Eaton's Neck, Elwood, Fort Salonga, Great River, Greenlawn, Halesite, Hauppauge, Holbrook, Huntington, Huntington Station, Islandia, Islip, Islip Terrace, Jericho, King's Park, Lindenhurst, Lloyd Harbor, Melville, North Amityville, Northport, Oakdale, Ocean Beach, Old Bethpage, Plainview, Ronkonkoma, Sayville, Smithtown, South Huntington, Syosset, West Babylon, West Hills, West Islip, West Sayville, Wheatley Heights, Woodbury and Wyandanch. Population (2000), 654,360.

ZIP Codes: 11701, 11703–06, 11714–18, 11721–22, 11724–26, 11729–31, 11735, 11737, 11739–43, 11746–47, 11749–54, 11757, 11760, 11767–70, 11772, 11775, 11779, 11782, 11787–88, 11791, 11796–98, 11801, 11803–04

* * *

THIRD DISTRICT

PETER T. KING, Republican, of Seaford, NY; born in Manhattan, NY, April 5, 1944; education: B.A., St. Francis College, NY, 1965; J.D., University of Notre Dame Law School, IN, 1968; military service: served, U.S. Army Reserve National Guard, specialist 5, 1968–73;

admitted to New York bar, 1968; professional: attorney; Deputy Nassau County Attorney, 1972–74, executive assistant to the Nassau County Executive, 1974–76; general counsel, Nassau Off-Track Betting Corporation, 1977; Hempstead Town Councilman, 1978–81; Nassau County Comptroller, 1981–92; member: Ancient Order of Hiberians, Long Island Committee for Soviet Jewry, Sons of Italy, Knights of Columbus, 69th Infantry Veterans Corps, American Legion; married: Rosemary Wiedl King, 1967; children: Sean and Erin; committees: Financial Services; Homeland Security; International Relations; subcommittees: chair, Emergency Preparedness, Service, and Technology; elected on November 3, 1992 to the 103rd Congress; reelected to each succeeding Congress.

Office Listings

http://www.house.gov/king

436 Cannon House Office Building, Washington, DC 20515	(202) 225–7896
Chief of Staff.—Robert O'Connor.	FAX: 226–2279
Legislative Director / Press Secretary.—Kevin Fogarty.	
Special Assistant.—Ryan Travis.	
1003 Park Boulevard, Massapequa Park, NY 11762	(516) 541–4225
District Director.—Anne Rosenfeld.	
Suffolk County	(631) 541–4225

Counties: NASSAU (part), SUFFOLK (part). CITIES AND TOWNSHIPS: Amityville, Babylon, Baldwin, Bayshore, Bayville, Bellmore, Bethpage, Brightwaters, Brookville, Cedar Beach, Centre Island, Copiague, Cove Neck, East Islip, East Norwich, Farmingdale, Freeport, Gilgo Beach, Glen Cove, Glen Head, Glenwood Landing, Greenvale, Harbor Isle, Hicksville, Island Park, Islip, Jericho, Lattingtown, Laurel Hollow, Levittown, Lido Beach, Lindenhurst, Locust Grove, Locust Valley, Long Beach, Massapequa, Massapequa Park, Matinecock, Merrick, Mill Neck, Muttontown, North Babylon, North Bellmore, North Lindenhurst, Oak Beach, Oceanside, Old Bethpage, Old Brookville, Old Westbury, Oyster Bay, Oyster Bay Cove, Plainview, Point Lookout, Sea Cliff, Seaford, Syosset, Wantagh, West Babylon, West Bayshore, Westbury, West Islip, and Woodbury. Population (2000), 654,361.

ZIP Codes: 11510, 11520, 11542, 11545, 11547–48, 11558, 11560–61, 11566, 11568–69, 11572, 11576, 11579, 11590, 11599, 11701–04, 11706, 11709–10, 11714, 11718, 11724, 11726, 11730, 11732, 11735–37, 11751, 11753, 11756–58, 11762, 11765, 11771, 11773–74, 11783, 11791, 11793, 11795, 11797, 11801–04, 11815, 11819, 11854–55

* * *

FOURTH DISTRICT

CAROLYN McCARTHY, Democrat, of Mineola, NY; born in Brooklyn, NY, January 5, 1944; education: graduated, Mineola High School, 1962; graduated, nursing school, 1964; professional: licensed practical nurse in ICU Section, Glen Cove Hospital; married: Dennis McCarthy, 1967; widowed on December 7, 1993, when her husband was killed and her only son, Kevin, severely wounded in the Long Island Railroad Massacre; turned personal nightmare into a crusade against violence—speaking out with other families of the Long Island tragedy, not just to the victims of the shooting but to crime victims across the country; board of directors, New Yorkers Against Gun Violence; board of directors, New York City "Stop the Violence" campaign; committees: Education and the Workforce; Financial Services; subcommittees: Capital Markets, Insurance and Government Sponsored Enterprises; Employer-Employee Relations; Financial Institutions and Consumer Credit; 21st Century Competitiveness; elected to the 105th Congress; reelected to each succeeding Congress.

Office Listings

http://www.house.gov/carolynmccarthy

106 Cannon House Office Building, Washington, DC 20515	(202) 225–5516
Chief of Staff.—Jim Hart.	FAX: 225–5758
District Director.—Mary Ellen Mendelsohn.	
Executive Assistant.—Christopher Hoven.	
Communications Director.—Mark Sokolove.	
200 Garden City Plaza, Suite 320, Garden City, NY 11530	(516) 739–3008

Counties: NASSAU (part). CITIES AND TOWNSHIPS: Atlantic Beach, Baldwin, Bellerose, Carle Place, Cedarhurst, East Meadow, East Rockaway, East Williston, Elmont, Floral Park, Franklin Square, Freeport, Garden City, Garden City Park, Hempstead, Hewlett, Inwood, Lakeview, Lawrence, Lynbrook, Malverne, Merrick, Mineola, New Cassel, New Hyde Park, North Bellmore, North New Hyde Park, Oceanside, Rockville Centre, Roosevelt, Salisbury, Stewart Manor, South Floral Park, South Valley Stream, Uniondale, Valley Stream, West Hempstead, Westbury, Williston Park, Woodmere, and Woodsburgh. Population (2000) 654,360.

ZIP Codes: 11001–03, 11010, 11040, 11042, 11096, 11501, 11509–10, 11514, 11516, 11518, 11520, 11530–31, 11535–36, 11549–57, 11559, 11561, 11563–66, 11568, 11570–72, 11575, 11577, 11580–83, 11588, 11590, 11592–99, 11710, 11793

FIFTH DISTRICT

GARY L. ACKERMAN, Democrat, of Queens, NY; born in Brooklyn, NY, November 19, 1942; education: graduate, Queens College, Flushing, NY; attended St. John's University, Jamaica, NY; professional: public school teacher; newspaper editor; businessman; New York State Senate, 1979–83; married: the former Rita Tewel; children: Lauren, Corey, and Ari; committees: Financial Services; International Relations; elected by special election on March 1, 1983, to the 98th Congress, to fill the vacancy caused by the death of Representative Benjamin Rosenthal; reelected to each succeeding Congress.

Office Listings
http://www.house.gov/ackerman

2243 Rayburn House Office Building, Washington, DC 20515 .... (202) 225–2601
   Chief of Staff.—Jedd Moskowitz.
   Deputy Chief of Staff.—Lisa Baranello.
   Legislative Director.—Howard Diamond.
   Press Secretary.—Jordan Goldes.
218–14 Northern Boulevard, Bayside, NY 11361 .... (718) 423–2154
   District Office Administrator.—Moya Berry.

Counties: NASSAU (part), QUEENS (part). CITIES AND TOWNSHIPS: Auburndale, Bay Terrace, Bayside, Bell Park Gardens, Bell Park Manor, Centre Island, Clearview, Corona, Deepdale, Douglaston, Douglaston Manor, East Elmhurst, East Hills, Flushing, Fresh Meadows, Glen Oaks, Great Neck, Great Neck Estates, Great Neck Gardens, Great Neck Plaza, Greenvale, Herricks, Hillcrest, Hollis Court Gardens, Hollis Hills, Jackson Heights, Jamaica Estates, Kensington, Kew Gardens Hills, Kings Point, Lake Success, Lefrak City, Linden Hill, Little Neck, Malba, Manor Haven, North Shore Towers, Oakland Gardens, Pomonok, Port Washington, Port Washington North, Queensboro Hill, Roslyn, Roslyn Estates, Roslyn Harbor, Roslyn Heights, Russell Gardens, Saddle Rock, Saddle Rock Estates, Sands Point, Searington, Thomaston, University Gardens, West Neck, and Windsor Park. Population (2000), 654,361.

ZIP Codes: 11004–05, 11020–24, 11030, 11040, 11042, 11050–55, 11351–52, 11354–58, 11360–66, 11368–69, 11372–73, 11375, 11379, 11423, 11426–27, 11432, 11507, 11542, 11548, 11560, 11568, 11576–77, 11596

* * *

SIXTH DISTRICT

GREGORY W. MEEKS, Democrat, of Far Rockaway, NY; born in Harlem, NY, September 25, 1953; married: Simone-Marie Meeks, 1997; children: Aja, Ebony, and Nia-Ayana; education: P.S. 183; Robert F. Wagner Junior High School; Julia Richman High School, New York, NY; bachelor degree, Adelphi University, 1971–75; J.D., Howard University School of Law, 1975–78; professional: lawyer, admitted to bar, 1979; Queens District Attorney's Office, 1978–83, serving as Assistant District Attorney; Judge, New York State Workers' Compensation Board; public service: New York State Assemblyman, 1992–97; organizations: Alpha Phi Alpha Fraternity; Congressional Black Caucus; Council of Black-Elected Democrats; National Bar Association; Task Force on Financial Services; committees: Financial Services; International Relations; subcommittees: Capital Markets, Insurance, and Government Sponsored Enterprises; Financial Institutions and Consumer Credit; Africa, Global Human Rights and International Operations; Western Hemisphere; active member of the Congressional Black Caucus; elected to the 105th Congress on February 3, 1998; reelected to each succeeding Congress.

Office Listings
http://www.house.gov/meeks

1710 Longworth House Office Building, Washington, DC 20515 .... (202) 225–3461
   Chief of Staff.—Jameel Aalim-Johnson.   FAX: 226–4169
   Legislative Director.—Sophia King.
   Office Manager/Scheduler.—Patricia Fisher.
196–06 Linden Boulevard, St. Albans, NY 11412 .... (718) 949–5600
   District Director.—Patrick Jenkins.
1931 Mott Avenue, Room 305, Far Rockaway, NY 11691 .... (718) 327–9791
   Community Liaison.—Edward Williams.

Counties: QUEENS COUNTY (part). CITIES AND TOWNSHIPS: Arverne, Cambria Heights, Edgemere, Far Rockaway, Floral Park, Glen Oaks, Hammels, Hollis, Howard Beach, Jamaica, Jamaica Estates, Kew Gardens, Laurelton, New Hyde Park, Ozone Park, Queens Village, Richmond Hill, Rosedale, St. Albans, South Jamaica, South Ozone Park, Springfield Gardens, and Woodhaven. Population (2000), 654,361.

ZIP Codes: 11001, 11004, 11040, 11405, 11411–20, 11422–23, 11425–36, 11439, 11451, 11484, 11690–93

SEVENTH DISTRICT

JOSEPH CROWLEY, Democrat, of Elmhurst, Queens, NY; born in New York, NY, March 16, 1962; education: graduated, Power Memorial High School, 1981; B.A., Queens College, 1985; professional: elected to the New York State Assembly, 1986–98; Assembly Committees: Racing and Wagering; Banking, Consumer Affairs, and Protection; Election Law; Labor and Housing; religion: Roman Catholic; married: Kasey Nilson; committees: Financial Services; International Relations; subcommittees: Capital Markets, Insurance and Government-Sponsored Enterprises; Domestic and International Monetary Policy, Trade and Technology; Financial Institutions and Consumer Credit; International Terrorism and Nonproliferation; Middle East and Central Asia; elected to the 106th Congress; reelected to each succeeding Congress.

Office Listings

http://house.gov/crowley

312 Cannon House Office Building, Washington, DC 20510	(202) 225–3965
Chief of Staff.—Christopher McCannell.	FAX: 225–1909
Office Manager.—Shawn Hodjati.	
Legislative Director.—Kevin Casey.	
3425 East Tremont Avenue, Suite 1–3, Bronx, NY 10465	(718) 931–1400
82–11 37th Avenue, Suite 705, Jackson Heights, NY 10372	(718) 779–1400
177 Dreiser Loop, Room 3, Bronx, NY 10475	(718) 320–2314

Counties: BRONX (part), QUEENS (part). Population (2000), 654,360.

ZIP Codes: 10458, 10460–62, 10464–67, 10469, 10472–75, 10805, 11103–04, 11354, 11356, 11368–73, 11377–78, 11380

* * *

EIGHTH DISTRICT

JERROLD NADLER, Democrat, of New York, NY; born in Brooklyn, NY, June 13, 1947; education: graduated from Stuyvesant High School, 1965; B.A., Columbia University, 1970; J.D., Fordham University, 1978; professional: New York State Assembly, 1977–92; member: American Jewish Congress; ACLU; National Abortion Rights Action League; AIPAC; National Organization for Women; Assistant Whip; married: 1976; one child; committees: Judiciary; Transportation and Infrastructure; elected to the 102nd Congress on November 3, 1992, to fill the vacancy caused by the death of Representative Ted Weiss; at the same time elected to the 103rd Congress; reelected to each succeeding Congress.

Office Listings

http://www.house.gov/nadler

2334 Rayburn House Office Building, Washington, DC 20515	(202) 225–5635
Legislative Director.—Lisette Morton.	FAX: 225–6923
Director, Washington office.—John Doty.	
201 Varick Street, Suite 669, New York, NY 10014	(212) 367–7350
Chief of Staff.—Amy Rutkin.	
445 Neptune Avenue, Brooklyn, NY 11224	(718) 373–3198
Brooklyn Director.—Robert Gottheim.	

Counties: KINGS (part), NEW YORK (part). Population (2000), 654,360.

ZIP Codes: 10001–08, 10010–14, 10016, 10018–20, 10023–24, 10036, 10038, 10041, 10043, 10047–48, 10069, 10072, 10080–81, 10101–02, 10108–09, 10113–14, 10116–17, 10119–24, 10129, 10132–33, 10149, 10199, 10209, 10213, 10242, 10249, 10256, 10260, 10265, 10268–70, 10272–82, 10285–86, 10292, 11204, 11214–15, 11218–20, 11223–24, 11228, 11230–32, 11235

* * *

NINTH DISTRICT

ANTHONY D. WEINER, Democrat, of Brooklyn, NY; born in Brooklyn, September 4, 1964; education: graduated, Brooklyn Tech High School; B.A., State University of New York at Plattsburgh, 1985; professional: served in the New York City Council, 1992–98; selected to serve as Freshman Whip, 106th Congress; committees: Judiciary; Transportation and Infrastructure; subcommittees: Aviation; Courts, the Internet, and Intellectual Property; Crime, Terrorism and Homeland Security; Coast Guard and Maritime Transportation; Highways, Transit and Pipelines; elected to the 106th Congress; reelected to each succeeding Congress.

Office Listings
http://www.house.gov/weiner

1122 Longworth House Office Building, Washington, DC 20515	(202) 225–6616
Chief of Staff/Legislative Director.—Marc Dunkelman.	FAX: 226–7253
Executive Assistant.—Michael Marcy.	
Special Assistant.—Matthew McKenna.	
80–02 Kew Gardens Road, Suite 5000, Kew Gardens, NY 11415	(718) 520–9001
90–16 Rockaway Beach Boulevard, Rockaway, NY 11693	(718) 318–9255
1800 Sheepshead Bay Road, Brooklyn, NY 11235	(718) 743–0441
District Director.—Marc Dunkelman.	

Counties: KINGS COUNTY (part). CITIES AND TOWNSHIPS: Bergen Beach, Brighton Beach, Canasie, Flatbush, Flatlands, Gerritsen Beach, Georgetowne, Kensington, Manhattan Beach, Marine Park, Midwood, Mill Basin, Park Slope, Parkville, Sheepshead Bay, Windsor Terrace. QUEENS COUNTY (part). CITIES AND TOWNSHIPS: Belle Harbor, Breezy Point, Briarwood, Broad Channel, Corona, Elmhurst, Far Rockaway, Forest Hills, Glendale, Hamilton Beach, Howard Beach, Kew Gardens, Lindenwood, Middle Village, Neponsit, Ozone Park, Rego Park, Richmond Hill, Ridgewood, Rockway Point, Roxbury, West Lawrence, and Woodhaven. Population (2000), 654,360.

ZIP Codes: 11204, 11208, 11210, 11218, 11223, 11229–30, 11234–36, 11358, 11361, 11364–67, 11373–75, 11378–79, 11381, 11385, 11414–18, 11421, 11424, 11427, 11432, 11435, 11693–95, 11697

* * *

TENTH DISTRICT

EDOLPHUS TOWNS, Democrat, of Brooklyn, NY; born in Chadbourn, NC, July 21, 1934; graduated, West Side High School, Chadbourn, 1952; B.S., North Carolina A&T State University, Greensboro, 1956; master's degree in social work, Adelphi University, Garden City, NY, 1973; U.S. Army, 1956–58; teacher, Medgar Evers College, Brooklyn, NY, and for the New York City public school system; deputy hospital administrator, 1965–71; deputy president, Borough of Brooklyn, 1976–82; member: Kiwanis, Boy Scouts Advisory Council, Salvation Army, Phi Beta Sigma Fraternity; married the former Gwendolyn Forbes in 1960; two children: Darryl and Deidra; committees: Energy and Commerce; Government Reform; subcommittees: Commerce, Trade and Consumer Protection; ranking member, Government Management, Finance, and Accountability; Health; Telecommunications and the Internet; elected on November 2, 1982, to the 98th Congress; reelected to each succeeding Congress.

Office Listings
http://www.house.gov/towns

2232 Rayburn House Office Building, Washington, DC 20515	(202) 225–5936
Chief of Staff.—Brenda Pillors.	FAX: 225–1018
Legal Counsel.—Cherri Branson.	
Office Manager/Scheduler.—Gerri Taylor.	
1110 Pennsylvania Avenue, Store #5, Brooklyn, NY 11207	(718) 272–1175
26 Court Street, Suite 1510, Brookyln, NY 11241	(718) 855–8018
District Director.—Karen Johnson.	
1670 Fulton Street, Brooklyn, NY 11213	(718) 774–5682

Counties: KINGS COUNTY (part). Population (2000), 654,361.

ZIP Codes: 11201–03, 11205–08, 11210–13, 11216–17, 11221, 11230, 11233–34, 11236, 11238–39, 11245, 11247–48, 11251, 11256

* * *

ELEVENTH DISTRICT

MAJOR R. OWENS, Democrat, of Brooklyn, NY; born in Memphis, TN, June 28, 1936; education: attended Hamilton High School, Memphis, TN; B.A., with high honors Morehouse College, 1956; M.S., Atlanta University, 1957; chairman, Brooklyn Congress of Racial Equality; vice president, Metropolitan Council of Housing, 1964; community coordinator, Brooklyn Public Library, 1965; executive director, Brownsville Community Council, 1966; commissioner, New York City Community Development Agency, 1968–73; director, community media library program at Columbia University, 1974; New York State Senate, 1974–82; chairman, Senate Democratic Operations Committee; Brooklyn borough president declared September 10, 1971, "Major R. Owens Day"; served on International Commission on Ways of Implementing Social Policy to Ensure Maximum Public Participation and Social Justice for Minorities at The Hague, the Netherlands, 1972; published author and lecturer on library science; featured speaker, White House Conference on Libraries, 1979; recognized authority in community development; married: Maria A. Owens of New York City; the children of their blended family are Christopher, Geoffrey, Millard, Carlos, and Cecelia; appointed chairman of the House Subcommittee on Select Education and Civil Rights, 1987; chairman of the Congressional Black Caucus Budget Task Force; appointed chairman of the Congressional Black Caucus Education Braintrust from the 98th Congress to the present; committees: Education and the Workforce; Government Reform; elected to the 98th Congress, November 2, 1982; reelected to each succeeding Congress.

Office Listings

2309 Rayburn House Office Building, Washington, DC 20515 .... (202) 225–6231
Chief of Staff / Administrative Assistant.—Theda Zawaiza. FAX: 226–0112
Legislative Director.—Norman Meyer.
Legislative Assistant / Scheduler.—Lauren Thompson.
Office Manager.—Lisa Williams.
289 Utica Avenue, Brooklyn, NY 11213 .... (718) 773–3100
1414 Cortelyou Road, Brooklyn, NY 11226 .... (718) 940–3213

Counties: KINGS COUNTY (part). Population (2000), 654,361.

ZIP Codes: 11201, 11203, 11210, 11212–13, 11215–18, 11225–26, 11230–31, 11233–34, 11236, 11238, 11241–42

* * *

TWELFTH DISTRICT

NYDIA M. VELÁZQUEZ, Democrat, of New York, NY; born in Yabucoa, Puerto Rico, March 28, 1953; education: University of Puerto Rico, B.A. in political science, 1974; New York University, M.A. in political science, 1976; professional: faculty member, University of Puerto Rico, 1976–81; adjunct professor, Hunter College of the City University of New York, 1981–83; special assistant to Congressman Ed Towns, 1983; member, City Council of New York, 1984–86; national director of Migration Division Office, Department of Labor and Human Resources of Puerto Rico, 1986–89; director, Department of Puerto Rican Community Affairs in the United States, 1989–92; committees: Financial Services; ranking member, Small Business; elected on November 3, 1992, to the 103rd Congress; reelected to each succeeding Congress.

Office Listings
http://www.house.gov/velazquez

2241 Rayburn House Office Building, Washington, DC 20515 .... (202) 225–2361
Chief of Staff.—Michael Day. FAX: 226–0327
Press Secretary.—Kate Davis.
268 Broadway, 2nd Floor, Brooklyn, NY 11211 .... (718) 599–3658
16 Court Street, Suite 1006, Brooklyn, NY 11241 .... (718) 222–5819
173 Avenue B, New York, NY 10009 .... (212) 673–3997

Counties: KINGS (part), NEW YORK (part), QUEENS (part). Population (2000), 654,360.

ZIP Codes: 10002, 10009, 10012–13, 10038, 11104, 11201, 11205–08, 11211, 11215, 11219–22, 11231–32, 11237, 11251, 11377–78, 11385, 11416, 11421

* * *

THIRTEENTH DISTRICT

VITO FOSSELLA, Republican, of Staten Island, NY; born in Staten Island, March 9, 1965; education: Public School 39, South Beach; Intermediate School 2, Midland Beach; Monsignor Farrell High School; B.S., University of Pennsylvania Wharton School; Fordham University School of Law; professional: lawyer, admitted to New York bar, 1994; New York City Council, 1994–97; married: Mary Pat Fossella, 1990; children: Dylan, Griffin, and Rowan; organizations: Ancient Order of Hibernians; South Shore Rotary; Staten Island Bucks; committees: Energy and Commerce; Financial Services; elected to the 105th Congress, by special election, on November 4, 1997; reelected to each succeeding Congress.

Office Listings
http://www.house.gov/fossella

1239 Longworth House Office Building, Washington, DC 20515 .... (202) 225–3371
   Chief of Staff.—Tom Quaadman.   FAX: 226–1272
   Office Manager.—Vicki J. Hook.
   Legislative Director.—Brendon Weiss.
4434 Amboy Road, Second Floor, Staten Island, NY 10312 .... (718) 356–8400
   District Director.—Sherry Diamond.
9818 4th Avenue, Brooklyn, NY 11209 .... (718) 630–5277
   Office Manager.—Eileen Long.

Counties: KINGS (part), RICHMOND. Population (2000), 654,361.

ZIP Codes: 10301–10, 10312–14, 11204, 11209, 11214, 11219–20, 11223, 11228, 11252

* * *

FOURTEENTH DISTRICT

CAROLYN B. MALONEY, Democrat, of New York City, NY; born in Greensboro, NC, February 19, 1948; education: B.A., Greensboro College, Greensboro, NC, 1968; professional: various positions, New York City Board of Education, 1970–77; legislative aide, New York State Assembly, senior program analyst, 1977–79; executive director of advisory council, 1979–82; director of special projects, New York State Senate Office of the Minority Leader; New York City council member, 1982–93; chairperson, New York City Council Committee on Contracts; member: Council Committee on Aging, National Organization of Women, Common Cause, Sierra Club, Americans for Democratic Action, New York City Council Committee on Housing and Buildings, Citizens Union, Grand Central Business Improvement District, Harlem Urban Development Corporation (1982–91), Commission on Early Childhood Development Programs, Council of Senior Citizen Centers of New York City, 1982–87; married: Clifton H. W. Maloney, 1976; children: Virginia Marshall Maloney and Christina Paul Maloney; committees: Financial Services; Government Reform; senior House Democratic member, Joint Economic Committee; subcommittees: ranking member, Domestic and International Monetary Policy, Trade and Technology; elected on November 3, 1992, to the 103rd Congress; reelected to each succeeding Congress.

Office Listings
http://www.house.gov/maloney

2331 Rayburn House Office Building, Washington, DC 20515 .... (202) 225–7944
   Administrative Assistant.—Ben Chevat.   FAX: 225–4709
   Legislative Director.—Orly Isaacson.
1651 Third Avenue, Suite 311, New York, NY 10128 .... (212) 860–0606
28–11 Astoria Boulevard, Long Island City, NY 11102 .... (718) 932–1804

Counties: NEW YORK (part), QUEENS (part). CITIES AND TOWNSHIPS: Astoria, Manhattan, Queens, Long Island City, Roosevelt Island, Sunnyside, and Woodside. Population (2000), 654,361.

ZIP Codes: 10012, 10016–24, 10026, 10028–29, 10036, 10044, 10055, 10103–07, 10110–12, 10126, 10128, 10138, 10150–60, 10162–79, 11101–06, 11375, 11377

* * *

FIFTEENTH DISTRICT

CHARLES B. RANGEL, Democrat-Liberal, of New York, NY; born in Harlem, NY, June 11, 1930; attended DeWitt Clinton High School; served in U.S. Army, 1948–52; awarded the Purple Heart, Bronze Star for Valor, U.S. and Korean presidential citations, and three battle stars while serving in combat with the Second Infantry Division in Korea; honorably discharged with rank of staff sergeant; after military duty, completed high school, 1953; graduated from New York University School of Commerce, student under the G.I. bill; 1957 dean's list; graduated from St. John's University School of Law, dean's list student under a full three-year scholarship, 1960; lawyer; admitted to practice in the courts of the State of New York, U.S. Federal Court, Southern District of New York, and U.S. Customs Court; appointed assistant U.S. attorney, Southern District of New York, 1961; legal counsel, New York City Housing and Redevelopment Board, Neighborhood Conservation Bureau; general counsel, National Advisory Commission on Selective Service, 1966; served two terms in the New York State Assembly, 1966–70; active in 369th Veterans Association; Community Education Program; and Martin Luther King, Jr., Democratic Club; married Alma Carter; two children: Steven and Alicia; committees: ranking member, Ways and Means; Joint Committee on Taxation; subcommittees: Trade; elected to the 92nd Congress, November 3, 1970; reelected to each succeeding Congress.

Office Listings
http://www.house.gov/rangel

2354 Rayburn House Office Building, Washington, DC 20515	(202) 225–4365
Administrative Assistant.—George A. Dalley.	FAX: 225–0816
163 West 125th Street, New York, NY 10027	(212) 663–3900
District Administrator.—Vivian E. Jones.	

Counties: BRONX (part), NEW YORK (part), QUEENS (part). Population (2000), 654,361.

ZIP Codes: 10023–27, 10029–35, 10037, 10039–40, 10115–16, 10169, 10463, 11105

* * *

SIXTEENTH DISTRICT

JOSÉ E. SERRANO, Democrat, of Bronx, NY; born in Mayagüez, PR, October 24, 1943; education: Dodge Vocational High School, Bronx, NY; attended Lehman College, City University of New York, NY; served with the U.S. Army Medical Corps, 1964–66; employed by the Manufacturers Hanover Bank, 1961–69; Community School District 7, 1969–74; New York State Assemblyman, 1974–90; chairman, Consumer Affairs Committee, 1979–83; chairman, Education Committee, 1983–90; married in 1987 to the former Mary Staucet; five children: Lisa, Jose Marco, Justine, Jonathan and Benjamin; committees: Appropriations; subcommittees: Homeland Security; Science, The Departments of State, Justice, and Commerce, and Related Agencies; elected to the 101st Congress, by special election, March 28, 1990, to fill the vacancy caused by the resignation of Robert Garcia; reelected to each succeeding Congress.

Office Listings
http://www.house.gov/serrano

2227 Rayburn House Office Building, Washington, DC 20515	(202) 225–4361
Executive Assistant.—Pichy Marty.	
Legislative Director.—Nadine Berg.	
Scheduler.—Elisa Howie.	
788 Southern Boulevard, Bronx, NY 10455	(718) 620–0084
Chief of Staff.—Paul Lipson.	

Counties: BRONX COUNTY (part). CITIES AND TOWNSHIPS: Bronx. Population (2000), 654,360.

ZIP Codes: 10451–60, 10463, 10468, 10472–74

* * *

SEVENTEENTH DISTRICT

ELIOT L. ENGEL, Democrat, of Bronx, NY; born in Bronx, February 18, 1947; education: B.A., Hunter-Lehman College, 1969; M.A., City University of New York, 1973; New York Law School, 1987; professional: teacher and counselor in the New York City public school system, 1969–77; elected to the New York legislature, 1977–88; chaired the Assembly Committee on Alcoholism and Substance Abuse and subcommittee on Mitchell-Lama Housing (twelve years prior to his election to Congress); member: Congressional Human Rights Caucus; Democratic Study Group on Health; Long Island Sound Caucus; co-chairman, Albanian Issues Caucus; board member, Congressional Ad Hoc Committee on Irish Affairs; married: Patricia Ennis, 1980; children: Julia, Jonathan, and Philip; committees: Energy and Commerce; International Relations; subcommittees: Energy and Air Quality; Telecommunications and the Internet; Middle East and Central Asia; Europe and Emerging Threats; elected on November 8, 1988, to the 101st Congress; reelected to each succeeding Congress.

Office Listings

http://www.house.gov/engel

2161 Rayburn House Office Building, Washington, DC 20515 .... (202) 225–2464
    Administrative Assistant/Legal Counsel.—Jason Steinbaum.
    Office Manager.—Michelle Shwimer.
3655 Johnson Avenue, Bronx, NY 10463 .... (718) 796–9700
    Chief of Staff.—William Weitz.
6 Gramatan Avenue, Mt. Vernon, NY 10550 .... (914) 699–4100
261 West Nyack Road, West Nyack, NY 10994 .... (845) 358–7800

Counties: BRONX (part), WESTCHESTER (part). CITIES AND TOWNSHIPS: Parts of Bronx, Yonkers, Mount Vernon, New Rochelle and Pelham. Population (2000), 654,360.

ZIP Codes: 10458, 10463, 10466–71, 10475, 10522, 10533, 10550–53, 10557–58, 10591, 10701, 10704–06, 10708, 10901, 10913, 10920, 10931, 10952, 10954, 10956, 10960, 10962, 10964–65, 10968, 10970, 10974, 10976–77, 10983, 10989, 10994

* * *

EIGHTEENTH DISTRICT

NITA M. LOWEY, Democrat, of Harrison, NY; born in New York, NY, July 5, 1937; education: graduated, Bronx High School of Science, 1955; B.S., Mount Holyoke College, 1959; assistant to Secretary of State for Economic Development and Neighborhood Preservation, and deputy director, Division of Economic Opportunity, 1975–85; Assistant Secretary of State, 1985–87; member: boards of directors, Close-Up Foundation; Effective Parenting Information for Children; Windward School, Downstate (New York Region); Westchester Jewish Conference; Westchester Opportunity Program; National Committee of the Police Corps; Women's Network of the YWCA; Legal Awareness for Women; National Women's Political Caucus of Westchester; American Jewish Committee of Westchester; married: Stephen Lowey, 1961; children: Dana, Jacqueline, and Douglas; committees: Appropriations; Homeland Security; elected on November 8, 1988, to the 101st Congress; reelected to each succeeding Congress.

Office Listings

http://www.house.gov/lowey

2329 Rayburn House Office Building, Washington, DC 20515 .... (202) 225–6506
    Chief of Staff.—Clare Coleman.   FAX: 225–0546
    Executive Assistant.—Katie Papa.
Suite 310, 222 Mamaroneck Avenue, White Plains, NY 10605 .... (914) 428–1707
    District Administrator.—Patricia Keegan.

Counties: ROCKLAND (part), WESTCHESTER (part). CITIES AND TOWNSHIPS: Ardsley, Ardsley on the Hundson, Briarcliff Manor; Bronxville, Chappaqua, Congers, Crestwood, Dobbs Ferry, Eastchester, Elmsford, Harrison, Hartsdale, Hasting-on-Hudson, Haverstraw, Hawthorne, Irvington, Larchmont, Mamaroneck, Maryknoll, Millwood, Mt. Kisco, New City, New Rochelle, North Castle, Ossining, Pelham, Pleasantville, Port Chester, Purchase, Rye, Rye Brook, Scarsdale, Sleepy Hollow, Tarrytown, Thornwood, Tuckahoe, Valhalla, Valley Cottage, West Harrison, West Haverstraw, White Plains, and Yonkers. Population (2000), 654,360.

ZIP Codes: 10502, 10504, 10506, 10510, 10514, 10522–23, 10528, 10530, 10532–33, 10538, 10543, 10546, 10549, 10562, 10570, 10573, 10577, 10580, 10583, 10591, 10594–95, 10601–07, 10610, 10650, 10701–10, 10801–05, 10920, 10923, 10927, 10956, 10989, 10993–94

* * *

NINETEENTH DISTRICT

SUE W. KELLY, Republican, of Katonah, NY; born in Lima, OH, September 26, 1936; graduated, Lima Central High School; B.A., Denison University, Granville, OH, 1958; M.A., Sarah Lawrence College, Bronxville, NY, 1985; educator; small business owner; patient advocate; rape crisis counselor; community leader; member: League of Women Voters; American Association of University Women; PTA; Bedford Recreation Committee; Bedford Presbyterian Church; married Edward W. Kelly, 1960; four children: Eric, Sean, Charity, and Tim; committees: Financial Services; Small Business; Transportation and Infrastructure; elected to the 104th Congress; reelected to each succeeding Congress.

Office Listings
http://www.house.gov/suekelly

2182 Rayburn House Office Building, Washington, DC 20515 .... (202) 225–5441
   Chief of Staff.—Mike Giuliani.
   Deputy Chief of Staff.—Nick Curran.
   Press Secretary.—Kevin Callahan.
21 Old Main Street, Room 107, Fishkill, NY 12524 .... (845) 897–5200
   District Director.—Jerry Nappi.
255 Main Street, 3rd Floor, Goshen, NY 10924 .... (845) 291–4100
2025 Crompond Road, Yorktown Heights, NY 10598 .... (914) 962–0761

Counties: DUTCHESS COUNTY (part). CITIES AND TOWNSHIPS: Beacon, Castle Point, Chelsea, Dover Plains, Fishkill, Glenham, Holmes, Hopewell Junction, Hughsonville, Pawling, Poughkeepsie, Poughquag, Stormville, Wappingers Falls, Wingdale. ORANGE COUNTY (part). CITIES AND TOWNSHIPS: Amity, Arden, Bear Mountain, Bellvale, Blooming Grove, Burnside, Campbell Hall, Central Valley, Chester, Cornwall, Cornwall-on-Hudson, Craigville, Cuddebackville, Durlandville, Eagle Valley, Edenville, Finchville, Finnegan's Corner, Firthcliff, Florida, Fort Montgomery, Gardnerville, Goddefroy, Goshen, Greenwood Lake, Guymard, Harriman, Highland Falls, Highland Mills, Huguenot, Johnson, Kiryas Joel, Little Britain, Little York, Maybrook, Middletown, Monroe, Montgomery, Mountainville, New Hampton, New Milford, New Vernon, New Windsor, Newburgh, Otisville, Oxford Depot, Phillipsburg, Pine Island, Port Jervis, Ridgebury, Rock Tavern, Salisbury Mills, Slate Hill, Sloatsburg, Southfields, Sparrowbush, Sterling Forest, Stony Ford, Suffern, Sugarloaf, Tuxedo, Tuxedo Park, Unionville, Vails Gate, Wallkill, Warwick, Washingtonville, West Point, Westbrookville, Westtown, Wickham Village. PUTNAM COUNTY. CITIES AND TOWNSHIPS: Baldwin Place, Brewster, Carmel, Cold Spring, Garrison, Kent, Lake Peekskill, Mahopac, Mahopac Falls, Patterson, Putnam Valley. ROCKLAND COUNTY. CITIES AND TOWNSHIPS: Garnerville, Haverstraw, Pomona, Stony Point, Thiells, Tomkins Cove. WESTCHESTER COUNTY. CITIES AND TOWNSHIPS: Amawalk, Baldwin Place, Bedford, Bedford Hills, Buchanan, Cortlandt Manor, Crompound, Cross River, Croton Falls, Croton-on-Hudson, Golden's Bridge, Jefferson Valley, Katonah, Lincolndale, Mohegan Lake, Montrose, Mt. Kisco, North Salem, Peekskill, Pound Ridge, Purdys, Shenorock, Shrub Oak, Somers, South Salem, Verplanck, Waccabuc, and Yorktown Heights. Population (2000), 654,361.

ZIP Codes: 10501, 10504–07, 10509, 10511–12, 10516–21, 10524, 10526–27, 10530, 10535–37, 10540–42, 10545, 10547–49, 10551, 10558, 10560, 10562, 10566–67, 10571–72, 10576, 10578–79, 10587–90, 10596–98, 10602, 10911, 10916–18, 10921–26, 10928, 10930, 10940–41, 10943, 10950, 10953, 10958, 10963, 10969–70, 10973, 10975, 10979–80, 10984, 10986–87, 10990, 10992, 10996–98, 11518, 11542, 11568, 11572, 11701–02, 11704, 11706–09, 11721, 11724, 11730–31, 11740, 11757, 11768, 11797, 12508, 12510–12, 12518, 12520, 12522, 12524, 12527, 12531, 12533, 12537–38, 12540, 12543, 12549, 12552–53, 12555, 12563–64, 12570, 12575, 12577–78, 12582, 12584, 12590, 12592, 12594, 12601–04, 12729, 12746, 12771, 12780, 12785

* * *

TWENTIETH DISTRICT

JOHN E. SWEENEY, Republican, of Clifton Park, NY; born in Troy, NY, August 9, 1955; education: B.A., Russell Sage College, Troy, NY, 1981; J.D., Western New England School of Law, 1990; professional: attorney, New York; New York State Commissioner of Labor, 1995–97; Deputy Secretary to the Governor, 1997–98; children: Kelly, John, and Mary; committees: Appropriations; subcommittees: Foreign Operations, Export Financing, and Related Programs; Homeland Security; vice-chair, Transportation, Treasury, HUD, The Judiciary, District of Columbia, and Independent Agencies; elected to the 106th Congress; reelected to each succeeding Congress.

Office Listings
http://www.house.gov/sweeney

416 Cannon House Office Building, Washington, DC 20515 .... (202) 225–5614
   Chief of Staff.—Martin Torrey.   FAX: 225–6234
   Press Secretary.—Demetrios Karoutsos.
939 Route 146, Suite 430, Clifton Park, NY 12065 .... (518) 371–8839
Senator Charles D. Cook Office Building, 111 Main Street, Delhi, NY 13753 .... (607) 746–9700
560 Warren Street, Room 302, Hudson, NY 12534 .... (518) 828–0181
21 Bay Street, Glens Falls, NY 12801 .... (518) 792–3031

Counties: COLUMBIA, DELAWARE (part), DUTCHESS (part), ESSEX (part), GREENE, RENSSELAER (part), SARATOGA (part), OTSEGO (part), WARREN, and WASHINGTON. Population (2000), 654,360.

ZIP Codes: 12010, 12015, 12017–20, 12022, 12024–25, 12027–29, 12033, 12037, 12040, 12042, 12046, 12050–52, 12057–60, 12062, 12065, 12074–76, 12083, 12086–87, 12089–90, 12093–94, 12106, 12115, 12118, 12123–25, 12130, 12132–34, 12136, 12138, 12140, 12143, 12148, 12151, 12153–56, 12165, 12167–70, 12172–74, 12176, 12180, 12182, 12184–85, 12192, 12195–96, 12198, 12405–07, 12413–14, 12418, 12421–24, 12427, 12430–31, 12434, 12438–39, 12442, 12444, 12450–51, 12454–55, 12459–60, 12463, 12468–70, 12473–74, 12480, 12482, 12485, 12492, 12496, 12501–03, 12507, 12513–14, 12516–17, 12521–23, 12526, 12529, 12533–34, 12538, 12540, 12545–46, 12565, 12567, 12569–72, 12578, 12580–81, 12583, 12585, 12590, 12592, 12594, 12601, 12603, 12776, 12801, 12803–04, 12808–11, 12814–17, 12819–24, 12827–28, 12831–39, 12841, 12843–46, 12848–50, 12853–56, 12859–63, 12865–66, 12870–74, 12878, 12883–87, 12942–43, 12946, 12977, 12983, 13326, 13450, 13488, 13731, 13739–40, 13750, 13752–53, 13755, 13757, 13775, 13782, 13786, 13788, 13804, 13806–07, 13820, 13838, 13842, 13846, 13849, 13856, 13860

TWENTY-FIRST DISTRICT

MICHAEL R. McNULTY, Democrat, of Green Island, NY; born in Troy, Rensselaer County, NY, September 16, 1947; education: graduated St. Joseph's Institute, Barrytown, NY, 1965; attended Loyola University, Rome Center, Rome, Italy, 1967–68; B.A., Holy Cross College, Worcester, MA, 1969; attended Hill School of Insurance, New York City, 1970; professional: insurance broker; town supervisor, Green Island, NY, 1969–77; Mayor, village of Green Island, 1977–83; New York State Assembly, 1983–88; member: Albany County Democratic Executive Committee; Green Island Democratic Committee; New York State Democratic Committee; board of directors, Capital Region Technology Development Council; delegate, Democratic National Convention, 1972; married: the former Nancy Ann Lazzaro, 1971; children: Michele, Angela, Nancy, and Maria; committees: Ways and Means; subcommittees: Oversight; ranking member, Select Revenue Measures; elected on November 8, 1988, to the 101st Congress; reelected to each succeeding Congress.

Office Listings

http://www.house.gov/mcnulty

2210 Rayburn House Office Building, Washington, DC 20515	(202) 225–5076
Chief of Staff.—David Torian.	FAX: 225–5077
Press Secretary.—Michael Wojnar.	
Legislative Director.—Jim Glenn.	
Leo W. O'Brien Federal Building, Albany, NY 12207	(518) 465–0700
U.S. Office, Schenectady, NY 12305	(518) 374–4547
33 Second Street, Troy, NY 12180	(518) 271–0822
2490 Riverfront Center, Amsterdam, NY 12010	(518) 843–3400
233 West Main Street, Room 10, Johnstown, NY 12095	(518) 762–3568

Counties: ALBANY, FULTON (part), MONTGOMERY, RENSSELAER (part), SARATOGA (part), SCHOHARIE, and SCHENECTADY. Population (2000), 654,361.

ZIP Codes: 12007–10, 12016, 12019, 12027, 12031, 12033, 12035–36, 12041, 12043, 12045–47, 12053–54, 12056, 12061, 12063–64, 12066–73, 12077–78, 12082–87, 12092–93, 12095, 12107, 12110, 12116, 12120–23, 12128, 12131, 12137, 12141, 12143–44, 12147, 12149–50, 12157–61, 12166–67, 12175, 12177, 12179–83, 12186–89, 12193–94, 12197–98, 12201–12, 12214, 12220, 12222–40, 12242–50, 12252, 12255–57, 12260–61, 12288, 12301–09, 12325, 12345, 12434, 12469, 13317, 13320, 13339, 13410, 13428, 13452, 13459

* * *

TWENTY-SECOND DISTRICT

MAURICE D. HINCHEY, Democrat, of Hurley, NY; born in New York, NY, October 27, 1938; education: graduated, Saugerties High School, 1956; B.S., State College, New Paltz, NY, 1968; M.A., State College, New Paltz, 1969; professional: Seaman First Class, U.S. Navy, 1956–59; teacher; public administrator; elected to the New York State Assembly, 1975–92; member: New York Council of State Governments; National Conference of State Legislatures; three children: Maurice Scott, Josef, and Michelle Rebecca; committees: Appropriations; Joint Economic Committee; elected on November 3, 1992 to the 103rd Congress; reelected to each succeeding Congress.

Office Listings

http://www.house.gov/hinchey

2431 Rayburn House Office Building, Washington, DC 20515	(202) 225–6335
Chief of Staff.—Wendy Darwell.	
Legislative Director.—Mike Iger.	
Communications Director.—Jeff Lieberson.	
291 Wall Street, Kingston, NY 12401	(845) 331–4466
100A Federal Building, Binghamton, NY 13901	(607) 773–2768
123 S. Cayuga Street, Suite 201, Ithaca, NY 14850	(607) 273–1388
16 James Street, Middletown, NY 10940	(845) 344–3211

Counties: BROOME COUNTY (part); CITIES AND TOWNS OF: Binghamton, Conklin, Kirkwood, Sanford, Union (includes villages of Endicott and Johnson City), Vestal, and Windsor. DELAWARE COUNTY (part); TOWNS OF: Deposit, Hancock, and Tompkins. DUTCHESS COUNTY (part). CITIES: Poughkeepsie. ORANGE COUNTY (part); CITIES AND TOWNS OF: Crawford, Middletown, Montgomery (includes village of Walden), Newburgh, and Wallkill. SULLIVAN COUNTY; CITIES AND TOWNS OF: Bethel, Callicoon, Cochecton, Delaware, Fallsburg, Forestburgh, Fremont, Highland, Liberty, Lumberland, Mamakating, Neversink, Rockland, Thompson, and Tusten. TIOGA COUNTY (part). CITIES AND TOWNS: Barton, Nichols, Owego, and Spencer. TOMPKINS COUNTY (part). CITIES AND TOWNS: Danby, and Ithaca. ULSTER COUNTY. CITIES AND TOWNS: Denning, Esopus, Gardiner, Hardenburgh, Hurley, Kingston, Lloyd, Marbletown, Marlborough, New Paltz, Olive, Plattekill, Rochester, Rosendale, Saugerties, Shandaken, Shawangunk, Ulster, Wawarsing (includes village of Ellenville), and Woodstock. Population (2000), 654,361.

ZIP Codes: 10915, 10919, 10932, 10940–41, 10985, 12401–02, 12404, 12406, 12409–12, 12416, 12419–20, 12428–29, 12432–33, 12435–36, 12440–41, 12443, 12446, 12448–49, 12451–53, 12455–58, 12461, 12464–66, 12469,

12471–72, 12475, 12477, 12480–81, 12483–84, 12486–87, 12489–91, 12493–95, 12498, 12504, 12506, 12515, 12525, 12528, 12530, 12541–44, 12547–51, 12561, 12566, 12568, 12574–75, 12583, 12586, 12588–89, 12601, 12603, 12701, 12719–27, 12729, 12732–34, 12736–38, 12740–43, 12745, 12747–52, 12754, 12758–60, 12762–70, 12775–84, 12786–92, 12814, 12853, 12857–58, 12879, 12883, 12928, 12983, 13068, 13501, 13730, 13732, 13734, 13737, 13743, 13748–49, 13754, 13756, 13760, 13774, 13783, 13790, 13795, 13811–13, 13820, 13826, 13850, 13856, 13864–65, 13901–05, 14817, 14850–51, 14853, 14859, 14867, 14883, 14889, 14892

* * *

TWENTY-THIRD DISTRICT

JOHN M. McHUGH, Republican, of Pierrepoint Manor, NY; born in Watertown, NY, September 29, 1948; education: graduated from Watertown High School, 1966; B.A., Utica College of Syracuse University; M.A., Nelson A. Rockefeller Graduate School of Public Affairs; professional: assistant to the city manager, Watertown; liaison with local governments for New York State Senator H. Douglas Barclay; New York State Senate, 1984–92; co-chair, Army Caucus; committees: Armed Services; Government Reform; Permanent Select Committee on Intelligence; subcommitees: Energy and Resources; Intelligence Policy; chair, Military Personnel; National Security, Emerging Threats and International Relations; Readiness; Technical and Tactical Intelligence; Terrorism, Human Intelligence, Analysis and Counterintelligence; chair, Special Panel on Postal Reform and Oversight; elected on November 3, 1992, to the 103rd Congress; reelected to each succeeding Congress.

Office Listings

http://www.house.gov/mchugh

2333 Rayburn House Office Building, Washington, DC 20515	(202) 225–4611
Chief of Staff.—Robert Taub.	
Administrative Secretary.—Donna M. Bell.	
205 South Peterboro Street, Canastota, NY 13032	(315) 697–2063
28 North School Street, P.O. Box 800, Mayfield, NY 12117	(518) 661–6486
104 Federal Building, Plattsburgh, NY 12901	(518) 563–1406
120 Washington Street, Suite 200, Watertown, NY 13601	(315) 782–3150

Counties: CLINTON, ESSEX (part), FRANKLIN, FULTON (part), HAMILTON, JEFFERSON, LEWIS, MADISON, ONEIDA (part), OSWEGO, ST. LAWRENCE. Population (2000), 654,361.

ZIP Codes: 12010, 12023, 12025, 12032, 12036, 12070, 12078, 12086, 12095, 12108, 12117, 12134, 12139, 12164, 12167, 12190, 12812, 12842, 12847, 12851–52, 12857, 12864, 12883, 12901, 12903, 12910–24, 12926–30, 12932–37, 12939, 12941, 12944–46, 12949–50, 12952–53, 12955–62, 12964–67, 12969–70, 12972–76, 12978–81, 12983, 12985–87, 12989, 12992–93, 12996–98, 13028, 13030, 13032–33, 13035–37, 13042–44, 13052, 13061, 13064, 13069, 13072, 13074, 13076, 13082–83, 13093, 13103–04, 13107, 13111, 13114–15, 13121–23, 13126, 13131–32, 13134–36, 13142, 13144–45, 13156, 13158, 13163, 13167, 13301–04, 13308–10, 13313–16, 13318–19, 13321–23, 13325–29, 13332–35, 13337–43, 13345–46, 13348, 13350, 13352, 13354–55, 13357, 13360–65, 13367–68, 13401–03, 13406–11, 13413, 13415, 13417–18, 13421, 13424–25, 13428, 13431, 13433, 13435–41, 13449–50, 13452, 13455–57, 13460–61, 13465, 13468–69, 13471, 13473, 13475, 13477–80, 13482–86, 13488–95, 13501–05, 13599, 13601–03, 13605–08, 13611–28, 13630–43, 13645–52, 13654–62, 13664–85, 13687–88, 13690–97, 13699

* * *

TWENTY-FOURTH DISTRICT

SHERWOOD BOEHLERT, Republican, of New Hartford, NY; born in Utica, NY, September 28, 1936; education: graduated from Whitesboro Central High School; Utica College, B.A., 1961; military service: served in the U.S. Army, 1956–58; professional: manager of Public Relations, Wyandotte Chemicals Corporation, 1961–64; chief of staff for Congressman Alexander Pirnie, 1964–72; chief of staff for Congressman Donald J. Mitchell, 1973–79; elected 1979, Oneida County Executive; member: board of directors, Utica College Foundation; St. John the Evangelist Church, New Hartford; numerous awards including honorary doctoral degrees from Syracuse University, Colgate University and Cazenovia College; married: the former Marianne Willey; four children; committees: chairman, Science; Transportation and Infrastructure; elected on November 2, 1982 to the 98th Congress; reelected to each succeeding Congress.

Office Listings

http://www.house.gov/boehlert

2246 Rayburn House Office Building, Washington, DC 20515	(202) 225–3665
Chief of Staff.—Dean D'Amore.	
Executive Assistant.—John Konkus.	

Alexander Pirnie Federal Office Building, Room 200, 10 Broad Street, Utica, NY 13501 .... (315) 793–8146
District Director.—Jeanne Donalty.

Counties: BROOME (part), CAYUGA (part), CHENANGO, CORTLAND, HERKIMER (part), ONEIDA (part), ONTARIO (part), OTSEGO (part), SENECA, TIOGA (part), TOMPKINS (part). Population (2000), 654,361.

ZIP Codes: 13021–22, 13024, 13026, 13032–34, 13040, 13042, 13045, 13052–54, 13056, 13062, 13065, 13068, 13071–74, 13077, 13080–81, 13083, 13087, 13092, 13101–02, 13117–18, 13124, 13136, 13139–41, 13147–48, 13152, 13155, 13157–60, 13162, 13165–66, 13302–05, 13308–09, 13312, 13315, 13317–20, 13322–29, 13331–33, 13335, 13337–40, 13342–43, 13345, 13348, 13350, 13353–54, 13357, 13360–61, 13363, 13365, 13367–68, 13403–04, 13406–07, 13411, 13413, 13415–17, 13420–21, 13424–26, 13431, 13433, 13436–42, 13452, 13454, 13456, 13460–61, 13464, 13468–73, 13475–78, 13480, 13485–86, 13489–93, 13495, 13501–02, 13601, 13603, 13605–08, 13611–26, 13628, 13630, 13632–43, 13645–52, 13654–56, 13658–62, 13664–69, 13672–85, 13687, 13690–97, 13699, 13730, 13733–34, 13736, 13738, 13743–47, 13752–54, 13758, 13760, 13776–78, 13780, 13784, 13787, 13790, 13794, 13796–97, 13801–03, 13807–11, 13813–15, 13820, 13825–27, 13830, 13832–33, 13835, 13838, 13840–41, 13843–45, 13848–49, 13856, 13859, 13861–64, 14433, 14443, 14456, 14468–69, 14489, 14504, 14521, 14532, 14541, 14548, 14571, 14588, 14817, 14841, 14847, 14850–52, 14854, 14860, 14867, 14881–83, 14886

* * *

TWENTY-FIFTH DISTRICT

JAMES T. WALSH, Republican, of Syracuse, NY; born in Syracuse, June 19, 1947; son of U.S. Representative William F. Walsh; education: B.A., St. Bonaventure University, Olean, NY, 1970; professional: marketing executive; president, Syracuse Common Council; member: Syracuse Board of Estimates; board of trustees of Erie Canal Museum; advisory council of the Catholic Schools Drug-Free Schools and Communities Consortium; Valley Men's Club; South Side Businessmen's Club; Nine Mile Republican Club; Onondaga Anglers Association; Oneida Lake Association; Otisco Lake Association; married: the former Diane Elizabeth Ryan, 1974; children: James (Jed), Benjamin, and Maureen; committees: Appropriations; subcommittees: Labor, Health and Human Sciences, Education, and Related Agencies; chair, Military Quality of Life and Veterans' Affairs, and Related Agencies; elected on November 8, 1988, to the 101st Congress; reelected to each succeeding Congress.

Office Listings

http://www.house.gov/walsh

2369 Rayburn House Office Building, Washington, DC 20515 .... (202) 225–3701
Chief of Staff.—Art Jutton.   FAX: 225–4042
Executive Assistant.—Kristin Calabrese.
Appropriations Associate.—Ron Anderson.
P.O. Box 7306, Syracuse, NY 13261 .... (315) 423–5657
District Representative.—Virginia Carmody.
1180 Canandaigua Road, Palmyra, NY 14522 .... (315) 597–6138

Counties: CAYUGA (part), MONROE (part), ONONDAGA, and WAYNE. CITIES AND TOWNSHIPS: Arcadia, Butler, Camillus, Cato, Cicero, Clay, Conquest, DeWitt, Elbridge, Fabius, Galen, Geddes, Huron, Ira, Irondequoit, LaFayette, Lyons, Lysander, Macedon, Manlius, Marcellus, Marion, Onondaga, Ontario, Otisco, Palmyra, Penfield, Pompey, Rose, Salina, Savannah, Skaneateles, Sodus, Spafford, Sterling, Syracuse, Tully, Van Buren, Victory, Walworth, Webster, Williamson, and Wolcott. Population (2000), 654,361.

ZIP Codes: 13020–21, 13027, 13029–31, 13033, 13035, 13037, 13039–41, 13051–53, 13057, 13060, 13063–64, 13066, 13068–69, 13077–78, 13080, 13082, 13084, 13088, 13090, 13104, 13108, 13110–13, 13116–17, 13119–20, 13122, 13126, 13135, 13137–38, 13140–41, 13143, 13146, 13148, 13152–54, 13156, 13159, 13164–66, 13201–12, 13214–15, 13217–21, 13224–25, 13235, 13244, 13250–52, 13261, 13290, 14413, 14432–33, 14449–50, 14489, 14502, 14505, 14513, 14516, 14519–20, 14522, 14526, 14537–38, 14542, 14551, 14555, 14563–64, 14568, 14580, 14589–90, 14609, 14617, 14621–22, 14625

* * *

TWENTY-SIXTH DISTRICT

THOMAS M. REYNOLDS, Republican, of Springville, NY; born in Springville, September 3, 1950; education: attended Kent State University; professional: Erie County legislator, 1982–88; New York State Assembly, 1988–98; former director, Better Business Bureau; Cooperative Extension and Central Referral Service; married: Donna; children: four; committees: House Administration; Ways and Means; chair, National Republican Congressional Committee; elected to the 106th Congress; reelected to each succeeding Congress.

Office Listings

http://www.house.gov/reynolds

332 Cannon House Office Building, Washington, DC 20515 .... (202) 225–5265
Chief of Staff.—Michael Brady.   FAX: 225–5910
Executive Assistant.—Karen Kaumeier.
Legislative Director.—Tina Mufford.
500 Essjay Road, Suite 260, Williamsville, NY 14221 .... (716) 634–2324
1577 Ridge Road West, Rochester, NY 14615 .... (585) 663–5570

Counties: ERIE (part), GENESEE, LIVINGSTON, MONROE (part), NIAGARA (part), ORLEANS (part), WYOMING. Population (2000), 654,361.

ZIP Codes: 14001, 14004–05, 14008–09, 14011–13, 14020–21, 14024, 14026, 14030–32, 14036, 14038–39, 14043, 14051, 14054, 14056, 14058–59, 14066–68, 14082–83, 14086, 14094–95, 14098, 14103, 14105, 14113, 14120, 14125, 14130–32, 14139, 14143, 14145, 14167, 14215, 14221, 14224–26, 14228, 14231, 14260, 14304, 14410–11, 14414, 14416, 14420, 14422–23, 14427–30, 14435, 14437, 14452, 14454, 14462, 14464, 14466, 14468, 14470–72, 14476–77, 14479–82, 14485–88, 14510–12, 14514–15, 14517, 14525, 14530, 14533, 14536, 14539, 14545–46, 14549–50, 14556–60, 14569, 14571–72, 14591–92, 14606, 14612, 14615–16, 14624, 14626, 14822, 14836, 14846

* * *

TWENTY-SEVENTH DISTRICT

BRIAN HIGGINS, Democrat, of Buffalo, NY; born in Buffalo, October 6, 1959; education: B.A., Buffalo State College, NY, 1984; M.A., Buffalo State College, 1985; M.P.A., Harvard University, Cambridge, MA, 1996; professional: lecturer, Buffalo State College; member of the Buffalo Common Council, 1988–1994; member of the New York state assembly, 1999–2004; married: Mary Jane Hannon; two children: John and Maeve; committees: Government Reform; Transportation and Infrastructure; elected to the 109th Congress on November 2, 2004.

Office Listings

http://www.house.gov/higgins

431 Cannon House Office Building, Washington, DC 20515 .... (202) 225–3306
Chief of Staff.—Charles Eaton.   FAX: 226–0347
Administrative Assistant / Communications Director.—Suzanne Anziska.
Legislative Director.—Moira Campion.
Larkin Building, 726 Exchange Street, Suite 601, Buffalo, NY 14210 .... (716) 852–3501
Fenton Building, 2 E. 2nd Street, Suite 300, Jamestown, NY 14701 .... (716) 484–0729

Counties: CHAUTAUQUA, ERIE (part). CITIES AND TOWNSHIPS: Boston, Brant, Buffalo, Cheektowaga, Colden, Concord, Collins, East Aurora, Eden, Elma, Evans, Hamburg, Holland, Lackawanna, North Boston, North Collins, Orchard Park, Sardinia, and Seneca. Population (2000), 654,361.

ZIP Codes: 14004, 14006, 14010, 14025–27, 14030, 14033–35, 14037, 14040, 14043, 14047–48, 14052, 14055, 14057, 14059, 14061–63, 14069–70, 14075, 14080–81, 14085–86, 14091, 14102, 14110–12, 14127, 14134–36, 14138–41, 14145, 14166, 14169–70, 14201–03, 14206–16, 14218–22, 14224–27, 14233, 14240–41, 14264–65, 14267, 14269, 14272, 14276, 14280, 14504, 14701–04, 14710, 14712, 14716, 14718, 14720, 14722–24, 14726, 14728, 14732–33, 14736, 14738, 14740, 14742, 14747, 14750, 14752, 14756–58, 14767, 14769, 14775, 14781–82, 14784–85, 14787

* * *

TWENTY-EIGHTH DISTRICT

LOUISE McINTOSH SLAUGHTER, Democrat, of Fairport, NY; born in Harlan County, KY, August 14, 1929; education: graduated from University of Kentucky with a B.S. in bacteriology; master's degree in public health; professional: elected to Monroe County legislature, two terms, 1976–79; elected to New York State Assembly, two terms, 1982–86; Distinguished Public Health Legislation Award, American Public Health Association, 1998; married: Robert Slaughter; three daughters; four grandchildren; committees: ranking member, Rules; elected to the 100th Congress on November 4, 1986; reelected to each succeeding Congress.

Office Listings

http://www.house.gov/slaughter

2469 Rayburn House Office Building, Washington, DC 20515 .... (202) 225–3615
Chief of Staff.—Cynthia Pellegrini.
Legislative Director.—Sally Schaeffer.
Communications Director.—Megan Thompson.

3120 Federal Building, 100 State Street, Rochester, NY 14614 .... (716) 232–4850
465 Main Street, Suite 105, Buffalo, NY 14203 .... (716) 853–5813
1910 Pine Avenue, Niagara Falls, NY 14301 .... (716) 282–1274

Counties: Erie (part), Monroe (part), Niagara (part), Orleans (part). CITIES AND TOWNSHIPS: Appleton, Barker, Brighton, Buffalo, Burt, East Rochester, Fairport, Grand Island, Greece, Hamlin, Hilton, Irondequoit, Kendall, Kent, Lewiston, Lyndonville, Model City, Morton, Newfane, Niagara Falls, Olcott, Penfield, Perinton, Ransomville, Rochester, Sanborn, Stella Niagara, Tonawanda, Waterport, Wilson and Youngstown. Population (2000), 654,361.

ZIP Codes: 14008, 14012, 14028, 14067, 14072, 14092, 14094, 14098, 14107–09, 14126, 14131–32, 14144, 14150–51, 14172, 14174, 14202–03, 14205–12, 14214–15, 14217, 14222–23, 14225–26, 14263, 14270, 14273, 14301–05, 14411, 14420, 14445, 14450, 14464, 14468, 14470, 14476–77, 14508, 14526, 14534, 14571, 14602–25, 14627, 14638–39, 14642–47, 14649–53, 14660, 14664, 14673

* * *

TWENTY-NINTH DISTRICT

JOHN R. (RANDY) KUHL, JR., Republican, of Hammondsport, NY; born in Bath, NY, April 19, 1943; education: graduated, Hammondsport Central School; B.S., Civil Engineering, Union College; J.D., Syracuse University College of Law; professional: lawyer; member, New York Assembly, 1981–87; member, New York Senate, 1987–2004; former State Chairman of the American Legislative Exchange Council (ALEC); former vice chairman, National Conference of State Legislatures' (NCSL) Wine Industry Task Force; Hammondsport Rotary Club; BPOE 1547; Advisory Committee of the Steuben Area Council of the Boy Souts of America; Branchport Rod and Gun Club; Executive Committee of the Steuben County Republican Committee; President of the Board of Directors of the Reginald Wood Scouting Memorial; member of the board of Directors of the Alliance for Manufacturing and Technology; communicant, St. James Episcopal; family: three children; committees: Agriculture; Education and the Workforce; Transportation and Infrastructure; elected to the 109th Congress on November 2, 2004.

Office Listings
http://www.house.gov/kuhl

1505 Longworth House Office Building, Washington, DC 20515 .... (202) 225–3161
    Chief of Staff.—Brian Fitzpatrick.   FAX: 226–6599
    Deputy Chief of Staff / Press Secretary / Legislative Director.—
        Bob Van Wicklin.
    Scheduling Coordinator.—Sarah Bitting.
    Legislative Assistants: Krista Heckler, Chelsi Stevens, Ira Treuhaft.
P.O. Box 153, Bath, NY 14810 .... (607) 937–3333

Counties: ALLEGANY, CATTARAUGUS, CHEMUNG, MONROE (part), ONTARIO (part), SCHUYLER, STEUBEN, YATES. Population (2000), 654,361.

ZIP Codes: 14009, 14024, 14029–30, 14041–42, 14060, 14065, 14070, 14081, 14101, 14129, 14133, 14138, 14141, 14168, 14171, 14173, 14414–15, 14418, 14423–25, 14428, 14432, 14437, 14441, 14445, 14450, 14453, 14456, 14461, 14463, 14466–67, 14469, 14471–72, 14475, 14478, 14482, 14485, 14487, 14489, 14502, 14504, 14506–07, 14512–14, 14518, 14522, 14526–27, 14529, 14532, 14534, 14536, 14543–44, 14546–48, 14559–61, 14564, 14572, 14585–86, 14606, 14610, 14618, 14620, 14623–25, 14706–09, 14711, 14714–15, 14717, 14719, 14721, 14726–27, 14729–31, 14735, 14737–39, 14741, 14743–45, 14747–48, 14751, 14753–55, 14760, 14766, 14770, 14772, 14774, 14777–79, 14783, 14786, 14788, 14801–10, 14812–16, 14818–27, 14830–31, 14836–46, 14855–59, 14861, 14863–65, 14867, 14869–74, 14876–80, 14884–87, 14889, 14891–95, 14897–98, 14901–05, 14925

NORTH CAROLINA

(Population 2000, 8,049,313)

SENATORS

ELIZABETH H. DOLE, Republican, of North Carolina; born in Salisbury, NC, July 29, 1936; education: B.A., Duke University, 1958; M.A., Harvard University, 1960; J.D., Harvard University, 1965; Phi Beta Kappa; public service: Deputy Assistant to President Nixon for Consumer Affairs, 1971–73; member, Federal Trade Commission, 1973–79; Assistant to President Reagan for Public Liaison, 1981–83; Secretary of Transportation, 1983–87, under President Reagan; Secretary of Labor, 1989–91, under President George H.W. Bush; President, American Red Cross, 1991–99; awards: National Safety Council's Distinguished Service Award; National Commission Against Drunk Driving Humanitarian Award; Women Executives in State Government Lifetime Achievement Award; North Carolina Award; National Religious Broadcasters' Board of Directors Award; League of Women Voters Leadership Award; organizations: Duke University Board of Trustees, 1974–85; Harvard University Board of Overseers, 1990–96; married to former Senator Bob Dole (R–KS); committees: Armed Services; Banking, Housing, and Urban Affairs; Special Committee on Aging; elected to the U.S. Senate on November 5, 2002.

Office Listings

htttp://dole.senate.gov

120 Russell Senate Office Building, Washington, DC 20510	(202) 224–6342
Chief of Staff.—Greg Gross.	FAX: 224–1100
Legislative Counsel / Policy Director.—Scott Quesenberry.	
Scheduler.—Amanda Dawson	
Communications Director.—Lindsay Taylor.	
310 New Bern Avenue, Suite 122, Raleigh NC 27601	(919) 856–4630
225 North Main Street, Suite 404, Salisbury, NC 28144	(704) 633–5011
State Director.—Margaret Klutta.	
401 N. Main Street, Suite 200, Hendersonville, NC 28792, ...	(828) 698–3747
306 South Evans Street, Greenville, NC 27835	(252) 329–1093

* * *

RICHARD BURR, Republican, of Winston-Salem, NC; born in Charlottesville, VA, November 30, 1955; education: R.J. Reynolds High School, Winston-Salem, NC, 1974; B.A., Communications, Wake Forest University, Winston-Salem, NC, 1978; professional: sales manager, Carswell Distributing; member: Reynolds Rotary Club; board member, Brenner Children's Hospital; public service: U.S. House of Representatives, 1995–2005; served as vice-chairman of the Energy and Commerce Committee; married: Brooke Fauth, 1984; children: two sons; committees: Energy and Natural Resources; Health, Education, Labor, and Pensions; Indian Affairs; Veterans' Affairs; elected to the U.S. Senate on November 2, 2004.

Office Listings

http://burr.senate.gov

217 Russell Senate Office Building, Washington, DC 20510	(202) 224–3154
Chief of Staff.—Alicia Peterson Clark.	FAX: 228–2981
Legislative Director.—Donald Dempsey.	
Policy Director.—Chris Joyner.	
2000 West First Street, Suite 508, Winston-Salem, NC 27104	(336) 631–5125
State Director.—Dean Myers.	

REPRESENTATIVES

FIRST DISTRICT

G.K. BUTTERFIELD, Democrat, of Wilson County, NC; born, April 27, 1947; education: North Carolina Central University, graduated in 1971, with degrees in Sociology and Political Science; North Carolina Central University School of Law, graduated in 1974, with a Juris Doctor degree; military service: U.S. Army, 1968–1970; served as a Personnel Specialist; discharged with the rank of Specialist E–4; professional: attorney; private practice, 1974–1988; public service: elected to the North Carolina Superior Court bench in November, 1988; appointed on February 8, 2001, by Governor Michael F. Easley to the North Carolina Supreme Court; after leaving the Supreme Court, following the 2002 election, Governor Easley appointed

Justice Butterfield as a Special Superior Court Judge; served until his retirement on May 7, 2004; organizations: North Carolina Bar Association; North Carolina Association of Black Lawyers; Wilson Opportunities Industrialization Center; religion: Baptist; committees: Agriculture; Armed Services; subcommittees: Conservation, Credit, Rural Development and Research; Department Operations, Oversight, Nutrition and Forestry; General Farm Commodities and Risk Management; Readiness; Tactical Air and Land Forces; Assistant Whip; Democratic Committee on Steering and Policy; elected to the 108th Congress, by special election, on July 20, 2004; elected to the 109th Congress on November 2, 2004.

Office Listings

413 Cannon House Office Building, Washington, DC 20515 .... (202) 225–3101
    Chief of Staff.—Corliss Clemonts-James.
    Communications Director.—Ken Willis.
    Legislative Assistant.—Adria Crutchfield.
415 East Boulevard, Suite 100, Williamston, NC 27892 .... (252) 789–4939

Counties: BEAUFORT (part), BERTIE, CHOWAN, CRAVEN (part), EDGECOMBE, GATES, GRANVILLE VANCE (part), GREENE, HALIFAX, HARTFORD, JONES (part), MARTIN, NORTHAMPTON, PASQUOTANK, PERQUIMANS, PITT (part), WARREN, WASHINGTON, WAYNE (part), WILSON (part). Population (2000), 619,178.

ZIP Codes: 27507, 27530–31, 27533–34, 27536–37, 27551, 27553, 27556, 27563, 27565, 27570, 27584, 27586, 27589, 27594, 27801, 27803–06, 27809, 27811–14, 27817–23, 27825, 27827–29, 27831–35, 27837, 27839–47, 27849–50, 27852–55, 27857–58, 27860–64, 27866–67, 27869–74, 27876–77, 27879, 27881, 27883–84, 27886–95, 27897, 27906–07, 27909–10, 27919, 27922, 27924, 27926, 27928, 27930, 27932, 27935, 27937–38, 27942, 27944, 27946, 27957, 27962, 27967, 27969–70, 27979–80, 27983, 27985–86, 28216, 28226, 28502–04, 28513, 28523, 28526, 28530, 28538, 28551, 28554–55, 28560–63, 28573, 28580, 28585–86, 28590, 28645

* * *

SECOND DISTRICT

BOB ETHERIDGE, Democrat, of Lillington, NC; born in Sampson County, NC, August 7, 1941; B.S., business administration, 1965, Campbell University, NC; graduate studies in economics, North Carolina State University, 1967; U.S. Army, 1965–67; businessman, bank director, licensed realtor; North Carolina General Assembly, 1978–88; North Carolina Superintendent of Public Instruction, 1988–96; Harnett County commissioner, 1972–76, serving as chairman of the board in 1974–76; past member: National Council of Chief State School Officers; Governor's Executive Cabinet; advisory board, Mathematics/Science Education Network; Board of the North Carolina Council on Economic Education; board of trustees, North Carolina Symphony; board of trustees, University of North Carolina Center for Public Television; Harnett County Mental Health Board; North Carolina Law and Order Commission; member and past president, Occoneechee Boy Scout Council; received Lillington Jaycees Distinguished Service Award and Lillington Community Service Award; elder, Presbyterian Church; married the former Faye Cameron in 1965; three children: Brian, Catherine, and David; committees: Agriculture; Homeland Security; elected to the 105th Congress; reelected to each succeeding Congress.

Office Listings

http://www.house.gov/etheridge

1533 Longworth House Office Building, Washington, DC 20515 .... (202) 225–4531
    Chief of Staff.—Julie Dwyer.   FAX: 225–5662
    Legislative Director.—Pat Devlin.
    Press Secretary.—Sara Lang.
    Executive Assistant.—Leigh Ann Smith.
225 Hillsborough Street, Suite 490, Raleigh, NC 27603 .... (919) 829–9122
609 North First Street, Lillington, NC 27564 .... (910) 814–0335

Counties: CHATHAM, CUMBERLAND, FRANKLIN, HARNETT, JOHNSTON, LEE, NASH, SAMPSON (part), VANCE, and WAKE (part). Population (2000), 619,178.

ZIP Codes: 27207–08, 27213, 27237, 27252, 27256, 27298, 27312, 27325, 27330–32, 27344, 27349, 27355, 27405, 27501, 27504–06, 27508, 27520–21, 27524–26, 27529, 27536–37, 27540, 27542–44, 27546, 27549, 27552, 27555, 27557, 27559, 27562, 27564, 27568–70, 27576–77, 27589, 27591–93, 27596–97, 27601–03, 27605–07, 27610, 27614, 27625, 27698, 27801–04, 27807, 27809, 27816, 27822, 27829, 27850, 27856, 27863, 27878, 27880, 27882, 27891, 27893–94, 27896, 28301, 28303, 28307–08, 28310–11, 28314, 28323, 28326, 28328, 28334–35, 28339, 28341, 28355–56, 28365–66, 28368, 28382, 28385, 28390, 28393, 28441, 28444, 28447, 28453, 28458, 28466, 28478

THIRD DISTRICT

WALTER B. JONES, Republican, of Farmville, NC; born in Farmville, February 10, 1943; education: graduated Hargrave Military Academy, Chatham, VA, 1961; B.A., Atlantic Christian College, Wilson, NC, 1966; served in North Carolina National Guard; self-employed, sales; member: North Carolina House of Representatives, 1983–92; married: Joe Anne Whitehurst Jones; one child, Ashley Elizabeth Jones Scarborough; committees: Armed Services; Financial Services; Resources; elected to the 104th Congress; reelected to each succeeding Congress.

Office Listings

422 Cannon House Office Building, Washington, DC 20515 .... (202) 225–3415
   Chief of Staff.—Glen Downs.   FAX: 225–3286
   Office Manager.—Emily Chapman.
   Press Secretary.—Kristen Quigley.
1105 C Corporate Drive, Greenville, NC 27858 .... (252) 931–1003
   District Office Manager.—Millicent A. Lilley.

Counties: BEAUFORT (part), CAMDEN, CARTERET, CRAVEN (part), CURRITUCK, DARE, DUPLIN (part), HYDE, JONES (part), LENOIR (part), MARTIN (part), ONSLOW (part), PAMLICO, PENDER (part), PITT (part), SAMPSON, TYRRELL and WAYNE (part). CITIES: Atlantic Beach, Ayden, Beaufort, Belhaven, Burgaw, Clinton, Emerald Isle, Fremont, Goldsboro, Greenville, Havelock, Jacksonville, Kill Devil Hills, Kinston, Kitty Hawk, Morehead City, Mount Olive, Nags Head, New Bern, Newport, River Bend, Trent Woods, Wallace, Washington, and Winterville. Population (2000), 619,178.

ZIP Codes: 27530–32, 27534, 27542, 27557, 27569, 27803–04, 27807–10, 27814, 27817, 27822, 27824, 27826, 27828–30, 27834, 27836–37, 27851–52, 27856, 27858, 27860, 27863, 27865, 27868, 27871, 27875, 27879, 27880, 27882–83, 27885, 27888–89, 27892–93, 27896, 27909, 27915–17, 27920–21, 27923, 27925, 27927–29, 27936, 27939, 27941, 27943, 27947–50, 27953–54, 27956, 27958–60, 27962, 27964–66, 27968, 27972–74, 27976, 27978, 27981–82, 28333, 28341, 28445, 28454, 28460, 28501, 28504, 28508–13, 28515–16, 28518–22, 28524–29, 28531–33, 28537, 28539–47, 28551–53, 28555–57, 28560, 28562, 28564, 28570–72, 28574–75, 28577–87, 28589–90, 28594

* * *

FOURTH DISTRICT

DAVID E. PRICE, Democrat, of Chapel Hill, NC; born in Erwin, TN, August 17, 1940; education: B.A., Morehead Scholar, University of North Carolina; Bachelor of Divinity, 1964, and Ph.D., political science, 1969, Yale University; professor of political science and public policy, Duke University; author of four books on Congress and the American political system; served North Carolina's Fourth District in the U.S. House of Representatives, 1987–94; in the 102nd Congress, wrote and pushed to passage the Scientific and Advanced Technology Bill and sponsored the Home Ownership Assistance Act; past chairman and executive director, North Carolina Democratic Party; Hubert Humphrey Public Service Award, American Political Science Association, 1990; member, North Carolina's Transit 2001 Commission; past chairman of the board and Sunday School teacher, Binkley Memorial Baptist Church; married: Lisa Price; children: Karen and Michael; committees: Appropriations; subcommittees: Homeland Security; Legislative; VA-HUD; elected to the 100th–103rd Congresses; elected to the 105th Congress; reelected to each succeeding Congress.

Office Listings
http://www.house.gov/price

2162 Rayburn House Office Building, Washington, DC 20515 .... (202) 225–1784
   Chief of Staff.—Jean-Louise Beard.   FAX: 225–2014
   Legislative Director.—Darek Newby.
   Executive Assistant.—Elizabeth Gottschalk.
   Systems Manager.—Catherine Liao.
5400 Trinity Place, Suite 205, Raleigh, NC 27607 .... (919) 859–5999
   District Director.—Rose Auman.
88 Vilcom Circle, Suite 140, Chapel Hill, NC 27514 .... (919) 967–7924
411 W. Chapel Hill Street, Durham, NC 27701 .... (919) 688–3004

Counties: CHATHAM (part), DURHAM, ORANGE, WAKE (part). Population (2000), 619,178.

ZIP Codes: 27228, 27231, 27243, 27278, 27302, 27312, 27330, 27501–03, 27510–17, 27519, 27523, 27526, 27529, 27539–41, 27560, 27562, 27572, 27583, 27592, 27599, 27603, 27606–07, 27610, 27612–15, 27617, 27623–24, 27656, 27675–76, 27690, 27695, 27699, 27701–05, 27707–13, 27715, 27717, 27722

FIFTH DISTRICT

VIRGINIA FOXX, Republican, of Banner Elk, NC; born in New York, NY, June 29, 1943; education: B.A., University of North Carolina, Chapel Hill, NC, 1968; M.A.C.T., University of North Carolina, Chapel Hill, NC, 1972; Ed.D., University of North Carolina, Greensboro, NC, 1985; professional: professor, Caldwell Community College, Hudson, NC; professor, Appalachian State University, Boone, NC; Assistant Dean, Appalachian State University, Boone, NC; president, Mayland Community College, Spruce Pine, NC, 1987–1994; nursery operator; deputy secretary for management, North Carolina Department of Administration; organizations: member, Watauga County board of education, 1967–1988; member, North Carolina State Senate, 1994–2004; Executive Committee of North Carolina Citizens for Business and Industry; Z. Smith Reynolds Foundation Advisory Panel; National Advisory Council for Women's Educational Programs; Board of Directors of the NC Center for Public Research; UNC–Chapel Hill Board of Visitors; National Conference of State Legislatures' Blue Ribbon Advisory Panel on Child Care; Foscoe-Grandfather Community Center Board; family: married to Tom Foxx; one daughter; committees: Agriculture; Education and the Workforce; Government Reform; elected to the 109th Congress on November 2, 2004.

Office Listings

http://www.house.gov/foxx

503 Cannon House Office Building, Washington, DC 20515	(202) 225–2071
Chief of Staff.—Richard Hudson.	FAX: 225–2995
Legislative Director.—Deana Funderburk.	
Press Secretary.—Amy Auth.	
6000 Meadowbrook Mall, Suite 3, Clemmons, NC 27012	(336) 778–0173
240 Highway 105 Extension, Suite 200, Boone, NC 28607.	

Counties: ALEXANDER COUNTY. CITIES: Bethlehem, Hiddenite, Stony Point, Taylorsville. ALLEGANY COUNTY. CITIES: Ennice, Glade Valley, Laurel Springs, Sparta. ASHE COUNTY. CITIES: Crumpler, Glendale Springs, Grassy Creek, Jefferson, Lansing, Scottville, Todd, Warrensville, West Jefferson. DAVIE COUNTY. CITIES: Advance, Cooleemee, Mocksville. FORSYTH COUNTY (part). CITIES: Bethania, Clemmons, Kernersville, King, Lewisville, Pfafftown, Rural Hall, Tobaccoville, Walkertown, Winston-Salem. IREDELL COUNTY (part). CITIES: Harmony, Love Valley, Mooresville, Olin, Statesville, Turnersburg, Troutman. ROCKINGHAM COUNTY (part). CITIES: Madison, Stokesdale. STOKES COUNTY. CITIES: Danbury, Germanton, Lawsonville, King, Pine Hall, Pinnacle, Sandy Ridge, and Walnut Cove. SURRY COUNTY. CITIES: Ararat, Dobson, Elkin, Flat Rock, Mount Airy, Pilot Mountain, Siloam, Toast, Westfield, White Plains. WATAUGA COUNTY. CITIES: Beech Mountain, Blowing Rock, Boone, Deep Gap, Seven Devils, Sugar Grove, Triplett, Vilas, Zionville. WILKES COUNTY. CITIES: Boomer, Cricket, Hays, Fairplains, Ferguson, Millers Creek, Moravian Falls, Mulberry, N. Wilkesboro, Olin, Pleasant Hill, Roaring River, Ronda, Thurmond, Traphill, Wilkesboro. YADKIN COUNTY. CITIES: Arlington, Booneville, East Bend, Hamptonville, Jonesville, Turnersburg, and Yadkinville. Population (2000), 619,178.

ZIP Codes: 27006–07, 27009–14, 27016–25, 27028, 27030, 27040–43, 27045–47, 27049–53, 27055, 27094, 27098–99, 27101–09, 27111, 27113–17, 27120, 27127, 27130, 27150–51, 27155–57, 27199, 27201–02, 27235, 27244, 27265, 27284–85, 27305, 27314–15, 27320, 27326, 27343, 27357–58, 27360, 27379, 27565, 27582, 27893, 28115, 28125, 28166, 28601, 28604–08, 28615, 28617–18, 28621–27, 28629–31, 28634–36, 28640, 28642–45, 28649, 28651, 28654, 28656, 28659–60, 28663, 28665, 28668–70, 28672, 28675–79, 28681, 28683–85, 28688–89, 28691–94, 28697–99

* * *

SIXTH DISTRICT

HOWARD COBLE, Republican, of Greensboro, NC; born in Greensboro, March 18, 1931; education: Appalachian State University, Boone, NC, 1949–50; A.B., history, Guilford College, Greensboro, NC, 1958; J.D., University of North Carolina School of Law, Chapel Hill, 1962; military service: U.S. Coast Guard as a seaman recruit, 1952; active duty, 1952–56 and 1977–78; reserve duty, 1960–82; presently holds rank of captain; last reserve duty assignment, commanding officer, U.S. Coast Guard Reserve Unit, Wilmington, NC; professional: attorney; admitted to North Carolina bar, 1966; field claim representative and superintendent, auto insurance, 1961–67; elected to North Carolina House of Represenives, 1969; assistant U.S. attorney, Middle District of North Carolina, 1969–73; commissioner (secretary), North Carolina Department of Revenue, 1973–77; North Carolina House of Representatives, 1979–83; practiced law with law firm of Turner, Enochs and Sparrow, Greensboro, NC, 1979–84; member: Alamance Presbyterian Church, American Legion, Veterans of Foreign Wars of the United States, Lions Club, Greensboro Bar Association, North Carolina Bar Association, North Carolina State Bar; North Carolina State co-chairman, American Legislative Exchange Council, 1983–84; committees: Judiciary; Transportation and Infrastructure; elected to the 99th Congress on November 6, 1984; reelected to each succeeding Congress.

Office Listings

http://www.house.gov/coble   howard.coble@mail.house.gov

2468 Rayburn House Office Building, Washington, DC 20515	(202) 225–3065
Chief of Staff / Press Secretary.—Ed McDonald.	FAX: 225–8611
Executive Assistant.—Mary Elizabeth Tillman.	

2102 North Elm Street, Suite B, Greensboro, NC 27408–5100 .... (336) 333–5005
    Office Manager.—Chris Beaman.
155 Northpoint Avenue, Suite 200B, High Point, NC 27262–7723 .... (336) 886–5106
    District Representative.—Nancy Mazza.
241 Sunset Avenue, Suite 101, Asheboro, NC 27203–5658 .... (336) 626–3060
    District Representative.—Rebecca Redding.
2727D Old Concord Road, Salisbury, NC 28146–8388 .... (704) 645–8082
    District Representative.—Terri Welch.
124 West Elm Street, P.O. Box 812, Graham, NC 27253–0812 .... (336) 229–0159
    District Representative.—Janine Osborne.

Counties: ALAMANCE (part), DAVIDSON (part), GUILFORD (part), MOORE, RANDOLPH, ROWAN (part). Population (2000), 620,590.

ZIP Codes: 27201–05, 27208–09, 27214–17, 27220, 27230, 27233, 27235, 27239, 27242, 27244, 27248–49, 27252–53, 27258–65, 27281–84, 27288–89, 27292, 27295, 27298–99, 27301–02, 27310, 27312–13, 27316–17, 27325, 27330, 27340–42, 27344, 27349–50, 27355–61, 27370–71, 27373–74, 27376–77, 27401–10, 27415–17, 27419–20, 27425, 27427, 27429, 27435, 27438, 27455, 27495, 27498–99, 27607, 27612–13, 27640, 27803–04, 28023, 28041, 28071–72, 28081, 28083, 28088, 28125, 28127, 28137–38, 28144, 28146–47, 28315, 28326–27, 28347, 28350, 28370, 28373–74, 28387–88, 28394

* * *

SEVENTH DISTRICT

MIKE McINTYRE, Democrat, of Lumberton, NC; born in Robeson County, August 6, 1956; education: B.A., Phi Beta Kappa Morehead Scholar, 1978, and J.D., 1981, University of North Carolina; upon graduation, received the Algernon Sydney Sullivan Award for "unselfish interest in the welfare of his fellow man"; professional: attorney; past president, Lumberton Economic Advancement for Dowtown; formerly on board of directors of Lumberton Rotary Club, Chamber of Commerce and a local group home for the mentally handicapped; active in the Boy Scouts of America, and Lumberton PTA; married: the former Dee Strickland; two children; committees: Agriculture; Armed Services; subcommittees: Conservation, Credit, and Rural Development; Specialty Crops and Foreign Agriculture Programs; Tactical Air and Land Forces; Terrorism, Unconventional Threats and Capabilities; elected to the 105th Congress; reelected to each succeeding Congress.

Office Listings

http://www.house.gov/mcintyre

2437 Rayburn House Office Building, Washington, DC 20515 .... (202) 225–2731
    Chief of Staff/Press Secretary.—Dean Mitchell.   FAX: 225–5773
    Deputy Chief of Staff.—Audrey Lesesne.
    Chief of Constituent Services.—Vivian Lipford.
    Legislative Director.—Jeff Hogg.
Federal Building, 301 Green Street, Room 218, Fayetteville, NC 28401 .... (910) 323–0260
201 North Front Street, Suite 440, Wilmington, NC 28401 .... (910) 815–4959
701 Elm Street, Lumberton, NC 28358 .... (910) 671–6223
    District Director.—Marie Thompson.

Counties: BLADEN, BRUNSWICK, COLUMBUS, CUMBERLAND (part), DUPLIN (part), NEW HANOVER, PENDER, ROBESON, SAMPSON (part). Population (2000), 619,178.

ZIP Codes: 28301–06, 28309, 28311–12, 28318–20, 28325, 28328, 28331–32, 28334, 28337, 28340–42, 28344, 28348–49, 28356–60, 28362, 28364–66, 28369, 28371–72, 28375, 28377–78, 28383–86, 28390–93, 28395, 28398–99, 28401–12, 28420–25, 28428–36, 28438–39, 28441–59, 28461–70, 28472, 28478–80, 28513, 28518, 28521, 28572, 28574

* * *

EIGHTH DISTRICT

ROBIN HAYES, Republican, of Concord, NC; born in Concord, NC, August 14, 1945; education: B.A., history, Duke University, 1967; professional: owner and operator, Mt. Pleasant Hosiery Mill; member, North Carolina House of Representatives, 1992–96; married: Barbara Weiland, 1968; children: Winslow and Bob; appointed to the Armed Services Committee Panel on Morale, Welfare, and Recreation for the 106th Congress; appointed to Special Oversight Panel on Terrorism for the 107th Congress; committees: Agriculture; Armed Services; Transportation and Infrastructure; chairman, Congressional Sportsmen's Caucus; chairman, Special Operations Forces Caucus; Assistant Majority Whip; elected to the 106th Congress; reelected to each succeeding Congress.

Office Listings
http://www.hayes.house.gov

130 Cannon House Office Building, Washington, DC 20515 .... (202) 225–3715
  Administrative Assistant.—Andrew Duke.   FAX: 225–4036
  Legislative Director.—Jennifer Thompson.
  Scheduler.—Andy Munn.
137 Union Street South, Concord, NC 28025 .... (704) 786–1612
  District Director.—Gary Mitchell.
230 East Franklin Street, Rockingham, NC 28379 .... (910) 997–2070

Counties: ANSON, CABARRUS (part), CUMBERLAND (part), HOKE, MECKLENBURG (part), MONTGOMERY, RICHMOND, SCOTLAND (part), STANLY, UNION (part). Population (2000), 619,178.

ZIP Codes: 27209, 27215, 27229, 27247, 27253, 27281, 27284, 27306, 27312, 27320, 27341, 27356, 27358, 27371, 27405, 27534, 27803–04, 27893, 28001–02, 28007, 28009, 28025–27, 28036, 28071, 28075, 28081–83, 28091, 28097, 28102–04, 28107–12, 28119, 28124, 28127–29, 28133, 28135, 28137–38, 28159, 28163, 28167, 28170, 28174, 28204–05, 28209–13, 28215, 28217–18, 28220, 28223, 28227, 28229, 28262, 28270, 28278, 28301, 28303–06, 28308, 28311, 28314–15, 28325, 28329–30, 28338, 28343, 28345, 28347, 28349, 28351–53, 28357, 28361, 28363–64, 28367, 28371, 28376–77, 28379–80, 28382, 28386, 28396

* * *

NINTH DISTRICT

SUE WILKINS MYRICK, Republican, of Charlotte, NC; born in Tiffin, OH, August 1, 1941; education: graduated Port Clinton High School, Port Clinton, OH; attended Heidelberg College; professional: former president and CEO, Myrick Advertising and Myrick Enterprises; mayor of Charlotte, NC, 1987–91; Charlotte City Council, 1983–85; active with the National League of Cities and the U.S. Conference of Mayors; served on former President Bush's Affordable Housing Commission; member: Charlotte Chamber of Commerce; Muscular Dystrophy Association; March of Dimes; Elks Auxiliary; PTA; Cub Scout den mother; United Methodist Church; founder, Charitable Outreach Society; married Ed Myrick, 1977; five children; committee: Energy and Commerce; elected to the 104th Congress; reelected to each succeeding Congress.

Office Listings
http://www.myrick.house.gov

230 Cannon House Office Building, Washington, DC 20515 .... (202) 225–1976
  Administrative Assistant.—Ashley Hoy.   FAX: 225–3389
  Executive Assistant.—Hollie Arnold.
6525 Morrison Boulevard, Suite 402, Charlotte, NC 28211 .... (704) 362–1060
197 W. Main Avenue, Gastonia, NC 28052 .... (704) 861–1976

Counties: GASTON (part), MECKLENBURG (part), UNION. Population (2000), 619,178.

ZIP Codes: 28006, 28012, 28016–17, 28031–34, 28036, 28042, 28052–56, 28070, 28077–80, 28086, 28092–93, 28098, 28101, 28103–07, 28110, 28112, 28114, 28120, 28126, 28130, 28134, 28136, 28150–52, 28164, 28169, 28173–74, 28201, 28203–04, 28206–11, 28213–17, 28222, 28226–27, 28241, 28247, 28250, 28253, 28261–62, 28269–71, 28273–74, 28277–78, 28287

* * *

TENTH DISTRICT

PATRICK T. McHENRY, Republican, of Cherryville, NC; born in Charlotte, October 22, 1975; education: graduated Ashbrook High School, Gastonia, NC; attended North Carolina State University, Raleigh, NC; B.A., Belmont Abbey College, Belmont, NC, 1999; professional: realtor; media executive; appointed special assistant to the U.S. Secretary of Labor by President George W. Bush in 2001; member, North Carolina House of Representatives, 2002–2004; organizations: Gaston Chamber of Commerce, Gastonia Rotary Club, the National Rifle Association, Saint Michael Church, board of directors of the United Way's Success by Six Youth Program; committees: Budget; Financial Services; Government Reform; elected to the 109th Congress on November 2, 2004.

Office Listings

http://www.house.gov/mchenry

224 Cannon House Office Building, Washington, DC 20515 .... (202) 225-2576
    Chief of Staff.—Dee Stewart.   FAX: 225-0316
    Legislative Director.—Jon Causey.
    Communications Director.—Jonathan Collegio.
    Scheduler.—Cendy Gonzalez.
87 Fourth Street, NW., Suite A, P.O. Box 1830, Hickory, NC 28603 .... (828) 327-6100

Counties: AVERY, BURKE, CALDWELL, CATAWBA, CLEVELAND, GASTON (part), IREDELL (part), LINCOLN, MITCHELL, and RUTHERFORD (part). CITIES AND TOWNSHIPS: Hickory, Lenoir, Morganton, Shelby, and Mooresville. Population (2000), 619,178.

ZIP Codes: 28006, 28010, 28016–21, 28024, 28033, 28036–38, 28040, 28042–43, 28052, 28073–74, 28076, 28080, 28086, 28089–90, 28092, 28114–15, 28117, 28139, 28150, 28152, 28164, 28166–69, 28601–07, 28609–13, 28616, 28619, 28621–22, 28624–25, 28628–30, 28633, 28635–38, 28641, 28645–47, 28650, 28652–55, 28657–58, 28661–62, 28664, 28666–67, 28671, 28673, 28676–78, 28680–82, 28687, 28690, 28699, 28705, 28720, 28740, 28746, 28752, 28761, 28765, 28777

* * *

ELEVENTH DISTRICT

CHARLES H. TAYLOR, Republican, of Brevard, NC; born in Brevard, January 23, 1941; graduated from Brevard High School; B.A., Wake Forest University, 1963; J.D., Wake Forest University, 1966; tree farmer; member: North Carolina Board of Transportation, North Carolina Energy Policy Council; vice chairman, Western North Carolina Environmental Council; chairman, North Carolina Parks and Recreation Council; member, North Carolina State House, 1967–73; minority leader, 1969–73; North Carolina State Senator and minority leader, 1973–75; married to the former Elizabeth Owen; three children: Owen, Bryan, and Charles Robert; member, Board of Visitors to the Military Academy; committees: Appropriations; subcommittees: Commerce, State, Justice and the Judiciary; chairman, Interior; elected to the 102nd Congress on November 6, 1990; reelected to each succeeding Congress.

Office Listings

339 Cannon House Office Building, Washington, DC 20515 .... (202) 225-6401
    Chief of Staff.—Sean Dalton.
    Scheduler.—Michael Calvo.
22 South Pack Square, Suite 330, Asheville, NC 28801 .... (828) 251-1988
303 Fairground Road, Spindale, NC 28160 .... (828) 286-8750
211 Seventh Avenue West, Hendersonville, NC 28791 .... (828) 697-8539
Cherokee County Courthouse, Murphy, NC 28906 .... (828) 837-3249
515 South Haywood Street, Suite 118, Waynesville, NC 28787 .... (828) 456-7559

Counties: BUNCOMBE, CHEROKEE, CLAY, GRAHAM, HAYWOOD, HENDERSON, JACKSON, MCDOWELL, MACON, MADISON, POLK, RUTHERFORD (part), SWAIN, TRANSYLVANIA, YANCEY. Population (2000), 619,177.

ZIP Codes: 28043, 28114, 28139, 28160, 28701–02, 28704, 28707–45, 28747–58, 28760–63, 28766, 28768, 28770–79, 28781–93, 28801–06, 28810, 28813–16, 28901–06, 28909

* * *

TWELFTH DISTRICT

MELVIN L. WATT, Democrat, of Charlotte, NC; born in Charlotte, August 26, 1945; education: graduated, York Road High School, Charlotte, 1963; B.S., business adminisration, University of North Carolina, Chapel Hill, 1967; J.D., Yale University Law School, New Haven, CT, 1970; professional: attorney; admitted to the District of Columbia bar, 1970, admitted to the North Carolina bar, 1971; began practice with Chambers, Stein, Ferguson and Becton, 1971–92; North Carolina State Senate, 1985–86; life member: NAACP; member: Mount Olive Presbyterian Church; Mecklenburg County Bar Association, past president; Johnston C. Smith University Board of Visitors; Central Piedmont Community College Foundation; North Carolina Association of Black Lawyers; North Carolina Association of Trial Lawyers; Legal Aid of Southern Piedmont; NationsBank Community Development Corporation; Charlotte Chamber of Commerce; Sports Action Council; Auditorium-Coliseum-Civic Center Authority; United Way; Mint Museum; Inroads, Inc.; Family Housing Services; Public Education Forum; Dilworth Community Development Association; Cities in Schools; West Charlotte Business Incubator;

Housing Authority Scholarship Board; Morehead Scholarship Selection Committee, Forsyth Region; married: the former Eulada Paysour, 1968; children: Brian and Jason; committees: Financial Services; Judiciary; elected on November 3, 1992, to the 103rd Congress; reelected to each succeeding Congress.

Office Listings
http://www.house.gov/watt

2236 Rayburn House Office Building, Washington, DC 20515 .... (202) 225–1510
    Chief of Staff.—Joyce Brayboy.   FAX: 225–1512
1230 West Morehead Street, Suite 306, Charlotte, NC 28208 .... (704) 344–9950
301 South Greene Street, Suite 210, Greensboro, NC 27401 .... (336) 275–9950
    District Director.—Pam Stubbs.

Counties: CABARRUS COUNTY (part). DAVIDSON COUNTY (part). CITIES AND TOWNSHIPS: Lexington, and Thomasville. FORSYTH COUNTY (part). CITIES AND TOWNSHIPS: Winston-Salem. GUILFORD COUNTY (part). CITIES AND TOWNSHIPS: High Point, Greensboro. MECKLENBURG COUNTY. CITIES AND TOWNSHIPS: Charlotte. ROWAN COUNTY. CITIES: Salisbury. Population (2000), 619,178.

ZIP Codes: 27010, 27012–13, 27019, 27040, 27045, 27051, 27054, 27101, 27103–07, 27110, 27127, 27214, 27260, 27262–63, 27265, 27282, 27284, 27292–95, 27299, 27310, 27320, 27351, 27360, 27401, 27403, 27405–11, 27534, 27803–04, 27893, 28023, 28027, 28035–36, 28039, 28078, 28081, 28115, 28123, 28125, 28134, 28144–47, 28159, 28202–17, 28219, 28221, 28224, 28226–28, 28230–37, 28240, 28242–43, 28254–56, 28258, 28260, 28262, 28265–66, 28269–70, 28272–73, 28275, 28278, 28280–82, 28284–85, 28289–90, 28296–97

* * *

THIRTEENTH DISTRICT

BRAD MILLER, Democrat, of Raleigh, NC; born in Fayetteville, NC, May 19, 1953; education: B.A., Political Science, University of North Carolina, 1975; Master's Degree, Political Science, London School of Economics, 1978; J.D., Columbia University Law School, 1979; professional: attorney; law clerk to Circuit Court of Appeals Judge J. Dickson Phillips, Jr., 1979–80; has practiced law in Raleigh since 1980, and has been in private practice since 1991; public service: North Carolina House of Representatives, 1992–94; North Carolina State Senate, 1996–2002; religion: Episcopal; family: married to Esther Hall; committees: Financial Services; Science; elected to the 108th Congress on November 5, 2002; reelected to each succeeding Congress.

Office Listings
http://www.house.gov/bradmiller

1722 Longworth House Office Building, Washington, DC 20515 .... (202) 225–3032
    Chief of Staff.—Mark Harkins.   FAX: 225–0181
    Legislative Director.—Thomas Koonce.
    Press Secretary.—Joe Bonfiglio.
    Scheduler.—Eleanor Blaine.
1300 St. Mary's Street, Suite 504, Raleigh, NC 27605 .... (919) 836–1313
400 West Market Street, Suite 104, Greensboro, NC 27401 .... (336) 574–2909

Counties: ALAMANCE (part), CASWELL, GRANVILLE (part), GUILFORD (part), PERSON, ROCKINGHAM (part), WAKE (part). Population (2000), 619,178.

ZIP Codes: 27025, 27027, 27046, 27048, 27212, 27214–17, 27231, 27244, 27249, 27253, 27258, 27288–89, 27291, 27301–02, 27305, 27311–12, 27314–15, 27320, 27323, 27326, 27343, 27375, 27379, 27401, 27403, 27405–10, 27412, 27455, 27507, 27509, 27511, 27522, 27525–26, 27541, 27544–45, 27565, 27571–74, 27581–83, 27587–88, 27591, 27596–97, 27601, 27603–17, 27619–20, 27622, 27625, 27627–29, 27634–36, 27640, 27650, 27658, 27661, 27668, 27690, 27698

NORTH DAKOTA

(Population 2000, 642,200)

SENATORS

KENT CONRAD, Democrat, of Bismarck, ND; born in Bismarck, March 12, 1948; education: graduated from Wheelus High School, Tripoli, Libya, 1966; attended the University of Missouri, Columbia, 1967; B.A., Stanford University, CA, 1971; M.B.A., George Washington University, Washington, DC, 1975; professional: assistant to the Tax Commissioner, Bismarck, 1974–80; director, Management Planning and Personnel, North Dakota Tax Department, March–December 1980; Tax Commissioner, State of North Dakota, 1981–86; married Lucy Calautti, February 1987; one child by former marriage: Jessamyn Abigail; elected to the U.S. Senate on November 4, 1986; was not a candidate for a second term on Senate seat he had won in 1986; subsequently elected by special election on December 4, 1992, to fill the vacancy caused by the death of Senator Quentin Burdick, whose term would have expired on January 3, 1995; took the oath of office on December 14, 1992, and continued his Senate service without interruption; committees: Agriculture, Nutrition and Forestry; ranking member, Budget; Finance; Indian Affairs; reelected to each succeeding Senate term.

Office Listings
http://conrad.senate.gov

530 Hart Senate Office Building, Washington, DC 20510	(202) 224–2043
Chief of Staff.—Bob Van Heuvelen.	FAX: 224–7776
Legislative Director.—Tom Mahr.	
220 East Rosser Avenue, Room 228, Bismarck, ND 58501	(701) 258–4648
State Director.—Lynn Clancy.	
657 Second Avenue North, Room 306, Fargo, ND 58102	(701) 232–8030
	TDD: 232–2139
102 North Fourth Street, Suite 104, Grand Forks, ND 58203	(701) 775–9601
100 First Street, SW, Room 105, Minot, ND 58701	(701) 852–0703

* * *

BYRON L. DORGAN, Democrat, of Bismarck, ND; born in Dickinson, ND, May 14, 1942; education: graduated, Regent High School, 1961; B.S., University of North Dakota, 1965; M.B.A., University of Denver, 1966; professional: North Dakota State Tax Commissioner, 1969–80, the only elected state tax commissioner in the nation; received 80 percent of the vote in 1976 tax commissioner reelection bid; chairman, Multi-State Tax Commission, 1972–74; executive committee member, National Association of Tax Administrators, 1972–75; selected by the *Washington Monthly* as one of the outstanding state officials in the United States, 1975; chosen by one of North Dakota's leading newspapers as the individual with the greatest influence on State government, 1977; elected to Congress, 1980; elected president of Democratic freshman class during first term; reelected, 1982, with 72 percent of the vote; reelected to Congress in 1984 with 78.5 percent of the vote, setting three election records in North Dakota—largest vote ever received by a statewide candidate, largest vote by a U.S. House candidate, and largest majority by a U.S. House candidate; his 242,000 votes in 1984 were the most received anywhere in the nation by an opposed House candidate; reelected to each succeeding Congress; served on three congressional committees during first term in Congress: Agriculture, Small Business, and Veterans' Affairs; named to the Ways and Means Committee, January 1983; called the real successor to Bill Langer and the State's most exciting office holder in generations, by the 1983 *Book of America*; 1990 *New York Times* editorial said, "Mr. Dorgan sets an example for political statesmanship"; named to Select Committee on Hunger in 1985; chairman, International Task Force on Select Committee on Hunger; chairman, Democratic Policy Committee, 106th thru 109th Congresses; assistant Democratic Leader for Policy, 106th and 107th Congresses; assistant Democratic Floor Leader, 104th and 105th Congresses; assistant Democratic Floor Leader, ex officio, 106th and 107th Congresses; married: Kim Dorgan; children: Scott, Shelly (deceased), Brendon, and Haley; committees: Appropriations; Commerce, Science and Transportation; Energy and Natural Resources; Indian Affairs; elected to the U.S. Senate on November 3, 1992; first sworn in on December 15, 1992, to fill the remainder of the term in North Dakota's open Senate seat, then sworn in January 5, 1993, for six-year term; reelected to each succeeding Senate term.

Office Listings

http://dorgan.senate.gov

322 Hart Senate Office Building, Washington, DC 20510 .... (202) 224–2551
Chief of Staff.—Jim Messina.   FAX: 224–1193
Communications Director.—Barry E. Piatt.
Office Manager.—Dana McCallum.
State Director.—Bob Valeu.
220 East Rosser Avenue, Room 312, Bismarck, ND 58502 .... (701) 250–4618
1802 32nd Avenue S., Suite B, P.O. Box 9060, Fargo, ND 58106 .... (701) 239–5389
102 North Fourth Street, Room 108, Grand Forks, ND 58201 .... (701) 746–8972
100 First Street SW, Suite 105, Minot, ND 58701 .... (701) 852–0703

REPRESENTATIVE

AT LARGE

EARL POMEROY, Democrat-NPL, of Valley City, ND; born in Valley City, September 2, 1952; education: B.A. and J.D., University of North Dakota, Grand Forks, 1974, 1979; graduate research in legal history at the University of Durham, England, 1975–76; professional: attorney; admitted to North Dakota bar, 1979; North Dakota House of Representatives, 1980–84; Insurance Commissioner of North Dakota, 1985–92; president, National Association of Insurance Commissioners, 1990; children: Kathryn and Scott; committees: Agriculture; Ways and Means; elected to the 103rd Congress on November 3, 1992; reelected to each succeeding Congress.

Office Listings

http://www.house.gov/pomeroy

1501 Longworth House Office Building, Washington, DC 20515 .... (202) 225–2611
Chief of Staff.—Bob Siggins.   FAX: 226–0893
Legislative Director.—Aleta Botts.
Press Secretary.—Mac Schneider.
Federal Building, 220 East Rosser Avenue, Room 328, Bismarck, ND 58501 .... (701) 224–0355
3003 32nd Avenue South, Suite 6, Fargo, ND 58103 .... (701) 235–9760
State Director.—Gail Skaley.

Population (2000), 642,200.

ZIP Codes: 58001–02, 58004–09, 58011–13, 58015–18, 58021, 58027, 58029, 58030–33, 58035–36, 58038, 58040–43, 58045–49, 58051–54, 58056–65, 58067–69, 58071–72, 58074–79, 58081, 58102–09, 58121–22, 58124–26, 58201–06, 58208, 58210, 58212, 58214, 58216, 58218–20, 58222–25, 58227–31, 58233, 58235–41, 58243–44, 58249–51, 58254–62, 58265–67, 58269–78, 58281–82, 58301, 58310–11, 58313, 58316–19, 58321, 58323–25, 58327, 58329–32, 58335, 58338–39, 58341, 58343–46, 58348, 58351–53, 58355–57, 58359, 58361–63, 58365–70, 58372, 58374, 58377, 58379–82, 58384–86, 58401–02, 58405, 58413, 58415–16, 58418, 58420–26, 58428–31, 58433, 58436, 58438–45, 58448, 58451–52, 58454–56, 58458, 58460–61, 58463–64, 58466–67, 58472, 58474–84, 58486–88, 58490, 58492, 58494–97, 58501–07, 58520–21, 58523–24, 58528–33, 58535, 58538, 58540–42, 58544–45, 58549, 58552, 58554, 58558–66, 58568–73, 58575–77, 58579–81, 58601–02, 58620–23, 58625–27, 58630–32, 58634, 58636, 58638–47, 58649–56, 58701–05, 58707, 58710–13, 58716, 58718, 58721–23, 58725, 58727, 58730–31, 58733–37, 58740–41, 58744, 58746–48, 58750, 58752, 58755–63, 58765, 58768–73, 58775–76, 58778–79, 58781–85, 58787–90, 58792–95, 58801–02, 58830–31, 58833, 58835, 58838, 58843–45, 58847, 58849, 58852–54, 58856

OHIO

(Population 2000, 11,353,140)

SENATORS

MIKE DeWINE, Republican, of Columbus, OH; born in Springfield, OH, January 5, 1947; Yellow Springs High School; B.S., Miami University, Oxford, OH, 1969; graudated, J.D., Ohio Northern University, 1972; attorney, admitted to the Ohio State bar, 1972; Greene County assistant and prosecuting attorney, 1976–80; Ohio State Senator, 1980–82; U.S. Representative, 1983–91; Lieutenant Governor of Ohio, 1991–95; married the former Frances Struewing, 1967; eight children: Patrick, Jill, Becky, John, Brian, Alice, Mark, and Anna; committees: **Appropriations; Health, Education, Labor, and Pensions; Judiciary; Select Committee on Intelligence**; elected to the U.S. Senate on November 8, 1994; reelected to each succeeding Senate term.

Office Listings
http://dewine.senate.gov

140 Russell Senate Office Building, Washington, DC 20510	(202) 224–2315
Chief of Staff.—Laurel Dawson.	FAX: 224–6519
Communications Director.—Mike Dawson.	
Legislative Director.—Paul Palagyi.	
Press Secretary.—Amanda Flaig.	
312 Walnut Street, Room 2030, Cincinnati, OH 45202	(513) 763–8260
Regional Director.—Scott Noyes.	
600 Superior Avenue East, Room 2450, Cleveland, OH 44114	(216) 522–7272
Regional Director.—Michelle Gillcrest.	
37 West Broad Street, Room 300, Columbus, OH 43215	(614) 469–5186
Regional Director.—Scott Corbitt.	
121 Putnam Street, Suite 102, Marietta, OH 45750	(614) 373–2317
District Representative.—Karen Sloan.	
420 Madison Avenue, Room 1225, Toledo, OH 43604	(419) 259–7535
District Representative.—Diane Miller.	
100 West Main Street, 2nd Floor, Xenia, OH 45385	(937) 376–3080
State Director.—Barbara Schenck.	

* * *

GEORGE V. VOINOVICH, Republican, of Cleveland, OH; born in Cleveland, July 15, 1936; B.A., Ohio University, 1958; J.D., College of Law, Ohio State University, 1961; Honorary Doctorate of Law, Ohio University, 1981; Honorary Doctorate of Public Administration, Findlay University, 1993; public service: Assistant Attorney General, Ohio, 1963; member, Ohio House of Representatives, 1967–71; Cuyahoga County Auditor, 1971–76; Cuyahoga County Commissioner, 1977–78; Lieutenant Governor, Ohio, 1979; Mayor, Cleveland, OH, 1979–86; 65th Governor of Ohio, 1990–98; President, National League of Cities, 1985; chairman, National Governor's Association, 1997–98; Catholic; married: Janet Voinovich; three children: George, Betsy, and Peter; committees: **Environment and Public Works; Foreign Relations; Homeland Security and Governmental Affairs; chair, Select Committee on Ethics**; elected to the U.S. Senate on November 3, 1998; reelected to each succeeding Senate term.

Office Listings
http://voinovich.senate.gov

524 Hart Senate Office Building, Washington, DC 20510	(202) 224–3353
Chief of Staff.—Aric Newhouse.	FAX: 228–1382
Legislative Director.—Phil Park.	
Press Secretary.—Scott Milburn.	
Office Manager.—Melanie Worth.	
1240 East Ninth Street, Suite 2955, Cleveland, OH 44199	(216) 522–7095
Regional Representative.—Dora Pruce.	
37 West Broad Street, Suite 310, Columbus, OH 43215	(614) 469–6774
State Director.—Beth Hansen.	
36 East 7th Street, Room 2615, Cincinnati, OH 45202	(513) 684–3265
District Representative.—Tony Condia.	
420 Madison Avenue, Room 1210, Toledo, OH 43604	(419) 259–3895
District Representative.—Dennis Fligor.	
37 West Broad Street, Suite 320, Columbus, OH 43215	(614) 409–6774
Constituent Services Director.—Michael Dustman.	
417 Second Avenue, Gallipolis, OH 45631	(740) 441–6410
District Representative.—Cara Dingus.	

REPRESENTATIVES

FIRST DISTRICT

STEVE CHABOT, Republican, of Cincinnati, OH; born in Cincinnati, January 22, 1953; attended LaSalle High School, Cincinnati; B.A., College of William and Mary, Williamsburg, VA, 1975; J.D., Salmon P. Chase College of Law, 1978; former school teacher; private practice lawyer, 1978–94; Hamilton County commissioner, 1990–94; member, Cincinnati City Council, 1985–90; chairman, County Council's Urban Development and Law and Public Safety committees; married: Donna Chabot, 1973; children: Randy and Erica; committees: International Relations; Judiciary; Small Business; subcommittees: chairman, The Constitution; Middle East and Central Asia; Asia and the Pacific; Crime, Terrorism, and Homeland Security; Commercial and Administrative Law; Tax, Finance, and Exports; elected to the 104th Congress; reelected to each succeeding Congress.

Office Listings

129 Cannon House Office Building, Washington, DC 20515 .... (202) 225–2216
    Chief of Staff.—Gary Lindgren.   FAX: 225–3012
    Legislative Director.—Kevin Fitzpatrick.
    Office Manager.—Angela Oswald.
Carew Tower, 441 Vine Street, Room 3003, Cincinnati, OH 45202 .... (513) 684–2723
    District Director.—Mike Cantwell.

Counties: BUTLER (part), HAMILTON (part). Population (2000), 630,730.

ZIP Codes: 45001–02, 45013–14, 45030, 45033, 45040–41, 45051–54, 45056, 45070, 45201–21, 45223–25, 45229, 45231–34, 45236–41, 45246–48, 45250–53, 45258, 45262–64, 45267–71, 45273–74, 45277, 45280, 45296, 45298–99

* * *

SECOND DISTRICT

VACANT

Counties: ADAMS, BROWN, CLERMONT, HAMILTON (part), PIKE, SCIOTO (part), WARREN (part). Population (2000), 630,730.

ZIP Codes: 45034, 45036, 45039–40, 45054, 45065, 45068, 45101–03, 45105–07, 45111–13, 45115, 45118–22, 45130–31, 45133, 45140, 45142, 45144–45, 45147–48, 45150, 45152–54, 45156–58, 45160, 45162, 45167–68, 45171, 45174, 45176, 45202, 45206–09, 45212–13, 45222, 45226–27, 45230, 45235–37, 45241–46, 45249, 45254–55, 45601, 45612–13, 45616, 45618, 45624, 45630, 45642, 45646, 45648, 45650, 45652, 45657, 45660–63, 45671, 45679, 45683–84, 45687, 45690, 45693, 45697

* * *

THIRD DISTRICT

MICHAEL R. TURNER, Republican, of Dayton, OH; born in Dayton, January 11, 1960; education: B.A., Ohio Northern University, 1982; J.D., Case Western Reserve University Law School, 1985; M.B.A., University of Dayton, 1992; professional: attorney; president, JMD Development (real estate company); corporate counsel, MTC International (holding company); organizations: Ohio Bar Association; California Bar Association; public service: Mayor of Dayton, 1994–2002; family: married to Lori; children: Jessica and Carolyn; committees: Armed Services; Government Reform; Veterans' Affairs; elected to the 108th Congress on November 5, 2002; reelected to each succeeding Congress.

Office Listings
http://www.house.gov/miketurner

1740 Longworth House Office Building, Washington, DC 20515 .... (202) 225–6465
    Chief of Staff.—Stacy Palmer-Barton.   FAX: 225–6754
    Legislative Director.—Neil Siefring.
120 West Third Street, Suite 305, Dayton, OH 45402 .... (937) 225–2843

Counties: CLINTON, HIGHLAND, MONTGOMERY (part), WARREN (part). Population (2000), 630,730.

ZIP Codes: 45005, 45032, 45036, 45040, 45042, 45044, 45054, 45066, 45068, 45107, 45110, 45113–14, 45118, 45123, 45132–33, 45135, 45138, 45140, 45142, 45146, 45148, 45155, 45159, 45164, 45166, 45169, 45177, 45206, 45240–

41, 45309, 45315, 45322, 45325, 45327, 45335, 45338, 45342–45, 45354, 45371, 45377, 45381, 45401–10, 45412–20, 45422, 45426–29, 45431–32, 45437, 45439–41, 45448–49, 45454, 45458–59, 45463, 45469–70, 45475, 45479, 45481–82, 45490, 45612, 45660, 45679, 45697

* * *

FOURTH DISTRICT

MICHAEL G. OXLEY, Republican, of Findlay, OH; born in Findlay, February 11, 1944, son of George Garver and Marilyn Maxine; education: graduated, Findlay Senior High School, 1962; B.A., government, Miami University, Oxford, OH, 1966; J.D., Ohio State University College of Law, Columbus, 1969; admitted to Ohio bar, 1969; professional: FBI special agent, Washington, DC, Boston, and New York City, 1969–72; attorney, Oxley, Malone, Fitzgerald, Hollister, 1972–81; elected to Ohio House of Representatives, 1972, from 82nd District, which includes all or parts of four northwestern Ohio counties; reelected, 1974, 1976, 1978, and 1980; member: financial institutions committee and State government committee; ranking minority member, judiciary and criminal justice committee; member: Trinity Lutheran Church, Findlay, OH; American, Ohio, and Findlay Bar Associations; Sigma Chi Fraternity; Omicron Delta Kappa Men's Honorary Fraternity; Society of Former Special Agents of the FBI; Rotary International; Ohio Association of Township Trustees and Clerks; Ohio Farm Bureau; Findlay Area Chamber of Commerce; married: the former Patricia Pluguez of Philadelphia, 1971; children: Chadd; committees: chairman, Financial Services; elected to the 97th Congress, June 25, 1981, in a special election to fill the vacancy caused by the death of Tennyson Guyer; reelected to each succeeding Congress.

Office Listings

http://oxley.house.gov

2308 Rayburn House Office Building, Washington, DC 20515 .... (202) 225–2676
    Administrative Assistant.—Jim Conzelman.
    Legislative Director/Press Secretary.—Timothy M. Johnson.
    Office Manager/Personal Secretary.—Debi Deimling.
3121 West Elm Plaza, Lima, OH 45805–2516 .... (419) 999–6455
100 East Main Cross Street, Findlay, OH 45840–3311 .... (419) 423–3210
24 West Third Street, Room 314, Mansfield, OH 44902–1299 .... (419) 522–5757

Counties: ALLEN, AUGLAIZE, CHAMPAIGN, HANCOCK, HARDIN, LOGAN, MARION, MORROW, RICHLAND, SHELBY, WYANDOT (part). Population (2000), 630,730.

ZIP Codes: 43003, 43009, 43011, 43019, 43044–45, 43047, 43050, 43060, 43067, 43070, 43072, 43074, 43078, 43083–84, 43301–02, 43306, 43310–11, 43314–26, 43330–38, 43340–51, 43356–60, 43516, 44802, 44804–05, 44813, 44817, 44822, 44827, 44830, 44833, 44837, 44843, 44849, 44862, 44864–65, 44875, 44878, 44901–07, 44999, 45013, 45302, 45306, 45312, 45317, 45326, 45333–34, 45336, 45340, 45344, 45353, 45356, 45360, 45363, 45365, 45380, 45388–89, 45404, 45414, 45420, 45424, 45431–32, 45502, 45801–02, 45804–10, 45812, 45814, 45816–17, 45819–20, 45822, 45830, 45833, 45835–36, 45839–41, 45843–45, 45850, 45854, 45856, 45858–59, 45862, 45865, 45867–72, 45877, 45881, 45884–85, 45887–90, 45894–97

* * *

FIFTH DISTRICT

PAUL E. GILLMOR, Republican, of Old Fort, OH; born in Tiffin, OH, February 1, 1939; education: graduated, Old Fort High School, Old Fort, OH, 1957; B.A., Ohio Wesleyan University, Delaware, 1961; J.D., University of Michigan Law School, Ann Arbor, 1964; military service: served in the U.S. Air Force, captain, 1965–66; professional: attorney; admitted to the Ohio bar, 1965; commenced practice in Tiffin, OH; Ohio State Senate, 1967–88; minority leader and president, Ohio State Senate; married the former Karen Lako, 1983; five children: Linda, Julie, Paul Michael, Adam, and Connor; committees: Energy and Commerce; Financial Services; subcommittees: chairman, Environment and Hazardous Materials; elected to the 101st Congress on November 8, 1988; reelected to each succeeding Congress.

Office Listings

http://gillmor.house.gov

1203 Longworth House Office Building, Washington, DC 20515 .... (202) 225–6405
    Administrative Assistant.—Mark Wellman.
    Executive Assistant/Scheduler.—Kelley Kurtz.
56 South Washington St., Suite 400, Tiffin, OH 44883 .... (419) 448–9016
613 West Third Street, Defiance, OH 43512 .... (419) 782–1996
130 Shady Lane Drive, Norwalk, OH 44857 .... (419) 668–0206

Counties: ASHLAND (part), CRAWFORD, DEFIANCE, FULTON, HENRY, HURON, LUCAS (part), MERCER (part), PAULDING, PUTNAM, SANDUSKY, SENECA, VAN WERT, WILLIAMS, WOOD, WYANDOT (part). Population (2000), 630,730.

ZIP Codes: 43302, 43314, 43316, 43323, 43337, 43351, 43402–03, 43406–07, 43410, 43413–14, 43416, 43420, 43430–31, 43435, 43437, 43441–43, 43447, 43449–51, 43457, 43460, 43462–67, 43469, 43501–02, 43504–06, 4351012, 43515–27, 43529–36, 43540–43, 43545, 43547–58, 43565–67, 43569–71, 43605, 43619, 43654, 44035, 44235, 44287, 44802, 44805, 44807, 44809, 44811, 44815, 44817–18, 44820, 44825–28, 44830, 44833, 44836–37, 44841, 44844–51, 44853–57, 44859–61, 44865–67, 44874–75, 44878, 44880–83, 44887–90, 45813, 45815, 45817, 45821–22, 45827–28, 45830–33, 45837–38, 45844, 45846, 45848–49, 45851, 45853, 45855–56, 45858, 45861–64, 45868, 45872–77, 45879–80, 45882, 45886–87, 45889, 45891, 45893–94, 45898–99

* * *

SIXTH DISTRICT

TED STRICKLAND, Democrat, of Lisbon, OH: born in Lucasville, August 4, 1941; education: B.A., history, Asbury College, 1963; M. Div., Asbury College, 1967; M.A., 1967; M.A., Ph.D. (1980), counseling psychology, University of Kentucky; professional: psychologist and educator; director of a Methodist children's home; professor at Shawnee State University; and consulting psychologist at Southern Ohio Correctional Facility; married: Francis Smith Strickland; committees: Energy and Commerce; Veterans' Affairs; elected to the 103rd and 105th Congresses; reelected to each succeeding Congress.

Office Listings

336 Cannon House Office Building, Washington, DC 20515	(202) 225–5705
Chief of Staff.—John Haseley.	FAX: 225–5907
Legislative Director.—Michelle Dallafior.	
Press Secretary.—Chad Tanner.	
Scheduler.—Joan Gregory.	
11692 Gallia Pike, Wheelersburg, OH 45694	(740) 574–2676
Toll Free Number.	(888) 706–1833
254 Front Street, Marietta, OH 45750	(740) 376–0868
District Director.—Jess Goode.	
374 Boardman-Poland Road, Boardman, OH 44512	(330) 965–4220
35 South Fifth Street, Martins Ferry, OH 43935	(740) 633–2275

Counties: ATHENS (part), BELMONT, COLUMBIANA, GALLIA, JEFFERSON, LAWRENCE, MAHONING (part), MEIGS, MONROE, NOBLE, SCIOTO (part), WASHINGTON. Population (2000), 630,730.

ZIP Codes: 43711, 43713, 4371619, 43724, 43728, 43732, 43747, 43752, 43754, 43757, 43759, 43772–73, 43778–80, 43786–89, 43793, 43901–03, 43905–10, 43917–18, 43920, 43925–26, 43930–35, 43937–48, 43950–53, 43961–64, 43967–68, 43970–71, 43973, 43977, 43983, 43985, 44401, 44406, 44408, 44412–13, 44415–16, 44422–23, 44427, 44429, 44431–32, 44441–45, 44449, 44451–52, 44454–55, 44460, 44481, 44490, 44492–93, 44502, 44507, 44511–15, 44601, 44609, 44619, 44625, 44634, 44657, 44665, 44672, 45014, 45040, 45054, 45065, 45067–68, 45107, 45110, 45113–14, 45123, 45132–33, 45135, 45138, 45140, 45142, 45146, 45148, 45155, 45159, 45162, 45164, 45166, 45172, 45177, 45419, 45614, 45619–20, 45623, 45629, 45631, 45636, 45638, 45643, 45645, 45648, 45653, 45656, 45658–59, 45662, 45669, 45674–75, 45677–78, 45680, 45682, 45685–86, 45688, 45694, 45696, 45699, 45701, 45710–15, 45720–21, 45723–24, 45727, 45729, 45732, 45734–35, 45739, 45741–46, 45750, 45760–61, 45764, 45766–73, 45775–80, 45783–84, 45786–89

* * *

SEVENTH DISTRICT

DAVID L. HOBSON, Republican, of Springfield, OH; born in Cincinnati, OH, October 17, 1936; education: graduated from Withrow High School, Cincinnati, 1954; B.A., Ohio Wesleyan University, Delaware, OH, 1958; J.D., Ohio State College of Law, Columbus, 1963; admitted to the Kentucky bar, 1965; airman, Ohio Air National Guard, 1958–63; businessman; member: VFW Post No. 1031, Springfield Rotary, Shrine Club No. 5121, Moose No. 536, Elks No. 51; member: board of Ohio Wesleyan University; appointed to Ohio State Senate, 1982; Ohio State Senator, 1982–90; majority whip, 1986–88; president pro tempore, 1988–90; married: the former Carolyn Alexander, 1958; children: Susan Marie, Lynn Martha, Douglas Lee; six grandchildren; committees: Appropriations; elected to the 102nd Congress on November 6, 1990; reelected to each succeeding Congress.

Office Listings

http://www.house.gov/hobson

2346 Rayburn House Office Building, Washington, DC 20515	(202) 225–4324
Chief of Staff.—Wayne Struble.	
Legislative Director.—Kenny Kraft.	
Washington Scheduler.—Ginny Gano.	
Press Secretary.—Sara Perkins.	
5 West North Street, Suite 200, P.O. Box 269, Springfield, OH 45501–0269	(937) 325–0474
212 South Broad Street, Room 55, Lancaster, OH 43130–4389	(740) 654–5149

Counties: CLARK, FAIRFIELD, FAYETTE, FRANKLIN (part), GREENE, PERRY, PICKAWAY, ROSS (part). Population (2000), 630,730.

ZIP Codes: 43009–10, 43044, 43046, 43062, 43068, 43076, 43078, 43102–03, 43105–07, 43109–10, 43112–13, 43115–17, 43125, 43128, 43130, 43135–38, 43140, 43142–43, 43145–48, 43150, 43153–57, 43160, 43163–64, 43199, 43207, 43213, 43217, 43227, 43232, 43314, 43730–31, 43739, 43748, 43758, 43760–61, 43764, 43766, 43777, 43782–83, 45123, 45135, 45169, 45301, 45305, 45307, 45314, 45316, 45319, 45323–24, 45335, 45341, 45344, 45349, 45368–70, 45372, 45384–85, 45387, 45424, 45430–35, 45440, 45458–59, 45501–06, 45601, 45628, 45644, 45671, 45732

* * *

EIGHTH DISTRICT

JOHN A. BOEHNER, Republican, of West Chester, OH; born in Reading, OH, November 17, 1949; education: graduated, Moeller High School, Cincinnati, OH, 1968; B.S., Xavier University, 1977; president, Nucite Sales, Inc.; Ohio House of Representatives, 1984–90; ranking Republican member, Commerce and Labor Committee; Energy and Environment Committee; Judiciary and Criminal Justice; elected, Union Township Trustees, 1981; elected, president, Union Township Board of Trustees, 1984; member: St. John Catholic Church; Ohio Farm Bureau; Lakota Hills Homeowners Association; Knights of Columbus, Pope John XXIII; Union Chamber of Commerce; American Heart Association Board; Butler County Mental Health Association; YMCA Capital Campaign; Union Elementary School PTA; Middletown Chamber of Commerce; American Legion Post 218 of Middletown Butler County Trustees and Clerks Association; married the former Deborah Gunlack, 1973; two children: Lindsay, Tricia; committees: Agriculture; chairman, Education and the Workforce; subcommittees: Employer-Employee Relations; General Farm Commodities and Risk Management; Livestock and Horticulture; 21st Century Competitiveness; elected to the 102nd Congress; reelected to each succeeding Congress.

Office Listings

http://johnboehner.house.gov

1011 Longworth House Office Building, Washington, DC 20515	(202) 225–6205
Chief of Staff.—Mike Sommers.	FAX: 225–0704
Press Secretary.—Don Seymour.	
7969 Cincinnati-Dayton road, Suite B, West Chester, OH 45069	(513) 779–5400
12 South Plum Street, Troy, Ohio 45373	(937) 339–1524

Counties: BUTLER (part), DARKE, MERCER (part), MIAMI, MONTGOMERY (part), PREBLE. Population (2000), 630,730.

ZIP Codes: 45003–05, 45011–15, 45018, 45025–26, 45036, 45042–44, 45050, 45055–56, 45061–64, 45067, 45069, 45071, 45073, 45099, 45241, 45246, 45303–04, 45308–12, 45317–18, 45320–22, 45325–28, 45330–32, 45337–39, 45344, 45346–48, 45350–52, 45356, 45358–59, 45361–62, 45365, 45371, 45373–74, 45378, 45380–83, 45388, 45390, 45402–04, 45406, 45414, 45424, 45431–32, 45822, 45826, 45828, 45845–46, 45860, 45865–66, 45869, 45883, 45885

* * *

NINTH DISTRICT

MARCY KAPTUR, Democrat, of Toledo, OH; born in Toledo, June 17, 1946; education: graduated, St. Ursula Academy, Toledo, 1964; B.A., University of Wisconsin, Madison, 1968; Master of Urban Planning, University of Michigan, Ann Arbor, 1974; attended University of Manchester, England, 1974; professional: urban planner; assistant director for urban affairs, domestic policy staff, White House, 1977–79; member: American Planning Association and American Institute of Certified Planners board of directors; National Center for Urban Ethnic Affairs advisory committee; University of Michigan Urban Planning Alumni Association; NAACP; Urban League; Polish Museum; Polish American Historical Association; Lucas County Democratic Party Executive Committee; Democratic Women's Campaign Association; Little Flower Parish Church; co-chair, Congressional Competitiveness Caucus; House Auto Parts Task Force; Ukrainian Caucus; religion: Roman Catholic; committees: Appropriations; subcommittees: Agriculture, Rural Development, Food and Drug Administration, and Related Agencies; Defense; elected on November 2, 1982, to the 98th Congress; reelected to each succeeding Congress.

Office Listings

http://www.house.gov/kaptur

2366 Rayburn House Office Building, Washington, DC 20515	(202) 225–4146
Chief of Staff.—Roger Szemraj.	FAX: 225–7711
Office Manager / Scheduler.—Norma Olsen.	
One Maritime Plaza, Suite 600, Toledo, OH 43604	(419) 259–7500
Administrative Assistant.—Steve Katich.	

Counties: ERIE COUNTY. CITIES AND TOWNSHIPS: Bellevue, Berlin Heights, Berlinville, Birmingham, Bloomingville, Bronson, Castalia, Chatham, Clarksfield, Collins, East Townsend, Fitchville, Hartland, Huron, Kimball, Litchfield, Milan, Mitiwanga, Monroeville, New London, Norwalk, Nova, Olena, Ridgefield, River Corners, Ruggles, Ruggles Beach, Sandusky, Shinrock, Spencer, Steuben, Sullivan, Wakeman, West Clarksfield. LORAIN COUNTY. CITIES AND TOWNSHIPS: Amherst, Beaver Park, Belden, Beulah Beach, Brownhelm, Columbia Station, Elyria, Grafton, Henrietta, Kipton, Lagrange, Linwood Park, Lorain, North Eaton, Oberlin, Ridgeville, Rochester, South Amherst, Vermilion, Wellington. LUCAS COUNTY (part). CITIES AND TOWNSHIPS: Berkey, Curtice, Gypsum, Harbor View, Holland, Maumee, Monclova, Northwood, Oregon, Swanton, Sylvania, Toledo, Waterville, Whitehouse, Woodville. OTTAWA COUNTY. CITIES AND TOWNSHIPS: Bay Shore, Bono, Catawba Island, Clay Center, Danbury, Eagle Beach, Elliston, Elmore, Gem Beach, Genoa, Graytown, Hessville, Isle St. George, Kelleys Island, Lacarne, Lakeside, Lindsey, Marblehead, Martin, Oak Harbor, Port Clinton, Portage, Put-in-Bay, Rocky Ridge, Springbrook, Vickery, Washington, Wayne, Whites Landing, and Williston. Population (2000), 630,730.

ZIP Codes: 43408, 43412, 43416, 43430, 43432–34, 43436, 43438–40, 43442, 43445–47, 43449, 43452, 43456, 43458, 43464, 43468–69, 43504, 43528, 43537, 43542, 43558, 43560, 43566, 43571, 43601–18, 43620, 43623–24, 43635, 43652, 43656–57, 43659–61, 43666–67, 43681–82, 43697, 43699, 44001, 44028, 44035, 44044, 44049–50, 44053, 44074, 44089–90, 44253, 44256, 44275, 44280, 44811, 44814, 44816, 44824, 44826, 44839, 44846–47, 44851, 44857, 44859, 44870–71, 44880, 44889

* * *

TENTH DISTRICT

DENNIS J. KUCINICH, Democrat, of Cleveland, OH; born in Cleveland, October 8, 1946; B.A., M.A., speech and communications, Case Western Reserve University, 1973; editor, professor; Ohio Senate, 1994–96; named outstanding Ohio Senator by National Association of Social Workers for his work on health and social welfare issues; Mayor of Cleveland, 1977–79; Clerk of the Municipal Court, 1975–77; Cleveland City Councilman, 1969–75; one child, Jackie; committees: Education and the Workforce; Government Reform; subcommittees: ranking member, National Security, Emerging Threats and International Relations; Education Reform; Energy Policy, Natural Resources, and Regulatory Affairs; Workforce Protections; elected to the 105th Congress; reelected to each succeeding Congress.

Office Listings

http://www.house.gov/kucinich

1730 Longworth House Office Building, Washington, DC 20515	(202) 225–5871
Administrative Director.—Doug Gordon.	FAX: 225–5745
14400 Detroit Avenue, Lakewood, OH 44107	(216) 228–8850

Counties: CUYAHOGA COUNTY (part). CITIES AND TOWNSHIPS: Bay Village, Berea, Brooklyn, Brooklyn Heights, Cleveland, Cuyahoga Heights, Fairview Park, Lakewood, Newberg Heights, North Olmsted, Olmsted Falls, Olmsted Township, Parma, Rocky River, Seven Hills, Strongsville, and Westlake. Population (2000), 630,730.

ZIP Codes: 44017, 44070, 44102, 44105, 44107, 44109, 44111, 44113, 44115–16, 44125–27, 44129–31, 44134–42, 44144–46, 44149, 44181

* * *

ELEVENTH DISTRICT

STEPHANIE TUBBS JONES, Democrat, of Cleveland, OH; born in Cleveland, September 10, 1949; B.A., Case Western Reserve University, 1971; J.D., Case Western Reserve University, 1974; Prosecutor, Cuyahoga County, OH; Judge of Common Pleas and Municipal Courts; Baptist; married to Mervyn; one child; committees: Standards of Official Conduct; Ways and Means; elected to the 106th Congress; reelected to each succeeding Congress.

Office Listings

http://www.house.gov/tubbsjones

1009 Longworth House Office Building, Washington, DC 20515	(202) 225–7032
Chief of Staff.—Patrice Willoughby.	FAX: 225–1339
Legislative Director.—Melvenia Gueye.	
Communications Director.—Nicole Williams.	
Scheduler.—Hannah Ramsey.	
3645 Warrensville Center Road, Suite 204, Shaker Heights, OH 44122	(216) 522–4900

Counties: CUYAHOGA COUNTY (part). CITIES: Beachwood, Bedford Heights, Brooklyn, Cleveland, Cleveland Heights, East Cleveland, Euclid, Garfield Heights, Linndale, Maple Heights, Oakwood, Orange, Richmond Heights, Shaker Heights, South Euclid, University Heights, Warrensville Heights, and Woodmere. Population (2000), 630,730.

ZIP Codes: 44022, 44101–06, 44108–10, 44112–15, 44117–25, 44127–28, 44132, 44137, 44143, 44146, 44178, 44185, 44188–95, 44197–99

TWELFTH DISTRICT

PATRICK J. TIBERI, Republican, of Columbus, OH; born in Columbus, October 21, 1962; education: B.A., Ohio State University, 1985; professional: real estate agent; assistant to Representative John Kasich (R–OH); public service: Ohio House of Representatives, 1992–2000; served as Majority Leader; organizations: American Red Cross Columbus Chapter Advisory Board; Westerville Chamber of Commerce; Columbus Board of Realtors; Military Veterans and Community Service Commission; Sons of Italy; awards: Fraternal Order of Police Outstanding Legislator; Watchdog of the Treasury Award; American Red Cross Volunteer Service Award; married: Denice; committees: Education and the Workforce; Financial Services; elected to the 107th Congress on November 7, 2000; reelected to each succeeding Congress.

Office Listings

http://www.house.gov/tiberi

113 Cannon House Office Building, Washington, DC 20515 .... (202) 225–5355
    Chief of Staff.—Chris Zeigler.   FAX: 226–4523
    Legislative Director.—Adam Francis.
    Communications Director.—Bruce Cuthbertson.
2700 East Dublin-Granville Road, Suite 525, Columbus, OH 43231 .... (614) 523–2555
    District Director.—Sally Testa.

Counties: DELAWARE, FRANKLIN (part), LICKING (part). Population (2000), 630,730.

ZIP Codes: 43001–04, 43011, 43013, 43015–18, 43021, 43023, 43025–27, 43031–33, 43035, 43040, 43046, 43054–56, 43061–62, 43064–66, 43068, 43071, 43073–74, 43080–82, 43085–86, 43105, 43147, 43201, 43203, 43205–07, 43209, 43211, 43213–15, 43218–19, 43224, 43226–27, 43229–32, 43235–36, 43240, 43334, 43342, 43344, 43356

* * *

THIRTEENTH DISTRICT

SHERROD BROWN, Democrat, of Lorain, OH; born in Mansfield, OH, November 9, 1952; education: B.A., Yale University, 1974; M.A., education, Ohio State University, 1979; M.A., Public Administration, Ohio State University, 1981; Ohio House of Representatives, 1975–83; Ohio Secretary of State, 1983–91; Eagle Scout, Boy Scouts of America; married: Connie Schultz; children: Emily and Elizabeth; committees: Energy and Commerce; International Relations; elected to the 103rd Congress; reelected to each succeeding Congress.

Office Listings

http://www.house.gov/sherrodbrown

2332 Rayburn House Office Building, Washington, DC 20515 .... (202) 225–3401
    Chief of Staff.—Jack Dover.   FAX: 225–2266
    Press Secretary.—Joanna Kuebler.

205 W. 20th Street, M–230, Elyria, OH 44052 .... (440) 245–5350
1655 W. Market Street, Suite E, Akron, OH 44313 .... (330) 865–8450

Counties: CUYAHOGA (part), LORAIN (part), MEDINA (part), SUMMIT (part). CITIES AND TOWNSHIPS: Akron, Lorain, Elyria, N. Ridgeville, Brunswick, Strongsville, and N. Royalton. Population (2000), 630,730.

ZIP Codes: 44001, 44011–12, 44028, 44035–36, 44039, 44044, 44052–55, 44133, 44136, 44141, 44147, 44149, 44203, 44210, 44212, 44216, 44221–24, 44230, 44233, 44253, 44256, 44264, 44280–81, 44286, 44301–04, 44306–14, 44317, 44319–22, 44325–26, 44328, 44333–34, 44372, 44393, 44398–99, 44614, 44645, 44685, 44720

* * *

FOURTEENTH DISTRICT

STEVEN C. LATOURETTE, Republican, of Concord, OH; born, July 22, 1954; education: graduated, Cleveland Heights High School, 1972; B.A., University of Michigan, 1976; J.D., Cleveland State University, 1979; professional: assistant public defender, Lake County, OH, Public Defender's Office, 1980–83; associated with Painesville firm of Cannon, Stern, Aveni and Krivok, 1983–86; Baker, Hackenberg and Collins, 1986–88; prosecuting attorney, Lake County, OH, 1988–94; served on the Lake County Budget Commission; executive board of the Lake County Narcotics Agency; chairman, County Task Force on Domestic Violence; trustee, Cleveland Policy Historical Society; director, Regional Forensic Laboratory; member: Lake

County Association of Police Chiefs, Ohio Prosecuting Attorneys Association, and National District Attorneys Association; appointed to serve as a fellow of the American College of Prosecuting Attorneys; married: Jennifer; children: Sarah, Sam, Clare, and Amy; committees: Financial Services; Government Reform; Transportation and Infrastructure; subcommittees: chair, Railroads; Financial Institutions and Consumer Credit; Government Efficiency and Financial Management; Highways, Transit and Pipelines; National Security, Emerging Threats and International Relations; Oversight and Investigations; Water Resources and the Environment; elected to the 104th Congress; reelected to each succeeding Congress.

Office Listings
http://www.house.gov/latourette

2453 Rayburn House Office Building, Washington, DC 20515 .... (202) 225–5731
    Chief of Staff.—Matt Wallen.   FAX: 225–3307
    Communications Director.—Deborah Setliff.
    Executive Assistant / Scheduler.—Kathy Kato.
1 Victoria Place, Room 320, Painesville, OH 44077 .... (440) 352–3939

Counties: ASHTABULA, CUYAHOGA (part), GEAUGA, LAKE, PORTAGE (part), SUMMIT (part), TRUMBULL (part). Population (2000), 630,730.

ZIP Codes: 44003–05, 44010, 44021–24, 44026, 44030, 44032–33, 44040–41, 44045–48, 44056–57, 44060–62, 44064–65, 44067–68, 44072–73, 44076–77, 44080–82, 44084–88, 44092–97, 44099, 44124, 44139, 44141, 44143, 44202, 44221, 44223–24, 44231, 44234, 44236–37, 44240, 44255, 44262, 44264, 44278, 44404, 44410, 44417–18, 44428, 44439, 44450, 44470, 44491

* * *

FIFTEENTH DISTRICT

DEBORAH PRYCE, Republican, of Columbus, OH; born in Warren, OH, July 29, 1951; education: B.A., *cum laude,* Ohio State University, Columbus, 1973; J.D., Capital University Law School, Columbus, OH, 1976; attorney; admitted to the Ohio bar in 1976; administrative law judge, Ohio Department of Insurance, 1976–78; first assistant city prosecutor, senior assistant city attorney, and assistant city attorney, Columbus City Attorney's Office, 1978–85; judge, Franklin County Municipal Court, presiding judge for two terms; Ohio Supreme Court Victims of Crime Award, 1986–92; member, Ohio Supreme Court Committee on Dispute Resolution; chairperson, Municipal Court Subcommittee; YWCA Woman of the Year Award, 1995; 2001 Ohio Women's Hall of Fame Inductee; Board member, National Fund for the U.S. Botanic Garden; Board member, John F. Kennedy Center for the Performing Arts; American Council of Young Political Leaders, delegate to Australia, 1986; session member, former deacon and stewardship chair, Indianola Presbyterian Church; children: Caroline (deceased), and Mia; 103rd Congress freshman class policy director; 104th Congress transition team; elected Republican Conference Secretary for the 105th Congress; elected Republican Conference vice chairman, 107th Congress; elected Republican Conference chair, 108th and 109th Congresses; committee: Financial Services; subcommittees: chair, Domestic and International Monetary Policy, Trade, and Technology; Deputy Whip, NRCC Executive Committee; elected to the 103rd Congress; reelected to each succeeding Congress.

Office Listings
http://www.house.gov/pryce

204 Cannon House Office Building, Washington, DC 20515 .... (202) 225–2015
    Chief of Staff.—Lori Salley.
    Legislative Director.—Shiloh Reiher.
    Executive Assistant.—Sara Rogers.
500 S. Front Street, Room1130,Columbus, OH 43215 .... (614) 469–5614
    District Director.—Marcee McCreary.

Counties: FRANKLIN (part), MADISON, UNION. Population (2000), 630,730.

ZIP Codes: 43007, 43015–17, 43026, 43029, 43036, 43040–41, 43044–45, 43060–61, 43064–67, 43077, 43084–85, 43110, 43119, 43123, 43125–26, 43137, 43140, 43143, 43146, 43151, 43153, 43162, 43196, 43198, 43201–04, 43206–07, 43210–12, 43214–16, 43220–24, 43228–29, 43231–32, 43234–35, 43251, 43260, 43265–66, 43268, 43270–72, 43279, 43287, 43291, 43299, 43302, 43319, 43340, 43342, 43344, 43358, 45368–69

SIXTEENTH DISTRICT

RALPH REGULA, Republican, of Navarre, OH; born in Beach City, OH, December 3, 1924; education: B.A., Mount Union College, Alliance, OH, 1948; LL.B., William McKinley School of Law, Canton, OH, 1952; military service: U.S. Navy, 1944–46; professional: attorney at law; admitted to Ohio bar and began practice in Navarre, OH, 1952; Ohio House of Representatives, 1965–66, and Ohio Senate, 1967–72; member: Ohio State Board of Education, 1960–64; Saint Timothy Episcopal Church, Massillon, OH; board of trustees, Mount Union College; honorary member, board of advisors, Walsh College; Kiwanis; Grange; trustee, Stark County Historical Society; married: Mary Ann Rogusky, 1950; children: Martha, David, and Richard; committee: vice-chairman, Appropriations; subcommittees: chairman, Labor, Health and Human Services, Education, and Related Agencies; Transportation, Treasury, HUD, The Judiciary, District of Columbia, and Independent Agencies; elected to the 93rd Congress, November 7, 1972; reelected to each succeeding Congress.

Office Listings
http://www.house.gov/regula

2306 Rayburn House Office Building, Washington, DC 20515	(202) 225–3876
Chief of Staff / Press Secretary.—Lori Rowley.	FAX: 225–3059
Executive Assistant.—Sylvia Snyder.	
Legal Counsel.—Karen Buttaro.	
Assistant.—Viquar Ahmad.	
4150 Belden Village Street NW, Suite 408, Canton, OH 44718	(330) 489–4414
District Staff Director.—Robert Mullen.	
124 West Washington Street, Suite 1A, Medina, OH 44256	(330) 722–3793

Counties: ASHLAND (part), MEDINA (part), STARK, WAYNE. Population (2000), 630,730.

ZIP Codes: 44090, 44201, 44203, 44214–17, 44230, 44233, 44235, 44251, 44253–54, 44256, 44258, 44260, 44270, 44273–76, 44280–82, 44287, 44321, 44333, 44601, 44606, 44608, 44611–14, 44618, 44624, 44626–27, 44630, 44632, 44634, 44636, 44638, 44640–41, 44643, 44645–48, 44650, 44652, 44657, 44659, 44662, 44666–67, 44669–70, 44676–77, 44680, 44685, 44688–89, 44691, 44701–12, 44714, 44718, 44720–21, 44730, 44735, 44750, 44760, 44767, 44799, 44805, 44822, 44838, 44840, 44842–43, 44864, 44866, 44878, 44880, 44903

* * *

SEVENTEENTH DISTRICT

TIM RYAN, Democrat, of Niles, OH; born, July 16, 1973; education: B.S., Bowling Green University, 1995; J.D., Franklin Pierce Law Center, 2000; awarded a National Italian American Foundation Scholarship; professional: attorney; internship, Trumbull County Prosecutor's Office; also worked as a congressional legislative aide in Washington, DC; organizations: former president, Trumbull County Young Democrats; former chairman, Earning by Learning Program in Warren, OH; public service: Ohio State Senate, 2000–2002; religion: Catholic; committees: Armed Services; Education and the Workforce; elected to the 108th Congress on November 5, 2002; reelected to each succeeding Congress.

Office Listings
http://timryan.house.gov

222 Cannon House Office Building, Washington, DC 20515	(202) 225–5261
Chief of Staff.—Mary Anne Walsh.	FAX: 225–3719
Scheduler.—Erin Isenberg.	
Legislative Director.—John Stephan.	
197 West Market Street, Warren, OH 44481	(330) 373–0074
241 Federal Plaza West, Youngstown, OH 44503	(330) 740–0193

Counties: MAHONING (part), PORTAGE (part), SUMMIT (part), TRUMBULL (part). Population (2000), 630,730.

ZIP Codes: 44201, 44211, 44221, 44223–24, 44231–32, 44236, 44240–43, 44250, 44255, 44260, 44265–66, 44272, 44278, 44285, 44288, 44302–06, 44308, 44310–13, 44315–16, 44319, 44402–06, 44410–12, 44417–18, 44420, 44424–25, 44429–30, 44436–38, 44440, 44444, 44446, 44449–50, 44453, 44470–71, 44473, 44481–86, 44488, 44491, 44501–07, 44509–12, 44514–15, 44555, 44599, 44632, 44685, 44720

* * *

EIGHTEENTH DISTRICT

ROBERT W. NEY, Republican, of St. Clairsville, OH; born in Wheeling, WV, July 5, 1954; education: graduated, St. John's High School, Bellaire, OH; B.S., Ohio State University, Columbus, OH; Ohio House of Representatives, 1981–82, and Ohio Senate, 1984–94; Ohio Senate Chairman, Finance Committee; member: Elks, Lions, Kiwanis, and NRA; married: Elizabeth Ney; children: Robert William II, and Kayla Marie; committees: Financial Services; chairman, House Administration; Transportation and Infrastructure; vice-chairman, Joint Committee on Printing; chairman, Joint Committee on the Library of Congress; subcommittees: chairman, Housing and Community Opportunity; Deputy Majority Whip; elected to the 104th Congress; relected to each succeeding Congress.

Office Listings

http://www.house.gov/ney   bobney@mail.house.gov

2438 Rayburn House Office Building, Washington, DC 20515 .... (202) 225–6265
  Chief of Staff.—Will Heaton.   FAX: 225–3394
  Legislative Director.—Chris Otillio.
  Scheduler.—Jennie Vollor.
  Legislative Assistants: Brian Petersen, Jason Spence.
146 A West Main Street, St. Clairsville, OH 43950 .... (740) 699–2704
  Toll-free, Ohio only.   (866) 464–4618
  District Director.—Matthew Parker.
126 East Second Street, Suite D, Chillicothe, OH 45601 .... (740) 779–1634
200 Broadway, Jackson, OH 45640 .... (740) 288–1430
152 Second Street, NE., Hilton-Fairfield Building #200, New Philadelphia, OH
  44663 .... (330) 364–6380
  District Representative.—Lesley Applegarth.
Masonic Temple Building, 38 North Fourth Street, Room 502, Zanesville, OH
  43701 .... (614) 452–7023
  District Representative.—Annmarie O'Grady.

Counties: ATHENS (part), BELMONT (PART), CARROLL, COSHOCTON, GUERNSEY, HARRISON, HOCKING, HOLMES, JACKSON, KNOX, LICKING (part), MORGAN, MUSKINGUM, ROSS (part), TUSCARAWAS, VINTON. Population (2000), 630,730.

ZIP Codes: 43005–06, 43008, 43011, 43014, 43019, 43022–23, 43025, 43028, 43030, 43037, 43048, 43050, 43055–56, 43058, 43071, 43076, 43080, 43093, 43098, 43101–02, 43107, 43111, 43127, 43130, 43135, 43138, 43144, 43149, 43152, 43155, 43158, 43160, 43701–02, 43718, 43720–25, 43727–28, 43730–36, 43738–40, 43746, 43749–50, 43755–56, 43758, 43760, 43762, 43766–68, 43771–73, 43777–78, 43780, 43787, 43791, 43802–05, 43811–12, 43821–22, 43824, 43828, 43830, 43832, 43836–37, 43840, 43842–45, 43901, 43903, 43906–08, 43910, 43927–28, 43933, 43945, 43950, 43972–74, 43976–77, 43981, 43983–84, 43986, 43988, 44427, 44607–08, 44610–12, 44615, 44617, 44620–22, 44624–29, 44631, 44633, 44637–39, 44643–44, 44651, 44653–54, 44656–57, 44660–61, 44663, 44671, 44675–76, 44678–83, 44687–90, 44693, 44695, 44697, 44699, 44730, 44813, 44822, 44842, 45123, 45601, 45612–13, 45617, 45621–22, 45628, 45633–34, 45640, 45644, 45647, 45651, 45653–54, 45656, 45672–73, 45681–82, 45685, 45690, 45692, 45695, 45698, 45701, 45710–11, 45715–16, 45719, 45732, 45740–41, 45761, 45764, 45766, 45780, 45782, 45786

OKLAHOMA

(Population 2000, 3,450,654)

SENATORS

JAMES M. INHOFE, Republican, of Tulsa, OK; born in Des Moines, IA, November 17, 1934; education: graduated Central High School, Tulsa, OK, 1953; B.A., University of Tulsa, OK, 1959; military service: served in the U.S. Army, private first class, 1957–58; professional: businessman; active pilot; president, Quaker Life Insurance Company; Oklahoma House of Representatives, 1967–69; Oklahoma State Senate, 1969–77; Mayor of Tulsa, OK, 1978–84; religion: member, First Presbyterian Church of Tulsa; married: the former Kay Kirkpatrick; children: Jim, Perry, Molly, and Katy; eleven grandchildren; committees: Armed Services; chairman, Environment and Public Works; elected to the 100th Congress on November 4, 1986; reelected to each succeeding Congress; elected to the U.S. Senate on November 8, 1994, finishing the unexpired term of Senator David Boren; reelected to each succeeding Senate term.

Office Listings

http://inhofe.senate.gov

453 Russell Senate Office Building, Washington, DC 20510	(202) 224–4721
Chief of Staff.—Glenn Powell.	
Legislative Director.—Aloysius Hogan.	
Press Secretary.—Ryan Thompson.	
Scheduler.—Wendi Price.	
Suite 530, 1924 South Utica, Tulsa, OK 74104	(918) 748–5111
1900 N.W. Expressway, Suite 1210, Oklahoma City, OK 73118	(405) 608–4381
Suite 104, 302 North Independence, Enid, OK 73701	(405) 234–5104
Suite 106, 215 East Choctaw, McAlester, OK 74501	(918) 426–0933

* * *

TOM COBURN, Republican, of Muskogee, OK; born in Casper, WY, March 14, 1948; education: Central High School, Muskogee, OK, 1955; B.S., Oklahoma State University, 1970; Oklahoma University Medical School, 1983; professional: manufacturing manager, Coburn Ophthalmic Division, Coburn Optical Industries, 1970–78; family physician, 1983–present; member, American Medical Association, Oklahoma State Medical Association, East Central County Medical Society, American Academy of Family Practice; religion: First Baptist Church, ordained deacon; member, Promise Keepers; public service: U.S. House of Representatives, 1995–2001; married: Carolyn Denton Coburn, 1968; children: Callie, Katie, and Sarah; committees: Homeland Security and Governmental Affairs; Indian Affairs; Judiciary; elected to the U.S. Senate on November 2, 2004.

Office Listings

http://coburn.senate.gov

172 Russell Hart Senate Office Building, Washington, DC 20510	(202) 224–5754
Chief of Staff.—Michael Schwartz.	FAX: 224–6008
Legislative Director.—Roland Foster.	
Communications Director.—John Hart.	
Scheduler.—Courtney Cox.	
3310 Mid-Continent Tower, 401 South Boston, Tulsa, OK 74103	(918) 581–7651
100 North Broadway, Suite 1820, Oklahoma City, OK 73102	(405) 231–4941

REPRESENTATIVES

FIRST DISTRICT

JOHN SULLIVAN, Republican, of Tulsa, OK; born in Tulsa, January 1, 1965; education: B.B.A., Northeastern State University, 1992; professional: fuel sales, Love's Country Stores; Real Estate, McGraw, Davison, Stewart; public service: Oklahoma House of Representatives, 1995–2002; organizations: member, St. Mary's Church; member, National Rifle Association; member, Tulsa County Republican Men's Club; U.S. House of Representatives Assistant Majority Whip; family: married to Judy; children: Thomas, Meredith, Sydney, Daniel; committees: Energy and Commerce; elected to the 107th Congress, by special election, on January 8, 2002; reelected to each succeeding Congress.

Office Listings
http://sullivan.house.gov

114 Cannon House Office Building, Washington, DC 20510 .... (202) 225–2211
Chief of Staff.—Elizabeth Bartheld. FAX: 225–9187
Scheduler.—Brooke Stegall.
5727 S. Lewis, Suite 520, Tulsa, OK 74105 .... (918) 749–0014
Chief of Staff.—Richard Hedgecock.

Counties: CREEK (part), ROGERS (part), TULSA, WAGONER, WASHINGTON. Population (2000), 690,131.

ZIP Codes: 74003–06, 74008, 74011–14, 74021–22, 74029, 74033, 74037, 74039, 74041, 74043, 74047–48, 74050–51, 74053, 74055, 74061, 74063, 74066, 74070, 74073, 74080, 74082–83, 74101–08, 74110, 74112, 74114–17, 74119–21, 74126–30, 74132–37, 74141, 74145–50, 74152–53, 74155–59, 74169–72, 74182–84, 74186–87, 74189, 74192–94, 74337, 74352, 74403, 74429, 74434, 74436, 74446, 74454, 74458, 74467, 74477

* * *

SECOND DISTRICT

DANIEL DAVID BOREN, Democrat, of Muskogee, OK; born in Shawnee, OK, August 2, 1973; education: B.S., Texas Christian University, Fort Worth, TX, 1997; M.B.A., University of Oklahoma, 2001; professional: president, Seminole State College Educational Foundation; vice-president, Robbins Energy Corporation; loan processor, Banc First Corporation; staff for United States Representative Wesley Watkins; education administrator; bank teller; aide, Oklahoma Corporation Commission; member of the Oklahoma State House of Representatives, 2002–04; organizations: Big Brothers Big Sisters Board; The Jasmine Moran Children's Museum Board; KIPP Foundation Board Member; committees: Armed Services; Resources; elected to the 109th Congress on November 2, 2004.

Office Listings
http://www.house.gov/boren

216 Cannon House Office Building, Washington, DC 20515 .... (202) 225–2701
Chief of Staff.—Peter J. Regan. FAX: 225–3038
Legislative Director.—Karen Kuhlman.
Press Secretary.—Michael Allen.
Executive Assistant.—Beth Barefoot.
431 W. Broadway, Muskogee, OK 74401 .... (918) 687–2533
District Coordinator.—Ward Curtin.
309 W. 1st Street, Claremore, OK 74017 .... (918) 341–9336
Field Representative.—Marguerite McKinney.
321 South Third, Suite 4, McAlester, OK 74501 .... (918) 423–5951
Case Worker.—Janice Beatty.

Counties: ADAIR, ATOKA, BRYAN, CANADIAN, CHEROKEE, CHOCTAW, COAL, CRAIG, CREEK, DELAWARE, HASKELL, HUGHES, JOHNSTON, LATIMER, LEFLORE, MAYES, MCCURTAIN, MCINTOSH, MUSKOGEE, NOWATA, OKFUSKEE, OTTAWA, PAWNEE, PITTSBURG, PUSHMATAHA, ROGERS, SEMINOLE, SEQUOYAH. Population (2000), 690,130.

ZIP Codes: 73014, 73036, 73064, 73078, 73085, 73090, 73447, 73449–50, 73455, 73460–62, 74010, 74015–16, 74018, 74020, 74027–28, 74030–31, 74034, 74036, 74038–39, 74041–42, 74044–45, 74047–49, 74052–53, 74058, 74067–68, 74071–72, 74080–81, 74083, 74085, 74101, 74103, 74301, 74330–33, 74335, 74337–40, 74343–44, 74346–47, 74349–50, 74352, 74355, 74358–63, 74365–67, 74369–70, 74401–02, 74421–23, 74425–26, 74428, 74430–32, 74434–38, 74441–42, 74445, 74447, 74450, 74455, 74459, 74461–64, 74468–70, 74472, 74502, 74521–23, 74525, 74530–31, 74533–34, 74536, 74538, 74546–47, 74552–54, 74556, 74560–63, 74565, 74569–72, 74576, 74578, 74650, 74701, 74720, 74723, 74726–30, 74733, 74735–36, 74740–41, 74743, 74745, 74747–48, 74750, 74756, 74759, 74764, 74766, 74829–30, 74833, 74837, 74839, 74845, 74848–50, 74856, 74859–60, 74867–68, 74880, 74883–85, 74901–02, 74930, 74932, 74935–37, 74940–42, 74944–46, 74948, 74951, 74953–56, 74959–60, 74962, 74964–66

* * *

THIRD DISTRICT

FRANK D. LUCAS, Republican, of Cheyenne, OK; born in Cheyenne, January 6, 1960; education: B.S., Agricultural Economics, Oklahoma State University, 1982; professional: rancher and farmer; served in Oklahoma State House of Representatives, 1989–94; secretary, Oklahoma House Republican Caucus, 1991–94; member: Oklahoma Farm Bureau, Oklahoma Cattlemen's Association, and Oklahoma Shorthorn Association; married: Lynda Bradshaw Lucas; children: Jessica, Ashlea, and Grant; committees: Agriculture; Financial Services; Science; elected to the 103rd Congress, by special election, in May 1994; reelected to each succeeding Congress.

Office Listings
http://www.house.gov/lucas

2342 Rayburn House Office Building, Washington, DC 20515 .... (202) 225–5565
Deputy Chief of Staff.—Nicole Scott.   FAX: 225–8698
Communications Director.—Jim Luetkemeyer.
Scheduler / Office Manager.—Jessica Reinsch.
Legislative Assistants: Richard Blackwood, Marna Harris, Micah Zomer, Courtney Box.
10952 Northwest Expressway, Suite B, Yukon, OK 73099 .... (405) 373–1958
Chief of Staff.—Stacey Glasscock.
720 South Husband, Suite 7, Stillwater, OK 74075 .... (405) 624–6407
Field Representative.—Julie Arntz.
2728 Williams Avenue, Suite F, Woodward, OK 73801 .... (580) 256–5752
Field Representative.—Bryce Marlatt.

Counties: ALFALFA, BEAVER, BECKHAM, BLAINE, CADDO, CANADIAN (part), CIMARRON, CREEK (part), CUSTER, DEWEY, ELLIS, GARFIELD, GRANT, GREER, HARMON, HARPER, JACKSON, KINGFISHER, KAY, KIOWA, LINCOLN, LOGAN, MAJOR, NOBLE, OSAGE, PAWNEE, PAYNE, ROGER MILLS, TEXAS, WASHITA, WOODS, AND WOODWARD. CITIES: Altus, Clinton, El Reno, Elk City, Enid, Guthrie, Guymon, Oklahoma City, Perry, Ponce City, Sapulpa, Stillwater, Tulsa, Weatherford, Woodward and Yukon. Population (2000), 690,131.

ZIP Codes: 73001, 73003, 73005–07, 73009, 73014–17, 73021–22, 73024, 73027–29, 73033–34, 73036, 73038, 73040–45, 73047–48, 73050, 73053–54, 73056, 73058–59, 73061–64, 73073, 73077–79, 73085, 73090, 73092, 73094, 73096–97, 73099, 73127, 73437, 73501, 73521–23, 73526, 73532, 73537, 73539, 73544, 73547, 73549–50, 73554, 73556, 73559–60, 73564, 73566, 73571, 73601, 73620, 73622, 73624–28, 73632, 73638–39, 73641–42, 73644–48, 73650–51, 73654–55, 73658–64, 73666–69, 73673, 73701–03, 73705–06, 73716–20, 73722, 73724, 73726–31, 73733–39, 73741–44, 73746–47, 73749–50, 73753–64, 73766, 73768, 73770–73, 73801–02, 73832, 73834–35, 73838, 73840–44, 73847–48, 73851–53, 73855, 73857–60, 73901, 73931–33, 73937–39, 73942, 73944–47, 73949–51, 74001–03, 74010, 74020, 74022–23, 74026, 74028, 74030, 74032, 74034–35, 74038–39, 74044–47, 74051–52, 74054, 74056, 74058–60, 74062–63, 74066–68, 74070–71, 74073–79, 74081, 74084–85, 74106, 74126–27, 74131–32, 74601–02, 74604, 74630–33, 74636–37, 74640–41, 74643–44, 74646–47, 74650–53, 74824, 74832, 74834, 74851, 74855, 74859, 74864, 74869, 74875, 74881

* * *

FOURTH DISTRICT

TOM COLE, Republican, of Moore, OK; born in Shreveport, LA, April 28, 1949; education: B.A., Grinnell College, 1971; M.A. Yale University, 1974; Ph.D., University of Oklahoma, 1984; Watson Fellow, 1971–72; and a Fulbright Fellow, 1977–78; professional: former college professor of history and politics; President, Cole Hargrave Snodgrass & Associates (political consulting firm); public service: Oklahoma State Senate, 1988–91; Oklahoma Secretary of State, 1995–99; has served as Chairman, and Executive Director, of the Oklahoma Republican Party; Executive Director, National Republican Congressional Committee; and Chief of Staff of the Republican National Committee; family: married to Ellen; one child: Mason; religion: United Methodist; committees: Rules; Standards of Conduct; elected to the 108th Congress on November 5, 2002; reelected to each succeeding Congress.

Office Listings
http://www.house.gov/cole

236 Cannon House Office Building, Washington, DC 20515 .... (202) 225–6165
Chief of Staff.—Pete Kirkham.   FAX: 225–3512
Legislative Director / Rules Associate.—Chris Caron.
Press Secretary.—Julie Shutley.
2420 Springer Drive, Suite 120, Norman, OK 73069 .... (405) 329–6500
711 SW., D Avenue, Suite 201, Lawton, OK 73501 .... (580) 357–2131
104 East 12th, Ada, OK 74820 .... (580) 436–5375

Counties: CANADIAN (part), CARTER, CLEVELAND, COMANCHE, COTTON, GARVIN, GRADY, JEFFERSON, LOVE, MARSHALL, MCCLAIN, MURRAY, OKLAHOMA (part), PONTOTOC, STEPHENS, TILLMAN. Population (2000), 690,131.

ZIP Codes: 73002, 73004, 73006, 73010–11, 73017–20, 73023, 73026, 73030–32, 73036, 73051–52, 73055, 73057, 73059, 73064–65, 73067–72, 73074–75, 73079–80, 73082, 73086, 73089, 73092–93, 73095, 73098–99, 73110, 73115, 73127–30, 73135, 73139–40, 73145, 73149–50, 73153, 73159–60, 73165, 73169–70, 73173, 73179, 73189, 73401–03, 73425, 73430, 73433–44, 73446, 73448, 73453, 73456, 73458–59, 73463, 73476, 73481, 73487–88, 73491, 73501–03, 73505–07, 73520, 73527–31, 73533–34, 73536, 73538, 73540–43, 73546, 73548, 73551–53, 73555, 73557, 73559, 73561–62, 73564–70, 73572–73, 74820–21, 74825, 74831, 74842–44, 74851, 74857, 74865, 74871–72

FIFTH DISTRICT

ERNEST J. ISTOOK, JR., Republican, of Oklahoma City, OK; born in Fort Worth, TX, February 11, 1950; education: graduated, Castleberry High School, Ft. Worth, 1967; B.A., Baylor University, 1971; J.D., Oklahoma City University, 1976; emploment: attorney; admitted to the Oklahoma bar, 1977; reporter, WKY, KOMA, 1972–77; city councilman, Warr Acres, 1982–86; library board chairman, Oklahoma City, 1985–86; director, Warr Acres Chamber of Commerce, 1986–92; Oklahoma State House of Representatives, 1986–92; married: the former Judy Bills, 1973; children: Butch, Chad, Amy, Diana, and Emily; committees: Appropriations; subcommittees: Homeland Security; vice-chair, Interior and Related Agencies; Labor, Health and Human Services, Education, and Related Agencies; elected on November 3, 1992, to the 103rd Congress; reelected to each succeeding Congress.

Office Listings

http://www.house.gov/istook

2404 Rayburn House Office Building, Washington, DC 20515	(202) 225–2132
Chief of Staff.—John Albaugh.	FAX: 226–1463
Legislative Director.—Kurt Conrad.	
Office Manager / Scheduler.—Kim Rubin.	
Press Secretary.—Micah Leydorf.	
120 North Robinson Avenue, Suite 100, Oklahoma City, OK 73102	(405) 234–9900
District Director.—Devery Youngblood.	
23 East 9th Street, Suite 301, Shawnee, OK 74801	(405) 273–6202
211 East Broadway, Seminole, OK 74868	(405) 303–2868

Counties: OKLAHOMA (part), POTTAWATOMIE, and SEMINOLE. CITIES: Arcadia, Asher, Aydelotte, Bethany, Bethel Acres, Bowlegs, Brooksville, Choctaw, Cromwell, Del City, Earlsboro, Edmond, Forrest Park, Harrah, Johnson, Jones, Konawa, Lake Aluma, Lima, Luther, Macomb, Maud, McLoud, Midwest City, Newalla, Nichols Hills, Nicoma Park, Oklahoma City, Pink, Sasakwa, Seminole, Shawnee, Smith Village, Spencer, St. Louis, Tecumesh, The Village, Tribbey, Valley Brook, Wanette, Warr Acres, Wewoka, and Woodlawn Park. Population (2000), 690,131.

ZIP Codes: 73003, 73007–08, 73013, 73020, 73034, 73045, 73049, 73054, 73066, 73078, 73083–84, 73097, 73099, 73101–32, 73134–37, 73139, 73141–49, 73151–52, 73154–57, 73159–60, 73162, 73164, 73169, 73172–73, 73178–79, 73184–85, 73190, 73194–96, 73198, 74587, 74801–02, 74804, 74818, 74826, 74830, 74837, 74840, 74849, 74851–52, 74854–55, 74857, 74859, 74866–68, 74873, 74878, 74884

OREGON

(Population 2000, 3,421,399)

SENATORS

RON WYDEN, Democrat, of Portland, OR; born in Wichita, KS, May 3, 1949; education: graduated from Palo Alto High School, 1967; B.A. in political science, with distinction, Stanford University, 1971; J.D., University of Oregon Law School, 1974; professional: attorney; member, American Bar Association; former director, Oregon Legal Services for the Elderly; former public member, Oregon State Board of Examiners of Nursing Home Administrators; cofounder and codirector, Oregon Gray Panthers, 1974–80; children: Adam David and Lilly Anne; elected to the 97th Congress, November 4, 1980; reelected to each succeeding Congress; committees: Budget; Energy and Natural Resources; Finance; Special Committee on Aging; Select Committee on Intelligence; elected to the U.S. Senate on February 6, 1996, to fill the unexpired term of Senator Bob Packwood; reelected to each succeeding Senate term.

Office Listings
http://wyden.senate.gov

230 Dirksen Senate Office Building, Washington, DC 20510	(202) 224–5244
Chief of Staff.—Josh Kardon.	
Legislative Director.—Carole Grunberg.	
Communications Director.—Carol Guthrie.	
Scheduler.—Sallie Derr.	
700 NE Multnomah Street, Suite 450, Portland, OR 97232	(503) 326–7525
151 West Seventh Avenue, Suite 435, Eugene, OR 97401	(541) 431–0229
The Federal Courthouse, 310 West Sixth Street, Room 118, Medford, OR 97501	(541) 858–5122
The Jamison Building, 131 NW Hawthorne Avenue, Suite 107, Bend, OR 97701	(541) 330–9142
SAC Annex Building, 105 Fir Street, Suite 201, LaGrande, OR 97850	(541) 962–7691
777 13th Street, SE, Suite 110, Salem, OR 97310	(503) 589–4555

* * *

GORDON HAROLD SMITH, Republican, of Pendleton, OR; born in Pendleton, May 25, 1952; B.A., 1976, Brigham Young University; LL.B, 1979, Southwestern University; served as law clerk to Justice H. Vernon Payne of the New Mexico Supreme Court and practiced law in Arizona; elected to State of Oregon Senate, 1993; elected Oregon Senate President, 1994; president/owner of Smith Frozen Foods, Inc., since 1981; married: Sharon Lankford Smith, 1975; three children: Brittany, Garrett, and Morgan; committees: Commerce, Science, and Transportation; Energy and Natural Resources; Finance; Indian Affairs; chair, Special Committee on Aging; elected to the U.S. Senate on November 5, 1996; reelected to each succeeding Senate term.

Office Listings
http://gsmith.senate.gov

404 Russell Senate Office Building, Washington, DC 20510	(202) 224–3753
Chief of Staff.—John Easton.	
Legislative Director.—Rob Epplin.	
Director of Administration.—Sue Keenom.	
Communications Director.—Chris Matthews.	
121 S.W. Salmon, Suite 1250, Portland, OR 97204	(503) 326–3386
Jager Building, 116 S. Main Street, Suite 3, Pendleton, OR 97801	(541) 278–1129
Federal Building, 211 E. 7th Avenue, Room 202, Eugene, OR 97401	(541) 465–6750
Security Plaza, 1175 E. Main Street, Suite 2D, Medford, OR 97504	(541) 608–9102
Jamison Building, 131 NW Hawthorne Avenue, Suite 107, Bend, OR 97701	(541) 318–1298

REPRESENTATIVES

FIRST DISTRICT

DAVID WU, Democrat, of Portland, OR; born in Taiwan, April 8, 1955; moved to the United States, with his family, in October, 1961; education: B.S., Stanford University, 1977; attended, Harvard University Medical School; law degree, Yale University, 1982; professional: lawyer; co-founder of Cohen & Wu (law firm), 1988; first Chinese American member of the U.S. House of Representatives; past chairman, Congressional Asian Pacific American Caucus; member, New Democrat Coalition; married: Michelle; two children: Matthew, Sarah; committees: Education and the Workforce; Science; subcommittees: ranking member, Environment, Technology and Standards; 21st Century Competiveness; Employer-Employee Relations; Space and Aeronautics; elected to the 106th Congress; reelected to each succeeding Congress.

Office Listings
http://www.house.gov/wu

1023 Longworth House Office Building, Washington, DC 20515	(202) 225–0855
Chief of Staff.—Julie Tippens.	FAX: 225–9497
Executive Assistant.—Ajah Maloney.	
Press Secretary.—Patrick Morris.	
620 SW Main Street, Suite 606, Portland, OR 97205	(503) 326–2901

Counties: CLATSOP, COLUMBIA, MULTNOMAH (part), WASHINGTON, YAMHILL. Population (2000), 684,277.

ZIP Codes: 97005–08, 97016, 97018, 97035, 97048, 97051, 97053–54, 97056, 97062, 97064, 97070, 97075–78, 97101–03, 97106, 97109–11, 97113–17, 97119, 97121, 97123–25, 97127–28, 97132–33, 97138, 97140, 97144–46, 97148, 97201, 97204–05, 97207–10, 97219, 97221, 97223–25, 97228–29, 97231, 97239–40, 97251, 97253–55, 97258, 97272, 97280–81, 97291, 97296, 97298, 97378, 97396, 97498

* * *

SECOND DISTRICT

GREG WALDEN, Republican, of Hood River, OR; born in The Dalles, OR, January 10, 1957; married: Mylene Walden; one child: Anthony David Walden; education: graduated from the University of Oregon, 1981; B.S. in Journalism; owner, Columbia Gorge Broadcasters, Inc.; member, and Assistant Majority Leader, Oregon State Senate; 1995–97; member, Oregon State House of Representatives, 1989–95, and Majority Leader, 1991–93; National Republican Legislators Association Legislator of the Year, 1993; Oregon Jaycees Outstanding Young Oregonian, 1991; member, Associated Oregon Industries; Oregon Health Sciences Foundation; Hood River Rotary Club; Hood River Elk's Club; National Federation of Independent Business; Hood River Chamber of Commerce; Hood River Memorial Hospital; Columbia Bancorp; committees: Energy and Commerce; Resources; subcommittees: vice chairman, Oversight and Investigations; Energy and Air Quality; Telecommunications and the Internet; Water and Power; elected to the 106th Congress; reelected to each succeeding Congress.

Office Listings
http://www.walden.house.gov

1210 Longworth House Office Building, Washington, DC 20515	(202) 225–6730
Chief of Staff.—Brian MacDonald.	FAX: 225–5774
Legislative Director.—Brian Hard.	
Executive Assistant.—Jill Wyman.	
843 East Main, Suite 400, Medford, OR 97504	(541) 776–4646
District Director.—John Snider.	(800) 533–3303
131 NW Hawthorne Street, Suite 201, Bend, OR 97701	(541) 389–4408

Counties: BAKER, CROOK, DESCHUTES, GILLIAM, GRANT, HARNEY, HOOD RIVER, JACKSON, JEFFERSON, JOSEPHINE (part), KLAMATH, LAKE, MALHEUR, MORROW, SHERMAN, UMATILLA, UNION, WALLOWA, WASCO, WHEELER. Population (2000), 684,280.

ZIP Codes: 97001, 97014, 97021, 97029, 97031, 97033, 97037, 97039–41, 97044, 97050, 97057–58, 97063, 97065, 97116, 97425, 97501–04, 97520, 97522, 97524–28, 97530, 97533, 97535–37, 97539–41, 97544, 97601–04, 97620–27, 97630, 97632–41, 97701–02, 97707–12, 97720–22, 97730–39, 97741, 97750–54, 97756, 97758–61, 97801, 97810, 97812–14, 97817–20, 97823–28, 97830, 97833–46, 97848, 97850, 97856–57, 97859, 97861–62, 97864–65, 97867–70, 97873–77, 97880, 97882–86, 97901–11, 97913–14, 97917–18, 97920

* * *

THIRD DISTRICT

EARL BLUMENAUER, Democrat, of Portland, OR; born in Portland, August 16, 1948; education: graduated from Centennial High School; Lewis and Clark College; J.D., Northwestern School of Law; professional: assistant to the president, Portland State University; served in Oregon State Legislature 1973–78; chaired Revenue and School Finance Committee; Multnomah County Commissioner, 1978–85; Portland City Commissioner 1986–96; served on Governor's Commission on Higher Education; National League of Cities Transportation Committee; National Civic League Board of Directors; Oregon Environmental Council; Oregon Public Broadcasting; married: Margaret Kirkpatrick; children: Jon and Anne; committees: International Relations; Transportation and Infrastructure; elected to the U.S. House of Representatives on May 21, 1996, to fill the vacancy created by Representative Ron Wyden's election to the U.S. Senate; reelected to each succeeding Congress.

Office Listings
http://blumenauer.house.gov

2446 Rayburn House Office Building, Washington, DC 20515	(202) 225–4811
Administrative Assistant.—Mariia Zimmerman.	FAX: 225–8941
Communications Director.—Tim Daly.	
Legislative Director.—James Koski.	
729 Northeast Oregon Street, Suite 115, Portland, OR 97232	(503) 231–2300
District Director.—Julia Pomeroy.	

Counties: MULTNOMAH (part), CLAKAMUS (part). Population (2000), 684,279.

ZIP Codes: 97004, 97009, 97011, 97014–15, 97017, 97019, 97022–24, 97028, 97030, 97035, 97045, 97049, 97055, 97060, 97067, 97080, 97124, 97133, 97202–03, 97206, 97210–18, 97220, 97222, 97227, 97229–33, 97236, 97238, 97242, 97256, 97266–67, 97269, 97282–83, 97286, 97290, 97292–94, 97299

* * *

FOURTH DISTRICT

PETER A. DeFAZIO, Democrat, of Springfield, OR; born in Needham, MA, May 27, 1947; B.A., Tufts University, 1969; M.S., University of Oregon, 1977; aide to Representative Jim Weaver, 1977–82; Lane County commissioner, 1983–86; married: Myrnie Daut; committees: Homeland Security; Resources; Transportation and Infrastructure; elected to the 100th Congress, November 4, 1986; reelected to each succeeding Congress.

Office Listings
http://www.house.gov/defazio

2134 Rayburn House Office Building, Washington, DC 20515	(202) 225–6416
Administrative Assistant.—Penny Dodge.	
Legislative Director.—Tom Vinson.	
151 West Seventh Avenue, Suite 400, Eugene, OR 97401	(541) 465–6732
District Director.—Karmen Fore.	(800) 944–9603
125 Central Avenue, Room 350, Coos Bay, OR 97420	(541) 269–2609
612 SE Jackson Street, Room 9, Roseburg, OR 97470	(541) 440–3523

Counties: BENTON (part), COOS, CURRY, DOUGLAS, JOSEPHINE (part), LANE, LINN. CITIES: Eugene, Roseburg, and Coos Bay. Population (2000), 684,280.

ZIP Codes: 97321–22, 97324, 97326–27, 97329–30, 97333, 97335–36, 97345–46, 97348, 97350, 97352, 97355, 97358, 97360–61, 97370, 97374, 97377, 97383, 97386, 97389, 97401–17, 97419–20, 97423–24, 97426–32, 97434–44, 97446–59, 97461–67, 97469–70, 97472–73, 97476–82, 97484, 97486–99, 97523, 97526–27, 97530–34, 97537–38, 97543–44

* * *

FIFTH DISTRICT

DARLENE HOOLEY, Democrat, of West Linn, OR; born in Williston, ND, April 4, 1939; education: B.S., Oregon State University; professional: teacher; past member: Oregon House of Representatives, West Linn City Council, Clackamas County Board of Commissioners; children: Chad and Erin; committees: Financial Services; Science; Veterans' Affairs; subcommittees: Capital Markets, Insurance and Government Sponsored Enterprises; Economic Opportunity; Financial Institutions and Consumer Credit; ranking member, Research; elected to the 105th Congress; reelected to each succeeding Congress.

Office Listings
http://www.house.gov/hooley

2430 Rayburn House Office Building, Washington, DC 20515	(202) 225–5711
Chief of Staff / Press.—Joan Mooney-Evans.	FAX: 225–5699
Executive Assistant / Scheduler.—Anne Marie Feeney.	
Legislative Director.—Mark Dedrick.	

315 Mission Street, Suite 101, Salem, OR 97302 .... (503) 588–9100
　　District Co-Director.—Travis Brouwer.
21570 Williamette Drive West, Linn, OR 97068 .... (503) 557–1324
　　District Co-Director.—Suzanne Kunse.

Counties: BENTON (part); CLACKAMAS (part); LINCOLN; MARION; MULTNOMAH (part); POLK; TILLAMOOK. CITIES: Corvallis, Portland, Salem, and Tillamook. Population (2000), 684,333.

ZIP Codes: 97002, 97004, 97010, 97013, 97015, 97017, 97020, 97023, 97026–27, 97032, 97034–36, 97038, 97042, 97045, 97062, 97068, 97070–71, 97101, 97107–08, 97112, 97118, 97122, 97130–31, 97134–37, 97140–41, 97143, 97147, 97149, 97201, 97219, 97222, 97239, 97267–68, 97301–14, 97321, 97324–25, 97330–31, 97333, 97338–39, 97341–44, 97346–47, 97350–52, 97357–62, 97364–73, 97375–76, 97380–81, 97383–85, 97388, 97390–92, 97394, 97396, 97498

PENNSYLVANIA

(Population 2000, 12,281,054)

SENATORS

ARLEN SPECTER, Republican, of Philadelphia, PA; born in Wichita, KS, February 12, 1930; education: graduated, Russell High School, Russell, KS, 1947; University of Pennsylvania, 1951, B.A., international relations, Phi Beta Kappa; Yale Law School, LL.B., 1956; board of editors, *Law Journal*; military service: served in U.S. Air Force, 1951–53, attaining rank of first lieutenant; professional: member, law firm of Dechert, Price and Rhoads before and after serving two terms as district attorney of Philadelphia, 1966–74; married: former Joan Levy, who was elected to the city council of Philadelphia in 1979; children: Shanin and Stephen; served as assistant counsel to the Warren Commission, 1964; served on Pennsylvania's State Planning Board, The White House Conference on Youth, The National Commission on Criminal Justice, and the Peace Corps National Advisory Council; committees: Appropriations; chairman, Judiciary; Veterans' Affairs; subcommittees: chairman, Labor, Health and Human Services, Education and Related Agencies; elected to the U.S. Senate on November 4, 1980; reelected to each succeeding Senate term.

Office Listings

http://specter.senate.gov   arlen_specter@specter.senate.gov

711 Hart Senate Office Building, Washington, DC 20510	(202) 224–4254
Chief of Staff.—David Brog.	FAX: 228–1229
Legislative Director.—Tom Dower.	
Administrative Director.—Reagan Blewett.	
600 Arch Street, Suite 9400, Philadelphia, PA 19106	(215) 597–7200
Regional Enterprise Tower, Suite 1450, Pittsburgh, PA 15219–1837	(412) 644–3400
Federal Building, Suite B–120, 17 South Park Row, Erie, PA 16501	(814) 453–3010
Federal Building, Room 1104, 228 Walnut Street, Harrisburg, PA 17101	(717) 782–3951
Federal Building, Suite 3814, 504 West Hamilton Street, Allentown, PA 18101	(610) 434–1444
310 Spruce Street, Suite 201, Scranton, PA 18503	(570) 346–2006
7 North Wilkes Barre Boulevard, Stegmaier Building, Room 377M, Wilkes Barre, PA 18702	(570) 826–6265

* * *

RICHARD JOHN SANTORUM, Republican, of Penn Hills, PA; born in Winchester, VA, May 10, 1958; graduated Carmel High School, 1976; B.A., Pennsylvania State University, 1980; M.B.A., University of Pittsburgh, 1981; J.D., Dickinson School of Law, 1986; admitted to the Pennsylvania bar; administrative assistant to State Senator J. Doyle Corman (R–Centre), 1981–86: director of the Senate Local Government Committee, 1981–84; director of the Senate Transportation Committee, 1984–86; associate attorney, Kirkpatrick and Lockhart, Pittsburgh, PA, 1986–90; married Karen Garver Santorum, 1990; six children: Elizabeth Anne, Richard John, Jr., Daniel James, Sarah Maria, Peter Kenneth, Patrick Francis; committees: Agriculture, Nutrition, and Forestry; Banking, Housing, and Urban Affairs; Finance; Rules and Administration; Special Committee on Aging; subcommittee chair, Social Security and Family Policy; chair, Senate Republican Conference; elected to the 102nd Congress; reelected to each succeeding Congress; elected to the U.S. Senate on November 8, 1994; reelected to each succeeding Senate term.

Office Listings

http://santorum.senate.gov

511 Dirksen Senate Office Building, Washington, DC 20510	(202) 224–6324
Chief of Staff.—Wayne Palmer.	FAX: 228–0604
Executive Assistant.—Ramona Ely.	
Legislative Director.—Zack Moore.	
Office Manager.—Jeff Stoltzfoos.	
1705 West 26th Street, Erie, PA 16508	(814) 454–7114
555 Walnut Street, Harrisburg, PA 17101	(717) 231–7540
Federal Building, Suite 3802, 504 West Hamilton Street, Allentown, PA 18101	(610) 770–0142
Regency Square, Suite 202, Route 220 North, Altoona, PA 16001	(814) 946–7023
Widener Building, One South Penn Square, Suite 960, Philadelphia, PA 19107	(215) 864–6900
Landmarks Building, One Station Square, Suite 250, Pittsburgh, PA 15219	(412) 562–0533
527 Linden Street, Scranton, PA 18503	(717) 344–8799

REPRESENTATIVES

FIRST DISTRICT

ROBERT A. BRADY, Democrat, of Philadelphia, PA; born in Philadelphia, April 7, 1945; education: graduated from St. Thomas More High School; professional: carpenter; union official; assistant Sergeant-At-Arms, Philadelphia City Council, 1975–83; Deputy Mayor for Labor, W. Wilson Goode Administration; consultant to Pennsylvania State Senate; Pennsylvania Turnpike Commissioner; board of director's, Philadelphia Redevelopment Authority; Democratic Party Executive; ward leader; chairman, Philadelphia Democratic Party; member of Pennsylvania Democratic State Committee, and Democratic National Committee; Catholic; married; Debra Brady; children: Robert and Kimberly; committees: Armed Services; House Administration; Joint Committee on Printing; elected to the 105th Congress on May 21, 1998, to fill the unexpired term of Representative Tom Foglietta; reelected to each succeeding Congress.

Office Listings
http://www.house.gov/robertbrady

206 Cannon House Office Building, Washington, DC 20515	(202) 225–4731
Chief of Staff.—Stan White.	FAX: 225–0088
Legislative Director.—Teri Morgan.	
Appointments Secretary.—Kristie Muchnok.	
Press Secretary.—Karen Warrington.	
1907 South Broad Street, Philadelphia, PA 19148	(215) 389–4627
The Colony Building, 511–13 Welsh Street, 1st Floor, Chester, PA 19103	(610) 874–7094

Counties: PHILADELPHIA (part). CITIES AND TOWNSHIPS: Chester City, Chester Township, Eddystone Borough, Colwyn Borough, Ridley Township, Tinicum Township, Darby Township, and Yeadon Borough. Population (2000), 630,730.

ZIP Codes: 19012–16, 19018, 19022–23, 19029, 19032, 19036, 19050, 19078–79, 19086, 19092–93, 19101, 19105–09, 19111–13, 19120, 19122–26, 19130–34, 19137–51, 19153–54, 19160–62, 19170–73, 19175, 19177–78, 19181–82, 19185, 19187–88

* * *

SECOND DISTRICT

CHAKA FATTAH, Democrat, of Philadelphia, PA; born in Philadelphia, November 21, 1956; education: attended Overbrook High School, Community College of Philadelphia, University of Pennsylvania's Wharton School; M.A., University of Pennsylvania's Fels School of State and Local Government, 1986; Harvard University's John F. Kennedy School of Government; recognized for outstanding leadership in *Time* magazine, and in *Ebony* magazine as one of 50 Future Leaders; recipient, Pennsylvania Public Interest Coalition's State Legislator of the Year Award; Pennsylvania State Senate, 1988–94; State House of Representatives, 1982–88; created the Jobs Project; in Pennsylvania House of Representatives, sponsored 1987 Employment Opportunities Act; supported Ben Franklin Technology Center, a conduit for securing government contracts for African-American and women-owned businesses; founded Graduate Opportunities Conference; chairman of the executive committee of the Pennsylvania Higher Education Assistance Agency; convened and led a task force, Child Development Initiative; supported measures to reform the Philadelphia Housing Authority; formed the Drug-Free Program; founded the American Cities Foundation; trustee, Lincoln University and Community College of Philadelphia; member, Mt. Carmel Baptist Church; married: the former Renée Chenault; four children; committees: Appropriations; subcommittees: Foreign Operations, Export Financing, and Related Programs; Science, The Departments of State, Justice and Commerce, and Related Agencies; elected to the 104th Congress; reelected to each succeeding Congress.

Office Listings
http://www.house.gov/fattah

2301 Rayburn House Office Building, Washington, DC 20515	(202) 225–4001
Chief of Staff.—Michelle Anderson Lee.	
Legislative Director.—Jerome Murray.	
Communications Director.—Debra Anderson.	
4104 Walnut Street, Philadelphia, PA 19104	(215) 387–6404
6632 Germantown Avenue, Philadelphia, PA 19119	(215) 848–9386

Counties: MONTGOMERY (part), PHILADELPHIA. Population (2000), 630,730.

ZIP Codes: 19004, 19012, 19027, 19038, 19046, 19093, 19095, 19101–04, 19107, 19109–11, 19118–24, 19126–32, 19138–41, 19143–48, 19150, 19161–62, 19170–71, 19173, 19178, 19184, 19187, 19191–93, 19196–97

THIRD DISTRICT

PHIL ENGLISH, Republican, of Erie, PA; born in Erie, June 20, 1956; B.A., University of Pennsylvania, political science; chief of staff, State Senator Melissa Hart; executive director, State Senate Finance Committee; married Christiane Weschler-English, 1992; committees: Joint Economic Committee; Ways and Means; subcommittees: Health; Human Resources; Trade; elected to the 104th Congress; reelected to each succeeding Congress.

Office Listings
http://www.house.gov/english

1410 Longworth House Office Building, Washington, DC 20515	(202) 225–5406
Chief of Staff.—Bob Holste.	FAX: 225–3103
Office Manager.—Nancy Billet.	
Press Secretary.—Idil Oyman.	
Legislative Director.—David Stewart.	
208 East Bayfront Parkway, Suite 102, Erie, PA 16507	(814) 456–2038
312 Chestnut Street, Suite 114, Meadville, PA 16335	(814) 724–8414
City Annex Building, 900 North Hermitage Road, Suite 6, Hermitage, PA 16148 ..	(724) 342–6132
101 East Dramond Street, Suite 213, Butler PA 16001	(724) 285–7005

Counties: ARMSTRONG (part), BUTLER (part), CRAWFORD (part), ERIE, MERCER (part), VENANGO (part), WARREN (part). Population (2000), 630,730.

ZIP Codes: 16001–03, 16016–18, 16020, 16022–23, 16025, 16027–30, 16033–35, 16037–41, 16045–46, 16048–53, 16055–57, 16059, 16061, 16110–11, 16113–14, 16124–25, 16127, 16130–31, 16133–34, 16137, 16142–43, 16145–46, 16148, 16150–51, 16153–54, 16156, 16159, 16201, 16210, 16218, 16222–24, 16226, 16229, 16232, 16242, 16244–45, 16249–50, 16253, 16259, 16261–63, 16311–12, 16314, 16316–17, 16319, 16323, 16327, 16329, 16335, 16340, 16342, 16345, 16350–51, 16354, 16360, 16362, 16365–69, 16371–74, 16388, 16401–07, 16410–13, 16415, 16417, 16420–24, 16426–28, 16430, 16432–36, 16438, 16440–44, 16475, 16501–12, 16514–15, 16522, 16530–34, 16538, 16541, 16544, 16546, 16550, 16553–54, 16563, 16565

* * *

FOURTH DISTRICT

MELISSA A. HART, Republican, of Bradford Woods, PA; born in Pittsburgh, PA, April 4, 1962; education: B.A., Washington and Jefferson College; J.D., University of Pittsburgh; professional: attorney; Doepken, Keevican & Weiss (law firm); public service: elected to the Pennsylvania State Senate, 1990; reelected in 1994, and 1998; served as chairman of the State Senate Finance Committee; House committees: Standards of Official Conduct; Ways and Means; subcommittees: Human Resources; Select Revenue Measures; elected to the 107th Congress on November 7, 2000; reelected to each succeeding Congress.

Office Listings
http://www.house.gov/hart

1024 Longworth House Office Building, Washington, DC 20515	(202) 225–2565
Administrative Assistant.—William Ries.	FAX: 226–2274
Legislative Director.—William Rys.	
Press Secretary.—Lee Cohen.	
501 Lawrence Avenue, Ellwood City, PA 16117	(724) 752–0490
District Director.—Kevin McGavick.	
4655 Route 8, Suite 124G, Coventry Square Shopping Center, Allison Park, PA 15101	(412) 492–0161
District Director.—Kevin McGavick.	

Counties: ALLEGHENY (part), BEAVER, BUTLER (part), LAWRENCE, MERCER (part), WESTMORELAND (part). Population (2000), 630,730.

ZIP Codes: 15001, 15003, 15005–07, 15009–10, 15014–15, 15024, 15026–27, 15030, 15032, 15042–44, 15046, 15049–52, 15056, 15059, 15061, 15065–66, 15068–69, 15074, 15076–77, 15081, 15084–86, 15090–91, 15095–96, 15101, 15108, 15116, 15127, 15139, 15143–44, 15146, 15202, 15209, 15212, 15214–15, 15223, 15229, 15235, 15237–39, 15601, 15626, 15632, 15650, 15668, 16002, 16024–25, 16033, 16037, 16040, 16046, 16051–52, 16055–57, 16059, 16061, 16063, 16066, 16101–03, 16105, 16107–08, 16112, 16115–17, 16120–21, 16123, 16127, 16132, 16136, 16140–43, 16148, 16155–57, 16159–61, 16172, 16229

* * *

FIFTH DISTRICT

JOHN E. PETERSON, Republican, of Pleasantville, PA; born in Titusville, PA, December 25, 1938; education: attended Pennsylvania State University; military service: served in U.S. Army, 1958–64; professional: past owner of supermarket; served in Pennsylvania House of Representatives, 1977–84, and in Pennsylvania Senate, 1985–96; Pleasantville Borough Councilman, 1968–77; past president: Pleasantville Lions Club, Titusville Chamber of Commerce, Pleasantville PTA, and Pleasantville Borough Council; formerly served on: board of directors of Titusville Hospital; and University of Pittsburgh's Titusville and Bradford campuses; advisory board of Pennsylvania State University School of Forest Resources; and advisory committee of the University of Pittsburgh Graduate School of Public Health; married: Saundra J. Watson in 1966; children: Richard; committees: Appropriations; Resources; elected to the 105th Congress; reelected to each succeeding Congress.

Office Listings

123 Cannon House Office Building, Washington, DC 20515 .... (202) 225–5121
Chief of Staff.—Jordan Clark.   FAX: 225–5796
Legislative Director.—Jeff Vorberger.
Senior Legislative Assistant.—Brian Sowa.
Communications Director.—Chris Tucker.
127 West Spring Street, Suite C, Titusville, PA 16354 .... (814) 827–3985
1524 West College Avenue, State College, PA 16801 .... (814) 238–1776

Counties: CAMERON, CENTRE, CLARION, CLEARFIELD (part), CLINTON, CRAWFORD (part), ELK, FOREST, JEFFERSON, LYCOMING (part), McKEAN, MIFFLIN (part), POTTER, TIOGA, VENANGO (part), WARREN (part). Population (2000), 630,730.

ZIP Codes: 15711, 15715, 15730, 15733, 15744, 15753, 15757, 15764, 15767, 15770, 15772, 15776, 15778, 15780–81, 15784, 15801, 15821, 15823–25, 15827–29, 15831–32, 15834, 15840–41, 15845–49, 15851, 15853, 15856–57, 15860–61, 15863–66, 15868, 15870, 16028, 16036, 16049, 16054, 16058, 16153, 16213–14, 16217, 16220–22, 16224–26, 16230, 16232–35, 16239–40, 16242, 16248, 16254–58, 16260, 16301, 16311, 16313–14, 16317, 16319, 16321–23, 16326–29, 16331–34, 16340–47, 16351–54, 16361–62, 16364–65, 16370–71, 16373–75, 16404, 16416, 16434, 16620, 16627, 16645, 16651, 16661, 16663, 16666–77, 16681, 16686, 16701, 16720, 16724–35, 16738, 16740, 16743–46, 16748–50, 16801–05, 16820–23, 16825–30, 16832–41, 16843–45, 16847–56, 16858–61, 16863–66, 16868, 16870–79, 16881–82, 16901, 16911–12, 16914–15, 16917–18, 16920–23, 16927–30, 16932–33, 16935–40, 16942–43, 16946–48, 16950, 17004, 17009, 17029, 17044, 17051, 17063, 17084, 17099, 17701–02, 17720–21, 17723–24, 17726–27, 17729, 17738–40, 17744–45, 17747–48, 17750–52, 17754, 17759–60, 17764–65, 17767, 17769, 17773, 17776–79, 17810, 17841

* * *

SIXTH DISTRICT

JIM GERLACH, Republican, of West Whiteland Township, PA; born in Ellwood City, PA, February 25, 1955; education: B.A., Dickinson College, 1977; J.D., Dickinson School of Law, 1980; professional: attorney; former special counsel to the regional law firm of Fox, Rothschild, O'Brien & Frankel; community service: Brandywine Hospital and Trauma Center, board of directors; MECA (Mission for Educating Children with Autism), board of directors; Dickinson College Board of Trustees; Chester County Agricultural Development Council; West Brandywine Township Zoning Hearing Board; public service: Pennsylvania House of Representatives, 1991–1994; Pennsylvania State Senate, 1995–2002; children: Katie, Jimmy, and Robby; committees: Financial Services; Transportation and Infrastructure; elected to the 108th Congress on November 5, 2002; reelected to each succeeding Congress.

Office Listings
http://www.house.gov/gerlach

308 Cannon House Office Building, Washington, DC 20515 .... (202) 225–4315
Chief of Staff.—Linda Pedigo.   FAX: 225–8440
Legislative Director.—Bill Tighe.
Communications Director.—John Gentzel.
111 East Uwchlan Avenue, Exton, PA 19341 .... (610) 594–1415
501 North Park Road, Wyomissing, PA 19610 .... (610) 376–7630
580 Main Street, Suite #4, Trappe, PA 19426 .... (610) 409–2780

Counties: BERKS (part), CHESTER (part), LEHIGH (part), MONTGOMERY (part). Population (2000), 630,730.

ZIP Codes: 17527, 17555, 17569, 18011, 18031, 18041, 18056, 18062, 18070, 18092, 19003–04, 19010, 19025, 19031, 19034–35, 19041, 19066, 19072, 19085, 19087, 19096, 19131, 19151, 19301, 19310, 19312, 19316, 19320, 19333, 19335, 19341, 19343–45, 19353–55, 19358, 19365–67, 19369, 19371–72, 19376, 19380, 19382, 19401, 19403–04, 19409, 19421, 19423, 19425–26, 19428, 19430, 19432, 19438, 19442, 19444, 19446, 19457, 19460, 19462, 19464–65, 19468, 19470, 19473–75, 19480–85, 19490, 19493–96, 19503–05, 19508, 19511–12, 19518–20, 19522–23, 19525, 19530, 19535, 19538–40, 19542–43, 19545, 19547–48, 19562, 19565, 19601–02, 19604–12

SEVENTH DISTRICT

CURT WELDON, Republican, of Thornbury, PA; born in Marcus Hook, PA, July 22, 1947; education: B.A., West Chester State College, PA, 1969; graduate work, Cabrini College, Wayne, PA; Temple and St. Joseph's Universities, Philadelphia, PA; professional: business executive; administrator and teacher; mayor of Marcus Hook Borough, 1977–82; member, Delaware County Council, 1981–86; chairman, Delaware Valley Regional Planning Commission; member: Lower Delco Lions Club, United Way of Southeastern Pennsylvania, American Red Cross in Media, Marcus Hook Fire Company, Viscose Fire Company, Sacred Heart Medical Center, Neumann College, Delaware County Industrial Development Authority, Delaware County Community Action Agency, Delaware County Hero Scholarship Fund, Boy Scout Troop No. 418, Darby-Colwyn-William Penn School District Education Association; awards: 1984 Man of the Year from Delaware County Irish-American Association; 1984 Man of the Year from the Chester Business and Professional Association; married: the former Mary Gallagher in 1972; children: Karen, Kristen, Kimberly, Curt, and Andrew; committees: Armed Services; Homeland Security; Science; elected to the 100th Congress on November 4, 1986; reelected to each succeeding Congress.

Office Listings

http://www.house.gov/curtweldon   curtpa07@mail.house.gov

2466 Rayburn House Office Building, Washington, DC 20515	(202) 225–2011
Administrative Assistant.—Russell Caso.	FAX: 225–8137
Scheduler.—Margaret Lemmerman.	
Legislative Director.—Xenia Horczakiwskyj.	
1554 Garrett Road, Upper Darby, PA 19082	(610) 259–0700
District Representative.—Kelly Colvin.	

Counties: CHESTER (part), DELAWARE (part), MONTGOMERY (part). Population (2000), 630,730.

ZIP Codes: 19008, 19010, 19014–15, 19017–18, 19022–23, 19026, 19028–29, 19032–33, 19036–37, 19039, 19041, 19043, 19050, 19052, 19061, 19063–65, 19070, 19073–74, 19076, 19078–79, 19081–83, 19085–87, 19094, 19312, 19317, 19319, 19331, 19333, 19339–40, 19342, 19355, 19373, 19380, 19382, 19395, 19403, 19405–06, 19426, 19428, 19468

* * *

EIGHTH DISTRICT

MICHAEL G. FITZPATRICK, Republican, of Doylestown, PA; born in Philadelphia, PA, June 28, 1963; education: graduated, Bishop Egan High School; B.A., with honors, St. James University, Miami, FL, 1985; J.D., Dickinson School of Law, Pennsylvania State University, 1988; professional: admitted to the practice of law in Pennsylvania and New Jersey; special counsel at the Philadelphia law firm of Saul Ewing LLP; organizations: member of the Bucks County, Pennsylvania, and American Bar Associations; past president of the Bucks County Council; Boy Scouts of America; Temple Lower Bucks Hospital Board of Directors; Conwell-Egan Catholic Board of Advisors; Knights of Columbus; Levittown Bristol Kiwanis Club; Ancient Order of Hibernians; Brehon Law Society; five-county anti-terrorism task force; member of the Board of Commissioners since January, 1995; awards: Red Cross Citizen of the Year, 2000; A Woman's Place M.J. Kirkpatrick Award for Leadership, 2001; Bucks County Council, B.S.A. Distinguished Scouter, 2002; Conwell-Egan Catholic Wall of Fame, 2003; married: Kathleen; six children; committees: Financial Services; Small Business; subcommittees: Capital Markets, Insurance and Government-Sponsored Enterprises; Housing and Community Opportunity; Oversight and Investigation; Tax, Finance, and Exports; Workforce, Empowerment and Government Programs; elected to the 109th Congress on November 2, 2004.

Office Listings

http://www.house.gov/fitzpatrick

1516 Longworth House Office Building, Washington, DC 20515	(202) 225–4276
Chief of Staff.—Mike Conallen.	FAX: 225–9511
Senior Legislative Assistant.—Greg Calhoun.	
Executive Assistant.—Faith Leichliter.	
60 North Main Street, Doylestown, PA 18901	(215) 348–7511
District Director.—Chris Brennan.	
One Oxford Valley, Suite 800, Langhorne, PA 19047	(215) 752–7711
Deputy District Director.—Valerie Mihalek.	

Counties: BUCKS, MONTGOMERY (part), PHILADELPHIA (part). Population (2000), 630,730.

ZIP Codes: 18036, 18039, 18041–42, 18054–55, 18073, 18077, 18081, 18901, 18910–17, 18920–23, 18925–35, 18938, 18940, 18942–44, 18946–47, 18949–51, 18953–56, 18960, 18962–64, 18966, 18968–70, 18972, 18974, 18976–77, 18980–

81, 18991, 19001–02, 19006–08, 19020–21, 19025, 19030, 19034, 19038, 19040, 19044, 19047–49, 19053–59, 19067, 19075, 19090, 19114, 19116, 19154–55, 19440, 19454

* * *

NINTH DISTRICT

BILL SHUSTER, Republican, of Hollidaysburg, PA; born in McKeesport, PA, January 10, 1961; education: Everett High School, Bedford County, PA; B.A., Dickinson College; M.B.A., American University; professional: businessman; Goodyear Tire & Rubber Corp.; Bandag, Inc.; Shuster Chrysler (President and General Manager); organizations: Member, Zion Lutheran Church; National Federation of Independent Business; National Rifle Association; Y.M.C.A.; Precious Life, Inc.; Rotary Club; Director, Pennsylvania Automotive Association; Board of Trustees, Homewood Home Retirement Community; Sigma Chi Fraternity; family: married to Rebecca; two children: Ali and Garrett; committees: Armed Services; Small Business; Transportation and Infrastructure; elected to the 107th Congress, by special election, on May 15, 2001; reelected to each succeeding Congress.

Office Listings

http://www.house.gov/shuster

1108 Longworth House Office Building, Washington, DC 20515	(202) 225–2431
Chief of Staff.—Alex Mistri.	FAX: 225–2486
Legislative Director.—Joel Brubaker.	
Scheduler.—Robbe Diehl.	
310 Penn Street, Hollidaysburg, PA 16648	(814) 696–6318
100 Lincoln Way East, Chambersburg, PA 17201	(717) 264–8308
645 Philadelphia Street, Suite 303, Indiana, PA 15701	(724) 463–0516
118 West Main Street, Suite 104, Somerset, PA 15501	(814) 443–3918

Counties: BEDFORD, BLAIR, CAMBRIA (part), CLEARFIELD (part), CUMBERLAND (part), FAYETTE (part), FRANKLIN, FULTON, HUNTINGDON, INDIANA (part), JUNIATA, MIFFLIN, PERRY (part), SOMERSET (part). Population (2000), 630,730.

ZIP Codes: 15411, 15416, 15421, 15424–25, 15431, 15436–37, 15440, 15445, 15451, 15459, 15462, 15464–65, 15469–70, 15478–79, 15501, 15510, 15521–22, 15530, 15532–42, 15545, 15549–54, 15557–60, 15562–65, 15681, 15701, 15712–14, 15716–17, 15720–25, 15727–29, 15731–32, 15734, 15738–39, 15741–42, 15746–48, 15750, 15752–54, 15756–59, 15763, 15765, 15767, 15771–72, 15774–75, 15777, 15783, 15840, 15920, 15924, 15926, 15929, 15931, 15936, 15940, 15944, 15946, 15949, 15954, 15961, 15963, 16211, 16222, 16246, 16256, 16601–03, 16611, 16613, 16616–17, 16619, 16621–25, 16627, 16629–31, 16633–41, 16644, 16646–48, 16650–52, 16654–57, 16659–62, 16664–65, 16667–75, 16678–80, 16682–86, 16689, 16691–95, 16823, 16833, 16844, 16861, 16865, 16871, 16877, 17002, 17004, 17006, 17013–14, 17021, 17024, 17035, 17037, 17040, 17044–45, 17047, 17049, 17051–54, 17056, 17058–60, 17062, 17065–66, 17068, 17071, 17074–76, 17081–82, 17086, 17090, 17094, 17201, 17210–15, 17217, 17219–25, 17228–29, 17231–33, 17235–41, 17243–44, 17246–47, 17249–57, 17260–68, 17270–72, 17307, 17324

* * *

TENTH DISTRICT

DON SHERWOOD, Republican, of Tunkhannock, PA; born in Nicholson, PA, March 5, 1941; education: Nicholson Elementary School; Lackawanna Trail High School; Wyoming Seminary Preparatory School; Dartmouth College, degree in Economics; military: U.S. Army, 1963–65, active duty service as a 1st Lieutenant; professional: small businessman; owner and chief executive officer of Sherwood Chevrolet and Horiacher-Sherwood Forestry Equipment; business organizations: vice president, Northeastern Pennsylvania Chevrolet Dealers Association; director, Pennsylvania Chevrolet Dealers Area Marketing Group; Pennsylvania Hardware Lumber Manufacturing Association; Pennsylvania Farmers Association; married: Carol Evans, 1972; three children: Jesse, Dana, and Maria; public service: Tunkhannock Area School Board, 1975–98; committees: Appropriations; elected to the 106th Congress; reelected to each succeeding Congress.

Office Listings

http://www.house.gov/sherwood

1131 Longworth House Office Building, Washington, DC 20515	(202) 225–3731
Chief of Staff.—John Enright.	FAX: 225–9594
Press Secretary.—Jake O'Donnell.	
Scheduler.—Matt Allen.	
1146 Northern Boulevard, Clarks Summit, PA 18411	(570) 585–8190
District Director.—Jerry Morgan.	
330 Pine Street, Suite 202, Williamsport, PA 17701	(570) 327–9359
106 Arch Street, Sunbury, PA 17801	(570) 286–1723

Counties: BRADFORD, LACKAWANNA (part), LUZERNE (part), LYCOMING (part), MONTOUR, NORTHUMBERLAND, PIKE, SNYDER, SULLIVAN, SUSQUEHANNA, TIOGA (part), UNION, WAYNE, WYOMING. Population (2000), 630,730.

ZIP Codes: 16910, 16914, 16925–26, 16930, 16932, 16936, 16945, 16947, 17017, 17045, 17063, 17086, 17701, 17703, 17705, 17724, 17728, 17730, 17731, 17735, 17737, 17742, 17749, 17756, 17758, 17762–63, 17765, 17768, 17771–72, 17774, 17777, 17801, 17810, 17812–15, 17820–24, 17827, 17829–37, 17840–42, 17844–45, 17847, 17850–51, 17853, 17855–57, 17860–62, 17864–68, 17870, 17872, 17876–77, 17880–87, 17889, 18301, 18324–26, 18328, 18336–37, 18340, 18371, 18403, 18405, 18407, 18410–11, 18413–17, 18419–21, 18424–28, 18430–31, 18433–41, 18443–49, 18451–65, 18469–73, 18512, 18612, 18614–16, 18618–19, 18622–23, 18625–30, 18632, 18636, 18640–41, 18653–54, 18656–57, 18704, 18708, 18801, 18810, 18812–18, 18820–34, 18837, 18840, 18842–48, 18850–51, 18853–54

* * *

ELEVENTH DISTRICT

PAUL E. KANJORSKI, Democrat, of Nanticoke, PA; born in Nanticoke, April 2, 1937; U.S. Capitol Page School, Washington, DC, 1954; attended, Wyoming Seminary, Kingston, PA, Temple University, Philadelphia, PA, Dickinson School of Law, Carlisle, PA; served in U.S. Army, private, 1960–61; attorney, admitted to Pennsylvania State bar, 1966; began practice in Wilkes Barre, PA, November 7, 1966; married to the former Nancy Marie Hickerson; one daughter, Nancy; committees: Financial Services; Government Reform; subcommittees: ranking member, Capital Markets, Insurance, and Government-Sponsored Enterprises; elected to the 99th Congress on November 6, 1984; reelected to each succeeding Congress.

Office Listings

http://kanjorski.house.gov

2188 Rayburn House Office Building, Washington, DC 20515	(202) 225–6511
Chief of Staff.—Karen Feather.	FAX: 225–0764
Legislative Director.—Todd Harper.	
Executive Assistant.—Donna Giobbi.	
Press Secretary.—Gretchen M. Wintermantel.	
The Stegmaier Building, 7 North Wilkes Barre Boulevard, Suite 400–M, Wilkes Barre, PA 18702–5283	(570) 825–2200
546 Spruce Street, Scranton, PA 18503	(570) 496–1011

Counties: CARBON, COLUMBIA, LACKAWANNA (part), LUZERNE (part), MONROE. Population (2000), 630,730.

ZIP Codes: 17814–15, 17820–21, 17824, 17839, 17846, 17858–59, 17878, 17888, 17920, 17985, 18012, 18030, 18058, 18071, 18201–02, 18210–12, 18216, 18219, 18221–25, 18229–30, 18232, 18234–35, 18237, 18239–41, 18244, 18246–47, 18249–51, 18254–56, 18301, 18320–23, 18325–27, 18330–35, 18341–42, 18344, 18346–50, 18352–57, 18360, 18370, 18372, 18424, 18434, 18445, 18447, 18466, 18501–05, 18507–10, 18512, 18514–15, 18517–19, 18522, 18540, 18577, 18601–03, 18610–12, 18617, 18621–22, 18624, 18631, 18634–35, 18640–44, 18651, 18655, 18660–61, 18690, 18701–11, 18761–67, 18769, 18773–74

* * *

TWELFTH DISTRICT

JOHN P. MURTHA, Democrat, of Johnstown, PA; graduated, Ramsey High School, Mount Pleasant, PA; Kiskiminetas Spring School; B.A. in economics, University of Pittsburgh; graduate study at Indiana University of Pennsylvania; married Joyce Bell; three children: Donna Sue and twin sons, John and Patrick; served in Marine Corps as an enlisted Marine commissioned as an officer; discharged as a first lieutenant; maintained active reserve officer status; volunteered for one year of active duty in Vietnam as a major; served with 1st Marines, a Marine infantry regiment, 1966–67, south of Danang; awarded Bronze Star Medal with combat "V", two Purple Heart medals, Vietnamese Cross of Gallantry, and service medals; retired colonel, U.S. Marine Corps Reserves; elected to Pennsylvania House of Representatives in 1969, served continuously until elected to U.S. House of Representatives; recipient of Pennsylvania Distinguished Service Medal and Pennsylvania Meritorious Service Medal (the commonwealth's two highest honors); first Vietnam veteran to be elected to Congress; received 9 honorary doctorate degrees from colleges and universities; committee: Appropriations; elected to the 93rd Congress, February 5, 1974; reelected to each succeeding Congress.

Office Listings

http://www.house.gov/murtha

2423 Rayburn House Office Building, Washington, DC 20515	(202) 225–2065
Administrator / Director.—Winifred Frederick.	
Legislative Director.—Debra Tekavac.	
Schedule Coordinator.—Jane Phipps.	
Appropriations Staff.—Gabrielle Carruth.	

P.O. Box 780, Johnstown, PA 15907 .... (814) 535–2642
Chief of Staff.—John Hugya.
District Director.—Brad Clemenson.

Counties: ALLEGHENY COUNTY (part). CITIES AND TOWNSHIPS: East Deer, and Tarentum; ARMSTRONG COUNTY (part). CITIES AND TOWNSHIPS: Apollo, Bethel, Burrell, Elderton, Ford City, Ford Cliff, Freeport, Gilpin, Kiskiminetas, Kittanning, Leechburg, Manor, Manorville, North Apollo, North Buffalo, Parks, Plumcreek, South Bend, and South Buffalo; CAMBRIA COUNTY (part). CITIES AND TOWNSHIPS: Adams, Barr, Blacklick, Brownstown, Cambria, Carrolltown, Cassandra, Conemaugh, Cresson, Croyle, Daisytown, Dale, East Carroll, East Conemaugh, East Taylor, Ebensburg, Ehrenfeld, Ferndale, Franklin, Geistown, Jackson, Johnstown, Lilly, Lorain, Lower Yoder, Middle Taylor, Munster, Nanty Glo, Portage, Richland, Sankertown, Scalp Level, South Fork, Southmonth, Stonycreek, Summerhill, Susquehanna, Upper Yoder, Vintondale, Washington, Westmont, West Carroll, West Taylor, Wilmore. FAYETTE COUNTY (part). CITIES AND TOWNSHIPS: Belle Vernon, Brownsville, Bullskin, Connellsville, Dawson, Dunbar, Everson, Fayette City, Franklin, Georges, German, Jefferson, Lower Tyrone, Luzerne, Masontown, Menallen, Newell, Nicholson, North Union, Perry, Perryopolis, Point Marion, Redstone, Saltlick, South Union, Springhill, Upper Tyrone, Uniontown, Vanderbilt, Washington. GREENE COUNTY, INDIANA COUNTY (part). CITIES AND TOWNSHIPS: Cherryhill, Clymer, Indiana, Pine, White. SOMERSET COUNTY (part). CITIES AND TOWNSHIPS: Benson, Boswell, Conemaugh, Hooversville, Jefferson, Jenner, Jennerstown, Lincoln, Middlecreek, Paint, Quemahoning, Seven Springs, Stoystown, Windber. WASHINGTON COUNTY (part). CITIES AND TOWN-SHIPS: Allenport, Beallsville, Bentleyville, California, Canonsburg, Canton, Carroll, Centerville, Charleroi, Chartier, Coal Center, Cokeburg, Deemston, Donora, Dunlevy, East Bethlehem, East Washington, Elco, Ellsworth, Fallowfield, Finleyville, Houston, Long Branch, Marianna, Monongahela, New Eagle, North Bethlehem, North Charleroi, North Strabane, Roscoe, Somerset, South Strabane, Speers, Stockdale, Twilight, Union, Washington, West Bethlehem, West Brownsville, West Pike Run. WESTMORELAND COUNTY (part). CITIES AND TOWNSHIPS: Allegheny, Arnold, Avonmore, Bell, Bessemer, Bolivar, Bovard, Bridgeport, Crabtree, Derry, Dorothy, Duncan, East Herminie, East Huntingdon, East Vandergrift, Fairfield, Hannastown, Heccla, Hempfield, Hugus, Hyde Park, Jacobs Creek, Latrobe, Laurel Run, Lloydsville, Lowber, Lower Burrell, Loyalhanna, Luxor, Mammoth, Mechlings, Mineral, Monessen, Mount Pleasant, New Alexandria, New Florence, New Kensington, North Belle Vernon, North Washington, Oklahoma, Paulton, Port Royal, Rillton, Rostraver, Salem, Scottdale, Seward, Sewickley, Smithton, South Huntingdon, Spring Garden, St. Clair, United, Unity, Upper Burrell, Vandergrift, Washington, Wayne, Westmoreland, West Herminie, West Leechburg, West Newton, Wyano, and Yukon. Population (2000), 630,730.

ZIP Codes: 15012, 15022, 15030, 15033, 15038, 15062–63, 15067–68, 15072, 15083, 15087, 15089, 15301, 15310, 15313–17, 15320, 15322, 15324–25, 15327, 15329–34, 15336–38, 15341–42, 15344–49, 15351–54, 15357–60, 15362–64, 15366, 15368, 15370, 15377, 15380, 15401, 15410–13, 15415, 15417, 15419–20, 15422–25, 15427–36, 15438, 15442–44, 15446–47, 15449–51, 15454–56, 15458, 15460, 15463, 15466–68, 15472–77, 15479–80, 15482–86, 15488–90, 15492, 15501–02, 15520, 15531, 15541, 15544, 15547–48, 15551, 15555, 15557, 15561, 15563, 15601, 15610, 15613, 15618, 15620–22, 15624–25, 15627, 15629, 15631, 15633, 15635, 15637, 15641–42, 15644, 15646, 15650, 15655–56, 15660–62, 15664, 15666, 15670–71, 15673–74, 15677–78, 15680–90, 15701, 15705, 15710, 15714, 15717, 15722, 15724, 15728, 15732, 15736–37, 15745, 15748, 15760–62, 15765, 15773–74, 15779, 15901–02, 15904–07, 15909, 15921–23, 15925, 15927–28, 15930–31, 15934–38, 15940, 15942–46, 15948, 15951–63, 16055, 16201, 16215, 16226, 16228–29, 16236, 16238, 16240, 16249, 16630, 16641, 16646, 16668–69

* * *

THIRTEENTH DISTRICT

ALLYSON Y. SCHWARTZ, Democrat, of Jenkintown, PA; born in Queens County, NY, October 3, 1948; education: graduated from the Calhoun School, New York, NY, 1966; B.A., Simmons College, Boston, MA, 1970; M.S.W., Bryn Mawr College, Bryn Mawr, PA, 1972; professional: executive director of the Elizabeth BlackwellCenter, 1977–1988; Deputy Commissioner of the Philadelphia Department of Human Services, 1988–1990; elected to the Pennsylvania state Senate, 1991–2004; member: Pennsylvania State Board of Education; Pennsylvania Council on Higher Education; Education Commission of the States; married: Dr. David Schwartz; children: Daniel and Jordan; committees: Budget; Transportation and Infrastructure; subcommittees: Highways, Transit and Pipelines; Water Resources and Environment; elected to the 109th Congress on November 2, 2004.

Office Listings

http://www.house.gov/schwartz

423 Cannon House Office Building, Washington, DC 20515 .... (202) 225–6111
Chief of Staff.—Daniel McElhatton.   FAX: 226–0611
Legislative Director.—Kate Winkler.
Communications Director.—Rachel Leed.
Executive Assistant / Scheduler.—Vanessa Menaged.
706 West Avenue, Jenkintown, PA 19046 .... (215) 517–6572
District Director.—Julie Slavet.
7219 Frankford Avenue, Philadelphia, PA 19135 .... (215) 335–3355

County: MONTGOMERY COUNTY; CITIES AND TOWNSHIPS: Abington Wards, Hatfield, Horsham, Lower Frederick, Lower Gwynedd, Lower Moreland, Lower Salford, Malborough, Montgomery, New Hanover, Plymouth, Springfield, Towamencin, Upper Dublin, Upper Frederick, Upper Gwynedd, Upper Moreland, Upper Salford, Whitemarsh, Whitpain. Boroughs of Ambler, Bryn Athyn, Green Lane, Hatboro, Hatfield, Jenkintown, Lansdale, North Wales, Rockledge, Schwenksville. PHILADELPHIA COUNTY; CITY OF: Philadelphia. Population (2000), 630,730.

ZIP Codes: 18054, 18074, 18914–15, 18932, 18936, 18957–58, 18964, 18969, 18979, 19001–02, 19006, 19009, 19019, 19025, 19027, 19038, 19040, 19044, 19046, 19075, 19090, 19096, 19111, 19114–16, 19118, 19120, 19124, 19128,

19134–37, 19149, 19152, 19154–55, 19244, 19255, 19422, 19424, 19428, 19435–38, 19440–41, 19443–44, 19446, 19450–51, 19454–55, 19462, 19464, 19473, 19477–78, 19486–87, 19489, 19492, 19504, 19512, 19525

* * *

FOURTEENTH DISTRICT

MICHAEL F. DOYLE, Democrat, of Swissvale, PA; born in Swissvale, PA, August 5, 1953; graduated, Swissvale Area High School, 1971; B.S., Pennsylvania State University, 1975; co-owner, Eastgate Insurance Agency, Inc., 1983; elected and served as finance and recreation chairman, Swissvale, Borough Council, 1977–81; member: Leadership Pittsburgh Alumni Association, Lions Club, Ancient Order of the Hibernians, Italian Sons and Daughters of America, and Penn State Alumni Association; member: Democratic Caucus, Democratic Study Group, Pennsylvania Democratic Delegation, Congressional Steel Caucus, Travel and Tourism CMO, Ad Hoc Committee on Irish Affairs, and National Italian-American Foundation; married Susan Beth Doyle, 1975; four children: Michael, David, Kevin, and Alexandra; committees: Energy and Commerce; Standards of Official Conduct; founder and co-chair, Coalition for Autism Research and Education; elected November 8, 1994, to the 104th Congress; reelected to each succeeding Congress.

Office Listings

http://www.house.gov/doyle   rep.doyle@mail.house.gov

401 Cannon House Office Building, Washington, DC 20515	(202) 225–2135
Administrative Assistant.—David Lucas.	
Legislative Director.—Pat Cavanagh.	
Office Manager / Scheduler.—Ellen Young.	
225 Ross Street, Pittsburgh, PA 15219	(412) 261–5091
11 Duff Road, Penn Hills, PA 15235	(412) 241–6055
District Director.—Paul D'Alesandro.	
627 Lysle Boulevard, McKeesport, PA 15132	(412) 664–4049

County: ALLEGHENY COUNTY (part); CITIES AND TOWNSHIPS OF: Avalon, Baldwin Borough, Baldwin Township, Blawnox, Braddock, Braddock Hills, Chalfant, Clairton, Coraopolis, Dravosburg, Duquesne, E. McKeesport, E. Pittsburgh, Edgewood, Elizabeth Borough, Elizabeth Township, Etna, Forest Hills, Glassport, Ingram, Kennedy, Liberty, Lincoln, McKees Rocks, McKeesport, Millvale, Monroeville, Mt. Oliver, Munhall, Neville, North Braddock, North Versailles, O'Hara Township, Penn Hills, Pitcairn, Pittsburgh, Port Vue, Rankin, Reserve, Robinson, Stowe, Swissvale, Sharpsburg, Turtle Creek, Verona, Versailles, Wall, West Homestead, West Mifflin, Whitaker, Wilkins, Wilkinsburg, and Wilmerding. Population (2000), 630,730.

ZIP Codes: 15025, 15034–35, 15037, 15044–45, 15063, 15104, 15106, 15108, 15110, 15112, 15116, 15120, 15122, 15132–37, 15140, 15145–48, 15201–19, 15221–27, 15230, 15232–36, 15238–40, 15242, 15244, 15250–51, 15253, 15255, 15257–62, 15264–65, 15267–68, 15272, 15274, 15278–79, 15281–83, 15285–86, 15290, 15295

* * *

FIFTEENTH DISTRICT

CHARLES W. DENT, Republican, of Allentown, PA, born in Allentown, May 24, 1960; education: M.A., Public Administration, Lehigh University, 1993; B.A., Foreign Service and International Politics, Pennsylvania State University, 1982; professional: Legislator Development Officer, Lehigh University, 1986–1990; sales representative, P.A. Peters, Inc.; Pennsylvania State House, District 132, 1991–1998; Representative, Pennsylvania State Senate, 1998–2004; religion: First Presbyterian Church; married: Pamela Jane Serfass; children: Karthryn Elizabeth, William Reed, and Charles John (Jack); committees: Government Reform; Homeland Security; Transportation and Infrastructure; elected to the 109th Congress on November 2, 2004.

Office Listings

http://www.house.gov/dent

502 Cannon House Office Building, Washington, DC 20515	(202) 225–6411
Administrative Assistant.—George McElwee.	FAX: 226–0778
Legislative Director.—Peter Richards.	
701 West Broad Street, Suite 200, Bethlehem, PA 18018	(610) 861–9734

Counties: BERKS (part), LEHIGH, MONTGOMERY (part), NORTHAMPTON. POPULATION (2000), 630,730.

ZIP Codes: 18001–03, 18010–11, 18013–18, 18020, 18025, 18031–32, 18034–38, 18040–46, 18049–55, 18059–60, 18062–70, 18072–74, 18076–80, 18083–88, 18091–92, 18098–99, 18101–06, 18109, 18175, 18195, 18343, 18351, 18918, 18924, 18951, 18960, 18964, 18969, 18971, 19438, 19440, 19464, 19472, 19504–05, 19512, 19525, 19529–30, 19539

SIXTEENTH DISTRICT

JOSEPH R. PITTS, Republican, of Kennett Square, PA; born in Lexington, KY, October 10, 1939; education: B.A., philosophy and religion, Asbury College, KY; military service: served in U.S. Air Force, 1963–69, rising from second lieutenant to captain; professional: nursery business owner and operator; math and science teacher, Great Valley High School, Malvern, PA, 1969–72; teacher, Mortonsville Elementary School, Versailles, KY; member: Pennsylvania House of Representatives, 1972–96, serving as chairman of Appropriations Committee, 1989–96, and of Labor Relations Committee, 1981–88; married: the former Virginia M. Pratt in 1961; children: Karen, Carol, and Daniel; committees: Energy and Commerce; elected to the 105th Congress; reelected to each succeeding Congress.

Office Listings

http://www.house.gov/pitts

221 Cannon House Office Building, Washington, DC 20515	(202) 225–2411
Chief of Staff.—Gabe Neville.	
Legislative Director.—Ken Miller.	
Press Secretary.—Derek Karchner.	
P.O. Box 837, Unionville, PA 19375	(610) 444–4581
50 North Duke Street, Lancaster, PA 17602	(717) 393–0667

Counties: LANCASTER, BERK (part). CITIES AND TOWNSHIPS: Reading, Bern, Lower Heidelberg, South Heidelberg, Spring. BOROUGH OF: Wernersville. CHESTER COUNTY (part). CITIES AND TOWNSHIPS: Birmingham, East Bradford, East Fallowfield, East Marlborough, East Nottingham, Elk, Franklin, Highland, Kennett, London Britain, London Grove, Londonderry, Lower Oxford, New Garden, New London, Newlin, Penn, Pennsbury, Upper Oxford, West Fallowfield, West Marlborough, West Nottingham. BOROUGHS OF: Avondale, Kennett Square, Oxford, Parkesburg, West Chester, and West Grove. Population (2000), 630,730.

ZIP Codes: 17501–09, 17512, 17516–22, 17527–29, 17532–38, 17540, 17543, 17545, 17547, 17549–52, 17554–55, 17557, 17560, 17562–70, 17572–73, 17575–76, 17578–85, 17601–08, 19106, 19310–11, 19317–20, 19330, 19342, 19346–48, 19350–52, 19357, 19360, 19362–63, 19365, 19374–75, 19380–83, 19390, 19395, 19464, 19501, 19540, 19543, 19565, 19601–02, 19604–05, 19608–11

* * *

SEVENTEENTH DISTRICT

TIM HOLDEN, Democrat, of St. Clair, PA; born in Pottsville, PA, March 5, 1957; education: attended St. Clair High School, St. Clair; Fork Union Military Academy; University of Richmond, Richmond, VA; B.A., Bloomsburg State College, 1980; professional: sheriff of Schuylkill County, PA, 1985–93; licensed insurance broker and real estate agent, John J. Holden Insurance Agency and Holden Realty Company, St. Clair; member: Pennsylvania Sheriffs Association; Fraternal Order of Police; St. Clair Fish and Game Association; Benevolent and Protective Order of the Elks Lodge 1533; co-chair, Correctional Officers Caucus; co-chair, House Mining Caucus; co-chair, Northeast Agriculture Caucus; Ad-Hoc Committee for Irish Affairs; Alzheimer's Caucus; Arts Caucus; Autism Caucus; Blue Dog Coalition; Congressional 4–H Caucus; Congressional Beef Caucus; Congressional Cement Caucus; Congressional Hellenic Caucus; Diabetes Caucus; Firefighter's Caucus; Friends of Ireland; House Baltic Caucus; House Commuter Caucus; House Nursing Caucus; Law Enforcement Caucus; National Guard and Reserve Components Caucus; Rural Caucus; Rural Health Care Caucus; Home Health Care Working Group; Sportsmens Caucus; Steel Caucus; Water Infrastructure Caucus; Wine Caucus; Congressional Caucus on Armenian Issues; House Auto Caucus; Special Operations Forces Caucus; Mental Health Caucus; Homeland Security Caucus; Iraq Fallen Heroes Caucus; Appalachian Region Commission Caucus; committees: Agriculture; Transportation and Infrastructure; elected to the 103rd Congress; reelected to each succeeding Congress.

Office Listings

2417 Rayburn House Office Building, Washington, DC 20515	(202) 225–5546
Chief of Staff.—Trish Reilly-Hudock.	FAX: 226–0996
Legislative Director.—Ari Strauss.	
Projects Director.—Bill Hanley.	
Scheduler.—Rebecca Spangler.	
1721 North Front Street, Suite 105, Harrisburg, PA 17102	(717) 234–5904
4918 Kutztown Road, Temple, PA 19560	(610) 921–3502
47 South 8th Street, Lebanon, PA 17042	(717) 270–1395
101 North Centre Street, Suite 303, Pottsville, PA 17901	(570) 622–4212

Counties: BERKS (part), DAUPHIN, LEBANON, PERRY (part), SCHUYLKILL. Population (2000), 630,730.

ZIP Codes: 17003, 17005, 17010, 17016–18, 17020, 17022–24, 17026, 17028, 17030, 17032–34, 17036, 17038–39, 17041–42, 17045–46, 17048, 17053, 17057, 17061–62, 17064, 17067–69, 17073–74, 17077–78, 17080, 17083, 17085, 17087–

88, 17097–98, 17101–13, 17120–30, 17140, 17177, 17502, 17830, 17836, 17901, 17921–23, 17925, 17929–36, 17938, 17941–46, 17948–49, 17951–54, 17957, 17959–61, 17963–68, 17970, 17972, 17974, 17976, 17978–83, 17985, 18211, 18214, 18218, 18220, 18231, 18237, 18240–42, 18245, 18248, 18250, 18252, 18255, 19506–07, 19510, 19512, 19516, 19518, 19522, 19526, 19529–30, 19533–34, 19536, 19541, 19544, 19547, 19549–51, 19554–55, 19559–60, 19564–65, 19567, 19601, 19604–06

* * *

EIGHTEENTH DISTRICT

TIM MURPHY, Republican, of Upper St. Clair, PA; born in Cleveland, OH, September 12, 1952; education: B.S., Wheeling Jesuit University, 1974; M.A., Cleveland State University, 1976; Ph.D., University of Pittsburgh, 1979; professional: Psychologist; holds two adjunct faculty positions at the University of Pittsburgh; Associate Professor in the Department of Public Health, and in the Department of Pediatrics; public service: Pennsylvania State Senate, 1996–2002; religion: Catholic; family: married to Nan Missig; children: Bevin; committees: Energy and Commerce; elected to the 108th Congress on November 5, 2002; reelected to each succeeding Congress.

Office Listings

http://murphy.house.gov

322 Cannon House Office Building, Washington, DC 20515 .... (202) 225–2301
    Chief of Staff.—Susan Mosychuk.
    Legislative Director.—Kelly Gosselin.
    Executive Assistant / Scheduler.—Pat Koch.
    Press Secretary.—Mark Carpen.
504 Washington Road, Pittsburgh, PA 15228 .... (412) 344–5583

Counties: ALLEGHENY (part), WASHINGTON (part), WESTMORELAND (part). CITIES AND TOWNSHIPS: Pittsburgh (part), Greensburg, and Jeannette. Population (2000), 630,730.

ZIP Codes: 15001, 15004, 15017–22, 15025–26, 15028, 15031, 15033, 15036–37, 15044, 15046–47, 15053–55, 15057, 15060, 15063–64, 15071, 15075, 15078, 15082–83, 15085, 15088–89, 15102, 15106, 15108, 15126, 15129, 15131, 15136, 15142, 15146, 15205, 15209, 15212, 15215–16, 15220–21, 15226–28, 15231, 15234–36, 15238, 15241, 15243, 15270, 15277, 15301, 15311–12, 15314, 15317, 15321, 15323, 15329–30, 15332, 15339–40, 15342, 15345, 15350, 15361, 15363, 15365, 15367, 15376–79, 15448, 15501, 15601, 15605–06, 15611–12, 15615–17, 15619, 15622–23, 15626, 15628, 15632, 15634, 15636–40, 15642, 15644, 15647, 15650, 15655, 15658, 15663, 15665, 15668, 15672, 15675–76, 15679, 15683, 15687–88, 15691–93, 15695–97

* * *

NINETEENTH DISTRICT

TODD RUSSELL PLATTS, Republican, of York County, PA; born in York County, March 5, 1962; education: York Suburban High School, 1980; Shippensburg University of Pennsylvania; 1984, B.S. in Public Administration; Pepperdine University School of Law, 1991, Juris Doctorate; professional: Attorney; married: Leslie; children: T.J. and Kelsey; organizations: York County Transportation Coalition; Statewide Children's Health Insurance Program Advisory Council; York Metropolitan Planning Organization; public service: Pennsylvania House of Representatives, 1992–2000; committees: Education and the Workforce; Government Reform; Transportation and Infrastructure; subcommittees: chairman, Government Management, Finance, and Accountability; elected to the 107th Congress on November 7, 2000; reelected to each succeeding Congress.

Office Listings

http://www.house.gov/platts

1032 Longworth House Office Building, Washington, DC 20515 .... (202) 225–5836
    Chief of Staff.—Scott E. Miller.   FAX: 226–1000
2209 East Market Street, York, PA 17402 .... (717) 600–1919
    Deputy Chief of Staff.—Bob Reilly.
22 Chambersburg Street, Gettysburg, PA 17325 .... (717) 338–1919
59 West Louther Street, Carlisle, PA 17013 .... (717) 249–0190

Counties: ADAMS COUNTY. CITIES OF: Abbottstown, Arendtsville, Aspers, Bendersville, Biglerville, East Berlin, Fairfield, Gardners, Gettysburg, Littlestown, McKnightstown, McSherrystown, New Oxford, Orrtanna. CUMBERLAND COUNTY. CITIES OF: Boiling Springs, Carlisle, Camp Hill, East Pennsboro, Enola, Grantham, Lemoyne, Mechanicsburg, Mt. Holly Springs, Newburg, New Cumberland, Newville, Shippensburg, Shiremanstown, Summerdale, Walnut Bottom, West Fairview, Wormleysburg; TOWNSHIPS OF Hampden, Lower Allen, Middlesex, Monroe, Shippensburg, Silver Spring, South Newton, Southamption, Upper Allen, the boroughs of Camp Hill, Carlisle, Lemoyne, Mt. Holly Springs, New Cumberland, Shippensburg, Shiremanstown, Wormleysburg. YORK COUNTY. CITIES AND TOWNSHIPS: Airville, Brodbecks, Brogue, Dallastown, Delta, Dillsburg, Dover, Emigsville, East Prospect, Etters, Felton, Fawn Grove, Glen Rock, Hanover,

Hellam, Jacobus, Lewisberry, Loganville, Manchester, Mount Wolf, New Freedom, New Park, Red Lion, Spring Grove, Shrewsbury, Stewartstown, Seven Valleys, Thomasville, Wellsville, Windsor, Wrightsville, York, York Haven, York New Salem, Yoe, and York Springs. Population (2000), 647,065.

ZIP Codes: 17001, 17007–08, 17011–13, 17019, 17025, 17027, 17043, 17050, 17053, 17055, 17065, 17070, 17072, 17089–90, 17093, 17222, 17257, 17301–04, 17306–07, 17309–27, 17329, 17331–33, 17337, 17339–40, 17342–45, 17347, 17349–50, 17352–56, 17358, 17360–66, 17368, 17370–72, 17401–07, 17415

RHODE ISLAND

(Population 2000, 1,048,319)

SENATORS

JACK REED, Democrat, of Cranston, RI; born in Providence, RI, November 12, 1949; graduated, La Salle Academy, Providence, RI, 1967; B.S., U.S. Military Academy, West Point, NY, 1971; M.P.P., Kennedy School of Government, Harvard University, 1973; J.D., Harvard Law School, 1982; served in the U.S. Army, 1967–79; associate professor, Department of Social Sciences, U.S. Military Academy, West Point, NY, 1978–79; 2nd BN (Abn) 504th Infantry, 82nd Airborne Division, Fort Bragg, NC; platoon leader, company commander, battalion staff officer, 1973–77; military awards: Army commendation medal with Oak Leaf Cluster, ranger, senior parachutist, jumpmaster, expert infantryman's badge; lawyer; admitted to the Washington, DC bar, 1983; elected to the Rhode Island State Senate, 1985–90; committees: Armed Services; Banking, Housing, and Urban Affairs; Health, Education, Labor, and Pensions; Joint Economic Committee; elected to the 102nd Congress on November 6, 1990; served three terms in the U.S. House of Representatives; elected to the U.S. Senate, November 5, 1996; reelected to each succeeding Senate term.

Office Listings

http://reed.senate.gov

728 Hart Senate Office Building, Washington, DC 20510 .... (202) 224–4642
 Administrative Assistant.—Neil Campbell.
 Administrative Manager.—Cathy Nagle.
 Press Secretary.—Greg McCarthy.
201 Hillside Road, Suite 200, Cranston, RI 02920 .... (401) 943–3100
 Chief of Staff.—Raymond Simone.
U.S. District Courthouse, One Exchange Terrace, Suite 408, Providence, RI 02903   (401) 528–5200

* * *

LINCOLN D. CHAFEE, Republican, of Warwick, RI; born in Warwick, March 26, 1953; education: Brown University, B.A. degree in Classics, 1975; after graduation he attended horseshoeing school in Bozeman, MT; professional: blacksmith; Cranston Print Works; Rhode Island Forging Steel; and General Dynamics' Electric Boat; public service: elected to the Rhode Island Constitutional Convention, 1985; Warwick, RI, City Council, 1986; and Warwick, RI, Mayor, 1992; in 1998 he was elected by his peers as President of the Rhode Island League of Cities and Towns; married: the former Stephanie Danforth; children: Louisa, Caleb, and Thea; committees: Environment and Public Works; Foreign Relations; Homeland Security and Governmental Affairs; appointed to the U.S. Senate on November 4, 1999; elected to the U.S. Senate on November 7, 2000.

Office Listings

http://chafee.senate.gov

141A Russell Senate Office Building, Washington, DC 20510 .... (202) 224–2921
 Chief of Staff.—David A. Griswold.   FAX: 228–2853
 Appointments Secretary.—Betty Dudik.
 Press Secretary.—Stephen Hourahan.
320 Thames Street, Newport, RI 02840 .... (401) 845–0700
170 Westminster Street, Providence, RI 02903 .... (401) 453–5294

REPRESENTATIVES

FIRST DISTRICT

PATRICK J. KENNEDY, Democrat, of Providence, RI; born in Brighton, MA, July 14, 1967; education: graduated, Phillips Academy, Andover, MA; B.A., Providence College, Providence, RI, 1991; public service: Rhode Island State Legislature, 1988–94; member: Rhode Island Special Olympics (board of directors), Rhode Island March of Dimes, Rhode Island Lung Association, Rhode Island Mental Health Association, Rhode Island Chapter of National Committee for the Prevention of Child Abuse; committees: Appropriations; elected to the 104th Congress; reelected to each succeeding Congress.

Office Listings
http://www.house.gov/patrickkennedy

407 Cannon House Office Building, Washington, DC 20515 .... (202) 225–4911
    Chief of Staff.—Sean Richardson.   FAX: 225–3290
    Legislative Director.—Kimber Colton.
    Executive Assistant.—Terri Alford.
    Press Secretary.—Ernesto Anguilla.
249 Roosevelt Avenue, Suite 200, Pawtucket, RI 02860 .... (401) 729–5600
    District Director.—George Zainyeh.

Counties: BRISTOL, NEWPORT, PROVIDENCE (part). CITIES AND TOWNSHIPS: Barrington, Bristol, Burrillville, Central Falls, Cumberland, East Providence, Jamestown, Lincoln, Little Compton, Middleton, Newport, North Providence, North Smithfield, Providence, Pawtucket, Portsmouth, Smithfield, Tiverton, Warren, and Woonsocket. Population (2000), 524,157.

ZIP Codes: 02801, 02802, 02806, 02809, 02824, 02826, 02828, 02830, 02835, 02837, 02838, 02839, 02840, 02841, 02842, 02858, 02859, 02860, 02861, 02862, 02863, 02864, 02865, 02871, 02872, 02876, 02878, 02885, 02895, 02896, 02903, 02904, 02906, 02908, 02909, 02911, 02912, 02914, 02915, 02916, 02917, 02918, 02940

* * *

SECOND DISTRICT

JAMES R. LANGEVIN, Democrat, of Warwick, RI; born in Providence, RI, April 22, 1964; education: Rhode Island College, B.A., Political Science / Public Administration, 1990; Harvard University, Masters of Public Administration, 1994; community service: American Red Cross; March of Dimes; Lions Club of Warwick; PARI Independent Living Center; Knights of Columbus; public service: Secretary, 1986 Rhode Island Constitutional Convention; Rhode Island State Representative, 1989–95; Rhode Island Secretary of State, 1995–2000; committees: Armed Services; Homeland Security; elected to the 107th Congress; reelected to each succeeding Congress.

Office Listings
http://www.house.gov/langevin

109 Cannon House Office Building, Washington, DC 20515 .... (202) 225–2735
    Chief of Staff.—Kristin Nicholson.   FAX: 225–5976
    Office Manager.—Stu Rose.
The Summit South, 300 Centerville Road, Suite 200, Warwick, RI 02886 .... (401) 732–9400
    District Director.—Ken Wild.

Counties: KENT, PROVIDENCE (part), WASHINGTON. CITIES AND TOWNSHIPS: Charleston, Coventry, Cranston, Exeter, Foster, Glocester, Greenwich (East and West), Hopkinton, Johnston, Kingstown (North and South), Narragansett, New Shoreham, Providence, Richmond, Warwick, West Warwick, Westerly, and Scituate. Population (2000), 538,032.

ZIP Codes: 02804, 02807–08, 02812–18, 02822–23, 02825, 02827–29, 02831–33, 02836, 02852, 02857, 02873–75, 02877, 02879–83, 02886–89, 02891–94, 02898, 02901–05, 02907–11, 02917, 02919–21

SOUTH CAROLINA

(Population 2000, 4,012,012)

SENATORS

LINDSEY O. GRAHAM, Republican, of Seneca, SC; born in Seneca, July 9, 1955; education: graduated, Daniel High School, Central, SC; B.A., University of South Carolina, 1977; awarded J.D., 1981; military service: joined the U.S. Air Force, 1982; served in the Base Legal Office and as Area Defense Counsel; assigned to Rhein Main Air Force Base, Germany, 1984; circuit trial counsel, U.S. Air Forces; Meritorious Service Medal for Active Duty Tour in Europe; Base Staff Judge Advocate in McEntire Air National Guard Base, SC, 1989–1994; presently a Colonel in the Air Force Reserves; professional: established private law practice, 1988; former member, South Carolina House of Representatives; Assistant County Attorney for Oconee County, 1988–92; City Attorney for Central, SC, 1990–94; member: Walhalla Rotary; American Legion Post 120; appointed to the Judicial Arbitration Commission by the Chief Justice of the Supreme Court; religion: attends Corinth Baptist Church; committees: Armed Services; Budget; Judiciary; Veterans' Affairs; subcommittees: Airland; Antitrust, Competition Policy and Consumer Rights; Constitution, Civil Rights and Property Rights; chairman, Crime and Drugs; Emerging Threats and Capabilities; Intellectual Property; chairman, Personnel; Strategic Forces; Terrorism, Technology and Homeland Security; elected to the 104th Congress on November 8, 1994; reelected to each succeeding Congress; elected to the U.S. Senate on November 5, 2002.

Office Listings

http://lgraham.senate.gov

290 Russell Senate Office Building, Washington, DC 20510	(202) 224–5972
Chief of Staff.—Richard Perry.	FAX: 224–3808
Legislative Director.—Jen Olson.	
Scheduler.—Ellen Bradley.	
101 East Washington Street, Suite 220, Greenville, SC 29601	(864) 250–1417
530 Johnnie Dodds Boulevard, Suite 203, Mt. Pleasant, SC 29464	(843) 849–3887
508 Hampton Street, Suite 202, Columbia, SC 29201	(803) 933–0112
401 West Evans Street, Suite 226B, Florence, SC 29501	(843) 669–1505
140 East Main Street, Suite 110, Rock Hill, SC 29730	(803) 366–2828

* * *

JIM DeMINT, Republican, of Greenville, SC; born in Greenville, September 2, 1951; education: West Hampton High School, Greenville, SC, 1969; B.S., University of Tennessee, 1973; M.B.A., Clemson University, 1981; certified management consultant and certified quality trainer; advertising and marketing businessman; started his own company, DeMint Marketing; active in Greenville, SC, business and educational organizations; U.S. House of Representatives, 1999–2005; religion: Presbyterian; family: married to Debbie; four children; committees: Commerce, Science and Transportation; Environment and Public Works; Joint Economic Committee; Special Commitee on Aging; elected to the U.S. Senate on November 2, 2004.

Office Listings

http://demint.senate.gov

340 Russell Senate Office Building, Washington, DC 20510	(202) 224–6121
Chief of Staff.—Bret Bernhardt.	FAX: 228–5143
Policy Director.—Matt Hoskins.	
Executive Assistant / Office Manager.—Ellen Weaver.	
Communications Director.—Wesley Denton.	
105 North Spring Street, Suite 109, Greenville, SC 29601	(864) 233–5366
112 Customs House, 200 East Bay Street, Charleston, SC 29401	(843) 727–4525

REPRESENTATIVES

FIRST DISTRICT

HENRY E. BROWN, JR., Republican, of Hanahan, SC; born in Lee County, SC, December 20, 1935; education: Berkeley High School; Baptist College; and The Citadel; professional: Businessman; Piggly Wiggly Carolina Co., Inc.; helped develop the Lowcountry Investment Corp.; awards: National Republican Legislator of the Year; South Carolina Taxpayers Watchdog Award; South Carolina Association of Realtors Legislator of the Year; honorary degree, Doctor of Business Administration, The Citadel; married: Billye; three children; public service:

Hanahan City Council, 1981–85; South Carolina House of Representatives, 1985–2000; committees: Resources; Transportation and Infrastructure; Veterans' Affairs; subcommittees: Aviation; Forests and Forest Health; Highways, Transit and Pipelines; National Parks, Recreation and Public Lands; Water Resources and Environment; elected to the 107th Congress on November 7, 2000; reelected to each succeeding Congress.

Office Listings
http://www.house.gov/henrybrown

1124 Longworth House Office Building, Washington, DC 20515 .... (202) 225–3176
  Chief of Staff.—Delores Dacosta.
  Legislative Director.—Chris Berardini.
  Press Secretary.—Sharon Axson.
5900 Core Avenue, Suite 401, North Charleston, SC 29406 .... (843) 747–4175
  District Director.—Kathy Crawford.
1800 North Oak Street, Suite C, Myrtle Beach, SC 29577 .... (843) 445–6459

Counties: BERKELEY (part), CHARLESTON (part), DORCHESTER (part), GEORGETOWN (part), HORRY. Population (2000), 668,668.

ZIP Codes: 29401–07, 29410, 29412–14, 29416–20, 29422–25, 29429, 29436, 29439–40, 29442, 29445, 29449, 29451, 29455–58, 29461, 29464–66, 29469–70, 29472, 29474–75, 29482–85, 29487, 29511, 29526–28, 29544–45, 29566, 29568–69, 29572, 29575–79, 29581–82, 29585, 29587–88, 29597–98

* * *

SECOND DISTRICT

JOE WILSON, Republican, of Springdale, SC; born in Charleston, SC, July 31, 1947; education: graduated, Washington & Lee University, Lexington, VA; University of South Carolina School of Law; professional: attorney; Kirkland, Wilson, Moore, Taylor & Thomas (law firm); served on the staff of Senator Strom Thurmond and Congressman Floyd Spence; former Deputy General Counsel for the U.S. Department of Energy; former Judge of the town of Springdale, SC; military service: U.S. Army Reserves, 1972–1975; currently a Colonel in the South Carolina Army National Guard as a Staff Judge Advocate for the 218th Mechanized Infantry Brigade; organizations: Cayce-West Columbia Rotary Club; Sheriff's Department Law Enforcement Advisory Council; Reserve Officers Association; Lexington County Historical Society; Columbia Home Builders Association; County Community and Resource Development Committee; American Heart Association; Mid-Carolina Mental Health Association; Cayce-West Columbia Jaycees; Kidney Foundation; South Carolina Lung Association; Alston-Wilkes Society; Cayce-West Metro Chamber of Commerce; Columbia World Affairs Council; Fellowship of Christian Athletes, Sinclair Lodge 154; Jamil Temple; Woodmen of the World; Sons of Confederate Veterans; Military Order of the World Wars; Lexington, Greater Irmo, Chapin, Columbia, West Metro, and Batesburg-Leesville Chambers of Commerce; West Metro and Dutch Fork Women's Republican Clubs; and Executive Council of the Indian Waters Council, Boy Scouts of America; awards: U.S. Chamber of Commerce Spirit of Enterprise Award, 2001; Americans for Tax Reform Friend of the Taxpayer Award, 2001; public service: South Carolina State Senate, 1984-2001; family: married to Roxanne Dusenbury McCrory; four sons; committees: Armed Services; Education and the Workforce; International Relations; elected to the 107th Congress, by special election, on December 18, 2001; reelected to each succeeding Congress.

Office Listings
http://joewilson.house.gov

212 Cannon House Office Building, Washington, DC 20515 .... (202) 225–2452
  Chief of Staff.—Eric Dell.   FAX: 225–2455
  Press Secretary.—Emily Lawrimore.
  Legislative Director.—Laurin Groover.
903 Port Republic Street, P.O. Box 1538, Beaufort, SC 29901 .... (843) 521–2530
1700 Sunset Boulevard (U.S. 378), Suite 1, West Columbia, SC 29169 .... (803) 939–0041

Counties: AIKEN (part), ALLENDALE, BARNWELL, BEAUFORT, CALHOUN (part), HAMPTON, JASPER, LEXINGTON, ORANGEBURG (part), RICHLAND (part). CITIES AND TOWNSHIPS: Aiken, Allendale, Ballentine, Barnwell, Batesburg, Beaufort, Blackville, Bluffton, Blythewood, Brunson, Cayce, Chapin, Columbia, Coosawhatchie, Cope, Cordova, Crocketville, Daufuskie Island, Early Branch, Elko, Estill, Fairfax, Furman, Garnett, Gaston, Gifford, Gilbert, Hampton, Hardeeville, Hilda, Hilton Head Island, Irmo, Islandston, Kline, Leesville, Lexington, Livingston, Luray, Martin, Miley, Montmorenci, Neeses, North, Norway, Orangeburg, Pelion, Pineland, Port Royal, Ridgeland, Ruffin, Scotia, Springfield, St. Helena Island, St. Matthews, State Park, Swansea, Sycamore, Tillman, Ulmer, Varnville, West Columbia, White Rock, Williams, Williston, Windsor, and Yemassee. Population (2000), 668,668.

ZIP Codes: 29002, 29006, 29016, 29033, 29036, 29045, 29053–54, 29063, 29070–73, 29075, 29078, 29107, 29112–13, 29115–16, 29118, 29123, 29128, 29130, 29135, 29137, 29142, 29146–47, 29160, 29164, 29169–72, 29177, 29180,

29203–07, 29209–10, 29212, 29219, 29221, 29223–24, 29226–27, 29229, 29260, 29290, 29292, 29405, 29412–13, 29436, 29470, 29472, 29801, 29803, 29805, 29810, 29812–13, 29817, 29826–27, 29836, 29839, 29843, 29846, 29849, 29853, 29901–07, 29909–11, 29913–16, 29918, 29920–28, 29932–36, 29938–41, 29943–45

* * *

THIRD DISTRICT

J. GRESHAM BARRETT, Republican, of Westminster, SC; born in Oconee, SC, February 14, 1961; education: B.S., Business Administration, The Citadel, 1983; military service: U.S. Army, 1983–1987; professional: small businessman; organizations: Westminster Rotary Club; Oconee County Boy Scouts; Westminster Chamber of Commerce; Oconee County Red Cross; religion: Baptist; attends Westminster Baptist Church; public service: South Carolina House of Representatives, 1987–2002; family: married to Natalie; children: Madison, Jeb, and Ross; committees: Budget; Financial Services; International Relations; elected to the 108th Congress on November 5, 2002; reelected to each succeeding Congress.

Office Listings
http://www.house.gov/barrett

1523 Longworth House Office Building, Washington, DC 20515	(202) 225–5301
Chief of Staff.—William (Lance) Williams.	FAX: 225–3216
Legislative Director.—Sandra Campbell.	
315 South McDuffie Street, Anderson, SC 29622	(864) 224–7401
115 Enterprise Court, Suite B, Greenwood, SC 29649	(864) 223–8251
233 Pendleton Street, NW., Aiken, SC 29801	(803) 649–5571

Counties: ABBEVILLE, AIKEN (part), ANDERSON, EDGEFIELD, GREENWOOD, LAURENS (part), MCCORMICK, OCONEE, PICKENS, SALUDA. Population (2000), 668,669.

ZIP Codes: 29006, 29037, 29070, 29105, 29127–29, 29138, 29166, 29178, 29325, 29332, 29334–35, 29351, 29355, 29360, 29370, 29384, 29388, 29406, 29611, 29620–28, 29630–33, 29635, 29638–49, 29653–59, 29661, 29664–67, 29669–73, 29675–79, 29682, 29684–86, 29689, 29691–93, 29695–97, 29801–05, 29808–09, 29816, 29819, 29821–22, 29824, 29828–29, 29831–32, 29834–35, 29838, 29840–42, 29844–45, 29847–48, 29850–51, 29853, 29856, 29860–61

* * *

FOURTH DISTRICT

BOB INGLIS, Republican, of Travelers Rest, SC; born in Savannah, GA, October 11, 1959; native of Bluffton, SC; education: May River Academy, Bluffton, SC, 1977; Duke University, Durham, NC, 1981; University of Virginia Law School, Charlottesville, VA, 1984; professional: attorney; admitted to the South Carolina Bar, 1984; Leatherwood, Walker, Todd & Mann (law firm), 1986–92 and 1999–2004; Hunger, Maclean, Exley & Dunn (law firm), 1984–86; religion: Presbyterian; member, Redeemer Presbyterian Church; married: the former Mary Anne Williams, 1982; five children; U.S. House of Representatives, 1993–98; committees: Education and the Workforce; Judiciary; Science; elected to the 109th Congress on November 2, 2004.

Office Listings
http://www.house.gov/inglis

330 Cannon House Office Building, Washington, DC 20515	(202) 225–6030
Chief of Staff.—Wayne Roper.	FAX: 226–1177
Legislative Director.—Jason Morris.	
Legislative Assistants: Brenda Ballard, Flynn Cratty, Garth Van Meter.	
Executive Assistant.—Barbara Grogan.	
105 North Spring Street, Suite 111, Greenville, SC 29601	(864) 232–1141
Communications Director.—Price Atkinson.	
145 North Church Street, BTC #56, Spartanburg, SC 29306	(864) 582–6422
Constituent Liaison.—Dwayne Hatchett.	

Counties: GREENVILLE, LAURENS (part), SPARTANBURG, UNION. Population (2000), 668,669.

ZIP Codes: 29031, 29178, 29301–07, 29316, 29318–24, 29329–31, 29333–36, 29338, 29346, 29348–49, 29353, 29356, 29364–65, 29368–69, 29372–79, 29385–86, 29388, 29390–91, 29395, 29564, 29601–17, 29627, 29635–36, 29644–45, 29650–52, 29654, 29661–62, 29669, 29673, 29680–81, 29683, 29687–88, 29690, 29698

FIFTH DISTRICT

JOHN M. SPRATT, JR., Democrat, of York, SC; born in Charlotte, NC, November 1, 1942; education: graduated, York High School, 1960; A.B., Davidson College, 1964; president of student body and Phi Beta Kappa, Davidson College; M.A., economics, Oxford University, Corpus Christi College (Marshall Scholar), 1966; LL.B., Yale Law School, 1969; admitted to the South Carolina Bar in 1969; military service: active duty, U.S. Army, 1969–71, discharged as captain; served as member of Operations Analysis Group, Office of the Assistant Secretary of Defense (Comptroller), received Meritorious Service Medal; professional: private practice of law 1971–82, Spratt, McKeown and Spratt in York, SC; York County attorney, 1973–82; president, Bank of Fort Mill, 1973–82; president, Spratt Insurance Agency, Inc.; president, York Chamber of Commerce; chairman, Winthrop College Board of Visitors; chairman, Divine Saviour Hospital Board; board of visitors, Davidson and Coker Colleges; president, Western York County United Fund; board of directors, Piedmont Legal Services; House of Delegates, South Carolina bar; elder, First Presbyterian Church, York; married: Jane Stacy Spratt, 1968; children: Susan, Sarah, and Catherine; committees: Armed Services; ranking member, Budget; elected to the 98th Congress, November 2, 1982; reelected to each succeeding Congress.

Office Listings

http://www.house.gov/spratt

1401 Longworth House Office Building, Washington, DC 20515	(202) 225–5501
Chief of Staff.—Ellen Buchanan.	FAX: 225–0464
Press Secretary.—Chuck Fant.	
P.O. Box 350, Rock Hill, SC 29731	(803) 327–1114
District Administrator.—Robert Hopkins.	
39 East Calhoun Street, Sumter, SC 29150	(803) 773–3362
88 Public Square, Darlington, SC 29532–0025	(843) 393–3998

Counties: CHEROKEE, CHESTER, CHESTERFIELD, DARLINGTON, DILLON, FAIRFIELD, FLORENCE (part), KERSHAW, LANCASTER, LEE (part), MARLBORO, NEWBERRY, SUMTER (part), YORK. Population (2000), 668,668.

ZIP Codes: 29009–10, 29014–16, 29020, 29031–32, 29036–37, 29040, 29045, 29055, 29058, 29065, 29067, 29069, 29074–75, 29078–79, 29101–02, 29104, 29106, 29108, 29122, 29126–28, 29130, 29132, 29145, 29150–54, 29161, 29163, 29175–76, 29178, 29180, 29203, 29218, 29307, 29323, 29330, 29332, 29340–42, 29355, 29372, 29501, 29506, 29512, 29516, 29520, 29525, 29532, 29536, 29540, 29543, 29547, 29550–51, 29563, 29565, 29567, 29570, 29573–74, 29581, 29584, 29592–94, 29596, 29654, 29702–04, 29706, 29708–10, 29712, 29714–18, 29720–22, 29724, 29726–32, 29734, 29741–45

* * *

SIXTH DISTRICT

JAMES E. CLYBURN, Democrat, of Columbia, SC; born in Sumter, SC, July 21, 1940; education: graduated, Mather Academy, Camden, SC, 1957; B.S., South Carolina State University, Orangeburg, 1962; attended University of South Carolina Law School, Columbia, 1972–74; professional: South Carolina State Human Affairs Commissioner; Assistant to the Governor for Human Resource Development; executive director, South Carolina Commission for Farm Workers, Inc.; director, Neighborhood Youth Corps and New Careers; counselor, South Carolina Employment Security Commission; member: NAACP, lifetime member; Southern Regional Council; Omega Psi Phi Fraternity, Inc.; Arabian Temple, No. 139; Nemiah Lodge No. 51 F&AM; married: the former Emily England; children: Mignon, Jennifer and Angela; elected Vice Chairman, Democratic Caucus, 2002; committees: Appropriations; elected on November 3, 1992, to the 103rd Congress; reelected to each succeeding Congress.

Office Listings

http://www.house.gov/clyburn

2135 Rayburn House Office Building, Washington, DC 20515	(202) 225–3315
Administrative Assistant.—Yelberton Watkins.	FAX: 225–2313
Legislative Director.—Danny Cromer.	
Legislative Assistant.—Barvetta Singletary.	
Policy Advisor.—Jaime Harrison.	
1703 Gervais Street, Columbia, SC 29201	(803) 799–1100
District Director.—Robert Nance.	
181 East Evans Street, Suite 314, Post Office Box 6286, Florence, SC 29502	(803) 662–1212
8833 Old Highway Number Six, Santee, SC 29142	(843) 965–5578

Counties: BAMBERG COUNTY. CITIES AND TOWNSHIPS: Bamberg, Denmark, Erhardt, Olar. BERKELEY COUNTY (part). CITIES AND TOWNSHIPS: Bethera, Cross, Daniel Island, Huger, Jamestown, Pineville, Russellville, Saint Stephen, Wando. CALHOUN COUNTY (part). CITY OF: Cameron, Creston, Fort Motte, St. Matthews. CHARLESTON COUNTY (part). CITIES

AND TOWNSHIPS: Adams Run, Charleston, Edisto Island, Hollywood, Johns Island, Ravenel, Wadmalaw Island. CLARENDON COUNTY. CITIES AND TOWNSHIPS: Alcolu, Davis Station, Gable, Manning, New Zion, Rimini, Summerton, Turbeville. COLLETON COUNTY. CITIES AND TOWNSHIPS: Ashton, Cottageville, Green Pond, Hendersonville, Islandton, Jacksonboro, Lodge, Ritter, Round O, Smoaks, Walterboro, Williams. DORCHESTER COUNTY (part). CITIES AND TOWN-SHIPS: Dorchester, Harleyville, Reevesville, Ridgeville, Rosinville, Saint George. FLORENCE COUNTY (part). CITIES AND TOWNSHIPS: Coward, Effingham, Florence, Johnsonville, Lake City, Olanta, Pamplico, Quinby, Scranton, Timmonsville. GEORGETOWN COUNTY (part). CITIES AND TOWNSHIPS: Andrews, Outland, Sampit. MARION COUNTY. CITIES AND TOWN-SHIPS: Centenary, Gresham, Marion, Mullins, Nichols, Rains, Sellers. LEE COUNTY (part). CITIES AND TOWNSHIPS: Elliott, Lynchburg. ORANGEBURG COUNTY (part). CITIES AND TOWNSHIPS: Bowman, Branchville, Cardova, Cope, Elloree, Eutawville, Holly Hill, Norway, Orangeburg, Rowesville, Santee, Vance. RICHLAND COUNTY (part). CITIES AND TOWN-SHIPS: Blythewood, Columbia, Eastover, Gadsden, Hopkins. SUMTER COUNTY (part). CITIES AND TOWNSHIPS: Mayesville, Oswego, Pinewood, Sumter. WILLIAMSBURG COUNTY. CITIES AND TOWNSHIPS: Cades, Greeleyville, Hemingway, Kingstree, Lane, Nesmith, Salters, and Trio. Population (2000), 668,670.

ZIP Codes: 29001, 29003, 29006, 29010, 29018, 29030, 29038–42, 29044–48, 29051–52, 29056, 29059, 29061–62, 29078, 29080–82, 29102, 29104, 29107, 29111, 29113–15, 29117–18, 29125, 29128, 29130, 29133, 29135, 29142–43, 29146, 29148, 29150, 29153–54, 29161–63, 29168, 29201–05, 29208–09, 29211, 29214–17, 29220, 29223, 29225, 29228, 29230, 29240, 29250, 29403, 29405–06, 29409, 29415, 29418, 29426, 29430–38, 29440, 29446–50, 29452–53, 29461, 29466, 29468, 29470–72, 29474–77, 29479, 29481, 29488, 29492–93, 29501–06, 29510, 29518–19, 29530, 29541, 29546, 29554–56, 29560, 29565, 29571, 29574, 29580–81, 29583, 29589–92, 29817, 29843, 29929, 29931, 29945

SOUTH DAKOTA

(Population 2000, 754,844)

SENATORS

TIM JOHNSON, Democrat, of Vermillion, SD, born in Canton, SD, December 28, 1946; education: B.A., University of South Dakota, 1969; Phi Beta Kappa; M.A., political science, University of South Dakota, 1970; post-graduate study in political science, Michigan State University, 1970–71; J.D., University of South Dakota, 1975; married: Barbara Brooks, 1969; children: Brooks, Brendan and Kelsey Marie; Lutheran; budget advisor to the Michigan State Senate Appropriations Committee, 1971–72; admitted to the South Dakota bar in 1975 and began private law practice in Vermillion; served as Clay County Deputy State's Attorney, 1985; elected to the South Dakota House of Representatives, 1978; reelected, 1980; elected to the South Dakota State Senate, 1982; reelected, 1984; served on the Joint Appropriations Committee and the Senate Judiciary Committee; named Outstanding Citizen of Vermillion (1983); received South Dakota Education Association's "Friend of Education" Award (1983); Billy Sutton Award for Legislative Achievement (1984); elected to the U.S. House of Representatives, 1986; reelected to each succeeding Congress; delegate, Democratic National Convention, 1988–92; member: President's Export Council, 1999; committees: Appropriations; Banking, Housing and Urban Affairs; Budget; Energy and Natural Resources; Indian Affairs; Select Committee on Ethics; elected to the U.S. Senate on November 5, 1996; reelected to each succeeding Senate term.

Office Listings

http://johnson.senate.gov

136 Hart Senate Office Building, Washington, DC 20510	(202) 224–5842
Chief of Staff.—Drey Samuelson.	
Legislative Director.—Todd Stubbendieck.	
Communications Director.—Julianne Fisher.	
715 S. Minnesota Avenue, Sioux Falls, SD 57104	(605) 332–8896
State Director.—Sharon Boysen.	
320 S. First Street, Suite 103, Aberdeen, SD 57401	(605) 226–3440
405 E. Omaha Street, Suite B, Rapid City, SD 57701	(605) 341–3990

* * *

JOHN THUNE, Republican, of Pierre, SD; born in Pierre, January 7, 1961; education: Jones County High School, 1979; B.S., Business Administration, Biola University, CA; M.B.A., University of South Dakota, 1984; professional: executive director, South Dakota Municipal League; board of directors, National League of Cities; executive director, South Dakota Republican Party, 1989–1991; appointed, State Railroad Director, 1991; former congressional legislative assistant, and deputy staff director; elected, U.S. House of Representatives, 1997–2003; married: Kimberly Weems, 1984; children: Brittany and Larissa; committees: Armed Services; Environment and Public Works; Small Business and Entrepreneurship; Veterans' Affairs; elected to the U.S. Senate on November 2, 2004.

Office Listings

http://thune.senate.gov

383 Russell Senate Office Building, Washington, DC 20510	(202) 224–2321
Chief of Staff.—Matt Zabel.	FAX: 228–5429
Executive Director.—Summer Pitlick.	
Legislative Director.—Bob Taylor.	
Office Manager.—Pamela Fleming.	
320 N. Main Avenue, Suite B, Sioux Falls, SD 57104	(605) 334–9596
1312 West Main Street, Rapid City, SD 57701	(605) 348–7551
320 S. First Street, Suite 101, Aberdeen, SD 57401	(605) 225–8823

REPRESENTATIVE

AT LARGE

STEPHANIE HERSETH, Democrat, of Brookings, SD; born, December 3, 1970; education: graduated, Valedictorian, Groton High School; graduated, *summa cum laude* and Phi Beta Kappa, with a B.A. in Government, Georgetown University; graduated with honors, with a J.D., from the Georgetown University Law Center, and was a senior editor of the law review; professional: attorney; member, South Dakota Bar; served on the faculty of Georgetown University Law Center; worked on telecommunications and energy issues for the South Dakota Public Utilities Commission; organized commission meetings with Indian tribal leaders regarding utility regulation on Indian reservations; worked with U.S. District Court Judge Charles B. Kornmann; also served as a law clerk on the U.S. Court of Appeals for the Fourth Circuit; Executive Director, South Dakota Farmers Union Foundation; committees: Agriculture; Resources; Veterans' Affairs; elected to the 108th Congress by special election, on June 1, 2004; reelected to the 109th Congress on November 2, 2004.

Office Listings

331 Cannon House Office Building, Washington, DC 20515 .... (202) 225–2801
    Chief of Staff.—Jeff Navin.   FAX: 225–5823
    Communications Director.—Russ Levsen.
    Legislative Director.—Ryan Stroschein.
    Scheduler.—McLean Thompson.
2600 South Minnesota Avenue, Suite 100, Sioux Falls, SD 57105 .... (605) 367–8371
    District Director.—Tessa Gould.
1823 West Main Street, Rapid City, SD 57702 .... (605) 394–5280
    Outreach Director.—Ira Taken Alive.
10 Sixth Avenue, SW., Aberdeen, SD 57401 .... (605) 626–3440
    Northeast Director.—Scott Herreid.

Population (2000), 754,844.

ZIP Codes: 57001–07, 57010, 57012–18, 57020–22, 57024–59, 57061–73, 57075–79, 57101, 57103–10, 57117–18, 57186, 57188–89, 57192–98, 57201, 57212–14, 57216–21, 57223–27, 57231–39, 57241–43, 57245–49, 57251–53, 57255–66, 57268–74, 57276, 57278–79, 57301, 57311–15, 57317, 57319, 57321–26, 57328–32, 57334–35, 57337, 57339–42, 57344–46, 57348–50, 57353–56, 57358–59, 57361–71, 57373–76, 57379–86, 57399, 57401–02, 57420–22, 57424, 57426–30, 57432–42, 57445–46, 57448–52, 57454–57, 57460–61, 57465–77, 57479, 57481, 57501, 57520–23, 57528–29, 57531–34, 57536–38, 57540–44, 57547–48, 57551–53, 57555, 57559–60, 57562–64, 57566–72, 57574, 57576–77, 57579–80, 57584–85, 57601, 57620–23, 57625–26, 57630–34, 57636, 57638–42, 57644–46, 57648–52, 57656–61, 57701–03, 57706, 57709, 57714, 57716–20, 57722, 57724–25, 57730, 57732, 57735, 57737–38, 57741, 57744–45, 57747–48, 57750–52, 57754–56, 57758–64, 57766–67, 57769–70, 57772–73, 57775–77, 57779–80, 57782–83, 57785, 57787–88, 57790–94, 57799

TENNESSEE

(Population 2000, 5,689,283)

SENATORS

WILLIAM H. (BILL) FRIST, Republican, of Nashville, TN; born in Nashville, February 22, 1952; education: graduated, Montgomery Bell Academy, Nashville, 1970; A.B., Princeton University, Woodrow Wilson School of Public and International Affairs, 1974; M.D., Harvard Medical School, 1978, with honors; residency in general surgery (1978–84) and thoracic surgery (1983–84), Massachusetts General Hospital; cardiovascular and transplant fellowship, Stanford University Medical Center, 1985–86; heart and lung transplant surgeon; founding director, Vanderbilt Transplant Center; teaching faculty, Vanderbilt University Medical Center, 1986–93; staff surgeon, Nashville Veterans' Administration Hospital; board certified in both general surgery and cardiothoracic surgery; Medical Center Ethics Committee, 1991–93; chairman, Tennessee Medicaid Task Force, 1992–93; recipient: Distinguished Service Award, Tennessee Medical Association; president, Middle Tennessee Heart Association; member: Smithsonian Institution's Board of Regents, Princeton University Board of Trustees, American College of Surgeons, Society of Thoracic Surgeons, Southern Thoracic Surgical Association, American College of Chest Physicians; American Medical Association, Tennessee Medical Association, American Society of Transplant Surgeons, Association of Academic Surgery, International Society for Heart and Lung Transplantation, Tennessee Transplant Society, Alpha Omega Alpha, Rotary Club, United Way de Tocqueville Society; board member: YMCA Foundation of Metropolitan Nashville, Sergeant York Historical Association; commercial pilot; author of 100 scientific articles, chapters and abstracts (subjects: fibroblast growth factor, thoracic surgery, artificial heart, transplantation, immunosuppression); author of *Transplant* (Atlantic Monthly Press, 1989); co-editor, *Grand Rounds in Transplantation* (Chapman and Hall, 1995); married Karyn McLaughlin Frist, 1981; three children: Harrison, Jonathan, and Bryan; committees: Finance; Health, Education, Labor, and Pensions; Rules and Administration; Senate Majority Leader; elected to the U.S. Senate on November 8, 1994; reelected to each succeeding Senate term.

Office Listings
http://frist.senate.gov

509 Hart Senate Office Building, Washington, DC 20510	(202) 224–3344
Chief of Staff.—Andrea Becker.	
Deputy Chief of Staff.—Nick Smith.	
Legislative Director.—Jim Hippe.	
Executive Assistant / Scheduler.—Ramona Lessen.	
28 White Bridge Road, Suite 211, Nashville, TN 37205	(615) 352–9411
State Director.—Bart VerHulst.	
5100 Poplar Avenue, Suite 514, Memphis, TN 38137	(901) 683–1910
James Building, 735 Broad Street, Suite 701, Chattanooga, TN 37402	(423) 894–2203
200 East Main Street, Suite 111, Jackson, TN 38301	(731) 424–9655
10368 Wallace Alley Street, Suite 7, Kingsport, TN 37663	(423) 323–1252
Howard Baker Federal Building, 800 Market Street, Suite 121, Knoxville, TN 37902	(865) 637–4180

* * *

LAMAR ALEXANDER, Republican, of Nashville, TN; born in Maryville, TN, July 3, 1940; education: Vanderbilt University, graduating Phi Beta Kappa, with honors in Latin American history; New York University Law School; served as Law Review editor; professional: clerk to Judge John Minor Wisdom, U.S. Court of Appeals in New Orleans; legislative assistant to Senator Howard Baker (R–TN), 1967; executive assistant to Bryce Harlow, counselor to President Nixon, 1969; President, University of Tennessee, 1988–1991; Co-Director, Empower America, 1994–1995; helped found a company that is now the nation's largest provider of worksite day care, Bright Horizons; public service: Republican nominee for Governor of Tennessee, 1974; elected Governor of Tennessee in 1978, and reelected in 1982, serving from 1979–1987; U.S. Secretary of Education, 1991–1993; community service: chairman, Salvation Army Red Shield Family Initiative; and the Museum of Appalachia in Norris, TN; received Tennessee Conservation League Conservationist of the Year Award; family: married to Honey Alexander; four children; committees: Budget; Energy and Natural Resources; Foreign Relations; Health, Education, Labor, and Pensions; Special Committee on Aging; elected to the U.S. Senate on November 5, 2002.

Office Listings

http://alexander.senate.gov

302 Hart Senate Office Building, Washington, DC 20510 .... (202) 224–4944
    Chief of Staff.—Tom Ingram.   FAX: 228–3398
    Communications Director.—Alexia Poe.
    Administrative Assistant.—Trina Tyrer.
    Executive Assistant / Scheduler.—Bonnie Sansonetti.
3322 West End Avenue, Suite 120, Nashville, TN 37203 .... (615) 736–5129
Howard H. Baker, Jr. U.S. Courthouse; 800 Market Street, Suite 112, Knoxville,
    TN 37902 .... (865) 545–4253
Federal Building, 167 North Main Street, Suite 1068, Memphis, TN 38103 .... (901) 544–4224
Federal Building, 109 South Highland Street, Suite B–9, Jackson, TN 38301 .... (731) 423–9344
Joel E. Solomon Federal Building, 900 Georgia Avenue, Suite 260, Chattanooga,
    TN 37402 .... (423) 752–5337
Tri-Cities Regional Airport, Terminal Building, Suite 101, Blountville, TN 37617   (423) 325–6240

REPRESENTATIVES

FIRST DISTRICT

WILLIAM L. JENKINS, Republican, of Rogersville, TN; born in Detroit, MI, November 29, 1936; education: graduated from Rogersville High School, 1954; B.B.A from Tennessee Tech, Cookville, 1957; military service: served in the U.S. Army Military Police, second lieutenant, 1959–60; J.D., University of Tennessee College of Law, Knoxville, TN, 1961; admitted to the Tennessee bar, 1962; professional: attorney; farmer; Commissioner of Conservation; Circuit Judge; energy advisor to Governor Lamar Alexander; TVA board member; State Representative to Tennessee General Assembly, 1962–70; Speaker of the House, 1968–70; delegate to the Republican National Convention, 1988; member: American Legion, Masonic Lodge, Tennessee Bar Association, Tennessee Farm Bureau; married: Mary Kathryn Jenkins, 1959; children: Rebecca, Georgeanne Price, William, Jr., Douglas; committees: Agriculture; Judiciary; subcommittees: chair, Specialty Crops and Foreign Agriculture Programs; elected to the 105th Congress; reelected to each succeeding Congress.

Office Listings

1207 Longworth House Office Building, Washington, DC 20515 .... (202) 225–6356
    Chief of Staff.—Brenda J. Otterson.   FAX: 225–5714
    Scheduler.—Dennis LeNard.
    Legislative Director.—Richard Vaughn.
320 West Center Street, Kingsport, TN 57660 .... (423) 247–8161

Counties: CARTER, COCKE, GREENE, HAMBLEN, HANCOCK, HAWKINS, JEFFERSON, JOHNSON, SEVIER, SULLIVAN, UNICOI, WASHINGTON. Population (2000), 632,143.

ZIP Codes: 37601–02, 37604–05, 37614–18, 37620–21, 37625, 37640–45, 37650, 37656–60, 37662–65, 37680–84, 37686–88, 37690–92, 37694, 37699, 37711, 37713, 37722, 37725, 37727, 37731, 37738, 37743–45, 37752–53, 37760, 37764–65, 37778, 37809–11, 37813–16, 37818, 37821–22, 37843, 37857, 37860, 37862–65, 37868–69, 37873, 37876–77, 37879, 37881, 37890–91

* * *

SECOND DISTRICT

JOHN J. DUNCAN, JR., Republican, of Knoxville, TN; born in Lebanon, TN, July 21, 1947; education: University of Tennessee, B.S. degree in journalism, 1969; National Law Center, George Washington University, J.D. degree, 1973; served in both the Army National Guard and the U.S. Army Reserves, retiring with the rank of captain; private law practice in Knoxville, 1973–81; appointed State Trial Judge by Governor Lamar Alexander in 1981 and elected to a full eight-year term in 1982 without opposition, receiving the highest number of votes of any candidate on the ballot that year; member: American Legion 40 and 8, Elks, Sertoma Club, Masons, Scottish Rite and Shrine; present or past board member: Red Cross, Girl's Club, YWCA, Sunshine Center for the Mentally Retarded, Beck Black Heritage Center, Knoxville Union Rescue Mission, Senior Citizens Home Aid Service; religion: active elder at Eastminster Presbyterian Church; married: the former Lynn Hawkins; children: Tara, Whitney, John J. III, and Zane; committees: Government Reform; Resources; Transportation and Infrastructure; elected to both the 100th Congress (special election) and the 101st Congress in separate elections held on November 8, 1988; reelected to each succeeding Congress.

Office Listings
http://www.house.gov/duncan

2267 Rayburn House Office Building, Washington, DC 20515	(202) 225–5435
Chief of Staff.—Bob Griffitts.	FAX: 225–6440
Deputy Chief of Staff.—Don Walker.	
Press Secretary.—Matt Lehigh.	
6 East Madison Avenue, Athens, TN 37303	(423) 745–4671
800 Market Street, Suite 100, Knoxville, TN 37902	(423) 523–3772
District Director.—Bob Griffitts.	
262 East Broadway, Maryville, TN 37804	(423) 984–5464

Counties: BLOUNT, KNOX (part), LOUDON, MCMINN, MONROE. CITIES AND TOWNSHIPS: Alcoa, Athens, Englewood, Etowah, Farragut, Halls (Knox Co.), Knoxville, Lenoir City, Loudon, Madisonville, Maryville, Powell, Seymour, and Sweetwater. Population (2000), 632,144.

ZIP Codes: 37303, 37309, 37311–12, 37314, 37322–23, 37325, 37329, 37331, 37353–54, 37369–71, 37385, 37701, 37709, 37721, 37725, 37737, 37742, 37754, 37764, 37771–72, 37774, 37777, 37779, 37801–04, 37806–07, 37820, 37826, 37830, 37846, 37849, 37853, 37865, 37871, 37874, 37876, 37878, 37880, 37882, 37885–86, 37901–02, 37909, 37912, 37914–24, 37927–33, 37938–40, 37950, 37990, 37995–98

* * *

THIRD DISTRICT

ZACH WAMP, Republican, of Chattanooga, TN; born in Fort Benning, GA, October 28, 1957; graduated, McCallie School, Chattanooga, 1976; attended University of North Carolina at Chapel Hill and University of Tennessee; member, Red Bank Baptist Church; commercial and industrial real estate broker; named Chattanooga Business Leader of the Year; chairman, Hamilton County Republican Party; regional director, Tennessee Republican Party; received Tennessee Jaycees' Outstanding Young Tennessean Award in 1996, U.S. Chamber of Commerce Spirit of Enterprise Award, Citizens Against Government Waste "A" Rating, National Taxpayers Union Friend of the Taxpayers Award; recognized by the Citizens Taxpayers Association of Hamilton County, the National Federation of Independent Business and the Concord Coalition for casting tough votes to reduce spending; married Kimberly Watts Wamp, 1985; two children: Weston and Coty; committees: Appropriations; subcommittees: Energy and Water Development, and Related Agencies; Homeland Security; Interior, Environment, and Related Agencies; elected to the 104th Congress; reelected to each succeeding Congress.

Office Listings
http://www.house.gov/wamp

2447 Rayburn House Office Building, Washington, DC 20515	(202) 225–3271
Chief of Staff.—Helen Hardin.	FAX: 225–3494
Deputy Chief of Staff.—Rob Hobart.	
Press Secretary.—Rachel Carter.	
Scheduler.—Randy Forrester.	
900 Georgia Avenue, Suite 126, Chattanooga, TN 37402	(423) 756–2342
District Director.—Doug Fisher.	
Federal Building, Suite 100, 200 Administration Road, Oak Ridge, TN 37830	(865) 576–1976
District Director.—Linda Ponce.	

Counties: ANDERSON, BRADLEY, CLAIBORNE, GRAINGER, HAMILTON, JEFFERSON (part), MEIGS, POLK, RHEA, ROANE (part), UNION. Population (2000), 632,143.

ZIP Codes: 37302, 37304, 37307–12, 37315–17, 37320–23, 37325–26, 37332–33, 37336–38, 37341, 37343, 37350–51, 37353, 37361–64, 37369, 37373, 37375, 37377, 37379, 37381, 37384, 37391, 37397, 37401–12, 37414–16, 37419, 37421–22, 37424, 37450, 37705, 37707–10, 37715–17, 37719, 37721, 37724–26, 37730, 37752, 37754, 37760, 37763–64, 37769, 37771, 37774, 37779, 37806–07, 37811, 37820–21, 37824–26, 37828, 37830–31, 37840, 37846, 37848–49, 37851, 37861, 37866, 37869–71, 37874, 37876–77, 37879–81, 37888, 37890, 37931, 37938

* * *

FOURTH DISTRICT

LINCOLN DAVIS, Democrat, of Pall Mall, TN; born in Pall Mall, September 13, 1943; education: Alvin C. York Agricultural Institute, 1962; B.S., Agronomy, Tennessee Technological University, 1966; professional: farmer and general contractor; civic organizations: Tennessee State Jaycees; Pickett County Chamber of Commerce; Upper Cumberland Developmental District; Boy Scouts; public service: Mayor of Byrdstown, TN, 1978–1982; Tennessee State

Representative, 1980–1984; Tennessee State Senator, 1996–2002; religion: Baptist; married: Lynda; children: Larissa, Lynn, and Libby; committees; Agriculture; Science; Transportation and Infrastructure; elected to the 108th Congress on November 5, 2002; reelected to each succeeding Congress.

Office Listings

http://www.house.gov/lincolndavis

410 Cannon House Office Building, Washington, DC 20515	(202) 225–6831
Chief of Staff.—Beecher Frasier.	FAX: 226–5172
Legislative Director.—Brandi McBride.	
Press Secretary.—Tom Hayden.	
1064 North Gateway Avenue, Rockwood, TN 37854	(865) 354–3323
629 North Main Street, Jamestown, TN 38556	(931) 879–2361
1804 Carmack Boulevard, Suite A, Columbia, TN 38401	(931) 490–8699
477 North Chancery Street, Suite A–1, McMinnville, TN 37110	(931) 473–7251

Counties: BLEDSOE, CAMPBELL, COFFEE, CUMBERLAND, FENTRESS, FRANKLIN, GILES, GRUNDY, HICKMAN (part), LAWRENCE, LEWIS, LINCOLN, MARION, MAURY, MOORE, MORGAN, PICKETT, ROANE (part), SCOTT, SEQUATCHIE, VAN BUREN, WARREN, WHITE, WILLIAMSON (part). Population (2000), 632,143.

ZIP Codes: 37018, 37025–26, 37033, 37037, 37047, 37062, 37064, 37078, 37091, 37096, 37098, 37110–11, 37129–33, 37137, 37144, 37160, 37166, 37171, 37174, 37179, 37183, 37190, 37301, 37305–06, 37313, 37318, 37324, 37327–28, 37330, 37334–35, 37337, 37339–40, 37342, 37345, 37347–49, 37352, 37355–57, 37359–60, 37365–67, 37374–83, 37387–89, 37394, 37396–98, 37419, 37714–15, 37719, 37721, 37723, 37726, 37729, 37732–33, 37748, 37755–57, 37762–63, 37766, 37769–71, 37773, 37778, 37819, 37829, 37840–41, 37845, 37847, 37852, 37854, 37867, 37869–70, 37872, 37880, 37887, 37892, 38370, 38401–02, 38449, 38451, 38453–57, 38459–64, 38468–69, 38472–78, 38481–83, 38486–88, 38504, 38506, 38549–50, 38553, 38555–59, 38565, 38571–72, 38574, 38577–79, 38581, 38583, 38585, 38587, 38589

* * *

FIFTH DISTRICT

JIM COOPER, Democrat, of Nashville, TN; born in Nashville, June 19, 1954; education: University of North Carolina at Chapel Hill, B.A., History & Economics, 1975; Rhodes Scholar, Oxford University, 1977; J.D., Harvard Law School, 1980; admitted to Tennessee bar, 1980; professional: attorney; Waller, Lansden, Dortch, and Davis (law firm), 1980–1982; Managing Director, Equitable Securities, 1995–1999; Adjunct Professor, Vanderbilt University Owen School of Management, 1995–2002; partner, Brentwood Capital Advisors LLC, 1999–2002; married: Martha Hays; children: Mary, Jamie, and Hayes; committees: Armed Services; Budget; elected to the U.S. House of Representatives, 1982–95; elected to the 108th Congress on November 5, 2002; reelected to each succeeding Congress.

Office Listings

http://www.cooper.house.gov

1536 Longworth House Office Building, Washington, DC 20515	(202) 225–4311
Chief of Staff.—Greg Hinote.	FAX: 226–1035
Legislative Director.—Thomas Fields.	
706 Church Street, Suite 101, Nashville, TN 37203	(615) 736–5295

Counties: CHEATHAM (part), DAVIDSON, WILSON (part). Population (2000), 632,143.

ZIP Codes: 37011, 37013, 37015, 37027, 37032, 37034–35, 37064, 37070–72, 37076, 37080, 37082, 37086–88, 37090, 37115–16, 37121–22, 37135, 37138, 37143, 37146, 37189, 37201–22, 37224, 37227–30, 37232, 37234–36, 37238–50

* * *

SIXTH DISTRICT

BART GORDON, Democrat, of Murfreesboro, TN; born in Murfreesboro, January 24, 1949; graduated, Central High School, Murfreesboro, 1967; B.S. *cum laude*, Middle Tennessee State University, Murfreesboro, 1971; J.D., University of Tennessee College of Law, Knoxville, 1973; admitted to the Tennessee State bar, 1974; opened private law practice in Murfreesboro, 1974; elected to the Tennessee Democratic Party's executive committee, 1974; appointed executive director of the Tennessee Democratic Party, 1979; elected the first full-time chairman of the Tennessee Democratic Party, 1981; resigned chairmanship, 1983, to successfully seek congressional seat; member, St. Mark's Methodist Church, Murfreesboro; past chairman: Rutherford County United Givers Fund and Rutherford County Cancer Crusade; board member: Rutherford

County Chamber of Commerce, MTSU Foundation; married: Leslie Peyton Gordon; children: Peyton Margaret; committees: Energy and Commerce; ranking member, Science; elected to the 99th Congress on November 6, 1984; reelected to each succeeding Congress.

Office Listings

http://www.house.gov/gordon

2304 Rayburn House Office Building, Washington, DC 20515	(202) 225–4231
Chief of Staff.—Chuck Atkins.	FAX: 225–6887
Executive Assistant / Scheduler.—Julie Eubank.	
P.O. Box 1986, 305 W. Main Street, Murfreesboro, TN 37133	(615) 896–1986
District Chief of Staff.—Kent Syler.	
P.O. Box 1140, 15 South Jefferson, Cookeville, TN 38501	(931) 528–5907
Sumner County Courthouse, Room B–100, Gallatin, TN 37066	(615) 451–5174

Counties: BEDFORD, CANNON, CLAY, DEKALB, JACKSON, MACON, MARSHALL, OVERTON, PUTNAM, ROBERTSON, RUTHERFORD, SMITH, SUMNER, TROUSDALE, WILSON (part). CITIES AND TOWNSHIPS: Cookeville, Gallatin, Hendersonville, Lafayette, Lebanon, Lewisburg, Livingston, Murfreesboro, Shelbyville, and Springfield. Population (2000), 632,143.

ZIP Codes: 37010, 37012, 37014, 37016, 37018–20, 37022, 37026, 37030–32, 37034, 37037, 37046–49, 37057, 37059–60, 37063, 37066, 37072–75, 37077, 37080, 37083, 37085–87, 37090–91, 37095, 37110, 37118–19, 37122, 37127–28, 37135–36, 37141, 37144–46, 37148–53, 37160–62, 37166–67, 37172, 37174, 37180, 37183–84, 37186, 37188, 37190, 37357, 37360, 37388, 38451, 38472, 38501–03, 38505–06, 38541–45, 38547–48, 38551–52, 38554, 38560, 38562–64, 38567–70, 38573–75, 38580–83, 38588–89

* * *

SEVENTH DISTRICT

MARSHA BLACKBURN, Republican, of Franklin, TN; born in Laurel, MS, June 6, 1952; education: B.S., Mississippi State University, 1973; professional: retail marketing; public service: American Council of Young Political Leaders; executive director, Tennessee Film, Entertainment, and Music Commission; chairman, Governor's Prayer Breakfast; Tennessee State Senate, 1998–2002; minority whip; community service: Rotary Club; Chamber of Commerce; Arthritis Foundation; Nashville Symphony Guild Board; Tennessee Biotechnology Association; March of Dimes; American Lung Association; awards: Chi Omega Alumnae Greek Woman of the Year, 1999; Middle Tennessee 100 Most Powerful People, 1999–2002; married: Chuck; children: Mary Morgan Ketchel and Chad; committees: Energy and Commerce; elected to the 108th Congress on November 5, 2002; reelected to each succeeding Congress.

Office Listings

http://www.house.gov/blackburn

509 Cannon House Office Building, Washington, DC 20515	(202) 225–2811
Chief of Staff.—Steve Brophy.	FAX: 225–3004
Legislative Director.—Michael Platt.	
Executive Assistant.—Joshua Mullen.	
7975 Stage Hill Boulevard, Suite 1, Memphis, TN 38133	(901) 382–5811
City Hall Mall, 201 3rd Avenue S., Suite 117, Franklin, TN 37064	(615) 591–5161

Counties: CHEATHAM (part), CHESTER, DAVIDSON (part), DECATUR, FAYETTE, HARDEMAN, HARDIN, HENDERSON, HICKMAN (part), MCNAIRY, MONTGOMERY (part), PERRY, SHELBY (part), WAYNE, WILLIAMSON (part). Population (2000), 632,139.

ZIP Codes: 37010, 37014–15, 37024–25, 37027, 37032–33, 37035–36, 37040–43, 37046, 37052, 37055, 37060, 37062, 37064–65, 37067–69, 37079, 37082, 37096–98, 37101, 37135, 37137, 37140, 37155, 37174, 37179, 37187, 37191, 37211, 37215, 37220–21, 38002, 38004, 38008, 38010–11, 38014, 38016–18, 38027–29, 38036, 38039, 38042, 38044–46, 38048–49, 38052–53, 38057, 38060–61, 38066–69, 38075–76, 38088, 38128, 38133–34, 38138–39, 38141, 38163, 38183–84, 38310–11, 38315, 38321, 38326–29, 38332, 38334, 38339–41, 38345, 38347, 38351–52, 38356–57, 38359, 38361, 38363, 38365–68, 38370–72, 38374–76, 38379–81, 38388, 38390, 38392–93, 38425, 38450, 38452, 38463, 38471, 38475, 38485–86

* * *

EIGHTH DISTRICT

JOHN S. TANNER, Democrat, of Union City, TN; born at Dyersburg Army Air Base, Halls, TN, September 22, 1944; attended elementary and high school in Union City; B.S., University of Tennessee at Knoxville, 1966; J.D., University of Tennessee at Knoxville, 1968; served, U.S. Navy, lieutenant, 1968–72; Tennessee Army National Guard, colonel, 1974–2000; attorney; admitted to the Tennessee bar in 1968 and commenced practice in Union City; member, Elam,

Glasgow, Tanner and Acree law firm until 1988; businessman; elected to Tennessee House of Representatives, 1976–88; chairman, House Committee on Commerce, 1987–88; member: Obion County Chamber of Commerce; Obion County Cancer Society; Union City Rotary Club, Paul Harris Fellow; Obion County Bar Association; American Legion; Masons; First Christian Church (Disciples of Christ) of Union City; married: the former Betty Ann Portis; children: Elizabeth Tanner Atkins and John Portis; two grandchildren; committees: Ways and Means; member: Blue Dog Coalition; Congressional Sportsmen's Caucus; elected to the 101st Congress on November 8, 1988; reelected to each succeeding Congress.

Office Listings
http://www.house.gov/tanner

1226 Longworth House Office Building, Washington, DC 20515 .... (202) 225–4714
   Administrative Assistant.—Vickie Walling.   FAX: 225–1765
   Legislative Director.—Douglas Thompson.
   Press Secretary.—Randy Ford.
   Personal Secretary.—Kathy Becker.
203 West Church Street, Union City, TN 38261 .... (731) 885–7070
   District Director.—Joe Hill.
Federal Building, Room B–7, Jackson, TN 38301 .... (731) 423–4848
8120 Highway 51 North, Suite 3, Millington, TN 38053 .... (901) 873–5690

Counties: BENTON, CARROLL, CROCKETT, DICKSON, DYER, GIBSON, HAYWOOD, HENRY, HOUSTON, HUMPHREYS, LAKE, LAUDERDALE, MADISON, MONTGOMERY (part), OBION, SHELBY (part), STEWART, TIPTON, WEAKLEY. Population (2000), 632,142.

ZIP Codes: 37015, 37023, 37025, 37028–29, 37036, 37040, 37043–44, 37050–52, 37055–56, 37058, 37061–62, 37078–79, 37097, 37101, 37134, 37142, 37165, 37171, 37175, 37178, 37181, 37185, 37187, 38001, 38004, 38006–07, 38011–12, 38015, 38019, 38021, 38023–25, 38030, 38034, 38037, 38040–41, 38047, 38049–50, 38053–55, 38058–59, 38063, 38069–71, 38075, 38077, 38079–80, 38083, 38127–29, 38135, 38201, 38220–26, 38229–33, 38235–38, 38240–42, 38251, 38253–61, 38271, 38281, 38301–03, 38305, 38308, 38313–14, 38316–18, 38320–21, 38324, 38330–31, 38333, 38336–38, 38341–44, 38346, 38348, 38355–56, 38358, 38362, 38366, 38369, 38378, 38380, 38382, 38387, 38389–92

* * *

NINTH DISTRICT

HAROLD E. FORD, JR., Democrat, of Memphis, TN; born in Memphis, May 11, 1970; son of the Honorable Harold E. Ford (D, TN–09, 1974–96) and Dorothy Bowles Ford; B.A. in American History, University of Pennsylvania, 1992; cofounded monthly newspaper, "The Vision" while at the University of Pennsylvania; J.D., University of Michigan School of Law, 1996; special assistant, Department of Commerce Economic Development Administration; Special Assistant, Justice/Civil Rights Cluster, President Clinton's 1992 transition team; aide to U.S. Senator James Sasser, Senate Budget Committee; coordinator of 1992 and 1994 reelection campaigns of U.S. Representative Harold E. Ford; member: Mt. Moriah-East Baptist Church; committees: Budget; Financial Services; subcommittees: Capital Markets, Insurance, and Government Sponsored Enterprises; Financial Institutions and Consumer Credit; elected to the 105th Congress; reelected to each succeeding Congress.

Office Listings
http://www.house.gov/ford

325 Cannon House Office Building, Washington, DC 20515 .... (202) 225–3265
   Chief of Staff.—Mark Schuermann.   FAX: 225–5663
   Deputy Chief of Staff/Executive Assistant.—Amy Mollenkamp.
   Legislative Director.—Scott Keefer.
   Communications Director.—Zac Wright.
Federal Office Building, Suite 369, 167 North Main Street, Memphis, TN 38103 ... (901) 544–4131

County: SHELBY COUNTY (part). CITY OF: Memphis. Population (2000), 632,143.

ZIP Codes: 37501, 38016–18, 38101, 38103–09, 38111–20, 38122, 38124–28, 38130–37, 38139, 38141–42, 38145–48, 38151–52, 38157, 38159, 38161, 38165–68, 38173–75, 38177, 38181–82, 38186–88, 38190, 38193–95, 38197

TEXAS

(Population 2000, 20,851,820)

SENATORS

KAY BAILEY HUTCHISON, Republican, of Dallas, TX; raised in La Marque, TX; education: graduate of The University of Texas at Austin, and University of Texas School of Law; Texas House of Representatives, 1972–76; appointed vice chair of the National Transportation Safety Board, 1976; senior vice president and general counsel, RepublicBank Corporation, and later co-founded Fidelity National Bank of Dallas; owned McCraw Candies, Inc.; political and legal correspondent for KPRC–TV, Houston; religion: Episcopalian, married: Ray Hutchison; member: development boards of SMU and Texas A&M schools of business; trustee of The University of Texas Law School Foundation; elected Texas State Treasurer, 1990; committees: Appropriations; Commerce, Science and Transportation; Rules and Administration; Veterans' Affairs; elected to the U.S. Senate, by special election, on June 5, 1993, to fill the vacancy caused by the resignation of Senator Lloyd Bentsen; reelected to each succeeding Senate term.

Office Listings
http://hutchison.senate.gov

284 Russell Senate Office Building, Washington, DC 20510	(202) 224–5922
Counsel.—David Beckwith.	FAX: 224–0776
Legislative Director.—J. Harley Walsh.	
Deputy Legislative Director.—James Christoferson.	
Press Secretary.—Chris Paulitz.	
961 Federal Building, 300 East 8th Street, Austin, TX 78701	(512) 916–5834
Chief of Staff.—Lindsey Howe Parham.	
10440 North Central Expressway, Suite 1160, LB 606, Dallas, Texas 75231	(214) 361–3500
1919 Smith Street, Suite 800, Houston, TX 77024	(713) 653–3456
222 E. Van Buren, Suite 404, Harlingen, TX 77002	(956) 423–2253
500 Chestnut Street, Suite 1570, Abilene, Texas 79602	(325) 676–2839
145 Duncan Drive, Suite 120, San Antonio, Texas 78230	(210) 340–2885

* * *

JOHN CORNYN, Republican, of San Antonio, TX; born in Houston, TX, February 2, 1952; education: graduated, Trinity University, and St. Mary's School of Law, San Antonio, TX; Masters of Law, University of Virginia, Charlottesville, VA; professional: attorney; public service: Bexar County District Court Judge; Presiding Judge, Fourth Administrative Judicial Region; Texas Supreme Court, 1990–1997; Texas Attorney General, 1999–2002; community service: Salvation Army Adult Rehabilitation Council; World Affairs Council of San Antonio; Lutheran General Hospital Board; awards: Outstanding Texas Leader Award, 2000; James Madison Award, 2001; committees: Armed Services; Budget; Judiciary; Small Business and Entrepreneurship; Joint Economic Committee; elected to the U.S. Senate on November 5, 2002.

Office Listings
http://cornyn.senate.gov

517 Hart Senate Office Building, Washington, DC 20510	(202) 224–2934
Chief of Staff.—Pete Olson.	FAX: 228–2856
Legislative Director.—Beth Jafari.	
5300 Memorial Drive, Houston, TX 77007	(713) 572–3337
Occidental Tower, 5005 LBJ Freeway, Suite 1150, Dallas, TX 75244	(972) 239–1310
100 East Ferguson Street, Suite 1004, Tyler, TX 75702	(903) 593–0902
221 West 6th Street, Suite 1530, Austin, TX 78701	(512) 469–6034
3405 22nd Street, Suite 203, Lubbock, TX 79410	(806) 472–7533
222 East Van Buren, Suite 404, Harlingen, TX 78550	(956) 423–0162

REPRESENTATIVES

FIRST DISTRICT

LOUIE GOHMERT, Republican, of Tyler, TX; born in Pittsburg, TX, August 18, 1953; education: B.A., Texas A&M University, 1975; J.D., Baylor University, Waco, TX, 1977; professional: United States Army, 1978–82; district judge, Smith County, 1992–2002; appointed by Governor Rick Perry to complete an unexpired term as Chief Justice of the 12th Court of

Appeals, 2002–03; Brigade Commander of the Corps of Cadets, Texas A&M; organizations: President of the South Tyler Rotary Club; Boy Scout District Board of Directors; religion: deacon at Green Acres Baptist Church; director of Leadership Tyler; director of Centrepoint Ministries; married: Kathy; children: Katy, Caroline, Sarah; committees: Judiciary; Resources; Small Business; subcommittees: Commercial and Administrative Law; Crime, Terrorism, and Homeland Security; Energy and Mineral Resources; Immigration, Border Security, and Claims; Regulatory Reform and Oversight; Water and Power; elected to the 109th Congress on November 2, 2004.

Office Listings
http://www.house.gov/gohmert

508 Cannon House Office Building, Washington, DC 20515 .... (202) 225–3035
    Chief of Staff.—Samantha Jordan.   FAX: 226–1230
    Legislative Director.—Michael Tomberlin.
    Press Secretary.—Amos Snead.
1121 E.S.E. Loop 323, Suite 206, Tyler, TX 75701 .... (903) 561–6349

Counties: ANGELINA, CASS (part), GREGG, HARRISON, MARION, NACOGDOCHES, PANOLA, RUSK, SABINE, SAN AUGUSTINE, SHELBY, SMITH, UPSHUR. Population (2000), 651,619.

ZIP Codes: 75551, 75555, 75562, 75564–65, 75601–08, 75615, 75631, 75633, 75637, 75639–45, 75647, 75650–54, 75657–63, 75666–67, 75669–72, 75680, 75682–85, 75687–89, 75691–94, 75701–13, 75750, 75755, 75757, 75760, 75762, 75771, 75788–89, 75791–92, 75797–99, 75901–04, 75915, 75929–31, 75935, 75937, 75941, 75943–44, 75946–49, 75954, 75958–59, 75961–65, 75968–69, 75972–75, 75978, 75980

* * *

SECOND DISTRICT

TED POE, Republican, of Humble, TX; born in Temple, TX, October 13, 1948; education: B.A., Political Science, Abilene Christian University, Abilene, TX, 1970; J.D., University of Houston, TX, 1973; professional: United States Air Force, 1970–1976; Felony Court Judge, 1981–2004; Trainer, Federal Bureau of Investigations National Academy; Chief Felony Prosecutor, District Attorney, Harris County, TX; United States Air Force Reserves Instructor, University of Houston; organizations: Board of the National Children's Alliance; Child Abuse Prevention Council; family: married to Carol; children: Kim, Kara, Kurt, and Kellee; committees: International Relations; Small Business; Transportation and Infrastructure; elected to the 109th Congress on November 2, 2004.

Office Listings
http://www.house.gov/poe

1605 Longworth House Office Building, Washington, DC 20515 .... (202) 225–6565
    Chief of Staff.—Heather Ramsey.   FAX: 225–5547
    Legislative Director.—Alan Knapp.
    Press Secretary.—Anouck McCall.
    Scheduler.—Rebecca Baca.
20202 US Highway 59 North, Suite 105, Humble, TX 77338–2400 .... (281) 446–0242

Counties: ANGELINA, CHEROKEE, GRIMES, HARDIN, HOUSTON, JASPER, LIBERTY, MONTGOMERY (part), NACOGDOCHES (part), NEWTON, ORANGE, POLK, SABINE, SAN AUGUSTINE, SAN JACINTO, TRINITY, TYLER, WALKER. Population (2000), 651,619.

ZIP Codes: 75757, 75759, 75764, 75766, 75772, 75780, 75784–85, 75789, 75834–35, 75839, 75844–45, 75847, 75849, 75851–52, 75856, 75858, 75862, 75865, 75901–04, 75915, 75925–26, 75928–34, 75936–39, 75941–42, 75944, 75947–49, 75951, 75956, 75959–61, 75965–66, 75968–69, 75972, 75976–80, 77301–03, 77306, 77320, 77326–28, 77331–32, 77334–35, 77340–42, 77350–51, 77354, 77356–60, 77363–64, 77367–69, 77371–72, 77374, 77376, 77378, 77399, 77519, 77533, 77535, 77538, 77561, 77564, 77574–75, 77582, 77585, 77611–12, 77614–17, 77624–26, 77630–32, 77639, 77656–57, 77659, 77660, 77662–64, 77670, 77830–31, 77861, 77868, 77872, 77875–76

* * *

THIRD DISTRICT

SAM JOHNSON, Republican, of Dallas, TX; born in San Antonio, TX, October 11, 1930; education: B.S., business administration, Southern Methodist University, Dallas, TX, 1951; M.A., international affairs, George Washington University, Washington, DC, 1974; military service: served in Air Force, 29 years: Korea and Vietnam (POW in Vietnam, six years, ten months); director, Air Force Fighter Weapons School; flew with Air Force Thunderbirds Precision Flying Demonstration Team; graduate of Armed Services Staff College and National War College; military awards: two Silver Stars, two Legions of Merit, Distinguished Flying Cross, one Bronze Star with Valor, two Purple Hearts, four Air Medals, and three Outstanding Unit awards; ended career with rank of colonel and Air Division commander; retired, 1979; professional: opened homebuilding company, 1979; served seven years in Texas House of Representatives; Smithsonian Board of Regents; U.S./Russian Joint Commission on POW/MIA; member: Executive Board of Dedman College, Southern Methodist University; Associated Texans Against Crime; Texas State Society; married the former Shirley L. Melton, 1950; three children, Dr. James Robert Johnson, Shirley Virginia (Gini) Mulligan, Beverly Briney; elected to Texas State House of Representatives, 1984; committees: Education and the Workforce; Ways and Means; elected to the 102nd Congress by special election on May 18, 1991, to fill the vacancy caused by the resignation of Steve Bartlett; reelected to each succeeding Congress.

Office Listings
http://www.house.gov/samjohnson

1211 Longworth House Office Building, Washington, DC 20515	(202) 225–4201
Chief of Staff.—Cody Lusk.	
Legislative Director.—Layton Skelly.	
Executive Assistant.—Ellie Mae Harrison.	
2929 North Central Expressway, Suite 240, Richardson, TX 75080	(972) 470–0892

Counties: COLLIN (part), DALLAS, (part). CITIES AND TOWNSHIPS: Allen, Dallas, Frisno, Garland, McKinney, Plano, Richardson, Rowlett, and Sachse. Population (2000), 651,620.

ZIP Codes: 75002, 75007, 75009, 75013, 75023–26, 75030, 75034–35, 75040–42, 75044–48, 75069–71, 75074–75, 75078, 75080–82, 75085–86, 75088–89, 75093–94, 75098, 75228, 75238, 75245, 75248, 75252, 75287, 75355, 75367, 75370, 75378, 75382, 75409, 75424, 75442, 75454, 78243

* * *

FOURTH DISTRICT

RALPH M. HALL, Republican, of Rockwall, TX; born in Fate, TX, May 3, 1923; education: graduated, Rockwall High School, 1941; attended Texas Christian University, University of Texas, and received LL.B., Southern Methodist University, 1951; professional: lieutenant (senior grade), U.S. Navy, carrier pilot, 1942–45; lawyer; admitted to the Texas bar in 1951 and commenced practice in Rockwall; former president and chief executive officer, Texas Aluminum Corporation; past general counsel, Texas Extrusion Company, Inc.; past organizer, chairman, board of directors, now chairman of board, Lakeside National Bank of Rockwall (now Lakeside Bancshares, Inc.); past chairman, board of directors, Lakeside News, Inc.; past vice chairman, board of directors, Bank of Crowley; president, North and East Trading Company; vice president, Crowley Holding Co.; county judge, Rockwall County, 1950–62; member, Texas State Senate, 1962–72; member: First Methodist Church; American Legion Post 117; VFW Post 6796, Rockwall Rotary Club, and Rotary Clubs International; married: the former Mary Ellen Murphy, 1944; three sons: Hampton, Brett and Blakeley; committees: Energy and Commerce; Science; elected to the 97th Congress, November 4, 1980; reelected to each succeeding Congress.

Office Listings
http://www.house.gov/ralphhall

2405 Rayburn House Office Building, Washington, DC 20515	(202) 225–6673
Chief of Staff.—Janet Perry Poppleton.	FAX: 225–3332
Legislative Director.—Grace Warren.	
104 North San Jacinto Street, Rockwall, TX 75087–2508	(972) 771–9118
District Assistant.—Tom Hughes.	
101 East Pecan Street, Suite 114, Sherman, TX 75090–5989	(903) 892–1112
District Assistant.—Judy Rowton.	
U.S. P.O., 320 Church Street, Suite 132, Sulphur Springs, TX 75482–2606	(903) 885–8138
Bowie County Courthouse, 700 James Bowie Dr., New Boston, TX 75570–2328 ...	(903) 628–8309

Counties: BOWIE COUNTY. CITIES AND TOWNSHIPS: De Kalb, Hooks, Leary, Maud, Nash, New Boston, Red Lick, Redwater, Texarkana, Wake Village. CAMP COUNTY, CITIES AND TOWNSHIPS: Pittsburg, Rocky Mound. CASS COUNTY. CITIES AND TOWNSHIPS: Atlanta, Avinger, Bloomburg, Domino, Douglassville, Hughes Springs, Linden, Marietta, Queen City. COLLIN COUNTY. CITIES AND TOWNSHIPS: Allen, Anna, Blue Ridge, Celina, Fairview, Farmersville, Frisco, Josephine, Lavon, Lowry Crossing, Lucas, McKinney, Melissa, Nevada, New Hope, Parker, Princeton, Prosper, Royse City, Sachse, St. Paul, Van Alstyne, Westminster, Weston, Wylie, Winfield. DELTA COUNTY. CITIES AND TOWNSHIPS: Cooper, Pecan Gap. FANNIN COUNTY. CITIES AND TOWNSHIPS: Bailey, Bonham, Dodd City, Ector, Honey Grove, Ladonia, Leonard, Pecan Gap, Ravenna, Savoy, Trenton, Whitewright, Windom. FRANKLIN COUNTY. CITIES AND TOWNSHIPS: Mount Vernon, Winnsboro. GRAYSON COUNTY. CITIES AND TOWNSHIPS: Bells, Collinsville, Denison, Dorchester, Gunter, Howe, Knollwood, Pottsboro, Sadler, Sherman, Southmayd, Tioga, Tom Bean, Van Alstyne, Whitesboro, Whitewright. HOPKINS COUNTY. CITIES AND TOWNSHIPS: Como, Cumby, Sulphur Springs, Tira. HUNT COUNTY. CITIES AND TOWNSHIPS: Caddo Mills, Campbell, Celeste, Commerce, Greenville, Hawk Cove, Josephine, Lone Oak, Neylandville, Quinlan, West Tawakoni, Wolfe City. LAMAR COUNTY. CITIES AND TOWNSHIPS: Blossom, Deport, Paris, Reno, Roxton, Sun Valley, Toco. MORRIS COUNTY. CITIES AND TOWNSHIPS: Daingerfield, Hughes Springs, Lone Star, Naples, Omaha.

RAINS COUNTY. CITIES AND TOWNSHIPS: Alba, East Tawakoni, Emory, Point. RED RIVER COUNTY. CITIES AND TOWN-SHIPS: Annona, Avery, Bogata, Clarksville, Deport, Detroit. ROCKWALL COUNTY. CITIES AND TOWNSHIPS: Fate, Garland, Heath, McLendon-Chisholm, Mobile City, Rockwall, Rowlett, Royse City, Wylie. TITUS COUNTY. CITIES AND TOWNSHIPS: Miller's Cove, Mount Pleasant, Talco.

ZIP Codes: 75002, 75009, 75013, 75019, 75030, 75032, 75034–35, 75040–41, 75058, 75069, 75071, 75074, 75076, 75078, 75087–88, 75090, 75094, 75097–98, 75132, 75135, 75164, 75166, 75173, 75189, 75407, 75409, 75413–14, 75416–18, 75422–24, 75426, 75428–29, 75431–33, 75435–36, 75438–40, 75442, 75446, 75449, 75452–55, 75457, 75459, 75460, 75462, 75469, 75472–73, 75474, 75476, 75477, 75479, 75482, 75486–87, 75489, 75490–95, 75501, 75550–51, 75554, 75556, 75559–61, 75563, 75566–73, 75572, 75630, 75638, 75656, 75668, 75686, 75855, 76233, 76264, 76268, 76271, 76273

* * *

FIFTH DISTRICT

JEB HENSARLING, Republican, of Dallas, TX; born in Stephenville, TX, May 29, 1957; education: B.A., economics, Texas A&M University, 1979; J.D., University of Texas School of Law, 1982; professional: businessman; vice president, Maverick Capital, 1993–1996; owner, San Jacinto Ventures, 1996–2002; vice president, Green Mountain Energy Co., 1999–2001; community service: American Cancer Society for the Dallas Metro Area; Children's Education Fund; Habitat for Humanity; religion: Christian; married: Melissa; children: Claire; committees: Budget; Financial Services; elected to the 108th Congress on November 5, 2002; reelected to each succeeding Congress.

Office Listings

http://www.house.gov/hensarling

132 Cannon House Office Building, Washington, DC 20515	(202) 225–3484
Chief of Staff.—Dee Buchanan.	FAX: 226–4888
Legislative Director.—Gerry O'Shea.	
Press Secretary.—Mike Walz.	
10675 East Northwest Highway, Suite 1685, Dallas, TX 75238	(214) 349–9996
100 East Corsicana Street, Suite 208, Athens, TX 77571	(903) 675–8288

Counties: ANDERSON, CHEROKEE, DALLAS (part), HENDERSON, KAUFMAN, VAN ZANDT, WOOD. Population (2000), 651,620.

ZIP Codes: 75030, 75032, 75041, 75043, 75047, 75049, 75088, 75103, 75114, 75117–18, 75124, 75126–27, 75140, 75142–43, 75147–50, 75156–61, 75163, 75169, 75180–82, 75185, 75187, 75214, 75218, 75227–28, 75231, 75238, 75243, 75253, 75336, 75355, 75357, 75359, 75374, 75382, 75390, 75393–94, 75410, 75444, 75474, 75480, 75494, 75497, 75751–52, 75754, 75756–59, 75763–66, 75770, 75772–73, 75778–80, 75782–85, 75789–90, 75801–03, 75832, 75839, 75844, 75853, 75861, 75880, 75882, 75884, 75886, 75925, 75976

* * *

SIXTH DISTRICT

JOE BARTON, Republican, of Ennis, TX; born in Waco, TX, September 15, 1949; education: graduated Waco High School, 1968; B.S., industrial engineering, Texas A&M University, College Station, 1972; M.S., industrial administration, Purdue University, West Lafayette, IN, 1973; professional: plant manager, assistant to the vice president, Ennis Business Forms, Inc., 1973–81; awarded White House Fellowship, 1981–82; served as aide to James B. Edwards, Secretary, Department of Energy; member, Natural Gas Decontrol Task Force in the Office of Planning, Policy and Analysis; worked with the Department of Energy task force in support of the President's Private Sector Survey on Cost Control; natural gas decontrol and project cost control consultant, Atlantic Richfield Company; cofounder, Houston County Volunteer Ambulance Service, 1976; vice president, Houston County Industrial Development Authority, 1980; chairman, Crockett Parks and Recreation Board, 1979–80; vice president, Houston County Chamber of Commerce, 1977–80; member, Dallas Energy Forum; religion: Methodist; married: Terri; children: Brad, Alison and Kristin, from a previous marriage; stepchildren: Lindsay and Cullen; committees: chair, Energy and Commerce; elected to the 99th Congress on November 6, 1984; reelected to each succeeding Congress.

Office Listings

http://www.joebarton.house.gov

2109 Rayburn House Office Building, Washington, DC 20515	(202) 225–2002
Chief of Staff.—Heather Couri.	FAX: 225–3052
Legislative Director.—Theresa Lavery.	
Press Secretary.—Brooks Landgraf.	
Scheduler.—Linda Gillespie.	
6001 West I–20, Suite 200, Arlington, TX 76107	(817) 543–1000
2106A West Ennis Avenue, Ennis, TX 75119	(972) 875–8488

Counties: ELLIS, FREESTONE, HOUSTON, LEON, LIMESTONE, NAVARRO, TARRANT, TRINITY. CITIES AND TOWNSHIPS: Arlington, Bardwell, Buffalo, Centerville, Corsicana, Crockett, Crowley, Dawson, Ennis, Fairfield, Ferris, Fort Worth, Frost, Grapeland, Groveton, Italy, Kerens, Lovelady, Mansfield, Maypearl, Mexia, Midlothian, Milford, Oak Leaf, Palmer, Pecan Hill, Red Oak, Rice, Richland, and Waxahachie. Population (2000), 651,620.

ZIP Codes: 75050, 75052, 75054, 75101–02, 75104–06, 75109–10, 75119–20, 75125, 75144, 75146, 75151–55, 75165, 75167–68, 75831, 75833–35, 75838, 75840, 75844–52, 75855–56, 75858–60, 75862, 75865, 75926, 76001–07, 76010–19, 76028, 76036, 76040–41, 76050, 76055, 76060, 76063–65, 76084, 76094, 76096–97, 76119–20, 76123, 76126, 76132–34, 76140, 76155, 76162–63, 76623, 76626, 76635, 76639, 76641–42, 76651, 76667, 76670, 76679, 76681, 76686, 76693, 77850, 77855, 77865, 77871

* * *

SEVENTH DISTRICT

JOHN ABNEY CULBERSON, Republican, of Harris County, TX; born in Houston, TX, August 24, 1956; education: B.A., Southern Methodist University; J.D., South Texas College of Law; professional: attorney; awards: Citizens for a Sound Economy Friend of the Taxpayer Award; Texas Eagle Forum Freedom and Family Award; Houston Jaycees Outstanding Young Houstonian Award; public service: Texas House of Representatives, 1987–2000; married: Belinda Burney, 1989; children: Caroline; committees: Appropriations; elected to the 107th Congress on November 7, 2000; reelected to each succeeding Congress.

Office Listings

http://www.house.gov/culberson

1728 Longworth House Office Building, Washington, DC 20515	(202) 225–2571
Chief of Staff.—Bill Crow.	FAX: 225–4381
Legislative Director.—Tony Essalih.	
Office Manager.—Jamie Gahun.	
10000 Memorial Drive, Suite 620, Houston, TX 77024–3490	(713) 682–8828
District Director.—Nick Swyka.	

County: HARRIS COUNTY (part). Population (2000), 651,620.

ZIP Codes: 77002, 77004–08, 77019, 77024–25, 77027, 77030, 77035–36, 77040–43, 77046, 77055–57, 77063–65, 77070, 77074, 77077, 77079–81, 77084, 77086, 77094–96, 77098, 77215, 77218–19, 77224–25, 77227, 77241–44, 77255–57, 77265–66, 77269, 77277, 77279–82, 77284, 77401–02, 77429, 77433

* * *

EIGHTH DISTRICT

KEVIN BRADY, Republican, of The Woodlands, TX; born in Vermillion, SD, April 11, 1955; education: B.S., business, University of South Dakota; professional: served in Texas House of Representatives, 1991–96, the first Republican to capture the 15th District seat since the 1800s; awards: Achievement Award, Texas Conservative Coalition; Outstanding Young Texan (one of five), Texas Jaycees; Ten Best Legislators for Families and Children, State Bar of Texas; Legislative Standout, Dallas Morning News; Scholars Achievement Award for Excellence in Public Service, North Harris Montgomery Community College District; Victims Rights Equalizer Award, Texans for Equal Justice Center; Support for Family Issues Award, Texas Extension Homemakers Association; chair, Council of Chambers of Greater Houston; president, East Texas Chamber Executive Association; president, South Montgomery County Woodlands Chamber of Commerce, 1985–present; director, Texas Chamber of Commerce Executives; Rotarian; religion: attends Saints Simon and Jude Catholic Church; married: Cathy Brady; committees: Ways and Means; Joint Economic Committee; subcommittees: Social Security, Trade; elected to the 105th Congress; reelected to each succeeding Congress.

Office Listings

http://www.house.gov/brady

428 Cannon House Office Building, Washington, DC 20515	(202) 225–4901
Chief of Staff.—Doug Centilli.	
Press Secretary.—Sarah Stephens.	
Legislative Director.—David Malech.	
200 River Pointe Drive, Suite 304, Conroe, TX 77304	(936) 441–5700
District Director.—Heather Montgomery.	
1202 Sam Houston Avenue, Suite 7, Huntsville, TX 77340	(936) 439–9542
420 Green Avenue, Orange, TX 77630	(409) 883–4197

COUNTIES: HARDIN, JASPER, LIBERTY (part), MONTGOMERY, NEWTON, ORANGE, POLK, SAN JACINTO, TRINTY (part), TYLER, WALKER. CITIES AND TOWNSHIPS: Bevil Oaks, Bridge City, Browndell, Buna, Chester, Coldspring, Conroe, Colmesneil,

Corrigan, Cut and Shoot, Dayton Lakes, Deweyville, Evadale, Goodrich, Hardin, Huntsville, Jasper, Kenefick, Kirbyville, Kountze, Lake Livingston, Lumberton, Magnolia, Mauriceville, Montgomery, New Waverly, Newton, Oak Ridge North, Oakhurst, Onalaska, Orange, Palton Village, Panorama Village, Pine Forest, Pinehurst, Pinewood Estates, Point Blank, Porter Heights, Roman Fores, Rose City, Rose Hill Acres, Seven Oaks, Shenandoah, Shepherd, Silshee, Sour Lake, South Toledo Bend, Splendora, Stagecoach, The Woodlands, Trinity, Vidor, West Livingston, West Orange, Willis, Woodbranch, and Woodville. Population (2000), 651,619.

ZIP Codes: 75931, 75951, 75956, 75966, 77318, 77320, 77340–44, 77348–49, 77350–51, 77355, 77359–60, 77364, 77367, 77371, 77378, 77399, 77561, 77611, 77614, 77630–32, 77656, 77659, 77862, 77939

* * *

NINTH DISTRICT

AL GREEN, Democrat, of Houston, TX; born in New Orleans, LA, September 1, 1947; raised in Florida; education: A&M University, 1966–71; attended Tuskegee University, Tuskegee, AL; J.D., Texas Southern University, Houston, TX, 1974; professional: co-founded and co-managed the law firm of Green, Wilson, Dewberry and Fitch; Justice of the Peace, Precinct 7, Position 2, 1977–2004; organizations: former president of the Houston NAACP; Houston Citizens Chamber of Commerce; awards: Distinguished Service Award, 1978; Black Heritage Society, Outstanding Leadership Award, 1981; American Federation of Teachers, Citation for Service as a "Courageous Defender of Due Process for Educators," 1983; committees: Financial Services; Science; elected to the 109th Congress on November 2, 2004.

Office Listings

http://www.house.gov/algreen

1529 Longworth House Office Building, Washington, DC 20515	(202) 225–7508
Chief of Staff.—Jacqueline Ellis.	FAX: 225–2947
Legislative Director.—Oscar Ramirez.	
Senior Legislative Assistant.—Jessica Swafford.	
Communications Director.—Ashley Etienne.	
3003 South Loop West, Suite 460, Houston, TX 77054	(713) 383–9234
District Director.—Lucinda Daniels.	

Counties: FORT BEND, HARRIS. Population (2000), 651,619.

ZIP Codes: 77004–05, 77021, 77025, 77030–31, 77033, 77035–36, 77042, 77045, 77047–48, 77051, 77053–54, 77056–57, 77061, 77063, 77071–72, 77074, 77077, 77081–83, 77085, 77087, 77096, 77099, 77230–31, 77233, 77235–37, 77251, 77254, 77263, 77271–72, 77274, 77401, 77411, 77469, 77477–78, 77489

* * *

TENTH DISTRICT

MICHAEL T. McCAUL, Republican, of Austin, TX; born in Dallas, TX, January 14, 1962; education: B.S., Trinity University, San Antonio, TX, 1984; J.D., St. Mary's University, San Antonio, TX, 1987; professional: lawyer, private practice; deputy attorney general, office of Texas state attorney general; committees: Homeland Security; International Relations; Science; elected to the 109th Congress on November 2, 2004.

Office Listings

http://www.house.gov/mccaul

415 Cannon House Office Building, Washington, DC 20515	(202) 225–2401
Chief of Staff.—Matt Miller.	FAX: 225–5955
Deputy Chief of Staff / Legislative Director.—Gene Irisari.	
Scheduler / Office Manager.—Kelly Richardson.	
300 East 8th Street, LBJ Suite, Ninth Floor, Austin, TX 78701	(512) 473–2357
Rosewood Professional Bldg., 990 Village Square, Suite B, Tomball, TX 77375	(281) 733–0999

Counties: AUSTIN, BASTROP, BURLESON, HARRIS, LEE, TRAVIS, WALLER, WASHINGTON. Population (2000), 651,619.

ZIP Codes: 77070, 77084, 77094–95, 77218, 77269, 77284, 77375, 77377, 77379, 77383, 77388–89, 77391, 77410, 77413, 77418, 77423, 77426, 77429, 77433, 77445–47, 77449–50, 77452, 77466, 77473–74, 77476, 77484–85, 77491–94, 77833–36, 77838, 77852–53, 77863, 77868, 77878–80, 78602, 78615, 78621, 78650–51, 78653, 78659–60, 78664, 78682–83, 78691, 78703, 78705, 78708, 78710, 78713, 78716, 78718, 78720, 78724, 78727–31, 78733, 78746, 78751–59, 78761, 78763, 78765–66, 78779–80, 78785, 78788–89, 78931–33, 78940, 78942, 78944, 78946–48, 78950

ELEVENTH DISTRICT

K. MICHAEL CONAWAY, Republican, of Midland, TX; born in Borger, TX, June 11, 1948; education: B.B.A., Texas A&M–Commerce, 1970; professional: owner, K. Conaway CPA, 1993–present; Senior Vice President, Texas Commerce Bank, 1990–92; Senior Vice President/ Chief Financial Officer, United Bank, 1987–90; Chief Financial Officer, Spectrum 7 Energy Corporation, 1984–86; Chief Financial Officer, Bush Exploration Company, 1982–84; Chief Financial Officer, Keith D. Graham & Lantern Petroleum Company, 1980–81; tax manager, Price Waterhouse & Company, 1972–80; Spec 5 United States Army, 1970–72; religion: Baptist; married: Suzanne; children: Brian, Erin, Kara, and Stephanie; Assistant Whip; committees: Agriculture; Armed Services; Budget; elected to the 109th Congress on November 2, 2004.

Office Listings
http://www.house.gov/conaway

511 Cannon House Office Building, Washington, DC 20515 .... (202) 225–3605
  Chief of Staff.—Jeff Burton.   FAX: 225–1783
  Legislative Director.—Michael Beckerman:
  Scheduler.—Cassandra Harrison.
6 Desta Drive, Suite 2000, Midland, TX 79705 .... (432) 687–2390
  District Scheduler.—Patsy Bain.
33 East Twohig, Room 307, San Angelo, TX 76903 .... (325) 659–4010
  Regional Director.—Joanne Powell.

Counties: ANDREWS, BROWN, BURNET, COKE, COLEMAN, COMANCHE, CONCHO, CRANE, DAWSON, ECTOR, GILLESPIE, MENARD, MIDLAND, MILLS, GLASSCOCK, IRION, KIMBLE, LAMPASAS, LLANO, LOVING, MARTIN, MASON, MCCULLOCH, SUTTON (part), TOM GREEN, UPTON, MITCHELL, NOLAN (part), REAGAN, RUNNELS, SAN SABA, SCHLEICHER, SCURRY, STERLING, WARD, WINKLER. POPULATION (2000), 651,620.

ZIP Codes: 76246, 76432, 76442, 76444, 76455, 76550, 76801–04, 76821, 76823, 76825, 76834, 76837, 76844, 76853, 76856, 76859, 76861, 76864, 76866, 76872–73, 76877, 76901–04, 76932–33, 76935–36, 76941, 76945, 76950–51, 76957, 77381–82, 77393, 78611, 78624, 78643, 78654–69, 79331, 79512, 79532, 79545, 79549–50, 79556, 79565, 79567, 79605–09, 79714, 79760–69, 79701–13, 79739, 79742, 79745, 79756, 79778, 79789

* * *

TWELFTH DISTRICT

KAY GRANGER, Republican, of Fort Worth, TX; born in Greenville, TX, January 18, 1943; education: B.S., *magna cum laude*, 1965, and Honorary Doctorate of Humane Letters, 1992, Texas Wesleyan University; professional: owner, Kay Granger Insurance Agency, Inc.; former public school teacher; elected Mayor of Fort Worth, 1991, serving three terms; during her tenure, Fort Worth received All-America City Award from the National Civic League; former Fort Worth Councilwoman; past chair, Fort Worth Zoning Commission; past board member: Dallas-Fort Worth International Airport; North Texas Commission; Fort Worth Convention and Visitors Bureau; U.S. Conference of Mayors Advisory Board; Business and Professional Women's Woman of the Year, 1989; three grown children: J.D., Brandon and Chelsea; first woman Republican to represent Texas in the U.S. House; committees: Appropriations; Deputy Republican Whip; elected to the 105th Congress; reelected to each succeeding Congress.

Office Listings
http://www.house.gov/granger

440 Cannon House Office Building, Washington, DC 20515 .... (202) 225–5071
  Deputy Chief of Staff.—Robert Head.   FAX: 225–5683
  Legislative Director.—Darin Gardner.
  Scheduler.—Stacey Kounelias.
  Staff Assistant.—Andrew Acker.
1701 River Run Road, Suite 407, Fort Worth, TX 76107 .... (817) 338–0909
  District Director.—Barbara Ragland.   (817) 335–5852

Counties: PARKER, TARRANT (part), WISE. Population (2000), 651,619.

ZIP Codes: 76008, 76020, 76023, 76035–36, 76049, 76052, 76066–68, 76071, 76073, 76078, 76082, 76085–88, 76098, 76101–02, 76104, 76106–11, 76113–18, 76121–23, 76126–27, 76129–37, 76147–48, 76161–64, 76177, 76179–82, 76185, 76191–93, 76195–99, 76225, 76234, 76244, 76246, 76248, 76262, 76267, 76270, 76299, 76426, 76431, 76439, 76462, 76485–87, 76490

THIRTEENTH DISTRICT

MAC THORNBERRY, Republican, of Clarendon, TX; born in Clarendon, July 15, 1958; education: graduate, Clarendon High School; B.A., Texas Tech University; University of Texas, law degree; professional: rancher, attorney; admitted to the Texas bar, 1983; member: Texas and Southwestern Cattle Raisers; co-chair of the Congressional Oil and Gas Forum; Rural Health Care Coalition, and co-founder/co-chair of Defense Study Group; married: Sarah Adams, 1986; children: Will and Mary Kemp; committees: Armed Services; Permanent Select Committee on Intelligence; subcommittees: chairman, Oversight; Terrorism, Unconventional Threats and Capabilities; Strategic Forces; elected to the 104th Congress; reelected to each succeeding Congress.

Office Listings

http://www.house.gov/thornberry

2457 Rayburn House Office Building, Washington, DC 20515	(202) 225–3706
Administrative Assistant.—Kim Kotlar.	FAX: 225–3486
Office Manager.—Erin Dowd.	
905 South Filmore, Suite 520, Amarillo, TX 79101	(806) 371–8844
Chief of Staff.—Bill Harris.	
4245 Kemp, Suite 506, Wichita Falls, TX 76308	(940) 692–1700

Counties: ARCHER (part), ARMSTRONG, BAYLOR, BRISCOE, CARSON, CHILDRESS, CLAY, COLLINGSWORTH, COOKE (part), COTTLE, CROSBY, DALLAM, DICKENS, DONLEY, FOARD, GRAY, HALL, HANSFORD, HARDEMAN, HARTLEY, HASKELL, HEMPHILL, HUTCHINSON, JACK, JONES, KING, KNOX, LIPSCOMB, MONTAGUE, MOORE, MOTLEY, OCHILTREE, OLDHAM, PALO PINTO, POTTER, RANDALL, ROBERTS, SHERMAN, STONEWALL, SWISHER, THROCKMORTON, WHEELER, WICHITA, WILBARGER. Population (2000), 651,619.

ZIP Codes: 76066, 76067–68, 76228, 76230, 76234, 76238–40, 76250–53, 76255, 76261, 76263, 76265–66, 76270, 76272, 76301–02, 76305–11, 76352, 76354, 76357, 76360, 76363–67, 76369, 76371–73, 76377, 76379–80, 76384–85, 76388–89, 76427, 76430, 76449–50, 76453, 76458–59, 76462–63, 76472, 76475, 76483–84, 76486–87, 76491, 79001–03, 79005, 79007–08, 79010–16, 79018–19, 79022, 79024, 79029, 79033–34, 79036, 79039–40, 79042, 79044, 79046, 79051–52, 79054, 79056–59, 79061–62, 79065–66, 79068, 79070, 79077–81, 79083–84, 79086–88, 79091–97, 79101–11, 79116–21, 79124, 79159, 79166, 79168, 79172, 79174, 79178, 79185, 79187, 79189, 79201, 79220, 79223, 79225–27, 79229–30, 79233–34, 79236–37, 79239, 79243–45, 79247–48, 79251–52, 79255–57, 79259, 79261, 79322, 79343, 79357, 79370, 79501–03, 79505, 79520–21, 79525, 79529, 79533, 79536, 79539–40, 79544, 79547–48, 79553, 79560, 79601

* * *

FOURTEENTH DISTRICT

RON PAUL, Republican, of Surfside Beach, TX; born in Pittsburgh, PA, August 20, 1935; education: B.A., Gettysburg College, 1957; M.D., Duke College of Medicine, North Carolina, 1961; professional: captain, U.S. Air Force, 1963–68; obstetrician and gynecologist; represented Texas' 22nd District in the U.S. House of Representatives, 1976–1977, and 1979–85; married: the former Carol Wells, 1957; children: Ronnie, Lori, Pyeatt, Rand, Robert and Joy LeBlanc; committees: Financial Services; International Relations; Joint Economic Committee; elected to the 105th Congress; reelected to each succeeding Congress.

Office Listings

http://www.house.gov/paul

203 Cannon House Office Building, Washington, DC 20515	(202) 225–2831
Chief of Staff.—Tom Lizardo.	
Legislative Director.—Norman Singleton.	
Press Secretary.—Jeff Deist.	
312 South Main, Suite 228, Victoria, TX 77901	(361) 576–1231
200 W. 2nd Street, Suite 210, Freeport, TX 77541	(979) 230–0000

Counties: ARANSAS, BRAZORIA (part), CALHOUN, CHAMBERS, FORT BEND (part), GALVESTON (part), JACKSON, MATAGORDA, VICTORIA, WHARTON. Population (2000), 651,619.

ZIP Codes: 77082, 77404, 77414–15, 77417, 77419–20, 77422–23, 77428, 77430–32, 77435–37, 77440–41, 77443–44, 77448, 77450–51, 77453–58, 77461, 77463–65, 77467–69, 77471, 77476, 77480, 77482–83, 77485–86, 77488, 77493–94, 77510–12, 77514–18, 77520–21, 77531, 77534–35, 77539, 77541–42, 77546, 77549–55, 77560, 77563, 77565–66, 77568, 77571, 77573–74, 77577–78, 77580–81, 77583–84, 77590–92, 77597, 77617, 77623, 77650, 77661, 77665, 77901–05, 77951, 77957, 77961–62, 77968–71, 77973, 77976–79, 77982–83, 77988, 77991, 77995, 78336, 78358, 78381–82

FIFTEENTH DISTRICT

RUBÉN HINOJOSA, Democrat, of Mercedes, TX; born in Mercedes, August 20, 1940; education: B.B.A., 1962, and M.B.A., 1980, University of Texas; professional: president and chief financial officer, H&H Foods, Inc.; board of directors, National Livestock and Meat Board and Texas Beef Industry Council, 1989–93; past president and past chairman of the board of directors, Southwestern Meat Packers Association; chairman and member of board of trustees, South Texas Community College, 1993–96; past public member, Texas State Bar Board of Directors; former adjunct professor, Pan American University School of Business; elected member, Texas State Board of Education, 1975–84; past director, Rio Grande Valley Chamber of Commerce; Knapp Memorial Hospital Board of Trustees; and Our Lady of Mercy Church Board of Catholic Advisors; past member, board of trustees, Mercedes Independent School District; former U.S. Jaycee Ambassador to Colombia and Ecuador; married: Martha; children: Ruben, Jr., Laura, Iliana, Kaitlin, and Karen; committees: Education and the Workforce; Financial Services; elected to the 105th Congress; reelected to each succeeding Congress.

Office Listings

http://www.house.gov/hinojosa

2463 Rayburn House Office Building, Washington, DC 20515 .... (202) 225–2531
Chief of Staff.—Rita Jaramillo. FAX: 225–5688
Legislative Director.—Connie Humphrey.
Senior Advisor.—Greg Davis.
Press Secretary.—Ciaran Clayton.
311 North 15th Street, McAllen, TX 78501 .... (956) 682–5545
District Director.—Salomon Torres.
107 South St. Mary's Street, Beeville, TX 78102 .... (361) 358–8400
District Director.—Judy McAda.

Counties: BEE, BROOKS, GOLIAD, HIDALGO (part), KLEBERG (part), LIVE OAK, NUECES (part), SAN PATRICIO. CITIES AND TOWNSHIPS: Agua Dulce, Alamo, Beeville, Bishop, Donna, Driscoll, Edcouch, Edinburg, Elroy, Elsa, Goliad, Gregory, Kingsville, LaVilla, Mathis, McAllen, Mercedes, Mission, Odem, Pharr, Portland, Robstown, San Juan, Sinton, Taft, Three Rivers, and Weslaco. Population: (2000) 651,619.

ZIP Codes: 77905, 77954, 77960, 77963, 77967, 77974, 77989, 77993–94, 78022, 78060, 78071, 78075, 78102, 78104, 78107, 78119, 78125, 78142, 78145–46, 78151, 78162, 78330, 78332, 78335–36, 78343, 78350, 78352–53, 78355, 78359, 78362–64, 78368, 78370, 78372, 78374, 78380, 78383, 78387, 78389–91, 78501–05, 78516, 78537–41, 78543, 78549, 78557–58, 78561–63, 78565, 78569–70, 78572–74, 78577, 78579–80, 78589, 78595–96, 78599

* * *

SIXTEENTH DISTRICT

SILVESTRE REYES, Democrat, of El Paso, TX; born in Canutillo, TX, November 10, 1944; education: graduated, Canutillo High School, 1964; associate degree, El Paso Community College, 1976; attended University of Texas, Austin, 1964–65, and El Paso, 1965–66; served in U.S. Army, 1966–68, Vietnam combat veteran; U.S. Border Patrol, chief patrol agent, 26½ years, retired December 1, 1995; member: Canutillo School Board, 1968–69, 21st Century Democrats, El Paso County Democrats, and Unite El Paso; married: the former Carolina Gaytan, 1968; children: Monica, Rebecca and Silvestre Reyes, Jr.; committees: Armed Services; Veterans' Affairs; Permanent Select Committee on Intelligence; elected on November 5, 1996, to the 105th Congress; reelected to each succeeding Congress.

Office Listings

http://www.house.gov/reyes

2433 Rayburn House Office Building, Washington, DC 20515 .... (202) 225–4831
Chief of Staff.—Perry Finney Brody. FAX: 225–2016
Press Secretary.—Kira Maas.
Scheduler / Office Manager.—Liza Lynch.
Suite 400, 310 North Mesa, El Paso, TX 79901 .... (915) 534–4400
Deputy Chief of Staff.—Sal Payan.

Counties: EL PASO (part). CITIES AND TOWNSHIPS: Anthony, Canutillo, Clint, El Paso, Fabens, Horizon City, San Elizario, Socorro, Vinton, and Westway. Population (2000), 651,619.

ZIP Codes: 79821, 79835–36, 79838–39, 79849, 79901–08, 79910, 79912–18, 79920, 79922–27, 79929–32, 79934–38, 79940–55, 79958, 79960–61, 79968, 79976, 79978, 79980, 79995–99, 88510–21, 88523–36, 88538–50, 88553–63, 88565–90, 88595

SEVENTEENTH DISTRICT

CHET EDWARDS, Democrat, of Waco, TX; born in Corpus Christi, TX, November 24, 1951; education: graduated Memorial High School, Houston, TX, 1970; B.A., Texas A&M University, College Station, 1974; M.B.A., Harvard Business School, Boston, MA, 1981; professional: served as legislative assistant to Texas Congressman Olin "Tiger" Teague, 1974–77; marketing representative, Trammell Crow Company, 1981–85; president, Edwards Communications, Inc.; member, Texas State Senate, 1983–90; married: the former Lea Ann Wood; children: John Thomas and Garrison Alexander; committees: Appropriations; Budget; elected to the 102nd Congress, November 6, 1990; reelected to each succeeding Congress.

Office Listings

http://edwards.house.gov

2264 Rayburn House Office Building, Washington, DC 20515	(202) 225–6105
Administrative Assistant.—Chris Chwastyk.	FAX: 225–0350
Press Secretary.—Joshua Taylor.	
600 Austin Avenue, Suite 29, Waco, TX 76710	(254) 752–9600
District Director.—Sam Murphey.	
Wright Plaza, 115 South Main Street, Suite 202, Cleburne, TX 76033	(817) 645–4743
Deputy District Director.—Chris Turner.	
111 University Drive East, Suite 216, College Station, TX 77840	(979) 691–8797

Counties: BOSQUE, BRAZOS, BURLESON (part), GRIMES (part), HILL, HOOD, JOHNSON, LIMESTONE (part), MADISON, MCLENNAN, ROBERTSON (part), SOMMERVELL. CITIES OF: Anderson, Bryan, Cleburne, College Station, Glen Rose, Granbury, Groesbeck, Hillsboro, Madisonville, Miami, Valley Mills, and Waco. Population (2005), 651,786.

ZIP Codes: 75846, 75852, 76009, 76028, 76031, 76033, 76035–36, 76043–44, 76048–50, 76055, 76058–59, 76061, 76063, 76070, 76077, 76084, 76087, 76093, 76097, 76433, 76439, 76462, 76465, 76467, 76476, 76524, 76557, 76561, 76596, 76621–22, 76624, 76627–31, 76633–38, 76640, 76642–45, 76648–50, 76652–55, 76657, 76660, 76664–66, 76670–71, 76673, 76676, 76678, 76682, 76684, 76687, 76689–92, 76701–08, 76710–12, 76714–16, 76795, 76797–99, 77333, 77356, 77363, 77801–03, 77805–08, 77830–31, 77836–38, 77840–45, 77852, 77856, 77859, 77861–64, 77866–68, 77870, 77872–73, 77875–76, 77878–79, 77881–82

* * *

EIGHTEENTH DISTRICT

SHEILA JACKSON LEE, Democrat, of Houston, TX; born in Queens, NY, January 12, 1950; education: graduated, Jamaica High School; B.A., Yale University, New Haven, CT, 1972; J.D., University of Virginia Law School, 1975; professional: practicing attorney for 12 years; AKA Sorority; Houston Area Urban League; American Bar Association; staff counsel, U.S. House Select Committee on Assassinations, 1977–78; admitted to the Texas bar, 1975; city council (at large), Houston, 1990–94; Houston Municipal Judge, 1987–90; married Dr. Elwyn Cornelius Lee, 1973; two children: Erica Shelwyn and Jason Cornelius Bennett; committees: Homeland Security; Judiciary; Science; elected to the 104th Congress; reelected to each succeeding Congress.

Office Listings

http://www.jacksonlee.house.gov

2435 Rayburn Cannon House Office Building, Washington, DC 20515	(202) 225–3816
Chief of Staff.—Leon Buck.	
Administrative Assistant.—Matt Haist.	
Senior Legislative Counsel.—Dana Thompson.	
Scheduler.—Jeanette Lenoir.	
1919 Smith Street, Suite 1180, Mickey Leland Building, Houston, TX 77002	(713) 655–0050
District Director.—Cynthia Buggage.	
420 West 19th Street, Houston, TX 77008	(713) 861–4070

Counties: HARRIS COUNTY (part). CITY OF: Houston. Population (2000), 651,620.

ZIP Codes: 77001–10, 77013, 77016, 77018–24, 77026, 77028–30, 77033, 77035, 77038, 77040–41, 77045, 77047–48, 77051–52, 77054–55, 77064, 77066–67, 77076, 77078, 77080, 77086–88, 77091–93, 77097–98, 77201–06, 77208, 77210, 77212, 77216, 77219, 77221, 77226, 77230, 77233, 77238, 77240–41, 77251–53, 77255, 77265–66, 77277, 77288, 77291–93, 77297–99

NINETEENTH DISTRICT

RANDY NEUGEBAUER, Republican, of Lubbock, TX; born in St. Louis, MO, December 24, 1949; education: Texas Tech University, 1972; professional: small businessman (home building industry); organizations: West Texas Home Builders Association; Land Use and Developers Council; Texas Association of Builders; National Association of Home Builders; Campus Crusade for Christ; public service: Lubbock City Council, 1992–1998; served as Mayor Pro Tempore, 1994–1996; leader of coalition to create the Ports-to-Plains Trade Corridor; awards: Lubbock Chamber of Commerce Distinguished Service Award; Reese Air Force Base Friend of Reese Award; religion: Baptist; married: to Dana; two children; committees: Agriculture; Financial Services; elected to the 108th Congress, by special election, on June 3, 2003; reelected to the 109th Congress on November 2, 2004.

Office Listings

429 Cannon House Office Building, Washington, DC 20515	(202) 225–4005
Chief of Staff.—Gayland Barksdale.	FAX: 225–9615
Communications Director.—Josh Noland.	
Federal Building, 1205 Texas Avenue, Room 810, Lubbock, TX 79401	(806) 763–1611
District Director.—Jimmy Clark.	

Counties: ARCHER, BAILEY, BORDEN, CALLAHAN, CASTRO, COCHRAN, DEAF SMITH, EASTLAND, FISHER, FLOYD, GAINES, GARZA, HALE, HOCKLEY, HOWARD, KENT, LAMB, LUBBOCK, LYNN, NOLAN, PARMER, SHACKELFORD, STEPHENS, TAYLOR, TERRY, YOAKUM, YOUNG. Population (2000), 651,619.

ZIP Codes: 76302, 76305, 76308, 76310, 76351, 76360, 76366, 76370, 76372, 76374, 76379, 76389, 76424, 76427, 76429–30, 76435, 76437, 76442–43, 76445, 76448, 76450, 76454, 76459–60, 76462–64, 76466, 76469–70, 76475, 76481, 76491, 79009, 79021, 79025, 79027, 79031–32, 79035, 79041, 79043, 79045, 79053, 79063–64, 79072–73, 79082, 79085, 79221, 79231, 79235, 79241, 79250, 79258, 79311–14, 79316, 79320, 79323–26, 79329–30, 79336, 79338–39, 79342, 79344–47, 79350–51, 79353, 79355–56, 79358–60, 79363–64, 79366–67, 79369–73, 79376, 79378–83, 79401–16, 79423–24, 79430, 79452–53, 79457, 79464, 79490–91, 79493, 79499, 79504, 79506, 79508, 79510–11, 79518–20, 79526, 79528, 79530, 79532–37, 79541, 79543, 79545–46, 79549, 79556, 79560–63, 79566–67, 79601–05, 79720–21, 79733, 79738, 79748

* * *

TWENTIETH DISTRICT

CHARLES A. GONZALEZ, Democrat, of San Antonio, TX; born in San Antonio, May 5, 1945; son of former Representative Henry Gonzalez, who served the 20th district from 1961–99; education: Thomas A. Edison High School, 1965; B.A., University of Texas at Austin, 1969; J.D., St. Mary's School of Law, 1972; elementary school teacher; private attorney, 1972–82; Municipal Court Judge; County Court at Law Judge, 1983–87; District Judge, 1989–97; committees: Energy and Commerce; Democratic Regional Whip; chair, Congressional Hispanic Caucus Civil Rights Task Force; elected to the 106th Congress; reelected to each succeeding Congress.

Office Listings

327 Cannon House Office Building, Washington, DC 20515	(202) 225–3236
Chief of Staff.—Kevin Kimble.	FAX: 225–1915
Executive Assistant.—Rose Ann Maldonado.	
Legislative Director.—Tony Zaffirini.	
Communications Director.—Adrian Saenz.	
Federal Building, B–124, 727 East Durango Boulevard, San Antonio, TX 78206 ...	(210) 472–6195

Counties: BEXAR COUNTY (part). CITIES OF: Alamo Heights, Balcones Heights, Converse, Kirby, Lackland AFB, Leon Valley, and San Antonio. Population (2000), 651,619.

ZIP Codes: 78073, 78109, 78201–19, 78225–31, 78233, 78236–46, 78250, 78252, 78254

* * *

TWENTY-FIRST DISTRICT

LAMAR S. SMITH, Republican, of San Antonio, TX; born in San Antonio, November 19, 1947; education: graduated from Texas Military Institute, San Antonio, 1965; B.A., Yale University, New Haven, CT, 1969; management intern, Small Business Administration, Washington, DC, 1969–70; business and financial writer, *The Christian Science Monitor*, Boston, MA, 1970–72; J.D., Southern Methodist University School of Law, Dallas, TX, 1975; admitted to the State bar of Texas, 1975, and commenced practice in San Antonio with the firm of Maebius and Duncan, Inc.; elected chairman of the Republican Party of Bexar County, TX, 1978 and 1980; elected District 57–F State Representative, 1981; elected Precinct 3 Commissioner of Bexar County, 1982 and 1984; partner, Lamar Seeligson Ranch, Jim Wells County, TX; married: Beth Schaefer; children: Nell Seeligson and Tobin Wells; committees: Homeland Security; Judiciary; Science; Standards of Official Conduct; subcommittees: chairman, Courts, the Internet, and Intellectual Property; elected to the 100th Congress on November 4, 1986; reelected to each succeeding Congress.

Office Listings
http://lamarsmith.house.gov

2184 Rayburn House Office Building, Washington, DC 20515 .... (202) 225–4236
    Chief of Staff / Assistant to the Chairman.—Joseph Gibson.   FAX: 225–8628
    Administrative Assistant / Scheduler.—Jennifer Brown.
Guaranty Federal Building, Suite 640, 1100 North East Loop 410, San Antonio,
    TX 78209 .... (210) 821–5024
    District Director.—O'Lene Stone.
5608 Parkcrest Drive, Suite 260, Austin, TX 78731 .... (512) 402–9743

Counties: BEXAR (part), BLANCO, COMAL, HAYS (part), TRAVIS (part). Population (2000), 651,619.

ZIP Codes: 78006, 78015, 78070, 78135, 78148, 78150, 78154, 78163, 78209, 78213, 78216–18, 78239, 78247, 78258–61, 78266, 78270, 78280, 78606, 78610–11, 78613, 78618–20, 78623, 78630–31, 78635–36, 78641, 78645–46, 78652, 78654, 78663, 78666, 78669, 78676, 78726, 78730, 78732–39, 78746, 78749–50, 78759, 78780

* * *

TWENTY-SECOND DISTRICT

TOM DeLAY, Republican, of Sugar Land, TX; born in Laredo, TX, April 8, 1947; education: graduated Calallan High School, Corpus Christi, 1965; attended Baylor University, Waco, TX, 1967; B.S., University of Houston, TX, 1970; businessman; Texas House of Representatives, 1979–84; member: Oyster Creek Rotary; Fort Bend 100 Club; Chamber of Commerce; board member, Youth Opportunities Unlimited; married to the former Christine Furrh; one child: Danielle; elected by colleagues to the No. 3 leadership post as Majority Whip for the 104th through the 107th Congresses; elected as Majority Leader for the 108th and 109th Congresses; elected to the 99th Congress on November 6, 1984; reelected to each succeeding Congress.

Office Listings
http://tomdelay.house.gov

242 Cannon House Office Building, Washington, DC 20515 .... (202) 225–5951
    Chief of Staff.—Tim Berry.   FAX: 225–5241
    Administrative Assistant / Legislative Director.—David James.
    Director of Communications.—Dan Allen.
    Legislative Assistants: Hope Henry, Ryan Flood.
    Director of Finance / Special Events.—Amy Lorenzini.
    Legislative Correspondents: Keagan Resler, Matthew Wolf.
10701 Corporate Drive, Stafford, TX 77477 .... (281) 240–3700
    District Director.—Barkley Peschel.
711 W. Bay Area Boulevard, Suite 410, Webster, TX 77598 .... (281) 557–8855
    Regional Director.—Ben Jones.

Counties: BRAZORIA COUNTY. CITIES AND TOWNSHIPS: Brookside Village, Pearland. FORT BEND COUNTY. CITIES AND TOWNSHIPS: Arcola, Beasley, Fairchilds, Fresno, Houston, Meadows Place, Missouri City, Needville, Pleak, Richmond, Rosenberg, Stafford, Sugar Land, Thompsons. GALVESTON COUNTY. CITIES AND TOWNSHIPS: Friendswood, Hitchcock, La Marque, Santa Fe, Texas City. HARRIS COUNTY. CITIES AND TOWNSHIPS: Deer Park, El Lago, Friendswood, Houston, LaPorte, League City, Nassau Bay, Pasadena, Seabrook, Shoreacres, Taylor Lake Village, and Webster. Population (2000), 651,619.

ZIP Codes: 77031, 77034, 77048, 77053, 77058–59, 77061–62, 77075, 77089, 77099, 77216, 77234, 77245, 77258–59, 77263, 77271, 77275, 77289, 77406, 77411, 77417, 77430–31, 77441, 77444, 77451, 77459, 77461, 77464, 77469, 77471, 77477–79, 77481, 77487, 77489, 77496–97, 77502–05, 77507–08, 77510–12, 77517, 77536, 77539, 77545–46, 77549, 77554, 77563, 77568, 77571–72, 77578, 77581, 77583–84, 77586, 77588, 77591, 77598

TWENTY-THIRD DISTRICT

HENRY BONILLA, Republican, of San Antonio, TX; born in San Antonio, January 2, 1954; education: graduated from South San Antonio High School, 1972; B.J., University of Texas, Austin, 1976; Executive Producer for Public Affairs, KENS–TV, San Antonio; Executive News Producer, KENS–TV, San Antonio; co-chair of Congressional Border Caucus; vice-chair of U.S./Mexico Congressional Caucus; founding member of Congressional Hispanic Conference; co-chair of Community Health Center Causus; awards: American Cancer Society Public Policy Leadership Award; American Diabetes Association Public Policy Leadership Award; 60 Plus Associations, Hero of the American Tax Payer Award; Champion of Small Business; National Job Corps Award, Policymaker of the Year; National Retail Federation Retail Champion of the Year; National Association of Manufacturers, Free Trade Alliance Award; National Federation of Independent Business Guardian of Small Business; U.S. Chamber of Commerce Spirit of Enterprise Award; U.S. Hispanic Chamber of Commerce President's Award; U.T. Health Science Center at San Antonio Star Award; married: former Deborah JoAnn Knapp, 1981; children: Alicia Knapp and Austin Elliot; committees: Appropriations; subcommittees: chairman, Agriculture, Rural Development, Food and Drug Administration and Related Agencies; Defense; Foreign Operations, Export Financing and Related Programs; elected to the 103rd Congress; reelected to each succeeding Congress.

Office Listings
http://www.house.gov/bonilla

2458 Rayburn House Office Building, Washington, DC 20515	(202) 225–4511
Chief of Staff.—Marcus Lubin.	FAX: 225–2237
Press Secretary.—Taryn Fritz.	
District Director.—Richard Martinez.	
11120 Wurzbach, Suite 300, San Antonio, TX 78230	(210) 697–9055
1300 Matamoros Street, Suite 113B, Laredo, TX 78040	(956) 726–4682
111 East Broadway, Suite 101, Del Rio, TX 78840	(830) 774–6547
107 W. Avenue E., Suite 14, Alpine, TX 79830	(432) 837–1313

Counties: BANDERA COUNTY. CITIES AND TOWNSHIPS: Bandera, Lake Hills, Medina, Pipe Creek, Tarpley, Vanderpool. BEXAR COUNTY. CITIES AND TOWNSHIPS: Boerne, Cross Mountain, Dominion, Fair Oaks Ranch, Grey Forest, Helotes, Hill Country Village, Hollywood Park, Leon Springs, Leon Valley, San Antonio, Scenic Oaks, Shavano Park, Timberwood Park. BREWSTER COUNTY. CITIES AND TOWNSHIPS: Alpine, Big Bend National Park, Castolon, Chisos Basin, Lajitas, Marathon, Rio Grande Village, Study Butte, Terlingua. CROCKETT COUNTY. CITY OF: Ozona. CULBERSON COUNTY. CITIES AND TOWNSHIPS: Kent, Lobo, Nickle Creek, Pine Springs, and Van Horn. DIMMIT COUNTY. CITIES AND TOWNSHIPS: Asherton, Big Wells, Brundage, Carrizo Springs, Catarina, Valley Wells, and Winter Haven. EDWARDS COUNTY. CITIES AND TOWNSHIPS: Barksdale, Carta Valley, Rocksprings. EL PASO COUNTY. CITIES AND TOWNSHIPS: Clint, El Paso, Fabens, Fort Bliss, Homestead Meadows, Horizon City, San Azario, Socorro, Sparks, Tornillo. HUDSPETH COUNTY. CITIES AND TOWNSHIPS: Acala, Allamore, Cornudas, Dell City, Esperanza, Finlay, Fort Hancock, Hot Wells, Hueca, McNary, Salt Flat, Sierra Blanca. JEFF DAVIS COUNTY. CITIES AND TOWNSHIPS: Fort Davis, Valentine. KERR COUNTY. CITIES AND TOWNSHIPS: Camp Verde, Center Point, Comfort, Hunt, Ingram, Kerrville. KINNEY COUNTY. CITIES AND TOWNSHIPS: Brackettville, Fort Clark Springs, Spofford. KURDALL CO. CITIES AND TOWNSHIPS: Bergheim, Boerne, Sisterdale, Vendalia, Waring. MAVERICK COUNTY. CITIES AND TOWNSHIPS: Eagle Pass, El India, Normandy, Quemado. MEDINA COUNTY. CITIES AND TOWNSHIPS: Castroville, Devine, D'Hanis, Dunlay, Honda, Lacoste, Mico, Natalia, Riomedina, Lytle, and Yancey. PECOS COUNTY. CITIES AND TOWNSHIPS: Bakersfield, Buena Vista, Coyanosa, Fort Stockton, Girvin, Imperial, Iraan, Sheffield. PRESIDIO COUNTY. CITIES AND TOWNSHIPS: Adobes, Candelaria, Casa Pierda, Fort Leaton State Park, Marfa, Presidio, Redford, Ruidosa, Shafter. REAL COUNTY. CITIES AND TOWNSHIPS: Leakey, Camp Wood. REEVES COUNTY. CITIES AND TOWNSHIPS: Arno, Balmorhea, Orla, Pecos, Saragosa, Toyah, Toyahvale, Verhalen. SUTTON COUNTY. CITY OF: Sonora. TERRELL COUNTY. CITIES AND TOWNSHIPS: Dryden, Sanderson. UVALDE COUNTY. CITIES AND TOWNSHIPS: Blewett, Cline, Concan, Dabney, Knippa, Montell, Reagan Wells, Sabinal, Utopia. VAL VERDE COUNTY. CITIES AND TOWNSHIPS: Comstock, Del Rio, Juno, Langtry, Laughlin AFB, Loma Alta, Pandale, Pumpville. WEBB COUNTY. CITIES AND TOWNSHIPS: Callaghan, Chupadero Springs, Laredo, Webb. ZAVALA COUNTY. CITIES AND TOWNSHIPS: Batesville, Crystal City, and La Pryor. Population (2000) 651,619.

ZIP Codes: 76943, 76950, 78003–04, 78006, 78009–10, 78013, 78015–16, 78023–25, 78027–29, 78039–46, 78049, 78052, 78055–57, 78059, 78063, 78066, 78074, 78216, 78230–33, 78240, 78245–51, 78253–58, 78260, 78269, 78278, 78801– 02, 78827–30, 78832–34, 78836–43, 78847, 78850–53, 78860–61, 78870–73, 78877, 78879–81, 78883–86, 79718, 79730, 79734–35, 79740, 79743–44, 79770, 79772, 79780–81, 79785–86, 79830–32, 79834, 79836–37, 79839, 79842–43, 79845–49, 79851–55, 79927–28, 79938

* * *

TWENTY-FOURTH DISTRICT

KENNY MARCHANT, Republican, of Coppell, TX; born in Bonham, TX, February 23, 1951; education: B.A., Southern Nazarene University, Bethany, OK, 1974; attended Nazarene Theological Seminary, Kansas City, MO, 1975–1976; professional: real estate developer; member of the Carrollton, TX, city council, 1980–1084; mayor of Carrollton, TX, 1984–1987; member of the Texas state House of Representatives, 1987–2004; member, Advisory Board of Children's Medical Center; married: Donna; four children; committees: Education and the Workforce; Government Reform; Transportation and Infrastructure; elected to the 109th Congress on November 2, 2004.

Office Listings
http://www.house.gov/marchant

501 Cannon House Office Building, Washington, DC 20515 .... (202) 225–6605
   Chief of Staff.—Brian Thomas.   FAX: 225–0074
   Scheduler.—Sarah Phipps.
9901 East Valley Ranch Parkway, Suite 3035, Irving, TX 75063 .... (972) 556–0162

Counties: DALLAS (part), TARRANT (part). CITIES AND TOWNSHIPS: Bedford, Carrollton, Cedar Hill, Colleyville, Coppell, Dallas, Duncanville, Euless, Farmer's Branch, Fort Worth, Grand Prairie, Irving, and Southlake. Population (2000), 651,619.

ZIP Codes: 75006–07, 75010–11, 75014–17, 75019, 75024, 75027, 75029, 75037, 75038, 75050–54, 75056–57, 75060–63, 75067, 75093, 75099, 75104, 75106, 75116, 75137–38, 75211, 75234, 75236, 75244, 75249, 75261, 75287, 75368, 75370, 75379, 75381, 75387, 75396, 75398, 76005–06, 76011, 76021–22, 76034, 76039, 76040, 76051, 76054, 76092, 76095, 76099, 76155, 76262, 76299

* * *

TWENTY-FIFTH DISTRICT

LLOYD DOGGETT, Democrat, of Austin, TX; born in Austin, October 6, 1946; education: graduated, Austin High School; B.B.A., University of Texas, Austin, 1967; J.D., University of Texas, 1970; president, University of Texas Student Body; associate editor, *Texas Law Review*; Outstanding Young Lawyer, Austin Association of Young Lawyers; president, Texas Consumer Association; religion: member, First United Methodist Church; admitted to the Texas State bar, 1971; Texas State Senate, 1973–85, elected at age 26; Senate author of 124 state laws and Senate sponsor of 63 House bills enacted into law; elected president pro tempore of Texas Senate; served as acting governor; named Outstanding Young Texan by Texas Jaycees; Arthur B. DeWitty Award for outstanding achievement in human rights, Austin NAACP; honored for work by Austin Rape Crisis Center, Planned Parenthood of Austin; Austin Chapter, American Institute of Architects; Austin Council on Alcoholism; Disabled American Veterans; justice on Texas Supreme Court, 1989–94; chairman, Supreme Court Task Force on Judicial Ethics, 1992–94; Outstanding Judge (Mexican-American Bar of Texas), 1993; adjunct professor, University of Texas School of Law, 1989–94; James Madison Award, Texas Freedom of Information Foundation, 1990; First Amendment Award, National Society of Professional Journalists, 1990; member: co-founder, House Information Technology Roundtable; Democratic Caucus Task Force on Education; Congressional Task Force on Tobacco and Health; Democratic Caucus Task Force on Child Care; married: Libby Belk Doggett, 1969; children: Lisa and Cathy; committees: Ways and Means; subcommittees: Health; Select Revenue Measures; elected to the 104th Congress; reelected to each succeeding Congress.

Office Listings
http://www.house.gov/doggett

201 Cannon House Office Building, Washington, DC 20515 .... (202) 225–4865
   Chief of Staff.—Michael J. Mucchetti.
   Systems Administrator.—Luke George.
   Press Secretary.—Jess Fassler.
   Staff Assistant.—Diana Ramirez.
300 East 8th Street, Suite 763, Austin, TX 78701 .... (512) 916–5921
   District Director.—Tom Weber.

Counties: CALDWELL, DUVAL, GONZALES, HIDALGO (part), JIM HOGG, KARNES, LIKE OAK, STARR, TRAVIS (part). Population (2000), 651,619.

ZIP Codes: 73301, 73344, 78008, 78022, 78060, 78071, 78075, 78102, 78111, 78113, 78116–19, 78122, 78125, 78140, 78144, 78151, 78159, 78341, 78349–50, 78357, 78360–61, 78368, 78376, 78383–84, 78501–05, 78536, 78545, 78547–48, 78557, 78560, 78565, 78572–74, 78576–77, 78582, 78584–85, 78588, 78591, 78595, 78604, 78610, 78612, 78614, 78616–17, 78621–22, 78629, 78632, 78640, 78644, 78648, 78653, 78655–56, 78658, 78661, 78666, 78677, 78702, 78704–05, 78713, 78715, 78719, 78721–25, 78741–42, 78744–45, 78747–48, 78751–52, 78760–62, 78764–65, 78772, 78781, 78783, 78785, 78799, 78953, 78959

* * *

TWENTY-SIXTH DISTRICT

MICHAEL C. BURGESS, Republican, of Denton County, TX; born, December 23, 1950; education: North Texas State University, Bachelor and Masters degrees in Physiology; received his M.D. from the University of Texas Medical School in Houston; and received a Masters degree in Medical Management from the University of Texas in Dallas; completed medical residency programs at Parkland Hospital in Dallas; professional: founder of Private Practice

264 *Congressional Directory* TEXAS

Specialty Group for Obstetrics and Gynecology; former Chief of Staff and Chief of Obstetrics for Lewisville Medical Center; organizations: past president, Denton County Medical Society; Denton County delegate to the Texas Medical Association; alternate delegate to the American Medical Association; married: Laura; three children; committees: Energy and Commerce; elected to the 108th Congress on November 5, 2002; reelected to each succeeding Congress.

Office Listings
http://www.house.gov/burgess

1721 Longworth House Office Building, Washington, DC 20515 .... (202) 225–7772
Chief of Staff.—Barry Brown.   FAX: 225–2919
Legislative Director.—Josh Martin.
Press Secretary.—Michelle Stein.
1660 South Stemmons Freeway, Suite 230, Lewisville, TX 75067 .... (972) 434–9700

Counties: COOKE (part), DALLAS (part), DENTON (part), TARRANT (part). Population (2000) 651,619.

ZIP Codes: 75009, 75019, 75022, 75028, 75034, 75056–57, 75063, 75067–68, 75077–78, 75261, 76012–13, 76021–22, 76034, 76040, 76051–54, 76092, 76102–05, 7610–12, 76115, 76117–20, 76134, 76140, 76148, 76177, 76180, 76201, 76205, 76207–10, 76226–27, 76233–34, 76240, 76247–49, 76258–59, 76262, 76266, 76272, 76273

* * *

TWENTY-SEVENTH DISTRICT

SOLOMON P. ORTIZ, Democrat, of Corpus Christi, TX; born in Robstown, TX, June 3, 1937; education: attended Robstown High School; attended Del Mar College, Corpus Christi; officers certificate, Institute of Applied Science, Chicago, IL, 1962; officers certificate, National Sheriffs Training Institute, Los Angeles, CA, 1977; served in U.S. Army, Sp4c. 1960–62; professional: insurance agent; Nueces County constable, 1965–68; Nueces County commissioner, 1969–76; Nueces County sheriff, 1977–82; member: Congressional Hispanic Caucus (chairman, 102nd Congress); Congressional Hispanic Caucus Institute (chairman of the board, 102nd Congress); Army Caucus; Depot Caucus; Sheriffs' Association of Texas; National Sheriffs' Association; Corpus Christi Rotary Club; American Red Cross; United Way; honors: *Who's Who Among Hispanic Americans;* Man of the Year, International Order of Foresters (1981); Conservation Legislator of the Year for the Sportsman Clubs of Texas (1986); Boss of the Year by the American Businesswomen Association (1980); National Government Hispanic Business Advocate, U.S. Hispanic Chamber of Commerce (1992); Leadership Award, Latin American Management Association (1991); National Security Leadership Award, American Security Council (1992); Tree of Life Award, Jewish National Fund (1987); Quality of Life Award (USO) 2001; children: Yvette and Solomon, Jr.; committees: Armed Services; Resources; elected on November 2, 1982, to the 98th Congress; reelected to each succeeding Congress.

Office Listings

2470 Rayburn House Office Building, Washington, DC 20515 .... (202) 225–7742
Chief of Staff.—Florencio H. Rendon.   FAX: 226–1134
Executive Assistant / Scheduling.—Rhiannon Burruss.
Legislative Director.—Nando Gomez.
Press Secretary.—Cathy Travis.
3649 Leopard, Suite 510, Corpus Christi, TX 78408 .... (361) 883–5868
3505 Boca Chica Boulevard, Suite 200, Brownsville, TX 78521 .... (956) 541–1242

Counties: CAMERON (part), KENNEDY, KLEBERG, NUECES, SAN PATRICO, (part), WILLACY. Population (2000), 651,619.

ZIP Codes: 78330, 78335–36, 78338–39, 78343, 78347, 78351, 78359, 78362–64, 78373–74, 78379–80, 78383, 78385, 78390, 78401–19, 78426–27, 78460, 78463, 78465–78, 78480, 78520–23, 78526, 78550, 78552, 78559, 78561, 78566–67, 78569, 78575, 78578, 78580, 78583, 78586, 78590, 78592, 78594, 78597–98

* * *

TWENTY-EIGHTH DISTRICT

HENRY CUELLAR, Democrat, of Laredo, TX; born in Laredo, September 19, 1955; education: A.A., Laredo Community College, Laredo, TX, 1976; B.S., Georgetown University, Washington, DC, 1978; J.D., University of Texas, 1981; M.A., Texas A&M University, Laredo, TX, 1982; PhD., University of Texas, Austin, TX, 1998; professional: lawyer, private practice; Licensed United States Customs Broker, 1983–present; attorney, Law Office of Henry Cuellar, 1981–present; Adjunct Professor, International Commercial Law, Texas A&M international,

1984–86; Instructor, Department of Government; Laredo Community College, Laredo, TX, 1982–86; Arbitrator/Mediator Businessman; Representative, Texas State House of Representatives, 1986–2001; Secretary of State, State of Texas, 2001; Texas Delegate, National Democratic Convention, 1992; sustaining member, Texas Democratic Party, 1984; Board of Advisors, Texas Hispanic Journal of Law and Policy, University of Texas Law School, 2002; Texas Lyceum, 1997 member, College of the State Bar of Texas, 1994; member, International Trade Association, Laredo State University, 1988; legal advisor, American GI, local chapter, 1986–87; advisory board member, Stop Child Abuse and Neglect, 1984; president, Laredo Young Lawyers Association, 1983–84; president, board of directors, Laredo Legal Aid Society Incorporated, 1982–84; board of directors, Kiwanis Club of Laredo, TX, 1982–83; co-founder/president, Laredo Volunteers Lawyers Program, Incorporated, 1982–83; co-founder/treasurer, Stop Child Abuse and Neglect, 1982–83; board of directors, United Way, 1982–83; member, American Bar Association; member, Inter-American Bar Association; president, board of directors, International Good Neighbor Council; Texas Bar Association member; Webb County/Laredo Bar Association; religion: Catholic; married: Imelda; children: Christina Alexandra, Catherine Ann; committees: Agriculture; Budget; elected to the 109th Congress on November 2, 2004.

Office Listings
http://www.house.gov/cuellar

1404 Longworth House Office Bulding, Washington, DC 20515 .... (202) 225–1640
    Chief of Staff.—Colin Strother.   FAX: 225–1641
    Legislative Director.—Billy Peche.
    Executive Assistant / Scheduler.—Jennifer Milek.
1149 E. Commerce Street, Suite 210, San Antonio, TX 78205 .... (210) 271–2851
111 E. San Antonio, Suite 205, San Marcos, TX 78666 .... (512) 392–2364
1300 Matamoros, Suite 210, Laredo, TX 78040 .... (956) 725–0639

Counties: ATASCOSA, BEXAR, COMAL, FRIO, GUADALUPE, HAYS, LA SALLE, MCMULLEN, WEBB, WILSON, ZAPATA. Population (2000), 651,620.

ZIP Codes: 78001–02, 78005, 78007–09, 78011–12, 78014, 78017, 78019, 78021, 78026, 78039, 78040–41, 78043, 78045–46, 78050, 78052, 78054, 78057, 78061–62, 78064–65, 78069, 78072–73, 78076, 78108–09, 78112–13, 78115, 78121, 78123, 78131–32, 78140, 78143, 78152, 78154–56, 78161, 78202–03, 78205, 78210–11, 78214, 78218–22, 78223–26, 78235, 78242, 78244, 78252, 78263–64, 78369, 78371, 78564, 78610, 78638, 78640, 78648, 78655–56, 78666–67

* * *

TWENTY-NINTH DISTRICT

GENE GREEN, Democrat, of Houston, TX; born in Houston, October 17, 1947; education: B.A., University of Houston, 1971; admitted, Texas bar, 1977; professional: business manager; attorney; Texas State Representative, 1973–85; Texas State Senator, 1985–92; member: Houston Bar Association; Texas Bar Association; American Bar Association; Communications Workers of America; Aldine Optimist Club; Gulf Coast Conservation Association; Texas Historical Society; Lindale Lions Club; Democratic Deputy Whip; member: Congressional Steel Caucus; Urban Caucus; Sportsmen's Caucus; co-chair, Congressional Urban Healthcare Caucus; Vision Caucus; married: January 23, 1970, to Helen Albers; children: Angela and Christopher; committees: Energy and Commerce; Standards of Official Conduct; subcommittees: Commerce, Trade, and Consumer Protection; Energy and Air Quality; Environment and Hazardous Materials; Health; elected on November 3, 1992, to the 103rd Congress; reelected to each succeeding Congress.

Office Listings
http://www.house.gov/green

2335 Rayburn House Office Building, Washington, DC 20515 .... (202) 225–1688
    Chief of Staff / Administrative Assistant.—Rhonda Jackson.   FAX: 225–9903
    Legislative Director.—Andrew Wallace.
    Press Secretary.—Celinda Gonzalez.
    Legislative Assistants: Lantie Ferguson, Vince Jesaitis, Leo Munoz.
256 North Sam Houston Parkway East, Suite 29, Houston, TX 77060 .... (281) 999–5879
11811 I–10 East, Suite 430, Houston, TX 77029 .... (713) 330–0761

Counties: HARRIS COUNTY (part). CITIES AND TOWNSHIPS: Baytown, Channelview, Galena Park, Houston, Humble, Jacinto City, La Porte, Pasadena, and South Houston. Population (2000), 651,620.

ZIP Codes: 77003, 77009, 77011–13, 77015–18, 77020–23, 77026, 77029, 77032, 77034, 77037, 77039, 77044, 77049–50, 77060–61, 77075–76, 77087, 77091, 77093, 77205–07, 77213, 77216–17, 77220–23, 77226, 77229, 77234, 77249, 77261–62, 77275, 77287, 77291–93, 77315, 77396, 77501–04, 77506, 77520–22, 77530, 77536, 77547, 77562, 77571–72, 77580, 77587

THIRTIETH DISTRICT

EDDIE BERNICE JOHNSON, Democrat, of Dallas, TX; born in Waco, TX, December, 3, 1935; education: nursing diploma, St. Mary's at Notre Dame, 1955; B.S., nursing, Texas Christian, 1967; M.P.A, Southern Methodist, 1976; proprietor, Eddie Bernice Johnson and Associates consulting and airport concession management; Texas House of Representatives, 1972–77; Carter administration appointee, 1977–81; Texas State Senate, 1986–92; member, St. John Baptist Church, Dallas; member, American Nurses Association; member, Links, Inc., Dallas Chapter; member, Dallas Black Chamber of Commerce; life member, NAACP; member, Charter 100 of Dallas; member, Girlfriends, Inc.; honorary member, Delta Kappa Gama Society International Women Educators Organization, Epsilon Chapter; life member, YWCA; executive committee member, United Way of Metropolitan Dallas; member, Women's Council of Dallas; member and past president, National Council of Negro Women; member, Democratic Women of Dallas County; member, Dallas Urban League; member, Dallas County Democratic Progressive Voters League; member, past national vice president and past national secretary, National Order of Women Legislators; member, National Black Nurses Association; member, Goals for Dallas; Emma V. Kelly Achievement Award, Grant Temple Daughters of IBPOE of W, 1973; first woman to chair a major House committee in the Texas Legislature; Libertarian of the Year, ACLU, 1978; Women Helping Women Award, Soroptimist International of Dallas and Southwest Region, 1979; Outstanding Citizenship Award, National Conference of Christians and Jews, 1985; NAACP Juanita Craft Award in Politics, NAACP, Dallas Chapter, 1989; Legislative Action Award, Texas Association of Community Action Agencies, 1989; "She Knows Where She is Going," Girls Inc., 1990; Distinguished Public Service Award, Prairie View A&M University, 1990; Eartha M.M. White Award, outstanding achievement as a businesswoman, National Business League, 1990; Outstanding Service Award, KKDA Radio, 1991; National Association of Negro Business and Professional Women and Clubs Achievement in Government, 1991; Outstanding Service Award, Sigma Pi Phi Fraternity, 1991; Certificate of Commendation, City of Dallas, 1991; Outstanding Service Award, the Child Care Group, 1991; Legislator of the Year Award, Dallas Alliance for the Mentally Ill, 1991; Mental Health Association of Greater Dallas Prism Award, 1991; member, Alpha Kappa Alpha Sorority, Inc., Dallas Chapter; 1993 Meritorious Award, the National Black Nurses Foundation, Inc.; 1993 Award for Achievement in Equal Employment Opportunity, U.S. Department of Energy; NAACP–Arlington Branch, Special Service Award, 1993; South Dallas Business & Professional Women's Club, Inc., President's Award, 1993; 1994 Leadership Commendation, Campaign To Keep America Warm; Texas Senate Black Caucus Mickey Leland Award, 1994, U.S. Department of Energy Hall of Fame Black History Month, 1995; U.S. Department of Energy Leadership Award, 1999; Zeta Phi Beta Sorority Governmental Affairs Award, 1999; NABTP Mickey Leland Award for Excellence in Diversity, 2000; National Association of School Nurses, Inc., Legislative Award, 2000; The State of Texas Honorary Texan issued by the Governor of Texas, 2000; Links, Inc., Co-Founders Award, 2000; 100 Black Men of America, Inc., Woman of the Year, 2001; National Black Caucus of State Legislators Image Award, 2001; National Conference of Black Mayors, Inc. President's Award, 2001; 2002 Alpha Kappa Alpha Trailblazer; Thurgood Marshall Scholarship Community Leader 2002; Phi Beta Sigma Fraternity Woman of the Year 2002; CBCF Outstanding Leadership 2002; chair, (107th Congress), Congressional Black Caucus; Congressional Womens' Caucus; congressional caucuses: Asian-Pacific; Airpower; Army; Arts; Biomedical Research; Women's Issues; Children's Working Group; Fire Services; Oil & Gas Educational Forum; Study Group on Japan; co-chair, Task Force on International HIV/AIDS; Urban; Medical Technology; Livable Communities Task Force; Congressional Human Rights Caucus; Congressional Korean Caucus; Congressional Singapore Caucus; Tex-21 Transportation Caucus; children: Dawrence Kirk; committees: Science; Transportation and Infrastructure; elected on November 3, 1992, to the 103rd Congress; reelected to each succeeding Congress.

Office Listings

http://www.house.gov/ebjohnson

1511 Longworth House Office Building, Washington, DC 20515	(202) 225–8885
Chief of Staff / Legislative Director.—Murat Gokcigdem.	FAX: 226–1477
Scheduler / Executive Assistant.—Julie Reistrup.	
Communications Director.—Lisa Hanna.	
Legislative Assistants: Ron Hall, Cathleen Harrington, Lisa Sherrod.	
3102 Maple Avenue, Suite 600, Dallas, TX 75201	(214) 922–8885
District Director.—Roscoe Smith.	
8344 East R.L. Thornton Freeway, Suite 222, Dallas, TX 75228	(214) 324–0080
Special Assistant.—Mardi Chev.	

Counties: DALLAS (part). CITIES AND TOWNSHIPS: Cedar Hill, Dallas, De Soto, Duncanville, Glenn Heights, Hutchins, Lancaster, Ovilla, and Wilmer. Population (2000), 651,620.

ZIP Codes: 75104, 75115–16, 75125, 75134, 75137, 75141, 75146, 75149, 75154, 75159, 75172, 75201–04, 75206–10, 75212, 75214–20, 75223–24, 75226–28, 75232–33, 75235–37, 75239, 75241, 75246–47, 75253

THIRTY-FIRST DISTRICT

JOHN R. CARTER, Republican, of Round Rock, TX; born in Houston, TX, November 6, 1941; education: Texas Tech University, 1964; University of Texas Law School, 1969; professional: attorney; private law practice; public service: appointed and elected a Texas District Court Judge, 1981–2001; awards: recipient and namesake of the Williamson County "John R. Carter Lifetime Achievement Award"; family: married to Erika Carter; children: Gilianne, John, Theodore, and Erika Danielle; committees: Appropriations; elected to 108th Congress on November 5, 2002; reelected to each succeeding Congress.

Office Listings
http://www.house.gov/carter

408 Cannon House Office Building, Washington, DC 20515	(202) 225–3864
Administrative Assistant.—Jason Fenton.	FAX: 225–5886
Scheduler.—Brooke McWhirter.	
1717 North IH 35, Round Rock, TX 78664	(512) 246–1600
116 South East Street, Belton, TX 76513	(979) 846–6068

Counties: BELL, CORYELL, ERATH, FALLS, HAMILTON, MILIAM, SOUTHERN ROBERTSON, WILLIAMSON. POPULATION (2000), 651,209.

ZIP Codes: 76401, 76436, 76446, 76457, 76501–05, 76508, 76511, 76513, 76518–20, 76522–28, 76530–31, 76533–34, 76537–38, 76540–44, 76547–49, 76554, 76557–59, 76561, 76564–67, 76569–71, 76573–74, 76577–79, 76596–99, 76632, 76656, 76680, 76685, 76689, 77410, 77426, 77466, 77473, 77492, 77805–07, 77834, 77836, 77838, 77841, 77852, 77857, 77862, 77866, 77878–79, 77881, 78363, 78602, 78613, 78615, 78626, 78628, 78634, 78641–42, 78646, 78673–74, 78664, 78681, 78717, 78729, 78931, 78933, 78940, 78942, 78944, 78948, 78950

* * *

THIRTY-SECOND DISTRICT

PETE SESSIONS, Republican, of Dallas, TX; born, March 22, 1955; education: graduate, Southwestern University, 1978; worked for Southwestern Bell, and Bell Communications Research (formerly Bell Labs), 1978–94, rising to the position of district manager; past vice president for public policy, National Center for Policy Analysis, 1994–95; board member, East Dallas YMCA; past chairman, East Dallas Chamber of Commerce; past district chairman, White Rock Council of the Boy Scouts of America; member, East Dallas Rotary Club; married to Juanita Sessions; two children, Bill and Alex; committees: Budget; Rules; chairman, Results Caucus; elected on November 5, 1996, to the 105th Congress; reelected to each succeeding Congress.

Office Listings
http://www.house.gov/sessions

1514 Longworth House Office Building, Washington, DC 20515	(202) 225–2231
Chief of Staff.—Guy Harrison.	FAX: 225–5878
Communications Director.—Gina Vaughn.	
Legislative Director.—Tucker Anderson.	
Park Central VII, 12750 Merit Drive, Suite 1434, Dallas, TX 75251	(972) 392–0505

County: DALLAS (part). CITIES AND TOWNSHIPS: Addison, Cockrell Hill, Dallas, Grand Prairie, Highland Park, Irving, Richardson, and University Park. Population (2000), 651,619.

ZIP Codes: 75001, 75038–39, 75050–51, 75060–63, 75080–81, 75203–06, 75208–09, 75211–12, 75214, 75219–20, 75222, 75224–25, 75229–31, 75233, 75240, 75244, 75248, 75251, 75254, 75262

UTAH

(Population 2000, 2,233,169)

SENATORS

ORRIN G. HATCH, Republican, of Salt Lake City, UT; born in Pittsburgh, PA, March 22, 1934; education: B.S., Brigham Young University, Provo, UT, 1959; LL.B., University of Pittsburgh, 1962; practiced law in Salt Lake City, UT, and Pittsburgh, PA; senior partner, Hatch and Plumb law firm, Salt Lake City; worked his way through high school, college, and law school at the metal lathing building trade; member, AFL–CIO; holds "AV" rating in Martindale-Hubbell Law Directory; member, Salt Lake County Bar Association, Utah Bar Association, American Bar Association, Pennsylvania Bar Association, Allegheny County Bar Association, numerous other professional and fraternal organizations; member, Church of Jesus Christ of Latter-Day Saints; honorary doctorate, University of Maryland; honorary doctor of laws: Pepperdine University and Southern Utah State University; honorary national ski patroller; Help Eliminate Litter and Pollution (HELP) Association; author of numerous national publications; married: Elaine Hansen of Newton, UT; children: Brent, Marcia, Scott, Kimberly, Alysa and Jess; committees: Finance; Health, Education, Labor, and Pensions; Judiciary; Select Committee on Intelligence; Joint Committee on Taxation; elected to the U.S. Senate on November 2, 1976; reelected to each succeeding Senate term.

Office Listings
http://hatch.senate.gov

104 Hart Senate Office Building, Washington, DC 20510 .... (202) 224–5251
    Chief of Staff.—Patricia Knight.
    Communications Director.—Adam Elggren.
Federal Building, Suite 8402, Salt Lake City, UT 84138 .... (801) 524–4380
    State Director.—Melanie Bowen.
Federal Building, 324 25th Street, Suite 1006, Ogden, UT 84401 .... (801) 625–5672
51 South University Avenue, Suite 320, Provo, UT 84606 .... (801) 375–7881
197 East Tabernacle, Room 2, St. George, UT 84770 .... (435) 634–1795
2390 West Highway 56, P.O. Box 99, Cedar City, UT 84720 .... (435) 586–8435

* * *

ROBERT F. BENNETT, Republican, of Salt Lake City, UT; born in Salt Lake City, September 18, 1933; education: B.S., University of Utah, 1957; chief executive officer of Franklin Quest, Salt Lake City; chief congressional liaison; U.S. Department of Transportation chairman of Utah Education Strategic Planning Commission; awards: "Entrepreneur of the Year," *Inc.* magazine, 1989, Light of Learning Award, 1989; High-Tech Legislator of the Year; author, *Gaining Control*; member, Church of Jesus Christ of Latter-Day Saints; honorary doctorates: Westminster College; Salt Lake Community College; married: Joyce McKay; children: James, Julie, Robert, Wendy, Heather, and Heidi; committees: Appropriations; Banking, Housing, and Urban Affairs; Homeland Security and Governmental Affairs; Rules and Administration; Joint Economic Committee; elected to the U.S. Senate on November 3, 1992; reelected to each succeeding Senate term.

Office Listings
http://bennett.senate.gov

431 Dirksen Senate Office Building, Washington, DC 20510 .... (202) 224–5444
    Chief of Staff.—Chip Yost.
    Legislative Director.—Mark Morrison.
    Office Manager.—Sandy Knickman.
    Communications Director.—Mary Jane Collipriest.
Wallace F. Bennett Federal Building, Suite 4225, Salt Lake City, UT 84138 .... (801) 524–5933
    State Director.—Tim Sheehan.
Federal Building, 324 25th Street, Suite 1410, Ogden, UT 84401 .... (801) 625–5675
51 South University Avenue, Provo, UT 84601–4424 .... (801) 379–2525
Federal Building, 196 E. Tabernacle Street, St. George, UT 84770–3474 .... (435) 628–5514
2390 West Highway 56, Suite 4B, Cedar City, UT 84720 .... (435) 865–1335

REPRESENTATIVES

FIRST DISTRICT

ROB BISHOP, Republican, of Brigham City, UT; born in Kaysville, UT, July 13, 1951; education: B.A., Political Science, University of Utah, 1974; graduated *magna cum laude;* professional: high-school teacher; public service: Utah House of Representatives, 1979–1994;

served as Speaker of the House his last two years; elected, chairman of the Utah Republican Party, 1997, and served for two terms; religion: Church of Jesus Christ of Latter-day Saints; family: married to Jeralynn Hansen; children: Shule, Jarom, Zenock, Maren and Jashon; committees: Rules; elected to the 108th Congress on November 5, 2002; reelected to each succeeding Congress.

Office Listings
http://www.house.gov/robbishop

124 Cannon House Office Building, Washington, DC 20515	(202) 225–0453
Chief of Staff.—Scott Parker.	FAX: 225–5857
Legislative Assistants: Justin Harding, Miriam Harmer.	
Scheduler/Office Manager.—Jennifer Griffith.	
1017 Federal Building, 324 25th Street, Ogden, UT 84401	(801) 625–0107

Counties: Box Elder, Cache, Davis, Juab (part), Morgan, Rich, Salt Lake (part), Summit, Tooele, Weber. Population (2000), 744,389.

ZIP Codes: 84010–11, 84014–18, 84022, 84024–25, 84028–29, 84033–34, 84036–38, 84040–41, 84044, 84050, 84054–56, 84060–61, 84064, 84067–69, 84071, 84074–75, 84080, 84083, 84086–87, 84089, 84098, 84101–06, 84110–11, 84114–16, 84119–20, 84122, 84125–28, 84130–31, 84133–34, 84136, 84138–39, 84141, 84144–45, 84147, 84150–51, 84180, 84189–90, 84199, 84201, 84244, 84301–02, 84304–41, 84401–05, 84407–09, 84412, 84414–15, 84628

* * *

SECOND DISTRICT

JIM MATHESON, Democrat, of Salt Lake City, UT; born in Salt Lake City, March 21, 1960; education: B.A., Harvard University; M.B.A., University of California at Los Angeles (UCLA); professional: energy consultant; Bonneville Pacific; Energy Strategies, Inc.; The Matheson Group; organizations: Environmental Policy Institute; Salt Lake Public Utilities Board; Scott M. Matheson Leadership Forum; religion: Mormon; married: Amy; children: Will; committees: Financial Services; Science; Transportation and Infrastructure; elected to the 107th Congress on November 7, 2000; reelected to each succeeding Congress.

Office Listings
http://www.house.gov/matheson

1222 Longworth House Office Building, Washington, DC 20515	(202) 225–3011
Chief of Staff.—Stacey Alexander.	FAX: 225–5638
Executive Assistant.—Wendy Ware.	
240 E. Morris Avenue, #235, Salt Lake City, UT 84115	(801) 486–1236
District Director.—Alene Bentley.	
321 North Mall Drive, #E101B, St. George, UT 84790	(435) 627–0880

Counties: Carbon, Daggett, Duchensne, Emery, Garfield, Grand, Iron, Kane, Piute, Salt Lake (part), San Juan, Unitah, Utah (part), Wasatch, Washington, Wayne. Population (2000), 744,390.

ZIP Codes: 84001–04, 84007–08, 84020–21, 84023, 84026–27, 84031–32, 84035, 84039, 84043, 84046–47, 84049, 84051–53, 84062–63, 84066, 84070, 84072–73, 84076, 84078–79, 84082, 84085, 84090–94, 84102–03, 84105–09, 84112–13, 84115–17, 84119, 84121, 84123–24, 84132, 84143, 84148, 84152, 84157–58, 84165, 84171, 84501, 84510–13, 84515–16, 84518, 84520–23, 84525–26, 84528–37, 84539, 84540, 84542, 84604, 84710, 84712, 84714–23, 84725–26, 84729, 84732–38, 84740–43, 84745–47, 84749–50, 84753, 84755–65, 84767, 84770–76, 84779–84, 84790–91

* * *

THIRD DISTRICT

CHRIS CANNON, Republican, of Mapleton, UT; born in Salt Lake City, UT, October 20, 1950; education: B.S., University Studies, Brigham Young University, 1974; graduate work at Harvard School of Business, 1974–75; J.D., Brigham Young University, 1977–80; professional: admitted to the Utah bar in 1980 and began practice in Provo, UT; attorney, Robinson, Seiler and Glazier; former associate solicitor and deputy associate solicitor, Department of the Interior; cofounder, Geneva Steel, Provo; founder, Cannon Industries, Salt Lake City; president and, subsequently, chairman, of Cannon Industries, Salt Lake City; member, Utah Republican Party Elephant Club and Finance Committee; Utah Chairman, Lamar Alexander for President; Utah Finance Chairman, Bush-Quayle '92; married: the former Claudia Ann Fox in 1978; religion: Church of Jesus Christ of Latter-day Saints; children: Rachel, Jane, Laura, Emily, Elizabeth, Jonathan, Matthew, Katherine; committees: Government Reform; Judiciary; Resources; elected to the 105th Congress; reelected to each succeeding Congress.

Office Listings

http://chriscannon.house.gov   cannon.ut03@mail.house.gov

2436 Cannon House Office Building, Washington, DC 20515 .... (202) 225–7751
    Executive Assistant.—Jenny Davis.   FAX: 225–5629
    Legislative Director / Administrative Assistant.—Todd Thorpe.
    Legislative Assistants: Rachel Dresen, Matt Iandoli, Maury Litwack, Cody
      Stewart.
    Communications Director.—Charles Isom.
51 South University Avenue, Suite 319, Provo, UT 84606 .... (801) 851–2500
    Chief of Staff.—Joe Hunter.

Counties: BEAVER, JUAB (part), MILLARD, SALT LAKE (part), SANPETE, SEVIER, UTAH (part). Population (2000), 744,390.

ZIP Codes: 84003, 84006, 84013, 84042–44, 84047, 84057–59, 84062, 84065, 84070, 84084, 84088, 84095, 84097, 84107,
    84118–20, 84123, 84128, 84170, 84184, 84199, 84601–06, 84620–24, 84626–27, 84629–40, 84642–57, 84660,
    84662–65, 84667, 84701, 84711, 84713, 84724, 84728, 84730–31, 84739, 84744, 84751–52, 84754, 84766

VERMONT

(Population 2000, 608,827)

SENATORS

PATRICK J. LEAHY, Democrat, of Middlesex, VT; born in Montpelier, VT, March 31, 1940, son of Howard and Alba Leahy; education: graduate of St. Michael's High School, Montpelier, 1957; B.A., St. Michael's College, 1961; J.D., Georgetown University, 1964; professional: attorney, admitted to the Vermont bar, 1964; admitted to the District of Columbia bar, 1979; admitted to practice before the U.S. Supreme Court, 1968, the Second Circuit Court of Appeals in New York, 1966, the Federal District Court of Vermont, 1965, and the Vermont Supreme Court, 1964; State's Attorney, Chittenden County, 1966–74; vice president, National District Attorneys Association, 1971–74; married: the former Marcelle Pomerleau, 1962; children: Kevin, Alicia and Mark; first Democrat and youngest person in Vermont to be elected to the U.S. Senate; committees: Agriculture, Nutrition and Forestry; Appropriations; ranking member, Judiciary; subcommittees: Antitrust, Competition Policy and Consumer Rights; Commerce, Justice, Science, and Related Agencies; Corrections and Rehabilitation; Defense; Forestry, Conservation and Rural Revitalization; Homeland Security; ranking member, Intellectual Property; Interior and Related Agencies; Production and Price Competitiveness; ranking member, Research, Nutrition and General Legislation; ranking member, State, Foreign Operations, and Related Programs; Transportation, Treasury, the Judiciary, HUD, and Related Agencies; elected to the Senate on November 5, 1974; reelected to each succeeding Senate term.

Office Listings
http://leahy.senate.gov

433 Russell Senate Office Building, Washington, DC 20510	(202) 224–4242

    Chief of Staff.—Luke Albee.
    Deputy Chief of Staff.—Clara Kircher.
    Legislative Director.—John P. Dowd.
    Press Secretary.—David Carle.

Federal Building, Room 338, Montpelier, VT 05602	(802) 229–0569

    Office Director.—Robert G. Paquin.

199 Main Street, Courthouse Plaza, Burlington, VT 05401	(802) 863–2525

    State Director.—Chuck Ross.

* * *

JAMES M. JEFFORDS, Independent, of Shrewsbury, VT; born in Rutland, VT, May 11, 1934; education: attended public schools in Rutland; received B.S.I.A. degree from Yale, New Haven, CT, 1956; graduate work, Harvard, Cambridge, MA, 1962, LL.B.; served in the U.S. Navy as lieutenant (jg.); captain, U.S. Naval Reserves (retired June 1990); admitted to the Vermont bar, 1962, and began practice in Rutland; State Senator, 1967–68; Attorney General, State of Vermont, 1969–73; married: Elizabeth Daley; children: Leonard and Laura; Northeast-Midwest Coalition; committees: ranking member, Environment and Public Works; Finance; Health, Education, Labor, and Pensions; Veterans' Affairs; Special Committee on Aging; elected to the 94th Congress, November 5, 1974; reelected to each succeeding Congress; elected to the U.S. Senate on November 8, 1988; reelected to each succeeding Senate term.

Office Listings
http://jeffords.senate.gov

413 Dirksen Senate Office Building, Washington, DC 20510	(202) 224–5141

    Chief of Staff.—Bill Kurtz.
    Legislative Director.—Sherry Kaiman.
    Office Manager.—Jim Eismeier.
    Scheduler/Personal Assistant.—Trecia McEvoy.

453 Stone Cutters Way, Suite 1, Montpelier, VT 05602	(802) 223–5273
2 South Main Street, Rutland, VT 05701	(802) 773–3875
30 Main Street, Suite 350, Burlington, VT 05401	(802) 658–6001

REPRESENTATIVE

AT LARGE

BERNARD SANDERS, Independent, of Burlington, VT; born in Brooklyn, NY, September 8, 1941; education: graduated from Madison High School, Brooklyn; B.S., Political Science, University of Chicago, 1964; professional: carpenter, writer, college professor; Mayor of Burlington, VT, 1981–89; married: the former Jane O'Meara, 1988; children: Levi, Heather, Carina and David; committees: Financial Services; Government Reform; subcommittees: Domestic and International Monetary Policy, Trade and Technology; Financial Services and Consumer Credit; Housing and Community Opportunity; National Security, Emerging Threats and International Relations; Wellness and Human Rights; elected to the 102nd Congress on November 6, 1990; reelected to each succeeding Congress.

Office Listings
http://bernie.house.gov

2233 Rayburn House Office Building, Washington, DC 20515 .... (202) 225–4115
    Chief of Staff.—Jeff Weaver.   FAX: 225–6790
    Executive Assistant.—Roxanne Scott.
    Legislative Director.—Warren Gunnels.
    Communications Director.—Joel Barkin.
1 Church Street, Second Floor, Burlington, VT 05401 .... (802) 862–0697

Population (2000), 608,827.

ZIP Codes: 05001, 05009, 05030–43, 05045–56, 05058–62, 05065, 05067–77, 05079, 05081, 05083–86, 05088–89, 05091, 05101, 05141–43, 05146, 05148–56, 05158–59, 05161, 05201, 05250–55, 05257, 05260–62, 05301–04, 05340–46, 05350–63, 05401–07, 05439–66, 05468–74, 05476–79, 05481–83, 05485–92, 05494–95, 05601–04, 05609, 05620, 05633, 05640–41, 05647–58, 05660–67, 05669–82, 05701–02, 05730–48, 05750–51, 05753, 05757–70, 05772–78, 05819–30, 05832–33, 05836–43, 05845–51, 05853, 05855, 05857–63, 05866–68, 05871–75, 05901–07

VIRGINIA

(Population 2000, 7,078,515)

SENATORS

JOHN W. WARNER, Republican, of Alexandria, VA; born, February 18, 1927; grandson of John W. and Mary Tinsley Warner of Amherst County, VA, son of the late Dr. John W. Warner and Martha Budd Warner; education: left high school in 1944 to serve in the U.S. Navy, released from active duty, third class electronics technician, July 1946; graduated Washington and Lee University (engineering), 1949; entered University of Virginia Law School, 1949; U.S. Marine Corps, second tour of active military duty as a first lieutenant, September, 1950 to May, 1952, with service in Korea, October, 1951 to May, 1952 as a ground communications officer with Marine Air Group 33, 1st Marine Air Wing; received LL.B. from University of Virginia, 1953; former owner and operator of Atoka, a cattle and crops farm, 1961–94; law clerk to E. Barrett Prettyman, late chief judge for the U.S. Court of Appeals for D.C. Circuit, 1953–54; private law practice, 1954–56; assistant U.S. attorney, 1956–60; private law practice, 1960–69; trustee, Protestant Episcopal Cathedral, Mount St. Albans, 1967–72; member, board of trustees, Washington and Lee University, 1968–79; presidential appointments: Under Secretary, U.S. Navy, February 1969–April 1972; Secretary, U.S. Navy, May 1972–April 1974; Department of Defense delegate to Law of Sea Conferences, 1969–72, head of U.S. delegation for Incidents at Sea Conference, treaty signed in Moscow, May 1972; administrator, American Revolution Bicentennial Administration, April 1974–October 1976; National Security Working Group; Commission on Roles and Capabilities of U.S. Intelligence; U.S. Delegate to the 12th special session of the U.N. General Assembly devoted to disarmament, 1982; appointed in 1985 as a Senate observer to the Geneva arms control talks with the Soviet Union; committees: chairman, Armed Services; Environment and Public Works; Homeland Security and Governmental Affairs; ex-officio, Select Committee on Intelligence; elected to the U.S. Senate on November 7, 1978, and took the oath of office in Richmond, VA, on January 2, 1979; reelected to each succeeding Senate term.

Office Listings

http//warner.senate.gov

225 Russell Senate Office Building, Washington, DC 20510	(202) 224–2023
Chief of Staff.—Susan Magill.	
Executive Assistant / Scheduler.—Anna Reilly.	
Communications Director.—John Ullyot.	
Office Manager.—Kristin White.	
235 Federal Building, 180 West Main Street, Abingdon, VA 24210	(276) 628–8158
5309 Commonwealth Centre Parkway, Midlothian, VA 23112	(804) 739–0247
4900 World Trade Center, Norfolk, VA 23510	(757) 441–3079
1003 First Union Bank Building, 213 South Jefferson Street, Roanoke, VA 24011..	(540) 857–2676

* * *

GEORGE ALLEN, Republican, of Chesterfield County, VA; born in Whittier, CA, March 8, 1952; education: B.A., University of Virginia, 1974; Juris Doctorate, University of Virginia, 1977; professional: attorney; businessman: Commonwealth Biotechnologies, Inc.; Xybernaut Corp.; organizations: Virginia Council on Economic Education; Virginia-Israel Advisory Board; Richmond Historic Riverfront Foundation; Atlantic Rural Exposition Board; Boy Scouts of America, Stonewall Jackson Council; public service: Virginia House of Delegates, 1983–1991; U.S. House of Representatives, 1991–1993; Governor of Virginia, 1994–1998; married: Susan; children: Forrest, Brooke, and Tyler; committees: Commerce, Science and Transportation; Energy and Natural Resources; Foreign Relations; Small Business and Entrepreneurship; elected to the U.S. Senate on November 7, 2000.

Office Listings

http://allen.senate.gov

204 Russell Senate Office Building, Washington, DC 20510	(202) 224–4024
Chief of Staff.—Michael Thomas.	FAX: 224–5432
Deputy Chief of Staff.—Teresa DeRoco.	
Legislative Director.—Paul Unger.	
Scheduler.—Carlos Munoz.	
507 E. Franklin Street, Richmond, VA 23219	(804) 771–2221
3140 Chaparral Drive, Building C, Suite 101, Roanoke, VA 24018	(540) 772–4236
2214 Rock Hill Road, Suite 100, Herndon, VA 20170	(703) 435–0039
222 Central Park Avenue, Suite 120, Virginia Beach, VA 23462	(757) 518–1674

REPRESENTATIVES

FIRST DISTRICT

JO ANN DAVIS, Republican, of Yorktown, VA; born in Rowan County, NC, June 29, 1950; education: Kecoughtan High School, Hampton, VA; Hampton Roads Business College; professional: Real Estate Broker; established Davis Management Co., 1988; and Jo Ann Davis Realty, 1990; organizations: Peninsula Chamber of Commerce; Better Business Bureau; National Association of Realtors; Mothers Against Drunk Driving; York County Business Association; married: Chuck Davis; children: Charlie and Chris; public service: Virginia House of Delegates, 1997–2000; committees: Armed Services; International Relations; Permanent Select Committee on Intelligence; elected to the 107th Congress on November 7, 2000; reelected to each succeeding Congress.

Office Listings

http://www.house.gov/joanndavis

1123 Longworth House Office Building, Washington, DC 20515	(202) 225–4261
Chief of Staff.—Chris Connelly.	
Legislative Director/Deputy Chief of Staff.—Mary Springer.	
Scheduler/Office Manager.—Jenny Stein.	
4904–B George Washington Memorial Highway, Yorktown, VA 23692	(757) 874–6687
District Director.—Joe Schumacher.	
4500 Plank Road, Suite 105, Fredericksburg, VA 22407	(540) 548–1086
508 Church Lane, Tappahannock, VA 22560	(804) 443–0668

Counties: CAROLINE (part), ESSEX, FAUQUIER (part), GLOUCESTER, JAMES CITY, KING AND QUEEN, KING GEORGE, KING WILLIAM, LANCASTER, MATHEWS, MIDDLESEX, NORTHUMBERLAND, PRINCE WILLIAM (part), RICHMOND, SPOTSYLVANIA (part), STAFFORD, WESTMORELAND, YORK. CITIES AND TOWNSHIPS: Bowling Green, Chancellorsville, Cobbs Creek, Colonial Beach, Dumfries, Falmouth, Fredericksburg, Hampton, Kilmarnock, Lightfoot, Montross, Newport News, Poquoson, Quantico, Saluda, Seaford, Tappahannock, Toano, Triangle, Warsaw, West Point, White Stone, Williamsburg, and Yorktown. Population (2000), 643,514.

ZIP Codes: 20106, 20112, 20115, 20119, 20128, 20138–39, 20181, 20186–87, 22026, 22134–35, 22172, 22191, 22193, 22401–08, 22412, 22427, 22430, 22432, 22435–38, 22442–43, 22446, 22448, 22451, 22454, 22456, 22460, 22463, 22469, 22471–73, 22476, 22480–82, 22485, 22488, 22501, 22503–04, 22507–09, 22511, 22513–14, 22517, 22520, 22523–24, 22526, 22528–30, 22535, 22538–39, 22544–48, 22552–56, 22558, 22560, 22570, 22572, 22576–81, 22639, 22712, 22720, 22728, 22734, 22739, 22742, 23001, 23003, 23009, 23011, 23017–18, 23021, 23023–25, 23031–32, 23035, 23043, 23045, 23050, 23056, 23061–62, 23064, 23066, 23068–72, 23076, 23079, 23081, 23085–86, 23089–92, 23106–10, 23115, 23117, 23119, 23125–28, 23130–31, 23138, 23148–49, 2315356, 23161, 23163, 23168–69, 23175–78, 23180–81, 23183–88, 23190–91, 23354, 23601–03, 23605–06, 23608–09, 23612, 23662–63, 23665–67, 23669–70, 23681, 23690–94, 23696

* * *

SECOND DISTRICT

THELMA D. DRAKE, Republican, of Norfolk, VA; born in Elyria, OH, November 20, 1949; education: graduated, Elyria High School; professional: realtor; Delegate, Virginia House of Delegates, 1995–2004; Concerned Citizens for Effective Government; Lee's Friends Bay View PTA; board member, East Ocean View Civic League; Northside Civic League; Bay View Civic League; Norfolk Republican Women; Housing and Community Development Board; awards: Crime Prevention Association Award; Tidewater Association of Realtors Circle of Excellence Award; Coldwell Banker's Presidents Circle, Sales and Marketing Executives Award; religion: United Church of Christ; married: Thomas E. (Ted); children: Lynn Sorey and J. Mark Sawyers; committees: Armed Services; Education and the Workforce; Resources; subcommittees: Energy and Mineral Resources; Fisheries, Conservation, Wildlife, and Oceans; Military Personnel; Projection Forces; 21st Century Competitiveness; Workforce Protections; elected to the 109th Congress on November 2, 2004.

Office Listings
http://www.house.gov/drake

1208 Longworth House Office Building, Washington, DC 20515	(202) 225–4215
Chief of Staff.—Tom Gordy.	FAX: 225–4218
Press Secretary.—Jim Jeffries.	
Executive Assistant/Scheduler.—Jennifer Lawrence.	
4772 Euclid Road, Suite E, Virginia Beach, VA 23462	(757) 497–6859
23386 Front Street, Accomac, VA 23301	(757) 787–7836

Counties: ACCOMACK, NORTHAMPTON. CITIES: Hampton, Norfolk, and Virginia Beach. Population (2000), 643,510.

ZIP Codes: 23301–03, 23306–08, 23310, 23313, 23316, 23336–37, 23341, 23345, 23347, 23350, 23354, 23356–59, 23389, 23395, 23398–99, 23401, 23404–05, 23407–10, 23412–23, 23426–27, 23429, 23440–43, 23450–67, 23471, 23479–

80, 23482–83, 23486, 23488, 23502–03, 23505–08, 23511–13, 23515, 23518–19, 23521, 23529, 23541, 23551, 23605, 23651, 23661, 23663–66, 23669

* * *

THIRD DISTRICT

ROBERT C. SCOTT, Democrat, of Newport News, VA; born in Washington, DC, April 30, 1947; education: graduated from Groton High School; B.A., Harvard University; J.D., Boston College Law School; professional: served in the Massachusetts National Guard; attorney; admitted to the Virginia bar; Virginia House of Representatives, 1978–83; Virginia State Senate, 1983–92; member: Sigma Pi Phi Fraternity; Peninsula Chamber of Commerce; NAACP; Alpha Phi Alpha Fraternity; March of Dimes Board of Directors; Peninsula Legal Aid Center Board of Directors; committees: Education and the Workforce; Judiciary; subcommittees: ranking member, Crime, Terrorism and Homeland Security; The Constitution; elected on November 3, 1992 to the 103rd Congress; reelected to each succeeding Congress.

Office Listings

wttp://www.house.gov/scott

1201 Longworth House Office Building, Washington, DC 20515	(202) 225–8351
Chief of Staff.—Joni L. Ivey.	
Special Assistant.—Randi Estes.	
Legislative Counsels: Ilana Fisher, LaQuita Honeysucker.	
2600 Washington Avenue, Suite 1010, Newport News, VA 23607	(757) 380–1000
501 North Second Street, Suite 401, Richmond, VA 23219–1321	(804) 644–4845

Counties: CHARLES CITY, HENRICO (part), NEW KENT, SURRY. CITIES: Hampton, Norfolk, Portsmouth and Richmond. Population (2000), 643,476.

ZIP Codes: 23011, 23030, 23059–60, 23075, 23089, 23111, 23124, 23140–41, 23147, 23150, 23181, 23185, 23218–25, 23227–28, 23230–32, 23234, 23240–41, 23249–50, 23260–61, 23269–70, 23272, 23274–76, 23278–79, 23282, 23284– 86, 23290–93, 23295, 23298, 23501–02, 23504–05, 23507–10, 23513–14, 23517–18, 23520, 23523, 23530, 23601– 09, 23628, 23630–31, 23653, 23661, 23663–64, 23666–70, 23701–05, 23707–09, 23839, 23842, 23846, 23860, 23875, 23881, 23883, 23888, 23898–99

* * *

FOURTH DISTRICT

J. RANDY FORBES, Republican, of Chesapeake, VA; born in Chesapeake, February 17, 1952; education: B.A., Randolph-Macon College; J.D., University of Virginia School of Law; professional: attorney; religion: Baptist; public service: Virginia House of Delegates, 1990–97; Virginia State Senate, 1997–2001; Republican House Floor Leader, 1994–97; Republican Senate Floor Leader, 1998–2001; Chairman of the Republican Party of Virginia, 1996–2000; married: Shirley; children: Neil, Jamie, Jordan, and Justin; committees: Armed Services; Judiciary; Science; elected to the 107th Congress, by special election, on June 19, 2001; reelected to each succeeding Congress.

Office Listings

307 Cannon House Office Building, Washington, DC 20515	(202) 225–6365
Chief of Staff.—Dee Gilmore.	FAX: 226–1170
Press Secretary.—Christy Boardman.	
Legislative Director.—Andy Halataei.	
636 Cedar Road, Suite 200, Chesapeake, VA 23322	(757) 382–0080
District Representative.—Ryan K. Mottley.	
2903 Boulevard, Suite B, Colonial Heights, VA 23834	(804) 526–4969
District Representative.—Jason Gray.	
425 H. South Main Street, Emporia, VA 23847	(434) 634–5575
District Field Representative.—Rick Franklin.	

Counties: AMELIA, BRUNSWICK (part), CHESTERFIELD (part), DINWIDDIE, GREENSVILLE, ISLE OF WIGHT (part), NOTTOWAY, POWHATAN, PRINCE GEORGE (part), SOUTHAMPTON, SUSSEX. Population (2000), 643,477.

ZIP Codes: 23002, 23083, 23101, 23105, 23112–14, 23120, 23139, 23234, 23236–37, 23304, 23314–15, 23320–28, 23397, 23424, 23430–39, 23487, 23501, 23801, 23803–06, 23821, 23824, 23827–34, 23836–38, 23840–42, 23844–45, 23847, 23850–51, 23856–57, 23860, 23866–67, 23872–76, 23878–79, 23882, 23884–85, 23887–91, 23894, 23897–98, 23920, 23922, 23930, 23938, 23950, 23955

FIFTH DISTRICT

VIRGIL H. GOODE, JR., Republican, of Rocky Mount, VA; born in Richmond, VA, October 17, 1946; education: B.A., University of Richmond, 1969; J.D., University of Virginia Law School, 1973; served in Virginia Army National Guard; professional: attorney; admitted to the Virginia bar in 1973; member, Virginia State Senate, 1973–97; former member: Ruritan Chamber of Commerce; Jaycees; married: Lucy Dodson Goode, 1991; children: Catherine; committees: Appropriations; elected to the 105th Congress; reelected to each succeeding Congress.

Office Listings
http://www.house.gov/goode

1520 Longworth House Office Building, Washington, DC 20515	(202) 225–4711
Chief of Staff.—Jerr Rosenbaum.	FAX: 225–5681
Legislative Director.—David Jennings.	
70 East Court Street, Suite 215, Rocky Mount, VA 24151	(540) 484–1254
437 Main Street, Danville, VA 24541	(434) 792–1280
Scheduler.—Judy Mattox.	
104 South First Street, Charlottesville, VA 22902	(434) 295–6372
P.O. Box 366, Farmville, VA 23901	(434) 392–8331

Counties: ALBEMARLE COUNTY. CITIES AND TOWNSHIPS: Charlotteville, Batesville, Covesville, Esmont, Greenwood, Hatton, Ivy, Keene, Keswick, North Garden, Scottsville. APPOMATTOX COUNTY. CITIES AND TOWNSHIPS: Appomattox, Evergreen, Pamplin, Spout Spring. BEDFORD COUNTY. CITIES AND TOWNSHIPS: Bedford, Big Island, Goodview, Coleman Falls, Forest, Goode, Huddleston, Lowry, Thaxton. BRUNSWICK COUNTY. BUCKINGHAM COUNTY. CITIES AND TOWNSHIPS: Andersonville, Arvonia, Buckingham, Dillwyn, Buckingham, New Canton. CAMPBELL COUNTY. CITIES AND TOWNSHIPS: Altavista, Brookneal, Concord, Evington, Gladys, Long Island, Lynch Station, Naruna, Rustburg. CHARLOTTE COUNTY. CITIES AND TOWNSHIPS: Barnesville, Charlotte Court House, Cullen, Drakes Branch, Keysville, Phenix, Randolph, Red House, Red Oak, Saxe, Wylliesburg. CUMBERLAND COUNTY. CITIES AND TOWNSHIPS: Carterville, Cumberland. DANVILLE COUNTY. CITY: Danville. FLUVANNA COUNTY. CITIES AND TOWNSHIPS: Bremo Bluff, Bybee, Carysbrook, Columbia, Fort Union, Kents Store, Palmyra, Troy. FRANKLIN COUNTY. CITIES AND TOWNSHIPS: Boones Mill, Callaway, Ferrum, Glade Hill, Henry, Redwood, Penhook, Rocky Mount, Union Hall, Waidsboro, Wirtz. GREENE COUNTY. HALIFAX COUNTY. CITIES AND TOWNSHIPS: Alton, Clover, Cluster Springs, Crystal Hall, Denniston, Halifax, Ingram, Lennig, Mayo, Nathalie, Republican Grove, Scottsburg, Turbeville, Vernon Hill, Virgilina. HENRY COUNTY. CITIES AND TOWNSHIPS: Axton, Bassett, Collinsville, Fieldale, Ridgeway, Spencer, Stanleytown. LUNENBURG COUNTY. CITIES AND TOWNSHIPS: Tamworth, Dundas, Fort Mitchell, Kenbridge, Lunenburg, Rehoboth, Victoria. MARTINSVILLE COUNTY. CITY: Martinsville. MECKLENBURG COUNTY. CITIES AND TOWNSHIPS: Baskerville, Blackridge, Boydton, Bracey, Chase City, Clarksville, Forksville, LaCross, Palmer Springs, Skipwith, South Hill, Union Level Buffalo Junction, Nelson. NELSON COUNTY. CITIES AND TOWNSHIPS: Afton, Arrington, Faber, Lovingston, Massies Mill, Nellysford, Montebello, Gladstone, Norwood, Piney River, Roseland, Schuyler, Shipman, Tye River, Tyro, Wingina. PITTSYLVANIA COUNTY. CITIES AND TOWNSHIPS: Blairs, Callands, Cascade, Chatham, Pittsville, Sandy Level, Dry Fork, Gretna, Hurt, Java, Keeling, Ringgold, Sutherlin. PRINCE EDWARD COUNTY. CITIES AND TOWNSHIPS: Green Bay, Farmville, Darlington, Heights, Green Bay, Hampden-Sydney, Meherrin, Prospect, Rice, and South Boston. Population (2000), 643,497.

ZIP Codes: 22901–11, 22920, 22922–24, 22931–32, 22935–38, 22940, 22942–43, 22945–47, 22949, 22952, 22954, 22958–59, 22963–65, 22967–69, 22971, 22973–74, 22976, 22987, 23004, 23022, 23027, 23038, 23040, 23055, 23084, 23093, 23123, 23139, 23821, 23824, 23843, 23845, 23856–57, 23868, 23887, 23889, 23893, 23901, 23909, 23915, 23917, 23919–24, 23927, 23934, 23936–39, 23941–44, 23947, 23950, 23952, 23954, 23958–60, 23962–64, 23966–68, 23970, 23974, 23976, 24012, 24053–55, 24059, 24064–65, 24067, 24069, 24076, 24078–79, 24082, 24088–89, 24091–92, 24095, 24101–02, 24104, 24112–15, 24120–22, 24133, 24137, 24139, 24146, 24148, 24151, 24153, 24161, 24168, 24171, 24174, 24176–77, 24179, 24184–85, 24312, 24464, 24483, 24501–02, 24504, 24517, 24520, 24522–23, 24527–31, 24534–35, 24538–41, 24543–44, 24549–51, 24553–54, 24556–58, 24562–63, 24565–66, 24569–71, 24574, 24576–77, 24580–81, 24585–86, 24588–90, 24592–94, 24597–99

* * *

SIXTH DISTRICT

BOB GOODLATTE, Republican, of Roanoke, VA; born in Holyoke, MA, September 22, 1952; education: B.A., Bates College, Lewiston, ME, 1974; J.D., Washington and Lee University, 1977; Massachusetts bar, 1977, Virginia bar, 1978; professional: began practice in Roanoke, VA, 1979; district director for Congressman M. Caldwell Butler, 1977–79; attorney, sole practitioner, 1979–81; partner, 1981–92; chairman, sixth district, VA, Republican Committee, 1983–88; member, Civitan Club of Roanoke (president, 1989–90); former member, Building Better Boards Advisory Council; member, Parent Teachers Association, Fishburn Park Elementary School; married: Maryellen Flaherty, 1974; children: Jennifer and Robert; committees: chairman, Agriculture; Judiciary; House Republican Policy Committee; subcommittees: Courts, the Internet, and Intellectual Property; Immigration, Border Security, and Claims; deputy majority whip; elected on November 3, 1992, to the 103rd Congress; reelected to each succeeding Congress.

Office Listings
http://www.house.gov/goodlatte

2240 Rayburn House Office Building, Washington, DC 20515 .... (202) 225–5431
  Chief of Staff.—Shelley Husband.   FAX: 225–9681
  Legislative Counsel.—Branden Ritchie.
  Press Secretary.—Kathryn Rexrode.
10 Franklin Road, SE, 540 Crestar Plaza, Roanoke, VA 24011 .... (540) 857–2672
  District Director.—Pete Larkin.
919 Main Street, Suite 300, Lynchburg, VA 24504 .... (804) 845–8306
7 Court Square, Staunton, VA 24401 .... (540) 885–3861
2 South Main Street, First Floor, Suite A, Harrisonburg, VA 22801 .... (540) 432–2391

Counties: ALLEGHANY (part), AMHERST, AUGUSTA, BATH, BEDFORD (part), BOTETOURT, HIGHLAND, ROANOKE (part), ROCKBRIDGE, ROCKINGHAM (part), SHENANDOAH. CITIES: Buena Vista, Covington, Harrisonburg, Lexington, Lynchburg, Roanoke, Salem, Staunton, and Waynesboro. Population (2000), 643,504.

ZIP Codes: 22626, 22641, 22644–45, 22652, 22654, 22657, 22660, 22664, 22801–03, 22807, 22810–12, 22815, 22820–21, 22824, 22827, 22830–34, 22840–48, 22850, 22853, 22920, 22922, 22939, 22952, 22967, 22980, 24001–20, 24022–38, 24040, 24042–44, 24048, 24053, 24059, 24064–66, 24070, 24077, 24079, 24083, 24085, 24087, 24090, 24101, 24121–22, 24130, 24153, 24156, 24174–75, 24178–79, 24401–02, 24411–13, 24415–16, 24421–22, 24426, 24430–33, 24435, 24437–42, 24445, 24450, 24458–60, 24463, 24465, 24467–69, 24471–73, 24476–77, 24479, 24482–87, 24501–06, 24512–15, 24521, 24523, 24526, 24533, 24536, 24550–51, 24553, 24555–56, 24572, 24574, 24578–79, 24595

* * *

SEVENTH DISTRICT

ERIC CANTOR, Republican, of Henrico County, VA; born in Henrico County, VA, June 6, 1963; education: George Washington University, Bachelor's Degree, 1985; College of William and Mary, Law Degree, 1988; Columbia University, Masters Degree, 1989; professional: attorney; organizations: Western Henrico Rotary; Henrico County Republican Committee; President, Virginia-Israel Foundation; Virginia Holocaust Museum Board of Trustees; Elk Hill Farm Board of Trustees; elected to the Virginia House of Delegates, 1991; appointed Chief Deputy Majority Whip, December, 2002; married: Diana; three children; committees: Ways and Means; elected to the 107th Congress on November 7, 2000; reelected to each succeeding Congress.

Office Listings
http://www.house.gov/cantor

329 Cannon House Office Building, Washington, DC 20515 .... (202) 225–2815
  Chief of Staff.—Rob Collins.   FAX: 225–0011
  Legislative Director.—Colleen Maloney.
  Press Secretary.—Geoff Embler.
5040 Sadler Place, Suite 110, Glen Allen, VA 23060 .... (804) 747–4073
763 Madison Road, Suite 207, Culpeper, VA 22701 .... (540) 825–8960

Counties: CAROLINE (part), CHESTERFIELD (part), CULPEPER, GOOCHLAND, HANOVER, HENRICO (part), LOUISA, MADISON, ORANGE, PAGE, RAPPAHANNOCK, SPOTSYLVANIA (part). CITIES: Richmond. Population (2000), 643,499.

ZIP Codes: 20106, 20119, 20186, 22407, 22433, 22508, 22534, 22542, 22546, 22553, 22565, 22567, 22580, 22610, 22623, 22627, 22630, 22640, 22650, 22701, 22709, 22711, 22713–16, 22718–19, 22721–27, 22729–38, 22740–41, 22743, 22746–49, 22827, 22835, 22849, 22851, 22903, 22923, 22942, 22947–48, 22957, 22960, 22972, 22974, 22989, 23005, 23015, 23024, 23038–39, 23047, 23058–60, 23063, 23065, 23067, 23069, 23084, 23093, 23102–03, 23111–14, 23116–17, 23120, 23124, 23129, 23146, 23153, 23160, 23162, 23170, 23173, 23192, 23221–30, 23233–36, 23242, 23255, 23273, 23280, 23288–89, 23294–95

* * *

EIGHTH DISTRICT

JAMES P. MORAN, Democrat, of Alexandria, VA; born in Buffalo, NY, May 16, 1945; education: College of Holy Cross, B.A.; Bernard Baruch Graduate School of Finance—City University of New York; University of Pittsburgh Graduate School of Public and International Affairs, M.P.A.; served on City Council of Alexandria, 1979–82; Vice Mayor of Alexandria from 1982–84, Mayor from 1985–90; founding member of the New Democrat Coalition, a group of more than 75 centrist House Democrats committed to fiscal responsibility, improvements to education, and maintaining America's economic competitiveness; co-chair of the Congressional Prevention Coalition; named as one of two "High Technology Legislators of the Year" by the Information Technology Industry Council; in 2000 named to the "Legislative Hall of Fame'' by the American Electronics Association for his work on technology issues; married: LuAnn; children: James, Michael, Patrick, Mary, and Dorothy; committees: Appropriations; subcommittees: Defense; Interior; elected to the 102nd Congress on November 6, 1990; reelected to each succeeding Congress.

Office Listings

http://www.house.gov/moran

2239 Rayburn House Office Building, Washington, DC 20515	(202) 225–4376
Chief of Staff/Administrative Assistant.—Melissa Koloszar.	FAX: 225–0017
Legislative Director.—Tim Aiken.	
5115 Franconia Road, Suite B, Alexandria, VA 22310	(703) 971–4700
District Director.—Susie Warner.	
1760 Reston Parkway, Suite 312, Reston, VA 20190	(703) 481–4339

Counties: ARLINGTON, FAIRFAX (part). CITIES: Alexandria, and Falls Church. Population (2000), 643,503.

ZIP Codes: 20170–71, 20190–91, 20194–96, 20206, 20231, 20301, 20310, 20330, 20350, 20406, 20453, 22003, 22027, 22031, 22037, 22040–44, 22046–47, 22060, 22079, 22101–03, 22107–09, 22122, 22124, 22150–51, 22159, 22180–82, 22201–07, 22209–17, 22219, 22222, 22225–27, 22229–30, 22234, 22240–45, 22301–07, 22310–15, 22320–21, 22331–34, 22336

* * *

NINTH DISTRICT

RICK BOUCHER, Democrat, of Abingdon, VA; born in Washington County, VA, August 1, 1946; education: graduated from Abingdon High School in 1964; B.A. degree from Roanoke College in 1968; J.D. degree from the University of Virginia School of Law in 1971; professional: associate, Milbank, Tweed, Hadley and McCloy, New York, NY; partner, Boucher and Boucher, Abingdon, VA; elected to the Virginia State Senate in 1975 and reelected in 1979; former chairman of the Oil and Gas Subcommittee of the Virginia Coal and Energy Commission; former member: Virginia State Crime Commission; Virginia Commission on Interstate Cooperation; Law and Justice Committee of the National Conference of State Legislatures; member: board of directors of the First Virginia Bank, Damascus; Abingdon United Methodist Church; Kappa Alpha order; Phi Alpha Delta legal fraternity; American Bar Association; Virginia Bar Association; Association of the Bar of the City of New York; recipient of the Abingdon Jaycees Outstanding Young Businessman Award, 1975; committees: Energy and Commerce; Judiciary; assistant whip; elected to the 98th Congress on November 2, 1982; reelected to each succeeding Congress.

Office Listings

http://www.house.gov/boucher   ninthnet@mail.house.gov

2187 Rayburn House Office Building, Washington, DC 20515	(202) 225–3861
Chief of Staff.—Becky Coleman.	FAX: 225–0442
Deputy Chief of Staff/Comunications Director.—Sharon Ringley.	
188 East Main Street, Abingdon, VA 24210	(540) 628–1145
District Administrator.—Linda Di Yorio.	
1 Cloverleaf Square, Suite C–1, Big Stone Gap, VA 24219	(540) 523–5450
112 North Washington Avenue, P.O. Box 1268, Pulaski, VA 24301	(540) 980–4310

Counties: ALLEGHANY (part), BLAND, BUCHANAN, CARROLL, CRAIG, DICKENSON, FLOYD, GILES, GRAYSON, HENRY (part), LEE, MONTGOMERY, PATRICK, PULASKI, ROANOKE (part), RUSSELL, SCOTT, SMYTH, TAZEWELL, WASHINGTON, WISE, WYTHE. CITIES: Bristol, Covington, Galax, Norton, and Radford. Population (2000), 643,514.

ZIP Codes: 24018–19, 24053, 24055, 24058–64, 24068, 24070, 24072–73, 24076, 24079, 24082, 24084, 24086–87, 24089, 24091, 24093–94, 24104–05, 24111–12, 24120–22, 24124, 24126–29, 24131–34, 24136, 24138, 24141–43, 24147–50, 24153, 24162, 24165, 24167, 24171, 24175, 24177, 24185, 24201–03, 24209–12, 24215–21, 24224–26, 24228, 24230, 24236–37, 24239, 24243–46, 24248, 24250–51, 24256, 24258, 24260, 24263, 24265–66, 24269–73, 24277, 24279–83, 24290, 24292–93, 24301, 24311–19, 24322–28, 24330, 24333, 24340, 24343, 24347–48, 24350–52, 24354, 24360–61, 24363, 24366, 24368, 24370, 24374–75, 24377–78, 24380–82, 24422, 24426, 24448, 24457, 24474, 24502, 24526, 24550–51, 24556, 24601–09, 24612–14, 24618–20, 24622, 24624, 24627–28, 24630–31, 24634–35, 24637, 24639–41, 24646–47, 24649, 24651, 24656–58

* * *

TENTH DISTRICT

FRANK R. WOLF, Republican, of Vienna, VA; born in Philadelphia, PA, January 30, 1939; education: B.A., Pennsylvania State University, 1961; LL.B., Georgetown University Law School, 1965; served in the U.S. Army Signal Corps (Reserves); professional: lawyer, admitted to the Virginia State bar; legislative assistant for former U.S. Congressman Edward G. Biester,

Jr., 1968–71; assistant to Secretary of the Interior Rogers C.B. Morton, 1971–74; Deputy Assistant Secretary for Congressional and Legislative Affairs, Department of the Interior, 1974–75; member, Vienna Presbyterian Church; married: the former Carolyn Stover; children: Frank, Jr., Virginia, Anne, Brenda, and Rebecca; committees: Appropriations; elected to the 97th Congress, November 4, 1980; reelected to each succeeding Congress.

Office Listings
http://www.house.gov/wolf

241 Cannon House Office Building, Washington, DC 20515 .... (202) 225–5136
   Chief of Staff / Press Secretary.—Dan Scandling.   FAX: 225–0437
   Legislative Director.—Janet Shaffron.
13873 Park Center Road, Suite 130, Herndon, VA 20171 .... (703) 709–5800
   Director of Constituent Services.—Judy McCary.
110 North Cameron Street, Winchester, VA 22601 .... (540) 667–0900

Counties: CLARKE, FAIRFAX (part), FAUQUIER (part), FREDERICK, LOUDOUN, PRINCE WILLIAM (part), WARREN. CITIES: Manassas, Manassas Park, and Winchester. Population (2000), 643,512.

ZIP Codes: 20101–05, 20107–13, 20115–18, 20120–22, 20129–32, 20134–35, 20137, 20140–44, 20146–49, 20151–53, 20158–60, 20163–67, 20170–72, 20175–78, 20180, 20184–90, 20194, 20197–98, 22026, 22033, 22043–44, 22046, 22066–67, 22101, 22106, 22184–85, 22193, 22207, 22556, 22601–04, 22610–11, 22620, 22622, 22624–25, 22630, 22637, 22639, 22642–43, 22645–46, 22649, 22654–57, 22663

* * *

ELEVENTH DISTRICT

TOM DAVIS, Republican, of Falls Church, VA; born in Minot, ND, January 5, 1949; education: graduated, U.S. Capitol Page School; graduated, Amherst College with honors in political science; law degree, University of Virginia; attended officer candidate school; served in the U.S. Army Reserves; member: Fairfax County Board of Supervisors, 1980–94, Chairman, 1992–94; vice president and general counsel of PRC, Inc., McLean, VA; past president, Washington Metropolitan Council of Governments; founding member and past president, Bailey's Crossroads Rotary Club; married Jeannemarie Devolites, 2004; three children: Carlton, Pamela, and Shelley; committees: chairman, Government Reform; Homeland Security; elected to the 104th Congress; reelected to each succeeding Congress.

Office Listings
http://www.house.gov/tomdavis

2348 Rayburn House Office Building, Washington, DC 20515 .... (202) 225–1492
   Chief of Staff.—David Thomas.   FAX: 225–3071
   Legislative Director.—Bill Womack.
   Executive Assistant.—Gabriele Forsyth.
4415 Annandale Road, Annandale, VA 22003 .... (703) 916–9610
   District Director.—Dave Foreman.
Telecommuting District Office .... (703) 437–1726
   Constituent Service Director.—Ann Rust.
Dominion Center, 13554 Minnieville Road, Woodbridge, VA 22192 .... (703) 590–4599
   Constituent Service Director.—Ryan Kelly.

Counties: FAIRFAX (part), PRINCE WILLIAM (part). CITIES: Alexandria, Annandale, Burke, Centreville, Clifton, Fairfax, Fairfax Station, Herndon, Lorton, Manassas, Oakton, Occoquan, Springfield, Vienna, and Woodbridge. Population (2000), 643,509.

ZIP Codes: 20069–70, 20109–10, 20112, 20119–22, 20124, 20136–37, 20155–56, 20168–69, 20171, 20181–82, 22003, 22009, 22015, 22027, 22030–33, 22035, 22038–39, 22044, 22060, 22079, 22081–82, 22102, 22116, 22118–21, 22124–25, 22150–53, 22156, 22158–61, 22180–83, 22185, 22191–95, 22199, 22308–09, 22312

WASHINGTON

(Population 2000, 5,894,121)

SENATORS

PATTY MURRAY, Democrat, of Seattle, WA; born in Seattle, October 11, 1950; education: B.A., Washington State University, 1972; professional: teacher; lobbyist; Shoreline Community College; parent education instructor for Crystal Springs, 1984–87; citizen lobbyist for environmental and educational issues, 1983–88; school board member, 1985–89; elected Board of Directors, Shoreline School District, 1985–89; Washington State Senate, 1988–92; Democratic Whip, 1990–92; State Senate committees: Education; Ways and Means; Commerce and Labor; Domestic Timber Processing Select Committee; Open Government Select Committee; School Transportation Safety Task Force chairperson; Washington State Legislator of the Year, 1990; married: Rob Murray; children: Randy and Sara; committees: Appropriations; Budget; Health, Education, Labor and Pensions; Veterans' Affairs; elected to the U.S. Senate on November 3, 1992; reelected to each succeeding Senate term.

Office Listings

http://murray.senate.gov

173 Russell Senate Office Building, Washington, DC 20510	(202) 224–2621
Chief of Staff.—Rick Desimone.	FAX: 224–0238
Deputy Chief of Staff.—Tovah Ravitz-Meehn.	TDD: 224–4430
Legislative Director.—Leslie Turner.	
Communications Director.—Alex Glass.	
2988 Jackson Federal Building, 915 Second Avenue, Seattle, WA 98174	(206) 553–5545
State Director.—John Engber.	
The Marshall House, 1323 Officer's Row, Vancouver, WA 98661	(360) 696–7797
District Director.—Mindi Linquist.	
601 West Main Avenue, Suite 1213, Spokane, WA 99201	(509) 624–9515
District Director.—Judy Olson.	
2930 Wetmore Avenue, Suite 903, Everett, WA 98201	(425) 259–6515
District Director.—Rachelle Hein.	
402 E. Yakima Avenue, Suite 390, Yakima, WA 98901	(509) 453–7462
District Director.—Mary McBride.	

* * *

MARIA CANTWELL, Democrat, of Edmonds, WA; born in Indianapolis, IN, October 13, 1958; education: B.A., Miami University, Miami, OH, 1980; professional: businesswoman; RealNetworks, Inc.; organizations: South Snohomish County Chamber of Commerce; Alderwood Rotary; Mountlake Terrace Friends of the Library; public service: Washington State House of Representatives, 1987–1992; U.S. House of Representatives, 1992–1994; religion: Roman Catholic; committees: Commerce, Science and Transportation; Energy and Natural Resources; Indian Affairs; Small Business and Entrepreneurship; elected to the U.S. Senate on November 7, 2000.

Office Listings

http://cantwell.senate.gov

717 Hart Senate Office Building, Washington, DC 20510	(202) 224–3441
Chief of Staff.—Kurt Beckett.	FAX: 228–0514
Deputy Chief of Staff.—Jennifer Griffith.	
Legislative Director.—Mary Frances Repko.	
Office Manager.—Michael Hill.	
915 Second Avenue, Suite 3206, Seattle, WA 98174	(206) 220–6400
The Marshall House, 1313 Officers Row, Vancouver, WA 98661	(360) 696–7838
950 Pacific Avenue, Suite 615, Tacoma, WA 98402	(253) 572–2281
U.S. Federal Courthouse, W. 920 Riverside, Suite 697, Spokane, WA 99201	(509) 353–2507
825 Jadwin Avenue, 204/204A, Richland, WA 99352	(509) 946–8106
2930 Wetmore Avenue, Suite 9B, Everett, WA 98201	(425) 303–0114

REPRESENTATIVES

FIRST DISTRICT

JAY INSLEE, Democrat, of Bainbridge Island, WA; born in Seattle, WA, February 9, 1951; education: graduated, Ingraham High School, 1969; B.A., University of Washington, 1973; J.D., Willamette School of Law, 1976; professional: attorney, 1976–92; Washington State House of

Representatives, 1988–92, 14th Legislative District; served on Appropriations; Housing; Judiciary; and Financial Institutions and Insurance Committees; represented the 4th District in the U.S. House of Representatives, 1993–95; attorney, 1995–96; Regional Director, U.S. Department of Health and Human Services, 1997–98; married: Trudi; three children: Jack, Connor, and Joe; committees: Energy and Commerce; Resources; subcommittees: Environment and Hazardous Materials; Oversight and Investigations; Telecommunications and the Internet; elected to the U.S. House of Representatives, from the 1st District, for the 106th Congress; reelected to each succeeding Congress.

Office Listings
http://www.house.gov/inslee

403 Cannon House Office Building, Washington, DC 20515	(202) 225–6311
Chief of Staff.—Joby Shimomura.	(800) 422–5521
Legislative Director/Deputy Chief of Staff.—Brian Bonlender.	
Scheduler.—Kate Kriner.	
Communications Director.—Sara O'Connell.	
21905 64th Avenue West, Suite 101, Mountlake Terrace, WA 98043	(425) 640–0233
17701 Fjord Drive NE, Suite A–112, Liberty Bay Marina, Poulsbo, WA 98370	(360) 598–2342
District Director.—Kennie Endelman.	

Counties: KING (part), KITSAP (part), SNOHOMISH (part). CITIES AND TOWNSHIPS: Bainbridge Island, Bothell, Bremerton, Brier, Duvall, Edmonds, Everett, Hansville, Indianola, Kenmore, Keyport, Kingston, Kirkland, Lake Forest, Lynnwood, Mill Creek, Monroe, Mountlake Terrace, Mukilteo, Port Gamble, Poulsbo, Redmond, Rollingbay, Seabeck, Seattle, Shoreline, Silverdale, Snohomish, Suquamish, and Woodinville. Population (2000), 654,904.

ZIP Codes: 98011–12, 98019–20, 98021, 98026, 98028, 98033–34, 98036–37, 98041, 98043, 98046, 98052, 98061, 98072–74, 98077, 98082–83, 98110, 98133, 98155, 98160, 98177, 98204, 98208, 98272, 98275, 98290, 98296, 98311–12, 98315, 98340, 98342, 98345–46, 98364, 98370, 98380, 98383, 98392–93

* * *

SECOND DISTRICT

RICK LARSEN, Democrat, of Lake Stevens, WA; born in Arlington, WA, June 15, 1965; education: B.A., Pacific Lutheran University; M.P.A., University of Minnesota; professional: economic development official at the Port of Everett; worked as a Director of Public Affairs for a health provider association; public service: Snohomish County Council; religion: Methodist; married: Tiia Karlen; children: Robert and Per; committees: Agriculture; Armed Services; Transportation and Infrastructure; elected to the 107th Congress on November 7, 2000; reelected to each succeeding Congress.

Office Listings
http:/www.house.gov/larsen

107 Cannon House Office Building, Washington, DC 20515	(202) 225–2605
Deputy Chief of Staff/Legislative Director.—Jennifer Pharaoh.	FAX: 225–4420
Press Secretary.—Abbey Blake.	
2930 Wetmore Avenue, Suite 9E, Everett, WA 98201	(425) 252–3188
Chief of Staff.—Jeff Bjornstad.	
104 West Magnolia, Room 303, Bellingham, WA 98225	(360) 733–4500

Counties: ISLAND, KING (part), SAN JUAN, SKAGIT, SNOHOMISH (part), WHATCOM. CITIES AND TOWNSHIPS: Bellingham, Everett, and Mount Vernon. Population (2000), 654,903.

ZIP Codes: 98201, 98203–08, 98213, 98220–33, 98235–41, 98243–45, 98247–53, 98255–64, 98266–67, 98270–84, 98286–88, 98290–97

* * *

THIRD DISTRICT

BRIAN BAIRD, Democrat, of Vancouver, WA; born in Chauma, NM, March 7, 1956; education: B.S., University of Utah, 1977; M.S., University of Wyoming, 1980; Ph.D., University of Wyoming, 1984; professional: licensed clincial psychologist; has practiced in Washington State and Oregon; Professor and former Chairman of the Department of Psychology at Pacific Lutheran University; has worked in a variety of medical environments prior to election to the U.S. Congress; elected President of the Democratic Freshman Class for the 106th Congress; Democratic Regional Whip; committees: Budget; Science; Transportation and Infrastructure; elected to the 106th Congress; reelected to each succeeding Congress.

Office Listings
http://www.house.gov/baird

1421 Longworth House Office Building, Washington, DC 20515 .... (202) 225–3536
Chief of Staff.—Lisa Boyd. FAX: 225–3478
Press Secretary.—Meghan O'Shaughnessy.
Executive Assistant.—Rachel Brehm.
750 Anderson Street, Suite B, Vancouver, WA 98661 .... (360) 695–6292
District Director.—Pam Browkaw.
120 Union Avenue, Suite 105, Olympia, WA 98501 .... (360) 352–9768

Counties: CLARK COUNTY. CITIES AND TOWNSHIPS: Amboy, Ariel, Battle Ground, Brush Prairie, Camas, Heisson, La Center, Ridgefield, Vancouver, Washougal, Woodland, Yacolt. COWLITZ COUNTY. CITIES AND TOWNSHIPS: Carrolls, Castle Rock, Cougar, Kalama, Kelso, Longview, Ryderwood, Silverlake, Toutle. LEWIS COUNTY. CITIES AND TOWNSHIPS: Adna, Centralia, Chehalis, Cinebar, Curtis, Doty, Ethel, Galvin, Glenoma, Mineral, Morton, Mossyrock, Napavine, Onalaska, Packwood, Pe Ell, Randle, Salkum, Silver Creek, Toledo, Vader, Winlock. PACIFIC COUNTY. CITIES AND TOWNSHIPS: Bay Center, Chinook, Ilwaco, Lebam, Long Beach, Menlo, Nahcotta, Naselle, Ocean Park, Oysterville, Raymond, Seaview, South Bend, Tokeland. PIERCE COUNTY. CITIES AND TOWNSHIPS: Elbe. SKAMANIA COUNTY (part). CITIES AND TOWNSHIPS: Carson, North Bonneville, Stevenson, Underwood. THURSTON COUNTY (part). CITIES AND TOWNSHIPS: Buroda, Littlerock, Olympia, Tenino, and Rochester. WAHKIAKUM COUNTY. CITIES AND TOWNSHIPS: Cathlamet, Grays River, Rosburg, and Skamokawa. Population (2000), 654,898.

ZIP Codes: 98304, 98328, 98330, 98336, 98355–56, 98361, 98377, 98501–09, 98511–13, 98522, 98527, 98531–33, 98537–39, 98541–42, 98544, 98547, 98554, 98556–57, 98559, 98561, 98564–65, 98568, 98570, 98572, 98576–77, 98579, 98581–83, 98585–86, 98589–91, 98593, 98595–97, 98601–04, 98606–07, 98609–12, 98614, 98616, 98621–22, 98624–26, 98628–29, 98631–32, 98635, 98637–45, 98647–51, 98660–66, 98668, 98671–72, 98674–75, 98682–87

* * *

FOURTH DISTRICT

DOC HASTINGS, Republican, of Pasco, WA; born in Spokane, WA, February 7, 1941; education: graduated, Pasco High School, 1959; attended Columbia Basin College and Central Washington State University, Ellensburg, WA; military service: U.S. Army Reserves, 1963–69; professional: president, Columbia Basin Paper and Supply; board of directors, Yakima Federal Savings and Loan; member: Washington State House of Representatives, 1979–87; Republican Caucus chairman, assistant majority leader, and National Platform Committee, 1984; president: Pasco Chamber of Commerce; Pasco Downtown Development Association; Pasco Jaycees (chamber president); chairman, Franklin County Republican Central Committee, 1974–78; delegate, Republican National Convention, 1976–84; married: Claire Hastings, 1967; children: Kirsten, Petrina and Colin; committees: Rules; chairman, Standards of Official Conduct; subcommittees: chairman, Rules and Organization of the House; Legislative and Budget Process; elected to the 104th Congress; reelected to each succeeding Congress.

Office Listings
http://www.house.gov/hastings

1323 Longworth House Office Building, Washington, DC 20515 .... (202) 225–5816
Administrative Assistant.—Ed Cassidy. FAX: 225–3251
Scheduler / Office Manager.—Ilene Clauson.
Press Secretary.—Jessica Gleason.
2715 St. Andrews Loop, Suite D, Pasco, WA 99302 .... (509) 543–9396
302 East Chestnut, Yakima, WA 98901 .... (509) 452–3243

Counties: ADAMS COUNTY (part). CITIES: Othello. BENTON COUNTY. CITIES AND TOWNSHIPS: Benton City, Kennewick, Paterson, Plymouth, Prosser, Richland, West Richland. CHELAN COUNTY. CITIES AND TOWNSHIPS: Ardenvoir, Cashmere, Chelan, Chelan Falls, Dryden, Entiat, Leavenworth, Malaga, Manson, Monitor, Peshastin, Stehekin, Wenatchee. DOUGLAS COUNTY. CITIES AND TOWNSHIPS: Bridgeport, East Wenatchee, Leahy, Mansfield, Orondo, Palisades, Rock Island, Waterville. FRANKLIN COUNTY. CITIES AND TOWNSHIPS: Basin City, Connell, Eltopia, Kahlotus, Mesa, Pasco, Windust. GRANT COUNTY. CITIES AND TOWNSHIPS: Beverly, Coulee City, Desert Aire, Electric City, Ephrata, George, Grand Coulee, Hartline, Marlin, Mattawa, Moses Lake, Quincy, Royal City, Soap Lake, Stratford, Warden, Wilson Creek. KITTITAS COUNTY. CITIES AND TOWNSHIPS: Cle Elum, Easton, Ellensburg, Hyak, Kittitas, Ronald, Roslyn, Snoqualmic Pass, South Cle Elum, Thorp, Vantage. KLICKITAT COUNTY. CITIES AND TOWNSHIPS: Alderdale, Appleton, Bickleton, Bingen, Centerville, Cook, Dallesport, Glenwood, Goldendale, Husum, Klickitat, Lyle, Roosevelt, Trout Lake, Wahkiacus, White Salmon, Wishram, Wishram Heights. SKAMANIA COUNTY (part), YAKIMA COUNTY. CITIES AND TOWNSHIPS: Brownstown, Buena, Carson, Cowiche, Grandview, Granger, Harrah, Mabton, Moxee, Naches, Outlook, Parker, Selah, Sunnyside, Tieton, Toppenish, Underwood, Wapato, White Swan, Yakima, and Zillah. Population (2000), 654,901.

ZIP Codes: 98068, 98602, 98605, 98610, 98613, 98617, 98619–20, 98623, 98628, 98635, 98648, 98650–51, 98670, 98672–73, 98801–02, 98807, 98811–13, 98815–17, 98819, 98821–24, 98826, 98828–32, 98834, 98836–37, 98843, 98845, 98847–48, 98850–53, 98857–58, 98860, 98901–04, 98907–09, 98920–23, 98925–26, 98929–30, 98932–44, 98946–48, 98950–53, 99103, 99115–16, 99123–24, 99133, 99135, 99155, 99301–02, 99320–22, 99326, 99330, 99335–38, 99343–46, 99349–50, 99352–54, 99356–57

FIFTH DISTRICT

CATHY McMORRIS, Republican, of Colville, WA; born in Salem, OR, May 22, 1969; education: B.A., Pensacola Christian College, Pensacola, FL, 1990; M.B.A., University of Washington, Seattle, WA, 2002; professional: fruit orchard worker; member, Washington State House of Representatives, 1994–2004; minority leader, 2002–03; organizations: member, Grace Evangelical Free Church; committees: Armed Services; Education and the Workforce; Resources; subcommittees: Forests and Forest Health; Readiness; vice-chair, Select Education; Strategic Forces; Water and Power; 21st Century Competitiveness; elected to the 109th Congress on November 2, 2004.

Office Listings

http://www.house.gov/mcmorris

1708 Longworth House Office Building, Washington, DC 20515	(202) 225–2006
Chief of Staff.—Connie Partoyan.	FAX: 225–3392
Legislative Director.—Jack Silzel.	
Scheduler.—Julie Blackorby.	
10 N. Post Street, 6th floor, Spokane, WA 99201	(509) 353–2374
District Director.—David Condon.	
555 S. Main Street, Colville, WA 99114	(509) 684–3481
29 S. Palouse Street, Walla Walla, WA 99362	(509) 529–9358

Counties: ADAMS (part), ASOTIN, COLUMBIA, FERRY, GARFIELD, LINCOLN, PEND OREILLE, OKANAGAN, SPOKANE, STEVENS, WALLA WALLA, WHITMAN. Population (2000), 654,901.

ZIP Codes: 98812, 98814, 98819, 98827, 98829, 98832–34, 98840–41, 98844, 98846, 98849, 98855–57, 98859, 98862, 99001, 99003–06, 99008–09, 99011–14, 99016–23, 99025–27, 99029–34, 99036–37, 99039–40, 99101–05, 99107, 99109–11, 99113–14, 99116–19, 99121–22, 99125–26, 99128–31, 99133–41, 99143–44, 99146–61, 99163–67, 99169–71, 99173–74, 99176, 99179–81, 99185, 99201–20, 99223–24, 99228, 99251–52, 99256, 99258, 99260, 99302, 99323–24, 99326, 99328–29, 99333, 99335, 99341, 99344, 99347–48, 99356, 99359–63, 99371, 99401–03

* * *

SIXTH DISTRICT

NORMAN D. DICKS, Democrat, of Bremerton, WA; born in Bremerton, December 16, 1940; education: graduated, West Bremerton High School, 1959; B.A., political science, University of Washington, 1963; J.D., University of Washington School of Law, 1968; admitted to Washington bar, 1968; joined the staff of Senator Warren G. Magnuson in 1968 as legislative assistant and appropriations assistant, named administrative assistant in 1973, and held that post until he resigned to campaign for Congress in February 1976; member: Democratic Caucus; Washington, DC, and Washington State Bars; Puget Sound Naval Bases Association; Navy League of the United States; married: the former Suzanne Callison, 1967; children: David and Ryan; committees: Appropriations; Homeland Security; subcommittees: Intelligence and Counterterrorism; Infrastructure and Border Security; Defense; ranking member, Interior, Environment, and Related Agencies; elected to the 95th Congress; reelected to each succeeding Congress.

Office Listings

2467 Rayburn House Office Building, Washington, DC 20515	(202) 225–5916
Chief of Staff / Press Secretary.—George Behan.	
Legislative Director.—Pete Modaff.	
Scheduler.—Alyson Daly.	
1717 Pacific Avenue, Suite 2244, Tacoma, WA 98402	(253) 593–6536
District Director.—Tom Luce.	
Norm Dicks Government Ctr., 345 6th Street, Suite 500, Bremerton, WA 98337 ...	(360) 479–4011
Deputy District Director.—Cheri Williams.	
322 E. 5th Street, Port Angeles, WA 98362	(360) 452–3370
District Representative.—Mary Schuneman.	

Counties: CLALLAM COUNTY. CITIES AND TOWNSHIPS: Forks, Port Angeles, La Push, Sequim, Sekiu, Neah Bay. GRAYS HARBOR COUNTY. CITIES AND TOWNSHIPS: Aberdeen, Hoquiam, Montesano, Ocean City, Ocean Shores, Moclips, Westport. JEFFERSON COUNTY. CITIES AND TOWNSHIPS: Port Townsend, Quilcene. KITSAP COUNTY (part). CITIES AND TOWNSHIPS: Bremerton, Port Orchard, Gorst. MASON COUNTY. CITIES AND TOWNSHIPS: Shelton, Belfair, Allyn, Union. PIERCE COUNTY (part). CITIES AND TOWNSHIPS: Tacoma, Gig Harbor, Lakebay, and Lakewood. Population (2000), 654,902.

ZIP Codes: 98305, 98310–12, 98314, 98320, 98322, 98324–26, 98329, 98331–33, 98335, 98337, 98339, 98343, 98349–51, 98353, 98357–59, 98362–63, 98365–68, 98373, 98376, 98378, 98380–82, 98384, 98386, 98394–95, 98401–09, 98411–13, 98415–16, 98418, 98442, 98444–45, 98464–67, 98471, 98477, 98481, 98492, 98497–99, 98502, 98520, 98524, 98526, 98528, 98535–37, 98541, 98546–48, 98550, 98552, 98555, 98557, 98560, 98562–63, 98566, 98568–69, 98571, 98575, 98584, 98587–88, 98592, 98595

SEVENTH DISTRICT

JIM McDERMOTT, Democrat, of Seattle, WA; born in Chicago, IL, December 28, 1936; education: B.S., Wheaton College, Wheaton, IL, 1958; M.D., University of Illinois Medical School, Chicago, 1963; residency in adult psychiatry, University of Illinois Hospitals, 1964–66; residency in child psychiatry, University of Washington Hospitals, Seattle, 1966–68; served, U.S. Navy Medical Corps, lieutenant commander, 1968–70; psychiatrist; Washington State House of Representatives, 1971–72; Washington State Senate, 1975–87; Democratic nominee for governor, 1980; regional medical officer, Sub-Saharan Africa, U.S. Foreign Service, 1987–88; practicing psychiatrist and assistant clinical professor of psychiatry, University of Washington, Seattle, 1970–83; member: Washington State Medical Association; King County Medical Society; American Psychiatric Association; religion: St. Mark's Episcopal Church, Seattle; children: Katherine and James; committees: Ways and Means; subcommittees: ranking, Human Resources; Trade; elected on November 8, 1988, to the 101st Congress; reelected to each succeeding Congress.

Office Listings

1035 Longworth House Office Building, Washington, DC 20515	(202) 225–3106
Chief of Staff.—Jan Shinpoch.	FAX: 225–6197
Executive Assistant.—Beverly Swain.	
1809 Seventh Avenue, Suite 1212, Seattle, WA 98101–1313	(206) 553–7170
District Administrator.—Jane Sanders.	

Counties: KING COUNTY (part). CITIES AND TOWNSHIPS: Vashon, Burton, Dockton, and Seattle. Population (2000), 654,902.

ZIP Codes: 98013, 98055, 98070, 98101–09, 98111–19, 98121–22, 98124–27, 98129, 98131, 98133–34, 98136, 98139, 98141, 98144–46, 98151, 98154–55, 98161, 98164–66, 98168, 98171, 98174–75, 98177–78, 98181, 98184–85, 98190–91, 98194–95, 98199

* * *

EIGHTH DISTRICT

DAVID G. REICHERT, Republican, of Auburn, WA; born in Detroit Lakes, MI, August 29, 1950; education: graduated, Kent Meridian High School, Renton, WA, 1968; B.A., Concordia Lutheran College, Portland, OR, 1970; professional: U.S. Air Force Reserve, 1971–76; U.S. Air Force, 1976; police officer, King County, WA, 1972–97; sheriff, King County, WA, 1997–2004; member: president of the Washington State Sheriff's Association; executive board member of the Washington Association of Sheriffs and Police Chiefs; co-chair of the Washington State Partners in Crisis; awards: recipient of the 2004 National Sheriff's Association's "Sheriff of the Year"; two-time Medal of Valor Award Recipient from the King County sheriff's office; Washington Policy Center's Champion of Freedom Award; Families Northwest Public Policy Award; married: Julie; children: Angela, Tabitha, and Daniel; committees: Homeland Security; Science; Transportation and Infrastructure; elected to the 109th Congress on November 2, 2004.

Office Listings

http://www.house.gov/reichert

1223 Longworth House Office Building, Washington, DC 20515	(202) 225–7761
Chief of Staff.—Mike Shields.	FAX: 225–4282
Legislative Director.—Chris Miller.	
Executive Assistant / Scheduler.—Nichole Robison.	
Press Secretary.—Heather Janik.	
2737 78th Avenue, SE, Suite 202, Mercer Island, WA 98040	(206) 275–3438
District Director.—Mariana Parks.	

Counties: KING COUNTY (part). CITIES AND TOWNSHIPS: Auburn, Baring, Beaux Arts Village, Bellevue, Black Diamond, Carnation, Duvall, Enumclaw, Fall City, Issaquah, Kent, Mercer Island, Maple Valley, New Castle, North Bend, Preston, Redmond, Renton, Skykomish, Snoqualmie, Summit, Woodinville. PIERCE COUNTY. CITIES AND TOWNSHIPS: Ashford, Bonney Lake, Buckley, Carbonado, Eatonville, Elbe, Graham, Orting, Roy, South Prairie, Spanaway, and Wilkeson. Population (2000), 654,905.

ZIP Codes: 98002, 98004–10, 98014–15, 98019, 98022, 98024–25, 98027, 98029–31, 98033, 98035, 98038–40, 98042, 98045, 98050–53, 98055–56, 98058–59, 98064–65, 98068, 98074–75, 98077, 98092, 98304, 98321, 98323, 98328, 98330, 98338, 98344, 98348, 98352, 98360, 98372–75, 98385, 98387, 98390, 98396–98, 98446

NINTH DISTRICT

ADAM SMITH, Democrat, of Tacoma, WA; born in Washington, DC, June 15, 1965; education: graduated from Tyee High School, 1983; graduated from Fordham University, NY, 1987; law degree, University of Washington, 1990; admitted to the Washington bar in 1991; prosecutor for the city of Seattle; Washington State Senate, 1990–96; member, Kent Drinking Driver Task Force; board member, Judson Park Retirement Home; married Sara Smith, 1993; committees: Armed Services; International Relations; elected to the 105th Congress; reelected to each succeeding Congress.

Office Listings

227 Cannon House Office Building, Washington, DC 20515 .... (202) 225–8901
    Chief of Staff.—John Mulligan.   FAX: 225–5893
    Office Manager.—Katie Kuciemba.
    Communications Director.—Lars Anderson.
1717 Pacific Avenue, #2135, Tacoma, WA 98402 .... (253) 593–6600
    District Director.—Linda Danforth.

Counties: KING (part), PIERCE (part), THURSTON (part). CITIES: Algona, Auburn, Des Moines, Dupont, Edgewood, Federal Way, Fife, Kent, Lacey, Lakewood, Milton, Muckleshoot Indian Reservation, Nisqually Indian Reservation, Normandy Park, Pacific, Puyallup, Puyallup Indian Reservation, Renton, Roy, SeaTac, Spanaway, Tacoma, and Yelm. Population (2000), 654,902.

ZIP Codes: 98001–03, 98023, 98030–32, 98047, 98054–58, 98062–63, 98071, 98089, 98092–93, 98131–32, 98138, 98148, 98158, 98166, 98168, 98171, 98178, 98188, 98198, 98303, 98327–28, 98338, 98354, 98371–75, 98387–88, 98390, 98402, 98404, 98421–22, 98424, 98430–31, 98433, 98438–39, 98443–46, 98467, 98493, 98497–99, 98501, 98503, 98506, 98509, 98513, 98516, 98558, 98576, 98580, 98597

WEST VIRGINIA

(Population 2000, 1,808,344)

SENATORS

ROBERT C. BYRD, Democrat, of Sophia, WV; born, November 20, 1917; Baptist; married Erma Ora James; two daughters: Mrs. Mohammad (Mona Byrd) Fatemi and Mrs. Jon (Marjorie Byrd) Moore; six grandchildren: Erik, Darius and Fredrik Fatemi, and Michael (deceased), Mona and Mary Anne Moore; and six great-grandchildren; committees: ranking member, Appropriations; Armed Services; Budget; Rules and Administration; sworn in to the U.S. Senate on January 3, 1959; reelected to each succeeding Senate term.

Office Listings

http://byrd.senate.gov

311 Hart Senate Office Building, Washington, DC 20510	(202) 224–3954
Chief of Staff.—Barbara Videnieks.	
Administrative Assistant.—Gail John.	
Press Secretary.—Tom Gavin.	
300 Virginia Street East, Suite 2630, Charleston, WV 25301	(304) 342–5855
State Director.—Anne Barth.	

* * *

JOHN D. ROCKEFELLER IV, Democrat, of Charleston, WV; born in New York City, NY, June 18, 1937; education: graduated, Phillips Exeter Academy, Exeter, NH, 1954; A.B., Harvard University, Cambridge, MA, 1961; honorary degrees: J.D., West Virginia University; Marshall University; Davis and Elkins College; Dickinson College; University of Alabama; University of Cincinnati; doctor of humanities, West Virginia Institute of Technology; doctor of public service, Salem College; Vista volunteer, Emmons, WV, 1964; West Virginia House of Delegates, 1966–68; elected Secretary of State of West Virginia, 1968; president, West Virginia Wesleyan College, 1973–76; Governor of West Virginia, 1976–84; married: the former Sharon Percy; children: John, Valerie, Charles and Justin; committees: Commerce, Science, and Transportation; Finance; Veterans' Affairs; Select Committee on Intelligence; Joint Committee on Taxation; elected to the U.S. Senate on November 6, 1984; reelected to each succeeding Senate term.

Office Listings

http://rockefeller.senate.gov

531 Hart Senate Office Building, Washington, DC 20510	(202) 224–6472
Chief of Staff.—Kerry Ates.	FAX: 224–7665
Legislative Director.—Ellen Doneski.	
Communications Director.—Wendy Morigi.	
405 Capitol Street, Suite 308, Charleston, WV 25301	(304) 347–5372
207 Prince Street, Beckley, WV 25801	(304) 253–9704
118 Adams Street, Suite 301, Fairmont, WV 26554	(304) 367–0122
225 W. King Street, Suite 307, Martinsburg, WV 25401	(304) 262–9285

REPRESENTATIVES

FIRST DISTRICT

ALAN B. MOLLOHAN, Democrat, of Fairmont, WV; born in Fairmont, May 14, 1943; son of former Congressman Robert H. Mollohan and Helen Holt Mollohan; education: graduated, Greenbrier Military School, Lewisburg, WV, 1962; A.B., College of William and Mary, Williamsburg, VA, 1966; J.D., West Virginia University College of Law, Morgantown, 1970; captain, U.S. Army Reserves, 1970–83; professional: attorney; admitted to the West Virginia bar in 1970 and commenced practice in Fairmont; admitted to the District of Columbia bar in 1975; religion: member, First Baptist Church, Fairmont; married: the former Barbara Whiting, 1976; children: Alan, Robert, Andrew, Karl and Mary Kathryn; committees: Appropriations; ranking member, Standards of Official Conduct; elected on November 2, 1982, to the 98th Congress; reelected to each succeeding Congress.

Office Listings

2302 Rayburn House Office Building, Washington, DC 20515 .... (202) 225–4172
    Chief of Staff.—Colleen McCarty.
    Scheduler.—Jill Butash.
    Legislative Director.—Angela Ohm.
    Press Secretary.—Ron Hudok.
209 Post Office Building, P.O. Box 1400, Clarksburg, WV 26302–1400 .... (304) 623–4422
Federal Building, Room 232, P.O. Box 720, Morgantown, WV 26507–0720 .... (304) 292–3019
Federal Building, Room 2040, 425 Juliana Street, Parkersburg, WV 26101–0145 ... (304) 428–0493
Federal Building, 1125 Chapline Street, Wheeling, WV 26003–2900 .... (304) 232–5390

Counties: BARBOUR, BROOKE, DODDRIDGE, GILMER, GRANT, HANCOCK, HARRISON, MARION, MARSHALL, MINERAL, MONONGALIA, OHIO, PLEASANTS, PRESTON, RITCHIE, TAYLOR, TUCKER, TYLER, WETZEL, WOOD. CITIES AND TOWNSHIPS: Albright, Alma, Alvy, Anmoore, Arthur, Arthurdate, Auburn, Aurora, Baldwin, Barrackville, Baxter, Bayard, Beech Bottom, Belington, Belleville, Belleville, Bellview, Belmont, Bens Run, Benwood, Berea, Bethany, Big Run, Blacksville, Blandville, Booth, Brandonville, Bretz, Bridgeport, Bristol, Brownton, Bruceton Mills, Burlington, Burnt House, Burton, Cabins, Cairo, Cameron, Carolina, Cassville, Cedarville, Center Point, Central Station, Century, Chester, Clarksburg, Coburn, Colfax, Colliers, Core, Corinth, Cove, Coxs Mills, Cuzzart, Dallas, Davis, Davisville, Dawmont, Dellslow, Dorcas, Eglon, Elk Garden, Ellenboro, Elm Grove, Enterprise, Eureka, Everettville, Fairmont, Fairview, Farmington, Flemington, Flower, Follansbee, Folsom, Fort Ashby, Fort Neal, Four states, Friendly, Galloway, Gilmer, Glen Dale, Glen Easton, Glenville, Goffs, Gormania, Grafton, Grant Town, Granville, Greenwood, Gypsy, Hambleton, Harrisville, Hastings, Haywood, Hazelton, Hebron, Hendricks, Hepzibah, Highland, Hundred, Idamay, Independence, Industrial, Jacksonburg, Jere, Jordan, Junior, Keyser, Kingmont, Kingwood, Knob Fork, Lahmansville, Letter Gap, Lima, Linn, Littleton, Lockney, Lost Creek, Lumberport, MacFarlan, Mahone, Maidsville, Mannington, Masontown, Maysville, McMechen, McWhorter, Meadowbrook, Medley, Metz, Middlebourne, Mineralwells, Moatsville, Monongah, Montana Mines, Morgantown, Moundsville, Mount Clare, Mount Storm, Mountain, New Creek, New Cumberland, New England, New Manchester, New Martinsville, New Milton, Newberne, Newburg, Newell, Normantown, North Parkersburg, Nutter Fort, Osage, Owings, Paden City, Parkersburg, Parsons, Pennsboro, Pentress, Perkins, Petersburg, Petroleum, Philippi, Piedmont, Pine Grove, Porters Falls, Proctor, Pullman, Pursglove, Rachel, Reader, Red Creek, Reedsville, Reynoldsville, Riegeley, Rivesville, Rocket Center, Rockport, Rosedale, Rosemont, Rowlesburg, Saint George, Saint Marys, Salem, Sand Fork, Shinnston, Shirley, Shocks, Short Creek, Simpson, Sistersville, Smithburg, Smithfield, Smithville, Spelter, Stonewood, Stouts Mill, Stumptown, Tanner, Terra Alta, Thomas, Thornton, Toll Gate, Troy, Triadelphia, Tunnelton, Valley Grove, Vienna, Volga, Wadestown, Walker, Wallace, Wana, Warwood, Washington, Watson, Waverly Weirton, Wellsburg, Wendel, West Liberty, West Milford, West Union, Westover, Wheeling Wick, Wilbur, Wiley Ford, Wileyville, Williamstown, Wilson, Wilsonburg, Windsor Heights, Wolf Summit, Worthington, and Wyatt. Population (2000), 602,543.

ZIP Codes: 25258, 25267, 26003, 26030–41, 26047, 26050, 26055–56, 26058–60, 26062, 26070, 26074–75, 26101–06, 26120–21, 26133–34, 26142–43, 26146–50, 26155, 26159, 26161–62, 26164, 26167, 26169–70, 26175, 26178, 26180–81, 26184, 26186–87, 26201, 26238, 26250, 26254, 26260, 26263, 26269, 26271, 26275–76, 26283, 26287, 26289, 26292, 26301–02, 26306, 26320–21, 26323, 26325, 26327, 26330, 26332, 26334–35, 26337, 26339, 26342, 26346–49, 26351, 26354, 26361–62, 26366, 26369, 26374, 26377–78, 26384–86, 26404–05, 26408, 26410–12, 26415–16, 26419, 26421–22, 26424–26, 26430–31, 26434–38, 26440, 26443–44, 26448, 26451, 26456, 26463, 26501–02, 26504–08, 26519–21, 26524–25, 26527, 26529, 26531, 26534, 26537, 26541–44, 26546–47, 26554–55, 26559–63, 26566, 26568, 26570–72, 26574–76, 26578, 26581–82, 26585–88, 26590–91, 26611, 26623, 26636, 26638, 26705, 26710, 26716–17, 26719–20, 26726, 26731, 26734, 26739, 26743, 26750, 26753, 26764, 26767, 26833, 26847, 26852, 26855

* * *

SECOND DISTRICT

SHELLEY MOORE CAPITO, Republican, of Charleston, WV; born in Glen Dale, WV, November 26, 1953; education: B.S., Duke University; M.Ed., University of Virginia; professional: career counselor; West Virginia State College; West Virginia Board of Regents; organizations: Community Council of Kanawha Valley; YWCA; West Virginia Interagency Council for Early Intervention; Habitat for Humanity; public service: elected to the West Virginia House of Delegates, 1996; reelected in 1998; awards: Coalition for a Tobacco-Free West Virginia Legislator of the Year; religion: Presbyterian; married: to Charles L., Jr.; three children; committees: Rules; subcommittees: Rules and Organization of the House; elected to the 107th Congress on November 7, 2000; reelected to each succeeding Congress.

Office Listings

http://www.house.gov/capito

1431 Longworth House Office Building, Washington, DC 20515 .... (202) 225–2711
    Chief of Staff.—Martin Baker.
    Office Manager.—Alison Bibbee.
    Legislative Director.—Robert Steptoe.
4815 MacCorkle Avenue, Southeast, Charleston, WV 25304 .... (304) 925–5964
300 Foxcroft Avenue, Suite 102, Martinsburg, WV 25401 .... (304) 264–8810

Counties: BERKELEY, BRAXTON, CALHOUN, CLAY, HAMPSHIRE, HARDY, JACKSON, JEFFERSON, KANAWHA, LEWIS, MASON, MORGAN, PENDLETON, PUTNAM, RANDOLPH, ROANE, UPSHUR, WIRT. Population (2000), 602,245.

ZIP Codes: 25002–03, 25005, 25011, 25015, 25019, 25025–26, 25030, 25033, 25035, 25039, 25043, 25045–46, 25054, 25059, 25061, 25063–64, 25067, 25070–71, 25075, 25079, 25081–83, 25085–86, 25088, 25102–03, 25106–07, 25109–13, 25123–26, 25132–34, 25136, 25139, 25141, 25143, 25147, 25150, 25156, 25159–60, 25162, 25164, 25168, 25177,

25187, 25201–02, 25211, 25213–14, 25231, 25234–35, 25239, 25241, 25243–45, 25247–48, 25251–53, 25259–62, 25264–68, 25270–71, 25275–76, 25279, 25281, 25285–87, 25301–06, 25309, 25311–15, 25317, 25320–39, 25350, 25356–58, 25360–62, 25364–65, 25375, 25392, 25396, 25401–02, 25410–11, 25413–14, 25419–23, 25425, 25427–32, 25434, 25437–38, 25440–44, 25446, 25502–03, 25510, 25515, 25520, 25523, 25526, 25541, 25550, 25560, 25569, 26133, 26136–38, 26141, 26143, 26147, 26151–52, 26160–61, 26164, 26173, 26180, 26201–02, 26205, 26210, 26215, 26218, 26224, 26228–30, 26234, 26236–38, 26241, 26253–54, 26257, 26259, 26261, 26263, 26267–68, 26270, 26273, 26276, 26278, 26280, 26282–83, 26285, 26293–94, 26296, 26321, 26335, 26338, 26342–43, 26351, 26372, 26376, 26378, 26384–85, 26412, 26430, 26443, 26447, 26452, 26546, 26590, 26601, 26610–11, 26615, 26617, 26619, 26621, 26623–24, 26627, 26629, 26631, 26636, 26638–39, 26641, 26651, 26656, 26660, 26662, 26667, 26671, 26675–76, 26678–79, 26681, 26684, 26690–91, 26704–05, 26707, 26710–11, 26714, 26717, 26722, 26731, 26739, 26743, 26750, 26755, 26757, 26761, 26763–64, 26801–02, 26804, 26807–08, 26810, 26812, 26814–15, 26817–18, 26823–24, 26836, 26838, 26845, 26847, 26851–52, 26865–66, 26884, 26886

* * *

THIRD DISTRICT

NICK J. RAHALL II, Democrat, of Beckley, WV; born in Beckley, May 20, 1949; education: graduated, Woodrow Wilson High School, Beckley, 1967; A.B., Duke University, Durham, NC, 1971; graduate work, George Washington University, Washington, DC; colonel in U.S. Air Force Civil Air Patrol; president of the West Virginia Society of Washington, DC; business executive; sales representative, WWNR radio station; president, Mountaineer Tour and Travel Agency, 1974; president, West Virginia Broadcasting; named: Coal Man of the Year, *Coal Industry News,* 1979; "Young Democrat of the Year", Young Democrats, 1980; 1984 West Virginia American Legion Distinguished Service Award recipient; delegate, Democratic national conventions, 1972, 1976, 1980, 1984; member: Rotary; Elks; Moose; Eagles; NAACP; National Rifle Association; AF & AM; RAM; Mount Hope Commandery; Shrine Club; Benie Kedeem Temple in Charleston; Beckley Presbyterian Church; chairman and founder, Congressional Coal Group; Democratic Leadership Council; Congressional Arts Caucus; Congressional Black Caucus; Congressional Fitness Caucus; International Workers' Rights Caucus; ITS Caucus; Qatar Caucus; Congressional Rural Caucus; Congressional Steel Caucus; Congressional Textile Caucus; Congressional Travel and Tourism Caucus; Congressional Truck Caucus; Wine Caucus; Automobile Task Force; Democratic Congressional Campaign Committee; Democratic Study Group; Energy and Environment Study Conference; married: the former Melinda Ross; children: Rebecca Ashley, Nick Joe III, and Suzanne Nicole; committees: ranking member, Resources; Transportation and Infrastructure; elected to the 95th Congress, November 2, 1976; reelected to each succeeding Congress.

Office Listings

nrahall@mail.house.gov   http://www.house.gov/rahall

2307 Rayburn House Office Building, Washington, DC 20515	(202) 225–3452
Administrative Assistant.—Kent Keyser.	FAX: 225–9061
Chief Counsel.—Jim Zoia.	
Legislative Staff: Stefan Bailey, Erika Young, Ben Zogby.	
Press Secretary.—Kevin Baker.	
815 Fifth Avenue, Huntington, WV 25701	(304) 522–6425
106 Main Street, Beckley, WV 25801	(304) 252–5000
220 Dingess Street, Logan, WV 25601	(304) 752–4934
1005 Federal Building, Bluefield, WV 24701	(304) 325–6222

Counties: BOONE, CABELL, FAYETTE, GREENBRIER, LINCOLN, LOGAN, MCDOWELL, MERCER, MINGO, MONROE, NICHOLAS, POCAHONTAS, RALEIGH, SUMMERS, WAYNE, WEBSTER, WYOMING. Population (2000), 603,556.

ZIP Codes: 24701, 24712, 24714–16, 24719, 24724, 24726, 24729, 24731–33, 24736–40, 24747, 24751, 24801, 24808, 24811, 24813, 24815–18, 24820–31, 24834, 24836, 24839, 24842–57, 24859–62, 24866–74, 24878–82, 24884, 24887–88, 24892, 24894–99, 24901–02, 24910, 24915–18, 24920, 24924–25, 24927, 24931, 24934–36, 24938, 24941, 24943–46, 24950–51, 24954, 24957, 24961–63, 24966, 24970, 24974, 24976–77, 24981, 24983–86, 24991, 24993, 25002–04, 25007–10, 25021–22, 25024, 25028, 25031, 25036, 25040, 25043–44, 25047–49, 25051, 25053, 25057, 25059–60, 25062, 25076, 25081, 25083, 25085, 25090, 25093, 25108, 25114–15, 25118–19, 25121, 25130, 25136, 25139–40, 25142, 25148–49, 25152, 25154, 25161, 25165, 25169, 25173–74, 25180–81, 25183, 25185–86, 25193, 25202–06, 25208–09, 25213, 25501, 25504–08, 25510–12, 25514, 25517, 25520–21, 25523–24, 25526, 25529–30, 25534–35, 25537, 25540–41, 25544–45, 25547, 25555, 25557, 25559, 25562, 25564–65, 25567, 25570–73, 25601, 25606–08, 25611–12, 25614, 25617, 25621, 25624–25, 25628, 25630, 25632, 25634–39, 25644, 25646–47, 25649–54, 25661, 25665–67, 25669–71, 25674, 25676, 25678, 25682, 25685–88, 25690–92, 25694, 25696, 25699, 25701–29, 25755, 25770–79, 25801–02, 25810–13, 25816–18, 25820, 25823, 25825–27, 25831–33, 25836–37, 25839–41, 25843–49, 25851, 25853–57, 25859–60, 25862, 25864–66, 25868, 25870–71, 25873, 25875–76, 25878–80, 25882, 25901–02, 25904, 25906–09, 25911, 25913–22, 25927–28, 25931–32, 25934, 25936, 25938, 25942–43, 25951, 25958, 25961–62, 25965–67, 25969, 25971–72, 25976–79, 25981, 25984–86, 25989, 26202–03, 26205–06, 26208–09, 26217, 26222, 26230, 26234, 26261, 26264, 26266, 26288, 26291, 26294, 26298, 26610, 26617, 26639, 26651, 26656, 26660, 26662, 26674, 26676, 26678–81, 26684, 26690–91

WISCONSIN

(Population 2000, 5,363,675)

SENATORS

HERB KOHL, Democrat, of Milwaukee, WI; born in Milwaukee, February 7, 1935; education: graduated, Washington High School, Milwaukee, 1952; B.A., University of Wisconsin, Madison, 1956; M.B.A., Harvard Graduate School of Business Administration, Cambridge, MA, 1958; LL.D., Cardinal Stritch College, Milwaukee, WI, 1986 (honorary); served, U.S. Army Reserves, 1958–64; businessman; president, Herbert Kohl Investments; owner, Milwaukee Bucks NBA basketball team; past chairman, Milwaukee's United Way Campaign; State Chairman, Democratic Party of Wisconsin, 1975–77; honors and awards: Pen and Mike Club Wisconsin Sports Personality of the Year, 1985; Wisconsin Broadcasters Association Joe Killeen Memorial Sportsman of the Year, 1985; Greater Milwaukee Convention and Visitors Bureau Lamplighter Award, 1986; Wisconsin Parkinson's Association Humanitarian of the Year, 1986; Kiwanis Milwaukee Award, 1987; committees: Appropriations; Judiciary; Special Committee on Aging; elected to the U.S. Senate on November 8, 1988; reelected to each succeeding Senate term.

Office Listings

http://kohl.senate.gov

330 Hart Senate Office Building, Washington, DC 20510	(202) 224–5653
Chief of Staff.—Paul Bock.	
Legislative Director.—Kate Sparks.	
Communications Director.—Lynn Becker.	
Executive Assistant.—Arlene Branca.	
310 W. Wisconsin Avenue, Suite 950, Milwaukee, WI 53203	(414) 297–4451
14 West Muffin Street, Suite 207, Madison, WI 53703	(608) 264–5338
402 Graham Avenue, Suite 206, Eau Claire, WI 54701	(715) 832–8424
4321 West College Avenue, Suite 235, Appleton, WI 54914	(920) 738–1640
425 State Street, Suite 202, LaCrosse, WI 54601	(608) 796–0045

* * *

RUSSELL FEINGOLD, Democrat, of Middleton, WI; born in Janesville, WI, March 2, 1953; education: graduated from Craig High School, Janesville, WI, 1971; B.A., University of Wisconsin-Madison, 1975; Rhodes Scholar, Oxford University, 1977; J.D., Harvard Law School, 1979; practicing attorney with Foley and Lardner, and with LaFollette and Sinykin, both in Madison, WI, 1979–85; Wisconsin State Senate, January 1983 to January 1993; married: Mary Feingold; four children: daughters Jessica and Ellen, and stepsons Sam Speerschneider and Ted Speerschneider; committees: Budget; Foreign Relations; Judiciary; Special Committee on Aging; subcommittees: Security and Cooperation in Europe; elected to the U.S. Senate on November 3, 1992; reelected to each succeeding Senate term.

Office Listings

http://feingold.senate.gov

506 Hart Senate Office Building, Washington, DC 20510	(202) 224–5323
Administrative Assistant.—Mary Irvine.	
Legislative Director.—Paul Weinberger.	
Press Secretary.—Trevor Miller.	
517 East Wisconsin Avenue, Room 408, Milwaukee, WI 53202	(414) 276–7282
1600 Aspen Commons, Room 100, Middleton, WI 53562	(608) 828–1200
State Coordinator.—Jay Robaidek.	
401 Fifth Street, Room 410, Wausau, WI 54401	(715) 848–5660
425 State Street, Room 225, LaCrosse, WI 54603	(608) 782–5585
1640 Main Street, Green Bay, WI 54302	(920) 465–7508

REPRESENTATIVES

FIRST DISTRICT

PAUL RYAN, Republican, of Janesville, WI; born in Janesville, January 29, 1970; education: Joseph A. Craig High School; economic and political science degrees, Miami University in Ohio; professional: marketing consultant, Ryan Inc., Central (construction firm); aide to former U.S. Senator Bob Kasten (R–WI); advisor to former Vice Presidential candidate Jack Kemp, and U.S. Drug Czar Bill Bennett; also served as a legislative director in the U.S. Senate; organizations: Janesville Bowmen, Inc.; Ducks Unlimited; committees: Budget; Ways and Means; Joint Economic Committee; elected to the 106th Congress; reelected to each succeeding Congress.

Office Listings

http://www.house.gov/ryan

1217 Longworth House Office Building, Washington, DC 20515 .... (202) 225–3031
    Administrative Assistant.—Joyce Meyer.   FAX: 225–3393
    Legislative Director.—Peter Fotos.
    Scheduler.—Maureen Mitchell.
20 South Main Street, Suite 10, Janesville, WI 53545 .... (608) 752–4050
5712 7th Avenue, Kenosha, WI 53140 .... (262) 654–1901
304 6th Street, Racine, WI 53403 .... (262) 637–0510

Counties: KENOSHA, MILWAUKEE (part), RACINE, ROCK (part), WALWORTH (part), WAUKESHA (part). Population (2000), 670,458.

ZIP Codes: 53101–05, 53108–09, 53114–15, 53119–21, 53125–26, 53128–30, 53132, 53138–44, 53146–54, 53156–59, 53167–68, 53170–72, 53176–77, 53179, 53181–82, 53184–85, 53189–92, 53194–95, 53207, 53219–21, 53228, 53401–08, 53501, 53505, 53511, 53525, 53534, 53538, 53545–48, 53563, 53585

* * *

SECOND DISTRICT

TAMMY BALDWIN, Democrat, of Madison, WI; born in Madison, WI, February 11, 1962; education: graduated from Madison West High School, 1980; A.B., mathematics and government, Smith College, 1984; J.D., University of Wisconsin Law School, 1989; professional: attorney, 1989–92; elected to the Dane County Board of Supervisors, 1986–94; elected to the State Assembly from the 78th district, 1993–99; committees: Energy and Commerce; elected to the 106th Congress; reelected to each succeeding Congress.

Office Listings

http://tammybaldwin.house.gov

1022 Longworth House Office Building, Washington, DC 20515 .... (202) 225–2906
    Chief of Staff.—Bill Murat.   FAX: 225–6942
    Legislative Director.—Kris Pratt.
    Appointment Secretary.—Maureen Hekmat.
    Press Secretary.—Jerilyn Goodman. .... (608) 258–9800
10 East Doty Street, Suite 405, Madison, WI 53703 .... (608) 258–9800
    District Director.—Curt Finkelmeyer.
400 East Grand Avenue, Suite 402, Beloit, WI 53511 .... (608) 362–2800

Counties: COLUMBIA, DANE, GREEN, JEFFERSON (part), ROCK (part), SAUK (part), WALWORTH (part). Population (2000), 670,457.

ZIP Codes: 53038, 53094, 53098, 53190, 53501–02, 53504, 53508, 53511–12, 53515–17, 53520–23, 53527–29, 53531–32, 53534, 53536–38, 53542, 53544–46, 53548–51, 53555, 53558–63, 53566, 53570–72, 53574–76, 53578, 53581–83, 53589–91, 53593–94, 53596–98, 53701–08, 53711, 53713–19, 53725–26, 53744, 53777–79, 53782–94, 53901, 53911, 53913, 53916, 53923, 53925–26, 53928, 53932–33, 53935, 53951, 53954–57, 53959–60, 53965, 53968–69

* * *

THIRD DISTRICT

RON KIND, Democrat, of La Crosse, WI; born in La Crosse, March 16, 1963; education: B.A., Harvard University, 1985; M.A., London School of Economics, 1986; J.D., University of Minnesota Law School, 1990; admitted to the Wisconsin bar, 1990; state prosecutor, La Crosse County District Attorney's Office; board of directors, La Crosse Boys and Girls Club; Coulee Council on Alcohol and Drug Abuse; Wisconsin Harvard Club; Wisconsin Bar Association; La Crosse County Bar Association; married: Tawni Zappa in 1994; two sons, Jonathan, Matthew; committees: Budget; Education and the Workforce; Resources; elected to the 105th Congress; reelected to each succeeding Congress.

Office Listings

1406 Longworth House Office Building, Washington, DC 20515 .... (202) 225–5506
   Chief of Staff.—Cindy Brown.   FAX: 225–5739
   Press Secretary.—Stephanie Lundberg.
   Legislative Director.—Sherry Harper.
   Scheduler.—Dan Guilbeault.
205 5th Avenue South, Suite 227, La Crosse, WI 54601 .... (608) 782–2558
   District Director.—Loren Kannenberg.
131 S. Barstow Street, Suite 301, Eau Claire, WI 54701 .... (715) 831–9214
   Staff Assistant/Case Worker.—Mark Aumann.

Counties: BUFFALO, CLARK (part), CRAWFORD, DUNN, EAU CLAIRE, GRANT, IOWA, JACKSON, JUNEAU, LA CROSSE, LAFAYETTE, MONROE, PEPIN, PIERCE, RICHLAND, SAUK (part), ST. CROIX, TREMPEALEAU, VERNON. Population (2000), 670,462.

ZIP Codes: 53503–04, 53506–07, 53510, 53516–18, 53522, 53526, 53530, 53533, 53535, 53540–41, 53543–44, 53553–54, 53556, 53560, 53565, 53569, 53573, 53577–78, 53580–84, 53586–88, 53595, 53599, 53801–13, 53816–18, 53820–21, 53824–27, 53913, 53924, 53929, 53937, 53940–44, 53948, 53950–51, 53958–59, 53961–62, 53965, 53968, 54001–05, 54007, 54009–11, 54013–17, 54020–28, 54082, 54420, 54436–37, 54446, 54449, 54456–57, 54460, 54466, 54479, 54488, 54493, 54601–03, 54610–12, 54614–16, 54618–32, 54634–46, 54648–62, 54664–67, 54669–70, 54701–03, 54720–30, 54733–43, 54746–47, 54749–51, 54754–65, 54767–73

* * *

FOURTH DISTRICT

GWEN MOORE, Democrat, of Milwaukee, WI; born in Racine, WI, April 18, 1951; education: graduated North Division High School, Milwaukee; B.A., Political Science, Marquette University, Milwaukee, WI, 1978; professional: Program and Planning Analyst for the State of Wisconsin Services; housing officer, Wisconsin Housing and Development Authority; member: Wisconsin state assembly, 1989–92; Wisconsin state senate, 1993–2004; president pro tempore, 1997–98; family: three children; committees: Financial Services; Small Business; elected to the 109th Congress on November 2, 2004.

Office Listings

http://www.house.gov/moore

1408 Longworth House Office Building, Washington, DC 20515 .... (202) 225–4572
   Legislative Director.—Winfield Boerckel.   FAX: 225–8135
   Legislative Assistant.—Andrew Stevens.
   Scheduler/Executive Assistant.—Kendra Murray.
5032 West Forest Home Avenue, Milwaukee, WI 53219 .... (414) 297–1140
   Chief of Staff.—Shirley Elllis.

Counties: MILWAUKEE (part). CITIES AND TOWNSHIPS: Milwaukee, Cudahy, South Milwaukee, St. Francis, West Allis, and West Milwaukee. Population (2000), 670,458.

ZIP Codes: 53110, 53154, 53172, 53201–28, 53233–35, 53237, 53268, 53270, 53277–78, 53280–81, 53284–85, 53288, 53290, 53293, 53295

* * *

FIFTH DISTRICT

F. JAMES SENSENBRENNER, JR., Republican, of Menomonee Falls, WI; born in Chicago, IL, June 14, 1943; education: graduated from Milwaukee Country Day School, 1961; A.B., Stanford University, 1965; J.D., University of Wisconsin Law School, 1968; admitted to the Wisconsin bar, 1968; commenced practice in Cedarburg, WI; admitted to practice before the U.S. Supreme Court in 1972; attorney; elected to the Wisconsin Assembly in 1968, reelected in 1970, 1972, and 1974; elected to Wisconsin Senate in a special election in 1975, and reelected in 1976, serving as assistant minority leader; staff member of former U.S. Congressman J. Arthur Younger of California in 1965; member: Waukesha County Republican Party; Wisconsin Bar Association; Riveredge Nature Center; Friends of Museums; and American Philatelic Society; married: the former Cheryl Warren, 1977; children: Frank James III, and Robert Alan; committees: chairman, Judiciary; elected to the 96th Congress, November 7, 1978; reelected to each succeeding Congress.

Office Listings

http://www.house.gov/sensenbrenner   sensenbrenner@mail.house.gov

2449 Rayburn House Office Building, Washington, DC 20515 .... (202) 225–5101
Chief of Staff.—Tom Schreibel.
Deputy Chief of Staff/Press Secretary.—Raj Bharwani.
Scheduler/Office Manager.—Emily Sanders.
Room 154, 120 Bishops Way, Brookfield, WI 53005 .... (262) 784–1111
Chief of Staff.—Tom Schreibel.

Counties: JEFFERSON (part), MILWAUKEE (part), OZAUKEE, WASHINGTON, WAUKESHA (part). Population (2000), 670,458.

ZIP Codes: 53002, 53004–05, 53007–08, 53012–13, 53017–18, 53021–22, 53024, 53027, 53029, 53033, 53037–38, 53040, 53045–46, 53051–52, 53056, 53058, 53060, 53064, 53066, 53069, 53072, 53074, 53076, 53080, 53085–86, 53089–90, 53092, 53095, 53097–98, 53118, 53122, 53127, 53137, 53146, 53151, 53156, 53178, 53183, 53186–90, 53208–14, 53217, 53219, 53222–23, 53225–28, 53263, 53538, 53549

* * *

SIXTH DISTRICT

THOMAS E. PETRI, Republican, of Fond du Lac, WI; born in Marinette, WI, May 28, 1940; education: graduated, Lowell P. Goodrich High School, 1958; B.A., Harvard University, Cambridge, MA, 1962; J.D., Harvard Law School, 1965; professional: admitted to the Wisconsin state and Fond du Lac county bar associations, 1965; commenced practice in Fond du Lac in 1970; lawyer; law clerk to Federal Judge James Doyle, 1965; Peace Corps volunteer, 1966–67; White House aide, 1969; elected to the Wisconsin State Senate in 1972; reelected in 1976, and served until April, 1979; married; one daughter; committees: Education and the Workforce; Transportation and Infrastructure; elected to the 96th Congress, by special election, on April 3, 1979, to fill the vacancy caused by the death of William A. Steiger; reelected to each succeeding Congress.

Office Listings

http://www.house.gov/petri

2462 Rayburn House Office Building, Washington, DC 20515 .... (202) 225–2476
Administrative Assistant/Legislative Director.—Debra Gebhardt.
Communications Director.—Niel Wright.
Office Manager.—Linda Towse.
490 West Rolling Meadows Drive, Suite B, Fond du Lac, WI 54937 .... (920) 922–1180
District Director.—David G. Anderson.
2390 State Road, Suite B, Oshkosh, WI 54904 .... (920) 231–6333

Counties: ADAMS, CALUMET (part), DODGE, FOND DU LAC, GREEN LAKE, JEFFERSON (part), MANITOWOC, MARQUETTE, OUTAGAMIE (part), SHEBOYGAN, WAUSHARA, WINNEBAGO. Population (2000), 670,459.

ZIP Codes: 53001, 53003, 53006, 53010–11, 53013–16, 53019–21, 53023, 53026–27, 53031–32, 53034–36, 53039, 53042, 53044, 53047–50, 53057, 53059, 53061–63, 53065–66, 53070, 53073, 53075, 53078–79, 53081–83, 53085, 53088, 53091, 53093–94, 53098–99, 53137, 53205, 53207, 53215, 53221, 53557, 53579, 53594, 53901, 53910, 53916–17, 53919–20, 53922–23, 53925–27, 53930–34, 53936, 53939, 53946–47, 53949–50, 53952–54, 53956, 53963–65, 53968, 54110, 54115, 54123, 54126, 54129–30, 54136, 54140, 54160, 54169, 54207–08, 54214–16, 54220–21, 54227–28, 54230, 54232, 54240–41, 54245, 54247, 54413, 54457, 54486, 54494, 54499, 54613, 54619, 54638, 54648, 54660, 54755, 54901–04, 54906, 54909, 54911, 54913–15, 54921–23, 54927, 54930, 54932–37, 54941, 54943–44, 54947, 54950, 54952, 54956–57, 54960, 54963–68, 54970–71, 54974, 54976, 54979–86

* * *

SEVENTH DISTRICT

DAVID R. OBEY, Democrat, of Wausau, WI; born in Okmulgee, OK, October 3, 1938; education: graduated Wausau High School, 1956; M.A. in political science, University of Wisconsin, 1960 (graduate work in Russian government and foreign policy); elected to the Wisconsin Legislature from Marathon County's 2nd District at the age of 24; reelected three times; assistant Democratic floor leader; married: Joan Lepinski of Wausau, WI, 1962; children: Craig David and Douglas David; committees: ranking member, Appropriations; subcommittees: ranking member, Labor, Health and Human Services, and Education; ex officio member of all subcommittees; former chairman, Joint Economic Committee; elected to the 91st Congress, by special election, on April 1, 1969, to fill the vacancy created by the resignation of Melvin R. Laird; reelected to each succeeding Congress.

Office Listings

http://www.house.gov/obey

2314 Rayburn House Office Building, Washington, DC 20515 .... (202) 225–3365
  Chief of Staff.—William H. Stone.
  Scheduler.—Carly M. Burns.
  Press Secretary.—Dan Sanchez.
401 5th Street, Suite 406A, Wausau, WI 54403 .... (715) 842–5606
  District Representative.—Doug Hill.
1401 Tower Avenue, Suite 307, Superior, WI 54880 .... (715) 398–4426

Counties: ASHLAND, BARRON, BAYFIELD, BURNETT, CHIPPEWA, CLARK (part), DOUGLAS, IRON, LANGLADE (part), LINCOLN, MARATHON, ONEIDA (part), POLK, PORTAGE, PRICE, RUSK, SAWYER, TAYLOR, WASHBURN, WOOD. Population (2000), 670,462.

ZIP Codes: 54001, 54004–07, 54009, 54017, 54020, 54024, 54026, 54401–12, 54414–15, 54417–18, 54420–29, 54432–35, 54437, 54439–43, 54447–49, 54451–52, 54454–55, 54457–60, 54462–63, 54466–67, 54469–76, 54479–81, 54484–85, 54487–90, 54492, 54494–95, 54498–99, 54501, 54513–15, 54517, 54524–27, 54529–32, 54534, 54536–38, 54545–47, 54550, 54552, 54555–56, 54559, 54563–65, 54703, 54724, 54726–33, 54739, 54745, 54748, 54757, 54762–63, 54766, 54768, 54771, 54774, 54801, 54805–06, 54810, 54812–14, 54816–22, 54824, 54826–30, 54832, 54834–50, 54853–59, 54861–62, 54864–65, 54867–68, 54870–76, 54880, 54888–91, 54893, 54895–96, 54909, 54921, 54945, 54966, 54977, 54981

* * *

EIGHTH DISTRICT

MARK GREEN, Republican, of Green Bay, WI; born in Boston, MA, June 1, 1960; education: B.A., University of Wisconsin-Eau Claire; J.D., University of Wisconsin Law School-Madison, 1987; attorney; elected to Wisconsin State Assembly, 4th District, 1992–98; he and his wife Sue have three children: Rachel, Anna, and Alex; committees: International Relations; Judiciary; Republican Policy Committee; Assistant Majority Whip; elected to the 106th Congress; reelected to each succeeding Congress.

Office Listings

http://ww.house.gov/markgreen   mark.green@mail.house.gov

1314 Longworth House Office Building, Washington, DC 20515 .... (202) 225–5665
  Chief of Staff.—Chris Tuttle.   FAX: 225–5729
  Press Secretary.—Luke Punzenberger.
  Executive Assistant.—Nicole Vernon.
700 East Walnut Street, Green Bay, WI 54301 .... (920) 437–1954
  District Director.—Chad Weininger.
609–A W. College Avenue, Appleton, WI 54911 .... (920) 380–0061
  Regional Representative.—Rebecca Deschane.

Counties: BROWN, CALUMET (part), DOOR, FLORENCE, FOREST, KEWAUNEE, LANGLADE (part), MARINETTE, MENOMINEE, OCONTO, ONEIDA (part), OUTAGAMIE (part), SHAWANO, VILAS, WAUPACA. Population (2000), 670,461.

ZIP Codes: 54101–04, 54106–07, 54110–15, 54119–21, 54124–28, 54130–31, 54135, 54137–41, 54143, 54149–57, 54159, 54161–62, 54165–66, 54169–71, 54173–75, 54177, 54180, 54182, 54201–02, 54204–05, 54208–13, 54216–17, 54226–27, 54229–30, 54234–35, 54241, 54246, 54301–08, 54311, 54313, 54324, 54344, 54408–09, 54414, 54416, 54418, 54424, 54427–28, 54430, 54435, 54450, 54452, 54462–65, 54485–87, 54491, 54499, 54501, 54511–12, 54519–21, 54529, 54531, 54538–43, 54545, 54548, 54554, 54557–58, 54560–62, 54564, 54566, 54568, 54911–15, 54919, 54922, 54926, 54928–29, 54931, 54933, 54940, 54942, 54944–50, 54952, 54956, 54961–62, 54965, 54969, 54975, 54977–78, 54981, 54983, 54990

WYOMING

(Population 2000, 493,782)

SENATORS

CRAIG THOMAS, Republican, of Casper, WY; born in Cody, WY, February 17, 1933; education: graduated from Cody High School; B.S., University of Wyoming, 1955; military service: served in the U.S. Marine Corps, captain, 1955–59; small businessman; vice president, Wyoming Farm Bureau, 1959–66; American Farm Bureau, 1966–75; general manager, Wyoming Rural Electric Association, 1975–89; member: Wyoming House of Representatives, 1984–89; married: Susan Thomas; children: Peter, Paul, Lexi and Patrick; elected to the U.S. House of Representatives, by special election, on April 25, 1989, to fill the vacancy caused by the resignation of Dick Cheney; reelected to each succeeding Congress; committees: Agriculture, Nutrition, and Forestry; Energy and Natural Resources; Finance; Indian Affairs; Select Committee on Ethics; elected to the U.S. Senate in November, 1994; reelected to each succeeding Senate term.

Office Listings

http://thomas.senate.gov

307 Dirksen Senate Office Building, Washington, DC 20510	(202) 224–6441
Chief of Staff.—Shawn Whitman.	FAX: 224–1724
Legislative Director.—Bryn Stewart.	
Press Secretary.—Cameron Hardy.	
Administrative Director.—David Brewster.	
2201 Federal Building, Casper, WY 82601	(307) 261–6413
State Director.—Bobbi Brown.	
2120 Capitol Avenue, Suite 2013, Cheyenne, WY 82001	(307) 772–2451
Field Representative.—Mary Paxson.	
2632 Foothills Boulevard, Suite 101, Rock Springs, WY 82901	(307) 362–5012
Field Representative.—Pati Smith.	
325 West Main, Suite F, Riverton, WY 82501	(307) 856–6642
Field Representative.—Pam Buline.	
2 North Main Street, Suite 206, Sheridan, WY 82801	(307) 672–6456
Field Representative.—Matt Jones.	

* * *

MICHAEL B. ENZI, Republican, of Gillette, WY; born in Bremerton, WA, February 1, 1944; education: B.S., accounting, George Washington University, 1966; M.B.A., Denver University, 1968; professional: served in Wyoming National Guard, 1967–73; accounting manager and computer programmer, Dunbar Well Service, 1985–97; director, Black Hills Corporation, a New York Stock Exchange company, 1992–96; member, founding board of directors, First Wyoming Bank of Gillette, 1978–88; owner, with wife, of NZ Shoes; served in Wyoming House of Representatives, 1987–91, and in Wyoming State Senate, 1991–96; Mayor of Gillette, 1975–82; commissioner, Western Interstate Commission for Higher Education, 1995–96; served on the Education Commission of the States, 1989–93; president, Wyoming Association of Municipalities, 1980–82; president, Wyoming Jaycees, 1973–74; member: Lions Club; elder, Presbyterian Church; Eagle Scout; married: Diana Buckley, 1969; children: Amy, Brad, and Emily; committees: Banking, Housing, and Urban Affairs; Budget; chair, Health, Education, Labor and Pensions; Small Business and Entrepreneurship; elected to the U.S. Senate in November, 1996; reelected to each succeeding Senate term.

Office Listings

http://enzi.senate.gov   senator@enzi.senate.gov

379–A Russell Senate Office Building, Washington, DC 20510	(202) 224–3424
Chief of Staff.—Flip McConnaughey.	
Legislative Director.—Randi Reid.	
Press Secretary.—Coy Knobel.	
Office Manager.—Christen Petersen.	
Federal Center, Suite 2007, 2120 Capitol Avenue, Cheyenne, WY 82001	(307) 772–2477
400 S. Kendrick, Suite 303, Gillette, WY 82716	(307) 682–6268
100 East B Street, Room 3201, P.O. Box 33201, Casper, WY 82602	(307) 261–6572
1285 Sheridan Avenue, Suite 210, Cody, WY 82414	(307) 527–9444
P.O. Box 12470, Jackson, WY 83002	(307) 739–9507

REPRESENTATIVE

AT LARGE

BARBARA CUBIN, Republican, of Casper, WY; graduated, Natrona County High School; B.S., Creighton University, 1969; manager; substitute teacher; social worker; chemist; founding member of the Casper Suicide Prevention League; Casper Service League; president, Southridge Elementary School Parent/Teacher Organization; Mercer House, president and executive member; Casper Self Help Center, board member; Seton House, board member; Central Wyoming Rescue Mission, volunteer cook and server; Wyoming State Choir; Casper Civic Chorale; Cub Scout leader; Sunday School teacher at Saint Stephen's Episcopal Church; past memberships: executive committee of the Energy Council; chairman, Center for Legislators Energy and Environment Research (CLEER); National Council of State Legislatures; vice chairman, Energy Committee; 1994 Edison Electric Institutes' Wyoming Legislator of the Year and Toll Fellowship from the Council of State Governments, 1990; Wyoming House of Representatives committees, 1987–92: Minerals, Business and Economic Development; Revenue; Transportation; chair, Joint Interim Economic Development Subcommittee; Wyoming Senate committees, 1993–94: Travel, Recreation, Wildlife, and Cultural Resources; Revenue; Republican activities: chair, Wyoming Senate Conference, 1992–94; precinct committeewoman, 1988–94; legislative liaison and member, Natrona County Republican Women; 1992 Wyoming State Convention Parliamentarian; delegate, Wyoming State Convention, 1990, 1992, and 1994; State Legislative Candidate Recruitment Committee for the Wyoming Republican Party in 1988, 1990, and 1992; married: Frederick W. (Fritz) Cubin; children: William (Bill) and Frederick III (Eric); committees: Energy and Commerce; Resources; subcommittees: Energy and Mineral Resources; Water and Power; Commerce, Trade, and Consumer Protection; Telecommunications and the Internet; Health; Deputy Majority Whip; elected to the 104th Congress; reelected to each succeeding Congress.

Office Listings
http://www.house.gov/cubin

1114 Longworth House Office Building, Washington, DC 20515	(202) 225–2311
Chief of Staff.—Tom Wiblemo.	FAX: 225–3057
Legislative Director.—Rick Axthelm.	
Senior Legislative Assistant.—Jonni McCrann.	
Press Secretary.—Joe Milczewski.	
100 East B Street, Suite 4003, Casper, WY 82601	(307) 261–6595
State Director.—Jackie King.	
2120 Capitol Avenue, Suite 2015, Cheyenne, WY 82001	(307) 772–2595
District Representative.—Katie Legerski.	
2515 Foothill Boulevard, Suite 204, Rock Springs, WY 82901	(307) 362–4095
District Representative.—Bonnie Cannon.	

Population (2000), 493,782.

ZIP Codes: 82001, 82003, 82005–10, 82050–55, 82058–61, 82063, 82070–73, 82081–84, 82190, 82201, 82210, 82212–15, 82217–19, 82221–25, 82227, 82229, 82240, 82242–44, 82301, 82310, 82321–25, 82327, 82329, 82331–32, 82334–36, 82401, 82410–12, 82414, 82420–23, 82426, 82428, 82430–35, 82440–43, 82450, 82501, 82510, 82512–16, 82520, 82523–24, 82601–02, 82604–05, 82609, 82615, 82620, 82630, 82633, 82635–40, 82642–44, 82646, 82648–49, 82701, 82710–12, 82714–18, 82720–21, 82723, 82725, 82727, 82729–32, 82801, 82831–40, 82842, 82844–45, 82901–02, 82922–23, 82925, 82929–39, 82941–45, 83001–02, 83011–14, 83025, 83101, 83110–16, 83118–24, 83126–28

AMERICAN SAMOA

(Population 2000, 57,291)

DELEGATE

ENI F.H. FALEOMAVAEGA, Democrat, of Vailoatai, AS; education: graduate of Kahuku High School, Hawaii, 1962; B.A., Brigham Young University, 1966; J.D., University of Houston Law School, 1972; LL.M., University of California, Berkeley, 1973; military service: enlisted in U.S. Army, 1966–69, Vietnam veteran; captain, USAR, Judge Advocate General Corps, 1982–92; professional: adminstrative assistant to American Samoa's Delegate to Washington, 1973–75; staff counsel, Committee on Interior and Insular Affairs, 1975–81; deputy attorney general, American Samoa, 1981–84; elected Lieutenant Governor, American Samoa, 1984–89; Congressional Human Rights Caucus; Congressional Travel and Tourism Caucus; Democratic Study Group; Congressional Arts Caucus; Congressional Hispanic Caucus; admitted to U.S. Supreme Court and American Samoa bars; National Conference of Lieutenant Governors; National Association of Secretaries of State; Veterans of Foreign Wars; Navy League of the United States; National American Indian Prayer Breakfast Group; Pago Pago Lions Club; committees: International Relations; Resources; Small Business; married: Hinanui Bambridge Cave of Tahiti; five children; committees: International Relations; Resources; Small Business; elected as the American Samoan Delegate to the 101st Congress on November 8, 1988; reelected to each succeeding Congress.

Office Listings

http://www.house.gov/faleomavaega

2422 Rayburn House Office Building, Washington, DC 20515 .... (202) 225–8577
Deputy Chief of Staff.—Lisa Williams.   FAX: 225–8757
Office Manager.—Vili Lei.
Legislative Director.—David Richmond.
P.O. Drawer X, Pago Pago, AS 96799 .... (684) 633–1372

ZIP Codes: 96799

* * *

DISTRICT OF COLUMBIA

(Population 2000, 572,059)

DELEGATE

ELEANOR HOLMES NORTON, Democrat, of Washington, DC; born in Washington, DC, June 13, 1937; education: graduated from Dunbar High School, 1955; B.A., Antioch College, 1960; M.A., Yale Graduate School, 1963; J.D., Yale Law School, 1964; honorary degrees: Tougalvo University, 1992; University of Southern Connecticut, 1992; Fisk University, 1991; University of Hartford, 1990; Ohio Wesleyan University, 1990; Wake Forest University, 1990; Colgate University, 1989; Drury College, 1989; Florida International University, 1989; St. Lawrence University, 1989; University of Wisconsin, 1989; Rutgers University, 1988; St. Joseph's College, 1988; University of Lowell, 1988; Sojourner-Douglas College, 1987; Salem State College, 1987; Haverford College, 1986; Lesley College, 1986; New Haven University, 1986; University of San Diego, 1986; Bowdoin College, 1985; Antioch College, 1985; Tufts University, 1984; University of Massachusetts, 1983; Smith College, 1983; Medical College of Pennsylvania, 1983; Spelman College, 1982; Syracuse University, 1981; Yeshiva University, 1981; Lawrence University, 1981; Emanuel College, 1981; Wayne State University, 1980; Gallaudet College, 1980; Denison University, 1980; New York University, 1978; Howard University, 1978; Brown University, 1978; Wilberforce University, 1978; Georgetown University, 1977; City College of New York, 1975; Marymount College, 1974; Princeton University, 1973; Bard College, 1971; Cedar Crest College, 1969; chair, Equal Employment Opportunity Commission, 1977–81; professor of law, Georgetown University, 1982–90; chair, New York Commission on Human Rights, 1970–76; executive assistant to the mayor of New York City (concurrent appointment); law clerk, Judge A. Leon Higginbotham, Federal District Court, 3rd Circuit; attorney, admitted to practice by examination in the District of Columbia and Pennsylvania and in the U.S. Supreme Court; One Hundred Most Important Women (*Ladies Home Journal*, 1988); One Hundred Most Powerful Women in Washington (The *Washingtonian* magazine, September 1989); Ralph E. Shikes Bicentennial Fellow, Harvard Law School, 1987; Visiting Phi Beta Kappa Scholar, 1985; Visiting Fellow, Harvard University, John F. Kennedy School of Government, spring 1984; Distinguished Public Service Award, Center for National Policy, 1985;

Chancellor's Distinguished Lecturer, University of California Law School (Boalt Hall) at Berkeley, 1981; Yale Law School Association Citation of Merit Medal to the Outstanding Alumnus of the Law School, 1980; Harper Fellow, Yale Law School, 1976, (for "a person . . . who has made a distinguished contribution to the public life of the nation . . ."); Rockefeller Foundation, trustee, 1982–90; Community Foundation of Greater Washington, board; Yale Corporation, 1982–88; Council on Foreign Relations; Overseas Development Council; U.S. Committee to Monitor the Helsinki accords; Carter Center, Atlanta, Georgia; boards of Martin Luther King, Jr. Center for Social Change and Environmental Law Institute; Workplace Health Fund; divorced; two children: John and Katherine; committees: Government Reform; Homeland Security; Transportation and Infrastructure; subcommittees: Aviation; Civil Service and Agency Organization; Criminal Justice, Drug Policy and Human Resources; ranking member, Economic Development, Public Buildings and Emergency Management; Emergency Preparedness and Response; Intelligence and Counterterrorism; elected to the 102nd Congress on November 6, 1990; reelected to each succeeding Congress.

Office Listings

http://www.house.gov/norton

2136 Rayburn House Office Building, Washington, DC 20515 .... (202) 225–8050
    Chief of Staff.—Julia Hudson.   FAX: 225–3002
    Legislative Director.—Rosalind Parker.
    Executive Assistant.—Raven Roddey.
    Communications Director.—Doxie McCoy.

ZIP Codes: 20001–13, 20015–20, 20024, 20026–27, 20029–30, 20032–33, 20035–45, 20047, 20049–53, 20055–71, 20073–77, 20080, 20088, 20090–91, 20099, 20201–04, 20206–08, 20210–13, 20215–24, 20226–33, 20235, 20237, 20239–42, 20244–45, 20250, 20254, 20260, 20268, 20270, 20277, 20289, 20301, 20303, 20306–07, 20310, 20314–15, 20317–19, 20330, 20340, 20350, 20370, 20372–76, 20380, 20388–95, 20398, 20401–16, 20418–29, 20431, 20433–37, 20439–42, 20444, 20447, 20451, 20453, 20456, 20460, 20463, 20469, 20472, 20500, 20503–10, 20515, 20520–27, 20530–36, 20538–44, 20546–49, 20551–55, 20557, 20559–60, 20565–66, 20570–73, 20575–77, 20579–81, 20585–86, 20590–91, 20593–94, 20597, 20599

* * *

GUAM

(Population 2000, 154,805)

DELEGATE

MADELEINE Z. BORDALLO, Democrat, of Tamuning, Guam, born in Graceville, MN, May 31, 1933; education: Associate Degree in Music, St. Katherine's College, St. Paul, MN, 1953; professional: First Lady of Guam 1975–78, and 1983–86; Guam Senator, five terms, 1981–82, and 1987–94; two term Lt. Governor of Guam 1995–2002; National Committee Chairwoman for the National Democratic Party 1964–2004; family: Ricardo J. Bordallo (deceased); daughter Deborah, and granddaughter Nicole; committees: Armed Services; Resources; Small Business; elected to the 108th Congress on November 5, 2002; reelected to each succeeding Congress.

Office Listings

http://www.house.gov/bordallo   madeleine.bordallo@mail.house.gov

427 Cannon House Office Building, Washington, DC 20515 .... (202) 225–1188
    Chief of Staff/Legislative Director.—John Whitt.   FAX: 226–0341
    Press Secretary.—Neil Weare.
    Scheduler.—Rosanne Meno.
120 Father Duenas Avenue, Suite 107, Hagåtña, GU 96910 .... (671) 477–4272

ZIP Codes: 96910, 96912–13, 96915–17, 96919, 96921, 96923, 96926, 96928–29, 96931–32

* * *

PUERTO RICO

(Population 2000, 3,808,610)

RESIDENT COMMISSIONER

LUIS G. FORTUÑO, Republican, of Guaynabo, PR; born in San Juan, PR, October 31, 1960; education: B.S., Georgetown University, School of Foreign Service; J.D., University of Virginia

Law School; professional: attorney; public service: Secretary of Economic Development and Commerce for Puerto Rico, 1994–1997; member, New Progressive Party; religion: Catholic; family: married to Lucé; three children: Luis, Guillermo, and Maria; committees: Education and the Workforce; Resources; Transportation and Infrastructure; elected to the 109th Congress on November 2, 2004.

Office Listings

http://www.house.gov/fortuno

126 Cannon House Office Building, Washington, DC 20515 .... (202) 225–2615
    Chief of Staff.—Luis A. Baco.   FAX: 225–2154
    Deputy Chief of Staff.—Nicole Guillemard.
    Senior Policy Advisor.—Jaime Gonzalez.
    Senior Legislative Counsel.—Carmen Feliciano.
250 Calle Fortaleza, Old San Juan, PR 00901 .... (787) 723–6333

ZIP Codes: 00601–06, 00610–14, 00616–17, 00622–25, 00627, 00631, 00636–38, 00641, 00646–48, 00650, 00652–62, 00664, 00667, 00669–70, 00674, 00676–78, 00680–83, 00685, 00687–88, 00690, 00692–94, 00698, 00701, 00703–05, 00707, 00714–21, 00723, 00725–42, 00744–45, 00751, 00754, 00757, 00765–69, 00771–73, 00775, 00777–78, 00780, 00782–86, 00791–92, 00794–95, 00901–36, 00938, 00940, 00949–63, 00965–66, 00968–71, 00975–79, 00981–88

* * *

VIRGIN ISLANDS

(Population 2000, 108,612)

DELEGATE

DONNA M. CHRISTENSEN, Democrat, of St. Croix, VI; B.S., St. Mary's College, Notre Dame, IN, 1966; M.D., George Washington University School of Medicine, 1970; physician, family medicine; Acting Commissioner of Health, 1994–95; medical director, St. Croix Hospital, 1987–88; founding member and vice president, Virgin Islands Medical Institute; trustee, National Medical Association; past secretary and two-time past president, Virgin Islands Medical Society; founding member and trustee, Caribbean Youth Organization; member: Democratic National Committee; Virgin Islands Democratic Territorial Committee (past vice chair); Substance Abuse Coalition; St. Dunstan's Episcopal School Board of Directors; Caribbean Studies Association; Women's Coalition of St. Croix; St. Croix Environmental Association; past chair, Christian Education Committee; Friedensthal Moravian Church; past member: Virgin Islands Board of Education; Democratic Platform Committee; cohost, Straight Up TV interview program, 1993; married Chris Christensen; children: two daughters: Rabiah Layla and Karida Yasmeen; member: Congressional Black Caucus; Congressional Women's Caucus; committees: Homeland Security; Resources; Small Business; elected to the 105th Congress; reelected to each succeeding Congress.

Office Listings

1510 Longworth House Office Building, Washington, DC 20515 .... (202) 225–1790
    Chief of Staff.—Monique Clendinen Watson.   FAX: 225–5517
    Legislative Director.—Brian Modeste.
    Office Manager.—Steven Steele.
    Executive Assistant / Scheduler.—Shelley Thomas.
Nisky Center, 2nd Floor, Suite 207, St. Thomas, VI 00802 .... (340) 774–4408
    Office Assistant.—Joyce Jackson.
Sunny Isle Shopping Center, Space No. 25, P.O. Box 5980, St. Croix, VI 00823 ... (340) 778–5900
    District Manager.—Claire Roker.

ZIP Codes: 00801–05, 00820–24, 00830–31, 00840–41, 00850–51

STATE DELEGATIONS

Number before names designates Congressional district. Republicans in roman; Democrats in *italic*; Independents in SMALL CAPS; Resident Commissioner and Delegates in **boldface**.

ALABAMA

SENATORS
Richard C. Shelby
Jeff Sessions

REPRESENTATIVES
[Republicans 5, Democrats 2]
1. Jo Bonner

2. Terry Everett
3. Mike Rogers
4. Robert B. Aderholt
5. *Robert E. (Bud) Cramer, Jr.*
6. Spencer Bachus
7. *Artur Davis*

ALASKA

SENATORS
Ted Stevens
Lisa Murkowski

REPRESENTATIVE
[Republican 1]
At Large - Don Young

ARIZONA

SENATORS
John McCain
Jon Kyl

REPRESENTATIVES
[Republicans 6, Democrats 2]
1. Rick Renzi

2. Trent Franks
3. John B. Shadegg
4. *Ed Pastor*
5. J.D. Hayworth
6. Jeff Flake
7. *Raúl M. Grijalva*
8. Jim Kolbe

ARKANSAS

SENATORS
Blanche L. Lincoln
Mark Pryor

REPRESENTATIVES
[Republicans 1, Democrats 3]

1. *Marion Berry*
2. *Vic Snyder*
3. John Boozman
4. *Mike Ross*

CALIFORNIA

SENATORS
Dianne Feinstein
Barbara Boxer

REPRESENTATIVES
[Republicans 20, Democrats 33]
1. *Mike Thompson*
2. Wally Herger

3. Daniel E. Lungren
4. John T. Doolittle
5. *Doris O. Matsui*
6. *Lynn Woolsey*
7. *George Miller*
8. *Nancy Pelosi*
9. *Barbara Lee*
10. *Ellen O. Tauscher*

11. Richard W. Pombo
12. *Tom Lantos*
13. *Fortney Pete Stark*
14. *Anna G. Eshoo*
15. *Michael M. Honda*
16. *Zoe Lofgren*
17. *Sam Farr*
18. *Dennis A. Cardoza*
19. George Radanovich
20. *Jim Costa*
21. Devin Nunes
22. William M. Thomas
23. *Lois Capps*
24. Elton Gallegly
25. Howard P. (Buck) McKeon
26. David Dreier
27. *Brad Sherman*
28. *Howard L. Berman*
29. *Adam B. Schiff*
30. *Henry A. Waxman*
31. *Xavier Becerra*
32. *Hilda L. Solis*

33. *Diane E. Watson*
34. *Lucille Roybal-Allard*
35. *Maxine Waters*
36. *Jane Harman*
37. *Juanita Millender-McDonald*
38. *Grace F. Napolitano*
39. *Linda T. Sánchez*
40. Edward R. Royce
41. Jerry Lewis
42. Gary G. Miller
43. *Joe Baca*
44. Ken Calvert
45. Mary Bono
46. Dana Rohrabacher
47. *Loretta Sanchez*
48. Christopher Cox
49. Darrell E. Issa
50. Randy (Duke) Cunningham
51. *Bob Filner*
52. Duncan Hunter
53. *Susan A. Davis*

COLORADO

SENATORS
Wayne Allard
Ken Salazar

REPRESENTATIVES
[Republicans 4, Democrats 3]
1. *Diana DeGette*

2. *Mark Udall*
3. *John T. Salazar*
4. *Marilyn N. Musgrave*
5. Joel Hefley
6. Thomas G. Tancredo
7. Bob Beauprez

CONNECTICUT

SENATORS
Christopher J. Dodd
Joseph I. Lieberman

REPRESENTATIVES
[Republicans 3, Democrats 2]
1. *John B. Larson*

2. Rob Simmons
3. *Rosa L. DeLauro*
4. Christopher Shays
5. Nancy L. Johnson

DELAWARE

SENATORS
Joseph R. Biden, Jr.
Thomas Carper

REPRESENTATIVE
[Republican 1]
At Large - Michael N. Castle

FLORIDA

SENATORS
Bill Nelson
Mel Martinez

REPRESENTATIVES
[Republicans 18, Democrats 7]
1. Jeff Miller
2. *Allen Boyd*
3. *Corrine Brown*
4. Ander Crenshaw

5. Ginny Brown-Waite
6. Cliff Stearns
7. John L. Mica
8. Ric Keller
9. Michael Bilirakis
10. C.W. Bill Young
11. *Jim Davis*
12. Adam H. Putnam
13. Katherine Harris
14. Connie Mack

15. Dave Weldon
16. Mark Foley
17. *Kendrick B. Meek*
18. Ileana Ros-Lehtinen
19. *Robert Wexler*
20. *Debbie Wasserman Schultz*

21. Lincoln Diaz-Balart
22. E. Clay Shaw, Jr.
23. *Alcee L. Hastings*
24. Tom Feeney
25. Mario Diaz-Balart

GEORGIA

SENATORS
Saxby Chambliss
Johnny Isakson

REPRESENTATIVES
[Republicans 7, Democrats 6]
1. Jack Kingston
2. *Sanford D. Bishop, Jr.*
3. *Jim Marshall*
4. *Cynthia McKinney*

5. *John Lewis*
6. Tom Price
7. John Linder
8. Lynn A. Westmoreland
9. Charlie Norwood
10. Nathan Deal
11. Phil Gingrey
12. *John Barrow*
13. *David Scott*

HAWAII

SENATORS
Daniel K. Inouye
Daniel K. Akaka

REPRESENTATIVES
[Democrats 2]
1. *Neil Abercrombie*
2. *Ed Case*

IDAHO

SENATORS
Larry Craig
Michael Crapo

REPRESENTATIVES
[Republicans 2]
1. C.L. (Butch) Otter
2. Michael K. Simpson

ILLINOIS

SENATORS
Richard J. Durbin
Barack Obama

REPRESENTATIVES
[Republicans 9, Democrats 10]
1. *Bobby L. Rush*
2. *Jesse L. Jackson, Jr.*
3. *Daniel Lipinski*
4. *Luis V. Gutierrez*
5. *Rahm Emanuel*
6. Henry J. Hyde
7. *Danny K. Davis*

8. *Melissa L. Bean*
9. *Janice D. Schakowsky*
10. Mark Steven Kirk
11. Jerry Weller
12. *Jerry F. Costello*
13. Judy Biggert
14. J. Dennis Hastert
15. Timothy V. Johnson
16. Donald A. Manzullo
17. *Lane Evans*
18. Ray LaHood
19. John Shimkus

INDIANA

SENATORS
Richard G. Lugar
Evan Bayh

REPRESENTATIVES
[Republicans 7, Democrats 2]
1. *Peter J. Visclosky*
2. Chris Chocola

3. Mark E. Souder
4. Steve Buyer
5. Dan Burton
6. Mike Pence
7. *Julia Carson*
8. John N. Hostettler
9. Michael E. Sodrel

IOWA

SENATORS
Charles E. Grassley
Tom Harkin

REPRESENTATIVES
[Republicans 4, Democrats 1]
1. Jim Nussle

2. James A. Leach
3. *Leonard L. Boswell*
4. Tom Latham
5. Steve King

KANSAS

SENATORS
Samuel Dale Brownback
Pat Roberts

REPRESENTATIVES
[Republicans 3, Democrats 1]
1. Jerry Moran

2. Jim Ryun
3. *Dennis Moore*
4. Todd Tiahrt

KENTUCKY

SENATORS
Mitch McConnell
Jim Bunning

REPRESENTATIVES
[Republicans 5, Democrats 1]
1. Ed Whitfield

2. Ron Lewis
3. Anne M. Northup
4. Geoff Davis
5. Harold Rogers
6. *Ben Chandler*

LOUISIANA

SENATORS
Mary Landrieu
David Vitter

REPRESENTATIVES
[Republicans 5, Democrats 2]
1. Bobby Jindal

2. *William J. Jefferson*
3. *Charlie Melancon*
4. Jim McCrery
5. Rodney Alexander
6. Richard H. Baker
7. Charles W. Boustany, Jr.

MAINE

SENATORS
Olympia J. Snowe
Susan Collins

REPRESENTATIVES
[Democrats 2]

1. *Thomas H. Allen*
2. *Michael H. Michaud*

MARYLAND

SENATORS
Paul S. Sarbanes
Barbara A. Mikulski

REPRESENTATIVES
[Republicans 2, Democrats 6]
1. Wayne T. Gilchrest

2. *C.A. Dutch Ruppersberger*
3. *Benjamin L. Cardin*
4. *Albert Russell Wynn*
5. *Steny H. Hoyer*
6. Roscoe G. Bartlett
7. *Elijah E. Cummings*
8. *Chris Van Hollen*

MASSACHUSETTS

SENATORS
Edward M. Kennedy
John F. Kerry

REPRESENTATIVES
[Democrats 10]
1. *John W. Olver*
2. *Richard E. Neal*

3. *James P. McGovern*
4. *Barney Frank*
5. *Martin T. Meehan*
6. *John F. Tierney*
7. *Edward J. Markey*
8. *Michael E. Capuano*
9. *Stephen F. Lynch*
10. *William D. Delahunt*

MICHIGAN

SENATORS
Carl Levin
Debbie Stabenow

REPRESENTATIVES
[Republicans 9, Democrats 6]
1. *Bart Stupak*
2. Peter Hoekstra
3. Vernon J. Ehlers
4. Dave Camp
5. *Dale E. Kildee*

6. Fred Upton
7. John J.H. (Joe) Schwarz
8. Mike Rogers
9. Joe Knollenberg
10. Candice S. Miller
11. Thaddeus G. McCotter
12. *Sander M. Levin*
13. *Carolyn C. Kilpatrick*
14. *John Conyers, Jr.*
15. *John D. Dingell*

MINNESOTA

SENATORS
Mark Dayton
Norm Coleman

REPRESENTATIVES
[Republicans 4, Democrats 4]
1. Gil Gutknecht

2. John Kline
3. Jim Ramstad
4. *Betty McCollum*
5. *Martin Olav Sabo*
6. Mark R. Kennedy
7. *Collin C. Peterson*
8. *James L. Oberstar*

MISSISSIPPI

SENATORS
Thad Cochran
Trent Lott

REPRESENTATIVES
[Republicans 2, Democrats 2]
1. Roger F. Wicker
2. *Bennie G. Thompson*
3. Charles W. (Chip) Pickering
4. *Gene Taylor*

MISSOURI

SENATORS
Christopher S. Bond
James Talent

REPRESENTATIVES
[Republicans 5, Democrats 4]
1. *Wm. Lacy Clay*
2. W. Todd Akin

3. *Russ Carnahan*
4. *Ike Skelton*
5. *Emanuel Cleaver*
6. Sam Graves
7. Roy Blunt
8. Jo Ann Emerson
9. Kenny C. Hulshof

MONTANA

SENATORS
Max Baucus
Conrad Burns

REPRESENTATIVE
[Republican 1]
At Large - Dennis R. Rehberg

NEBRASKA

SENATORS
Chuck Hagel
E. Benjamin Nelson

REPRESENTATIVES
[Republicans 3]
1. Jeff Fortenberry
2. Lee Terry
3. Tom Osborne

NEVADA

SENATORS
Harry Reid
John Ensign

REPRESENTATIVES
[Republicans 2, Democrats 1]
1. *Shelley Berkley*
2. Jim Gibbons
3. Jon C. Porter

NEW HAMPSHIRE

SENATORS
Judd Gregg
John Sununu

REPRESENTATIVES
[Republicans 2]
1. Jeb Bradley
2. Charles F. Bass

NEW JERSEY

SENATORS
Jon S. Corzine
Frank Lautenberg

REPRESENTATIVES
[Republicans 6, Democrats 7]
1. *Robert E. Andrews*
2. Frank LoBiondo
3. Jim Saxton
4. Christopher H. Smith
5. Scott Garrett
6. *Frank Pallone, Jr.*
7. Mike Ferguson
8. *Bill Pascrell, Jr.*
9. *Steven R. Rothman*
10. *Donald M. Payne*
11. Rodney P. Frelinghuysen
12. *Rush D. Holt*
13. *Robert Menendez*

NEW MEXICO

SENATORS
Pete V. Domenici
Jeff Bingaman

REPRESENTATIVES
[Republicans 2, Democrats 1]
1. Heather Wilson
2. Stevan Pearce
3. *Tom Udall*

NEW YORK

SENATORS
Charles E. Schumer
Hillary Rodham Clinton

REPRESENTATIVES
[Republicans 9, Democrats 20]
1. *Timothy H. Bishop*
2. *Steve Israel*
3. Peter T. King
4. *Carolyn McCarthy*
5. *Gary L. Ackerman*
6. *Gregory W. Meeks*
7. *Joseph Crowley*
8. *Jerrold Nadler*
9. *Anthony D. Weiner*
10. *Edolphus Towns*
11. *Major R. Owens*
12. *Nydia M. Velázquez*
13. Vito Fossella
14. *Carolyn B. Maloney*

15. *Charles B. Rangel*
16. *José E. Serrano*
17. *Eliot L. Engel*
18. *Nita M. Lowey*
19. Sue W. Kelly
20. John E. Sweeney
21. *Michael R. McNulty*
22. *Maurice D. Hinchey*

23. John M. McHugh
24. Sherwood Boehlert
25. James T. Walsh
26. Thomas M. Reynolds
27. *Brian Higgins*
28. *Louise McIntosh Slaughter*
29. John R. (Randy) Kuhl, Jr.

NORTH CAROLINA

SENATORS
Elizabeth Dole
Richard Burr

REPRESENTATIVES
[Republicans 7, Democrats 6]

1. *G.K. Butterfield*
2. *Bob Etheridge*
3. Walter B. Jones
4. *David E. Price*

5. Virginia Foxx
6. Howard Coble
7. *Mike McIntyre*
8. Robin Hayes
9. Sue Wilkins Myrick
10. Patrick T. McHenry
11. Charles H. Taylor
12. *Melvin L. Watt*
12. *Brad Miller*

NORTH DAKOTA

SENATORS
Kent Conrad
Byron L. Dorgan

REPRESENTATIVE
[Democrat 1]
At Large - *Earl Pomeroy*

OHIO

SENATORS
Mike DeWine
George V. Voinovich

REPRESENTATIVES
[Republicans 11, Democrats 6]

1. Steve Chabot
2. [Vacancy]
3. Michael R. Turner
4. Michael G. Oxley
5. Paul E. Gillmor
6. *Ted Strickland*

7. David L. Hobson
8. John A. Boehner
9. *Marcy Kaptur*
10. *Dennis J. Kucinich*
11. *Stephanie Tubbs Jones*
12. Patrick J. Tiberi
13. *Sherrod Brown*
14. Steven C. LaTourette
15. Deborah Pryce
16. Ralph Regula
17. *Timothy J. Ryan*
18. Robert W. Ney

OKLAHOMA

SENATORS
James M. Inhofe
Tom Coburn

REPRESENTATIVES
[Republicans 4, Democrats 1]

1. John Sullivan

2. *Dan Boren*
3. Frank D. Lucas
4. Tom Cole
5. Ernest J. Istook, Jr.

OREGON

SENATORS
Ron Wyden
Gordon Smith

REPRESENTATIVES
[Republican 1, Democrats 4]

1. *David Wu*

2. Greg Walden
3. *Earl Blumenauer*

4. *Peter A. DeFazio*
5. *Darlene Hooley*

PENNSYLVANIA

SENATORS
Arlen Specter
Rick Santorum

REPRESENTATIVES
[Republicans 12, Democrats 7]

1. *Robert A. Brady*
2. *Chaka Fattah*
3. Phil English
4. Melissa A. Hart
5. John E. Peterson
6. Jim Gerlach
7. Curt Weldon

8. Michael G. Fitzpatrick
9. Bill Shuster
10. Don Sherwood
11. *Paul E. Kanjorski*
12. *John P. Murtha*
13. *Allyson Y. Schwartz*
14. *Michael F. Doyle*
15. Charles W. Dent
16. Joseph R. Pitts
17. *Tim Holden*
18. Tim Murphy
19. Todd Russell Platts

RHODE ISLAND

SENATORS
Jack Reed
Lincoln D. Chafee

REPRESENTATIVES
[Democrats 2]

1. *Patrick J. Kennedy*
2. *James R. Langevin*

SOUTH CAROLINA

SENATORS
Lindsey Graham
Jim DeMint

REPRESENTATIVES
[Republicans 4, Democrats 2]
1. Henry E. Brown, Jr.

2. Joe Wilson
3. J. Gresham Barrett
4. Bob Inglis
5. *John M. Spratt, Jr.*
6. *James E. Clyburn*

SOUTH DAKOTA

SENATORS
Tim Johnson
John Thune

REPRESENTATIVE
[Democrat 1]

At Large - *Stephanie Herseth*

TENNESSEE

SENATORS
William H. (Bill) Frist
Lamar Alexander

REPRESENTATIVES
[Republicans 4, Democrats 5]
1. William L. Jenkins
2. John J. Duncan, Jr.

3. Zach Wamp
4. *Lincoln Davis*
5. *Jim Cooper*
6. *Bart Gordon*
7. Marsha Blackburn
8. *John S. Tanner*
9. *Harold E. Ford, Jr.*

TEXAS

SENATORS
Kay Bailey Hutchison
John Cornyn

REPRESENTATIVES
[Republicans 21, Democrats 11]
1. Louie Gohmert
2. Ted Poe
3. Sam Johnson
4. Ralph M. Hall
5. Jeb Hensarling
6. Joe Barton
7. John Abney Culberson
8. Kevin Brady
9. *Al Green*
10. Michael T. McCaul
11. K. Michael Conaway
12. Kay Granger
13. Mac Thornberry
14. Ron Paul
15. *Rubén Hinojosa*
16. *Silvestre Reyes*
17. *Chet Edwards*
18. *Sheila Jackson Lee*
19. Randy Neugebauer
20. *Charles A. Gonzalez*
21. Lamar S. Smith
22. Tom DeLay
23. Henry Bonilla
24. Kenny Marchant
25. *Lloyd Doggett*
26. Michael C. Burgess
27. *Solomon P. Ortiz*
28. *Henry Cuellar*
29. *Gene Green*
30. *Eddie Bernice Johnson*
31. John R. Carter
32. Pete Sessions

UTAH

SENATORS
Orrin G. Hatch
Robert F. Bennett

REPRESENTATIVES
[Republicans 2, Democrats 1]
1. Rob Bishop
2. *Jim Matheson*
3. Christopher B. Cannon

VERMONT

SENATORS
Patrick J. Leahy
JAMES M. JEFFORDS

REPRESENTATIVE
[Independent 1]
At Large - BERNARD SANDERS

VIRGINIA

SENATORS
John W. Warner
George Allen

REPRESENTATIVES
[Republicans 8, Democrats 3]
1. Jo Ann Davis
2. Thelma D. Drake
3. *Robert C. Scott*
4. J. Randy Forbes
5. Virgil H. Goode, Jr.
6. Robert W. Goodlatte
7. Eric Cantor
8. *James P. Moran*
9. *Rick Boucher*
10. Frank R. Wolf
11. Tom Davis

WASHINGTON

SENATORS
Patty Murray
Maria Cantwell

REPRESENTATIVES
[Republicans 3, Democrats 6]
1. *Jay Inslee*
2. *Rick Larsen*
3. *Brian Baird*
4. Doc Hastings
5. Cathy McMorris
6. *Norman D. Dicks*
7. *Jim McDermott*
8. David G. Reichert
9. *Adam Smith*

WEST VIRGINIA

SENATORS
Robert C. Byrd
John D. Rockefeller IV

REPRESENTATIVES
[Republicans 1, Democrats 2]
1. *Alan B. Mollohan*
2. Shelley Moore Capito
3. *Nick J. Rahall II*

WISCONSIN

SENATORS
Herb Kohl
Russell D. Feingold

REPRESENTATIVES
[Republicans 4, Democrats 4]
1. Paul Ryan

2. *Tammy Baldwin*
3. *Ron Kind*
4. *Gwen Moore*
5. F. James Sensenbrenner, Jr.
6. Thomas E. Petri
7. *David R. Obey*
8. Mark Green

WYOMING

SENATORS
Craig Thomas
Michael B. Enzi

REPRESENTATIVE
[Republican 1]
At Large - Barbara Cubin

AMERICAN SAMOA

DELEGATE
[Democrat 1]

Eni F.H. Faleomavaega

DISTRICT OF COLUMBIA

DELEGATE
[Democrat 1]

Eleanor Holmes Norton

GUAM

DELEGATE
[Democrat 1]

Madeleine Z. Bordallo

PUERTO RICO

RESIDENT COMMISSIONER
[Republican 1]

Luis G. Fortuño

VIRGIN ISLANDS

DELEGATE
[Democrat 1]

Donna M. Christensen

ALPHABETICAL LIST

SENATORS

Alphabetical list of Senators, Representatives, Delegates, and Resident Commissioner.
Republicans in roman (55); Democrats in *italic* (44); Independent in SMALL CAPS (1).

Akaka, Daniel K., HI
Alexander, Lamar, TN
Allard, Wayne, CO
Allen, George, VA
Baucus, Max, MT
Bayh, Evan, IN
Bennett, Robert F., UT
Biden, Joseph R., Jr., DE
Bingaman, Jeff, NM
Bond, Christopher S., MO
Boxer, Barbara, CA
Brownback, Sam, KS
Bunning, Jim, KY
Burns, Conrad, MT
Burr, Richard, NC
Byrd, Robert C., WV
Cantwell, Maria, WA
Carper, Thomas R., DE
Chafee, Lincoln D., RI
Chambliss, Saxby, GA
Clinton, Hillary Rodham, NY
Coburn, Tom, OK
Cochran, Thad, MS
Coleman, Norm, MN
Collins, Susan M., ME
Conrad, Kent, ND
Cornyn, John, TX
Corzine, Jon S., NJ
Craig, Larry E., ID
Crapo, Michael, ID
Dayton, Mark, MN
DeMint, Jim, SC
DeWine, Mike, OH
Dodd, Christopher J., CT
Dole, Elizabeth, NC
Domenici, Pete V., NM
Dorgan, Byron L., ND
Durbin, Richard J., IL
Ensign, John, NV
Enzi, Mike, WY
Feingold, Russell D., WI
Feinstein, Dianne, CA
Frist, William H. (Bill), TN
Graham, Lindsey O., SC
Grassley, Charles E., IA
Gregg, Judd, NH
Hagel, Chuck, NE
Harkin, Tom, IA
Hatch, Orrin G., UT
Hutchison, Kay Bailey, TX

Inhofe, James M., OK
Inouye, Daniel K., HI
Isakson, Johnny, GA
JEFFORDS, JAMES M., VT
Johnson, Tim, SD
Kennedy, Edward M., MA
Kerry, John F., MA
Kohl, Herb, WI
Kyl, Jon, AZ
Landrieu, Mary L., LA
Lautenberg, Frank, NJ
Leahy, Patrick J., VT
Levin, Carl, MI
Lieberman, Joseph I., CT
Lincoln, Blanche L., AR
Lott, Trent, MS
Lugar, Richard G., IN
McCain, John, AZ
McConnell, Mitch, KY
Martinez, Mel, FL
Mikulski, Barbara A., MD
Murkowski, Lisa, AK
Murray, Patty, WA
Nelson, Bill, FL
Nelson, E. Benjamin, NE
Obama, Barack, IL
Pryor, Mark, AR
Reed, Jack, RI
Reid, Harry, NV
Roberts, Pat, KS
Rockefeller, John D., IV, WV
Salazar, Ken, CO
Santorum, Rick, PA
Sarbanes, Paul S., MD
Schumer, Charles E., NY
Sessions, Jeff, AL
Shelby, Richard C., AL
Smith, Gordon, OR
Snowe, Olympia J., ME
Specter, Arlen, PA
Stabenow, Debbie, MI
Stevens, Ted, AK
Sununu, John E., NH
Talent, James M., MO
Thomas, Craig, WY
Thune, John, SD
Vitter, David, LA
Voinovich, George V., OH
Warner, John W., VA
Wyden, Ron, OR

REPRESENTATIVES

Republicans in roman (231); Democrats in *italic* (202); Independents in SMALL CAPS (1);
Vacancy (1); Resident Commissioner and Delegates in **boldface** (5); total, 440.

Abercrombie, Neil, HI (1st)
Ackerman, Gary L., NY (5th)
Aderholt, Robert B., AL (4th)
Akin, W. Todd, MO (2nd)
Alexander, Rodney, LA (5th)
Allen, Thomas H., ME (1st)
Andrews, Robert E., NJ (1st)
Baca, Joe, CA (43rd)
Bachus, Spencer, AL (6th)
Baird, Brian, WA (3rd)
Baker, Richard H., LA (6th)
Baldwin, Tammy, WI (2nd)
Barrett, J. Gresham, SC (3rd)
Barrow, John, GA (12th)
Bartlett, Roscoe G., MD (6th)
Barton, Joe, TX (6th)
Bass, Charles F., NH (2nd)
Bean, Melissa L., IL (8th)
Beauprez, Bob, CO (7th)
Becerra, Xavier, CA (31st)
Berkley, Shelley, NV (1st)
Berman, Howard L., CA (28th)
Berry, Marion, AR (1st)
Biggert, Judy, IL (13th)
Bilirakis, Michael, FL (9th)
Bishop, Rob, UT (1st)
Bishop, Sanford D., Jr., GA (2nd)
Bishop, Timothy H., NY (1st)
Blackburn, Marsha, TN (7th)
Blumenauer, Earl, OR (3rd)
Blunt, Roy, MO (7th)
Boehlert, Sherwood, NY (24th)
Boehner, John A., OH (8th)
Bonilla, Henry, TX (23rd)
Bonner, Jo, AL (1st)
Bono, Mary, CA (45th)
Boozman, John, AR (3rd)
Boren, Dan, OK (2nd)
Boswell, Leonard L., IA (3rd)
Boucher, Rick, VA (9th)
Boustany, Charles W., Jr., LA (7th)
Boyd, Allen, FL (2nd)
Bradley, Jeb, NH (1st)
Brady, Kevin, TX (8th)
Brady, Robert A., PA (1st)
Brown, Corrine, FL (3rd)
Brown, Henry E., Jr., SC (1st)
Brown, Sherrod, OH (13th)
Brown-Waite, Ginny, FL (5th)
Burgess, Michael C., TX (26th)
Burton, Dan, IN (5th)
Butterfield, G.K., NC (1st)
Buyer, Steve, IN (4th)

Calvert, Ken, CA (44th)
Camp, Dave, MI (4th)
Cannon, Christopher B., UT (3rd)
Cantor, Eric, VA (7th)
Capito, Shelley Moore, WV (2nd)
Capps, Lois, CA (23rd)
Capuano, Michael E., MA (8th)
Cardin, Benjamin L., MD (3rd)
Cardoza, Dennis A., CA (18th)
Carnahan, Russ, MO (3rd)
Carson, Julia M., IN (7th)
Carter, John R., TX (31st)
Case, Ed, HI (2nd)
Castle, Michael N., DE (At Large)
Chabot, Steve, OH (1st)
Chandler, Ben, KY (6th)
Chocola, Chris, IN (2nd)
Clay, Wm. Lacy, MO (1st)
Cleaver, Emanuel, MO (5th)
Clyburn, James E., SC (6th)
Coble, Howard, NC (6th)
Cole, Tom, OK (4th)
Conaway, Michael K., TX (11th)
Conyers, John, Jr., MI (14th)
Cooper, Jim, TN (5th)
Costa, Jim, CA (20th)
Costello, Jerry F., IL (12th)
Cox, Christopher, CA (48th)
Cramer, Robert E. (Bud), Jr., AL (5th)
Crenshaw, Ander, FL (4th)
Crowley, Joseph, NY (7th)
Cubin, Barbara, WY (At Large)
Cuellar, Henry, TX (28th)
Culberson, John Abney, TX (7th)
Cummings, Elijah E., MD (7th)
Cunningham, Randy (Duke), CA (50th)
Davis, Artur, AL (7th)
Davis, Danny K., IL (7th)
Davis, Geoff, KY (4th)
Davis, Jim, FL (11th)
Davis, Jo Ann, VA (1st)
Davis, Lincoln, TN (4th)
Davis, Susan A., CA (53rd)
Davis, Tom, VA (11th)
Deal, Nathan, GA (10th)
DeFazio, Peter A., OR (4th)
DeGette, Diana, CO (1st)
Delahunt, William D., MA (10th)
DeLauro, Rosa L., CT (3rd)
DeLay, Tom, TX (22nd)
Dent, Charles W., PA (15th)
Diaz-Balart, Lincoln, FL (21st)
Diaz-Balart, Mario FL (25th)

Dicks, Norman D., WA (6th)
Dingell, John D., MI (15th)
Doggett, Lloyd, TX (25th)
Doolittle, John T., CA (4th)
Doyle, Michael F., PA (14th)
Drake, Thelma D., VA (2nd)
Dreier, David, CA (26th)
Duncan, John J., Jr., TN (2nd)
Edwards, Chet, TX (17th)
Ehlers, Vernon J., MI (3rd)
Emanuel, Rahm, IL (5th)
Emerson, Jo Ann, MO (8th)
Engel, Eliot L., NY (17th)
English, Phil, PA (3rd)
Eshoo, Anna G., CA (14th)
Etheridge, Bob, NC (2nd)
Evans, Lane, IL (17th)
Everett, Terry, AL (2nd)
Farr, Sam, CA (17th)
Fattah, Chaka, PA (2nd)
Feeney, Tom, FL (24th)
Ferguson, Mike, NJ (7th)
Filner, Bob, CA (51st)
Fitzpatrick, Michael G., PA (8th)
Flake, Jeff, AZ (6th)
Foley, Mark, FL (16th)
Forbes, J. Randy, VA (4th)
Ford, Harold E., Jr., TN (9th)
Fortenberry, Jeff, NE (1st)
Fossella, Vito, NY (13th)
Foxx, Virginia, NC (5th)
Frank, Barney, MA (4th)
Franks, Trent, AZ (2nd)
Frelinghuysen, Rodney P., NJ (11th)
Gallegly, Elton, CA (24th)
Garrett, Scott, NJ (5th)
Gerlach, Jim, PA (6th)
Gibbons, Jim, NV (2nd)
Gilchrest, Wayne T., MD (1st)
Gillmor, Paul E., OH (5th)
Gingrey, Phil, GA (11th)
Gohmert, Louie, TX (1st)
Gonzalez, Charles A., TX (20th)
Goode, Virgil H., Jr., VA (5th)
Goodlatte, Bob, VA (6th)
Gordon, Bart, TN (6th)
Granger, Kay, TX (12th)
Graves, Sam, MO (6th)
Green, Al, TX (9th)
Green, Gene, TX (29th)
Green, Mark, WI (8th)
Grijalva, Raúl M., AZ (7th)
Gutierrez, Luis V., IL (4th)
Gutknecht, Gil, MN (1st)
Hall, Ralph M., TX (4th)
Harman, Jane, CA (36th)
Harris, Katherine, FL (13th)
Hart, Melissa A., PA (4th)
Hastert, J. Dennis, IL (14th)
Hastings, Alcee L., FL (23rd)
Hastings, Doc, WA (4th)
Hayes, Robin, NC (8th)
Hayworth, J.D., AZ (5th)
Hefley, Joel, CO (5th)
Hensarling, Jeb, TX (5th)
Herger, Wally, CA (2nd)

Herseth, Stephanie, SD (At Large)
Higgins, Brian, NY (27th)
Hinchey, Maurice D., NY (22nd)
Hinojosa, Rubén, TX (15th)
Hobson, David L., OH (7th)
Hoekstra, Peter, MI (2nd)
Holden, Tim, PA (17th)
Holt, Rush D., NJ (12th)
Honda, Michael M., CA (15th)
Hooley, Darlene, OR (5th)
Hostettler, John N., IN (8th)
Hoyer, Steny H., MD (5th)
Hulshof, Kenny C., MO (9th)
Hunter, Duncan, CA (52nd)
Hyde, Henry J., IL (6th)
Inglis, Bob, SC (4th)
Inslee, Jay, WA (1st)
Israel, Steve, NY (2nd)
Issa, Darrell E., CA (49th)
Istook, Ernest J., Jr., OK (5th)
Jackson, Jesse L., Jr., IL (2nd)
Jackson Lee, Sheila, TX (18th)
Jefferson, William J., LA (2nd)
Jenkins, William L., TN (1st)
Jindal, Bobby, LA (1st)
Johnson, Eddie Bernice, TX (30th)
Johnson, Nancy L., CT (5th)
Johnson, Sam, TX (3rd)
Johnson, Timothy V., IL (15th)
Jones, Stephanie Tubbs, OH (11th)
Jones, Walter B., NC (3rd)
Kanjorski, Paul E., PA (11th)
Kaptur, Marcy, OH (9th)
Keller, Ric, FL (8th)
Kelly, Sue W., NY (19th)
Kennedy, Mark R., MN (6th)
Kennedy, Patrick J., RI (1st)
Kildee, Dale E., MI (5th)
Kilpatrick, Carolyn C., MI (13th)
Kind, Ron, WI (3rd)
King, Peter T., NY (3rd)
King, Steve, IA (5th)
Kingston, Jack, GA (1st)
Kirk, Mark Steven, IL (10th)
Kline, John, MN (2nd)
Knollenberg, Joe, MI (9th)
Kolbe, Jim, AZ (8th)
Kucinich, Dennis J., OH (10th)
Kuhl, John R. (Randy), Jr., NY (29th)
LaHood, Ray, IL (18th)
Langevin, James R., RI (2nd)
Lantos, Tom, CA (12th)
Larsen, Rick, WA (2nd)
Larson, John B., CT (1st)
Latham, Tom, IA (4th)
LaTourette, Steven C., OH (14th)
Leach, James A., IA (2nd)
Lee, Barbara, CA (9th)
Levin, Sander M., MI (12th)
Lewis, Jerry, CA (41st)
Lewis, John, GA (5th)
Lewis, Ron, KY (2nd)
Linder, John, GA (7th)
Lipinski, Daniel, IL (3rd)
LoBiondo, Frank A., NJ (2nd)
Lofgren, Zoe, CA (16th)

Lowey, Nita M., NY (18th)
Lucas, Frank D., OK (3rd)
Lungren, Daniel E., CA (3rd)
Lynch, Stephen F., MA (9th)
McCarthy, Carolyn, NY (4th)
McCaul, Michael, T., TX (10th)
McCollum, Betty, MN (4th)
McCotter, Thaddeus G., MI (11th)
McCrery, Jim, LA (4th)
McDermott, Jim, WA (7th)
McGovern, James P., MA (3rd)
McHenry, Patrick T., NC (10th)
McHugh, John M., NY (23rd)
McIntyre, Mike, NC (7th)
McKeon, Howard P. (Buck), CA (25th)
McKinney, Cynthia, GA (4th)
McMorris, Cathy, WA (5th)
McNulty, Michael R., NY (21st)
Mack, Connie, FL (14th)
Maloney, Carolyn B., NY (14th)
Manzullo, Donald A., IL (16th)
Marchant, Kenny, TX (24th)
Markey, Edward J., MA (7th)
Marshall, Jim, GA (3rd)
Matheson, Jim, UT (2nd)
Matsui, Doris O., CA (5th)
Meehan, Martin T., MA (5th)
Meek, Kendrick B., FL (17th)
Meeks, Gregory W., NY (6th)
Melancon, Charlie, LA (3rd)
Menendez, Robert, NJ (13th)
Mica, John L., FL (7th)
Michaud, Michael H., ME (2nd)
Millender-McDonald, Juanita, CA (37th)
Miller, Brad, NC (13th)
Miller, Candice S., MI (10th)
Miller, Gary G., CA (42nd)
Miller, George, CA (7th)
Miller, Jeff, FL (1st)
Mollohan, Alan B., WV (1st)
Moore, Dennis, KS (3rd)
Moore, Gwen, WI (4th)
Moran, James P., VA (8th)
Moran, Jerry, KS (1st)
Murphy, Tim, PA (18th)
Murtha, John P., PA (12th)
Musgrave, Marilyn N., CO (4th)
Myrick, Sue Wilkins, NC (9th)
Nadler, Jerrold, NY (8th)
Napolitano, Grace F., CA (38th)
Neal, Richard E., MA (2nd)
Neugebauer, Randy, TX (19th)
Ney, Robert W., OH (18th)
Northup, Anne M., KY (3rd)
Norwood, Charlie, GA (9th)
Nunes, Devin, CA (21st)
Nussle, Jim, IA (1st)
Oberstar, James L., MN (8th)
Obey, David R., WI (7th)
Olver, John W., MA (1st)
Ortiz, Solomon P., TX (27th)
Osborne, Tom, NE (3rd)
Otter, C.L. (Butch), ID (1st)
Owens, Major R., NY (11th)
Oxley, Michael G., OH (4th)
Pallone, Frank, Jr., NJ (6th)

Pascrell, Bill, Jr., NJ (8th)
Pastor, Ed, AZ (4th)
Paul, Ron, TX (14th)
Payne, Donald M., NJ (10th)
Pearce, Stevan, NM (2nd)
Pelosi, Nancy, CA (8th)
Pence, Mike, IN (6th)
Peterson, Collin C., MN (7th)
Peterson, John E., PA (5th)
Petri, Thomas E., WI (6th)
Pickering, Charles W. (Chip), MS (3rd)
Pitts, Joseph R., PA (16th)
Platts, Todd Russell, PA (19th)
Poe, Ted, TX (2nd)
Pombo, Richard W., CA (11th)
Pomeroy, Earl, ND (At Large)
Porter, Jon C., NV (3rd)
Price, David E., NC (4th)
Price, Tom, GA (6th)
Pryce, Deborah H., OH (15th)
Putnam, Adam H., FL (12th)
Radanovich, George, CA (19th)
Rahall, Nick J. II, WV (3rd)
Ramstad, Jim, MN (3rd)
Rangel, Charles B., NY (15th)
Regula, Ralph, OH (16th)
Rehberg, Dennis, MT (At Large)
Reichert, David G., WA (8th)
Renzi, Rick, AZ (1st)
Reyes, Silvestre, TX (16th)
Reynolds, Thomas M., NY (26th)
Rogers, Harold, KY (5th)
Rogers, Mike, AL (3rd)
Rogers, Mike, MI (8th)
Rohrabacher, Dana, CA (46th)
Ros-Lehtinen, Ileana, FL (18th)
Ross, Mike, AR (4th)
Rothman, Steven R., NJ (9th)
Roybal-Allard, Lucille, CA (34th)
Royce, Edward R., CA (40th)
Ruppersberger, C.A. Dutch, MD (2nd)
Rush, Bobby L., IL (1st)
Ryan, Paul, WI (1st)
Ryan, Tim, OH (17th)
Ryun, Jim, KS (2nd)
Sabo, Martin Olav, MN (5th)
Salazar, John T., CO (3rd)
Sánchez, Linda T., CA (39th)
Sanchez, Loretta, CA (47th)
SANDERS, BERNARD, VT (At Large)
Saxton, Jim, NJ (3rd)
Schakowsky, Janice D., IL (9th)
Schiff, Adam B., CA (29th)
Schwartz, Allyson Y., PA (13th)
Schwarz, John J.H. (Joe), MI (7th)
Scott, David, GA (13th)
Scott, Robert C., VA (3rd)
Sensenbrenner, F. James, Jr., WI (5th)
Serrano, José E., NY (16th)
Sessions, Pete, TX (32nd)
Shadegg, John B., AZ (3rd)
Shaw, E. Clay, Jr., FL (22nd)
Shays, Christopher, CT (4th)
Sherman, Brad, CA (27th)
Sherwood, Don, PA (10th)
Shimkus, John, IL (19th)

Shuster, Bill, PA (9th)
Simmons, Rob, CT (2nd)
Simpson, Michael K., ID (2nd)
Skelton, Ike, MO (4th)
Slaughter, Louise McIntosh, NY (28th)
Smith, Adam, WA (9th)
Smith, Christopher H., NJ (4th)
Smith, Lamar S., TX (21st)
Snyder, Vic, AR (2nd)
Sodrel, Michael E., IN (9th)
Solis, Hilda L., CA (32nd)
Souder, Mark E., IN (3rd)
Spratt, John M., Jr., SC (5th)
Stark, Fortney Pete, CA (13th)
Stearns, Cliff, FL (6th)
Strickland, Ted, OH (6th)
Stupak, Bart, MI (1st)
Sullivan, John, OK (1st)
Sweeney, John E., NY (20th)
Tancredo, Thomas G., CO (6th)
Tanner, John S., TN (8th)
Tauscher, Ellen O., CA (10th)
Taylor, Charles H., NC (11th)
Taylor, Gene, MS (4th)
Terry, Lee, NE (2nd)
Thomas, William M., CA (22nd)
Thompson, Bennie G., MS (2nd)
Thompson, Mike, CA (1st)
Thornberry, Mac, TX (13th)
Tiahrt, Todd, KS (4th)
Tiberi, Patrick J., OH (12th)
Tierney, John F., MA (6th)
Towns, Edolphus, NY (10th)
Turner, Michael R., OH (3rd)
Udall, Mark, CO (2nd)
Udall, Tom, NM (3rd)
Upton, Fred, MI (6th)

Van Hollen, Chris, MD (8th)
Velázquez, Nydia M., NY (12th)
Visclosky, Peter J., IN (1st)
Walden, Greg, OR (2nd)
Walsh, James T., NY (25th)
Wamp, Zach, TN (3rd)
Wasserman Schultz, Debbie, FL (20th)
Waters, Maxine, CA (35th)
Watson, Diane E., CA (33rd)
Watt, Melvin L., NC (12th)
Waxman, Henry A., CA (30th)
Weiner, Anthony D., NY (9th)
Weldon, Curt, PA (7th)
Weldon, Dave, FL (15th)
Weller, Jerry, IL (11th)
Westmoreland, Lynn A., GA (8th)
Wexler, Robert, FL (19th)
Whitfield, Ed, KY (1st)
Wicker, Roger F., MS (1st)
Wilson, Heather, NM (1st)
Wilson, Joe, SC (2nd)
Wolf, Frank R., VA (10th)
Woolsey, Lynn C., CA (6th)
Wu, David, OR (1st)
Wynn, Albert Russell, MD (4th)
Young, C.W. Bill, FL (10th)
Young, Don, AK (At Large)

DELEGATES
Bordallo, Madeleine Z., GU
Christensen, Donna M., VI
Faleomavaega, Eni F.H., AS
Norton, Eleanor Holmes, DC

RESIDENT COMISSIONER
Fortuño, Luis G., PR

109th Congress
Nine-Digit Postal ZIP Codes

Senate Post Office (20510): The four-digit numbers in these tables were assigned by the Senate Committee on Rules and Administration. Mail to all Senate offices is delivered by the main Post Office in the Dirksen Senate Office Building.

Senate Committees

Committee on Agriculture, Nutrition, and Forestry	−6000	Committee on Governmental Affairs	−6250
Committee on Appropriations	−6025	Committee on Health, Education, Labor and Pensions.	−6300
Committee on Armed Services	−6050		
Committee on Banking, Housing, and Urban Affairs.	−6075	Committee on Indian Affairs	−6450
		Committee on the Judiciary	−6275
Committee on the Budget	−6100	Committee on Rules and Administration	−6325
Committee on Commerce, Science, and Transportation.	−6125	Committee on Small Business and Entrepreneurship.	−6350
Committee on Energy and Natural Resources	−6150	Committee on Veterans' Affairs	−6375
Committee on Environment and Public Works	−6175	Committee on Aging (Special)	−6400
Committee on Finance	−6200	Committee on Ethics (Select)	−6425
Committee on Foreign Relations	−6225	Committee on Intelligence (Select)	−6475

Joint Committee Offices, Senate Side

Joint Economic Committee	−6602	Joint Committee on Printing	−6650
Joint Committee on the Library	−6625	Joint Committee on Taxation	−6675

Senate Leadership Offices

President Pro Tempore	−7000	Secretary for the Minority	−7024
Chaplain	−7002	Democratic Policy Committee	−7050
Majority Leader	−7010	Republican Conference	−7060
Assistant Majority Leader	−7012	Secretary to the Republican Conference	−7062
Secretary for the Majority	−7014	Republican Policy Committee	−7064
Minority Leader	−7020	Republican Steering Committee	−7066
Assistant Minority Leader	−7022	Arms Control Observer Group	−7070

Senate Officers

Secretary of the Senate	−7100	Facilities	−7204
Curator of Art and Antiquities	−7102	Finance Division	−7205
Disbursing Office	−7104	Hair Care Services	−7206
Document Room	−7106	Procurement	−7207
Historian	−7108	Capitol Guides	−7209
Interparliamentary Services	−7110	Parking	−7210
Senate Library	−7112	Employee Assistance Program Office	−7211
Office of Senate Security	−7114	Human Resources	−7212
Office of Public Records	−7116	Health Promotion Seminars	−7213
Office of Official Recorders of Debates	−7117	Placement	−7214
Stationery Room	−7118	Senate Office of Education and Training	−7215
Office of Printing Services	−7120	Photographic Studio	−7261
U.S. Capitol Preservation Commission	−7122	Capitol Police	−7218
Office of Conservation and Preservation	−7124	Senate Post Office	−7263
Senate Gift Shop	−7128	Senate Recording Studio	−7222
Legal Counsel, Employment Management Relations.	−7130	Congressional Special Services Office	−7228
Senate Sergeant at Arms	−7200	Customer Relations	−7230
General Counsel	−7201	CR-Customer Support	−7231

Other Offices on the Senate Side

Senate Legal Counsel	−7250	OO-IT / Telecom Support	−7281
Central Operations (CO)—Administration	−7260	OO-Equipment Services	−7282
CO-Photo Studio	−7261	OO-Communication Installation & Support	−7283
CO-Parking / ID	−7262	OO-Desktop / LAN Support	−7284
CO-Post Office	−7263	OO-State Office Liasion	−7285
CO-Printing Graphics & Direct Mail—Production.	−7264	Technical Operations (TO)—Administration	−7290
		TO-Applications Development	−7291
CO-Recording	−7265	TO-Web & Technology Assessment	−7292
CO-Printing Graphics & Direct Mail—Reprographics.	−7266	TO-Network Engineering & Management	−7293
		TO-Enterprise It Systems	−7294
Chief of Operations	−7270	TO-Voice & RF Systems	−7295
Deputy Chief of Operations	−7271	TO-Inter / Intranet Services	−7296
Senate Legislative Counsel	−7275	Architect of the Capitol	−8000
Program Management	−7276	Superintendent of Senate Buildings	−8002
Systems Architecture	−7277	Restaurant	−8050
Office Operations (OO)—Administration	−7280	Office of Technology Assessment	−8025

315

Amtrak Ticket Office	–9010
Airlines Ticket Office (CATO)	–9014
Child Care Center	–9022
Credit Union	–9026
Periodical Press Gallery	–7234
Press Gallery	–7238
Press Photo Gallery	–7242
Radio and TV Gallery	–7246
Webster Hall	–7248
Office of Compliance	–9061
Social Security Liaison	–9064
Veterans Liaison	–9054
Western Union	–9058
Office of Senate Fair Employment Practices	–9060
Frank Delano Roosevelt Memorial Commission	–9066
Caucus on International Narcotics Control	–9070
Army Liaison	–9082
Air Force Liaison	–9083
Coast Guard Liaison	–9084
Navy Liaison	–9085
Marine Liaison	–9087

House Post Office (20515): Mail to all House offices is delivered by the main Post Office in the Longworth House Office Building.

House Committees, Leadership and Officers

U.S. House of Representatives	–0001
Cannon House Office Building	–0002
Rayburn House Office Building	–0003
Longworth House Office Building	–0004
O'Neill House Office Building	–0005
Ford House Office Building	–0006
The Capitol	–0007
Office of the Chaplain	–6655
Committee on Agriculture	–6001
Committee on Appropriations	–6015
Committee on Armed Services	–6035
Committee on the Budget	–6065
Committee on Education and the Workforce	–6100
Committee on Energy and Commerce	–6115
Committee on Financial Services	–6050
Committee on Government Reform	–6143
Committee on House Administration	–6157
Committee on International Relations	–6128
Committee on the Judiciary	–6216
Committee on Resources	–6201
Committee on Rules	–6269
Committee on Science	–6301
Committee on Small Business	–6315
Committee on Standards of Official Conduct	–6328
Committee on Transportation and Infrastructure	–6256
Committee on Veterans' Affairs	–6335
Committee on Ways and Means	–6348
Select Committee on Homeland Security	–6480
Select Committee on Intelligence	–6415

Joint Committee Offices, House Side

Joint Economic Committee	–6432
Joint Committee on the Library of Congress	–6439
Joint Committee on Printing	–6445
Joint Committee on Taxation	–6453

House Leadership Offices

Office of the Speaker	–6501
Office of the Majority Leader	–6502
Office of the Majority Whip	–6503
Office of the Deputy Majority Whip	–6504
Democratic Caucus	–6524
Democratic Congressional Campaign Committee	–6525
Democratic Personnel Committee	–6526
Democratic Steering and Policy Committee	–6527
Democratic Cloakroom	–6528
Office of the Democratic Leader	–6537
Office of the Democratic Whip	–6538
House Republican Conference	–6544
House Republican Research Committee	–6545
Legislative Digest (Republican Conference)	–6546
Republican Congressional Committee, National	–6547
Republican Policy Committee	–6549
Republican Cloakroom	–6650

House Officers

Office of the Clerk	–6601
Office of History and Preservation	–6612
Office of Employment and Counsel	–6622
House Page School	–9996
House Page Dorm	–6606
Legislative Computer Systems	–6618
Office of Legislative Operations	–6602
Legislative Resource Center	–6612
Official Reporters	–6615
Office of Publication Services	–6611
Office of Interparliamentary Affairs	–6579
Office of the House Historian	–6701
Office of the Parliamentarian	–6731
Chief Administrative Officer	–6861
First Call	–6660
Administrative Counsel	–6660
Periodical Press Gallery	–6624
Press Gallery	–6625
Radio/TV Correspondents' Gallery	–6627
HIR Call Center	–6165
HIR Information Systems Security	–6165
Outplacement Services	–9920
Office of Employee Assistance	–6619
ADA Services	–6860
Personnel and Benefits	–9980
Child Care Center	–0001
Payroll	–9920
Members' Services	–9970
Office Supply Service	–6860
House Gift Shop	–6860
Mail List/Processing	–6860
Mailing Services	–6860
Contractor Management	–6860
Photography	–6623
House Recording Studio	–6613
Furniture Support Services	–6610
House Office Service Center	–6860
Budget	–6604
Financial Counseling	–6604
Procurement Desktop Help	–9940
Office of the Sergeant at Arms	–6611

House Commissions and Offices

Congressional-Executive Commission on the People's Republic of China.	–0001
Commission on Security and Cooperation in Europe.	–6460
Commission on Congressional Mailing Standards	–6461
Office of the Law Revision Counsel	–6711
Office of Emergency Planning, Preparedness and Operations.	–6462
Office of the Legislative Counsel	–6721
Office of the Parliamentarian	–6731
General Counsel	–6532
Architect of the Capitol	–6906
Attending Physician	–6907
Congressional Budget Office	–6925

Liaison Offices

Air Force	–6854
Army	–6855
Coast Guard	–6856
Navy	–6857
Office of Personnel Management	–6858
Veterans' Administration	–6859

TERMS OF SERVICE

EXPIRATION OF THE TERMS OF SENATORS

CLASS I.—SENATORS WHOSE TERMS OF SERVICE EXPIRE IN 2007

[33 Senators in this group: Democrats, 17; Republicans, 15; Independents, 1]

Name	Party	Residence
Akaka, Daniel K.[1]	D.	Honolulu, HI.
Allen, George	R.	Chesterfield County, VA.
Bingaman, Jeff	D.	Santa Fe, NM.
Burns, Conrad R.	R.	Billings, MT.
Byrd, Robert C.	D.	Sophia, WV.
Cantwell, Maria	D.	Edmonds, WA.
Carper, Thomas	D.	Wilmington, DE.
Chafee, Lincoln D.[2]	R.	Warwick, RI.
Clinton, Hillary Rodham	D.	Chappaqua, NY.
Conrad, Kent[3]	D.	Bismarck, ND.
Corzine, Jon S.	D.	Summit, NJ.
Dayton, Mark	D.	Minneapolis, MN.
DeWine, Mike	R.	Cedarville, OH.
Ensign, John	R.	Las Vegas, NV.
Feinstein, Dianne[4]	D.	San Francisco, CA.
Frist, William H. (Bill)	R.	Nashville, TN.
Hatch, Orrin G.	R.	Salt Lake City, UT.
Hutchison, Kay Bailey[5]	R.	Dallas, TX.
Jeffords, James M.[6]	I.	Shrewsbury, VT.
Kennedy, Edward M.	D.	Boston, MA.
Kohl, Herb	D.	Milwaukee, WI.
Kyl, Jon	R.	Phoenix, AZ.
Lieberman, Joseph I.	D.	New Haven, CT.
Lott, Trent	R.	Pascagoula, MS.
Lugar, Richard G.	R.	Indianapolis, IN.
Nelson, Ben	D.	Omaha, NE.
Nelson, Bill	D.	Tallahassee, FL.
Santorum, Rick	R.	Pittsburgh, PA.
Sarbanes, Paul S.	D.	Baltimore, MD.
Snowe, Olympia J.	R.	Auburn, ME.
Stabenow, Debbie	D.	Lansing, MI.
Talent, James M.[7]	R.	Chesterfield, MO.
Thomas, Craig	R.	Casper, WY.

[1] Senator Akaka was appointed Apr. 28, 1990 by the Governor of Hawaii to fill the vacancy caused by the death of Senator Spark M. Matsunaga, and took the oath of office on May 16, 1990. He was elected in a special election on Nov. 6, 1990, for the remainder of the unexpired term.

[2] Senator Lincoln D. Chafee was appointed on November 2, 1999, by the Governor of Rhode Island, to fill the vacancy caused by the death of Senator John H. Chafee. He was then elected to a full term on November 7, 2000.

[3] Senator Conrad resigned his term from Class III after winning a special election on Dec. 4, 1992. Senator Conrad's seniority in the Senate continues without a break in service. He took the oath of office on Dec. 15, 1992.

[4] Senator Feinstein won the special election held on Nov. 3, 1992, to fill the vacancy caused by the resignation of Senator Pete Wilson. She took the oath of office on Nov. 10, 1992. This seat was filled, pending the election, by Senator John Seymour who was appointed by the Governor of California on January 7, 1991.

[5] Senator Hutchison won the special election held on June 5, 1993, to fill remainder of the term of Senator Lloyd Bentsen. She took the oath of office on June 14, 1993. She won the seat from Senator Bob Krueger, who had been appointed by the Governor of Texas on Jan. 21, 1993.

[6] Senator Jeffords changed party affiliation from Republican to Independent on June 6, 2001.

[7] Senator Talent won the special election held on November 5, 2002, against Senator Jean Carnahan, who had been appointed on January 3, 2001.

CLASS II.—SENATORS WHOSE TERMS OF SERVICE EXPIRE IN 2009

[33 Senators in this group: Republicans, 21; Democrats, 12]

Name	Party	Residence
Alexander, Lamar	R.	Nashville, TN.
Allard, Wayne	R.	Loveland, CO.
Baucus, Max	D.	Missoula, MT.
Biden, Joseph R., Jr.	D.	Hockessin, DE.
Chambliss, Saxby	R.	Moultrie, GA.
Cochran, Thad	R.	Jackson, MS.
Coleman, Norm	R.	St. Paul, MN.
Collins, Susan	R.	Bangor, ME.
Cornyn, John	R.	San Antonio, TX.
Craig, Larry E.	R.	Boise, ID.
Dole, Elizabeth H.	R.	Salisbury, NC.
Domenici, Pete V.	R.	Albuquerque, NM.
Durbin, Richard J.	D.	Springfield, IL.
Enzi, Michael B.	R.	Gillette, WY.
Graham, Lindsey	R.	Seneca, SC.
Hagel, Chuck	R.	Omaha, NE.
Harkin, Tom	D.	Cumming, IA.
Inhofe, James M.[1]	R.	Tulsa, OK.
Johnson, Tim	D.	Vermillion, SD.
Kerry, John F.	D.	Boston, MA.
Landrieu, Mary	D.	Baton Rouge, LA.
Lautenberg, Frank R.[2]	D.	Cliffside Park, NJ.
Levin, Carl	D.	Detroit, MI.
McConnell, Mitch	R.	Louisville, KY.
Pryor, Mark	D.	Little Rock, AR.
Reed, Jack	D.	Cranston, RI.
Roberts, Pat	R.	Dodge City, KS.
Rockefeller, John D., IV	D.	Charleston, WV.
Sessions, Jeff	R.	Mobile, AL.
Smith, Gordon	R.	Pendleton, OR.
Stevens, Ted[3]	R.	Anchorage, AK.
Sununu, John E.	R.	Bedford, NH.
Warner, John W.	R.	Middleburg, VA.

[1] Senator James Inhofe was elected November 8, 1994 to fill unexpired term ending January 2, 1997.
[2] Senator Frank Lautenberg replaced Senator Robert Torricelli as the Democratic candidate for the U.S. Senate in October 2002.
[3] Senator Ted Stevens was elected November 3, 1970 to fill vacancy in term ending January 2, 1978.

CLASS III.—SENATORS WHOSE TERMS OF SERVICE EXPIRE IN 2011

[34 Senators in this group: Republicans, 19; Democrats, 15]

Name	Party	Residence
Bayh, Evan	D.	Indianapolis, IN.
Bennett, Robert F.	R.	Salt Lake City, UT.
Bond, Christopher S.	R.	Mexico, MO.
Boxer, Barbara	D.	Greenbrae, CA.
Brownback, Samuel Dale [1]	R.	Topeka, KS.
Bunning, Jim	R.	Southgate, KY.
Burr, Richard M.	R,	Winston-Salem, NC.
Coburn, Tom	R.	Muskogee, OK.
Crapo, Michael D.	R.	Idaho Falls, ID.
DeMint, Jim	R.	Greenville, SC.
Dodd, Christopher J.	D.	Norwich, CT.
Dorgan, Byron L.[2]	D.	Bismarck, ND.
Feingold, Russell D.	D.	Middleton, WI.
Grassley, Charles E.	R.	New Hartford, IA.
Gregg, Judd	R.	Greenfield, NH.
Inouye, Daniel K.	D.	Honolulu, HI.
Isakson, Johnny	R.	Marietta, GA.
Leahy, Patrick J.	D.	Burlington, VT.
Lincoln, Blanche L.	D.	Hughes, AR.
McCain, John	R.	Phoenix, AZ.
Mel Martinez	R.	Orlando, FL.
Mikulski, Barbara A.	D.	Baltimore, MD.
Murkowski, Lisa[3]	R.	Anchorage, AK.
Murray, Patty	D.	Seattle, WA.
Obama, Barack	D.	Chicago, IL.
Reid, Harry	D.	Las Vegas, NV.
Salazar, Ken	D.	Denver, CO.
Schumer, Charles E.	D.	Brooklyn, NY.
Shelby, Richard C.[4]	R.	Tuscaloosa, AL.
Specter, Arlen	R.	Philadelphia, PA.
Thune, John	R.	Pierre, SD.
Vitter, David	R	Metairie, LA.
Voinovich, George V.	R.	Cleveland, OH.
Wyden, Ron[5]	D.	Portland, OR.

[1] Senator Brownback was elected on November 5, 1996 to fill the remainder of the term of Senator Bob Dole. He took the oath of office on November 27, 1996. This seat was filled by Senator Sheila Frahm, who had been appointed, ad interim, on June 11, 1996 by the Governor.

[2] Senator Dorgan was elected to a 6-year term on Nov. 3, 1992, and subsequently was appointed by the Governor Dec. 14, 1992 to fill the vacancy caused by the resignation of Senator Kent Conrad.

[3] Senator Lisa Murkowski was appointed on December 20, 2002 by the Governor of Alaska to fill the vacancy caused by the resignation of Senator Frank Murkowski who was elected Governor on November 5, 2002.

[4] Senator Shelby changed parties on November 5, 1994.

[5] Senator Wyden was elected on January 30, 1996, to fill the vacancy caused by the resignation of Senator Bob Packwood.

CONTINUOUS SERVICE OF SENATORS

[Republicans in roman (55); Democrats in *italic* (44); Independents in SMALL CAPS (1); total, 100]

Rank	Name	State	Beginning of present service
1	*Byrd, Robert C.*†	West Virginia	Jan. 3, 1959.
2	*Kennedy, Edward M.*[1]	Massachusetts	Nov. 7, 1962. ‡
3	*Inouye, Daniel K.*†	Hawaii	Jan. 3, 1963.
5	Stevens, Ted [2]	Alaska	Dec. 24, 1968.
6	*Biden, Joseph R., Jr.*	Delaware	Jan. 3, 1973.
	Domenici, Pete V.	New Mexico	
7	*Leahy, Patrick J.*	Vermont	Jan. 3, 1975.
8	Hatch, Orrin G.	Utah	Dec. 30, 1976.
	Lugar, Richard G.	Indiana	
9	*Sarbanes, Paul S.*†	Maryland	Jan. 3, 1977.
10	*Baucus, Max* †[3]	Montana	Dec. 15, 1978.
11	Cochran, Thad †[4]	Mississippi	Dec. 27, 1978.
12	Warner, John W.[5]	Virginia	Jan. 2, 1979.
13	*Levin, Carl*	Michigan	Jan. 3, 1979.
14	*Dodd, Christopher J.*†	Connecticut	Jan. 3, 1981.
	Grassley, Charles E.†	Iowa	
	Specter, Arlen	Pennsylvania	
15	*Bingaman, Jeff*	New Mexico	Jan. 3, 1983.
16	*Kerry, John F.*[6]	Massachusetts	Jan. 2, 1985.
17	*Harkin, Tom* †	Iowa	
	McConnell, Mitch	Kentucky	
18	*Rockefeller, John D., IV*[7]	West Virginia	Jan. 15, 1985.
19	Bond, Christopher S.	Missouri	Jan. 3, 1987.
	Conrad, Kent	North Dakota	
	McCain, John †	Arizona	
	Mikulski, Barbara A.†	Maryland	
	Reid, Harry †	Nevada	
	Shelby, Richard C.†	Alabama	
20	Burns, Conrad	Montana	Jan. 3, 1989.
	JEFFORDS, JAMES M.†[8]	Vermont	
	Kohl, Herb	Wisconsin	
	Lieberman, Joseph I.	Connecticut	
	Lott, Trent †	Mississippi	
21	*Akaka, Daniel K.*†[9]	Hawaii	Apr. 28, 1990.
22	Craig, Larry E.†	Idaho	Jan. 3, 1991.
23	*Feinstein, Dianne*[10]	California	Nov. 10, 1992.‡
24	*Dorgan, Byron* † [11]	North Dakota	Dec. 14, 1992.
25	Bennett, Robert F.	Utah	Jan. 3, 1993.
	Boxer, Barbara †	California	
	Feingold, Russell	Wisconsin	
	Gregg, Judd †	New Hampshire ..	
	Murray, Patty	Washington	
26	Hutchison, Kay Bailey [12]	Texas	June 5, 1993.
27	Inhofe, James M. † [13]	Oklahoma	Nov. 16, 1994. ‡
28	DeWine, Mike †	Ohio	Jan. 3, 1995
	Frist, William H. (Bill)	Tennessee	
	Kyl, Jon †	Arizona	
	Santorum, Rick †	Pennsylvania	
	Snowe, Olympia J.†	Maine	
	Thomas, Craig †	Wyoming	
29	*Wyden, Ron* † [14]	Oregon	Feb. 6, 1996.‡
30	Brownback, Samuel Dale † [15]	Kansas	Nov. 6, 1996. ‡
31	Hagel, Chuck	Nebraska	Jan. 3, 1997.
	Allard, Wayne †	Colorado	

CONTINUOUS SERVICE OF SENATORS—CONTINUED

[Republicans in roman (55); Democrats in *italic* (44); Independents in SMALL CAPS (1); total, 100]

Rank	Name	State	Beginning of present service
	Collins, Susan	Maine	
	Durbin, Richard J. †	Illinois	
	Enzi, Michael B.	Wyoming	
	Johnson, Tim †	South Dakota	
	Landrieu, Mary	Louisiana	
	Reed, Jack †	Rhode Island	
	Roberts, Pat †	Kansas	
	Sessions, Jeff	Alabama	
	Smith, Gordon	Oregon	
32	*Bayh, Evan*	Indiana	Jan. 3, 1999.
	Bunning, Jim †	Kentucky	
	Crapo, Michael D.†	Idaho	
	Lincoln, Blanche L. †	Arkansas	
	Schumer, Charles E. †	New York	
	Voinovich, George V.	Ohio	
33	Chafee, Lincoln D.[16]	Rhode Island	Nov. 2, 1999.
35	Allen, George †	Virginia	Jan. 3, 2001.
	Cantwell, Maria †	Washington	
	Carper, Thomas †	Delaware	
	Clinton, Hillary Rodham	New York	
	Corzine, Jon S.	New Jersey	
	Dayton, Mark	Minnesota	
	Ensign, John †	Nevada	
	Nelson, Ben	Nebraska	
	Nelson, Bill †	Florida	
	Stabenow, Debbie †	Michigan	
36	Talent, James M. † [17]	Missouri	Nov. 6, 2002. ‡
37	Cornyn, John [18]	Texas	Dec. 2, 2002.
38	Murkowski, Lisa [19]	Alaska	Dec. 20, 2002.
39	Alexander, Lamar	Tennessee	Jan. 3, 2003.
	Chambliss, Saxby †	Georgia	
	Coleman, Norm	Minnesota	
	Dole, Elizabeth H.	North Carolina ...	
	Graham, Lindsey †	South Carolina ...	
	Lautenberg, Frank R. [20]	New Jersey	
	Pryor, Mark	Arkansas	
	Sununu, John †	New Hampshire ..	
40	Burr, Richard M. †	North Carolina ...	Jan. 3, 2005.
	Coburn, Tom †	Oklahoma	
	DeMint, Jim †	South Carolina ...	
	Isakson, Johnny †	Georgia	
	Martinez, Mel	Florida	
	Obama, Barack	Illinois	
	Salazar, Ken	Colorado	
	Thune, John †	South Dakota	
	Vitter, David †	Louisiana	

† Served in the House of Representatives previous to service in the Senate.
‡ Senators elected to complete unexpired terms begin their terms on the day following the election.
[1] Senator Kennedy was elected Nov. 6, 1962, to complete the unexpired term caused by the resignation of Senator John F. Kennedy.
[2] Senator Stevens was appointed Dec. 23, 1968 by the Governor to fill the vacancy caused by the death of Senator Edward L. Bartlett.
[3] Senator Baucus was elected Nov. 7, 1978, for the 6-year term commencing Jan. 3, 1979; subsequently appointed Dec. 15, 1978, to fill the vacancy caused by the resignation of Senator Paul Hatfield.
[4] Senator Cochran was elected Nov. 6, 1978, for the 6-year term commencing Jan. 3, 1979; subsequently appointed Dec. 27, 1978, to fill the vacancy caused by the resignation of Senator James Eastland.

⁵ Senator Warner was elected Nov. 6, 1978, for the 6-year term commencing Jan. 3, 1979; subsequently appointed Jan. 2, 1979, to fill the vacancy caused by the resignation of Senator William Scott.

⁶ Senator Kerry was elected Nov. 6, 1984, for the 6-year term commencing Jan. 3, 1985; subsequently appointed Jan. 2, 1985, to fill the vacancy caused by the resignation of Senator Paul E. Tsongas.

⁷ Senator Rockefeller was elected Nov. 6, 1984, for the 6-year term commencing Jan. 3, 1985; did not take his seat until Jan. 15, 1985.

⁸ Senator Jeffords changed party affiliation from Republican to Independent on June 6, 2001.

⁹ Senator Akaka was appointed Apr. 28, 1990 by the Governor to fill the vacancy caused by the death of Senator Spark M. Matsunaga. Subsequently elected on Nov. 6, 1990 to complete the unexpired term.

¹⁰ Senator Feinstein was elected on Nov. 3, 1992 to fill the vacancy caused by the resignation of Senator Pete Wilson. She replaced appointed Senator John Seymour when she took the oath of office on Nov. 10, 1992.

¹¹ Senator Dorgan was elected to a 6-year term on Nov. 3, 1992 and subsequently was appointed by the Governor on Dec. 14, 1992 to complete the unexpired term of Senator Kent Conrad.

¹² Senator Hutchison won a special election on June 5, 1993 to fill the vacancy caused by the resignation of Senator Lloyd Bentsen. She won the seat from Senator Bob Krueger, who had been appointed on Jan. 21, 1993 by the Governor.

¹³ Senator Inhofe was elected to fill an unexpired term until January 3, 1997.

¹⁴ Senator Wyden was elected on January 30, 1996 to fill the vacancy caused by the resignation of Senator Bob Packwood.

¹⁵ Senator Brownback was elected on November 5, 1996 to fill the vacancy caused by the resignation of Senator Bob Dole. He replaced appointed Senator Sheila Frahm when he took the oath of office on November 27, 1996.

¹⁶ Senator Lincoln D. Chafee was appointed on November 2, 1999, by the Governor of Rhode Island, to fill the vacancy caused by the death of Senator John H. Chafee. He was then elected to a full term on November 7, 2000.

¹⁷ Senator Talent was elected to fill an unexpired term until January 3, 2007.

¹⁸ Senator Cornyn was appointed on December 2, 2002 to fill the vacancy caused by the resignation of Senator Phil Gramm.

¹⁹ Senator Lisa Murkowski was appointed on December 20, 2002 to fill the vacancy caused by the resignation of Senator Frank Murkowski; reelected to the 109th Congress..

²⁰ Senator Lautenberg previously served in the Senate from December 27, 1982 until January 3, 2001.

CONGRESSES IN WHICH REPRESENTATIVES HAVE SERVED, WITH BEGINNING OF PRESENT SERVICE

[*Elected to fill a vacancy; Republicans in roman (231); Democrats in *italic* (202); Independents in SMALL CAPS (1); Vacancy (1); Resident Commissioner and Delegates in **boldface** (5); total, 440]

Name	State	Congresses (inclusive)	Beginning of present service
26 terms, consecutive			
Dingell, John D.	MI	*84th to 109th	Dec. 13, 1955
21 terms, consecutive			
Conyers, John, Jr.	MI	89th to 109th	Jan. 3, 1965
19 terms, consecutive			
Obey, David R.	WI	*91st to 109th	Apr. 1, 1969
18 terms, consecutive			
Rangel, Charles B.	NY	92d to 109th	Jan. 3, 1971
Young, C.W. Bill	FL	92d to 109th	Jan. 3, 1971
17 terms, consecutive			
Murtha, John P.	PA	*93d to 109th	Feb. 5, 1974
Regula, Ralph	OH	93d to 109th	Jan. 3, 1973
Stark, Fortney Pete	CA	93d to 109th	Jan. 3, 1973
Young, Don	AK	*93d to 109th	Mar. 6, 1973
16 terms, consecutive			
Hyde, Henry J.	IL	94th to 109th	Jan. 3, 1975
Markey, Edward J.	MA	*94th to 109th	Nov. 2, 1976
Miller, George	CA	94th to 109th	Jan. 3, 1975
Oberstar, James L.	MN	94th to 109th	Jan. 3, 1975
Waxman, Henry A.	CA	94th to 109th	Jan. 3, 1975
15 terms, consecutive			
Dicks, Norman D.	WA	95th to 109th	Jan. 3, 1977
Kildee, Dale E.	MI	95th to 109th	Jan. 3, 1977
Leach, James A.	IA	95th to 109th	Jan. 3, 1977
Rahall, Nick J. II	WV	95th to 109th	Jan. 3, 1977
Skelton, Ike	MO	95th to 109th	Jan. 3, 1977
14 terms, consecutive			
Lewis, Jerry	CA	96th to 109th	Jan. 3, 1979
Petri, Thomas E.	WI	*96th to 109th	Apr. 3, 1979
Sabo, Martin Olav	MN	96th to 109th	Jan. 3, 1979
Sensenbrenner, F. James, Jr.	WI	96th to 109th	Jan. 3, 1979
Thomas, Bill	CA	96th to 109th	Jan. 3, 1979
13 terms, consecutive			
Dreier, David	CA	97th to 109th	Jan. 3, 1981
Frank, Barney	MA	97th to 109th	Jan. 3, 1981
Hall, Ralph M.	TX	97th to 109th	Jan. 3, 1981
Hoyer, Steny H.	MD	*97th to 109th	May 19, 1981
Hunter, Duncan	CA	97th to 109th	Jan. 3, 1981
Lantos, Tom	CA	97th to 109th	Jan. 3, 1981
Oxley, Michael G.	OH	*97th to 109th	June 25, 1981
Rogers, Harold	KY	97th to 109th	Jan. 3, 1981

CONGRESSES IN WHICH REPRESENTATIVES HAVE SERVED, WITH BEGINNING OF PRESENT SERVICE—CONTINUED

[*Elected to fill a vacancy; Republicans in roman (231); Democrats in *italic* (202); Independents in SMALL CAPS (1); Vacancy (1); Resident Commissioner and Delegates in **boldface** (5); total, 440]

Name	State	Congresses (inclusive)	Beginning of present service
Shaw, E. Clay, Jr.	FL	97th to 109th	Jan. 3, 1981
Smith, Christopher H.	NJ	97th to 109th	Jan. 3, 1981
Wolf, Frank R.	VA	97th to 109th	Jan. 3, 1981
12 terms, consecutive			
Ackerman, Gary L.	NY	*98th to 109th	Mar. 1, 1983
Berman, Howard L.	CA	98th to 109th	Jan. 3, 1983
Bilirakis, Michael	FL	98th to 109th	Jan. 3, 1983
Boehlert, Sherwood	NY	98th to 109th	Jan. 3, 1983
Boucher, Rick	VA	98th to 109th	Jan. 3, 1983
Burton, Dan	IN	98th to 109th	Jan. 3, 1983
Evans, Lane	IL	98th to 109th	Jan. 3, 1983
Johnson, Nancy L.	CT	98th to 109th	Jan. 3, 1983
Kaptur, Marcy	OH	98th to 109th	Jan. 3, 1983
Levin, Sander M.	MI	98th to 109th	Jan. 3, 1983
Mollohan, Alan B.	WV	98th to 109th	Jan. 3, 1983
Ortiz, Solomon P.	TX	98th to 109th	Jan. 3, 1983
Owens, Major R.	NY	98th to 109th	Jan. 3, 1983
Saxton, Jim	NJ	*98th to 109th	Nov. 6, 1984
Spratt, John M., Jr.	SC	98th to 109th	Jan. 3, 1983
Towns, Edolphus	NY	98th to 109th	Jan. 3, 1983
11 terms, consecutive			
Barton, Joe	TX	99th to 109th	Jan. 3, 1985
Coble, Howard	NC	99th to 109th	Jan. 3, 1985
DeLay, Tom	TX	99th to 109th	Jan. 3, 1985
Gordon, Bart	TN	99th to 109th	Jan. 3, 1985
Kanjorski, Paul E.	PA	99th to 109th	Jan. 3, 1985
Kolbe, Jim	AZ	99th to 109th	Jan. 3, 1985
Visclosky, Peter J.	IN	99th to 109th	Jan. 3, 1985
10 terms, consecutive			
Baker, Richard H.	LA	100th to 109th	Jan. 3, 1987
Cardin, Benjamin L.	MD	100th to 109th	Jan. 3, 1987
Costello, Jerry F.	IL	*100th to 109th	Aug. 9, 1988
DeFazio, Peter A.	OR	100th to 109th	Jan. 3, 1987
Duncan, John J., Jr.	TN	*100th to 109th	Nov. 8, 1988
Gallegly, Elton	CA	100th to 109th	Jan. 3, 1987
Hastert, J. Dennis	IL	100th to 109th	Jan. 3, 1987
Hefley, Joel	CO	100th to 109th	Jan. 3, 1987
Herger, Wally	CA	100th to 109th	Jan. 3, 1987
Lewis, John	GA	100th to 109th	Jan. 3, 1987
McCrery, Jim	LA	*100th to 109th	Apr. 16, 1988
Pallone, Frank, Jr.	NJ	*100th to 109th	Nov. 8, 1988
Pelosi, Nancy	CA	*100th to 109th	June 2, 1987
Shays, Christopher	CT	*100th to 109th	Aug. 18, 1987
Slaughter, Louise McIntosh	NY	100th to 109th	Jan. 3, 1987
Smith, Lamar S.	TX	100th to 109th	Jan. 3, 1987
Upton, Frederick S.	MI	100th to 109th	Jan. 3, 1987
Weldon, Curt	PA	100th to 109th	Jan. 3, 1987

CONGRESSES IN WHICH REPRESENTATIVES HAVE SERVED, WITH BEGINNING OF PRESENT SERVICE—CONTINUED

[* Elected to fill a vacancy; Republicans in roman (231); Democrats in *italic* (202); Independents in SMALL CAPS (1); Vacancy (1); Resident Commissioner and Delegates in **boldface** (5); total, 440]

Name	State	Congresses (inclusive)	Beginning of present service
9 terms, consecutive			
Andrews, Robert E.	NJ	*101st to 109th	Nov. 6, 1990
Cox, Christopher	CA	101st to 109th	Jan. 3, 1989
Engel, Eliot L.	NY	101st to 109th	Jan. 3, 1989
Gillmor, Paul E.	OH	101st to 109th	Jan. 3, 1989
Lowey, Nita M.	NY	101st to 109th	Jan. 3, 1989
McDermott, Jim	WA	101st to 109th	Jan. 3, 1989
McNulty, Michael R.	NY	101st to 109th	Jan. 3, 1989
Neal, Richard E.	MA	101st to 109th	Jan. 3, 1989
Payne, Donald M.	NJ	101st to 109th	Jan. 3, 1989
Rohrabacher, Dana	CA	101st to 109th	Jan. 3, 1989
Ros-Lehtinen, Ileana	FL	*101st to 109th	Aug. 29, 1989
Serrano, José E.	NY	*101st to 109th	Mar. 20, 1990
Stearns, Cliff	FL	101st to 109th	Jan. 3, 1989
Tanner, John S.	TN	101st to 109th	Jan. 3, 1989
Taylor, Gene	MS	*101st to 109th	Oct. 17, 1989
Walsh, James T.	NY	101st to 109th	Jan. 3, 1989
9 terms, not consecutive			
Abercrombie, Neil	HI	*99th, 102d to 109th.	Jan. 3, 1991
Paul, Ron	TX	94th, 96th to 98th, 105th to 109th.	Jan. 3, 1997
Price, David E.	NC	100th to 103d, 105th to 109th.	Jan 3. 1997
8 terms, consecutive			
Boehner, John A.	OH	102d to 109th	Jan. 3, 1991
Camp, Dave	MI	102d to 109th	Jan. 3, 1991
Cramer, Robert (Bud), Jr.	AL	102d to 109th	Jan. 3, 1991
Cunningham, Randy (Duke)	CA	102d to 109th	Jan. 3, 1991
DeLauro, Rosa L.	CT	102d to 109th	Jan. 3, 1991
Doolittle, John T.	CA	102d to 109th	Jan. 3, 1991
Edwards, Chet	TX	102d to 109th	Jan. 3, 1991
Gilchrest, Wayne T.	MD	102d to 109th	Jan. 3, 1991
Hobson, David L.	OH	102d to 109th	Jan. 3, 1991
Jefferson, William J.	LA	102d to 109th	Jan. 3, 1991
Johnson, Sam	TX	*102d to 109th	May 18, 1991
Moran, James P.	VA	102d to 109th	Jan. 3, 1991
Nadler, Jerrold	NY	*102d to 109th	Nov. 4, 1992
Nussle, Jim	IA	102d to 109th	Jan. 3, 1991
Olver, John W.	MA	*102d to 109th	June 4, 1991
Pastor, Ed	AZ	*102d to 109th	Sep. 24, 1991
Peterson, Collin C.	MN	102d to 109th	Jan. 3, 1991
Ramstad, Jim	MN	102d to 109th	Jan. 3, 1991
SANDERS, BERNARD	VT	102d to 109th	Jan. 3, 1991
Taylor, Charles H.	NC	102d to 109th	Jan. 3, 1991
Waters, Maxine	CA	102d to 109th	Jan. 3, 1991
8 terms, not consecutive			
Cooper, Jim	TN	98th to 103d, 108th and 109th.	Jan. 3, 2003

CONGRESSES IN WHICH REPRESENTATIVES HAVE SERVED, WITH BEGINNING OF PRESENT SERVICE—CONTINUED

[* Elected to fill a vacancy; Republicans in roman (231); Democrats in *italic* (202); Independents in SMALL CAPS (1); Vacancy (1); Resident Commissioner and Delegates in **boldface** (5); total, 440]

Name	State	Congresses (inclusive)	Beginning of present service
7 terms, consecutive			
Bachus, Spencer	AL	103d to 109th	Jan. 3, 1993
Bartlett, Roscoe G.	MD	103d to 109th	Jan. 3, 1993
Becerra, Xavier	CA	103d to 109th	Jan. 3, 1993
Bishop, Sanford D., Jr.	GA	103d to 109th	Jan. 3, 1993
Bonilla, Henry	TX	103d to 109th	Jan. 3, 1993
Brown, Corrine	FL	103d to 109th	Jan. 3, 1993
Brown, Sherrod	OH	103d to 109th	Jan. 3, 1993
Buyer, Steve	IN	103d to 109th	Jan. 3, 1993
Calvert, Ken	CA	103d to 109th	Jan. 3, 1993
Castle, Michael N.	DE	103d to 109th	Jan. 3, 1993
Clyburn, James E.	SC	103d to 109th	Jan. 3, 1993
Deal, Nathan	GA	103d to 109th	Jan. 3, 1993
Diaz-Balart, Lincoln	FL	103d to 109th	Jan. 3, 1993
Ehlers, Vernon	MI	103d to 109th	Dec. 7, 1993
Eshoo, Anna G.	CA	103d to 109th	Jan. 3, 1993
Everett, Terry	AL	103d to 109th	Jan. 3, 1993
Farr, Sam	CA	*103d to 109th	June 8, 1993
Filner, Bob	CA	103d to 109th	Jan. 3, 1993
Goodlatte, Robert W. (Bob)	VA	103d to 109th	Jan. 3, 1993
Green, Gene	TX	103d to 109th	Jan. 3, 1993
Gutierrez, Luis V.	IL	103d to 109th	Jan. 3, 1993
Hastings, Alcee L.	FL	103d to 109th	Jan. 3, 1993
Hinchey, Maurice D.	NY	103d to 109th	Jan. 3, 1993
Hoekstra, Peter	MI	103d to 109th	Jan. 3, 1993
Holden, Tim	PA	103d to 109th	Jan. 3, 1993
Istook, Ernest J., Jr.	OK	103d to 109th	Jan. 3, 1993
Johnson, Eddie Bernice	TX	103d to 109th	Jan. 3, 1993
King, Peter T.	NY	103d to 109th	Jan. 3, 1993
Kingston, Jack	GA	103d to 109th	Jan. 3, 1993
Knollenberg, Joseph	MI	103d to 109th	Jan. 3, 1993
Lewis, Ron	KY	*103d to 109th	May 17, 1994
Linder, John	GA	103d to 109th	Jan. 3, 1993
Lucas, Frank	OK	*103d to 109th	May 10, 1994
McHugh, John M.	NY	103d to 109th	Jan. 3, 1993
McKeon, Howard P. (Buck)	CA	103d to 109th	Jan. 3, 1993
Maloney, Carolyn B.	NY	103d to 109th	Jan. 3, 1993
Manzullo, Donald A.	IL	103d to 109th	Jan. 3, 1993
Meehan, Martin T.	MA	103d to 109th	Jan. 3, 1993
Menendez, Robert	NJ	103d to 109th	Jan. 3, 1993
Mica, John L.	FL	103d to 109th	Jan. 3, 1993
Pombo, Richard W.	CA	103d to 109th	Jan. 3, 1993
Pomeroy, Earl	ND	103d to 109th	Jan. 3, 1993
Pryce, Deborah	OH	103d to 109th	Jan. 3, 1993
Roybal-Allard, Lucille	CA	103d to 109th	Jan. 3, 1993
Royce, Ed	CA	103d to 109th	Jan. 3, 1993
Rush, Bobby L.	IL	103d to 109th	Jan. 3, 1993
Scott, Robert C. (Bobby)	VA	103d to 109th	Jan. 3, 1993
Stupak, Bart	MI	103d to 109th	Jan. 3, 1993
Thompson, Bennie G.	MS	*103d to 109th	Apr. 13, 1993
Velázquez, Nydia M.	NY	103d to 109th	Jan. 3, 1993

CONGRESSES IN WHICH REPRESENTATIVES HAVE SERVED, WITH BEGINNING OF PRESENT SERVICE—CONTINUED

[* Elected to fill a vacancy; Republicans in roman (231); Democrats in *italic* (202); Independents in SMALL CAPS (1); Vacancy (1); Resident Commissioner and Delegates in **boldface** (5); total, 440]

Name	State	Congresses (inclusive)	Beginning of present service
Watt, Melvin L.	NC	103d to 109th	Jan. 3, 1993
Woolsey, Lynn	CA	103d to 109th	Jan. 3, 1993
Wynn, Albert Russell.	MD	103d to 109th	Jan. 3, 1993
6 terms, consecutive			
Bass, Charles F.	NH	104th to 109th	Jan. 3, 1995
Blumenauer, Earl	OR	*104th to 109th	May 21, 1996
Chabot, Steve	OH	104th to 109th	Jan. 3, 1995
Cubin, Barbara	WY	104th to 109th	Jan. 3, 1995
Cummings, Elijah E.	MD	*104th to 109th	Apr. 16, 1996
Davis, Tom	VA	104th to 109th	Jan. 3, 1995
Doggett, Lloyd	TX	104th to 109th	Jan. 3, 1995
Doyle, Michael F.	PA	104th to 109th	Jan. 3, 1995
Emerson, Jo Ann	MO	*104th to 109th	Nov. 5, 1996
English, Phil	PA	104th to 109th	Jan. 3, 1995
Fattah, Chaka	PA	104th to 109th	Jan. 3, 1995
Foley, Mark	FL	104th to 109th	Jan. 3, 1995
Frelinghuysen, Rodney P.	NJ	104th to 109th	Jan. 3, 1995
Gutknecht, Gil	MN	104th to 109th	Jan. 3, 1995
Hastings, Doc	WA	104th to 109th	Jan. 3, 1995
Hayworth, J.D.	AZ	104th to 109th	Jan. 3, 1995
Hostettler, John N.	IN	104th to 109th	Jan. 3, 1995
Jackson Lee, Sheila	TX	104th to 109th	Jan. 3, 1995
Jackson, Jesse, Jr.	IL	*104th to 109th	Dec. 12, 1995
Jones, Walter B.	NC	104th to 109th	Jan. 3, 1995
Kelly, Sue	NY	104th to 109th	Jan. 3, 1995
Kennedy, Patrick J.	RI	104th to 109th	Jan. 3, 1995
LaHood, Ray	IL	104th to 109th	Jan. 3, 1995
Latham, Tom	IA	104th to 109th	Jan. 3, 1995
LaTourette, Steven	OH	104th to 109th	Jan. 3, 1995
LoBiondo, Frank	NJ	104th to 109th	Jan. 3, 1995
Lofgren, Zoe	CA	104th to 109th	Jan. 3, 1995
Millender-McDonald, Juanita	CA	*104th to 109th	Mar. 26, 1996
Myrick, Sue Wilkins	NC	104th to 109th	Jan. 3, 1995
Ney, Robert W.	OH	104th to 109th	Jan. 3, 1995
Norwood, Charlie	GA	104th to 109th	Jan. 3, 1995
Radanovich, George	CA	104th to 109th	Jan. 3, 1995
Ryun, Jim	KS	*104th to 109th	Nov. 27, 1996
Shadegg, John	AZ	104th to 109th	Jan. 3, 1995
Souder, Mark E.	IN	104th to 109th	Jan. 3, 1995
Thornberry, Mac	TX	104th to 109th	Jan. 3, 1995
Tiahrt, Todd	KS	104th to 109th	Jan. 3, 1995
Wamp, Zachary Paul	TN	104th to 109th	Jan. 3, 1995
Weldon, Dave	FL	104th to 109th	Jan. 3, 1995
Weller, Jerry	IL	104th to 109th	Jan. 3, 1995
Whitfield, Ed	KY	104th to 109th	Jan. 3, 1995
Wicker, Roger	MS	104th to 109th	Jan. 3, 1995
6 terms, not consecutive			
Harman, Jane	CA	103d to 105th, 107th to 109th.	Jan. 3, 2001

CONGRESSES IN WHICH REPRESENTATIVES HAVE SERVED, WITH BEGINNING OF PRESENT SERVICE—CONTINUED

[* Elected to fill a vacancy; Republicans in roman (231); Democrats in *italic* (202); Independents in SMALL CAPS (1); Vacancy (1); Resident Commissioner and Delegates in **boldface** (5); total, 440]

Name	State	Congresses (inclusive)	Beginning of present service
Lungren, Dan	CA	96th to 100th and 109th.	Jan. 3, 2005
McKinney, Cynthia	GA	103d to 107th and 109th.	Jan. 3, 2005
Strickland, Ted	OH	103d, 105th to 109th.	Jan. 3, 1997
5 terms			
Aderholt, Robert	AL	105th to 109th	Jan. 3, 1997
Allen, Thomas H.	ME	105th to 109th	Jan. 3, 1997
Berry, Marion	AR	105th to 109th	Jan. 3, 1997
Blunt, Roy	MO	105th to 109th	Jan. 3, 1997
Bono, Mary	CA	*105th to 109th	Apr. 7, 1998
Boswell, Leonard L.	IA	105th to 109th	Jan. 3, 1997
Boyd, Allen	FL	105th to 109th	Jan. 3, 1997
Brady, Kevin	TX	105th to 109th	Jan. 3, 1997
Brady, Robert A.	PA	*105th to 109th	May. 19, 1998
Cannon, Christopher B.	UT	105th to 109th	Jan. 3, 1997
Capps, Lois	CA	*105th to 109th	Mar. 10, 1998
Carson, Julia M.	IN	105th to 109th	Jan. 3, 1997
Davis, Danny K.	IL	105th to 109th	Jan. 3, 1997
Davis, Jim	FL	105th to 109th	Jan. 3, 1997
DeGette, Diana	CO	105th to 109th	Jan. 3, 1997
Delahunt, William D.	MA	105th to 109th	Jan. 3, 1997
Etheridge, Bob	NC	105th to 109th	Jan. 3, 1997
Ford, Harold E., Jr.	TN	105th to 109th	Jan. 3, 1997
Fossella, Vito	NY	*105th to 109th	Nov. 4, 1997
Gibbons, Jim	NE	105th to 109th	Jan. 3, 1997
Goode, Virgil H., Jr.	VA	105th to 109th	Jan. 3, 1997
Granger, Kay	TX	105th to 109th	Jan. 3, 1997
Hinojosa, Rubén	TX	105th to 109th	Jan. 3, 1997
Hooley, Darlene	OR	105th to 109th	Jan. 3, 1997
Hulfshof, Kenny	MO	105th to 109th	Jan. 3, 1997
Jenkins, William L. (Bill)	TN	105th to 109th	Jan. 3, 1997
Kilpatrick, Carolyn C.	MI	105th to 109th	Jan. 3, 1997
Kind, Ron	WI	105th to 109th	Jan. 3, 1997
Kucinich, Dennis J.	OH	105th to 109th	Jan. 3, 1997
Lee, Barbara	CA	*105th to 109th	Apr. 7, 1998
McCarthy, Carolyn	NY	105th to 109th	Jan. 3, 1997
McGovern, James P.	MA	105th to 109th	Jan. 3, 1997
McIntyre, Mike	NC	105th to 109th	Jan. 3, 1997
Meeks, Gregory W.	NY	*105th to 109th	Feb. 3, 1998
Moran, Jerry	KS	105th to 109th	Jan. 3, 1997
Northup, Anne M.	KY	105th to 109th	Jan. 3, 1997
Pascrell, Bill, Jr.	NJ	105th to 109th	Jan. 3, 1997
Peterson, John E.	PA	105th to 109th	Jan. 3, 1997
Pickering, Charles W. (Chip), Jr.	MS	105th to 109th	Jan. 3, 1997
Pitts, Joseph R.	PA	105th to 109th	Jan. 3, 1997
Reyes, Silvestre	TX	105th to 109th	Jan. 3, 1997
Rothman, Steven R.	NJ	105th to 109th	Jan. 3, 1997
Sanchez, Loretta	CA	105th to 109th	Jan. 3, 1997
Sessions, Pete	TX	105th to 109th	Jan. 3, 1997

CONGRESSES IN WHICH REPRESENTATIVES HAVE SERVED, WITH BEGINNING OF PRESENT SERVICE—CONTINUED

[* Elected to fill a vacancy; Republicans in roman (231); Democrats in *italic* (202); Independents in SMALL CAPS (1); Vacancy (1); Resident Commissioner and Delegates in **boldface** (5); total, 440]

Name	State	Congresses (inclusive)	Beginning of present service
Sherman, Brad	CA	105th to 109th	Jan. 3, 1997
Shimkus, John	IL	105th to 109th	Jan. 3, 1997
Smith, Adam	WA	105th to 109th	Jan. 3, 1997
Snyder, Vic	AR	105th to 109th	Jan. 3, 1997
Tauscher, Ellen O.	CA	105th to 109th	Jan. 3, 1997
Tierney, John	MA	105th to 109th	Jan. 3, 1997
Wexler, Robert	FL	105th to 109th	Jan. 3, 1997
Wilson, Heather	NM	*105th to 109th	Jun. 23, 1998
5 terms, not consecutive			
Inslee, Jay	WA	*103d, 106th to 109th.	Jan. 3, 1999
4 terms			
Baca, Joe	CA	*106th to 109th	Nov. 17, 1999
Baird, Brian	WA	106th to 109th	Jan. 3, 1999
Baldwin, Tammy	WI	106th to 109th	Jan. 3, 1999
Berkley, Shelley	NV	106th to 109th	Jan. 3, 1999
Biggert, Judy	IL	106th to 109th	Jan. 3, 1999
Capuano, Michael E.	MA	106th to 109th	Jan. 3, 1999
Crowley, Joseph	NY	106th to 109th	Jan. 3, 1999
Gonzalez, Charles A.	TX	106th to 109th	Jan. 3, 1999
Green, Mark	WI	106th to 109th	Jan. 3, 1999
Hayes, Robin	NC	106th to 109th	Jan. 3, 1999
Holt, Rush D.	NJ	106th to 109th	Jan. 3, 1999
Jones, Stephanie Tubbs	OH	106th to 109th	Jan. 3, 1999
Larson, John B.	CT	106th to 109th	Jan. 3, 1999
Miller, Gary G.	CA	106th to 109th	Jan. 3, 1999
Moore, Dennis	KS	106th to 109th	Jan. 3, 1999
Napolitano, Grace F.	CA	106th to 109th	Jan. 3, 1999
Reynolds, Thomas M.	NY	106th to 109th	Jan. 3, 1999
Ryan, Paul	WI	106th to 109th	Jan. 3, 1999
Schakowsky, Janice D.	IL	106th to 109th	Jan. 3, 1999
Sherwood, Don	PA	106th to 109th	Jan. 3, 1999
Simpson, Michael K.	ID	106th to 109th	Jan. 3, 1999
Sweeney, John E.	NY	106th to 109th	Jan. 3, 1999
Tancredo, Thomas G.	CO	106th to 109th	Jan. 3, 1999
Terry, Lee	NE	106th to 109th	Jan. 3, 1999
Thompson, Mike	CA	106th to 109th	Jan. 3, 1999
Udall, Mark	CO	106th to 109th	Jan. 3, 1999
Udall, Tom	NM	106th to 109th	Jan. 3, 1999
Walden, Greg	OR	106th to 109th	Jan. 3, 1999
Weiner, Anthony D.	NY	106th to 109th	Jan. 3, 1999
Wu, David	OR	106th to 109th	Jan. 3, 1999
3 terms			
Akin, W. Todd	MO	107th to 109th	Jan. 3, 2001
Boozman, John	AR	*107th to 109th	Nov. 20, 2001
Brown, Henry E., Jr.	SC	107th to 109th	Jan. 3, 2001
Cantor, Eric	VA	107th to 109th	Jan. 3, 2001
Capito, Shelley Moore	WV	107th to 109th	Jan. 3, 2001

CONGRESSES IN WHICH REPRESENTATIVES HAVE SERVED, WITH BEGINNING OF PRESENT SERVICE—CONTINUED

[* Elected to fill a vacancy; Republicans in roman (231); Democrats in *italic* (202); Independents in SMALL CAPS (1); Vacancy (1); Resident Commissioner and Delegates in **boldface** (5); total, 440]

Name	State	Congresses (inclusive)	Beginning of present service
Case, Ed	HI	*107th to 109th	Nov. 30, 2002
Clay, Wm. Lacy	MO	107th to 109th	Jan. 3, 2001
Crenshaw, Ander	FL	107th to 109th	Jan. 3, 2001
Culberson, John	TX	107th to 109th	Jan. 3, 2001
Davis, Jo Ann	VA	107th to 109th	Jan. 3, 2001
Davis, Susan	CA	107th to 109th	Jan. 3, 2001
Ferguson, Mike	NJ	107th to 109th	Jan. 3, 2001
Flake, Jeff	AZ	107th to 109th	Jan. 3, 2001
Forbes, J. Randy	VA	*107th to 109th	June 19, 2001
Graves, Samuel	MO	107th to 109th	Jan. 3, 2001
Hart, Melissa A.	PA	107th to 109th	Jan. 3, 2001
Honda, Mike	CA	107th to 109th	Jan. 3, 2001
Israel, Steve	NY	107th to 109th	Jan. 3, 2001
Issa, Darrell	CA	107th to 109th	Jan. 3, 2001
Johnson, Timothy V.	IL	107th to 109th	Jan. 3, 2001
Keller, Ric	FL	107th to 109th	Jan. 3, 2001
Kennedy, Mark	MN	107th to 109th	Jan. 3, 2001
Kirk, Mark	IL	107th to 109th	Jan. 3, 2001
Langevin, James	RI	107th to 109th	Jan. 3, 2001
Larsen, Rick	WA	107th to 109th	Jan. 3, 2001
Lynch, Stephen F.	MA	*107th to 109th	Oct. 16, 2001
McCollum, Betty	MN	107th to 109th	Jan. 3, 2001
Matheson, Jim	UT	107th to 109th	Jan. 3, 2001
Miller, Jeff	FL	*107th to 109th	Oct. 16, 2001
Osborne, Tom	NE	107th to 109th	Jan. 3, 2001
Otter, C.L. (Butch)	ID	107th to 109th	Jan. 3, 2001
Pence, Mike	IN	107th to 109th	Jan. 3, 2001
Platts, Todd Russell	ID	107th to 109th	Jan. 3, 2001
Putnam, Adam	FL	107th to 109th	Jan. 3, 2001
Rehberg, Dennis	MT	107th to 109th	Jan. 3, 2001
Rogers, Mike	MI	107th to 109th	Jan. 3, 2001
Ross, Mike	AR	107th to 109th	Jan. 3, 2001
Schiff, Adam	CA	107th to 109th	Jan. 3, 2001
Shuster, Bill	PA	*107th to 109th	May 15, 2001
Simmons, Rob	CT	107th to 109th	Jan. 3, 2001
Solis, Hilda	CA	107th to 109th	Jan. 3, 2001
Sullivan, John	OK	*107th to 109th	Feb. 27, 2002
Tiberi, Patrick	OH	107th to 109th	Jan. 3, 2001
Watson, Diane E.	CA	*107th to 109th	June 5, 2001
Wilson, Joe	SC	*107th to 109th	Dec. 18, 2001
3 terms, not consecutive			
Inglis, Bob	SC	103d, 104th and 109th.	Jan. 3, 1993
2 terms			
Alexander, Rodney	LA	108th and 109th	Jan. 3, 2003
Barrett, Gresham	SC	108th and 109th	Jan. 3, 2003
Beauprez, Bob	CO	108th and 109th	Jan. 3, 2003
Bishop, Rob	UT	108th and 109th	Jan. 3, 2003
Bishop, Timothy H.	NY	108th and 109th	Jan. 3, 2003
Blackburn, Marsha	TN	108th and 109th	Jan. 3, 2003

CONGRESSES IN WHICH REPRESENTATIVES HAVE SERVED, WITH BEGINNING OF PRESENT SERVICE—CONTINUED

[* Elected to fill a vacancy; Republicans in roman (231); Democrats in *italic* (202); Independents in SMALL CAPS (1); Vacancy (1); Resident Commissioner and Delegates in **boldface** (5); total, 440]

Name	State	Congresses (inclusive)	Beginning of present service
Bonner, Jo	AL	108th and 109th	Jan. 3, 2003
Bradley, Jeb	NH	108th and 109th	Jan. 3, 2003
Brown-Waite, Ginny	FL	108th and 109th	Jan. 3, 2003
Burgess, Michael	TX	108th and 109th	Jan. 3, 2003
Butterfield, G.K.	NC	* 108th and 109th ..	July 20, 2004
Cardoza, Dennis	CA	108th and 109th	Jan. 3, 2003
Carter, John R.	TX	108th and 109th	Jan. 3, 2003
Chandler, Ben	KY	* 108th and 109th ..	Feb. 17, 2004
Chocola, Chris	IN	108th and 109th	Jan. 3, 2003
Cole, Tom	OK	108th and 109th	Jan. 3, 2003
Davis, Artur	AL	108th and 109th	Jan. 3, 2003
Davis, Lincoln	TN	108th and 109th	Jan. 3, 2003
Diaz-Balart, Mario	FL	108th and 109th	Jan. 3, 2003
Emanuel, Rahm	IL	108th and 109th	Jan. 3, 2003
Feeney, Tom	FL	108th and 109th	Jan. 3, 2003
Franks, Trent	AZ	108th and 109th	Jan. 3, 2003
Garrett, Scott	NJ	108th and 109th	Jan. 3, 2003
Gerlach, Jim	PA	108th and 109th	Jan. 3, 2003
Gingrey, Phil	GA	108th and 109th	Jan. 3, 2003
Grijalva, Raúl M.	AZ	108th and 109th	Jan. 3, 2003
Harris, Katherine	FL	108th and 109th	Jan. 3, 2003
Hensarling, Jeb	TX	108th and 109th	Jan. 3, 2003
Herseth, Stephanie	SD	* 108th and 109th ..	June 1, 2004
King, Steve	IA	108th and 109th	Jan. 3, 2003
Kline, John	MN	108th and 109th	Jan. 3, 2003
Marshall, Jim	GA	108th and 109th	Jan. 3, 2003
McCotter, Thaddeus G.	MI	108th and 109th	Jan. 3, 2003
Meek, Kendrick B.	FL	108th and 109th	Jan. 3, 2003
Michaud, Michael H.	ME	108th and 109th	Jan. 3, 2003
Miller, Brad	NC	108th and 109th	Jan. 3, 2003
Miller, Candice S.	MI	108th and 109th	Jan. 3, 2003
Murphy, Tim	PA	108th and 109th	Jan. 3, 2003
Musgrave, Marilyn N.	CO	108th and 109th	Jan. 3, 2003
Neugebauer, Randy	TX	*108th and 109th ...	June 3, 2003
Nunes, Devin	CA	108th and 109th	Jan. 3, 2003
Pearce, Stevan	NM	108th and 109th	Jan. 3, 2003
Porter, Jon C.	NV	108th and 109th	Jan. 3, 2003
Renzi, Rick	AZ	108th and 109th	Jan. 3, 2003
Rogers, Mike	AL	108th and 109th	Jan. 3, 2003
Ruppersberger, C.A. Dutch	MD	108th and 109th	Jan. 3, 2003
Ryan, Timothy J.	OH	108th and 109th	Jan. 3, 2003
Sánchez, Linda	CA	108th and 109th	Jan. 3, 2003
Scott, David	GA	108th and 109th	Jan. 3, 2003
Turner, Mike	OH	108th and 109th	Jan. 3, 2003
Van Hollen, Chris	MD	108th and 109th	Jan. 3, 2003
1 term			
Barrow, John	GA	109th	Jan. 3, 2005
Bean, Melissa	IL	109th	Jan. 3, 2005
Boren, Dan	OK	109th	Jan. 3, 2005
Boustany, Charles W., Jr.	LA	109th	Jan. 3, 2005
Carnahan, Russ	MO	109th	Jan. 3, 2005

CONGRESSES IN WHICH REPRESENTATIVES HAVE SERVED, WITH BEGINNING OF PRESENT SERVICE—CONTINUED

[* Elected to fill a vacancy; Republicans in roman (231); Democrats in *italic* (202); Independents in SMALL CAPS (1); Vacancy (1); Resident Commissioner and Delegates in **boldface** (5); total, 440]

Name	State	Congresses (inclusive)	Beginning of present service
Cleaver, Emanuel	MO	109th	Jan. 3, 2005
Conaway, Mike	TX	109th	Jan. 3, 2005
Costa, Jim	CA	109th	Jan. 3, 2005
Cuellar, Henry	TX	109th	Jan. 3, 2005
Davis, Geoff	KY	109th	Jan. 3, 2005
Dent, Charles W.	PA	109th	Jan. 3, 2005
Drake, Thelma D.	VA	109th	Jan. 3, 2005
Fitzpatrick, Michael G.	PA	109th	Jan. 3, 2005
Fortenberry, Jeff	NE	109th	Jan. 3, 2005
Foxx, Virginia	NC	109th	Jan. 3, 2005
Gohmert, Louie	TX	109th	Jan. 3, 2005
Green, Al	TX	109th	Jan. 3, 2005
Higgins, Brian	NY	109th	Jan. 3, 2005
Jindal, Bobby	LA	109th	Jan. 3, 2005
Kuhl, John R., Jr., (Randy)	NY	109th	Jan. 3, 2005
Lipinski, Daniel	IL	109th	Jan. 3, 2005
McCaul, Michael T.	TX	109th	Jan. 3, 2005
McHenry, Patrick T.	NC	109th	Jan. 3, 2005
McMorris, Cathy	WA	109th	Jan. 3, 2005
Mack, Connie	FL	109th	Jan. 3, 2005
Marchant, Kenny	TX	109th	Jan. 3, 2005
Matsui, Doris O.	FL	109th	Mar. 10, 2005
Melancon, Charlie	LA	109th	Jan. 3, 2005
Moore, Gwen	WI	109th	Jan. 3, 2005
Poe, Ted	TX	109th	Jan. 3, 2005
Price, Tom	GA	109th	Jan. 3, 2005
Reichert, David G.	WA	109th	Jan. 3, 2005
Salazar, John T.	CO	109th	Jan. 3, 2005
Schwartz, Allyson Y.	PA	109th	Jan. 3, 2005
Schwarz, John J.H. (Joe)	MI	109th	Jan. 3, 2005
Sodrel, Michael E.	IN	109th	Jan. 3, 2005
Wasserman Schultz, Debbie	FL	109th	Jan. 3, 2005
Westmoreland, Lynn A.	GA	109th	Jan. 3, 2005
RESIDENT COMMISSIONER			
Fortuño, Luis	PR	109th	Jan. 3, 2005
DELEGATES			
Faleomavaega, Eni F.H.	AS	101st to 109th	Jan. 3, 1989
Norton, Eleanor Holmes	DC	102d to 109th	Jan. 3, 1991
Christensen, Donna M.	VI	105th to 109th	Jan. 3, 1997
Bordallo, Madeleine Z.	GU	108th and 109th	Jan. 3, 2003

NOTE: Members elected by special election are considered to begin service on the date of the election, except for those elected after a sine die adjournment. If elected after the Congress has adjourned for the session, Members are considered to begin their service on the day after the election.

STANDING COMMITTEES OF THE SENATE

[Republicans in roman; Democrats in *italic*; Independents in SMALL CAPS]

[Room numbers beginning with SD are in the Dirksen Building, SH in the Hart Building, SR in the Russell Building, and S in The Capitol]

Agriculture, Nutrition, and Forestry

328A Russell Senate Office Building 20510–6000

phone 224–2035, fax 224–1725, TTY / TDD 224–2587

http://agriculture.senate.gov

meets first and third Wednesdays of each month

Saxby Chambliss, of Georgia, *Chair*

Richard G. Lugar, of Indiana.	*Tom Harkin,* of Iowa.
Thad Cochran, of Mississippi.	*Patrick J. Leahy,* of Vermont.
Mitch McConnell, of Kentucky.	*Kent Conrad,* of North Dakota.
Pat Roberts, of Kansas.	*Max Baucus,* of Montana.
James M. Talent, of Missouri.	*Blanche L. Lincoln,* of Arkansas.
Craig Thomas, of Wyoming.	*Debbie Stabenow,* of Michigan.
Rick Santorum, of Pennsylvania.	*E. Benjamin Nelson,* of Nebraska.
Norm Coleman, of Minnesota.	*Mark Dayton,* of Minnesota.
Mike Crapo, of Idaho.	*Ken Salazar,* of Colorado.
Charles E. Grassley, of Iowa.	

SUBCOMMITTEES

[The chairman and ranking minority member are ex officio (non-voting) members of all subcommittees on which they do not serve.]

Forestry, Conservation, and Rural Revitalization

Mike Crapo, of Idaho, *Chair*

Richard G. Lugar, of Indiana.	*Blanche L. Lincoln,* of Arkansas.
Thad Cochran, of Mississippi.	*Patrick J. Leahy,* of Vermont.
James M. Talent, of Missouri.	*E. Benjamin Nelson,* of Nebraska.
Craig Thomas, of Wyoming.	*Mark Dayton,* of Minnesota.
Norm Coleman, of Minnesota.	*Ken Salazar,* of Colorado.

Marketing, Inspection, and Product Promotion

James M. Talent, of Missouri, *Chair*

Mitch McConnell, of Kentucky.	*Max Baucus,* of Montana.
Craig Thomas, of Wyoming.	*E. Benjamin Nelson,* of Nebraska.
Pat Roberts, of Kansas.	*Ken Salazar,* of Colorado.
Charles E. Grassley, of Iowa.	*Kent Conrad,* of North Dakota.
Richard Lugar, of Indiana.	*Debbie Stabenow,* of Michigan.

Production and Price Competitiveness

Mitch McConnell, of Kentucky, *Chair*

Thad Cochran, of Mississippi.
Pat Roberts, of Kansas.
Rick Santorum, of Pennsylvania.
Norm Coleman, of Minnesota.
Charles E. Grassley, of Iowa.

Kent Conrad, of North Dakota.
Mark Dayton, of Minnesota.
Max Baucus, of Montana.
Patrick Leahy, of Vermont.
Blanche L. Lincoln, of Arkansas.

Research, Nutrition, and General Legislation

Rick Santorum, of Pennsylvania, *Chair*

Richard G. Lugar, of Indiana.
Mike Crapo, of Idaho.
Thad Cochran, of Mississippi.
Mitch McConnell, of Kentucky.
Pat Roberts, of Kansas.

Patrick J. Leahy, of Vermont.
Debbie Stabenow, of Michigan.
Blanche Lincoln, of Arkansas.
Max Baucus, of Montana.
E. Benjamin Nelson, of Nebraska.

STAFF

Committee on Agriculture, Nutrition, and Forestry (SR–328A), 224–2035, fax 224–1725.
  Majority Staff Director.—Martha Scott Poindexter.
    Chief Counsel.—David L. Johnson.
    Counsel.—Vernie Hubert.
    Chief Economist.—Andrew Morton.
    Executive Assistant.—Jane Anna Harris.
    Senior Professional Staff: Betsy Croker, Andy Johnson, Hayden Milberg, Christy Seyfert.
    Professional Staff: Cameron Bruett, Graham Harper, Eric Steiner.
    Legislative Correspondent/Staff Assistant.—Rich Horne.
    Hearing Clerk.—Jacob Chaney.
    Chief Clerk.—Robert Sturm.
    GPO Editor.—Natoshka Faxio-Douglas.
  Minority Staff Director/Counsel.—Mark Halverson, 4–6702, fax 8–4576.
    Counsels: Eric Juzenas, Susan Keith.
    Legislative Staff Assistant.—Dave Townsend.
    Professional Staff: Richard Bender, Phil Buchan, John Ferrell, Derek Miller, Lloyd Ritter.
    Economist.—Stephanie Mercier.

Appropriations

S–128 The Capitol 20510–6025, phone 224–7363

http://appropriations.senate.gov

meets upon call of the chair

Thad Cochran, of Mississippi, *Chair*

Ted Stevens, of Alaska.	*Robert C. Byrd*, of West Virginia.
Arlen Specter, of Pennsylvania.	*Daniel K. Inouye*, of Hawaii.
Pete V. Domenici, of New Mexico.	*Patrick J. Leahy*, of Vermont.
Christopher S. Bond, of Missouri.	*Tom Harkin*, of Iowa.
Mitch McConnell, of Kentucky.	*Barbara A. Mikulski*, of Maryland.
Conrad Burns, of Montana.	*Harry Reid*, of Nevada.
Richard C. Shelby, of Alabama.	*Herb Kohl*, of Wisconsin.
Judd Gregg, of New Hampshire.	*Patty Murray*, of Washington.
Robert F. Bennett, of Utah.	*Byron L. Dorgan*, of North Dakota.
Larry Craig, of Idaho.	*Dianne Feinstein*, of California.
Kay Bailey Hutchison, of Texas.	*Richard J. Durbin*, of Illinois.
Mike DeWine, of Ohio.	*Tim Johnson*, of South Dakota.
Sam Brownback, of Kansas.	*Mary L. Landrieu*, of Louisiana.
Wayne Allard, of Colorado.	

SUBCOMMITTEES

[The chairman and ranking minority member are ex officio members of all subcommittees on which they do not serve.]

Agriculture, Rural Development, and Related Agencies

Robert F. Bennett, of Utah, *Chair*

Thad Cochran, of Mississippi.	*Herb Kohl*, of Wisconsin.
Arlen Specter, of Pennsylvania.	*Tom Harkin*, of Iowa.
Christopher S. Bond, of Missouri.	*Byron L. Dorgan*, of North Dakota.
Mitch McConnell, of Kentucky.	*Dianne Feinstein*, of California.
Conrad Burns, of Montana.	*Richard J. Durbin*, of Illinois.
Larry Craig, of Idaho.	*Tim Johnson*, of South Dakota.
Sam Brownback, of Kansas.	*Mary L. Landrieu*, of Louisiana.

Commerce, Justice, Science, and Related Agencies

Richard C. Shelby, of Alabama, *Chair*

Judd Gregg, of New Hampshire.	*Barbara A. Mikulski*, of Maryland.
Ted Stevens, of Alaska.	*Daniel K. Inouye*, of Hawaii.
Pete V. Domenici, of New Mexico.	*Patrick J. Leahy*, of Vermont.
Mitch McConnell, of Kentucky.	*Herb Kohl*, of Wisconsin.
Kay Bailey Hutchison, of Texas.	*Patty Murray*, of Washington.
Sam Brownback, of Kansas.	*Tom Harkin*, of Iowa.
Christopher S. Bond, of Missouri.	*Byron L. Dorgan*, of North Dakota.

Defense

Ted Stevens, of Alaska, *Chair*

Thad Cochran, of Mississippi.
Arlen Specter, of Pennsylvania.
Pete V. Domenici, of New Mexico.
Christopher S. Bond, of Missouri.
Mitch McConnell, of Kentucky.
Richard C. Shelby, of Alabama.
Judd Gregg, of New Hampshire.
Kay Bailey Hutchison, of Texas.
Conrad Burns, of Montana.

Daniel K. Inouye, of Hawaii.
Robert C. Byrd, of West Virginia.
Patrick J. Leahy, of Vermont.
Tom Harkin, of Iowa.
Byron L. Dorgan, of North Dakota.
Richard J. Durbin, of Illinois.
Harry Reid, of Nevada.
Dianne Feinstein, of California.
Barbara A. Mikulski, of Maryland.

District of Columbia

Sam Brownback, of Kansas, *Chair*

Mike DeWine, of Ohio.
Wayne Allard, of Colorado.

Mary L. Landrieu, of Louisiana.
Richard J. Durbin, of Illinois.

Energy and Water, and Related Agencies

Pete V. Domenici, of New Mexico, *Chair*

Thad Cochran, of Mississippi.
Mitch McConnell, of Kentucky.
Robert F. Bennett, of Utah.
Conrad Burns, of Montana.
Larry Craig, of Idaho.
Christopher S. Bond, of Missouri.
Kay Bailey Hutchison, of Texas.
Wayne Allard, of Colorado.

Harry Reid, of Nevada.
Robert C. Byrd, of West Virginia.
Patty Murray, of Washington.
Byron L. Dorgan, of North Dakota.
Dianne Feinstein, of California.
Tim Johnson, of South Dakota.
Mary L. Landrieu, of Louisiana.
Daniel K. Inouye, of Hawaii.

Homeland Security

Judd Gregg, of New Hampshire, *Chair*

Thad Cochran, of Mississippi.
Ted Stevens, of Alaska.
Arlen Specter, of Pennsylvania.
Pete V. Domenici, of New Mexico.
Richard C. Shelby, of Alabama.
Larry Craig, of Idaho.
Robert F. Bennett, of Utah.
Wayne Allard, of Colorado.

Robert C. Byrd, of West Virginia.
Daniel K. Inouye, of Hawaii.
Patrick J. Leahy, of Vermont.
Barbara A. Mikulski, of Maryland.
Herb Kohl, of Wisconsin.
Patty Murray, of Washington.
Harry Reid, of Nevada.
Dianne Feinstein, of California.

Interior and Related Agencies

Conrad Burns, of Montana, *Chair*

Ted Stevens, of Alaska.
Thad Cochran, of Mississippi.
Pete V. Domenici, of New Mexico.
Robert F. Bennett, of Utah.
Judd Gregg, of New Hampshire.
Larry Craig, of Idaho.
Wayne Allard, of Colorado.

Byron L. Dorgan, of North Dakota.
Robert C. Byrd, of West Virginia.
Patrick J. Leahy, of Vermont.
Harry Reid, of Nevada.
Dianne Feinstein, of California.
Barbara A. Mikulski, of Maryland.
Herb Kohl, of Wisconsin.

Labor, Health and Human Services, Education, and Related Agencies

Arlen Specter, of Pennsylvania, *Chair*

Thad Cochran, of Mississippi.
Judd Gregg, of New Hampshire.
Larry Craig, of Idaho.
Kay Bailey Hutchison, of Texas.
Ted Stevens, of Alaska.
Mike DeWine, of Ohio.
Richard C. Shelby, of Alabama.

Tom Harkin, of Iowa.
Daniel K. Inouye, of Hawaii.
Harry Reid, of Nevada.
Herb Kohl, of Wisconsin.
Patty Murray, of Washington.
Mary L. Landrieu, of Louisiana.
Richard J. Durbin, of Illinois.

Legislative Branch

Wayne Allard, of Colorado, *Chair*

Thad Cochran, of Mississippi.
Mike DeWine, of Ohio.

Richard J. Durbin, of Illinois.
Tim Johnson, of South Dakota.

Military Construction and Veterans Affairs, and Related Agencies

Kay Bailey Hutchison, of Texas, *Chair*

Conrad Burns, of Montana.
Larry Craig, of Idaho.
Mike DeWine, of Ohio.
Sam Brownback, of Kansas.
Wayne Allard, of Colorado.
Mitch McConnell, of Kentucky.

Dianne Feinstein, of California.
Daniel K. Inouye, of Hawaii.
Tim Johnson, of South Dakota.
Mary L. Landrieu, of Louisiana.
Robert C. Byrd, of West Virginia.
Patty Murray, of Washington.

State, Foreign Operations, and Related Programs

Mitch McConnell, of Kentucky, *Chair*

Arlen Specter, of Pennsylvania.
Judd Gregg, of New Hampshire.
Richard C. Shelby, of Alabama.
Robert F. Bennett, of Utah.
Christopher S. Bond, of Missouri.
Mike DeWine, of Ohio.
Sam Brownback, of Kansas.

Patrick J. Leahy, of Vermont.
Daniel K. Inouye, of Hawaii.
Tom Harkin, of Iowa.
Barbara A. Mikulski, of Maryland.
Richard J. Durbin, of Illinois.
Tim Johnson, of South Dakota.
Mary L. Landrieu, of Louisiana.

Transportation, Treasury, the Judiciary, Housing and Urban Development, and Related Agencies

Christopher S. Bond, of Missouri, *Chair*

Richard C. Shelby, of Alabama.
Arlen Specter, of Pennsylvania.
Robert F. Bennett, of Utah.
Kay Bailey Hutchison, of Texas.
Mike DeWine, of Ohio.
Sam Brownback, of Kansas.
Ted Stevens, of Alaska.
Pete V. Domenici, of New Mexico.
Conrad Burns, of Montana.

Patty Murray, of Washington.
Robert C. Byrd, of West Virginia.
Barbara A. Mikulski, of Maryland.
Harry Reid, of Nevada.
Herb Kohl, of Wisconsin.
Richard J. Durbin, of Illinois.
Byron L. Dorgan, of North Dakota.
Patrick J. Leahy, of Vermont.
Tom Harkin, of Iowa.

STAFF

Committee on Appropriations (S–128), 224–7363.
  Majority Staff Director.—J. Keith Kennedy.
    Deputy Staff Director/General Counsel.—Clayton Heil.
    Chief Clerk.—Robert W. Putnam.

Communications Director.—Jenny Manley.
Professional Staff: John J. Conway (SD–114); Carolyn E. Apostolou (S–128); Hong Nguyen (SD–114); Les Spivey (S–128); Fred Pagan (S–128); Mimi Braniff (SD–120).
Security Manager.—Kristin Jepson (SD–118).
Assistant Chief Clerk.—Mazie R. Mattson (SD–119).
Staff Assistants: Wendi D. Dow, Christen Taylor.
Minority Staff Director.—Terrence E. Sauvain (S–125A), 4–7292.
Deputy Staff Director.—Charles Kieffer.
Chief Clerk.—Edie Stanley (S–112).
Communications Director.—Tom Gavin.
Professional Staff: Suzanne Bentzel (S–112); Nora Martin (SD–134); Leslie Staples (S–112); Chris Watkins (SH–123).
Staff Assistant.—Elnora Harvey (SH–123).
Subcommittee on Agriculture, Rural Development, and Related Agencies (SD–188), 4–5270.
Majority Clerk.—John Ziolkowski.
Professional Staff.—Fitz Elder, Hunter Moorhead.
Staff Assistant.—Dianne Preece.
Minority Clerk.—Galen Fountain (SH–123), 4–8090.
Professional Staff: Jessica Arden Frederick, William Simpson, Tom Gonzales.
Subcommittee on Commerce, Justice, Science, and Related Agencies (S–146A), 4–7277.
Majority Clerk.—Katherine Hennessey.
Professional Staff: Jill Shapiro Long, Jessica Roberts, Allen Cutler, Nancy Perkins.
Minority Clerk.—Paul Carliner (SD–144), 4–5202.
Professional Staff: Gabrielle A. Batkin, Alexa Sewell.
Staff Assistant.—Kate Fitzpatrick.
Subcommittee on Defense (SD–119), 4–7255.
Majority Clerk.—Sid Ashworth.
Professional Staff: Jennifer Chartrand, Alycia Farrell, Mark Haaland, Lesley Kalan, Kate Kaufer, Mazie R. Mattson, Brian Potts, Brian Wilson.
Staff Assistant.—Janelle Treon.
Minority Clerk.—Charles J. Houy (SD–117), 4–6688.
Professional Staff: Nicole Rutberg Di Resta, Betsy Schmid (SD–115).
Staff Assistant.—Kate Fitzpatrick (SD–144).
Subcommittee on District of Columbia (SD–127), 4–7643.
Majority Clerk.—Mary Dietrich.
Professional Staff.—Emily Brunini (SD–133).
Minority Clerk.—Kate Eltrich (SH–123), 4–6933.
Subcommittee on Energy and Water, and Related Agencies (SD–133), 4–7260.
Majority Clerk.—Scott O'Malia.
Professional Staff.—Roger Cockrell, Emily Brunini.
Minority Clerk.—Drew Willison (SD–156), 4–8119.
Professional Staff.—Nancy Olkewicz.
Subcommittee on Homeland Security (SD–135), 4–4319.
Majority Clerk.—Rebecca Davies.
Professional Staff: James Hayes, Carol Cribbs, Kimberly Nelson, Tammy Cameron.
Staff Assistant.—Avery Forbes.
Minority Clerk.—Charles Kieffer (S–125A), 4–8244.
Professional Staff: Chip Walgren, Scott Nance, Drenan E. Dudley, (SD–196).
Subcommittee on Interior and Related Agencies (SD–132), 4–7233.
Majority Clerk.—Bruce Evans.
Professional Staff: Ginny James, Leif Fonnesbeck, Ryan Thomas, Rebecca Benn.
Staff Assistant.—Ellis Fisher.
Minority Clerk.—Peter Kiefhaber (SH–123), 8–0774.
Professional Staff.—Brooke Thomas.
Subcommittee on Labor, Health and Human Services, Education, and Related Agencies (SD–184), 4–7230.
Majority Clerk.—Bettilou Taylor.
Professional Staff: Jim Sourwine, Mark Laisch, Sudip Shrikant Parikh, Candice Rogers.
Staff Assistant.—Rachel Jones.
Minority Clerk.—Ellen Murray (SH–123), 4–7288.
Professional Staff.—Erik Fatemi, Adrienne Hallett.
Subcommittee on the Legislative Branch (S–128) 4–7238.
Majority Clerk.—Carolyn E. Apostolou.
Staff Assistant.—Christen Taylor.
Minority Clerk.—Terrence E. Sauvain (S–125A), 4–0335.
Professional Staff.—Drew Willison, Nancy Olkewicz (SD–156).

Subcommittee on Military Construction and Veterans Affairs, and Related Agencies (SD–127), 4–5245.
  Majority Clerk.—Dennis Ward.
    Professional Staff: Sean Knowles, Dennis Balkham.
  Minority Clerk.—Christina Evans (SH–123), 4–8224.
    Professional Staff.—B.G. Wright, Chad Schulken.
Subcommittee on State, Foreign Operations, and Related Programs (SD–142), 4–2104.
  Majority Clerk.—Paul Grove.
    Professional Staff.—Tom Hawkins.
    Staff Assistant.—LaShawnda Smith.
  Minority Clerk.—Tim Rieser (SH–123), 4–7284.
    Professional Staff.—Mark Lippert, Kate Eltrich.
Subcommittee on Transportation, Treasury, the Judiciary, Housing and Urban Development, and Related Agencies (SD–130), 4–5310.
  Majority Clerk.—Jon Kamarck.
    Professional Staff.—Paul Doerrer, Lula Edwards, Cheh Kim, Josh Manley.
    Staff Assistant.—Matthew McCardle.
  Minority Clerk.—Peter Rogoff (SD–128), 4–7281.
    Professional Staff.—Kate Hallahan, Diana Gourlay Hamilton, William Simpson, Meaghan L. McCarthy.
  Editorial and Printing (SD–126): Richard L. Larson, 4–7265; Wayne W. Hosier (GPO), 4–7267; Heather Crowell (GPO), 4–7266; Doris Jackson (GPO), 4–7217.
  Clerical Assistant.—George Castro (SD–120), 4–5433.

Armed Services

228 Russell Senate Office Building 20510–6050

phone 224–3871, http://www.senate.gov/~armed__services

meets every Tuesday and Thursday

John Warner, of Virginia, *Chair*

John McCain, of Arizona.
James M. Inhofe, of Oklahoma.
Pat Roberts, of Kansas.
Jeff Sessions, of Alabama.
Susan M. Collins, of Maine.
John Ensign, of Nevada.
James M. Talent, of Missouri.
Saxby Chambliss, of Georgia.
Lindsey O. Graham, of South Carolina.
Elizabeth Dole, of North Carolina.
John Cornyn, of Texas.
John Thune, of South Dakota.

Carl Levin, of Michigan.
Edward M. Kennedy, of Massachusetts.
Robert C. Byrd, of West Virginia.
Joseph I. Lieberman, of Connecticut.
Jack Reed, of Rhode Island.
Daniel K. Akaka, of Hawaii.
Bill Nelson, of Florida.
E. Benjamin Nelson, of Nebraska.
Mark Dayton, of Minnesota.
Evan Bayh, of Indiana.
Hillary Rodham Clinton, of New York.

SUBCOMMITTEES

[The chairman and the ranking minority member are ex officio (non-voting) members of all subcommittees on which they do not serve.]

Airland

John McCain, of Arizona, *Chair*

James M. Inhofe, of Oklahoma.
Jeff Sessions, of Alabama
John Ensign, of Nevada.
James M. Talent, of Missouri.
Saxby Chambliss, of Georgia.
Lindsey O. Graham, of South Carolina.
Elizabeth Dole, of North Carolina.

Joseph I. Lieberman, of Connecticut.
Jack Reed, of Rhode Island.
Daniel K. Akaka, of Hawaii.
Bill Nelson, of Florida.
Mark Dayton, of Minnesota.
Evan Bayh, of Indiana.
Hillary Rodham Clinton, of New York.

Emerging Threats and Capabilities

John Cornyn, of Texas, *Chair*

Pat Roberts, of Kansas.
Susan M. Collins, of Maine.
John Ensign, of Nevada.
James M. Talent, of Missouri.
Lindsey O. Graham, of South Carolina.
Elizabeth Dole, of North Carolina.
John Thune, of South Dakota.

Jack Reed, of Rhode Island.
Edward M. Kennedy, of Massachusetts.
Robert C. Byrd, of West Virginia.
Bill Nelson, of Florida.
E. Benjamin Nelson, of Nebraska.
Evan Bayh, of Indiana.
Hillary Rodham Clinton, of New York.

Personnel

Lindsey O. Graham, of South Carolina, *Chair*

John McCain, of Arizona.
Susan M. Collins, of Maine.
Saxby Chambliss, of Georgia.
Elizabeth Dole, of North Carolina.

E. Benjamin Nelson, of Nebraska.
Edward M. Kennedy, of Massachusetts.
Joseph I. Lieberman, of Connecticut.
Daniel K. Akaka, of Hawaii.

Committees of the Senate

Readiness and Management Support

John Ensign, of Nevada, *Chair*

John McCain, of Arizona.	Daniel K. Akaka, of Hawaii.
James M. Inhofe, of Oklahoma.	Robert C. Byrd, of West Virginia.
Pat Roberts, of Kansas.	Bill Nelson, of Florida.
Jeff Sessions, of Alabama.	E. Benjamin Nelson, of Nebraska.
Saxby Chambliss, of Georgia.	Mark Dayton, of Minnesota.
John Cornyn, of Texas.	Evan Bayh, of Indiana.
John Thune, of South Dakota.	Hillary Rodham Clinton, of New York.

Seapower

James M. Talent, of Missouri, *Chair*

John McCain, of Arizona.	Edward M. Kennedy, of Massachusetts.
Susan M. Collins, of Maine.	Joseph I. Lieberman, of Connecticut.
Saxby Chambliss, of Georgia.	Jack Reed, of Rhode Island.

Strategic Forces

Jeff Sessions, of Alabama, *Chair*

James M. Inhofe, of Oklahoma.	Bill Nelson, of Florida.
Pat Roberts, of Kansas.	Robert C. Byrd, of West Virginia.
Lindsey O. Graham, of South Carolina.	Jack Reed, of Rhode Island.
John Cornyn, of Texas.	E. Benjamin Nelson, of Nebraska.
John Thune, of South Dakota.	Mark Dayton, of Minnesota.

STAFF

Committee on Armed Services (SR–228), 224–3871.
  Majority Staff Director.—Judith A. Ansley.
    Chief Clerk.—Marie Fabrizio Dickinson.
    Assistant Chief Clerk and Security Manager.—Cindy Pearson.
    General Counsel.—Scott W. Stucky.
    Counsels: David M. Morriss, Richard F. Walsh.
    Professional Staff Members: Charles W. Alsup, William C. Greenwalt, Ambrose R. Hock, Gregory T. Kiley, Thomas L. MacKenzie, Elaine A. McCusker, Lucian L. Niemeyer, Stanley R. O'Connor, Jr., Paula J. Philbin, Lynn F. Rusten, Joseph T. Sixeas, Robert M. Soofer, Kristine L. Svinicki, Diana G. Tabler.
    Research Assistant.—Regina A. Dubey.
    Nominations and Hearings Clerk.—Leah C. Brewer.
    Systems Administrator.—Gary J. Howard.
    Printing and Documents Clerk.—June M. Borawski.
    Security Clerk.—Jennifer Key.
    Special Assistant.—Jennifer D. Cave.
    Staff Assistants: Alison E. Brill, Andrew W. Florell, Benjamin L. Rubin, Catherine E. Sendak, Nicholas W. West, Pendred K. Wilson.
    Receptionist.—Jessica L. Kingston.
  Minority Staff Director.—Richard D. DeBobes.
    Administrative Assistant to the Minority.—Christine E. Cowart.
    Counsels: Madelyn R. Creedon, Gerald J. Leeling, Peter K. Levine, William G.P. Monahan.
    Professional Staff: Daniel J. Cox, Jr., Evelyn N. Farkas, Richard W. Fieldhouse, Creighton Greene, Michael J. Kuiken, Michael J. McCord, Arun A. Seraphin.
    Research Assistants: Gabriella Eisen, Bridget W. Higgins.
  Subcommittee on Airland:
    Majority Professional Staff: Ambrose R. Hock, Stanley R. O'Connor, Jr.
    Minority Professional Staff: Daniel J. Cox, Jr., Creighton Greene.
  Subcommittee on Emerging Threats and Capabilities:
    Majority Professional Staff: Charles W. Alsup, Elaine A. McCusker, Paula J. Philbin, Lynn F. Rusten.
    Minority Professional Staff: Madelyn R. Creedon, Richard W. Fieldhouse, Evelyn N. Farkas, Peter K. Levine, Arun A. Seraphin.

Subcommittee on Personnel:
  Majority Professional Staff: David M. Morriss, Diana G. Tabler, Richard F. Walsh.
  Minority Professional Staff.—Gerald J. Leeling.
Subcommittee on Readiness and Management Support:
  Majority Professional Staff: William C. Greenwalt, Gregory T. Kiley, David M. Morriss, Lucian L. Niemeyer, Joseph T. Sixeas.
  Minority Professional Staff: Peter K. Levine, Michael J. McCord.
Subcommittee on Seapower:
  Majority Professional Staff: Ambrose R. Hock, Thomas L. MacKenzie, Stanley R. O'Connor, Jr.
  Minority Professional Staff: Daniel J. Cox, Jr., Creighton Greene.
Subcommittee on Strategic Forces:
  Majority Professional Staff: Charles W. Alsup, William C. Greenwalt, Stanley R. O'Connor, Jr., Robert M. Soofer, Kristine L. Svinicki.
  Minority Professional Staff: Madelyn R. Creedon, Richard W. Fieldhouse.
Majority Professional Staff for:
  Acquisition Policy.—William C. Greenwalt.
  Arms Control/Counterproliferation.—Lynn F. Rusten.
  Army Programs.—Ambrose R. Hock.
  Aviation Systems.—Stanley R. O'Connor, Jr.
  Budget Tracking.—Gregory T. Kiley.
  Civilian Nominations: Scott W. Stucky, Richard F. Walsh.
  Combating Terrorism/Domestic Preparedness.—Paula J. Philbin.
  Counterdrug Programs.—Charles W. Alsup.
  Defense Security Assistance.—Lynn F. Rusten.
  Energy Issues.—Kristine L. Svinicki.
  Environmental Issues.—David M. Morriss.
  Export Controls: William C. Greenwalt.
  Foreign Policy: Charles W. Alsup, Lynn F. Rusten.
  Information Assurance.—Paula J. Philbin.
  Intelligence Issues.—Charles W. Alsup.
  Military Construction/Base Closures.—Lucian L. Niemeyer.
  Military Health Care.—Diana G. Tabler.
  Military Nominations.—Richard F. Walsh.
  Military Strategy.—Charles W. Alsup.
  Missile Defense.—Robert M. Soofer.
  Personnel Issues: David M. Morriss, Diana G. Tabler, Richard F. Walsh.
  Readiness/Operations and Maintenance: William C. Greenwalt, Gregory T. Kiley, Joseph T. Sixeas.
  Science and Technology.—Elaine A. McCusker.
  Shipbuilding Programs.—Thomas L. MacKenzie.
  Special Operations Forces.—Charles W. Alsup.
  Strategic Programs.—Robert M. Soofer.
  Threat Reduction Programs.—Lynn F. Rusten.
Minority Professional Staff for:
  Acquisition Policy.—Peter K. Levine.
  Arms Control/Counterproliferation.—Richard W. Fieldhouse.
  Army Programs.—Daniel J. Cox, Jr.
  Aviation Systems.—Creighton Greene.
  Budget Tracking.—Michael J. McCord.
  Civilian Nominations.—Peter K. Levine.
  Combating Terrorism/Domestic Preparedness.—Evelyn N. Farkas.
  Counterdrug Programs.—Evelyn N. Farkas.
  Defense Security Assistance.—Evelyn N. Farkas.
  Energy Issues: Madelyn R. Creedon.
  Environmental Issues.—Peter K. Levine.
  Export Controls.—Evelyn N. Farkas.
  Foreign Policy: Richard D. DeBobes, Evelyn N. Farkas, William G.P. Monahan.
  Homeland Defense.—Evelyn N. Farkas.
  Information Security.—Creighton Greene.
  Intelligence Issues.—Creighton Greene.
  Marine Corps Ground Procurement and R&D Issues.—Daniel J. Cox, Jr.
  Military Construction/Base Closures.—Michael J. McCord.
  Military Health Care.—Gerald J. Leeling.
  Military Nominations.—Gerald J. Leeling.
  Military Strategy.—Richard D. DeBobes.
  Missile Defense: Richard W. Fieldhouse.

Morale, Welfare, Recreation.—Gerald J. Leeling.
Personnel Issues.—Gerald J. Leeling.
Readiness and Training / Operations and Maintenance.—Michael J. McCord.
Readiness Logistics / Operations and Maintenance.—Michael J. McCord.
Science and Technology.—Arun A. Seraphin.
Shipbuilding Programs.—Creighton Greene.
Space Issues.—Madelyn R. Creedon.
Special Operations Forces.—Evelyn N. Farkas.
Strategic Programs.—Madelyn R. Creedon.
Threat Reduction Programs.—Madelyn R. Creedon.

Banking, Housing, and Urban Affairs

534 Dirksen Senate Office Building 20510

phone 224–7391, http://banking.senate.gov

Richard C. Shelby, of Alabama, *Chair*

Robert F. Bennett, of Utah.	*Paul S. Sarbanes, of Maryland.*
Wayne Allard, of Colorado.	*Christopher J. Dodd, of Connecticut.*
Michael B. Enzi, of Wyoming.	*Tim Johnson, of South Dakota.*
Chuck Hagel, of Nebraska.	*Jack Reed, of Rhode Island.*
Rick Santorum, of Pennsylvania.	*Charles E. Schumer, of New York.*
Jim Bunning, of Kentucky.	*Evan Bayh, of Indiana.*
Mike Crapo, of Idaho.	*Thomas R. Carper, of Delaware.*
John E. Sununu, of New Hampshire.	*Debbie Stabenow, of Michigan.*
Elizabeth Dole, of North Carolina.	*Jon S. Corzine, of New Jersey.*
Mel Martinez, of Florida.	

SUBCOMMITTEES

[The chairman and ranking minority member are ex officio members of all subcommittees.]

Economic Policy

Jim Bunning, of Kentucky, *Chair*

Richard Shelby, of Alabama.	*Charles E. Schumer, of New York.*

Financial Institutions

Robert F. Bennett, of Utah, *Chair*

Wayne Allard, of Colorado.	*Tim Johnson, of South Dakota.*
Rick Santorum, of Pennsylvania.	*Thomas R. Carper, of Delaware.*
John Sununu, of New Hampshire.	*Christopher J. Dodd, of Connecticut.*
Mel Martinez, of Florida.	*Jack Reed, of Rhode Island.*
Chuck Hagel, of Nebraska.	*Debbie Stabenow, of Michigan.*
Jim Bunning, of Kentucky.	*Evan Bayh, of Indiana.*
Mike Crapo, of Indiana.	

Housing and Transportation

Wayne Allard, of Colorado, *Chair*

Rick Santorum, of Pennsylvania.	*Jack Reed, of Rhode Island.*
Elizabeth Dole, of North Carolina.	*Debbie Stabenow, of Michigan.*
Michael B. Enzi, of Wyoming.	*Jon S. Corzine, of New Jersey.*
Robert F. Bennett, of Utah.	*Christopher J. Dodd, of Connecticut.*
Mel Martinez, of Florida.	*Thomas R. Carper, of Delaware.*
Richard C. Shelby, of Alabama.	*Charles E. Schumer, of New York.*

International Trade and Finance

Mike Crapo, of Idaho, *Chair*

Chuck Hagel, of Nebraska.	*Evan Bayh, of Indiana.*
Michael B. Enzi, of Wyoming.	*Tim Johnson, of South Dakota.*
John E. Sununu, of New Hampshire.	*Jon S. Corzine, of New Jersey.*
Elizabeth Dole, of North Carolina.	

Securities and Investment

Chuck Hagel, of Nebraska, *Chair*

Michael B. Enzi, of Wyoming.	*Christopher J. Dodd,* of Connecticut.
John E. Sununu, of New Hampshire.	*Tim Johnson,* of South Dakota.
Mel Martinez, of Florida.	*Jack Reed,* of Rhode Island.
Robert F. Bennett, of Utah.	*Charles E. Schumer,* of New York.
Jim Bunning, of Kentucky.	*Evan Bayh,* of Indiana.
Mike Crapo, of Idaho.	*Debbie Stabenow,* of Michigan.
Elizabeth Dole, of North Carolina.	*Jon S. Corzine,* of New Jersey.
Wayne Allard, of Colorado.	*Thomas R. Carper,* of Delaware.
Rick Santorum, of Pennsylvania.	

STAFF

Committee on Banking, Housing, and Urban Affairs (SD–534), 224–7391.
  Majority Staff Director.—Kathy Casey.
    Chief Counsel.—Doug Nappi.
    Counsel.—Mark Oesterle.
    Deputy Press Secretary.—Andrew Gray.
    Legislative Assistant.—Sherry Little.
    Special Assistant.—Genevieve deSanctis.
  Subcommittee Staff Directors:
    Majority Economic Policy.—Steve Patterson.
    Financial Institutions.—Mike Nielsen.
    Housing and Transportation.—Tewana Wilkerson.
    International Trade and Finance.—Gregg Richard.
    Securities and Investment.—Joe Cwiklinski.
  Minority Staff Director/Chief Counsel.—Steven Harris.
    Senior Counsel.—Martin Gruenberg.
    Counsels: Jennifer Fogel-Bublick, Lynsey Graham, Sarah Kline, Dean Shahinian, Patience Singleton.
    Professional Staff.—Jonathan Miler.
    Economist.—Aaron Klein.
    Legislative Assistants: Sarah Garrett, Genevieve Herreria, Ellen Weis.
    Communications Director.—Jesse Jacobs.
    Chief Clerk/Systems Administrator.—Joseph Kolinski.
    Deputy Chief Clerk.—Liz Hackett.
    Editor.—George Whittle.
    Editorial Assistant.—Jim Crowell.

Budget

624 Dirksen Senate Office Building 20510–6100

phone 224–0642, http://budget.senate.gov

meets first Thursday of each month

Judd Gregg, of New Hampshire, *Chair*

Pete V. Domenici, of New Mexico.
Charles E. Grassley, of Iowa.
Wayne Allard, of Colorado.
Michael Enzi, of Wyoming.
Jeff Sessions, of Alabama.
Jim Bunning, of Kentucky.
Mike Crapo, of Idaho.
John Ensign, of Nevada.
John Cornyn, of Texas.
Lamar Alexander, of Tennessee.
Lindsey Graham, of South Carolina.

Kent Conrad, of North Dakota.
Paul S. Sarbanes, of Maryland.
Patty Murray, of Washington.
Ron Wyden, of Oregon.
Russell D. Feingold, of Wisconsin.
Tim Johnson, of South Dakota.
Robert C. Byrd, of West Virginia.
Bill Nelson, of Florida.
Debbie Stabenow, of Michigan.
Jon Corzine, of New Jersey.

(No Subcommittees)

STAFF

Committee on Budget (SD–624), 224–0642.
  Majority Staff Director.—Scott Gudes, 4–0856.
    Policy Director.—Vince Ventimiglia, 4–4471.
    Counsel.—Allison Parent, 4–0857.
    General Counsel.—Gail Millar, 4–0531.
    Chief Economist.—Dan Brandt, 4–0797.
    Communications Director.—Gayle Osterberg, 4–6011.
    Director for—
      Budget Review/Revenues.—Cheri Reidy, 4–0557.
      Federal Programs and Budget Process.—Jim Hearn, 4–2370.
    Professional Staff: Kevin Bargo, 4–8695; Don Dempsey, 4–0543; David Fisher, 4–6988; Katie Friesen, 8–5831; Vanessa Green, 4–4999; Matt Howe, 4–0865; Mike Lofgren, 4–9373; Bill Lucia, 4–5369; Seema Mittal, 4–0838; Kim Monk, 4–6744; David Myers, 4–0843; Shannon O'Keefe, 4–0539; Maureen O'Neill, 4–1602; David Pappone, 4–0564; Steve Richardson, 4–6815; Richard Weiblinger, 4–1107.
    Press Secretary.—Cara Duckworth, 4–2574.
    Detailees: Peggy Binzer, 4–0566; Mara Browne, 8–5846; Elissa Konove, 4–0857; Jennifer Pollom, 4–3023.
    Non-designated:
      Chief Clerk.—Lynne Seymour, 4–0191.
      Computer Systems Administrator.—George Woodall, 4–6576.
      Publications Department.—Letitia Fletcher, 4–0855.
      Staff Assistants: Sarah Eyster, 4–0565; Andrew Kermick, 4–0796.
  Minority Staff Director.—Mary Naylor, 4–0862.
    Deputy Staff Director.—Sue Nelson, 4–0560.
    General Counsel.—Lisa Konwinski, 4–2757.
    Senior Analyst for—
      Agriculture and Trade.—Jim Miller, 4–8463.
      Education and Appropriations.—Shelley Amdur, 4–9731.
      Revenues.—Steve Bailey, 4–2835.
    Analyst for—
      Appropriations, General Government.—John Righter, 4–0544.
      Budget, Energy and Environment.—Cliff Isenberg, 4–0835.
      General Government.—John Righter, 4–0544.
      Income Security and Medicaid.—Jim Esquea, 4–5811.
      International Affairs, National Security.—Jamie Morin, 4–0872.
      Justice, Homeland Security, Community, and Regional Development.—Mike Jones, 4–0833.
      Social Security, Transportation.—Sarah Kuehl, 4–0559.

Director, Strategic Planning and Outreach.—David Vandivier, 4–8604.
Executive Assistant.—Anne Page, 4–0533.
Communications Director.—Stu Nagurka, 4–7436.
Deputy Communications Director.—Steve Posner, 4–7925.
Graphics Production Coordinator.—Kobye Noel, 4–3728.
Chief Economist.—Jim Klumpner, 4–6588.
Webmaster/Junior Analyst for Science and International Affairs.—Rock Cheung, 4–0538.
Staff Assistants: Tyler Haskell, 4–0547; Matthew Havlik, 4–0581.

Commerce, Science, and Transportation

508 Dirksen Senate Office Building 20510–6125
phone 224–5115, TTY / TDD 224–8418 http://commerce.senate.gov

meets first and third Tuesdays of each month

Ted Stevens, of Alaska, *Chair*

John McCain, of Arizona.
Conrad R. Burns, of Montana.
Trent Lott, of Mississippi.
Kay Bailey Hutchison, of Texas.
Olympia J. Snowe, of Maine.
Gordon H. Smith, of Oregon.
John Ensign, of Nevada.
George Allen, of Virginia.
John E. Sununu, of New Hampshire.
Jim DeMint, of South Carolina.
David Vitter, of Louisiana.

Daniel K. Inouye, of Hawaii.
John D. Rockefeller IV, of West Virginia.
John F. Kerry, of Massachusetts.
Byron L. Dorgan, of North Dakota.
Barbara Boxer, of California.
Bill Nelson, of Florida.
Maria Cantwell, of Washington.
Frank Lautenberg, of New Jersey.
E. Benjamin Nelson, of Nebraska.
Mark Pryor, of Arkansas.

SUBCOMMITTEES

Aviation

Conrad R. Burns, of Montana, *Chair*

Ted Stevens, of Alaska.
John McCain, of Arizona.
Trent Lott, of Mississippi.
Kay Bailey Hutchison, of Texas.
Olympia J. Snowe, of Maine.
Gordon H. Smith, of Oregon.
John Ensign, of Nevada.
George Allen, of Virginia.
John E. Sununu, of New Hampshire.
Jim DeMint, of South Carolina.

John D. Rockefeller IV, of West Virginia.
Daniel K. Inouye, of Hawaii.
Byron L. Dorgan, of North Dakota.
Barbara Boxer, of California.
Maria Cantwell, of Washington.
Frank Lautenberg, of New Jersey.
Bill Nelson, of Florida.
E. Benjamin Nelson, of Nebraska.
Mark Pryor, of Arkansas.

Consumer Affairs, Product Safety, and Insurance

George Allen, of Virginia, *Chair*

Ted Stevens, of Alaska.
Conrad R. Burns, of Montana.
Jim DeMint, of South Carolina.
David Vitter, of Louisiana.

Mark Pryor, of Arkansas.
Daniel K. Inouye, of Hawaii, *ex officio.*
Barbara Boxer, of California.

Disaster Prevention and Prediction

Jim DeMint, of South Carolina, *Chair*

Ted Stevens, of Alaska.
Gordon H. Smith, of Oregon.
David Vitter, of Louisiana.

E. Benjamin Nelson, of Nebraska.
Maria Cantwell, of Washington.
Bill Nelson, of Florida.

Fisheries and the Coast Guard

Olympia J. Snowe, of Maine, *Chair*

Ted Stevens, of Alaska.
Trent Lott, of Mississippi.
Gordon H. Smith, of Oregon.
John E. Sununu, of New Hampshire.
David Vitter, of Louisiana.

Maria Cantwell, of Washington.
Daniel K. Inouye, of Hawaii.
John F. Kerry, of Massachusetts.
Frank Lautenberg, of New Jersey.

Global Climate Change and Impacts

David Vitter, of Louisiana, *Chair*

Ted Stevens, of Alaska.
John McCain, of Arizona.
Olympia J. Snowe, of Maine.

Frank Lautenberg, of New Jersey.
John F. Kerry, of Massachusetts.

National Ocean Policy Study

John E. Sununu, of New Hampshire, *Chair*

Ted Stevens, of Alaska.
Trent Lott, of Mississippi.
Kay Bailey Hutchison, of Texas.
Olympia J. Snowe, of Maine.
Gordon H. Smith, of Oregon.
Jim DeMint, of South Carolina.
David Vitter, of Louisiana.

Barbara Boxer, of California.
Daniel K. Inouye, of Hawaii.
John F. Kerry, of Massachusetts.
Maria Cantwell, of Washington.
Frank Lautenberg, of New Jersey.

Science and Space

Kay Bailey Hutchison, of Texas, *Chair*

Ted Stevens, of Alaska.
Conrad R. Burns, of Montana.
Trent Lott, of Mississippi.
John Ensign, of Nevada.
George Allen, of Virginia.
John E. Sununu, of New Hampshire.

Bill Nelson, of Florida.
John D. Rockefeller IV, of West Virginia.
Byron L. Dorgan, of North Dakota.
E. Benjamin Nelson, of Nebraska.
Mark Pryor, of Arkansas.

Surface Transportation and Merchant Marine

Trent Lott, of Mississippi, *Chair*

Ted Stevens, of Alaska.
John McCain, of Arizona.
Conrad R. Burns, of Montana.
Kay Bailey Hutchison, of Texas.
Olympia J. Snowe, of Maine.
Gordon H. Smith, of Oregon.
George Allen, of Virginia.
John E. Sununu, of New Hampshire.
David Vitter, of Louisiana.

Daniel K. Inouye, of Hawaii.
John D. Rockefeller IV, of West Virginia.
Byron Dorgan, of North Dakota.
Barbara Boxer, of California.
Maria Cantwell, of Washington.
Frank Lautenberg, of New Jersey.
E. Benjamin Nelson, of Nebraska.
Mark Pryor, of Arkansas.

Technology, Innovation, and Competitiveness

John Ensign, of Nevada, *Chair*

Ted Stevens, of Alaska.
Conrad R. Burns, of Montana.
Trent Lott, of Mississippi.
Kay Bailey Hutchison, of Texas.
George Allen, of Virginia.
John E. Sununu, of New Hampshire.
Jim DeMint, of South Carolina.

John F. Kerry, of Massachusetts.
Daniel K. Inouye, of Hawaii, *ex officio.*
John D. Rockefeller IV, of West Virginia.
Byron L. Dorgan, of North Dakota.
E. Benjamin Nelson, of Nebraska.
Mark Pryor, of Arkansas.

Trade, Tourism, and Economic Development

Gordon H. Smith, of Oregon, *Chair*

Ted Stevens, of Alaska.
John McCain, of Arizona.
Conrad R. Burns, of Montana.
John Ensign, of Nevada.
George Allen, of Virginia.
John E. Sununu, of New Hampshire.
Jim DeMint, of South Carolina.
David Vitter, of Louisiana.

Byron L. Dorgan, of North Dakota.
Daniel K. Inouye, of Hawaii, *ex officio.*
John D. Rockefeller IV, of West Virginia.
John F. Kerry, of Massachusetts.
Maria Cantwell, of Washington.
Frank Lautenberg, of New Jersey.
Bill Nelson, of Florida.
E. Benjamin Nelson, of Nebraska.
Mark Pryor, of Arkansas.

STAFF

Committee on Commerce, Science, and Transportation (SD–508), 224–5115.
 Majority Staff Director.—Lisa Sutherland.
  Deputy Staff Director.—Christine Kurth.
  Chief Counsel.—David Russell.
  Senior Counsel for Maritime, Oceans, and Atmosphere.—Matthew Paxton.
  Senior Counsel for TSA, Port Security, Sports, Consumer, Trade, Technology.—Ken Nahigian.
  Senior Advisor.—Floyd DesChamps.
  Communications Director.—Melanie Alvord.
  Deputy Communications Director.—Aaron Saunders.
  Counsels: Paul Nagle, Harry Wingo.
  Professional Staff.—Mark Davis.
  Research Assistant.—Mark Delich.
  Scheduler.—Theresa Eugene.
 Minority Staff Director / Chief Counsel.—Margaret Cummisky.
  Deputy Staff Director / General Counsel.—Sam Whitehorn.
  Policy Director.—Lila Helms.
  Communications Director.—Andy Davis.
  Senior Counsel.—James Assey.
  Counsel.—Rachel Welch.
  Staff Assistant.—Jamie Gillespie.
 Aviation, Surface Transportation, and Transportation Security Policy Staff
  Majority Staff Director, Aviation.—Jarrod Thompson.
   Staff Director, Surface Transportation and Merchant Marine.—Chris Bertram.
   Professional Staff, Surface Transportation and Merchant Marine.—Dave Wonnenburg.
   Transportation Detailee.—Susan Kirinich.
   Staff Assistant.—Mike Blank.
  Minority Senior Professional Staff, Aviation.—Gael Sullivan.
   Professional Staff: Stephen Gardner, Dabney Hegg.
   Staff Assistant.—Channon Clements.
 Consumer Affairs, Product Safety, Insurance, Trade, Tourism, Economic Development and Sports Policy Staff
  Majority Staff Director, Trade, Tourism, and Economic Development.—Wally Hsueh.
   Staff Director, Consumer Affairs, Product Safety and Insurance.—Frank Cavaliere.
  Minority Senior Counsel.—David Strickland.
   Counsel.—Catherine McCullough.
   Professional Staff.—Matthew Morrissey.
   Staff Assistant.—Alexsis Horowitz.
 Oceans, Fisheries, Coast Guard, NOPS, Climate Change Policy Staff
  Majority Staff Director, Fisheries and Coast Guard.—Drew Minkiewicz.
   Staff Director, Disaster Prevention and Preparedness.—Thomas Jones.
   Staff Director, Global Climate Change and Impacts.—Garrett Graves.
   Professional Staff.—Kris Lynch.
   SeaGrant Fellow.—Chad English.
   Coast Guard Fellow.—Joe Malinauskas.
   NOAA Fellow.—Rori Marston.
  Minority Senior Counsel.—Margaret Spring.
   Counsel.—Amy Fraenkel.
   SeaGrant Fellow.—Whitley Saumweber.
   Staff Assistant.—Helen Colosimo.

Science, Technology, and Space Policy Staff
    Majority Staff Director, Science and Space.—Jeff Bingham.
        NASA Detailee.—Tom Cremins.
        Staff Director, Technology, Innovation, and Competitiveness.—Jason Mulvihill.
    Minority Senior Professional Staff.—Jean Toal Eisen.
        Professional Staff.—Chan D. Lieu.
        Staff Assistant.—Ivy Shannon.
Bipartisan Staff:
    Chief Clerk.—Debbie Paul.
    Professional Staff/Hearing Clerk.—Susan MacDonald.
    Systems Administrator.—Rebecca Kojm.
    GPO Detailees: Jack Fulmer, Mark Moore.
Bipartisan Staff, Legislative Counsel's Office:
    Legislative Counsel.—Lloyd Ator.
    Staff Assistant.—Jessica Dutton.
Bipartisan Staff, Public Information Office:
    Professional Staff.—Robert Foster.
    Public Information Staff.—Yvonne Gowdy, Joani Wales.
    Staff Assistant.—Stephanie Lieu.

Energy and Natural Resources

364 Dirksen Senate Office Building 20510

phone 224–4971, fax 224–6163, http://energy.senate.gov

meets third Wednesday of each month

Pete V. Domenici, of New Mexico, *Chair*

Larry E. Craig, of Idaho.	*Jeff Bingaman, of New Mexico.*
Craig Thomas, of Wyoming.	*Daniel K. Akaka, of Hawaii.*
Lamar Alexander, of Tennessee.	*Byron L. Dorgan, of North Dakota.*
Lisa Murkowski, of Alaska.	*Ron Wyden, of Oregon.*
Richard Burr, of North Carolina.	*Tim Johnson, of South Dakota.*
Mel Martinez, of Florida.	*Mary L. Landrieu, of Louisiana.*
James M. Talent, of Missouri.	*Dianne Feinstein, of California.*
Conrad Burns, of Montana.	*Maria Cantwell, of Washington.*
George Allen, of Virginia.	*Jon Corzine, of New Jersey.*
Gordon H. Smith, of Oregon.	*Ken Salazar, of Colorado.*
Jim Bunning, of Kentucky.	

SUBCOMMITTEES

[The chairman and the ranking minority member are ex officio members of all subcommittees.]

Energy

Lamar Alexander, of Tennessee, *Chair*

Richard Burr, of North Carolina	*Byron L. Dorgan, of North Dakota.*
Mel Martinez, of Florida.	*Daniel K. Akaka, of Hawaii.*
James M. Talent, of Missouri.	*Tim Johnson, of South Dakota.*
George Allen, of Virginia	*Mary L. Landrieu, of Louisiana.*
Jim Bunning, of Kentucky.	*Dianne Feinstein, of California.*
Lisa Murkowski, of Alaska.	*Maria Cantwell, of Washington.*
Larry E. Craig, of Idaho.	*Jon Corzine, of New Jersey.*
Craig Thomas, of Wyoming.	*Ken Salazar, of Colorado.*
Conrad Burns, of Montana.	

National Parks

Craig Thomas, of Wyoming, *Chair*

Lamar Alexander, of Tennessee.	*Daniel K. Akaka, of Hawaii.*
George Allen, of Virginia.	*Ron Wyden, of Oregon.*
Richard Burr, of North Carolina.	*Mary L. Landrieu, of Louisiana.*
Mel Martinez, of Florida.	*Jon Corzine, of New Jersey.*
Gordon H. Smith, of Oregon.	*Ken Salazar, of Colorado.*

Public Lands and Forests

Larry E. Craig, of Idaho, *Chair*

Conrad Burns, of Montana.	*Ron Wyden, of Oregon.*
Craig Thomas, of Wyoming.	*Daniel K. Akaka, of Hawaii.*
James M. Talent, of Missouri.	*Byron L. Dorgan, of North Dakota.*
Gordon H. Smith, of Oregon.	*Tim Johnson, of South Dakota.*
Lamar Alexander, of Tennessee.	*Mary L. Landrieu, of Louisiana.*
Lisa Murkowski, of Alaska.	*Dianne Feinstein, of California.*
George Allen, of Virginia.	*Maria Cantwell, of Washington.*

Water and Power

Lisa Murkowski, of Alaska, *Chair*

Gordon H. Smith, of Oregon.
Larry E. Craig, of Idaho.
Richard Burr, of North Carolina.
Mel Martinez, of Florida.
Conrad Burns, of Montana.
Jim Bunning, of Kentucky.
James M. Talent, of Missouri.

Tim Johnson, of South Dakota.
Byron L. Dorgan, of North Dakota.
Ron Wyden, of Oregon.
Dianne Feinstein, of California.
Maria Cantwell, of Washington.
Jon Corzine, of New Jersey.
Ken Salazar, of Colorado.

STAFF

Committee on Energy and Natural Resources (SD–364), 224–4971, fax 224–6163.
  Majority Staff Director.—Alex Flint, 4–1004.
    Deputy Staff Director.—Carole McGuire, 4–0537.
    Chief Counsel.—Judy Pensabene, 4–1327.
    Counsels: Kellie Donnelly, 4–9360; Lisa Epifani, 4–5269; Nate Gentry, 4–2179; Frank Macchiarola, 4–1219.
    Deputy Chief Counsel.—Karen Billups, 4–2576.
    Chief Clerk.—Carol Craft, 4–7153.
    Communications Director.—Marnie Funk, 4–6977.
    Deputy Communications Director.—Angela Harper, 4–7875.
    Professional Staff: Dick Bouts, 4–7545; Frank Gladies, 4–2878; Thomas Lillie, 4–5161; Pete Lyons, 4–5861; John Peschke, 4–4797; Clint Williamson, 4–7556.
    Executive Assistant.—Colin Hayes, 4–5305.
    Staff Assistants: David Marks, 4–9313; Amy Millet, 4–8276; Shane Perkins, 4–7555; Justin Tillinghast, 4–2694.
    Bevinetto Fellow.—Brian Carlstrom, 4–6293.
    Fellow.—Erik Webb, 4–4756.
  Minority Staff Director.—Robert Simon, 4–9201.
    Chief Clerk.—Vicki Thorne, 4–3607.
    Chief Counsel.—Sam Fowler, 4–7571.
    Senior Counsels: Patty Beneke, 4–5451; David Brooks, 4–9863.
    Counsels: Michael Carr, 4–8164; Mike Connor, 4–5479; Deborah Estes, 4–5360; Scott Miller, 4–5488.
    Communications Director.—Bill Wicker, 4–5243.
    Professional Staff: Leon Lowery, 4–2209; Jennifer Michael, 4–7143; Al Stayman, 4–7865.
    Legislative Assistant.—Jonathan Black, 4–6722.
    Staff Assistants: Amanda Goldman, 4–6836; Mark Wilson, 4–8046.
    Calendar Clerk.—Mia Bennett, 4–7147.
    Financial Clerk.—Nancy Hall, 4–3606.
    Systems Administrator.—Kathleen Hacker, 4–7163.
    Printer/Editor.—Richard Smit, 4–3118.
    Printer.—Paul Maiorana, 4–7302.
    AAAS Fellows: Sreela Nandi, 4–6689; Adam Rosenberg, 4–5915.

Environment and Public Works

410 Dirksen Senate Office Building 20510–6175

phone 224–6176, www.senate.gov/~epw

meets first and third Thursdays of each month

James M. Inhofe, of Oklahoma, *Chair*

John W. Warner, of Virginia.
Christopher S. Bond, of Missouri.
George V. Voinovich, of Ohio.
Lincoln Chafee, of Rhode Island.
Lisa Murkowski, of Alaska.
John Thune, of South Dakota.
Jim DeMint, of South Carolina.
Johnny Isakson, of Georgia.
David Vitter, of Louisiana.

JAMES M. JEFFORDS, of Vermont.
Max Baucus, of Montana.
Joseph I. Lieberman, of Connecticut.
Barbara Boxer, of California.
Thomas R. Carper, of Delaware.
Hillary Rodham Clinton, of New York.
Frank Lautenberg, of New Jersey.
Barack Obama, of Illinois.

SUBCOMMITTEES

[The chairman and the ranking minority member are ex officio (non-voting) members of all subcommittees on which they do not serve.]

Clean Air, Climate Change, and Nuclear Safety

George V. Voinovich, of Ohio, *Chair*

Christopher S. Bond, of Missouri.
Jim DeMint, of South Carolina.
Johnny Isakson, of Georgia.
David Vitter, of Louisiana.

Thomas R. Carper, of Delaware.
Joseph I. Lieberman, of Connecticut.
Frank Lautenberg, of New Jersey.
Barack Obama, of Illinois.

Fisheries, Wildlife, and Water

Lincoln Chafee, of Rhode Island, *Chair*

John W. Warner, of Virginia.
Lisa Murkowski, of Alaska.
Jim DeMint, of South Carolina.
David Vitter, of Louisiana.

Hillary Rodham Clinton, of New York.
Joseph I. Lieberman, of Connecticut.
Frank Lautenberg, of New Jersey.
Barack Obama, of Illinois.

Superfund and Waste Management

John Thune, of South Dakota, *Chair*

Johnny Isakson, of Georgia.
John W. Warner, of Virginia.
Christopher S. Bond, of Missouri.

Barbara Boxer, of California.
Max Baucus, of Montana.
Frank Lautenberg, of New Jersey.

Transportation and Infrastructure

Christopher S. Bond, of Missouri, *Chair*

John W. Warner, of Virginia.
George V. Voinovich, of Ohio.
Lincoln Chafee, of Rhode Island.
Lisa Murkowski, of Alaska.
John Thune, of South Dakota.

Max Baucus, of Montana.
Joseph I. Lieberman, of Connecticut.
Barbara Boxer, of California.
Thomas R. Carper, of Delaware.
Hillary Rodham Clinton, of New York.

STAFF

Committee on Environment and Public Works (SD–410), phone 224–6176; Recording
for Committee Agenda, 224–1179; Majority fax (SD–410), 224–5167; (SH–415),
224–2322.
Majority Staff Director.—Andrew Wheeler.
Deputy Staff Director for Environment.—Marty Hall.
Deputy Staff Director for Transportation.—Ruth Van Mark.
Counsels: Katherine English, Frank Fannon, Ryan Jackson, Nathan Richmond, John
Shanahan.
Chief Clerk.—Alicia Butler.
Executive Assistant.—Nancy Kate Ryder.
Systems Administrator.—RaeAnn Phipps.
Communications Director.—Will Hart.
Deputy Communications Director.—Matt Dempsey.
Senior Professional Staff.—Michele Nellenbach.
Professional Staff: Mary Anne Dolbeare, Angelina Giancarlo, James O'Keeffe, Jonathan
Tolman.
Editorial Director.—Corinne Lucero.
Legislative Correspondents: Steve Higley, Suzanne Matwyshen-Gillen.
Legislative Fellow.—James Gentry, Greg Murrill.
GPO Detailee.—Brenda Samuels.
Staff Assistants: Kristen Buie, Alex Herrgott, Shawn Ryan.
Research Analyst.—Stephen Aaron.
Minority fax (SD–456), 224–1273; (SH–508), 224–0574.
Minority Staff Director.—Ken Connolly.
Deputy Staff Director.—Jeff Squires.
Executive Assistant.—Carolyn Dupree.
Chief Counsel.—Alison Taylor.
Counsels: J.C. Sandberg, Malcolm Woolf.
Senior Policy Advisors: Jo-Ellen Darcy, Chris Miller.
Office Manager.—Carolyn Dupree.
Professional Staff: Geoff Brown, Catharine Ransom, Margaret Wetherald.
Legislative Correspondent.—Cara Cookson.
Research Assistants: Patrick Rankin, Malia Somerville.
Fellows: Caroline Ahearn, Lauren Michal.
Chief Clerk.—Alicia Butler.
Systems Administrator.—RaeAnn Phipps.
Editorial Director.—Corinne Lucero.
Staff Assistant.—Tom Ashley.
Communications Director.—Eric Smulson.

Finance

219 Dirksen Senate Office Building 20510
phone 224–4515, fax 224–0554, http://finance.senate.gov

meets second and fourth Tuesdays of each month

Charles E. Grassley, of Iowa, *Chair*

Orrin G. Hatch, of Utah.
Trent Lott, of Mississippi.
Olympia J. Snowe, of Maine.
Jon Kyl, of Arizona.
Craig Thomas, of Wyoming.
Rick Santorum, of Pennsylvania.
William H. (Bill) Frist, of Tennessee.
Gordon H. Smith, of Oregon.
Jim Bunning, of Kentucky.
Mike Crapo, of Idaho.

Max Baucus, of Montana.
John D. Rockefeller IV, of West Virginia.
Kent Conrad, of North Dakota.
JAMES M. JEFFORDS, of Vermont.
Jeff Bingaman, of New Mexico.
John F. Kerry, of Massachusetts.
Blanche L. Lincoln, of Arkansas.
Ron Wyden, of Oregon.
Charles E. Schumer, of New York.

SUBCOMMITTEES

[The chairman and the ranking minority member are ex officio (non-voting) members of all subcommittees on which they do not serve.]

Health Care

Orrin G. Hatch, of Utah, *Chair*

Olympia J. Snowe, of Maine.
William H. (Bill) Frist, of Tennessee.
Jon Kyl, of Arizona.
Craig Thomas, of Wyoming.
Rick Santorum, of Pennsylvania.
Jim Bunning, of Kentucky.

John D. Rockefeller IV, of West Virginia.
JAMES M. JEFFORDS, of Vermont.
Jeff Bingaman, of New Mexico.
John F. Kerry, of Massachusetts.
Ron Wyden, of Oregon.

International Trade

Craig Thomas, of Wyoming, *Chair*

Mike Crapo, of Idaho.
Trent Lott, of Mississippi.
Gordon H. Smith, of Oregon.
Jim Bunning, of Kentucky.
Orrin G. Hatch, of Utah.
Olympia J. Snowe, of Maine.
William H. (Bill) Frist, of Tennessee.

Jeff Bingaman, of New Mexico.
Max Baucus, of Montana.
John D. Rockefeller IV, of West Virginia.
Kent Conrad, of North Dakota.
Ron Wyden, of Oregon.
Charles E. Schumer, of New York.

Long-Term Growth and Debt Reduction

Gordon H. Smith, of Oregon, *Chair*

Charles E. Grassley, of Iowa.

John F. Kerry, of Massachusetts.

Social Security and Family Policy

Rick Santorum, of Pennsylvania, *Chair*

Charles E. Grassley, of Iowa.
Jim Bunning, of Kentucky.
William H. (Bill) Frist, of Tennessee.
Trent Lott, of Mississippi.
Jon Kyl, of Arizona.
Gordon H. Smith, of Oregon.
Mike Crapo, of Idaho.

Kent Conrad, of North Dakota.
John D. Rockefeller IV, of West Virginia.
JAMES M. JEFFORDS, of Vermont.
Jeff Bingaman, of New Mexico.
John F. Kerry, of Massachusetts.
Blanche L. Lincoln, of Arkansas.

Taxation and IRS Oversight

Jon Kyl, of Arizona, *Chair*

Trent Lott, of Mississippi.
Orrin G. Hatch, of Utah.
Olympia J. Snowe, of Maine.
Mike Crapo, of Idaho.
Craig Thomas, of Wyoming.
Rick Santorum, of Pennsylvania.

JAMES M. JEFFORDS, of Vermont.
Max Baucus, of Montana.
Kent Conrad, of North Dakota.
Blanche L. Lincoln, of Arkansas.
Charles E. Schumer, of New York.

STAFF

Committee on Finance (SD–219), 224–4515, fax 228–0554.
Majority Staff Director/Chief Counsel.—Kolan Davis.
 Deputy Staff Director.—Ted Totman.
 Special Counsel to the Chair/Chief Investigator.—Emilia Disanto.
 Investigative Counsel.—Dan Donovan.
 Investigative Staff Assistant.—Tom Novelli.
 Chief Tax Counsel.—Mark Prater.
 Tax Counsel/Senior Counsel to the Chair.—Dean Zerbe.
 Tax Counsels: Ed McClellan, Christy Mistr, John O'Neill, Elizabeth Paris.
 Legislative Aide/Assistant Investigator.—Adam Freed.
 Chief Health Counsel.—Mark Hayes.
 Health Policy Advisors: Colette Desmarais, Joelle Oishi, Becky Shipp.
 Legislative Aide.—Mollie Zito.
 Chief Trade Counsel.—Everett Eissenstat.
 Trade Counsels: David Johanson, Stephen Schaefer.
 Trade Staff Assistant.—Zach Paulsen.
 Trade Professional Staff Member.—Tiffany McCullen-Atwood.
 Archivist.—Josh Levasseur.
 Chief Editor.—Bob Merulla.
 Chief Clerk.—Carla Martin.
 Deputy Clerk.—Amber Williams.
 Hearing Clerk.—Mark Blair.
 Communications Director.—Jill Kozeny.
 Press Secretary.—Jill Gerber.
 Senior Staff Assistant.—Jewel Harper.
 Staff Assistants: John Good, Regina Sherrick.
 System Administrator.—Geoffery Burrell.
 Detailee.—Daniel Shepherdson.
Minority Staff Director.—Russ Sullivan.
 Deputy Staff Director.—Bill Dauster.
 Senior Advisor.—John Angell.
 Executive Assistant to the Minority Staff Director.—Wendy Carey.
 Chief Tax Counsel.—Pat Heck.
 Tax Counsels: Matt Genasci, Matt Jones, Judy Miller, Anita Horn Rizek, Jonathan Selib.
 Tax Research Assistant.—Ryan Abraham.
 Chief International Trade Counsel.—Brian Pomper.
 Trade Counsels: Shara Aranoff, John Gilliland.
 Trade Research Assistant.—Sara Andrews.
 Chief Health Counsel.—Liz Fowler.
 Health Investigative Counsel.—Kate Hahn.
 Health Research Assistant.—Daniel Stein.
 Senior Budget Advisor.—Alan Cohen.
 Professional Staff Members of:
  Medicare.—Pat Bousliman.
  Social Security.—Tom Klouda.
 Detailee.—David Schwartz.

Foreign Relations

450 Dirksen Senate Office Building 20510–6225

phone 224–4651, http://foreign.senate.gov

meets each Tuesday

Richard G. Lugar, of Indiana, *Chair*

Chuck Hagel, of Nebraska.
Lincoln D. Chafee, of Rhode Island.
George Allen, of Virginia.
Norm Coleman, of Minnesota.
George V. Voinovich, of Ohio.
Lamar Alexander, of Tennessee.
John E. Sununu, of New Hampshire.
Lisa Murkowski, of Alaska.
Mel Martinez, of Florida.

Joseph R. Biden Jr., of Delaware.
Paul S. Sarbanes, of Maryland.
Christopher J. Dodd, of Connecticut.
John F. Kerry, of Massachusetts.
Russell D. Feingold, of Wisconsin.
Barbara Boxer, of California.
Bill Nelson, of Florida.
Barack Obama, of Illinois.

SUBCOMMITTEES

[The chairman and ranking minority member are ex officio (non-voting) members of all subcommittees on which they do not serve.]

African Affairs

Mel Martinez, of Florida, *Chair*

Lamar Alexander, of Tennessee.
Norm Coleman, of Minnesota.
John E. Sununu, of New Hampshire.
Lisa Murkowski, of Alaska.

Russell D. Feingold, of Wisconsin.
Paul S. Sarbanes, of Maryland.
Christopher J. Dodd, of Connecticut.
Barack Obama, of Illinois.

East Asian and Pacific Affairs

Lisa Murkowski, of Alaska, *Chair*

Lamar Alexander, of Tennessee.
Chuck Hagel, of Nebraska.
Lincoln D. Chafee, of Rhode Island.
George Allen, of Virginia.

John F. Kerry, of Massachusetts.
Joseph R. Biden Jr., of Delaware.
Russell D. Feingold, of Wisconsin.
Barack Obama, of Illinois.

European Affairs

George Allen, of Virginia, *Chair*

George V. Voinovich, of Ohio.
Lisa Murkowski, of Alaska.
Chuck Hagel, of Nebraska.
Lincoln D. Chafee, of Rhode Island.

Joseph R. Biden Jr., of Delaware.
Paul S. Sarbanes, of Maryland.
Christopher J. Dodd, of Connecticut.
Russell D. Feingold, of Wisconsin.

International Economic Policy, Export and Trade Promotion

Chuck Hagel, of Nebraska, *Chair*

Lamar Alexander, of Tennessee.
Lisa Murkowski, of Alaska.
Mel Martinez, of Florida.
George V. Voinovich, of Ohio.

Paul S. Sarbanes, of Maryland.
Christopher J. Dodd, of Connecticut.
John F. Kerry, of Massachusetts.
Barack Obama, of Illinois.

International Operations and Terrorism

John E. Sununu, of New Hampshire, *Chair*

George V. Voinovich, of Ohio.
George Allen, of Virginia.
Norm Coleman, of Minnesota.
Lamar Alexander, of Tennessee.

Bill Nelson, of Florida.
Joseph R. Biden Jr., of Delaware.
John F. Kerry, of Massachusetts.
Barbara Boxer, of California.

Near Eastern and South Asian Affairs

Lincoln D. Chafee, of Rhode Island, *Chair*

Chuck Hagel, of Nebraska.
Norm Coleman, of Minnesota.
George V. Voinovich, of Ohio.
John E. Sununu, of New Hampshire.

Barbara Boxer, of California.
Paul S. Sarbanes, of Maryland.
Bill Nelson, of Florida.
Barack Obama, of Illinois.

Western Hemisphere, Peace Corps, and Narcotics Affairs

Norm Coleman, of Minnesota, *Chair*

Lincoln D. Chafee, of Rhode Island.
George Allen, of Virginia.
Mel Martinez, of Florida.
John E. Sununu, of New Hampshire.

Christopher J. Dodd, of Connecticut.
John F. Kerry, of Massachusetts.
Barbara Boxer, of California.
Bill Nelson, of Florida.

STAFF

Committee on Foreign Relations (SD–450), 224–4651.
Staff Director.—Kenneth A. Myers, Jr.
　Deputy Staff Director.—Daniel C. Diller.
　Chief Counsel.—Paul F. Clayman.
　Democratic Staff Director.—Antony J. Blinken.
　Democratic Counsel.—Brian P. McKeon.
　Chief Clerk.—Susan Oursler.
Republican Staff (SD–450), 224–4651.
　Republican Administrative Director.—Katherine E. Maloney.
　Counsels: Chris Ann Kechner, Manisha Singh.
　Legislative Assistants: Cristina L. Tallarigo, Ellona Wilner.
　Staff Assistants: Kristen C. Armitage, Caitlin Davitt.
　Legislative Aide.—D. Derick Stowe.
　Professional Staff: Jay Branegan, Lisa A. Curtis, Paul S. Foldi, Jessica S. Fugate, Patrick
　　Garvey, Mark Helmke, Mary Locke, W. Keith Luse, Carl E. Meacham, Thomas C.
　　Moore, Kenneth A. Myers, III, Michael V. Phelan, Nilmini G. Rubin, Kim Savit.
Democratic Staff (SD–439), 224–3953.
　Special Assistant to the Democratic Staff Director.—Jessica S. Dalton.
　Staff Assistant.—Sylvia Renner.
　Research Assistant.—Gabriel J. Bitol.
　Professional Staff: Jonah B. Blank, Heather D. Flynn, Michael H. Haltzel, Frank S.
　　Jannuzi, Edward P. Levine, Erin M. Logan, Janice M. O'Connell, Diana L. Ohlbaum,
　　Jennifer Simon, Nancy H. Stetson, Puneet Talwar.
Undesignated Staff (SD–450), 224–4651.
　Office Manager.—Joanna Woodard.
　Executive/Legislative Clerk.—Angie Evans.
　Executive Assistant to the Chief Clerk.—Megan A. McCray.
　Director for Protocol/Foreign Travel.—Sandra S. Mason (S–116).
　Deputy Director for Protocol/Foreign Travel.—Margaret Brooks (S–116).
　Hearing Coordinator.—Bertie H. Bowman.
　Systems Administrator.—Alan Browne.
　Staff Assistants: Matt Dixson, Matthew McMillan.
　Archivist Research Assistant.—Deborah M. Johnson.
　Printing Clerks: Michael W. Bennett, David L. Evans.

Health, Education, Labor, and Pensions

428 Dirksen Senate Office Building 20510–6300

phone 224–5375, http://help.senate.gov

meets second and fourth Wednesdays of each month

Michael B. Enzi, of Wyoming, *Chair*

Judd Gregg, of New Hampshire.
William H. (Bill) Frist, of Tennessee.
Lamar Alexander, of Tennessee.
Richard Burr, of North Carolina.
Johnny Isakson, of Georgia.
Mike DeWine, of Ohio.
John Ensign, of Nevada.
Orrin Hatch, of Utah.
Jeff Sessions, of Alabama.
Pat Roberts, of Kansas.

Edward M. Kennedy, of Massachusetts.
Christopher J. Dodd, of Connecticut.
Tom Harkin, of Iowa.
Barbara A. Mikulski, of Maryland.
JAMES M. JEFFORDS, of Vermont.
Jeff Bingaman, of New Mexico.
Patty Murray, of Washington.
Jack Reed, of Rhode Island.
Hillary Rodham Clinton, of New York.

SUBCOMMITTEES

[The chairman and ranking minority member are ex officio members of all subcommittees
on which they do not serve.]

Bioterrorism and Public Health Preparedness

Richard Burr, of North Carolina, *Chair*

Judd Gregg, of New Hampshire.
William H. (Bill) Frist, of Tennessee.
Lamar Alexander, of Tennessee.
Mike DeWine, of Ohio.
John Ensign, of Alabama.
Orrin Hatch, of Utah.
Pat Roberts, of Kansas.

Edward M. Kennedy, of Massachusetts.
Christopher J. Dodd, of Connecticut.
Tom Harkin, of Iowa.
Barbara A. Mikulski, of Maryland.
Jeff Bingaman, of New Mexico.
Patty Murray, of Washington.
Jack Reed, of Rhode Island.

Education and Early Childhood Development

Lamar Alexander, of Tennessee, *Chair*

Judd Gregg, of New Hampshire.
Richard Burr, of North Carolina.
Johnny Isakson, of Georgia.
Mike DeWine, of Ohio.
John Ensign, of Nevada.
Orrin Hatch, of Utah.
Jeff Sessions, of Alabama.

Christopher J. Dodd, of Connecticut.
Tom Harkin, of Iowa.
JAMES M. JEFFORDS, of Vermont.
Jeff Bingaman, of New Mexico.
Patty Murray, of Washington.
Jack Reed, of Rhode Island.
Hillary Rodham Clinton, of New York.

Employment and Workplace Safety

Johnny Isakson, of Georgia, *Chair*

Lamar Alexander, of Tennessee.
Richard Burr, of North Carolina.
John Ensign, of Nevada.
Jeff Sessions, of Alabama.
Pat Roberts, of Kansas.

Patty Murray, of Washington.
Christopher J. Dodd, of Connecticut.
Tom Harkin, of Iowa.
Barbara A. Mikulski, of Maryland.
JAMES M. JEFFORDS, of Vermont.

Retirement Security and Aging

Mike DeWine, of Ohio, *Chair*

Johnny Isakson, of Georgia.
Orrin Hatch, of Utah.
Jeff Sessions, of Alabama.
Pat Roberts, of Kansas.

Barbara A. Mikulski, of Maryland.
JAMES M. JEFFORDS, of Vermont.
Jeff Bingaman, of New Mexico.
Hillary Rodham Clinton, of New York.

STAFF

Committee on Health, Education, Labor, and Pensions (SH–835), 224–6770, fax 224–6510, TDD 224–1975.

Majority Staff Director.—Katherine B. McGuire.
  Chief Counsel.—Ilyse W. Schuman.
  General Counsel.—Greg Dean.
  Office Administrator.—Christina W. Sink.
  Communications Director.—Craig Orfield.
    Senior Communications Advisor.—Ron Hindle.
    Communications Assistant.—Ryan J. Taylor.
  Chief Investigative Counsel.—Lauren Fuller (SH–615), 4–7229.
    Investigative Advisor.—Adam Briddell.
    Investigative Associate.—Kori Forster.
    Senior Policy Advisor.—Amy E. Angelier.
  Health Policy Director.—Stephen J. Northrup (SH–725), 4–0623.
    Senior Health Counsel.—Andrew W. Patzman.
    Professional Staff Members: Katy Barr, Shana Christrup, Amy Muhlberg.
    Research Assistant.—Michelle Dirst.
    CMS Fellow.—Devona Delach.
    NIH Detailee.—Dave Schmickel.
    RWJ Fellow.—John Ring.
  Education Policy Director.—Beth B. Buehlmann (SH–833), 4–8484.
    Professional Staff Member.—Scott Flemming.
    Kennedy Foundation Fellow.—Tec Champman.
    DOE Detailee.—Ann Clough.
    Research Assistant.—Courtney Brown.
    Staff Assistant.—Will Green.
  Labor Policy Director.—Brian Hayes (SH–608), 4–6770.
    Labor Counsel.—Kyle Hicks.
    Professional Staff Member.—Aaron Bishop.
    Pensions Counsels: David L. Thompson, Diann Howland (SH–608), 4–6770.
  Chief Clerk.—Denis P. O'Donovan (SD–426), 4–5375.
    Deputy Chief Clerk.—John Edward Dutton.
    Clerks: Kimberly G. Kirkpatrick, Chris Schron, Erin E. Shea.
  Editor.—Denise L. Lowery.
    Assistant Editor.—Stephen L. Chapman.
  Senior Staff Assistant/Hearing Clerk.—Mary M. Smith.
  Professional Staff Member.—Uwe E. Timpke.
  Director, Information Systems.—Jizhu Zhang.
Minority Staff Director/Chief Counsel.—Michael J. Myers (SD–644), 4–0767.
  Health Staff Director.—David Bowen (SH–527), 4–7675.
  Deputy Health Staff Director.—Dora Hughes (SH–527).
  Chief Counsel/Policy.—Jeffrey Teitz.
  Policy Director for Disabilities and Public Health.—Constance M. Garner.
  Labor Counsel.—Portia Wu (SH–639), 4–5441.
  Chief Counsel/Labor.—Holly B. Fechner.
  Senior Counsel/Education: Michael Dannenberg (SH–622B), 4–5501; Roberto Rodriguez (SH–622B), 4–5501.
  Chief Counsel/Education.—Carmel Martin.
  Labor Policy Advisor.—Julie P. Kashen (SH–639), 4–0767.
  Education Advisor.—Jane Oates (SH–622B), 4–5501.
  Legislative Aide/Disability.—Kent Mitchell.
  Staff Assistants: Annick Febrey (SH–527), 4–7675; Cody S. Keenan (SD–644), 4–0767; Elizabeth Maher (SH–622B), 4–5501; Erin McLaughlin (SH–639), 4–5441.

Subcommittee on Bioterrorism Preparedness and Public Health (SD–424), 4–3154.
  Majority Staff Director.—Dr. Robert Kadlec.
    Health Policy Director.—Jenny Hansen.
    Staff Assistant.—Kendall Byrum.
    Professional Staff.—Celia Sims.
  Minority Staff Director.—David Bowen (SH–527), 4–7675.
    Deputy Staff Director.—Dora Hughes.
Subcommittee on Education and Early Childhood Development (SH–632), 4–5800.
  Majority Staff Director.—Christine Dodd.
    Health/Labor Policy Advisor.—Page Kranbuhl.
    Education Policy Advisor.—Kristen Bannerman.
    Professional Staff.—John Grant.
    Clerk.—Erin Shea.
  Minority Staff Director.—Grace A. Reef (SH–404), 4–5630.
    Professional Staff: Benjamin B. Berwick, James Fenton, Julius Lloyd Horwich.
Subcommittee on Employment and Workplace Safety (SH–132), 4–3643.
  Majority Staff Director.—Glee Smith.
    Professional Staff Members: Ed Egee, Brittany Espy.
  Minority Staff Director.—William Kamela (SH–801B), 4–4925.
    Staff Assistant.—Heather Honaker.
Subcommittee on Retirement Security and Aging (SH–607), 4–7900.
  Majority Staff Director.—Karla Carpenter.
    Professional Staff: Abby Kral, Lindsay Morris.
    Clerk.—Chris Schron.
  Minority Staff Director.—Rhonda Richards (SH–113), 4–9243.
    Professional Staff.—Stephanie Sterling.

Homeland Security and Governmental Affairs

340 Dirksen Senate Office Building 20510

phone 224–4751, http://hsgac.senate.gov

Hearing Room—SD–342 Dirksen Senate Office Building

meets first Thursday of each month

Susan M. Collins, of Maine, *Chair*

Ted Stevens, of Alaska.
George V. Voinovich, of Ohio.
Norm Coleman, of Minnesota.
Tom Coburn, of Oklahoma.
Lincoln D. Chafee, of Rhode Island.
Robert F. Bennett, of Utah.
Pete V. Domenici, of New Mexico.
John W. Warner, of Virginia.

Joseph I. Lieberman, of Connecticut.
Carl Levin, of Michigan.
Daniel K. Akaka, of Hawaii.
Thomas R. Carper, of Delaware.
Mark Dayton, of Minnesota.
Frank Lautenberg, of New Jersey.
Mark Pryor, of Arkansas.

SUBCOMMITTEES

[The chairman and the ranking minority member are ex officio members of all subcommittees.]

Federal Financial Management, Government Information, and International Security (FFM)

Tom Coburn, of Oklahoma, *Chair*

Ted Stevens, of Alaska.
George V. Voinovich, of Ohio.
Lincoln D. Chafee, of Rhode Island.
Robert F. Bennett, of Utah.
Pete V. Domenici, of New Mexico.
John W. Warner, of Virginia.

Thomas R. Carper, of Delaware.
Carl Levin, of Michigan.
Daniel K. Akaka, of Hawaii.
Mark Dayton, of Minnesota.
Frank Lautenberg, of New Jersey.

Oversight of Government Management, the Federal Workforce and the District of Columbia (OGM)

George V. Voinovich, of Ohio, *Chair*

Ted Stevens, of Alaska.
Norm Coleman, of Minnesota.
Tom Coburn, of Oklahoma.
Lincoln D. Chafee, of Rhode Island.
Robert F. Bennett, of Utah.
Pete V. Domenici, of New Mexico.
John W. Warner, of Virginia.

Daniel K. Akaka, of Hawaii.
Carl Levin, of Michigan.
Thomas R. Carper, of Delaware.
Mark Dayton, of Minnesota.
Frank Lautenberg, of New Jersey.
Mark Pryor, of Arkansas.

Permanent Subcommittee on Investigations (PSI)

Norm Coleman, of Minnesota, *Chair*

Ted Stevens, of Alaska.
Tom Coburn, of Oklahoma.
Lincoln D. Chafee, of Rhode Island.
Robert F. Bennett, of Utah.
Pete V. Domenici, of New Mexico.
John W. Warner, of Virginia.

Carl Levin, of Michigan.
Daniel K. Akaka, of Hawaii.
Thomas R. Carper, of Delaware.
Mark Dayton, of Minnesota.
Frank Lautenberg, of New Jersey.
Mark Pryor, of Arkansas.

STAFF

Committee on Homeland Security and Governmental Affairs (SD–340), 224–4751.
　Majority Staff Director/Chief Counsel.—Michael Bopp.
　　Deputy Staff Director.—Ann Fisher.
　　Deputy Staff Director for Investigations.—Michael Stern.
　　Senior Counsels: Tom Eldridge, Jason A. Foster, Johanna Hardy, Lesley Leger-Kelley,
　　　Jon Nass, Alec D. Rogers.
　　Counsels: Allison Boyd, James McKay.
　　Professional Staff: Jane Alonso, Priscilla Hanley, Jennifer Hemingway, Bruce Kyle.
　　Executive Assistant.—Jennifer Gagnon.
　　Chief Clerk.—Amy B. Newhouse.
　　Financial Clerk.—John Gleason.
　　Publications Clerk.—Pat Hogan.
　　Systems Administrator/Webmaster.—Dan Muchow.
　　Archivist/Librarian.—Elisabeth Butler.
　　Press Secretary.—Elissa Davidson.
　　Staff Assistants: Jayne McCullough, Kate Scontras, Amber Smith, Heather Smith, Sarah
　　　Taylor, Monica Wickey.
　　Detailees: Don Bumgardner (GAO), Keith Janssen (Coast Guard), Edward Priestap (FBI).
　Minority Staff Director/Counsel.—Joyce Rechtschaffen (SH–604), 224–2627.
　　Chief Counsel.—Laurie Rubenstein.
　　Office Manager/Executive Assistant.—Janet Burrell.
　　Communications Director.—Leslie Phillips.
　　Communications Advisor.—Scott Campbell.
　　Assistant Press Secretary.—Sarah Wachtel.
　　Counsels: Beth Grossman, Holly Idelson, Kevin Landy, Lawrence B. Novey, Mary Beth
　　　Schultz.
　　Professional Staff: Michael L. Alexander, David Barton, David M. Berick, Donny R.
　　　Williams, Leslie Woolley, Jason M. Yanussi.
　　Research Assistant.—Adam Sedgewick.
　　Staff Assistants: Kristine Lam, Alysha Liljeqvist.
　*Subcommittee on Federal Financial Management, Government Information and International
　　Security (FFM)* (SH–439), 4–2254.
　　Majority Staff Director.—Chris Gacek.
　　Minority Staff Director.—Sheila Murphy (SD–326), 4–7155.
　　　Deputy Staff Director.—John Kilvington.
　*Subcommittee on Oversight of Government Management, The Federal Workforce, and the
　　District of Columbia (OGM)* (SH–442), 4–3682.
　　Majority Staff Director.—Andrew Richardson.
　　　Professional Staff: David Cole, Theresa Prych, John Salamone.
　　　Clerk.—Tara Baird.
　　Minority Staff Director.—Richard J. Kessler (SH–446), 4–4551.
　　　Deputy Staff Director.—Nanci Langley.
　　　Counsel.—Jennifer Tyree.
　　　Professional Staff.—Deborah Parkinson.
　　　Staff Assistant.—Patrick Driscoll.
　　　Fellow.—Norman Schneidewind.
　　　Detailee.—Robert Westbrooks.
　Permanent Subcommittee on Investigations (PSI) (SR–199), 4–3721.
　　Majority Staff Director.—Raymond Shepherd.
　　　General Counsel.—Joseph Kennedy.
　　　Counsels: Leland B. Erickson, Mark L. Greenblatt, Steven A. Groves.
　　　Investigator.—C. Jay Jennings.
　　　Clerk.—Mary Robertson.
　　　Detailees: Gregory C. Coats (IRS), Richard Fahy (ICE), Jeffrey G. James (IRS), Katherine
　　　　Russell (FBI), Phillip Thomas (GAO).
　　Minority Staff Director/Chief Counsel.—Elise J. Bean, (SR–199), 4–9505.
　　　Counsel/Chief Investigator.—Robert L. Roach.
　　　Counsels: Dan M. Berkovitz, Laura E. Stuber.
　　　Professional Staff: Joe Bryan, Zachary Schram.
　　　Fellow.—Kathleen Trainor (CIA).

Committee on Indian Affairs

836 Hart Senate Office Building 20510–2251

phone 224–2251, fax 224–5429, http://indian.senate.gov

[Created pursuant to S. Res. 4, 95th Congress; amended by S. Res. 71, 103d Congress]

meets first Tuesday of each month

John McCain, of Arizona, *Chair*

Byron Dorgan, of North Dakota, *Vice Chair*

Pete V. Domenici, of New Mexico.
Craig Thomas, of Wyoming.
Gordon H. Smith, of Oregon.
Lisa Murkowski, of Alaska.
Mike Crapo, of Idaho.
Richard Burr, of North Carolina.
Tom Coburn, of Oklahoma.

Daniel K. Inouye, of Hawaii.
Kent Conrad, of North Dakota.
Daniel K. Akaka, of Hawaii.
Tim Johnson, of South Dakota.
Maria Cantwell, of Washington.

(No Subcommittees)

STAFF

Majority Staff Director.—Jeanne Bumpus.
   Deputy Staff Director.—John Tahsuda.
   General Counsel.—David Mullon.
   Chief Investigative Counsel.—Pablo Carrillo.
      Deputy Chief Investigative Counsel.—Bryan Parker.
   Senior Counsel.—Rhonda Harjo.
   Professional Staff.—Patrick McMullen.
   Executive Assistant.—Katherine Rossi.
Minority Staff Director.—Sara G. Garland.
   Senior Policy Advisor.—Cindy Darcy.
   Counsel.—Janet Erickson.
   Legislative Aide.—David Montes.

Judiciary

224 Dirksen Senate Office Building 20510–6275
phone 224–5225, fax 224–9102, http://www.senate.gov/~judiciary
meets upon call of the chair

Arlen Specter, of Pennsylvania, *Chair*

Orrin G. Hatch, of Utah.
Charles E. Grassley, of Iowa.
Jon Kyl, of Arizona.
Mike DeWine, of Ohio.
Jeff Sessions, of Alabama.
Lindsey Graham, of South Carolina.
John Cornyn, of Texas.
Sam Brownback, of Kansas.
Tom Coburn, of Oklahoma.

Patrick Leahy, of Vermont.
Edward M. Kennedy, of Massachusetts.
Joseph R. Biden, Jr., of Delaware.
Herbert H. Kohl, of Wisconsin.
Dianne Feinstein, of California.
Russell D. Feingold, of Wisconsin.
Charles E. Schumer, of New York.
Richard Durbin, of Illinois.

SUBCOMMITTEES

Administrative Oversight and the Courts

Jeff Sessions, of Alabama, *Chair*

Arlen Specter, of Pennsylvania.
Charles E. Grassley, of Iowa.
Jon Kyl, of Arizona.

Charles E. Schumer, of New York.
Dianne Feinstein, of California.
Russell D. Feingold, of Wisconsin.

Antitrust, Competition Policy and Consumer Rights

Mike DeWine, of Ohio, *Chair*

Arlen Specter, of Pennsylvania.
Orrin G. Hatch, of Utah.
Charles E. Grassley, of Iowa.
Lindsey Graham, of South Carolina.
Sam Brownback, of Kansas.

Herbert H. Kohl, of Wisconsin.
Patrick Leahy, of Vermont.
Joseph R. Biden, Jr., of Delaware.
Russell D. Feingold, of Wisconsin.
Charles E. Schumer, of New York.

Constitution, Civil Rights and Property Rights

Sam Brownback, of Kansas, *Chair*

Arlen Specter, of Pennsylvania.
Lindsey Graham, of South Carolina.
John Cornyn, of Texas.
Tom Coburn, of Oklahoma.

Russell D. Feingold, of Wisconsin.
Edward M. Kennedy, of Massachusetts.
Dianne Feinstein, of California.
Richard Durbin, of Illinois.

Corrections and Rehabilitation

Tom Coburn, of Oklahoma, *Chair*

Arlen Specter, of Pennsylvania.
Jeff Sessions, of Alabama.
John Cornyn, of Texas.
Sam Brownback, of Kansas.

Richard Durbin, of Illinois.
Patrick Leahy, of Vermont.
Joseph R. Biden, Jr., of Delaware.
Russell D. Feingold, of Wisconsin.

Crime and Drugs

Lindsey Graham, of South Carolina, *Chair*

Charles E. Grassley, of Iowa.
Jon Kyl, of Arizona.
Mike DeWine, of Ohio.
Jeff Sessions, of Alabama.
Tom Coburn, of Oklahoma.

Joseph R. Biden, Jr., of Delaware.
Herbert H. Kohl, of Wisconsin.
Dianne Feinstein, of California.
Russell D. Feingold, of Wisconsin.
Charles E. Schumer, of New York.

Immigration, Border Security and Citizenship

John Cornyn, of Texas, *Chair*

Charles E. Grassley, of Iowa.
Jon Kyl, of Arizona.
Mike DeWine, of Ohio.
Jeff Sessions, of Alabama.
Sam Brownback, of Kansas.
Tom Coburn, of Oklahoma.

Edward M. Kennedy, of Massachusetts.
Joseph R. Biden, Jr., of Delaware.
Dianne Feinstein, of California.
Russell D. Feingold, of Wisconsin.
Charles E. Schumer, of New York.
Richard Durbin, of Illinois.

Intellectual Property

Orrin G. Hatch, of Utah, *Chair*

Jon Kyl, of Arizona.
Mike DeWine, of Ohio.
Lindsey Graham, of South Carolina.
John Cornyn, of Texas.
Sam Brownback, of Kansas.
Tom Coburn, of Oklahoma.

Patrick Leahy, of Vermont.
Edward M. Kennedy, of Massachusetts.
Joseph R. Biden, Jr., of Delaware.
Dianne Feinstein, of California.
Herbert H. Kohl, of Wisconsin.
Richard Durbin, of Illinois.

Terrorism, Technology and Homeland Security

Jon Kyl, of Arizona, *Chair*

Orrin G. Hatch, of Utah.
Charles E. Grassley, of Iowa.
John Cornyn, of Texas.
Mike DeWine, of Ohio.
Jeff Sessions, of Alabama.
Lindsey Graham, of South Carolina.

Dianne Feinstein, of California.
Edward M. Kennedy, of Massachusetts.
Joseph R. Biden, Jr., of Delaware.
Herbert H. Kohl, of Wisconsin.
Russell D. Feingold, of Wisconsin.
Richard Durbin, of Illinois.

STAFF

Committee on the Judiciary (SD–224), 224–5225, fax 224–9102.
  Majority Chief of Staff/Staff Director.—David Brog.
    Assistant to the Chief of Staff.—Maria Plakoudas.
    Deputy Staff Director/Senior Counsel.—Joe Jacquot.
    Chief Counsel.—Mike O'Neill.
    Assistant to the Chief Counsel.—Lissa Camacho.
    Counsels: Ken Cohen, Dimple Gupta, Mark Heilbrun, Ivy Johnson, Juria Jones, Evan Kelly, Hannibal Kemerer, Kathy Michalko, Greg Nunziata, Nick Rossi, Carolyn Short, Seema Singh, Tim Strachan, Frank Scaturro, Ryan Triplette.
    Senior Nominations Counsel.—Peter Jensen.
    Chief Civil Counsel.—Harold Kim.
    Civil Staff Assistant.—Nathan Morris.
    Chief Crime Counsel.—Brett Tolman.
    Investigative Counsel/Nomination Clerk.—Mike Thorpe.
    Crime Staff Assistant.—Viana Cabral.
    Chief Clerk.—Jane Butterfield, 4–1444.
    Deputy Chief Clerk.—Roslyne Turner, 4–6928.
    Hearings Clerk/Systems Administrator.—Barr Huefner, 4–9376.
    Librarian.—Kurt Carroll, 4–9250.
    Legal Fellow.—Adam Turner.
    Press Secretary.—Blain Rethmeier.
    Archivist.—Stuart Paine.
    Stenographer.—Paula Carroll.
    Staff Assistants: Damion Nielsen, Tom Robins.
    GPO Printers.—Preble Marmion, Cecilia Morcombe.
  Minority Staff Director/Chief Counsel.—Bruce Cohen (SD–152), 224–7703, fax 224–9516.
    Legislative Staff Assistant to Chief Counsel.—Kathryn Neal.
    Senior Counsels: Susan Davies, Julie Katzman, Ed Pagano.
    Legislative Staff Assistant to Ed Pagano.—Jessica Berry.
    Counsels: Kristine Lucius, Tim Lynch, Tara Magner.
    Senior Nominations Counsel.—Helaine Greenfield.
    Nominations Counsels: Noah Bookbinder, Jeremy Paris.

Nominations Clerk.—Mona Lewandowski.
Legislative Correspondents: Jessica Bashford, Mary Kate Meyer.
Legislative Staff Assistant.—Dan Fine.
Staff Assistants: Julia Franklin, Maggie Gage.
Subcommittee on Administrative Oversight and the Courts (SD–335) 224–7572.
Majority Chief Counsel.—William Smith.
Deputy Chief Counsel.—Cindy Hayden.
Legislative Counsels: Amy Blakenship, Wendy Fleming.
Minority Chief Counsel.—Preet Bharara, 224–6542.
Counsel.—Josh Levy.
Legislative Correspondent.—Derek Lindblom.
Subcommittee on Antitrust, Competition Policy, and Consumer Rights (SD–161) 224–9494.
Majority Chief Counsel/Staff Director.—Peter Levitas.
Counsel.—Rob Steinbuch.
Legislative Aide.—Robin Blackwell.
Minority Chief Counsel.—Jeffrey Miller, 224–3406.
Counsels: Seth Bloom, Jon Schwantes.
Subcommittee on the Constitution, Civil Rights, and Property Rights (SD–303) 224–6521.
Majority Chief Counsel.—Ajit Pai.
Legislative Assistant.—Courtney Anderson.
Minority Chief Counsel.—Bob Schiff, 224–5573.
Subcommittee on Corrections and Rehabilitation (SR–170) 224–5754.
Majority Chief Counsel.—Mary Chesser.
Minority Chief Counsel/Staff Director.—Neil McBride, 224–0558.
Counsels: Jonathan Meyer, Eric Rosen.
Senior Advisor.—Marcia Lee.
Subcommittee on Crime and Drugs (SR–290) 224–5972.
Majority Chief Counsel/Staff Director.—James Galyean.
Clerk/Research Assistant.—Ed Bonapfel.
Clerk.—Scott Burris.
Subcommittee on Immigration, Border Security, and Citizenship (SH–517) 224–2934.
Majority Chief Counsel.—James Ho.
Legislative Director.—Beth Jafari.
Legal Assistant.—Lindsey Kiser.
Counsels: Reed O'Connor, Chip Roy.
Minority Chief Counsel.—Jim Flug, 224–7878.
Counsels: Janice Kaguyutan, Esther Olavarria.
Subcommittee on Intellectual Property (SH–104) 224–5251.
Majority Chief Counsel.—Bruce Artim.
Professional Staff Member.—Brendan Dunn.
Counsels: David Jones, Kevin O'Scannlain.
Subcommittee on Terrorism, Technology, and Homeland Security (SH–325) 224–6791.
Majority Chief Counsel.—Stephen Higgins.
Counsels: Mike Dougherty, Joe Matal, Andrea Sander.
Legislative Correspondent/Clerk.—Amy Tyra.
Minority Chief Counsel/Staff Director.—Steve Cash, 224–4933.
Legislative Aide.—Jason Knapp.

Rules and Administration

305 Russell Senate Office Building 20510–6325

phone 224–6352, http://rules.senate.gov

[Legislative Reorganization Act of 1946]

meets second and fourth Wednesday of each month

Trent Lott, of Mississippi, *Chair*

Ted Stevens, of Alaska.
Mitch McConnell, of Kentucky.
Thad Cochran, of Mississippi.
Rick Santorum, of Pennsylvania.
Kay Bailey Hutchison, of Texas.
William H. (Bill) Frist, of Tennessee.
Saxby Chambliss, of Georgia.
Robert Bennett, of Utah.
Chuck Hagel, of Nebraska.

Christopher J. Dodd, of Connecticut.
Robert C. Byrd, of West Virginia.
Daniel K. Inouye, of Hawaii.
Dianne Feinstein, of California.
Charles E. Schumer, of New York.
Mark Dayton, of Minnesota.
Richard J. Durbin, of Illinois.
E. Benjamin Nelson, of Nebraska.

(No Subcommittees)

STAFF

Committee on Rules and Administration (SR–305), 224–6352.
Majority Staff Director.—Susan Wells, 4–6352.
 Deputy Staff Director.—LuraNell Mitchell, 4–6352.
 Legislative Director.—Alexander Polinsky, 4–1966.
 Director for Administration and Policy.—Chris Shunk, 4–9528.
 Chief Clerk.—Sue Wright, 4–2536.
 Professional Staff: Leann Alwood, 4–7569; Mayvis Caldwell, 4–6913; Tom Hogdahl, 4–6282; Matthew McGowan, 4–0281.
 Publications Assistant.—Cami Ragland, 4–0284.
 Executive Assistants: Lauren Stanton, 4–1208; Galey Tatum, 4–4508.
 Staff Assistants: Caroline Bryant, 4–3879; Cooper Dawson, 4–8925.
Minority Staff Director/Chief Counsel.—Kennie Gill, 4–6351.
 Elections Counsel.—Veronica Gillespie, 4–5648.
 Administrative Assistant to Democratic Staff Director.—Carole Blessington, 4–0278.
 Professional Staff.—Candace Chin, 4–0279.

Small Business and Entrepreneurship

428A Russell Senate Office Building 20510

phone 224–5175, fax 224–6619, http://www.senate.gov/~sbc

[Created pursuant to S. Res. 58, 81st Congress]

meets first Wednesday of each month

Olympia J. Snowe, of Maine, *Chair*

Christopher S. Bond, of Missouri.
Conrad Burns, of Montana.
George Allen, of Virginia.
Norm Coleman, of Minnesota.
John Thune, of South Dakota.
Johnny Isakson, of Georgia.
David Vitter, of Louisiana.
Michael Enzi, of Wyoming.
John Cornyn, of Texas.

John F. Kerry, of Massachusetts.
Carl Levin, of Michigan.
Tom Harkin, of Iowa.
Joseph I. Lieberman, of Connecticut.
Mary Landrieu, of Louisiana.
Maria Cantwell, of Washington.
Evan Bayh, of Indiana.
Mark Pryor, of Arkansas.

(No Subcommittees)

STAFF

Committee on Small Business and Entrepreneurship (SR–428A), 224–5175, fax 224–6619.
   Majority Staff Director.—Weston J. Coulam
      Banking and Finance Counsel.—Greg Wach.
      Oversight Counsel.—Matthew Walker.
      Regulatory Counsel.—Alex Hecht.
      Tax and Finance Counsel.—Fred Hartman.
      Counsels: Max Kidalov, Jennifer Perkins.
      Executive Assistant.—Michele Pendleton.
      Professional Staff Member.—Jackie Sierodzinski.
      Research Assistants: Linda Le, Matt Reid, Jamie Suzor.
      System Administrator.—John Falls.
      Staff Assistants: Christian Berle, Kaitlin Sighinolfi.
      Chief Clerk.—Lena Lawrence.
   Minority Staff Director.—Kevin Wheeler (acting).
      Assistant to the Staff Director.—Gail Steinberg.
      Counsels: Mirah Horowitz, Barry La Sala.
      Social Security and Tax Counsel.—Kathleen Kerrigan.
      Professional Staff: Marc Comer, John Phillips, Nigel Stevens.
      Research Assistant.—Casey Scott.
      Staff Assistant.—Alison Matela.
      Committee Aide.—Salvatore Ciolino.

Veterans' Affairs

SR–412 Russell Senate Office Building 20510
phone 224–9126, http://veterans.senate.gov

meets first Wednesday of each month

Larry E. Craig, of Idaho, *Chair*

Arlen Specter, of Pennsylvania.
Kay Bailey Hutchison, of Texas.
Lindsey O. Graham, of South Carolina
Richard Burr, of North Carolina.
John Ensign, of Nevada.
John Thune, of South Dakota.
Johnny Isakson, of Georgia.

Daniel K. Akaka, of Hawaii.
John D. Rockefeller IV, of West Virginia.
JAMES M. JEFFORDS, of Vermont.
Patty Murray, of Washington.
Barack Obama, of Illinois.
Ken Salazar, of Colorado.

(No Subcommittees)

STAFF

Committee on Veterans' Affairs (SR–412), 224–9126.
　Majority Staff Director.—Lupe Wissel.
　　Chief Counsel.—William F. Tuerk.
　　Benefits Counsel.—Ronald C. Crump.
　　Health Policy Counsel.—William T. Cahill.
　　Health Policy Advisor.—Lisa A. (Toni) Lawson.
　　Communications Director.—Jeffrey A. Schrade.
　　Press.—Iris Amador.
　　Professional Staff Member.—Jonathan A. Towers.
　　Staff Assistant.—Elizabeth Fox.
　　Legislative Correspondent.—Sara Hofstetter.
　Minority Staff Director.—Noe Kalipi (SH–143), 224–2074.
　　Deputy Staff Director for Health Programs.—Kim E. Lipsky.
　　Legislative Assistant.—Amanda Krohn.
　　Counsel.—Dahlia Melendrez.
　　Staff Assistants: Patrick Driscoll, Michelle A. Moreno.
　　Professional Staff Members: Edward B. Pusey, Alexandra Sardegna.
　Non-Designated:
　　Chief Clerk.—Zola McMurray.
　　Publications Assistant/Legislative Clerk/IT.—Matthew Lawrence.

SELECT AND SPECIAL COMMITTEES OF THE SENATE

Select Committee on Ethics

220 Hart Senate Office Building 20510, phone 224–2981, fax 224–7416

[Created pursuant to S. Res. 338, 88th Congress; amended by S. Res. 110, 95th Congress]

George V. Voinovich, of Ohio, *Chair*

Tim Johnson, of South Dakota, *Vice Chair*

Pat Roberts, of Kansas.
Craig Thomas, of Wyoming.

Daniel K. Akaka, of Hawaii.
Mark Pryor, of Arkansas.

STAFF

Staff Director/Chief Counsel.—Robert L. Walker.
  Counsels: Kenyen Brown, Katja Eichinger, Lydia Griggsby.
  Chief Clerk.—Annette M. Gillis.
  Professional Staff.—John Lewter.
  Systems Administrator.—Danny Remington.
  Staff Assistants: Charles Brown, Krystyna Rejrat, Dawne Vernon.

Select Committee on Intelligence

211 Hart Senate Office Building 20510–6475, phone 224–1700

http://www.senate.gov/~intelligence

[Created pursuant to S. Res. 400, 94th Congress]

Pat Roberts, of Kansas, *Chair*

John D. Rockefeller IV, of West Virginia, *Vice Chair*

Orrin G. Hatch, of Utah.
Mike DeWine, of Ohio.
Christopher S. Bond, of Missouri.
Trent Lott, of Mississippi.
Olympia J. Snowe, of Maine.
Chuck Hagel, of Nebraska.
Saxby Chambliss, of Georgia.

Carl Levin, of Michigan.
Dianne Feinstein, of California.
Ron Wyden, of Oregon.
Evan Bayh, of Indiana.
Barbara A. Mikulski, of Maryland.
Jon S. Corzine, of New Jersey

Ex Officio

William H. (Bill) Frist, of Tennessee.
John W. Warner, of Virginia

Harry Reid, of Nevada.

STAFF

Majority Staff Director.—Bill Duhnke.
Minority Staff Director.—Andy Johnson.
  Chief Clerk.—Kathleen P. McGhee.

375

Special Committee on Aging

G–31 Dirksen Senate Office Building 20510, phone 224–5364, fax 224–8660

http://aging.senate.gov

[Reauthorized pursuant to S. Res. 4, 95th Congress]

Gordon H. Smith, of Oregon, *Chair*

Richard C. Shelby, of Alabama.
Susan M. Collins, of Maine.
James M. Talent, of Missouri.
Elizabeth Dole, of North Carolina.
Mel Martinez, of Florida.
Larry E. Craig, of Idaho.
Rick Santorum, of Pennsylvania.
Conrad Burns, of Montana.
Lamar Alexander, of Tennessee.
Jim DeMint, of South Carolina.

Herb Kohl, of Wisconsin.
JAMES M. JEFFORDS, of Vermont.
Russell D. Feingold, of Wisconsin.
Ron Wyden, of Oregon.
Blanche L. Lincoln, of Arkansas.
Evan Bayh, of Indiana.
Thomas R. Carper, of Delaware.
Bill Nelson, of Florida.
Hillary Rodham Clinton, of New York.

STAFF

Majority Staff Director.—Catherine Finley.
    Legislative Assistant.—Tara Ward.
    Systems Administrator.—Michael Poteat.
    Professional Staff: Kara Getz, Mike Smith, Ken Van Pool.
    Staff Assistants: Carley Dillon, Jon Moss, Paul Perkins.
    Chief Clerk.—Patricia Hameister.
    Health Counsel.—Steve Irizarry.
    Legislative Correspondent.—Ali Burket.
Minority Staff (SH–628), 224–5364, fax 224–9926.
    Staff Director.—Julie Cohen.
    Senior Counsel.—Cecil Swamidoss.
    Senior Policy Advisors: Topher Spiro, Stacy Stordahl.
    Policy Advisor.—Mary Beth Stanton.
    Research Assistant.—Brad Wolters.

National Republican Senatorial Committee

425 Second Street NE., 20002, phone 675–6000, fax 675–6058

Elizabeth Dole, of North Carolina, *Chair*

STAFF

Executive Director.—Mark Stephens.
    Treasurer.—Stan Huckaby.
    Director of:
        Administration.—Mindy Anderson.
        Communications.—Brian Nick.
        Finance.—Nicole Sexton.
        Legal Counsel.—Steve Hoersting.
    Political Director.—Blaise Hazelwood.
        Research.—Gary Feld.

Erik Ablin	Jonathan Finger	Mike Kroeger
Todd Bachman	Megan Foran	Josh Kvernan
Ted Borie	Blair Foutch	Rachel Lavender
Thomas Breen	Will Fulgeras	Alex Lawhon
Keith Carter	Leslie Grabias	Chris Maiorana
Jamieson Clem	Tricia Hall	Andrew Maletz
Taylor Craig	Kelly Holdway	Jim Martin
Teresa DeRoco	Daniel Kayede	Helen Mathews

Thomas Maxwell
Megan Morgan
Joseph Osborn
Steve Pavlick
Meghann Peterlin

Amy Powers
Doug Robinson
Chris Scully
Emily Walton
David Welch

Emily Wiley
Gina Williams
Lindsey Williams
Whitney Williams
Kevin Wright

Republican Policy Committee
347 Russell Senate Office Building, phone 224–2946
fax 224–1235, http://rpc.senate.gov

Jon Kyl, of Arizona, *Chair*

STAFF

Staff Director.—Lawrence Willcox.
  Deputy Staff Director.—Katie Altshuler.
  Administrative Director.—Craig Cheney.
  Analysts:
    Defense Policy.—Mark Gaspers.
    Foreign Policy.—Daniel Fata.
    Natural Resources, Energy, and Environmental Policy.—Paul Georgia.
    Judiciary Issues.—Steven J. Duffield.
    Labor, Education, Welfare Policy.—Dana Barbieri.
    Health Care Policy.—Diane Major.
    Tax, Budget, and Economic Policy.—Mark Warren.
    Economic Policy.—Jason Thomas.
  Professional Staff:
    Editor.—Judy Gorman Prinkey.
    System Administrator/RVA Analyst.—Tom Pulju.
    Station Manager/Special Projects.—Carolyn Laird.
    Station Operators/Project Assistants: Julia Crouch, Natalie Farr.

Senate Republican Conference
405 Hart Senate Office Building, phone 224–2764
http://src.senate.gov

Chair.—Rick Santorum, of Pennsylvania.
Vice Chair.—Kay Bailey Hutchison, of Texas.
Committee Chairmen:
  Policy.—Jon Kyl, of Arizona.
  NRSC.—Elizabeth Dole, of North Carolina.

STAFF

Conference of the Majority (SH–405), 224–2764.
  Staff Director.—Mark Rodgers.
    Assistant to the Staff Director.—Kate Harris.
    Deputy Staff Director/Communications Director.—Robert Traynham.
    Assistant to Deputy Staff Director/Staff Assistant.—Katharine Gonzalez.
    Art Director.—Chris Angrisani.
    Senior Graphic Designer.—Laura Gill.
    Graphic Designer.—Nick Schweich.
    Director of Information Technology.—Tim Petty.
    Technology Specialist.—Aaron Broughton.
    Systems Administrator.—Eric Miller.
    Television Services Director.—Henry Peterson, Jr.
    Photographer.—Chris Ahlberg.
    Producer.—Cyrus Pearson.
    Radio Services Director.—Dave Hodgdon.
    Assistant Radio Services Director.—John Rankin.
    Director of Coalitions.—Barbara Ledeen.
    Senior Communications Advisor.—Elizabeth Keys.
    Office Manager.—Garrett Fahy.

Communications Managers: Dan Ronayne, Melissa Seckora.
Staff Assistant.—Jennifer Mahurin.
Vice Chair of the Conference Staff (SR–287), 224–1326
    Staff Director.—David Davis.
    Professional Staff Member.—Jeffrey Lee.

Democratic Policy Committee

419 Hart Senate Office Building, phone 224–3232

Byron Dorgan, of North Dakota, *Chair*

Patty Murray, of Washington, Regional Chair.
Evan Bayh, of Indiana, Regional Chair.
Jack Reed, of Rhode Island, Regional Chair.
Mary L. Landrieu, of Louisiana, Regional
  Chair.
Harry Reid, of Nevada, ex officio.
John D. Rockefeller IV, of West Virginia.
Daniel K. Akaka, of Hawaii.
Russell D. Feingold, of Wisconsin.
Joseph I. Lieberman, of Connecticut.
Dianne Feinstein, of California.

Ron Wyden, of Oregon.
Tim Johnson, of South Dakota.
Charles E. Schumer, of New York.
Blanche L. Lincoln, of Arkansas.
Bill Nelson, of Florida.
Thomas R. Carper, of Delaware.
Jon S. Corzine, of New Jersey.
Mark Dayton, of Minnesota.
Richard J. Durbin, of Illinois, ex officio.
Debbie Stabenow, of Michigan, ex officio.

STAFF

Staff Director.—Chuck Cooper.
    Assistant to the Staff Director.—Kathryn Copeland.
    Research Director.—Tim Gaffaney.
    Research Analyst.—Laura Fenimore.
    Policy Advisors: Brian Hickey, Tommy Ross.
    Publications Director.—Doug Connelly.
    Votes Analyst.—Michael Mozden.

Steering and Outreach Committee

712 Hart Senate Office Building, phone 224–9048

Hillary Rodham Clinton, of New York, *Chair*

John F. Kerry, of Massachusetts.
Daniel K. Inouye, of Hawaii.
Robert C. Byrd, of West Virginia.
Edward M. Kennedy, of Massachusetts.
Joseph R. Biden, Jr., of Delaware.
Patrick J. Leahy, of Vermont.
Christopher J. Dodd, of Connecticut.
Tom Harkin, of Iowa.
Max Baucus, of Montana.

Kent Conrad, of North Dakota.
Carl Levin, of Michigan.
Herbert H. Kohl, of Wisconsin.
Barbara Boxer, of California.
Jeff Bingaman, of New Mexico.
Paul Sarbanes, of Maryland.
Harry Reid, of Nevada.
Richard J. Durbin, of Illinois.
Mark Pryor, of Arkansas.

STAFF

Staff Director.—Dana E. Singiser.
    Associate Directors: Leslie Brown, Sabrina deSantiago, Andrea Minkow.
    Staff Assistant.—Jessica MacLeman.

Senate Democratic Communications Center

619 Hart Senate Office Building, phone 224–1430

Harry Reid, of Nevada, *Chair*

STAFF

Staff Director.—Jim Manley.
  Administrator.—Mary Helen Fuller.
  Radio Producer.—Ian Shifrin.
  Editors: Ike Blake, Toby Hayman, Mike Million.
  TV Producer.—Nathan Ackerman.
  Internet Technology Adviser.—Brian Barrie.
  Videographers: Clare Flood, Brian Jones, Kevin Kelleher.
  Press Assistant/Translator.—Carolina Alban.
  Graphic Design Specialist.—Lisa Pettibone.

Senate Democratic Conference

133 Hart Senate Office Building, phone 224–4822, fax 228–0325

Secretary.—*Debbie Stabenow,* of Michigan.
  Liaison to Leadership.—Sander Lurie.

Democratic Senatorial Campaign Committee

120 Maryland Avenue, NE., 20002, phone 224–2447

Charles Schumer, of New York, *Chair*

Barbara Boxer, of California, *Vice Chair*

Barack Obama, of Illinois, *Midwest Vice Chair*

Mark Pryor, of Arkansas, *Southern Vice Chair*

Jack Reed, of Rhode Island, *Northeast Vice Chair*

Ron Wyden, of Oregon, *Western Vice Chair*

Harry Reid, of Nevada, *Democratic Leader*

STAFF

Executive Director.—J.B. Poersch.
  Communications Director.—Phil Singer.
  PAC Director.—Eli Joseph.
    PAC Deputy Director.—Alison Dooley.
  Political Director.—Guy Cecil.
  Information Systems Director.—Jude Meche.
  Direct Marketing Director.—Robin Brunstrum.
  Research Director.—Katie Barge.
  Finance Director.—Julianna Smoot.
    Finance Chief of Staff.—Chris Koob.
    Special Assistant to Finance Director.—Stacy Koo.
    Finance Assistants: Michael Dykes, Allie Eichenbaum, Meredith Levine, Erica Price.
  Southern Finance Director.—Jen Medley.
    Southern Finance Deputy Director.—Jill McCarthy.
  Mid Atlantic Finance Director.—Meg Jongeward.
  Mid West Finance Director.—Michael O'Neil.
  Western Regional Finance Deputy Director.—Jessica Straus.
  Director of Information Systems.—Jude Meche.
  Comptroller.—Darlene Setter.
    Deputy Comptrollers: Dominique King Ancheta, Len Lloyd.

Special Assistant to the Chairman.—David Nurnberg.
Assistant to the Executive Director.—Nicki Sacco.
Chief Operating Officer.—Karen Hancox.
Copywriter.—Julie Chon.
Senior Consultant, Political.—Joe Hansen.
Legal Counsel.—Marc Elias.
Direct Marketing.—Todd Plants.
Systems.—Tim Nelson.
Senate Services.—Ryan Ramsey.
Events Planner.—Patti Ogle.
Call Time Manager.—Lateisha Garrett.
Receptionist.—Marisol Ponce de Leon.

OFFICERS AND OFFICIALS OF THE SENATE

Capitol Telephone Directory, 224–3121
Senate room prefixes:
Capitol—S, Russell Senate Office Building—SR
Dirksen Senate Office Building—SD, Hart Senate Office Building—SH

PRESIDENT OF THE SENATE

Vice President of the United States and President of the Senate.—Richard B. Cheney.

The Ceremonial Office of the Vice President is S–212 in the Capitol. The Vice President has offices in the Dirksen Office Building, Eisenhower Executive Office Building (EEOB) and the White House (West Wing).

Chief of Staff.—Lewis Libby, EEOB, Room 276, 456–9000.
  Deputy Chief of Staff.—Dean McGrath, EEOB, Room 276, 456–9000.
  Counsel to the Vice President.—David Addington, EEOB, Room 268, 456–9089.
  Counselor to the Vice President.—Steve Schmidt, EEOB, Room 272, 456–3880.
  Principal Deputy, National Security Advisor to the Vice President.—Victoria Nuland, EEOB, Room 298, 456–9501.
  Assistant to the Vice President for Legislative Affairs.—Brenda Becker, EEOB, Room 285, 456–6774.
  Assistant to the Vice President for Domestic Policy.—Kevin O'Donovan, EEOB, Room 286, 456–2728.
  Executive Assistant to the Vice President.—Debra Heiden, West Wing, 456–7549.
  Assistant to the Vice President and Deputy Chief of Staff of Operations.—Claire O'Donnell, EEOB, Room 272, 456–6770.
  Chief of Staff to Mrs. Cheney.—Stephanie Lundberg, EEOB, Room 200, 456–7458.
  Deputy Assistant to the Vice President and Director of Scheduling.—Elizabeth Kleppe, EEOB, Room 279, 456–6773.
  Director of Correspondence.—Cecelia Boyer, EEOB, Room 265, 456–9002.

PRESIDENT PRO TEMPORE

S–237 The Capitol, phone 224–1034

President Pro Tempore of the Senate.—Ted Stevens.
  Director.—Jennifer Mies Lowe.
  Staff Assistant.—Claire Jolly, 224–5811.

MAJORITY LEADER

S–230 The Capitol, phone 224–3135, fax 228–1264

Majority Leader.—William H. (Bill) Frist.
  Chief of Staff.—Eric Ueland.
    Assistant to the Chief of Staff.—Meg Gregory.
  Chief Counsel.—Allen Hicks.
  Legislative Counsel.—Brandi Wilson White.
  Policy Advisor and Counsel.—Rohit Kumar.
  Policy Advisors: Bill Hoagland, Amy Holmes, Libby Jarvis, Dean Rosen, Bill Witcherman.
  Administrative Director.—Darla Cassell.
  Communications Director.—Bob Stevenson.
    Deputy Communications Director.—Nick Smith.

Policy Director for National Security Affairs.—Mark Esper.
Director of Special Projects.—Holly Hammond Nass.
Director of Speechwriting and Chief Speechwriter.—Rob Hoppin.
Systems Administrator.—Judson Blewett.
Press Secretary.—Amy (Well) Call.
Executive Assistant.—Ramona Lessen.
Special Assistant.—Brook Whitfield.
Personal Assistant.—Brendan Kelly.
Speechwriter.—Eli Lehrer.
Staff Assistants: Valerie Edwards, Louise Riley.
Legislative Correspondent.—Steve Kline.
Consultant.—Johannes (Hanns) Kuttner.

MAJORITY WHIP

S–208 The Capitol, phone 224–2708

Majority Whip.—Mitch McConnell.
  Chief of Staff.—Kyle Simmons.
  Policy Director.—Michael Solon.
  Legal Counsel.—John Abegg.
  Floor Counsel.—Brian Lewis.
  Whip Liaisons: Malloy McDaniel, Laura Pemberton.
  Floor Assistant.—Serena Underwood.
  Director of Administration.—Nan Mosher.
  Personal Assistant.—Brad Sullivan.
  Staff Assistant.—Anneke Green.

DEMOCRATIC LEADER

S–221 The Capitol, phone 224–2158, fax 224–7362

Democratic Leader.—Harry Reid.
  Chief of Staff.—Susan McCue.
    Deputy Chief of Staff.—Gary Myrick.
  Senior Legislative and Policy Director.—Randy Devalk.
  Chief Counsel.—Kevin Keyes.
  Scheduler.—Callie Fuselier.
  Executive Assistant to the Senator.—Janice Shelton.
  Executive Assistant to the Chief of Staff.—Erin Eagan.
  Staff Director.—Jim Manley.
  Press Secretary.—Tessa Hafen.

ASSISTANT DEMOCRATIC LEADER

S–321 The Capitol, phone 224–9447

Assistant Democratic Leader.—Dick Durbin.
  Staff Director.—Pat Souders.
  Director of Operations.—Sally Brown-Shaklee.
  Personal Assistant/Scheduler.—Andrea Del'Aguila.
  Communications Director.—Joe Shoemaker.
  Press Secretaries: Angela Benander, Bill Burton.
  Speechwriter.—Molly Rowley.
  Senior Floor Counsel.—Anne McGuire.
  Floor Counsel.—Chris Kang.
  Special Assistant.—Michael Delich.
  Staff Assistant.—Puja Mehta.

OFFICE OF THE SECRETARY

S–312 The Capitol, phone 224–3622

EMILY J. REYNOLDS, Secretary of the Senate; elected and sworn in as the 31st Secretary of the Senate on January 7, 2003; born and raised in the State of Tennessee; graduate of Stephens College, Columbia, MO; Chief of Staff to U.S. Senator Bill Frist, 2001–2002; State Director for U.S. Senator Bill Frist, 1995–2000; Deputy Campaign Manager and Finance Director, Dr. Bill Frist for U.S. Senate, 1994; Active in several U.S. Senate campaigns, and Bush/Quayle, 1992; served as Deputy Director of National Coalitions, 1985–1993; Special Assistant, U.S. Senate Majority Leader, Howard H. Baker, Jr., 1980–1984; Associate Director of Admissions, Stephens College, 1978–1980.

Secretary of the Senate.—Emily J. Reynolds (S–312), 224–3622.
  Chief of Staff.—Sammie G. Young, Jr. (S–333), 224–5636.
  Capitol Offices Liaison.—Gerald Thompson (SB–36), 224–1483.
Assistant Secretary of the Senate.—Mary Suit Jones (S–414C), 224–2114.
  General Counsel.—Adam Bramwell (S–333), 224–8789.
  Executive Accounts Administrator.—Zoraida Torres (S–414B), 224–7099.
  Director (LIS Project Office).—Marsha Misenhimer (SD–B44A), 224–2500.
Bill Clerk.—Mary Anne Clarkson (S–123), 224–2120.
Director of:
  Captioning Services.—JoEllen R. Dicken (ST–54), 224–4321.
  Conservation and Preservation.—Carl Fritter, (S–416), 224–4550.
Curator.—Diane Skvarla (S–411), 224–2955.
Daily Digest, Editor.—Linda E. Sebold (S–421 & S–421A), 224–2658.
  Assistant Editor.—Ken Dean, 224–2658.
Disbursing Office, Financial Clerk.—Timothy S. Wineman (SH–1?7), 224–3205.
  Assistant Financial Clerk.—Chris J. Doby, 224–3208.
Enrolling Clerk.—Joe Monahan (S–139), 224–7108.
  Assistant Enrolling Clerk.—Margarida Curtis, 224–8427.
Executive Clerk.—Michelle Haynes (S–138), 224–4341.
  Assistant Executive Clerk.—Chad Klutts, 224–1918.
Historian.—Richard A. Baker (SH–201), 224–6900.
  Associate Historian.—Donald A. Ritchie, 224–6816.
  Assistant Historian.—Betty K. Koed, 224–0753.
Human Resources, Director.—Michelle Jezycki (SH–231B), 224–3625.
Information Systems, Systems Administrator.—Dan Kulnis (S–422), 224–4883.
Webmaster.—Cheri Allen, 224–2020.
Interparliamentary Services, Director.—Sally Walsh (SH–808), 224–3047.
Journal Clerk.—Scott Sanborn (S–135), 224–4650.
Legislative Clerk.—David J. Tinsley (S–134), 224–4350.
  Assistant Legislative Clerk.—Kathleen Alvarez, 224–3630.
Librarian.—Gregory C. Harness (SR–B15), 224–3313.
Official Reporters of Debates, Chief Reporter.—Jerald D. Linell (S–410A), 224–7525.
Coordinator of the Record.—Petie Gallacher, 224–1238.
Morning Business Editor.—Jack Hickman (S–123), 224–3079.
Parliamentarian.—Alan S. Frumin (S–133), 224–6128.
  Senior Assistant Parliamentarian.—Peter Robinson, 224–5133.
Printing and Document Services, Director.—Karen Moore (SH–B04), 224–0205.
  Assistant to the Director.—Bud Johnson, 224–2555.
Public Records, Superintendent.—Pamela B. Gavin (SH–232), 224–0762.
  Assistant Superintendent.—Elizabeth Williams, 224–0329.
Information Specialist for—
  Campaign Finance.—Raymond Davis, 224–0761.
  Ethics and Disclosure.—Jennifer Terrill, 224–0763.
Lobbying and Foreign Travel.—Erica Omorogieva, 224–0758.
Senate Chief Counsel for Employment.—Jean Manning (SH–103), 224–5424.
Senate Gift Shop, Director.—Ernie LePire (SDG–42), 224–7308.
Senate Page School, Principal.—Kathryn S. Weeden, 224–3926.
Senate Security, Director.—Michael P. DiSilvestro (S–407), 224–5632.
  Deputy Director.—Margaret Garland, 224–5632.
Stationery, Keeper of the Stationery.—Michael V. McNeal, 224–3381.
  Assistant Keeper of the Stationery.—Tony Super, 224–4846.
Joint Office of Education and Training, Director.—Peggy Greenberg (SH–121), 224–5969.

OFFICE OF THE CHAPLAIN

S–332 The Capitol, phone 224–2510, fax 224–9686

BARRY C. BLACK, Chaplain, U.S. Senate; born in Baltimore, MD, on November 1, 1948; education: Bachelor of Arts, Theology, Oakwood College, 1970; Master of Divinity, Andrews Theological Seminary, 1973; Master of Arts, Counseling, North Carolina Central University, 1978; Doctor of Ministry, Theology, Eastern Baptist Seminary, 1982; Master of Arts, Management, Salve Regina University, 1989; Doctor of Philosophy, Psychology, United States International University, 1996; military service: U.S. Navy, 1976–2003; rising to the rank of Rear Admiral; Chief of Navy Chaplains, 2000–2003; awards: Legion of Merit Medal; Defense Meritorious Service Medal; Meritorious Service Medals (two awards); Navy and Marine Corps Commendation Medals (two awards); 1995 NAACP Renowned Service Award; family: married to Brenda; three children: Barry II, Brendan, and Bradford.

Chaplain of the Senate.—Barry C. Black.
  Chief of Staff.—Alan N. Keiran, 224–7456.
  Communications Director.—Meg Saunders, 224–3894.
  Program/Office Manager.—Carlynne Alberts, 224–2048.

OFFICE OF THE SERGEANT AT ARMS

S–151 The Capitol, phone 224–2341, fax 224–7690

WILLIAM H. PICKLE, Sergeant at Arms, U.S. Senate; elected and sworn in as 37th Sergeant at Arms on March 17, 2003; education: attended American University; B.A., Metro State College, Denver, CO; military service: First Air Cavalry Division in Vietnam; infantry sergeant, and MedEvac helicopter door gunner, 1968–1969; awards: Bronze Star, Purple Heart, two Army Commendation Medals, Combat Infantryman Badge, seven Air Medals; professional: U.S. Secret Service, 26 years, attaining the positions of Deputy Assistant Director for Human Resources and Training, and as Special Agent in Charge of the Vice Presidential Protective Division; Deputy Inspector General for the Department of Labor; first Federal Security Director of the Transportation Security Administration; family: married, with two children.

Sergeant at Arms.—William H. Pickle.
  Deputy Sergeant at Arms.—Lynne M. Halbrooks.
  Administrative Assistant.—Rick Edwards, SB–8.
  Executive Assistant.—Nancy Erickson, ST–39, 224–1047.
  Assistant Sergeant at Arms for Police Operations.—Al V. Concordia, SD–150, 224–7027.
  Assistant Sergeant at Arms for Operations.—Esther L. Gordon (Postal Square), 224–7747.
  Assistant Sergeant at Arms and Chief Information Officer.—J. Greg Hanson, Ph.D., (Postal Square), 224–9430.
  Assistant Sergeant at Arms for Security and Emergency Prepardness.—Chuck Kaylor (Postal Square), 224–1404.

EXECUTIVE OFFICE

Appointment Desk Manager.—Joy Ogden, North Door Capitol Building, 1st Floor, 224–6304.
Capitol Information Officer.—Laura Parker, S–151, 224–2341.
Doorkeeper Supervisor.—Myron J. Fleming, SB–6, 224–1879.
Employee Assistance Program Administrator.—Christy Prietsch, Hart Senate Office Building, 228–3902.
Protocol Officer.—Becky Daugherty, S–151, 224–2341.

CAPITOL FACILITIES

Capitol Facilities Manager.—Skip Rouse, ST–62, 224–4171.

CENTRAL OPERATIONS

Director of Central Operations.—Juanita Rilling, SD–G61A, 224–8587.
  Administrative Services Manager.—Joann Soults, SD–G84, 224–4716.
  Hair Care Manager.—Mario D'Angelo, SR–B70, 224–4560.
  Parking and ID Manager.—Ron Fritts, SD–G58, 224–9200.

Photo Studio Manager.—Bill Allen, SD–G85, 224–6000.
Printing, Graphics and Direct Mail Manager.—Hazel Getty, SD–G82, 224–5981.

FINANCIAL MANAGEMENT

Chief Financial Officer.—Christopher Dey (Postal Square), 224–6292.
Accounting and Budget Manager.—Peter DuBois, 224–1499.
Accounts Payable Manager.—Roy McElwee, 224–6074.
Financial Analysis Manager.—David Salem, 224–8844.
Procurement Manager.—David Baker, 224–2547.

HUMAN RESOURCES

Director of Human Resources.—Doug Fertig, SH–142, 224–2889.
Director of Human Resources.—Jean McComish (acting), 224–2797.
SAA Safety Office Officer.—Irvin Queja, 228–0823.
Senate Placement Officer Manager.—Brian Bean, 224–9167.
Workers' Compensation Office Manager.—Catherine Modeste Brooks, 224–3796.

IT SUPPORT SERVICES

Director of IT Support Services.—Kimball Winn (Postal Square), 224–0459.
Desktop/LAN Support Manager.—Tim Dean, 224–3564.
Office Equipment Services Manager.—Dave Saville, 224–6779.
Telecom Services Manager.—Rick Kauffman, 224–9293.

MEDIA GALLERIES

Director of the Daily Press Gallery.—S. Joseph Keenan, S–316, 224–0241.
Director of the Periodical Press Gallery.—Edward V. Pesce, S–320, 224–0265.
Director of the Press Photographers Gallery.—Jeff Kent, S–317, 224–6548.
Director of the Radio and Television Gallery.—Michael Mastrian, S–325, 224–7610.

OFFICE OF EDUCATION AND TRAINING

Director of the Office of Education and Training.—Peggy Greenberg, SH–121, 224–5969.

OFFICE OF SECURITY AND EMERGENCY PREPARDNESS

Deputy Assistant Sergeant at Arms for Security and Emergency Preparedness.—Michael Johnson (Postal Square), 224–1969.
Continuity Programs Executive Manager.—Curtis Bartell, 228–4045.
Security Planning and Operations Executive Manager.—Dick Attridge, 224–3691.

OFFICE SUPPORT SERVICES

Administrative Services Executive Manager.—Barbara Graybill (Postal Square), 224–5402.
Customer Support Manager.—Dave Cape, SD–180, 224–0310.
State Office Liaison.—Jeanne Tessieri (Postal Square), 224–5409.

PAGE PROGRAM

Director of the Page Program.—Elizabeth Roach (Webster Hall), 228–1291.

POLICE OPERATIONS

Deputy Assistant Sergeant at Arms for Police Operations.—Bret Swanson, SD–150, 224–7052.

PROCESS MANAGEMENT & INNOVATION

Director of Process Management & Innovation.—Ed Jankus (Postal Square), 224–7780.
  IT Research & Deployment Manager.—Steve Walker, 224–1768.
  Program Management Manager.—Joe Eckert, 224–2982.

RECORDING STUDIO

Recording Studio Manager.—Dave Bass, ST–29, 224–4979.

SENATE POST OFFICE

Senate Postmaster.—Joe Collins, SD–B23, 224–5675.
  Superintendent of Mails.—Alan Stone, SD–B28, 224–1060.

TECHNOLOGY DEVELOPMENT

Director of Technology Development.—Tracy Williams (Postal Square), 224–8157.
  Enterprise IT Operations Manager.—Karlos Davis, 224–3322.
  Information Technology Security Manager.—Paul Grabow, 224–4966.
  Inter/Intranet & Research Branch Manager.—Tom Meenan, 224–8620.
  Network Engineering & Management Manager.—Jim Harrell, 224–4181.
  Systems Development Services Manager.—Jay Moore, 224–0092.

OFFICE OF THE MAJORITY SECRETARY
S–337 The Capitol, phone 224–3835, fax 224–2860

Secretary for the Majority.—David Schiappa (S–337).
  Assistant Secretary for the Majority.—Laura Dove (S–229).

S–226 Majority Cloakroom, phone 224–6191

Cloakroom Assistants: Conner Collins, Robert Duncan, Noelle Ringel, Robert White.

S–335 Republican Legislative Scheduling, phone 224–5456

Legislative Scheduler.—Caroline Johnson.
  Floor Assistant.—Dan Dukes (S–226), phone 224–6191.
  Administrative Assistant.—Marilyn J. Sayler (S–337).

OFFICE OF THE MINORITY SECRETARY
S–309 The Capitol, phone 224–3735

Secretary for the Minority.—Martin P. Paone.
  Assistant Secretary for the Minority.—Lula J. Davis (S–118), 224–5551.
  Administrative Assistant to the Secretary.—Nancy Iacomini.

S–225 Democratic Cloakroom, phone 224–4691

Cloakroom Assistants: Joe Lapia, Stacy Rich, Ben Vaughn, Bret Wincup.

OFFICE OF THE LEGISLATIVE COUNSEL
668 Dirksen Senate Office Building, phone 224–6461, fax 224–0567

Legislative Counsel.—James W. Fransen.
  Deputy Legislative Counsel.—William F. Jensen III.
  Senior Counsels: Anthony C. Coe, Polly W. Craighill, Gary L. Endicott, Mark J. Mathiesen.

Assistant Counsels: Charles E. Armstrong, Laura M. Ayoud, William R. Baird, Heather L. Burnham, Darcie E. Chan, Kevin M. Davis, Stephanie Easley, Ruth A. Ernst, Amy E. Gaynor, John A. Goetcheus, Elizabeth Aldridge King, Mark S. Koster, Matthew D. McGhie, Mark M. McGunagle.
Staff Attorneys: Heather L. Arpin, Robert A. Grant, John A. Henderson, Michelle L. Johnson-Weider, Stacy E. Kern, Kelly J. Malone, Kristin K. Romero.
*Systems Integrator.—*Thomas E. Cole.
*Office Manager.—*Donna L. Pasqualino.
Staff Assistants: Kimberly Bourne-Goldring, Patricia E. Harris, Ahmika V. Isaac, Barbara J. Lyskawa, Rebekah J. Musgrove, Diane E. Nesmeyer, Gretchen E. Walter.

OFFICE OF SENATE LEGAL COUNSEL
642 Hart Senate Office Building, phone 224–4435, fax 224–3391

*Senate Legal Counsel.—*Patricia Mack Bryan.
*Deputy Senate Legal Counsel.—*Morgan J. Frankel.
Assistant Senate Legal Counsels: Thomas E. Caballero, Grant R. Vinik.
*Systems Administrator/Legal Assistant.—*Sara Fox Jones.
*Administrative Assistant.—*Kathleen M. Parker.

STANDING COMMITTEES OF THE HOUSE

[Republicans in roman; Democrats in *italic*; Independents in SMALL CAPS; Resident Commissioner and Delegates in **boldface**]

[Room numbers beginning with H are in the Capitol, with CHOB in the Cannon House Office Building, with LHOB in the Longworth House Office Building, with RHOB in the Rayburn House Office Building, with H1 in O'Neill House Office Building, and with H2 in the Ford House Office Building]

Agriculture

1301 Longworth House Office Building, phone 225–2171, fax 225–0917

http://www.house.gov/agriculture

meets first Wednesday of each month

Bob Goodlatte, of Virginia, *Chair*

John A. Boehner, of Ohio.
Richard W. Pombo, of California.
Terry Everett, of Alabama.
Frank D. Lucas, of Oklahoma.
Jerry Moran, of Kansas.
William L. Jenkins, of Tennessee.
Gil Gutknecht, of Minnesota.
Robin Hayes, of North Carolina.
Timothy V. Johnson, of Illinois.
Tom Osborne, of Nebraska.
Mike Pence, of Indiana.
Sam Graves, of Missouri.
Jo Bonner, of Alabama.
Mike Rogers, of Alabama.
Steven King, of Iowa.
Marilyn N. Musgrave, of Colorado.
Devin Nunes, of California.
Randy Neugebauer, of Texas.
Charles W. Boustany, Jr., of Louisiana.
John J.H. (Joe) Schwarz, of Michigan.
John R. (Randy) Kuhl, Jr., of New York.
Virginia Foxx, of North Carolina.
K. Michael Conaway, of Texas.
Jeff Fortenberry, of Nebraska.

Collin C. Peterson, of Minnesota.
Tim Holden, of Pennsylvania.
Mike McIntyre, of North Carolina.
Bob Etheridge, of North Carolina.
Joe Baca, of California.
Ed Case, of Hawaii.
Dennis A. Cardoza, of California.
David Scott, of Georgia.
Jim Marshall, of Georgia.
Stephanie Herseth, of South Dakota.
G.K. Butterfield, of North Carolina.
Henry Cuellar, of Texas.
Charlie Melancon, of Louisiana.
Jim Costa, of California.
John T. Salazar, of Colorado.
John Barrow, of Georgia.
Earl Pomeroy, of North Dakota.
Leonard L. Boswell, of Iowa.
Rick Larsen, of Washington.
Lincoln Davis, of Tennessee.
Ben Chandler, of Kentucky.

SUBCOMMITTEES

[The chairman and ranking minority member are ex officio (voting) members of all subcommittees on which they do not serve.]

Conservation, Credit, Rural Development, and Research

Frank D. Lucas, of Oklahoma, *Chair*

Jerry Moran, of Kansas.	*Tim Holden, of Pennsylvania.*
Tom Osborne, of Nebraska.	*Henry Cuellar, of Texas.*
Sam Graves, of Missouri.	*Mike McIntyre, of North Carolina.*
Mike Rogers, of Alabama.	*Bob Etheridge, of North Carolina.*
Steven King, of Iowa.	*Ed Case, of Hawaii.*
Charles W. Boustany, Jr., of Louisiana.	*Lincoln Davis, of Tennessee.*
John J.H. (Joe) Schwarz, of Michigan.	*Stephanie Herseth, of South Dakota.*
Jeff Fortenberry, of Nebraska.	*G.K. Butterfield, of North Carolina.*

Department Operations, Oversight, Dairy, Nutrition, and Forestry

Gil Gutknecht, of Minnesota, *Chair*

Richard W. Pombo, of California.	*Joe Baca, of California.*
Jerry Moran, of Kansas.	*Dennis A. Cardoza, of California.*
Jo Bonner, of Alabama.	*G.K. Butterfield, of North Carolina.*
Devin Nunes, of California.	*Tim Holden, of Pennsylvania.*
Virginia Foxx, of North Carolina.	*Henry Cuellar, of Texas.*
Jeff Fortenberry, of Nebraska.	*Jim Costa, of California.*

General Farm Commodities and Risk Management

Jerry Moran, of Kansas, *Chair*

John A. Boehner, of Ohio.	*Bob Etheridge, of North Carolina.*
Terry Everett, of Alabama.	*John T. Salazar, of Colorado.*
Frank D. Lucas, of Oklahoma.	*Jim Marshall, of Georgia.*
William L. Jenkins, of Tennessee.	*Stephanie Herseth, of South Dakota.*
Timothy V. Johnson, of Illinois.	*G.K. Butterfield, of North Carolina.*
Mike Pence, of Indiana.	*Charlie Melancon, of Louisiana.*
Sam Graves, of Missouri.	*John Barrow, of Georgia.*
Jo Bonner, of Alabama.	*Earl Pomeroy, of North Dakota.*
Steven King, of Iowa.	*Leonard L. Boswell, of Iowa.*
Marilyn N. Musgrave, of Colorado.	*Rick Larsen, of Washington.*
Randy Neugebauer, of Texas.	*Ben Chandler, of Kentucky.*
Charles W. Boustany, Jr., of Louisiana.	*David Scott, of Georgia.*
K. Michael Conaway, of Texas.	*Jim Costa, of California.*
Jeff Fortenberry, of Nebraska.	

Livestock and Horticulture

Robin Hayes, of North Carolina, *Chair*

John A. Boehner, of Ohio.	*Ed Case, of Hawaii.*
Richard W. Pombo, of California.	*David Scott, of Georgia.*
Tom Osborne, of Nebraska.	*Stephanie Herseth, of South Dakota.*
Mike Pence, of Indiana.	*Jim Costa, of California.*
Mike Rogers, of Alabama.	*Dennis A. Cardoza, of California.*
Steven King, of Iowa.	*John T. Salazar, of Colorado.*
Devin Nunes, of California.	*Leonard L. Boswell, of Iowa.*
Randy Neugebauer, of Texas.	*Rick Larsen, of Washington.*
John R. (Randy) Kuhl, Jr., of New York.	*Earl Pomeroy, of North Dakota.*
Virginia Foxx, of North Carolina.	*John Barrow, of Georgia.*
K. Michael Conaway, of Texas.	

Specialty Crops and Foreign Agriculture Programs

William L. Jenkins, of Tennessee, *Chair*

Terry Everett, of Alabama.
Gil Gutknecht, of Minnesota.
Robin Hayes, of North Carolina.
Mike Rogers, of Alabama.
Randy Neugebauer, of Texas.
John J.H. (Joe) Schwarz, of Michigan.
Virginia Foxx, of North Carolina.

Mike McIntyre, of North Carolina.
Jim Marshall, of Georgia.
Charlie Melancon, of Louisiana.
John Barrow, of Georgia.
David Scott, of Georgia.
Ben Chandler, of Kentucky.
Henry Cuellar, of Texas.

STAFF

Committee on Agriculture (1301 LHOB), 225–2171, fax 225–0917.
  Majority Staff Director.—William E. O'Conner, Jr.
    Deputy Chief of Staff.—Brent W. Gattis.
    Chief Clerk.—Callista Gingrich.
    Administrator.—Diane Keyser.
    Printing Editor.—James Cahill.
    Director, Information Systems.—Merrick Munday.
    Chief Counsel.—Kevin J. Kramp.
    Associate Counsels: Jen Daulby, Stephanie Myers.
    Legislative Clerk.—Debbie Smith.
    Deputy Communications Director.—Alise Kowalski.
    Chief Economist.—Craig Jagger.
    Senior Professional Staff: Dave Ebersole, Lynn Gallagher, Alan Mackey, Pete Thomson.
    Professional Staff: John Goldberg, Bill Imbergamo, Elizabeth Parker.
    Legislative Assistants: Claire Folbre, Matt Schertz.
    Staff Assistants: Jeremy Carter, Mike Dunlap, Brandon Farris, Josh Maxwell, Matt Smith.
  Subcommittee Staff Directors:
    Conservation, Credit, Rural Development and Research.—Ryan Weston.
    Department Operations, Oversight, Dairy, Nutrition and Forestry.—Benjamin Anderson.
    General Farm Commodities and Risk Management.—Tyler Wegmeyer.
    Livestock and Horticulture.—Pam Miller.
    Specialty Crops and Foreign Agriculture Programs.—Pelham Straughn.
  Minority Staff Director.—Rob Larew (1305 LHOB), 5–0317.
    Office Manager.—Sharon Rusnak.
    Press Secretary.—April Demert, 5–6878.
    Counsel.—Andy Baker (1010 LHOB), 5–3069.
    Assistant Counsel.—Tony Jackson (1002 LHOB), 5–8903.
    Economist.—Howard (Chip) Conley (1041 LHOB), 5–2349.
    Professional Staff: Chandler Goule (1010 LHOB), 5–8407; Russell Middleton (1010 LHOB), 5–1496; John Riley (1305 LHOB), 5–7987; Anne Simmons (1010 LHOB), 5–1494.
  Subcommittee Minority Consultants:
    Conservation, Credit, Rural Development and Research.—Anne Simmons.
    Department Operations, Oversight, Dairy, Nutrition and Forestry.—Tony Jackson.
    General Farm Commodities and Risk Management.—John Riley.
    Livestock and Horticulture.—Chandler Goule.
    Specialty Crops and Foreign Agriculture Programs.—Russell Middleton.

Appropriations

H–218 The Capitol, phone 225–2771

http://www.house.gov/appropriations

meets first Wednesday of each month

Jerry Lewis, of California, *Chair*

C.W. Bill Young, of Florida.
Ralph Regula, of Ohio.
Harold Rogers, of Kentucky.
Frank R. Wolf, of Virginia.
Jim Kolbe, of Arizona.
James T. Walsh, of New York.
Charles H. Taylor, of North Carolina.
David L. Hobson, of Ohio.
Ernest J. Istook, Jr., of Oklahoma.
Henry Bonilla, of Texas.
Joe Knollenberg, of Michigan.
Jack Kingston, of Georgia.
Rodney P. Frelinghuysen, of New Jersey.
Roger F. Wicker, of Mississippi.
Randy (Duke) Cunningham, of California.
Todd Tiahrt, of Kansas.
Zach Wamp, of Tennessee.
Tom Latham, of Iowa.
Anne M. Northup, of Kentucky.
Robert B. Aderholt, of Alabama.
Jo Ann Emerson, of Missouri.
Kay Granger, of Texas.
John E. Peterson, of Pennsylvania.
Virgil H. Goode, Jr., of Virginia.
John T. Doolittle, of California.
Ray LaHood, of Illinois.
John E. Sweeney, of New York.
Don Sherwood, of Pennsylvania.
Dave Weldon, of Florida.
Michael K. Simpson, of Idaho.
John Abney Culberson, of Texas.
Mark Steven Kirk, of Illinois.
Ander Crenshaw, of Florida.
Dennis R. Rehberg, of Montana.
John Carter, of Texas.
Rodney Alexander, of Louisiana.

David R. Obey, of Wisconsin.
John P. Murtha, of Pennsylvania.
Norman D. Dicks, of Washington.
Martin Olav Sabo, of Minnesota.
Steny H. Hoyer, of Maryland.
Alan B. Mollohan, of West Virginia.
Marcy Kaptur, of Ohio.
Peter J. Visclosky, of Indiana.
Nita M. Lowey, of New York.
José E. Serrano, of New York.
Rosa L. DeLauro, of Connecticut.
James P. Moran, of Virginia.
John W. Olver, of Massachusetts.
Ed Pastor, of Arizona.
David E. Price, of North Carolina.
Chet Edwards, of Texas.
Robert E. (Bud) Cramer, Jr., of Alabama.
Patrick J. Kennedy, of Rhode Island.
James E. Clyburn, of South Carolina.
Maurice D. Hinchey, of New York.
Lucille Roybal-Allard, of California.
Sam Farr, of California.
Jesse L. Jackson, Jr., of Illinois.
Carolyn C. Kilpatrick, of Michigan.
Allen Boyd, of Florida.
Chaka Fattah, of Pennsylvania.
Steven R. Rothman, of New Jersey.
Sanford D. Bishop, Jr., of Georgia.
Marion Berry, of Arkansas.

SUBCOMMITTEES

[The chairman and ranking minority member are ex officio (voting) members of all
subcommittees on which they do not serve.]

Agriculture, Rural Development, Food and Drug Administration, and Related Agencies

Henry Bonilla, of Texas, *Chair*

Jack Kingston, of Georgia.
Tom Latham, of Iowa.
Jo Ann Emerson, of Missouri.
Virgil H. Goode, Jr., of Virginia.
Ray LaHood, of Illinois.
John T. Doolittle, of California.
Rodney Alexander, of Louisiana.

Rosa L. DeLauro, of Connecticut.
Maurice D. Hinchey, of New York.
Sam Farr, of California.
Allen Boyd, of Florida.
Marcy Kaptur, of Ohio.

Defense

C.W. Bill Young, of Florida, *Chair*

David L. Hobson, of Ohio.
Henry Bonilla, of Texas.
Randy (Duke) Cunningham, of California.
Rodney P. Frelinghuysen, of New Jersey.
Todd Tiahrt, of Kansas.
Roger F. Wicker, of Mississippi.
Jack Kingston, of Georgia.
Kay Granger, of Texas.

John P. Murtha, of Pennsylvania.
Norman D. Dicks, of Washington.
Martin Olav Sabo, of Minnesota.
Peter J. Visclosky, of Indiana.
James P. Moran, of Virginia.
Marcy Kaptur, of Ohio.

Energy and Water Development, and Related Agencies

David L. Hobson, of Ohio, *Chair*

Rodney P. Frelinghuysen, of New Jersey.
Tom Latham, of Iowa.
Zach Wamp, of Tennessee.
Jo Ann Emerson, of Missouri.
John T. Doolittle, of California.
Michael K. Simpson, of Idaho.
Dennis R. Rehberg, of Montana.

Peter J. Visclosky, of Indiana.
Chet Edwards, of Texas.
Ed Pastor, of Arizona.
James E. Clyburn, of South Carolina.
Marion Berry, of Arkansas.

Foreign Operations, Export Financing, and Related Programs

Jim Kolbe, of Arizona, *Chair*

Joe Knollenberg, of Michigan.
Mark Steven Kirk, of Illinois.
Ander Crenshaw, of Florida.
Don Sherwood, of Pennsylvania.
John E. Sweeney, of New York.
Dennis R. Rehberg, of Montana.
John Carter, of Texas.

Nita M. Lowey, of New York.
Jesse L. Jackson, Jr., of Illinois.
Carolyn C. Kilpatrick, of Michigan.
Steven R. Rothman, of New Jersey.
Chaka Fattah, of Pennsylvania.

Homeland Security

Harold Rogers, of Kentucky, *Chair*

Zach Wamp, of Tennessee.
Tom Latham, of Iowa.
Jo Ann Emerson, of Missouri.
John E. Sweeney, of New York.
Jim Kolbe, of Arizona.
Ernest J. Istook, Jr., of Oklahoma.
Ray LaHood, of Illinois.
Ander Crenshaw, of Florida.
John Carter, of Texas.

Martin Olav Sabo, of Minnesota.
David E. Price, of North Carolina.
José E. Serrano, of New York.
Lucille Roybal-Allard, of California.
Sanford D. Bishop, Jr., of Georgia.
Marion Berry, of Arkansas.
Chet Edwards, of Texas.

Interior, Environment, and Related Agencies

Charles H. Taylor, of North Carolina, *Chair*

Zach Wamp, of Tennessee.
John E. Peterson, of Pennsylvania.
Don Sherwood, of Pennsylvania.
Ernest J. Istook, Jr., of Oklahoma.
Robert B. Aderholt, of Alabama.
John T. Doolittle, of California.
Michael K. Simpson, of Idaho.

Norman D. Dicks, of Washington.
James P. Moran, of Virginia.
Maurice D. Hinchey, of New York.
John W. Olver, of Massachusetts.
Alan B. Mollohan, of West Virginia.

Labor, Health and Human Services, Education, and Related Agencies

Ralph Regula, of Ohio, *Chair*

Ernest J. Istook, Jr., of Oklahoma.
Roger F. Wicker, of Mississippi.
Anne M. Northup, of Kentucky.
Randy (Duke) Cunningham, of California.
Kay Granger, of Texas.
John E. Peterson, of Pennsylvania.
Don Sherwood, of Pennsylvania.
Dave Weldon, of Florida.
James T. Walsh, of New York.

David R. Obey, of Wisconsin.
Steny H. Hoyer, of Maryland.
Nita M. Lowey, of New York.
Rosa L. DeLauro, of Connecticut.
Jesse L. Jackson, Jr., of Illinois.
Patrick J. Kennedy, of Rhode Island.
Lucille Roybal-Allard, of California.

Military Quality of Life and Veterans' Affairs, and Related Agencies

James T. Walsh, of New York, *Chair*

Robert B. Aderholt, of Alabama.
Anne M. Northup, of Kentucky.
Michael K. Simpson, of Idaho.
Ander Crenshaw, of Florida.
C.W. Bill Young, of Florida.
Mark Steven Kirk, of Illinois.
Dennis R. Rehberg, of Montana.
John Carter, of Texas.

Chet Edwards, of Texas.
Sam Farr, of California.
Allen Boyd, of Florida.
Sanford D. Bishop, Jr., of Georgia.
David E. Price, of North Carolina.
Robert E. (Bud) Cramer, Jr., of Alabama.

Science, The Departments of State, Justice, and Commerce, and Related Agencies

Frank R. Wolf, of Virginia, *Chair*

Charles H. Taylor, of North Carolina.
Mark Steven Kirk, of Illinois.
Dave Weldon, of Florida.
Virgil H. Goode, Jr., of Virginia.
Ray LaHood, of Illinois.
John Abney Culberson, of Texas.
Rodney Alexander, of Louisiana.

Alan B. Mollohan, of West Virginia.
José E. Serrano, of New York.
Robert E. (Bud) Cramer, Jr., of Alabama.
Patrick J. Kennedy, of Rhode Island.
Chaka Fattah, of Pennsylvania.

Transportation, Treasury, HUD, The Judiciary, District of Columbia, and Independent Agencies

Joe Knollenberg, of Michigan, *Chair*

Frank R. Wolf, of Virginia.
Harold Rogers, of Kentucky.
Todd Tiahrt, of Kansas.
Anne M. Northup, of Kentucky.
Robert B. Aderholt, of Alabama.
John E. Sweeney, of New York.
John Abney Culberson, of Texas.
Ralph Regula, of Ohio.

John W. Olver, of Massachusetts.
Steny H. Hoyer, of Maryland.
Ed Pastor, of Arizona.
Carolyn C. Kilpatrick, of Michigan.
James E. Clyburn, of South Carolina.
Steven R. Rothman, of New Jersey.

STAFF

Committee on Appropriations (H–218), 225–2771.
Majority Clerk and Staff Director.—Frank M. Cushing.
　　Staff Assistants: Sandy Farrow, John Howard, Di Kane, Dave LesStrang, Jennifer Miller,
　　Dale Oak, Theodore Powell, Jeff Shockey.
　　Communications Director.—John Scofield, 6–5828.
　　Legislative Issues (H–147), 6–7252: Liz Dawson, Kathy Rohan, Chuck Turner.
　　Editors: (B–301A RHOB), 5–2851: Larry Boarman, Cathy Edwards.
　　Computer Operations (B–305 RHOB), 5–2718: Carrie Campbell, Vernon Hammett, Linda
　　Muir, Jay Sivulich.

Minority Staff Director.—Rob Nabors (1016 LHOB), 5–3481.
Professional Staff.—Christina Hamilton, William Stone.
Communications Director.—Chris Fitzgerald.
Press Secretary.—David Helfert.
Administrative Aides: Beth Houser, Heather Wilson.
Surveys and Investigations Staff (283 FHOB), 5–3881.
   Chief and Director.—Robert H. Pearre, Jr.
   Deputy Director.—L. Michael Welsh.
   Associate Director.—H.C. Young.
   Assistant Directors: Susan G. Joseph, Richard M. Potocek.
   Investigators: Mary A. Dyess, Douglas D. Nosik, Johannah P. O'Keeffe, George N. Walne.
   Administrative Assistant.—Victoria V. Decatur-Brodeur.
   Administrative Aides: Joyce C. Stover, Tracey E. Russell, Shanna D. Walker, L. Celia Vismale.
   System Administrator.—Jesse F. Sanderson.
Subcommittee on Agriculture, Rural Development, Food and Drug Administration, and Related Agencies (2362–A RHOB), 5–2638.
   Staff Assistants: Leslie Barrack, Martin Delgado, Maureen Holohan, Joanne Perdue.
   Minority Professional Staff.—Martha Foley (1016 LHOB), 5–3481.
Subcommittee on Defense (H–149), 5–2847.
   Staff Assistants: Leslie Albright, Doug Disrud, Rich Efford, Douglas Gregory, Alicia Jones, Kevin Jones, Paul Juola, Greg Lankler, Kris Mallard, Callie Michael, Steven Nixon, John Shank, Paul Terry, Sherry Young.
   Minority Professional Staff: David Morrison, Linda Pagelsen (1016 LHOB), 5–3481.
Subcommittee on Energy and Water Development, and Related Agencies (2362–B RHOB), 5–3421.
   Staff Assistants: John Blazey, Scott Burnison, Kevin Cook, Tracy LaTurner, Terry Tyborowski.
   Minority Professional Staff.—Dixon Butler (1016 LHOB), 5–3481.
Subcommittee on Foreign Operations, Export Financing, and Related Programs (H–26), 5–2041.
   Staff Assistants: Rodney Bent, Rob Blair, Alice Hogans, Lori Maes, Betsy Phillips.
   Minority Professional Staff.—Mark W. Murray (1016 LHOB), 5–3481.
Subcommittee on Homeland Security (B–307 RHOB), 5–5834.
   Staff Assistants: Jeff Ashford, Tad Gallion, Stephanie Gupta, Tom McLemore, Michelle Mrdeza, Kelly Wade.
   Minority Professional Staff.—Beverly Pheto (1016 LHOB), 5–3481.
Subcommittee on Interior, Environment, and Related Agencies (B–308 RHOB), 5–3081.
   Staff Assistants: Loretta C. Beaumont, Greg Knadle, Andria Oliver, Christopher Topik, Deborah A. Weatherly.
   Minority Professional Staff.—Mike Stephens (1016 LHOB), 5–3481.
Subcommittee on Labor, Health and Human Services, Education, and Related Agencies (2358 RHOB), 5–3508.
   Staff Assistants: Susan Firth, Craig Higgins, Nicole Kunko, Sue Quantius, Francine Salvador, Meg Thompson.
   Minority Professional Staff: David Reich, Cheryl Smith (1016 LHOB), 5–3481.
Subcommittee on Military Quality of Life and Veterans' Affairs, and Related Agencies (H–143), 5–3047.
   Staff Assistants: Mary Arnold, Walter Hearne, Carol Murphy, Tim Peterson, Sarah Young.
   Minority Professional Staff: Bob Bonner, Tom Forhan (1016 LHOB), 5–3481.
Subcommittee on Science, The Departments of State, Justice, and Commerce, and Related Agencies (H–309), 5–3351.
   Staff Assistants: Clelia Alvarado, Anne Marie Goldsmith, Joel Kaplan, Christine Kojac, John Martens, Mike Ringler.
   Minority Professional Staff: Michelle Burkett, David Pomerantz (1016 LHOB), 5–3481.
Subcommittee on Transportation, Treasury, HUD, The Judiciary, District of Columbia, and Independent Agencies (2358 RHOB), 5–2141.
   Staff Assistants: Dena Baron, Steve Crane, David Gibbons, Tammy Hughes, David Napoliello, Cheryle Tucker.
   Minority Professional Staff: Mike Malone, Lesley Turner (1016 LHOB), 5–3481.

Armed Services

2120 Rayburn House Office Building, phone 225–4151, fax 225–9077

http://www.house.gov/hasc

Duncan Hunter, of California, *Chair*

Curt Weldon, of Pennsylvania.
Joel Hefley, of Colorado.
Jim Saxton, of New Jersey.
John M. McHugh, of New York.
Terry Everett, of Alabama.
Roscoe G. Bartlett, of Maryland.
Howard P. (Buck) McKeon, of California.
Mac Thornberry, of Texas.
John N. Hostettler, of Indiana.
Walter B. Jones, of North Carolina.
Jim Ryun, of Kansas.
Jim Gibbons, of Nevada.
Robin Hayes, of North Carolina.
Ken Calvert, of California.
Rob Simmons, of Connecticut.
Jo Ann Davis, of Virginia.
W. Todd Akin, of Missouri.
J. Randy Forbes, of Virginia.
Jeff Miller, of Florida.
Joe Wilson, of South Carolina.
Frank A. LoBiondo, of New Jersey.
Jeb Bradley, of New Hampshire.
Michael Turner, of Ohio.
John Kline, of Minnesota.
Candice S. Miller, of Michigan.
Mike Rogers, of Alabama.
Trent Franks, of Arizona.
Bill Shuster, of Pennsylvania.
Thelma Drake, of Virginia.
Joe Schwarz, of Michigan.
Cathy McMorris, of Washington.
Michael Conaway, of Texas.
Geoff Davis, of Kentucky.

Ike Skelton, of Missouri.
John M. Spratt, Jr., of South Carolina.
Solomon P. Ortiz, of Texas.
Lane Evans, of Illinois.
Gene Taylor, of Mississippi.
Neil Abercrombie, of Hawaii.
Marty Meehan, of Massachusetts.
Silvestre Reyes, of Texas.
Vic Snyder, of Arkansas.
Adam Smith, of Washington.
Loretta Sanchez, of California.
Mike McIntyre, of North Carolina.
Ellen O. Tauscher, of California.
Robert A. Brady, of Pennsylvania.
Robert Andrews, of New Jersey.
Susan A. Davis, of California.
James R. Langevin, of Rhode Island.
Steve Israel, of New York.
Rick Larsen, of Washington.
Jim Cooper, of Tennessee.
Jim Marshall, of Georgia.
Kendrick B. Meek, of Florida.
Madeleine Z. Bordallo, of Guam.
Tim Ryan, of Ohio.
Mark Udall, of Colorado.
G.K. Butterfield, of North Carolina.
Cynthia McKinney, of Georgia.
Dan Boren, of Oklahoma.

SUBCOMMITTEES

Military Personnel

John M. McHugh, of New York, *Chair*

Jo Ann Davis, of Virginia.
John Kline, of Minnesota.
Thelma Drake, of Virginia.
Michael Conaway, of Texas.
Jim Saxton, of New Jersey.
Walter B. Jones, of North Carolina.
Jim Ryun, of Kansas.
Robin Hayes, of North Carolina.

Vic Snyder, of Arkansas.
Marty Meehan, of Massachusetts.
Loretta Sanchez, of California.
Robert Andrews, of New Jersey.
Susan A. Davis, of California.
Mark Udall, of Colorado.
Cynthia McKinney, of Georgia.

Projection Forces

Roscoe G. Bartlett, of Maryland, *Chair*

Rob Simmons, of Connecticut.
Jo Ann Davis, of Virginia.
Jeff Miller, of Florida.
Thelma Drake, of Virginia.
Curt Weldon, of Pennsylvania.
Jim Saxton, of New Jersey.
John N. Hostettler, of Indiana.
Ken Calvert, of California.

Gene Taylor, of Mississippi.
Ellen O. Tauscher, of California.
James R. Langevin, of Rhode Island.
Steve Israel, of New York.
Jim Marshall, of Georgia.
Madeleine Z. Bordallo, of Guam.
Dan Boren, of Oklahoma.

Readiness

Joel Hefley, of Colorado, *Chair*

John N. Hostettler, of Indiana.
Walter B. Jones, of North Carolina.
Jim Ryun, of Kansas.
J. Randy Forbes, of Virginia.
Jeff Miller, of Florida.
Mike Rogers, of Alabama.
Joe Schwarz, of Michigan.
Cathy McMorris, of Washington.
John M. McHugh, of New York.
Howard P. (Buck) McKeon, of California.
Robin Hayes, of North Carolina.
Rob Simmons, of Connecticut.
Jeb Bradley, of New Hampshire.
Candice S. Miller, of Michigan.
Trent Franks, of Arizona.

Solomon P. Ortiz, of Texas.
Lane Evans, of Illinois.
Gene Taylor, of Mississippi.
Neil Abercrombie, of Hawaii.
Silvestre Reyes, of Texas.
Vic Snyder, of Arkansas.
Robert A. Brady, of Pennsylvania.
Susan A. Davis, of California.
Jim Marshall, of Georgia.
Kendrick B. Meek, of Florida.
Madeleine Z. Bordallo, of Guam.
Tim Ryan, of Ohio.
Mark Udall, of Colorado.
G.K. Butterfield, of North Carolina.

Strategic Forces

Terry Everett, of Alabama, *Chair*

Mac Thornberry, of Texas.
Trent Franks, of Arizona.
Michael Turner, of Ohio.
Mike Rogers, of Alabama.
Joe Schwarz, of Michigan.
Cathy McMorris, of Washington.
Geoff Davis, of Kentucky.

Silvestre Reyes, of Texas.
John M. Spratt, Jr., of South Carolina.
Loretta Sanchez, of California.
Ellen O. Tauscher, of California.
Rick Larsen, of Washington.
Jim Cooper, of Tennessee.

Tactical Air and Land Forces

Curt Weldon, of Pennsylvania, *Chair*

Howard P. (Buck) McKeon, of California.
Jim Gibbons, of Nevada.
Ken Calvert, of California.
Frank A. LoBiondo, of New Jersey.
Jeb Bradley, of New Hampshire.
Michael Turner, of Ohio.
Michael Conaway, of Texas.
Terry Everett, of Alabama.
Roscoe G. Bartlett, of Maryland.
Walter B. Jones, of North Carolina.
Jim Ryun, of Kansas.
W. Todd Akin, of Missouri.
J. Randy Forbes, of Virginia.
Joe Wilson, of South Carolina.
Bill Shuster, of Pennsylvania.

Neil Abercrombie, of Hawaii.
Ike Skelton, of Missouri.
John M. Spratt, Jr., of South Carolina.
Solomon P. Ortiz, of Texas.
Lane Evans, of Illinois.
Adam Smith, of Washington.
Mike McIntyre, of North Carolina.
Robert A. Brady, of Pennsylvania.
Steve Israel, of New York.
Jim Cooper, of Tennessee.
Kendrick B. Meek, of Florida.
Tim Ryan, of Ohio.
G.K. Butterfield, of North Carolina.
Dan Boren, of Oklahoma.

Terrorism, Unconventional Threats and Capabilities

Jim Saxton, of New Jersey, *Chair*

Robin Hayes, of North Carolina.
W. Todd Akin, of Missouri.
Joe Wilson, of South Carolina.
John Kline, of Minnesota.
Bill Shuster, of Pennsylvania.
Geoff Davis, of Kentucky.
Joel Hefley, of Colorado.
Mac Thornberry, of Texas.
Jim Gibbons, of Nevada.
Jeff Miller, of Florida.
Frank A. LoBiondo, of New Jersey.

Marty Meehan, of Massachusetts.
Adam Smith, of Washington.
Mike McIntyre, of North Carolina.
Ellen O. Tauscher, of California.
Robert Andrews, of New Jersey.
James R. Langevin, of Rhode Island.
Rick Larsen, of Washington.
Jim Cooper, of Tennessee.
Jim Marshall, of Georgia.
Cynthia McKinney, of Georgia.

STAFF

Committee on Armed Services (2120 RHOB), 225–4151; fax 225–9077.
  Staff Director.—Robert S. Rangel.
    Executive Assistant.—Jennifer E. Giglio.
  Deputy Staff Director.—Hugh N. Johnston, Jr.
  Counsels: Uyen T. Dinh, Mary Ellen Fraser, Jeffrey A. Green, William C. Ostendorff, Henry J. Schweiter.
  Professional Staff: Paul Arcangeli, Hugh P. Brady, John D. Chapla, Erin C. Conaton, Joseph V. Fengler, James W. Godwin, Jr., Joshua T. Hartman, Thomas E. Hawley, Michael R. Higgins, Jeanette S. James, Robert W. Lautrup, Mark R. Lewis, Bill R. Marck, Jr., William H. Natter, Dick Pawloski, Jean D. Reed, Douglas C. Roach, Robert L. Simmons, Eric R. Sterner, John F. Sullivan, B. Ryan Vaart, Debra S. Wada, Nancy M. Warner, Brenda J. Wright.
  Communications Director.—Harald Stavenas.
  Communications Assistant.—Loren L. Dealy.
  Communications Advisor.—Miriam Wolff.
  Press Secretary.—Carrie M. Sloan.
  Legislative Operations Clerk.—W. Holly Neal.
  Analyst.—Alexis R. Lasselle.
  Research Assistant.—Jesse D. Tolleson.
  Staff Assistants: Brian R. Anderson, E. Hayes Arendall, Frank A. Barnes, Diane W. Bowman, Taylor L. Clukey, Katherine A. Croft, Claire E. Dunn, Curtis B. Flood, Betty B. Gray, Chandler T. Lockhart, Ernest B. Warrington, Jr., Lindsay D. Young.
  Assistant.—Heather L. Messera.
  Printing Clerk.—Linda M. Burnette.
  Intern.—Jordan Redmond.

Budget

309 Cannon House Office Building 20515–6065, phone 226–7270, fax 226–7174

http://www.house.gov/budget

meets second Wednesday of each month

Jim Nussle, of Iowa, *Chair*

Jim Ryun, of Kansas.
Ander Crenshaw, of Florida.
Adam Putnam, of Florida.
Roger Wicker, of Mississippi.
Kenny C. Hulshof, of Missouri.
Jo Bonner, of Alabama.
Scott Garrett, of New Jersey.
J. Gresham Barrett, of South Carolina.
Thaddeus McCotter, of Michigan.
Mario Diaz-Balart, of Florida.
Jeb Hensarling, of Texas.
Dan Lungren, of California.
Pete Sessions, of Texas.
Paul Ryan, of Wisconsin.
Michael Simpson, of Idaho.
Ileana Ros-Lehtinen, of Florida.
Jeb Bradley, of New Hampshire.
Patrick McHenry, of North Carolina.
Connie Mack, of Florida.
Mike Conaway, of Texas.

John M. Spratt, Jr., of South Carolina.
Dennis Moore, of Kansas.
Richard E. Neal, of Massachusetts.
Rosa DeLauro, of Connecticut.
Chet Edwards, of Texas.
Harold E. Ford, Jr., of Tennessee.
Lois Capps, of California.
Brian Baird, of Washington.
Jim Cooper, of Tennessee.
Artur Davis, of Alabama.
Willliam Jefferson, of Louisiana.
Thomas Allen, of Maine.
Ed Case, of Hawaii.
Cynthia McKinney, of Georgia.
Henry Cuellar, of Texas.
Ron Kind, of Wisconsin.
Allyson Schwartz, of Pennsylvania.

(No Subcommittees)

Committee on Budget (309 CHOB), 226–7270; fax 226–7174.
  Majority Chief of Staff.—Jim Bates.
    Executive Assistant.—Jon Romito.
    Administrative Officer.—Marsha Douglas.
    Special Assistants: Irina Antochkina, Derrick Landwehr-Brown.
    Information Systems Manager.—Richard E. Magee.
    Systems Administrator.—José Guillen.
    Chief Counsel.—Paul Restuccia.
    Chief Economist.—John Kitchen.
    Director of Communications.—Sean M. Spicer.
      Deputy Director of Communications.—Angela Kuck.
    Director of Electronic Communications.—Steve Webber.
    Coalitions and Media Coordinator.—L.D. Platt.
    Director of—
      Budget Policy.—Patrick L. Knudsen.
      Strategic Planning.—Kimber H. Boyer, Jr.
      Analysts: Jim Cantwell, Bret Coulson, Chauncey Goss, Jeff Hopkins, Roger Mahan, Jason McKitrick, Otto J. Mucklo, Edward Puccerella.
    Director of Budget Review.—Dan Kowalski.
    Analysts: Tiffany R. Blair, Takako Tsuji.
    Counsels: George A. Callas, Charlene Smith.
  Minority Staff Director/Chief Counsel.—Tom Kahn, (B71 Cannon), 226–7200, fax 225–9905.
    Executive Assistant to Staff Director.—Linda Bywaters.
    Counsel.—Lisa Venus.
    Director of Policy/Chief Economist.—Pat Ruggles.
    Office Manager.—Shelia McDowell.
    Project Manager/Budget Analyst.—Arthur Burris.
    Analysts: Sarah Abernathy, Dan Ezrow, Jennifer Friedman, Jason Lumia, Diana Meredith, Kimberly Overbeek, Scott Russell, Andrea Weathers.

Education and the Workforce

2181 Rayburn House Office Building, phone 225–4527, fax 225–9571

http://edworkforce.house.gov

meets second Wednesday of each month

John A. Boehner, of Ohio, *Chair*

Thomas E. Petri, of Wisconsin.
Howard P. (Buck) McKeon, of California.
Michael N. Castle, of Delaware.
Sam Johnson, of Texas.
Mark E. Souder, of Indiana.
Charlie Norwood, of Georgia.
Vernon J. Ehlers, of Michigan.
Judy Biggert, of Illinois.
Todd Russell Platts, of Pennsylvania.
Patrick J. Tiberi, of Ohio.
Ric Keller, of Florida.
Tom Osborne, of Nebraska.
Joe Wilson, of South Carolina.
Jon C. Porter, of Nevada.
John Kline, of Minnesota.
Marilyn N. Musgrave, of Colorado.
Bob Inglis, of South Carolina.
Cathy McMorris, of Washington.
Kenny Marchant, of Texas.
Tom Price, of Georgia.
Luis G. Fortuño, of Puerto Rico.
Bobby Jindal, of Louisiana.
Charles W. Boustany, Jr., of Louisiana.
Virginia Foxx, of North Carolina.
Thelma D. Drake, of Virginia.
John R. (Randy) Kuhl, Jr., of New York.

George Miller, of California.
Dale E. Kildee, of Michigan.
Major R. Owens, of New York.
Donald M. Payne, of New Jersey.
Robert E. Andrews, of New Jersey.
Robert C. Scott, of Virginia.
Lynn C. Woolsey, of California.
Rubén Hinojosa, of Texas.
Carolyn McCarthy, of New York.
John F. Tierney, of Massachusetts.
Ron Kind, of Wisconsin.
Dennis J. Kucinich, of Ohio.
David Wu, of Oregon.
Rush D. Holt, of New Jersey.
Susan Davis, of California.
Betty McCollum, of Minnesota.
Danny K. Davis, of Illinois.
Raúl M. Grijalva, of Arizona.
Chris Van Hollen, of Maryland.
Timothy J. Ryan, of Ohio.
Timothy H. Bishop, of New York.
John Barrow, of Georgia.

SUBCOMMITTEES

[The chairman and ranking minority member are ex officio (non-voting) members of all subcommittees on which they do not serve.]

Education Reform

Michael N. Castle, of Delaware, *Chair*

Tom Osborne, of Nebraska.
Mark E. Souder, of Indiana.
Vernon J. Ehlers, of Michigan.
Judy Biggert, of Illinois.
Todd Russell Platts, of Pennsylvania.
Ric Keller, of Florida.
Joe Wilson, of South Carolina.
Marilyn N. Musgrave, of Colorado.
Bobby Jindal, of Louisiana.
John R. (Randy) Kuhl, Jr., of New York.

Lynn C. Woolsey, of California.
Danny K. Davis, of Illinois.
Raúl M. Grijalva, of Arizona.
Robert E. Andrews, of New Jersey.
Robert C. Scott, of Virginia.
Rubén Hinojosa, of Texas.
Ron Kind, of Wisconsin.
Dennis J. Kucinich, of Ohio.
Susan Davis, of California.

Employer-Employee Relations

Sam Johnson, of Texas, *Chair*

John Kline, of Minnesota.
John A. Boehner, of Ohio.
Howard P. (Buck) McKeon, of California.
Todd Russell Platts, of Pennsylvania.
Patrick J. Tiberi, of Ohio.
Joe Wilson, of South Carolina.
Marilyn N. Musgrave, of Colorado.
Kenny Marchant, of Texas.
Bobby Jindal, of Louisiana.
Charles W. Boustany, Jr., of Louisiana.
Virginia Foxx, of North Carolina.

Robert E. Andrews, of New Jersey.
Dale E. Kildee, of Michigan.
Donald M. Payne, of New Jersey.
Carolyn McCarthy, of New York.
John F. Tierney, of Massachusetts.
David Wu, of Oregon.
Rush D. Holt, of New Jersey.
Betty McCollum, of Minnesota.
Raúl M. Grijalva, of Arizona.

Select Education

Patrick J. Tiberi, of Ohio, *Chair*

Cathy McMorris, of Washington.
Mark E. Souder, of Indiana.
Jon C. Porter, of Nevada.
Bob Inglis, of South Carolina.
Luis G. Fortuño, of Puerto Rico.

Rubén Hinojosa, of Texas.
Danny K. Davis, of Illinois.
Chris Van Hollen, of Maryland.
Timothy J. Ryan, of Ohio.

21st Century Competitiveness

Howard P. (Buck) McKeon, of California, *Chair*

Jon C. Porter, of Nevada.
John A. Boehner, of Ohio.
Thomas E. Petri, of Wisconsin.
Michael N. Castle, of Delaware.
Sam Johnson, of Texas.
Vernon J. Ehlers, of Michigan.
Patrick J. Tiberi, of Ohio.
Ric Keller, of Florida.
Tom Osborne, of Nebraska.
Bob Inglis, of South Carolina.
Cathy McMorris, of Washington.
Tom Price, of Georgia.
Luis G. Fortuño, of Puerto Rico.
Charles W. Boustany, Jr., of Louisiana.
Virginia Foxx, of North Carolina.
Thelma D. Drake, of Virginia.
John R. (Randy) Kuhl, Jr., of New York.

Dale E. Kildee, of Michigan.
Donald M. Payne, of New Jersey.
Carolyn McCarthy, of New York.
John F. Tierney, of Massachusetts.
Ron Kind, of Wisconsin.
David Wu, of Oregon.
Rush D. Holt, of New Jersey.
Betty McCollum, of Minnesota.
Chris Van Hollen, of Maryland.
Timothy J. Ryan, of Ohio.
Robert C. Scott, of Virginia.
Susan Davis, of California.
Timothy H. Bishop, of New York.
John Barrow, of Georgia.
Major R. Owens, of New York.

Workforce Protections

Charlie Norwood, of Georgia, *Chair*

Judy Biggert, of Illinois.
Ric Keller, of Florida.
John Kline, of Minnesota.
Kenny Marchant, of Texas.
Tom Price, of Georgia.
Thelma D. Drake, of Virginia.

Major R. Owens, of New York.
Dennis J. Kucinich, of Ohio.
Lynn C. Woolsey, of California.
Timothy H. Bishop, of New York.
John Barrow, of Georgia.

STAFF

Committee on Education and the Workforce (2181 RHOB), 225–4527.
Majority Staff Director.—Paula Nowakowski.
  Deputy to the Staff Director.—Amy Lozupone.
  General Counsel.—Jo-Marie St. Martin.
  Counselor to the Chair.—George Canty.
  Director of Workforce Policy.—Ed Gilroy.
  Deputy Director of Workforce Policy.—Molly Salmi (B–346A RHOB), 5–7101.
  Workforce Policy Counsel.—Jim Paretti (B–346A RHOB), 5–7101.
  Coalitions Director.—Greg Maurer.
  Director of Education and Human Resources Policy.—Sally G. Lovejoy.
  Deputy Director of Education and Human Resources Policy.—Krisann Pearce (H2–230 FHOB), 5–6558.
  Assistant Deputy Director of Education and Human Resources Policy.—Rich Stombres (H2–230 FHOB), 5–6558;
  Coalitions Director for Education Policy.—Emily Porter.
  Chief Clerk/Assistant to the General Counsel.—Linda Stevens.
  Committee Clerk/Intern Coordinator.—Deborah L. Samantar.
  Financial Administrator.—Dianna J. Ruskowsky (2257A RHOB), 5–4527.
  Senior Budget Analyst.—Cindy Herrle (B–346A RHOB), 5–7101.
  Web/Information Technology Manager.—Cindy Von Gogh (2178 RHOB), 5–4527.
  Senior Systems Administrator.—Dray Thorne (2178 RHOB), 5–4527.
  Systems Administrator.—Billy Benjamin (2178 RHOB), 5–4527.
  Communications Director.—Dave Schnittger.
  Senior Communications Advisor.—Kevin Smith.
  Communications Assistant.—Todd Shriber.
  Communications Staff Assistant.—Jennifer Daniels.
  Press Secretary.—Alexa Marrero.
  Director, Media Affairs.—Joshua Holly.
  Financial Assistant.—Holli Traud (2257A RHOB), 5–4527.
  Professional Staff: David Cleary, Pam Davidson, Amanda Farris, Alison Griffin, Kate Houston, Melanie Looney, Amy Raaf, Whitney Rhoades, Robert Sweet (H2–230 FHOB), 5–6558; Danielle English (B–345D RHOB), 5–7101; Steven Perrotta (B–345B RHOB), 5–7101; Stacey Dion, Kevin Frank, Aron Griffin, Stephanie Milburn, Stephen Settle, Loren Sweatt (B–346A RHOB), 5–7101.
  Administrative Staff: Billie Irving (B–346A RHOB), 5–7101; Lisa Paschal (H2–230 FHOB), 5–6558.
  Editor/Printer/Administrative Staff.—Natalie Nixon (2181 RHOB), 5–4527.
  Executive Assistants: Nancy DeLuca; Kim Proctor.
  Legislative Assistants: Jessica Gross, Lucy House, Brad Thomas (H2–230 FHOB), 5–6558; Donald McIntosh (B–346A RHOB), 5–7101.
  Staff Assistant.—Richard Hoar (B–346A RHOB), 5–7101.
  Receptionist.—Kimberly Ketchel.
Minority Staff Director/General Counsel.—Mark Zuckerman, (2101 RHOB), 5–3725.
  Administrative Assistant.—Ann Owens.
  Staff Assistants: Tylease Fitzgerald, Joycelyn Johnson.
  Special Assistant to the Ranking Member.—Daniel Weiss (2205 RHOB), 5–2095.
  Counsel/Education and Oversight.—Cheryl Johnson (1040 LHOB), 5–3725.
  Legislative Associates/Education: Ellynne Bannon, Denise Forte, Ruth Friedman, Alex Nock (1107 LHOB), 6–2068; Alice Johnson Cain, Lloyd Horwich, Ricardo Martinez (1040 LHOB), 5–3725.
  Legislative Assistant/Education.—Joe Novotny (1107 LHOB), 6–2068.
  Senior Legislative Associate/Labor.—Peter Rutledge (1040 LHOB), 5–3725.
  Legislative Associate/Labor.—Marsha Renwanz (112 CHOB), 6–1881.
  Legislative Assistant/Labor.—Margo Hennigan (112 CHOB), 6–1881.
  Special Assistant for Policy.—Amy Rosenbaum (2101 RHOB), 5–3725.
  Counsel/Employer-Employee Relations.—Jody Calemine (112 CHOB), 6–1881.
  Labor Counsel/Coordinator.—Michele Varnhagen (112 CHOB), 6–1881.
  Press Secretary.—Tom Kiley (2205 RHOB), 5–2095.

Energy and Commerce

2125 Rayburn House Office Building, phone 225–2927

http://www.house.gov/commerce

meets fourth Tuesday of each month

Joe Barton, of Texas, *Chair*

Ralph M. Hall, of Texas.
Michael Bilirakis, of Florida.
Fred Upton, of Michigan.
Cliff Stearns, of Florida.
Paul E. Gillmor, of Ohio.
Nathan Deal, of Georgia.
Ed Whitfield, of Kentucky.
Charlie Norwood, of Georgia.
Barbara Cubin, of Wyoming.
John Shimkus, of Illinois.
Heather Wilson, of New Mexico.
John B. Shadegg, of Arizona.
Charles W. (Chip) Pickering, of Mississippi.
Vito Fossella, of New York.
Roy Blunt, of Missouri.
Steve Buyer, of Indiana.
George Radanovich, of California.
Charles F. Bass, of New Hampshire.
Joseph R. Pitts, of Pennsylvania.
Mary Bono, of California.
Greg Walden, of Oregon.
Lee Terry, of Nebraska.
Mike Ferguson, of New Jersey.
Mike Rogers, of Michigan.
C.L. (Butch) Otter, of Idaho.
Sue Myrick, of North Carolina.
John Sullivan, of Oklahoma.
Tim Murphy, of Pennsylvania.
Michael Burgess, of Texas.
Marsha Blackburn, of Tennessee.

John D. Dingell, of Michigan.
Henry A. Waxman, of California.
Edward J. Markey, of Massachusetts.
Rick Boucher, of Virginia.
Edolphus Towns, of New York.
Frank Pallone, Jr., of New Jersey.
Sherrod Brown, of Ohio.
Bart Gordon, of Tennessee.
Bobby L. Rush, of Illinois.
Anna G. Eshoo, of California.
Bart Stupak, of Michigan.
Eliot L. Engel, of New York.
Albert Russell Wynn, of Maryland.
Gene Green, of Texas.
Ted Strickland, of Ohio.
Diana DeGette, of Colorado.
Lois Capps, of California.
Michael F. Doyle, of Pennsylvania.
Thomas H. Allen, of Maine.
Jim Davis, of Florida.
Janice D. Schakowsky, of Illinois.
Hilda L. Solis, of California.
Charles A. Gonzalez, of Texas.
Jay Inslee, of Washington.
Tammy Baldwin, of Wisconsin.
Mike Ross, of Arkansas.

SUBCOMMITTEES

[The chairman and ranking minority member are ex officio (voting) members of all subcommittees on which they do not serve.]

Commerce, Trade, and Consumer Protection

Cliff Stearns, of Florida, *Chair*

Fred Upton, of Michigan.
Nathan Deal, of Georgia.
Barbara Cubin, of Wyoming.
George Radanovich, of California.
Charles F. Bass, of New Hampshire.
Joseph R. Pitts, of Pennsylvania.
Mary Bono, of California.
Lee Terry, of Nebraska.
Mike Ferguson, of New Jersey.
Mike Rogers, of Michigan.
C.L. (Butch) Otter, of Idaho.
Sue Myrick, of North Carolina.
Tim Murphy, of Pennsylvania.
Marsha Blackburn, of Tennessee.

Janice D. Schakowsky, of Illinois.
Mike Ross, of Arkansas.
Edward J. Markey, of Massachusetts.
Edolphus Towns, of New York.
Sherrod Brown, of Ohio.
Bobby L. Rush, of Illinois.
Gene Green, of Texas.
Ted Strickland, of Ohio.
Diana DeGette, of Colorado.
Jim Davis, of Florida.
Charles A. Gonzalez, of Texas.
Tammy Baldwin, of Wisconsin.

Energy and Air Quality

Ralph M. Hall, of Texas, *Chair*

Michael Bilirakis, of Florida.
Ed Whitfield, of Kentucky.
Charlie Norwood, of Georgia.
John Shimkus, of Illinois.
Heather Wilson, of New Mexico.
John B. Shadegg, of Arizona.
Charles W. (Chip) Pickering, of Mississippi.
Vito Fossella, of New York.
George Radanovich, of California.
Mary Bono, of California.
Greg Walden, of Oregon.
Mike Rogers, of Michigan.
C.L. (Butch) Otter, of Idaho.
John Sullivan, of Oklahoma.
Tim Murphy, of Pennsylvania.
Michael Burgess, of Texas.

Rick Boucher, of Virginia.
Mike Ross, of Arkansas.
Henry A. Waxman, of California.
Edward J. Markey, of Massachusetts.
Eliot L. Engel, of New York.
Albert Russell Wynn, of Maryland.
Gene Green, of Texas.
Ted Strickland, of Ohio.
Lois Capps, of California.
Michael F. Doyle, of Pennsylvania.
Thomas H. Allen, of Maine.
Jim Davis, of Florida.
Hilda L. Solis, of California.
Charles A. Gonzalez, of Texas.

Environment and Hazardous Materials

Paul E. Gillmor, of Ohio, *Chair*

Ralph M. Hall, of Texas.
Nathan Deal, of Georgia.
Heather Wilson, of New Mexico.
John B. Shadegg, of Arizona.
Vito Fossella, of New York.
Charles F. Bass, of New Hampshire.
Joseph R. Pitts, of Pennsylvania.
Mary Bono, of California.
Lee Terry, of Nebraska.
Mike Rogers, of Michigan.
C.L. (Butch) Otter, of Idaho.
Sue Myrick, of North Carolina.
John Sullivan, of Oklahoma.
Tim Murphy, of Pennsylvania.

Hilda L. Solis, of California.
Frank Pallone, Jr., of New Jersey.
Bart Stupak, of Michigan.
Albert Russell Wynn, of Maryland.
Lois Capps, of California.
Michael F. Doyle, of Pennsylvania.
Thomas H. Allen, of Maine.
Janice D. Schakowsky, of Illinois.
Jay Inslee, of Washington.
Gene Green, of Texas.
Charles A. Gonzalez, of Texas.
Tammy Baldwin, of Wisconsin.

Health

Nathan Deal, of Georgia, *Chair*

Ralph M. Hall, of Texas.
Michael Bilirakis, of Florida.
Fred Upton, of Michigan.
Paul E. Gillmor, of Ohio.
Charlie Norwood, of Georgia.
Barbara Cubin, of Wyoming.
John Shimkus, of Illinois.
John B. Shadegg, of Arizona.
Charles W. (Chip) Pickering, of Mississippi.
Steve Buyer, of Indiana.
Joseph R. Pitts, of Pennsylvania.
Mary Bono, of California.
Mike Ferguson, of New Jersey.
Mike Rogers, of Michigan.
Sue Myrick, of North Carolina.
Michael Burgess, of Texas.

Sherrod Brown, of Ohio.
Henry A. Waxman, of California.
Edolphus Towns, of New York.
Frank Pallone, Jr., of New Jersey.
Bart Gordon, of Tennessee.
Bobby L. Rush, of Illinois.
Anna G. Eshoo, of California.
Gene Green, of Texas.
Ted Strickland, of Ohio.
Diana DeGette, of Colorado.
Lois Capps, of California.
Thomas H. Allen, of Maine.
Jim Davis, of Florida.
Tammy Baldwin, of Wisconsin.

Oversight and Investigations

Ed Whitfield, of Kentucky, *Chair*

Cliff Stearns, of Florida.
Charles W. (Chip) Pickering, of Mississippi.
Charles F. Bass, of New Hampshire.
Greg Walden, of Oregon.
Mike Ferguson, of New Jersey.
Michael Burgess, of Texas.
Marsha Blackburn, of Tennessee.

Bart Stupak, of Michigan.
Diana DeGette, of Colorado.
Janice D. Schakowsky, of Illinois.
Jay Inslee, of Washington.
Tammy Baldwin, of Wisconsin.
Henry A. Waxman, of California.

Telecommunications and the Internet

Fred Upton, of Michigan, *Chair*

Michael Bilirakis, of Florida.
Cliff Stearns, of Florida.
Paul E. Gillmor, of Ohio.
Ed Whitfield, of Kentucky.
Barbara Cubin, of Wyoming.
John Shimkus, of Illinois.
Heather Wilson, of New Mexico.
Charles W. (Chip) Pickering, of Mississippi.
Vito Fossella, of New York.
George Radanovich, of California.
Charles F. Bass, of New Hampshire.
Greg Walden, of Oregon.
Lee Terry, of Nebraska.
Mike Ferguson, of New Jersey.
John Sullivan, of Oklahoma.
Marsha Blackburn, of Tennessee.

Edward J. Markey, of Massachusetts.
Eliot L. Engel, of New York.
Albert Russell Wynn, of Maryland.
Michael F. Doyle, of Pennsylvania.
Charles A. Gonzalez, of Texas.
Jay Inslee, of Washington.
Rick Boucher, of Virginia.
Edolphus Towns, of New York.
Frank Pallone, Jr., of New Jersey.
Sherrod Brown, of Ohio.
Bart Gordon, of Tennessee.
Bobby L. Rush, of Illinois.
Anna G. Eshoo, of California.
Bart Stupak, of Michigan.

STAFF

Committee on Energy and Commerce (2125 RHOB), 225–2927; fax 225–1919.
Majority Staff Director.—C.H. (Bud) Albright.
  Deputy Staff Director of:
    Communications.—Lawrence Neal.
    Policy.—Andrew Black.
  Communications Director.—Kevin Schweers.
    Deputy Communications Directors: Lisa Miller, Jon Tripp.
  Chief Counsel, Oversight and Investigations.—Mark Paoletta.
    Deputy Chief Counsel, Oversight and Investigations.—Alan Slobodin.
  Chief Counsel of:
    Commerce, Trade, and Consumer Protection.—David Cavicke.
    Energy and Air Quality/Environment and Hazardous Materials.—Mark Menezes.
    Health.—Charles Clapton.
    Telecommunications and the Internet.—Howard Waltzman.
  Counsels: Kelli Andrews, Melissa Bartlett, Kurt Bilas, Margaret Caravelli, Kelly Cole, Brad Conway, Anthony Cooke, Thomas Feddo, Joseph Fortson, Neil Fried, Thomas Hassenboehler, Rebecca Hemard, Shannon Jacquot, Nandan Kenkeremath, Clayton Matheson, David Rosenfeld, Maryam Sabbaghian, Andrew Snowdon.
  Professional Staff: Annie Caputo, William Carty, Dwight Cates, Julie Cordell, Jeanne Haggerty, Cheryl Jaeger, Ryan Long, Brian McCullough, Robert Simison, Peter Spencer.
  Policy Coordinators: Brandon Clark, Gerald Couri, John Halliwell, Christopher Leahy, William Nordwind, Elizabeth Stack.
  Legislative Analysts: Jaylyn Jensen, Clayton Matheson, William O'Brien.
  Legislative Clerks: Michael Abraham, Eugenia Edwards, Chad Grant, Peter Kielty, William Harvard, Anh Nguyen.
  Director, External Affairs.—Jacqueline Walker.
  Administrative and Human Resources Coordinator.—Linda Walker.
    Assistant to the Administrative Coordinator.—Audrey Murdoch.
  Comptroller.—Anthony Sullivan.
  Director of Information Technology.—Jean McGinley.
  Printer.—Joseph Patterson.
  Archivist.—Jerome Sikorski.

Special Assistant.—Julie Fields.
Energy Assistant.—Eric Hutchins.
Press Assistant.—Elizabeth Hill.
Staff Assistants: Michael Green, Matthew Owen, Christine Sequenzia.
Minority Staff Director/Chief Counsel.—Reid P.F. Stuntz (2322 RHOB), 225–3641.
Deputy Staff Director/General Counsel.—David R. Schooler.
Chief Clerk.—Sharon E. Davis.
Senior Counsels: Richard A. Frandsen, Consuela M. Washington, Sue D. Sheridan.
Counsels: Jonathan J. Cordone, Peter J. Filon, John P. Ford, Michael L. Goo, Edith Holleman, Purvee Parekh Kempf, Johanna Mikes Shelton.
Professional Staff: Amy B. Hall, Bruce C. Harris, Bridgett E. Taylor.
Investigator.—Christopher Knauer.
Investigator/Economist.—David W. Nelson.
Press Secretary.—Jodi Bennett Seth.
Deputy Chief Clerk/LAN Administrator.—Candace E. Butler.
Assistant Clerk/Assistant LAN Administrator.—Carla R. Hultberg.
Finance Assistant.—Raymond R. Kent, Jr.
Research Assistants: Voncille Trotter Hines, Jessica A. McNiece, Robert T. (Turney) Hall, David A. Vogel.
Research/Press Assistant.—Ashley R. Groesbeck.
Secretary.—Angela E. Davis-West.
Staff Assistant.—John Alexander (Alec) Gerlach.

Financial Services

2129 Rayburn House Office Building, phone 225–7502

http://www.house.gov/financialservices

meets first Tuesday of each month

Michael G. Oxley, of Ohio, *Chair*

James A. Leach, of Iowa.	*Barney Frank, of Massachusetts.*
Richard H. Baker, of Louisiana.	*Paul E. Kanjorski, of Pennsylvania.*
Deborah Pryce, of Ohio.	*Maxine Waters, of California.*
Spencer Bachus, of Alabama.	*Carolyn B. Maloney, of New York.*
Michael N. Castle, of Delaware.	*Luis V. Gutierrez, of Illinois.*
Peter T. King, of New York.	*Nydia M. Velázquez, of New York.*
Edward R. Royce, of California.	*Melvin L. Watt, of North Carolina.*
Frank D. Lucas, of Oklahoma.	*Gary L. Ackerman, of New York.*
Robert W. Ney, of Ohio.	*Darlene Hooley, of Oregon.*
Sue W. Kelly, of New York.	*Julia Carson, of Indiana.*
Ron Paul, of Texas.	*Brad Sherman, of California.*
Paul E. Gillmor, of Ohio.	*Gregory W. Meeks, of New York.*
Jim Ryun, of Kansas.	*Barbara Lee, of California.*
Steven C. LaTourette, of Ohio.	*Dennis Moore, of Kansas.*
Donald A. Manzullo, of Illinois.	*Michael E. Capuano, of Massachusetts.*
Walter B. Jones, of North Carolina.	*Harold E. Ford, Jr., of Tennessee.*
Judy Biggert, of Illinois.	*Rubén Hinojosa, of Texas.*
Christopher Shays, of Connecticut.	*Joseph Crowley, of New York.*
Vito Fossella, of New York.	*Wm. Lacy Clay, of Missouri.*
Gary G. Miller, of California.	*Steve Israel, of New York.*
Patrick J. Tiberi, of Ohio.	*Carolyn McCarthy, of New York.*
Mark R. Kennedy, of Minnesota.	*Joe Baca, of California.*
Tom Feeney, of Florida.	*Jim Matheson, of Utah.*
Jeb Hensarling, of Texas.	*Stephen F. Lynch, of Massachusetts.*
Scott Garrett, of New Jersey.	*Brad Miller, of North Carolina.*
Ginny Brown-Waite, of Florida.	*David Scott, of Georgia.*
J. Gresham Barrett, of South Carolina.	*Artur Davis, of Alabama.*
Katherine Harris, of Florida.	*Al Green, of Texas.*
Rick Renzi, of Arizona.	*Emanuel Cleaver, of Missouri.*
Jim Gerlach, of Pennsylvania.	*Melissa L. Bean, of Illinois.*
Stevan Pearce, of New Mexico.	*Debbie Wasserman Schultz, of Florida.*
Randy Neugebauer, of Texas.	*Gwen Moore, of Wisconsin.*
Tom Price, of Georgia.	
Michael G. Fitzpatrick, of Pennsylvania.	BERNARD SANDERS, of Vermont.
Geoff Davis, of Kentucky.	
Patrick T. McHenry, of North Carolina.	

SUBCOMMITTEES

[The chairman and ranking minority member are ex officio (voting) members of all subcommittees on which they do not serve.]

Capital Markets, Insurance, and Government-Sponsored Enterprises

Richard H. Baker, of Louisiana, *Chair*

Jim Ryun, of Kansas.
Christopher Shays, of Connecticut.
Paul E. Gillmor, of Ohio.
Spencer Bachus, of Alabama.
Michael N. Castle, of Delaware.
Peter T. King, of New York.
Frank D. Lucas, of Oklahoma.
Donald A. Manzullo, of Illinois.
Edward R. Royce, of California.
Sue W. Kelly, of New York.
Robert W. Ney, of Ohio.
Vito Fossella, of New York.
Judy Biggert, of Illinois.
Gary G. Miller, of California.
Mark R. Kennedy, of Minnesota.
Patrick J. Tiberi, of Ohio.
J. Gresham Barrett, of South Carolina.
Ginny Brown-Waite, of Florida.
Tom Feeney, of Florida.
Jim Gerlach, of Pennsylvania.
Katherine Harris, of Florida.
Jeb Hensarling, of Texas.
Rick Renzi, of Arizona.
Geoff Davis, of Kentucky.
Michael G. Fitzpatrick, of Pennsylvania.

Paul E. Kanjorski, of Pennsylvania.
Gary L. Ackerman, of New York.
Darlene Hooley, of Oregon.
Brad Sherman, of California.
Gregory W. Meeks, of New York.
Dennis Moore, of Kansas.
Michael E. Capuano, of Massachusetts.
Harold E. Ford, Jr., of Tennessee.
Rubén Hinojosa, of Texas.
Joseph Crowley, of New York.
Steve Israel, of New York.
Wm. Lacy Clay, of Missouri.
Carolyn McCarthy, of New York.
Joe Baca, of California.
Jim Matheson, of Utah.
Stephen F. Lynch, of Massachusetts.
Brad Miller, of North Carolina.
David Scott, of Georgia.
Nydia M. Velázquez, of New York.
Melvin L. Watt, of North Carolina.
Artur Davis, of Alabama.
Melissa L. Bean, of Illinois.
Debbie Wasserman Schultz, of Florida.

Domestic and International Monetary Policy, Trade and Technology

Deborah Pryce, of Ohio, *Chair*

Judy Biggert, of Illinois.
James A. Leach, of Iowa.
Michael N. Castle, of Delaware.
Frank D. Lucas, of Oklahoma.
Ron Paul, of Texas.
Steven C. LaTourette, of Ohio.
Donald A. Manzullo, of Illinois.
Mark R. Kennedy, of Minnesota.
Katherine Harris, of Florida.
Jim Gerlach, of Pennsylvania.
Randy Neugebauer, of Texas.
Tom Price, of Georgia.
Patrick T. McHenry, of North Carolina.

Carolyn B. Maloney, of New York.
BERNARD SANDERS, of Vermont.
Melvin L. Watt, of North Carolina.
Maxine Waters, of California.
Barbara Lee, of California.
Paul E. Kanjorski, of Pennsylvania.
Brad Sherman, of California.
Luis V. Gutierrez, of Illinois.
Melissa L. Bean, of Illinois.
Debbie Wasserman Schultz, of Florida.
Gwen Moore, of Wisconsin.
Joseph Crowley, of New York.

Financial Institutions and Consumer Credit

Spencer Bachus, of Alabama, *Chair*

Walter B. Jones, of North Carolina.
Richard H. Baker, of Louisiana.
Michael N. Castle, of Delaware.
Edward R. Royce, of California.
Frank D. Lucas, of Oklahoma.
Sue W. Kelly, of New York.
Ron Paul, of Texas.
Paul E. Gillmor, of Ohio.
Jim Ryun, of Kansas.
Steven C. LaTourette, of Ohio.
Judy Biggert, of Illinois.
Vito Fossella, of New York.
Gary G. Miller, of California.
Patrick J. Tiberi, of Ohio.
Tom Feeney, of Florida.
Jeb Hensarling, of Texas.
Scott Garrett, of New Jersey.
Ginny Brown-Waite, of Florida.
J. Gresham Barrett, of South Carolina.
Rick Renzi, of Arizona.
Randy Neugebauer, of Texas.
Tom Price, of Georgia.
Patrick T. McHenry, of North Carolina.

BERNARD SANDERS, of Vermont.
Carolyn B. Maloney, of New York.
Melvin L. Watt, of North Carolina.
Gary L. Ackerman, of New York.
Brad Sherman, of California.
Gregory W. Meeks, of New York.
Luis V. Gutierrez, of Illinois.
Dennis Moore, of Kansas.
Paul E. Kanjorski, of Pennsylvania.
Maxine Waters, of California.
Darlene Hooley, of Oregon.
Julia Carson, of Indiana.
Harold E. Ford, Jr., of Tennessee.
Rubén Hinojosa, of Texas.
Joseph Crowley, of New York.
Steve Israel, of New York.
Carolyn McCarthy, of New York.
Joe Baca, of California.
Al Green, of Texas.
Gwen Moore, of Wisconsin.
Wm. Lacy Clay, of Missouri.
Jim Matheson, of Utah.

Housing and Community Opportunity

Robert W. Ney, of Ohio, *Chair*

Gary G. Miller, of California.
Richard H. Baker, of Louisiana.
Peter T. King, of New York.
Walter B. Jones, of North Carolina.
Christopher Shays, of Connecticut.
Patrick J. Tiberi, of Ohio.
Ginny Brown-Waite, of Florida.
Katherine Harris, of Florida.
Rick Renzi, of Arizona.
Randy Neugebauer, of Texas.
Michael G. Fitzpatrick, of Pennsylvania.
Geoff Davis, of Kentucky.

Maxine Waters, of California.
Nydia M. Velázquez, of New York.
Julia Carson, of Indiana.
Barbara Lee, of California.
Michael E. Capuano, of Massachusetts.
BERNARD SANDERS, of Vermont.
Stephen F. Lynch, of Massachusetts.
Brad Miller, of North Carolina.
David Scott, of Georgia.
Artur Davis, of Alabama.
Emanuel Cleaver, of Missouri.
Al Green, of Texas.

Oversight and Investigations

Sue W. Kelly, of New York, *Chair*

Ron Paul, of Texas.
Steven C. LaTourette, of Ohio.
Mark R. Kennedy, of Minnesota.
Scott Garrett, of New Jersey.
J. Gresham Barrett, of South Carolina.
Tom Price, of Georgia.
Michael G. Fitzpatrick, of Pennsylvania.
Geoff Davis, of Kentucky.
Patrick T. McHenry, of North Carolina.

Luis V. Gutierrez, of Illinois.
Dennis Moore, of Kansas.
Carolyn B. Maloney, of New York.
Stephen F. Lynch, of Massachusetts.
Artur Davis, of Alabama.
Emanuel Cleaver, of Missouri.
David Scott, of Georgia.
Debbie Wasserman Schultz, of Florida.
Gwen Moore, of Wisconsin.

STAFF

Committee on Financial Services (2129 RHOB), 225–7502.
  *Majority Chief of Staff.—*Robert Foster.
    *Deputy Chief of Staff/Communications Director.—*Peggy Peterson.
    *General Counsel.—*Tom Duncan.
    *Chief Counsel.—*Carter McDowell.
    *Counselor to the Chair.—*James Conzelman.
    *Assistant Communications Director.—*Sarah Morgan.
    Senior Counsels: Jonathan Blackmer, James Clinger, Justin Daly, Dina Ellis, Robert
      Gordon, Clinton Jones, Kevin MacMillan, Barbara Matthews, Frank Tillotson, Scott
      Wilber.
    Counsels: Peter Barrett, David Eppstein, Kristen Jaconi, Glenn Westrick.
    Senior Professional Staff: John Butler, Cindy Chetti, Paul Kangas, Joe Pinder.
    Professional Staff: Tucker Foote, Tallman Johnson, Mike McEleney, Christopher Rosello.
    *Administrative Assistant.—*Angela Gambo.
    *Executive Assistant.—*Dale Dorr.
    *Systems Administrator.—*Kim Trimble.
    *Executive Staff Assistant.—*Rosemary Keech.
    *Clerk.—*Lois Richerson.
    Staff Assistants: Marisol Garibay, Dave Oxner, Beverly Price, Frank Scardena, Heather
      Wheeler, Earnestine Worelds.
  *Minority Staff Director.—*Jeanne Roslanowick (B–301C RHOB), 225–4247.
    Counsels: Todd Cranford, Ricardo Delfin, Erika Jeffers, Dominique McCoy, Jeff Riley,
      Lawranne Stewart, Ken Swab.
    *Communications Director.—*S. Kay Gibbs.
    *Press Secretary.—*Jennifer Gore.
    *Senior Policy Analyst.—*Dean Sagar.
    *Economist.—*Scott Morris.
    *Senior Professional Staff.—*Jaime Lizarraga.
    Professional Staff: Eleni Constantine, Timothy Dehnhoff, Gary Goldberg, Warren Gunnels,
      Todd Harper, Kellie Larkin, Patricia Lord, Daniel McGlinchey, Scott Olson.
    *Legislative Assistant.—*Jonathan Obee.

Government Reform

2154 Rayburn House Office Building, phone 225–5074, fax 225–3974, TTY 225–6852

http://reform.house.gov

meets second Tuesday of each month

Tom Davis, of Virginia, *Chair*

Christopher Shays, of Connecticut.
Dan Burton, of Indiana.
Ileana Ros-Lehtinen, of Florida.
John M. McHugh, of New York.
John L. Mica, of Florida.
Gil Gutknecht, of Minnesota.
Mark E. Souder, of Indiana.
Steven C. LaTourette, of Ohio.
Todd Russell Platts, of Pennsylvania.
Chris Cannon, of Utah.
John J. Duncan, Jr., of Tennessee.
Candice S. Miller, of Michigan.
Michael R. Turner, of Ohio.
Darrell E. Issa, of California.
Ginny Brown-Waite, of Florida.
Jon C. Porter, of Nevada.
Kenny Marchant, of Texas.
Lynn A. Westmoreland, of Georgia.
Patrick T. McHenry, of North Carolina.
Charles W. Dent, of Pennsylvania.
Virginia Foxx, of North Carolina.

Henry A. Waxman, of California.
Tom Lantos, of California.
Major R. Owens, of New York.
Edolphus Towns, of New York.
Paul E. Kanjorski, of Pennsylvania.
Carolyn B. Maloney, of New York.
Elijah E. Cummings, of Maryland.
Dennis J. Kucinich, of Ohio.
Danny K. Davis, of Illinois.
Wm. Lacy Clay, of Missouri.
Diane E. Watson, of California.
Stephen F. Lynch, of Massachusetts.
Chris Van Hollen, of Maryland.
Linda T. Sánchez, of California.
C.A. Dutch Ruppersberger, of Maryland.
Brian Higgins, of New York.
Eleanor Holmes Norton, of the District of
   Columbia.

BERNARD SANDERS, of Vermont.

SUBCOMMITTEES

[The chairman and ranking minority member are ex officio (voting) members of all subcommittees]

Criminal Justice, Drug Policy, and Human Resources

Mark E. Souder, of Indiana, *Chair*

Patrick T. McHenry, of North Carolina.
Dan Burton, of Indiana.
John L. Mica, of Florida.
Gil Gutknecht, of Minnesota.
Steven C. LaTourette, of Ohio.
Chris Cannon, of Utah.
Candice S. Miller, of Michigan.
Ginny Brown-Waite, of Florida.
Virginia Foxx, of North Carolina.

Elijah E. Cummings, of Maryland.
BERNARD SANDERS, of Vermont.
Danny K. Davis, of Illinois.
Diane E. Watson, of California.
Linda T. Sánchez, of California.
C.A. Dutch Ruppersberger, of Maryland.
Major R. Owens, of New York.
Eleanor Holmes Norton, of the District of
   Columbia.

Energy and Resources

Darrell E. Issa, of California, *Chair*

Lynn A. Westmoreland, of Georgia.
Ileana Ros-Lehtinen, of Florida.
John M. McHugh, of New York.
Patrick T. McHenry, of North Carolina.
Kenny Marchant, of Texas.

Diane E. Watson, of California.
Brian Higgins, of New York.
Tom Lantos, of California.
Dennis J. Kucinich, of Ohio.

412 *Congressional Directory*

Federal Workforce and Agency Organization

Jon C. Porter, of Nevada, *Chair*

John L. Mica, of Florida.
Tom Davis, of Virginia.
Darrell E. Issa, of California.
Kenny Marchant, of Texas.
Patrick T. McHenry, of North Carolina.

Danny K. Davis, of Illinois.
Major R. Owens, of New York.
Eleanor Holmes Norton, of the District of Columbia.
Elijah E. Cummings, of Maryland.
Chris Van Hollen, of Maryland.

Federalism and the Census

Michael R. Turner, of Ohio, *Chair*

Charles W. Dent, of Pennsylvania.
Christopher Shays, of Connecticut.
Virginia Foxx, of North Carolina.

Wm. Lacy Clay, of Missouri.
Paul E. Kanjorski, of Pennsylvania.
Carolyn B. Maloney, of New York.

Government Management, Finance, and Accountability

Todd Russell Platts, of California, *Chair*

Virginia Foxx, of North Carolina.
Tom Davis, of Virginia.
Gil Gutknecht, of Minnesota.
Mark E. Souder, of Indiana.
John J. Duncan, Jr., of Tennessee.

Edolphus Towns, of New York.
Major R. Owens, of New York.
Paul E. Kanjorski, of Pennsylvania.
Carolyn B. Maloney, of New York.

National Security, Emerging Threats and International Relations

Christopher Shays, of Connecticut, *Chair*

Kenny Marchant, of Texas.
Dan Burton, of Indiana.
Ileana Ros-Lehtinen, of Florida.
John M. McHugh, of New York.
Steven C. LaTourette, of Ohio.
Todd Russell Platts, of Pennsylvania.
John J. Duncan, Jr., of Tennessee.
Michael R. Turner, of Ohio.
Jon C. Porter, of Nevada.
Charles W. Dent, of Pennsylvania.

Dennis J. Kucinich, of Ohio.
Tom Lantos, of California.
BERNARD SANDERS, of Vermont.
Carolyn B. Maloney, of New York.
Chris Van Hollen, of Maryland.
Linda T. Sánchez, of California.
C.A. Dutch Ruppersberger, of Maryland.
Stephen F. Lynch, of Massachusetts.
Brian Higgins, of New York.

Regulatory Affairs

Candice S. Miller, of Michigan, *Chair*

Ginny Brown-Waite, of Florida.
Chris Cannon, of Utah.
Michael R. Turner, of Ohio.
Lynn A. Westmoreland, of Georgia.

Stephen F. Lynch, of Massachusetts.
Wm. Lacy Clay, of Missouri.
Chris Van Hollen, of Maryland.

STAFF

Committee on Government Reform (2157 RHOB), 225–5074.
>*Majority Staff Director.*—Melissa Wojciak.
>>*Deputy Staff Director/Communications Director.*—David Marin.
>>*Chief Counsel.*—Keith Ausbrook.
>>*Legislative Director/Senior Policy Counsel.*—Ellen Brown.
>>*Deputy Legislative Director.*—Mason Alinger.
>>*Chief Counsel for Oversight and Investigations.*—Jennifer Safavian.
>>*Senior Counsel/Parliamentarian.*—Robert Borden.
>>*Special Assistant.*—Amy Laudeman.
>>*Counsels:* John Callender, Howie Denis, John Hunter, Jim Moore, Ann Marie Turner.
>>*Press Secretary.*—Rob White.
>>*Deputy Director of Communications.*—Drew Crockett.
>>*Senior Professional Staff Member.*—Victoria Proctor.
>>*Professional Staff:* Brien Beattie, Jaime Hjort, Edward Kidd, Shalley Kim, Scott Kopple, Michael Layman, Susie Schulte, Brian Stout, Grace Washbourne.
>>*Chief Clerk.*—Teresa Austin.
>>*Deputy Clerk.*—Sarah D'Orsie.
>>*Financial Administrator.*—Robin Butler.
>>*Office Manager.*—Allyson Blandford.
>>*Chief Information Officer.*—Corinne Zaccagnini.
>>*Computer Systems Manager.*—Leneal Scott.
>>*Legislative Correspondent.*—Kristina Sherry.
>>*Staff Assistants:* Todd Greenwood, Andrew James.
>*Minority Staff Director/Chief Counsel.*—Phil Barnett (B–350A RHOB), 225–5051.
>>*Deputy Chief Counsels:* Kristin Amerling, Christopher Lu, Michael Yeager.
>>*Senior Legislative Counsel.*—Michelle Ash.
>>*Counsels:* Jeff Baran, Krista Boyd, Sarah Despres, Greg Dotson, Althea Gregory, Tony Haywood, Rosalind Parker, David Rapallo, Naomi Seiler, Alexandra Teitz, Tim Westmoreland.
>>*Senior Policy Advisor/Communications Director.*—Karen Lightfoot.
>>>*Communications/Policy Assistant.*—Anna Laitin.
>>*Senior Investigator/Policy Advisor.*—Brian Cohen.
>>*Office Manager.*—Cecelia Morton.
>>*Special Assistant.*—Therese Foote.
>>*Investigator.*—Christopher Davis.
>>*Professional Staff:* Adam Bordes, Richard Butcher, David McMillan, Nancy Scola, Tania Shand, Josh Sharfstein, Mark Stephenson, Andrew Su, Denise Wilson.
>>*Research Assistant.*—Chris Traci.
>>*Staff Assistant.*—Isaac Brown.
>>*Chief Clerk.*—Earley Green.
>>*Assistant Clerks:* Teresa Coufal, Jean Gosa.
>*Subcommittee on Criminal Justice, Drug Policy, and Human Resources* (B–377 RHOB), 5–2577.
>>*Staff Director.*—Marc Wheat.
>>*Counsel.*—Nicholas Coleman.
>>*Professional Staff.*—Brandon Lerch.
>>*Detailees:* Pat DeQuattro, David Thomasson.
>>*Clerk.*—Malia Holst.
>*Subcommittee on Energy and Resources* (B–349C RHOB), 5–6472.
>>*Staff Director.*—Larry Brady.
>>*Professional Staff.*—Steve Cima.
>>*Clerk.*—Lori Gavaghan.
>*Subcommittee on Federal Workforce and Agency Organization* (B–373A RHOB), 5–5147.
>>*Staff Director.*—Ronald Martinson.
>>*Deputy Staff Director/Chief Counsel.*—Chad Bungard.
>>*Professional Staff:* Christopher Barkley, Shannon Meade.
>>*Legislative Assistant/Clerk.*—Reid Voss.
>*Subcommittee on Federalism and the Census* (B–349A RHOB), 5–6751.
>>*Staff Director.*—John Cuaderes.
>>*Deputy Counsel/Professional Staff.*—Shannon Weinberg.
>>*Professional Staff.*—Ursula Wojciechowski.
>>*Clerk.*—Juliana French.

Subcommittee on Government Management, Finance, and Accountability (B–371C RHOB), 5–3741.
  Staff Director.—Michael Hettinger.
    Communications Director/Professional Staff.—Tabetha Mueller.
    Counsel.—Dan Daly.
    Professional Staff.—Jessica Friedman.
    Clerk.—Nate Berry.
Subcommittee on National Security, Emerging Threats, and International Relations (B–372 RHOB), 5–2548.
  Staff Director/Counsel.—Lawrence J. Halloran.
    Senior Policy Analyst.—R. Nicholas Palarino.
    Chief Investigator.—Vincent Chase.
    Professional Staff: Thomas Costa, Kristine McElroy.
    Clerk.—Robert Briggs.
Subcommittee on Regulatory Affairs (B–373B RHOB), 5–4407.
  Staff Director.—Ed Schrock.
    Professional Staff.—Erik Glavich.
    Clerk.—Lauren Jacobs.

Homeland Security

phone 226–8417, fax 226–3399

Christopher Cox, of California, *Chair*

Don Young, of Alaska.
Lamar S. Smith, of Texas.
Curt Weldon, of Pennsylvania.
Christopher Shays, of Connecticut.
Peter T. King, of New York.
John Linder, of Georgia.
Mark E. Souder, of Indiana.
Tom Davis, of Virginia.
Daniel E. Lungren, of California.
Jim Gibbons, of Nevada.
Rob Simmons, of Connecticut.
Mike Rogers, of Alabama.
Stevan Pearce, of New Mexico.
Katherine Harris, of Florida.
Bobby Jindal, of Louisiana.
Dave G. Reichert, of Washington.
Michael McCaul, of Texas.
Charlie Dent, of Pennsylvania.

Bennie G. Thompson, of Mississippi.
Loretta Sanchez, of California.
Edward J. Markey, of Massachusetts.
Norman D. Dicks, of Washington.
Jane Harman, of California.
Peter A. DeFazio, of Oregon.
Nita M. Lowey, of New York.
Eleanor Holmes Norton, of the District of Columbia.
Zoe Lofgren, of California.
Sheila Jackson Lee, of Texas.
Bill Pascrell, Jr., of New Jersey.
Donna M. Christensen, of the Virgin Islands.
Bob Etheridge, of North Carolina.
James R. Langevin, of Rhode Island.
Kendrick B. Meek, of Florida.

SUBCOMMITTEES

[The chairman and ranking minority member are ex officio (voting) members of all subcommittees on which they do not serve.]

Economic Security, Infrastructure Protection, and Cybersecurity

Daniel E. Lungren, of California, *Chair*

Don Young, of Alaska.
Lamar S. Smith, of Texas.
John Linder, of Georgia.
Mark E. Souder, of Indiana.
Tom Davis, of Virginia.
Mike Rogers, of Alabama.
Stevan Pearce, of New Mexico.
Katherine Harris, of Florida.
Bobby Jindal, of Louisiana.

Loretta Sanchez, of California.
Edward J. Markey, of Massachusetts.
Norman D. Dicks, of Washington.
Peter A. DeFazio, of Oregon.
Zoe Lofgren, of California.
Sheila Jackson Lee, of Texas.
Bill Pascrell, Jr., of New Jersey.
James R. Langevin, of Rhode Island.

Emergency Preparedness, Science, and Technology

Peter T. King, of New York, *Chair*

Lamar S. Smith, of Texas.
Curt Weldon, of Pennsylvania.
Rob Simmons, of Connecticut.
Mike Rogers, of Alabama.
Stevan Pearce, of New Mexico.
Katherine Harris, of Florida.
Dave G. Reichert, of Washington.
Michael McCaul, of Texas.
Charlie Dent, of Pennsylvania.

Bill Pascrell, Jr., of New Jersey.
Loretta Sanchez, of California.
Norman D. Dicks, of Washington.
Jane Harman, of California.
Nita M. Lowey, of New York.
Eleanor Holmes Norton, of the District of Columbia.
Donna M. Christensen, of the Virgin Islands.
Bob Etheridge, of North Carolina.

Intelligence, Information Sharing, and Terrorism Risk Assessment

Rob Simmons, of Connecticut, *Chair*

Curt Weldon, of Pennsylvania.
Peter T. King, of New York.
Mark E. Souder, of Indiana.
Daniel E. Lungren, of California.
Jim Gibbons, of Nevada.
Stevan Pearce, of New Mexico.
Bobby Jindal, of Louisiana.
Dave G. Reichert, of Washington.
Charlie Dent, of Pennsylvania.

Zoe Lofgren, of California.
Loretta Sanchez, of California.
Jane Harman, of California.
Nita M. Lowey, of New York.
Sheila Jackson Lee, of Texas.
Bob Etheridge, of North Carolina.
James R. Langevin, of Rhode Island.
Kendrick B. Meek, of Florida.

Management, Integration and Oversight

Mike Rogers, of Alabama, *Chair*

Christopher Shays, of Connecticut.
John Linder, of Georgia.
Tom Davis, of Virginia.
Katherine Harris, of Florida.
Dave G. Reichert, of Washington.
Michael McCaul, of Texas.
Charlie Dent, of Pennsylvania.

Kendrick B. Meek, of Florida.
Edward J. Markey, of Massachusetts.
Zoe Lofgren, of California.
Sheila Jackson Lee, of Texas.
Bill Pascrell, Jr., of New Jersey.
Donna M. Christensen, of the Virgin Islands.

Prevention of Nuclear and Biological Attack

John Linder, of Georgia, *Chair*

Don Young, of Alaska.
Christopher Shays, of Connecticut.
Daniel E. Lungren, of California.
Jim Gibbons, of Nevada.
Rob Simmons, of Connecticut.
Bobby Jindal, of Louisiana.
Michael McCaul, of Texas.

James R. Langevin, of Rhode Island.
Edward J. Markey, of Massachusetts.
Norman D. Dicks, of Washington.
Jane Harman, of California.
Eleanor Holmes Norton, of the District of Columbia.
Donna M. Christensen, of the Virgin Islands.

STAFF

Committee on Homeland Security (Library of Congress LA–202 John Adams Building), 226–8417, fax 226–3399.
  Majority Chief of Staff.—Benedict Cohen.
    Deputy Chief of Staff.—Steve DeVine.
    Chief Financial Officer.—Dawn M. Criste.
    Communications Director.—Paul Wilkinson.
    Press Secretary.—Bailey Wood.
    Assistant Press Secretary.—Ryan Patmintra.
    Press Assistant.—Nadra Harrison.
    Chief Counsel.—Thomas DiLenge.
    Senior Counsels: Michael Geffroy, Linda Solheim, Andrew Weis.
    Counsels: Patricia DeMarco, Mark Klaassen.
    Chief Clerk.—Michael Twinchek.
    Deputy Clerk.—Joseph Windrem.
    Staff Assistant.—Ammani Nagesh.
    Executive Assistant.—Elizabeth Burgess.
    Deputy Policy Director.—Mike Russell.
    Senior Advisor.—Josh Weerasinghe.
    Professional Staff Members: Kimberly Baronof, Mandy Bowers, Donovan Chau, Josh Dozer, Sterling Marchand, Deron McElroy, Winsome Packer, Margaret Peterlin, Brian White.
  Minority Staff Director.—Calvin Humphrey (228 John Adams Building), 226–2616, fax 226–4499.
    Chief Counsel/Deputy Staff Director.—Jessica Herrera.
    Deputy Chief Counsel.—Sue Ramanathan.
    Counsel/Senior Policy Advisor.—Todd Gee.
    Counsel.—Carla Buckner.

Special Assistant.—Joshua Magarik.
Staff Assistant.—Kandis Gibson.
Legal Clerk.—Christopher Espy.
Professional Staff Member/Subcommittee Policy Coordinator.—Jerry Ross.
Professional Staff.—Allen Thompson.

House Administration

1309 Longworth House Office Building, phone 225–8281, fax 225–9957

http://www.house.gov/cha

meets second Wednesday of each month

Robert W. Ney, of Ohio, *Chair*

Vernon J. Ehlers, of Michigan.
John L. Mica, of Florida.
John T. Doolittle, of California.
Thomas M. Reynolds, of New York.
Candice Miller, of Michigan.

Juanita Millender-McDonald, of California.
Robert A. Brady, of Pennsylvania.
Zoe Lofgren, of California.

(No Subcommittees)

STAFF

Committee on House Administration (1309 LHOB), 225–8281.
  Majority Staff Director.—Paul Vinovich.
    General Counsel.—Fred Hay.
    Counsel.—Matthew Petersen.
    Technology Director.—John Clocker.
    Advisors to the Chairman: Lynne Crow, Will Heaton, Patrick Sweeney.
    Professional Staff Members: Owen Beetham, Claire Cowart, Bryan Dorsey, David Duncan,
      Diane Giannini, George Hadijski, Alec Hoppes, Jeff Janas, Jennifer Mohtarez, Matthew
      Skipper, Donald Zelaya.
    Office Manager.—Darren Feist.
    Communications Director.—Brian Walsh.
    Systems Administrator.—Tim Torres.
    Executive Assistant to the Chair.—Chris Krueger.
    Staff Assistants: Samantha Dredge, Brett Pahler.
  Minority Staff Director.—George F. Shevlin IV (1216 LHOB), 225–2061.
    Chief Counsel.—Charles T. Howell.
    Professional Staff: Connie Goode, Michael L. Harrison, Thomas Hicks, Ellen A. McCarthy,
      Monica M.N. McCollin, Brian M. McCue, Mary Elizabeth McHugh, Matt Pinkus,
      Diana Rodriguez.
    Technology Director.—Sterling Spriggs.
Franking Commission (1338 LHOB), 5–9337.
  Majority Staff Director.—Jack Dail.
    Professional Staff.—Richard Landon.
  Minority Staff Director.—Ellen A. McCarthy.
    Professional Staff.—Connie Goode.

International Relations

2170 Rayburn House Office Building, phone 225–5021

http://www.house.gov/international__relations

meets first Tuesday of each month

Henry J. Hyde, of Illinois, *Chair*

James A. Leach, of Iowa.
Christopher H. Smith, of New Jersey.
Dan Burton, of Indiana.
Elton Gallegly, of California.
Ileana Ros-Lehtinen, of Florida.
Dana Rohrabacher, of California.
Edward R. Royce, of California.
Peter T. King, of New York.
Steve Chabot, of Ohio.
Thomas G. Tancredo, of Colorado.
Ron Paul, of Texas.
Darrell Issa, of California.
Jeff Flake, of Arizona.
Jo Ann Davis, of Virginia.
Mark Green, of Wisconsin.
Jerry Weller, of Illinois.
Mike Pence, of Indiana.
Thaddeus G. McCotter, of Michigan.
Katherine Harris, of Florida.
Joe Wilson, of South Carolina.
John Boozman, of Arkansas.
J. Gresham Barrett, of South Carolina.
Connie Mack, of Florida.
Jeff Fortenberry, of Nebraska.
Michael McCaul, of Texas.
Ted Poe, of Texas.

Tom Lantos, of California.
Howard L. Berman, of California.
Gary L. Ackerman, of New York.
Eni F.H. Faleomavaega, of American Samoa.
Donald M. Payne, of New Jersey.
Robert Menendez, of New Jersey.
Sherrod Brown, of Ohio.
Brad Sherman, of California.
Robert Wexler, of Florida.
Eliot L. Engel, of New York.
William D. Delahunt, of Massachusetts.
Gregory W. Meeks, of New York.
Barbara Lee, of California.
Joseph Crowley, of New York.
Earl Blumenauer, of Oregon.
Shelley Berkley, of Nevada.
Grace F. Napolitano, of California.
Adam B. Schiff, of California.
Diane E. Watson, of California.
Adam Smith, of Washington.
Betty McCollum, of Minnesota.
Ben Chandler, of Kentucky.
Dennis A. Cardoza, of California.

SUBCOMMITTEES

[The chairman and ranking minority member are ex officio (non-voting) members of all
subcommittees on which they do not serve.]

Africa, Global Human Rights and International Operations

Christopher H. Smith, of New Jersey, *Chair*

Thomas G. Tancredo, of Colorado.
Jeff Flake, of Arizona.
Mark Green, of Wisconsin.
John Boozman, of Arkansas.
Jeff Fortenberry, of Nebraska.
Edward R. Royce, of California.

Donald M. Payne, of New Jersey.
Barbara Lee, of California.
Betty McCollum, of Minnesota.
Brad Sherman, of California.
Gregory W. Meeks, of New York.
Diane E. Watson, of California.

Asia and the Pacific

James A. Leach, of Iowa, *Chair*

Dan Burton, of Indiana.
Elton Gallegly, of California.
Dana Rohrabacher, of California.
Steve Chabot, of Ohio.
Ron Paul, of Texas.
Joe Wilson, of South Carolina.

Eni F.H. Faleomavaega, of American Samoa.
Sherrod Brown, of Ohio.
Earl Blumenauer, of Oregon.
Diane E. Watson, of California.
Adam Smith, of Washington.
Gary L. Ackerman, of New York.

Europe and Emerging Threats

Elton Gallegly, of California, *Chair*

Jo Ann Davis, of Virginia.
Peter T. King, of New York.
Thaddeus G. McCotter, of Michigan.
Darrell Issa, of California.
Ted Poe, of Texas.
J. Gresham Barrett, of South Carolina.

Robert Wexler, of Florida.
Eliot L. Engel, of New York.
Shelley Berkley, of Nevada.
Grace F. Napolitano, of California.
Adam Smith, of Washington.
Ben Chandler, of Kentucky.

International Terrorism and Nonproliferation

Edward R. Royce, of California, *Chair*

Peter T. King, of New York.
Thomas G. Tancredo, of Colorado.
Darrell Issa, of California.
Michael McCaul, of Texas.
Ted Poe, of Texas.
Jerry Weller, of Illinois.
J. Gresham Barrett, of South Carolina.

Brad Sherman, of California.
Robert Menendez, of New Jersey.
Robert Wexler, of Florida.
Joseph Crowley, of New York.
Betty McCollum, of Minnesota.
Dennis A. Cardoza, of California.
Diane Watson, of California.

The Middle East and Central Asia

Ileana Ros-Lehtinen, of Florida, *Chair*

Steve Chabot, of Ohio.
Thaddeus G. McCotter, of Michigan.
John Boozman, of Arkansas.
Connie Mack, of Florida.
Jeff Fortenberry, of Nebraska.
Jo Ann Davis, of Virginia.
Mike Pence, of Indiana.
Katherine Harris, of Florida.
Darrell Issa, of California.

Gary L. Ackerman, of New York.
Howard L. Berman, of California.
Eliot L. Engel, of New York.
Joseph Crowley, of New York.
Shelley Berkley, of Nevada.
Adam B. Schiff, of California.
Ben Chandler, of Kentucky.
Dennis A. Cardoza, of California.

Oversight and Investigations

Dana Rohrabacher, of California, *Chair*

Edward R. Royce, of California.
Jeff Flake, of Arizona.
Mark Green, of Wisconsin.
Mike Pence, of Indiana.
Joe Wilson, of South Carolina.

William D. Delahunt, of Massachusetts.
Howard L. Berman, of California.
Earl Blumenauer, of Oregon.
Adam B. Schiff, of California.

The Western Hemisphere

Dan Burton, of Indiana, *Chair*

Ron Paul, of Texas.
Jerry Weller, of Illinois.
Katherine Harris, of Florida.
James A. Leach, of Iowa.
Christopher H. Smith, of New Jersey.
Ileana Ros-Lehtinen, of Florida.
Connie Mack, of Florida.
Michael McCaul, of Texas.

Robert Menendez, of New Jersey.
Grace F. Napolitano, of California.
Gregory W. Meeks, of New York.
Eni F.H. Faleomavaega, of American Samoa.
Donald M. Payne, of New Jersey.
William D. Delahunt, of Massachusetts.
Barbara Lee, of California.

STAFF

Committee on International Relations (2170 RHOB), 225–5021.
Majority Staff Director/General Counsel.—Thomas Mooney.
Deputy Staff Director.—John Walker Roberts.
Chief Counsel.—Jonathan Scharfen.

Investigative Counsel.— John Mackey.
Counsels: Frank Cotter, Kirsti Garlock.
Counsel/Parliamentarian.—Dan Freeman.
Senior Professional Staff/Counsel.—Hillel Weinberg.
Senior Professional Staff: Kristen Gilley, Sam Stratman.
Professional Staff: Blaine Aaron, Lara Alameh, Renee Austell, Joan Condon, Dennis Halpin, Caleb McCarry, Matthew McLean, Patrick Murphy, Doug Seay, Sarah Tillemann.
Senior Policy Advisor for Transatlantic Relations.—John Lis.
Security Officer.—Laura Rush.
Administrative Director/Executive Assistant to General Counsel.—Sheila Klein.
Financial Administrator.—Jim Farr.
Travel Coordinator/Staff Associate.—Jeff Cox.
Information Resource Manager.—Vlad Cerga.
Senior Staff Associate/Intern Coordinator.—Marilyn Owen.
Legislative Correspondence Manager.—Elizabeth Singleton.
Protocol Officer.—Linda Solomon.
Printing Manager/Web Assistant.—Shirley Alexander.
Full Committee Hearing Coordinator.—Jean Carroll.
Staff Associates: David Bacci, Genell Brown, Fran Marcucci.
Minority Staff Director.—Robert King (B–360 RHOB), 225–6735.
Deputy Staff Director.—Peter Yeo.
Chief Counsel.—David Abramowitz.
Deputy Chief Counsel.—Paul Oostburg Sanz.
Senior Policy Advisor.—Kay King.
Professional Staff: Doug Campbell, David Fite, Hans Hogrefe, David Killion, Alan Makovsky, Pearl Alice Marsh, Robin Roizman, Guido Zucconi.
Press Secretary.—Lynne Weil.
Special Assistant.—Candace Bryan-Abbey.
Clerk.—Melilssa Adamson.
Subcommittee on Africa, Global Human Rights and International Operations (255 FHOB), 226–7812.
Majority Staff Director.—Mary Noonan.
Minority Professional Staff.—Noelle Lusane.
Staff Associate.—Lindsey Plumley.
Subcommittee on Asia and the Pacific (B–358 RHOB), 226–7825.
Majority Staff Director.—Jamie McCormick.
Minority Professional Staff.—Lisa Williams.
Professional Staff/Counsel.—Douglas Anderson.
Staff Associate.—Tiernen Miller Donald.
Subcommittee on Europe and Emerging Threats (2401A RHOB), 226–7820.
Majority Staff Director.—Richard Mereu.
Minority Professional Staff.—Jonathan Katz.
Professional Staff.—Patrick Prisco.
Staff Associate.—Beverly Hallock.
Subcommittee on International Terrorism and Nonproliferation (256 FHOB), 226–1500.
Majority Staff Director.—Tom Sheehy.
Minority Professional Staff.—Don MacDonald.
Professional Staff.—Malik Chaka.
Staff Associate.—Greg Galvin.
Subcommittee on the Middle East and Central Asia (257 FHOB), 225–3345.
Majority Staff Director.—Yleem Poblete.
Minority Professional Staff: David Adams, Matthew Zweig.
Subcommittee on Oversight and Investigations (253 FHOB), 226–6434.
Majority Staff Director.—Gregg Rickman.
Minority Professional Staff.—Cliff Stammerman.
Professional Staff.—Gregory McCarthy.
Special Assistant.—Tod Hull.
Subcommittee on the Western Hemisphere (259 FHOB), 226–9980.
Majority Staff Director.—Mark Walker.
Minority Professional Staff.—Jessica Lewis.
Professional Staff.—Daniel Getz.
Staff Associate.—Brian Wanko.

Judiciary

2138 Rayburn House Office Building, phone 225–3951

http://www.house.gov/judiciary

meets every Tuesday

F. James Sensenbrenner, Jr., of Wisconsin, *Chair*

Henry J. Hyde, of Illinois.
Howard Coble, of North Carolina.
Lamar S. Smith, of Texas.
Elton Gallegly, of California.
Bob Goodlatte, of Virginia.
Steve Chabot, of Ohio.
Daniel E. Lungren, of California.
William L. Jenkins, of Tennessee.
Chris Cannon, of Utah.
Spencer Bachus, of Alabama.
Robert D. Inglis, of South Carolina.
John N. Hostettler, of Indiana.
Mark Green, of Wisconsin.
Ric Keller, of Florida.
Darrell E. Issa, of California.
Jeff Flake, of Arizona.
Mike Pence, of Indiana.
J. Randy Forbes, of Virginia.
Steve King, of Iowa.
Tom Feeney, of Florida.
Trent Franks, of Arizona.
Louie Gohmert, of Texas.

John Conyers, Jr., of Michigan.
Howard L. Berman, of California.
Rick Boucher, of Virginia.
Jerrold Nadler, of New York.
Robert C. Scott, of Virginia.
Melvin L. Watt, of North Carolina.
Zoe Lofgren, of California.
Sheila Jackson Lee, of Texas.
Maxine Waters, of California.
Martin T. Meehan, of Massachusetts.
William D. Delahunt, of Massachusetts.
Robert Wexler, of Florida.
Anthony Weiner, of New York.
Adam B. Schiff, of California.
Linda Sánchez, of California.
Chris Van Hollen, of Maryland.

SUBCOMMITTEES

[The chairman and the ranking minority member are ex officio (non-voting) members of all subcommittees on which they do not serve.]

Commercial and Administrative Law

Chris Cannon, of Utah, *Chair*

Howard Coble, of North Carolina.
Trent Franks, of Arizona.
Steve Chabot, of Ohio.
Mark Green, of Wisconsin.
J. Randy Forbes, of Virginia.
Louie Gohmert, of Texas.

Melvin L. Watt, of North Carolina.
William D. Delahunt, of Massachusetts.
Chris Van Hollen, of Maryland.
Jerrold Nadler, of New York.

The Constitution

Steve Chabot, of Ohio, *Chair*

Trent Franks, of Arizona.
William L. Jenkins, of Tennessee.
Spencer Bachus, of Alabama.
John N. Hostettler, of Indiana.
Mark Green, of Wisconsin.
Steve King, of Iowa.
Tom Feeney, of Florida.

Jerrold Nadler, of New York.
John Conyers, Jr., of Michigan.
Robert C. Scott, of Virginia.
Melvin L. Watt, of North Carolina.
Chris Van Hollen, of Maryland.

Courts, the Internet, and Intellectual Property

Lamar S. Smith, of Texas, *Chair*

Henry J. Hyde, of Illinois.
Elton Gallegly, of California.
Bob Goodlatte, of Virginia.
William L. Jenkins, of Tennessee.
Spencer Bachus, of Alabama.
Robert D. Inglis, of South Carolina.
Ric Keller, of Florida.
Darrell E. Issa, of California.
Chris Cannon, of Utah.
Mike Pence, of Indiana.
J. Randy Forbes, of Virginia.

Howard L. Berman, of California.
John Conyers, Jr., of Michigan.
Rick Boucher, of Virginia.
Zoe Lofgren, of California.
Maxine Waters, of California.
Martin T. Meehan, of Massachusetts.
Robert Wexler, of Florida.
Anthony Weiner, of New York.
Adam B. Schiff, of California.
Linda Sánchez, of California.

Crime, Terrorism, and Homeland Security

Howard Coble, of North Carolina, *Chair*

Daniel E. Lungren, of California.
Mark Green, of Wisconsin.
Tom Feeney, of Florida.
Steve Chabot, of Ohio.
Ric Keller, of Florida.
Jeff Flake, of Arizona.
Mike Pence, of Indiana.
J. Randy Forbes, of Virginia.
Louie Gohmert, of Texas.

Robert C. Scott, of Virginia.
Sheila Jackson Lee, of Texas.
Maxine Waters, of California.
Martin T. Meehan, of Massachusetts.
William D. Delahunt, of Massachusetts.
Anthony Weiner, of New York.

Immigration, Border Security, and Claims

John N. Hostettler, of Indiana, *Chair*

Steve King, of Iowa.
Louie Gohmert, of Texas.
Lamar S. Smith, of Texas.
Elton Gallegly, of California.
Bob Goodlatte, of Virginia.
Daniel E. Lungren, of California.
Jeff Flake, of Arizona.
Robert D. Inglis, of South Carolina.
Darrell E. Issa, of California.

Sheila Jackson Lee, of Texas.
Howard L. Berman, of California.
Zoe Lofgren, of California.
Linda Sánchez, of California.
Jerrold Nadler, of New York.
Maxine Waters, of California.

STAFF

Committee on the Judiciary (2138 RHOB), 225–3951.
Majority Chief of Staff/General Counsel.—Philip Kiko.
 Deputy Chief of Staff/Deputy General Counsel.—Sean McLaughlin.
 Chief Legislative Counsel/Parliamentarian.—Robert Tracci.
 Counsel.—Thad Bingel.
 Chief Clerk/Administrator.—Tish Schwartz.
 Executive Assistant.—Christine Layman.
 Legislative Assistant.—Chris Cylke.
 Office Manager.—Michele Manon Utt.
 Communications Director.—Jeff Lungren.
 Press Secretary.—Terry Shawn.
 Finance Clerk.—Diane Hill.
 Legislative Clerk.—James David Binsted.
 Information Systems Specialist.—Seth Ciango.
 Calendar Clerk.—Jennifer Noll (B–29 CHOB), 6–1790.
 Publications Clerk.—Joe McDonald (B–29 CHOB), 5–0408.
 Staff Assistant.—Andrew Meehan.
 Printing Clerk.—Douglas Alexander.
 Oversight Counsel: Mindy Barry, Luke Bellocchi, Jason Cervanek, James Daley.
 Senior Investigator.—Brian Zimmer.

Coalition and Projects Director.—Paul Zanowski.
Information Systems Manager.—Kerli Philippe.
Editor.—Anne M. Binsted.
Legislative Correspondent.—Anthony Grossi.
Minority Chief Counsel.—Perry Apelbaum (2142 RHOB), 5–6504.
Financial and Administrative Officer.—Anita Johnson.
Senior Counsel.—Burt Wides.
General Counsel.—Ted Kalo.
Counsels: Gregory Barnes, Kanya Bennett, Stacey Dansky, Sampak Garg, Lillian German, Michone Johnson, Keenan Keller, Stephanie Moore, Michelle Persaud, Nolan Rappaport, Michele Richardson, Bobby Vassar, Kirsten Wells.
Professional Staff: Danielle Brown, David G. Lachmann.
Chief Clerk/Web Administrator.—Teresa Vest.
Staff Assistants: Veronica Eligan, Susanna Gutierrez.
Subcommittee on Commercial and Administrative Law (B–353 RHOB), 5–2825.
Majority Chief Counsel.—Raymond V. Smietanka.
Counsel.—Susan Jensen.
Staff Assistant.—Chris Slinker.
Minority Counsel.—Stephanie Moore (B–351C RHOB), 5–6906.
Subcommittee on the Constitution (H2–362 FHOB), 6–7680.
Majority Chief Counsel.—Paul Taylor.
Minority Professional Staff.—David Lachmann (B–336 RHOB), 5–2022.
Subcommittee on Courts, the Internet, and Intellectual Property (B–351A RHOB), 5–5741.
Majority Chief Counsel.—Blaine Merritt.
Counsels: Debra Laman Rose, David Whitney.
Staff Assistant.—Eunice Goldring.
Subcommittee on Crime, Terrorism, and Homeland Security (207 CHOB), 5–3926.
Majority Chief Counsel.—Jay Apperson.
Deputy Chief Counsel.—Michael Volkov.
Counsels: Katy Crooks, Beth Sokul.
Staff Assistant.—Latoya McBeam.
Minority Counsel.—Bobby Vassar (B–336 RHOB), 5–2329.
Subcommittee on Immigration, Border Security, and Claims (B–370B RHOB), 5–5727.
Majority Chief Counsel.—George Fishman.
Counsel.—Art Arthur.
Professional Staff.—Cynthia Blackston.
Staff Assistant.—Leilani Pallares.
Minority Counsel.—Nolan Rappaport (B–336 RHOB), 5–2329.

Resources

1324 Longworth House Office Building, phone 225-2761

http://www.house.gov/resources

meets each Wednesday

Richard W. Pombo, of California, *Chair*

Don Young, of Alaska.	*Nick J. Rahall II,* of West Virginia.
Jim Saxton, of New Jersey.	*Dale E. Kildee,* of Michigan.
Elton Gallegly, of California.	***Eni F.H. Faleomavaega***, of American Samoa.
John J. Duncan, Jr., of Tennessee.	*Neil Abercrombie,* of Hawaii.
Wayne T. Gilchrest, of Maryland.	*Solomon P. Ortiz,* of Texas.
Ken Calvert, of California.	*Frank Pallone, Jr.,* of New Jersey.
Barbara Cubin, of Wyoming.	***Donna M. Christensen***, of the Virgin Islands.
George P. Radanovich, of California.	*Ron Kind,* of Wisconsin.
Walter B. Jones, of North Carolina.	*Grace F. Napolitano,* of California.
Chris Cannon, of Utah.	*Tom Udall,* of New Mexico.
John E. Peterson, of Pennsylvania.	*Raúl M. Grijalva,* of Arizona.
Jim Gibbons, of Nevada.	***Madeleine Z. Bordallo***, of Guam.
Greg Walden, of Oregon.	*Jim Costa,* of California.
Thomas G. Tancredo, of Colorado.	*Charlie Melancon,* of Louisiana.
J.D. Hayworth, of Arizona.	*Dan Boren,* of Oklahoma.
Jeff Flake, of Arizona.	*George Miller,* of California.
Rick Renzi, of Arizona.	*Edward J. Markey,* of Massachusetts.
Stevan Pearce, of New Mexico.	*Peter DeFazio,* of Oregon.
Devin Nunes, of California.	*Jay Inslee,* of Washington.
Henry Brown, of South Carolina.	*Mark Udall,* of Colorado.
Thelma Drake, of Virginia.	*Dennis A. Cardoza,* of California.
Luis G. Fortuño, of Puerto Rico.	*Stephanie Herseth,* of South Dakota.
Cathy McMorris, of Washington.	
Bobby Jindal, of Louisiana.	
Louie Gohmert, of Texas.	
Marilyn Musgrave, of Colorado.	

SUBCOMMITTEES

[The chairman and ranking minority member are ex officio (non-voting) members of all subcommittees on which they do not serve.]

Energy and Mineral Resources

Jim Gibbons, of Nevada, *Chair*

Don Young, of Alaska.	*Raúl M. Grijalva,* of Arizona.
Barbara Cubin, of Wyoming.	***Eni F.H. Faleomavaega***, of American Samoa.
Chris Cannon, of Utah.	*Solomon P. Ortiz,* of Texas.
John E. Peterson, of Pennsylvania.	*Jim Costa,* of California.
Stevan Pearce, of New Mexico.	*Charlie Melancon,* of Louisiana.
Thelma Drake, of Virginia.	*Dan Boren,* of Oklahoma.
Bobby Jindal, of Louisiana.	*Edward J. Markey,* of Massachusetts.
Louie Gohmert, of Texas.	

Fisheries Conservation, Wildlife, and Oceans

Wayne T. Gilchrest, of Maryland, *Chair*

Don Young, of Alaska.	*Frank Pallone, Jr.,* of New Jersey.
Jim Saxton, of New Jersey.	***Eni F.H. Faleomavaega***, of American Samoa.
Walter B. Jones, of North Carolina.	*Neil Abercrombie,* of Hawaii.
Thelma Drake, of Virginia.	*Solomon P. Ortiz,* of Texas.
Luis G. Fortuño, of Puerto Rico.	*Ron Kind,* of Wisconsin.
Bobby Jindal, of Louisiana.	***Madeleine Z. Bordallo***, of Guam.

Forests and Forest Health

Greg Walden, of Oregon, *Chair*

John J. Duncan, Jr., of Tennessee.
Wayne T. Gilchrest, of Maryland.
Chris Cannon, of Utah.
John E. Peterson, of Pennsylvania.
Thomas G. Tancredo, of Colorado.
J.D. Hayworth, of Arizona.
Jeff Flake, of Arizona.
Rick Renzi, of Arizona.
Henry Brown, of South Carolina.
Cathy McMorris, of Washington.

Tom Udall, of New Mexico.
Dale E. Kildee, of Michigan.
Neil Abercrombie, of Hawaii.
Dan Boren, of Oklahoma.
Peter DeFazio, of Oregon.
Jay Inslee, of Washington.
Mark Udall, of Colorado.
Dennis A. Cardoza, of California.
Stephanie Herseth, of South Dakota.

National Parks, Recreation, and Public Lands

Devin Nunes, of California, *Chair*

Jim Saxton, of New Jersey.
Elton Gallegly, of California.
John J. Duncan, Jr., of Tennessee.
George P. Radanovich, of California.
Walter B. Jones, of North Carolina.
Henry Brown, of South Carolina.
Luis G. Fortuño, of Puerto Rico.

Donna M. Christensen, of the Virgin Islands.
Dale E. Kildee, of Michigan.
Neil Abercrombie, of Hawaii.
Ron Kind, of Wisconsin.
Tom Udall, of New Mexico.
Madeleine Z. Bordallo, of Guam.
Charlie Melancon, of Louisiana.

Water and Power

George P. Radanovich, of California, *Chair*

Ken Calvert, of California.
Barbara Cubin, of Wyoming.
Greg Walden, of Oregon.
Thomas G. Tancredo, of Colorado.
J.D. Hayworth, of Arizona.
Stevan Pearce, of New Mexico.
Devin Nunes, of California.
Cathy McMorris, of Washington.
Louie Gohmert, of Texas.

Grace F. Napolitano, of California.
Raúl M. Grijalva, of Arizona.
Jim Costa, of California.
George Miller, of California.
Mark Udall, of Colorado.
Dennis A. Cardoza, of California.

STAFF

Committee on Resources (1324 LHOB), 225–2761.
   Majority Chief of Staff.—Steve Ding.
      Executive Assistant to the Chief of Staff.—Tammy McDougald.
      Director of External Affairs.—Kristin Schrader.
      Chief Counsel.—Lisa Pittman (1320 LHOB), 225–7800.
         Deputy Chief Counsel.—Vince Sampson.
         Legislative Assistant to the Chief Counsel.—Joanna MacKay.
      Chief Financial Officer.—Lisa Wallace (1327A LHOB), 225–2761.
      Communications Director.—Brian Kennedy (1333 LHOB), 226–9019.
         Deputy Communications Director.—Matthew Streit.
      Press Secretary.—Jennifer Zuccarelli.
         Deputy Press Secretary.—Amanda Lawson.
      Chief Clerk.—Nancy Laheeb (1328 LHOB), 225–2761.
      Legislative Calendar Clerk.—Ann Vogt.
      Executive Assistant.—Linda Livingston.
      Systems Administrators: Matt Vaccaro, Ed Van Scoyoc (1322 LHOB).
      Senior Advisors: Dan Kish (1322A LHOB); Matt Miller (1324 LHOB).
      Senior Policy Director.—Todd Willens (1331 LHOB).
      Professional Staff: Tom Brierton, Kurt Christensen (1413P LHOB), 225–2761; Rob Gordon (1334 LHOB), 226–0987; Carrie Weaver (1324 LHOB), 225–2761.
      Staff Assistants: Jennifer Jacobs, Sophia Varnasidis.
      Editor and Printer.—Kathleen Miller (H2–550 Ford).

Minority Staff Director.—James H. Zoia (1329 LHOB), 225–6065.
   Chief Counsel.—Jeffrey Petrich.
   Policy Advisor.—Ann Adler.
   Administrator.—Linda Booth.
   Staff Assistants: Whitney Smith (1329 LHOB), 225–6065; David Zacher (186 LHOB), 226–2311.
   Press Secretary.—Kristen Bossi (269 FHOB), 226–2311.
Subcommittee on Energy and Mineral Resources (1626 LHOB), 225–9297.
   Majority Staff Director.—Jay Cranford.
   Legislative Staff.—Kathy Benedetto.
   Clerk.—Lucas Frances.
   Minority Professional Staff.—Deborah van Hoffman Lanzone (186 FHOB), 226–2311.
Subcommittee on Fisheries Conservation, Wildlife, and Oceans (H2–188 FHOB), 226–0200.
   Majority Staff Director.—Harry Burroughs.
   Legislative Staff: Bonnie Bruce, Dave Whaley.
   Clerk.—Michael Correia.
   Minority Professional Staff: Dave Jansen, Amelia Jenkins (186 FHOB), 226–2311.
Subcommittee on Forests and Forest Health (1337 LHOB), 225–0691.
   Majority Staff Director.—Doug Crandall.
   Legislative Staff.—Erica Tergeson.
   Clerk.—Ryan Yates.
   Minority Professional Staff: Meghan Conklin, Amelia Jenkins (186 FHOB), 226–2311.
Subcommittee on National Parks, Recreation, and Public Lands (1333 LHOB), 226–7736.
   Majority Staff Director.—Rob Howarth.
   Legislative Staff.—Casey Hammond.
   Minority Professional Staff: Richard Healy, David Watkins, (186 FHOB), 226–2311.
Subcommittee on Water and Power (1522 LHOB), 225–8331.
   Majority Staff Director.—Kiel Weaver.
   Clerk.—Daisy Minter.
   Minority Professional Staff: Steve Lanich (186 FHOB); Lori Sonken, (269 FHOB), 226–2311.
Office of Native American and Insular Affairs (140 CHOB), 226–9725.
   Majority Staff Director.—Christopher Fluhr (140 CHOB), 225–6523.
   Legislative Staff: Cynthia Ahwinona, Jim Hall.
   Insular Affairs.—Chris Foster.
   Clerk.—Laura Hylden.
   Minority Professional Staff: Tony Babauta, Marie Howard Fabrizio, Tracey Parker, (186 FHOB), 226–2311.

Rules

H–312 The Capitol, phone 225–9191

http://www.house.gov/rules

meets every Tuesday

David Dreier, of California, *Chair*

Lincoln Diaz-Balart, of Florida.
Doc Hastings, of Washington.
Pete Sessions, of Texas.
Adam Putnam, of Florida.
Shelley Moore Capito, of West Virginia.
Tom Cole, of Oklahoma.
Rob Bishop, of Utah.
Phil Gingrey, of Georgia.

Louise M. Slaughter, of New York.
James P. McGovern, of Massachusetts.
Alcee L. Hastings, of Florida.
Doris O. Matsui, of California.

SUBCOMMITTEES

Legislative and Budget Process

Lincoln Diaz-Balart, of Florida, *Chair*

Pete Sessions, of Texas.
Rob Bishop, of Utah.
Phil Gingrey, of Georgia.
David Dreier, of California.

Alcee Hastings, of Florida.
Louise Slaughter, of New York.
Doris O. Matsui, of California.

Rules and Organization of the House

Doc Hastings, of Washington, *Chair*

Adam Putnam, of Florida.
Shelley Moore Capito, of West Virginia.
Tom Cole, of Oklahoma.
David Dreier, of California.

James P. McGovern, of Massachusetts.
Louise Slaughter, of New York.

STAFF

Committee on Rules (H–312 The Capitol), 225–9191.
  Majority Staff Director.—Hugh Halpern.
    Press Secretary.—Jo Maney.
    Policy Director.—Amy Heerink.
    Professional Staff: Eileen Harley, Adam Jarvis, George Rogers, Celeste West, Kathy White.
    Legislative Clerk.—Donald Sisson.
    Staff Assistant.—Bettie Antrim.
  Minority Staff Director.—John Daniel (H–152), 5–9091.
    Professional Staff: Sophie Hayford, Shannon Meissner, John Williams (2460 RHOB, 5–9486); Askia Sunuma (H–152).
    Associate Staff: Keith Stern (430 CHOB), Fred Turner (2235 RHOB).
Subcommittee on Legislative and Budget Process (1627 LHOB), 5–4211.
    Staff Director.—Steve Cote (Diaz-Balart).
Subcommittee on Rules and Organization of the House (1627 LHOB), 5–5816.
    Staff Director.—Todd Young (Doc Hastings).

Science

2320 Rayburn House Office Building, phone 225–6371, fax 226–0113
http://www.house.gov/science

meets second and fourth Wednesdays of each month

Sherwood Boehlert, of New York, *Chair*

Ralph M. Hall, of Texas.	*Bart Gordon, of Tennessee.*
Lamar S. Smith, of Texas.	*Jerry F. Costello, of Illinois.*
Curt Weldon, of Pennsylvania.	*Eddie Bernice Johnson, of Texas.*
Dana Rohrabacher, of California.	*Lynn C. Woolsey, of California.*
Ken Calvert, of California.	*Darlene Hooley, of Oregon.*
Roscoe G. Bartlett, of Maryland.	*Mark Udall, of Colorado.*
Vernon J. Ehlers, of Michigan.	*David Wu, of Oregon.*
Gil Gutknecht, of Minnesota.	*Michael M. Honda, of California.*
Frank D. Lucas, of Oklahoma.	*Brad Miller, of North Carolina.*
Judy Biggert, of Illinois.	*Lincoln Davis, of Tennessee.*
Wayne T. Gilchrest, of Maryland.	*Russ Carnahan, of Missouri.*
W. Todd Akin, of Missouri.	*Daniel Lipinski, of Illinois.*
Timothy V. Johnson, of Illinois.	*Sheila Jackson Lee, of Texas.*
J. Randy Forbes, of Virginia.	*Brad Sherman, of California.*
Jo Bonner, of Alabama.	*Brian Baird, of Washington.*
Tom Feeney, of Florida.	*Jim Matheson, of Utah.*
Bob Inglis, of South Carolina.	*Jim Costa, of California.*
Dave G. Reichert, of Washington.	*Al Green, of Texas.*
Michael E. Sodrel, of Indiana.	*Charlie Melancon, of Louisiana.*
John J.H. (Joe) Schwarz, of Michigan.	
Michael T. McCaul, of Texas.	

SUBCOMMITTEES

[The chairman and ranking minority member are ex officio (voting) members of all subcommittees on which they do not serve.]

Energy

Judy Biggert, of Illinois, *Chair*

Ralph M. Hall, of Texas.	*Michael M. Honda, of California.*
Curt Weldon, of Pennsylvania.	*Lynn C. Woolsey, of California.*
Roscoe G. Bartlett, of Maryland.	*Lincoln Davis, of Tennessee.*
Vernon J. Ehlers, of Michigan.	*Jerry F. Costello, of Illinois.*
W. Todd Akin, of Missouri.	*Eddie Bernice Johnson, of Texas.*
Jo Bonner, of Alabama.	*Daniel Lipinski, of Illinois.*
Bob Inglis, of South Carolina.	*Jim Matheson, of Utah.*
Dave G. Reichert, of Washington.	*Sheila Jackson Lee, of Texas.*
Michael E. Sodrel, of Indiana.	*Brad Sherman, of California.*
John J.H. (Joe) Schwarz, of Michigan.	*Al Green, of Texas.*

Environment, Technology, and Standards

Vernon J. Ehlers, of Michigan, *Chair*

Gil Gutknecht, of Minnesota.	*David Wu, of Oregon.*
Judy Biggert, of Illinois.	*Brad Miller, of North Carolina.*
Wayne T. Gilchrest, of Maryland.	*Mark Udall, of Colorado.*
Timothy V. Johnson, of Illinois.	*Lincoln Davis, of Tennessee.*
Dave G. Reichert, of Washington.	*Brian Baird, of Washington.*
John J.H. (Joe) Schwarz, of Michigan.	*Jim Matheson, of Utah.*

430   *Congressional Directory*

Research

Bob Inglis, of South Carolina, *Chair*

Lamar S. Smith, of Texas.
Curt Weldon, of Pennsylvania.
Dana Rohrabacher, of California.
Gil Gutknecht, of Minnesota.
Frank D. Lucas, of Oklahoma.
W. Todd Akin, of Missouri.
Timothy V. Johnson, of Illinois.
Dave G. Reichert, of Washington.
Michael E. Sodrel, of Indiana.
Michael T. McCaul, of Texas.

Darlene Hooley, of Oregon.
Russ Carnahan, of Missouri.
Daniel Lipinski, of Illinois.
Brian Baird, of Washington.
Charlie Melancon, of Louisiana.
Eddie Bernice Johnson, of Texas.
Brad Miller, of North Carolina.

Space and Aeronautics

Ken Calvert, of California, *Chair*

Ralph M. Hall, of Texas.
Lamar S. Smith, of Texas.
Dana Rohrabacher, of California.
Roscoe G. Bartlett, of Maryland.
Frank D. Lucas, of Oklahoma.
J. Randy Forbes, of Virginia.
Jo Bonner, of Alabama.
Tom Feeney, of Florida.
Michael T. McCaul, of Texas.

Mark Udall, of Colorado.
David Wu, of Oregon.
Michael M. Honda, of California.
Brad Miller, of North Carolina.
Sheila Jackson Lee, of Texas.
Brad Sherman, of California.
Jim Costa, of California.
Al Green, of Texas.
Charlie Melancon, of Louisiana.

STAFF

Committee on Science (2320 RHOB), 225–6371, fax 226–0113.
 Majority Chief of Staff.—David Goldston, 5–8772.
  Deputy Chief of Staff: John Mimikakis (Environment, Technology, and Standards; Space), 5–7950, Peter Rooney (Research; Energy), 6–3281.
  Chief Counsel.—Mike Bloomquist, 5–0125.
  Counsel.—Tim Hughes, 6–0354.
  Communications Director.—Joe Pouliot, 5–0581.
  Projects Director.—Tim Clancy, 5–0585.
  Financial Administrator.—Dave Laughter, 5–5977.
  Legislative Clerk.—Vivian Tessieri, 5–8121.
  Systems Administrator.—Larry Whittaker, 5–4414.
  Special Assistant to the Chief of Staff/Administrative Clerk.—David Mayorga, 5–0584.
  Printer.—Jude Ruckel, 5–6371.
  Press Assistant.—Nathaniel Sillin, 6–1430.
  Staff Assistants: Leslie Caudle, 5–1456; Rachel Jagoda, 5–8123; Zach Kurz, 6–4955.
  Shared Professional Staff.—Amy Chiang, 5–3665.
 Minority Staff Director.—Chuck Atkins (394 FHOB), 5–6375, fax 5–3895.
  Chief Counsel.—Jim Turner, 5–8128.
  Counsel: Mike Lynch, 6–3096; Marsha Shasteen, 5–1569.
  Professional Staff: James Paul, 6–3639; Dan Pearson, 5–4494; Christal Sheppard, 5–6375.
  Communications Director.—Alisha Prather, 5–6375.
  Staff Assistant.—Leigh Ann Brown, 5–6375.
 Subcommittee on Energy (390 FHOB) 5–9662, fax 6–6983.
  Majority Staff Director.—Kevin Carroll, 5–9816.
   Fellow.—Dahlia Sokolov, 5–2157.
   Staff Assistant.—Colin Hubbell, 6–8665.
   Professional Staff: Eli Hopson, 5–0302; Tina Kaarsburg, 6–8948.
  Minority Professional Staff: Charlie Cooke, 5–8896; Chris King, 5–7255.

Subcommittee on Environment, Technology, and Standards (2319 RHOB), 5–8844, fax 5–4438.
  Majority Staff Director.—Eric Webster, 6–4851.
    Professional Staff, Chair's Designee.—Amy Carroll, 6–5342.
    Professional Staff: Susannah Foster, 6–2179; Olwen Huxley, 6–3614; Marty Spitzer, 5–7223.
    Staff Assistant.—Jamie Brown, 5–7593.
  Minority Professional Staff: Jean Frucci, 6–0697; Mike Quear, 5–6917.
Subcommittee on Research (B–374 RHOB), 5–7858, fax 5–7815.
  Majority Staff Director.—Dan Byers, 5–5064.
    Professional Staff: Elizabeth Grossman, 5–7284; Kara Haas, 5–8115.
    Staff Assistant.—Jimmy Hague, 5–9011.
  Minority Professional Staff.—Jim Wilson, 5–2634.
Subcommittee on Space and Aeronautics (B–374 RHOB), 5–7858, fax 5–6415.
  Majority Staff Director.—Bill Adkins, 5–2070.
    Professional Staff, Chair's Designee.—Roselee Roberts, 5–8459.
    Professional Staff: Ed Feddeman, 5–0587; Johannes Loschnigg, 6–0584; Ken Monroe, 6–3660; Chris Shank, 5–2656.
    Staff Assistant.—Tom Hammond, 6–2177.
  Minority Professional Staff.—Dick Obermann, 5–4482.

Small Business

2361 Rayburn House Office Building, phone 225–5821, fax 225–3587
http://www.house.gov/smbiz

meets second Thursday of each month

Donald A. Manzullo, of Illinois, *Chair*

Roscoe G. Bartlett, of Maryland.	*Nydia M. Velázquez,* of New York.
Sue W. Kelly, of New York.	*Juanita Millender-McDonald,* of California.
Steve Chabot, of Ohio.	*Tom Udall,* of New Mexico.
Sam Graves, of Missouri.	*Daniel Lipinski,* of Illinois.
W. Todd Akin, of Missouri.	*Eni Faleomavaega,* of American Samoa.
Bill Shuster, of Pennsylvania.	*Donna M. Christensen,* of Virgin Islands.
Marilyn N. Musgrave, of Colorado.	*Danny K. Davis,* of Illinois.
Jeb Bradley, of New Hampshire.	*Ed Case,* of Hawaii.
Steve King, of Iowa.	*Madeleine Bordallo,* of Guam.
Thaddeus McCotter, of Michigan.	*Raúl Grijalva,* of Arizona.
Ric Keller, of Florida.	*Michael Michaud,* of Maine.
Ted Poe, of Texas.	*Linda Sánchez,* of California.
Michael Sodrel, of Indiana.	*John Barrow,* of Georgia.
Jeff Fortenberry, of Nebraska.	*Melissa Bean,* of Illinois.
Michael Fitzpatrick, of Pennsylvania.	*Gwen Moore,* of Wisconsin.
Lynn Westmoreland, of Georgia.	
Louie Gohmert, of Texas.	

SUBCOMMITTEES

[The chairman and ranking minority member are ex officio (non-voting) members of all
subcommittees on which they do not serve.]

Regulatory Reform and Oversight

W. Todd Akin, of Missouri, *Chair*

Michael Sodrel, of Indiana.	*Madeleine Bordallo,* of Guam.
Lynn Westmoreland, of Georgia.	*Eni Faleomavaega,* of American Samoa.
Louie Gohmert, of Texas.	*Donna M. Christensen,* of Virgin Islands.
Sue W. Kelly, of New York.	*Ed Case,* of Hawaii.
Steve King, of Iowa.	
Ted Poe, of Texas.	

Rural Enterprises, Agriculture, and Technology

Sam Graves, of Missouri, *Chair*

Steve King, of Iowa.	*John Barrow,* of Georgia.
Roscoe G. Bartlett, of Maryland.	*Tom Udall,* of New Mexico.
Michael Sodrel, of Indiana.	*Ed Case,* of Hawaii.
Jeff Fortenberry, of Nebraska.	*Michael Michaud,* of Maine.
Marilyn N. Musgrave, of Colorado.	

Tax, Finance, and Exports

Jeb Bradley, of New Hampshire, *Chair*

Sue W. Kelly, of New York.	*Juanita Millender-McDonald,* of California.
Steve Chabot, of Ohio.	*Daniel Lipinski,* of Illinois.
Thaddeus McCotter, of Michigan.	*Eni Faleomavaega,* of American Samoa.
Ric Keller, of Florida.	*Danny K. Davis,* of Illinois.
Ted Poe, of Texas.	*Ed Case,* of Hawaii.
Jeff Fortenberry, of Nebraska.	*Michael Michaud,* of Maine.
Michael Fitzpatrick, of Pennsylvania.	*Melissa Bean,* of Illinois.

Workforce, Empowerment, and Government Programs

Marilyn N. Musgrave, of Colorado, *Chair*

Roscoe G. Bartlett, of Maryland.	*Daniel Lipinski,* of Illinois.
Bill Shuster, of Pennsylvania.	*Tom Udall,* of New Mexico.
Michael Fitzpatrick, of Pennsylvania.	*Danny K. Davis,* of Illinois.
Lynn Westmoreland, of Georgia.	*Raúl Grijalva,* of Arizona.
Thaddeus McCotter, of Michigan.	*John Barrow,* of Georgia.
Jeb Bradley, of New Hampshire.	*Melissa Bean,* of Illinois.

STAFF

Committee on Small Business (2361 RHOB), 225–5821, fax 225–3587.
  Majority Chief of Staff/Chief Counsel.—Matt Szymanski.
    Deputy Chief of Staff/Policy Director.—Phil Eskeland.
    Subcommittee Director/General Counsel.—Nelson Crowther.
    Special Counsel.—Rich Beutel.
    Counsels: Greg Dean (Finance); Barry Pineles (Regulatory).
    Communications Director.—Rich Carter.
    Chief Clerk/Deputy Communications Director.—Mike Arlinsky.
    Director of Coalitions/Senior Counsel.—Patrick Wilson.
    Deputy Director of Coalitions.—Dan Horowitz.
    Director of Operations/Special Assistant to the Chief of Staff.—Christy Markva.
    Senior Trade Advisor.—Jim Meenan.
    Professional Staff/Special Assistant to the Chief of Staff.—Sean Deverey.
    Systems Administrator & Professional Staff.—Ken Shaw.
    Professional Staff: Thomas Bezas, Joe Hartz, Piper Largent
    Chief Counsel.—Brad Knox.
    Chief Tax Counsel.—John Westmoreland.
    Regulatory Counsel.—Barry Pineles.
    Staff Assistant.—Nathan Berkeley.
    Commerce Detailee.—Mike Fullerton.
  Minority Staff Director.—Michael Day (B–343C RHOB), 225–4038, fax 225–7209.
    Office Manager.—Mory Garcia.
    Communications Director.—Kate Davis.
    Professional Staff: LeAnn Delaney, Jordan Haas, Adam Minehardt, Russell Orban, Michael Robinovich, Tim Slattery.

Standards of Official Conduct

HT–2 The Capitol, phone 225–7103, fax 225–7392

Doc Hastings, of Washington, *Chair*

Judy Biggert, of Illinois.
Lamar Smith, of Texas.
Melissa Hart, of Pennsylvania.
Tom Cole, of Oklahoma.

Alan B. Mollohan, of West Virginia.
Stephanie Tubbs Jones, of Ohio.
Gene Green, of Texas.
Lucille Roybal-Allard, of California.
Michael F. Doyle, of Pennsylvania.

(No Subcommittees)

STAFF

Acting Chief Counsel.—Kenneth E. Kellner.
Advisor to the Chair.—Ed Cassidy.
Assistant to the Ranking Minority Member.—Colleen McCarty.
Counsels: Carol E. Dixon, Susan Olson, John C. Sassaman, Jr., Peter Van Hartesveldt.
System Administrator.—Pete Johnson.
Staff Assistant.—Briana M. Nord.
Administrative Assistant.—Joanne White.

Transportation and Infrastructure

2165 Rayburn House Office Building, phone 225–9446, fax 225–6782

http://www.house.gov/transportation

meets first Wednesday of each month

Don Young, of Alaska, *Chair*

Thomas E. Petri, of Wisconsin.
Sherwood Boehlert, of New York.
Howard Coble, of North Carolina.
John J. Duncan, Jr., of Tennessee.
Wayne T. Gilchrest, of Maryland.
John L. Mica, of Florida.
Peter Hoekstra, of Michigan.
Vernon J. Ehlers, of Michigan.
Spencer Bachus, of Alabama.
Steven C. LaTourette, of Ohio.
Sue W. Kelly, of New York.
Richard H. Baker, of Louisiana.
Robert W. Ney, of Ohio.
Frank A. LoBiondo, of New Jersey.
Jerry Moran, of Kansas.
Gary G. Miller, of California.
Robin Hayes, of North Carolina.
Rob Simmons, of Connecticut.
Henry E. Brown, Jr., of South Carolina.
Timothy V. Johnson, of Illinois.
Todd Russell Platts, of Pennsylvania.
Sam Graves, of Missouri.
Mark R. Kennedy, of Minnesota.
Bill Shuster, of Pennsylvania.
John Boozman, of Arkansas.
Jim Gerlach, of Pennsylvania.
Mario Diaz-Balart, of Florida.
Jon C. Porter, of Nevada.
Tom Osborne, of Nebraska.
Kenny Marchant, of Texas.
Michael E. Sodrel, of Indiana.
Charles W. Dent, of Pennsylvania.
Ted Poe, of Texas.
David G. Reichert, of Washington.
Connie Mack, of Florida.
John R. (Randy) Kuhl, Jr., of New York.
Luis G. Fortuño, of Puerto Rico.
Lynn A. Westmoreland, of Georgia.
Charles W. Boustany, Jr., of Louisiana.

James L. Oberstar, of Minnesota.
Nick J. Rahall II, of West Virginia.
Peter A. DeFazio, of Oregon.
Jerry F. Costello, of Illinois.
***Eleanor Holmes Norton**, of the District of*
Columbia.
Jerrold Nadler, of New York.
Robert Menendez, of New Jersey.
Corrine Brown, of Florida.
Bob Filner, of California.
Eddie Bernice Johnson, of Texas.
Gene Taylor, of Mississippi.
Juanita Millender-McDonald, of California.
Elijah E. Cummings, of Maryland.
Earl Blumenauer, of Oregon.
Ellen O. Tauscher, of California.
Bill Pascrell, Jr., of New Jersey.
Leonard L. Boswell, of Iowa.
Tim Holden, of Pennsylvania.
Brian Baird, of Washington.
Shelley Berkley, of Nevada.
Jim Matheson, of Utah.
Michael M. Honda, of California.
Rick Larsen, of Washington.
Michael E. Capuano, of Massachusetts.
Anthony D. Weiner, of New York.
Julia Carson, of Indiana.
Timothy H. Bishop, of New York.
Michael H. Michaud, of Maine.
Lincoln Davis, of Tennessee.
Ben Chandler, of Kentucky.
Brian Higgins, of New York.
Russ Carnahan, of Missouri.
Allyson Y. Schwartz, of Pennsylvania.
John T. Salazar, of Colorado.

SUBCOMMITTEES

[The chairman and ranking minority member are ex officio (voting) members of all subcommittees on which they do not serve.]

Aviation

John L. Mica, of Florida, *Chair*

Thomas E. Petri, of Wisconsin.
Howard Coble, of North Carolina.
John J. Duncan, Jr., of Tennessee.
Vernon J. Ehlers, of Michigan.
Spencer Bachus, of Alabama.
Sue W. Kelly, of New York.
Richard H. Baker, of Louisiana.
Robert W. Ney, of Ohio.
Frank A. LoBiondo, of New Jersey.
Jerry Moran, of Kansas.
Robin Hayes, of North Carolina.
Henry E. Brown, Jr., of South Carolina.
Timothy V. Johnson, of Illinois.
Sam Graves, of Missouri.
Mark R. Kennedy, of Minnesota.
John Boozman, of Arkansas.
Jim Gerlach, of Pennsylvania.
Mario Diaz-Balart, of Florida.
Jon C. Porter, of Nevada.
Charles W. Dent, of Pennsylvania.
Ted Poe, of Texas.
John R. (Randy) Kuhl, Jr., of New York.
Lynn A. Westmoreland, of Georgia.

Jerry F. Costello, of Illinois.
Leonard L. Boswell, of Iowa.
Peter A. DeFazio, of Oregon.
Eleanor Holmes Norton, of the District of Columbia.
Corrine Brown, of Florida.
Eddie Bernice Johnson, of Texas.
Juanita Millender-McDonald, of California.
Ellen O. Tauscher, of California.
Bill Pascrell, Jr., of New Jersey.
Tim Holden, of Pennsylvania.
Shelley Berkley, of Nevada.
Jim Matheson, of Utah.
Michael M. Honda, of California.
Rick Larsen, of Washington.
Michael E. Capuano, of Massachusetts.
Anthony D. Weiner, of New York.
Ben Chandler, of Kentucky.
Russ Carnahan, of Missouri.
John T. Salazar, of Colorado.
Nick J. Rahall II, of West Virginia.
Bob Filner, of California.

Coast Guard and Maritime Transportation

Frank A. LoBiondo, of New Jersey, *Chair*

Howard Coble, of North Carolina.
Wayne T. Gilchrest, of Maryland.
Peter Hoekstra, of Michigan.
Rob Simmons, of Connecticut.
Mario Diaz-Balart, of Florida.
David G. Reichert, of Washington.
Connie Mack, of Florida.
Luis G. Fortuño, of Puerto Rico.
Charles W. Boustany, Jr., of Louisiana.

Bob Filner, of California.
Corrine Brown, of Florida.
Gene Taylor, of Mississippi.
Juanita Millender-McDonald, of California.
Michael M. Honda, of California.
Anthony D. Weiner, of New York.
Brian Higgins, of New York.
Brian Baird, of Washington.

Economic Development, Public Buildings, and Emergency Management

Bill Shuster, of Pennsylvania, *Chair*

Jim Gerlach, of Pennsylvania.
Kenny Marchant, of Texas.
Charles W. Dent, of Pennsylvania.
John R. (Randy) Kuhl, Jr., of New York.

Eleanor Holmes Norton, of the District of Columbia.
Michael H. Michaud, of Maine.
Lincoln Davis, of Tennessee.
Julia Carson, of Indiana.

Highways, Transit and Pipelines

Thomas E. Petri, of Wisconsin, *Chair*

Sherwood Boehlert, of New York.
Howard Coble, of North Carolina.
John J. Duncan, Jr., of Tennessee.
John L. Mica, of Florida.
Peter Hoekstra, of Michigan.
Spencer Bachus, of Alabama.
Steven C. LaTourette, of Ohio.
Sue W. Kelly, of New York.
Richard H. Baker, of Louisiana.
Robert W. Ney, of Ohio.
Frank A. LoBiondo, of New Jersey.
Jerry Moran, of Kansas.
Gary G. Miller, of California.
Robin Hayes, of North Carolina.
Rob Simmons, of Connecticut.
Henry E. Brown, Jr., of South Carolina.
Timothy V. Johnson, of Illinois.
Todd Russell Platts, of Pennsylvania.
Sam Graves, of Missouri.
Mark R. Kennedy, of Minnesota.
Bill Shuster, of Pennsylvania.
John Boozman, of Arkansas.
Mario Diaz-Balart, of Florida.
Jon C. Porter, of Nevada.
Tom Osborne, of Nebraska.
Kenny Marchant, of Texas.
Michael E. Sodrel, of Indiana.
David G. Reichert, of Washington.

Peter A. DeFazio, of Oregon.
Nick J. Rahall II, of West Virginia.
Jerrold Nadler, of New York.
Gene Taylor, of Mississippi.
Juanita Millender-McDonald, of California.
Elijah E. Cummings, of Maryland.
Earl Blumenauer, of Oregon.
Ellen O. Tauscher, of California.
Bill Pascrell, Jr., of New Jersey.
Tim Holden, of Pennsylvania.
Brian Baird, of Washington.
Shelley Berkley, of Nevada.
Jim Matheson, of Utah.
Michael M. Honda, of California.
Rick Larsen, of Washington.
Michael E. Capuano, of Massachusetts.
Anthony D. Weiner, of New York.
Julia Carson, of Indiana.
Timothy H. Bishop, of New York.
Michael H. Michaud, of Maine.
Lincoln Davis, of Tennessee.
Ben Chandler, of Kentucky.
Brian Higgins, of New York.
Russ Carnahan, of Missouri.
Allyson Y. Schwartz, of Pennsylvania.

Railroads

Steven C. LaTourette, of Ohio, *Chair*

Thomas E. Petri, of Wisconsin.
Sherwood Boehlert, of New York.
John L. Mica, of Florida.
Spencer Bachus, of Alabama.
Jerry Moran, of Kansas.
Gary G. Miller, of California.
Rob Simmons, of Connecticut.
Todd Russell Platts, of Pennsylvania.
Sam Graves, of Missouri.
Jon C. Porter, of Nevada.
Tom Osborne, of Nebraska.
Michael E. Sodrel, of Indiana.
Lynn A. Westmoreland, of Georgia.

Corrine Brown, of Florida.
Nick J. Rahall II, of West Virginia.
Jerrold Nadler, of New York.
Robert Menendez, of New Jersey.
Bob Filner, of California.
Elijah E. Cummings, of Maryland.
Earl Blumenauer, of Oregon.
Leonard L. Boswell, of Iowa.
Julia Carson, of Indiana.
Peter A. DeFazio, of Oregon.
Jerry F. Costello, of Illinois.
Eddie Bernice Johnson, of Texas.

Water Resources and Environment

John J. Duncan, Jr., of Tennessee, *Chair*

Sherwood Boehlert, of New York.
Wayne T. Gilchrest, of Maryland.
Vernon J. Ehlers, of Michigan.
Steven C. LaTourette, of Ohio.
Sue W. Kelly, of New York.
Richard H. Baker, of Louisiana.
Robert W. Ney, of Ohio.
Gary G. Miller, of California.
Henry E. Brown, Jr., of South Carolina.
Bill Shuster, of Pennsylvania.
John Boozman, of Arkansas.
Jim Gerlach, of Pennsylvania.
Tom Osborne, of Nebraska.
Ted Poe, of Texas.
Connie Mack, of Florida.
Luis G. Fortuño, of Puerto Rico.
Charles W. Boustany, Jr., of Louisiana.

Eddie Bernice Johnson, of Texas.
Robert Menendez, of New Jersey.
John T. Salazar, of Colorado.
Jerry F. Costello, of Illinois.
Gene Taylor, of Mississippi.
Brian Baird, of Washington.
Timothy H. Bishop, of New York.
Brian Higgins, of New York.
Allyson Y. Schwartz, of Pennsylvania.
Earl Blumenauer, of Oregon.
Ellen O. Tauscher, of California.
Bill Pascrell, Jr., of New Jersey.
Russ Carnahan, of Missouri.
Nick J. Rahall II, of West Virginia.
Eleanor Holmes Norton, of the District of Columbia.

STAFF

Committee on Transportation and Infrastructure (2165 RHOB), 225–9446, fax 225–6782.
  Majority Chief of Staff.—Lloyd Jones.
    Administrator.—Christine Kennedy.
    Chief Counsel.—Elizabeth Megginson.
    Deputy Chief Counsel/Parliamentarian.—Charles Ziegler.
    Legislative Staff Assistant to the Chief Counsel.—Kevin McColaugh.
    Director of Committee Facilities/Travel.—Jimmy Miller.
    Special Counsel.—Mark Zachares.
    Executive Assistant to Chief of Staff.—Debbie Callis.
    Policy Director.—Fraser Verrusio.
    Financial Administrator.—Wynn Bott.
    Communications Director.—Steve Hansen.
    Deputy Communications Director.—Justin Harclerode.
    Information Systems Manager.—Keven Sard.
    Assistant Systems Administrator.—Sonia Tutiven.
    Web and Graphics Editor.—Christopher Hewett.
    Staff Assistants: Andrew Forbes, Kendall Yow.
    Senior Counsel, Investigations.—Bob Faber (586 FHOB), 5–5504.
    Investigative Counsel.—Richard Stanton.
    Legislative Staff Assistant, Investigations.—William Barnes.
    Professional Staff Member, Investigations.—Joseph Graziano.
    Editor/Assistant Legislative Calendar Clerk.—Gilda Shirley.
    Legislative Calendar Clerk/Assistant Editor.—Tracy Mosebey.
  Minority Committee Staff (2163 RHOB), 225–4472, fax 226–1270.
    Staff Director.—David Heymsfeld.
    Chief Counsel.—Ward McCarragher.
    Counsel.—Kathleen Donnelly Zern.
    Administrator.—Dara Schlieker.
    Director of Communications.—Jim Berard (2167–A RHOB), 5–6260.
    Counsel, Investigations.—Trinita Brown (585 FHOB), 6–4697.
    Executive Assistant.—Jennifer Walsh.
  Subcommittee on Aviation (2251 RHOB), 6–3220, fax 5–4629.
    Majority Staff Director.—Jim Coon.
    Counsel.—Holly E. Woodruff Lyons.
    Legislative Staff Assistant.—John Bressler.
    Professional Staff: Sharon Barkeloo, Adam Tsao.
    Minority Staff Director.—Stacie Soumbeniotis, 5–9161.
    Counsel.—Giles Giovinazzi.
    Staff Assistant.—Pam Keller.

Subcommittee on Coast Guard and Maritime Transportation (507 FHOB), 6–3552, fax 6–2524.
   Majority Staff Director.—John Rayfield.
   Senior Legislative Staff Assistant.—Marsha Canter.
   Professional Staff.—Garrett Graves.
   Fellows: Eric Nagel, Howard Shaw.
   Minority Staff Director.—John Cullather (585 FHOB), 6–3587.
   Staff Assistant.—Rose Hamlin.
Subcommittee on Economic Development, Public Buildings, and Emergency Management (591 FHOB), 5–3014, fax 6–1898.
   Majority Staff Director.—Dan Mathews.
   Counsel.—Dan Schulman.
   Legislative Staff Assistant.—Amanda Newman.
   Minority Staff Director.—Susan Brita (585 FHOB), 5–9961.
   Counsel, Emergency Management.—Trinita Brown.
   Staff Assistant.—Rose Hamlin.
Subcommittee on Highways, Transit and Pipelines (B–370A RHOB), 5–6715, fax 5–4623.
   Majority Staff Director/Counsel.—Graham Hill.
   Counsel.—Derek Miller.
   Legislative Staff Assistants: Will Bland, Bailey Edwards.
   Professional Staff: Joyce Rose, James Tymon.
   Minority Staff Director for:
     Transit Issues.—Kenneth House (B–375 RHOB), 5–9989, fax 4–4627.
     Hazardous Materials and Pipelines.—Jennifer Esposito (2251 RHOB), 5–3274.
   Legislative Assistant.—Eric Van Schyndle.
   Chief Economist.—Art Chan.
   Senior Policy Staff.—Stephanie Manning.
Subcommittee on Railroads (589 FHOB), 6–0727, fax 6–3475.
   Majority Staff Director/Senior Counsel.—Glenn Scammel.
   Counsel.—John Brennan.
   Legislative Staff Assistant.—Travis Johnson.
   Minority Staff Director.—Jennifer Esposito (2251 RHOB), 5–3274, fax 5–4629.
   Staff Assistant.—Pam Keller.
Subcommittee on Water Resources and Environment (B–376 RHOB), 5–4360, fax 6–5435.
   Majority Staff Director/Senior Counsel.—Susan Bodine.
   Counsel.—Jonathan Pawlow.
   Senior Legislative Staff Assistant.—Donna Campbell.
   Legislative Staff Assistant.—Fess Cassels.
   Professional Staff: John Anderson, Geoff Bowman.
   Minority Staff Director.—Kenneth Kopocis (B–375 RHOB), 5–0060, fax 5–4627.
   Counsel.—Ryan Seiger.
   Staff Assistant.—Beth Goldstein.

Veterans' Affairs

335 Cannon House Office Building, phone 225–3527, fax 225–5486

http://www.veterans.house.gov

meets second Wednesday of each month

Steve Buyer, of Indiana, *Chair*

Mike Bilirakis, of Florida.
Terry Everett, of Alabama.
Cliff Stearns, of Florida.
Dan Burton, of Indiana.
Jerry Moran, of Kansas.
Richard H. Baker, of Louisiana.
Henry E. Brown, Jr., of South Carolina.
Jeff Miller, of Florida.
John Boozman, of Arkansas.
Jeb Bradley, of New Hampshire.
Ginny Brown-Waite, of Florida.
Devin Nunes, of California.
Michael R. Turner, of Ohio.

Lane Evans, of Illinois.
Bob Filner, of California.
Luis V. Gutierrez, of Illinois.
Corrine Brown, of Florida.
Vic Snyder, of Arkansas.
Michael H. Michaud, of Maine.
Stephanie Herseth, of South Dakota.
Ted Strickland, of Ohio.
Darlene Hooley, of Oregon.
Silvestre Reyes, of Texas.
Shelley Berkley, of Nevada.
Tom Udall, of New Mexico.

SUBCOMMITTEES

Disability Assistance and Memorial Affairs

Jeff Miller, of Florida, *Chair*

Jerry Moran, of Kansas.
Jeb Bradley, of New Hampshire.
Ginny Brown-Waite, of Florida.

Shelley Berkley, of Nevada.
Tom Udall, of New Mexico.
Lane Evans, of Illinois.

Economic Opportunity

John Boozman, of Arkansas, *Chair*

Richard H. Baker, of Louisiana.
Ginny Brown-Waite, of Florida.
Devin Nunes, of California.

Stephanie Herseth, of South Dakota.
Darlene Hooley, of Oregon.
Lane Evans, of Illinois.

Health

Henry E. Brown, Jr., of South Carolina, *Chair*

Cliff Stearns, of Florida.
Richard H. Baker, of Louisiana.
Jerry Moran, of Kansas.
Jeff Miller, of Florida.
Devin Nunes, of California.
Michael R. Turner, of Ohio.

Michael H. Michaud, of Maine.
Bob Filner, of California.
Luis V. Gutierrez, of Illinois.
Corrine Brown, of Florida.
Vic Snyder, of Arkansas.

Oversight and Investigations

Mike Bilirakis, of Florida, *Chair*

Terry Everett, of Alabama.
John Boozman, of Arkansas.
Jeb Bradley, of New Hampshire.

Ted Strickland, of Ohio.
Silvestre Reyes, of Texas.

STAFF

Committee on Veterans' Affairs (335 CHOB), 225–3527, fax 225–5486.
  Majority Staff Director.—Mike Copher.
    Deputy Staff Director.—Kelly Craven.
    Chief Counsel.—Kingston Smith.
    Legislative Coordinator.—Jeannie McNally.
    Legislative Assistant.—Holly Palmer.
    Press Secretary.—Brooke Adams.
    Director of Information Systems.—Steve Kirkland.
    Office Manager.—Bernadine Dotson.
    Printing Editor.—Jerry Tan.
  Minority Staff Director.—Jim Holley (333 CHOB), 5–9756.
    Professional Staff Member.—Kevin Gash.
    Communications Director.—Geoffrey Collover.
  Subcommittee on Disability Assistance and Memorial Affairs (337 CHOB), 225–9164.
  Majority Staff Director.—Paige McManus.
    Professional Staff Member.—Chris McNamee.
  Minority Staff Director.—Mary Ellen Mc Dermott.
    Executive Assistant.—Leah Booth.
  Subcommittee on Economic Opportunity (337 CHOB), 225–9164.
  Majority Staff Director.—Mike Brinck.
    Professional Staff Member.—Devon Seibert.
  Minority Staff Director.—Geoffrey Collover.
    Executive Assistant.—Leah Booth.
  Subcommittee on Health (338 CHOB), 225–9154.
  Majority Professional Staff: Dolores Dunn, Kathleen Greve.
  Minority Staff Director.—Susan Edgerton (333 CHOB), 5–9756.
    Executive Assistant.—Leah Booth.
  Subcommittee on Oversight and Investigations (337A CHOB), 225–3569.
  Majority Staff Director.—Arthur Wu.
    Professional Staff Member.—Veronica Crowe.
  Minority Staff Director.—Len Sistek (333 CHOB), 5–9756.
    Executive Assistant.—Virginia Richardson.
    Administrative Assistant/Executive Assistant.—Debbie Smith.

Ways and Means

1102 Longworth House Office Building, phone 225–3625

http://waysandmeans.house.gov

William M. Thomas, of California, *Chair*

E. Clay Shaw, Jr., of Florida.
Nancy L. Johnson, of Connecticut.
Wally Herger, of California.
Jim McCrery, of Louisiana.
Dave Camp, of Michigan.
Jim Ramstad, of Minnesota.
Jim Nussle, of Iowa.
Sam Johnson, of Texas.
Phil English, of Pennsylvania.
J.D. Hayworth, of Arizona.
Jerry Weller, of Illinois.
Kenny C. Hulshof, of Missouri.
Ron Lewis, of Kentucky.
Mark Foley, of Florida.
Kevin Brady, of Texas.
Thomas M. Reynolds, of New York.
Paul Ryan, of Wisconsin.
Eric Cantor, of Virginia.
John Linder, of Georgia.
Bob Beauprez, of Colorado.
Melissa A. Hart, of Pennsylvania.
Chris Chocola, of Indiana.

Charles B. Rangel, of New York.
Fortney Pete Stark, of California.
Sander M. Levin, of Michigan.
Benjamin L. Cardin, of Maryland.
Jim McDermott, of Washington.
John Lewis, of Georgia.
Richard E. Neal, of Massachusetts.
Michael R. McNulty, of New York.
William J. Jefferson, of Louisiana.
John S. Tanner, of Tennessee.
Xavier Becerra, of California.
Lloyd Doggett, of Texas.
Earl Pomeroy, of North Dakota.
Stephanie Tubbs Jones, of Ohio.
Mike Thompson, of California.
John B. Larson, of Connecticut.
Rahm Emanuel, of Illinois.

SUBCOMMITTEES

[The chairman and ranking minority member are ex officio (non-voting) members of all subcommittees.]

Health

Nancy L. Johnson, of Connecticut, *Chair*

Jim McCrery, of Louisiana.
Sam Johnson, of Texas.
Dave Camp, of Michigan.
Jim Ramstad, of Minnesota.
Phil English, of Pennsylvania.
J.D. Hayworth, of Arizona.
Kenny C. Hulshof, of Missouri.

Fortney Pete Stark, of California.
John Lewis, of Georgia.
Lloyd Doggett, of Texas.
Mike Thompson, of California.
Rahm Emanuel, of Illinois.

Human Resources

Wally Herger, of California, *Chair*

Nancy L. Johnson, of Connecticut.
Bob Beauprez, of Colorado.
Melissa A. Hart, of Pennsylvania.
Chris Chocola, of Indiana.
Jim McCrery, of Louisiana.
Dave Camp, of Michigan.
Phil English, of Pennsylvania.

Jim McDermott, of Washington.
Benjamin L. Cardin, of Maryland.
Fortney Pete Stark, of California.
Xavier Becerra, of California.
Rahm Emanuel, of Illinois.

Oversight
Jim Ramstad, of Minnesota, *Chair*

Eric Cantor, of Virginia
Bob Beauprez, of Colorado.
Thomas M. Reynolds, of New York.
John Linder, of Georgia.
E. Clay Shaw, Jr., of Florida.
Sam Johnson, of Texas.

John Lewis, of Georgia.
Earl Pomeroy, of North Dakota.
Michael R. McNulty, of New York.
John S. Tanner, of Tennessee.
Charles B. Rangel, of New York.

Select Revenue Measures
Dave Camp, of Michigan, *Chair*

Jerry Weller, of Illinois.
Mark Foley, of Florida.
Thomas M. Reynolds, of New York.
Eric Cantor, of Virginia.
John Linder, of Georgia.
Melissa A. Hart, of Pennsylvania.
Chris Chocola, of Indiana.

Michael R. McNulty, of New York.
Lloyd Doggett, of Texas.
Stephanie Tubbs Jones, of Ohio.
Mike Thompson, of California.
John B. Larson, of Connecticut.

Social Security
Jim McCrery, of Louisiana, *Chair*

E. Clay Shaw, Jr., of Florida.
Sam Johnson, of Texas.
J.D. Hayworth, of Arizona.
Kenny C. Hulshof, of Missouri.
Ron Lewis, of Kentucky.
Kevin Brady, of Texas.
Paul Ryan, of Wisconsin.

Sander M. Levin, of Michigan.
Earl Pomeroy, of North Dakota.
Xavier Becerra, of California.
Stephanie Tubbs Jones, of Ohio.
Richard E. Neal, of Massachusetts.

Trade
E. Clay Shaw, Jr., of Florida, *Chair*

Wally Herger, of California.
Phil English, of Pennsylvania.
Jim Nussle, of Iowa.
Jerry Weller, of Illinois.
Ron Lewis, of Kentucky.
Mark Foley, of Florida.
Kevin Brady, of Texas.

Benjamin L. Cardin, of Maryland.
Sander M. Levin, of Michigan.
William J. Jefferson, of Louisiana.
John S. Tanner, of Tennessee.
John B. Larson, of Connecticut.
Jim McDermott, of Washington.

STAFF

Committee on Ways and Means (1102 LHOB), 225–3625.
Majority Chief of Staff.—Allison Giles.
  Assistant to Chief of Staff.—Stephanie Johnson.
  Senior Advisor to the Chair.—Shahira Knight.
  Director of IS.—Melody Buras.
  Deputy Director of IS.—Darren Gunlock.
  Senior Economist.—Alex Brill.
  Assistant Economic Analyst.—Jonathan Lieber.
  Senior Staff Assistants: Brandon Audap, Matt Turkstra.
  Chief Tax Counsel.—Bob Winters (1135 LHOB), 5–5522.
  Tax Counsels: Jim Lyons, Lisa Schultz.
  Senior Tax Staff Assistant.—Austin Clark.
  Professional Tax Staff.—Chris Giosa.
  Tax Staff Assistant.—Phillips Hinch.
  Professional Staff.—Peter Sloan.
  Committee Administrator.—Julie Hasler.
  Communications Director.—Christin Tinsworth.
  Press Secretary.—Ianthe Jackson.
  Deputy Press Secretary.—Robert Vandenheuvel.

Office Manager.—Adam Martinez.
Calendar Clerk.—Carren Turko.
Committee Hearing Clerk.—Kevin Herms.
Committee Clerk.—Michael Morrow.
Webmaster/Committee Clerk.—Diane Kirkland.
Documents Clerk.—Reggie Greene.
Minority Staff Director/Chief Counsel.—Janice Mays (1106 LHOB), 5–4021.
   Chief Tax Counsel.—John Buckley.
   Tax Counsels: Mildeen Worrell, Beth Kuntz Vance.
   Chief Economist.—Diane Rogers.
   Communications Director.—Daniel Maffei.
   Deputy Communications Director.—Jennifer Adams.
   Professional Staff Assistants: David Burke, Jennifer Gould, Aruna Kalyanam, Anthony
      Tait.
   Systems Administrator.—Antoine Walker.
Subcommittee on Health (1136 LHOB), 5–3943.
   Majority Staff Director.—Joel White.
      Professional Staff: Ken Serafin, Madeleine Smith, Kathleen Weldon.
      Senior Staff Assistant.—Caitlin Horton.
   Minority Professional Staff: Cybele Bjorklund, Deborah Veres.
Subcommittee on Human Resources (B–317 RHOB), 5–1025.
   Majority Staff Director.—Matt Weidinger.
      Professional Staff: Christine Devere, Margo Smith.
      Senior Staff Assistant.—Risa Salsburg.
   Minority Professional Staff: Nick Gwyn, Sonja Nesbit.
Subcommittee on Oversight (1136 LHOB), 5–7601.
   Tax Counsel.—Payson Peabody.
      Professional Staff: Pete Davila, Deborah Williams.
      Senior Staff Assistant.—Scott Berman.
Subcommittee on Social Security (B–316 RHOB), 5–9263.
   Majority Staff Director.—Kim Hildred.
      Professional Staff: Rachel Forward, Sophia Wright.
      Senior Staff Assistant.—Amber Crockett.
   Minority Professional Staff: Karlin McNeill, Kathryn Olson, Ted Zegers.
Subcommittee on Trade (1104 LHOB), 5–6649.
   Majority Staff Director.—Angela Ellard.
      General Counsel/Professional Staff.—David Kavanaugh.
      Professional Staff.—Stephanie Lester.
      Senior Staff Assistant.—Ian Steff.
      Staff Assistant.—Ken Barbic.
   Minority Chief Trade Counsel.—Timothy Reif (1106 LHOB), 5–4021.
      Trade Counsel.—Julie Herwig.

SELECT AND SPECIAL COMMITTEES OF THE HOUSE

Permanent Select Committee on Intelligence
H–405 The Capitol, phone 225–4121
[Created pursuant to H. Res. 658, 95th Congress]

Peter Hoekstra, of Michigan, *Chair*

Ray LaHood, of Illinois.
Randy (Duke) Cunningham, of California.
Terry Everett, of Alabama.
Elton Gallegly, of California.
Heather Wilson, of New Mexico.
Jo Ann Davis, of Virginia.
Mac Thornberry, of Texas.
John McHugh, of New York.
Todd Tiahrt, of Kansas.
Mike Rogers, of Michigan.
Rick Renzi, of Arizona.

Jane Harman, of California.
Alcee L. Hastings, of Florida.
Silvestre Reyes, of Texas.
Leonard L. Boswell, of Iowa.
Robert E. (Bud) Cramer, Jr., of Alabama.
Anna G. Eshoo, of California.
Rush D. Holt, of New Jersey.
C.A. Dutch Ruppersberger, of Maryland.
John Tierney, of Massachusetts.

SUBCOMMITTEES

[The Speaker and Minority Leader are ex officio (non-voting) members of the committee.]

Intelligence Policy

Jo Ann Davis, of Virginia, *Chair*

Heather Wilson, of New Mexico.
John McHugh, of New York.
Mike Rogers, of Michigan.
Rick Renzi, of Arizona.

Rush D. Holt, of New Jersey.
Anna G. Eshoo, of California.
John Tierney, of Massachusetts.

Oversight

Mac Thornberry, of Texas, *Chair*

Ray LaHood, of Illinois
Terry Everett, of Alabama.
Heather Wilson, of New Mexico.
Todd Tiahrt, of Kansas.
Mike Rogers, of Michigan.
Rick Renzi, of Arizona.

Robert E. (Bud) Cramer, Jr., of Alabama.
Alcee L. Hastings, of Florida.
Silvestre Reyes, of Texas.
C.A. Dutch Ruppersberger, of Maryland.
John Tierney, of Massachusetts.

Technical and Tactical Intelligence

Heather Wilson, of New Mexico, *Chair*

Randy (Duke) Cunningham, of California.
Terry Everett, of Alabama.
Elton Gallegly, of California.
Mac Thornberry, of Texas.
John McHugh, of New York.

Anna G. Eshoo, of California.
Robert E. (Bud) Cramer, Jr., of Alabama.
Rush D. Holt, of New Jersey.
C.A. Dutch Ruppersberger, of Maryland.

Terrorism, Human Intelligence, Analysis and Counterintelligence

Randy (Duke) Cunningham, of California, *Chair*

Ray LaHood, of Illinois.
Elton Gallegly, of California.
Jo Ann Davis, of Virginia.
John McHugh, of New York.
Todd Tiahrt, of Kansas.
Rick Renzi, of Arizona.

Leonard L. Boswell, of Iowa.
Alcee L. Hastings, of Florida.
Silvestre Reyes, of Texas.
C.A. Dutch Ruppersberger, of Maryland.

STAFF

Majority Staff Director.—Mike Meermans.
    Deputy Staff Director/General Counsel.—Chris Donesa.
    Chief Clerk.—Larry Denton.
    Executive Assistant to the Staff Director.—Julie Mitchell.
    Director of Security.—Bill McFarland.
    Systems Administrator.—Brandon Smith.
    Staff Assistants: Katrina Gammon, Carolyn Lyons, Meghann Peterlin, Sam White.
    Professional Staff: David Abruzzino, Bruce Allen, Mike Ennis, Kelly Gaffney, Michele Lang, Beth Larson, Riley Perdue, Kevin Schmidt, Don Stone, John Stopher.
Minority Staff Director.—David Buckley.
    Deputy Staff Director.—Chuck Gault.
    Executive Assistant.—Karen Brooke.
    Professional Staff: Jeremy Bash, Larry Hanauer, Pam Moore, Wyndee Parker, Christine York.

National Republican Congressional Committee

320 First Street, SE., 20003, phone 479-7000

Thomas M. Reynolds, of New York, *Chair*

Chair, Executive Committee.—Sue Wilkins Myrick, of North Carolina.
  Chair of:
    Candidate Recruitment.—Candice Miller, of Michigan.
    Finance.—Kay Granger, of Texas.
    Get-out-the-vote.—Howard P. (Buck) McKeon, of California.
    Communications-Message.—Patrick McHenry, of North Carolina.
    Community Partnerships.—Jerry Weller, of Illinois.
    Incumbent Development.—Don Sherwood, of Pennsylvania.
    Incumbent Retention.—Pete Sessions, of Texas.
    Incumbent Support: Kevin Brady, of Texas, and Melissa A. Hart, of Pennsylvania.

EXECUTIVE COMMITTEE MEMBERS

Marsha Blackburn, of Tennessee.
John A. Boehner, of Ohio.
Eric Cantor, of Virginia.
Tom Cole, of Oklahoma.
Mike Conaway, of Texas.
Ander Crenshaw, of Florida.
John Abney Culberson, of Texas.
Geoff Davis, of Kentucky.
Mario Diaz-Balart, of Florida.
David Dreier, of California.
Phil English, of Pennsylvania.
Tom Feeney, of Florida.
Mike Ferguson, of New Jersey.
Kay Granger, of Texas.
Sam Graves, of Missouri.
Jeb Hensarling, of Texas.
David L. Hobson, of Ohio.
Sue W. Kelly, of New York.
Mark Steven Kirk, of Illinois.
Jim McCrery, of Louisiana.
Patrick McHenry, of North Carolina.
Howard P. (Buck) McKeon, of
California.

Cathy McMorris, of Washington.
Candice S. Miller, of Michigan.
Jerry Moran, of Kansas.
Sue Wilkins Myrick, of North Carolina.
Robert W. Ney, of Ohio.
Tom Price, of Georgia.
Adam Putnam, of Florida.
Mike Rogers, of Alabama.
Mike Rogers, of Michigan.
Ed Royce, of California.
Pete Sessions, of Texas.
Don Sherwood, of Pennsylvania.
John E. Sweeney, of New York.
Todd Tiahrt, of Kansas.
Patrick J. Tiberi, of Ohio.
Fred Upton, of Michigan.
Greg Walden, of Oregon.
Zach Wamp, of Tennessee.
Jerry Weller, of Illinois.
Roger F. Wicker, of Mississippi.
Joe Wilson, of South Carolina.

Ex Officio Members from the Leadership
J. Dennis Hastert, of Illinois.
Tom Delay, of Texas.
Roy Blunt, of Missouri.

Deborah Pryce, of Ohio.
Chris Cox, of California.

STAFF

Executive Director.—Sally Vastola.
Political Director.—Mike McElwain.
Director of:
  Communications.—Carl Forti.
  Finance.—Tara Snow.
  Research.—Matt Lowe.
Counsel.—Don McGahn.

House Policy Committee

2471 Rayburn House Office Building, phone, 225–6168

http://policy.house.gov

meets at the call of the Chair or the Speaker

John Shadegg, of Arizona, *Chair*

Republican Leadership:
  Speaker.—J. Dennis Hastert, of Illinois.
  Majority Leader.—Tom DeLay, of Texas.
  Majority Whip.—Roy Blunt, of Missouri.
  Conference Chair.—Deborah Pryce, of Ohio.
  Conference Vice Chair.—Jack Kingston, of Georgia.
  Conference Secretary.—John Doolittle, of California.
  NRCC Chair.—Thomas Reynolds, of New York.

Committee Chairmen:
  Appropriations Committee.—Jerry Lewis, of California.
  Budget Committee.—Jim Nussle, of Iowa.
  Energy and Commerce Committee.—Joe Barton, of Texas.
  Rules Committee.—David Dreier, of California.
  Ways and Means Committee.—Bill Thomas, of California.

At Large Representatives (Appointed by the Speaker of the House):
John Boozman, of Arkansas.
Michael Burgess, of Texas.
Shelley Moore Capito, of West Virginia.
Ander Crenshaw, of Florida.
Virginia Foxx, of Virginia.
Phil Gingrey, of Georgia.
Louie Gohmert, of Texas.
Katherine Harris, of Florida.
Melissa Hart, of Pennsylvania.
Kenny Hulshof, of Missouri.
Joe Knollenberg, of Michigan.
Ron Lewis, of Kentucky.
Bob Ney, of Ohio.
Jerry Weller, of Illinois.
Joe Wilson, of South Carolina.

Class Representatives:
Sophomore Class.—Bob Beauprez, of Colorado.
Freshman Class.—Thelma Drake, of Virginia.

STAFF

House Policy Committee (2471 RHOB), 225–6168.
Executive Director.—Elise Finley.
Director of Policy.—Douglas Stoss.
Chief Counsel.—Caroline Lynch.
CPA.—Thomas Anfinson.
Clerk.—Kristin Nelthorpe.
Press.—Michael Steel.

House Republican Conference

1010 Longworth House Office Building, phone 225–5107, fax 225–0809

Deborah Pryce, of Ohio, *Chair*

Jack Kingston, of Georgia, *Vice Chair*

John Doolittle, of California, *Secretary*

STAFF

Chief of Staff.—Kathryn Lehman.
Deputy Chief of Staff.—Lori Salley.
Assistant to the Chief of Staff.—Genevieve Hillis.
Director of Policy and Coalitions.—Andrew Shore.
Senior Policy Advisor.—Shalla Ross.
Policy Advisors: Kelly Bulliner, Jackie Moran.
Assistant to Policy and Coalitions.—Matt Sturges.
Scheduler.—Sara Rogers.
Special Assistant to the Chair.—John DeStefano.
Systems Administrator.—Jennifer Parks.
Conference Coordinator.—Steven Frank.
Staff Assistant.—Sam Porter.
Communications Director.—Greg Crist.
Deputy Communications Director.—Anne Buresh.
Press Secretary.—Andrea Tantaros.
Deputy Press Secretary.—Jessica Ferguson.
Speechwriter.—Arthur Berg-Bochner.
Press Assistant.—Kathryn Staczek, 226–9000.
Floor Debate Coordinator.—Steven Martinko.
Committee Liaison.—Larissa Pennington.
Managing Editor, GOP.gov.—Matt Lira.

House Republican Steering Committee
H–209 The Capitol, phone, 225–2204

J. Dennis Hastert, of Illinois, *Chair*

Tom DeLay, of Texas.
Roy Blunt, of Missouri.
Eric Cantor, of Virginia.
Deborah Pryce, of Ohio.
John B. Shadegg, of Arizona.
Jack Kingston, of Georgia.
John T. Doolittle, of California.
Thomas M. Reynolds, of New York.
Jerry Lewis, of California.
Joe Barton, of Texas.
David Dreier, of California.
Bill Thomas, of California.
Ken Calvert, of California.
Lamar Smith, of Texas.

Adam H. Putnam, of Florida.
Doc Hastings, of Washington.
Marilyn Musgrave, of Colorado.
Tom Latham, of Iowa.
Dave Camp, of Michigan.
John McHugh, of New York.
Curt Weldon, of Pennsylvania.
Ralph Regula, of Ohio.
Hal Rogers, of Kentucky.
Spencer Bachus, of Alabama.
Don Young, of Alaska.
John R. Carter, of Texas.
Cathy McMorris, of Washington.

Democratic Congressional Campaign Committee
430 South Capitol Street SE., 20003, phone (202) 863–1500

Executive Committee:
Rahm Emanuel, of Illinois, *Chair.*
Nancy Pelosi, of California, *Democratic Leader.*
Nita Lowey, of New York, *Chair Emeritus/Committee Vice Chair.*
Patrick J. Kennedy, of Rhode Island, *Chair Emeritus.*
John D. Dingell, of Michigan, *Chair's Council.*
Charles B. Rangel, of New York, *Executive Board Chair.*
Ed Markey, of Massachusetts, *Committee Vice Chair.*
Kendrick Meek, of Florida, *Committee Vice Chair.*
Lucille Roybal-Allard, of California, *Committee Vice Chair.*
Zoe Lofgren of California, *Committee Vice Chair.*
Joe Crowley, of New York, *Business Council Chair.*
Mike Thompson, of California, *Frontline Democrats Chair.*
Chris Van Hollen, of Maryland, *Recruitment Chair.*
Janice D. Schakowsky, of Illinois, *Women LEAD Chair.*
Steve Israel, of New York, *National Jewish Outreach Chair.*
Adam Schiff, of California, *Regional Recruitment Chair.*
Hilda Solis, of California, *Regional Recruitment Chair.*
Mark Udall, of Colorado, *Regional Recruitment Chair.*
Betty McCollum, of Minnesota, *Regional Recruitment Chair.*
Tim Ryan, of Ohio, *Regional Recruitment Chair.*
Artur Davis, of Alabama, *Regional Recruitment Chair.*
Debbie Wasserman Schultz, of Florida, *Regional Recruitment Chair.*
Michael Capuano, of Massachusetts, *Regional Recruitment Chair.*
John Murtha, of Pennsylvania, *Regional Recruitment Chair.*
Mike Ross, of Arkansas, *Regional Recruitment Chair.*

STAFF

Executive Director.—John Lapp, 485–3424, fax 485–3512.
  Deputy Executive Director.—Brian Wolff, 485–3425, fax 485–3427.
  Chief Operating Officer.—Ann Marie Habershaw, 485–3529, fax 741–7353.
  Political Director.—Dave Hamrick, 485–3507, fax 741–7351.
  Communications Director.—Bill Burton, 485–3442, fax 741–7340.
  National Field Director.—Glenn Rushing, 485–3434, fax 741–7374.
  National Finance Director.—Nicole Runge, 485–3526, fax 485–3427.
  Marketing and Membership Director.—Meaghan Burdick, 485–3418, fax 741–7378.
  Member Services Director.—Beverly Gilyard, 485–3516, fax 485–3522.

Research Director.—Christina Reynolds, 485–3428, fax 741–7354.
Campaign Director.—Alixandra Wade, 485–3449, fax 485–3512.
Press Secretary.—Sarah Feinberg, 485–3446, fax 741–7359.

Democratic Steering and Policy Committee

H–204 The Capitol, phone 225–0100

Chair.—Nancy Pelosi, Representative from California.
Co-Chairs:
    Steering.—Rosa DeLauro, Representative from Connecticut.
    Policy.—George Miller, Representative from California.

STAFF

Democratic Steering Committee 225–0100, fax 225–4188.
    Steering Advisors: George Kundanis, Jonathan Stivers, Ashley Turton.

Democratic Policy Committee (H–130), 225–0100, fax 226–0938.
    Policy Advisors: George Kundanis, John Lawrence.

Democratic Caucus

1420 Longworth House Office Building, phone 226–3210, fax 225–9253

democratic.caucus@mail.house.gov

Robert Menendez, of New Jersey, *Chair*

James E. Clyburn, of South Carolina, *Vice Chair*

STAFF

Executive Director.—Andrew Kauders.
    Deputy Executive Director/Policy Director.—Karissa Willhite.
    Communications Director.—Matthew Miller.
    Director of Member Services.—Allie Neill.
    Caucus Planning Director.—Wendy Hartman.
    General Counsel.—George Henry.
    Special Assistant to the Executive Director.—Justin Field.
    Staff Assistant.—Tomica Burke.
    Parliamentarian.—Matt Pinkus.
    Chief of Staff to the Vice Chair.—Yelberton Watkins.
    Legislative Director to the Vice Chair.—Danny Cromer.
    Legislative Assistant to the Vice Chair.—Barvetta Singletary.
    Special Assistant to the Vice Chair.—Jaime Harrison.
    Press Secretary for the Vice Chair.—Hope Derrick.

OFFICERS AND OFFICIALS OF THE HOUSE

OFFICE OF THE SPEAKER
H–232 The Capitol, phone 225–0600, fax 226–1996
http://speaker.house.gov

The Speaker.—J. Dennis Hastert.
  Chief of Staff.—Scott B. Palmer, H–228, The Capitol, 225–5555.
    Assistant to the Chief of Staff.—John Russell.
  Deputy Chief of Staff.—Michael Stokke, H–227, The Capitol, 225–0305.
    Chief Counsel.—Theodore Van Der Meid.
    Special Assistant.—Tim Kennedy.
  Director of Special Events.—Rachel Perry, H–419C, The Capitol, 225–0600.
    Staff Assistant (Room Reservations).—Courtney Franke.
    Staff Assistant.—Erin Mitchell.
  Policy Director.—Bill Hughes, 225–0510.
    Assistants to the Speaker for Policy.—Sally Canfield, Kevin Fromer, Kiki Kless, Bill
      Koetzle, Margaret Peterlin, Andy Tiongson, Chris Walker.
    Assistant to the Director of Policy.—Tripp Guess.
    Staff Assistant.—Ja'Ron Smith.
  Director of Speaker Operations.—Samuel Lancaster, H–232, The Capitol, 225–6398.
    Executive Assistant.—Kathleen O'Connor.
    Executive Staff Assistant.—Luke Hatzis.
  Scheduler.—Helen Morrell, H–229, The Capitol, 225–2774.
    Assistant Scheduler.—Chris Stottman.

SPEAKER'S PRESS OFFICE
H–326 The Capitol, phone 225–2800

Communications Director.—Ron Bonjean.
  Assistant to the Speaker for Communications and Outreach.—Charles Chamberlayne.
  Speechwriter.—Larry Farnsworth.

SPEAKER'S FLOOR OFFICE
H–210 The Capitol, phone 225–2204

Senior Floor Director.—Seth Webb.
  Floor Assistants: Dave Bellis, Karen Haas, Jay Pierson.

OFFICE OF THE MAJORITY LEADER
H–107 The Capitol, phone 225–4000, fax 225–5117

Majority Leader.—Tom DeLay.
  Chief of Staff.—Tim Berry.
  Special Assistant to the Chief of Staff.—Elizabeth Pauls.
  Deputy Chief of Staff.—Dan Flynn.
  Policy Director.—Brett Shogren.
  Communications Director.—Dan Allen.

Press Secretary.—Jonathan Grella.
Deputy Press Secretary.—Shannon Flaherty.
Speechwriter.—Michael Connolly.
Senior Policy Advisor.—Cassie Bevan.
Senior Advisor, Director of National Security Policy.—Brett Shogren.
Policy Advisor.—Jack Victory.
Deputy Chief of Staff/Legislative Operations.—Brett Loper.
Senior Floor Assistant.—Danielle Simonetta.
Floor Assistant.—Jonathan Robilotto.
Director of Finance and Special Events.—Amy Lorenzini.
Scheduler.—Dawn Loffredo.
Staff Assistants: Mary Katherine Ascik, Sara Diaz.
Director of Information Technology.—Ed Mullen.
Deputy Director of Information Technology.—Josh Shultz.

OFFICE OF THE MAJORITY WHIP

H–329 The Capitol, phone 225–0197

Majority Whip.—Roy Blunt.
 Chief of Staff.—Brian Gaston.
 Deputy Chief of Staff/Director of Member Services.—Mildred Webber.
 Director of Policy Analysis & Management/Deputy Chief of Staff.—Neil Bradley.
 Director of Floor Operations.—Amy Steinmann.
 Chief Floor Assistant.—Kyle Nevins.
 Communications Director.—Burson Taylor.
 Press Secretary.—Jessica Boulanger.
 Deputy Press Secretary.—Laurent Crenshaw.
 Director of Scheduling.—Richard Eddings.
 Director of Coalitions.—Sam Geduldig.

OFFICE OF THE CHIEF DEPUTY MAJORITY WHIP

H–330 The Capitol, phone 225–0197

Chief Deputy Majority Whip.—Eric Cantor.
 Chief of Staff.—Steve Stombres.
 Special Assistant.—Matt Lakin.

OFFICE OF THE DEMOCRATIC LEADER

H–204 The Capitol, phone 225–0100

Democratic Leader.—Nancy Pelosi.
 Chief of Staff.—John Lawrence.
 Executive Assistant/Director of Scheduling.—Cortney Bright.
 Senior Advisor/Deputy Chief of Staff.—George Kundanis.
 Communications Director.—Brendan Daly.
 Deputy Communications Director.—Jennifer Crider.
 Office Manager.—Paula Short.
 Deputy Scheduler.—Kate Jensen.
 Assistant to the Chief of Staff.—Deborah Spriggs.
 Floor Assistant.—Catlin O'Neill.
 Executive Floor Assistant.—Jerry Hartz.
 Senior Policy Advisor, Member Support Program.—Howard Moon.
 Counsel to the Leader.—Bernie Raimo.
 Director of Intergovernmental Relations.—Lorraine Miller.

OFFICE OF THE DEMOCRATIC WHIP

H-306 The Capitol, phone 225-3130, fax 226-0663

http://democraticwhip.house.gov

Democratic Whip.—Steny Hoyer.
  Chief of Staff.—Cory Alexander.
  Executive Assistant/Appointments.—Kathy May.
  Office Manager.—Alexis Covey-Brandt.
  Floor Director.—Rob Cogorno.
  Floor Assistant/Member Services Director.—Brian Romick.
  Communications Director.—David Ransom.
  Press Secretary.—Stacey Farnen.
  Senior Policy Advisors: Keith Aboucher, Scott DeFife, Gina Mahony.
  Director of Information Technology.—Stephen Dwyer.

CHIEF DEPUTY DEMOCRATIC WHIPS

Deputy Democratic Whips:

John Lewis.	Diana DeGette.
Ed Pastor.	Jan Schakowsky.
Joseph Crowley.	Ron Kind.
John Tanner.	Maxine Waters.

OFFICE OF THE CLERK

H-154 The Capitol, phone 225-7000

JEFF TRANDAHL, native of Spearfish, South Dakota; 1983 Graduate of Spearfish High School; Bachelor of Arts in Government/Politics, English emphasis, from the University of Maryland, 1987. Professional experience includes: Office of United States Senator James Abdnor (R–SD) from 1983 to 1987; Office of Congresswoman Virginia Smith (R–NE) and the House Committee on Appropriations from 1987 to 1990; Office of Congressman Pat Roberts (R–KS) and the Committee on House Administration from 1990 to 1995; Assistant to the Clerk of the U.S. House of Representatives from 1995 to 1996; Chief Administrative Officer (acting) for the U.S. House of Representatives from 1996 to 1997; Deputy Clerk of the House of Representatives from 1997 to 1999; appointed Clerk of the House of Representatives on January 1, 1999, and elected Clerk of the House of Representatives on January 6, 1999. Involved in various social and professional organizations.

Clerk.—Jeff Trandahl.
  Deputy Clerk.—Gerasimos C. Vans.
    Assistants to the Clerk: Marjorie C. Kelaher, Daniel J. Strodel.
    Chief of—
      Legislative Computer Systems.—Joe Carmel, (2401 RHOB), 225-1182.
      Legislative Operations.—Frances Chiappardi, (HT–13), 225-7925.
      Legislative Resource Center.—Deborah Turner, (B–106 CHOB), 226-5200.
      Office of Publication Services.—Janice Wallace-Robinson, (B–28 CHOB), 225-1908.
      Office of History and Preservation.—Kenneth Kato, (B–53 CHOB), 226-1300.
      Official Reporter.—Susan Hanback, (1718 LHOB), 225-2627.
    Service Groups—
      Majority Chief of Pages.—Peggy Sampson, 225-7350.
      Minority Chief of Pages.—Wren Ivester, 225-7330.
      Congresswoman's Suite.—225-4196.
      Members and Family Committee.—225-0622.
      Prayer Room.—225-8070.
    Office of House Employment Counsel.—Gloria Lett, (1036 LHOB), 225-7075.

CHIEF ADMINISTRATIVE OFFICER

HB–30 The Capitol, phone 225–6969

[Authorized by House Resolution 423, 102nd Congress, enacted April 9, 1992]

JAMES M. EAGEN III, Chief Administrative Officer of the House of Representatives; native of Clarks Summit, PA; B.A. in History, Gettysburg College, Gettysburg, PA, 1979; M.A. in International Relations, American University School of International Services, Washington, D.C., 1982; Congressman Steve Gunderson (R–WI), Legislative Assistant, 1982–83; Administrative Assistant, 1983–85; Congressman William F. Goodling (R–PA), Administrative Assistant, 1985–1991; House Committee on Education and Labor, Minority Staff Director, 1991–94; House Committee on Education and the Workforce, Majority Staff Director, 1995–97; elected August 1, 1997, as Chief Administrative Officer of the House of Representatives.

Chief Administrative Officer.—James M. Eagen III.
    Deputy Chief Administrative Officer for Operations.—Will Plaster, H2–217 FHOB, 225–6969.
    Deputy Chief Administrative Officer for Strategy.—Philip Flewallen, H2–217 FHOB, 225–6969.
    Administrative Counsel.—Bill Cable, H2–217 FHOB, 225–6969.
    Executive Assistant.—Jordana Zobkoff, HB–30 The Capitol, 225–6969.
    Associate Administrator for—
        House Information Resources.—Dan Doody, H2–631 FHOB, 225–9276.
        House Support Services.—Helene Flanagan, H2–B29, 225–2033.
        Human Resources.—Kathy Wyszynski, H2–B29, 225–2450.
        Procurement.—Bill Dellar, H2–359A FHOB, 225–2921.

CHAPLAIN

HB–25 The Capitol, phone 225–2509, fax 225–0204

DANIEL P. COUGHLIN, Chaplain, House of Representatives; residence: St. Clement Parish, Chicago, IL; attended St. Mary of the Lake University, Mundelein, IL, and received a degree in Sacred Theology; ordained a Roman Catholic Priest on May 3, 1960; also attended Loyola University, Chicago, IL, and received a degree in Pastoral Studies; Director of the Office for Divine Worship, Archdiocese of Chicago, under John Cardinal Cody, 1969–1984; Director of the Cardinal Stritch Retreat House, Mundelein, IL, 1990–1995; Vicar for Priests under Francis Cardinal George, and Joseph Cardinal Bernardin, Archbishops of Chicago, 1995–2000; elected House Chaplain on March 23, 2000.

Chaplain of the House.—Daniel P. Coughlin.
    Assistant to the Chaplain.—Don Myhill.

OFFICE OF THE HOUSE HISTORIAN

243 Cannon House Office Building, phone 226–5525

House Historian.—Dr. Robert Remini.

OFFICE OF INTERPARLIAMENTARY AFFAIRS

HB–28 Capitol, phone 226–1766

Director.—Martha C. Morrison.
Assistant Director.—Janet McKinney.

HOUSE INFORMATION RESOURCES
Ford House Office Building, H2–630, 20515, phone 225–9276, fax 226–6150

Associate Administrator.—Dan Doody.

OFFICE OF THE ATTENDING PHYSICIAN
H–166 The Capitol, phone 225–5421
(After office hours, call Capitol Operator 224–2145)

Attending Physician.—Dr. John F. Eisold.
 Chief of Staff.—Christopher R. Picaut.
 Administrative Officer.—Keith Pray.

OFFICE OF INSPECTOR GENERAL
Ford House Office Building, H2–385, phone 226–1250

Inspector General.—[Vacant.]
 Deputy Inspector General.—James J. Cornell.
 Administrative Director.—Susan M. Kozubski.
 Secretary.—Monique Holliday.
 Director, Performance and Financial Audits.—G. Kenneth Eichelman.
  Assistant Directors: Opal Marie Hughes, Gary A. Muller.
  Auditors: Stephen M. Connard, Stuart W. Josephs, Julie A. Poole.
 Director, Information Systems Audits.—Steven L. Johnson.
  Auditors: Donna K. Hughes, Stephen D. Lockhart, Walter F. McClean, Keith A. Sullenberger.
 Director, Computer Assisted Audit Techniques.—Michael E. Benner.
 Director, Management Advisory Services.—Theresa M. Grafenstine.
  Assistant Director.—Susan L. Sharp.

OFFICE OF THE LAW REVISION COUNSEL
Ford House Office Building, H2–304, 20515–6711, phone 226–2411, fax 225–0010

Law Revision Counsel.—Peter G. LeFevre.
 Deputy Counsel.—Jerald J. Director.
 Senior Counsels: Kenneth I. Paretzky, Richard B. Simpson.
 Assistant Counsels: Ray Kaselonis, James Aaron Kirkpatrick, Edward T. Mulligan, Ralph V. Seep, Alan G. Skutt, Robert M. Sukol, Timothy D. Trushel, John Wagner.
 Staff Assistants: Charlotte Connolly, Debra L. Johnson.
 Printing Editors.—Terisa L. Allison, Robert E. Belcher.
 Senior Systems Engineer.—Eric Loach.

OFFICE OF THE LEGISLATIVE COUNSEL
136 Cannon House Office Building, phone 225–6060

Legislative Counsel.—Pope Barrow.
 Deputy Legislative Counsel.—Douglass Bellis.
 Senior Counsels: Wade Ballou, Timothy Brown, Sherry Criss, Steven Cope, Robert Cover, Ira Forstater, Edward Grossman, James Grossman, Jean Harmann, Lawrence Johnston, Edward Leong, David Mendelsohn, Sandra Strokoff, Robert Weinhagen, James Wert.
 Assistant Counsels: Philip Bayer, Warren Burke, Paul C. Callen, Henry Christrup, Lisa M. Daly, Tobias A. Dorsey, Matthew Eckstein, Susan Fleishman, Rosemary Gallagher, Pete Goodloe, Curt C. Haensel, Nicole Isaac, Gregory M. Kostka, Molly Lothamer, Pierre Poisson, Hadley Ross, Hank Savage, Kate Sawyer, Jessica Shapiro, Mark A. Synnes, Noah L. Wofsy, Brady Young.
 Office Administrator.—Renate Stehr.
 Assistant Office Administrator.—Nancy Cassavechia.
 Staff Assistants: Ashley Anderson, Debra Birch, Elonda Blount, Pamela Griffiths, Kelly Meryweather, Tom Meryweather, David Topper, Melissa Weiss.

Information Systems Analyst.—Willie Blount.
Publications Coordinator.—Craig Sterkx.

OFFICE OF THE PARLIAMENTARIAN
H–209 The Capitol, phone 225–7373

Parliamentarian.—John V. Sullivan.
  Deputy Parliamentarian.—Thomas J. Wickham.
    Associate Parliamentarian.— Muftiah M. McCartin.
    Assistant Parliamentarians: Ethan B. Lauer, Tara R. Sarathy.
  Chief Clerk.—Gay S. Topper.
    Assistant Clerk.—Brian C. Cooper.
  Precedent Consultant.—Charles W. Johnson III.
  Precedent Editor.—Deborah W. Khalili.
  Information Technology Manager.—Bryan J. Feldblum.

OFFICE OF THE SERGEANT AT ARMS
H–124 The Capitol, phone 225–2456

WILSON (BILL) LIVINGOOD, Sergeant at Arms of the U.S. House of Representatives; born on October 1, 1936 in Philadelphia, PA; B.S., Police Administration, Michigan State University; career record: special agent, U.S. Secret Service's Dallas Field Office, 1961–69; assistant to the special agent in charge of the Presidential Protective Division, 1969; special agent in charge of the Office of Protective Forces, 1970; inspector, Office of Inspection, 1978–82; special agent in charge, Houston Field Office, 1982–86; deputy assistant director, Office of Training, 1986–89; executive assistant to the Director of Secret Service, 1989–95; elected 36th Sergeant at Arms of the U.S. House of Representatives on January 4, 1995, for the 104th Congress; reelected for each succeeding Congress.

Sergeant at Arms.—Wilson (Bill) Livingood.
  Deputy Sergeant at Arms.—Kerri Hanley.
  Executive Assistant.—Kathleen Joyce.
  Staff Assistants: Doris Boyd, Karen Forriest, KaSandra Greenhow, Susan Lowe, Tanya McBride, Micaela Fernandez.
  Directors—
    Police Services/Special Events.—Don Kellaher.
    Identification Services.—Melissa Franger.
  Chamber Security.—Bill Sims.
    Assistant Supervisor.—Richard Wilson.
  House Garages and Parking Security.—Rod Myers.
  Assistants to the Sergeant at Arms: Stefan Bieret, Kevin Brennan, Kara Carlson, Ted Daniel, Teresa Johnson, Tripp Jones, Jim Kaelin, Jack Kelliher, Nina Parini, Alissa Strawcutter.
  Appointments/Public Information Center: Sam Jeffries, Robin Pegues.

OFFICE OF EMERGENCY PLANNING, PREPAREDNESS, AND OPERATIONS
H2–192 Ford House Office Building, phone 226–0950

Director.—Curt Coughlin.
  Deputy Director.—Lawrence Himmelsbach.
  Special Assistant to the Director.—Sara K. Sahm.
  Assistant Director for—
    Operations.—Michael P. Susalla.
    Planning.—Eric M. Kruse.
    Preparedness.—John E. Veatch.
    Special Projects.—W. Lee Trolan.
  Executive Assistant.—Linda R. Shealy.
  Senior Program Manager.—Traci L. Brasher.
  Program Analyst.—Lynsi P. Pfleegor.
  Senior Systems Engineer.—Eddie X. Tutivene.
  Homeland Security Liaison.—Grant A. Dillon.
  USCP Liaison.—Michael D. Shaffer.

JOINT COMMITTEES

Joint Economic Committee

G01 Dirksen Senate Office Building 20510–6432, phone 224–5171

[Created pursuant to sec. 5(a) of Public Law 304, 79th Congress]

Jim Saxton, Representative from New Jersey, *Chair*

Robert F. Bennett, Senator from Utah, *Vice Chair*

HOUSE

Paul Ryan, of Wisconsin.
Phil English, of Pennsylvania.
Ron Paul, of Texas.
Kevin Brady, of Texas.
Thaddeus G. McCotter, of Michigan.

Carolyn B. Maloney, of New York.
Maurice D. Hinchey, of New York.
Loretta Sanchez, of California.
Elijah E. Cummings, of Maryland.

SENATE

Sam Brownback, of Kansas.
John E. Sununu, of New Hampshire.
Jim DeMint, of South Carolina.
Jeff Sessions, of Alabama.
John Cornyn, of Texas.

Jack Reed, of Rhode Island.
Edward M. Kennedy, of Massachusetts.
Paul S. Sarbanes, of Maryland.
Jeff Bingaman, of New Mexico.

STAFF

Joint Economic Committee (SDG–01), 224–5171, fax 224–0240.
  Majority Executive Director.—Chris Frenze (433 CHOB), 5–3923.
    Finance Director.—Colleen Healy (SDG–01), 4–0370.
    Chief Macroeconomist.—Robert Keleher (368 FHOB), 6–3227.
    Senior Economists: Jason Fichtner (433 CHOB), 5–0371; Joe Kennedy (SDG–03),
      4–0368; Dan Miller (433 CHOB), 5–2223; Robert O'Quinn (246 FHOB), 6–4065;
      Timothy Slaper (SDG–05), 4–0376.
    Analyst.—Brian Higginbotham (433 CHOB), 5–0370.
    Executive Assistant.—Connie Foster (433 CHOB), 6–3231.
    Systems Administrator.—Bernard Readmond (SDG–01), 4–0374.
    Staff Assistant.—John Kachtik (SDG–01), 4–5171.
    Director of Vice Chair's Staff.—Jeff Schlagenhauf (SDG–09), 4–3922.
    Senior Economist to Vice-Chair.—Jeff Wrase (SDG–07), 4–2335.
    Chief Economist to Vice Chair.—Ike Brannon (SDG–07), 4–0378.
    Senior Health Economist to Vice-Chair.—Tom Miller (SH–805), 4–3915.
    Economist to Vice-Chair.—Natasha Moore (SH–805), 4–2944.
    Research Assistants to Vice-Chair: Michael Ashton, 4–0364; Suzanne Stewart
      (SDG–07), 4–0367.
    Professional Staff to Vice-Chair.—Trish Kent (SH–805), 4–2989.
  Minority Staff Director.—Chad Stone (SH–804)4–2675.
    Deputy Staff Director/Chief Economist.—Frank Sammartino (SH–804), 4–7056.
    Deputy Staff Director for Communications.—Nan Gibson (SH–804), 4–0377.
    Principal Economist.—Matthew Salomon (SH–804), 4–0373.

Senior Economist.—Daphne V. Clones-Federing (244 FHOB), 6–7108.
Economist.—John McInerney (244 FHOB), 6–2487.
Policy Analysts: Christina FitzPatrick (SH–804), 4–7683; Kasia Murray (244 FHOB), 5–6024.
Senior Research Assistant.—Mindy Levit (SH–804), 4–7998.
Research Assistant.—Wuryati Morris (SH–804), 4–9065.
Staff Assistant.—Pamela Wilson (SH–804), 4–0372.

Joint Committee on the Library of Congress
S–240 The Capitol, 20515, phone 224–1034

Robert W. Ney, Representative from Ohio, *Chair*
Ted Stevens, Senator from Alaska, *Vice-Chair*

SENATE

Trent Lott, of Mississippi.
Thad Cochran, of Mississippi.

Christopher J. Dodd, of Connecticut.
Charles E. Schumer, of New York.

HOUSE

Vernon J. Ehlers, of Michigan.
Candice Miller, of Michigan.

Juanita Millender-McDonald, of California.
Zoe Lofgren, of California.

STAFF

Senate Staff Director.—Jennifer Mies Lowe.
House Staff Director.—Bryan T. Dorsey.

Joint Committee on Printing
SR–305 Russell Senate Office Building, 20510, phone 224–6352
[Created by act of August 3, 1846 (9 Stat. 114); U.S. Code 44, Section 101]

Trent Lott, Senator from Mississippi, *Chair*
Robert W. Ney, Representative from Ohio, *Vice-Chair*

SENATE

Thad Cochran, of Mississippi.
Saxby Chambliss, of Georgia.

Daniel K. Inouye, of Hawaii.
Mark Dayton, of Minnesota.

HOUSE

John T. Doolittle, of California.
Thomas M. Reynolds, of New York.

Juanita Millender-McDonald, of California.
Robert A. Brady, of Pennsylvania.

STAFF

Staff Director.—Susan Wells.
Senior Staff.—Matthew McGowan.
Deputy Staff Director.—Bryan T. Dorsey.
Minority Staff Director.—Michael Harrison.

Joint Committee on Taxation

1015 Longworth House Office Building 20515–6453, phone 225–3621
http://www.house.gov/jct

[Created by Public Law 20, 69th Congress]

William M. Thomas, Representative from California, *Chair*
Clarles E. Grassley, Senator from Iowa, *Vice Chair*

HOUSE

E. Clay Shaw, Jr., of Florida.
Nancy Johnson, of Connecticut.

Charles B. Rangel, of New York.
Fortney Pete Stark, of California.

SENATE

Orrin G. Hatch, of Utah.
Trent Lott, of Mississippi.

Max Baucus, of Montana.
John D. Rockefeller IV, of West Virginia.

STAFF

Joint Committee on Taxation (1015 LHOB), 225–3621.
Chief of Staff.—George K. Yin.
   Deputy Chiefs of Staff: Bernard A. Schmitt (594 FHOB), 6–7575; Mary M. Schmitt (1620 LHOB), 5–7377.
   Associate Deputy Chiefs of Staff: Thomas F. Koerner (595 FHOB), 6–7575; Carolyn E. Smith (1620 LHOB), 5–7377.
   Administrative Director.—Bonnie Johnson (1015 LHOB), 5–3621.
   Chief Clerk.—John H. Bloyer (1620 LHOB), 5–7377.
   Senior Legislation Counsels: Harold E. Hirsch (1620 LHOB), 5–7377; Laurie A. Matthews (1620 LHOB), 5–7377; Cecily W. Rock (1620 LHOB), 5–7377; Melvin C. Thomas, Jr. (1620 LHOB), 5–7377.
   Legislation Counsels: Ray Beeman (SD–204), 4–5561; Roger Colinvaux (SD–204), 4–5561; Gordon Cray (SD–204), 4–5561; Nikole Flax (1604 LHOB), 5–7377; Deirdre James (1620 LHOB), 5–7377; David Lenter (1604 LHOB), 5–7377; Trisha McDermott (SD–204), 4–5561; Joseph W. Nega (1620 LHOB), 5–7377; David Noren (1604 LHOB), 5–7377; Kashi Way (1620 LHOB), 5–7377; Allison Wielobob (1620 LHOB), 5–7377.
   Senior Economists: Thomas A. Barthold (1620 LHOB), 5–7377; Patrick A. Driessen (560A FHOB), 6–7575; Ronald A. Jeremias (593 FHOB), 6–7575; Pamela H. Moomau (593 FHOB), 6–7575; William T. Sutton (560B FHOB), 6–7575.
   Economists: Timothy Dowd (578 FHOB), 6–7575; Robert P. Harvey (561 FHOB), 6–7575; Thomas Holtmann (578 FHOB), 6–7575; Gary Koenig (595 FHOB), 6–7575; John F. Navratil (1620 LHOB), 5–7377; Christopher Overend (574B FHOB), 6–7575; Michael A. Udell (574A FHOB), 6–7575; Susan Yang (593 FHOB), 6–7575.
   Accountants: Tara Fisher, Gray Fontenot (1604 LHOB), 5–7377.
   Chief Statistical Analyst.—Melani M. Houser (966 FHOB), 6–7575.
   Statistical Analyst.—Tanya Butler (596 FHOB), 6–7575.
   Tax Resources Specialist.—Melissa A. O'Brien (SD–462), 4–0494.
   Senior Refund Counsel.—Norman J. Brand (3565 IRS), 622–3580.
   Refund Counsel.—Chase Gibson (3565 IRS) 622–3580; Robert C. Gotwald (3565 IRS), 622–3580.
   Document Production Specialist.—Christine J. Simmons (1620 LHOB), 5–7377.
   Executive Assistants: B. Jean Best (596 LHOB), 6–7575; Emily Collins (1015 LHOB), 5–3621; Jayne Northern (SD–204), 4–5561; Lucia J. Rogers (1015 LHOB), 5–3621; Patricia C. Smith (1620 LHOB), 5–7377; Sharon Watts (3565 IRS), 662–3580.
   Senior Computer Specialist.—Damion Jedlicka (577 FHOB), 6–7575.
   Computer Specialist.—Hal G. Norman (577 FHOB), 6–7575.
   Data Research Analyst.—Brent Trigg (561 FHOB), 6–7575.
   Senior Staff Assistant.—Debra L. McMullen (1620 LHOB), 5–2647.
   Staff Assistants: Sean R. Corcoran (1620 LHOB), 5–2647; Neval E. McMullen (1620 LHOB), 5–2647; Kristine Means (1620 LHOB), 5–2647.

ASSIGNMENTS OF SENATORS TO COMMITTEES

[Republicans in roman (55); Democrats in *italic* (44); Independent in SMALL CAPS (1); total, 100]

Senator	Committees (Standing, Joint, Special, Select)
Akaka	Armed Services. Energy and Natural Resources. Homeland Security and Governmental Affairs. Indian Affairs. Veterans' Affairs. Select Committee on Ethics.
Alexander	Budget. Energy and Natural Resources. Foreign Relations. Health, Education, Labor, and Pensions. Special Committee on Aging.
Allard	Appropriations. Banking, Housing, and Urban Affairs. Budget.
Allen	Commerce, Science, and Transportation. Energy and Natural Resources. Foreign Relations. Small Business and Entrepreneurship.
Baucus	Agriculture, Nutrition, and Forestry. Environment and Public Works. Finance. Joint Committee on Taxation.
Bayh	Armed Services. Banking, Housing, and Urban Affairs. Small Business and Entrepreneurship. Select Committee on Intelligence. Special Committee on Aging.
Bennett	Appropriations. Banking, Housing, and Urban Affairs. Homeland Security and Governmental Affairs. Rules and Administration. Joint Economic Committee.
Biden	Foreign Relations. Judiciary.
Bingaman	Energy and Natural Resources. Finance. Health, Education, Labor, and Pensions. Joint Economic Committee.
Bond	Appropriations. Environment and Public Works. Small Business and Entrepreneurship. Select Committee on Intelligence.
Boxer	Commerce, Science, and Transportation. Environment and Public Works. Foreign Relations.

Senator	Committees (Standing, Joint, Special, Select)
Brownback	Appropriations. Judiciary. Joint Economic Committee.
Bunning	Banking, Housing, and Urban Affairs. Budget. Energy and Natural Resources. Finance.
Burns	Appropriations. Commerce, Science, and Transportation. Energy and Natural Resources. Small Business and Entrepreneurship. Special Committee on Aging.
Burr	Energy and Natural Resources. Health, Education, Labor, and Pensions. Indian Affairs. Veterans' Affairs.
Byrd	Appropriations. Armed Services. Budget. Rules and Administration.
Cantwell	Commerce, Science, and Transportation. Energy and Natural Resources. Indian Affairs. Small Business and Entrepreneurship.
Carper	Banking, Housing, and Urban Affairs. Environment and Public Works. Homeland Security and Governmental Affairs. Special Committee on Aging.
Chafee	Environment and Public Works. Foreign Relations. Homeland Security and Governmental Affairs.
Chambliss	Agriculture, Nutrition, and Forestry, *chairman.* Armed Services. Rules and Administration. Joint Committee on Printing. Select Committee on Intelligence.
Clinton	Armed Services. Environment and Public Works. Health, Education, Labor, and Pensions. Special Committee on Aging.
Coburn	Homeland Security and Governmental Affairs. Indian Affairs. Judiciary.
Cochran	Appropriations, *chairman.* Agriculture, Nutrition, and Forestry. Rules and Administration. Joint Committee on the Library of Congress. Joint Committee on Printing.
Coleman	Agriculture, Nutrition, and Forestry. Foreign Relations. Homeland Security and Governmental Affairs. Small Business and Entrepreneurship.
Collins	Homeland Security and Governmental Affairs, *chairman.* Armed Services. Special Committee on Aging.

Senator	Committees (Standing, Joint, Special, Select)
Conrad	Agriculture, Nutrition, and Forestry. Budget. Finance. Indian Affairs.
Cornyn	Armed Services. Budget. Judiciary. Small Business and Entrepreneurship. Joint Economic Committee.
Corzine	Banking, Housing, and Urban Affairs. Budget. Energy and Natural Resources. Select Committee on Intelligence.
Craig	Veterans' Affairs, *chairman.* Appropriations. Energy and Natural Resources. Special Committee on Aging.
Crapo	Agriculture, Nutrition, and Forestry. Banking, Housing, and Urban Affairs. Budget. Finance. Indian Affairs.
Dayton	Agriculture, Nutrition, and Forestry. Armed Services. Homeland Security and Governmental Affairs. Rules and Administration. Joint Committee on Printing.
DeMint	Commerce, Science, and Transportation. Environment and Public Works. Joint Economic Committee. Special Committee on Aging.
DeWine	Appropriations. Health, Education, Labor, and Pensions. Judiciary. Select Committee on Intelligence.
Dodd	Banking, Housing, and Urban Affairs. Foreign Relations. Health, Education, Labor, and Pensions. Rules and Administration. Joint Committee on the Library of Congress.
Dole	Armed Services. Banking, Housing, and Urban Affairs. Special Committee on Aging.
Domenici	Energy and Natural Resources, *chairman.* Appropriations. Budget. Homeland Security and Governmental Affairs. Indian Affairs.
Dorgan	Appropriations. Commerce, Science, and Transportation. Energy and Natural Resources. Indian Affairs.
Durbin	Appropriations. Judiciary. Rules and Administration.

Senator	Committees (Standing, Joint, Special, Select)
Ensign	Armed Services. Budget. Commerce, Science, and Transportation. Health, Education, Labor, and Pensions. Veterans' Affairs.
Enzi	Health, Education, Labor, and Pensions, *chairman.* Banking, Housing, and Urban Affairs. Budget. Small Business and Entrepreneurship.
Feingold	Budget. Foreign Relations. Judiciary. Special Committee on Aging.
Feinstein	Appropriations. Energy and Natural Resources. Judiciary. Rules and Administration. Select Committee on Intelligence.
Frist	Finance. Health, Education, Labor, and Pensions. Rules and Administration. Select Committee on Intelligence.
Graham	Armed Services. Budget. Judiciary. Veterans' Affairs.
Grassley	Finance, *chairman.* Agriculture, Nutrition, and Forestry. Budget. Judiciary. Joint Committee on Taxation.
Gregg	Budget, *chairman.* Appropriations. Health, Education, Labor, and Pensions.
Hagel	Banking, Housing, and Urban Affairs. Foreign Relations. Rules and Administration. Select Committee on Intelligence.
Harkin	Agriculture, Nutrition, and Forestry. Appropriations. Health, Education, Labor, and Pensions. Small Business and Entrepreneurship.
Hatch	Finance. Health, Education, Labor, and Pensions. Judiciary. Joint Committee on Taxation. Select Committee on Intelligence.
Hutchison	Appropriations. Commerce, Science, and Transportation. Rules and Administration. Veterans' Affairs.
Inhofe	Environment and Public Works, *chairman.* Armed Services.
Inouye	Appropriations. Commerce, Science, and Transportation. Indian Affairs.

Senator	Committees (Standing, Joint, Special, Select)
	Rules and Administration. Joint Committee on Printing.
Isakson	Environment and Public Works. Health, Education, Labor, and Pensions. Small Business and Entrepreneurship. Veterans' Affairs.
JEFFORDS	Environment and Public Works. Finance. Health, Education, Labor, and Pensions. Veterans' Affairs. Special Committee on Aging.
Johnson	Appropriations. Banking, Housing, and Urban Affairs. Budget. Energy and Natural Resources. Indian Affairs. Select Committee on Ethics.
Kennedy	Armed Services. Health, Education, Labor, and Pensions. Judiciary. Joint Economic Committee.
Kerry	Commerce, Science, and Transportation. Finance. Foreign Relations. Small Business and Entrepreneurship.
Kohl	Appropriations. Judiciary. Special Committee on Aging.
Kyl	Finance. Judiciary.
Landrieu	Appropriations. Energy and Natural Resources. Small Business and Entrepreneurship.
Lautenberg	Commerce, Science, and Transportation. Environment and Public Works. Homeland Security and Governmental Affairs.
Leahy	Agriculture, Nutrition, and Forestry. Appropriations. Judiciary.
Levin	Armed Services. Homeland Security and Governmental Affairs. Small Business and Entrepreneurship. Select Committee on Intelligence.
Lieberman	Armed Services. Environment and Public Works. Homeland Security and Governmental Affairs. Small Business and Entrepreneurship.
Lincoln	Agriculture, Nutrition, and Forestry. Finance. Special Committee on Aging.
Lott	Rules and Administration, *chairman.* Joint Committee on Printing, *chairman.* Commerce, Science, and Transportation. Finance.

Senator	Committees (Standing, Joint, Special, Select)
	Joint Committee on the Library of Congress. Joint Committee on Taxation. Select Committee on Intelligence.
Lugar	Foreign Relations, *chairman.* Agriculture, Nutrition, and Forestry.
McCain	Indian Affairs, *chairman.* Armed Services. Commerce, Science, and Transportation.
McConnell	Agriculture, Nutrition, and Forestry. Appropriations. Rules and Administration.
Martinez	Banking, Housing, and Urban Affairs. Energy and Natural Resources. Foreign Relations. Special Committee on Aging.
Mikulski	Appropriations. Health, Education, Labor, and Pensions. Select Committee on Intelligence.
Murkowski	Energy and Natural Resources. Environment and Public Works. Foreign Relations. Indian Affairs.
Murray	Appropriations. Budget. Health, Education, Labor, and Pensions. Veterans' Affairs.
Nelson, Bill, of Florida	Armed Services. Budget. Commerce, Science, and Transportation. Foreign Relations. Special Committee on Aging.
Nelson, E. Ben, of Nebraska ...	Agriculture, Nutrition, and Forestry. Armed Services. Commerce, Science, and Transportation. Rules and Administration.
Obama	Environment and Public Works. Foreign Relations. Veterans' Affairs.
Pryor	Commerce, Science and Transportation. Homeland Security and Governmental Affairs. Small Business and Entrepreneurship. Select Committee on Ethics.
Reed, of Rhode Island	Armed Services. Banking, Housing, and Urban Affairs. Health, Education, Labor, and Pensions. Joint Economic Committee.
Reid, of Nevada	Appropriations.
Roberts	Select Committee on Intelligence, *chairman.* Agriculture, Nutrition, and Forestry. Armed Services. Health, Education, Labor, and Pensions. Select Committee on Ethics.

Senator	Committees (Standing, Joint, Special, Select)
Rockefeller	Commerce, Science, and Transportation. Finance. Veterans' Affairs. Joint Committee on Taxation. Select Committee on Intelligence.
Salazar	Agriculture, Nutrition, and Forestry. Energy and Natural Resources. Veterans' Affairs.
Santorum	Agriculture, Nutrition, and Forestry. Banking, Housing, and Urban Affairs. Finance. Rules and Administration. Special Committee on Aging.
Sarbanes	Banking, Housing, and Urban Affairs. Budget. Foreign Relations. Joint Economic Committee.
Schumer	Banking, Housing, and Urban Affairs. Finance. Judiciary. Rules and Administration. Joint Committee on the Library of Congress.
Sessions	Armed Services. Budget. Health, Education, Labor, and Pensions. Judiciary. Joint Economic Committee.
Shelby	Banking, Housing, and Urban Affairs, *chairman.* Appropriations. Special Committee on Aging.
Smith	Special Committee on Aging, *chairman.* Commerce, Science, and Transportation. Energy and Natural Resources. Finance. Indian Affairs.
Snowe	Small Business and Entrepreneurship, *chairman.* Commerce, Science, and Transportation. Finance. Select Committee on Intelligence.
Specter	Judiciary, *chairman.* Appropriations. Veterans' Affairs.
Stabenow	Agriculture, Nutrition, and Forestry. Banking, Housing, and Urban Affairs. Budget.
Stevens	Commerce, Science, and Transportation, *chairman.* Appropriations. Homeland Security and Governmental Affairs. Rules and Administration. Joint Committee on the Library of Congress.
Sununu	Banking, Housing, and Urban Affairs. Commerce, Science, and Transportation. Foreign Relations. Joint Economic Committee.

Senator	Committees (Standing, Joint, Special, Select)
Talent	Agriculture, Nutrition, and Forestry. Armed Services. Energy and Natural Resources. Special Committee on Aging.
Thomas	Agriculture, Nutrition, and Forestry. Energy and Natural Resources. Finance. Indian Affairs. Select Committee on Ethics.
Thune	Armed Services. Environment and Public Works. Small Business and Entrepreneurship. Veterans' Affairs.
Vitter	Commerce, Science, and Transportation. Environment and Public Works. Small Business and Entrepreneurship.
Voinovich	Select Committee on Ethics, *chairman.* Environment and Public Works. Foreign Relations. Homeland Security and Governmental Affairs.
Warner	Armed Services, *chairman.* Environment and Public Works. Homeland Security and Governmental Affairs. Select Committee on Intelligence.
Wyden	Budget. Energy and Natural Resources. Finance. Select Committee on Intelligence. Special Committee on Aging.

ASSIGNMENTS OF REPRESENTATIVES TO COMMITTEES

[Republicans in roman (231); Democrats in *italic* (202); Independents in SMALL CAPS (1); Vacancy (1); Resident Commissioner and Delegates in **boldface** (5); total, 440]

Representative	Committees (Standing, Joint, Special, and Select)
Abercrombie	Armed Services. Resources.
Ackerman	Financial Services. International Relations.
Aderholt	Appropriations.
Akin	Armed Services. Science. Small Business.
Alexander	Appropriations.
Allen	Budget. Energy and Commerce.
Andrews	Armed Services. Education and the Workforce.
Baca	Agriculture. Financial Services.
Bachus	Financial Services. Judiciary. Transportation and Infrastructure.
Baird	Budget. Science. Transportation and Infrastructure.
Baker	Financial Services. Transportation and Infrastructure. Veterans' Affairs.
Baldwin	Energy and Commerce.
Barrett	Budget. Financial Services. International Relations.
Barrow	Agriculture. Education and the Workforce. Small Business.
Bartlett	Armed Services. Science. Small Business.
Barton	Energy and Commerce, *chairman.*
Bass	Energy and Commerce.
Bean	Financial Services. Small Business.
Beauprez	Ways and Means.

Representative	Committees (Standing, Joint, Special, and Select)
Becerra	Ways and Means.
Berkley	International Relations. Transportation and Infrastructure. Veterans' Affairs.
Berman	International Relations. Judiciary.
Berry	Appropriations.
Biggert	Education and the Workforce. Financial Services. Science. Standards of Official Conduct.
Bilirakis	Energy and Commerce. Veterans' Affairs.
Bishop, Rob, of Utah	Rules.
Bishop, Sanford D., Jr., of Georgia.	Appropriations.
Bishop, Timothy H., of New York.	Education and the Workforce. Transportation and Infrastructure.
Blackburn	Energy and Commerce.
Blumenauer	International Relations. Transportation and Infrastructure.
Blunt	Majority Whip. Energy and Commerce.
Boehlert	Science, *chairman.* Transportation and Infrastructure.
Boehner	Education and the Workforce, *chairman.* Agriculture.
Bonilla	Appropriations.
Bonner	Agriculture. Budget. Science.
Bono	Energy and Commerce.
Boozman	International Relations. Transportation and Infrastructure. Veterans' Affairs.
Bordallo	Armed Services. Resources. Small Business.
Boren	Armed Services. Resources.
Boswell	Agriculture. Transportation and Infrastructure. Permanent Select Committee on Intelligence.
Boucher	Energy and Commerce. Judiciary.
Boustany	Agriculture. Education and the Workforce. Transportation and Infrastructure.

Representative	Committees (Standing, Joint, Special, and Select)
Boyd	Appropriations.
Bradley	Armed Services. Budget. Small Business. Veterans' Affairs.
Brady, Kevin, of Texas	Ways and Means. Joint Economic Committee.
Brady, Robert A., of Pennsylvania.	Armed Services. House Administration. Joint Committee on Printing.
Brown, Corrine, of Florida	Transportation and Infrastructure. Veterans' Affairs.
Brown, Henry E., Jr., of South Carolina.	Resources. Transportation and Infrastructure. Veterans' Affairs.
Brown, Sherrod, of Ohio	Energy and Commerce. International Relations.
Brown-Waite	Financial Services. Government Reform. Veterans' Affairs.
Burgess	Energy and Commerce.
Burton	Government Reform. International Relations. Veterans' Affairs.
Butterfield	Agriculture. Armed Services.
Buyer	Veterans' Affairs, *chairman*. Energy and Commerce.
Calvert	Armed Services. Resources. Science.
Camp	Ways and Means.
Cannon	Government Reform. Judiciary. Resources.
Cantor	Ways and Means.
Capito	Rules.
Capps	Budget. Energy and Commerce.
Capuano	Financial Services. Transportation and Infrastructure.
Cardin	Ways and Means.
Cardoza	Agriculture. International Relations. Resources.
Carnahan	Science. Transportation and Infrastructure.

Representative	Committees (Standing, Joint, Special, and Select)
Carson	Financial Services. Transportation and Infrastructure.
Carter	Appropriations.
Case	Agriculture. Budget. Small Business.
Castle	Education and the Workforce. Financial Services.
Chabot	International Relations. Judiciary. Small Business.
Chandler	Agriculture. International Relations. Transportation and Infrastructure.
Chocola	Ways and Means.
Christensen	Homeland Security. Resources. Small Business.
Clay	Financial Services. Government Reform.
Cleaver	Financial Services.
Clyburn	Appropriations.
Coble	Judiciary. Transportation and Infrastructure.
Cole	Rules. Standards of Conduct.
Conaway	Agriculture. Armed Services. Budget.
Conyers	Judiciary.
Cooper	Armed Services. Budget.
Costa	Agriculture. Resources. Science.
Costello	Science. Transportation and Infrastructure.
Cox	Homeland Security, *chairman*.
Cramer	Appropriations. Permanent Select Committee on Intelligence.
Crenshaw	Appropriations. Budget.
Crowley	Financial Services. International Relations.
Cubin	Energy and Commerce. Resources.

Representative	Committees (Standing, Joint, Special, and Select)
Cuellar	Agriculture. Budget.
Culberson	Appropriations.
Cummings	Government Reform. Transportation and Infrastructure. Joint Economic Committee.
Cunningham	Appropriations. Permanent Select Committee on Intelligence.
Davis, Artur, of Alabama	Budget. Financial Services.
Davis, Danny K., of Illinois	Education and the Workforce. Government Reform. Small Business.
Davis, Geoff, of Kentucky	Armed Services. Financial Services.
Davis, Jim, of Florida	Energy and Commerce.
Davis, Jo Ann, of Virginia	Armed Services. International Relations. Permanent Select Committee on Intelligence.
Davis, Lincoln, of Tennessee	Agriculture. Science. Transportation and Infrastructure.
Davis, Susan A., of California ...	Armed Services. Education and the Workforce.
Davis, Tom, of Virginia	Government Reform, *chairman.* Homeland Security.
Deal	Energy and Commerce.
DeFazio	Homeland Security. Resources. Transportation and Infrastructure.
DeGette	Energy and Commerce.
Delahunt	International Relations. Judiciary.
DeLauro	Appropriations. Budget.
DeLay	Majority Leader.
Dent	Government Reform Homeland Security. Transportation and Infrastructure.
Diaz-Balart, Lincoln, of Florida.	Rules.
Diaz-Balart, Mario, of Florida ...	Budget. Transportation and Infrastructure.
Dicks	Appropriations. Homeland Security.
Dingell	Energy and Commerce.
Doggett	Ways and Means.

Representative	Committees (Standing, Joint, Special, and Select)
Doolittle	Appropriations. House Administration. Joint Committee on Printing.
Doyle	Energy and Commerce. Standards of Official Conduct.
Drake	Armed Services. Education and the Workforce. Resources.
Dreier	Rules, *chairman.*
Duncan	Government Reform. Resources. Transportation and Infrastructure.
Edwards	Appropriations. Budget.
Ehlers	Education and the Workforce. House Administration. Science. Transportation and Infrastructure. Joint Committee on the Library of Congress.
Emanuel	Ways and Means.
Emerson	Appropriations.
Engel	Energy and Commerce. International Relations.
English	Ways and Means. Joint Economic Committee.
Eshoo	Energy and Commerce. Permanent Select Committee on Intelligence.
Etheridge	Agriculture. Homeland Security.
Evans	Armed Services. Veterans' Affairs.
Everett	Agriculture. Armed Services. Veterans' Affairs. Permanent Select Committee on Intelligence.
Faleomavaega	International Relations. Resources. Small Business.
Farr	Appropriations.
Fattah	Appropriations.
Feeney	Financial Services. Judiciary. Science.
Ferguson	Energy and Commerce.
Filner	Transportation and Infrastructure. Veterans' Affairs.
Fitzpatrick	Financial Services. Small Business.

Representative	Committees (Standing, Joint, Special, and Select)
Flake	International Relations. Judiciary. Resources.
Foley	Ways and Means.
Forbes	Armed Services. Judiciary. Science.
Ford	Budget. Financial Services.
Fortenberry	Agriculture. International Relations. Small Business.
Fortuño	Education and the Workforce. Resources. Transportation and Infrastructure.
Fossella	Energy and Commerce. Financial Services.
Foxx	Agriculture. Education and the Workforce. Government Reform.
Frank	Financial Services.
Franks	Armed Services. Judiciary.
Frelinghuysen	Appropriations.
Gallegly	International Relations. Judiciary. Resources. Permanent Select Committee on Intelligence.
Garrett	Budget. Financial Services.
Gerlach	Financial Services. Transportation and Infrastructure.
Gibbons	Armed Services. Homeland Security. Resources.
Gilchrest	Resources. Science. Transportation and Infrastructure.
Gillmor	Energy and Commerce. Financial Services.
Gingrey	Rules.
Gohmert	Judiciary. Resources. Small Business.
Gonzalez	Energy and Commerce.
Goode	Appropriations.
Goodlatte	Agriculture, *chairman.* Judiciary.

Representative	Committees (Standing, Joint, Special, and Select)
Gordon	Energy and Commerce. Science.
Granger	Appropriations.
Graves	Agriculture. Small Business. Transportation and Infrastructure.
Green, Al, of Texas	Financial Services. Science.
Green, Gene, of Texas	Energy and Commerce. Standards of Official Conduct.
Green, Mark, of Wisconsin	International Relations. Judiciary.
Grijalva	Education and the Workforce. Resources. Small Business.
Gutierrez	Financial Services. Veterans' Affairs.
Gutknecht	Agriculture. Government Reform. Science.
Hall	Energy and Commerce. Science.
Harman	Homeland Security. Permanent Select Committee on Intelligence.
Harris	Financial Services. Homeland Security. International Relations.
Hart	Standards of Official Conducts. Ways and Means.
Hastert	Speaker of the House. Permanent Select Committee on Intelligence.
Hastings, Alcee L., of Florida	Rules. Permanent Select Committee on Intelligence.
Hastings, Doc, of Washington ...	Standards of Official Conduct, *chairman.* Rules.
Hayes	Agriculture. Armed Services. Transportation and Infrastructure.
Hayworth	Resources. Ways and Means.
Hefley	Armed Services.
Hensarling	Budget. Financial Services.
Herger	Ways and Means.
Herseth	Agriculture. Resources. Veterans' Affairs.

Representative	Committees (Standing, Joint, Special, and Select)
Higgins	Government Reform. Transportation and Infrastructure.
Hinchey	Appropriations. Joint Economic Committee.
Hinojosa	Education and the Workforce. Financial Services.
Hobson	Appropriations.
Hoekstra	Permanent Select Committee on Intelligence, *chairman*. Transportation and Infrastructure.
Holden	Agriculture. Transportation and Infrastructure.
Holt	Education and the Workforce. Permanent Select Committee on Intelligence.
Honda	Science. Transportation and Infrastructure.
Hooley	Financial Services. Science. Veterans' Affairs.
Hostettler	Armed Services. Judiciary.
Hoyer	Appropriations. Democratic Whip.
Hulshof	Budget. Ways and Means.
Hunter	Armed Services, *chairman*.
Hyde	International Relations, *chairman*. Judiciary.
Inglis	Education and the Workforce. Judiciary. Science.
Inslee	Energy and Commerce. Resources.
Israel	Armed Services. Financial Services.
Issa	Government Reform. International Relations. Judiciary.
Istook	Appropriations.
Jackson	Appropriations.
Jackson Lee	Homeland Security. Judiciary. Science.
Jefferson	Budget. Ways and Means.
Jenkins	Agriculture. Judiciary.

Representative	Committees (Standing, Joint, Special, and Select)
Jindal	Education and the Workforce. Homeland Security. Resources.
Johnson, Eddie Bernice, of Texas.	Science. Transportation and Infrastructure.
Johnson, Nancy L., of Connecticut.	Ways and Means. Joint Committee on Taxation.
Johnson, Sam, of Texas	Education and the Workforce. Ways and Means.
Johnson, Timothy V., of Illinois.	Agriculture. Science. Transportation and Infrastructure.
Jones, Stephanie Tubbs, of Ohio.	Standards of Official Conduct. Ways and Means.
Jones, Walter B., of North Carolina.	Armed Services. Financial Services. Resources.
Kanjorski	Financial Services. Government Reform.
Kaptur	Appropriations.
Keller	Education and the Workforce. Judiciary. Small Business.
Kelly	Financial Services. Small Business. Transportation and Infrastructure.
Kennedy, Mark R., of Minnesota.	Financial Services. Transportation and Infrastructure.
Kennedy, Patrick J., of Rhode Island.	Appropriations.
Kildee	Education and the Workforce. Resources.
Kilpatrick	Appropriations.
Kind	Budget. Education and the Workforce. Resources.
King, Peter T., of New York	Financial Services. Homeland Security. International Relations.
King, Steve, of Iowa	Agriculture. Judiciary. Small Business.
Kingston	Appropriations.
Kirk	Appropriations.
Kline	Armed Services. Education and the Workforce.
Knollenberg	Appropriations.

Representative	Committees (Standing, Joint, Special, and Select)
Kolbe	Appropriations.
Kucinich	Education and the Workforce. Government Reform.
Kuhl	Agriculture. Education and the Workforce. Transportation and Infrastructure.
LaHood	Appropriations. Permanent Select Committee on Intelligence.
Langevin	Armed Services. Homeland Security.
Lantos	Government Reform. International Relations.
Larsen	Agriculture. Armed Services. Transportation and Infrastructure.
Larson	Ways and Means.
Latham	Appropriations.
LaTourette	Financial Services. Government Reform. Transportation and Infrastructure.
Leach	Financial Services. International Relations.
Lee	Financial Services. International Relations.
Levin	Ways and Means.
Lewis, Jerry, of California	Appropriations, *chairman.*
Lewis, John, of Georgia	Ways and Means.
Lewis, Ron, of Kentucky	Ways and Means.
Linder	Homeland Security. Ways and Means. Joint Committee on Printing.
Lipinski	Science. Small Business.
LoBiondo	Armed Services. Transportation and Infrastructure.
Lofgren	Homeland Security. House Administration. Judiciary. Joint Committee on the Library of Congress.
Lowey	Appropriations. Homeland Security.
Lucas	Agriculture. Financial Services. Science.
Lungren	Budget. Homeland Security. Judiciary.

Representative	Committees (Standing, Joint, Special, and Select)
Lynch	Financial Services. Government Reform.
McCarthy	Education and the Workforce. Financial Services.
McCaul	Homeland Security. International Relations. Science.
McCollum	Education and the Workforce. International Relations.
McCotter	Budget. International Relations. Small Business. Joint Economic Committee.
McCrery	Ways and Means.
McDermott	Ways and Means.
McGovern	Rules.
McHenry	Budget. Financial Services. Government Reform.
McHugh	Armed Services. Government Reform. Permanent Select Committee on Intelligence.
McIntyre	Agriculture. Armed Services.
McKeon	Armed Services. Education and the Workforce.
McKinney	Armed Services. Budget.
McMorris	Armed Services. Education and the Workforce. Resources.
McNulty	Ways and Means.
Mack	Budget. International Relations. Transportation and Infrastructure.
Maloney	Financial Services. Government Reform. Joint Economic Committee.
Manzullo	Small Business, *chairman*. Financial Services.
Marchant	Education and the Workforce. Government Reform. Transportation and Infrastructure.
Markey	Energy and Commerce. Homeland Security. Resources.
Marshall	Agriculture. Armed Services.

Representative	Committees (Standing, Joint, Special, and Select)
Matheson	Financial Services. Science. Transportation and Infrastructure.
Matsui, Doris	Rules.
Meehan	Armed Services. Judiciary.
Meek	Armed Services. Homeland Security.
Meeks	Financial Services. International Relations.
Melancon	Agriculture. Resources. Science.
Menendez	International Relations. Transportation and Infrastructure.
ica	Government Reform. House Administration. Transportation and Infrastructure.
chaud	Small Business. Transportation and Infrastructure. Veterans' Affairs.
llender-McDonald	House Administration. Small Business. Transportation and Infrastructure. Joint Committee on the Library of Congress.
iller, Brad, of North Carolina.	Financial Services. Science.
Miller, Candice S., of Michigan.	Armed Services. Government Reform. House Administration. Joint Committee on the Library of Congress.
Miller, Gary G., of California	Financial Services. Transportation and Infrastructure.
Miller, George, of California	Education and the Workforce. Resources.
Miller, Jeff, of Florida	Armed Services. Veterans' Affairs.
Mollohan	Appropriations. Standards of Official Conduct.
Moore, Dennis, of Kansas	Budget. Financial Services.
Moore, Gwen, of Wisconsin	Financial Services. Small Business.
Moran, James P., of Virginia	Appropriations.
Moran, Jerry, of Kansas	Agriculture. Transportation and Infrastructure. Veterans' Affairs.
Murphy	Energy and Commerce.
Murtha	Appropriations.

Representative	Committees (Standing, Joint, Special, and Select)
Musgrave	Agriculture. Education and the Workforce. Resources. Small Business.
Myrick	Energy and Commerce.
Nadler	Judiciary. Transportation and Infrastructure.
Napolitano	International Relations. Resources.
Neal	Budget. Ways and Means.
Neugebauer	Agriculture. Financial Services.
Ney	House Administration, *chairman*. Financial Services. Transportation and Infrastructure. Joint Committee on the Library of Congress, *chairman*. Joint Committee on Printing.
Northup	Appropriations.
Norton	Government Reform. Homeland Security. Transportation and Infrastructure.
Norwood	Education and the Workforce. Energy and Commerce.
Nunes	Agriculture. Resources. Veterans' Affairs.
Nussle	Budget, *chairman*. Ways and Means.
Oberstar	Transportation and Infrastructure.
Obey	Appropriations.
Olver	Appropriations.
Ortiz	Armed Services. Resources.
Osborne	Agriculture. Education and the Workforce. Transportation and Infrastructure.
Otter	Energy and Commerce.
Owens	Education and the Workforce. Government Reform.
Oxley	Financial Services, *chairman*.
Pallone	Energy and Commerce. Resources.
Pascrell	Homeland Security. Transportation and Infrastructure.
Pastor	Appropriations.

Representative	Committees (Standing, Joint, Special, and Select)
Paul	Financial Services. International Relations. Joint Economic Committee.
Payne	Education and the Workforce. International Relations.
Pearce	Financial Services. Homeland Security. Resources.
Pelosi	Democratic Leader. Permanent Select Committee on Intelligence.
Pence	Agriculture. International Relations. Judiciary.
Peterson, Collin C., of Minnesota.	Agriculture.
Peterson, John E., of Pennsylvania.	Appropriations. Resources.
Petri	Education and the Workforce. Transportation and Infrastructure.
Pickering	Energy and Commerce.
Pitts	Energy and Commerce.
Platts	Education and the Workforce. Government Reform. Transportation and Infrastructure.
Poe	International Relations. Small Business. Transportation and Infrastructure.
Pombo	Resources, *chairman.* Agriculture.
Pomeroy	Agriculture. Ways and Means.
Porter	Education and the Workforce. Government Reform. Transportation and Infrastructure.
Price, David E., of North Carolina.	Appropriations.
Price, Tom of Georgia	Education and the Workforce. Financial Services.
Pryce	Financial Services.
Putnam	Budget. Rules.
Radanovich	Energy and Commerce. Resources.
Rahall	Resources. Transportation and Infrastructure.
Ramstad	Ways and Means.

Representative	Committees (Standing, Joint, Special, and Select)
Rangel	Ways and Means. Joint Committee on Taxation.
Regula	Appropriations.
Rehberg	Appropriations.
Reichert	Homeland Security. Science. Transportation and Infrastructure.
Renzi	Financial Services. Resources. Permanent Select Committee on Intelligence.
Reyes	Armed Services. Veterans' Affairs. Permanent Select Committee on Intelligence.
Reynolds	House Administration. Ways and Means.
Rogers, Harold, of Kentucky	Appropriations.
Rogers, Mike, of Alabama	Agriculture. Armed Services. Homeland Security.
Rogers, Mike, of Michigan	Energy and Commerce. Permanent Select Committee on Intelligence.
Rohrabacher	International Relations. Science.
Ros-Lehtinen	Budget. Government Reform. International Relations.
Ross	Energy and Commerce.
Rothman	Appropriations.
Roybal-Allard	Appropriations. Standards of Official Conduct.
Royce	Financial Services. International Relations.
Ruppersberger	Government Reform. Permanent Select Committee on Intelligence.
Rush	Energy and Commerce.
Ryan, Paul, of Wisconsin	Budget. Ways and Means. Joint Economic Committee.
Ryan, Tim, of Ohio	Armed Services. Education and the Workforce.
Ryun	Armed Services. Budget. Financial Services.
Sabo	Appropriations.
Salazar	Agriculture. Transportation and Infrastructure.

Representative	Committees (Standing, Joint, Special, and Select)
Sánchez, Linda T., of California.	Government Reform. Judiciary. Small Business.
Sanchez, Loretta, of California...	Armed Services. Homeland Security. Joint Economic Committee.
SANDERS	Financial Services. Government Reform.
Saxton	Joint Economic Committee, *chairman.* Armed Services. Resources.
Schakowsky	Energy and Commerce.
Schiff	International Relations. Judiciary.
Schwartz, of Pennsylvania	Budget. Transportation and Infrastructure.
Schwarz, of Michigan	Agriculture. Armed Services. Science.
Scott, David, of Georgia	Agriculture. Financial Services.
Scott, Robert C., of Virginia	Education and the Workforce. Judiciary.
Sensenbrenner	Judiciary, *chairman.*
Serrano	Appropriations.
Sessions	Budget. Rules.
Shadegg	Energy and Commerce.
Shaw	Ways and Means. Joint Committee on Taxation.
Shays	Financial Services. Government Reform. Homeland Security.
Sherman	Financial Services. International Relations. Science.
Sherwood	Appropriations.
Shimkus	Energy and Commerce.
Shuster	Armed Services. Small Business. Transportation and Infrastructure.
Simmons	Armed Services. Homeland Security. Transportation and Infrastructure.
Simpson	Appropriations. Budget.
Skelton	Armed Services.
Slaughter	Rules.

Representative	Committees (Standing, Joint, Special, and Select)
Smith, Adam, of Washington	Armed Services. International Relations. Judiciary.
Smith, Christopher H., of New Jersey.	International Relations.
Smith, Lamar S., of Texas	Homeland Security. Judiciary. Science. Standards of Official Conduct.
Snyder	Armed Services. Veterans' Affairs.
Sodrel	Science. Small Business. Transportation and Infrastructure.
Solis	Energy and Commerce.
Souder	Education and the Workforce. Government Reform. Homeland Security.
Spratt	Armed Services. Budget.
Stark	Ways and Means. Joint Committee on Taxation.
Stearns	Energy and Commerce. Veterans' Affairs.
Strickland	Energy and Commerce. Veterans' Affairs.
Stupak	Energy and Commerce.
Sullivan	Energy and Commerce.
Sweeney	Appropriations.
Tancredo	International Relations. Resources.
Tanner	Ways and Means.
Tauscher	Armed Services. Transportation and Infrastructure.
Taylor, Charles H., of North Carolina.	Appropriations.
Taylor, Gene, of Mississippi	Armed Services. Transportation and Infrastructure.
Terry	Energy and Commerce.
Thomas	Ways and Means, *chairman*. Joint Committee on Taxation, *chairman*.
Thompson, Bennie G., of Mississippi.	Homeland Security.
Thompson, Mike, of California ..	Ways and Means.
Thornberry	Armed Services. Permanent Select Committee on Intelligence.

CONGRESSIONAL ADVISORY BOARDS
COMMISSIONS, AND GROUPS

BOARD OF VISITORS TO THE AIR FORCE ACADEMY
[Title 10, U.S.C., Section 9355(a)]

Wayne Allard, of Colorado.
Larry E. Craig, of Idaho.
Mark Pryor, of Arkansas.

Joel Hefley, of Colorado.
Kay Granger, of Texas.
Carolyn C. Kilpatrick, of Michigan.

BOARD OF VISITORS TO THE MILITARY ACADEMY
[Title 10, U.S.C., Section 4355(a)]

Jeff Sessions, of Alabama.
Mike DeWine, of Ohio.
Jack Reed, of Rhode Island.
Mary Landrieu, of Louisiana.

Charles H. Taylor, of North Carolina.
Sue Kelly, of New York.
John M. McHugh, of New York.
Maurice D. Hinchey, of New York.
Ellen O. Tauscher, of California.

BOARD OF VISITORS TO THE NAVAL ACADEMY
[Title 10, U.S.C., Section 6968(a)]

John McCain, of Arizona.
Thad Cochran, of Mississippi.
Paul Sarbanes, of Maryland.
Barbara Mikulski, of Maryland.

Wayne T. Gilchrest, of Maryland.
Randy (Duke) Cunningham, of California.
Steny Hoyer, of Maryland.
John S. Tanner, of Tennessee.
Mike McIntyre, of North Carolina.

BOARD OF VISITORS TO THE COAST GUARD ACADEMY
[Title 14 U.S.C., Section 194(a)]

John McCain, of Arizona.
Peter G. Fitzgerald, of Illinois.
Patty Murray, of Washington.

Rob Simmons, of Connecticut.
Don Young, of Alaska.
Howard Coble, of North Carolina.
Bob Filner, of California.
Frank LoBiondo, of New Jersey.

CANADA–UNITED STATES INTERPARLIAMENTARY GROUP

Senate Hart Building, Room 808, 224–3047

[Created by Public Law 86–42, 22 U.S.C., 1928a–1928d, 276d–276g]

Senate Delegation:
  Chairman.—Mike Crapo, Senator from Idaho.
  Vice Chairman.—[Vacancy].
  Director, Interparliamentary Services.—Sally Walsh.

COMMISSION ON CONGRESSIONAL MAILING STANDARDS

1338 Longworth House Office Building, phone 225–9337

[Created by Public Law 93–191]

Chairman.—Robert W. Ney, Representative from Ohio.
Robert B. Aderholt, Representative from Alabama.
John E. Sweeney, Representative from New York.
Juanita Millender-McDonald, Representative from California.
Rush D. Holt, Representative from New Jersey.
Brad Sherman, Representative from California.

STAFF

Staff Director.—Jack Dail, 225–9337.
  Professional Staff.—Richard Landon.
  Counsel.—Matt Petersen.

COMMISSION ON SECURITY AND COOPERATION IN EUROPE

234 Ford House Office Building, phone 225–1901, fax 226–4199

http://www.csce.gov

Sam Brownback, of Kansas, *Chairman.*

Christopher H. Smith, of New Jersey, *Co-Chairman.*

LEGISLATIVE BRANCH COMMISSIONERS

Senate

Gordon H. Smith, of Oregon.
Kay Bailey Hutchison, of Texas.
Saxby Chambliss, of Georgia.

Christopher J. Dodd, of Connecticut.
Russell D. Feingold, of Wisconsin.
Hillary Rodham Clinton, of New York.

House

Frank R. Wolf, of Virginia.
Joseph R. Pitts, of Pennsylvania.
Robert B. Aderholt, of Alabama.
Mike Pence, of Indiana.

Benjamin L. Cardin, of Maryland.
Louise McIntosh Slaughter, of New York.
Alcee L. Hastings, of Florida.

EXECUTIVE BRANCH COMMISSIONER

Department of Commerce.—William Henry Lash III.

COMMISSION STAFF

Chief of Staff.—Sean H. Woo.
    Deputy Chief of Staff.—Dorothy Douglas Taft.
    Communications Director.—James Geoffrey.
    Staff Assistants: Quena Gonzalez, Justin Johnson.
    Senior Advisor.—Elizabeth B. Pryor.
    Staff Advisors: Orest Deychakiwsky, John Finerty, Chadwick R. Gore, Robert Hand, Janice Helwig, Michael Ochs.
    Counsel for International Law.—Erika B. Schlager.
    General Counsel.—Maureen T. Walsh.
    Counsels: Marlene Kaufmann, H. Knox Thames.
    International Policy Director.—Ronald J. McNamara.

CONGRESSIONAL AWARD FOUNDATION
379 Ford House Office Building 20515, phone (202) 226–0130, fax (202) 226–0131
[Created by Public Law 96–114]

Chairman.—John M. Falk, Esq., Compressus, Inc. (202) 742–4307.
    Vice Chairmen:
        Linda Mitchell, Mississippi State University Extension Service (662) 534–7776.
        Paxton Baker, BET (202) 608–2052.
    Secretary.—Michael Cohen, Esq., Heller Ehrman White & McAuliffe LLP (202) 912–2515.
    Treasurer.—Robert Clements, Compressus, Inc. (202) 742–4297.
    National Director.—Erica Wheelan Heyse (202) 226–0130.

Members:
    Paxton Baker, BET (202) 608–2052.
    Bridget Barrus (208) 375–3628.
    Max Baucus, Senator from Montana (202) 224–2651.
    Dolores M. Beilenson, Chevy Chase, MD (301) 652–9125.
    Dr. Clinton Bristow, Jr., Alcorn State University (601) 877–6131.
    Mary Bunning (202) 224–4343.
    Michael Carozza, Bristol-Myers Squibb Company (202) 783–8659.
    Robert Clements, Compressus, Inc. (202) 742–4297.
    Michael Cohen, Heller Ehrman White & McAuliffe LLP (202) 912–2515.
    Larry E. Craig, Senator from Idaho (202) 224–2752.
    Barbara Cubin, Representative from Wyoming (202) 225–2311.
    Kathy Didawick, Blue Cross Blue Shield (202) 626–4804.
    Brad Enzi, South Park Development (307) 778–0400.
    John M. Falk, Esq., Compressus, Inc. (202) 742–4307.
    George B. Gould, National Association of Letter Carriers (202) 662–2833.
    J. Steven Hart, Esq., Williams & Jensen, P.C. (202) 659–8201.
    David W. Hunt, Esq., White & Case, L.L.P. (202) 626–3604.
    Sheila Jackson Lee, Representative from Texas (202) 225–3816.
    Gayle Kildee (202) 225–3611.
    Kevin B. Lefton, XO Communications (703) 547–2664.
    Reynaldo L. Martinez, Strategic Dimensions (703) 941–4420.
    Linda Mitchell, Mississippi State University Extension Service (662) 534–7776.
    Marc Monyek, McDonald's Corporation (630) 623–3795.
    Sir James Murray K.C.M.G., New York, NY (718) 852–3320.
    Andrew F. Ortiz, J.D., M.P.A., Arizona Cleaning the Air (602) 224–0524 ext. 2055.
    Altagracia Ramos, Hispanic Youth Foundation, (937) 427–3565.
    Galen J. Reser, Pepsi Co., Inc. (914) 253–2862.
    Felix R. Sanchez, TerraCom, Inc. (202) 965–5151.
    Daniel B. Scherder, The Willard Group (703) 893–8409.
    William F. Sittmann, National Association of Chain Drug Stores (703) 837–4161.

Charles F. Smithers, UBS (800) 223–0170.
Debbie Snyder, Kintera (972) 342–8429.
Kimberly Talley Norman, Affiliated Computer Systems, Inc. (214) 584–5403.
Rex B. Wackerle, Prudential Insurance Co. (202) 293–1141.
Greg Walker, Foundation Coal (410) 689–7602.

CONGRESSIONAL CLUB

2001 New Hampshire Avenue, NW., 20008, phone 332–1155, fax 797–0698

President.—Vicki Tiahrt.
  Vice Presidents:
    (1st) Vivian Bishop.
    (2d) Vicki Miller.
    (3d) Carolyn Barry.
    (4th) Cynthia Pearce.
    (5th) Jan English.
    (6th) Marilyn King.
  Treasurer.—Belinda Culberson.
  Corresponding Secretary.—Cissy Marshall.
  Recording Secretary.—Freda Manzullo.

HOUSE OFFICE BUILDING COMMISSION

H–232 The Capitol, phone 225–0600

[Title 40, U.S.C. 175–176]

Chairman.—J. Dennis Hastert, Speaker of the House of Representatives.
Tom DeLay, House Majority Leader.
Nancy Pelosi, House Minority Leader.

HOUSE OF REPRESENTATIVES PAGE BOARD

H–154 The Capitol, phone 225–7000

[Established by House Resolution 611, 97th Congress]

Chairman.—John Shimkus, Representative from Illinois.
Members:
  Heather Wilson, Representative from New Mexico.
  Dale Kildee, Representative from Michigan.
  Jeff Trandahl, Clerk of the House.
  Wilson (Bill) Livingood, Sergeant at Arms of the House.
Staff Contact:
  Grace Crews, Office of the Clerk, Page Program Coordinator.

JAPAN–UNITED STATES FRIENDSHIP COMMISSION

1201 15th Street, NW., Suite 330, phone 653–9800, fax 653–9802

[Created by Public Law 94–118]

Chairman.—Dr. Richard J. Samuels, Massachusetts Institute of Technology.
  Vice Chairman.—Dr. Amy Y. Heinrich, Columbia University.
  Executive Director.—Dr. Eric J. Gangloff.
  Assistant Executive Director.—Margaret P. Mihori.
  Assistant Executive Director, CULCON.—Pamela L. Fields.
  Secretary.—Sylvia L. Dandridge.
Members:
  The Honorable Dana Gioia, Chairman, National Endowment for the Arts.
  Bruce Cole, Chairman, National Endowment for the Humanities.
  The Honorable Thomas Petri, U.S. House of Representatives.
  The Honorable John D. Rockefeller IV, U.S. Senate.

Dr. Patricia Steinhoff, University of Hawaii.
Dr. Linda Kerber, University of Iowa.
Theodore R. Life, Filmmaker.
The Honorable James McDermott, U.S. House of Representatives.
Dr. Richard E. Dyck, President, TCS Japan, KK
The Honorable Patricia De Stacy Harrison, Assistant Secretary of State for Educational and Cultural Affairs.
Frank P. Stanek, President, International Business Development, Universal Studios Recreation Group, Universal Studios.
The Honorable Sally Stroup, Assistant Secretary of Education for Post-Secondary Education.
The Honorable Christopher R. Hill, Assistant Secretary of State for East Asian and Pacific Affairs, U.S. Department of State.
The Honorable Lisa Murkowski, U.S. Senate.
Willard G. Clark, Founder, Center for Japanese Art and Culture.

MEXICO–UNITED STATES INTERPARLIAMENTARY GROUP

Senate Hart Building, Room 808, phone 224–3047

[Created by Public Law 82–420, 22 U.S.C. 276h–276k]

Senate Delegation:
 Chairman.—John Cornyn, of Alabama.
 Vice Chairman.—Christopher J. Dodd, of Connecticut.
House Delegation:
 Chairman.—Jim Kolbe, of Arizona.

MIGRATORY BIRD CONSERVATION COMMISSION

4401 North Fairfax Drive, Room 622, Arlington, VA 22203

phone (703) 358–1716 fax (703) 358–2223

[Created by act of February 18, 1929, 16 U.S.C. 715a]

Chairman.—Gale Norton, Secretary of the Interior.
Blanche Lincoln, Senator from Arkansas.
Thad Cochran, Senator from Mississippi.
John D. Dingell, Representative from Michigan.
Curt Weldon, Representative from Pennsylvania.
Mike Johanns, Secretary of Agriculture.
Stephen L. Johnson (acting), Administrator of Environmental Protection Agency.
 Secretary.—A. Eric Alvarez.

NATO PARLIAMENTARY ASSEMBLY

Headquarters: Place du Petit Sablon 3, B–1000 Brussels, Belgium

[Created by Public Law 84–689, 22 U.S.C., 1928z]

Senate Delegation:
 Chairman.—Gordon Smith, Senator from Oregon.
 Vice Chairman.—Joseph Biden, Senator from Delaware.
House of Representatives Delegation:
 Chairman.—Joel Hefley, Representative from Colorado.

STAFF

Secretary, Senate Delegation.—Julia Hart Reed, Interparliamentary Services, SH–808, 224–3047.
Secretary, House Delegation.—Susan Olsen, 226–8806.

PERMANENT COMMITTEE FOR THE OLIVER WENDELL HOLMES DEVISE FUND

Library of Congress 20540, phone 707–1082

[Created by act of Congress approved Aug. 5, 1955 (Public Law 246, 84th Congress), to administer Oliver Wendell Holmes Devise Fund, established by same act]

Chairman ex officio.—James H. Billington.
Administrative Officer for the Devise.—James H. Hutson.

SENATE NATIONAL SECURITY WORKING GROUP

113 Dirksen Senate Office Building 20510, phone 224–3941

Administrative Co-Chairman.—Bill Frist, Senator from Tennessee.
Administrative Co-Chairman.—*Robert C. Byrd*, Senator from West Virginia.
Co-Chairman.—Thad Cochran, Senator from Mississippi.
Co-Chairman.—Jon Kyl, Senator from Arizona.
Co-Chairman.—Trent Lott, Senator from Mississippi.
Co-Chairman.—*Harry Reid*, Senator from Nevada.
Co-Chairman.—*Carl Levin*, Senator from Michigan.
Co-Chairman.—*Joseph R. Biden, Jr.*, Senator from Delaware.

Members:

Ted Stevens, Senator from Tennessee.
Richard G. Lugar, Senator from Indiana.
John Warner, Senator from Virginia.
Jeff Sessions, Senator from Alabama.
Gordon Smith, Senator from Oregon.
Lincoln Chafee, Senator from Rhode Island.

Edward M. Kennedy, Senator from Massachusetts.
Paul S. Sarbanes, Senator from Maryland.
Richard J. Durbin, Senator from Illinois.
Bryon L. Dorgan, Senator from North Dakota.
Bill Nelson, Senator from Florida.
Mark Dayton, Senator from Minnesota.

STAFF

Republican Staff Director.—Mark Esper, 224–3135.
Democratic Staff Director.—Christina Evans, 224–3088.

U.S. ASSOCIATION OF FORMER MEMBERS OF CONGRESS

233 Pennsylvania Avenue SE., Suite 200, 20003–1107

phone (202) 543–8676, fax 543–7145

The nonpartisan United States Association of Former Members of Congress was founded in 1970 as a nonprofit, educational, research and social organization. It has been chartered by the United States Congress and has approximately 600 members who represented American citizens in both the U.S. Senate and House of Representatives. The Association promotes improved public understanding of the role of Congress as a unique institution as well as the crucial importance of representative democracy as a system of government, both domestically and internationally.

President.—Jack Buechner, of Missouri.
  Vice President.—Jim Slattery, of Kansas.
  Treasurer.—John J. Rhodes III, of Arizona.
  Secretary.—Dennis M. Hertel, of Michigan.
  Immediate Past President.—Larry LaRocco, of Idaho.
  Honorary Co-Chairmen: Gerald R. Ford, of Michigan; Walter F. Mondale, of Minnesota.
  Executive Director.—Peter M. Weichlein.
  Counselors: Mark Andrews, of North Dakota; J. Glenn Beall, Jr., of Maryland; Robert Kastenmeier, of Wisconsin; Matthew F. McHugh, of New York; Philip E. Ruppe, of Michigan; Carlton R. Sickles, of Maryland; James W. Symington, of Missouri.

U.S. CAPITOL HISTORICAL SOCIETY

200 Maryland Avenue NE., 20002, phone 543–8919, fax 544–8244

[Congressional Charter, October 20, 1978, Public Law 95–493, 95th Congress, 92 Stat. 1643]

Chairman of the Board.—The Honorable E. Thomas Coleman.
  President.—The Honorable Ron Sarasin.
  Treasurer.—L. Neale Cosby.
  General Secretary.—Suzanne C. Dicks.
  Vice Presidents of:
    Finance and Administration.—Paul E. McGuire.
    Membership and Development.—Rebecca A. Evans.
    Merchandising.—Diana E. Wailes.
    Scholarship and Education.—Donald R. Kennon, Ph.D.

EXECUTIVE COMMITTEE

Steve Chaudet
The Honorable E. Thomas Coleman
L. Neale Cosby
Brenda Day
Curtis C. Deane
Suzanne C. Dicks

Michael Dineen
The Honorable Thomas S. Foley
Susan Fritschler
Robert W. Lively
The Honorable Robert H. Michel
The Honorable Ron Sarasin

STAFF

Director of:
  Education and Outreach.—Felicia Bell.
  Marketing.—Mary Hughes.
  Retail Sales.—Chuck Keyton.
Manager of:
  Accounting Department.—Sheri Williams.
  Corporate Committee.—Marilyn Green.
  Member Programs.—Diana Friedman.
  Public Programs and Chief Guide.—Steve Livengood.
Associate Historian.—Lauren Borchard
Development Associate.—Chris Leibundguth.
Operations Manager.—Randy Groves.
Receiving Supervisor.—Vince Scott.
Receptionist.—Ann McNeil.

U.S. CAPITOL PRESERVATION COMMISSION

[Created pursuant to Public Law 100–696]

Co-Chairmen:
  J. Dennis Hastert, Speaker of the House.
  Ted Stevens, Senate President Pro Tempore.

House Members:
Tom DeLay, Majority Leader.
Nancy Pelosi, Minority Leader.
Jerry Lewis.
Robert W. Ney.
Bill Shuster.
John Mica.
Marcy Kaptur.
Juanita Millender-McDonald.

Senate Members:
William H. (Bill) Frist, Majority Leader.
Harry Reid, Minority Leader.
Trent Lott.
Christopher J. Dodd.
Robert Bennett.
Richard J. Durbin.
Thad Cochran.

Architect of the Capitol.—Alan M. Hantman.

U.S. HOUSE OF REPRESENTATIVES FINE ARTS BOARD
1309 Longworth House Office Building, phone 225–8281
[Created by Public Law 101–696]

Chairman.—Robert W. Ney, of Ohio.

Members:
Vernon Ehlers, of Michigan.
Candice Miller, of Michigan.
Juanita Millender-McDonald, of California.
Zoe Lofgren, of California.

U.S. SENATE COMMISSION ON ART
S–411 The Capitol, phone 224–2955
[Created by Public Law 100–696]

Chairman.—William H. (Bill) Frist, of Tennessee.
Vice Chairman.—Harry Reid, of Nevada.

Members:
Ted Stevens, of Alaska.
Christopher J. Dodd, of Connecticut.
Trent Lott, of Mississippi.

STAFF

Executive Secretary.—Emily J. Reynolds.
Curator.—Diane K. Skvarla.
Administrator.—Scott M. Strong.
Associate Curator.—Melinda K. Smith.
Collections Manager.—Deborah Wood.
Museum Specialist.—Richard L. Doerner.
Registrar.—Jamie Arbolino.
Associate Registrar.—Theresa Manalum.
Curatorial Assistant.—Amy Burton.
Historical Preservation Officer.—Kelly Steele.
Staff Assistant.—Claire Hobson.

OTHER CONGRESSIONAL OFFICIALS AND SERVICES

ARCHITECT OF THE CAPITOL

ARCHITECT'S OFFICE

SB–15 The Capitol, phone 228–1793, fax 228–1893, http://www.aoc.gov

Architect of the Capitol.—Alan M. Hantman.
   Assistant Architect of the Capitol.—Michael G. Turnbull, 228–1221.
   Administrative Assistant.—Amita Poole, 228–1701.
   Director of:
      Administrative Operations.—Hector Suarez, 228–1205.
      Engineering.—Scott Birkhead, 226–5630.
      Safety, Fire & Environmental Programs.—Susan Adams, 226–0630.
   Chief Financial Officer.—Gary Glovinsky, 228–1819.
   Budget Officer.—Marilyn Wiles, 228–1793.
   Communications Officer.—Eva Malecki, 228–1793.
   General Counsel.—Peter Kushner, 228–1793.
   Executive Officer, U.S. Botanic Garden.—Holly Shimizu, 225–6670.
   Landscape Architect.—Matthew Evans, 224–6645.
   Curator.—Barbara Wolanin, 228–1222.

U.S. CAPITOL

HT–42, Capitol Superintendent's Service Center, phone 228–8800, fax 225–7351

Superintendent.—Carlos Elias, 226–4859.
   Assistant Superintendents: Larry Brown, 228–1793; Don White, 228–1875.

SENATE OFFICE BUILDINGS

G45 Dirksen Senate Office Building, phone 224–3141, fax 224–0652

Superintendent.—Lawrence Stoffel, 224–5023.
   Deputy Superintendent.—Robin Morey, 224–6951.
   Assistant Superintendents: Mark Sciarritta, Marvin Simpson, 224–7686.

HOUSE OFFICE BUILDINGS

B–341 Rayburn House Office Building, phone 225–4141, fax 225–3003

Superintendent.—Frank Tiscione, 225–7012.
   Deputy Superintendent.—Robert Gleich, 225–4142.
   Assistant Superintendents: Peter Aitcheson, Sterling Thomas, Bill Wood, 225–4142.

CAPITOL TELEPHONE EXCHANGE

6110 Postal Square Building, phone 224–3121

Supervisor.—Joan Sartori.

CHILD CARE CENTERS

HOUSE OF REPRESENTATIVES CHILD CARE CENTER

147 Ford House Office Building,
Virginia Avenue and 3rd Street SW., 20515,
phone 225–9684, fax 225–6908

Director.—Lisa Bryant.

SENATE EMPLOYEES' CHILD CARE CENTER

United States Senate, Washington, DC 20510
phone 224–1461, fax 228–3686

Director.—Christine Wauls.

COMBINED AIRLINES TICKET OFFICES (CATO)

**1800 N. Kent Street, Suite 950, Arlington VA 22209
phone (703) 522–8664, fax (703) 522–0616**

General Manager.—Charles A. Dinardo.
Administrative Assistant.—Cathy Meyer.

B–222 Longworth House Office Building
phone (703) 522–2286, fax (202) 226–5992

Supervisor.—Michelle Gelzer.

B–24 Russell Senate Office Building
phone (703) 522–2286, fax (202) 393–1981

Supervisor.—Sandra Hishmeh.

CONGRESSIONAL DAILY DIGEST

HOUSE SECTION

HT–13 The Capitol, phone 225–2868 (committees), 225–7497 (chamber)

Editors for—
Committee Meetings.—Maura Patricia Kelly.
Chamber Action.—Wendy Kirkpatrick.

SENATE SECTION

S–421 The Capitol, phone 224–2658, fax 224–1220

Editor.—Linda E. Sebold.
Assistant Editor.—Ken Dean.

CONGRESSIONAL RECORD INDEX OFFICE

**U.S. Government Printing Office, Room C–738
North Capitol and H Streets NW., 20401, phone 512–0275**

Director.—Marcia Oleszewski, 512–2010, ext. 3–1975.
Deputy Director.—Philip C. Hart, 512–2010, ext. 3–1973.

Historian of Bills.—Barbre A. Brunson, 512–2010, ext. 3–1957.
Editors: Grafton J. Daniels, Jason Parsons.
Indexers: Ytta B. Carr, Joel K. Church.

CAPITOL GUIDE SERVICE AND CONGRESSIONAL SPECIAL SERVICES OFFICE
ST–13 The Capitol 20510, Recorded Information 225–6827
Special Services 224–4048, TTY 224–4049

Director.—Tom Stevens, 224–3235.
  Assistant Director (Administration).—Sharon Nevitt, 224–3235.
  Assistant Director (Special Services Office).—David Hauck, Crypt, 224–4048.
  Assistant Director (Tours).—Jeff Aaron, 224–3235.
  Assistant Director (Training).—Tina Pearson, 224–3235.

LIAISON OFFICES

AIR FORCE
B–322 Rayburn House Office Building, phone 225–6656, fax 685–2592

Chief.—COL Randy O'Boyle.
  Deputy Chief.—LTC Mark Ross.
  Action Officers: MAJ Jim Drape, MAJ Stella Smith.
  Legislative Liaison Specialist.—Alice Geishecker.
  Legislative Liaison Assistant.—SSgt Lloyd Jenkins.

182 Russell Senate Office Building, phone 224–2481, fax 685–2575

Chief.—COL Tony Lazarski.
  Deputy Chief.—LTC Eric Fick.
  Liaison Officers: MAJ Cathy Haverstock, Dolores Toni, MAJ Rico Vaca.

ARMY
B–325 Rayburn House Office Building, phone 225–3853, fax 685–2674

Chief.—COL Michael DeYoung.
  Liaison Officers: MAJ Trudy Caldwell, LTC Larnell Exum, LTC Carl Grunow, LTC Michael Legg, MAJ Carolyn Walford.
  Administrative Assistant.—SGT Kenneth Boles.
  Chief Congressional Caseworker.— Gail Warren.
  Congressional Caseworker—Bob Nelson, Jr.

183 Russell Senate Office Building, phone 224–2881, fax 685–2570

Chief.—COL Mike Barbero.
  Deputy Chief.—LTC Lon Pribble.
  Liaison Officer.—MAJ Gean McGinnis.
  Administrative Assistant.—SSG Tammy Marshall.
  Chief, Casework Liaison.—Margaret T. Tyler.
  Casework Liaison Officer.—Cynthia Gray.

COAST GUARD
B–320 Rayburn House Office Building, phone 225–4775, fax 426–6081

Liaison Officer.—CDR William Milne.
  Assistant Liaison Officers: LT Heath Brown, LT Sara Moser.

183 Russell Senate Office Building, phone 224–2913, fax 755–1695

Liaison Officer.—CDR Anthony Popiel.
Liaison Assistant.—LTC Mike Cribbs, Liz Moses.

NAVY / MARINE CORPS

B–324 Rayburn House Office Building, phone Navy 685–6079; Marine Corps 225–7124

Director.—CAPT Earl Gay, USN.
Deputy Director.—CDR Drew Wannamaker, USN.
USN Liaison Officers: LCDR John Gilliland, USN (contracts); LT Pete Giambastiani, USN; LT Kevin Hernandez, USN; LT Brian Jaskot, USN; LT Colby Miller, USN; LT Jennifer Seguin, USN; LT Roy Zaletski, USN.
Director USMC.—COL Richard Simcock, USMC.
USMC Liaison Officers: MAJ Christopher Lauer, USMC; CAPT Brian Sharp, USMC.
Office Manager/Administrative Clerk.—SGT Claire Buffington, USMC.
House Staff NCO.—SGT Lorence Chance.

182 Russell Senate Office Building, phone: Navy 224–4682; Marine Corps 224–4681

Director.—CAPT Thomas Copeman, USN.
Deputy Director.—CAPT Jim Stein, USN.
USN Liaison Officers: LT Neil Lapointe, LT Jennifer Navarro, LT Joshua Teylor.
Assistant Liaison Officer.—YNC(SW) James Evans.
Director, USMC.—COL Carl Mundy.
Deputy Director, USMC.—MAJ Pete McAleer.
Assistant Liaison Officers: SGT Daisy Espinosa, USMC; SSGT Thomas Poenitske, USMC.

GENERAL ACCOUNTING OFFICE

Room 7125, 441 G Street 20548, phone 512–4400

Congressional Relations Director.—Gloria L. Jarmon.
Legislative Advisers: Doris Cannon, 512–4507; Rosa Harris, 512–9492; Elizabeth Johnston, 512–6345; Larry Malenich, 512–9399; Elizabeth Sirois, 512–8989; Jerry Skelly, 512–9918; Mary Frances Widner, 512–3804.
Associate Legislative Adviser.—Carolyn McCowan, 512–3503.

OFFICE OF PERSONNEL MANAGEMENT

B–332 Rayburn House Office Building, phone 225–4955

Chief.—Charlene E. Luskey.
Senior Civil Service Representative.—Carlos Tingle.
Administrative Assistant.—Kirk H. Brightman.

VETERANS' AFFAIRS

B–328 Rayburn House Office Building, phone 225–2280, fax 453–5225

Director.—Patricia Covington.
Assistant Director.—Paul Downs.
Liaison Assistant.—Jewell Knight.
Representatives: Richard Armstrong, Pamela Mugg, Rick Shannon.

321 Hart Senate Office Building, phone 224–5351, fax 453–5218

Director.—Patricia Covington.
  Assistant Director.—Paul Downs.
  Representatives: Erica Jones, Stuart Weiner.

PAGE SCHOOLS

SENATE

Daniel Webster Senate Page Residence 20510, fax 224–1838

Principal.—Kathryn S. Weeden, 224–3926.
  English.—Frances Owens, 8–1024.
  Mathematics.—Raymond Cwalina, 8–1018.
  Science.—John Malek, 8–1025.
  Social Studies.—Michael Bowers, 8–1012.
  Administrative Assistant.—Lorraine Foreman, 4–3927.

HOUSE OF REPRESENTATIVES

LJ–A11 Library of Congress 20540–9996, phone 225–9000, fax 225–9001

Principal.—Linda G. Miranda.
  Administrative Assistant.—Robin Bridges.
  English.—Lona Carwile-Klein.
  Guidance.—Donna D. Wilson.
  Languages: Sebastian Hobson, French; Linda G. Miranda, Spanish.
  Mathematics.—Barbara R. Bowen.
  Science.—Walter Cuirle.
  Social Studies.—Ronald L. Weitzel.
  Technology.—Darryl Gonzalez.

U.S. CAPITOL POLICE
119 D Street, NE., 20510–7218
**Office of the Chief 224–9806, Command Center 224–0908
Communications 224–5151, Emergency 224–0911**

U.S. CAPITOL POLICE BOARD

Sergeant at Arms, U.S. Senate.—William H. Pickle.
Sergeant at Arms, U.S. House of Representatives.—Wilson (Bill) Livingood.
Architect of the Capitol.—Alan M. Hantman.

OFFICE OF THE CHIEF

Chief of Police.—Terrance W. Gainer.
  Administrative Assistant.—LT Michael A. Spochart.
  General Counsel.—John T. Caulfield.
  Deputy Counsel.—Gretchen DeMar; William Emory.
  Office of:
    Strategic Planning / Inspections.—SGT Ricardo Anderson.
    Internal Affairs.—Insp. Yancey Garner.
    Public Information.—Officer Michael J. Lauer.
    Chief of Staff.—Kristan Trugman.

CHIEF OF OPERATIONS

Assistant Chief.—James P. Rohan.
  Administration Assistant.—Insp. Matthew R. Verderosa.
  Command Center: Insp. Edward Bailor, Insp. Gregory Parman, CAPT Mark Sullivan, CAPT William Uber.
  Special Events.—LT Kathryn Stillman.

OPERATIONAL SERVICES BUREAU

Bureau Commander.—Deputy Chief Vickie Frye.
  Hazardous Incident Response Division.—CAPT Shirley Johnson.
  Patrol/Mobile Response Division.—Insp. Greg Parmen (acting).

PROTECTIVE SERVICES BUREAU

Bureau Commander.—Deputy Chief Christopher McGaffin.
  Investigations Division.—CAPT Donald Rouiller.
  Dignitary Protection Division.—Insp. David Calloway.

SECURITY SERVICES BUREAU

Bureau Commander.—Robert M. Greeley.
  Physical Security Division.—Robert F. Ford.
  Technical Countermeasures Division.—Michael Marinucci.
  Construction Security Division.—CAPT Lawrence Loughery.

UNIFORM SERVICES BUREAU

Bureau Commander.—Deputy Chief Larry D. Thompson.
  Executive Assistant.—LT Brett Neeld.
  Capitol Division Commander.—Insp. Phillip Morris.
  House Division Commander.—Insp. Daniel Nichols.
  Senate Division Commander.—Insp. Fred Rogers.

CHIEF ADMINISTRATIVE OFFICER

Chief Administrative Officer.—Anthony J. Stamilio.
  Deputy Chief Administrative Officer.—Richard Braddock.
  Director, Office of:
    Financial Management.—Mary Jean Jablonicky.
    Human Resources.—Jan Jones.
    Information Systems.—James R. Getter.
    Logistics.—J. Bruce Holmberg.
  Commander, Training Services Bureau.—Deputy Chief Michael A. Jarboe.

WESTERN UNION TELEGRAPH CO.

B–244 Longworth House Office Building, phone 225–4553/4554, fax 225–5499

Manager.—Gladys R. Crockett.

STATISTICAL INFORMATION

VOTES CAST FOR SENATORS IN 2000, 2002, and 2004

[Compiled from official statistics obtained by the Clerk of the House. Figures in the last column, for the 2004 election, may include totals for more candidates than the ones shown.]

State	Vote 2000 Republican	Vote 2000 Democrat	Vote 2002 Republican	Vote 2002 Democrat	Vote 2004 Republican	Vote 2004 Democrat	Total vote cast in 2004
Alabama			792,561	538,878	1,242,200	595,018	1,839,066
Alaska			179,438	24,133	149,773	140,424	308,315
Arizona	1,108,196				1,505,372	404,507	1,961,677
Arkansas			370,735	433,386	458,036	580,973	1,039,349
California	3,886,853	5,932,522			4,555,922	6,955,728	12,053,295
Colorado			717,893	648,130	980,668	1,081,188	2,107,472
Connecticut	448,077	828,902			457,749	945,347	1,424,726
Delaware	142,891	181,566	94,793	135,253			
Florida	2,705,348	2,989,487			3,672,864	3,590,201	7,429,894
Georgia	920,478	1,413,224	1,071,352	932,422	1,864,202	1,287,690	3,220,981
Hawaii	84,701	251,215			87,172	313,629	415,347
Idaho			266,215	132,975	499,796		503,932
Illinois			1,325,703	2,103,766	1,390,690	3,597,456	5,141,520
Indiana	1,427,944	683,273			903,913	1,496,976	2,428,233
Iowa			447,892	554,278	1,038,175	412,365	1,479,228
Kansas			641,075		780,863	310,337	1,129,022
Kentucky			731,679	399,634	873,507	850,855	1,724,362
Louisiana			596,642	638,654[1]	943,014	877,482	1,848,056
Maine	437,689	197,183	295,041	209,858			
Maryland	715,178	1,230,013			783,055	1,504,691	2,321,931
Massachusetts	334,341	1,889,494		1,605,976			
Michigan	1,994,693	2,061,952	1,185,545	1,896,614			
Minnesota	1,047,474	1,181,553	1,116,697	1,078,627			
Mississippi	654,941	314,090	533,269				
Missouri	1,142,852	1,191,812	935,032	913,778	1,518,089	1,158,261	2,706,402
Montana	208,082	194,430	103,611	204,853			
Nebraska	337,977	353,093	397,438	70,290			
Nevada	330,687	238,260			284,640	494,805	810,068
New Hampshire			227,229	207,478	434,847	221,549	657,086
New Jersey	1,420,267	1,511,237	928,439	1,138,193			
New Mexico	225,517	363,744	314,193	168,863			
New York	2,724,589	3,562,415			1,625,069	4,384,907	7,447,818
North Carolina			1,248,664	1,047,983	1,791,450	1,632,527	3,472,082
North Dakota	111,069	176,470			98,553	212,143	310,696
Ohio	2,665,512	1,595,066			3,464,356	1,961,171	5,425,823
Oklahoma			583,579	369,789	763,433	596,750	1,446,846
Oregon			712,287	501,898	565,254	1,128,728	1,780,550
Pennsylvania	2,481,962	2,154,908			2,925,080	2,334,126	5,559,105
Rhode Island	222,588	161,023	69,808	253,774			
South Carolina			600,010	487,359	857,167	704,384	1,597,221
South Dakota			166,949	167,481	197,848	193,340	391,188
Tennessee	1,255,444	621,152	891,498	728,232			
Texas	4,078,954	2,025,024	2,496,243	1,955,758			
Utah	504,803	242,569			626,640	258,955	911,726
Vermont	189,133	73,352			75,398	216,972	307,208
Virginia	1,420,460	1,296,093	1,229,894				
Washington	1,197,208	1,199,437			1,204,584	1,549,708	2,818,651
West Virginia	121,635	469,215	160,902	275,281			
Wisconsin	940,744	1,563,238			1,301,183	1,632,697	2,949,743
Wyoming	157,622	47,087	133,710	49,570			

[1] Louisiana law requires a runoff election between the top two candidates in the general election if none of the candidates receives 50 percent of the total votes cast. The runoff election was held on December 7, 2002.

VOTES CAST FOR REPRESENTATIVES, RESIDENT COMMISSIONER, AND DELEGATES IN 2000, 2002, and 2004

[The figures, compiled from official statistics obtained by the Clerk of the House, show the votes for the Republican and Democratic nominees, except as otherwise indicated. Figures in the last column, for the 2004 election, may include totals for more candidates than the ones shown. The 2002 congressional districts reflect changes in apportionments resulting from the 2000 census.]

State and district	Vote cast in 2000 Republican	Vote cast in 2000 Democrat	State and district	Vote cast in 2002 Republican	Vote cast in 2002 Democrat	State and district	Vote cast in 2004 Republican	Vote cast in 2004 Democrat	Total vote cast in 2004
AL:			AL:			AL:			
1st	151,188	....	1st	108,102	67,507	1st	161,067	93,938	255,164
2d	151,830	64,958	2d	129,233	55,495	2d	177,086	70,562	247,947
3d	147,317	....	3d	91,169	87,351	3d	150,411	95,240	245,784
4th	140,009	86,400	4th	139,705	....	4th	191,110	64,278	255,724
5th	186,059	....	5th	48,226	143,029	5th	74,145	200,999	275,459
6th	212,751	....	6th	178,171	....	6th	264,819	....	268,043
7th	46,134	148,243	7th	....	153,735	7th	61,019	183,408	244,638
AK:			AK:			AK:			
At large ..	190,862	45,372	At large ..	169,685	39,357	At large ..	213,216	67,074	299,996
AZ:			AZ:			AZ:			
1st	123,289	97,455	1st	85,967	79,730	1st	148,315	91,776	253,351
2d	32,990	84,034	2d	100,359	61,217	2d	165,260	107,406	279,303
3d	198,367	94,676	3d	104,847	47,173	3d	181,012	....	225,974
4th	140,396	71,803	4th	18,381	44,517	4th	28,238	77,150	110,027
5th	172,986	101,564	5th	103,870	61,559	5th	159,455	102,363	268,007
6th	186,687	108,317	6th	103,094	49,355	6th	202,882	....	255,577
			7th	38,474	61,256	7th	59,066	108,868	175,437
			8th	126,930	67,328	8th	183,363	109,963	303,769
AR:			AR:			AR:			
1st	79,437	120,266	1st	64,357	129,701	1st	81,556	162,388	243,944
2d	93,692	126,957	2d	....	142,752	2d	115,655	160,834	276,493
3d	(1)	....	3d	141,478	....	3d	160,629	103,158	270,803
4th	104,017	108,143	4th	77,904	119,633	4th	....	(1)	(1)
CA:			CA:			CA:			
1st	66,987	155,638	1st	60,013	118,669	1st	79,970	189,366	282,971
2d	168,172	72,075	2d	117,747	52,455	2d	182,119	90,310	272,429
3d	129,254	93,067	3d	121,732	67,136	3d	177,738	100,025	287,073
4th	197,503	97,974	4th	147,997	72,860	4th	221,926	117,443	339,369
5th	55,945	147,025	5th	34,749	92,726	5th	45,120	138,004	193,387
6th	80,169	182,116	6th	62,052	139,750	6th	85,244	226,423	311,667
7th	44,154	159,692	7th	36,584	97,849	7th	52,446	166,831	219,277
8th	25,298	181,847	8th	20,063	127,684	8th	31,074	224,017	270,064
9th	21,033	182,352	9th	25,333	135,893	9th	31,278	215,630	255,039
10th	134,863	160,429	10th	....	126,390	10th	95,349	182,750	278,099
11th	120,635	79,539	11th	104,921	69,035	11th	163,582	103,587	267,169
12th	44,162	158,404	12th	38,381	105,597	12th	52,593	171,852	252,599
13th	44,499	129,012	13th	26,852	86,495	13th	48,439	144,605	201,921
14th	59,338	161,720	14th	48,346	117,055	14th	69,564	182,712	261,888
15th	99,866	128,545	15th	41,251	87,482	15th	59,953	154,385	214,338
16th	37,213	115,118	16th	32,182	72,370	16th	47,992	129,222	182,281
17th	51,557	143,219	17th	40,334	101,632	17th	65,117	148,958	223,225
18th	56,465	121,003	18th	47,528	56,181	18th	49,973	103,732	153,705
19th	144,517	70,578	19th	106,209	47,403	19th	155,354	64,047	235,264
20th	57,563	66,235	20th	25,628	47,627	20th	53,231	61,005	114,236
21st	142,539	49,318	21st	87,544	32,584	21st	140,721	51,594	192,315
22d	113,094	135,538	22d	120,473	38,988	22d	209,384	....	209,384
23d	119,479	89,918	23d	62,604	95,752	23d	83,926	153,980	244,297
24th	70,169	155,398	24th	120,585	58,755	24th	178,660	96,397	284,378
25th	138,628	73,921	25th	80,775	38,674	25th	145,575	80,395	225,970
26th	96,500	....	26th	95,360	50,081	26th	134,596	107,522	251,207
27th	94,518	113,708	27th	48,996	79,815	27th	66,946	125,296	201,198
28th	116,557	81,804	28th	23,926	73,771	28th	37,868	115,303	162,510
29th	45,784	180,295	29th	40,616	76,036	29th	62,871	133,670	206,832
30th	11,788	83,223	30th	54,989	130,604	30th	87,465	216,682	304,147
31st	89,600	....	31st	12,674	54,569	31st	22,048	89,363	111,411
32d	19,924	137,447	32d	23,366	58,530	32d	....	119,144	140,146
33d	8,260	60,510	33d	16,699	97,779	33d	....	166,801	188,314
34th	33,445	105,980	34th	17,090	48,734	34th	28,175	82,282	110,457
35th	12,582	100,569	35th	18,094	72,401	35th	23,591	125,949	156,407
36th	111,199	115,651	36th	50,328	88,198	36th	81,666	151,208	244,044
37th	12,762	93,269	37th	20,154	63,445	37th	31,960	118,823	158,318
38th	87,266	85,498	38th	23,126	62,600	38th	....	116,851	116,851
39th	129,294	64,398	39th	38,925	52,256	39th	64,832	100,132	164,964
40th	151,069	....	40th	92,422	40,265	40th	147,617	69,684	217,301
41st	104,695	66,361	41st	91,326	40,155	41st	181,605	....	218,937
42d	53,239	90,585	42d	98,476	42,090	42d	167,632	78,393	246,025
43d	140,201	....	43d	20,821	45,374	43d	44,004	86,830	130,834
44th	123,738	79,302	44th	76,686	38,021	44th	138,768	78,796	225,123
45th	136,275	71,066	45th	87,101	43,692	45th	153,523	76,967	230,490
46th	40,928	70,381	46th	108,807	60,890	46th	171,318	90,129	276,690
47th	181,365	83,186	47th	24,346	42,501	47th	43,099	65,684	108,783
48th	160,627	74,073	48th	122,884	51,058	48th	189,004	93,525	290,872
49th	105,515	113,400	49th	94,594	....	49th	141,658	79,057	226,466
50th	38,526	95,191	50th	111,095	55,855	50th	169,025	105,590	289,328

VOTES CAST FOR REPRESENTATIVES, RESIDENT COMMISSIONER, AND DELEGATES IN 2000, 2002, and 2004—CONTINUED

[The figures, compiled from official statistics obtained by the Clerk of the House, show the votes for the Republican and Democratic nominees, except as otherwise indicated. Figures in the last column, for the 2004 election, may include totals for more candidates than the ones shown. The 2002 congressional districts reflect changes in apportionments resulting from the 2000 census.]

State and district	Vote cast in 2000 Republican	Vote cast in 2000 Democrat	State and district	Vote cast in 2002 Republican	Vote cast in 2002 Democrat	State and district	Vote cast in 2004 Republican	Vote cast in 2004 Democrat	Total vote cast in 2004
51st	172,291	81,408	51st	40,430	59,541	51st	63,526	111,441	180,879
52d	131,345	63,537	52d	118,561	43,526	52d	187,799	74,857	271,438
			53d	43,891	72,252	53d	63,897	146,449	221,436
CO:			CO:			CO:			
1st	56,291	141,831	1st	49,884	111,718	1st	58,659	177,077	240,929
2d	109,338	155,725	2d	75,564	123,504	2d	94,160	207,900	309,364
3d	199,204	87,921	3d	143,433	68,160	3d	141,376	153,500	303,646
4th	209,078		4th	115,359	87,499	4th	155,958	136,812	305,509
5th	253,330		5th	128,118	45,587	5th	193,333	74,098	274,058
6th	141,410	110,568	6th	158,851	71,327	6th	212,778	139,870	357,741
			7th	81,789	81,668	7th	135,571	106,026	247,764
CT:			CT:			CT:			
1st	59,331	151,932	1st	66,968	134,698	1st	73,601	198,802	272,403
2d	114,380	111,520	2d	117,434	99,674	2d	166,412	140,536	307,078
3d	60,037	156,910	3d	54,757	121,557	3d	69,160	200,638	276,980
4th	119,155	84,472	4th	113,197	62,491	4th	152,493	138,333	290,830
5th	98,229	118,932	5th	113,626	90,616	5th	168,268	107,438	281,447
6th	143,698	75,471							
DE:			DE:			DE:			
At large	211,797	96,488	At large	164,605	61,011	At large	245,978	105,716	356,045
FL:			FL:			FL:			
1st	(2)		1st	152,635	51,972	1st	236,604	72,506	309,110
2d	71,754	185,579	2d	75,275	152,164	2d	125,399	201,577	326,987
3d	75,228	102,143	3d	60,747	88,462	3d		172,833	174,156
4th	203,090	94,587	4th	171,152		4th	256,157		257,327
5th	100,244	180,338	5th	121,998	117,758	5th	240,315	124,140	364,488
6th	(2)		6th	141,570	75,046	6th	211,137	116,680	327,853
7th	171,018	99,531	7th	142,147	96,444	7th	(2)		(2)
8th	125,253	121,295	8th	123,497	66,099	8th	172,232	112,343	284,575
9th	210,318		9th	169,369	67,623	9th	284,035		284,278
10th	146,799		10th	(2)		10th	207,175	91,658	298,833
11th	149,465		11th		(2)	11th		191,780	223,481
12th	125,224	94,395	12th	(2)		12th	179,204	96,965	276,169
13th	175,918	99,568	13th	139,048	114,739	13th	190,477	153,961	344,438
14th	242,614		14th	(2)		14th	226,662	108,672	335,334
15th	176,189	117,511	15th	146,414	85,433	15th	210,388	111,538	321,926
16th	176,153	108,782	16th	176,171		16th	215,563	101,247	316,810
17th		(2)	17th		113,749	17th		178,690	179,424
18th	(2)		18th	103,512	42,852	18th	143,647	78,281	221,928
19th	67,789	171,080	19th	60,477	156,747	19th		(2)	(2)
20th		(2)	20th		(2)	20th	81,213	191,195	272,408
21st	(2)		21st			21st	146,507		201,243
22d	105,855	105,256	22d	131,930	83,265	22d	192,581	108,258	306,726
23d	27,630	89,179	23d	27,986	96,347	23d		(2)	(2)
			24th	135,576	83,667	24th	(2)		(2)
			25th	81,845	44,757	25th	(2)		(2)
GA:			GA:			GA:			
1st	131,684	58,776	1st	103,661	40,026	1st	188,347		188,347
2d	83,870	96,430	2d		102,925	2d	64,645	129,984	194,629
3d	150,200	86,309	3d	73,866	75,394	3d	80,435	136,273	216,708
4th	90,277	139,579	4th	35,202	118,045	4th	89,509	157,461	246,970
5th	40,606	137,333	5th		116,259	5th		201,773	201,773
6th	256,595	86,666	6th	163,525	41,204	6th	267,542		267,619
7th	126,312	102,272	7th	138,997	37,124	7th	258,982		258,982
8th	113,380	79,051	8th	142,505	39,422	8th	227,524	73,632	301,156
9th	183,171	60,360	9th	123,313	45,974	9th	197,869	68,462	266,331
10th	122,590	71,309	10th	129,242		10th	219,136		219,136
11th	199,652		11th	69,427	65,007	11th	120,696	89,591	210,287
			12th	77,479	62,904	12th	105,132	113,036	218,168
			13th	47,405	70,011	13th		170,657	170,657
HI:			HI:			HI:			
1st	44,989	108,517	1st	45,032	131,673	1st	69,371	128,567	204,181
2d	65,906	112,856	2d	71,661	100,671	2d	79,072	133,317	212,389
ID:			ID:			ID:			
1st	173,743	84,080	1st	120,743	80,269	1st	207,662	90,927	298,589
2d	158,912	58,265	2d	135,605	57,769	2d	193,704	80,133	273,837
IL:			IL:			IL:			
1st	23,915	172,271	1st	29,776	149,068	1st	37,840	212,109	249,949
2d	19,906	175,995	2d	32,567	151,443	2d		207,535	234,525
3d	47,005	145,498	3d		156,042	3d	57,845	167,034	229,956
4th		89,487	4th	12,778	67,339	4th	15,536	104,761	125,142
5th		142,161	5th	46,008	106,514	5th	49,530	158,400	207,930
6th	133,327	92,880	6th	113,174	60,698	6th	139,627	110,470	250,097
7th	26,872	164,155	7th	25,280	137,933	7th	35,603	221,133	256,736
8th	141,918	90,777	8th	95,275	70,626	8th	130,601	139,792	270,393

VOTES CAST FOR REPRESENTATIVES, RESIDENT COMMISSIONER, AND DELEGATES IN 2000, 2002, and 2004—CONTINUED

[The figures, compiled from official statistics obtained by the Clerk of the House, show the votes for the Republican and Democratic nominees, except as otherwise indicated. Figures in the last column, for the 2004 election, may include totals for more candidates than the ones shown. The 2002 congressional districts reflect changes in apportionments resulting from the 2000 census.]

State and district	Vote cast in 2000 Republican	Vote cast in 2000 Democrat	State and district	Vote cast in 2002 Republican	Vote cast in 2002 Democrat	State and district	Vote cast in 2004 Republican	Vote cast in 2004 Democrat	Total vote cast in 2004
9th	45,344	147,002	9th	45,307	118,642	9th	56,135	175,282	231,417
10th	121,582	115,924	10th	128,611	58,300	10th	177,493	99,218	276,711
11th	132,384	102,485	11th	124,192	68,893	11th	173,057	121,903	294,960
12th		183,208	12th	58,440	131,580	12th	82,677	198,962	286,435
13th	193,250	98,768	13th	139,546	59,069	13th	200,472	107,836	308,312
14th	188,597	66,309	14th	135,198	47,165	14th	191,618	87,590	279,208
15th	125,943	110,679	15th	134,650	64,131	15th	178,114	113,625	291,739
16th	178,174	88,781	16th	133,339	55,488	16th	204,350	91,452	295,806
17th	108,853	132,494	17th	76,519	127,093	17th	111,680	172,320	284,000
18th	173,706	85,317	18th	192,567		18th	216,047	91,548	307,595
19th	85,137	155,101	19th	133,956	110,517	19th	213,451	94,303	307,754
20th	161,393	94,382							
IN:			**IN:**			**IN:**			
1st	56,200	148,683	1st	41,909	90,443	1st	82,858	178,406	261,264
2d	106,023	80,885	2d	95,081	86,253	2d	140,496	115,513	259,355
3d	98,822	107,438	3d	92,566	50,509	3d	171,389	76,232	247,621
4th	131,051	74,492	4th	112,760	41,314	4th	190,445	77,574	274,136
5th	132,051	81,427	5th	129,442	45,283	5th	228,718	82,637	318,363
6th	199,207	74,881	6th	118,436	63,871	6th	182,529	85,123	272,049
7th	135,869	66,764	7th	64,379	77,478	7th	97,491	121,303	223,175
8th	116,879	100,488	8th	98,952	88,763	8th	145,576	121,522	272,778
9th	102,219	126,420	9th	87,169	96,654	9th	142,197	140,772	287,510
10th	62,233	91,689							
IA:			**IA:**			**IA:**			
1st	164,972	96,283	1st	112,280	83,779	1st	159,993	125,490	290,054
2d	139,906	110,327	2d	108,130	94,767	2d	176,684	117,405	299,881
3d	83,810	156,327	3d	97,285	115,367	3d	136,099	168,007	304,319
4th	169,267	101,112	4th	115,430	90,784	4th	181,294	116,121	297,566
5th	159,367	67,593	5th	113,257	68,853	5th	168,583	97,597	266,341
KS:			**KS:**			**KS:**			
1st	214,328		1st	189,976		1st	239,776		264,293
2d	164,951	71,709	2d	127,477	79,160	2d	165,325	121,532	294,436
3d	144,672	154,505	3d	102,882	110,095	3d	145,542	184,050	335,739
4th	131,871	101,980	4th	115,691	70,656	4th	173,151	81,388	261,915
KY:			**KY:**			**KY:**			
1st	132,115	95,806	1st	117,600	62,617	1st	175,972	85,229	261,387
2d	160,800	74,537	2d	122,773	51,431	2d	185,394	87,585	272,979
3d	142,106	118,875	3d	118,228	110,846	3d	197,736	124,040	328,154
4th	100,943	125,872	4th	81,651	87,776	4th	160,982	129,876	295,927
5th	145,980	52,495	5th	137,986	38,254	5th	177,579		177,579
6th	142,971	94,167	6th	115,622		6th	119,716	175,355	299,217
LA:			**LA:**			**LA:**			
1st	191,379	29,935	1st	174,614		1st	233,683	54,214	287,897
2d		(3)	2d	15,440	122,927	2d	46,097	173,510	219,607
3d	143,446		3d	130,323		3d	57,042	57,611	114,653
4th	122,678	43,600	4th	114,649	42,340	4th	(3)		(3)
5th	123,975	42,977	5th	85,744	86,718	5th	179,466	58,591	238,057
6th	165,637	72,192	6th	146,932		6th	189,106	72,763	261,869
7th		152,796	7th		138,659	7th	75,039	61,493	136,532
ME:			**ME:**			**ME:**			
1st	123,915	202,823	1st	97,931	172,646	1st	147,663	219,077	366,740
2d	79,522	219,783	2d	107,849	116,868	2d	135,547	199,303	343,436
MD:			**MD:**			**MD:**			
1st	165,293	91,022	1st	192,004	57,986	1st	245,149	77,872	323,021
2d	178,556	81,591	2d	88,954	105,718	2d	75,812	164,751	247,071
3d	53,827	169,347	3d	75,721	145,589	3d	97,008	182,066	286,969
4th	24,973	172,624	4th	34,890	131,644	4th	52,907	196,809	261,607
5th	89,019	166,231	5th	60,758	137,903	5th	87,189	204,867	298,129
6th	168,624	109,136	6th	147,825	75,575	6th	206,076	90,108	305,508
7th	19,773	134,066	7th	49,172	137,047	7th	60,102	179,189	244,018
8th	156,241	136,840	8th	103,587	112,788	8th	71,989	215,129	287,197
MA:			**MA:**			**MA:**			
1st	73,580	169,375	1st	66,061	137,841	1st		229,465	295,208
2d		196,670	2d		153,387	2d		217,682	287,871
3d		213,065	3d		155,697	3d	80,197	192,036	285,996
4th	56,553	200,638	4th		166,125	4th		219,260	299,783
5th		199,601	5th	69,337	122,562	5th	88,232	179,652	280,310
6th	83,501	205,324	6th	75,462	162,900	6th	91,597	213,458	321,736
7th		211,543	7th		170,968	7th	60,334	202,399	292,187
8th		144,031	8th		111,861	8th		165,852	215,800
9th	48,672	193,020	9th		168,055	9th		218,167	297,826
10th	81,192	234,675	10th	79,624	179,238	10th	114,879	222,013	350,738
MI:			**MI:**			**MI:**			
1st	117,300	169,649	1st	69,254	150,701	1st	105,706	211,571	322,674
2d	186,762	96,370	2d	156,937	61,749	2d	225,343	94,040	325,005

VOTES CAST FOR REPRESENTATIVES, RESIDENT COMMISSIONER, AND DELEGATES IN 2000, 2002, and 2004—CONTINUED

[The figures, compiled from official statistics obtained by the Clerk of the House, show the votes for the Republican and Democratic nominees, except as otherwise indicated. Figures in the last column, for the 2004 election, may include totals for more candidates than the ones shown. The 2002 congressional districts reflect changes in apportionments resulting from the 2000 census.]

State and district	Vote cast in 2000 Republican	Vote cast in 2000 Democrat	State and district	Vote cast in 2002 Republican	Vote cast in 2002 Democrat	State and district	Vote cast in 2004 Republican	Vote cast in 2004 Democrat	Total vote cast in 2004
3d	179,539	91,309	3d	153,131	61,987	3d	214,465	101,395	322,103
4th	182,128	78,019	4th	149,090	65,950	4th	205,274	110,885	318,924
5th	59,274	184,048	5th		158,709	5th	96,934	208,163	309,915
6th	159,373	68,532	6th	126,936	53,793	6th	197,425	97,978	302,158
7th	147,369	86,080	7th	121,142	78,412	7th	176,053	109,527	301,642
8th	145,179	145,019	8th	156,525	70,920	8th	207,925	125,619	340,694
9th	92,926	158,184	9th	141,102	96,856	9th	199,210	134,764	340,799
10th	93,713	181,818	10th	137,339	77,053	10th	227,720	98,029	331,868
11th	170,790	124,053	11th	126,050	87,402	11th	186,431	134,301	327,216
12th	78,795	157,720	12th	61,502	140,970	12th	88,256	210,827	304,134
13th	79,445	160,084	13th		120,859	13th	40,935	173,246	221,654
14th	17,582	168,982	14th	26,544	145,285	14th	35,089	213,681	254,580
15th	14,336	140,609	15th	48,626	136,518	15th	81,828	218,409	307,963
16th	62,469	167,142							
MN:			**MN:**			**MN:**			
1st	159,835	117,946	1st	163,570	92,165	1st	193,132	115,088	324,055
2d	138,957	138,802	2d	152,970	121,121	2d	206,313	147,527	365,945
3d	222,571	98,219	3d	213,334	82,575	3d	231,871	126,665	358,892
4th	83,852	130,403	4th	89,705	164,597	4th	105,467	182,387	317,299
5th	58,191	176,629	5th	66,271	171,572	5th	76,600	218,434	313,526
6th	170,900	176,340	6th	164,747	100,738	6th	203,669	173,309	377,224
7th	79,175	185,771	7th	90,342	170,234	7th	106,349	207,628	314,257
8th	79,890	210,094	8th	88,673	194,909	8th	112,693	228,586	350,483
MS:			**MS:**			**MS:**			
1st	145,967	59,763	1st	95,404	32,318	1st	219,328		277,584
2d	54,090	112,777	2d	69,711	89,913	2d	107,647	154,626	264,869
3d	153,899	54,151	3d	139,329	76,184	3d	234,874		293,368
4th	79,218	115,732	4th	34,373	121,742	4th	96,740	179,979	280,382
5th	35,309	153,264							
MO:			**MO:**			**MO:**			
1st	42,730	149,173	1st	51,755	133,946	1st	64,791	213,658	283,771
2d	164,926	126,441	2d	167,057	77,223	2d	228,725	115,366	349,867
3d	100,967	147,222	3d	80,551	122,181	3d	125,422	146,894	277,916
4th	84,406	180,634	4th	64,451	142,204	4th	93,334	190,800	288,226
5th	66,439	159,826	5th	60,245	122,645	5th	123,431	161,727	293,025
6th	138,925	127,792	6th	131,151	73,202	6th	196,516	106,987	307,855
7th	202,305	65,510	7th	149,519	45,964	7th	210,080	84,356	298,205
8th	162,239	67,760	8th	135,144	50,686	8th	194,039	71,543	268,711
9th	172,787	111,662	9th	146,032	61,126	9th	193,429	101,343	299,447
MT:			**MT:**			**MT:**			
At large	211,418	189,971	At large	214,100	108,233	At large	286,076	145,606	444,230
NE:			**NE:**			**NE:**			
1st	155,485	72,859	1st	133,013		1st	143,756	113,971	265,072
2d	148,911	70,268	2d	89,917	46,843	2d	152,608	90,292	249,764
3d	182,117	34,944	3d	163,939		3d	218,751	26,434	250,136
NV:			**NV:**			**NV:**			
1st	101,276	118,469	1st	51,148	64,312	1st	63,005	133,569	202,436
2d	229,608	106,379	2d	149,574	40,189	2d	195,466	79,978	291,079
			3d	100,378	66,659	3d	162,240	120,365	297,918
NH:			**NH:**			**NH:**			
1st	150,609	128,387	1st	128,993	85,426	1st	204,836	118,226	323,372
2d	152,581	110,367	2d	125,804	90,479	2d	191,188	125,280	328,194
NJ:			**NJ:**			**NJ:**			
1st	46,455	167,327	1st		121,846	1st	66,109	201,163	268,203
2d	155,187	74,632	2d	116,834	47,735	2d	172,779	86,792	265,442
3d	157,053	112,848	3d	123,375	64,364	3d	195,938	107,034	308,862
4th	158,515	87,956	4th	115,293	55,967	4th	192,671	92,826	287,553
5th	175,546	81,715	5th	118,881	76,504	5th	171,220	122,259	297,425
6th	62,454	141,698	6th	42,479	91,379	6th	70,942	153,981	230,151
7th	128,434	113,479	7th	106,055	74,879	7th	162,597	119,081	285,847
8th	60,606	134,074	8th	40,318	88,101	8th	62,747	152,001	218,820
9th	61,984	140,462	9th	42,088	97,108	9th	68,564	146,038	216,251
10th	18,436	133,073	10th	15,913	86,433	10th		155,697	160,713
11th	186,140	80,958	11th	132,938	48,477	11th	200,915	91,811	296,002
12th	145,511	146,162	12th	62,938	104,806	12th	115,014	171,691	289,785
13th	27,849	117,856	13th	16,852	72,605	13th	35,288	121,018	159,541
NM:			**NM:**			**NM:**			
1st	107,296	92,187	1st	95,711	77,234	1st	147,372	123,339	270,905
2d	100,742	72,614	2d	79,631	61,916	2d	130,498	86,292	216,790
3d	65,979	135,040	3d		122,921	3d	79,935	175,269	255,204
NY:			**NY:**			**NY:**			
1st	111,003	97,299	1st	64,999	81,325	1st	110,786	140,878	313,966
2d	65,880	90,438	2d	48,239	75,845	2d	72,953	147,197	283,480
3d	122,820	91,948	3d	98,874	46,022	3d	151,323	100,737	316,125
4th	75,650	128,688	4th	61,473	85,496	4th	85,505	148,615	284,530

VOTES CAST FOR REPRESENTATIVES, RESIDENT COMMISSIONER, AND DELEGATES IN 2000, 2002, and 2004—CONTINUED

[The figures, compiled from official statistics obtained by the Clerk of the House, show the votes for the Republican and Democratic nominees, except as otherwise indicated. Figures in the last column, for the 2004 election, may include totals for more candidates than the ones shown. The 2002 congressional districts reflect changes in apportionments resulting from the 2000 census.]

State and district	Vote cast in 2000		State and district	Vote cast in 2002		State and district	Vote cast in 2004		Total vote cast in 2004
	Republican	Democrat		Republican	Democrat		Republican	Democrat	
5th	56,046	127,233	5th		68,773	5th	43,002	114,132	206,533
6th		117,194	6th		68,718	6th		125,127	184,957
7th	24,592	78,207	7th	16,460	48,983	7th	21,843	100,382	177,452
8th	27,057	139,936	8th	18,623	71,996	8th	35,177	154,098	251,650
9th	40,866	96,348	9th	27,882	57,104	9th	39,648	108,577	202,558
10th	6,852	118,812	10th		72,313	10th	11,099	130,265	195,241
11th	7,088	105,321	11th	9,250	67,967	11th		134,175	202,027
12th	10,052	81,699	12th		43,809	12th	15,697	100,402	163,344
13th	95,696	55,763	13th	62,520	27,304	13th	102,713	72,180	217,895
14th	45,453	143,809	14th	30,053	85,029	14th	41,936	175,886	274,043
15th	6,906	124,415	15th	8,790	77,036	15th	12,355	153,099	218,608
16th	3,943	100,891	16th	3,916	48,411	16th	4,917	106,739	148,123
17th	11,513	112,748	17th	35,389	73,569	17th	40,524	135,344	230,261
18th	52,923	126,878	18th		95,396	18th	73,975	159,072	290,215
19th	133,963	82,082	19th	102,848	44,967	19th	152,051	87,429	306,733
20th	136,016	87,602	20th	125,335	45,878	20th	163,343	96,630	324,160
21st	60,333	157,773	21st	53,525	128,584	21st	80,121	167,247	311,854
22d	153,997	72,640	22d	52,499	92,336	22d	81,881	148,588	287,401
23d	110,634	38,049	23d	110,042		23d	136,222	66,448	265,012
24th	128,513	41,719	24th	108,017		24th	128,493	85,140	286,686
25th	132,120	64,533	25th	113,914	53,290	25th	155,163		315,880
26th	78,103	124,862	26th	105,807	41,140	26th	137,425	116,484	321,080
27th	144,011	69,870	27th	105,946	45,060	27th	125,275	127,267	299,699
28th	67,251	151,688	28th	45,125	94,209	28th	48,981	150,431	262,220
29th	68,958	115,685	29th	116,245	37,128	29th	136,883	104,555	306,070
30th	113,638	62,378							
31st	143,584	45,193							
NC:			NC:			NC:			
1st	62,198	124,171	1st	50,907	93,157	1st	77,508	137,667	215,175
2d	103,011	146,733	2d	50,965	100,121	2d	87,811	145,079	232,890
3d	121,940	74,058	3d	131,448		3d	171,863	71,227	243,090
4th	119,412	200,885	4th	78,095	132,185	4th	121,717	217,441	339,234
5th	172,489		5th	137,879	58,558	5th	167,546	117,271	284,817
6th	195,727		6th	151,430		6th	207,470	76,153	283,623
7th	66,463	160,185	7th	45,537	118,543	7th	66,084	180,382	246,466
8th	111,950	89,505	8th	80,298	66,819	8th	125,070	100,101	225,171
9th	181,161	79,382	9th	140,095	49,974	9th	210,783	89,318	300,101
10th	164,182	70,877	10th	102,768	65,587	10th	157,884	88,233	246,117
11th	146,677	112,234	11th	112,335	86,664	11th	159,709	131,188	290,897
12th	69,596	135,570	12th	49,588	98,821	12th	76,898	154,908	231,806
			13th	77,688	100,287	13th	112,788	160,896	273,684
ND:			ND:			ND:			
At large	127,251	151,173	At large	109,957	121,073	At large	125,684	185,130	310,814
OH:			OH:			OH:			
1st	116,768	98,328	1st	110,760	60,168	1st	173,430	116,235	289,863
2d	204,184	64,091	2d	139,218	48,785	2d	227,102	89,598	316,760
3d		177,731	3d	111,630	78,307	3d	197,290	119,448	316,738
4th	156,510	67,330	4th	120,001	57,726	4th	167,807	118,538	286,345
5th	169,857	62,138	5th	126,286	51,872	5th	196,649	96,656	293,305
6th	96,966	138,849	6th	77,643	113,972	6th		223,842	223,987
7th	163,646	60,755	7th	113,252	45,568	7th	186,534	100,617	287,151
8th	179,756	66,293	8th	119,947	49,444	8th	201,675	90,574	292,249
9th	49,446	168,547	9th	46,481	132,236	9th	95,983	205,149	301,132
10th	48,930	167,063	10th	41,778	129,997	10th	96,463	172,406	287,212
11th	21,630	164,134	11th	36,146	116,590	11th		222,371	222,371
12th	139,242	115,432	12th	116,982	64,707	12th	198,912	122,109	321,046
13th	84,295	170,058	13th	55,357	123,025	13th	97,090	201,004	298,094
14th	71,432	149,184	14th	134,413	51,846	14th	201,652	119,714	321,366
15th	156,792	64,805	15th	108,193	54,286	15th	166,520	110,915	277,435
16th	162,294	62,709	16th	129,734	58,644	16th	202,544	101,817	304,361
17th	54,751	120,333	17th	62,188	94,441	17th	62,871	212,800	275,671
18th	152,325	79,232	18th	125,546		18th	177,600	90,820	268,420
19th	206,639	101,842							
OK:			OK:			OK:			
1st	138,528	58,493	1st	119,566	90,649	1st	187,145	116,731	310,934
2d	81,672	107,273	2d	51,234	146,748	2d	92,963	179,579	272,542
3d	137,826		3d	148,206		3d	215,510		262,131
4th	114,000	54,808	4th	106,452	91,322	4th	198,985		255,854
5th	134,159	53,275	5th	121,374	63,208	5th	180,430	92,719	273,149
6th	95,635	63,106							
OR:			OR:			OR:			
1st	115,303	176,902	1st	80,917	149,215	1st	135,164	203,771	354,338
2d	220,086	78,101	2d	181,295	64,991	2d	248,461	88,914	346,865
3d	64,128	181,049	3d	62,821	156,851	3d	82,045	245,559	346,560

VOTES CAST FOR REPRESENTATIVES, RESIDENT COMMISSIONER, AND DELEGATES IN 2000, 2002, and 2004—CONTINUED

[The figures, compiled from official statistics obtained by the Clerk of the House, show the votes for the Republican and Democratic nominees, except as otherwise indicated. Figures in the last column, for the 2004 election, may include totals for more candidates than the ones shown. The 2002 congressional districts reflect changes in apportionments resulting from the 2000 census.]

State and district	Vote cast in 2000 Republican	Vote cast in 2000 Democrat	State and district	Vote cast in 2002 Republican	Vote cast in 2002 Democrat	State and district	Vote cast in 2004 Republican	Vote cast in 2004 Democrat	Total vote cast in 2004
4th	88,950	197,998	4th	90,523	168,150	4th	140,882	228,611	374,909
5th	118,631	156,315	5th	113,441	137,713	5th	154,993	184,833	349,634
PA:			**PA:**			**PA:**			
1st	19,920	149,621	1st	17,444	121,076	1st	33,266	214,462	248,585
2d		180,021	2d	20,988	150,623	2d	34,411	253,226	287,637
3d	59,343	130,528	3d	116,763		3d	166,580	110,684	277,264
4th	145,390	100,995	4th	130,534	71,674	4th	204,329	116,303	323,917
5th	147,570		5th	124,942		5th	192,852		219,091
6th	71,227	140,084	6th	103,648	98,128	6th	160,348	153,977	314,325
7th	172,569	93,687	7th	146,296	75,055	7th	196,556	134,932	334,527
8th	154,090	100,617	8th	127,475	76,178	8th	183,229	143,427	331,264
9th	184,401		9th	124,184	50,558	9th	184,320	80,787	265,107
10th	124,830	112,580	10th	152,017		10th	191,967		206,772
11th	66,699	131,948	11th	71,543	93,758	11th		171,147	181,252
12th	56,575	145,538	12th	44,818	124,201	12th		204,504	204,504
13th	126,501	146,026	13th	100,295	107,945	13th	127,205	171,763	308,124
14th		147,533	14th		123,323	14th		220,139	220,139
15th	118,307	103,864	15th	98,493	73,212	15th	170,634	114,646	291,134
16th	162,403	80,177	16th	119,046		16th	183,620	98,410	285,299
17th	166,236	66,190	17th	97,802	103,483	17th	113,592	172,412	291,786
18th	68,798	156,131	18th	119,885	79,451	18th	197,894	117,420	315,314
19th	168,722	61,538	19th	143,097		19th	224,274		245,094
20th	80,312	145,131							
21st	135,164	87,018							
RI:			**RI:**			**RI:**			
1st	61,522	123,442	1st	59,370	95,286	1st	69,819	124,923	195,010
2d	27,932	123,805	2d	37,767	129,390	2d	43,139	154,392	207,165
SC:			**SC:**			**SC:**			
1st	139,597	82,622	1st	127,562		1st	186,448		212,308
2d	154,338	110,672	2d	144,149		2d	181,862	93,249	279,870
3d	150,180	64,917	3d	119,644	55,743	3d	191,052		191,999
4th	150,436		4th	122,422	51,462	4th	188,795	78,376	270,594
5th	85,247	126,877	5th		121,912	5th	89,568	152,867	242,518
6th	50,005	138,053	6th	55,760	116,586	6th	75,443	161,987	241,829
SD:			**SD:**			**SD:**			
At large	231,083	78,321	At large	180,023	153,551	At large	178,823	207,837	389,468
TN:			**TN:**			**TN:**			
1st	157,828		1st	127,300		1st	172,543	56,361	233,560
2d	187,154		2d	146,887	37,035	2d	215,795	52,155	272,928
3d	139,840	75,785	3d	112,254	58,824	3d	166,154	84,295	256,636
4th	133,622	67,165	4th	85,680	95,989	4th	109,993	138,459	252,646
5th	50,386	149,277	5th	56,825	108,903	5th	74,978	168,970	243,963
6th	97,169	168,861	6th	57,397	117,119	6th	87,523	167,448	260,642
7th	171,056	71,587	7th	138,314	51,790	7th	232,404		232,404
8th	54,929	143,127	8th	45,853	117,811	8th	59,853	173,623	233,567
9th		143,298	9th		120,904	9th	41,578	190,648	232,392
TX:			**TX:**			**TX:**			
1st	91,912	118,157	1st	66,654	86,384	1st	157,068	96,281	255,507
2d		162,891	2d	53,656	85,492	2d	139,951	108,156	252,038
3d	187,436	67,233	3d	113,974	37,503	3d	180,099		210,352
4th	91,574	145,887	4th	67,939	97,304	4th	182,866	81,585	267,942
5th	100,487	82,629	5th	81,439	56,330	5th	148,816	75,911	230,845
6th	222,685		6th	115,396	45,404	6th	168,767	83,609	255,627
7th	183,712	60,694	7th	96,795		7th	175,440	91,126	273,651
8th	233,848		8th	140,575		8th	179,599	77,324	260,628
9th	87,165	130,143	9th	59,635	86,710	9th	42,132	114,462	158,566
10th		203,628	10th		114,428	10th	182,113		231,643
11th	85,546	105,782	11th	68,236	74,678	11th	177,291	50,339	230,977
12th	117,739	67,612	12th	121,208		12th	173,222	66,316	239,538
13th	117,995		13th	119,401	31,218	13th	189,448		205,241
14th	137,370	92,689	14th	102,905	48,224	14th	173,668		173,668
15th	106,570		15th		66,311	15th	67,917	96,089	166,358
16th	40,921	92,649	16th		72,383	16th	49,972	108,577	160,773
17th	72,535	120,670	17th	77,622	84,136	17th	116,049	125,309	244,748
18th	38,191	131,857	18th	27,980	99,161	18th		136,018	152,988
19th	170,319		19th	117,092		19th	136,459	93,531	233,514
20th		107,487	20th		68,685	20th	54,976	112,480	171,804
21st	251,049	73,326	21st	161,836	56,206	21st	209,774	121,129	341,119
22d	154,662	92,645	22d	100,499	55,716	22d	150,386	112,034	272,620
23d	119,679	78,274	23d	77,573	71,067	23d	170,716	72,480	246,503
24th	61,235	103,152	24th	38,332	73,002	24th	154,435	82,599	241,374
25th	68,010		25th	50,041	63,590	25th	49,252	108,309	160,217
26th	214,025	75,601	26th	123,195	37,485	26th	180,519	89,809	274,539
27th	54,660	102,088	27th	41,004	68,559	27th	61,955	112,081	177,536
28th		123,104	28th	26,973	71,393	28th	69,538	106,323	180,166

VOTES CAST FOR REPRESENTATIVES, RESIDENT COMMISSIONER, AND DELEGATES IN 2000, 2002, and 2004—CONTINUED

[The figures, compiled from official statistics obtained by the Clerk of the House, show the votes for the Republican and Democratic nominees, except as otherwise indicated. Figures in the last column, for the 2004 election, may include totals for more candidates than the ones shown. The 2002 congressional districts reflect changes in apportionments resulting from the 2000 census.]

State and district	Vote cast in 2000		State and district	Vote cast in 2002		State and district	Vote cast in 2004		Total vote cast in 2004
	Repub-lican	Demo-crat		Repub-lican	Demo-crat		Repub-lican	Demo-crat	
29th	29,606	84,665	29th		55,760	29th		78,256	83,124
30th		109,163	30th	28,981	88,980	30th		144,513	155,334
			31st	111,556	44,183	31st	160,247	80,292	247,427
			32d	100,226	44,886	32d	109,859	89,030	202,236
UT:			UT:			UT:			
1st	180,591	71,229	1st	109,265	66,104	1st	199,615	85,630	293,961
2d	107,114	145,021	2d	109,123	110,764	2d	147,778	187,250	341,968
3d	138,943	88,547	3d	103,598	44,533	3d	173,010	88,748	272,928
VT:			VT:			VT:			
At large	4 51,977	14,918	At large	5 72,813		At large	6 74,271	21,684	305,008
VA:			VA:			VA:			
1st	151,344	97,399	1st	113,168		1st	225,071		286,534
2d	97,856	90,328	2d	104,081		2d	132,946	108,180	241,380
3d		137,527	3d		87,521	3d	70,194	159,373	229,892
4th		189,787	4th	108,733		4th	182,444	100,413	283,027
5th		7 65,387	5th	95,360	54,805	5th	172,431	98,237	270,758
6th	153,338		6th	105,530		6th	206,560		213,648
7th	192,652	94,935	7th	113,658	49,854	7th	230,765		305,658
8th	88,262	164,178	8th	64,121	102,759	8th	106,231	171,986	287,919
9th	59,335	137,488	9th		100,075	9th	98,499	150,039	252,947
10th	238,817		10th	115,917	45,464	10th	205,982	116,654	323,011
11th	150,395	83,455	11th	135,379		11th	186,299	118,305	309,233
WA:			WA:			WA:			
1st	121,823	155,820	1st	84,696	114,087	1st	117,850	204,121	327,769
2d	134,660	146,617	2d	92,528	101,219	2d	106,333	202,383	316,682
3d	114,861	159,428	3d	74,065	119,264	3d	119,027	193,626	312,653
4th	143,259	87,585	4th	108,257	53,572	4th	154,627	92,486	247,113
5th	144,038	97,703	5th	126,757	65,146	5th	179,600	121,333	300,933
6th	79,215	164,853	6th	61,584	126,116	6th	91,228	202,919	294,147
7th		193,470	7th	46,256	156,300	7th	65,226	272,302	337,528
8th	183,255	104,944	8th	121,633	75,931	8th	173,298	157,148	336,499
9th	76,766	135,452	9th	63,146	95,805	9th	88,304	162,433	256,671
WV:			WV:			WV:			
1st		170,974	1st		110,941	1st	79,196	166,583	245,779
2d	108,769	103,003	2d	98,276	65,400	2d	147,676	106,131	257,025
3d		146,807	3d	37,229	87,783	3d	76,170	142,682	218,852
WI:			WI:			WI:			
1st	177,612	88,885	1st	140,176	63,895	1st	233,372	116,250	356,976
2d	154,632	163,534	2d	83,694	163,313	2d	145,810	251,637	397,724
3d	97,741	173,505	3d	69,955	131,038	3d	157,866	204,856	363,008
4th	101,811	163,622	4th		122,031	4th	85,928	212,382	305,142
5th	49,296	173,893	5th	191,224		5th	271,153	129,384	407,291
6th	179,205	96,125	6th	169,834		6th	238,620	107,209	355,995
7th	100,264	173,007	7th	81,518	146,364	7th		241,306	281,752
8th	211,388	71,575	8th	152,745	50,284	8th	248,070	105,513	353,725
9th	239,498	83,720							
WY:			WY:			WY:			
At large	141,848	60,638	At large	110,229	65,961	At large	132,107	99,989	239,163

[Table continues on next page]

VOTES CAST FOR REPRESENTATIVES, RESIDENT COMMISSIONER, AND DELEGATES IN 2000, 2002, and 2004—CONTINUED

[The figures, compiled from official statistics obtained by the Clerk of the House, show the votes for the Democratic and Republican nominees, except as otherwise indicated. Figures in the last column, for the 2004 election, may include totals for more candidates than the ones shown.]

Commonwealth of Puerto Rico	Vote						Total vote cast in 2004
	2000		2002		2004		
	New Progressive	Popular Democrat	New Progressive	Popular Democrat	New Progressive	Popular Democrat	
Resident Commissioner (4-year term)	905,690	983,488	....	....	956,828	945,691	1,959,108

District of Columbia	Vote						Total vote cast in 2004
	2000		2002		2004		
	Republican	Democrat	Republican	Democrat	Republican	Democrat	
Delegate	10,258	158,824	....	119,268	18,296	202,027	221,213

Guam	Vote						Total vote cast in 2004
	2000		2002		2004		
	Republican	Democrat	Republican	Democrat	Republican	Democrat	
Delegate	8,167	29,099	14,836	27,081	....	31,051	31,888

Virgin Islands	Vote						Total vote cast in 2004
	2000		2002		2004		
	Democrat	Independent	Democrat	Republican	Democrat	Republican	
Delegate	9,512	1,270	4,286	20,414	17,379	1,512	26,431

American Samoa	Vote						Total vote cast in 2004
	2000		2002		2004		
	Democrat	Republican	Democrat	Republican	Democrat	Republican	
Delegate	[8] 5,505	....	[9] 4,959	....	6,656	5,472	12,128

[1] According to Arkansas law, it is not required to tabulate votes for unopposed candidates.
[2] Under Florida law, the names of those with no opposition are not printed on the ballot.
[3] Under Louisiana law, the names of those with no opposition are not printed on the ballot.
[4] The Independent candidate was elected with 196,118 votes.
[5] The Independent candidate was elected with 144,880 votes.
[6] The Independent candidate was elected with 186,540 votes.
[7] The Independent candidate was elected with 143,312 votes.
[8] A runoff election was held on November 21, 2000.
[9] A runoff election was held on November 19, 2002.

SESSIONS OF CONGRESS

[Closing date for this table was July 11, 2005.]

MEETING DATES OF CONGRESS: Pursuant to a resolution of the Confederation Congress in 1788, the Constitution went into effect on March 4, 1789. From then until the 20th amendment took effect in January 1934, the term of each Congress began on March 4th of each odd-numbered year; however, Article I, section 4, of the Constitution provided that "The Congress shall assemble at least once in every Year, and such Meeting shall be on the first Monday in December, unless they shall by law appoint a different day." The Congress therefore convened regularly on the first Monday in December until the 20th amendment became effective, which changed the beginning of Congress's term as well as its convening date to January 3rd. So prior to 1934, a new Congress typically would not convene for regular business until 13 months after being elected. One effect of this was that the last session of each Congress was a "lame duck" session. After the 20th amendment, the time from the election to the beginning of Congress's term as well as when it convened was reduced to two months. Recognizing that the need might exist for Congress to meet at times other than the regularly scheduled convening date, Article II, section 3 of the Constitution provides that the President "may, on extraordinary occasions, convene both Houses, or either of them"; hence these sessions occur only if convened by Presidential proclamation. Except as noted, these are separately numbered sessions of a Congress, and are marked by an E in the session column of the table. Until the 20th amendment was adopted, there were also times when special sessions of the Senate were convened, principally for confirming Cabinet and other executive nominations, and occasionally for the ratification of treaties or other executive business. These Senate sessions were also called by Presidential proclamation (typically by the outgoing President, although on occasion by incumbents as well) and are marked by an S in the session column. MEETING PLACES OF CONGRESS: Congress met for the first and second sessions of the First Congress (1789 and 1790) in New York City. From the third session of the First Congress through the first session of the Sixth Congress (1790 to 1800), Philadelphia was the meeting place. Congress has convened in Washington since the second session of the Sixth Congress (1800).

Congress	Session	Convening Date	Adjournment Date	Length in days [1]	Recesses [2] Senate	Recesses [2] House of Representatives	President pro tempore of the Senate [3]	Speaker of the House of Representatives
1st	1	Mar. 4, 1789	Sept. 29, 1789	210			John Langdon, of New Hampshire	Frederick A.C. Muhlenberg, of Pennsylvania.
	2	Jan. 4, 1790	Aug. 12, 1790	221			......do.	
	3	Dec. 6, 1790	Mar. 3, 1791	88			......do.	
2d	S	Mar. 4, 1791	Mar. 4, 1791	1			......do.	
	1	Oct. 24, 1791	May 8, 1792	197			Richard Henry Lee, of Virginia.	Jonathan Trumbull, of Connecticut.
	2	Nov. 5, 1792	Mar. 2, 1793	119			John Langdon, of New Hampshire.	
3d	S	Mar. 4, 1793	Mar. 4, 1793	1			......do.	
	1	Dec. 2, 1793	June 9, 1794	190			John Langdon, of New Hampshire; Ralph Izard, of South Carolina.	Frederick A.C. Muhlenberg, of Pennsylvania.
4th	1	Nov. 3, 1794	Mar. 3, 1795	121			Henry Tazewell, of Virginia.	Jonathan Dayton, of New Jersey.
	S	June 8, 1795	June 26, 1795	19			Henry Tazewell, of Virginia; Samuel Livermore, of New Hampshire.	
	1	Dec. 7, 1795	June 1, 1796	177			......do.	
5th	1	Dec. 5, 1796	Mar. 3, 1797	89			William Bingham, of Pennsylvania.	
	S	Mar. 4, 1797	Mar. 4, 1797	1				
	1-E	May 15, 1797	July 10, 1797	57			William Bradford, of Rhode Island	Do.
	2	July 17, 1798	July 19, 1798	3			Jacob Read, of South Carolina; Theodore Sedgwick, of Massachusetts.	
	S	Nov. 13, 1797	July 16, 1798	246			John Laurance, of New York; James Ross, of Pennsylvania.	
6th	3	Dec. 3, 1798	Mar. 3, 1799	91			Samuel Livermore, of New Hampshire.	
	1	Dec. 2, 1799	May 14, 1800	164			Uriah Tracy, of Connecticut.	Theodore Sedgwick, of Massachusetts.
	2	Nov. 17, 1800	Mar. 3, 1801	107	Dec. 23–Dec. 30, 1800	Dec. 23–Dec. 30, 1800	John E. Howard, of Maryland; James Hillhouse, of Connecticut.	
7th	S	Mar. 4, 1801	Mar. 5, 1801	2			Abraham Baldwin, of Georgia	Nathaniel Macon, of North Carolina.
	1	Dec. 7, 1801	May 3, 1802	148				

Congress	Sess.	Assembled	Adjourned	No.	Special session of the Senate	President pro tempore of the Senate	Speaker of the House of Representatives
	2	Dec. 6, 1802	Mar. 3, 1803	88		Stephen R. Bradley, of Vermont.	Do.
8th	1	Oct. 17, 1803	Mar. 27, 1804	163		John Brown, of Kentucky; Jesse Franklin, of North Carolina.	
	2	Nov. 5, 1804	Mar. 3, 1805	119		Joseph Anderson, of Tennessee.	
9th	1	Dec. 2, 1805	Apr. 21, 1806	141		Samuel Smith, of Maryland	Do.
	2	Dec. 1, 1806	Mar. 3, 1807	93		do.	
10th	1	Oct. 26, 1807	Apr. 25, 1808	182		Stephen R. Bradley, of Vermont; John Milledge, of Georgia.	Joseph B. Varnum, of Massachusetts.
	2	Nov. 7, 1808	Mar. 3, 1809	117			
11th	spec.	Mar. 4, 1809	Mar. 7, 1809	4			
	1	May 22, 1809	June 28, 1809	38		Andrew Gregg, of Pennsylvania	Do.
	2	Nov. 27, 1809	May 1, 1810	156		John Gaillard, of South Carolina.	
	3	Dec. 3, 1810	Mar. 3, 1811	91		John Pope, of Kentucky.	
12th	1	Nov. 4, 1811	July 6, 1812	245		William H. Crawford, of Georgia	Henry Clay, of Kentucky.
	2	Nov. 2, 1812	Mar. 3, 1813	122		do.	
13th	1	May 24, 1813	Aug. 2, 1813	71		Joseph B. Varnum, of Massachusetts; John Gaillard, of South Carolina.	Do.[4]
	2	Dec. 6, 1813	Apr. 18, 1814	134		John Gaillard, of South Carolina.	
	3	Sept. 19, 1814	Mar. 3, 1815	166		do.	Langdon Cheves, of South Carolina.[4]
14th	1	Dec. 4, 1815	Apr. 30, 1816	148		do.	Henry Clay, of Kentucky.
	2	Dec. 2, 1816	Mar. 3, 1817	92		do.	
15th	spec.	Mar. 4, 1817	Mar. 6, 1817	3		do.	
	1	Dec. 1, 1817	Apr. 20, 1818	141	Dec. 24–Dec. 29, 1817	do.	Do.
	2	Nov. 16, 1818	Mar. 3, 1819	108		James Barbour, of Virginia.	
16th	1	Dec. 6, 1819	May 15, 1820	162		James Barbour, of Virginia; John Gaillard, of South Carolina.	Do.[5]
	2	Nov. 13, 1820	Mar. 3, 1821	111		John Gaillard, of South Carolina	John W. Taylor, of New York.[5]
17th	1	Dec. 3, 1821	May 8, 1822	157		do.	Philip P. Barbour, of Virginia.
	2	Dec. 2, 1822	Mar. 3, 1823	92		do.	
18th	1	Dec. 1, 1823	May 27, 1824	178		do.	Henry Clay, of Kentucky.
	2	Dec. 6, 1824	Mar. 3, 1825	88		do.	
19th	spec.	Mar. 4, 1825	Mar. 9, 1825	6			
	1	Dec. 5, 1825	May 22, 1826	169		Nathaniel Macon, of North Carolina	John W. Taylor, of New York.
	2	Dec. 4, 1826	Mar. 3, 1827	90		do.	
20th	1	Dec. 3, 1827	May 26, 1828	175		Samuel Smith, of Maryland	Andrew Stevenson, of Virginia.
	2	Dec. 1, 1828	Mar. 3, 1829	93	Dec. 24–Dec. 29, 1828	do.	
21st	spec.	Mar. 4, 1829	Mar. 17, 1829	14			
	1	Dec. 7, 1829	May 31, 1830	176		do.	Do.
	2	Dec. 6, 1830	Mar. 3, 1831	88		do.	
22d	1	Dec. 5, 1831	July 16, 1832	225		Littleton Waller Tazewell, of Virginia	Do.
	2	Dec. 3, 1832	Mar. 2, 1833	91		Hugh Lawson White, of Tennessee.	
23d	1	Dec. 2, 1833	June 30, 1834	211		Hugh Lawson White, of Tennessee; George Poindexter, of Mississippi.	Do.[6]
	2	Dec. 1, 1834	Mar. 3, 1835	93		John Tyler, of Virginia	John Bell, of Tennessee.[6]
24th	1	Dec. 7, 1835	July 4, 1836	211		William R. King, of Alabama	James K. Polk, of Tennessee.
	2	Dec. 5, 1836	Mar. 3, 1837	89		do.	
25th	spec.	Mar. 4, 1837	Mar. 10, 1837	7			
	1	Sept. 4, 1837	Oct. 16, 1837	43		do.	Do.
	2	Dec. 4, 1837	July 9, 1838	218		do.	
	3	Dec. 3, 1838	Mar. 3, 1839	91		do.	
26th	1	Dec. 2, 1839	July 21, 1840	233		do.	Robert M.T. Hunter, of Virginia.
	2	Dec. 7, 1840	Mar. 3, 1841	87		do.	
27th	spec.	Mar. 4, 1841	Mar. 15, 1841	12		William R. King, of Alabama; Samuel L. Southard, of New Jersey.	

SESSIONS OF CONGRESS—CONTINUED

[Closing date for this table was July 11, 2005.]

MEETING DATES OF CONGRESS: Pursuant to a resolution of the Confederation Congress in 1788, the Constitution went into effect on March 4, 1789. From then until the 20th amendment took effect in January 1934, the term of each Congress began on March 4th of each odd-numbered year; however, Article I, section 4, of the Constitution provided that ''The Congress shall assemble at least once in every Year, and such Meeting shall be on the first Monday in December, unless they shall by law appoint a different day.'' The Congress therefore convened regularly on the first Monday in December until the 20th amendment became effective, which changed the beginning of Congress's term as well as its convening date to January 3rd. So prior to 1934, a new Congress typically would not convene for regular business until 13 months after being elected. One effect of this was that the last session of each Congress was a ''lame duck'' session. After the 20th amendment, the time from the election to the beginning of Congress's term as well as when it convened was reduced to two months. Recognizing that the need might exist for Congress to meet at times other than the regularly scheduled convening date, Article II, section 3 of the Constitution provides that the President ''may, on extraordinary occasions, convene both Houses, or either of them''; hence these sessions occur only if convened by Presidential proclamation. Except as noted, these are separately numbered sessions of a Congress, and are marked by an E in the session column of the table. Until the 20th amendment was adopted, there were also times when special sessions of the Senate were convened, principally for confirming Cabinet and other executive nominations, and occasionally for the ratification of treaties or other executive business. These Senate sessions were also called by Presidential proclamation (typically by the outgoing President, although on occasion by incumbents as well) and are marked by an S in the session column. MEETING PLACES OF CONGRESS: Congress met for the first and second sessions of the First Congress (1789 and 1790) in New York City. From the third session of the First Congress through the first session of the Sixth Congress (1790 to 1800), Philadelphia was the meeting place. Congress has convened in Washington since the second session of the Sixth Congress (1800).

Congress	Session	Convening Date	Adjournment Date	Length in days [1]	Recesses [2]		President pro tempore of the Senate [3]	Speaker of the House of Representatives
					Senate	House		
	1–E	May 31, 1841	Sept. 13, 1841	106			Samuel L. Southard, of New Jersey	John White, of Kentucky.
	2	Dec. 6, 1841	Aug. 31, 1842	269			Willie P. Mangum, of North Carolina.	
	3	Dec. 5, 1842	Mar. 3, 1843	89			....do.	
28th	1	Dec. 4, 1843	June 17, 1844	196			....do.	John W. Jones, of Virginia.
	2	Dec. 2, 1844	Mar. 3, 1845	92			....do.	
29th	S	Mar. 4, 1845	Mar. 20, 1845	17				
	1	Dec. 1, 1845	Aug. 10, 1846	253			Ambrose H. Sevier; David R. Atchison, of Missouri.	John W. Davis, of Indiana.
	2	Dec. 7, 1846	Mar. 3, 1847	87			David R. Atchison, of Missouri.	
30th	1	Dec. 6, 1847	Aug. 14, 1848	254			....do.	Robert C. Winthrop, of Massachusetts.
	2	Dec. 4, 1848	Mar. 3, 1849	90			....do.	
31st	S	Mar. 5, 1849	Mar. 23, 1849	19			William R. King, of Alabama	
	1	Dec. 3, 1849	Sept. 30, 1850	302			....do.	Howell Cobb, of Georgia.
	2	Dec. 2, 1850	Mar. 3, 1851	92			....do.	
32d	S	Mar. 4, 1851	Mar. 13, 1851	10			David R. Atchison, of Missouri.	
	1	Dec. 1, 1851	Aug. 31, 1852	275			....do.	Linn Boyd, of Kentucky.
	2	Dec. 6, 1852	Mar. 3, 1853	88				
33d	S	Mar. 4, 1853	Apr. 11, 1853	39			Lewis Cass, of Michigan; Jesse D. Bright, of Indiana.	
	1	Dec. 5, 1853	Aug. 7, 1854	246			Charles E. Stuart, of Michigan; Jesse D. Bright, of Indiana.	Do.
	2	Dec. 4, 1854	Mar. 3, 1855	90			Jesse D. Bright, of Indiana.	
34th	1	Dec. 3, 1855	Aug. 18, 1856	260			James M. Mason, of Virginia.	Nathaniel P. Banks, of Massachusetts.
	2–E	Aug. 21, 1856	Aug. 30, 1856	10			James M. Mason, of Virginia; Thomas J. Rusk, of Texas.	
	3	Dec. 1, 1856	Mar. 3, 1857	93				
35th	S	Mar. 4, 1857	Mar. 14, 1857	11				
	1	Dec. 7, 1857	June 14, 1858	189	Dec. 23, 1857–Jan. 4, 1858	Dec. 23, 1857–Jan. 4, 1858	Benjamin Fitzpatrick, of Alabama	James L. Orr, of South Carolina.

Congress	Sess.	Date of assembling	Days	Period	Period	President of the Senate	President pro tempore of the Senate	Speaker of the House of Representatives
36th	s	June 15, 1858	2		Dec. 23, 1858–Jan. 4, 1859	do.	Benjamin Fitzpatrick, of Alabama; Jesse D. Bright, of Indiana.	William Pennington, of New Jersey.
	2	Dec. 6, 1858	88	Dec. 23, 1858–Jan. 4, 1859		do.	Benjamin Fitzpatrick, of Alabama.	
	1	Mar. 4, 1859	7			do.	Solomon Foot, of Vermont.	
37th	s	June 26, 1860	202					Galusha A. Grow, of Pennsylvania.
	2	Dec. 3, 1860	3			do.		
	1-E	Mar. 4, 1861	93			do.		
	3	July 4, 1861	25					
	1	Dec. 2, 1861	34					
38th	2	Mar. 4, 1863	228	Dec. 23, 1862–Jan. 5, 1863	Dec. 23, 1862–Jan. 5, 1863	do.	Solomon Foot, of Vermont; Daniel Clark, of New Hampshire.	Schuyler Colfax, of Indiana.
	s	Dec. 1, 1862	93	Dec. 23, 1863–Jan. 5, 1864	Dec. 23, 1863–Jan. 5, 1864	do.	Daniel Clark, of New Hampshire.	
39th	2	Mar. 4, 1863	11	Dec. 22, 1864–Jan. 5, 1865	Dec. 22, 1864–Jan. 5, 1865	do.	Lafayette S. Foster, of Connecticut.	Do.
	s	Dec. 7, 1863	209	6–Dec. 11, 1865	6–Dec. 11, 1865	do.		
	1	Mar. 3, 1865	89	Dec. 21, 1865–Jan. 5, 1866	Dec. 21, 1865–Jan. 5, 1866			
40th	2	Mar. 11, 1865	8	Dec. 20, 1866–Jan. 3, 1867	Dec. 20, 1866–Jan. 3, 1867	do.	Benjamin F. Wade, of Ohio.	Do.[7]
	1	July 28, 1866	237	Mar. 30–July 3, 1867	Mar. 30–July 3, 1867	do.		
		Dec. 3, 1866	91	July 20–Nov. 21, 1867	July 20–Nov. 21, 1867			
	2	Mar. 4, 1867	273	Dec. 20, 1867–Jan. 6, 1868	Dec. 20, 1867–Jan. 6, 1868			
	1	Apr. 1, 1867	20	July 27–Sept. 21, 1868	July 27–Sept. 21, 1868			
		Nov. 10, 1868	345	Sept. 21–Oct. 16, 1868	Sept. 21–Oct. 16, 1868			
41st	s	Mar. 3, 1869	87	Dec. 21, 1868–Jan. 5, 1869	Dec. 21, 1868–Jan. 5, 1869	do.	Henry B. Anthony, of Rhode Island.	Theodore M. Pomeroy, of New York.[7]
	3	Apr. 10, 1869	38			do.		James G. Blaine, of Maine.
	1	Apr. 22, 1869	11			do.		
42d	s	July 15, 1870	222	Dec. 22, 1869–Jan. 10, 1870	Dec. 22, 1869–Jan. 10, 1870	do.		Do.
	2	Mar. 3, 1871	89	Dec. 23, 1870–Jan. 4, 1871	Dec. 23, 1870–Jan. 4, 1871	do.		
	3	Apr. 20, 1871	48					
43d	1	May 10, 1871	18					Do.
	s	June 10, 1872	190	Dec. 21, 1871–Jan. 8, 1872	Dec. 21, 1871–Jan. 8, 1872	do.	Matthew H. Carpenter, of Wisconsin.	
	3	Mar. 3, 1873	92	Dec. 20, 1872–Jan. 6, 1873	Dec. 20, 1872–Jan. 6, 1873	do.		
	1	Mar. 26, 1873	23					
44th	2	June 23, 1874	204	Dec. 19, 1873–Jan. 5, 1874	Dec. 19, 1873–Jan. 5, 1874	do.	Matthew H. Carpenter, of Wisconsin; Henry B. Anthony, of Rhode Island.	Michael C. Kerr, of Indiana.[8]
	s	Mar. 3, 1875	87	Dec. 23, 1874–Jan. 5, 1875	Dec. 23, 1874–Jan. 5, 1875	do.		Samuel J. Randall, of Pennsylvania.[8]
45th	1	Mar. 5, 1875	20				Thomas W. Ferry, of Michigan.	
	2	Aug. 15, 1876	254	Dec. 21, 1875–Jan. 5, 1876	Dec. 21, 1875–Jan. 5, 1876	do.		Do.
	3	Mar. 3, 1877	90			do.		
	1-E	Mar. 17, 1877	13			do.		
46th	2	Oct. 15, 1877	50					Do.
	3	Dec. 3, 1877	200	Dec. 15, 1877–Jan. 10, 1878	Dec. 15, 1877–Jan. 10, 1878	do.	Allen G. Thurman, of Ohio.	
	1-E	Mar. 3, 1878	92	Dec. 20, 1878–Jan. 7, 1879	Dec. 20, 1878–Jan. 7, 1879	do.		
	2	Mar. 18, 1879	106					
	3	July 1, 1879	199	Dec. 19, 1879–Jan. 6, 1880	Dec. 19, 1879–Jan. 6, 1880	do.		
47th	s	June 1, 1880	88	Dec. 23, 1880–Jan. 5, 1881	Dec. 23, 1880–Jan. 5, 1881	do.	Thomas F. Bayard, of Delaware; David Davis, of Illinois.	J. Warren Keifer, of Ohio.
		Mar. 3, 1881	78			do.	David Davis, of Illinois.	
		May 20, 1881	20					
		Oct. 10, 1881						
	1	Dec. 5, 1881	247	Dec. 22, 1881–Jan. 5, 1882	Dec. 22, 1881–Jan. 5, 1882			

SESSIONS OF CONGRESS—CONTINUED

[Closing date for this table was July 11, 2005.]

MEETING DATES OF CONGRESS: Pursuant to a resolution of the Confederation Congress in 1788, the Constitution went into effect on March 4, 1789. From then until the 20th amendment took effect in January 1934, the term of each Congress began on March 4th of each odd-numbered year; however, Article I, section 4, of the Constitution provided that "The Congress shall assemble at least once in every Year, and such Meeting shall be on the first Monday in December, unless they shall by law appoint a different day." The Congress therefore convened regularly on the first Monday in December until the 20th amendment became effective, which changed the beginning of Congress's term as well as its convening date to January 3rd. So prior to 1934, a new Congress typically would not convene for regular business until 13 months after being elected. One effect of this was that the last session of each Congress was a "lame duck" session. After the 20th amendment, the time from the election to the beginning of Congress's term is reduced to two months. Recognizing that the need might not exist for Congress to meet at times other than the regularly scheduled convening date, Article II, section 3 of the Constitution provides that the President "may, on extraordinary occasions, convene both Houses, or either of them"; hence these sessions occur only if convened by Presidential proclamation. Except as noted, these are separately numbered sessions of a Congress, and are marked by an E in the session column of the table. Until the 20th amendment was adopted, there were also times when special sessions of the Senate were convened, principally for confirming Cabinet and other executive nominations, and occasionally for the ratification of treaties or other executive business. These Senate sessions were also called by Presidential proclamation (typically by the outgoing President, although on occasion by incumbents as well) and are marked by an S in the session column. MEETING PLACES OF CONGRESS: Congress met for the first and second sessions of the First Congress (1789 and 1790) in New York City. From the third session of the First Congress through the first session of the Sixth Congress (1790 to 1800), Philadelphia was the meeting place. Congress has convened in Washington since the second session of the Sixth Congress (1800).

Congress	Session	Convening Date	Adjournment Date	Length in days [1]	Recesses [2] Senate	Recesses [2] House of Representatives	President pro tempore of the Senate [3]	Speaker of the House of Representatives
48th	2	Dec. 4, 1882	Mar. 3, 1883	90			George F. Edmunds, of Vermont.	J. Warren Keifer, of Ohio.
	1	Dec. 3, 1883	July 7, 1884	218	Dec. 24, 1883–Jan. 7, 1884	Dec. 24, 1883–Jan. 7, 1884	do.	John G. Carlisle, of Kentucky.
	2	Dec. 1, 1884	Mar. 3, 1885	93	Dec. 24, 1884–Jan. 5, 1885	Dec. 24, 1884–Jan. 5, 1885	do.	
49th	S	Mar. 4, 1885	Apr. 2, 1885	30			John Sherman, of Ohio.	
	1	Dec. 7, 1885	Aug. 5, 1886	242	Dec. 21, 1885–Jan. 5, 1886	Dec. 21, 1885–Jan. 5, 1886	John J. Ingalls, of Kansas.	Do.
	2	Dec. 6, 1886	Mar. 3, 1887	88	Dec. 22, 1886–Jan. 4, 1887	Dec. 22, 1886–Jan. 4, 1887	do.	
50th	1	Dec. 5, 1887	Oct. 20, 1888	321	Dec. 22, 1887–Jan. 4, 1888	Dec. 22, 1887–Jan. 4, 1888	do.	Do.
	2	Dec. 3, 1888	Mar. 3, 1889	91	Dec. 21, 1888–Jan. 2, 1889	Dec. 21, 1888–Jan. 2, 1889	do.	
51st	S	Mar. 4, 1889	Apr. 2, 1889	30			Charles F. Manderson, of Nebraska.	
	1	Dec. 2, 1889	Oct. 1, 1890	304	Dec. 21, 1889–Jan. 6, 1890	Dec. 21, 1889–Jan. 6, 1890	do.	Thomas B. Reed, of Maine.
	2	Dec. 1, 1890	Mar. 3, 1891	93				
52d	1	Dec. 7, 1891	Aug. 5, 1892	251			Charles F. Manderson, of Nebraska; Isham G. Harris, of Tennessee.	Charles F. Crisp, of Georgia.
	2	Dec. 5, 1892	Mar. 3, 1893	89	Dec. 22, 1892–Jan. 4, 1893	Dec. 22, 1892–Jan. 4, 1893	Isham G. Harris, of Tennessee.	
53d	S	Mar. 4, 1893	Apr. 15, 1893	43				
	1-E	Aug. 7, 1893	Nov. 3, 1893	89				
	2	Dec. 4, 1893	Aug. 28, 1894	268		Dec. 21, 1893–Jan. 3, 1894	Matt W. Ransom, of North Carolina; Isham G. Harris, of Tennessee.	Do.
	3	Dec. 3, 1894	Mar. 3, 1895	97		Dec. 23, 1894–Jan. 3, 1895		
54th	1	Dec. 2, 1895	June 11, 1896	193			William P. Frye, of Maine.	Thomas B. Reed, of Maine.
	2	Dec. 7, 1896	Mar. 3, 1897	87	Dec. 22, 1896–Jan. 5, 1897	Dec. 22, 1896–Jan. 5, 1897	do.	
55th	S	Mar. 4, 1897	Mar. 10, 1897	11			do.	
	1-E	Mar. 15, 1897	July 24, 1897	131			do.	
	2	Dec. 6, 1897	July 8, 1898	215	Dec. 18, 1897–Jan. 5, 1898	Dec. 18, 1897–Jan. 5, 1898	do.	Do.
	3	Dec. 5, 1898	Mar. 3, 1899	89	Dec. 21, 1898–Jan. 4, 1899	Dec. 21, 1898–Jan. 4, 1899	do.	
56th	1	Dec. 4, 1899	June 7, 1900	186	Dec. 20, 1899–Jan. 3, 1900	Dec. 20, 1899–Jan. 3, 1900	do.	David B. Henderson, of Iowa.
	2	Dec. 3, 1900	Mar. 3, 1901	91	Dec. 20, 1900–Jan. 3, 1901	Dec. 21, 1900–Jan. 3, 1901	do.	
57th	S	Mar. 4, 1901	Mar. 9, 1901	6			do.	

Congress	Session	Date of beginning	Date of adjournment	Length in days	Recess	Recess	President pro tempore of the Senate	Speaker of the House of Representatives
57th	1	Dec. 2, 1901	July 1, 1902	212	Dec. 19, 1901–Jan. 6, 1902	Dec. 19, 1901–Jan. 6, 1902	do.	Do.
	2	Dec. 1, 1902	Mar. 3, 1903	93	Dec. 20, 1902–Jan. 5, 1903	Dec. 20, 1902–Jan. 5, 1903	do.	
	S	Mar. 5, 1903	Mar. 19, 1903	15			do.	
58th	1-E	Nov. 9, 1903	Dec. 7, 1903	29			do.	Joseph G. Cannon, of Illinois.
	1	Dec. 7, 1903	Apr. 28, 1904	144	Dec. 19, 1903–Jan. 4, 1904	Dec. 19, 1903–Jan. 4, 1904	do.	
	2	Dec. 5, 1904	Mar. 3, 1905	89	Dec. 21, 1904–Jan. 4, 1905	Dec. 21, 1904–Jan. 4, 1905	do.	
59th	S	Mar. 4, 1905	Mar. 18, 1905	15			do.	Do.
	1	Dec. 4, 1905	June 30, 1906	209	Dec. 21, 1905–Jan. 4, 1906	Dec. 21, 1905–Jan. 4, 1906	do.	
	2	Dec. 3, 1906	Mar. 3, 1907	91	Dec. 20, 1906–Jan. 3, 1907	Dec. 20, 1906–Jan. 3, 1907	do.	
60th	1	Dec. 2, 1907	May 30, 1908	181	Dec. 21, 1907–Jan. 6, 1908	Dec. 21, 1907–Jan. 6, 1908	do.	Do.
	2	Dec. 7, 1908	Mar. 3, 1909	87	Dec. 19, 1908–Jan. 4, 1909	Dec. 19, 1908–Jan. 4, 1909	do.	
61st	S	Mar. 4, 1909	Mar. 6, 1909	3			do.	Do.
	1-E	Mar. 15, 1909	Aug. 5, 1909	144			do.	
	2	Dec. 6, 1909	June 25, 1910	202	Dec. 21, 1909–Jan. 4, 1910	Dec. 21, 1909–Jan. 4, 1910	do.	
	3	Dec. 5, 1910	Mar. 3, 1911	89	Dec. 21, 1910–Jan. 5, 1911	Dec. 21, 1910–Jan. 5, 1911	do.	
62d	1-E	Apr. 4, 1911	Aug. 22, 1911	141			do.[9]	Champ Clark, of Missouri.
	2	Dec. 4, 1911	Aug. 26, 1912	267	Dec. 21, 1911–Jan. 3, 1912	Dec. 21, 1911–Jan. 3, 1912	Charles Curtis, of Kansas; Augustus O. Bacon, of Georgia; Jacob H. Gallinger, of New Hampshire; Henry Cabot Lodge, of Massachusetts; Frank B. Brandegee, of Connecticut.	
	3	Dec. 2, 1912	Mar. 3, 1913	92	Dec. 19, 1912–Jan. 2, 1913	Dec. 19, 1912–Jan. 2, 1913		
63d	S	Mar. 4, 1913	Mar. 17, 1913	14			Augustus O. Bacon, of Georgia; Jacob H. Gallinger, of New Hampshire.	Do.
	1-E	Apr. 7, 1913	Dec. 1, 1913	239			do.	
	2	Dec. 1, 1913	Oct. 24, 1914	328	Dec. 23, 1913–Jan. 12, 1914	Dec. 23, 1913–Jan. 12, 1914	do.	
	3	Dec. 7, 1914	Mar. 3, 1915	87	Dec. 23–Dec. 28, 1914	Dec. 23–Dec. 28, 1914	do.	
64th	1	Dec. 6, 1915	Sept. 8, 1916	278	Dec. 17, 1915–Jan. 4, 1916	Dec. 17, 1915–Jan. 4, 1916	James P. Clarke, of Arkansas.	Do.
	2	Dec. 4, 1916	Mar. 3, 1917	90	Dec. 22, 1916–Jan. 2, 1917	Dec. 22, 1916–Jan. 2, 1917	do.	
65th	S	Mar. 5, 1917	Mar. 16, 1917	12			do.[10]	Do.
	1-E	Apr. 2, 1917	Oct. 6, 1917	188			Willard Saulsbury, of Delaware[10]	
	2	Dec. 3, 1917	Nov. 21, 1918	354	Dec. 18, 1917–Jan. 3, 1918	Dec. 18, 1917–Jan. 3, 1918	do.	
	3	Dec. 2, 1918	Mar. 3, 1919	92			do.	
66th	1-E	May 19, 1919	Nov. 19, 1919	185	July 1–July 8, 1919	July 1–July 8, 1919	Albert B. Cummins, of Iowa	Frederick H. Gillett, of Massachusetts.
	2	Dec. 1, 1919	June 5, 1920	188	Dec. 20, 1919–Jan. 5, 1920	Dec. 20, 1919–Jan. 5, 1920	do.	
	3	Dec. 6, 1920	Mar. 3, 1921	88			do.	
67th	S	Mar. 4, 1921	Mar. 15, 1921	12			do.	Do.
	1-E	Apr. 11, 1921	Nov. 23, 1921	227	Aug. 24–Sept. 21, 1921	Aug. 24–Sept. 21, 1921	do.	
	2	Dec. 5, 1921	Sept. 22, 1922	292	Dec. 22, 1921–Jan. 3, 1922	Dec. 22, 1921–Jan. 3, 1922	do.	
	3-E	Nov. 20, 1922	Dec. 4, 1922	15			do.	
	4	Dec. 4, 1922	Mar. 4, 1923	90			do.	
68th	1	Dec. 3, 1923	June 7, 1924	188	Dec. 20, 1923–Jan. 3, 1924	Dec. 20, 1923–Jan. 3, 1924	do.	Do.
	2	Dec. 1, 1924	Mar. 3, 1925	93	Dec. 20–Dec. 29, 1924	Dec. 20–Dec. 29, 1924	do.	
69th	S	Mar. 4, 1925	Mar. 18, 1925	15			Albert B. Cummins, of Iowa; George H. Moses, of New Hampshire.	Nicholas Longworth, of Ohio.
	1	Dec. 7, 1925	July 3, 1926	209	Dec. 22, 1925–Jan. 4, 1926	Dec. 22, 1925–Jan. 4, 1926	do.	
	2	Dec. 6, 1926	Mar. 4, 1927	88	Dec. 22, 1926–Jan. 3, 1927	Dec. 22, 1926–Jan. 3, 1927	do.	
70th	1	Dec. 5, 1927	May 29, 1928	177	Dec. 21, 1927–Jan. 4, 1928	Dec. 21, 1927–Jan. 4, 1928	do.	Do.
	2	Dec. 3, 1928	Mar. 4, 1929	91	Dec. 22, 1928–Jan. 3, 1929	Dec. 22, 1928–Jan. 3, 1929	do.	
71st	S	Mar. 4, 1929	Mar. 5, 1929	2			do.	Do.
	1-E	Apr. 15, 1929	Nov. 22, 1929	222	June 19–Sept. 23, 1929	June 19–Sept. 23, 1929	do.	
	2	Dec. 2, 1929	July 3, 1930	214	Dec. 21, 1929–Jan. 6, 1930	Dec. 21, 1929–Jan. 6, 1930	do.	
	S	July 7, 1930	July 21, 1930	15			do.	

SESSIONS OF CONGRESS—CONTINUED

[Closing date for this table was July 11, 2005.]

MEETING DATES OF CONGRESS: Pursuant to a resolution of the Confederation Congress in 1788, the term of each Congress began on March 4th of each odd-numbered year; however, Article I, section 4, of the Constitution provided that "The Congress shall assemble at least once in every Year, and such Meeting shall be on the first Monday in December, unless they shall by law appoint a different day." The Congress therefore convened regularly on the first Monday in December until the 20th amendment became effective, which changed the beginning of Congress's term as well as its convening date to January 3rd. So prior to 1934, a new Congress typically would not convene for regular business until 13 months after being elected. One effect of this was that the last session of each Congress was a "lame duck" session. After the 20th amendment, the time from the election to the beginning of Congress's term as well as when it convened was reduced to two months. Recognizing that the need might exist for Congress to meet at times other than the regularly scheduled convening date, Article II, section 3 of the Constitution provides that the President "may, on extraordinary occasions, convene both Houses, or either of them"; hence these sessions occur only if convened by Presidential proclamation. Except as noted, these are separately numbered sessions of a Congress, and are marked by an E in the session column of the table. Until the 20th amendment was adopted, there were also times when special sessions of the Senate were convened, principally for confirming Cabinet and other executive nominations, and occasionally for the ratification of treaties or other executive business. These Senate sessions were also called by Presidential proclamation (typically by the outgoing President, although on occasion by incumbents as well) and are marked by an S in the session column. MEETING PLACES OF CONGRESS: Congress met for the first and second sessions of the First Congress (1789 and 1790) in New York City. From the third session of the First Congress through the first session of the Sixth Congress (1790 to 1800), Philadelphia was the meeting place. Congress has convened in Washington since the second session of the Sixth Congress (1800).

Congress	Session	Convening Date	Adjournment Date	Length in days [1]	Recesses [2]		President pro tempore of the Senate [3]	Speaker of the House of Representatives
					Senate	House of Representatives		
72d	3	Dec. 1, 1930	Mar. 3, 1931	93	Dec. 20, 1930–Jan. 5, 1931	Dec. 20, 1930–Jan. 5, 1931	George H. Moses, of New Hampshire	Nicholas Longworth, of Ohio.
	1	Dec. 7, 1931	July 16, 1932	223	Dec. 22, 1931–Jan. 4, 1932	Dec. 22, 1931–Jan. 4, 1932	do.	John N. Garner, of Texas.
	2	Dec. 5, 1932	Mar. 3, 1933	89			do.	
73d	S	Mar. 4, 1933	Mar. 6, 1933	3			Key Pittman, of Nevada	
	1-E	Mar. 9, 1933	June 15, 1933	99			do.	Henry T. Rainey, of Illinois.
	2	Jan. 3, 1934	June 18, 1934	167			do.	
74th	1	Jan. 3, 1935	Aug. 26, 1935	236			do.	Joseph W. Byrns, of Tennessee.[11]
	2	Jan. 3, 1936	June 20, 1936	170	June 8–June 15, 1936	June 8–June 15, 1936	do.	William B. Bankhead, of Alabama.[11]
75th	1	Jan. 5, 1937	Aug. 21, 1937	229			do.	Do.
	2-E	Nov. 15, 1937	Dec. 21, 1937	37			do.	
	3	Jan. 3, 1938	June 16, 1938	165			do.	
76th	1	Jan. 3, 1939	Aug. 5, 1939	215			do.	Do.[12]
	2-E	Sept. 21, 1939	Nov. 3, 1939	44			do.	
	3	Jan. 3, 1940	Jan. 3, 1941	366	July 11–July 22, 1940	July 11–July 22, 1940	Key Pittman, of Nevada;[13] William H. King, of Utah.[13]	Sam Rayburn, of Texas.[12]
77th	1	Jan. 3, 1941	Jan. 2, 1942	365			Pat Harrison, of Mississippi;[14] Carter Glass, of Virginia.[14]	Do.
	2	Jan. 5, 1942	Dec. 16, 1942	346			Carter Glass, of Virginia.	
78th	1	Jan. 6, 1943	Dec. 21, 1943	350	July 8–Sept. 14, 1943	July 8–Sept. 14, 1943	do.	Do.
	2	Jan. 10, 1944	Dec. 19, 1944	345	Apr. 1–Apr. 12, 1944	Apr. 1–Apr. 12, 1944	do.	
					June 23–Aug. 1, 1944	June 23–Aug. 1, 1944		
					Sept. 21–Nov. 14, 1944	Sept. 21–Nov. 14, 1944		
79th	1	Jan. 3, 1945	Dec. 21, 1945	353	Aug. 1–Sept. 5, 1945	Aug. 1–Sept. 5, 1945	Kenneth McKellar, of Tennessee	Do.
	2	Jan. 14, 1946	Aug. 2, 1946	201		Apr. 18–Apr. 30, 1946		
80th	1 [15]	Jan. 3, 1947	Dec. 19, 1947	351	July 27–Nov. 17, 1947	July 27–Nov. 17, 1947	Arthur H. Vandenberg, of Michigan	Joseph W. Martin, Jr., of Massachusetts.
	2 [15]	Jan. 6, 1948	Dec. 31, 1948	361	June 20–July 26, 1948	June 20–July 26, 1948	do.	
					Aug. 7–Dec. 31, 1948	Aug. 7–Dec. 31, 1948		

Congress	Session	Date of beginning	Date of adjournment	Length in days			President pro tempore of the Senate	Speaker of the House of Representatives
81st	1	Jan. 3, 1949	Oct. 19, 1949	290		Apr. 6-Apr. 18, 1950	Kenneth McKellar, of Tennessee	Sam Rayburn, of Texas.
	2	Jan. 3, 1950	Jan. 2, 1951	365	Sept. 23-Nov. 27-1950	Sept. 23-Nov. 27, 1950	.....do	Do.
82d	1	Jan. 3, 1951	Oct. 20, 1951	291		Aug. 23-Sept. 12, 1951	.....do	
	2	Jan. 8, 1952	July 7, 1952	182			.....do	
83d	1	Jan. 3, 1953	Aug. 3, 1953	213		Apr. 2-Apr. 13, 1953	Styles Bridges, of New Hampshire	Joseph W. Martin, Jr., of Massachusetts.
	2	Jan. 6, 1954	Dec. 2, 1954	331	Aug. 20-Nov. 8, 1954 Nov. 18-Nov. 29, 1954	Apr. 15-Apr. 22, 1954 Adjourned sine die Aug. 20, 1954	.....do	
84th	1	Jan. 5, 1955	Aug. 2, 1955	210	Apr. 4-Apr. 13, 1955	Apr. 4-Apr. 13, 1955	Walter F. George, of Georgia	Sam Rayburn, of Texas.
	2	Jan. 3, 1956	July 27, 1956	207	Mar. 29-Apr. 9, 1956	Mar. 29-Apr. 9, 1956	.....do	
85th	1	Jan. 3, 1957	Aug. 30, 1957	239	Apr. 18-Apr. 29, 1957	Apr. 18-Apr. 29, 1957	Carl Hayden, of Arizona	Do.
	2	Jan. 7, 1958	Aug. 24, 1958	230	Apr. 3-Apr. 14, 1958	Apr. 3-Apr. 14, 1958	.....do.	
86th	1	Jan. 7, 1959	Sept. 15, 1959	252	Mar. 26-Apr. 7, 1959	Mar. 26-Apr. 7, 1959	.....do.	Do.
	2	Jan. 6, 1960	Sept. 1, 1960	240	Apr. 14-Apr. 18, 1960 May 27-May 31, 1960 July 3-Aug. 8, 1960	Apr. 14-Apr. 18, 1960 May 27-May 31, 1960 July 3-Aug. 15, 1960	.....do	
87th	1	Jan. 3, 1961	Sept. 27, 1961	268		Mar. 30-Apr. 10, 1961	.....do.	Do.[16] John W. McCormack, of Massachusetts.[16]
	2	Jan. 10, 1962	Oct. 13, 1962	277		Apr. 19-Apr. 30, 1962	.....do.	
88th	1	Jan. 9, 1963	Dec. 30, 1963	356		Apr. 11-Apr. 22, 1963	.....do.	Do.
	2	Jan. 7, 1964	Oct. 3, 1964	270	July 10-July 20, 1964 Aug. 21-Aug. 31, 1964	Mar. 26-Apr. 6, 1964 July 2-July 20, 1964 Aug. 21-Aug. 31, 1964	.....do.	
89th	1	Jan. 4, 1965	Oct. 23, 1965	293			.....do.	Do.
	2	Jan. 10, 1966	Oct. 22, 1966	286	Apr. 7-Apr. 13, 1966 June 30-July 11, 1966	Apr. 7-Apr. 18, 1966 June 30-July 11, 1966	.....do.	
90th	1	Jan. 10, 1967	Dec. 15, 1967	340	Mar. 23-Apr. 3, 1967 June 29-July 10, 1967 Aug. 31-Sept. 11, 1967 Nov. 22-Nov. 27, 1967	Mar. 23-Apr. 3, 1967 June 29-July 10, 1967 Aug. 31-Sept. 11, 1967 Nov. 22-Nov. 27, 1967	.....do.	Do.
	2	Jan. 15, 1968	Oct. 14, 1968	274	Apr. 11-Apr. 17, 1968 May 29-June 3, 1968 June 3-July 8, 1968 Aug. 2-Sept. 4, 1968	Apr. 11-Apr. 22, 1968 May 29-June 3, 1968 June 3-July 8, 1968 Aug. 2-Sept. 4, 1968	.....do.	
91st	1	Jan. 3, 1969	Dec. 23, 1969	355	Feb. 7-Feb. 17, 1969 Apr. 3-Apr. 14, 1969 July 2-July 7, 1969 Aug. 13-Sept. 3, 1969 Nov. 26-Dec. 1, 1969	Feb. 7-Feb. 17, 1969 Apr. 3-Apr. 14, 1969 May 28-June 2, 1969 July 2-July 7, 1969 Aug. 13-Sept. 3, 1969 Nov. 6-Nov. 12, 1969 Nov. 26-Dec. 1, 1969	Richard B. Russell, of Georgia	Do.
	2	Jan. 19, 1970	Jan. 2, 1971	349	Feb. 10-Feb. 16, 1970 Mar. 26-Mar. 31, 1970 Sept. 2-Sept. 8, 1970 Oct. 14-Nov. 16, 1970 Nov. 25-Nov. 30, 1970 Dec. 22-Dec. 28, 1970	Feb. 10-Feb. 16, 1970 Mar. 26-Mar. 31, 1970 May 27-June 1, 1970 July 1-July 6, 1970 Aug. 14-Sept. 9, 1970 Oct. 14-Nov. 16, 1970 Nov. 25-Nov. 30, 1970 Dec. 22-Dec. 29, 1970	.....do.	

SESSIONS OF CONGRESS—CONTINUED

[Closing date for this table was July 11, 2005.]

MEETING DATES OF CONGRESS: Pursuant to a resolution of the Confederation Congress in 1788, the Constitution went into effect on March 4, 1789. From then until the 20th amendment took effect in January 1934, the term of each Congress began on March 4th of each odd-numbered year, however, Article I, section 4, of the Constitution provided that "The Congress shall assemble at least once in every Year, and such Meeting shall be on the first Monday in December, unless they shall by law appoint a different day." The Congress therefore convened regularly on the first Monday in December until the 20th amendment became effective, which changed the beginning of Congress's term as well as its convening date to January 3rd. So prior to 1934, a new Congress typically would not convene for regular business until 13 months after being elected. One effect of this was that the last session of each Congress was a "lame duck" session. After the 20th amendment, the time from the election to the beginning of Congress's term as well as when it convened was reduced to two months. Recognizing that the need might exist for Congress to meet at times other than the regularly scheduled convening date, Article II, section 3 of the Constitution provides that the President "may, on extraordinary occasions, convene both Houses, or either of them"; hence these sessions occur only if convened by Presidential proclamation. Except as noted, these are separately numbered sessions of a Congress, and are marked by an E in the session column of the table. Until the 20th amendment was adopted, there were also times when special sessions of the Senate were convened, principally for confirming Cabinet and other executive nominations, and occasionally for the ratification of treaties or other executive business. These Senate sessions were also called by Presidential proclamation (typically by the outgoing President, although on occasion by incumbents as well) and are marked by an S in the session column. MEETING PLACES OF CONGRESS: Congress met for the first and second sessions of the First Congress (1789 and 1790) in New York City. From the third session of the First Congress through the first session of the Sixth Congress (1790 to 1800), Philadelphia was the meeting place. Congress has convened in Washington since the second session of the Sixth Congress (1800).

Congress	Session	Convening Date	Adjournment Date	Length in days[1]	Recesses[2] — Senate	Recesses[2] — House of Representatives	President pro tempore of the Senate[3]	Speaker of the House of Representatives
92d	1	Jan. 21, 1971	Dec. 17, 1971	331	Feb. 11–Feb. 17, 1971 Apr. 7–Apr. 14, 1971 May 26–June 1, 1971 June 30–July 6, 1971 Aug. 6–Sept. 8, 1971 Oct. 21–Oct. 26, 1971 Nov. 24–Nov. 29, 1971	Feb. 10–Feb. 17, 1971 Apr. 7–Apr. 19, 1971 May 27–June 1, 1971 July 1–July 6, 1971 Aug. 6–Sept. 8, 1971 Oct. 7–Oct. 12, 1971 Oct. 21–Oct. 26, 1971 Nov. 19–Nov. 29, 1971	Richard B. Russell, of Georgia;[17] Allen J. Ellender, of Louisiana.[17]	Carl B. Albert, of Oklahoma.
	2	Jan. 18, 1972	Oct. 18, 1972	275	Feb. 9–Feb. 14, 1972 Mar. 30–Apr. 4, 1972 May 25–May 30, 1972 June 30–July 17, 1972 Aug. 18–Sept. 5, 1972	Feb. 9–Feb. 16, 1972 Mar. 29–Apr. 10, 1972 May 24–May 30, 1972 June 30–July 10, 1972 Aug. 18–Sept. 5, 1972	Allen J. Ellender, of Louisiana;[18] James O. Eastland, of Mississippi.[18]	
93d	1	Jan. 3, 1973	Dec. 22, 1973	354	Feb. 8–Feb. 15, 1973 Apr. 18–Apr. 30, 1973 May 23–May 29, 1973 June 30–July 9, 1973 Aug. 3–Sept. 5, 1973 Oct. 18–Oct. 23, 1973 Nov. 21–Nov. 26, 1973	Feb. 8–Feb. 19, 1973 Apr. 19–Apr. 30, 1973 May 24–May 29, 1973 June 30–July 10, 1973 Aug. 3–Sept. 5, 1973 Oct. 18–Oct. 23, 1973 Nov. 15–Nov. 26, 1973	James O. Eastland, of Mississippi	Do.
	2	Jan. 21, 1974	Dec. 20, 1974	334	Feb. 8–Feb. 18, 1974 Mar. 13–Mar. 19, 1974 Apr. 11–Apr. 22, 1974 May 23–May 28, 1974 Aug. 22–Sept. 4, 1974 Oct. 17–Nov. 18, 1974 Nov. 26–Dec. 2, 1974	Feb. 7–Feb. 13, 1974 Mar. 13–Mar. 19, 1974 Apr. 11–Apr. 22, 1974 May 23–May 28, 1974 Aug. 22–Sept. 11, 1974 Oct. 17–Nov. 18, 1974 Nov. 26–Dec. 3, 1974	do.	

Congress	Session	Date of assembling	Date of adjournment	Length in days	Recesses	Recesses	President pro tempore of the Senate	Speaker of the House
94th	1	Jan. 14, 1975	Dec. 19, 1975	340	Mar. 26–Apr. 7, 1975 May 22–June 2, 1975 June 27–July 7, 1975 Aug. 1–Sept. 3, 1975 Oct. 9–Oct. 20, 1975 Oct. 23–Oct. 28, 1975 Nov. 20–Dec. 1, 1975	Mar. 26–Apr. 7, 1975 May 22–June 2, 1975 June 26–July 8, 1975 Aug. 1–Sept. 3, 1975 Oct. 9–Oct. 20, 1975 Oct. 23–Oct. 28, 1975 Nov. 20–Dec. 1, 1975	do	Do.
	2	Jan. 19, 1976	Oct. 1, 1976	257	Feb. 6–Feb. 16, 1976 Apr. 14–Apr. 26, 1976 May 28–June 2, 1976 July 2–July 19, 1976 Aug. 10–Aug. 23, 1976 Sept. 1–Sept. 7, 1976	Feb. 11–Feb. 16, 1976 Apr. 14–Apr. 26, 1976 May 27–June 1, 1976 July 2–July 19, 1976 Aug. 10–Aug. 23, 1976 Sept. 2–Sept. 8, 1976	do.	
95th	1	Jan. 4, 1977	Dec. 15, 1977	346	Feb. 11–Feb. 21, 1977 Apr. 7–Apr. 18, 1977 May 27–June 6, 1977 July 1–July 11, 1977 Aug. 6–Sept. 7, 1977	Feb. 9–Feb. 16, 1977 Apr. 6–Apr. 18, 1977 May 26–June 1, 1977 June 30–July 11, 1977 Aug. 5–Sept. 7, 1977 Oct. 6–Oct. 11, 1977	do	Thomas P. O'Neill, Jr., of Massachusetts.
	2	Jan. 19, 1978	Oct. 15, 1978	270	Feb. 10–Feb. 20, 1978 Mar. 23–Apr. 3, 1978 May 26–June 5, 1978 June 29–July 10, 1978 Aug. 25–Sept. 6, 1978	Feb. 9–Feb. 14, 1978 Mar. 22–Apr. 3, 1978 May 25–May 31, 1978 June 29–July 10, 1978 Aug. 17–Sept. 6, 1978	do.	
96th	1	Jan. 15, 1979	Jan. 3, 1980	354	Feb. 9–Feb. 19, 1979 Apr. 10–Apr. 23, 1979 May 24–June 4, 1979 June 27–July 9, 1979 Aug. 3–Sept. 5, 1979 Nov. 20–Nov. 26, 1979 Adjourned sine die, Dec. 20, 1979	Feb. 8–Feb. 13, 1979 Apr. 10–Apr. 23, 1979 May 24–May 30, 1979 June 29–July 9, 1979 Aug. 2–Sept. 5, 1979 Nov. 20–Nov. 26, 1979	Warren G. Magnuson, of Washington	Do.
	2	Jan. 3, 1980	Dec. 16, 1980	349	Apr. 3–Apr. 15, 1980 May 22–May 28, 1980 July 2–July 21, 1980 Aug. 6–Aug. 18, 1980 Aug. 27–Sept. 3, 1980 Oct. 1–Nov. 12, 1980 Nov. 25–Dec. 1, 1980	Feb. 13–Feb. 19, 1980 Apr. 2–Apr. 15, 1980 May 22–May 28, 1980 July 2–July 21, 1980 Aug. 1–Aug. 18, 1980 Aug. 28–Sept. 3, 1980 Oct. 2–Nov. 12, 1980 Nov. 21–Dec. 1, 1980	Warren G. Magnuson, of Washington; Milton Young, of North Dakota;[19] Warren G. Magnuson, of Washington.[19]	
97th	1	Jan. 5, 1981	Dec. 16, 1981	347	Feb. 6–Feb. 16, 1981 Apr. 10–Apr. 27, 1981 June 25–July 8, 1981 Aug. 3–Sept. 9, 1981 Oct. 1–Oct. 14, 1981 Nov. 24–Nov. 30, 1981	Feb. 6–Feb. 17, 1981 Apr. 10–Apr. 27, 1981 June 26–July 8, 1981 Aug. 4–Sept. 9, 1981 Oct. 1–Oct. 13, 1981 Nov. 23–Nov. 30, 1981	Strom Thurmond, of South Carolina	Do.
	2	Jan. 25, 1982	Dec. 23, 1982	333	Feb. 11–Feb. 22, 1982 Apr. 1–Apr. 13, 1982 May 27–June 8, 1982 July 1–July 12, 1982 Aug. 20–Sept. 8, 1982 Oct. 1–Nov. 29, 1982	Feb. 10–Feb. 22, 1982 Apr. 6–Apr. 20, 1982 May 27–June 2, 1982 July 1–July 12, 1982 Aug. 20–Sept. 8, 1982 Oct. 1–Nov. 29, 1982	do	

SESSIONS OF CONGRESS—CONTINUED

[Closing date for this table was July 11, 2005.]

MEETING DATES OF CONGRESS: Pursuant to a resolution of the Confederation Congress in 1788, the term of each Congress began on March 4th of each odd-numbered year; however, Article I, section 4, of the Constitution provided that "The Congress shall assemble at least once in every Year, and such Meeting shall be on the first Monday in December, unless they shall by law appoint a different day." The Congress therefore convened regularly on the first Monday in December until the 20th amendment became effective, which changed the beginning of Congress's term as well as its convening date to January 3rd. So prior to 1934, a new Congress typically would not convene for regular business until 13 months after being elected. One effect of this was that the last session of each Congress was a "lame duck" session. After the 20th amendment, the time from the election to the beginning of Congress's term as well as when it convened was reduced to two months. Recognizing that the need might exist for Congress to meet at times other than the regularly scheduled convening date, Article II, section 3 of the Constitution provides that the President "may, on extraordinary occasions, convene both Houses, or either of them"; hence these sessions occur only if convened by Presidential proclamation. Except as noted, these are separately numbered sessions of a Congress, and are marked by an E in the session column of the table. Until the 20th amendment was adopted, there were also times when special sessions of the Senate were convened, principally for confirming Cabinet and other executive nominations, and occasionally for the ratification of treaties or other executive business. These Senate sessions were also called by Presidential proclamation (typically by the outgoing President, although on occasion by incumbents as well) and are marked by an S in the session column. MEETING PLACES OF CONGRESS: Congress met for the first and second sessions of the First Congress (1789 and 1790) in New York City. From the third session of the First Congress through the first session of the Sixth Congress (1790 to 1800), Philadelphia was the meeting place. Congress has convened in Washington since the second session of the Sixth Congress (1800).

Congress	Session	Convening Date	Adjournment Date	Length in days[1]	Recesses[2] Senate	Recesses[2] House of Representatives	President pro tempore of the Senate[3]	Speaker of the House of Representatives
98th	1	Jan. 3, 1983	Nov. 18, 1983	320	Jan. 3–Jan. 25, 1983 Feb. 3–Feb. 14, 1983 Mar. 24–Apr. 5, 1983 May 26–June 6, 1983 June 29–July 11, 1983 Aug. 4–Sept. 12, 1983 Oct. 7–Oct. 17, 1983	Jan. 6–Jan. 25, 1983 Feb. 17–Feb. 22, 1983 Mar. 24–Apr. 5, 1983 May 26–June 1, 1983 June 30–July 11, 1983 Aug. 4–Sept. 12, 1983 Oct. 6–Oct. 17, 1983	Strom Thurmond, of South Carolina	Thomas P. O'Neill, Jr., of Massachusetts.
	2	Jan. 23, 1984	Oct. 12, 1984	264	Feb. 9–Feb. 20, 1984 Apr. 12–Apr. 24, 1984 May 24–May 31, 1984 June 29–July 23, 1984 Aug. 10–Sept. 5, 1984	Feb. 9–Feb. 21, 1984 Apr. 12–Apr. 24, 1984 May 24–May 30, 1984 June 29–July 23, 1984 Aug. 10–Sept. 5, 1984	do.	Do.
99th	1	Jan. 3, 1985	Dec. 20, 1985	352	Jan. 7–Jan. 21, 1985 Feb. 7–Feb. 18, 1985 Apr. 4–Apr. 15, 1985 May 9–May 14, 1985 May 24–June 3, 1985 June 27–July 8, 1985 Aug. 1–Sept. 9, 1985 Nov. 23–Dec. 2, 1985	Jan. 3–Jan. 21, 1985 Feb. 7–Feb. 19, 1985 Mar. 7–Mar. 19, 1985 Apr. 4–Apr. 15, 1985 May 23–June 3, 1985 June 27–July 8, 1985 Aug. 1–Sept. 4, 1985 Nov. 21–Dec. 2, 1985	do.	
	2	Jan. 21, 1986	Oct. 18, 1986	278	Feb. 7–Feb. 17, 1986 Mar. 27–Apr. 8, 1986 May 21–June 2, 1986 June 26–July 7, 1986 Aug. 15–Sept. 8, 1986	Feb. 6–Feb. 18, 1986 Mar. 25–Apr. 8, 1986 May 22–June 3, 1986 June 26–July 14, 1986 Aug. 16–Sept. 8, 1986	do.	

							President pro tempore	Speaker
100th	1	Jan. 6, 1987	Dec. 22, 1987	351	Jan. 6–Jan. 12, 1987 Feb. 5–Feb. 16, 1987 Apr. 10–Apr. 21, 1987 May 21–May 27, 1987 July 1–July 7, 1987 Aug. 7–Sept. 9, 1987 Nov. 20–Nov. 30, 1987	Jan. 8–Jan. 20, 1987 Feb. 11–Feb. 18, 1987 Apr. 9–Apr. 21, 1987 May 21–May 27, 1987 July 1–July 7, 1987 July 15–July 20, 1987 Aug. 7–Sept. 9, 1987 Nov. 10–Nov. 16, 1987 Nov. 20–Nov. 30, 1987	John C. Stennis, of Mississippi	James C. Wright, Jr., of Texas.
	2	Jan. 25, 1988	Oct. 22, 1988	272	Feb. 4–Feb. 15, 1988 Mar. 4– Mar. 14, 1988 Mar. 31–Apr. 11, 1988 Apr. 29–May 9, 1988 May 27–June 6, 1988 July 14–July 25, 1988 Aug. 11–Sept. 7, 1988	Feb. 9–Feb. 16, 1988 Mar. 31–Apr. 11, 1988 May 26–June 1, 1988 June 30–July 7, 1988 July 14–July 26, 1988 Aug. 11–Sept. 7, 1988	....do.	
101st	1	Jan. 3, 1989	Nov. 22, 1989	324	Jan. 4–Jan. 20, 1989 Jan. 20–Jan. 25, 1989 Feb. 9–Feb. 21, 1989 Mar. 17–Apr. 4, 1989 Apr. 19–May 1, 1989 May 18–May 31, 1989 June 23–July 11, 1989 Aug. 4–Sept. 6, 1989	Jan. 4–Jan. 19, 1989 Feb. 9–Feb. 21, 1989 Mar. 23–Apr. 3, 1989 Apr. 18–Apr. 25, 1989 May 25–May 31, 1989 June 29–July 10, 1989 Aug. 5–Sept. 6, 1989	Robert C. Byrd, of West Virginia	James C. Wright, Jr., of Texas;[20] Thomas S. Foley, of Washington.[20]
	2	Jan. 23, 1990	Oct. 28, 1990	260	Feb. 8–Feb. 20, 1990 Mar. 9–Mar. 20, 1990 Apr. 5–Apr. 18, 1990 May 24–June 5, 1990 June 28–July 10, 1990 Aug. 4–Sept. 10, 1990	Feb. 7–Feb. 20, 1990 Apr. 4–Apr. 18, 1990 May 25–June 5, 1990 June 28–July 10, 1990 Aug. 4–Sept. 5, 1990	....do.	
102d	1	Jan. 3, 1991	Jan. 3, 1992	366	Feb. 7–Feb. 19, 1991 Mar. 22–Apr. 9, 1991 Apr. 25–May 6, 1991 May 24–June 3, 1991 June 28–July 8, 1991 Aug. 2–Sept. 10, 1991 Nov. 27, 1991–Jan. 3, 1992	Feb. 6–Feb. 19, 1991 Mar. 22–Apr. 9, 1991 May 23–May 29, 1991 June 27–July 9, 1991 Aug. 2–Sept. 11, 1991 Nov. 27, 1991–Jan. 3, 1992	...do	Thomas S. Foley, of Washington.
	2	Jan. 3, 1992	Oct. 9, 1992	281	Jan. 3–Jan. 21, 1992 Feb. 7–Feb. 18, 1992 Apr. 10–Apr. 28, 1992 May 21–June 1, 1992 July 2–July 20, 1992 Aug. 12–Sept. 8, 1992	Jan. 3–Jan. 22, 1992 Feb. 7–Feb. 18, 1992 Apr. 10–Apr. 28, 1992 May 21–May 26, 1992 July 2–July 7, 1992 July 9–July 21, 1992 Aug. 12–Sept. 9, 1992	....do.	

SESSIONS OF CONGRESS—CONTINUED

[Closing date for this table was July 11, 2005.]

MEETING DATES OF CONGRESS: Pursuant to a resolution of the Confederation Congress in 1788, the Constitution went into effect on March 4, 1789. From then until the 20th amendment took effect in January 1934, the term of each Congress began on March 4th of each odd-numbered year; however, Article I, section 4, of the Constitution provided that "The Congress shall assemble at least once in every Year, and such Meeting shall be on the first Monday in December, unless they shall by law appoint a different day." The Congress therefore convened regularly on the first Monday in December until the 20th amendment became effective, which changed the beginning of Congress's term as well as its convening date to January 3rd. So prior to 1934, a new Congress typically would not convene for regular business until 13 months after being elected. One effect of this was that the last session of each Congress was a "lame duck" session. After the 20th amendment, the time from the election to the beginning of Congress's term as well as when it convened was reduced to two months. Recognizing that the need might exist for Congress to meet at times other than the regularly scheduled convening date, Article II, section 3 of the Constitution provides that the President "may, on extraordinary occasions, convene both Houses, or either of them"; hence these sessions occur only if convened by Presidential proclamation. Except as noted, these are separately numbered sessions of a Congress, and are marked by an E in the session column of the table. Until the 20th amendment was adopted, there were also times when special sessions of the Senate were convened, principally for confirming Cabinet and other executive nominations, and occasionally for the ratification of treaties or other executive business. These Senate sessions were also called by Presidential proclamation (typically by the outgoing President, although on occasion by incumbents as well) and are marked by an S in the session column. MEETING PLACES OF CONGRESS: Congress met for the first and second sessions of the First Congress (1789 and 1790) in New York City. From the third session of the First Congress through the first session of the Sixth Congress (1790 to 1800), Philadelphia was the meeting place. Congress has convened in Washington since the second session of the Sixth Congress (1800).

Congress	Session	Convening Date	Adjournment Date	Length in days[1]	Recesses[2]		President pro tempore of the Senate[3]	Speaker of the House of Representatives
					Senate	House of Representatives		
103d	1	Jan. 5, 1993	Nov. 26, 1993	326	Jan. 7–Jan. 20, 1993 Feb. 4–Feb. 16, 1993 Apr. 7–Apr. 19, 1993 May 28–June 7, 1993 July 1–July 13, 1993 Aug. 7–Sept. 7, 1993 Oct. 7–Oct. 13, 1993 Nov. 11–Nov. 16, 1993	Jan. 6–Jan. 20, 1993 Jan. 27–Feb. 2, 1993 Feb. 4–Feb. 16, 1993 Apr. 7–Apr. 19, 1993 May 27–June 8, 1993 July 1–July 13, 1993 Aug. 6–Sept. 8, 1993 Sept. 15–Sept. 21, 1993 Oct. 7–Oct. 12, 1993 Nov. 10–Nov. 15, 1993	Robert C. Byrd, of West Virginia	Thomas S. Foley, of Washington.
	2	Jan. 25, 1994	Dec. 1, 1994	311	Feb. 11–Feb. 22, 1994 Mar. 26–Apr. 11, 1994 May 25–June 7, 1994 July 1–July 11, 1994 Aug. 25–Sept. 12, 1994 Oct. 8–Nov. 30, 1994	Jan. 26–Feb. 1, 1994 Feb. 11–Feb. 22, 1994 Mar. 24–Apr. 12, 1994 May 26–June 8, 1994 June 30–July 12, 1994 Aug. 26–Sept. 12, 1994 Oct. 8–Nov. 29, 1994	....do.	
104th	1	Jan. 4, 1995	Jan. 3, 1996	365	Feb. 16–Feb. 22, 1995 Apr. 7–Apr. 24, 1995 May 26–June 5, 1995 June 30–July 10, 1995 Aug. 11–Sept. 5, 1995 Sept. 29–Oct. 10, 1995 Nov. 20–Nov. 27, 1995	Feb. 16–Feb. 21, 1995 Mar. 16–Mar. 21, 1995 Apr. 7–May 1, 1995 May 3–May 9, 1995 May 25–June 6, 1995 June 30–July 10, 1995 Aug. 4–Sept. 6, 1995 Sept. 29–Oct. 6, 1995 Nov. 20–Nov. 28, 1995	Strom Thurmond, of South Carolina	Newt Gingrich, of Georgia.

Congress	Session	Convened	Adjourned	Days	Recess dates	Recess dates	President pro tempore of the Senate	Speaker of the House
	2	Jan. 3, 1996	Oct. 4, 1996	276	Jan. 10–Jan. 22, 1996 Mar. 29–Apr. 15, 1996 May 24–June 3, 1996 June 28–July 8, 1996 Aug. 2–Sept. 3, 1996	Jan. 9–Jan. 22, 1996 Mar. 29–Apr. 15, 1996 May 23–May 29, 1996 June 28–July 8, 1996 Aug. 2–Sept. 4, 1996	do.	Do.
105th	1	Jan. 7, 1997	Nov. 13, 1997	311	Jan. 9–Jan. 21, 1997 Feb. 13–Feb. 24, 1997 Mar. 21–Apr. 7, 1997 June 27–July 7, 1997 July 31–Sept. 2, 1997 Oct. 9–Oct. 20, 1997	Jan. 9–Jan. 20, 1997 Feb. 1–Feb. 4, 1997 Feb. 13–Feb. 25, 1997 Mar. 21–Apr. 8, 1997 June 26–July 8, 1997 Aug. 1–Sept. 3, 1997 Oct. 9–Oct. 21, 1997	do	
	2	Jan. 27, 1998	Dec. 19, 1998	327	Feb. 13–Feb. 23, 1998 Apr. 3–Apr. 20, 1998 May 22–June 1, 1998 June 26–July 6, 1998 July 31–Aug. 31, 1998 Adjourned sine die, Oct. 21, 1998.	Feb. 13–Feb. 23, 1998 Apr. 3–Apr. 20, 1998 May 22–June 1, 1998 June 26–July 6, 1998 July 31–Aug. 31, 1998	do.	
106th	1	Jan. 6, 1999	Nov. 22, 1999	321	Feb. 12–Feb. 22, 1999 Mar. 25–Apr. 12, 1999 May 27–June 7, 1999 July 1–July 12, 1999 Aug. 5–Sept. 8, 1999	Jan. 6–Jan. 19, 1999 Jan. 19–Feb. 2, 1999 Feb. 12–Feb. 23, 1999 Mar. 25–Apr. 12, 1999 May 27–June 7, 1999 July 1–July 12, 1999 Aug. 6–Sept. 8, 1999	do	J. Dennis Hastert, of Illinois.
	2	Jan. 24, 2000	Dec. 15, 2000	326	Feb. 10–Feb. 22, 2000 Mar. 9–Mar. 20, 2000 Apr. 13–Apr. 25, 2000 May 25–June 6, 2000 June 30–July 10, 2000 July 27–Sept. 5, 2000 Nov. 14–Dec. 5, 2000	Feb. 16–Feb. 29, 2000 Apr. 13–May 2, 2000 May 25–June 6, 2000 June 30–July 10, 2000 July 27–Sept. 6, 2000 Nov. 3–Nov. 13, 2000 Nov. 14–Dec. 4, 2000	do.	
107th	1	Jan. 3, 2001	Dec. 20, 2001	352	Jan. 8–Jan. 20, 2001 Feb. 15–Feb. 26, 2001 Apr. 6–Apr. 23, 2001 May 26–June 5, 2001 June 29–July 9, 2001 Aug. 3–Sept. 4, 2001 Oct. 18–Oct. 23, 2001 Nov. 16–Nov. 27, 2001	Jan. 6–Jan. 20, 2001 Jan. 20–Jan. 30, 2001 Jan. 31–Feb. 6, 2001 Feb. 14–Feb. 26, 2001 Apr. 4–Apr. 24, 2001 May 26–June 5, 2001 May 28–July 10, 2001 Aug. 2–Sept. 5, 2001 Oct. 17–Oct. 23, 2001 Nov. 19–Nov. 27, 2001	Robert C. Byrd, of West Virginia;[21] Strom Thurmond, of South Carolina;[21] Robert C. Byrd, of West Virginia.[21]	Do.
	2	Jan. 23, 2002	Nov. 22, 2002	304	Jan. 29–Feb. 4, 2002 Feb. 15–Feb. 25, 2002 Mar. 22–Apr. 8, 2002 May 23–June 3, 2002 June 28–July 8, 202 Aug. 1–Sept. 3, 2002	Jan. 29–Feb. 4, 2002 Feb. 14–Feb. 26, 2002 Mar. 20–Apr. 9, 2002 May 24–June 4, 2002 June 28–July 8, 2002 July 27–Sept. 4, 2002	Robert C. Byrd, of West Virginia.	

SESSIONS OF CONGRESS—CONTINUED

[Closing date for this table was July 11, 2005.]

MEETING DATES OF CONGRESS: Pursuant to a resolution of the Confederation Congress in 1788, the term of each Congress began on March 4th of each odd-numbered year; however, Article I, section 4, of the Constitution provided that "The Congress shall assemble at least once in every Year, and such Meeting shall be on the first Monday in December, unless they shall by law appoint a different day." The Congress therefore convened regularly on the first Monday in December until the 20th amendment became effective, which changed the beginning of Congress's term as well as its convening date to January 3rd. So prior to 1934, a new Congress typically would not convene for regular business until 13 months after being elected. One effect of this was that the last session of each Congress was a "lame duck" session. After the 20th amendment, the time from the election to the beginning of Congress's term as well as when it convened was reduced to two months. Recognizing that the need might exist for Congress to meet at times other than the regularly scheduled convening date, Article II, section 3 of the Constitution provides that the President 'may, on extraordinary occasions, convene both Houses, or either of them'; hence these sessions occur only if convened by Presidential proclamation. Except as noted, these are separately numbered sessions of a Congress, and are marked by an E in the session column of the table. Until the 20th amendment was adopted, there were also times when special sessions of the Senate were convened, principally for confirming Cabinet and other executive nominations, and occasionally for the ratification of treaties or other executive business. These Senate sessions were also called by Presidential proclamation (typically by the outgoing President, although on occasion by incumbents as well) and are marked by an S in the session column. MEETING PLACES OF CONGRESS: Congress met for the first and second sessions of the First Congress (1789 and 1790) in New York City. From the third session of the First Congress through the first session of the Sixth Congress (1790 to 1800), Philadelphia was the meeting place. Congress has convened in Washington since the second session of the Sixth Congress (1800).

Congress	Session	Convening Date	Adjournment Date	Length in days [1]	Recesses [2] Senate	Recesses [2] House of Representatives	President pro tempore of the Senate [3]	Speaker of the House of Representatives
108th..	1	Jan. 7, 2003	Dec. 9, 2003	337	Feb. 14–Feb. 24, 2003 Apr. 11–Apr. 28, 2003 May 23–June 2, 2003 June 27–July 7, 2003 Aug. 1–Sept 2, 2003 Oct. 3–Oct. 14, 2003 Nov. 25–Dec. 9, 2003	Jan. 8–Jan. 27, 2003 Feb. 13–Feb. 25, 2003 Apr. 12–Apr. 29, 2003 May 23–June 2, 2003 June 27–July 7, 2003 July 29–Sept. 3, 2003 Nov. 25–Dec. 8, 2003	Ted Stevens, of Alaska	J. Dennis Hastert, of Illinois.
	2	Jan. 20, 2004	Dec. 8, 2004	324	Feb. 12–Feb. 23, 2004 Mar. 12–Mar. 22, 2004 Apr. 8–Apr. 19, 2004 May 21–June 1, 2004 June 9–June 14, 2004 June 25–July 6, 2004 July 22–Sept. 7, 2004 Oct. 11–Nov. 16, 2004 Nov. 24–Dec. 7, 2004	Feb. 11–Feb. 24, 2004 Apr. 2–Apr. 20, 2004 May 20–June 1, 2004 June 9–June 14, 2004 June 25–July 6, 2004 July 22–Sept. 7, 2004 Nov. 24–Dec. 6, 2004	....do	
109th..	1	Jan. 4, 2005			Jan. 6–Jan. 20, 2005 Jan. 26–Jan. 31, 2005 Feb. 18–Feb. 28, 2005 Mar. 20–Apr. 4, 2005 Apr. 29–May 9, 2005 May 26–June 6, 2005 July 1–July 11, 2005	Jan. 6–Jan. 20, 2005 Jan. 20–Jan. 25, 2005 Jan. 26–Feb. 1, 2005 Feb. 2–Feb. 8, 2005 Feb. 17–Mar. 1, 2005 Mar. 21–Apr. 5, 2005 May 26–June 7, 2005 July 1–July 11, 2005	....do	Do.

[1] For the purposes of this table, a session's "length in days" is defined as the total number of calendar days from the convening date to the adjournment date, inclusive. It does not mean the actual number of days that Congress met during that session.

2 For the purposes of this table, a "recess" is defined as any period of three or more complete days—excluding Sundays—when either the House of Representatives or the Senate is not in session. As listed, the recess periods also are inclusive of days only partially in the recess, i.e., the day (or days) when the House and Senate each adjourn to begin the recess, as well as the day (or days) when each body reconvenes at the end of the recess.

3 The election and role of the President pro tempore has evolved considerably over the Senate's history. "Pro tempore is Latin for 'for the time being'; thus, the post was conceived as a temporary presiding officer. In the eighteenth and nineteenth centuries, the Senate frequently elected several Presidents pro tempore during a single session. Since Vice Presidents presided routinely, the Senate thought it necessary to choose a President pro tempore only for the limited periods when the Vice President might be ill or otherwise absent." Since no provision was in place (until the 25th amendment was adopted in 1967) for replacing the Vice President if he died or resigned from office, or if he assumed the Presidency, the President pro tempore would continue under such circumstances to fill the duties of the chair until the next Vice President was elected. Since Mar. 12, 1890, however, Presidents pro tempore have served until "the Senate otherwise ordered." Since 1949, while still elected, the position has gone to the most senior member of the majority party (see footnote 19 for a minority party exception). To gain a more complete understanding of this position, see Robert C. Byrd's *The Senate 1789–1989: Addresses on the History of the United States Senate*, vol. 2, ch. 6 "The President Pro Tempore," pp. 167–183, from which the quotes in this footnote are taken. Also, a complete listing of the dates of election of the Presidents pro tempore is in vol. 4 of the Byrd series (*The Senate 1789–1989: Historical Statistics, 1789–1992*), table 6–2, pp. 647–653.

4 Henry Clay resigned as Speaker on Jan. 19, 1814. He was succeeded by Langdon Cheves who was elected on that same day.

5 Henry Clay resigned as Speaker on Oct. 28, 1820, after the sine die adjournment of the first session of the 16th Congress. He was succeeded by John W. Taylor who was elected at the beginning of the second session.

6 Andrew Stevenson resigned as Speaker on June 2, 1834. He was succeeded by John Bell who was elected on that same day.

7 Speaker Schuyler Colfax resigned as Speaker on the last day of the 40th Congress, Mar. 3, 1869, in preparation for becoming Vice President of the United States on the following day. Theodore M. Pomeroy was elected Speaker on Mar. 3, and served for only that one day.

8 Speaker Michael C. Kerr died on Aug. 19, 1876, after the sine die adjournment of the first session of the 44th Congress. Samuel J. Randall was elected Speaker at the beginning of the second session.

9 William P. Frye resigned as President pro tempore on Apr. 27, 1911.

10 President pro tempore James P. Clarke died on Oct. 1, 1916, after the sine die adjournment of the first session of the 64th Congress. Willard Saulsbury was elected President pro tempore during the second session.

11 Speaker Joseph W. Byrns died on June 4, 1936. He was succeeded by William B. Bankhead who was elected Speaker on that same day.

12 Speaker William B. Bankhead died on Sept. 15, 1940. He was succeeded by Sam Rayburn who was elected Speaker on that same day.

13 President pro tempore Key Pittman died on Nov. 10, 1940. He was succeeded by William H. King who was elected President pro tempore on Nov. 19, 1940.

14 President pro tempore Pat Harrison died on June 22, 1941. He was succeeded by Carter Glass who was elected President pro tempore on July 10, 1941.

15 President Harry S. Truman called the Congress into extraordinary session twice, both times during the 80th Congress. Each time Congress had essentially wrapped up its business for the year, but for technical reasons had not adjourned sine die, so in each case the extraordinary session is considered an extension of the regularly numbered session rather than a separately numbered one. The dates of these extraordinary sessions were Nov. 17 to Dec. 19, 1947, and July 26 to Aug. 7, 1948.

16 Speaker Sam Rayburn died on Nov. 16, 1961, after the sine die adjournment of the first session of the 87th Congress. John W. McCormack was elected Speaker at the beginning of the second session.

17 President pro tempore Richard B. Russell died on Jan. 21, 1971. He was succeeded by Allen J. Ellender who was elected to that position on Jan. 22, 1971.

18 President pro tempore Allen J. Ellender died on July 27, 1972. He was succeeded by James O. Eastland who was elected President pro tempore on July 28, 1972.

19 Milton Young was elected President pro tempore for one day, Dec. 5, 1980, which was at the end of his 36-year career in the Senate. He was Republican, which was the minority party at that time. Warren G. Magnuson resumed the position of President pro tempore on Dec. 6, 1980.

20 James C. Wright, Jr., resigned as Speaker on June 6, 1989. He was succeeded by Thomas S. Foley who was elected on that same day.

21 The 2000 election resulted in an even split in the Senate between Republicans and Democrats. From the date the 107th Congress convened on Jan. 3, 2001, until Inauguration Day on Jan. 20, 2001, Vice President Albert Gore tipped the scale to a Democratic majority, hence Robert C. Byrd served as President pro tempore during this brief period. When Vice President Richard B. Cheney took office on Jan. 20, the Republicans became the majority party, and Strom Thurmond was elected President pro tempore. On June 6, 2001, Republican Senator James Jeffords became an Independent, creating a Democratic majority, and Robert C. Byrd was elected President pro tempore on that day.

CEREMONIAL MEETINGS OF CONGRESS

The following ceremonial meetings of Congress occurred on the following dates, at the designated locations, and for the reasons indicated. Please note that Congress was not in session on these occasions.

July 16, 1987, 100th Congress, Philadelphia, Pennsylvania, Independence Hall and Congress Hall—In honor of the bicentennial of the Constitution, and in commemoration of the Great Compromise of the Constitutional Convention which was agreed to on July 16, 1787.

September 6, 2002, 107th Congress, New York City, New York, Federal Hall—In remembrance of the victims and heroes of September 11, 2001, and in recognition of the courage and spirit of the City of New York.

JOINT SESSIONS AND MEETINGS, ADDRESSES TO THE SENATE OR THE HOUSE, AND INAUGURATIONS

1st–109th CONGRESSES, 1789–2005 [1]

The parliamentary difference between a joint session and a joint meeting has evolved over time. In recent years the distinctions have become clearer: a joint session is more formal, and occurs upon the adoption of a concurrent resolution; a joint meeting occurs when each body adopts a unanimous consent agreement to recess to meet with the other legislative body. Joint sessions typically are held to hear an address from the President of the United States or to count electoral votes. Joint meetings typically are held to hear an address from a foreign dignitary or visitors other than the President.

The Speaker of the House of Representatives usually presides over joint sessions and joint meetings; however, the President of the Senate does preside over joint sessions where the electoral votes are counted, as required by the Constitution.

In the earliest years of the Republic, 1789 and 1790, when the national legislature met in New York City, joint gatherings were held in the Senate Chamber in Federal Hall. In Philadelphia, when the legislature met in Congress Hall, such meetings were held in the Senate Chamber, 1790–1793, and in the Hall of the House of Representatives, 1794–1799. Once the Congress moved to the Capitol in Washington in 1800, the Senate Chamber again was used for joint gatherings through 1805. Since 1809, with few exceptions, joint sessions and joint meetings have occurred in the Hall of the House.

Presidential messages on the state of the Union were originally known as the "Annual Message," but since the 80th Congress, in 1947, have been called the "State of the Union Address." After President John Adams's Annual Message on November 22, 1800, these addresses were read by clerks to the individual bodies until President Woodrow Wilson resumed the practice of delivering them to joint sessions on December 2, 1913.

In some instances more than one joint gathering has occurred on the same day. For example, on January 6, 1941, Congress met in joint session to count electoral votes for President and Vice President, and then met again in joint session to receive President Franklin Delano Roosevelt's Annual Message.

Whereas in more recent decades, foreign dignitaries invited to speak before Congress have typically done so at joint meetings, in earlier times (and with several notable exceptions), such visitors were received by the Senate and the House separately, or by one or the other singly, a tradition begun with the visit of General Lafayette of France in 1824. At that time a joint committee decided that each body would honor Lafayette separately, establishing the precedent. (See footnote 7 for more details.) Not all such occasions included formal addresses by such dignitaries (e.g., Lafayette's reception by the Senate in their chamber, at which he did not speak before they adjourned to greet him), hence the "occasions" listed in the third column of the table include not only addresses, but also remarks (defined as brief greetings or off-the-cuff comments often requested of the visitor at the last minute) and receptions. Relatively few foreign dignitaries were received by Congress before World War I.

Congress has hosted inaugurations since the first occasion in 1789. They always have been formal joint gatherings, and sometimes they also were joint sessions. Inaugurations were joint sessions when both houses of Congress were in session, and they processed to the ceremony as part of the business of the day. In many cases, however, one or both houses were not in session or were in recess at the time of the ceremony. In this table, inaugurations that were not joint sessions are listed in the second column. Those that were joint sessions are so identified and described in the third column.

JOINT SESSIONS AND MEETINGS, ADDRESSES TO THE SENATE OR THE HOUSE, AND INAUGURATIONS

[See notes at end of table]

Congress & Date	Type	Occasion, topic, or inaugural location	Name and position of dignitary (where applicable)
		NEW YORK CITY	
1st CONGRESS			
Apr. 6, 1789	Joint session	Counting electoral votes	N.A.
Apr. 30, 1789	......do	Inauguration and church service [2]	President George Washington; Right Reverend Samuel Provoost, Senate-appointed Chaplain.
Jan. 8, 1790	...do	Annual Message	President George Washington.
		PHILADELPHIA	
Dec. 8, 1790	...do	......do	Do.
2d CONGRESS			
Oct. 25, 1791	......do	......do	Do.
Nov. 6, 1792	......do	......do	Do.
Feb. 13, 1793	......do	Counting electoral votes	N.A.
3d CONGRESS			
Mar. 4, 1793	Inauguration	Senate Chamber	President George Washington.
Dec. 3, 1793	Joint session	Annual Message	Do.
Nov. 19, 1794	......do	......do	Do.
4th CONGRESS			
Dec. 8, 1795	...do	......do	Do.
Dec. 7, 1796	Joint session	Annual Message	Do.
Feb. 8, 1797	...do	Counting electoral votes	N.A.
5th CONGRESS			
Mar. 4, 1797	Inauguration	Hall of the House	President John Adams.
May 16, 1797	Joint session	Relations with France	Do.
Nov. 23, 1797	...do	Annual Message	Do.
Dec. 8, 1798	...do	......do	Do.
6th CONGRESS			
Dec. 3, 1799	...do	......do	Do.
Dec. 26, 1799	...do	Funeral procession and oration in memory of George Washington.[3]	Representative Henry Lee.
		WASHINGTON	
Nov. 22, 1800	......do	Annual Message	President John Adams.
Feb. 11, 1801	......do	Counting electoral votes [4]	N.A.
7th CONGRESS			
Mar. 4, 1801	Inauguration	Senate Chamber	President Thomas Jefferson.
8th CONGRESS			
Feb. 13, 1805	Joint session	Counting electoral votes	N.A.
9th CONGRESS			
Mar. 4, 1805	Inauguration	Senate Chamber	President Thomas Jefferson.
10th CONGRESS			
Feb. 8, 1809	Joint session	Counting electoral votes	N.A.
11th CONGRESS			
Mar. 4, 1809	Inauguration	Hall of the House	President James Madison.
12th CONGRESS			
Feb. 10, 1813	Joint session	Counting electoral votes	N.A.
13th CONGRESS			
Mar. 4, 1813	Inauguration	Hall of the House	President James Madison.
14th CONGRESS			
Feb. 12, 1817	Joint session	Counting electoral votes [5]	N.A.
15th CONGRESS			
Mar. 4, 1817	Inauguration	In front of Brick Capitol	President James Monroe.
16th CONGRESS			
Feb. 14, 1821	Joint session	Counting electoral votes [6]	N.A.
17th CONGRESS			
Mar. 5, 1821	Inauguration	Hall of the House	President James Monroe.
18th CONGRESS			
Dec. 9, 1824	Senate	Reception	General Gilbert du Motier, Marquis de Lafayette, of France.

JOINT SESSIONS AND MEETINGS, ADDRESSES TO THE SENATE OR THE HOUSE, AND INAUGURATIONS—CONTINUED

[See notes at end of table]

Congress & Date	Type	Occasion, topic, or inaugural location	Name and position of dignitary (where applicable)
Dec. 10, 1824	House [7]	Address	Speaker Henry Clay; General Gilbert du Motier, Marquis de Lafayette, of France.
Feb. 9, 1825	Joint session	Counting electoral votes [8]	N.A.
19th CONGRESS Mar. 4, 1825	Inauguration	Hall of the House	President John Quincy Adams.
20th CONGRESS Feb. 11, 1829	Joint session	Counting electoral votes	N.A.
21st CONGRESS Mar. 4, 1829	Inauguration	East Portico [9]	President Andrew Jackson.
22d CONGRESS Feb. 13, 1833	Joint session	Counting electoral votes	N.A.
23d CONGRESS Mar. 4, 1833 .... Dec. 31, 1834	Inauguration ...... Joint session	Hall of the House [10] .... Lafayette eulogy	President Andrew Jackson. Representative and former President John Quincy Adams; ceremony attended by President Andrew Jackson.
24th CONGRESS Feb. 8, 1837	.....do	Counting electoral votes	N.A.
25th CONGRESS Mar. 4, 1837	Inauguration	East Portico	President Martin Van Buren.
26th CONGRESS Feb. 10, 1841	Joint session	Counting electoral votes	N.A.
27th CONGRESS Mar. 4, 1841	Inauguration	East Portico	President William Henry Harrison.
28th CONGRESS Feb. 12, 1845	Joint session	Counting electoral votes	N.A.
29th CONGRESS Mar. 4, 1845	Inauguration	East Portico	President James Knox Polk.
30th CONGRESS Feb. 14, 1849	Joint session	Counting electoral votes	N.A.
31st CONGRESS Mar. 5, 1849 .... July 10, 1850	Inauguration ...... Joint session	East Portico .... Oath of office to President Millard Fillmore. [11]	President Zachary Taylor. N.A.
32d CONGRESS Jan. 5, 1852	Senate	Reception	Louis Kossuth, exiled Governor of Hungary.
Jan. 7, 1852 .... Feb. 9, 1853	House .... Joint session	Remarks and Reception .... Counting electoral votes	Do. N.A.
33d CONGRESS Mar. 4, 1853	Inauguration	East Portico	President Franklin Pierce.
34th CONGRESS Feb. 11, 1857	Joint session	Counting electoral votes	N.A.
35th CONGRESS Mar. 4, 1857	Inauguration	East Portico	President James Buchanan.
36th CONGRESS Feb. 13, 1861	Joint session	Counting electoral votes	N.A.
37th CONGRESS Mar. 4, 1861 .... Feb. 22, 1862	Inauguration ...... Joint session	East Portico .... Reading of Washington's farewell address.	President Abraham Lincoln. John W. Forney, Secretary of the Senate.
38th CONGRESS Feb. 8, 1865	.....do	Counting electoral votes	N.A.
39th CONGRESS Mar. 4, 1865 .... Feb. 12, 1866	Inauguration ...... Joint session	East Portico .... Memorial to Abraham Lincoln	President Abraham Lincoln. George Bancroft, historian; ceremony attended by President Andrew Johnson.

JOINT SESSIONS AND MEETINGS, ADDRESSES TO THE SENATE OR THE HOUSE, AND INAUGURATIONS—CONTINUED

[See notes at end of table]

Congress & Date	Type	Occasion, topic, or inaugural location	Name and position of dignitary (where applicable)
40th CONGRESS June 9, 1868	House	Address	Anson Burlingame, Envoy to the U.S. from China, and former Representative.
Feb. 10, 1869	Joint session	Counting electoral votes	N.A.
41st CONGRESS Mar. 4, 1869	Inauguration	East Portico	President Ulysses S. Grant.
42d CONGRESS Mar. 6, 1872	House	Address	Tomomi Iwakura, Ambassador from Japan.
Feb. 12, 1873	Joint session	Counting electoral votes [12]	N.A.
43d CONGRESS Mar. 4, 1873	Inauguration	East Portico	President Ulysses S. Grant.
Dec. 18, 1874	Joint meeting	Reception and Remarks	Speaker James G. Blaine; David Kalakaua, King of the Hawaiian Islands.[13]
44th CONGRESS Feb. 1, 1877 .... Feb. 10, 1877 Feb. 12, 1877 Feb. 19, 1877 Feb. 20, 1877 Feb. 21, 1877 Feb. 24, 1877 Feb. 26, 1877 Feb. 28, 1877 Mar. 1, 1877 Mar. 2, 1877	Joint session	Counting electoral votes [14]	N.A.
45th CONGRESS Mar. 5, 1877	Inauguration	East Portico	President Rutherford B. Hayes.
46th CONGRESS Feb. 2, 1880	House	Address	Charles Stewart Parnell, member of Parliament from Ireland.
Feb. 9, 1881	Joint session	Counting electoral votes	N.A.
47th CONGRESS Mar. 4, 1881	Inauguration	East Portico	President James A. Garfield.
Feb. 27, 1882	Joint session	Memorial to James A. Garfield	James G. Blaine, former Speaker, Senator, and Secretary of State; ceremony attended by President Chester A. Arthur.
48th CONGRESS Feb. 11, 1885	Joint session	Counting electoral votes	N.A.
Feb. 21, 1885	......do	Completion of Washington Monument	Representative John D. Long; Representative-elect John W. Daniel,[15] ceremony attended by President Chester A. Arthur.
49th CONGRESS Mar. 4, 1885	Inauguration	East Portico	President Grover Cleveland.
50th CONGRESS Feb. 13, 1889	Joint session	Counting electoral votes	N.A.
51st CONGRESS Mar. 4, 1889	Inauguration	East Portico	President Benjamin Harrison.
Dec. 11, 1889	Joint session	Centennial of George Washington's first inauguration.	Melville W. Fuller, Chief Justice of the United States; ceremony attended by President Benjamin Harrison.
52d CONGRESS Feb. 8, 1893	......do	Counting electoral votes	N.A.
53d CONGRESS Mar. 4, 1893	Inauguration	East Portico	President Grover Cleveland.
54th CONGRESS Feb. 10, 1897	Joint session	Counting electoral votes	N.A.
55th CONGRESS Mar. 4, 1897	Inauguration	In front of original Senate Wing of Capitol.	President William McKinley.

JOINT SESSIONS AND MEETINGS, ADDRESSES TO THE SENATE OR THE HOUSE, AND INAUGURATIONS—CONTINUED

[See notes at end of table]

Congress & Date	Type	Occasion, topic, or inaugural location	Name and position of dignitary (where applicable)
56th CONGRESS			
Dec. 12, 1900	Joint meeting	Centennial of the Capital City	Representatives James D. Richardson and Sereno E. Payne, and Senator George F. Hoar; ceremony attended by President William McKinley.
Feb. 13, 1901	Joint session	Counting electoral votes	N.A.
57th CONGRESS			
Mar. 4, 1901	Inauguration	East Portico	President William McKinley.
Feb. 27, 1902	Joint session	Memorial to William McKinley	John Hay, Secretary of State; ceremony attended by President Theodore Roosevelt and Prince Henry of Prussia.
58th CONGRESS			
Feb. 8, 1905	......do	Counting electoral votes	N.A.
59th CONGRESS			
Mar. 4, 1905	Inauguration	East Portico	President Theodore Roosevelt.
60th CONGRESS			
Feb. 10, 1909	Joint session	Counting electoral votes	N.A.
61st CONGRESS			
Mar. 4, 1909	Inauguration	Senate Chamber [16]	President William Howard Taft.
Feb. 9, 1911	House	Address	Count Albert Apponyi, Minister of Education from Hungary.
62d CONGRESS			
Feb. 12, 1913	Joint session	Counting electoral votes	N.A.
Feb. 15, 1913	......do	Memorial for Vice President James S. Sherman.[17]	Senators Elihu Root, Thomas S. Martin, Jacob H. Gallinger, John R. Thornton, Henry Cabot Lodge, John W. Kern, Robert M. LaFollette, John Sharp Williams, Charles Curtis, Albert B. Cummins, George T. Oliver, James A. O'Gorman; Speaker Champ Clark; President William Howard Taft.
63d CONGRESS			
Mar. 4, 1913	Inauguration	East Portico	President Woodrow Wilson.
Apr. 8, 1913	Joint session	Tariff message	Do.
June 23, 1913	......do	Currency and bank reform message	Do.
Aug. 27, 1913	......do	Mexican affairs message	Do.
Dec. 2, 1913	......do	Annual Message	Do.
Jan. 20, 1914	......do	Trusts message	Do.
Mar. 5, 1914	......do	Panama Canal tolls	Do.
Apr. 20, 1914	......do	Mexico message	Do.
Sept. 4, 1914	......do	War tax message	Do.
Dec. 8, 1914	......do	Annual Message	Do.
64th CONGRESS			
Dec. 7, 1915	......do	......do	Do.
Aug. 29, 1916	Joint session	Railroad message (labor-management dispute).	Do.
Dec. 5, 1916	......do	Annual Message	Do.
Jan. 22, 1917	Senate	Planning ahead for peace	Do.
Feb. 3, 1917	Joint session	Severing diplomatic relations with Germany.	Do.
Feb. 14, 1917	......do	Counting electoral votes	N.A.
Feb. 26, 1917	......do	Arming of merchant ships	President Woodrow Wilson.
65th CONGRESS			
Mar. 5, 1917	Inauguration	East Portico	Do.
Apr. 2, 1917	Joint session	War with Germany	Do.
May 1, 1917	Senate	Address	René Raphaël Viviani, Minister of Justice from France; Jules Jusserand, Ambassador from France; address attended by Marshal Joseph Jacques Césaire Joffre, member of French Commission to U.S.
May 3, 1917	House	......do	Do.
May 5, 1917	......do	......do	Arthur James Balfour, British Secretary of State for Foreign Affairs.
May 8, 1917	Senate	......do	Do.
May 31, 1917	......do	......do	Ferdinando di'Savoia, Prince of Udine, Head of Italian Mission to U.S.
June 2, 1917	House	......do	Ferdinando di'Savoia, Prince of Udine, Head of Italian Mission to U.S.; Guglielmo Marconi, member of Italian Mission to U.S.

JOINT SESSIONS AND MEETINGS, ADDRESSES TO THE SENATE OR THE HOUSE, AND INAUGURATIONS—CONTINUED

[See notes at end of table]

Congress & Date	Type	Occasion, topic, or inaugural location	Name and position of dignitary (where applicable)
June 22, 1917	Senate	.....do	Baron Moncheur, Chief of Political Bureau of Belgian Foreign Office at Havre.
June 23, 1917	House	.....do	Boris Bakhmetieff, Ambassador from Russia.[18]
June 26, 1917	Senate	.....do	Do.
June 27, 1917	House	.....do	Baron Moncheur, Chief of Political Bureau of Belgian Foreign Office at Havre.
Aug. 30, 1917	Senate	.....do	Kikujirō Ishii, Ambassador from Japan.
Sept. 5, 1917	House	.....do	Do.
Dec. 4, 1917	Joint session	Annual Message/War with Austria-Hungary.	President Woodrow Wilson.
Jan. 4, 1918	.....do	Federal operation of transportation systems.	Do.
Jan. 5, 1918	Senate	Address	Milenko Vesnic, Head of Serbian War Mission.
Jan. 8, 1918	House	Address	Milenko Vesnic, Head of Serbian War Mission.
Do	Joint session	Program for world's peace	President Woodrow Wilson.
Feb. 11, 1918	.....do	Peace message	Do.
May 27, 1918	.....do	War finance message	Do.
Sept. 24, 1918	Senate	Address and Reception [19]	Jules Jusserand, Ambassador from France; Vice President Thomas R. Marshall.
Sept. 30 1918	.....do	Support of woman suffrage	President Woodrow Wilson.
Nov. 11, 1918	Joint session	Terms of armistice signed by Germany	Do.
Dec. 2, 1918	.....do	Annual Message	Do.
Feb. 9, 1919	.....do	Memorial to Theodore Roosevelt	Senator Henry Cabot Lodge, Sr.; ceremony attended by former President William Howard Taft.
66th CONGRESS			
June 23, 1919	Senate	Address	Epitácio da Silva Pessoa, President-elect of Brazil.
July 10, 1919	.....do	Versailles Treaty ....:...............	President Woodrow Wilson.
Aug. 8, 1919	Joint session	Cost of living message	Do.
Sept. 18, 1919	.....do	Address	President pro tempore Albert B. Cummins; Speaker Frederick H. Gillett; Representative and former Speaker Champ Clark; General John J. Pershing.
Oct. 28, 1919	Senate	.....do	Albert I, King of the Belgians.
Do	House	.....do	Do.
Feb. 9, 1921	Joint session	Counting electoral votes	N.A.
67th CONGRESS			
Mar. 4, 1921	Inauguration	East Portico	President Warren G. Harding.
Apr. 12, 1921	Joint session	Federal problem message	Do.
July 12, 1921	Senate	Adjusted compensation for veterans of the World War[20].	Do.
Dec. 6, 1921	Joint session	Annual Message	Do.
Feb. 28, 1922	.....do	Maintenance of the merchant marine	Do.
Aug. 18, 1922	.....do	Coal and railroad message	Do.
Nov. 21, 1922	.....do	Promotion of the American merchant marine.	Do.
Dec. 8, 1922	.....do	Annual Message[21]	Do.
Feb. 7, 1923	.....do	British debt due to the United States	Do.
68th CONGRESS			
Dec. 6, 1923	.....do	Annual Message	President Calvin Coolidge.
Feb. 27, 1924	.....do	Memorial to Warren G. Harding	Charles Evans Hughes, Secretary of State; ceremony attended by President Calvin Coolidge.
Dec. 15, 1924	.....do	Memorial to Woodrow Wilson	Dr. Edwin Anderson Alderman, President of the University of Virginia; ceremony attended by President Calvin Coolidge.
Feb. 11, 1925	.....do	Counting electoral votes	N.A.
69th CONGRESS			
Mar. 4, 1925	Inauguration	East Portico	President Calvin Coolidge.
Feb. 22, 1927	Joint session	George Washington birthday message ..	Do.
70th CONGRESS			
Jan. 25, 1928	House	Reception and Address	William Thomas Cosgrave, President of Executive Council of Ireland.
Feb. 13, 1929	Joint session	Counting electoral votes	N.A.

JOINT SESSIONS AND MEETINGS, ADDRESSES TO THE SENATE OR THE HOUSE, AND INAUGURATIONS—CONTINUED

[See notes at end of table]

Congress & Date	Type	Occasion, topic, or inaugural location	Name and position of dignitary (where applicable)
71st CONGRESS			
Mar. 4, 1929	Inauguration	East Portico	President Herbert Hoover.
Oct. 7, 1929	Senate	Address	James Ramsay MacDonald, Prime Minister of the United Kingdom.
Jan. 13, 1930	......do	Reception	Jan Christiaan Smuts, former Prime Minister of South Africa.
72d CONGRESS			
Feb. 22, 1932	Joint session	Bicentennial of George Washington's birth.	President Herbert Hoover.
May 31, 1932	Senate	Emergency character of economic situation in U.S.	Do.
Feb. 6, 1933	Joint meeting	Memorial to Calvin Coolidge	Arthur Prentice Rugg, Chief Justice of the Supreme Judicial Court of Massachusetts; ceremony attended by President Herbert Hoover.
Feb. 8, 1933	Joint session	Counting electoral votes	N.A.
73d CONGRESS			
Mar. 4, 1933	Inauguration	East Portico	President Franklin Delano Roosevelt.
Jan. 3, 1934	Joint session	Annual Message	President Franklin Delano Roosevelt.
May 20, 1934	......do	100th anniversary, death of Lafayette	André de Laboulaye, Ambassador of France; President Franklin Delano Roosevelt; ceremony attended by Count de Chambrun, great-grandson of Lafayette.
74th CONGRESS			
Jan. 4, 1935	......do	Annual Message	President Franklin Delano Roosevelt.
May 22, 1935	......do	Veto message	Do.
Jan. 3, 1936	......do	Annual Message	Do.
75th CONGRESS			
Jan. 6, 1937	......do	Counting electoral votes	N.A.
Do	......do	Annual Message	President Franklin Delano Roosevelt.
Jan. 20, 1937	Inauguration	East Portico	President Franklin Delano Roosevelt; Vice President John Nance Garner.[22]
Apr. 1, 1937	Senate	Address	John Buchan, Lord Tweedsmuir, Governor General of Canada.
Do	House	......do	Do.
Jan. 3, 1938	Joint session	Annual Message	President Franklin Delano Roosevelt.
76th CONGRESS			
Jan. 4, 1939	......do	......do	Do.
Mar. 4, 1939	......do	Sesquicentennial of the 1st Congress	Do.
May 8, 1939	Senate	Address	Anastasio Somoza Garcia, President of Nicaragua.
Do	House	......do	Do.
June 9, 1939	Joint meeting	Reception [23]	George VI and Elizabeth, King and Queen of the United Kingdom.
Sept. 21, 1939	Joint session	Neutrality address	President Franklin Delano Roosevelt.
Jan. 3, 1940	......do	Annual Message	Do.
May 16, 1940	......do	National defense message	Do.
77th CONGRESS			
Jan. 6, 1941	......do	Counting electoral votes	N.A.
Do	......do	Annual Message	President Franklin Delano Roosevelt.
Jan. 20, 1941	......do	Inauguration, East Portico	President Franklin Delano Roosevelt; Vice President Henry A. Wallace.
Dec. 8, 1941	......do	War with Japan	President Franklin Delano Roosevelt.
Dec. 26, 1941	Joint meeting [24]	Address	Winston Churchill, Prime Minister of the United Kingdom.
Jan. 6, 1942	Joint session	Annual Message	President Franklin Delano Roosevelt.
May 11, 1942	Senate	Address	Manuel Prado, President of Peru.
Do	House	......do	Do.
June 2, 1942	......do	......do	Manuel Luis Quezon, President of the Philippines.[25]
June 4, 1942	Senate	......do	Do.
June 15, 1942	......do	......do	George II, King of Greece.[26]
Do	House	......do	Do.
June 25, 1942	Senate	......do	Peter II, King of Yugoslavia.[26]
Do	House	......do	Do.
Aug. 6, 1942	Senate [27]	......do	Wilhelmina, Queen of the Netherlands.[26]
Nov. 24, 1942	House	......do	Carlos Arroyo del Río, President of Ecuador.
Nov. 25, 1942	Senate	......do	Do.
Dec. 10, 1942	House	......do	Fulgencio Batista, President of Cuba.
78th CONGRESS			
Jan. 7, 1943	Joint session	Annual Message	President Franklin Delano Roosevelt.

JOINT SESSIONS AND MEETINGS, ADDRESSES TO THE SENATE OR THE HOUSE, AND INAUGURATIONS—CONTINUED

[See notes at end of table]

Congress & Date	Type	Occasion, topic, or inaugural location	Name and position of dignitary (where applicable)
Feb. 18, 1943	Senate	Remarks	Madame Chiang Kai-shek, of China.
Do	House	Address	Do.
May 6, 1943	Senate	......do	Enrique Peñaranda, President of Bolivia.
Do	House	......do	Do.
May 13, 1943	Senate	......do	Edvard Beneš, President of Czechoslovakia.[26]
Do	House	......do	Do.
May 19, 1943	Joint meeting	Address	Winston Churchill, Prime Minister of the United Kingdom.
May 27, 1943	Senate	Remarks	Edwin Barclay, President of Liberia.
Do	House	Address	Do.
June 10, 1943	Senate	......do	President Hininio Moríñigo M., President of Paraguay.
Do	House	......do	Do.
Oct. 15, 1943	Senate	......do	Elie Lescot, President of Haiti.
Nov. 18, 1943	Joint meeting	Moscow Conference	Cordell Hull, Secretary of State.
Jan. 20, 1944	Senate	Address	Isaías Medina Angarita, President of Venezuela.
Do	House	......do	Do.
79th CONGRESS			
Jan. 6, 1945	Joint session	Counting electoral votes	N.A.
Jan. 6, 1945	Joint session	Annual Message	President Roosevelt was not present. His message was read before the Joint Session of Congress.
Jan. 20, 1945	Inauguration	South Portico, The White House [28]	President Franklin Delano Roosevelt; Vice President Harry S. Truman.
Mar. 1, 1945	Joint session	Yalta Conference	President Franklin Delano Roosevelt.
Apr. 16, 1945	......do	Prosecution of the War	President Harry S. Truman.
May 21, 1945	......do	Bestowal of Congressional Medal of Honor on Tech. Sgt. Jake William Lindsey.	General George C. Marshall, Chief of Staff, U.S. Army; President Harry S. Truman.
June 18, 1945	Joint meeting	Address	General Dwight D. Eisenhower, Supreme Commander, Allied Expeditionary Force.
July 2, 1945	Senate	United Nations Charter	President Harry S. Truman.
Oct. 5, 1945	Joint meeting	Address	Admiral Chester W. Nimitz, Commander-in-Chief, Pacific Fleet.
Oct. 23, 1945	Joint session	Universal military training message	President Harry S. Truman.
Nov. 13, 1945	Joint meeting	Address	Clement R. Attlee, Prime Minister of the United Kingdom.
May 25, 1946	Joint session	Railroad strike message	President Harry S. Truman.
July 1, 1946	......do	Memorial to Franklin Delano Roosevelt	John Winant, U.S. Representative on the Economic and Social Council of the United Nations; ceremony attended by President Harry S. Truman and Mrs. Franklin Delano Roosevelt.
80th CONGRESS			
Jan. 6, 1947	......do	State of the Union Address [29]	President Harry S. Truman.
Mar. 12, 1947	......do	Greek-Turkish aid policy	Do.
May 1, 1947	Joint meeting	Address	Miguel Alemán, President of Mexico.
Nov. 17, 1947	Joint session	Aid to Europe message	President Harry S. Truman.
Jan. 7, 1948	......do	State of the Union Address	Do.
Mar. 17, 1948	......do	National security and conditions in Europe.	Do.
Apr. 19, 1948	......do	50th anniversary, liberation of Cuba	President Harry S. Truman; Guillermo Belt, Ambassador of Cuba.
July 27, 1948	......do	Inflation, housing, and civil rights	President Harry S. Truman.
81st CONGRESS			
Jan. 5, 1949	......do	State of the Union Address	Do.
Jan. 6, 1949	......do	Counting electoral votes	N.A.
Jan. 20, 1949	......do	Inauguration, East Portico	President Harry S. Truman; Vice President Alben W. Barkley.
May 19, 1949	Joint meeting	Address	Eurico Gaspar Dutra, President of Brazil.
Aug. 9, 1949	House	......do	Elpidio Quirino, President of the Philippines.
Do	Senate	......do	Do.
Oct. 13, 1949	......do	......do	Jawaharlal Nehru, Prime Minister of India.
Do	House	......do	Do.
Jan. 4, 1950	Joint session	State of the Union Address	President Harry S. Truman.
Apr. 13, 1950	Senate	Address	Gabriel González-Videla, President of Chile.
May 4, 1950	......do	......do	Liaquat Ali Khan, Prime Minister of Pakistan.
Do	House	......do	Do.

JOINT SESSIONS AND MEETINGS, ADDRESSES TO THE SENATE OR THE HOUSE, AND INAUGURATIONS—CONTINUED

[See notes at end of table]

Congress & Date	Type	Occasion, topic, or inaugural location	Name and position of dignitary (where applicable)
May 31, 1950	Joint meeting	Address	Dean Acheson, Secretary of State.
July 28, 1950	Senate	......do	Chōjirō Kuriyama, member of Japanese Diet.
July 31, 1950	House	......do	Tokutarō Kitamura, member of Japanese Diet.
Aug. 1, 1950	......do	......do	Robert Gordon Menzies, Prime Minister of Australia.
Do	Senate	......do	Do.
82d CONGRESS			
Jan. 8, 1951	Joint session	State of the Union Address	President Harry S. Truman.
Feb. 1, 1951	Joint meeting [30]	North Atlantic Treaty Organization	General Dwight D. Eisenhower.
Apr. 2, 1951	Joint meeting	Address	Vincent Auriol, President of France.
Apr. 19, 1951	......do	Return from Pacific Command	General Douglas MacArthur.
June 21, 1951	......do	Address	Galo Plaza, President of Ecuador.
July 2, 1951	Senate	Addresses	Tadao Kuraishi, and Aisuke Okamoto, members of Japanese Diet.
Aug. 23, 1951	......do	Address	Zentarō Kosaka, member of Japanese Diet.
Sept. 24, 1951	Joint meeting	......do	Alcide de Gasperi, Prime Minister of Italy.
Jan. 9, 1952	Joint session	State of the Union Address	President Harry S. Truman.
Jan. 17, 1952	Joint meeting	Address	Winston Churchill, Prime Minister of the United Kingdom.
Apr. 3, 1952	Joint meeting	Address	Juliana, Queen of the Netherlands.
May 22, 1952	......do	Korea	General Matthew B. Ridgway.
June 10, 1952	Joint session	Steel industry dispute	President Harry S. Truman.
83d CONGRESS			
Jan. 6, 1953	......do	Counting electoral votes	N.A.
Jan. 20, 1953	......do	Inauguration, East Portico	President Dwight D. Eisenhower; Vice President Richard M. Nixon.
Feb. 2, 1953	......do	State of the Union Address	President Dwight D. Eisenhower.
Jan. 7, 1954	......do	......do	Do.
Jan. 29, 1954	Joint meeting	Address	Celal Bayar, President of Turkey.
May 4, 1954	......do	......do	Vincent Massey, Governor General of Canada.
May 28, 1954	......do	......do	Haile Selassie I, Emperor of Ethiopia.
July 28, 1954	......do	......do	Syngman Rhee, President of South Korea.
Nov. 12, 1954	Senate	Remarks	Shigeru Yoshida, Prime Minister of Japan.
Nov. 17, 1954	......do	Address [31]	Sarvepalli Radhakrishnan, Vice President of India.
Nov. 18, 1954	......do	Remarks	Pierre Mendès-France, Premier of France.
84th CONGRESS			
Jan. 6, 1955	Joint session	State of the Union Address	President Dwight D. Eisenhower.
Jan. 27, 1955	Joint meeting	Address	Paul E. Magliore, President of Haiti.
Mar. 16, 1955	Senate	......do	Robert Gordon Menzies, Prime Minister of Australia.
Do	House	......do	Do.
Mar. 30, 1955	Senate	......do	Mario Scelba, Prime Minister of Italy.
Do	House	......do	Do.
May 4, 1955	Senate	......do	P. Phibunsongkhram, Prime Minister of Thailand.
Do	House	......do	Do.
June 30, 1955	Senate	......do	U Nu, Prime Minister of Burma.
Do	House	......do	Do.
Jan. 5, 1956	Senate	......do	Juscelino Kubitschek de Oliverira, President-elect of Brazil.
Feb. 2, 1956	......do	......do	Anthony Eden, Prime Minister of the United Kingdom.
Do	House	......do	Do.
Feb. 29, 1956	Joint meeting ...:	......do	Giovanni Gronchi, President of Italy.
Mar. 15, 1956	Senate	......do	John Aloysius Costello, Prime Minister of Ireland.
Do	House	......do	Do.
Apr. 30, 1956	Senate	......do	João Goulart, Vice President of Brazil.
May 17, 1956	Joint meeting	......do	Sukarno, President of Indonesia.
85th CONGRESS			
Jan. 5, 1957	Joint session	Middle East message	President Dwight D. Eisenhower.
Jan. 7, 1957	......do	Counting electoral votes	N.A.
Jan. 10, 1957	......do	State of the Union Address	President Dwight D. Eisenhower.
Jan. 21, 1957	......do	Inauguration, East Portico	President Dwight D. Eisenhower; Vice President Richard M. Nixon.
Feb. 27, 1957	House	Address	Guy Mollet, Premier of France.
Do	Senate	......do	Do.

JOINT SESSIONS AND MEETINGS, ADDRESSES TO THE SENATE OR THE HOUSE, AND INAUGURATIONS—CONTINUED

[See notes at end of table]

Congress & Date	Type	Occasion, topic, or inaugural location	Name and position of dignitary (where applicable)
May 9, 1957	Joint meeting	......do	Ngo Dinh Diem, President of Vietnam.
May 28, 1957	House	......do	Konrad Adenauer, Chancellor of West Germany.
Do	Senate	......do	Do.
June 20, 1957	......do	......do	Nobusuke Kishi, Prime Minister of Japan.
Do	House	......do	Do.
July 11, 1957	Senate	......do	Husseyn Shaheed Suhrawardy, Prime Minister of Pakistan.
Jan. 9, 1958	Joint session	State of the Union Address	President Dwight D. Eisenhower.
June 5, 1958	Joint meeting	Address	Theodor Heuss, President of West Germany.
June 10, 1958	Senate	......do	Harold Macmillan, Prime Minister of the United Kingdom.
June 18, 1958	Joint meeting	......do	Carlos F. Garcia, President of the Philippines.
June 25, 1958	House	......do	Muhammad Daoud Khan, Prime Minister of Afghanistan.
Do	Senate	......do	Do.
July 24, 1958	......do	......do	Kwame Nkrumah, Prime Minister of Ghana.
July 25, 1958	House	......do	Do.
July 29, 1958	Senate	......do	Amintore Fanfani, Prime Minister of Italy.
Do	House	......do	Do.
86th CONGRESS			
Jan. 9, 1959	Joint session	State of the Union Address	President Dwight D. Eisenhower.
Jan. 21, 1959	Joint meeting	Address	Arturo Frondizi, President of Argentina.
Feb. 12, 1959	Joint session	Sesquicentennial of Abraham Lincoln's birth.	Fredric March, actor; Carl Sandburg, poet.
Mar. 11, 1959	Joint meeting	Address	Jose Maria Lemus, President of El Salvador.
Mar. 18, 1959	......do	......do	Sean T. O'Kelly, President of Ireland.
May 12, 1959	......do	......do	Baudouin, King of the Belgians.
Jan. 7, 1960	Joint session	State of the Union Address	President Dwight D. Eisenhower.
Mar. 30, 1960	Senate	Address	Harold Macmillan, Prime Minister of the United Kingdom.
Apr. 6, 1960	Joint meeting	......do	Alberto Lleras-Camargo, President of Colombia.
Apr. 25, 1960	......do	......do	Charles de Gaulle, President of France.
Apr. 28, 1960	......do	......do	Mahendra, King of Nepal.
June 29, 1960	......do	......do	Bhumibol Adulyadej, King of Thailand.
87th CONGRESS			
Jan. 6, 1961	Joint session	Counting electoral votes	N.A.
Jan. 20, 1961	......do	Inauguration, East Portico	President John F. Kennedy; Vice President Lyndon B. Johnson.
Jan. 30, 1961	......do	State of the Union Address	President John F. Kennedy.
Apr. 13, 1961	Senate	Remarks	Konrad Adenauer, Chancellor of West Germany.
Apr. 18, 1961	House	Address	Constantine Karamanlis, Prime Minister of Greece.
May 4, 1961	Joint meeting	......do	Habib Bourguiba, President of Tunisia.
May 25, 1961	Joint session	Urgent national needs: foreign aid, defense, civil defense, and outer space.	President John F. Kennedy.
June 22, 1961	Senate	Remarks	Hayato Ikeda, Prime Minister of Japan.
Do	House	Address	Do.
July 12, 1961	Joint meeting	......do	Mohammad Ayub Khan, President of Pakistan.
July 26, 1961	House	......do	Abubakar Tafawa Balewa, Prime Minister of Nigeria.
Sept. 21, 1961	Joint meeting	......do	Manuel Prado, President of Peru.
Jan. 11, 1962	Joint session	State of the Union Address	President John F. Kennedy.
Feb. 26, 1962	Joint meeting	Friendship 7: 1st United States orbital space flight.	Lt. Col. John H. Glenn, Jr., USMC; Friendship 7 astronaut.
Apr. 4, 1962	......do	Address	João Goulart, President of Brazil.
Apr. 12, 1962	......do	......do	Mohammad Reza Shah Pahlavi, Shahanshah of Iran.
88th CONGRESS			
Jan. 14, 1963	Joint session	State of the Union Address	President John F. Kennedy.
May 21, 1963	Joint meeting	Flight of Faith 7 Spacecraft	Maj. Gordon L. Cooper, Jr., USAF, Faith 7 astronaut.
Oct. 2, 1963	Senate	Address	Haile Selassie I, Emperor of Ethiopia.
Nov. 27, 1963	Joint session	Assumption of office	President Lyndon B. Johnson.
Jan. 8, 1964	......do	State of the Union Address	Do.
Jan. 15, 1964	Joint meeting	Address	Antonio Segni, President of Italy.
May 28, 1964	......do	......do	Eamon de Valera, President of Ireland.

JOINT SESSIONS AND MEETINGS, ADDRESSES TO THE SENATE OR THE HOUSE, AND INAUGURATIONS—CONTINUED

[See notes at end of table]

Congress & Date	Type	Occasion, topic, or inaugural location	Name and position of dignitary (where applicable)
89th CONGRESS			
Jan. 4, 1965	Joint session	State of the Union Address	President Lyndon B. Johnson.
Jan. 6, 1965	......do	Counting electoral votes	N.A.
Jan. 20, 1965	......do [32]	Inauguration, East Portico	President Lyndon B. Johnson; Vice President Hubert H. Humphrey.
Mar. 15, 1965	Joint session	Voting rights	President Lyndon B. Johnson.
Sept. 14, 1965	Joint meeting	Flight of Gemini 5 Spacecraft	Lt. Col. Gordon L. Cooper, Jr., USAF; and Charles Conrad, Jr., USN; Gemini 5 astronauts.
Jan. 12, 1966	Joint session	State of the Union Address	President Lyndon B. Johnson.
Sept. 15, 1966	Joint meeting	Address	Ferdinand E. Marcos, President of the Philippines.
90th CONGRESS			
Jan. 10, 1967	Joint session	State of the Union Address	President Lyndon B. Johnson.
Apr. 28, 1967	Joint meeting	Vietnam policy	General William C. Westmoreland.
Aug. 16, 1967	Senate	Address	Kurt George Kiesinger, Chancellor of West Germany.
Oct. 27, 1967	Joint meeting	......do	Gustavo Diaz Ordaz, President of Mexico.
Jan. 17, 1968	Joint session	State of the Union Address	President Lyndon B. Johnson.
91st CONGRESS			
Jan. 6, 1969	......do	Counting electoral votes [33]	N.A.
Jan. 9, 1969	Joint meeting	Apollo 8: 1st flight around the moon ...	Col. Frank Borman, USAF; Capt. James A. Lowell, Jr., USN; Lt. Col. William A. Anders, USAF; Apollo 8 astronauts.
Jan. 14, 1969	Joint session	State of the Union Address	President Lyndon B. Johnson.
Jan. 20, 1969	Joint session [32] ..	Inauguration, East Portico	President Richard M. Nixon; Vice President Spiro T. Agnew.
Sept. 16, 1969	Joint meeting	Apollo 11: 1st lunar landing	Neil A. Armstrong; Col. Edwin E. Aldrin, Jr., USAF; and Lt. Col. Michael Collins, USAF; Apollo 11 astronauts.
Nov. 13, 1969	House	Executive-Legislative branch relations and Vietnam policy.	President Richard M. Nixon.
Do	Senate	......do	Do.
Jan. 22, 1970	Joint session	State of the Union Address	Do.
Feb. 25, 1970	Joint meeting	Address	Georges Pompidou, President of France.
June 3, 1970	......do	......do	Rafael Caldera, President of Venezuela.
Sept. 22, 1970	......do	Report on prisoners of war	Col. Frank Borman, Representative to the President on Prisoners of War.
92d CONGRESS			
Jan. 22, 1971	Joint session	State of the Union Address	President Richard M. Nixon.
Sept. 9, 1971	......do	Economic policy	Do.
Do	Joint meeting	Apollo 15: lunar mission	Col. David R. Scott, USAF; Col. James B. Irwin, USAF; and Lt. Col. Alfred M. Worden, USAF; Apollo 15 astronauts.
Jan. 20, 1972	Joint session	State of the Union Address	President Richard M. Nixon.
June 1, 1972	......do	European trip report	Do.
June 15, 1972	Joint meeting	Address	Luis Echeverria Alvarez, President of Mexico.
93d CONGRESS			
Jan. 6, 1973	Joint session	Counting electoral votes	N.A.
Jan. 20, 1973	Inauguration	East Portico	President Richard M. Nixon; Vice President Spiro T. Agnew.
Dec. 6, 1973	Joint meeting	Oath of office to, and Address by Vice President Gerald R. Ford.	Vice President Gerald R. Ford; ceremony attended by President Richard M. Nixon.
Do	Senate	Remarks and Reception	Vice President Gerald R. Ford.
Jan. 30 1974	Joint session	State of the Union Address	President Richard M. Nixon.
Aug. 12, 1974	......do	Assumption of office	President Gerald R. Ford.
Oct. 8, 1974	......do	Economy	Do.
Dec. 19, 1974	Senate	Address [34]	Vice President Nelson A. Rockefeller.
94th CONGRESS			
Jan. 15, 1975	Joint session	State of the Union Address	President Gerald R. Ford.
Apr. 10, 1975	......do	State of the World message	Do.
June 17, 1975	Joint meeting	Address	Walter Scheel, President of West Germany.
Nov. 5, 1975	......do	......do	Anwar El Sadat, President of Egypt.
Jan. 19, 1976	Joint session	State of the Union Address	President Gerald R. Ford.
Jan. 28, 1976	Joint meeting	Address	Yitzhak Rabin, Prime Minister of Israel.
Mar. 17, 1976	......do	......do	Liam Cosgrave, Prime Minister of Ireland.

JOINT SESSIONS AND MEETINGS, ADDRESSES TO THE SENATE OR THE HOUSE, AND INAUGURATIONS—CONTINUED

[See notes at end of table]

Congress & Date	Type	Occasion, topic, or inaugural location	Name and position of dignitary (where applicable)
May 18, 1976	......do	......do	Valery Giscard d'Estaing, President of France.
June 2, 1976	......do	......do	Juan Carlos I, King of Spain.
Sept. 23, 1976	......do	......do	William R. Tolbert, Jr., President of Liberia.
95th CONGRESS			
Jan. 6, 1977	Joint session	Counting electoral votes	N.A.
Jan. 12, 1977	......do	State of the Union Address	President Gerald R. Ford.
Jan. 20, 1977	Inauguration	East Portico	President Jimmy Carter; Vice President Walter F. Mondale.
Feb. 17, 1977	House	Address	José López Portillo, President of Mexico.
Feb. 22, 1977	Joint meeting	Address	Pierre Elliot Trudeau, Prime Minister of Canada.
Apr. 20, 1977	Joint session	Energy	President Jimmy Carter.
Jan. 19, 1978	......do	State of the Union Address	Do.
Sept. 18, 1978	......do	Middle East Peace agreements	President Jimmy Carter; joint session attended by Anwar El Sadat, President of Egypt, and by Menachem Begin, Prime Minister of Israel.
96th CONGRESS			
Jan. 23, 1979	......do	State of the Union Address	Do.
June 18, 1979	......do	Salt II agreements	Do.
Jan. 23, 1980	......do	State of the Union Address	Do.
97th CONGRESS			
Jan. 6, 1981	......do	Counting electoral votes	N.A.
Jan. 20, 1981	Joint session [32]	Inauguration, West Front	President Ronald Reagan; Vice President George Bush.
Feb. 18, 1981	Joint session	Economic recovery	President Ronald Reagan.
Apr. 28, 1981	......do	Economic recovery—inflation	Do.
Jan. 26, 1982	......do	State of the Union Address	Do.
Jan. 28, 1982	Joint meeting	Centennial of birth of Franklin Delano Roosevelt.	Dr. Arthur Schlesinger, historian; Senator Jennings Randolph; Representative Claude Pepper; Averell Harriman, former Governor of New York [35]; former Representative James Roosevelt, son of President Roosevelt.
Apr. 21, 1982	......do	Address	Beatrix, Queen of the Netherlands.
98th CONGRESS			
Jan. 25, 1983	Joint session	State of the Union Address	President Ronald Reagan.
Apr. 27, 1983	......do	Central America	Do.
Oct. 5, 1983	Joint meeting	Address	Karl Carstens, President of West Germany.
Jan. 25, 1984	Joint session	State of the Union Address	President Ronald Reagan.
Mar. 15, 1984	Joint meeting	Address	Dr. Garett FitzGerald, Prime Minister of Ireland.
Mar. 22, 1984	......do	......do	François Mitterand, President of France.
May 8, 1984	......do	Centennial of birth of Harry S. Truman	Representatives Ike Skelton and Alan Wheat; former Senator Stuart Symington; Margaret Truman Daniel, daughter of President Truman; and Senator Mark Hatfield.
May 16, 1984	......do	Address	Miguel de la Madrid, President of Mexico.
99th CONGRESS			
Jan. 7, 1985	Joint session	Counting electoral votes	N.A.
Jan. 21, 1985	Inauguration	Rotunda [36]	President Ronald Reagan; Vice President George Bush.
Feb. 6, 1985	Joint session	State of the Union Address	President Ronald Reagan.
Feb. 20, 1985	Joint meeting	Address	Margaret Thatcher, Prime Minister of the United Kingdom.
Mar. 6, 1985	......do	......do	Bettino Craxi, President of the Council of Ministers of Italy.
Mar. 20, 1985	......do	......do	Raul Alfonsin, President of Argentina.
June 13, 1985	......do	......do	Rajiv Gandhi, Prime Minister of India.
Oct. 9, 1985	......do	......do	Lee Kuan Yew, Prime Minister of Singapore.
Nov. 21, 1985	Joint session	Geneva Summit	President Ronald Reagan.
Feb. 4, 1986	......do	State of the Union Address	Do.
Sept. 11, 1986	Joint meeting	Address	Jose Sarney, President of Brazil.
Sept. 18, 1986	......do	......do	Corazon C. Aquino, President of the Philippines.
100th CONGRESS			
Jan. 27, 1987	Joint session	State of the Union Address	President Ronald Reagan.

JOINT SESSIONS AND MEETINGS, ADDRESSES TO THE SENATE OR THE HOUSE, AND INAUGURATIONS—CONTINUED

[See notes at end of table]

Congress & Date	Type	Occasion, topic, or inaugural location	Name and position of dignitary (where applicable)
Nov. 10, 1987	Joint meeting	Address	Chaim Herzog, President of Israel.
Jan. 25, 1988	Joint session	State of the Union Address	President Ronald Reagan.
Apr. 27, 1988	Joint meeting	Address	Brian Mulroney, Prime Minister of Canada.
June 23, 1988	......do	......do	Robert Hawke, Prime Minister of Australia.
101st CONGRESS			
Jan. 4, 1989	Joint session	Counting electoral votes	N.A.
Jan. 20, 1989	Inauguration	West Front	President George Bush; Vice President Dan Quayle.
Feb. 9, 1989	Joint session	Building a Better America	President George Bush.
Mar. 2, 1989	Joint meeting	Bicentennial of the 1st Congress	President Pro Tempore Robert C. Byrd; Speaker James C. Wright, Jr.; Representatives Lindy Boggs, Thomas S. Foley, and Robert H. Michel; Senators George Mitchell and Robert Dole; Howard Nemerov, Poet Laureate of the United States; David McCullough, historian; Anthony M. Frank, Postmaster General; former Senator Nicholas Brady, Secretary of the Treasury.
Apr. 6, 1989	Senate [37]	Addresses on the 200th anniversary commemoration of Senate's first legislative session.	Former Senators Thomas F. Eagleton and Howard H. Baker, Jr..
June 7, 1989	Joint meeting	Address	Benazir Bhutto, Prime Minister of Pakistan.
Oct. 4, 1989	......do	......do	Carlos Salinas de Gortari, President of Mexico.
Oct. 18, 1989	......do	......do	Roh Tae Woo, President of South Korea.
Nov. 15, 1989	Joint meeting	Address	Lech Walesa, chairman of Solidarność labor union, Poland.
Jan. 31, 1990	Joint session	State of the Union Address	President George Bush.
Feb. 21, 1990	Joint meeting	Address	Vaclav Hável, President of Czechoslovakia.
Mar. 7, 1990	......do	......do	Giulio Andreotti, President of the Council of Ministers of Italy.
Mar. 27, 1990	......do	Centennial of birth of Dwight D. Eisenhower.	Senator Robert Dole; Walter Cronkite, television journalist; Winston S. Churchill, member of British Parliament and grandson of Prime Minister Churchill; Clark M. Clifford, former Secretary of Defense; James D. Robinson III, chairman of Eisenhower Centennial Foundation; Arnold Palmer, professional golfer; John S.D. Eisenhower, former Ambassador to Belgium and son of President Eisenhower; Representatives Beverly Byron, William F. Goodling, and Pat Roberts.
June 26, 1990	......do	Address	Nelson Mandela, Deputy President of the African National Congress, South Africa.
Sept. 11, 1990	Joint session	Invasion of Kuwait by Iraq	President George Bush.
102d CONGRESS			
Jan. 29, 1991	......do	State of the Union Address	Do.
Mar. 6, 1991	......do	Conclusion of Persian Gulf War	Do.
Apr. 16, 1991	Joint meeting	Address	Violeta B. de Chamorro, President of Nicaragua.
May 8, 1991	House [38]	......do	General H. Norman Schwarzkopf.
May 16, 1991	Joint meeting	Address	Elizabeth II, Queen of the United Kingdom; joint meeting also attended by Prince Philip.
Nov. 14, 1991	......do	......do	Carlos Saul Menem, President of Argentina.
Jan. 28, 1992	Joint session	State of the Union Address	President George Bush.
Apr. 30, 1992	Joint meeting	Address	Richard von Weizsäcker, President of Germany.
June 17, 1992	......do	......do	Boris Yeltsin, President of Russia.
103d CONGRESS			
Jan. 6, 1993	Joint session	Counting electoral votes	N.A.
Jan. 20, 1993	Inauguration	West Front	President William J. Clinton; Vice President Albert Gore.
Feb. 17, 1993	Joint session	Economic Address [39]	President William J. Clinton.
Sept. 22, 1993	......do	Health care reform	Do.
Jan. 25, 1994	Joint session	State of the Union Address	Do.

JOINT SESSIONS AND MEETINGS, ADDRESSES TO THE SENATE OR THE HOUSE, AND INAUGURATIONS—CONTINUED

[See notes at end of table]

Congress & Date	Type	Occasion, topic, or inaugural location	Name and position of dignitary (where applicable)
May 18, 1994	Joint meeting	Address	Narasimha Rao, Prime Minister of India.
July 26, 1994	......do	Addresses	Hussein I, King of Jordan; Yitzhak Rabin, Prime Minister of Israel.
Oct. 6, 1994	......do	Address	Nelson Mandela, President of South Africa.
104th CONGRESS			
Jan. 24, 1995	Joint session	State of the Union Address	President William J. Clinton.
July 26, 1995	Joint meeting	Address	Kim Yong-sam, President of South Korea.[40]
Oct. 11, 1995	......do	Close of the Commemoration of the 50th Anniversary of World War II.	Speaker Newt Gingrich; Vice President Albert Gore; President Pro Tempore Strom Thurmond; Representatives Henry J. Hyde and G. V. "Sonny" Montgomery; Senators Daniel K. Inouye and Robert Dole; former Representative Robert H. Michel; General Louis H. Wilson (ret.), former Commandant of the Marine Corps.
Dec. 12, 1995	......do	Address	Shimon Peres, Prime Minister of Israel.
Jan. 30, 1996	Joint session	State of the Union Address	President William J. Clinton.
Feb. 1, 1996	Joint meeting	Address	Jacques Chirac, President of France.
July 10, 1996	......do	......do	Benyamin Netanyahu, Prime Minister of Israel.
Sept. 11, 1996	......do	......do	John Bruton, Prime Minister of Ireland.
105th CONGRESS			
Jan. 9, 1997	Joint session	Counting electoral votes	N.A.
Jan. 20, 1997	Inauguration	West Front	President William J. Clinton; Vice President Albert Gore.
Feb. 4, 1997	Joint session	State of the Union Address[41]	President William J. Clinton.
Feb. 27, 1997	Joint meeting	Address	Eduardo Frei, President of Chile.
Jan. 27, 1998	Joint session	State of the Union Address	President William J. Clinton.
June 10, 1998	Joint meeting	Address	Kim Dae-jung, President of South Korea.
July 15, 1998	......do	......do	Emil Constantinescu, President of Romania.
106th CONGRESS			
Jan. 19, 1999	Joint session	State of the Union Address	President William J. Clinton.
Jan. 27, 2000	......do	......do	Do.
Sept. 14, 2000	Joint meeting	Address	Atal Bihari Vajpayee, Prime Minister of India.
107th CONGRESS			
Jan. 6, 2001	Joint session	Counting electoral votes	N.A.
Jan. 20, 2001	Inauguration	West Front	President George W. Bush; Vice President Richard B. Cheney.
Feb. 27, 2001	Joint session	Budget message[39]	President George W. Bush.
Sept. 6, 2001	Joint meeting	Address	Vicente Fox, President of Mexico.
Sept. 20, 2001	Joint session	War on terrorism	President George W. Bush; joint session attended by Tony Blair, Prime Minister of the United Kingdom, by Tom Ridge, Governor of Pennsylvania, by George Pataki, Governor of New York, and by Rudolph Giuliani, Mayor of New York City.
Jan. 29, 2002	......do	State of the Union Address	President George W. Bush; joint session attended by Hamid Karzai, Chairman of the Interim Authority of Afghanistan.
108th CONGRESS			
Jan. 28, 2003	......do	......do	President George W. Bush.
July 17, 2003	Joint meeting	Address	Tony Blair, Prime Minister of the United Kingdom; joint meeting attended by Mrs. George W. Bush.
Jan. 20, 2004	Joint session	State of the Union Address	President George W. Bush.
Feb. 4, 2004	Joint meeting	Address	Jose Maria Aznar, President of the Government of Spain.
June 15, 2004	......do	......do	Hamid Karzai, President of Afghanistan.
Sept. 23, 2004	......do	......do	Ayad Allawi, Interim Prime Minister of Iraq.
109th CONGRESS			
Jan. 6, 2005	Joint session	Counting electoral votes[42]	N.A.
Jan. 20, 2005	Inauguration	West Front	President George W. Bush; Vice President Richard B. Cheney.
Feb. 2, 2005	Joint session	State of the Union Address	President George W. Bush.
Apr. 6, 2005	Joint meeting	Address	Viktor Yushchenko, President of Ukraine.
July 19, 2005	......do	......do	Dr. Manmohan Singh, Prime Minister of India.

[1] Closing date for this table was July 19, 2005.

[2] The oath of office was administered to George Washington outside on the gallery in front of the Senate Chamber, after which the Congress and the President returned to the chamber to hear the inaugural address. They then proceeded to St. Paul's Chapel for the "divine service" performed by the Chaplain of the Congress. Adjournment of the ceremony did not occur until the Congress returned to Federal Hall.

[3] Funeral oration was delivered at the German Lutheran Church in Philadelphia.

[4] Because of a tie in the electoral vote between Thomas Jefferson and Aaron Burr, the House of Representatives had to decide the election. Thirty-six ballots were required to break the deadlock, with Jefferson's election as President and Burr's as Vice President on February 17. The Twelfth Amendment was added to the Constitution to prevent the 1800 problem from recurring.

[5] During most of the period while the Capitol was being reconstructed following the fire of 1814, the Congress met in the "Brick Capitol," constructed on the site of the present Supreme Court building. This joint session took place in the Representatives' chamber on the 2d floor of the building.

[6] The joint session to count electoral votes was dissolved because the House and Senate disagreed on Missouri's status regarding statehood. The joint session was reconvened the same day and Missouri's votes were counted.

[7] While this occasion has historically been referred to as the first joint meeting of Congress, the Journals of the House and Senate indicate that Lafayette actually addressed the House of Representatives, with some of the Senators present as guests of the House (having been invited at the last minute to attend). Similar occasions, when members of the one body were invited as guests of the other, include the Senate address by Queen Wilhelmina of the Netherlands on Aug. 6, 1942, and the House address by General H. Norman Schwarzkopf on May 8, 1991.

[8] Although Andrew Jackson won the popular vote by a substantial amount and had the highest number of electoral votes from among the several candidates, he did not receive the required majority of the electoral votes. The responsibility for choosing the new President therefore devolved upon the House of Representatives. As soon as the Senators left the chamber, the balloting proceeded, and John Quincy Adams was elected on the first ballot.

[9] The ceremony was moved outside to accommodate the extraordinarily large crowd of people who had come to Washington to see the inauguration.

[10] The ceremony was moved inside because of cold weather.

[11] Following the death of President Zachary Taylor, Vice President Millard Fillmore took the Presidential oath of office in a special joint session in the Hall of the House.

[12] The joint session to count electoral votes was dissolved three times so that the House and Senate could resolve several electoral disputes.

[13] Because of a severe cold and hoarseness, the King could not deliver his speech, which was read by former Representative Elisha Hunt Allen, then serving as Chancellor and Chief Justice of the Hawaiian Islands.

[14] The contested election between Rutherford B. Hayes and Samuel J. Tilden created a constitutional crisis. Tilden won the popular vote by a close margin, but disputes concerning the electoral vote returns from four states deadlocked the proceedings of the joint session. Anticipating this development, the Congress had created a special commission of five Senators, five Representatives, and five Supreme Court Justices to resolve such disputes. The Commission met in the Supreme Court Chamber (the present Old Senate Chamber) as each problem arose. In each case, the Commission accepted the Hayes electors, securing his election by one electoral vote. The joint session was convened on 15 occasions, with the last on March 2, just three days before the inauguration.

[15] The speech was written by former Speaker and Senator Robert C. Winthrop, who could not attend the ceremony because of ill health.

[16] Because of a blizzard, the ceremony was moved inside, where it was held as part of the Senate's special session. President William Howard Taft took the oath of office and gave his inaugural address after Vice President James S. Sherman's inaugural address and the swearing-in of the new senators.

[17] Held in the Senate Chamber.

[18] Bakhmetieff represented the provisional government of Russia set up after the overthrow of the monarchy in March 1917 and recognized by the United States. The Bolsheviks took over in November 1917.

[19] The address and reception were in conjunction with the presentation to the Senate by France of two Sèvres vases in appreciation of the United States' involvement in World War I. The vases are today in the Senate lobby, just off the Senate floor. Two additional Sèvres vases were given without ceremony to the House of Representatives, which today are in the Rayburn Room, not far from the floor of the House.

[20] Senators later objected to President Harding's speech (given with no advance notice to most of the Senators) as an unconstitutional effort to interfere with the deliberations of the Senate, and Harding did not repeat visits of this kind.

[21] This was the first Annual Message broadcast live on radio.

[22] This was the first inauguration held pursuant to the Twentieth Amendment, which changed the date from March 4 to January 20. The Vice Presidential oath, which previously had been given earlier on the same day in the Senate Chamber, was added to the inaugural ceremony as well, but the Vice Presidential inaugural address was discontinued.

[23] A joint reception for the King and Queen of the United Kingdom was held in the Rotunda, authorized by Senate Concurrent Resolution 17, 76th Congress. Although the concurrent resolution was structured to establish a joint meeting, the Senate, in fact, adjourned rather than recessed as called for by the resolution.

[24] Held in the Senate Chamber.

[25] At this time, the Philippines was still a possession of the United States, although it had been made a self-governing commonwealth in 1935, in preparation for full independence in 1946. From 1909 to 1916, Quezon had served in the U.S. House of Representatives as the resident commissioner from the Philippines.

[26] In exile.

[27] For this Senate Address by Queen Wilhelmina, the members of the House of Representatives were invited as guests. This occasion has sometimes been mistakenly referred to as a joint meeting.

[28] The oaths of office were taken in simple ceremonies at the White House because the expense and festivity of a Capitol ceremony were thought inappropriate because of the war. The Joint Committee on Arrangements of the Congress was in charge, however, and both the Senate and the House of Representatives were present.

[29] This was the first time the term "State of the Union Address" was used for the President's Annual Message. Also, it was the first time the address was shown live on television.

[30] This was an informal meeting in the Coolidge Auditorium of the Library of Congress.

[31] Presentation of new ivory gavel to the Senate.

[32] According to the Congressional Record, the Senate adjourned prior to the inaugural ceremonies, even though the previously adopted resolution had stated the adjournment would come immediately following the inauguration. The Senate Journal records the adjournment as called for in the resolution, hence this listing as a joint session.

[33] The joint session to count electoral votes was dissolved so that the House and Senate could each resolve the dispute regarding a ballot from North Carolina. The joint session was reconvened the same day and the North Carolina vote was counted.

[34] Rockefeller was sworn in as Vice President by Chief Justice Warren E. Burger, after which, by unanimous consent, he was allowed to address the Senate.

[35] Because the Governor had laryngitis, his speech was read by his wife, Pamela.

[36] The ceremony was moved inside because of extremely cold weather.

[37] These commemorative addresses were given in the Old Senate Chamber during a regular legislative session.

[38] For this House Address by General Schwarzkopf, the members of the Senate were invited as guests.

[39] This speech was mislabeled in many sources as a State of the Union Address.

[40] President Kim Yong-sam was in Washington for the dedication of the Korean Veterans' Memorial, held the day after this joint meeting.

[41] This was the first State of the Union Address carried live on the Internet.

[42] The joint session to count electoral votes was dissolved so that the House and Senate could each discuss the dispute regarding the ballots from Ohio. The joint session was reconvened the same day and the Ohio votes were counted.

REPRESENTATIVES UNDER EACH APPORTIONMENT

State	Constitutional apportionment	First Census, 1790	Second Census, 1800	Third Census, 1810	Fourth Census, 1820	Fifth Census, 1830	Sixth Census, 1840	Seventh Census, 1850	Eighth Census, 1860	Ninth Census, 1870	Tenth Census, 1880	Eleventh Census, 1890	Twelfth Census, 1900	Thirteenth Census, 1910 [1]	Fifteenth Census, 1930	Sixteenth Census, 1940	Seventeenth Census, 1950	Eighteenth Census, 1960	Nineteenth Census, 1970	Twentieth Census, 1980	Twenty-First Census, 1990	Twenty-Second Census, 2000
AL				[2]	3	5	7	7	6	8	8	9	9	10	9	9	9	8	7	7	7	7
AK																	[2,3]	1	1	1	1	1
AZ													[2]	[4]1	1	2	2	3	4	5	6	8
AR						[2]	1	2	3	4	5	6	7	7	7	7	6	4	4	4	4	4
CA							[2]	[4]2	3	4	6	7	8	11	20	23	30	38	43	45	52	53
CO										[2]	1	2	3	4	4	4	4	4	5	6	6	7
CT	5	7	7	7	6	6	4	4	4	4	4	4	5	5	6	6	6	6	6	6	6	5
DE	1	1	1	2	1	1	1	1	1	1	1	1	1	1	1	1	1	1	1	1	1	1
FL							[2]	1	1	2	2	2	3	4	5	6	8	12	15	19	23	25
GA	3	2	4	6	7	9	8	8	7	9	10	11	11	12	10	10	10	10	10	10	11	13
HI																	[2,3]	2	2	2	2	2
ID											[2]	1	1	2	2	2	2	2	2	2	2	2
IL				[2]	1	3	7	9	14	19	20	22	25	27	27	26	25	24	24	22	20	19
IN				[2]	3	7	10	11	11	13	13	13	13	13	12	11	11	11	11	10	10	9
IA							[2]	2	6	9	11	11	11	11	9	8	8	7	6	6	5	5
KS									[2]	3	7	8	8	8	7	6	6	5	5	5	4	4
KY	[2]	[4]2	6	10	12	13	10	10	9	10	11	11	11	11	9	9	8	7	7	7	6	6
LA				[2]	3	3	4	4	5	6	6	6	7	8	8	8	8	8	8	8	7	7
ME				[5]	7	8	7	6	5	5	4	4	4	4	3	3	3	2	2	2	2	2
MD	6	8	9	9	9	8	6	6	5	6	6	6	6	6	6	6	7	8	8	8	8	8
MA	8	14	17	[5]20	13	12	10	11	10	11	12	13	14	16	15	14	14	12	12	11	10	10
MI						[2]	3	4	6	9	11	12	12	13	17	17	18	19	19	18	16	15
MN								[2]	2	3	5	7	9	10	9	9	9	8	8	8	8	8
MS				[2]	1	2	4	5	5	6	7	7	8	8	7	7	6	5	5	5	5	4
MO				[2]	[4]1	2	5	7	9	13	14	15	16	16	13	13	11	10	10	9	9	9
MT											[2]	1	1	2	2	2	2	2	2	2	1	1
NE									[2]	1	3	6	6	6	5	4	4	3	3	3	3	3
NV									[2]	1	1	1	1	1	1	1	1	1	1	2	2	3
NH	3	4	5	6	6	5	4	3	3	3	2	2	2	2	2	2	2	2	2	2	2	2
NJ	4	5	6	6	6	6	5	5	5	7	7	8	10	12	14	14	14	15	15	14	13	13
NM													[2]	[4]1	1	2	2	2	2	3	3	3
NY	6	10	17	27	34	40	34	33	31	33	34	34	37	43	45	45	43	41	39	34	31	29
NC	5	10	12	13	13	13	9	8	7	8	9	9	10	10	11	12	12	11	11	11	12	13
ND											[2]	1	2	3	2	2	2	2	1	1	1	1
OH			[2]	6	14	19	21	21	19	20	21	21	21	22	24	23	23	24	23	21	19	18
OK													[2]	8	9	8	6	6	6	6	6	5
OR								[2]	1	1	1	2	2	3	3	4	4	4	4	5	5	5
PA	8	13	18	23	26	28	24	25	24	27	28	30	32	36	34	33	30	27	25	23	21	19
RI	1	2	2	2	2	2	2	2	2	2	2	2	2	3	2	2	2	2	2	2	2	2
SC	5	6	8	9	9	9	7	6	4	5	7	7	7	7	6	6	6	6	6	6	6	6
SD											[2]	2	2	3	2	2	2	2	2	1	1	1
TN		[2]	3	6	9	13	11	10	8	10	10	10	10	10	9	10	9	9	8	9	9	9
TX							[2]	2	4	6	11	13	16	18	21	21	22	23	24	27	30	32
UT												[2]	1	2	2	2	2	2	2	3	3	3
VT	[2]	[4]2	4	6	5	5	4	3	3	3	2	2	2	2	1	1	1	1	1	1	1	1
VA	10	19	22	23	22	21	15	13	[6]11	9	10	10	10	10	9	9	10	10	10	10	11	11
WA											[2]	2	3	5	6	6	7	7	7	8	9	9
WV									[6]3	3	4	4	5	6	6	6	6	5	4	4	3	3
WI							[2]	3	6	8	9	10	11	11	10	10	10	10	9	9	9	8
WY											[2]	1	1	1	1	1	1	1	1	1	1	1
Total	65	105	141	181	213	240	223	234	241	292	325	356	386	435	435	435	435	435	435	435	435	435

NOTE: The original apportionment of Representatives was assigned in 1787 in the Constitution and remained in effect for the 1st and 2d Congresses. Subsequent apportionments based on the censuses over the years have been figured using several different methods approved by Congress, all with the goal of dividing representation among the states as equally as possible. After each census up to and including the Thirteenth in 1910, Congress would enact a law designating the specific changes in the actual number of Representatives as well as the increase in the ratio of persons-per-Representative. After having made no apportionment after the Fourteenth census in 1920, Congress by statute in 1929 fixed the total number of Representatives at 435 (the number attained with the apportionment after the 1910 census), and since that time, only the ratio of persons-per-Representative has continued to increase, in fact, significantly so. Since the total is now fixed, the specific number of Representatives per state is adjusted after each census to reflect its percentage of the entire population. Since the Sixteenth Census in 1940, the "equal proportions" method of apportioning Representatives within the 435 total has been employed. A detailed explanation of the entire apportionment process can be found in The Historical Atlas of United States Congressional Districts, 1789–1983. Kenneth C. Martis, The Free Press, New York, 1982.

[1] No apportionment was made after the 1920 census.

[2] The following Representatives were added after the indicated apportionments when these states were admitted in the years listed. The number of these additonal Representatives for each state remained in effect until the next census's apportionment (with the exceptions of California and New Mexico, as explained in footnote 4). They are not included in the total for each column. In reading this table, please remember that the apportionments made after each census took effect with the election two years after the census date. As a result, in the table footnote 2 is placed for several states under the decade preceding the one in which it entered the Union, since the previous decade's apportionment was still in effect at the time of statehood. Constitutional: Vermont (1791), 2; Kentucky (1792), 2; First: Tennessee (1796), 1; Second: Ohio (1803), 1; Third: Louisiana (1812), 1; Indiana (1816), 1; Mississippi (1817), 1; Illinois (1818), 1; Alabama (1819), 1; Missouri (1821), 1; Fifth: Arkansas (1836), 1; Michigan (1837), 1; Sixth: Florida (1845), 1; Texas (1845), 2; Iowa (1846), 2; Wisconsin (1848), 1; California (1850), 2; Seventh: Minnesota (1858), 2; Oregon (1859), 1; Kansas (1861), 1; Eighth: Nevada (1864), 1; Nebraska (1867), 1; Ninth: Colorado (1876), 1; Tenth: North Dakota (1889), 1; South Dakota (1889), 2; Montana (1889), 1; Washington (1889), 1; Idaho (1890), 1; Wyoming (1890), 1; Eleventh: Utah (1896), 1; Twelfth: Oklahoma (1907), 5; New Mexico (1912), 2; Arizona (1912), 1; Seventeenth: Alaska (1959), 1; Hawaii (1959), 1.

[3] When Alaska and then Hawaii joined the Union in 1959, the law was changed to allow the total membership of the House of Representatives to increase to 436 and then to 437, apportioning one new Representative for each of those states. The total returned to 435 in 1963, when the 1960 census apportionment took effect.

544

[4] Even though the respective censuses were taken before the following states joined the Union, Representatives for them were apportioned either because of anticipation of statehood or because they had become states in the period between the census and the apportionment, hence they are included in the totals of the respective columns. *First:* Vermont (1791); Kentucky (1792); *Fourth:* Missouri (1821); *Seventh:* California (1850); *Eighth:* Kansas (1861); *Thirteenth:* New Mexico (1912); Arizona (1912). (Please note: These seven states are also included in footnote 2 because they became states while the previous decade's apportionment was still in effect for the House of Representatives.) California's situation was unusual. It was scheduled for inclusion in the figures for the 1850 census apportionment; however, when the apportionment law was passed in 1852, California's census returns were still incomplete so Congress made special provision that the state would retain "the number of Representatives [two] prescribed by the act of admission * * * into the Union until a new apportionment [i.e., after the 1860 census]" would be made. The number of Representatives from California actually increased before the next apportionment to three when Congress gave the state an extra Representative during part of the 37th Congress, from 1862 to 1863. Regarding New Mexico, the 1911 apportionment law, passed by the 62d Congress in response to the 1910 census and effective with the 63d Congress in 1913, stated that "if the Territor[y] of * * * New Mexico shall become [a State] in the Union before the apportionment of Representatives under the next decennial census [it] shall have one Representative * * *." When New Mexico became a state in 1912 during the 62d Congress, it was given two Representatives. The number was decreased to one beginning the next year in the 63d.

[5] The "Maine District" of Massachusetts became a separate state during the term of the 16th Congress, in 1820. For the remainder of that Congress, Maine was assigned one "at large" Representative while Massachusetts continued to have 20 Representatives, the number apportioned to it after the 1810 census. For the 17th Congress (the last before the 1820 census apportionment took effect), seven of Massachusetts's Representatives were reassigned to Maine, leaving Massachusetts with 13.

[6] Of the 11 Representatives apportioned to Virginia after the 1860 census, three were reassigned to West Virginia when that part of Virginia became a separate state in 1863. Since the Virginia seats in the House were vacant at that time because of the Civil War, all of the new Representatives from West Virginia were able to take their seats at once. When Representatives from Virginia reentered the House in 1870, only eight members represented it.

IMPEACHMENT PROCEEDINGS

The provisions of the United States Constitution which apply specifically to impeachments are as follows: Article I, section 2, clause 5; Article I, section 3, clauses 6 and 7; Article II, section 2, clause 1; Article II, section 4; and Article III, section 2, clause 3.

For the officials listed below, the date of impeachment by the House of Representatives is followed by the dates of the Senate trial, with the result of each listed at the end of the entry.

WILLIAM BLOUNT, a Senator of the United States from Tennessee; impeached July 7, 1797; tried Monday, December 17, 1798, to Monday, January 14, 1799; charges dismissed for want of jurisdiction.

JOHN PICKERING, judge of the United States district court for the district of New Hampshire; impeached March 2, 1803; tried Thursday, March 3, 1803, to Monday, March 12, 1804; removed from office.

SAMUEL CHASE, Associate Justice of the Supreme Court of the United States; impeached March 12, 1804; tried Friday, November 30, 1804, to Friday, March 1, 1805; acquitted.

JAMES H. PECK, judge of the United States district court for the district of Missouri; impeached April 24, 1830; tried Monday, April 26, 1830, to Monday, January 31, 1831; acquitted.

WEST H. HUMPHREYS, judge of the United States district court for the middle, eastern, and western districts of Tennessee; impeached May 6, 1862; tried Wednesday, May 7, 1862, to Thursday, June 26, 1862; removed from office and disqualified from future office.

ANDREW JOHNSON, President of the United States; impeached February 24, 1868; tried Tuesday, February 25, 1868, to Tuesday, May 26, 1868; acquitted.

WILLIAM W. BELKNAP, Secretary of War; impeached March 2, 1876; tried Friday, March 3, 1876, to Tuesday, August 1, 1876; acquitted.

CHARLES SWAYNE, judge of the United States district court for the northern district of Florida; impeached December 13, 1904; tried Wednesday, December 14, 1904, to Monday, February 27, 1905; acquitted.

ROBERT W. ARCHBALD, associate judge, United States Commerce Court; impeached July 11, 1912; tried Saturday, July 13, 1912, to Monday, January 13, 1913; removed from office and disqualified from future office.

GEORGE W. ENGLISH, judge of the United States district court for the eastern district of Illinois; impeached April 1, 1926; tried Friday, April 23, 1926, to Monday, December 13, 1926; resigned office Thursday, November 4, 1926; Court of Impeachment adjourned to December 13, 1926, when, on request of House managers, the proceedings were dismissed.

HAROLD LOUDERBACK, judge of the United States district court for the northern district of California; impeached February 24, 1933; tried Monday, May 15, 1933, to Wednesday, May 24, 1933; acquitted.

HALSTED L. RITTER, judge of the United States district court for the southern district of Florida; impeached March 2, 1936; tried Monday, April 6, 1936, to Friday, April 17, 1936; removed from office.

HARRY E. CLAIBORNE, judge of the United States district court of Nevada; impeached July 22, 1986; tried Tuesday, October 7, 1986, to Thursday, October 9, 1986; removed from office.

ALCEE L. HASTINGS, judge of the United States district court for the southern district of Florida; impeached August 3, 1988; tried Wednesday, October 18, 1989, to Friday, October 20, 1989; removed from office.

WALTER L. NIXON, judge of the United States district court for the southern district of Mississippi; impeached May 10, 1989; tried Wednesday, November 1, 1989, to Friday, November 3, 1989; removed from office.

WILLIAM JEFFERSON CLINTON, President of the United States; impeached December 19, 1998; tried Thursday, January 7, 1999, to Friday, February 12, 1999; acquitted.

DELEGATES, REPRESENTATIVES, AND SENATORS SERVING IN THE 1st–109th CONGRESSES [1]

As of February 1, 2005, 11,751 individuals have served: 9,867 only in the House of Representatives, 1,243 only in the Senate, and 641 in both Houses. Total serving in the House of Representatives (including individuals serving in both bodies) is 10,508. Total for the Senate (including individuals serving in both bodies) is 1,884. [2]

State	Date Became Territory	Date Entered Union	Delegates	Representatives Only	Senators Only	Both Houses	Total, Not Including Delegates
Alabama	Mar. 3, 1817	Dec. 14, 1819 (22d)	1	166	24	15	205
Alaska	Aug. 24, 1912	Jan. 3, 1959 (49th)	9	4	6	0	10
Arizona	Feb. 24, 1863	Feb. 14, 1912 (48th)	11	25	7	4	36
Arkansas	Mar. 2, 1819	June 15, 1836 (25th)	3	83	23	9	115
California		Sept. 9, 1850 (31st)		324	32	11	366
Colorado	Feb. 28, 1861	Aug. 1, 1876 (38th)	3	54	24	9	87
Connecticut		Jan. 9, 1788 (5th)		188	28	25	241
Delaware		Dec. 7, 1787 (1st)		47	35	14	96
Florida	Mar. 30, 1822	Mar. 3, 1845 (27th)	5	102	26	6	134
Georgia		Jan. 2, 1788 (4th)		248	37	22	307
Hawaii	June 14, 1900	Aug. 21, 1959 (50th)	10	6	2	3	11
Idaho	Mar. 3, 1863	July 3, 1890 (43d)	9	25	19	6	50
Illinois	Feb. 3, 1809	Dec. 3, 1818 (21st)	3	431	29	22	482
Indiana	May 7, 1800	Dec. 11, 1816 (19th)	3	295	27	17	339
Iowa	June 12, 1838	Dec. 28, 1846 (29th)	2	168	22	11	201
Kansas	May 30, 1854	Jan. 29, 1861 (34th)	2	104	22	9	135
Kentucky		June 1, 1792 (15th)		309	36	29	374
Louisiana	Mar. 24, 1804	Apr. 30, 1812 (18th)	2	144	34	14	192
Maine		Mar. 15, 1820 (23d)		141	18	18	177
Maryland		Apr. 28, 1788 (7th)		252	28	27	307
Massachusetts		Feb. 6, 1788 (6th)		383	20	28	431
Michigan	Jan. 11, 1805	Jan. 26, 1837 (26th)	7	246	24	14	285
Minnesota	Mar. 3, 1849	May 11, 1858 (32d)	3	119	25	11	155
Mississippi	Apr. 17, 1798	Dec. 10, 1817 (20th)	5	109	27	16	152
Missouri	June 4, 1812	Aug. 10, 1821 (24th)	3	291	34	9	334
Montana	May 26, 1864	Nov. 8, 1889 (41st)	5	26	13	6	45
Nebraska	May 30, 1854	Mar. 1, 1867 (37th)	6	86	28	7	121
Nevada	Mar. 2, 1861	Oct. 31, 1864 (36th)	2	25	19	6	50
New Hampshire		June 21, 1788 (9th)		117	35	26	178
New Jersey		Dec. 18, 1787 (3d)		297	48	14	359
New Mexico	Sept. 9, 1850	Jan. 6, 1912 (47th)	13	21	12	3	36
New York		July 26, 1788 (11th)		1,398	36	23	1,457
North Carolina		Nov. 21, 1789 (12th)		305	35	18	358
North Dakota [3]	Mar. 2, 1861	Nov. 2, 1889 (39th)	11	21	15	6	42
Ohio [4]		Mar. 1, 1803 (17th)	2	617	36	18	671
Oklahoma	May 2, 1890	Nov. 16, 1907 (46th)	4	71	11	6	88
Oregon	Aug. 14, 1848	Feb. 14, 1859 (33d)	2	56	31	5	92
Pennsylvania		Dec. 12, 1787 (2d)		995	32	21	1,047
Rhode Island		May 29, 1790 (13th)		61	36	10	107
South Carolina		May 23, 1788 (8th)		195	39	16	250
South Dakota [3]	Mar. 2, 1861	Nov. 2, 1889 (40th)	11	25	16	10	51
Tennessee		June 1, 1796 (16th)	2	242	39	18	299
Texas		Dec. 29, 1845 (28th)		236	21	10	267
Utah	Sept. 9, 1850	Jan. 4, 1896 (45th)	7	33	12	3	48
Vermont		Mar. 4, 1791 (14th)		80	24	15	119
Virginia		June 25, 1788 (10th)		380	25	26	431
Washington	Mar. 2, 1853	Nov. 11, 1889 (42d)	10	68	13	10	91
West Virginia		June 20, 1863 (35th)		91	22	8	121
Wisconsin	Apr. 20, 1836	May 29, 1848 (30th)	6	170	19	7	196
Wyoming	July 25, 1868	July 10, 1890 (44th)	4	14	17	3	34

[1] March 4, 1789 until February 1, 2005.

[2] Some of the larger states split into smaller states as the country grew westward (e.g., part of Virginia became West Virginia); hence, some individuals represented more than one state in the Congress.

[3] North and South Dakota were formed from a single territory on the same date, and they shared the same delegates before statehood.

[4] The Territory Northwest of the Ohio River was established as a district for purposes of temporary government by the Act of July 13, 1787. Virginia ceded the land beyond the Ohio River, and delegates representing the district first came to the 6th Congress on March 4, 1799.

NOTE: Information was supplied by the Congressional Research Service.

POLITICAL DIVISIONS OF THE SENATE AND HOUSE FROM 1855 TO 2005

[All Figures Reflect Immediate Result of Elections. Figures Supplied by the Clerk of the House]

Congress	Years	SENATE					HOUSE OF REPRESENTATIVES				
		No. of Senators	Republicans	Democrats	Other parties	Vacancies	No. of Representatives	Republicans	Democrats	Other parties	Vacancies
34th	1855–1857	62	15	42	5	....	234	108	83	43	....
35th	1857–1859	64	20	39	5	....	237	92	131	14	....
36th	1859–1861	66	26	38	2	....	237	113	101	23	....
37th	1861–1863	50	31	11	7	1	178	106	42	28	2
38th	1863–1865	51	39	12	....	....	183	103	80	....	....
39th	1865–1867	52	42	10	....	....	191	145	46	....	....
40th	1867–1869	53	42	11	....	....	193	143	49	....	1
41st	1869–1871	74	61	11	....	2	243	170	73	....	....
42d	1871–1873	74	57	17	....	....	243	139	104	....	....
43d	1873–1875	74	54	19	....	1	293	203	88	....	2
44th	1875–1877	76	46	29	....	1	293	107	181	3	2
45th	1877–1879	76	39	36	1	....	293	137	156	....	....
46th	1879–1881	76	33	43	....	....	293	128	150	14	1
47th	1881–1883	76	37	37	2	....	293	152	130	11	....
48th	1883–1885	76	40	36	....	....	325	119	200	6	....
49th	1885–1887	76	41	34	....	1	325	140	182	2	1
50th	1887–1889	76	39	37	....	....	325	151	170	4	....
51st	1889–1891	84	47	37	....	....	330	173	156	1	....
52d	1891–1893	88	47	39	2	....	333	88	231	14	....
53d	1893–1895	88	38	44	3	3	356	126	220	10	....
54th	1895–1897	88	44	39	5	....	357	246	104	7	....
55th	1897–1899	90	46	34	10	....	357	206	134	16	1
56th	1899–1901	90	53	26	11	....	357	185	163	9	....
57th	1901–1903	90	56	29	3	2	357	198	153	5	1
58th	1903–1905	90	58	32	....	....	386	207	178	....	1
59th	1905–1907	90	58	32	....	....	386	250	136	....	....
60th	1907–1909	92	61	29	....	2	386	222	164	....	....
61st	1909–1911	92	59	32	....	1	391	219	172	....	....
62d	1911–1913	92	49	42	....	1	391	162	228	1	....
63d	1913–1915	96	44	51	1	....	435	127	290	18	....
64th	1915–1917	96	39	56	1	....	435	193	231	8	3
65th	1917–1919	96	42	53	1	....	435	216	[1]210	9	....
66th	1919–1921	96	48	47	1	....	435	237	191	7	....
67th	1921–1923	96	59	37	....	....	435	300	132	1	2
68th	1923–1925	96	51	43	2	....	435	225	207	3	....
69th	1925–1927	96	54	40	1	1	435	247	183	5	....
70th	1927–1929	96	48	47	1	....	435	237	195	3	....
71st	1929–1931	96	56	39	1	....	435	267	163	1	4
72d	1931–1933	96	48	47	1	....	435	218	[2]216	1	....
73d	1933–1935	96	36	59	1	....	435	117	313	5	....
74th	1935–1937	96	25	69	2	....	435	103	322	10	....
75th	1937–1939	96	17	75	4	....	435	89	333	13	....
76th	1939–1941	96	23	69	4	....	435	169	262	4	....
77th	1941–1943	96	28	66	2	....	435	162	267	6	....
78th	1943–1945	96	38	57	1	....	435	209	222	4	....
79th	1945–1947	96	38	57	1	....	435	190	243	2	....
80th	1947–1949	96	51	45	....	....	435	246	188	1	....
81st	1949–1951	96	42	54	....	....	435	171	263	1	....
82d	1951–1953	96	47	48	1	....	435	199	234	2	....
83d	1953–1955	96	48	46	2	....	435	221	213	1	....
84th	1955–1957	96	47	48	1	....	435	203	232	....	....
85th	1957–1959	96	47	49	....	....	435	201	234	....	....
86th	1959–1961	98	34	64	....	....	[3]436	153	283	....	....
87th	1961–1963	100	36	64	....	....	[4]437	175	262	....	....
88th	1963–1965	100	33	67	....	....	435	176	258	....	1
89th	1965–1967	100	32	68	....	....	435	140	295	....	....
90th	1967–1969	100	36	64	....	....	435	187	248	....	....
91st	1969–1971	100	42	58	....	....	435	192	243	....	....
92d	1971–1973	100	44	54	2	....	435	180	255	....	....
93d	1973–1975	100	42	56	2	....	435	192	242	1	....
94th	1975–1977	100	37	60	2	....	435	144	291	1	....
95th	1977–1979	100	38	61	1	....	435	143	292	....	....
96th	1979–1981	100	41	58	1	....	435	158	277	....	....
97th	1981–1983	100	53	46	1	....	435	192	242	1	....
98th	1983–1985	100	54	46	....	....	435	166	269	....	....
99th	1985–1987	100	53	47	....	....	435	182	253	....	....
100th	1987–1989	100	45	55	....	....	435	177	258	....	....
101st	1989–1991	100	45	55	....	....	435	175	260	....	....
102d	1991–1993	100	44	56	....	....	435	167	267	1	....
103d	1993–1995	100	43	57	....	....	435	176	258	1	....
104th	1995–1997	100	52	48	....	....	435	230	204	1	....
105th	1997–1999	100	55	45	....	....	435	226	207	2	....
106th	1999–2001	100	55	45	....	....	435	223	211	1	....
107th	2001–2003	100	50	50	....	....	435	221	212	2	....
108th	2003–2005	100	51	48	1	....	435	229	204	1	1
109th	2005–2007	100	55	44	1	....	435	232	202	1	....

[1] Democrats organized House with help of other parties.
[2] Democrats organized House because of Republican deaths.
[3] Proclamation declaring Alaska a State issued January 3, 1959.
[4] Proclamation declaring Hawaii a State issued August 21, 1959.

GOVERNORS OF THE STATES, COMMONWEALTH, AND TERRITORIES—2005

State, Commonwealth, or Territory	Capital	Governor	Party	Term of service	Expiration of term
STATE				*Years*	
Alabama	Montgomery	Bob Riley	Republican	c 4	Jan. 2007
Alaska	Juneau	Frank Murkowski	Republican	c 4	Dec. 2006
Arizona	Phoenix	Janet Napolitano	Democrat	c 4	Jan. 2007
Arkansas	Little Rock	Mike Huckabee	Republican	e 4	Jan. 2007
California	Sacramento	Arnold Schwarzenegger	Republican	c 4	Jan. 2007
Colorado	Denver	Bill Owens	Republican	c 4	Jan. 2007
Connecticut	Hartford	M. Jodi Rell	Republican	b 4	Jan. 2007
Delaware	Dover	Ruth Ann Minner	Democrat	c 4	Jan. 2009
Florida	Tallahassee	Jeb Bush	Republican	c 4	Jan. 2007
Georgia	Atlanta	Sonny Perdue	Republican	c 4	Jan. 2007
Hawaii	Honolulu	Linda Lingle	Republican	c 4	Dec. 2006
Idaho	Boise	Dirk Kempthorne	Republican	b 4	Jan. 2007
Illinois	Springfield	Rod R. Blagojevich	Democrat	b 4	Jan. 2007
Indiana	Indianapolis	Mitch Daniels	Republican	f 4	Jan. 2009
Iowa	Des Moines	Tom Vilsack	Democrat	b 4	Jan. 2007
Kansas	Topeka	Kathleen Sebelius	Democrat	c 4	Jan. 2007
Kentucky	Frankfort	Ernie Fletcher	Republican	c 4	Dec. 2007
Louisiana	Baton Rouge	Kathleen Blanco	Democrat	c 4	Jan. 2008
Maine	Augusta	John Baldacci	Democrat	c 4	Jan. 2007
Maryland	Annapolis	Robert L. Ehrlich, Jr.	Republican	c 4	Jan. 2007
Massachusetts	Boston	Mitt Romney	Republican	b 4	Jan. 2007
Michigan	Lansing	Jennifer Granholm	Democrat	b 4	Jan. 2007
Minnesota	St. Paul	Tim Pawlenty	Republican	b 4	Jan. 2007
Mississippi	Jackson	Haley Barbour	Republican	c 4	Jan. 2008
Missouri	Jefferson City	Matt Blunt	Republican	c 4	Jan. 2009
Montana	Helena	Brian Schweitzer	Democrat	c 4	Jan. 2009
Nebraska	Lincoln	Dave Heineman	Republican	c 4	Jan. 2007
Nevada	Carson City	Kenny C. Guinn	Republican	c 4	Jan. 2007
New Hampshire	Concord	John Lynch	Democrat	b 2	Jan. 2007
New Jersey	Trenton	Richard Codey	Democrat	c 4	Jan. 2006
New Mexico	Santa Fe	Bill Richardson	Democrat	c 4	Jan. 2007
New York	Albany	George E. Pataki	Republican	b 4	Jan. 2007
North Carolina	Raleigh	Mike Easley	Democrat	c 4	Jan. 2009
North Dakota	Bismarck	John Hoeven	Republican	b 4	Dec. 2008
Ohio	Columbus	Bob Taft	Republican	c 4	Jan. 2007
Oklahoma	Oklahoma City	Brad Henry	Democrat	c 4	Jan. 2007
Oregon	Salem	Ted Kulongoski	Democrat	f 4	Jan. 2007
Pennsylvania	Harrisburg	Ed Rendell	Democrat	c 4	Jan. 2007
Rhode Island	Providence	Donald Carcieri	Republican	c 4	Jan. 2007
South Carolina	Columbia	Mark Sanford	Republican	c 4	Jan. 2007
South Dakota	Pierre	Mike Rounds	Republican	c 4	Jan. 2007
Tennessee	Nashville	Phil Bredesen	Democrat	c 4	Jan. 2007
Texas	Austin	Rick Perry	Republican	b 4	Jan. 2007
Utah	Salt Lake City	Jon Huntsman, Jr.	Republican	b 4	Jan. 2009
Vermont	Montpelier	Jim Douglas	Republican	b 2	Jan. 2007
Virginia	Richmond	Mark R. Warner	Democrat	a 4	Jan. 2006
Washington	Olympia	Christine Gregoire	Democrat	d 4	Jan. 2009
West Virginia	Charleston	Joe Manchin III	Democrat	c 4	Jan. 2009
Wisconsin	Madison	Jim Doyle	Democrat	b 4	Jan. 2007
Wyoming	Cheyenne	Dave Freudenthal	Democrat,	c 4	Jan. 2007
COMMONWEALTH OF					
Puerto Rico	San Juan	Anibal Acevedo-Vila	1 P.D.P.	b 4	Jan. 2009
TERRITORIES					
Guam	Agana	Felix Camacho	Republican	c 4	Jan. 2007
Virgin Islands	Charlotte Amalie	Charles W. Turnbull	Democrat	c 4	Jan. 2007
American Samoa	Pago Pago	Togiola T.A. Tulafono	Democrat	c 4	Jan. 2009
Northern Mariana Islands.	Saipan	Juan N. Babauta	Republican	c 4	Jan. 2006

a Cannot succeed himself.   b No limit.   c Can serve 2 consecutive terms.   d Can serve 3 consecutive terms.
e Can serve 4 consecutive terms.   f Can serve no more than 8 years in a 12-year period.
1 Popular Democratic Party.

PRESIDENTS AND VICE PRESIDENTS AND THE CONGRESSES
COINCIDENT WITH THEIR TERMS [1]

President	Vice President	Service	Congresses
George Washington	John Adams	Apr. 30, 1789–Mar. 3, 1797	1, 2, 3, 4.
John Adams	Thomas Jefferson	Mar. 4, 1797–Mar. 3, 1801	5, 6.
Thomas Jefferson	Aaron Burr	Mar. 4, 1801–Mar. 3, 1805	7, 8.
Do	George Clinton	Mar. 4, 1805–Mar. 3, 1809	9, 10.
James Madison	......do.[2]	Mar. 4, 1809–Mar. 3, 1813	11, 12.
Do	Elbridge Gerry[3]	Mar. 4, 1813–Mar. 3, 1817	13, 14.
James Monroe	Daniel D. Tompkins	Mar. 4, 1817–Mar. 3, 1825	15, 16, 17, 18, 19
John Quincy Adams	John C. Calhoun	Mar. 4, 1825–Mar. 3, 1829	19, 20.
Andrew Jackson	......do.[4]	Mar. 4, 1829–Mar. 3, 1833	21, 22.
Do	Martin Van-Buren	Mar. 4, 1833–Mar. 3, 1837	23, 24.
Martin Van Buren	Richard M. Johnson	Mar. 4, 1837–Mar. 3, 1841	25, 26.
William Henry Harrison[5]	John Tyler	Mar. 4, 1841–Apr. 4, 1841	27.
John Tyler		Apr. 6, 1841–Mar. 3, 1845	27, 28.
James K. Polk	George M. Dallas	Mar. 4, 1845–Mar. 3, 1849	29, 30.
Zachary Taylor[5]	Millard Fillmore	Mar. 5, 1849–July 9, 1850	31.
Millard Fillmore		July 10, 1850–Mar. 3, 1853	31, 32.
Franklin Pierce	William R. King[6]	Mar. 4, 1853–Mar. 3, 1857	33, 34.
James Buchanan	John C. Breckinridge	Mar. 4, 1857–Mar. 3, 1861	35, 36.
Abraham Lincoln	Hannibal Hamlin	Mar. 4, 1861–Mar. 3, 1865	37, 38.
Do.[5]	Andrew Johnson	Mar. 4, 1865–Apr. 15, 1865	39.
Andrew Johnson		Apr. 15, 1865–Mar. 3, 1869	39, 40.
Ulysses S. Grant	Schuyler Colfax	Mar. 4, 1869–Mar. 3, 1873	41, 42.
Do	Henry Wilson[7]	Mar. 4, 1873–Mar. 3, 1877	43, 44.
Rutherford B. Hayes	William A. Wheeler	Mar. 4, 1877–Mar. 3, 1881	45, 46.
James A. Garfield[5]	Chester A. Arthur	Mar. 4, 1881–Sept. 19, 1881	47.
Chester A. Arthur		Sept. 20, 1881–Mar. 3, 1885	47, 48.
Grover Cleveland	Thomas A. Hendricks[8]	Mar. 4, 1885–Mar. 3, 1889	49, 50.
Benjamin Harrison	Levi P. Morton	Mar. 4, 1889–Mar. 3, 1893	51, 52.
Grover Cleveland	Adlai E. Stevenson	Mar. 4, 1893–Mar. 3, 1897	53, 54.
William McKinley	Garret A. Hobart[9]	Mar. 4, 1897–Mar. 3, 1901	55, 56.
Do.[5]	Theodore Roosevelt	Mar. 4, 1901–Sept. 14, 1901	57.
Theodore Roosevelt		Sept. 14, 1901–Mar. 3, 1905	57, 58.
Do	Charles W. Fairbanks	Mar. 4, 1905–Mar. 3, 1909	59, 60.
William H. Taft	James S. Sherman[10]	Mar. 4, 1909–Mar. 3, 1913	61, 62.
Woodrow Wilson	Thomas R. Marshall	Mar. 4, 1913–Mar. 3, 1921	63, 64, 65, 66, 67.
Warren G. Harding[5]	Calvin Coolidge	Mar. 4, 1921–Aug. 2, 1923	67.
Calvin Coolidge		Aug. 3, 1923–Mar. 3, 1925	68.
Do	Charles G. Dawes	Mar. 4, 1925–Mar. 3, 1929	69, 70.
Herbert C. Hoover	Charles Curtis	Mar. 4, 1929–Mar. 3, 1933	71, 72.
Franklin D. Roosevelt	John N. Garner	Mar. 4, 1933–Jan. 20, 1941	73, 74, 75, 76, 77.
Do	Henry A. Wallace	Jan. 20, 1941–Jan. 20, 1945	77, 78, 79.
Do.[5]	Harry S. Truman	Jan. 20, 1945–Apr. 12, 1945	79.
Harry S. Truman		Apr. 12, 1945–Jan. 20, 1949	79, 80, 81.
Do	Alben W. Barkley	Jan. 20, 1949–Jan. 20, 1953	81, 82, 83.
Dwight D. Eisenhower	Richard M. Nixon	Jan. 20, 1953–Jan. 20, 1961	83, 84, 85, 86, 87.
John F. Kennedy[5]	Lyndon B. Johnson	Jan. 20, 1961–Nov. 22, 1963	87, 88, 89.
Lyndon B. Johnson		Nov. 22, 1963–Jan. 20, 1965	88, 89.
Do	Hubert H. Humphrey	Jan. 20, 1965–Jan. 20, 1969	89, 90, 91.
Richard M. Nixon	Spiro T. Agnew[11]	Jan. 20, 1969–Dec. 6, 1973	91, 92, 93.
Do.[13]	Gerald R. Ford[12]	Dec. 6, 1973–Aug. 9, 1974	93.
Gerald R. Ford		Aug. 9, 1974–Dec. 19, 1974	93.
Do	Nelson A. Rockefeller[14]	Dec. 19, 1974–Jan. 20, 1977	93, 94, 95.
James Earl (Jimmy) Carter	Walter F. Mondale	Jan. 20, 1977–Jan. 20, 1981	95, 96, 97.
Ronald Reagan	George Bush	Jan. 20, 1981–Jan. 20, 1989	97, 98, 99, 100, 101.
George Bush	Dan Quayle	Jan. 20, 1989–Jan. 20, 1993	101, 102, 103.
William J. Clinton	Albert Gore	Jan. 20, 1993–Jan. 20, 2001	103, 104, 105, 106, 107.
George W. Bush	Richard B. Cheney	Jan. 20, 2001–	107, 108, 109.

[1] From 1789 until 1933, the terms of the President and Vice President and the term of the Congress coincided, beginning on March 4 and ending on March 3. This changed when the 20th amendment to the Constitution was adopted in 1933. Beginning in 1934 the convening date for Congress became January 3, and beginning in 1937 the starting date for the Presidential term became January 20. Because of this change, the number of Congresses overlapping with a Presidential term increased from two to three, although the third only overlaps by a few weeks.

[2] Died Apr. 20, 1812.

[3] Died Nov. 23, 1814.

[4] Resigned Dec. 28, 1832, to become a United States Senator from South Carolina.

[5] Died in office.

[6] Died Apr. 18, 1853.

[7] Died Nov. 22, 1875.

[8] Died Nov. 25, 1885.

[9] Died Nov. 21, 1899.

[10] Died Oct. 30, 1912.

[11] Resigned Oct. 10, 1973.

[12] Nominated to be Vice President by President Richard M. Nixon on Oct. 12, 1973; confirmed by the Senate on Nov. 27, 1973; confirmed by the House of Representatives on Dec. 6, 1973; took the oath of office on Dec. 6, 1973 in the Hall of the House of Representatives. This was the first time a Vice President was nominated by the President and confirmed by the Congress pursuant to the 25th amendment to the Constitution.

[13] Resigned from office.

[14] Nominated to be Vice President by President Gerald R. Ford on Aug. 20, 1974; confirmed by the Senate on Dec. 10, 1974; confirmed by the House of Representatives on Dec. 19, 1974; took the oath of office on Dec. 19, 1974, in the Senate Chamber.

CAPITOL BUILDINGS AND GROUNDS

UNITED STATES CAPITOL

OVERVIEW OF THE BUILDING AND ITS FUNCTION

The United States Capitol is among the most architecturally impressive and symbolically important buildings in the world. It has housed the chambers of the Senate and the House of Representatives for more than two centuries. Begun in 1793, the Capitol has been built, burnt, rebuilt, extended, and restored; today, it stands as a monument not only to its builders but also to the American people and their government.

As the focal point of the government's legislative branch, the Capitol is the centerpiece of the Capitol Complex, which includes the six principal congressional office buildings and three Library of Congress buildings constructed on Capitol Hill in the 19th and 20th centuries.

In addition to its active use by Congress, the Capitol is a museum of American art and history. Each year, it is visited by millions of people from around the world.

A fine example of 19th-century neoclassical architecture, the Capitol combines function with aesthetics. Its design was derived from ancient Greece and Rome and evokes the ideals that guided the nation's founders as they framed their new republic. As the building was expanded from its original design, harmony with the existing portions was carefully maintained.

Today, the Capitol covers a ground area of 175,170 square feet, or about 4 acres, and has a floor area of approximately 16½ acres. Its length, from north to south, is 751 feet 4 inches; its greatest width, including approaches, is 350 feet. Its height above the base line on the east front to the top of the Statue of Freedom is 288 feet; from the basement floor to the top of the dome is an ascent of 365 steps. The building contains approximately 540 rooms and has 658 windows (108 in the dome alone) and approximately 850 doorways.

The building is divided into five levels. The first, or ground, floor is occupied chiefly by committee rooms and the spaces allocated to various congressional officers. The areas accessible to visitors on this level include the Hall of Columns, the Brumidi Corridor, the restored Old Supreme Court Chamber, and the Crypt beneath the Rotunda, where historical exhibits are presented.

The second floor holds the chambers of the House of Representatives (in the south wing) and the Senate (in the north wing) as well as the offices of the congressional leadership. This floor also contains three major public areas. In the center under the dome is the rotunda, a circular ceremonial space that also serves as a gallery of paintings and sculpture depicting significant people and events in the nation's history. The rotunda is 96 feet in diameter and rises 180 feet 3 inches to the canopy. The semicircular chamber south of the rotunda served as the Hall of the House until 1857; now designated National Statuary Hall, it houses part of the Capitol's collection of statues donated by the states in commemoration of notable citizens. The Old Senate Chamber northeast of the rotunda, which was used by the Senate until 1859, has been returned to its mid-19th-century appearance.

The third floor allows access to the galleries from which visitors to the Capitol may watch the proceedings of the House and the Senate when Congress is in session. The rest of this floor is occupied by offices, committee rooms, and press galleries.

The fourth floor and the basement/terrace level of the Capitol are occupied by offices, machinery rooms, workshops, and other support areas.

LOCATION OF THE CAPITOL

The Capitol is located at the eastern end of the Mall on a plateau 88 feet above the level of the Potomac River, commanding a westward view across the Capitol Reflecting Pool to the Washington Monument 1.4 miles away and the Lincoln Memorial 2.2 miles away. The geographic location of the head of the Statue of Freedom that surmounts the Capitol dome is described by the National Geodetic Survey as latitude 38°53'23.31098" north and longitude 77°00'32.62262" west.

551

Before 1791, the Federal Government had no permanent site. The early Congresses met in eight different cities: Philadelphia, Baltimore, Lancaster, York, Princeton, Annapolis, Trenton, and New York City. The subject of a permanent capital for the government of the United States was first raised by Congress in 1783; it was ultimately addressed in Article I, Section 8 of the Constitution (1787), which gave the Congress legislative authority over "such District (not exceeding ten Miles square) as may, by Cession of Particular States, and the Acceptance of Congress, become the Seat of the Government of the United States. . . ."

In 1788, the state of Maryland ceded to Congress "any district in this State, not exceeding ten miles square," and in 1789 the State of Virginia ceded an equivalent amount of land. In accordance with the "Residence Act" passed by Congress in 1790, President Washington in 1791 selected the area that is now the District of Columbia from the land ceded by Maryland (private landowners whose property fell within this area were compensated by a payment of £25 per acre); that ceded by Virginia was not used for the capital and was returned to Virginia in 1846. Also under the provisions of that Act, he selected three commissioners to survey the site and oversee the design and construction of the capital city and its government buildings. The commissioners, in turn, selected the French-American engineer Peter Charles L'Enfant to plan the new city of Washington. L'Enfant's plan, which was influenced by the gardens at Versailles, arranged the city's streets and avenues in a grid overlaid with baroque diagonals; the result is a functional and aesthetic whole in which government buildings are balanced against public lawns, gardens, squares, and paths. The Capitol itself was located at the elevated east end of the Mall, on the brow of what was then called Jenkins' Hill. The site was, in L'Enfant's words, "a pedestal waiting for a monument."

SELECTION OF A PLAN

L'Enfant was expected to design the Capitol and to supervise its construction. However, he refused to produce any drawings for the building, claiming that he carried the design "in his head"; this fact and his refusal to consider himself subject to the commissioners' authority led to his dismissal in 1792. In March of that year the commissioners announced a competition, suggested by Secretary of State Thomas Jefferson, that would award $500 and a city lot to whoever produced "the most approved plan" for the Capitol by mid-July. None of the 17 plans submitted, however, was wholly satisfactory. In October, a letter arrived from Dr. William Thornton, a Scottish-trained physician living in Tortola, British West Indies, requesting an opportunity to present a plan even though the competition had closed. The commissioners granted this request.

Thornton's plan depicted a building composed of three sections. The central section, which was topped by a low dome, was to be flanked on the north and south by two rectangular wings (one for the Senate and one for the House of Representatives). President Washington commended the plan for its "grandeur, simplicity and convenience," and on April 5, 1793, it was accepted by the commissioners; Washington gave his formal approval on July 25.

BRIEF CONSTRUCTION HISTORY
1793–1829

The cornerstone was laid by President Washington in the building's southeast corner on September 18, 1793, with Masonic ceremonies. Work progressed under the direction of three architects in succession. Stephen H. Hallet (an entrant in the earlier competition) and George Hadfield were eventually dismissed by the commissioners because of inappropriate design changes that they tried to impose; James Hoban, the architect of the White House, saw the first phase of the project through to completion.

Construction was a laborious and time-consuming process: the sandstone used for the building had to be ferried on boats from the quarries at Aquia, Virginia; workers had to be induced to leave their homes to come to the relative wilderness of Capitol Hill; and funding was inadequate. By August 1796 the commissioners were forced to focus the entire work effort on the building's north wing so that it at least could be ready for government occupancy as scheduled. Even so, some third-floor rooms were still unfinished when the Congress, the Supreme Court, the Library of Congress, and the courts of the District of Columbia occupied the Capitol in late 1800.

In 1803, Congress allocated funds to resume construction. A year earlier, the office of the Commissioners had been abolished and replaced by a superintendent of the city of Washington. To oversee the renewed construction effort, B. Henry Latrobe was appointed surveyor of public buildings. The first professional architect and engineer to work in America, Latrobe modified Thornton's plan for the south wing to include space for offices and committee rooms; he also introduced alterations to simplify the construction work. Latrobe began work by removing a squat, oval, temporary building known as "the Oven," which had been erected in 1801 as a meeting place for the House of Representatives. By 1807 construction on the south wing was sufficiently advanced that the House was able to occupy its new legislative chamber, and the wing was completed in 1811.

In 1808, as work on the south wing progressed, Latrobe began the rebuilding of the north wing, which had fallen into disrepair. Rather than simply repair the wing, he redesigned the interior of the building to increase its usefulness and durability; among his changes was the addition of a chamber for the Supreme Court. By 1811, he had completed the eastern half of this wing, but funding was being increasingly diverted to preparations for a second war with Great Britain. By 1813, Latrobe had no further work in Washington and so he departed, leaving the north and south wings of the Capitol connected only by a temporary wooden passageway.

The War of 1812 left the Capitol, in Latrobe's later words, "a most magnificent ruin": on August 24, 1814, British troops set fire to the building, and only a sudden rainstorm prevented its complete destruction. Immediately after the fire, Congress met for one session in Blodget's Hotel, which was at Seventh and E Streets, NW. From 1815 to 1819, Congress occupied a building erected for it on First Street, NE, on part of the site now occupied by the Supreme Court Building. This building later came to be known as the Old Brick Capitol.

Latrobe returned to Washington in 1815, when he was rehired to restore the Capitol. In addition to making repairs, he took advantage of this opportunity to make further changes in the building's interior design (for example, an enlargement of the Senate Chamber) and introduce new materials (for example, marble discovered along the upper Potomac). However, he came under increasing pressure because of construction delays (most of which were beyond his control) and cost overruns; finally, he resigned his post in November 1817.

On January 8, 1818, Charles Bulfinch, a prominent Boston architect, was appointed Latrobe's successor. Continuing the restoration of the north and south wings, he was able to make the chambers for the Supreme Court, the House, and the Senate ready for use by 1819. Bulfinch also redesigned and supervised the construction of the Capitol's central section. The copper-covered wooden dome that topped this section was made higher than Bulfinch considered appropriate to the building's size (at the direction of President James Monroe and Secretary of State John Quincy Adams). After completing the last part of the building in 1826, Bulfinch spent the next few years on the Capitol's decoration and landscaping. In 1829, his work was done and his position with the government was terminated. In the 38 years following Bulfinch's tenure, the Capitol was entrusted to the care of the commissioner of public buildings.

1830–1868

The Capitol was by this point already an impressive structure. At ground level, its length was 351 feet 7½ inches and its width was 282 feet 10½ inches. Up to the year 1827— records from later years being incomplete—the project cost was $2,432,851.34. Improvements to the building continued in the years to come (running water in 1832, gas lighting in the 1840s), but by 1850 its size could no longer accommodate the increasing numbers of senators and representatives from newly admitted states. The Senate therefore voted to hold another competition, offering a prize of $500 for the best plan to extend the Capitol. Several suitable plans were submitted, some proposing an eastward extension of the building and others proposing the addition of large north and south wings. However, Congress was unable to decide between these two approaches, and the prize money was divided among five architects. Thus, the tasks of selecting a plan and appointing an architect fell to President Millard Fillmore.

Fillmore's choice was Thomas U. Walter, a Philadelphia architect who had entered the competition. On July 4, 1851, in a ceremony whose principal oration was delivered by Secretary of State Daniel Webster, the president laid the cornerstone in the northeast corner of the House wing. Over the next 14 years, Walter supervised the construction of the extension, ensuring their compatibility with the architectural style of the existing building. However, because the Aquia Creek sandstone used earlier had deteriorated noticeably, he chose to use marble for the exterior. For the veneer, Walter selected marble quarried at Lee, MA, and for the columns he used marble from Cockeysville, MD.

Walter faced several significant challenges during the course of construction. Chief among these was the steady imposition by the government of additional tasks without additional pay. Aside from his work on the Capitol extension, Walter designed the wings of the Patent Office building, extensions to the Treasury and Post Office buildings, and the Marine barracks in Pensacola and Brooklyn. When the Library of Congress in the Capitol's west central section was gutted by a fire in 1851, Walter was commissioned to restore it. He also encountered obstacles in his work on the Capitol extensions. His location of the legislative chambers was changed in 1853 at the direction of President Franklin Pierce, based on the suggestions of the newly appointed supervising engineer, Captain Montgomery C. Meigs. In general, however, the project progressed rapidly: the House of Representatives was able to meet in its new chamber on December 16, 1857, and the Senate first met in its present chamber on January 4, 1859. The old House chamber was later designated National Statuary Hall. In 1861 most construction was suspended because of the Civil War, and the Capitol was used briefly as a military barracks, hospital, and bakery. In 1862 work on the entire building was resumed.

As the new wings were constructed, more than doubling the length of the Capitol, it became apparent that the dome erected by Bulfinch no longer suited the building's proportions. In 1855 Congress voted for its replacement based on Walter's design for a new, fireproof cast-iron dome. The old dome was removed in 1856–56, and 5,000,000 pounds of new masonry was placed on the existing rotunda walls. Iron used in the dome construction had an aggregate weight of 8,909,200 pounds and was lifted into place by steam-powered derricks.

In 1859, Thomas Crawford's plaster model for the Statue of Freedom, designed for the top of the dome, arrived from the sculptor's studio in Rome. With a height of 19 feet 6 inches, the statue was almost 3 feet taller than specified, and Walter was compelled to make revisions to his design for the dome. When cast in bronze by Clark Mills at his foundry on the outskirts of Washington, it weighed 14,985 pounds. The statue was lifted into place atop the dome in 1863, its final section being installed on December 2 to the accompaniment of gun salutes from the forts around the city.

The work on the dome and the extension was completed under the direction of Edward Clark, who had served as Walter's assistant and was appointed Architect of the Capitol in 1865 after Walter's resignation. In 1866, the Italian-born artist Constantino Brumidi finished the canopy fresco, a monumental painting entitled *The Apotheosis of George Washington*. The Capitol extension was completed in 1868.

1869–1902

Clark continued to hold the post of Architect of the Capitol until his death in 1902. During his tenure, the Capitol underwent considerable modernization. Steam heat was gradually installed in the old Capitol. In 1874 the first elevator was installed, and in the 1880s electric lighting began to replace gas lights.

Between 1884 and 1891, the marble terraces on the north, west, and south sides of the Capitol were constructed. As part of the landscape plan devised by Frederick Law Olmsted, these terraces not only added over 100 rooms to the Capitol but also provided a broader, more substantial visual base for the building.

On November 6, 1898, a gas explosion and fire in the original north wing dramatically illustrated the need for fireproofing. The roofs over the Statuary Hall wing and the original north wing were reconstructed and fireproofed, the work being completed in 1902 by Clark's successor, Elliott Woods. In 1901 the space in the west central front vacated by the Library of Congress was converted to committee rooms.

1903–1970

During the remainder of Woods's service, which ended with his death in 1923, no major structural work was required on the Capitol. The activities performed in the building were limited chiefly to cleaning and refurbishing the interior. David Lynn, the Architect of the Capitol from 1923 until his retirement in 1954, continued these tasks. Between July 1949 and January 1951, the corroded roofs and skylights of both wings and the connecting corridors were replaced with new roofs of concrete and steel, covered with copper. The cast-iron and glass ceilings of the House and Senate chambers were replaced with ceilings of stainless steel and plaster, with a laylight of carved glass and bronze in the middle of each. The House and Senate chambers were completely redecorated, modern lighting was added, and acoustical problems were solved. During this renovation program, the House and Senate vacated their chambers on several occasions so that the work could progress.

The next significant modification made to the Capitol was the east front extension. This project was carried out under the supervision of Architect of the Capitol J. George Stewart, who served from 1954 until his death in 1970. Begun in 1958, it involved the construction of a new east front 32 feet 6 inches east of the old front, faithfully reproducing the sandstone structure in marble. The old sandstone walls were not destroyed; rather, they were left in place to become a part of the interior wall and are now buttressed by the addition. The marble columns of the connecting corridors were also moved and reused. Other elements of this project included repairing the dome, constructing a subway terminal under the Senate steps, reconstructing those steps, cleaning both wings, birdproofing the building, providing furniture and furnishings for 90 new rooms created by the extension, and improving the lighting throughout the building. The project was completed in 1962.

1971–PRESENT

During the nearly 25-year tenure (1971–1995) of Architect of the Capitol George M. White, FAIA, the building was both modernized and restored. Electronic voting equipment was installed in the House chamber in 1973; facilities were added to allow television coverage of the House and Senate debates in 1979 and 1986, respectively; and improved climate control, electronic surveillance systems, and new computer and communications facilities have been added to bring the Capitol up-to-date. The Old Senate Chamber, National Statuary Hall, and the Old Supreme Court Chamber, on the other hand, were restored to their mid-19th-century appearance in the 1970s.

In 1983, work began on the strengthening, renovation, and preservation of the west front of the Capitol. Structural problems had developed over the years because of defects in the original foundations, deterioration of the sandstone facing material, alterations to the basic building fabric (a fourth-floor addition and channeling of the walls to install interior utilities), and damage from the fires of 1814 and 1851 and the 1898 gas explosion

To strengthen the structure, over one thousand stainless steel tie rods were set into the building's masonry. More than 30 layers of paint were removed, and damaged stonework was repaired or replicated. Ultimately, 40 percent of the sandstone blocks were replaced with limestone. The walls were treated with a special consolidant and then painted to match the marble wings. The entire project was completed in 1987.

A related project, completed in January 1993, effected the repair of the Olmsted terraces, which had been subject to damage from settling, and converted the terrace courtyards into several thousand square feet of meeting space.

As the Capitol enters its third century, restoration and modernization work continues. Major projects completed in recent years include; repair and restoration of the House monumental stairs; conservation of the Statue of Freedom atop the Capitol dome; completion of the murals in the first-floor House corridors; preparation and publication of a new book on the artist Constantino Brumidi, whose paintings decorate much of the Capitol; preparation of a telecommunications plan for the Legislative Branch agencies; installation of an improved Senate subway system; construction of the Thurgood Marshall Federal Judiciary Building; construction of new House and Senate child care facilities and a new Senate Page school; and renovation, restoration, and modification of the interiors and exteriors of the Thomas Jefferson and John Adams Buildings of the Library of Congress.

The present Architect of the Capitol, Alan M. Hantman, FAIA, was appointed in January 1997. New and ongoing projects under his direction include rehabilitation of the Capitol dome; conservation of murals; improvement of speech-reinforcement, electrical, and fire-protection systems in the Capitol and the Congressional office buildings; work on security improvements within the Capitol Complex; restoration of the U.S. Botanic Garden Conservatory; the design and construction of the National Garden adjacent to the Botanic Garden Conservatory; renovation of the building systems in the Dirksen Senate Office Building; preparation and publication of the first comprehensive history of the Capitol to appear in a century; and construction of a new Capitol Visitor Center.

Work is now underway on the Capitol Visitor Center, which will make the U.S. Capitol more accessible, comfortable, secure, and informative for all visitors. Preparatory construction activities began in the fall of 2001, including relocation of utilities and visitor screening facilities, and implementation of a comprehensive tree preservation program. Major construction started in July 2002 and is scheduled to be completed in 2006.

The CVC will be located underground on the East Front of the Capitol, so as to enhance rather than detract from the appearance of the Capitol and its historic Frederick Law Olmsted landscape. When completed, the CVC will contain 580,000 square feet on three levels, requiring a 196,000-square-foot excavation, or "footprint," on the East Front of the Capitol. (For purposes of comparison, the Capitol itself encompasses 775,000 square feet.)

The project will include space for exhibits, visitor comfort, food service, two orientation theaters, an auditorium, gift shops, security, a service tunnel for truck loading and deliveries, mechanical facilities, storage, and much needed space for the House and Senate. When completed, the CVC will preserve and maximize public access to the Capitol while greatly enhancing the experience for the millions who walks its historic corridors and experience its monumental spaces every year.

All activities related to the Capitol Visitor Center take place under the direction of the Capitol Preservation Commission.

HOUSE OFFICE BUILDINGS

Cannon House Office Building

An increased membership of the Senate and House resulted in a demand for additional rooms for the accommodations of the Senators and Representatives. On March 3, 1903, the Congress authorized the erection of a fireproofed office building for the use of the House. It was designed by the firm of Carrere & Hastings of New York City in the Beaux Arts style. The first brick was laid July 5, 1905, in square No. 690, and formal exercises were held at the laying of the cornerstone on April 14, 1906, in which President Theodore Roosevelt participated. The building was completed and occupied January 10, 1908. A subsequent change in the basis of congressional representation made necessary the building of an additional story in 1913–14. The total cost of the building, including site, furnishings, equipment, and the subway connecting it with the U.S. Capitol, amounted to $4,860,155. This office building contains about 500 rooms, and was considered at the time of its completion fully equipped for all the needs of a modern building for office purposes. A garage was added in the building's courtyard in the 1960s.

Pursuant to authority in the Second Supplemental Appropriations Act, 1955, and subsequent action of the House Office Building Commission, remodeling of the Cannon Building began in 1966. The estimated cost of this work was $5,200,000. Pursuant to the provisions of Public Law 87–453, approved May 21, 1962, the building was named in honor of Joseph G. Cannon of Illinois, who was Speaker at the time the building was constructed.

Longworth House Office Building

Under legislation contained in the authorization act of January 10, 1929, and in the urgent deficiency bill of March 4, 1929, provisions were made for an additional House office building, to be located on the west side of New Jersey Avenue (opposite the first House office building). The building was designed by the Allied Architects of Washington in the Neoclassical Revival style.

The cornerstone was laid June 24, 1932, and the building was completed on April 20, 1933. It contains 251 two-room suites and 16 committee rooms. Each suite and committee room is provided with a storeroom. Eight floors are occupied by members. The basement and subbasement contain shops and mechanical areas needed for the maintenance of the building. A cafeteria was added in the building's courtyard in the 1960s. The cost of this building, including site, furnishings, and equipment, was $7,805,705. Pursuant to the provisions of Public Law 87–453, approved May 21, 1962, the building was named in honor of Nicholas Longworth of Ohio, who was Speaker when the second House office building was constructed.

Rayburn House Office Building and Other Related Changes and Improvements

Under legislation contained in the Second Supplemental Appropriations Act, 1955, provision was made for construction of a fireproof office building for the House of Representatives.

All work was carried forward by the Architect of the Capitol under the direction of the House Office Building Commission at a cost totaling $135,279,000.

The Rayburn Building is connected to the Capitol by a subway from the center of the Independence Avenue upper garage level to the southwest corner of the Capitol. Designs for the building were prepared by the firm of Harbeson, Hough, Livingston & Larson of Philadelphia, Associate Architects. The building contains 169 congressional suites; full-committee hearing rooms for 9 standing committees, 16 subcommittee hearing rooms, committee staff rooms and other committee facilities; a large cafeteria and other restaurant facilities; an underground garage accommodating 1,600 automobiles; and a variety of liaison offices, press and television facilities, maintenance and equipment shops or rooms, and storage areas. This building has nine stories and a penthouse for machinery.

The cornerstone was laid May 24, 1962, by John W. McCormack, Speaker of the House of Representatives. President John F. Kennedy participated in the cornerstone laying and delivered the address.

A portion of the basement floor was occupied beginning March 12, 1964, by House of Representatives personnel moved from the George Washington Inn property. Full occupancy of the Rayburn Building, under the room-filing regulations, was begun February 23, 1965, and completed April 2, 1965. Pursuant to the provisions of Public Law 87–453, approved May 21, 1962, the building was named in honor of Sam Rayburn of Texas.

Two buildings have been purchased and adapted for office use by the House of Representatives. The eight-story Congressional Hotel, across from the Cannon on C Street SE. was acquired in 1957 and subsequently altered for office use and a dormitory for the Pages. It has 124,000 square feet. It was known as House Office Building Annex No. 1, until it was named the "Thomas P. O'Neill, Jr. House of Representatives Office Building" in honor of the former Speaker of the House, pursuant to House Resolution 402, approved September 10, 1990. It was demolished in 2002 and the site made into a parking lot. House Office Building Annex No. 2, named the "Gerald R. Ford House of Representatives Office Building" by the same resolution, was acquired in 1975 from the General Services Administration. The structure, located at Second and D Streets SW., was built in 1939 for the Federal Bureau of Investigation as a fingerprint file archives. This building has approximately 432,000 square feet of space.

SENATE OFFICE BUILDINGS

RICHARD BREVARD RUSSELL SENATE OFFICE BUILDING

In 1891 the Senate provided itself with office space by the purchase of the Maltby Building, then located on the northwest corner of B Street (now Constitution Avenue) and New Jersey Avenue, NW. When it was condemned as an unsafe structure, senators needed safer and more commodious office space. Under authorization of the Act of April 28, 1904, square 686 on the northeast corner of Delaware Avenue and B Street NE. was purchased as a site for the Senate Office Building. The plans for the House Office Building were adapted for the Senate Office Building by the firm of Carrere & Hastings, with the exception that the side of the building fronting on First Street NE. was temporarily omitted. The cornerstone was laid without special exercises on July 31, 1906, and the building was occupied March 5, 1909. In 1931, the completion of the fourth side of the building was commenced. In 1933 it was completed, together with alterations to the C Street facade, and the construction of terraces, balustrades, and approaches. The cost of the completed building, including the site, furnishings, equipment and the subway connecting it with the United States Capitol, was $8,390,892.

The building was named the "Richard Brevard Russell Senate Office Building" by Senate Resolution 296, 92nd Congress, agreed to October 11, 1972, as amended by Senate Resolution 295, 96th Congress, agreed to December 3, 1979.

EVERETT MCKINLEY DIRKSEN SENATE OFFICE BUILDING

Under legislation contained in the Second Deficiency Appropriations Act, 1948, Public Law 80–785, provision was made for an additional office building for the United States Senate with limits of cost of $1,100,000 for acquisition of the site and $20,600,000 for constructing and equipping the building.

The construction cost limit was subsequently increased to $24,196. All work was carried forward by the Architect of the Capitol under the direction of the Senate Office Building Commission. The New York firm of Eggers & Higgins served as the consulting architect.

The site was acquired and cleared in 1948–49 at a total cost of $1,011,492.

A contract for excavation, concrete footings and mats for the new building was awarded in January 1955, in the amount of $747,200. Groundbreaking ceremonies were held January 26, 1955.

A contract for the superstructure of the new building was awarded September 9, 1955, in the amount of $17,200,000. The cornerstone was laid July 13, 1956.

As a part of this project, a new underground subway system was installed from the Capitol to both the Old and New Senate Office Buildings.

An appropriation of $1,000,000 for furniture and furnishings for the new building was provided in 1958. The building was accepted for beneficial occupancy October 15, 1958.

The building was named the "Everett McKinley Dirksen Senate Office Building" by Senate Resolution 296, 92nd Congress, agreed to October 11, 1972, and Senate Resolution 295, 96th Congress, agreed to December 3, 1979.

PHILIP A. HART SENATE OFFICE BUILDING

Construction as an extension to the Dirksen Senate Office Building was authorized on October 31, 1972; legislation enacted in subsequent years increased the scope of the project and established a total cost ceiling of $137,700,400. The firm of John Carl Warnecke & Associates served as Associate Architect for the project.

Senate Resolution 525, passed August 30, 1976, amended by Senate Resolution 295, 96th Congress, agreed to December 3, 1979, provided that upon completion of the extension it would be named the "Philip A. Hart Senate Office Building" to honor the senator from Michigan.

The contract for clearing of the site, piping for utilities, excavation, and construction of foundation was awarded in December 1975. Groundbreaking took place January 5, 1976. The contract for furnishing and delivery of the exterior stone was awarded in February 1977, and the contract for the superstructure, which included wall and roof systems and the erection of all exterior stonework, was awarded in October 1977. The contract for the first portion of the interior and related work was awarded in December 1978. A contract for interior finishing was awarded in July 1980. The first suite was occupied on November 22, 1982. Alexander Calder's mobile/stabile *Mountains and Clouds* was installed in the building's atrium in November 1986.

CAPITOL POWER PLANT

During the development of the plans for the Cannon and Russell Buildings, the question of heat, light, and power was considered. The Senate and House wings of the Capitol were heated by separate heating plants. The Library of Congress also had a heating plant for that building. It was determined that needs for heating and lighting and electrical power could be met by a central power plant.

A site was selected in Garfield Park. Since this park was a Government reservation, an appropriation was not required to secure title. The determining factors leading to the selection of this site were its proximity to the tracks of what is now the Penn Central Railroad and to the buildings to be served.

The dimensions of the Capitol Power Plant, which was authorized on April 28, 1904, and completed in 1910, were 244 feet 8 inches by 117 feet. There are two radial brick chimneys 174 feet in height (reduced from 212 feet to 174 feet in 1951–52) and 11 feet in diameter at the top.

The buildings originally served by the Capitol Power Plant were connected to it by a reinforced-concrete steam tunnel 7 feet high by 4½ feet wide, with walls approximately 12 inches thick. This tunnel originated at the Capitol Power Plant and terminated at the Senate Office Building, with connecting tunnels for the Cannon House Office Building, the Capitol, and the Library of Congress. Subsequently it was extended to the Government Printing Office and the Washington City Post Office, with steam lines extended to serve the Longworth House Office Building, the Supreme Court Building, the John Adams Building of the Library of Congress, and the Botanic Garden.

In September 1951, when the demand for electrical energy was reaching the maximum capacity of the Capitol Power Plant, arrangements were made to purchase electrical service from the local public utility company and to discontinue electrical generation. The heating and cooling functions of the Capitol Power Plant were expanded in 1935, 1939, 1958, 1973, and 1980. A new modernization and expansion project is now underway.

U.S. CAPITOL GROUNDS

A DESCRIPTION OF THE GROUNDS

Originally a wooded wilderness, the U.S. Capitol Grounds today provide a parklike setting for the Nation's Capitol, offering a picturesque counterpoint to the building's formal architecture. The grounds immediately surrounding the Capitol are bordered by a stone wall and cover an area of 58.8 acres. Their boundaries are Independence Avenue on the south, Constitution Avenue on the north, First Street NE./SE. on the east, and First Street NW./SW. on the west. Over 100 varieties of trees and bushes are planted around the Capitol, and thousands of flowers are used in seasonal displays. In contrast to the building's straight, neoclassical lines, most of the walkways in the grounds are curved. Benches along the paths offer pleasant spots for visitors to appreciate the building, its landscape, and the surrounding areas, most notably the Mall to the west.

The grounds were designed by Frederick Law Olmsted (1822–1903), who planned the landscaping of the area that was performed from 1874 to 1892. Olmsted, who also designed New York's Central Park, is considered the greatest American landscape architect of his day. He was a pioneer in the development of public parks in America, and many of his designs were influenced by his studies of European parks, gardens, and estates. In describing his plan for the Capitol grounds, Olmsted noted that "The ground is in design part of the Capitol, but in all respects subsidiary to the central structure." Therefore, he was careful not to group trees or other landscape features in any way that would distract the viewer from the Capitol. The use of sculpture and other ornamentation has also been kept to a minimum.

Many of the trees on the Capitol grounds have historic or memorial associations. Among the oldest is the "Cameron Elm" near the House entrance. This tree was named in honor of the Pennsylvania Senator who ensured its preservation during Olmsted's landscaping project. Other trees commemorate members of Congress and other notable citizens, national organizations, and special events. In addition, over 30 states have made symbolic gifts of their state trees to the Capitol grounds. Many of the trees on the grounds bear plaques that identify their species and their historic significance. The eastern part of the grounds contains the greatest number of historic and commemorative trees.

At the East Capitol Street entrance to the Capitol plaza are two large rectangular stone fountains. The bottom levels now contain plantings, but at times in the past they have been used to catch the spillover from the fountains. At other times, both levels have held plantings. Six massive red granite lamp piers topped with light fixtures in wrought-iron cages, and 16 smaller bronze light fixtures, line the paved plaza. Seats are placed at intervals along the sidewalks. Three sets of benches are enclosed with wrought-iron railings and grilles; the roofed bench was originally a shelter for streetcar passengers.

The northern part of the grounds offers a shaded walk among trees, flowers, and shrubbery. A small, hexagonal brick structure named the Summer House may be found in the northwest corner of the grounds. This structure contains shaded benches, a central ornamental fountain, and three public drinking fountains. In a small grotto on the eastern side of the Summer House, a stream of water flows and splashes over rocks to create a pleasing sound and cool the summer breezes.

A Brief History of the Grounds Before Olmsted

The land on which the Capitol stands was first occupied by the Manahoacs and the Monacans, who were subtribes of the Algonquin Indians. Early settlers reported that these tribes occasionally held councils not far from the foot of the hill. This land eventually became a part of Cerne Abbey Manor, and at the time of its acquisition by the Federal Government it was owned by Daniel Carroll of Duddington.

The "Residence Act" of 1790 provided that the federal government should be established in a permanent location by the year 1800. In early March 1791 the commissioners of the city of Washington, who had been appointed by President George Washington, selected the French engineer Peter Charles L'Enfant to plan the new federal city. L'Enfant decided to locate the Capitol at the elevated east end of the Mall (on what was then called Jenkins' Hill); he described the site as "a pedestal waiting for a monument."

At this time the site of the Capitol was a relative wilderness partly overgrown with scrub oak. Oliver Wolcott, a signer of the Declaration of Independence, described the soil as an "*exceedingly stiff* clay, becoming dust in dry and mortar in rainy weather."

In 1825, a plan was devised for imposing order on the Capitol grounds, and it was carried out for almost 15 years. The plan divided the area into flat, rectangular grassy areas bordered by trees, flower beds, and gravel walks. The growth of the trees, however, soon deprived the other plantings of nourishment, and the design became increasingly difficult to maintain in light of sporadic and small appropriations. John Foy, who had charge of the grounds during most of this period, was "superseded for political reasons," and the area was then maintained with little care or forethought. Many rapidly growing but short-lived trees were introduced and soon depleted the soil; a lack of proper pruning and thinning left the majority of the area's vegetation ill-grown, feeble, or dead. Virtually all was removed by the early 1870's, either to make way for building operations during Thomas U. Walter's enlargement of the Capitol or as required by changes in grading to accommodate the new work on the building or the alterations to surrounding streets.

THE OLMSTED PLAN

The mid-19th-century extension of the Capitol, in which the House and Senate wings and the new dome were added, required also that the Capitol grounds be enlarged, and in 1874 Frederick Law Olmsted was commissioned to plan and oversee the project. As noted above, Olmsted was determined that the grounds should complement the building. In addition, he addressed an architectural problem that had persisted for some years: from the west (the growth of the city had nothing to do with the terraces)—the earthen terraces at the building's base made it seem inadequately supported at the top of the hill. The solution, Olmsted believed, was to construct marble terraces on the north, west, and south sides of the building, thereby causing it to "gain greatly in the supreme qualities of stability, endurance, and repose." He submitted his design for these features in 1875, and after extensive study it was approved.

Work on the grounds began in 1874, concentrating first on the east side and then progressing to the west, north, and south sides. First, the ground was reduced in elevation. Almost 300,000 cubic yards of earth and other material were eventually removed, and over 200 trees were removed. New sewer, gas, and water lines were installed. The soil was then enriched with fertilizers to provide a suitable growth medium for new plantings. Paths and roadways were graded and laid.

By 1876, gas and water service was completed for the entire grounds, and electrical lamp-lighting apparatuses had been installed. Stables and workshops had been removed from the northwest and southwest corners. A streetcar system north and south of the west grounds had been relocated farther from the Capitol, and ornamental shelters were in place at the north and south car-track termini. The granite and bronze lamp piers and ornamental bronze lamps for the east plaza area were completed.

Work accelerated in 1877. By this time, according to Olmsted's report, "altogether 7,837 plants and trees [had] been set out." However, not all had survived: hundreds were stolen or destroyed by vandals, and, as Olmsted explained, "a large number of cattle [had] been caught trespassing." Other work met with less difficulty. Foot-walks were laid with artificial stone, a mixture of cement and sand, and approaches were paved with concrete. An ornamental iron trellis had been installed on the northern east-side walk, and another was under way on the southern walk.

The 1878 appointment of watchmen to patrol the grounds was quite effective in preventing further vandalism, allowing the lawns to be completed and much shrubbery to be added. Also in that year, the roads throughout the grounds were paved.

Most of the work required on the east side of the grounds was completed by 1879, and effort thus shifted largely to the west side. The Pennsylvania Avenue approach was virtually finished, and work on the Maryland Avenue approach had begun. The stone walls on the west side of the grounds were almost finished, and the red granite lamp piers were placed at the eastward entrance from Pennsylvania Avenue.

In the years 1880–82, many features of the grounds were completed. These included the walls and coping around the entire perimeter, the approaches and entrances, and the Summer House. Work on the terraces began in 1882, and most work from this point until 1892 was concentrated on these structures.

In 1885, Olmsted retired from superintendency of the terrace project; he continued to direct the work on the grounds until 1889. Landscaping work was performed to adapt the surrounding areas to the new construction, grading the ground and planting shrubs at the bases of the walls, as the progress of the masonry work allowed. Some trees and other types of vegetation were removed, either because they had decayed or as part of a careful thinning-out process.

In 1888, the wrought-iron lamp frames and railings were placed at the Maryland Avenue entrance, making it the last to be completed. In 1892, the streetcar track that had extended into grounds from Independence Avenue was removed.

THE GROUNDS AFTER OLMSTED

In the last years of the 19th century, work on the grounds consisted chiefly of maintenance and repairs as needed. Trees, lawns, and plantings were tended, pruned, and thinned to allow their best growth. This work was quite successful: by 1894, the grounds were so deeply shaded by trees and shrubs that Architect of the Capitol Edward Clark recommended an all-night patrol by watchmen to ensure public safety. A hurricane in September 1896 damaged or destroyed a number of trees, requiring extensive removals in the following year. Also in 1897, electric lighting replaced gas lighting in the grounds.

Between 1910 and 1935, 61.4 acres north of Constitution Avenue were added to the grounds. Approximately 100 acres was added in subsequent years, bringing the total area to 274 acres. In 1981, the Architect of the Capitol developed the Master Plan for future development of the U.S. Capitol grounds and related areas.

Since 1983, increased security measures have been put into effect, including the installation of barriers at vehicular entrances. However, the area still functions in many ways as a public park, and visitors are welcome to use the walks to tour the grounds. Demonstrations and ceremonies are often held on the grounds. During the spring, many high-school bands perform in front of the Capitol, and a series of evening concerts by the bands of the Armed Forces is offered free of charge on the west front plaza. On various holidays, concerts by the National Symphony Orchestra are held on the west front lawn.

LEGISLATIVE BRANCH AGENCIES

CONGRESSIONAL BUDGET OFFICE

H2–405 Ford House Office Building, Second and D Streets SW., 20515
phone 226–2600, http://www.cbo.gov

[Created by Public Law 93–344]

Director.—Douglas Holtz-Eakin, 6–2700.
  Deputy Director.—Elizabeth M. Robinson, 6–2702.
  General Counsel.—Robert P. Murphy, 5–1971.
  Assistant Director for—
    Budget Analysis.—Robert A. Sunshine, 6–2800.
    Health and Human Resources.—Bruce Vavrichek, 6–2666.
    Macroeconomic Analysis.—Robert A. Dennis, 6–2784.
    Management, Business and Information Services.—Stephen A. Weigler, 6–2600.
    Microeconomic and Financial Studies.—Roger Hitchner, 6–2940.
    National Security.—J. Michael Gilmore, 6–2900.
    Tax Analysis.—G. Thomas Woodward, 6–2687.

GOVERNMENT ACCOUNTABILITY OFFICE

441 G Street NW., 20548, phone 512–3000

www.gao.gov

Comptroller General of the United States.—David M. Walker, 512–5500, fax 512–5500.
  Chief Operating Officer.—Gene Dodaro, 512–5600.
  Chief Administrative Officer.—Sallyanne Harper, 512–5800.
  General Counsel.—Tony Gamboa, 512–5400.
  Deputy General Counsel and Ethics Counselor.—Gary Kepplinger, 512–5207.
  Office of Special Investigations.—Robert Cramer, 512–7455.

TEAMS

Applied Research and Methods.—Nancy Kingsbury, 512–2700.
Acquisition and Sourcing Management.—Katherine Schinasi, 512–4841.
Defense Capabilities and Management.—Butch Hinton, 512–4300.
Education Workforce and Income Security.—Cindy Fagnoni, 512–7215.
Financial Management and Assurance.—Jeff Steinhoff, 512–2600.
Financial Markets and Community Investments.—Tom McCool, 512–8678.
Health Care.—Marjorie Kanof, 512–7114.
Homeland Security and Justice/National Preparedness.—Norm Rabkin, 512–9110.
Information Technology.—Joel Willemssen, 512–6408.
International Affairs and Trade.—Jacquie Williams-Bridgers, 512–3101.
Natural Resources and Environment.—Bob Robinson, 512–3841.
Physical Infrastructure.—Pat Dalton, 512–6737.
Strategic Issues.—J. Christophe Mihm, 512–6806.

SUPPORT FUNCTIONS

Congressional Relations.—Gloria Jarmon, 512–4400.
Strategic Planning and External Liaison.—Helen Hsing, 512–2639.
Field Offices.—John Anderson, 512–8024.
Inspector General (IG).—Frances Garcia, 512–5748.
Opportunity and Inclusiveness.—Ron Stroman, 512–6388.

Personnel Appeals Board.—Anne Wagner, 512–6137.
Public Affairs.—Paul L. Anderson, 512–3823.
Quality and Continuous Improvement.—Tim Bowling, 512–6100.

MISSION SUPPORT OFFICES

Deputy Chief Administrative Officer/Chief Information Officer.—Tony Cicco, 512–6623.
Controller.—Stan Czerwinski, 512–6520.
Human Capital Officer.—Jesse Hoskins, 512–5533.
Knowledge Services Officer.—Catherine Teti, 512–9255.
Professional Development Program.—Mark Gebicke, 512–4126.

U.S. GOVERNMENT PRINTING OFFICE
732 North Capitol Street NW., 20401
phone 512–0000, www.gpo.gov

OFFICE OF THE PUBLIC PRINTER

Public Printer of the United States.—Bruce R. James, 512–1000, fax 512–1347.
  Deputy Public Printer.—William H. Turri, 512–2036, fax 512–1347.
  Chief of Staff.—Robert C. Tapella, 512–1100, fax 512–1896.
    Deputy Chief of Staff.—Maria S. Robinson, 512–1100, fax 512–1896.
  Inspector General.—Gregory A. Brower, 512–0039, fax 512–1352.
  Director, Office of Equal Employment Opportunity.—Nadine L. Elzy, 512–2014, fax 512–0521.
  Chief, Acquisition Officer.—Kerry L. Miller, 512–0008, fax 512–1517.
  General Counsel.—Anthony J. Zagami, 512–0033, fax 512–0076.
    Deputy General Counsel.—Drew Spalding, 512–0033, fax 512–0076.
  Co-Director, Innovation and New Technology.—Scott Stovall, 512–1080, fax 512–1076.
  Chief Technical Officer and Co-Director, Innovation and New Technology.—Michael Wash, 512–1080, fax 512–1076.
  Director, Congressional Relations.—Andrew M. Sherman, 512–1991, fax 512–1293.
  Director, Public Relations.—Veronica Meter, 512–1957, fax 512–1293.
  Director, New Business Development.—Charles C. Cook, Sr., 512–2004, fax 512–1101.

CUSTOMER SERVICES

Managing Director.—Jim Bradley, 512–0111, fax 512–1795.
  Deputy Managing Director.—Davita Vance-Cooks, 512–0014, fax 512–1795.
    Chief Acquisition Officer.—Kerry L. Miller, 512–0008, fax 512–1517.
      Director, Acquisition Policy and Planning Staff.—Jim Davidson (acting), 512–0376, fax 512–1848.
      Chief, Acquisiton Services.—Herbert H. Jackson, 512–0937, fax 512–1354.
    Director, Sales and Marketing Office.—Jim Bradley (acting), 512–0111, fax 512–1795.
    Director, Program and Operations Management Office.—Patty Hammond, 512–0271, fax 512–0007.
    Director, Office of Development and Program Support.—Sandy Zanko, 512–0559, fax 512–1463.
    Director, Congressional Publishing Services (formerly Congressional Printing Management Division).—Jerry Hammond, 512–0224, fax 512–1101.
    Director, Creative Services (formerly Typography & Design Division).—Janice Sterling, 512–0212, fax 512–1737.
    Assistant Director, Agency Publishing Services.—Emery A. Dilda, 512–0528, fax 512–1612.
    Assistant Director, Agency Publishing Services.—Spurgeon F. Johnson, Jr., 512–0238, fax 512–1260,
    Assistant Director, Agency Publishing Services.—Raymond T. Sullivan, 512–0320, fax 512–1567.
    Assistant Director, Agency Publishing Services.—Larry Vines (acting), 512–0485, fax 512–1364.
    Director, Institute for Federal Printing and Electronic Publishing.—Carol F. Cini, 512–1116, fax 512–1255.
    Assistant Director, Regional Operations Office.—Julie Hasenfus, 512–0412, fax 512–0381.

GPO OFFICES NATIONWIDE

Atlanta: 1888 Emery Street, Suite 110, Atlanta, GA 30318–2542,
(404) 605–9160, fax (404) 605–9185.
Manager.—Gary C. Bush.
> **Charleston Satellite Office:** 2825 Noisette Boulevard, Charleston, SC 29405–1819, (843) 743–2036, fax (843) 743–2068.
> *Assistant Manager.*—John Robert Mann.
Boston: 28 Court Square, Boston, MA 02108–2504, (617) 720–3680, fax (617) 720–0281.
Manager.—Fred W. Garlick.
Chicago: 200 North La Salle Street, Suite 810, Chicago, IL 60601–1055, (312) 353–3916, fax (312) 886–3163.
Assistant Manager.—Clint Mixon.
Columbus: 1335 Dublin Road, Suite 112–B, Columbus, OH 43215–7034, (614) 488–4616, fax (614) 488–4577.
Manager.—Aurelio E. Morales.
Dallas: U.S. Courthouse and Federal Office Building, 1100 Commerce Street, Room 731, Dallas, TX 75242–0395, (214) 767–0451, fax (214) 767–4101.
Manager.—Arthur Jacobson.
> **San Antonio Satellite Office:** 1531 Connally Street, Suite 2, Lackland AFB, TX 78236–5514, (210) 675–1480, fax (210) 675–2429.
> *Manager.*—Arthur Jacobson.
> **New Orleans Satellite Office:** U.S. Customs Building, 423 Canal Street, Room 310, New Orleans, LA 70130–2352, (504) 589–2538, fax (504) 589–2542.
> *Assistant Manager.*—Gerard J. Finnegan.
> **Oklahoma City Satellite Office:** 3420 D Avenue, Suite 100, Tinker Air Force Base, OK 73145–9188, (405) 610–4146, fax (405) 610–4125.
> *Assistant Manager.*—Timothy J. Ashcraft.
Denver: Denver Federal Center, Building 53, Room D–1010, Denver, CO 80225–0347, (303) 236–5292, fax (303) 236–5304.
Assistant Manager.—Barbara Lessans.
Hampton, VA: 11836 Canon Boulevard, Suite 400, Newport News, VA 23606–2555, (757) 873–2800, fax (757) 873–2805.
Assistant Manager.—John Robert Mann.
Los Angeles: 12501 East Imperial Highway, Suite 110, Norwalk, CA 90650–3136, (562) 863–1708, fax (562) 863–8701.
Manager.—John J. O'Connor.
> **San Diego Satellite Office:** Valley Center Office Building, 2221 Camino Del Rio S., Suite 109, San Diego, CA 92108–3609, (619) 497–6050, fax (619) 497–6055.
> *Manager.*—John J. O'Connor.
New York: 201 Varick Street, Room 709, Seventh Floor, New York, NY 10014–4879, (212) 620–3321, fax (212) 620–3378.
Manager.—Ira Fishkin.
Philadelphia: Southampton Office Park, 928 Jaymore Road, Suite A190, Southampton, PA 18966–3820, (215) 364–6465, fax (215) 364–6479.
Manager.—Ira Fishkin.
San Francisco: 536 Stone Road, Suite 1, Benicia, CA 94510–1170, (707) 748–1970, fax (707) 748–1980.
Manager.—John J. O'Connor.
Seattle: Federal Center South, 4735 East Marginal Way S., Seattle, WA 98134–2397, (206) 764–3726, fax (206) 764–3301.
Manager.—Michael J. Atkins.
St. Louis: 1222 Spruce Street, Room 1–205, St. Louis, MO 63103–2822, (314) 241–0349, fax (314) 241–4154.
Manager.—James A. Davidson.
Washington, DC: Rapid Response Center, Building 136, SE. Federal Center, 3rd and M Street, SE., Washington, DC 20403, (202) 755–2110, fax (202) 755–0287.
Assistant Manager.—Melvin R. Allen.

INFORMATION DISSEMINATION

Superintendent of Documents.—Judith C. Russell, 512–0571, fax 512–1434.
> *Deputy Superintendent of Documents.*—Thomas C. Evans III, 512–1524.
> *Library Services and Customer Relations Director.*—Kevin O'Toole, 512–1006, fax 512–2484.
> *Program Development Service Director.*—Richard G. Davis, 512–1622, fax 512–1262.

GPO BOOKSTORE

Washington, DC, Metropolitan Area: GPO Bookstore, 710 North Capitol Street NW., Washington, DC 20401, (202) 512–0132, fax (202) 512–1355.

TO ORDER PUBLICATIONS:

Phone toll free (866) 512–1800 [DC area: (202) 512–1800], fax (202) 512–2250, mail orders to Superintendent of Documents, P.O. Box 371954, Pittsburgh PA 15250–7954, or order online from http://bookstore.gpo.gov. *GPO Access* technical support: gpoaccess@gpo.gov or toll free (888) 293–6498 [DC area (202) 512–1530].

PLANT OPERATIONS

Managing Director.—Robert E. Schwenk, 512–0707, fax 512–0740.
  Deputy Managing Director of Plant Operations.—Olivier Girod, 512–1097, fax 512–0740.
    Production Manager.—Jeffrey J. Bernazzoli, 512–0707.
      Assistant Production Manager (night).—William C. Krakat, 512–0688, fax 512–0740.
      Assistant to the Production Manager (night).—David N. Boddie, 512–0688.
    Superintendent of:
      Binding Division.—John W. Crawford, 512–0593, fax 512–1830.
      Electronic Photocomposition Division.—Dannie E. Young, 512–0625, fax 512–1730.
      Press Division.—George M. Domarasky, 512–0673, fax 512–1754.
      Production Planning Division.—Philip J. Markett, Jr., 512–0233, fax 512–1569.
    Manager, Quality Control and Technical Department.—Sylvia S.Y. Subt, 512–0766, fax 512–0015.
    Engineering Service.—Dennis J. Carey (acting), 512–1031, fax 512–1418.

INFORMATION TECHNOLOGY AND SYSTEMS

Chief Information Officer.—Reynold Schweickhardt, 512–1913, fax 512–1840.
  Manager of:
    Systems Architecture Director.—Richard G. Leeds, Jr., 512–0029, fax 512–1756.
    Plans/Policy/Program Support Director.—Melvin C. Eley, 512–0731, fax 512–1840.

HUMAN CAPITAL

Chief Human Capital Officer.—William T. Harris (acting), 512–1111, fax 512–2139.
  Director of Labor and Employee Relations.—Neal H. Fine, 512–0200, fax 512–1150.

FINANCE AND ADMINISTRATION

Chief Financial Officer.—Steven T. Shedd, 512–2073, fax 512–1520.
  Comptroller.—William L. Boesch, Jr., 512–2073, fax 512–1520.
  Director of Budget.—William M. Guy, 512–0832, fax 512–1736.

LIBRARY OF CONGRESS

10 First Street SE., 20540, phone 707–5000, fax 707–5844

http://www.loc.gov

OFFICE OF THE LIBRARIAN, LM 608

Librarian of Congress.—James H. Billington, 707–5205.
  Confidential Assistant to the Librarian.—Timothy L. Robbins.
  Deputy Librarian/Chief Operating Officer.—Donald L. Scott, 707–5215.
  Chief of Staff.—Jo Ann C. Jenkins, 707–0351.
  Director, Congressional Relations Office.—Geraldine Otremba, LM 611, 707–6577.
  Director, Development Office.—Charles V. Stanhope, LM 605, 707–2777.
  Special Events Officer.—Larry Stafford, LM 605, 707–1523.
  Director, Communications Office.—Jill D. Brett, LM 105, 707–2905.

Editor, Calendar of Events.—Helen W. Dalrymple, 707–1940.
Editor, Library of Congress Information Bulletin.—Helen W. Dalrymple, 707–1940.
Editor, The Gazette.—Gail Fineberg, 707–9194.
General Counsel.—Elizabeth Pugh, LM 601, 707–6316.
Inspector General.—Karl W. Schornagel, LM 630, 707–6314.
Chief of Contracts and Grants Management.—Nydia Coleman, LA 325, 707–6109.

OFFICE OF SECURITY AND EMERGENCY PREPAREDNESS, LM G03

Director.—Kenneth Lopez, 707–8708.

OFFICE OF WORKFORCE DIVERSITY, LM 624

Director.—Gilbert Sandate, 707–4170.
Affirmative Action and Special Programs Office (LM 623), 707–5479.
Dispute Resolution Center, 707–4170.
Equal Employment Opportunity Complaints Office (LM 626), 707–6024.

OFFICE OF THE DIRECTOR FOR HUMAN RESOURCES SERVICES, LM 645

Director.—Teresa A. Smith, LM 645, 707–5659.
Special Assistants: Timothy W. Cannon, 707–6544; Michaline Dobrzeniecki, 707–7191.
Director, Office of:
  Strategic Planning and Automation.—Dennis Hanratty, 707–0029.
  Workforce Acquisitions.—William Ayers, Jr. (acting), 707–0289.
  Workforce Management.—Charles Carron, LM 653, 707–6637.
  Worklife Services Center.—Rafael E. Landrau, 707–8072.

OFFICE OF THE CHIEF FINANCIAL OFFICER, LM 613

Accounting Operations Officer.—Nicole N. Sims, LM 617, 707–5547.
  Budget Officer.—Kathryn B. Murphy, 707–5186.
  Disbursing Officer.—Nicholas Roseto, 707–5202.
  Financial Systems Officer.—Jamie L. McCullough, LM 617, 707–4160.

OFFICE OF THE DIRECTOR FOR INTEGRATED SUPPORT SERVICES, LM 327

Director.—Mary Berghaus Levering, 707–1393.
  Facility Services Officer.—Neal Graham (acting), 707–7512.
  Health Services Officer.—Sandra Charles, LM G40, 707–8035.
  Safety Services Officer.—Robert Browne, LM B28, 707–6204.

OFFICE OF STRATEGIC INITIATIVES, LM 637

Associate Librarian for Strategic Initiatives/Chief Information Officer.—Laura E. Campbell, 707–3300.
  Confidential Assistant to the Associate Librarian.—George Coulbourne, 707–7856.
  Director, Digital Resource Managemant and Planning.—Molly H. Johnson, 707–0809.
  Senior Advisor, Integration Management.—Elizabeth S. Dulabahn, 707–2369.
  Director for Information Technology Services.—James M. Gallagher, LM G51, 707–5114.
    Special Assistant to the Director.—Karen Caldwell, 707–3797.

LAW LIBRARY, OFFICE OF THE LAW LIBRARIAN, LM 240

Law Librarian.—Rubens Medina, 707–5065.
  Director, Directorate of Law Library Services.—Donna Scheeder, 707–8939.
    Chief, Public Services.—Robert N. Gee, LM 201, 707–0638.
  Director, Directorate of Legal Research.—Walter Gary Sharp, 707–9148.
    Chief, Eastern Law Division.—Tao-tai Hsia, LM 235, 707–5085.
    Chief, Western Law Division.—Kersi B. Shroff, LM 235, 707–7850.

LIBRARY SERVICES, OFFICE OF THE ASSOCIATE LIBRARIAN FOR LIBRARY SERVICES, LM 642

Associate Librarian.—Deanna Marcum, 707–6240.
  Director for Acquisitions.—Beacher Wiggins, 707–5333.
    Fiscal Operations Officer.—Sylvia M. Csiffary, LM 633, 707–9444.
  Director, Office for Collections and Services.—Carolyn T. Brown, LJ 100, 707–1902.
    Chief of:
      African and Middle Eastern Division.—Beverly Ann Gray, LJ 220, 707–2933.
      Asian Division.—Hwa-Wei Lee, LJ 149, 707–5919.
      European Division.—John Van Oudenaren, LJ 250, 707–4543.
      Federal Research Division.—Robert L. Worden, LA 5282, 707–3909.
      Hispanic Division.—Georgette M. Dorn, LJ 240, 707–2003.
  Director, Office of Scholarly Programs.—Prosser Gifford, LJ 120, 707–1517.
  Director of Bibliographic Access.—Judith A. Mansfield (acting), 707–5333.
    Chief, Cataloging Distribution Service.—Kathryn M. Mendenhall (acting), LA 206, 707–6121.
  Director, Center for the Book.—John Y. Cole, Jr., LM 650, 707–5221.
  Executive Director, Federal Library and Information Center Committee.—Susan M. Tarr, LA 217, 707–4801.
    Interpretive Programs Officer.—Irene U. Chambers, LA G25, 707–5223.
  Director, Office of National Library Service for the Blind and Physically Handicapped, TSA.—Frank K. Cylke, 707–5104.
    Chief, Photoduplication Service.—Sandra M. Lawson (acting), LA 130, 707–5650.
  Director, Publishing Office.—W. Ralph Eubanks, LM 602, 707–3892.
    Retail Marketing Officer.—Anna S. Lee, LM 225Q, 707–7715.
    Visitor Services Officer.—Teresa V. Sierra, 707–5277.
  Director for Preservation.—Dianne Van Der Reyden, 707–5213.
  Director of:
    American Folklife Center.—Peggy Bulger, LJ G59, 707–1745.
    Veterans History Project.—Diane Kresh, LA 144, 707–4916.
    Chief of:
      Children's Literature Center.—Sybille A. Jagusch, LJ 100, 707–5535.
      Collections Access, Loan and Management.—Steven J. Herman, LJ G02, 707–7400.
      Geography and Map Division.—John R. Hebert, LM B02, 707–8530.
      Humanities and Social Sciences Divisions.—Stephen E. James, LJ 139A, 707–5530.
      Manuscript Division.—James H. Hutson, LM 102, 707–5383.
    Assistant Chief, Motion Picture, Broadcasting and Recorded Sound Division.—Gregory A. Lukow, LM 338, 707–5709.
    Chief of:
      Music Division.—Jon W. Newsom, LM 113, 707–5503.
      Prints and Photographs Division.—Jeremy E. Adamson, LM 339, 707–5836.
      Rare Book and Special Collections Division.—Mark G. Dimunation, LJ Dk A, 707–5434.
      Science Technology and Business Division.—William J. Sittig, LA 5203, 707–5664.
      Serial and Government Publications Division.—Karen Renninger, LM 133, 707–5096.

CONGRESSIONAL RESEARCH SERVICE, LM 203

Director.—Daniel P. Mulhollan, 707–5775.
  Associate Directors for the offices of:
    Congressional Affairs and Counselor to the Director.—Kent M. Ronhovde, 707–7090.
    Finance and Administration.—Kathy A. Williams, LM 208, 707–6698.
    Legislative Information.—Jeffrey C. Griffith, LM 208, 707–2475.
    Research.—Roger S. White, LM–203, 707–7844.
    Workforce Development.—Bessie E.H. Alkisswani, LM 208, 707–8835.
  Assistant Directors of:
    American Law Division.—Richard C. Ehlke, LM 227, 707–6006.
    Domestic Social Policy Division.—Royal Shipp, LM 323, 707–6228.
    Foreign Affairs, Defense and Trade Division.—Charlotte P. Preece, LM 315, 707–7654.
    Government and Finance Division.—Robert J. Dilger, LM 303, 707–3110.
    Knowledge Services Group.—Stephanie V. Williams, LM 221, 707–5804.
    Resources, Science and Industry Division.—John L. Moore, LM 423, 707–7232.

U.S. COPYRIGHT OFFICE, LM 403

Register of Copyrights and Associate Librarian for Copyright Services.—Marybeth Peters, 707–8350.
General Counsel.—David Carson, 707–8380.
Associate General Counsel.—Tanya M. Sandros.
Chief Operating Officer.—Julia B. Huff, 707–8350.
Special Legal Advisor for Reengineering.—Nanette Petruzzelli, 707–8350.
Chief of:
　Cataloging Division.—Joanna Roussis (acting), LM 513, 707–8040.
　Information and Reference Division.—James P. Cole, LM 453, 707–6800.
　Receiving and Processing Division.—Melissa Dadant, LM 435, 707–7700.
　Copyright Acquisitions Division.—Jewel Player, LM 438C, 707–7125.

UNITED STATES BOTANIC GARDEN

245 First Street, SW., Washington, DC 20024

(202) 225–8333 (information); (202) 226–8333 (receptionist)

http://www.usbg.gov

Director.—Alan M. Hantman, Architect of the Capitol, 228–1204.
　Executive Director.—Holly H. Shimizu, 225–6670.
　Administrative Officer.—Elizabeth A. Spar, 225–5002.
　Public Programs Coordinator.—Christine A. Flanagan, 225–1269.
　Horticulture Division Manager.—Robert Pennington, 225–6647.
　Operations Division Manager.—John M. Gallagher, 225–6646.

THE CABINET

Vice President of the United States	RICHARD B. CHENEY.
Secretary of State	CONDOLEEZZA RICE.
Secretary of the Treasury	JOHN W. SNOW.
Secretary of Defense	DONALD H. RUMSFELD.
Attorney General	ALBERTO GONZALES.
Secretary of the Interior	GALE NORTON.
Secretary of Agriculture	MICHAEL JOHANNS.
Secretary of Commerce	CARLOS GUTIERREZ.
Secretary of Labor	ELAINE CHAO.
Secretary of Health and Human Services	MICHAEL O. LEAVITT.
Secretary of Housing and Urban Development	ALPHONSO JACKSON.
Secretary of Transportation	NORMAN Y. MINETA.
Secretary of Energy	SAMUEL W. BODMAN.
Secretary of Education	MARGARET SPELLINGS.
Secretary of Veterans Affairs	JAMES NICHOLSON.
Secretary of Homeland Security	MICHAEL CHERTOFF.
Chief of Staff	ANDREW H. CARD, JR.
Director, Office of Management and Budget	JOSHUA B. BOLTEN.
U.S. Trade Representative	ROB PORTMAN.
Administrator, Environmental Protection Agency	STEPHEN L. JOHNSON.
Director, Office of National Drug Control Policy	JOHN P. WALTERS.

EXECUTIVE BRANCH

THE PRESIDENT

GEORGE W. BUSH, Republican, of Texas; born on July 6, 1946; raised in Midland and Houston, TX; education: Yale University (Bachelor's Degree); Harvard University (M.B.A.); military service: Texas Air National Guard; occupations: businessman (energy industry); Managing General Partner of the Texas Rangers (Major League Baseball team); public service: elected Governor of Texas on November 8, 1994; reelected as Governor on November 3, 1998; became the first Governor in Texas history to be elected to consecutive four-year terms; religion: Methodist; family: married to Laura; two children, Barbara and Jenna; elected President of the United States on November 7, 2000; took the oath of office on January 20, 2001; reelected November 2, 2004.

EXECUTIVE OFFICE OF THE PRESIDENT

THE WHITE HOUSE OFFICE

1600 Pennsylvania Avenue, NW., 20500

Eisenhower Executive Office Building (EEOB), 17th Street and Pennsylvania Avenue, NW., 20500, phone 456–1414, http://www.whitehouse.gov

The President of the United States.—George W. Bush.
    Deputy Assistant to the President and Director of Oval Office Operations.—Linda Gambatesa.
    Personal Secretary to the President.—Karen Keller.
    Personal Aide to the President.—Blake Gottesman.

CABINET LIAISON
phone 456–2572

Special Assistant to the President for Cabinet Liaison.—Heidi Smith.

CHIEF OF STAFF
phone 456–6798

Assistant to the President and Chief of Staff—Andrew H. Card, Jr.

COMMUNICATIONS AND SPEECHWRITING
phone 456–7910, speechwriting phone 456–2763

Assistant to the President for Communications.—Nicolle Devenish.
    Assistant to the President for Speechwriting.—William McGurn.
    Counselor to the President.—Dan Bartlett.

OFFICE OF THE PRESS SECRETARY
Upper Press Office phone 456–2673, Lower Press Office phone 456–2580

Assistant to the President and White House Press Secretary.—Scott McClellan.

CORRESPONDENCE
phone 456–7610

Director of Presidential Correspondence.—Marguerite A. Murer (acting).

Deputy Director of Presidential Correspondence.—Marguerite A. Murer, 456–6779.
Editor/Quality Control.—Nathaniel Kraft, 456–5867.
Director of:
  Agency Liaison.—Richard Henry, 456–5485.
  Gift Unit.—Christa Bailey, 456–5457.
  Mail Analysis.—Trudy Roddick, 456–5490.

WHITE HOUSE COUNSEL
phone 456–2632

Assistant to the President and White House Counsel.—Harriet Miers.
  Executive Assistant to the Counsel.—Heather Roebke.
  Deputy Assistant to the President and Deputy Counsel to the President.—David Leitch.
  Special Assistants to the President and Associate Counsels to the President: Jennifer
    Brosnahan, Reg Brown, Grant Dixton, Charles Duggan, Nanette Everson, Leslie
    Fahrenkopf, Dabney Friedrich, Thomas Monheim, Benjamin Powell.

DOMESTIC POLICY COUNCIL
phone 456–5594

Assistant to the President for Domestic Policy.—Claude Allen.

NATIONAL AIDS POLICY
phone 456–7320

Director.—Carol Thompson.

OFFICE OF FAITH-BASED AND COMMUNITY INITIATIVES
phone 456–6708

Assistant to the President and Director.—Jim Towey.
  Special Assistant to the President and Deputy Director.—Dennis Grace.

STRATEGIC INITIATIVES
phone 456–2369

Deputy Chief of Staff for Policy and Senior Advisor to the President.—Karl Rove.
  Deputy Assistant to the President and Assistant to the Senior Advisor.—Israel Hernandez.
  Executive Assistant to the Senior Advisor.—Taylor Hughes.

FIRST LADY'S OFFICE
phone 456–7064

The First Lady.—Laura Bush.
  Deputy Assistant to the President and Chief of Staff to the First Lady.—Anita McBride.
  Special Assistant to the President and White House Social Secretary.—Janet Lea Smith.

INTERGOVERNMENTAL AFFAIRS
phone 456–2896

Deputy Assistant to the President and Director for Intergovernmental Affairs.—Ruben Barrales.
  Special Assistants to the President for Intergovernmental Affairs: Toby Burke, Maggie
    Grant, James M. Kelly.

LEGISLATIVE AFFAIRS

phone 456–2230

Assistant to the President for Legislative Affairs.—Candida Wolff.
Deputy Assistant to the President for Legislative Affairs.—Doug Badger.
Special Assistant to the Assistant to the President for Legislative Affairs.—Lindley Kratovil.
Deputy Assistant to the President for—
  House Legislative Affairs.—Brian Conklin.
  Senate Legislative Affairs.—Matt Kirk.
Director of Legislative Correspondence.—Brooke Manning.

MANAGEMENT AND ADMINISTRATION

phone 456–5400

Deputy Assistant to the President for Management Administration, and Oval Office Operations.—Linda Gambatesa.

NATIONAL ECONOMIC COUNCIL

phone 456–2800

Assistant to the President for Economic Policy and Director, National Economic Council.—Allan B. Hubbard.
Deputy Assistant to the President for Economic Policy and Deputy Director, National Economic Council.—Keith Hennessey.
Executive Assistant to the Director.—Dougie Simmons.
Special Assistants to the President for Economic Policy: Charles Blahous, Charles Conner, Cathie Martin, Brian Reardon, Kevin Warsh.

OFFICE OF THE VICE PRESIDENT

phone 456–1414

The Vice President.—Richard B. Cheney.
  Chief of Staff.—Lewis Libby, EEOB, Room 276, 456–9000.
  Deputy Chief of Staff.—Dean McGrath, EEOB, Room 276, 456–9000.
  Counsel to the Vice President.—David Addington, EEOB, Room 268, 456–9089.
  Counselor to the Vice President.—Steve Schmidt, EEOB, Room 272, 456–3880.
  Principal Deputy National Security Advisor to the Vice President.—Victoria Nuland, EEOB, Room 298, 456–9501.
  Assistant to the Vice President for Legislative Affairs.—Brenda Becker, EEOB, Room 285, 456–6774.
  Assistant to the Vice President for Domestic Policy.—Kevin O'Donovan, EEOB, Room 286, 456–2728.
  Executive Assistant to the Vice President.—Debra Heiden, West Wing, 456–7549.
  Assistant to the Vice President and Deputy Chief of Staff (Operations).—Claire O'Donnell, EEOB, Room 272, 456–6770.
  Chief of Staff to Mrs. Cheney.—Stephanie Lundberg, EEOB, Room 200, 456–7458.
  Deputy Assistant to the Vice President and Director of Scheduling.—Elizabeth Kleppe, EEOB, Room 279, 456–6773.
  Director of Correspondence.—Cecelia Boyer, EEOB, Room 265, 456–9002.

POLITICAL AFFAIRS

phone 456–6257

Deputy Assistant to the President and Director of Political Affairs.—Sara Taylor.
Executive Assistant.—Henley MacIntyre.
Special Assistant to the President and Deputy Director of Political Affairs.—Tim Griffin.
Associate Political Directors: Glynda Becker, Raul Damas, Mike Davis, Jonathon Felts, Scott Jennings, Annie Mayol.
Political Coordinators: Luke Frans, Nathan Hollifield.

PRESIDENTIAL PERSONNEL

phone 456–6676

Assistant to the President for Presidential Personnel.—Dina Powell.
  Executive Assistant to the President for Presidential Personnel.—Brian Cossiboom.
  Special Assistants to the President and Associate Directors.—Amanda Becker, Katja Bullock,
    Eric Burgeson, Monica Kladakis, Eric Motley, Ed Moy, Julie Myers, Liza Wright.

OFFICE OF PUBLIC LIAISON

phone 456–2380

Deputy Assistant to the President and Director of Public Liaison.—Lezlee Westine.

SCHEDULING

phone 456–5323

Deputy Assistant to the President for Appointments and Scheduling.—Melissa Bennett.
  Deputy Director of Appointments and Scheduling.—Ashley Drummond.
  Staff Assistant.—Sarah Keith.
  Deputy Director of:
    Scheduling.—Meredith Terpeluk.
    Scheduling-Research.—James Waters.
  Research Assistant.—John Powell.
  Schedulers: Julia Newton, Jennifer Wray.
  Associate Directors of Scheduling for Invitations and Correspondence: Nathan Atlas, Ashley
    Selph.
  Presidential Diarist.—Ellen McCathran.
  Assistant to the Presidential Diarist.—Angela Fritz.

ADVANCE

phone 456–5309

Deputy Assistant to the President and Director of Advance.—Todd Beyer.
  Special Assistant to the President and Deputy Director of Advance—Press.—Chris Edwards.
  Special Assistant to the President and Tour Director.—Steve Atkiss.

STAFF SECRETARY

phone 456–2702

Assistant to the President and Staff Secretary.—Brett Kavanaugh.
  Deputy Assistant to the President and Deputy Staff Secretary.—Bill Burck.
  Assistant Staff Secretaries: Leslie Drogin, David Sherzer, Lauren Vestewig.
  Special Assistants to the Staff Secretary: Molly Houser, Kristen Slaughter.

WHITE HOUSE MILITARY OFFICE

phone 757–2151

Director.—CAPT Mark I. Fox (acting), USN.
  Deputy Director.—George Mulligan (acting).
  Air Force Aide to the President.—LTC John Quintas.
  Army Aide to the President.—MAJ Steve Fischer.
  Coast Guard Aide to the President.—LCDR John Daly.
  Marine Corps Aide to the President.—MAJ Christian Cabaniss.
  Naval Aide to the President.—LCDR Keith Davids.
  Director of:
    Admission.—LT Mike Chapman, USN.
    Financial Management.—LTC David Zorzi, USAF.

Information and Technology Management.—Karin Mills.
Operations.—COL Rick Antaya, USAF.
Policy, Plans and Requirements.—Paul J. Jackson.
Presidential Food Service.—LT Jonathan Oringdulph, USN.
Security.—LTC Peter Coughlin, USA.
White House Transportation Agency.—Leroy Borden.
White House Medical Unit.—COL Richard J. Tubb, USAF.
Presidential Pilot's Office.—COL Mark Tillman, USAF.

COUNCIL OF ECONOMIC ADVISERS

1800 G Street, NW., 8th floor, phone (202) 395–5084
www.whitehouse.gov/cea

Chair.—N. Gregory Mankiw.
  Chief of Staff.—Phillip Swagel.
  Member.—Randall S. Kroszner.

COUNCIL ON ENVIRONMENTAL QUALITY

730 Jackson Place, NW., phone (202) 456–6224, www.whitehouse.gov/ceq

Chair.—James Connaughton.
  Chief of Staff.—Phil Cooney.
  Special Assistant to the Chair.—Khary Cauthen.
  Deputy Director for Communications.—William Holbrook.
  Associate Director for—
    Agriculture and Public Lands.—David Anderson.
    Congressional Affairs.—Heather Pearce.
    Energy and Transportation.—Bryan Hannegan.
    Environmental Policy.—Kameran Onley.
    Global Environmental Affairs.—Kenneth Peel.
    Natural Resources.—William Leary.
    NEPA Oversight.—Horst Greczmiel.
    Toxics and Environmental Protection.—Elizabeth Stolpe.
  General Counsel.—Dinah Bear.
    Deputy General Counsel.—Edward Boling.
  Legal Assistant.—William (Bill) Perhach.
  Administrative Officer.—Angela Stewart.
  Secretaries: Quesean Rice, Essence Washington.
  Records Clerk.—Shaffers Rawlings.

CENTRAL INTELLIGENCE AGENCY

phone (703) 482–1100

Director.—Porter Goss.
  Director of Congressional Affairs.—Joseph Wippl.
  General Counsel.—John Rizzo (acting).

FOREIGN INTELLIGENCE ADVISORY BOARD

phone 456–2352

Executive Director.—Joan Dempsey.

NATIONAL SECURITY COUNCIL

Eisenhower Executive Office Building, phone 456–9491

MEMBERS

The President.—George W. Bush.
  The Vice President.—Richard Cheney.

The Secretary of State.—Condoleezza Rice.
The Secretary of Defense.—Donald Rumsfeld.

STATUTORY ADVISERS

Director of Central Intelligence.—Porter Goss.
  Chairman, Joint Chiefs of Staff.—Gen. Richard B. Myers, USAF.
  Assistant to the President for National Security Affairs.—Stephen J. Hadley.
  Assistant to the President and Deputy National Security Advisor.—J.D. Crouch II.

HOMELAND SECURITY COUNCIL

phone 456–1700

Assistant to the President and Homeland Security Advisor.—Frances Fragos Townsend.

POLICY AND STRATEGIC PLANNING

phone 456–0170

Assistant to the President for Policy and Strategic Planning.—Mike Gerson.
  Special Assistant to the Director.—Emily Kropp.

OFFICE OF ADMINISTRATION

Eisenhower Executive Office Building, room 148, phone 456–2861

Special Assistant to the President/Director of Administration.—John Straub.
  Chief, Office of:
    Equal Employment Opportunity.—Linda Sites.
    Finance.—John Straub (acting).
    General Counsel.—Vic Bernson.
    Information.—John Straub (acting).
    Operations.—Sandy Evans.
    Security.—Jim Knodell.

OFFICE OF MANAGEMENT AND BUDGET

Eisenhower Executive Office Building, phone 395–4840

Director.—Joshua B. Bolten.
  Deputy Director.—Joel D. Kaplan.
  Deputy Director for Management.—Clay Johnson III.
  Executive Associate Director.—Austin Smythe.
  Administrator, Office of:
    Federal Procurement Policy.—David Safavian.
    Information and Regulatory Affairs.—John Graham.
  Assistant Director for—
    Budget.—Richard Emery.
    Legislative Reference.—James J. Jukes.
  Associate Director for—
    Communications.—Noam Neusner.
    Economic Policy.—J.D. Foster.
    Human Resources Programs.—Dean Clancy.
    General Government Programs.—Steve McMillin.
    Legislative Affairs.—Beth Rossman (acting).
    National Security Programs.—Robin Cleveland.
    Natural Resources, Energy and Science Programs.—Marcus Peacock.
  General Counsel.—Jennifer Newstead.

OFFICE OF NATIONAL DRUG CONTROL POLICY

750 17th Street, NW., phone 395–6738, fax 395–7251

Director.—John P. Walters, room 805, 395–6700.
  Deputy Director.—Mary Ann Solberg, room 836, 395–6710.
  Chief of Staff.—Stephen A. Katsurinis, room 809, 395–6732.
    Assistant Deputy Director.—Addison Davis, room 610, 395–4992.
    Assistant Deputy Director, Office of Supply Reduction.—Lennard Wolfson, room 714, 395–6645.
  Deputy Director, Office of State and Local Affairs.—Scott M. Burns, room 661, 395–7252.
    Assistant Deputy Director.—Joseph Keefe, room 659, 395–6755.
  General Counsel, Office of the General Counsel.—Edward H. Jurith, room 518, 395–6709.
  Director, Counterdrug Technology Assessment Center.—David Rivait (acting), room 846, 395–5505.
  Associate Director, National Youth Anti-drug Media Campaign.—Robert Denniston, room 560, 395–4653.
  Associate Director, Office of:
    Legislative Affairs.—Christine E. Morden, room 825, 395–6655.
    Management and Administration.—Michele C. Marx, room 326, 395–6883.
    Planning and Budget.—David Rivait, room 846, 395–5505.
    Public Affairs.—Thomas A. Riley, room 842, 395–6627.

OFFICE OF SCIENCE AND TECHNOLOGY POLICY

Eisenhower Executive Office Building, phone 456–7116, fax 456–6021
www.ostp.gov

Director.—John H. Marburger III.
  Associate Director for—
    Science.—Kathie Olsen.
    Technology.—Richard Russell.
  Chief of Staff and General Counsel.—Shana Dale.
  Executive Secretary for—
    National Science and Technology Council.—Christopher Flaherty.
  Executive Director for President's Committee of Advisors on Science and Technology.—Stan Sokul.

OFFICE OF THE UNITED STATES TRADE REPRESENTATIVE

600 17th Street NW., phone 395–3230, www.ustr.gov

United States Trade Representative.—Rob Portman.
  Deputy United States Trade Representative.—Peter F. Allgeier.
  Deputy U.S. Trade Representative, Geneva.—Linnett F. Deily.
  Associate U.S. Trade Representative.—Sheeran Shiner.
  Special Textile Negotiator.—David Spooner.
  Chief Agricultural Negotiator.—Allen F. Johnson.
  General Counsel.—James Mendenhall (acting).
  Assistant U.S. Trade Representative for—
    Administration.—Lorraine Green (acting).
    Africa.—Florie Liser.
    Agricultural Affairs.—James Murphy.
    China Affairs.—Charles Freeman.
    Congressional Affairs.—Matt Niemeyer.
    Economic Affairs.—David Walters.
    Environment and Natural Resources.—Mark Linscott.
    Europe and the Mediterranean.—Cathy Novelli.
    Industry.—Meredith Broadbent.
    Intergovernmental Affairs and Public Liaison.—Christopher Padilla.
    Japan, Korea and APEC Affairs.—Wendy Cutler.
    Monitoring and Enforcement.—Dan Brinza
    Office of the Americas.—Regina Vargo.
    Policy Coordination.—Carmen Suro-Bredie.
    Public/Media Affairs.—E. Richard Mills.

Services, Investment and Intellectual Property.—James Mendenhall.
South Asian Affairs.—E. Ashley Wills.
Southeast Asia, Pacific and Pharmaceutical Policy.—Barbara Weisel.
Trade and Labor.—William Clatanoff.
World Trade Organization (WTO) and Multilateral Affairs.—Dorothy Dwoskin.

PRESIDENT'S COMMISSION ON WHITE HOUSE FELLOWSHIPS
phone 395–4522

Director.—Janet Eissenstat.
   Associate Director.—Lauren McCord.
   Administrative Officer.—Pandoria Nobles-Jones.
   Education Director.—Susan Salmini.
   Staff Assistant.—Nikki Lewis.

USA FREEDOM CORPS

1600 Pennsylvania Avenue, NW., 1–877–USA–CORPS, www.usafreedomcorps.gov

Deputy Assistant to the President and Director of USA Freedom Corps.—Desiree Sayle.

DEPARTMENT OF STATE

2201 C Street NW., 20520, phone 647–4000

CONDOLEEZZA RICE, Secretary of State; born in Birmingham, AL, November 14, 1954; education: B.A., *cum laude*, Phi Beta Kappa, University of Denver, 1974; M.A., University of Notre Dame, 1975; Ph.D., Graduate School of International Studies, University of Denver, 1981; professional: professor of political science; Provost, Stanford University, 1993–99; National Security Advisor for President George W. Bush, 2001–04; founding board member, Center for a New Generation; senior fellow, American Academy of Arts and Sciences; member, Center for International Security and Arms Control; senior fellow, Institute for International Studies; fellow, Hoover Institution; awards: Walter J. Gores Award for Excellence in Teaching, 1984; School of Humanities and Sciences Dean's Award for Distinguished Teaching, 1993; author, *Germany Unified and Europe Transformed*, 1995 (with Philip Zelikow); *The Gorbachev Era*, 1986 (with Alexander Dallin); *Uncertain Allegiance: The Soviet Union and the Czechoslovak Army*, 1984; nominated by President George W. Bush to become the 66th Secretary of State, and was confirmed by the U.S. Senate on January 26, 2005.

OFFICE OF THE SECRETARY

Secretary of State.—Condoleezza Rice, 647–5291.
    Executive Assistant.—Steve Beecroft, 647–9572.

OFFICE OF THE DEPUTY SECRETARY

Deputy Secretary of State.—Robert B. Zoellick, room 7220, 647–9641.
    Executive Assistant.—Ross Wilson, 647–8931.

EXECUTIVE SECRETARIAT

Special Assistant and Executive Secretary.—Karl Hofmann, room 7224, 647–5301.
    Deputy Executive Secretaries: Douglas C. Greene, 647–5302; John D. Feeley, 647–8448; Marcia K. Wong, 647–5302.

POLICY PLANNING STAFF

Director.—Dr. Stephen Krasner, room 7311, 647–2972.
    Principal Deputy Director.—Barry Lowenkron, 647–2372.

AMBASSADOR-AT-LARGE FOR WAR CRIMES ISSUES

Ambassador-at-Large.—Pierre-Richard Prosper, room 7419A, 647–5074.
    Deputy.—Elizabeth Richard, 647–5072.

UNDER SECRETARY FOR POLITICAL AFFAIRS

Under Secretary.—Nicholas Burns, room 7240, 647–2471.
    Executive Assistant.—Marsha Yovanovitch (acting), 647–1598.

UNDER SECRETARY FOR ECONOMIC, BUSINESS, AND AGRICULTURAL AFFAIRS

Executive Assistant.—Anna Borg, 647–7674.

UNDER SECRETARY FOR ARMS CONTROL AND INTERNATIONAL SECURITY

Under Secretary.—John Bolton, room 7208, 647–1049.
Executive Assistant.—Fred Fleitz, 647–1749.

UNDER SECRETARY FOR MANAGEMENT

Under Secretary.—Christopher B. Burnham (acting), room 7207, 647–1500.
Executive Assistant.—Lynwood Dent, 647–1501.

UNDER SECRETARY FOR GLOBAL AFFAIRS

Under Secretary.—Paula Dobriansky, room 7250, 647–6240.
Executive Assistant.—Jeff Miotke, 647–7609.

UNDER SECRETARY FOR PUBLIC DIPLOMACY AND PUBLIC AFFAIRS

Under Secretary.—Patricia S. Harrison (acting), 647–9199.
Executive Assistant.—Jeremy Curtin.

BUREAUS

AFRICAN AFFAIRS

Assistant Secretary.—Constance Berry Newman, room 6234, 647–4440.
  Principal Deputy Assistant Secretary.—Michael Ranneberger, 647–4493.
  Deputy Assistant Secretaries: Thomas Woods, 647–4485; Don Yamamoto, 647–1819.

EAST ASIAN AND PACIFIC AFFAIRS

Assistant Secretary.—Ambassador Christopher Hill, 647–9596.
  Principal Deputy Assistant Secretary.—Evans Revere, 647–4393.
  Deputy Assistant Secretaries: Joseph Detrani, 647–8929; Marie Huhtala, 647–6904; Lauren Moriarty, 647–7266; Randall Schriver, 647–6910.

EUROPEAN AFFAIRS

Assistant Secretary.—Robert Bradtke (acting), room 6226, 647–9626.
  Principal Deputy Assistant Secretary.—Robert Bradtke, 647–6402.
  Deputy Assistant Secretaries: Heather Conley, 647–6233; Glyn Davies, 647–6402; Laura Kennedy, 647–5447; Kathleen Stephens, 647–6145; John Tefft, 647–5174.

NEAR-EASTERN AFFAIRS

Assistant Secretary.—C. David Welch, room 6242, 647–7209.
  Principal Deputy Assistant Secretary.—Elizabeth Cheney, 647–7207.
  Deputy Assistant Secretary.—Elizabeth Dibble, 647–7170.

WESTERN HEMISPHERE AFFAIRS

Assistant Secretary.—Roger Noriega, room 6262, 647–8386.
  Principal Deputy Assistant Secretary.—James Derham, 647–8562.
  Deputy Assistant Secretaries: Daniel Fisk, 647–7337; Linda Jewel, 647–8387; Charles Shapiro, 647–6754.

SOUTH ASIAN AFFAIRS

Assistant Secretary.—Christina Rocca, room 6254, 736–4325.
  Principal Deputy Assistant Secretary.—Donald A. Camp, 736–4331.
  Deputy Assistant Secretary.—John A. Gastright.

ADMINISTRATION

Assistant Secretary.—William A. Eaton, room 6330, 647–1492.
Procurement Executive.—Cory Reinder, (703) 516–1684.
Deputy Assistant Secretaries: Vince Chaverini, 647–1638; Frank Coulter (703) 875–6956; Lee R. Lohman, 663–2217.

ARMS CONTROL

Assistant Secretary.—Stephen Rademaker, room 6820, 647–9610.
Principal Deputy Assistant Secretary.—Francis Record, 647–7992.
Deputy Assistant Secretary.—Ambassador Donald Mahley, 647–5999.

CONSULAR AFFAIRS

Assistant Secretary.—Maura Harty, room 6811, 647–9576.
Principal Deputy Assistant Secretary.—Daniel B. Smith, 647–9577.

COORDINATOR FOR COUNTERTERRORISM

Ambassador-at-Large.—Karen Aguilara, room 2509, 647–9892.
Deputy Coordinator.—Karl Wycoff, 647–8536.

DEMOCRACY, HUMAN RIGHTS AND LABOR

Assistant Secretary.—Michael Kozak (acting), room 7802, 647–2126.
Principal Deputy Assistant Secretary.—Michael Butler (acting), 647–3315.
Deputy Assistant Secretary.—Gretchen Birkle, 647–1783.

DIPLOMATIC SECURITY

Assistant Secretary.—Joe Morton (acting), room 6316, 647–6290.
Principal Deputy Assistant Secretary.—Joe Morton, (571) 345–3815.
Deputy Assistant Secretary.—John Arndt (acting), 647–3417.

DIRECTOR GENERAL OF THE FOREIGN SERVICE AND DIRECTOR OF PERSONNEL

Director General.—W. Robert Pearson, room 6218, 647–9898.
Principal Deputy Assistant Secretary.—Ruth A. Whiteside, 647–9438.
Deputy Assistant Secretaries: John O'Keefe, 647–5942; Linda Taglialatela, 647–5152.

ECONOMIC AND BUSINESS AFFAIRS

Assistant Secretary.—E. Anthony Wayne, room 6828, 647–7971.
Principal Deputy Assistant Secretary.—Shaun Donnelly, 647–5991.
Deputy Assistant Secretaries: C. Lawrence Greenwood, 647–9496; Paul Simons, 647–1498.

EDUCATIONAL AND CULTURAL AFFAIRS

Assistant Secretary.—Patricia de Stacy Harrison, 203–5118.
Principal Deputy Assistant Secretary.—C. Miller Crouch, 203–5122.
Deputy Assistant Secretaries: Tom Farrell, 453–8111; Travis Horel, 205–2159.

OFFICE OF CIVIL RIGHTS

Deputy Assistant Secretary.—Gregory Smith (acting), room 7428, 647–9295.

FINANCE AND MANAGEMENT POLICY

Chief Financial Officer.—Christopher B. Burnham, room 7427, 647–7490.
Deputy Chief Financial Officer.—Christopher Flaggs, 261–8620.

OFFICE OF FOREIGN MISSIONS

Deputy Assistant Secretary.—John Arndt (acting), 647–3417.

FOREIGN SERVICE INSTITUTE

Director.—Katherine H. Peterson, room F2102 (703) 302–6703.
Deputy Director.—Barry Wells (703) 302–6707.

INTELLIGENCE AND RESEARCH

Assistant Secretary.—Thomas Fingar, room 6531, 647–9177.
Principal Deputy Assistant Secretary.—Carol Rodley, 647–7826.
Deputy Assistant Secretaries: Paula Causey, 647–7754; Bill Wood, 647–9633.

INTERNATIONAL INFORMATION PROGRAMS

Coordinator.—Alexander C. Feldman, 736–4405.
Principal Deputy Coordinator.—Francis Ward, 736–4651.

INTERNATIONAL NARCOTICS AND LAW ENFORCEMENT AFFAIRS

Assistant Secretary.—Nancy Powell, room 7333, 647–8464.
Principal Deputy Assistant Secretary.—William Todd, 647–6642.
Deputy Assistant Secretaries: Jonathan Farrar, 647–9822; Elizabeth Verville (acting), 647–9822.

INTERNATIONAL ORGANIZATION AFFAIRS

Assistant Secretary.—Kim R. Holmes, room 6323, 647–9600.
Principal Deputy Assistant Secretary.—Philo L. Dibble, 647–9602.
Deputy Assistant Secretary.—Mark Lagon, 647–9431; Richard Miller, 647–9604.

LEGAL ADVISER

The Legal Advisor.—John B. Bellinger III, room 6423, 647–9598.
Principal Deputy Legal Adviser.—James H. Thessin, 647–8460.
Deputy Legal Advisers: Ronald J. Bettauer, 647–7942; Jonathan B. Schwartz, 647–5036; Samuel M. Witten, 647–7942.

LEGISLATIVE AFFAIRS

Assistant Secretary.—Matthew Reynolds (acting), room 7325, 647–4204.
Deputy Assistant Secretary for Global Affairs.—James Terry, 647–1048.
Deputy Assistant Secretary (Senate).—Matthew Reynolds, 647–2140.
Deputy Assistant Secretary (House).—Carl N. Raether, 647–2623.

NONPROLIFERATION

Head.—Stephen Rademaker, room 7531, 647–8699.
Deputy Assistant Secretaries: Mark Fitzpatrick (acting), 647–6977; Andrew Semmel, 647–5122.

OCEANS AND INTERNATIONAL ENVIRONMENTAL AND SCIENTIFIC AFFAIRS

Assistant Secretary.—John F. Turner, room 7831, 647–1554.
Principal Deputy Assistant Secretary.—Anthony Rock, 647–3004.
Deputy Assistant Secretaries: David A. Balton, 647–2396; Claudia A. McMurray, 647–2232.

OFFICE OF THE INSPECTOR GENERAL

Inspector General.—Cameron R. Hume (acting), room 8100, 663–0361.
Deputy Inspector General.—John E. Lange.
Assistant Inspector General.—Robert Peterson.

POLITICAL–MILITARY AFFAIRS

Assistant Secretary.—Ambassador Rose M. Likins (acting), room 6212, 647–9022.
Principal Deputy Assistant Secretary.—Kara Bue (acting), 647–9023.
Deputy Assistant Secretaries: Ambassador Robert Loftis (acting), 647–9023; Gregory M. Suchan, 663–2861.

POPULATION, REFUGEES AND MIGRATION

Assistant Secretary.—Arthur E. Dewey, room 5824, 647–5767.
Principal Deputy Assistant Secretary.—Richard L. Greene, 647–5982.
Deputy Assistant Secretaries: Linda Thomas-Greenfield, 647–5822; Kelly Ryan, 647–5767.

PROTOCOL

Chief of Protocol.—Donald Ensenat, room 1232, 647–4543.
Deputy Chief.—Jeffrey Eubank, 647–4120.

PUBLIC AFFAIRS

Assistant Secretary.—Richard Boucher, room 6800, 647–6607.
Principal Deputy Assistant Secretary.—Robert Tappan, 647–6088.
Deputy Assistant Secretary.—Betsy Murphy, 647–6088.

UNITED STATES DIPLOMATIC OFFICES—FOREIGN SERVICE

(C= Consular Office, N= No Embassy or Consular Office)

LIST OF CHIEFS OF MISSION

AFGHANISTAN (Kabul).
  Hon. Zalmay Khalilzad.
ALBANIA (Tirana).
  Hon. Marcie B. Ries.
ALGERIA (Algiers).
  Hon. Richard W. Erdman.
ANGOLA (Luanda).
  Hon. Cynthia G. Efird.
ANTIGUA AND BARBUDA
(St. John's) (N).
  Hon. Mary Kramer.
ARGENTINA (Buenos Aires).
  Hon. Lino Gutierrez.
ARMENIA (Yerevan).
  Hon. John Marshall Evans.
AUSTRALIA (Canberra).
  Hon. John Thomas Schieffer.
AUSTRIA (Vienna).
  Hon. Lyons Brown, Jr.
AZERBAIJAN REPUBLIC (Baku).
  Hon. Reno L. Harnish III.
BAHAMAS (Nassau).
  Hon. John D. Rood.
BAHRAIN (Manama).
  Hon. William T. Monroe.

BANGLADESH (Dhaka).
  Hon. Harry K. Thomas, Jr.
BARBADOS (Bridgetown) (N).
  Hon. Mary Kramer.
BELARUS (Minsk).
  Hon. George A. Krol.
BELGIUM (Brussels).
  Hon. Tom C. Korologos.
BELIZE (Belize City).
  Hon. Russell F. Freeman.
BENIN (Cotonou).
  Hon. Wayne E. Neill.
BOLIVIA (La Paz).
  Hon. David N. Greenlee.
BOSNIA-HERZEGOVINA (Sarajevo).
  Hon. Douglas L. McElhaney.
BOTSWANA (Gaborone).
  Hon. Joseph Huggins.
BRAZIL (Brasilia).
  Hon. John J. Danilovich.
BRUNEI DARUSSALAM
(Bandar Seri Begawan).
  Hon. Gene B. Christy.
BULGARIA (Sofia).
  Hon. James W. Pardew.

BURKINA FASO (Ouagadougou).
 Hon. J. Anthony Holmes.
BURMA (Rangoon).
 Hon. Carmen Martinez.
BURUNDI (Bujumbura).
 Hon. James Howard Yellin.
CAMBODIA (Phnom Penh).
 Hon. Charles Aaron Ray.
CAMEROON (Yaounde).
 Hon. R. Niels Marquardt.
CANADA (Ottawa).
 Hon. Argeo Paul Celluci.
CAPE VERDE (Praia).
 Hon. Donald C. Johnson.
CHAD (N'Djamena).
 Hon. Marc McGowan Wall.
CHILE (Santiago).
 Hon. Craig A. Kelly.
CHINA (Beijing).
 Hon. Clark T. Randt, Jr.
COLOMBIA (Bogota).
 Hon. William B. Wood.
COMOROS (Moroni) (N).
 Hon. John Price.
CONGO, REPUBLIC OF (Brazzaville).
 Hon. Robin Renee Sanders.
CONGO, DEMOCRATIC
REPUBLIC OF (Kinshasa).
 Hon. Roger A. Meece.
COTE D'IVOIRE (Abidjan).
 Hon. Aubrey Hooks.
CROATIA (Zagreb).
 Hon. Ralph Frank.
CUBA (Havana) (N).
 Hon. James C. Cason.
CURACAO (Willemstad).
 Hon. Robert Earl Sorenson.
CYPRUS (Nicosia).
 Hon. Michael Klosson.
CZECH REPUBLIC (Prague).
 Hon. William J. Cabaniss.
DJIBOUTI, REPUBLIC OF (Djibouti).
 Hon. Marguerita Dianne Ragsdale.
DOMINICAN REPUBLIC (Santo Domingo).
 Hon. Hans H. Hertell.
EAST TIMOR (Dili).
 Hon. Grover Joseph Rees III.
ECUADOR (Quito).
 Hon. Kristie Anne Kenney.
EGYPT (Cairo).
 Hon. C. David Welch.
EL SALVADOR (San Salvador).
 Hon. H. Douglas Barclay.
EQUATORIAL GUINEA (Malabo) (N).
 Hon. R. Niels Marquardt.
ERITREA (Asmara).
 Hon. Scott H. DeLisi.
ESTONIA (Tallinn).
 Hon. Aldona Wos.
ETHIOPIA (Addis Ababa).
 Hon. Aurelia E. Brazeal.
FIJI (Suva) (N).
 Hon. David L. Lyon.
FINLAND (Helsinki).
 Hon. Earle I. Mack.
FRANCE (Paris).
 Hon. Howard H. Leach.
GABONESE REPUBLIC (Libreville) (N).
 Hon. R. Barrie Walkley.
GAMBIA (Banjul).
 Hon. Joseph D. Stafford III.
GEORGIA (Tbilisi).
 Hon. Richard Monroe Miles.
GERMANY (Berlin).
 Hon. Daniel R. Coats.
GHANA (Accra).
 Hon. Mary Carlin Yates.
GREECE (Athens).
 Hon. Charles P. Ries.
GRENADA (St. George) (N).
 Hon. Mary Kramer.
GUATEMALA (Guatemala).
 Hon. John Randle Hamilton.
GUINEA (Conakry).
 Hon. Jackson McDonald.
GUINEA-BISSAU (Bissau).
 Hon. Richard Allan Roth.
GUYANA (Georgetown).
 Hon. Roland W. Bullen.
HAITI (Port-au-Prince).
 Hon. James B. Foley.
HOLY SEE (Vatican City).
 Hon. Jim Nicholson.
HONDURAS (Tegucigalpa).
 Hon. Larry Leon Palmer.
HONG KONG (Hong Kong) (C).
 Hon. James R. Keith.
HUNGARY (Budapest).
 Hon. George H. Walker.
ICELAND (Reykjavik).
 Hon. James Irvin Gadsden.
INDIA (New Delhi).
 Hon. David C. Mulford.
INDONESIA (Jakarta).
 Hon. B. Lynn Pascoe.
IRAQ (Baghdad)
 Hon. John D. Negroponte.
IRELAND (Dublin).
 Hon. James Casey Kenny.
ISRAEL (Tel Aviv).
 Hon. Daniel C. Kurtzer.
ITALY (Rome).
 Hon. Melvin Sembler.
JAMAICA (Kingston).
 Hon. Sue McCourt Cobb.
JAPAN (Tokyo).
 Hon. Howard H. Baker, Jr.
JERUSALEM (C).
 Hon. David Duane Pearce.
KAZAKHSTAN (Almaty).
 Hon. John M. Ordway.
KENYA (Nairobi).
 Hon. William M. Bellamy.
KIRIBATI (Tarawa) (N).
 Hon. David L. Lyon.
KOREA, REPUBLIC OF (Seoul).
 Hon. Christopher R. Hill.
KOSOVO (Pristina) (N).
 Hon. Philip S. Goldberg.

KYRGYZ REPUBLIC (Bishkek).
   Hon. Stephen M. Young.
KUWAIT (Kuwait City).
   Hon. Richard LeBaron.
LAOS PEOPLE'S DEMOCRATIC
REPUBLIC (Vientiane).
   Hon. Patricia M. Haslach.
LATVIA (Riga).
   Hon. Catherine Todd Bailey.
LEBANON (Beirut).
   Hon. Jeffrey D. Feltman.
LESOTHO (Maseru).
   Hon. June Carter Perry.
LIBERIA (Monrovia).
   Hon. John W. Blaney.
LIECHTENSTEIN (Vaduz) (N).
   Pamela P. Willeford.
LITHUANIA (Vilnius).
   Hon. Stephen D. Mull.
LUXEMBOURG (Luxembourg).
   Hon. Peter Terpeluk, Jr.
MACEDONIA (Skopje).
   Hon. Lawrence E. Butler.
MADAGASCAR
(Antananarivo).
   Hon. James D. McGee.
MALAYSIA (Kuala Lumpur).
   Hon. Christopher J. LeFleur.
MALDIVES (Male) (N).
   Hon. Jeffrey Lunstead.
MARSHALL ISLANDS (Majuro).
   Hon. Greta N. Morris.
MAURITANIA (Nouakchott).
   Hon. Joseph LeBaron.
MAURITIUS (Port Louis).
   Hon. John Price.
MEXICO (Mexico City).
   Hon. Antonio O. Garza, Jr.
MICRONESIA (Kolonia).
   Hon. Suzanne Hale.
MOLDOVA (Chisinau).
   Hon. Heather M. Hodges.
MONGOLIA (Ulaanbaatar).
   Hon. Pamela J.H. Slutz.
MOROCCO (Rabat).
   Hon. Thomas T. Riley.
MOZAMBIQUE (Maputo).
   Hon. Helen R. Meagher La Lime.
NAMIBIA (Windhoek).
   Hon. Joyce A. Barr.
NAURU (Yaren) (N).
   Hon. David L. Lyon.
NEPAL (Kathmandu).
   Hon. James Francis Moriarty.
NETHERLANDS (The Hague).
   Hon. Clifford M. Sobel.
NEW ZEALAND (Wellington).
   Hon. Charles J. Swindells.
NICARAGUA (Managua).
   Hon. Barbara C. Moore.
NIGER (Niamey).
   Hon. Gail Dennise Thomas Mathieu.
NIGERIA (Abuja).
   Hon. John Campbell.
NORWAY (Oslo).
   Hon. John D. Ong.

OMAN (Muscat).
   Hon. Richard Lewis Baltimore III.
PAKISTAN (Islamabad).
   Hon. Ryan C. Crocker.
PALAU (Koror).
   Hon. Francis Joseph Ricciardone, Jr.
PANAMA (Panama).
   Hon. Linda Ellen Watt.
PAPUA NEW GUINEA (Port Moresby).
   Hon. Robert W. Fitts.
PARAGUAY (Asunción).
   Hon. John F. Keane.
PERU (Lima).
   Hon. James Curtis Struble.
PHILIPPINES (Manila).
   Hon. Francis J. Ricciardone, Jr.
POLAND (Warsaw).
   Hon. Victor Henderson Ashe.
QATAR (Doha).
   Hon. Charles Graves Untermeyer.
ROMANIA (Bucharest).
   Hon. Jack Dyer Crouch II.
RUSSIAN FEDERATION (Moscow).
   Hon. Alexander R. Vershbow.
SAINT KITTS AND NEVIS
(Basseterrie) (N).
   Hon. Mary Kramer.
SAINT LUCIA (Castries) (N).
   Hon. Mary Kramer.
SAINT VINCENT AND THE
GRENADINES (Kingstown) (N).
   Hon. Mary Kramer.
SAMOA (Apia) (N).
   Hon. Charles J. Swindells.
SAO TOME AND PRINCIPE
(Sao Tome) (N).
   Hon. R. Barrie Walkley.
SAUDI ARABIA (Riyadh).
   Hon. James C. Oberwetter.
SENEGAL (Dakar).
   Hon. Richard Allan Roth.
SERBIA AND MONTENEGRO (Belgrade)
   Hon. Michael Christian Polt.
SEYCHELLES (Victoria).
   Hon. John Price.
SIERRA LEONE (Freetown).
   Hon. Thomas Neil Hull III.
SINGAPORE (Singapore).
   Hon. Franklin L. Lavin.
SLOVENIA (Ljubljana).
   Hon. Thomas Bolling Robertson.
SOLOMON ISLANDS (Honiara) (N).
   Hon. Robert W. Fitts.
SOUTH AFRICA (Pretoria).
   Hon. Jendayi Elizabeth Frazer.
SRI LANKA (Colombo) (N).
   Hon. Jeffrey Lunstead.
SURINAME (Paramaribo).
   Hon. Marsha E. Barnes.
SWAZILAND (Mbabane).
   Hon. Lewis W. Lucke.
SWEDEN (Stockholm).
   Hon. Miles T. Bivins.
SWITZERLAND (Bern).
   Pamela P. Willeford.

SYRIAN ARAB REPUBLIC (Damascus).
Hon. Margaret Scobey.
TAJIKISTAN (Dushanbe).
Hon. Richard E. Hoagland.
THAILAND (Bangkok).
Hon. Ralph Leo Boyce, Jr.
TOGOLESE REPUBLIC (Lome).
Hon. Gregory W. Engle.
TONGA (Nuku'alofe) (N).
Hon. David L. Lyon.
TRINIDAD AND TOBAGO
(Port-of-Spain).
Hon. Roy L. Austin.
TUNISIA (Tunis).
Hon. William J. Hudson.
TURKEY (Ankara).
Hon. Eric S. Edelman.
TURKMENISTAN (Ashgabat).
Hon. Tracey Ann Jacobson.
TUVALU (Funafuti) (N).
Hon. David L. Lyon.
UGANDA (Kampala).
Hon. Jimmy Kolker.

UKRAINE (Kiev).
Hon. John E. Herbst.
UNITED ARAB EMIRATES (Abu Dhabi).
Hon. Michele J. Sison.
URUGUAY (Montevideo).
Hon. Martin J. Silverstein.
UZBEKISTAN (Tashkent).
Hon. Jon R. Purnell.
VANUATU (Port Vila) (N).
Hon. Robert W. Fitts.
VENEZUELA (Caracas).
Hon. William R. Brownfield.
VIETNAM, SOCIALIST REPUBLIC OF
(Hanoi).
Hon. Michael W. Marine.
YEMEN (Sanaa).
Hon. Thomas Charles Krajeski.
ZAMBIA (Lusaka).
Hon. Martin George Brennan.
ZIMBABWE (Harare).
Hon. Christopher William Dell.

UNITED STATES PERMANENT DIPLOMATIC MISSIONS TO INTERNATIONAL ORGANIZATIONS

ORGANIZATION OF AMERICAN
STATES (Washington, DC).
Hon. John F. Maisto.
ORGANIZATION FOR SECURITY AND
COOPERATION IN EUROPE (Vienna).
Hon. Stephan Michael Minikes.
NORTH ATLANTIC TREATY
ORGANIZATION (Brussels).
Hon. R. Nicholas Burns.

ORGANIZATION FOR
ECONOMIC COOPERATION
AND DEVELOPMENT (Paris).
Hon. Constance Albanese Morella.
UNITED NATIONS (Geneva).
Hon. Kevin E. Moley.
EUROPEAN UNION (Brussels).
Hon. Rockwell A. Schnabel.

DEPARTMENT OF THE TREASURY

15th and Pennsylvania Ave., NW., 20220, phone 622–2000, http://www.ustreas.gov

JOHN W. SNOW, Secretary of the Treasury; born on August 2, 1939, in Toledo, OH; education: Kenyon College, University of Toledo, B.A., 1962; University of Virginia, Ph.D. in Economics, 1965; George Washington University School of Law, LL.B., 1967; Kenyon College, Honorary Degree, LL.D., 1993; professional: Attorney; Assistant Professor of Economics, University of Maryland, 1965–67; Wheeler & Wheeler (law firm), 1967–72; Adjunct Professor of Law, George Washington University Law School, 1972–75; Assistant General Counsel, U.S. Department of Transportation (DOT), 1972–73; Deputy Assistant Secretary for Policy Plans, and International Affairs, DOT, 1973–74; Assistant Secretary for Governmental Affairs, DOT, 1974–75; Deputy Undersecretary, DOT, 1975–76; Administrator, National Highway Traffic Safety Administration, 1976–77; Visiting Professor of Economics, University of Virginia, 1977; Visiting Fellow, American Enterprise Institute, 1977; Vice President for Governmental Affairs, Chessie System, Inc., 1977–80; Senior Vice President for Corporate Services, CSX Corp., 1980–84; Executive Vice President, CSX Corp., 1984–85; President and Chief Executive Officer, Chessie System Railroads, 1985–86; President and Chief Executive Officer, CSX Rail Transport, 1986–87; President and Chief Executive Officer, CSX Transportation, 1987–88; President and Chief Operating Officer, CSX Corp., 1988–89; President and Chief Executive Officer, CSX Corp., 1989–91; Chairman, President, and Chief Executive Officer, CSX Corp., 1991–2002; religion: Episcopal; family: married to Carolyn Kalk Snow; children: Bradley, Ian, and Christopher; nominated by President George W. Bush to become the 73rd Secretary of the Treasury on December 9, 2002; and was confirmed by the U.S. Senate on January 30, 2003.

OFFICE OF THE SECRETARY

Secretary of the Treasury.—John W. Snow, room 3330, 622–1100.
    Executive Assistant.—Deborah Grubbs, 622–2147.
    Confidential Assistant.—Cheryl Matera, 622–0190.

OFFICE OF THE DEPUTY SECRETARY

    Executive Assistant.—Annabella Mejia, room 3326, 622–1080.,

OFFICE OF THE CHIEF OF STAFF

Chief of Staff.—Chris Smith, room 3408, 622–1906.
    Review Analyst.—Shirley Gathers.
    Deputy Chief of Staff.—[Vacancy].
    Senior Advisor to the Secretary.—Kimberly Reed, 622–0520.

OFFICE OF THE EXECUTIVE SECRETARY

Executive Secretary.—Paul Curry, room 3408, 622–1700.
    Special Assistant to the Executive Secretary.—Amanda Biedrzycki, 622–5575.

OFFICE OF THE GENERAL COUNSEL

General Counsel.—Arnold I. Havens, room 4312, 622–0283.
    Deputy General Counsel.—James W. Carroll, room 4000, 622–6362.
    Counselor to the General Counsel.—Stephen Larson, room 4308, 622–1143.
    Senior Advisor to the General Counsel.—Sean Thornton, room 4310, 622–9880.
    Administrative Officer.—Linda Mathis, room 4312, 622–0285.

Assistant General Counsels:
  Banking and Finance.—Roberta McInerney, room 4019, 622–1988.
  General Law and Ethics.—Kenneth R. Schmalzbach, room 2020, 622–1137.
  International Affairs.—Russell L. Munk, room 2224, 622–1899.
Deputy Assistant General Counsels: Peter Bieger, room 4027, 622–1975; Marilyn L. Muench, room 2218, 622–1986.
Chief Counsel, Foreign Assets Control.—Mark Monborne (acting), room 3122 Annex, 622–1286.

OFFICE OF THE INSPECTOR GENERAL

Inspector General.—Dennis S. Schindel (acting), room 1022, 622–1090.
  Deputy Inspector General.—Dennis S. Schindel.
  Counsel to the Inspector General.—Richard Delmar, suite 510, 927–0650.
  Assistant Inspector General for Investigations.—Nick Swanstrom, room 500, 927–5260.
    Deputy Assistant Inspector General for Investigations.—Carl Hoecker.
  Assistant Inspector General for Management Services.—Adam Silverman, room 510, 927–5200.
  Assistant Inspector General for Audit.—Marla Freedman, room 600, 927–5400.
    Deputy Assistant Inspector General for Audit.—Robert Taylor, 927–5400.
    Deputy Assistant Inspector General for Audit (CFO).—William Pugh, 927–5400.
  Director of Asset Management.—Debra McGruder, room 510, 927–5229.

OFFICE OF THE ASSISTANT SECRETARY FOR LEGISLATIVE AFFAIRS

Assistant Secretary.—John Duncan, room 3134, 622–1900.
  Deputy to the Assistant Secretary.—Tim Keeler, room 3464, 622–1900.
  Legislative Assistant.—Cherry Grayson, room 3134, 622–0555.
  Deputy Assistant Secretary for—
    Appropriations and Management.—Andy Fishburn, room 2464, 622–1900.
    Banking and Finance.—Courtney C. Geduldig, room 3128, 622–1900.
    International Affairs.—David Merkel, room 3462, 622–1900.
    Tax and Budget.—John Emling, room 3132, 622–1900.

OFFICE OF THE ASSISTANT SECRETARY FOR PUBLIC AFFAIRS

Assistant Secretary.—Robert Nichols, room 3438, 622–2920.
  Deputy Assistant Secretary.—Tony Fratto, room 3446, 622–2910.
  Deputy Assistant Secretary (Public Liaison).—Becky Relic.
  Senior Advisor to the Assistant Secretary.—Betsy Holahan.
  Director, Public Affairs, Tax Policy.—Taylor Griffin, room 1208, 622–2960.
  Review Analyst and Scheduling Coordinator.—Carmen Alvarado, room 3442.
  Public Affairs Specialist for—
    Economic Policy.—Brookly McLaughlin.
    Enforcement.—Molly Millerwise.
    Social Security.—Mary Diamond.
  Senior Advisor, Public Liaison.—Kirstie Tucker.
  Senior Writer.—Jean Card.

OFFICE OF THE UNDER SECRETARY FOR INTERNATIONAL AFFAIRS

Under Secretary.—John Taylor, room 4448 MT, 622–0656.
  Senior Advisor.—Sonja Renander (acting), room 4453 MT, 622–0395.
  Staff Assistant.—Lenora Culley, room 4448 MT, 622–0656.

OFFICE OF THE ASSISTANT SECRETARY FOR INTERNATIONAL AFFAIRS

Assistant Secretary.—Randal K. Quarles, room 4460 MT, 622–1270.
  Senior Advisor.—John D. Ciorciari, room 4453 MT, 622–0659.
  Staff Assistant.—Clara M. Robinson, room 4460 MT, 622–1270.
  Deputy Assistant Secretaries for—
    Africa, Broader MidEast, South & Southeast Asia, East Asia.—David Loevinger, room 3204 MT, 622–0138.

Development Policy, Multilateral Development Institutions Debt Policy.—Bobby Pittman, room 3205 MT, 622–0070.
Europe/Eurasia, Western Hemisphere.—Nancy Lee, room 3204 MT, 622–2916.
International Monetary, Policy, Banking & Securities.—Mark Sobel, room 3034 MT, 622–0168.
Technical Assistance Policy.—James H. Fall III, room 3041 MT, 622–0667.
Trade Investment & Trade Finance.—Charles Schott, room 3205 MT, 622–0237.
Directors for International Affairs:
    Africa.—John Ralyea, room 5466 MT, 622–0716.
    Broader Middle East.—Alpita Shah (acting), room 3212 MT, 622–9398.
    East Asia.—Robert Dohner, room 5221 MT, 622–7222.
    Europe & Eurasia.—Brian Cox, room 5441 MT, 622–0603.
    Quantitative Policy Analysis.—Lawrence Goodman, room 5132 MT, 622–2876.
    Reconstruction & Stabilization.—Lawrence McDonald, room 5008 MT, 622–5504.
    Western Hemisphere.—Ramin Toloui, room 5466 MT, 622–0763.
Directors for International Affairs, 1440 New York Avenue, NW.:
    Banking and Securities.—William Murden, room 3121, 622–2775.
    Development Finance.—Sara Paulson, room 3501, 622–1231.
    Development Policy.—John Hurley, room 3427, 622–9124.
    International Debt Policy.—Stephen Donovan, room 4423, 622–0159.
    International Monetary Policy.—Michael Kaplan, room 3101, 622–6865.
    Investment.—Gay Sills, room 4201, 622–9066.
    Multilateral Development Banks.—Mark Jaskowiak, room 3317, 622–2052.
    South and Southeast Asia.—Andrew Baukol, room 3105, 622–2129.
    Trade Finance.—Steven Tvardek, room 4311, 622–1749.
    Trade Office.—Whittier Warthin, room 4401, 622–1733.
Director, Technical Assistance.—Van Jorstad, 740 15th Street, NW., 622–2886.

OVERSEAS

U.S. Director of:
    African Development Bank and Fund (Tunisia).—Ambassador Cynthia Shepard Perry, 9–011–216–71–10–2810.
    Asian Development Bank (Manila, Philippines).—Paul W. Speltz, 9–011–632–632–6050.
    European Bank for Reconstruction and Development.—Mark Sullivan, 9–011–44–207–338–6503.
U.S. Executive Director of:
    Inter-American Development Bank.—Hector Morales, 9–623–1075.
    International Bank for Reconstruction and Development.—Bob Holland (acting), 9–458–0115/6.
    International Monetary Fund.—Nancy P. Jacklin, 9–623–7759.

OFFICE OF THE UNDER SECRETARY FOR DOMESTIC FINANCE

Under Secretary.—Donald V. Hammond (acting), room 2112, 622–1703.
    Review Analyst.—Diana Ridgway, room 1205, 622–1703.

OFFICE OF THE FISCAL ASSISTANT SECRETARY

Fiscal Assistant Secretary.—Donald Hammond, room 2112, 622–0560.
    Deputy Assistant, Secretary of:
        Fiscal Operations and Policy.—Kenneth Carfine, room 2064, 622–0570.
        Accounting Policy.—Robert Reid, room 2108, 622–0550.
    Director, Office of Fiscal Projections.—David Monroe, room 2044, 622–0580.

FINANCIAL MANAGEMENT SERVICE
401 14th Street, SW., 20227, phone 874–6750, fax 874–7016

Commissioner.—Richard L. Gregg.
    Deputy Commissioner.—Kenneth R. Papaj.
        Assistant Commissioner for—
            Debt Management Services.—Martin Mills.
            Federal Finance.—Gary Grippo.

Financial Operations.—Wanda J. Rogers.
   Governmentwide Accounting.—D. James Sturgill.
   Information Resources (Chief Information Officer).—Nancy C. Fleetwood.
   Management (Chief Financial Officer).—Scott Johnson.
   Regional Operations.—Judith R. Tillman.
   Treasury Agency Services.—Kerry Lanham.
Chief Counsel.—Margaret Marquette.
Director for Legislative and Public Affairs.—Alvina M. McHale.

BUREAU OF THE PUBLIC DEBT

799 9th Street, NW., 20239, phone 504–3500, fax 504–3630

[Codified under U.S.C. 31, section 306]

Commissioner.—F. Van Zeck.
   Deputy Commissioner.—Anne Meister.
   Assistant Commissioner for—
      Administration.—Glenn E. Ball (304) 480–8101.
      Office of Information Technology.—Cynthia Springer (304) 480–6988.
      Financing.—Carl Locken, 504 3550.
      Public Debt Accounting.—Debra Hines (304) 480–5101.
      Office of Securities Operations.—John Swales (304) 480–6516.
      Office of Investor Services.—Frederick Pyatt (304) 480–7730.
   Chief Counsel.—Brian Ferrell, 504–3520.
   Executive Director, Marketing Office.—Paul T. Vogelzang, 504–3535.

OFFICE OF THE ASSISTANT SECRETARY FOR ECONOMIC POLICY

Assistant Secretary.—Mark Warshawsky, room 3454, 622–2200.
   Deputy Assistant Secretary for—
      Macroeconomics Analysis.—Robert Stein, room 3449, 622–2584.
      Policy Coordination.—James Carter, room 3445, 622–2220.
   Director, Office of Microeconomic Analysis.—John Worth, room 2449, 622–2683.
   Director, Office of Macroeconomic Analysis.—Karen Hendershot (acting), room 2450, 622–1683.

OFFICE OF THE ASSISTANT SECRETARY FOR FINANCIAL INSTITUTIONS

Assistant Secretary.—Greg Zerzan (acting), room 2326, 622–2610.
   Deputy Assistant Secretary, Office of:
      Critical Infrastructure Protection and Compliance Policy.—D. Scott Parsons, room 3170, 622–0101.
      Financial Education.—Dan Iannicola, Jr., room 2414, 622–5770.
      Financial Institutions Policy.—Greg Zerzan, room 2010, 622–0430.
   Director, Office of:
      Community Development Financial Institutions Fund.—Arthur A. Garcia, room 601, 622–8530.
      Financial Education.—Edward W. Christovich (acting).
      Financial Institutions Policy.—Mario Ugoletti (acting), room 3160, 622–2792.
      Sallie Mae Oversight.—Philip Quinn, room 5015, 622–0270.
      Terrorism Risk Insurance Program.—Jeffrey S. Bragg.

OFFICE OF THE ASSISTANT SECRETARY FOR FINANCIAL MARKETS

Assistant Secretary.—Timothy Bitsberger, room 2000, 622–2245.
   Deputy Assistant Secretary, Office of:
      Accounting Operation.—Robert Reid, room 2108, 622–0550.
      Fiscal Operations and Policy.—Ken Caefine, room 2064, 622–0570.
      Government Financial Policy.—Roger Kodat, room 2001, 622–7073.
   Director, Office of:
      Advanced Counterfeit Deterrence.—Reese Fuller, room 5310, 622–1882.
      Cash and Debt Management.—David Monroe, room 5308, 622–1813.
      Debt Management.—Jeff Huther, room 4138, 622–1868.
      Federal Lending.—Brian Jackson, 1120 Vermont Avenue, room 951, 622–0706.

Financial Market Policy.—Heidilynne Schultheiss, room 5016, 622–2692.
Policy and Legislative Review.—Paula Farrell, 1120 Vermont Avenue, room 934, 622–2450.

OFFICE OF THE ASSISTANT SECRETARY FOR TAX POLICY

Deputy Assistant Secretary for—
 Regulatory Affairs.—Eric Solomon, room 3104, 622–0868.
 Tax Analysis.—Robert Carroll, room 3064–A, 622–0120.
 Tax Policy.—Eric Solomon (acting), room 3112, 622–0140.
 Tax, Trade and Tariff Policy.—Tim Skud, room 3060, 622–0220.
Tax Legislative Counsel.—Helen Hubbard, room 3040, 622–1776.
 Deputy Tax Legislative Counsel.—John Parcell (acting), room 4224, 622–2578.
Deputy, International Tax Counsel.—Patricia Brown, room 5064, 622–1781.
Director, Office of:
 Business Taxation.—Geraldine A. Gerardi, room 4221, 622–1782.
 Economic Modeling and Computer Applications.—Paul Dobbins, room 4039, 622–0846.
 Individual Taxation.—James R. Nunns, room 4043, 622–1328.
 International Taxation.—William Randolph, room 5117, 622–0471.
 Revenue Estimating.—Joel Platt, room 4112, 622–0259.
 Tax Analysis.—Donald Kiefer, room 4116, 622–0269.

OFFICE OF THE ASSISTANT SECRETARY FOR MANAGEMENT / CHIEF FINANCIAL OFFICER

Assistant Secretary for Management.—Jesus Delgado-Jenkins (acting), room 1308, 622–0410.
 Deputy Assistant Secretary for Management and Budget.—Jesus Delgado-Jenkins, 622–0021.
 Deputy Assistant Secretary for Human Resources and Chief Human Capital Officer.—Patricia Pointer (acting), 1750 Pennsylvania Avenue, NW., room 8119, 622–5206.
 Deputy Chief Financial Officer.—Barry K. Hudson, room 6253, 622–0750.
Director of:
 Accounting and Internal Control.—James R. Lingebach, room 6263, 622–0818.
 Asset Management.—Carolyn Austin-Diggs, room 6179, 622–0500.
 Budget.—Mark Olechowski, room 6118, 622–1479.
 Conference Events and Meeting Services.—Lucinda Gooch, room 3094, Annex, 622–2071.
 Departmental Budget Execution.—Chantale Wong, room 6123, Met Square, 622–5475.
 Disclosure Services.—Alana Johnson, room 6200, Annex, 622–0876.
 Environmental Safety and Health.—Gary Adams, room 6001, 622–1712.
 Equal Opportunity and Diversity.—Mariam Harvey, room 8139, 622–1160.
 Facilities Management.—Wesley L. Hawley, room 1155, 622–0505.
 Facilities Support Services.—James Thomas, room 6100, Annex, 622–4080.
 Financial Management.—Mary Menefee, room 6202, Met Square, 622–2218.
 Human Resource Strategy and Solutions.—Dennis Cannon, room 8121, 622–1109.
 Human Resources Operations.—Barbara McWhirter, room 5202, 622–1577.
 Information Services.—Veronica Marco, room 6904, 622–2477.
 Printing and Graphics.—Craig Larsen, room 6100, Annex, 622–1409.
 Procurement Services.—Ernest Dilworth, room 2154, New York Avenue, 622–1066.
 Small and Disadvantaged Business Utilization.—Virginia Bellamy-Graham, room 6099, Met Square, 622–2826.
 Strategic Planning and Performance Management.—Jay Hoffman, room 6129, Met Square, 622–8614.
 Treasury Building.—Polly Dietz, room 1041, 622–7067.
 Senior Procurement Executive.—Thomas Sharpe, room 6111, Met Square, 622–1039.
 Budget Officer.—Carol Bryant, room 6075, Met Square, 622–7346.
 Accounting Officer.—David Legge, room 6070, Met Square, 622–1167.
 Facilities Support Services DD.—MelIssa Hartman, room 6100, Annex, 622–4901.

OFFICE OF THE TREASURER OF THE UNITED STATES

Treasurer.—Anna Escobedo Cabral, 622–0100.
 Special Assistant.—Jessica Garcia.

UNITED STATES MINT

801 9th Street, NW., 20002, phone 354–7200, fax 756–6160

Director.—Henrietta Holsman Fore.
Executive Assistant to the Director.—Arnetta Cain.
 Deputy Director.—David A. Lebryk.
 Staff Assistant to the Deputy Director.—Pamela Carr.
  Chief Counsel.—Dan Shaver.
  Director of Legislative and Intergovernmental Affairs.—Madelyn Simmons.
  Director of Public Affairs.—Becky Bailey.
 Associate Director (Protection Strategic Business Unit).—William F. Daddio.
  Deputy Director (Protection Strategic Business Unit).—Bill R. Bailey.
 Associate Director/Chief Information Officer.—Jerry Horton.
  Deputy Associate Director/Chief Information Officer.—Jay Mahanand.
 Associate Director/Chief Financial Officer.—Robert Byrd.
 Associate Director (Numismatic Strategic Business Unit).—Gloria Eskridge.
  Deputy Associate Director (Numismatic Strategic Business Unit).—Jim Riedford.
 Associate Director (Circulating Strategic Business Unit).—Scott Myers.

BUREAU OF ENGRAVING AND PRINTING

14th and C Streets, NW., 20228, phone 874–2000

[Created by act of July 11, 1862; codified under U.S.C. 31, section 303]

Director.—Thomas A. Ferguson, 874–2000, fax 874–3879.
 Chief Counsel.—Michael Davidson, 874–5363, fax 874–5710.
 Associate Directors:
  Chief Financial Officer.—Gregory D. Carper, 874–2020, fax 874–2025.
  Chief Information Officer.—Ronald W. Falter, 874–3000, fax 927–1757.
  Chief Operating Officer.—William W. Wills, 874–2030, fax 874–2034.
 Associate Director for—
  Management.—Joel C. Taub, 874–2040, fax 874–2043.
  Technology.—Lenore Clarke (acting), 874–2008, fax 874–2009.

OFFICE OF THE COMPTROLLER OF THE CURRENCY

250 E Street, SW., 20219, phone 874–5000

Comptroller.—Julie L. Williams (acting), 874–4900.
 Chief of Staff/Sr. Deputy Comptroller (Public Affairs).—Mark A. Nishan, 874–4880.
 Chief Counsel.—Daniel P. Stipano, 874–5200.
 Director for Congressional Liaison.—Carolyn Z. McFarlane, 874–4840.
 Senior Deputy Comptroller of:
  Midsize/Community Bank Supervision.—Timothy W. Long, 874–5020.
  International and Economic Affairs.—Jeffrey A. Brown, 874–5010.
  Management.—Thomas R. Bloom, 874–5080.
  Large Bank Supervision.—Douglas W. Roeder, 874–4610.
  Chief National Bank Examiner.—Emory W. Rushton, 874–2870.
 Ombudsman.—Samuel P. Golden (713) 336–4350.
 Chief Information Officer.—Jackie Fletcher, 874–4480.

INTERNAL REVENUE SERVICE

Internal Revenue Building, 1111 Constitution Avenue, NW., 20224, phone 622–5000

[Created by act of July 1, 1862; codified under U.S.C. 26, section 7802]

Commissioner.—Mark W. Everson, 622–9511.
 Deputy Commissioner, Services and Enforcement.—Mark Matthews, 622–4255.
  Commissioner of:
  Large and Mid-Size Business.—Deborah Nolan, 283–8710.
  Small Business/Self-Employed.—Kevin M. Brown, 622–0600.

Tax Exempt and Government Entities.—Steven T. Miller, 283–2500.
    Wage and Investment.—Henry O. Lamar, Jr., 622–6860.
Chief, Criminal Investigation.—Nancy Jardini, 622–3200.
Director, Office of Professional Responsibility.—Cono Namorato, 927–3397.
Deputy Commissioner, Operations Support.—John M. Dalrymple, 622–6860.
    Chief:
        Agency-Wide Shared Services.—Carl Froehlich, 622–7500.
        Appeals.—David Robison, 435–5600.
        Communications and Liaison.—Frank Keith, 622–5440.
        EEO and Diversity.—John M. Robinson, 622–5400.
        Financial Officer.—Janice Lambert, 622–6400.
        Human Capital Officer.—Beverly Babers, 622–7676.
        Information Officer/Modernization & Information Technology Services.—W. Todd Grams, 622–6800.
        Mission Assurance and Security Services.—Daniel Galik, 622–8910.
        Office of Privacy.—Barbra E. Symonds.
Chief Counsel.—Donald L. Korb, 622–3300.
National Taxpayer Advocate.—Nina E. Olson, 622–6100.
Director, Research, Analysis and Statistics.—Mark J. Mazur, 874–0100.
Office of Legislative Affairs.—Floyd L. Williams, 622–3720.
Inspector General TIGTA.—Russell George, 622–6500.

OFFICE OF THRIFT SUPERVISION

1700 G Street, NW., 20552, phone 906–6000, fax 906–5660

[Codified in U.S.C. 12, section 1462a]

Director.—James Gilleran, 906–6590.
    Deputy Director.—Richard M. Riccobono, 906–6853.
    Chief Counsel.—John Bowman, 906–6372.
    Managing Director of:
        Examinations, Supervision and Consumer Protection.—Scott M. Albinson, 906–7984.
        External Affairs.—Kevin Petrasic, 906–6288.
    Chief Information and Financial Officer.—Timothy T. Ward, 906–5666.

DEPARTMENT OF DEFENSE

The Pentagon 20301–1155, phone (703) 545–6700

fax (703) 695–3362/693–2161, www.defenselink.mil

DONALD H. RUMSFELD, Secretary of Defense; born on July 9, 1932, in Chicago, IL; education: A.B., Princeton University, 1954; military service: U.S. Navy, 1954–1957, served as a Naval aviator; professional: congressional assistant, 1958–1959; investment broker, 1960–1962; elected to the U.S. House of Representatives, 1963–1969; Assistant to the President, and Director of the Office of Economic Opportunity, 1969–1970; Counselor to the President, and Director of the Economic Stabilization Program, 1971–1972; U.S. Ambassador to NATO, 1973–1974; Chief of Staff for President Gerald R. Ford, 1974–1975; Secretary of Defense, 1975–1977; CEO, President, and then Chairman of G.D. Searle & Co., 1977–1985; private business, 1985–1990; Chairman and CEO of General Instrument Corp., 1990–1993; Chairman, Gilead Sciences, Inc., 1997–2000; nominated by President George W. Bush to become the 21st Secretary of Defense, and was confirmed by the U.S. Senate on January 20, 2001.

OFFICE OF THE SECRETARY

Pentagon, Room 3E880, 20301–1000, phone (703) 692–7100, fax (703) 697–9080

Secretary of Defense.—Donald H. Rumsfeld.

OFFICE OF THE DEPUTY SECRETARY

Pentagon, Room 3E944, 20301–1010, phone (703) 692–7150

Deputy Secretary of Defense.—Paul Wolfowitz.

EXECUTIVE SECRETARIAT

Pentagon, Room 3E880, 20301–1000, phone (703) 692–7125, fax (703) 697–9080

Executive Secretary.—CAPT William P. Marriott, USN.

UNDER SECRETARY OF DEFENSE FOR ACQUISITION AND TECHNOLOGY

Pentagon, Room 3E1006, 20301, phone (703) 693–7021

Under Secretary.—Michael Wynne (acting).
  Deputy Under Secretary for—
    Industrial Policy.—Suzanne Patrick.
    Installations and Environment.—Philip W. Grone.
    Logistics.—Brad Berkson.
  Director, Small and Disadvantaged Business Utilization.—Frank M. Ramos.
  Director, Defense Research and Engineering.—Ron Sega.
  Deputy Under Secretary for—
    Advanced Systems and Concepts.—Sue Payton.
    Science and Technology.—Charles Holland.
    Assistant to the Secretary of Defense for Nuclear and Chemical and Biological Defense Programs.—Dale Klein.

JOINT STRIKE FIGHTER PROGRAM OFFICE

200 12th Street South, Suite 600, Arlington, VA 22202–5402, phone 602–7640, fax 602–7649

Program Executive Officer.—RADM Steven L. Enewold.

UNDER SECRETARY OF DEFENSE FOR POLICY
Pentagon, Room 4E830, 20301–2000, phone (703) 697–7200

Under Secretary.—Douglas Feith.
  Principal Deputy Under Secretary.—Ryan Henry.
  Assistant Secretary of Defense for—
    International Security Affairs.—Peter Rodman.
    International Security Policy.—Mira Ricardel.
    Homeland Defense.—Paul McHale.
    Special Operations and Low-Intensity Conflict.—Tom O'Connell.
  Deputy Under Secretary (Technology Security Policy).—Lisa Bronson.

UNDER SECRETARY OF DEFENSE (COMPTROLLER) AND CHIEF FINANCIAL OFFICER

Pentagon, Room 3E602, 20301–1100, phone (703) 695–3237

Under Secretary/Chief Financial Officer.—Tina W. Jonas.
  Principal Deputy Under Secretary.—Robert J. Henke.

PERSONNEL AND READINESS
Pentagon, Room 3E764, 20301–4000, phone (703) 695–5254

Under Secretary.—David S.C. Chu.
  Principal Deputy Under Secretary.—Charles Abell.
  Assistant Secretary for—
    Health Affairs.—William Winkenwerder.
    Reserve Affairs.—Thomas Hall.
  Deputy Under Secretary for—
    Personnel and Readiness.—Paul Mayberry.
    Program Integration.—Jeanne Fites.

GENERAL COUNSEL
Pentagon, Room 3E980, 20301–1600, phone (703) 695–3341, fax (703) 693–7278

General Counsel.—William J. Haynes.
  Principal Deputy.—Daniel J. Dell'Orto (703) 697–7248.

OPERATIONAL TEST AND EVALUATION
Pentagon, Room 3A1073, 20301–1700, phone (703) 697–3654, fax (703) 693–5248

Director.—David Duma (acting).

INSPECTOR GENERAL
400 Army Navy Drive, Room 1000, Arlington VA 22202, phone (703) 604–8300 fax 604–8310, hotline 1–800–424–9098, hotline fax 604–8567

Inspector General.—Joseph Schmitz.

ASSISTANT SECRETARY FOR NETWORKS AND INFORMATION INTEGRATION (NII)
Pentagon, Room 3E172, 20301–6000, phone (703) 695–0348

Assistant Secretary.—Linton Wells (acting).

ASSISTANT SECRETARY FOR LEGISLATIVE AFFAIRS

Pentagon, Room 3E966, 20301–1300, phone (703) 697–6210, fax (703) 697–8299

Assistant Secretary.—Powell Moore.
   Assistant Secretary of Defense for Legislative Affairs.—Daniel Stanley (acting).

ASSISTANT TO THE SECRETARY OF DEFENSE
FOR INTELLIGENCE OVERSIGHT

Pentagon, Room 2E253, 20301–7200, phone (703) 275–6550.

Assistant to the Secretary.—George B. Lotz II.

ASSISTANT SECRETARY FOR PUBLIC AFFAIRS

**Pentagon, Room 2E556, 20301–1400, phone (703) 697–9312, fax (703) 695–4299
public inquiries (703) 697–5737**

Principal Deputy Assistant Secretary.—Larry DiRita (acting).

ADMINISTRATION AND MANAGEMENT

Pentagon, phone (703) 692–7138

Director.—692–7138.

DEPARTMENT OF DEFENSE FIELD ACTIVITIES

AMERICAN FORCES INFORMATION SERVICE

**601 North Fairfax Street, Room 300, EFC Plaza, Alexandria, VA 22314
phone (703) 428–1200**

Director.—Larry DiRita (acting), (703) 697–9312.
   Director for American Forces Radio and Television Services.—Melvin W. Russell, room
360 (703) 428–0617.

DEPARTMENT OF DEFENSE EDUCATION ACTIVITY

4040 North Fairfax Drive, Arlington, VA 22203

school information (703) 588–3030

Director.—Dr. Joseph Tafoya, 588–3050.
   Principal Deputy Director.—Elizabeth Middlemiss, 588–3104.
   Associate Director for Management and Business Operations.—Irma Finocchiaro, 588–3300.
   General Counsel.—Maxanne Witkin, 588–3060.

DEPARTMENT OF DEFENSE HUMAN RESOURCES ACTIVITY

4040 Fairfax Drive, Arlington, VA 22209, phone (703) 696–1036

Director.—David S.C. Chu.
   Deputy Director.—Jeanne Fites.
   Assistant Director.—Sharon Cooper, 696–0909.

TRICARE MANAGEMENT ACTIVITY

5111 Leesburg Pike, Suite 810, Falls Church, VA 22041, phone (703) 681–6909

Director.—Dr. William Winken Werder, Jr.
   Deputy Director.—RADM Richard Mayo.

DEFENSE PRISONER OF WAR / MISSING PERSONNEL OFFICE

241 18th Street, Arlington, VA 22202, phone (703) 699–1100

Director.—Jerry D. Jennings.

OFFICE OF ECONOMIC ADJUSTMENT

400 Army Navy Drive, Suite 200, Arlington, VA 22202, phone (703) 604–6020

Director.—Patrick J. O'Brien.
Deputy Director.—Dave Larson, 604–4828.
Assistant to Director.—Martha Sands 604–6131, fax 604–5843.
Sacramento Region Manager.—Anthony Gallegos (916) 557–7365.

WASHINGTON HEADQUARTERS SERVICES

Pentagon, phone (703) 693–7995

Director.—693–7995.
Director for—
  Administrative Services and Program Support.—601–2553.
  Defense Facilities.—697–7241.
  Executive Services and Communications.—693–7704.
  Financial Management.—614–0971.
  General Counsel.—693–7374.
  Human Resources.—588–0404.
  Information Technology.—604–4569.
  Pentagon Renovation and Construction Program Office.—693–5507.
  Planning and Evaluation Office.—588–8140.
  Procurement and Contracting.—697–4504.

JOINT CHIEFS OF STAFF

OFFICE OF THE CHAIRMAN

Pentagon, Room 2E872, 20318–0001, phone (703) 697–9121

Chairman.—GEN Richard B. Myers, USAF.
  Vice Chairman.—GEN Peter Pace, USMC, room 2E860 (703) 614–8948 (703) 614–2500.
  Assistant to Chairman, Joint Chiefs of Staff.—LTG Raymond T. Odierno, USA, room 2E868 (703) 695–4605.

JOINT STAFF

Director.—LTG Norton A. Schwartz, USAF, room 2E936 (703) 614–5221.
  Vice Director.—MG Michael D. Maples, USA, room 2E936 (703) 614–5223.
  Director for—
  Manpower and Personnel, J–1.—RADM Donna L. Crisp, USN, room 1E948 (703) 697–6098.
  Intelligence, J–2.—MG Ronald L. Burgess, Jr., USA, room 1E880 (703) 697–9773.
  Operations, J–3.—LTG James T. Conway, USMC, room 2D874 (703) 697–3702.
  Logistics, J–4.—LTG Duncan J. McNabb, USAF, room 2E828 (703) 697–7000.
  Strategic Plans and Policy, J–5.—LTG Walter Sharp, USA, room 2E996 (703) 695–5618.
  Command, Control, Communications and Computer Systems, J–6.—LTG Robert M. Shea, USMC, room 2D860 (703) 695–6478.
  Operational Plans and Interoperability, J–7.—MG Jack J. Catton, USMC, room 2B865 (703) 697–9031.
  Force Structure, Resource, and Assessment, J–8.—VADM Robert F. Willard, USN, room 1E962 (703) 697–8853.

DEFENSE AGENCIES

MISSILE DEFENSE AGENCY

7100 Defense Pentagon, Washington, DC 20301–7100,
phone (703) 695–6344

Director.—LTG Henry A. (Trey) Obering III, USAF.
Deputy Director.—MG John Holly (703) 697–6228.
Chief, Media Relations and Plans.—LTC Catherine A. Reardon, USAF (703) 697–8491.

DEFENSE ADVANCED RESEARCH PROJECTS AGENCY

3701 North Fairfax Drive, Arlington, VA 22203, phone (703) 696–2444

Director.—Anthony Tether.
Deputy Director.—Dr. Robert Leheny (703) 696–2402.

DEFENSE COMMISSARY AGENCY

1300 E Avenue, Fort Lee, VA 23801–1800, phone (804) 734–8718/8330

Chief Executive Officer.—Patrick B. Nixon, 734–8720.
Chief Operating Officer.—Scott E. Simpson, 734–8330.
Chief Support Officer.—Edward S. Jones, 734–8718.

WASHINGTON OFFICE

Pentagon, Room 2E335, 20301–4100, phone (703) 614–9225

Director.—Daniel W. Schlater.

DEFENSE CONTRACT AUDIT AGENCY

8725 John J. Kingman Road, Suite 2135, Fort Belvoir, VA 22060
phone (703) 767–3200

Director.—William H. Reed.
Deputy Director.—Michael J. Thibault (703) 767–3272.

DEFENSE FINANCE AND ACCOUNTING SERVICE

1851 S. Bell Street, Suite 920, Crystal Mall Building No. 3, Arlington, VA 22240
phone (703) 607–2616

Director.—Zack E. Gaddy.
Deputy Director.—BG Jan D. Eakle, USAF, 607–3803.

DEFENSE INFORMATION SYSTEMS AGENCY

P.O. Box 4502, Arlington, VA 22204, phone (703) 607–6020

Director.—LTG Harry D. Raduege, Jr., USAF, room 4222 (703) 607–6001.
Vice Director.—MG Marilyn Quagliotti, USA, room 4235 (703) 607–6010.

DEFENSE INTELLIGENCE AGENCY

Pentagon, Room 3E258, 20340–7400, phone (703) 695–0071

Director.—VADM Lowell Jacoby, USN.
Deputy Director.—Mark W. Ewing, room 3E258 (703) 697–5128.

DEFENSE SECURITY SERVICE

1340 Braddock Place, Alexandria, VA 22314–1651, phone (703) 325–5364

Director.—Heather A. Anderson (acting).
Chief Operating and Information Officer.—Janice C. Haith.

DEFENSE LEGAL SERVICES AGENCY

Pentagon, Room 3E980, 20301–1600, phone (703) 695–3341, fax 693–7278

Director/General Counsel.—William J. Haynes.
Principal Deputy Director.—Daniel Dell'Orto (703) 697–7248.

DEFENSE LOGISTICS AGENCY

**8725 John J. Kingman Road, Suite 2533, Ft. Belvoir, VA 22060
phone (703) 767–5264**

Director.—VADM Keith W. Lippert, USN (703) 767–5200.
Vice Director.—MG Mary L. Saunders, USAF (703) 767–5222.

DEFENSE SECURITY COOPERATION AGENCY

201 12th Street South, Suite 203, Arlington, VA 22202–5408, phone (703) 604–6604

Director.—LTG Jeffrey B. Kohler, USAF.
Deputy Director.—Richard Millies (703) 604–6606.

NATIONAL GEOSPATIAL—INTELLIGENCE AGENCY

4600 Sangamore Road, Bethesda, MD 20816, phone (301) 227–7400

Director.—LTG James R. Clapper, Jr., USAF (Ret.).
Deputy Director.—Joanne Isham.

NATIONAL SECURITY AGENCY/CENTRAL SECURITY SERVICE

Ft. George G. Meade, MD 20755, phone (301) 688–6524

Director.—LTG Michael V. Hayden, USAF.
Deputy Director.—William B. Black, Jr.

DEFENSE THREAT REDUCTION AGENCY

8725 John J. Kingman Road, Ft. Belvoir, VA 22060, phone (703) 325–2102

Director.—Dr. James A. Tegnelia.
Deputy Director.—MG Trudy H. Clark, USAF.

JOINT SERVICE SCHOOLS

9820 Belvoir Road, Ft. Belvoir, VA 22060, phone (800) 845–7606

DEFENSE ACQUISITION UNIVERSITY

President.—Frank J. Anderson, Jr. (703) 805–3660.

DEFENSE SYSTEMS MANAGEMENT COLLEGE—SCHOOL OF PROGRAM MANAGERS

Commandant.—COL Mary Kringer, USAF (703) 805–2436.

JOINT MILITARY INTELLIGENCE COLLEGE

President.—A. Denis Clift (202) 231–3344.

NATIONAL DEFENSE UNIVERSITY

Bldg. 62, 300 Fifth Avenue, Fort McNair, Washington, DC 20319
phone (202) 685–3912

President.—LTG Michael M. Dunn, USAF, room 308 (202) 685–3922.
Senior Vice President.— Ambassador Johnnie Carson (202) 685–3923.

INFORMATION RESOURCES MANAGEMENT COLLEGE

Dean of the College.— Dr. Robert D. Childs (202) 685–3884.

JOINT FORCES STAFF COLLEGE

7800 Hampton Boulevard, Norfolk, VA 23511–1702, phone (757) 443–6200

Commandant.—MG Kenneth J. Quinlan, USA, room A201.

INDUSTRIAL COLLEGE OF THE ARMED FORCES

Commandant.—MG Frances C. Wilson, USMC, room 200 (202) 685–4337.

NATIONAL WAR COLLEGE

Commandant.—RADM Richard D. Jaskot, USN, room 113 (202) 685–4312.

UNIFORMED SERVICES UNIVERSITY OF THE HEALTH SCIENCES

4301 Jones Bridge Road, Bethesda, MD 20814

President.—Larry Laughlin, M.D., Ph.D., room A1018 (301) 295–3013.

DEPARTMENT OF THE AIR FORCE

Pentagon, 1670 Air Force, Washington, DC 20330–1670

phone (703) 697–7376, fax 693–7553

SECRETARY OF THE AIR FORCE

Secretary of the Air Force.—Pete Geren (acting), room 4E874.
  Confidential Assistant.—Debbie Henderson, room 4E871.
  Senior Military Assistant.—COL Janet Therianos, room 4E864.
    Deputy Military Assistant.—LTC Mark T. Beierle, room 4E864, 697–8141.
    Military Aid.—MAJ Robert Armfield.
  Protocol.—Karen Tibus, room 4E871.

SECAF/CSAF EXECUTIVE ACTION GROUP

Chief.—COL Paul Schafer, room 4E941, 697–5540.
  Deputy Chief.—LTC Geo Frasier.

UNDER SECRETARY OF THE AIR FORCE

Pentagon, 1670 Air Force, Room 4E886, Washington, DC 20330, phone 697–1361

Confidential Assistant.—Elizabeth Owen.
Senior Military Assistant.—COL James Horton.
Military Assistant.—LTC Alec Robinson.
Executive Assistant.—MSgt Stuart Lemon.

DEPUTY UNDER SECRETARY FOR INTERNATIONAL AFFAIRS

Pentagon, 1080 Air Force, Room 4E236, Washington, DC 20330–1080

Rosslyn, 1500 Wilson Blvd., 8th Floor, Arlington, VA 22209

Deputy Under Secretary.—Bruce S. Lemkin, 695–7262.
  Assistant Deputy.—MG John L. Hudson, 588–8855.
  Director of Policy.—Richard A. Genaille (acting), 588–8860.
  Director of Regional Affairs.—BG Ronald D. Yaggi, 588–8820.
    Executive Secretary.—Georgia Smothers, 685–7261.
  Senior Executive Officer.—LTC Michael J. McCarthy, 697–7262.
    Executive Officers: LTC James Federwisch, 588–8833; MAJ Hal Brown, 588–8828.

DIRECTOR FOR SMALL AND DISADVANTAGED BUSINESS UTILIZATION

Pentagon, 1060 Air Force, SAF/SB, Washington, DC 20330–1060

Director.—Joseph G. Diamond, 696–1103.

DEPUTY ASSISTANT SECRETARY FOR ENVIRONMENT, SAFETY AND OCCUPATIONAL HEALTH

Deputy Assistant Secretary.—Maureen T. Koetz, room 5C866, 697–9297.
  Deputy for—
    Cleanup, Munitions, and Environmental Technology.—LTC Jeff Cornell, 693–9544.
    Environmental Health and Conservation.—MAJ Ron Lahti, 695–5978.
    Environmental Policy.—Robert McCann, 697–1019.

ESOH Integration.—LTC Rodney Croslen, 697–0997.
Force Health Protection, Occupational Health.—LTC Rebecca Brown 693–7705.
Policy and Planning.—COL Richard Ashworth, 697–1016.
Workforce Infrastructure, Safety.—Vance E. Lineberger, 693–7706.

DEPUTY ASSISTANT SECRETARY FOR BASING AND
INFRASTRUCTURE ANALYSIS

Deputy Assistant Secretary.—Gerald F. Pease, Jr., room 5C283, 697–2524.
Chief, Joint Cross Service Analysis.—COL Thomas Fleming, room 5D260, 692–9515.
Chief, Infrastructure Analysis.—COL Chris Kapellas, room 5C266, 692–9510.

DIRECTORATE OF LOGISTICS

Director.—Mark Van Gilst, room 4D284, 692–9090.
Chief, Depot Operations and Strategy Planning.—LTC John Migyanko, room 4D284, 693–2185.
Chief, Weapons System Integration.—Sandra Meckley, room 4D284, 695–6716.

DEPUTY ASSISTANT SECRETARY FOR INSTALLATIONS

Deputy Assistant Secretary.—Fred W. Kuhn, room 4C940, 695–3592.
Assistant for Installation Management.—John E.B. Smith, room 4C940, 593–9327.
Director for—
  Installation Policy.—LTC Terri L. Toppin, room 4C940, 695–6456.
  Planning and Resources.—Marriane Serrano, room 4C940, 697–7244.
  Real Estate Policy.—Barbara J. Jenkins, room 4C940, 697–7070.
  Reserve Affairs.—COL Joe Morganti, room 4C940, 693–9328.
Assistant for the Air National Guard Affairs.—COL Ron Sachse, room 4C940, 693–9339.
Secretary.—Pamela L. Coghill, room 4C940, 695–3592.
Administrative Assistant.—Everette Dewaine Longus, room 4C940, 697–4391.

AIR FORCE REAL PROPERTY AGENCY

Director.—Kathryn M. Halvorson (703) 696–5501.
  Secretary.—LaShelle M. Taylor, 696–5503.696–5532.
Program Managers of:
  Division A.—Andrea Ziemian (acting), 696–5255.
  Division B.—Chips Johnson, 696–5546.
  Division C.—Jean Reynolds, 696–5260.
  Division EV.—Gerald Johnson, 696–5534.
Chief of:
  Real Estate Division.—Richard D. Jenkins, 696–5552.
  Legal Counsel Division.—Derry Fivehouse, 696–5522.
  Executive Services Division.—Joyce Truett, 696–5505.
  Financial Management Division.—Kathy Peters, 696–5559.

AIR FORCE REVIEW BOARDS AGENCY

Director.—Joe G. Lineberger, AAFB, Building 1535 (240) 857–3137.
  Confidential Assistant.—Donna Atchison, 857–3137.
Chief, Review Boards Management.—CMSgt. Susan Ayala, 857–3119.

AIR FORCE BOARD FOR CORRECTION OF MILITARY RECORDS (AFBCMR)

Executive Director.—Mack M. Burton, AAFB, Building 1535 (240) 857–3502.
  Deputy Executive Director.—Raymond H. Weller.
Chief Examiners; John J. D'Orazio; Rose Kirkpatrick; Donna Pittenger; Ralph Prete.
Superintendent, AFBCMR Information Management.—TSgt Gabrielle Allaway, USAF, 857–3502.

AIR FORCE PERSONNEL COUNCIL

Director.—COL Joseph Marchino, AAFB Building 1535 (240) 857–3138.
Senior Legal Advisor.—COL Thomas Jaster, 857–9043.
Senior Medical Advisor.—COL Horace Carson, 857–5353.
Chief, Air Force Discharge Review Board.—COL Tom Hammen, 857–3504.
Air National Guard Advisor.—COL Tom Hammen.
Decoration/Air Force Reserve Advisor.—COL Lee Tucker, 857–5342.
Chair/Attorney Advisor on Clemency/Parole Board.—James D. Johnston, 857–5329.
Executive Secretary, DOD Civilian/Military Service Review Board.—James D. Johnston.

AIR FORCE CIVILIAN APPELLATE REVIEW OFFICE

Director.—Rita Looney, AAFB Building 1535 (240) 857–7071.
Assistant Director.—J. Hayward Kight, 857–3168.

ASSISTANT SECRETARY FOR MANPOWER AND RESERVE AFFAIRS

1660 Air Force Pentagon (4E1020), Washington, DC 20330

Assistant Secretary.—Hon. Michael L. Dominguez, (703) 697–2302.
MA.—MG Peter K. Sullivan, 693–9312.
Confidential Assistant.—Ruth N. Thornton, 695–6677.
Military Assistant.—COL Francis L. Hendricks, 697–2303.
Executive Officer.—MAJ Jerome Williams, 697–1258.
Superintendent.—TSgt Henry Lopez, 697–5828.

DEPUTY ASSISTANT SECRETARY FOR FORCE MANAGEMENT INTEGRATION

Executive Secretary.—Dottie A. Baltimore, 614–4751.
Assistant Deputy for—
  Civilian Personnel.—Charlene M. Bradley, 614–4753.
  Family Programs.—Linda Stephens-Jones, 693–9574.
  Health Affairs.—Carol J. Thompson, 693–9764.
  USAFA Affairs.—David A. French, 693–9333.
  Services and Force Support.—LTC Sanda Adams, 693–9765.
Program Analyst.—Thomas E. Booth, 697–7783.

DEPUTY ASSISTANT SECRETARY FOR RESERVE AFFAIRS

Deputy Assistant Secretary.—John C. Truesdell, room 5C938.
Secretary.—Rosa R. Ramirez, 697–6375.
IMA.—COL Melissa Planert, 693–9505.
Assistant for—
  Air Force Reserve Affairs Matters.—COL Kevin Bushey, 697–6431.
  ANG Matters.—COL Ronald Gionta, 693–9504.
  Enlisted Matters.—CMSgt. Gail Paich, 697–6429.
  Military Executive for Air Reserve Forces Policy Division Committee.—LTC Laura Hunter, 697–6430.

DEPUTY ASSISTANT SECRETARY FOR EQUAL OPPORTUNITY

Deputy Assistant Secretary.—Shirley A. Martinez, room 5D973, 697–6586.
Secretary.—Karen Sauls, 697–6586.
Program Manager.—Diane C. Wakeham, 614–1619.
Assistant Deputy for Military EO.—LTC Mary Quinn, 697–6583.

ASSISTANT SECRETARY FOR FINANCIAL MANAGEMENT AND COMPTROLLER OF THE AIR FORCE

Pentagon, 1130 Air Force, Washington, DC 20330

CGN, Air Force Cost Analysis Agency, Crystal Gateway North

1111 Jefferson Davis Highway, Suite 403, Arlington, VA 22202

Assistant Secretary.—John G. Vonglis (acting), room 4E984, 693–6457.
  Military Assistant.—COL Barbara J. Gilchrist, 695–0837.
  Chief, Enlisted Matters.—CMSgt Jeannie McLean, 614–5437.

PRINCIPAL DEPUTY ASSISTANT SECRETARY FOR FINANCIAL MANAGEMENT

Principal Deputy Assistant Secretary.—John G. Voglis, 697–4464.
  Military Assistant.—LTC Antonio (Tony) Douglas, 695–0829.

EXECUTIVE SUPPORT

Chief.—LTC Dallas N. Newsome, room 4C138, 695–3589.

DEPUTY ASSISTANT SECRETARY FOR BUDGET (Room 4D131)

Deputy Assistant Secretary.—MG Stephen Lorenz, 695–1875.
  Executive Officer.—LTC Luke Carter, 695–1876.
  Deputy.—Robert D. Stuart, 695–1877.

DIRECTORATE OF BUDGET AND APPROPRIATIONS LIAISON (Room 5D911)

Director.—COL Pete Bunce, 614–8114.
  Division Chief for—
    Appropriations Liaison.—LTC Doug Carney, 614–8044.
    Budget Liaison.—Garry G. Sauner, 614–8112.

DIRECTORATE OF BUDGET MANAGEMENT AND EXECUTION (Room 4D120)

Director.—Marilyn Thomas, 697–1220.
  Executive Officer.—LTC Patrice Solorzano, 695–1220.
  Assistant for—
    Policy and Fiscal Control.—Marti A. Maust, 695–0305.
    Revolving Funds.—Mike Cerda, 693–4708.
    Special Programs.—Clai Ellett, 614–1319.

DIRECTORATE OF BUDGET INVESTMENT (Room 4D120)

Director.—Ann McDermott, 695–9737.
  Executive Officer.—LTC Patrice Solorzano.
  Assistant for—
    Aircraft Procurement and Technology Programs.—COL Mike Benjamin, 614–5701.
    Military Construction and Family Housing.—Mike J. Novel, 697–0166.
    Missile, Munitions, Space and Other Procurement.—Carolyn Gleason, 614–4996.
    Security Assistance.—Patricia Vestal, 697–2511.

DIRECTORATE OF BUDGET OPERATIONS AND PERSONNEL (Room 4D120)

Director.—BG Sandra A. Gregory, 697–0627.
  Executive Officer.—MAJ Derren Burrell, 697–0627.

Assistant for—
 Integration.—COL Robbie Lowe, 614–4097.
 Mission Operations.—Augie Doddato, 614–3801.
 Personnel and Training.—LTC Jim O'Brien, 695–4865.

DIRECTORATE OF BUDGET PROGRAMS (Room 4C239)

Director.—COL Dan Barnett, 614–7883.
Deputy Director.—Cindy Fuller, 614–3113.

DEPUTY ASSISTANT SECRETARY FOR COST AND ECONOMICS

Deputy Assistant Secretary.—Richard K. Hartley, room 4D159, 697–5311.
Associate Deputy Assistant Secretary.—BJ White-Olson, 697–5313.
Executive Officer.—MAJ Michael Welborn, 697–5312.
Technical Director for Cost and Economics.—Jay Jordan, CGN, room 403, 604–0404.
Director, Economics and Business Management.—Stephen M. Connair, room 4D167, 693–0347.

DEPUTY ASSISTANT SECRETARY FOR FINANCIAL OPERATIONS

Deputy Assistant Secretary.—James E. Short, room 5E989, 697–2905.
Associate Deputy Assistant Secretary.—Richard (Gus) Gustafson, 693–7066.
Military Assistant.—CAPT Craig Harding, 697–3831.
Director for—
 AF Accounting and Financial Office.—COL Patrick Coe, DFAS–DE (303) 676–5853.
 Financial Accounting and Reporting.—Anthony Colucci, room 4E139, 697–6465.
 FM Workforce Management.—Todd Schafer, room 4D160, 697–2657.

ASSISTANT SECRETARY FOR ACQUISITION

Pentagon, 1060 Air Force, Washington, DC 20330

Rosslyn, 1500 Wilson Blvd., Arlington, VA 22209

Arlington, 1745 Jefferson Davis Highway, Suite 307, Arlington, VA 22202

Military Assistant.—COL Robert Saxer, 697–6990.
Executive Officer.—LTC Bill Leister, 697–6362.

AIR FORCE PROGRAM EXECUTIVE OFFICERS

Program Executive Officer for—
 Airlift and Trainers.—LTG William Looney (937) 255–5714.
 Combat and Mission Support.—Ron Poussard, 588–7190.
 Command and Control/Combat Support Systems.—LTG Charles Johnson (781) 377–5102.
 Fighters and Bombers.—BG Rick Lewis, Rosslyn, 11th Floor, 588–7310.
 Weapons.—MG Robert Chedister (850) 882–5422.

PRINCIPAL DEPUTY ASSISTANT SECRETARY FOR ACQUISITION

Principal Deputy Assistant Secretary.—LTG John D.W. Corley, room 4E964, 697–6363.
Executive Officer.—LTC Duke Richardson, 695–7311.
Chief Enlisted Manager.—CMSgt Christopher Nelson, room 4E959, 697–8331.

DEPUTY ASSISTANT SECRETARY FOR CONTRACTING

Deputy Assistant Secretary.—Charlie E. Williams, Jr., Rosslyn, 7th Floor, 588–7070.
Associate Deputy Assistant Secretary.—COL William David McKinney, 588–7010.
Chief of:
 Contracting Mission Support Division.—COL Denean Rivera, 588–7029.
 Contracting Operations Division.—COL Phil W. Parker, 588–7050.
 Policy and Implementation Division.—Mike Maglio, 588–7077.

DEPUTY ASSISTANT SECRETARY FOR ACQUISITION INTEGRATION

Deputy Assistant Secretary.—Blaise J. Durante, Rosslyn, 16th Floor, 588–7211.
  Associate Deputy Assistant Secretary.—Richard W. Lombardi, 16th Floor, 696–0082.
  Division of:
    Acquisition Center for Excellence.—COL Ralph DiCicco, 9th Floor, 253–5656.
    Acquisition Information.—Terry Balven, 16th Floor, 588–7240.
    Career Management and Resources.—Carolyn Willis, 17th Floor, 588–7120.
    Management Policy.—Janet Hassan, 17th Floor, 588–7110.
    Operations Support.—Joe Casso, 16th Floor, 588–7124.
    Program Integration.—COL Charles Porter, 16th Floor, 588–7232.

CAPABILITY DIRECTORATE FOR INFORMATION DOMINANCE

Director.—Bobby W. Smart, Rosslyn, 12th Floor, 588–6346.
  Deputy.—COL Scott Grunwald, 12th Floor, 588–6350.
  Division Chief for—
    Airborne Reconnaissance.—COL Jerry Jankowiak, 15th Floor, 588–2645.
    C2 and Combat Support.—John Whitmore, 12th Floor, 588–6461.
    C2 Platforms and ATC Systems.—LTC Ken Fielding, 12th Floor, 588–6360.
    C4ISR Future Capabilities.—COL Craig Bendorf, 12th Floor, 588–6430.
    Congressional/Budget and Program Integration.—COL Mary A. Seibel (acting), 12th Floor, 588–6370.

CAPABILITY DIRECTORATE FOR GLOBAL REACH PROGRAMS

Director.—BG Wendell L. Griffin, Rosslyn, 14th Floor, 588–7752.
  Deputy Director.—COL Paul M. Stipe, 14 Floor, 588–7756.
  Division Chief for—
    Mobility.—COL John Brunderman, 14th Floor, 588–7757.
    Program, Budget and Congressional.—COL Rockford Reiners, 15th Floor, 588–8330.
    Tactical Airlift, SOF, and Trainer.—COL Tye Bo, 14th Floor, 588–7740.

CAPABILITY DIRECTORATE FOR SPECIAL PROGRAMS

Director.—COL David Bujold, Rosslyn, 15th Floor (703) 588–1631.
  Deputy Director.—COL John Gibbons.
  Associate Director.—Ryan Dow.
  Division Chief for—
    Advance Aircraft Survivability.—COL Randy Petyak, 588–2117.
    Advanced Sensors and Weapons.—LTC Chad Stephensen, 588–1463.
    Operational and Export Policy.—LTC Roderick Cregier, 588–2083.

DIRECTORATE FOR AIR FORCE RAPID CAPABILITIES

Director.—David E. Hamilton, Rosslyn, 15th Floor (703) 696–2407.
  Technical Director.—Randall G. Walden.
  Program Integration.—LTC Stephen Uyehata.

CAPABILITY DIRECTORATE FOR GLOBAL POWER PROGRAMS

Director.—MG Mark A. Welsh III, Rosslyn, 11th Floor, 588–7171.
  Deputy Director.—COL C.D. Moore, 11th Floor, 588–7177.
  Division Chief for—
    Air Dominance Division.—COL Russ Walden, 10th Floor, 588–6510.
    Figher Bomber Division.—COL Roy Cleland, 10th Floor, 588–1201.
    Program Integration Division.—Sue A. Lumpkins, 588–7181.
    Weapons Division.—COL Doug Cooke, 11th Floor, 588–1260.

DEPUTY ASSISTANT SECRETARY FOR
SCIENCE, TECHNOLOGY, AND ENGINEERING

Deputy Assistant Secretary.—Jim Engle, Rosslyn, 6th Floor, 588–7766.
Associate Deputy Assistant Secretary.—Terry Jaggers, 588–7768.

GENERAL COUNSEL
Pentagon, 1740 Air Force, Washington, DC 20330

General Counsel.—Mary L. Walker.
  Principal Deputy.—Daniel Ramos.
  Military Assistant/Special Counsel.—COL Kevin Baron (703) 697–8418.
  Deputy General Counsel for—
    Acquisition.—James Hughes, room 4D980, 697–3900.
    Contractor Responsibility.—Steven A. Shaw, Ballston, 588–0057.
    Dispute Resolution.—Joseph McDade, room 4D1000, 693–7286.
    Fiscal and Administrative Law.—Don W. Fox, room 4C916, 693–9291.
    Installations and Environment.—J. Steven Rogers, room 4C921, 695–4691.
    International Affairs.—Michael W. Zehner, room 4C941, 697–5196.
    Military Affairs.—W. Kipling Atlee, room 4C948, 695–5663.

INSPECTOR GENERAL
Pentagon, 1140 Air Force, Washington, DC 20330

Inspector General.—LTG Steven R. Polk, room 4E1076, 697–6733.
  Deputy Inspector General.—MG Jeff M. Musfeldt, 697–4351.
  Executive Officer.—LTC Kristine Blackwell, 697–4787.
  Advisor for—
    Reserve Matters.—COL Ray Joinson, room 4E1082, 697–0066.
    Air National Guard Matters.—LTC Thelma Jones, 588–1559.

OFFICE OF THE INSPECTOR GENERAL

Director of:
  Inquiries Directorate.—COL Dann McDonald, room 110, 588–1558.
  Inspections.—COL Pat Ward, room 4E1081, 697–7050.
  Special Investigations.—COL Scott Deacon, room 4E1081, 697–0411.
  Senior Officials Inquiries.—Tim Timmons, room 4E119, 693–3579.

ADMINISTRATIVE ASSISTANT TO THE SECRETARY
Pentagon, 1720 Air Force, Washington, DC 20330
2221 South Clark Street, Arlington, VA 22202 (CP6)
220 Brookley Avenue, Bolling AFB, Washington, DC 20032 (BAFB1)
200 McChord Street, Box 94, Bolling AFB, Washington, DC 20032 (BAFB2)

Administrative Assistant.—William A. Davidson, Pentagon, room 4D881, 695–9492.
  Deputy Administrative Assistant.—Robert E. Corsi, Jr., 695–9492.
  Senior Executive Assistant.—LTC Frank Malafarina, 695–8806.
  Executive Assistant.—MAJ Jeff Spinnanger, 695–8807.
  Deputy Executive Assistant.—TSgt Kim Rabon, 695–9492.
  Executive Administrator.—Rita Evaristo.

AIR FORCE ART PROGRAM OFFICE

Director.—Russell Kirk, room 5E271, 697–2858.

AIR FORCE CENTRAL ADJUDICATION FACILITY

Director.—COL Joseph Schott, BAFB1 (202) 767–9236.

AIR FORCE DECLASSIFICATION OFFICE

Director.—Linda Smith, CP6, Suite 600, 604–4665.

AIR FORCE DEPARTMENTAL PUBLISHING OFFICE

Director.—Jessica Spencer-Gallucci, BAFB2 (202) 404–2380.

AIR FORCE EXECUTIVE DINING FACILITY

General Manager.—Alfonso Sisneros, room 4C854, 697–1112.

FACILITIES SUPPORT DIVISION

Director.—Hector Dittamo, room 5E1083, 697–8222.

HUMAN RESOURCES AND MANPOWER DIVISION

Director.—Patricia Robey, room 4C882, 697–1806.

POLICY, PLANS AND RESOURCES DIVISION

Director.—Carolyn Lunsford, room 5E117, 695–4007.

SECURITY, COUNTERINTELLIGENCE AND SPECIAL PROGRAMS OVERSIGHT DIVISION

Director.—Barry Hennessey, room 5D972, 693–2013.

AIR FORCE PENTAGON COMMUNICATIONS AGENCY

Director.—COL Gerald Alexander, room 1D1000, 697–4264.

AUDITOR GENERAL

Pentagon, 1120 Air Force, Washington, DC 20330

4170 Hebble Creek Road, Building 280, Room 1,
Wright-Patterson AFB, OH 45433 (WPAFB)

5023 Fourth Street, March ARB, CA 95218 (MARB)

2000 North 15th Street, Suite 506, Arlington, VA 22201 (ARLINGTON)

2509 Kennedy Circle, Brooks City-Base, TEXAS 78235

Auditor General.—Robert E. Dawes, room 4E168, 614–5626.

AIR FORCE AUDIT AGENCY

Deputy Auditor General and Director of Operations.—Cathy Sparks, room 4E168 (703) 614–5738.
Assistant Deputy Auditor General.—Michael V. Barbino, Arlington (703) 696–8038.
Assistant Auditor General for—
   Financial and Systems Audits.—Donna L. Edsall, MARB (909) 655–7011.
   Acquisition and Logistics Audits.—Theodore J. Williams, WPAFB (937) 257–6355.
   Support and Personnel Audits.—James W. Salter, Jr., Brooks City-Base (210) 536–1999.

DIRECTORATE OF LEGISLATIVE LIAISON
Pentagon, 1160 Air Force, Washington, DC 20330
Rayburn House Office Building, Washington, DC 20515 (RHOB)
Russell Senate Office Building, Washington, DC 20510 (RSOB)

Director.—BG Scott S. Custer, Pentagon, room 4D927, 697–8153.
  Military Assistant to the Director.—COL Christine Turner, 695–2650.
  Executive Officer.—CAPT Pualani Zuniga, 697–4142.
  Deputy Executive Assistant.—SMSgt Darryl Moorer, 695–2650.
  Chief of:
      House Liaison Office.—COL Randy O'Boyle, RHOB, room B322 (202) 685–4531.
      Senate Liaison Office.—COL Anthony Lazarski, RSOB, room SR182 (202) 685–2573.
      Weapons Systems Liaison.—COL John Taylor, room 4D961, 697–6711.
      Programs and Legislation.—COL Eden Murrie, room 5D927, 697–7950.
      Congressional Action.—Daniel Sitterly, room 5D928, 695–1292.
      Air Operations.—Sandi J. Esty, room 5D912, 697–1500.
      Congressional Inquiries.—COL Darrell Adams, room 5D883, 697–3783.

DIRECTORATE OF PUBLIC AFFAIRS
Pentagon, 1690 Air Force, Washington, DC 20330
Arlington, 901 N. Stuart Street, Suite 803, Arlington, VA 22203

Director.—BG Frederick Roggero, room 4D922, 697–6061.
  Deputy Director.—COL James DeFrank.
  Executive Officer.—LTC Robyn Chumley, 695–2074.

MEDIA OPERATIONS

Chief.—COL Dewey Ford, room 5C879, 695–9085.
  Deputy.—Jean Schaefer, 695–9402.
  Media Desk.—LTC Frank Smolinsky, 697–5147.

STRATEGIC COMMUNICATION

Chief.—Larry Clavette, room 4A120, 697–6715.

RESOURCES AND READINESS

Chief.—Sherry Medders, room 4A120, 695–8563.
  Deputy.—LTC Tom Gilroy, 697–6702.

SECURITY REVIEW

Chief.—Devalee Pridgen, room 4A120, 697–3222.
  Deputy.—Stephanie VanDevander, 697–3994.

AIR FORCE NEWS AGENCY

Commander.—CPT Mike Strickler, Arlington, Suite 605, 696–9146.
  Superintendent.—SMSgt Anne Proctor, 696–9148.

NATIONAL OUTREACH AND COMMUNICATION

Chief.—June Forte (acting), room 5D227, 693–9094.
  Deputy.—LTC Mary MacLeod, 614–1196.

EXECUTIVE ISSUES GROUP

Chief.—COL Christopher Burne, room 5C945, 695–9425.

CHIEF OF STAFF

Pentagon, 1670 Air Force, Washington, DC 20330

Chief of Staff.—GEN John P. Jumper, room 4E925, 697–9225.
Executive Officer.—COL Judy Fedder.
Director, Operations Group.—COL Paul Schafer, room 4E941, 697–5540.
Vice Chief of Staff.—GEN Teed M. Moseley, room 4E936, 695–7911.
Assistant Vice Chief of Staff.—MG Kevin P. Chilton, room 4E944, 695–7913.
Chief Master Sergeant of the Air Force.—CMSAF Gerald R. Murray, room 4B948, 695–0498.

AIR FORCE STUDIES AND ANALYSIS AGENCY

Pentagon, 1570 Air Force, Washington, DC 20330

Rosslyn, 1777 North Kent Street, 6th, 7th, and 8th Floors, VA 22209

Director.—Dr. Jacqueline R. Henningsen, PhD, SES, 588–6966.
Vice Director.—COL James Brooks, 588–6966.
Technical Director.—Daniel Barker, 588–6944.
Technical Advisor.—Dr. Francis McDonald, 588–8880.
Chief Analyst.—COL Roxann A. Oyler, 588–6910.

CHIEF OF SAFETY

Pentagon, 1400 Air Force, Washington, DC 20330–1400

Chief of Safety/Commander, Air Force Safety Center.—MG Maurice L. McFann, 5E161 (703) 693–7281.

SAFETY ISSUES DIVISION (PENTAGON LIAISON)

Pentagon, 1400 Air Force, Washington, DC 20330

Director.—COL Daniel Stanton, room 5E161, 693–7333.

SCIENTIFIC ADVISORY BOARD

Pentagon, 1180 Air Force, Washington, DC 20330

Chair.—Dr. Daniel E. Hastings, room 5D982 (703) 697–4811.
Vice Chair.—Heidi Shyu, room 5D982, 697–4811.
Military Director.—LTG John D.W. Corley, room 4E964, 697–6363.
Executive Director.—COL Charles D. Bowker, room 5D982, 697–8288.
Deputy Executive Director.—LTC Lionel Mellott, room 5D982, 697–8652.
Military Assistants: MAJ Christopher Berg, room 5D982, 697–4648; MAJ Kyle Gresham, room 5D982, 697–4808.
Executive Assistants: TSgt Ramon Powell, SSgt Ebony Rodriguez, room 5D982, 697–4811.

DIRECTORATE OF TEST AND EVALUATION

Pentagon, 1650 Air Force, Washington, DC 20330

Director.—John Manclark, room 4E995, 697–4774.
Deputy Director.—David Hamilton, room 4D866.
Executive Officer.—John Miller, room 4E995, 697–5067.

AIR FORCE HISTORY OFFICE

3 Brookley Avenue, Box 94, Bolling Air Force Base, Washington, DC 20032–5000 (BAFB)

Director.—C.R. (Dick) Andcregg, room 401 (202) 404–2167.
Executive Officer.—MAJ Beverly Sloan (703) 697–2289.
Director, Air Force Historical Research Agency, Maxwell AFB, AL.—Dr. Charles O'Connell (334) 953–5342.

AIR FORCE SCIENTIST

Pentagon, 1075 Air Force, Washington, DC 20330

Chief Scientist.—Dr. Mark J. Lewis, room 4E288, 697–7842.
Military Assistant.—COL Daniel L. DeForest, room 4E288, 697–7842.

AIR FORCE RESERVE

Pentagon, 1150 Air Force, Washington, DC 20330

Chief, Air Force Reserve/Commander, Air Force Reserve Command.—LTG John A. Bradley,
room 4E160, 695–9225.
Deputy.—BG Charles D. Ethredge, room 4E160, 614–7307.

NATIONAL GUARD BUREAU

1411 Jefferson Davis Highway, Arlington, VA 22202

Chief.—LTG H. Steven Blum, JP–1, Pentagon, Washington, DC, 2A514B (703) 614–3117.
Director, Air National Guard.—LTG Daniel James III, JP–1, Crystal City, Suite 12200,
607–2408.
Deputy Director.—BG Ickes, JP–1, Crystal City, Suite 12200, 607–2409.

SURGEON GENERAL

Pentagon, 1780 Air Force Pentagon, Washington, DC 20330–1780

Bolling AFB, 110 Luke Avenue, Building 5681, Suite 400, Washington, DC 20332–7050

Surgeon General.—LTG George Peach Taylor, Jr. (703) 692–6800.
Deputy Surgeon General.—MG James Roudebush (202) 767–4766.
Executive Officers: COL Mark Hamilton (703) 692–6990; MAJ Brian Goviea, (202)
767–4759.
Director for—
  Congressional and Public Affairs.—Donna Tinsley (202) 767–4797.
  Financial Management.—Allen Middleton (703) 681–6330.
  Expeditionary Operations.—MG Joseph Kelley (202) 767–0020.
  Force Development.—MG Barbara Brannon (202) 767–4498.
  Plans and Programs.—BG (Sel) Patricia Lewis (202) 767–4915.
  Modernization.—COL Peter Demitry (703) 681–7055.
Corps Directors for—
  Medical.—COL Mike Spatz (202) 767–4492.
  Biomedical Sciences.—COL Martha Davis (202) 767–4499.
  Nursing.—COL Linda Kisner (202) 767–4462.
  Medical Services.—COL Brian Acker (202) 767–4432.

CHIEF OF CHAPLAINS

Bolling AFB, 112 Luke Avenue, Building 5683, Washington, DC 20032

Chief.—Chaplain (MG) Charles Baldwin, room 316 (202) 767–4577.
Deputy Chief.—Chaplain (BG) Cecil Richardson, room 313 (202) 767–4599.

JUDGE ADVOCATE GENERAL

Pentagon, 1420 Air Force, Washington, DC 20330

1501 Wilson Boulevard, Suite 810, Rosslyn, VA 22209 (ROSSLYN)

172 Luke Avenue, Suite 343, Bolling AFB, Washington, DC 20032 (BAFB)

Deputy Judge Advocate General.—MG Jack L. Rives.
Director for—
  Civil Law and Litigation.—COL Evan Haberman, Rosslyn, room 810, 696–9040.
  USAF Judiciary.—COL Rebecca Weeks, BAFB, room 336 (202) 767–1535.
  General Law.—Harlan G. Wilder, room 5E279, 614–4075.
  International Law.—COL Jeanna Rueth, room 5C269, 695–9631.

LEGAL SERVICES

Commander, Air Force Legal Services Agency.—COL David Ehrhart, BAFB, room 336 (202) 404–8758.

DEPUTY CHIEF OF STAFF FOR AIR AND SPACE OPERATIONS
Pentagon, 1630 Air Force, Washington, DC 20330
GAL PL, 624 9th Street, NW., Suite 300, Washington, DC 20001

Deputy Chief of Staff.—LTG Howie Chandler, room 4E1032, 697–9991.
  Assistant Deputy.—MG Robert D. Bishop, 697–9881.
  Mobilization Assistant.—BG Michael K. Lynch, room 4D1086, 697–3087.
  Director, Security Forces.—BG (Sel) Robert Holmes, room 4C166, 693–5494.
    Deputy Director.—COL Robert Tirevold.
  Director, Strategic Security.—MG Roger Burg, room 4E1048, 693–9747.
    Deputy Director.—BG (Sel) Suzanne Vautrinot.
  Associate Director.—SES Dr. Billy Mullins, room 4E1041, 697–0152.
  Director, Intelligence, Surveillance and Reconnaissance.—MG Ronald F. Sams, room 4A932, 695–5613.
    Deputy Director.—BG Kevin Kennedy.
  Director, Operations and Training.—MG Marne Peterson, room 4E1046, 695–9067.
    Deputy Director.—BG William Holland.
  Director, Operational Capability Requirements.—MG Stanley Gorenc, room 4E1021, 695–3018.
    Deputy Director.—SES Harry C. Disbrow, Jr.
  Director, Operational Plans and Joint Matters.—BG R. Mike Worden, room 4E1047, 614–2711.
    Deputy Directors.—COL Marc Felman.
  Director, Executive Support.—LTC Brian Bellacicco, room 5C1072, 697–7823.

DEPUTY CHIEF OF STAFF FOR PERSONNEL
Pentagon, 1040 Air Force, Washington, DC 20330

Deputy Chief of Staff.—LTG Roger A. Brady, room 4E194, 697–6088.
  Assistant Deputy.—Roger M. Blanchard.
  Chief, Personnel Issues Team.—LTC Steven B. Johnson, room 4E185, 695–4212.
  Director of:
    Air Force Senior Leader Management Office.—BG Richard S. Hassan, Crystal Plaza 6, Suite 500, 604–8126.
    Airmen Development and Sustainment.—BG William A. Chambers, room 4E144, 695–2144.
    Executive Services.—CAPT Julie Newlin, room 4E207, 697–1125.
    Force Management Policy.—BG Glenn Spears, room 4E228, 695–6770.
    Manpower and Organization.—BG Marshall K. Sabol, room 5A328, 692–1601.
    Plans and Integration.— Timothy Beyland, room 4E178, 697–5222.

DEPUTY CHIEF OF STAFF FOR INSTALLATIONS AND LOGISTICS
Pentagon, 1030 Air Force, Washington, DC 20330
Crystal Gateway North, 1111 Jefferson Davis Highway, Arlington, VA 22202 (CGN)
Crystal Gateway 1, 1235 Jefferson Davis Highway, Arlington, VA 22202 (CG1)
Rosslyn, 1500 Wilson Boulevard, Arlington, VA 22209 (ROS)

Deputy Chief of Staff.—LTG Donald J. Wetekam, Pentagon, room 4E260, 695–3153.
  Assistant Deputy.—Michael A. Aimone, Pentagon, room 4E260, 695–6236.
  Director of:
    Communication Operations.—BG Ronnie D. Hawkins, ROS, Suite 220, 588–6100.
    Innovation and Transformation.—Grover L. Dunn, Pentagon, room 5D967, 697–6559.
    Logistics Readiness.—BG Ron Ladmier, Pentagon, room 4B283, 697–1429.

Maintenance.—BG David Gillett, Pentagon, room 4E278, 695–4900.
Resources.—BG Arthur B. Morrill, Pentagon, room 4A272, 697–2822.
Services.—Arthur J. Myers, CGN, room 413, 604–0010.
The Civil Engineer.—MG L. Dean Fox, CG1, room 1000, 607–0200.

ARMY AND AIR FORCE EXCHANGE SERVICE

3911 S. Walton Walker Boulevard, Dallas, TX 75236, phone 1–800–527–6790

Commander.—MG Bill Essex, USAF.
Vice Commander.—BG Toreaser A. Steele, USAF.
Chief Operating Officer.—Marilyn Iverson.

WASHINGTON OFFICE/OFFICE OF THE BOARD OF DIRECTORS

National Center 1 (NC1), 2511 Jefferson Davis Highway, Suite 11600

Arlington, VA 22202, phone (703) 604–7523, DSN 664–7523

Director/Executive Secretary.—Gregg Cox.
Deputy Director/Executive Assistant.—Richard G. Struss.

DEPUTY CHIEF OF STAFF FOR PLANS AND PROGRAMS

AF/XP, 1070 Air Force Pentagon, Washington DC 20330–1070

Deputy Chief of Staff.—LTG Stephen Wood, room 4E124, 697–9472.
Director of Programs.—MG Raymond Johns, room 5B279, 697–2405.
Deputy Director.—BG Winifield Scott, room 5B279, 697–2405.
Director for Strategic Planning.—MG Ronald Bath, room 5E171, 697–3117.

OFFICE OF THE CHIEF INFORMATION OFFICER

Pentagon, 1155 Air Force, Washington, DC 20330

1401 Wilson Boulevard, Suite 600, Arlington, VA 22202

Chief Information Officer.—John M. Gilligan (703) 695–9698.
Executive Officer.—COL Jeff Mercer, 614–7891.
Director, Systems and Technology.—COL Michael Harper, 696–7373.
Deputy Director.—LTC Remy Acevedo, 696–6920.
Director, Plans and Policy.—COL Anne Leary, 696–7711.
Deputy Director.— Al Bodnar, 696–6327.
Director, Resources and Operation.—COL Michael Crane, 696–7557.
Deputy Director.—James Brown, 696–6518.
Chief Architect.—Gerald Friedman, 696–7670.

DEPUTY CHIEF OF STAFF FOR WARFIGHTING INTEGRATION

Pentagon, 1800 Air Force Pentagon, Washington, DC 20330

Deputy Chief of Staff.—LTG William T. Hobbins, room 4E212 (703) 695–6829.
Assistant.—Rob Thomas II, 697–1605.
Director of:
  C4IER Infostructure.—MG Charles C. Croom, room 4B1060, 697–1326.
  C4ISR Integration.—MG Greg Power, room 4C1059, 695–1835.
  C4ISR Architecture and Operational Support Modernization.—David Tillotson, room 4C1059, 695–1839.
  Resource Planning.—COL Brenda Gregory, room 4B1060, 697–3957.

DEPARTMENT OF THE ARMY

The Pentagon, 20310, phone (703) 695–2442

OFFICE OF THE SECRETARY

Pentagon, Room 3E560, 20310, phone (703) 695–3211, fax 697–8036

Secretary of the Army.—Dr. Francis J. Harvey.
Executive Officer.—COL Joseph Anderson, 695–1717.

OFFICE OF THE UNDER SECRETARY

Pentagon, Room 3E588, 20310–0102, phone (703) 695–4311

Under Secretary of the Army.—Raymond DuBois (acting).
Executive Officer.—COL Daniel Gerstein, 697–6806.

ASSISTANT SECRETARY FOR CIVIL WORKS

Pentagon, Room 3E446, 20310–0108, phone (703) 697–8986, fax 697–7401

Principal Deputy Assistant Secretary.—John Paul Woodley, Jr.
Executive Officer.—COL James Balocki, 697–9809.
Military Assistant.—LTC David Press, 695–0482.
Deputy Assistant Secretary for—
  Policy and Legislation.—George Dunlop, 695–1370.
  Management and Budget.—Claudia L. Tornblom, 695–1376.

ASSISTANT SECRETARY FOR FINANCIAL MANAGEMENT AND COMPTROLLER

Pentagon, Room 3E324, 20310–0109, phone (703) 614–4356

Assistant Secretary.—Valerie L. Baldwin.
  Executive Officer.—COL William Ford, 614–4337.
  Deputy Assistant Secretary for—
    Financial Operations.—John Argodale, room 3A320A, 693–2741.
    Resource Analysis and Business Practices.—Sharon Weinhold, room 3A712, 697–7399.
    Army Budget.—MG Edgar Stanton, room 3A314, 614–4035.
    Director for U.S. Cost and Economic Analysis Center.—Steve Bagby, room 3E352.

ASSISTANT SECRETARY FOR INSTALLATIONS AND ENVIRONMENT

Pentagon, Room 3E464, 20310–0110, phone (703) 692–9801

Principal Deputy Assistant Secretary.—Geoffrey G. Prosch, 692–9802.
  Executive Officer.—COL Michael Conrad, 692–9804.
  Deputy Assistant Secretary for—
    Installations and Housing.—Joseph Whitaker, 697–8161, room 3E475.
    Environment, Safety and Occupational Health.—Raymond J. Fatz, room 3D453, 697–1913.
    Infrastructure and Analysis.—Craig College, room 3D453, 697–3388.
    Privatizations and Partnerships.—William Armbruster, room 3D453, 692–9890.

ASSISTANT SECRETARY FOR MANPOWER AND RESERVE AFFAIRS

Pentagon, Room 2E468, 20310–0111, phone (703) 697–9253

Assistant Secretary.—Daniel B. Denning (acting).
   Principal Deputy Assistant Secretary.—Daniel B. Benning, room 2E460, 692–1292.
   Executive Officer.—COL Heid V. Brown, 695–1375.
   Deputy Assistant Secretary for—
      Force Management, Manpower and Resources.—Sarah White, room 2E460, 695–9652.
      Review Boards.—Karl Schneider, Crystal City #4, 607–1597.
      Training, Readiness, and Mobility.—Daniel B. Denning, room 2E460, 692–1292.
      Human Resources.—John P. McLaurin III, room 2E482, 697–2631.

ASSISTANT SECRETARY FOR ARMY ACQUISITION,
LOGISTICS AND TECHNOLOGY

Pentagon, Room 2E532, 20310–0103, phone (703) 695–6153, fax 697–4003

Assistant Secretary.—Claude M. Bolton, Jr., 693–6153.
   Chief of Staff.—COL Mary Fuller, 695–5749.
   Military Assistant.—LTC Kirk F. Vollmecke, 695–6742.
   Military Deputy.—LTG Joseph L. Yakovac, Jr., 697–0397.
      Secretary to the Military Deputy.—Sandy Schruggs.
      Executive to Military Deputy.—LTC Paul R. Lepine, 697–0356.
   Deputy Assistant Secretary for—
      Plans, Programs and Resources.—Don Damstetter, room 2E673, 697–0387.
      Policy and Procurement.—Earnestine Ballard, room 2E661, 695–2488.
      Science and Technology.—Dr. Thomas H. Killion, room 3E620, 692–1830.
   Deputy Assistant Secretary for Defense, Exports and Cooperation.—Craig D. Hunter, 1777 N. Kent Street, North Plaza, 8th Floor, Rosslyn VA 22332, 588–8070.

GENERAL COUNSEL

Pentagon, Room 2E722, 20310–0104, phone (703) 697–9235, fax 697–6553

General Counsel.—Avon N. Williams III (acting).
   Principal Deputy General Counsel.—Avon N. Williams III.
   Executive Officer/Special Counsel.—COL Manuel E.F. Supervielle.
   Senior Deputy General Counsel.—Thomas W. Taylor, room 3D546, 695–0562.
   Deputy General Counsel for—
      Acquisition.—Levator Norsworthy, Jr., room 3D546, 697–5120.
      Civil Works and Environment.—Craig R. Schmauder, room 3D546, 695–3024.
      Ethics and Fiscal Law.—Matt Reres, room 3D546, 695–5105.

ADMINISTRATIVE ASSISTANT

Pentagon, Room 3E585, 20310–0105, phone (703) 695–2442, fax 697–6194

Administrative Assistant.—Sandra R. Riley.
   Deputy Administrative Assistant.—George A. Sullivan (acting), Taylor Building, room 13178, 602–5541.
   Executive Officer.—COL Larry Stubblefield, 695–7444.
   Deputy for Organizational Management & Planning.—Mary Costa (acting), 697–7741.
   Chief, Executive Support & Planning Office.—W. Anthony Tatum, room 3E591, 697–3061.
   Chief, Organizational Management Office.—Susan Baskin (acting), Taylor Building, room 13038, 602–5615.
   Special Assistant.—MG Robert Diamond, Taylor Building, room 13176, 602–6969.
   Chief, Strategic Planning Office.—Gem Loranger, Taylor Building, room 13140, 602–7181.
   Executive Director, U.S. Army Resources and Programs Agency.—George A. Sullivan (acting), Taylor Building, room 13178, 602–5541.
   Pentagon Chaplain.—COL Ralph Benson, room 1E443, 692–9377.
   HQDA Resource Management.—Robert Jaworski, Taylor Building, room 8122, 602–1503.
   Defense Contracting Command (Washington).—COL Joe Conley, room 1E230, 695–2005.
   Human Resources Management.—Sherri Ward, Taylor Building, room 8016, 602–2220.
   Equal Employment Opportunity.—Debra Muse, Taylor Building, room 8202, 604–2736.
   Chief Attorney & Legal Services.—COL Nathaniel Causey, room 1C242, 697–5423.
   Internal Review.—Donald Friend, Taylor Building, room 13204, 602–1774.

Administrative Services (NCR).—Fritz Kirklighter, Taylor Building, room 8088, 602–3511.
The Institute for Heraldry.—Fred Eichorn, Ft. Belvoir, Building 1466, room S–103, 806–4969.
Records Management & Declassification Agency.—Steve Raho, 7701 Telegraph Road, room 102, 428–6462.
Executive Director, U.S. Army Services and Operations Agency.—Thomas Scullen (acting), Taylor Building, room 13116, 602–2027.
Army Publishing.—John Czekner, Hoffman I, room 1010, 325–6801.
Army Multimedia Visual Information.—Edward Jonas, room 5A928, 697–1798.
Security and Safety.—David Beltz, Taylor Building, room 1E16, 602–9752.
Support Services (Washington).—I.E. Washburn (acting), room 1A125, 692–4857.
Support Estate & Facilities, Pentagon (Army).—Lacy Saunders, room 1A125, 695–7555.
Logistics (Washington).—Walt Myers (acting), Taylor Building, room 10088, 604–3227.
U.S. Army Priority Air Transport.—LTC Lorenzo Riddick, Andrews AFB, (240) 857–6667.
Executive Director, U.S. Army Information Technology Agency.—Ron Bechtold, Taylor Building, room 13094, 602–6811.
Network Security Services (Pentagon).—Rick Anderson, Rosslyn Plaza North 8200, 588–8050.
Defense Telecommunications Services (Washington).—Larry Miller, Taylor Building, room 10202, 602–1574.
Army Information Management Support Center.—Jeffrey Riplinger (acting), Taylor Building, room 9088, 602–4197.
Network Infrastructure Services & Operations (Pentagon).—Virginia Arreguin, room ME882, 614–5761.
Pentagon Data Center Services.—Susan Fisher (acting), room BF849D, 692–0312.
Pentagon Telecommunications Center.—Marvin Owens, room 5A910, 697–8840.
Information Technology Integration (Pentagon).—Paul Beardsley, Rosslyn Plaza North, room S4100, 588–8730.

THE OFFICE OF THE CHIEF INFORMATION OFFICER / G–6

Pentagon, Room 1A271, 20310–0107, phone (703) 695–4366, fax 695–3091

Chief Information Officer.—LTG Steven W. Boutelle.
Deputy Chief Information Officer.—Vernon Bettencourt, 695–6604.
Executive Officer.—COL James Lien, 697–5503.
Director of:
　Resource Integration.—Ms. Diane Armstrong, room 1A310, 614–0439.
　Information Operations, Networks and Space.—MG Dennis Moran, room 2B855, 614–5666.
　Enterprise Integration.—Gary Winkler, room 7178, Taylor Building, Crystal City, VA.

INSPECTOR GENERAL

Pentagon, Room 5D561, 20310–1700, phone (703) 695–1500, fax 614–5628

Inspector General.—MG Stanley E. Green.
Executive Officer.—COL Robert C. Faille, Jr., 695–1502.

AUDITOR GENERAL

3101 Park Center Drive, Alexandria, VA 22302, phone (703) 681–9809, fax 681–4602

Auditor General.—Joyce E. Morrow.
Principal Deputy Auditor General.—Patrick J. Fitzgerald.
Deputy Auditor General for—
　Acquisition and Logistics Audits.—Thomas Druzgal, 681–9860.
　Forces and Financial Audits.—Benjamin J. Piccolo, 681–9585.
　Policy and Operations Management.—Joseph P. Mizzoni, 681–9593.

DEPUTY UNDER SECRETARY OF THE ARMY

101 Army Pentagon, Room 3E573, 20310–0001, phone (703) 697–5075

Deputy Under Secretary.—Jack Bell.
Executive Officer.—Jeffrey S. White, 695–4392.

DEPUTY UNDER SECRETARY OF THE ARMY (OPERATIONS RESEARCH)

Pentagon, Room 5D565, phone (703) 695–0083, fax 697–4488

Deputy Under Secretary.—Walter W. Hollis.
Executive Officer.—COL Walter Barge, 697–0366.
Executive Assistant.—Cynthia C. Mafnas, 693–4488

LEGISLATIVE LIAISON

Pentagon, Room 1E416, 20310–1600, phone (703) 697–6767, fax 614–7599

Chief.—MG Guy C. Swan III, room 1E428.
Deputy Chief.—COL (P) Richard McCabe, room 1E428, 695–1235.
Special Assistant for Legislative Affairs for Intelligence.—Robert J. Winchester, room 1E428, 695–3918.
Executive Officer.—COL John L. Goetchius, Jr., room 1E428, 695–3524.
Chief of:
  Congressional Inquiry.—Janet Fagan, room 1E423, 697–8381.
  House Liaison.—COL Michael DeYoung, room B325, Rayburn House Office Building, Washington DC (202) 225–3853.
  Senate Liaison.—COL Michael Barbero, room SR183, Senate Russell Office Building, Washington DC (202) 224–2881.
  Investigation and Legislative.—COL Joseph Frisk, room 1E433, 697–2106.
  Programs.—COL John Peabody, room 1E385, 693–8766.

OFFICE OF THE CHIEF OF PUBLIC AFFAIRS

Pentagon, Room 1E484, 20310–1500, phone (703) 695–5135, fax 693–8362

Chief.—BG Vincent K. Brooks.
Deputy Chief.—BG Mary K. Eder.
Executive Officer.—LTC Robert Ali.
Chief of Plans.—COL James Pullen.
Chief of:
  Media Relations Division.—COL Joseph Curtin.
  Strategic Communications Division.—COL Garrie Dornan.
  Community Relations and Outreach Division.—COL Richard Breen.
  Resource Management Division.—Randa Vagnerini.

SMALL AND DISADVANTAGED BUSINESS UTILIZATION

Pentagon, Room 3B514, 20310–0106, phone (703) 697–2868, fax 693–3898

Director.—Tracey L. Pinson.
Deputy Director.—Paul L. Gardner.

ARMED RESERVE FORCES POLICY COMMITTEE

Pentagon, Room 2D484, 20310–0111, phone (703) 695–5129, fax 695–6967

Chairman.—MG Claude A. Williams.
Deputy Chairman.—MG David E. Kratzer.

ARMY STAFF AND SELECTED AGENCIES

Pentagon, 20310–0200, phone (703) 695–2077

Chief of Staff.—GEN Peter J. Schoomaker, room 3E528.
Vice Chief of Staff—GEN Richard A. Cody, 695–4371.
Director, CSA's Staff Group.—COL Kim Kadesch, 697–4120.
Director of Army Staff.—LTG James L. Campbell, 695–6636.
Director, Office of:
  Executive Commission and Control.—COL Richard E. Arnold, 697–5280.
  Army Protocol.—Arlene York, 697–0692.

Program Analysis and Evaluation.—MG N. Ross Thompson III, room 3E362, 695–4697.
Test and Evaluation Management Agency.—Richard A. Sayre (acting), 695–8998.
Sergeant Major.—SMA Kenneth O. Preston, 695–2150.

INTELLIGENCE

Pentagon, Room 2E408, 20310–1000, phone (703) 695–3033

Deputy Chief of Staff.—LTG Keith B. Alexander.
  Executive Officer.—COL Clyde T. Harthcock.
  Assistant Deputy Chiefs: MG George R. Fay, 693–5851; Terrance M. Ford, 697–4644;
    COL (P) Julia A. Kraus, 695–3929.
  Director, Office of:
    Counterintelligence/HUMINT.—Thomas Gandy, 695–2374.
    Foreign Intelligence.—COL Anthony Lieto, 695–2186.
    Foreign Liaison.—COL David Allwine, 692–1467.
    Information Management.—COL Lynn Schnurr, 693–7019.
    Intel, Surveillance and Recon Integration.—Collin Agee, 695–4202.
    Plans and Operations.—COL Christopher Munn, 695–1623.
    Resource Integration.—Jean Bennett, 695–1233.

LOGISTICS

Pentagon, Room 1E394, 20310–0500, phone (703) 695–4102, fax 614–6702

Deputy Chief of Staff.—LTG Claude V. Christianson.
  Assistant Deputy Chiefs of Staff: MG Jeanette Edmunds.
  Director, Office of:
    Force Projection.—BG Kathleen Gainey, room 1E384.
    Logistics Integration Agency.—Mark O'Konski.
    Logistics Integration Services.—Wimpy Pybus, room 3C652.
    Plans, Operations, and Readiness.—COL (P) Michael Terry, room 1E367.
    Program Development.—Robert Turzak, room 1E369.

OPERATIONS AND PLANS

Pentagon, Room 2E366, 20310–0400, phone (703) 695–2904

Deputy Chief of Staff.—LTG James J. Lovelace.
  Assistant Deputy Chiefs of Staff: Kathryn A. Condon. 692–7883; MG Robert Wilson,
    697–5180.

PERSONNEL

Pentagon, Room 2E446, 20310–0300, phone (703) 697–8060

Deputy Chief of Staff, G–1.—LTG F.L. Hagenbeck.
  Assistant Deputy Chief of Staff, G–1.—Mark Lewis, room 2E446, 692–1585.
  Assistant Deputy Chief of Staff for Mobilization and Reserve Affairs, G–1.—MG John
    Hawkins, room 1D449, 695–5868.
  Director, Office of:
    Military Personnel Management.—BG Sean Byrne, room 1D429, 695–5871.
    Plans, Resources and Operations.—Roy Wallace, room 2B453, 697–5263.
    Human Resources.—COL (P) Robert Woods, room 2C453, 693–1850.
    Civilian Personnel.—Melinda Darby, room 2C453, 695–5701.
    MANPRINT.—Dr. Michael Drillings, room 2C485, 695–6761.
    Army Research Institute.—Dr. Zita Simutis, 602–7798.

ASSISTANT CHIEF OF STAFF INSTALLATION MANAGEMENT

Pentagon, Room 3E474, 20310–0600, phone (703) 693–3233, fax 693–3507

Assistant Chief of Staff.—MG Geoffrey D. Miller.
  Deputy Assistant.—J.C. Menig.

CORPS OF ENGINEERS

GAO Building, 441 G Street, NW., Washington, DC 20314, phone (202) 761–0001

fax 761–4463

Commander/Chief of Engineers.—LTG Carl A. Strock
  Deputy Commander.—MG Robert H. Griffin.
  Director of Civil Works.—MG Don T. Riley, 761–0099.
    Deputy Director for Civil Works.—Fred Caver, 761–0100.
  Director of Military Programs.—MG James Cheatham, 761–0379.
    Deputy Director of Military Programs.—Dwight Beranek, 761–0382.
  Chief, Program Integration Division.—Robert Vining, 761–4100.

SURGEON GENERAL

Skyline Place 6, Suite 672, 5109 Leesburg Pike, Falls Church, VA 22041–3258

phone (703) 681–3000, fax 681–3167

Surgeon General.—LTG Kevin C. Kiley.
  Deputy Surgeon General.—MG Joseph G. Webb, Jr., 681–3002.

NATIONAL GUARD BUREAU

1411 Jefferson Davis Highway, Arlington, VA 22202–3231, phone (703) 614–3087

Chief.—LTG H. Steven Blum.
  Director, Army National Guard.—LTG Roger Schultz, 607–7000.
  Director, Joint Staff.—MG Paul Sullivan, 607–2204.

ARMY RESERVE

Pentagon, Room 2B548, 20310–2400, phone (703) 697–1784

Chief.—LTG James R. Helmly.
  Deputy Chief.—BG Gary M. Profit, 697–1260.
  Deputy Chief (IMA).—MG Collis N. Phillips, 695–1913.

JUDGE ADVOCATE GENERAL

Pentagon, Room 2B514, 20310–2200, phone (703) 697–5151, fax 693–0600

Judge Advocate General.—MG Thomas J. Romig.
  Assistant Judge Advocate General.—MG Michael J. Marchand, 693–5112.
  Assistant Judge Advocate General for Military Law and Operations.—BG Daniel V. Wright, Rosslyn, VA, 588–6768.
  Commander, United States Army Legal Services Agency.—BG David P. Carey, Ballston, VA, 588–6269.
  Commander/Commandant, USA The Judge Advocate General's Legal Center and School.— BG Scott C. Black, Charlottesville, VA (434) 971–3301.

CHIEF OF CHAPLAINS

Pentagon, Room 2A514A, 20310–2700, phone (703) 695–1133, fax 695–9834

Chief.—MG Gaylord T. Gunhus.
  Deputy Chief.—BG David H. Hicks, 695–1135.

LIAISON OFFICES

Pentagon, Room 2A474, 20310–2200, phone (703) 695–1327, fax 695–8370

U.S. Army, Europe (USAREUR).—Dr. Bryan T. van Sweringen; David Dull, 692–6886, fax 614–9714.
  U.S. Army Accessions Command.—LTC Alissa Turner, 603–4034, fax 603–4036.

U.S. Army Forces Command (FORSCOM)/US Army Training and Doctrine Command (TRADOC).—SFC David Cleveland; SSG Jemse L. Cruz; Laverne De Sett; Celeste Johnson, 697–2552, 2588, fax 697–5725.

U.S. Army, Pacific (USARPAC).—Robert Ralston, 693–4032, fax 693–4036.

U.S. Forces Korea (USFK).—Ronald R. Rollison; Cathy Abell; SFC David Cleveland; Harrison J. Parker III; Sharon L. Smith, 693–4038, fax 695–4576.

MAJOR ARMY COMMANDS

U.S. Army.—Sandra R. Riley, Headquarters, Department of the Army, Pentagon, Washington, DC 20310–0105 (703) 695–2442.

U.S. Army Materiel Command.—GEN Benjamin Griffin, 9301 Chapek Road, Building 1459, Ft. Belvoir, VA 22060–5527 (703) 806–8250.

U.S. Army Corps of Engineers.—LTG Carl A. Strock, 441 G Street, NW, Washington, DC 20314–1000 (202) 761–0000.

U.S. Army Criminal Investigation Command.—MG Donald J. Ryder, 6010 6th Street, Fort Belvoir, VA 22060–5506 (703) 806–0400.

U.S. Army Forces Command.—GEN Dan K. McNeill, 1777 Hardee Avenue SW., Fort McPherson, GA 30330–1062 (404) 464–5054.

U.S. Army Intelligence and Security Command.—MG John F. Kimmons, 8825 Beulah Street, Fort Belvoir, VA 22060–5246 (703) 706–1603.

U.S. Army Medical Command/The Surgeon General.—LTG Kevin C. Kiley, 5109 Leesburg Pike, Falls Church, VA 22041–3258 (703) 681–3000.

U.S. Army Military District of Washington.—MG Galen B. Jackson, 103 3rd Avenue, Building 32, Fort Lesley J. McNair, Washington, DC 20319–5000 (202) 685–2807.

U.S. Army Surface Deployment and Distribution Command.—BG (P) Charles W. Fletcher, Jr., 200 Stovall Street, Hoffman Bldg. II, Alexandria, VA 22332–5000 (703) 428–3210.

U.S. Army Special Operations Command.—LTG Philip R. Kensinger, Fort Bragg, NC 28310–5200 (910) 432–3000.

U.S. Army Training and Doctrine Command.—GEN Kevin P. Byrnes, 7 Fenwick Road, Building 37, Fort Monroe, VA 23651–1049 (757) 788–3514.

U.S. Army South.—MG Jack Gardner, 2450 Stanley Road, Suite 700, Ft. Sam Houston, TX 78234–7517 (210) 295–6334.

Eighth U.S. Army.—LTG Charles C. Campbell, APO AP 96205.

U.S. Army Pacific.—LTG John M. Brown III, Fort Shafter, Hawaii 96858–5100 (808) 438–2206.

U.S. Army Europe and 7th Army.—GEN B.B. Bell, APO AE 09014.

U.S. Army Space and Missile Defense Command.—LTG Larry J. Dodgen, 1901 South Bell Street, Suite 900, Arlington, VA 22202 (703) 607–1873.

DEPARTMENT OF THE NAVY

Pentagon 20350–1000, phone (703) 695–3131

OFFICE OF THE SECRETARY OF THE NAVY

Pentagon, Room 4E686, phone (703) 695–3131

Secretary of the Navy.—Gordon R. England.
  Confidential Assistant.—J. Drennan, 695–4884.
  Senior Military Assistant.—RADM Allen Myers, USN.
  Executive Assistant and Marine Aide.—COL Fred Hudson, USMC.
  Special Assistant for Business Initiatives.—SES4 Robert Earl, room 4E775, 693–0258.
  Administrative Aide.—CDR Lawrence Vasquez, USN, room 4E687, 695–5410.
  Personal Aide.—CAPT L. Krsulich, USMC.
  Special Assistant for—
    Administrative Matters.—Herman Raybon, Jr., room 4E687, 697–3334.
    Legislation.—CDR J. Hannink, room 4D730, 697–6935.
    Public Affairs.—CAPT K. Wensing, room 4D745, 697–7491.
  Director, Division of:
    Congressional Liaison Office.—YN1 K. Nixon, USN, room 4D514, 695–3834.
    Sensitive Correspondence.—YNC (SW) W. Ball, USN, room 4C729, 695–3800.

OFFICE OF THE UNDER SECRETARY OF THE NAVY

Pentagon, Room 4E576, phone (703) 695–3141

Under Secretary of the Navy.—Dionel M. Aviles.
  Executive Assistant and Naval Aide.—CAPT Terence McKnight, 695–9233.
  Confidential Assistant.—Jean C. Rowan, 695–2002.
  Military Assistant and Marine Aide.—COL John E. Mitchell, USMC.
  Assistant for Administration.—John H. LaRaia, room 4D572, 697–0047.
    Administration Assistant.—SSGT Michael G. Johnson.
  Facilities and Support Services Division.—B. O'Donnell, room 5B731, 614–4290.
  Director of:
    Financial Management.—D. Nugent, AA/2507, 693–0321.
    OPTI.—G. Wyckoff, room AA/4101, 695–6191.
    SADBU.—Paulette Widmann (acting) (202) 685–6485.
    SHHRO.—W. Mann, room AA/2510, 693–0888.
    Special Programs.—J. Moore, room AA/2517, 693–0933.
  EEO Manager.—R. McGee, room AA/2052, 693–0202.

GENERAL COUNSEL

Pentagon, Room 4E635

Washington Navy Yard, Bldg. 36, 720 Kennon Street, SE., Washington, DC 20374

phone (703) 614–1994

General Counsel.—Hon. A.J. Mora.
  Principal Deputy General Counsel.—F. Jimenez, 614–5066.
  Deputy General Counsel.—W. Molzahn.
  Executive Assistant and Special Counsel.—CAPT B. Bill, JAGC, USN.
  Associate General Counsel for—
    Litigation.—F. Phelps, WNY/36, 685–6989.
    Management.—A. Hildebrandt, room 4D644, 614–5066.
  Assistant General Counsel for—
    Ethics.—D. Grimord, room NC–1, 604–8211.
    Manpower and Reserve Affairs.—R. Cali, room 4D730, 614–5066.
    Research, Development and Acquisition.—S. Krasik, room 4C748, 614–6985.
  Military Assistant.—LTC D. Neesen, USMC, 614–5066.
  Administrative Assistant.—LT S. Wartell, USNR, room 4D644, 614–4472.

INSPECTOR GENERAL

1254 9th Street, SE, Bldg 172, Washington Navy Yard, DC 20374, phone (202) 433–2000

Inspector General.—VADM Ronald Route.
Deputy Naval Inspector General.—Jill Vines-Loftus.

LEGISLATIVE AFFAIRS

Room 4C549, phone (703) 697–7146, fax 697–1009

Chief.—RADM Barry Costello.
  Deputy Chief.—CAPT S.W. Gray.
  Executive Assistant.—LCDR Jim Kirk.
  Congressional Travel.—Paul B. Backe, room 5C765, 693–3764.
  Public Affairs and Congressional Notifications.—CDR Chris Dour, Sandra Latta, Virgil
    Smith, YN1 (SW/AW), 614–3710, Dan Vernon.
  Director for Senate Liaison.—CAPT Thomas Copeman III, room 182 (202) 685–6006.
  Assistant Director for Senate Liaison.—CAPT James C. Stein (202) 685–6007.
  Director for House Liaison.—CAPT Earl Gay, room B324 (202) 225–7808.
  Assistant Director for House Liaison.—CDR Andrew Wannamaker (202) 225–3075.
  Director for Naval Programs.—CAPT Stephen Honan, 693–2919.
  Director for Legislation.—CDR Jeff Horwitz, JAGC, 695–2776.

OFFICE OF INFORMATION

Pentagon, Room 4B463, phone (703) 697–7391

Chief.—RADM T. McCreary.
  Deputy Chief.—CAPT Bruce Cole.
  Executive Assistant.—CDR Lydia Robertson.
  Assistant Chief for—
    Administration and Resource Management.—William Mason (703) 692–4747.
    Media Operations.—CDR Conrad Chun (703) 697–5342.
    Naval Media Center.—CAPT Joseph Gradisher (202) 433–5764.
    Plans, Policy, and Community Programs.—CDR Anthony Cooper (703) 697–0250.
    Technology Integration.—Alan Goldstein (703) 695–1887.

JUDGE ADVOCATE GENERAL

Pentagon, Room 5D834

Washington Navy Yard, 1322 Patterson Avenue, Suite 3000, Washington, DC 20374–5066
phone (703) 697–4610

Judge Advocate General.—RADM James E. McPherson.
  Executive Assistant.—CAPT Christopher N. Morin (703) 614–7420.
  Deputy Judge Advocate General.—RADM Bruce E. MacDonald.
  Executive Assistant to the Deputy Judge Advocate General.—CDR Erin E. Stone (703)
    614–7420, fax 697–4610.
  Assistant Judge Advocate General for Civil Law.—CAPT Jane G. Dalton, WNY, Bldg.
    33 (202) 685–5190 fax 685–5461.
  Deputy Assistant Judge Advocate General for—
    Administrative Law.—CAPT Eric E. Geiser (703) 604–8200.
    Admiralty.—CDR Gregg Cervi (202) 685–5075.
    Claims, Investigations and Tort Litigation.—CAPT Paul M. Delaney (202) 685–5920,
      fax 685–5484.
    General Litigation.—CAPT Alex Whitaker (202) 685–5075, fax 685–5472.
    International and Operational Law.—Joe Baggett (acting) (703) 697–9161.
    Legal Assistance.—CDR Jeffrey Fischer, fax (202) 685–5486.
    National Security Litigation and Intelligence Law.—CDR George E. Reilly (202)
      685–5464, fax 685–5467.
  Assistant Judge Advocate General for Military Justice.—COL Kevin H. Winters, USMC,
    Building 111, 1st Floor, Washington Navy Yard, 20374–1111 (202) 685–7050,
    fax 685–7084.
    Deputy Assistant Judge Advocate General for Criminal Law.—CAPT Kenneth R. Bryant,
      USMC (202) 685–7060, fax 685–7687.

Assistant Judge Advocate General for Operations and Management.—CAPT James F. Duffy (202) 685–5190, fax 685–5461.
Deputy Assistant Judge Advocate General for—
　Management and Plans.—CDR Jon E. Nelson (202) 685–5218, fax 685–5479.
　Military Personnel.—CDR Ann M. Delaney (202) 685–5185, fax 685–5489.
　Reserve and Retired Personnel Programs.—CDR Ingrid Turner (202) 685–5216, fax 685–5489.
Special Assistants to the Judge Advocate General—
　Command Master Chief.—LNCM Stephen S. Distefano (202) 685–5194, fax 685–5461.
　Comptroller.—Dennis J. Oppman (202) 685–5274, fax 685–5455.
　Inspector General.—Joseph Scranton (202) 685–5192, fax 685–5461.

OFFICE OF THE ASSISTANT SECRETARY OF THE NAVY FOR MANPOWER AND RESERVE AFFAIRS

Pentagon, Room 4E615, phone (703) 697–2180

Assistant Secretary.—Hon. William A. Navas, Jr.
　Executive Assistant and Naval Aide.—LTC Marc Riccio, USMC, 695–4537.
　Military Assistant and Marine Aide.—LCDR Robert O'Neill, USN, 697–0975.
　Special Assistant for Military Law.—LCDR Robert O'Neill, USN, room 4C636, 695–4367.
　Administrative Assistant.—CAPT Terry Horton, USMC, 614–8288.
　Director of Personnel Readiness Community Support.—B. Tate, room 4C637, 614–3553.
　Deputy of:
　　Civilian Human Resources.—P. Adams, room 4D648, 695–2633.
　AGC.—R. Cali, room 4C648, 692–6162.
　　Manpower Analysis and Assessment.—R. Beland, room 4D648, 695–4350.
　　Military Manpower Personnel & Total Force Transformation.—A. Blair, room 4E611, 693–7700.
　　Reserve Affairs.—H. Barnum, room 4D648, 614–1327.
　Staff Directors: C. Donovan, room 4C648, 614–3053; CDR S. Hartsel, USN, room 4D648, 695–4356; CAPT Layne Smith, USN, room 4D648, 695–5302; CAPT R. Mohr, USN, room 4E611, 693–7715; M. Roberts, room 4D648, 695–2634; CAPT M. Thomas, USNRC, room 4D633, 693–0697.

NAVAL COUNCIL OF REVIEW BOARDS

Washington Navy Yard, 720 Kennon Street SE., Room 309, Washington, DC 20374–5023
phone (202) 685–6407, fax 685–6610

Director.—COL Marsha L. Culver, USMC.
Counsel.—Roger R. Claussen.
Special Correspondence Officer.—Frank A. Walker, Jr.
Physical Evaluation Board.—Paul D. Williamson.
Naval Clemency and Parole Board.—LTCOL David C. Francis, USMC.
Naval Discharge Review Board.—COL Thomas B. Galvin, USMC.

BOARD FOR CORRECTION OF NAVAL RECORDS

Arlington Annex Room 2432, Arlington, VA 20370–5100, phone (703) 614–9800
fax 614–9857

Executive Director.—W. Dean Pfeiffer.
Deputy Executive Director.—Robert D. Zsalman.
Administrative Officer.—Ev Sellers.

BOARD FOR DECORATIONS AND MEDALS

720 Kennon Street, SE., Building 36, room 135, Washington Navy Yard,
Washington, DC 20374, phone (202) 685–6378

Senior Member.—VADM Ronald Route.
Secretary to the Board.—LCDR Lesley Priest.

OFFICE OF THE ASSISTANT SECRETARY OF THE NAVY FOR RESEARCH, DEVELOPMENT AND ACQUISITION

Pentagon, Room 4E741, phone (703) 695–6315

Assistant Secretary.—Hon. J. Young, Jr, 4E589.
  Executive Assistant and Naval Aide.—CAPT James P. McManamon, USN.
  Military Assistant and Marine Aide.—COL Mark Savarese, USMC.
  Deputy Assistant Secretary of the Navy for—
    Acquisition Management.—RADM Martin Brown, USN, room BF999, 614–9445.
    Air Programs.—B. Balderson, room 5B549, 614–7794.
    C4I/Space Program.—Dr. Gary A. Federici, room BF963, 914–6619.
    Integrated Warfare Programs.—Anne Sandel, room 5B546, 614–8806.
    International Programs.—RADM Mark Milliken, Nebraska Avenue, Washington, DC (202) 764–2800.
    Littoral and Mine Warfare Programs.—Roger Smith, room 5B514, 614–4794.
    Logistics.—Nick Kunesh, room 5B546, 697–1799.
    Management and Budget.—CAPT Eric Wilson, USN (acting), room 5C547, 697–1091.
    RDT&E.—Dr. M. McGrath, room 5B546, 695–2204.
    Ship Programs.—Allison Stiller, room 5B546, 697–1710.
    Acquisition and Career Management.—C. Stelloh-Garner, room BF992, 614–0522.
    Manpower and Administration.—CAPT Eric Wilson, USN (acting) room 5C547, 697–1091.

ASSISTANT SECRETARY FOR FINANCIAL MANAGEMENT AND COMPTROLLER

Pentagon, Room 4E569, phone (703) 697–2325

Assistant Secretary.—Hon. R. Greco.
  Executive Assistant and Naval Aide.—CDR S. Strano, USN.
  Military Assistant and Marine Aide.—CAPT C. Ybarra, USMC.
  Director, Office of:
    Budget.—RADM B. Engelhart, USN, room 4E348, 697–7105.
    Financial Operations.—M. Easton, WNY, 685–6701.

ASSISTANT SECRETARY FOR INSTALLATIONS AND ENVIRONMENT

Pentagon, Room 4E523, phone (703) 693–4530

Assistant Secretary.—Hon. B.J. Penn.
  Executive Assistant and Naval Aide.—CAPT J. Heffernan, USN.
  Deputy of:
    Environment.—D. Schregardus, Pentagon, 614–5080.
    Infrastructure Analysis.—A. Davis, Crystal City, 602–6500.
    Installations and Facilities.—Wayne Arny, room 4D573, 693–4527.
    Safety.—C. DeWitte, Pentagon, 614–5179.
  Assistant General Counsel for Installations and Environment.—T. Ledvina, room BF986, 614–1097.
  Confidential Assistant.—Corry Robb.
  Special Assistant/Scheduler.—SSgt T. Robinson, room 4E523, 693–4527.

DEPARTMENT OF THE NAVY CHIEF INFORMATION OFFICER

Chief Information Officer.—D. Wennergren, room PT1/2100, 602–1800.
  Deputy CIO for Policy and Integration.—R. Carey.

CHIEF OF NAVAL OPERATIONS

Pentagon, Room 4E660, phone (703) 695–0532, fax 693–9408

Chief.—ADM V.E. Clark.
  Vice Chief.—ADM J.B. Nathman.
  Director, Naval Nuclear Propulsion Program.—ADM K.H. Donald.
  Special Assistant for—
    Inspection Support.—VADM R.A. Route.

Legal Services.—RADM J.E. McPherson.
Legislative Support.—RADM B.M. Costello.
Material Inspections and Surveys.—RADM C.A. Kemp.
Naval Investigative Matters and Security.—D. Brant.
Public Affairs Support.—RADM T.L. McCreary.
Safety Matters.—RADM R.E. Brooks.
Deputy Chief of Naval Operations for—
  Logistics.—VADM J.D. McCarthy.
  Manpower.—VADM G.L. Hoewing.
  Plans, Policy, and Operations.—VADM J.G. Morgan, Jr.
  Resources, Warfare Requirements, and Assessments.—VADM L.W. Crenshaw, Jr.
  Warfare Requirements and Programs.—VADM J.A. Sestak, Jr.
Director, Office of:
  Naval Intelligence.—RADM R.B. Porterfield.
  Naval Medicine and Surgery.—VADM D.C. Arthur, Jr.
  Naval Reserve.—VADM J.G. Cotton.
  Naval Training.—VADM J.K. Moran.
  Naval Network Warfare.—VADM J.D. McArthur, Jr.
  Test and Evaluation and Technology Requirements.—RADM J.M. Cohen.
Chief of Chaplains.—RADM L.V. Iasiello.
Oceanographer.—RADM S.J. Tomaszeski.

BUREAU OF MEDICINE AND SURGERY

2300 E Street, NW., Washington, DC 20372, phone (202) 762–3701
fax 762–3750

Chief.—VADM D.C. Arthur, MC, USN.

NAVAL AIR SYSTEMS COMMAND

47123 Buse Road, Building 2272, Patuxent River, MD 20670
phone (301) 757–1487

Commander.—VADM Wally Massenburg.

NAVAL SEA SYSTEMS COMMAND

1333 Isaac Hull Avenue, SE., Stop 1010, Washington Navy Yard, 20376–1010,
phone (202) 781–0100

Commander.—VADM Phillip M. Balisle.

NAVAL SUPPLY SYSTEMS COMMAND

Mechanicsburg, PA, phone (717) 605–3433

Commander.—RADM D.H. Stone.

NATIONAL NAVAL MEDICAL CENTER

Commander.—RADM Adam M. Robinson, Jr. (National Naval Medical Command), Bethesda,
MD 20889 (301) 295–5800/5802, fax 295–5336.

NAVAL FACILITIES ENGINEERING COMMAND

1322 Patterson Avenue, SE., Suite 1000, Washington Navy Yard, DC 20374
phone (202) 685–9003, fax 685–1463

Commander.—RADM Mike K. Loose.

OFFICE OF NAVAL INTELLIGENCE

4251 Suitland Road, Washington, DC 20395, phone (301) 669–3001, fax 669–3099

Commander.—CAPT Tony L. Cothron.

NAVAL CRIMINAL INVESTIGATIVE SERVICE COMMAND

716 Sicard Street SE, Suite 2000, Washington, DC 20388, phone (202) 433–8800, fax 433–9619

Director.—David L. Brant.

MILITARY SEALIFT COMMAND

Building No. 210, Washington Navy Yard, 9th and M Streets SE., Washington, DC 20398, phone (202) 685–5001, fax 685–5020

Commander.—VADM David L. Brewer.

NAVAL NETWORK AND SPACE OPERATIONS COMMAND

Building 1700, 5280 Fourth Street, Dahlgren, VA 22448, phone (540) 653–6100

Commander.—RADM Gerald R. Beaman.

SPACE AND NAVAL WARFARE SYSTEMS COMMAND

14675 Lee Road, Chantilly, VA 20151, phone (703) 808–3000
fax 808–2779

Commander.—RADM Victor C. See, Jr.

NAVAL DISTRICT OF WASHINGTON

1343 Dahlgren Avenue, SE., Washington, DC 20374–5001, phone 433–2777, fax 433–2207

Commandant.—RADM Jan Gaudio.
Deputy Commandant.—CAPT Albert Shimkus.

U.S. NAVAL ACADEMY

Annapolis, MD 21402, phone (410) 293–1000

Superintendent.—RADM Rodney P. Rempt, 293–1500.
Commandant of Midshipmen.—CAPT Joe Leidig, 293–7005.

U.S. MARINE CORPS HEADQUARTERS

Pentagon, Room 4E586, Washington, DC, phone (703) 614–2500

Commandant.—GEN M.W. Hagee.
 Assistant Commandant.—GEN W.L. Nyland.
 Aide-de-Camp.—LTC F.W. Simonds.
 Military Secretary.—COL J.C. Walker.
 Sergeant Major of the Marine Corps.—SMAJ J. Estrada.
 Legislative Assistant.—BG J.F. Kelly.
 Inspector General of the Marine Corps.—MG David Biu.
 Fiscal Director of the Marine Corps.—W.J. Wallhenhorst.
 Chaplain.—RADM R.F. Burt, USN.
 Dental Officer.—COL A. Williams, US Army.
 Judge Advocate.—BG K.M. Sandkuhler.

Medical Officer.—RADM (LH) R.D. Hufstader.
Deputy Chief of Staff for—
  Aviation.—LTG M.A. Hough.
  Installations and Logistics.—LTG R.L. Kelly.
  Manpower and Reserve Affairs.—LTG H.P. Osman.
  Plans, Policies, and Operations.—LTG J.C. Huly.
  Public Affairs.—BG M.A. Krusa-Dossin.
  Programs and Resources.—LTG R. Mangus (703) 614–3435.
Director of:
  Intelligence.—BG M.E. Ennis.
  Marine Corps History and Museums.—COL (Ret) J.W. Ripley.

MARINE BARRACKS

Eighth and I Streets SE., Washington DC 20390, phone (202) 433–4094

Commanding Officer.—COL T.M. Lockard.

TRAINING AND EDUCATION COMMAND

3300 Russell Road, Quantico, VA 22134, phone (703) 784–3730, fax 784–3724

Commanding General.—MG Thomas S. Jones.

DEPARTMENT OF JUSTICE

Main Justice Building

Robert F. Kennedy Department of Justice Building, 950 Pennsylvania Avenue, NW., Washington, DC 20530, phone (202) 514–2000
http://www.usdoj.gov

ALBERTO R. GONZALES, Attorney General, born in San Antonio, TX, August 4, 1955; education: Rice University, 1979; Harvard Law School, 1982; United States Air Force Academy, 1977; military service: U.S. Air Force, 1973–75; professional: partner with law firm of Vinson & Elkins L.L.P., 1982–94; taught law at University of Houston Law Center; President of the Houston Hispanic Bar Association, 1990–91; Texas General Counsel, 1994–97; Texas Secretary of State, 1997–99; Justice of the Texas Supreme Court, 1999–2001; Counsel to President George W. Bush, 2001–05; married: Rebecca Turner; children: Jared, Graham and Gabriel; nominated by George W. Bush to become the Attorney General of the United States on November 10, 2004, and was confirmed by the U.S. Senate on February 3, 2005.

OFFICE OF THE ATTORNEY GENERAL

Main Justice Building, Room 5111

Pennsylvania Avenue, NW., 20530, phone (202) 514–2001

Attorney General.—Alberto R. Gonzales.
    Chief of Staff.—Ted W. Ullyot, room 5115, 514–3892.
    Deputy Chief of Staff and Counselor.—Kyle Sampson, room 5112, 514–1061.
    Senior Counselor to the Attorney General.—Raul Yanes, room 5110, 514–2291.
    Counselors to the Attorney General: Courtney Elwood, room 5123, 514–2267; Jeff Taylor, room 5116, 514–2107.
    Director of Scheduling and Advance.—Andrew A. Beach, room 5131, 514–4195.
    Deputy White House Liaison.—John Eddy, room 5224, 616–7740.
    Confidential Assistant to the Attorney General.—Carrie Nelson, room 5111, 514–2001.

OFFICE OF THE DEPUTY ATTORNEY GENERAL

Main Justice Building, Room 4111, phone (202) 514–2101

Deputy Attorney General.—James Comey.
    Chief of Staff.—Chuck Rosenberg, room 4206, 514–2269.
    Associate Deputy Attorneys General: John Davis, room 4119, 514–0049; Uttam Dhillon, room 4214, 514–6753; David Margolis, room 4113, 514–4945; Catherine O'Neil, room 4212, 307–2090; Patrick Philbin, room 4222, 514–3744.
    Senior Counsels to the Deputy Attorney General: Chad Boudreaux, room 4116, 514–8086; Timothy J. Coleman, room 4121, 514–0020; Francesco Isgro, room 4112, 353–1957; James McAtamney, room 4311, 514–6907; Patrick O'Brien, room 4115, 305–3481; Stuart Nash, room 4131, 514–8694; Robert Tronto, room 4129, 514–8500.
    Counsels to the Deputy Attorney General: Dawn Burton, room 4210, 305–0091; Wendell Taylor, room 4220.
    Special Assistants to the Deputy Attorney General: Blair Birkeland, room 4215, 353–8878; James Rybicki, room 4216, 514–0438.
    Confidential Assistant to the Deputy Attorney General.—Linda Long, room 4111, 514–1904.
    Director, Faith Based and Community Initiatives Task Force.—Patrick Purtill, room 4409, 305–8283.
    Chief Science Advisor.—Vahid Majidi, room 4217, 305–7848.

OFFICE OF THE ASSOCIATE ATTORNEY GENERAL

Robert F. Kennedy Department of Justice Building, Room 5706, phone (202) 514–9500

Associate Attorney General.—Robert D. McCallum, Jr., room 5706, 514–9500.
    Principal Deputy Associate Attorney General.—Brian D. Boyle, room 5708, 305–1434.
    Deputy Associate Attorneys General: Elizabeth Kessler, room 5722; Mike Wiggins, room 5724.

Counsels to the Associate Attorney General: Luis Reyes, room 5732; Jeffrey Senger, room 5726.
Confidential Assistant.—Currie Gunn, room 5706, 514–9500.

OFFICE OF DISPUTE RESOLUTION

Director/Senior Counsel.—Linda Cinciotta, room 5734, 514–8910.

OFFICE OF THE SOLICITOR GENERAL
Main Justice Building, Room 5143, phone (202) 514–2201
www.usdjoj.gov.osg

Solicitor General.—Paul D. Clement (acting), 514–2206.
  Deputy Solicitors General: Edwin S. Kneedler, room 5137, 514–3261; Michael R. Dreeben, room 5623, 514–4285; Thomas G. Hungar, room 5137, 514–2211.
  Tax Assistant.—Malcolm Stewart, room 5633, 514–4218.
  Executive Officer.—Robert J. Faurot, room 5142, 514–5507.
  Executive Assistant.—Janet Potter, 514–2399.
  Legal Administrative Officer, Case Management Section.—Emily C. Spadoni, room 5614, 514–2218.
  Chief, Research and Publications Section.—G. Shirley Anderson, room 6636, 514–3914.

OFFICE OF THE INSPECTOR GENERAL
Robert F. Kennedy Department of Justice Building, Room 4322, 950 Pennsylvania Avenue, NW., 20530 phone (202) 514–3435
1425 New York Avenue, NW., 20530

Inspector General.—Glenn A. Fine.
  Deputy Inspector General.—Paul K. Martin.
  Counselor to the Inspector General.—Paul K. Martin.
  Special Counsel.—Scott S. Dahl.
  General Counsel.—Howard L. Sribnick (NYAV), Suite 6000, 616–0646.
  Assistant Inspectors General:
    Audit.—Guy K. Zimmerman (NYAV), Suite 5000, 616–4633.
    Evaluation and Inspections.—Paul A. Price (NYAV), Suite 6100, 616–4620.
    Investigations.—Thomas F. McLaughlin (NYAV), Suite 7100, 616–4760.
    Management and Planning.—Gregory T. Peters (NYAV), Suite 7000, 616–4550.
    Oversight and Review.—Carol F. Ochoa (RFK), Room 4722, 616–0645.

OFFICE OF OVERSIGHT AND REVIEW

Director.—Carol F. Ochoa, room 4726, 616–0645.

REGIONAL AUDIT OFFICES

Washington: Troy M. Meyer, 1300 N. 17th Street, Suite 3400, Arlington, VA 22209 (202) 616–4686.
  Computer Security and Information Technology Audit Office: Norman Hammonds, room 5000 (202) 616–3801.
  Financial Statement Audit Office: Marilyn A. Kessinger, 1110 Vermont Avenue, NW., 8th Floor, Washington, DC 20530 (202) 616–4660.
Atlanta: Ferris B. Polk, Suite 1130, 75 Spring Street, Atlanta, GA 30303 (404) 331–5928.
Chicago: Carol S. Taraszka, Suite 3510, Citicorp Center, 500 West Madison Street, Chicago, IL 60661 (312) 353–1203.
Dallas: Robert J. Kaufman, Room 575, Box 4, 207 South Houston Street, Dallas, TX 75202–4724 (214) 655–5000.
Denver: David M. Sheeren, Suite 1603, Chancery Building, 1120 Lincoln Street, Denver, CO 80203 (303) 864–2000.
Philadelphia: Richard A. McGeary, Suite 201, 701 Market Street, Philadelphia, PA 19106 (215) 580–2111.
San Francisco: David J. Gaschke, Suite 201, 1200 Bayhill Drive, San Bruno, CA 94066 (650) 876–9220.

REGIONAL INVESTIGATIONS OFFICES

Atlanta: Eddie D. Davis, 60 Forsyth Street, SW., Room 8M45, Atlanta, GA 30303 (404) 562–1980.
Boston: Thomas M. Hopkins, P.O. Box 2134, Boston, MA 02106 (617) 748–3218.
Chicago: Edward M. Dyner, P.O. Box 1802, Chicago, IL 60690 (312) 886–7050.
Colorado Springs: Craig Trautner, Suite 312, 111 S. Tejon Street, Colorado Springs, CO 80903 (719) 635–2366.
Dallas: James H. Mahon, Suite 551, Box 5, 207 S. Houston Street, Dallas, TX 75202 (214) 655–5076.
Detroit: Nicholas V. Candela, Suite 2001, 211 West Fort Street, Detroit, MI 48226 (313) 226–4005.
El Paso: Stephen P. Beauchamp, Suite 200, 4050 Rio Bravo, El Paso, TX 79902 (915) 577–0102.
Houston: Fred C. Ball, Jr., P.O. Box 610071, Houston, TX 77208 (713) 718–4888.
Los Angeles: Steve F. Turchek, Suite 655, 330 N. Brand Street, Glendale, CA 91203 (818) 543–1172.
McAllen: Wayne D. Beaman, Suite 510, Bentsen Tower, 1701 W. Business Highway 83, McAllen, TX 78501 (956) 618–8145.
Miami: Alan J. Hazen, Suite 312, 3800 Inverrary Boulevard, Ft. Lauderdale, FL 33319 (954) 535–2859.
New York: Ralph F. Paige, JFK Airport, P.O. Box 300999, Jamaica, NY 11430 (718) 553–7520.
Philadelphia: Kenneth R. Connaughton, Jr., P.O. Box 43508, Philadelphia, PA 19106 (215) 861–8755.
San Francisco: Norman K. Lau, Suite 220, 1200 Bayhill Drive, San Bruno, CA 94066 (650) 876–9058.
Seattle: Wayne Hawney, Suite 104, 620 Kirkland Way, Kirkland, WA 98033 (425) 828–3998.
Tucson: William L. King, Jr., P.O. Box 471, Tucson, AZ 85702 (520) 670–5243.
Washington: Charles T. Huggins, 1425 New York Avenue, NW., Suite 7100, Washington, DC 20530 (202) 616–4766.
Fraud Detection Office.—David R. Glendinning, room 7100 (202) 616–4766.

OFFICE OF LEGAL COUNSEL

Main Justice Building, Room 5218, phone (202) 514–2051

Principal Deputy Assistant Attorney General.—Steven G. Bradbury, 514–2046.
Deputy Assistant Attorney General—.Howard C. Nielson, Jr., room 5238, 514–2069.
Special Counsels: Paul P. Colborn, room 5240, 514–2048; Daniel L. Koffsky, room 5268, 514–2030.
Senior Counsel.—Rosemary A. Hart, room 5242, 514–2027.
Chief of Staff.—Frits H. Geurtsen, room 5245, 305–9250.

OFFICE OF LEGAL POLICY

Main Justice Building, Room 4234, phone (202) 514–4601

Assistant Attorney General.—Daniel J. Bryant (acting).
Principal Deputy Assistant Attorney General.—Rachel Brand, room 4238, 616–0038.
Deputy Assistant Attorneys General: Richard Hertling, room 4226, 514–9114; Kevin Jones, room 4250, 514–4604; Kristi Remington, room 4237, 514–8356; Frank Campbell, room 4245, 514–2283.
Staff Director/Senior Counsel.—Erin Nealy Cox, room 4228, 305–0180.

OFFICE OF PUBLIC AFFAIRS

Main Justice Building, Room 1220, phone (202) 514–2007

Director.—Tasia Scolinos.
Deputy Directors: Kevin Madden, Gina M. Talamona.
Senior Counsel.—John A. Nowacki.

OFFICE OF INFORMATION AND PRIVACY

Flag Building, Suite 570, phone (202) 514-3642

Co-Directors: Richard L. Huff and Daniel J. Metcalfe.
*Deputy Director.—*Melanie Ann Pustay.
*Associate Director.—*Kirsten J. Moncada.
*Senior Counsel.—*Janice G. McLeod.
*Chief, Initial Request Staff.—*Carmen L. Mallon.
*Counsel, Initial Request Staff.—*Tricia S. Wellman.

OFFICE OF INTELLIGENCE POLICY AND REVIEW

Robert F. Kennedy Building, Room 6150, phone (202) 514-5600

*Counsel.—*James A. Baker.
Deputy Counsels: Margaret A. Skelly-Nolen, Mark A. Bradley.
*Chief of Staff.—*Sheryl Walter.

OFFICE OF PROFESSIONAL RESPONSIBILITY

Robert F. Kennedy Department of Justice Building, 950 Pennsylvania Avenue, NW., room 3266, phone (202) 514-3365

*Counsel.—*H. Marshall Jarrett.
*Deputy Counsel.—*Judith B. Wish.
Associate Counsels: William J. Birney, Paul L. Colby, James G. Duncan, Mary Anne Hoopes.
Senior Assistant Counsels: Neil C. Hurley, Alexander S. White.
Assistant Counsels: Kathleen Brandon, Mark G. Fraase, Lisa Griffin, Lyn A. Hardy, Tamara J. Kessler, Frederick C. Leiner, James Meade, Margaret S. McCarty, Simone E. Ross, Robert Thomson, Marlene M. Wahowiak, Barbara L. Ward, Karen A. Wehner.

PROFESSIONAL RESPONSIBILITY ADVISORY OFFICE

1325 Pennsylvania Avenue, National Theater Building, Suite 500, phone (202) 514-0458

*Director.—*Claudia J. Flynn.
*Senior Advisor.—*Barbara Kammerman.

OFFICE OF LEGISLATIVE AFFAIRS

Main Justice Building, Room 1145, phone (202) 514-2141

*Assistant Attorney General.—*William E. Moschella.
*Special Counsel to the Assistant Attorney General.—*M. Faith Burton.
Deputy Assistant Attorney Generals: Crystal Roberts, Rebecca Seidel.

OFFICE OF INTERGOVERNMENTAL AND PUBLIC LIAISON

Main Justice Building, Room 1629, phone (202) 514-3465

*Director.—*Greg Harris (acting).
Associate Directors: Denise Gitsham, Ebony Lee, Lindsey de la Torre.

OFFICE OF THE FEDERAL DETENTION TRUSTEE

1331 Pennsylvania Avenue, National Place Building, Suite 1210, phone (202) 353-4601

*Trustee.—*Stacia A. Hylton.
*Deputy Trustee.—*David Musel.

JUSTICE MANAGEMENT DIVISION

**Robert F. Kennedy Department of Justice Building,
950 Pennsylvania Avenue, NW., 20530**

Rockville Building (ROC), 1151–D Seven Locks Road, Rockville, MD 20854

Bicentennial Building (BICN), 600 E Street NW., 20004

National Place Building (NPB), 1331 Pennsylvania Avenue, NW., 20530

Liberty Place Building (LPB), 325 7th Street NW., 20530

20 Massachusetts Avenue, NW., 20530

Patrick Henry Building (PHB), 601 D Street NW., 20530

Assistant Attorney General/Administration.—Paul R. Corts, room 1111, 514–3101.
   Deputy Assistant Attorney General/Policy, Management and Planning.—Michael H. Allen, room 1111, 514–3101.
   Staff Directors for—
      Department Ethics Office.—Keith Simmons (acting), 1331 F Street, 514–8196.
      Management and Planning.—David Orr (NPB), room 1400, 307–1800.
      Audit Liaison Group.—Richard Theis (acting), 1331 F Street, 514–0469.
      Office of General Counsel.—Stuart Frisch, General Counsel (NPB), room 520, 514–3452.
      Security and Emergency Planning.—James Dunlap, room 6217, 514–2094.
      Procurement Executive.—Michael H. Allen, room 1111, 514–3101.
      Office of Small and Disadvantaged Business Utilization.—David Sutton (NPB), room 1010, 616–0521.
   Deputy Assistant Attorney General/Controller.—Leon J. Lofthaus, room 1112, 514–1843.
   Staff Directors for—
      Budget.—Jolene Laurie Sullens, room 7601, 514–4082.
      Finance.—Melinda Morgan (BICN), room 4070, 616–5800.
      Procurement Services.—James Johnston (NPB), room 1000, 307–2000.
      Asset Forfeiture Management Staff.—Michael Perez, room 6400, 20 Massachusetts Avenue, 616–8000.
      Debt Collection Management.—Kathleen Haggerty (Liberty Place), 2nd Floor, 514–5343.
   Deputy Assistant Attorney General, Human Resources/Administration.—Blaine Dessy (acting), room 1112, 514–5501.
   Associate Assistant Attorney General for Federal Law Enforcement Training.—Thomas G. Milburn, Glynco, GA 31524 (912) 267–2914.
   Staff Directors for—
      Facilities and Administrative Services.—Ronald Deacon, (NPB), room 1050, 616–2995.
      Library.—Blaine Dessy, room 7535, 514–2133.
      Personnel.—Debra Tomchek (NPB), room 1110, 514–6788.
      Equal Employment Opportunity.—Ted McBurrows, 620 VT2, 616–4800.
      Office of Attorney Recruitment and Management.—Louis DeFalaise, Suite 5200, 20 Massachusetts Avenue, 514–8900.
      Consolidated Executive Office.—Cyntoria Carter, room 7113, 514–5537.
      DOJ Executive Secretariat.—Dana Paige, room 4412, 514–2063.
   Deputy Assistant Attorney General/Information Resources Management and CIO.—Vance Hitch, room 1310–A, 514–0507.
   Staff Directors for—
      E-Government Services.—Mike Duffy, room 1314, 514–0507.
      Policy and Planning.—Justin Lindsey, room 1310, 514–4292.
      Enterprise Solutions.—John Murray (PHB), room 4606, 514–0507.
      IT Security.—Dennis Heretick (PHB), room 1600, 514–0507.
      Operation Services.—Roger Beasley (acting), room 1315, 514–3404.

ANTITRUST DIVISION

Robert F. Kennedy Department of Justice Building,
950 Pennsylvania Avenue NW., 20530

City Center Building, 1401 H Street NW., 20530 (CCB)

Bicentennial Building, 600 E Street NW., 20530 (BICN)

Liberty Place Building, 325 Seventh Street NW., 20530 (LPB)

Patrick Henry Building, 601 D Street NW., 20530 (PHB)

Assistant Attorney General.—R. Hewitt Pate, room 3109, 514–2401.
Deputy Assistant Attorneys General: Thomas O. Barnett, room 3117, 514–0731; Makan Delrahim, room 3121, 305–4517; Scott M. Hammond, room 3214, 514–3543; J. Bruce McDonald, room 3210, 514–1157.
Director of:
    Criminal Enforcement.—Marc Siegel, room 3217, 514–3543.
    Economics Enforcement.—Kenneth Heyer, room 3112, 514–6995.
    Operations.—Robert J. Kramer, room 3118, 514–3544.
Freedom of Information Act Officer.—Ann Lea Harding (LPB), room 200, 514–2692.
Executive Officer.—Thomas D. King (PHB), room 10150, 514–4005.
Section Chiefs:
    Appellate.—Catherine G. O'Sullivan (PHB), room 3222, 514–2413.
    Competition Policy.—Robert Majure (acting), (BICN), room 10900, 307–6341.
    Economic Litigation.—Norman Familant (BICN), room 10800, 307–6323.
    Economic Regulatory.—George A. Rozanski (BICN), room 10100, 307–6591.
    Foreign Commerce.—Edward T. Hand, room 3623, 514–2464.
    Legal Policy.—Robert A. Potter, room 3236, 514–2512.
    Litigation I.—Mark J. Botti (CCB), room 4000, 307–0827.
    Litigation II.—Maribeth Petrizzi (CCB), room 3000, 307–0924.
    Litigation III.—John R. Read (LPB), room 300, 616–5935.
    National Criminal Enforcement.—Lisa M. Phelan (CCB), room 3700, 307–6694.
    Networks and Technology.—Renata B. Hesse (BICN), room 9300, 514–5634.
    Telecommunications and Media.—Nancy M. Goodman (CCB), room 8000, 514–5621.
    Transportation, Energy, and Agriculture.—Roger W. Fones (LPB), room 500, 307–6351.

FIELD OFFICES

California: Phillip H. Warren, 450 Golden Gate Avenue, Room 10–0101, Box 36046, San Francisco, CA 94102 (415) 436–6660.
Georgia: Nezida S. Davis, Richard B. Russell Building, 75 Spring Street SW., Suite 1176, Atlanta, GA 30303 (404) 331–7100.
Illinois: Marvin N. Price Jr., Rookery Building, 209 South LaSalle Street, Suite 600, Chicago, IL 60604 (312) 353–7530.
New York: Ralph T. Giordano, 26 Federal Plaza, Room 3630, New York, NY 10278 (212) 264–0391.
Ohio: Scott M. Watson, Plaza 9 Building, 55 Erieview Plaza, Suite 700, Cleveland, OH 44114 (216) 522–4070.
Pennsylvania: Robert E. Connolly, Curtis Center, One Independence Square West, 7th and Walnut Streets, Suite 650, Philadelphia, PA 19106 (215) 597–7405.
Texas: Duncan S. Currie, Thanksgiving Tower, 1601 Elm Street, Suite 4950, Dallas, TX 75201 (214) 880–9401.

CIVIL DIVISION

Robert K. Kennedy Department of Justice Building, 950 Pennsylvania Avenue, NW.,
20530, (202) 514–3301 (MAIN)

20 Massachusetts Avenue, NW., 20530 (20MASS)

1100 L Street NW., 20530 (L ST)

National Place Building, 1331 Pennsylvania Avenue NW., 20530 (NATP)

1425 New York Avenue NW., 20530 (NYAV)

Patrick Henry Building, 601 D Street NW., 20530 (PHB)

Assistant Attorney General.—Peter D. Keisler (MAIN), room 3141, 514–3301.
Principal Deputy Assistant Attorney General.—Daniel Meron (MAIN), room 3605, 353–2793.

FEDERAL PROGRAMS BRANCH

Deputy Assistant Attorney General.—Carl J. Nichols (MAIN), room 3137, 514–3310.
  Directors: Felix Baxter (20MASS), room 7100, 514–4651; Joseph H. Hunt, room 7348,
    514–1259; Jennifer D. Rivera (20MASS), room 6100, 514–3671.
  Deputy Directors: Vincent M. Garvey (20MASS), room 7346, 514–3449; Sheila M.
    Lieber (20MASS), room 7102, 514–3786.

COMMERCIAL LITIGATION BRANCH

Deputy Assistant Attorney General.—Stuart E. Schiffer (MAIN), room 3607, 514–3306.
  Directors: David M. Cohen, L Street, room 12124, 514–7300; John N. Fargo, L Street,
    room 11116, 514–7223; Michael F. Hertz (PHB), room 9902, 514–7179; J. Christopher
    Kohn, L Street, room 10036, 514–7450.
  Office of Foreign Litigation.—Robert Hollis, L Street, room 11006, 514–7455.
    Deputy Directors: Joyce R. Branda (PHB), room 9904, 307–0231; Jeanne Davidson,
      L Street, room 12132, 307–0290; James M. Kinsella, L Street, room 12008,
      307–1011; Sandra P. Spooner, L Street, room 10052, 514–7194.
    Legal Officer.—Donna C. Maizel, Esq., U.S. Department of Justice, Civil Division Euro-
      pean Office, The American Embassy, London, England, PSC 801, Box 42, FPO AE,
      09498–4042, 9+011–44–20–7894–0840.
    Attorney-in-Charge.—Barbara Williams, Suite 359, 26 Federal Plaza, New York, NY
      10278 (212) 264–9240.

TORTS BRANCH

Deputy Assistant Attorney General.—Jeffrey S. Bucholtz (MAIN), room 3127, 514–3045.
  Directors: Gary W. Allen (NYAV), room 10122, 616–4000; Sharon Y. Eubanks (NATP),
    room 1150–02, 616–8280; Timothy P. Garren (NYAV), room 8122, 616–4171; J.
    Patrick Glynn (NATP), room 8028S, 616–4200; Phyllis J. Pyles (NATP), room 8098N,
    616–4252;
  Deputy Directors: JoAnn J. Bordeaux (NATP), room 8024S, 616–4204; Paul F. Figley
    (NATP), room 8096N, 616–4248; Stephen D. Brody (NATP), room 1150–04,
    616–1437.
  Attorneys-in-Charge: Philip A. Berns, 450 Golden Gate Avenue, 10/6610, Box 36028,
    San Francisco, CA 94102–3463, FTS: (415) 436–6630; [Vacant], Suite 320, 26 Federal
    Plaza, New York, NY 10278–0140, FTS: (212) 264–0480.

APPELLATE STAFF

Deputy Assistant Attorney General.—Gregory G. Katsas (MAIN), room 3135, 514–4015.
  Director.—Robert E. Kopp (MAIN), room 7519, 514–3311.
  Deputy Director.—William Kanter (MAIN), room 7517, 514–4575.

CONSUMER LITIGATION

Deputy Assistant Attorney General.—Jeffrey S. Bucholtz (MAIN), room 3127, 514–3045.
  Director.—Eugene M. Thirolf (NATP), room 950N, 307–3009.
  Deputy Director.—Lawrence G. McDade (NATP), room 950N, 307–0138.

IMMIGRATION LITIGATION

Deputy Assistant Attorney General.—Jonathan F. Cohn (MAIN), room 3131, 514–1258.
  Director.—Thomas W. Hussey (NATP), room 7026S, 616–4852.
  Deputy Directors: Donald E. Keener (NATP), room 7022S, 616–4878; David J. Kline
    (NATP), room 7006N, 616–4856; David M. McConnell (NATP), room 7260N,
    616–4881.

MANAGEMENT PROGRAMS

Director.—Kenneth L. Zwick (MAIN), room 3140, 514–4552.
  Directors, Office of:
    Administration.—Shirley Lloyd, L Street, room 9008, 307–0016.
    Planning, Budget, and Evaluation.—Linda S. Liner, L Street, room 9042, 307–0034.

Management Information.—Dorothy Bahr, L Street, room 8044, 616–8026.
Litigation Support.—Clarisse Abramidis, L Street, room 9126, 616–5014.
Policy and Management Operations.—Kevin Burket, L Street, room 8128, 616–8073.

CIVIL RIGHTS DIVISION

Main Justice Building, Room 5623 (202) 514–2151 (MAIN)

1425 New York Avenue, NW., 20035 (NYAV)

601 D Street, NW., 20004 (PHB)

100 Indiana Avenue, NW., 20004 (NALC)

1800 G Street, NW., 20004 (NWB)

www.usdoj.gov/crt

Assistant Attorney General.—R. Alexander Acosta, room 5623, 514–2151.
　Principal Deputy Assistant Attorney General.—Sheldon Bradshaw, room 5748, 514–2151.
　Deputy Assistant Attorneys General: Loretta King, room 5744, 616–1278; Brad Schlozman, room 5541, 305–8060; Wan Kim, room 5740, 353–0742.
　Counsels to the Assistant Attorney General for Civil Rights: Cynthia McKnight, room 5535, 305–0864; Hans von Spakovsky, room 5539, 305–9750.
　Executive Officer.—DeDe Greene (NYAV), room 5058, 514–4224.
　Section Chiefs:
　　Appellate.—David K. Flynn (MAIN), room 3647, 514–2195.
　　Coordination and Review.—Merrily A. Friedlander (NYAV), room 6001, 307–2222.
　　Criminal.—Albert N. Moskowitz (PHB), room 5802, 514–3204.
　　Disability Rights.—John L. Wodatch (NYAV), room 4055, 307–2227.
　　Educational Opportunities.—Jeremiah Glassman (PHB), room 4002, 514–4092.
　　Employment Litigation.—David Palmer (PHB), room 4040, 514–3831.
　　Housing and Civil Enforcement.—Steven H. Rosenbaum (NWB), room 7002, 514–4713.
　　Special Counsel for Immigration Related Unfair Employment Practices.—William Sanchez (MAIN), room 9032, 616–5528.
　　Special Litigation.—Shanetta Brown Cutler (acting) (PHB), room 5114, 514–6255.
　　Voting.—Joseph D. Rich (NWB), room 7254, 307–2767.

CRIMINAL DIVISION

Robert F. Kennedy Department of Justice Building, 950 Pennsylvania Avenue, NW., 20530 Room 2107 (202) 514–2601 (RFK)

Bond Building, 1400 New York Avenue NW., 20530 (BB)

1331 F Street NW. (F Street)

1301 New York Avenue, NW., 20530 (1301 NY)

Patrick Henry Building, 601 D Street, NW. (PHB)

Assistant Attorney General.—Christopher A. Wray, room 2107, 514–7200.
　Principal Deputy Assistant Attorney General.—John C. Keeney, room 2109, 514–2621.
　Deputy Assistant Attorneys General: Joseph Bianco, room 2212, 616–5777; Laura Parksy, room 2113, 616–3928; Bruce C. Swartz, room 2119, 514–2333; Mary Lee Warren, room 2115, 514–3729.
　Chief of Staff to the Assistant Attorney General.—John C. Richter, room 2100, 353–3600.
　Deputy Chief of Staff to the Assistant Attorney General.—Rena J. Comisac, room 2208, 353–9065.
　Counselor to the Assistant Attorney General.—Deborah J. Rhodes, room 2218, 514–9351.
　Senior Counsels to the Assistant Attorney General: James S. Reynolds, room 2313, 616–8664; Richard M. Rogers, room 2110, 307–0030; Bruce A. Taylor, room 2311, 514–2535.
　Counsels to the Assistant Attorney General: Robert K. Hur, Monique Perez Roth, J. Patrick Rowan.
　Special Assistant to the Assistant Attorney General.—Bryan Sierra, room 2228, 515–4389.
　Executive Officer.—Steve J. Parent (BB), room 5100, 514–2641.
　Section Chiefs/Office Directors:
　　Appellate.—Patty M. Stemler (PHB), room 2606, 514–3521.
　　Asset Forfeiture and Money Laundering.—Joseph Lester (acting), (BB), room 10100, 514–1263.

Capital Case Unit.—Margaret P. Griffey (PHB), room 6140, 353–9779.
Child Exploitation and Obscenity.—Andrew G. Oosterbaan (BB), room 6000, 514–5780.
Computer Crime and Intellectual Property.—Martha Stansell-Gramm (1301 NY), suite 600, 514–1026.
Counterespionage.—John Dion (BB), room 9100, 514–1187.
Counterterrorism.—Barry Sabin (PHB), room 6500, 514–5000.
Domestic Security.—Teresa McHenry (acting) (1301 NY), suite 6500, 514–0849.
Enforcement Operations.—Maureen Killion (1301 NY), suite 1200, 514–6809.
Fraud.—Joshua R. Hochberg (BB), room 4100, 514–7023.
International Affairs.—Mary Ellen Warlow (1301 NY), suite 900, 514–0000.
International Criminal Investigative Training Assistance Program.—Joseph Jones (acting) (1331 F Street), suite 500, 514–8881.
Narcotics and Dangerous Drugs.—Michael Walther (acting), (BB), room 11100, 514–0917.
Overseas Prosecutorial Development, Assistance and Training.—Carl Alexandre (1331 F Street), room 400, 514–1323.
Organized Crime and Racketeering.—Bruce Ohr (1301 NY), suite 700, 514–3594.
Policy and Legislation: Julie E. Samuels (1301 NY), suite 1000.
Public Integrity.—Noel Hillman (BB), room 12000, 514–1412.
Special Investigations.—Eli M. Rosenbaum (1301 NY), suite 200, 616–2492.

ENVIRONMENT AND NATURAL RESOURCES DIVISION
Main Justice Building, Room 2143 (202) 514–2701 (MAIN)
601 Pennsylvania Avenue, 20044 (PENN)
1425 New York Avenue NW., 20530 (NYAV)
501 D Street (PHB)

Assistant Attorney General.—Thomas L. Sansonetti (MAIN), room 2143, 514–2701.
Principal Deputy Assistant Attorney General.—Kelly A. Johnson (MAIN), room 2141, 514–4760.
Deputy Assistant Attorneys General: Jeffrey Bossert Clark (MAIN), room 2607, 514–3370; John Cruden (MAIN), room 2611, 514–2718; Eileen Sobeck (MAIN), room 2135, 514–0943.
Counsels to the Assistant Attorney General: Andrew C. Emrich (MAIN), room 2607, 514–0624; Mary Neumayr (MAIN), room 2129, 514–0624.
Executive Officer.—Robert L. Bruffy (PHB), room 2038, 616–3147.
Section Chiefs:
  Appellate.—James C. Kilbourne (PHB), room 8046, 514–2748.
  Environmental Crimes.—David M. Uhlmann (PHB), room 2102, 305–0337.
  Environmental Defense.—Letitia J. Grishaw (PHB), room 8002, 514–2219.
  Environmental Enforcement.—Bruce Gelber (NYAV), room 13063, 514–4624.
  General Litigation.—K. Jack Haugrud (PHB), room 3102, 305–0438.
  Indian Resources.—Craig Alexander (PHB), room 3016, 514–9080.
  Land Acquisition.—Virginia P. Butler (PHB), room 3638, 305–0316.
  Policy, Legislation, and Special Litigation.—Pauline M. Milius (PHB), room 8022, 514–2586.
  Wildlife and Marine Resources.—Jean E. Williams (PHB), room 3902, 305–0210.

FIELD OFFICES
801 B Street, Suite 504, Anchorage, AK 99501–3657

Trial Attorneys: Regina Belt (907) 271–3456; Dean Dunsmore (907) 271–5457; Bruce Landon (907) 271–5948.

999 18th Street, Suite 945, North Tower, Denver, CO 80202

Trial Attorneys: David Askman (303) 312–7247; Bruce Bernard (303) 312–7319; Bradley Bridgewater (303) 312–7318; Dave Carson (303) 312–7309; Jerry Ellington (303) 312–7321; Robert Foster (303) 312–7320; Jim Freeman (303) 312–7376; Dave Gehlert (303) 312–7352; Mike Gheleta (303) 312–7303; Alan Greenberg (303) 312–7324; David

Harder (303) 312–7328; Robert Homiak (303) 312–7353; Heidi Kukis (303) 312–7354; Lee Leininger (303) 312–7322; John Moscato (303) 312–7346; Mark Nitcynski (303) 312–7388; Terry Petrie (303) 312–7327; Daniel Pinkston (303) 312–7397; Susan Schneider (303) 312–7308; Andrew Smith (303) 312–7326; Andrew Walch (303) 312–7316.

Administrative Officer.—David Jones (303) 312–7387.

501 I Street, Suite 9–700, Sacramento, CA 95814–2322

Trial Attorneys: Maria Iizuka (916) 930–2202; Stephen Macfarlane (916) 930–2204; Charles Shockey (916) 930–2203.

301 Howard Street, Suite 1050, San Francisco, CA 94105–2001

Trial Attorneys: Matt Fogelson (415) 744–6470; David Glazer (415) 744–6477; Herb Johnson (415) 436–7159; Robert Mullaney (415) 744–6483; Bradley O'Brien (415) 744–6484; Angela O'Connell (415) 744–6485; Thomas Pacheco (415) 744–6480; Judith Rabinowitz (415) 744–6486; Mark Rigau (415) 744–6487; Noel Wise (415) 744–6471.

c/o NOAA/DARCNW, 7600 San Point Way NE, Seattle, WA 98115–0070

Trial Attorneys: Sean Carman (206) 526–6617; James Nicoli (206) 526–6616; David Spohr (206) 526–4603; Mike Zevenbergen (206) 526–6607.

One Gateway Center, Suite 6116, Newton Corner, MA 02158

Trial Attorneys: Catherine Fiske (617) 450–0444; Donald Frankel (617) 450–0442.

c/o U.S. Attorney's Office, 555 Pleasant Street, Suite 352, Concord, NH 03301

Trial Attorney.— Kristine Tardiff (603) 225–1562, ext. 283.

c/o U.S. Attorney's Office, 201 Third Street, NW., Suite 900, Albuquerque, NM 87102

Trial Attorney.—Andrew Smith (505) 224–1468.

161 East Mallard Drive, Suite A, Boise, ID 83706

Trial Attorney.—David Negri (208) 331–5943.

c/o U.S. Attorney's Office, 105 E. Pine Street, 2nd Floor, Missoula, MT 59802

Trial Attorney.—Robert Anderson (406) 829–3322.

c/o U.S. Attorney's Office, Room 6–100, PJKK Federal Building, 300 Ala Moana Boulevard, Honolulu, HI 96850

Trial Attorney.—Sila DeRoma (808) 541–2850.

483 Doe Run Road, Sequim, WA 98382

Appraiser.—James Eaton (360) 582–0038.

1205 Via Escalante, Chula Vista, CA 91910

Trial Attorney.—Mike Reed (619) 656–2273.

TAX DIVISION

Robert F. Kennedy Department of Justice Building, 950 Pennsylvania Avenue NW., Room 4141 (202) 514–2901

Judiciary Center Building, 555 Fourth Street NW., 20001 (JCB)

Maxus Energy Tower, 7717 N. Harwood Street, Suite 400, Dallas, TX 75242 (MAX)

Patrick Henry Building, 601 D Street NW., 20004 (PHB)

Assistant Attorney General.—Eileen J. O'Connor, room 4601, 514–2901.
  Deputy Assistant Attorneys General: Claire Fallon, room 4137, 514–5109 (Civil Matters); Patrick F. Hofer, room 4609, 514–8665 (Policy and Management Matters); Richard T. Morrison, room 4613, 514–2901 (Appellate and Review); Rod J. Rosenstein, room 4603, 514–2915 (Criminal Matters).
  Senior Legislative Counsel.—Stephen J. Csontos (MAIN), room 4134, 307–6419.
  Section Chiefs:
    Central Region, Civil Trial.—Seth Heald (acting) (JCB), room 8921–B, 514–6502.
    Eastern Region, Civil Trial.—David A. Hubbert (JCB) room 6126, 307–6426.
    Northern Region, Civil Trial.—D. Patrick Mullarkey (JCB), room 7804–A, 307–6533.
    Southern Region, Civil Trial.—Michael Kearns (JCB), room 6243–A, 514–5905.
    Southwestern Region, Civil Trial.—Louise P. Hytken (MAX), room 4100 (214) 880–9725.
    Western Region, Civil Trial.—Robert S. Watkins (JCB), room 7907–B, 307–6413.
    Court of Federal Claims.—Mildred L. Seidman (JCB), room 8804–A, 307–6440.
    Office of Review.—John DiCicco (JCB), room 6846, 307–6567.
    Appellate.—Gilbert S. Rothenberg (PHB), room 7038, 514–3361.
    Criminal Enforcement, Northern Region.—Rosemary E. Paguni (BICN), room 5824, 514–2323.
    Criminal Enforcement, Southern Region.—Gregory E. Gallagher (acting), (PHB), room 7640, 514–5112.
    Criminal Enforcement, Western Region.—Ronald Cimino (PHB), room 7038, 514–5762.
    Criminal Appeals and Tax Enforcement Policy.—Alan Hechtkopf (acting), (PHB), room 7002, 514–3011.
  Executive Officer.—Joseph E. Young (PHB), room 7802, 616–0010.

DRUG ENFORCEMENT ADMINISTRATION

Lincoln Place-1 (East), 600 Army-Navy Drive, Arlington, VA 22202 (LP–1)

Lincoln Place-2 (West), 700 Army-Navy Drive, Arlington, VA 22202 (LP–2)

Administrator.—Karen P. Tandy, room W–12060, 307–8000.
  Chief of Staff.—Jodi L. Avergun, room W–12060–E, 307–8003.
  Deputy Administrator.—Michele M. Leonhart, room W–12058–F, 307–7345.
  Executive Assistant.—Joel K. Fries, room W–12058–E, 307–8770.
  Chief, Office of Congressional and Public Affairs.—Mary Irene Cooper, room W–12228, 307–7363.
  Chief, Executive Policy and Strategic Planning.—Elizabeth W. Kempshall, room W–11100, 307–7420.
  Section Chiefs:
    Congressional Affairs.—Eric Akers, room W–12104, 307–7423.
    Demand Reduction.—Catherine Harnett, room W–9049–E, 307–7936.
    Public Affairs.—William Grant (acting), 307–7979.
    Information Services.—Donald E. Joseph, room W–12232, 307–7967.
  Chief Counsel.—Wendy H. Goggin, room W–12142–C, 307–7322.
  Deputy Chief Counsel.—Robert C. Gleason, room E–12375, 307–8020.
  Chief, Office of Administrative Law Judges.—Mary Ellen Bittner, room E–2129, 307–8188.

FINANCIAL MANAGEMENT DIVISION

Chief Financial Officer.—Frank M. Kalder, room W–12138, 307–7330.
  Deputy Assistant Administrators for—
    Acquisition Management.—Christinia K. Sisk, room W–5100, 307–7888.
    Finance.—Alison Doone, room E–7397, 307–7002.
    Resource Management.—Charlotte A. Saunders, room E–7399, 307–4800.

Section Chiefs:
   Acquisition Management.—Michele Allen, room W–5028, 307–7802.
   Controls and Coordination.—John Osterday, room E–7395, 307–7080.
   Evaluations and Planning.—Donna Wilson, room E–850P, 307–7463.
   Financial Integrity.—William S. Truitt, room E–7101, 307–7082.
   Financial Operations.—Tammy Balas, room E–7165, 307–9933.
   Financial Reports.—Sherri Woodle, room E–7297, 307–7040.
   Financial Systems.—Daniel G. Gillette, room E–7205, 307–7031.
   Organization and Staffing Management.—Donna Ciccolella, room E–7331, 307–7077.
   Policy and Transportation.—Barbara J. Joplin, room W–5018, 307–7808.
   Program Liaison and Analysis.—Karin O'Leary, room E–7225, 305–9149.
   Statistical Services.—Patrick R. Gartin, room W–6300, 307–8276.

INSPECTIONS DIVISION

Chief Inspector.—Rogelio E. Guevara, room W–12042A, 307–7358.
   Deputy Chief Inspector, Office of:
     Inspections.—Gerard P. McAleer, room W–4348, 307–8200.
     Professional Responsibility.—Stephen G. Griswold, room W–4176, 307–8235.
     Security Programs.—Mark S. Johnson, room W–2340, 307–3465.

OPERATIONS DIVISION

Chief of Operations.—Michael A. Braun, room W–12050, 307–7340.
   Chiefs of:
     Enforcement Operations.—Thomas M. Harrigan, room W–11070, 307–7927.
       Deputy Chief, Enforcement Operations.—Joseph T. Rannazzisi, room W–11064, 307–7159.
     Financial Operations.—Donald C. Semesky, room W–10190, 353–9574.
     International Programs.—Kevin C. Whaley, room W–11024, 307–4233.
     Operations Management.—Ava Cooper-Davis, room W–11148, 307–4200.
   Deputy Assistant Administrator, Office of Diversion Control.—William J. Walker, room E–6295, 307–7165.
   Special Agent in Charge, Aviation Division.—William C. Brown, Ft. Worth, TX (817) 837–2004.
   Special Agent in Charge, Special Operations Division.—Derek S. Maltz, Chantilly, VA (703) 488–4205.

INTELLIGENCE DIVISION

Assistant Administrator.—Anthony P. Pacido (acting), room W–12020A, 307–3607.
   Special Agent in Charge, El Paso Intelligence Center.—James S. Mavromatis, Building 11339, SSG Sims Street, El Paso, TX 79908–8098 (915) 760–2011.
   Deputy Associate Administrator, Office of Intelligence.—Judith E. Bertini, room W–12020C, 307–3607.
   Section Chief, Office of Management and Production Section.—James A. Curtin, room W–7268, 307–7534.
   Deputy Assistant Administrator, Office of Strategic Intelligence.—Linda Crume (acting), room W–8072, 307–8243.
   Section Chiefs:
     Regional Strategic Section.—Linda Crume, room W–8258, 307–5442.
     Special Strategic Intelligence Section A.—Lourdes P. Border. room 8066, 307–4358.
   Deputy Assistant Administrator, Office of Investigative Intelligence.—Jill Webb (acting), room W–10190, 307–8050.
   Section Chief of Worldwide Investigative Intelligence.—Craig Estancona, room W–10280, 307–8431.
   Deputy Assistant Administrator, Special Intelligence.—Anthony P. Pacido, room E–5075A, 307–8369.
   Section Chiefs:
     Operational Support.—Benjamin J. Sanborn, room E–5015, 307–3645.
     Technical Support.—Gisele Gatjanis, room E–5121A, 307–4872.

OPERATIONAL SUPPORT DIVISION

Assistant Administrator.—William B. Simpkins, room W–12142, 307–4730.
Deputy Assistant Administrator, Office of Administration.—Mary E. Colarusso (acting), room W–9088, 307–7708.
Section Chiefs:
  Administrative Operations.—Emmett T. Ridley, Jr., room W–5100–A, 307–7766.
  Facilities and Finance.—William A. Kopitz, room W–5244, 307–7792.
Deputy Assistant Administrator, Office of Forensic Sciences.—Thomas J. Janovsky, room W–7342, 307–8866.
Associate Deputy Assistant Administrators, Office of Forsenic Sciences: Alan B. Clark, room W–7344, 307–8866; Rhesa G. Gilliland, room W–7346, 307–8868.
Section Chiefs:
  Hazardous Waste Disposal.—John Patrick, room W–7308, 307–8872.
  Laboratory Operations.—Steven M. Sottolano, room W–7310, 307–8880.
  Laboratory Support.—Richard P. Meyers, room W–7348, 307–8785.
Deputy Assistant Administrator, Office of Investigative Technology.—Dale Zeisset, Lorton, VA (703) 495–6500.
Section Chiefs:
  Surveillance Support.—Jon J. Sugrue, Lorton, VA (703) 495–6575.
  Telecommunications Intercept Support.—Donald Torres, Lorton, VA (703) 495–6550.
Deputy Assistant Administrator, Office of Information Systems.—Dennis R. McCrary, room E–3105, 307–7454.
Associate Deputy Assistant Administrator, Office of Information Systems.—Julie Jones, room E–3005, 307–5269.
Section Chiefs:
  Operations and Support.—Larry Castleberry, room E–4111, 307–9481.
  Program Planning and Control Staff.—Maria Hughes, room E–3163, 307–9885.
  Special Projects.—Michelle M. Bower, room E–3206, 307–9896.
  Systems Applications.—Ruth Torres, room E–3285, 307–9883.
  Technology Officer.—Mark Shafernich, room E–3101, 353–9691.

HUMAN RESOURCES DIVISION

Assistant Administrator.—Catherine J. Kasch, room W–12020, 307–4177.
Section Chiefs:
  Management & Employee Services.—Margaret A. Hager, room W–3058, 307–4015.
  Recruitment and Placement.—Margie Aira, room W–3242, 307–4055.
Equal Employment Opportunity Officer.—Margaret Norman, room E–11275, 307–8888.
Career Board Executive Secretary.—Jerry A. Heard, room W–2268, 307–7349.
Chairman, Board of Professional Conduct.—Pat Dunn, room E–9333, 307–8980.
Special Agent-in-Charge, Office of Training.—John R. McCarty, 2500 Investigation Parkway, DEA Academy, Quantico, VA 22135 (703) 632–5010.
Assistant Special Agents-in-Charge:
  Domestic Training Section 1.—Bill Faiella (703) 632–5110.
  Domestic Training Section 2.—Richard Inscore (703) 632–5310.
  International Training Section.—Dominick D. Braccio, Jr. (703) 632–5330.

FIELD OFFICES

ATLANTA DIVISION:
  Special Agent-in-Charge.—Sherri Strange, Room 800, 75 Spring Street SW, Atlanta, GA 30303 (404) 893–7000.
BOSTON DIVISION:
  Special Agent-in-Charge.—June Stansbury, JFK Federal Building, Room E–400, 15 New Sudsbury Street, Boston, MA 02203–0402 (617) 557–2100.
CARIBBEAN DIVISION:
  Special Agent-in-Charge.—Jerome M. Harris, P.O. Box 2167, San Juan, PR 00922–2167 (787) 775–1815.
CHICAGO DIVISION:
  Special Agent-in-Charge.—Richard W. Sanders, Suite 1200, John C. Kluczynski Federal Building, 230 South Dearborn Street, Chicago, IL 60604 (312) 353–7875.
DALLAS DIVISION:
  Special Agent-in-Charge.—Gary G. Olenkiewicz, 10160 Technology Boulevard East, Dallas, TX 75220 (214) 366–6900.

DENVER DIVISION:
  Special Agent-in-Charge.—Jeffrey D. Sweetin, 115 Inverness Drive, East, Englewood, CO 80112–5116 (303) 705–7300.
DETROIT DIVISION:
  Special Agent-in-Charge.—John J. Arvanitis (acting), 431 Howard Street, Detroit, MI 48226 (313) 234–4000.
EL PASO DIVISION:
  Special Agent-in-Charge.—Zoran Yankovich, 660 Mesa Hills Drive, Suite 2000, El Paso, TX 79912 (915) 832–6000.
HOUSTON DIVISION:
  Special Agent-in-Charge.—James T. Craig, 1433 West Loop South, Suite 600, Houston, TX 77027–9506 (713) 693–3000.
LOS ANGELES DIVISION:
  Special Agent-in-Charge.—Stephen Delgado, 255 East Temple Street, 20th Floor, Los Angeles, CA 90012 (213) 621–6700.
MIAMI DIVISION:
  Special Agent-in-Charge.—Mark Trouville, Phoenix Building, 8400 NW. 53rd Street, Miami, FL 33166 (305) 994–4870.
NEWARK DIVISION:
  Special Agent-in-Charge.—Michael Pasterchick, Jr., 80 Mulberry Street, Second Floor, Newark, NJ 07102–4206 (973) 273–5000.
NEW ORLEANS DIVISION:
  Special Agent-in-Charge.—William J. Renton, Jr., Suite 1800, 3838 North Causeway Boulevard, Metaire, LA 70002 (504) 840–1100.
NEW YORK DIVISION:
  Special Agent-in-Charge.—John P. Gilbride, 99 10th Avenue, New York, NY 10011 (212) 337–3900.
PHILADELPHIA DIVISION:
  Special Agent-in-Charge.—James M. Kasson, William J. Green Federal Building, 600 Arch Street, Room 10224, Philadelphia, PA 19106 (215) 861–3474.
PHOENIX DIVISION:
  Special Agent-in-Charge.—Timothy J. Landrum, Suite 301, 3010 North Second Street, Phoenix, AZ 85012 (602) 664–5600.
SAN DIEGO DIVISION:
  Special Agent-in-Charge.—John S. Fernandes, 4560 Viewridge Avenue, San Diego, CA 92123–1672 (858) 616–4100.
SAN FRANCISCO DIVISION:
  Special Agent-in-Charge.—Javier F. Pena, 450 Golden Gate Avenue, P.O. Box 36035, San Francisco, CA 94102 (415) 436–7900.
SEATTLE DIVISION:
  Special Agent-in-Charge.—Rodney G. Benson, 400 Second Avenue West, Seattle, WA 98119 (206) 553–5443.
ST. LOUIS DIVISION:
  Special Agent-in-Charge.—Preston Gubbs, 317 South 16th Street, St. Louis, MO 63103 (314) 538–4600.
WASHINGTON, DC DIVISION:
  Special Agent-in-Charge.—Shawn A. Johnson, 800 K Street, NW., Suite 520, Washington, DC 20001 (202) 305–8500.

OTHER DEA OFFICES

Special Agents-in-Charge:
  James S. Mavromatis, El Paso Intelligence Center, Building 11339, SSG Sims Street, El Paso, TX 79908 (915) 760–2000.
  William C. Brown, Aviation Operations Division, 2300 Horizon Drive, Fort Worth, TX 76177 (817) 837–2000.
  Derek S. Maltz, Special Operations Division, 14560 Avion Parkway, Chantilly, VA 20151 (703) 488–4200.
  John R. McCarty, Training Office, P.O. Box 1475, Quantico, VA 22134 (703) 632–5000.

FOREIGN OFFICES

Ankara, Turkey: DEA/Justice, American Embassy Ankara, PSC 93, Box 5000, APO AE 09823, 9–011–90–312–468–6136.

Asuncion, Paraguay: DEA/Justice, American Embassy, Unit 4740, APO AA 34036, 9–011–595–21–210–738.

Athens, Greece: DEA/Justice, American Embassy Athens, PSC 108, Box 14, AA/RE/FPO APO AE 09842, 9–011–30–1–643–4328.

Bangkok, Thailand: DEA/Justice, American Embassy Bangkok, APO AP 96546–0001, 9–011–662–205–4987.

Beijing, China: DEA/Justice, American Embassy Beijing, PSC 461, Box 50, FPO AP 96521–0002, 9–011–8610–8529–6880.

Belize, Country Office: DEA/Justice, American Embassy, PSC 120, Unit 7405, APO AA 34025, 9–011–501–233–3857.

Berlin, Germany: DEA/Justice, Berlin Country Office, PSC 120, Box 3000, APO AE 09265, 9–011–49–30–8305–1460.

Bern, Switzerland: DEA/Justice, American Embassy, Department of State (Bern), Washington, DC 20521, 9–011–41–31–357–7367.

Bogota, Columbia: DEA/Justice, American Embassy, Unit 5116, APO AA 34038, 9–011–571–315–2121.

Brasilia, Brazil: DEA/Justice, American Embassy, Unit 3500, APO AA 34030, 9–011–55–61–312–7498.

Bridgetown, Barbados: DEA/Justice, American Embassy, CMR 1014, APO AA 34055, 9–1–246–437–6337.

Brussels, Belgium: DEA/Justice, Brussels Country Office, PSC 82, Box 002, APO AE 09710, 9–011–32–2–508–2420.

Buenos Aires, Argentina: DEA/Justice, American Embassy, Unit 4309, APO AA 34034, 9–011–5415–114949.

Cairo, Egypt: DEA/Justice, Cairo Country Office, American Embassy, Unit 64900, Box 25, APO AE 09839–4900, 9–011–20–2–357–2461.

Canberra, Australia: DEA/Justice, American Embassy Canberra, APO AP 96549, 9–011–61–2–6214–5903.

Caracas, Venezuela: DEA/Justice, American Embassy, Unit 4962, APO AA 34037, 9–011–582–12–975–8910.

Cartagena, Resident Office: DEA/Justice, American Consulate, Unit 5116, APO AA 34038, 9–011–575–655–1423.

Chiang-Mai, Resident Office: DEA/Justice, American Consulate, Box C, APO AP 96546, 9–011–66–53–217–285.

Chimore Post of Duty: DEA/Justice, American Embassy, Unit 3913 (Chimore), APO AA 34032, 301–985–9399.

Cochabamba, Resident Office: DEA/Justice, American Embassy, Unit 3913 (Cochabamba), APO AA 34032, 9–011–591–428–8896.

Copenhagen, Denmark: DEA/Justice, American Embassy Copenhagen, PSC 73, APO AE 09716, 9–011–45–35–42–26–80.

Curacao, Netherlands Antilles: DEA/Justice, American Consulate, Washington, DC 20521, 9–011–5999–461–6985.

Frankfurt, Resident Office: DEA/Justice, American Consulate General, PSC 115, Frankfurt/DEA, APO AE 09213, 9–011–49–69–7535–3770.

Freeport, Resident Office: DEA Freeport-Airport, 22400 Ft. Lauderdale, FL 33335, 1–242–352–5353.

Guadalajara, Resident Office: DEA/Justice, Guadalajara Resident Office, P.O. Box 9001, Brownsville, TX 78520–0901, 9–011–523–825–3064.

Guatemala City, Guatemala: DEA/Justice, American Embassy, Unit 3311, APO AA 34024, 9–011–502–331–4389.

Guayaquil, Resident Office: DEA/Justice, American Embassy Quito, Unit 5350, APO AA, 34039, 9–011–593–42–327–862.

The Hague, Netherlands: DEA/Justice, American Embassy, Unit 6707, Box 8, APO AE 09715, 9–011–31–70–310–9327.

Hanoi, Vietnam: DEA/Justice, American Embassy Vietnam, Department of State, Attn: DEA/Justice, Washington, DC 20521 9–011–772–1500, ext. 2357/9.

Hermosillo, Resident Office: DEA/Justice, Hermosillo Resident Office, P.O. Box 1689, Nogales, AZ 85628, 9–011–526–289–0220.

Hong Kong: DEA/Justice, American Consulate General, PSC 461, Box 16, FPO AP 96521, 9–852–2521–4536.

Istanbul: DEA/Justice, American Consulate General, PSC 97, Box 0002, APO AE 09327, 9–011–90–212–251–0160.

Juarez, Resident Office: P.O. Box 10545, El Paso, TX 79995, 9–011–52–656–611–1179.
Kingston, Jamaica: Kingston Country Office, Department of State, 3210 Kingston Place, Washington, DC 20521, 9–1–876–929–4956.
Kuala Lumpur, Malaysia: DEA/Justice, American Embassy Kuala Lumpur, APO AP 96535, 9–011–603–248–7951.
Lagos, Nigeria: DEA/Justice, American Embassy Lagos, Department of State, Attn: DEA/Justice, 8300 Lagos Place, Washington, DC 20521, 9–011–234–1–261–9837.
La Paz, Bolivia: DEA/Justice, American Embassy, Unit 3913, APO AA 34032, 9–011–591–2–431481.
Lima, Peru: DEA/Justice, American Embassy, Unit 3810, APO AA 34031, 9–011–511–434–3058.
London, England: DEA/Justice, American Embassy, PSC 801, Box 08, FPO AE 09498, 9–011–441–71–403–8026.
Lyon (INTERPOL): American Embassy Paris, DEA/Interpol, Lyon, PSC 116, APO AE 09777, 9–011–33–4–7244–7086.
Madrid, Spain: DEA/Justice, American Embassy Madrid, PSC 61, Box 0014, APO AE 09642, 9–011–34–91–587–2280.
Managua, Nicaragua: DEA/Justice, American Embassy Nicaragua, Unit 2701, Box 21, APO AA 34021, 9–011–505–268–2148.
Manila, Philippines: DEA/Justice, American Embassy, PSC 500, Box 11, FPO AP 96515, 9–011–632–523–1219.
Mazatlan, Resident Office: DEA/Justice, Mazatlan Resident Office, P.O. Box 9006, Brownsville, TX 78520, 9–011–52–69–82–1659.
Merida: DEA/Justice, U.S. Consulate-Merida, P.O. Box 9003, Brownsville, TX 78520, 9–011–529–925–8013.
Mexico City, Mexico: DEA/Justice, U.S. Embassy Mexico City, P.O. Box 9000–DEA, Brownsville, TX 78520, 9–011–52–55–5080–2600.
Milan, Resident Office: DEA/Justice, American Consulate Milan, c/o American Embassy Rome, PSC 59, Box 60–M, APO AE 09624, 9–011–39–02–655–5766.
Monterrey, Resident Office: DEA/Justice, Monterrey Road, P.O. Box 9002, Brownsville, TX 78520–0902, 9–011–528–340–1299.
Moscow, Russia: DEA/Justice, American Embassy Moscow, PSC 77, APO AE 09721, 9–011–7–095–956–8066.
Nassau: Nassau Country Office, 3370 Nassau Place, Washington, DC 20521, 9–1–242–322–1700.
New Delhi, India: DEA/Justice, New Delhi Country Office, Department of State, 9000 New Delhi Place, Attn: DEA/Justice, Washington, DC 20521, 9–011–91–11–419–0008.
Nicosia, Cyprus: DEA/Justice, American Embassy, PSC 815, Box 1, FPO AE 09836, 9–011–357–2–777–086.
Ottawa, Canada: DEA/Justice, American Embassy Ottawa, P.O. Box 13669, Ogdensburg, New York 13669, 9–1–613–238–5633.
Panama City, Panama: DEA/Justice, American Embassy, Unit 0945, APO AA 34002, 9–011–507–225–9685.
Paris, France: Justice, American Embassy Paris, PSC 116, Box D–401, APO AE 09777, 9–011–33–1–4312–7332.
Peshawar: DEA/Justice, American Consulate General Peshawar, Unit 62217, APO AE 09812–2217, 9–011–92–521–840–424.
Port-Au-Prince, Haiti: U.S. Department of State, DEA Port-au-Prince, 3400 Port-au-Prince Place, Washington, DC 20521, 9–011–509–223–8888.
Port of Spain, Trinidad and Tobago: DEA/Justice, Port of Spain, Department of State, Port of Spain Country Office, 3410 Port of Spain Place, Washington, DC 20537, 9–1–868–628–8136.
Pretoria, South Africa: DEA/Justice, Pretoria Country Office, Department of State, Washington, DC 20521, 9–011–27–12–362–5009.
Quito, Ecuador: DEA/Justice, American Embassy, Unit 5338, APO AA 34039, 9–011–593–22–231–547.
Rangoon, Burma: DEA/Justice, American Embassy Rangoon, Box B, APO AP 96546, 9–011–95–1–282055.
Rome, Italy: DEA/Justice, American Embassy Rome, PSC 59, Box 22, APO AE 09624, 9–011–39–06–4674–2319.
San Jose, Costa Rica: DEA/Justice, American Embassy, Unit 2506, APO AA 34020, 9–011–506–220–2433.
San Salvador, El Salvador: American Embassy, Unit 3130, APO AA 34023, 9–011–503–278–6005.
Santa Cruz, Resident Office: DEA/Justice, American Embassy, Unit 3913 (Santa Cruz), APO AA 34032, 9–011–591–3–32–7152.

Santiago, Chile: DEA/Justice, American Embassy, Unit 4119, APO AA 34033, 9–011–591–3–345–1841.
Santo Domingo, Dominican Republic: DEA/Justice, American Embassy, Unit 5514, APO AA 34041, 809–687–3754.
Sao Paulo, Resident Office: DEA/Justice, American Embassy, Unit 3502, AP0 AA 34030, 9–011–55–11–3062–6962.
Seoul, Korea: DEA/Justice, American Embassy Seoul, Unit 15550, APO AP 96205, 9–011–82–2–397–4260.
Singapore: DEA/Justice, American Embassy Singapore, PSC 470 DEA FPO 96507, 9–011–65–476–9021.
Songkhla, Resident Office: DEA/Justice, American Embassy, APO AP 96546, 9–011–66–74–324–236.
Tashkent: Uzbekistan Country Office, DEA/Justice, 7110 Tashkent Place, Washington, DC 20521, 9–011–998–71120–5450.
Tegucigalpa, Honduras: DEA/Justice, American Embassy, Unit 2912, APO AA 34022, 9–011–504–236–6780.
Tijuana, Resident Office: P.O. 439039, San Diego, CA 92143, 9–011–52–664–622–7452.
Tokyo, Japan: DEA/Justice, American Embassy Tokyo, Unit 45004, Box 224, APO AP 96337, 9–011–81–3–3224–5452.
Trinidad, Resident Office: DEA/Justice, American Embassy, Unit 3913 (Trinidad), TRO, APO AA 34032, 301–985–9368.
Udorn, Resident Office: DEA/Justice, American Embassy (Udorn), Box UD, APO AP 96546, 9–011–66–42–247–636.
Vancouver Resident Office: United States Consulate, DEA/Justice, Vancouver, P.O. Box 5002, Point Roberts, WA 98281.
Vienna, Austria: American Embassy Vienna, Department of State, Attn: DEA/Justice, Washington, DC 20521, 9–011–43–1–514–2251.
Vientiane, Laos: American Embassy Vientiane, Box V, APO AP 96546, 9–011–856–2121.

FEDERAL BUREAU OF ALCOHOL, TOBACCO, FIREARMS, AND EXPLOSIVES (ATF)

650 Massachusetts Avenue, NW., 20226

OFFICE OF THE DIRECTOR

Director.—Carl J. Truscott (202) 927–8700.
  Deputy Director.—Edgar A. Domenech, 927–8710.
  Chief of Staff.—Tina L. Street, 927–8309.

OFFICE OF OMBUDSMAN

Ombudsman.—Marianne Ketels, 927–3538.

STRATEGIC PLANNING OFFICE

Chief.—E. Wayne Miller, 927–7720.

OFFICE OF EQUAL OPPORTUNITY

Executive Assistant.—Anthony Torres, 927–8154.
  Deputy Executive Assistant.—Oliver C. Allen, Jr., 927–8263.

OFFICE OF CHIEF COUNSEL

Chief Counsel.—Stephen R. Rubenstein, 927–8224.
  Deputy Chief Counsel.—Melanie S. Stinnett, 927–8211.

OFFICE OF ENFORCEMENT PROGRAMS AND SERVICES

Assistant Director.—Lewis P. Raden, 927–7940.
  Deputy Assistant Director.—Wally Nelson.

Special Assistant.—Enrique Perez. 927–8489.
Chief of Staff.—Mary Jo Hughes, 927–7940.
Director of NIBIN Program.—Steve Pugmire, 927–5660.
Chief, Division of:
  Arson and Explosives.—Joseph Riehl, 927–7930.
  FEA Services.—Audrey Stucko, 927–8300.
  Firearms Program.—John Spurgeon, 927–7770.
  National Tracing Center.—Charles Houser (304) 274–4100.
Deputy Chief, Division of:
  Arson and Explosives.—Mark Siebert, 927–7930.
  Firearms Programs.—Nick Colucci, 927–7770.

OFFICE OF SCIENCE AND TECHNOLOGY/CIO

Assistant Director / Chief Information Officer.—Gregg D. Bailey, 927–8390.
Deputy Assistant Director.—Linda Y. Cureton.

OFFICE OF TRAINING AND PROFESSIONAL DEVELOPMENT

Assistant Director.—Mark Logan, 927–9380.
Deputy Assistant Director.—Steve L. Mathis.

OFFICE OF FIELD OPERATIONS

Assistant Director.—Michael R. Bouchard, 927–7970.
Deputy Assistant Director for—
  Central.—Carson F. Carroll, 927–7980.
  East.—Hugo Barrera.
  West.—J. Dewey Webb.
  Industry Operations.—James A. Zamillo, Sr.

OFFICE OF PUBLIC AND GOVERNMENTAL AFFAIRS

Assistant Director.—W. Larry Ford, 927–8500.
Executive Assistant for Legislative Affairs.—David Grothaus, 927–8490.

OFFICE OF PROFESSIONAL RESPONSIBILITY AND SECURITY OPERATIONS

Assistant Director.—Richard E. Chase, 927–7800.
Deputy Assistant Director.—Jeffrey Roehm.

OFFICE OF MANAGEMENT/CFO

Assistant Director / Chief Financial Officer.—Marguerite Moccia, 927–8400.
Deputy Assistant Director.—Candace E. Moberly.

OFFICE OF STRATEGIC INTELLIGENCE AND INFORMATION

Assistant Director.—James E. McDermond, 927–6500.
Deputy Assistant Director.—Virginia T. O'Brien, 927–6500.

FEDERAL BUREAU OF INVESTIGATION

J. Edgar Hoover Building, 935 Pennsylvania Avenue NW., Washington, DC 20535–0001, phone (202) 324–3000, http://www.fbi.gov

Director.—Robert S. Mueller III, 324–3444.
Deputy Director.—John S. Pistole, 324–3315.
Chief of Staff.—Charles M. Steele, 324–3444.

Executive Assistant Directors of:
  Administration.—Jonathan I. Solomon, 324–7101.
  Counterterrorism/Counterintelligence.—Gary M. Bald, 324–7045.
  Intelligence.—Maureen A. Baginski, 324–9213.
  Law Enforcement Services.—Grant D. Ashley, 324–4880.
Assistant Director of Administrative Services Division.—Mark S. Bullock, 324–3514.
  Deputy Assistant Directors: Mary B. Hannagan, 324–5364; J.P. Weis, 324–3516.
Assistant Director of Counterintelligence Division.—David Szady, 324–4614.
  Deputy Assistant Directors: Beverly Andress, 324–8912; Timothy D. Bereznay, 324–4883.
Assistant Director of Counterterrorism Division.—Willie T. Hulon, 324–2770.
  Deputy Assistant Directors: Thomas J. Harrington (703) 280–5505; John E. Lewis, 324–7055; Donald N. Van Duyn, 324–2013.
Assistant Director of Criminal Investigative Division.—Chris Swecker, 324–4260.
  Deputy Assistant Directors: James H. Burrus, Jr., 324–5740; Deborah Strebel Pierce, 324–4262.
Assistant Director of Criminal Justice Information Services Division.—Thomas E. Bush III (304) 625–2700.
  Deputy Assistant Directors: Jerome M. Pender (304) 625–4400; Monte C. Strait (acting) (304) 625–2900.
Assistant Director of Cyber Division.—Louis M. Reigel III, 324–6615.
  Deputy Assistant Director.—Steven M. Martinez, 324–1380.
Assistant Director of Finance Division.—Joseph L. Ford, 324–1345.
  Deputy Assistant Director.—Richard L. Haley, 324–4104.
Assistant Director of Information Technology Operations Division.—James A. Loudermilk II (acting), 324–4507.
  Deputy Assistant Director.—James A. Loudermilk II, 324–4840.
Assistant Director of Inspection Division.—Charlene B. Thornton, 324–2901.
  Deputy Assistant Director.—Andrew R. Bland III, 324–2903.
Assistant Director of Investigative Technology Division.—Kerry E. Haynes (703) 632–6100.
  Deputy Assistant Director.—Marcus C. Thomas.
Assistant Director of Laboratory Division.—Dwight E. Adams (703) 632–7000.
  Deputy Assistant Directors: Joseph A. Di Zinno (703) 632–7003; Tod Alan Hildebrand (703) 632–7010.
Chief Information Officer.—Zalmai Azmi, 324–6165.
Assistant Director, Office of Congressional Affairs.—Eleni P. Kalisch, 324–5051.
Equal Employment Opportunity Officer.—Veronica Venture, 324–4128.
  Assistant Equal Employment Opportunity Officers: Janis Famous, 324–8162; Maximo De Lancer, 324–4128.
General Counsel.—Valerie Caproni, 324–6829.
  Deputy General Counsels.—John Curran, 324–8528; Anne M. Gulyassy, 324–5020; Patrick W. Kelley, 324–8067.
Assistant Director, Office of Intelligence.—Kevin R. Brock, 324–7605.
  Deputy Assistant Directors: Robert E. Casey, Jr., 324–0740; Janet C. Keys, 324–8287.
Office of International Operations.—Thomas V. Fuentes, special agent in charge, 324–5292.
Assistant Director, Office of Law Enforcement Coordination.—Louis F. Quijas, 324–7126.
Office of the Ombudsman.—Sarah Zeigler, 324–2156.
Assistant Director of:
  Professional Responsibility.—Candice M. Will, 324–8284,
  Public Affairs.—Cassandra M. Chandler, 324–5352.
Assistant Director, Records Management Division.—William L. Hooton, 324–7141.
  Deputy Assistant Director.—Harold M. Hendershot, 324–7141.
  Executive Secretariat.—Marilyn Moore, 324–6565.
Assistant Director, Security Division.—Charles S. Phalen, Jr., 324–7112.
  Deputy Assistant Director.—Jeffrey Berkin, 324–2121.
Assistant Director, Training Division.—James A. Trinka, 324–2506.

FIELD DIVISIONS

Albany: 200 McCarty Avenue, Albany, NY 12209 (518) 465–7551.
Albuquerque: 415 Silver Avenue SW., Suite 300, Albuquerque, NM 87102 (505) 224–2000.
Anchorage: 101 East Sixth Avenue, Anchorage, AK 99501 (907) 258–5322.
Atlanta: 2635 Century Center Parkway, NE., Suite 400, Atlanta, GA 30345 (404) 679–9000.
Baltimore: 7142 Ambassador Road, Baltimore, MD 21244 (410) 265–8080.

Birmingham: 2121 Eighth Avenue North, Room 1400, Birmingham, AL 35203 (205) 326–6166.

Boston: One Center Plaza, Suite 600, Boston, MA 02108 (617) 742–5533.

Buffalo: One FBI Plaza, Buffalo, NY 14202 (716) 856–7800.

Charlotte: Wachovia Building, 400 South Tryon Street, Suite 900, Charlotte, NC 28285 (704) 377–9200.

Chicago: E.M. Dirksen Federal Office Building, 219 South Dearborn Street, Room 905, Chicago, IL 60604 (312) 431–1333.

Cincinnati: Federal Office Building, 550 Main Street, Room 9000, Cincinnati, OH 45202 (513) 421–4310.

Cleveland: 1501 Lakeside Avenue, Cleveland, OH 44114 (216) 522–1400.

Columbia: 151 Westpark Boulevard, Columbia, SC 29210 (803) 551–4200.

Dallas: J. Gordon Shanklin Building, One Justice Way, Dallas, TX 75220 (972) 559–5000.

Denver: Federal Office Building, 1961 Stout Street, Room 1823, Denver, CO 80294 (303) 629–7171.

Detroit: P.V. McNamara Federal Office Building, 477 Michigan Avenue, 26th Floor, Detroit, MI 48226 (313) 965–2323.

El Paso: 660 South Mesa Hills Drive, Suite 3000, El Paso, TX 79912 (915) 832–5000.

Honolulu: Kalanianaole Federal Office Building, 300 Ala Moana Boulevard, Room 4–230, Honolulu, HI 96850 (808) 566–4300.

Houston: 2500 East T.C. Jester, Suite 200, Houston, TX 77008 (713) 693–5000.

Indianapolis: Federal Office Building, 575 North Pennsylvania Street, Room 679, Indianapolis, IN 46204 (371) 639–3301.

Jackson: Federal Office Building, 100 West Capitol Street, Suite 1553, Jackson, MS 39269 (601) 948–5000.

Jacksonville: 7820 Arlington Grove Expressway, Suite 200, Jacksonville, FL 32211 (904) 721–1211.

Kansas City: 1300 Summit, Kansas City, MO 64105 (816) 512–8200.

Knoxville: John J. Duncan Federal Office Building, 710 Locust Street, Room 600, Knoxville, TN 37902 (423) 544–0751.

Las Vegas: John Lawrence Bailey Building, 700 East Charleston Boulevard, Las Vegas, NV 89104 (702) 385–1281.

Little Rock: #24 Shackleford West Boulevard, Little Rock, AR 72211 (501) 221–9100.

Los Angeles: Federal Office Building, 11000 Wilshire Boulevard, Suite 1700, Los Angeles, CA 90024 (310) 477–6565.

Louisville: 600 Martin Luther King, Jr. Place, Room 500, Louisville, KY 40202 (502) 583–2941.

Memphis: Eagle Crest Building, 225 North Humphreys Boulevard, Suite 3000, Memphis, TN 38120 (901) 747–4300.

Miami: 16320 Northwest Second Avenue, Miami, FL 33169 (305) 944–9101.

Milwaukee: 330 East Kilbourn Avenue, Suite 600, Milwaukee, WI 53202 (414) 276–4684.

Minneapolis: 111 Washington Avenue South, Suite 100, Minneapolis, MN 55401 (612) 376–3200.

Mobile: 200 North Royal Street, Mobile, AL 36602 (334) 438–3674.

New Haven: 600 State Street, New Haven, CT 06511 (203) 777–6311.

New Orleans: 2901 Leon C. Simon Boulevard, New Orleans, LA 70126 (504) 816–3122.

New York: 26 Federal Plaza, 23rd Floor, New York, NY 10278 (212) 384–1000.

Newark: Claremont Tower Building, 11 Centre Place, Newark, NJ 07102 (973) 792–3000.

Norfolk: 150 Corporate Boulevard, Norfolk, VA 23502 (757) 455–0100.

Oklahoma City: 3301 West Memorial, Oklahoma City, OK 73134 (405) 290–7770.

Omaha: 10755 Burt Street, Omaha, NE 68114 (402) 493–8688.

Philadelphia: William J. Green, Jr., Federal Office Building, 600 Arch Street, Eighth Floor, Philadelphia, PA 19106 (215) 418–4000.

Phoenix: 201 East Indianola Avenue, Suite 400, Phoenix, AZ 85012 (602) 279–5511.

Pittsburgh: Martha Dixon Building, 3311 East Carson Street, Pittsburgh, PA 15203 (412) 432–4000.

Portland: Crown Plaza Building, 1500 Southwest First Avenue, Suite 401, Portland, OR 97201 (503) 224–4181.

Richmond: 1970 East Parham Road, Richmond, VA 23228 (804) 261–1044.

Sacramento: 4500 Orange Grove Avenue, Sacramento, CA 95841 (916) 481–9110.

Salt Lake City: 257 Towers Building, 257 East 200 South, Suite 1200, Salt Lake City, UT 84111 (801) 579–1400.

San Antonio: U.S. Post Office and Courthouse Building, 614 East Houston Street, Room 200, San Antonio, TX 78205 (210) 225–6741.

San Diego: Federal Office Building, 9797 Aero Drive, San Diego, CA 92123 (858) 565–1255.

San Francisco: 450 Golden Gate Avenue, 13th Floor, San Francisco, CA 64102 (415) 553–7400.

San Juan: U.S. Federal Office Building, 150 Chardon Avenue, Room 526, Hato Rey, PR 00918 (787) 754–6000.
Seattle: 1110 Third Avenue, Seattle, WA 98101 (206) 622–0460.
Springfield: 400 West Monroe Street, Suite 400, Springfield, IL 62704 (217) 522–9675.
St. Louis: 2222 Market Street, St. Louis, MO 63103 (314) 241–5357.
Tampa: Federal Office Building, 500 Zack Street, Room 610, Tampa, FL 33602 (813) 273–4566.
Washington Field Office: 601 Fourth Street NW., Washington, DC 20535 (202) 278–3400.

FEDERAL BUREAU OF PRISONS (BOP)
320 1st Street, NW., 20534
General Information Number (202) 307–3198

Director.—Harley G. Lappin, room 654, HOLC, 307–3250.
  Director, National Institute of Corrections.—Morris L. Thigpen, Sr., 7th floor, 500 FRST, 307–3106 (0).
  Assistant Director of:
    Administration.—Bruce K. Sasser, 9th floor, 500 FRST, 307–3123.
    Correctional Programs.—John M. Vanyur, Ph.D., room 554, HOLC, 307–3226.
    General Counsel.—Kathleen M. Kenney, room 958C, HOLC, 307–3062.
    Health Services.—MaryEllen Thomas, room 1054, HOLC, 307–3055.
    Human Resources Management.—W. Elaine Chapman (acting), room 454, HOLC, 307–3082.
    Industries, Education, and Vocational Training.—Steve Schwalb, 8th floor, 400 FRST, 305–3500.
    Information, Policy and Public Affairs.—Thomas R. Kane, Ph.D., room 641, HOLC, 514–6537.
  Regional Director for—
    Mid-Atlantic.—K.M. White (301) 317–3100.
    North Central.—Michael K. Nalley (913) 621–3939.
    Northeast.—D. Scott Dodrill (215) 521–7300.
    South Central.—Ronald G. Thompson (214) 224–3389.
    Southeast.—R.E. Holt (678) 686–1200.
    Western.—Joseph E. Gunja (925) 803–4700.
  Telephone Directory Coordinator.—Jerry Vroegh, 307–3250.

OFFICE OF JUSTICE PROGRAMS (OJP)
810 7th Street, NW., 20531

Assistant Attorney General.—Tracy A. Henke (acting), room 6400, 307–5933.
  Deputy Assistant Attorney Generals: Lizette Benedi, room 6355; Cheri Nolan, room 6422.
  Senior Counsel to the Assistant Attorney General.—Beth McGarry, room 6224.
  Manager, Equal Employment Opportunity.—Stacie Brockman, room 6109, 307–6013.

BUREAU OF JUSTICE ASSISTANCE

Director.—Domingo S. Herraiz, room 4427, 353–2720.
  Deputy Directors of:
    Planning.—Hope D. Janke (acting), room 4429, 514–6094.
    Policy.—James H. Burch II, room 4207, 307–5910.
    Programs.—Eileen Garry, room 4345, 307–6226.
  Associate Deputy Directors of:
    Policy.—Elizabeth Griffith, room 4121, 307–6226; James Patrick McCreary, room 4124, 616–0532.
    Programs.—Timothy Wight, room 4428, 514–2190.

BUREAU OF JUSTICE STATISTICS

Director.—Lawrence A. Greenfeld, room 2413, 307–0765.
  Chiefs of:
    Corrections Statistics.—Allen Beck, room 2239, 616–3277.
    Criminal Statistics Improvement Program.—Gerard Ramker, room 2323, 307–0759.

Law Enforcement, Adjudication, and Federal Statistics.—Steven K. Smith, room 2338, 616–3485.
Law Enforcement and Pretrial Statistics.—Brian Reaves, room 2320, 616–3287.
Planning, Management and Budget.—Maureen A. Henneberg, room 2402, 616–3282.
Publication and Electronic Dissemination.—Marianne Zawitz, room 2249, 616–3499.
Publication Development and Verification.—Tom Hester, room 2247, 616–3283.
Victimization Statistics.—Michael Rand, room 2215, 616–3494.
Senior Statistician, Research and Public Policy Issues.—Patrick A. Langan, room 2326, 616–3490.

NATIONAL INSTITUTE OF JUSTICE

Director.—Sara V. Hart, room 7422, 307–2942.
Chief of Staff.—Kirsten Baumgarten Rowe, room 7412, 305–7560.
Assistant Directors of:
Research and Evaluation.—Thomas Feucht (acting), room 7330, 307–2949.
Science and Technology.—John Morgan, room 7234, 305–0995.
Division Chiefs of:
Communications.—Gerald Soucy, room 7118, 616–3808.
Crime Control and Prevention Research.—Bryan Vila, room 7344, 307–2951.
Evaluations.—Betty Chemers, room 7440, 307–3677.
Investigative and Forensic Sciences.—Susan Narveson (acting), room 7123, 305–4884.
Justice Systems Research.—Christopher Innes, room 7333, 307–2955.
Planning and Management.—Doug Horner, room 7423, 307–2942.
Research and Technology Development.—Stanley Erickson, room 7131, 305–4686.
Technology Assistance.—Marc Caplan, room 7224, 307–2956.
Violence and Victimization Research.—Angela Moore Parmley, room 7355, 307–0145.

OFFICE OF JUVENILE JUSTICE AND DELINQUENCY PREVENTION

Administrator.—J. Robert Flores, room 3345, TWC, 307–5911.
Deputy Administrator for Policy.—William Woodruff, room 3347, TWC, 514–8053.
Deputy Administrator for Programs.—Marilyn Roberts, room 3349, TWC, 616–9055.
Associate Administrators of:
Child Protection.—Ronald C. Laney, room 3135, TWC, 616–7323.
Communications Policy Advisor.—Catherine Doyle, room 3319, TWC, 514–9208.
Demonstrations Program Division.—Jeffrey Slowikowski, room 3141, TWC, 616–3646.
State Relations and Assistance Division.—Gregory Thompson, room 3411, TWC, 616–3663.

OFFICE FOR VICTIMS OF CRIME

Director.—John W. Gillis, room 8322, 307–5983.
Principal Deputy Director.—Carolyn A. Hightower, room 8328, 616–3586.
Deputy Director.—Dennis Greenhouse, room 8261, 616–9971.
Directors of:
Federal, State and Tribal Victim Program.—Cathy Sanders, room 8241, 616–3578.
Program Development and Dissemination.—Joye Whatley, room 8338, 305–1715.
State Compensation and Assistance.—Toni Thomas, room 8242, 616–3579.
Terrorism and International Victim Assistance Services.—Barbara Johnson, room 8340, 307–0012.
Training and Information Dissemination.—Pamela Leupen, room 8323, 307–0711.

COMMUNITY CAPACITY DEVELOPMENT OFFICE

Director.—Nelson Hernandez, 616–1152.

OFFICE OF POLICE CORPS AND LAW ENFORCEMENT EDUCATION

Director.—Michael J. Costigan, room 3227, TWC, 305–8273.

OFFICE OF CHIEF INFORMATION OFFICER

Chief Information Officer.—Gerald Fralick, room 8411, 305–9071.
Deputy Chief Information Officer.—Sandra Borden, room 8425, 305–9071.

OFFICE OF ADMINISTRATION

Director.—Gary N. Silver, room 3424, 307–0087.
  Director of:
    Acquisition Management.—Patrick R. Fanning, room 3605, 307–0608.
    Building and Support Services.—Bobby J. Railey, room 3418, 305–1549.
    Personnel.—Jerry Peterson, room 3330, 616–3272.

OFFICE FOR CIVIL RIGHTS

Director.—Michael Alston, room 8124, 307–0690.

OFFICE OF THE COMPTROLLER

Comptroller.—Cynthia Schwimer, room 5248, 307–3186.
  Deputy Comptroller.—James J. McKay, room 5252, 616–2687.
  Directors of:
    Accounting.—Marsha Barton, room 5322, 514–5579.
    External Oversight.—Angel Conty (acting), room 8240, 514–7934.
    Financial Management.—Larry Hailes, room 5254, 514–7925.
    Training and Policy.—Joanne Suttington, room 5112, 305–2122.

OFFICE OF COMMUNICATIONS

Director.—Nancy Segerdahl, room 6338, 307–0703.
  Deputy Director of:
    Congressional Affairs.—Glenda Kendrick, room 6118.
    Information Resources.—Jim Pinkelman, room 6317.
    Public Affairs.—Pete Pierce, room 6346.

OFFICE OF GENERAL COUNSEL

General Counsel.—Rafael A. Madan, room 5418, 307–0790.
  Principal Deputy General Counsel.—Gregory C. Brady, room 5328, 616–3254.
  Deputy General Counsel.—John L. Pensinger, room 5420, 616–2370.

OFFICE OF BUDGET AND MANAGEMENT SERVICES

Director.—Jill R. Meldon, room 6248, (202) 307–5980.

UNITED STATES MARSHALS SERVICE (USMS)
Washington, DC 20530–1000

[Use (202) for 307 exchange and (703) for 557, 603, 416 and 285 exchanges]

fax (202) 307–5040

Director.—Benigno G. Reyna, 307–9001.
  Deputy Director.—Donald A. Gambatesa, 307–9489.
  Chief of Staff.—Lisa Dickinson (acting), 307–9004.
  Equal Employment Opportunity Officer.—Lisa Dickinson, 307–9048, fax 307–8765.

OFFICE OF DISTRICT AFFAIRS

Chief.—Arthur D. Roderick, Jr., 307–9494.

MANAGEMENT AND BUDGET DIVISION

Assistant Director.—Broadine M. Brown, 307–9032, fax 307–8340.
  Chief Financial Officer.—Edward Dolan, 307–9193, fax 353–8340.
  Chief Information Officer.—Diane Litman (acting), 307–9677, fax 307–5130.

OFFICE OF FINANCE

Chief.—Robert A. Whiteley, 307–9320, fax (703) 603–0386.
Program Review.—Michael Urenko, 307–9749, fax 307–9773.
Security Programs.—James R. Ogan, 307–9696, fax 307–9780.

INVESTIGATIVE SERVICES DIVISION

24 Hour Communications Center, 307–9000, fax 307–9177

Assistant Director.—Robert Finan II, 307–9707, fax 307–9299.
Protective Operations.—Kearn Knowles, 307–9150, fax 307–9337.
Office of Inspections.—Yvonne Bonner, 307–9155, fax 307–9779.

JUDICIAL SECURITY DIVISION

Court Security, 307–9500, fax 307–5047

Assistant Director.—Marc Farmer, 307–9860, fax 307–5206.

PRISONER SERVICES DIVISION

Assistant Director.—Sylvester Jones (acting), 307–5100, fax 305–9434.

JUSTICE PRISONER AND ALIEN TRANSPORTATION SYSTEM (JPATS)

Assistant Director.—Kenneth Pakarek, Kansas City, MO (816) 374–6060, fax 374–6040.
Air Operations.—Alexandria, LA (318) 473–7536, fax (318) 473–7522.
Air Operations, OIC.—Jerry Hurd, Oklahoma City, OK (405) 680–3404, fax 680–3466.

OFFICE OF THE GENERAL COUNSEL

Chief.—Gerald M. Auerbach (acting), 307–9054, fax 307–9456.
Deputy General Counsel.—Luci Roberts.

BUSINESS SERVICES DIVISION

Assistant Director.—Gary Mead, 307–9395, fax 307–5026.
Director, Asset Forfeiture.—Katherine Deoudes, 307–9221, fax (703) 557–9751.
Central Courthouse Management Group.—Dave Barnes, 353–8767, fax 353–7827.
National Procurement.—Pat Hanson, 307–8640.

HUMAN RESOURCES DIVISION

Assistant Director.—Suzanne Smith, 307–9625, fax 307–9461.
Training.—Brian R. Beckwith, FLETC Building 70, Glynco, GA (912) 267–2731, fax (912) 267–2882.

EXECUTIVE SERVICES DIVISION

Assistant Director.—Michael Pearson (acting), 307–9105, fax 307–9831.
Congressional Affairs.—John J. McNulty III, 307–9220, fax 307–5228.
Public Affairs.—Don C. Hines, 307–9065, fax 307–8729.
Telephone Directory Coordinator.—David M. Green, 307–5050.

OFFICE OF THE PARDON ATTORNEY

500 First Street, NW., Suite 400, 20530, phone (202) 616–6070

Pardon Attorney.—Roger C. Adams.
Deputy Pardon Attorney.—Susan M. Kuzma.
Executive Officer.—William J. Dziwura.

U.S. PAROLE COMMISSION

5550 Friendship Boulevard, Suite 420, Chevy Chase, MD 20815, phone (301) 492–5990
fax (301) 492–6694

Chairman.—Edward F. Reilly, Jr.
  Vice Chairman.—Cranston J. Mitchell.
  Commissioners: Patricia K. Cushwa, Isaac Fulwood, Jr., Deborah K. Spagnoli.
  Chief of Staff.—Thomas W. Hutchinson.
  Case Operations Administrator.—Stephen J. Husk.
  Case Service Administrator.—Shelley L. Witenstein.
  Research Administrator.—James L. Beck.
  General Counsel.—Rockne J. Chickinell.
  Executive Officer.—Judy I. Carter.
  Staff Assistant to the Chairman.—Patricia W. Moore.

EXECUTIVE OFFICE FOR UNITED STATES TRUSTEES

20 Massachusetts Avenue NW., Washington, DC 20530, phone (202) 307–1391

www.usdoj.gov/ust

Director.—Lawrence A. Friedman, room 8000.
  Deputy Director.—Clifford J. White III.
  Associate Director.—Jeffrey M. Miller.
  General Counsel.—Donald F. Walton (acting), 307–1399, room 8100.
    Deputy General Counsel.—Esther I. Estryn, room 8102, 307–1320.
  Assistant Directors Office of:
    Administration.—Santal Manos, room 8200, 307–2926.
    Research and Planning.—Steven Pillingham, room 8310, 307–2605.
    Review and Oversight.—W. Clarkson McDow, Jr., room 8338, 305–0550.

U.S. TRUSTEES:

Region I:
  Room 1184, 10 Causeway Street, Boston, MA 02222–1043 (617) 788–0400.
  Suite 303, 537 Congress Street, Portland, ME 04101 (207) 780–3564.
  14th Floor, 446 Main Street, Worcester, MA 01608 (508) 793–0555.
  Suite 302, 66 Hanover Street, Manchester, NH 03101 (603) 666–7908.
  Suite 910, 10 Dorrance Street, Providence, RI 02903 (401) 528–5551.

Region II:
  21st floor, 33 Whitehall Street, New York, NY 10004 (212) 510–0500.
  Suite 200, 74 Chapel Street, Albany, NY 12207 (518) 434–4553.
  Suite 100, 42 Delaware Avenue, Buffalo, NY 14202 (716) 551–5541.
  Long Island Federal Courthouse, 560 Federal Plaza, Central Islip, NY 11722–4456 (631) 715–7800.
  Suite 1103, 265 Church Street, New Haven, CT 06510 (203) 773–2210.
  Room 609, 100 State Street, Rochester, NY 14614 (716) 263–5812.
  Room 105, 10 Broad Street, Utica, NY 13501 (315) 793–8191.

Region III:
  Suite 500, 833 Chestnut Street, Philadelphia, PA 19107 (215) 597–4411.
  Suite 2100, One Newark Center, Newark, NJ 07102 (973) 645–3014.
  Suite 970, 1001 Liberty Avenue, Pittsburgh, PA 15222 (412) 644–4756.
  Suite 1190, 228 Walnut Street, Harrisburg, PA 17101 or P.O. Box 969, Harrisburg, PA 17101 (717) 221–4515.
  Suite 2313, 844 King Street, Wilmington, DE 19801 (302) 573–6491.

Region IV:
  Suite 953, 1835 Assembly Street, Columbia, SC 29201 (803) 765–5250.
  Room 210, 115 S. Union Street, Alexandria, VA 22314 (703) 557–7176.
  Room 625, 200 Granby Street, Norfolk, VA 23510 (757) 441–6012.
  Room 2025, 300 Virginia Street East, Charleston, WV 25301 (304) 347–3400.
  First Campbell Square Building, 210 First Street SW., Suite 505, Roanoke, VA 24011 (540) 857–2806.
  Suite 301, 600 East Main Street, Richmond, VA 23219 (804) 771–2310.
  Suite 600, 6305 Ivy Lane, Greenbelt, MD 20770 (301) 344–6216.
  Suite 350, 300 West Pratt Street, Baltimore, MD 21201 (410) 962–3910.

Region V:
Suite 2110, 400 Poydras Street, New Orleans, LA 70130 (504) 589–4018.
Suite 3196, 300 Fannin Street, Shreveport, LA 71101–3099 (318) 676–3456.
Suite 706, 100 West Capitol Street, Jackson, MS 39269 (601) 965–5241.

Region VI:
Room 976, 1100 Commerce Street, Dallas, TX 75242 (214) 767–8967.
Room 300, 110 North College Avenue, Tyler, TX 75702 (903) 590–1450.

Region VII:
Suite 3516, 515 Rusk Avenue, Houston, TX 77002 (713) 718–4650.
Room 230, 903 San Jacinto, Austin, TX 78701 (512) 916–5328.
Suite 533, 615 East Houston Street, San Antonio, TX 78205 (210) 472–4640.
Suite 1107, 606 N. Carancahua Street, Corpus Christi, TX 78476 (361) 888–3261.

Region VIII:
Suite 400, 200 Jefferson Avenue, Memphis, TN 38103 (901) 544–3251.
Suite 512, 601 W. Broadway, Louisville, KY 40202 (502) 582–6000.
Fourth floor, 31 East 11th Street, Chattanooga, TN 37402 (423) 752–5153.
Room 318, 701 Broadway, Nashville, TN 37203 (615) 736–2254.
Suite 803, 100 East Vine Street, Lexington, KY 40507 (859) 233–2822.

Region IX:
Suite 20–3300, BP Building, 200 Public Square, Cleveland, OH 44114 (216) 522–7800.
Suite 200, Schaff Building, 170 North High Street, Columbus, OH 43215–2403 (614) 469–7411.
Suite 2030, 36 East Seventh Street, Cincinnati, OH 45202 (513) 684–6988.
Suite 700, 211 W. Fort Street, Detroit, MI 48226 (313) 226–7999.
Suite 202, 330 Ionia NW. Grand Rapids, MI 49503 (616) 456–2002.

Region X:
Room 1000, 101 West Ohio Street, Indianapolis, IN 46204 (317) 226–6101.
Suite 1100, 401 Main Street, Peoria, IL 61602 (309) 671–7854.
Suite 555, 100 East Wayne Street, South Bend, IN 46601 (219) 236–8105.

Region XI:
Suite 3350, 227 West Monroe Street, Chicago, IL 60606 (312) 886–5785.
Room 430, 517 East Wisconsin Avenue, Milwaukee, WI 53202 (414) 297–4499.
Suite 304, 780 Regent Street, Madison, WI 53715 (608) 264–5522.

Region XII:
Suite 1015, U.S. Courthouse, 300 S. Fourth Street, Minneapolis, MN 55415 (612) 664–5500.
Suite 400, 225 Second Street SE., Cedar Rapids, IA 52401 (319) 364–2211.
Room 793, 210 Walnut Street, Des Moines, IA 50309–2108 (515) 284–4982.
Suite 502, 230 S. Philips Avenue, Sioux Falls, SD 57102–6321 (605) 330–4450.

Region XIII:
Suite 3440, 400 East 9th Street, Kansas City, MO 64106–1910 (816) 512–1940.
Suite 6353, 111 South 10th Street, St. Louis, MO 63102 (314) 539–2976.
Suite 1200, 200 West Capital Avenue, Little Rock, AR 72201–3344 (501) 324–7357.
Suite 1148, 111 South 18th Plaza, Omaha, NE 68102 (402) 221–4300.

Region XIV:
Suite 204, 230 North First Avenue, Phoenix, AZ 85003 or P.O. Box 36170, Phoenix, AZ 85067 (602) 682–2600.

Region XV:
Suite 600, 402 West Broadway Street, San Diego, CA 92101–8511 (619) 557–5013.
Suite 602, 1132 Bishop Street, Honolulu, HI 96813–2836 (808) 522–8150.

Region XVI:
725 South Figueroa, 26th floor, Los Angeles, CA 90017 (213) 894–6811.
Suite 9041, 411 W. Fourth Street, Santa Ana, CA 92701–8000 (714) 338–3401.
Suite 300, 3685 Main Street, Riverside, CA 92501 (909) 276–6990.
Suite 115, 21051 Warner Center Lane, Woodland Hills, CA 91367 (818) 716–8800.

Region XVII:
Suite 700, 235 Pine Street, San Francisco, CA 94104–3401 (415) 705–3300.
Suite 7–500, U.S. Courthouse, 501 I Street, Sacramento, CA 95814–2322 (916) 930–2100.
Suite 1110, 1130 O Street, Fresno, CA 93721 (559) 498–7400.
Suite 690N, 1301 Clay Street, Oakland, CA 94612–5217 (510) 637–3200.
Room 4300, 300 Las Vegas Boulevard South, Las Vegas, NV 89101 (702) 388–6600.
Suite 2129, 300 Booth Street, Reno, NV 89502 (775) 784–5335.
Room 268, 280 South First Street, San Jose, CA 95113 (408) 535–5525.

Region XVIII:
Suite 5103, 700 Stewart Street, Seattle, WA 98101 (206) 553–2000.
Suite 213, 620 S.W. Main Street, Portland, OR 97205 (503) 326–4000.
Suite 220, 720 Park Boulevard, Boise, ID 83712 (208) 334–1300.
Room 593, 920 West Riverside, Spokane, WA 99201 (509) 353–2999.
Suite 204, 301 Central Avenue, Great Falls, MT 59401 (406) 761–8777.
Suite 258, 605 West Fourth Avenue, Anchorage, AK 99501 (907) 271–2600.
Room 285, 211 East Seventh Avenue, Eugene, OR 97401 (541) 465–6330.

Region XIX:
Suite 1551, 999 Eighteenth Street, Denver, CO 80202 (303) 312–7230.
Suite 203, 308 West 21st Street, Cheyenne, WY 82001 (307) 772–2790.
Suite 100, 9 Exchange Place, Salt Lake City, UT 84111 (801) 524–5734.

Region XX:
Room 500, Epic Center, 301 North Main Street, Wichita, KS 67202 (316) 269–6637.
Suite 112, 421 Gold Street SW., Albuquerque, NM 87102 (505) 248–6544.
Suite 408, 215 Northwest Dean A. McGee Avenue, Oklahoma City, OK 73102 (405) 231–5950.
Suite 225, 224 S. Boulder Avenue, Tulsa, OK 74103 (918) 581–6670.

Region XXI:
Room 362, 75 Spring Street SW., Atlanta, GA 30303 (404) 331–4437.
Suite 301, 500 Tanca Street, San Juan, PR 00901 (787) 729–7444.
Room 1204, 51 Southwest First Avenue, Miami, FL 33130 (305) 536–7285.
Suite 302, 222 West Oglethorpe Avenue, Savannah, GA 31401 (912) 652–4112.
Suite 1200, 501 E. Polk Street, Tampa, FL 33602 (813) 228–2000.
Suite 510, 433 Cherry Street, Macon, GA 31201 (478) 752–3544.
Suite 128, 110 East Park Avenue, Tallahassee, FL 32301 (850) 521–5050.
Suite 620, 135 West Central Boulevard, Orlando, FL 32801 (407) 648–6301.

COMMUNITY RELATIONS SERVICE

**600 E Street NW, Suite 6000, Washington, DC 20530, phone (202) 305–2935
fax 305–3009 (BICN)**

Director.—Sharee M. Freeman.
Deputy Associate Director.—Stephen N. Thom.
Special Assistant to the Director.—Julie Warren.
Attorney Advisor.—George Henderson, 305–2964.
Media Affairs Officer.—Daryl Borgquist, 305–2966.

REGIONAL DIRECTORS

New England.—Frances Amoroso, 408 Atlantic Avenue, Suite 222, Boston, MA 02110–1032 (617) 424–5715.
Northeast Region.—Reinaldo Rivera, 26 Federal Plaza, Suite 36–118, New York, NY 10278 (212) 264–0700.
Mid-Atlantic Region.—Vermont McKinney, Customs House, Second and Chestnut Streets, Suite 208, Philadelphia, PA 19106 (215) 597–2344.
Southeast Region.—Thomas Battles, Citizens Trust Company Bank Building, Suite 900, 75 Piedmont Avenue NE., Atlanta, GA 30303 (404) 331–6883.
Midwest Region.—Jesse Taylor, Xerox Center Building, 55 West Monroe Street, Suite 420, Chicago, IL 60603 (312) 353–4391.
Southwest Region.—Carmelita P. Freeman, 1420 West Mockingbird Lane, Suite 250, Dallas, TX 75247 (214) 655–8175.
Central Region.—Pascual Marquez, 1100 Maine Street, Suite 320, Kansas City, MO 64106 (816) 426–7433.
Rocky Mountain Region.—Philip Arreola, 1244 Speer Boulevard, Suite 650, Denver, CO 80204–3584 (303) 844–2973.
Northwest Region.—Rosa Melendez, Federal Office Building, 915 Second Avenue, Suite 1808, Seattle, WA, 98174 (206) 220–6700.
Western Region.—Ron Wakabayashi, 888 South Figueroa Street, Suite 1880, Los Angeles, CA 90017 (213) 894–2941.

FOREIGN CLAIMS SETTLEMENT COMMISSION

Bicentennial Building, 600 E Street NW., Suite 6002, 20579, phone (202) 616–6975 (BICN)

Chair.—Mauricio J. Tamargo.
   Chief Counsel.—David E. Bradley.
   Special Assistant.—Elizabeth Nodal.
   Commissioner.—Jeremy H.G. Ibrahim.
   Administrative Officer.—Judith H. Lock, 616–6986.

OFFICE OF COMMUNITY ORIENTED POLICING SERVICES

1110 Vermont Avenue NW., Washington, DC 20530

DIRECTOR'S OFFICE

Director.—Carl Peed, 616–2888.
   Special Assistant.—Laurel Matthews.
   Administrative Assistant.—Sharon Baker.
   Chief of Staff.—Timothy Quinn.
   Deputy Director for—
      Community Policing Development.—Pam Cammarata, 514–5793.
      Management.—Timothy Quinn.
      Operations.—Robert Phillips.

ADMINISTRATIVE DIVISION

Assistant Director.—Diane Hughes, 4th floor, 353–2500.
   Financial Officer.—Vivian Perry, 3rd floor, 514–3973.
   Human Resources Program Manager.—Debbie Brown, 4th floor, 514–8956.
   Management Information Technology Specialist.—Andy Taylor, 4th floor, 305–2391.
   Supervisory Administrative Services Specialist.—Vicki Ellison, 4th floor, 353–3361.

AUDIT DIVISION

Assistant Director.—Cynthia Bowie, 6th floor, 514–7022.

COMMUNICATIONS DIVISION

Assistant Director.—Maria Carolina Rozas, 6th floor, 616–1728.

EXTERNAL AFFAIRS DIVISION

Assistant Director.—David Buchanan, 11th floor, 514–9079.

GRANTS ADMINISTRATION DIVISION

Assistant Director.—Robert Phillips, 10th floor, 616–2888.
   Grant Regional Supervisors:
Jamie French, 7th floor, 616–9767.   Michael Dame, 8th floor, 305–7541.
Keesha Thompson, 5th floor, 616–1902.   Andy Dorr, 9th floor, 353–9736.

GRANT MONITORING DIVISION

Assistant Director.—Juliette White, 6th floor, 514–9195.
   Grant Monitoring Regional Supervisors: David Neely, 514–8553; Marcia Samuels, 514–8507.

LEGAL DIVISION

General Counsel.—Lani Lee, 12th floor, 514–3750.
Deputy General Counsel.—Charlotte C. Grzebien, 616–2899.
Associate General Counsel.—Jenny Wu, 514–9424.

PROGRAM / POLICY SUPPORT AND EVALUATION

Assistant Director.—Matthew Scheider (acting), 6th floor, 514–2301.

TECHNICAL ASSISTANCE AND TRAINING DIVISION

Assistant Director.—Beverly Alford, 6th floor, 514–2301.

EXECUTIVE OFFICE FOR IMMIGRATION REVIEW (EOIR)

Director.—Kevin D. Rooney, 2600 SKYT (703) 305–0169.
  Deputy Director.—Kevin A. Ohlson.
  Associate Director / Chief of Staff.—Paula Nasca.
  Executive Secretariat.—Terry Samuels.
  Assistant Director / General Counsel.—MaryBeth Keller, 305–0470.
  Assistant Director of:
    Administration.—Lawrence M. D'Elia, 2300 SKYT, 305–1171.
    Management Programs.—Frances A. Mooney, 305–0289.
    Planning, Analysis and Technology.—Amy Dale, 605–0445.
  Chairman, Board of Immigration Appeals.—Lori L. Scialabba, 2400 SKYT, 305–1194.
  Chief, Office of the Chief Administrative Hearing Officer.—MaryBeth Keller (acting), 2600 SKYT, 305–0470.
  Chief Judge, Office of the Chief Immigration Judge.—Michael J. Creppy, 2500 SKYT, 305–1247.
  Deputy Chiefs, Immigration Judge.—Brian M. O'Leary, Thomas L. Pullen, 2500 SKYT, 305–1247.
  Telephone Directory Coordinator.—Annette Thomas (703) 605–1336.

EXECUTIVE OFFICE FOR UNITED STATES ATTORNEYS (EOUSA)
Robert F. Kennedy Department of Justice Building, 950 Pennsylvania Avenue, NW., Room 2621, 20530, phone 514–2121

Director.—Mary Beth Buchanan.
  Deputy Director.—Robin C. Ashton, room 2621.
  Chief of Staff.—Richard Byrne.
  Editor, AGAC Liaison and United States Attorney's Manual.—Judith A. Beeman, room 2335, 514–4633.
  Office of Tribal Justice.—Tracy Toulou, room 2229A, 514–8812.
  Assistant Director of:
    Case Management.—Siobhan Sperin, room 7500, BICN, 616–6919.
    Data Analysis Staff.—Barbara Tone, room 2000, BICN, 616–6779.
    Equal Employment Opportunity Staff.—Juan E. Milanes, room 524, NPB, 514–3982.
    Evaluation and Review Staff.—Chris Barnes, room 8500, BICN, 616–6776.
    Budget Execution.—Mary Ellen Wagner, room 8000, BICN, 616–6886.
    Facilities Management and Support Service.—Trisha M. Bursey, room 2400, BICN, 616–6425.
    FOIA and Privacy.—Marie O'Rourke, room 7300, BICN, 616–6757.
    Information Systems Security Staff.—Ted Shelkey, room 2300, BICN, 616–6973.
    Office Automation.—Vance Allen, room 9100, BICN, 616–6969.
    Personnel Management Staff.—Linda Schwartz, room 8017, BICN, 616–6873.
    Security Programs Staff.—Tommie Barnes, room 2600, BICN, 616–6878.
  Employee Assistance Program Administrator.—Bob Norton, room 6800, BICN, 514–1036.
  General Counsel.—Scott Schools, room 2200, BICN, 514–4024.
  Director, Legal Education.—Michael W. Bailie, National Advocacy Center, 1620 Pendleton Street, Columbia, SC 29201 (803) 544–5100.

Chief Financial Officers: Michael W. Bailie (acting); Lisa Bevels, room 8000, BICN, 616–6886.
Chief Operating Officer.—David Downs, room 8105, BICN, 616–6600.
Associate Directors.—Gail Williamson, room 8105, BICN, 616–6600.
Telecommunications and Technology Development.—Danny Ko, room 6012, BICN, 616–6439.
Counsel, Legal Programs and Policy.—Dan Villegas, room 7600, BICN, 616–6444.
Assistant Director, District Assistance Program.—Debora Cottrell, room 8105, BICN, 353–9394.
Telephone Directory Coordinator.—Mary Kay Benavente, room 8200, BICN, 616–6900.

INTERPOL—U.S. NATIONAL CENTRAL BUREAU

phone 616–9000

Director.—James M. Sullivan, 616–9700.
Deputy Director.—Martin Renkiewicz, 616–9700.
Information Resources Manager.—Wayne Towson, 616–3855.
General Counsel.—Kevin Smith, 616–4103.
Assistant Director, Division of:
  Administrative Services.—Aaron A. BoBo (acting), 616–7983.
  Alien/Fugitive.—Esteban Soto, 616–0310.
  Drug Investigations.—Frank Marrero, 616–3379.
  Economic Crimes.—John Sinnen, 616–5466.
  State Liaison.—Michael D. Muth, 616–8272.
  Terrorism and Violent Crimes.—Paul Cha (acting), 616–7258.

NATIONAL DRUG INTELLIGENCE CENTER (NDIC)

319 Washington Street, Johnstown, PA 15901, phone (814) 532–4601

Email: NDIC.contacts@usdoj.gov

Liaison Office, 8201 Greensboro Drive, Suite 1001, McLean, VA 22102

phone (703) 556–8970

Director.—Martin W. Pracht (acting), (814) 532–4607.
Special Assistant to the Director.—John K. Wallace (703) 556–8984.
Legal Counsel.—Manuel A. Rodriguez (703) 556–8975.
Chief of:
  Congressional, Public, and Interagency Relations.—Charles F. Miller (703) 556–8986.
  Security and Classified Programs.—Steven R. Frank (814) 532–4728.
Supervisor, Policies and Procedures.—Suzanne L. Craft (814) 532–4649.
Assistant Director, Intelligence.—Robert J. Rae (acting), (814) 532–4069.
Deputy Assistant Director, Intelligence.—Robert J. Rae (814) 532–4069.
Deputy Assistant Director for Intelligence Policy.—Gregory T. Gatjanis (703) 556–8997.
Chief of:
  Domestic Strategic Branch.—Matthew G. Maggio (acting), (814) 532–4989.
  National Issues Branch.—Dean T. Scott (acting), (814) 532–4577.
Assistant Director, Document Exploitation.—Dennis A. Morton (814) 532–4761.
  Deputy Assistant Director, Document Exploitation.—Irene S. Hernandez (814) 532–4675.
Chief of:
  Document Exploitation Branch A.—Charles J. Rivetti (814) 532–4654.
  Document Exploitation Branch B.—Randy A. Weaver (814) 532–4552.
  Document Exploitation Branch C.—Vance W. Stacy (814) 532–4066.
Assistant Director, Intelligence Support.—David J. Mrozowski (814) 532–4087.
Chief of:
  Administrative Services Branch.—Karl F. Wenger, Jr. (814) 532–4628.
  Intelligence Services Branch.—Bruce I. Merchant (814) 532–4558.
  Technical Services Branch.—David J. Bonski (814) 532–4795.
Telephone Directory Coordinator.—Kelly Creighton (703) 556–8982.

OFFICE ON VIOLENCE AGAINST WOMEN
800 K Street, NW., Suite 920, Washington, DC 20530

Director.—Diane M. Stuart, room 9327, TWC, 307–0728.
  Chief of Staff.—Kristina Rose, room 9325, TWC, 307–0466.
  Deputy Director.—Catherine Pierce, room 9212, TWC, 307–3913.
  Counsel to the Director.—Natalie Voris, room 9306, TWC, 514–5076.
  Assistant Directors: Darlene Johnson, room 9424, TWC, 307–6795; Lauren Nassikas, room 9225, TWC, 305–1792; Nadine Neufville, room 9425, TWC, 305–2590.

DEPARTMENT OF THE INTERIOR

Interior Building, 1849 C Street 20240, phone (202) 208–3100, http://www.doi.gov

GALE NORTON, Secretary of the Interior; education: B.A., University of Denver, 1975; law degree, University of Denver, 1978; professional: Senior Attorney, Mountain States Legal Foundation, 1979–1983; Assistant to the Deputy Secretary of Agriculture, 1984–1985; Associate Solicitor at the Department of the Interior, 1985–1990; Colorado Attorney General, 1991– 1999; Chair, Environment Committee for the Republican National Lawyers Association; General Counsel, Colorado Civil Justice League; awards: National Federalist Society Young Lawyer of the Year; and Colorado Women's Bar Association Mary Lathrop Trailblazer Award; family: married to John Hughes; nominated by President George W. Bush to become the 48th Secretary of the Interior, and was confirmed by the U.S. Senate on January 30, 2001.

OFFICE OF THE SECRETARY

Interior Building, Room 6156, phone 208–7351, fax 208–5048

Secretary of the Interior.—Gale Norton.
  Special Assistant to the Secretary.—Patricia Connally.
  Chief of Staff.—Brian Waidmann.
  Deputy Chief of Staff.—David L. Bernhardt, 208–5504.
  Director of External and Intergovernmental Affairs.—Kit Kimball, 208–1923.
  Senior Adviser for Alaska Affairs.—Drue Pearce, 208–4177.

OFFICE OF THE DEPUTY SECRETARY

Interior Building, Room 6117, phone 208–6291

Deputy Secretary.—P. Lynn Scarlett.
  Associate Deputy Secretary.—James E. Cason.
  Assistant Deputy Secretary.—Abraham E. Haspel.
  Counselor to the Deputy Secretary.—Daniel Jorjani.

OFFICE OF THE SPECIAL TRUSTEE FOR AMERICAN INDIANS

Interior Building, Room 5140, phone 208–4866, fax 208–7545

Special Trustee.—Ross O. Swimmer.

EXECUTIVE SECRETARIAT

Interior Building, Room 7212, phone 208–3181, fax 219–2100

Director.—Fay Iudicello.
  Acting Deputy Director.—Dick Stephan, room 7217, 208–5257.

CONGRESSIONAL AND LEGISLATIVE AFFAIRS

Interior Building, Room 6256, phone 208–7693

Director and Counselor to the Secretary.—Matthew Eames.
  Deputy Director of the Senate.—Chad Calvert.
  Deputy Director, House of Representatives.—Teresa Davies.
  Legislative Counsel.—Jane Lyder, Room 6245, 208–6706.

OFFICE OF COMMUNICATIONS

Interior Building, Room 6213, phone 208–6416

Director.—Tina Kreisher.
 Speech Writer.—Charles Russo.
 Press Secretary.—Dan Dubray, room 6217.
 Information Officers: Steve Brooks, Stephanie Hanna, Joan Moody, Frank Quimby, Hugh Vickery, John E. Wright, 208–6416.

OFFICE OF THE SOLICITOR

Interior Building, Room 6352, phone 208–4423

Solicitor.—Sue Ellen Wooldridge.
 Deputy Solicitor.—Roderick E. Walston.
 Associate Solicitor for—
  Administration.—Edward Keable.
  General Law.—Hugo Teufel.
  Indian Affairs.—Edith Blackwell.
  Land and Water.—Matthew J. McKeown.
  Mineral Resources.—Fred Ferguson.
  Parks and Wildlife.—Charles (Pete) Raynor.

OFFICE OF THE INSPECTOR GENERAL

Interior Building, Room 539, phone 208–5745, fax 219–3856

Inspector General.—Earl Devaney, room 5359.
 Deputy Inspector General.—Mary Kendall Adler.
 Association Inspector General for Whistle Blower Protection.—Richard Trinidad.
 Assistant Inspector General for—
  Administrative Service and Information Management.—Michael F. Wood.
  Audits.—Roger La Rouche, 208–4252.
  Investigations.—David A. Montoya, 208–6752.

ASSISTANT SECRETARY FOR POLICY, MANAGEMENT AND BUDGET

Interior Building, Room 5110, phone 208–4203

Senior Advisor.—Robert Lamb.
 Director, Office of Budget.—John D. Trezise, room 4100, 208–5308.
 Deputy Assistant Secretary for—
  Business Management and Wildland Fire.—Nina Hatfield, 208–7966.
  Insular Affairs.—David Cohen, room 4328, 208–4736.
  Law Enforcement and Security.—Larry Parkinson, room 7352, 208–5773.
  Performance, Accountability, and Human Resources.—Scott Cameron, room 5120, 208–1738.
  Policy and International Affairs.—Chris Kearney, room 5124, 208–3219.
 Human Capitol Officer.—Kathleen Wheeler, room 5129, 208–4727.

ASSISTANT SECRETARY FOR FISH AND WILDLIFE AND PARKS

Interior Building, Room 3156, phone 208–5347

Assistant Secretary.—Harold Craig Manson.
 Deputy Assistant Secretary.—Paul D. Hoffman, 208–4416.
 Deputy Assistant Secretary and Counselor.—P. David Smith, room 3154, 208–5378.
 Senior Advisor to the Assistant Secretary.—Julie A. MacDonald, room 3144, 208–3928.

U.S. FISH AND WILDLIFE SERVICE

Interior Building, phone 208–4717, fax 208–6965

Director.—Steven A. Williams, 208–4717.
 Deputy Directors: Matthew J. Hogan, Marshall P. Jones, Jr., 208–4545.

Chief, Office of Law Enforcement.—Kevin Adams, 208–3809.
Assistant Director for External Affairs.—Thomas O. Melius, 208–3809.
  Chief, Division of:
    Congressional and Legislative Affairs.—Alexandra Pitts, 208–5403.
    Public Affairs.—Mitch Snow (acting), 208–4131.
Assistant Director for Migratory Birds and State Programs.—Paul Schmidt, 208–1050.
  Chief, Office of Federal Aid.—Kris LaMontagne (703) 358–2156.
Assistant Director for—
  Budget, Planning, and Human Resources.—Denise Sheehan, 208–3736.
    Chief, Division of Human Resources.—Kent Baum (703) 358–1776.
  Business Management and Operations.—Paul Henne (703) 358–1822.
  Endangered Species.—Gary Frazer, 208–4646.
  Fisheries and Habitat Conservation.—Mamie Parker, 208–6394.
  International Affairs.—Kenneth P. Stansell, 208–6393.
  National Wildlife Refuge System.—William Hartwig, 208–5333.
Regional Directors:
  Region 1.—David B. Allen, Eastside Federal Complex, 911 Northeast 11th Avenue, Portland, OR 97232 (503) 231–6118, fax 872–2716.
    California/Nevada Operations.—Steve Thompson, 2800 Cottage Way, Suite W2606, Sacramento, CA 95823 (916) 414–6486.
  Region 2.—Dale Hall, PO Box 1306, Room 1306, 500 Gold Avenue SW., Albuquerque, NM 87103 (505) 248–6845.
  Region 3.—Robyn Thorson, Federal Building, Fort Snelling, Twin Cities, MN 55111 (612) 713–5301.
  Region 4.—Samuel D. Hamilton, 1875 Century Boulevard, Atlanta, GA 30345 (404) 679–4000, fax 679–4006.
  Region 5.—Marvin Moriarty, 300 Westgate Center Drive, Hadley, MA 01035 (413) 253–8300, fax 253–8308.
  Region 6.—Ralph Morgenweck, PO Box 25486, Denver Federal Center, Denver, CO 80225 (303) 236–7920, fax 236–8295.
  Region 7.—Rowan Gould, 1011 East Tudor Road, Anchorage, AK 99503 (907) 786–3542, fax 786–3306.

NATIONAL PARK SERVICE

Interior Building, Room 3104, phone 208–4621, fax 208–7625

Director.—Fran Mainella, room 3112.
  Deputy Director.—Randy Jones, room 3113.
  Associate Director for—
    Cultural Resources, Stewardship and Partnership.—Kate Stevenson, room 3128, 208–7625.
    Natural Resources Stewardship and Science.—Mike Soukup, room 3125, 208–3884.
    Park Operations and Education.—Richard Ring, room 3130, 208–5651.
    Professional Services.—Terrell Emmons, room 3127, 208–3264.
  Assistant Director for Legislative and Congressional Affairs.—P. Daniel Smith, room 3210A, 208–5655.
  Chief, Office of Public Affairs.—Dave Barna, room 3043, 208–6843.
  Regional Directors:
    Alaska Region.—Rob Arnberger, 2525 Gambell Street, Anchorage, AK 99503 (907) 257–2690, fax 257–2510.
    Northeast Region.—Marie Rust, 200 Chestnut Street, Philadelphia, PA 19106 (215) 597–7013, fax 597–0815.
    Midwest Region.—Ernest Quintana, 1709 Jackson Street, Omaha, NE, 68102 (402) 221–3448, fax 341–2039.
    National Capital Region.—Terry R. Carlstrom (acting), 1100 Ohio Drive SW, Washington, DC 20242 (202) 619–7005, fax 619–7220.
    Intermountain Region.—Karen Wade, PO Box 25287, Denver, CO 80225 (303) 969–2500, fax 969–2785.
    Southeast Region.—William Schnek, 75 Spring Street SW., Atlanta, GA 30303 (404) 562–3100, fax 331–3263.
    Pacific Western Region.—Jon Jarvis, 600 Harrison Street, Suite 600, San Francisco, CA 94107 (415) 744–3876, fax 744–4050.

668 *Congressional Directory*

ASSISTANT SECRETARY FOR INDIAN AFFAIRS
Interior Building, Room 4160, phone 208–7163

Counselors to the Assistant Secretary: Mike Olsen, Theresa Rosier.

BUREAU OF INDIAN AFFAIRS
Interior Building, Room 4160, phone 208–5116

Director.—William (Pat) Ragsdale.
Director, Office of:
 Administration.—Debbie Clark.
 Trust Responsibilities.—Jeff Lowman.
 Tribal Services.—Michael Smith.
Director, Office of Indian Education Programs.—William Mehojah.
Regional Directors:
 Alaska Region.—Niles Cesar, Federal Building, 3rd floor, PO Box 25520, Juneau, AK 99802 (907) 586–7177, fax 586–7169.
 Eastern Oklahoma Region.—Janet Hanna, Fifth and West Okmulgee, Muskogee, OK 74401 (918) 687–2296, fax 687–2571.
 Eastern Region.—Franklin Keel, 711 Stewarts Ferry Pike, Nashville, TN 37214 (615) 467–1700, fax 467–1701.
 Great Plains Region.—William Benjamin, 115 Fourth Avenue SE, Aberdeen, SD 57401 (605) 226–7343, fax (602) 226–7446.
 Midwest Region.—Terry Virden, 331 Second Avenue South, Minneapolis, MN 55401 (612) 713–4400, fax 713–4401.
 Navajo Region.—Elouise Chicharello, PO Box 1060, Gallup, NM 87305 (505) 863–8314, fax 863–8245.
 Northwest Region.—Stanley Speaks, 911 11th Avenue NE, Portland, OR 97232 (503) 231–6702, fax 231–2201.
 Pacific Region.—Clay Gregory, 2800 Cottage Way, Sacramento, CA 95835 (916) 978–6000, fax 978–6099.
 Rocky Mountain Region.—Keith Beartusk, 316 North 26th Street, Billings, MT 58101 (406) 247–7943, fax 247–7976.
 Southern Plains Region.—Daniel J. Deerinwater, WCD Office Complex, Box 368, Anadarko, OK 73005 (405) 247–6673 Ext 314, fax 247–2242.
 Southwest Region.—Larry Morrin, 615 First Street NW., Box 26567, Albuquerque, NM 87125 (505) 563–3100, fax 563–3101.
 Western Region.—Wayne C. Nordwall, One North First Street, PO Box 10, Phoenix, AZ 85001 (602) 379–6600, fax 379–4413.

ASSISTANT SECRETARY FOR LAND AND MINERALS MANAGEMENT
Interior Building, Room 7312, phone 208–6734, fax 208–3144

Assistant Secretary.—Rebecca W. Watson.
Deputy Assistant Secretary.—Patricia Morrison.

BUREAU OF LAND MANAGEMENT
Interior Building, Room 3314, phone 208–3801, fax 208–5242

Director.—Kathleen Clark, room 5660.
Deputy Director of:
 Fire and Aviation.—Anne Jeffrey, room 5633, 208–4717.
 Operations.—Francis R. Cherry, room 5660.
 Programs and Policy.—James Hughes.
State Directors:
 Alaska.—Henri Bisson, 222 West Seventh Avenue No. 13, Anchorage, AK 99513 (907) 271–5080, fax 271–4596.
 Arizona.—Elaine Y. Zielinski, 222 North Central Avenue, Phoenix, AZ 85004 (602) 417–9500, fax 417–9398.
 California.—Mike Pool, 2800 Cottage Way, Suite W1834, Sacramento, CA 95825 (916) 978–4600, fax 978–4699.
 Colorado.—Ron Wenker, 2850 Youngfield Street, Lakewood, CO 80215 (303) 239–3700, fax 239–3934.

Eastern States.—Mike Nedd, 7450 Boston Boulevard, Springfield, VA 22153 (703) 440–1700, fax 440–1701.
Idaho.—K. Lynn Bennett, 1387 South Vinnell Way, Boise, ID 83709 (208) 373–4000, fax 373–3919.
Montana.—Thomas P. Lonnie, 5001 Southgate Drive, Billings, MT 59101 (406) 896–5012, fax 896–5004.
Nevada.—Robert V. Abbey, P.O. Box 12000, Reno, NV 89520 (775) 861–6590, fax 861–6601.
New Mexico.—Linda S.C. Rundell, P.O. Box 27115, Sante Fe, NM 87502 (505) 438–7501, fax 438–7452.
Oregon.—Elaine Marquis-Brong, 333 SW 1st Avenue, Portland, OR 97204 (503) 808–6024, fax 808–6308.
Utah.—Sally Wisely, 324 South State Street, 4th Floor, Salt Lake City, UT 84111 (801) 539–4010, fax 539–4013.
Wyoming.—Bob Bennett, 5353 Yellowstone Road, PO Box 1828, Cheyenne, WY 82003 (307) 775–6001, fax 775–6028.

MINERALS MANAGEMENT SERVICE
Interior Building, MS 4230 MIB, phone 208–3500, fax 208–7242

Director.—R.M. (Johnnie) Burton.
Deputy Director.—Walter D. Cruickshank.
Associate Director for—
  Administration and Budget.—Robert E. Brown, 208–3220.
  Offshore Minerals Management.—Thomas Readinger, 208–3530.
  Policy and Management Improvement.—George Triebsch, 208–3398.
  Royalty Management.—Lucy Querques Denett, 208–3515.
Other Continental Shelf Regions:
  Alaska.—John T. Goll, 949 East 36th Avenue, Suite 300, Anchorage, AK 99508 (907) 271–6010.
  Gulf of Mexico.—Chris C. Oynes, 1201 Elmwood Park Boulevard, New Orleans, LA 70123 (504) 736–2589, fax 736–2589.
  Pacific.—J. Lisle Reed, 770 Paseo Camarillo, Camarillo, CA 93010 (805) 389–7502.

SURFACE MINING RECLAMATION AND ENFORCEMENT
South Interior Building, Room 233, phone 208–4006, fax 219–3106

Director.—Jeffrey D. Jarrett.
Deputy Director.—Glenda Owens, room 233, SIB, 208–2807.
Assistant Director for Finance and Administration.—Carol Sampson, 208–2560.
Regional Director for—
  Appalachian Coordinating Center.—Allen Klein, Three Parkway Center, Pittsburgh, PA 15220 (412) 937–2828, fax 937–2903.
  Mid-Continent Coordinating Center.—Charles Sandberg, 501 Belle Street, Room 216, Alton, IL 62002 (618) 463–6463, fax 463–6470.
  Western Coordinating Center.—Brent T. Walquist, 1999 Broadway, Suite 3320, Denver, CO 80202 (303) 844–1401, fax 844–1522.
Field Office Director for—
  Alabama.—Arthur Abbs, 135 Gemini Circle, Suite 215, Homewood, AL 35209 (205) 290–7282, fax 290–7280.
  Indiana.—Andrew Gilmore, Minton-Capehart Federal Building, 575 North Pennsylvania Street, Room 301, Indianapolis, IN 46204 (317) 226–6700, fax 226–6182.
  Kentucky.—William Kovacic, 2675 Regency Road, Lexington, KY 40503 (606) 233–2894, fax 233–2898.
  New Mexico.—Willis Gainer, 505 Marquette Avenue NW, Suite 1200, Albuquerque, NM 87102 (505) 248–5070, fax 248–5081.
  Oklahoma.—Michael Wolfrom, 5100 East Skelley Drive, Suite 470, Tulsa, OK 74135 (918) 581–6430, fax 581–6419.
  Pennsylvania.—Beverly Brock (acting), Transportation Center, 415 Market Street, Suite 3C, Harrisburg, PA 17101 (717) 782–4036, fax 782–3771.
  Tennessee.—George Miller, 530 Gay Street, Suite 500, Knoxville, TN 37902 (423) 545–4103, fax 545–4111.
  Virginia.—Robert Penn, PO Drawer 1216, Big Stone Gap, VA 24219 (540) 523–0001, fax 523–5053.

West Virginia.—Roger Calhoun, 1027 Virginia Street East, Charleston, WV 25301 (304) 347–7162, fax 347–7170.
Wyoming.—Guy Padgett, 100 East B Street, Room 2128, Casper, WY 82601 (307) 261–6550, fax 261–6552.

ASSISTANT SECRETARY FOR WATER AND SCIENCE

Interior Building, Room 7414, phone 208–3186, fax 208–6948

Assistant Secretary.—R. Thomas Weimer (acting).
Deputy Assistant Secretary.—R. Thomas Weimer, room 6654, 208–3136.

U.S. GEOLOGICAL SURVEY

The National Center, 12201 Sunrise Valley Drive, Reston, VA 20192

phone (703) 648–7411, fax 648–4454

Director.—Charles G. Groat.
Deputy Director.—Robert E. Doyle, 648–7412.
Office of:
  Administrative Policy and Services.—Carol Aten (703) 648–7200.
  Geographic Information Officer.—Karen Siderelis (703) 648–5747.
Associate Directors for—
  Biology.—Susan D. Haseltine (703) 648–4050.
  Geology.—P. Patrick Leahy (703) 648–6600.
  Geography.—Barbara J. Ryan (703) 648–7413.
  Water.—Robert M. Hirsch (703) 648–5215.
Eastern Regional Director.—Bonnie A. McGregor, 1700 Leetown Road, Kearneysville, WV 25430 (304) 724–4521.
Central Regional Director.—Thomas J. Casadevall, P.O. Box 25046, Denver Federal Center, Building 810, Denver, CO 80225 (303) 202–4740.
Western Regional Director.—John (Doug) Buffington, 909 First Avenue, Suite 704, Seattle, WA 98104 (206) 220–4578.

BUREAU OF RECLAMATION

Interior Building, Room 7554, phone 513–0501, fax 513–0309

Commissioner.—John W. Keys III, room 7654.
Chief of Staff.—Robert J. Quint, room 7657.
Director of:
  Congressional and Legislative Affairs.—David McCarthy, 513–0565.
  External and Intergovernmental Affairs.—Mark Limbaugh, 513–0615.
  Public Affairs.—Trudy Harlow, room 7642, 513–0575.
Director, Operations.—Jack Garner, room 7645, 513–0615.
Regional Directors:
  Great Plains.—Maryanne Bach, P.O. Box 36900, Billings, MT 59107 (406) 247–7600, fax 247–7793.
  Lower Colorado.—Robert W. Johnson, P.O. Box 61470, Boulder City, NV 89006 (702) 293–8411, fax 293–8416.
  Mid-Pacific Region.—Kirk C. Rodgers, Federal Office Building, 2800 Cottage Way, Sacramento, CA 95825 (916) 978–5000, fax 978–5599.
  Pacific Northwest.—Bill McDonald, 1150 North Curtis Road, Suite 100, Boise, ID 83706 (208) 378–5012, fax 378–5019.
  Upper Colorado.—Rick Gold, 125 South State Street, room 6107, Salt Lake City, UT 84138 (801) 524–3600.

DEPARTMENT OF AGRICULTURE

Jamie L. Whitten Building, 1400 Independence Avenue, SW, Washington, DC 20250
phone (202) 720–3631, http://www.usda.gov

MIKE JOHANNS, Secretary of Agriculture; born in Osage, IA; education: B.A., St. Mary's University, Minnesota; J.D., Creighton University; professional: Governor, Nebraska, 1999–2005; Mayor, Lincoln, Nebraska, 1991–98; Lancaster County Board, 1982–88; Lincoln City Council, 1989–90; Practicing attorney, 1975–91; member: National Governors' Association; Western Governors' Association; married: Stephanie; two children; nominated by President George W. Bush to become the 28th Secretary of Agriculture, and was confirmed by the U.S. Senate on January 20, 2005.

OFFICE OF THE SECRETARY

Secretary of Agriculture.—Mike Johanns, room 200–A (202) 720–3631.
 Deputy Secretary.—Charles F. Conner.
 Chief of Staff.—Dale Moore.
 Counsel for Trade.—David Hegwood.
 Special Assistant to the President/Personnel.—Drew DeBerry.
 Executive Secretariat.—Bruce Bundick, room 116–A, 720–7100.
 General Counsel.—James Michael Kelly (acting), room 107–W, 720–3351.
 Inspector General.—Phyllis Fong, room 117–W, 720–8001.
 Chief Economist.—Keith Collins, room 227–E, 720–4164.
 Chief Information Officer.—Scott Charbo, room 416–W, 720–3152.
 Director of Communications.—Terri Teuber, room 402–A, 720–4623.
 Press Secretary.—Ed Loyd, 720–4623.
 Under Secretary for Natural Resources and Environment.—Mark Rey.
 Chief of:
  Forest Service.—Dale Bosworth, Sidney R. Yates Building, 205–1661.
  Natural Resources Conservation Service.—Bruce Knight, room 5105–S, BG, 720–4526.
 Under Secretary for Farm and Foreign Agricultural Services.—J.B. Penn, room 205–E, 720–3111.
 Administrator for—
  Farm Services Agency.—James Little, room 3086–S, BG, 720–3467.
  Foreign Agricultural Service.—A. Ellen Terpstra, room 5071–S, BG, 720–3935.
 Under Secretary for Rural Development.—Gilbert Gonzalez (acting).
 Administrator for—
  Rural Business-Cooperative Service.—Peter Thomas, room 5045–S, 690–4730.
  Rural Housing Service.—Russell Davis, 690–1533.
  Rural Utilities Service.—Curtis Anderson (acting), 720–9540.
 Under Secretary for Food, Nutrition and Consumer Services.—Eric Bost, room 240–E, 720–7711.
 Administrator for Food and Nutrition Service.—Roberto Salazar, room 803, Park Center, 305–2062.
 Under Secretary for Food Safety.—Merle D. Pierson (acting), 720–0350.
 Administrator for Food Safety and Inspection Service.—Barbara Masters, room 331–E, 720–7025.
 Under Secretary for Research, Education and Economics.—Joseph Jen, room 217–W, 720–8885.
 Administrator for—
  Agricultural Research Service.—Edward B. Knipling, room 302–A, 720–3656.
  Cooperative State Research, Education, and Extension Service.—Colien Hefferan, room 304–A, 720–4423.
  Economic Research Service.—Susan Offutt, room 4145, M. Street, 694–5000.
  National Agricultural Statistics Service.—Ron Bosecker, room 417–S, BG, 720–2707.
 Under Secretary for Marketing and Regulatory Service.—William Hawks, room 228–W, 720–4256.

Administrator for—
  Agricultural Marketing Service.—Kenneth Clayton (acting), room 3071–S, 720–5115.
  Animal and Plant Health Inspection Service.—Ron DeHaven, room 313–E, 720–3668.
  Grain Inspection, Packers and Stockyards.—David Shipman (acting), room 1094–S, 720–0219.
Assistant Secretary for—
  Administration.—Michael Harrison, 720–3291.
  Civil Rights.—Vernon Parker, room 240–W, 720–3808.
  Congressional and Intergovernmental Relations.—Arlen Lancaster, room 213–A, 720–7095.
Director of:
  Ethics.—Ray Sheehan, room 347–W, 720–2251.
  Human Resources Management.—Ruthie Jackson, room 316–W, 720–3585.
  Operations.—Priscilla Carey, room 1575–S, 720–3937.
  Outreach.—Gladys Vaughn, 1575 Reporters Building, 720–6350.
  Procurement and Property Management.—Warren R. Ashworth, Reporters Building, room 302, 720–9448.
  Small and Disadvantaged Business Utilization.—Jim House, room 1566–S, 720–7117.
Office of Administrative Law Judges, Chief Judge.—Marc Hillson, room 1070–S, 720–6368.
Board of Contract Appeals.—Judge Howard Pollack, Chairman, room 2916–S, 720–7023.
Office of the Judicial Officer.—William Jensen, room 1449–S, 720–7664.
Director, Office of:
  Budget and Program Analysis.—Stephen B. Dewhurst, room 101–A, 720–7323.
  Executive Secretariat.—Bruce Bundick, room 116–A, 720–7100.
  National Appeals Division.—Roger J. Klurfeld, room 1100–Park Center (703) 305–2708.

GENERAL COUNSEL
Jamie L. Whitten Building, Room 107–W, phone 720–3351

General Counsel.—James Michael Kelly (acting).
Deputy General Counsel.—James Michael Kelly.
Associate General Counsel for—
  Civil Rights.—Arlean Leland, 720–1760.
  International Affairs: Commodity Programs and Food Assistant Programs.—Thomas V. Conway, 720–6883.
  Legislation, Litigation, General Law.—James Michael Kelly, 720–3351.
  Marketing, Regulatory and Food Safety Programs.—John Golden, 720–3155.
  Natural Resources.—Jan Poling, 720–9311.
  Rural Development.—David P. Grahn, 720–6187.
Deputy Associate General Counsel, Division of:
  Civil Rights Litigation.—Inga Bumbary-Langston, 720–3955.
  Community Development.—Paul Loizeaux, 720–4591.
  Conservation and Environment.—Stuart L. Shelton, 720–7121.
Assistant General Counsel, Division of:
  Food and Nutrition.—Ronald W. Hill, 720–6181.
  General Law.—Kenneth E. Cohen, 720–5565.
  International Affairs and Commodity Programs.—Ralph A. Linden, 720–9246.
  Legislation.—Michael J. Knipe, 720–5354.
  Litigation.—Margaret M. Breinholt, 720–4733.
  Marketing.—Kenneth H. Vail, 720–5935.
  Natural Resources.—Thomas Millet, 720–7121.
  Regulatory.—Tom M. Walsh, 720–5550.
  Rural Utilities.—Terence M. Brady, 720–2764.
  Trade Practices.—Mary K. Hobbie, 720–5293.
Resource Management Specialist.—Deborah L. Vita, 720–4861.

INSPECTOR GENERAL
Jamie L. Whitten Building, Room 117–W, phone 720–8001, fax 690–1278

Inspector General.—Phyllis K. Fong.
Deputy Inspector General.—Joyce Fleischmann, room 117–W, 720–7431.

Assistant Inspector General for—
    Audit.—Robert Young, room 403–E, 720–6945.
    Investigations.—Mark Woods, room 507–A, 720–3306.
    Planning and Special Projects.—Tracy LaPoint (acting), room 403–E, 720–6945.
    Policy Development and Resources Management.—Suzanne Murrin, room 5–E, 720–6979.

ASSISTANT SECRETARY FOR ADMINISTRATION
Jamie L. Whitten Building, Room 209–A, phone 720–3291

Assistant Secretary for Administration.—Michael J. Harrison.
    Deputy Assistant Secretary for Administration.—John Surina.
    Special Assistant.—Jennifer Cervantes-Eggers.
    Executive Assistant.—Eileen Kurtz.

BOARD OF CONTRACT APPEALS
South Agriculture Building, Room 2916–S, phone 720–7023

Chairman and Administrative Judge.—Howard A. Pollack.
    Administrative Judges: Anne W. Westbrook, 720–7242; Joseph A. Vergilio, 720–2066.
    Recorder.—Elaine M. Hillard, 720–7023.
    Deputy Recorder.—Alice Vincent, 720–7023.
    Legal Technician.—Natalie Krolczyk, room 2914–S, 720–7023.

OFFICE OF ADMINISTRATIVE LAW JUDGES
South Agriculture Building, Room 1070–S, phone 720–6383

Chief Administrative Law Judge.—Marc Hillson.
    Secretary to the Chief Administrative Law Judge.—Diane Green.
    Administrative Law Judge.—Jill S. Clifton, 720–8161.
    Hearing Clerk.—Joyce A. Dawson, 720–4443.

OFFICE OF THE JUDICIAL OFFICER
South Agriculture Building, Room 1449–S, phone 720–4764

Judicial Officer.—William G. Jensen.
    Attorney Examiner.—Michael J. Stewart, 720–9268.

OFFICE OF SMALL AND DISADVANTAGED BUSINESS UTILIZATION
South Agriculture Building, Room 1566–S, phone 720–7117

Director.—James E. House.

OFFICE OF OPERATIONS
South Agriculture Building, Room 1456–S, phone 720–3937

Director.—Priscilla Carey.
    Deputy Director.—Christopher A. Gomez, 720–1762.
    Medical Officer.—Oleh Jacykewycw, room 1039, 720–3893.

OFFICE OF HUMAN CAPITAL MANAGEMENT
Jamie L. Whitten Building, Room 302–W, phone 720–3585

Director.—Ruthie Jackson.
    Division Directors:
        Performance Management and Policy.—Denise Leger-Lee, 720–3327.
        Safety and Health Management.—James Stevens, 720–8248.

OFFICE OF PROCUREMENT AND PROPERTY MANAGEMENT
Reporters Building, Room 302, phone 720–9448

Director.—Warren R. Ashworth.
  Deputy Director.—Glenn Haggstrom.
  Division Directors:
    Procurement Policy.—David Shea, 720–6206.
    Property Management.—Denise Hayes, 720–7283.

ASSISTANT SECRETARY FOR CIVIL RIGHTS
Jamie L. Whitten Building Room 240–W, phone 720–3808

Assistant Secretary.—Vernon Parker.
  Deputy Assistant Secretary.—Paul Gutierrez.
  Associate Assistant Secretary.—Clyde Thompson.

OFFICE OF THE CHIEF FINANCIAL OFFICER
Jamie L. Whitten Building, Room 143–W, phone 720–5539

Deputy Chief Financial Officer.—Pat Healy, room 143–W, 720–0727.
  Associate Chief Financial Officer.—Wendy Snow, room 3057–S, 619–7636.
  Division Chiefs:
    Accounting Policy and Consolidated Reporting.—Kevin Close (202) 720–0990.
    Administrative Management.—Gaye Cook, 720–1011.
    Budget Division.—William King, room 3440–S, 720–1885.
    Credit, Travel and Grants Policy.—Matt Faulkner, 720–1307.
    Planning and Accountability.—Ava Lee, room 3436–S, 720–1179.
    Working Capital Fund.—Dwight Tayman, 720–1203.
  Director, National Finance Center.—Jerry Lohfink, PO Box 60000, New Orleans LA 70160 (504) 426–0120, fax (504) 426–9700.

OFFICE OF THE CHIEF INFORMATION OFFICER
Jamie L. Whitten Building, Room 414–W, phone 720–8833

Chief Information Officer.—Scott Charbo.
  Deputy Chief Information Officer.—Dave Combs (acting), room 414–W, 720–8833.
  Associate Chief Information Officers for—
    Cyber Security.—Gregory Parham (acting), 690–0048.
    E-Government.—Chris Niedermayer, 690–2118.
    Information Resources Management.—Greg Parham, 720–5865.
    National Information Technology Center.—Kathleen Rundle, P.O. Box 205, 8930 Ward Parkway, Kansas City, MO 64114 (816) 926–6501.
    Telecommunications Services and Operations.—Jan Lilja, 720–8695.
  Senior Policy Advisor for Field Service Center Oversight.—Richard Roberts (acting), 720–3482.
  Supervisory Computer Specialist.—Ed Troup, 3825 East Mulberry Street, Fort Collins, CO 80524 (303) 498–1510.

OFFICE OF THE CHIEF ECONOMIST
Jamie L. Whitten Building, Room 112–A, phone 720–4164

Chief Economist.—Keith Collins.
  Deputy Chief Economist.—Joseph Glauber, 720–6185.
  Chairperson of the World Agricultural Outlook Board.—Gerald A. Bange, room 4419–S, 720–6030.
  Chief Meteorologist.—Ray Motha, room 4441–S, 720–8651.
  National Weather Service, Supervisory Meteorologist.—David Miskus, room 4443–S, 720–6030.

Global Change Program Office.—William Hohenstein, room 4407–S, 720–6698.
Office of Energy Policy and New Uses.—Roger Conway, room 4059–S, 401–0461.
Office of Risk Assessment and Cost Benefit Analysis.—James Schaub, room 4032–S, 720–8022.
Office of Sustainable Development.—Adela Backiel, room 112–A, 720–2456.

OFFICE OF BUDGET AND PROGRAM ANALYSIS

Jamie L. Whitten Building, Room 101–A, phone 720–3323

Director.—Lawrence Wachs (acting).
Associate Director.—Lawrence Wachs, 720–5303.
Deputy Director, Budget, Legislative and Regulatory Systems.—Dennis Kaplan, room 102–E, 720–6667.
Deputy Director Program Analysis.—Scott Steele, room 126–W, 720–3396.

OFFICE OF THE EXECUTIVE SECRETARIAT

Jamie L. Whitten Building, Room 116–A, phone 720–7100

Director.—Bruce Bundick.
Deputy Director.—MaryAnn Swigart.

NATIONAL APPEALS DIVISION

3101 Park Center Drive, Room 1100, Alexandria VA 22302

Director.—Roger J. Klurfeld (703) 305–2708.
Deputy Director.—M. Terry Johnson.

OFFICE OF COMMUNICATIONS

Jamie L. Whitten Building, Room 402–A, phone 720–4623

Director.—Terri Teuber.
Deputy Press Secretary.—Ed Loyd.
Assistant Director.—Larry Quinn.
Center Directors:
  Broadcast Media and Technology.—David Black.
  Budget and Operations Services.—Ron DeMunbrun.
  Constituent Affairs.—Patricia Klintberg.
  Web Services and Distribution.—Kim Taylor.

UNDER SECRETARY FOR NATURAL RESOURCES AND ENVIRONMENT

Jamie L. Whitten Building, Room 21709–E, phone 720–7173

Under Secretary.—Mark Rey.
Deputy Under Secretary of Forestry.—Dave Tenny.

FOREST SERVICE

Sydney R. Yates Building, Fourth Floor, Auditors Building, 201 14th Street, SW., 20250 phone 205–1661

Chief.—Dale N. Bosworth.
Associate Chief.—Sally Collins.
Staff Directors:
  International Programs.—Valdis E. Mezainis, 205–1650.
  Office of Communications.—George Lennon, 205–8333.

BUDGET AND FINANCE
Sydney R. Yates Building, First Floor, phone 205–1784

CFO.—Jessie King, 205–1784.
Staff Director for Program Development and Budget.—Hank Kashdan, 205–0987.

BUSINESS OPERATIONS
Sydney R. Yates Building, Second Floor, phone 205–1709

Deputy Chief.—Chris Pyron, 205–1655.
Associate Deputy Chief.—Irving Thomas, 205–1707.
Staff Assistant.—Ron Hooper.
Staff Directors:
  Civil Rights.—Kathy Gause, 205–1585.
  Freedom of Information/Privacy Act.—Naomi Charboneau (703) 605–4910.
  Human Resources Management.—John Lopez (703) 605–4532.
  Senior, Youth and Volunteer Programs.—Art Bryant (703) 605–4830.

NATIONAL FOREST SYSTEM
Sydney R. Yates Building, Third Floor, phone 205–1665

Deputy Chief.—Joel Holtrop.
Associate Deputy Chiefs: Gloria Manning, Fred Norbury, 205–1465.
Staff Directors of:
  Ecosystem Management Coordination.—Fred Norbury, 205–0895.
  Engineering.—Vaughn Stokes, 205–1400.
  Forest Management.—Jeanette Raiser.
  Lands.—Greg Smith, 205–1248.
  Minerals and Geology.—Skip Underwood, 205–1224.
  Recreation.—Dave Holland, 205–1643.
  Watershed and Air Management.—Anne Zimmermann, 205–1473.

PROGRAMS AND LEGISLATION
Sydney R. Yates Building, Fifth Floor, phone 205–1663

Deputy Chief.—Elizabeth Estill.
Staff Assistant.—Eurial Turner, 205–1265.
Staff Chiefs of:
  Legislative Affairs.—Tim DeCoster, 205–1637.
  Policy Analysis.—Matiland Sharpe, 205–1775.
  Strategic Planning and Resource Assessment.—Paul Brouha, 205–1235.

RESEARCH AND DEVELOPMENT
Sydney R. Yates Building, First Floor, phone 205–1665

Deputy Chief.—Ann Bartuska, 205–1665.
Associate Deputy Chief.—Bov Eav, 205–1702.
Staff Assistant.—Hao Tran, 205–1293.
Staff Directors of:
  Science Policy, Planning, Inventory and Information.—Richard W. Guldin, 205–1507.
  Vegetation Management and Protection Research.—Jim Reaves, 205–1561.

STATE AND PRIVATE FORESTRY
Sydney R. Yates Building, Second Floor, phone 205–1567

Associate Deputy Chief.—Robin Thompson, 205–1331.
Staff Assistant.—Stana Federighi, 205–1470.
Staff Directors of:
  Cooperative Forestry.—Larry Payne, 205–1389.
  Fire and Aviation Management.—Tom Harbour, 205–1483.
  Forest Health Protection.—Rob Nangold, 205–1600.

NATURAL RESOURCES CONSERVATION SERVICE
South Building, Room 5105–S, 720–4525

Chief.—Bruce I. Knight, 720–7246.
  Associate Chief.—Dana D. York, 720–4531.
  Director of:
    Civil Rights Division.—Andrew Johnson (301) 504–2180.
    Conservation Communication Staff.—Terry Bish, 720–3210.
    Legislative Affairs.—Douglas McKalip, 720–2771.
  Strategic Natural Resource Issues Staff:
    Special Assistants to the Chiefs: Dave Gagner, 720–2534; Gary A. Margheim, 690–2877 / 720–9480; Taylor Oldroyd, 720–1882.
  Deputy Chief of Management.—P. Dwight Holman, 720–6297.
  Director & CIO, Information Technology Division.—Mary Thomas (301) 504–2232.
  Director of:
    Correspondence Management.—Stephanie I. Edelen, 690–0023.
    Financial Management Division.—Joseph O'Leska, 720–5904.
    Human Resources Management Division.—Karen Karlinchak, 720–2227.
    Information Technology Center.—Jack Carlson (970) 295–5576.
    Management Services Division.—Edward M. Biggers, Jr., 720–4102.
    National Employee Development Center.—Charles K. Adams (817) 509–3241.
  Deputy Chief, Programs.—Thomas W. Christensen, 720–4527.
  Director, Division of:
    Conservation Planning and Technical Assistance.—Carlos F. Henning, 720–8851.
    Easement Programs.—Leonard Jordan, 720–1854.
    Financial Assistance.—Kevin Brown, 720–1845.
    Resource Conservation and Community Development.—Anne Dubey, 720–2847.
  Associate Deputy Chief.—Carol Jett, 720–6580.
  Director of Outreach Division.—Larry Holmes (301) 504–2229.
Science and Technology:
  Deputy Chief.—Lawrence E. Clark, 720–4630.
  Director of:
    Animal Husbandry and Clean Water.—Tom Christensen (301) 504–2196.
    Conservation Engineering Division.—David Thackeray (acting), 720–2520.
    Conservation Operations Division.—Charles Whitmore, 720–1845.
    Ecological Sciences Division.—Diane F. Gelburd, 720–2587.
    Resource Economics and Social Sciences Division.—Doug Lawrence (acting), 720–5235.
Soil Survey and Resources Assessment:
  Deputy Chief.—William E. Puckett, 690–4616.
    Special Assistant to the Director.—Jeri I. Bere, 720–1881.
  Director of:
    Resource Inventory Division.—Wayne Maresch (301) 504–2271.
    Soil Survey Division.—Michael L. Golden, 720–1820.
Strategic Planning and Accountability:
  Deputy Chief.—Katherine C. Gugulis, 720–7847.
  Director, Operations Management and Oversight Division.—Steve Probst (acting), 720–8388.
  Budget Planning and Analysis.—Dan Runnels, 720–4533.
  Strategic and Performance Planning Division.—Dan Lawson, 690–0467.

UNDER SECRETARY FOR FARM AND FOREIGN AGRICULTURE SERVICES

Under Secretary.—Dr. J.B. Penn, 720–3111.
  Deputy Under Secretaries: Jim Butler, Floyd Gaibler, 720–7107.

FARM SERVICE AGENCY
South Building, Room 3086–S, 720–3467.

Administrator.—James R. Little.
  Associate Administrators:
    Operations and Management.—Thomas B. Hofellar.
    Programs.—Michael Yost.
  Civil Rights.—Johnny Toles, 410–7197.
  Legislative Liaison Staff.—Mary Helen Askins, room 3613–S, 720–3865.

Public Affairs Staff.—Eric Parsons, room 3624–S, 720–5237.
Economic and Policy Analysis Staff.—Ed Rall (acting), room 3741–S, 720–3451.
Deputy Administrator for Farm Programs.—John Johnson, room 3612–S, 720–3175.
   Assistant Deputy Administrator for Farm Programs.—Steve Connelly, 720–2070.
   Production, Emergencies and Compliance Division.—Diane Sharp, room 4754, 720–7641.
   Price Support Division.—Grady Bilberry, room 4095–S, 720–7901.
   Conservation and Environmental Programs Division.—Robert Stephenson, room 4714–S, 720–6221.
   Tobacco and Peanuts Division.—John Truluck, room 5724, 720–8120.
Deputy Administrator for Loan Programs.—Carolyn Cooksie, room 3605–S, 720–4671.
   Program Development and Economic Enhancement Division.—Bobby Reynolds, room 4919–S, 720–3647.
   Loan Making Division.—James Radintz, room 5438–S, 720–1632.
   Loan Servicing and Property Management Division.—Veldon Hall, room 5449–S, 720–4572.
Deputy Administrator for Field Operations.—Doug Frago, room 3092, 690–2807.
   Assistant Deputy Administrator.—John W. Chott, Jr., room 8092, 690–2807.
   Operations Review and Analysis Staff.—Thomas McCann, room 2720–S, 690–2532.
Deputy Administrator for Commodity Operations.—Bert Farrish, room 3080–S, 720–3217.
   Kansas City Commodity Office.—George Aldaya (816) 926–6301.
   Procurement and Donations Division.—Cleveland Marsh, room 5755, 720–5074.
   Warehouse and Inventory Division.—Steve Gill (acting), room 5962–S, 720–2121.
Deputy Administrator for Management.—John Williams, room 3095–S, 720–3438.
   Budget Division.—Dennis Taitano, room 4720–S, 720–3674.
   Financial Management Division.—Kristine Chadwick, room 1208 POC, 305–1386.
   Human Resources Division.—Patricia Farmer, room 5200 (L-St), 418–8950.
   Information Technology Services Division.—Steve Sanders, room 5768–S, 720–5320.
   Management Services Division.—Chris Reagan, room 6603–S, 720–3138.

RISK MANAGEMENT AGENCY
South Building, Room 6092–S, 690–2803

Administrator.—Ross J. Davidson, Jr.
   Associate Administrators: Byron E. Anderson, David C. Hatch.
   Deputy Administrator for—
      Compliance.—Michael Hand, room 4619–S, 720–0642.
      Insurance Services.—David C. Hatch (acting), room 6709–S, 720–5290.
      Research and Development.—Timothy Witt, Kansas City (816) 926–7394/7822.

FOREIGN AGRICULTURAL SERVICE
South Building, 14th and Independence Avenue, SW., room 5071, 20250
phone 720–3935, fax 690–2159

Administrator.—A. Ellen Terpstra, room 5071–S.
   Associate Administrator.—Kenneth J. Roberts.
   Chief of Staff.—JonAnn Flemings.
   General Sales Manager.—W. Kirk Miller.
   Director of:
      Budget Staff.—Hall G. Wynne, Jr., room 6083–S, 690–4052.
      Civil Rights Staff.—Mae Johnson, room 6504–S, 720–7233.
      Compliance Review Staff.—Robert Huttenlocker, room 4957–S, 720–6713.
      Correspondence Unit.—Kenneth Naylor, room 6627–S, 720–7631.
      External Affairs.—Roy Henwood, room 5071, 720–3935.
      Information Division.—Maureen Quinn, room 5074–S, 720–3448.
      Legislative Affairs Staff.—Dana Johnson, room 5931–S, 720–6829.

FOREIGN AGRICULTURAL AFFAIRS

Deputy Administrator.—Lyle Sebranek, room 5702–S, 720–6138.
   Assistant Deputy Administrator for—
      International Operations.—Charles Alexander, room 5702–S, 720–3253.
      International Services.—Kathy Ting, room 6075–S, 720–7781.

Field Communications Officer.—Kathy Ting (acting), room 6072–S, 205–2930.
Representation and Foreign Visitors Protocol Staff Chief.—Allen Alexander, room 5088–S, 720–6725.
Area Officers:
Africa, Middle East, and Western Hemisphere.—Alan Hrapsky, room 5094–S, 720–7053.
Eastern Europe and Eurasia.—James Dever, room 5099–S, 690–4053.
Western Europe.—Scott Bleggi, room 5098–S, 690–3412.
North Asia.—Susan Schayes, room 5095–S, 720–3080.
South Asia and Oceania.—Michael Conlon, room 5095–S,
Western Hemisphere.—Jeanne Bailey, room 5094–S, 720–3221.

INTERNATIONAL TRADE POLICY

Deputy Administrator.—Patricia Sheikh, room 5910–S, 720–6887.
Assistant Deputy Administrator.—Robert Macke, room 5910–S, 720–4434.
Director of:
Asia and Americas Division.—Brian Grunenfelder, room 5507–S, 720–2056.
Deputy Directors: Brenda Freeman, room 5511–S, 720–2337; Gary Meyer, room 5508–S, 720–1064.
Europe, Africa, Middle East Division.—Thomas Pomeroy, room 5514–S, 720–1340.
Deputy Directors: Lara Bennett (acting), room 5515, 720–1277; David Young, room 5517–S, 720–1322.
Food Safety and Technical Services Division.—Daryl Brehm, room 5545–S, 690–0929.
Deputy Directors: Cathy McKinnell, room 5547–S, 690–4898; Audrey Talley, room 5552–S, 720–9408.
Import Policies and Programs Division.—Robert Curtis, room 5529–S, 720–1330.
Deputy Director.—Ronald Lord, room 5535–S, 720–6939.
Multilateral Trade Negotiations Division.—Debra Henke, room 5530–S, 720–1324.
Deputy Directors: Charles Bertsch, room 5524–S, 720–6278; Sara Schwartz, room 5538–S, 720–0022.

EXPORT CREDITS

Deputy Administrator.—Mary T. Chambliss, room 4083–S, 720–6301.
Assistant Deputy Administrator.—Robin Tilsworth, room 4083–S, 720–4274.
Director of:
Operations Division.—Mark Rowse, room 4521–S, 720–6211.
Program Administration Division.—William Hawkins, room 4077–S, 720–3241.
Programming Division.—Ron Croushorn, room 4506–S, 720–4221.
Chief of:
Africa and Middle East Branch.—Judy Phillips, room 4543, 720–0732.
Asia and Central Asia Branch.—Joe Lopez, room 4574–S, 720–2637.
Europe and Latin American Branch.—Ken Naylor, room 4543–S, 720–2465.

COMMODITY AND MARKETING PROGRAMS

Deputy Administrator.—Franklin D. Lee, room 5089A–S, 720–4761.
Assistant Deputy Administrators: Kent Sisson, room 5089A–S, 720–7791; Randy Zeitner, room 5087–S, 720–1590.
Director of:
Cotton, Oilseeds, Tobacco and Seeds Division.—J. Lawrence Blum, room 5646–S, 720–9516.
Dairy, Livestock and Poultry Division.—Howard Wetzel, room 5935–S, 720–2579.
Grain and Feed Division.—Robert Riemenschneider, room 5603–S, 720–6219.
Horticultural and Tropical Products.—Sharon McClore (acting), room 5649, 720–6590.
Marketing Operations Staff.—Denise Huttenlocker, room 4932–S, 720–4327.
Planning and Evaluation.—John Nuttall, room 6615–S, 690–1198.
Production Estimates and Assessment Division.—Allen Vandergriff, room 6541–S, 720–0888.

INTERNATIONAL COOPERATION AND DEVELOPMENT

Deputy Administrator.—William L. Brant, room 3008–S, 690–0776.
  Assistant Deputy Administrators: Jocelyn Brown, room 3010–S, 690–0775; Christian Foster, room 3002–S, 690–0776.
  Directors for—
    Development Resources Division.—Grant Pettrie, room 3208–S, 690–1924.
      Deputy Director.—Betsy Davis, room 3208–S, 690–1924.
    Food Industries Division.—Merritt Chesley, room 3241–S, 690–1339.
    International Organization Affairs Division.—Lynne Reich, room 3005–S, 690–1823.
    Research and Scientific Exchanges Division.—Susan Owens, room 3229–S, 690–4872.
  Center Managers for—
    Business Management Center.—Peter Benson, 690–1943.
    Project Development and Management Center.—Mark Holt, 690–2922.
    RSSA Management Center.—Bruce Crossan, 690–2928.
  Leaders of:
    Cochran Fellowship Program.—Margaret McDaniel, room 3846–S, 690–1734.
    Food Security Branch.—Leanne Hogie, room 3234–S, 720–3320.
    Professional Development Program.—Virginia Wolf, room 3245–S, 690–1141.
    Science and Trade Branch.—Gary Laidig, room 3236–S, 720–7481.
    Sustainable Agriculture and Resource Management Branch.—Rao Achutuni, room 3215–S, 720–2036.
    Trade Investment Program.—Joe Hain, room 3250–S, 720–1818.

UNDER SECRETARY FOR RURAL DEVELOPMENT
Jamie L. Whitten Building, phone 720–4581

Under Secretary.—Gilbert Gonzalez (acting).
  Deputy Under Secretary for—
    Operations and Management.—Timothy Ryan (acting).
    Policy and Planning.—Gilbert Gonzalez.

RURAL HOUSING SERVICE
South Agriculture Building, Room 5014–S, phone 690–1533

Administrator.—Russell Davis.
  Associate Administrator.—Rodney Hood.
  Director, Program Support Staff.—Richard A. Davis, 720–9619.
  Deputy Director.—Keith Suerdieck, 720–9619.
  Deputy Administrator for Single Family.—David J. Vilano, 720–5177.
  Director of:
    Family Housing Direct Loan Division.—Philip Stetson, 720–1474.
    Family Housing Guaranteed Loan Division.—Roger Glendenning, 720–1452.
  Deputy Administrator for Multi-Family Housing.—Jackie J. Gleason, 720–3773.
    Deputy Director.—Sue Harris-Green, 720–1606.
  Director of:
    Guaranteed Loan Division.—Glenn Walden, 720–1505.
    Direct Loan and Grant Processing Division.—Chadwick Parker, 720–1502.
    Multi-Family Housing Portfolio Management Division, Direct Housing.—Stephanie White, 720–1600.
  Deputy Director.—Janet Stouder, 720–9728.

RURAL BUSINESS-COOPERATIVE SERVICE
South Building, Room 5045–S, phone 690–4730

Administrator.—Peter Thomas, 690–4730.
  Deputy Administrator for Business Programs.—William F. Hagy III, 720–7287.
  Director of:
    Business and Industry Division.—Carolyn Parker, 690–4103.
    Cooperative Development Division.—John H. Wells, 720–3350.
    Cooperative Marketing Division.—Thomas H. Stafford, 690–0368.

Cooperative Resources Management Division.—John R. Dunn, 690–1374.
Deputy Administrator for Cooperative Services.—Roberta Purcell, 720–7558.
Statistics.—Eldon Erversull (acting), 720–3189.

OFFICE OF COMMUNITY DEVELOPMENT

Director of:
  Community Resource Development.—Rick Wetherill (acting), room 266, 619–7983.
  Empowerment Division.—Rick Wetherill, room 266, 619–7983.
Executive Director, National Sheep Industry Improvement Center.—Jay B. Wilson, 690–0632.

OPERATIONS AND MANAGEMENT
NASA Building, Third Floor, phone 692–0200

Deputy Administrator.—Sherie Hinton-Henry, 692–0200.
Director of:
  Budget Division.—Deborah Lawrence, 692–0122.
  Civil Rights Staff.—Cheryl Prejean Greaux, 692–0204.
  Financial Management Division.—John Purcell, 692–0080.
  Legislative and Public Affairs.—Allan Johnson, 720–1019.
  Policy and Analysis Division.—William French, 690–9824.
  Chief Financial Officer.—Barbara Stanhaus (acting) (314) 457–4152.
  Chief Information Officer.—Tom Hannah, 692–0212.
Assistant Administrator for—
  Human Resources.—William J. Fleming, 692–0222.
  Procurement and Administration Services.—Sharon Randolph, 692–0207.
Program Manager for Alternate Dispute Resolution.—Bob Lovan, 690–2583.
Coordinator for Native American Affairs.—David Saffert, 720–0400.

RURAL UTILITIES SERVICE
South Building, Room 4051–S, phone 720–9540

Administrator.—Curtis M. Anderson (acting), 720–9540.
Deputy Administrator.—Curtis M. Anderson, room 4048–S, 720–0962.
Assistant Administrator for—
  Electric Division.—Jim Newby, room 4037–S, 720–9545.
  Program Accounting and Regulatory Analysis.—Kenneth M. Ackerman, room 4063–S, 720–9450.
  Telecommunications.—Jonathan Claffey (acting).
  Water and Environmental Programs.—Gary J. Morgan, room 4048–S, 690–2670.
Director of:
  Advanced Services Division.—Orren E. Cameron, room 2845–S, 690–4493.
  Broadband Division.—Kenneth Kuchno, room 2846–S, 690–4673.
  Electric Staff Division.—George J. Bagnall, room 1246–S, 720–1900.
  Northern Regional Electric Division.—Nivin Elgohary, room 0243–S, 720–1420.
  Northern Area, Telecommunications Program.—Jerry H. Brent, room 2835–S, 720–1025.
  Power Supply Division.—Victor T Vu, room 270–S, 720–6436.
  Southern Regional Electric Division.—Robert O. Ellinger, room 221–S, 720–0848.
  Southern Area, Telecommunications Program.—Ken B. Chandler, room 2808–S, 720–0800.
  Telecommunications Standards Division.—John Schnell (acting), room 2868–S, 720–8663.
Chief, Portfolio Management Branch.—Susan Card, room 2231–S, 720–9631.
Engineering and Environmental Staff.—Glenn Deal.

UNDER SECRETARY FOR FOOD, NUTRITION AND CONSUMER SERVICES
Jamie L. Whitten Building, Room 240–E, phone 720–7711, fax 690–3100

Under Secretary.—Eric M. Bost.
Deputy Under Secretary.—Kate Coler.
Executive Director, Center for Nutrition, Policy and Promotion.—Dr. Eric Hentges.

FOOD AND NUTRITION SERVICE

3101 Park Center Drive, Alexandria, VA 22302, phone (703) 305–2062

Administrator.—Roberto Salazar, room 906, 305–2062.
Associate Administrator.—George A. Braley, room 906, 305–2060.

COMMUNICATIONS AND GOVERNMENTAL AFFAIRS

Deputy Administrator.—Steve Savage, room 920, 305–2281.
  Director of:
  Consumer and Community Affairs.—Pam Phillips, room 912, 305–2000.
  Governmental Affairs.—Frank Ippolito, room 910, 305–2010.
  Public Affairs.—Susan Acker, room 920, 305–2286.

MANAGEMENT

Deputy Administrator.—Gloria Gutierrez, room 314 (703) 305–2030.
  Associate Deputy Administrator.—Tim O'Connor, room 314 (703) 305–2032.
  Director of:
  Administrative Services Division.—Cherie Stallman, room 202 (703) 305–2231.
  Human Resources Division.—Laura Wilmot, room 614, 305–2326.
  Information Technology Division.—Lenore Siwiec, room 304, 305–2754.

FINANCIAL MANAGEMENT

Deputy Administrator.—Gary Maupin, room 712, 305–2046.
  Divisional Directors:
  Accounting.—Rose McClyde, room 724, 305–2447.
  Budget.—David Burr, room 708, 305–2189.

FOOD STAMP PROGRAM

Deputy Administrator.—Clarence Carter, room 808, 305–2026.
  Associate Deputy Administrator.—Jessica Shahin, room 808, 305–2022.
  Division Directors of:
  Benefit Redemption.—Jeff Cohen, room 400, 305–2756.
  Program Accountability.—Karen Walker.
  Program Development.—Arthur T. Foley, room 814, 305–2490.

SPECIAL NUTRITION PROGRAMS

Deputy Administrator.—Steve Christensen, room 628, 305–2052.
  Associate Administrator.—Ron Vogel, 305–2054.
  Division Directors:
  Child Nutrition.—Stan Garnets, room 620, 305–2590.
  Food Distribution.—Cathie McCullough, room 500, 305–2680.
  Supplemental Food Programs.—Patricia Daniels, room 520, 305–2746.

CENTER FOR NUTRITION POLICY AND PROMOTION

3101 Park Center Drive, Room 1032, Alexandria, VA 22302
phone (703) 305–7600, fax 305–3400

Executive Director.—Dr. Eric Hentges.
  Director for—
  Nutrition Policy and Analysis Staff.—Peter Basiotis.
  Nutrition Promotion Staff.—Carole Davis.
  Public Information and Governmental Affairs—John Webster.

UNDER SECRETARY FOR FOOD SAFETY

Under Secretary.—Merle D. Pierson (acting), 720–0350.
Deputy Under Secretary.—Merle D. Pierson.
Special Assistant to the Under Secretary.—Cheryn Evans.

FOOD SAFETY AND INSPECTION SERVICE
Jamie L. Whitten Building, Room 331–E, phone 720–7025, fax 690–0550

Administrator.—Dr. Barbara Masters (acting).
Deputy Administrator.—Barbara Masters, 720–7900.
U.S. Manager for Codex.—Dr. F. Ed. Scarbrough, room 4861–S, 720–2057.

OFFICE OF FOOD SECURITY & EMERGENCY PREPAREDNESS (OFSEP)

Assistant Administrator.—Dr. Carol A. Maczka, room 3130–S, 720–5643.
Deputy Assistant Administrator.—Dr. Perfecto Santiago, 205–0452.
Executive Associate.—Suzanne Rigby, 720–5643.
Director, Scientific & Technical Support Staff.—Daniel J. Vitiello, room 0205–S, 720–8524.
Director, Emergency Preparedness Staff.—Roberta Wedge, 411 Aero Building, 690–6486.

PROGRAM EVALUATION, ENFORCEMENT & REVIEW (OPEER)

Assistant Administrator.—Ronald F. Hicks, room 3133–S, 720–8609.
Director, Program Evaluation & Improvement Staff.—Jane Roth, room 3831–S, 720–6735.
Director, Compliance & Investigations Division.—Zygmunt Sala, room 300, WEC, 418–8874.

PUBLIC AFFAIRS, EDUCATION & OUTREACH (OPAEO)

Assistant Administrator.—Bryce Quick, room 350–E, 720–8217.
Deputy Assistant Administrators: Terri Nintemann, room 3137–S, 720–3884; Daniel Puzo, 720–4832.
Director, Congressional & Public Affairs Staff.—Terri Nintemann (acting), room 1175–S, 720–3897 or 9113.
Director, Executive Correspondence & Issues Management Staff.—Jonathan Theodule (acting), room 1167–S, 690–3882.

INTERNATIONAL AFFAIRS (OIA)

Assistant Administrator.—Karen Stuck, room 3143–S, 720–3473.
Deputy Assistant Administrator.—Dr. William James, 720–5362.
Director, Import Inspection Division.—Mary Stanley, room 3843–S, 720–9904.

PUBLIC HEALTH SCIENCE (OPHS)

Assistant Administrator.—Dr. David Goldman, room 341–E, 720–2644.
Deputy Assistant Administrator.—Loren Lange, 205–0293.

MANAGEMENT

Assistant Administrator.—William P. (Billy) Milton, Jr., room 347–E, 720–4425.
Deputy Assistant Administrator.—Karen A. Messmore, 720–4744.

FIELD OPERATIONS (OFO)

Assistant Administrator.—William C. (Bill) Smith, room 344–E, 720–8803.
Deputy Assistant Administrator.—Dr. Kenneth Petersen (acting), 720–5190.

Executive Associates, Regulatory Operations: Jeanne O. Axtell, room 3155–S, 720–5397; Dr. John C. Prucha, room 3161–S, 720–4863, Judith Riggins, room 3154–S, 720–5768.
Chief Veterinary Public Health Officer.—Bonnie Buntain, DVM, room 3133–S, 690–1276.
Director, Recall Management Staff.—Dr. Hany Sidrak, room 0008–S, 690–6389.
Director, State Program Liaison Staff.—Dr. Murli M. Prasad, room 329–WEC, 418–8897.

POLICY, PROGRAM & EMPLOYEE DEVELOPMENT (OPPED)

Assistant Administrator.—Philip Derfler, room 350–E, 720–2709.
Deputy Assistant Administrator.—Daniel Engeljohn, room 3147–S, 205–0495.
Director, Labeling & Consumer Protection Staff.—Robert Post, room 602 Annex, 205–0279.
Director, New Technology Staff.—Shaukat Syed, room 2934–S, 205–0675.

UNDER SECRETARY FOR RESEARCH, EDUCATION, AND ECONOMICS

Under Secretary.—Joseph J. Jen, 720–5923.
Deputy Under Secretary.—Rodney J. Brown, 720–8885.
Executive Assistant.—Maureen Wood.
Director, Legislative and Intergovernmental Affairs.—Terry Van Doren, 690–0826.
Budget Coordinator.—Sara Mazie, 720–4110.

AGRICULTURAL RESEARCH SERVICE

Administration Building, Room 303–A, phone 720–3656, fax 720–5427

Administrator.—Edward B. Knipling, room 302–A, 720–3656.
Associate Administrator, Research and Operations.—Antoinette Betschart, 720–3658.
Director of:
  ARS Information Staff.—Sandy M. Hays, room 2251–G (301) 504–1638.
  Budget and Program Management Staff.—Joseph S. Garbarino, room 358–A, 720–4421.
  Civil Rights Staff.—Korona I. Prince, room 3552–S, 690–2244.
  International Research Programs.—Richard V. Greene, room 4–1139 (301) 504–4542.
Assistant Administrator, Office of Technology Transfer.—Richard J. Brenner, room 4–1156 (301) 504–6905.

ADMINISTRATIVE AND FINANCIAL MANAGEMENT

5601 Sunnyside Avenue, Beltsville, MD 20705–5108, Room 3–2154, phone (301) 504–1008

Deputy Administrator.—James H. Bradley, room 323 Whitten (202) 690–2575.
Director of:
  Acquisition, Property, and Telecommunications Division.—Larry Cullumber, room 2102–G (301) 504–1695.
  Facilities Division.—Patrick Barry, room 1294 (301) 504–1151.
  Financial Management Division.—Steven M. Helmrich, room 2190–G (301) 504–1257.
  Human Resources Division.—Karen M. Brownell, room 1143–G (301) 504–1317.

NATIONAL AGRICULTURE LIBRARY

Route 1, Beltsville, MD 20705, phone (301) 504–5248, fax (301) 504–7042

Director.—Peter Young, room 200 (301) 504–5248.
Deputy Director.—Eleanor G. Frierson, room 200, 504–6780.
Director of:
  Administrative Officer.—Linda Mooney, room 201, 504–5570.
  Information Systems Division.—Gary McCone, room 204 (301) 504–5018.
  Public Affairs.—Len Carey, room 204, 504–6778.
  Public Services Division.—Maria G. Pisa, room 203, 504–5834.
  Technical Services Division.—Christopher Cole, room 203, 504–7294.

NATIONAL PROGRAM STAFF

5601 Sunnyside Avenue, Room 4–2152, Beltsville MD 20705–5134

phone (301) 504–5084

Associate Administrator.—Caird E. Rexroad, room 4–2152, 504–5084.
  Program Planning Advisor.—David Rust, room 4–2144, 504–6233.
  Deputy Administrator for—
    Animal Production and Protection.—Dr. Steven Kappas, room 4–2188, 504–7050.
    Crop Production and Protection.—Judith St. John, room 4–2204, 504–6252.
    Natural Resources and Sustainable Agricultural Systems.—Dr. Jean Steiner (acting), room 4–2288, 504–7987.
    Nutrition, Food Safety, and Quality.—Dr. Joseph Spence.

AREA OFFICES

Director, Beltsville Area.—Phyllis E. Johnson, room 223, Building 003, BARC–West, Beltsville MD 20705 (301) 504–6078.
Director, Beltsville Human Nutrition Research Center.—David Granstrom (acting).
  Assistant Director, Beltsville Human Nutrition Research Center.—Ellen W. Harris, room 117 B–005 (301) 504–0610.
Director, U.S. National Arboretum.—Thomas S. Elias, room 100 (202) 245–4539.
Division Deputy Area Director of Facilities Management and Operations.—John Van de Vaarst, room 203 B–003 (301) 504–5664.
Director of:
  North Atlantic Area.—Wilda Martinez, 600 East Mermaid Lane, Wyndmoor, PA 19038 (215) 233–6593.
  South Atlantic Area.—Darrell Cole, PO Box 5677, College Station Road, Athens, GA 30604–5677 (706) 546–3311.
  Mid South Area.—Edgar King, Jr., PO Box 225, Stoneville, MS 38776 (601) 686–5265.
  Midwest Area.—Adrianna Hewings, room 2004, 1815 North University Street, Peoria, IL 61604–0000 (309) 681–6602.
  Pacific West Area.—Dwayne R. Buxton, room 2030, 800 Buchanan Street, Albany, CA 94710 (510) 559–6060.
  Northern Plains Area.—Wilbert H. Blackburn, room S–150, 1201 Oakridge Road, Fort Collins, CO 80525–5562 (970) 229–5557.
  Southern Plains Area.—Charles A. Onstad, Suite 230, 7607 Eastmark Drive, College Station, TX 77840 (409) 260–9346.

REGIONAL RESEARCH CENTERS

Director, Eastern Regional Research Center.—John P. Cherry, 600 East Mermaid Lane, Wyndmoor, PA 19038 (215) 233–6595.
Director, Western Regional Research Center.—James N. Seiber, 800 Buchanan Street, Albany, CA 94710–0000 (510) 559–5600.
Director, Southern Regional Research Center.—John Patrick Jordan, 1100 Robert E. Lee Boulevard, New Orleans, LA 70179–0000 (504) 286–4212.
Director, National Center for Agricultural Utilization Research.—Peter B. Johnsen, room 2038, 1815 North University Street, Peoria, IL 61604–0000 (309) 681–6541.

COOPERATIVE STATE RESEARCH, EDUCATION AND EXTENSION SERVICE

Jamie L. Whitten Building, Room 305–A, phone (202) 720–4423, fax 720–8987

Administrator.—Colien Heffernan.
  Associate Administrator.—Gary Cunningham, 720–7441.
  Deputy Administrator for—
    Budget.—Tina Buch, room 332–A, 720–2675.
    Communiucations.—Janet Allen, room 4231, 720–2677.
    Economic and Community Systems.—Frank Boteler, room 4343, 720–5305.
    Equal Opportunity Staff.—Curt DeVille, room 1230, 720–5843.
    Extramural Programs.—Louise M. Ebaugh, room 2250, 401–6021.

Families, 4–H and Nutrition.—Mary Gray, room 4329, 720–2326.
Information Systems and Technology Management.—Michel Desbois (acting), room 4122, 720–1766.
Natural Resources and Environment.—Dan Kugler, room 3231, 720–0740.
Planning and Accountability.—Cheryl Oros, room 1315, 690–1297.
Plant and Animal Systems.—Ralph Otto, room 3359, 401–5877.
Science and Education Resources Development.—George Cooper, room 3310, 401–2855.

ECONOMIC RESEARCH SERVICE

Administrator.—Susan E. Offutt, room N4145 (202) 694–5000.
 Associate Administrator.—Philip Fulton, room N4150, 694–5000.
 Division Directors:
  Food and Rural Economics.—Betsey A. Kuhn, room N2168, 694–5400.
  Information Services.—Ron Bianchi, room S2032, 694–5100.
  Market and Trade Economics.—Neilson Conklin, room N5119, 694–5200.
  Resource Economics.—Katherine R. Smith, room S4186, 694–5500.

NATIONAL AGRICULTURAL STATISTICS SERVICE
South Agriculture Building, Room 4117–S, phone 720–2707, fax 720–9013

Administrator.—R. Ronald Bosecker.
 Associate Administrator.—Carol House, 720–2702.
 Deputy Administrator for—
  Field Operations.—Joseph T. Reilly, room 4133, 720–3638.
  Programs and Products.—Richard D. Allen, room 5095, 690–8141.
 Division Directors for—
  Census and Survey.—Marshall Dantzler, room 6306, 720–4557.
  Information Technology.—John P. Nealon, room 5847, 720–2984.
  Research and Development.—George A. Hanuschak, room 305, Fairfax CBG (703) 235–5211.
  Statistics.—Steven D. Wiyatt, room 5810, 720–3896.

UNDER SECRETARY FOR MARKETING AND REGULATORY PROGRAMS
Jamie A. Whitten Building, Room 228–W, phone (202) 720–4256, fax 720–5775

Under Secretary.—Bill Hawks.
 Deputy Under Secretary.—Chuck Lambert, 720–4256.
 Special Assistant to the Under Secretary.—Tim Cansler, 720–5759.
 Confidential Assistant to the Under Secretary.—Kelly Porter, 720–4031.

AGRICULTURAL MARKETING SERVICE
South Agriculture Building, Room 3071–S, phone (202) 720–5115, fax 720–8477

Associate Administrator.—Kenneth C. Clayton (acting), room 3064–S, 720–4276.
 Deputy Associate Administrator.—Charles R. Martin, room 3064–S, 720–4024.

MARKETING PROGRAMS

Deputy Administrator for Compliance and Analysis Programs.—David N. Lewis, room 3529–S, 720–6766.
 Deputy Administrator for—
  Cotton Programs.—Darryl Earnest (acting), room 2641–S, 720–3193.
  Dairy Programs.—Dana Cole, room 2968–S, 720–4392.
  Fruit and Vegetable Programs.—Robert C. Keeney, room 2077–S, 720–4722.
  Livestock and Seed Programs.—Barry L. Carpenter, room 2092–S, 720–5705.
  Poultry Programs.—Craig Morse, room 3932–S, 720–4476.
  Science and Technology.—Robert L. Epstein, room 3507–S, 720–5231.
  Tobacco Programs.—William Coats (acting), room 502 Annex, 205–0567.
  Transportation and Marketing.—Barbara C. Robinson, room 2510–S, 690–1300.

ANIMAL AND PLANT HEALTH INSPECTION SERVICE (APHIS)

Jamie L. Whitten Building, Room 312–E, phone (202) 720–3668, fax 720–3054

OFFICE OF THE ADMINISTRATOR

Administrator.—W. Ron DeHaven.
  Associate Administrator.—Peter Fernandez.
  Chief Operating Officer.—Kevin Shea, room 308–E.
  Director of Civil Rights Enforcement and Compliance.—Anna P. Grayson, room 1137–S, 720–6312, fax 720–2365.

LEGISLATIVE AND PUBLIC AFFAIRS

South Building, Room 1147–S, phone (202) 720–2511, fax 720–3982

Director.—Courtney R. Billet.
  Deputy Director.—Bethany Jones.
  Assistant Director of:
    Public Affairs.—Ed Curlett (301) 734–7799.
    Executive Correspondence.—Christina Myers (301) 734–7776.
    Freedom of Information.—Lesia Banks (301) 734–8296.

POLICY AND PROGRAM DEVELOPMENT

4700 River Road, Riverdale, MD 20737, phone (301) 734–5136, fax 734–5899

Deputy Administrator.—Michael Gregoire.
  Assistant Deputy Administrator.—Shannon Hamm.
  Unit Chiefs:
    Planning, Evaluation and Monitoring.—Christine Zakarka, 734–8512.
    Policy Analysis and Development.—Janet W. Berls, 734–8667.
    Regulatory Analysis and Development.—Cynthia Howard, 734–0682.
    Risk Analysis.—Richard Fite, 734–3634.

WILDLIFE SERVICES

South Building, Room 1624, phone (202) 720–2054, fax 690–0053

Deputy Administrator.—William H. Clay.
  Assistant Deputy Administrator.—Martin Mendoza.
  Director for Operational Support.—Joanne Garrett (301) 734–7921.

VETERINARY SERVICES

Jamie L. Whitten Building, Room 317–E, phone (202) 720–5193, fax 690–4171

Deputy Administrator.—John Clifford.
  Administrative Assistant.—James Newton, 720–5793.
  Associate Deputy Administrator for Regional Operations.—Dr. Andrea Morgan, 720–5193.
  Assistant Deputy Administrator.—Dr. Valerie Ragan (301) 734–3754.
  Director for—
    Emergency Programs.—Randall Crom (301) 734–8073.
    Inspection and Compliance.—Steven A. Karli (Ames) (515) 232–5785.
    National Center of Import and Export.—Gary S. Colgrave (301) 734–4356.
    Outreach Liaison.—Joseph Annelli (301) 794–8073.
    Policy, Evaluation and Licensing.—Richard E. Hill, Jr. (515) 232–5785.
  Chief Staff Veterinarian for National Animal Health Programs.—Michael Gilsdorf (301) 734–6954.

INTERNATIONAL SERVICES

Jamie L. Whitten Building, Room 324–E, phone (202) 720–7593, fax 690–1484

Deputy Administrator.—Dan Sheesley.
  Associate Deputy Administrator.—Nick Gutierrez, 720–7021.
  Division Directors: Freida Skaggs (301) 734–5214; John Wyss, 734–3779.
  Trade Support Team.—John Greifer, room 1128, 720–7677.

MARKETING AND REGULATORY PROGRAMS BUSINESS SERVICES

Jamie L. Whitten Building, Room 308–E, phone (202) 720–5213, fax 690–0686

Deputy Administrator.—William Hudnall.
  Associate Deputy Administrator.—Joanne Munno.
  Division Directors:
    Financial Management.—Laura MacKenzie, 720–7865.
    Investigative and Enforcement Services.—Alan Christian (301) 734–6491.
    Management Services.—Howard Price (301) 734–6502.
    MRP Human Resources: Karen Benham, Ellen King, room 1709–S, 720–6377.

PLANT PROTECTION AND QUARANTINE

Jamie L. Whitten Building, Room 302–E, phone (202) 720–5601, fax 690–0472

Deputy Administrator.—Richard L. Dunkle.
  Associate Deputy Administrator.—Paul Eggert, 720–4441.
  Assistant to the Deputy Administrator.—John H. Payne, 720–5601.
  Director of:
    Biocontrol.—Dale Meyerdirk (301) 734–5667.
    Center for Plant Health Science and Technology.—Gordon Gordh (919) 513–2400.
    Phytosanitary Issues Management.—Cathleen Enright (301) 734–5291.
    Resource Management Support.—Terri Burrell (301) 734–7764.
    Technical Information Systems.—Allison Young (301) 734–5518.

ANIMAL CARE

4700 River Road, Riverdale, MD 20737, phone (301) 734–4980, fax 734–4328

Deputy Administrator.—Chester Gipson.
  Assistant Deputy Administrator.—Allan Hogue.

BIOTECHNOLOGY REGULATORY SERVICES

4700 River Road, Riverdale, MD 20737, phone (301) 734–7324, fax 734–8724

Deputy Administrator.—Cindy Smith.
  Associate Deputy Administrator.—Rebecca Bech, 734–5716.
  Directors of:
    Regulatory Division.—Neil Hoffman, 734–5716.

GRAIN INSPECTION, PACKERS AND STOCKYARDS ADMINISTRATION

South Agriculture Building, Room 2055, phone (202) 720–0219, fax 205–9237

Administrator.—David R. Shipman (acting), room 2063, 720–9170.
  Director of:
    Enterprise Architecture Program Management.—Charles E. Smith, room 0009, 205–4366.
    Executive Resource Staff.—Patricia Donohue-Galvin, room 2047, 720–0231.
    Civil Rights.—Eugene Bass, room 0623, 720–0216.
    Information Technology Staff.—Gerald Bromley, room 2446, 720–3204.

Deputy Administrator for Federal Grain Inspection Service.—David R. Shipman, room 2063, 720–9170.

Director of:
   Field Management Division.—David Orr, room 2409, 720–0228.
   Office of International Affairs.—John Pitchford, room 1629, 720–0226.
   Compliance.—John Sharpe, room 1647, 720–8262.
   Technical Services.—Steven Tanner, Kansas City, MO (816) 891–0401.

Deputy Administrator for Packers and Stockyards Programs.—JoAnn Waterfield, room 2055, 720–7051.

Director of:
   Field Operations.—William Crutchfield, room 1641, 720–7063.
   Economic/Statistical Support.—Gary McBryde (acting), room 1644, 720–7455.
   Office of Policy/Litigation Support.—Brett Offutt, room 2420, 720–7363.

Regional Supervisors:
   Atlanta, GA.—Elkin Parker (404) 562–5840.
   Denver, CO.—John Barthel (303) 375–4240.
   Des Moines, IA.—Jay Johnson (515) 323–2579.

DEPARTMENT OF COMMERCE

Herbert C. Hoover Building

14th Street between Pennsylvania and Constitution Avenues 20230

phone 482–2000, http://www.doc.gov

CARLOS M. GUTIERREZ, Secretary of Commerce; born in Havana, Cuba, in 1953; came to the United States in 1960; education: studied business administration, Monterrey Institute of Technology, Queretaro, Mexico; professional: Chairman of the Board, and Chief Executive Officer, Kellogg Company; married: Edilia; children: Carlos, Erika, and Karina; nominated by President George W. Bush to become the 35th Secretary of Commerce, and was confirmed by the U.S. Senate on January 24, 2005.

OFFICE OF THE SECRETARY

Secretary of Commerce.—Carlos M. Gutierrez, room 5858, 482–2112.
  Deputy Secretary.—Theodore W. Kassinger, room 5838, 482–4625.
  Chief of Staff.—Claire Buchan, room 5858, 482–4246.
  Chief of Protocol.—Aimee Strudwick, room 5847, 482–3225.
  Director, Office of:
    Business Liaison.—Dan McCardell, room 5062, 482–1360.
    Chief Information Officer.—Tom Pyke, room 5029B, 482–4797.
    Executive Secretariat.—Fred Schwien, room 5516, 482–3934.
    External Affairs.—Darren Grubb, room 5858, 482–2158.
    Policy and Strategic Planning.—David Bohigian, room 5865, 482–3520.
    Public Affairs.—Christine Iverson, room 5413, 482–4883.
    Scheduling.—Marilyn Abel, room 5883, 482–5880.
    White House Liaison.—Christy Simon, room 5835, 482–1684.

GENERAL COUNSEL

General Counsel.—Jane T. Dana (acting), room 5870, 482–4772.
  Deputy General Counsel.—Jane T. Dana.

ASSISTANT SECRETARY FOR LEGISLATIVE AND INTERGOVERNMENTAL AFFAIRS

Assistant Secretary.—Brett Palmer, room 5421, 482–3663.
  Deputy Assistant Secretary for Trade Legislation.—Nat Wienecke, room 5419, 482–5631.
  Director for—
    Legislative and Intergovernmental Affairs.—Karen A. Swanson-Woolf, room 5414, 482–4556.
    Intergovernmental Affairs.—Elizabeth Dial, room 5422, 482–8017.

CHIEF FINANCIAL OFFICER (CFO) AND ASSISTANT SECRETARY FOR ADMINISTRATION

Herbert C. Hoover Building, Room 5830, 482–4951

Chief Financial Officer and Assistant Secretary.—Otto Wolff, room 5830.
  Deputy Chief Financial Officer, Financial Management.—James Taylor, room 6827, 482–1207.
  Deputy Assistant Secretary for Administration.—Jeffery Nulf.
  Director for—
    Acquisition Management.—Michael S. Sade, room 6422, 482–2773.
    Administrative Services.—Denise Wells, room 6316, 482–1200.
    Budget.—Barbara A. Retzlaff, room 5818, 482–4648.
    Civil Rights.—Suzan J. Aramaki, room 6012, 482–0625.

Human Resources Management.—Deborah A. Jefferson, room 5001, 482–4807.
Management and Organization.—John J. Phelan III, room 5327, 482–3707.
Security.—Richard Yamamoto, room 1067, 482–4371.
Small and Disadvantaged Business Utilization.—LaJuene Desmukes (acting), room 6411, 482–1472.

INSPECTOR GENERAL

Herbert C. Hoover Building, Room 7898–C, 482–4661

Inspector General.—Johnnie E. Frazier.
  Deputy Inspector General.—Edward Blansitt, room 7898C, 482–3516.
  Legislative and Intergovernmental Affairs Officer.—Susan Carnohan, room 7898C, 482–2187.
  Counsel to Inspector General.—Carey Croak (acting), room 7892, room 482–0038.
  Assistant Inspector General, Office of:
    Auditing.—Alexis Stefani, room 7721, 482–3606.
    Compliance and Administration.—Jessica Rickenbach, room 7099C, 482–3052.
    Inspections and Program Evaluations.—Jill A. Gross, room 7886–B, 482–2754.
    Investigations.—Elizabeth T. Barlow, room 7087, 482–3860.
    Systems Evaluation.—Judith J. Gordon, room 7876, 482–6186.

ECONOMICS AND STATISTICS ADMINISTRATION AFFAIRS

Herbert C. Hoover Building, Room 4848, phone 482–3727

Under Secretary for Economic Affairs.—Kathleen B. Cooper.
  Chief Counsel.—Roxie Jamison Jones, room 4868A, 482–5394.
  Chief Economist.—Keith Hall, room 4842, 482–3523.
  Associate Under Secretary for—
    Communications.—Elizabeth R. Anderson, room 4836, 482–2760.
    Congressional and Intergovernmental Affairs Specialist.—Clark L. Reid, room 4842, 482–3331.
    Economic Information Officer.—Jane A. Callen, room 4855, 482–2235.
  Director, Office of:
    Economic Conditions.—Carl E. Cox, room 4861, 482–4871.
    Policy Development.—Jane Molloy, room 4858, 482–5926.
  Management.—James K. White, room 4834, 482–2405.
    Chief Information Officer and Director.—Kenneth S. Taylor, room 4880, 482–2853.
    STAT–USA.—Forrest B. Williams, room 4886, 482–3429.
  Chief Financial Officer, Finance and Administration.—Suzette Kern, room 4842, 482–4885.

BUREAU OF ECONOMIC ANALYSIS

1441 L Street NW., room 6006, Washington, DC 20230, phone (202) 606–9600

Director.—J. Steven Landefeld.
  Deputy Director.—Rosemary Marcuss, room 6005, 606–9602.
  Chief Economist.—Barbara Fraumeni, room 6063, 606–9603.
  Chief Statistician.—Dennis J. Fixler, room 6060, 606–9607.
  Chief Information Officer.—Alan C. Lorish, Jr., room 3050, 606–9910.
  Associate Director for—
    Industry Accounts.—Sumiye Okubo, room 6004, 606–9612.
    International Economics.—Ralph H. Kozlow, room 6065, 606–9604.
    National Economic Accounts.—Brent R. Moulton, room 6064, 606–9606.
    Regional Economics.—John W. Ruser, room 6062, 606–9605.
  Division Chiefs:
    Administrative Services.—C. Brian Grove, room 3003, 606–9624.
    Balance of Payments.—Christopher L. Bach, room 8024, 606–9545.
    Communications.—Michael D. Moore, room 3029, 606–9630.
    Government.—Brooks B. Robinson, room 4067, 606–9778.
    Industry Economics.—Ann M. Lawson, room 4006, 606–9462.
    International Investment.—Obie G. Wichard, room 7006, 606–9890.
    National Income and Wealth.—Carol E. Moylan, room 5006, 606–9711.
    Regional Economic Analysis.—John R. Kort, room 9018, 606–9221.
    Regional Economic Measurement.—Robert L. Brown, room 8066, 606–9246.

THE CENSUS BUREAU
Federal Office Building 3, Silver Hill and Suitland Roads, Suitland, MD 20746

Director.—Charles Louis Kincannon, room 2049 (301) 763–2135.
Deputy Director and Chief Operating Officer.—Hermann Habermann, room 2049, 763–2138.
Associate Director for—
  Administration and Chief Financial Officer.—Theodore A. Johnson, room 2025, 763–3464.
  Communications.—Jefferson Taylor, room 2069, 763–2164.
  Comptroller.—Andrew H. Moxam, room 3586, 763–9575.
  Decennial Census.—Preston Jay Waite, room 2037, 763–3968.
  Demographic Programs.—Nancy M. Gordon, room 2061, 763–2126.
  Economic Programs.—Thomas L. Mesenbourg (acting), room 2069, 763–2932.
  Field Operations.—Marvin D. Raines, room 2027, 763–2072.
  Information Technology.—Richard W. Swartz, room 2065, 763–2117.
Assistant Director for—
  Decennial Census and American Community Survey.—Teresa Angueira, room 2016–2, 763–1764.
  Decennial IT and Geographic Systems.—Arnold A. Jackson, room 2018–2, 763–8626.
  Economic Programs.—Thomas L. Mesenbourg, room 2069, 763–2932.
  Information Technology.—Douglas Clift, room 1031, 763–5499.
Division and Office Chiefs for—
  Acquisition Division.—Michael L. Palensky, room G–314, 763–1818.
  Administrative and Customer Services.—Walter C. Odom, Jr., room 2150, 763–2228.
  Administrative and Management Systems Division.—James Aikman, room 3102, 763–3149.
  American Community Survey Office.—Lawrence S. McGinn, room 1657, 763–8050.
  Budget Division.—Andrew H. Moxam (acting), room 3586, 763–9575.
  Center for Economic Studies.—Daniel H. Weinberg, room 206, 763–6460.
  Client Support Office.—Ronald R. Swank, room 1373, 763–6846.
  Company Statistics Division.—Ewen M. Wilson, room 1182, 763–3388.
  Computer Services Division.—Kenneth A. Riccini, Bowie Computer Center, 763–3922.
  Congressional Affairs Office.—Joanne Caldwell (acting), room 2073, 763–2171.
  Customer Liaison Office.—Stanley J. Rolark, room 3634, 763–1305.
  Decennial Management Division.—Edison Gore (acting), room 2012–2, 763–3998.
  Decennial Statistical Studies Division.—Rajendra Singh, room 2024, 763–9295.
  Decennial Systems and Contract Management Office.—Michael J. Longini, room 2301, 763–2933.
  Demographic Statistical Methods Division.—Alan Tupek, room 3705, 763–4287.
  Demographic Surveys Division.—Chester E. Bowie, room 3324, 763–3773.
  Economic Planning and Coordination Division.—Shirin A. Ahmed, room 2584, 763–2558.
  Economic Statistical Methods and Programming Division.—Howard Hogan, room 3015, 763–5870.
  Equal Employment Opportunity Office.—Roy P. Castro, room 1229, 763–2853.
  Field Division.—Brian Monaghan, room 1111–2, 763–7879.
  Finance Division.—Joan P. Johnson, room 3582, 763–6803.
  Foreign Trade Division.—C. Harvey Monk, Jr., room 2104, 763–2255.
  Geography Division.—Robert A. LaMacchia, WP1, 763–2131.
  Governments Division.—Stephanie H. Brown, room 407, 763–1489.
  Human Resources Division.—Tyra Dent Smith, room 3260, 763–5863.
  Information Systems Support and Review Office.—J. Jerry Bell, room 1023, 763–1881.
  Information Technology Security Office.—Timothy P. Ruland, room 1537, 763–2869.
  International Relations Office.—Jay Keller, room 2068, 763–2883.
  Manufacturing and Construction.—William G. Bostic, Jr., room 2102–4, 763–4593.
  Marketing Services Office.—John C. Kavaliunas, room 3023, 763–4090.
  Planning Research and Evaluation.—Ruth Ann Killion, room 1107–2, 763–2048.
  Population.—John F. Long, room 2011, 763–2071.
  Privacy Office.—Gerald W. Gates, room 2430, 763–2515.
  Public Information Office.—Kenneth C. Meyer, room 2705, 763–3100.
  Security Office.—Harold L. Washington, Jr., room 1631, 763–1716.
  Service Sector Statistics.—Mark E. Wallace, room 2633, 763–2683.
  Statistical Research Division.—Tommy Wright, room 3203–4, 763–1702.
  Systems Support.—Robert G. Munsey, room 1342, 763–2999.
  Technologies Management Office.—Barbara M. LoPresti, room 1757, 763–7765.
  Telecommunications Office.—Kenneth A. Riccini (acting), room 1101, 763–1793.

BUREAU OF INDUSTRY AND SECURITY

Herbert C. Hoover Building, Room 3898, phone (202) 482–1455

Under Secretary.—Peter Lichtenbaum (acting).
　Deputy Under Secretary.—Mark Foulon, room 3892, 482–1427.
　Senior Advisor, Office of International Programs.—Mi-Yong Kim, room 4515, 482–8345.
　Comptroller—Gay Shrum, room 6883, 482–1058.
　Chief Information Officer.—Dawn Leaf, room 6092, 482–4848.
　Chief Counsel.—Roman Slowiewsky (acting), room 3839, 482–5301.
　Deputy Chief Counsel.—Roman Slowiewsky, room 3839, 482–5301.
　Assistant Secretary for Export Administration.—Peter Lichtenbaum, room 3886–C, 482–5491.
　Deputy Assistant Secretary for Export Administration.—Matthew S. Borman, room 3886–C, 482–5711.
　Assistant Secretary for Export Enforcement.—Wendy Wysong (acting), room 3721, 482–5914.
　Deputy Assistant Secretary.—Wendy Wysong, room 3721, 482–5914.
　Director, Office of:
　　Administration.—Mike Carroll, room 3889, 482–1900.
　　Antiboycott Compliance.—Ned Weant (acting), room 6098, 482–5914.
　　Congressional, Public and Intergovernmental Affairs.—Scott Kamins, room 3897, 482–0097.
　　Enforcement Analysis.—Thomas Andrukonis, room 4065, 482–4255.
　　Export Enforcement.—Mike Turner, room 4525, 482–2252.
　　Exporter Services.—Eileen Albanese, room 1093, 482–0436.
　　Nonproliferation Controls and Treaty Compliance.—Steven C. Goldman, room 2093, 482–3825.
　　Planning, Evaluation and Management.—Jeannette Chiari, room 6883, 482–2117.
　　Strategic Industries and Economic Security.—Dan Hill, room 3878, 482–4506.
　　Strategic Trade and Foreign Policy Controls.—Joan Roberts (acting), room 2628, 482–4196.
　Divisional Directors for—
　　South Asia/Europe Division.—Carol Bryant, room 4065, 482–4255.
　　China/Hong Kong Division.—Kimberly A. Smith, room 4065, 482–4255.
　　Middle East/Russia Division.—Elizabeth Rosenkranz, room 4065, 482–4255.

ECONOMIC DEVELOPMENT ADMINISTRATION

Herbert C. Hoover Building, Room 7800, phone (202) 482–5081

Office of the Assistant Secretary (OAS)
　Assistant Secretary.—David A. Sampson.
　　Deputy Assistant Secretary.—David Bearden.
　　Chief of Staff.—Sandy Baruah.
Office of Chief Counsel (OCC)
　Chief Counsel.—Ben Erulkar, room 7005, 482–5671.
Office of External Affairs and Communications (OEAC)
　Deputy Assistant Secretary for External Affairs and Communications.—Alicia Davis, room 7822, 482–2900.
　Director, Division of:
　　Intergovernmental Affairs (IAD).—Paul Pisano, room 7816, 482–2900.
　　Public Affairs (PAD).—Matt Crow, room 7826, 482–4085.
Office of Information Technology (OIT)
　Chief Information Officer.—Louise McGlathery, room 7112, 482–2507.
Office of Management Services (OMS)
　Deputy Assistant Secretary for Management Services/Chief Financial Officer.—Mary Pleffner, room 7015, 482–2838.
Director, Office of:
　Administrative and Support Services (ASSD).—Sandra Walters (acting), room 7217, 482–0548.
　Budgeting and Performance Evaluation(BPED).—Vicki Hendershot (acting), room 7106, 482–0547.

Department of Commerce

695

INTERNATIONAL TRADE ADMINISTRATION

Under Secretary.—Rhonda Keenum (acting), room 3850, 482–2867.
Deputy Under Secretary.—Timothy J. Hauser, room 3842, 482–3917.
Legislative and Intergovernmental Affairs.—Lori Harju, room 3424, 482–1389.
Public Affairs.—Victoria Park (acting), room 3416, 482–3809.
Trade Promotion Coordinating Committee.—Jeri Jensen-Moran, room 3051, 482–5455.

ADMINISTRATION

Director and Chief Financial Officer.—Linda Moye Cheatham, room 3827, 482–5855.
Deputy Chief Financial Officer.—Jim Donahue, room 4112, 482–0210.
Director, Office of:
  Human Resources Management.—Doris Brown, room 7060, 482–3505.
  Organization and Management Support.—Mary Ann McFate, room 4001, 482–5436.

TRADE PROMOTION AND U.S. AND FOREIGN COMMERCIAL SERVICE

Assistant Secretary for Trade Promotion and Director General of the Commercial Service.—
  Rhonda Keenum, room 3802, 482–5777.
Deputy Director General.—Thomas Moore, room 3802, 482–0725.
Career Development and Assignment.—Rebecca Mann, room 1222, 482–5208.
Deputy Assistant Secretary for—
  Domestic Operations.—Neal Burnham, room 3810, 482–4767.
  International Operations.—Barry Friedman, room 3128, 482–6228.
  Office of Global Trade Program.—Timothy Thompson, room 2810, 482–6220.
Director for—
  Africa, Near East and South Asia.—Daniel Harris, room 1223, 482–4836.
  East Asia and Pacific.—Ann Bacher, room 1223, 482–0423.
  Europe.—Bobette Orr, room 3122, 482–1599.
  Western Hemisphere.—Danny DeVito, room 1202, 482–2736.

ASSISTANT SECRETARY FOR IMPORT ADMINISTRATION

Assistant Secretary.—Joseph A. Spetrini (acting), room 3099, 482–1780.
  Chief Counsel.—John D. McInerney, room 3622, 482–5589.
  Foreign Trade Zones Executive Secretary.—Dennis Puccinelli, room 4008, 482–2862.
  Director for—
    Office of Accounting.—Neal Halper, room 3087–B, 482–2210.
    Office of Policy.—Ronald Lorentzen, room 3713, 482–4412.
    Policy and Analysis.—Roland MacDonald, room 3713, 482–1768.
    Statutory Import Programs Staff.—Faye Robinson, room 4100W, 482–1660.
  Deputy Assistant Secretary for—
    Antidumping Countervailing Duty Operations.—Barbara Tillman (acting), room 3095, 482–5497.
    Antidumping Countervailing Duty Policy and Negotiations.—Joseph Spetrini, room 3075, 482–2104.
    Textiles and Apparel.—James C. Leonard III, room 3001A, 482–3737.
  Chairman for Committee for the Implementation of Textile Agreements.—James C. Leonard, room 3100, 482–3737.

ASSISTANT SECRETARY FOR MARKET ACCESS AND COMPLIANCE

Assistant Secretary.—William Henry Lash III, room 3868, 482–3022.
  Deputy Assistant Secretary for—
    Agreements Compliance.—Stephen Jacobs, room 3043, 482–5767.
    Asia and the Pacific.—Hank Levine, room 2038, 482–4527.
    Europe.—Eric Stewart, room 3863, 482–5638.
    Middle East and Africa.—Holly Vineyard, room 2329, 482–4651.
    Western Hemisphere.—Walter Bastian, room 3826, 482–5324.
  Director, Office of:
    Africa.—Kevin Boyd, room 2037, 482–4227.
    APEC (Asian and Asia-Pacific Economic Cooperation) Affairs.—Brenda Fisher, room 2308, 482–5334.

BISNIS (Business Information Service for the Newly Independent States).—Tanya Shuster, room 800, 482–2036.
CEEBIC (Central and Eastern Europe Business Information Center).—Jennifer Gothard, room 800, 482–2645.
China Economic Area.—Cheryl McQueen, room 3024, 482–5527.
Eastern Europe, Russia and the Newly Independent States.—Susanne Lotarski, room 3319, 482–1104.
European Union and Regional Affairs.—Penelope Naas, room 3513, 482–4498.
Japan.—Nicole Melcher, room 2322, 482–2515.
Latin America and the Caribbean.—John Anderson, room 3203, 482–2436.
Middle East and North Africa.—Cherie Loustanau, room 2031, 482–4442.
Multilateral Affairs.—Steward L. (Skip) Jones, Jr., room 3027, 482–2307.
NAFTA Secretariat.—Caratina Alston, room 2061, 482–5438.
North American Free Trade Agreement and Inter-American Affairs.—Andrew Rudman, room 3024, 482–0507.

ASSISTANT SECRETARY FOR MANUFACTURING

Assistant Secretary.—Albert Frink, room 3832, 482–1461.
  Chief of Staff.—Rebecca Bernier, room 3832, 482–1112.
  Deputy Assistant Secretary for—
    Industry Analysis.—Jack McDougle, room 2815, 482–5145.
    Manufacturing.—Joseph Bogosian, room 2800A, 482–1872.
    Services.—Douglas B. Baker, room 1128, 482–5261.

PRESIDENT'S EXPORT COUNCIL

Room 2015, Department of Commerce 20230, phone (202) 482–1124.

[Authorized by Executive Orders 12131, 12534, 12551, 12610, 12692, 12774, 12869, and 12974 (May through September 1995)]

Executive Director, Under Secretary of International Trade.—Rhonda Keenum (acting).
Executive Secretary/Staff Director.—Mark Chittum.

MINORITY BUSINESS DEVELOPMENT AGENCY

Director.—Ronald N. Langston, room 5055 (202) 482–5061.
  Associate Director.—Edith McCloud, room 5088, 482–6224.
  Chief Counsel.—Meena Elliot, room 5069, 482–5045.
  Budget Division Chief.—Ronald Marin, room 5089, 482–3341.

NATIONAL OCEANIC AND ATMOSPHERIC ADMINISTRATION

Under Secretary for Oceans and Atmosphere.—VADM Conrad C. Lautenbacher, Jr., room 5128 (202) 482–3436.
  Deputy Under Secretary.—BG John (Jack) Kelly, Jr., USAF (Ret.), room 6811, 482–4569.
  Assistant Secretary/Deputy Administrator.—James R. Mahoney, room 5804, 482–3567.
  Chief Financial Officer.—Maureen Wylie, room 6805, 482–0917.
  Chief Administrative Officer.—William (Bill) Broglie, SSMC4, room 8431, Suite 8443, (301) 713–0836 ext. 105.
  General Counsel.—James Walpole, room 5814, 482–4080.
  Director, Office of:
    Education and Sustainable Development.—Dr. Marlene Kaplan (acting), room 6869, 482–3384.
    International Affairs.—William Brennan, room 6228, 482–6196.
    Legislative Affairs.—Debbie Larson, room 5225, 482–4981.
    Marine and Aviation Operations Center.—RADM Samuel P. DeBow, Jr., room 12837 (301) 713–1045.
    Public and Constituent Affairs.—Jordan St. John, room 6217, 482–6090.

NATIONAL MARINE FISHERIES SERVICE

1315 East-West Highway, Silver Spring, MD 20910

Assistant Administrator.—William T. Hogarth, Ph.D., room 14636 (301) 713–2239.
Deputy Assistant Administrator for—
    Operations.—John Oliver, room 14743.
    Regulatory Programs.—Rebecca Lent, Ph.D., room 14657.
Director, Office of:
    Constituent Services.—Gordon Helm (acting), room 9553, 713–2379.
    Habitat Conservation.—Rolland A. Schmitten, room 14828, 713–2325.
    Law Enforcement.—Dale Jones, room 415, 427–2300.
    Management and Budget.—Gary Reisner, room 14450, 713–2259.
    Protected Resources.—Laurie Allen, room 13821, 713–2332.
    Science and Technology.—Steven Murawski, Ph.D., room 12450, 713–2367.
    Scientific Programs.—Michael Sissenwine, Ph.D., room 14659, 713–2239.
    Seafood Inspection Program.—Richard Cano, room 10837, 713–2351.
    Sustainable Fisheries.—Jack Dunnigan, room 13362, 713–2334.
Chief Information Officer.—Larry Tyminski, room 3657, 713–2372.

NATIONAL OCEAN SERVICE

Assistant Administrator.—Richard W. Spinrad, room 13632 (301) 713–3074.
    Director, Office of Operational Oceanographic Products and Services.—Michael Szabados, room 6633, 713–2981.
    Deputy Director.—Rick Edwing, room 662, 713–2981.
    Chief Financial Officer.—Mitchell Luxenberg (acting), room 13430, 713–3056.
Director, Office of:
    Coast Survey.—CAPT Roger L. Parsons, room 6147, 713–2770.
    International Programs.—Charles Ehler, room 10414, 713–3078.
    National Centers for Coastal Ocean Science.—Gary C. Matlock, room 8211, 713–3020.
    National Geodetic Survey.—Charles W. Challstrom, room 8657, 713–3222.
    NOAA Coastal Services.—Margaret A. Davidson, room 842, 740–1220.
    Ocean and Coastal Resource Management.—Eldon Hout, room 10413, 713–3155.
    Response and Restoration.—David Kennedy, room 10102, 713–2989.
    Special Projects.—Daniel Farrow, room 9515, 713–3000.

NATIONAL ENVIRONMENTAL SATELLITE, DATA AND INFORMATION SERVICE

Assistant Administrator.—Gregory W. Withee, room 8338 (301) 713–3578.
    International and Interagency Affairs Chief.—D. Brent Smith, room 7315, 713–2024.
Director, Office of:
    Chief Financial Officer.—Charles S. Baker, room 8338, 713–9476.
    Chief Information.—Richard Brooks (acting), room 8110, 713–9220.
    Coastal Ocean Laboratory.—Wayne Wilmot, room 4651, 713–3272.
    Environmental Information Services.—Ida Hakkarinen, room 7232, 713–0813.
    Management Operations and Analysis.—Christine Carpino, room 8132, 713–9210.
    National Climatic Data.—Thomas R. Karl, room 557–C (828) 271–4476.
    National Geophysical Data Center.—Christopher Fox, room 1B148 (303) 497–6215.
    National Oceanographic Data Center.—Kurt Schnebele, room 4820, 713–3270.
    National Polar Orbiting Operational Environmental Satellite System Integrated Program.—John D. Cunningham, room 1450, 427–2070.
    Research and Applications.—Marie Colton, room 701, 763–8127.
    Satellite Data Processing and Distribution.—Richard Barazotto, room 1069, 457–5120.
    Satellite Operations.—Kathleen A. Kelly, room 0135, 457–5130.
    Systems Development.—Gary K. Davis, room 3301, 457–5277.

NATIONAL WEATHER SERVICE

Assistant Administrator.—David L. Johnson, room 18150 (301) 713–9095.
    Chief Financial Officer.—Matt Jadacki, room 18176, 713–0397.
    Deputy Chief Financial Officer.—John Van Kuren (acting), room 18212, 713–0718.
    Chief Information Officer.—Dr. Paul Chan, room 18122, 713–1360.

Director, Office of:
  Climate, Water and Weather Services.—Dennis H. McCarthy (acting), room 14348, 713–0700.
  Hydrologic Development.—Gary M. Carter, room 8212, 713–1658.
  National Centers for Environmental Prediction.—Louis W. Uccellini, room 101, 763–8016.
  Operational Systems.—John McNulty, room 16212, 713–0165.
  Science and Technology.—Gregory A. Mandt, room 15146, 713–1746.

OCEANIC AND ATMOSPHERIC RESEARCH

Assistant Administrator.—Richard D. Rosen (301) 713–2458.
  Director of:
    Aeronomy Laboratory.—Daniel L. Albritton (303) 497–3134.
    Air Resources Laboratory.—Bruce B. Hicks (301) 713–0684.
    Atlantic Oceanographic and Meteorological Laboratory.—Judy Gray (acting), (305) 361–4300.
    Climate Diagnostic Center.—Randall M. Dole (303) 497–6878.
    Climate Monitoring and Diagnostics Laboratory.—David Hofmann (303) 497–6074.
    Environmental Technology Laboratory.—William Neff (acting), (303) 497–6291.
    Forecast Systems Laboratory.—Alexander MacDonald (303) 497–6818.
    Geophysical Fluid Dynamics Laboratory.—Ants Leetmaa (609) 452–6503.
    Great Lakes Environmental Research Laboratory.—Stephen E. Brandt (734) 741–2245.
    National Sea Grant College Program.—Ronald Baird, room 11716 (301) 713–1031.
    National Severe Storms Laboratory.—James Kimpel (405) 366–0429.
    National Undersea Research Program.—Barbara S.P. Moore, room 11359 (301) 713–2427.
    Pacific Marine Environmental Laboratory.—Eddie N. Bernard (206) 526–6800.
    Space Environmental Center.—Ernest Hildner, room 2C–108 (303) 497–3311.
  Director, Office of:
    Arctic Research.—John Calder (301) 713–2518.
    Global Programs.—Chester Koblinsky (301) 427–2089.
    Ocean Exploration.—Stephen Hammond (acting); (301) 713–9444.

PATENT AND TRADEMARK OFFICE
P.O. Box 1450, 600 Dulany Street, Arlington, VA 22313–1450
phone (571) 272–8600

Under Secretary of Commerce for Intellectual Property and Director of U.S. Patent and Trade Office.—Jon W. Dudas.
  Deputy Under Secretary of Commerce for Intellectual Property and Deputy Director of the U.S. Patent and Trademark Office.—Stephen M. Pinkos, 272–8700.
  Chief of Staff.—Eleanor Meltzer.
  Director of Public Affairs.—Richard Maulsby, 272–8400.
    Deputy Director.—Brigid Quinn.

COMMISSIONER FOR PATENTS

Commissioner.—Nicholas P. Godici (571) 272–8800.
  Deputy Commissioner for Patent Examination Policy.—Joseph J. Rolla.
  Director, Office of:
    Patent Cooperation Treaty Legal Administration.—Charles Pearson, 272–3224.
    Patent Legal Administation.—Robert J. Spar, 272–7700.
  Deputy Commissioner for Patent Operations.—Margaret A. Focarino, 272–8800.
  Patent Examining Group Directors:
    Technology Center 1600 (biotechnology and organic chemistry): Jasemine Chambers, 272–0500; Bruce Kisliuk, 272–0700.
    Technology Center 1700/2900 (chemical and materials engineering/design): Michael Ball, 272–1300; Mary Lee, 272–1100; Jacqueline Stone, 272–1200.
    Technology Center 2100 (computer architecture, software and information security): Steward J. Levy, 272–0900; Peter Wong, 272–1400.
    Technology Center 2600 (telecommunications): Jin F. Ng, 272–3050; Mark R. Powell, 272–4550.
    Technology Center 2800 (semiconductors, electrical and optical systems and components): James L. Dwyer, 272–1950; Janice A. Falcone, 272–1550; Sharon Gibson, 272–1650; Howard M. Goldberg, 272–1750; Richard Seidel, 272–1850.

Technology Center 3600 (transportation, construction, electronic commerce, agriculture, national security, and license and review): Donald T. Hajec, 272–5150; John Love, 272–5250; Robert Oberleitner, 272–5350.

Technology Center 3700 (mechanical engineering, manufacturing, and products and designs): Richard Bertsch, 272–3750; Edward (Kaz) Kazenske, 272–4050; Esther Kepplinger, 272–2975.

Director, Patent Quality Assurance.—George C. Elliott, 272–5018.

Deputy Commissioner for Patent Resources and Planning.—John J. Doll, 272–8800.

Director, Office of:
  Initial Patent Examination.—Thomas I. Koontz (703) 308–9210.
  Patent Classification.—Harold P. Smith, 272–7850.
  Patent Cooperation Treaty Operations.—Donald Levin (acting), (703) 308–9290.
  Patent Financial Management.—John Mielcarek, 272–8110.
  Patent Publications.—Richard A. Bawcombe (703) 308–6789.
Administrator, Office of:
  Patent Resources Administration.—Karen M. Young, 272–7900.
  Search and Information Resources Administration.—Frederick R. Schmidt, 272–3398.
Director, Scientific and Technical Information Center.—Kristin Vajs, 272–3512.

COMMISSIONER FOR TRADEMARKS

Commissioner.—Lynne Beresford (acting), (571) 272–8900.
Deputy Commissioner for Trademark Operation.—Lynne Beresford.
Trademark Examination Law Office Managing Attorneys:
  Law Office 102.—Thomas Shaw, 272–9261.
  Law Office 103.—Michael Hamilton, 272–9278.
  Law Office 105.—Thomas G. Howell, 272–9302.
  Law Office 106.—Mary Sparrow, 272–9332.
  Law Office 108.—David Shallant, 272–9351.
  Law Office 110.—Chris Pedersen, 272–9371.
  Law Office 111.—Craig Taylor, 272–9395.
  Law Office 112.—Jancie O'Lear, 272–9415.
  Law Office 113.—Odette Bonnet, 272–9426.
  Law Office 114.—Margaret Le, 272–9456.
  Law Office 115.—Thomas Vlcek, 272–9485.
  Law Office 116.—Meryl Hershkowitz, 272–9173.
Director, Office of Trademark Program Control.—Gary Cannon, 272–9671.
Deputy Commissioner for Trademark Examination Policy.—Sharon Marsh (acting), 272–8901.
Director, Office of Trademark Quality Review.—Kevin Peska, 272–9658.

ADMINISTRATOR FOR EXTERNAL AFFAIRS

Administrator for External Affairs and Director, Office of International Relations.—Lois Boland (571) 272–9300.
Director, Office of:
  Congressional Relations.—Chris Katopis.
  Enforcement.—Robert L. Stoll.

CHIEF FINANCIAL OFFICER AND CHIEF ADMINISTRATIVE OFFICER

Chief Financial Officer/Administrative Officer.—JoAnne Bernard (571) 272–9200.
Senior Advisor on:
  Planning and Financial Management.—Frances Michalkewicz.
  Process Design and Improvement.—Bo Bounkong.
Director of:
  Administration.—John Hassett, 282–8183.
  Civil Rights.—Patricia Boylan, 272–8095.
  Corporate Planning.—Arpie Balian, 272–6280.
  Finance.—Michele Picard (703) 305–8360.
  Human Resources.—Jim Matthews, 272–6200.
  Procurement.—Page A. Etzel, 272–6579.
  Space Acquisition.—Carl Winters, 272–6535.

OFFICE OF GENERAL COUNSEL

General Counsel.—James A. Toupin (571) 272–7000.
  Deputy General Counsel for—
    General Law.—Bernard J. Knight, Jr., 272–3000.
    Intellectual Property Law and Solicitor.—John M. Whealan, 272–9035.
  Chief Administrative Law Judge for—
    Board of Patent Appeals and Interferences.—Gary Harkcom (acting), 272–9797.
    Trademark Trial and Appeal Board.—J. David Sams, 272–4304.
  Director, Office of Enrollment and Discipline.—Harry Moatz, 272–4097.

CHIEF INFORMATION OFFICER

Chief Information Officer.—David J. Freeland (571) 272–9400.
  Executive for Systems Development and Maintenance Services.—Tom Kenton, 272–9075.
  Director, Office of Systems Development and Maintenance.—Robert Porter, 272–6217.
  Executive for Customer Information Services.—Kay Melvin, 272–9025.
  Director, Office of:
    Electronic Information Products.—Trish Michel, 272–5450.
    Information Services.—Martha Sneed, 272–5486.
    Public Records.—Ted Parr (703) 308–9743.
  Executive for Architecture Engineering and Technical Services.—Connie Davis, 272–9050.
  Director, Office of Data Architecture and Services.—Holly Higgins, 272–5437.
  Executive for IT Operations and Customer Support Services.—Ron Hack, 272–9095.
  Web Services.—Glen Brown, 272–5846.
  Deputy Chief Information Officer.—Larry Cogut (acting), 272–5411.
  Internal Auditor.—Ken Giese, 272–8995.
  Director, Office of System Product Assurance.—Jeffery Wolfe, 272–5631.

TECHNOLOGY ADMINISTRATION

Under Secretary.—Phillip J. Bond (202) 482–1575.
Deputy Under Secretary.—Benjamin H. Wu.

OFFICE FOR TECHNOLOGY POLICY

Assistant Secretary.—Bruce P. Mehlman (202) 482–5687.
  Director, Office of Technology Competitiveness.—Karen Laney-Cummings (acting), 482–6101.

NATIONAL INSTITUTE OF STANDARDS AND TECHNOLOGY

Director.—Dr. Hratch G. Semerjian (acting), (301) 975–2300.
  Deputy Director.—Dr. Richard F. Kayser (acting).
    Baldrige National Quality Program.—Harry S. Hertz, 975–2360.
    International and Academic Affairs.—B. Stephen Carpenter, 975–4119.
    NIST/Boulder Laboratories.—Zelda C. Bailey (303) 497–3237.
  Chief of Staff.—Matthew Heyman, 975–2759.
    Congressional and Legislative Affairs.—Verna B. Hines, 975–3080.
    Program Office.—Eric Steel (acting), 975–2667.
    Public and Business Affairs.—Sharon Shaffer (acting), 975–2758.
  Chief Financial Officer.—Douglas K. Day, 975–5000.
    Acquisition Management.—Phyllis A. Bower, 975–6336.
    Budget.—Thomas P. Klausing, 975–2669.
    Business Systems.—Teresa Coppolino, 975–2290.
    Grants and Agreements Management.—Angela McNerney, 975–8006.
    Finance.—Jon Alexander, 975–8204.
  Chief Human Capital Officer.—Marilia A. Matos, 975–2389.
    Civil Rights and Diversity.—Mirta-Marie M. Keys (acting), 975–2042.
    Human Resources Management.—Ellen M. Dowd, 975–3000.
    Management and Organization.—Sharon E. Bisco, 975–4074.
    Safety, Health and Environment.—Rosamond A. Rutledge-Burns, 975–5818.
  Chief Information Officer.—Cita M. Furlani, 975–6500.
    Applications Systems.—Harris Liebergot, 975–8292.
    Customer Access and Support.—Tim Halton, 975–8920.

Enterprise Systems.—James Fowler, 975–6888.
Information Technology Security and Networking.—Robert Glenn, 975–3667.
Telecommunications and CIO Support.—Bruce Rosen, 975–3622.
Chief Facilities Management Officer.—Robert F. Moore, 975–8836.
  Administration Services.—Robert F. Moore (acting), 975–8836.
  Emergency Services.—Benjamin Overbey, 975–8247.
  Engineering, Maintenance, and Support Services.—Stephen S. Salber, (303) 497–5680.
  Plant.—John Bollinger, 975–6900.
Director, Technology Services.—Belinda L. Collins (acting), 975–4500.
  Deputy Director.—James Adams (acting), 975–4510.
    Information Services.—Mary-Deirdre Coraggio, 975–5158.
    Measurement Services.—Robert L. Watters, Jr. (acting), 975–4122.
    Standards Services.—Mary H. Saunders, 975–4000.
    Technology Partnerships.—Bruce E. Mattson, 975–6501.
    Weights and Measures.—Henry V. Oppermann, 975–5507.
Director, Advanced Technology Program.—Marc G. Stanley, 975–2161.
  Deputy Director.—Lorel Wisniewski (acting), 975–2162.
    Chemistry and Life Sciences.—Linda Beth Schilling, 975–2887.
    Economic Assessment.—Stephanie Shipp, 975–8978.
    Information Technology and Electronics.—Elissa Sobolewski, 975–3620.
Director, Hollings Manufacturing Extension Partnership.—Kevin Carr, 975–5454.
  Deputy Director.—Roger Kilmer, 975–4676.
    Center Operations Office.—Phillip Wadsworth, 975–3945.
    Program Development Office.—Stephen J. Thompson, 975–5042.
    Systems Operation Office.—Michael J. Simpson, 975–6147.
Director, Electronics and Electrical Engineering Laboratory.—William E. Anderson, 975–2220.
  Deputy Director.—Alan Cookson.
    Electromagnetics.—Dennis S. Friday, (303) 497–3131.
    Optoelectronics.—Kent Rochford, (303) 497–5285.
    Quantum Electrical Metrology.—James K. Olthoff, 975–2431.
    Semiconductor Electronics.—David G. Seiler, 975–2054.
Director, Manufacturing Engineering Laboratory.—Dale E. Hall, 975–3400.
  Deputy Director.—Howard Harary, 975–3401.
    Fabrication Technology.—Mark E. Luce, 975–2159.
    Intelligent Systems.—Albert Wavering, 975–3418.
    Manufacturing Metrology.—Kevin K. Jurrens (acting), 975–6600.
    Manufacturing Systems Integration.—Steven R. Ray, 975–3508.
    Precision Engineering.—Dennis A. Swyt, 975–3463.
Director, Chemical Science and Technology Laboratory.—Willie E. May, 975–8300.
  Deputy Director.—William Koch, 975–8301.
    Analytical Chemistry.—Stephen A. Wise, 975–3108.
    Biotechnology.—Vincent L. Vilker, 975–2629.
    Physical and Chemical Properties.—Gregory J. Rosasco, 975–2483.
    Process Measurements.—James R. Whetstone, 975–2609.
    Surface and Microanalysis Science.—Richard R. Cavanagh, 975–2368.
Director, Physics Laboratory.—Katharine B. Gebbie, 975–4201.
  Deputy Director.—William Ott, 975–4202.
    Atomic Physics.—Carl J. Williams, 975–3531.
    Electron and Optical Physics.—Charles W. Clark, 975–3709.
    Ionizing Radiation.—Lisa R. Karam (acting), 975–5561.
    Optical Technology.—Albert C. Parr, 975–2316.
    Quantum Physics.—Steven T. Cundiff, (303) 492–7858.
    Time and Frequency.—Thomas R. O'Brian, (303) 497–3295.
Director, Materials Science and Engineering Laboratory.—Leslie E. Smith, 975–5658.
  Deputy Director.—Stephen Freiman.
    Ceramics.—Debra Kaiser, 975–6119.
    Materials Reliability.—Thomas A. Siewert (acting), (303) 497–3523.
    Metallurgy.—Carol A. Handwerker, 975–6158.
    NIST Center for Neutron Research.—Patrick D. Gallagher, 975–6210.
    Polymers.—Eric J. Amis, 975–6681.
Director, Building and Fire Research Laboratory.—James E. Hill, 975–5900.
  Deputy Director.—S. Shyam-Sunder (acting), 975–6850.
    Building Environment.—George Kelly, 975–5850.
    Fire Research.—William L. Grosshandler, 975–2310.
    Materials and Construction Research.—James St. Pierre (acting), 975–4124.

Director, Information Technology Laboratory.—Shashi Phoha, 975–2900.
  Deputy Director.—Kathleen Roberts (acting), 975–2144.
    Advanced Network Technologies.—David Su, 975–6194.
    Computer Security.—Edward Roback, 975–2934.
    Information Access.—Martin Herman, 975–4495.
    Mathematical and Computational Sciences.—Ronald F. Boisvert, 975–3800.
    Software Diagnostics and Conformance Testing.—Mark W. Skall, 975–3262.
    Statistical Engineering.—Nell Sedransk, 975–2853.

NATIONAL TELECOMMUNICATIONS AND INFORMATION ADMINISTRATION

Herbert C. Hoover Building, Room 4898 (202) 482–1840

Assistant Secretary for Communications and Information.—Michael D. Gallagher.
  Deputy Assistant Secretary.—John M.R. Kneuer.
  Director, Office of:
    Chief Counsel.—Kathy Smith, 482–1816.
    Communications and Information Infrastructure Assurance.—Daniel Hurley, 482–1116.
    Congressional Affairs.—Jim Wasilewski, 482–1551.
    Public Affairs.—Ranjit deSilva, 482–7002.
  Associate Administrator of:
    International Affairs.—Robin Layton, 482–1866.
    Policy Analysis and Development.—Joseph Watson, 482–1880.
    Spectrum Management.—Frederick R. Wentland, 482–1850.
    Telecommunications and Information Applications.—Bernadette McGuire–Rivera, 482–5802.
  Associate Administrator/Director, Institute for Telecommunications Sciences.—Al Vincent (303) 497–3500.

NATIONAL TECHNICAL INFORMATION SERVICE

Sills Building, 5285 Port Royal Road, Room 200, Springfield, VA 22161

Director.—Benjamen H. Wu (acting), (202) 482–1091.
  Director, Office of:
    Accounting.—Mary O. Houff, (703) 605–6611.
    Administration.—Vicki Buttram, 605–6133.
    Budget and Financial Analysis.—Wayne J. Gallant, 605–6471.
    Chief Information Officer.—Keith Sinner, 605–6310.
    Customer Relations.—Wendy Stone, 605–6083.
    Database Services.—Jean Bowers, 605–6227.
    Liaison Services.—Patricia Gresham, 605–6123.
    Policy Analyst.—Steven Needle, 605–6404.
    Product Services.—Douglas Campion, 605–6214.
  Associate Director for—
    Business Development.—Janice Long Coe, 605–6181.
    Customer Services.—Sandra M. Rigby, 605–6100.

DEPARTMENT OF LABOR

Frances Perkins Building, Third Street and Constitution Avenue, NW., 20210

phone (202) 693–5000, http://www.dol.gov

ELAINE L. CHAO, Secretary of Labor; education: B.A., Mount Holyoke College, 1975; M.B.A., Harvard University, 1979; she also studied at the Massachusetts Institute of Technology, Dartmouth College, and Columbia University; employment: Citicorp, 1979–1983; BankAmerica Capital Markets Group, 1984–1986; Distinguished Fellow, Heritage Foundation, 1996–2001; public service: White House Fellow, Office of Policy Development, 1983–1984; Deputy Maritime Administrator, Department of Transportation, 1986–1988; Chairwoman, Federal Maritime Commission, 1988–1989; Deputy Secretary of Transportation, 1989–1991; Peace Corps Director, 1991–1992; President and Chief Executive Officer of the United Way of America, 1992–1996; family: married to U.S. Senator Mitch McConnell (R–KY); recipient of many awards for her community service and professional accomplishments; and recipient of 11 honorary doctorate degrees from numerous colleges and universities; nominated by President George W. Bush to become the 24th Secretary of Labor, and was confirmed by the U.S. Senate on January 29, 2001.

OFFICE OF THE SECRETARY

phone 693–6000

Secretary of Labor.—Elaine L. Chao.
  Executive Assistant.—Connie Johnston.
  Executive Secretariat.—Ruth D. Knouse, 693–6100.
  Director of Operations (Scheduling and Advance).—Leah Levy, 693–6003.

OFFICE OF THE DEPUTY SECRETARY

Deputy Secretary.—Steven Law, 693–6002.

OFFICE OF THE 21ST CENTURY WORKFORCE

Director.—Karen Czarnecki, 693–6490.
  Deputy Director.—Bettye Samuels.
  Special Assistant.—Alan Severson.

OFFICE OF FAITH BASED INITIATIVES

Director.—Brent Orrell, 693–6450.
  Deputy Director.—Jacqueline Halbig.

ADMINISTRATIVE LAW JUDGES

Techworld, 800 K Street, NW., Suite 4148 20001–8002

Chief Administrative Law Judge.—John M. Vittone, 693–7542.

BENEFITS REVIEW BOARD

Chair.—Nancy S. Dolder, room N5101, 693–6300.

EMPLOYEES COMPENSATION APPEALS BOARD

Chairman.—Alec Koromilas, room N–2613, 693–6420.

ADMINISTRATIVE REVIEW BOARD

Chairman.—M. Cynthia Douglass, room S4309, 693–6200.

OFFICE OF SMALL BUSINESS PROGRAMS

Director.—Jose Lira, room C2318, 693–6460.

OFFICE OF DISABILITY EMPLOYMENT POLICY
Frances Perkins Building, Room S–1303, 693–7880, TTY 693–7881

Assistant Secretary.—W. Roy Grizzard, Ed.D.
  Chief of Staff.—J. Kim Cook, 693–7880.
  Executive Assistant.—Nancy Skaggs.
  Special Assistants: Robert Brostrom, Alice O'Steen.
  Director of:
    Office of Policy and Research.—Susan Parker.
    Office of Operations.—John Davey.

ASSISTANT SECRETARY FOR CONGRESSIONAL AND INTERGOVERNMENTAL AFFAIRS
Frances Perkins Building, Room S2006, phone 693–4601

Assistant Secretary.—Kristine Iverson.
  Staff Assistant.—Glenda Manning.
  Deputy Assistant Secretary, Congressional.—Adam Sullivan, room S–2220, 693–4600.
  Deputy Assistant Secretary, Intergovernmental.—Karen Czarnecki, room S–2235, 693–6490.
  Senior Legislative Officers:
    Budget and Appropriations.—Eric Mondero, room S–2220, 693–4600.
    Employment Standards.—Sheila Greenwood, Elizabeth Keelan, room S–2220, 693–4600.
    Employment and Training: Blake Hanlon, room S–2220, 693–4600.
    Employee Benefits.—Alice Joe, room S–2220, 693–4600.
    Workplace Safety and Health.—Bryan Little, room S–2220, 693–4600.
  Legislative Officers: Brewster Bevis, Peter Dugas, room S–2220, 693–4600.
  Congressional Research Assistants: Jana Hoisington, Michael McCarlie, room S–2220, 693–4600.
  Senior Intergovernmental Officer.—Laura Caliguiri, room S–2220, 693–4600.
  Intergovernmental Officers: Todd Dupler, Maria Fuentes, room S–2220, 693–4600.
  Intergovernmental Assistants: Aaron Coats, Cristina Reyna, room S–2220, 693–4600.
  Administrative Officer.—Joycelyn Daniels, room S–1318, 693–4600.

REGIONAL OFFICES

Region I, Boston.—Connecticut, Maine, Massachusetts, New Hampshire, Rhode Island, Vermont.
  Regional Representative.—Kathleen Summers, John F. Kennedy Federal Building, Suite 335, Boston, MA 02203 (617) 565–2282.
Region II, New York.—New York, New Jersey, Puerto Rico, Virgin Islands.
  Regional Representative.—Angelica O. Tang, 201 Varick Street, Suite 605, New York, NY 10014–4811 (212) 337–2387.
Region III, Philadelphia.—Pennsylvania, Delaware, District of Columbia, Maryland, Virginia, West Virginia.
  Regional Representative.—Patrick Marano, The Curtis Center, 170 S. Independence Mall West, Suite 637 East, Philadelphia, PA 19106 (215) 861–5027.
Region IV, Atlanta.—Alabama, Georgia, Florida, Kentucky, Mississippi, North Carolina, South Carolina, Tennessee.
Region V, Chicago.—Illinois, Indiana, Michigan, Minnesota, Ohio, Wisconsin.
  Regional Representative.—Robert (Bob) Athey, 230 South Dearborn Street, Suite 3810, Chicago, IL 60604 (312) 353–4591.

Region VI, Dallas.—Texas, Arkansas, Louisiana, New Mexico, Oklahoma.
Region VII, Kansas City.—Iowa, Kansas, Nebraska, Missouri.
Regional Representatives: Bruce Cornett, City Center Square, 1100 Main Street, Suite 1225, Kansas City, MO 64105 (816) 426–6371; Jack Rife, 210 Walnut Street, Room 275, Des Moines, IA 50309 (515) 284–4740.
Region VIII, Denver.—Colorado, Montana, North Dakota, South Dakota, Wyoming.
Regional Representative.—Rick Collins, 1801 California Street, Suite 945, Denver, CO 80202 (303) 844–1256.
Region IX, San Francisco.—California, Hawaii, Nevada, Arizona, Guam.
Regional Representative.—Judy Bioviani Lloyd, 71 Stevenson Street, Suite 1035, San Francisco, CA 94119 (415) 975–4042.
Region X, Seattle.—Alaska, Idaho, Oregon, Washington.
Regional Representative.—Walter Liang, 1111 Third Avenue, Suite 920, Seattle, WA 98101–3212 (206) 553–0574.

ASSISTANT SECRETARY FOR PUBLIC AFFAIRS
Frances Perkins Building, Room S2514, phone 693–4676

Assistant Secretary.—Lisa M. Kruska.
Deputy Assistant Secretaries: Jane Norris, Robert Zachariasiewicz.

REGIONAL OFFICES

Region I.—Connecticut, Maine, Massachusetts, New Hampshire, Rhode Island, Vermont.
Public Affairs Director.—John Chavez, JFK Federal Building, Government Center, Room E–120, Boston, MA 02203 (617) 565–2075.
Region IIA.—New York, Puerto Rico, Virgin Islands.
Regional Representative.—John Chavez, JFK Federal Building, Government Center, Room E–120, Boston, Massachusetts 02203 (617) 565–2075.
Region IIB.—New Jersey.
Regional Representative.—Kate Dugan, 170 S. Independence Mall West, Philadelphia, PA 19106–3306 (215) 596–1147.
Region III.—Delaware, District of Columbia, Maryland, Pennsylvania, Virginia, West Virginia.
Public Affairs Director.—Kate Dugan, 170 S. Independence Mall West, Philadelphia, PA 19106–3306 (215) 596–1147.
Region IV.—Alabama, Florida, Georgia, Kentucky, Mississippi, North Carolina, South Carolina, Tennessee.
Public Affairs Director.—Dan Fuqua, Atlanta Federal Center, 61 Forsyth SW, Suite 6B75, Atlanta, GA 30303 (404) 562–2078.
Region V.—Illinois, Indiana, Michigan, Minnesota, Ohio, Wisconsin.
Public Affairs Director.—Bradley Mitchell, Room 3192, 230 South Dearborn Street, Room 3192, Chicago, IL 60604 (312) 353–6976.
Region VI.—Arkansas, Louisiana, New Mexico, Oklahoma, Texas.
Public Affairs Director.—Diana Petterson, Room 734, 525 Griffin Street, Dallas, TX 75202 (214) 767–4777.
Region VII.—Iowa, Kansas, Missouri, Nebraska.
Public Affairs Specialist.—Norma Conrad, City Center Square, 11000 Main Street, Suite 1220, Kansas City, MO 64105 (816) 426–5490.
Region VIII.—Colorado, Montana, North Dakota, South Dakota, Utah, Wyoming.
Public Affairs Director.—Rich Kulczewski, 1999 Broadway, Suite 1640, Denver, CO 80202 (303) 844–1303.
Region IX.—Arizona, California, Guam, Hawaii, Nevada.
Public Affairs Director.—Deanne Amaden, Suite 1035, 71 Stevenson Street, San Francisco, CA 94119–3766 (415) 975–4742.
Region X.—Alaska, Idaho, Oregon, Washington.
Public Affairs Director.—Mike Shimizu, Building B, Room 930, 1111 Third Avenue, Seattle WA, 98101 (206) 553–7620.

BUREAU OF INTERNATIONAL LABOR AFFAIRS
Frances Perkins Building, phone 693–4770

Deputy Under Secretary.—Arnold Levine.
Associate Deputy Under Secretaries: Martha Newton, Jorge Perez-Lopez.

Chief of Staff.—Donald Robert Owen.
Director, Office of:
  Foreign Relations.—Gary Russell (acting), 693–4785.
  International Child Labor Programs.—Marcia Eugenio (acting), 693–4843.
  International Economic Affairs.—Jorge Perez-Lopez, 693–4888.
  International Organizations.—Robert Shepard, 693–4855.
  Trade Agreement Implementation.—Lewis Karesh (acting), 693–4900.

INSPECTOR GENERAL
Frances Perkins Building, Room S–5502, phone 693–5100

Inspector General.—Gordon S. Heddell.
  Deputy Inspector General.—George J. Opfer.
  Chief of Staff.—Nancy Ruiz de Gamboa.
  Assistant Inspector General for—
    Audit.—Elliot P. Lewis, room S–5518, 693–5170.
    Inspection and Special Investigations.—Richard S. Clark, room S–5021, 693–5211.
    Labor Racketeering and Fraud Investigations.—Stephen J. Cossu, room S–5014, 693–7034.
    Legal Services.—Howard L. Shapiro, room S–5506, 693–5116.
    Management and Policy.—Nancy Ruiz de Gamboa, room S–5020, 693–5191.

WOMEN'S BUREAU
Frances Perkins Building, Room S–3002, phone 693–6710

Director.—Shinae Chun.
  Chief of Staff.—Beth Gable Hicks.
  National Office Manager.—Karen Furia.
  Regional Office Manager.—Delores Crockett, (404) 562–2336.
  Chief of:
    Information and Support Services.—Catherine Brietenbach.
    Policy and Programs.—Collis Phillips.

EMPLOYEE BENEFITS SECURITY ADMINISTRATION
Frances Perkins Building, Room S–2524, phone 693–8300

Assistant Secretary.—Ann L. Combs.
  Deputy Assistant Secretary for Policy.—Bradford P. Campbell.
  Deputy Assistant Secretary.—Alan D. Lebowitz, room N–5677, 693–8315.
  Chief of Staff.—Thomas Alexander, room S–2524, 693–8300.
  Executive Assistant to the Deputy Assistant Secretary.—Sue Ugelow, 693–8315.
  Confidential Assistant.—Holly Katherine Winthrop.
  Special Assistant.—Christine Heatley.
  Senior Director for Policy and Legislative Analysis.—Morton Klevan, room N–5677, 693–8315.
  Director of:
    Program, Planning, Evaluation and Management.—Brian C. McDonnell, room N–5668, 693–8480.
    Chief Accountant.—Ian Dingwall, room N–5459, 693–8360.
    Enforcement.—Virginia Smith, room N–5702, 693–8440.
    Exemption Determinations.—Ivan L. Strasfeld, room N–5649, 693–8540.
    Information Management.—John Helms, room N–5459, 693–8600.
    Program Services.—Sharon Watson, room N–5625, 693–8630.
    Regulations and Interpretations.—Robert Doyle, room N–5669, 693–8500.
    Policy and Research.—Joseph Piacentini, room N–5718, 693–8410.

EMPLOYMENT STANDARDS ADMINISTRATION
Frances Perkins Building, Room S–2321, phone 693–0200

Assistant Secretary.—Victoria Lipnic.
  Deputy Assistant Secretary.—D. Mark Wilson.

Chief of Staff.—Horace Cooper.
Special Assistant.—Nicolee Ambrose.
Deputy Administrator for Policy.—Alfred B. Robinson, Jr.
Deputy Administrator for Operations.—Russell Harris.
Chief of Staff.—Dave Minsky.
Director, Office of:
  External Affairs.—Rae E. Glass.
  Planning and Analysis.—Nancy M. Flynn.
  Wage Determinations.—William M. Gross.
Deputy Assistant Secretary, Office of Federal Contract Compliance Programs.—Charles
  E. James, Sr., 693–0101.
Deputy Director.—Bill Doyle.
Chief of Staff.—Shawn Hooper.
Director of Workers' Compensation Programs.—Shelby Hallmark, 693–0031.
Director, Division of:
  Coal Mine Worker's Compensation.—James DeMarce.
  Energy Employees Occupational Illness Compensation Program.—Peter Turcic.
  Federal Employees Compensation.—Deborah Sanford.
  Longshore and Harbor Worker's Compensation.—Michael Niss.
Director, Office of Management, Administration and Planning.—Anne Baird-Bridges,
  693–0608.
  Deputy Director.—Patricia J. Vastano.
Coordinator, Equal Employment Opportunity Unit.—Kate Dorrell, 693–0024.

OFFICE OF THE ASSISTANT SECRETARY FOR ADMINISTRATION AND MANAGEMENT

Frances Perkins Building, Room S–2203, phone 693–4040

Assistant Secretary.—Patrick Pizzella.
  Deputy Assistant Secretary for—
    Budget and Strategic and Performance Planning.—James McEntire.
    Operations.—Edward C. Hugler.
    Security and Emergency Management.—Kenneth McCreless, room S–1229G, 693–7990.
  Special Assistants: Cesar DeGuzman, Jeff Koch, John Pallasch, Terrance Wear.
  Administrative Officer.—Noelia Fernandez.
  Staff Assistant.—Rawnette Murray.

DEPARTMENTAL BUDGET CENTER

Director.—Kimberly Taylor-Locey, room S–4020, 693–4090.
  Deputy Director.—Mark P. Wichlin.
  Staff Assistant.—Patricia Smith.
  Office of:
    Agency Budget Programs.—William C. Keisler, 693–4068.
    Financial Management Operations.—Geoffrey Kenyon, S–5526, 693–4490.

CENTER FOR PROGRAM PLANNING AND RESULTS

Director.—Richard French, room S–3317, 693–4088.
  Office of:
    Performance Monitoring.—Karen Pane, 693–7121.
    Planning.—Mark Davis, 693–7126.

SECURITY CENTER

Director.—Robert Rouse, room S–1519, 693–7200.
  Deputy Director.—Tom Holman.

EMERGENCY MANAGEMENT CENTER

Deputy Director.—Greg Rize, 800 K Street, NW., Suite 450 North, 20001–8002, 693–7555.

BUSINESS OPERATIONS CENTER

Director.—Al Stewart, room S–1524, 693–4028.
Deputy Director.—John Saracco (acting), room S–1524, 693–4026.
Office of:
   Acquisition and Management Support Services.—Pauline Perrow (acting), room S–1512, 693–7272.
   Administrative Services.—Leonard Pettiford, room S–1521, 693–6665.
   Procurement Services.—Valerie Veatch, room N–5416, 693–4570.
   Safety and Health Services.—Laurie Hileman, room C–3317, 693–6670.
   Wirtz Labor Library.—Linda Parker, room N–2455, 693–6600.
   Special Assistant.—Linda Hunt, room S–1511, 693–4032.

CIVIL RIGHTS CENTER

Director.—Annabelle T. Lockhart, room N–4123, 693–6500.
Staff Assistant.—Vicky Best-Morris.
Office of:
   Compliance Assistance and Planning.—Gregory Shaw, 693–6501.
   EEO Coordinator of Counselors.—Lillian Winstead, 693–6504.
   Enforcement External.—Willie Alexander, 693–6501.
   Enforcement Internal.—Naomi Berry Perez, 693–6502.
   Reasonable Accommodation Hotline.—Dawn Murray-Johnson, room N–4309, 693–6569.

HUMAN RESOURCES CENTER

Director.—Daliza Salas, room S–5526, 693–7600.
Deputy Director.—Jerry Lelchook, C–5526, 693–7600.
Office of:
   Administration, Events Management and Assistive Services.—Tracey Schaeffer, C–5515, 693–7612.
   Continuous Learning and Career Management.—Kim Green, room N–5460, 693–7630.
   Employee Labor Management Relations.—Sandra Keppley, room N–5470, 693–7670.
   Executive Resources and Personnel Security.—Anne Bartels, room C–5508, 693–7628.
   Human Resources Policy and Accountability.—Susan Barker, room C–5470, 693–7725.
   Human Resources Service Center.—Violet R. Parker, room C–5516, 693–7718.
   Workforce Planning and Diversity.—Dennis Sullivan, room C–5522, 693–7739.
   Worklife and Benefits Programs.—Brooke Brewer, room N–5454, 693–7616.

INFORMATION TECHNOLOGY CENTER

Director.—Thomas Wiesner, room N–1301, 693–4567.
Administrative Officer.—Kathy Fox, 693–4215.
Director, Office of:
   Chief Information Officer Programs.—Peter Sullivan, 693–4211.
   Customer Support and Field Operations.—Cornelius Johnson, 693–4170.
   Government Benefits/Government.—Jeff Koch (acting), N–4309, 693–4205.
   Systems Development and Integration.—Richard Lewis, 693–4149.
   Technical Services.—Cornelius Johnson (acting), 693–4170.
IT Help Desk.—8 a.m. to 6:30 p.m., room N–1505, 693–4444.

ASSISTANT SECRETARY FOR POLICY

Frances Perkins Building, Room S–2312, phone 693–5959

Assistant Secretary.—Veronica V. Stidvent.
Deputy Assistant Secretary.—Susan (Suey) Howe.
Chief of Staff.—John Britton.
Staff Assistant.—Kristina Rivas.
Director, Office of:
   Compliance Assistance Policy.—Barbara Bingham, 693–5080.
   Programmatic Policy.—Ruth Samardick, 693–5075.
   Regulatory Policy.—Kathleen Franks, 693–5072.

Department of Labor

OFFICE OF THE SOLICITOR
Frances Perkins Building, phone 693–5260

Solicitor.—Howard M. Radzely.
  Deputy Solicitor.—Gregory M. Jacob.
    Confidential Assistant.—Tina McCants.
    Special Assistant.—Sam J. Saad III.
  Associate Solicitor for Legal Counsel.—Robert A. Shapiro, 693–5500.
  Deputy Solicitor for National Operations.—Carol A. DeDeo, 693–5261.
    Special Assistants: Craig W. Hukill, Nancy M. Rooney, 693–5261.
  Associate Deputy Solicitor for Legal Policy.—Gary M. Buff, 693–5260.
  Associate Deputy Solicitor for Appellate and Supreme Court Advice.—Allen H. Feldman, 693–5760.
  Deputy Solicitor for Regional Operations.—Ronald G. Whiting, 693–5262.

OFFICE OF MANAGEMENT AND ADMINISTRATIVE LEGAL SERVICES

Associate Solicitor.—James E. Culp (acting), room N–2414, 693–5405.
  Deputy Associate Solicitor.—Rae Ellen James (acting).
  Director.—Cecilia M. Holmes.
  Counsel for:
    Administrative Law.—April E. Nelson, 693–5500.
    Appropriations and Contracts.—Dennis A. Adelson, 695–5710; Myron G. Zeitz, 693–5500.
    FOIA/FACA.—Miriam McD. Miller, 693–5500.
    Human Resourcesz; Peter J. Constantine, Neilda C. Lee, 693–5405.
    Financial Manager.—June M. Groft, room N–2427, 693–5433.
    Legal Technology.—Alice L. Rapport, room N–2414, 693–5430.

DIVISION OF BLACK LUNG AND LONGSHORE LEGAL SERVICES

Associate Solicitor.—Donald S. Shire, room N–2605, 693–5660.
  Deputy Associate Solicitor.—Christian P. Barber (acting).
  Counsel for—
    Administrative Litigation and Legal Advice.—Michael J. Rutledge.
    Appellate Litigation: Christian Barber; Patricia M. Nece.
    Enforcement.—Edward Waldman.
    Longshore.—Mark A. Reinhalter.

DIVISION OF CIVIL RIGHTS AND LABOR-MANAGEMENT

Associate Solicitor.—Katherine E. Bissell, room N–2474, 693–5740.
  Deputy Associate Solicitor.—Andrew D. Auerbach.
  Counsel for—
    Civil Rights Interpretations and Advice.—Suzan Chastain.
    Litigation: Beverly Dankowitz, Richard Gilman.
    Labor-Management Advice.—Alexandra A. Tsiros.
    Labor-Management Programs.—Sharon E. Hanley.

DIVISION OF EMPLOYMENT AND TRAINING LEGAL SERVICES

Associate Solicitor.—Charles D. Raymond, room N–2101, 693–5710.
  Deputy Associate Solicitor.—Jonathan H. Waxman, 693–5730.
  Counsel for—
    Employment and Training Advise.—Robert P. Hines.
    Immigration Programs.—Bruce W. Alter.
    International Affairs and USERRA.—Donald D. Carter, Jr.
    Litigation.—Harry L. Sheinfeld.

DIVISION OF FEDERAL EMPLOYEE AND ENERGY WORKERS COMPENSATION

Associate Solicitor.—Jeffrey L. Nesvet, room S–4325, 693–5320.
  Deputy Associate Solicitor.—Craig W. Hukill (acting).

Counsel for—
  Claims and Compensation.—Catherine P. Carter.
  Energy Employees Compensation.—Sheldon G. Turley, Jr.

DIVISION OF FAIR LABOR STANDARDS

Associate Solicitor.—Steve Mandel, room N–2716, 693–5555.
  Deputy Associate Solicitor.—William Lesser.
  Counsel for—
  Appellate Litigation.—Paul L. Frieden, 693–5552.
  Legal Advice.—Diane Heim.
  Trial Litigation.—Jonathan M. Kronheim.
  Trial Litigation (Contract Labor Standards).—Ford F. Newman.

DIVISION OF MINE SAFETY AND HEALTH

1100 Wilson Boulevard, 22nd Floor, Arlington, VA 22209

Associate Solicitor.—Edward P. Clair, room 2222 (202) 693–9333.
  Deputy Associate Solicitor.—Thomas A. Mascolino, room 2221.
  Counsel for—
  Appellate Litigation.—W. Christian Schumann, room 2220.
  Standards and Legal Advice.—Heidi W. Strassler, room 2224.
  Trial Litigation.—Mark R. Malecki, room 2226.

DIVISION OF OCCUPATIONAL SAFETY AND HEALTH

Associate Solicitor.—Joseph M. Woodward, room S–4004, 693–5452.
  Deputy Associate Solicitor.—Alexander Fernández.
  Counsel for—
  Appellate Litigation: Charles F. James, Ann Rosenthal.
  General Legal Advice.—Robert W. Swain, 693–5445.
  Health Standards.—Claudia Thurber, 693–5479.
  Safety Standards.—Bradford E. Hammock.
  Trial and OSHRC Litigation.—Daniel Mick, 693–5445.

DIVISION OF PLAN BENEFITS SECURITY

Associate Solicitor.—Timothy D. Hauser, room N–4611, 693–5600.
  Deputy Associate Solicitor.—Karen L. Handorf.
  Counsel for—
  Appellate and Special Litigation.—Elizabeth Hopkins.
  Fiduciary Litigation.—Risa D. Sandler.
  General Litigation.—Leslie Candied Perlman.
  Regulation.—William White Taylor.
  Senior Trial Attorneys: Michael A. Schloss, William Scott, William P. Tedesco, William E. Zuckerman.

OCCUPATIONAL SAFETY AND HEALTH ADMINISTRATION
Frances Perkins Building, Room S–2315, phone 693–2000

Assistant Secretary.—Johnathan Snare (acting).
  Deputy Assistant Secretary.—Steve Witt (acting).
  Director, Office of:
  Equal Employment Opportunity.—Betty Gillis-Robinson, 693–2150.
  Public Affairs.—George Shaw (acting), 693–1999.
  Director of:
  Administrative Programs.—David Zeigler, 693–1600.
  Construction and Engineering.—Russell B. Swanson, 693–2345.
  Cooperative and State Programs.—Paula White.
  Enforcement Programs.—Richard Fairfax, 693–2100.
  Evaluation and Analysis.—Keith Goddard (acting), 693–2400.
  Information Technology.—Cheryl Greeangh, 693–2400.

Science, Technology.—Ruth McCully, 693–2300.
Standards and Guidance.—Steven Witt, 693–1950.

EMPLOYMENT AND TRAINING ADMINISTRATION
Frances Perkins Building, Room S–2307, phone 693–2700

Assistant Secretary.—Emily Stover DeRocco.
Deputy Assistant Secretaries: Mason M. Bishop, Thomas M. Dowd.
Administrator, Office of:
  Apprenticeship Training, Employer and Labor Services.—Anthony Swoope, room N–4671, 693–2796.
  Business Relations Group.—Jennifer McNelly, N–4643, 693–3949.
  EEO.—Jan T. Austin, N–4306, 693–3370.
  Financial and Administrative Management.—Anna Goddard, room N–4653, 693–2800.
  Job Corps.—Grace A. Kilbane, room N–4463, 693–3000.
  National Programs.—John R. Beverly III, room C–4312, 693–3840.
  National Response.—Shirley M. Smith, room N–5422, 693–3500.
  Performance and Technology.—Esther R. Johnson, room S–5206, 693–3420.
  Policy Development and Research.—Maria Kniesler Flynn, room N–5637, 693–3700.
  Regional Operations.—Jack Rapport, room C–4517, 693–3690.
  Workforce Investment.—Gay Gilbert, room S–4231, 693–3980.
  Workforce Security.—Cheryl Atkinson, room S–4231, 693–3029.

MINE SAFETY AND HEALTH ADMINISTRATION
1100 Wilson Boulevard, Arlington, VA 22209–3939, phone (202) 693–9414, fax 693–9401, http://www.msha.gov

Deputy Assistant Secretaries: John R. Correll, David G. Dye.
Chief of Staff.—Loretta M. Herrington.
Director, Office of Information and Public Affairs.—Layne Lathram, 693–9422.
Administrator for—
  Coal Mine Safety and Health.—Ray McKinney, 693–9502.
  Metal and Nonmetal Mine Safety and Health.—Robert M. Friend, 693–9603.
Director for—
  Administration and Management Office.—David L. Meyer, 693–9802.
  Assessments Office.—Neal Merrifield, 693–9702.
  Educational Policy and Development Office.—Jeffrey A. Duncan, 693–9572.
  Program Evaluation and Information Resources.—George M. Fesak, 693–9752.
  Standards, Regulations and Variances.—Rebecca Smith (acting), 693–9442.
  Technical Support.—Mark E. Skiles, 693–9472.

VETERANS' EMPLOYMENT AND TRAINING SERVICE
Frances Perkins Building, Room S–1313, phone 693–4700

Assistant Secretary.—Frederico Juarbe, Jr.
Deputy Assistant Secretaries: Charles S. Ciccolella, John McWilliam.
Executive Assistant.—John Muckelbauer.
Special Assistants: Daniel Nichols, Vicki Sinnett.
Director, Management, Budget, and Agency Adminisrative Officer.—Paul Briggs, 693–4713.
  Operations and Programs.—Gordon Burke, 693–4707.
Chief of:
  Compliance Assistance and Investigations Branch.—Robert Wilson, 693–4719.
  Employment and Training Program Division.—Pamela Langley, 693–4708.
Director, Strategic Planning.—Ronald Drach, 693–4749.
President's National Hire Veterans Committee.—William Offutt, 693–4717.

REGIONAL OFFICES

Boston:
  Administrator.—David Houle (617) 565–2080.
Philadelphia:
  Administrator.—John W. Hortiz, Jr. (215) 861–5390.

Atlanta:
   Administrator.—William J. Bolls, Jr. (404) 562–2305.
Chicago/Kansas City:
   Administrator.—Ronald J. Bachman (312) 353–4942.
Dallas/Denver:
   Administrator.—Lester L. Williams, Jr. (214) 767–4987.
Seattle/San Francisco:
   Administrator.—Alex Cuevas (316) 654–8178.

BUREAU OF LABOR STATISTICS

Postal Square Building, Suite 4040, 2 Massachusetts Avenue NE 20212, phone 691–7800

Commissioner.—Kathleen P. Utgoff, suite 4040, 691–7800.
   Deputy Commissioner.—Philip L. Rones, 691–7802.
   Associate Commissioners, Office of:
      Administration.—Daniel J. Lacey, suite 4060, 691–7777.
      Compensation and Working Conditions.—Katrina Reut, suite 4130, 691–6300.
      Employment and Unemployment Statistics.—John M. Galvin, suite 4945, 691–6400.
      Field Operations.—Robert A. Gaddie (acting), suite 2935, 691–5800.
      Prices and Living Conditions.—John Greenlees, suite 3120, 691–6960.
      Productivity and Technology.—Marilyn E. Manser, suite 2150, 691–5600.
      Publications and Special Studies.—William Parks, suite 4110, 691–5900.
      Survey Methods Research.—Stephen H. Cohen, suite 4080, 691–7372.
      Technology and Survey Processing.—Fernando Burbano, suite 5025, 691–7603.
   Assistant Commissioner, Office of:
      Compensation Levels and Trends.—Mary McCarthy, suite 4130, 691–6302.
      Consumer Prices and Price Indexes.—David Johnson, suite 3130, 691–6950.
      Current Employment Analysis.—Thomas Nadone, suite 4675, 691–6388.
      Industrial Prices and Price Indexes.—Michael Horrigan, suite 3840, 691–7700.
      Industry Employment Statistics.—George S. Werking, suite 4840, 691–6528.
      Occupational Statistics and Employment Projections.—Charles Bowman (acting).
   Director of:
      Survey Processing.—Richard L. Schroeder (acting), suite 5025, 691–7603.
      Technology and Computing Services.—Rick Kryger (acting), suite 5025, 691–7606.

DEPARTMENT OF HEALTH AND HUMAN SERVICES

200 Independence Avenue SW 20201, http://www.hhs.gov

MICHAEL O. LEAVITT, Secretary of Health and Human Services; born in Cedar City, UT, February 11, 1951; education: B.S., Southern Utah University, 1978; professional: served as Administrator of the U.S. Environmental Protection Agency; Governor of Utah for 11 years; organizations: chairman, National Governors Association; Western Governors Association; Republican Governors Association; married: Jacalyn; five children; nominated by President George W. Bush to become the 20th Secretary of Health and Human Services, and was confirmed by the U.S. Senate on January 26, 2005.

OFFICE OF THE SECRETARY

Secretary of Health and Human Services.—Michael O. Leavitt (202) 690–7000.
  Staff Assistant to the Secretary.—Denise Schwartz.
  Counselor to the Secretary.—Natalie Gochnour, 690–5400.

OFFICE OF THE DEPUTY SECRETARY

Chief of Staff.—Richard McKeown, 690–8157.
  Deputy Chiefs of Staff: Laura Lawlor, Kerry Weems, 690–5400.
  Executive Secretary.—Ann Agnew, 690–5627.
  Deputy Executive Secretary.—Dick Eisinger, 690–5627.
  Director, Office of:
    Global Health Affairs.—William Steiger, 690–6174.
    Intergovernmental Affairs.—Regina Schofield, 690–6060.
  Chair, Departmental Appeals Board.—Cecilia Sparks Ford, 690–5501.

ASSISTANT SECRETARY FOR LEGISLATION

Assistant Secretary—Legislation.—Jennifer Young, 690–5621.
  Director, Congressional Liaison.—Matt Hughes, 690–6786.
  Deputy Assistant Secretary for—
    Budget and Science.—Craig Burton, 690–7627.
    Human Services.—Laura O. Ott, 690–6311.

ASSISTANT SECRETARY FOR BUDGET, TECHNOLOGY AND FINANCE

Principal Deputy Assistant Secretary.—Kerry Weems, 690–6396.
  Deputy Assistant Secretary for—
    Budget.—William Beldon, 690–7393.
    Finance.—George H. Strader, 690–7084.
    Information Resources Management.—Charles Havekost, 690–6162.
    Grants.—Charles Havekost (acting), 690–6162.

ASSISTANT SECRETARY FOR PLANNING AND EVALUATION

Assistant Secretary.—Michael O'Grady, Ph.D., 690–7858.
  Principal Deputy Assistant Secretary.—Donald A. Young, M.D.
  Deputy Assistant Secretary for—
    Disability, Aging, & Long Term Care Policy.—Ruth Katz (acting), 690–6443.
    Health Policy.—Donald A. Young, M.D., 690–6870.
    Human Services Policy.—Barbara Broman (acting), 690–7409.
    Science and Data Policy.—Jim Scanlon (acting), 690–5874.

ASSISTANT SECRETARY FOR ADMINISTRATION AND MANAGEMENT

Assistant Secretary.—Ed Sontag, 690–7431, fax 401–5207.
  Principal Deputy Assistant Secretary.—Evelyn M. White.
  Special Assistant.—Catherine Tyrell.

Deputy Assistant Secretary for Human Resources.—Robert Hosenfeld, 690–6191.
Executive Officer, Office of the Secretary Executive Office.—Sharon Jenkins, 690–6340.
Director, Office of:
   Acquisition Management and Policy.—Marc Weisman (acting), 690–8554.
   Competitive Sourcing.—Robert Noonan (acting), 205–4650.
   Grants Management Policy.—Charles Havekost (acting), 690–8443.
   Secretary Equal Employment Office.—Barbara Barski-Carrow, 619–3677.

ASSISTANT SECRETARY FOR PUBLIC AFFAIRS

Assistant Secretary.—Kevin Keane, 690–7850.
Deputy Assistant Secretary for Media.—Bill Pierce, 690–6343; fax 690–6247.
Director, Division of Freedom of Information/Privacy.—Ross Cirrincione, 690–7453.

OFFICE FOR CIVIL RIGHTS

Director.—Richard Campanelli, 619–0403.
Principal Deputy Director.—Robinsue Frohboese, 619–0403.
Director for Management Operations.—David Young, 619–0553.
   Toll Free Voice Number (Nationwide)—1–800–368–1019.
   Toll Free TDD Number (Nationwide)—1–800–527–7697.

OFFICE OF PUBLIC HEALTH AND SCIENCE

Assistant Secretary for Health.—Christina V. Beato, M.D. (acting) (202) 690–7694.
The Surgeon General.—Richard H. Carmona, M.D., M.P.H., F.A.C.S. (301) 443–4000.
Principal Deputy Assistant Secretary for Health.—Christina V. Beato, M.D., 690–7694.
Deputy Assistant Secretary, Office of:
   Disease Prevention and Health Promotion.—Penelope Royall, P.T., M.S.W. (202) 401–6295.
   HIV/AIDS Policy.—Christopher Bates (acting), (202) 690–5560.
   Minority Health.—Garth Graham, M.D., M.P.H. (301) 443–5084.
   Population Affairs.—Alma Golden, M.D., F.A.A.P. (301) 594–4001.
   President's Council on Physical Fitness and Sports.—Melissa Johnson, M.S. (202) 690–9000.
   Research Integrity.—Christopher Pascal, J.D. (301) 443–3400.
   Science, Technology, and Medicine.—Howard Zucker, M.D. (202) 260–9123.
   Women's Health.—Dr. Wanda Jones, Ph.D. (202) 690–7650.
Director, Office of:
   Commissioned Corps Force Management.—CAPT Lawrence Furman, D.D.S., M.P.H. (202) 205–4859.
   National Vaccine Programs.—Bruce Gellin, M.D., (202) 205–5294.
Regional Administrators for—
   Region I: CT, ME, MA, NH, RI, VT.—Michael Milner, PA–C (617) 565–4999.
   Region II: NJ, NY, PR, VI.—Robert W. Amler, M.D., M.S. (212) 264–2560.
   Region III: DE, DC, MD, PA, VA, WV.—Dalton G. Paxman, Ph.D. (215) 861–4631.
   Region IV: AL, FL, GA, KY, MS, NC, SC, TN.—Clara H. Cobb, M.S., R.N. (404) 562–7894.
   Region V: IL, IN, MI, MN, OH, WI.—Steven R. Potsic, M.D., M.P.H., FACPM (312) 353–1385.
   Region VI: AR, LA, NM, OK, TX.—Ronald Banks, M.D., M.P.H. (214) 767–3879.
   Region VII: IA, KS, MO, NE.—Linda Vogel (816) 426–3291.
   Region VIII: CO, MT, ND, SD, UT, WY.—Jane Wilson, M.S. (303) 844–7859.
   Region IX: AZ, CA, HI, NV, Guam, American Samoa, CNMI, FSMI, RMI, Palau.—Ronald Banks, M.D., M.P.H. (415) 437–8096.
   Region X: AK, ID, OR, WA.—Patrick O'Carroll, M.D., M.P.H., FACPM (206) 615–2469.

ASSISTANT SECRETARY FOR PUBLIC HEALTH EMERGENCY PREPAREDNESS

Assistant Secretary.—Stewart Simonson, 205–2882, fax 690–6512.
Principal Deputy Assistant Secretary.—Dr. William Raub.
Director, Office of:
   Emergency Operations and Security Programs.—Robert Blitzer, 205–8387.
   Mass Casualty Planning.—Dr. Robert Claypool, 260–1198.

Medicine, Science and Public Health.—Dr. Stuart Nightingale, 205–2882.
Research and Development Coordination.—Dr. Noreen Hynes, 401–4862.

OFFICE OF THE GENERAL COUNSEL

fax [Immediate Office] 690–7998, fax [Admin. Office] 690–5452

General Counsel.—Alex M. Azar, 690–7741.
  Deputy General Counsel.—David S. Cade, 690–7721.
  Legal Counsel.—E. Peter Urbanowicz, 690–7741.
  Program Review.—Paula Stannard.
  Regulations.—Stewart G. Simonson.
  Associate General Counsel for—
    Centers for Medicare and Medicaid Division.—Sheree Kanner, 619–0300.
    Children, Family and Aging Division.—Robert Keith, 690–8005.
    Civil Rights Division.—George Lyon, 619–0900.
    Ethics Division/Special Counsel for Ethics.—Edgar Swindell, 690–7258.
    Food and Drug Division.—Daniel Troy (301) 827–1137.
    General Law Division.—Katherine Drews, 619–0150.
    Legislation Division.—Sondra Steigen Wallace, 690–7773.

OFFICE OF THE INSPECTOR GENERAL

330 Independence Avenue, SW., 20201

Inspector General.—Daniel R. Levinson, 619–3148.
  Principal Deputy Inspector General.—Larry J. Goldberg (acting), 619–3148.
  Chief Counsel to the Inspector General.—Lewis Morris, 619–0335.
  Deputy Inspector General for—
    Audit Services.—Joseph Vengrin, 619–3155.
    Evaluation and Inspections.—George Grob (acting), 619–0480.
    Investigations.—Michael Little, 619–3208.
    Management and Policy.—Don Dille (acting), 619–3081.
  Director, External Affairs.—Stuart Wright, 619–1343.

ADMINISTRATION ON AGING

1 Massachusetts Avenue, SW., 20001

Assistant Secretary for Aging.—Josefina G. Carbonell (202) 401–4541.
  Deputy Assistant Secretary for—
    Policy and Programs.—Edwin Walker, 401–4634.
    Management.—John Wren (acting), 357–3430.
    Center for Wellness and Community-Based Services.—Frank Burns, 357–3516.
  Director for:
    Center for Communications and Consumer Services.—Carol Crecy, 401–4541.
    Center for Planning and Policy Development.—Mary Guthrie, 357–3460.
    Executive Secretariat.—Harry Posman, 357–3540.
    Office of Evaluation.—Saadia Greenberg, 357–3516.

ADMINISTRATION FOR CHILDREN AND FAMILIES

370 L'Enfant Promenade SW., 20447

Assistant Secretary.—Wade F. Horn, Ph.D., (202) 401–9200.
  Deputy Assistant Secretary for Administration.—Curtis L. Coy, 401–9238.
  Senior Advisor to the Assistant Secretary.—Martin Dannefelser, 401–6947.
  Director, Regional Operations Staff.—Diann Dawson, 401–4802.
  Commissioner for Administration on:
    Children, Youth, and Families.—Joan E. Ohl, 205–8347.
    Developmental Disabilities.—Patricia Morrissey, 690–6590.
    Native Americans.—Quanah Stamps, 401–5590.
  Associate Commissioner for—
    Child Care Bureau.—Shannon Christian, 690–6782.
    Children's Bureau.—Susan Orr, 205–8618.

Family and Youth Services Bureau.—Harry Wilson, 205–8102.
Head Start Bureau.—Wendy Hill, 205–8573.
Director, Office of:
Community Services.—Josephine Robinson, 401–9333.
Family Assistance.—Andrew Bush, 401–9275.
Legislative Affairs and Budget.—Madeline Mocko, 401–9223.
Planning, Research and Evaluation.—Noami Goldstein, 401–9220.
Public Affairs.—Christopher Downing, 401–9215.
Refugee Resettlement.—Nguyen Van Hanh, 401–9246.

AGENCY FOR TOXIC SUBSTANCES AND DISEASE REGISTRY

1600 Clifton Road NE, Atlanta, GA 30333

Administrator.—Julie L. Gerberding (404) 639–7000.
Deputy Administrator.—Dixie E. Snider.
Assistant Administrator.—Thomas Sinks (acting), 498–0004.

CENTERS FOR DISEASE CONTROL AND PREVENTION

1600 Clifton Road NE, Atlanta, GA 30333

Director.—Julie L. Gerberding (404) 639–7000.
Deputy Director for Public Health Service.—F.E.(Ed) Thompson.
Deputy Director for Public Health Science.—Dixie E. Snider.
Chief Operating Officer.—William H. Gimson.
Chief of Staff.—Robert Delaney.
Staff Offices—
CDC Washington.—Donald E. Shriber (202) 690–8598.
Enterprise Communication.—Donna Garland, 639–7540.
Equal Employment Opportunity.—Murray Kampf (acting), 371–5931.
Strategy and Innovation.—Lonnie King, 639–7000.
Workforce and Career Development.—Stephen B. Thacker, 498–6010.
Coordinating Office for—
Global Health.—Steven Blount, 639–7420.
Terrorism Preparedness and Response.—Charles Schable, 639–7405.
Coordinating Center for Environmental Health and Injury Prevention.—Henry Falk, 498–0004.
National Center for Environmental Health.—Thomas Sinks (acting), 498–0004.
National Center for Injury Prevention and Control.—Ileana Arias (acting), (770) 488–4696.
Coordinating Center for Health Information and Services.—Blake Caldwell (acting), 488–8320; Edward J. Sondik (301) 458–4500.
National Center for Health Marketing.—Steve Solomon (acting), (770) 488–8320.
National Center for Health Statistics.—Edward J. Sondik (301) 458–4500.
National Center for Public Health Informatics.—John Loonsk (acting), 639–7600.
Coordinating Center for Health Promotion.—Donna Stroup (770) 488–5971.
National Center for Birth Defects and Developmental Disabilities.—Jose Cordero, 498–3800.
National Center for Chronic Disease Prevention and Health Promotion.—George Mensah (acting), (770) 488–5401.
Office of Genomics and Disease Prevention.—Muin J. Khoury (acting), 498–1420.
Coordinating Center for Infectious Diseases.—Mitchell Cohen, 498–2580.
National Center for HIV, STD, and TB Prevention.—Janet Collins (acting), 639–8005.
National Center for Infectious Disease.—Ann Schuachat (acting), 639–3401.
National Institute for Occupational Safety and Health.—John Howard (202) 401–6997.

CENTERS FOR MEDICARE AND MEDICAID SERVICES

200 Independence Avenue, SW., 20201

Administrator.—Mark B. McClellan, M.D., Ph.D., (202) 690–6726.
Deputy Administrator.—Leslie Norwalk.
Chief Operating Officer.—John R. Dyer (410) 786–3151.
Chief, Office of Actuary.—Rick Foster, 786–6374.

Director, Office of:
  Acquisitions and Grants Management.—Rodney Benson (410) 786–8853.
  Clinical Standards and Quality.—Sean Tunis (410) 786–6841.
  Equal Opportunity and Civil Rights.—Patricia Lamond (acting), (410) 786–5110.
  External Affairs.—Kathleen Harrington, 401–3135.
  Legislation.—Linda Fishman, 690–5960.
  Research, Development, and Information.—Stu Guterman (410) 786–0948.
  Strategic Operations and Regulatory Support.—Jacqueline White, 690–8390.
Director, Center for—
  Beneficiary Choices.—Leslie Norwalk (acting), 690–6726.
  Medicaid and State Operations.—Dennis Smith, 690–7428.
  Medicare Management.—Herb Kuhn, 205–2505.
Director, Office of:
  Financial Management.—Tim Hill (410) 786–5448.
  Information Services.—Tim Love (410) 786–1800.
  Operations Management.—Karen O'Steen (410) 786–1051.
Regional Administrator for—
  Atlanta.—Rose Crum-Johnson (404) 562–7150.
  Boston.—Charlotte Yeh, M.D. (617) 565–1188.
  Chicago.—Jackie Garner (312) 886–6432.
  Dallas.—Randy Farris, M.D. (214) 767–6427.
  Denver.—Alex Trujillo (303) 844–2111.
  Kansas City.—Tom Lenz (acting), (816) 426–5925.
  New York.—James Kerr (212) 616–2205.
  Philadelphia.—Nancy O'Connor (215) 861–4140.
  San Francisco.—Jeff Flick (415) 744–3501.
  Seattle.—R.J. Ruff (206) 615–2306.

FOOD AND DRUG ADMINISTRATION
5600 Fishers Lane, Rockville, MD 20857

Commissioner.—Lester M. Crawford, D.V.M., Ph.D. (acting), (301) 827–2410.
  Deputy Commissioner for International and Special Programs.—Murray M. Lumpkin, M.D. (acting), 827–5709.
  Deputy Commissioner for Operations.—Janet Woodcock, M.D. (acting), 827–3310.
  Chief Counsel.—Gerald Mausodi (acting), (301) 827–1137.
  Director of Scientific Policy and Development.—Susan Bond, 827–1622.
Associate Commissioner for—
  External Relations.—Sheila Walcoff, 827–3330.
  Management.—Kathleen Heuer, 255–6762.
  Policy and Planning.—William K. Hubbard, 827–3370.
  Regulatory Affairs.—John Taylor, 827–3101.
Assistant Commissioner for—
  International Programs.—Melinda Plaisier, 827–4480.
  Legislation.—Patrick Ronan, 827–0087.
  Planning.—Theresa Mullin, Ph.D., 827–5292.
  Policy.—Jeffrey Shuren, M.D., 827–3360.
  Public Affairs.—Bradford Stone (acting), 827–6250.
  Special Health Issues.—Theresa A. Toigo, 827–4460.
  Women's Health.—Susan Wood, Ph.D., 827–0305.
Director, Center for—
  Biologics Evaluation and Research.—Jesse Goodman, M.D., 827–0372.
  Devices and Radiological Health.—Daniel Schultz, M.D., 827–7975.
  Drug Evaluation and Research.—Steven Galson, M.D. (acting), 594–5400.
  Food Safety and Applied Nutrition.—Robert E. Brackett, Ph.D., 436–1600.
  Veterinary Medicine.—Stephen Sundlof, D.V.M., Ph.D., 827–2950.
Director, National Center for Toxicological Research.—Daniel E. Casciano, Ph.D. (870) 543–7517.
Director, Office of:
  Executive Secretariat.—LaJuana Caldwell, 827–4450.
  Executive Operations.—Linda Brna, 827–3440.
  Equal Opportunity and Diversity Management.—Georgia Coffey, 827–4840.
  Financial Management.—Helen Horn, 827–5001.
  Management Programs.—Kimberly Holden, 827–4120.
  Orphan Products Development.—Marlene Haffner, M.D., 827–3666.

HEALTH RESOURCES AND SERVICES ADMINISTRATION
5600 Fishers Lane, Rockville, MD 20857

Administrator.—Elizabeth M. Duke (301) 443–2216.
Deputy Administrator.—Dennis P. Williams, 443–2194.
Principal Advisor to the Administrator.—Steve Smith, 443–2216.
Chief Medical Officer.—William A. Robinson, 443–9776.
Associate Administrator for Administration and Financial Management.—Steve Pelovitz, 443–2053.
Associate Administrator for—
  Health Professions.—Kerry Nesseler, 443–5794.
  Healthcare Systems.—Joyce Somsak (acting), 443–3300.
  HIV/AIDS.—Deborah Parham-Hopson, 443–1993.
  Maternal and Child Health.—Peter C. van Dyck, 443–2170.
  Primary Health Care.—Michelle Snyder, 594–4110.
Director, Office of:
  Communications.—Kay Templeton Garvey, 443–3376.
  Equal Opportunity and Civil Rights.—Patricia Mackey, 443–5636.
  Information Technology.—Catherine Flickinger, 443–6846.
  Legislation.—Patricia Stroup, 443–1890.
  Minority Health and Health Disparities.—William A. Robinson, 443–9776.
  Planning and Evaluation.—Lyman Van Nostrand, 443–1891.
  Rural Health Policy.—Marcia Brand, 443–0835.

INDIAN HEALTH SERVICE
801 Thompson Avenue, Rockville, MD 20852

Director.—Charles W. Grim, DDS, MHSA, (301) 443–1083.
Deputy Director.—Robert McSwain.
Deputy Director of:
  Indian Health Policy.—Mary Lou Stanton (acting).
  Management Operations.—Phyllis Eddy.
Chief Medical Officer.—W. Craig Vanderwagen, M.D. (acting).
Director of:
  Equal Employment Opportunity.—Vernon Mabry (acting), 443–1108.
  Legislative Affairs.—Michael Mahsetky, 443–7261.
  Urban Indian Health Program.—Robert Harry, DDS (acting), 443–4680.
Director, Office of:
  Public Affairs.—Athena Elliott (acting), 443–3593.
  Tribal Programs.—Douglas P. Black, 443–1104.
  Tribal Self-Governance.—Paula K. Williams, 443–7821.

NATIONAL INSTITUTES OF HEALTH
9000 Rockville Pike, Bethesda, MD 20892

Director.—Elias A. Zerhouni, M.D. (301) 496–2433.
Deputy Director.—Raynard S. Kington, M.D., Ph.D., 496–7322.
Senior Advisor to the Director.—Ruth L. Kirschstein, M.D., 496–1096.
Director/Executive Secretriat.—E. Dale Johnson, Ph.D., J.D., 496–1461.
Executive Officer, Office of the Director.—Wendy A. Liffers, J.D., M.A., 594–8231.
Legal Advisor, Office of the General Counsel.—Barbara M. McGarey, J.D., 496–4108.
Deputy Director, Office of:
  Extramural Research.—Norka Ruiz Bravo, Ph.D., 496–1096.
  Intramural Research.—Michael M. Gottesman, M.D., 496–1921.
  Management.—Colleen Barros, 496–3271.
Associate Director for—
  Administration.—Diane Frasier (acting) 496–4422.
  AIDS Research.—Jack E. Whitescarver, Ph.D., 496–0357.
  Behavioral and Social Sciences Research.—David B. Abrams, Ph.D., 402–1146.
  Budget.—Richard J. Turman, 496–4477.
  Communications and Public Liaison.—John T. Burklow, 496–4461.
  Disease Prevention.—Barnett S. Kramer, M.D., M.P.H., 496–1508.
  Legislative Policy and Analysis.—Marc Smolonsky, 496–3471.

Research on Women's Health.—Vivian W. Pinn, M.D., 402–1770.
Research Services.—Shirl Eller (acting), 496–2215.
Science Policy.—Lana R. Skirboll, Ph.D., 496–2122.
Director, Office of:
  Community Liaison.—John T. Burklow (acting), 496–4461.
  Equal Opportunity.—Lawrence N. Self, 496–6301.
  Human Resource.—Chris Steyer (acting), 496–3592.
  Technology Transfer.—Mark L. Rohrbaugh, Ph.D., J.D., 594–7700.
Director of:
  Fogarty International Center.—Sharon Hrynkow, Ph.D. (acting), 496–1415.
  Warren Grant Magnuson Clinical Center.—John I. Gallin, M.D., 496–4114.
  National Library of Medicine.—Donald A.B. Lindberg, M.D., 496–6221.
Director, National Center for—
  Complementary and Alternative Medicine.—Stephen E. Straus, M.D., 435–6826.
  Minority Health and Health Disparities.—John Ruffin, Ph.D., 402–1366.
  Research Resources.—Barbara Alving, M.D. (acting), 496–5793.
Director, Center for—
  Information Technology.—Alan S. Graeff, 496–5703.
  Scientific Review.—Brent Stanfield, Ph.D. (acting), 435–1114.
Director, National Institute for—
  Aging.—Richard J. Hodes, M.D., 496–9265.
  Alcohol Abuse and Alcoholism.—Ting-Kai Li, M.D., 443–3885.
  Allergy and Infectious Diseases.—Anthony S. Fauci, M.D., 496–2263.
  Arthritis, Musculoskeletal and Skin Diseases.—Stephen I. Katz, M.D., Ph.D., 496–4353.
  Biomedical Imaging and Bioengineering.—Roderic I. Pettigrew, Ph.D., M.D., 496–8859.
  Cancer.—Andrew von Eschenbach, M.D., 496–5615.
  Child Health and Human Development.—Duane F. Alexander, M.D., 496–3454.
  Deafness and Other Communication Disorders.—James F. Battey, Jr., M.D., Ph.D., 402–0900.
  Dental and Craniofacial Research.—Lawrence Tabak, D.D.S., Ph.D., 496–3571.
  Diabetes, Digestive and Kidney Diseases.—Allen M. Spiegel, M.D., 496–5877.
  Drug Abuse.—Nora Volkow, M.D., 443–6480.
  Environmental Health Sciences.—Kenneth Olden, Ph.D. (919) 541–3201.
  Eye.—Paul A. Sieving, M.D., Ph.D., 496–2234.
  General Medical Sciences.—Jeremy M. Berg, Ph.D., 594–2172.
  Heart, Lung and Blood.—Elizabeth G. Nabel, M.D., 496–5166.
  Human Genome Research.—Francis Collins, M.D., Ph.D., 496–0844.
  Mental Health.—Thomas Insel, M.D., 443–3673.
  Neurological Disorders and Stroke.—Story C. Landis, M.D., 496–9746.
  Nursing Research.—Patricia A. Grady, Ph.D., R.N., 496–8230.

PROGRAM SUPPORT CENTER

5600 Fishers Lane, Rockville, MD 20857

Deputy Assistant Secretary.—Philip VanLandingham (301) 443–3921.
  Administrative Operations Service.—John Aguirre, 443–2516.
  Business Technology Optimization.—Ann Speyer, 443–2365.
  Federal Operational Health.—John Hisle, 594–0250.
  Financial Management Service.—Larry Bedker, 443–1478.
  Human Resources Service.—Carol Arbogast, 443–1200.
  Strategic Acquisition Service.—Marc Weisman (202) 690–8554.

SUBSTANCE ABUSE AND MENTAL HEALTH SERVICES ADMINISTRATION

1 Choke Cherry Road, Rockville, MD 20857

Administrator.—Charles Curie (240) 276–2000.
  Deputy Administrator.—Andy Knapp (acting).
  Director, Equal Employment Opportunity.—Donald Inniss (301) 443–1976.
Associate Administrator for—
  Communications.—Mark Weber, 276–2130.
  Policy Planning and Budget.—Daryl Kade, 276–2200.

Director, Center for—
  Mental Health Services.—A. Kathryn Power, 276–1310.
  Substance Abuse Prevention.—Beverly Watts Davis, 276–2420.
  Substance Abuse Treatment.—H. Westley Clark, 276–1670.
Director, Office of:
  Applied Studies.—Charlene Lewis (acting), 276–1241.
  Program Services.—Anna Marsh, 276–1110.

DEPARTMENT OF HOUSING AND URBAN DEVELOPMENT

Robert C. Weaver Federal Building, 451 Seventh Street, SW., 20410
phone (202) 708–1112, http://www.hud.gov

ALPHONSO JACKSON, Secretary of Housing and Urban Development; born on September 9, 1945; education: received a Bachelor's Degree in Political Science, and a Master's Degree in Education Administration, from Truman State University; received a Law Degree from Washington University School of Law; professional: Director of Consultant Services for the accounting firm of Laventhol and Horwath-St. Louis; Special Assistant to the Chancellor, and Assistant Professor, at the University of Missouri; President of American Electric Power-Texas, 1996–2001; public service: Director of Public Safety, St. Louis, MO; Executive Director, St. Louis, MO, Housing Authority; Director, Department of Public and Assisted Housing, Washington, DC; Chairperson, District of Columbia Redevelopment Land Agency Board; President and CEO, Dallas, TX, Housing Authority, 1989–1996; Deputy Secretary of Housing and Urban Development, 2001–2004; nominated by President George W. Bush to become the 13th Secretary of Housing and Urban Development, and was confirmed by the U.S. Senate on March 31, 2004.

OFFICE OF THE SECRETARY

Secretary of Housing and Urban Development.—Alphonso Jackson, room 10000, 708–0417.
Chief of Staff.—Camille Pierce, 708–2713.
Special Assistant.—Kimberly Snyder, 708–0417.
Deputy Chief of Staff.—Scott Kellerr, 708–1781.
Director, Center for Faith Based and Community Initiatives.—Ryan Streeter, 708–2404.
Executive Office for Administrative Operations and Management.—Marcella Belt, 708–3750.
Administrative Officer.—Marianne C. DeConti, 708–3750.

OFFICE OF THE DEPUTY SECRETARY

Deputy Secretary.—Roy A. Bernardi, room 10100, 708–0123.
Senior Advisor to the Deputy Secretary.—Jim Parenti.

ASSISTANT TO THE DEPUTY SECRETARY FOR FIELD POLICY AND MANAGEMENT

Assistant Deputy Secretary.—Pamela H. Patenaude, room 7106, 708–2426.

SMALL AND DISADVANTAGED BUSINESS UTILIZATION

Director.—Valerie T. Hayes (acting), room 3130, 708–1428.

OFFICE OF FAIR HOUSING AND EQUAL OPPORTUNITY

Assistant Secretary.—Carolyn Y. Peoples, room 5100, 708–4252.
General Deputy Assistant Secretary.—Floyd May.
Director, Office of Policy, Legislative Initiatives, and Outreach.—Bryan Greene, 708–1145.
Deputy Assistant Secretary for—
  Enforcement Programs.—Jon Gant, 619–8046.
  Operations and Management.—Karen A. Newton, 708–0768.

OFFICE OF ADMINISTRATION

General Deputy Assistant Secretary for Administration.—Darlene Williams.
  Chief Technology Officer.—Lisa Schlosser, 708–0306.
  Director, Office of the Executive Secretariat.—Cynthia A. O'Connor, 708–3054.
  Chief Procurement Officer.—A. Jo Baylor, 708–0600.
  Deputy Assistant Secretary for—
    Human Resource Management.—Barbara Edwards, 708–3946.
    Operations.—Sherman R. Lancefield, 708–2268.

OFFICE OF GENERAL COUNSEL

General Deputy General Counsel.—George L. Weidenfeller, 708–2804.
  Deputy General Counsel for—
    Equal Opportunity and Administrative Law.—Kathleen Koch, 708–3250.
    Housing Finance Operations.—George L. Weidenfeller, 708–2864.
  Associate General Counsel for—
    Assisted Housing and Community Development.—Robert S. Kenison, 708–0212.
    Finance and Regulatory Compliance.—John P. Kennedy, 708–2203.
    Human Resources.—Sam E. Hutchinson, 708–0888.
    Insured Housing.—Angelo Aiosa, 708–1042.
    Legislation and Regulations.—Camille E. Acevedo, 708–1793.
    Litigation.—Carole W. Wilson, 708–0300.
    Fair Housing.—Harry L. Carey, 708–0570.
  Director, Departmental Enforcement Center.—Margarita Maisonet, 708–3354.

OFFICE OF COMMUNITY PLANNING AND DEVELOPMENT

General Deputy Assistant Secretary.—Nelson Bregon (acting).
  Deputy Assistant Secretary for—
    Economic Development.—Donald Mains, 708–4091.
    Grant Programs.—Anna Maria Farias, 708–2111.
    Operations.—William Eargle, Jr., 401–6367.
    Special Needs.—Patricia Carlile, 708–1590.

OFFICE OF THE CHIEF FINANCIAL OFFICER

Chief Financial Officer.—Carin M. Barth, room 10234, 708–1946.
  Assistant Chief Financial Officer for—
    Accounting.—Mary Sally Matiella, 708–3601.
    Budget.—David M. Gibbons, 708–3296.
    Financial Management.—James M. Martin, 708–0638.
    Systems.—Hartley M. Jones, 708–4474.

OFFICE OF THE INSPECTOR GENERAL

Inspector General.—Kenneth M. Donohue, Sr., room 8256, 708–0430.
  Deputy Inspector General.—Michael P. Stephens.
  Assistant Inspector General, Office of Audit.—James Heist, 708–0364.
  Counsel to the Inspector General, Office of Legal Counsel.—Bryan Saddler, 708–1613.
  Assistant Inspector General, Office of:
    Investigation.—R. Joe Haban, 708–0390.
    Management and Policy.—Dennis A. Raschka, 708–0006.

OFFICE OF HOUSING

Assistant Secretary/Federal Housing Commissioner.—John C. Weicher, 708–2601.
  General Deputy Assistant Secretary.—Frank L. Davis.
  Deputy Assistant Secretary for—
    Affordable Housing Preservation.—Charles H. Williams, 708–0001.
    Finance and Budget.—Margaret A. Young, 708–2601.

Housing Operations.—Michael F. Hill, room 9138, 708–1104.
Office of Affordable Housing Preservation.—Charles H. Williams, 708–0001.
Single Family Housing.—Joe McCloskey, 708–3175.

ASSISTANT SECRETARY FOR CONGRESSIONAL AND INTERGOVERNMENTAL RELATIONS

Assistant Secretary.—Steven B. Nesmith, room 10120, 708–0005.
  Deputy Assistant Secretary for—
  Congressional Relations.—Mark Studdert, 708–0380.
  Intergovernmental Relations.—Gregory Y. Hill.
  Legislation.—L. Carter Cornick, 708–0005.

OFFICE OF LEAD HAZARD CONTROL

Director.—Joseph Smith (acting), room P3206, 755–1785.

OFFICE OF PUBLIC AND INDIAN HOUSING

Assistant Secretary.—Michael Liu, room 4100, 708–0950.
  General Deputy Assistant Secretary.—Paula Blunt.
  Deputy Assistant Secretary, for—
  Administration and Budget/Chief Financial Officer.—George K. Dickey, 708–0440.
  Field Operations.—David R. Ziaya (acting), 708–4016.
  Native American Programs.—Rodger J. Boyd, 708–7914.
  Office of Field Operations.—Deborah Hernandez, 708–4016.
  Policy, Programs and Legislative Initiatives.—Bessie Kong (acting), 708–0713.
  Public Housing Investments.—Milan Ozdinec, 708–8812.
  Public Housing and Voucher Programs.—William Russell, 708–1380.
  Director, Office of:
  Real Estate Assessment Center.—Elizabeth A. Hanson, 708–4924.

OFFICE OF POLICY DEVELOPMENT AND RESEARCH

Assistant Secretary.—Dennis C. Shea, room 8100, 708–1600.
  General Deputy Assistant Secretary.—Darlene F. Williams.
  Deputy Assistant Secretary for—
  Economic Affairs.—Harold Bunce 708–3080.
  International Affairs.—Shannon Sorzano, 708–0770.

ASSISTANT SECRETARY FOR PUBLIC AFFAIRS

Assistant Secretary.—Catherine M. Macfarland, room 10130, 708–0980.
  Director of Press Relations.—Nicole Larourene, 708–0685.

GOVERNMENT NATIONAL MORTGAGE ASSOCIATION

President.—Ronald A. Rosenfeld, room 6100, 708–0926.
  Senior Vice President, Office of:
  Management Operations.—Cheryl W. Owens, 708–2648.
  Finance.—Michael J. Najjum, Jr., 401–2064.
  Vice President, Office of:
  Capital Markets.—Michael J. Frenz, 401–8970.
  Mortgage-Backed Securities.—Theodore B. Foster, 708–4141.
  Program Operations.—Thomas R. Weakland, 708–2884.

OFFICE OF DEPARTMENTAL OPERATIONS AND COORDINATION

Director.—Inez Banks-Dubose (acting), room 2124, 708–2806.
  Deputy Director.—Inez Banks-DuBose.
  Coordinator, Southwest Border region, Colonias & Migrant/Farmworker Initiatives.—Maria
  S. Ortiz, 708–3086.

OFFICE OF DEPARTMENTAL EQUAL EMPLOYMENT OPPORTUNITY

Deputy Director.—Linda Bradford Washington, 708–3362.

OFFICE OF FIELD POLICY AND MANAGEMENT

Assistant Secretary.—Pamela H. Patenaude, 708–2426.
Supervisory Field Management Officer.—Robert Etchinson, 708–1123.

FIELD OFFICES

Boston, MA.—Jim Barnes, Regional Director, Federal Building, Room 301, 10 Causeway Street, Boston, MA 02222–1092 (617) 994–8200.

Bangor, ME.—Loren W. Cole, Field Office Director, 202 Harlow Street, Chase Building, Suite 101, Bangor, ME 04402–1384 (207) 945–0467.

Burlington, VT.—Michael McNamara, Field Office Director, 159 Bank Street, Burlington, VT 05401 (802) 951–6290.

Hartford, CT.—Julie Fagan, Field Office Director, One Corporate Center, 19th Floor, Hartford, CT 06103–3220 (860) 240–4800, ext. 3100.

Manchester, NH.—Greg Carson, Field Office Director, 1000 Elm Street, 8th Floor, Manchester, NH 03101–1730 (603) 666–7510, ext. 3903.

Providence, RI.—Nancy D. Smith, Field Office Director, Sixth Floor, 10 Weybosset Street, Providence, RI 02903–2818 (401) 528–5230.

New York, NY Regional.—Frank McKay, Regional Director, 26 Federal Plaza, Suite 3541, New York, NY 10278–0068 (212) 264–8000.

Albany, NY.—Bob Scofield, Field Office Director, 52 Corporate Circle, Albany, NY 12203–5121 (518) 464–4200.

Buffalo, NY.—Stephen Banko, Field Office Director, Lafayette Court, Fifth Floor, 465 Main Street, Buffalo, NY 14203–1780 (716) 551–5755.

Camden, NJ.—Michael Worth, Field Office Director, Hudson Building, 800 Hudson Square, Second Floor, Camden, NJ 08102–1156 (856) 757–5081.

Newark, NJ.—Diane Johnson, Field Office Director, One Newark Center, 13th Floor, Newark, NJ 07102–5260 (973) 622–7900.

Syracuse, NY.—Stephen Banko, Field Office Director, 128 Jefferson Street, Syracuse, NY 13202 (315) 477–0616.

Philadelphia, PA Regional.—Milton R. Pratt, Director, Wanamaker Building, 100 Penn Square East, Philadelphia, PA 19107–3380 (215) 656–0500.

Baltimore, MD.—James Kelly, Field Office Director, City Crescent Building, 10 South Howard Street, Fifth Floor, Baltimore, MD 21201–2505 (410) 962–2520.

Charleston, WV.—George H. Rodriguez, Field Office Director, Suite 708, 405 Capitol Street, Charleston, WV 25301–1795 (304) 347–7000.

Pittsburgh, PA.—Cheryl E. Campbell, Field Office Director, U.S. Post Office and Courthouse Building, 339 Sixth Avenue, Pittsburgh, PA 15222–2515 (412) 644–6436.

Richmond, VA.—William P. Miles, Field Office Director, 600 East Broad Street, Richmond, VA 23219–4920 (804) 771–2100.

Washington, DC.—James David Reeves, Field Office Director, 820 First Street, NE., Washington, DC 20002–4205 (202) 275–9200.

Wilmington, DE.—Diane Lello, Field Office Director, Suite 404, 920 King Street, Wilmington, DE 19801–3016 (302) 573–6300.

Atlanta, GA.—John W. Meyers, Regional Director, 40 Marietta St., Five Points Plaza, Atlanta, GA 30303–2806 (404) 331–4111.

Birmingham, AL.—Cindy Yarbrough, Field Office Director, 950 22nd St. N., Ste. 900, Birmingham, AL 35203–5302 (205) 731–2617.

Miami, FL.—Ramando Fana, Field Office Director, 909 SE, First Avenue, Miami, FL 33131 (305) 536–4456.

Columbia, SC.—William Dudley Gregory, Field Office Director, Strom Thurmond Federal Building, 1835 Assembly Street, Columbia, SC 29201–2480 (803) 765–5592.

Greensboro, NC.—Edward Ellis, Acting Field Office Director, Koger Building, 2306 West Meadowview Road, Greensboro, NC 27401–3707 (336) 547–4001.

Jackson, MS.—Patricia Hoban-Moore, Field Office Director, McCoy Federal Building, Room 910, 100 West Capitol Street, Jackson, MS 39269–1016 (601) 965–4757.

Jacksonville, FL.—J. Nicholas Shelly, Field Office Director, Southern Bell Tower, 301 West Bay Street, Suite 2200, Jacksonville, FL 32202–5121 (904) 232–2627.

Louisville, KY.—Krista Mills, Field Office Director, 601 West Broadway, Louisville, KY 40202 (502) 585–5251.

Knoxville, TN.—William Dirl Field Office Director, Suite 300, John J. Duncan Federal Building, 710 Locust Street, Knoxville, TN 37902–2526 (865) 545–4384.
Memphis, TN.—Yvonne F. Leander, Field Office Director, 200 Jefferson Ave, Suite 1200, Memphis, TN 38103–2335 (901) 544–3367.
Nashville, TN.—William Dirl, Field Office Director, Suite 200, 235 Cumberland Bend Drive, Nashville, TN 37228–1803 (615) 736–5213.
Tampa, FL.—Karen Jackson Sims, Field Office Director, 500 Zack Street, Suite 402, Tampa, FL 33602 (813) 228–2026.
Orlando, FL.—Paul C. Ausley, Jr., Field Office Director, Langley Building, Suite 270, 3751 Maguire Boulevard, Orlando, FL 32803–3032 (407) 648–6441.
Caribbean.—Michael A. Colon, Field Office Director, New San Juan Building, 171 Carlos E. Chardon Avenue, San Juan, PR 00918–0903 (787) 766–5201.
Chicago, IL.—Joseph Galvan, Regional Director, Ralph H. Metcalfe Federal Building, 77 West Jackson Boulevard, Chicago, IL 60604–3507 (312) 353–5680.
Cincinnati, OH.—James Cunningham, Field Office Director, 15 E. Seventh St, Cincinnati, OH 45202–2401 (513) 684–3451.
Cleveland, OH.—Douglas W. Shelby, Field Office Director, Renaissance Building, 1350 Euclid Avenue, Suite 500, Cleveland, OH 44115–1815 (216) 522–4058.
Columbus, OH.—Thomas Leach, Field Office Director, 200 North High Street, Columbus, OH 43215–2463 (614) 469–2540.
Detroit, MI.—Toni Schmiegelow, Field Office Director, Patrick V. McNamara Federal Building, 477 Michigan Avenue, Detroit, MI 48226–2592 (313) 226–7900.
Grand Rapids, MI.—Louis M. Berra, Field Office Director, Trade Center Building, 50 Louis Street, NW., Grand Rapids, MI 49503–2633 (616) 456–2100.
Indianapolis, IN.—John Hall, Field Office Director, 151 North Delaware Street, Suite 1200, Indianapolis, IN 46204–2526 (317) 226–6303.
Milwaukee, WI.—Delbert F. Reynolds, Field Office Director, Henry S. Reuss Federal Plaza, Suite 1380, 310 West Wisconsin Avenue, Milwaukee, WI 53203–2289 (414) 297–3214.
Flint, MI.—Jason Gamlin, Field Office Director, Phoenix Building, 801 South Saginaw, 4th Floor, Flint, MI 48502 (810) 755–5122.
Minneapolis, MN.—Dexter Sidney, Field Office Director, 920 Second Street South, Minneapolis, MN 55402 (612) 370–3000.
Springfield, IL.—Naomi J. Lear, Field Office Director, 500 W. Monroe Street, Suite 1SW, Springfield, IL 62704 (217) 492–4120.
Fort Worth, TX.—Cynthia Leon, Regional Director, 801 Cherry St., P.O. Box 2905, Fort Worth, TX 76113–2905 (817) 978–5980.
Albuquerque, NM.—Edward L. Floss, Field Office Director, 625 Silver Avenue, SW., Suite 100, Albuquerque, NM 87102 (505) 346–7320.
Dallas, TX.—Michael Backman, Room 860, 525 Griffin Street, Dallas, TX 75202–5007 (214) 767–8300.
Houston, TX.—Ed Pringle, Field Office Director, 1301 Fannin, Suite 2200, Houston, TX 77002 (713) 718–3199.
Little Rock, AR.—Bessie Jackson, Field Office Director, 425 W. Capitol Avenue, Suite 900, Little Rock, AR 72201–3488 (501) 324–5931.
Lubbock, TX.—Miguel C. Rincon, Field Office Director, George H. Mahon Federal Building and United States Courthouse, Room 511, 1205 Texas Avenue, Lubbock, TX 79401–4093 (806) 472–7265.
New Orleans, LA.—Maravel Robertson, Field Office Director, Hale Boggs Federal Building, 501 Magazine Street, 9th Floor, New Orleans, LA 70130–3099 (504) 589–7201.
Oklahoma City, OK.—Kevin McNeely, Field Office Director, 301 NW 6th Street, Suite 200, Oklahoma City, OK 73102 (405) 609–8509.
San Antonio, TX.—Luz Day, Field Office Director, One Alamo Center, 106 South St. Mary's Street, San Antonio, TX 78205 (210) 475–6806.
Shreveport, LA.—Martha N. Sakre, Field Office Director, 401 Edwards Street, Suite 1510, Shreveport, LA 71101–5513 (318) 676–3440.
Tulsa, OK.—Ronald Miles, Field Office Director, 1516 S. Boston Ave., Ste. 100, Tulsa, OK 74119–4030 (918) 581–7434.
Kansas City, KS.—Macie Houston, Regional Director, Gateway Tower II, 400 State Avenue, Room 200, Kansas City, KS 66101–2406 (913) 551–5462.
Des Moines, IA.—Bruce Ray, Field Office Director, Room 239, 210 Walnut Street, Des Moines, IA 50309–2155 (515) 284–4512.
Omaha, NE.—Stan Quy, Field Office Director, 10909 Mill Valley Road, Suite 100, Omaha, NE 68154–3955 (402) 492–3101.
St. Louis, MO.—James Heard, Field Office Director, 1222 Spruce Street, Suite 3207, St. Louis, MO 63103–2836 (314) 539–6583.
Denver, CO.—John K. Carson, Regional Director, 1670 Broadway, 23rd Floor, Denver, CO 80202–3607 (303) 672–5440.

Casper, WY.—Chris Stearns, Field Office Director, 150 East B Street, Room 1010, Casper, WY 82601–1969 (307) 261–6250.

Fargo, ND.—Joel Manske, Field Office Director, Federal Building, 657 Second Avenue North, Room 366, Fargo, ND 58108 (701) 239–5136.

Helena, MT.—Tom Friesen, Field Office Director, 7 W. 6th Ave, Helena, MT 59601 (406) 449–5050.

Salt Lake City, UT.—Dwight A. Peterson, Director, 125 South State Street, Suite 3001, Salt Lake City, UT 84138 (801) 524–6070.

Sioux Falls, SD.—Sheryl Miller, Field Office Director, 2400 W. 49th Street, Suite I–201, Sioux Falls, SD 57105–6558 (605) 330–4223.

San Francisco, CA.—Richard K. Rainey, Regional Director, 600 Harrison Street, 3rd Floor, San Francisco, CA 94107–1300 (415) 489–6400.

Fresno, CA.—Roland Smith, Field Office Director, 2135 Fresno St., Ste. 100, Fresno, CA, 93721–1718 (559) 487–5033.

Honolulu, HI.—Gordan Y. Furutani, Field Office Director, 500 Ala Moana Boulevard, Suite 3A, Honolulu, HI 96813–4918 (808) 522–8175.

Los Angeles, CA.—Theresa Camling, Field Office Director, AT&T Center, 611 West Sixth Street, Suite 800, Los Angeles, CA 90017 (213) 894–8007.

Phoenix, AZ.—Rebecca Flanagan, Field Office Director, One N. Central Avenue, Suite 600, Phoenix, AZ 85004 (602) 379–7100.

Reno, NV.—Tony Ramirez, Field Office Director, 3702 S. Virginia St., Reno, NV 89502–6581 (775) 784–5383.

Sacramento, CA.—Cynthia Abbott, Field Office Director, 925 L Street, Sacramento, CA 95814 (916) 498–5220.

San Diego, CA.—Frances Y. Riley, Field Office Director, Symphony Towers, 750 B St., Ste. 1600, San Diego, CA 92101–8131 (619) 557–5310.

Santa Ana, CA.—Jill Hurt, Field Office Director, 1600 N. Broadway, Suite 101, Santa Ana, CA 92706–3927 (714) 796–5577.

Las Vegas, NV.—Ken Lobene, Field Office Director, 300 S Las Vegas Boulevard, Suite 2900, Las Vegas, NV 89101–5833 (720) 355–2100.

Tucson, AZ.—Sharon K. Atwell, Field Office Director, Security Pacific Bank Plaza, 160 North Stone Avenue, Suite 100, Tucson, AZ 85701–1467 (520) 670–6000.

Seattle, WA.—John W. Meyers, Regional Director, Seattle Federal Office Building, 909 First Avenue, Suite 200, Seattle, WA 98104–1000 (206) 220–5101.

Anchorage, AK.—Colleen Bickford, Field Office Director, 3000 C. Street, Suite 401, Anchorage, AK 99503 (907) 677–9800.

Boise, ID.—Constance Hogland, Field Office Director, Plaza IV, Suite 220, 800 Park Boulevard, Boise, ID 83712–7743 (208) 334–1990.

Portland, OR.—Thomas C. Cusack, Field Office Director, 400 Southwest Sixth Avenue, Suite 700, Portland, OR 97204–1632 (503) 326–2561.

Spokane, WA.—Arlene Patton, Field Office Director, U.S. Courthouse Bldg., 920 W. Riverside, Ste. 588, Spokane, WA 99201–1010 (509) 353–0674.

DEPARTMENT OF TRANSPORTATION

400 Seventh Street SW., 20590

phone 366–4000, http://www.dot.gov

NORMAN Y. MINETA, Secretary of Transportation, born on November 12, 1931, in San Jose, CA; education: University of California, Berkeley, CA, 1953; military service: U.S. Army, 1953–56, served as an intelligence officer; professional: Mineta Insurance Agency; Lockheed Martin Corp.; public service: San Jose City Council, 1967–71; San Jose Mayor, 1971–1974; U.S. House of Representatives, 1975–1995; Chairman, National Civil Aviation Review Commission; Secretary of Commerce, 2000–2001; awards: Martin Luther King, Jr., Commemorative Medal, awarded by George Washington University, for contributions in the field of civil rights; family: married to Danealia (Deni) Mineta; he has two sons, David and Stuart Mineta, and two stepsons, Robert and Mark Brantner; nominated by President George W. Bush to become the 14th Secretary of Transportation, and was confirmed by the U.S. Senate on January 25, 2001.

OFFICE OF THE SECRETARY

Room 10200, phone 366–1111, fax 366–4508

[Created by the act of October 15, 1966; codified under U.S.C. 49]

Secretary of Transportation.—Norman Y. Mineta.
  Chief of Staff.—John Flaherty, 366–1103.
    Deputy Chief of Staff.—Shane Karr, 366–6800.
  Under Secretary of Transportation for Policy.—Jeffrey N. Shane, 366–1815.
  Chairman, Board of Contract Appeals (Chief Administrative Judge).—Thaddeus V. Ware, room 5101, 366–4305.
  Director, Office of:
    Civil Rights.—Michael Trujillo, room 10215, 366–4648.
    Executive Secretariat.—Michael Dannenhauer, room 10205, 366–4277.
    Intelligence and Security.—Tom Falvey, room 10401, 366–6525.
    Small and Disadvantaged Business Utilization.—Sean M. Moss, room 9414, 366–1930.

GENERAL COUNSEL

General Counsel.—Jeffrey A. Rosen, room 10428, 366–4702.
  Deputy General Counsel.—Rosalind A. Knapp, 366–4713.
  Special Counsel.—James Ray.
  Assistant General Counsel for—
    Aviation Enforcement and Proceedings.—Samuel Podberesky, room 4116, 366–9342.
    Environmental, Civil Rights and General Law.—Roberta D. Gabel, room 10102, 366–4710.
    International Law.—Donald H. Horn, room 10105, 366–2972.
    Legislation.—Thomas W. Herlihy, room 10100, 366–4687.
    Litigation.—Paul M. Geier, room 4102, 366–4731.
    Regulation and Enforcement.—Neil R. Eisner, room 10424, 366–4723.

INSPECTOR GENERAL

Inspector General.—Kenneth M. Mead, room 9210, 366–1959.
  Deputy Inspector General.—Todd J. Zinser, room 9210, 366–6767.
  Senior Counsel for Legal, Legislative and External Affairs.—Brian Dettelbach, room 9208, 366–8751.

Assistant Inspector General for—
   Aviation Audits.—David A. Dobbs, room 9217, 366–0500.
   Competition and Economic Analysis.—Mark Dayton, room 9134, 366–9970.
   Financial and Information Technology Audits.—Ted Alves.
   Investigations.—Charles H. Lee, Jr., room 9210, 366–1967.
Deputy Assistant Inspector General for—
   Information Technology and Computer Security.—Rebecca Leng, room 9288, 366–1488.
   Investigations.—Cecelia Rosser, room 9200, 366–8081.
   Transportation Security and Hazardous Material.—Robin Hunt, 201 Mission Street, Suite
      2130, San Francisco, CA (415) 744–3090.
Director, Office of Human Resources.—Vivian Jarcho, room 7107, 366–1441.
Chief Technology Officer.—James Heminger, room 7117, 366–1968.
Chief Financial Officer and Chief Information Officer.—Jackie Weber, room 7117,
   366–1495.

REGIONAL AUDIT OFFICES

Regional Program Directors:
   Region II.—Michael E. Goldstein, Room 3134, 26 Federal Plaza, New York, NY 10278
      (212) 264–8701.
   Region III.—Earl Hedges, Suite 4500, City Cresent Building, 10 South Howard Street,
      Baltimore, MD 21201 (410) 962–3612.
   Region IV.—Lou Dixon, Suite 17T60, 61 Forsythe Street, SW, Atlanta, GA 30303 (404)
      562–3770.
   Region IX.—Scott Macey, 201 Mission Street, Suite 2310, San Francisco, CA 94105
      (415) 744–3090.
   Region X.—Darren Murphy, Room 644, 915 Second Avenue, Seattle WA, 98174 (206)
      220–7754.

REGIONAL INVESTIGATIVE OFFICES

Special Agents-In-Charge:
   Region I.—Ted Doherty, Room 1055, Kendall Square, 55 Broadway, Cambridge, MA
      02142, (617) 494–2701.
   Region II.—Ned E. Schwartz, Room 3134, 26 Federal Plaza, New York, NY 10278 (212)
      264–8700.
   Region IV.—John Long, Suite 17T60, 61 Forsythe Street, SW, Atlanta, GA 30303 (404)
      562–3850.
   Region V.—Michelle McVicker, 200 W. Adams Street, Suite 300, Chicago, IL 60606
      (312) 353–0106.
   Region VI.—Max Smith, Room 13A42, Federal Office Building, 819 Taylor Street, Fort
      Worth, TX 76102 (817) 978–3236.
   Region VII.—Barbara Barnet, Suite 295, Corporate Park of Miami, 7789 NW 48th Street,
      Miami, FL 33166 (305) 716–3120.
   Region IX.—Hank W. Smedley, Suite 2310, 201 Mission Street, San Francisco, CA 94105
      (415) 744–3090.
   Region X.—Michelle Ward McGee, Room 644, Jackson Federal Building, 915 Second
      Avenue, Seattle, WA 98174 (206) 220–7754.

ASSISTANT SECRETARY FOR TRANSPORTATION POLICY

Assistant Secretary.—Tyler D. Duvall (acting), room 10228, (202) 366–0582.
   Deputy Assistant Secretaries: Tyler D. Duvall, George E. Schoener, 366–4067.

ASSISTANT SECRETARY FOR AVIATION AND INTERNATIONAL AFFAIRS

Assistant Secretary.—Karen K. Bhatia, room 10232, 366–8822.
   Deputy Assistant Secretary.—Susan McDermott, room 10232, 366–4551.
      Director, Office of:
         Aviation Analysis.—Randall Bennett, room 6401, 366–5903.
         International Aviation.—Paul Gretch, room 6402, 366–2423.
         International Transportation and Trade.—Bernestine Allen, room 10300, 366–4398.

ASSISTANT SECRETARY FOR ADMINISTRATION

Assistant Secretary.—Vincent T. Taylor, room 10320, 366–2332.
Deputy Assistant Secretary.—Linda J. Washington.
Director, Office of:
  Building Management and Space.—George Fields, room 10314, 366–9284.
  Financial Management.—Marie Petrosino-Woolverton, room 10320, 366–9427.
  Hearings, Chief Administrative Law Judge.—Judge Ronnie A. Yoder, room 5411C, 366–2142.
  Human Resource Management.—Patricia Prosperi, room 7411, 366–4088.
  Information Services.—Dorothy Beard, room 2317, 366–3944.
  Security and Administrative Management.—Lee A. Privett, room 7404H, 366–4676.
  Senior Procurement Executive.—David J. Litman, room 7101D, 366–4263.

ASSISTANT SECRETARY FOR BUDGET AND PROGRAMS

Assistant Secretary.—Phyllis F. Scheinberg (acting), room 10101, 366–9191.
Deputy Assistant Secretary.—Phyllis F. Scheinberg, 366–9192.
Deputy Chief Financial Officer.—A. Thomas Park, 366–9192.
Director, Office of:
  Budget and Program Performance.—Lana Hurdle.
  Financial Management.—Lawrence Neff, room 6101, 366–1306.

ASSISTANT SECRETARY FOR GOVERNMENTAL AFFAIRS

Assistant Secretary.—Nicole R. Nason, room 10408, 366–4573.
Deputy Assistant Secretaries.—David Kelly, Michael Wascom.
Associate Directors for—
  FAA, FRA, X, Security.—Simon Gros.
  NHTSA, IGA, PIGS, AMTRAK.—Brian Elson.
  FTA, MARAD, SLSDC.—Jessie Torres.
  FMCSA.—Ross Mellor.
  Approps, PHMSA.—Kelly Kolb.
  FHWA, RITA.—Suhail Khan.

OFFICE OF PUBLIC AFFAIRS

Assistant to the Secretary and Director of Public Affairs.—Robert Johnson, room 10414, 366–4570.
Deputy Director.—Brian Turmail, 366–4531.
Assistant Director for—
  Speech Writing and Research Division.—Terri Hauser, room 10413, 366–5580.
  Media Relations Division.—William Adams, 366–5580.

BUREAU OF TRANSPORTATION STATISTICS

400 Seventh Street SW., Room 3103, 20590, phone 366–3282

Director.—Rick Kowaleski (acting), 366–6268.
Deputy Director.—Rick Kowaleski.

FEDERAL AVIATION ADMINISTRATION

800 Independence Avenue SW, 20591, phone 267–3484

Administrator.—Marion C. Blakey, 267–3111.
  Chief of Staff.—David Mandell.
  Senior Counsel to the Administrator.—Louise E. Maillett, 267–7417.
  Executive Assistant to the Administrator.—Derra Brown, 267–3111.
    Deputy Administrator.—Bobby Sturgell, 267–8111.
  Senior Advisor to the Deputy Administrator.—Howard Swancy.

Assistant Administrator for Financial Services.—Ramesh K. Punwani 267–9105.
 Deputy Assistant Administrator.—John F. Hennigan, 267–8928.
Director of:
 Budget.—Alex Keenan, 267–8010.
 Financial Controls.—Carl Burrus (acting), 267–7140.
 Financial Management.—Timothy Lawler, 267–3018.
Assistant Administrator for Civil Rights.—Fanny Rivera, 267–3254.
 Deputy Assistant Administrator.—Barbara A. Edwards, 267–3264.
Assistant Administrator for Aviation Policy, Planning and Environment.—Sharon L.
  Pinkerton, 267–3927.
 Deputy Assistant Administrator.—Nancy LoBue, 267–7954.
Director of:
 Aviation Policy and Plans.—Nan Shellabarger, 267–3274.
 Environment and Energy.—Carl Burleson, 267–3576.
Chief Counsel.—Andrew B. Steinberg, 267–3222.
 Deputy Chief Counsel.—James W. Whitlow, 267–3773.
Assistant Administrator for Government and Industry Affairs.—David Balloff, 267–3277.
 Deputy Assistant Administrator.—Daniel Hickey, 267–8211.
Assistant Administrator for Human Resource Management.—Ventris C. Gibson, 267–3456.
 Deputy Assistant Administrator.—Mary Ellen Dix, 267–3850.
Director of:
 Accountability Board.—Maria Fernandez-Greczmiel, 267–3065.
 Center for Management Devleopment.—Barbara J. Smith (386) 446–7136.
 Corporate, Learning and Development.—Darlene Freeman (acting), 267–9041.
 Labor and Employee Relations.—Melvin Harns, 267–3979.
 Personnel.—Sue Engelhardt, 267–3850.
Assistant Administrator for Information Services.—Daniel J. Mehan, 493–4570.
 Deputy Assistant Administrator.—Walter Iwanow, 493–4570.
Director of Information Systems Security.—Michael F. Brown, 267–7104.
Assistant Administrator for Public Affairs.—Greg Martin, 267–3883.
 Deputy Assistant Administrator.—Laura J. Brown, 267–3883.
Assistant Administrator for International Aviation.—Douglas E. Lavin, 267–3033.
Director of:
 Asia-Pacific.—Elizabeth E. Erickson, 65–6540–4114.
 Europe, Africa, and Middle East.—Paul Feldman (322) 508–2700.
 International Aviation.—John R. Hancock (acting), 267–3213.
 Latin America-Caribbean.—Joaquin Archilla (305) 716–3300.
Assistant Administrator for Regions and Center Operations.—Ruth Leverenz, 267–7369
 Deputy Assistant Administrator.—John R. Block, 267–7369.
Regional Administrator for—
 Alaskan.—Patrick N. Poe (907) 271–5645.
 Central.—Christopher Blum (816) 329–3050.
 Eastern.—Arlene B. Feldman (718) 553–3000.
 Great Lakes.—Christopher Blum (acting), (847) 294–7294.
 New England.—Amy Lind Corbett (781) 238–7020.
 Northwest Mountain.—Douglas R. Murphy (425) 227–2001.
 Southern.—Carolyn Blum (404) 305–5000.
 Southwest.—Ava L. Wilkerson (817) 222–5001.
 Western-Pacific.—William C. Withycombe (310) 725–3550.
Director, Mike Monroney Aeronautical Center.—Lindy Ritz (405) 954–4521.
Assistant Administrator for Security & Hazardous Materials.—Lynne A. Osmus, 267–7211.
 Deputy Assistant Administrator.—Claudio Manno (acting), 267–7211.
Director of:
 Emergency Operations and Communications.—Claudio Manno, 267–8979.
 Hazardous Materials.—William Wilkening, Jr., 267–9864.
 Internal Security.—Barbara Bilodeau (acting), 366–9241.
 Investigation.—Eddie Gibson (acting), 366–1246.
 Operations.—Thomas D. Ryan (acting), 267–7211.
Chief Operating Officer for Air Traffic Services.—Russell G. Chew, 493–5602.
Vice President for—
 Acquisition & Business Services.—Dennis DeGaetano, 267–7222.
 Communications Services.—Sandra M. Sanchez, 267–8507.
 En Route & Oceanic Services.—Richard Day (acting), 385–8501.
 Flight Services.—James H, Washington, 385–7500.

Operations Planning Services.—Charles E. Keegan, 267–7111.
Safety Services.—William S. Davis (acting), 493–5882.
Systems Operations Services.—Michael A. Cirillo, 267–8558.
Technical Operations Services.—Steven B. Zaidman, 267–8181.
Terminal Services.—David B. Johnson, 385–8801.
Senior Vice President for Finance Services.—Eugene D. Juba, 267–3022.
Director, Joint Planning and Development Office.—Charles E. Keegan, 2203310.
Director, William J. Hughes Technical Center.—Dr. Anne Harlan (609) 485–6641.
Associate Administrator for Airports.—Woodie Woodward, 267–9471.
Deputy Associate Administrator.—Catherine Lang, 267–8738.
Director of:
    Airport Planning and Programming.—Dennis E. Roberts, 267–8775.
    Airport Safety and Standards.—David L. Bennett, 267–3053.
Associate Administrator for Commercial Space Transportation.—Patricia Grace Smith, 267–7793.
Deputy Associate Administrator.—Dr. George C. Nield, 267–7848.
Associate Administrator for Aviation Safety.—Nicholas A. Sabatini, 267–3131.
Deputy Associate Administrator.—Peggy Gilligan, 267–7804.
Director of:
    Accident Investigation.—Steven B. Wallace, 267–9612.
    Air Traffic Oversight.—J. David Canoles, 267–5202.
    Aircraft Certification Service.—John J. Hickey, 267–8235.
    Flight Standards Service.—James Ballough, 267–8237.
    Quality and Integration.—Vi Lipski, 493–5860.
    Rulemaking.—Anthony F. Fazio, 267–9677.
Federal Air Surgeon.—Dr. Jon L. Jordan, 267–3535.

FEDERAL HIGHWAY ADMINISTRATION

Washington Headquarters, Nassif Building, 400 Seventh Street SW, 20590

Turner-Fairbank Highway Research Center (TFHRC)

6300 Georgetown Pike, McLean, VA 22201

Administrator.—Mary E. Peters, 366–0650.
Deputy Administrator.—J. Richard Capka, 366–2240.
Executive Director.—Frederick G. (Bud) Wright, 366–2242.
Chief Counsel.—James A. Rowland, room 4213, 366–0740.
Associate Administrator for—
    Administration.—Michael J. Vecchietti, room 4316, 366–0604.
    Civil Rights.—Edward W. Morris, Jr., room 4132, 366–0693.
    Corporate Management.—Ronald C. Marshall, room 4208, 366–9393.
    Federal Lands Highway.—Arthur E. Hamilton, room 6311, 366–9494.
    Infrastructure.—King W. Gee, room 3212, 366–0371.
    Operations.—Jeffrey F. Paniati, room 3401, 366–0408.
    Planning, Environment, and Realty.—Cynthia J. Burbank, room 3212, 366–0116.
    Policy.—Charles D. Nottingham, room 3317, 366–0585.
    Professional Development.—Joseph S. Toole, room 800, 235–0500.
    Public Affairs.—Brian Keeter, room 4211, 366–0660.
    Turner-Fairbank Highway Research Center.—Dennis C. Judycki, room T–306, 493–3999.

FIELD SERVICES

Organizationally report to Executive Director (HOA–3), Washington, DC

Eastern Field Office
    Director.—Gene K. Fong, 10 S. Howard Street, Suite 4000, Baltimore, MD 21201 (410) 962–0093.
Southern Field Office
    Director.—Eugene W. Cleckley, 61 Forsyth Street, SW., Suite 17T26, Atlanta, GA 30303 (404) 562–3570.
Western Field Office
    Director.—Christine M. Johnson, 2520 West 4700 South, Suite 9C, Salt Lake City, UT 84114 (801) 967–5979.

RESOURCE CENTERS

Eastern Resource Center
Manager.—Joyce A. Curtis, 10 S. Howard Street, Suite 4000, Baltimore, MD 21201 (410) 962–0093
Midwestern Resource Center
Manager.—William R. Gary White, 19900 Governors Drive, Suite 301, Olympia Fields, IL 60461 (708) 283–3510.
Southern Resource Center
Manager.—Garrett (Gary) Corino, 61 Forsyth Street, SW., Suite 17T26, Atlanta, GA 30303 (404) 562–3570.
Western Resource Center
Manager.—C. Glenn Clinton, 201 Mission Street, Suite 2100, San Francisco, CA 94105 (415) 744–3102.

FEDERAL RAILROAD ADMINISTRATION

1120 Vermont Avenue, NW., 20590 (202) 493–6000, www.fra.dot.gov

Administrator.—Robert Jamison (acting), room 7089, 493–6014.
  Associate Administrator for—
    Administration and Finance.—Margaret Reid, room 6077, 493–6110.
    Policy and Program Development.—Jane H. Bachner (acting), room 7074, 493–6400.
    Railroad Development.—Mark E. Yachmetz, room 0729, 493–6381.
    Safety.—Dan Smith, room 6014, 493–6300.
  Chief Counsel.—Mark Lindsey, room 7022, 493–6052.
  Director of:
    Budget.—DJ Stadler, room 6124, 493–6150.
    Civil Rights.—Carl-Martin Ruiz, room 7096, 493–6010.
    Public Affairs.—Steven W. Kulm, room 7086, 493–6024.

REGIONAL OFFICES (RAILROAD SAFETY)

Region 1.—Northeastern. Connecticut, Maine, Massachusetts, New Hampshire, New Jersey, New York, Rhode Island, Vermont.
  Regional Administrator.—Mark H. McKeon, Room 1077, 55 Broadway, Cambridge, MA 02142 (617) 494–2302.
Region 2.—Eastern. Delaware, District of Columbia, Maryland, Pennsylvania, Virginia, West Virginia, Ohio.
  Regional Administrator.—David Myers, International Plaza, Suite 550, Philadelphia, PA 19113 (610) 521–8200.
Region 3.—Southern. Kentucky, Tennessee, Mississippi, North Carolina, South Carolina, Georgia, Alabama, Florida.
  Regional Administrator.—Fred Denin, 61 Forsyth Street, NW., Suite 16T20, Atlanta, GA 30303 (404) 562–3800.
Region 4.—Central. Minnesota, Illinois, Indiana, Michigan, Wisconsin.
  Regional Administrator.—Lawrence Hasvold, 200 W. Adams Street, Chicago, IL 60606 (312) 353–6203.
Region 5.—Southwestern. Arkansas, Louisiana, New Mexico, Oklahoma, Texas.
  Regional Administrator.—Bonnie Murphy, 4100 International Plaza, Suite 450, Ft. Worth, TX 96109 (817) 862–2200.
Region 6.—Midwestern. Iowa, Missouri, Kansas, Nebraska, Colorado.
  Regional Administrator.—Darrell J. Tisor, DOT Building, 901 Locust Street, Suite 464, Kansas City, MO 64106 (816) 329–3840.
Region 7.—Western. Arizona, California, Nevada, Utah.
  Regional Administrator.—Alvin L. Settle, 801 I Street, Suite 466, Sacramento, CA 95814 (916) 498–6540.
Region 8.—Northwestern. Idaho, Oregon, Wyoming, Montana, North Dakota, South Dakota, Washington, Alaska.
  Regional Administrator.—Dave Brooks, 500 Broadway, Murdock Executive Plaza, Suite 240, Vancouver, WA 98660 (360) 696–7536.

NATIONAL HIGHWAY TRAFFIC SAFETY ADMINISTRATION
400 Seventh Street SW, 20590

Administrator.—Jeffrey W. Runge, M.D., room 5220, 366–1836.
Senior Associate Administrator for—
  Policy and Operation.—Gregory Walter, 366–2330.
  Traffic Injury Control.—Brian McLaughlin, 366–1755.
  Vehicle Safety.—Ronald Medford, 366–9700.
Associate Administrator for—
  Administration.—Delmas Johnson, 366–1788.
  Development and Delivery.—Marilena Amoni, 366–1755.
  External Affairs.—Michael Harrington, 366–2111.
  Operation and Resource.—Marlene Markinson, 366–2121.
  Rulemaking.—Stephen R. Kratzke, 366–1810.
  Vehicle Safety Research Program.—Joseph Kanathra, 366–4862.
Director, Office of:
  Civil Rights.—George B. Quick, 366–0972.
  Communication and Consumer Information.—Susan Gorcowski, 366–9550.
  Legislative Affairs.—Wilfred Otero, 366–9263.
Chief Counsel.—Jacqueline Glassman, 366–9511.
Director, Executive Correspondence.—Tammie White, 366–1936.

REGIONAL OFFICES

Region I. Connecticut, Maine, Massachusetts, New Hampshire, Rhode Island, Vermont.
  Regional Administrator.—Philip J. Weiser, (617) 494–3427.
Region II. New York, New Jersey, Puerto Rico, Virgin Islands.
  Regional Administrator.—Thomas M. Louizou, Suite 204, 222 Mamaroneck Avenue, White Plains, NY 10605 (914) 682–6239. ,
Region III. Delaware, District of Columbia, Maryland, Pennsylvania, Virginia, West Virginia.
  Regional Administrator.—Elizabeth Baker, The Cresent Building, 10 South Howard Street, Suite 4000, Baltimore, MD 21201 (410) 962–0090.
Region IV. Alabama, Florida, Georgia, Kentucky, Mississippi, North Carolina, South Carolina, Tennessee.
  Regional Administrator.—Terrance D. Schiavone, 100 Alabama Street SW, Suite 17T30, Atlanta, GA 30303–3106 (404) 562–3739.
Region V. Illinois, Indiana, Michigan, Minnesota, Ohio, Wisconsin.
  Regional Administrator.—Donald J. McNamara, 19900 Governors Drive, Suite 201, Olympia Fields, IL 60461 (708) 503–8892.
Region VI. Arkansas, Louisiana, New Mexico, Oklahoma, Texas.
  Regional Administrator.—George S. Chakiris, Room 8A38, 819 Taylor Street, Fort Worth, TX 76102–6177 (817) 978–3653.
Region VII. Iowa, Kansas, Missouri, Nebraska.
  Regional Administrator.—Romell Cooks, PO Box 412515, Kansas City, MO 64141 (816) 822–7233.
Region VIII. Colorado, Montana, North Dakota, South Dakota. Utah, Wyoming.
Region IX. American Samoa, Arizona, California, Guam, Hawaii, Nevada.
  Regional Administrator.—David Manning (acting), Suite 2230, 201 Mission Street, San Francisco, CA 94105 (415) 744–3089.
Region X. Alaska, Idaho, Oregon, Washington.
  Regional Administrator.—Curtis Winston, Federal Building, Room 3140, 915 Second Avenue, Seattle, WA 98174 (206) 220–7640.

FEDERAL TRANSIT ADMINISTRATION
400 Seventh Street SW, 20590, phone 366–4040

Administrator.—Jennifer L. Dorn.
Deputy Administrator.—Robert Jamison.
Chief Counsel.—Judith Kaleta, 366–4063.
Director, Office of:
  Civil Rights.—Michael Winter.
Associate Administrator for—
  Administration.—Rita Wells.
  Program Management.—Susan Schruth.

Deputy Associate Administrator for—
  Budget and Policy.—Bob Tuccillo, 366–4050.
  Research, Demonstration and Innovation.—Barbara Sisson.

REGIONAL OFFICES

Region 1.—Connecticut, Maine, Massachusetts, New Hampshire, Rhode Island, Vermont.
  Regional Administrator.—Richard H. Doyle, Transportation Systems Center, Kendall Square, Suite 920, 55 Broadway, Cambridge, MA 02142.
Region 2.—New Jersey, New York, Virgin Islands.
  Regional Administrator.—Letitia Thompson, One Bowling Green, room 429, New York, NY 10004.
Region 3.—Delaware, District of Columbia, Maryland, North Carolina, Pennsylvania, Tennessee, Virginia, West Virginia.
  Regional Administrator.—Susan Borinsky, Suite 500, 1760 Market Street, Philadelphia, PA 19103.
Region 4.—Alabama, Florida, Georgia, Kentucky, Mississippi, North Carolina, Puerto Rico, South Carolina, Tennessee.
  Regional Administrator.—Hiram Walker, 61 Forsyth Street, SW, Suite 17T50, Atlanta, GA 30303.
Region 5.—Illinois, Indiana, Michigan, Minnesota, Ohio, Wisconsin.
Region 6.—Arkansas, Louisiana, New Mexico, Oklahoma, Texas.
  Regional Administrator.—Robert C. Patrick, Fritz Lanham Federal Building, 819 Taylor Street, room 8A36, Fort Worth, TX 76102.
Region 7.—Iowa, Kansas, Missouri, Nebraska.
  Regional Administrator.—Mohktee Altmad, 901 Locust Street, Suite 404, Kansas City, MO 64131.
Region 8.—Colorado, Montana, North Dakota, South Dakota, Utah, Wyoming.
  Regional Administrator.—Lee O. Waddleton, Columbine Place, 216 16th Street, Denver, CO 80202.
Region 9.—Arizona, California, Guam, Hawaii, Nevada, American Samoa.
  Regional Administrator.—Leslie T. Rogers, Suite 2210, 201 Mission Street, San Francisco, CA 94105.
Region 10.—Alaska, Idaho, Oregon, Washington.
  Regional Administrator.—Rick Krochalis, Suite 3142, 915 Second Avenue, Seattle, WA 98174.

SAINT LAWRENCE SEAWAY DEVELOPMENT CORPORATION

400 Seventh Street SW 20590, phone 366–0091, fax 366–7147

Administrator.—Albert Jacquez.
  Director, Office of:
    Budget and Logistics.—Kevin P. O'Malley.
    Chief Counsel.—Craig H. Middlebrook (acting).
    Trade Development and Public Affairs.—Rebecca McGill.

SEAWAY OPERATIONS

180 Andrews Street, PO Box 520, Massena, NY 13662–0520

phone (315) 764–3200, fax (315) 764–3235

Associate Administrator.—Salvatore L. Pisani.
  Deputy Associate Administrator.—Carol A. Fenton.
  Assistant.—Mary C. Fregoe.
  Chief Financial Officer.—Edward Margosian.
  Director, Office of:
    Engineering.—Thomas A. Lavigne.
    Financial Management and Administration.—Mary Ann Hazel.
    Lock Operations and Marine Services.—Lori K. Curran.
    Maintenance.—Jesse Hinojosa.

Department of Transportation

MARITIME ADMINISTRATION

400 Seventh Street SW, 20590, phone 366–5812

Maritime Administrator and Chairman, Maritime Subsidy Board.—John E. Jamian (acting), room 7206, 366–5823.
Deputy Administrator.—John E. Jamian, room 7208, 366–1719.
Secretary, Maritime Administration and Maritime Subsidy Board.—Joel Richard, room 7210, 366–5746.
Chief Counsel and Member, Maritime Subsidy Board.—Robert B. Ostrom, room 7232, 366–5711.
Director, Office of:
  Congressional and Public Affairs.—John Irvin, room 7206, 366–1707.
Associate Administrator for Administration.—Eileen S. Roberson, room 7216, 366–5802.
Director, Office of:
  Accounting.—John G. Hoban, room 7325, 366–5852.
  Acquisition.—Tim Roark, room 7310, 366–5757.
  Budget.—John Portel, room 7217, 366–5778.
  Management and Information Services.—Richard A. Weaver, room 7301, 366–5816.
  Personnel.—Raymond A. Pagliarini, room 2109, 366–4141.
Associate Administrator for Policy, International Trade.—Bruce J. Carlton, room 7218, 366–5772.
Director of:
  International Activities.—Gregory Hall, room 7119, 366–5773.
  Policy and Plans.—Janice G. Weaver, room 7123, 366–4468.
Associate Administrator for Financial Approvals and Cargo Preference.—James J. Zok, room 8114, 366–0364.
Director, Office of:
  Cargo Preference.—Thomas W. Harrelson, room 8118, 366–4610.
  Financial and Rate Approvals.—Michael P. Ferris, room 8117, 366–2324.
  Insurance and Shipping Analysis.—Edmond J. Fitzgerald, room 8117, 366–2400.
Associate Administrator for National Security.—James E. Caponiti, room 7300, 366–5400.
Director, Office of:
  National Security Plans.—Thomas M.P. Christensen, room 7130, 366–5900.
  Sealift Support.—Taylor E. Jones, II, room 7304, 366–2323.
  Ship Operations.—William H. Cahill (acting), room 2122, 366–1875.
Associate Administrator for Shipbuilding.—Jean E. McKeever, room 8126, 366–5737.
Director of:
  Insurance and Shipping Analysis.—Edmond J. Fitzgerald, room 8117, 366–2400.
  Ship Financing.—Mitchell D. Lax, room 8122, 366–5744.
  Shipbuilding and Marine Technology.—Joseph A. Byrne, room 8101, 366–1931.
Associate Administrator for Port, Intermodal and Environmental Activities.—Margaret D. Blum, room 7214, 366–4721.
Director, Office of:
  Environmental Activities.—Michael C. Carter, room 7209, 366–8887.
  Intermodal Development.—Richard L. Walker, room 7209, 366–8888.
  Ports and Domestic Shipping.—Richard Lolich (acting), room 7201, 366–4357.

FIELD ACTIVITIES

North Atlantic Region: *Director.*—Robert F. McKeon, 1 Bowling Green, room 418, New York, NY 10004 (212) 668–3330.
Great Lakes Region: *Director.*—Doris J. Bautch, Suite 185, 2860 S. River Road, Des Plaines, IL 60018 (847) 298–4535.
Western Region: *Director.*—Francis Johnston III, Suite 2200, 201 Mission Street, San Francisco, CA 94105 (415) 744–2580.
South Atlantic Region: *Director.*—M. Nuns Jain, Building 4D, Room 211, 7737 Hampton Boulevard, Norfolk, VA 23505 (757) 441–6393.

U.S. MERCHANT MARINE ACADEMY

Superintendent.—RADM Joseph D. Stewart, Kings Point, NY 11024 (516) 773–5000.
  Assistant Superintendent for Academic Affairs (Academic Dean).—Dr. Warren F. Mazek.

PIPELINE AND HAZARDOUS MATERIALS SAFETY ADMINISTRATION

400 Seventh Street SW, 20590, phone 366–4433

Chief Safety Officer.—Stacey Gerard (acting), room 2103.
  Chief Counsel.—Elaine Joost, room 8407, 366–4400.
  Director, Office of Civil Rights.—Helen E. Hagin, room 8419, 366–9638.
  Associate Administrator for—
    Hazardous Materials Safety.—Robert A. McGuire, room 8421, 366–0656.
    Management and Administration.—Edward A. Brigham, room 7128, 366–4347.
    Pipeline Safety.—Stacey Gerard, room 7128, 366–4595.

HAZARDOUS MATERIALS SAFETY OFFICES

Eastern Region: *Chief.*—Colleen D. Abbenhaus, 820 Bear Tavern Road, Suite 306, West Trenton, NJ 08628 (609) 989–2256.
Central Region: *Chief.*—Kevin Boehne, Suite 478, 2350 East Devon Avenue, Des Plaines, IL 60018 (847) 294–8580.
Western Region: *Chief.*—Daniel Derwey, 3401 Centre Lake Drive, Suite 550–B, Ontario, CA 91764 (909) 937–3279.
Southern Region: *Chief.*—John Heneghan, 1701 Columbia Avenue, Suite 520, College Park, GA 30337 (404) 305–6120.
Southwest Region: *Chief.*—Billy Hines, 2320 LaBranch Street, room 2100, Houston, TX 77004 (713) 718–3950.

PIPELINE SAFETY OFFICES

Eastern Region: *Director.*—William H. Gute, 409 3rd Street, SW., Suite 300, Washington, DC 20024 (202) 260–8500.
Central Region: *Director.*—Ivan A. Huntoon, 901 Locust Street, Room 462, Kansas City, MO 64106 (816) 329–3800.
Western Region: *Director.*—Chris Hoidal, 12600 West Colfax Avenue, Suite A250, Lakewood, CO 80215 (303) 231–5701.
Southwest Region: *Director.*—Rodrick M. Seeley, 2320 LaBranch Street, Suite 2100, Houston, TX 77004 (713) 718–3748.
Southern Region: *Director.*—Linda Dougherty, 61 Forsyth Street, Suite 6T15, Atlanta, GA 30303 (404) 562–3530.

RESEARCH AND INNOVATIVE TECHNOLOGY ADMINISTRATION (RITA)

400 Seventh Street, SW, room 3103, phone (202) 366–7582

Deputy Administrator.—Eric Peterson.

BUREAU OF TRANSPORTATION STATISTICS

400 Seventh Street SW., 20590, Room 7412, phone 366–1270

Deputy Director.—Rick Kowaleski.

TRANSPORTATION SAFETY INSTITUTE

Director.—Frank Tupper, 6500 South MacArthur Boulevard, Oklahoma City, OK 73125 (405) 954–2222.

VOLPE NATIONAL TRANSPORTATION SYSTEMS CENTER

Associate Administrator.—Dr. Curtis J. Tompkins, 55 Broadway, Kendall Square, Cambridge, MA 02142 (617) 494–2222.

SURFACE TRANSPORTATION BOARD

1925 K St. NW., 20423–0001, phone 565–1500

http://www.stb.dot.gov

Chairman.—Roger Nober, 565–1510.
  Vice Chairman.—W. Douglas Buttrey, 565–1505.
  Office of:
    Commissioner.—Francis P. Mulvey, 565–1525.
    Compliance and Enforcement.—Melvin F. Clemens, 565–1573.
    Congressionl and Public Services.—Dan G. King, 565–1594.
    Economics, Environmental Analysis, and Administration.—Leland L. Gardner, 565–1526.
    General Counsel.—Ellen D. Hanson, 565–1558.
    Proceedings.—David M. Konschnik, 565–1600.
    Secretary.—Vernon A. Williams, 565–1650.

DEPARTMENT OF ENERGY

James Forrestal Building, 1000 Independence Avenue SW 20585
phone (202) 586–5000, http://www.doe.gov

SAMUEL WRIGHT BODMAN, Secretary of Energy; born on November 26, 1938, in Chicago, IL; education: BChE., Cornell University, 1961; ScD, Massachusetts Institute of Technology, 1965; professional: Associate Professor of Chemical Engineering at Massachusetts Institute of Technology; Technical Director of the American Research and Development Corporation; President and Chief Operating Officer of Fidelity Investments and Director of the Fidelity Group of Mutual Funds; Chairman, CEO and Director of the Cabot Corporation; public service: Deputy Secretary, Department of Commerce, 2001–04; Deputy Secretary, Department of the Treasury, 2004; organizations: member, American Academy of Arts and Sciences; Former Director of School of Engineering Practice, Executive and Investment Committees at Massachusetts Institute of Technology; Trustee of the Isabella Stewart Gardner Museum and the New England Aquarium; married: M. Diane Bodman; three children, two stepchildren, and eight grandchildren; nominated by President George W. Bush to become the 11th Secretary of Energy, and was confirmed by the U.S. Senate on January 31, 2005.

OFFICE OF THE SECRETARY

Secretary of Energy.—Samuel Wright Bodman, 586–6210.
  Deputy Secretary.—Jeffrey Clay Sell, 586–5500.
  Under Secretary for National Nuclear Security Administration.—Linton F. Brooks, 586–5555.
  Inspector General.—Gregory H. Friedman, 586–4393.
  General Counsel.—Eric Fygi (acting), 586–5281.
  Secretary of Energy Advisory Board.—Richard Burrow (acting), 586–7092.
  Assistant Secretary for—
    Congressional and Intergovernmental Affairs.—Jill Sigal (acting), 586–5450.
    Energy Efficiency and Renewable Energy.—David K. Garman, 586–9220.
    Environment, Safety and Health.—John Shaw, 586–6151.
    Environmental Management.—Paul Golan (acting), 586–7709.
    Fossil Energy.—mark Maddox (acting), 586–6660.
    Policy and International Affairs.—Karen Harbert, 586–5800.
  Administrator for Energy Information Administration.—Guy F. Caruso, 586–4361.
  Director, Office of:
    Civilian Radioactive Waste Management.—Theodore J. Garrish (acting), 586–6842.
    Counterintelligence.—Stephen W. Dillard, 586–5901.
    Economic Impact and Diversity.—Theresa Alvillar-Speake, 586–8383.
    Fissile Materials Disposition.—Kenneth Bromberg (acting), 586–2695.
    Hearings and Appeals.—George B. Breznay, 287–1566.
    Intelligence.—John Russack, 586–2610.
    Legacy Management.—Michael W. Owen, 586–7550.
    Management, Budget and Evaluation.—Bruce Carnes, 586–4171.
    Nuclear Energy, Science and Technology.—William D. Magwood IV, 586–6630.
    Public Affairs.—Anne Womack Kolton, 586–4940.
    Science.—Dr. Raymond L. Orbach, 586–5430.

MAJOR FIELD ORGANIZATIONS
OPERATIONS OFFICES

Managers:
  Chicago.—Marvin Gunn (708) 972–2110.
  Idaho.—Elizabeth D. Sellers (208) 526–5665.
  Oak Ridge.—Gerald Boyd (865) 576–4444.

Richland.—Keith Klein (509) 376–7395.
Savannah River.—Jeffrey Allison (803) 725–2405.

SITE OFFICES

Director, Oakland.—Camille Yuan-Soo Hoo (925) 422–2572.
Manager, Nevada.—Kathleen A. Carlson (702) 295–3211.

NNSA SERVICE CENTER

Director, Albuquerque.—Karen Boardman (505) 845–6050.

FIELD OFFICES

Managers:
  Golden.—John Kerston (303) 275–4792.
  Ohio.—Robert Warther (513) 246–0180.
  Rocky Flatts.—Frazer R. Lockhart (303) 966–2025.

ENERGY EFFICIENCY REGIONAL OFFICES

Directors:
  Atlanta.—James R. Powell (404) 562–0555.
  Boston.—Christine Reinselds (acting), (617) 565–9700.
  Chicago.—Peter Dreyfuss (312) 353–6749.
  Denver.—Jeff Baker (acting), (303) 275–4826.
  Philadelphia.—Ellen D. Lutz (215) 656–6954.
  Seattle.—Julie A. Riel (206) 553–2875.

POWER MARKETING ADMINISTRATIONS

Administrator, Power Administration:
  Bonneville.—Stephen J. Wright (503) 230–5101.
  Southeastern Area.—Charles A. Borchardt (706) 213–3805.
  Southwestern Area.—Michael A. Diehl (918) 595–6601.
  Western Area.—Michael S. Hacskaylo (720) 962–7077.

OFFICE OF SCIENTIFIC AND TECHNICAL INFORMATION

Director.—Walter L. Warnick (301) 903–7996.
  Deputy Director.—R.L. Scott (865) 576–1193.

NAVAL REACTORS OFFICES

Managers:
  Pittsburgh.—Henry A. Cardinali (412) 476–7200.
  Schenectady.—Phil E. Salm (518) 395–4690.

OFFICE OF CIVILIAN RADIOACTIVE WASTE MANAGEMENT

Las Vegas.—W. John Arthur III (702) 794–1300.
Washington, DC.—Theodore J. Garrish (202) 586–6850.

FOSSIL ENERGY FIELD OFFICES

Directors:
  Albany Research Center (Oregon).—George J. Dooley III (541) 967–5893.
  National Energy Technology Lab.—Carl O. Bauer (acting), (304) 285–4511.
Project Manager, Strategic Petroleum Reserve Project Office.—William C. Gibson Jr. (504) 734–4201.

NAVAL PETROLEUM RESERVES

Directors:
  California.—James Curtis Killen (661) 837–5000.
  Colorado, Utah, Wyoming (Oil Shale Reserves).—Clarke D. Turner (307) 261–5161.

FEDERAL ENERGY REGULATORY COMMISSION
Washington DC 20426

Chair.—Pat Wood III (202) 502–8000.
  Commissioners:
    Nora Mead Brownell (202) 502–8383.
    Joseph T. Kelliher (202) 502–8377.
    Suedeen G. Kelly (202) 502–6501.
  Executive Director and Chief Financial Officer.—Thomas R. Herlihy (202) 502–8300.
  Director, Office of External Affairs.—McLane Layton (202) 502–8004.

DEPARTMENT OF EDUCATION

400 Maryland Avenue SW 20202

phone 401–3000, fax 401–0596, http://www.ed.gov

MARGARET SPELLINGS, Secretary of Education; born in Ann Arbor, MI, November 30, 1957; education: B.A., University of Houston, 1979; professional: education reform commissioner under Texas Governor William P. Clements; associate executive director, Texas Association of School Boards, 1988–94; senior advisor to George W. Bush during his term as Governor of Texas, 1994–2000; as senior adviser, Secretary Spellings created the Texas Reading Initiative, the Student Success Initiative to eliminate social promotion, and the nation's strongest school assessment and accountability system; Domestic Policy Adviser, 2001–05; one of the principal authors of the 2001 No Child Left Behind Act; first mother of school children to serve as Secretary of Education; children: Mary and Grace; nominated by President George W. Bush to become the 8th Secretary of Education on November 17, 2004; confirmed on January 20, 2005.

OFFICE OF THE SECRETARY

Room 7W301, phone 401–3000, fax 401–0596

Secretary of Education.—Margaret Spellings.
  Chief of Staff.—David Dunn, 205–9694.
  Interim Director, Public Affairs.—DJ Nordquist, room 7C105, 401–8459, fax 401–3130.

OFFICE OF THE DEPUTY SECRETARY

Room 7W310, phone 401–1000, fax 401–3095

Office of Educational Technology.—Susan Patrick, 205–4274.

OFFICE FOR CIVIL RIGHTS

550 12th Street SW, Room 5000, 20202–1100, phone 245–6800, fax 245–6840 or 6844

Assistant Secretary.—James Manning (acting).
  Deputy Assistant Secretary for Enforcement.—David Black (acting).
  Special Assistant/Legal.—Kimberly Richey, room 6142, 245–6819.
  Director of:
    Enforcement, East.—Susan Bowers, room 6094, 245–6798.
    Enforcement, West.—Susan Bowers (acting).
    Program Legal Group.—Sandra Battle, room 6125, 245–6767.
    Resource Management Group.—Lester Slayton, room 6117, 245–6753.

OFFICE OF THE UNDER SECRETARY

400 Maryland Avenue, SW., Federal Office Building 6, Room 7E307, phone 401–1000, fax 260–7113 or 401–4353 or 205–7655

Under Secretary.—Edward R. McPherson.

743

OFFICE OF INSPECTOR GENERAL

550 12th Street, SW., 8th Floor, 20024, phone 245–6900, fax 245–6993

Inspector General.—John P. Higgins, Jr..
  Deputy Inspector General.—Thomas A. Carter.
  Counsel to the Inspector General.—Mary Mitchelson.
  Assistant Inspector General for—
    Audit Services.—Helen Lew, 245–7050.
    Cyber Audit and Computer Crime Investigations.—Charles E. Coe, 245–7034.
    Evaluation, Inspection and Management Services.—Cathy H. Lewis, 245–7007.
    Investigations.—Thomas Sipes, 245–6966.

OFFICE OF THE GENERAL COUNSEL

Room 6E301, phone 401–6000, fax 205–2689

General Counsel.—Kent Talbert (acting).
  Chief of Staff.—Charles R. Hokanson.
  Senior Counsel.—Robert Wexler.
  Deputy General Counsel of Departmental and Legislative Service.—Kent Talbert.
  Executive Officer.—J. Carolyn Adams, 401–8340.

OFFICE OF SPECIAL EDUCATION AND REHABILITATIVE SERVICES

Potomac Center Placa (PCP), 550 12th Street SW., 5th Floor 20202, phone 245–7468, fax 245–7636

Assistant Secretary.—John Hager.
  Executive Administrator.—Andrew J. Pepin, room 3110, 245–7632.
  Director of National Institute on Disability and Rehabilitation Research.—Steve Tingus, 245–7640.

OFFICE OF THE CHIEF INFORMATION OFFICER

Room 2W301, phone 401–5848, fax 260–3761

Chief Information Officer.—William J. Leidinger, room 2W311, 260–0563 or 401–5848.
  Deputy Chief Information Officer/Chief Technology Officer.—Stephen Fletcher, PCP, room 9112, 245–6677.
  Director of:
    Information Assurance Services.—Jerry Davis, PCP, room 9009, 245–6441.
    Information Technology Operations and Maintenance.—Robert Leach, PCP, room 2W307, 260–2645.
    Regulatory Information Management Services.—Jeanne Van Vlandren, PCP, room 9150, 245–6611.

OFFICE OF LEGISLATION AND CONGRESSIONAL AFFAIRS

Room 6W301, phone 401–0020, fax 401–1438

Assistant Secretary.—Karen C. Quarles (acting), 205–3530.
  Deputy Assistant Secretary.—Karen C. Quarles.
  Chief of Staff.—Marc DeCourcey, 260–2434.
  Congressional Affairs Liaisons:
    Central Region.—Steven Tisher, 260–7008.
    Mountain Region.—Clinton Manning, 260–0268.
    Northeast Region.—Jonathan Keeling, 401–0023.
    Pacific Region.—William Knudsen, 401–3743.
    Southeast Region.—Robertson Dickens, 401–2035.

OFFICE OF INTERGOVERNMENTAL AND INTERAGENCY AFFAIRS
Room 5E313, phone 401–0404, fax 401–8607

Assistant Secretary.—Christina Culver (acting).
  Chief of Staff.—Jeff Sims (acting), room 5E329, 401–0026.
  Deputy Assistant Secretary for—
    Intergovernmental and Constituent Services.—Ken Meyer, 205–5158.
    Regional Services.—Christina Culver, 205–0678.
    Corporate Liaison.—Kimberly Strycharz, 401–3728.
    Senior Director for Community Services.—John McGrath, 401–1309.

OFFICE OF THE CHIEF FINANCIAL OFFICER
Room 4E313, phone 401–0085, fax 401–0006

Chief Financial Officer.—Jack Martin, 401–0477.
  Deputy Chief Financial Officer.—Danny A. Harris, Ph.D., room 4E314, 401–0896.
  Chief of Staff.—William M. McCabe, room 4E311, 205–0707.
  Executive Officer.—Michael Holloway, room 4E231, 401–0322.
  Director of:
    Contracts and Acquisitions Management.—Glenn Perry, room 7153, 550 12th Street, SW., 20202, 245–6289.
    Financial Improvement and Post Audit Operations.—Charles Miller (acting), room 21C5, 830 First Street, NE., 377–3819.
    Financial Management Operations.—Terry Bowie, room 4W202, 401–4144.
    Financial Systems Operations.—Danny Harris (acting), room 4E314, 401–0896.
    Grants Policy and Oversight Staff.—Blanca Rodriguez, room 7065, 550 12th Street SW., 20202, 245–6121.

OFFICE OF MANAGEMENT
Room 2W301, phone 401–5848, fax 260–3761

Assistant Secretary/Chief Information Officer.—William J. Leidinger, room 2W311, 260–0563 or 401–5848, fax 260–3761.
  Deputy Assistant Secretary.—Michell Clark, room 2W307, 260–7337, fax 260–3761.
  Chief of Staff.—Nina Aten, room 2W309, 401–5846, fax 260–3761.
  Executive Officer.—Keith Berger, room 2W227, 401–0693, fax 401–3513.
  Group Director of:
    Facility Services.—Steve Moore, room 2E315, 401–2349, fax 732–1534.
    Human Resource Services.—Veronica D. Trietsch, room 2E314, 401–0553, fax 401–0520.
    Management Services.—George F. Green, room 2W226, 401–5931.
    Office of Hearings and Appeals.—Frank J. Furey, L'Enfant Plaza–2134, 619–9701, fax 619–9726.
    Process Performance Improvement Services.—Michell Clark (acting), room 2W307, 260–7337.
    Security Services.—Winona Varnon, room 2W330, 401–1583, fax 260–3761.

OFFICE OF FEDERAL STUDENT AID
830 First Street, NE., 20202, phone 377–3000, fax 275–5000

Chief Operating Officer.—Terri Shaw.
  Chief of Staff.—James Manning.
  Ombudsman.—Deb Wiley, room 41I1, 377–3801.
  Chief Financial Officer.—Vicki Bateman, room 42G3, 377–3401.
  Chief Information Officer.—Jerry Schubert, room 102E3, 377–3009.
  Program Manager, Policy Liaison and Implementation Staff.—Jeff Baker, room 93G3, 377–4009.
  General Manager of:
    Administration and Workforce Support Services.—Marianna O'Brien (acting), room 22D1, 377–3095.
    Borrower Services.—Sue Szabo, room 42G2, 377–3437.
    Communications Management Services.—Marianna O'Brien, room 11, 377–3095.
    Enterprise Performance Management Services.—John Fare, room 92G2, 377–3707.

Financial Partners Services.—Kristie Hansen, room 112F1, 377–3301.
FSA Application and Delivery Services.—Kay Jacks, room 82E1, 377–4286.

OFFICE OF POSTSECONDARY EDUCATION

1990 K Street, NW., 20006, phone 502–7750, fax 502–7677

Assistant Secretary.—Sally Stroup.
   Chief of Staff.—Tara Porter.
   Deputy Assistant Secretary for Higher Education Programs.—Wilbert Bryant, 502–7555.

INSTITUTE OF EDUCATION SCIENCES

555 New Jersey Avenue, NW., Room 600, 20208, phone 219–1385, fax 219–1466

Director.—Grover J. (Russ) Whitehurst.
   Deputy Director for—
   Administration and Policy.—Sue Betka.
   Science.—Lynn Okagaki, 219–2006.
   National Center for Education Statistics.—Grover J. (Russ) Whitehurst (acting), 502–7300.
   National Center for Education Research.—Barbara Foorman, 219–2369.
   National Center for Education Evaluation and Regional Assistance.—Phoebe Cottingham, 219–2484.

OFFICE OF ELEMENTARY AND SECONDARY EDUCATION

400 Maryland Avenue, SW., Room 3W315, 20202, phone 401–0113, 205–0303

Assistant Secretary.—Raymond Simon, 401–0113.
   Deputy Assistant Secretary.—Darla Marburger, 260–2032.
   Chief of Staff.—Christopher Doherty, 401–0113.
   Director of:
   Impact Aid Programs.—Catherine Schagh, room 3E105, 260–3858, fax 205–0088.
   Office of Migrant Education.—Francisco Garcia, room 3E317, 260–1164, fax 205–0089.
   Office of Indian Education.—Victoria Vasques, 205–3687.
   Student Achievement and School Accountability Programs.—Jackie Jackson, 260–0826.
   School Support and Technology Programs.—Jenelle Leonard (acting), 401–3641.
   Academic Improvement and Teacher Quality Programs.—Joseph Conaty, 260–8230.
   Reading First.—Christopher Doherty, 401–4877.

OFFICE OF ENGLISH LANGUAGE ACQUISITION

550 12th Street, SW., 10th Floor, 20202, phone 245–7100, fax 245–7168

Primary Associate Assistant Deputy Secretary.—Marina Tse.
   Associate Assistant Deputy Secretary.—Kathleen Leos.

OFFICE OF VOCATIONAL AND ADULT EDUCATION

550 12th Street, SW., Room 1100, 20202, phone 245–7700, fax 245–7171

Assistant Secretary.—Susan Selafani.
   Deputy Assistant Secretary.—Richard LaPointe.
   Special Assistant.—Joan Athen.
   Confidential Assistant.—Iris Oliver.

OFFICE OF SAFE AND DRUG-FREE SCHOOLS

400 Maryland Avenue, SW., phone 205–4169, fax 205–5005

Assistant Deputy Secretary.—Deborah A. Price, room 1E110, 260–7497.
   Associate Assistant Deputy Secretary.—Bill Modzeleski, room 3E314, 260–1856.

OFFICE OF INNOVATION AND IMPROVEMENT
400 Maryland Avenue, SW., 20202, phone 205–4500

Assistant Deputy Secretary.—Nina Rees, 205–4484.
  Associate Assistant Deputy Secretary for Policy: Michael Petrilli, 205–0653.
  Chief of Staff.—Marcie Brown, 401–1857.
  Confidential Assistant.—Joshua Venable, 205–4516.

DEPARTMENT OF VETERANS AFFAIRS

Mail should be addressed to 810 Vermont Avenue, Washington DC 20420

http://www.va.gov

R. JAMES (JIM) NICHOLSON, Secretary of Veterans Affairs; education: graduate, U.S. Military Academy, West Point, NY, 1961; M.A., Columbia University; J.D., University of Denver; military service: paratrooper and Ranger-qualified Army officer, U.S. Army; Vietnam War veteran; military awards: Bronze Star Medal, Combat Infantryman Badge, the Meritorious Service Medal, Republic of Vietnam Cross of Gallantry, and two Air Medals; professional: founded Nicholson Enterprises, Inc., 1978; owner, Renaissance Homes, 1987–present; chairman, Republican National Committee, 1997–2000; U.S. Ambassador to the Holy See, 2001–04; married: Suzanne Marie Ferrell; three children; nominated by President George W. Bush to become the 5th Secretary of Veterans Affairs, and was confirmed by the U.S. Senate on January 26, 2005.

OFFICE OF THE SECRETARY

Secretary of Veterans Affairs.—R. James Nicholson, 273–4800.
  Chief of Staff.—Claude M. Kicklighter, 273–4808.
  Deputy Chief of Staff.—Thomas G. Bowman.
  Special Assistant for Veterans Service Organizations Liaison.—Allen (Gunner) Kent, 273–4835.
  General Counsel.—Tim S. McClain, 273–6660.
  Inspector General.—Richard J. Griffin, 801 I Street, NW., 565–8620.
  Chairman, Board of:
    Contract Appeals.—Gary J. Krump, 1800 G Street, NW., 273–6743.
    Veterans Appeals.—Ron Garvin (acting), 811 Vermont Avenue, NW., 565–5001.

OFFICE OF THE DEPUTY SECRETARY

Deputy Secretary of Veterans Affairs.—Gordon H. Mansfield, 273–4817.
  Director of:
    Center for Minority Veterans.—Charles W. Nesby, 273–6708.
    Center for Women Veterans.—Irene Trowell-Harris, 273–6193.
    Employment Discrimination Complaint Adjudication.—Charles R. Delobe, 1722 I Street, NW., 254–0065.
    Regulation Policy and Management.—Robert C. McFetridge (acting), 273–9515.
    Small and Disadvantaged Business Utilization.—Scott Denniston, 801 I Street, NW., 565–8124.

ASSISTANT SECRETARY FOR CONGRESSIONAL AND LEGISLATIVE AFFAIRS

Assistant Secretary.—Pamela M. Iovino, 273–5611.
  Executive Assistant.—Harriet Singleton, 273–5611.
  Director for—
    Congressional and Legislative Affairs.—Gloria Bennett, 273–5628.
    Congressional Liaison.—Patricia Covington, 224–5321 or 225–2280.

ASSISTANT SECRETARY FOR PUBLIC AND INTERGOVERNMENTAL AFFAIRS

Assistant Secretary.—Cynthia R. Church, 273–5750.
  Deputy Assistant Secretary for—
    Intergovernmental and International Affairs.—William McLemore, 273–5121.
    Public Affairs.—Robert Klear (acting), 273–5710.

ASSISTANT SECRETARY FOR POLICY, PLANNING, AND PREPAREDNESS

Assistant Secretary.—Dennis M. Duffy (acting), 273–5033.
 Principal Deputy Assistant Secretary.—Dennis M. Duffy.
 Deputy Assistant Secretary for—
 Planning and Evaluation.—H. Raymond Wilburn (acting), 273–5068.
 Policy.—Michael McLendon, 273–5182.
 Security and Law Enforcement.—John H. Baffa, 273–5500.
 Director, Operations and Readiness.—R. Tom Sizemore (acting), 273–5287.

ASSISTANT SECRETARY FOR MANAGEMENT

Deputy Assistant Secretary for—
 Acquisition and Materiel Management.—Ford Heard (acting), 273–6029.
 Budget.—Rita Reed, 273–5289.
 Finance.—Edward Murray, 273–5504.

ASSISTANT SECRETARY FOR INFORMATION AND TECHNOLOGY

Assistant Secretary.—Bob McFarland, 273–8842.
 Deputy Assistant Secretary for Information and Technology Management.—Edward F. Meagher, 273–8855.

ASSISTANT SECRETARY FOR HUMAN RESOURCES AND ADMINISTRATION

Assistant Secretary.—R. Allen Pittman, 273–4901.
 Principal Deputy Assistant Secretary.—Gary A. Steinberg.
 Deputy Assistant Secretary for—
 Diversity Management and EEO.—Susan C. McHugh, 1575 I Street, NW., 501–1970.
 Human Resources Management.—Thomas J. Hogan, 273–4920.
 Resolution Management.—James S. Jones, 1575 I Street, NW., 501–2800.
 Director, Office of Administration.—C.G. (Deno) Verenes, 273–5356.
 Associate Deputy for Labor-Management Relations.—Ronald E. Cowles, 273–5369.
 Associate Deputy Assistant Secretary for Human Resources Management.—Willie L. Hensley, 273–4920.

NATIONAL CEMETERY ADMINISTRATION

Under Secretary.—Richard A. Wannemacher, Jr. (acting), 273–5146.
 Deputy Under Secretary.—Steve Muro (acting), 273–5235.
 Senior Advisor.—Richard A. Wannemacher, Jr., 273–5235
 Director of:
 Communications Management Service.—Peggy McGee, 273–5175.
 Construction Management.—Robert B. Holbrook, 565–4830.
 Field Programs.—Steve Muro, 273–5235.
 Finance and Planning.—Dan Tucker, 273–5157.
 Information Systems Service.—Joseph Nosari, 273–5205.
 Management Support Service.—Robert Kline (acting), 273–5232.
 Memorial Programs Service.—David Schettler, 501–3100.
 State Cemetery Grants Service.—G. William Jayne, 565–6152.

VETERANS BENEFITS ADMINISTRATION

Under Secretary.—Daniel L. Cooper, 1800 G Street, NW., 273–6761.
 Deputy Under Secretary.—Ronald Aument.
 Chief of Staff.—Lois Mittelstaedt.
 Associate Deputy Under Secretary for—
 Field Operations.—Michel Walcoff, 273–7259.
 Policy and Program Management.—Robert J. Epley, 273–6851.
 Chief Financial Officer.—James Bohmbach, 273–6728.
 VA Deputy Chief Information Officer for Benefits.—K. Adair Martinez, 273–7004.

Director of:
  Compensation and Pension.—Renee Szybala, 273–7203.
  Education.—Jack McCoy, 273–7132.
  Employee Development and Training.—Dorothy Mackay, 273–5446.
  Insurance.—Thomas Lastowka, 215–381–3100.
  Loan Guaranty.—R. Keith Pedigo, 273–7331.
  Vocational Rehabilitation and Employment.—Judith Caden, 273–7419.

VETERANS HEALTH ADMINISTRATION

Under Secretary.—Jonathan B. Perlin (acting), M.D., Ph.D., MSHA, FACP, 273–5781.
  Deputy Under Secretary.—Michael J. Kussman (acting), M.D., MS, MACP, 273–5878.
  Deputy Under Secretary for Health (DUSH) for Operations and Management.—Laura J. Miller, 273–5826.
  Officer for—
    Patient Care Services.—Madhulika Agarwal (acting), M.D., MPH, 273–8474.
    Public Health and Environmental Hazards.—Susan H. Mather, M.D., 273–8575.
    Research and Development.—Stephan D. Fihn (acting), 254–0183.

DEPARTMENT OF HOMELAND SECURITY

U.S. Naval Security Station, 3801 Nebraska Avenue, NW., Washington, DC 20393

phone 282–8000

MICHAEL CHERTOFF, Secretary of Homeland Security; born on November 28, 1953, in Elizabeth, NJ; education: Harvard College, *magna cum laude*, 1975; Harvard Law School, *magna cum laude*, 1978; public service: clerk to Supreme Court Justice William Brennan, Jr., 1979–80; U.S. Attorney for the District of New Jersey; First Assistant U.S. Attorney for the District of New Jersey; Assistant U.S. Attorney for the Southern District of New York; former partner, law firm of Latham & Watkins; Special Counsel, U.S. Senate Whitewater Committee, 1994–96; United States Circuit Judge for the Third Circuit Court of Appeals; confirmed by the President George W. Bush as Assistant Attorney General for the Criminal Division, Department of Justice, March 5, 2003; family: married to Meryl Justin Chertoff; children: two; nominated by President George W. Bush to become the 2nd Secretary of Homeland Security on January 11, 2005, and was confirmed by the U.S. Senate on February 15, 2005.

OFFICE OF THE SECRETARY

Secretary of Homeland Security.—Michael Chertoff.

OFFICE OF THE DEPUTY SECRETARY

Deputy Secretary of Homeland Security.—Michael P. Jackson.

OFFICE OF THE CHIEF OF STAFF

Chief of Staff.—John Wood.

MANAGEMENT DIRECTORATE

Under Secretary.—Janet Hale.
  Chief Financial Officer.—Andrew Maner.
  Chief Information Officer.—Steven Cooper.
  Chief Human Capital Officer.—Ronald James.

BORDER AND TRANSPORTATION SECURITY DIRECTORATE

Under Secretary.—Randy Beardsworth (acting).
  Assistant Secretary for Immigration and Customs Enforcement.—Michael J. Garcia.
  Commissioner, Customs and Border Protection.—Robert Bonner.
  Administrator, Transportation Security Administration.—David Stone.

SCIENCE AND TECHNOLOGY DIRECTORATE

Under Secretary.—Charles E. McQueary.

753

INFORMATION ANALYSIS AND INFRASTRUCTURE PROTECTION DIRECTORATE

Under Secretary.—Matthew Broderick (acting).

EMERGENCY PREPAREDNESS AND RESPONSE DIRECTORATE

Under Secretary.—Michael Brown.

UNITED STATES SECRET SERVICE

Director.—W. Ralph Basham.

UNITED STATES COAST GUARD

Commandant.—ADM Thomas H. Collins.

U.S. CITIZENSHIP AND IMMIGRATION SERVICES

Director.—Eduardo Aguirre.

OFFICE OF COUNTERNARCOTICS

Counternarcotics Officer / U.S. Interdiction Coordinator.—Ralph Utley (acting).

OFFICE OF STATE AND LOCAL GOVERNMENT COORDINATION AND PREPAREDNESS

Director.—Matt Mayer (acting).

OFFICE OF NATIONAL CAPITAL REGION COORDINATION

Director.—Tom Lockwood.

OFFICE OF THE INSPECTOR GENERAL

Inspector General.—Richard Skinner (acting).

OFFICE OF THE GENERAL COUNSEL

General Counsel.—Joe Whitley.

OFFICE OF THE PRIVACY OFFICER

Privacy Officer.—Nuala O'Connor Kelly.

OFFICE OF CIVIL RIGHTS AND CIVIL LIBERTIES

Civil Rights and Civil Liberties Officer.—Daniel Sutherland.

OFFICE OF THE PRIVATE SECTOR LIAISON

Special Assistant to the Secretary.—Al Martinez-Fonts.

OFFICE OF LEGISLATIVE AFFAIRS

Assistant Secretary.—Pam Turner.

OFFICE OF PUBLIC AFFAIRS

Assistant Secretary.—Brian Besanceney.

OFFICE OF INTERNATIONAL AFFAIRS

Director.—Cresencio Arcos.

INDEPENDENT AGENCIES, COMMISSIONS, BOARDS

ADVISORY COUNCIL ON HISTORIC PRESERVATION

1100 Pennsylvania Avenue NW, Suite 809, 20004

phone 606–8503, http://www.achp.gov

[Created by Public Law 89–665, as amended]

Chairman.—John L. Nau III, Houston, Texas.
  Vice Chairman.—Bernadette Castro, Albany, New York.
  Expert Members:
    Bruce D. Judd, San Francisco, California.
    Susan Snell Barnes, Aurora, Illinois.
    Ann Alexander Pritzlaff, Denver, Colorado.
    Julia A. King, St. Leonard, Maryland.
  Citizen Members:
    Emily Summers, Dallas, Texas.
    Carolyn J. Brackett, Nashville, Tennessee.
  Native Hawaiian Member:
    Raynard C. Soon, Honolulu, Hawaii.
  Governor.—Hon. Tim Pawlenty, St. Paul, Minnesota.
  Mayor.—Hon. Bob Young, Augusta, Georgia.
  Architect of the Capitol.—Hon. Alan M. Hantman, FAIA.
  Secretary, Department of:
    Agriculture.—Hon. Mike Johanns.
    Interior.—Hon. Gale A. Norton.
    Defense.—Hon. Donald H. Rumsfeld.
    Transportation.—Hon. Norman Y. Mineta.
  Administrator:
    Environmental Protection Agency.—Hon. Stephen L. Johnson (acting).
    General Services Administration.—Hon. Stephen A. Perry.
  National Trust for Historic Preservation.—Jonathan Kemper, Chairman,
    Kansas City, Missouri.
  National Conference of State Historic Preservation Officers.—Jay D. Vogt,
    President, Pierre, South Dakota.

AFRICAN DEVELOPMENT FOUNDATION

1400 Eye Street NW, Suite 1000, 20005–2248, phone 673–3916, fax 673–3810

E-mail: info@adf.gov; Wb: www.adf.gov

[Created by Public Law 96–533]

BOARD OF DIRECTORS

Chair.—Edward W. Brehm.
  Vice Chair.—Willie Grace Campbell.
  Private Members: Ephraim Batambuze, John W. Leslie, Jr.
  Public Members: Constance Newman, Lloyd O. Pierson.

STAFF

President and CEO.—Nathaniel Fields.
  Advisory Committee Management.—[Inactive].
  Congressional Liaison Officer.—Roger M. Ervin II.
  General Counsel.—Doris Mason Martin.
  Chief Financial Officer.—Martha C. Edmondson.

Chief Management Officer.—Larry P. Bevan.
Director of Human Resources.—Stephanie A. Wrightson.
Program and Field Operations:
    Region 1: Rama Bah.
    Region 2: Richard C. Day.
    Region 3: Christine S. Fowles.

AMERICAN BATTLE MONUMENTS COMMISSION

Courthouse Plaza II, Suite 500, 2300 Clarendon Blvd., Arlington, VA 22201–3367

phone (703) 696–6902

[Created by Public Law 105–225]

Chairman.—GEN Frederick M. Franks, Jr.,, U.S. Army (ret.).
  Commissioners:

LTG Julius Becton, Jr., U.S. Army (ret.).	Honorable Sara A. Sellers.
MG Patrick H. Brady, U.S. Army (ret.).	Honorable Alan K. Simpson.
Honorable James B. Francis, Jr.	MG Will Hill Tankersley, U.S. Army
Honorable Antonio Lopez.	(ret.).
Honorable Joseph E. Persico.	BG Sue E. Turner, U.S. Air Force (ret.).

  Secretary.—BG John W. Nicholson, U.S. Army (ret.).
    Executive Director.—BG William J. Leszczynski, Jr., U.S. Army (ret.).
    Director for—
      Engineering, Maintenance, and Operations.—Thomas R. Sole.
      Finance.—Richard M. Holcomb.
      Personnel and Administration.—Theodore Gloukoff.
      Public Affairs.—Michael G. Conley.

(Note: Public law changed to 105–225, August 1998; H.R. 1085).

AMERICAN NATIONAL RED CROSS

National Headquarters, 2025 E Street, NW., 20006, phone (202) 737–8300

HONORARY OFFICERS

Honorary Chairman.—George W. Bush, President of the United States.

CORPORATE OFFICERS

Chairman.—Bonnie McElveen-Hunter.
  President & CEO.—Marsha J. Evans.
  General Counsel/Secretary.—Mary S. Elcano.

BOARD OF GOVERNORS

C=Elected by the Chartered Units

L=Elected by Board as Member-at-Large

P=Appointed by the President of the United States

Gina F. Adams (L).	Karen K. Goodman (C)
Chris Allen (C).	William F. Grinnan, Jr. (C).
Sanford A. Belden (C).	Hon. Carlos M. Gutierrez (P).
Hon. John L. Braxton (C).	Carol Ann Haake (C).
Julie J. Burger (C).	Dr. Susan B. Hassmiller (C).
Steven E. Carr (C).	Michael W. Hawkins (C).
Hon. Michael Chertoff (P).	Edward A. Heidt, Jr. (C).
Dr. Nita Clyde (L).	Joyce N. Hoffman (C).
Douglas H. Dittrick (C).	Judith Richards Hope (L).
Bill J. Gagliano (C).	Jon M. Huntsman (L).
Dr. Lee A. Goldstein (C).	Ann F. Kaplan (L).

Gregory Kozmetsky (L).
Sherry Lansing (L).
Hon. Michael O. Leavitt (P).
Dr. William V. Lewis, Jr. (C).
Rex K. Linder (C).
William Lucy (L).
Elaine M. Lyerly (C).
Dr. Allen W. Mathies, Jr. (C).
William F. McConnell, Jr. (C).
Bonnie McElveen-Hunter (P).
Gen. Richard B. Myers (P).
Hon. R. James Nicholson (P).

Richard M. Niemiec (C).
Ross H. Ogden (C).
Theodore Parrish (C).
Pat M. Powers (C).
Hon. Condoleezza Rice (P).
Glenn A. Sieber (C).
Brian G. Skotko (C).
Maj. Gen. Robert L. Smolen (L).
Hon. Margaret Spellings (P).
E. Francine Stokes (C).
Dr. Christine K. Wilkinson (C).
Maurice W. Worth (C).

ADMINISTRATIVE OFFICERS

National Chair of Volunteers.—Kate Forbes.
   Chief Diversity Officer.—David Wilkins.
   Chief Financial Officer.—Robert P. McDonald.
   Executive Vice President for Chapter and International Operations.—Alan McCurry.
   Executive Vice President & CEO, Biomedical Services.—Jack McGuire.
   General Auditor.—Timothy Holmes.
Senior Vice President for—
   Communications and Marketing.—Charles Connor.
   Growth and Integrated Development.—Skip Seitz.
   Human Resources.—Rick Pogue.
   Quality and Regulatory.—Bill Cherry.
Vice President for—
   Finance and Business Planning.—Brian Rhoa.
   Products, Health and Safety Services.—Scott Conner.
   Public Policy and Partner Relations.—Jan Lane.

APPALACHIAN REGIONAL COMMISSION
1666 Connecticut Avenue NW 20235, phone (202) 884–7660, fax 884–7691

Federal Co-Chairman.—Anne B. Pope.
   Alternate Federal Co-Chairman.—Richard J. Peltz.
   States' Washington Representative.—Cameron Whitman.
   Executive Director.—Thomas M. Hunter.
   Congressional Affairs Officer.—Guy Land.

ARMED FORCES RETIREMENT HOME
3700 N. Capitol Street, NW., Box 1303, Washington, DC 20011–8400
phone (202) 730–3077, fax 730–3166

Chief Operating Officer.—Timothy C. Cox.
   Chief Financial Officer.—Steven G. McManus.
   Chief Support Services.—Nancy C. Duran.

ARMED FORCES RETIREMENT HOME—WASHINGTON
3700 N. Capitol Street, NW., Washington, DC 20011–8400
phone (202) 730–3229, fax 730–3127

Director.—CAPT Jerald Ulmer, Sr., USN (acting).
   Deputy Director.—CAPT Paul Soares, USN.

ARMED FORCES RETIREMENT HOME—GULFPORT
1800 Beach Drive, Gulfport, MS 39507, phone (228) 897–4003, fax 897–4017

Director.—CAPT Jerald Ulmer, Sr., USN.
   Deputy Director.—LCOL Wendy Van Dyke, USAF.

BOARD OF GOVERNORS OF THE FEDERAL RESERVE SYSTEM
Constitution Avenue and 20th Street 20551, phone (202) 452–3000

Chairman.—Alan Greenspan.
Vice Chair.—Roger W. Ferguson, Jr.
Members: Ben S. Bernanke; Susan Schmidt Bies; Edward M. Gramlich; Donald L. Kohn, Mark W. Olson.
Assistant to the Board and Director.—Michelle A. Smith.
Assistant to the Board.—Winthrop P. Hambley.
Special Assistants to the Board: Laricke D. Blanchard, Rosanna Pianalto-Cameron, Robert M. Pribble, Dave Skidmore,

DIVISION OF INTERNATIONAL FINANCE

Director.—Karen H. Johnson.
Deputy Director.—David H. Howard.
Associate Director.—Thomas A. Conners.
Deputy Associate Directors: Richard T. Freeman, Steven B. Kamin.
Assistant Directors: Jon W. Faust, Joseph E. Gagnon, Michael P. Leahy, D. Nathan Sheets, Ralph W. Tryon.
Senior Advisers: Dale W. Henderson, William L. Helkie.
Adviser.—Willene A. Johnson.

DIVISION OF RESEARCH AND STATISTICS

Director.—David J. Stockton.
Deputy Directors: Edward C. Ettin, David Wilcox.
Associate Directors: Myron L. Kwast, Stephen D. Oliner, Patrick M. Parkinson, Lawrence Slifman, Charles S. Struckmeyer.
Deputy Associate Directors: David L. Reifschneider, William L. Wascher, III, A. Patricia White, Joyce K. Zickler.
Assistant Directors: J. Nellie Liang, S. Wayne Passmore, Janice Shack-Marquez, Daniel Sichel, Mary M. West.
Assistant Directors/Chiefs: Douglas Elmendorf, Michael Gibson, Diana Hancock.
Senior Advisers: Glenn B. Canner, David S. Jones, Thomas D. Simpson.

DIVISION OF MONETARY AFFAIRS

Director.—Vincent Reinhart.
Deputy Director.—Brian F. Madigan.
Special Assistant to the Board.—Deborah J. Danker.
Deputy Associate Directors: James A. Clouse, William C. Whitesell.
Assistant Directors: Cheryl Edwards, William B. English.
Adviser.—Athansios Orphanides.

DIVISION OF BANKING SUPERVISION AND REGULATION

Director.—Richard Spillenkothen.
Deputy Director.—Stephen M. Hoffman, Jr.
Senior Advisor.—Michael G. Martinson.
Advisor.—Steve Roberts.
Senior Associate Directors: Herbert A. Biern, Roger T. Cole, Angela Desmond.
Associate Directors: Deborah P. Bailey, Norah Barber, Betsy Cross, Gerald A. Edwards, Jr., James V. Houpt, Jack P. Jennings, Peter J. Purcell, Molly S. Wassom, David M. Wright.
Deputy Associate Directors: Barbara J. Bouchard, James A. Embersit, Charles H. Holm, William G. Spaniel.
Assistant Directors: Stacy Coleman, Jon D. Greenlee, Walt H. Miles, William C. Schneider, Jr., William F. Treacy.

LEGAL DIVISION

General Counsel.—Scott G. Alvarez.
  Deputy General Counsels: Richard M. Ashton, Kathleen M. O'Day.
  Associate General Counsels: Stephanie Martin, Anne E. Misback, Katherine H. Wheatley.
  Assistant General Counsels: Kieran J. Fallon, Stephen H. Meyer, Patricia A. Robinson,
    Cary K. Williams.

DIVISION OF CONSUMER AND COMMUNITY AFFAIRS

Director.—Sandra F. Braunstein.
  Deputy Director.—Glenn E. Loney.
  Associate Counsel and Advisor.—Adrienne D. Hurt.
  Senior Advisor.—Irene Shawn McNulty.
  Associate Directors: Mary T. Johnsen, Tonda E. Price.
  Assistant Director.— Suzanne Killian.
  Assistant Consumer Counsel.—James A. Michaels.

OFFICE OF THE SECRETARY

Secretary.—Jennifer J. Johnson.
  Deputy Secretary.—Robert deV. Frierson.
  Assistant Secretary.—Margaret McCloskey Shanks.

STAFF DIRECTOR FOR MANAGEMENT

Staff Director.—Stephen R. Malphrus.
  EEO Programs Director.—Sheila Clark.
  Senior Adviser.—Lynn S. Fox.

MANAGEMENT DIVISION

Director.—H. Fay Peters.
  Deputy Director.—Darrell R. Pauley.
  Senior Associate Director.—Stephen J. Clark.
  Associate Directors: Christine M. Fields, Marsha Reidhill, Billy J. Sauls, Donald A. Spicer.

DIVISION OF INFORMATION TECHNOLOGY

Director.—Marianne M. Emerson.
  Deputy Director.—Maureen T. Hannan.
  Assistant Directors: Tillena G. Clark, Geary L. Cunningham, Wayne A. Edmondson, Po
    Kyung Kim, Susan F. Marycz, Sharon L. Mowry, Raymond Romero.

INSPECTOR GENERAL

Inspector General.—Barry R. Snyder.
  Deputy Inspector General.—Donald L. Robinson.

DIVISION OF FEDERAL RESERVE BANK OPERATIONS AND PAYMENT SYSTEMS

Director.—Louise L. Roseman.
  Deputy Director.—Jeffrey C. Marquardt.
  Senior Associate Director.—Paul W. Bettge.
  Associate Directors: Kenneth D. Buckley, Jack K. Walton II.
  Deputy Associate Director.—Dorothy B. LaChapelle.
  Assistant Directors: Gregory L. Evans, Joseph H. Hayes, Jr., Lisa Hoskins, Michael J.
    Lambert, Jeff J. Stehm.

BROADCASTING BOARD OF GOVERNORS

330 Independence Avenue SW, Suite 3360, 20237, phone (202) 203–4545, fax 203–4568

Chairman.—Kenneth Y. Tomlinson.

INTERNATIONAL BROADCASTING BUREAU

[Created by Public Law 103–236]

The International Broadcasting Bureau (IBB) is composed of the Voice of America, and Radio and TV Marti. The Broadcasting Board of Governors oversees the operation of the IBB and provides yearly funding grants approved by Congress to three non-profit grantee corporations, Radio Free Europe/Radio Liberty, Radio Free Asia, and the Middle East Broadcasting Networks.

Director, International Broadcasting Bureau.—Brian Conniff (acting) (202) 203–4515, fax 203–4587.
Director of:
  Cuba Broadcasting.—Pedro Roig (305) 437–7010, fax 437–7016.
  Voice of America.—David Jackson (202) 203–4500, fax 203–4513.
President, Radio Free Asia.—Richard Richter.
President, Radio Free Europe.—Thomas Dine.
President, Middle East Broadcasting Networks.—Herbert Kleinman (acting).

GOVERNORS

Edward E. Kaufman
Norman J. Pattiz
Joaquin F. Blaya
Blanquita Walsh Cullum

D. Jeffrey Hirschberg
Steven J. Simmons
Condoleezza Rice
  (ex officio)

STAFF

Executive Director.—Brian T. Conniff.
  Legal Counsel.—Carol Booker.
  Program Review Officer.—Bruce Sherman.
  Congressional Coordinator.—Susan Andross.
  Senior Adviser.—Howard Mortman.
  Chief Financial Officer.—Janet Stormes.
  Executive Assistant.—Brenda Hardnett.
  Management and Program Analyst.—John Giambalvo.
  Program Review and Planning Officer.—Jim Morrow.
  Special Projects Officer.—Oanh Tran.
  Special Assistants.—Clark Pearson, Humaira Wakili.

COMMISSION OF FINE ARTS

401 F Street NW., Suite 312, National Building Museum, 20001–2728

phone (202) 504–2200, fax 504–2195, http://www.cfa.gov

Commissioners:
  David M. Childs, New York, NY, Chair.
  Earl A. Powell III, Washington, DC., Vice-Chair.
  Witold Rybczynski, Philadelphia, PA.

Barbaralee Diamonstein-Spielvogel, New York, NY.
Pamela Nelson, Dallas, TX.
Diana Balmori, New York, NY.
Elyn Zimmerman, New York, NY.

Secretary.—Frederick J. Lindstrom (acting).

BOARD OF ARCHITECTURAL CONSULTANTS FOR THE OLD GEORGETOWN ACT

Mary Oehrlein, FAIA, Chair.
John McCartney, FAIA.

Heather Willson Cass, FAIA.

COMMITTEE FOR PURCHASE FROM PEOPLE WHO ARE BLIND OR SEVERELY DISABLED
1421 Jefferson Davis Highway, Suite 10800, Jefferson Plaza 2
Arlington, VA 22202–3259, phone (703) 603–7740, fax 603–0655

Chairperson.—Steven B. Schwalb, Department of Justice.
Vice Chairperson.—LeRoy F. Saunders, private citizen (knowledgeable about obstacles to employment of persons who are blind).
Members:
  John Surina, Department of Agriculture.
  Frederick R. Beaman, Department of the Air Force.
  Sandra O. Sieber, Department of the Army.
  Michael Sade, Department of Commerce.
  Steven R. Bernett, Department of Defense.
  W. Roy Grizzard, Jr., Department of Labor.
  Felipe Mendoza, General Services Administration.
  Andrew D. Houghton and Robert T. Kelly, Jr., private citizens (representing nonprofit agency employees with other severe disabilities).
  James H. Omvig, private citizen (representing nonprofit agency employees who are blind).

COMMODITY FUTURES TRADING COMMISSION
Three Lafayette Centre, 1155 21st Street NW 20581, phone 418–5000
fax 418–5521, http://www.cftc.gov

Chairman.—Sharon Brown-Hruska (acting), 418–5050.
Chief of Staff.—Gregory Kuserk.
Commissioners:
  Michael V. Dunn, 418–5070.
  Frederick W. Hatfield, 418–5060.
  Walter L. Lukken, 418–5014.
Executive Director.—Madge A. Bolinger, 418–5160.
General Counsel.—Patrick McCarty, 418–5120.
Office of the Chief Economist.—James A. Overdahl, 418–5656.
Director, Division of:
  Clearing and Intermediary Oversight.—James Carley (acting), 418–5430.
  Enforcement.—Gregory Mocek, 418–5320.
  Market Oversight.—Rick Shilts (acting), 418–5260.
Director, Office of:
  External Affairs.—Alan C. Sobba, 418–5080.
  Inspector General.—A. Roy Lavik, 418–5110.
  International Affairs.—Andrea M. Corcoran, 418–5645.
  Secretary.—Jean A. Webb, 418–5100.

REGIONAL OFFICES

Chicago: 525 West Monroe Street, Suite 1100, Chicago, IL 60601 (312) 596–0700, fax 596–0716.
Kansas City: Two Emanuel Cleaver II Boulevard, Suite 300, Kansas City, MO 64112, (816) 960–7700, fax 960–7750.
Minneapolis: 510 Grain Exchange Building, 400 South 4th Street, Minneapolis, MN 55415, (612) 370–3255, fax 370–3257.
New York: 140 Broadway, Nineteenth floor, New York, NY 10005 (646) 746–9700, fax 746–9938.

CONSUMER PRODUCT SAFETY COMMISSION

4330 East West Highway, Bethesda, MD 20814, phone (301) 504–7923

fax 504–0124, http://www.cpsc.gov

[Created by Public Law 92–573]

Chairperson.—Hal Stratton, 504–7900.
  Commissioner.—Thomas H. Moore, 504–7902.
  Executive Director.—Patricia M. Semple, 504–7907.
  Deputy Executive Director.—Thomas W. Murr, Jr., 504–7907.
  Director, Office of:
    The Secretary.—Todd A. Stevenson, 504–7923.
    Congressional Relations.—Jack Horner, 504–7660.
  General Counsel.—Page C. Faulk, 504–7922.

CORPORATION FOR NATIONAL AND COMMUNITY SERVICE

1201 New York Avenue NW 20525, phone (202) 606–5000

http://www.cns.gov

[Executive Order 11603, June 30, 1971; codified in 42 U.S.C., section 4951]

Chief Executive Officer.—David Eisner.
  Chief of Staff.—Amy Mack.
  Chief Financial Officer.—Andrew Kleine (acting), ext. 564.
  Inspector General.—Carol Bates (acting), ext. 390.
  Director of:
    AmeriCorps/State and National.—Rosie Mauk, ext. 386.
    AmeriCorps/National Civilian Community Corps.—Merlene Mazyck, ext. 137.
    AmeriCorps/VISTA.—Kathie Ferguson (acting).
    National Senior Service Corps.—Tess Scannell, ext 300.
    Learn and Serve America.—Dr. Amy Cohen, ext. 484.
    Office of Government Relations.—Kathy Ott, ext. 228.
  General Counsel.—Frank Trinity, ext. 256.

DEFENSE NUCLEAR FACILITIES SAFETY BOARD

625 Indiana Avenue NW., Suite 700, 20004, phone 694–7000

fax 208–6518, http://www.dnfsb.gov

Chairman.—John T. Conway.
  Vice Chairman.—A.J. Eggenberger.
  Members: Joseph F. Bader, John E. Mansfield, R. Bruce Matthews.
  General Counsel.—Richard A. Azzaro.
  General Manager.—Kenneth M. Pusateri.
  Technical Director.—Kent Fortenberry.

DELAWARE RIVER BASIN COMMISSION

25 State Police Drive, PO Box 7360, West Trenton, NJ 08628–0360

phone (609) 883–9500, fax (609) 883–9522, http://www.drbc.net

FEDERAL REPRESENTATIVES

Federal Commissioner.—BG Merdith W.B. Temple, Commander, U.S. Army Corps of Engineers, North Atlantic Division (NAD) (718) 765–7000.
First Alternate.—COL Francis X. Kosich, Deputy Commander, U.S. Army Corps of Engineers, North Atlantic Division (NAD) (718) 765–7001.
Second Alternate.—LTC Robert J. Ruch, District Engineer, U.S. Army Corps of Engineers (215) 656–6501.

STAFF

Executive Director.—Carol R. Collier, ext. 200.
  Deputy Executive Director.—Robert Tudor, ext. 208.
  Commission Secretary/Assistant General Counsel.—Pamela M. Bush, Esq., ext. 203.
  Communications Manager.—Clarke Rupert, ext. 260.

DELAWARE REPRESENTATIVES

State Commissioner.—Ruth Ann Minner, Governor (302) 577–3210.
First Alternate.—John A. Secretary, Secretary, DE Department of Natural Resources and Environmental Control (302) 739–4403.
Second Alternate.—Kevin C. Connelly, Director, Office of the Director, Division of Water Resources (302) 739–4860.
Third Alternate.—Dr. Harry W. Otto, Senior Science Advisor, Office of the Director, Division of Water Resources (302) 739–5726.

NEW JERSEY REPRESENTATIVES

State Commissioner.—Richard J. Codey, Governor (acting) (609) 292–6000.
First Alternate.—Bradley M. Campbell, Commissioner, New Jersey Department of Environmental Protection (609) 292–2885.
Second Alternate.—Samuel A. Wolfe, Assistant Commissioner, Environmental Regulation (609) 292–2795.
Third Alternate.—Lisa Jackson, Assistant Commissioner, Land Use Management (609) 292–1932.

NEW YORK REPRESENTATIVES

State Commissioner.—George E. Pataki, Governor (518) 474–8390.
First Alternate.—Lynette M. Stark, Commissioner (acting), New York State Department of Environmental Conservation (518) 402–8540.
Second Alternate.—Sandra Allen, Director, Division of Water (518) 402–8233.
Third Alternate.—Fred Nuffer, Assistant Director, Division of Water (518) 402–8228.

PENNSYLVANIA REPRESENTATIVES

State Commissioner.—Edward G. Rendell, Governor (717) 787–2500.
First Alternate.—Cathy Curran Myers, Esq., Deputy Secretary for Water Management, Office of Water Management, Pennsylvania Department of Environmental Protection (717) 787–4686.
Second Alternate.—William A. Gast, Chief, Division of Water use Planning, Bureau of Watershed Management (717) 772–5671.

ENVIRONMENTAL PROTECTION AGENCY

1200 Pennsylvania Avenue, NW., 20460 (202) 564–4700, http://www.epa.gov

Administrator.—Stephen Johnson (acting).
  Deputy Administrator.—Stephen Johnson.
  Environmental Appeals Board: Scott Fulton, Edward Reich, Kathie Stein, Anna Wolgast, 233–0122.
  Associate Administrator for—
    Congressional and Intergovernmental Relations.—Charles Ingebretson, 564–5200.
    Policy, Economics and Innovation.—Stephanie Daigle (acting), 564–4332.
  Staff Offices, Director for—
    Regional Operations.—Judy Kertcher, 564–3103.
    Children's Health Protection.—William Sanders (acting), 564–2188.
    Civil Rights.—Karen Higginbotham, 564–7272.
    Science Advisory Board.—Vanessa Vu, 343–9999.
  Director, Office of:
    Small and Disadvantaged Business Utilization.—Jeanette Brown, 564–4100.
    Cooperative Environmental Management.—Dalva Balkus, 233–0066.
    Executive Secretariat.—Brian Hope, 564–7311.
    Executive Support.—Diane Bazzle, 564–0444.
  Administrative Law Judges.—Chief Judge Susan L. Biro, 564–6255.

ADMINISTRATION AND RESOURCES MANAGEMENT

Assistant Administrator.—David J. O'Connor (acting), 564–4600.
  Deputy Assistant Administrator.—Sherry A. Kaschak (acting), 564–1861.

Director, Office of:
  Acquisition Management.—Judy S. Davis, 564–4310.
  Administration and Resources Management: William M. Henderson, Cincinnati, OH (513)
    487–2026; William G. Laxton, Research Triangle Park, NC (919) 541–2258.
  Administrative Services.—Richard Lemley, 564–8400.
  Grants and Debarment.—Howard F. Corcoran, 564–5310.
  Human Resources.—Rafael DeLeon, 564–4606.
  Policy and Resources Management.—John L. Showman (acting), 564–1861.

OFFICE OF ENVIRONMENTAL INFORMATION

Assistant Administrator.—Kimberly T. Nelson, 564–6665.
  Deputy Assistant Administrator.—Linda Travers.
  Director, Office of:
    Information, Analysis, and Access.—Mike Flynn, 566–0600.
    Information Collection.—Mark Luttner, 566–1360.
    Planning, Resources, and Outreach.—Maggie Mitchell, 564–0284.
    Technology Operations and Planning.—Mark Day, 566–0300.

AIR AND RADIATION

Assistant Administrator.—Jeffrey (Jeff) Holmstead, 564–7404.
  Deputy Assistant Administrators: John Beale, 564–6229; Robert D. Brenner, 564–1666;
    Elizabeth Craig, 564–7403.
  Director, Office of:
    Air Quality Planning and Standards.—Steve Page, Research Triangle Park, NC (919)
      541–5616.
    Atmospheric Programs.—Brian J. McLean, 343–9140.
    Policy Analysis and Review.—Robert D. Brenner, 564–1677.
    Program Management Operations.—Jerry A. Kurtzweg, 564–1234.
    Radiation and Indoor Air.—Elizabeth Cotsworth, 564–9320.
    Transportation and Air Quality.—Margo T. Oge, 564–1682.

ENFORCEMENT AND COMPLIANCE ASSURANCE

Assistant Administrator.—Thomas V. Skinner (acting), 564–2440.
  Principal Deputy Assistant Administrator.—Phyllis P. Harris.
  Director, Office of:
    Administration and Resources Management Support.—David Swack, 564–2455.
    Civil Enforcement.—Walker B. Smith, 564–2220.
    Compliance.—Michael M. Stahl, 564–2280.
    Criminal Enforcement, Forensics, and Training.—Peter J. Murtha, 564–2480.
    Environmental Justice.—Barry Hill, 564–2515.
    Federal Activities.—Anne Miller, 564–5400.
    Federal Facilities Enforcement.—David Kling, 564–2510.
    Planning Policy Analysis and Communications.—Caroline Petti (acting), 564–2530.
    Site Remediation Enforcement.—Susan E. Bromm, 564–5110.

CHIEF FINANCIAL OFFICER

Chief Financial Officer.—Charles E. Johnson, 564–1151.
  Director Office of:
    Comptroller.—Joseph Dillon, 564–9673.
    Planning, Analysis, and Accountability.—Kathy Sedlack Obrien (acting), 564–9327.

GENERAL COUNSEL

General Counsel.—Ann R. Klee, 564–8040.
  Deputy General Counsel.—Kenneth von Schaumburg.
  Principal Deputy General Counsel.—Brenda Mallory, 564–8064.
  Designated Agency Ethics Officials: Peggy Love, 564–1784; Ken Wernick, 564–1763.
  Associate General Counsel for—
    Air and Radiation Law Office.—Rich Ossias (acting), 564–7606.
    Civil Rights Law Office.—Stephen Pressman, 564–2738.

Cross-Cutting Issues Law Office.—James C. Nelson, 564–7622.
Finance and Operations Law Office.—Marla E. Diamond, 564–5323.
International Environmental Law Office.—Peter Lallas, 564–1810.
Pesticides and Toxic Substances Law Office.—Bob Perlis, 564–5375.
Solid Waste and Emergency Response Law Office.—Scott Sherman, 564–7706.
Water Law Office.—Susan G. Lepow, 564–7700.

INSPECTOR GENERAL

Inspector General.—Nikki L. Tinsley, 566–0847.
Deputy Inspector General.—Michael J. Speedling, 566–0848.
Assistant Inspector General for—
    Audit.—Melissa Heist, 566–0824.
    Congressional and Public Liaison.—Eileen McMahon, 566–2391.
    Counsel to the Inspector General.—Mark Bialek, 566–0863.
    Human Capital.—Sandra Wiggins, 566–0914.
    Investigations.—Stephen Nesbitt, 566–0819.
    Mission Systems.—Patricia Hill, 566–2683.
    Planning Analysis and Results.—Michael Binder (acting), 566–2615.
    Program Evaluation.—Kwai Chan, 566–0832.

INTERNATIONAL AFFAIRS

Assistant Administrator.—Judith E. Ayres, 564–6600.
Deputy Assistant Administrator.—Jerry Clifford, 564–6442.
Director, Office of:
    International Environmental Policy.—Paul F. Cough, 564–6458.
    Management Operations.—Kathy Petruccilli, 564–6605.
    Technology Cooperation and Assistance.—Martin Dieu, 564–6439.
    Western Hemisphere and Bilateral Affairs.—Joan Fidler, 564–6611.

PREVENTION, PESTICIDES AND TOXIC SUBSTANCES

Assistant Administrator.—Susan B. Hazen (acting), 564–2902.
Principal Deputy Assistant Administrator.—Susan B. Hazen.
Associate Assistant Administrator for Program Management Operations.—Marylouise Uhlig, 564–0523.
Director, Office of:
    Pesticide Program.—Jim Jones (703) 305–7090.
    Pollution Prevention and Toxics.—Charles Auer, 564–3810.
    Science Coordination Policy.—Clifford Gabriel, 564–8430.

RESEARCH AND DEVELOPMENT

Assistant Administrator for Research and Development.—E. Timothy Oppelt (acting), 564–6620.
Director, Administrator for—
    Resources Management and Administration.—Lek G. Kadeli, 564–6700.
    Science.—William Farland, M.D. (acting), 564–6620.
    Science Policy.—Kevin Teichman (acting), 564–6705.
Director, Office of:
    National Center for Environmental Assessment.—George Alapas (acting), 564–3322.
    National Center for Environmental Research.—Peter W. Preuss, 564–6825.
    National Exposure Research Laboratory.—Gary J. Foley, Ph.D., 919–541–2106.
    National Health and Environmental Effects Research Laboratory.—Lawrence W. Reiter, Ph.D., 919–541–2281.
Associate Director for—
    Health.—Harold Zenich, Ph.D., 919–541–2283.
National Risk Management Research Laboratory.—E. Timothy Oppelt, 513–569–7418.

SOLID WASTE AND EMERGENCY RESPONSE

Principal Deputy Assistant Administrator.—Barry Breen, 566–0200.
Deputy Assistant Administrator.—Thomas P. Dunne.

Director, Office of:
  Brownsfields Cleanup and Redevelopment.—Linda Garczynski, 566–2777.
  Emergency Management.—Debbie Y. Dietrich, 564–8600.
  Federal Facilities Restoration and Reuse.—James E. Woolford (703) 603–9089.
  Innovation Partnership and Communication.—Marsha Minter (acting), 566–0205.
  Land Revitalization Staff.—Ed Chu, 566–2743.
  Organizational Management and Integrity Staff.—Lora Culver (acting), 566–1897.
  Program Management.—Devereaux Barnes, 566–1884.
  Solid Waste.—Matt Hale (703) 308–8895.
  Superfund Remediation and Technology Innovation.—Michael B. Cook (703) 308–8790.
  Underground Storage Tanks.—Cliff Rothenstein (703) 603–9900.

WATER

Assistant Administrator.—Benjamin H. Grumbles, 564–5700.
Deputy Assistant Administrators: Michael H. Shapiro.
Director, Office of:
  American Indian Environmental.—Carol Jorgensen, 564–0303.
  Ground Water and Drinking Water.—Cynthia C. Dougherty, 564–3750.
  Science and Technology.—Geoffrey Grubbs, 566–0430.
  Wastewater Management.—James A. Hanlon, 564–0748.
  Wetlands, Oceans and Watersheds.—Diane Regas, 566–1146.

REGIONAL ADMINISTRATION

Region I (Boston): *Regional Administrator.*—Robert W. Varney, One Congress Street, Suite 1100, Boston, MA 02114 (617) 918–1010.
  Congressional Liaisons: Rudy Brown (617) 918–1031, Michael Ochs (617) 918–1066.
  Public Affairs.—Nancy Grantham (617) 918–1101.
Region II (New York): *Regional Administrator.*—Kathleen Callahan (acting), 290 Broadway, New York, NY 10007 (212) 637–5000.
  Congressional Liaisons: Pat Carr (212) 637–3652; Barry Shore (212) 637–3657.
  Intergovernmental and Community Affairs.—Peter B. Brandt (212) 687–3654.
  Public Outreach.—Mary Mears (212) 637–3673.
Region III (Philadelphia): *Regional Administrator.*—Donald S. Welsh, 1650 Arch Street, Philadelphia, PA 19103–2029 (215) 814–2900.
  Congressional Liaison.—Catherine Libertz (215) 814–2737.
  Public Out-Reach.—Thomas Damm (215) 814–8075.
Region IV (Atlanta): *Regional Administrator.*—James I. Palmer, Jr., 61 Forsyth Street SW, Atlanta, GA 30303–8960 (404) 562–8357.
  Gulf of Mexico Program.—Bryon Griffith (228) 688–3726.
  Congressional Liaison.—Allison Wise (404) 562–8327.
  Public Affairs.—Carl Terry (404) 562–8327.
Region V (Chicago): *Regional Administrator.*—Bharat Mathur, 77 West Jackson Boulevard, Chicago, IL 60604–3507 (312) 886–3000.
  Congressional Liaison.—Mary Canavan (312) 886–4957.
  Public Affairs.—Elissa Speizman (312) 353–3018.
Region VI (Dallas): *Regional Administrator.*—Richard Greene, Fountain Place, 1445 Ross Avenue, 12th Floor, Suite 1200, Dallas, TX 75202–2733 (214) 665–2100.
  Congressional Liaison.—Carmen Henning (AR, LA, OK), Virginia Vietti (TX, NM), (214) 665–2200.
  Intergovernmental Liaison.—Deborah Ponder.
  External Affairs.—David W. Gray.
Region VII (Kansas City): *Regional Administrator.*—James B. Gulliford, 901 N. 5th Street, Kansas City, MO 66101 (913) 551–7006.
  Congressional Liaisons: Janette Lambert (913) 551–7768; LaTonya Sanders (913) 551–7555.
  External Affairs.—Patrick Bustos (913) 551–7969.
Region VIII (Denver): *Regional Administrator.*—Robert E. Roberts, 999 18th Street, Suite 300, Denver, CO 80202–2466 (303) 312–6308.
  Congressional Liaison.—Sandra Johnston-Fells (303) 312–6604.
  External Affairs.—Sonya S. Pennock (303) 312–6600.
  Office of Communications and Public Involvement.—Nola Cooke (303) 312–6599.
Region IX (San Francisco): *Regional Administrator.*—Wayne Nastri, 75 Hawthorne Street, San Francisco, CA 94105 (415) 947–8702.
  Director, Office of Planning and Public Affairs.—Sally Seymour (415) 947–3592.

Congressional Liaisons: Sunny Nelson (Southern CA, HI, Pacific Islands), (415) 947–4255; Brent Maier (NV, AZ, U.S./Mexico Border), (415) 947–4256; Jim Vreeland (Northern and Central CA), (415) 947–4298.

Region X (Seattle): *Regional Administrator.*—Ronald A. Kreizenbeck, 1200 Sixth Avenue, Seattle, WA 98101 (206) 553–1234.

Congressional Liaison.—Marianne Deppman (206) 553–1237.

External Affairs.—Michelle Pirzadeh (206) 553–1272.

EQUAL EMPLOYMENT OPPORTUNITY COMMISSION

1801 L Street 20507, phone (202) 663–4900

Chair.—Cari M. Dominguez, room 10006, 663–4001, fax 663–4110.

Chief Operating Officer.—Leonora Guarraia, room 10008, 663–4001.

Attorney Advisor.—Richard Roscio, room 10010, 663–4655.

Confidential Assistant.—Monica Barnhart, room 10012, 663–4002.

Senior Advisor.—Michael Richards, room 10127, 663–4010.

Special Assistants: Terrie Dandy, room 10038, 663–4816; Sandra Hobson, room 10042, 663–4009; Susan Murphy, room 10040, 663–4687.

Staff Assistant.—Cynthia Matthews, room 10016, 663–4026.

Vice Chair.—Naomi C. Earp, room 10103, 663–4027, fax 663–7121.

Senior Advisor.—Anthony Kaminski, room 10115, 663–4033.

Special Assistant.—Lynn Clements, room 10118, 663–4624.

COMMISSIONERS

Commissioners: Stuart Ishimaru, room 10133, 663–4052, fax 663–4108; Leslie Silverman, room 10305, 663–4099, fax 663–7086.

Special Assistants: Antoinette M. Eates, room 10127, 663–4067; Naomi Levin, room 10305, 663–4099; Jacinta Ma, room 10125, 663–4970; Sharyn Tejani, room 10123, 663–4022; Mindy Weinstein, room 10315, 663–4058.

Secretary.—Melissa Fenwick (acting), room 10129, 663–4062.

Executive Officer.—Stephen Llewellyn (acting), room 10426, 663–4073, fax 663–4114.

General Counsel.—Eric Dreiband, room 7000, 663–4702, fax 663–4196.

Deputy General Counsel.—James Lee, room 7003, 663–7034.

Legal Counsel.—Peggy Mastroianni (acting), room 6001, 663–4638, fax 663–4639.

Inspector General.—Aletha L. Brown, room 3001, 663–4327, fax 663–7204.

Director, Office of:
   Communications and Legislative Affairs.—Karen Pedrick (acting), room 9027, 663–4011, fax 663–4912.
   Equal Opportunity.—Jean M. Watson, room 9024, 663–4012, fax 663–7003.
   Field Programs.—Nicholas Inzeo, room 8002, 663–4801, fax 663–7190.

Attorney Advisors: Susan Adams, room 7002, 663–4743; Douglas Gallegos, room 5009, 663–4615; Stephen Llewellyn, room 10426, 663–4073; Lisa Morelli, room 4760, 663–4760.

EXPORT-IMPORT BANK OF THE UNITED STATES

811 Vermont Avenue NW 20571, phone (800) 565–EXIM, fax 565–3380

President and Chairman.—Philip Merrill, room 1215, 565–3500.
   Vice President and Vice Chairman.—April H. Foley, room 1229, 565–3540.
   Executive Vice President.—James Lambright, room 1214, 565–3515.
   Directors: Max Cleland, room 1257, 565–3520; Linda Conlin, room 1209, 565–3535; J. Jospeh Grandmaison, room 1241, 565–3530.

Chief Operating Officer/General Counsel.—Peter Saba, room 947, 565–3430.

Chief Financial Officer.—James K. Hess, room 1055, 565–3240.

Chief Information Officer.—Fernanda Young, room 1045, 565–3798.

Senior Vice President of:
   Congressional Affairs.—Thomas C. Montgomery, room 1261, 565–3216.
   Credit Risk Management.—John McAdams, room 919, 565–3222.
   Export Finance.—Jeffrey L. Miller, room 1121, 565–3601.
   Policy and Planning.—James C. Cruse, room 1243, 565–3761.
   Resource Management.—Michael Cushing, room 1017, 565–3561.

Vice President and Deputy Head of Export Finance.—John Emens, room 1115, 565–3701.

Vice President of:
   Country Risk and Economic Analysis.—William Marsteller, room 701, 565–3739.
   Credit Underwriting.—Kenneth M. Tinsley, room 919, 565–3668.
   Domestic Business Developoment.—Wayne L. Gardella, room 1137, 565–3787.
   Engineering and Environment.—James Mahoney, room 1169, 565–3573.
   International Business Development.—C. Michael Forgione, room 1107, 565–3224.
   Operations.—Raymond J. Ellis, room 719, 565–3674.
   Policy.—Piper P. Starr, room 1240, 565–3626.
   Policy Analysis.—Michael Kuester, room 1243, 565–3766.
   Structured Finance.—Barbara A. O'Boyle, room 1005, 565–3694.
   Trade Finance and Insurance.—Richard Maxwell, room 931, 565–3633.
   Transportation.—Robert A. Morin, room 1035, 565–3453.
Directors of:
   Human Resources.—Elliot Davis, room 771, 565–3316.
   Employee Development and Training.—Sherry Beyers, room 767, 565–3592.

FARM CREDIT ADMINISTRATION
1501 Farm Credit Drive, McLean, VA 22102–5090
phone (703) 883–4000, fax 734–5784
[Reorganization pursuant to Public Law 99–205, December 23, 1985]

Chair.—Nancy C. Pellett.
Members:
   Douglas L. Flory.
   Dallas Tonsager.
Secretary.—Jeanette Brinkley.
Chief of Staff.—Keith Hefferman.
Chief, Office of:
   Administration.—Philip Shebest, 883–4130.
   Finance.—W.B. Erwin, 883–4099.
   Information.—Doug Valcour, 883–4166.
Director, Office of:
   Communication and Public Affairs.—Carl A. Clinefelter (acting), 883–4056, fax 790–3260.
   Congressional and Legislative Affairs.—Martha Schober, 883–4056, fax 790–3260.
   Ombudsman.—Eric Howard, 883–4144.
   Policy and Analysis.—Ed Harshbarger, 883–4414.
   Secondary Market Oversight.—Andrew Jacob, 883–4280.
General Counsel.—Charles R. Rawls, 883–4020.
Inspector General.—Stephen Smith, 883–4030.
Chief Examiner and Director, Office of Examination.—Thomas G. McKenzie, 883–4160.
Manager, Equal Employment Opportunity.—Eric Howard, 883–4144.

FEDERAL COMMUNICATIONS COMMISSION
445 12th Street SW, Washington, DC 20554, phone (202) 418–0200, http://www.fcc.gov

Chairman.—Kevin J. Martin, room 8–B201, 418–1000.
   Confidential Assistant.—Lori Alexiou.
   Senior Legal Advisor.—Daniel Gonzalez.
   Legal Advisors: Catherine Bohigian, Samuel Feder.
Commissioner.—Jonathan S. Adelstien, room 8–C302, 418–2300.
   Confidential Assistant.—Geraldine Taylor.
   Senior Legal Advisor.—Barry Ohlson.
   Legal Advisor.—Scott Bergman.
Commissioner.—Kathleen Q. Abernathy, room 8–B115, 418–2400.
   Confidential Assistant.—Elizabeth (Ann) Monahan.
   Senior Legal Advisor.—Matthew Brill.
   Legal Advisors: Jennifer Manner, Stacey Robinson.
Commissioner.—Michael Copps, room 8–A302, 418–2000.
   Confidential Assistant.—Carolyn Conyers.
   Senior Legal Advisor.—Jordan Goldstein.
   Legal Advisors: Paul Margie, Jessica Rosenworcel.
FCC National Consumer Center, 1–888–225–5322; 1–888–835–5322 (TTY).

OFFICE OF STRATEGIC PLANNING AND POLICY ANALYSIS

Chief.—Linda Blair (acting), room 7–C452, 418–2030.
Chief of Staff.—Maureen C. McLaughlin.

OFFICE OF MEDIA RELATIONS

Director.—David H. Fiske, room CY–C314, 418–0500.

OFFICE OF LEGISLATIVE AFFAIRS

Director.—Anthony Dale (acting), room 8–C432, 418–1900.

OFFICE OF COMMUNICATIONS BUSINESS OPPORTUNITIES

Director.—Carolyn Fleming Williams, room 7–C204, 418–0990.

OFFICE OF ADMINISTRATIVE LAW JUDGES

Administrative Law Judges: Richard L. Sippel, room 1–C768, 418–2280; Arthur I. Steinberg, room 1–C861, 418–2255.

OFFICE OF GENERAL COUNSEL

General Counsel.—Austin Schlick (acting), room 8–C723, 418–1700.
Deputy General Counsel.—P. Michele Ellison.
Associate General Counsel.—Linda Kinney.

OFFICE OF INSPECTOR GENERAL

Inspector General.—H. Walker Feaster, room 2–C762, 418–0470.
Assistant Inspector General for Audits.—Thomas D. Bennett.

OFFICE OF MANAGING DIRECTOR

Managing Director.—Andrew S. Fishel, room 1–C144, 418–1919.
Deputy Managing Directors: Renee Licht, William Spencer.
Secretary.—Marlene Dortch, room TW–B204, 418–0300.
Deputy Secretary.—William F. Caton.
Associate Managing Director for Human Resources Management.—Kent Baum, room 1–A100, 418–0137; 418–0126 (TTY); 418–0150 (Employment Verification).
Deputy Director.—Carol Nichols, room 1–A130, 418–0134.
Senior Policy Advisor.—Thomas Green, room 1–A161, 418–0116.

OFFICE OF ENGINEERING AND TECHNOLOGY

Chief.—Ed Thomas, room 7–C155, 418–2470.
Deputy Chiefs: Bruce A. Franca, Julius P. Knapp.

OFFICE OF WORKPLACE DIVERSITY

Director.—Barbara J. Douglas, room 5–C750, 418–1799.
Deputy Director.—Harvey Lee, room 5–C751.

MEDIA BUREAU

Chief.—Debra Klein, room 3–C740, 418–7200.
Deputy Bureau Chiefs: William H. Johnson, room 3–C742; Robert H. Ratcliffe, room 3–C486.

Audio Services Division, 418–2700
   Chief.—Peter H. Doyle, room 2–A360.
   Deputy Chief.—Nina Shafran, room 2–A267.
Video Services Division, 418–1600.
   Chief.—Barbara A. Kreisman, room 2–A666.
   Deputy Chief.—James J. Brown, room 2–A663.

WIRELINE COMPETITION BUREAU

Senior Deputy Chiefs: Michelle Carey, room 5–C356; Lisa Gelb, room 5–C451, 418–1500.
Associate Bureau Chief.—Jane Jackson, room 5–C354, 418–1500.

ENFORCEMENT BUREAU

Deputy Bureau Chiefs: Linda Blair, Anne L. Weismann, room 7–C751, 418–7450.
   Investigations and Hearing Division, 418–1420.
      Chief.—Maureen F. Del Duca, room 3–B431.
   Market Disputes Resolution Division, 418–7330.
      Chief.—Alex Starr, room 5–848, 418–7248.
         Deputy Chiefs: Lisa Griffin, room 5–C828, 418–7273; Radhika Karmarkar, room
         5–A847, 418–1628.
   Technical and Public Safety Division, 418–1160.
      Chief.—Joseph P. Casey, room 7–A843, 418–1111.
         Deputy Chiefs: Ricardo M. Durham, room 7–A744, 418–1160; James Dailey, room
         7–C831, 418–1113.
   Telecommunications Consumer Division, 418–7320.
      Chief.—Colleen Heitkamp, room 3–C365, 418–0974.
      Deputy Chief.—Kurt Schroeder, room 3–C366, 418–0966.
   North East Region: Chicago, IL
      Director.—Russell (Joe) D. Monie (847) 376–2984.
      Deputy Director.—Barry A. Bohoe.
   South Central Region: Kansas City, MO
      Director.—Dennis (Denny) P. Carlton (816) 316–1243.
   Western Region: San Diego, CA
      Director.—Rebecca L. Dorch (925) 416–9661.

INTERNATIONAL BUREAU

Chief.—Donald Abelson, room 6–C750, 418–0437.
   Deputy Chiefs: Anna Gomez, room 6–C475, 418–0438; Roderick K. Porter, room 6–C752.
   Satellite Division:
      Chief.—Thomas S. Tycz, room 6–A665, 418–0719.
      Deputy Chiefs: Fern Jarmulnek, room 6–A760; Cassandra Thomas, room 6–A666.

WIRELESS TELECOMMUNICATIONS BUREAU

Chief.—John B. Muleta, room 3–C252, 418–0600.
   Deputy Bureau Chiefs: James D. Schlichting, room 3–C254; Gerald P. Vaughan, room
   3–C250, 418–0600.
   Commercial Wireless Division:
      Chief.—William Kunze, room 4–C224, 418–7887.
         Deputy Chiefs: Kathy Harris, room 4–C236, 418–0609; Roger Noel, room 4–B115,
         418–0698; Jeffrey Steinberg, room 4–C222, 418–0896.
   Public Safety & Private Wireless Division:
      Chief.—D'Wana Terry, room 4–C321, 418–0680.
         Deputy Chiefs: Jeanne Kowalski (Public Safety), room 4–C324, 418–0680; Ramona
         Melson (Legal), room 4–C322, 418–0680; Herbert W. Zeiler (Technical), room
         4–C343, 418–0686.

CONSUMER AND GOVERNMENTAL AFFAIRS BUREAU

Chief.—Jay Keithley (acting), room 5–C758, 418–1400.
   Deputy Chief.—Kris Monteith, room 5–C755.

Consumer Inquiries and Complaints Division:
 Chief.—Thomas D. Wyatt, room 5–A844.
  Deputy Chief.—Sharon Bowers (Gettysburg) (717) 338–2531.
 Reference Information Center Director.—Bill Cline, room CY–B533, 418–0267.
Consumer Affairs and Outreach Division:
 Chief.—Martha Contee, room CY–B523, 418–2513.
  Deputy Chief.—Irshad Abdal-Haqq, room 6–C466, 418–1444.

FIELD OFFICES

Atlanta: Director.—Fred L. Broce, Koger Center, 3575 Koger Boulevard, Ste. 320, Duluth, GA 30096 (707) 935–3373.

Boston: Director.—Dennis Loria, One Batterymarch Park, Quincy, MA 02169 (617) 786–7746.

Chicago: Director.—George M. Moffitt, Park Ridge Office Center, Room 306, 1550 Northwest Highway, Park Ridge, IL 60068 (847) 813–4661.

Columbia: Director.—Charles C. Magin, 9300 East Hampton Drive, Capitol Heights, MD 20743 (301) 725–1996.

Dallas: Director.—James D. Wells, 9330 LBJ Freeway, Room 1170, Dallas, TX 75243 (214) 575–6361.

Denver: Director.—Rebecca Dorch, 215 S. Wadsworth Blvd., Suite 303, Lakewood, CO 80226 (303) 407–8708.

Detroit: Director.—James A. Bridgewater, 24897 Hathaway Street, Farmington Hills, MI 48335 (248) 471–5661.

Kansas City: Director.—Robert C. McKinney, 520 NE Colbern Road, Second Floor, Lee's Summit, MO 64086 (816) 316–1248.

Los Angeles: Director.—Catherine Deaton, Cerritos Corporate Towers, 18000 Studebaker Road, Room 660, Cerritos, CA 90701 (562) 860–7474.

New Orleans: Director.—James C. Hawkins, 2424 Edenborn Avenue, Room 460, Metarie, LA 70001 (504) 589–4966.

New York: Director.—Dan Noel, 201 Varick Street, Room 1151, New York, NY 10014 (212) 337–1865.

Philadelphia: Director.—John Rahtes, One Oxford Valley Office Building, Room 404, 2300 East Lincoln Highway, Langhorne, PA 19047 (215) 752–8549.

San Diego: Director.—Bill Zears, Interstate Office Park, 4542 Ruffner Street, Room 370, San Diego, CA 92111 (858) 496–5111.

San Francisco: Director.—Thomas N. Van Stavern, 5653 Stoneridge Drive, Suite 105, Pleasanton, CA 94588 (925) 416–9717.

Seattle: Director.—Kris McGowan, 11410 Northeast 122nd Way, Room 312, Kirkland, WA 98034 (425) 820–6271.

Tampa: Director.—Ralph M. Barlow, 2203 North Lois Avenue, Room 1215, Tampa, FL 33607 (813) 348–1741.

FEDERAL DEPOSIT INSURANCE CORPORATION
550 17th Street NW., 20429
phone (202) 736–0000, http://www.fdic.gov

Chairman.—Donald E. Powell.
 Deputy to the Chairman and Chief Operating Officer.—John F. Bovenzi, 898–6949.
Vice Chairman.—John Reich, 898–3888.
 Deputy.—Robert W. Russell, 898–8952.
Director.—Thomas J. Curry.
 Special Assistant to the Director.—John Vogel.
Director.—Julie Williams (acting), 874–4900.
 Deputy.—Tom Zemke, 898–6960.
Director.—James E. Gilleran, 906–6280.
 Deputy.—Walter B. Mason, Jr., 898–6965.
Director, Office of Legislative Affairs.—Alice C. Goodman, 898–7055, fax 898–3745/7062.

FEDERAL ELECTION COMMISSION

999 E Street, NW., 20463

phone (202) 694–1000, Toll Free (800) 424–9530, fax 219–3880, http://www.fec.gov

Chairman.—Scott E. Thomas, 694–1055.
  Vice Chairman.—Michael Toner, 694–1045.
  Commissioners:
    Danny Lee McDonald, 694–1020.
    Bradley Mason, 694–1050
    Bradley A. Smith, 694–1011.
    Ellen L. Weintraub, 694–1035.
  Inspector General.—Lynne A. McFarland, 694–1015.
  Staff Director.—James A. Pehrkon, 694–1007, fax 219–2338.
    Deputy Staff Director for—
      Audit and Review.—Robert J. Costa, 694–1200.
      Information Technology.—Alec Palmer, 694–1250.
      Management.—John C. O'Brien (acting), 694–1215.
    Assistant Staff Director for—
      Audit.—Joe Stoltz, 694–1200.
      Disclosure.—Patricia K. Young, 694–1120.
      Information Services.—Greg Scott, 694–1100.
      Reports Analysis.—John D. Gibson, 694–1130.
  Director for—
    Congressional Affairs.—Tina VanBrakle, 694–1006.
    Personnel and Labor Management Relation.—Scotty McBride (acting), 694–1080.
    Planning and Management.—John C. O'Brien, 694–1216.
  General Counsel.—Lawrence H. Norton, 694–1650.
    Deputy General Counsel.—James A. Kahl.
    Associate General Counsel for—
      Enforcement.—Rhonda Vosdingh.
      General Law and Advice.—Thomasenia P. Duncan.
      Litigation.—Richard B. Bader.
      Policy.—Rosemary Smith.
  Administrative Officer.—Sylvia E. Butler, 694–1240.
  Accounting Officer.—Brian Duffy, 694–1230.
  EEO Director.—Kevin Salley (acting), 694–1100.
  Library Director (Law).—Leta L. Holley, 694–1600.
  Press Officer.—Bob Biersack, 694–1220.

FEDERAL HOUSING FINANCE BOARD

1777 F Street NW 20006, phone 408–2500, fax 408–1435

[Created by the Financial Institutions Reform, Recovery, and Enforcement Act of

August 9, 1989, 103 Stat. 354, 415]

Chairman.—Ronald A. Rosenfeld, 408–2838.
  Board of Directors:
    John C. Weicher,* 708–3600.
    Franz S. Leichter, 408–2986.
    Allan I. Mendelowitz, 408–2587.
    Alicia Castaneda, 408–2542.
  Inspector General.—Edward Kelley, 408–2570.
  General Counsel.—Mark Tenhundfeld, 408–2536.
  Director of Resource Management.—Judith L. Hofmann, 408–2586.
  Director of Supervision.—Stephen M. Cross, 408–2980.

---

*The Secretary of Housing and Urban Development is one of the five Directors of the Federal Housing Finance Board. Secretary Jackson has designated John C. Weicher, the Assistant Secretary for Housing/Federal Housing Commissioner, to act for him on the Board of Directors of the Federal Housing Finance Board.

Independent Agencies

775

FEDERAL LABOR RELATIONS AUTHORITY
1400 K Street, NW., 20424–0001, phone (202) 218–7000, fax 482–6659

Chair.—Dale Cabaniss, 218–7900.
   Chief of Staff.—Jill Crumpacker, 218–7945.
   Chief Counsel.—Kirk Underwood.
   Director, Case Control.—Gail Reinhart, 218–7776.
Members:
   Carol Waller Pope, 218–7920.
     Chief Counsel.—Susan D. McCluskey.
   Tony Armendariz, 218–7930.
     Chief Counsel.—Steven H. Svartz.
Assistant General Counsel for Appeals.—Richard Zorn.
Chief Administrative Law Judge.—Eli Nash, 218–7918.
Executive Director.—David M. Smith (acting), 218–7907.
Solicitor.—David M. Smith, 218–7907.
Inspector General.—Francine Eichler, 218–7744.
Collaboration and Alternative Dispute Resolution Program.—Andy Pizzi, 218–7933.
Federal Service Impasses Panel.—Becky Norton Dunlop, 218–7746.
   Special Assistant to the Chairman.—Victoria Dutcher, 218–7746.
   Executive Director.—H. Joseph Schimansky, 218–7991.
Foreign Service Impasse Disputes Panel.—Peter Tredick, 218–7746.
Foreign Service Labor Relations Board.—Dale Cabaniss, 218–7900.

REGIONAL OFFICES

Regional Directors:
   Atlanta: Nancy A. Speight, Marquis Two Tower, Suite 701, 285 Peachtree Center Avenue, Atlanta, GA 30303 (404) 331–5212, fax (404) 331–5280.
   Boston: Richard D. Zaiger, 10 Causeway Street, Suite 472, Boston, MA 02222 (617) 424–5731, fax 424–5743.
   Chicago: Peter Sutton (acting), Suite 1150, 55 West Monroe, Chicago, IL 60603 (312) 886–3485, fax 886–5977.
   Dallas: James E. Petrucci, Suite 926, LB 107, 525 Griffin Street, Dallas, TX 75202 (214) 767–4996, fax 767–0156.
   Denver: Matthew Jarvinen (acting), Suite 100, 1244 Speer Boulevard, Denver, CO 80204 (303) 844–5226, fax 844–2774.
   San Francisco: Gerald M. Cole, Suite 220, 901 Market Street, San Francisco, CA 94103 (415) 356–5002, fax 356–5017.
   Washington, DC: Robert Hunter, 1400 K Street, NW., Suite 200, Washington, DC 20005 (202) 482–6700, fax (202) 482–6724.

FEDERAL MARITIME COMMISSION
800 North Capitol Street NW., 20573, phone (202) 523–5725, fax 523–0014

OFFICE OF THE CHAIRMAN

Chairman.—Steven R. Blust, room 1000, 523–5911.
   Counsel—Cory R. Cinque.
Commissioner.—Harold J. Creel, Jr., room 1044, 523–5712.
   Counsel.—David R. Miles.
Commissioner.—Joseph E. Brennan, room 1032, 523–5723.
   Counsel.—Steven D. Najarian.
Commissioner.—Rebecca F. Dye, room 1038, 523–5715.
   Counsel.—Edward L. Lee, Jr.
Commissioner.—A. Paul Anderson, room 1026, 523–5721.
   Special Assistant.—Lucille A. Streeter.

OFFICE OF THE SECRETARY

Secretary.—Bryant L. VanBrakle, room 1046, 523–5725.
   Assistant Secretary.—Karen V. Gregory.
Librarian.—Charlotte C. White, room 1085, 523–5762.

Director, Office of Consumer Affairs and Dispute Resolution.—Ronald D. Murphy, room 972, 523–5807.

OFFICE OF THE GENERAL COUNSEL

General Counsel.—Amy W. Larson, room 1018, 523–5740.
Deputy General Counsel.—Christopher Hughey.

OFFICE OF ADMINISTRATIVE LAW JUDGES

Chief Judge.—Norman D. Kline, room 1089, 523–5750.

OFFICE OF THE INSPECTOR GENERAL

Inspector General.—Tony P. Kominoth, room 1054, 523–5863.

OFFICE OF ADMINISTRATION

Director.—Bruce A. Dombrowski, room 1082, 523–5800.
Deputy Director/CIO.—Derek O. Scarbrough.
Director of:
  Budget and Financial Management.—Karon E. Douglass, room 916, 523–5770.
  Human Resources.—Hatsie H. Charbonneau, room 924, 523–5773.
  Information Technology.—Stephanie Y. Burwell, room 904, 523–5835.
  Management Services.—Michael H. Kilby, room 924, 523–5900.

OFFICE OF OPERATIONS

Director.—Austin L. Schmitt, room 1078, 523–0988.
Deputy Director.—Rachel E. Dickon.
Area Representatives:
  Los Angeles.—Oliver E. Clark (310) 514–4905.
  New Orleans.—Alvin N. Kellogg (504) 589–6662.
  New York.—Emanuel J. Mingione (718) 553–2228.
  Seattle.—Michael A. Moneck (206) 553–0221.
  South Florida.—Andrew Margolis (954) 963–5362; Eric O. Mintz (954) 963–5284.
Director of Certification and Licensing.—Sandra L. Kusumoto, room 970, 523–5787.
  Deputy Director.—Peter J. King.
Director of:
  Passenger Vessels and Information Processing.—Anne E. Trotter, room 970, 523–5818.
  Transportation Intermediaries.—Ralph W. Freibert, room 970, 523–5843.
Director of Enforcement.—Vern W. Hill, room 900, 523–5783.
  Deputy Director.—George A. Quadrino.
Director of Trade Analysis.—Florence A. Carr, room 940, 523–5796.
  Deputy Director.—Frank J. Schwarz.
Director of:
  Agreements.—Jeremiah D. Hospital, room 940, 523–5793.
  Service Contracts and Tariffs.—Mamie H. Black, room 940, 523–5856.

BUREAU OF CONSUMER COMPLAINTS AND LICENSING

Director.—Sandra L. Kusumoto, room 970, 523–5787.
Deputy Director.—Ronald D. Murphy.
Director of:
  Consumer Complaints.—Joseph T. Farrell, 523–5807.
  Passenger Vessels and Information Processing.—Anne E. Trotter, 523–5818.
  Transportation Intermediaries.—Ralph W. Freibert, 523–5843.

BUREAU OF ENFORCEMENT

Director.—Vern W. Hill, room 900, 523–5783 or 523–5860.
Deputy Director.—Peter J. King.

AREA REPRESENTATIVES

Los Angeles.—Oliver E. Clark (310) 514–4905.
Miami.—Andrew Margolis (305) 536–4316, Eric O. Mintz (305) 536–5529.
New Orleans.—Alvin N. Kellogg (504) 589–6662.
New York.—Emanuel J. Mingione (212) 637–2929.
Seattle.—Michael A. Moneck (206) 553–0221.

FEDERAL MEDIATION AND CONCILIATION SERVICE

2100 K Street NW., Washington, DC 20427, phone (202) 606–8100, fax 606–4251

[Codified under 29 U.S.C. 172]

Director.—Scot L. Beckenbaugh (acting).
Deputy Director.—C. Richard Barnes.
Chief of Staff.—John Toner.
General Counsel.—Arthur Pearlstein, 606–5444.
Director for—
  Arbitration Services.—Vella M. Traynham, 606–5111.
  Budget and Finance.—Fran L. Leonard, 606–3661.
  FMCS Institute.—Gary R. Hattal (206) 553–2282.
  Grants.—Jane A. Lorber, 606–8181.
  Human Resources.—Dan Ellerman, 606–5460.
  Information Systems and Administrative Services.—Dan W. Funkhouser, 606–5477.
  Regional Director.—John F. Buettner (216) 522–4800.

FEDERAL MINE SAFETY AND HEALTH REVIEW COMMISSION

601 New Jersey Avenue, NW., Suite 9500, Washington, DC 20001

phone (202) 434–9900, fax 434–9944

[Created by Public Law 95–164]

Chairperson.—Michael F. Duffy, room 9515, 434–9924.
  Commissioners: Mary Lu Jordan, room 9527, 434–9926; Stanley C. Suboleski, room 9531, 434–9921; Michael Young, room 9517, 434–9914.
Executive Director.—Richard L. Baker, room 9507, 434–9905.
Chief Administrative Law Judge.—Robert J. Lesnick, room 8515, 434–9958.
General Counsel.—Thomas Stock, room 9547, 434–9935.

FEDERAL RETIREMENT THRIFT INVESTMENT BOARD

1250 H Street NW 20005, phone (202) 942–1600, fax 942–1676

[Authorized by 5 U.S.C. 8472]

Executive Director.—Gary A. Amelio, 942–1601.
General Counsel.—Elizabeth S. Woodruff, 942–1660.
Director, Office of:
  Accounting.—David L. Black, 942–1610.
  Administration.—Susan Smith (acting), 942–1670.
  Automated Systems.—Lawrence Stiffler, 942–1440.
  External Affairs.—Thomas J. Trabucco, 942–1640.
  Investments.—James B. Petrick, 942–1630.
  Participant Services.—Pamela J. Moran, 942–1450.

Chairman.—Andrew M. Saul, 942–1660.
Board Members:
  Thomas A. Fink.
  Alejandro M. Sanchez.
  Gordon J. Whiting.
  Terrence A. Duffy.

FEDERAL TRADE COMMISSION

600 Pennsylvania Avenue NW., 20580, phone 326–2222, http://www.ftc.gov

Chairman.—Deborah Platt Majoras, room 440, 326–2100.
  Executive Assistant.—Martha Schoenborn, room 442, 326–2673.
  Chief of Staff.—Maryanne Kane, room 444, 326–2450.
  Commissioners: Pamela Jones Harbour, room 328, 326–2907; Thomas B. Leary, room 528, 326–2142; Jonathan Leibowitz, room 340, 326–3400; Orson Swindle, room 540, 326–2150.
  Director, Office of:
    Competition.—Susan A. Creighton, room 374, 326–2946.
    Congressional Relations.—Anna Holmquist Davis, room 404, 326–3680.
    Consumer Protection.—Lydia Parnes (acting), room 472, 326–2676.
    Economics.—Luke Froeb, room 268, 326–2827.
    Policy Planning.—Maureen Ohlhausen (acting), room 492, 326–2632.
    Public Affairs.—Nancy Ness Judy, room 423, 326–2180.
  Executive Director.—Judy Bailey (acting), room 426, 326–3609.
  General Counsel.—John D. Graubert (acting), room 570, 326–2186.
  Secretary.—Donald S. Clark, room 172, 326–2514.
  Inspector General.—Adam Trzeciak (acting), room 1117NJ, 326–2435.
  Chief Administrative Law Judge.—Stephen J. McGuire, room 112, 326–3637.

REGIONAL DIRECTORS

East Central Region: John Mendenhall, Eaton Center, Suite 200, 1111 Superior Avenue, Cleveland, OH 44114 (216) 263–3455.
Midwest Region: C. Steve Baker, 55 East Monroe Street, Suite 1860, Chicago, IL 60603 (312) 960–5634.
Northeast Region: Barbara Anthony, One Bowling Green, Suite 318, New York, NY 10004 (212) 607–2829.
Northwest Region: Charles A. Harwood, 915 Second Avenue, Suite 2896, Seattle, WA 98174 (206) 220–6350.
Southeast Region: Andrea Foster, 60 Forsyth Street, Midrise Building, Suite 5M35, Atlanta, GA 30303 (404) 656–1390.
Southwest Region: Bradley Elbein, 1999 Bryan Street, Suite 2150, Dallas, TX 75201 (214) 979–9350.
Western Region—Los Angeles: Jeffrey Klurfeld, 18077 Wilshire Boulevard, Suite 700, Los Angeles, CA 90024–3679 (310) 824–4320.
Western Region—San Francisco: Jeffrey Klurfeld, 901 Market Street, Suite 570, San Francisco, CA 94103 (415) 848–5100.

FOREIGN–TRADE ZONES BOARD

1099 14th Street, NW., Franklin Court Building, Suite 4100W, Washington, DC 20005 phone (202) 482–2862, fax 482–0002

Chairman.—Carlos Gutierrez, Secretary of Commerce.
Member.—John W. Snow, Secretary of the Treasury.
Executive Secretary.—Dennis Puccinelli.

GENERAL SERVICES ADMINISTRATION

1800 F Street NW 20405, phone (202) 501–0800, http://www.gsa.gov

Administrator.—Stephen A. Perry, 501–0800.
  Deputy Administrator.—David L. Bibb, 501–1226.
    Chief of Staff.—Ed Fielder (acting), 501–1216.
  Associate Administrator, Office of Small Business Utilization.—Felipe Mendoza (acting), 501–1021.
  Associate Administrator, Office of Civil Rights.—Madeline Caliendo, 501–0767.
    Deputy Associate Administrator.—Regina Budd.
  Associate Administrator, Office of Congressional and Intergovernmental Affairs.—Clinton Robinson, 501–0563.
    Deputy Associate Administrator.—Thomas Dryer.

Associate Administrator, Office of Citizen Services and Communications.—M.J. Jameson, 501–0705.
Deputy Associate Administrator.—David Bethel.
Inspector General.—Daniel R. Levinson, 501–0450.
Deputy Inspector General.—Joel S. Gallay, 501–1362.
Counsel to the Inspector General.—Kathleen S. Tighe, 501–1932.
Assistant Inspector General for Auditing.—Eugene L. Waszily, 501–0374.
Deputy Assistant Inspector General for Auditing.—Andrew Patchan, Jr., 501–0374.
Assistant Inspector General for Investigations.—James E. Henderson, 501–1397.
Deputy Assistant Inspector General for Investigations.—Charles J. Augone, 501–1397.
Deputy Counsel.—Virginia S. Grebasch, 501–1932.
Assistant Inspector General for Administration.—John C. Lebo, Jr. (acting), 501–2319.
Chairman, Board of Contract Appeals.—Stephen M. Daniels, 501–0585.
Vice Chairman.—Robert W. Parker, 501–0890.
Chief Counsel.—Margaret S. Pfunder, 501–0272.
Clerk.—Beatrice Jones, 501–0116.
Board Judges:
Anthony S. Borwick, 501–1852.
Stephen M. Daniels, 501–0585.
Martha H. DeGraff, 208–7922.
Allan H. Goodman, 501–0352.
Catherine B. Hyatt, 501–4594.
Edwin B. Neill, 501–0435.
Robert W. Parker, 501–0890.
Chief People Officer.—Gail T. Lovelace, 501–0398.
Deputy Chief People Officer/Director of Information Management.—June V. Huber, 501–0796.
Director of Human Resources Policy.—William A. Kelly, 501–0885.
General Counsel.—George Barclay (acting), 501–2200.
Associate General Counsel for—
General Law.—Eugenia D. Ellison, 501–1460.
Personal Property.—George N. Barclay, 501–1156.
Real Property.—Samuel J. Morris III, 501–0430.
Chief Financial Officer (B).—Kathleen M. Turco, 501–1721.
Director of:
Budget (BB).—Deborah Schilling, 501–0719.
Finance (BC).—Douglas Glenn, 501–0562.
Financial Management Systems (BD).—Christopher Smith, 208–6968.
Controller (BE).—Ellen Warren, 501–0562.
Chief Information Officer.—Michael Carleton, 501–1000.
Director of Internetworking.—Eugene McNerney, 501–2812.
Chief Technology Officer.—Christopher Fornicker, 219–3393.
Associate Administrator, Office of Governmentwide Policy (M).—G. Martin Wagner, 501–8880.
Deputy Associate Administrator (M).—John G. Sindelar, 501–8880.
Executive Officer, Office of Governmentwide Policy (M).—Nancy Wong, 501–8880.
Deputy Associate Administrator for—
Acquisition Policy (MV).—David A. Drabkin, 501–1043.
Electronic Government and Technology (ME).—Mary J. Mitchell, 501–0202.
Real Property (MP).—Ed Felder (acting), 501–0856.
Transportation and Personal Property (MT).—Rebecca R. Rhodes, 501–1777.
Chief Information Officer for Governmentwide Policy (MJ).—Jack Finley, 501–1500.
Executive Director, Regulatory Information Service Center (MI).—Ronald C. Kelly, 482–7340.
Director, Committee Management Secretariat (MC).—James L. Dean, 273–3563.
Commissioner, Public Buildings Service.—F. Joseph Moravec, 501–1100.
Deputy Commissioner.—Anthony Costa, 501–1100.
Chief of Staff.—Mary Mitschow, 501–1100.
Chief Financial Officer.—William Brady, 501–0658.
Chief Information Officer.—Diane Herdt (acting), 501–9100.
Assistant Commissioner for—
Organizational Resources.—Kay McNew, 501–0971.
Portfolio Management.—William H. Matthews, 501–0658.
Property Disposal.—Brian K. Polly, 501–0084.
Chief Architect.—Leslie Shepherd (acting), 501–1888.
Director, Energy Center of Expertise.—Mark Ewing, 708–9296.

Commissioner, Federal Technology Service.—Barbara L. Shelton (acting) (703) 306–6020.
Deputy Commissioner.—James A. Williams (703) 306–6046.
Chief Financial Officer.—Robin Short (acting) (703) 306–6369.
Assistant Commissioner for—
　Acquisition.—T. Keith Sandridge (acting) (703) 306–7800.
　Chief Information Officer.—Casey Coleman (703) 306–6150.
　Information Technology Solutions.—Robert E. Suda (703) 306–6101.
　Regional Services.—Margaret C. Binns (703) 306–6508.
　Sales.—Mary Davie (703) 306–6031.
　Service Delivery.—John C. Johnson (acting) (703) 306–6200.
　Service Development.—John C. Johnson (703) 306–6007.
Commissioner, Federal Supply Service.—Donna D. Bennett (703) 605–5400.
Deputy Commissioner.—Lester D. Gray (703) 605–5400.
Chief of Staff.—Amanda G. Fredriksen (703) 605–5400.
Assistant Commissioner, Office of:
　Acquisition Management.—Roger Waldron (acting) (703) 605–1888.
　Business Management and Marketing.—Gary Feit (703) 605–5640.
　Commercial Acquisition.—Neal Fox (703) 305–7901.
　Controller.—Jon A. Jordan (703) 605–5505.
　Enterprise Planning.—John R. Roehmer (703) 605–5480.
　Global Supply.—Joseph Jeu (703) 605–5515.
　Information Chief Officer.—Elizabeth Delnegro (acting) (703) 305–5670.
　Vehicle Acquisition and Leasing.—Barnaby Brasseux (703) 605–5500.

REGIONAL OFFICES

National Capital Region: 7th and D Streets SW, Washington, DC 20407 (202) 708–9100.
Regional Administrator.—Donald C. Williams, 708–9100.
　Deputy Administrator.—Ann Everett, 708–9100.
　Assistant Regional Administrator for—
　　Federal Technology Service.—Craig F. Kennedy, 708–6100.
　　Public Buildings Service.—Linda Garvin, 708–5891.
　Regional Counsel.—Sharon A. Roach, 708–5155.
New England Region: Thomas P. O'Neill Federal Building, 10 Causeway Street, Boston, MA 02222 (617) 565–5860.
Regional Administrator.—Dennis R. Smith, 565–5860.
　Assistant Regional Administrator for—
　　Federal Technology Service.—Sharon Wall, 565–5760.
　　Public Buildings Service.—Glenn Rotundo (acting), 565–5694.
Northeast and Caribbean Region: 26 Federal Plaza, New York, NY 10278 (212) 264–2600.
Regional Administrator.—Eileen Long-Chelales, 264–2600.
　Deputy Regional Administrator.—Steve Ruggiero, 264–2600.
　Assistant Regional Administrator for—
　　Federal Supply Service.—Charles Weill, 264–3590.
　　Federal Technology Service.—Kerry Blette, 264–1257.
　　Public Buildings Service.—John Scorcia (acting), 264–4282.
Mid-Atlantic Region: The Strawbridge's Building, 20 N. Eighth Street, Philadelphia, PA 19107 (215) 446–5100.
Regional Administrator.—John Kvistad (acting), 446–4900.
　Deputy Regional Administrator.—Linda C. Chero, 446–4900.
　Assistant Regional Administrator for—
　　Federal Supply Service.—Jack R. Williams, 446–5000.
　　Federal Technology Service.—Paul J. McDermott, 446–5800.
　　Public Buildings Service.—Celeste Martins (acting), 446–4500.
　Regional Counsel.—Robert J. McCall, 446–4946.
Southeast Sunbelt Region: 77 Forsyth Street, Suite 600, Atlanta, GA 30303 (404) 331–3200.
Regional Administrator.—Jimmy H. Bridgeman (acting), 331–3200.
　Deputy Regional Administrator.—Jimmy H. Bridgeman, 331–3200.
　Assistant Regional Administrator for—
　　Federal Supply Service.—William (Bill) Sisk, 331–5114.
　　Federal Technology Service.—Randall Witty, 331–5104.
　　Public Buildings Service.—Thomas Walker, 562–0262.
Great Lakes Region: 230 South Dearborn Street, Chicago, IL 60604 (312) 353–5395.
Regional Administrator.—James C. Handley, 353–5395.
　Deputy Regional Administrator.—Michael Gelber, 353–5395.

Assistant Regional Administrator for—
  Federal Supply Service.—Michael Gelber, 353–5504.
  Federal Technology Service.—Frank Hoeft, 886–3824.
  Public Buildings Service.—J. David Hood, 353–5572.
Heartland Region: 1500 East Bannister Road, Kansas City, MO 64131 (816) **926–7201**.
Regional Administrator.—Brad Scott, 926–7201.
Deputy Regional Administrator.—James Ogden, 926–7217.
Assistant Regional Administrator for—
  Federal Supply Service.—Steve Triplett, 926–7245.
  Federal Technology Service.—Jimmy Parker, 926–5192.
  Public Buildings Service.—Mary Ruwwe, 926–7231.
Staff Support Service Directors:
  Human Resources.—Nick Cave (816) 926–7401.
  Regional Counsel.—Samm Skare (816) 926–7212.
  Regional EEO Office.—Pinkie Mason (816) 926–7349.
  Finance Center.—Ed Nasalik (816) 926–7625.
Office of Inspector General:
  Audits.—Larry Elkin (816) 926–7052.
  Investigations.—John Kolze (816) 926–7214.
Greater Southwest Region: 819 Taylor Street, Fort Worth, TX 76102 (817) **978–2321**.
Regional Administrator.—Scott Armey, 978–2321.
Assistant Regional Administrator for—
  Federal Supply Service.—Tyree Varnado, 978–2516.
  Federal Technology Service.—Marcella F. Banks, 978–2871.
  Public Buildings Service.—Jim Weller, 978–2522.
Rocky Mountain Region: Building 41, Denver Federal Center, Denver, CO 80225 (303) 236–7329.
Regional Administrator.—Larry Trujillo, 236–7329.
Deputy Regional Administrator.—Benjamin F. Gonzales, 236–7329.
Assistant Regional Administrator for—
  Federal Supply Service.—Tyree Varnado, 236–7547.
  Federal Technology Service.—Benjamin F. Gonzales (acting), 236–7319.
  Public Buildings Service.—Paul F. Prouty, 236–7245.
Pacific Rim Region: 450 Golden Gate Avenue, room 5–2690, San Francisco, CA 94102 (415) 522–3001.
Regional Administrator.—Peter G. Stamison, 522–3001.
Deputy Regional Administrator.—Peter T. Glading, 522–3001.
Public Information Officer.—Bethany Rich, 522–3001.
Administrative Officer.—Kathryne McInturff, 522–3001.
Assistant Regional Administrator for—
  Federal Supply Service.—John Boyan, 522–2777.
  Federal Technology Service.—Maria Jamini-Rameriz, 522–4500.
  Public Buildings Service.—Jeffrey Neely, 522–3001.
Northwest/Arctic Region: GSA Center, 400 15th Street SW, Auburn, WA 98001 (253) 931–7000.
Regional Administrator.—Robin G. Graf (acting), 931–7000.
Deputy Regional Administrator.—Bill DuBray, 931–7000.
Assistant Regional Administrator for—
  Federal Supply Service.—Gary G. Casteel, 931–7115.
  Federal Technology Service.—Gary G. Casteel (acting), 931–7115.
  Public Buildings Service.—Carole Diamond (acting), 931–7200.

HARRY S. TRUMAN SCHOLARSHIP FOUNDATION

712 Jackson Place NW., 20006, phone (202) 395–4831, fax 395–6995

[Created by Public Law 93–642]

BOARD OF TRUSTEES

President.—Madeleine K. Albright.
  Chairman Emeritus.—Elmer B. Staats.
  Vice Chairman.—Ike Skelton, Representative from Missouri.
  Vice President.—Max Sherman.
  General Counsel.—C. Westbrook Murphy.
  Treasurer.—Frederick G. Slabach, Dean, Texas Wesleyan University School of Law.

Members:
    Margaret Spellings, Secretary of Education.
    Christopher S. Bond, Senator from Missouri.
    Max Baucus, Senator from Montana.
    Todd Akin, Representative from Missouri.
    Scott O. Wright, U.S. District Judge, Western District of Missouri.
    Juanita Vasquez-Gardner, Judge, 399th District Court of Texas.
    Patrick Lloyd McCrory, Mayor, City of Charlotte, North Carolina.
    Sharon (Nyota) Tucker, Assistant Professor, Albany State University.
    Executive Secretary.—Louis H. Blair.
    Associate Executive Secretary.—Tara Kneller.
    Program Officers: Christina Kleinbeck, Tonji Wade.
    Administrative Officer.—Ruth Keen.
    Financial Desk Officer.—Elise Hofer.

INTER-AMERICAN FOUNDATION
901 North Stuart Street, 10th Floor, Arlington, VA 22203, phone (703) 306–4301

Chair, Board of Directors.—Roger W. Wallace.
    Vice Chair, Board of Directors.—Nadine Hogan.
    President.—Linda Kolko (interim).
    General Counsel.—Jocelyn Nieva (acting).
    Vice President for Programs.—Ramón Daubón.

JOHN F. KENNEDY CENTER FOR THE PERFORMING ARTS
Washington, DC 20566, phone 416–8000, fax 416–8205

BOARD OF TRUSTEES

Honorary Chairs:
    Mrs. Laura Bush
    Senator Hillary Rodham Clinton
    Mrs. George Bush
    Mrs. Ronald Reagan

    Mrs. Jimmy Carter
    Mrs. Gerald R. Ford
    Mrs. Lyndon B. Johnson

Officers:
    Chairman.—Stephen A. Schwarzman.
    Vice Chairman.—Alma Johnson Powell.
    President.—Michael M. Kaiser.
    Secretary.—Jean Kennedy Smith.
        Assistant Secretary.—Ann Stock.
    Treasurer.—Roland Betts.
    General Counsel.—Maria Kersten.
    Members Appointed by the President of the United States:

Smith Bagley	Vinod Gupta	Catherine B. Reynolds
Lois Phifer Betts	Anne Sewell Johnson	Gabrielle B. Reynolds
Ronald W. Burkle	Brenda LaGrange Johnson	David M. Rubenstein
Bo Derek	James V. Kimsey	Stephen A. Schwarzman
Elisabeth Dee DeVos	Kathi Koll	Jean Kennedy Smith
Ronald I. Dozoretz	Marlene A. Malek	Alex G. Spanos
Melvyn J. Estrin	Dorothy Swann McAuliffe	Jay Stein
George Farias	William F. McSweeney	Catherine A. Stevens
Thomas C. Foley	Mary V. Mochary	Alexander F. Treadwell
David F. Girard-diCarlo	Mary M. Ourisman	Mark S. Weiner
Albert B. Glickman	Frank H. Pearl	Beatrice W. Welters
Roy Goodman	Alma Johnson Powell	Thomas E. Wheeler

Ex Officio Members Designated by Act of Congress:
    Dr. Condoleezza Rice, Secretary of State.
    Michael O. Leavitt, Secretary of Health and Human Services.
    Margaret Spellings, Secretary of Education.
    Edward M. Kennedy, Senator from Massachusetts.
    James M. Jeffords, Senator from Vermont.
    James Inhofe, Senator from Oklahoma.
    William (Bill) Frist, Senate Republican Leader from Tennessee.
    Kay Bailey Hutchison, Senator from Texas.
    Harry Reid, Senator from Nevada.

Thad Cochran, Senator from Mississippi.
James L. Oberstar, Representative from Minnesota.
J. Dennis Hastert, Speaker of the U.S. House of Representatives from Illinois.
Don Young, Representative from Alaska.
Jim Kolbe, Representative from Arizona.
Patrick J. Kennedy, Representative from Rhode Island.
Deborah Pryce, Representative from Ohio.
Nancy Pelosi, House Minority Leader from California.
Anthony A. Williams, Mayor, District of Columbia.
Lawrence M. Small, Secretary, Smithsonian Institution.
James H. Billington, Librarian of Congress.
David M. Childs, Chairman, Commission of Fine Arts.
Fran P. Mainella, Director, National Park Service.

Honorary Trustees:

Buffy Cafritz	Alma Gildenhorn	Henry Strong
Kenneth M. Duberstein	Melvin R. Laird	
James H. Evans	Leonard L. Silverstein	

Senior Counsel.—Robert Barnett.
Founding Chairman.—Roger L. Stevens (deceased).
Chairmen Emeriti: James A. Johnson, James D. Wolfensohn.

LEGAL SERVICES CORPORATION

3333 K Street, NW., 3rd Floor, 20007, phone (202) 295–1500 fax 337–6797

BOARD OF DIRECTORS

Frank B. Strickland, *Chair*	Michael D. McKay
Lillian R. BeVier, *Vice Chair*	Thomas R. Meites
Robert J. Dieter	Maria L. Mercado
Thomas A. Fuentes	Florentino Subia
Herbert S. Garten	Ernestine P. Watlington
David Hall	

President.—Helaine M. Barnett.
Vice President, Legal Affairs, General Counsel and Corporate Secretary.—Victor M. Fortuno.
Comptroller/Treasurer.—David L. Richardson.
Director of:
  Compliance and Enforcement.—Danilo Cardona.
  Governmental Relations and Public Affairs.—Thomas C. Polgar.
Inspector General.—Kirt West.

NATIONAL AERONAUTICS AND SPACE ADMINISTRATION

300 E Street SW., 20546, phone 358–0000 http://www.nasa.gov

OFFICE OF THE ADMINISTRATOR

Code AA000, Room 9F44, phone: 358–1010

Administrator.—Frederick D. Gregory (acting).
Deputy Administrator.—Frederick D. Gregory, 358–1020.
Executive Assistants: Susan Fenn, 358–1020; Denise Stewart, 358–1827.
Chief of Staff.—John D. Schumacher, 358–1827.
White House Liaison.—J.T. Jezierski, 358–2198.
Assistant Deputy Administrator for Internal Operations.—Suzanne Hilding, 358–1821.
Chief Scientist.—Dr. James Garvin, room 6V87, 358–4509.
Chief Health and Medical Officer.—Dr. Richard S. Williams, room 7P13, 358–2390.

OFFICE OF THE CHIEF FINANCIAL OFFICER (CFO)

Code 1A000, Room 8E39–A, phone: 358–0978

Chief Financial Officer/Chief Acquisition Officer.—Gwendolyn Sykes.
Deputy Chief Financial Officer.—Daphne Jefferson (acting), 358–1135.

OFFICE OF HEADQUARTERS OPERATIONS
Code LD000, Room 6T80, phone: 358–2100

Director for Headquarters Operations.—Christopher Jedrey.

OFFICE OF DIVERSITY AND EQUAL OPPORTUNITY PROGRAMS
Code LF000, Room 4Y23, phone: 358–2167

Assistant Administrator for Equal Opportunity Programs.—Dr. Dorothy Hayden-Watkins.
Deputy Assistant Administrator.—Kenny Aguilar.

OFFICE OF HUMAN CAPITAL MANAGEMENT
Code LE000–A, Room 4V84, phone: 358–0520

Assistant Administrator.—Vicki A. Novak.

OFFICE OF THE GENERAL COUNSEL
Mail Code MA000, Room 9V39, phone: 358–2450

General Counsel.—Michael Wholley.
Deputy General Counsel.—John G. Mannix.
Deputy General Counsel for Administrative and Management.—Keith T. Sefton.

OFFICE OF PROCUREMENT
Code ID000, Room 3A70, phone: 358–2090

Director.—Thomas S. Luedtke.

OFFICE OF EXTERNAL RELATIONS
Code ND000, Room 7V30, phone: 358–0400

Assistant Administrator.—Michael F. O'Brien.
Deputy Assistant Administrator.—Al Condes.

OFFICE OF INFRASTRUCTURE AND ADMINISTRATION
Code LD000, Room 6W31, phone: 358–2800

Assistant Administrator.—Jeffrey E. Sutton.
Deputy Assistant Administrator.—Olga Dominguez.

OFFICE OF SMALL AND DISADVANTAGED BUSINESS UTILIZATION
Code IG000, Room 9K70, phone: 358–2088

Assistant Administrator.—Ralph C. Thomas III.

OFFICE OF LEGISLATIVE AFFAIRS
Code NC000, Room 9L39, phone: 358–1948

Assistant Administrator.—D. Lee Forsgren.
Deputy Assistant Administrator.—Angela Phillips Diaz.

OFFICE OF PUBLIC AFFAIRS
Code NB000, Room 9P39, phone: 358–1400

Assistant Administrator.—Glenn Mahone.
Deputy Assistant Administrator.—Dean Acosta.

EXPLORATION SYSTEMS MISSSION DIRECTORATE
Code BA000, Room 8G17, phone: 358–1523

Associate Administrator.—ADM Craig Steidle.
Deputy Associate Administrator.—Steve Isakowitz.

Deputy Associate Administrator for—
Development Programs.—Jim Nehman.
Research.—Dr. Terri Lomax.
Systems Integration.—Doug Cooke.

SPACE OPERATIONS MISSION DIRECTORATE

Code CA000, Room 7K39, phone: 358–2015

Associate Administrator.—William F. Readdy.
Deputy Associate Administrator.—Lynn F.H. Cline
Deputy Associate Administrator for—
Exploration Operations.—Michael Foale.
International Space Station and Space Shuttle.—Michael C. Kostelnik.
Systems Integration and Program Management.—Michael Hawes.

SCIENCE MISSION DIRECTORATE

Code DA000, room 3K39, phone: 358–3889

Associate Administrator.—Al Diaz.
Deputy Associate Administrator.—Ghassem Asrar.
Deputy Associate Administrator for—
Management.—Alison McNally.
Programs.—Orlando Figueroa.

AERONAUTICS RESEARCH MISSION DIRECTORATE

Code EA000, Room 6D39–A, phone: 358–4600

Associate Administrator.—Dr. J. Victor Lebacqz.
Deputy Associate Administrator.—Dr. Jaiwon Shin.

OFFICE OF INSPECTOR GENERAL

Code W, Room 8U79, phone: 358–1220

Inspector General.—Robert W. Cobb.
Deputy Inspector General.—Thomas Howard.

OFFICE OF SECURITY AND PROGRAM PROTECTION

Code LG000, Room 9U70, phone: 358–2010

Associate Administrator.—David Saleeba.
Deputy Associate Administrator.—Clint Herbert.

SAFETY AND MISSION ASSURANCE

Code GA000, Room 5W21, phone: 358–2406

Chief Officer.—Bryan D. O'Connor.
Deputy Chief Officer.—James D. Lloyd.

NASA NATIONAL OFFICES

Air Force Space Command/XPX (NASA): Peterson Air Force Base, CO 80914.
NASA Senior Representative.—Stan Newberry (719) 554–4900.
Ames Research Center: Moffett Field, CA 94035.
Director.—G. Scott Hubbard (650) 604–5000.
Dryden Flight Research Center: P.O. Box 273, Edwards, CA 93523.
Director.—Kevin L. Petersen (661) 276–3311.
Glenn Research Center at Lewisfield: 21000 Brookpark Road, Cleveland, OH 44135.
Director.—Dr. Julian Earls (216) 433–4000.
Goddard Institute for Space Studies: Goddard Space Flight Center, 2880 Broadway, New York, NY 10025.
Head.—Dr. James E. Hansen (212) 678–5500.

Goddard Space Flight Center: 8800 Greenbelt Road, Greenbelt, MD 20771.
  Director.—Dr. Ed Weiler (301) 286–2000.
Jet Propulsion Laboratory: 4800 Oak Grove Drive, Pasadena, CA 91109.
  Director.—Dr. Charles Elachi (818) 354–4351.
Lyndon B. Johnson Space Center: Houston, TX 77058–3696.
  Director.—Gen. Jefferson D. Howell, Jr. (281) 483–0123.
John F. Kennedy Space Center: Kennedy Space Center, FL 32899.
  Director.—John T. Kennedy (321) 867–5000.
Langley Reseach Center: Hampton, VA 23681.
  Director.—GEN Roy D. Bridges (757) 864–1000.
George C. Marshall Space Flight Center: Marshall Space Flight Center, AL 35812.
  Director.—David A. King (256) 544–2121.
Michoud Assembly Facility: P.O. Box 29300, New Orleans, LA 70189.
  Manager.—John K. White (504) 257–3311.
NASA IV & V Facility: NASA Independent Verification and Validation Facility, 100 University Drive, Fairmont, WV 26554.
  Director.—Nelson H. Keeler (304) 367–8200.
NASA Management Office: Jet Propulsion Laboratory, 4800 Oak Grove Drive, Pasadena, CA 91109.
  Director.—Dr. Robert A. Parker (818) 354–5359.
John C. Stennis Space Center: Stennis Space Center, MS 39529.
  Director.—ADM Thomas Donaldson (228) 688–2211.
Vandenberg AFB: P.O. Box 425, Lompoc, CA 93438.
  Manager.—Ted L. Oglesby (805) 866–5859.
Wallops Flight Facility: Goddard Space Flight Center, Wallops Island, VA 23337.
  Director.—Arnold Torres (757) 824–1000.
White Sands Test Facility: Johnson Space Center, P.O. Drawer MM, Las Cruces, NM 88004.
  Manager.—Joseph Fries (505) 524–5771.

NASA OVERSEAS REPRESENTATIVES

Australia: APO AP 96549.
  NASA Representative.—Neal Newman, phone: 011–61–2–6281–8501.
Europe: U.S. Embassy, Paris, PSC 116 APO AE 09777.
  NASA Representative.—Karen C. Feldstein, phone: 011–33–1–4312–2100.
Japan: U.S. Embassy, Tokyo, Unit 45004, Box 235, APO AP, 96337–5004.
  NASA Representative.—William Jordan, phone: 011–81–3–3224–5827.
Russia: U.S. Embassy, Moscow, PSC 77/NASA APO AE 09721.
  NASA Representative.—Phillip Cleary, phone: (256) 961–6333.
Spain: PSC No. 61, Box 0037, APO AE 09642.
  NASA Representative.—Ms. Ingrid Desilvestre, phone: 011–34–91–548–9250.

NATIONAL ARCHIVES AND RECORDS ADMINISTRATION
8601 Adelphi Road, College Park, MD 20740–6001
phone (301) 837–1600, http://www.nara.gov
[Created by Public Law 98–497]

Archivist of the United States.—Dr. Allen Weinstein, fax (202) 208–3267.
  Deputy Archivist of the United States and Chief of Staff.—Lewis J. Bellardo, fax (301) 837–3218.
  Congressional and Public Affairs.—John A. Constance (202) 501–5506, fax (202) 208–2404.
  General Counsel.—Gary M. Stern (301) 837–1750, fax (301) 837–0293.
  Equal Employment Opportunity and Diversity Programs.—Robert Jew (301) 837–1550, fax (301) 837–0869.
  Policy and Communications Staff.—MaryAnn Hadyka (acting) (301) 837–1850, fax (301) 837–0319.
  Information Security Oversight Office.—J. William Leonard (202) 219–5250, fax (202) 219–5385.
  National Historical Publications and Records Commission.—Max J. Evans (202) 501–5600, fax (202) 501–5601.

Mayoral Appointees:
   Arrington Dixon.
   Dr. Patricia Elwood, *Vice Chair.*
Ex Officio Members:
   Anthony A. Williams, Mayor of the District of Columbia.
      Alternate.—Ellen M. McCarthy.
   Linda W. Cropp, Chairman, Council of the District of Columbia.
      First Alternate.—Robert E. Miller, Esq.
      Second Alternate.—Christopher Murray.
   Gale A. Norton, Secretary of the Interior.
      First Alternate.—Fran P. Mainella.
      Second Alternate.—Joseph A. Lawler.
      Third Alternate.—John G. Parsons.
   Donald H. Rumsfeld, Secretary of Defense.
      First Alternate.—Raymond F. DuBois.
      Second Alternate.—Jerry R. Shiplett.
   Stephen A. Perry, Administrator, General Services Administration.
      First Alternate.—F. Joseph Moravec.
      Second Alternate.—Donald Williams.
      Third Alternate.—William J. Guerin.
      Fourth Alternate.—Michael S. McGill.
   Susan Collins, Chairman, Senate Committee on Homeland Security and
      Governmental Affairs.
      Alternate.—Johanna Hardy.
   Tom Davis, Chairman, House Committee on Government Reform.
      First Alternate.—Melissa Wojciak.
      Second Alternate.—Victoria Proctor.
      Third Alternate.—Shalley Kim.

EXECUTIVE STAFF

Executive Director.—Patricia E. Gallagher, 482–7212.
   Deputy Executive Director.—Marcel C. Acosta, 482–7221.
   Executive Officer.—Barry S. Socks, 482–7209.
   Secretariat.—Deborah B. Young, 482–7228.
   Executive Assistant.—Priscilla A. Brown, 482–7212.
   Management Assistant.—LaWan L. Jenkins, 482–7225.
   General Counsel.—Wayne E. Costa, 482–7231.
   Director, Office of:
      Plan and Project Implementation.—William G. Dowd, 482–7240.
      Planning Research and Policy.—Julia A. Koster, 482–7211.
      Public Affairs.—Lisa N. MacSpadden, 482–7263.
      Technology Development and Applications Support.—Michael Sherman, 482–7254.
      Urban Design and Plans Review.—Christine L. Saum, 482–7245.

NATIONAL COMMISSION ON LIBRARIES AND INFORMATION SCIENCE
1800 M Street, NW., Suite 350, North Tower 20036–5841
phone 606–9200, fax 606–9203, http://www.nclis.gov
[Created by Public Law 91–345]

Chair.—Beth Fitzsimmons, Ph.D., Ann Arbor, MI.
   Vice Chair.—Bridget L. Lamont, Springfield, IL.
   Members:
      José A. Aponte, Colorado Springs, CO.
      Sandra F. Ashworth, Bonners Ferry, ID.
      Edward L. Bertorelli, Boston, MA.
      James H. Billington, Ph.D., Librarian of Congress, Washington, DC.
   Serves for the Librarian of Congress:
      Carolyn T. Brown, Ph.D., The Library of Congress, Washington, DC.
      Joan R. Challinor, Ph.D., Washington, DC.
      Carol L. Diehl, Neenah, WI.
      Allison Druin, Ph.D., College Park, MD.
      Jack E. Hightower, Austin, TX.

Patricia M. Hines, Mayesville, SC.
Colleen E. Huebner, Ph.D., Seattle, WA.
Stephen M. Kennedy, Dunbarton, NH.
Robert S. Martin, Ph.D., Director, Institute of Museum and Library Services, Washington, DC.
Mary H. Perdue, Salisbury, MD.
Herman L. Totten, Ph.D., Denton, TX.

Chairpersons Emeritus:
Charles Benton.
Frederick Burkhardt.
Elinor M. Hashim.
Jerald C. Newman.
Charles E. Reid.

EXECUTIVE STAFF

Executive Director.—Trudi Bellardo Hahn, Ph.D.
  Director of Operations.—Madeleine C. McCain.
    Special Assistant.—Kim Miller.
    Administrative Officer.—Kathleen Lannon.

NATIONAL COUNCIL ON DISABILITY

1331 F Street NW., Suite 850, 20004, phone 272–2004, fax 272–2022

Chairperson.—Lex Frieden, Houston, TX.
  First Vice Chairperson.—Patricia Pound, Austin, TX.
  Second Vice Chairperson.—Glenn Anderson, Ph.D., Little Rock, AR.
  Executive Director.—Ethel D. Briggs.
Members:

Milton Aponte, J.D., Cooper City, FL.
Robert R. Davila, Ph.D., Pittsford, NY.
Barbara Gillcrist, Santa Fe, NM.
Graham Hill, Arlington, VA.
Joel I. Kahn, Ph.D., Wyoming, OH.
Young Woo Kang, Ph.D., Munster, IN.
Kathleen Martinez, Oakland, CA.
Carol Novak, Tampa, FL.
Marco Rodriguez, Elk Grove, CA.
David Wenzel, Scranton, PA.
Linda Wetters, Columbus, OH.
Kate Pew Wolters, Grand Rapids, MI.

NATIONAL CREDIT UNION ADMINISTRATION

1775 Duke Street, Alexandria, VA 22314–3428, phone (703) 518–6300, fax 518–6319

Chairman.—JoAnn Johnson.
  Chief of Staff and Counsel to Acting Chairman.—Holly Herman.
  Special Assistant to the Chairman/Director of External Affairs.—Nicholas Owens, 518–6330, fax 518–6671.
  Secretary to the Board.—Mary Rupp.
Board Member.—Deborah Matz.
Executive Director.—J. Leonard Skiles, 518–6320, fax 518–6661.
  Deputy Executive Director.—Owen Cole, 518–6320.
Deputy Director Inspector General.—William DeSarno, 518–6350.
Director, Office of:
  Capital Markets and Planning.—James L. Patrick, 518–6320, fax 518–6663.
  Chief Financial Officer.—Dennis Winans, 518–6570, fax 518–6664.
  Chief Information Officer.—Doug Verner, 518–6440, fax 518–6669.
  Corporate Credit Unions.—Kent Buckham, 518–6640, fax 518–6665.
  EEO.—Marilyn G. Gannon, 518–6325.
  Examination and Insurance.—David M. Marquis, 518–6360, fax 518–6666.
  General Counsel.—Robert M. Fenner, 518–6540, fax 518–6667.
    Deputy General Counsel.—Michael McKenna.
  Human Resources.—Sherry Turpenoff, 518–6510, fax 518–6668.
  Public and Congressional Affairs.—Clifford R. Northup, 518–6330.
  Small Credit Union Initiatives.—Tawana James, 518–6610.
  Training and Development.—Leslie Armstrong, 518–6630, fax 518–6672.

REGIONAL OFFICES

Director, Office of:
   Region I (Albany).—Mark A. Treichel, 9 Washington Square, Washington Avenue Extension, Albany, NY 12205 (518) 862–7400, fax 862–7420.
   Region II (National Capital Region).—Edward Dupcak, Suite 4206, 1775 Duke Street, Alexandria, VA 22314 (703) 519–4600, fax 519–4620.
   Region III (Atlanta).—Alonzo A. Swann III, Suite 1600, 7000 Central Parkway, Atlanta, GA 30328 (678) 443–3000, fax 443–3020.
   Region IV (Austin).—Jane Walters, Suite 5200, 4807 Spicewood Springs Road, Austin, TX 78759–8490 (512) 342–5600, fax 342–5620.
   Region V (Tempe).—Melinda Love, Suite 301, 1230 West Washington Street, Tempe, AZ 85281 (602) 302–6000, fax 302–6024.
President, Asset Management and Assistance Center (Austin).—Mike Barton, Suite 5100, 4807 Spicewood Springs Road, Austin, TX 78759–8490 (512) 231–7900, fax 231–7920.

NATIONAL FOUNDATION ON THE ARTS AND THE HUMANITIES

Old Post Office Building, 1100 Pennsylvania Avenue, NW., 20506

NATIONAL ENDOWMENT FOR THE ARTS

http://www.arts.gov

Chairman.—Dana Gioia, 682–5414.
   Senior Deputy Chairman.—Eileen B. Mason, 682–5415.
   Deputy Chairman for—
      Grants and Awards.—Tony Chauveaux, 682–5441.
      Management and Budget.—Laurence Baden, 682–5408.
   Government Affairs/Congressional and White House Liaison.—Ann Guthrie Hingston, 682–5434.
   General Counsel.—Claudia Nadig, 682–5418.
   Research and Analysis.—Mark Bauerlein, 682–5424.
   Inspector General.—Daniel Shaw, 682–5402.
   Communications Director.—Felicia Knight, 682–5570.

THE NATIONAL COUNCIL ON THE ARTS

Chairman.—Dana Gioia.
   Members:

James K. Ballinger	James McBride	Karen Lias Wolff
Don V. Cogman	Maribeth Walton	*Ex Officio Members:*
Mary D. Costa	McGinley	Hon. Harry Reid
Katharine Cramer DeWitt	Jerry Pinkney	Hon. Buck McKeon
Makoto Fujimura	Deedie Potter Rose	Hon. Robert F. Bennett
David H. Gelernter	Gerard Schwarz	Hon. Mike DeWine
Teresa Lozano Long	Terry Teachout	Hon. Betty McCullom

NATIONAL ENDOWMENT FOR THE HUMANITIES

phone (202) 606–8400, info@neh.gov, www.neh.gov

Chairman.—Bruce Cole, 606–8310.
   Deputy Chairman.—Lynne Munson, 606–8273.
   Inspector General.—Sheldon L. Bernstein, 606–8350.
   General Counsel.—Daniel Schneider, 606–8322.
   Governmental Affairs.—Cherie Harder, 606–8328.
   Communications.—Erik Lokkesmoe, 606–8446.
   Public Information Officer.—Joy Evans, 606–8446.
   Public Affairs.—Noel Milan, 606–8446.
   Strategic Planning.—Larry Myers, 606–8428.

NATIONAL COUNCIL ON THE HUMANITIES

Members:

Herman Belz
Jewel Spears Brooker
Celeste Colgan
Dario Fernandez-Morera
Elizabeth Fox-Genovese
Craig Haffner
Nathan Hatch
David Hertz

James Davison Hunter
Tamar Jacoby
Harvey Klehr
Andrew Ladis
Wright Lassiter
Thomas Lindsay
Iris Cornelia Love
Wilfred McClay

Steven McKnight
Lawrence Okamura
Ricardo J. Quinones
James Stoner
Marguerite Sullivan
Stephan Thernstrom
Jeffrey Wallin

FEDERAL COUNCIL ON THE ARTS AND THE HUMANITIES

Federal Council Members:
Dana Gioia, Chairman, National Endowment for the Arts.
Bruce Cole, Chairman, National Endowment for the Humanities.
Robert S. Martin, Director, Institute for Museum and Library Services.
Margaret Spellings, Secretary, Department of Education.
Earl A. Powell III, Director, National Gallery of Art.
David M. Childs, Chairman, Commission of Fine Arts.
James H. Billington, Librarian of Congress, Library of Congress.
Allen Weinstein, Archivist of the United States, National Archives and
    Records Administration.
F. Joseph Moravec, Commissioner, Public Buildings Service, General
    Services Administration.
Gale Norton, Secretary, Department of the Interior.
Arden L. Bement, Jr., Director, National Science Foundation.
Emily Reynolds, Secretary of the Senate.
Lawrence M. Small, Secretary, Smithsonian Institution.
Fortney Pete Stark, Member, U.S. House of Representatives.
Carlos M. Gutierrez, Secretary, Department of Commerce.
Norman Y. Mineta, Secretary, Department of Transportation.
Alphonso Jackson, Secretary, Department of Housing and Urban Development.
Elaine L. Chao, Secretary, Department of Labor.
R. James Nicholson, Secretary, Department of Veterans Affairs.
Josefina G. Carbonell, Assistant Secretary for Aging, Department of Health and
    Human Services.
Staff Contact.—Alice M. Whelihan, Indemnity Administrator, National Endowment
    for the Arts, 682–5574.

INSTITUTE OF MUSEUM AND LIBRARY SERVICES
phone (202) 653–4657, fax 202–653–4625, http://www.imls.gov

[The Institute of Museum and Library Services was created by the Museum and Library
Services Act of 1996, Public Law 104–208]

Director.—Robert S. Martin, PhD, (202) 653–4645.
Deputy Director for—
    Library Services.—Mary Chute, 653–4700.
    Museum Services.—Schroeder Cherry, PhD, 653–4789.
Director of:
    Administration and Budget.—Teresa M. LaHaie, 653–4657.
    Public and Legislative Affairs.—Mamie Bittner, 653–4757.
    Research and Technology.—Rebecca Danvers, 653–4767.
Associate Deputy Director for—
    Library Services.—Joyce Ray, PhD, 653–4700.
    Museum Services.—Mary Estelle Kennelly, 653–4789.
    State Programs.—George Smith, 653–4650.

NATIONAL MUSEUM AND LIBRARY SERVICES BOARD

Members:

Robert S. Martin
Beverly E. Allen

John E. Buchanan, Jr.
Schroeder Cherry

Mary Chute
Gail M. Daly

David A. Donath
Nancy S. Dwight
Beth Fitzsimmons, PhD
A. Wilson Greene
Mariam Mercedes
  Guillemard
Peter Hero

Donald S. Leslie
Thomas E. Lorentzen
Terry L. Maple
Amy Owen
Sandra Pickett
Judith Ann Rapanos
Edwin Rigaud

Harry Robinson, Jr.
Margaret Webster
  Scarlett
Katina Strauch
Renee Becker Swartz
Kim Wang

NATIONAL GALLERY OF ART
Sixth Street and Constitution Avenue, NW., Washington, DC 20565,
phone (202) 737–4215, http://www.nga.gov
[Under the direction of the Board of Trustees of the National Gallery of Art]

Board of Trustees:
  William H. Rehnquist, Chief Justice of the United States, ex officio.
  Condoleezza Rice, Secretary of State, ex officio.
  John W. Snow, Secretary of the Treasury, ex officio.
  Lawrence M. Small, Secretary of the Smithsonian Institution, ex officio.
  Robert F. Erburu, Chairman.
  Victoria P. Sant, President.
  Julian Ganz, Jr.
  David O. Maxwell.
  John C. Fontaine.
Trustee Emerita.—Ruth Carter Stevenson.
Trustees Emeritus: Alexander M. Laughlin, Robert H. Smith.
  Director.—Earl A. Powell III.
    Deputy Director.—Alan Shestack.
    Dean, Center for Advanced Study in the Visual Arts.—Elizabeth Cropper.
    Administrator.—Darrell Willson.
    Treasurer.—James E. Duff.
    Secretary-General Counsel.—Elizabeth A. Croog.
    External Affairs Officer.—Joseph J. Krakora.

NATIONAL LABOR RELATIONS BOARD
1099 14th Street, NW., 20570–0001
Personnel Locator (202) 273–1000

Chairman.—Robert J. Battista, 273–1770, fax 273–4270.
  Chief Counsel.—Harold Datz.
  Deputy Chief Counsel.—Kathleen Nixon.
  Executive Assistant.—William B. Cowen.
  Members:
    Wilma B. Liebman, 273–1700.
      Chief Counsel.—John F. Colwell.
    Peter C. Schaumber, 273–1790.
      Chief Counsel.—Terence Flynn.
    Chief Counsels: Gary W. Shinners, 273–1740; Peter Winkler (acting), 273–1070.
  Executive Secretary.—Lester A. Heltzer, 273–1940, fax 273–4270.
    Deputy Executive Secretary.—David B. Parker.
    Associate Executive Secretaries: Hollace J. Enoch, 273–1938; Richard D. Hardick, 273–1935; Enid W. Weber, 273–1937.
  Solicitor.—Hank Breiteneicher (acting), 273–2914, fax 273–1962.
  Inspector General.—Jane E. Altenhofen, 273–1960, fax 273–3244.
  Director, Representation Appeals.—Lafe E. Solomon, 273–1980, fax 273–1962.
  Associate Director, Division of Information.—Patricia M. Gilbert, 273–1991, fax 273–1789.
  Chief Administrative Law Judge.—Robert A. Giannasi, 501–8800, fax 501–8686.
    Deputy Chief Administrative Law Judge.—Richard A. Scully.
    Associate Chief Administrative Law Judges:
    Joel P. Biblowitz, 120 West 45th Street, 11th Floor, New York, NY 10036–5503 (212) 944–2943, fax 944–4904.
    William N. Cates, 401 West Peachtree Street NW, Atlanta, GA 30308–3510 (404) 331–6654, fax 331–2061.
    Mary Miller Cracraft, 901 Market Street, Suite 300, San Francisco, CA 94103–1779 (415) 356–5255, fax 356–5254.

GENERAL COUNSEL

General Counsel.—Arthur F. Rosenfeld, 273–3700, fax 273–4483.
  Deputy General Counsel.—John E. Higgins, Jr., 273–3700.
  Assistant General Counsel.—Joseph F. Frankl, 273–3700.
Associate General Counsel, Division of Operations Management.—Richard Siegel, 273–2900, fax 273–4274.
  Deputy Associate General Counsel.—Anne Purcell, 273–2900.
  Assistant General Counsels: Shelley S. Korch, 273–2889; Nelson Levin, 273–2893; James G. Paulsen, 273–2882.
  Executive Assistant.—Carole K. Coleman, 273–2901.
  Special Counsels: Elizabeth Bach, 273–2918, fax 273–0864; Joseph M. Davis, Jennifer S. Kovachich, Barry F. Smith.
Associate General Counsel, Division of Advice.—Barry J. Kearney, 273–3800, fax 273–4275.
  Deputy Associate General Counsel.—Ellen A. Farrell, 273–3800.
  Assistant General Counsels:
    Injunction Litigation Branch.—Judith I. Katz, 273–3812.
    Regional Advice Branch.—David Colangelo, 273–3831.
    Research and Policy Planning Branch.—Jacqueline A. Young, 273–3825.
Associate General Counsel, Division of Enforcement Litigation.—John H. Ferguson, 273–2950, fax 273–4244.
  Appellate Court Branch:
    Deputy Associate General Counsel.—Aileen Armstrong, 273–2960, fax 273–0191.
  Supreme Court Branch:
    Assistant General Counsel.—Linda Dreeben, 273–2977, fax 273–4244.
  Special Litigation Branch:
    Assistant General Counsel.—Margery E. Lieber, 273–2930, fax 273–1799.
  Contempt Litigation and Compliance Branch:
    Assistant General Counsel.—Stanley R. Zirkin, 273–3739, fax 273–4244.
    Deputy Assistant General Counsels: Daniel F. Collopy, 273–3745; Kenneth J. Shapiro, 273–3741.
  Director, Office of Appeals.—Yvonne T. Dixon, 273–3760, 273–4283.
  Director, Division of Administration.—Gloria J. Joseph, 273–3890, fax 273–4266.
  Deputy Director.—Frank V. Battle, 273–3890.

NATIONAL MEDIATION BOARD

1301 K Street NW., Suite 250 East, 20572, phone (202) 692–5000, fax 692–5080

Chairman.—Harry R. Hoglander, 692–5022.
  Board Members: Edward Fitzmaurice, 692–5016; Read Van de Water, 692–5019.
  Director, Office of:
    Administration.—June D.W. King, 692–5010.
    Alternative Dispute Resolution Services.—Daniel Rainey, 692–5051.
    Arbitration Services.—Roland Watkins, 692–5055.
    Mediation Services.—Larry Gibbons, 692–5060.
  General Counsel, Office of Legal Affairs.—Mary L. Johnson, 692–5040.

NATIONAL RESEARCH COUNCIL—NATIONAL ACADEMY OF SCIENCES
NATIONAL ACADEMY OF ENGINEERING—INSTITUTE OF MEDICINE

2101 Constitution Avenue NW 20418, phone (202) 334–2000

The National Research Council, National Academy of Sciences, National Academy of Engineering, and Institute of Medicine, serves as an independent adviser to the Federal Government on scientific and technical questions of national importance. Although operating under a congressional charter granted the National Academy of Sciences in 1863, the National Research Council and its three parent organizations are private organizations, not agencies of the Federal Government, and receive no appropriations from Congress.

NATIONAL RESEARCH COUNCIL

Chairman.—Bruce M. Alberts, President, National Academy of Sciences, 334–2100.
  Vice Chairman.—Wm. A. Wulf, President, National Academy of Engineering, 334–3200.

Executive Officer.—E. William Colglazier, 334–3000.
Director, Office of Congressional and Government Affairs.—James E. Jensen, 334–1601.

NATIONAL ACADEMY OF SCIENCES

President.—Ralph Cicerone, 334–2100.
  Vice President.—James S. Langer, University of California, Santa Barbara.
  Home Secretary.—John I. Brauman, Stanford University.
  Foreign Secretary.—M.T. Clegg, University of California, Irvine.
  Treasurer.—Ronald L. Graham, University of California, San Diego.
  Executive Officer.—E. William Colglazier, 334–3000.

NATIONAL ACADEMY OF ENGINEERING

President.—Wm. A. Wulf, 334–3200.
  Chairman.—Craig R. Barrett (retired), Intel Corporation.
  Vice President.—Sheila E. Widnall, Massachusetts Institute of Technology.
  Home Secretary.—W. Dale Compton, Purdue University.
  Foreign Secretary.—George Bugliarello (retired), Polytechnic University.
  Executive Officer.—Lance Davis, 334–3677.
  Treasurer.—William L. Friend, National Labs.

INSTITUTE OF MEDICINE

President.—Harvey V. Fineberg, M.D., 334–3300.
  Executive Officer.—Susanne Stoiber, 334–2177.

NATIONAL SCIENCE FOUNDATION

4201 Wilson Boulevard, Suite 1245, Arlington, VA 22230, http://www.nsf.gov

Director.—Arden L. Bement, Jr. (703) 292–8000.
  Deputy Director.—Joseph Bordogna (703) 292–8000.
  Inspector General.—Christine C. Boesz (703) 292–7100.
  Equal Opportunity Coordinator.—Ronald D. Branch (703) 292–8020.
  Director, Office of:
    Legislative and Public Affairs.—Curt Suplee (703) 292–8070.
    Integrative Activities.—Nathaniel G. Pitts (703) 292–8040.
    Polar Programs.—Karl Erb (703) 292–8030.
  General Counsel.—Lawrence Rudolph (703) 292–8060.
  Assistant Director for—
    Biological Sciences.—Mary E. Clutter (703) 292–8500.
    Computer and Information Science and Engineering.—Peter Freeman (703) 292–8900.
    Education and Human Resources.—Donald Thompson (acting) (703) 292–8300.
    Engineering.—John Brighton (703) 292–8300.
    Geosciences.—Margaret S. Leinen (703) 292–8500.
    Mathematical and Physical Sciences.—Michael Turner (703) 292–8800.
    Social, Behavorial, and Economic Sciences.—David W. Lightfoot (703) 292–8700.
  Director, Office of:
    Budget, Finance, and Award Management.—Thomas N. Cooley (703) 292–8200.
    Information and Resource Management.—Anthony Arnolie (703) 292–8100.

NATIONAL SCIENCE BOARD

Chairman.—Warren M. Washington (703) 292–7000.
  Vice Chairman.—Diana Natalicio.
  Executive Officer.—Michael Crosby.

MEMBERS

Dan E. Arvizu	G. Wayne Clough	Pamela A. Ferguson
Barry C. Barish	Kelvin K. Droegemier	Kenneth M. Ford
Steven C. Beering	Delores M. Etter	Daniel Hastings
Ray M. Bowen	Nina V. Fedoroff	Elizabeth Hoffman

Louis J. Lanzerotti
Alan I. Leshner
Jane Lubchenco
Douglas D. Randall

Michael G. Rossmann
Daniel Simberloff
Jon C. Strauss
Kathryn D. Sullivan

JoAnne Vasquez
John A. White, Jr.
Mark S. Wrighton

NATIONAL TRANSPORTATION SAFETY BOARD
490 L'Enfant Plaza, SW., 20594, phone (202) 314–6000

Chairman.—Ellen G. Engleman, 314–6010, fax 314–6018.
  Vice Chairman.—Mark V. Rosenker, 314–6004, fax 314–6027.
  Members:
    Richard Healing, 314–6058, fax 314–6035.
    Debbie Hersman, 314–6660, fax 314–6665.
    Carol J. Carmody, 314–6020, fax 314–6027.
Managing Director.—Daniel Campbell, 314–6091, fax 314–6090.
General Counsel.—Ronald Battocchi, 314–6616, fax 314–6090.
Chief Administrative Law Judge.—William W. Fowler, Jr., 314–6150, fax 314–6158.
Chief Financial Officer.—Steven Goldberg, 314–6212, fax 314–6261.
Director, Office of:
  Aviation Safety.—John Clark, 314–6301, fax 314–6309.
  Government Affairs.—Cheryl McCullough (acting), 314–6121, fax 314–6110.
  Highway Safety.—Joseph Osterman, 314–6441, fax 314–6482.
  Marine Safety.—Majorie Murtagh, 314–6450, fax 314–6454.
  Public Affairs.—Ted Lopatkiewicz, 314–6100, fax 314–6110.
  Railroad, Pipeline and Hazardous Materials Investigations.—Bob Chipkevich, 314–6461,
    fax 314–6482.
  Research and Engineering.—Vernon Ellingstad, 314–6501, fax 314–6599.
  Safety Recommendations/Accomplishments.—Elaine Weinstein, 314–6171, fax 314–6717.
  Transportation Disaster Assistance.—Sharon Bryson, 314–6185, fax 314–6638.

NEIGHBORHOOD REINVESTMENT CORPORATION
1325 G Street, NW., Suite 800, 20005, phone (202) 220–2300, fax 376–2600

BOARD OF DIRECTORS

Chair.—Edward M. Gramlich, Member, Board of Governors, Federal Reserve System.
  Vice Chair.—Deborah Matz, Board Member, National Credit Union Administration.
  Members:
    Thomas J. Curry, Director, Federal Deposit Insurance Corporation.
    James E. Gilleran, Director, Office of Thrift Supervision.
    Julie Williams (acting), Comptroller, Comptroller of the Currency.
    Alphonso Jackson, Secretary, U.S. Department of Housing and Urban Development.
    John C. Weicher (designate), Assistant Secretary, U.S. Department of Housing and Urban
      Development.
Chief Executive Director.—Kenneth D. Wade, 220–2410.
General Counsel/Secretary.—Jeffrey T. Bryson, 220–2372.
Interim Chief Operating Officer.—Paul Kealey, 220–2375.
Treasurer.—Steven J. Tuminaro, 220–2415.
Director for—
  Finance and Administration.—Allan Martin, 223–2390.
  Internal Audit.—Frederick Udochi, 220–2409.
  Public Policy and Legislative Affairs.—Steven J. Tuminaro, 220–2415.
Manager, Congressional Affairs.—Michael Butchko, 220–2362.

NUCLEAR REGULATORY COMMISSION

Washington, DC 20555, phone (301) 415–7000, http//www.nrc.gov
[Authorized by 42 U.S.C. 5801 and U.S.C. 1201]

OFFICE OF THE CHAIRMAN

Chairman.—Nils J. Diaz, 415–1759.
  Executive Assistant.—Janet R. Schlueter, 415–1759.

Chief of Staff.—Richard P. Croteau, 415–1750.
Administration and Communications Assistant.—Robert B. McOsker, 415–1750.
Counsel.—Roger K. Davis, 415–1750.
Administrative Assistant.—Vicki M. Bolling, 415–1759.

COMMISSIONERS

Edward McGaffigan, Jr.—415–1800.
  Executive Assistant.—Jeffry Sharkey.
  Technical Assistants for Reactors.—James E. Beall.
  Technical Assistant for Materials.—Heather Astwood.
  Legal Assistant.—Bradley Jones.
  Special Assistant.—Linda D. Lewis.
Jeffrey S. Merrifield—415–1855.
  Chief of Staff/Materials.—John Thoma.
  Special Assistant.—Spiros Droggitis.
  Technical Assistants for Reactors.—David Skeen.
  Legal Assistant.—Kathryn Nolan.
  Administrative Assistant.—Lorna Kipfer.
Gregory B. Jaczko.—415–1820.
  Chief of Staff.—Josh Batkin.
  Legal Assistant.—Angela Coggins.
  Administrative Assistant.—Jackie Raines.
Peter B. Lyons, 415–8420.
  Executive Assistant.—Josie Piccone.
  Technical Assistant for Reactors.—John Jolicoeur.
  Technical Assistant for Materials.—Rebecca Tadesse.
  Legal Assistant.—Catherine Marco.
  Administrative Assistant.—Vicki Ibarra.

STAFF OFFICES OF THE COMMISSION

Secretary.—Annette L. Vietti-Cook, 415–1969, fax 415–1672.
  Commission Appellate Adjudication.—John F. Cordes, 415–1600, fax 415–1672.
  Congressional Affairs.—William N. Outlaw (acting), 415–1776 or 415–1897, fax 415–8571.
  General Counsel.—Karen D. Cyr, 415–1743, fax 415–3725.
  International Programs.—Janice Dunn Lee, 415–1780, fax 415–2400.
  Public Affairs.—Eliot B. Brenner, 415–8200, fax 415–3324.

ADVISORY COMMITTEE ON NUCLEAR WASTE

Chairman.—Michael T. Ryan, 415–7360.
  (Contact: John T. Larkins, Executive Director, ACRS/ACNW, 415–7360, fax 415–5589.)

ADVISORY COMMITTEE ON MEDICAL USES OF ISOTOPES

Committee Coordinator.—Angela McIntosh, 415–5030.

ADVISORY COMMITTEE ON REACTOR SAFEGUARDS

Chairman.—Graham B. Wallis, 415–7360,
  (Contact: John T. Larkins, Executive Director, ACRS/ACNW, 415–7360, fax 415–5589.)

ATOMIC SAFETY AND LICENSING BOARD PANEL

Chief Administrative Judge.—G. Paul Bollwerk III, 415–7454, fax 415–5599.

INSPECTOR GENERAL

Inspector General.—Hubert Bell, 415–5930, fax 415–5091.
  Deputy Inspector General.—David C. Lee, 415–5930.

OFFICE OF INFORMATION SERVICES

Director, Information Services.—Edward T. Baker III, 415–8700, fax 415–4246.
  Deputy Director.—James B. Schaeffer.

CHIEF FINANCIAL OFFICER

Chief Financial Officer.—Jesse L. Funches, 415–7322, fax 415–4236.
  Deputy Chief Financial Officer.—Peter J. Rabideau.

OFFICE OF THE EXECUTIVE DIRECTOR FOR OPERATIONS

Executive Director for Operations.—Luis A. Reyes, 415–1700, fax 415–2162.
  Deputy Executive Director for—
    Homeland Protection and Preparedness.—William F. Kane, 415–1713, fax 415–2162.
    Information Services and Administration and Chief Information Officer.—Jacqueline E.
      Silber, 415–7443, fax 415–2162.
    Materials, Research and State Programs.—Martin J. Virgilio, 415–1705, fax 415–2162.
    Reactor Programs.—Ellis W. Merschoff, 415–8710, fax 415–2162.

STAFF OFFICES OF THE EXECUTIVE DIRECTOR FOR OPERATIONS

Director, Office of:
  Administration.—Timothy F. Hagan, 415–6222, fax 415–5400.
  Enforcement.—Frank J. Congel, 415–2741, fax 415–3431.
  Human Resources.—Paul E. Bird, 415–7516, fax 415–5106.
  Investigations.—Guy P. Caputo, 415–2373, fax 415–2370.
  Small Business and Civil Rights.—Corenthis B. Kelley, 415–7380, fax 415–5953.
  State and Tribal Programs.—Paul H. Lohaus, 415–3340, fax 415–3502.

OFFICE OF NUCLEAR MATERIAL SAFETY AND SAFEGUARDS

Director.—Jack R. Strosnider, 415–7800, fax 415–5371.
  Deputy Director.—Margaret V. Federline, 415–7358.
  Divisional Directors:
    Fuel Cycle Safety and Safeguards (FCSS).—Robert C. Pierson, 415–7212.
    High-Level Waste Repository Safety (HLWRS).—C. William Reamer, 415–7437.
    Industrial and Medical Nuclear Safety (IMNS).—Charles L. Miller, 415–7197.
    Spent Fuel Project Office (SFPO).—E. William Brach, 415–8500.
    Waste Management and Environmental Protection (DWMEP).—Lawrence Camper,
      415–7319.

OFFICE OF NUCLEAR REACTOR REGULATION

Director.—James E. Dyer, 415–1270, fax 415–1887.
  Deputy Director.—R. William Borchardt, 415–1284.
  Associate Director for Project Licensing and Technical Analysis.—Brian Sheron, 415–1274.
  Divisional Directors:
    Engineering.—Michael Mayfield, 415–3298.
    Inspection Program Management.—Bruce A. Boger, 415–1004.
    Licensing Project Management.—Ledyard (Tad) Marsh, 415–1453.
    Regulory Improvement Programs.—David B. Matthews, 415–1199.
    Systems Safety and Analysis.—Suzanne Black, 415–2884.

OFFICE OF NUCLEAR REGULATORY RESEARCH

Director.—Carl J. Paperiello, 415–6641, fax 415–5153.
  Deputy Director.—John W. Craig, 415–6045.
  Divisional Directors:
    Engineering Technology.—Richard Barrett, 415–5678.
    Risk Analysis and Applications.—Charles Ader, 415–5790.
    Systems Analysis and Regulatory Effectiveness.—Farouk Eltawila, 415–7499.

Independent Agencies

REGIONAL OFFICES

Region I: Samuel J. Collins, 475 Allendale Road, King of Prussia, PA 19406 (610) 337–5299, fax 337–5324.
Deputy Regional Administrator.—James T. Wiggins, 337–5359.
Divisional Directors:
Nuclear Materials Safety.—George C. Pangburn, 337–5281.
Reactor Projects.—A. Rancy Blough, 337–5229.
Reactor Safety.—Wayne D. Lanning, 337–5126.
Region II: William D. Travers, 61 Forsyth Street SE, Atlanta, GA 30303 (404) 562–4410, fax 562–4766.
Deputy Regional Administrator.—Loren R. Plisco, 562–4411.
Divisional Directors:
Fuel Facility Inspection.—Douglas M. Collins, 562–4700.
Reactor Projects.—Victor M. McCree, 562–4500.
Reactor Safety.—Charles Casto, 562–4600.
Region III: James L. Caldwell, 2443 Warrensville Road, Suite 210, Lisle, IL 60532 (630) 829–9657, fax 515–1096.
Deputy Regional Administrator.—Geoffrey E. Grant, 829–9658.
Divisional Directors:
Nuclear Materials Safety.—Mark L. Dapas, 829–9802.
Reactor Projects.—Mark A. Satorius, 829–9634.
Reactor Safety.—Cynthia D. Pederson, 829–9702.
Region IV: Bruce S. Mallett, Suite 400, 611 Ryan Plaza Drive, Arlington, TX 76011 (817) 860–8225, fax 860–8210.
Deputy Regional Administrator.—Thomas P. Gwynn, 860–8226.
Divisional Directors:
Nuclear Materials Safety.—Patricia Holahan, 860–8106.
Reactor Projects.—Arthur T. Howell, 860–8248.
Reactor Safety.—Dwight D. Chamberlain, 860–8180.

OCCUPATIONAL SAFETY AND HEALTH REVIEW COMMISSION
1120 20th Street, NW., 20036, phone (202) 606–5398
[Created by Public Law 91–596]

Chairman.—W. Scott Railton, 606–2082.
Commissioners: Thomasina V. Rogers, James M. Stephens, 606–5374.
Counsel to the Commissioner.—Richard L. Huberman.
Administrative Law Judges:
James Barkley, 425 Ivanhoe Street, Denver, CO 80220.
Sidney Goldstein, 1880 Arapahoe Street, Number 2608, Denver, CO 80202–1858.
Benjamin Loye, 3810 Marshall Street, Wheat Ridge, CO 80033.
Irving Sommer, 1951 Hopewood Drive, Falls Church, VA 22043.
Nancy L. Spies, 1365 Peachtree Street, NE, Room 240, Atlanta, GA 30309–3119.
Robert A. Yetman, McCormack Post Office and Courthouse, Room 420, Boston, MA 02109–4501.
Covette Rooney, 1120 20th Street, NW, 9th Floor, Washington, DC 20036–3419.
Marvin G. Bober, 1120 20th Street, NW, 9th Floor, Washington, DC 20036–3419.
Ken S. Welsch, 100 Alabama Street, SW, Building 1924, Room 2R90, Atlanta, GA 30303–3104.
Stephen J. Simko, 100 Alabama Street, SW, Building 1924, Room 2R90, Atlanta, GA 30303–3104.
Deputy General Counsel.—Patrick E. Moran, 606–5410.
Executive Director.—Patricia A. Randle, 606–5380.
Executive Secretary.—Ray H. Darling, Jr.
Public Information Officer.—Linda A. Gravely, 606–5398.

OFFICE OF GOVERNMENT ETHICS
1201 New York Avenue NW, Suite 500, 20005, phone (202) 482–9300, fax 482–9238
[Created by Act of October 1, 1989; codified in 5 U.S.C. app., section 401]

Director.—Marilyn L. Glynn (acting).
Special Assistant.—James O'Sullivan.

Confidential Assistant.—Marilyn L. Bennett (acting).
General Counsel.—Marilyn L. Glynn.
Deputy General Counsel.—Stuart Rick.
Deputy Director for—
  Administration and Information Management (CIO).—Daniel D. Dunning.
  Agency Programs.—Jack Covaleski.
  Government Relations and Special Projects.—Jane S. Ley.
Associate Director for—
  Education Division.—Carolyn W. Chapman.
  Information Resources Management.—James V. Parle.
  Program Review Division.—Edward W. Pratt.
  Program Services Division.—Patricia C. Zemple.

OFFICE OF PERSONNEL MANAGEMENT

Theodore Roosevelt Building, 1900 E Street NW 20415–0001, phone (202) 606–1800
http://www.opm.gov

OFFICE OF THE DIRECTOR

Director.—Dan G. Blair (acting) (202) 606–1000.
  Deputy Director.—Dan G. Blair.
    Special Assistant to the Deputy Director.—Tricia Hollis.
  Chief of Staff.—Tricia Hollis (acting).
    Deputy Chief of Staff/Executive Secretariat.—Richard B. Lowe.
    Deputy Chief of Staff.—Amber Roseboom.
    White House Liaison.—Carrie B. Cabelka.
    Special Assistant.—Benjamin D. Allen.
  Senior Policy Advisor to the Director.—Doris Hausser.
    Special Assistant.—Gay L. Gardner.
  Senior Policy Advisor on the Department of Defense.—George Nesterczuk.
  Senior Advisor for Investigative Operations and Agency Planning.—Eric M. Thorson.
  Executive Director, Chief Human Capital Officers Council.—Michael D. Dovilla.
  Director of Combined Federal Campaign Operations.—Mara T. Patermaster, 606–2564.

OFFICE OF E-GOVERNMENT INITIATIVES

Program Director.—Norman Enger, 606–4185.
Deputy Director.—Jeff T.H. Pon, 606–8632.

FEDERAL PREVAILING RATE ADVISORY COMMITTEE

Chair.—Mary R. Rose, 606–1500.

OFFICE OF THE INSPECTOR GENERAL

Inspector General.—Patrick E. McFarland, 606–1200.
  Executive Assistant.—A. Paulette Berry.
  Deputy Inspector General.—Joseph R. Willever.
  Assistant Inspector General, Legal Affairs Program.—E. Jeremy Hutton, 606–3807.
  Counsel to the Inspector General.—Timothy C. Watkins, 606–2030.
  Assistant Inspector General, Policy, Resources Management, and Oversight Program.—
    Daniel K. Marella, 606–2638.
  Assistant Inspector General, Audits Programs.—Harvey D. Thorp, 606–1200.
    Deputy Assistant Inspector General, Audits Programs.—Dennis K. Black, 606–4711.
  Assistant Inspector General, Investigations Program.—Norbert E. Vint, 606–1200.
    Deputy Assistant Inspector General, Investigations Program.—Charles W. Focarino,
      606–3809.

OFFICE OF THE GENERAL COUNSEL

General Counsel.—Mark A. Robbins, 606–1700.
  Secretary.—Althea D. Elam.
  Deputy General Counsel.—Kathie Ann Whipple.
  Administrative Officer (OGC Administration).—Gloria V. Clark.
  Associate General Counsel (Compensation, Benefits, Products, and Services).—James S. Green.
  Assistant General Counsel (Merit Systems and Accountability Division).—Steve E. Abow.

OFFICE OF CONGRESSIONAL RELATIONS

Director.—John C. Gartland, 606–1300.
  Chief of:
    House Affairs.—Jonathan J. Blyth.
    Senate Affairs.—Dino L. Carluccio.
    Capitol Hill.—Charlene E. Luskey, B332 Rayburn House Office Building (202) 632–6296, fax 632–0832.
    Legislative Analysis.—Harry A. Wolf, 606–1424.
    Administration and Confidential Assistant to the Director.—Kathi D. Ladner.

OFFICE OF COMMUNICATIONS AND PUBLIC LIAISON

Director.—Scott Hatch, 606–2402.
  Deputy Director.—Susan Bryant.
    Special Assistant.—Eldon Girdner.
  Director of:
    Administration / Budget.—Teresa Gilbert.
    Press Relations.—Chad Cowan.
    Web Design and Publications.—Vivian Mackey.
  Speech Writers: Hans B. Petersen, Harry Phillips.

DIVISION FOR MANAGEMENT AND CHIEF FINANCIAL OFFICER

Associate Director.—Clarence C. Crawford, 606–1918.
  Director of Operations.—Gisele D. Jones.
  Administrative Officer.—Patrice W. Mendonca, 606–2204.
  Deputy Associate Director, Center for—
    Contracting, Facilities, and Administrative Services Group.—Ronald C. Flom, 606–2200.
    Financial Services and Deputy Chief Financial Officer.—Evelyn A. Brown, 606–1101.
    Human Capital Management Services Group.—William A. Jackson, 606–1402.
    Information Services and Chief Information Officer.—Janet L. Barnes, 606–2150.
  Chief, Center for—
    Equal Employment Opportunity.—Steve Shih, 606–2460.
    Security and Emergency Actions.—Thomas L. Forman, 606–0939.

OFFICE OF HUMAN RESOURCES PRODUCTS AND SERVICES

Associate Director.—Stephen C. Benowitz, 606–0600.
  Staff Assistant.—Rodney E. Leonard.
  Resource Management Group.—Rich Liebl (acting), 606–2871.
  Deputy Associate Director, Center for—
    Eastern Management Development Group.—John R. O'Shea (304) 879–8000.
    Federal Executive Institute.—Thomas J. Towberman (434) 980–6200.
    Investigations Services.—Kathy Dillaman (724) 794–5612.
    Leadership Capacity Services.—Robert F. Danbeck, 606–2100.
    Retirement and Insurance Services Program.—Kathleen M. McGettigan, 606–0462.
    Talent Services.—Nancy Randa, 606–0142.
    Western Management Development Group.—Myhre (Bud) Paulson (303) 671–1010.
  Assistant Director for—
    Examining and Consulting Services.—Linda M. Petersen (acting), 606–1029.
    Insurance Services Programs.—Frank D. Titus, 606–0745.
    Operations.—Winona H. Varnon, 606–1042.

Retirement Services Programs.—Joseph E. McDonald, Jr., 606–0300.
RIS Support Services Program.—Maurice O. Duckett, 606–8089.

DIVISION FOR STRATEGIC HUMAN RESOURCES POLICY

Associate Director.—Ronald P. Sanders, 606–6500.
  Executive Assistant.—Mekaela Nelson.
  Deputy Associate Director, Center for—
    Employee and Family Support Policy.—Mary Ellen Wilson (acting), 606–0770.
    HR Systems Requirements and Strategies.—David Anderson, 606–1343.
    Leadership and Executive Resources Policy.—Hughes Turner, 606–8046.
    Pay and Performance Policy.—Donald J. Winstead, 606–2880.
    Talent and Capacity Policy.—Mark Doboga, 606–8097.
    Workforce Planning and Policy Analysis.—Nancy H. Kichak, 606–0722.
    Workforce Relations and Accountability Policy.—Ana Mazzi, 606–2930.

DIVISION FOR HUMAN CAPITAL LEADERSHIP AND MERIT SYSTEM ACCOUNTABILITY

Associate Director.—Marta Brito Perez, 606–1575.
  Deputy Associate Director, Center for—
    General Government.—Kevin E. Mahoney, 606–2015.
    Human Capital Implementation and Assessment.—Ann Ludwig, 606–2840.
    Human Resources.—Solly J. Thomas (acting), 606–1959.
    Merit System Compliance.—Michael J. Wilkin, 606–2980.
    National Security.—Ray Decker, 606–2511.
    Natural Resources Management.—Solly J. Thomas, 606–1959.
    Small Agencies.—David M. Amaral, 606–2530.

OFFICE OF THE SPECIAL COUNSEL
1730 M Street, NW., Suite 300, 20036–4505, phone (202) 254–3600
[Authorized by 5 U.S.C. 1101 and 5 U.S.C. 1211]

Special Counsel.—Scott J. Bloch.
  Deputy Special Counsel.—James Renne.
    Outreach Director and Counsel.—James McVay.
    Congressional and Public Affairs Division.—Catherine Deeds
    Legal Counsel and Policy Division.—Erin McDonnell.
    Investigation and Prosecution Division.—Leonard Dribinsky.
    Director of Field Operations.—William Reukauf.

PEACE CORPS
1111 20th Street, NW., 20526, phone (202) 692–2000

Toll-Free Number (800) 424–8580, http://www.peacecorps.gov

[Created by Public Law 97–113]

OFFICE OF THE DIRECTOR
fax 692–2101

Director.—Gaddi H. Vasquez.
  Deputy Director.—Josephine K. Olsen.
  Chief of Staff/Chief of Operations.—Marie Wheat.
  Congressional Relations Director.—Michelle Brooks.
  General Counsel.—Tyler Posey.
  Communications Director.—Ellen Field.
  Marketing Strategist.—Linda Isaac.
  Press Director.—Barbara Daly.
  Director of Planning, Policy and Analysis.—Kyo (Paul) Jhin.
  American Diversity Program Manager.—Shirley Everest.
  Office of Private Sector Initiatives.—Nanci Brannan.

Overseas Executive Selection and Support Director.—Lou Barnett.
Printing Officer.—Susan Bloomer.
Inspector General.—Allan Gall (acting).

OFFICE OF PLANNING, BUDGET, AND FINANCE

Chief Financial Officer.—Gopal Khanna.
Budget Officer.—Janice Hagginbothom.
Office of Contracts Director.—George Schutter.
Office of Financial Services Director.—Stephanie Mitchell.

VOLUNTEER SUPPORT

Associate Director for Volunteer Support.—Steven Weinberg.
Director of:
  Medical Services.—Steven Weinberg.
  Special Services.—Robert L. Kirkhorn, Jr.

CRISIS CORPS

Director.—Mary Angelini.

CENTER FOR FIELD ASSISTANCE AND APPLIED RESEARCH

Director.—Elizabeth D. Shays.

AFRICA OPERATIONS

Regional Director.—Henry McKoy.

EUROPE, MEDITERRANEAN, AND ASIA OPERATIONS

Regional Director.—Jay K. Katzen.

INTER-AMERICA AND PACIFIC OPERATIONS

Regional Director.—Allene Zanger.

ASSOCIATE DIRECTOR FOR MANAGEMENT

Associate Director/Management.—Gilbert Smith.
Office of Human Resource Management Director.—Walter Kreamer.
Office of Human Resource Management Deputy Director.—Catherine A. Pearson.

CHIEF INFORMATION OFFICER

CIO.—Edward Anderson.

VOLUNTEER RECRUITMENT AND SELECTION

Associate Director for Volunteer Recruitment and Selection.—Chuck Brooks.
  Director of Minority Recruitment.—Wilfredo Sauri.
  Office of Domestic Programs Director.—Michele Titi (acting).
  Office of Domestic Programs Assistant Director for—
    Fellows/USA Programs.—Michele Titi.
    Returned Volunteer Services.—Patricia Licata.

PEACE CORPS REGIONAL OFFICES

Atlanta: 100 Alabama Street, Building 1924, Suite 2R70, Atlanta, GA 30303 (404)
562–3451, fax (404) 562–3455 (FL, GA, TN, MS, AL, SC, PR, VI).

Manager.—John Eaves.
Public Affairs Specialist.—Carmellia Kenner.
Boston: Tip O'Neill Federal Building, 10 Causeway Street, Suite 450, Boston, MA 02222–1099 (617) 565–5555, fax (617) 565–5539 (MA, VT, NH, RI, ME).
Manager.—James Arena-DeRosa.
Public Affairs Specialist.—Joanna Shea.
Chicago: 55 West Monroe Street, Suite 450, Chicago, IL 60603 (312) 353–4990, fax (312) 353–4192 (IL, IN, MO, MI, OH, KY).
Manager.—Virginia Koch.
Public Affairs Specialist.—Scot Roskelley.
Dallas: 207 South Houston Street, Room 527, Dallas, TX 75202 (214) 253–5400, fax (214) 253–5401 (TX, OK, LA, NM, AR).
Manager.—Sharon Sugarek.
Public Affairs Specialist.—Jesus Garcia.
Denver: 1999 Broadway, Suite 2205, Denver, CO 80202–3050 (303) 844–7020, fax (303) 844–7010 (CO, KS, NE, UT, WY).
Manager.—Ann Conway.
Public Affairs Specialist.—Jill Thiare.
Los Angeles: 2361 Rosecrans Avenue, Suite 155, El Segundo, CA 90245–0916 (310) 356–1100, fax (310) 356–1125 (Southern CA, AZ).
Manager.—Jill Andrews.
Minneapolis: 330 Second Avenue South, Suite 420, Minneapolis, MN 55401 (612) 348–1480, fax (612) 348–1474 (MN, WI, SD, ND, IA).
Manager.—Allan Gerber.
Public Affairs Specialist.—Gary Lore.
New York: 201 Varick Street, Suite 1025, New York, NY 10014 (212) 352–5440, fax (212) 352–5442 (NY, NJ, CT, PA).
Manager.—Edwin Jorge.
Public Affairs Specialist.—Bartel Kendrick.
Rosslyn: 1525 Wilson Boulevard, Suite 100, Arlington, VA 22209 (703) 235–9191, fax (703) 235–9189 (DC, MD, NC, WV, DE, VA).
Manager.—Lynn Kneedler.
San Francisco: 333 Market Street, Suite 600, San Francisco, CA 94105; (415) 977–8800, fax (415) 977–8803 (Northern CA, NV, HI).
Manager.—Harris Bostic II.
Public Affairs Specialist.—Dennis McMahon.
Seattle: 1601 5th Avenue, Suite 605, Seattle, WA 98101 (206) 553–5490, fax (206) 553–2343 (WA, OR, ID, AK, MT).
Manager.—Wayne Blackwelder.
Public Affairs Specialist.—James Aquirre.

PENSION BENEFIT GUARANTY CORPORATION
1200 K Street 20005–4026 (202) 326–4000

BOARD OF DIRECTORS

Chairman.—Elaine L. Chao, Secretary of Labor.
Members:
John W. Snow, Secretary of the Treasury.
Carlos M. Gutierrez, Secretary of Commerce.

OFFICIALS

Executive Director.—Bradley D. Belt, 326–4010.
Deputy Executive Director.—Vincent Snowbarger, 326–4010.
Chief Officer for—
Finance.—Theodore Winter (acting), 326–4060.
Management and Human Capital.—John Seal, 326–4180.
Operations.—Joseph H. Grant, 326–4010.
Technology.—Richard W. Hartt, 326–4010.
Department Director for—
Benefits Administration and Payment.—Bennie Hagans, 326–4050.
Budget.—Henry Thompson, 326–4120.
Communications and Public Affairs.—Randolph Clerihue, 326–4040.

Contracts and Controls Review.—Marty Boehm, 326–4161.
Facilities and Services.—Patricia Davis, 326–4150.
Financial Operations.—Theodore Winter, 326–4060.
General Counsel.—Phillip Hertz (acting), 326–4020.
Human Resources.—Michelle Pilipovich, 326–4110.
Insurance Program.—Terrence Deneen, 326–4050.
Legislative and Regulatory Affairs.—James Armbruster (acting), 326–4130.
Policy, Research and Analysis.—David Gustafson (acting), 326–4080.
Process Change Consulting Group.—Wilmer Graham, 326–4180.
Procurement.—Robert W. Herting, 326–4160.
Chief Counsel.—Jeffrey B. Cohen, 326–4020.
Inspector General.—Robert Emmons, 326–4030.

POSTAL RATE COMMISSION
1333 H Street NW., Suite 300, 20268–0001, phone (202) 789–6800, fax 789–6886

Chairman.—George A. Omas, 789–6801.
Vice Chairman.—Tony Hammond, 789–6805.
Commissioners:
 Dana B. Covington, 789–6868.
 Ruth Y. Goldway, 789–6810.
 Dawn Tisdale, 789–6813.
Chief Administrative Officer and Secretary.—Steven W. Williams, 789–6840.
General Counsel.—Stephen L. Sharfman, 789–6820.
Director, Office of:
 Consumer Advocate.—Shelley S. Dreifuss, 789–6830.
 Rates, Analysis and Planning.—John Waller, 789–6850.

SECURITIES AND EXCHANGE COMMISSION
**450 Fifth Street NW 20549, phone (202) 942–8088, TTY Relay Service 1–800–877–8339
fax 942–9628, http://www.sec.gov**

THE COMMISSION

Chairman.—William Donaldson, 942–0100, fax 942–9646.
Counselor to the Chairman.—Martha Peterson.
Counsel to the Chairman: Anil Abraham, David Huntington, Jeffrey Minton.
Managing Executive for—
 Operations.—Peter Derby.
 Policy and Staff.—Joseph Hall.
Commissioners:
 Paul Atkins, 952–0700, fax 942–9521.
  Counsel to the Commissioner: Susan Ameel, David Nason, Hester Peirce.
 Roel Campos, 942–0500, fax 942–9647.
  Counsel to the Commissioner: Scot Draeger, Keir Gumbs, Heather Traeger.
 Cynthia A. Glassman, 942–0600, fax 942–9666.
  Counsel to the Commissioner: Julie Bell, Mark Berman, Mary Head.
 Harvey Goldschmid, 942–0800, fax 942–9563.
  Counsel to the Commissioner: Tracey Aronson, Daphne Chisolm, Luis DeLatorre.

OFFICE OF THE SECRETARY

Secretary.—Jonathan G. Katz, 942–7070.
Deputy Secretary.—Margaret H. McFarland, 942–7070.
Library Director.—Cindy Plisch, 942–7086.

OFFICE OF INVESTOR EDUCATION AND ASSISTANCE

Director.—Susan Ferris-Wyderko, 942–7040, fax 942–9634.

OFFICE OF EQUAL EMPLOYMENT OPPORTUNITY

Director.—Deborah K. Balducchi, 551–6006, fax 942–9547.

OFFICE OF FREEDOM OF INFORMATION AND PRIVACY ACT OPERATIONS

FOIA Officer.—Celia Winter, 551–7900.
  FOIA/PA Branch Chiefs: Brenda Fuller, Ligia Glass, Frank Henderson.

OFFICE OF THE CHIEF ACCOUNTANT

Chief Accountant.—Carol Stacey, 942–2960.
  Deputy Chief Accountant.—Craig Olinger, 942–2960.
  Chief Counsel.—Paula Dubberly, 942–2900.

OFFICE OF ECONOMIC ANALYSIS

Chief Economist.—Chester Spatt, 551–6600.
  Deputy Chief Economist.—Jonathan Sokobin.

OFFICE OF THE GENERAL COUNSEL

General Counsel.—Giovanni P. Prezioso, 942–0900, fax 942–9625.
  Special Assistant for Management.—Virginia A. Mayberry, 942–0832.
  Deputy General Counsel.—Meyer Eisenberg, 942–0966.
  Ethics Counsel.—William Lenox, 942–0970.
  Solicitor, Appellate Litigation and Bankruptcy.—Jacob H. Stillman, 942–0930.
  Assistant General Counsels: Eric Summergrad (Principal Assistant), 942–0911; Katharine Gresham (Bankruptcy and Appellate Litigation), 942–0810; Randall Quinn (Appellate Litigation), 942–0933.
  Associate General Counsel for Litigation and Administrative Practice.—Richard M. Humes, 942–0875.
  Assistant General Counsels: Melinda Hardy, 942–0877, Samuel Forstein, 942–0871; (Litigation and Administrative Practice); George C. Brown (Litigation and Contracting), 942–0828.
  Principal Associate General Counsel for Legal Policy.—Meredith Mitchell, 942–0834.
  Assistant General Counsels: Arthur Laby (Investment Management, PUHCA and Administrative Law), 942–0958; Janice Mitnick (Market Regulation), 942–0935; David Fredrickson (Corporation Finance and Accounting), 942–0916; Stephen Jung (Legislation and Financial Services), 942–0927; Richard Levine (Enforcement), 942–0886.
  Associate General Counsel for Counseling and Regulatory Policy.—Diane Sanger, 942–0960.
  Associate General Counsel for Adjudication.—Anne E. Chafer, 942–0950.
  Counselor for Adjudication.—William S. Stern, 942–0949.
  Assistant General Counsels: Joan Loizeaux (Principal Assistant), 942–0990; Joan McCarthy (Adjudication), 942–0950.

DIVISION OF INVESTMENT MANAGEMENT

Director.—Paul F. Roye, 551–6720, fax 942–9659.
  Senior Adviser to the Director.—Jennifer B. McHugh, 551–6720.
  Associate Director, Chief Counsel.—Douglas J. Scheidt, 551–6701.
  Assistant Chief Counsels: Alison M. Fuller (International Issues), 551–6825; Elizabeth G. Osterman (Financial Institutions), 551–6825.
  Associate Director, Office of:
    Disclosure & Insurance Product Regulation.—Susan Nash, 551–6742.
    Legal and Disclosure.—Barry D. Miller, 551–6725.
    Public Utility & Investment Company Regulation.—David B. Smith, 551–6746.
    Regulatory Policy & Investment Adviser Regulation.—Robert E. Plaze, 551–6702.
  Assistant Director, Office of:
    Disclosure and Review No. 1.—Michael A. Lainoff, 551–6921.
    Disclosure and Review No. 2.—Frank J. Donaty, 551–6925.
    Enforcement Liaison.—Barbara Chretien-Dar, 551–6785.
    Financial Analysis.—Paul B. Goldman, 551–6715.
    Insurance Products.—William J. Kotapish, 551–6795.
    Investment Adviser Regulation.—Jennifer L. Sawin, 551–6787.
    Investment Company Regulation.—Nadya B. Roytblat, 551–6821.
    Public Utility Regulation.—Catherine A. Fisher, 551–6944.
    Regulatory Policy.—C. Hunter Jones, 551–6792.
  Chief Accountant, Office of Chief Accountant.—Brian D. Bullard, 551–6918.

DIVISION OF CORPORATION FINANCE

Director.—Alan Beller, 942–2929, fax 942–9525.
Deputy Director of:
  Disclosure Operations.—Shelley E. Parratt, 942–2830.
  Legal and Regulatory.—Martin Dunn, 942–2890.
Associate Directors:
  Legal Office.—Paula Dubberly, 942–2900.
  Regulatory.—Mauri L. Osheroff, 942–2840.
  Chief Accountant.—Carol Stacey, 942–2960.
  Disclosure Operations.—Paul Belvin, 942–8978; James Daly, 942–2881; Barry Summer, 942–7875.
Chief, Office of:
  Chief Counsel.—David Lynn, 942–2900.
  EDGAR, Information and Analysis.—Herbert D. Scholl, 942–2930.
  Enforcement Liaison.—Mary Kosterlitz, 824–5600.
  International Corporate Finance.—Paul Dudek, 942–2990.
  Mergers and Acquisitions.—Brian Breheny, 942–2920.
  Rulemaking.—Elizabeth Murphy, 942–2910.
  Small Business Policy.—Gerald Laporte, 942–2950.
  Assistant Directors: Karen Garnett, 942–1960; Peggy Fisher, 942–1880; Barbara Jacobs, 942–1800; Pamela Long, 942–1950; H. Christopher Owings, 942–1900; Jeffrey Reidler, 942–1840; John Reynolds, 942–2999; Todd Schiffman, 942–1760; H. Roger Schwall, 942–1870; Larry Spirgel, 942–1990; Max Webb, 942–1850.

DIVISION OF ENFORCEMENT

Director.—Stephen M. Cutler, 942–4500, fax 942–9636.
Senior Advisor.—Donna Norman, 942–4947.
Deputy Director.—Linda C. Thomsen, 942–4501.
Senior Advisor.—Pauline Calande, 824–5688.
Associate Director.—Peter H. Bresnan, 942–4550.
  Assistant Directors: Cheryl J. Scarboro, 942–4583; Josh Fekler, 942–4897.
Chief, Office of Internet Enforcement.—John R. Stark, 942–4803.
Associate Director.—Scott Friestad, 942–4732.
  Assistant Directors: James T. Coffman, 942–4574; Laura Josephs, 942–7872.
Chief, Market Surveillance.—Joseph J. Cella, 942–4559.
Associate Director.—Paul R. Berger, 942–4854.
  Assistant Directors: Timothy N. England, 942–7109; Richard W. Grime, 942–4863; Robert Kaplan, 942–2803; Mark Kreitman, 942–4677.
Associate Director.—Lawrence A. West, 942–4631.
  Assistant Directors: Gregory Faragasso, 942–4601; Kenneth Lench, 942–4755; Richard Firestone, 942–4640.
Associate Director.—Antonia Chion, 942–4567.
  Assistant Directors: Christopher R. Conte, 942–4579; Yuri B. Zelinsky, 942–4890.
Chief Counsel.—Joan E. McKown, 942–4530.
Associate Chief Counsel.—Gretta J. Powers, 942–4756.
  Assistant Chief Counsels: Nancy A. Doty, 942–4536; Charlotte L. Buford, 942–4758; Kenneth H. Hall, 942–4635; Sarah Bessin, 942–7160; John Polise, 942–0068.
Chief Litigation Counsel.—David L. Kornblau, 942–4818.
  Deputy Chief Litigation Counsel.—Mark A. Adler, 942–4770.
Chief Accountant.—Susan G. Markel, 942–4871.
  Associate Chief Accountants: Regina M. Barrett, 942–4524; Dwayne Brown, 942–4547; David M. Estabrook, 942–4814; Pierron Leef, 942–4687.
Director, Regional Office Operations.—James A. Clarkson, 942–4580.

DIVISION OF MARKET REGULATION

Director.—Annette L. Nazareth, 942–0090, fax 942–9643.
Deputy Director.—Robert L.D. Colby, 942–0094.
Chief of Operations.—Herbert Brooks, 942–0150.
Associate Director, Market Supervision.—Elizabeth King, 942–0140.
Assistant Directors, Office of:
  Broker Dealer.— James Brigagliano, 942–0772; Jerry Carpenter, 942–4187; Thomas McGowan, 942–0177; JoAnne Swindler, 942–0750.

Markets.—Ira Brandriss, 942–0148; Katherine England, 942–0154; Terri Evans, 942–4162; Deborah L. Flynn, 942–0075; John Roeser, 942–0762; Nancy Sanow, 942–0796.
Associate Directors, Office of Broker Dealer: Larry Bergmann, 942–0770; Michael A. Macchiaroli, 942–0132.
Associate Director, Chief Counsel.—Catherine McGuire, 942–0061.
Deputy Chief Counsel.—Paula Jenson, 942–0073.

OFFICE OF INTERNATIONAL AFFAIRS

Director.—Ethiopis Tafara, 551–6690, fax 942–9524.
Deputy Director.—Elizabeth Jacobs.
Assistant Directors: Sherman Boone, Robert D. Strahota, Susan Yashar.

OFFICE OF LEGISLATIVE AFFAIRS

Director.—Jane Cobb, 942–0010, fax 942–9650.
Deputy Director.—Peter Kiernan.

OFFICE OF THE INSPECTOR GENERAL

Inspector General.—Walter J. Stachnik, 551–6060, fax 942–9653.
Deputy Inspector General.—Nelson N. Egbert.

OFFICE OF FILINGS AND INFORMATION SERVICES

Associate Executive Director.—Kenneth A. Fogash, 551–7200, fax (703) 914–1005.
Deputy Director.—Cecilia Wilkerson.
Associate Director.—Margaret Favor, 551–8204; Shirley Slocum.
Assistant Director.—Ronnette McDaniel, 551–8378.

OFFICE OF PUBLIC AFFAIRS

Director.—Matthew Well, 942–0020, fax 942–9654.
Deputy Directors: Amy Best, John D. Heine.

OFFICE OF FINANCIAL MANAGEMENT

Associate Executive Director.—Margaret J. Carpenter, 551–7854, fax (703) 914–0172.

OFFICE OF INFORMATION TECHNOLOGY

Associate Executive Director/Chief Information Officer.—Corey Booth, 551–8800; fax (703) 914–2621.

OFFICE OF ADMINISTRATIVE AND PERSONNEL MANAGEMENT

Associate Executive Director.—Anne O'Donoghue, 551–7500.

REGIONAL OFFICES

Northeast Regional Office: The Woolworth Building, 233 Broadway, New York, NY 10279 (646) 428–1500, fax (646) 428–1981.
Regional Director.—Mark Schonfeld, 748–1650.
Associate Regional Directors, Enforcement: Robert B. Blackburn, 428–1610; Andrew Calamari, 428–1659; Helene T. Glotzer, 428–1736; David Rosenfeld, 428–1869.
Assistant Regional Directors, Enforcement: Doria Bachenheimer, 428–1911; Alistaire Bambach, 428–1636; Robert DeLeonardis, 428–1688; Gerald Gross, 428–1743; Bruce

Karpati, 428–1775; Leslie Kazon, 428–1778; Kay Lackey, 428–1790; David Markowitz, 428–1806; George Stepaniuk, 428–1910; Scott York, 428–1946.

Associate Regional Director, Investment Management and Corporate Reorganization.— Douglas Scarff, 428–1660.

Assistant Regional Directors: Dawn Blankenship, 428–1600; Joseph Dimaria, 426–1692; William Delmage, 428–1689; Dorothy Eschwie, 428–1700.

Associate Regional Director, Broker/Dealer.—Robert A. Sollazzo, 428–1620; Richard D. Lee, 428–1520.

Assistant Regional Directors, Broker/Dealer Examinations: Richard A. Heapy, 428–1753; Linda Lettieri, 428–1797; John M. Nee, 428–1831; Rosanne R. Smith, 428–1901.

Boston District Office: 73 Tremont Street, Suite 600, Boston, MA 02108 (617) 573–8900, fax 424–5945.

District Administrator.—Walter G. Ricciardi, 573–8934.

Associate District Administrator, Enforcement.—David Bergers, 424–5927.

Assistant District Administrators, Enforcement: John Dugan, 573–8936; Martin Healey, 573–8952.

Assistant District Administrators, Investment Adviser/Investment Company Examinations: Diane Gillies, 573–8947; Edward A. Ryan, Jr., 573–8935; Elizabeth Salini, 573–8931.

Assistant District Administrator, Broker/Dealer Examinations.—Lucile Corkery, 573–8932.

Philadelphia District Office: Mellon Independence Center, 701 Market Street, Suite 2000, Philadelphia, PA 19106 (215) 597–3100, fax 597–5885.

District Administrator.—Arthur Gabinet, 597–3106.

Associate District Administrator, Examinations.—Joy G. Thompson, 597–6135.

Associate District Administrator, Enforcement.—Daniel G. Hawke, 597–3191.

Assistant District Administrators, Enforcement: Elaine C. Greenberg, 597–3107; David Horowitz, 597–3107.

Senior Assistant District Administrators, Investment Company/Investment Adviser Examinations: Paul T. Hee, 597–8307; William R. Meck, 597–0789.

Assistant District Administrator, Regulation.—A. Laurence Ehrhart, 597–2983.

Southeast Regional Office: 801 Brickell Avenue, Suite 1800, Miami, FL 33131 (305) 982–6300, fax (305) 536–6300.

Regional Director.—David Nelson, 982–4120.

Assistant Regional Directors, Enforcement: Ivan Harris, 982–6342; John C. Mattimore, 982–6357.

Assistant Regional Director.—John D. Mahoney, 982–6303.

Atlanta District Office: 3475 Lenox Road NE., Suite 1000, Atlanta, GA 30326 (404) 842–7600, fax 842–7666.

District Administrator.—Richard P. Wessel, 842–7610.

Senior Associate District Administrator, Enforcement.—Ronald L. Crawford, 842–7630.

Associate District Administrator, Enforcement.—Katherine Addleman, 842–7682.

Assistant District Administrators, Enforcement: Stephen E. Donahue, 842–7618; Richard P. Murphy, 842–7665.

Associate Administrator, Examinations.—Francis P. McGing, 842–7645.

Assistant District Administrator, Broker/Dealer Examinations.—Howard Dennis, Jr., 842–7643.

Assistant District Administrators, Investment Company/Investment Advisers Examinations: Diane S. Eckert, 842–7655; Lillian A. Wilcox, 842–7653.

Midwest Regional Office: 175 West Jackson Boulevard, Suite 900, Chicago, IL 60604 (312) 353–7390, fax 353–7398.

Regional Director.—Merri Jo Gillette, 353–9338.

Associate Regional Directors, Enforcement: Robert J. Burson, 353–7428; Timothy L. Warren, 353–7394 .

Associate Regional Directors, Examinations: John R. Brissman, 353–7436; Jeannette L. Lewis, 353–0525.

Assistant Regional Directors, Enforcement: Peter Chan, 353–7410; Daniel R. Gregus, 353–7423; Scott J. Hlavacek, 353–1679; Jane Jarcho, 353–5479; John R. Lee, 886–2247; Paul A. Montoya, 353–7429; John J. Sikora, 353–7418.

Assistant Regional Directors, Examinations: Doug R. Adams, 353–7402; Maureen Dempsey, 886–1496; Lewis A. Garcia, 353–6888; J. Gary Hopkins, 886–8511; Lawrence Kendra, 886–8508; Thomas Kirk, 886–3956; David J. Mueller, 353–7404; Thomas Murphy, 886–8513; Larry P. Perdue, 353–7219.

Central Regional Office: 1801 California Street, Suite 1500, Denver, CO 80202 (303) 844–1000, fax 844–1010.

Regional Director.—Randall J. Fons, 844–1042.

Associate Regional Director.—Donald M. Hoerl, 844–1060.

Assistant Regional Directors, Enforcement: Mary S. Brady, 844–1023; Laura Metcalfe, 844–1092; Amy Norwood, 844–1029.

Assistant Regional Director, Broker/Dealer Examinations.—Edward A. Lewkowski, 844–1050.
Assistant Regional Director, Investment Company/Investment Adviser Examinations.—Dale E. Coffin, 844–1040.
Fort Worth District Office: 801 Cherry Street, 19th Floor, Fort Worth, TX 76102 (817) 978–3821, fax 978–2700.
District Administrator.—Harold F. Degenhardt, 978–3821.
  Assistant District Administrators, Enforcement: Alan Buie, 978–0581; Jeffrey Cohen, 978–6480; Stephen Webster, 978–6459.
  Associate District Associate Administrator, Examinations.—Hugh M. Wright, 978–6474.
  Assistant District Administrators, Broker/Dealer Examinations: Julie Preuitt, 978–6428; Jim Perry, 978–6439.
  Assistant District Administrator, Investment Company/Investment Adviser Examinations.—Robert Pike, 978–6444.
Salt Lake District Office: 15 West South Temple Street, Suite 1800, Salt Lake City, UT 84101 (801) 524–5796, fax 524–3558.
District Administrator.—Kenneth D. Israel, 524–6745.
Pacific Regional Office: 5670 Wilshire Boulevard, 11th Floor, Los Angeles, CA 90036 (213) 965–3998, fax 965–3816.
Regional Director.—Randall R. Lee, 965–3807.
  Associate Regional Directors, Enforcement: Sandra J. Harris, 965–3962; Briane Nelson Mitchel, 965–3864.
  Assistant Regional Directors, Enforcement: Kelly C. Bowers, 965–3924; Michele Wein Layne, 965–3850; Diana Tani, 965–3991.
  Associate Regional Director, Examinations.—Rosalind R. Tyson, 965–3893.
  Associate Regional Directors, Investment Company/Investment Adviser Examinations: Michael P. Levitt, 525–2684; Paula Weiser, 525–3252.
  Assistant Regional Directors, Broker/Dealer Examinations: Martin Murphy, 965–3859; Cindy S. Wong, 965–3927.
San Francisco District Office: 44 Montgomery Street, Suite 2600, San Francisco, CA 94104 (415) 705–2500, fax 705–2501.
District Administrator.—Helane L. Morrison, 705–2450.
  Associate District Administrator.—Marc J. Fagel, 705–2449.
  Assistant District Administrators, Enforcement: Kathleen K. Bisaccia, 705–2350; Michael S. Dicke, 705–2458.
  Assistant District Administrators, Investment Company/Investment Adviser Examinations: Daryl Hagel, 705–2340; John D. Swayze, 705–2466.
  Assistant District Administrator, Broker/Dealer Examinations.—Jennet Leong, 705–2452.

SELECTIVE SERVICE SYSTEM

1515 Wilson Boulevard, 4th Floor, Arlington, VA 22209–2425

phone (703) 605–4000, fax 605–4133, http://www.sss.gov

Director.—William A. Chatfield, 605–4010.
  Deputy Director.—S. Eric Benson.
  Chief of Staff.—COL Richard A. Moore.
  Office of General Counsel.—Rudy Sanchez, 605–4012.
  Inspector General.—Carlo Verdino, 605–4022.
  Director for—
    Operations.—Willie L. Blanding, Jr., 605–4066.
    Information Management.—Scott Campbell, 605–4110.
    Resource Management.—Edward A. Blackadar, Jr., 605–4032.
    Public and Intergovernmental Affairs.—Richard S. Flahavan, 605–4017, fax 605–4106.
    Financial Management.—William Reese, 605–4028.
Registration Information Office, P.O. Box 94638, Palatine, IL 60094–4638, phone (847) 688–6888, fax (847) 688–2860.

SMALL BUSINESS ADMINISTRATION

409 Third Street, SW 20416

phone (202) 205–6600, fax (202) 205–7064, http://www.sbaonline.sba.gov

Administrator.—Hector V. Barreto, 205–6605.
Deputy Administrator.—Melanie Sabelhaus.

Chief of Staff.—Stephen Galvan, 205–6605.
Director of Executive Secretariat.—Don Swain, 205–2410.
General Counsel.—David Javdan, 205–6642.
Chief Counsel for Advocacy.—Thomas M. Sullivan, 205–6533.
Inspector General.—Harry Damelin, 205–6580.
Chief Financial Officer.—Thomas Dumaresq, 205–6449.
Director, National Advisory Council.—Balbina Caldwell, 205–6914.
Associate Administrator for—
  Disaster Assistant.—Herb Mitchell, 205–6734.
  Field Operations.—Michael Pappas, 205–6808.
  Public Communications.—Raul Cisneros, 205–6740.
Assistant Administrator for—
  Congressional and Legislative Affairs.—Anthony Bedell, 205–6700.
  Equal Employment Opportunity and Compliance.—Loyola Trujillo (acting), 205–6750.
  Hearings and Appeals.—Delorice Ford, 205–7340.
Associate Deputy Administrator for Management and Administration.—Lewis Andrews, 205–6610.
Assistant Administrator for—
  Administration.—Darryl Hariston, 205–6642.
  Chief Information Officer.—Jerry Williams (acting), 205–6706.
  Human Capital Management.—Richard Brechbiel, 205–6784.
Associate Deputy Administrator for Capital Access.—Michael Barrera (acting), 205–6557.
Associate Administrator for—
  Business and Community Initiatives.—Ellen Thrasher (acting), 205–6665.
  Financial Assistance.—James Riviera, 205–6490.
  Investment.—Jaime Guzman, 205–6510.
  Small Business Development Centers.—Antonio Doss, 205–6766.
  Surety Guarantees.—Diane Neal (acting), 205–6540.
Assistant Administrator for—
  International Trade.—Manuel Rosales, 205–6720.
  Veterans' Affairs.—William Elmore, 205–6773.
  Women's Business Ownership.—Wilma Goldstein, 205–6673.
Associate Deputy Administrator for Government Contracting and Business Development.—Allegra McCullough, 205–6459.
Associate Administrator for—
  Business Development.—Luz Hopewell, 205–6463.
  Government Contracting.—Denise Benjamin (acting), 205–6460.
Assistant Administrator for—
  Size Standard.—Gary Jackson, 205–6618.
  Technology.—Edison Brown (acting), 205–6450.

SMITHSONIAN INSTITUTION

Smithsonian Institution Building—The Castle (SIB), 1000 Jefferson Drive, SW., 20560

phone 357–2700, http://www.smithsonian.org

The Smithsonian Institution is an independent trust instrumentality created in accordance with the terms of the will of James Smithson of England who in 1826 bequeathed his property to the United States of America "to found at Washington under the name of the Smithsonian Institution an establishment for the increase and diffusion of knowledge among men." Congress pledged the faith of the United States to carry out the trust in 1836 (Act of July 1, 1836, C. 252, 5 Stat. 64), and established the Institution in its present form in 1846 (August 10, 1846, C. 178, 9 Stat. 102), entrusting the management of the institution to its independent Board of Regents.

THE BOARD OF REGENTS

ex officio

Chief Justice of the United States.—William H. Rehnquist, Chancellor.
Vice President of the United States.—Richard B. Cheney.

Appointed by the President of the Senate	*Appointed by the Speaker of the House*
Hon. Thad Cochran	Hon. Sam Johnson
Hon. William H. (Bill) Frist	Hon. Ralph Regula
Hon. Patrick Leahy	Hon. Xavier Becerra

Appointed by Joint Resolution of Congress

Eli Broad	Dr. Manuel L. Ibáñez	Alan G. Spoon
Anne d'Harnoncourt	Dr. Walter E. Massey	Roger Sant
Dr. Hanna H. Gray	Dr. Patty Stonesifer	Wesley S. Williams, Jr.

OFFICE OF THE SECRETARY

Secretary.—Lawrence M. Small, 357–1846.
　Executive Assistant to the Secretary.—James M. Hobbins, 357–1869.
　Inspector General.—Debroah Ritt, 275–2154.
　Director of:
　　Policy and Analysis.—Carole M.P. Neves, 633–8065.
　　External Affairs.—Virginia Clark, 786–2710.
　General Counsel.—John Huerta, 357–2583.

OFFICE OF THE DEPUTY SECRETARY AND CHIEF OPERATING OFFICER

Deputy Secretary.—Sheila P. Burke, 357–7033.
　Director of:
　　Government Relations.—Nell Payne, 357–2962.
　　Communications and Public Affairs.—Evelyn Lieberman, 357–2627.
　　Special Events and Protocol.—Nicole L. Krakora, 357–2284.
　　National Programs.—Richard Kurin (acting), 357–7037.
　　Arts and Industries Building.—Ellen Dorn, 786–9199.
　　Quadrangle Building.—Ronald W. Hawkins, 633–4025.
　　Accessibility Program.—Elizabeth Ziebarth, 786–2942.

MUSEUMS

　Director of:
　　Anacostia Museum.—James Early (acting), 610–3378.
　　National Museum of American History.—Brent Glass, 633–3435.
　　National Museum of the American Indian.—W. Richard West, 633–6990.
　　National Postal Museum.—Allen Kane, 633–5500.

PAN-INSTITUTIONAL PROGRAMS

　Director of:
　　Asian Pacific American Program.—Franklin Odo, 786–2963.
　　Center for Folklife Programs and Cultural Heritage.—Richard Kurin, 275–1138.
　　Smithsonian Center for Latino Initiatives.—Luben Montoya (acting), 633–1240.
　　Smithsonian Institution Archives.—Thomas Soapes (acting), 357–3080.
　　Smithsonian Institution Libraries.—Nancy Gwinn, 633–2240.

NATIONAL PROGRAMS

　Director of:
　　Smithsonian Affiliations Program.—Harold Closter, 633–9157.
　　Smithsonian Associates Program.—Barbara Tuceling (acting), 357–2696.
　　Smithsonian Center for Education and Museum Studies.—Stephanie L. Norby, 357–2624.
　　Smithsonian Institution Traveling Exhibition Service.—Anna Cohn, 633–3136.

Independent Agencies

813

OPERATING UNITS

Director, Office of:
  Equal Employment and Minority Affairs.—Era Marshall, 275–0146.
  Exhibits Central.—Michael Headley, 357–1556.
  Facilities Engineering and Operations.—William Brubaker, 357–1873.
  Human Resources.—James Douglas, 275–1100.
Chief, Office of:
  Finance.—Alice Maroni, 275–2020.
  Information.—Dennis Shaw, 633–2800.
Ombudsman.—Chandra Heilman, 357–3261.

OFFICE OF THE UNDER SECRETARY FOR SCIENCE

Under Secretary.—David Evans, 357–2903.
  Director of:
  International Relations.—Francine Berkowitz, 357–4795.
  National Air and Space Museum.—Jack Dailey, 633–2350.
  National Museum of Natural History.—Cristian Samper, 633–2664.
  National Science Resources Center.—Sally Goetz Shuler, 357–4892.
  National Zoological Park.—David Evans (acting), 673–4666.
  Smithsonian Astrophysical Observatory.—Charles Alcock (617) 495–7100.
  Smithsonian Center for Materials Research and Education.—Robert Koestler (301) 238–1205.
  Smithsonian Environmental Research Center.—Ross Simons (443) 482–2205.
  Smithsonian Tropical Research Institute.—Ira Rubinoff, 011–507–212–8110.

OFFICE OF THE UNDER SECRETARY FOR ART

Under Secretary.—Ned Rifkin, 633–2824.
  Director of:
  Archives of American Art.—Richard Wattenmaker, 275–1874.
  Cooper Hewitt, National Design Museum.—Paul Thompson (212) 849–8370.
  Freer and Sackler Galleries.—Julian Raby, 633–0456.
  Hirshhorn Musem and Sculpture Garden.—Ned Rifkin, 633–2824.
  National Museum of African Art.—Sharon Patton, 633–4610.
  National Portrait Gallery.—Marc Pachter, 275–1740.
  Smithsonian American Art Museum.—Elizabeth Broun, 275–1515.
  Office of Fellowships.—Catherine Harris, 275–0655.
Senior Curator for Photography.—Merry Foresta, 275–1176.

SMITHSONIAN BUSINESS VENTURES

Chief Executive Officer.—Gary M. Beer, 786–9141.
  Publisher, Smithsonian Magazine.—Amy Wilkins (212) 916–1313.
  Editor, Smithsonian Magazine.—Carey Winfrey, 275–2202.

SOCIAL SECURITY ADMINISTRATION

International Trade Commission Building, 500 E Street SW, Washington, DC 20254 (ITCB)

Altmeyer Building, 6401 Security Boulevard, Baltimore, MD 21235 (ALTMB)

Annex Building, 6401 Security Boulevard, Baltimore, MD 21235 (ANXB)

National Computer Center, 6201 Security Boulevard, Baltimore, MD 21235 (NCC)

West High Rise Building, 6401 Security Boulevard, Baltimore, MD 21235 (WHRB)

East High Rise Building, 6401 Security Boulevard, Baltimore, MD 21235 (EHRB)

Gwynn Oak Building, 1710 Gwynn Oak Avenue, Baltimore, MD 21207 (GWOB)

Operations Building, 6401 Security Boulevard, Baltimore, MD 21235 (OPRB)

Metro West Tower Building, 300 North Greene Street, Baltimore, MD 21201 (MWTB)

Security West Tower, 1500 Woodlawn Drive, Baltimore, MD 21241 (SWTB)

One Skyline Tower, 5107 Leesburg Pike, Falls Church, VA 22041 (SKY)

http://www.ssa.gov

OFFICE OF THE COMMISSIONER

Commissioner.—Jo Anne Barnhart, ITCB, room 850 (202) 358–6000 or ALTMB, room 900 (410) 965–3120.
Deputy Commissioner.—James B. Lockhart III, ITCB, room 874 (202) 358–6041 or ALTMB, room 960 (410) 965–9000.
Chief of Staff.—Larry W. Dye, ITCB, room 858 (202) 358–6013 or ALTMB, room 900 (410) 966–8323.

OFFICE OF THE CHIEF ACTUARY

Chief Actuary.—Stephen C. Goss, ALTMB, room 700 (410) 965–3000.
Deputy Chief Actuary for—
Long Range.—Alice H. Wade, ALTMB, room 700 (410) 965–3002.
Short Range.—Eli N. Donkar, OPRB, room 4–N–29 (410) 965–3004.

OFFICE OF THE CHIEF INFORMATION OFFICER

Chief Information Officer.—Thomas P. Hughes, ALTMB, room 500 (410) 966–5738.
Deputy Chief Information Officer.—Dean Mesterham, ALTMB, room 500 (410) 965–4721.

OFFICE OF COMMUNICATION

Deputy Commissioner for Communications/Press Officer.—Jim Courtney, ALTMB, room 460 (410) 965–1720, or ITCB, room 866, (202) 358–6131.
Assistant Deputy Commissioner.—Philip Gambino, ALTMB, room 460 (410) 965–1720.
Associate Commissioner, Office of:
Communication, Planning, Evaluation and Measurement.—Jean Venable, ANXB, room 3505 (410) 965–1334.
Communications Policy and Technology.—Tom Tobin, ANXB, room 3165 (410) 965–4029.
External Affairs.—Janice Mosby, WHRB, room 4300 (410) 965–7138.
Public Inquiries.—Annie B. White, WHRB, room 4200 (410) 965–2739.

OFFICE OF THE DEPUTY COMMISSIONER FOR DISABILITY AND INCOME SECURITY PROGRAMS

Deputy Commissioner for Disability and Income Security Programs.—Martin H. Gerry, ALTMB, room 100 (410) 965–0100.

Assistant Deputy Commissioner.—Fritz G. Streckewald, ALTMB, room 100 (410) 965–6212.
Associate Commissioner, Office of:
  Disability Determinations.—Lenore Carlson, ANXB, room 3570 (410) 965–1250.
  Disability Programs.—Glenn Sklar, ANXB, room 4555 (410) 965–6247.
  Employment Support Programs.—Sue Suter, OPRB, room 4–A–16 (410) 965–1352.
  Hearings and Appeals.—A. Jacy Thurmond, Jr., SKY, room 1600 (703) 605–8200.
  Income Security Programs.—Nancy Veillon, ALTMB, room 252 (410) 965–5961.
  International Programs.—Rogelis Gomez, ALTMB, room 142 (410) 966–1541.
  Program Development and Research.—Pamela Mazerski, ALTMB, room 128 (410) 965–2161.

OFFICE OF FINANCE, ASSESSMENT AND MANAGEMENT

Deputy Commissioner for Finance, Assessment and Management.—Dale W. Sopper, ALTMB, room 800 (410) 965–2910.
Assistant Deputy Commissioner.—Tony Dinoto, ALTMB, room 800 (410) 965–2914.
Associate Commissioner, Office of:
  Budget.—Robert M. Rothenberg, WHRB, room 2126 (410) 965–3501.
  Facilities Management.—Andria Childs, ALTMB, room 860 (410) 965–6789.
  Financial Policy and Operations.—Tony Dinoto (acting), EHRB, room 2150 (410) 965–3098.
  Publications and Logistics Management.—Gary Arnold, ANXB, room 1540 (410) 965–4272.
  Quality Assurance and Performance Assessment.—Thomas C. Evans, EHRB, room 600 (410) 965–3815.

OFFICE OF THE GENERAL COUNSEL

General Counsel.—Lisa deSoto, ALTMB, room 600 (410) 965–0600.
Deputy General Counsel.—Thomas W. Crawley, ALTMB, room 600 (410) 965–3414.
Associate General Counsel for—
  General Law.—Michael G. Gallagher, ALTMB, room 560 (410) 965–3148.
  Program Law.—John B. Watson, ALTMB, room 616 (410) 965–3137.
  Program Litigation.—Charlotte Hardnett, ALTMB, room 624 (410) 965–3114.
Regional Chief Counsel for—
  Boston: Robert J. Triba, JFK Federal Building, Room 625, Boston, MA 02203 (617) 565–4277.
  New York: Barbara L. Spivak, 26 Federal Plaza, Suite 3904, New York, NY 12078 (212) 264–3650, ext. 222.
  Philadelphia: James A. Winn, 300 Spring Garden Street, 6th Floor, Philadelphia, PA 19123 (215) 597–3300.
  Atlanta: Mary Ann Sloan, Atlanta Federal Center, 61 Forsyth Street, SW, Suite 20T45, Atlanta, GA 30303 (404) 562–1010.
  Chicago: Kim Leslie Bright, 200 West Adams Street, 30th Floor, Chicago, IL 60606 (312) 353–8201.
  Dallas: Tina M. Waddell, 1301 Young Street, Suite 430, Dallas, TX 75202 (214) 767–3212.
  Kansas City: Frank V. Smith, Federal Office Building, 601 East 12th Street, Room 535, Kansas City, MO 64106 (816) 936–5750.
  Denver: Yvette G. Keesee (acting), Federal Office Building, 1961 Stout Street, Room 327, Denver, CO 80294 (303) 844–5459.
  San Francisco: Janice L. Walli, 333 Market Street, Suite 1500, San Francisco, CA 94105 (415) 977–8943.
  Seattle: Lucille Meis, 701 Fifth Avenue, Suite 2900, M/S 901, Seattle, WA 98104 (206) 615–2539.

OFFICE OF HUMAN RESOURCES

Deputy Commissioner for Human Resources.—Dr. Reginald F. Wells, ALTMB, room 200 (410) 965–1900.
Assistant Deputy Commissioner.—Feli Sola-Carter, ALTMB, room 200 (410) 965–7642.
Associate Commissioner, Office of Personnel.—Sander K. Eckert, ANXB, room 4170 (410) 965–3324.

Director, Office of:
   Civil Rights and Equal Opportunity.—Mark A. Anderson, ANXB, room 2571 (410)
      965–3318.
   Labor Management and Employee Relations.—David L. Feder, ANXB, room 2170 (410)
      965–0066.
   Training.—Wayne Harmon, EHRB, room 100 (410) 966–8193.

OFFICE OF THE INSPECTOR GENERAL

Inspector General.—Patrick P. O'Carroll, ALTMB, room 300 (410) 966–8385.
   Counsel to the Inspector General.—Kathy A. Buller, OPRB, room 4–M–1 (410)
      965–6211.
Assistant Inspector General for—
   Audit.—Steven L. Schaeffer, OPRB, room 4–L–1 (410) 965–9701.
   Communications.—Paul Wood, ALTMB, room 310 (410) 965–7840.
   Executive Operations.—Stephanie J. Palmer, ALTMB, room 300 (410) 965–9704.
   Investigations.—Richard A. Rohde (acting), OPRB, room 4–S–1 (410) 966–2436.

OFFICE OF LEGISLATION AND CONGRESSIONAL AFFAIRS

Deputy Commissioner for Legislation and Congressional Affairs.—Robert M. Wilson, ITCB,
   room 826 (202) 358–6030, or ALTMB, room 152 (410) 965–2386.
Assistant Deputy Commissioner.—Diane B. Garro, ALTMB, room 152 (410) 965–2386,
   or ITCB, room 818 (202) 358–6080.
Associate Commissioner for Legislative Development.—Webster Phillips, ITCB, room 813
   (202) 358–6027 or ALTMB, room 146 (410) 965–3735.
Director for—
   Disability Insurance Program.—Amy Snurr, WHRB, room 3216 (410) 965–1835.
   Legislative Research and Congressional Constituent Relations.—Sharon A. Wilsin, WHRB,
      room 3120 (410) 965–3531.
   Old Age and Survivors Insurance Benefits.—Timothy J. Kelley, WHRB, room 3322 (410)
      965–3293.
   Program Administration and Financing.—Sallie B. Whitney, WHRB, room 3210 (410)
      965–3288.
   Supplemental Security Income Program.—Thomas M. Parrott, WHRB, room 3227 (410)
      965–2617.

OFFICE OF OPERATIONS

Deputy Commissioner for Operations.—Linda S. McMahon, WHRB, room 1204 (410)
   965–3143.
Assistant Deputy Commissioner.—Mary Glenn-Croft, WHRB, room 1204 (410) 965–1880.
Associate Commissioner, Office of:
   Automation Support.—Mark Blatchford, ANXB, room 4705 (410) 965–4844.
   Central Operations.—W. Burnell Hurt, SWTB, room 7000 (410) 966–7000.
   Electronic Services.—James Kissko, ANXB, room 3845 (410) 965–2850.
   Public Service and Operations Support.—Roger McDonnell, WHRB, room 1224 (410)
      965–4292.
   Telephone Services.—Donnell Adams, ANXB, room 4845 (410) 966–7758.
Regional Commissioner for—
   Boston: Manny Vaz (acting), JFK Federal Building, Room 1900, Boston, MA 02203
      (312) 575–4000.
   New York: Beatrice Disman, 26 Federal Plaza, Room 40–102, New York, NY 10278
      (312) 575–4000.
   Philadelphia: Larry G. Massanari, P.O. Box 8788, 300 Spring Garden Street, Philadelphia,
      PA 19123 (312) 575–4000.
   Atlanta: Paul Barnes, 61 Forsyth Street, Suite 23T30, Atlanta, GA 30303 (404)
      562–5600.
   Chicago: James F. Martin, Harold Washington Social Security Center, 600 West Madison
      Street, Chicago, IL 60661 (312) 575–4000.
   Dallas: Horace Dickerson, 1301 Young Street, Suite 500, Dallas, TX 75202–5433 (214)
      767–4210.
   Kansas City: Michael Grochowski, Federal Office Building, 601 East 12th Street, Room
      436, Kansas City, MO 64106 (816) 936–5700.

Denver: James Everett, Federal Office Building, 1961 Stout Street, Room 325, Denver, CO 80294 (303) 844–2388.
San Francisco: Pete Spencer, 75 Hawthorne Street, San Francisco, CA 94105 (415) 744–4676.
Seattle: Carmen M. Keller, 2201 Sixth Street, Mail Stop RX–50, Seattle, WA 98121 (206) 615–2103.

OFFICE OF POLICY

Deputy Commissioner for Policy.—Larry Love (acting), ITCB, room 845 (202) 358–6014.
Assistant Deputy Commissioner.—Paul Van de Water, ITCB, room 830 (202) 358–6137.
Associate Commissioner, Office of:
    Research, Evaluation and Statistics.—Edward J. DeMarco, ITCB, room 828 (202) 358–6020.
    Retirement Policy.—Andrew Biggs, ITCB, room 819 (202) 358–6064.

OFFICE OF SYSTEMS

Deputy Commissioner for Systems.—William Gray, ALTMB, room 400 (410) 965–7747.
Assistant Deputy Commissioner.—Kelly Croft, ALTMB, room 400 (410) 965–7481.
Associate Commissioner, Office of:
    Disability and Supplemental Security Income Systems.—Peter V. Herrera, Jr., WHRB, room 3224 (410) 965–0413.
    Earnings, Enumeration and Administrative Systems.—Judy Ziolkowski, WHRB, room 3124 (410) 965–5311.
    Enterprise Support, Architecture and Engineering.—Charles M. Wood, WHRB, room 3100 (410) 965–3780.
    Retirement and Survivors Insurance Systems.—Carl Couchoud, WHRB, room 4–K–5 (410) 965–6290.
    Systems Electronic Services.—Marsha R. Rydstrom, OPRB, room 3–A–8 (410) 965–3400.
    Telecommunications and Systems Operations.—James E. Preissner, NCC, room 541 (410) 965–1500.
Director, Office of:
    Client/Server Configuration.—John Standridge (acting), NCC, room 553 (410) 965–6453.
    Computer Operations Production Control.—Lillian (Bunny) Burnett, NCC, room 471 (410) 965–2297.
    Integrated Telecommunications Management.—Nadine Tracht, NCC, room 258 (410) 965–7121.
    Integration and Environmental Testing.—Roland Washington, NCC, room 593 (410) 965–6485.
    National Network Services and Operations.—Roderick Hairston, NCC, room 354 (410) 966–3838.
    Network Engineering.—Gina Kotowski, NCC, room 560 (410) 965–2197.
    Operational Capacity Performance Management.—Patrick Mooney, NCC, room 250 (410) 965–2116.
    Operational Software Suport.—Nelson J. Brenneman, NCC, room 490 (410) 965–2241.
    Resource Management and Acquisition.—Neil Whaley, NCC, room 570 (410) 965–6365.
    Systems User Services and Facilities.—James Strickler, NCC, room 472 (410) 965–1536.
    Telecommunications Security and Standards.—Ronald Burdinkski, NCC, room 252 (410) 965–1233.

SUSQUEHANNA RIVER BASIN COMMISSION
COMMISSIONERS AND ALTERNATES

Federal Government.—BG Merdith (Bo) Temple (Vice-Chair); COL Robert J. Davis, Jr. (Alternate); COL Francis X. Kosich (Alternate).
New York.—Kenneth P. Lynch (Alternate); Scott J. Foti (Alternate).
Pennsylvania.—Kathleen A. McGinty (Commissioner); Cathleen C. Myers (Alternate); William A. Gast (Alternate).
Maryland.—Kendl P. Philbrick (Chair); Dr. Robert Summers (Alternate); Matthew G. Pajerowski (Alternate).

STAFF

1721 North Front Street, Harrisburg, PA 17102, phone (717) 238–0423,
srbc@srbc.net, www.srbc.net

Executive Director.—Paul O. Swartz.
 Deputy Director.—Thomas W. Beauduy.
 Chief Administrative Officer.—Duane A. Friends.
 Secretary to the Commission.—Richard A. Cairo.
 Chief, Watershed Assessment and Protection.—David W. Heicher.
 Chief, Water Resources Management.—Michael G. Brownell.
 Director of Communications.—Susan S. Obleski.

STATE JUSTICE INSTITUTE

1650 King Street, Suite 600, Alexandria, VA 22314, phone (703) 684–6100

http://www.statejustice.org

BOARD OF DIRECTORS

Chairman.—Robert A. Miller.
Vice Chairman.—Joseph F. Baca.
Secretary.—Sandra A. O'Connor.
Executive Committee Member.—Keith McNamara.
Members:

Terrence B. Adamson
Robert N. Baldwin
Carlos R. Garza

Sophia H. Hall
Tommy Jewell
Arthur A. McGiverin

Officers:
 Executive Director.—Kevin Linskey.
 Deputy Director.—Kathy Schwartz.

TENNESSEE VALLEY AUTHORITY

One Massachusetts Avenue 20444, phone (202) 898–2999

Knoxville, TN 37902, phone (865) 632–2101

Chattanooga, TN 37401, phone (423) 751–0011

Muscle Shoals, AL 35660, phone (202) 386–2601

BOARD OF DIRECTORS

Chairman.—Glenn L. McCullough, Jr. (865) 632–2600 (Knoxville).
 Directors: Skila Harris (865) 632–3871 (Knoxville); William Baxter (865) 632–2535 (Knoxville).
 Chief Operating Officer.—Tom D. Kilgore (865) 632–2366 (Knoxville).
 Chief Nuclear Officer.—Karl W. Singer (423) 751–8682 (Chattanooga).
 Chief Financial Officer.—Michael E. Rescoe (865) 632–4049 (Knoxville).

CORPORATE VICE PRESIDENTS

Executive Vice Presidents:
 Human Resources.—John E. Long (865) 632–6307 (Knoxville).
 Administration.—LeAnne Stribley (865) 632–4352 (Knoxville).
 Communications and Government Relations.—Ellen Robinson (865) 632–3199 (Knoxville).
 Customer Service and Marketing.—Kenneth R. Breeden (615) 232–6011 (Nashville).
General Counsel.—Maureen Dunn (865) 632–4131 (Knoxville).
Inspector General.—Richard W. Moore (865) 621–4120 (Knoxville).

CHIEF OPERATING OFFICER ORGANIZATION

Bulk Power Trading.—Amy T. Burns (423) 751–3907 (Chattanooga).
Performance Initiatives.—Anda A. Ray (423) 751–8511 (Chattanooga).
Fossil Power Group.—Joseph R. Bynum (423) 751–2601 (Chattanooga).

River System Operations and Environment.—Kathryn J. Jackson (865) 632–3141 (Knoxville).
TVA Nuclear.—Karl W. Singer (423) 751–8682 (Chattanooga).
Transmission/Power Supply.—W. Terry Boston (423) 751–6000 (Chattanooga).
Power Resources & Operations Planning.—Jack A. Bailey (423) 751–3922 (Chattanooga).

WASHINGTON OFFICE

(202) 898–2995, fax (202) 898–2991

Vice President, Government Affairs.—Linda Whitestone.
Washington Representatives: Justin Maierhofer, Cicely Simpson, Juliet H. Wells.

U.S. ADVISORY COMMISSION ON PUBLIC DIPLOMACY

301 Fourth Street SW., Room 600, 20547

phone (202) 203–7880, fax 203–7886

[Created by Executive Order 12048 and Public Law 96–60]

Chairman.—Barbara M. Barrett.
  Members: Maria Sophia Aguirre, Amb. Elizabeth Bagley, Tre Charles Evers III, Harold C. Pachios, Amb. Penne Korth Peacock, Jay T. Snyder.
  Executive Director.—Razvigor Bazala.
  Administrative Officer.—Jamice Clayton.

U.S. AGENCY FOR INTERNATIONAL DEVELOPMENT

1300 Pennsylvania Avenue NW., Washington, DC 20523 phone (202) 712–0000

http://www.usaid.gov

Administrator.—Andrew S. Natsios, room 6.09, 712–4040, fax 216–3455.
  Deputy Administrator.—Frederick Schieck, room 6.09, 712–4070.
  Chief of Staff.—Douglas J. Aller, room 6.08, 712–0700.
  Counselor.—Carol Peasley, room 6.08, 712–5010.
  Executive Secretary.—Douglas J. Aller, room 6.08, 712–0700.
  Assistant Administrator for—
    Africa.—Lloyd Pierson, room 4.08, 712–0500.
    Asia and the Near East.—James Kunder, room 4.09, 712–0200.
    Europe and Eurasia.—Kent Hill, room 5.06, 712–0290.
    Latin America and the Caribbean.—Adolfo Franco, room 5.09, 712–4800.
    Program and Policy Coordination.—Edward D. Menarchik, room 6.08, 712–5820.
    Democracy, Conflict and Humanitarian Assistance.—William Garvelink (acting), room 8.06, 712–0100.
    Economic Growth, Agriculture, and Trade.—James Smith (acting), room 3.09, 712–0670.
    Global Health.—Kent Hill (acting), room 3.09, 712–1325.
    Management.—Steve Wisecarver (acting), room 6.09, 712–1200.
    Legislative and Public Affairs.—J. Edward Fox, room 6.10, 712–4300.
  Director of Equal Opportunity Programs.—Jessalyn L. Pendarvis, room 2.09, 712–1110.
  Director of Small and Disadvantaged Business Utilization.—Marilyn Marton, room 7.08, 712–1500.
  General Counsel.—John Gardner, room 6.06, 712–4476.
  Inspector General.—James R. Ebbitt (acting), room 6.06, 712–1150.

U.S. COMMISSION ON CIVIL RIGHTS

624 Ninth Street NW., 20425, phone (202) 376–7700, fax (202) 376–7672

(Codified in 42 U.S.C., section 1975)

Chairperson.—Gerald A. Reynolds.
  Vice Chairperson.—Abigail Thernstrom.
  Commissioners: Jennifer C. Braceras, Peter N. Kirsanow, Ashley L. Taylor, Jr., Michael Yaki.
  Staff Director.—Kenneth L. Marcus.
  Office of Civil Rights Evaluation.—Terri Dickerson, 376–8582.

U.S. HOLOCAUST MEMORIAL COUNCIL

The United States Holocaust Memorial Museum, 100 Raoul Wallenberg Place SW., 20024
phone 488–0400, fax (202) 488–2690

Officials:
Chair.—Fred S. Zeidman, Houston, TX.
Vice Chair.—Ruth B. Mandel, Princeton, NJ.
Director.—Sara J. Bloomfield, Washington, DC.

Members:
James M. Abroms, Birmingham, AL.
Sheldon G. Adelson, Las Vegas, NV.
Ivan E. Becker, Princeton, NJ.
Dottie Bennett, Falls Church, VA.
Frank R. Berman, Edina, MN.
Tom A. Bernstein, New York, NY.
Rudy A. Boschwitz, Fridley, MN.
Gila J. Bronner, Chicago, IL.
Norman Brownstein, Denver, CO.
Myron M. Cherry, Chicago, IL.
Stanley M. Chesley, Cincinnati, OH.
Debra Lerner Cohen, Washington, DC.
William J. Danhof, Lansing, MI.
Sam M. Devinki, Kansas City, MO.
Kitty Dukakis, Brookline, MA.
Donald Etra, Los Angeles, CA.
David M. Flaum, Rochester, NY.
Pam Fleischaker, Oklahoma City, OK.
Howard L. Ganek, New York, NY.
Joel M. Geiderman, Los Angeles, CA.
Tony B. Gelbart, Boca Raton, FL.
Michael C. Gelman, Bethesda, MD.
Harold Gershowitz, Chicago, IL.
William H. Gray III, Vienna, VA.
Barbara W. Grossman, Newton, MA.
Phyllis G. Heideman, Bethesda, MD.

Arlene Herson, Boca Raton, FL.
Harlan D. Hockenberg, Des Moines, IA.
Alice A. Kelikian, Cambridge, MA.
John F. Kordek, Chicago, IL.
M. Ronald Krongold, Coral Gables, FL.
Frank R. Lautenberg, Newark, NJ.
Stuart P. Levine, Deerfield, IL.
Deborah E. Lipstadt, Atlanta, GA.
Leo Melamed, Chicago, IL.
Harvey M. Meyerhoff, Baltimore, MD.
Set C. Momjian, Huntington Valley, PA.
Mervin G. Morris, Menlo Park, CA.
Harry Reicher, Philadelphia, PA.
Burton P. Resnick, New York, NY.
Alvin H. Rosenfeld, Bloomington, IN.
Jack Rosen, New York, NY.
Eric F. Ross, West Orange, NJ.
Richard S. Sambol, Toms River, NJ.
Nathan Shapell, Beverly Hills, CA.
Mickey Shapiro, Farmington Hills, MI.
Ronald G. Steinhart, Dallas, TX.
Nechama Tec, Stamford, CT.
Merryl H. Tisch, New York, NY.
Sonia Weitz, Peabody, MA.
Elie Wiesel, Boston, MA.
Karen B. Winnick, Los Angeles, CA.

Former Chairs:
Irving Greenberg, 2000–02.
Miles Lerman, 1993–2000.
Harvey M. Meyerhoff, 1987–93.
Elie Wiesel, 1980–86.

Former Vice Chairs:
William J. Lowenberg, 1986–93.
Mark E. Talisman, 1980–86.

Congressional Members:
Senate:
Barbara Boxer, from California.
Norm Coleman, from Minnesota.
Susan Collins, from Maine.
Orrin G. Hatch, from Utah.
Harry Reid, from Nevada.

House of Representatives:
Christopher B. Cannon, from Utah.
Eric I. Cantor, from Virginia.
Tom Lantos, from California.
Steven LaTourette, from Ohio.

Ex Officio Members:
U.S. Department of:
Education.—Susan Sclafani.
Interior.—Sue Ellen Wooldridge.
State.—Edward B. O'Donnell, Jr.

Council Staff:
General Counsel.—Gerard Leval.
Secretary of the Council.—Jane M. Rizer.

U.S. INSTITUTE OF PEACE

1200 17th Street NW, Suite 200, 20036
phone (202) 457–1700, fax (202) 429–6063

BOARD OF DIRECTORS

Public Members:
Chairman.—J. Robinson West.
Vice Chairman.—Maria Otero.

Members:

Betty Bumpers
Holly Burkhalter
Chester Crocker
Laurie Fulton

Charles Horner
Seymour Martin Lipset
Mora McLean
Barbara Snelling

Ex Officio:
  Assistant Secretary of Defense.—Peter Rodman (Secretary's Designate).
  Assistant Secretary of State.—Arthur Dewey (Secretary's Designate).
  National Defense University.—Michael Dunn.
Officials:
  President.—Richard H. Solomon.
  Executive Vice President.—Michael Graham.
Vice President for—
  Education.—Pamela Aall.
  Grants.—Judy Barsalou.
  Headquarters Project.—Charles Nelson.
  Management.—Erin Singshinsuk.
  Peace and Stability Operations.—Daniel Serwer.
  Research and Studies.—Paul Stares.
  Training.—George Ward.
Associate Vice President for—
  Library, Fellowships, Information Resources.—Sheryl Brown.
  Religion and Peacemaking.—David Smock.
  Rule of Law.—Neil Kritz.
Director of Congressional and Public Affairs.—Kay King.

U.S. INTERNATIONAL TRADE COMMISSION

500 E Street, SW., 20436

phone (202) 205–2000, fax 205–2798, http://www.usitc.gov

COMMISSIONERS

Chairman.—Stephen Koplan, Democrat, Virginia; term ending June 16, 2006; entered duty on August 4, 1998; designated Chairman for the term ending June 17, 2004 through June 16, 2006.

Vice Chairman.—Deanna Tanner Okun, Republican, Idaho; term ending June 16, 2008; entered duty on November 19, 1999; designated Vice Chairman for the term June 16, 2004 through June 16, 2006.

Commissioners:

Marcia E. Miller, Democrat, Indiana; term ending December 16, 2003; entered duty on August 5, 1996.

Jennifer A. Hillman, Democrat, Indiana; term ending December 16, 2006; entered duty on June 17, 2002.

Charlotte R. Lane, Republican, West Virginia; term ending December 16, 2009, entered duty on November 21, 2004.

Daniel R. Pearson, Republican, Minnesota; June 16, 2011, entered duty on November 21, 2004.

Congressional Relations Officer.—Nancy M. Carman, 205–3151.
Secretary.—Marilyn R. Abbott, 205–2799.
Director, Office of External Relations.—Lyn M. Schlitt, 205–3141.
Administrative Law Judges: Robert L. Barton, Jr., 708–4051; Charles E. Bullock, 205–2681; Sidney Harris, 205–2692; Paul J. Luckern, 205–2694.
General Counsel.—James M. Lyons, 205–3101.
Inspector General.—Kenneth Clarke, 205–2210.
Chief Information Officer.—Stephen A. McLaughlin, 205–3131.
Director, Office of:
  Administration.—Stephen A. McLaughlin, 205–3131.
  Economics.—Robert B. Koopman, 205–3216.
  Equal Employment Opportunity.—Jacqueline A. Waters, 205–2240.
  Finance.—Patricia Katsouros, 205–2682.
  Industries.—Karen Laney-Cummings, 205–3296.
  Investigations.—Robert Carpenter, 205–3160.
  Operations.—Robert A. Rogowsky, 205–2230.
  Human Resources.—Jeri L. Buchholz, 205–2651.

Tariff Affairs and Trade Agreements.—David Beck, 205–2595.
Unfair Import Investigations.—Lynn I. Levine, 205–2561.
Facilities Management.—Jonathan Brown, 205–2745.
Publishing.—Pamela Dyson, 205–2768.

U.S. MERIT SYSTEMS PROTECTION BOARD
1615 M Street, NW., 20419
phone (202) 653–7220, toll-free (800) 209–8960, fax 653–7130
[Created by Public Law 95–454]

Chairman.—Neil Anthony Gordon McPhie.
 Member.—Barbara J. Sapin.
 Chief of Staff.—Tracey Watkins.
 General Counsel.—Martha Schneider.
 Appeals Counsel.—Lynore Carnes.

REGIONAL OFFICES

Regional Directors:
 Atlanta Regional Office: Covering Alabama, Florida, Georgia, Mississippi, South Carolina, Tennessee.—Thomas J. Lamphear, 10th Floor, 401 West Peachtree Street NW, Atlanta, GA 30308 (404) 730–2755, fax 730–2767.
 Central Regional Office: Covering Illinois, Iowa, Kanas City, Kansas, Kentucky, Indiana, Michigan, Minnesota, Missouri, Ohio, Wisconsin.—Martin Baumgaertner, 31st Floor, 230 South Dearborn Street, Chicago, IL 60604 (312) 353–2923, fax 886–4231.
 Dallas Regional Office: Covering Arkansas, Louisiana, Oklahoma, Texas.—Sharon Jackson, Chief Administrative Judge, Room 620, 1100 Commerce Street, Dallas, TX 75242 (214) 767–0555, fax 767–0102.
 Northeastern Regional Office: Covering Connecticut, Delaware, Maryland (except Montgomery and Prince Georges counties), Massachusetts, New Hampshire, New Jersey (except the counties of Bergen, Essex, Hudson, and Union), Pennsylvania, Rhode Island, Vermont, West Virginia.—William L. Boulden, U.S. Customhouse, Room 501, Second and Chestnut Streets, Philadelphia, PA 19106 (215) 597–9960, fax 597–3456.
   New York Field Office: Covering New York, Puerto Rico, Virgin Islands, the following counties in New Jersey: Bergen, Essex, Hudson, Union.—Arthur Joseph, Chief Administrative Judge, Room 3137, 26 Federal Plaza, New York, NY 10278 (212) 264–9372, fax 264–1417.
 Western Regional Office: Covering Alaska, California, Hawaii, Idaho, Nevada, Oregon, Washington, and Pacific Overseas.—Amy Dunning, 250 Montgomery Street, Suite 400, 4th Floor, San Francisco, CA 94104 (415) 705–2935, fax (415) 705–2945.
   Denver Field Office: Covering Arizona, Colorado, Kansas (except Kansas City), Montana, Nebraska, New Mexico, North Dakota, South Dakota, Utah, Wyoming.—Joseph H. Hartman, Chief Administrative Judge, 165 South Union Boulevard, Suite 318, Lakewood, CO 80228 (303) 969–5101, fax (303) 969–5109.
 Washington Regional Office: Covering Washington, DC, Maryland (counties of Montgomery and Prince Georges, North Carolina, all overseas areas not otherwise covered), Virginia.—P.J. Winzer, 1811 Diagonal Road, Suite 205, Alexandria, VA 22314 (703) 756–6250, fax (703) 756–7112.

U.S. OVERSEAS PRIVATE INVESTMENT CORPORATION
1100 New York Avenue NW, Washington, DC 20527 (202) 336–8400

President and Chief Executive Officer.—Ross J. Connelly (acting).
 Executive Vice President and Chief Operating Officer.—Ross J. Connelly.
 Chief of Staff.—Joseph E. Flynn.
 Vice President and General Counsel.—Mark Garfinkel.
 Vice President for—
   External Affairs.—Christopher Coughlin.
   Finance.—Robert B. Drumheller.
   Insurance.—Michael T. Lempres.
   Investment Development and Economic Growth.—Daniel A. Nichols.
   Investment Funds.—Cynthia L. Hostetler.
   Investment Policy.—Virginia D. Green.
 Director, Congressional Affairs.—Richard C. Horanburg, 336–8417.

BOARD OF DIRECTORS

Government Directors:
Andrew S. Natsios, Administrator, Agency for International Development.
Josette Sheeran Shiner, Deputy United States Trade Representative.
Ross J. Connelly (acting), President and Chief Executive Officer, Overseas Private Investment Corporation.
Grant D. Aldonas, Under Secretary of Commerce for International Trade, U.S. Department of Commerce.
Randal K. Quarles, Assistant Secretary for International Affairs, U.S. Department of Treasury.
Patrick Pizzella, Assistant Secretary of Labor for Administration and Management, U.S. Department of Labor.
Private Sector Directors:
Samuel E. Ebbesen, President and CEO, Virgin Island Telephone Corporation, St. Thomas, Virgin Islands.
Sanford L. Gottesman, President, The Gottesman Company, Austin, TX.
Collister Johnson, Jr., Senior Consultant, Mercer Management Consulting, Inc., Washington, DC.
John L. Morrison, Chairman, Highland Capital, Minneapolis, Minnesota.
Diane M. Ruebling, President, The Ruebling Group, Midvale, Utah.
Ned L. Siegel, President, The Siegel Group, Boca Raton, Florida.
C. William Swank, Retired Executive Vice President, Ohio Farm Bureau Federation, Westerville, Ohio.
Staff:
Board Counsel.—Mark Garfinkel, 336–8410.
Corporate Secretary.—Connie M. Downs, 336–8438.

U.S. POSTAL SERVICE
475 L'Enfant Plaza SW 20260–0010, phone (202) 268–2000

BOARD OF GOVERNORS

Chairman.—James C. Miller III.
Vice Chairman.—Alan Kessler.
Postmaster General/CEO.—John E. Potter.
Deputy Postmaster General/Chief Operating Officer.—Patrick R. Donahoe.

MEMBERS

LeGree S. Daniels	Robert F. Rider
Carolyn Lewis Gallagher	John F. Walsh
Louis J. Guiliano	

OFFICERS OF THE BOARD OF GOVERNORS

Secretary to the Board of Governors.—William T. Johnstone, 268–4800.
Deputy Secretary to the Board of Governors.—John Reynolds.

OFFICERS OF THE POSTAL SERVICE

Postmaster General, Chief Executive Officer.—John E. Potter, 268–2550.
Deputy Postmaster General/Chief Operating Officer.—Patrick R. Donahoe, 268–2525.
Chief Financial Officer and Executive Vice President.—Richard J. Strasser, Jr., 268–5272.
Chief Postal Inspector.—Lee R. Heath, 268–5615.
Judicial Officer.—James A. Cohen (703) 812–1902.
Senior Vice Presidents:
  Chief Technology Officer.—Robert L. Otto, 268–6900.
  Chief Marketing Officer.—Anita J. Bizzotto, 268–4400.
  Consumer Advocate.—Michael F. Spates (acting), 268–2281.
  Controller.—Lynn Malcolm, 268–4177.
  Delivery and Retail.—William P. Galligan, 268–5100.
  Diversity Development.—Susan LaChance (acting), 268–6566.

Emergency Preparedness.—Henry A. Pankey, 268–5394.
Employee Resource Management.—DeWitt Harris, 268–3783.
Engineering.—Thomas G. Day (703) 280–7001.
Facilities.—Rudoloph K. Umscheid (703) 526–2727.
General Counsel.—Mary Anne Gibbons, 268–2950.
Government Relations.—Ralph J. Moden, 268–2506.
Human Resources.—Suzanne Medvidovich, 268–4000.
Intelligent Mall and Address Quality.—Charles E. Bravo, 268–6200.
International Business.—James P. Wade (703) 292–3834.
Labor Relations.—Anthony Vegliante, 268–7852.
Network Operations Management.—Paul Vogel, 268–7666.
Pricing and Classification.—Stephen M. Kearney, 268–2244.
Product Development.—Nicholas F. Barranca, 268–7301.
Public Affairs and Communications.—Azeezaly S. Jaffer, 268–2143.
Sales.—Jerry Whalen (703) 292–3679.
Service and Market Development.—John R. Wargo, 268–5300.
Strategic Planning.—Linda A. Kingsley, 268–2252.
Supply Management.—Keith Strange, 268–4040.
Treasury.—Robert J. Pedersen, 268–2875.
Area Operations, Vice Presidents:
 Eastern.—Alexander Lazaroff (412) 494–2510.
 Great Lakes.—Jo Ann Feldnt (630) 539–5858.
 New York Metro.—David L. Solomon (718) 321–5823.
 Northeast.—Megan J. Brennan (860) 285–7040.
 Pacific.—Al Iniguez (858) 674–3100.
 Southeast.—William J. Brown (901) 747–7333.
 Southwest.—George L. Lopez (214) 819–8650.
 Western.—Sylvester Black (303) 313–5100.
Manager, Capital Metro Operations.—Jerry D. Lane (301) 548–1403.

U.S. RAILROAD RETIREMENT BOARD

844 North Rush Street, Chicago, IL 60611, phone (312) 751–4500, fax 751–7136
http://www.rrb.gov
Office of Legislative Affairs, 1310 G Street, Suite 500, 20005
phone (202) 272–7742, fax 272–7728, e-mail ola@rrb.gov

Chairman—Michael S. Schwartz (312) 751–4900, fax 751–7193.
 Assistant to the Chairman.—Nancy S. Pittman.
 Counsel to the Chairman.—Rachel L. Simmons.
Labor Member.—V.M. Speakman, Jr. (312) 751–4905, fax 751–7194.
 Assistants to the Labor Member: James C. Boehner, Geraldine L. Clark, Michael J.
 Collins.
 Counsel to the Labor Member.—Thomas W. Sadler.
Management Member.—Jerome F. Kever (312) 751–4910, fax 751–7189.
 Assistant to the Management Member.—Joseph M. Waechter.
 Counsel to the Management Member.—Robert M. Perbohner.
 Attorney-Advisor to the Management Member.—Ann L. Chaney.
Inspector General.—Martin J. Dickman (312) 751–4690, fax 751–4342.
General Counsel.—Steven A. Bartholow (202) 272–7742, fax 272–7728.
 Assistant General Counsel.—Marguerite P. Dadabo (312) 751–4945, fax 751–7102.
Director of:
 Assessment and Training.—Catherine A. Leyser (312) 751–4757, fax 751–7190.
 Equal Opportunity.—Lynn E. Cousins (312) 751–4925, fax 751–7179.
 Field Service.—Martha M. Barringer (312) 751–4515, fax 751–3360.
 Hearings and Appeals.—Arthur A. Arfa (312) 751–4346, fax 751–7159.
 Human Resources.—Keith B. Earley (312) 751–4392, fax 751–7164.
 Legislative Affairs.—Margaret A. Lindsley (202) 272–7742, fax 272–7728.
 Operations.—Robert J. Duda (312) 751–4698, fax 751–7157.
 Policy and Systems.—Ronald Russo (312) 751–4984, fax 751–4650.
 Programs.—Dorothy A. Isherwood (312) 751–4980, fax 751–4333.
 Resource Management Center.—Cecilia A. Freeman (312) 751–4392, fax 751–7161.
Supervisor of:
 Acquisition Management.—Karen A. Bentall (acting) (312) 751–4526, fax 751–4998.
 Congressional Inquiry.—Richard M. Konopka (312) 751–4974, fax 751–7154.
 Public Affairs.—Anita J. Rogers (312) 751–4737, fax 751–7154.

Chief of:
  Actuary.—Frank J. Buzzi (312) 751–4915, fax 751–7129.
  Benefit and Employment Analysis.—Marla L. Huddleston (312) 751–4779, fax 751–7129.
  Finance.—Kenneth P. Boehne (312) 751–4930, fax 751–4931.
  Information.—Terri S. Morgan (312) 751–4851, fax 751–7169.
Librarian.—Katherine Tsang (312) 751–4926, fax 751–4924.
SEO/Director of Administration.—Henry M. Valiulis (312) 751–4990, fax 751–7197.

REGIONAL OFFICES

Atlanta: Patricia R. Lawson, Suite 1703, 401 West Peachtree Street, Atlanta, GA 30308 (404) 331–2691, fax (404) 331–7234.
Denver: Louis E. Austin, Suite 3300, 1999 Broadway, Box 7, Denver, CO 80202 (303) 844–0800, fax (303) 844–0806.
Philadelphia: Richard D. Baird, 900 Market Street, Suite 304, Philadelphia, PA 19107 (215) 597–2647, fax (215) 597–2794.

U.S. SENTENCING COMMISSION

One Columbus Circle NE, Suite 2–500, South Lobby, 20002–8002

phone (202) 502–4500, fax (202) 502–4699

Chair.—Ricardo H. Hinojosa.
Vice Chairs:
  Ruben Castillo, William K. Sessions III, John R. Steer.
Commissioners: Michael E. Horowitz, Beryl A. Howell.
Commissioners, ex officio: Edward F. Reilly, Jr., Deborah J. Rhodes.
Staff Director.—Timothy B. McGrath, 502–4510.
General Counsel.—Charles R. Tetzlaff, 502–4520.
Director of:
  Administration.—Susan L. Winarsky, 502–4610.
  Policy Analysis.—Louis W. Reedt (acting), 502–4530.
  Monitoring.—J. Deon Haynes (acting), 502–4620.
Director and Chief Counsel of Office of Training.—Pamela G. Montgomery, 502–4540.
Special Counsel.—Judith M. Sheon, 502–4666.
Public Affairs Officer.—Michael Courlander, 502–4627.
Director of Legislative and Governmental Affairs.—Kenneth P. Cohen, 502–4627.
Public Information: 502–4590.
Publications Request Line: 502–4568.
Guideline Application Assistance HelpLine: 502–4545.

U.S. TRADE AND DEVELOPMENT AGENCY

1000 Wilson Boulevard, Suite 1600, Arlington, VA 22209, phone (703) 875–4357

Director.—Thelma J. Askey.
Deputy Director.—Barbara Bradford.
Chief of Staff.—Thomas R. Hardy.
General Counsel.—Leocadia I. Zak.
Policy and Planning Director.—Geoffrey Jackson.
Resource Advisor.—Micheal Hillier.
Congressional Relations Advisor.—Jennifer Wolff.
Communications and Policy Advisor.—Donna Thiessen.
Regional Directors:
  Asia.—Henry Steingass.
  Eastern Europe/Eurasia.—Daniel D. Stein.
  Latin America and Caribbean.—Albert W. Angulo.
  North Africa/Middle East/South Asia.—Carl B. Kress.
  Sub-Saharan Africa.—Ned Cabot.
Economist/Evaluation Officer.—David Denny.
Grants Administrator.—Patricia Smith.
Financial Manager.—Noreen St. Louis.
Contracting Officer.—Della Glenn.
Administrative Officer.—Carolyn Hum.

WASHINGTON METROPOLITAN AREA TRANSIT AUTHORITY

600 Fifth Street, NW., 20001, phone (202) 637–1234

General Manager/CEO.—Richard A. White.
  Assistant General Manager for Operations.—James J. Hughes.
  General Counsel.—Carol B. O'Keeffe (acting).
  Chief of Staff/Secretary.—Harold M. Bartlett.
  Chief Operation Officer for—
    Bus Service.—Jack Requa.
    Rail Service.—Steve Feil.
  Assistant General Manager for—
    Capital Projects Management.—P. Takis Salpeas.
    Communications.—Leona Agouridis.
    Planning and Strategic Programs.—Edward L. Thomas.
    System Safety and Risk Protection.—Frederick C. Goodine.
    Workforce Development and Diversity Program.—William F. Scott.
  Chief of:
    Finances.—Peter Benjamin.
    Transit Police Department.—Polly Hanson.
  Director, Office of:
    Intergovernmental Relations.—Deborah S. Lipman.
    Media Relations.—Raymond Feldmann.

WASHINGTON NATIONAL MONUMENT SOCIETY

[Organized 1833; chartered 1859; amended by Acts of August 2, 1876, October, 1888]

President Ex Officio.—George W. Bush, President of the United States.
  First Vice President.—James W. Symington, 1666 K Street, NW., Suite 500, Washington,
    DC 20006–2107 (202) 778–2107.
  Treasurer.—Henry Ravenel, Jr.
  Secretary.—Fran Mainella, National Park Service, Department of the Interior.
  Assistant Secretary.—Vikki Keys, Superintendent of the National Mall and Memorial Parks,
    900 Ohio Drive, SW., Washington, DC 20024–2000, phone (202) 485–9875

Members:
  Christopher Addison
  Vincent C. Burke, Jr.
  Robert W. Duemling
  Gilbert M. Grosvenor
  Mrs. Potter Stewart

  Richard P. Williams
  C. Boyden Gray
  George B. Hartzog, Jr.
  John D.H. Kane
  John A. Washington

Member Emeritus:
  Harry F. Byrd, Jr.

WOODROW WILSON INTERNATIONAL CENTER FOR SCHOLARS

One Woodrow Wilson Plaza, phone 691–4000, fax 691–4001

1300 Pennsylvania Avenue NW., Washington, DC 20004–3027

(Under the direction of the Board of Trustees of
Woodrow Wilson International Center for Scholars)

Director.—Lee H. Hamilton, 691–4202.
  Deputy Director.—Michael Van Dusen, 691–4055.
  Administrative Management and Human Resources.—Leslie Johnson.
  Financial Management.—John Dysland.

Board of Trustees:
  Chairman.—Joseph B. Gildenhorn.
  Vice Chairman.—David A. Metzner.

Private Members:
  Joseph A. Cari, Jr.
  Carol Cartwright
  Robin Cook
  Donald E. Garcia

  Bruce S. Gelb
  Charles L. Glazer
  Tami Longaberger

JUDICIARY

SUPREME COURT OF THE UNITED STATES

One First Street NE 20543, phone 479-3000

WILLIAM HUBBS REHNQUIST, Chief Justice of the United States; born in Milwaukee, WI, October 1, 1924; son of William Benjamin and Margery Peck Rehnquist; married to Natalie Cornell of San Diego, CA; children: James, Janet, and Nancy, member of Faith Lutheran Church, Arlington, VA; served in the U.S. Army Air Corps in this country and overseas from 1943–46; discharged with the rank of sergeant; Stanford University, B.A., M.A., 1948; Harvard University, M.A., 1950; Stanford University, LL.B., 1952, ranking first in class; Order of the Coif; member of the Board of Editors of the Stanford Law Review; law clerk for Justice Robert H. Jackson, Supreme Court of the United States, 1952–53; private practice of law, Phoenix, AZ, 1953–69; engaged in a general practice of law with primary emphasis on civil litigation; appointed Assistant Attorney General, Office of Legal Counsel, by President Nixon in January 1969; nominated Associate Justice of the Supreme Court of the United States by President Nixon on October 21, 1971, confirmed December 10, 1971, sworn in on January 7, 1972; nominated by President Reagan as Chief Justice of the United States on June 17, 1986; sworn in on September 26, 1986.

JOHN PAUL STEVENS, Associate Justice of the Supreme Court of the United States; born in Chicago, IL, April 20, 1920; son of Ernest James and Elizabeth Street Stevens; A.B., University of Chicago, 1941, Phi Beta Kappa, Psi Upsilon; J.D. (*magna cum laude*), Northwestern University, 1947, Order of the Coif, Phi Delta Phi, co-editor, Illinois Law Review; married to Maryan Mulholland; children: John Joseph, Kathryn Jedlicka, Elizabeth Jane Sesemann, and Susan Roberta Mullen; entered active duty U.S. Navy in 1942, released as Lt. Commander in 1945 after WW II service, Bronz Star; law clerk to U.S. Supreme Court Justice Wiley Rutledge, 1947–48; admitted to Illinois bar, 1949; practiced law in Chicago, Poppenhusen, Johnston, Thompson and Raymond, 1949–52; associate counsel, Subcommittee on the Study of Monopoly Power, Judiciary Committee of the U.S. House of Representatives, 1951–52; partner, Rothschild, Stevens, Barry and Myers, Chicago, 1952–70; member of the Attorney General's National Committee to Study Antitrust Laws, 1953–55; lecturer in Antitrust Law, Northwestern University School of Law, 1950–54, and University of Chicago Law School, 1955–58; chief counsel, Illinois Supreme Court Special Commission to Investigate Integrity of the Judgment of *People* v. *Isaacs*, 1969; appointed U.S. Circuit Judge for the Seventh Circuit, October 14, 1970, entering on duty November 2, 1970, and serving until becoming an Associate Justice of the Supreme Court; nominated to the Supreme Court December 1, 1975, by President Ford; confirmed by the Senate December 17, 1975; sworn in on December 19, 1975.

SANDRA DAY O'CONNOR, Associate Justice of the Supreme Court of the United States; born in El Paso, TX, March 26, 1930; daughter of Harry A. and Ada Mae Wilkey Day; A.B. (with great distinction), Stanford University, 1950; LL.B., Stanford Law School, 1952; Order of the Coif, Board of Editors, Stanford Law Review; married to John Jay O'Connor III, 1952; children: Scott, Brian, and Jay; deputy county attorney, San Mateo County, CA, 1952–53; civilian attorney for Quartermaster Market Center, Frankfurt, Germany, 1954–57; private practice of law in Maryvale, AZ, 1958–60; assistant attorney general, Arizona, 1965–69; elected to the Arizona State senate, 1969–75; senate majority leader, 1974 and 1975; chairman of the State, County, and Municipal Affairs Committee in 1972 and 1973; also served on the Legislative Council, on the Probate Code Commission, and on the Arizona Advisory Council on Intergovernmental Relations; elected judge of the Maricopa County Superior Court, Phoenix, AZ, 1975–79; appointed to the Arizona Court of Appeals by Gov. Bruce Babbitt, 1979–81; nominated by President Reagan as Associate Justice of the U.S.

Supreme Court on July 7, 1981; confirmed by the U.S. Senate on September 22, 1981; and sworn in on September 25, 1981; member, National Board of Smithsonian Associates, 1981–present; president, board of trustees, The Heard Museum, 1968–74, 1976–81; member: Salvation Army Advisory Board, 1975–81, board of trustees, Stanford University, 1976–81, Board of Colonial Williamsburg Foundation, 1988 to present.

ANTONIN SCALIA, Associate Justice of the Supreme Court of the United States; born in Trenton, NJ, March 11, 1936; LL.B., Harvard Law School, 1960; note editor, Harvard Law Review; Sheldon fellow, Harvard University, 1960–61; married to Maureen McCarthy, September 10, 1960; children: Ann Forrest; Eugene, John Francis, Catherine Elisabeth, Mary Clare, Paul David, Matthew, Christopher James, and Margaret Jane; admitted to practice in Ohio (1962) and Virginia (1970); in private practice with Jones, Day, Cockley, and Reavis (Cleveland, OH), 1961–67; professor of law, University of Virginia Law School, 1967–74 (on leave 1971–74); general counsel, Office of Telecommunications Policy, Executive Office of the President, 1971–72; chairman, Administrative Conference of the United States, 1972–74; Assistant Attorney General, Office of Legal Counsel, U.S. Department of Justice, 1974–77; scholar in residence, American Enterprise Institute, 1977; professor of law, University of Chicago, 1977–82; appointed by President Reagan as Circuit Judge of the U.S. Court of Appeals for the District of Columbia Circuit; sworn in on August 17, 1982; appointed by President Reagan as Associate Justice of the U.S. Supreme Court; sworn in on September 26, 1986.

ANTHONY M. KENNEDY, Associate Justice of the Supreme Court of the United States; born in Sacramento, CA, July 23, 1936; son of Anthony James and Gladys McLeod Kennedy; married to Mary Davis, June 29, 1963; children: Justin Anthony, Gregory Davis, and Kristin Marie; Stanford University, 1954–57; London School of Economics, 1957–58; B.A., Stanford University, 1958; LL.B., Harvard Law School, 1961; associate, Thelen, Marrin, Johnson and Bridges, San Francisco, 1961–63; sole practitioner, Sacramento, 1963–67; partner, Evans, Jackson and Kennedy, Sacramento, 1967–75; professor of constitutional law, McGeorge School of Law, University of the Pacific, 1965–88; California Army National Guard, 1961; member: the Judicial Conference of the United States' Advisory Panel on Financial Disclosure Reports and Judicial Activities (subsequently renamed the Advisory Committee of Codes of Conduct), 1979–87; Committee on Pacific Territories, 1979–90 (chairman, 1982–90); board of the Federal Judicial Center, 1987–88; nominated by President Ford to U.S. Court of Appeals for the Ninth Circuit; sworn in on May 30, 1975; nominated by President Reagan as Associate Justice of the U.S. Supreme Court; sworn in on February 18, 1988.

DAVID HACKETT SOUTER, Associate Justice of the Supreme Court of the United States; born in Melrose, MA, September 17, 1939; son of Joseph Alexander and Helen Adams Hackett Souter; Harvard College, A.B., 1961, Phi Beta Kappa, selected Rhodes Scholar; Magdalen College, Oxford, 1963, A.B. in Jurisprudence, 1989, M.A., 1989; Harvard Law School, LL.B., 1966; associate, Orr and Reno, Concord, NH, 1966–68; assistant attorney general of New Hampshire, 1968–71; Deputy Attorney General of New Hampshire, 1971–76; Attorney General of New Hampshire, 1976–78; Associate Justice, New Hampshire Superior Court, 1978–83; Associate Justice, New Hampshire Supreme Court, 1983–90; member: Maine-New Hampshire Interstate Boundary Commission, 1971–75; New Hampshire Police Standards and Training Council, 1976–78; New Hampshire Governor's Commission on Crime and Delinquency, 1976–78; 1979–83; New Hampshire Judicial Council, 1976–78; Concord Hospital Board of Trustees, 1972–85 (president, 1978–84); New Hampshire Historical Society, 1968–present, (vice-president, 1980–85, trustee, 1976–85); Dartmouth Medical School, Board of Overseers, 1981–87; Merrimack County Bar Association, 1966–present; New Hampshire Bar Association, 1966–present; Honorary Fellow, American Bar Foundation; Honorary Fellow, American College of Trial Lawyers; Honorary Master of the Bench, Gray's Inn, London; Honorary Fellow, Magdalen College, Oxford; Associate, Lowell House, Harvard College; nominated by President Bush to U.S. Court of Appeals for the First Circuit; took oath May 25, 1990; nominated by President Bush as Associate Justice of the U.S. Supreme Court; took oath of office October 9, 1990.

CLARENCE THOMAS, Associate Justice of the Supreme Court of the United States; born in Pin Point, GA (near Savannah), June 23, 1948; son of M.C. and Leola Thomas; raised by his grandparents, Myers and Christine Anderson; married to Virginia Lamp, May 30, 1987; son Jamal Adeen by previous marriage; attended Conception Seminary, 1967–68; A.B. (*cum laude*), Holy Cross College, 1971; J.D., Yale Law School, 1974; admitted to practice in Missouri, 1974; assistant attorney general of Missouri, 1974–77; attorney in the law department of Monsanto Company, 1977–79; legislative assistant to Senator John Danforth, 1979–81; Assistant Secretary for Civil Rights, U.S. Department of Education, 1981–82; chairman, U.S. Equal Employment Opportunity Commission, 1982–90; nominated by President Bush to U.S. Court of Appeals for the District of Columbia Circuit; took oath March 12, 1990; nominated by President Bush as Associate Justice of the U.S. Supreme Court; took the constitutional oath on October 18, 1991 and the judicial oath on October 23, 1991.

RUTH BADER GINSBURG, Associate Justice of the Supreme Court of the United States; born March 15, 1933, Brooklyn, N.Y., the daughter of Nathan and Celia Amster Bader; married Martin Ginsburg, 1954; two children: Jane C. and James S.; B.A., Phi Beta Kappa, Cornell University, 1954; attended Harvard Law School, 1956–58; LL.B., Columbia Law School, 1959; law clerk to Edmund L. Palmieri, U.S. District Court, Southern District of New York, 1959–61; Columbia Law School Project on International Procedure, 1961–62, associate director, 1962–63; professor, Rutgers University School of Law, 1963–72; professor, Columbia Law School, 1972–80; Fellow, Center for Advanced Study in Behavioral Sciences, 1977–78; American Civil Liberties Union, general counsel, 1973–80; National Board of Directors, 1974–80; Women's Rights Project, founder and Counsel, 1972–80; American Bar Foundation Board of Directors, executive committee, secretary, 1979–89; American Bar Association Board of Editors, 1972–78; ABA Section on Individual Rights and Responsibilities, council member, 1975–81; American Law Institute, council member, 1978–93; American Academy of Arts and Sciences, Fellow, 1982–present; Council on Foreign Relations, 1975–present; nominated by President Carter as a Judge, U.S. Court of Appeals for the District of Columbia Circuit, sworn in on June 30, 1980; nominated Associate Justice by President Clinton, June 14, 1993, confirmed by the Senate, August 3, 1993, and sworn in August 10, 1993.

STEPHEN G. BREYER, Associate Justice of the Supreme Court of the United States; born in San Francisco, CA, August 15, 1938; son of Irving G. and Anne R. Breyer; married Joanna Hare, 1967, three children: Chloe, Nell, and Michael; A.B., Stanford University, 1959; B.A., Oxford University, Magdalen College, Marshall Scholar, 1961; LL.B., Harvard Law School, 1964; law clerk to Associate Justice Arthur J. Goldberg of the Supreme Court of the United States, 1964–65; special assistant to the Assistant Attorney General (Antitrust), Department of Justice, 1965–67; Assistant Special Prosecutor of the Watergate Special Prosecution Force, 1973; Special Counsel of the U.S. Senate Judiciary Committee, Subcommittee on Administrative Practices, 1974–75; Chief Counsel of the U.S. Senate Judiciary Committee, 1979–80; Professor of Law, Harvard Law School, 1970–80; (assistant professor, 1967–70; lecturer, 1980–94); professor, Kennedy School of Government, Harvard University, 1977–80; Nominated by President Carter as a Judge, U.S. Court of Appeals for the First Circuit, sworn in on December 10, 1980; Chief Judge, 1990–94; member, U.S. Sentencing Commission, 1985–89; member, Judicial Conference of the United States, 1990–94; nominated Associate Justice by President Clinton May 13, 1994, confirmed by the Senate July 29, 1994, and sworn in on August 3, 1994.

Officers of the Supreme Court

Clerk.—William K. Suter.
Librarian.—Judith Gaskell.
Marshal.—Pamela Talkin.
Reporter of Decisions.—Frank D. Wagner.
Counsel.—Scott Harris.
Curator.—Catherine Fitts.
Budget and Personnel Officer.—Cyril A. Donnelly.
Public Information Officer.—Kathleen L. Arberg.
Director of Data Systems.—Donna Clement.
Administrative Assistant to the Chief Justice.—Sally M. Rider.

UNITED STATES COURTS OF APPEALS

First Judicial Circuit (Districts of Maine, Massachusetts, New Hampshire, Puerto Rico, and Rhode Island).—*Chief Judge:* Michael Boudin. *Circuit Judges:* Juan R. Torruella; Bruce M. Selya; Sandra L. Lynch; Kermit V. Lipez; Jeffrey R. Howard. *Senior Circuit Judges:* Frank M. Coffin; Levin H. Campbell; Conrad K. Cyr; Norman H. Stahl. *Circuit Executive:* Gary H. Wente, (617) 748–9613. *Clerk:* Richard C. Donovan, (617) 748–9057, John Joseph Moakley U.S. Courthouse, One Courthouse Way, Suite 2500, Boston, MA 02210.

Second Judicial Circuit (Districts of Connecticut, New York, and Vermont).—*Chief Judge:* John M. Walker, Jr. *Circuit Judges:* Dennis Jacobs; Guido Calabresi; José A. Cabranes; Rosemary S. Pooler; Chester J. Straub; Robert D. Sack; Sonia Sotomayor; Robert A. Katzmann; Barrington D. Parker, Jr.; Reena Raggi. *Senior Circuit Judges:* Wilfred Feinberg; James L. Oakes; Thomas J. Meskill; Jon O. Newman; Richard J. Cardamone; Ralph K. Winter; Roger J. Miner; Joseph M. McLaughlin; Amalya L. Kearse; Pierre N. Leval. *Circuit Executive:* Karen Greve Milton, (212) 857–8700. *Clerk:* Roseann B. MacKechnie, (212) 857–8500, Thurgood Marshall United States Courthouse, 40 Foley Square, New York, NY 10007–1581.

Third Judicial Circuit (Districts of Delaware, New Jersey, Pennsylvania, and Virgin Islands).— *Chief Judge:* Anthony J. Scirica. *Circuit Judges:* Dolores K. Sloviter; Richard L. Nygaard; Samuel H. Alito, Jr.; Jane R. Roth; Theodore A. McKee; Marjorie O. Rendell; Maryanne Trump Barry; Thomas L. Ambro; Julio M. Fuentes; D. Brooks Smith; D. Michael Fisher; Franklin S. Van Antwerpen. *Senior Circuit Judges:* Ruggero J. Aldisert; Max Rosenn; Joseph F. Weis, Jr.; Leonard I. Garth; Edward R. Becker; Walter K Stapleton; Morton I. Greenberg; Robert E. Cowen. *Circuit Executive:* Toby D. Slawsky, (215) 597–0718. *Clerk:* Marcia M. Waldron, (215) 597–2995, U.S. Courthouse, 601 Market Street, Philadelphia, PA 19106.

Fourth Judicial Circuit (Districts of Maryland, North Carolina, South Carolina, Virginia, and West Virginia).—*Chief Judge:* William W. Wilkins. *Circuit Judges:* H. Emory Widener, Jr.; Paul V. Niemeyer; J. Harvie Wilkinson III; J. Michael Luttig; Karen J. Williams; M. Blane Michael; Diana Gribbon Motz; William B. Traxler, Jr.; Robert B. King; Roger L. Gregory; Dennis W. Shedd; Allyson K. Duncan. *Senior Circuit Judge:* Clyde H. Hamilton. *Circuit Executive:* Samuel W. Phillips, (804) 916–2184. *Clerk:* Patricia S. Connor, (804) 916–2700, Lewis F. Powell, Jr., U.S. Courthouse Annex, 1100 E. Main Street, Richmond, VA 23219.

Fifth Judicial Circuit (Districts of Louisiana, Mississippi, and Texas).—*Chief Judge:* Carolyn Dineen King. *Circuit Judges:* E. Grady Jolly; Patrick E. Higginbotham; W. Eugene Davis; Edith H. Jones; Jerry E. Smith; Jacques L. Wiener, Jr.; Rhesa H. Barksdale; Emilio M. Garza; Harold R. DeMoss, Jr.; Fortunato P. Benavides; Carl E. Stewart; James L. Dennis; Edith Brown Clement; Edward C. Prado. *Senior Circuit Judges:* Thomas M. Reavley; Will Garwood. *Circuit Executive:* Gregory A. Nussel, (504) 310–7777. *Clerk:* Charles R. Fulbruge III, (504) 310–7700, John Minor Wisdom, U.S. Court of Appeals Building, 600 Camp Street, New Orleans, LA 70130–3425.

Sixth Judicial Circuit (Districts of Kentucky, Michigan, Ohio, and Tennessee).—*Chief Judge:* Danny J. Boggs; *Circuit Judges:* Boyce F. Martin, Jr.; Alice M. Batchelder; Martha Craig Daughtrey; Karen Nelson Moore; R. Guy Cole, Jr.; Eric Lee Clay; Ronald Lee Gilman; Julie Smith Gibbons; John M. Rogers; Jeffrey S. Sutton; Deborah L. Cook. *Senior Circuit Judges:* Damon J. Keith; Gilbert S. Merritt; Cornelia G. Kennedy; Ralph B. Guy, Jr.; David A. Nelson; James L. Ryan; Alan E. Norris; Richard F. Suhrheinrich; Eugene E. Siler, Jr. *Circuit Executive:* James A. Higgins, (513) 564–7200. *Clerk:* Leonard Green, (513) 564–7000, Potter Stewart U.S. Courthouse, 100 E. Fifth Street, Cincinnati, OH 45202.

Seventh Judicial Circuit (Districts of Illinois, Indiana, and Wisconsin).—*Chief Judge:* Joel M. Flaum. *Circuit Judges:* Richard A. Posner; Frank H. Easterbrook; Kenneth F. Ripple; Daniel A. Manion; Michael S. Kanne; Ilana Diamond Rovner; Diane P. Wood; Terence T. Evans; Ann Claire Williams; Diane S. Sykes. *Senior Circuit Judges:* Thomas E. Fairchild; William J. Bauer; Richard D. Cudahy; John L. Coffey. *Circuit Executive:* Collins T. Fitzpatrick, (312) 435–5803. *Clerk:* Gino J. Agnello, (312) 435–5850, 2722 U.S. Courthouse, 219 S. Dearborn Street, Chicago, IL 60604.

Eighth Judicial Circuit (Districts of Arkansas, Iowa, Minnesota, Missouri, Nebraska, North Dakota, and South Dakota).—*Chief Judge:* James B. Loken. *Circuit Judges:* Theodore McMillian; Pasco M. Bowman II; Roger L. Wollman; Morris S. Arnold; Diana E. Murphy; Kermit E. Bye; William Jay Riley; Michael J. Melloy; Lavenski R. Smith. *Senior Circuit Judges:* Donald P. Lay; Gerald W. Heaney; Myron H. Bright; Richard S. Arnold; John R. Gibson; George G. Fagg; Frank J. Magill; C. Arlen Beam; David R. Hansen. *Circuit Executive:* Millie Adams, (314) 244–2600. *Clerk:* Michael E. Gans, (314) 244–2400, 111 S. Tenth Street, Suite 24.327, St. Louis, MO 63102.

Ninth Judicial Circuit (Districts of Alaska, Arizona, Central California, Eastern California, Northern California, Southern California, Guam, Hawaii, Idaho, Montana, Nevada, Northern Mariana Islands, Oregon, Eastern Washington and Western Washington).—*Chief Judge:* Mary M. Schroeder. *Circuit Judges:* Harry Pregerson; Stephen Reinhardt; Alex Kozinski; Diarmuid F. O'Scannlain; Pamela Ann Rymer; Andrew J. Kleinfeld; Michael Daly Hawkins; Sidney R. Thomas; Barry G. Silverman; Susan P. Graber; M. Margaret McKeown; Kim McLane Wardlaw; William A. Fletcher; Raymond C. Fisher; Ronald M. Gould; Richard A. Paez; Marsha S. Berzon; Richard C. Tallman; Johnnie B. Rawlinson; Richard R. Clifton; Jay S. Bybee; Consuelo M. Callahan; Carlos T. Bea. *Senior Circuit Judges:* James R. Browning; Alfred T. Goodwin; J. Clifford Wallace; Joseph Tyree Sneed III; Procter Hug, Jr.; Otto R. Skopil, Jr.; Betty Binns Fletcher; Jerome Farris; Authur L. Alarcon; Warren J. Ferguson; Dorothy W. Nelson; William C. Canby, Jr.; Robert Boochever; Robert R. Beezer; Cynthia Holcomb Hall; Melvin Brunetti; John T. Noonan, Jr.; David R. Thompson; Edward Leavy; Stephen Trott; Ferdinand F. Fernandez; Thomas G. Nelson; A. Wallace Tashima. *Circuit Executive:* Gregory B. Walters, (415) 556–6162. *Clerk:* Cathy A. Catterson, (415) 556–9890, P.O. Box 193939, San Francisco, CA 94119–3939.

Tenth Judicial Circuit (Districts of Colorado, Kansas, New Mexico, Oklahoma, Utah, and Wyoming).—*Chief Judge:* Deanell R. Tacha. *Circuit Judges:* David M. Ebel; Paul J. Kelly, Jr.; Robert H. Henry; Mary Beck Briscoe; Carlos F. Lucero; Michael R. Murphy; Harris L. Hartz; Terrence L. O'Brien; Michael W. McConnell; Timothy Tymkovich. *Senior Circuit Judges:* William J. Holloway, Jr.; Robert H. McWilliams; Monroe G. McKay; John C. Porfilio; Stephen H. Anderson; Bobby R. Baldock; Wade Brorby; Stephanie K. Seymour. *Circuit Executive:* David Tighe, (303) 844–2067. *Clerk:* Patrick J. Fisher, (303) 844–3157, Byron White Courthouse, 1823 Stout Street, Denver, CO 80257.

Eleventh Judicial Circuit (Districts of Alabama, Florida, and Georgia).—*Chief Judge:* J.L. Edmondson. *Circuit Judges:* Gerald Bard Tjoflat; R. Lanier Anderson III; Stanley F. Birch, Jr.; Joel F. Dubina; Susan Harrell Black; Edward E. Carnes; Rosemary Barkett; Frank Mays Hull; Stanley Marcus; Charles Reginald Wilson; William H. Pryor Jr. *Senior Circuit Judges:* John C. Godbold; Paul H. Roney; James C. Hill; Peter T. Fay; Phyllis A. Kravitch; Emmett Ripley Cox. *Circuit Executive:* Norman E. Zoller, (404) 335–6535. *Clerk:* Thomas K. Kahn, (404) 335–6100, 56 Forsyth Street NW., Atlanta, GA 30303.

UNITED STATES COURT OF APPEALS

FOR THE DISTRICT OF COLUMBIA CIRCUIT

333 Constitution Avenue 20001, phone 216–7300

DOUGLAS HOWARD GINSBURG, chief judge; born in Chicago, IL, May 25, 1946; education: diploma, Latin School of Chicago, 1963; B.S., Cornell University, 1970 (Phi Kappa Phi, Ives Award); J.D., University of Chicago, 1973 (Mecham Prize Scholarship 1970–73, Casper Platt Award, 1973, Order of Coif, Articles and Book Rev. Ed., 40 U. Chi. L. Rev.); bar admissions: Illinois (1973), Massachusetts (1982), U.S. Supreme Court (1984), U.S. Court of Appeals for the Ninth Circuit (1986). Member: Mont Pelerin Society, American Economic Association, American Law and Economics Association, Honor Society of Phi Kappa Phi, American Bar Association, Antitrust Section, Council, 1985–86 (ex officio), 2000–03 (judicial liaison); Advisory Boards: Competition Policy International; Harvard Journal of Law and Public Policy; Journal of Competition Law and Economics; Law and Economics Center, George Mason University School of Law; Supreme Court Economic Review; University of Chicago Law Review; Board of Directors: Foundation for Research in Economics and the Environment, 1991–present; Rappahannock County Conservation Alliance, 1998–2004; Rappahannock Hunt, Inc., 2000–01; Rappahannock Association for Arts and Community, 1997–99; Committees: Judicial Conference of the United States, 2002–present, Budget Committee, 1997–2001, Committee on Judicial Resources, 1987–96; Boston University Law School, Visiting Committee, 1994–97; University of Chicago Law School, Visiting Committee, 1985–88; law clerk to: Judge Carl McGowan, U.S. Court of Appeals for the District of Columbia Circuit, 1973–74; Associate Justice Thurgood Marshall, U.S. Supreme Court, 1974–75; previous positions: assistant professor, Harvard University Law School, 1975–81; Professor 1981–83; Deputy Assistant Attorney General for Regulatory Affairs, Antitrust Division, U.S. Department of Justice, 1983–84; Administrator for Information and Regulatory Affairs, Executive Office of the President, Office of Management and Budget, 1984–85; Assistant Attorney General, Antitrust Division, U.S. Department of Justice, 1985–86; visiting professor of law, Columbia University, New York City, 1987–88; lecturer on law, Harvard University, Cambridge, MA, 1988–89; distinguished professor of law, George Mason University, Arlington, VA, 1988–; Charles J. Merriam visiting scholar, senior lecturer, University of Chicago Law School, 1990, 1992, 1994, 1996, 1998, and 2000. Appointed to U.S. Court of Appeals for the District of Columbia Circuit by President Ronald Reagan on October 14, 1986, taking the oath of office on November 10, 1986, becoming Chief Judge on July 16, 2001.

HARRY T. EDWARDS, circuit judge; born in New York, NY, November 3, 1940; son of George H. Edwards and Arline (Ross) Lyle; B.S., Cornell University, 1962; J.D. (with distinction), University of Michigan Law School, 1965; associate with Seyfarth, Shaw, Fairweather and Geraldson, 1965–70; professor of law, University of Michigan, 1970–75 and 1977–80; professor of law, Harvard University, 1975–77; visiting professor of law, Free University of Brussels, 1974; arbitrator of labor/management disputes, 1970–80; vice president, National Academy of Arbitrators, 1978–80; member (1977–79) and chairman (1979–80), National Railroad Passenger Corporation (Amtrak); Executive Committee of the Association of American Law Schools, 1979–80; public member of the Administrative Conference of the United States, 1976–80; International Women's Year Commission, 1976–77; American Bar Association Commission of Law and the Economy; coauthor of four books: *Labor Relations Law in the Public Sector, The Lawyer as a Negotiator, Higher Education and the Law,* and *Collective Bargaining and Labor Arbitration*; recipient of the Judge William B. Groat Alumni Award, 1978, given by Cornell University; the Society of American Law Teachers Award (for "distinguished contributions to teaching and public service"); the Whitney North Seymour Medal presented by the American Arbitration Association for outstanding contributions to the use of arbitration; Recipient of the 2004 Robert J. Kutak Award, presented by the American Bar Association Selection of Legal Education and Admission to the Bar "to a person who meets the highest standards of professional responsibility and demonstrates substantial achievement toward increased understanding between legal education and the active practice of law", and several Honorary Doctor of Laws degrees. Judge Edwards teaches law on

HALDANE ROBERT MAYER, circuit judge; born in Buffalo, NY, February 21, 1941; son of Haldane and Myrtle Mayer; educated in the public schools of Lockport, NY; B.S., U.S. Military Academy, West Point, NY, 1963; and J.D., Marshall-Wythe School of Law, The College of William and Mary in Virginia, 1971; editor-in-chief, *William and Mary Law Review*, Omicron Delta Kappa; admitted to practice in Virginia and the District of Columbia; board of directors, William and Mary Law School Association, 1979–85; served in the U.S. Army, 1963–75, in the Infantry and the Judge Advocate General's Corps; awarded the Bronze Star Medal, Meritorious Service Medal, Army Commendation Medal with Oak Leaf Cluster, Combat Infantryman Badge, Parachutist Badge, Ranger Tab, Ranger Combat Badge, Campaign and Service Ribbons; resigned from Regular Army and was commissioned in the U.S. Army Reserve, currently Lieutenant Colonel, retired; law clerk for Judge John D. Butzner, Jr., U.S. Court of Appeals for the Fourth Circuit, 1971–72; private practice with McGuire, Woods and Battle in Charlottesville, VA, 1975–77; adjunct professor, University of Virginia School of Law, 1975–77, 1992–94, George Washington University National Law Center, 1992–96; Special Assistant to the Chief Justice of the United States, Warren E. Burger, 1977–80; private practice with Baker and McKenzie in Washington, DC, 1980–81; Deputy and Acting Special Counsel (by designation of the President), U.S. Merit Systems Protection Board, 1981–82; appointed by President Reagan to the U.S. Claims Court, 1982; appointed by President Reagan to the U.S. Court of Appeals for the Federal Circuit, June 15, 1987; assumed duties of the office, June 19, 1987; elevated to the position of Chief Judge on December 25, 1997; relinquished that position on December 24, 2004, after having held it for seven years; Judicial Conference of the U.S. Committee on the International Appellate Judges Conference, 1988–91, Committee on Judicial Resources, 1990–97; member of the Judicial Conference of the United States, 1997–2004; married Mary Anne McCurdy, August 13, 1966; two daughters, Anne Christian and Rebecca Paige.

ALAN D. LOURIE, circuit judge; born January 13, 1935, in Boston, MA; son of Joseph Lourie and Rose; educated in public schools in Brookline, MA; A.B., Harvard University, (1956); M.S., University of Wisconsin, (1958); Ph.D., University of Pennsylvania, (1965); and J.D., Temple University, (1970); married to the former L. Elizabeth D. Schwartz; children, Deborah L. Rapoport and Linda S. Lourie; employed at Monsanto Company (chemist, 1957–59); Wyeth Laboratories (chemist, literature scientist, patent liaison specialist, 1959–64); SmithKline Beecham Corporation, (Patent Agent, 1964–70; assistant director, Corporate Patents, 1970–76; director, Corporate Patents, 1976–77; vice president, Corporate Patents and Trademarks and Associate General Counsel, 1977–90); vice chairman of the Industry Functional Advisory Committee on Intellectual Property Rights for Trade Policy Matters (IFAC 3) for the Department of Commerce and the Office of the U.S. Trade Representative (1987–90); Treasurer of the Association of Corporate Patent Counsel (1987–89); President of the Philadelphia Patent Law Association (1984–85); member of the board of directors of the American Intellectual Property Law Association (formerly American Patent Law Association) (1982–85); member of the U.S. delegation to the Diplomatic Conference on the Revision of the Paris Convention for the Protection of Industrial Property, October–November 1982, March 1984; chairman of the Patent Committee of the Law Section of the Pharmaceutical Manufacturers Association (1980–85); member of Judicial Conference Committee on Financial Disclosure, 1990–98; member of the American Bar Association, the American Chemical Society, the Cosmos Club, and the Harvard Club of Washington; recipient of Jefferson Medal of the New Jersey Intellectual Property Law Association for outstanding contributions to intellectual property law, 1998; admitted to: Supreme Court of Pennsylvania, U.S. District Court for the Eastern District of Pennsylvania, U.S. Court of Appeals for the Third Circuit, U.S. Court of Appeals for the Federal Circuit, U.S. Supreme Court; nominated January 25, 1990, by President George Bush to be circuit judge, U.S. Court of Appeals for the Federal Circuit, confirmed by Senate on April 5, 1990, and assumed duties of the office on April 11, 1990.

RAYMOND C. CLEVENGER, III, circuit judge; born August 27, 1937, in Topeka, KS; son of R. Charles and Mary Margaret Clevenger; educated in the public schools in Topeka, Kansas, and at Phillips Academy, Andover, MA; B.A., Yale University, 1959; LL.B., Yale University, 1966; law clerk to Justice White, October term, 1966; practice of law at Wilmer, Cutler and Pickering, Washington, DC, 1967–90. Nominated by President George Bush on January 24, 1990, confirmed on April 27, 1990 and assumed duties on May 3, 1990.

RANDALL R. RADER, circuit judge; born April 21, 1949 in Hastings, NE, son of Raymond A. and Gloria R. Rader; higher education: B.A., Brigham Young University, 1971–74, (*magna cum laude*), Phi Beta Kappa; J.D., George Washington University Law Center, 1974–78; married the former Victoria Semenyuk: legislative assistant to Representative Virginia Smith; 1978–81: legislative director, counsel, House Committee on Ways and Means to Representative

Philip M. Crane; 1981–86: General Counsel, Chief Counsel, Subcommittee on the Constitution; 1987–88, Minority Chief Counsel, Staff Director, Subcommittee on Patents, Trademarks and Copyrights, Senate Committee on Judiciary; 1988–90: Judge, U.S. Claims Court; 1990–present, Circuit Judge, U.S. Court of Appeals for the Federal Circuit, nominated by President George Bush on June 12, 1990; confirmed by Senate August 3, 1990, sworn in August 14, 1990, recipient: Outstanding Young Federal Lawyer Award by Federal Bar Association, 1983; recipient: Jefferson Medal Award 2003; bar member: District of Columbia, 1978, Supreme Court of the United States, 1984, U.S. Claims Court, 1988, U.S. Court of Appeals for the Federal Circuit, 1990.

ALVIN A. SCHALL, circuit judge; born April 4, 1944, in New York City, NY; son of Gordon W. Schall and Helen D. Schall; preparatory education: St. Paul's School, Concord, NH, 1956–62, graduated *cum laude*; higher education: B.A., Princeton University, 1962–66; J.D., Tulane Law School, 1966–69; married to the former Sharon Frances LeBlanc, children: Amanda and Anthony. 1969–73: associate with the law firm of Shearman and Sterling in New York City; 1973–78: Assistant United States Attorney, Office of the United States Attorney for the Eastern District of New York; Chief of the Appeals Division, 1977–78; 1978–87: Trial Attorney, Senior Trial Counsel, Civil Division, United States Department of Justice, Washington, DC; 1987–88: member of the Washington, DC law firm of Perlman and Partners; 1988–92: Assistant to the Attorney General of the United States; 1992–Present: Circuit Judge, United States Court of Appeals for the Federal Circuit, appointed by President George Bush on August 17, 1992, sworn in on August 19, 1992. Author: "Federal Contract Disputes and Forums," Chapter 9 in Construction Litigation: Strategies and Techniques, published by John Wiley and Sons (Wiley Law Publications), 1989. Bar memberships: State of New York (1970), District of Columbia (1980), Supreme Court of the United States (1989), U.S. Court of Appeals for the Second Circuit (1974), U.S. District Courts for the Eastern and Southern Districts of New York (1973), U.S. Court of Appeals for the District of Columbia Circuit (1991), United States District Court for the District of Columbia (1991), U.S. Court of Appeals for the Federal Circuit (1982), and U.S. Court of Federal Claims, formerly the U.S. Claims Court (1978).

WILLIAM CURTIS BRYSON, circuit judge; born August 19, 1945, in Houston, TX; A.B., Harvard University, 1969; J.D., University of Texas School of Law, 1973; married with two children; law clerk to Hon. Henry J. Friendly, circuit judge, U.S. Court of Appeals for the Second Circuit (1973–74), and Hon. Thurgood Marshall, associate justice, U.S. Supreme Court (1974–75); associate, Miller, Cassidy, Larroca and Lewin, Washington, DC (1975–78); Department of Justice, Criminal Division (1979–86), Office of Solicitor General (1978–79, 1986–94), and Office of the Associate Attorney General (1994); nominated in June 1994 by President Clinton to be circuit judge, U.S. Court of Appeals for the Federal Circuit, and assumed duties of the office on October 7, 1994.

ARTHUR J. GAJARSA, circuit judge; born March 1, 1941 in Norcia (Pro. Perugia), Italy; married to Melanie Gajarsa; five children; education: Rensselaer Polytechnic Institute, Troy, NY, 1958–62, B.S.E.E., Bausch and Lomb Medal, 1958, Benjamin Franklin Award, 1958; Catholic University of America, Washington, DC, 1968; M.A. in economics, graduate studies; J.D., Georgetown University Law Center, Washington, DC, 1967; career record: 1962–63, patent examiner, U.S. Patent Office, Department of Commerce; 1963–64, patent Adviser, U.S. Air Force, Department of Defense; 1964–67, patent adviser, Cushman, Darby and Cushman; 1967–68, law clerk to Judge Joseph McGarraghy, U.S. District Court for the District of Columbia, Washington, DC; 1968–69, attorney, Office of General Counsel, Aetna Life and Casualty Co.; 1969–71, special counsel and assistant to the Commissioner of Indian Affairs, Bureau of Indian Affairs, Department of Interior; 1971–72, associate, Duncan and Brown; 1972–78, partner, Gajarsa, Liss and Sterenbuch; 1978–80, partner, Garjarsa, Liss and Conroy; 1980–86, partner, Wender, Murase and White; 1987–97, partner and officer, Joseph Gajarsa, McDermott and Reiner, P.C.; registered patent agent, registered patent attorney, 1963; admitted to the D.C. Bar, U.S. District Court for the District of Columbia, and U.S. Court of Appeals for the District of Columbia, 1968; Connecticut State Bar, 1969; U.S. Supreme Court, 1971; Superior Court for D.C., Court of Appeals for D.C., 1972; U.S. Courts of Appeals for the Ninth and Federal Circuits, 1974; U.S. District Court for the Northern District of New York, 1980; awards: Sun and Balance Medal, Rensselaer Polytechnic Institute, 1990; Gigi Pieri Award, Camp Hale Association, Boston, MA, 1992; Rensselaer Key Alumni Award, 1992; 125th Anniversary Medal, Georgetown University Law Center, 1995; Order of Commendatore, Republic of Italy, 1995; Alumni Fellow Award, Rensselaer Alumni Association, 1996; Board of Directors: National Italian American Foundation, 1976–97, serving as general counsel, 1976–89, president, 1989–92, and vice chair, 1993–96; Rensselaer Neuman Foundation, trustee, 1973-present; Foundation for Improving Understanding of the Arts, trustee,

1982–96; Outward Bound, U.S.A., trustee, 1987–2002; John Carroll Society, Board of Governors, 1992–96; Rensselaer Polytechnic Institute, trustee, 1994–present; Georgetown University, regent, 1995–2001; Georgetown University Board of Directors, 2001–present; member: Federal, American, Federal Circuit, and D.C. Bar Associations; American Judicature Association; nominated for appointment on April 18, 1996 by President Clinton; confirmed by the Senate on July 31, 1997; entered service September 12, 1997.

RICHARD LINN, circuit judge; born in Brooklyn, NY, April 13, 1944; son of Marvin and Enid Linn; graduated in 1961 from Polytechnic Preparatory County Day School, Brooklyn, NY; received Bachelor of Electrical Engineering degree from Rensselaer Polytechnic Institute in 1965, and J.D. from Georgetown University Law Center in 1969; served as patent examiner at the U.S. Patent and Trademark Office, 1965–68; member of the founding Board of Governors of the Virginia State Bar Section on Patent, Trademark and Copyright Law, chairman, 1975; member of the American Bar Association Intellectual Property Law Section; the American Intellectual Property Law Association; the District of Columbia Bar Association Intellectual Property Section; the Virginia Bar Intellectual Property Law Section; and the Federal Circuit Bar Association; admitted to the Virginia Bar in 1969, the District of Columbia Bar in 1970, and the New York Bar in 1994; admitted to practice before the U.S. Supreme Court, the U.S. Courts of Appeals for the Fourth, Sixth, District of Columbia, and Federal Circuits, and the U.S. District Courts for the Eastern District of Virginia and the District of Columbia; partner, Marks and Murase, L.L.P., 1977–97, and member of the Executive Committee, 1987–97; partner, Foley and Lardner, 1997–99, Practice Group Leader, Electronics Practice Group, and Intellectual Property Department, 1997–99; recipient, Rensselaer Alumni Association Fellows Award for 2000; adjunct professor of law, George Washington University Law School, 2001–present; member, Advisory Board of the George Washington University Law School, 2001–present; Master, Giles S. Rich American Inn of Court, 2000–present; nominated to be Circuit Judge by President William J. Clinton on September 28, 1999, and confirmed by the Senate on November 19, 1999; assumed duties of the office on January 1, 2000.

TIMOTHY B. DYK, circuit judge; nominated for appointment on April 1, 1998 by President Clinton; confirmed by the Senate on May 24, 2000; entered on duty June 9, 2000; education: Harvard College, A.B. (*cum laude*), 1958; Harvard Law School, LL.B. (*magna cum laude*), 1961; prior employment: law clerk to Justices Reed and Burton (retired), 1961–62; law clerk to Chief Justice Warren, 1962–63; special assistant to Assistant Attorney General, Louis F. Oberdorfer, 1963–64; associate and partner, Wilmer, Cutler & Pickering, 1964–90; partner, and chair, of Issues & Appeals Practice area (until nomination) with Jones, Day, Reavis and Pogue, 1990–2000; and Adjunct Professor at Yale, University of Virginia and Georgetown Law Schools.

SHARON PROST, circuit judge; born Newburyport, MA; daughter of Zyskind and Ester Prost; educated in Hartford, CT; B.S., Cornell University, 1973; M.B.A., George Washington University, 1975; J.D., Washington College of Law, American University, 1979; admitted to practice in Washington, DC, 1979; LL.M., George Washington University School of Law, 1984; Labor Relations Specialist, U.S. Civil Service Commission, 1973–76; Labor Relations Specialist/Auditor, U.S. General Accounting Office, 1976–79; Trial Attorney, Federal Labor Relations Authority, 1979–82; Chief Counsel's Office, Department of Treasury, 1982–84; Assistant Solicitor, Associate Solicitor, and then Acting Solicitor, National Labor Relations Board, 1984–89; Adjunct Professor of Labor Law, George Mason University School of Law, 1986–87; Chief Labor Counsel, Senate Labor Committee—minority, 1989–93; Chief Counsel, Senate Judiciary Committee—minority, 1993–95; Deputy Chief Counsel, Senate Judiciary Committee—majority, 1995–2001; Chief Counsel, Senate Judiciary Committee—majority, 2001; appointed by President George W. Bush to the U.S. Court of Appeals for the Federal Circuit, September 21, 2001; assumed duties of the office, October 3, 2001; two sons, Matthew and Jeffrey.

DANIEL M. FRIEDMAN, senior judge; born New York, NY, February 8, 1916; son of Henry M. and Julia (Freedman) Friedman; attended the Ethical Culture Schools in New York City; A.B., Columbia College, 1937; LL.B., Columbia Law School, 1940; married to Leah L. Lipson (deceased), January 16, 1955; married to Elizabeth M. Ellis (deceased), October 18, 1975; admitted to New York bar, 1941; private practice, New York, NY, 1940–42; legal staff, Securities and Exchange Commission, 1942, 1946–51; served in the U.S. Army, 1942–46; Appellate Section, Antitrust Division, U.S. Department of Justice, 1951–59; assistant to the Solicitor General, 1959–62; second assistant to the Solicitor General, 1962–68; First Deputy Solicitor General, 1968–78; Acting Solicitor General, January–March 1977; nominated by President Carter as chief judge of the U.S. Court of Claims, March 22, 1978; confirmed by the Senate, May 17, 1978, and assumed duties of the office on May 24, 1978; as of October 1, 1982, continued in office as judge of the U.S. Court of Appeals for the Federal Circuit, pursuant to section 165, Federal Courts Improvement Act of 1982, Public Law 97–164, 96 Stat. 50.

GLENN LEROY ARCHER, JR., senior judge; born March 21, 1929, in Densmore, KS; son of Glenn L. and Ruth Agnes Archer; educated in Kansas public schools; B.A., Yale University, 1951; J.D., with honors, George Washington University Law School, 1954; married to Carole Joan Thomas; children: Susan, Sharon, Glenn III, and Thomas; First Lieutenant, Judge Advocate General's Office, U.S. Air Force, 1954–56; associate (1956–60) and partner (1960–81), Hamel, Park, McCabe and Saunders, Washington, DC; nominated in 1981 by President Ronald Reagan to be Assistant Attorney General for the Tax Division, U.S. Department of Justice, and served in that position from December 1981 to December 1985; nominated in October 1985 by President Ronald Reagan to be circuit judge, U.S. Court of Appeals for the Federal Circuit; took the oath of office as a Circuit Judge in December 1985; elevated to the position of Chief Judge on March 18, 1994, served in that capacity until December 24, 1997; took senior status beginning December 25, 1997.

S. JAY PLAGER, senior judge; born May 16, 1931, son of A.L. and Clara Plager; educated public schools, Long Branch, NJ; A.B., University of North Carolina, 1952; J.D., University of Florida, with high honors, 1958; LL.M., Columbia University, 1961; Phi Beta Kappa, Phi Kappa Phi, Order of the Coif, Holloway fellow, University of North Carolina; Editor-in-Chief, University of Florida Law Review; Charles Evans Hughes Fellow, Columbia University; three children; commissioned, Ensign U.S. Navy, 1952; active duty Korean conflict; honorable discharge as Commander, USNR, 1971; professor, Faculty of Law, University of Florida, 1958–64; University of Illinois, 1964–77; Indiana University School of Law, Bloomington, 1977–89; visiting research professor of law, University of Wisconsin, 1967–68; visiting fellow, Trinity College and visiting professor, Cambridge University, 1980; visiting scholar, Stanford University Law School, 1984–85; dean and professor, Indiana University School of Law, Bloomington, 1977–84; counselor to the Under Secretary, U.S. Department of Health and Human Services, 1986–87; Associate Director, Office of Management and Budget, Executive Office of the President of the United States, 1987–88; Administrator, Office of Information and Regulatory Affairs, Office of Management and Budget, Executive Office of the President of the United States, 1988–89; circuit judge, U.S. Court of Appeals for the Federal Circuit, appointed by President George Bush, November 1989.

OFFICERS OF THE UNITED STATES COURT OF APPEALS

FOR THE FEDERAL CIRCUIT

Circuit Executive and Clerk of Court.—Jan Horbaly, (202) 312–5520.
Senior Technical Assistant.—Melvin L. Halpern, 312–3484.
Senior Staff Attorney.—Eleanor M. Thayer, 312–3490.
Assistant Circuit Executive for Administrative Services.—Ruth A. Butler, 312–3464.
Circuit Librarian.—Patricia M. McDermott, 312–5500.
Assistant Circuit Executive for Automation Technology.—Larry Luallen, 312–3475.
Operations Officer.—Dale Bosley, 312–5517.
Chief Deputy Clerk for Administration.—Edward W. Hosken, Jr., 312–5521.
Chief Deputy Clerk for Operations.—Pamela Twiford, 312–5522.

UNITED STATES DISTRICT COURT FOR THE DISTRICT OF COLUMBIA

E. Barrett Prettyman U.S. Courthouse, 333 Constitution Avenue, Room 4106, 20001
phone (202) 354–3320, fax 354–3412

THOMAS F. HOGAN, chief judge; born in Washington, DC, May 31, 1938; son of Adm. Bartholomew W. (MC) (USN) Surgeon Gen., USN, 1956–62, and Grace (Gloninger) Hogan; Georgetown Preparatory School, 1956; A.B., Georgetown University (classical), 1960; master's program, American and English literature, George Washington University, 1960–62; J.D., Georgetown University, 1965–66; Honorary Degree, Doctor of Laws, Georgetown University Law Center, May 1999; St. Thomas More Fellow, Georgetown University Law Center, 1965–66; American Jurisprudence Award: Corporation Law; member: bars of the District of Columbia and Maryland; law clerk to Hon. William B. Jones, U.S. District Court for the District of Columbia, 1966–67; counsel, Federal Commission on Reform of Federal Criminal Laws, 1967–68; private practice of law in the District of Columbia and Maryland, 1968–82; adjunct professor of law, Potomac School of Law, 1977–79; adjunct professor of law, Georgetown University Law Center, 1986–88; public member, officer evaluation board, U.S. Foreign Service, 1973; member: American Bar Association, State Chairman, Maryland Drug Abuse Education Program, Young Lawyers Section, 1970–73, District of Columbia Bar Association, Bar Association of the District of Columbia, Maryland State Bar Association, Montgomery County Bar Association, served on many committees, National Institute for Trial Advocacy, Defense Research Institute; chairman, board of directors, Christ Child Institute for Emotionally Ill Children, 1971–74; member, The Barristers, The Lawyers Club, USDC Executive Committee; Conference Committee on Administration of Federal Magistrates System 1988–91; Chairman Inter-Circuit Assignment Committee, 1990–; appointed judge of the U.S. District Court for the District of Columbia by President Ronald Reagan on October 4, 1982. Chief Judge June 19, 2001; member: Judicial Conference of the United States 2001–; Executive Committee of the Judicial Conference July 2001–present.

ROYCE C. LAMBERTH, judge; born in San Antonio, TX, July 16, 1943; son of Nell Elizabeth Synder and Larimore S. Lamberth, Sr.; South San Antonio High School, 1961; B.A., University of Texas at Austin, 1966; LL.B., University of Texas School of Law, 1967; permanent president, class of 1967, University of Texas School of Law; 1967–74, U.S. Army (Captain, Judge Advocate General's Corps, 1968–74; Vietnam Service Medal, Air Medal, Bronze Star with Oak Leaf Cluster, Meritorious Service Medal with Oak Leaf Cluster); 1974–87, assistant U.S. attorney, District of Columbia (chief, civil division, 1978–87); President's Reorganization Project, Federal Legal Representation Study, 1978–79; honorary faculty, Army Judge Advocate General's School, 1976; Attorney General's Special Commendation Award; Attorney General's John Marshall Award, 1982; vice chairman, Armed Services and Veterans Affairs Committee, Section on Administrative Law, American Bar Association, 1979–82, chairman, 1983–84; chairman, Professional Ethics Committee, 1989–91; co-chairman, Committee of Article III Judges, Judiciary Section 1989–present; chairman, Federal Litigation Section, 1986–87; chairman, Federal Rules Committee, 1985–86; deputy chairman, Council of the Federal Lawyer, 1980–83; chairman, Career Service Committee, Federal Bar Association, 1978–80; appointed judge, U.S. District Court for the District of Columbia by President Ronald Reagan, November 16, 1987; appointed by Chief Justice Rehnquist to be Presiding Judge of the United States Foreign Intelligence Surveillance Court, May 1995–2002.

GLADYS KESSLER, judge; born in New York, NY, January 22, 1938; Education: B.A., Cornell University, 1959; LL.B. Harvard Law School, 1962; member: American Judicature Society (board of directors, 1985–89); National Center for State Courts (board of directors, 1984–87); National Association of Women Judges (president, 1983–84); Women Judges' Fund for Justice, (president, 1980–82); Fellows of the American Bar Foundation; President's Council of Cornell Women; American Law Institute; American Bar Association—committees: Alternative Dispute Resolution, Bioethics and AIDS; Executive Committee, Conference of Federal Trial Judges; private law practice—partner, Roisman, Kessler and Cashdan, 1969–77; associate judge, Superior Court of the District of Columbia, 1977–94; court administrative activities: District of Columbia Courts Joint Committee on Judicial Administration, 1989–94; Domestic Violence Coordinating Council (chairperson, 1993–94); Multi-Door Dispute Resolution Program (supervising judge, 1985–90); family division, D.C. Superior Court (presiding judge,

1981–85); Einshac Institute Board of Directors; appointed judge, U.S. District Court for the District of Columbia by President Bill Clinton, June 16, 1994, and took oath of office, July 18, 1994; U.S. Judicial Conference Committee on Court Administration and Court Management; Frederick B. Abramson Memorial Foundation Board of Directors; Our Place Board of Directors; Vice Chair, District of Columbia Judicial Disabilities and Tenure Commission.

PAUL L. FRIEDMAN, judge; born in Buffalo, NY, February 20, 1944; son of Cecil A. and Charlotte Wagner Friedman; education: B.A. (political science), Cornell University, 1965; J.D., *cum laude,* School of Law, State University of New York at Buffalo, 1968; admitted to the bars of the District of Columbia, New York, U.S. Supreme Court, and U.S. Courts of Appeals for the D.C., Federal, Fourth, Fifth, Sixth, Seventh, Ninth and Eleventh Circuits; Law Clerk to Judge Aubrey E. Robinson, Jr., U.S. district court for the District of Columbia, 1968–69; Law Clerk to Judge Roger Robb, U.S. Court of Appeals for the District of Columbia Circuit, 1969–70; Assistant U.S. Attorney for the District of Columbia, 1970–74; assistant to the Solicitor General of the United States, 1974–76; associate independent counsel, Iran-Contra investigation, 1987–88; private law practice, White and Case (partner, 1979–94; associate, 1976–79); member: American Bar Association, Commission on Multidisciplinary Practice (1998–2000), District of Columbia bar (president, 1986–87), American Law Institute (1984) and ALI Council, 1998, American Academy of Appellate Lawyers, Bar Association of the District of Columbia, Women's Bar Association of the District of Columbia, Washington Bar Association, Hispanic Bar Association, Assistant United States Attorneys Association of the District of Columbia (president, 1976–77), Civil Justice Reform Act Advisory Group (chair, 1991–94), District of Columbia Judicial Nomination Commission (member, 1990–94; chair, 1992–94), Advisory Committee on Procedures, U.S. Court of Appeals for the D.C. Circuit (1982–88), Grievance Committee; U.S. District Court for the District of Columbia (member, 1981–87; chair, 1983–85); fellow, American College of Trial Lawyers; fellow, American Bar Foundation; board of directors: Frederick B. Abramson Memorial Foundation (president, 1991–94), Washington Area Lawyers for the Arts (1988–92), Washington Legal Clinic for the Homeless (member, 1987–92; vice-president 1988–91), Stuart Stiller Memorial Foundation (1980–94), American Judicature Society (1990–94), District of Columbia Public Defender Service (1989–92); member: Cosmos Club, Lawyers Club of Washington; appointed judge, U.S. District Court for the District of Columbia by President William Clinton, June 16, 1994, and took oath of office August 1, 1994; U.S. Judicial Conference Advisory Committee on Federal Criminal Rules.

RICARDO M. URBINA, judge; 59, sits on the United States District Court for the District of Columbia; born of an Honduran father and Puerto Rican mother in Manhattan, New York; attended Georgetown University and Georgetown Law Center before working as a staff attorney with the D.C. Public Defender Service; after a period of private practice with an emphasis on commercial litigation, joined the faculty of Howard University School of Law, during which time he maintained a private practice; directed the university's criminal justice clinic and taught criminal law, criminal procedure and torts; voted Professor of the Year by the Howard Law School student body, 1978; nominated to the D.C. Superior Court by President Carter, 1980; appointed to the bench as President Reagan's first presidential judicial appointment and the first Hispanic judge in the history of the District of Columbia, 1981; during his thirteen years on the Superior Court, Judge Urbina served as Chief Presiding Judge of the Family Division for three years and chaired the committee that drafted the Child Support Guidelines later adopted as the District of Columbia's child support law; managed a criminal calendar 1989–90 that consisted exclusively of first degree murder, rape and child molestation cases; designated by the Chief Judge to handle a special calendar consisting of complex civil litigation; twice recognized by the United States Department of Health and Human Services for his work with children and families; selected one of the Washingtonians of the Year by *Washington Magazine,* 1986; received Hugh Johnson Memorial Award for his many contributions to ". . . the creation of harmony among diverse elements of the community and the bar by D.C. Hispanic Bar Association;" received the Hispanic National Bar Association's 1993 award for demonstrated commitment to the "Preservation of Civil and Constitutional Rights of All Americans", and the 1995 NBC-Hispanic Magazine National VIDA Award in recognition of lifetime community service; adjunct professor at the George Washington University Law School since 1993; served as a visiting instructor of trial advocacy at the Harvard Law School, 1996–97; appointment by President Clinton to the U.S. District Court for the District of Columbia in 1994 made him the first Latino ever appointed to the federal bench in Washington, D.C.; Latino Civil Rights Center presented him with the Justice Award in 1999; conferred Distinguished Adjunct Teacher Award by George Washington University Law School in 2001 and in 2005 has been awarded the David Seidlson Chair for Trial Advocacy.

EMMET G. SULLIVAN, judge; born in Washington, DC; graduated McKinley High School, 1964; B.A., Howard University, 1968; J.D., Howard University Law School, 1971; law clerk to Judge James A. Washington, Jr.; joined the law firm of Houston and Gardner, 1973–80, became a partner; thereafter was a partner with Houston, Sullivan and Gardner; board of directors of the D.C. Law Students in Court Program; D.C. Judicial Conference Voluntary Arbitration Committee; Nominating Committee of the Bar Association of the District of Columbia; U.S. District Court Committee on Grievances; adjunct professor at Howard University School of Law; member: National Bar Association, Washington Bar Association, Bar Association of the District of Columbia; appointed by President Reagan to the Superior Court of the District of Columbia as an associate judge, 1984; deputy presiding judge and presiding judge of the probate and tax division; chairperson of the rules committees for the probate and tax divisions; member: Court Rules Committee and the Jury Plan Committee; appointed by President George Bush to serve as an associate judge of the District of Columbia Court of Appeals, 1991; chairperson for the nineteenth annual judicial conference of the District of Columbia, 1994. The Conference theme was "Rejuvenating Juvenile Justice—Responses to the Problems of Juvenile Violence in the District of Columbia"; appointed by chief judge Wagner, to chair the "Task Force on Families and Violence for the District of Columbia Courts"; nominated to the U.S. District Court by President William Clinton on March 22, 1994; and confirmed by the U.S. Senate on June 15, 1994. Appointed by Chief Justice Rehnquist to serve on the Federal Judicial Conference Committee on Criminal Law, 1998; District of Columbia Judicial Disabilities and Tenure Commission, 1996–2001; presently serving on the District of Columbia Judicial Nomination Commission; first person in the District of Columbia to have been appointed to three judicial positions by three different U.S. Presidents.

JAMES ROBERTSON, judge; born Cleveland, OH, May 18, 1938; son of Frederick Irving and Doris (Byars) Robertson; educated at Western Reserve Academy, Hudson, OH; A.B., Princeton University, 1959 (Woodrow Wilson School); served as an officer in the U.S. Navy, on destroyers and in the Office of Naval Intelligence, 1959–64; LL.B., George Washington University, 1965 (editor-in-chief, George Washington Law Review); admitted to the bar of the District of Columbia, 1966; associate, Wilmer, Cutler and Pickering, 1965–69; chief counsel, litigation office, Lawyers' Committee for Civil Rights Under Law, Jackson, MS, 1969–70; executive director, Lawyers' Committee for Civil Rights Under Law, Washington, DC, 1971–72; partner, Wilmer, Cutler and Pickering, 1973–94; co-chair, Lawyers' Committee for Civil Rights Under Law, 1985–87; president, Southern Africa Legal Services and Legal Education Project, Inc., 1989–94; president, District of Columbia bar, 1991–92; fellow, American College of Trial Lawyers; fellow, American Bar Foundation; member, American Law Institute; appointed U.S. District Judge for the District of Columbia by President Clinton on October 11, 1994 and took oath of office on December 31, 1994; Member, Judicial Conference Committee on Information Technology, 1996–present, chair, 2002–present. Member, Foreign Intelligence Surveillance Court, 2001–present.

COLLEEN KOLLAR–KOTELLY, judge; born in New York City; daughter of Konstantine and Irene Kollar; attended bilingual schools in Mexico, Ecuador and Venezuela, and Georgetown Visitation Preparatory School in Washington, D.C.; received B.A. degree in English at Catholic University (Delta Epsilon Honor Society); received J.D. at Catholic University's Columbus School of Law (Moot Court Board of Governors); law clerk to Hon. Catherine B. Kelly, District of Columbia Court of Appeals, 1968–69; attorney, United States Department of Justice, Criminal Division, Appellate Section (1969–72); chief legal counsel, Saint Elizabeths Hospital, Department of Health and Human Services, 1972–84; received Saint Elizabeths Hospital Certificate of Appreciation, 1981; Meritorious Achievement Award from Alcohol, Drug Abuse and Mental Health Administration (ADAMHA), Department of Health and Human Services, 1981, appointed judge, Superior Court of the District of Columbia by President Ronald Reagan, October 3, 1984, took oath of office October 21, 1984; served as Deputy Presiding Judge, Criminal Division, January 1996–April 1997; received Achievement Recognition Award, Hispanic Heritage CORO Awards Celebration, 1996; appointed judge, U.S. District Court for the District of Columbia by President William Jefferson Clinton on March 26, 1997, took oath of office May 12, 1997; appointed by Chief Justice Rehnquist to serve on the Financial Disclosure Committee, 2000–2002; Presiding Judge of the United States Foreign Intelligence Surveillance Court, 2002–present.

HENRY H. KENNEDY, Jr., judge; born in Columbia, South Carolina, February 22, 1948; son of Henry and Rachel Kennedy; A.B., Princeton University, 1970; J.D., Harvard University, 1973; admitted to the bar of the District of Columbia, 1973; Reavis, Pogue, Neal and Rose, 1972 and 1973; Assistant United States Attorney for the District of Columbia, 1973–76; United States Magistrate for the District of Columbia, April 1976–79; Judge, Superior Court of the District of Columbia, appointed by President Jimmy Carter, December 17,

1979; member: American Bar Foundation; District of Columbia Bar; Washington Bar Association; Bar Association of the District of Columbia; American Law Institute; member: The Barristers; Sigma Pi Phi; Epsilon Boule; Trustee, Princeton University; appointed judge, United States District Court for the District of Columbia, by President William Jefferson Clinton on September 18, 1997.

RICHARD W. ROBERTS, judge; born in New York, NY; son of Beverly N. Roberts and Angeline T. Roberts; graduate of the High School of Music and Art, 1970; A.B. Vassar College, 1974; M.I.A. School for International Training, 1978; J.D., Columbia Law School, 1978; Honors Program trial attorney, Criminal Section, Civil Rights Division, U.S. Department of Justice, Washington, D.C., 1978–1982; Associate, Covington and Burling, Washington, D.C., 1982–1986; Assistant U.S. Attorney, Southern District of NY, 1986–1988; Assistant U.S. Attorney, 1988–1993, then Principal Assistant U.S. Attorney, District of Columbia, 1993–1995; Chief, Criminal Section, Civil Rights Division, U.S. Department of Justice, Washington, DC, 1995–1998; adjunct professor of trial practice, Georgetown University Law Center, Washington, DC, 1983–1984; Guest faculty, Harvard Law School, Trial Advocacy Workshop, 1984 to present; admitted to bars of NY (1979) and DC (1983); U.S. District Court for District of Columbia, 1983; U.S. Court of Appeals for the D.C. Circuit, 1984; U.S. Supreme Court, 1985; U.S. District Court for the Southern District of NY and U.S. Court of Appeals for the Second Circuit, 1986; past or present member or officer of National Black Prosecutors Association; Washington Bar Association; National Conference of Black Lawyers; Department of Justice Association of Black Attorneys; Department of Justice Association of Hispanic Employees for Advancement and Development; DC Bar, Committee on Professionalism and Public Understanding About the Law; American Bar Association Criminal Justice Section Committees on Continuing Legal Education, and Race and Racism in the Criminal Justice System; ABA Task Force on the Judiciary; DC Circuit Judicial Conference Arrangements Committee; D.C. Judicial Conference Planning Committee; Edward Bennett Williams Inn of Court, Washington, DC, master; board of directors, Alumnae and Alumni of Vassar College; African American Alumni of Vassar College; Vassar Club of Washington, DC; Concerned Black Men, Inc., Washington DC Chapter; Sigma Pi Phi, Epsilon Boule; Council on Foreign Relations; DC Coalition Against Drugs and Violence; Murch Elementary School Restructuring Team; nominated as U.S. District Judge for the District of Columbia by President Clinton on January 27, 1998 and confirmed by the Senate on June 5, 1998. Took oath of office on July 31, 1998.

ELLEN SEGAL HUVELLE, judge; born in Boston, Massachusetts, June 3, 1948; daughter of Robert M. Segal, Esquire and Sharlee Segal; B.A., Wellesley College, 1970; Masters in City Planning, Yale University, 1972; J.D., *magna cum laude*, Boston College Law School, 1975 (Order of the Coif; Articles Editor of the law review); law clerk to Chief Justice Edward F. Hennessey, Massachusetts Supreme Judicial Court, 1975–1976; associate, Williams & Connolly, 1976–1984; partner, Williams & Connolly, 1984–1990; associate judge, Superior Court of the District of Columbia 1990–1999; member: American Bar Association, District of Columbia Bar; Women's Bar Association, Fellow of the American Bar Foundation, Master in the Edward Bennett Williams Inn of Court and member of the Inn's Executive Committee; instructor of Trial Advocacy at the University of Virginia Law School; member of Visiting Faculty at Harvard Law School's Trial Advocacy Workshop; Boston College Law School Board of Overseers; appointed judge, U.S. District Court for the District of Columbia by President Clinton in October 1999, and took oath of office on February 25, 2000.

REGGIE B. WALTON, judge; born in Donora, Pennsylvania, February 8, 1949; son of the late Theodore and Ruth (Garard) Walton; B.A., West Virginia State College, 1971; J.D., American University, Washington College of Law, 1974; admitted to the bars of the Supreme Court of Pennsylvania, 1974; United States District Court for the Eastern District of Pennsylvania, 1975; District of Columbia Court of Appeals, 1976; United States Court of Appeals for the District of Columbia Circuit, 1977; Supreme Court of the United States, 1980; United States District Court for the District of Columbia; Staff Attorney, Defender Association of Philadelphia, 1974–1976; Assistant United States Attorney for the District of Columbia, 1976–1980; Chief, Career Criminal Unit, Assistant United States Attorney for the District of Columbia, 1979–1980; Executive Assistant United States Attorney for the District of Columbia, 1980–1981; Associate Judge, Superior Court of the District of Columbia, 1981–1989; Deputy Presiding Judge of the Criminal Division, Superior Court of the District of Columbia, 1986–1989; Associate Director, Office of National Drug Control Policy, Executive Office of the President, 1989–1991; Senior White House Advisor for Crime, The White House, 1991; Associate Judge, Superior Court of the District of Columbia, 1991–2001; Presiding Judge of the Domestic Violence Unit, Superior Court of the District of Columbia, 2000; Presiding Judge of the Family Division, Superior Court of the District of Columbia, 2001;

Instructor: National Judicial College, Reno, Nevada, 1999–present; Harvard University Law School, Trial Advocacy Workshop, 1994–present; National Institute of Trial Advocacy, Georgetown University Law School, 1983–present; Co-author, Pretrial Drug Testing—an Essential component of the National Drug Control Strategy, Brigham Young University Law Journal of Public Law (1991); Distinguished Alumnus Award, American University, Washington College of Law (1991); The William H. Hastie Award, The Judicial Council of the National Bar Association (1993); Commissioned as a Kentucky Colonel by the Governor (1990, 1991); Governor's Proclamation declaring April 9, 1991, Judge Reggie B. Walton Day in the State of Louisiana; The West Virginia State College National Alumni Association James R. Waddy Meritorious Service Award (1990); Secretary's Award, United States Department of Veterans Affairs (1990); Outstanding Alumnus Award, Ringgold High School (1987); Director's Award for Superior Performance as an Assistant United States Attorney (1980); Profiled in book entitled "Black Judges on Justice: Prospectives From The Bench" by Linn Washington (1995); appointed district judge, United States District Court for the District of Columbia by President George W. Bush, September 24, 2001, and took oath of office October 29, 2001. Judge Walton was also appointed by President Bush in June of 2004 to serve as the Chairperson of the National Prison Rape Reduction Commission, a two-year commission created by the United States Congress that is tasked with the mission of identifying methods to curb the incidents of prison rape.

JOHN D. BATES, judge; born in Elizabeth, NJ, October 11, 1946; son of Richard D. and Sarah (Deacon) Bates; B.A., Wesleyan University, 1968; J.D., University of Maryland School of Law, 1976; U.S. Army (1968–71, 1st Lt., Vietnam Service Medal, Bronze Star); law clerk to Hon. Roszel Thomsen, U.S. District Court for the District of Maryland, 1976–77; 1980–97, Assistant U.S. Attorney, District of Columbia (Chief, Civil Division, 1987–97); Director's Award for Superior Performance (1983); Attorney General's Special commendation Award (1986); Deputy Independent Counsel, Whitewater Investigation, 1995–1997; private practice of law, Miller & Chevalier (partner, 1998–2001), Chair of Government Contracts Litigation Department and member of Executive Committee), Steptoe & Johnson (associate, 1977–80); District of Columbia Circuit Advisory Committee for Procedures (1989–93); Civil Justice Reform Committee of the U.S. District Court for the District of Columbia (1996–2001); Treasurer, D.C. Bar (1992–93); Publications Committee, D.C. Bar (1991–97, Chair 1994–97); D.C. Bar Special Committee on Government Lawyers (1990–91); D.C. Bar Task Force on Civility in the Profession (1994–96); D.C. Bar Committee on Examination of Rule 49 (1995–96); Chairman, Litigation Section, Federal Bar Association (1986–89); Board of Directors, Washington Lawyers Committee for Civil Rights and Urban Affairs (1999–2001).

RICHARD J. LEON, judge; 55, born in South Natick, Massachusetts on December 3, 1949; son of Silvano B. Leon and Rita (O'Rorke) Leon; A.B., Holy Cross College, 1971, J.D., *cum laude*, Suffolk Law School, 1974; LL.M. Harvard Law School, 1981; Law Clerk to Chief Justice McLaughlin and the Associate Justices, Superior Court of Massachusetts, 1974–75; Law Clerk to Hon. Thomas F. Kelleher, Supreme Court of Rhode Island, 1975–76; admitted to bar, Rhode Island, 1975 and District of Columbia, 1991; Special Assistant U.S. Attorney, Southern District of New York, 1977–1978; Assistant Professor of Law, St. John's Law School, New York, 1979–1983; Senior Trial Attorney, Criminal Section, Tax Division, U.S. Department of Justice, 1983–1987; Deputy Chief Minority Counsel, U.S. House Select "Iran-Contra" Committee, 1987–1988; Deputy Assistant U.S. Attorney General, Environment Division, 1988–1989; Partner, Baker & Hostetler, Washington, DC, 1989–1999; Commissioner, The White House Fellows Commission, 1990–1992; Chief Minority Counsel, U.S. House Foreign Affairs Committee "October Suprise" Task Force, 1992–1993; Special Counsel, U.S. House Banking Committee "Whitewater" Investigation, 1994; Special Counsel, U.S. House Ethics Reform Task Force, 1997; Adjunct Professor, Georgetown University Law Center, 1997–present; Partner, Vorys, Sater, Seymour and Pease, Washington, DC, 1999–2002; Commissioner, Judicial Review Commission on Foreign Asset Control, 2000–2001; Master, Edward Bennett Williams Inn of Court; appointed U.S. District Judge for the District of Columbia by President George W. Bush on February 19, 2002; took oath of office on March 20, 2002.

ROSEMARY M. COLLYER, judge; born in White Plains, NY, November 19, 1945; daughter of Thomas C. and Alice Henry Mayers; educated in parochial and public schools in Stamford, Connecticut; B.A., Trinity College, Washington, DC, 1968; J.D., University of Denver College of Law, 1977; practiced with Sherman & Howard, Denver, Colorado, 1977–1981; Chairman, Federal Mine Safety and Health Review Commission, 1981–1984 by appointment of President Ronald Reagan with Senate confirmation; General Counsel, National Labor Relations Board, 1984–1989 by appointment of President Ronald Reagan with Senate confirmation; private practice with Crowell & Moring LLP, Washington, DC 1989–2003; member and chairman of the firm's Management Committee; appointed U.S. District Judge for the District of Columbia by President George W. Bush and took oath of office on January 2, 2003.

SENIOR JUDGES

WILLIAM BENSON BRYANT, senior judge; born Wetumpka, AL, September 18, 1911; son of Benson and Alberta Bryant; married to Astaire A. Gonzalez (deceased), August 25, 1934; A.B., Howard University, 1932; LL.B., Howard University Law School, 1936; served in U.S. Army, World War II, 1943–47; member of the bar of the District of Columbia and of the Supreme Court of the United States; assistant U.S. attorney for the District of Columbia, 1951–54; private practice of law in District of Columbia as partner in firm of Houston, Bryant and Gardner, 1954–65; member: Committee on Admissions and Grievances of U.S. District Court for District of Columbia, 1959–65; District of Columbia Board of Appeals and Review, District of Columbia Special Police Trial Board, American Law Institute, National Lawyers' Club (honorary); appointed judge of the U.S. District Court for the District of Columbia Circuit by President Lyndon B. Johnson on July 11, 1965, and entered upon the duties of that office on August 16, 1965; served as chief judge, 1977–81; took senior judge status on January 31, 1982.

LOUIS FALK OBERDORFER, senior judge; born in Birmingham, AL, February 21, 1919; son of A. Leo and Stella Falk Oberdorfer; A.B., Dartmouth College, 1939; LL.B., Yale Law School, 1946 (editor in chief, Yale Law Journal, 1941); admitted to the bar of Alabama, 1947, District of Columbia, 1949; U.S. Army, rising from private to captain, 1941–45; law clerk to Justice Hugo L. Black, 1946–47; attorney, Paul Weiss, Wharton, Garrison, 1947–51; partner, Wilmer, Cutler and Pickering, and predecessor firms, 1951–61 and 1965–77; Assistant Attorney General, Tax Division, U.S. Department of Justice, 1961–65; president, District of Columbia Bar, 1977; transition chief executive officer, Legal Services Corp., 1975; co-chairman, Lawyers' Committee for Civil Rights Under Law, 1967–69; member, Advisory Committee on Federal Rules of Civil Procedure, 1963–84; visiting lecturer, Yale Law School, 1966, 1971; adjunct professor, Georgetown Law Center, 1993–present; appointed judge of the U.S. District Court for the District of Columbia by President Jimmy Carter on October 11, 1977, and took oath of office on November 1, 1977; senior status July 31, 1992.

JOHN GARRETT PENN, senior judge; born in Pittsfield, MA, March 19, 1932; son of John and Eugenie Heyliger Penn; A.B., University of Massachusetts (Amherst), 1954; LL.B., Boston University School of Law, 1957; admitted to the bars of Massachusetts, 1957 and District of Columbia, 1970; U.S. Army, first lieutenant, Judge Advocate General Corps, 1958–61; attorney, U.S. Department of Justice, Tax Division, 1961–70; trial attorney, 1961–65, reviewer, 1965–68, assistant chief, 1968–70; National Institute of Public Affairs Fellow, Woodrow Wilson School of Public and International Affairs, Princeton University, 1967–68; Awarded the Charles Hamilton Houston Medallion of Merit by the Washington Bar Association, May 1996; appointed judge, Superior Court of the District of Columbia by President Richard Nixon, October 1970; appointed judge, U.S. District Court for the District of Columbia by President Jimmy Carter, March 23, 1979, and took oath of office, May 15, 1979; Chief Judge March 1, 1992—July 21, 1997.

OFFICERS OF THE UNITED STATES DISTRICT COURT
FOR THE DISTRICT OF COLUMBIA

United States Magistrate Judges: Deborah A. Robinson; Alan Kay; John M. Facciola.
Clerk of Court.—Nancy Mayer-Whittington.
Administrative Assistant to the Chief Judge.—Sheldon L. Snook.
Bankruptcy Judge.—S. Martin Teel, Jr.
Bankruptcy Clerk of Court.—Denise Curtis.
Chief Probation Officer.—Richard A. Houck, Jr.

UNITED STATES COURT OF INTERNATIONAL TRADE

One Federal Plaza, New York NY 10278–0001, phone 212–264–2800

JANE A. RESTANI, chief judge, 2003–present; born February 27, 1948 in San Francisco, CA; parents, Emilia C. and Roy J. Restani; B.A., University of California at Berkeley, 1969; J.D., University of California at Davis, 1973; law review staff writer, 1971–72; articles editor, 1972–73; member, Order of the Coif; elected to Phi Kappa Phi Honor Society; admitted to the bar of the Supreme Court of the State of California, 1973; joined the civil division of the Department of Justice under the Attorney General's Honor Program, 1973 as a trial attorney; assistant chief commercial litigation section, civil division, 1976–80; director, commercial litigation branch, civil division, 1980–83; assumed the duties of a judge of the U.S. Court of International Trade on November 25, 1983; husband, Ira Bloom.

GREGORY W. CARMAN, Judge; born in Farmingdale, Long Island, NY, January 31, 1937; son of Nassau County District Court Judge Willis B. and Marjorie Sosa Carman; B.A., St. Lawrence University, Canton, NY, 1958; national exchange student, 1956–57, studying at the University of Paris through Sweet Briar College Junior Year in France Program; J.D., St. John's University School of Law (honors program), 1961; Member, St. John's Law Review; University of Virginia Law School, JAG (with honors), 1962; Master in Taxation Program, New York University School of Law; Captain, U.S. Army, 1958–64, stationed with the 2d Infantry Division, Fort Benning, GA; awarded Army Commendation Medal for Meritorious Service, 1964; admitted to the New York bar, 1961; practiced law with the firm of Carman, Callahan & Sabino, Farmingdale, NY; admitted to practice in U.S. Court of Military Appeals, 1962; certified by Judge Advocate General to practice at general court martial trials, 1962; admitted to practice in the U.S. District Courts, Eastern District of New York and Southern District of New York, 1965; Second Circuit Court of Appeals, 1966; Supreme Court of the United States, 1967; U.S. Court of Appeals, District of Columbia, 1982; Councilman for the Town of Oyster Bay, 1972–80; Member, U.S. House of Representatives, 97th Congress; appointed to Banking, Finance and Urban Affairs Committee and Select Committee on Aging, 1981–82; Member, International Trade, Investment and Monetary Policy Subcommittee of House Banking Committee, 1981–82; U.S. congressional Delegate, International I.M.F. Conference, 1982; nominated by President Ronald Reagan, confirmed and appointed Judge of the U.S. Court of International Trade, March 2, 1983; served as Acting Chief Judge, 1991; Chief Judge, 1996–2003; Statutory Member, Judicial Conference of the United States; Member, Executive Committee; Member, Judicial Branch Committee, and Subcommittees on Long Range Planning, Benefits, Civic Education, and Seminars, of the Judicial Conference of the United States; Member, Bicentennial Commission of Nassau County; Rotary International, 1964–present; named a Paul Harris Fellow of The Rotary Foundation of Rotary International; Chairman, United Way, Town of Oyster Bay, 1973–76; Member, Benevolent Protective Order of Elks; Past President, Savings and Loan League Committee, New York Chapter of the American Bar Association; Member: American Bar Association; Fellow, American Bar Foundation; Member, New York State Bar Association; Member, New York State Bar Association's Committee on Courts and the Community; recipient of 1996 Special Recognition Award from New York State Bar Association's Committee on Courts and the Community; Director and Member, Respect for Law Alliance, Inc.; former Member and Chair, Board of Directors of SUNSGLO, The Center for the Study of the United Nations System and the Global Legal Order; Member, Executive Board, The Theodore Roosevelt American Inn of Court, and President, 2003–04; Past President, Protestant Lawyers Association of Long Island; former Member, Vestry, St. Thomas's Episcopal Church, Farmingdale, NY, 1992–94; Fellow, American College of Mortgage Attorneys; Phi Delta Phi legal fraternity; District Committee Member, Nassau County Council of Boy Scouts of America; Past vice-chair, Paumanok Boy Scout District; former District Chair, United Cerebral Palsy; Member, Holland Society; Recipient of 1999 Gold Medal for Distinguished Achievement in Jurisprudence from The Holland Society of New York; Doctor of Laws, *honoris causa*, Nova Southeastern University, 1999; Distinguished Jurist in Residence, Touro College Law Center, 2000; Doctor of Laws, *honoris causa*, St. John's University, 2002; Inaugural Lecturer, The Honorable Dominick L. DiCarlo U.S. Court of International Trade Lecture, John Marshall Law School, 2003;

Distinguished Alumni Citation, St. Lawrence University, 2003; Public Service Award, Italian Board of Guardians, 2003; Sigma Chi, social fraternity; married to Nancy Endruschat (deceased); children: Gregory Wright Carman, Jr., John Frederick Carman, James Matthew Carman, and Mira Catherine Carman; married to Judith L. Dennehy, 1995.

DONALD C. POGUE, was appointed a Judge of the United States Court of International Trade (USCIT) by President Clinton in 1995; one of the nine members of the Court, he serves as chair of the Court's Budget and Long Range Planning Committee; served as judge in Connecticut's Superior Court, appointed to the bench in 1994; served as chairman of Connecticut's Commission on Hospitals and Health Care; appointed as Commissioner by Governor O'Neill in 1989, and named chairman by Governor Weicker; practiced law in Hartford for 15 years with the firm of Kestell, Pogue, & Gould; lectured on labor law, at the University of Connecticut School of Law; assisted in teaching the Harvard Law School's program on negotiations and dispute resolution for lawyers; chaired the Connecticut Bar Association's Labor and Employment Law Section; graduated *magna cum laude,* Phi Beta Kappa from Dartmouth College; graduate work at the University of Essex, England; J.D., from Yale Law School; Masters of Philosophy, Yale University; listed in Martindale-Hubbell and in the Best Lawyers in America; resides in Connecticut with wife, Susan, since their marriage in 1971.

EVAN J. WALLACH, judge; born in Superior, AZ, November 11, 1949; son of Albert A. and Sara F. Wallach; married to Katherine Colleen Tobin, 1992; graduate of Acalanes High School, Lafayette, CA, 1967; attended Diablo Valley Junior College, Pleasant Hill, CA, 1967–68; news editor Viking Reporter; member Alfa Gamma Sigma, National Junior College Honor Society, member Junior Varsity Wrestling Team; enlisted United States Army, January, 1969, PVT–SGT, served as Recognizance Sergeant 8th Engineer Bn., 1st Calvary Division (Air Mobile), Republic of Vietnam, 1970–71, Bronze Star Medal, Air Medal, Valorous Unit Citation, Good Conduct Medal; attended University of Arizona, 1971–73, graduated B.A., Journalism (high honors), Phi Beta Kappa, Phi Kappa Phi, Kappa Tau Alfa, Rufenacht French language prize, Douglas Martin Journalism Scholarship; attended University of California, Berkeley, 1973–76, graduated J.D., 1976, research assistant to Prof. Melvin Eisenberg, member of University of California Honor Society; Associate (1976–82) and Partner (1983–95) Lionel Sawyer and Collins, Las Vegas, NV with emphasis on media representation; attended Cambridge University, Cambridge, England, LL.B. (international law) (honors), 1981, member Hughes Hall College Rowing Club, Cambridge University Tennis Club; General Counsel and Public Policy Advisor to U.S. Senator Harry Reid (D) of Nevada, 1987–88; served CAPT–MAJ Nevada Army National Guard, 1989–95; served as Attorney/Advisor, International Affairs Division; Office of the Judge Advocate General of the Army, February–June, 1991–92; Meritorious Service Medal (oak leaf cluster); Nevada Medal of Merit; General Counsel, Nevada Democratic Party, 1978–80, 1982–86; General Counsel, Reid for Congress campaign, 1982, 1984; Reid for Senate campaign, 1986, 1992; General Counsel, Bryan for Senate campaign, 1988; Nevada State Director, Mondale for President campaign, 1984; State Director, Nevada and Arizona Gore for President campaign, 1988; General Counsel Nevada Assembly Democratic Caucus, 1990–95; General Counsel, Society for Professional Journalists, 1988–95; General Counsel, Nevada Press Association, 1989–95; awarded American Bar Association Liberty Bell Award, 1993; Nevada State Press Association President's Award, 1994; Clark County School Librarians Intellectual Freedom Award, 1995; Law of War, Adjunct Professor, New York Law School, 1997–present; Brooklyn Law School 2000 to present; member Nevada Bar, 1977; District of Columbia, 1988; U.S. District Court, District of Nevada, 1977; Ninth Circuit Court of Appeals, 1989; author, Legal Handbook for Nevada Reporters (1994); Comparison of British and American Defense Based Prior Restraint, ICLQ (1984); Treatment of Crude Oil As A War Munition, ICLQ (1992); Three Ways Nevada Unconstitutionally Chills The Media; Nevada Lawyer (1994); Co-Editor, Nevada Civil Practice Handbook (1993). Extradition to the Rwandan War Crimes Tribunal: Is Another Treaty Required, USCLA Journal of International Law and Foreign Affairs, Spring/Summer, 1998. The Procedural and Evidentiary Rules of the Post World War II War Crimes Trials: Did They Provide An Outline For International Criminal Procedure? Columbia Journal of Translational Law, Spring, 1999; Webmaster, International Law of War Association, lawofwar.org; Afghanistan, Yamashita and Uchiyama: Does the Sauce Suit the Gander? The Army Lawyer, June 2003. The Logical Nexus Between the Decision to Deny Application of the Third Geneva Convention to the Taliban and Al Queda and the Mistreatment of Prisoners of War in Abu Ghraib, Case Western Reserve Journal of International Law, April, 2005.

JUDITH M. BARZILAY, judge, U.S. Court of International Trade; born January 3, 1944, Russell, KS; husband, Sal (Doron) Barzilay; children, Ilan and Michael; parents, Arthur and Hilda Morgenstern; B.A., Wichita State University, 1965; M.L.S., Rutgers University School of Library and Information Science, 1971; J.D., Rutgers University School of Law, 1981, Moot Court Board, 1980–1981; trial attorney, U.S. Department of Justice (International Trade

Field OFfice), 1983 to 1986; litigation associate, Siegel, Mandell and Davidson, New York, NY, 1986 to 1988; Sony Corporation of America, 1988 to 1998; customs and international trade counsel, 1988–1989; vice-president for import and export operations, 1989–1996; vice-president for government affairs, 1996–1998; executive board of the American Association of Exporters and Importers, 1993–1998; appointed by Treasury Secretary Robert Rubin to the Advisory Committee on Commercial Operations of the United States Customs Service, 1995–1998; nominated for appointment January 27, 1998 by President Clinton (D); sworn-in as judge June 3, 1998.

DELISSA A. RIDGWAY, judge; born June 28, 1955 in Kirksville, MO; B.A. (honors), University of Missouri-Columbia, 1975; graduate work, University of Missouri-Columbia, 1975–76; J.D., Northeastern University School of Law, 1979; Shaw Pittman Potts & Trowbridge (Washington, D.C.), 1979–94; Chair, Foreign Claims Settlement Commission of the U.S. (1994–98); U.S. Court of International Trade (1998-Present); Adjunct Professor of Law, Cornell Law School (1999–Present); Adjunct Professor of Law, Washington College of Law/The American University (1992–94); District of Columbia Bar, Secretary (1991–92), Board of Governors (1992–98); President, Women's Bar Association (1992–93); American Bar Association, Commission on Women in the Profession (2002–present); Federal Bar Association, National Council (1993–2002, 2003–present), Government Relations Committee (1996–present), Public Relations Committee Chair (1998–99); Executive Committee, National Conference of Federal Trial Judges (2004–present); Founding Member of Board, D.C. Conference on Opportunities for Minorities in the Legal Profession (1992–93); Chair, D.C. Bar Summit on Women in the Legal Profession (1995–98); Fellow, American Bar Foundation; Member, American Law Institute; Fellow, Federal Bar Foundation; Earl W. Kintner Award of the Federal Bar Association (2000); Woman Lawyer of the Year, Washington, DC (2001); Distinguished Visiting Scholar-in-Residence, University of Missouri-Columbia (2003).

RICHARD K. EATON, judge; born, Walton, NY, August 22, 1948; married to Susan Henshaw Jones; two children: Alice and Elizabeth; attended Walton public schools; received B.A., Ithaca College, 1970; J.D., Union University Albany Law School, 1974; professional experience: Eaton and Eaton, partner (1975–76); Mudge Rose Guthrie Alexander & Ferdon, New York, NY, associate (1983–91) and partner (1993–95); Stroock & Stroock & Lavan, partner (1995–2000); served on the staff of Senator Daniel Patrick Moynihan (1977–79, 1980–83, 1991–93); confirmed by the United States Senate October 22, 1999.

TIMOTHY C. STANCEU was appointed to the U.S. Court of International Trade by President George W. Bush and began serving on April 15, 2003. In assuming this responsibility, he returned to public service after a thirteen-year career in private practive in Washington, DC with the law firm Hogan & Hartson L.L.P, during which he represented clients in a variety of matters involving customs and international trade law. During the fifteen years prior to his law practice, Judge Stanceu's career in the Federal Government included a term as Deputy Director of the Office of Trade and Tariff Affairs at the U.S. Department of the Treasury, where his responsibilities involved the regulatory and enforcement matters of the U.S. Customs Service and other agencies. Prior to that position, he served as Special Assistant to the Treasury Department's Assistant Secretary for Enforcement and in several positions at the U.S. Environmental Protection Agency, where he concentrated on the development and review of regulations on various environmental subjects. Judge Stanceu is a native of Canton, Ohio. He is a 1973 graduate of Colgate University and received a law degree from the Georgetown University Law Center in 1979.

THOMAS J. AQUILINO, JR., senior judge; born in Mount Kisco, NY, December 7, 1939; son of Thomas J. and Virginia B. (Doughty) Aquilino; attended Cornell University, 1957–59; B.A., Drew University, 1959–60, 1961–62; University of Munich, Germany, 1960–61; Free University of Berlin, Germany, 1965–66; J.D., Rutgers University School of Law, 1966–69; research assistant, Prof. L.F.E. Goldie (Resources for the Future—Ford Foundation) (1967–69); administrator, Northern Region, 1969 Jessup International Law Moot Court Competition; served in the U.S. Army, 1962–65; law clerk, Hon. John M. Cannella, U.S. district court for the Southern District of New York, 1969–71; attorney with Davis Polk & Wardwell, New York, 1971–85; admitted to practice New York, U.S. Supreme Court, U.S. Courts of Appeals for Second and Third Circuits, U.S. Court of International Trade, U.S. Court of Claims, U.S. district courts for Eastern, Southern and Northern Districts of New York, Interstate Commerce Commission; adjunct professor of law, Benjamin N. Cardozo School of Law, 1984–95; Mem., Drew University Board of Visitors, 1997–present; appointed by President Reagan on February 22, 1985; confirmed by U.S. Senate, April 3, 1985; assumed senior status on December 10, 2004; married to Edith Berndt Aquilino; children: Christopher Thomas, Philip Andrew, Alexander Berndt.

NICHOLAS TSOUCALAS, senior judge; born August 24, 1926 in New York, NY; one of five children of George M. and Maria (Monogenis) Tsoucalas; received B.S. degree from Kent State University, 1949; received LL.B. from New York Law School, 1951; attended New York University Law School; entered U.S. Navy, 1944–46; reentered Navy, 1951–52 and served on the carrier, *U.S.S. Wasp;* admitted to New York bar, 1953; appointed Assistant U.S. Attorney for the Southern District of New York, 1955–59; appointed in 1959 as supervisor of 1960 census for the 17th and 18th Congressional Districts; appointed chairman, Board of Commissioners of Appraisal; appointed judge of Criminal Court of the City of New York, 1968; designated acting Supreme Court Justice, Kings and Queens Counties, 1975–82; resumed service as judge of the Criminal Court of the City of New York until June 1986; appointed judge of the U.S. Court of International Trade by President Ronald Reagan on September 9, 1985, and confirmed by U.S. Senate on June 6, 1986; assumed senior status on September 30, 1996; former chairman: Committee on Juvenile Delinquency, Federal Bar Association, and the Subcommittee on Public Order and Responsibility of the American Citizenship Committee of the New York County Lawyers' Association; member of the American Bar Association, New York State Bar Association; founder of Eastern Orthodox Lawyers' Association; former president: Greek-American Lawyers' Association, and Board of Directors of Greek Orthodox Church of "Evangelismos", St. John's Theologos Society, and Parthenon Foundation; member, Order of Ahepa, Parthenon Lodge, F.A.M.; married to Catherine Aravantinos; two daughters: Stephanie (Mrs. Daniel Turriago) and Georgia (Mrs. Christopher Argyrople); five grandchildren.

R. KENTON MUSGRAVE, senior judge, U.S. Court of International Trade; born Clearwater, FL, September 7, 1927. Attended Augusta Academy (Virginia); B.A., University of Washington, 1948; editorial staff, Journal of International Law, Emory University; J.D., with distinction, Emory University, 1953; assistant general counsel, Lockheed Aircraft and Lockheed International, 1953–62; vice president and general counsel, Mattel, Inc., 1963–71; director, Ringling Bros. and Barnum and Bailey Combined Shows, Inc., 1968–72; commissioner, BSA (Atlanta), 1952–55; partner, Musgrave, Welbourn and Fertman, 1972–75; assistant general counsel, Pacific Enterprises, 1975–81; vice president, general counsel and secretary, Vivitar Corporation, 1981–85; vice president and director, Santa Barbara Applied Research Corp., 1982–87; trustee, Morris Animal Foundation, 1981–; director Emeritus, Pet Protection Society, 1981–; director, Dolphins of Shark Bay (Australia) Foundation, 1985–; trustee, The Dian Fossey Gorilla Fund, 1987–; trustee, The Ocean Conservancy, 2000–present; vice president and director, South Bay Social Services Group, 1963–70; director, Palos Verdes Community Arts Association, 1973–79; member, Governor of Florida's Council of 100, 1970–73; director, Orlando Bank and Trust, 1970–73; counsel, League of Women Voters, 1964–66; member, State Bar of Georgia, 1953–; State Bar of California, 1962–; Los Angeles County Bar Association, 1962–87 and chairman, Corporate Law Departments Section, 1965–66; admitted to practice before the U.S. Supreme Court, 1962; Supreme Court of Georgia, 1953; California Supreme Court, 1962; U.S. Customs Court, 1967; U.S. Court of International Trade, 1980. Married May 7, 1949 to former Ruth Shippen Hoppe, of Atlanta, GA. Three children: Laura Marie Musgrave (deceased), Ruth Shippen Musgrave, Esq., and Forest Kenton Musgrave. Nominated by President Ronald Reagan on July 1, 1987; confirmed by the Senate on November 9, and took oath of office on November 13, 1987.

RICHARD W. GOLDBERG, senior judge; born September 23, 1927 in Fargo, ND; J.D. from the University of Miami, 1952; served on active duty as an Air Force Judge Advocate, 1953–56; admitted to Washington, DC bar, Florida bar and North Dakota bar; from 1959 to 1983, owned and operated a regional grain processing firm in North Dakota; served as State Senator from North Dakota for eight years; taught military law for the Army and Air Force ROTC at North Dakota State University; was vice-chairman of the board of Minneapolis Grain Exchange; joined the Reagan administration in 1983 in Washington at the U.S. Department of Agriculture. Served as Deputy Under Secretary for International Affairs and Commodity Programs and later as Acting Under Secretary; in 1990 joined the Washington, DC law firm of Anderson, Hibey and Blair; appointed judge of the U.S. Court of International Trade in 1991; assumed senior status in 2001; married: two children, a daughter and a son.

OFFICERS OF THE UNITED STATES COURT OF INTERNATIONAL TRADE

Clerk.—Leo M. Gordon (212) 264–2814.

UNITED STATES COURT OF FEDERAL CLAIMS

Lafayette Square, 717 Madison Place NW 20005, phone (202) 219–9657

EDWARD J. DAMICH, chief judge; born in Pittsburgh, PA, June 19, 1948; son of John and Josephine (Lovrencic) Damich; A.B., St. Stephen's College, 1970; J.D., Catholic University, 1976; professor of law at Delaware School of Law of Widener University, 1976–84; served as a Law and Economics Fellow at Columbia University School of Law, where he earned his L.L.M. in 1983 and his J.S.D. in 1991; professor of law at George Mason University, 1984–98; appointed by President Bush to be a Commissioner of the Copyright Royalty Tribunal, 1992–93; Chief Intellectual Property Counsel for the Senate Judiciary Committee, 1995–98; appointed by President Clinton as judge, U.S. Court of Federal Claims, October 22, 1998; appointed by President Bush as chief judge, U.S. Court of Federal Claims, May 13, 2002; admitted to the Bars of the District of Columbia and Pennsylvania; member of the District of Columbia Bar Association, Pennsylvania Bar Association, American Bar Association, Supreme Court of the United States, the Federal Circuit and *Association litteraire et artistique internationale;* president of the National Federation of Croatian Americans, 1994–95. At present Judge Damich is an adjunct professor of law at the Georgetown University Law Center.

LAWRENCE M. BASKIR, judge; born in Brooklyn, NY, January 10, 1938; married to Marna Tucker, two children; graduated *magna cum laude,* Princeton University; A.B., Woodrow Wilson School of Public and International Affairs, 1959; LL.B., Harvard Law School, 1962; Principal Deputy General Counsel, Department of the Army, 1994–1998; private practice and Editor-In-Chief, Military Law Reporter, 1981–1994; Legislative Director to Senator Bill Bradley, 1979–1981; Deputy Assistant Secretary (Legislation), Office of the Secretary, Department of the Treasury, 1977–1979; Director, Vietnam Offender Study; Faculty Fellow, University of Notre Dame Law School, 1975–1977; Director, Presidential (Ford) Clemancy Board, White House, 1974–1975; Chief Counsel, Subcommittees on Constitutional Rights and Separation of Powers, Senate Judiciary Committee, Senator Sam J. Ervin, Chairman, 1967–1974; publications include *Chance and Circumstances: The Draft, the War and the Vietnam Generation;* consultant to Information Intelligence Committees, U.S. Congress; Adjunct Professor and Lecturer, Georgetown, Notre Dame, Catholic Law Schools, and American University; appointed judge of the U.S. Court of Federal Claims on October 22, 1998; chief judge, July 11, 2000 to May 10, 2002.

CHRISTINE ODELL COOK (O.C.) MILLER, judge; born in Oakland, CA, August 26, 1944; married to Dennis F. Miller; B.A., Stanford University, 1966; J.D., University of Utah College of Law, 1969; Comment Editor, Utah Law Review; Member, Utah Chapter Order of the Coif; Clerk to Chief Judge David T. Lewis, U.S. Court of Appeals for the 10th Circuit; trial attorney, Civil Division, U.S. Department of Justice; trial attorney, Federal Trade Commission, Bureau of Consumer Protection; Hogan and Hartson, litigation section; Pension Benefit Guaranty Corporation, Special Counsel; U.S. Railway Association, Assistant General Counsel; Shack and Kimball P.C., litigation; member of the Bars of the State of California and District of Columbia; Judge Miller was appointed by President Reagan on December 10, 1982, and confirmed as Christine Cook Nettsheim. She is a member of the University Club and the Cosmos Club. Judge Miller was reappointed by President Clinton on February 4, 1998.

MARIAN BLANK HORN, judge; born in New York, NY, 1943; daughter of Werner P. and Mady R. Blank; married to Robert Jack Horn; three daughters; attended Fieldston School, New York, NY, Barnard College, Columbia University and Fordham University School of Law; admitted to practice U.S. Supreme Court, 1973, Federal and State courts in New York, 1970, and Washington, DC, 1973; assistant district attorney, Deputy Chief Appeals Bureau, Bronx County, NY, 1969–72; attorney, Arent, Fox, Kintner, Plotkin and Kahn, 1972–73; adjunct professor of law, Washington College of Law, American University,

Congressional Directory

1973–76; litigation attorney, Federal Energy Administration, 1975–76; senior attorney, Office of General Counsel, Strategic Petroleum Reserve Branch, Department of Energy, 1976–79; deputy assistant general counsel for procurement and financial incentives, Department of Energy, 1979–81; deputy associate solicitor, Division of Surface Mining, Department of the Interior, 1981–83; associate solicitor, Division of General Law, Department of the Interior, 1983–85; principal deputy solicitor and acting solicitor, Department of Interior, 1985–86; adjunct professor of law, George Washington University National Law Center, 1991–present; Woodrow Wilson Visiting Fellow, 1994; assumed duties of judge, U.S. Court of Federal Claims in 1986 and confirmed for a second term in 2003.

ROBERT HAYNE HODGES, JR., judge; born in Columbia, SC, September 11, 1944, son of Robert Hayne and Mary (Lawton) Hodges; educated in the public schools of Columbia, SC; attended Wofford College, Spartanburg, SC; B.S., University of South Carolina, 1966; J.D., University of South Carolina Law School, 1969; married to Ruth Nicholson (Lady) Hodges, August 23, 1963; three children; judge, U.S. Court of Federal Claims, March 12, 1990.

LYNN J. BUSH, judge; born in Little Rock, AR, December 30, 1948; daughter of John E. Bush III and Alice (Saville) Bush; one son, Brian Bush Ferguson; B.A., Antioch College, 1970, Thomas J. Watson Fellow; J.D., Georgetown University Law Center, 1976; admitted to the Arkansas Bar in 1976 and to the District of Columbia Bar in 1977; trial attorney, Commercial Litigation Branch, Civil Division, U.S. Department of Justice, 1976–1987; senior trial attorney, Naval Facilities Engineering Command, Department of the Navy, 1987–1989; counsel, Engineering Field Activity Chesapeake, Naval Facilities Engineering Command, Department of the Navy, 1989–1996; administrative judge, U.S. Department of Housing and Urban Development Board of Contract Appeals, 1996–1998; nominated by President William Jefferson Clinton as judge, U.S. Court of Federal Claims, June 22, 1998; and assumed duties of the office on October 26, 1998.

NANCY B. FIRESTONE, judge; born October 17, 1951, in Manchester, NH; B.A., Washington University, 1973; J.D., University of Missouri, Kansas City, 1977; one child: Amanda Leigh; attorney, Appellate Section and Environmental Enforcement Section, U.S. Department of Justice, Washington, D.C., 1977–1984; Assistant Chief, Policy Legislation and Special Litigation, Environment and Natural Resources Division, Department of Justice, Washington, D.C., 1984–1985; Deputy Chief, Environmental Enforcement Section, Department of Justice, Washington, D.C., 1985–1989; Associate Deputy Administrator, Environmental Protection Agency, Washington, D.C., 1989–1992; Judge, Environmental Appeals Board, Environmental Protection Agency, Washington, D.C., 1992–1995; Deputy Assistant Attorney General, Environment and Natural Resources Division, Department of Justice, Washington, D.C., 1995–1998; Adjunct Professor, Georgetown University Law Center, 1985–current; judge, U.S. Court of Federal Claims, December 4, 1998.

EMILY CLARK HEWITT, judge; born in Baltimore, MD, May 26, 1944; appointed Judge of the United States Court of Federal Claims on October 22, 1998; entered duty on November 10, 1998; educated at the Roland Park Country School, Baltimore, MD (1949–1962); Cornell University (A.B. 1966); Union Theological Seminary (M. Phil. 1975); Harvard Law School (J.D. c.1. 1978); ordained minister in the Episcopal Church (diaconate 1972; priesthood 1974); member, Bar of the Supreme Judicial Court of The Commonwealth of Massachusetts (1978); administrator, Cornell/Hofstra Upward Bound Program (1967–1969); lecturer, Union Theological Seminary (1972–1973; 1974–1975); assistant professor, Andover Newton Theological School (1973–1975); private practice of law, Hill & Barlow (1978–1993); council member, Real Property Section, Massachusetts Bar Association (1983–1986); member, Executive Committee and chair, Practice Standards Committee, Massachusetts Conveyancers Association (1990–1992); General Counsel, U.S. General Services Administration (1993–1998); member, Administrative Conference of the United States (1993–1995); member, President's Interagency Council on Women (1995–1998).

FRANCIS M. ALLEGRA, judge; born October 14, 1957, in Cleveland, Ohio; married to Regina Allegra; one child (Domenic); B.A., Borromeo College of Ohio, 1978; J.D., Cleveland State University, 1981; judicial clerk to Chief Trial Judge Philip R. Miller, U.S. Court of Claims, 1981–82; associate, Squire, Sanders & Dempsey (Cleveland), 1982–84; line attorney, Appellate Section, then 1984–89, Counselor to the Assistant Attorney General, both with Tax Division, U.S. Department of Justice; 1994, Counselor to the Associate Attorney General then 1994–98, Deputy Associate Attorney General, both with the U.S. Department of Justice; judge, U.S. Court of Federal Claims, since October 22, 1998.

LAWRENCE J. BLOCK, judge, born in New York City, March 15, 1951; son of Jerome Block and Eve Silver; B.A., *magna cum laude,* New York University, 1973; J.D., The John Marshall Law School, 1981; law clerk for Hon. Roger J. Miner, United States District Court Judge for Northern District of New York, 1981–83; Associate, New York office of Skadden, Arps, Slate, Meagher and Flom, 1983–86; Attorney, Commercial Litigation Branch, U.S. Department of Justice, 1986; Senior Attorney-Advisor, Office of Legal Policy and Policy Development, U.S. Department of Justice, 1987–90; adjunct professor, George Mason University School of Law, 1990–91; acting general counsel for legal policy and deputy assistant general counsel for legal policy, U.S. Department of Energy, 1990–94; senior counsel, Senate Judiciary Committee, 1994–02; appointed by President George W. Bush on October 3, 2002, to a 15-years term as judge, U.S. Court of Federal Claims; admitted to the bar of Connecticut; admitted to practice in the U.S. Supreme Court, 1982, the U.S. Court of Appeals for the Eleventh Circuit, 1985, the United States District Court for the Eastern District of New York, 1985, the United States District Court for the northern district of New York, 1982.

SUSAN G. BRADEN, judge, born in Youngstown, OH, November 8, 1948, married to Thomas M. Susman, daughter (Daily); graduated Case Western Reserve University, B.A., 1970; Case Western Reserve University School of Law, J.D., 1973; Post graduate study Harvard Law School, Summer, 1979. Private practice, 1985–2003 (1997–2003 Baker & McKenzie); Federal Trade Commission: Special Counsel to Chairman, 1984–1985, Senior Attorney Advisor to Commissioner and Acting Chairman, 1980–1983; U.S. Department of Justice, Antitrust Division, Senior Trial Attorney, Energy Section, 1978–1980; Cleveland Field Office, 1973–1978. Special Assistant Attorney General for the State of Alabama, 1990; Consultant to the Administrative Conference of the United States, 1984–1985; 2000 Co-Chair, Lawyers for Bush-Cheney; General Counsel Presidential Debate for Dole-Kemp Campaign, 1996; Counsel to RNC Platform, 1996; Coordinator for Regulatory Reform and Antitrust Policy, Dole Presidential Campaign, 1995–1996; National Steering Committee, Lawyers for Bush-Quayle, 1992; Assistant General Counsel, Republican National Convention, 1988, 1992, 1996, 2000. Elected At-Large Member, D.C. Republican National Committee, 2000–2002; admitted to the Supreme Court of Ohio, 1973, U.S. District Court for the District of Columbia, 1980, U.S. Supreme Court, 1980; U.S. Court of Appeals for the District of Columbia, 1992; U.S. Court of Appeals for the Second Circuit, 1993, U.S. Court of Appeals for the Federal Circuit, 2001. Member of the American Bar Association (Council Member, Section on Administrative Law and Regulatory Practice, 1996–1999), Federal Circuit Bar Association, District of Columbia Bar Association, Computer Law Bar Association.

CHARLES F. LETTOW, judge, born in Iowa Falls, Iowa, February 10, 1941; son of Carl F. and Catherine Lettow; B.S.Ch.E. Iowa State University, 1962; LL.B. Stanford University, 1968, Order of the Coif; M.A. Brown University, 2001; Note Editor, Stanford Law Review; married to B. Sue Lettow; children: Renee Burnett, Carl Frederick II, John Stangland, and Paul Vorbeck; served U.S. Army, 1963–1965; law clerk to Judge Ben C. Duniway, U.S. Court of Appeals for the Ninth Circuit, 1968–1969, and Chief Justice Warren E. Burger, Supreme Court of the United States, 1969–1970; counsel, Council on Environmental Quality, Executive Office of the President, 1970–1973; associate (1973–1976) and partner (1976–2003), Cleary, Gottlieb, Steen & Hamilton, Washington, DC; admitted to practice before the U.S. Supreme Court, the U.S. Courts of Appeals for the D.C., Second, Third, Fourth, Fifth, Sixth, Eighth, Ninth, Tenth, and Federal Circuits, the U.S. District Courts for the District of Columbia, the Northern District of California, and the District of Maryland, and the U.S. Court of Federal Claims; member: American Law Institute, the American Bar Association, the D.C. Bar, the California State Bar, the Iowa State Bar Association, and the Maryland State Bar; nominated by President George W. Bush in 2001 and confirmed and took office in 2003.

MARY ELLEN COSTER WILLIAMS, judge; born in Flushing, NY, April 3, 1953; married to Mark Calhoun Williams; son: Justin; daughter: Jacquelyn; B.A. *summa cum laude* (Greek and Latin); MA (Latin), Catholic University, 1974; J.D. Duke University; Editorial Board, *Duke Law Journal,* 1976–1977; Admitted to the District of Columbia Bar. Associate, Fulbright and Jaworski, 1977–1979; Associate, Schnader, Harrison, Segal and Lewis, 1979–1983; Assistant U.S. Attorney, Civil Division, District of Columbia, 1983–1987; Partner—Janis, Schuelke, and Wechsler, 1987–1989; Administrative Judge, General Services Board of Contract Appeals March, 1989–July, 2003; Secretary, District of Columbia Bar, 1988–1989; Fellow, American Bar Foundation, Elected, 1985; Board of Directors, Bar Association of District of Columbia, 1985–1988; Chairman, Young Lawyers Section, Bar Association of District of Columbia, 1985–1986; Chair, Public Contract Law Section of American Bar Association 2002–03; Chair-Elect, Vice-Chair, Secretary, Council, 1995–2002; Delegate, Section of Public Contract Law, ABA House of Delegates 2003–04; Lecturer, Government Contract Law, 1989–Present.

VICTOR JOHN WOLSKI, judge; born in New Brunswick, NJ, November 14, 1962; son of Vito and Eugenia Wolski; B.A., B.S., University of Pennsylvania, 1984; J.D., University of Virginia School of Law, 1991; married to Lisa Wolski, June 3, 2000; admitted to Supreme Court of the United States, 1995; California Supreme Court, 1992; Washington Supreme Court, 1994; Oregon Supreme Court, 1996; District of Columbia Court of Appeals, 2001; U.S. Court of Appeals for the Ninth Circuit, 1993; U.S. Court of Appeals for the Federal Circuit, 2001; U.S. District Court for the Eastern District of California, 1993; U.S. District Court for the Northern District of California, 1995; U.S. Court of Federal Claims, 2001; U.S. District Court for the District of Columbia, 2002; research assistant, Center for Strategic and International Studies, 1984–85; research associate, Institute for Political Economy, 1985–88; Confidential Assistant and Speechwriter to the Secretary, U.S. Dept. of Agriculture, 1988; paralegal specialist, Office of the General Counsel, U.S. Dept. of Energy, 1989; law clerk to Judge Vaughn R. Walker, U.S. District Court for the Northern District of California, 1991–92; attorney, Pacific Legal Foundation, 1992–97; General Counsel, Sacramento County Republican Central Committee, 1995–97; Counsel to Senator Connie Mack, Vice-Chairman of the Joint Economic Committee, U.S. Congress, 1997–98; General Counsel and Chief Tax Adviser, Joint Economic Committee, U.S. Congress, 1999–2000; associate, Cooper, Carvin & Rosenthal, 2000–01; associate, Cooper & Kirk, 2001–03; nominated by President George W. Bush as judge, U.S. Court of Federal Claims, September 12, 2002, renominated January 7, 2003, confirmed by U.S. Senate July 9, 2003.

SENIOR JUDGES

THOMAS J. LYDON, senior judge; born June 3, 1927 in Portland, ME; educated in the parochial and public schools in Portland; attended University of Maine, 1948–52, B.A.; Georgetown University Law Center, 1952–55, LL.B., 1956–57, LL.M.; trial attorney, Civil Division, Department of Justice, 1955–67; Chief, Court of Claims Section, Civil Division, 1967–72; trial commissioner (trial judge), U.S. Court of Claims, 1972 to September 30, 1982; judge, U.S. Claims Court, October 1, 1982–July 31, 1987; senior judge, August 1, 1987–present.

JAMES F. MEROW, senior judge; born in Salamanca, NY, March 16, 1932; educated in the public schools of Little Valley, NY and Alexandria, VA; A.B. (with distinction), The George Washington University, 1953; J.D. (with distinction), The George Washington University Law School, 1956; member: Phi Beta Kappa, Order of the Coif, Omicron Delta Kappa; officer, U.S. Army Judge Advocate General's Corps, 1956–59; trial attorney-branch director, Civil Division, U.S. Department of Justice, 1959–78; trial judge, U.S. Court of Claims, 1978–82; judge, U.S. Court of Federal Claims since October 1, 1982 (reappointed by President Reagan to a 15-year term commencing August 5, 1983); member of Virginia State Bar, District of Columbia Bar, American Bar Association, and Federal Bar Association; married.

REGINALD W. GIBSON, senior judge; born in Lynchburg, VA, July 31, 1927; son of McCoy and Julia Gibson; son, Reginald S. Gibson, Jr.; educated in the public schools of Washington, DC; served in the U.S. Army, 1946–47; B.S., Virginia Union University, 1952; Wharton Graduate School of Business Administration, University of Pennsylvania, 1952–53; LL.B., Howard University School of Law, 1956; admitted to the District of Columbia Bar in 1957 and to the Illinois Bar in 1972; Internal Revenue agent, Internal Revenue Service, Washington, DC, 1957–61; trial attorney, tax division, criminal section, Department of Justice, Washington, DC, 1961–71; senior and later general tax attorney, International Harvester Co., Chicago, IL, 1971–82; judge, U.S. Court of Federal Claims, December 15, 1982–August 15, 1995; senior status, August 15, 1995–present.

JOHN PAUL WIESE, senior judge; born in Brooklyn, NY, April 19, 1934; son of Gustav and Margaret Wiese; B.A., *cum laude*, Hobart College, 1962, Phi Beta Kappa; LL.B., University of Virginia School of Law, 1965; married to Alice Mary Donoghue, June, 1961; one son, John Patrick; served U.S. Army, 1957–59; law clerk: U.S. Court of Claims, trial division, 1965–66, and Judge Linton M. Collins, U.S. Court of Claims, appellate division, 1966–67; private practice in District of Columbia, 1967–74 (specializing in government contract litigation); trial judge, U.S. Court of Claims, 1974–82; designated in Federal Courts Improvement Act of 1982 as judge, U.S. Court of Federal Claims, reappointed by President Reagan on October 14, 1986, to 15-year term as judge, U.S. Court of Federal Claims; admitted to bar of the District of Columbia, 1966; admitted to practice in the U.S. Supreme Court, the U.S. Court of Appeals for the Federal Circuit, the U.S. Court of Federal Claims; member: District of Columbia Bar Association and American Bar Association.

ROBERT J. YOCK, senior judge; born in St. James, MN, January 11, 1938; son of Dr. William J. and Erma Yock; B.A. St. Olaf College, 1959; J.D. University of Michigan Law School, 1962; married to Carla M. Moen, June 13, 1964; children: Signe Kara and Torunn Ingrid; admitted to the Minnesota Supreme Court in 1962; Court of Military Appeals, 1964; U.S. Supreme Court, 1965; U.S. District Court for the District of Minnesota, 1966; U.S. District Court for the District of Columbia, 1972; U.S. Court of Claims, 1979; and U.S. Court of Federal Claims, 1982; member: Minnesota State Bar Association, and District of Columbia Bar Association; served in the U.S. Navy, Judge Advocate General's Corps, 1962–66; private practice, St. Paul, MN, 1966–69; entered Government service as chief counsel to the National Archives and Record Services of the General Services Administration, 1969–70; executive assistant and legal advisor to the Administrator of General Services, 1970–72; assistant general counsel at GSA, 1972–77; trial judge, U.S. Court of Claims, 1977–82; designated by Public Law 97–164 as judge, U.S. Court of Federal Claims, 1982–83; renominated by President Reagan as judge, U.S. Court of Federal Claims, June 20, 1983, confirmed by U.S. Senate, August 4, 1983, reappointed to 15-year term, August 5, 1983.

LAWRENCE S. MARGOLIS, senior judge; born in Philadelphia, PA, March 13, 1935; son of Reuben and Mollie Margolis; B.A., Central High School, Philadelphia, PA; B.S. in mechanical engineering from the Drexel Institute of Technology (now Drexel University), 1957; J.D., George Washington University Law School, 1961; admitted to the District of Columbia Bar; patent examiner, U.S. Patent Office, 1957–62; patent counsel, Naval Ordnance Laboratory, White Oak, MD, 1962–63; assistant corporation counsel for the District of Columbia, 1963–66; attorney, criminal division, U.S. Department of Justice and special assistant U.S. attorney for District of Columbia, 1966–68; assistant U.S. attorney for the District of Columbia, 1968–71; appointed U.S. magistrate for District of Columbia in 1971; reappointed for a second 8-year term in 1979 and served until December, 1982 when appointed a judge, U.S. Court of Federal Claims; chairman, U.S. Court of Federal Claims: Security Committee, Building Committee, and Alternative Dispute Resolution Committee; chairman, American Bar Association, judicial administration division, 1980–81; chairman, National Conference of Special Court Judges, 1977–78; board of directors, Bar Association of the District of Columbia, 1970–72; editor: DC Bar Journal, 1966–73, Young Lawyers Newspaper editor, 1965–66; executive council, Young Lawyers Section, 1968–69; board of editors, The Judges' Journal and The District Lawyer; president, George Washington University National Law Association, 1983–84; president, George Washington Law Association, District of Columbia Chapter, 1975–76; board of governors, George Washington University General Alumni Association, 1978–85; fellow, Institute of Judicial Administration, 1993–; member, District of Columbia Judicial Conference; former member, board of directors, National Council of U.S. Magistrates; former president, Federal Bar Toastmasters; former technical editor, Federal Bar Journal; faculty, Federal Judicial Center; trustee, Drexel University, 1983–91; member, Rotary Club; Board of Managers, Central High (Philadelphia, PA); president, Washington, D.C. Rotary Club, 1988–89, District governor, 1991–92; American Bar Association Judicial Administration Division Award for distinguished service as chairman for 1980–81; Drexel University and George Washington University Distinguished Alumni Achievement Awards; Drexel University 100 (one of top 100 graduates); Center for Public Resources Alternative Dispute Resolution Achievement Award, 1987; George Washington University Community Service Award; married to Doris May Rosenberg, January 30, 1960; children: Mary Aleta and Paul Oliver; nominated by President Ronald Reagan as a judge on the U.S. Court of Federal Claims on September 27, 1982, confirmed by the Senate and received Commission on December 10, 1982, took oath of office on December 15, 1982.

LOREN ALLAN SMITH, senior judge; born December 22, 1944, in Chicago, IL; son of Alvin D. and Selma (Halpern) Smith; B.A., Northwestern University, 1966; J.D., Northwestern University School of Law, 1969; admitted to the Bars of the Illinois Supreme Court; the Court of Military Appeals; the U.S. Court of Appeals, District of Columbia Circuit; the U.S. Court of Appeals for the Federal Circuit; the U.S. Supreme Court; the U.S. Court of Federal Claims; honorary member: The University Club; consultant, Sidley and Austin Chicago, 1972–73; general attorney, Federal Communications Commission, 1973; assistant to the Special Counsel to the President, 1973–74; Special Assistant U.S. Attorney, District of Columbia, 1974–75; chief counsel, Reagan for President campaigns, 1976 and 1980; professor, Delaware Law School, 1976–84; distinguished lecturer at Columbus School of Law, The Catholic University of America and distinguished adjunct professor at George Mason University School of Law; deputy director, Executive Branch Management Office of Presidential Transition, 1980–81; Chairman, Administrative Conference of the Unites States, 1981–85; served as a member of the President's Cabinet Councils on Legal Policy and on Management and Administration; appointed judge of the U.S. Court of Federal Claims on July 11, 1985; entered on duty September 12, 1985; served as chief judge from January 14, 1986, until July 11, 2000; married.

ERIC G. BRUGGINK, senior judge; born in Kalidjati, Indonesia, September 11, 1949; naturalized U.S. citizen, 1961; married to Melinda Harris Bruggink; sons: John and David; B.A., *cum laude* (sociology), Auburn University, AL, 1971; M.A. (speech), 1972; J.D., University of Alabama, 1975; Hugo Black Scholar and Note and Comments Editor of Alabama Law Review; member, Alabama State Bar and District of Columbia Bar; served as law clerk to chief judge Frank H. McFadden, Northern District of Alabama, 1975–76; associate, Hardwick, Hause and Segrest, Dothan, AL, 1976–77; assistant director, Alabama Law Institute, 1977–79; director, Office of Energy and Environmental Law, 1977–79; associate, Steiner, Crum and Baker, Montgomery, AL, 1979–82; Director, Office of Appeals Counsel, Merit Systems Protection Board, 1982–86; judge, U.S. Court of Federal Claims, April 15, 1986.

BOHDAN A. FUTEY, senior judge; born in Ukraine, June 28, 1939; B.A., Western Reserve University, 1962; M.A., 1964; J.D., Cleveland Marshall Law School, 1968; partner, Futey and Rakowsky, 1968–72; chief assistant police prosecutor, city of Cleveland, 1972–74; executive assistant to the mayor of Cleveland, 1974–75; partner, Bazarko, Futey and Oryshkewych, 1975–84; chairman, U.S. Foreign Claims Settlement Commission, May, 1984–87; nominated judge of the U.S. Court of Federal Claims on January 30, 1987, and entered on duty, May 29, 1987; married to the former Myra Fur; three children: Andrew, Lidia, and Daria; member: District of Columbia Bar Association, the Ukrainian American Bar Association; Judge Futey is actively involved with Democratization and Rule of Law programs organized by the Judicial Conference of the United States, the Department of State, and the American Bar Association in Ukraine and Russia. He has participated in judicial exchange programs, seminars, and workshops and has been a consultant to the working group on Ukraine's Constitution and Ukrainian Parliament; Judge Futey is an advisor to the International Foundation for Election Systems (IFES); and the International Republican Institutes (IRI) democracy programs for Ukraine. He served as an official observer during the parliamentary and presidential elections in 1994 and 1998 and conducted briefings on Ukraine's election law for international observers; Judge Futey has lectured on Constitutional Law at the Ukrainian Free University in Munich and Passau University, Germany; also at Kyiv State University and Lviv University in Ukraine.

UNITED STATES TAX COURT

400 Second Street, NW., Washington, DC 20217, phone (202) 606–8754

JOEL GERBER, chief judge, Virginia; born in Chicago, IL, July 16, 1940; married to Judith Smilgoff, 1963; three sons: Jay Lawrence, Jeffrey Mark, and Jon Victor; B.S., business administration, Roosevelt University, 1962; J.D., DePaul University, 1965; LL.M., taxation, Boston University Law School, 1968; admitted to the Illinois Bar, 1965; Georgia Bar, 1974; Tennessee Bar, 1978; member American Bar Association (section of taxation); served with U.S. Treasury Department, Internal Revenue Service as: trial attorney, Boston, MA, 1965–72; staff assistant, regional counsel/senior trial attorney, Atlanta, GA, 1972–76; district counsel, Nashville, TN, 1976–80; deputy chief counsel, Internal Revenue Service, Washington, DC, 1980–84; acting chief counsel, Internal Revenue Service, May 1983 to March 1984; recipient of a Presidential Meritorious Rank Award, 1983 and the Secretary of the Treasury's Exceptional Service Award, 1984; lecturer, law, Vanderbilt University, 1976–80; appointed to the Tax Court for a 15-year term, beginning June 18, 1984, to succeed Senior Judge C. Moxley Featherston.

MARY ANN COHEN, judge, California; born July 16, 1943, Albuquerque, NM; B.A., University of California at Los Angeles, 1964; J.D., University of Southern California, 1967; admitted to California Bar, 1967; private practice of law, Los Angeles, with firm of Abbott and Cohen, a professional corporation (and predecessors), 1967–82; member: American Bar Association (sections of taxation, litigation, and criminal justice), American Judicature Society, Attorney General's Advisory Committee on Tax Litigation, U.S. Department of Justice (1979–80); appointed to U.S. Tax Court, July 1982 to succeed Cynthia H. Hall; term expires September 24, 1997.

STEPHEN J. SWIFT, judge, California; born September 7, 1943, Salt Lake City, UT, son of Edward A. Swift and Maurine Jensen; married to Lorraine Burnell Facer, 1972; children: Carter, Stephanie, Spencer, Meredith, and Hunter; graduated, Menlo Atherton High School, Atherton, CA, 1961; B.A., Brigham Young University, political science, 1967; George Washington Law School, J.D. (with honors), 1970; trial attorney (honors program), tax division, U.S. Department of Justice, 1970–74; assistant U.S. attorney, tax division, U.S. attorney's office, San Francisco, CA 1974–77; vice president and senior tax counsel, tax department, BankAmerica N.T. and S.A., San Francisco, CA, 1977–83; adjunct professor, Graduate Tax Program, Golden Gate University, San Francisco, CA 1978–83; member: California Bar, District of Columbia Bar, and American Bar Association (section of taxation); appointed August 16, 1983 to the U.S. Tax Court for a 15-year term expiring August 16, 1998.

ROBERT PAUL RUWE, judge, Virginia; born July 3, 1941, Cincinnati, Ohio; married to Mary Kay Sayer, Cincinnati, Ohio, 1967; children: Paul, Michael, Christian, and Stephen; graduated Roger Bacon High School, St. Bernard, OH, 1959, Xavier University, Cincinnati, OH, 1963; J.D., Salmon P. Chase College of Law, 1970; admitted to Ohio bar, 1970; joined Office of Chief Counsel, Internal Revenue Service in 1970 and held the following positions, Trial Attorney (Indianapolis), Director, Criminal Tax Division, Deputy Associate Chief Counsel (Litigation), and Director, Tax Litigation Division; member, American Bar Association (Section of taxation); took oath of office as a judge of the U.S. Tax Court, November 20, 1987 for a 15-year term to succeed Judge Charles R. Simpson.

JOHN O. COLVIN, judge, Virginia; born November 17, 1946, Canton, OH; married Ava M. Belohlov in 1970; one son: Timothy; graduated from the University of Missouri (A.B., 1968), and Georgetown University Law Center (J.D., Masters of Law in Taxation, 1978). During college and law school, employed by Niedner, Niedner, Nack and Bodeux, St. Charles, MO; Missouri Attorney General John C. Danforth and Missouri State Representative Richard C. Marshall, Jefferson City, MO; and U.S. Senator Mark O. Hatfield and Congressman Thomas B. Curtis, Washington, DC; admitted to the practice of law in Missouri, 1971 and District

859

of Columbia, 1974. Office of the Chief Counsel, U.S. Coast Guard, Washington, DC, 1971–75; served as tax counsel, Senator Bob Packwood, 1975–84; chief counsel, 1985–87, and chief minority counsel, 1987–88, U.S. Senate Finance Committee; officer of the Tax Section, Federal Bar Association since 1978, and adjunct professor of law, Georgetown University Law Center since 1987. Numerous civic and community activities; Judge Colvin was nominated by President Reagan and confirmed by the Senate as a Judge of the U.S. Tax Court for a term of 15 years beginning September 1, 1988 and expiring August 31, 2003. Judge Colvin filled a vacancy due to the resignation of Judge Samuel B. Sterrett.

JAMES S. HALPERN, judge, District of Columbia; born 1945, New York City; married to Nancy A. Nord; two children: W. Dyer and Hilary Ann; graduated from Hackley School, Terrytown, New York, 1963; Wharton School, University of Pennsylvania, B.S. 1967; Law School, University of Pennsylvania, J.D., 1972; Law School, New York University, LL.M. (in taxation) 1975; associate attorney, Mudge, Rose, Guthrie and Alexander, New York City, 1972–74; assistant professor of law, Law School, Washington and Lee University, 1975–76; assistant professor of law, St. John's University, New York City, 1976–78, visiting professor, Law School, New York University, 1978–79; associate attorney, Roberts and Holland, New York City, 1979–80; Principal Technical Advisor, Assistant Commissioner (Technical) and Associate Chief Counsel (Technical), Internal Revenue Service, Washington, DC, 1980–83; partner, Baker and Hostetler, Washington, DC, 1983–90; adjunct professor, Law School, George Washington University, Washington, DC, 1984–90; Colonel, U.S. Army Reserves; appointed to the U.S. Tax Court on July 3, 1990.

CAROLYN P. CHIECHI, judge, Maryland; born December 6, 1943, Newark, New Jersey; B.S., Georgetown, University, Washington, DC, *magna cum laude,* 1965 (Class Rank: 1); J.D., 1969 (Class Rank: 9); LL.M. (Taxation), 1971; admitted to the bar of the District of Columbia, 1969; served as attorney-advisor to Judge Leo H. Irwin, United States Tax Court, 1969–1971; practiced with the law firm of Sutherland, Asbill and Brennan, Washington, D.C. and Atlanta, Georgia (partner, 1976–1992; associate, 1971–1976); member, District of Columbia Bar (served as taxation section Tax Audits and Litigation Committee chairperson, 1987–1988); American Bar Association (Section of Taxation); Federal Bar Association (Section of Taxation); Women's Bar Association of the District of Columbia; elected fellow, American College of Tax Counsel; fellow, American Bar Foundation; member, Board of Regents, Georgetown University; member, National Law Alumni Board, Georgetown University; member, Stuart Stiller Memorial Foundation; appointed by the President to the U.S. Tax Court for a 15–year term beginning October 1, 1992.

DAVID LARO, judge, Michigan; born Flint, MI, March 3, 1942; married to the former Nancy Lynn Wolf on June 18, 1967; two children: Rachel Lynn and Marlene Ellen; graduated from the University of Michigan in 1964 with a B.A.; the University of Illinois Law School in 1967 with a J.D.; and New York University Law School in 1970 with an LL.M. in taxation; admitted to the bar of Michigan in 1968 and the United States District Court (Eastern District) Michigan in 1968, United States Tax Court, 1971; former partner of Winegarden, Booth, Shedd, and Laro, Flint, MI, 1970–75; principal member, Laro and Borgeson, Flint, MI, 1975–86; principal member, David Laro, Attorney at Law, P.C., Flint, MI, 1986–92; of counsel to Dykema Gossett, Ann Arbor, MI, 1989–90; former president and chief executive officer of Durakon Industries, Inc., Lapeer, MI, 1989–91, and former chairman of the board of Durakon Industries, Inc., 1991–92; former chairman of the board of Republic Bank, Ann Arbor, MI, 1986–92, and vice chairman and co-founder of Republic Bancorp, Inc., Ann Arbor, MI, 1986–92. Regent, University of Michigan Board of Regents, Ann Arbor, MI, 1975–81; former member of the Michigan State Board of Education, 1982–83; former chairman of the Michigan State Tenure Commission, 1972–75; former commissioner, Civil Service Commission, Flint, MI, 1984–1985. Former Commissioner of Police, Flint Township, 1972–74; former member of the Political Leadership Program, the Institute for Public Policy and Social Research, Lansing, MI; frequent speaker and lecturer on tax matters for the Michigan Association of Certified Public Accountants, and the Michigan Institute of Continuing Legal Education and other professional and business groups and organizations; author of numerous articles on taxation; former member of the Ann Arbor Art Association Board of Directors, board member of the Holocaust Foundation (Ann Arbor); appointed to the Tax Court for a 15–year term beginning November 2, 1992, to fill vacancy created by Judge Jules G. Körner III, who assumed senior status.

MAURICE B. FOLEY, judge, Illinois; born March 28, 1960, Belleville, Illinois; married Cassandra LaNel Green; three children: Malcolm, Corinne, and Nathan; received a Bachelor of Arts degree from Swarthmore College, a Juris Doctor from Boalt Hall School of Law at the University of California at Berkeley, and a Master of Laws in Taxation from Georgetown University Law Center; prior to the appointment to the Court was an attorney for the Legislation and Regulations Division of the Internal Revenue Service, tax counsel for the United States Senate Committee on Finance and Deputy Tax Legislative Counsel in the Treasury's Office of Tax Policy; appointed to the Tax Court for a 15-year term beginning April 10, 1995 to succeed Judge Charles E. Clapp, II.

JUAN F. VASQUEZ, judge, Texas; born in San Antonio, TX on June 24, 1948; married to Mary Theresa (Terry) Schultz in 1970; two children: Juan, Jr. and Jaime; attended Fox Tech High School and San Antonio Junior College, A.D. (Data Processing); received B.B.A (Accounting) from the University of Texas in Austin in 1972; attended State University of New York in Buffalo, 1st year law school in 1975; graduate of University of Houston Law Center in 1977 with a J.D. and New York University Law School in 1978 with an LL.M. in Taxation. Certified in Tax Law by Texas Board of Legal Specialization in 1984; Certified Public Account Certificate from Texas in 1976 and California in 1974; admitted to the bar of Texas in 1977; United States Tax Court in 1978, United States District Court, Southern District of Texas in 1982 and Western District of Texas in 1985, Fifth Circuit Court of Appeals in 1982; private practice of Tax Law, 1987–April 1995; partner, Leighton, Hood and Vasquez, 1982–87, San Antonio, Texas; Trial Attorney, Office of Chief Counsel, Internal Revenue Service, Houston, TX, 1978–82; accountant, Coopers and Lybrand, Los Angeles, California, 1972–74; member American Bar Association (Tax Section); Texas State Bar (Tax and Probate Sections); Fellow of Texas and San Antonio Bar Foundations, Mexican American Bar Association (MABA) of San Antonio (Treasurer); Houston MABA; Texas MABA (Treasurer), National Association of Hispanic CPA's; San Antonio Chapter (founding member), College of State Bar of Texas, National Hispanic Bar Association, Member of Greater Austin Tax Litigation Association; served on Austin Internal Revenue Service District Director's Practitioner Liaison Committee, 1990–91, chairman, 1991; Judge Vasquez was nominated by President Clinton on September 14, 1994, and confirmed by the Senate on March 17, 1995, as a Judge of the United States Tax Court for a term of 15 years beginning on May 1, 1995 to succeed Judge Perry Shields who took senior status.

JOSEPH H. GALE, judge, Virginia; born August 26, 1953, in Smithfield, VA; received A.B., Philosophy, Princeton University, Princeton, New Jersey, 1976; J.D., University of Virginia School of Law, Charlottesville, VA, 1980, where he was a Dillard Fellow; practiced law as an associate attorney at Dewey Ballantine, Washington, DC, and New York, New York, 1980–83, and Dickstein, Shapiro and Morin, Washington, DC, 1983–85; served as Tax Legislative Counsel for Senator Daniel Patrick Moynihan (D–NY), 1985–88; administrative assistant and Tax Legislative Counsel, 1989; chief counsel, 1990–93; chief tax counsel, Committee on Finance, U.S. Senate, 1993–95; minority chief tax counsel, Senate Finance Committee, January 1995-July 1995; minority staff director and chief counsel, Senate Finance Committee, July 1995–January 1996; admitted to the District of Columbia Bar; member: American Bar Association, Section of Taxation; frequent speaker at professional conferences and seminars on various Federal income tax topics; appointed to Tax Court for a 15-year term beginning February 9, 1996, to succeed Judge Edna G. Parker, who assumed senior status.

MICHAEL B. THORNTON, judge; born February 9, 1954, in Hattiesburg, Mississippi. Married Alexandra Deane Thornton in 1992 and has two daughters, Michaela and Camille. Graduated from University of Southern Mississippi, B.S. in Accounting, summa cum laude, 1976, and M.S. in Accounting, 1997; University of Tennessee, M.A. in English Literature, 1979; Duke University School of Law, J.D. with distinction, 1982 (Order of the Coif, Duke Law Journal Editorial Board). Served as law clerk to the Honorable Charles Clark, Chief Judge, U.S. Court of Appeals for the Fifth Circuit (1983–1984). Practiced law as an Associate Attorney at Sutherland, Asbill and Brennan, Washington, D.C. (1982–1983 and summer 1981); and Miller and Chevalier, Chartered, Washington, D.C. (1985–1988). Served as Tax Counsel, U.S. House Committee on Ways and Means (1988–1993); Chief Minority Tax Counsel, U.S. House Committee on Ways and means (January 1995); Attorney-Adviser, U.S. Treasury Department (February-April 1995); and Deputy Tax Legislative Counsel (Tax Legislation) in the Office of Tax Policy, United States Treasury Department (April 1995-February 1998). Recipient of Treasury Secretary's Annual Award, U.S. Department of the Treasury, 1997; Meritorious Service Award, U.S. Department of the Treasury, 1998. Admitted to the District of Columbia Bar (1982). Appointed to the Tax Court for a 15-year term beginning March 8, 1998, to succeed Judge Lapsley W. Hamblen, Jr., who assumed senior status.

L. PAIGE MARVEL, judge, Baltimore, Maryland; born December 6, 1949, in Easton, Maryland. Education: College of Notre Dame, Baltimore, Maryland, B.A. *magna cum laude*, 1971; University of Maryland School of Law, Baltimore, Maryland, J.D. with honors, 1974. Member, Order of the Coif. Professional Experience: Garbis & Schwait, PA (Associate 1974–76; Shareholder 1976–1985); Garbis, Marvel & Junghans, PA (Shareholder 1985–1986); Melnicove, Kaufman, Weiner, Smouse & Garbis, PA (Shareholder 1986–1988); Venabel, Baetjer & Howard LLP (Partner 1988–1998). Practice concentrated in the areas of federal and state tax litigation (civil and criminal). Bar Associations: American Bar Association, Section of Taxation (Vice-Chair, Committee Operations 1993–95; Council Director 1989–92; Chair, Court Procedure Committee 1985–87); Maryland State Bar Association (Member, Board of Governors 1988–90, 1996–98; Chair, Taxation Section 1982–83); Federal Bar Association, Section of Taxation (Member, Section Council). Affiliations: Fellow, American Bar Foundation; Fellow, Maryland Bar Foundation; Fellow and Regent, American College of Tax Counsel; Member, American Law Institute; Advisor, ALI Restatement of Law Third-The Law Governing Lawyers 1988–1998; Member, University of Maryland Board of Visitors; Member, Loyola/Notre Dame Library, Inc. Board of Trustees; Co-editor, Procedure Department, *The Journal of Taxation* 1990–1998; member, Commissioner's Review Panel on IRS Integrity 1989–91; Member and Chair, Procedure Subcommittee, Commission to Revise the Annotated Code of Maryland; (Tax Provisions). Author of various articles and book chapters on tax and tax litigation topics. Frequent lecturer on tax and tax controversy topics. Married to Robert H. Dyer, Jr.; two children—Alex and Kelly Dyer. Appointed to the Tax Court for a 15-year term beginning April 6, 1998 to succeed Judge Lawrence A. Wright who assumed senior status.

HARRY A. HAINES, judge, Montana; married to the former Janet Meyers; three children: Eric, Rob, and Jeanne; B.A., St. Olaf College in Northfield, Minnesota; J.D., University of Montana Law School; LL.M., New York University School of Law, in taxation; practiced law with the firm of Worden, Thane & Haines, P.C., in Missoula, Montana; appointed April 22, 2003 as a judge of the United States Tax Court; appointed by President George W. Bush to the Tax Court for a 15-year term to succeed Judge Renato Beghe who assumed senior status.

JOSEPH ROBERT GOEKE, judge, Illinois; married to the former Linda Powers; three children: Robert, Benjamin, and Elizabeth; B.S., Xavier University in Cincinnati, OH; J.D., University of Kentucky College of Law; initially, with the Chief Counsel of the Internal Revenue Service and since 1998 with Mayer, Brown, Rowe and Maw in Chicago; appointed April 22, 2003 as a judge of the United States Tax Court; appointed by President George W. Bush to the Tax Court for a 15-year term to succeed Judge Herbert L. Chabot who assumed senior status.

ROBERT A. WHERRY, JR., judge, Colorado; married to the former Leslie Ross; two children: Richard and Marsha; B.S., J.D., University of Colorado at Boulder; LL.M., New York University in taxation; practiced law for 30 years with Lentz, Evans, and King, P.C., in Denver, Colorado; appointed April 23, 2003, as a judge of the United States Tax Court; appointed by President George W. Bush to the Tax Court for a 15-year term to succeed Judge Laurence J. Whalen who assumed senior status.

THOMAS B. WELLS, judge; born Akron, OH, July 2, 1945; married Mary Josephine Graham of Vidalia, GA in 1974; children: Kathryn and Graham; received B.S. degree from Miami University, Oxford, OH in 1967; J.D. degree from Emory University School of Law, Atlanta, GA in 1973; LL.M. degree (in Taxation) from New York University Graduate School of Law, New York, NY in 1978; attended Ohio Northern University School of Law, Ada, OH, served as managing editor of the law review until he transferred to Emory University School of Law in 1972; completed active duty in 1970 as a supply corps officer in the U.S. Naval Reserve after tours in Morocco and Vietnam; admitted to the practice of law in the State of Georgia and practiced law in Vidalia, GA with the law firm of Graham and Wells, P.C., served as county attorney for Toombs County, GA and city attorney for the city of Vidalia, GA until 1977, and in Atlanta with the law firm of Hurt, Richardson, Garner, Todd and Cadenhead until 1981 and with the law firm of Shearer and Wells, P.C. until his appointment to the U.S. Tax Court in 1986; member; American Bar Association (section of taxation); State Bar of Georgia, served as a member of its Board of Governors; Board of Editors of the Georgia State Bar Journal; active in the Atlanta Bar Association, served as editor of The Atlanta Lawyer; active in various tax organizations such as the Atlanta Tax Forum; the Atlanta Estate Planning Council, served as a director; and the North

Atlanta Tax Council, served as a director; nominated by President Reagan and confirmed by the Senate as a judge of the U.S. Tax Court for a term of 15 years beginning October 12, 1986 to succeed Judge Richard C. Wilbur who retired.

SENIOR JUDGES

HOWARD A. DAWSON, JR., senior judge, Arkansas; born October 23, 1922, Okolona, AR, married to Marianne Atherholt; two daughters, Amy and Suzanne; graduated from University of North Carolina, B.S. in business administration, 1946; George Washington University Law School, J.D. with honors, 1949; president, Case Club; secretary-treasurer, Student Bar Association; private practice of law, Washington, DC, 1949–50; served with the U.S. Treasury Department, Internal Revenue Service, as follows: attorney, civil division, Office of Chief Counsel, 1950–53; civil advisory counsel, Atlanta District, 1953–57; regional counsel, Atlanta Region, 1958; personal assistant to Chief Counsel, December 1, 1958 to June 1, 1959; and assistant chief counsel (administration), June 1, 1959 to August 19, 1962; military service: U.S. Army Finance Corps, 1942–45; served 2 years in European theater; captain, Finance Corps, U.S. Army Reserve; member of District of Columbia Bar, Georgia Bar, American Bar Association (Section of Taxation), Federal Bar Association, National Lawyers Club, Delta Theta Phi Legal Fraternity, George Washington University Law Alumni Association; appointed on August 21, 1962, to the U.S. Tax Court for term expiring June 1, 1970; reappointed on May 21, 1970, to the U.S. Tax Court for a 15-year term expiring June 1, 1985; elected chief judge for a 2-year term beginning July 1, 1973; reelected chief judge for a 2-year term beginning July 1, 1975; again elected chief judge for a 2-year term beginning July 1, 1983. Assumed status as a senior judge on June 2, 1985. David L. Brennan Distinguished Visiting Professor of Law, University of Akron School of Law, spring term, 1986, professor of law and director, Graduate Tax Program, University of Baltimore School of Law, 1986–89; presently serving on senior status.

ARTHUR L. NIMS III, senior judge, New Jersey; elected chief judge for a 2-year term beginning June 1, 1988, re-elected chief judge beginning June 1, 1990; born January 3, 1923, Oklahoma City, OK; married to Nancy Chloe Keyes; two daughters; Deerfield Academy, Deerfield, MA; B.A., Williams College; LL.B., University of Georgia Law School; LL.M. (Tax), New York University Law School; served as an officer, lieutenant (jg.), U.S. Naval Reserve, on active duty in the Pacific theater during World War II; admitted to the bar of Georgia, 1949; and practiced in Macon, GA, 1949–51; served as special attorney, Office of the District Counsel, Internal Revenue Service, New York, NY, 1951–54; attorney, Legislation and Regulations Division, Chief Counsel's Office, Washington, DC, 1954–55; admitted to the bar of New Jersey, 1955; was with the law firm of McCarter and English, Newark, NJ, until 1979, having become a partner in 1961; served as secretary, Section of Taxation, American Bar Association, 1977–79; served as chairman, Section of Taxation, New Jersey State Bar Association, 1969–71; member, American Law Institute; appointed by the President to the U.S. Tax Court, June 21, 1979, to succeed Judge Arnold Raum, who assumed senior status; took office on June 29, 1979; assumed senior status June 1, 1992.

JULIAN I. JACOBS, senior judge, Maryland; born in Baltimore, MD, August 13, 1937; children: Richard and Jennifer; residence: Bethesda, MD; B.A., University of Maryland, 1958; LL.B., University of Maryland Law School, 1960; LL.M. (taxation), Georgetown Law Center, 1965; began legal career with the Internal Revenue Service, first in Washington, DC, drafting tax legislation and regulations from 1961–65, and then in Buffalo, NY, as a trial attorney in the regional counsel's office from 1965–67; entered private practice of law Baltimore City, 1967; partner, Baltimore law firm of Gordon, Feinblatt, Rothman, Hoffberger and Hollander, 1967, and remained until his appointment to the Tax Court on March 30, 1984, for a 15-year term to succeed Senior Judge Theodore Tannenwald, Jr.; chairman, study commission to improve the quality of the Maryland Tax Court, 1978, appointed by Maryland Gov. Blair Lee; member, several study groups to consider changes in the Maryland tax laws and as a commissioner on a commission to reorganize and recodify that article of Maryland law dealing with taxation, 1980, appointed by Maryland Gov. Harry Hughes; lecturer, tax seminars and professional programs; chairman, section of taxation, Maryland State Bar Association.

HERBERT L. CHABOT, senior judge, Maryland; born July 17, 1931, Bronx County, NY; married to Aleen Kerwin, 1951; four children: Elliot C., Donald J., Lewis A., and Nancy Jo; graduated, Stuyvesant High School, 1948; B.A. (*cum laude*), C.C.N.Y., 1952; LL.B., Columbia University, 1957; LL.M. (taxation), Georgetown University, 1964; enlisted in U.S. Army for 2 years and Army Reserves (civil affairs units), 8 years; served on legal staff, American Jewish Congress, 1957–61; law clerk to tax court Judge Russell E. Train, 1961–65; served on staff of Congressional Joint Committee on Taxation, 1965–78; elected delegate, Maryland Constitutional Convention, 1967–68; adjunct professor, National Law Center, George Washington University, 1974–83; member, American Bar (tax section) and Federal Bar Associations; appointed to the U.S. Tax Court for a 15-year term, beginning April 3, 1978; reappointed for a second 15-year term in 1993.

LAURENCE J. WHALEN, judge, Oklahoma; born 1944, Philadelphia, PA; married Donna L. Whalen; son: E. Holmes Whalen, daughter: Kaitlyn Rose Whalen; A.B., Georgetown University, 1967; J.D., Georgetown University Law Center, 1970; LL.M., 1971; special assistant to the Assistant Attorney General, 1971–72; trial attorney, tax division, 1971–75; private practice in Washington, DC, with Hamel and Park (now Hopkins, Sutter, Hamel and Park), 1977–84; also in Oklahoma City, OK, with Crowe and Dunlevy, 1984–87; member: Oklahoma Bar Association, District of Columbia Bar Association, American Bar Association, and Bar Association of the District of Columbia; appointed to the U.S. Tax Court, November 23, 1987.

RENATO BEGHE, judge, Illinois; born 1933, Chicago, Illinois; married to Bina House; four children and one grandchild; University of Chicago (A.B. 1951; J.D. 1954); Phi Beta Kappa; Order of the Coif and Law Review co-managing editor; Phi Gamma Delta; admitted New York bar 1955; practiced law with Carter, Ledyard and Milburn, New York City (associate 1954–65; partner 1965–83) and Morgan, Lewis and Bockius, New York City (1983–89); bar associations; Association of the Bar of the City of New York (Chairman, Art Law Committee, 1980–83); New York State Bar Association (tax section chairman 1977–78; Joint Practice Committee of Lawyers and Accountants, co-chairman, 1989–90); American Bar Association (Tax Section); International Bar Association; International Fiscal Association; member American Law Institute and American College of Tax Counsel; member America-Italy Society, Inc. and Honorable Order of Kentucky Counsel; appointed to the Tax Court for 15-year term beginning March 26, 1991, to fill vacancy created by resignation of Judge B. John Williams, Jr.

SPECIAL TRIAL JUDGES OF THE COURT

Robert N. Armen, Jr.; Lewis R. Carluzzo; D. Irvin Couvillion; John F. Dean; Stanley J. Goldberg; Peter J. Panuthos (chief special trial judge); Carleton D. Powell.

OFFICERS OF THE COURT

Clerk.—Lynne L. Glasser, 606–2754.
Deputy Clerk.—Hazel Keahey.
Budget and Accounting Officer.—Kristi Greenslade.
Librarian.—Elsa Silverman.
Reporter.—John T. Fee.

UNITED STATES COURT OF APPEALS
FOR THE ARMED FORCES [1]

450 E Street NW 20442–0001, phone 761–1448, fax 761–4672

H.F. "SPARKY" GIERKE, chief judge; born March 13, 1943, in Williston, ND; son of Herman F. Gierke, Jr., and Mary Kelly Gierke; children: Todd, Scott, Craig, and Michelle; B.A., University of North Dakota, 1964; J.D., University of North Dakota, 1966; graduated basic course, the Judge Advocate General's School, Charlottesville, VA, 1967; graduated military judge course, the Judge Advocate General's School, Charlottesville, VA, 1969; active duty, U.S. Army judge advocate general's corps, 1967–71; private practice of law, 1971–83; served as a justice of the North Dakota supreme court from October 1, 1983 until appointment to U.S. Court of Military Appeals. Admitted to the North Dakota Bar, 1966; admitted to practice law before all North Dakota Courts, U.S. District Court for the District of North Dakota, U.S. District Court for the Southern District of Georgia, U.S. Court of Military Appeals, and U.S. Supreme Court; served as president of the State Bar Association of North Dakota in 1982–83; served as president of the North Dakota State's Attorneys Association in 1979–80; served on the board of governors of the North Dakota Trial Lawyers Association from 1977–83; served on the board of governors of the North Dakota State Bar Association from 1977–79 and from 1981–84; served as vice chairman and later chairman of the North Dakota Judicial Conference from June 1989 until November 1991. Fellow of the American Bar Foundation and the American College of Probate Counsel; member of the American Bar Association, American Judicature Society, Association of Trial Lawyers of America, Blue Key National Honor Fraternity, Kappa Sigma Social Fraternity, University of North Dakota President's Club; in 1984, received the Governor's Award from Governor Allen I. Olson for outstanding service to the State of North Dakota; in 1988 and again in 1991, awarded the North Dakota National Leadership Award of Excellence by Governor George A. Sinner; in 1989, selected as the Man of the Year by the Delta Mu Chapter of the Kappa Sigma Fraternity and as Outstanding Greek Alumnus of the University of North Dakota; also awarded the University of North Dakota Sioux Award (UND's alumni association's highest honor); in 1983–84, served as the first Vietnam era state commander of the North Dakota American Legion; in 1988–89, served as the first Vietnam era national commander of the American Legion; nominated by President Bush, October 1, 1991; confirmed by the Senate, November 14, 1991; sworn-in and assumed office on the U.S. Court of Military Appeals, November 20, 1991. On October 1, 2004, he became the Chief Judge until his retirement on September 30, 2006.

SUSAN J. CRAWFORD, associate judge; born April 22, 1947, in Pittsburgh, PA; daughter of William E. and Joan B. Crawford; married to Roger W. Higgins of Geneva, NY, September 8, 1979; one child, Kelley S. Higgins; B.A., Bucknell University, Pennsylvania, 1969; J.D. (*cum laude*), Dean's Award, Arthur McClean Founder's Award, New England School of Law, Boston, MA, 1977; Career record: history teacher and coach of women's athletics, Radnor High School, Pennsylvania, 1969–74; associate, Burnett and Eiswert, Oakland, MD, 1977–79; Assistant State's Attorney, Garrett County, Maryland, 1978–1980; partner, Burnett, Eiswert and Crasford, 1979–81; instructor, Garrett County Community College, 1979–81; deputy general counsel, 1981–83, and general counsel, Department of the Army, 1983–89; special counsel to Secretary of Defense, 1989; inspector general, Department of Defense, 1989–91; member: bar of the Supreme Court of the United States; bar of the U.S. Court of Military Appeals, Maryland Bar Association, District of Columbia Bar Association, American Bar Association, Federal Bar Association, and the Edward Bennett Williams American Inn of Court; member: board of trustees, 1989–present, and Corporation, 1992–present, of New England School of Law; board of trustees, 1988–present, Bucknell University; nominated by President Bush as judge, U.S. Court of Military Appeals, February 19, 1991, for a term

---

[1] Prior to October 5, 1994, United States Court of Military Appeals.

of 15 years; confirmed by the Senate on November 14, 1991, sworn in and officially assumed her duties on November 19, 1991. On October 1, 1999, she became the Chief Judge for a term of five years.

ANDREW S. EFFRON, associate judge; born in Stamford, CT, September 18, 1948; education: A.B., Harvard College, 1970; J.D., Harvard Law School, 1975; The Judge Advocate General's School, U.S. Army, 1976, 1983; legislative aide to the late Representative William A. Steiger, 1970–76 (two years full-time, the balance between school semesters); judge advocate, Office of the Staff Judge Advocate, Fort McClellan, Alabama, 1976–77; attorney-adviser, Office of the General Counsel, Department of Defense, 1977–87; Counsel, General Counsel, and Minority Counsel, Committee on Armed Services, U.S. Senate, 1987–96; nominated by President Clinton to serve on the U.S. Court of Appeals for the Armed Forces, June 21, 1996; confirmed by the Senate, July 12, 1996; took office on August 1, 1996.

JAMES E. BAKER, associate judge; born in New Haven, CT, on March 25, 1960; education: BA., Yale University, 1982; J.D., Yale Law School, 1990; Attorney, Department of State, 1990–1993; Counsel, President's Foreign Intelligence Advisory Board/Intelligence Oversight Board, 1993–1994; Deputy Legal Advisor, National Security Counsel, 1994–1997; Special Assistant to the President and Legal Advisor, National Security Counsel, 1997–2000; military service: U.S. Marine Corps and U.S. Marine Corp Reserve; nominated by President Clinton to serve on the U.S. Court of Appeals for the Armed Forces; began service on September 19, 2000.

CHARLES E. ERDMANN, associate judge; born in Great Falls, Montana on June 26, 1946; Education: BA, Montana State University, 1972; JD, University of Montana Law School, 1975; Air Force Judge Advocate Staff Officers Course, 1981; Air Command and Staff College, 1992; Air War College, 1994; Military Service: U.S. Marine Corps, 1967–1970; Air National Guard, 1981–2002 (retired as a Colonel); Employment: Assistant Montana Attorney General, 1975–76; Chief Counsel, Montana State Auditor's Office, 1976–78; Chief Staff Attorney, Montana Attorney General's Office, Antitrust Bureau; Bureau Chief, Montana Medicaid Fraud Bureau, 1980–82; General Counsel, Montana School Boards Association, 1982–86; Private Practice of Law, 1986–95; Associate Justice, Montana Supreme Court, 1995–97; Office of High Representative of Bosnia and Herzegovina, Judicial Reform Coordinator, 1998–99; Office of High Representative of Bosnia and Herzegovina, Head of Human Rights and Rule of Law Department, 1999; Chairman and Chief Judge, Bosnian Election Court, 2000–01; Judicial Reform and International Law Consultant, 2001–2002; appointed by President George W. Bush to serve on the U.S. Court of Appeals for the Armed Forces on October 9, 2002, commenced service on October 15, 2002.

WILLIAM HORACE DARDEN, senior judge; born in Union Point, GA, May 16, 1923; son of William W. and Sara (Newsom) Darden; B.B.A., University of Georgia, 1946; LL.B., University of Georgia, 1948; admitted to bar of Georgia and to practice before the Georgia Supreme Court, 1948; active duty in U.S. Navy from July 1, 1943 to July 3, 1946, when released to inactive duty as lieutenant (jg.); married to Mary Parrish Viccellio of Chatham, VA, December 31, 1949; children: Sara Newsom, Martha Hardy, William H., Jr., Daniel Hobson; secretary to U.S. Senator Richard B. Russell, 1948–51; chief clerk of U.S. Senate Committee on Armed Services, 1951–53; professional staff member and later chief of staff, U.S. Senate Committee on Armed Services, February 1953 to November 1968; received recess appointment as judge of the U.S. Court of Military Appeals from President Johnson on November 5, 1968, to succeed the late Judge Paul J. Kilday; took oath of office on November 13, 1968; nominated by President Johnson for the unexpired part of the term of the late Judge Paul J. Kilday ending May 1, 1976; confirmed by Senate on January 14, 1969; designated chief judge by President Nixon on June 23, 1971; resigned December 29, 1973; elected to become senior judge on February 11, 1974.

ROBINSON O. EVERETT, senior judge; born in Durham, NC, March 18, 1928; son of Reuben O. and Kathrine (Robinson) Everett; A.B. (*magna cum laude*), Harvard College, 1947; J.D. (*magna cum laude*), Harvard Law School, 1950; LL.M., Duke University, 1959; active duty in U.S. Air Force, 1951–53; thereafter served in U.S. Air Force Reserve and retired as colonel, 1978; married to Linda McGregor of Greensboro, NC, August 27, 1966; children: Robinson O., Jr., McGregor, and Lewis Moore; commissioner, U.S. Court of Military Appeals, 1953–55; private law practice, Durham, NC, 1955–80; assistant professor of law, 1950–51; adjunct professor of law, 1963–66; professor of law, Duke Law School, 1967–present; chairman Durham Urban Redevelopment Commission, 1958–75; counsel, 1961–64; consultant, 1964–66; Subcommittee on Constitutional Rights, Senate Committee on the Judiciary; chairman, Standing Committee on Military Law, American Bar Association,

1977–79; president, Durham County Bar Association, 1976–77; commissioner, National Conference of Commissioners on Uniform State Laws, 1961–73, 1977–present; member, American Law Institute, 1966–present; councillor, North Carolina State Bar, 1978–83; nominated by President Carter as judge of U.S. Court of Military Appeals, February 14, 1980, for the remainder of the term expiring May 1, 1981; unanimously confirmed by the Senate and designated chief judge by President Carter, March 28, 1980; took oath of office, April 16, 1980; term of office extended until April 15, 1990, by Act of December 23, 1980, Public Law 96–579, section 12, 94 Stat. 3369; term of office further extended until Sep. 30, 1990 by Act of November 29, 1989, Public Law 101–189, section 1301, 103 Stat 1575–76. Immediately upon his retirement at the end of his term on September 30, 1990, assumed status of senior judge and returned to full active service until January 1, 1992.

WALTER THOMPSON COX III, senior judge; born August 13, 1942, in Anderson, SC; son of Walter T. Cox and Mary Johnson Cox; married to Vicki Grubbs of Anderson, SC, February 8, 1963; children: Lisa and Walter; B.S., Clemson University, 1964; J.D. (*cum laude*), University of South Carolina School of Law, 1967; graduated Defense Language Institute (German), 1969; graduated basic course, the Judge Advocate General's School, Charlottesville, VA, 1967; studied procurement law at that same school, 1968. Active duty, U.S. Army judge advocate general's corps, 1964–72 (1964–67, excess leave to U.S.C. Law School). Private law practice, 1973–78. Elected resident judge, 10th Judicial Circuit, South Carolina, 1978–84; also served as acting associate justice of South Carolina supreme court, on the judicial council, on the circuit court advisory committee, and as a hearing officer of the judicial standards commission; member: bar of the Supreme Court of the United States; bar of the U.S. Court of Military Appeals; South Carolina Bar Association; Anderson County Bar Association; the American Bar Association; the South Carolina Trial Lawyers Association; the Federal Bar Association; and the Bar Association of the District of Columbia; has served as a member of the House of Delegates of the South Carolina Bar, and the Board of Commissioners on Grievances and Discipline. Nominated by President Reagan, as judge of U.S. Court of Military Appeals, June 28, 1984, for a term of 15 years; confirmed by the Senate, July 26, 1984; sworn-in and officially assumed his duties on September 6, 1984; retired on September 30, 1999 and immediately assumed status of senior judge on October 1, 1999 and returned to full active service until September 19, 2000.

EUGENE R. SULLIVAN, senior judge; born August 2, 1941, in St. Louis, MO; son of Raymond V. and Rosemary K. Sullivan; married to Lis U. Johansen of Ribe, Denmark, June 18, 1966; children: Kim A. and Eugene R. II; B.S., U.S. Military Academy, West Point, 1964; J.D., Georgetown Law Center, Washington, DC, 1971; active duty with the U.S. Army, 1964–69; service included duty with the 3rd Armored Division in Germany, and the 4th Infantry Division in Vietnam; R&D assignments with the Army Aviation Systems Command; one year as an instructor at the Army Ranger School, Ft. Benning, GA; decorations include: Bronze Star, Air Medal, Army Commendation Medal, Ranger and Parachutist Badges, Air Force Exceptional Civilian Service Medal. Following graduation from law school, clerked with U.S. Court of Appeals (8th Circuit), St. Louis, 1971–72; private law practice, Washington, DC, 1972–74; assistant special counsel, White House, 1974; trial attorney, U.S. Department of Justice, 1974–82; deputy general counsel, Department of the Air Force, 1982–84; general counsel of the Department of Air Force, 1984–86; Governor of Wake Island, 1984–86; presently serves on the Board of Governors for the West Point Society of the District of Columbia; the American Cancer Society (Montgomery County Chapter); nominated by President Reagan, as judge, U.S. Court of Military Appeals on February 25, 1986, and confirmed by the Senate on May 20, 1986, and assumed his office on May 27, 1986. President Bush named him the chief judge of the U.S. Court of Military Appeals, effective October 1, 1990, a position he held for five years. He retired on September 30, 2001 and immediately assumed status of senior judge and returned to full active service until Sept. 30, 2002.

OFFICERS OF THE U.S. COURT OF APPEALS FOR THE ARMED FORCES

Clerk of the Court.—William A. DeCicco.
Chief Deputy Clerk of the Court.—David A. Anderson.
Deputy Clerk for Opinions.—Patricia Mariani.
Administrative Officer.—Robert J. Bieber.
Librarian.—Agnes Kiang.

UNITED STATES COURT OF APPEALS
FOR VETERANS CLAIMS

625 Indiana Avenue 20004, phone 501-5970

DONALD L. IVERS, judge; born on May 6, 1941, in San Diego, CA; A.A., New Mexico Military Institute, 1961; B.A., University of New Mexico, 1963; J.D., American University, 1971; active duty in the U.S. Army, 1963-68, U.S., Europe, and Vietnam; retired from U.S. Army Reserve with the rank of lieutenant colonel; clerk, District of Columbia Superior Court and the District of Columbia Court of Appeals; private practice of law with Brault, Graham, Scott and Brault, Washington, DC, 1972-78; chief counsel, Republican National Committee, 1978-81; chief counsel, Federal Highway Administration, 1981-85; director, Safety Review Task Force, U.S. Department of Transportation, 1984-85; general counsel, Veterans Administration, 1985-89; assistant to the Secretary, United States Department of Veterans Affairs, 1990; resides in Alexandria, VA; married, and the father of three children; nominated by President Bush, confirmed by the U.S. Senate in 1990; sworn in August 7, 1990.

JONATHAN ROBERT STEINBERG, judge; B.A., Cornell University, 1960; L.L.B., *cum laude*, University of Pennsylvania School of Law, 1963; research and note editor, University of Pennsylvania Law Review; Order of the Coif; research assistant, American Law Institute; law clerk for then Circuit Judge Warren E. Burger, U.S. Court of Appeals for the District of Columbia Circuit, 1963-64; attorney advisor, Peace Corps, 1964-68, and deputy general counsel, 1968-69; counsel, U.S. Senate Committee on Labor and Public Welfare (Subcommittee on Veterans' Affairs, Subcommittee on Railroad Retirement, and Special Subcommittee on Human Resources) 1969-77; chief counsel/staff director, U.S. Senate Committee on Veterans' Affairs, 1977-81 and 1987-90; minority chief counsel/staff director, Committee on Veterans' Affairs, 1981-87; admitted to bar of U.S. Court of Appeals for D.C. Circuit, May 1964; resides in the Washington, DC area, with his wife Shellie; two adult children: Andrew and Amy; nominated by President Bush in May 1990, confirmed by the U.S. Senate in August 1990; sworn in on September 13, 1990.

WILLIAM P. GREENE, Jr., judge; born on July 27, 1943, in Bluefield, WV, to William and Dorothy Greene; married to Madeline Sinkford of Bluefield, WV; two children; B.A., political science, West Virginia State College, 1965; J.D., Howard University, Washington, D.C., 1968; active duty in the United States Army Judge Advocate General's Corps following graduation from law school; as Judge Advocate, completed military education at the Basic, Advanced, and Military Judges' courses at The Judge Advocate General's School, the Army Command and General Staff College, Fort Leavenworth, KS, and the Army War College, Carlisle Barracks, PA; served as the Chief Prosecutor, Fort Knox, KY, 1969-70, and Chief Defense Counsel, Army Command, Hawaii, 1970-73; Army chief recruiter for lawyers 1974-77; Department Chair, Criminal Law Division, the Judge Advocate General's School, Charlottesville, VA, 1981-84; Deputy Staff Judge Advocate, Third Infantry Division, Germany 1977-80; Staff Judge Advocate, Second Infantry Division, Korea 1984-85; following graduation from the United States Army War College, selected to serve as the Staff Judge Advocate of the United States Military Academy at West Point, NY, 1986-90, followed by another selection as Staff Judge Advocate at Fort Leavenworth, KS; retired from the United States Army as Colonel, 1993, receiving several awards during this service, including three Legions of Merit, three Meritorious Service Medals, and two Army Commendation Medals; appointed by the Attorney General of the United States as an Immigration Judge, Department of Justice, presiding over immigration cases in Maryland and Pennsylvania, June 1993—November 1997; nominated for appointment by President Clinton May 16, 1997; confirmed by the U.S. Senate November 7, 1997; sworn in November 24, 1997.

BRUCE E. KASOLD, judge; born in New York, 1951; B.S., United States Military Academy, 1973; J.D., *cum laude*, University of Florida, 1979; LL.M., Georgetown University, 1982; Honors Graduate, the Judge Advocate General's School Graduate Program, 1984; admitted to the bars of the U.S. Supreme Court, the Florida Supreme Court, the District of Columbia Court of Appeals; member: Florida Bar, District of Columbia Bar, the Federal

Bar Association, Order of the Coif; retired from the U.S. Army, Lieutenant Colonel, Air Defense Artillery and Judge Advocate General's Corp, 1994; commercial litigation attorney, Holland & Knight Law Firm, 1994–95; Chief Counsel, U.S. Senate Committee on Rules and Administration, 1995–98; Chief Counsel, Secretary of the Senate and Senate Sergeant at Arms, 1998–2003; appointed by President George W. Bush to the U.S. Court of Appeals for Veterans Claims on December 13, 2003; sworn in December 31, 2003.

LAWRENCE B. HAGEL, judge; born in Washington, Indiana, 1947; B.S., United States Naval Academy, 1969; J.D., University of the Pacific McGeorge School of Law, 1976; LL.M. (Labor Law, with highest honors) The National Law Center, George Washington University, 1983; admitted to the bars of the U.S. Supreme Court, the United States Court of Appeals for the Fourth, Ninth, Tenth, D.C. and Federal Circuits, U.S. Court of Appeals for the Armed Forces, U.S. Court of Appeals for Veterans Claims, Supreme Court of the States of Iowa and California and the District of Columbia; commissioned in the U.S. Marine Corps, second lieutenant, infantry officer 1969–72 service in Vietnam and Puerto Rico; Marine Corps judge advocate 1973–90, assignments concentrated in criminal and civil litigation; Deputy General Counsel and General Counsel, Paralyzed Veterans of America, 1990–2003; confirmed by the U.S. Senate to the Court of Appeals on December 9, 2003; sworn in January 2, 2004.

WILLIAM A. MOORMAN, judge; of Arlington, VA; born January 23, 1945 in Chicago, IL; B.A., University of Illinois at Champaign-Urbana, 1967; J.D., University of Illinois College of Law, 1970; commissioned in the United States Air Force, second lieutenant, Reserve Officers Training Corps, 1970; entered active duty, 1971; Judge Advocate General's Corps, 1972–2002, serving as the senior attorney at every level of command, culminating his active military service with his appointment as the Judge Advocate General of the United States Air Force; military decorations include the Superior Service Medal with oak leaf cluster, the Legion of Merit with oak leaf cluster, the Joint Meritorious Service Medal, and the Meritorious Service Medal with four oak leaf clusters; retired from the Air Force in April 2002, in the grade of Major General; Counselor to the General Counsel, Department of Veterans Affairs, 2002; Assistant to the Secretary for Regulation Policy and Management, Department of Veterans Affairs, 2003; appointed by President George W. Bush as Acting Assistant Secretary of Management for the Department of Veterans Affairs, August 2004; author: "Executive Privilege and the Freedom of Information Act: Sufficient Protection for Aircraft Mishap Reports?", 21 Air Force Law Review 581 (1979); "Cross-Examination Techniques," 27 Air Force Law Review 105 (1987); "Fifty Years of Military Justice: Does the UCMJ Need to be Changed?", 48 Air Force Law Review 185 (2000); "Humanitarian Intervention and International Law in the Case of Kosovo," 36 New England Law Review 775 (2002); "Serving our Veterans Through Clearer Rules," 56 Administrative Law Review 207 (2004); recipient: Albert M. Kuhfeld Outstanding Young Judge Advocate of the Air Force Award 1979, Stuart R. Reichart Outstanding Senior Attorney of the Air Force Award 1992, University of Illinois College of Law Distinguished Alumnus Award 2001, Department of Veterans Affairs Exceptional Service Award 2004; nominated for appointment to the U.S. Court of Appeals for Veterans Claims on September 21, 2004, by President George W. Bush; confirmed by the U.S. Senate November 20, 2004; sworn in December 16, 2004.

ALAN G. LANCE, SR., judge; born April 27, 1949 in McComb, Ohio. Graduated from South Dakota State University, 1971, B.A. in English and History, distinguished military graduate; commissioned U.S. Army, June 1971; graduated University of Toledo School of Law and Law Review, 1973; admitted to the U.S. Supreme Court, U.S. Court of Military Appeals, State of Ohio, State of Idaho; commissioned U.S. Army, Judge Advocate Generals Corps, 1974 and served as Claims Officer, defense counsel, Chief of Defense Counsel, Legal Assistance Officer, Administrative Law Officer and in the absence of a military Judge, military Magistrate for the 172nd Infantry Brigade (Alaska) 1974–1977; Army Commendation Medal 1977; served as the Command Judge Advocate, Corpus Christi Army Depot, 1977–78; engaged in private practice of law, Ada County, Idaho, 1978–94; elected to the Idaho House of Representatives, 1990, and served as Majority Caucus chairman, 1992–94; elected as Idaho Attorney General (31st) in 1994 and 1998; Distinguished Alumnus Award, University of Toledo School of Law, 2002; inducted into the Ohio Veterans Hall of Fame, November 2004; confirmed by the U.S. Senate to the Court of Appeals for Veterans Claims, November 2004 and sworn in on December 17, 2004.

ROBERT N. DAVIS, judge; born September 20, 1953, in Kewanee, IL; graduated from Davenport Central High School, Davenport, IA, 1971; B.A., University of Hartford, 1975; J.D. Georgetown University Law Center, 1978; admitted to the bars of the U.S. Supreme Court, the Ninth Circuit Court of Appeals; the State of Virginia; and the State of Iowa; career record 1978–83 appellate attorney with the Commodity Futures Trading Commission; 1983–88 attorney with the United States Department of Education, Business and Administrative law division of the Office of General Counsel; 1983 Governmental exchange program with the United States Attorneys office, District of Columbia; Special Assistant United States Attorney; 1988–2001 Professor of Law, University of Mississippi School of Law; 2001–05 Professor of Law, Stetson University College of Law; Published extensively in the areas of constitutional law, administrative law, national security law and sports law. Founder and Faculty Editor-in-Chief, Journal of National Security Law, Arbitrator/mediator with the American Arbitration Association and the United States Postal Service. Gubernatorial appointment to the National Conference of Commissioners on Uniform State Laws 1993–2000. Joined the United States Navy Reserve Intelligence Program in 1988. Presidential recall to active duty in 1999, Bosnia and 2001 for the Global War on Terrorism. Military decorations include Joint Service Commendation Medal, Joint Service Achievement Medal, Navy Achievement Medal, NATO Medal, Armed Forces Expeditionary Medal, Armed Forces Reserve Medal with "M" device, Overseas Service Ribbon, National Defense Ribbon, Joint Meritorious Unit Award, and Global War on Terrorism Medal. Nominated for appointment by President George W. Bush on March 23, 2003; confirmed by the United States Senate on November 21, 2004; Commissioned on December 4, 2004 as a Judge, United States Court of Appeals for Veterans Claims.

MARY J. SCHOELEN, judge; B.A. in Political Science from the University of California at Irvine, 1990; J.D. from the George Washington University Law School, 1993. Admitted to the State Bar of California. Law clerk for the National Veterans Legal Services Project, 1992–93; legal intern to the U.S. Senate Committee on Veterans' Affairs, 1994; staff attorney for Vietnam Veterans of America's Veterans Benefits Program, 1994–97; Minority Counsel, U.S. Senate Committee on Veterans' Affairs, 1997–2001; Minority General Counsel, March 2001–June 2001; Deputy Staff Director, Benefits Programs/General Counsel, June 2001–03; Minority Deputy Staff Director, Benefits Programs/General Counsel, 2003–04; confirmed by the U.S. Senate to the United States Court of Appeals for Veterans Claims on November 20, 2004; sworn in December 20, 2004.

OFFICERS OF THE U.S. COURT OF VETERANS APPEALS

Clerk of the Court.—Norman Y. Herring, 501–5980.
Operations Manager.—Anne P. Stygles.
Counsel and Court Reporter of Decisions.—Jack F. Lane.
Senior Staff Attorney (Central Legal Staff).—Jeffery N. Luthi.
Deputy Executive Officer.—Marlene Davis.
Librarian.—Bernard J. Sussman.

JUDICIAL PANEL ON MULTIDISTRICT LITIGATION

Thurgood Marshall Federal Judiciary Building, Room G–255, North Lobby,

One Columbus Circle NE 20002, phone (202) 502–2800, fax 502–2888

(National jurisdiction to centralize related cases pending in multiple circuits and districts under 28 U.S.C. §§ 1407 & 2112)

Chairman.—Wm. Terrell Hodges, U.S. District Judge, Middle District of Florida.
Judges:
    John F. Keenan, U.S. District Judge, Southern District of New York.
    D. Lowell Jensen, U.S. District Judge, Northern District of California.
    J. Frederick Motz, U.S. District Judge, Chief Judge, District of Maryland.
    Robert L. Miller, Jr., U.S. District Judge, Northern District of Indiana.
    Kathryn H. Vratil, U.S. District Judge, District of Kansas.
    David R. Hansen, U.S. Court of Appeals Judge, Eighth Circuit.
Executive Attorney.—Robert A. Cahn.
Clerk.—Michael J. Beck.

ADMINISTRATIVE OFFICE OF THE U.S. COURTS

Thurgood Marshall Federal Judiciary Building

One Columbus Circle, NE 20544, phone (202) 502–2600

Director.—Leonidas Ralph Mecham, 273–3000.
   Associate Director, Management and Operations.—Clarence A. Lee, Jr., 273–3015.
   Deputy Associate Director.—Cathy A. McCarthy, 502–1300.
   Chief, Office of Audit.—Jeff Larioni, 502–1000.
   Management, Planning and Assessment Officer.—Cathy A. McCarthy, 502–1300.
   Chief, Long-Range Planning Office.—William M. Lucianovic, 502–1300.
   Associate Director and General Counsel.—William R. Burchill, Jr., 502–1100.
   Deputy General Counsel.—Robert K. Loesche, 502–1100.
   Assistant Director, Judicial Conference Executive Secretariat.—Laura C. Minor, 502–2400.
   Deputy Assistant Directors, Judicial Conference Executive Secretariat: Jeffrey A. Hennemuth, 502–2400; Wendy Jennis, 502–2400.
   Assistant Director, Legislative Affairs.—Michael W. Blommer, 502–1700.
   Deputy Assistant Director for Legislative Affairs.—Daniel A. Cunningham, 502–1700.
   Chief, Judicial Impact Office.—Richard A. Jaffe, 502–1700.
   Assistant Director, Public Affairs.—David A. Sellers, 502–2600.
   Assistant Director, Office of Court Administration.—Noel J. Augustyn, 502–1500.
   Deputy Assistant Director for Court Administration.—Glen K. Palman, 502–1500.
   Chief of—
      Appellate Court and Circuit Administration Division.—Gary Bowden, 502–1520.
      Bankruptcy Court Administration Division.—Glen K. Palman, 502–1540.
      Court Administration Policy Staff.—Abel J. Mattos, 502–1560.
      District Court Administration Division.—Robert Lowney, 502–1570.
      Electronic Public Access Program Office.—Mary Stickney, 502–1500.
      Technology Division.—Gary L. Bockweg, 502–2500.
   Assistant Director, Office of Defender Services.—Ted Lidz, 502–3030.
   Assistant Director for Facilities and Security.—Ross Eisenman, 502–1200.
   Deputy Assistant Director for Facilities and Security.—William J. Lehman, 502–1200.
   Chief of—
      Court Security Office.—Edward M. Templeman, 502–1280.
      Security and Facilities Policy Staff.—Melanie F. Gilbert, 502–1200.
      Space and Facilities Division.—William J. Lehman (acting), 502–1200.
   Assistant Director for Finance and Budget.—George H. Schafer, 502–2000.
   Chief of—
      Accounting and Financial Systems Division.—Philip L. McKinney, 502–2000.
      Budget Division.—James R. Baugher, 502–2100.
      Financial Liaison and Analysis Office.—Penny Jacobs Fleming, 502–2028.
   Assistant Director, Office of Human Resources.—Charlotte G. Peddicord, 502–1170.
   Chief of—
      Benefits Division.—Cynthia Roth (acting), 502–1160.
      Court Personnel Management Division.—E. Maxine Wright, 502–3100.
      Fair Employment Practices Office.—Trudi M. Morrison, 502–1380.
      HRMIS Program Office.—Cecilee A. Goldberg, 502–3210.
      Judges Compensation and Retirement Services Office.—Carol S. Sefren, 502–1380.
      Policy and Strategic Initiatives Office.—H. Allen Brown, 502–3185.
   Assistant Director for Information Technology.—Melvin J. Bryson, 502–2300.
   Deputy Assistant Director for Information Technology.—Barbara C. Macken, 502–2300.
   Chief, Technology Officer.—Richard D. Fennell, 502–2300.
   Chief of—
      IT Applications Development Office.—Wendy R. Lageman, 502–2730.
      IT Infrastructure Management Division.—Craig W. Jenkins, 502–2640.
      IT Policy Staff.—Terry A. Cain, 502–3300.
      IT Project Coordination Office.—Robert D. Morse, 502–2377.

IT Security Office.—Robert N. Sinsheimer, 502–2350.
IT Systems Deployment and Support Division.—Howard J. Grandier, 502–2700.
Assistant Director for Internal Services.—Doreen Bydume (acting), 502–4200.
Chief of—
    AO Administrative Services Division: Iris Guerra (acting), 502–1220; Evan D. Tausch (acting), 502–1220.
    AO Information Management Services Division.—John C. Chang, 502–2830.
    AO Personnel Division, Human Resources Officer.—Cheri Thompson Reid, 502–3800.
    AO Procurement Management Division.—William Roeder, 502–1330.
Assistant Director for Judges Programs.—Peter G. McCabe, 502–1800.
Deputy Assistant Director for Judges Programs.—R. Townsend Robinson, 502–1800.
Chief of—
    Article III Judges Division.—Margaret A. Irving, 502–1860.
    Bankruptcy Judges Division.—Francis F. Szczebak, 502–1900.
    Magistrate Judges Division.—Thomas C. Hnatowski, 502–1830.
    Rules Committee Support Office.—John K. Rabiej, 502–1820.
    Statistics Division.—Steven R. Schlesinger, 502–1440.
Assistant Director, Office of Probation and Pretrial Services.—John M. Hughes, 502–1610.
    Deputy Assistant Director, Office of Probation and Pretrial Services.—Matthew G. Roland, 502–1600.
Chief of—
    Policy and Operations Division.—Nancy Beatty Gregoire, 502–1600.
    Special Projects Office.—Nancy Lee Bradshaw, 502–1600.
    Technology Division.—Nicholas B. DiSabatino, 502–1600.

FEDERAL JUDICIAL CENTER

One Columbus Circle NE 20002–8003, phone (202) 502–4000

Director.—Judge Barbara J. Rothstein, 502–4160, fax 502–4099.
Deputy Director.—Russell R. Wheeler, 502–4164, fax 502–4099.
Director of—
    Communications Policy and Design Office.—Sylvan A. Sobel, 502–4250, fax 502–4077.
    Education Division.—John S. Cooke, 502–4060, fax 502–4299.
    Federal Judicial History Office.—Bruce A. Ragsdale, 502–4181, fax 502–4077.
    International Judicial Relations Office.—Mira Gur-Arie, 502–4191; fax 502–4099.
    Research Division.—James B. Eaglin, 502–4070, fax 502–4199.
    Systems Innovations and Development Office.—Ted Coleman, 502–4223, fax 502–4288.

DISTRICT OF COLUMBIA COURTS

phone 879–1010

Executive Officer.—Anne B. Wicks, 879–1700.
Deputy Executive Officer.—Cheryl R. Bailey, 879–1700; fax 879–4829.
Director, Legislative, Intergovernmental and Public Affairs.—Leah Gurowitz, 879–1700.

DISTRICT OF COLUMBIA COURT OF APPEALS

500 Indiana Avenue 20001, phone 879-1010

Chief Judge.—Annice M. Wagner, 879–2770.
    Associate Judges:

Michael W. Farrell, 879–2790.	John A. Terry, 879–2780.
Stephen H. Glickman, 879–2740.	Frank E. Schwelb, 879–2730.
Inez Smith Reid, 879–2726.	John M. Steadman, 879–2785.
Vanessa Ruiz, 879–2761.	Eric T. Washington, 879–2750.

Senior Judges: John W. Kern III, 879–2754; William C. Pryor, 879–2745; Theodore R. Newman, Jr., 879–2739; James A. Belson, 879–2760; Warren King, 626–8871; John M. Ferren, 879–2772; Frank Q. Nebeker, 879–2778.
Clerk.—Garland Pinkston, Jr., 879–2725.
  Chief Deputy Clerk.—Joy A. Chapper, 879–2722.
  Administration Director.—John Dyson, 879–2738.
  Admissions Director.—Jacqueline Smith, 879–2714.
  Public Office Operations Director.—Jeanette E. Togans, 879–2702.
  Senior Staff Attorney.—Rosanna M. Mason, 879–2718.

SUPERIOR COURT OF THE DISTRICT OF COLUMBIA

phone 879–1010

Chief Judge.—Rufus G. King III, 879–1600.

Associate Judges:

Geoffrey M. Alprin, 879–1577.
Judith Bartnoff, 879–1988.
John H. Bayly, Jr., 879–7874.
Ronna L. Beck, 879–1162.
James E. Boasberg, 879–4886.
Ana Blackburne-Rigsby, 879–0055.
Patricia A. Broderick, 879–8345.
A. Franklin Burgess, Jr., 879–1164.
Zoe Bush, 879–0023.
Jerry S. Byrd, 879–4797.
John M. Campbell, 879–1430.
Russell F. Canan, 879–1952.
Erik Christian, 879–1760.
Kaye K. Christian, 879–1668.
Jeanette Clark, 879–0417.
Natalia Combs Greene, 879–8350.
Harold L. Cushenberry, Jr., 879–4866.
Linda Kay Davis, 879–0050.
Rafael Diaz, 879–1125.
Herbert B. Dixon, Jr., 879–4808.
Stephanie Duncan-Peters, 879–1882.
Gerald I. Fisher, 879–8388.
Wendell P. Gardner, Jr., 879–1810.
Brook Hedge, 879–1886.
Brian Holeman, 879–7815.
Craig Iscoe, 879–7835.
Gregory Jackson, 879–1815.
William M. Jackson, 879–1909.
J. Ramsey Johnson, 879–8306.

Anita Josey-Herring, 879–1574.
Ann O'Regan Keary, 879–1863.
Noël A. Kramer, 879–1446.
Neal E. Kravitz, 879–8353.
Cheryl M. Long, 879–1200.
José M. López, 879–7877.
Lynn Lebowitz, 879–0441
Zinora Mitchell-Rankin, 879–7846.
Robert E. Morin, 879–1550.
Thomas J. Motley, 879–8377.
John M. Mott, 879–8393.
Hiram E. Puig-Lugo, 879–8370.
Michael L. Rankin, 879–1220.
Judith E. Retchin, 879–1866.
Robert I. Richter, 879–1422.
Robert Rigsby, 879–4344.
Maurice Ross, 879–1765.
Michael Ryan, 879–8322.
Fern Flanagan Saddler, 879–4854.
Lee F. Satterfield, 879–1918.
Mary A. Gooden Terrell, 879–1639.
Linda D. Turner, 879–1819.
Odessa F. Vincent, 879–0447.
Frederick H. Weisberg, 879–1066.
Susan R. Winfield, 879–1272.
Rhonda Reid Winston, 879–4750.
Melvin R. Wright, 879–8336.
Joan Zeldon, 879–1590.

Senior Judges:

Mary Ellen Abrecht, 879–7834.
Bruce D. Beaudin, 879–1575.
Leonard Braman, 879–1440.
Arthur L. Burnett, Sr., 879–4882.
Frederick D. Dorsey, 879–7837.
Stephen F. Eilperin, 879–1566.
George H. Goodrich, 879–1055.
Steffen W. Graae, 879–1244.
Henry F. Greene, 879–1455.
Eugene N. Hamilton, 879–1727.
John R. Hess, 879–1420.
Bruce S. Mencher, 879–1358.

Stephen G. Milliken, 879–1823.
Gregory E. Mize, 879–1395.
Truman A. Morrison III, 879–1060.
Tim Murphy, 879–1099.
Nan R. Shuker, 879–1207.
Robert S. Tignor, 879–1252.
Fred B. Ugast, 879–1890.
Paul R. Webber III, 879–1426.
Ronald P. Wertheim, 879–1170.
Peter H. Wolf, 879–1088.
Patricia A. Wynn, 879–4630.

Clerk of the Court.—Duane B. Delaney, 879–1400.

GOVERNMENT OF THE DISTRICT OF COLUMBIA

COUNCIL OF THE DISTRICT OF COLUMBIA

John A. Wilson Building, 1350 Pennsylvania Avenue, NW, 20004, phone 724–8000

Council Chairwoman (at Large).—Linda W. Cropp, Suite 504, 724–8032.
Chairman Pro Tempore.—Jack Evans.

Council Members:
  Jim Graham, Ward 1, Suite 105, 724–8181.
  Jack Evans, Ward 2, Suite 106, 724–8058.
  Kathleen Patterson, Ward 3, Suite 107, 724–8062.
  Adrian Fenty, Ward 4, Suite 408, 724–8052.
  Vincent B. Orange, Sr., Ward 5, Suite 108, 724–8028.
  Sharon Ambrose, Ward 6, Suite 102, 724–8072.
  Vincent C. Gray, Ward 7, Suite 506, 724–8068.
  Marion Barry, Ward 8, Suite 400, 724–8045.

Council Members (at Large):
  Kwame R. Brown, Suite 406, 724–8174.
  Phil Mendelson, Suite 402, 724–8064.
  Carol Schwartz, Suite 404, 724–8105.
  David A. Catania, Suite 110, 724–7772.
Secretary to the Council.—Phyllis Jones, Suite 5, 724–8080.
General Counsel.—Charlotte Brookins-Hudson, Suite 4, 724–8026.
Budget Director.—Arte Blitzstein, Suite 508, 724–8139.

EXECUTIVE OFFICE OF THE MAYOR

Mayor of the District of Columbia.—Anthony A. Williams.
  Chief of Staff.—Alfreda V. Davis, Suite 521, 727–2643, fax 727–2975.
  Executive Assistant to the Chief of Staff.—Karen Hubbard.
  Deputy Mayor for:
    Children, Youth, Families and Elders.—Neil Albert, Suite 307, 727–8001, fax 727–0246.
    Planning and Economic Development.—Stanley Jackson, Suite 317, 727–6365, fax 727–6703.
    Public Safety and Justice.—Edward Reiskin, Suite 327, 727–4036, fax 727–8527.
    Operations.—Herb Tillery, Suite 310, 727–3636, fax 727–9878.
  Deputy Chief of Staff for:
    Community Affairs.—Henry Stewart (acting), Suite 211, 442–8150, fax 727–5931.
    Policy and Legislative Affairs.—Gregory McCarthy, Suite 509, 727–6979, fax 727–3765.
  Special Assistant to the Mayor.—Dante Scott, 6th Floor, 727–6263, fax 727–6561.
  Confidential Assistant to the Mayor.—Leslie Pinkston, 6th Floor, 727–6263, fax 727–6561.
  Executive Assistant to the Mayor.—Tracee Brown, 6th Floor, 727–6263, fax 727–6561.
  Director, Scheduling and Advance.—Henry Stewart, 5th Floor, 727–1681, fax 727–2357.
  Director, Office of Communications.—Vincent Morris, Suite 533, 727–5011, fax 727–9561.
  Deputy Chief of Staff for Operations.—Nathan Francis, Suite 310, 727–3636, fax 727–9878.
  Secretary of the District of Columbia.—Sherryl Hobbs-Newman, Suite 419, 727–6306, fax 727–3582.
  General Counsel to the Mayor.—Leonard Becker, Suite 327, 727–0872, fax 727–7743.
  Inspector General.—Austin A. Anderson, Esq. (acting), 717 14th Street, NW., 5th Floor, 20005, 727–2540, fax 727–9846.
  Senior Advisor:
    Congressional Affairs.—Kevin Clinton, Suite 509, 727–7969, fax 727–3765.
    Education.—Michelle J. Walker, Suite 527, 727–7672, fax 727–8977.

Environmental Affairs.—Elizabeth Berry, Suite 512, 727–6979, fax 727–3765.
External and Regional Affairs.—Fonda Richardson, Suite 512, 727–2643, fax 727–7418.
Religious Affairs.—Dr. Susan Newman, Suite 211A, 727–1751, fax 727–5931.

OFFICE OF THE CITY ADMINISTRATOR

City Administrator.—Robert Bobb, 727–6053, fax 727–9878..
  Executive Assistant to City Administrator.—Ayanna Lee.
  Chief of Staff.—Alfreda Davis.
  Director, Neighborhood Services.—Tara Jones.

COMMISSIONS

Arts and Humanities, 410 8th Street, NW., 5th Floor, 20004, 724–5613, fax 727–4135.
  Executive Director.—Anthony Gittens.

National and Community Service (Serve DC), 441 4th Street, NW., Suite 1040S, 20001, 727–7925, fax 727–9198.
  Executive Director.—MaryAnn Miller (acting).

Taxicab Commission, 2041 Martin Luther King Jr. Avenue, SE., Suite 204, 20020, 645–6018, fax 889–3604.
  Chairperson.—Lee Williams.

US Parole Commission, 5550 Friendship Boulevard, Suite 420, Chevy Chase, MD 20815, (301) 492–5990.
  Chairperson.—Edward F. Reilly, Jr.

DEPARTMENTS

Asian and Pacific Islander Affairs, 441 4th Street, NW., Suite 805S, 20001, 727–3120, fax 727–9655.
  Executive Director.—G. Greg Chen.

Child and Family Services Agency, 400 6th Street, SW., 5th Floor, 20024, 442–6000, fax 442–6498.
  Director.—Brenda-Donna Walker.

Consumer and Regulatory Affairs, 941 North Capitol Street, NE., 9th Floor, 20002, 442–4400, fax 442–9445.
  Director.—David Clark.

Contracting and Procurement, 441 4th Street, Suite 700 South, 20001, 724–0252, fax 727–9385.
  Director.—Herbert Tillery (acting).

Corrections Department, 1923 Vermont Avenue, NW., Room 207N, 20001, 673–7316, fax 332–1470.
  Director.—S. Elwood York, Jr.

Employment Services, 609 H Street, NE., 20002, 724–7000, fax 724–5683.
  Director.—Gregory P. Irish.

Fire and Emergency Medical Services, 1923 Vermont Avenue, NW., Suite 201, 20001, 673–3331, fax 673–3188.
  Fire Chief.—Adrian Thompson.

Health Department, 825 North Capitol Street, NE., 20002, 671–5000, fax 442–4788.
  Director.—Greg Payne, M.D.

Housing and Community Development, 801 North Capitol Street, NE., 8th floor, 20002, 442–7200, fax 442–8391.
  Director.—Jalal Greene (acting).

Human Rights, 441 4th Street, NW., Suite 570N, 20001, 727–4559, fax 727–9589.
  Director.—Kenneth Saunders.

District of Columbia

Human Services, 64 New York Avenue, NE, 6th floor, 20002, 671–4200, fax 671–4325.
Director.—Yvonne Gilchrist.

Insurance Securities, and Banking, 810 1st Street, NE., Suite 701, 20002, 727–8000, fax 535–1196.
Commissioner.—Lawrence H. Mirel.

Local Business Development, 441 4th Street, NW., Suite 970N, 20001, 727–3900, fax 727–3786.
Director.—Jacquelyn Flowers.

Mental Health, 77 P Street, NE.; 4th Floor, 20002, phone 673–7440, fax 673–3433.
Director.—Martha Knisley (acting).

Metropolitan Police, 300 Indiana Avenue, NW., Room 5080, 20001, 737–4404, fax 727–9524.
Police Chief.—Charles H. Ramsey.

Motor Vehicles, 301 C Street, NW., Suite 1018, 20001, 727–5000, fax 727–5017.
Director.—Ann Witt.

Parks and Recreation, 3149 16th Street, NW., 20010, 673–7647, fax 673–6694.
Director.—Neil Stanley (acting).

Property Management, 441 4th Street, NW.; Suite 1100S, 20001, 724–4400, fax 727–9877.
Director.—Carol Mitten.

Public Works, 2000 14th Street, NW., 6th Floor, 20009, 673–6833, fax 671–0642.
Director.—William O. Howland, Jr.

Transportation Department, 2000 14th Street, NW., 6th Floor, 20009, 673–6813, fax 671–0642.
Director.—Dan Tangherlini.

OFFICES

Aging, 441 Fourth Street, NW., Suite 900S, 20001, 724–5622, fax 724–4979.
Executive Director.—E. Veronica Pace.

Attorney General, 1350 Pennsylvania Avenue, NW., Suite 407 and 409, 20004, 727–3400, fax 724–6590.
Attorney General.—Robert J. Spagnoletti.

Boards and Commissions, 441 4th Street, NW., Suite 530S, 20001, 727–1372, fax 727–2359.
Director.—Ron Collins.

Cable Television and Telecommunications, 3007 Tilden Street, POD P, 20008, 671–0066, fax 332–7020.
Executive Director.—James Brown.

Chief Financial Officer, 1350 Pennsylvania Avenue, NW., Suite 203, 20004, 727–2476, fax 727–1643.
Chief Financial Officer.—Natwar M. Gandhi.

Chief Medical Examiner, 1910 Massachusetts Avenue, SE., Building 27, 20003, 698–9000, fax 698–9100.
Chief Medical Examiner.—Dr. Marie-Lydie Pierre-Louis.

Chief Technology Officer, 441 4th Street, NW., Suite 930S, 20001, 727–2277, fax 727–6857.
Chief Technology Officer.—Suzanne J. Peck.

Communications Office, John A. Wilson Building, 1350 Pennsylvania Avenue, NW., Suite 533, 20004, 727–5011, fax 727–9561.
Director.—Vincent Morris.

Community Outreach, John A. Wilson Building, 1350 Pennsylvania Avenue, NW., Suite 211A, 20004, 442–8150, fax 727–5931.
Director.—Henry Stewart.

Emergency Management Agency, 2000 14th Street, 8th Floor, 20009, 727–6161, fax 673–2290.
Director.—Barbara Childs-Pair.

Labor Relations and Collective Bargaining, 441 4th Street, NW., Suite 820 North, 20001, 724–4953, fax 727–6887.
Director.—Mary E. Leary.

Latino Affairs, 2000 14th Street, NW., 2nd Floor, 20009, 671–2825, fax 673–4557.
Director.—Gustavo Velasquez.

Partnerships and Grants Development, 441 4th Street, NW., Suite 200S, 20001, 727–8900, fax 727–1652.
Director.—Lafayette Barnes.

Personnel Office, 441 4th Street, NW., Suite 300S, 20001, 442–9700, fax 727–6827.
Director.—Lisa Marin.

Planning Office, 801 North Capitol Street, NE., Suite 4000, 20002, 442–7600, fax 442–7638.
Director.—Ellen McCarthy (acting).

Office of Policy and Legislative Affairs, 1350 Pennsylvania Avenue, NW., Suite 511, 20004, 727–6979, fax 727–3765.
Director.—Elizabeth Lloyd.

State Education, 441 4th Street, NW., Suite 350N, 20001, 727–6436, fax 727–2019.
State Education Officer.—Deborah Gist (acting).

Veterans Affairs, 441 4th Street, NW., Suite 570S, 20001, 724–5454, fax 727–7117.
Director.—Kerwin E. Miller.

OTHER

District of Columbia Housing Authority, 1133 North Capitol Street, NE., 20001, 535–1500, fax 535–1740.
Executive Director.—Michael P. Kelly.

District of Columbia Public Libraries, Martin Luther King Memorial Library (Main Library), 901 G Street, NW., Suite 400, 20001, 727–1101, fax 727–1129.
Director and State Librarian.—Francis J. Buckley (acting).

District of Columbia Public Schools, 825 North Capitol Street, NW., Suite 9026, 20002, 724–4222, fax 442–5026.
Superintendent.—Clifford Janey.

District of Columbia Sports and Entertainment Commission, 2400 East Capitol Street, SE., 20003, 547–9077, fax 547–7460.
Executive Director.—Allen Lew.

District Lottery and Charitable Games, 2101 Martin Luther King Jr. Avenue, SE., 20020, 645–8000, fax 645–7914.
Executive Director.—Jeanette Michael.

Superior Court of the District of Columbia, H. Carl Moultrie I Courthouse, 500 Indiana Avenue, NW., 20001, 879–1010.
Chief Judge.—Rufus G. King, III.

University of the District of Columbia, 4200 Connecticut Avenue, NW., 20008, 274–5000, fax 274–5212.
President.—William L. Pollard, Ph.D.

Washington Convention Center, 801 Mount Vernon Place NW., 20001, 249–3012, fax 249–3133.
General Manager.—Tom Mobley.

DISTRICT OF COLUMBIA POST OFFICE LOCATIONS

900 Brentwood Road NE 20066–9998, General Information (202) 636–1200

Postmaster.—Delores D. Killett.

CLASSIFIED STATIONS

Station	Phone	Location / Zip Code
Anacostia	523–2119	2650 Naylor Rd. SE., 20020
Ben Franklin	523–2386	1200 Pennsylvania Ave. NW., 20044
B.F. Carriers	636–2289	900 Brentwood Rd. NE., 20004
Benning	523–2391	3937–½ Minnesota Ave. NE., 20019
Bolling AFB	767–4419	Bldg. 10, Brookley Avenue, 20332
Brightwood	726–8119	6323 Georgia Ave. NW., 20
Brookland	523–2126	3401 12th St. NE., 20017
Calvert	523–2908	2336 Wisconsin Ave. NW., 20007
Cleveland Park	523–2396	3430 Connecticut Ave. NW., 20008
Columbia Heights	523–2192	6510 Chillum Pl. NW., 20010
Congress Heights	523–2122	400 Southern Ave. SE., 20032
Customs House	523–2195	3178 Bladensburg Rd. NE., 20018
Dulles	(703) 471–9497	Dulles International Airport, 20041
Farragut	523–2507	1145 19th St. NW., 20033
Fort Davis	842–4964	3843 Pennsylvania Ave. SE., 20020
Fort McNair	523–2144	300 A. St. SW., 20319
Frederick Douglass	842–4959	Alabama Ave. SE., 20020
Friendship	523–2151	4005 Wisconsin Ave. NW., 20016
Georgetown	523–2406	1215 31st St. NW., 20007
Headsville	357–3029	Smithsonian Institute, 20560
Kalorama	523–2906	2300 18th St. NW., 20009
Lamond Riggs	523–2041	6200 North Capitol St. NW., 20
LeDroit Park	483–0973	416 Florida Ave. NW., 20001
L'Enfant Plaza	523–2014	458 L'Enfant Plaza SW., 20026
Martin L. King, Jr	523–2001	1400 L St. NW., 20043
McPherson	523–2394	1750 Pennsylvania Ave. NW, 20038
Mid City	....	Temporarily Closed
National Capitol	523–2368	2 Massachusetts Ave. NE., 20002
Naval Research Lab	767–3426	4565 Overlook Ave., 20390
Navy Annex	(703) 920–0815	1668 D Street, 20335
Northeast	388–5216	1563 Maryland Ave. NE., 20002
Northwest	523–2570	5632 Connecticut Ave. NW., 20015
Palisades	842–2291	5136 MacArthur Blvd. NW., 20016
Pavilion Postique	523–2571	1100 Pennsylvania Ave. NW., 20004
Pentagon	(703) 695–6835	900 Brentwood Rd. NE., 20066
Petworth	523–2681	4211 9th St. NW., 20
Postal Square	523–2022	2 Massachusetts Ave. NW., 20002
Randle	584–6807	2341 Pennsylvania Ave. SE., 20023
River Terrace	523–2884	3621 Benning Rd. NE., 20019
Southeast	523–2174	327 7th St. SE., 20003
Southwest	523–2597	45 L St. SW., 20024
State Department	523–2574	2201 C St. NW., 20520
T Street	232–6301	1915 14th St. NW., 20009
Tech World	523–2019	800 K St. NW., 20001
Temple Heights	523–2563	1921 Florida Ave. NW., 20009
Twentieth Street	523–2411	2001 M St. NW., 20036
U.S. Naval	433–2216	940 M St. SE., 20374
V Street	636–2273	900 Brentwood Rd. NE, 20018
Walter Reed	782–3768	6800 Georgia Ave. NW., 20012
Ward Place	523–5109	2121 Ward Pl. NW., 20037
Washington Main	636–2130	900 Brentwood Rd. NE., 20066
Washington Square	523–2632	1050 Connecticut Ave. NW., 20035
Watergate	965–4598	2512 Virginia Ave. NW., 20037
Woodridge	523–2195	2211 Rhode Island Ave. NE., 20018

INTERNATIONAL ORGANIZATIONS

EUROPEAN SPACE AGENCY (E.S.A.)

Headquarters: 8–10 Rue Mario Nikis, 75738 Paris Cedex 15, France
phone 011–33–1–5369–7654, fax 011–33–1–5369–7560

Chairman of the Council.—Per Tegnér.
Director General.—Jean-Jacques Dordain.
  Member Countries:

Austria	Greece	Spain
Belgium	Ireland	Sweden
Denmark	Italy	Switzerland
Finland	Netherlands	United Kingdom
France	Norway	
Germany	Portugal	

Cooperative Agreement.—Canada.

European Space Operations Center (E.S.O.C.), Robert-Bosch-Str. 5, D–64293 Darmstadt, Germany, phone 011–49–6151–900, fax 011–49–6151–90495.

European Space Research and Technology Center (E.S.T.E.C.), Keplerlaan 1, NL–2201, AZ Noordwijk, ZH, The Netherlands, phone 011–31–71–565–6565; Telex: 844–39098, fax 011–31–71–565–6040.

European Space Research Institute (E.S.R.I.N.), Via Galileo Galilei, Casella Postale 64, 00044 Frascati, Italy. Phone, 011–39–6–94–18–01; fax 011–39–6–9418–0280.

Washington Office (E.S.A.), Suite 7800, 955 L'Enfant Plaza SW. 20024.
  Head of Office.—Frederic Nordlund (202) 488–4158, fax 488–4930,
    Frederic.Nordlund@esa.int.

INTER-AMERICAN DEFENSE BOARD

2600 16th Street 20441, phone 939–6041, fax 387–2880

Chairman.—MG Keith M. Huber, U.S. Army.
  Vice Chairman.—MG Dardo Juan Antonio Parodi, Army, Argentina.
  Secretary.—CAPT Jaime Navarro, U.S. Navy.
    Deputy Secretary for—
      Administration.—MAJ Richard D. Phillips, U.S. Army.
      Conference.—C/F Jose Da Costa Monteiro, Brazil, Navy.
      Finance.—MAJ Dan McGreal, U.S. Army.
      Information Management.—LTC Thomas Riddle, U.S. Army.
      Protocol.—MAJ Ivonne Martens, U.S. Air Force.
      Staff Vice Director.—COL Zuniga, Army, Honduras.

CHIEFS OF DELEGATION

Antigua and Barbuda.—Col. Trevor Thomas, Army.
Argentina.—Contralmirante Guillermo Oscar Iglesias, Navy.
Barbados.—LtCol. Atheline Branch, Defense Force.
Bolivia.—Division General Felix Torrico Negrete, Army.
Brazil.—General de Brigada Jorge Armando de Almeida Ribeiro, Army.
Canada.—RADM Ian Mack, Navy.
Chile.—Contraalmirante Roberto Carvajal Gacitua, Navy.

882 Congressional Directory

Costa Rica.—Amb. Javier Sancho Bonilla.
Dominican Republic.—MG Hugo Rafael Gonzalez Borell, Army.
Ecuador.—Coronel Diego Alban Noboa, Army.
El Salvador.—General de Brigada Juan Manuel Grijalva Torres, Air Force.
Guyana.—Colonel Chabilall Ramsarup, Defense Force.
Honduras.—Coronel Carlos Humberto Ramos Nunez, Army.
Mexico.—BG Manuel Castro Gomez, Army.
Nicaragua.—BG Pedro Martinez Mejia, Air Force.
Paraguay.—General de Brigada Carlos Arnaldo Torales, Army.
Peru.—LTG Cesar D. Gallo Lale, Army.
Trinidad.—LTC Anthony Phillips-Spencer, Army.
United States.—RADM William D. Sullivan, Navy.
Uruguay.—Admiral Carlos Rafael Magliocca, Navy.
Venezuela.—MG Angel Valecillos, Army.

INTER-AMERICAN DEFENSE COLLEGE

Director.—MG Keith M. Huber, U.S. Army.
  Vice Director.—GB Aldofo Domínguez Martinez, Army, Mexico.
  Chief of Studies.—BG German Galvis, Army, Colombia.

INTER-AMERICAN DEVELOPMENT BANK

1300 New York Avenue 20577, phone 623–1000

http://www.iadb.org

OFFICERS

President.—Enrique V. Iglesias (Uruguay).
  Chief, Office of the President.—Euric A. Bobb.
Executive Vice President.—Dennis E. Flannery (United States).
  Chief Advisor.—Joseph Engelhard.
Vice President for Finance and Administration.—João Sayad.
Private Sector Coordinator.—Carlos Guimarães.
Director, Office of Evaluation and Oversight.—Stephen A. Quick.
Chief Economist.—Guillermo Calvo.
Auditor General.—Elizabeth Joy Folsom.
External Relations Advisor.—Mirna Liévano de Marques.
  Deputy Advisor.—Chris Sale.
Ombudsperson.—José Ignacio Estevez.
Manager, Office of:
  Multilateral Investment Fund.—Donald F. Terry.
  Regional Operations Department 1.—Ricardo L. Santiago.
    Deputy Manager.—Luisa C. Rains.
  Regional Operations Support Office.—Rosa Olivia Villa Lawson.
  Regional Operations Department 2.—Miguel E. Martínez.
    Deputy Manager.—Lionel Nicol.
  Regional Operations Department 3.—Ciro De Falco.
    Deputy Manager.—Camille E. Gaskin-Reyes.
  Finance Department.—John R. Hauge.
    Senior Deputy Manager-Treasurer.—Eloy B. Garcia.
  Integration and Regional Programs Department.—Nohra Rey de Marulanda.
    Deputy Manager.—Robert Devlin.
  Private Sector Department.—Hiroshi Toyoda.
    Deputy Manager.—Bernardo Frydman.
  Sustainable Development Department.—Carlos M. Jarque.
  Development Effectiveness and Strategic Planning Department.—Manuel Rapoport.
    Deputy Managers: Christian Gómez-Fabling, Martin Stabile.
  Human Resources.—Manuel Labrado.
  Budget and Corporate Procurement.—William E. Schuerch.
  General Counsel, Legal Department.—James Spinner.
    Deputy General Counsel: Ana-Mita Betancourt, J. Roberto Nolasco.
  Secretary.—Carlos Ferdinand.
    Deputy Secretary.—Máximo Jeria-Figueroa.

BOARD OF EXECUTIVE DIRECTORS

Colombia and Peru.—Luis Guillermo Echeverri.
   Alternate.—Jaime Pinto Tabini.
Bahamas, Barbados, Guyana, Jamaica, Trinidad and Tobago.—Havelock Brewster.
   Alternate.—Jerry Christopher Butler.
Dominican Republic and Mexico.—Agustín García-López.
   Alternate.—Roberto B. Saladín.
Belize, Costa Rica, El Salvador, Guatemala, Haiti, Honduras, and Nicaragua.—
   José Carlos Castañeda.
   Alternate.—Sandra Regina Midence.
Panama and Venezuela.—Adina Bastidas.
   Alternate.—Fernando Eleta Casanovas.
Canada.—Charles Bassett.
   Alternate.—Jill Johnson.
Belgium, Germany, Israel, Italy, The Netherlands, and Switzerland.—Giorgio Leccesi.
   Alternate.—Ina-Marlene Ruthenberg.
Argentina and Haiti.—Eugenio Díaz-Bonilla.
   Alternate.—Martín Bès.
United States.—Héctor E. Morales.
Brazil, and Suriname.—Rogério Studart.
   Alternate.—Arlindo Villaschi.
Austria, Denmark, Finland, France, Norway, Spain, and Sweden.—Michel Planque.
   Alternate.—Marta Blanco.
Bolivia, Paraguay, and Uruguay.—Jorge Crespo-Velasco.
   Alternate.—Juan E. Notaro.
Chile and Ecuador.—Germán Quintana.
   Alternate.—Byron Solís.
Croatia, Japan, Portugal, Slovenia, and United Kingdom.—Yoshihisa Ueda.
   Alternate.—Stewart Mills.

INTER-AMERICAN TROPICAL TUNA COMMISSION

8604 La Jolla Shores Drive, La Jolla, CA 92037–1508, phone (858) 546–7100
fax (858) 546–7133, www.iattc.org

Director.—Robin L. Allen.
   Costa Rican Commissioners:
   George E. Heigold, INCOPESCA/Instituto Costarricense de Pesca, P.O. Box 82,
     Puntarenas, Costa Rica (506) 661–3880, fax 661–1309.
   Ligia Castro Ulate, INCOPESCA/Instituto Costarricense de Pesca, Apdo. 333–5400,
     Puntarenas, Costa Rica (506) 661–0846, 248–2387, 661–3020, fax 661–2855; email:
     lcastro@gobnet.co.cr, lmcastrou@yahoo.com.
   Asdrubal Vásquez, INCOPESCA, Apartado 549–7050, San José, Costa Rica (506) 253–
     4321, 552–1317, 382–3109, fax 253–4321; email: vasqueza@racsa.co.cr.
   Ecuador Commissioners:
   Juan F. Ballén, COMEXI, Av. Eloy Alfaro y Amazonas Edif.MAG-MICIP 1er Piso,
     Quito, Ecuador (593–2) 254–3897, 223–9258, email: jfballen@micip.gov.ec.
   Iván Prieto, Ministerio de Comercio Exterior, Industrialización, Pesca y Competitividad,
     Av. 9 de Octubre 200 y Pichincha, Edificio Banco Central, 7o Piso, Guayaquil, Ecuador
     (593–4) 256–4300, fax 256–1489; email: subse01@subpesca.gov.ec.
   Luis N. Torres, Ministerio de Comercio Exterior, Industrialización, Pesca y Competitividad,
     Av. 9 de Octubre 200 y Pichincha, Edif. Banco Central, piso 7, Guayaquil,
     Ecuador (593–4) 256–0993, 256–4300, ext. 103, fax 256–1489; email:
     Asesor01@subpesca.gov.ec.
   Xavier Abad Vicuña, Ecuador.

   El Salvador Commissioners:
   Manuel Calvo, Luis Calvo Sanz, El Salvador, C/Boulevard del Hipódromo 111, Edif.
     Gran Plaza, Local 103, San Salvador, El Salvador (503) 244–4800, fax 224–4850,
     email: mane.calvo@grupocalvo.com.sv, mane.calvo@calvo.es.
   Manuel F. Oliva, CENDEPESCA, Final 1 Av. Norte Nueva San Salvador, San Salvador,
     El Salvador (503) 228–0034, 289–6124, fax 289–6124; email: moliva@mag.gob.sv.
   Sonia M. Salaverría, Ministerio de Agricultura y Ganadería, CENDEPESCA, Final 1a.
     Avenida Norte y Avenida Manuel Gallardo, Santa Tecla, San Salvador, El

Salvador (503) 228–0034, 228–1066, fax 228–0074, email: ssalaverría@mag.gob.sv, ssalaverria@hotmail.com.

José Emilio Suadi, Ministerio de Agricultura y Ganadcria, Final 1a. Norte y Av. Manuel Gallardo, Santa Tecla, El Salvador (503) 228–9302, fax 228–1938; email: jsuadi@mag.gob.sv.

French Commissioners:

Didier Ortolland, Ministry of Foreign Affairs, 5, rue Olivier Noyer, 75014 Paris, France (33–1) 43 17 53 39, fax 43 17 55 05; email: didier.ortolland@diplomatie.gouv.fr.

Daniel Silvestre, Secretariat d'etat a la Mer, 16 Boulevard Raspail, 75700 Paris, France; email:daniel.silvestre@sgmer.pm.gouv.fr.

Sven-Erik Sjoden, Ministere des Affairs Estrangeres, 37 Quai D'Orsay, 75351 Paris, France (33–1) 43 17 46 59, fax 43 17 55 58; email: sven-erik.sjoden@diplomatie.gouv.fr.

Xavier Vant, Min. de l'Agri., de l'Alimentation, de la Peche et des Affaires Rurales, 3 Place Fontenoy, 75007 Paris, France (33–1) 49 55 82 36, fax 49 55 82 00; email: xavier.VANT@agriculture.gouv.fr.

Guatemalan Commissioners:

Ing. Ricardo Santacruz Rubí, Ministerio de Agricultura, Ganadería y Alimentación, Km. 22, Carretera al Pacifico, Edificio La Ceiba, 3er Nivel, Guatemala, Guatemala (502) 6630–5883, fax 6630–3839; email: unipesca@c.net.gt.

Nicolás Acevedo Sandoval, MAGA / Ministerio de Agricultura, Ganadería y Alimentación, Km. 22, Carretera al Pacifico, Edif. La Ceiba, 3er Nivel, Barccnas Villa Nueva, Guatemala (502) 6630–5839, fax 5510–3000; email: coor_unipesca@c.net.gt.

Erik Villagran, MAGA / Ministerio de Agricultura, Ganadería y Alimentación, Km. 22, Carretera al Pacifico, Edificio La Ceiba, 3er Nivel, Guatemala, Guatemala (502) 2362–4762, fax 6630–5839; email: villagranerick@hotmail.com.

Félix R. Pérez Zarco, Ministerio de Agricultura, Ganadería y Alimentación, 7a. Ave. 12–90 Zona 13, Edif. Monja Blanca, 1er Nivel, 01013 Guatemala, Guatemala (502) 2362–4762, 2331–0201, fax 2334–2784; email: vicegana@intelnet.net.com.

Japanese Commissioners:

Katsuma Hanafusa, Fisheries Agency of Japan, 1–2–1 Chome Kasumigaseki, Chiyoda-ku, 100–8907 Tokyo, Japan (81–3) 3591–1086, fax 3502–0571; email: katsuma_hanafusa@nm.maff.go.jp.

Masahiro Ishikawa, Federation of Japan Tuna Fish Co-operative Associations, 2–3–22 Kudankita, Chiyoda-Ku, 102 Tokyo, Japan (81–3) 326–46167, 326–46161, fax 323–47455; email: section1@intldiv.japantuna.or.jp.

Toshiyuki Iwado, Ministry of Foreign Affairs, 2–11–1 Shibakouen Minato-Ku, 105–8519 Tokyo, Japan (81–3) 6402–2234, fax 6402–2233; email: toshiyuki.iwado@mofa.go.jp.

Mexican Commissioners:

Guillermo A. Compeán, Instituto Nacional de la Pesca, Pitágoras #1320, Sta Cruz Atoyac, D.F. 03310 México, México (52–55) 5422–3002, 5688–1469, fax 5604–9169; email: compean@correo.inp.sagarpa.gob.mx.

Dr. Ramón Corral, CONAPESCA / Comisión Nacional de Acuicultura y Pesca, Av. Camarón-Sabalo S/N Esquina Tiburón, SIN 82100 Mazatlán, México (52–669) 913–0904, fax 913–0904; email: rcorrala@sagarpa.gob.mx.

Michel Dreyfus, Instituto Nacional de la Pesca, Campus CICESE Carretera Tijuana-Ensenada, B.C.N. 22890 Ensenada, México (52–646) 174–5637, fax 174–5639; email: dreyfus@cicese.mx.

Nicaraguan Commissioners:

Miguel A. Marenco, ADPESCA, Apartado Postal 2020, Managua, Nicaragua (505) 270–0932, 270–0946, fax 270–0954; email: miguel.marenco@mific.gob.ni, mmarenco@ibw.com.ni.

Edward Weissman, Jorge Fishing, Inc., 2240 India St., San Diego, CA 92101 USA (619) 338–9984, fax 338–9986; email: eweissman@aol.com.

Panamanian Commissioners:

María Patricia Díaz, Autoridad Marítima de Panamá, Apartado 8062, Zona 7, Panamá, Panamá (507) 269–0233, fax 269–2731; email: mpdiaz@robleslaw.com.

Ing. Arnulfo L. Franco, Asociación de Atuneros Panameños, Clayton #404–A, Panamá, Panamá (507) 677–1000, fax 317–0547; email: email: afranco@cwpanama.net.

Leika Martínez, Autoridad Marítima de Panamá, Apartado 8062, Zona 7, Panamá, Panamá (507) 232–8570, 232–6117, fax 232–6477; email: lmartinez@amp.gob.pa.

George Novey, Autoridad Marítima de Panamá, Apartado Postal 8062, Zona 7, Panamá, Panamá (507) 232–7510, 232–6117, fax 232–6477; email: drmarinos@amp.gob.pa.

Peruvian Commissioners:

Jorge Vértiz Calderón, Ministerio de Producción (Pesquería), Calle 1 Oeste #60, Urb. Córpac, Lima 27, San Isidro, Perú (51–1) 224–3423, fax 224–2381; email: jvertiz@produce.gob.pe.

Gladys Cárdenas, Instituto del Mar del Perú, Apartado Postal 22, Lima, Callao, Perú (51–1) 429–7630, ext. 2, 420–2000, fax 420–0144; email: gcardenas@imarpe.gob.pe.

Alejandro Jimenez, Ministerio de la Producción, Calle Uno Oeste No. 60, Urb. Córpac, San Isidro, Lima 27 Perú (51–1) 224–3334, 224–3416, fax 616–2222; email: ajimenez@produce.gob.pe.

Elvira Velásquez, Ministerio de Relaciones Exteriores, Jr. Lampa 545, 7mo piso, Lima 1, Lima, Perú (51–1) 311–2657, fax 311–2659; email: evelasquez@rree.gob.pe.

Spanish Commissioners:

Rafael Centenera, Secretaría General de Relaciones Pesqueras Internacionales, C. Ortega y Gasset, 57, 28006 Madrid, Spain (34–91) 347–6040, 647–6041, fax 347–6042; email: acuintpm@mpa.es.

Fernando Curcio, Secretaría General de Pesca Marítima, José Ortega y Gasset, 57, 28006 Madrid, Spain (34–91) 347–6030, 347–6031, fax 347–6032; email: drpesmar@mapya.es.

Samuel Juarez, Embajada de España, 2375 Pennsylvania Ave. NW., Washington, DC 20037 USA (202) 728–2339, fax 728–2320; email: juarez@mapausa.org.

United States Commissioners:

Scott Burns, World Wildlife Fund, 1250 24th Street, NW., Washington, DC 20037 USA (202) 778–9547, 293–4800, fax 887–5293; email: scott.burns@wwfus.org.

Robert C. Fletcher, Sportfishing Association of California, 1084 Bangor Street, San Diego, CA 92106 USA (619) 226–6455, fax 226–0175; email: dart@sacemup.org.

Rodney McInnis, NMFS/National Marine Fisheries Services, 501 West Ocean Boulevard, Suite 4200, Long Beach, CA 90802–4213 USA (562) 980–4001, fax 980–4018; email: rod.mcinnis@noaa.gov.

Patrick Rose, P.O. Box 7242, Rancho Santa Fe, CA 92067 USA (858) 756–2733, fax 756–5850; email: skyline756@aol.com.

Vanuatuan Commissioners:

Moses Amos, Ministry of Agriculture, Quarentine * Inspection Service, Forestry and Fisheries, Private Mail Bag 9045, Port Vila, Vanuatu (678) 23119, 23621, fax 23641; email: mosesamos@vanuatu.com.vu.

Christophe Emele, Tuna Fishing (Vanuatu) Limited, P.O. Box 1640 Socapore Area, Lini Highway, Port Vila, Vanuatu (678) 25887, fax 25608; email: tunafishing@vanuatu.com.vu.

David Johnson, Vanuatu Monitoring and Management Servicxes Ltd., P.O. Box 1640 Socapore Area, Lini Highway, Port Vila, Vanuatu (678) 25887, fax 25608; email: djohnson@vmmsl.com.

Venezuelan Commissioners:

Alvin Delgado, FUNDATUN, Edif. San Pablo, P.H., Av. Ppal, El Dique, 6101 Cumaná, Venezuela (58–293) 433–0431, fax 433–0431; email: fundatunpnov@cantv.net, fundatunpnov@yahoo.com.

Nancy Tablante, Instituto Nacional de Pesca y Acuacultura, Torre Este, Piso 10, Parque Central, 1010 Caracas, Venezuela (58–212) 571–4889, fax 571–4889; email: ori@inapesca.gov.ve, heralica@cantv.net.

Oscar Lucentini Wozel, Instituto Nacional de Pesca y Acuacultura, Av. Páez del paraiso, Diagonal a la Plaza Washington Planta Baja, 1010 Caracas, Venezuela (58–212) 461–9225, 509–0384, fax 574–3587; email: presidencia@inapesca.gov.ve.

INTERNATIONAL BOUNDARY AND WATER COMMISSION, UNITED STATES AND MEXICO

UNITED STATES SECTION

The Commons, Building C, Suite 100, 4171 North Mesa, El Paso TX 79902–1441

phone (915) 832–4100, fax (915) 832–4190 www.ibwc.state.gov

Commissioner.—Arturo Q. Duran, 832–4101.
Deputy Commissioner.—Rick Porras, 832–4110.
Secretary.—Carlos Rivera, 832–4105.
Principal Engineers: Bernardino Olague 832–4118; Carlos Marin 832–4157.

Human Resources Director.—Fred Graf (acting), 832–4108.
General Counsel/Legal Advisor.—Susan Daniel, 832–4109.

MEXICAN SECTION

Avenida Universidad, No. 2180, Zona de El Chamizal, A.P. 1612–D, C.P. 32310,
Ciudad Juarez, Chihuahua, Mexico
PO Box 10525, El Paso TX 79995.
phone 011–52–16–13–7311 or 011–52–16–13–7363 (Mexico)

Commissioner.—Arturo Herrera Solis.
Secretary.—Jose de Jesus Luevano Grano.
Principal Engineers: L. Antonio Rascon Mendoza, Gilberto Elizalde Hernandez.

INTERNATIONAL BOUNDARY COMMISSION, UNITED STATES AND CANADA

UNITED STATES SECTION

1250 23rd Street, NW., Suite 100, 20037, phone (202) 736–9100

Commissioner.—Dennis Schorack.
Deputy Commissioner.—Kyle Hipsley.
Administrative Officer.—Tracy Morris.

CANADIAN SECTION

Room 555, 615 Booth Street, Ottawa ON, Canada K1A 0E9, phone (613) 995–4341

Commissioner.—Michael J. O'Sullivan.
Deputy Commissioner.—Al Arseneault.

INTERNATIONAL COTTON ADVISORY COMMITTEE

**Headquarters: 1629 K Street Suite 702, 20006, secretariat@icac.org
phone 463–6660, fax 463–6950**

(Permanent Secretariat of the Organization)

MEMBER COUNTRIES

Argentina	Greece	South Africa
Australia	India	Spain
Belgium	Iran	Sudan
Brazil	Israel	Switzerland
Burkina Faso	Italy	Syria
Cameroon	Korea, Republic of	Tanzania
Chad	Mali	Togo
China (Taiwan)	Netherlands	Turkey
Colombia	Nigeria	Uganda
Côte d'Ivoire	Pakistan	United Kingdom
Egypt	Paraguay	United States
Finland	Philippines	Uzbekistan
France	Poland	Zimbabwe
Germany	Russia	

Executive Director.—Terry P. Townsend.
Statistician.—Gerald Estur.
Economists: Carlos Valderrama; Andrei Guitchounts.
Head of Technical Information Section.—M. Rafiq Chaudhry.

Manager Information Systems.—John Mulligan.
Administrative Officer.—Federico R. Arriola.

INTERNATIONAL JOINT COMMISSION, UNITED STATES AND CANADA

UNITED STATES SECTION

1250 23rd Street, Suite 100, 20440, phone (202) 736–9000, fax 467–0746, www.ijc.org

Chairman.—Dennis L. Schornack.
  Commissioners: Irene B. Brooks, Allen I. Olson.
  Secretary.—Elizabeth C. Bourget.
  Legal Adviser.—James G. Chandler.
  Engineering Adviser.—Mark Colosimo.
  Environmental Adviser.—Joel L. Fisher.
  Public Information Officer.—Frank Bevacqua.
  Ecologist.—Kay Austin.

CANADIAN SECTION

234 Laurier Avenue West, Ottawa, Ontario Canada K1P 6K6, phone (613) 995–2984,
fax 993–5583

Chairman.—Rt. Hon. Herb Gray.
  Commissioners: Jack Blaney, Robert Gourd.
  Secretary.—Murray Clamen.
  Legal Adviser.—Michael Vechsler.
  Engineering Adviser.—Edward A. Bailey.
  Senior Environmental Adviser.—Joel Weiner.
  Public Relations Adviser.—Paula Fedeski-Koundakjian.
  Economics Adviser.—Ann MacKenzie.
  Research Adviser.—Rudy Koop.

GREAT LAKES REGIONAL OFFICE

Eighth Floor, 100 Ouellette Avenue, Windsor, Ontario Canada N9A 6T3, phone
(519) 257–6700 (Canada), (313) 226–2170 (U.S.)

Director.—Gail Krantzberg.
  Public Affairs Officer.—Jennifer Day.

INTERNATIONAL LABOR ORGANIZATION

Headquarters: Geneva, Switzerland, www.ilo.org

**Washington Office, 1828 L Street, Suite 600, 20036, phone (202) 653–7652,
fax 653–7687, washington@ilo.org**

Liaison Office with the United Nations

220 East 42nd Street, Suite 3101, New York NY 10017–5806

International Labor Office (Permanent Secretariat of the Organization)
  Headquarters Geneva:
    Director-General.—Juan Somavia.
  Washington:
    Director.—Larry Kohler (acting).
      Special Assistant to the Director.—Jesica Seacor.
    Senior Advisor/Public Affairs.—Mary W. Covington.
    Other Branch Offices: Bonn, London, Paris, Rome, Tokyo, Moscow.

INTERNATIONAL MONETARY FUND

700 19th Street 20431, phone (202) 623–7000

http://www.imf.org

MANAGEMENT AND SENIOR OFFICERS

Managing Director.—Rodrigo de Rato y Figaredo.
 First Deputy Managing Director.—Anne O. Krueger.
 Deputy Managing Directors: Agustín Carstens, Takatoshi Kato.
 Economic Counsellor.—Raghuram G. Rajan.
 IMF Institute Director.—Leslie Lipschitz.
 Legal Department General Counsel.—Sean Hagan.
 Departmental Directors:
  Administration.—Brian C. Stuart.
  African.—Abdoulaye Bio-Tchané.
  Asia and Pacific.—David Burton.
  European I.—Michael C. Deppler.
  External Relations.—Thomas C. Dawson II.
  Finance.—Michael Kuhn.
  Fiscal Affairs.—Teresa Ter-Minassian.
  Middle Eastern.—Mohsin S. Khan.
  Monetary and Exchange Affairs.—Stefan Ingves.
  Policy Development and Review.—Mark Allen.
  Research.—Raghuram G. Rajan.
  Secretary.—Shailendra J. Anjaria.
  Statistics.—Robert W. Edwards.
  Western Hemisphere.—Anoop Singh.
 Director Office of:
  Budget and Planning.—Barry Potter.
  Internal Audit and Inspection.—Alain Coune.
 Regional Office for Asia and the Pacific Director.—Hiroyuki Hino.
 Director and Special Representative to the United Nations.—Reinhard Munzberg.

EXECUTIVE DIRECTORS AND ALTERNATES

Executive Directors:
 Sulaiman M. Al-Turki, represents Saudi Arabia.
  Alternate.—Abudullah S. Al Azzuz.
 Pierre Duquesne, represents France.
  Alternate.—Olivier Cuny.
 Jon A. Solheim, represents Denmark, Estonia, Finland, Iceland, Latvia, Lithuania, Norway, Sweden.
  Alternate.—David Farelius.
 Moisés Schwartz, represents Costa Rica, El Salvador, Guatemala, Honduras, Mexico, Nicaragua, Spain, Venezuela, Republica Bolivariana de.
  Alternate.—Mary Dager.
 Kevin G. Lynch, represents Antigua and Barbuda, the Bahamas, Barbados, Belize, Canada, Dominica, Grenada, Ireland, Jamaica, St. Kitts and Nevis, St. Lucia, St. Vincent and the Grenadines.
  Alternate.—Charles X. O'Loghlin.
 Peter Ngumbullu, represents Angola, Botswana, Burundi, Eritrea, Ethiopia, Gambia, Kenya, Lesotho, Malawi, Mozambique, Namibia, Nigeria, Sierra Leone, South Africa, Sudan, Swaziland, Tanzania, Uganda, Zambia, Zimbabwe.
  Alternate.—Peter Gakunu.
 B.P. Misra, represents Bangladesh, Bhutan, India, Sri Lanka.
  Alternate.—Amal Uthum Herat.
 Hooi Eng Phang, represents Brunei Darussalam, Cambodia, Fiji, Indonesia, Lao People's Democratic Republic, Malaysia, Myanmar, Nepal, Singapore, Thailand, Tonga, Vietnam.
  Alternate.—Made Sukada.
 Fritz Zurbrügg, represents Azerbaijan, Kyrgyz Republic, Poland, Switzerland, Tajikistan, Turkmenistan, Uzbekistan, Serbia and Montenegro.
  Alternate.—Andrzej Raczko.

Murilo Portugal, represents Brazil, Colombia, Dominican Republic, Ecuador, Guyana, Haiti, Panama, Suriname, Trinidad and Tobago.
  Alternate.—Roberto Steiner.
Willy Kiekens, represents Austria, Belarus, Belgium, Czech Republic, Hungary, Kazakhstan, Luxembourg, Slovak Republic, Slovenia, Turkey.
  Alternate.—Johann Prader.
Damian Ondo Mañe, represents Benin, Burkina Faso, Cameroon, Cape Verde, Central African Republic, Chad, Comoros, Congo, Democratic Republic of, Congo, Republic of, Côte d'Ivoire, Djibouti, Equatorial Guinea, Gabon, Guinea, Guinea-Bissau, Madagascar, Mali, Mauritania, Mauritius, Niger, Rwanda, São Tomé and Principe, Senegal, Togo.
  Alternate.—Laurean W. Rutayisire.
Pier Carlo Padoan, represents Albania, Greece, Italy, Malta, Portugal, San Marino.
  Alternate.—Miranda Xafa.
Nancy P. Jacklin, represents United States.
  Alternate.—Meg Lundsager.
Shigeo Kashiwagi, represents Japan.
  Alternate.—Michio Kitahara.
Abbas Mirakhor, represents Afghanistan Islamic State of, Algeria, Ghana, Iran, Islamic Republic of, Morocco, Pakistan, Tunisia.
  Alternate.—Mohammed Daïri.
Héctor R. Torres, represents Argentina, Bolivia, Chile, Paraguay, Peru, Uruguay.
  Alternate.—Javier Silva-Ruete.
Karlheinz Bischofberger, represents Germany.
  Alternate.—Gert Meissner.
A. Shakour Shaalan, represents Bahrain, Egypt, Iraq, Jordan, Kuwait, Lebanon, Libya Arab, Jamahiriya, Maldives, Oman, Qatar, Syrian Arab Republic, United Arab Emirates, Yemen, Republic of.
  Alternate.—Oussama T. Kanaan.
Aleksei V. Mozhin, represents Russian Federation.
  Alternate.—Andrei Lushin.
Jong Nam Oh, represents Australia, Kiribati, Korea, Marshall Islands, Micronesia, Federated States of, Mongolia, New Zealand, Palau, Papua New Guinea, Philippines, Samoa, Seychelles, Solomon Islands, Vanuatu.
  Alternate.—Richard Murray.
Jeroen Kremers, represents Armenia, Bosnia and Herzegovina, Bulgaria, Croatia, Cyprus, Georgia, Israel, Macedonia, former Yugoslav Republic of, Moldova, Netherlands, Romania, Ukraine.
  Alternate.—Yuriy G. Yakusha.
Wang Xiaoyi, represents China.
  Alternate.—G.E. Huayong.
Tom Scholar, represents United Kingdom.
  Alternate.—Andrew Hauser.

INTERNATIONAL ORGANIZATION FOR MIGRATION

Headquarters: 17 Route Des Morillons (PO Box 71), CH1211, Geneva 19, Switzerland

Washington Mission: 1752 N Street, NW, Suite 700, 20036, phone (202) 862–1826

New York Mission: 122 East 42nd Street, Suite 1610, New York NY 10168–1610

phone (212) 681–7000

HEADQUARTERS

Director General.—Brunson McKinley (United States).
Deputy Director General.—Ndioro Ndiaye (Senegal).
Washington Regional Representative.—Frances E. Sullivan (United States).
New York Chief of Mission.—Michael Gray (United States).
Permanent Observer to the United Nations.—Luca Dall'Oglio (Italy).

MEMBER STATES

Afghanistan
Albania
Algeria
Angola
Argentina
Armenia
Australia
Austria
Azerbaijan
Bahamas
Bangladesh
Belgium
Belize
Benin
Bolivia
Brazil
Bulgaria
Burkina Faso
Cambodia
Canada
Cape Verde
Chile
Colombia
Congo
Costa Rica
Côte d'Ivoire
Croatia
Cyprus
Czech Republic
Democratic Republic of
  the Congo
Denmark
Dominican Republic
Ecuador
Egypt
El Salvador
Estonia
Finland

France
Gambia
Georgia
Germany
Greece
Guatemala
Guinea
Guinea-Bissau
Haiti
Honduras
Hungary
Iran, Islamic
  Republic of
Ireland
Israel
Italy
Japan
Jordan
Kazakhstan
Kenya
Kyrgyzstan
Latvia
Liberia
Libyan Arab Jamahiriya
Lithuania
Luxembourg
Madagascar
Mali
Malta
Mauritania
Mexico
Morocco
Netherlands
New Zealand
Nicaragua
Nigeria
Niger (the)
Norway

Pakistan
Panama
Paraguay
Peru
Philippines
Poland
Portugal
Republic of Korea
Republic of Moldova
Romania
Rwanda
Senegal
Serbia and Montenegro
Sierra Leone
Slovakia
Slovenia
South Africa
Sri Lanka
Sudan
Sweden
Switzerland
Tajikistan
Thailand
Tunisia
Turkey
Uganda
Ukraine
United Kingdom of
  Great Britain and
  Northern Ireland
United Republic of Tanzania
United States of America
Uruguay
Venezuela
Yemen
Zambia
Zimbabwe

STATES WITH OBSERVER STATUS

Belarus
Bhutan
Bosnia and Herzegovina
Burundi
China
Cuba
Ethiopia
Ghana
Holy See

India
Indonesia
Jamaica
Mozambique
Namibia
Nepal
Papua New Guinea
Russian Federation
San Marino

Sao Tomé and Principe
Somalia
Spain
The former Yugoslav
  Republic of Macedonia
Turkmenistan
Viet Nam

IOM OVERSEAS LIAISON AND OPERATIONAL OFFICES

Afghanistan, Herat, Kabul
Albania, Tirana
Angola, Luanda
Argentina, Buenos Aires *
Armenia, Yerevan
Australia, Canberra *

Austria, Wien *
Azerbaijan, Baku
Bangladesh, Dhaka *
Belarus, Minsk
Belgium/Luxembourg,
  Bruxelles *

Bolivia, La Paz
Bosnia and Herzegovina,
  Sarajevo
Bulgaria, Sofia
Cambodia, Phnom Penh
Canada, Ottawa, Ontario

Chile, Santiago de Chile
China, Hong Kong
Colombia, Santafé de Bogotá
Congo, Brazzaville
Congo, (Democratic
 Republic of), Gombe,
 Kinshasa
Costa Rica, San José *
Côte D'Ivoire, Abidjan
Croatia, Zagreb
Czech Republic, Praha
Dominican Republic,
 Santo Domingo
Ecuador, Quito
Egypt, Cairo *
El Salvador, San Salvador
Estonia, Tallinn
Ethiopia, Addis Ababa
Finland, Helsinki *
France, Paris
Gambia, Banjul
Georgia, Tbilisi
Germany, Berlin, Bonn
Ghana, Accra North
Greece, Athens
Guatemala, Ciudad
 de Guatemala
Guinea, Conakry
Guinea-Bissau,
 Guinea Bissau
Haita, Port au Prince
Honduras, Tegucigalpa
Hungary, Budapest *
India, Ahmedabad
Indonesia, Jakarta, Kupang

Iran, Tehran
Iraq, Amman
Ireland, Dublin
Italy, Roma *
Jamaica, Kingston
Japan, Tokyo
Jordan, Amman
Kazakhstan, Almaty
Kenya, Nairobi *
Korea (Republic of), Seoul
Kuwait, Kuwait City
Kyrgyzstan, Bishkek City
Latvia, Riga
Liberia, Monrovia
Lithuania, Vilnius
Macedonia, Skopje
Mali, Bamako
Mexico, Mexico DF
Moldova, (Republic of)
 Chisinau
Morocco, Rabat
Mozambique, Maputo
Namibia, Windhoek
Nauru (Republic of)
Netherlands, Den Haag
Nicaragua, Managua
Nigeria, Abuja
Norway, Oslo
Pakistan, Islamabad *
Papua New Guinea, Manus
Peru, Lima *
Philippines, Metro Manila *
Poland, Warszawa
Portugal, Lisboa
Romania, Bucharest

Russia, Moscow
Saudi Arabia, Riyadh
Senegal, Dakar *
Serbia and Montenegro,
 Belgrade, Prishtina
Sierra Leone, Freetown
Slovak Republic, Bratislava
Slovenia, Ljubljana
South Africa, Pretoria *
Spain, Madrid
Sri Lanka, Colombo
Sudan, Khartoum
Switzerland, Bern
Syrian Arab Republic,
 Damascus
Tajikistan, Dushanbe
Thailand, Bangkok *
Timor Leste, Dili
Tunisia, Tunis
Turkey, Ankara
Turkmenistan, Ashgabad
Uganda, Kampala
Ukraine, Kyiv
United Kingdom, London
United States of America,
 Washington*, New York*,
 Los Angeles, Miami,
 Rosemont
Uruguay, Montevideo
Uzbekistan, Tashkent
Venezuela, Caracas
Vietnam, Hanoi, Ho Chi
 Minh City
Zambia, Lusaka
Zimbabwe, Harare

INTERNATIONAL PACIFIC HALIBUT COMMISSION,

UNITED STATES AND CANADA

Headquarters: University of Washington, Seattle, WA 98195

phone (206) 634–1838, fax (206) 632–2983

Mailing address: PO Box 95009, Seattle WA 98145–2009

American Commissioners:
 Ralph G. Hoard, 4019 21st Avenue W., Seattle, WA 98199, (206) 282–0988, fax (206) 281–0329.
 Phillip Lestenkof, P.O. Box 288, St. Paul Island, AK 99660, (907) 546–2597.
 Dr. Jim Balsiger, National Marine Fisheries Service, PO Box 21668, Juneau, AK 99802, (907) 586–7221, fax (907) 586–7249.

Canadian Commissioners:
 Dr. Richard J. Beamish, Pacific Biological Station, PO Box 100, Nanaimo, B.C., Canada V9R 5K6, (250) 756–7029, fax (250) 756–7333.
 Cliff Atleo, PO Box 1218, Port Alberni, BC, Canada V9Y 7Ml, (250) 723–0188, fax (250) 723–1393.
 John Secord, #307, 3680 W. 7th Avenue, Vancouver, BC, Canada V6R 1W4 (604) 734–1019, fax (604) 734–6962.
Director and Secretary (ex officio).—Dr. Bruce M. Leaman, PO Box 95009, Seattle, WA 98145–2009.

---

* Mission with Regional Functions.

ORGANIZATION OF AMERICAN STATES

17th Street and Constitution Avenue, NW., 20006
phone (202) 458–3000, fax 458–3967

PERMANENT MISSIONS TO THE OAS

Antigua and Barbuda.—Ambassador Deborah Mae-Lovell, Permanent Representative, 3216 New Mexico Avenue NW., Washington DC 20016, phone (202) 362–5122, 5166 or 5211, fax 362–5225.

Argentina.—Ambassador Rodolfo Gil, Permanent Representative, 1816 Corcoran Street NW., Washington DC 20009, phone (202) 387–4142, 4146 or 4170, fax 328–1591.

The Bahamas.—Ambassador Joshua Sears, Permanent Representative, 2220 Massachusetts Avenue NW., Washington DC 20008, phone (202) 319–2660 to 2667, fax 319–2668.

Barbados.—Ambassador Michael I. King, Permanent Representative, 2144 Wyoming Avenue NW., Washington DC 20008, phone (202) 939–9200, 9201, 9202, fax 332–7467.

Belize.—Ambassador Lisa Shoman, Permanent Representative, 2535 Massachusetts Avenue NW., Washington DC 20008–3098, phone (202) 332–9636, ext. 3001, fax 332–6888.

Bolivia.—Ambassador María Tamavo, Permanent Representative, 1819 H Street, NW., Suite 419, Washington, DC 20006, phone (202) 785–0218, fax 296–0563.

Brazil.—Ambassador Jose Luiz Machado e Costa, Interim Representative, 2600 Virginia Avenue NW., Suite 412, Washington DC 20037, phone (202) 333–4224, 4225 or 4226, fax 333–6610.

Canada.—Ambassador Paul Durand, Permanent Representative, 501 Pennsylvania Avenue NW., Washington DC 20001, phone (202) 682–1768, Ext. 7267, fax 682–7624.

Chile.—Ambassador Esteban Tomic Errázuriz, 2000 L Street NW., Suite 720, Washington DC 20036, phone (202) 887–5475, 5476, fax 775–0713.

Colombia.—Ambassador Álvaro Tirado Mejía, Permanent Representative, 1609 22nd Street NW., Washington DC 20008, phone 332–8003 or 8004, fax 234–9781.

Costa Rica.—Ambassador Javier Sancho Bonilla, Permanent Representative, 2112 S Street NW., Suite 300, Washington DC 20008, phone (202) 234–9280, fax 986–2274.

Dominica.—Ambassador Swinburne A.S. Lestrade, Permanent Representative, 3216 New Mexico Avenue NW., Washington, DC 20016, phone (202) 364–6781, fax 364–6791.

Dominican Republic.—Ambassador Mayerlyn Cordero, Interim Representative, 1715 22nd Street NW., Washington DC 20008, phone (202) 332–9142, 6280, fax 232–5038.

Ecuador.—Ambassador Marcelo Hervas, Permanent Representative, 2535 15th Street NW., Washington DC 20009, phone (202) 234–1494 or 1692, fax 667–3482.

El Salvador.—Ambassador Abigail Castro de Perez, Permanent Representative, 1211 Connecticut Avenue NW. Suite 401, Washington DC 20036, phone (202) 467–0054 or 4290, fax 467–4261.

Grenada.—Ambassador Denis G. Antoine, Permanent Representative, 1701 New Hampshire Avenue NW., Washington DC 20009, phone (202) 265–2561, fax 265–2468.

Guatemala.—Ambassador Francisco Villagrán de León, Permanent Representative, 1507 22nd Street NW., Washington DC 20037, phone (202) 833–4015, 4016, or 4017, fax 833–4011.

Guyana.—Ambassador Bayney R. Karran, Permanent Representative, 2490 Tracy Place NW., Washington DC 20008, phone (202) 265–6900 or 6901, fax 232–1297.

Haiti.—Ambassador Duly Brutus, Permanent Representative, 2311 Massachusetts Avenue NW., Washington DC 20008, phone (202) 332–4090 or 4092, fax 518–8742.

Honduras.—Ambassador Salvador Rodezno, Permanent Representative, 5100 Wisconsin Avenue NW., Suite 403, Washington DC 20016, phone (202) 362–9656 or 9657, fax 537–7170.

Jamaica.—Ambassador Gordon Valentine Shirley, Permanent Representative, 1520 New Hampshire Avenue NW., Washington DC 20036, phone (202) 986–0121, 0123, 452–0660, fax 452–9395.

Mexico.—Ambassador Jorge Eduardo Chen, Permanent Representative, 2440 Massachusetts Avenue NW., Washington DC 20008, phone (202) 332–3663, 3664, 3984, fax 234–0602.

Nicaragua.—Ambassador Carmen Marina Gutierrez, Permanent Representative, 1627 New Hampshire Avenue NW., Washington DC 20009, phone (202) 332–1643 or 1644, fax 745–0710.

Panama.—Ambassador Aristides Royo, Permanent Representative, 2201 Wisconsin Avenue NW., Suite 240, phone (202) 965–4826 or 4819, fax 965–4836.

Paraguay.—Ambassador Manuel Maria Cáceres, Permanent Representative, 2022 Connecticut Avenue NW., Washington DC 20008, phone (202) 244–3003, fax 244–3005.

Peru.—Ambassador Alberto Alfonso Borea, Permanent Representative, 1901 Pennsylvania Avenue NW., Suite 402, Washington DC 20006, phone (202) 232–2281, fax 466–3068.

Saint Kitts and Nevis.—Ambassador Dr. Izben C. Williams, Permanent Representative, 3216 New Mexico Avenue NW., Washington DC 20016, phone (202) 686–2636, fax 686–5740.

Saint Lucia.—Ambassador Sonia M. Johnny, Permanent Representative, 3216 New Mexico Avenue NW., Washington, DC 20016, phone (202) 364–6792 thru 6795, fax 364–6723.

Saint Vincent and The Grenadines.— Ambassador Ellsworth I.A. John, Permanent Representative, 3216 New Mexico Avenue, NW., Washington DC 20016, phone (202) 364–6730, fax 364–6736.

Suriname.—Ambassador Henry Lothar Illes, Permanent Representative, 4301 Connecticut Avenue NW., Suite 462, Washington, DC 20008, phone (202) 244–7488, 7590, 7591 or 7592, fax 244–5878.

Trinidad and Tobago.—Ambassador Marina Valere, Permanent Representative, 1708 Massachusetts Avenue NW., Washington DC 20036, phone (202) 467–6490, fax 785–3130.

United States of America.—Ambassador John Maisto, Permanent Representative, ARA / USOAS Bureau of Inter-American Affairs, Department of State, Room 6494, Washington DC 20520, phone (202) 647–9430, fax 647–0911.

Uruguay.—Ambassador Juan Enrique Fischer, Permanent Representative, 2801 New Mexico Avenue NW., Suite 1210, Washington DC 20007, phone (202) 333–0588 or 0687, fax 337–3758.

Venezuela.—Ambassador Jorge Valero, Permanent Representative, 1099 30th Street NW., Second Floor, Washington, DC 20007, phone (202) 342–5837 or 5838, fax 625–5657.

GENERAL SECRETARIAT

Secretary General.—José Miguel Insulza, 458–3000.
Assistant Secretary General.—Luigi Einaudi, 458–6046, fax 458–3011.
Chief of Staff to the Assistant Secretary General.—Sandra Honore, 458–3497.
Director, Department for—
  Administration and Finance.—Frank Almaguer, 458–3436.
  Communications and External Relations.—Irene Klinger, 458–6072.
  Democratic and Political Affairs.—John Biehl, 458–3585.
  Legal Affairs and Services.—William M. Berenson, 458–3415.
Department of Multidimensional Security, Officer in Charge.—Steven Monblatt, 458–6852.
Executive Secretary, Executive Secretariat for—
  Integral Development.—Brian J.R. Stevenson, 458–3510.
  Inter-American Commission on Human Rights.—Santiago A. Canton, 458–6002.

ORGANIZATION FOR ECONOMIC COOPERATION AND DEVELOPMENT

Headquarters: 2 rue André-Pascal, 75775 Paris CEDEX 16, France

phone (331) 4524–8200, fax (331) 4524–8500

Secretary-General.—Donald J. Johnston.
  Deputy Secretaries General: Richard Hecklinger, Seiichi Kondo, Herwig Schloǵl.
Member Countries:

Australia	Hungary	Norway
Austria	Iceland	Poland
Belgium	Ireland	Portugal
Canada	Italy	Slovak Republic
Czech Republic	Japan	Spain
Denmark	Korea	Sweden
Finland	Luxembourg	Switzerland
France	Mexico	Turkey
Germany	Netherlands	United Kingdom
Greece	New Zealand	United States

OECD WASHINGTON CENTER

2001 L Street NW., Suite 650, 20036, phone (202) 785–6323, fax (202) 785–0350

http://www.oecdwash.org

Head of Center.—Sandra Wilson.

PAN AMERICAN SANITARY BUREAU
REGIONAL OFFICE OF THE WORLD HEALTH ORGANIZATION
525 23rd Street, NW., Washington DC 20037, phone (202) 974–3000,
fax (202) 974–3663

PAN AMERICAN SANITARY BUREAU

Director.—Dr. Mirta Roses Periago, 974–3408.
Deputy Director.—Dr. Joxel Garcia, 974–3178.
Assistant Director.—Carissa Etienne, 974–3404.
Director of:
  Administration.—Eric Boswell, 974–3412.
  Program Management.—Dr. Daniel López Acuña, 974–3221.

FIELD OFFICES

PAHO/WHO Caribbean Program Coordinator.—Veta Brown, PO Box 508, Dayralls and Navy Garden Roads, Christ Church, Bridgetown, Barbados, phone (246) 426–3860/3865, fax 436–9779.
Caribbean Program Coordination (CPC).—Antigua and Barbuda, Barbados, Dominica, Grenada, St. Kitts and Nevis, Saint Lucia, St. Vincent and the Grenadines. Eastern Caribbean: Anguilla, British Virgin Islands, Montserrat. French Antilles: Guadaloupe, Martinique, St. Martin and St. Bartholomew, French Guiana.
PAHO/WHO Representatives:
  Argentina, Dr. José Antonio Pagés, Oficina Sanitaria Panamericana, Marcelo T. de Alvear 684, 4o. piso, 1058 Buenos Aires, Argentina, phone (54–11) 4312–5301 to 5304, fax 4311–9151.
  Bahamas (Turks and Caicos), Lynda Rae Campbell, Union Court, Elizabeth Avenue, Nassau, Bahamas, phone (242) 326–7390, 7299, fax 326–7012.
  Belize, Dr. Kathleen P. Israel, No. 168 Newtown Barracks, P.O. Box 1834, Belize City, Belize, phone (501–2) 448–85, 52, fax 309–17.
  Bolivia, Dr. Christian Darras, Representante de la OPS/OMS en Bolivia, Calle Victor Sanjines 2678, (Plaza España), 6to, Piso, La Paz, Bolivia, phone (591–2) 412–465, 303, 313, 397, fax 412–598.
  Brazil, Dr. Antonio Horacio Toro, Representante da OPAS/OMS no Brasil, Setor de Embaixadas Norte, Lote 19, 70800–400, Brasilia, D.F., Brasil, phone (55–61) 426–9595, 9550, 9500, fax 321–1922.
  Chile, Dr. Juan Manuel Sotelo Figueiredo, Representante de la OPS/OMS en Chile, Avenida Providencia No. 1017, Piso 4 y 5, Santiago, Chile, phone (56–2) 264–9300, fax 264–9311.
  Colombia, Dr. Pier Paolo Balladelli, Representante de la OPS/OMS en Colombia, Carrera 7 Nr. 74–21, Piso 9, Edificio Seguros Aurora, Santa Fé de Bogotá, D.C., Colombia, phone (57–1) 347–8373, fax 254–7070.
  Costa Rica, Dr. Carlos Samayoa, Representante de la OPS/OMS en Costa Rica, Calle 16, Avenida 6 y 8, Distrito Hospital, San José, Costa Rica, phone (506) 258–5810, fax 258–5830.
  Cuba, Dra. Lea Guido, Representante de la OPS/OMS en Cuba, Oficina Sanitaria Panamericana, Calle 4 No. 407, entre 17 y 19 Vedado, La Habana, Cuba, phone (53–7), 552–526, 527, fax 662–075.
  Dominican Republic, Dra. Socorro Gross, Representante de la OPS/OMS en República Dominicana, Calle Pepillo Salcedo, Plaza de la Salud, Edificio Cruz Roja/OPS/OMS, 2da, Planta, Santo Domingo, D.N., República Dominicana, phone (809) 562–1519, 1582, 1638, 1693, fax 544–0322.
  Ecuador, Sr. Diego Victoria, Representante de la OPS/OMS en el Ecuador, Oficina Sanitaria Panamericana, Av. Amazonas 2889 y La Granja, Edificio Naciones Unidas Quito, Ecuador, phone (593–2) 246–0330, 0215, 0274, 0273, fax 246–0635.
  El Salvador, Dr. Juan Eduardo Guerrero, Representante de la OPS/OMS en El Salvador, 73 Avenida Sur No. 135, Colonia Escalón, San Salvador, El Salvador, phone (503) 298–3491, 3306, fax 298–1168.
  Guatemala, Dr. Joaquín Molina, Representante de la OPS/OMS en Guatemala, Oficina Sanitaria Panamericana, Avenida 15 de septiembre (7a avenida) 12–23, Zona 9, Edificio Etisa 3er. nivel, Plaza España, Guatemala, Guatemala, phone (011–502) 332–2032, fax 334–3804.
  Guyana, Dr. Bernadette Theodore-Gandi, Lot 8 Brickdam Stabroek, Georgetown, Guyana, phone (592) 225–3000, fax 226–6654.

Haití, Dr. Béatrice Bonnevaux, Représentante de l'OPS/OMS en Haiti, ali., No. 295 Avenue John Brown, Port-au-Prince, Haiti, phone (53–7) 552–526, 527, fax 662–075.

Honduras, Dr. José Fiusa Lima, Representante de la OPS/OMS en Honduras, Oficina Sanitaria Panamericana, Edificio Imperial–6o.y 7o.piso, Avenida República de Panamá frente a la Casa de Naciones Unidas, Tegucigalpa, MDC, Honduras, phone (504) 221–3721, 3705, 7718, fax 221–3706.

Jamaica (Bermuda and Cayman), Dr. Ernest Pate, Old Oceana Building, 7th Floor, 2–4 King St., Kingston, Jamaica, phone (876) 967–4626, 4691, fax 967–5189.

México, Dr. José Germán Rodríguez Tores, Representante Interino de la OPS/OMS en México, Oficina Sanitaria Panamericana, Edificio Torre Prisma, Horacio No. 1855, 3er piso, Of.305 Blvd. Manuel Avila Camacho 191).Colonia Los Morales Polanco, México D.F., 11510, México, phone (525) 52–55–5207–3009, fax 52–55–5207–2964.

Nicaragua, Dr. Patricio Rojas, Representante de la OPS/OMS en Nicaragua, Oficina Sanitaria Panamericana, Complejo Nacional de Salud, Camino a la Sabana, Apartado Postal 1309, Managua, Nicaragua, phone (505–2) 89–4200, 4800, fax 89–4999.

Panama, Dr. Guadalupe Verdejo, Representante de la OPS/OMS en Panamá, Ministerio de Salud, Avenida Gorgas, Edif. 261, 2 piso, Ancón, Panamá, Panamá, phone (507) 262–0030, fax 262–4052.

Paraguay, Dra. Carmen Rosa Serrano, Representant de la OPS/OMS en Paraguay, Edificio "Faro del Río" Mcal. López 957 Esq. Estados Unidos, Asunción, Paraguay, phone (595–21) 450–495, 496, 497, fax 450–498.

Peru, Dr. Manuel Peña, Representante de la OPS/OMS en Perú, Oficina Sanitaria Panamericana, Los Cedros 269, San Isidro, Lima 27, Perú, phone (51–1) 421–3030, fax 222–6405.

Suriname, Dr. Stephen Simon, PAHO/WHO Representative, Burenstraat #33, Paramaribo, Suriname, phone (597) 471–676, fax 471–568.

Trinidad and Tobago, Dr. Lilian Reneau-Vernon, 49 Jerningham Avenue, Port-of-Spain, Trinidad, phone (868) 624–7524, 4376, 5642, 5928, fax 624–5643.

Uruguay, Dr. José Fernando Dora, Representante de la OPS/OMS en Uruguay, Avenida Brasil 2697, Apts. 5, 6 y 8, 2do. Piso, 11300, Montevideo, Uruguay, phone (598–2) 707–3581, 3589, 3590, fax 707–3530.

Venezuela (Netherlands Antilles), Dr. Renato d'Affonseca Gusmão, Representante de la OPS/OMS en Venezuela, Oficina Sanitaria Panamericana, Avenida Sexta entre 5a y 6a, Transversal, Altamira, Caracas 1010, Venezuela, phone (212) 262–2085, fax 261–6069.

CENTERS

Caribbean Epidemiology Center (CAREC).—Dr. Carl James Hospedales, Director, 16–18 Jamaica Boulevard, Federation Park, Port-of Spain, Trinidad, phone (1–868) 622–4261, 4262, 3168, 3277, fax 622–2792.

Caribbean Food and Nutrition Institute (CFNI).—Dr. Fitzroy J. Henry, Director, University of the West Indies, Kingston 7, Jamaica, phone (1–876), 927–1540, 1541, 1927, fax 927–2657.

Field Office, United States-Mexico Border (FO/USMB).—Dr. Isaías Daniel Gutiérrez, Chief, Pan American Sanitary Bureau, 5400 Suncrest Dr., Suite C–4, El Paso, Texas, 79912, phone (915) 845–5950, fax 845–4361.

Institute of Nutrition of Central America and Panama (INCAP).—Dr. Hernán Delgado, Director, Carretera Roosevelt, Zona 11, Guatemala, Guatemala, phone (011–502) 471–5655, fax 473–6529.

Latin American Center and Caribbean Center on Health Sciences Information (BIREME).—Mr. Abel Laerte Packer, Director, Rua Botucatú 862, Vila Clementino, CEP.04023–062, São Paulo, SP, Brasil, phone (011–55–11) 576–9800, fax 571–1919, 575–8868.

Latin American Center for Perinatology and Human Development (CLAP).—Dr. José Fernando Dora, Director, Hospital de Clínicas, Piso 16, Montevideo, Uruguay, phone (011–598–2) 487–2929, 2930, 2931, 2933, fax 487–2593.

Pan American Institute for Food Protection and Zoonoses (INPPAZ).—Dr. Claudio Roberto Almeida, Director, Talcahuano 1660, B1640WAB–Martínez, Buenos Aires, Argentina, phone (011–54–11) 5789–4000, fax 4789–4013.

Pan American Center for Sanitary Engineering and Environmental Sciences (CEPIS).—Dr. Mauricio Pardón Ojeda, Director, Calle Los Pinos 259, Urbanización Camacho, Lima 12, Perú, phone 437–7019, fax 437–8289.

Pan American Foot-and-Mouth Disease Center (PANAFTOSA).—Dr. Eduardo Correa Melo, Director, Avenida Presidente Kennedy 7778, (Antiga Estrada Rio-Petrópolis), São Bento, Duque de Caxias, CEP 25040–000, Rio de Janeiro, Brasil, phone (011–55–21) 3661–9000, fax 3661–9001.

Regional Program on Bioethics.—Dr. Fernando Lolas Stepke, Director, Regional Program on Bioethics PAHO/WHO, Providencia 1017, Piso 7, Santiago de Chile, Chile, phone (011–56–2), 236–0330, fax 346–7219.

Pan American Health and Education Foundation.—Jess Gersky, Executive Director, 525 Twenty-Third Street, NW., Washington, DC 20037, phone (202) 974–3416, fax 974–3636.

PERMANENT JOINT BOARD ON DEFENSE, CANADA-UNITED STATES

CANADIAN SECTION

The Canadian Section can be contacted through the U.S. Military Secretary.

UNITED STATES SECTION

JCS J–5 North America Division, Pentagon, Room 2E973, Washington, DC 20318

phone (703) 695–4477

Members:
  Joint Staff.—RADM William D. Sullivan, Room 2E996, 697–9559.
  State Department.—Terry Breese, Room 3917, State Department, (202) 647–2273.
  OSD.—James Townsend, 697–7207.
  National Security Council.—Veronica Angulo, (202) 456–9135.
  USNORTHCOM.—BG Guy Dahlbeck, (719) 554–2200.
  Military Secretary.—LTC Patricia Dees, Room 2E973, 695–4477.
  Assistant Military Secretary.—TSgt Glen Burrick, Room 2E973, 695–4477.
  Political Secretary.—Felix Hernandez, Room 3917, State Department, (202) 647–2475.

SECRETARIAT OF THE PACIFIC COMMUNITY

B.P. D5, 98848 Noumea Cedex, New Caledonia, phone (687) 26.20.00, fax (687) 26.38.18, E-mail spc@spc.int, http://www.spc.int

Director-General.—Lourdes Pangelinan.
  Senior Deputy Director General, Suva.—Dr. Jimmie Rodgers.
  Deputy Director General, Noumea.—Yves Corbel.
  Director of Corporate Services.—Louni Hanipale Mose.
  Director of the Marine Resource Division.—Tim Adams.
  Head of the Planning Unit.—Richard Mann.

U.S. Contact: Bureau of East Asian and Pacific Affairs, Office of Australia, New Zealand and Pacific Island Affairs, Department of State, Washington, DC 20520, phone (202) 647–9690, fax (202) 647–0118

Countries and Territories Covered by the SPC:

American Samoa	Northern Mariana Islands
Australia	Palau
Cook Islands	Papua New Guinea
Federated States of Micronesia	Pitcairn Islands
Fiji	Samoa
France	Solomon Islands
French Polynesia	Tokelau
Guam	Tonga
Kiribati	Tuvalu
Marshall Islands	United Kingdom
Nauru	United States
New Caledonia	Vanuatu
New Zealand	Wallis and Futuna
Niue	

UNITED NATIONS

GENERAL ASSEMBLY

The General Assembly is composed of all 191 United Nations Member States.

SECURITY COUNCIL

The Security Council has 15 members. The United Nations Charter designates five States as permanent members, and the General Assembly elects 10 other members for two-year terms. The term of office for each non-permanent member of the Council ends on 31 December of the year indicated in parentheses next to its name.

The five permanent members of the Security Council are China, France, Russian Federation, United Kingdom and United States.

The 10 non-permanent members of the Council in 2005 are Algeria (2005), Argentina (2006), Benin (2005), Brazil (2005), Denmark (2006), Greece (2006), Japan (2006), Philippines (2005), Romania (2005), and United Republic of Tanzania (2006).

ECONOMIC AND SOCIAL COUNCIL

The Economic and Social Council has 54 members, elected for three-year terms by the General Assembly. The term of office for each member expires on 31 December of the year indicated in parentheses next to its name. Voting in the Council is by simple majority; each member has one vote. In 2005, the Council is composed of the following 54 States:

Albania (2007)	Japan (2005)
Armenia (2006)	Kenya (2005)
Australia (2007)	Lithuania (2007)
Azerbaijan (2005)	Malaysia (2005)
Bangladesh (2006)	Mauritius (2006)
Belgium (2006)	Mexico (2007)
Belize (2006)	Mozambique (2005)
Benin (2005)	Namibia (2006)
Brazil (2007)	Nicaragua (2005)
Canada (2006)	Nigeria (2006)
Chad (2007)	Pakistan (2007)
China (2007)	Panama (2006)
Colombia (2006)	Poland (2006)
Congo (2005)	Republic of Korea (2006)
Costa Rica (2007)	Russian Federation (2007)
Cuba (2005)	Saudi Arabia (2005)
Democratic Republic of the Congo (2007)	Senegal (2005)
Denmark (2007)	South Africa (2007)
Ecuador (2005)	Spain (2005)
France (2005)	Thailand (2007)
Germany (2005)	Tunisia (2006)
Guinea (2007)	Turkey (2005)
Iceland (2007)	United Arab Emirates (2006)
India (2007)	United Kingdom of Great Britain and
Indonesia (2006)	Northern Ireland (2007)
Ireland (2005)	United Republic of Tanzania (2006)
Italy (2006)	United States of America (2006)
Jamaica (2005)	

TRUSTEESHIP COUNCIL

The Trusteeship Council has five members: China, France, Russian Federation, United Kingdom and the United States. With the independence of Palau, the last remaining United Nations trust territory, the Council formerly suspended operation on 1 November 1994. By a resolution adopted on that day, the Council amended its rules of procedure to drop the obligation to meet annually and agreed to meet as occasion required—by its decision or the decision of its President, or at the request of a majority of its members or the General Assembly or the Security Council.

INTERNATIONAL COURT OF JUSTICE

The International Court of Justice has 15 members, elected by both the General Assembly and the Security Council. Judges hold nine-year terms.

The current composition of the court is as follows: President Shi Jiuyong (China); Vice-President Raymond Ranjeva (Madagascar). Judges: Ronny Abraham (France), Abdul G. Koroma (Sierra Leone), Vladlen S. Vereshchetin (Russian Federation), Rosalyn Higgins (United Kingdom), Gonzalo Parra-Aranguren (Venezuela), Pieter H. Kooijmans (Netherlands), Francisco Rezek (Brazil), Awn Shawkat Al-Khasawneh (Jordan), Thomas Buergenthal (United States of America), Nabil Elaraby (Egypt), Hisashi Owada (Japan), Bruno Simma (Germany), and Peter Tomka (Slovakia).

The Registrar of the Court is Mr. Philippe Couvreur (Belgium).

UNITED NATIONS SECRETARIAT

One United Nations Plaza, New York NY 10017, (212) 963–1234, http://www.un.org

Secretary General.—Kofi A. Annan (Ghana).
  Deputy Secretary.—Louise Fréchette (Canada).

EXECUTIVE OFFICE OF THE SECRETARY-GENERAL

Chief of Staff.—Mark Malloch Brown (UK).
  Assistant Secretary-General for Policy Planning.—Robert C. Orr (USA).
  Special Assistant.—Michael Moller.
  Spokesman.—Fred Eckhard (USA).

OFFICE OF INTERNAL OVERSIGHT SERVICES

Under-Secretary-General.—Inga-Britt Ahlenius (Sweden).

OFFICE OF LEGAL AFFAIRS

Under-Secretary-General and Legal Counsel.—Nicholas Michel (Switzerland).
  Assistant Secretary General.—Ralph Zacklin (United Kingdom).

DEPARTMENT OF POLITICAL AFFAIRS

Under-Secretary-General.—Sir Kieran Prendergast (United Kingdom).
  Assistant Secretary-General.—Tuliameni Kalomoh (Namibia).
  Assistant Secretary-General.—Danilo Türk (Slovenia).

DEPARTMENT FOR DISARMAMENT AFFAIRS

Under-Secretary-General.—Abe Nobugasu (Japan).

DEPARTMENT OF PEACE-KEEPING OPERATIONS

Under-Secretary-General.—Jean-Marie Guehenno (France).
  Assistant Secretary-General.—Hédi Annabi (Tunisia).
  Assistant Secretary-General.—Jane Holl Lute (USA).

OFFICE FOR THE COORDINATION OF HUMANITARIAN AFFAIRS

Under-Secretary-General, Emergency Relief Coordinator.—Jan Egeland (Norway).
  Deputy Emergency Relief Coordinator.—Yvette Stevens (Sierra Leone).
  Chief, Humanitarian Emergency Branch.—Kevin M. Kennedy (USA).

DEPARTMENT OF ECONOMIC AND SOCIAL AFFAIRS

Under-Secretary-General.—Jose Antonio Campo (Colombia).
  Assistant Secretary-General.—Patricio Civili (Italy).

DEPARTMENT OF GENERAL ASSEMBLY AND CONFERENCE MANAGEMENT

Under-Secretary-General.—Jian Chen (China).
  Assistant Secretary-General.—Angela Kane.

DEPARTMENT OF PUBLIC INFORMATION

Under-Secretary-General.—Shashi Tharoor (India).

DEPARTMENT OF MANAGEMENT

Under-Secretary-General.—Catherine Bertini (USA).
  Assistant Secretary-General, Controller.—Warren Sach (UK).
  Officer-in-Charge, Human Resources Management.—Dennis Beissel (USA).
  Officer-in-Charge, Central Support Services.—Andrew Toh (Singapore).

OFFICE OF THE SPECIAL REPRESENTATIVE OF THE SECRETARY–GENERAL FOR CHILDREN AND ARMED CONFLICT

Under-Secretary-General.—Olara Otunnu (Cote d'Ivoire).

UNITED NATIONS FUND FOR INTERNATIONAL PARTNERSHIPS

Executive Director.—Amir A. Dossal (United Kingdom).

UNITED NATIONS AT GENEVA (UNOG)

Palais des Nations, 1211 Geneva 10, Switzerland, phone (41–22) 917–1234.
  Director-General of UNOG.—Assistant Secretary-General Sergei A. Ordzhonikidze (Russian
  Federation).

UNITED NATIONS AT VIENNA (UNOV)

Vienna International Centre, PO Box 500, A–1400 Vienna, Austria, phone (43–1) 21345.
  Director-General.—Antonio Maria Costa (Italy).

UNITED NATIONS INFORMATION CENTRE

1775 K Street, NW., Suite 400, Washington, DC 20006

phone: (202) 331–8670, fax: (202) 331–9191, email: unicdc@unicwash.org

http://www.unicwash.org

Deputy Director.—David Smith (acting) (UK).

REGIONAL ECONOMIC COMMISSIONS

Economic Commission for Africa (ECA), Africa Hall, P.O. Box 3001, Addis Ababa Ethiopia,
  phone (251–1) 51–72–00, fax (251–1) 51–44–16.
  Executive Secretary.—K.Y. Amoako (Ghana).

Economic Commission for Europe (ECE) Palais des Nations, 1211 Geneva 10, Switzerland,
  phone (41–22) 917–2893.
  Executive Secretary.—Brigita Schmognerova (Slovakia).

Economic Commission for Latin America and the Caribbean (ECLAC), Casilla 179–D, Santiago, Chile, phone (56–2) 210–2000, fax (56–2) 208–0252.
Executive Secretary.—Jose Luis Machinea (Argentina).

Economic and Social Commission for Asia and the Pacific (ESCAP), United Nations Building, Réjdamnern Avenue, Bangkok, Thailand, phone (66–2) 288–1234, fax (66–2) 288–1000.
Executive Secretary.—Hak-Su Kim (Republic of Korea).

Economic and Social Commission for Western Asia (ESCWA), P.O. Box 11–8575, Riad El-Solh Square, Beirut, Lebanon, phone 9611–981301, fax 9611– 981510.
Executive Secretary.—Mervat Tallawy (Egypt).

Regional Commissions, New York Office, (ECE, ESCAP, ECLAC, ECA, ESCWA), fax 963–1500.
Chief.—Sulafa Al-Bassam (Saudi Arabia).
Senior Economic Affairs Officer.—Kazi Rahman (Bangladesh).
Liaison Officer.—Margaret McCaffery (USA).
Documentation.—Maria Baquero (Ecuador).

FUNDS, PROGRAMMES, AND BODIES OF THE UNITED NATIONS

Advisory Committee on Administrative and Budgetary Questions (ACABQ), One United Nations Plaza, New York NY 10017, phone (212) 963–7456.
Chairman.—Vladimir V. Kuznetsov.

Office of the High Commissioner for Human Rights, Palais des Nations, 8–14 Avenue de la Paix, 1211 Geneva 10, Switzerland, phone (41–22) 917–1234.
High Commissioner for Human Rights.—Louise Arbour (Canada).

International Civil Service Commission (ICSC), One United Nations Plaza, New York NY 10017, phone (212) 963–8464.
Chairman.—Mohsen Bel Hadj Amor (Tunisia).

Joint Inspection Unit (JIU), Palais des Nations, 1211 Geneva 10, Switzerland, phone (41–22) 917–1234.
Chairman.—Ion Gorita (Romania).

Panel of External Auditors of the UN, Specialized Agencies and International Atomic Energy Agency, One United Nations Plaza, New York NY 10017, phone (212) 963–1234.
Chairman.—Shauket A. Fakie (South Africa).

United Nations Human Settlements Programme (UN–HABITAT), UN Office at Nairobi, PO Box 30030, Nairobi Kenya, phone (254–2) 621–1234.
Executive Director: Anna Kajumulo Tibaijuka (UR of Tanzania).

United Nations Children's Fund (UNICEF), UNICEF House, 3 UN Plaza, New York NY 10017, phone (212) 326–7000.
Executive Director.—Ann Veneman (USA).

United Nations Conference on Trade and Development (UNCTAD), Palais des Nations, 8–14 Avenue de la Paix, 1211 Geneva 10, Switzerland, phone (41–22) 917–1234.
Officer-in-Charge.—Carlos Fortin (Chile).

United Nations Development Fund for Women (UNIFEM), 304 East 45th Street, Sixth Floor, New York NY 10017, phone (212) 906–6400.
Director.—Noeleen Heyzer (Singapore).

United Nations Development Programme (UNDP), 1 United Nations Plaza, New York NY 10017, phone (212) 906–5000.
Administrator.—Mark Malloch Brown (United Kingdom).

United Nations Development Programme (UNDP), Liaison Office, 1775 K Street, NW., Suite 420, Washington DC 20006, phone (202) 331–9130.
Director.—Michael Marek (USA).

United Nations Environment Programme (UNEP), PO Box 30552, Nairobi Kenya, phone (254–2) 621–1234.
Executive Director.—Klaus Topfer (Germany).

United Nations High Commissioner for Refugees (UNHCR), Case Postale 2500, CH–1211 Geneve 2 Depot, Switzerland, phone (41–22) 739–8111.
High Commissioner.—Wendy Chamberlin (acting).

United Nations High Commissioner for Refugees (UNHCR), Regional Office for the United States and the Caribbean, 1775 K Street, NW., Third Floor, Washington DC 20006, phone (202) 296–5191.
Regional Representative.—Kolude Doherty (Nigeria).

United Nations Institute for Disarmament Research (UNIDIR), Palais des Nations, 1211 Geneva 10, Switzerland, phone (41–22) 917–4292.
Director.—Patricia Lewis (United Kingdom).

United Nations Institute for Training and Research (UNITAR), Palais des Nations, 1211 Geneva 10, Switzerland, phone (41–22) 798–5850.
Executive Director.—Marcel A. Boisard (Switzerland).

United Nations International Drug Control Programme (UNODC), PO Box 500, A–1400 Vienna, Austria, phone (43–1) 21345 ext. 4251.
Executive Director.—Antonio Maria Costa (Italy).

United Nations International Research and Training Institute for the Advancement of Women (INSTRAW), PO Box 21747, Santo Domingo, Dominican Republic, phone (1–809) 685–2111.
Director.—Carmen Moreno (Mexico).

United Nations Interregional Crime and Justice Research Institute (UNICRI), Via Giulia 52, 00186 Rome, Italy, phone (39–6) 687–7437.
Director.—Alberto Bradanini (Italy).

United Nations Office for Project Services (UNOPS), Room 1442, 220 East 42nd Street, New York NY 10017, phone (212) 906–6500.
Executive Director.—Gerald Walzer (Austria).

United Nations Population Fund (UNFPA), 220 East 42nd Street, New York NY 10017, phone (212) 297–5000.
Executive Director.—Thoraya Ahmed Obaid (Saudi Arabia).

United Nations Relief and Works Agency for Palestine Refugees in the Near East (UNRWA), Vienna International Centre, PO Box 700, A–1400 Vienna Austria, phone (43–1) 21345 ext. 4531.
Commissioner-General.—Peter Hansen (Denmark).

United Nations Research Institute for Social Development (UNRISD), Palais des Nations, 1211 Geneva 10, Switzerland, phone (41–22) 798–8400.
Director.—Thandika Mkandawire (Sweden).

United Nations Volunteers Programme (UNV), Postfach 260111, D–53153 Bonn Germany, phone (49–228) 815–2000.
Executive Coordinator.—Ad de Raad (Netherlands).

World Food Programme (WFP), 426 Via Cristoforo Colombo, 00145 Rome Italy, phone (39–6) 552–2821.
Executive Director.—James Morris (USA).

United Nations University (UNU), 53–70, Jingumae 5–Chome, Shibuya-Ku, Tokyo 150, Japan, phone (81–3) 3499–2811.
Rector.—Hans van Ginkel (Netherlands).

SPECIALIZED AGENCIES

Food and Agriculture Organization (FAO), Via delle Terme di Caracalla, 00100 Rome, Italy, phone (39–6) 52251.
Director-General.—Jacques Diouf (Senegal).

Food and Agriculture Organization, Liaison Office for North America, Suite 300, 2175 K Street, NW., Washington DC 20437, phone (202) 653–2400.
Director.—Charles Riemenschneider (USA).

International Civil Aviation Organization (ICAO), 1000 Sherbrooke Street West, Montreal, Quebec H3A 2R2 Canada, phone (1–514) 285–8221.
Secretary-General.—Dr. Taïeb Chérif (Algeria).

International Fund for Agricultural Development (IFAD), Via del Serafico 107, 00142 Rome, Italy, phone (39–6) 54591.
President.—Lennart Bage (Sweden).
External Affairs Department, IFAD North American Liaison Office, Washington, DC, Suite 410, 1775 K Street, NW., Washington, DC 20006, phone (202) 331–9099.
Representative.—Cheryl Morden (USA).

International Labour Organization (ILO), 4, Routes des Morillons, Ch–1211 Geneva 22, Switzerland, phone (41–22) 799–6111.
Director-General.—Juan Somavia (Chile).
ILO Washington Branch Office, 1828 L Street, NW., Suite 801, Washington, DC 20036, phone (202) 653–7652.
Interim Director.—Larry Kohler (USA).

International Maritime Organization (IMO), 4 Albert Embankment, London SE1 7SR, England, phone (44–171) 735–7611.
Secretary-General.—Efthimios Mitropoulos (Greece).

International Monetary Fund (IMF), 700 19th Street NW, Washington, DC 20431, phone (202) 623–7000.
Managing Director.—Rodrigo de Rato y Figaredo (Spain).

International Telecommunications Union (ITU), Palais des Nations, 1211 Geneva 20, Switzerland, phone (41–22) 730–5111.
Secretary-General.—Yoshio Utsumi (Japan).

United Nations Educational, Scientific and Cultural Organization (UNESCO), 7 Place de Fontenoy, 75732 Paris, 07 SP France, phone (33–1) 4568–1000.
Director-General.—Koichiro Matsuura (Japan).

United Nations Industrial Development Organization (UNIDO), PO Box 300, Vienna International Centre, A–1400 Vienna, Austria, phone (43–1) 21131–0.
Director-General.—Carlos Alfredo Magarinos (Argentina).

Universal Postal Union (UPU), Weltpoststrasse 4, Case Postale, 3000 Berne 15, Switzerland, phone (41–31) 350–3111.
Director-General.—Edouard Dayan (France).

World Bank Group, 1818 H Street NW, Washington DC 20433, phone (202) 477–1234.
President.—Paul Wolfowitz (USA).

World Health Organization (WHO), 20 Avenue Appia, 1211 Geneva 27, Switzerland, phone (41–22) 791–2111.
Director-General.—Jong-Wook Lee (Republic of Korea).
World Health Organization Liaison Office, 1775 K Street NW, 4th Floor, Washington, DC 20006, phone (202) 331–9081.
Special Adviser to the Director-General.—Thomas Loftus (USA).

World Intellectual Property Organization (WIPO), 34 Chemin des Colombetts, 1211 Geneva 20, Switzerland, phone (41–22) 730–9111.
Director General.—Kamil Idris (Sudan).
World Intellectual Property Organization Coordination Office, 1775 K Street, NW., Washington, DC 20006, phone (202) 454–2460.
Coordinator.—Suzanne Stoll.

World Meteorological Organization (WMO), Case postale No.2300, CH–1211 Geneva 2, Switzerland, phone (41–22) 730–8111.
Secretary-General.—Michel Jarraud (France).

RELATED BODY

International Atomic Energy Agency (IAEA), PO Box 100, Vienna International Centre, A–1400 Vienna, Austria, phone (43–1) 2060–0.
Director General.—Mohamed Elbaradei (Egypt).
(The IAEA is an independent intergovernmental organization under the aegis of the UN).

SPECIAL AND PERSONAL REPRESENTATIVES AND ENVOYS OF THE SECRETARY–GENERAL

AFRICA

African Region:
Special Adviser for Special Assignments.—Ibrahim Gambari (Nigeria).
Special Adviser.—Mohamed Sahnoun (Algeria).
Burundi:
Special Representative.—Carolyn McAskie (Canada).

Principal Deputy Special Representative.—Nureldin Satti (Sudan).
Deputy Special Representative.—Ibrahima Fall (Senegal).

Central African Republic:
Representative.—General Lamine Cissé (Senegal).

Côte d'Ivoire:
Special Representative.—Pierre Schori (Sweden).
Principal Deputy Special Representative.—Alan Doss (United Kingdom).
Deputy Special Representative.—Abdoulaye Mar Dieye (Senegal).

Democratic Republic of the Congo:
Special Representative.—William Lacy Swing (United States).
Deputy Special Representative.—Ross Mountain (New Zealand).
Special Envoy.—Mustapha Niasse (Senegal).

Ethiopia/Eritrea:
Special Envoy.—Lloyd Axworthy (Canada).
Special Representative.—Legwaila Joseph Legwaila (Botswana).
Deputy Special Representative.—Sissel Ekaas (Norway).

Great Lakes Region:
Special Representative.—Ibrahima Fall (Senegal).

Guinea-Bissau:
Representative.—João Bernardo Honwana (Mozambique).

Horn of Africa:
Special Envoy.—Martti Ahtisaari (Finland).

Liberia:
Special Representative.—Jacques Paul Klein (United States).
Deputy Special Representative for Operations.—Steinar Bjornsson (Iceland).
Special Representative for Relief, Recovery and Rehabilitation.—Abou Moussa (Chad).

Sierra Leone:
Special Representative.—Daudi Ngelautwa Mwakawago (Tanzania).
Deputy Special Representative.—Victor da Silva Angelo (Portugal).

Somalia:
Representative.—Winston A. Tubman (Liberia).

Sudan:
Special Representative.—Jan Pronk (Netherlands).
Deputy Special Representative.—Taye-Brook Zerihoun (Ethiopia).
Deputy Special Representative.—Manuel Aranda da Silva (Mozambique).
Special Envoy.—Tom Eric Vraalsen (Norway).

West Africa:
Special Representative.—Ahmedou Ould-Abdallah (Mauritania).

Western Sahara:
Special Representative.—Alvaro de Soto (Perú).

THE AMERICAS

Latin American Region:
Special Adviser.—Diego Cordovez (Ecuador).

Colombia:
Special Adviser.—James LeMoyne (United States).

Guyana-Venezuela:
Personal Representative.—Oliver Jackman (Barbados).

Haiti:
Special Representative.—Juan Gabriel Valdés (Chile).
Principal Deputy Special Representative.—Hocine Medili (Algeria).
Deputy Special Representative.—Adama Guindo (Mali).
Special Adviser.—John Reginald Dumas (Trinidad and Tobago).

ASIA AND THE PACIFIC

Afghanistan:
Special Representative.—Jean Arnault (France).
Principal Deputy Special Representative.—Ameerah Haq (Bangladesh).
Deputy Special Representative.—Filippo Grandi (Italy).

East Timor:
Special Representative.—Sukehiro Hasegawa (Japan).
Deputy Special Representative.—Atul Khare (India).
Myanmar:
Special Envoy.—Razali Ismail (Malaysia).
Papua New Guinea:
Observer Mission.—Tor Stenbock (Norway).
Tajikistan:
Representative.—Vladimir Sotirov (Bulgaria).

EUROPE

European Region:
Special Adviser.—Jean-Bernard Merimee (France).
Cyprus:
Special Representative.—Zbigniew Wlosowicz (Poland).
Former Yugoslav Republic of Macedonia-Greece:
Personal Envoy.—Matthew Nimetz (United States).
Georgia:
Special Representative.—Heidi Tagliavini (Switzerland).
Kosovo:
Special Representative.—Soren Jessen-Petersen (Denmark).
　Principal Deputy Special Representative.—Lawrence Rossin (United States).
　Deputy Special Representative for Police and Justice.—Jean Dussourd (France).
　Deputy Special Representative for Civil Administration.—Francesco Bastagli (Italy).
　Deputy Special Representative for Institution Building (OSCE).—Pascal Fieschi (France).
　Deputy Special Representative for Reconstruction (European Union).—Joachim Rücker (Germany).

MIDDLE EAST

Middle East:
Special Envoy for the Implementation of Security Council Resolution 1559.—Terje Roed-Larsen (Norway).
Iraq:
Special Representative.—Ashraf Jehangir Qazi (Pakistan).
　Deputy Special Representative.—Staffan de Mistura (Sweden).
Southern Lebanon:
Personal Representative.—Geir O. Pedersen (Norway).

OTHER HIGH LEVEL APPOINTMENTS

Children and Armed Conflict:
Special Representative.—Olara Otunnu (Uganda).
Commonwealth of Independent States (CIS):
Special Envoy.—Yuli Vorontsov (Russian Federation).
Conference on Disarmament:
Personal Representative.—Sergei A. Ordzhonikidze (Russian Federation).
Gender Issues and Advancement of Women:
Special Adviser.—Rachel N. Mayanja (Uganda).
Global Compact:
Special Adviser.—John Ruggie (United States).
HIV / AIDS in Africa:
Special Envoy.—Stephen Lewis (Canada).
HIV / AIDS in Asia:
Special Envoy.—Nafis Sadik (Pakistan).
HIV / AIDS in the Caribbean Region:
Special Envoy.—George Alleyne (Barbados).
HIV / AIDS in Eastern Europe:
Special Envoy.—Lars O. Kallings (Sweden).

Human Rights:
Special Representative.—Hina Jilani (Pakistan).
Internally Displaced Persons:
Representative.—Walter Kälin (Switzerland).
Least Developed Countries, Landlocked Developing Countries, and Small Island Developing States:
High Representative.—Anwarul K. Chowdhury (Bangladesh).
Millennium Development Goals:
Special Adviser.—Jeffrey D. Sachs (United States).
Executive Coordinator.—Eveline Herfkens (Netherlands).
Prevention of Genocide:
Special Adviser.—Juan E. Méndez (Argentina).
Special Adviser.—Lakhdar Brahimi (Algeria).
Special Adviser.—Maurice Strong (Canada).
Sport for Development and Peace:
Special Adviser.—Adolf Ogi (Switzerland).
United Nations International School (UNIS):
Special Representative.—Silvia Fuhrman (United States).
World Summit on Information Society:
Special Adviser.—Nitin Desai (India).

WORLD BANK GROUP

The World Bank Group comprises five organizations: the International Bank for Reconstruction and Development (IBRD), the International Development Association (IDA), the International Finance Corporation (IFC), the Multilateral Investment Guarantee Agency (MIGA) and the International Centre for the Settlement of Investment Disputes (ICSID).

Headquarters: 1818 H Street NW., 20433, (202) 473–1000

INTERNATIONAL BANK FOR RECONSTRUCTION AND DEVELOPMENT

President.—James D. Wolfensohn.
Managing Director.—Shengman Zhang.
Senior Vice President and General Counsel.—Roberto Danino.
Senior Vice President, Development Economics, and Chief Economist.—Francois Bourguignon.
Senior Vice President and Head, Human Development Network.—Jean-Louis Sarbib.
Chief Financial Officer.—John Wilton (acting).
Vice President and Chief Information Officer and Head, Information Solutions Network.—Mohamed V. Muhsin.
Vice President and Controller.—Fayezul Choudhury.
Vice President and Corporate Secretary.—W. Paatii Ofusu-Amah.
Vice President and Treasurer.—Graeme P. Wheeler.
Vice President of:
 Africa.—Gobind Nankani.
 East Asia and Pacific.—Jemal-ud-din Kassum.
 Environmentally and Socially Sustainable Development Network.—Ian Johnson.
 Europe (External Affairs).—Jean-François Rischard.
 Europe and Central Asia.—Shigeo Katsu.
 External and UN Affairs.—Ian A. Goldin.
 Human Resources.—Xavier E. Coll.
 Infrastructure.—Katherine Sierra.
 Japan (External Affairs).—Yukio Yoshimura.
 Latin America and the Caribbean.—Pamela Cox.
 Middle East and North Africa.—Christiaan J. Poortman.
 Network, Operational Policy and Country Services.—James W. Adams.
 Poverty Reduction and Economic Management Network.—Danny Leipziger.
 Private Sector Development (World Bank and IFC) and Chief Economist (IFC).—Michael U. Klein.
 Resource Mobilization and Cofinancing.—Geoffrey B. Lamb.
 South Asia.—Praful Patel.

Strategy, Finance and Risk Management.—John Wilton.
World Bank Institute.—Frannie Leautier.
Director-General, Operations Evaluation.—Gregory K. Ingram.
Counselor to the President for U.S. Affairs.—Suzanne Rich Folsom.

OTHER WORLD BANK OFFICES

London: New Zealand House, 15th Floor, Haymarket, London SW1Y 4TE, England.
Geneva: 3, Chemin Louis Dunant, CP 66, CH 1211, Geneva 10, Switzerland.
Paris: 66, Avenue d'Iena, 75116 Paris, France.
Brussels: 10, rue Montoyer, B–1000 Brussels, Belgium.
Tokyo: Fukoku Seimei Building, 10th Floor, 2–2–2 Uchisawai-cho, Chiyoda-Ku, Tokyo 100, Japan.
Sydney: c/o South Pacific Project Facility, 89 York Street, Level 8, GPO Box 1612, Sydney, NSW 2000, Australia.
Frankfurt: Bockenheimer Landstrasse 109, 60325 Frankfurt am Main, Germany.

BOARD OF EXECUTIVE DIRECTORS

Bahrain, Egypt (Arab Republic of), Iraq, Jordan, Kuwait, Lebanon, Libya, Maldives, Oman, Qatar, Syrian Arab Republic, United Arab Emirates, Yemen (Republic of).
Executive Director.—Mahdy Ismail Aljazzaf.
Alternate.—Mohamed Kamel Amr.
Saudi Arabia.
Executive Director.—Yahya Abdullah M. Alyahya.
Alternate.—Abdulrahman M. Almofadhi.
Austria, Belarus, Belgium, Czech Republic, Hungary, Kazakhstan, Luxembourg, Slovak Republic, Slovenia, Turkey.
Executive Director.—Gino Alzetta.
Alternate.—Meliá Nemli.
Australia, Cambodia, Kiribati, Korea (Republic of), Marshall Islands, Micronesia (Federated States of), Mongolia, New Zealand, Palau, Papua New Guinea, Samoa, Solomon Islands, Vanuatu.
Executive Director.—John Austin.
Alternate.—Terry O'Brien.
Albania, Greece, Italy, Malta, Portugal, San Marino, Timor-Leste.
Executive Director.—Biagio Bossone.
Alternate.—Nuno Mota Pinto.
United States.
Executive Director.—Robert B. Holland III (acting).
Brazil, Colombia, Dominican Republic, Ecuador, Haiti, Panama, Philippines, Suriname, Trinidad and Tobago.
Executive Director.—Octaviano Canuto.
Alternate.—Jeremias N. Paul, Jr.
Germany.
Executive Director.—Eckhard Deutscher.
Alternate.—Walter Hermann.
Afghanistan, Algeria, Ghana, Iran (Islamic Republic of), Morocco, Pakistan, Tunisia.
Executive Director.—Sid Dib.
Alternate.—Tanwir Ali Agha.
France.
Executive Director.—Pierre Duquesne.
Alternate.—Anthony Requin.
Benin, Burkina Faso, Cameroon, Cape Verde, Central African Republic, Chad, Comoros, Congo (Democratic Republic of), Congo (Republic of), Cote d'Ivoire, Djibouti, Equatorial Guinea, Gabon, Guinea, Guinea-Bissau, Madagascar, Mali, Mauritania, Mauritius, Niger, Rwanda, Sao Tome and Principe, Senegal, Togo.
Executive Director.—Paulo F. Gomes.
Alternate.—Louis Philippe Ong Seng.
Brunei Darussalam, Fiji, Indonesia, Lao People's Democratic Republic, Malaysia, Myanmar, Nepal, Singapore, Thailand, Tonga, Vietnam.
Executive Director.—Herwidayatmo.
Alternate.—Nursiah Arshad.

Denmark, Estonia, Finland, Iceland, Latvia, Lithuania, Norway, Sweden.
  Executive Director.—Thorsteinn Ingolfsson.
    Alternate.—Svein Aass.
Russian Federation.
  Executive Director.—Alexey G. Kvasov.
    Alternate.—Eugene Miagkov.
Costa Rica, El Salvador, Guatemala, Honduras, Mexico, Nicaragua, Spain, Venezuela
  (Republica Bolivariana de).
  Executive Director.—Luis Marti.
    Alternate.—Jorge Familiar.
Antigua and Barbuda, Bahamas (The), Barbados, Belize, Canada, Dominica, Grenada, Guyana,
  Ireland, Jamaica, St. Kitts and Nevis, St. Lucia, St. Vincent and the Grenadines.
  Executive Director.—Marcel Masse.
    Alternate.—Gobind Ganga.
Armenia, Bosnia and Herzegovina, Bulgaria, Croatia, Cyprus, Georgia, Israel, Macedonia
  (former Yugoslav Republic of), Moldova, Netherlands, Romania, Ukraine.
  Executive Director.—Ad Melkert.
    Alternate.—Tamara Solyanyk.
Japan.
  Executive Director.—Yoshio Okubo.
    Alternate.—Toshio Oya.
Argentina, Bolivia, Chile, Paraguay, Peru, Uruguay.
  Executive Director.—Jaime Quijandria.
    Alternate.—Alieto Guadagni.
United Kingdom.
  Executive Director.—Tom Scholar.
    Alternate.—Caroline Sergeant.
Angola, Botswana, Burundi, Eritrea, Ethiopia, Gambia (The), Kenya, Lesotho, Liberia, Malawi,
  Mozambique, Namibia, Nigeria, Seychelles, Sierra Leone, South Africa, Sudan, Swaziland,
  Tanzania, Uganda, Zambia, Zimbabwe.
  Executive Director.—Mathias Sinamenye.
    Alternate.—Mulu Ketsela.
Bangladesh, Bhutan, India, Sri Lanka.
  Executive Director.—Chander Mohan Vasudev.
    Alternate.—Akbar Ali Khan.
Azerbaijan, Serbia and Montenegro, Kyrgyz Republic, Poland, Switzerland, Tajikistan,
  Turkmenistan, Uzbekistan, Yugoslavia (Fed. Rep. of).
  Executive Director.—Pietro Veglio.
    Alternate.—Jakub Karnowski.
China.
  Executive Director.—Jianyi Zou.
    Alternate.—Jinlin Yang.

INTERNATIONAL DEVELOPMENT ASSOCIATION

[The officers, executive directors, and alternates are the same as those of the International
Bank for Reconstruction and Development.]

INTERNATIONAL FINANCE CORPORATION

President.—James D. Wolfensohn.
Executive Vice President.—Assaad J. Jabre (acting).
  Vice President and Corporate Secretary.—W. Paatii Ofusu-Amah.
  Vice President:
    Finance and Treasurer.—Nina Shapiro.
    Human Resources and Administration.—Dorothy H. Berry.
    Operations.—Assaad J. Jabre.
    Portfolio and Risk Management.—Farida Khambata.
    Private Sector Development / Chief Economist.—Michael U. Klein.
  Director General, Operations Evaluation.—Gregory K. Ingram.
  Chief Information Officer and Corporate Business Informatics.—Guy-Pierre de Poerck.
  Compliance Advisor / Ombudsman.—Meg Taylor.

General Counsel.—Jennifer A. Sullivan.
Corporate Relations Unit Manager.—Joseph O'Keefe.
Director, Office of:
    Agribusiness.—Jean-Paul Pinard.
    Controller's and Budgeting.—Allen F. Shapiro.
    Corporate Portfolio and Risk Management.—Marc A. Babin.
    Credit Review.—Sakdiyiam Kupasrimonkol.
    Environment and Social Development.—Rachel Kyte.
    Financial Operations.—Avil Hofman.
    Global Financial Markets.—Jyrki Koskelo.
    Global Information and Communications Technologies.—Mohsen A. Khalil.
    Global Manufacturing and Services.—Dimitris Tsitsiragos.
    Health and Education.—Guy M. Ellena.
    Infrastructure.—Francisco A. Tourreilles.
    Municipal Fund.—Declan J. Duff.
    Oil, Gas, Mining and Chemicals.—Rashad-Rudolf Kaldany.
    Operations Evaluation Group.—William E. Stevenson.
    Private Equity and Investment Funds.—Haydee Celaya.
    Risk Management and Financial Policy.—Lakshmi Shyam-Sunder.
    Special Operations.—Maria Da Graca Domínguez.
    Trust Funds.—Mwaghazi Mwachofi.
Central and Eastern Europe.—Edward A. Nassim.
East Asia and Pacific.—Javed Hamid.
Latin America and Caribbean.—Atul Mehta.
Middle East and North Africa.—Sami Haddad.
South Asia.—Ivad M. Malas.
Southern Europe and Central Asia.—Khosrow K. Zamani.
Sub-Saharan Africa.—Richard L. Ranken.

MULTILATERAL INVESTMENT GUARANTEE AGENCY

President.—James D. Wolfensohn.
    Vice President and Corporate Secretary.—W. Paatii Ofosu-Amah.
    Executive Vice President.—Yukiko Omura.
    Vice President and General Counsel, Legal Affairs and Claims Group.—Luis Dodero.
    Compliance Advisor/Ombudsman (ICC & MIGA).—Meg Taylor.
    Director of:
        External Outreach and Partners Group.—Moina Varkie.
        Operations Evaluation Unit.—Aysegul Akin-Karasapan.
        Operations Group.—Tessie San Martin.
    Director and Chief Economist, Economics and Policy Group.—Frank Lysy.
    Director and Chief Financial Officer, Finance and Risk Management Group.—Amedee Prouvost.

FOREIGN DIPLOMATIC OFFICES
IN THE UNITED STATES

AFGHANISTAN

Embassy of Afghanistan
2341 Wyoming Avenue, NW., Washington, DC 20008
phone (202) 483–6410, fax (202) 483–6488
His Excellency Said Tayeb Jawad
Consular Office: New York, New York

ALBANIA

Embassy of the Republic of Albania
2100 S Street NW., Washington, DC 20008
phone (202) 223–4942, fax (202) 628–7342
His Excellency Dr. Fatos Tarifa
Ambassador E. and P.

ALGERIA

Embassy of the Democratic and Popular Republic of Algeria
2118 Kalorama Road NW., Washington, DC 20008
phone (202) 265–2800, fax (202) 667–2174
His Excellency Idriss Jazairy
Ambassador E. and P.

Iraqi Interests Section

1801 P Street NW., Washington, DC 20036
phone (202) 483–7500, fax (202) 462–5066

ANDORRA

Embassy of Andorra
Two United Nations Plaza, 25th Floor, New York, NY 10017
phone (212) 750–8064, fax (212) 750–6630
Ms. Jelena V. Pia-Comella
Minister Counselor

ANGOLA

Embassy of the Republic of Angola
2108 16th Street NW., Washington, DC 20009
phone (202) 785–1156, fax (202) 785–1258
Her Excellency Josefina Pitra Diakite
Ambassador E. and P.
Consular Offices:
New York, New York
Texas, Houston

ANTIGUA AND BARBUDA

Embassy of Antigua and Barbuda
3216 New Mexico Avenue, NW., Washington, DC 20016
phone (202) 362–5122/5166/5211, fax (202) 362–5225

Her Excellency Deborah Lovell
Ambassador E. and P.
Consular Office: Florida, Miami

ARGENTINA

Embassy of the Argentine Republic
1600 New Hampshire Avenue, NW., Washington, DC 20009
phone (202) 238–6400, fax (202) 332–3171
His Excellency José Octavio Bordon
Ambassador E. and P.
Consular Offices:
California, Los Angeles
Florida, Miami
Georgia, Atlanta
Illinois, Chicago
New York, New York
Texas, Houston

ARMENIA

Embassy of the Republic of Armenia
2225 R Street NW., Washington, DC 20008
phone (202) 319–1976, fax (202) 319–2982
His Excellency Arman John Kirakossian
Ambassador E. and P.
Consular Office: California, Los Angeles

AUSTRALIA

Embassy of Australia
1601 Massachusetts Avenue, NW., Washington, DC 20036–2273
phone (202) 797–3000, fax (202) 797–3168
His Excellency Michael Thawley
Ambassador E. and P.
Consular Offices:
California:
Los Angeles
San Francisco
Colorado, Denver
Georgia, Atlanta
Hawaii, Honolulu
Illinois, Chicago
Massachusetts, Boston
New York, New York

AUSTRIA

Embassy of Austria
3524 International Court NW., Washington, DC 20008–3027

phone (202) 895–6700, fax (202) 895–6750
Her Excellency Eva Nowotny
Ambassador E. and P.
Consular Offices:
 California:
  Los Angeles
  San Francisco
 Colorado, Denver
 Florida, Miami
 Georgia, Atlanta
 Hawaii, Honolulu
 Illinois, Chicago
 Louisiana, New Orleans
 Michigan, Detroit
 Minnesota, Minneapolis
 Missouri, Kansas City
 New York, New York
 Pennsylvania, Philadelphia
 Puerto Rico, San Juan
 Texas, Houston

AZERBAIJAN

Embassy of the Republic of Azerbaijan
2741 34th Street NW., Washington, DC 20008
phone (202) 337–3500, fax (202) 337–5911
His Excellency Hafiz Mir Jalal Pashayev
Ambassador E. and P.

BAHAMAS

Embassy of the Commonwealth of The Bahamas
2220 Massachusetts Avenue, NW., Washington, DC
 20008
phone (202) 319–2660, fax (202) 319–2668
His Excellency Joshua Sears
Ambassador E. and P.
Consular Offices:
 Florida, Miami
 New York, New York

BAHRAIN

Embassy of the State of Bahrain
3502 International Drive NW., Washington, DC
 20008
phone (202) 342–0741, fax (202) 362–2192
Sheikh Khalifa Ali Al-Khalifa
Ambassador E. and P.
Consular Offices:
 New York, New York

BANGLADESH

Embassy of the People's Republic of Bangladesh
3510 International Drive NW., Washington, DC
 20008
phone (202) 244–0183, fax (202) 244–2771
His Excellency Shamsher M. Cnowbhury
Ambassador E. and P.
Consular Offices:
 California, Los Angeles
 Hawaii, Honolulu

Louisiana, New Orleans
New York, New York

BARBADOS

Embassy of Barbados
2144 Wyoming Avenue, NW., Washington, DC
 20008
phone (202) 939–9200, fax (202) 332–7467
His Excellency Michael Ian King
Ambassador E. and P.
Consular Offices:
 California, Los Angeles
 Florida, Miami
 New York, New York

BELARUS

Embassy of the Republic of Belarus
1619 New Hampshire Avenue, NW., Washington,
 DC 20009
phone (202) 986–1604, fax (202) 986–1805
His Excellency Mikhail Khvostov
Ambassador E. and P.
Consular Office: New York, New York

BELGIUM

Embassy of Belgium
3330 Garfield Street NW., Washington, DC 20008
phone (202) 333–6900, fax (202) 333–3079
His Excellency Franciskus Van Daele
Ambassador E. and P.
Consular Offices:
 California, Los Angeles
 Georgia, Atlanta
 Illinois, Chicago
 New York, New York
 Texas, Houston

BELIZE

Embassy of Belize
2535 Massachusetts Avenue, NW., Washington, DC
 20008
phone (202) 332–9636, fax (202) 332–6888
Her Excellency Lisa Shoman
Ambassador E. and P.
Consular Offices:
 California, Los Angeles
 Puerto Rico, San Juan
 Texas, Houston

BENIN

Embassy of the Republic of Benin
2124 Kalorama Road NW., Washington, DC 20008
phone (202) 232–6656, fax (202) 265–1996
His Excellency Segbe Cyrille Oguin
Ambassador E. and P.

BHUTAN

Consular Office:
 New York, New York

BOLIVIA

Embassy of the Republic of Bolivia
3014 Massachusetts Avenue, NW., Washington, DC
  20008
phone (202) 483-4410, fax (202) 328-3712
Her Excellency Jaime Aparicio
Ambassador E. and P.
Consular Offices:
  California, San Francisco
  Florida, Miami
  Georgia, Atlanta
  Massachusetts, Boston
  New York, New York
  Texas, Houston

BOSNIA AND HERZEGOVINA

Embassy of Bosnia and Herzegovina
2109 E Street NW., Washington, DC 20037
phone (202) 337-1500, fax (202) 337-1502
His Excellency Igor Davidovic
Ambassador E. and P.
Consular Office: New York, New York

BOTSWANA

Embassy of the Republic of Botswana
1531-1533 New Hampshire Avenue, NW.,
  Washington, DC 20036
phone (202) 244-4990, fax (202) 244-4164
His Excellency Lapologang Caesar Lekoa
Ambassador E. and P.

BRAZIL

Brazilian Embassy
3006 Massachusetts Avenue, NW., Washington, DC
  20008
phone (202) 238-2700, fax (202) 238-2827
His Excellency Roberto Abdenur
Ambassador E. and P.
Consular Offices:
  California:
    Los Angeles
    San Francisco
  Florida, Miami
  Illinois, Chicago
  Massachusetts, Boston
  New York, New York
  Puerto Rico, San Juan
  Texas, Houston

BRUNEI

Embassy of the State of Brunei Darussalam
3520 International Court NW., Washington, DC
  20008
phone (202) 237-1838, fax (202) 885-0560
His Excellency Pengiran Anak Dato Puteh
Ambassador E. and P.

BULGARIA

Embassy of the Republic of Bulgaria
1621 22nd Street NW., Washington, DC 20008
phone (202) 387-0174, fax (202) 234-7973
Her Excellency Elena Poptodorova
Ambassador E. and P.
Consular Office: New York, New York

BURKINA FASO

Embassy of the Burkina Faso
2340 Massachusetts Avenue, NW., Washington, DC
  20008
phone (202) 332-5577, fax (202) 667-1882
His Excellency Tertius Zongo
Ambassador E. and P.

BURMA

Embassy of the Union of Burma
2300 S Street NW., Washington, DC 20008-4089
phone (202) 332-9044, fax (202) 332-9046
Ambassador E. and P.
Consular Office: New York, New York

BURUNDI

Embassy of the Republic of Burundi
2233 Wisconsin Avenue, NW., Suite 212,
  Washington, DC 20007
phone (202) 342-2574, fax (202) 342-2578
His Excellency Antoine Ntamobwa
Ambassador E. and P.

CAMBODIA

Royal Embassy of Cambodia
4530 16th Street NW., Washington, DC 20011
phone (202) 726-7742, fax (202) 726-8381
His Excellency Sercywath Ek
Ambassador E. and P.

CAMEROON

Embassy of the Republic of Cameroon
2349 Massachusetts Avenue, NW., Washington, DC
  20008
phone (202) 265-8790, fax (202) 387-3826
His Excellency Jerome Mendouga
Ambassador E. and P.

CANADA

Embassy of Canada
501 Pennsylvania Avenue, NW., Washington, DC
  20001
phone (202) 682-1740, fax (202) 682-7726
His Excellency Frank McKenna
Ambassador E. and P.

Consular Offices:
  California:
    Los Angeles
    San Francisco
    San Jose
  Florida, Miami
  Georgia, Atlanta
  Illinois, Chicago
  Massachusetts, Boston
  Michigan, Detroit
  Minnesota, Minneapolis
  New Jersey, Princeton
  New York:
    Buffalo
    New York
  Texas, Dallas
  Washington, Seattle

CAPE VERDE

Embassy of the Republic of Cape Verde
3415 Massachusetts Avenue, NW., Washington, DC
  20007
phone (202) 965–6820, fax (202) 965–1207
His Excellency Jose Brito
Ambassador E. and P.
Consular Office:
  Massachusetts, Boston

CENTRAL AFRICAN REPUBLIC

Embassy of Central African Republic
1618 22nd Street NW., Washington, DC 20008
phone (202) 483–7800, fax (202) 332–9893
His Excellency Emmanuel Touaboy
Ambassador E. and P.
Consular Office:
  California, Los Angeles

CHAD

Embassy of the Republic of Chad
2002 R Street NW., Washington, DC 20009
phone (202) 462–4009, fax (202) 265–1937
His Excellency Hassaballah Ahmat Soubiane
Ambassador E. and P.

CHILE

Embassy of the Republic of Chile
1732 Massachusetts Avenue, NW., Washington, DC
  20036
phone (202) 785–1746, fax (202) 887–5579
His Excellency Andrés Bianchi
Ambassador E. and P.
Consular Offices:
  California:
    Los Angeles
    San Francisco
  Florida, Miami
  Illinois, Chicago
  New York, New York

Pennsylvania, Philadelphia
Puerto Rico, San Juan
Texas, Houston

CHINA

Embassy of the People's Republic of China
2300 Connecticut Avenue, NW., Washington, DC
  20008
phone (202) 328–2500, fax (202) 588–0032
His Excellency Jiechi Jang
Ambassador E. and P.
Consular Offices:
  California:
    Los Angeles
    San Francisco
  Illinois, Chicago
  New York, New York
  Texas, Houston

COLOMBIA

Embassy of Colombia
2118 Leroy Place NW., Washington, DC 20008
phone (202) 387–8338, fax (202) 232–8643
His Excellency Luis Alberto Moreno
Ambassador E. and P.
Consular Offices:
  California:
    Los Angeles
    San Francisco
  Florida, Miami
  Georgia, Atlanta
  Illinois, Chicago
  Louisiana, New Orleans
  Massachusetts, Boston
  New York, New York
  Puerto Rico, San Juan
  Texas, Houston

COMOROS

Embassy of the Federal and Islamic Republic of
  the Comoros
420 East 50th Street, New York, NY 10022
phone (212) 972–8010, fax (202) 983–4712
[Ambassador departed January 31, 1999]
Consular Office: New York, New York

CONGO, DEMOCRATIC REPUBLIC OF

Embassy of the Democratic Republic of the Congo
1726 M Street, NW., Washington, DC 20036
phone (202) 234–7690, fax (202) 234–2609
Her Excellency Faida Mitifu
Ambassador E. and P.

CONGO, REPUBLIC OF

Embassy of the Republic of the Congo
4891 Colorado Avenue, NW., Washington, DC
  20011

phone (202) 726–5500, fax (202) 726–1860
His Excellency Serge Mombouli
Ambassador E. and P.

COOK ISLANDS

Consular Offices:
  California, Los Angeles
  Hawaii, Honolulu

COSTA RICA

Embassy of Costa Rica
2114 S Street NW., Washington, DC 20008
phone (202) 234–2945, fax (202) 265–4795
His Excellency Tomas Duena
Ambassador E. and P.
Consular Offices:
  California:
    Los Angeles
    San Francisco
  Florida:
    Miami
    Tampa
  Georgia, Atlanta
  Illinois, Chicago
  Louisiana, New Orleans
  Massachusetts, Boston
  New Mexico, Albuquerque
  New York, New York
  North Carolina, Durham
  Pennsylvania, Philadelphia
  Puerto Rico, San Juan
  Texas:
    Austin
    Houston
    San Antonio

CÔTE D'IVOIRE

Embassy of the Republic of Côte d'Ivoire
2424 Massachusetts Avenue, NW., Washington, DC
  20007
phone (202) 797–0300, fax (202) 462–9444
His Excellency Daouda Diabate
Ambassador E. and P.
Consular Offices:
  California, San Francisco

CROATIA

Embassy of the Republic of Croatia
2343 Massachusetts Avenue, NW., Washington, DC
  20008
phone (202) 588–5899, fax (202) 588–8937
His Excellency Neven Jurica
Ambassador E. and P.
Consular Offices:
  California, Los Angeles
  Illinois, Chicago
  Minnesota, St. Paul
  New York, New York

CYPRUS

Embassy of the Republic of Cyprus
2211 R Street NW., Washington, DC 20008
phone (202) 462–5772, fax (202) 483–6710
His Excellency Euripides L. Evriviades
Ambassador E. and P.
Consular Offices:
  California, Los Angeles
  New York, New York
  Texas, Houston

CZECH REPUBLIC

Embassy of the Czech Republic
3900 Spring of Freedom Street NW., Washington,
  DC 20008
phone (202) 274–9100, fax (202) 966–8540
His Excellency Martin Palous
Ambassador E. and P.
Consular Offices:
  California:
    Los Angeles
    San Francisco
  New York, New York
  Pennsylvania, Philadelphia

DENMARK

Royal Danish Embassy
3200 Whitehaven Street NW., Washington, DC
  20008–3683
phone (202) 234–4300, fax (202) 328–1470
His Excellency Ulrik A. Federspiel
Ambassador E. and P.
Consular Offices:
  California, Los Angeles
  Illinois, Chicago
  New York, New York

DJIBOUTI

Embassy of the Republic of Djibouti
1156 15th Street NW., Suite 515, Washington, DC
  20005
phone (202) 331–0270, fax (202) 331–0302
His Excellency Roble Olhaye
Ambassador E. and P.

DOMINICA

Embassy of the Commonwealth of Dominica
3216 New Mexico Avenue, NW., Washington, DC
  20016
phone (202) 364–6781, fax (202) 364–6791
[Ambassador departed October 12, 2001]
Consular Office: New York, New York

DOMINICAN REPUBLIC

Embassy of the Dominican Republic
1715 22nd Street NW., Washington, DC 20008
phone (202) 332–6280, fax (202) 265–8057
His Excellency Flavio Dario Spinal

Ambassador E. and P.
Consular Offices:
  Alabama, Mobile
  California, San Francisco
  Florida:
    Jacksonville
    Miami
  Illinois, Chicago
  Louisiana, New Orleans
  Massachusetts, Boston
  Minnesota, Minneapolis
  New York, New York
  Pennsylvania, Philadelphia
  Puerto Rico:
    Mayaguez
    Ponce
    San Juan

ECUADOR

Embassy of Ecuador
2535 15th Street NW., Washington, DC 20009
phone (202) 234–7200, fax (202) 667–3482
Andes Teran
Minister
Consular Offices:
  California:
    Los Angeles
    San Francisco
  Florida, Miami
  Illinois, Chicago
  Louisiana, New Orleans
  Nevada, Las Vegas
  New Jersey, Newark
  New York, New York
  Pennsylvania, Philadelphia
  Texas, Houston

EGYPT

Embassy of the Arab Republic of Egypt
3521 International Court NW., Washington, DC
  20008
phone (202) 895–5400, fax (202) 244–4319/5131
His Excellency M. Nabil Fahmy
Ambassador E. and P.
Consular Offices:
  California, San Francisco
  Illinois, Chicago
  New York, New York
  Texas, Houston

EL SALVADOR

Embassy of El Salvador
2308 California Street NW., Washington, DC 20008
phone (202) 265–9671, fax (202) 332–2225
His Excellency René Antonio Leon
Ambassador E. and P.

Consular Offices:
  California:
    Los Angeles
    San Francisco
  Florida, Miami
  Illinois, Chicago
  Louisiana, New Orleans
  Massachusetts, Boston
  New York, New York
  Puerto Rico, Bayamon
  Texas:
    Dallas
    Houston

EQUATORIAL GUINEA

Embassy of the Republic of Equatorial Guinea
2020 16th Street NW., Washington, DC 20009
phone (202) 518–5700, fax (202) 518–5252
His Excellency Teodoro Biyogo Nsue
Ambassador E. and P.

ERITREA

Embassy of the State of Eritrea
1708 New Hampshire Avenue, NW., Washington,
  DC 20009
phone (202) 319–1991, fax (202) 319–1304
His Excellency Girma Asmerom
Ambassador E. and P.
Consular Office: California, Oakland

ESTONIA

Embassy of Estonia
2131 Massachusetts Avenue, Washington, DC
  20008
phone (202) 588–0101, fax (202) 588–0108
His Excellency Juri Luik
Ambassador E. and P.
Consular Office: New York, New York

ETHIOPIA

Embassy of Ethiopia
3506 International Drive NW., Washington, DC
  20008
phone (202) 364–1200, fax (202) 587–0195
His Excellency Kassahun Ayele
Ambassador E. and P.

FIJI

Embassy of the Republic of the Fiji Islands
2233 Wisconsin Avenue, NW., Suite 240,
  Washington, DC 20007
phone (202) 337–8320, fax (202) 337–1996
Ambassador E. and P.

FINLAND

Embassy of Finland
3301 Massachusetts Avenue, NW., Washington, DC
  20008
phone (202) 298–5800, fax (202) 298–6030

His Excellency Jukka Valtasaari
Ambassador E. and P.
Consular Offices:
  California:
    Los Angeles
    San Francisco
  Massachusetts, Boston
  New York, New York

FRANCE

Embassy of France
4101 Reservoir Road NW., Washington, DC 20007
phone (202) 944–6000, fax (202) 944–6166
His Excellency Jean David Levitte
Ambassador E. and P.
Consular Offices:
  California:
    Los Angeles
    San Francisco
  Florida, Miami
  Georgia, Atlanta
  Illinois, Chicago
  Louisiana, New Orleans
  Massachusetts, Boston
  New York, New York
  Texas, Houston

GABON

Embassy of the Gabonese Republic
2034 20th Street NW., Washington, DC 20009
phone (202) 797–1000, fax (202) 332–0668
His Excellency Jules Marius Ogouebandja
Ambassador E. and P.
Consular Office: New York, New York

GAMBIA, THE

Embassy of The Gambia
1156 15th Street NW., Suite 905, Washington, DC 20005
phone (202) 785–1399, fax (202) 785–1430
DoDou B. Gagane
Minister-Counselor
Consular Office: California, Los Angeles

GEORGIA, REPUBLIC OF

Embassy of the Republic of Georgia
1101 15th Street, NW., Suite 602, Washington, DC 20005
phone (202) 387–2390, fax (202) 393–4537
His Excellency Levan Mikeladze
Ambassador E. and P.

GERMANY, FEDERAL REPUBLIC OF

Embassy of the Federal Republic of Germany
4645 Reservoir Road NW., Washington, DC 20007–1998
phone (202) 298–8140, fax (202) 298–4249

His Excellency Wolfgang Friedrich Ischinger
Ambassador E. and P.
Consular Offices:
  California:
    Los Angeles
    San Francisco
  Florida, Miami
  Georgia, Atlanta
  Illinois, Chicago
  Massachusetts, Boston
  Michigan, Detroit
  New York, New York
  Texas, Houston

GHANA

Embassy of Ghana
3512 International Drive NW., Washington, DC 20008
phone (202) 686–4520, fax (202) 686–4527
His Excellency Alan J. Kyerematen
Ambassador E. and P.
Consular Offices:
  Georgia, Atlanta
  New York, New York

GREAT BRITAIN

See United Kingdom of Great Britain and Northern Ireland

GREECE

Embassy of Greece
2221 Massachusetts Avenue, NW., Washington, DC 20008
phone (202) 939–5800, fax (202) 939–5824
His Excellency Alexandre Philon
Ambassador E. and P.
Consular Offices:
  California:
    Los Angeles
    San Francisco
  Georgia, Atlanta
  Illinois, Chicago
  Louisiana, New Orleans
  Massachusetts, Boston
  New York, New York
  Texas, Houston

GRENADA

Embassy of Grenada
1701 New Hampshire Avenue, NW., Washington, DC 20009
phone (202) 265–2561, fax (202) 265–2468
His Excellency Denis G. Antoine
Ambassador E. and P.
Consular Offices:
  Florida, Ft. Lauderdale
  New York, New York

GUATEMALA

Embassy of Guatemala
2220 R Street NW., Washington, DC 20008
phone (202) 745–4952, fax (202) 745–1908
His Excellency Guillermo Castillo
Ambassador E. and P.
Consular Offices:
  California:
    Los Angeles
    San Francisco
  Colorado, Denver
  Florida, Miami
  Illinois, Chicago
  New York, New York
  Texas, Houston

GUINEA

Embassy of the Republic of Guinea
2112 Leroy Place NW., Washington, DC 20008
phone (202) 483–9420, fax (202) 483–8688
His Excellency Alpha Oumar Rafiou Barry
Ambassador E. and P.

GUINEA-BISSAU

Embassy of the Republic of Guinea-Bissau
P.O. Box 33813, Washington, DC 20033
phone (301) 947–3958
Henrique Adriano Da Silva
Minister-Counselor

GUYANA

Embassy of Guyana
2490 Tracy Place NW., Washington, DC 20008
phone (202) 265–6900, fax (202) 232–1297
His Excellency Bayney Karran
Ambassador E. and P.
Consular Office: New York, New York

HAITI

Embassy of the Republic of Haiti
2311 Massachusetts Avenue, NW., Washington, DC 20008
phone (202) 332–4090, fax (202) 745–7215
Arymond Joseph
Minister-Counselor
Consular Offices:
  Florida, Miami
  Illinois, Chicago
  Massachusetts, Boston
  New York, New York
  Puerto Rico, San Juan

THE HOLY SEE (VATICAN CITY)

Apostolic Nunciature
3339 Massachusetts Avenue, NW., Washington, DC 20008
phone (202) 333–7121, fax (202) 337–4036

His Excellency The Most Reverend Gabriele
  Montalvo
Apostolic Nuncio

HONDURAS

Embassy of Honduras
3007 Tilden Street NW., Suite 4–M, Washington, DC 20008
phone (202) 966–7702, fax (202) 966–9751
His Excellency Mario Miguel Canahuati
Ambassador E. and P.
Consular Offices:
  Arizona, Phoenix
  California:
    Los Angeles
    San Francisco
  Florida:
    Jacksonville
    Miami
  Georgia, Atlanta
  Illinois, Chicago
  Louisiana, New Orleans
  Maryland, Baltimore
  Massachusetts, Boston
  Michigan, Detroit
  New York, New York
  Puerto Rico, San Juan
  Texas, Houston

HUNGARY

Embassy of the Republic of Hungary
3910 Shoemaker Street NW., Washington, DC 20008
phone (202) 362–6730, fax (202) 966–8135
His Excellency Andras Simonyi
Ambassador E. and P.
Consular Offices:
  California, Los Angeles
  Colorado, Denver
  Florida, Miami
  New York, New York
  Ohio, Cleveland

ICELAND

Embassy of the Republic of Iceland
1156 15th Street NW., Suite 1200, Washington, DC 20005
phone (202) 265–6653, fax (202) 265–6656
His Excellency Helgi Agustsson
Ambassador E. and P.
Consular Offices:
  California, Los Angeles
  Florida:
    Hollywood
    Tallahassee
  Georgia, Atlanta
  Illinois, Chicago

Minnesota, Minneapolis
New York, New York
Washington, Seattle

INDIA

Embassy of India
2107 Massachusetts Avenue, NW., Washington, DC
20008
phone (202) 939–7000, fax (202) 265–4351
His Excellency Ronen Sen
Ambassador E. and P.
Consular Offices:
  California, San Francisco
  Hawaii, Honolulu
  Illinois, Chicago
  New York, New York
  Texas, Houston

INDONESIA

Embassy of the Republic of Indonesia
2020 Massachusetts Avenue, NW., Washington, DC
20036
phone (202) 775–5200, fax (202) 775–5365
Soemadi Djoko M. Brotodiningrat
Ambassador E. and P.
Consular Offices:
  California:
    Los Angeles
    San Francisco
  Illinois, Chicago
  New York, New York
  Texas, Houston

IRAN

See Pakistan

IRAQ

See Algeria

IRELAND

Embassy of Ireland
2234 Massachusetts Avenue, NW., Washington, DC
20008
phone (202) 462–3939, ext. 232, fax (202)
232–5993
His Excellency Noel Fahey
Ambassador E. and P.
Consular Offices:
  California, San Francisco
  Illinois, Chicago
  Massachusetts, Boston
  New York, New York

ISRAEL

Embassy of Israel
3514 International Drive NW., Washington, DC
20008
phone (202) 364–5500, fax (202) 364–5610
His Excellency Daniel Ayalon

Ambassador E. and P.
Consular Offices:
  California:
    Los Angeles
    San Francisco
  Florida, Miami
  Georgia, Atlanta
  Illinois, Chicago
  Massachusetts, Boston
  New York, New York
  Pennsylvania, Philadelphia
  Texas, Houston

ITALY

Embassy of Italy
3000 Whitehaven Street NW., Washington, DC
20008
phone (202) 612–4400, fax (202) 518–2154
His Excellency Sergio Vento
Ambassador E. and P.
Consular Offices:
  California:
    Los Angeles
    San Francisco
  Florida, Miami
  Illinois, Chicago
  Massachusetts, Boston
  Michigan, Detroit
  New York, New York
  Pennsylvania, Philadelphia
  Texas, Houston

IVORY COAST

See Côte d'Ivoire

JAMAICA

Embassy of Jamaica
1520 New Hampshire Avenue, NW., Washington,
DC 20036
phone (202) 452–0660, fax (202) 452–0081
His Excellency Gordon Shirley
Ambassador E. and P.
Consular Offices:
  Florida, Miami
  New York, New York

JAPAN

Embassy of Japan
2520 Massachusetts Avenue, NW., Washington, DC
20008
phone (202) 238–6700, fax (202) 328–2187
His Excellency Royozo Kato
Ambassador E. and P.
Consular Offices:
  Alabama, Mobile
  Alaska, Anchorage
  Arizona, Phoenix

California:
  Los Angeles
  San Diego
  San Francisco
Colorado, Denver
Connecticut, Avon
Florida, Miami
Georgia, Atlanta
Guam, Agana
Hawaii, Honolulu
Illinois, Chicago
Indiana, Indianapolis
Louisiana, New Orleans
Massachusetts, Boston
Michigan, Detroit
Minnesota, Minneapolis
Missouri:
  Kansas City
  St. Louis
New York:
  Buffalo
  New York
North Carolina, High Point
Ohio, Columbus
Oklahoma, Oklahoma City
Oregon, Portland
Pennsylvania, Philadelphia
Puerto Rico, San Juan
Tennessee, Nashville
Texas, Houston
  Houston
  Mariana Islands
Washington, Seattle
Wyoming, Casper

JORDAN

Embassy of the Hashemite Kingdom of Jordan
3504 International Drive NW., Washington, DC 20008
phone (202) 966–2664, fax (202) 966–3110
His Excellency Karim Kawar
Ambassador E. and P.
Consular Offices:
  Illinois, Chicago
  Texas, Houston

KAZAKHSTAN

Embassy of the Republic of Kazakhstan
1401 16th Street NW., Washington, DC 20036
phone (202) 232–5488, fax (202) 232–5845
His Excellency Kanat B. Saudabayev
Ambassador E. and P.
Consular Office: New York, New York

KENYA

Embassy of the Republic of Kenya
2249 R Street NW., Washington, DC 20008
phone (202) 387–6101, fax (202) 462–3829

Telex: 197376
His Excellency Leonard Mgaitag
Ambassador E. and P.
Consular Offices:
  California, Los Angeles
  New York, New York

KIRIBATI

Consular Office: Hawaii, Honolulu

KOREA, REPUBLIC OF

Embassy of the Republic of Korea
2450 Massachusetts Avenue, NW., Washington, DC 20008
phone (202) 939–5600, fax (202) 232–0117
His Excellency Seokhyun Holg
Ambassador E. and P.
Consular Offices:
  Alaska, Anchorage
  California:
    Los Angeles
    San Francisco
  Florida, Miami
  Georgia, Atlanta
  Guam, Agana
  Hawaii, Honolulu
  Illinois, Chicago
  Louisiana, New Orleans
  Massachusetts, Boston
  Minnesota, Minneapolis
  New York, New York
  Oregon, Portland
  Puerto Rico, San Juan
  Texas, Houston
  Washington, Seattle

KUWAIT

Embassy of the State of Kuwait
2940 Tilden Street, NW., Washington, DC 20008
phone (202) 966–0702, fax (202) 966–0517
His Excellency Sheikh Salem Abdullah Al Jaber Al-Sabah
Ambassador E. and P.

KYRGYZSTAN

Embassy of the Kyrgyz Republic
1732 Wisconsin Avenue, NW., Washington, DC 20007
phone (202) 338–5141, fax (202) 338–5139
His Excellency Baktybek Abdrissaev
Ambassador E. and P.
Consular Offices:
  New York, New York
  Texas, Houston

LAOS

Embassy of the Lao People's Democratic Republic
2222 S Street NW., Washington, DC 20008

phone (202) 332–6416, fax (202) 332–4923
His Excellency Phanthong Phommahaxay
Ambassador E. and P.

LATVIA

Embassy of Latvia
4325 17th Street NW., Washington, DC 20011
phone (202) 726–8123, fax (202) 726–6785
His Excellency Aivis Ronis
Ambassador E. and P.

LEBANON

Embassy of Lebanon
2560 28th Street NW., Washington, DC 20008
phone (202) 939–6300, fax (202) 939–6324
His Excellency Farid Abboud
Ambassador E. and P.
Consular Offices:
   California, Los Angeles
   Michigan, Detroit
   New York, New York

LESOTHO

Embassy of the Kingdom of Lesotho
2511 Massachusetts Avenue, NW., Washington, DC
   20008
phone (202) 797–5533, fax (202) 234–6815
Her Excellency Molelekeng E. Rapolaki
Ambassador E. and P.
Consular Office:
   Louisiana, New Orleans

LIBERIA

Embassy of the Republic of Liberia
5201 16th Street NW., Washington, DC 20011
phone (202) 723–0437, fax (202) 723–0436
Aaron B. Kollie
Minister
Consular Offices:
   California:
      Los Angeles
      San Francisco
   Georgia, Atlanta
   Illinois, Chicago
   Michigan, Detroit
   New York, New York

LIECHTENSTEIN

Embassy of the Principality of Liechtenstein
888 17th Street, NW., Suite 1250, Washington, DC
   20016
phone (202) 331–0590, fax (202) 331–3221
His Excellency Charles A. Minor
Ambassador E. and P.

LITHUANIA

Embassy of the Republic of Lithuania
2622 16th Street NW., Washington, DC 20009

phone (202) 234–5860, fax (202) 328–0466
His Excellency Vygaudas Usackas
Ambassador E. and P.
Consular Offices:
   California, Los Angeles
   Illinois, Chicago
   New York, New York

LUXEMBOURG

Embassy of Grand Duchy of Luxembourg
2200 Massachusetts Avenue, NW., Washington, DC
   20008
phone (202) 265–4171, fax (202) 328–8270
Her Excellency Arlette Conzemius
Ambassador E. and P.
Consular Offices:
   California, San Francisco
   Illinois, Chicago
   Missouri, Kansas City
   New York, New York

MACEDONIA

Embassy of the Former Yugoslav Republic of
   Macedonia
1101 30th Street, NW., Suite 302, Washington, DC
   20007
phone (202) 337–3063, fax (202) 337–3093
His Excellency Nikola Dmitrov
Ambassador E. and P.
Consular Office: New York, New York

MADAGASCAR

Embassy of the Republic of Madagascar
2374 Massachusetts Avenue, NW., Washington, DC
   20008
phone (202) 265–5525, fax (202) 265–3034
His Excellency Narisoa Rajaonarivony
Ambassador E. and P.
Consular Office: New York, New York

MALAWI

Embassy of the Republic of Malawi
2408 Massachusetts Avenue, NW., Washington, DC
   20008
phone (202) 721–0274, fax (202) 265–0976
His Excellency Tony Kandiero
Ambassador E. and P.

MALAYSIA

Embassy of Malaysia
3516 International Court, NW., Washington, DC
   20008
phone (202) 572–9700, fax (202) 572–9882
His Excellency Sheikh Abdul Khalid Ghazzali
Ambassador E. and P.
Consular Offices:
   California, Los Angeles
   New York, New York

MALDIVES

Embassy of the Republic of Maldives
800 2nd Avenue, Suite 400E, New York, NY 10017
phone (212) 599–6195
His Excellency Dr. Mohamed Latheef
Ambassador E. and P.

MALI

Embassy of the Republic of Mali
2130 R Street NW., Washington, DC 20008
phone (202) 332–2249, fax (202) 332–6603
His Excellency Abdoulaye Diop
Ambassador E. and P.

MALTA

Embassy of Malta
2017 Connecticut Avenue, NW., Washington, DC
20008
phone (202) 462–3611/12, fax (202) 387–5470
His Excellency John Lowell
Ambassador E. and P.
Consular Offices:
California, San Francisco
Michigan, Detroit
Minnesota, St. Paul
New York, New York
Texas, Houston

MARSHALL ISLANDS

Embassy of the Republic of the Marshall Islands
2433 Massachusetts Avenue, NW., Washington, DC
20008
phone (202) 234–5414, fax (202) 232–3236
His Excellency Banny De Brum
Ambassador E. and P.
Consular Office: Hawaii, Honolulu

MAURITANIA

Embassy of the Islamic Republic of Mauritania
2129 Leroy Place NW., Washington, DC 20008
phone (202) 232–5700, fax (202) 319–2623
His Excellency Tijani Ould Kerim
Ambassador E. and P.

MAURITIUS

Embassy of the Republic of Mauritius
4301 Connecticut Avenue, NW., Suite 441,
Washington, DC 20008
phone (202) 244–1491/92, fax (202) 966–0983
His Excellency Usha Jeetah
Ambassador E. and P.

MEXICO

Embassy of Mexico
1911 Pennsylvania Avenue, NW., Washington, DC
20006
phone (202) 728–1600, fax (202) 833–4320
His Excellency Carlos De Icaza

Ambassador E. and P.
Consular Offices:
Arizona:
Douglas
Nogales
Phoenix
Tucson
Yuma
California:
Calexico
Fresno
Los Angeles
Oxnard
Sacramento
San Bernardino
San Diego
San Francisco
San Jose
Santa Ana
Colorado, Denver
Florida:
Miami
Orlando
Georgia, Atlanta
Illinois, Chicago
Indiana, Indianapolis
Louisiana, New Orleans
Massachusetts, Boston
Michigan, Detroit
Missouri, Kansas City
Nebraska, Omaha
Nevada, Las Vegas
New Mexico, Albuquerque
New York, New York
Oregon, Portland
Pennsylvania, Philadelphia
Puerto Rico, San Juan
Texas:
Austin
Brownsville
Corpus Christi
Dallas
Del Rio
Eagle Pass
El Paso
Houston
Laredo
McAllen
Midland
San Antonio
Utah, Salt Lake City
Washington:
Seattle

MICRONESIA

Embassy of the Federated States of Micronesia
1725 N Street NW., Washington, DC 20036
phone (202) 223–4383, fax (202) 223–4391

His Excellency Jesse Bibiano Marehalau
Ambassador E. and P.
Consular Offices:
Guam, Tamuning
Hawaii, Honolulu

MOLDOVA

Embassy of the Republic of Moldova
2101 S Street NW., Washington, DC 20008
phone (202) 667–1130, fax (202) 667–1240
His Excellency Mihail Manoli
Ambassador E. and P.

MONACO

Embassy of Monoco
866 United Nations Plaza, Suite 520, New York, New York 10017
phone (212) 832–0721, fax (212) 832–5358
Ambassador Gilles Noghes
Consular Offices:
California:
Los Angeles
San Francisco
Florida, Miami
Illinois, Chicago
Massachusetts, Boston
New York, New York
Texas, Dallas

MONGOLIA

Embassy of Mongolia
2833 M Street NW., Washington, DC 20007
phone (202) 333–7117, fax (202) 298–9227
His Excellency Bold Ravdan
Ambassador E. and P.
Consular Offices:
California, San Francisco
New York, New York

MOROCCO

Embassy of the Kingdom of Morocco
1601 21st Street NW., Washington, DC 20009
phone (202) 462–7979, fax (202) 462–7643
His Excellency Aziz Mekouar
Ambassador E. and P.
Consular Office:
New York, New York

MOZAMBIQUE

Embassy of the Republic of Mozambique
1990 M Street NW., Suite 570, Washington, DC 20036
phone (202) 293–7146, fax (202) 835–0245
His Excellency Armando Alexandre Panguene
Ambassador E. and P.

NAURU

Consular Office: Guam, Agana

NAMIBIA

Embassy of the Republic of Namibia
1605 New Hampshire Avenue, NW., Washington, DC 20009
phone (202) 986–0540, fax (202) 986–0443
His Excellency Hopelong Iping
Ambassador E. and P.
Consular Office: Michigan, Detroit

NEPAL

Royal Nepalese Embassy
2131 Leroy Place NW., Washington, DC 20008
phone (202) 667–4550, fax (202) 667–5534
His Excellency Kedar B. Shretra
Ambassador E. and P.
Consular Offices:
California:
Los Angeles
San Francisco
New York, New York
Ohio, Cleveland

NETHERLANDS

Royal Netherlands Embassy
4200 Linnean Avenue, NW., Washington, DC 20008
phone (202) 244–5300, fax (202) 362–3430
His Excellency Tinan Valk
Ambassador E. and P.
Consular Offices:
California:
Los Angeles
Florida, Miami
Illinois, Chicago
Massachusetts, Boston
New York, New York
Texas, Houston

NEW ZEALAND

Embassy of New Zealand
37 Observatory Circle NW., Washington, DC 20008
phone (202) 328–4800, fax (202) 667–5227
His Excellency John Wood
Ambassador E. and P.
Consular Offices:
California, Los Angeles
New York, New York

NICARAGUA

Embassy of the Republic of Nicaragua
1627 New Hampshire Avenue, NW., Washington, DC 20009
phone (202) 939–6570, fax (202) 939–6542
His Excellency Salvador Stadthagen
Ambassador E. and P.
Consular Offices:
California, Los Angeles
Florida, Miami

Louisiana, New Orleans
New York, New York
Puerto Rico, San Juan
Texas, Houston

NIGER

Embassy of the Republic of Niger
2204 R Street NW., Washington, DC 20008
phone (202) 483–4224, fax (202) 683–3169
His Excellency Joseph Diatta
Ambassador E. and P.

NIGERIA

Embassy of the Federal Republic of Nigeria
3519 International Court, NW., Washington, DC
20008
phone (202) 986–8400, fax (202) 775–1385
His Excellency George A. Oblozor
Ambassador E. and P.
Consular Offices:
Georgia, Atlanta
New York, New York

NORWAY

Royal Norwegian Embassy
2720 34th Street NW., Washington, DC
20008–2714
phone (202) 333–6000, fax (202) 333–0543
His Excellency Knut Vollebaek
Ambassador E. and P.
Consular Offices:
California:
Los Angeles
San Francisco
Florida, Miami
Illinois, Chicago
Minnesota, Minneapolis
New York, New York
Texas, Houston

OMAN

Embassy of the Sultanate of Oman
2535 Belmont Road NW., Washington, DC 20008
phone (202) 387–1980, fax (202) 745–4933
His Excellency Mohamed Ali Al Khusaiby
Ambassador E. and P.

PAKISTAN

Embassy of Pakistan
3517 International Court, NW., Washington, DC
20008
phone (202) 243–6500, fax (202) 686–1534
Her Excellency Jehangir Karamat
Ambassador E. and P.
Consular Offices:
California:
Los Angeles
Sunnyvale

Massachusetts, Boston
New York, New York

Iranian Interests Section

2209 Wisconsin Avenue, NW., Washington, DC
20007
phone (202) 965–4990

PALAU

Embassy of the Republic of Palau
1700 Pennsylvania Avenue, Suite 400, Washington,
DC 20006
phone (202) 452–6814, fax (202) 349–8597
His Excellency Hersey Kyota
Ambassador E. and P.
Consular Office: Guam, Tamuning

PANAMA

Embassy of the Republic of Panama
2862 McGill Terrace NW., Washington, DC 20008
phone (202) 483–1407, fax (202) 483–8413
His Excellency Federicio Humberh
Ambassador E. and P.
Consular Offices:
California, San Francisco
Florida:
Miami
Tampa
Georgia, Atlanta
Hawaii, Honolulu
Illinois, Chicago
Louisiana, New Orleans
Massachusetts, Boston
New York, New York
Pennsylvania, Philadelphia
Puerto Rico, San Juan
Texas, Houston

PAPUA NEW GUINEA

Embassy of Papua New Guinea
1779 Massachusetts Avenue, NW., Suite 805,
Washington, DC 20036
phone (202) 745–3680, fax (202) 745–3679
Graham Michael
Counselor
Consular Offices:
California, Los Angeles
Texas, Houston

PARAGUAY

Embassy of Paraguay
2400 Massachusetts Avenue, NW., Washington, DC
20008
phone (202) 483–6960, fax (202) 234–4508
His Excellency James Spalding
Ambassador E. and P.
Consular Offices:
California, Los Angeles
Florida, Miami

Kansas, Kansas City
Louisiana, New Orleans
New York, New York

PERU

Embassy of Peru
1700 Massachusetts Avenue, NW., Washington, DC
20036
phone (202) 833–9860, fax (202) 659–8124
His Excellency Edwardo Ferrero
Ambassador E. and P.
Consular Offices:
California:
Los Angeles
San Francisco
Colorado, Denver
Connecticut, Hartford
Florida, Miami
Illinois, Chicago
Massachusetts, Boston
New Jersey, Paterson
New York, New York
Puerto Rico, San Juan
Texas, Houston

PHILIPPINES

Embassy of the Philippines
1600 Massachusetts Avenue, NW., Washington, DC
20036
phone (202) 467–9300/63, fax (202) 328–7614,
467–9417
His Excellency Albert Ferreros Del Rosario
Ambassador E. and P.
Consular Offices:
California:
Los Angeles
San Diego
San Francisco
Georgia, Atlanta
Guam, Agana
Hawaii, Honolulu
Illinois, Chicago
Louisiana, New Orleans
New York, New York
Texas, Houston

POLAND

Embassy of the Republic of Poland
2640 16th Street NW., Washington, DC 20009
phone (202) 234–3800, fax (202) 328–6271
His Excellency Przemyslaw Grudzinski
Ambassador E. and P.
Consular Offices:
California, Los Angeles
Illinois, Chicago
New York, New York

PORTUGAL

Embassy of Portugal
2125 Kalorama Road NW., Washington, DC 20008
phone (202) 328–8610, fax (202) 462–3726
His Excellency Pedro Catarino
Ambassador E. and P.
Consular Offices:
California:
Los Angeles
San Francisco
Massachusetts:
Boston
New Bedford
New Jersey, Newark
New York, New York
Rhode Island, Providence

QATAR

Embassy of the State of Qatar
2555 M Street, NW., Suite 200, Washington, DC
20037
phone (202) 274–1603, fax (202) 237–0061
His Excellency Bader Omar Al Dafa
Ambassador E. and P.
Consular Office: Texas, Houston

ROMANIA

Embassy of Romania
1607 23rd Street NW., Washington, DC 20008
phone (202) 332–4846, fax (202) 232–4748
His Excellency Dumitru Sorin Ducaru
Ambassador E. and P.
Consular Offices:
California, Los Angeles
Illinois, Chicago
Massachusetts, Boston
Michigan, Detroit
New York, New York

RUSSIA

Embassy of the Russian Federation
2650 Wisconsin Avenue, NW., Washington, DC
20007
phone (202) 298–5700, fax (202) 298–5735
His Excellency Yury Viktorovich Ushakov
Ambassador E. and P.
Consular Offices:
Alaska, Anchorage
California, San Francisco
Hawaii, Honolulu
New York, New York
Utah, Salt Lake City
Washington, Seattle

RWANDA

Embassy of the Republic of Rwanda
1714 New Hampshire Avenue, NW., Washington,
DC 20009

phone (202) 232–2882, fax (202) 232–4544
His Excellency Zac Nsenga
Ambassador E. and P.
Consular Office: Illinois, Chicago

SAINT KITTS AND NEVIS

Embassy of Saint Kitts and Nevis
3216 New Mexico Avenue, NW., Washington, DC
  20016
phone (202) 686–2636, fax (202) 686–5740
His Excellency Izben Cordinal Williams
Ambassador E. and P.
Consular Offices:
  Georgia, Atlanta
  Texas, Dallas

SAINT LUCIA

Embassy of Saint Lucia
3216 New Mexico Avenue, NW., Washington, DC
  20016
phone (202) 364–6792, fax (202) 364–6723
Her Excellency Sonia Merlyn Johnny
Ambassador E. and P.
Consular Offices:
  Florida, Miami
  New York, New York

SAINT VINCENT AND THE GRENADINES

Embassy of Saint Vincent and the Grenadines
3216 New Mexico Avenue, NW., Washington, DC
  20016
phone (202) 364–6730, fax (202) 364–6736
His Excellency Ellsworth I.A. John
Ambassador E. and P.
Consular Offices:
  California, Los Angeles
  Louisiana, New Orleans
  New York, New York

SAMOA

Embassy of the Independent State of Samoa
800 2nd Avenue, Suite 400J, New York, NY 10017
phone (212) 599–6196, fax (212) 599–0797
His Excellency Aliioaga Feturi Elisaia
Ambassador E. and P.
Consular Office: Hawaii, Honolulu

SAN MARINO

Consular Office: New York, New York

SAO TOME AND PRINCIPE

Consular Office: Illinois, Chicago

SAUDI ARABIA

Embassy of Saudi Arabia
601 New Hampshire Avenue, NW., Washington,
  DC 20037
phone (202) 342–3800, fax (202) 944–5983
His Royal Highness Prince Bandar Bin Sultan

Ambassador E. and P.
Consular Offices:
  California, Los Angeles
  New York, New York
  Texas, Houston

SENEGAL

Embassy of the Republic of Senegal
2112 Wyoming Avenue, NW., Washington, DC
  20008
phone (202) 234–0540, fax (202) 332–6315
His Excellency Dr. Amadou Lamine Ba
Ambassador E. and P.
Consular Offices:
  Louisiana, New Orleans
  Massachusetts, Boston
  New York, New York

SERBIA & MONTENEGRO

Embassy of Serbia & Montenegro
2134 Kaloram road, NW., Washington, DC 20008
phone (202) 332–0333, fax (202) 332–3933
His Excellency Ivan Vujacic
Ambassador E. and P.
Consular Offices:
  Colorado, Denver
  Illinois, Chicago
  Wyoming, Cheyenne

SEYCHELLES

Embassy of the Republic of Seychelles
800 2nd Avenue, Suite 400C, New York, NY 10017
phone (212) 972–1785, fax (212) 972–1786
His Excellency Claude Sylvestre Morel
Ambassador E. and P.
Consular Office: Washington, Seattle

SIERRA LEONE

Embassy of Sierra Leone
1701 19th Street NW., Washington, DC 20009
phone (202) 939–9261, fax (202) 483–1793
His Excellency Ibrahim M. Kamara
Ambassador E. and P.

SINGAPORE

Embassy of the Republic of Singapore
3501 International Place NW., Washington, DC
  20008
phone (202) 537–3100, fax (202) 537–0876
Her Excellency Heng Chee Chan
Ambassador E. and P.
Consular Offices:
  California:
    Las Angeles
    San Francisco
  Illinois, Chicago
  New York, New York

SLOVAK REPUBLIC

Embassy of the Slovak Republic
3523 International Court NW., Washington, DC
20008
phone (202) 237–1054, fax (202) 237–6438
Peter Kmec
Counselor

SLOVENIA

Embassy of the Republic of Slovenia
1525 New Hampshire Avenue, NW., Washington,
DC 20036
phone (202) 667–5363, fax (202) 667–4563
His Excellency Sammuel Zbogar
Ambassador E. and P.
Consular Offices:
New York, New York
Ohio, Cleveland

SOLOMON ISLANDS

Embassy of the Solomon Islands
800 2nd Avenue, Suite 400L, New York, NY 10017
phone (212) 599–6192, fax (212) 661–8925
Collin Beck
Counselor

SOMALIA

Embassy of the Somali Democratic Republic
(Embassy ceased operations May 8, 1991)

SOUTH AFRICA

Embassy of the Republic of South Africa
3051 Massachusetts Avenue, NW., Washington, DC
20008
phone (202) 232–4400, fax (202) 265–1607
Minister
Consular Offices:
Alabama, Mobile
California, Los Angeles
Illinois, Chicago
New York, New York

SPAIN

Embassy of Spain
2375 Pennsylvania Avenue, NW., Washington, DC
20037
phone (202) 452–0100, fax (202) 833–5670
His Excellency Carlos Westendorp
Ambassador E. and P.
Consular Offices:
Alabama, Mobile
California:
Los Angeles
San Francisco
Florida, Miami
Illinois, Chicago
Louisiana, New Orleans
Massachusetts, Boston

New York, New York
Puerto Rico, San Juan
Texas, Houston

SRI LANKA

Embassy of the Democratic Socialist Republic of
Sri Lanka
2148 Wyoming Avenue, NW., Washington, DC
20008
phone (202) 483–4025, fax (202) 232–7181
His Excellency Devinda Rohan Subasinghe
Ambassador E. and P.
Consular Offices:
California, Los Angeles
Georgia, Atlanta
New York, New York

SUDAN

Embassy of the Republic of the Sudan
2210 Massachusetts Avenue, NW., Washington, DC
20008
phone (202) 338–8565, fax (202) 667–2406
Khidir Haroun Ahmed
Minister

SURINAME

Embassy of the Republic of Suriname
4301 Connecticut Avenue, NW., Suite 460,
Washington, DC 20008
phone (202) 244–7488, fax (202) 244–5878
His Excellency Henry L. Illes
Ambassador E. and P.
Consular Office: Florida, Miami

SWAZILAND

Embassy of the Kingdom of Swaziland
1712 New Hampshire Avenue, NW., Washington,
DC 20009
phone (202) 234–5002, fax (202) 234–8254
Her Excellency Mary M. Kanya
Ambassador E. and P.

SWEDEN

Embassy of Sweden
1501 M Street, NW., Suite 900, Washington, DC
20005
phone (202) 467–2600, fax (202) 467–2699
His Excellency Jan K. Eliasson
Ambassador E. and P.
Consular Offices:
California:
Los Angeles
San Francisco
Illinois, Chicago
Minnesota, Minneapolis
New York, New York

SWITZERLAND

Embassy of Switzerland
2900 Cathedral Avenue, NW., Washington, DC
20008
phone (202) 745–7900, fax (202) 387–2564
His Excellency Christian Blickenstorfer
Ambassador E. and P.
Consular Offices:
California:
  Los Angeles
  San Francisco
Georgia, Atlanta
Illinois, Chicago
Massachusetts, Boston
New York, New York
Texas, Houston

Cuban Interests Section

Embassy of Switzerland
2630 16th Street, NW 20009
phone (202) 797–8518
Dagoberto Rodriguez Barrera
Counselor

SYRIA

Embassy of the Syrian Arab Republic
2215 Wyoming Avenue, NW., Washington, DC
20008
phone (202) 232–6313, fax (202) 265–4585
His Excellency Dr. Rostom Al Zoubi
Ambassador E. and P.
Consular Offices:
California, Los Angeles
Michigan, Detroit
Texas, Houston

TAJIKISTAN

Embassy of the Republic of Tajikistan
1005 New Hampshire Avenue, NW., Washington,
DC 20037
phone (202) 223–6090, fax (202) 223–6091
His Excellency Khamrokhon Zaripov
Ambassador E. and P.

TANZANIA

Embassy of the United Republic of Tanzania
2139 R Street NW., Washington, DC 20008
phone (202) 939–6125, 884–1080, fax (202)
797–7408
His Excellency Andrew Mhando Daraja
Ambassador E. and P.

THAILAND

Royal Thai Embassy
1024 Wisconsin Avenue, NW., Suite 401,
Washington, DC 20007
phone (202) 944–3600, fax (202) 944–3611
His Excellency Sakthip Krairiksh

Ambassador E. and P.
Consular Offices:
Alabama, Montgomery
California, Los Angeles
Colorado, Denver
Florida, Coral Gables
Georgia, Atlanta
Hawaii, Honolulu
Illinois, Chicago
Massachusetts, Boston
New York, New York
Oklahoma, Tulsa
Puerto Rico, Hato Rey
Texas:
  Dallas
  El Paso
  Houston

TOGO

Embassy of the Republic of Togo
2208 Massachusetts Avenue, NW., Washington, DC
20008
phone (202) 234–4212, fax (202) 232–3190
His Excellency Akoussoulelou Bodjona
Ambassador E. and P.

TONGA

Embassy of the Kingdom of Tonga
250 East 51st Street, New York, NY 10022
phone (917) 369–1025, fax (917) 369–1024
Her Excellency Fekitamoeloa Utoikamanu
Ambassador E. and P.
Consular Office: California, San Francisco

TRINIDAD AND TOBAGO

Embassy of the Republic of Trinidad and Tobago
1708 Massachusetts Avenue, NW., Washington, DC
20036–1975
phone (202) 467–6490, fax (202) 785–3130
Her Excellency Marina Annette Valere
Ambassador E. and P.
Consular Offices:
Florida, Miami
New York, New York

TUNISIA

Embassy of Tunisia
1515 Massachusetts Avenue, NW., Washington, DC
20005
phone (202) 862–1850, fax (202) 862–1858
His Excellency Mohamed Nejib Hathana
Ambassador E. and P.
Consular Office: California, San Francisco

TURKEY

Embassy of the Republic of Turkey
2525 Massachusetts Avenue, NW., Washington, DC
20008
phone (202) 612–6700, fax (202) 612–6744

His Excellency Dr. Osman Faruk Logoglu
Ambassador E. and P.
Consular Offices:
  California:
    Los Angeles
    Oakland
  Georgia, Atlanta
  Illinois, Chicago
  Kansas, Mission Hills
  Maryland, Baltimore
  New York, New York
  Texas, Houston
  Washington, Seattle

TURKMENISTAN

Embassy of Turkmenistan
2207 Massachusetts Avenue, NW., Washington, DC 20008
phone (202) 588–1500, fax (202) 588–0697
His Excellency Meret Bairamovich Orazov
Ambassador E. and P.

UGANDA

Embassy of the Republic of Uganda
5911 16th Street, NW., Washington, DC 20011
phone (202) 726–7100, fax (202) 726–1727
Her Excellency Edith Grace Ssempala
Ambassador E. and P.

UKRAINE

Embassy of Ukraine
3350 M Street, NW., Washington, DC 20007
phone (202) 333–0606, fax (202) 333–0817
His Excellency Kostyantyn Gryshchenko
Ambassador E. and P.
Consular Offices:
  Illinois, Chicago
  New York, New York

UNITED ARAB EMIRATES

Embassy of the United Arab Emirates
3522 International Court NW., Washington, DC 20008
phone (202) 243–2400, fax (202) 243–2432
His Excellency Alasri Saeed Aldhahri
Ambassador E. and P.

UNITED KINGDOM OF GREAT BRITAIN AND NORTHERN IRELAND

British Embassy
3100 Massachusetts Avenue, NW., Washington, DC 20008
phone (202) 588–6500, fax (202) 588–7870
Sir David Manning
Minister
Consular Offices:
  California:
    Los Angeles
    San Francisco

  Colorado, Denver
  Florida:
    Miami
    Orlando
  Georgia, Atlanta
  Illinois, Chicago
  Massachusetts, Boston
  New York, New York
  Texas:
    Dallas
    Houston
  Washington, Seattle

URUGUAY

Embassy of Uruguay
1913 I Street, NW., Washington, DC 20006
phone (202) 331–1313, fax (202) 331–8142
His Excellency Ricardo Nario
Ambassador E. and P.
Consular Offices:
  California, Los Angeles
  Florida, Miami
  Illinois, Chicago
  New York, New York

UZBEKISTAN

Embassy of the Republic of Uzbekistan
1746 Massachusetts Avenue, NW., Washington, DC 20036
phone (202) 887–5300, fax (202) 293–6804
His Excellency Abdulaziz Kamilov
Ambassador E. and P.
Consular Offices:
  Colorado, Denver
  New York, New York
  Washington, Seattle

VENEZUELA

Embassy of the Republic of Venezuela
1099 30th Street, NW., Washington, DC 20007
phone (202) 342–2214, fax (202) 342–6820
His Excellency Bernardo Alvarez Herrera
Ambassador E. and P.
Consular Offices:
  California, San Francisco
  Florida, Miami
  Illinois, Chicago
  Louisiana, New Orleans
  Massachusetts, Boston
  New York, New York
  Puerto Rico, San Juan
  Texas, Houston

VIETNAM

Embassy of Vietnam
1233 20th Street, NW., Suite 400, Washington, DC 20036
phone (202) 861–0737, fax (202) 861–0917

His Excellency Chien Tam Nguyen
Ambassador E. and P.
Consular Office: California, San Francisco

YEMEN

Embassy of the Republic of Yemen
2319 Wyoming Avenue, NW., Washington, DC 20008
phone (202) 965–4760, fax (202) 337–2017
His Excellency Abdulwahab A. Al-Hajjri
Ambassador E. and P.
Consular Office: Michigan, Detroit

YUGOSLAVIA

Permanent Mission of the Federal Republic of
Yugoslavia to the U.N.
854 5th Avenue, New York, NY 10021
phone (212) 879–8700, fax (212) 879–8705
Nebojsa Kaludjerovic
Ambassador E. and P.

ZAMBIA

Embassy of the Republic of Zambia
2419 Massachusetts Avenue, NW., Washington, DC 20008
phone (202) 265–9717, fax (202) 332–0826
Her Excellency Inonge Mbikusita Lewanika
Ambassador E. and P.

ZIMBABWE

Embassy of the Republic of Zimbabwe
1608 New Hampshire Avenue, NW., Washington, DC 20009
phone (202) 332–7100, fax (202) 483–9326
His Excellency Simbi Veke Mubako
Ambassador E. and P.

EUROPEAN UNION

Delegation of the European Commission
2300 M Street, NW., Washington, DC 20037
(202) 862–9500, fax (202) 429–1766
His Excellency John Bruton
Ambassador E. and P. (Head of Delegation)

The following is a list of countries with which
diplomatic relations have been severed:

After each country, in parenthesis, is the name
of the country's protecting power in the United
States.

CUBA (Switzerland)
IRAN (Pakistan)
IRAQ (Algeria)

PRESS GALLERIES*

SENATE PRESS GALLERY

The Capitol, Room S–316, phone 224–0241

Director.—S. Joseph Keenan
 Deputy Director.—Joan McKinney
  Media Coordinators:
   Amy H. Gross
   Wendy A. Oscarson

James D. Saris

HOUSE PRESS GALLERY

The Capitol, Room H–315, phone 225–3945

Superintendent.—Jerry L. Gallegos
 Deputy Superintendent.—Justin J. Supon
  Assistant Superintendents:
   Laura Reed
   Ric Andersen

Drew Cannon
Molly Cain

STANDING COMMITTEE OF CORRESPONDENTS

Julie Hirschfeld Davis, The Baltimore Sun, Chairman
Chuck McCutcheon, Newhouse News Service, Secretary
Bart Jansen, Portland Press Herald/Maine Sunday Telegraph
Susan Milligan, Boston Globe
Bill Walsh, The Times Picayune

RULES GOVERNING PRESS GALLERIES

1. Administration of the press galleries shall be vested in a Standing Committee of Correspondents elected by accredited members of the galleries. The Committee shall consist of five persons elected to serve for terms of two years. Provided, however, that at the election in January 1951, the three candidates receiving the highest number of votes shall serve for two years and the remaining two for one year. Thereafter, three members shall be elected in odd-numbered years and two in even-numbered years. Elections shall be held in January. The Committee shall elect its own chairman and secretary. Vacancies on the Committee shall be filled by special election to be called by the Standing Committee.

2. Persons desiring admission to the press galleries of Congress shall make application in accordance with Rule VI of the House of Representatives, subject to the direction and control of the Speaker and Rule 33 of the Senate, which rules shall be interpreted and administered by the Standing Committee of Correspondents, subject to the review and an approval by the Senate Committee on Rules and Administration.

3. The Standing Committee of Correspondents shall limit membership in the press galleries to bone fide correspondents of repute in their profession, under such rules as the Standing Committee of Correspondents shall prescribe.

---

*Information is based on data furnished and edited by each respective gallery.

929

4. An applicant for press credentials through the Daily Press Galleries must establish to the satisfaction of the Standing Committee of Correspondents that he or she is a full-time, paid correspondent who requires on-site access to congressional members and staff. Correspondents must be employed by a news organization:

(a) with General Publication periodicals mailing privileges under U.S. Postal Service rules, and which publishes daily; or

(b) whose principal business is the daily dissemination of original news and opinion of interest to a broad segment of the public, and which has published continuously for 18 months.

The applicant must reside in the Washington, D.C. area, and must not be engaged in any lobbying or paid advocacy, advertising, publicity or promotion work for any individual, political party, corporation, organization, or agency of the U.S. government, or in prosecuting any claim before Congress or any federal government department, and will not do so while a member of the Daily Press Galleries.

Applicants' publications must be editorially independent of any institution, foundation or interest group that lobbies the federal government, or that is not principally a general news organization.

Failure to provide information to the Standing Committee for this determination, or misrepresenting information, can result in the denial or revocation of credentials.

5. Members of the families of correspondents are not entitled to the privileges of the galleries.

6. The Standing Committee of Correspondents shall propose no changes in the these rules except upon petition in writing signed by not less than 100 accredited members of the galleries.Dennis Hastert, Speaker of the House of Representatives.Trent Lott, Chairman, Senate Committee on Rules and Administration.The above rules have been approved by the Committee on Rules and Administration.

J. DENNIS HASTERT,
Speaker of the House of Representatives.

TRENT LOTT,
Chairman, Senate Committee on Rules and Administration.

MEMBERS ENTITLED TO ADMISSION

PRESS GALLERIES

Abbott, Charles: Reuters
Abell, John: Reuters
Abrahms, Douglas: Gannett News Service
Abrams, James: Associated Press
Abruzzese, Leo: Bloomberg News
Achenbach, Joel: Washington Post
Ackerman, Liza: Congressional Quarterly
Adair, William: St. Petersburg Times
Adams, Rebecca: Congressional Quarterly
Adcock, Beryl: Knight Ridder
Agres, Theodore: Washington Times
Ahearn, David: Defense Today
Aida, Hirotsugu: Kyodo News
Akita, Hiroyuki: Nikkei
Albanesius, Chloe: National Journal's Technology
  Daily
Alberts, Sheldon: Canwest News Service
Alconada, Hugo: La Nacion
Alday, Ricardo: Notimex Mexican News Agency
Alden, Edward: Financial Times
Aldinger, Charles: Reuters
Alexander, Charles: Reuters
Alexander, Andrew: Cox Newspapers
Ali, Syed: Congressional Quarterly
Allen, Michael: Washington Post
Allen, Ross: Argus Media
Allen, JoAnne: Reuters
Allen, Victoria: Reuters
Allen, Jonathan: Congressional Quarterly
Allison, Wes: St. Petersburg Times
Alonso-Zaldivar, Ricardo: Los Angeles Times
Alpert, Bruce: New Orleans Times-Picayune
Al-Sowayel, Naila: Saudi Press Agency
Anason, Dean: American Banker
Anderson, Mark: Dow Jones Newswires
Andrews, Caesar: Gannett News Service
Andrews, Edmund: New York Times
Angle, Martha: Congressional Quarterly
Anklam, Jr., Fred: USA Today
Aoki, Tadaoki: Nishi-Nippon Shimbun
Appleby, Julie: USA Today
Archibald, George: Washington Times
Arkell, Robert: Washington Examiner
Arnold, Laurence: Bloomberg News
Arthur, William: Bloomberg News
Arundel, Kara: LRP Publications
Asher, Julie: Catholic News Service
Asher, James: Knight Ridder
Ashizuka, Tomoko: Nikkei
Asseo, Laurie: Bloomberg News
Aukofer, Frank: Artists & Writers Syndicate

Aulston, Von: New York Times
Auster, Elizabeth: Cleveland Plain Dealer
Aversa, Jeannine: Associated Press
Azpiazu, Maria: EFE News Services
Babcock, Charles: Washington Post
Babington, Charles: Washington Post
Bachelet, Pablo: Knight Ridder/Miami Herald
Baer, Susan: Baltimore Sun
Bai, Matt: New York Times Magazine
Bailey, Anna: Washington Examiner
Bailey, Ruby: Knight Ridder/Detroit Free Press
Baker, Chris: Washington Times
Baker, Peter: Washington Post
Baker, Frank: Associated Press
Baldor, Lolita: Associated Press
Ball, Michael: Argus Media
Balls, Andrew: Financial Times
Baltimore, Chris: Reuters
Balz, Daniel: Washington Post
Banales, Jorge: EFE News Services
Banks, Adelle: Religion News Service
Barfield Berry, Deborah: Newsday
Barker, Jeffrey: Baltimore Sun
Barnett, James: Oregonian
Barollier, Pascal: Agence France-Presse
Barr, Gary: Washington Post
Barrera, Ruben: Notimex Mexican News Agency
Barrett, Randy: Communications Daily
Barrett, Devlin: Associated Press
Barrett, Randy: National Journal's Technology Daily
Barringer, Felicity: New York Times
Barry, Theresa: Bloomberg News
Barshay, Jill: Congressional Quarterly
Bartash, Jeffry: MarketWatch
Bashir, Mustafa: Saudi Press Agency
Basken, Paul: Bloomberg News
Bater, Jeffrey: Dow Jones Newswires
Batrawy, Aya: Kuwait News Agency
Batt, Tony: Stephens Media Group
Battaile, Janet: New York Times
Bauerlein, Valerie: Raleigh News & Observer
Baygents, Ronald: Kuwait News Agency
Bayot, James: Congressional Quarterly
Bazinet, Kenneth: New York Daily News
Beattie, Jeff: Energy Daily
Beck, Ellen: United Press International
Beck, Tobin: United Press International
Becker, Elizabeth: New York Times
Beckner, Steven: Market News International
Beddall, Katherine: Agence France-Presse

Congressional Directory

MEMBERS ENTITLED TO ADMISSION—Continued

Beech, Eric: Reuters
Behn, Sharon: Washington Times
Bellantoni, Christina: Washington Times
Belopotosky, Danielle: National Journal's
   Technology Daily
Bendavid, Naftali: Chicago Tribune
Bender, Bryan: Boston Globe
Benedetto, Richard: USA Today
Benenson, Robert: Congressional Quarterly
Benincasa, Robert: Gannett News Service
Benkelman, Susan: Congressional Quarterly
Bennet, James: New York Times
Benson, Miles: Newhouse News Service
Berardelli, Phil: United Press International
Berger, Matthew: Jewish Telegraphic Agency
Bergman, Hannah: American Banker
Berley, Max: Bloomberg News
Bernard, Jerome: Agence France-Presse
Berry, John: Bloomberg News
Bethel, Alison: Detroit News
Bettelheim, Adriel: Congressional Quarterly
Bicknell, John: Congressional Quarterly
Bilodeau, Otis: Bloomberg News
Bilski, Christina: Nikkei
Birnbaum, Jeffrey: Washington Post
Bishop, Sam: Fairbanks Daily News Miner
Biskupic, Joan: USA Today
Bivins, Larry: Gannett News Service
Bjerga, Alan: Wichita Eagle
Blackstone, Brian: Dow Jones Newswires
Blackwell, Rob: American Banker
Blakely, Andrei: Washington Examiner
Bland, Melissa: Reuters
Blazar, Laurie: Associated Press
Bliss, Jeffrey: Bloomberg News
Block, Robert: Wall Street Journal
Block, Donna: Daily Deal
Blum, Justin: Washington Post
Blumenthal, Les: McClatchy Newspapers
Bohan, Caren: Reuters
Bold, Michael: McClatchy Newspapers
Boliek, Brooks: Hollywood Reporter
Bonilla, Laura: Agence France-Presse
Bono, Agostino: Catholic News Service
Borak, Donna: United Press International
Borenstein, Seth: Knight Ridder
Borkowski, Monica: New York Times
Bosman, Julie: New York Times
Bostick, Romaine: Bloomberg News
Bosworth, Geoffrey: Congressional Quarterly
Botjer, Jordan: Asahi Shimbun
Boudreau, Wendy: Congressional Quarterly
Bourge, Christian: United Press International
Bouza, Teresa: EFE News Services
Bovee, Timothy: Associated Press
Bowers, Faye: Christian Science Monitor
Bowman, Tom: Baltimore Sun
Bowman, Curtis Lee: Scripps Howard News Service

Boyd, Robert: Knight Ridder
Brady, Erik: USA Today
Branch-Brioso, Karen: St. Louis Post Dispatch
Branson, Louise: USA Today
Brasher, Philip: Des Moines Register
Braun, Stephen: Los Angeles Times
Bravin, Jess: Wall Street Journal
Bredemeier, Kenneth: Chicago Tribune
Bremner, Faith: Gannett News Service
Bridis, Ted: Associated Press
Brinkley, Joel: New York Times
Bristol, Nellie: Health News Daily
Brock, Gregory: New York Times
Broder, Jonathan: Congressional Quarterly
Broder, David: Washington Post
Brodmann, Ronald: Congressional Quarterly
Brogan, Pamela: Gannett News Service
Brooks, Jennifer: Gannett News Service
Brooks, David: La Jornada
Brooks, David: New York Times
Brosnan, James: Scripps Howard News Service
Brown, Steve: LRP Publications
Brown, David: Washington Post
Brownstein, Ronald: Los Angeles Times
Brune, Thomas: Newsday
Bumiller, Elisabeth: New York Times
Bunis, Dena: Orange County Register
Burke, Alecia: Congressional Quarterly
Burns, Judith: Dow Jones Newswires
Burns, Susan: Cox Newspapers
Burns, Robert: Associated Press
Burt, Andy: Bloomberg News
Bush, Rudolph: Chicago Tribune
Buskirk, Howard: Communications Daily
Bustos, Sergio: Gannett News Service
Butler, Steven: Knight Ridder
Calamur, Krishnadev: United Press International
Calmes, Jackie: Wall Street Journal
Camia, Catalina: Gannett News Service
Camire, Dennis: Gannett News Service
Canas, Rafael: EFE News Services
Canellos, Peter: Boston Globe
Cantaloube, Thomas: Le Parisien
Cantlupe, Joe: Copley News Service
Capaccio, Anthony: Bloomberg News
Caplan, Abby: Argus Media
Cardman, Michael: LRP Publications
Caretto, Ennio: Il Corriere Della Sera
Carey, Mary Agnes: Congressional Quarterly
Carlson, Peter: Washington Post
Carmichael, Kevin: Bloomberg News
Carnevale, Mary: Wall Street Journal
Carney, Dan: USA Today
Carney, David: Tech Law Journal
Carr, Rebecca: Cox Newspapers
Carreno, Jose: El Universal
Carroll, James: Louisville Courier Journal

MEMBERS ENTITLED TO ADMISSION—Continued

Carroll, James: Congressional Quarterly
Carter, Charlene: Congressional Quarterly
Carter, Thomas: Washington Times
Cartwright, Linda: Congressional Quarterly
Casey, Winter: National Journal's Technology Daily
Cason, James: La Jornada
Caspar, Lucian: Basler Zeitung
Cass O'Connell, Connie: Associated Press
Cassata, Donna: Associated Press
Casteel, Chris: Daily Oklahoman
Ch. Savage, Luiza: New York Sun
Chaddock, Gail: Christian Science Monitor
Chang, Tsung-Chih: United Daily News
Charles, Deborah: Reuters
Chase, Katharine: LRP Publications
Chebium, Raju: Gannett News Service
Chen, Zhigang: Singtao Daily
Chen, Edwin: Los Angeles Times
Chen, Sammie: Gannett News Service
Chi, Wennie: Central News Agency
Chiacu, Doina: Reuters
Chiantaretto, Mariuccia: Il Giornale
Chipman, Kimberly: Bloomberg News
Christensen, Mike: Congressional Quarterly
Christie, Rebecca: Dow Jones Newswires
Chwallek, Gabriele: German Press Agency/DPA
Ciccone, Risa Akiyama: Nishi-Nippon Shimbun
Cindemir, Mehmet: Hurriyet
Clark, Drew: National Journal's Technology Daily
Clarke, David: Congressional Quarterly
Clemetson, Lynette: New York Times
Cloud, David: Wall Street Journal
Coache, Wendy: Associated Press
Cobb, Jr., Charles: AllAfrica.com
Cochran, John: Congressional Quarterly
Codrea, George: Congressional Quarterly
Cohen, Stephanie: MarketWatch
Cohen, Robert: Newark Star-Ledger
Cohn, Peter: CongressDaily
Cohn, D'Vera: Washington Post
Coile, Zachary: San Francisco Chronicle
Cole, Justin: Agence France-Presse
Collie, Kristen: Hearst Newspapers
Collins, Michael: Scripps Howard News Service
Condon, Jr., George: Copley News Service
Conkey, Christopher: Wall Street Journal
Conlon, Charles: Congressional Quarterly
Conners, Maureen: Congressional Quarterly
Connolly, Ceci: Washington Post
Connor, John: Dow Jones Newswires
Constantine, Gus: Washington Times
Cook, David: Christian Science Monitor
Cooper, Christopher: Wall Street Journal
Cooper, Catherine: Congressional Quarterly
Cooper, Patrick: USA Today
Cooper, Sonya: Bloomberg News
Cooper, Richard: Los Angeles Times

Cooper, Helene: New York Times
Cooper, Kent: Political Money Line
Cooperman, Alan: Washington Post
Copeland, Libby: Washington Post
Copeland, Peter: Scripps Howard News Service
Copp, Tara: Scripps Howard News Service
Corbett, Rebecca: New York Times
Corbett Dooren, Jennifer: Dow Jones Newswires
Corchado, Alfredo: Dallas Morning News
Cornwell, Susan Jean: Reuters
Cornwell, Rupert: London Independent
Cowan, Richard: Reuters
Cox, James: USA Today
Crabtree, Susan: Congressional Quarterly
Crane, Mark: USA Today
Cranford, John: Congressional Quarterly
Crawford, Craig: Congressional Quarterly
Crawley, John: Reuters
Crawley, James: Media General News Service
Crenshaw, Albert: Washington Post
Crewdson, John: Chicago Tribune
Crites, Alice: Washington Post
Crittenden, Michael: Congressional Quarterly
Crutsinger, Martin: Associated Press
Cubbison, Christopher: USA Today
Cummings, Jeanne: Wall Street Journal
Curl, Joseph: Washington Times
Curtius, Mary: Los Angeles Times
Cushman, Jr., John: New York Times
Czarniak, Chet: USA Today
DaCosta, Mario Navarro: ABIM News Agency
Dahne, Hans: German Press Agency/DPA
Dalglish, Arthur: Cox Newspapers
Dalrymple, Mary: Associated Press
Daly, Matthew: Associated Press
Daly, Dr. John: United Press International
Dangond, Silvia: El Columbiano
Daniel, Douglass: Associated Press
Dannheisser, Ralph: Congressional Quarterly
Dao, James: New York Times
Dart, Robert: Cox Newspapers
Davenport, Todd: American Banker
Davidson, Julie: LRP Publications
Davidson, Paul: USA Today
Davies, Frank: Miami Herald
Davila, Juan: Associated Press
Davis, Susan: CongressDaily
Davis, Tamainia: Denver Post
Davis, Robert: Wall Street Journal
Davis, David: Congressional Quarterly
Davis, Crystal: Knight Ridder
Davis, Julie: Baltimore Sun
Davis, Robert: USA Today
Day, Kathleen: Washington Post
de Borchgrave, Arnaud: United Press International
De LaCruz, Donna: Associated Press
de Toledano, Ralph: National News Research
  Syndicate

MEMBERS ENTITLED TO ADMISSION—Continued

Deans, Jr., Robert: Cox Newspapers
DeBose, Brian: Washington Times
Decker, Susan: Bloomberg News
DeFrank, Thomas: New York Daily News
Deibel, Mary: Scripps Howard News Service
Del Giudice, Vincent: Bloomberg News
Del Riccio, Cristiano: ANSA Italian News Agency
Delgado, Jose': El Nuevo Dia
Delollis, Barbara: USA Today
Delporte, Christopher: Medical Device Daily
DeMarco, Edward: Bloomberg News
Deogun, Nikhil: Wall Street Journal
Dermody, William: USA Today
Dermota, Kenneth: Agence France-Presse
DeSenne, Michael: SmartMoney.com
Deutsch, Jack: CongressDaily
DeWitt, Karen: Washington Examiner
Diamond, John: USA Today
Diaz, Kevin: Minneapolis Star Tribune
Dick, Jason: CongressDaily
Dillin, Jr., John: Christian Science Monitor
Dinan, Stephen: Washington Times
Dine, Philip: St. Louis Post-Dispatch
Dineen, John: Congressional Quarterly
Dinmore, Guy: Financial Times
Divis, Dee Ann: United Press International
Dlouhy, Jennifer: Hearst Newspapers
Dobbyn, Timothy: Reuters
Dodge, Robert: Dallas Morning News
Dodge, Catherine: Bloomberg News
Doering, Christopher: Reuters
Doggett, Tom: Reuters
Doherty, Robert: Reuters
Dolan, Michael: Reuters
Donmoyer, Ryan: Bloomberg News
Donnelly, John: Congressional Quarterly
Dono, Linda: Gannett News Service
Dooley-Young, Kerry: Bloomberg News
Dorell, Oren: USA Today
Dorning, Mike: Chicago Tribune
Doublet, Jean-Louis: Agence France-Presse
Doughty, Stuart: Reuters
Douglas, William: Knight Ridder
Dowd, Maureen: New York Times
Doyle, Michael: McClatchy Newspapers
Doyle, Timothy: Bloomberg News
Drajem, Mark: Bloomberg News
Drawbaugh, Kevin: Reuters
Dreazen, Yochi: Wall Street Journal
Drees, Caroline: Reuters
Drinkard, Jim: USA Today
Drogin, Robert: Los Angeles Times
Drummond, Bob: Bloomberg News
Duggan, Loren: Congressional Quarterly
Duin, Julia: Washington Times
Duke, Lynne: Washington Post
Duncan, Leslie: Congressional Quarterly

Dung, Duc Dong: Vietnam News Agency
Dunham, Will: Reuters
Dunphy, Harry: Associated Press
Duriez, Isabelle: Ouest/France
Eastham, Todd: Reuters
Easton, Nina: Boston Globe
Eaton, Sabrina: Cleveland Plain Dealer
Eckert, Paul: Reuters
Eckert, Toby: Copley News Service
Eckstrom, Kevin: Religion News Service
Edmonds, Sarah: Reuters
Edmonds, Jr., Ronald: Associated Press
Edsall, Thomas: Washington Post
Efron, Sonni: Los Angeles Times
Efstathiou, James: Bloomberg News
Eggen, Daniel: Washington Post
Eisler, Peter: USA Today
Eisman, Dale: Virginian-Pilot
El Hamti, Maribel: EFE News Services
El Nasser, Haya: USA Today
Elgood, Giles: Reuters
Ellicott, Val: Gannett News Service
Ellis, Kristi: Fairchild News Service
Elsner, Alan: Reuters
Enoch, Daniel: Bloomberg News
Epstein, Victor: Bloomberg News
Epstein, Keith: Tampa Tribune
Epstein, Edward: San Francisco Chronicle
Espo, David: Associated Press
Estevez, Dolia: El Financiero
Estill, Jerry: Associated Press
Evans, Ben: Congressional Quarterly
Eversley, Melanie: USA Today
Fabi, Randy: Reuters
Fagan, Amy: Washington Times
Faler, Brian: Washington Post
Fan, Maureen: Washington Post
Farah, Joseph: WorldNetDaily.com
Farrell, John: Denver Post
Farrell, Greg: USA Today
Fatsis, Stefan: Wall Street Journal
Fazzino, Elysa: Il Secolo XIX
Fears, Darryl: Washington Post
Fein, Geoff: Defense Daily
Feld, Karen: Capital Connections
Feldman, Carole: Associated Press
Feldmann, Linda: Christian Science Monitor
Feller, Ben: Associated Press
Felsenthal, Mark: Reuters
Fendrich, Howard: Associated Press
Ferguson, Alexander: Reuters
Ferguson, Ellyn: Gannett News Service
Fernandez, Manny: Washington Post
Ferrari, Francisco: Agence France-Presse
Ferraro, Thomas: Reuters
Ferrechio, Susan: Congressional Quarterly
Ferris, Craig: Bond Buyer

MEMBERS ENTITLED TO ADMISSION—Continued

Fetterman, Mindy: USA Today
Fialka, John: Wall Street Journal
Fibich, Linda: Newhouse News Service
Fields, Gary: Wall Street Journal
Files, John: New York Times
Filipczyk, Kathleen: LRP Publications
Filteau, Jerome: Catholic News Service
Finkel, David: Washington Post
Fiore, Faye: Los Angeles Times
Fireman, Kenneth: Newsday
Fischer, Leonard: Gannett News Service
Fitzgerald, Alison: Bloomberg News
Flamini, Roland: United Press International
Flanders, Gwen: USA Today
Flattau, Edward: Global Horizons Syndicate
Fletcher, Michael: Washington Post
Flippen, Charlie: Argus Media
Forrest, Bonnie: Congressional Quarterly
Forsythe, Michael: Bloomberg News
Foss, Brad: Associated Press
Foster-Simeon, Ed: USA Today
Fowle, Andrew: Associated Press
Fox, Margaret: Reuters
Fram, Alan: Associated Press
Frank, Thomas: USA Today
Fraze, Barbara: Catholic News Service
Frederick, Don: Los Angeles Times
Freedman, Jacob: Congressional Quarterly
Freedman, Dan: Hearst Newspapers
Freking, Kevin: Associated Press
Friedman, Robert: Scripps Howard News Service
Friedman, Lisa: Los Angeles Daily News
Friedman, Jeffrey: Congressional Quarterly
Friesner, Margery: ANSA Italian News Agency
Frommer, Frederick: Associated Press
Fu, Norman: China Times
Fuhrig, Frank: German Press Agency/DPA
Funk, Timothy: Charlotte Observer
Furlow, Robert: Associated Press
Galianese, Joseph: Associated Press
Gallagher, Brian: USA Today
Gallen, Claire: Agence France-Presse
Galloway, Joseph: Knight Ridder
Gamboa, Suzanne: Associated Press
Gambrell, Kathy: CongressDaily
Gamerman, Ellen: Baltimore Sun
Gaouette, K. Nicole: Los Angeles Times
Gardiner, Andrew: USA Today
Gay, Lance: Scripps Howard News Service
Gearan, Anne: Associated Press
Gedda, George: Associated Press
Geewax, Marilyn: Cox Newspapers
Gehrke, Robert: Salt Lake Tribune
Gelie, Philippe: Le Figaro
Gentry, Caroline: Argus Media
Geracimos, Ann: Washington Times
Gerber, Michael: Washington Examiner

Gerdts, Jennifer: Tokyo-Chunichi Shimbun
Gerhart, Ann: Washington Post
Gerstenzang, James: Los Angeles Times
Gerth, Jeff: New York Times
Gertz, William: Washington Times
Giacomo, Carol: Reuters
Gibson, Andreas: Associated Press
Gibson, William: South Florida Sun-Sentinel
Gienger, Viola: Bloomberg News
Gilbert, Craig: Milwaukee Journal Sentinel
Gillman, Todd: Dallas Morning News
Giroux, Gregory: Congressional Quarterly
Givens, David: Argus Media
Glanz, William: Washington Times
Glass, Robert: Associated Press
Glass, Pamela: Le Mauricien
Glasser, Susan: Washington Post
Glover, K. Daniel: National Journal's Technology
    Daily
Godfrey, John: Dow Jones Newswires
Goffe, Shelia: Congressional Quarterly
Goldbacher, Raymond: USA Today
Golden, Jim: Gannett News Service
Goldman, Seth: Congressional Quarterly
Goldstein, Daniel: Bloomberg News
Goldstein, David: Kansas City Star
Goldstein, Jacobo: La Tribuna Newspaper
Goldstein, Steven: Knight Ridder/Philadelphia
    Inquirer
Golle, Vince: Bloomberg News
Gomez, Sergio: El Tiempo
Goode, Darren: CongressDaily
Goodman, Adrianne: New York Times
Gordon, D. Craig: Newsday
Gordon, Greg: McClatchy Newspapers
Gordon, Marcy: Associated Press
Gorham, Elizabeth: Canadian Press
Gosselin, Peter: Los Angeles Times
Goto, Shihoko: United Press International
Govindarajan, Shweta: Congressional Quarterly
Gowen, Annie: Washington Post
Graham, Bradley: Washington Post
Graham, Jed: Investor's Business Daily
Gramaglia, Giampiero: ANSA Italian News Agency
Grant, Paul: Reuters
Green, Mark: Daily Oklahoman
Greenberg, Brigitte: Bloomberg News
Greenburg, Jan: Chicago Tribune
Greene, Robert: Bloomberg News
Greenhouse, Linda: New York Times
Greenlee, Steven: Restructuring Today
Grenz-Marcuse, Gabrielle: Agence France-Presse
Greve, Frank: Knight Ridder
Gribben, Kristin: Argus Media
Grier, Peter: Christian Science Monitor
Griffith, Stephanie: Agence France-Presse
Groppe, Maureen: Gannett News Service
Grove, Ben: Las Vegas Sun

Gruenwald, Juliana: CongressDaily
Guan, Jinyong: China Economic Daily
Guest, Justin: Houston Chronicle
Guggenheim, Ken: Associated Press
Gugliotta, Guy: Washington Post
Gulino, Denny: Market News International
Gundersen, Heather: Associated Press
Gunther, Markus: Westdeutsche Allgemeine
Guroian, Rafi: Cox Newspapers
Hackett, Laurel: Scripps Howard News Service
Haddix, Dar: United Press International
Hagenbaugh, Barbara: USA Today
Hager, George: USA Today
Haggerty, Maryann: Washington Post
Hall, Kevin: Knight Ridder
Hall, Mimi: USA Today
Hall, John: Media General News Service
Hallam, Kristen: Bloomberg News
Hallock, Kimberly: Congressional Quarterly
Halloran, Liz: Hartford Courant
Hallow, Ralph: Washington Times
Hamalainen, Aloysia: St. Louis Post-Dispatch
Hamann, Carlos: Agence France-Presse
Hamatani, Koji: Akahata
Hamburger, Thomas: Los Angeles Times
Hananel, Sam: Associated Press
Hand, Mark: Washington Examiner
Harden, Patrick: LRP Publications
Hardin, Peter: Richmond Times-Dispatch
Hargrove, Thomas: Scripps Howard News Service
Harland, Janis: New York Times
Harper, Tim: Toronto Star
Harper, Jennifer: Washington Times
Harrington, Caitlin: Congressional Quarterly
Harris, Hamil: Washington Post
Harris, Francis: London Daily Telegraph
Harris, Gardiner: New York Times
Harris, John: Washington Post
Hart, Daniel: Bloomberg News
Hartman, Carl: Associated Press
Hartnagel, Nancy: Catholic News Service
Hartson, Merrill: Associated Press
Harwood, John: Wall Street Journal
Hatch, David: National Journal's Technology Daily
Havemann, Joel: Los Angeles Times
Hawkings, David: Congressional Quarterly
Hayakawa, Toshiyuki: Sekai Nippo
Hazar, Hasan: Turkiye Daily
Healy, Robert: Congressional Quarterly
Healy, Melissa: Los Angeles Times
Heavey, Susan: Reuters
Hebert, H. Josef: Associated Press
Hedges, Stephen: Chicago Tribune
Hedges, Michael: Houston Chronicle
Heiber, Jordan: Asahi Shimbun
Heil, Emily: CongressDaily
Heilprin, John: Associated Press

Heller, Michele: American Banker
Heller, Marc: Watertown Daily Times
Hendel, John: United Press International
Hendel, Caitlin: Congressional Quarterly
Henderson, Joan: Restructuring Today
Henderson, Diedtra: Boston Globe
Henderson, Stephen: Knight Ridder
Hendren, John: Los Angeles Times
Hendrie, Paul: Congressional Quarterly
Henriksson, Karin: Svenska Dagbladet
Heo, Yongbom: Chosun Ilbo
Herman, Ken: Cox Newspapers
Herman, Edith: Communications Daily
Hernandez, Raymond: New York Times
Hess, David: CongressDaily
Hiebert, Murray: Wall Street Journal
Higgins, Sean: Investor's Business Daily
Higgins, Marguerite: Washington Times
Hill, Patrice: Washington Times
Hille, Karl: Washington Examiner
Hillman, G. Robert: Dallas Morning News
Hines, Cragg: Houston Chronicle
Hines, Elizabeth: New York Times
Hinton, Earl: Associated Press
Hirose, Eiji: Yomiuri Shimbun
Hirsch, Claudia: Market News International
Hisadome, Shinichi: Tokyo-Chunichi Shimbun
Hishinuma, Takao: Yomiuri Shimbun
Hitt, Greg: Wall Street Journal
Hodge, Nathan: Defense Today
Hoffecker, Leslie: Los Angeles Times
Hoffman, Lisa: Scripps Howard News Service
Holland, Jesse: Associated Press
Holland, Judy: Hearst Newspapers
Holland, Gina: Associated Press
Holly, Christopher: Energy Daily
Holmes, Charles: Cox Newspapers
Holzer, Linda: USA Today
Hook, Janet: Los Angeles Times
Hopkins, Andrea: Reuters
Hopkins, Cheyenne: Reuters
Horrigan, Caroline: United Press International
Horrock, Nicholas: Washington Examiner
Horwich, Lee: USA Today
Horwitz, Sari: Washington Post
Hoskinson, Jr., Charles: Agence France-Presse
Hotakainen, Rob: Minneapolis Star Tribune
House, Billy: Arizona Republic
Howell, Deborah: Newhouse News Service
Hoy, Anne: Congressional Quarterly
Hoyt, Clark: Knight Ridder
Hsu, Spencer: Washington Post
Hubler, David: LRP Publications
Hudson, Audrey: Washington Times
Hudson, Saul: Reuters
Hughes, Siobhan: Dow Jones Newswires
Hughes, John: Bloomberg News

MEMBERS ENTITLED TO ADMISSION—Continued

Hughey, Ann: Bloomberg News
Hujer, Marc: Sueddeutsche Zeitung
Hulse, Carl: New York Times
Hultman, Tamela: AllAfrica.com
Hume, Lynn: Bond Buyer
Hunley, Johnathan: Fredericksburg Freelance-Star
Hunt, Albert: Bloomberg News
Hunt, Terence: Associated Press
Hurlburt, Sid: USA Today
Hurley, Liam: Saudi Press Agency
Hurt, Charles: Washington Times
Hutcheson, Ron: Knight Ridder
Hyde, Justin: Reuters
Ikeda, Nestor: Associated Press
Ip, Gregory: Wall Street Journal
Iqbal, Anwar: United Press International
Ishiai, Tsutomu: Asahi Shimbun
Ito, Toshiyuki: Yomiuri Shimbun
Ivanovich, David: Houston Chronicle
Ives-Halperin, Benton: Congressional Quarterly
Jackler, Rosalind: USA Today
Jackson, David: Dallas Morning News
Jackson, Frankie: Los Angeles Times
Jaffe, Greg: Wall Street Journal
Jahn, Daniel: Agence France-Presse
Jalonick, Mary Clare: Congressional Quarterly
Janofsky, Michael: New York Times
Jansen, Bart: Portland Press Herald
Jarlenski, Marian: Congressional Quarterly
Jaspin, Elliot: Cox Newspapers
Jean-Robert, Alain: Agence France-Presse
Jehl, Douglas: New York Times
Jelinek, Pauline: Associated Press
Jensen, Kristin: Bloomberg News
Jing, Hui: Epoch Times
Jitsu, Tetsuya: Nikkei
Johnson, Kevin: USA Today
Johnson, Sandy: Associated Press
Johnson, Toni: Congressional Quarterly
Johnson, Carrie: Washington Post
Johnson, Glen: Associated Press
Johnston, Nicholas: Bloomberg News
Johnston, Margret: German Press Agency/DPA
Johnston, David: New York Times
Jones, Kerry: Congressional Quarterly
Jones, David: Washington Times
Jordan, Charles: CongressDaily
Jordan, Lara Jakes: Associated Press
Joshi, Jitendra: Agence France-Presse
Joy, Patricia: Congressional Quarterly
Joyce, Amy: Washington Post
Joyce, Stacey: Reuters
Justice, Glen: New York Times
Justsen, Klaus: Jyllands-Posten
Kady II, Martin: Congressional Quarterly
Kagawa, Aya: Asahi Shimbun
Kamalick, Joseph: Chemical News & Intelligence

Kamen, Al: Washington Post
Kammer, Jerry: Copley News Service
Kampeas, Ron: Jewish Telegraphic Agency
Kang, Insun: Chosun Ilbo
Kaplan, Peter: Reuters
Kapochunas, Rachel: Congressional Quarterly
Karey, Gerald: Platts News Service
Karube, Kensuke: Jiji Press
Kashiyama, Yukio: Sankei Shimbun
Kastner, Kevin: Market News International
Kato, Hidenaka: Nikkei
Katz, Jonathan: Congressional Quarterly
Keating, Dan: Washington Post
Keefe, Stephen: Nikkei
Keen, Judith: USA Today
Keil, Richard: Bloomberg News
Keller, Susan: New York Times
Kelley, Matthew: Associated Press
Kellogg, Sarah: Newhouse News Service
Kelly, Sarah: Washington Examiner
Kelly, Nancy: American Metal Market
Kelly, Dennis: USA Today
Kelly, Erin: Gannett News Service
Kemper, Bob: Cox Newspapers
Kendall, Brent: Los Angeles Daily Journal
Kendall, Jr., Charles: National News Research Syndicate
Kenen, Joanne: Reuters
Kercheval, Nancy: Bloomberg News
Kertes, Noella: Congressional Quarterly
Kertesz, Kata: Associated Press
Kesen, Hideo: Sankei Shimbun
Kessler, Glenn: Washington Post
Kesten, Lou: Associated Press
Keto, Alex: Dow Jones Newswires
Kiefer, Francine: Christian Science Monitor
Kiely, Kathy: USA Today
Kilian, Michael: Chicago Tribune
Kilian, Martin: Tages Anzeiger
Kim, Dae Young: Yonhap News Agency
Kimura, Jun: Mainichi Shimbun
King, Peter: Congressional Quarterly
King, Llewellyn: Energy Daily
King, Ledyard: Gannett News Service
King, Jr., Neil: Wall Street Journal
Kinoshita, Hideomi: Kyodo News
Kipling, Bogdan: Kipling News Service
Kirchgaessner, Stephanie: Financial Times
Kirchhoff, Suzanne: USA Today
Kirkland, Michael: United Press International
Kirsanov, Dmitry: Itar-Tass News Agency
Kishida, Yoshida: Jiji Press
Kiss, Veroaique: Agence France-Presse
Kivlan, Terence: Newhouse News Service
Klamper, Amy: CongressDaily
Klein, Richard: Boston Globe
Klein, Alyson: CongressDaily
Klein, Alec: Washington Post

MEMBERS ENTITLED TO ADMISSION—Continued

Klein Jr., Gilbert: Media General News Service
Klisz, Theresa: Gannett News Service
Kniazkov, Maxim: Agence France-Presse
Knowlton, Brian: International Herald Tribune
Knox, Olivier: Agence France-Presse
Koar, Juergen: Stuttgarter Zeitung
Koff, Stephen: Cleveland Plain Dealer
Koffler, Keith: CongressDaily
Kohn, Francis: Agence France-Presse
Kohrs, Cecile: Daily Deal
Kojin, Yuichi: Asahi Shimbun
Kolawole, Emi: Congressional Quarterly
Komarow, Steven: USA Today
Komori, Yoshihisa: Sankei Shimbun
Kondo, Toyokazu: Sankei Shimbun
Kopecki, Dawn: Dow Jones Newswires
Kornblut, Anne: New York Times
Kosseff, Jeffrey: Oregonian
Koszczuk, Jaculine: Congressional Quarterly
Kotake, Hiroyuki: Nikkei
Kralev, Nicholas: Washington Times
Kramer, Reed: AllAfrica.com
Kranish, Michael: Boston Globe
Krawzak, Paul: Copley News Service
Krebs, Brian: WashingtonPost.com
Kreisher, Otto: Copley News Service
Krim, Jonathan: Washington Post
Krishnaswami, Sridhar: Hindu
Kroepsch, Adrianne: Communications Daily
Kronholz, June: Wall Street Journal
Kuhn, Mary Ann: Washington Examiner
Kuhnhenn, James: Knight Ridder
Kuk, Kiyon: Segye Times
Kumar, Anita: St. Petersburg Times
Kumar, Dinesh: Communications Daily
Kwon, Soon-Taek: Dong-A Ilbo
La Franchi, Howard: Christian Science Monitor
Labaton, Stephen: New York Times
Labriny, Azeddine: Saudi Press Agency
Lagomarsino, Deborah: Dow Jones Newswires
Lakely, James: Washington Times
Lambrecht, William: St. Louis Post-Dispatch
Lambro, Donald: Washington Times
Lambros, Papantoniou: Eleftheros Typos
Landay, Jonathan: Knight Ridder
Landers, James: Dallas Morning News
Landry, Catherine: Platts News Service
Lane, Terry: Communications Daily
Langan, Michael: Agence France-Presse
Lanman, Scott: Bloomberg News
Larkin, Catherine: Bloomberg News
Law, Darrell: Reuters
Lawder, David: Reuters
Lawrence, Jill: USA Today
Layton, Lyndsey: Washington Post
Leary, Warren: New York Times
Leavitt, Paul: USA Today

Lebedev, Ivan: Itar-Tass News Agency
Lebling, Madonna: Washington Post
Lee, Christopher: Washington Post
Lee, Do Woon: Seoul Shinmun
Lee, Kristen: New York Times
Lee, Richard: Media General News Service
Lee, Mi Sook: Munwha Ilbo
Lefkow, Chris: Agence France-Presse
Lehmann, Evan: Lowell Sun
Lehming, Malte: Der Tagesspiegel
Leibovich, Mark: Washington Post
Leiby, Richard: Washington Post
Leinwand, Donna: USA Today
Lek Kee Low, Eugene: Singapore Straits Times
Lengel, Allan: Washington Post
Lerman, David: Newport News Daily Press
Lesparre, Michael: Roll Call Report Syndicate
Lester, William: Associated Press
Leubsdorf, Carl: Dallas Morning News
Lever, Robert: Agence France-Presse
Levin, Alan: USA Today
Levine, Samantha: Houston Chronicle
Lewis, Charles: Hearst Newspapers
Lewis, Finlay: Copley News Service
Lewis, Neil: New York Times
Lewis, Katherine: Dallas Morning News
Lewis, Katherine: Newhouse News Service
Li, Zhengxin: China Economic Daily
Lichtblau, Eric: New York Times
Lieberman, Brett: Harrisburg Patriot-News
Lightman, David: Hartford Courant
Lilleston, Thomas: USA Today
Lin, Wen-Chi: Central News Agency
Lin, Betty: World Journal
Lindell, Chuck: Austin American Statesman
Link, Daniel: Congressional Quarterly
Lipman, Laurence: Cox Newspapers
Lipowicz, Alice: Congressional Quarterly
Lipton, Eric: New York Times
Litvan, Laura: Bloomberg News
Liu, Kuen-yuan: Central News Agency
Liu, Ping: China Times
Liu, Haixin: China Economic Daily
Lizama, Orlando: EFE News Services
Lobe, James: Inter Press Service
Lobsenz, George: Energy Daily
Lochhead, Carolyn: San Francisco Chronicle
Locy, Toni: USA Today
Lomax, Simon: Argus Media
Lopez Zamorano, Jose: Notimex Mexican News Agency
Lorente, Rafael: South Florida Sun-Sentinel
Lorenzetti, Maureen: Congressional Quarterly
Lorenzo, Aaron: BioWorld Today
Loven, Jennifer: Associated Press
Lowy, Joan: Scripps Howard News Service
Lueck, Sarah: Wall Street Journal
Lumpkin, John: Associated Press

MEMBERS ENTITLED TO ADMISSION—Continued

Lyman, L. Peter: Syracuse Post Standard
Lyons, Jonathan: Reuters
Lytle, Tamara: Orlando Sentinel
MacDonald, David: McClendon News Service
Machacek, John: Gannett News Service
MacInnis, Laura: Reuters
Mackler, Peter: Agence France-Presse
MacMillan, Robert: WashingtonPost.com
MacPhersen, Karen: Pittsburgh Post-Gazette
Madden, Mark: Los Angeles Times
Madden, Mike: Gannett News Service
Madigan, Sean: Congressional Quarterly
Magnuson, Stewart: LRP Publications
Maier, Tim: Washington Examiner
Majano, Rosendo: EFE News Services
Maler, Sandra: Reuters
Malone, Julia: Cox Newspapers
Maloy, Timothy: United Press International
Malsang-Salles, Isabelle: Agence France-Presse
Mann, William: Associated Press
Mannion, James: Agence France-Presse
Mansfield, Stephanie: Washington Times
Marano, Louis: United Press International
Marchand, Ann: WashingtonPost.com
Marcy, Steven: Argus Media
Margasak, Lawrence: Associated Press
Marino, Jonathan: Washington Examiner
Marino, Marie: Gannett News Service
Marklein, Mary Beth: USA Today
Markoe Kolko, Lauren: Columbia State
Marolo, Bruno: L'Unita
Marre, Klaus: German Press Agency/DPA
Marshall, Tyler: Los Angeles Times
Marshall, Michael: United Press International
Marshall, Stephen: USA Today
Martin, Gary: San Antonio Express-News
Martin, Andrew: Chicago Tribune
Martinez, Ian: Communications Daily
Martinez, Gebe: Houston Chronicle
Mason, Julie: Houston Chronicle
Massie, Alex: Edinburgh Scotsman
Mathews, Anna: Wall Street Journal
Mathewson, Judith: Bloomberg News
Matusic, Karen: Dow Jones Newswires
May, Michaela: CongressDaily
Mayer, Caroline: Washington Post
Maynard, Michael: MarketWatch
Mazzetti, Mark: Los Angeles Times
McCaffrey, Shannon: Knight Ridder
McCarthy, Thomas: Los Angeles Times
McCarthy, Mike: German Press Agency/DPA
McCaslin, John: Washington Times
McConnell, Alison: Bond Buyer
McCrehan, Jeff: Christian Science Monitor
McCutcheon, Chuck: Newhouse News Service
McDonough, Siobhan: Associated Press
McFeatters, Dale: Scripps Howard News Service

McFeatters, Ann: Pittsburgh Post-Gazette
McGinley, Laurie: Wall Street Journal
McGough, Michael: Pittsburgh Post Gazette
McGuire, David: WashingtonPost.com
McIntyre, Allison: Los Angeles Times
McKeaney, Kristy: Bloomberg News
McKee, Michael: Bloomberg News
McKenzie, Lesley: Yomiuri Shimbun
McKinnon, John: Wall Street Journal
McLean, Demian: Bloomberg News
McLoone, Sharon: National Journal's Technology Daily
McManus, Doyle: Los Angeles Times
McMurray, Jeffrey: Associated Press
McNeil, Margaret: MarketWatch
McQuaid, John: New Orleans Times-Picayune
McQuillan, Mark: Bloomberg News
McQuillen, William: Bloomberg News
Meadows, Clifton: New York Times
Means, Marianne: Hearst Newspapers
Meek, James: New York Daily News
Meinert, Dori: Copley News Service
Mekay, Emad: Inter Press Service
Melendez, Michele: Newhouse News Service
Memmott, Mark: USA Today
Mentzer, Thomas: Scripps Howard News Service
Mercer, Marsha: Media General News Service
Mercier, Rick: Fredericksburg Free Lance-Star
Merry, Robert: Congressional Quarterly
Meszoly, Robin: Bloomberg News
Meyer, Joshua: Los Angeles Times
Michaels, Jim: USA Today
Michalski, Patty: USA Today
Middleton, Chris: Market News International
Miga, Andrew: Boston Herald
Mihailescu, Andrea: United Press International
Mikkelsen, Randall: Reuters
Milbank, Dana: Washington Post
Miller, Kevin: Bloomberg News
Miller, Alan: Los Angeles Times
Miller, Steven: Washington Times
Miller, Jeff: Allentown Morning Call
Miller, Greg: Los Angeles Times
Miller, David: Congressional Quarterly
Miller, Leslie: Associated Press
Miller, T. Christian: Los Angeles Times
Milligan, Susan: Boston Globe
Mills, Michael: Congressional Quarterly
Mills, Betty: Griffin-Larrabee News Service
Mitchell, Brian: Investor's Business Daily
Mitchell, Steve: United Press International
Mitchell, Charles: CongressDaily
Mitoma, Yoshio: Sekai Nippo
Mittelstadt, Michelle: Dallas Morning News
Mitton, Roger: Singapore Straits Times
Miyasaka, Yoshio: Kyodo News
Mohammad, Saad: Kuwait News Agency
Mohammed, Arshad: Reuters

MEMBERS ENTITLED TO ADMISSION—Continued

Mondics, Christopher: Philadelphia Inquirer
Moniz, Dave: USA Today
Montgomery, David: Fort Worth Star-Telegram
Montgomery, David: Washington Post
Montgomery, Lori: Washington Post
Moore, Pamela: LRP Publications
Moore, Evan: Mainichi Shimbun
Morales Lujan, Armando: Los Tiempos
Morgan, David: Reuters
Morgan, Dan: Washington Post
Moriarty, JoAnn: Springfield Republican
Morris, Ryan: Associated Press
Morris, David: CongressDaily
Morris, James: Congressional Quarterly
Morrison, Joanne: Reuters
Morrison, Blake: USA Today
Moscoso, Eunice: Cox Newspapers
Mueller, Sarah: Newsday
Mulkern, Anne: Denver Post
Mullen, Richard: Defense Today
Mulligan, John: Providence Journal
Mullins, Brody: Wall Street Journal
Munoz, Cesar: EFE News Services
Murayama, Kohei: Kyodo News
Murayama, Tomohiro: Asahi Shimbun
Murray, Shanon: Daily Deal
Murray, Brendan: Bloomberg News
Murray, Shailagh: Washington Post
Myers, Jim: Tulsa World
Myers, Michael: Myers News Service
Naganuma, Aki: Tokyo-Chunichi Shimbun
Nagourney, Adam: New York Times
Nakano, Tetsuya: Jiji Press
Nance, Scott: Defense Today
Nance, Rahkia: Washington Examiner
Narayanan, Vin: USA Today
Nather, David: Congressional Quarterly
N'Diaye, Yali: Market News International
Neibauer, Michael: Washington Examiner
Neikirk, William: Chicago Tribune
Nelson, Deborah: Los Angeles Times
Nesmith, Jeff: Cox Newspapers
Neubauer, Chuck: Los Angeles Times
Neuman, Johanna: Los Angeles Times
Newman, Emily: Bond Buyer
Newman, Christopher: Argus Media
Newton Small, Jay: Bloomberg News
Nghi, Hi Vu: Vietnam News Agency
Nguyen, Minh: Vietnam News Agency
Nichols, John: WashingtonPost.com
Nichols, Bill: USA Today
Nishimura, Yoichi: Asahi Shimbun
Nishimura, Takuya: Hokkaido Shimbun
Nkansah, E. Roy: Congressional Quarterly
Noel, Essex: Reuters
Nomiyama, Chizu: Reuters
Norman, Jane: Des Moines Register

Norton, C. JoAnne: Bloomberg News
Norton, Stephen: Congressional Quarterly
Novak, Robert: Chicago Sun-Times
Noyes, Andrew: Communications Daily
Nutting, Rex: MarketWatch
Nutting, Brian: Congressional Quarterly
Nyitray, Joseph: Congressional Quarterly
O'Brien, Nancy: Catholic News Service
O'Connell, James: Bloomberg News
O'Connor, Bette: Reuters
O'Donnell, Jayne: USA Today
Oelrich, Christiane: German Press Agency/DPA
Oh, Diane: Asahi Shimbun
O'Hara, Terence: Washington Post
O'Keefe, Mark: Religion News Service
Okuma, Yoshiaki: Jiji Press
Olchowy, Mark: Associated Press
Oleksyn, Veronika: Congressional Quarterly
Oliphant, Cortright: Oliphant News Service
Oliphant, Thomas: Boston Globe
Olmsted, Daniel: United Press International
Olson, Elizabeth: New York Times
O'Reilly II, Joseph: Bloomberg News
Orndorff, Mary: Birmingham News
Orol, Ron: Daily Deal
O'Rourke, Lawrence: McClatchy Newspapers
Orr, J. Scott: Newark Star-Ledger
Ortiz, Ximens: Washington Times
Ostermann, Dietmar: Frankfurter Rundschau
Ota, Alan: Congressional Quarterly
Ota, Masakatsu: Kyodo News
Ourlian, Robert: Los Angeles Times
Overberg, Paul: USA Today
Pace, David: Associated Press
Page, Susan: USA Today
Page, Clarence: Chicago Tribune
Paletta, Damian: American Banker
Palmer, J. Jioni: Newsday
Panczyk-Collins, Tania: Communications Daily
Parasuram, T.V.: Press Trust of India
Parker, Laura: USA Today
Parks, Daniel: Congressional Quarterly
Parnes, Amie: Scripps Howard News Service
Pasternak, Judy: Los Angeles Times
Pattison, Mark: Catholic News Service
Pear, Robert: New York Times
Pearl, Larry: Argus Media
Peck, Louis: CongressDaily
Pelofsky, Jeremy: Reuters
Pena, Maria: EFE News Services
Perine, Keith: Congressional Quarterly
Pesce, Carolyn: USA Today
Petersen, Rosemary: Copley News Service
Peterson, Molly: CongressDaily
Peterson, Jonathan: Los Angeles Times
Phelps, Timothy: Newsday
Phillips, Michael: Wall Street Journal

MEMBERS ENTITLED TO ADMISSION—Continued

Phillips, Kathleen: New York Times
Phillips, Zachary: Congressional Quarterly
Philpott, Thomas: Military Update
Pianin, Eric: Washington Post
Pickler, Nedra: Associated Press
Pine, Art: Bloomberg News
Piper, Greg: Communications Daily
Pleming, Sue: Reuters
Plocek, Joseph: Market News International
Plummer, Anne: Congressional Quarterly
Plungis, Jeff: Detroit News
Poirier, John: Reuters
Polyakova, Susan: Communications Daily
Ponnudurai, Parameswaran: Agence France-Presse
Pontarelli, Erika: Agence France-Presse
Poole, Janet: Agence France-Presse
Poole, Isaiah: Congressional Quarterly
Pope, Charles: Seattle Post-Intelligencer
Posner, Michael: CongressDaily
Powell, Stewart: Hearst Newspapers
Powelson, Richard: Scripps Howard News Service
Powers, Ronald: Associated Press
Pressley, Sue Ann: Washington Post
Price, Marc: Associated Press
Price, Elizabeth: Dow Jones Newswires
Price, Deborah: Detroit News
Priest, Dana: Washington Post
Pruden, Wesley: Washington Times
Pruitt, Claude: Gannett News Service
Puente, Maria: USA Today
Pugh, Anthony: Knight Ridder
Purce, Melinda: Associated Press
Purdum, Todd: New York Times
Purger, Tibor: Magyar Szo
Pusey, Allen: Dallas Morning News
Putman, Eileen: Associated Press
Putrich, Gayle: Congressional Quarterly
Puzzanghera, James: San Jose Mercury News
Quaid, Libby: Associated Press
Raab, Charlotte: Agence France-Presse
Raasch, Charles: Gannett News Service
Radelat, Ana: Gannett News Service
Radsch, Courtney: New York Times
Raffaelli, Jean: Agence France-Presse
Raimon, Marcelo: ANSA Italian News Agency
Raivio, Jyri: Helsingin Sanomat
Rajauopalan, Sethuraman: Hindustan Times
Rambourg, Gersende: Agence France-Presse
Ramey, Joanna: Fairchild News Service
Ramstack, Thomas: Washington Times
Randall, Maya: Dow Jones Newswires
Rankin, Robert: Knight Ridder
Rapp, David: Congressional Quarterly
Rater, Philippe: Agence France-Presse
Rauber, Marilyn: Media General
Raum, Thomas: Associated Press
Rauscher, Jr., Carl: Cox Newspapers

Ray, Eric: Congressional Quarterly
Raymond, Anthony: Political Money Line
Rebello, Joseph: Dow Jones Newswires
Reber, Paticia: German Press Agency/DPA
Recio, Maria: Knight Ridder/Fort Worth Star-Telegram
Reddy, Tarun: Saudi Press Agency
Rehm, Barbara: American Banker
Rehrmann, Laura: Gannett News Service
Reichard, John: Congressional Quarterly
Reilly, Sean: Mobile Register
Reinert-Mason, Patty: Houston Chronicle
Reiss, Cory: New York Times
Remez, Michael: Congressional Quarterly
Reston, Maeve: Pittsburgh Post-Gazette
Retter, Daphne: Congressional Quarterly
Reynolds, Maura: Los Angeles Times
Riccardi, Emenuele: ANSA Italian News Agency
Rich, Spencer: CongressDaily
Rich, Eric: Washington Post
Richardson, Betty: Congressional Quarterly
Riche, Pascal: Liberation
Richey, Warren: Christian Science Monitor
Richter, Joseph: Bloomberg News
Richter, Paul: Los Angeles Times
Richwine, Lisa: Reuters
Rickett, Keith: Associated Press
Ricks, Tom: Washington Post
Riechmann-Kepler, Deb: Associated Press
Rief, Norbert: Die Presse
Riley, John: USA Today
Rios, Delia: Newhouse News Service
Ripley, Neil: Congressional Quarterly
Riskind, Jonathan: Columbus Dispatch
Risser, William: USA Today
Rivet, Jerome: Agence France-Presse
Rizzo, Katherine: Congressional Quarterly
Robb, Gregory: MarketWatch
Robbins, Carla: Wall Street Journal
Roberts, Roxanne: Washington Post
Roberts, Kristin: Reuters
Roberts, Martin: Reuters
Roberts III, William: Bloomberg News
Robinson, John: Defense Daily
Robinson, James: Los Angeles Times
Robinson, Eugene: Washington Post
Roche, Jr., Walter: Los Angeles Times
Rodriguez, Antonio: Agence France-Presse
Roff, Peter: United Press International
Rogers, David: Wall Street Journal
Rogin, Joshua: Asahi Shimbun
Roland, Neil: Bloomberg News
Rood, Justin: Congressional Quarterly
Roosevelt, Ann: Defense Daily
Rosen, James: McClatchy Newspapers
Rosenbaum, David: New York Times
Rosenberg, Eric: Hearst Newspapers
Rosenkrantz, Holly: Bloomberg News

MEMBERS ENTITLED TO ADMISSION—Continued

Rosenthal, Peter: Argus Media
Ross, Sonya: Associated Press
Roth, Bennett: Houston Chronicle
Rothstein, Joel: Reuters
Rovner, Julie: CongressDaily
Rowley, James: Bloomberg News
Roxe, Hilary: Associated Press
Roybal, Peter: Congressional Quarterly
Rubin, James: Bloomberg News
Ruiz, Phillip: Los Angeles Times
Runningen, Roger: Bloomberg News
Ruskin, Liz: Anchorage Daily News
Russell, Alec: London Daily Telegraph
Ryan, Timothy: Reuters
Ryan, Richard: Detroit News
Ryerson-Cruz, Geraldine: Bloomberg News
Sadahiro, Takashi: Yomiuri Shimbun
Sakajiri, Nobuyoshi: Asahi Shimbun
Salant, Jonathan: Bloomberg News
Salhani, Claude: United Press International
Sammon, William: Washington Times
San Martin-Raedle, Nancy: Miami Herald
Sanchez, Humberto: Bond Buyer
Sandalow, Marc: San Francisco Chronicle
Sands, Derek: Kyodo News
Sands, David: Washington Times
Sands, Peggy: Congressional Quarterly
Sanger, David: New York Times
Santini, Jean-Louis: Agence France-Presse
Santos, Lori: Reuters
Sasazawa, Kyoichi: Yomiuri Shimbun
Satariano, Adam: Congressional Quarterly
Savage, Charles: Boston Globe
Savage, David: Los Angeles Times
Savic, Dubravka: Vecernje Novosti
Sawai, Toshimitsu: Kyodo News
Sawyer, Jon: St. Louis Post-Dispatch
Scally, William: William Scally Reports
Scarborough, Rowan: Washington Times
Schaefer-Munoz, Sara: Wall Street Journal
Schatz, Amy: Wall Street Journal
Schatz, Joseph: Congressional Quarterly
Scherer, Eric: Agence France-Presse
Schleicher, Al: Yomiuri Shimbun
Schlesinger, Jacob: Wall Street Journal
Schlisserman, Courtney: Bloomberg News
Schmick, William: Bloomberg News
Schmid, Randolph: Associated Press
Schmid, Sharon: Wall Street Journal
Schmidt, Susan: Washington Post
Schmidt, Robert: Bloomberg News
Schmitt, Eric: New York Times
Schmitt, Richard: Los Angeles Times
Schnakenberg, Lea Ann: German Press
  Agency/DPA
Schneider, Tal: Maariv
Schneider, Jodi: Congressional Quarterly
Schoof, Renee: Knight Ridder

Schrader, Esther: Los Angeles Times
Schroeder, Michael: Wall Street Journal
Schroeder, Robert: MarketWatch
Schuler, Kate: Congressional Quarterly
Schwed, Craig: Gannett News Service
Schweid, Barry: Associated Press
Scott, Katherine: Gannett News Service
Scott-Molleda, Heather: Market News International
Seeley, Tina: Energy Daily
Seeman, Bruce: Newhouse News Service
Sefton, Dru: Newhouse News Service
Seib, Gerald: Wall Street Journal
Seibel, Mark: Knight Ridder
Seper, Jerry: Washington Times
Serrano, Richard: Los Angeles Times
Settles, Mary: McClatchy Newspapers
Sevastopulo, Demetri: Financial Times
Shaffrey, Mary: Winston-Salem Journal
Shalal-Esa, Andrea: Reuters
Shane, Scott: New York Times
Shanker, Thomas: New York Times
Sharma, Amol: Congressional Quarterly
Sharn, Lori: CongressDaily
Shaw, John: Market News International
Shea, Patti: Washington Times
Sheehan, Theresa: Market News International
Sheikh, Nezar: Saudi Press Agency
Shek, Katherine: LRP Publications
Shelly, Nedra: Cleveland Plain Dealer
Shenon, Philip: New York Times
Shepard, Scott: Cox Newspapers
Sher, Andrew: Chattanooga Times Free Press
Sherman, Mark: Associated Press
Sherwell, Philip: London Daily Telegraph
Sherzai, Magan: Agence France-Presse
Shesgreen, Deirdre: St. Louis Post-Dispatch
Shields, Gerard: Baton Rouge Advocate
Shields, Mark: Creators Syndicate
Shiver, Jr., Jube: Los Angeles Times
Shrader, Katie: Associated Press
Sia, Richard: CongressDaily
Sidorov, Dmitry: Kommersant
Sidoti, Elizabeth: Associated Press
Sieff, Martin: United Press International
Sigurdson, Todd: Associated Press
Silva, Rodrigo: Associated Press
Silva, Mark: Chicago Tribune
Silverstein, Kenneth: Los Angeles Times
Simison, Robert: Bloomberg News
Simon, Richard: Los Angeles Times
Simpson, Cameron: Chicago Tribune
Siniff, John: USA Today
Sisk, Richard: New York Daily News
Sitov, Andrei: Itar-Tass News Agency
Skarzenski, Ronald: New York Times
Skiba, Katherine: Milwaukee Journal Sentinel
Skomial, Marcin: Argus Media

MEMBERS ENTITLED TO ADMISSION—Continued

Skorneck, Carolyn: Associated Press
Slater, James: Agence France-Presse
Slavin, Barbara: USA Today
Smith, Christopher: Salt Lake Tribune
Smith, Jeffrey: Washington Post
Smith, Sylvia: Fort Wayne Journal Gazette
Smith, Stephen: Houston Chronicle
Smith, Donna: Reuters
Smith, Elliot: USA Today
Smith, Brad: Reuters
Snider, Michael: USA Today
Sniffen, Michael: Associated Press
Snyder, Charles: Taipei Times
Sobczyk, Joseph: Bloomberg News
Solis Jr., Carlos: Jiji Press
Solomon, John: Associated Press
Solomon, Deborah: Wall Street Journal
Somerville, Glenn: Reuters
Soraghan, Michael: Denver Post
Sotero, Paulo: O Estado De S. Paulo
Spang, Thomas: Rheinische Post
Spangler, Jerry: Deseret News
Sparks, Sarah: LRP Publications
Sparshott, Jeffrey: Washington Times
Spasyk, Clarissa: LRP Publications
Spence, Timothy: Hearst Newspapers
Spencer, George: Restructuring Today
Spencer, Samuel: Restructuring Today
Sperry, Paul: WorldNetDaily.com
Sprengelmeyer, Michael: Scripps Howard News
    Service
Squeo, Anne Marie: Wall Street Journal
St. Onge, Jeffrey: Bloomberg News
Stainer, M. Maria: Washington Times
Stanton, John: CongressDaily
Starks, Tim: Congressional Quarterly
Stearns, Matthew: Kansas City Star
Steele, Stephen: Catholic News Service
Stein, Jeff: Congressional Quarterly
Steinman, Jon: Bloomberg News
Stempleman, Neil: Reuters
Stencel, Mark: Congressional Quarterly
Stephens, Angela: Orange County Register
Stern, Seth: Congressional Quarterly
Stern, Marcus: Copley News Service
Sternberg, Steve: USA Today
Sternberg, William: USA Today
Stevenson, Johnny: Wall Street Journal
Stevenson, Richard: New York Times
Stewart, Bruce Scott: Sankei Shimbun
Stinson, Jeffrey: USA Today
Stirland, Sarah: National Journal's Technology
    Daily
Stockman, Farah: Boston Globe
Stoddard, Alexandra: Congressional Quarterly
Stohr, Greg: Bloomberg News
Stolberg, Sheryl: New York Times
Stone, Andrea: USA Today

Storey, David: Reuters
Stout, David: New York Times
Strahan, Amy: Bloomberg News
Straub, Bill: Scripps Howard News Service
Straub, Noelle: Boston Herald
Straw, Joseph: New Haven Register
Streck, Michael: Die Tageszeitung
Strobel, Warren: Knight Ridder
Strong, Thomas: Associated Press
Struglinski, Suzanne: Las Vegas Sun
Suissa Zeimet, Corinne: Agence France-Presse
Sullivan, Bartholomew: Scripps Howard News
    Service
Sullivan, Andy: Reuters
Sumikawa, Yuriko: Kyodo News
Superville, Darlene: Associated Press
Surzhanskiy, Andrey: Itar-Tass News Agency
Swann, Christopher: Financial Times
Swindell, Bill: Congressional Quarterly
Swisher, Lawrence: Northwest Newspapers
Szekely, Peter: Reuters
Tackett, R. Michael: Chicago Tribune
Takahashi, Jun: Kyodo News
Takahashi, Hiroyuki: Jiji Press
Takahashi, Masaya: Kyodo News
Talev, Margaret: McClatchy Newspapers
Tanaka, Shinya: Kyodo News
Tanzi, Alex: Bloomberg News
Tatsumi, Tomoji: Kyodo News
Taubman, Philip: New York Times
Tavara, Santiago: Notimex Mexican News Agency
Taylor, Andrew: Congressional Quarterly
Taylor, Guy: Washington Times
Taylor, Cynthia: Boston Globe
Teitelbaum, Michael: Congressional Quarterly
Terada, Masaomi: Yomiuri Shimbun
Teskrat, Nadia: Agence France-Presse
Tessler, Joelle: Congressional Quarterly
Tetreault, Stephan: Stephens Media Group
Theimer, Sharon: Associated Press
Thomas, Helen: Hearst Newspapers
Thomas, Lisa: Kyodo News
Thomas, Richard: Roll Call Report Syndicate
Thomas, Ken: Associated Press
Thomasson, Dan: Scripps Howard News Service
Thomet, Laurent: Agence France-Presse
Thomma, Steven: Knight Ridder
Thompson, Jake: Omaha World-Herald
Thompson Osuri, Laura: American Banker
Tierney, John: New York Times
Tilove, Jonathan: Newhouse News Service
Timberg, Robert: Baltimore Sun
Timmons, Karen: Scripps Howard News Service
Tinsley, Elisa: USA Today
Tokito, Mineko: Yomiuri Shimbun
Toles, Tom: Washington Post
Tomkin, Robert: Congressional Quarterly
Tomkins, Richard: United Press International

MEMBERS ENTITLED TO ADMISSION—Continued

Tompson, Trevor: Associated Press
Toner, Robin: New York Times
Toppo, Gregory: USA Today
Torres, Carlos: Bloomberg News
Torres, Craig: Bloomberg News
Torry, Jack: Columbus Dispatch
Torry, Saundra: USA Today
Toshi, Eiji: Jiji Press
Toyoda, Yoichi: Tokyo-Chunichi Shimbun
Trankovits, Laszlo: German Press Agency/DPA
Trescott, Jacqueline: Washington Post
Trott, William: Reuters
Truslow, Hugh: New York Times
Tsao, Nadia Y.F.: Liberty Times
Tucker, Boyd Neely: Washington Post
Tumulty, Brian: Gannett News Service
Tunks, Larry: Congressional Quarterly
Turner, Douglas: Buffalo News
Tyson, Ann Scott: Washington Post
Tyson, James: Bloomberg News
Ullmann, Owen: USA Today
Urban, Peter: Connecticut Post
Urbina, Ian: New York Times
Usher, Anne: Cox Newspapers
Vadum, Matthew: Bond Buyer
Val Mitjavila, Eusebio: LA VANGUARDIA
Vande Hei, Jim: Washington Post
Vanden Brook, Tom: USA Today
Vander Haar, William: Associated Press
Vanichkin, Pavel: Itar-Tass News Agency
Vaughan, Martin: CongressDaily
Vedantam, Shankar: Washington Post
Veigle, Anne: Communications Daily
Vekshin, Alison: Stephens Media Group
Vergano, Dan: USA Today
Viccora, Andrew: LRP Publications
Vicini, James: Reuters
Vidal Liy, Macarena: EFE News Services
Vieth, Warren: Los Angeles Times
Vinas Diaz, Piedad: EFE News Services
Vineys, Kevin: Associated Press
Vitucci, Claire: Riverside Press-Enterprise
Vogt, Christophe: Agence France-Presse
Von Drehle, David: Washington Post
Vorman, Julie: Reuters
Wada, Hiroaki: Mainichi Shimbun
Waggoner, John: USA Today
Wagman, Robert: Newspaper Enterprise
Waitz, Nancy: Reuters
Walcott, John: Knight Ridder
Wald, Matthew: New York Times
Waldmeir, Patti: Financial Times
Walker, Martin: United Press International
Wallsten, Peter: Los Angeles Times
Walsh, Edmund: Dow Jones Newswires
Walsh, Bill: New Orleans Times-Picayune
Walton-James, Vickie: Chicago Tribune

Ward, Jon: Washington Times
Warminsky, Joseph: Congressional Quarterly
Watanabe, Tsutomu: Asahi Shimbun
Waterman, Shaun: United Press International
Waters, Donald: Associated Press
Watson, Traci: USA Today
Watson II, Ripley: Bloomberg News
Watters, Susan: Fairchild News Service
Wayne, Alexander: Congressional Quarterly
Wayne, Leslie: New York Times
Wegner, Mark: CongressDaily
Weintraub, Lisa: Congressional Quarterly
Weintraub, Stephanie: Congressional Quarterly
Weisman, Jonathan: Washington Post
Weisman, Steven: New York Times
Weiss, Eric: Washington Post
Weiss, Rick: Washington Post
Welch, James: USA Today
Welch, William: USA Today
Wells, Billie Jean: Gannett News Service
Wells, Robert: Dow Jones Newswires
Weng, Xiang: China Youth Daily
Werner, Erica: Associated Press
Wessel, David: Wall Street Journal
West, Paul: Baltimore Sun
Westbrook, Jesse: Bloomberg News
Westphal, David: McClatchy Newspapers
Wetzel, Hubert: Financial Times Deutschland
Wetzstein, Cheryl: Washington Times
Wheeler, Lawrence: Gannett News Service
White, Dina: Chicago Tribune
White, Keith: Congressional Quarterly
White, Gordon: Washington Telecommunications Services
White, Keith: CongressDaily
White, Josh: Washington Post
White, Jr., Joseph: Associated Press
Whitesides, John: Reuters
Whitmire, Richard: USA Today
Whitmire, Guy: Congressional Quarterly
Whitney, David: McClatchy Newspapers
Whittle, Richard: Dallas Morning News
Wienberger, Sharon: Defense Daily
Wiessler, David: Reuters
Wiggins, Clayton: Wall Street Journal
Wilber, Del: Washington Post
Wilke, John: Wall Street Journal
Wilkie, Dana: Copley News Service
Williams, Clarence: Washington Post
Williams, Vanessa: Washington Post
Williams, Jr., Joseph: Boston Globe
Willing, Richard: USA Today
Willis, Robert: Bloomberg News
Willman, David: Los Angeles Times
Wilson, Patricia: Reuters
Wingfield, Brian: New York Times
Wingfield, Frederick: Associated Press
Winicour, Daniel: Congressional Quarterly

MEMBERS ENTITLED TO ADMISSION—Continued

Winski, Joe: Bloomberg News
Witcher, Tim: Agence France-Presse
Witcover, Jules: Baltimore Sun
Witkowski, Nancy Benac: Associated Press
Witter, Willis: Washington Times
Wodele, Greta: CongressDaily
Wolf, Richard: USA Today
Wolf, Jim: Reuters
Wolfe, Kathryn: Congressional Quarterly
Wolfe, Elizabeth: Associated Press
Woo, Yee Ling: Congressional Quarterly
Wood, Winston: Wall Street Journal
Wood, David: Newhouse News Service
Woods, Michael: Pittsburgh Post-Gazette
Woodward, Cal: Associated Press
Woodward, Bob: Washington Post
Woutat, Donald: Los Angeles Times
Wright, Gregory: Gannett News Service
Wright, Ivan: Associated Press
Wright, Vevlyn: CongressDaily
Wroughton, Lesley: Reuters
Wutkowski, Karey: Reuters
Wynn, Randall: Congressional Quarterly
Wysocki, Jr., Bernard: Wall Street Journal
Yamagishi, Isao: Hokkaido Shimbun
Yamamoto, Rumiko: Nikkei
Yamasaki, Shinji: Akahata
Yancey, Matthew: Associated Press

Yaukey, John: Gannett News Service
Yen, Hope: Associated Press
Yoder, Eric: Washington Post
Yoshida, Toru: Nikkei
Yoshimoto, Akemi: Kyodo News
Yost, Pete: Associated Press
Young, Alison: Knight Ridder
Young, Samantha: Stephens Media Group
Yu, Donghui: China News Service
Yule, Robert: Asahi Shimbun
Yun, Dong Young: Yonhap News Agency
Yun, Linda: Yomiuri Shimbun
Zabarenko, Deborah: Reuters
Zacharia, Janine: Bloomberg News
Zagaroli, Lisa: Detroit News
Zajac, Andrew: Chicago Tribune
Zakaria, Tabassum: Reuters
Zamora, Amanda: WashingtonPost.com
Zapor, Patricia: Catholic News Service
Zeleny, Jeff: Chicago Tribune
Zeuthen, Kasper: Yomiuri Shimbun
Zhang, Mengjun: Science and Technology Daily
Ziegler, Julie: Bloomberg News
Zimmerman, Carol: Catholic News Service
Zitner, Aaron: Los Angeles Times
Zoroya, Gregg: USA Today
Zremski, Jerry: Buffalo News
Zuckman, Jill: Chicago Tribune

NEWSPAPERS REPRESENTED IN PRESS GALLERIES

ABIM News Agency—(703) 243–2104; 1344 Merrie Ridge Road, McLean, VA 22101: Mario Navarro DaCosta.

AGENCE FRANCE-PRESSE—(202) 414–0602; 1015 15th Street, Suite 500, Washington, DC 20005: Pascal Barollier, Katherine Beddall, Jerome Bernard, Laura Bonilla, Justin Cole, Kenneth Dermota, Jean-Louis Doublet, Francisco Ferrari, Claire Gallen, Gabrielle Grenz-Marcuse, Stephanie Griffith, Carlos Hamann, Charles Hoskinson, Jr., Daniel Jahn, Alain Jean-Robert, Jitendra Joshi, Veroaique Kiss, Maxim Kniazkov, Olivier Knox, Francis Kohn, Michael Langan, Chris Lefkow, Robert Lever, Peter Mackler, Isabelle Malsang-Salles, James Mannion, Parameswaran Ponnudurai, Erika Pontarelli, Janet Poole, Charlotte Raab, Jean Raffaelli, Gersende Rambourg, Philippe Rater, Jerome Rivet, Antonio Rodriguez, Jean-Louis Santini, Eric Scherer, Magan Sherzai, James Slater, Corinne Suissa Zeimet, Nadia Teskrat, Laurent Thomet, Christophe Vogt, Tim Witcher.

AKAHATA—(202) 393–5238; 978 National Press Building, Washington DC 20045: Koji Hamatani, Shinji Yamasaki.

ALLAFRICA.COM—(202) 546–0777; 920 M Street, SE., Washington, DC 20003: Charles Cobb, Jr., Tamela Hultman, Reed Kramer.

ALLENTOWN MORNING CALL—(202) 824–8216; 1325 G Street, Suite 200, Washington, DC 20005: Jeff Miller.

AMERICAN BANKER—(202) 434–0316; 1325 G Street, Suite 900, Washington, DC 20005: Dean Anason, Hannah Bergman, Rob Blackwell, Todd Davenport, Michele Heller, Damian Paletta, Barbara Rehm, Laura Osuri Thompson.

AMERICAN METAL MARKET—(202) 393–7750; 943 National Press Building, Washington, DC 20045: Nancy Kelly.

ANCHORAGE DAILY NEWS—(202) 383–0007; 420 National Press Building, Washington, DC 20045: Liz Ruskin.

ANSA ITALIAN NEWS AGENCY—(202) 628–3317; 1285 National Press Building, Washington, DC 20045: Cristiano Del Riccio, Margery Friesner, Giampiero Gramaglia, Marcelo Raimon, Emenuele Riccardi.

ARGUS MEDIA—(202) 349–2878; 1012 14th Street, Suite 1500, Washington, DC 20005: Ross Allen, Michael Ball, Abby Caplan, Charlie Flippen, Caroline Gentry, David Givens, Kristin Gribben, Simon Lomax, Steven Marcy, Christopher Newman, Larry Pearl, Peter Rosenthal, Marcin Skomial.

ARIZONA REPUBLIC—(202) 906–8136; 1100 New York Avenue, 2nd Floor, Washington, DC 20005: Billy House.

ARTISTS & WRITERS SYNDICATE—(703) 820–4232; 6325 Beachway Drive, Falls Church, VA 22044: Frank Aukofer.

ASAHI SHIMBUN—(202) 783–1000; 1022 National Press Building, Washington, DC 20045: Jordan Botjer, Jordan Heiber, Tsutomu Ishiai, Aya Kagawa, Yuichi Kojin, Tomohiro Murayama, Yoichi Nishimura, Diane Oh, Joshua Rogin, Nobuyoshi Sakajiri, Tsutomu Watanabe, Robert Yule.

ASSOCIATED PRESS—(202) 776–9480; 2021 K Street, 6th Floor, Washington, DC 20006: James Abrams, Jeannine Aversa, Frank Baker, Lolita Baldor, Devlin Barrett, Laurie Blazar, Timothy Bovee, Ted Bridis, Robert Burns, Connie Cass O'Connell, Donna Cassata, Wendy Coache, Martin Crutsinger, Mary Dalrymple, Matthew Daly, Douglass Daniel, Juan Davila, Donna De LaCruz, Harry Dunphy, Ronald Edmonds, Jr., David Espo, Jerry Estill, Carole Feldman, Ben Feller, Howard Fendrich, Brad Foss, Andrew Fowle, Alan Fram, Kevin Freking, Frederick Frommer, Robert Furlow, Joseph Galianese, Suzanne Gamboa, Anne Gearan, George Gedda, Andreas Gibson, Robert Glass, Marcy Gordon, Ken Guggenheim, Heather Gundersen, Sam Hananel, Carl Hartman, Merrill Hartson, H. Josef Hebert, John Heilprin, Earl Hinton, Jesse Holland, Gina Holland, Terence Hunt, Nestor Ikeda, Pauline Jelinek, Glen Johnson, Sandy Johnson, Lara Jakes Jordan, Matthew Kelley, Kata Kertesz, Lou Kesten, William Lester, Jennifer Loven, John Lumpkin, William Mann, Lawrence Margasak, Siobhan McDonough, Jeffrey McMurray, Leslie Miller, Ryan Morris, Mark Olchowy, David Pace, Nedra Pickler, Ronald Powers, Marc Price, Melinda Purce, Eileen Putman, Libby Quaid, Thomas Raum, Keith Rickett, Deb Riechmann-Kepler, Sonya Ross, Hilary Roxe, Randolph Schmid, Barry Schweid, Mark Sherman, Katie Shrader, Elizabeth Sidoti, Todd Sigurdson, Rodrigo Silva, Carolyn Skorneck, Michael Sniffen, John Solomon, Thomas Strong, Darlene Superville, Sharon Theimer, Ken Thomas, Trevor Tompson, William Vander Haar, Kevin Vineys, Donald Waters, Erica Werner, Joseph White, Jr., Frederick

NEWSPAPERS REPRESENTED—Continued

Wingfield, Nancy Benac Witkowski, Elizabeth Wolfe, Cal Woodward, Ivan Wright, Matthew Yancey, Hope Yen, Pete Yost.

AUSTIN AMERICAN STATESMAN—(202) 887–8329; 400 N. Capitol Street, Suite 750, Washington, DC 20001: Chuck Lindell.

BALTIMORE SUN—(202) 416–0250; 1627 K Street, Suite 1100, Washington, DC 20006: Susan Baer, Jeffrey Barker, Tom Bowman, Julie Davis, Ellen Gamerman, Robert Timberg, Paul West, Jules Witcover.

BASLER ZEITUNG—(202) 986–7542; 1526 Corcoran Street, NW., Washington, DC 20009: Lucian Caspar.

BATON ROUGE ADVOCATE—(202) 554–0458; 33 Overbrook Road, Catonsville, MD 21228: Gerard Shields.

BIOWORLD TODAY—(202) 719–7816; 4301 Connecticut Avenue, Suite 330, Washington, DC 20008: Aaron Lorenzo.

BIRMINGHAM NEWS—(202) 383–7837; 1101 Connecticut Avenue, Suite 300, Washington, DC 20036: Mary Orndorff.

BLOOMBERG NEWS—(202) 624–1966; 1399 New York Avenue, 11th Floor, Washington, DC 20005: Leo Abruzzese, Laurence Arnold, William Arthur, Laurie Asseo, Theresa Barry, Paul Basken, Max Berley, John Berry, Otis Bilodeau, Jeffrey Bliss, Romaine Bostick, Andy Burt, Anthony Capaccio, Kevin Carmichael, Kimberly Chipman, Sonya Cooper, Susan Decker, Vincent Del Giudice, Edward DeMarco, Catherine Dodge, Ryan Donmoyer, Kerry Dooley-Young, Timothy Doyle, Mark Drajem, Bob Drummond, James Efstathiou, Daniel Enoch, Victor Epstein, Alison Fitzgerald, Michael Forsythe, Viola Gienger, Daniel Goldstein, Vince Golle, Brigitte Greenberg, Robert Greene, Kristen Hallam, Daniel Hart, John Hughes, Ann Hughey, Albert Hunt, Kristin Jensen, Nicholas Johnston, Richard Keil, Nancy Kercheval, Scott Lanman, Catherine Larkin, Laura Litvan, Judith Mathewson, Kristy McKeaney, Michael McKee, Demian McLean, Mark McQuillan, William McQuillen, Robin Meszoly, Kevin Miller, Brendan Murray, Jay Newton Small, C. JoAnne Norton, James O'Connell, Joseph O'Reilly II, Art Pine, Joseph Richter, William Roberts III, Neil Roland, Holly Rosenkrantz, James Rowley, James Rubin, Roger Runningen, Geraldine Ryerson-Cruz, Jonathan Salant, Courtney Schlisserman, William Schmick, Robert Schmidt, Robert Simison, Joseph Sobczyk, Jeffrey St. Onge, Jon Steinman, Greg Stohr, Amy Strahan, Alex Tanzi, Carlos Torres, Craig Torres, James Tyson, Ripley Watson II, Jesse Westbrook, Robert Willis, Joe Winski, Janine Zacharia, Julie Ziegler.

BOND BUYER—(202) 434–0307; 1325 G Street, Suite 900, Washington, DC 20005: Craig Ferris, Lynn Hume, Alison McConnell, Emily Newman, Humberto Sanchez, Matthew Vadum.

BOSTON GLOBE—(202) 857–5060; 1130 Connecticut Avenue, Suite 520, Washington, DC 20036: Bryan Bender, Peter Canellos, Nina Easton, Diedtra Henderson, Richard Klein, Michael Kranish, Susan Milligan, Thomas Oliphant, Charles Savage, Farah Stockman, Cynthia Taylor, Joseph Williams, Jr.

BOSTON HERALD—(202) 638–1796; 988 National Press Building, Washington, DC 20045: Andrew Miga, Noelle Straub.

BUFFALO NEWS—(202) 737–3188; 1141 National Press Building, Washington, DC 20045: Douglas Turner, Jerry Zremski.

CANADIAN PRESS—(202) 638–3367; 1128 National Press Building, Washington, DC 20045: Elizabeth Gorham.

CANWEST NEWS SERVICE—(202) 662–7576; 1206 National Press Building, Washington, DC 20045: Sheldon Alberts.

CAPITAL CONNECTIONS—(202) 337–2044; 1698 32nd Street, NW., Washington, DC 20007: Karen Feld.

CATHOLIC NEWS SERVICE—(202) 541–3255; 3211 Fourth Street, NE., Washington, DC 20017: Julie Asher, Agostino Bono, Jerome Filteau, Barbara Fraze, Nancy Hartnagel, Nancy O'Brien, Mark Pattison, Stephen Steele, Patricia Zapor, Carol Zimmerman.

CENTRAL NEWS AGENCY—(202) 628–2738; 1173 National Press Building, Washington, DC 20045: Wennie Chi, Wen-Chi Lin, Kuen-yuan Liu.

CHARLOTTE OBSERVER—(202) 383–6057; 700 12th Street, NW., Suite 1000, Washington, DC 20005: Timothy Funk.

CHATTANOOGA TIMES FREE PRESS—(202) 662–7651; 1190 National Press Building, Washington, DC 20045: Andrew Sher.

CHEMICAL NEWS & INTELLIGENCE—(202) 776–1352 1150 18th Street, Suite 600, Washington, DC 20036: Joseph Kamalick.

CHICAGO SUN-TIMES—(202) 393–4340; 1750 Pennsylvania Avenue, #1203, Washington, DC 20006: Robert Novak.

CHICAGO TRIBUNE—(202) 824–8226; 1325 G Street, Suite 200, Washington, DC 20005: Naftali Bendavid, Kenneth Bredemeier, Rudolph Bush, John Crewdson, Mike Dorning, Jan Greenburg, Stephen Hedges, Michael Kilian, Andrew Martin, William Neikirk, Clarence Page, Mark Silva, Cameron Simpson, R. Michael Tackett, Vickie Walton-James, Dina White, Andrew Zajac, Jeff Zeleny, Jill Zuckman.

CHINA ECONOMIC DAILY—(703) 698–8579; 3305 Crest Haven Court, Falls Church, VA 22042: Jinyong Guan, Zhengxin Li, Haixin Liu.

CHINA NEWS SERVICE—(703) 527–5887; 1020 N Stafford Street, Suite 100, Arlington, VA 22201: Donghui Yu.

NEWSPAPERS REPRESENTED—Continued

CHINA TIMES—(202) 347–5670; 952 National Press Building, Washington, DC 20045: Norman Fu, Ping Liu.

CHINA YOUTH DAILY—(703) 534–3378; 251 Gundry Drive, Falls Church, VA 22046: Xiang Weng.

CHOSUN ILBO—(202) 841–3090; 1291 National Press Building, Washington, DC 20045: Yongbom Heo, Insun Kang.

CHRISTIAN SCIENCE MONITOR—(202) 481–6643; 910 16th Street, Suite 200, Washington, DC 20006: Faye Bowers, Gail Chaddock, David Cook, John Dillin, Jr., Linda Feldmann, Peter Grier, Francine Kiefer, Howard La Franchi, Jeff McCrehan, Warren Richey.

CLEVELAND PLAIN DEALER—(202) 638–1366; 930 National Press Building, Washington, DC 20045: Elizabeth Auster, Sabrina Eaton, Stephen Koff, Nedra Shelly.

COLUMBIA STATE—(202) 383–6032; 700 12th Street, NW., Suite 1000, Washington, DC 20005: Lauren Markoe Kolko.

COLUMBUS DISPATCH—(202) 824–6766; 400 North Capitol Street, Suite 850, Washington, DC 20001: Jonathan Riskind, Jack Torry.

COMMUNICATIONS DAILY—(202) 872–9200; 2115 Ward Court, NW., Washington, DC 20037: Randy Barrett, Howard Buskirk, Edith Herman, Adrianne Kroepsch, Dinesh Kumar, Terry Lane, Ian Martinez, Andrew Noyes, Tania Panczyk-Collins, Greg Piper, Susan Polyakova, Anne Veigle.

CONGRESSDAILY—(202) 739–8400; 600 New Hampshire Avenue, NW., Washington, DC 20037: Peter Cohn, Susan Davis, Jack Deutsch, Jason Dick, Kathy Gambrell, Darren Goode, Juliana Gruenwald, Emily Heil, David Hess, Charles Jordan, Amy Klamper, Alyson Klein, Keith Koffler, Michaela May, Charles Mitchell, David Morris, Louis Peck, Molly Peterson, Michael Posner, Spencer Rich, Julie Rovner, Lori Sharn, Richard Sia, John Stanton, Martin Vaughan, Mark Wegner, Keith White, Greta Wodele, Vevlyn Wright.

CONGRESSIONAL QUARTERLY—(202) 419–8334; 1255 22nd Street, Washington, DC 20037: Liza Ackerman, Rebecca Adams, Syed Ali, Jonathan Allen, Martha Angle, Jill Barshay, James Bayot, Robert Benenson, Susan Benkelman, Adriel Bettelheim, John Bicknell, Geoffrey Bosworth, Wendy Boudreau, Jonathan Broder, Ronald Brodmann, Alecia Burke, Mary Agnes Carey, James Carroll, Charlene Carter, Linda Cartwright, Mike Christensen, David Clarke, John Cochran, George Codrea, Charles Conlon, Maureen Conners, Catherine Cooper, Susan Crabtree, John Cranford, Craig Crawford, Michael Crittenden, Ralph Dannheisser, David Davis, John Dineen, John Donnelly, Loren Duggan, Leslie Duncan, Ben Evans, Susan Ferrechio, Bonnie Forrest, Jacob Freedman, Jeffrey Friedman, Gregory Giroux, Shelia Goffe, Seth Goldman, Shweta Govindarajan, Kimberly Hallock, Caitlin Harrington, David Hawkings, Robert Healy, Caitlin Hendel, Paul Hendrie, Anne Hoy, Benton Ives-Halperin, Mary Clare Jalonick, Marian Jarlenski, Toni Johnson, Kerry Jones, Patricia Joy, Martin Kady II, Rachel Kapochunas, Jonathan Katz, Noella Kertes, Peter King, Emi Kolawole, Jaculine Koszczuk, Daniel Link, Alice Lipowicz, Maureen Lorenzetti, Sean Madigan, Robert Merry, David Miller, Michael Mills, James Morris, David Nather, E. Roy Nkansah, Stephen Norton, Brian Nutting, Joseph Nyitray, Veronika Oleksyn, Alan Ota, Daniel Parks, Keith Perine, Zachary Phillips, Anne Plummer, Isaiah Poole, Gayle Putrich, David Rapp, Eric Ray, John Reichard, Michael Remez, Daphne Retter, Betty Richardson, Neil Ripley, Katherine Rizzo, Justin Rood, Peter Roybal, Peggy Sands, Adam Satariano, Joseph Schatz, Jodi Schneider, Kate Schuler, Amol Sharma, Tim Starks, Jeff Stein, Mark Stencel, Seth Stern, Alexandra Stoddard, Bill Swindell, Andrew Taylor, Michael Teitelbaum, Joelle Tessler, Robert Tomkin, Larry Tunks, Joseph Warminsky, Alexander Wayne, Lisa Weintraub, Stephanie Weintraub, Keith White, Guy Whitmire, Daniel Winicour, Kathryn Wolfe, Yee Ling Woo, Randall Wynn.

CONNECTICUT POST—(202) 662–8927; 1255 National Press Building, Washington, DC 20045: Peter Urban.

COPLEY NEWS SERVICE—(202) 737–7686; 1100 National Press Building, Washington, DC 20045: Joe Cantlupe, George Condon, Jr., Toby Eckert, Jerry Kammer, Paul Krawzak, Otto Kreisher, Finlay Lewis, Dori Meinert, Rosemary Petersen, Marcus Stern, Dana Wilkie.

COX NEWSPAPERS—(202) 887–8334; 400 N. Capitol Street, Suite 750, Washington, DC 20001: Andrew Alexander, Susan Burns, Rebecca Carr, Arthur Dalglish, Robert Dart, Robert Deans, Jr., Marilyn Geewax, Rafi Guroian, Ken Herman, Charles Holmes, Elliot Jaspin, Bob Kemper, Laurence Lipman, Julia Malone, Eunice Moscoso, Jeff Nesmith, Carl Rauscher, Jr., Scott Shepard, Anne Usher.

CREATORS SYNDICATE—(202) 662–1255; 1009 National Press Building, Washington, DC 20045: Mark Shields.

DAILY DEAL—(202) 429–2991; 1775 K Street, Suite 590, Washington, DC 20006: Donna Block, Cecile Kohrs, Shanon Murray, Ron Orol.

DAILY OKLAHOMAN—(202) 662–7543; 914 National Press Building, Washington, DC 20045: Chris Casteel, Mark Green.

DALLAS MORNING NEWS—(202) 661–8413; 1325 G Street, Suite 250, Washington, DC 20005: Alfredo Corchado, Robert Dodge, Todd Gillman, G. Robert Hillman, David Jackson, James Landers, Carl Leubsdorf, Katherine Lewis, Michelle Mittelstadt, Allen Pusey, Richard Whittle.

DEFENSE DAILY—(703) 522–5655; 1011 Arlington Blvd., Suite 131, Arlington, VA 22209: Geoff Fein, John Robinson, Ann Roosevelt, Sharon Wienberger.

NEWSPAPERS REPRESENTED—Continued

DEFENSE TODAY—(202) 662–9729; 1325 G Street, Suite 1003, Washington, DC 20005: David Ahearn, Nathan Hodge, Richard Mullen, Scott Nance.

DENVER POST—(202) 662–8908; 1255 National Press Building, Washington, DC 20045: Tamainia Davis, John Farrell, Anne Mulkern, Michael Soraghan.

DER TAGESSPIEGEL—(202) 234–2168; 766 A Chireh Street, NW., Washington, DC 20036: Malte Lehming.

DES MOINES REGISTER—(202) 906–8138; 1100 New York Avenue, Washington, DC 20005: Philip Brasher, Jane Norman.

DESERET NEWS—(202) 737–5311; 1061 National Press Building, Washington, DC 20045: Jerry Spangler.

DETROIT FREE PRESS—(202) 383–6036; 700 12th Street, NW., Suite 1000, Washington, DC 20005: Ruby Bailey.

DETROIT NEWS—(202) 906–8204; 1100 New York Avenue, Suite 200E, Washington, DC 20005: Alison Bethel, Jeff Plungis, Deborah Price, Richard Ryan, Lisa Zagaroli.

DIE PRESSE—(703) 931–9558; 3308 Peace Valley Lane, Falls Church, VA 22044: Norbert Rief.

DIE TAGESZEITUNG—(202) 462–6824; 1721 Newton Street, NW., Washington, DC 20020: Michael Streck.

DONG-A ILBO—(202) 347–4097; 974 National Press Building, Washington, DC 20045: Soon-Taek Kwon.

DOW JONES NEWSWIRES—(202) 862–9230; 1025 Connecticut Avenue, Suite 1100, Washington, DC 20036: Mark Anderson, Jeffrey Bater, Brian Blackstone, Judith Burns, Rebecca Christie, John Connor, Jennifer Corbett Dooren, John Godfrey, Siobhan Hughes, Alex Keto, Dawn Kopecki, Deborah Lagomarsino, Karen Matusic, Elizabeth Price, Maya Randall, Joseph Rebello, Edmund Walsh, Robert Wells.

EDINBURGH SCOTSMAN—(202) 248–9592; 2515 13th Street, Apt.#408, Washington, DC 20009: Alex Massie.

EFE NEWS SERVICES—(202) 745–7692; 1252 National Press Building, Washington, DC 20045: Maria Azpiazu, Jorge Banales, Teresa Bouza, Rafael Canas, Maribel El Hamti, Orlando Lizama, Rosendo Majano, Cesar Munoz, Maria Pena, Macarena Vidal Liy, Piedad Vinas Diaz.

EL COLUMBIANO—(703) 931–9538; 4770 West Braddock Road, Alexandria VA 22311: Silvia Dangond.

EL FINANCIERO—(703) 707–0236; 2300 Darius Lane, Reston, VA 20191: Dolia Estevez.

EL NUEVO DIA—(202) 662–7360; 1053 National Press Building, Washington, DC 20045: José Delgado.

EL TIEMPO—(202) 607–5929; 1102 National Press Building, Washington, DC 20045: Sergio Gomez.

EL UNIVERSAL—(202) 662–7190; 1193 National Press Building, Washington, DC 20045: Jose Carreno.

ELEFTHEROS TYPOS—(202) 675–0697; 1125 6th Street, NE., Washington, DC 20008: Papantoniou Lambros.

ENERGY DAILY—(202) 662–9739; 1325 G Street, Suite 1003, Washington, DC 20005: Jeff Beattie, Christopher Holly, Llewellyn King, George Lobsenz, Tina Seeley.

EPOCH TIMES—(301) 515–9447; 8927 Shady Grove Ct., Rockvile, MD 20877: Hui Jing.

FAIRBANKS DAILY NEWS MINER—(202) 662–8721; 1255 National Press Building, Washington, DC 20045: Sam Bishop.

FAIRCHILD NEWS SERVICE—(202) 496–4975; 1050 17th Street NW., Suite 600, Washington, DC 20036: Kristi Ellis, Joanna Ramey, Susan Watters.

FINANCIAL TIMES—(202) 434–0975; 700 13th Street, Suite 555, Washington, DC 20005: Edward Alden, Andrew Balls, Guy Dinmore, Stephanie Kirchgaessner, Demetri Sevastopulo, Christopher Swann, Patti Waldmeir, Hubert Wetzel.

FORT WAYNE JOURNAL GAZETTE—(202) 879–6710; 551 National Press Building, Washington, DC 20045: Sylvia Smith.

FORT WORTH STAR-TELEGRAM—(202) 383–6016; 700 12th Street, NW., Suite 1000, Washington, DC 20005: David Montgomery, Maria Recio.

FRANKFURTER RUNDSCHAU—(301) 762–9661; 1717 Sunrise Drive, Rockville, MD 20854: Dietmar Ostermann.

FREDERICKSBURG FREE LANCE-STAR—(540) 374–5000; 616 Amelia Street, Fredericksburg, VA 22401: Rick Mercier, Johnathan Hunley.

GANNETT NEWS SERVICE—(703) 854–5898; 7950 Jones Branch Drive, McClean, VA 22107: Caesar Andrews, Sammie Chen, Linda Dono, Leonard Fischer, Marie Marino, Craig Schwed.

GANNETT NEWS SERVICE—(202) 906–8124; 1100 New York Avenue, Washington, DC 20005: Douglas Abrahms, Robert Benincasa, Larry Bivins, Faith Bremner, Pamela Brogan, Jennifer Brooks, Sergio Bustos, Catalina Camia, Dennis Camire, Raju Chebium, Val Ellicott, Ellyn Ferguson, Jim Golden, Maureen Groppe, Erin Kelly, Ledyard King, Theresa Klisz, John Machacek, Mike Madden, Claude Pruitt, Charles Raasch, Ana Radelat, Laura Rehrmann, Katherine Scott, Brian Tumulty, Billie Jean Wells, Lawrence Wheeler, Gregory Wright, John Yaukey.

GERMAN PRESS AGENCY–DPA—(202) 662–1227; 969 National Press Building, Washington, DC 20045: Gabriele Chwallek, Hans Dahne, Frank Fuhrig, Margret Johnston, Klaus Marre, Mike McCarthy, Christiane Oelrich, Paticia Reber, Lea Ann Schnakenberg, Laszlo Trankovits.

GLOBAL HORIZONS SYNDICATE—(202) 659–1921; 1330 New Hampshire Avenue, NW., Washington, DC: 20036 Edward Flattau.

GRIFFIN–LARRABEE NEWS SERVICE—(202) 554–3579; 2404 Davis Avenue, Alexandria, VA 22302: Betty Mills.

NEWSPAPERS REPRESENTED—Continued

HARRISBURG PATRIOT–NEWS—(202) 383–7833; 1101 Connecticut Avenue, Suite 300, Washington, DC 20036: Brett Lieberman.

HARTFORD COURANT—(202) 824–8451; 1325 G Street, Suite 200, Washington, DC 20005: Liz Halloran, David Lightman.

HEALTH NEWS DAILY—(301) 657–9830; 5550 Friendship Boulevard, Suite 1, Chevy Chase, MD 20815: Nellie Bristol.

HEARST NEWSPAPERS—(202) 263–6413; 1850 K Street NW., Suite 1000, Washington, DC 20006: Kristen Collie, Jennifer Dlouhy, Dan Freedman, Judy Holland, Charles Lewis, Marianne Means, Stewart Powell, Eric Rosenberg, Timothy Spence, Helen Thomas.

HELSINGIN SANOMAT—(202) 955–7956; 1726 M Street, NW., Suite #700, Washington, DC 20036: Jyri Raivio.

HINDU—(301) 654–9038; 4701 Willard Avenue, #1531, Chevy Chase, MD 20815: Sridhar Krishnaswami.

HINDUSTAN TIMES—(703) 876–6149; 2731 Pleasantdale Road, #203, Vienna, VA 22180: Sethuraman Rajauopalan.

HOKKAIDO SHIMBUN—(202) 628–5374; 1012 National Press Building, Washington, DC 20045: Takuya Nishimura, Isao Yamagishi.

HOLLYWOOD REPORTER—(202) 833–8845; 910 17th Street, NW., Washington, DC 20006: Brooks Boliek.

HOUSTON CHRONICLE—(202) 263–6533; 1850 K Street, NW., Suite 1000, Washington, DC 20006: Justin Guest, Michael Hedges, Cragg Hines, David Ivanovich, Samantha Levine, Gebe Martinez, Julie Mason, Patty Reinert-Mason, Bennett Roth, Stephen Smith.

HURRIYET—(301) 564–6691; 16 Grove Ridge Court, Rockville, MD 20852: Mehmet Cindemir.

IL CORRIERE DELLA SERA—(202) 879–6733; 841 National Press Building, Washington, DC 20045: Ennio Caretto.

IL GIORNALE—(202) 237–1019; 2841 Arizona Terrace, Washington, DC 20016: Mariuccia Chiantaretto.

IL SECOLO XIX—(202) 957–8522; 5132 Tilden Street, NW., Washington, DC 20016: Elysa Fazzino.

INTER PRESS SERVICE—(202) 662–7160; 1293 National Press Building, Washington, DC 20045: James Lobe, Emad Mekay.

INTERNATIONAL HERALD TRIBUNE—(202) 862–0357; 1627 I Street, Suite 700, Washington, DC 20006: Brian Knowlton.

INVESTOR'S BUSINESS DAILY—(202) 728–2155; 1001 Connecticut Avenue, Suite 415, Washington, DC 20036: Jed Graham, Sean Higgins, Brian Mitchell.

ITAR–TASS NEWS AGENCY—(202) 662–7080; 1004 National Press Building, Washington, DC 20045: Dmitry Kirsanov, Ivan Lebedev, Andrei Sitov, Andrey Surzhanskiy, Pavel Vanichkin.

JEWISH TELEGRAPHIC AGENCY—(202) 737–0935; 1025 Vermont Avenue, NW., #504, Washington, DC 20005: Matthew Berger, Ron Kampeas.

JIJI PRESS—(202) 783–4330; 550 National Press Building, Washington, DC 20045: Kensuke Karube, Yoshida Kishida, Tetsuya Nakano, Yoshiaki Okuma, Carlos Solis Jr., Hiroyuki Takahashi, Eiji Toshi.

JYLLANDS–POSTEN—(301) 320–9079; 6405 Little Leigh Court, Cabin John, MD 20818: Klaus Justsen.

KANSAS CITY STAR—(202) 383–6105; 700 12th Street, NW., Suite 1000, Washington, DC 20005: David Goldstein, Matthew Stearns.

KIPLING NEWS SERVICE—(301) 929–0760; 12611 Farnell Drive, Silver Spring, MD 20906: Bogdan Kipling.

KNIGHT RIDDER—(202) 383–6056; 700 12th Street NW., Suite 1000, Washington, DC 20005: Beryl Adcock, James Asher, Seth Borenstein, Robert Boyd, Steven Butler, Crystal Davis, William Douglas, Joseph Galloway, Frank Greve, Kevin Hall, Stephen Henderson, Clark Hoyt, Ron Hutcheson, James Kuhnhenn, Jonathan Landay, Shannon McCaffrey, Anthony Pugh, Robert Rankin, Renee Schoof, Mark Seibel, Warren Strobel, Steven Thomma, John Walcott, Alison Young.

KOMMERSANT—(202) 248–8191; 3700 Massachusetts Avenue, Suite 317, NW., Washington, DC 20016: Dmitry Sidorov.

KUWAIT NEWS AGENCY—(202) 347–5554; 906 National Press Building, Washington, DC 20045: Aya Batrawy, Ronald Baygents, Saad Mohammad.

KYODO NEWS—(202) 347–5767; 400 National Press Building, Washington, DC 20045: Hirotsugu Aida, Hideomi Kinoshita, Yoshio Miyasaka, Kohei Murayama, Masakatsu Ota, Derek Sands, Toshimitsu Sawai, Yuriko Sumikawa, Jun Takahashi, Masaya Takahashi, Shinya Tanaka, Tomoji Tatsumi, Lisa Thomas, Akemi Yoshimoto.

LA JORNADA—(202) 547–5852; 132 North Carolina Avenue, SE., Washington, DC 20003: David Brooks, James Cason.

LA NACION—(202) 744–7737; 1193 National Press Building, Washington, DC 20045: Hugo Alconada.

LA TRIBUNA NEWSPAPER—(202) 737–5349; 1193 National Press Building, Washington, DC 20045: Jacobo Goldstein.

LA VANGUARDIA—(301) 229–1695; 6812 Algonquin Avenue, Bethesda, MD 20817: Eusebio Val Mitjavila.

LAS VEGAS SUN—(202) 662–7436; 529 National Press Building, Washington, DC 20045: Ben Grove, Suzanne Struglinski.

NEWSPAPERS REPRESENTED—Continued

LE FIGARO—(202) 342–3199; 1228 30th Street, NW., Washington, DC 20007: Philippe Gelie.

LE MAURICIEN—(301) 424–3884; 1084 Pipestem Place, Potomac, MD 20854: Pamela Glass.

LE PARISIEN—(202) 320–9546; 1841 Columbia Road, NW., #402, Washington, DC 20009: Thomas Cantaloube.

LIBERATION—(202) 249–9343; 4127 Harrison Street, Washington, DC 20015: Pascal Riche.

LIBERTY TIMES—(202) 879–6765; 1294 National Press Building, Washington, DC 20045: Nadia Y.F. Tsao.

LONDON DAILY TELEGRAPH—(202) 393–5195; 1310 G Street, NW., Suite 750, Washington, DC 20005: Francis Harris, Alec Russell, Philip Sherwell.

LONDON INDEPENDENT—(202) 467–4460; 1726 M Street, Suite 700, Washington, DC 20036: Rupert Cornwell.

LOS ANGELES DAILY JOURNAL—(202) 484–8255; 1 First Street, NE., Pressroom, Washington, DC 20543: Brent Kendall.

LOS ANGELES DAILY NEWS—(202) 662–8731; 1255 National Press Building, Washington, DC 20045: Lisa Friedman.

LOS ANGELES TIMES—(202) 293–4650; 1875 I Street, Suite 1100, Washington, DC 20006: Ricardo Alonso-Zaldivar, Stephen Braun, Ronald Brownstein, Edwin Chen, Richard Cooper, Mary Curtius, Robert Drogin, Sonni Efron, Faye Fiore, Don Frederick, K. Nicole Gaouette, James Gerstenzang, Peter Gosselin, Thomas Hamburger, Joel Havemann, Melissa Healy, John Hendren, Leslie Hoffecker, Janet Hook, Frankie Jackson, Mark Madden, Tyler Marshall, Mark Mazzetti, Thomas McCarthy, Allison McIntyre, Doyle McManus, Joshua Meyer, Alan Miller, Greg Miller, T. Christian Miller, Deborah Nelson, Chuck Neubauer, Johanna Neuman, Robert Ourlian, Judy Pasternak, Jonathan Peterson, Maura Reynolds, Paul Richter, James Robinson, Walter Roche, Jr., Phillip Ruiz, David Savage, Richard Schmitt, Esther Schrader, Richard Serrano, Jube Shiver, Jr., Kenneth Silverstein, Richard Simon, Warren Vieth, Peter Wallsten, David Willman, Donald Woutat, Aaron Zitner.

LOS TIEMPOS—(703) 536–9001; 6521 Arlington Blvd., Suite 214, Falls Church, VA 22042: Armando Morales Lujan.

LOUISVILLE COURIER JOURNAL—(202) 906–8141; 1100 New York Avenue, NW., Washington, DC 20005: James Carroll.

LOWELL SUN—(202) 662–8926; 1255 National Press Building, Washington, DC 20045: Evan Lehmann.

LRP PUBLICATIONS—(703) 516–7002; 1901 North Moore Street, Suite 1106, Arlington, VA 22209: Kara Arundel, Steve Brown, Michael Cardman, Katharine Chase, Julie Davidson, Kathleen Filipczyk, Patrick Harden, David Hubler, Stewart Magnuson, Pamela Moore, Katherine Shek, Sarah Sparks, Clarissa Spasyk, Andrew Viccora.

L'UNITA—(202) 237–1050; 2841 Arizona Terrace, Washington, DC 20016: Bruno Marolo.

MAARIV—(202) 210–6019; 11800 Seven Locks Road, Potomac, MD 20854: Tal Schneider.

MAGYAR SZO—(202) 904–4433; 1775 Massachusetts Avenue, Suite 207, Washington, DC 20036: Tibor Purger.

MAINICHI SHIMBUN—(202) 737–2817; 340 National Press Building, Washington, DC 20045: Jun Kimura, Evan Moore, Hiroaki Wada.

MARKET NEWS INTERNATIONAL—(202) 371–2121; 552 National Press Building, Washington, DC 20045: Steven Beckner, Denny Gulino, Claudia Hirsch, Kevin Kastner, Chris Middleton, Yali N'Diaye, Joseph Plocek, Heather Scott-Molleda, John Shaw, Theresa Sheehan.

MARKETWATCH—(202) 824–0548; 620 National Press Building, Washington, DC 20045: Jeffry Bartash, Stephanie Cohen, Michael Maynard, Margaret McNeil, Rex Nutting, Gregory Robb, Robert Schroeder.

McCLATCHY NEWSPAPERS—(202) 383–0008; 420 National Press Building, Washington, DC 20045: Les Blumenthal, Michael Bold, Michael Doyle, Greg Gordon, Lawrence O'Rourke, James Rosen, Mary Settles, Margaret Talev, David Westphal, David Whitney.

McCLENDON NEWS SERVICE—(202) 797–8467; 2933 28th Street, NW., Washington, DC 20008: David MacDonald.

MEDIA GENERAL—(202) 662–7660; 1214 National Press Building, Washington, DC 20045: Marilyn Rauber.

MEDIA GENERAL NEWS SERVICE—(202) 662–7677; 1214 National Press Building, Washington, DC 20045: James Crawley, John Hall, Gilbert Klein Jr., Richard Lee, Marsha Mercer.

MEDICAL DEVICE DAILY—(202) 719–7814; 4301 Connecticut Avenue, Suite 330, Washington, DC 20008: Christopher Delporte.

MIAMI HERALD—(202) 383–6019; 700 12th Street, NW., Suite 1000, Washington, DC 20005: Pablo Bachelet, Frank Davies, Nancy San Martin-Raedle.

MILITARY UPDATE—(703) 830–6863; P.O. Box 231111, Centreville, VA 20120: Thomas Philpott.

MILWAUKEE JOURNAL SENTINEL—(202) 662–7290; 940 National Press Building, Washington, DC 20045: Craig Gilbert, Katherine Skiba.

MINNEAPOLIS STAR TRIBUNE—(202) 383–0003; 420 National Press Building, Washington, DC 20045: Kevin Diaz, Rob Hotakainen.

MOBILE REGISTER—(202) 383–7815; 1101 Connecticut Avenue, Suite 300, Washington, DC 20036: Sean Reilly.

NEWSPAPERS REPRESENTED—Continued

MUNWHA ILBO—(202) 662–7342; 1148 National Press Building, Washington, DC 20045: Mi Sook Lee.

MYERS NEWS SERVICE—(202) 479–1130; 8213 Taunton Place, Springfield, VA 22152: Michael Myers.

NATIONAL JOURNAL'S TECHNOLOGY DAILY—(202) 261–0359; 600 New Hampshire, NW., Washington, DC 20037: Chloe Albanesius, Randy Barrett, Danielle Belopotosky, Winter Casey, Drew Clark, K. Daniel Glover, David Hatch, Sharon McLoone, Sarah Stirland.

NATIONAL NEWS RESEARCH SYNDICATE—(202) 223–1196; 500 23rd Street, NW., Washington, DC 20037: Ralph de Toledano, Charles Kendall, Jr.

NEW HAVEN REGISTER—(202) 737–5654; 1331 Pennsylvania Avenue NW., Suite 232, Washington, DC 20004: Joseph Straw.

NEW ORLEANS TIMES–PICAYUNE—(202) 383–7861; 1101 Connecticut Avenue, Suite 300, Washington, DC 20036: Bruce Alpert, John McQuaid, Bill Walsh.

NEW YORK DAILY NEWS—(202) 467–6770; 1050 Thomas Jefferson Street, #3100, Washington, DC 20007: Kenneth Bazinet, Thomas DeFrank, James Meek, Richard Sisk.

NEW YORK SUN—(202) 775–1542; 1101 17th Street, Suite 610, Washington, DC 20036: Luiza Ch. Savage.

NEW YORK TIMES—(202) 862–0370; 1627 I Street, Suite 700, Washington, DC 20006: Edmund Andrews, Von Aulston, Felicity Barringer, Janet Battaile, Elizabeth Becker, James Bennet, Monica Borkowski, Julie Bosman, Joel Brinkley, Gregory Brock, David Brooks, Elisabeth Bumiller, Lynette Clemetson, Helene Cooper, Rebecca Corbett, John Cushman, Jr., James Dao, Maureen Dowd, John Files, Jeff Gerth, Adrianne Goodman, Linda Greenhouse, Janis Harland, Gardiner Harris, Raymond Hernandez, Elizabeth Hines, Carl Hulse, Michael Janofsky, Douglas Jehl, David Johnston, Glen Justice, Susan Keller, Anne Kornblut, Stephen Labaton, Warren Leary, Kristen Lee, Neil Lewis, Eric Lichtblau, Eric Lipton, Clifton Meadows, Adam Nagourney, Elizabeth Olson, Robert Pear, Kathleen Phillips, Todd Purdum, Courtney Radsch, Cory Reiss, David Rosenbaum, David Sanger, Eric Schmitt, Scott Shane, Thomas Shanker, Philip Shenon, Ronald Skarzenski, Richard Stevenson, Sheryl Stolberg, David Stout, Philip Taubman, John Tierney, Robin Toner, Hugh Truslow, Ian Urbina, Matthew Wald, Leslie Wayne, Steven Weisman, Brian Wingfield.

NEW YORK TIMES MAGAZINE—(202) 237–1218; 3742 Appleton Street, NW., Washington, DC 20016: Matt Bai.

NEWARK STAR–LEDGER—(202) 383–7823; 1101 Connecticut Avenue, Suite 300, Washington, DC 20036: Robert Cohen, J. Scott Orr.

NEWHOUSE NEWS SERVICE—(202) 383–7812; 1101 Connecticut Avenue, Suite 300, Washington, DC 20036: Miles Benson, Linda Fibich, Deborah Howell, Sarah Kellogg, Terence Kivlan, Katherine Lewis, Chuck McCutcheon, Michele Melendez, Delia Rios, Bruce Seeman, Dru Sefton, Jonathan Tilove, David Wood.

NEWPORT NEWS DAILY PRESS—(202) 824–8224; 1325 G Street, NW., Suite 200, Washington, DC 20005: David Lerman.

NEWSDAY—(202) 393–5630; 1730 Pennsylvania Avenue, #850, Washington, DC 20006: Deborah Barfield Berry, Thomas Brune, Kenneth Fireman, D. Craig Gordon, Sarah Mueller, J. Jioni Palmer, Timothy Phelps.

NEWSPAPER ENTERPRISE—(301) 320–5559; 6008 Osceola Road, Bethesda, MD 20816: Robert Wagman.

NIKKEI—(202) 393–1388; 815 Connecticut Avenue, Suite 310, Washington, DC 20006: Hiroyuki Akita, Tomoko Ashizuka, Christina Bilski, Tetsuya Jitsu, Hidenaka Kato, Stephen Keefe, Hiroyuki Kotake, Rumiko Yamamoto, Toru Yoshida.

NISHI–NIPPON SHIMBUN—(202) 393–5812; 1012 National Press Building, Washington, DC 20045: Tadaoki Aoki, Risa Akiyama Ciccone.

NORTHWEST NEWSPAPERS—(202) 546–2547; 316 3rd Street, NE., Washington, DC 20002: Lawrence Swisher.

NOTIMEX MEXICAN NEWS AGENCY—(202) 347–5227; 975 National Press Building, Washington, DC 20045: Ricardo Alday, Ruben Barrera, Jose Lopez Zamorano, Santiago Tavara.

O ESTADO DE S. PAULO—(202) 628–3752; 700 13th Street, Suite 555, Washington, DC 20005: Paulo Sotero.

OLIPHANT NEWS SERVICE—(202) 298–7226; P.O. Box 9808, Washington, DC 20016: Cortright Oliphant.

OMAHA WORLD–HERALD—(202) 662–7270; 836 National Press Building, Washington, DC 20045: Jake Thompson.

ORANGE COUNTY REGISTER—(202) 628–6381; 1295 National Press Building, Washington, DC 20045: Dena Bunis, Angela Stephens.

OREGONIAN—(202) 383–7819; 1101 Connecticut Avenue, Suite 300, Washington, DC 20036: James Barnett, Jeffrey Kosseff.

ORLANDO SENTINEL—(202) 824–8255; 1325 G Street, Suite 200, Washington, DC 20005: Tamara Lytle.

OUEST–FRANCE—(202) 248–6945; 1841 Columbia Road NW., #402, Washington, DC 20009: Isabelle Duriez.

NEWSPAPERS REPRESENTED—Continued

PHILADELPHIA INQUIRER—(202) 383–6048; 700 12th Street, NW., Suite 1000, Washington, DC 20005: Steven Goldstein, Christopher Mondics.

PITTSBURGH POST–GAZETTE—(202) 662–7025; 955 National Press Building, Washington, DC 20045: Michael McGough, Maeve Reston, Karen MacPhersen, Ann McFeatters, Michael Woods.

PLATTS NEWS SERVICE—(202) 383–2250; 1200 G Street, Suite 1100, Washington, DC 20005: Gerald Karey, Catherine Landry.

POLITICAL MONEY LINE—(202) 237–2500; 6004 Nevada Avenue, NW., Washington, DC 20015: Kent Cooper, Anthony Raymond.

PORTLAND PRESS HERALD—(202) 488–1119; 1711 Massachusetts Avenue, NW., Washington, DC 20036: Bart Jansen.

PRESS TRUST OF INDIA—(301) 951–8657; 4450 South Park Avenue, Suite 1719, Chevy Chase, MD 20815: T.V. Parasuram.

PROVIDENCE JOURNAL—(202) 661–8423; 1325 G Street, Suite 250, Washington, DC 20005: John Mulligan.

RALEIGH NEWS & OBSERVER—(202) 662–4380; 420 National Press Building, Washington, DC 20005: Valerie Bauerlein.

RELIGION NEWS SERVICE—(202) 383–7863; 1101 Connecticut Avenue, Suite 350, Washington, DC 20036: Adelle Banks, Kevin Eckstrom, Mark O'Keefe.

RESTRUCTURING TODAY—(202) 298–8201; 4418 MacArthur Blvd., Washington, DC 20007: Steven Greenlee, Joan Henderson, George Spencer, Samuel Spencer.

REUTERS—(202) 898–8319; 1333 H Street, Suite 410, Washington, DC 20005: Charles Abbott, John Abell, Charles Aldinger, Charles Alexander, Victoria Allen, JoAnne Allen, Chris Baltimore, Eric Beech, Melissa Bland, Caren Bohan, Deborah Charles, Doina Chiacu, Susan Jean Cornwell, Richard Cowan, John Crawley, Timothy Dobbyn, Christopher Doering, Tom Doggett, Robert Doherty, Michael Dolan, Stuart Doughty, Kevin Drawbaugh, Caroline Drees, Will Dunham, Todd Eastham, Paul Eckert, Sarah Edmonds, Giles Elgood, Alan Elsner, Randy Fabi, Mark Felsenthal, Alexander Ferguson, Thomas Ferraro, Margaret Fox, Carol Giacomo, Paul Grant, Susan Heavey, Cheyenne Hopkins, Andrea Hopkins, Saul Hudson, Justin Hyde, Stacey Joyce, Peter Kaplan, Joanne Kenen, Darrell Law, David Lawder, Jonathan Lyons, Laura MacInnis, Sandra Maler, Randall Mikkelsen, Arshad Mohammed, David Morgan, Joanne Morrison, Essex Noel, Chizu Nomiyama, Bette O'Connor, Jeremy Pelofsky, Sue Pleming, John Poirier, Lisa Richwine, Kristin Roberts, Martin Roberts, Joel Rothstein, Timothy Ryan, Lori Santos, Andrea Shalal-Esa, Donna Smith, Brad Smith, Glenn Somerville, Neil Stempleman, David Storey, Andy Sullivan, Peter Szekely, William Trott, James Vicini, Julie Vorman, Nancy Waitz, John Whitesides, David Wiessler, Anna Willard, Patricia Wilson, Jim Wolf, Lesley Wroughton, Karey Wutkowski, Deborah Zabarenko, Tabassum Zakaria.

RHEINISCHE POST—(301) 641–3463; 10201 Windsor View Drive, Potomac, MD 20854: Thomas Spang.

RICHMOND TIMES–DISPATCH—(202) 662–7669; 1214 National Press Building, Washington, DC 20045: Peter Hardin.

RIVERSIDE PRESS–ENTERPRISE—(202) 661–8422; 1325 G Street, Suite 250, Washington, DC 20045: Claire Vitucci.

ROLL CALL REPORT SYNDICATE—(202) 737–1888; 960 A National Press Building, Washington, DC 20045: Michael Lesparre, Richard Thomas.

SALT LAKE TRIBUNE—(202) 549–8955; 1255 National Press Building, Washington, DC 20045: Robert Gehrke.

SALT LAKE TRIBUNE—(202) 662–8897; 1255 National Press Building, Washington, DC 20045: Christopher Smith.

SAN ANTONIO EXPRESS–NEWS—(202) 263–6451; 1850 K Street, NW., Washington, DC 20006: Gary Martin.

SAN FRANCISCO CHRONICLE—(202) 263–6577; 1850 K Street, NW., Suite 1000, Washington, DC 20006: Zachary Coile, Edward Epstein, Carolyn Lochhead, Marc Sandalow.

SAN JOSE MERCURY NEWS—(202) 383–6043; 700 12th Street, NW., Suite 1000, Washington, DC 20005: James Puzzanghera.

SANKEI SHIMBUN—(202) 347–2101; 330 Nationa Press Building, Washington, DC 20045: Yukio Kashiyama, Hideo Kesen, Yoshihisa Komori, Toyokazu Kondo, Bruce Scott Stewart.

SAUDI PRESS AGENCY—(202) 944–3890; 6012 New Hampshire Avenue, NW., Washington, DC 20037: Naila Al-Sowayel, Mustafa Bashir, Liam Hurley, Azeddine Labriny, Tarun Reddy, Nezar Sheikh.

SCIENCE AND TECHNOLOGY DAILY—(703) 734–9288; 1827 Barbee Street, McLean, VA 22101: Mengjun Zhang.

SCRIPPS HOWARD NEWS SERVICE—(202) 408–1484; 1090 Vermont Avenue, Suite 1000, Washington, DC 20005: Curtis Lee Bowman, James Brosnan, Michael Collins, Peter Copeland, Tara Copp, Mary Deibel, Robert Friedman, Lance Gay, Laurel Hackett, Thomas Hargrove, Lisa Hoffman, Joan Lowy, Dale McFeatters, Thomas Mentzer, Amie Parnes, Richard Powelson, Michael Sprengelmeyer, Bill Straub, Bartholomew Sullivan, Dan Thomasson, Karen Timmons.

SEATTLE POST–INTELLIGENCER—(202) 263–6461; 1850 K Street, NW., Washington, DC 20006: Charles Pope.

NEWSPAPERS REPRESENTED—Continued

SEGYE TIMES—(202) 637–0587; 909 National Press Building, Washington, DC 20045: Kiyon Kuk.
SEKAI NIPPO—(202) 898–8292; 1510 H Street, NW., Washington, DC 20005: Toshiyuki Hayakawa, Yoshio Mitoma.
SEOUL SHINMUN—(202) 393–4061; 1267 National Press Building, Washington, DC 20045: Do Woon Lee.
SINGAPORE STRAITS TIMES—(202) 662–8728; 916 National Press Building, Washington, DC 20045: Eugene Lek Kee Low, Roger Mitton.
SINGTAO DAILY—(202) 250–6130; 2201 L Street, NW., Apt. #307, Washington, DC 20037: Zhigang Chen.
SMARTMONEY.COM—(202) 828–3390; 1025 Conneticut Avenue, NW., Suite 1100, Washington, DC 20036: Michael DeSenne.
SOUTH FLORIDA SUN–SENTINEL—(202) 8248256; 1325 G Street, Suite 200, Washington, DC 20005: William Gibson, Rafael Lorente.
SPRINGFIELD REPUBLICAN—(202) 383–7859; 1101 Connecticut Avenue, Suite 300, Washington, DC 20036: JoAnn Moriarty.
ST. LOUIS POST DISPATCH—(202) 298–6880; 1025 Connecticut Avenue, Suite 1102, Washington, DC 20036: Karen Branch-Brioso, Philip Dine, Aloysia Hamalainen, William Lambrecht, Jon Sawyer, Deirdre Shesgreen.
ST. PETERSBURG TIMES—(202) 463–0575; 1100 Connecticut Avenue, #1300, Washington, DC 20036: William Adair, Wes Allison, Anita Kumar.
STEPHENS MEDIA GROUP—(202) 738–1760; 666 11th Street, Suite 535, Washington, DC 20001: Tony Batt, Stephan Tetreault, Alison Vekshin, Samantha Young.
STUTTGARTER ZEITUNG—(301) 983–0735; 11204 Powder Horn Drive, Potomac, MD 20854: Juergen Koar.
SUEDDEUTSCHE ZEITUNG—(202) 965–5253; 4715 Butterworth Place, NW., Washington, DC 20016: Marc Hujer.
SVENSKA DAGBLADET—(202) 362–8253; 3601 Connecticut Avenue, #622, Washington, DC 20008: Karin Henriksson.
SYRACUSE POST STANDARD—(202) 383–7817; 1101 Connecticut Avenue, Suite 300, Washington, DC 20036: L. Peter Lyman.
TAGES ANZEIGER—(202) 3328575; 2026 16th Street, NW., #5, Washington, DC 20009: Martin Kilian.
TAIPEI TIMES—(301) 942–2442; P.O. Box 571, Garrett Park, MD 20898: Charles Snyder.
TAMPA TRIBUNE—(202) 662–7673; 1214 National Press Building, Washington, DC 20045: Keith Epstein.
TECH LAW JOURNAL—(202) 364–8882; 3034 Newark Street, NW., Washington, DC 20008: David Carney.
TOKYO–CHUNICHI SHIMBUN—(202) 783–9479; 1012 National Press Building, Washington, DC 20007: Jennifer Gerdts, Shinichi Hisadome, Aki Naganuma, Yoichi Toyoda.
TORONTO STAR—(202) 662–7390; 982 National Press Building, Washington, DC 20045: Tim Harper.
TULSA WORLD—(202) 484–1424; 1417 North Inglewood Street, Arlington, VA 22205: Jim Myers.
TURKIYE DAILY—(202) 253–3289; 12704 Hallman Court, North Potomac, MD 20878: Hasan Hazar.
UNITED DAILY NEWS—(202) 737–6426; 835 National Press Building, Washington, DC 20045: Tsung-Chih Chang.
UNITED PRESS INTERNATIONAL—(202) 898–8238; 1510 H Street, Washington, DC 20005: Ellen Beck, Tobin Beck, Phil Berardelli, Donna Borak, Christian Bourge, Krishnadev Calamur, Dr. John Daly, Arnaud de Borchgrave, Dee Ann Divis, Roland Flamini, Shihoko Goto, Dar Haddix, John Hendel, Caroline Horrigan, Anwar Iqbal, Michael Kirkland, Timothy Maloy, Louis Marano, Michael Marshall, Andrea Mihailescu, Steve Mitchell, Daniel Olmsted, Peter Roff, Claude Salhani, Martin Sieff, Richard Tomkins, Martin Walker, Shaun Waterman.
USA TODAY—(703) 854–5579; 1100 New York Avenue, Washington, DC 20005: Fred Anklam, Jr., Richard Benedetto, Joan Biskupic, Louise Branson, James Cox, Christopher Cubbison, Paul Davidson, Robert Davis, Barbara Delollis, William Dermody, John Diamond, Oren Dorell, Jim Drinkard, Peter Eisler, Melanie Eversley, Greg Farrell, Gwen Flanders, Thomas Frank, Barbara Hagenbaugh, Mimi Hall, Linda Holzer, Lee Horwich, Kevin Johnson, Judith Keen, Kathy Kiely, Suzanne Kirchhoff, Steven Komarow, Jill Lawrence, Donna Leinwand, Alan Levin, Toni Locy, Dave Moniz, Bill Nichols, Susan Page, William Risser, Barbara Slavin, Andrea Stone, William Welch, Richard Wolf.
USA TODAY—(703) 854–5647; 7950 Jones Branch Drive, McLean, VA 22108: Julie Appleby, Erik Brady, Dan Carney, Patrick Cooper, Mark Crane, Chet Czarniak, Haya El Nasser, Mindy Fetterman, 20005 Ed Foster-Simeon, Brian Gallagher, Andrew Gardiner, Raymond Goldbacher, George Hager, Sid Hurlburt, Rosalind Jackler, Dennis Kelly, Paul Leavitt, Thomas Lilleston, Mary Beth Marklein, Stephen Marshall, Mark Memmott, Jim Michaels, Patty Michalski, Blake Morrison, Vin Narayanan, Jayne O'Donnell, Paul Overberg, Laura Parker, Carolyn Pesce, Maria Puente, John Riley, John Siniff, Elliot Smith, Michael Snider, William Sternberg, Steve Sternberg, Jeffrey Stinson, Elisa Tinsley, Gregory Toppo, Saundra Torry, Owen Ullmann, Tom Vanden Brook, Dan Vergano, John Waggoner, 20005 Traci Watson, James Welch, Richard Whitmire, Richard Willing, Gregg Zoroya.

NEWSPAPERS REPRESENTED—Continued

VECERNJE NOVOSTI—(301) 325–2043; 4615 North Park Ave., Apt. 618, Bethesda, MD 20815: Dubravka Savic.

VIETNAM NEWS AGENCY—(202) 879–6718; 990 National Press Building, Washington, DC 20045: Duc Dong Dung, Hi Vu Nghi, Minh Nguyen.

VIRGINIAN–PILOT—(703) 913–9872; 7802 Glenister Drive, Springfield, VA 22152: Dale Eisman.

WALL STREET JOURNAL—(202) 862–9200; 1025 Connecticut Avenue, Suite 800, Washington, DC 20036: Robert Block, Jess Bravin, Jackie Calmes, Mary Carnevale, David Cloud, Christopher Conkey, Christopher Cooper, Jeanne Cummings, Robert Davis, Nikhil Deogun, Yochi Dreazen, Stefan Fatsis, John Fialka, Gary Fields, John Harwood, Murray Hiebert, Greg Hitt, Gregory Ip, Greg Jaffe, Neil King, Jr., June Kronholz, Sarah Lueck, Anna Mathews, Laurie McGinley, John McKinnon, Brody Mullins, Michael Phillips, Carla Robbins, David Rogers, Sara Schaefer-Munoz, Amy Schatz, Jacob Schlesinger, Sharon Schmid, Michael Schroeder, Gerald Seib, Deborah Solomon, Anne Marie Squeo, Johnny Stevenson, David Wessel, Clayton Wiggins, John Wilke, Winston Wood, Bernard Wysocki, Jr.

WASHINGTON EXAMINER—(703) 627–3065; 6408 Edsall Road, Alexandria, VA 22312: Robert Arkell, Anna Bailey, Andrei Blakely, Karen DeWitt, Michael Gerber, Mark Hand, Karl Hille, Nicholas Horrock, Sarah Kelly, Mary Ann Kuhn, Tim Maier, Jonathan Marino, Rahkia Nance, Michael Neibauer.

WASHINGTON POST—(202) 334–7261; 1150 15th Street, Washington, DC 20071: Joel Achenbach, Michael Allen, Charles Babcock, Charles Babington, Peter Baker, Daniel Balz, Gary Barr, Jeffrey Birnbaum, Justin Blum, David Broder, David Brown, Peter Carlson, D'Vera Cohn, Ceci Connolly, Alan Cooperman, Libby Copeland, Albert Crenshaw, Alice Crites, Kathleen Day, Lynne Duke, Thomas Edsall, Daniel Eggen, Brian Faler, Maureen Fan, Darryl Fears, Manny Fernandez, David Finkel, Michael Fletcher, Ann Gerhart, Susan Glasser, Annie Gowen, Bradley Graham, Guy Gugliotta, Maryann Haggerty, John Harris, Hamil Harris, Sari Horwitz, Spencer Hsu, Carrie Johnson, Amy Joyce, Al Kamen, Dan Keating, Glenn Kessler, Alec Klein, Jonathan Krim, Lyndsey Layton, Madonna Lebling, Christopher Lee, Mark Leibovich, Richard Leiby, Allan Lengel, Caroline Mayer, Dana Milbank, David Montgomery, Lori Montgomery, Dan Morgan, Shailagh Murray, Terence O'Hara, Eric Pianin, Sue Ann Pressley, Dana Priest, Eric Rich, Tom Ricks, Roxanne Roberts, Eugene Robinson, Susan Schmidt, Jeffrey Smith, Tom Toles, Jacqueline Trescott, Boyd Neely Tucker, Ann Scott Tyson, Jim Vande Hei, Shankar Vedantam, David Von Drehle, Jonathan Weisman, Rick Weiss, Eric Weiss, Josh White, Del Wilber, Vanessa Williams, Clarence Williams, Bob Woodward, Eric Yoder.

WASHINGTON TELECOMMUNICATIONS SERVICES—(804) 776–7947; 1006 Harrison Circle, Alexandria, VA 22304: Gordon White.

WASHINGTON TIMES—(202) 636–3202; 3600 New York Avenue, NE., Washington, DC 20002: Theodore Agres, George Archibald, Chris Baker, Sharon Behn, Christina Bellantoni, Thomas Carter, Gus Constantine, Joseph Curl, Brian DeBose, Stephen Dinan, Julia Duin, Amy Fagan, Ann Geracimos, William Gertz, William Glanz, Ralph Hallow, Jennifer Harper, Marguerite Higgins, Patrice Hill, Audrey Hudson, Charles Hurt, David Jones, Nicholas Kralev, James Lakely, Donald Lambro, Stephanie Mansfield, John McCaslin, Steven Miller, Ximens Ortiz, Wesley Pruden, Thomas Ramstack, William Sammon, David Sands, Rowan Scarborough, Jerry Seper, Patti Shea, Jeffrey Sparshott, M. Maria Stainer, Guy Taylor, Jon Ward, Cheryl Wetzstein, Willis Witter.

WASHINGTONPOST.COM—(703) 469–3162; 1515 N. Courthouse Road, Arlington, VA 22201: Brian Krebs, Robert MacMillan, Ann Marchand, David McGuire, John Nichols, Amanda Zamora.

WATERTOWN DAILY TIMES—(202) 662–7085; 1001 National Press Building, Washington, DC 20045: Marc Heller.

WESTDEUTSCHE ALLGEMEINE—(202) 363–7791; 4611 47th Street, Washington, DC 20016: Markus Gunther.

WICHITA EAGLE—(202) 383–6055; 700 12th Street, NW., Suite 1000, Washington, DC 20005: Alan Bjerga.

WILLIAM SCALLY REPORTS—(202) 362–2382; 2918 Legation Street, NW., Washington, DC 20015: William Scally.

WINSTON–SALEM JOURNAL—(202) 662–7672; 1214 National Press Club, Washington, DC 20045: Mary Shaffrey.

WORLD JOURNAL—(202) 215–1710; 835 National Press Building, Washington, DC 20045: Betty Lin.

WORLDNETDAILY.COM—(703) 815–0685; 8665 Sudley Road, Suite 605, Manasses, VA 20110: Joseph Farah, Paul Sperry,

YOMIURI SHIMBUN—(202) 783–0363; 802 National Press Building, Washington, DC 20045: Eiji Hirose, Takao Hishinuma, Toshiyuki Ito, Lesley McKenzie, Takashi Sadahiro, Kyoichi Sasazawa, Al Schleicher, Masaomi Terada, Mineko Tokito, Linda Yun, Kasper Zeuthen.

YONHAP NEWS AGENCY—(202) 783–5539; 1299 National Press Building, Washington, DC 20045: Dae Young Kim, Dong Young Yun.

PRESS PHOTOGRAPHERS' GALLERY*

The Capitol, Room S–317, 224–6548

www.senate.gov/galleries/photo

Director.—Jeffrey S. Kent.
  Deputy Director.—Mark A. Abraham.
  Assistant Director.—Sonya Hebert.

STANDING COMMITTEE OF PRESS PHOTOGRAPHERS

Tim Dillon, *Chairman*
Dennis Brack, *Secretary-Treasurer*
Scott Applewhite
Khue Bui
Stephen Crowley
Robert Pearson

RULES GOVERNING PRESS PHOTOGRAPHERS' GALLERY

1. (a) Administration of the Press Photographers' Gallery is vested in a Standing Committee of Press Photographers consisting of six persons elected by accredited members of the Gallery. The Committee shall be composed of one member each from Associated Press Photos; Reuters News Pictures or AFP Photos; magazine media; local newspapers; agency or freelance member; and one at-large member. The at-large member may be, but need not be, selected from media otherwise represented on the Committee; however no organization may have more than one representative on the Committee.

(b) Elections shall be held as early as practicable in each year, and in no case later than March 31. A vacancy in the membership of the Committee occurring prior to the expiration of a term shall be filled by a special election called for that purpose by the Committee.

(c) The Standing Committee of the Press Photographers' Gallery shall propose no change or changes in these rules except upon petition in writing signed by not less than 25 accredited members of the gallery.

2. Persons desiring admission to the Press Photographers' Gallery of the Senate shall make application in accordance with Rule 33 of the Senate, which rule shall be interpreted and administered by the Standing Committee of Press Photographers subject to the review and approval of the Senate Committee on Rules and Administration.

3. The Standing Committee of Press photographers shall limit membership in the photographers' gallery to bona fide news photographers of repute in their profession and Heads of Photographic Bureaus under such rules as the Standing Committee of Press Photographers shall prescribe.

4. Provided, however, that the Standing Committee of Press Photographers shall admit to the gallery no person who does not establish to the satisfaction of the Committee all of the following:

(a) That any member is not engaged in paid publicity or promotion work or in prosecuting any claim before Congress or before any department of the Government, and will not become so engaged while a member of the gallery.

(b) That he or she is not engaged in any lobbying activity and will not become so engaged while a member of the gallery.

The above rules have been approved by the Committee on Rules and Administration.

J. DENNIS HASTERT,
Speaker, House of Representatives.

TRENT LOTT,
Chairman, Senate Committee on Rules and Administration.

MEMBERS ENTITLED FOR ADMISSION

PRESS PHOTOGRAPHERS' GALLERY

Alleruzzo, Maya: Washington Times
Alswang, Ralph: Freelance
Applewhite, J. Scott: Associated Press Photos
Archambault, Charles: U.S. News & World Report
Arias, Juana L.: Washington Post
Arrossi, Eddie: Freelance
Ashe, James F.: Freelance
Ashley, Douglas G.: Suburban Communications
  Corp.
Atlan, Jean-Louis: Paris-Match
Attlee, Tracey A.: Freelance
Augustino, Jocelyn: Freelance
Ballard, Karen: Freelance
Bandeira, Pedro: The Hill
Barouh, Stan: Freelance
Barrett, Steve E.: Freelance
Baughman, J. Ross: Washington Times
Baylen, Liz: Washington Times
Beals, Herman: Reuters News Pictures
Beiser, H. Darr: USA/Today
Bengiveno, Nicole: The New York Times
Benic, Patrick T.: United Press International
Berg, Lisa: Freelance
Biber, Mehmet: Hurriyet
Biddle, Susan: Washington Post
Bigwood, Jeremy: Freelance
Bingham, Mary (Molly): Freelance
Binks, Porter L.: Sports Illustrated
Blass, Eileen M.: USA/Today
Bloom, Richard: National Journal
Bochatey, Terry F.: Reuters News Pictures
Bogert, Jr., Jeremiah M.: The New York Times
Boitano, Stephen J.: Freelance
Boston, Bernard N.: Bryce Mountain Courier
Bouchard, Renee M.: Freelance
Bourg, Jim: Reuters News Pictures
Bowe, Christy: ImageCatcher News
Brack, William D.: Black Star
Brantley, James: Washington Times
Bridges, George S.: Knight Ridder Tribune News
  Service
Brooks, Dudley: Washington Post
Brown, Robert A.: Richmond Times Dispatch
Brown, Stephen R.: Freelance
Bui, Khue: Newsweek
Burke, Lauren V.: Freelance
Burnett, David: Contact Press Images
Burns, David S.: Photo Trends, Inc.
Calvert, Mary F.: Washington Times
Cameron, Gary A.: Reuters News Pictures
Carioti, Richard A.: Washington Post

Carrier, Jason M.: Freelance
Cavanaugh, Matthew T.: Freelance
Cedeno, Ken: Freelance
Ceneta, Manuel B.: Associated Press Photos
Chikwendiu, Jahi: Washington Post
Chung, Andre F.: Baltimore Sun
Clark, Bill: Gannett
Clark, Kevin: Washington Post
Clement, Richard: Reuters News Pictures
Clendenin, Jay L.: Freelance
Cohen, Marshall H.: Bigmarsh News Photos
Colburn, James E.: Lincoln Journal-Star
Connor, Michael: Washington Times
Conway, Stuart: Daily Telegraph (London)
Cook, Dennis: Associated Press Photos
Cooke, John: Credit Union Times
Coppage, Gary R.: Photo Press International
Corcoran, Thomas Michael: Freelance
Crandall, Bill: Freelance
Crandall, Rob: Freelance
Crowley, Stephen: The New York Times
Curtis, Rob: Army Times Publishing
Cutts, Peter J.: Freelance
D'Angelo, Rebecca: Freelance
DeArmas, Adrienne: Freelance
Devorah, Carrie: Freelance
Dharapak, Charles: Associated Press Photos
DiBari, Jr., Michael: Freelance
Dillon, Timothy P.: USA/Today
Douliery, Olivier: ABACA Press
Downing, Lawrence: Reuters News Pictures
Doyle, Kevin W.: Freelance
Du Cille, Michel: Washington Post
Dukehart, Coburn: USAToday.com
Eddins, Jr., Joseph M.: Washington Times
Edmonds, Ronald: Associated Press Photos
Elfers, Steve: Army Times Publishing
Ellis, Richard: Getty Images
Ellsworth, Katie: Time Magazine
Emanuel, Hector: Freelance
Ericsson, Hans: Freelance
Ernst, Jonathan: Freelance
Fabiano, Gary: Sipa Press
Falk, Steven M.: The Philadelphia Daily News
Falls, Jr., John W.: Freelance
Fenster, J. Adam: The Gazette
Ferraro, Beth: Newsweek
Ferrell, Scott: CQ Weekly
Ficara, John F.: Freelance
Fitz-Patrick, Bill: Freelance
Fiume, Gregory C: Freelance

959

MEMBERS ENTITLED FOR ADMISSION—Continued

Foster, Jacqueline Mia: Freelance
Francis, Lloyd: Army Times Publishing
Franko, Jeff: Gannett
Frazza, Luke: Agence France Presse
Fremson, Ruth: The New York Times
Frischling, Steven E: World Picture News
Gainer, Denny: USAToday.com
Gamarra, Ruben F.: Notimex
Gandhi, Pareshkumar A.: Rediff.com/India Abroad Pub.
Garcia, Mannie: Freelance
Gatty, Michael Robert: Periodical News Service
Geissinger, Michael A.: Freelance
Gifford, Porter: Freelance
Gilbert, Patrice J.: Freelance
Glenn, Larry S.: Freelance
Golden, Rachael: The Gazette
Goulait, Bert V.: Washington Times
Graham, Douglas: Roll Call
Graves, Thomas A: Freelance
Gripas, Yuri: Sipa Press
Gunther, Brendan: European Press Photo
Guzy, Carol: Washington Post
Hairston, Kim: Baltimore Sun
Hall, John: Associated Press Photos
Halstead, Dirck: The Digital Journalist
Hamburg, Harry: New York Daily News
Harnik, Andrew: The Journal Newspapers
Harrington, John H.: Black Star
Harris, Steven J.: Polaris Images
Hartmann, Paul: Freelance
Heasley, Shaun: Freelance
Helber, Stephen: Associated Press Photos
Herbert, Gerald: Associated Press Photos
Hershorn, Gary: Reuters News Pictures
Hittle, David E.: Freelance
Hobby, David C.: Baltimore Sun
Holloway, David S.: Freelance
Hosefros, Paul: The New York Times
Jackson, Lawrence: Associated Press Photos
Jacobs, Vancé: Freelance
Jennings, Stan: Jennings Publications
Johnson, Richard D.: Freelance
Jones, Peter: Reuters News Pictures
Joseph, Marvin: Washington Post
Juarez, Miguel: Reforma
Kahn, Nikki: Washington Post
Kang, Hyungwon: Reuters News Pictures
Katz, Martin I.: Chesapeake News Service
Kemper, Gary: European Press Photo
Kennedy, Chuck: Knight Ridder Tribune News Service
Kennerly, David H.: Newsweek
Kittner, Sam: Freelance
Kleinfeld, Michael: United Press International
Kleponis, Chris: Freelance
Kon, Toshiyuki: The Yomiuri Shimbun
Kossoff, Leslie: Freelance

Kozak, Richard: Army Times Publishing
Kraft, Brooks: Time Magazine
Lamarque, Kevin: Reuters News Pictures
Lamkey, Jr., Rod A.: Washington Times
LaVor, Martin L.: Freelance
Lee, Chang W.: The New York Times
Lee, David Y.: Freelance
Lee, James J.: Army Times Publishing
Lessig, Alan: Army Times Publishing
Lewis, Roy: Washington Informer
Lewter, Lani R.: Global News Photos
Lipski, Richard A.: Washington Post
Liss, Steve: Time Magazine
Lopossay, Monica: Baltimore Sun
LoScalzo, Jim: U.S. News & World Report
Lu, Mingxiang: Xinhua News Agency
Lutzky, Micheal: Washington Post
Lynaugh, Michael: Freelance
Lynch, Liz: National Journal
Lynch, M. Patricia: Frontiers News Magazine
MacMillan, Jeffrey G.: U.S. News & World Report
Maddaloni, Chris: Roll Call
Madrid, Michael: USA/Today
Mahaskey, Michael Scott: Army Times Publishing
Makely, John: Baltimore Sun
Mallin, Jay: Freelance
Mallory, Tyler: Freelance
Malonson, Jacqueline: Freelance
Mara, Melina: Washington Post
Markel, Brad: Capri
Marks, Donovan: Freelance
Martineau, Gerald: Washington Post
Martinez Monsivais, Pablo: Associated Press Photos
Mathieson, Greg E.: MAI Photo Agency
McDermid, Brendan: European Press Photo
McDonnell, John: Washington Post
McKay, Richard D.: Cox Newspapers
McNamee, Win: Getty Images
Meyers, Keith: The New York Times
Mills, Douglas: The New York Times
Mohin, Andrea: The New York Times
Morris, Christopher: Time Magazine
Morris, Larry E.: Washington Post
Morris, Ryan: Fauquier Times Democrat
Mosley, Leigh H: The Washington Blade
Murphy, Timothy A.: Freelance
Musi, Vincent J.: Time Magazine
Nelson, Andrew P.: Christian Science Monitor
Newton, Gregg: Reuters News Pictures
Newton, Jonathan: Washington Post
Nipp, Lisa: Freelance
Nisnevitch, Lev: The Weekly Standard
O'Leary, William P: Washington Post
Ommanney, Charles: Newsweek
Ono, Akira: Asahi Shimbun
Otfinowski, Danuta: Freelance
Pajic, Kamenko: Freelance

MEMBERS ENTITLED FOR ADMISSION—Continued

Panagos, Dimitrios: Greek American News Agency
Parcell, James A.: Washington Post
Parker, Howard (Hank) H: Freelance
Parsons, Nate: Washington Post
Pastor, Nancy: Washington Times
Patterson, Kathryn B.: USA/Today
Pearson, Robert L: Agence France Presse
Perkins, Lucien: Washington Post
Perry, William: Freelance
Petros, Bill: Freelance
Philpott, William: Freelance
Poggi, Jennifer: U.S. News & World Report
Poleski, David: Freelance
Powers, Carol T: Freelance
Price, Brian: Times Community Newspapers
Prichard, James W: Education Week
Pryke, John Donald: Reuters News Pictures
Purcell, Steven: Freelance
Raab, Susana A: Freelance
Raimondo, Lois: Washington Post
Rasmussen, Randy L.: Oregonian
Reed, Jason: Reuters News Pictures
Reeder, Robert A: Washington Post
Reinhard, Rick: Impact Digitals
Remsberg, Edwin H: Freelance
Ricardel, Vincent J.: Freelance
Richards, Paul J.: Agence France Presse
Richardson, Joel M.: Washington Post
Riecken, Astrid: Washington Times
Riley, Molly: Reuters News Pictures
Roberts, Nicholas: Freelance
Robinson, Scott: Freelance
Robinson-Chavez, Michael: Washington Post
Ronay, Vivian: Freelance
Rose, Jamie: Freelance
Rosenbaum, Daniel: Washington Times
Ryan, Patrick: The Hill
Sachs, Arnold: Consolidated News Pictures
Sachs, Ronald M.: Consolidated News Pictures
Salisbury, Barbara L.: The Gazette
Samperton, Kyle: Freelance
Savoia, Stephen: Associated Press Photos
Schaeffer, Sandra L.: MAI Photo Agency
Schumacher, Karl H.: Freelance
Schwartz, David S.: Freelance
Scull, David: Freelance
Shell, Mary: Time Magazine
Shelley, Allison: Education Week
Silverman, Joseph A.: Washington Times
Simon, Martin: Corbis
Sloan, Timothy: Agence France Presse
Smialowski, Brendan: Freelance
Smith, Dayna: Washington Post
Sommer, Emilie: Freelance
Somodevilla, Kenneth: Freelance
Souza, Peter J.: Chicago Tribune
Spillers, Linda J.: Freelance

Spoden, Leonard: Freelance
Springer, Mike: Zuma Press
Starr, Adele: Freelance
Steele, Rick: Post-Newsweek Media
Stephenson, Al: Freelance
Sudyatmiko, Karina: Saura Pembaruan
Sykes, Jack W.: Professional Pilot Magazine
Sypher, Mark F.: Fauquier Times Democrat
Takeda, Yasushi: Shukan Shincho, Shinchosha Co.
Talbott, Jay: Freelance
Temchine, Michael: Freelance
Theiler, Michael: Freelance
Thew, Shawn: European Press Photo
Thiessen, Mark: National Geographic
Thomas, Margaret: Washington Post
Thomas, Ronald W.: Freelance
Thresher, James M.: Washington Post
Tines, Charles V.: The Detroit News
Trippett, Robert: Freelance
Turner, Tyrone: Freelance
Usher, Chris: Freelance
Van Riper, Frank A.: WashingtonPost.com
Varias, Stelios A.: Reuters News Pictures
Visser, Robert: Photopress Washington
Voisin, Sarah L.: Washington Post
Votaw, Jr., Charles W.: Freelance
Vucci, Evan: Associated Press Photos
Wagreich, Ian: Freelance
Walker, Diana: Time Magazine
Walker, Harry E.: Knight Ridder Tribune News
    Service
Walsh, Susan: Associated Press Photos
Walter, Micah: Freelance
Wang, Ting-Li: The New York Times
Watkins, Jr., Frederick L.: Johnson Publishing Co.
Watson, James H.: Agence France Presse
Watson, Ricardo A.: Freelance
Westbrook, Roberto: Legal Times
Westcott, Jay: Freelance
Whitney-Wilkerson, Susan: The Gazette
Williams, Tom: Roll Call
Williamson, Michael: Washington Post
Wilson, Jamal A.: Freelance
Wilson, Jim: The New York Times
Wilson, Mark L.: Getty Images
Wines, Heather: Gannett
Wolf, Kevin: Freelance
Wolf, Lloyd: Freelance
Wollenberg, Roger L.: United Press International
Wong, Alex: Getty Images
Woodall, Andrea Bruce: Washington Post
Woodward, Tracy A.: Washington Post
Wright, Donald A.: Freelance
Yim, Heesoon: Hana
Yohai, Roey: Washington Times
Zachmanoglou, Nike: Freelance
Zaklin, Stefan: Freelance
Ziffer, Steve: Freelance

SERVICES REPRESENTED

(Service and telephone number, office address, and name of representative)

ABACA PRESS—(212) 244–8460; 28 West 36th Street, Suite 703, New York, NY 10018: Douliery, Olivier.

AGENCE FRANCE PRESSE—(202) 414–0551; 1015 15th Street, NW., Suite 500, Washington, DC 20005: Frazza, Luke; Pearson, Robert; Richards, Paul; Sloan, Timothy; Watson, James.

ARMY TIMES PUBLISHING—(703) 750–8170; 6883 Commercial Drive, Springfield, VA 22159: Curtis, Rob; Elfers, Steve; Kozak, Richard; Lee, James; Lessig, Alan; Francis, Lloyd; Mahaskey, Michael.

ASAHI SHIMBUN—(202) 783–1000; 1022 National Press Building, 529 14th Street, NW., Washington, DC 20045: Ono, Akira.

ASSOCIATED PRESS PHOTOS—(202) 776–9510; 2021 K Street, NW., Washington, DC 20006: Applewhite, J. Scott; Ceneta, Manuel; Cook, Dennis; Dharapak, Charles; Edmonds, Ronald; Hall, John; Helber, Stephen; Herbert, Gerald; Jackson, Lawrence; Martinez Monsivais, Pablo; Savoia, Stephen; Vucci, Evan; Walsh, Susan.

BALTIMORE SUN—(410) 332–6941; 501 North Calvert Street, Baltimore, MD 21278: Chung, Andre; Hairston, Kim; Hobby, David; Lopossay, Monica; Makely, John.

BIGMARSH NEWS PHOTOS—(202) 364–8332; 5131 52nd Street, NW., Washington, DC 20016: Cohen, Marshall.

BLACK STAR—(703) 547–1176; 7704 Tauxemont Rd, Alexandria, VA 22308: Brack, William; Harrington, John.

BRYCE MOUNTAIN COURIER—(540) 856–3255; P.O. Box 247, 68 Polk Street, Basye, VA 22810: Boston, Bernard.

CAPRI—(717) 757–2962; 485 Sundale Drive, York, PA 17402: Markel, Brad.

CHESAPEAKE NEWS SERVICE—(410) 484–3500; P.O. Box 141, Brooklandville, MD 21022: Katz, Martin.

CHICAGO TRIBUNE—(202) 824–8200; 1325 G Street, NW., Suite 200, Washington, DC 20005: Souza, Peter.

CHRISTIAN SCIENCE MONITOR—(617) 450–2000; 1 Norway Street, Boston, MA 02115: Nelson, Andrew.

CONSOLIDATED NEWS PICTURES—(202) 543–3203; 10305 Leslie Street, Silver Spring, MD 20902–4857: Sachs, Arnold; Sachs, Ronald.

CONTACT PRESS IMAGES—(212) 695–7750; 341 West 38th Street, 7th Floor, New York, NY 10018: Burnett, David.

CORBIS–902—Broadway, 4th Floor, New York, NY 10010: Simon, Martin.

COX NEWSPAPERS—(202) 331–0900; 400 North Capitol Street, Suite 750, Washington, DC 20001: McKay, Richard.

CQ WEEKLY—(202) 822–1431; 1414 22nd Street, NW., Washington, DC 20037: Ferrell, Scott.

CREDIT UNION TIMES—(301) 845–7820; 8507 Inspiration Avenue, Walkersville, MD 21793: Cooke, John.

DAILY TELEGRAPH (LONDON)—(202) 393–5195; 1310 G Street, NW., Suite 750, Washington, DC 20005: Conway, Stuart.

EDUCATION WEEK—(301) 280–3100; 6935 Arlington Road, Suite 100, Bethesda, MD 20814: Prichard, James; Shelley, Allison.

EUROPEAN PRESS PHOTO—(202) 347–4694; 1252 National Press Building, 529 14th Street, NW., Washington, DC 20045: Gunther, Brendan "CJ"; Kemper, Gary; McDermid, Brendan; Thew, Shawn.

FAUQUIER TIMES DEMOCRAT—39 Culpeper Street, Warrenton, VA 20186: Morris, Ryan; Sypher, Mark.

FRONTIERS NEWS MAGAZINE—(301) 229–0635; P.O. Box 634, Glen Echo, MD 20812: Lynch, M., Patricia.

GANNETT—(703) 854–5800; 7950 Jones Branch Drive, McLean, VA 22107: Clark, Bill; Franko, Jeff; Wines, Heather.

GETTY IMAGES—(646) 613–3703; One Hudson Place, 75 Varick Street, New York, NY 10013: Ellis, Richard; McNamee, Win; Wilson, Mark; Wong, Alex.

GLOBAL NEWS PHOTOS—P.O Box 0082 Homecrest, Brooklyn, NY 11229: Lewter, Lani.

GREEK AMERICAN NEWS AGENCY—(202) 332–2727; 107 Frederick Avenue, Babylon, NY 11702: Panagos, Dimitrios.

HANA—(202) 262–4541; 11311 Park Drive, Fairfax, VA 22030: Yim, Heesoon.

HURRIYET—(703) 978–8073; 8910 Moreland Lane, Annandale, VA 22003: Biber, Mehmet.

SERVICES REPRESENTED—Continued

IMAGECATCHER NEWS—4911 Hampden Lane, Apt #3, Bethesda, MD 20814: Bowe, Christy.

IMPACT DIGITALS—(212) 614 8406; 171 Thompson Stret, #9, New York, NY 10012: Reinhard, Rick.

JENNINGS PUBLICATIONS—(301) 946–5538; 2600 Plyers Mill Road, Silver Spring, MD 20902: Jennings, Stan.

JOHNSON PUBLISHING CO.—(202) 393–5860; 1750 Pennsylvania Avenue, NW., Washington, DC 20006: Watkins, Jr., Frederick.

KNIGHT RIDDER TRIBUNE NEWS SERVICE—(202) 383–6142; 700 12th Street, NW., Suite 1000, Washington, DC 20005: Bridges, George; Kennedy, Chuck; Walker, Harry.

LEGAL TIMES—(202) 457–0686; 1730 M Street, NW., Suite 802, Washington, DC 20036: Westbrook, Roberto.

LINCOLN JOURNAL–STAR—(402) 473–7482; 926 P Street, Lincoln, NE. 68508: Colburn, James.

MAI PHOTO AGENCY—(703) 968–0030; 6601 Ashmere Lane, Centreville, VA 20120: Mathieson, Greg; Schaeffer, Sandra.

NATIONAL GEOGRAPHIC—(202) 857–7000; 1145 17th Street, NW., Washington, DC 20036: Thiessen, Mark.

NATIONAL JOURNAL—(202) 739–8400; 1501 M Street, NW., Suite 300, Washington, DC 20005: Bloom, Richard; Lynch, Liz.

NEW YORK DAILY NEWS—(202) 467–6670; 1215 17th Street, NW., 3rd Floor, Washington, DC 20036: Hamburg, Harry.

NEWSWEEK—(202) 626–2085; 1750 Pennsylvania Ave., NW., Washington, DC 20006: Bui, Khue; Ferraro, Beth; Kennerly, David; Ommanney, Charles.

NOTIMEX—(202) 347–5227; 529 14th Street, NW., Suite 425, Washington, DC 20045–1401: Gamarra, Ruben.

PARIS–MATCH—2225 49th Street, NW., Washington, DC 20007: Atlan, Jean-Louis.

PERIODICAL NEWS SERVICE—9206 Vollmerhausen Road, Jessup, MD 20794: Gatty, Michael.

PHOTO PRESS INTERNATIONAL—(703) 548–7172: Coppage, Gary.

PHOTO TRENDS, INC.—548 8th Avenue, suite 401, New York, NY 10018: Burns, David.

PHOTOPRESS WASHINGTON—(202) 234–8787; National Press Building, Suite 2105, Washington, DC 20045: Visser, Robert.

POLARIS IMAGES—259 W. 30th Street, 13th Floor, New York, NY 10001: Harris, Steven.

POST–NEWSWEEK MEDIA—(301) 948–3120; 1200 Quince Orchard Blvd, Gaithersburg, MD 20878: Steele, Rick.

PROFESSIONAL PILOT MAGAZINE—3014 Colvin Street, Alexandria, VA 22314: Sykes, Jack.

REDIFF.COM / INDIA ABROAD PUB.—(646) 432–6054; 43 West 24th Street, 2nd Floor, New York, NY 10010: Gandhi, Pareshkumar.

REFORMA—(202) 628–0031; 1126 National Press Building, Washington, DC 20045: Juarez, Miguel.

REUTERS NEWS PICTURES—(202) 898–8333; 1333 H Street, NW., Suite 410, Washington, DC 20005: Beals, Herman; Bochatey, Terry; Bourg, Jim; Cameron, Gary; Clement, Richard; Downing, Lawrence; Hershorn, Gary; Jones, Peter; Kang, Hyungwon; Lamarque, Kevin; Newton, Gregg; Pryke, John; Reed, Jason; Riley, Molly; Varias, Stelios.

ROLL CALL—(202) 824–6800; 50 F Street, NW., 7th Floor, Washington, DC 20001: Graham, Douglas; Maddaloni, Chris; Williams, Tom.

SAURA PEMBARUAN—(703) 534–6014; 1908 Armand Court, Falls Church, VA 22043: Sudyatmiko, Karina.

SHUKAN SHINCHO, SHINCHOSHA CO.—(703) 243–1569; 2001 North Adams Street, #715, Arlington, VA 22201: Takeda, Yasushi.

SIPA PRESS—(212) 463–0150; 30 West 21st Street, New York, NY 10010: Fabiano, Gary.

SPORTS ILLUSTRATED—(212) 522–3325; 1271 Avenue of the Americas, Room 1970, New York, NY 10020: Binks, Porter.

SUBURBAN COMMUNICATIONS CORP.—(810) 645–5164; 872 Dursley Road, Bloomfield Hills, ME 48304: Ashley, Douglas.

THE DETROIT NEWS—(312) 222–2030; 615 West Lafayette Avenue, Photo Dept, Detroit, MI 48226: Tines, Charles.

THE DIGITAL JOURNALIST—Center for American History, University of Texas at Austin, Austin, TX 78712: Halstead, Dirck.

THE GAZETTE—(301) 948–3120; 1200 Quince Orchard Boulevard, Gaithersburg, MD 20878: Fenster, J. Adam; Golden, Rachael; Salisbury, Barbara; Whitney-Wilkerson, Susan.

THE HILL—(202) 628–8525; 733 15th Street, Washington, DC 20005: Bandeira, Pedro; Ryan, Patrick.

THE JOURNAL NEWSPAPERS—6408 Edsall Road, Alexandria, VA 22312: Harnik, Andrew.

THE NEW YORK TIMES—(202) 862–0300; 1627 Eye Street, NW., Washington, DC 20006: Bengiveno, Nicole; Bogert, Jr., Jeremiah; Crowley, Stephen; Fremson, Ruth; Hosefros, Paul; Lee, Chang; Meyers, Keith; Mills, Douglas; Mohin, Andrea; Wang, Ting-Li; Wilson, Jim.

THE OREGONIAN—(503) 221–8370; 1320 SW Broadway, Portland, OR 97201: Rasmussen, Randy.

THE PHILADELPHIA DAILY NEWS—400 N. Broad Street, Philadelphia, PA 19130: Falk, Steven.

SERVICES REPRESENTED—Continued

THE RICHMOND TIMES DISPATCH—(804) 649–6486; 300 E Franklin Street, Richmond, VA 23219: Brown, Robert.
THE WASHINGTON BLADE—1408 U Street, NW., 2nd Floor, Washington, DC 20009: Mosley, Leigh.
THE WASHINGTON INFORMER—(202) 561–4100; 3117 Martin L. King Avenue, SE., Washington, DC 20032: Lewis, Roy.
THE WASHINGTON POST—(202) 334–7380; 1150 15th Street, NW., Washington, DC 20071: Arias, Juana; Biddle, Susan; Brooks, Dudley; Carioti, Richard; Chikwendiu, Jahi; Clark, Kevin; Du Cille, Michel; Guzy, Carol; Joseph, Marvin; Kahn, Nikki; Lipski, Richard; Lutzky, Micheal; Mara, Melina; Martineau, Gerald; McDonnell, John; Morris, Larry; Newton, Jonathan; O'Leary, William; Parcell, James; Parsons, Nate; Perkins, Lucien; Raimondo, Lois; Reeder, Robert; Richardson, Joel; Robinson-Chavez, Michael; Smith, Dayna; Thomas, Margaret; Thresher, James; Voisin, Sarah; Williamson, Michael; Woodall, Andrea; Woodward, Tracy.
THE WASHINGTON TIMES—(202) 636–3000; 3600 New York Ave., NE., Washington, DC 20002: Alleruzzo, Maya; Baughman, J. Ross; Baylen, Liz; Brantley, James; Calvert, Mary; Connor, Michael; Eddins, Jr., Joseph; Goulait, Bert; Lamkey, Jr., Rod; Pastor, Nancy; Riecken, Astrid; Rosenbaum, Daniel; Silverman, Joseph; Yohai, Roey.
THE WEEKLY STANDARD—1150 17th Street, NW., Suite 505, Washington, DC 20036: Nisnevitch, Lev.
THE YOMIURI SHIMBUN—(212) 582–5827; 50 Rockefeller Plaza, #903, New York, NY 10020: Kon, Toshiyuki.
TIME MAGAZINE—(202) 861–4062; 555 12th Street, NW., Suite 600, Washington, DC 20004: Ellsworth, Katie; Kraft, Brooks; Liss, Steve; Morris, Christopher; Musi, Vincent; Shell, Mary; Walker, Diana;
TIMES COMMUNITY NEWSPAPERS—1760 Reston Parkway, Suite 411, Reston, VA 20190: Price, Brian.
U.S. NEWS & WORLD REPORT—(202) 955–2210; 1050 Thomas Jefferson Street, NW., Washington, DC 20007: Archambault, Charles; LoScalzo, Jim; MacMillan, Jeffrey; Poggi, Jennifer.
UNITED PRESS INTERNATIONAL—(202) 387–7965; 1510 H Street, NW., Washington, DC 20005: Benic, Patrick; Kleinfeld, Michael; Wollenberg, Roger.
USA/TODAY—(703) 854–5216; 7950 Jones Branch Road, McLean, VA 22107: Beiser, H. Darr; Blass, Eileen; Dillon, Timothy; Madrid, Michael; Patterson, Kathryn.
USATODAY.COM—(703) 854–7651; 7950 Jones Branch Drive, McLean, VA 22108: Dukehart, Coburn; Gainer, Denny.
WASHINGTONPOST.COM—3502 Quesada Street, NW., Washington, DC 20025: Van Riper, Frank.
WORLD PICTURE NEWS—(212) 871–1207; 62 White Street, Suite 3 East, New York, NY 10013: Frischling, Steven.
XINHUA NEWS AGENCY—(703) 875–0086; 1740N 14th Street, Arlington, VA 22209: Lu, Mingxiang.

FREELANCE

Freelance—Alswang, Ralph; Arrossi, Eddie; Ashe, James; Attlee, Tracey; Augustino, Jocelyn; Ballard, Karen; Barouh, Stan; Barrett, Steve; Berg, Lisa; Bigwood, Jeremy; Bingham, Mary (Molly); Boitano, Stephen; Bouchard, Renee; Brown, Stephen; Burke, Lauren; Carrier, Jason; Cavanaugh, Matthew; Cedeno, Ken; Clendenin, Jay; Corcoran, Thomas; Crandall, Rob; Crandall, Bill; Cutts, Peter; D'Angelo, Rebecca; DeArmas, Adrienne; Devorah, Carrie; DiBari, Jr., Michael; Doyle, Kevin; Emanuel, Hector; Ericsson, Hans; Ernst, Jonathan; Falls, Jr., John; Ficara, John; Fitz-Patrick, Bill; Fiume, Gregory; Foster, Jacqueline Mia; Garcia, Mannie; Geissinger, Michael; Gifford, Porter; Gilbert, Patrice; Glenn, Larry; Graves, Thomas; Gripas, Yuri; Hartmann, Paul; Heasley, Shaun; Hittle, David; Holloway, David; Jacobs, Vance; Johnson, Richard; Kittner, Sam; Kleponis, Chris; Kossoff, Leslie; LaVor, Martin; Lee, David; Lynaugh, Michael; Mallin, Jay; Mallory, Tyler; Malonson, Jacqueline; Marks, Donovan; Murphy, Timothy; Nipp, Lisa; Otfinowski, Danuta; Pajic, Kamenko; Parker, Howard (Hank); Perry, William; Petros, Bill; Philpott, William; Poleski, David; Powers, Carol; Purcell, Steven; Raab, Susana; Remsberg, Edwin; Ricardel, Vincent; Roberts, Nicholas; Robinson, Scott; Ronay, Vivian; Rose, Jamie; Samperton, Kyle; Schumacher, Karl; Schwartz, David; Scull, David; Smialowski, Brendan; Sommer, Emilie; Somodevilla, Kenneth; Spillers, Linda; Spoden, Leonard; Springer, Mike; Starr, Adele; Stephenson, Al; Talbott, Jay; Temchine, Michael; Theiler, Michael; Thomas, Ronald; Trippett, Robert; Turner, Tyrone; Usher, Chris; Votaw, Jr., Charles; Wagreich, Ian; Walter, Micah; Watson, Ricardo; Westcott, Jay; Wilson, Jamal; Wolf, Kevin; Wolf, Lloyd; Wright, Donald; Zachmanoglou, Nike; Zaklin, Stefan; Ziffer, Steve.

WHITE HOUSE NEWS PHOTOGRAPHERS' ASSOCIATION

PO 7119, Washington, DC 20044–7119

www.whnpa.org

OFFICERS

Susan A. Walsh, Associated Press, *President*
John Poole, WashingtonPost.com, *Vice President*
Nikki Kahn, Washington Post, *Secretary*
Jonathan Elswick, Associated Press, *Treasurer*

EXECUTIVE BOARD

Susan Biddle (Washington Post)
Dennis Brack (Black Star)
Cliff Owen (AOL)
Ed Eaves (NBC News)
Stu Cohen (Freelance)
Pierre Kattar, (Washingtonpost.com)
Pete Souza, Contest Chair (Chicago Tribune)
Contest Chair, Television (Open)
Leighton Mark, Education Chair (Associated Press)

MEMBERS REPRESENTED

Abraham, Mark: Freelance
Adlerblum, Robin: CBS News
Alberter Jr., William: CNN
Allen, Tom:
Alleruzzo, Maya: Washington Times
Apt Johnson, Roslyn: Freelance
Archambault, Charles: US News & World Report
Arias, Juana: Washington Post
Arrington, Clyde Steven: ABC News
Attlee, Tracey: Freelance
Auth, William: US News & World Report
Baker, David: ITN
Ballard, Karen: Freelance
Baughman, J. Ross: Washington Times
Baylen, Elizabeth Olivia: Washington Times
Beiser, H. Darr: USA Today
Biddle, Susan: Washington Post
Blair, James P.: Freelance
Bochatey, Terry: Reuters
Bodnar, John: CNN
Boswell Jr., Victor: Freelance
Bowe, Christy: ImageCatcher News
Brack, Dennis: Black Star
Brantley, James R.: Washington Times
Bridges, George S.: Knight Ridder/Tribune

Brisson, Stephane: CTV Television
Brooks, Dudley: Washington Post
Brown, Stephen:
Bruce Woodall, Andrea: Washington Post
Bryan, Beverly: WJLA–TV
Bui, Khue: Freelance
Burgess, Robert Harrison: Freelance
Burke, Lauren Victoria: Freelance
Burnett, David: Contact Press Images
Butler, Francis: Freelance
Cain, Stephen: ABC–TV
Calvert, Mary F.: Washington Times
Cameron, Gary: Reuters
Carioti, Ricky: Washington Post
Casey, Sean: NBC4
Cassetta, Guido: Freelance
Castner, Edward: Freelance
Castoro, Susan Mary: Associated Press
Cavanaugh, Matthew: Freelance
Cedeno, Ken: Freelance
Ceneta, Manuel Balce: Assocaited Press
Chang Crandall, Jennifer: Washingtonpost.com
Chase, David: Cox Broadcasting
Chikwendiu, Jahi: Washington Post
Clark, Bill: Gannett News Srevice

MEMBERS REPRESENTED—Continued

Clark, Kevin: Washington Post
Clendenin, Jay L.: Freelance
Cobb, Jodi: National Geographic
Cohen, Marshall: Big Marsh News Photos
Cohen, Stuart A.: Freelance
Colburn, James: Lincoln Journal Star
Collinson, Luke: ITN
Connor, Michael: Washington Times
Cook, Dennis: Associated Press
Corder, Chris: AOL
Crane, Arnold: The LaVor Group
Crawford, Walter: WJLA–TV
Crowley, Stephen: The New York Times
Cuong, Pham: CBS
Curran, Patrick J.: WTTG–TV
Curtis, Rob: Army Times Publishing
Curtiss, Cathaleen: America On Line
Dale, Bruce: Freelance
Daniell, Parker Parker: Freelance
Daugherty, Bob: Associated Press
de la Cruz, Benedict: Washingtonpost.com
Deslich, Steve: Knight Ridder Tribune Photo Service
Dharapak, Charles: Associated Press
Dillon, Tim: USA Today
Doane, Martin Call: WJLA–TV
Dodson, Richard: NBC
Douliery, Oliver: Abaca Press
Downing, Larry: Reuters
Drenner, Dennis: Freelance
duCille, Michel: Washington Post
Dukehart, Coburn A: USAToday.com
Dunmire, John: WTTG–TV
Eddins, Joseph M.: Washington Times
Edmonds, Ron: Associated Press
Elbert II, Joseph: Washington Post
Elfers, Stephen: Army Times Publishing Co.
Elswick, Jonathan: Associated Press
Epstein, Linda D.: Knight Ridder Tribune
Ernst, Jonathan M.: Freelance
Ewan, Julia: Washington Post
Ewing, David: Freelance
Feldman, Randy: Viewpoint Communications Inc.
Fiedler Jr., James: American Online
Figueroa, Noreen: AOL
Folwell, Frank: USA Today
Fox, Travis Gerard: Washingtonpost.com
Foy, Mary Lou: Washington Post
Frame, John: WTTG–TV
Franklin, Ross: Washington Times
Frazza, Luke: AFP
Freeman, Roland: Freelance
Frey, Katherine: Washington Post
Gainer, Dennis: USA Today
Garcia, Mannie: Freelance
Gibson, Craig: Freelance
Gilbert, Kevin T.: Blue Pixel
Gilgannon, Pege: WJLA

Gmiter, Bernard: ABC News
Goodman, Jeffrey: NBC/Freelance
Goulait, Bert: Washington Times
Goulding, David: Emotion Pictures
Goyal, Raghubir: Asia Today & India Globe/ATN News
Graham, Douglas: Roll Call
Guzy, Carol: Washington Post
Hall, Ellie M.: Associated Press
Hamburg, Harry: New York Daily News
Harrington, John: Freelance
Harvey, Alan: NBC
Herbert, Gerald: Associated Press
Hershorn, Gary: Reuters
Hillian, Vanessa Barnes: Washington Post
Hinds, Hugh: Freelance
Holloway, David Scott: Freelance
Hopkins, Gary: AOL
Hopkins, Brian Clark: WJLA–TV
Horan, Michael: WTTG–TV
Hoyt, Michael: Catholic Standard
Ing, Lance: WTTG–TV
Jackson, Karen Leslie: WJLA–TV Channel 7
Jackson, Lawrence: Associated Press
Jackson, Ryan Leon: Cox Broadcasting
Johnson, Krissanne: U.S. News & Wordl Report
Johnston, Frank: Washington Post
Jones, Nelson P.: WTTG–TV
Joseph, Marvin: Washington Post
Kahn, Nikki: Washington Post
Kang, Hyungwon: Reuters News Pictures
Kattar, Pierre: Washingtonpost.com
Katz, Marty: Chesapeake News Service
Kennedy, Thomas: Washington Post Newseek Interactive
Kennedy, Charles: Knight Ridder/Tribune
Kennerly, David Hume: Eagles Roar Inc.
Keres, Preston: Washington Post
Kiesow, Damon Michael: America Online
King Lopez, Daniel: CNN
Kittner, Sam: Freelance
Kobersteen, Kent: National Geographic
Koppelman, Mitch: Reuters Television
Korab, Alexandra: AOL
Kossoff, Leslie E.: LK Photos
Kozak, Rick:
Kraft, Brooks: Time Magazine
Krieger, Barbara: Freelance/Day Hire
Lamarque, Kevin: Reuters
Lamkey Jr., Rod A.: Washington Times
Larsen, Gregory: Freelance
Lavies, Bianca: Freelance
LaVor, Marty: Freelance
Lawrence, Jeffrey Dean: Knight-Ridder Tribune
Lessig, Alan: Army Times
Levy, Glenn Ann: Freelance
Lichtenfeld, Sara: AOL
Lipski, Richard: Washington Post

MEMBERS REPRESENTED—Continued

Lizik, Ronald: Associated Press
Lorek, Stanley: ABC
LoScalzo, James: US News & World Report
Lynaugh, Mike: Freelance
MacDonald, Charles Wayne: National Geographic Channel
MacDonald, Jim: Canadian TV Network
MacMillan, Jeffrey: US News & World Report
Maddaloni, Christopher Anthony: Roll Call
Madrid, Michael A.: USA Today
Maggiolo, Vito: CNN
Malonson, Jacqueline: Freelance AP
Manley, Jerold: Freelance
Mara, Melina: Washington Post
Mark, Leighton: Associated Press
Marquette, Joseph: European Press Photo Agency
Martin, David John: Australian Broadcasting Corporation
Martineau, Gerald: Washington Post
Martinez Monsivais, Pablo: Associated Press
Mason, Thomas: WTTG–TV
Mathieson, Greg E.: MAI Photo News Agency, Inc.
Mawyer, Steve: AOL
Mazariegos, Mark Anthony: CBS News
Mazer Field, Joni: Freelance
Mazzatenta, O. Louis: Freelance
McDonnell, John: Washington Post
McKay, Richard: Cox Newspapers
McKee, Staci: WashingtonPost.com
McKenna, William Horace: Freelance/BBC
McLaughlin, David W.: National Geographic Channel
McClendon, Jerome: AOL
McNamee, Win: Getty Images
Mendelsohn, Matthew: Freelance
Milenic, Alexander: Freelance
Mills, Doug: New York Times
Mole, Robert: NBC
Morris, Larry: Washington Post
Morris, Peter H.: CNN
Morris, Ryan Kent: Apix
Morrisette, Roland Guy: Bloomberg News
Moss, Lisa M.: AOL
Murphy, John: Freelance
Murphy, Timothy: Freelance
Murtaugh, Peter: Murtaugh Productions, LLC
Natoli, Sharon: freelance
Nelson, Andrew Paul: Christian Science Monitor
Newton, Jonathan A.: Washington Post
Norling, Richard A.: Freelance
Ochs, Rochelle: AOL
O'Leary, William: Washington Post
Ommanney, Charles: Newsweek
Panzer, Chester: NBC–WRC
Parcell, James: Washington Post
Parsons, Nathan Andrew: Washington Post
Partlow, Wayne: Associated Press

Pastor, Nancy: Washington Times
Patterson, Jay: ABC
Pearson, Robert: AFP
Pensinger, Douglas Alan: Getty Images
Perkins, Lucian: Washington Post
Peterson, Jr., Robert: Freelance
Petros, Bill: Freelance
Philpott, William: AFP
Pinczuk, Murray: Freelance
Pino-Marina, Christina: Washingtonpost.com
Poole, John: Washingtonpost.Newsweek Interactive
Potasznik, David: Point of View Production Services Inc.
Powell Jr., William: NBC
Powers, Carol: Freelance
Proser, Michael: ABC–News
Raab, Susana Alicia: Freelance
Rabbage, Mark: BBC TV
Raimondo, Lois: Washington Post
Raker, Lester Raymond: ABC News
Reed, Jason Ian: Reuters
Reeder, Robert: Washington Post
Rhodes, Charles C.: Washingtonpost.com
Richardson, Joel: Washington Post
Riecken, Astrid: Washington Times
Rittman, Anne: WashingtonPost.com
Robinson-Chavez, Michael: Washington Post
Rogowski, David: AOL
Ronay, Vivian: Freelance
Rosenbaum, Daniel: Washington Times
Rossetti, Amy: Potomac News/Media General
Roth Jr., Johnie: NBC
Rysak, F. David: WTTG–TV
Sachs, Ronald M.: Consolidated News Photos
Santoro, Giuliana: Washington Post
Saunders, Ray Keller: Washington Post
Schaeffer, Sandra Lynne: MAI Photo News Agency
Schule, James: Fox News Network
Scicchitano, Carmine D.: NBC
Scull, David: Freelance
Semiatin, Morris: Morris Semiatin-Photographer
Shannon, Dennis: CBS News
Shlemon, Christopher: Independent TV News
Singles, Phaedra: Washington Post.com
Sladen, Kristin: AOL
Smialowski, Brendan: Freelance
Smith, Dayna: Washington Post
Smith, Jason Harding: WTTG–TV
Snowden, Thomas R.: NBC News
Sommer, Emilie: Freelance
Souza, Peter: Chicago Tribune
Spillers, Linda Jean: Freelance
Stein III, Arthur: Freelance
Stephenson, Al: Freelance
Stewart, Samaruddin K.: AOL
Stoddard, Mark: Freelance
Suddeth, Rick: Freelance
Sweets, Fred: St. Louis American

MEMBERS REPRESENTED—Continued

Swenson, Gordon: ABC
Sykes, Jack: Professional Pilot Magazine
Tefft-Soraghan, Jessica: Freelance
Temchine, Michael: Freelance
Thalman, Mark: Across the Pond Productions
Thew, Shawn A.: European Pressphoto Agency
Thomas, Margaret: Washington Post
Thresher, James: Washington Post
Trippett, Robert: Sipa Press
Tuckson D.D.S., Coleman: Consolidated News
   Pictures
Usher, Chris R.: Freelance/APIX
Van Grack, Lee: AOL
Van Riper, Frank: Goodman/Van Riper
   Photography
Vennell, Vicki: ABC News
Verna, Tressa: NBC–News Dateline
Voisin, Sarah L.: Washington Post
Vucci, Evan: Associated Press
Walker, Diana: Time Magazine
Walsh, Susan: Associated Press

Walter, Charles A.: National Geographic
Walz, Mark Louis: CNN
Watrud, Donald: WTTG–TV
Weik, David: ABC Television News
Weller, George: Freelance
Wells, Jim: Freelance
Wilkes, Douglas: WTTG–TV
Williams, Milton: Freelance
Williams, Robert: NBC News
Williams, Thomas L: Roll Call Newspaper
Williamson, Michael: Washington Post
Wilson, Mark: Getty Images
Wollenberg, Roger: United Press International
Wong, Alex: Getty Images
Woodward, Tracy: Washington Post
Yaqubi, Wajmah: AOL
Yates II, H. William: CBS News Freelance
Zervos, Stratis: Freelance—Zervos Video
   Productions, LLC
Zlotky, Alan: AOL

RADIO AND TELEVISION CORRESPONDENTS' GALLERIES*

SENATE RADIO AND TELEVISION GALLERY
The Capitol, Room S–325, 224–6421

Director.—Michael Mastrian
Deputy Director.—Jane Ruyle
Senior Media Coordinator.—Michael Lawrence
Media Coordinator.—Sara Robertson

HOUSE RADIO AND TELEVISION GALLERY
The Capitol, Room H–321, 225–5214

Director.—Tina Tate
Deputy Director.—Olga Ramirez Kornacki
Assistant for Administrative Operations.—Gail Davis
Assistant for Technical Operations.—Andy Elias
Assistants: Gerald Rupert, Kimberly Oates

EXECUTIVE COMMITTEE OF THE RADIO AND TELEVISION CORRESPONDENTS' GALLERIES

Joe Johns, NBC News, *Chair*
Jerry Bodlander, Associated Press Radio
Bob Fuss, CBS News
Edward O'Keefe, ABC News
Dave McConnell, WTOP Radio
Richard Tillery, The Washington Bureau
David Wellna, NPR News

RULES GOVERNING RADIO AND TELEVISION CORRESPONDENTS' GALLERIES

1. Persons desiring admission to the Radio and Television Galleries of Congress shall make application to the Speaker, as required by Rule 34 of the House of Representatives, as amended, and to the Committee on Rules and Administration of the Senate, as required by Rule 33, as amended, for the regulation of Senate wing of the Capitol. Applicants shall state in writing the names of all radio stations, television stations, systems, or news-gathering organizations by which they are employed and what other occupation or employment they may have, if any. Applicants shall further declare that they are not engaged in the prosecution of claims or the promotion of legislation pending before Congress, the Departments, or the independent agencies, and that they will not become so employed without resigning from the galleries. They shall further declare that they are not employed in any legislative or executive department or independent agency of the Government, or by any foreign government or representative thereof; that they are not engaged in any lobbying activities; that they

---

*Information is based on data furnished and edited by each respective gallery.

do not and will not, directly or indirectly, furnish special information to any organization, individual, or group of individuals for the influencing of prices on any commodity or stock exchange; that they will not do so during the time they retain membership in the galleries. Holders of visitors' cards who may be allowed temporary admission to the galleries must conform to all the restrictions of this paragraph.

2. It shall be prerequisite to membership that the radio station, television station, system, or news-gathering agency which the applicant represents shall certify in writing to the Radio and Television Correspondents' Galleries that the applicant conforms to the foregoing regulations.

3. The applications required by the above rule shall be authenticated in a manner that shall be satisfactory to the Executive Committee of the Radio and Television Correspondents' Galleries who shall see that the occupation of the galleries is confined to bona fide news gatherers and/or reporters of reputable standing in their business who represent radio stations, television stations, systems, or news-gathering agencies engaged primarily in serving radio stations, television stations, or systems. It shall be the duty of the Executive Committee of the Radio and Television Correspondents' Galleries to report, at its discretion, violation of the privileges of the galleries to the Speaker or to the Senate Committee on Rules and Administration, and pending action thereon, the offending individual may be suspended.

4. Persons engaged in other occupations, whose chief attention is not given to—or more than one-half of their earned income is not derived from—the gathering or reporting of news for radio stations, television stations, systems, or news-gathering agencies primarily serving radio stations or systems, shall not be entitled to admission to the Radio and Television Galleries. The Radio and Television Correspondents' List in the Congressional Directory shall be a list only of persons whose chief attention is given to or more than one-half of their earned income is derived from the gathering and reporting of news for radio stations, television stations, and systems engaged in the daily dissemination of news, and of representatives of news-gathering agencies engaged in the daily service of news to such radio stations, television stations, or systems.

5. Members of the families of correspondents are not entitled to the privileges of the galleries.

6. The Radio and Television Galleries shall be under the control of the Executive Committee of the Radio and Television Correspondents' Galleries, subject to the approval and supervision of the Speaker of the House of Representatives and the Senate Committee on Rules and Administration.

Approved.

J. DENNIS HASTERT,
Speaker, House of Representatives.

TRENT LOTT,
Chairman, Senate Committee on Rules and Administration.

MEMBERS ENTITLED TO ADMISSION

RADIO AND TELEVISION CORRESPONDENTS' GALLERIES

Abad Serra, Ignasi: Catalunya Radio
Abbott, Stacey: National Public Radio
Abdalla, Hebah: Al-Jazeera TV/Peninsula
Abdallah, Khalil: CNN
Abe, Takaaki: Nippon TV Network
Abed, Nader: Al-Jazeera TV/Peninsula
Abrams, Mike: Radio One
Abramson, Larry: National Public Radio
Abtar, Rana: Middle East Television Network (Alhurra)
Abuelhawa, Daoud: Middle East Television Network (Alhurra)
Aburahma, Eyad: Al-Jazeera TV/Peninsula
Acharya, Niharika: Voice of America
Ackerman, Thomas: Belo Capital Bureau
Ackland, Matt: Freelance
Adams, Douglas A.: NBC News
Adams, James M.: WRC–TV/NBC–4
Adams, Jeff: ABC News
Adams, Larry: Native American Television
Adelhardt, Christine: German Television/ARD
Advani, Reena: National Public Radio
Afsharian, Maria: NBC News
Aguirre, Bertrand: TF1 French Television
Ahearn, Brian M.: East Coast Television
Ahlquist, Gregory E.: Fox News
Ahmad, Adriana: Voice of America
Ahmed, Lukman: MBC–TV (Middle East Broadcasting)
Ahmed, M. Anis: Voice of America
Ahn, Jaehoon: Radio Free Asia
Aitken, Cynthia L.: Tribune Broadcasting
Akassy, Hugues-Denver: Orbite Television, Inc.
Akkad, Reem: ABC News
Alami, Mohammed: Al-Jazeera TV/Peninsula
Albano, Thomas: CBS News
Alberter, William: CNN
Albright-Hanna, Kate: CNN
Alcott, Abigail K.: Fox News
Aldridge, William T.: Hearst-Argyle Television
Alexander, Clinton N.: CBS News
Alexander, Kenneth: C–SPAN
Alexanian, Nubar: National Public Radio
Al-Haj, Talal: MBC–TV (Middle East Broadcasting)
Ali, Shujaat: NBC News
Allard, John: ABC News
Alldredge, Thomas: C–SPAN
Allen, Darrell: Voice of America
Allen, Keith: Reuters Television
Allison, Lynn Quarles: WETA–TV
Al-Mirazi, Hafez: Al-Jazeera TV/Peninsula

Al-Moajil, Waleed: APTN
Alnwick, Melanie: WTTG–Fox Television
Alrawi, Khaldoun: APTN
Alvarez, Manuel: C–SPAN
Alvey, Jay: WRC–TV/NBC–4
Alvey, Jay D.: Diversified Communications, Inc. (DCI)
Ambinder, Marc: ABC News
Ammerman, Stuart: Freelance
Amperiadis, Dimitrios: Hellenic Broadcast Corp.
Anastasi, Patrick G.: NBC News
Anders, Jaroslaw: Voice of America
Anderson, Anne Davenport: Newshour with Jim Lehrer
Anderson, Charles: Freelance
Anderson, Kevin: BBC
Anderson, Scott: ABC News
Anderson, Shawn: WTOP Radio
Andonovski, Vedran: Voice of America
Andress, Jeannie Ohm: NBC News
Andrew, Jeffrey: WTTG–Fox Television
Andrews, Wyatt: CBS News
Angelini, Mark: Belo Capital Bureau
Angle, James L.: Fox News
Anglim, John: Freelance
Anthony, Karyn: CBS News
Antonie, Victor: Reuters Television
Aoun, Larissa: Middle East Television Network (Alhurra)
Apokis, Dimitrios: Hellenic Broadcast Corp.
Archer, Nelson: NBC News
Ardalan, Faraj: Voice of America
Arena, Bruno: Freelance
Arena, Kelli: CNN
Arenstein, Howard: CBS News
Argentieri, David: National Public Radio
Armfield, Robert: Fox News
Armstrong, Phyllis: WUSA–TV
Armwood, Adrian Conrad: Freelance
Arobaga-Reardon, Mary: Voice of America
Arrington, Percy: NBC News
Artesona, Eva: Catalan Television
Aryankalayil, Babu: Middle East Television Network
Asberg, Stefan: Swedish Television
Ashburn, Lauren: USA Today Live
Asher, Julie: Fox News
Aspery, Gregory: Tribune Broadcasting
Assuras, Thalia: CBS News
Attkisson, Sharyl: CBS News
Augenstein, Neal: WTOP Radio

971

MEMBERS ENTITLED TO ADMISSION—Continued

Austin, Kenneth L.: NBC News
Austin, Traci Mitchell: Hearst-Argyle Television
Autrey, Steven: CBN News
Avila, Viviana: Caracol TV
Azais, Jean-Pascal: TF1 French Television
Azzam, Heni: Al-Jazeera TV/Peninsula
Babington-Heina, Martin: Freelance
Bach, David: Radio Free Asia
Bach, Stephen: CNN
Bachenheimer, Stephan: Deutsche Welle Television
Bachmann, Thorsten: German Television/ARD
Bacon, Jason: WJLA–TV/Newschannel 8
Bagnato, Barry: CBS News
Baham, Todd: C–SPAN
Baier, Bret: Fox News
Bailor, Michelle: C–SPAN
Baird, Ashley Anne: CBS News
Baker, Cissy: Tribune Broadcasting
Baker, Craig: CNN
Baker, Dai: Independent Television News (ITN)
Baker, Les: Fox News
Baldwin, Lorna: Newshour with Jim Lehrer
Ballard, Carl: Newshour with Jim Lehrer
Ballenger, Katy: Fox News
Ballou, Jeffrey: WTTG–Fox Television
Balsamo, James: Diversified Communications, Inc. (DCI)
Baltimore, Dennis: Fox News
Banaszak, Brendan: National Public Radio
Banegas, Al: Belo Capital Bureau
Banks, James: Eurovision Americas, Inc.
Banks, Katherine: WRC–TV/NBC–4
Banks, Mark: ABC News
Bannigan, Michael A.: CNN
Barber, William: WETA–TV
Barbour, Lantz: Freelance
Barnard, Bob: WTTG–Fox Television
Barnes, Christopher: Fox News
Barnes, Audrey: WUSA–TV
Barnett, James: CNN
Barnette, Denley: WTTG–Fox Television
Barnhart, Marsha J.: Radio Free Asia
Barocas, Emily: National Public Radio
Barr, Bruce: CBS News
Barreda, Eric: Freelance
Barrett, Gene: ABC News
Barrett, Ted: CNN
Barry, Caitlin: CNN
Barthelemy, Maniko: Community TV of PG's
Bartlett, Stephen: Freelance
Bascom, Jon: ABC News
Basinger, Stuart: Fox News
Baskerville, Kia: CBS News
Bates, Timothy: Australian Broadcasting Corporation
Batten, Rodney: NBC News
Batties, Khepera: NBC News
Baumann, Robert: Diversified Communications, Inc.

Bavaud, Pierre: Swiss Broadcasting
Beahn, James P.: WUSA–TV
Beale, Jonathan: BBC
Beall, Gary Glenn: NBC News
Bearson, Sonya Crawford: ABC News
Beasley, David: Radio Free Asia
Beasley, Diane: CBS News
Beausoleil, Garry: SRN News
Becker, Bruce: Fox News
Becker, Farrel: CBS News
Becker, Frank K.: WJLA–TV/Newschannel 8
Becker, Regina M.: CBS News
Beery, Nic: Mobile Video Services
Belanger, Elizabeth: CNN
Bell, Bradley: WJLA–TV/Newschannel 8
Bell Kathuria, Afrika: C–SPAN
Bell, Ross: Capitol Pulse
Bellard, Joseph: Bloomberg Television
Bellman, Charles: Al-Jazeera TV/Peninsula
Belmar, Adam: ABC News
Bena, John: CNN
Bender, Bob: ABC News
Bender, Gary: WTTG–Fox Television
Bender, Sharon: Belo Capital Bureau
Benetato, Michael: NBC News
Benjoar, Jacques: NBC News
Bennett, Christine: Sinclair Broadcast Group
Bennett, Mark R.: CBS News
Bensen, Jackie: WRC–TV/NBC–4
Benson, Pamela S.: CNN
Bentley, David: Freelance
Bentz, Thomas: CNN
Benz, Kathy: CNN
Beraud, Anyck: CBC
Berbner, Thomas: German Television/ARD
Berkowitz, Elisa: WTTG–Fox Television
Bernardini, Laura: CNN
Berrou, Loick: TF1 French Television
Berry, Michael P.: WTTG–Fox Television
Bertelmann, James: Voice of America
Berti, Barbara: CNN
Betsill, Brett: C–SPAN
Beverly, Erin: Freelance
Bhatia, Varuna: Fox News
Bhungyal, Bhungyal: Radio Free Asia
Biddle, Michael: C–SPAN
Bintrim, Tim Raymond: Freelance
Birr, Emily: Newshour with Jim Lehrer
Bisney, John: CNN
Blackburn, Regina: NBC News
Blackman, Jay: NBC News
Blackwill, Sarah: NBC News
Blair, Elizabeth: National Public Radio
Blanchet, Sharon: BBC
Blandburg, Victor: USA Today Live
Blaszyk, Amy N.: National Public Radio
Blickstein, Adam: Freelance

MEMBERS ENTITLED TO ADMISSION—Continued

Block, Deborah: Voice of America
Block, Melissa: National Public Radio
Blooston, Victoria: NBC News
Blount, Jeffrey: NBC News
Blumberg, Sarah: Fox News
Bly, Dennis: WUSA–TV
Bodlander, Gerald: AP–Broadcast
Bodnar, John: CNN
Bohannon, Camille: AP–Broadcast
Bohannon, Joseph: NBC News
Bohn, Kevin: CNN
Bohrman, David: CNN
Bojadzievski, Jane: Voice of America
Bolter, Brian: WTTG–Fox Television
Bonzagni, George: SRN News
Bookhultz, Bruce: WUSA–TV
Boothby, Jim: Potomac Television
Borger, Gloria: CBS News
Borniger, Charles: Freelance
Borniger, Herta: German Television/ARD
Borrasso, Jennifer: SRN News
Bosch, Anna: T.V.E./Spanish Public Television
Boskent-Norris, Amanda: Freelance
Bost, Mark: WUSA–TV
Boughton, Bryan: Fox News
Bourar, Hisham: Middle East Television Network
  (Alhurra)
Bourgeois, Didier: Fox News
Bovim, Megan: Fox News
Bowen, Timothy: WETA–TV
Boyce, Nell: National Public Radio
Boyd, John D.: NBC News
Boyd, Wayne: Freelance
Bradley, Carlotta L.: AP–Broadcast
Bragale, Charles: WRC–TV/NBC–4
Bramson, Robert E.: ABC News
Branche, Glennwood: ABC News
Brandkamp, Jonathan D.: Voice of America
Brandt, John: Fox News
Brannock, Michael: C–SPAN
Bransford, Fletcher: Fox News
Braun, Joshua S.: CNN
Brawner, Donald: WETA–TV
Bream, Shannon D.: WRC–TV/NBC–4
Breed, Richard E.: Freelance
Breiterman, Charles: ABC News
Brieger, Annette: Freelance
Brinberg, Claire: CNN
Briski, Natasa: Pro Plus, Slovenia
Brisson, Stephane: CTV–Canadian Television
Britch, Ray: CNN
Britell, Penny: CBS News
Brittain, Rebecca: CNN
Brock, Alan Matthew: WJLA–TV/Newschannel 8
Brody, David: CBN News
Broffman, Craig A.: CNN
Broleman, Michael: Sinclair Broadcasting Group
Bromberger, Mike: Voice of America

Brookes, Adam: BBC
Brooks, Kurt: WUSA–TV
Brooks, Sam: ABC News
Brown, Daryl: WTTG–Fox Television
Brown, Jr., Edgar: Fox News
Brown, Henry M.: ABC News
Brown, Jeffrey: Newshour with Jim Lehrer
Brown, Jennifer: CBC
Brown, Jerome: Voice of America
Brown, Karen E.: WJLA–TV/Newschannel 8
Brown, Kristi: CBS News
Brown, Malcolm: Feature Story News
Brown, Melissa: WJLA–TV/Newschannel 8
Brown, Paul: C–SPAN
Brown, Tracy Ann: APTN
Bruce, Andrea: CBS News
Bruchas, John Michael: East Coast Television
Brulle, Ashley Huffman: CNN
Brunetti, Sara: CBC
Bruns, Aaron: Fox News
Bryant, Aubrey: WUSA–TV
Buchanan, Douglas: WUSA–TV
Buck, Melanie: CNN
Buckingham, Joseph: WETA–TV
Buehler, Paul: WTTG–Fox Television
Buel, Meredith S.: Voice of America
Buhrow, Tom: German Television/ARD
Bull, David John: ABC News
Bullard Harmon, Susan: CBS News
Bullard, Larry: WRC–TV/NBC–4
Bullock, Peter: Reuters Television
Bullock, Tom: National Public Radio
Bundock, Susan J.: C–SPAN
Bunyan, Maureen: WJLA–TV/Newschannel 8
Burch, Jennifer: CNN
Burdick, Leslie: C–SPAN
Burke, James: C–SPAN
Burketh, Ivan: National Public Radio
Burlij, Terence: Newshour with Jim Lehrer
Burns, Alison: Cox Broadcasting
Burton, Daniel: Potomac Television
Buschschluter, Vanessa: BBC
Buschschluter, Siegfried: Deutschland Radio
Butler, Norman: Belo Capital Bureau
Butterworth, David: Newshour with Jim Lehrer
Byrne, Jay: Talk Radio News Service
Byrne, Matthew: CNN
Byrne, Michaela T.: Independent Television News
  (ITN)
Cabral, Juan E.: CNN
Cacas, Max: CNC/Capitol News Connection
Cadoret-Manier, Remi: TF1 French Television
Caldwell, Traci L.: CBS News
Calfat, Marcel: CBC
Callan, Elizabeth: Newshour with Jim Lehrer
Calo-Christian, Nancy: C–SPAN
Cameron, Carl: Fox News
Cameron, Ian: ABC News

MEMBERS ENTITLED TO ADMISSION—Continued

Camp, Joseph: WETA–TV
Campbell, Arch: WRC–TV/NBC–4
Campbell, Barbara: National Public Radio
Campbell, Christopher: Al-Jazeera TV
Candia, Kirsten: German Television/ZDF
Canizales, Cesar A.: NBC Newschannel
Canning, Andrea: ABC News
Canton, Soyini: Hearst-Argyle Television
Canty, James: CBS News
Cao, Huidong: Radio Free Asia
Cao, Yang: C–SPAN
Caplan, Craig: C–SPAN
Capra, Anthony: NBC News
Capstick, Leslie: C–SPAN
Caravello, David: CBS News
Carden, Elizabeth D.: ABC News
Cardon, John Christophe: WETA–TV
Carey, Julie: WRC–TV/NBC–4
Carlson, Brett: Freelance
Carlson, Christopher: ABC News
Carlson, Steve: Fox News
Carlsson, Leif: Swedish Television
Carlsson, Lisa: Swedish Television
Carney, Keith: FedNet
Caronello, Sophie R.: Bloomberg Radio (WBBR)
Carpel, Michael: Fox News
Carr, Martin: WETA–TV
Carrillo, Silvio: CNN
Carroll, Theodore: Diversified Communications, Inc.
Carson, Charles: WTTG–Fox Television
Carter, Mone Sha: Fox News
Carter, Jr., Walter: Fox News
Casey, Sean: WRC–TV/NBC–4
Cassidy, David M.: Belo Capital Bureau
Castner, Edward: German Television/ARD
Castrilli, Anthony M.: WUSA–TV
Castro, Carlos: WTTG–Fox Television
Catanza, Damian: CNN
Catrett, David Keith: CNN
Cavaiola, Michael: C–SPAN
Cavin, Anthony: CBS News
Cecil, Brenda: East Coast Television
Centanni, Steve: Fox News
Cesar, Ronald: Voice of America
Cesarano, Ashley J.: NBC News
Cetta, Denise: CBS News
Chaggaris, Steven: CBS News
Chamberlain, Richard: Tribune Broadcasting
Chamberland, Bethany: CNN
Champ, Henry: CBC
Chan, Enoch: Voice of America
Chang, Young Joo: Seoul Broadcasting System
Changuris, Zeke: WJLA–TV/Newschannel 8
Chapman, Irwin: Bloomberg Television
Chappell, Jill: Freelance
Charbonneau, Melissa A.: CBN News
Charner, Flora: APTN

Charpa, Silvia: German Television/ARD
Charters, Nadia: MBC–TV (Middle East Broadcasting)
Chase, David: Cox Broadcasting
Chase, Marina: CNN
Chase, Melvin: WTOP Radio
Chattman, Tanya: C–SPAN
Chavez, Roby: WTTG–Fox Television
Chavis, Brandi: Sinclair Broadcast Group
Chaytor, David: WUSA–TV
Chen, Joie: CBS News
Chen, Yi Qiu: ETTV
Chenevey, Steve: WTTG–Fox Television
Chernenkoff, Kelly: Fox News
Chicca, Trish: CNN
Chick, Jane S.: CBS News
Childs, Lete M.: Newshour with Jim Lehrer
Ching, Nike: Broadcasting Corporation of China
Chmura, Christopher: AP–Broadcast
Chophel, Lobsang: Radio Free Asia
Chow, Lisa: National Public Radio
Chrisinger, Travis Renee: Freelance
Christensen, Jocelyn: CNN
Christian, George: CBS News
Chung, Chen-Fang Tina: Formosa TV
Chung, Hyun Duk: Seoul Broadcasting System
Chung, Linda: Bloomberg Television
Cilberti, David: Freelance
Clark, James: C–SPAN
Clark, Theodore E.: National Public Radio
Clark, Thomas L.: FedNet
Clark, Tom: CTV–Canadian Television
Clarke, Andrea: Reuters Television
Clemann, William: WUSA–TV
Clemons, Bobby: CNN America
Clendenon, Kelly: Metro Teleproductions
Clifford, Megan: CNN
Clogston, Juanita: Freelance
Clugston, Gregory: SRN News
Clune, Sarah: Newshour with Jim Lehrer
Cochran, John: ABC News
Cockerham, Richard A.: Fox News
Codispoti, Alika: To The Contrary (Persephone Productions)
Coffman, Mary: Medill News Service
Cofske, Harvey: Irish Radio and Television (RTE)
Cohan, Stacey: WUSA–TV
Cohen, Josh: C–SPAN
Cohen, Stuart: BBC
Cohencious, Robert: Native American Television
Cohn, Alan: Washington News Network
Coil, Holley: WTTG–Fox Television
Colby, Alfred: CBS News
Cole, Bryan: Fox News
Cole, Robert: Voice of America
Cole, Vernon: ABC News
Colella, Anthony: WTTG–Fox Television
Coleman, Major: NBC News

MEMBERS ENTITLED TO ADMISSION—Continued

Coles, David: Newshour with Jim Lehrer
Colgan, Jill: Australian Broadcasting Corporation
Colimore, Eric: Fox News
Collender, Howard: Mobile Video Services
Collingwood, Eloise: C–SPAN
Collins, Bruce: C–SPAN
Collins, Maxine: BBC
Collins, Michael J.: Voice of America
Collins, Pat: WRC–TV/NBC–4
Collinson, Luke: Independent Television News (ITN)
Colton, Michael: CBC
Comport, Caroline J.: Tribune Broadcasting
Compton, Woodrow: CNN
Conatser, Cynthia: NBC Newschannel
Conlin, Sheila: NBC Newschannel
Conner, Eric: Fox News
Connolly, Camille: Freelance
Connor, Gail: APTN
Connor, James T.: CNBC
Conover, William: C–SPAN
Conrad, Monique: BET Nightly News
Contreras, Felix J.: National Public Radio
Contreras, Jorge: Univision News
Contreras, Lainie: AP–Broadcast
Conway, Abigail: C–SPAN
Cook, James L.: C–SPAN
Cook, Leslie: National Public Radio
Cook, Peter: Bloomberg Television
Cooke, David M.: Freelance
Coolidge, Richard: ABC News
Coomarasamy, James: BBC
Cooper, Caroline: CBS News
Cooper, Jeffrey: FDCH E–Media, Inc.
Cooper, John: Freelance
Cooper, Rebecca J.: WJLA–TV/Newschannel 8
Corcoran, Patricia: WTTG–Fox Television
Corke, Kevin: NBC News
Cornish, Francine: ABC News
Correa, Pedro: Telemundo Network
Corum, Paul H.: CBS News
Costantini, Bob: Freelance
Costello, Thomas: NBC News
Coudoux, Sylvain: NHK–Japan Broadcasting
Coughlin, Thomas: Tribune Broadcasting
Coulter, Pam: ABC News
Courson, Paul S.: CNN
Cowman, Chris: East Coast Television
Cox, Alexis: Newshour with Jim Lehrer
Coyte, Benjamin: CNN
Craca, Thomas: Freelance
Craig, John: East Coast Television
Cratty, Carol A.: CNN
Craven, William C.: National Public Radio
Crawford, James: Channel One News
Crawford, Robert: ABC News
Crawford, Walter: WJLA–TV/Newschannel 8
Crawley, Plummer: CNBC

Crenshaw, Elizabeth: WRC–TV/NBC–4
Cridland, Jeffrey: WUSA–TV
Crites, Jeff: SRN News
Crook, Anthony W.: Freelance
Crosariol, Paul M.: Potomac Television
Crosswhite-Chigbue, Karla: CNN
Crouse, Mary (Bebe): National Public Radio
Crowley, Candy: CNN
Crowley, Dennis: United News and Information
Crum, John: CBS News
Crutchfield, Curtis: Community TV of PG's
Crystal, Lester M.: Newshour with Jim Lehrer
Cuddy, Matthew: CNBC
Culhane, Max: ABC News
Cullen, Michael: National Public Radio
Cunha, John: CNN
Cuong, Pham Gia: CBS News
Curran, Patrick J.: Freelance
Currier, Liam: C–SPAN
Curtis, Alexander: C–SPAN
Curwen, Lesley: BBC
Cyr, Emily: WUSA–TV
Czzowitz, Greg: C–SPAN
Dahl, Heather: CNC/Capitol News Connection
Dajani, Rula: Al-Jazeera TV/Peninsula
D'Alberto, Emily A.: CNN
Daly, John: CBS News
D'Amico, Daniel: APTN
D'Angelo, Sara: WTOP Radio
Daniels, Brady G.: NBC News
Daniels, Nerissa: National Public Radio
D'Annibale, Thomas J.: ABC News
Danilko, Derek: Tribune Broadcasting
Dao, Thao: Radio Free Asia
Das, Mousumi: CNN
Daschle, Kelly: APTN
Date, Jack: ABC News
Dauchess, Matthew: C–SPAN
Daugherty, Jeffery: Voice of America
Davalos, Anna: Freelance
Davenport, Anne: Newshour with Jim Lehrer
Davenport, Deborah: C–SPAN
David, Michael R.M.: CNN
Davidi, Avi: Voice of America
Davidson, Joe: BET.com
Davie, Bianca: Bloomberg Television
Davieaud, Helene: TF1 French Television
Davies, Rhydwyn: Washington Bureau News Service
Davies-Williams, Stephen: WTTG–Fox Television
Davis, Derek: CNN
Davis, Gail: RadioTV
Davis, Gordon: WJLA–TV/Newschannel 8
Davis, Kristin: CNN
Davis, Matthew: BBC
Davis, Mitch: Fox News Radio
Davis, Patrick A.: CNN
Davis, Rebecca: National Public Radio

MEMBERS ENTITLED TO ADMISSION—Continued

Davis, Sharia: NBC News
Davis, Stephanie: Sinclair Broadcast Group
Davis, Tiffani M.: ABC News
Davis, V. Allison: CBS News
Davis, William: SRN News
Dawson, Charlie: CBS News
Dawson, Wendy: Fox News
Day, Richard: WTOP Radio
de Guise, Louis: CBC
de Schaetzen, Emilie: Eurovision Americas, Inc.
de Sola, David: CNN
Dean, Antoinette: Newshour with Jim Lehrer
Decker, Jonathan P.: USA Radio Network
DeFrank, Debra: Fox News
Deger, Anne H.: Hamilton Productions
Delafield, Alyssa: NBC News
DeMar, Brian: National Public Radio
DeMark, Michael: Freelance
DeMoss, Gary: Freelance
Dennert, Mary Pat: Fox News
Densmore, Steven: ABC News
Dentzer, Susan: Newshour with Jim Lehrer
Depoortere, Yohan: NOS Dutch Public Broadcasting
DePuyt, Bruce: WJLA–TV/Newschannel 8
Deroche, Sylvie: TF1 French Television
DeSantis, Dominic: Freelance
DeSimone, Bridget: Newshour with Jim Lehrer
Detrow, Jon: AP–Broadcast
DeVito, Andrea: Fox News
Dhue, Stephaniea: Nightly Business Report
Dhuy, Hans-Peter: Finnish Broadcasting/YLE
Diakides, Anastasia: CNN
Diarra, Sofia: BBC
DiBella, Richard: Fox News
DiCarlo, Patricia: WTTG–Fox Television
Dietrich, Geoffrey: CNN
Dignan, Kellyanne E.: USA Today Live
Dillon, H. Estel: NBC Newschannel
DiMassimo, Richard: Native American Television
Dimmler, Erika: CNN
Dimsdale, John: Marketplace Radio
Dine, Laura: Newshour with Jim Lehrer
Disselkamp, Henry: ABC News
Dixon-Gumm, Penny: Voice of America
Dixson, Charles H.: CBS News
Doane, Martin C.: WJLA–TV/Newschannel 8
Dobbins, Colin: Freelance
Dockins, Pamela: AP–Broadcast
Dodson, Richard E.: NBC News
Doebele, Constance: C–SPAN
Doell, Michell: WTTG–Fox Television
Doherty, Brian: Fox News
Doherty, Peter M.: ABC News
Dolce, Stephen: CNN
Dolcimascolo, Carolyn: WTTG–Fox Television
Dolma, Dawa: Radio Free Asia
Dolma, Rigdhen: Radio Free Asia

Donahue, Edward: AP–Broadcast
Donald, William: Viewpoint Communications
Donaldson, Sam: ABC News
Donnelly, Julie: Feature Story News
Donovan, Brian: ABC News
Donovan, Christopher: NBC News
Dore, Maggie: Freelance
Dorf-Dolce, Heather: Irish Radio and Television (RTE)
Dorjee, Karma: Radio Free Asia
Dorn, Jason M.: Tribune Broadcasting
Dorsey, Tony: WRC–TV/NBC–4
Dougherty, Mark: WUSA–TV
Dougherty, Martin: CNN
Douglass, Linda D.: ABC News
Downer, Carlton: CNN
Doyle, Geoffrey C.: NBC News
Drummond, Steven: National Public Radio
Dubroff, Rich: NBC News
Duck, Jennifer: ABC News
Duitch, David: Belo Capital Bureau
Duke, Megan: CNN
Dukehart, Thomas: WUSA–TV
Dumpe, Megan: Fox News
Dunaway, John: CNN
Duncan, Michael J.: Potomac Radio News
Duncan, Robert: National Public Radio
Duncan, Victoria: NBC News
Dunkley, Michael: Native American Television
Dunlavey, Dennis: ABC News
Dunlavey, Thomas: CNN
Dunlop, Melissa: NBC News
Dunlop, William: Eurovision Americas, Inc.
Dunn, Lauren: WJLA–TV/Newschannel 8
Dunston, Andre: WJLA–TV/Newschannel 8
Dupree, Jamie: Cox Broadcasting
Durham, Deborah: Univision News
Durham, Lisa: CNN
Durkin, Edward: WRC–TV/NBC–4
Dyball, Kenneth: C–SPAN
Dyer, Lois: CBS News
Dyson, Kareen Wynter: CNN
Earnest, Jerry R.: Voice of America
Eaton, Hugh M.: National Public Radio
Ebinger, Jonathan: Freelance
Ebitty-Doro, Estelle: AP–Broadcast
Echevarria, Pedro L.: C–SPAN
Echols, Jerry: Fox News
Eck, Christina: Deutsche Press Agency
Eckert, Barton: WTOP Radio
Edmond, Danaj: Fox News
Edmonds, George: BBC
Edwards, Alicia: Freelance
Edwards, Brian: CBN News
Egy Rose, A. Christine: NBC News
Ehrenberg, Richard: ABC News
Eisenbarth, Ronald: C–SPAN
Eisenhuth, Alfred Scott: Freelance

MEMBERS ENTITLED TO ADMISSION—Continued

Elbadry, Hanan H.: Egyptian TV
Eldridge, James W.: Fox News
Eldridge, Mercedes: Washington Bureau News Service
Eldridge, Michael: FDCH/E–Media, Inc.
el-Hamalawy, Mahmoud: Al-Jazeera TV/Peninsula
El-Konayyesi, Hany: ABU–DHABI Television
Ellard, Nancy: NBC Newschannel
Ellenwood, Gary: C–SPAN
Ellis, Neal: National Public Radio
Elnour, Waiel: APTN
Elving, Ronald: National Public Radio
Elvington, D. Glenn: ABC News
Emanuel, Mike: Fox News
Emery, Edie: CNN
Empey, Duane: East Coast Television
Engel, Seth: C–SPAN
Enqvist, Benita: Finnish Broadcasting/YLE
Epatko, Larisa: Newshour with Jim Lehrer
Epstein, Steve: Freelance
Erbe, Bonnie: To the Contrary (Persephone Productions)
Ericson, Ken: AP–Broadcast
Ernst, Charlotte: TV2–Denmark
Ernst, Manuel: German Television/ZDF
Espinoza, Cholene: Talk Radio News Service
Evans, Laura: WTTG–Fox Television
Evans, Sheila Diane: ABC News
Everist, Michael: FDCH/E–Media Inc.
Everly, Thomas: Freelance
Eyasu, Adiam: CNN
Fabian, Tom: Diversified Communications, Inc.
Fabic, Greg: C–SPAN
Faerber, Fritz: AP–Broadcast
Faigen, Glenn: Freelance
Faison, Al: Freelance
Falcone, David: APTN
Fancher, William T.: American Family Radio
Fant, Barbara: NBC News
Fantacone, John L.: CBS News
Farag, Aziz Fahmy: MBC–TV (Middle East Broadcasting)
Farhoodi, Ali B.: Voice of America
Farkas, Danny: Middle East Television Network
Farkas, Mark: C–SPAN
Farley, Sabrina Fang: Tribune Broadcasting
Farnum, Douglas: NBC News
Farrell, Kathryn: CNN
Farrell, Molly: Newshour with Jim Lehrer
Farzam, Parichehr: Voice of America
Faulkner, Michael: CBS News
Fauntleroy, Julius Dumarr: WETA–TV
Faw, Robert: NBC News
Fay, Mary Elizabeth: Freelance
Federico, Hector: Voice of America
Feeney, Joseph: WTTG–Fox Television
Feeney, Susan: National Public Radio
Feig, Christy: CNN

Feist, Sam: CNN
Feldman, Elizabeth: WRC–TV/NBC–4
Feldman, Randy: Viewpoint Communications
Fendrick, Anne-Marie: Freelance
Ferder, Bruce: Freelance
Fessler, Pamela: National Public Radio
Fetzer, Robert: Diversified Communications, Inc. (DCI)
Fiedler, Stephan: German Television/ARD
Fiegel, Eric James: CNN
Field, Andrew: Freelance
Field, Joan Mazer: BBC
Fields, Matthew: NBC News
Fielman, Sheldon: NBC News
Fierro, Juan Martinez: COPE Radio
Finamore, Charles: ABC News
Finch, Mark: Fox News
Fincher, Leta Hong: Voice of America
Fingar, Craig: CNN
Finkel, Benjamin: Viewpoint Communications
Finland, Alexander Y.: Fox News
Finney, Richard: Radio Free Asia
Finnigan, Michael: Freelance
Fiorito, Daniel: Freelance
Fischer, Elizabeth: NBC News
Fischoff, Michael: WTTG–Fox Television
Fishel, Justin: Fox News
Fitzgerald, Tom: WTTG–Fox Television
Fitzmaurice, Frank: WETA–TV
Fitzpatrick, Craig: Voice of America
Flanagan, Danielle: WUSA–TV
Fleeson, Richard: C–SPAN
Fleming, Eileen: AP–Broadcast
Fletcher, Robley: CNN
Flood, Randolph: Native American Television
Flores, Cesar: Freelance
Flynn, Michael Francis: WRC–TV/NBC–4
Flynn, Michael W.: WUSA–TV
Flynn, Liz: CNN
Foellmer-Suchorski, Kristin: German Television/ZDF
Fogarty, Kevin: Reuters Television
Folkenflik, David B.: National Public Radio
Forcucci, Michael: WJLA–TV/Newschannel 8
Ford, Sam: WJLA–TV/Newschannel 8
Foreman, Thomas: CNN
Forman, David: NBC News
Forrest, James M.: WRC–TV/NBC–4
Forte, B.J.: WTTG–Fox Television
Fortenberry, Tom: C–SPAN
Foster, Carl: C–SPAN
Foster, Jamie L.: WJLA–TV/Newschannel 8
Foster, Kurt: Fox News
Foster, Lesli: WUSA–TV
Foster, Scott: NBC News
Foster, Tom: Freelance
Foty, Tom: Freelance
Fouladvand, Hida: Freelance

MEMBERS ENTITLED TO ADMISSION—Continued

Foundas, John: WTTG–Fox Television
Fowler, Kathy: WJLA–TV/Newschannel 8
Fowlin, Joy: To the Contrary (Persephone Productions)
Fox, Janet: WUSA–TV
Fox, Michael C.: Al-Jazeera TV/Peninsula
Fox, Peggy: WUSA–TV
Fox, Peter: Reuters Television
Frado, John E.: CBS News
Frame, John: WTTG–Fox Television
Francis, Elliott: WJLA–TV/Newschannel 8
Franco, Brian: WUSA–TV
Frank, Langfitt: National Public Radio
Frankel, Bruce: TF1 French Television
Franken, Robert: CNN
Fraser, Jr., Wilfred: NBC News
Frayer, Lauren: AP–Broadcast
Frazier, William: C–SPAN
Freeland, Eric: WJLA–TV/Newschannel 8
French, F. Patrick: Freelance
Freymann-Weyr, Jeffrey K.: National Public Radio
Friar, David J.: AP–Broadcast
Fridrich, George J.: Fox News
Frieden, Terry: CNN
Friedman, David: Freelance
Froseth, Gary: WTOP Radio
Frost, Lovisa: Talk Radio News Service
Fry, Jim: Belo Capital Bureau
Fullwood, Adrian: APTN
Fung, Teddy: Radio Free Asia
Furlow, Tony: CBS News
Furman, Hal E.: CBS News
Fuss, Brian: CBS News
Fuss, Robert J.: CBS News
Futrowsky, David: Fox News
Gabala, Rick: C–SPAN
Gabriel, Oscar Wells: AP–Broadcast
Gadsden, Ginger: USA Today Live
Gaetano, Lawrence: NBC News
Gaffney, Dennis: Freelance
Gaffney, Matt: WTTG–Fox Television
Gaffney, Suzanne Yee: APTN
Gafner, Randall: Freelance
Gahagan, Kendra: ABC News
Galdabini, Christian: Freelance
Galfetti, Michele: Swiss Broadcasting
Galindo, Michael Travis: Freelance
Gallagher, Joseph: Voice of America
Gallasch, Hillery: Deutsche Welle
Gallo, Dan: Fox News
Gallu, Joshua: Freelance
Gangel, Jamie: NBC News
Garcia, Gina: NBC News
Garcia, Jon: ABC News
Garcia, Robert: ABC News Radio
Gardella, Richard: NBC News
Gargiulo, Michael: WTTG–Fox Television
Garlock, John: C–SPAN

Garner, Nicole: Potomac Television
Garraty, Timothy C.: CNN
Garrett, Major: Fox News
Garske, Jennifer: AP–Broadcast
Gary, Garney: C–SPAN
Gassman, Mara: CNN
Gato, Pabloz; Telemundo Network
Gauss, Martina: Freelance
Gauthier, Arthur R.: ABC News
Gavin, Gregory: National Public Radio
Gawad, Atef: APTN
Gebhardt, William A.: NBC News
Geimann, Steve: Bloomberg Television
Geldon, Ben: CNN
Geleschun, Uwe: German Television/ARD
Gentile, Esther M.: Venezuelan Television
Gentilo, Richard: APTN
Gentry, Pamela: CBS/BET Nightly News
Gentry, Robert H.: TV Asahi
Gentzler, Doreen: WRC–TV/NBC–4
George, Maurice: CNN
Gergely, Valer: Voice of America
Germany, Michelle: NBC News
Gersh, Darren: Nightly Business Report
Getter, John: The Washington Bureau
Geyelin, Philip: Freelance
Giammetta, Max: WTTG–Fox Television
Gibbons, Gavin: Fox News
Gibbons, Sarah: Eurovision Americas, Inc.
Gibbons, Sean: CNN
Gibson, Jr., Frank L.: NBC News
Gibson, Jake: Fox News
Gibson, Sheri Lynn: NBC Newschannel
Giebel, Edward: Freelance
Gilbert, Benjamin: National Public Radio
Gilgannon, Pege: WJLA–TV/Newschannel 8
Gillette, David: WETA–TV
Gillon, Vanessa: ABC News
Gilman, Jeff: WTTG–Fox Television
Gilmour, Karen: CBS News
Ginsburg, Benson: CBS News
Girshman, Peggy: National Public Radio
Githui, Esther: Voice of America
Giusto, Thomas: ABC News
Gjelten, Tom: National Public Radio
Gladstone, Jennifer: Sinclair Broadcasting Group
Glass, Evan: CNN
Glassman, Matt: WRC–TV/NBC–4
Glennon, John: Freelance
Glover-James, Ian: Independent Television News (ITN)
Glynn, William: NBC Newschannel
Gmiter, Bernard: ABC News
Goddard, Lisa: AP–Broadcast
Godsick, Andrew Louis: NBC Newschannel
Golau, Adam R.: East Coast Television
Gold, Lawrence: APTN
Gold, Peter: Fuji Television

MEMBERS ENTITLED TO ADMISSION—Continued

Goldberg, Ari: C–SPAN
Goldfein, Michael: Belo Capital Bureau
Goldman, Jeff Scott: CBS News
Goldman, David: Community TV of PG's
Goldman, Heather: CNN
Goler, Wendell: Fox News
Goltzman, Alison Kosik: Sinclair Broadcast Group
Gomes, Karina: CNN
Gomez, Juan Carlos: National Public Radio
Gonsar, Dhondup Namgyal: Radio Free Asia
Gonyea, Don: National Public Radio
Gonzalez, Carlos Alberto: WTTG–Fox Television
Gonzalez, John: WJLA–TV/Newschannel 8
Gonzalez, Julio: Hispanic Radio Network
Goodknight, Charles A: WRC/NBC–4
Goodman, Jeffrey: Freelance
Goodman, Susan: WAMU–FM
Goodwin, Susan: National Public Radio
Gordon, Chris Herbert: WRC–TV/NBC–4
Gordon, Stuart: ABC News
Gorman, Gregory A.: Talk Radio News Service
Gorman, James W.: APTN
Gorsky, Edward: NBC News
Gottlieb, Brian: Newshour with Jim Lehrer
Gould, Robert: C–SPAN
Grace, Stewart: ABC News
Gracey, David: CNN
Granda, Marco: Univision News
Granena, Marc: Eurovision Americas, Inc.
Grant, Miles: WJLA–TV/Newschannel 8
Grasso, Neil: CBS News
Graves, Lindsay: Freelance
Graydon, James: CNN
Grayson, Gisele: National Public Radio
Green, Erin: NBC News
Green, Jessie J.: WTOP Radio
Green, Molette: Cox Broadcasting
Greenaway, Walter T.S.: Potomac Television
Greenback, William Henry: Voice of America
Greenbaum, Adam: NBC Newschannel
Greenblatt, Larry: Viewpoint Communications
Greene, David: National Public Radio
Greene, James M.: NBC News
Greene, Thomas: CNN
Greenfield, Heather: AP–Broadcast
Greenspon, Dana: Nightly Business Report
Greenwood, John K.: WRC–TV/NBC–4
Greenwood, William: ABC News
Greer, Peter P.: WTTG–Fox Television
Gregory, David: NBC News
Greiner, Nicholas: Freelance
Griffin, Eileen: WETA–TV
Griffitts, William: Mobile Video Services
Groome, Marsha: NBC News
Gross, Andrew F.: NBC News
Gross, David: CBS News
Gross, Jr., Eddie S.: CNN

Gross, Joshua D.: CBS News
Gruber, Ben: Reuters Television
Guastadisegni, Richard: WJLA–TV/Newschannel 8
Guiloff, Stephanie: Azteca America
Guise, Gregory: WUSA–TV
Gunning, Meredith: Hearst-Argyle Television
Gural, Kathleen: East Coast Television
Gursky, Gregg L.: Fox News
Gutmann, Hanna: Washington Radio & Press
    Service
Gutnikoff, Robert: APTN
Guzman, Armando: Azteca America
Guzman, Roberto: Azteca America
Gwadz, Joel: CBS News
Haan, Mike: CNN
Haberstick, Fred: Fox News
Hackett, Hunter: CNN
Hackett, Stephen: WJLA–TV/Newschannel 8
Hadi, Abdul Wahar: Voice of America
Hadley, Laura: ABC News
Haefeli, Brian: Fox News
Hafer, Michael: WTTG–Fox Television
Hager, Mary: CBS News
Hager, Nathaniel: WTOP Radio
Hagerty, Barbara Bradley: National Public Radio
Hagerty, Michael E.: WJLA–TV/Newschannel 8
Haggerty, Patrick B.: U.S. Farm Report/WGN Radio
Hahn, Stephen: ABC News
Hakel, Peter: WJLA–TV/Newschannel 8
Halkett, Kimberly: Global Television
Hall Bruner, Caroline: Fox News
Hall, Randy: CNSNews.com
Hall, Richard: C–SPAN
Hall, Sabrina: WJLA–TV/Newschannel 8
Hall, Sean: Freelance
Haller, Sylvia: NBC News
Halton, David: CBC
Hamberg, Steve: Viewpoint Communications
Hamilton, Christopher B.: Middle East Television
    Network
Hamilton, Jay: Hamilton Productions
Hamilton, John: Hamilton Productions
Hamilton, John: WJLA–TV/Newschannel 8
Hamilton, Jonathan: National Public Radio
Hamlin, Gregg K.: Tribune Broadcasting
Hammer, Michael J.: AP–Broadcast
Hammond, Donald: Sinclair Broadcast Group
Hammons, Cheryl: East Coast Television
Hampton, Cheryl: National Public Radio
Hamrick, Mark A.: AP–Broadcast
Handelsman, Steve: NBC Newschannel
Handleman, Michelle: WUSA–TV
Handly, James: WRC–TV/NBC–4
Hanka, Roland: German Television/ARD
Hanner, Mark: CBS News
Hannon, Thomas: CNN
Hansen, Eric: C–SPAN
Hanson, Chris: C–SPAN

MEMBERS ENTITLED TO ADMISSION—Continued

Hara, Seiki: NHK–Japan Broadcasting
Harb, Moufac: Middle East Television Network (Alhurra)
Harding, Alejandro: Video News Service
Harding, Claus: Freelance
Harding, William: USA Today Live
Hardy, Arthur: CNN
Harkness, Stephen: C–SPAN
Harlan, Jeremy: CNN
Harleston, Robb: C–SPAN
Harmon, Predi-Reko: CBS News
Harper, Ben: Medill News Service
Harper, Elizabeth: Newshour with Jim Lehrer
Harper, Steven: Freelance
Harrington, Craig J.: WTTG–Fox Television
Harris, Catherine Meade: BBC
Harris, Lanese: CNN
Harris, Leon: WJLA–TV/Newschannel 8
Harris, Richard: National Public Radio
Harris, Roy J.: Freelance
Harter, John R.: WJLA–TV/Newschannel 8
Hartge, John: Freelance
Hartman, Brian: ABC News
Harvey, Alan: NBC News
Hash, James: WUSA–TV
Hass, Thomas: Freelance
Hastings Wotring, Melanie: WJLA–TV/Newschannel 8
Hatcher, William P.: ABC News
Hawke, Anne: National Public Radio
Hawkins, Yvonne P.: East Coast Television
Hayes, Monique: Newshour with Jim Lehrer
Hayley, Jr., Harold Paul: NBC News
Haynes, Maurice: C–SPAN
Hays, Guerin: CNN
Hayward, Jacqueline: WUSA–TV
Haywood, Barry: Freelance
Headen, Greg: Fox News
Heffley, William: C–SPAN
Heik, Jens: Freelance
Helm, Ronald G.: CNN
Helskog, Gerhard: TV2–Norway
Hempen, Michael: AP–Broadcast
Henderson, Susan: APTN
Hendin, Robert: CBS News
Hendricks, Mark B.: CBN News
Henneberg, Mary Janne: Fox News
Henrehan, John: WTTG–Fox Television
Henry, Ed: CNN
Henry, Jonelle P.: C–SPAN
Henry, Patrick: CBN News
Henry, Patrick L.: CBN News
Herman, Emily: NBC News
Herman, Elia: Talk Radio News Service
Hermes, Troy Allen: Freelance
Hernandez, Carlos E.: WTTG–Fox Television
Hernandez, Eugenio: APTN
Herndon, Sarah: Fox News

Herrera, Ruben: German Television/ZDF
Herridge, Catherine: Fox News
Hess, Ione: Freelance
Hester, Deirdre: CBS News
Heyman, Douglas: C–SPAN
Heywood, Harry B.: ABC News
Hickey, Joseph: CNN
Hickman, Stacy: Fox News
Hidaka, Masano: Diversified Communications, Inc.
Hidaka, Yoshiki: Diversified Communications, Inc.
Higgins, Ricardo: NBC News
Hill, Benjamin F.: CNN
Hill, Dallas: C–SPAN
Hillard, Timothy, KOMO–TV
Hindes, Wally: AP–Broadcast
Hinds, Hugh: Freelance
Hino, Katsumi: Tokyo Broadcasting System
Hirsh, Stephen: Fox News
Hirzel, Conrad: CNN
Hitchcock, Jennifer: Hearst-Argyle Television
Hix, Leta: C–SPAN
Ho, King Man: Radio Free Asia
Ho, Stephanie J.: Voice of America
Hochman, Jordana: National Public Radio
Hoffman, Brian: AP–Broadcast
Hoffmaster, Robert: C–SPAN
Hofler, Julie: CNN
Hofstad, Elizabeth H.: FDCH E–Media, Inc.
Holden, Michael: C–SPAN
Holland, John F.: NBC News
Holland, Sarah B.: CNN
Hollenbeck, Paul: Freelance
Holly, Derrill: AP–Broadcast
Holman, Kwame: Newshour with Jim Lehrer
Holmes, Horace: WJLA–TV/Newschannel 8
Holtschneider, Joseph: Mobile Video Services
Holubar, John: Freelance
Hooper, Molly: Fox News
Hooven, Jill Sorenson: WTTG–Fox Television
Hoover, Toni: Freelance
Hopkins, Adrienne Moira: Fox News
Hopkins, Brian: WJLA–TV/Newschannel 8
Hopkins, Joseph L.R.: Voice of America
Hopper, David: Freelance
Horan, Michael: WTTG–Fox Television
Hormuth, Thomas: WJLA–TV/Newschannel 8
Horne, Jeffrey K.: NBC News
Horne, LaTanya E.: WJLA–TV/Newschannel 8
Hosford, Matthew A.: NBC News
Houston, Chris: WUSA–TV
Houston, Karen Gray: WTTG–Fox Television
Howard, Cory R.: Fox News
Howard, Stephen: WETA–TV
Howell, George: C–SPAN
Howell, Richard: Fox News
Hoye, Matthew: CNN
Hristova, Rozalia: BBC

MEMBERS ENTITLED TO ADMISSION—Continued

Hsia, Chia-Lu: CTI–TV (Taiwan)
Hssaini, Nasser: Al-Jazeera TV/Peninsula
Huang, Laura: Radio Free Asia
Hudson, Christian: CNN
Hudson, Ira John: WRC–TV/NBC–4
Huebler, Ryan: Freelance
Huff, Dan: APTN
Huff, Priscilla: Feature Story News
Hughes, Ann Compton: ABC News
Hughes, James: Freelance
Hughes, Sarah: WAMU–FM
Huh, In Koo: Seoul Broadcasting System
Hume, Brit: Fox News
Hume, Kim: Fox News
Hung, Shirley: CNN
Hunn, Johney Burke: National Public Radio
Hunter, Kathleen: Stateline.org
Hunter, Roger: C–SPAN
Hunter, Ryan: WUSA–TV
Hurley, Charles: CNN
Hurley, Karina: Hispanic Radio Network
Hurt, James: NBC Newschannel
Hutcherson, Trudy Marie: Freelance
Hwang, Rosa: CBC
Hyater, John: WETA–TV
Hylton, Winston: WJLA–TV/Newschannel 8
Ichikawa, Mina: Nippon TV Network
Ide, Charles: WETA–TV
Ifill, Gwen: Newshour with Jim Lehrer
Iida, Kaori: NHK–Japan Broadcasting
Iiyama, Laura: Feature Story News
Imaida, Aya: Nippon TV Network
Imdorf, Jennifer: C–SPAN
Ing, Lance: WTTG–Fox Television
Ingram, Shermaze: Newshour with Jim Lehrer
Inoue, Hitoshi: TV Asahi
Inskeep, Steve: National Public Radio
Irving, John: Metro Networks
Ishaq, Salim I.: NBC News
Ishida, Shingo: TV Asahi
Iverson, Matthew: Diversified Communications, Inc.
Jackson, Katherine: WJLA–TV/Newschannel 8
Jackson, Nicole: CNN
Jackson, Roberta: C–SPAN
Jackson, Ryan: Cox Broadcasting
Jackson, Susan: CNC/Capitol News Connection
Jackson, Taryn: C–SPAN
Jackson-Gewirtz, Andrea: National Public Radio
Jacobi, Steven C.: Hearst-Argyle Television
Jacobs, Adia: Freelance
Jacobs, Philip H.: WRC–TV/NBC–4
Jacobson, Murrey: Newshour with Jim Lehrer
Jaconi, Michelle: NBC News
Jacques, Andree-Lyne: TF1 French Television
Jacques, Virg: WTTG–Fox Television
Jaffe, Gary M.: Voice of America
Jafri, Syed: Voice of America

James, Karen L.: CNBC
Jamison, Dennis: CBS News
Jansen, Lesa: CNN
Japaridze, NuNu: CNN
Jarboe, Brian David: National Public Radio
Jarvis, Julie: NBC Newschannel
Jaskot, Sheila: WTTG–Fox Television
Jeffries, Katherine: C–SPAN
Jenkins, David: CNN
Jenkins, Rhonda J.: Fox News
Jenkins, William G.: Fox News Radio
Jennings, Alicia: NBC News
Jensen, Heidi: ABC News
Jermin, Ede R.: WRC–TV/NBC–4
Jessup, John: CBN News
Jimenez, Martin: Freelance
Johns, Joseph: CNN
Johnsen, Kyle: CNN
Johnson, Chester Bruce: WUSA–TV
Johnson, Darryl B.: Freelance
Johnson, Douglas: Voice of America
Johnson, Fletcher: ABC News
Johnson, Irene: WJLA–TV/Newschannel 8
Johnson, Jeffrey S.: CNSNews.com
Johnson, Jennifer: Freelance
Johnson, Jennifer L.: Free Speech Radio News
Johnson, Kenneth: ABC News
Johnson, Kevin: Cox Broadcasting
Johnson, Kia: Reuters Television
Johnson, Leroy: NBC News
Johnson, Micahz: Washington News Network
Johnson, Obin: CBS News
Johnson, Rolanda: Freelance
Johnson, Sasha: CNN
Johnson-McNeely, Helena: National Public Radio
Johnston, Derek: Freelance
Johnston, Jeffrey: CBS News
Jones, Alvin: FedNet
Jones, Gwyneth: NBC News
Jones, Kimberly: National Public Radio
Jones, Lyrone Steven: WTTG–Fox Television
Jones, Morris: Sinclair Broadcasting Group
Jones, Nelson: WTTG–Fox Television
Jones, Rachel: National Public Radio
Jones, Torrance: Fox News
Jones, Victoria: Talk Radio News Service
Joost, Nathalie: WTTG–Fox Television
Jordan, Rosiland: NBC News
Joseph, Akilah N.: ABC News
Joslyn, James: WUSA–TV
Jouffriault, Pascal: Freelance
Joya, Steve E.: ABC News
Joyce, Christopher: National Public Radio
Joyce, Christopher C.: NBC News
Juenger, Georg: German Television/ZDF
Juergens, Hans P.: NBC News
Juginovic, Jana: CTV–Canadian Television

MEMBERS ENTITLED TO ADMISSION—Continued

Kahn, Michael W.: AP–Broadcast
Kaminsky, Allison: NBC News
Kanawati, Balajia: MBC–TV (Middle East Broadcasting)
Kane, James F.: ABC News
Kanehira, Shigenori: Tokyo Broadcasting
Kaplan, William: Freelance
Kara-Murza, Vladimirz: RTVI
Kareem, Khaled Abdel: Al-Jazeera TV/Peninsula
Karimi, Nazira: Freelance
Karl, Jonathan: ABC News
Karson, Danielle: WAMU–FM
Kast, Sheilah A.: National Public Radio
Katkov, Mark: CBS News
Kato, Atsushi, NHK–Japan Broadcasting
Katz, Amy D.: Voice of America
Katz, Barry: C–SPAN
Katz, Craig: CBS News
Katz, Nai Chian: Phoenix Satellite Television
Kaubfeld, Brad: AP–Broadcast
Kaye, Matthew: The Berns Bureau
Kazama, Shin: Fuji Television
Kearly, Donald: WTTG–Fox Television
Keator, John C.: National Public Radio
Kehoe, Steven: C–SPAN
Kelemen, Michele: National Public Radio
Kelleher, Colleen: WTOP Radio
Kelleher, Kristine: APTN
Kellerman, Mike: SBS Radio (Australia)
Kelley, Alice: German Television/ZDF
Kelley, Daniela: Fox News
Kelley, Jonathan: C–SPAN
Kelley, Pamela: CNN
Kellogg-Wheeler, Ashley: Sinclair Broadcast Group
Kelly, Mary Louise: National Public Radio
Kendall, Megyn: Fox News
Kennedy, Robert: C–SPAN
Kennedy, Suzanne: WJLA–TV/Newschannel 8
Kenny, Christopher: CNN
Kenny, Justin: Reuters Television
Kenyon, Linda: SRN News
Kerchner, Eric: ABC News
Kerley, David: ABC News
Kerr, Roxane: C–SPAN
Kersey, Philip: Fox News
Kessler, Jonathan: Freelance
Kestenbaum, David: National Public Radio
Ketcham, Lew: C–SPAN
Kettlewell, Christian: APTN
Keyes, Charley: CNN
Khader, Abdel Kareem: MBC–TV (Middle East Broadcasting)
Khader, Ibrahim: Al-Jazeera TV/Peninsula
Khananayev, Grigory: Fox News
Kharel, Ram C.: Sagarmatha Television
Kidd, Sally F.: Hearst-Argyle Television
Kidd, Susan M.: WRC–TV/NBC–4
Kiernan, Ryan: NBC News

Kiker, Douglas: CBS News
Killion, Nikole: WJLA–TV/Newschannel 8
Kim, Caitlyn: CNC/Capitol News Connection
Kim, Sung Joon: Seoul Broadcasting System
Kim, Yonho: Radio Free Asia
Kindestin, Jared: CTV–Canadian Television
King, Gregory: WETA–TV
King, Kevin: C–SPAN
King, Kevin G.: WUSA–TV
Kinlaw, Worth: CNN
Kinney, George P.: CNN
Kinney, Laura: Hearst-Argyle Television
Kinney, Michael: Freelance
Kirk, Beverly: National Public Radio
Kirsch Burgess, Elizabeth: ABC News
Kistner, William: Marketplace Radio
Kitanovska, Lilica: Voice of America
Kiyasu, Adilson: CNN
Kizer, James S.: WRC–TV/NBC–4
Klayman, Elliot: Freelance
Klein, Christianne: WJLA–TV/Newschannel 8
Klein, Robert: Freelance
Knapp, Timothy: Sinclair Broadcast Group
Knight, Steve: AP–Broadcast
Knight, Terrence: National Public Radio
Knighton, David: C–SPAN
Knoller, Mark: CBS News
Knott, James: CNN
Knott, John: ABC News
Knuckles, Georgette: Newshour with Jim Lehrer
Koch, Kathleen: CNN
Kojovic, Predrag: Reuters Television
Kokufuda, Kaoru: Tokyo Broadcasting System
Koller, Frank: CBC
Kolodziejczak, Thomas: Tribune Broadcasting
Konrad, Monika: ABC News
Koolhof, Vanessa M.: WJLA–TV/Newschannel 8
Korff, Jay: WJLA–TV/Newschannel 8
Kornacki, Olga Ramirez: Radio–TV
Kornely, Michael: Belo Capital Bureau
Kornely, Sharon: Medill News Service
Kos, Martin A.: Freelance
Koslow, Marc: NBC News
Kosnar, Michael J.: NBC News
Kotatori, Beth Anne: CNN
Kotke, Wolfgang: Freelance
Kotuby, Stephanie: CNN
Kovach, Robert S.: CNN
Kozel, Sandy: AP–Broadcast
Krakower, Gary: CNN
Krebs, Joe: WRC–TV/NBC–4
Kreinbihl, Mary: Fox News
Kreindler, Virginia: NBC Newschannel
Kresse, Thaddeus: NBC News
Kretman, Lester A.: NBC News
Kreuz, Greta: WJLA–TV/Newschannel 8
Krupin, David: Freelance

MEMBERS ENTITLED TO ADMISSION—Continued

Kruse, Jan Espen: Norwegian Broadcasting
Kube, Courtney: NBC News
Kuczynski, Ronald: CNN
Kuhar, Ivana: Voice of America
Kuhn, Steve: AP–Broadcast
Kuleta, Gene: Metro Networks
Kulkarni, Rohit N.: Voice of America
Kulsziski, Peter: Freelance
Kupper, Carmen: Freelance
Kupperman, Tamara: NBC News
Kur, Robert E.: NBC News
Kurcias, Martin R.: National Public Radio
Kurpershoek, Wouter: NOS Dutch Public
    Broadcasting
Kwan, Vivian: Radio Free Asia
Kwisnek, Stephanie: Fox News Channel
Kyodo, Atsushi: Tokyo Broadcasting System
Kyungwook, Min: Korean Broadcasting System
Laboy, Felix: C–SPAN
Lacey, Donna: Fox News
LaFollette, Marianna: Freelance
Lai, Chun Bon: Radio Free Asia
Lamb, Brian P.: C–SPAN
Lambidakis, Stephanie: CBS News
Landay, Woodrow: Australian Broadcasting
    Corporation
Landwehr, Arthur: German Public Radio/ARD
Lane, Christopher: WETA–TV
Lane, Grant Kevin: FedNet
Lane, Lisa: NHK–Japan Broadcasting
Langley, Kevin D.: National Public Radio
Langmade, Brigette: Cox Broadcasting
Langton, Laurence: Freelance
Lanningham, Kyle: Danish Broadcasting
    Corporation
Larade, Darren: C–SPAN
Larsen, Gregory: Freelance
Larsen, Joar Hoel: Norwegian Broadcasting
LaSalla, Susan A.: NBC News
Lassen, Kim: Danish Broadcasting Corporation
Lau, Hiumei: Radio Free Asia
Laughlin, Ara: Community TV of PG's
Laurent, Arthur: National Public Radio
Lavallee, Michael, Tokyo Broadcasting System
Laville, Molly: C–SPAN
Lawlor, William: WUSA–TV
Lawrence, Mary: WETA–TV
Lazar, Robert: C–SPAN
Lazernik, Ira: WTTG–Fox Television
Leake, Myron A.: CNN
Leamy, Elisabeth: WTTG–Fox Television
LeBlanc, Bertin: CBC
LeCroy, Philip: Fox News
Lee, Daniel N.: Radio Free Asia
Lee, Donald A.: CBS News
Lee, Dong Hyuk: Radio Free Asia
Lee, Edward: WETA–TV
Lee, Jinhee: Radio Free Asia

Lee, Joong Wan: Korean Broadcasting System
Lee, Kwang Chool: Korean Broadcasting System
Lee, Kyu: Radio Free Asia
Lee, Min: Taiwan Television
Lee, Sun Jae: Korean Broadcasting System
Leeds, Larry: Native American Television
Lefebvre, Hilary: CNN
Lehman, Russell: National Public Radio
Lehrer, Jim: Newshour with Jim Lehrer
Lehrman, Margaret: NBC News
Leidelmeyer, Ronald: WRC–TV/NBC–4
Leiken, Katherine: Freelance
Leissner, Janet: CBS News
Leist, Elizabeth: NBC News
LeMay, Gabriel: WJLA–TV/Newschannel 8
Lendzian, Kay: German Television/ZDF
Lent, David: Freelance
Lentz, Ruediger: Deutsche Welle Television
Leong, Dexter: Freelance
Leong, H. Ming: WJLA–TV/Newschannel 8
Leshan, Bruce: WUSA–TV
Levine, Adam: CNN
Levine, Michael: Fox News
Levine, Solomon: Freelance
Levinson, Molly: CNN
Lewine, Frances L.: CNN
Lewis, Aaron T.: CNN
Lewis, Edward: Fox News
Lewis, Jerry S.: WETA–TV
Lewis, John B.: WJLA–TV/Newschannel 8
Lewis, Libby: National Public Radio
Lewnes, Lisa: Reuters Television
Li, Bing: Washington Chinese Television
Li, Denise: CBS News
Li, Yue: Radio Free Asia
Liao, Xiao Qiang: Radio Free Asia
Libretto, John: NBC News
Lien, Arthur: NBC News
Lien, Jonathan: CBS News
Likowski, Alexander: WJLA–TV/Newschannel 8
Lilleston, Kristi King: WTOP Radio
Lilling, Dave: Court TV (Metro Teleproductions)
Limbach, Francis J.: AP–Broadcast
Lincoln, Diane: Newshour with Jim Lehrer
Lindblom, Mark: C–SPAN
Linden, Kim: CNN
Lindesay, Mark A.: Belo Capital Bureau
Linker, Ron: NOS Dutch Public Broadcasting
Lisle, John D.: WJLA–TV/Newschannel 8
Liss, Sharon Kehnemui: Fox News
Little, Craig: WTTG–Fox Television
Little, Walter: Bloomberg Television
Littleton, Philip: CNN
Litzenblatt, Seth: KTUU–TV (NBC)
Litzinger, Samuel: WAMU–FM
Liu, Ted: Radio Free Asia
Liu, Wei-Ming: Washington Chinese Television

MEMBERS ENTITLED TO ADMISSION—Continued

Liu, Libo: Voice of America
Liushar, Cideng: Radio Free Asia
Lively, Lydia: NBC News
Lodoe, Kalden: Radio Free Asia
Loebach, Joseph W.: NBC News
Loeschke, Paul: C–SPAN
Loew, Raimund: Austrian Radio & TV/ORF
Loftus, Kevin: Freelance
Logan, Charles: C–SPAN
Lomax, Malik: Freelance
Londres, Eduardo: Bloomberg Television
Long, James V.: NBC News
Loomans, Kathryn: AP–Broadcast
Loomis, Joseph: Washington Bureau News Service
Loper, Catherine: Fox News
Lopez, Edwing: Azteca America
Lopez, Myra B.: AP–Broadcast
Lopez, Rene: KTUU–TV (NBC)
Lopez-Isa, Anthony S.: WRC–TV/NBC–4
Lora, Willie A.: CNN
Lord, Bill: WJLA–TV/Newschannel 8
Lorek, Stanley: ABC News
Lormand, John: SRN News
Loucks, William: CBC
Lowe, Matthew: CBS News
Lowman, Wayne: Fox News
Lu, Lucy: Radio Free Asia
Lucas, Dave: WJLA–TV/Newschannel 8
Lucas, Tony: Newshour with Jim Lehrer
Lucchini, Maria Rosa: Univision News
Luck, David: C–SPAN
Ludwig, Robert: WETA–TV
Ludwin, James: AP–Broadcast
Luhn, Laurie: Fox News
Lukas, Jayne: Freelance
Lumpkin, Beverley C: ABC News
Lurch, Jr., David L.: NBC News
Lutterbeck, Deborah: Reuters Television
Lutz, Ellsworth: ABC News
Luzquinos, Julio: Freelance
Ly, Sherri: WTTG–Fox Television
Lyles, Brigitte: Fox News
Lynch, Dotty: CBS News
Lynch, Kathryn: CNN
Lyon, Michael: Fox News
MacDonald, Jim: CTV–Canadian Television
MacDonald, Neil: CBC
MacHamer, Lessandra: NBC News
Machin, Carmelo: T.V.E./Spanish Public Television
Macholz, Wolfgang: German Television/ZDF
MacKay, Elizabeth: Middle East Television Network (Alhurra)
MacNeil, Lachlan Murdoch: ABC News
MacSpadden, Ian: Reuters Television
Madorma, Tracey: Fox News
Maeder, Rudolf: Swiss Broadcasting
Maer, Peter: CBS News
Maggiolo, Vito: CNN

Mahdawi, Nezam: ABU–DHABI Television
Mahoney, Simon: Eurovision Americas, Inc.
Majchrowitz, Michael: Cox Broadcasting
Makori, Vincent: Voice of America
Malakoff, David Aram: National Public Radio
Malbon, Joy: CTV–Canadian Television
Malkie, Paul: To the Contrary (Persephone Productions)
Malloy, Brian: CBC
Malone, Fred: NBC News
Malone, James: Voice of America
Maltas, Michael: CNN
Mancini, Elizabeth: WTTG–Fox Television
Mandelson, Adam: Eurovision Americas, Inc.
Mann, Jonathon: WJLA–TV/Newschannel 8
Manning, Jason: Newshour with Jim Lehrer
Mannos, Sofia: AP–Broadcast
Maranho, Jose: C–SPAN
Marantz, Michael: WTTG–Fox Television
Marchione, Mark Anthony: CNN
Marchitto, J. Thomas: Freelance
Marks, Simon: Feature Story News
Marlantes, Liz: ABC News
Marno, Michael: Fox News
Marquardt, Ursula: German Television/ZDF
Marques, Antonio: Freelance
Marquez, Laura: ABC News
Marriott, Mai: Freelance
Marriott, Marc: Freelance
Marriott, Michael: CBS News
Marshall, Steven: CBS News
Martin, David: CBS News
Martin Ewing, Samara: WUSA–TV
Martin, Gail: FDCH E–Media, Inc.
Martin, Jr., James: ABC News
Martin, Wisdom: WTTG–Fox Television
Martinez, Luis: ABC News
Martinez, Sandra: CNN
Martinez, Tina Marie: Fox News
Martinez-Bustos, Lilliam: Telemundo Network
Martino, Jeffrey: Freelance
Mason, Cecelia, W.V.: Public Broadcasting
Mathers, Alexandra: CBS News
Mathieu, Joe: CBS Marketwatch
Matkosky, Timothy: WBAL–TV
Matsuyama, Toshiyuki: Fuji Television
Mattesky, Thomas A.: CBS News
Matthews, Claude L.: Freelance
Matthews, Kathleen: WJLA–TV/Newschannel 8
Matthews, Lisa N.: AP–Broadcast
Matthews, Ronald H.: CBS News
Matthews, Valerie: C–SPAN
Maxwell, Darraine: ABC News
Mayer, Charles: National Public Radio
Mayer, Petra: National Public Radio
Mayes, Michael: WETA–TV
Maylett, Chris: Diversified Communications, Inc. (DCI)

MEMBERS ENTITLED TO ADMISSION—Continued

Mayr, Sonia, German Television/ARD
Mazariegos, Mark, BET Nightly News
McAllister, Ian: Community TV of PG's
McCaffrey, Frank: Fox News
McCann, Michael: C–SPAN
McCann, Sean: C–SPAN
McCannon, Patrice: Freelance
McCarren, Andrea: WJLA–TV/Newschannel 8
McCarty, Dennis: Freelance
McCarty, Jay: Freelance
McCarthy, Kate: C–SPAN
McCarthy, Lark: WTTG–Fox Television
McCash, Douglas: Freelance
McCaughan, Timothy: CNN
McClam, Kevin: Fox News
McCleery, Kathleen: Newshour with Jim Lehrer
McClellan, Max: CBS News
McCloskey, George: Fox News
McClure, Tipp K.: Reuters Television
McClurkin, Donald: WETA–TV
McConnell, Dave: WTOP Radio
McCown, Gregory W.: ABC News
McCrae, Angela: Freelance
McCutchen, Yolanda: NBC News
McDermott, Frank: WUSA–TV
McDermott, Richard: NBC Newschannel
McDermott, Todd: WUSA–TV
McDevitt, Rebecca: WJLA–TV/Newschannel 8
McDonald, Mark: CNC/Capitol News Connection
McEachin, Johnny: Freelance
McFadden, Kerith: CNN
McFarland, Patty: Freelance
McGarrity, Gerard: C–SPAN
McGarvy, Sean: WTTG–Fox Television
McGinn, Anne: Fox News
McGinty, Derek G.: WUSA–TV
McGlinchy, James: CBS News
McGrath, Megan: WRC–TV/NBC–4
McGrath, Patrick: WTTG–Fox Television
McGraw, William: CNN
McGreevy, Allen: BBC
McGriff, Kathryn: WJLA–TV/Newschannel 8
McGuire, Bradley: C–SPAN
McGuire, Lorna: WTTG–Fox Television
McGuire, Michael: CBS News
McHenry, Bob: Freelance
McIntosh, Denise: CNN
McKelway, Douglas: WJLA–TV/Newschannel 8
McKenna, Patrick T.: WRC–TV/NBC–4
McKinley, Karen: NBC News
McKinley, Robert: CBS News
McKnight, William: WUSA–TV
McLellan, Daniel J.: Freelance
McMahon, Robert: Radio Free Europe
McManamon, Erin T.: Hearst–Argyle Television
McManus, Kevin A.: Freelance
McManus, Michael: CNN

McManus, Nicole: NBC Newschannel
McMartin, Philip: AGDAY
McMichael IV, Samuel J.: CNN
McMinn, Nan Hee: Washington News Network
McMullan, Michael: Freelance
McNamara, Melissa: CNN
McQuay, William: National Public Radio
McQueen Martin, Michel: ABC News
Means, Jeffrey Wendell: Voice of America
Mears, Carroll Ann: NBC News
Mears, William: CNN
Mebane, Martinez: NBC News
Mebane, William T.: National Public Radio
Meeks, Brock: MSNBC
Meghani, Sagar: AP–Broadcast
Mehrpore, Abdul Rauf: Voice of America
Meier, Christiane: German Television/ARD
Meier, Markus: N–TV News Television
Melendy, David R.: AP–Broadcast
Melhem, Richard Y.: MBC–TV (Middle East Broadcasting)
Melia, Michael K.: Newshour with Jim Lehrer
Mellman, Ira: WTOP Radio
Meltzer, Ari: ABC News
Meluza, Lourdes: Univision News
Mercurio, John: CNN
Merideth, Lila: Fox News
Merobshoev, Seeno: C–SPAN
Merrill, Robert: MSNBC
Merritt II, Marshall D.: The Washington Bureau
Meserve, Jeanne: CNN
Messer, Christopher: Al-Jazeera TV/Peninsula
Metil, Adrienne: WTOP Radio
Metzger, Edward: CNN
Meyer, Jill Rosenbaum: CBS News
Meyer, Kerry: Diversified Communications, Inc.
Meyer, Lisa: AP–Broadcast
Meyer, Richard: CBS News
Meyerdirk, Kimberly Ann: FDCH E–Media, Inc.
Meyers, Karen: WTTG–Fox Television
Michael, Buchanan: WJLA–TV/Newschannel 8
Michael, Michelle M.: WRC–TV/NBC–4
Michaud, Robert: Belo Capital Bureau
Michel, Theresa: C–SPAN
Mie, Ayako: Tokyo Broadcasting System
Miklaszewski, James: NBC News
Mikus, Andrea: SRN News
Milenic, Alexander: Freelance
Miles Jackson, Dayna-Marie: CBN News
Milford, Robert H.: Mobile Video Services
Miliano, Rugiero: CBS RADIO
Miller, Andrew P.: C–SPAN
Miller, Annette L.: Newshour with Jim Lehrer
Miller, Avery: ABC News
Miller, Elizabeth P.: BBC
Miller, Michael: Fox News
Miller, Mitchell: WTOP Radio
Miller, Richard F.: Talk Radio News Service

MEMBERS ENTITLED TO ADMISSION—Continued

Miller-Muro, Gil: Freelance
Mills, Jim: Fox News
Mills, Kate: C–SPAN
Mills, Lyle Wayne: Sinclair Broadcasting Group
Mills, Susan L.: Newshour with Jim Lehrer
Milne, Claudia: BBC
Minard, Nathalie: Eurovision Americas, Inc.
Minner, Richard: NBC News
Minor, Rodney Lee: FedNet
Minott, Gloria: WPFW–FM
Mishkin, Jay: WJLA–TV/Newschannel 8
Misol, Hannah: National Public Radio
Mitchell, Andrea: NBC News
Mitchell, Russell James: Voice of America
Mitnick, Steven E.: Freelance
Miyake, Yuko: TV Tokyo
Mizell, Shannon Scott: NBC News
Mock, Thomas: C–SPAN
Mohen, Peter: CNN
Moire, Jennifer: C–SPAN
Molineaux, Diana: Radio Marti
Mollet, Melissa: WJLA–TV/Newschannel 8
Monack, David: C–SPAN
Mong, Bryan: Freelance
Monk, Kathleen: CTV–Canadian Television
Montague, William: Global TV Canada
Monte-Bovi, Paul: WUSA–TV
Montenegro, Lori: Telemundo Network
Montenegro, Norma: Univision News
Mooar, Brian: NBC Newschannel
Moolenaar, Marjan: NOS Dutch Public Broadcasting
Moore, Dennis: Need to Know News
Moore, Garrette: C–SPAN
Moore, Linwood: C–SPAN
Moore, Robert: Independent Television News (ITN)
Moore, Terrence: Metro Networks
Moore, W. Harrison: Middle East Television
  Network
Moorhead, Jeremy: CNN
Moran, Terence P.: ABC News
Morano, Marc, CNSNews.com
Morgan, Nancy Gerstman: WETA–TV
Morgan, Parris: National Public Radio
Morrell, Geoff: ABC News
Morris, Amy: WTOP Radio
Morris, Holly: WTTG–Fox Television
Morris, Peter: CNN
Morrisette, Roland: Bloomberg Television
Morrison, Bridget: C–SPAN
Morrison, Jill: CNC/Capitol News Connection
Morse, Rick: CNN
Morton, Bruce: CNN
Morton, Dan: C–SPAN
Mortreux, Vincent: TF1 French Television
Moser, Rebecca: Hearst-Argyle Television
Moses, Lester: NBC News
Mosettig, Michael D.: Newshour with Jim Lehrer
Mosley, Matthew: Fuji Television

Moubray, Virginia A.: Freelance
Mountcastle, Katharine: CBS News
Mueller, John: Middle East Television Network
  (Alhurra)
Muhammad, Askia: National Scene News
Muhammad, Seleena M.: Fox News
Muir, Robert: Reuters Television
Munoz, Luis: Middle East Television Network
Muratani, Tateki: Freelance
Murray, Andrew: C–SPAN
Murphy, Frederick R.: Freelance
Murphy, John: CBS News
Murphy, Kathleen: Stateline.org
Murphy, Kathy: C–SPAN
Murray, Mark: NBC News
Murray, Matthew: Tribune Broadcasting
Murphy, Richard D.: WTTG–Fox Television
Murphy, Terence: C–SPAN
Murphy, Thomas: CNN
Murphy, Victor: WUSA–TV
Mursa, Alexander: Freelance
Mursa, Christina Marie: APTN
Murtaugh, Peter: BBC
Muse, Lowell: National Public Radio
Muse, Pat Lawson: WRC–TV/NBC–4
Musha, Masami, NHK–Japan Broadcasting
Muskat, Steven: NBC Newschannel
Muturi, Muthoni: National Public Radio
Myers, Lisa M.: NBC News
Namgyal, Tseten: Radio Free Asia
Napier, Joyce: CBC
Napshin, Jeff: WRC–TV/NBC–4
Narahari, Priya: Eurovision Americas, Inc.
Nash, John C.: WETA–TV
Nason, Andrew: C–SPAN
Naylor, Brian: National Public Radio
Neal, Jason W.: NBC News
Neapolitan, Michael: Freelance
Neary, Lynn: National Public Radio
Neel, Joe R.: National Public Radio
Nelson, Christopher: National Public Radio
Nelson, Deborah: CNN
Nelson, James: Fox News
Nelson, Jeffrey: NBC News
Nelson, Joseph: Washington Bureau News Service
Nelson, Suzanne: CNN
Neto, Joaquim: Mobile Video Services
Neustadt, James J.: WRC–TV/NBC–4
Nevins, Elizabeth: NBC News
Newberry, Tom: NBC Newschannel
Ng, Louise: Radio Free Asia
Nguyen, An: Radio Free Asia
Nguyen, Anh: Freelance
Nguyen, Bich-Ha: Radio Free Asia
Nguyen, Dien M.: Radio Free Asia
Nichols, James R.: WUSA–TV
Nicolaidis, Virginia: CNN

MEMBERS ENTITLED TO ADMISSION—Continued

Nieuwendijk, Hans van den: NOS Dutch Public
Broadcasting
Niiler, Eric: Freelance
Nikuradze, David: Rustavi–2 Broadcasting
Company
Niland, Martin: AP–Broadcast
Nilsson, Marco: Swedish Broadcasting
Ninan, Reena: Fox News
Nishiumi, Setsu: Fuji Television
Nixon, Chuck: WETA–TV
Nocciolo, Ernest G.: CNN
Noce, Julie: Swiss Broadcasting
Nohelty, Russell: The Washington Bureau
Nolen, John: CBS News
Norins, Jamie: Potomac Television
Norland, Dean E.: ABC News
Norling, Richard: Freelance
Norris, Christopher: Nightly Business Report
Norris, Donna: C–SPAN
Norris, James: Middle East Television Network
(Alhurra)
Norris, James F.: Middle East Television Network
(Alhurra)
Norris, Michele: National Public Radio
Northam, Jackie: National Public Radio
Novack, Christopher: Tribune Broadcasting
Novy, Michele: Fox News
Nugroho, Irawan: Voice of America
Nurenberg, Gary: Freelance
Nurnberger, Lisa: WAMU–FM
Nwazota, Kristina: The Newshour with Jim Lehrer
Nyland, Andrew: WJLA–TV/Newschannel 8
Oberti, Ralf: Television Nacional De Chile (TVN)
O'Brien, David: Freelance
Och, P. Andrew: Fox News
O'Connell, Benjamin: C–SPAN
O'Connell, Mike: NBC Newschannel
O'Connor, Thomas W.: Freelance
Odom, Quillie: Fox News
O'Donnell, Barry: East Coast Television
O'Donnell, Norah: NBC News
O'Donnell, Patrick: Freelance
Offermann, Claudia: German Television/ZDF
Ogata, Kerry: CNN
O'Hanlon, Maikel: C–SPAN
O'Hara, Victoria: National Public Radio
Oko, Jennifer Cohen: CBS News
Okpotor, Faith: NBC News
O'Leary, Lizzie: National Public Radio
Olick, Diana, CNBC
Oliger, Brian: WTOP Radio
Oliver, LaFontaine: Radio One
Ong, Linh: German Television/ARD
Ono, Mari, NHK–Japan Broadcasting
O'Regan, Michael: WRC–TV/NBC–4
Orgel, Paul: C–SPAN
Orr, K. Robert: CBS News
Osborne, Kyle: WJLA–TV/Newschannel 8

O'Shea, Daniel J.: Freelance
O'Shea, Jennifer Lynn: Newshour with Jim Lehrer
Osinski, Krystyna: Freelance
Ota, Kazuhiko: TV Asahi
O'Toole, Quinn: National Public Radio
Otsuka, Mika: TV Tokyo
Overby, Peter: National Public Radio
Overdiek, Tim: NOS Dutch Public Broadcasting
Overgaard, Sidsel: WAMU–FM
Overton, Ivan: ABC News
Owen, Andrea: ABC News
Ozsancak, Hakan: APTN
Padilla-Cirino, Mercy: Hispanic Radio Network
Pagan, Louis: AP–Broadcast
Page, David: CBN News
Palacio, Zulima: Voice of America
Palca, Joe: National Public Radio
Pande, Aru: WJLA–TV/Newschannel 8
Panzer, Chester: WRC–TV/NBC–4
Papadopoulos, Alexander: Mobile Video Services
Pappas, Icarus N. (Ike): Washington News Network
Parenti, Alisa: WJLA–TV/Newschannel 8
Parham, Kyneesha: C–SPAN
Park, Sarah Lee: WJLA–TV/Newschannel 8
Parker, Andre: CNN
Parker, Beth: WTTG–Fox Television
Parker, Julie: WJLA–TV/Newschannel 8
Parker, Robert Geoffrey: CNN
Parker, Serena Ravenel: Voice of America
Parshall, Janet: SRN News
Parshall, Sam: SRN News
Pasternak, Douglas S.: NBC News
Pastre, Dominique: Fox News
Patel, Sital S.: CNN
Patricia McDonald, Natashka: Freelance
Patrick, Daniel: WJLA–TV/Newschannel 8
Patruznick, Michael: C–SPAN
Patterson, Jay E.: ABC News
Pauls, Hartmut: Freelance
Paxton, Bradford S.: Fox News
Payne, Aaron C.: CNN
Payne, Nathan: CNN
Payne, Scott: Freelance
Peacock, Grant: Freelance
Peaks, Gershon: Reuters Television
Pearlman, Shana: Fox News
Pearson, Alysia: CNN
Pearson, Bryan: CNN
Pearson, Hampton, CNBC
Peck, Lauren: CBS News
Peltier, Yves: CBC
Pena, Celinda: WUSA–TV
Penaloza, Marisa: National Public Radio
Penniman, Judy: ABC News
Pennybacker, Gail: WJLA–TV/Newschannel 8
Pergram, Chad: CNC/Capitol News Connection
Perkins, Douglas: Hearst-Argyle Television

MEMBERS ENTITLED TO ADMISSION—Continued

Perkins, Vernon: C–SPAN
Perlmeter, Alan: WETA–TV
Perry, Andrea: C–SPAN
Perry, Michelle: NBC News
Perry, Timothy: Newshour with Jim Lehrer
Persky, Anna: Fox News
Peters, Ron: WUSA–TV
Peterson, Gordon: WJLA–TV/Newschannel 8
Peterson, James P.: Freelance
Peterson, Karen: WUSA–TV
Peterson, Kavan: Stateline.org
Peterson, Michael: CBS News
Peterson, Rebecca: CBS News
Peterson, Robert: Freelance
Petras, William: NBC News
Pettigrew, Sharon Rae: WTOP Radio
Pettit, Debra: NBC News
Pettit, Susan: CNN
Peyton, Michael: CBS News
Pfotzer, Elizabeth: C–SPAN
Pham, Jacqueline: Fox News
Phillips, Gurvir Dhindsa: WTTG–Fox Television
Phillips, Steven: Reuters Television
Pickett, Paul: C–SPAN
Pickup, Michael: ABC News
Pierce, Maura: C–SPAN
Piette, Didier: Eurovision Americas, Inc.
Piltz, Eberhard: German Television/ZDF
Pimble, William H.: CBS Radio
Pinczuk, Murray: Freelance
Pinzon, Wingel, Telemundo Network
Pinzon, Wingel G., Telemundo Network
Pitocco, Nickolas: C–SPAN
Pitra, Katharine: NBC News
Pizarro, Fernando, Univision News
Placie, Jordan: CNN
Plante, Gilles: CBC
Plante, William: CBS News
Plater, Christopher: WJLA–TV/Newschannel 8
Plater, Roz: WTTG–Fox Television
Pless, Stephen: CNN
Pliszak, Richard K.: ABC News
Plotkin, Mark: WTOP Radio
Plummer, Keith: Freelance
Poduch, Shelby: Freelance
Poley, Michael: CNN
Polly, Fabio: Austrian Radio & TV/ORF
Popkin, James K.: NBC News
Popp, Rena: WTTG–Fox Television
Porsella, Claude L.: Radio France Internationale
Porter, Almon: C–SPAN
Porter, Catherine: ABC News
Porter, Christina: C–SPAN
Porter, Taylor: C–SPAN
Posey, Luther: CBS News
Potisk, Steven: AP–Broadcast
Potter, Deidre: C–SPAN

Potts, Tracie: NBC Newschannel
Powell, Dennis: ABC News
Powell, Shannon: WTTG–Fox Television
Pozniak, Stephen: WJLA–TV/Newschannel 8
Prakash, Snigdha: National Public Radio
Prasad, William: Freelance
Pratt, James: WUSA–TV
Preloh, Anne: C–SPAN
Press, Robert: Bloomberg Radio (WBBR)
Presto, Suzanne: Voice of America
Presutti, Carolyn: Cox Broadcasting
Primmer, Ryan: Potomac Television
Priscilla, Huff: Feature Story News
Pronko, Tony: C–SPAN
Puckett, Richard: Freelance
Pugh, Kari: WUSA–TV
Pugliese, Pat, CNBC
Quijano, Elaine: CNN
Quinn, Diana: CBS News
Quinn, Jacqueline D.: AP–Broadcast
Quinn, John D.: Voice of America
Quinn, Mary: ABC News
Quinnette, John J.: Freelance
Quinonez, Omar: Freelance
Quiroz, Silvana: Hispanic Radio Network
Rabbage, Mark: BBC
Rabin, Carrie: CBS News
Racki, Jason D.: Australian Broadcasting Corporation
Rad, Ali: Freelance
Raffaele, Robert: Voice of America
Raffaelli, Jr., Stephen A.: FedNet
Rager, Bryan: Reuters Television
Rahman, Syed Ziaur: Voice of America
Rahmati, Jeff: Bloomberg Television
Ramirez, Edwin, Univision News
Ramirez, Max: Telemundo Network
Ramon, Jr., Fausto: Middle East Television Network (Alhurra)
Ramos, Raul: Univision News
Rampy, R. Grant: Tribune Broadcasting
Randle, Jim: Voice of America
Rarey, Richard Howell: National Public Radio
Rathner, Jeffrey: WETA–TV
Ratliff, Walter: APTN
Ratner, Ellen: Talk Radio News Service
Ratner, Victor: ABC News
Raval, Nikhil: C–SPAN
Raviv, Daniel: CBS News
Ray, Alonzo: NBC News
Ray, Diana: BBC
Ray, Elizabeth: CNN
Ray, James D.: AP–Broadcast
Ray, John Christophe: C–SPAN
Ray, Nicholas J.: Al-Jazeera TV/Peninsula
Reagan, Cheryl: Federal News Service
Reals, Gary: WUSA–TV
Reals, Tucker: APTN

MEMBERS ENTITLED TO ADMISSION—Continued

Reaume, Gregory: CBC
Reaux, Richard J.: Freelance
Redding, William: ABC News
Reddy, Kankali: C–SPAN
Redisch, Stuart S.: CNN
Redman, Justine: CNN
Reeb, Troy: Global TV Canada
Reed, Josephine: Interfaith Voices
Reese, Orla: AP–Broadcast
Reeve, Richard: WJLA–TV/Newschannel 8
Regan, James: C–SPAN
Reich, Sharon: Freelance
Reid, Brian M.: WJLA–TV/Newschannel 8
Reid, Chip: NBC News
Reilly, Robert: C–SPAN
Reimann, Fritz: Swiss Broadcasting
Reinsel, Ed: Freelance
Reise, Hans-Peter: German Television/ARD
Remillard, Michele: Fox News
Renken, David: Fox News
Rensberger, Scott: TV2–Denmark
Repke, Amy: WUSA–TV
Reyes, Malissa: WJLA–TV/Newschannel 8
Reyes, Victor, Telemundo Network
Reynolds, Andrew: National Public Radio
Reynolds, Judy: Religion & Ethics Newsweekly
Reynolds, Robert: CNBC
Reynolds, Talesha: ABC News
Rhode, Leslie Cook: WJLA–TV/Newschannel 8
Rhodes, Elizabeth: Fox News
Ricciuti, Leah: ABC News
Rice, Alan: NBC News
Richard, Sylvain: CBC
Rickard, Michael: WTTG–Fox Television
Ridgeway, David: C–SPAN
Rieger, Wendy: WRC–TV/NBC–4
Riess, Steffanie: German Television/ZDF
Riesser, Daniel: Freelance
Riha, Anne Marie: Fox News
Riner, Corbett: Fox News
Rinne, Jessica: Hearst-Argyle Television
Ritchie, Thomas: APTN
Rivero, Raul Jorge: WUSA–TV
Rivers, Jerome: Community TV of PG's
Roach, Amy: C–SPAN
Roane-Skehan, Andrea: WUSA–TV
Robbins, Diana: ARD German Radio NDR/WDR
Robbins, Francisco: CBS News
Robbins, Mark: WETA–TV
Robbins, Michael: Fox News
Robbins, Sarah: BBC
Roberts, Corinne B.: ABC News
Roberts, Diane: Freelance
Roberts, Jean Pierre: Eurovision Americas, Inc.
Roberts, Nathan: WJLA–TV/Newschannel 8
Roberts, Susan: CBS News
Robertson, Greg: CNN

Robertson, John: CBS News
Robertson, Laura: CBN News
Robinson, Daniel: Voice of America
Robinson, David: CNN
Robinson, Douglas: Austrian Radio & TV/ORF
Robinson, Earle: Freelance
Robinson, Laura: CNN
Robinson, Margaret: Newshour with Jim Lehrer
Robinson, Querry: Fox News
Roca, Xavier, TVE/Television of Spain
Rochelle, Carl: Freelance
Rockler, Julia: The Washington Bureau
Rockwell, Kelly: CBS News
Rodriguez, Eduardo: T.V.E./Spanish Public
    Television
Rodriguez, Janet: CNN
Rodriguez, Martine: C–SPAN
Rogers, Lauren: ABC News
Rohrbeck, Douglas: Fox News
Rojas, Carlos: ABC News
Rokus, Brian: CNN
Roland, Abu Bakr: ABC News
Rollins, Bonnie: NBC Newschannel
Romilly, George: ABC News
Roof, Peter: Freelance
Rooney, Alissa: CNN
Root, Sean L.: WUSA–TV
Rose, Floyd T.: Freelance
Rose, Jeff: WJLA–TV/Newschannel 8
Rose, Joseph: WJLA–TV/Newschannel 8
Rose, Raymond: NBC News
Roselli, H. Michael: CNN
Rosen, Amy: Bloomberg Television
Rosen, James: Fox News
Rosen, Rachel: CNN
Rosenbaum, Peter: Mobile Video Services
Rosenbaum, Thea: German Television/ARD
Rosenberg, Gary: ABC News
Rosenberg, Howard L.: ABC News
Rosenberg, Jeffrey: National Public Radio
Rosenfelder, Michael: APTN
Rosewicz, Barbara: Stateline.org
Rosgaard, Jessica: CNN
Ross, Lee: Fox News
Rossetti-Meyer, Misa: Diversified Communications,
    Inc.
Roston, Aram: NBC News
Rotchford, Karin: Newshour with Jim Lehrer
Roth, Johnie F.: NBC News
Rowe, Hildrun: German Television/ZDF
Royce, Lindy: CNN
Roycraft, David: WUSA–TV
Ruby, Tracy: C–SPAN
Rucci, Susan Ruth: CBS News
Rudd, Michael: WJLA–TV/Newschannel 8
Rudin, Ken: National Public Radio
Rueggeberg, Claudia Anke: German
    Television/ZDF

MEMBERS ENTITLED TO ADMISSION—Continued

Ruff, David W.: CNN
Ruggiero, Diane: CNN
Rugman, Jonathan A.: Independent Television News (ITN)
Rupert, Jr., Gerald: House Radio–TV Gallery
Rushfield, Stuart: National Public Radio
Rushing, Ian: WJLA–TV/Newschannel 8
Russell, Angela: WJLA–TV/Newschannel 8
Russell, David A.: CNN
Russell, Roxanne: CBS News
Russert, Timothy: NBC News
Russo, Jay R.: ABC News
Rust, Emily: CNN
Rutherford, John H.: NBC News
Ryan, Jason: ABC News
Ryan, Jennifer: WUSA–TV
Ryan, Marty: Fox News
Ryan, Mike: Potomac Television
Rynn, Kathleen R.: WJLA–TV/Newschannel 8
Rysak, F. David: WTTG–Fox Television
Saad, Layelle: Al-Jazeera TV/Peninsula
Sabo, Lara: Belo Capital Bureau
Sacks, Howard: NBC News
Saffelle, Jeffrey Lynn: Global TV Canada
Sagalyn, Daniel: Newshour with Jim Lehrer
Saint-Rossy, Karen: CBS News
Sakota, Alija: WUSA–TV
Sala, Salvador: Catalunya TV/TV3 **
Sala, Salvador: Catalan Television
Sales, Leigh: Australian Broadcasting Corporation
Salih, Sharief: MBC–TV (Middle East Broadcasting)
Salkoff, Brooke Hart: NBC Newschannel
Sallette, Joseph: BBC
Saltz, Michael: The Newshour with Jim Lehrer
Salzman, Eric: CBS News
Samaniego, Stephen: CNN
Sampaio, Frederico: C–SPAN
Sampy, David: Independent Television News (ITN)
Samuel, Maia T.: NBC News
Sanchez, Claudio: National Public Radio
Sanchez, George D.: ABC News
Sanchez, Pablo: Univision News
Sandell, Clayton D.: ABC News
Sanders, Molly: C–SPAN
Sanders-Smith, Sherry: C–SPAN
Sandiford, Michele: C–SPAN
Sanfuentes, Jose A.: NBC News
Santer, Sarah: Fox News
Santos, Jeff: Hispanic Radio Network
Santos, Jose G.: CNN
Saray-Yim, Chanlee: Diversified Communications, Inc.. (DCI)
Sargent, Mark: WTTG–Fox Television
Sarkisian, Vatche: Middle East Television Network (Alhurra)
Sarvamaa, Petri: Finnish Broadcasting/YLE
Sasek, Robert J.: Freelance

Sasson, Aaron: NBC News
Satchell, David: WUSA–TV
Sato, Keiichi: Nippon TV Network
Sato, Setsuko: National Public Radio
Savage, Craig: Fox News
Sawka, Andrew: Nippon TV Network
Scanlon, Jason: Fox News
Scanlon, Mary: C–SPAN
Scanlan, William: C–SPAN
Scarrah, Kathie: Freelance
Schaff, Michael: CBN News
Schalch, Kathleen: National Public Radio
Schall, Fred: Freelance
Schantz, Douglas N.: CNN
Schantz, Kristine: CNN
Scharf, Jason: APTN
Scherer, David: CNN
Scheschkewitz, Daniel: Deutsche Welle Television
Scheuer, John: C–SPAN
Scheuer, Stefan: German Television/ARD
Schieffer, Bob: CBS News
Schindler, Max: NBC News
Schlachter, Terese: Freelance
Schlegel, Barry C.: CNN
Schleicher, Anne: The Newshour with Jim Lehrer
Schloemer, Hans-Peter: Freelance
Schlosberg, Andrew: TV Tokyo
Schmidt-Massey, Emily: WUSA–TV
Schmiester, Carsten: ARD German Radio NDR/WDR
Schoenholtz, Howard: ABC News
Schoenmann, Donald: Freelance
Scholl, Christopher: NBC News
Schonche, Didrik: National Public Radio
Schott, Soniaz: Radio Valera Venezuela
Schuiten, Jeroen: Eurovision Americas, Inc.
Schule, James R.: Fox News
Schulken, Sonja Deaner: Tribune Broadcasting
Schultz, Teri: Fox News
Schultz-Burkel, Gunnar: German Broadcasting Systems/ARD
Schultze, F. Kevin: WJLA–TV/Newschannel 8
Schumaker-Shokraei, Carrie: AP–Broadcast
Schur, Paul: Fox News
Schwarte, Georg: ARD German Radio NDR/WDR
Schweiger, Ellen: C–SPAN
Schweitzer, Murray H.: WRC–TV/NBC–4
Schweppe, Michael: National Public Radio
Scicchitano, Carmine: NBC News
Scott, Graham: Austrian Radio & TV/ORF
Scott, Harry Lee: Radio Free Asia
Scott, Ivan: Freelance
Scott, Ivan, KGO RADIO
Scott, Linda J.: Newshour with Jim Lehrer
Scott, Sarah: Freelance
Scruggs, Wesley: NBC News
Scully, Steven: C–SPAN
Seabrook, Willliam: WETA–TV

MEMBERS ENTITLED TO ADMISSION—Continued

Seabrook, Andrea: National Public Radio
Seaby, Gregory: WUSA–TV
Sears, Carl V.: NBC News
Seem, Thomas H.: CBS News
Segraves, Mark: WTOP Radio
Seidman, Joel: NBC News
Seium, Michael, Washington News Network
Seldin, Jeffrey: WTOP Radio
Selma, Reginald G.: CNN
Sera, Frederick: ABC News
Serensits, Joseph: ABC News
Sergueev, Vladimir: RTVI
Sermeus, Erin: CNN
Settele, Hanno: Austrian Radio & TV/ORF
Sewell, Leslie: Freelance
Seymour, Allison: WTTG–Fox Television
Shaffir, Gregory: CBS News
Shaffir, Kimberlee: CBS News
Shah, Sayed S.: Voice of America
Shah, Sima: C–SPAN
Shalhoup, Joseph: NBC News
Shand, Susan: Freelance
Shand, Christina: Fox News
Shannon, Dennis: CBS News
Shannon, Holly: WJLA–TV/Newschannel 8
Shapiro, Joseph: National Public Radio
Sharon, Adam: Talk Radio News Service
Shaughnessy, Lawrence: CNN
Shaw, Benjamin H.: CNC/Capitol News Connection
Shaw, Cathy: National Public Radio
Shaw, Larry: ABC News
Shedrick, Daniel: APTN
Shelton, Steve: Fox News
Shenk, Samantha: CBS News
Sheppard, Holly B.: WUSA–TV
Shepherd, Sarah: CNN
Shepherd, Shawna: CNN
Sheridan, Chris: CBS News
Sherwood, Tom: WRC–TV/NBC–4
Shifflet, Mandi: Fox News
Shih, Che-Wei: TVBS
Shikaki, Muna: MBC–TV (Middle East Broadcasting)
Shimada, Masaaki: TV Tokyo
Shine, Thomas Andrew: ABC News
Shipman, Claire: ABC News
Shire, Robert: Viewpoint Communications
Shively, Caroline: Fox News
Shlemon, Chris: Independent Television News (ITN)
Shockley, Milton T.: WRC–TV/NBC–4
Shoffner, Harry: Freelance
Shogren, Elizabeth: National Public Radio
Shon, Robert: WTTG–Fox Television
Shortt, Robert: Irish Radio and Television (RTE)
Shott, David: Fox News
Shovelan, John: Australian Broadcasting Corporation
Showalter, Misty: WTTG–Fox Television

Showell, Andre, BET Nightly News
Shukhin, Daniel: National Public Radio
Shull, Roger: Reuters Television
Sides, James E.: C–SPAN
Siegel, Robert C.: National Public Radio
Siegfriedt, Anita: Fox News
Sierra, Joann: CNN
Silberbrandt, Allan: TV2–Denmark
Silberner, Joanne: National Public Radio
Sileo, Thomas: Tribune Broadcasting
Sills, Cecil John: NBC Newschannel
Silman, Jimmie: WUSA–TV
Silva-Pinto, Lauren: Austrian Radio & TV/ORF
Silver, Darwin: WETA–TV
Silver, David: Freelance
Silver, Diane: The Newshour with Jim Lehrer
Silver, Janet E.: Australian Broadcasting Corporation
Silver, Tiffany: C–SPAN
Silver, Torri: Community TV of PG's
Silverberg, Hank: WTOP Radio
Silverman, Ari: National Public Radio
Silverstein, Matthew J.: Eurovision Americas, Inc.
Simeone, Nick: Fox News
Simeone, Ronald: Freelance
Simkins, Chris: Voice of America
Simkin, Mark: Australian Broadcasting Corporation
Simmons, Y. Sean: Freelance
Simms, Jeffery: CNN
Simpson, Gary: C–SPAN
Simpson, Shelley A.: WJLA–TV/Newschannel 8
Sirgany, Aleen: CBS News
Sisco, Paul: Freelance
Sisco, Paul: Voice of America
Sit, David C.: Newshour with Jim Lehrer
Skeans, Ronald M.: BBC
Skomal, Paul: Freelance
Slafka, Kristi: C–SPAN
Slattery, Julie: Bloomberg Television
Slawinska, Katarzyna: TVN Poland
Slen, Peter: C–SPAN
Slie, Charles: Freelance
Sloane, Ward C.: CBS News
Slobogin, Kathy: CNN
Slone, James: C–SPAN
Small, Matt: AP–Broadcast
Small, William: Bloomberg Radio (WBBR)
Smith, Ashley: Fox News
Smith, Cindy: ABC News
Smith, Cynthia: ABC News
Smith, Graham: National Public Radio
Smith, Heather: Fox News
Smith, Hedrick: Freelance
Smith, James E.: ABC News
Smith, Jason H.: WTTG–Fox Television
Smith, Mark S.: AP–Broadcast
Smith, Michael J.: Dispatch Broadcast Group
Smith, Phillip: Belo Capital Bureau

MEMBERS ENTITLED TO ADMISSION—Continued

Smith, Scott D.: WJLA–TV/Newschannel 8
Smith, Shirley O'Bryan: AP–Broadcast
Smith, Terence: Newshour with Jim Lehrer
Smith, William B.: Hearst-Argyle Television
Sneed, Kimberly: NBC News
Snow, Robbie B.: Washington Bureau News Service
Snow, Tony: Fox News
Sockowitz, Ira: Washington News Network
Soh, June: Voice of America
Solorzano, Gilbert: Freelance
Sonderegger, Evan: SRN News
Sorenson, Randall: Freelance
Soucy, Peggy: Eurovision Americas, Inc.
Southern, Joel L.: Alaska Public Radio Network
Southworth, Cal R.: National Public Radio
Speck, Alan: C–SPAN
Spector, Teresa: Fox News
Speer, John C.: National Public Radio
Speights, Eric: ABC News
Speiser, Matthew: CNN
Spektor, Eleanor: CNN
Spellman, Jim: CNN
Spence, Patrick: WTOP Radio
Spence, Robert: C–SPAN
Spencer, Darcy: Freelance
Spevak, Joe: WTTG–Fox Television
Spicer, Rebecca Miller: WJLA–TV/Newschannel 8
Spire, Richard H.: CBS News
Spoerry, Philip Scott: CNN
Sponder, Myron: Talk Radio News Service
Sproesser, James M.: East Coast Television
St. James, Gregory: C–SPAN
St. John, Jonathan: CNN
St. Pierre, Christine: CBC
Stadsing, Hans: Danish Broadcasting Corporation
Stafford, Ronald: SRN News
Stafford-Walter, Michael: WUSA–TV
Stamberg, Susan L.: National Public Radio
Stanford, David E.: CBS News
Stanford, Kenneth: CNN
Stang, Tim: Bloomberg Television
Stanke, Donald E.: WTTG–Fox Television
Stanley, Randal: WUSA–TV
Stapleton, Marjorie: AP–Broadcast
Stark, Lisa: ABC News
Starke, Angela B.: WJLA–TV/Newschannel 8
Starks, Bill: WRC–TV/NBC–4
Starling, Alison: WJLA–TV/Newschannel 8
Staton, Thomas: Freelance
Statter, Louis David: WUSA–TV
Staude, Linda: ARD German Radio NDR/WDR
Stavisky, Sandra Bechan: Voice of America
Stay, Daniel J.: Fox News
Stefany, Steve: ABC News
Steinhauser, Paul: CNN
Steo, Austin: Viewpoint Communications
Stepney, Eric: C–SPAN

Stevenson, James: Voice of America
Stevenson, Louis: WTTG–Fox Television
Steverson, Simone: National Public Radio
Stewart, Andrew: SRN News
Stewart, James D.: CBS News
Stewart, Norman: C–SPAN
Stix, Gabriel: CBS News
Stoddard, Rick: C–SPAN
Stone, Evie: National Public Radio
Stone, Jamie: WRC–TV/NBC–4
Stoner, Matthew: C–SPAN
Storper, David: C–SPAN
Stout, Matthew: Fox News
Strand, Paul L.: CBN News
Strass, Nina X.: AP–Broadcast
Straub, Terry: Diversified Communications, Inc. (DCI)
Strickland, Kenneth: NBC News
Strickler, Laura: CNC/Capitol News Connection
Stringer, Ashley: CNBC
Strong, Jennifer: WAMU–FM
Stubblefield, Abraham: WJLA–TV/Newschannel 8
Stumpo, Donald: WRC–TV
Styles, Julian: CNN
Suarez, Fernando J.: CBS News
Suarez, Rafael A.: Newshour with Jim Lehrer
Suddeth, Rick: Freelance
Sulasma, Olli-Pekka: Finnish Broadcasting/YLE
Sullivan, Virginia L.: National Public Radio
Summers, Elizabeth: Newshour with Jim Lehrer
Summers, Patrick: Fox News
Sumrell, John M.: Belo Capital Bureau
Surbey, Jason: C–SPAN
Sussman, Brian: CNC/Capitol News Connection
Sutherland, Leigh: NBC News
Suto, Ena: TV Asahi
Sutton, Todd: NBC Newschannel
Svolopoulos, Christina: Fox News
Swain, Susan M.: C–SPAN
Swain, Todd M.: Mobile Video Services
Swanier, Sherrell: CNN
Swann, Michael: WRC–TV/NBC–4
Sweeney, David: National Public Radio
Sweeney, Robert: WRC–TV/NBC–4
Sweetapple, Dan: Australian Broadcasting Corporation
Sylvester, Lisa: CNN
Syrjanen, Janne: Belo Capital Bureau
Szechenyi, Nicholas: Fuji Television
Szucs, George: Fox News
Tabata, Tadashi: TV Asahi
Tagliaferri, Kelly: C–SPAN
Tait, Ted: BBC
Takahashi, Yusuke: NHK–Japan Broadcasting
Tamboli, Jay: Talk Radio News Service
Tamerlani, George: Reuters Television
Tapper, Jake: ABC News
Tasillo, Mary Ellen: Fox News

MEMBERS ENTITLED TO ADMISSION—Continued

Tate, Deborah: Voice of America
Tate, Tiffany: BET Nightly News
Tatton, Abbi: CNN
Tavcar, Erik: CNN
Taylor, Allyson Ross: CBS News
Taylor, Brian: C–SPAN
Teboe, Mark E.: Freelance
Taylor, Kenneth: Newshour with Jim Lehrer
Teeples, Joseph: C–SPAN
Tejerina, Pilar: CNN
Tendencia, Editha: Freelance
Tennent, Gerald W.: National Public Radio
Teranishi, Kenji: Nippon TV Network
Terry, Janet: WUSA–TV
Teshima, Harue, NHK–Japan Broadcasting
Teshima, Ryuichi: NHK–Japan Broadcasting
Tevault, Neil David: National Public Radio
Thai, Xuan: CNBC
Theall, David J.: CNN
Thery, Samara: Newshour with Jim Lehrer
Thibault, David, CNSNews.com
Thoman, Eric: C–SPAN
Thomas, Amy Jo: ABC News
Thomas, Andrew: Freelance
Thomas, Bert: Fox News
Thomas, Evelyn: CBS News
Thomas III, James B.: CNN
Thomas, Pierre G.: ABC News
Thomas, Renu: The Newshour with Jim Lehrer
Thomas, Sharahn: National Public Radio
Thomas, Will: WTTG–Fox Television
Thompson, Charles: National Public Radio
Thompson, James: C–SPAN
Thompson, Jerry: CNN
Thompson, Jr., Joseph: Freelance
Thompson, Lisa: CNN
Thompson, Melissa A.: The Washington Bureau
Thompson, Nick: NBC Newschannel
Thompson, Ron: Radio One
Thorne, C. Patrick: Washington Bureau News Service
Thornton, Ronald: NBC News
Till, Morgan: Newshour with Jim Lehrer
Tiller, Arthur: C–SPAN
Tillery, Richard: The Washington Bureau
Tillman, Thomas E.: CBS News
Tilman, Ai: Nippon TV Network
Tilman, Brandon: C–SPAN
Timmons, Kyria: SRN News
Tin, Annie: C–SPAN
Tinnefeld, Norbert: German Television/ARD
Tipper, William: CNN
Toai, Ngo: Radio Free Asia
Tobias, Ed: AP–Broadcast
Todd, Brian: CNN
Todd, Deborah J.: Freelance
Tofani, Jeffrey T.: Voice of America
Tolliver, Terri: WTTG–Fox Television

Toman, George: Freelance
Tomko, Stephen: Video News Service
Tong, Scott: Marketplace Radio
Torgerson, Ande: Fox News
Torpey, Robert: Fox News
Totenberg, Nina: National Public Radio
Touhey, Emmanuel: C–SPAN
Toulouse, Anne: Radio France Internationale
Trammell, Michael: WUSA–TV
Traynham, Peter C.: CBS News
Tremblay, Stephanie: CBC
Trengrove, James: Newshour with Jim Lehrer
Triay, Andres P.: CBS News
Tschida, Stephen: WJLA–TV/Newschannel 8
Tso, Chakmo: Radio Free Asia
Tuan, Shih Yuan: TVBS
Tucker, Elke: German Television/ZDF
Tully, Andrew: Radio Free Europe
Tureck, Matthew: NBC Newschannel
Turner, Martin G.: Bloomberg Television
Turner, Al Douglas: ABC News
Turner, Patricia: Fox News
Turner, Renee: NBC News
Turnham, Steve: CNN
Turrell, Elizabeth Ann: ABC News
Tuss, Adam: WTOP Radio
Tutman, Dan D.: CBS News
Tutt, Corey: C–SPAN
Tyler, Brett: CNN
Ubeda, Anna: T.V.E./Spanish Public Television
Uchimiya, Ellen: Fox News
Udenans, Vija: ABC News
Uhl, Kim: CNN
Ulery, Brad: Freelance
Uliano, Richard J.: CNN
Ulloa, Victor: CBS News
Ulmer, Kenya S.: CNN
Ulzby, Neda: National Public Radio
Umeh, Maureen: WTTG–Fox Television
Umrani, Anthony R.: CNN
Urbina, Adrienne: Newshour with Jim Lehrer
Urbina, Luis: WRC–TV/NBC–4
Ure, Laurie: CNN
Usaeva, Nadia: Radio Free Asia
Vakili, Mohammad R.: Voice of America
Valcarrel, Gus: APTN
Vallese, Juliette: CNN
Van der Bellen, Erin: WRC–TV/NBC–4
Van Horn, Allan: NBC News
Van Susteren, Greta: Fox News
VanArsdale, Vicki: Bloomberg Radio (WBBR)
Vance, Denise: APTN
Vance, Jim: WRC–TV/NBC–4
Vance, Lauren: WUSA–TV
Vasa, Sampath: WETA–TV
Vassil, Christopher D.: Freelance
Vaughan, Scott: Reuters Television

MEMBERS ENTITLED TO ADMISSION—Continued

Vaughan, Vincent: WJLA–TV/Newschannel 8
Vaughn, Michael R.: WJLA–TV/Newschannel 8
Vega, Fernando: CNN
Velkovska, Julija: Voice of America
Vennell, Vicki: ABC News
Veronelli, Alessio: Swiss Broadcasting
Vicario, Virginia A.: ABC News
Vicary, Lauren H.: AP–Broadcast
Vigran, Anna: National Public Radio
Villone Garcia, Patricia: Community TV of PG's
Vinson, Bryce: Fox News
Viqueira, Michael J.: NBC News
Visioli, Todd: Fox News
Visley, Andrew G.: AP–Broadcast
Vitorovich, Susan: NBC News
Vizcarra, Mario: Univision News
Vlahos, Kelley Beaucar: Fox News
Vohar, Den: AP–Broadcast
Voth, Charles: WETA–TV
Vu, Tu H.: CNN
Vukmer, David: NBC News
Vyas, Amit: Fox News
Wack, Valerie: CBN News
Wagfi, Wajd: Al-Jazeera TV/Peninsula
Wagner, Martin: German Public Radio/ARD
Wagner, Paul: WTTG–Fox Television
Wahl, Tracy: National Public Radio
Wait, Kevin: National Public Radio
Walde, Thomas: German Television/ZDF
Walker, Brian: APTN
Walker, Darius: CNN
Walker, James William: WJLA–TV/News
  channel 8
Walker, Tom: Dispatch Broadcast Group
Walker, William: CBS News
Wallace, Chris: Fox News
Wallace, John L.: Fox News
Wallace, Zelda: Cox Broadcasting
Walsh, Deirdre: CNN
Walsh, Mary E.: CBS News
Walter, Charles: Freelance
Walter, Mike: WUSA–TV
Wang, Yau: Radio Free Asia
Waqfi, Wajd: Al-Jazeera TV/Peninsula
Warehime, Keith: C–SPAN
Warner, Craig: CBS News
Warner, Margaret: Newshour with Jim Lehrer
Warner, Tarik: WJLA–TV/Newschannel 8
Washburn, Kevin: C–SPAN
Washington, Erick: CBS News
Washington, Ervin: Nightly Business Report
Waters, Hunter: CNN
Watkins, Duane: WTTG–Fox Television
Watrel, Jane: WRC–TV/NBC–4
Watrud, Don: WTTG–Fox Television
Watson, Walter Ray: National Public Radio
Watts, Andrew M.: National Public Radio
Watts, Michael: CNN

Waxler, Gary: Freelance
Weakly, David: NBC News
Webb, David Allen: WJLA–TV/Newschannel 8
Webb, Justin: BBC
Webster, Aaron S.: Freelance
Wehinger, Amy: Fox News
Wei, Jing: Phoenix Satellite Television
Weidenbosch, Glenn E.: ABC News
Weilhammer, Francoise: Swiss Broadcasting
Weiner, Eric: Tokyo Broadcasting System
Weinfeld, Michael: AP–Broadcast
Weinstein, Richard: C–SPAN
Weisskopf, Arlene: Freelance
Weldon, Jody: Sinclair Broadcasting Group
Wells Shott, Courtney: Fox News
Welna, David: National Public Radio
Wendy, Carla: Fox News
Werdel, Paul: BBC
Wertheimer, Linda C.: National Public Radio
Wesson, Michael: WTOP Radio
West, Megan: Hearst-Argyle Television
Westervelt, Eric: National Public Radio
Westley, Brian: APTN
White, Edward: Tribune Broadcasting
White, Douglas: ABC News
White, Jason: Newshour with Jim Lehrer
Whiteman, Doug: AP–Broadcast
Whiteside, John: Freelance
Whiteside, John P.: Freelance
Whitley, John H.: CBS News
Whitley, Walter: Fox News
Whitney, Michael: Washington Bureau News
  Service
Whittington, Christopher: NBC News
Wicai, Hillary: Marketplace Radio
Widmer, Christopher: CBS News
Wiedenbauer, Heidi: Cox Broadcasting
Wiesen, Stefan: Freelance
Wiggins, Christopher: NBC Newschannel
Wik, Snorre: NBC Newschannel
Wilcox, Yuni: Voice of America
Wilk, Sherry: C–SPAN
Wilk, Wendy: Hearst-Argyle Television
Wilkes, Douglas H.: WTTG–Fox Television
Wilkins, Tracee: WRC–TV/NBC–4
Wilkinson, Wendla: NBC News
Williams, Candace A.: Voice of America
Williams, Colleen: Fox News
Williams, David E.: CNN
Williams, Derek: WTOP Radio
Williams, Jeffrey L.: Cox Broadcasting
Williams, John Flawn: National Public Radio
Williams, John A.: Freelance
Williams, Juan: National Public Radio
Williams, Keith: WUSA–TV
Williams, Kenneth E.: CBS News
Williams, Louis A.: NBC News
Williams, Robert T: NBC News

MEMBERS ENTITLED TO ADMISSION—Continued

Williams, Steven: WTTG–Fox Television
Williams, Wendell, Metro Networks
Willingham, Dave: WJLA–TV/Newschannel 8
Willis, Judith: Newshour with Jim Lehrer
Wilmeth, Mary Dorman: NBC News
Wilner, Elizabeth: NBC News
Wilp, Christian, N–TV News Television
Wilson, Brian: Fox News
Wilson, G. Edwin: WJLA–TV/Newschannel 8
Wilson, George: Radio One
Wilson, John: AP–Broadcast
Wilson, Stephanie: WUSA–TV
Wilson, Toni: ABC News
Wilson, Traci: Sinclair Broadcasting Group
Windham, Ronald: Tribune Broadcasting
Winslow, David: AP–Broadcast
Winterhalter, Ruthann: C–SPAN
Winters, Ronald: NBC News
Winthrop, Tony: Freelance
Witte, Joel: WTTG–Fox Television
Witten, Robert: NBC News
Wittstock, Melinda: CNC/Capitol News Connection
Wixted, Kathleen: C–SPAN
Wolf, Zachary B.: ABC News
Wolfe, Lisa: WTOP Radio
Wolfe, Randy: NBC Newschannel
Wolfson, Charles: CBS News
Wolfson, Paula: Voice of America
Wolfson, Scott: WTTG–Fox Television
Wood, A. Robin: CBS News
Wood, Christopher: C–SPAN
Woodhouse, Edward: C–SPAN
Woodley, Thomas: Fox News
Woodruff, Judy: CNN
Woodward, Thom J.: National Public Radio
Wordock, Colleen: Bloomberg Television
Wordock, John: CBS Marketwatch
Wright, Dale: WJLA–TV/Newschannel 8
Wright, Kelly: Fox News
Wright, Tracey Marie: Global TV Canada
Wygal, Scott: NBC News
Xiao, Yanz; Phoenix Satellite Television
Xie, Yanmei: CNC/Capitol News Connection

Yaklyvich, Brian: CNN
Yam, Raymond: Voice of America
Yamada, Nancy M.: WUSA–TV
Yancy, Shawn: WTTG–Fox Television
Yang, Carter: CBS News
Yang, John: ABC News
Yang, Sungwon: Radio Free Asia
Yarmuth, Floyd: CNN
Yates, H. William: CBS News
Ydstie, John: National Public Radio
Ye, Mary: Radio Free Asia
Yeshi, Lobsang: Radio Free Asia
Yoon, Robert: CNN
Young, Jeffrey A.: National Public Radio/Living on Earth
Young, Jerome: CBN News
Young, Melissa: ABC News
Young, Paul: Freelance
Young, Rick: Freelance
Young, Robert Latimer: C–SPAN
Young, Saundra: CNN
Yu, Tae Kyu: Korean Broadcasting System
Yui, Hideki: NHK–Japan Broadcasting
Zaidi, Huma: NBC News
Zajko, Robert T.: Diversified Communications, Inc. (DCI)
Zalatimo, Dima: MBC–TV (Middle East Broadcasting)
Zang, Guohua: CTI–TV
Zavarce, Pedro: CNN Newsource
Zechar, David: ABC News
Zerehi, Mariam: Fox News
Zervos, Stratis: Freelance
Zhou, Zhou: Phoenix Satellite Television
Zibel, Eve: Fox News
Ziegler, Julia: WTOP Radio
Zilberstein, Shirley: CNN
Zmidzinski, Andrew: WJLA–TV/Newschannel 8
Zongker, Brett M.: AP–Broadcast
Zosso, Elizabeth: Middle East Television Network
Zumwalt, Maya: Fox News
Zwerdling, Daniel: National Public Radio

NETWORKS, STATIONS, AND SERVICES REPRESENTED

Senate Gallery 224–6421   House Gallery 225–5214

ABC NEWS—(202) 222–7700; 1717 DeSales Street, NW., Washington, DC 20036: Jeff Adams, Reem Akkad, John Allard, Marc Ambinder, Scott Anderson, Jane Aylor, Mark Banks, Gene Barrett, Jon Bascom, Sonya Crawford Bearson, Adam Belmar, Bob Bender, Robert E. Bramson, Glennwood Branche, Charles Breiterman, Sam Brooks, Henry M. Brown, David John Bull, Elizabeth Kirsch Burgess, Ian Cameron, Andrea Canning, Elizabeth D. Carden, Christopher Carlson, John Cochran, Vernon Cole, Richard Coolidge, Francine Cornish, Pam Coulter, Merrilee Cox, Robert Crawford, Max Culhane, Thomas J. D'Annibale, Jack Date, Tiffani M. Davis, Steven Densmore, Henry Disselkamp, Peter M. Doherty, Sam Donaldson, Brian Donovan, Linda D. Douglass, Jennifer Duck, Dennis Dunlavey, Richard Ehrenberg, D. Glenn Elvington, Sheila Diane Evans, Charles Finamore, Kendra Gahagan, Jon Garcia, Robert Garcia, Arthur R. Gauthier, Vanessa Gillon, Thomas Giusto, Bernard Gmiter, Stuart Gordon, Stewart Grace, William Greenwood, Laura Hadley, Stephen Hahn, Brian Hartman, William P. Hatcher, Harry B. Heywood, Ann Compton Hughes, Heidi Jensen, Fletcher Johnson, Kenneth Johnson, Akilah N. Joseph, Steve E. Joya, James F. Kane, Jonathan Karl, Eric Kerchner, David Kerley, John Knott, Monika Konrad, Stanley Lorek, Beverley C. Lumpkin, Ellsworth Lutz, Lachlan Murdoch MacNeil, Loretta Marbury, Liz Marlantes, James Martin, Jr., Michel McQueen Martin, Laura Marquez, Luis Martinez, Darraine Maxwell, Gregory W. McCown, Ari Meltzer, Avery Miller, Terence P. Moran, Geoff Morrell, Dean E. Norland, Ivan Overton, Andrea Owen, Jay E. Patterson, Judy Penniman, Michael Pickup, Richard K. Pliszak, Catherine Porter, Dennis Powell, Mary Quinn, Victor Ratner, William Redding, Talesha Reynolds, Leah Ricciuti, Corinne B. Roberts, Lauren Rogers, Carlos Rojas, Abu Bakr Roland, George Romilly, Gary Rosenberg, Howard L. Rosenberg, Jay R. Russo, Jason Ryan, George D. Sanchez, Clayton D. Sandell, Howard Schoenholtz, Frederick Sera, Joseph Serensits, Larry Shaw, Thomas Andrew Shine, Claire Shipman, Cindy Smith, Cynthia Smith, James E. Smith, Eric Speight, Robin Sproul, Lisa Stark, Steve Stefany, Jake Tapper, Amy Jo Thomas, Pierre G. Thomas, Al Douglas Turner, Elizabeth Ann Turrell, Vija Udenans, Juan Ureta, Vicki Vennell, Virginia A. Vicario, Glenn E. Weidenbosch, Douglas White, Toni Wilson, Zachary B. Wolf, John Yang, Melissa Young, David Zechar.

ABU–DHABI TELEVISION—Hany El-Konayyesi, Nezam Mahdawi.

AGDAY—(574) 631–1302; 54516 Business U.S. 31 North, South Bend, IN 46637: James P. Dugan, Philip McMartin.

ALASKA PUBLIC RADIO NETWORK—(202) 488–1961; H–321 U.S. Capitol, NW., Washington, DC 20515:Joel L. Southern.

AL–JAZEERA TV/PENINSULA—(202) 223–4230; 1627 K Street, NW, #400, Washington, DC 20006: Hebah Abdalla, Nader Abed, Eyad Aburahma, Hafez Al-Mirazi, Mohammed Alami, Heni Azzam, Charles Bellman, Christopher Campbell, Rula Dajani, Mahmoud el-Hamalawy, Michael C. Fox, Nasser Hssaini, Khaled Abdel Kareem, Ibrahim Khader, Christopher Messer, Nicholas J. Ray, Layelle Saad, Wajd Waqfi.

AMERICAN FAMILY RADIO NEWS NETWORK—(703) 378–0942; 15250 Louis Mill Drive, Chantilly, VA 20151: William T. Fancher, Fred Jackson.

AP–BROADCAST—(202) 736–9500; 1825 K Street, NW., Washington, DC 20006: Gerald Bodlander, Camille Bohannon, Carlotta L. Bradley, Christopher Chmura, Lainie Contreras, Jon Detrow, Pamela Dockins, Edward Donahue, Estelle Ebitty-Doro, Ken Ericson, Fritz Faerber, Eileen Fleming, Lauren Frayer, David J. Friar, Oscar Wells Gabriel, Jennifer Garske, Lisa Goddard, Heather Greenfield, Michael J. Hammer, Mark A. Hamrick, Michael Hempen, Wally Hindes, Brian Hoffman, Derrill Holly, Michael W. Kahn, Brad Kaubfeld, Steve Knight, Sandy Kozel, Steve Kuhn, Francis J. Limbach, Kathryn Loomans, Myra B. Lopez, James Ludwin, Sofia Mannos, Lisa N. Matthews, Sagar Meghani, David R. Melendy, Lisa Meyer, Martin Niland, Louis Pagan, Steven Potisk, Jacqueline D. Quinn, James D. Ray, Orla Reese, Carrie Schumaker-Shokraei, Matt Small, Mark S. Smith, Shirley O'Bryan Smith, Marjorie Stapleton, Nina X. Strass, Ed Tobias, Lauren H. Vicary, Andrew G. Visleyk, Den Vohar, Michael Weinfeld, Doug Whiteman, John Wilson, David Winslow, Brett M. Zongker.

APTN—(202) 736–9598; 1825 K Street, NW., Suite 800, Washington,DC20006: Waleed Al-Moajil, Khaldoun Alrawi, Tracy Ann Brown, Flora Charner, Gail Connor, Daniel D'Amico, Kelly Daschle, Waiel Elnour, David Falcone, Adrian Fullwood, Suzanne Yee Gaffney, Atef Gawad, Richard Gentilo, Lawrence Gold, James W. Gorman, Robert Gutnikoff, Susan Henderson, Eugenio Hernandez, Dan Huff, Kristine Kelleher, Christian Kettlewell, Christina Marie Mursa, Hakan Ozsancak, Walter Ratliff, Tucker Reals, Thomas Ritchie, Michael Rosenfelder, Jason Scharf, Daniel Shedrick, Gus Valcarrel, Denise Vance, Brian Walker, Brian Westley.

NETWORKS, STATIONS, AND SERVICES REPRESENTED—Continued

ARD GERMAN RADIO NDR/WDR—(202) 298–6535; 3132 M Street, NW., Washington, DC 20007: Tom Buhrow, Diana Robbins, Carsten Schmiester, Georg Schwarte, Linda Staude, Mario Wittke.

ARTE TV—(202) 297–3651; 2000 M Street, NW., Suite 305,Washington, DC20033: M. Philippe Gassot.

AUDIO VIDEO NEWS—(703) 354–6795; 2622 Stanford Circle,Falls Church, VA 22041.

AUSTRALIAN BROADCASTING CORPORATION—(202) 466–8575; 2000 M Street, NW., Suite 660, Washington, DC 20036: Timothy Bates, Jill Colgan, Woodrow Landay, Jason D. Racki, Leigh Sales, John Shovelan, Janet E. Silver, Mark Simkin, Dan Sweetapple.

AUSTRIAN RADIO ORF—(202) 822–9570; 1206 Eton Court, NW., Washington, DC 20007: Raimund Loew, Fabio Polly, Douglas Robinson, Graham Scott, Hanno Settele, Lauren Silva-Pinto.

AZTECA AMERICA—(202) 419–6134;1919 M Street, NW., 2nd Floor,Washington, DC 20036: Stephanie, Guiloff, Armando, Guzman, Roberto Guzman, Edwing Lopez.

BBC—(202) 223–2050; 2030 M Street, NW., #350, Washington, DC 20036: Kevin Anderson, Jonathan Beale, Sharon Blanchet, Adam Brookes, Vanessa Buschschluter, Stuart Cohen, Maxine Collins, James Coomarasamy, Lesley Curwen, Matthew Davis, Sofia Diarra, George Edmonds, Joan Mazer Field, Catherine Meade Harris, Rozalia Hristova, Allen McGreevy, Elizabeth P. Miller, Claudia Milne, Peter Murtaugh, Mark Rabbage, Diana Ray, Sarah Robbins, Joseph Sallette, Ronald M. Skeans, Ted Tait, Martin Turner, Justin Webb, Paul Werdel.

BBC POLISH SECTION—(202) 841–3291; 400 North Capitol Street, NW.,Washington, DC 20001: Barbara Terlecka.

BELGIAN RADIO AND TV/VRT—(202) 466–8793; 2000 M Street, NW., #365,Washington, DC 20036: Charles Groenhuijsen.

BELO CAPITAL BUREAU—(202) 661–8400; 1325 G Street, NW., Suite 250,Washington, DC 20005: Thomas Ackerman, Mark Angelini, Al Banegas, Sharon Bender, Norman Butler, David M. Cassidy, David Duitch, Jim Fry, Michael Goldfein, Michael Kornely, Mark A. Lindesay, Robert Michaud, George P.Rodrigue, Lara Sabo, Phillip Smith, John M. Sumrell, Janne Syrjanen.

BERNS BUREAU—(202) 314–5165; SDG–36 Dirksen Senate Office Building, P.O. Box 2939, Washington, DC 20013: Matthew D. Kaye.

BET NIGHTLY NEWS—(202) 783–0537; 400 North Capitol Street, NW., Suite 361,Washington, DC 20001: Monique Conrad, Pamela J. Gentry, Mark Mazariegos, Andre Showell, Tiffany Tate.

BET.COM: Joe Davidson.

BLOOMBERG RADIO (WBBR)—(202) 624–1933;1399 New York Avenue, 11th Floor, Washington, DC 20005: Sophie R. Caronello, Robert Press, William Small, Vicki VanArsdale, Joe Winski.

BLOOMBERG TELEVISION—(202) 624–1820; 1399 New York Avenue, 11th Floor, Washington,DC 20005: Joseph Bellard, Irwin Chapman, Linda Chung, Peter Cook, Bianca Davie, Steve Geimann, Walter Little, Eduardo Londres, Roland Morrisette, Jeff Rahmati, Amy Rosen, Julie Slattery, Tim Stang, Martin G. Turner, Joe Winski, Colleen Wordock.

BROADCASTING CORPORATION OF CHINA—(703) 691–0091; 9328 Branchside Lane, Fairfax, VA 22031: Nike Chang.

BTV–BALKAN NEWS CORP—(703) 907–6800; 307 Yoakum Parkway, #305,Alexandria, VA 22304.

CADENA COPE (SPAIN)—(202) 686–1982; 4904 Belt Road, NW.,Washington, DC 20016: Blanca Maria Pol.

CAPITOL NEWS CONNECTION—(202) 479–4004; c/o WHUT TV, 2222 4th Street, NW., Washington, DC 20059:Max Cacas, Melinda Wittstock.

CAPITOL PULSE—(202) 454–5285; 209 Pennsylvania Avenue, SE., #207/600, Washington, DC 20003: Ross Bell.

CARACOL TV—(202) 419–6061; 1919 M Street, NW., 2nd Floor, Washington, DC 20036: Viviana Avila, Dario Patino.

CATALUNA RADIO—(202) 686–6558; 3001 Veazey Terrace, NW., #116,Washington, DC 20008: Jaume Peral, Ignasi Abad Serra.

CATALUNA TV/TV3—(202) 785–0580; 1620 I Street, NW., #150,Washington, DC 20006: Eva Artesona, Salvador Sala.

CBC—(202) 383–2900; 529 14 & F Street, NW., Washington, DC 20045:Genevieve Ast, Anyck Beraud, Jennifer Brown, Sara Brunetti, Marcel Calfat, Henry Champ, Michael Colton, Louis de Guise, David Halton, Rosa Hwang, Frank Koller, Bertin LeBlanc, William Loucks, Neil MacDonald, Brian Malloy, Joyce Napier, Yves Peltier, Gilles Plante, Gregory Reaume, Sylvain Richard, Christine St. Pierre, Stephanie Tremblay.

CBN NEWS—(202) 833–2707; 1111 19th Street, NW., #100, Washington, DC 20036: Michael Anthony, Steven Autrey, David Brody, Melissa A. Charbonneau, Brian Edwards, Mark B. Hendricks, Patrick L. Henry, Dayna-Marie Miles Jackson, John Jessup, Matthew Keedy, David Page, Laura Robertson, Michael Schaff, Paul L. Strand, Valerie Wack, Jerome Young.

CBS MARKETWATCH—(202) 824–0573; 529 14th Street, NW., Washington,DC: Joe Mathieu, John Wordock.

CBS NEWS—(202) 457–4444; 2020 M Street, NW., Washington, DC 20036: Thomas Albano, Clinton N. Alexander, Karyn Anthony, Wyatt Andrews, Howard Arenstein, Thalia Assuras, Sharyl Attkisson,

NETWORKS, STATIONS, AND SERVICES REPRESENTED—Continued

Barry Bagnato, Ashley Anne Baird, Benneh Bangura, Bruce Barr, Kia Baskerville, Diane Beasley, Farrel Becker, Regina M. Becker, Mark R. Bennett, Gloria Borger, Penny Britell, Kristi Brown, Andrea Bruce, Traci L. Caldwell,James Canty, David Caravello, Anthony Cavin, Denise Cetta, Steven Chaggaris, Joie Chen, Jane S. Chick, George Christian, Alfred Colby, Caroline Cooper, Paul H. Corum, John Crum, Pham Gia Cuong, John Daly, V. Allison Davis, Charlie Dawson, Charles H. Dixson, Lois Dyer, John L. Fantacone, Michael Faulkner, John E. Frado, Hal E. Furman, Tony Furlow, Brian Fuss, Robert J. Fuss, Pamela J. Gentry, Karen Gilmour, Benson Ginsburg, Jeff Scott Goldman, Neil Grasso, David Gross, Joshua D. Gross, Joel Gwadz, Mary Hager, Mark Hanner, Predi-Reko Harmon, Susan Bullard Harmon, Robert Hendin, Deirdre Hester, Dennis Jamison, Obin Johnson, Jeffrey Johnston, Mark Katkov, Craig Katz, Douglas Kiker, Mark Knoller, Stephanie Lambidakis, Donald A. Lee, Janet Leissner, Denise Li, Jonathan Lien, Matthew Lowe, Dotty Lynch, Peter Maer, Michael Marriott, Alexandra Mathers, Thomas A. Mattesky, Ronald H. Matthews, Steven Marshall, David Martin, Max McClellan, James McGlinchy, Michael McGuire, Robert McKinley, Jill Rosenbaum Meyer, Richard Meyer, Katharine Mountcastle, John Murphy, John Nolen,Jennifer Cohen Oko, K. Robert Orr, Lauren Peck, Michael Peterson, Rebecca Peterson, Michael Peyton, William Plante, Luther Posey, Diana Quinn, Carrie Rabin, Daniel Raviv, Francisco Robbins, Susan Roberts, John Robertson, Kelly Rockwell, Karen Saint-Rossy, Susan Ruth Rucci, Roxanne Russell, Eric Salzman, Bob Schieffer, Thomas H. Seem, Gregory Shaffir, Kimberlee Shaffir, Dennis Shannon, Samantha Shenk, Chris Sheridan, Aleen Sirgany, Ward C. Sloane, Richard H. Spire, David E. Stanford, James D. Stewart, Gabriel Stix, Fernando J. Suarez, Allyson Ross Taylor, Evelyn Thomas, Thomas E. Tillman, Peter C. Traynham, Andres P. Triay, Dan D. Tutman, Victor Ulloa, William Walker, Mary E. Walsh, Craig Warner, Erick Washington, John H. Whitley, Christopher Widmer, Kenneth E. Williams, Charles Wolfson, A. Robin Wood, Carter Yang, H. William Yates.
CBS RADIO—Rugiero Miliano, William H. Pimble.
CENTER FOR INVESTIGATIVE REPORTING—(202) 637–8885; 529 14th Street, NW., #837,Washington, DC 20015.
CHANNEL ONE NEWS—(202) 296–5937; 1825 K Street, NW., #501,Washington, DC 20006: James Crawford, Sharon McGill.
CLEAR CHANNEL COMMUNICATIONS—(301) 255–4399; 1801 Rockville Pike, 6th Floor,Rockville, MD 20852: Bennett Zier.
CMI TELEVISION (COLOMBIA)—(571) 337–7500; Diagonal 22A N 43–65,Bogota, Columbia: Yamit Ahmad Ruiz.
CNBC—(202) 467–5400; 1025 Connecticut Avenue, NW., Washington, DC 20036: James T. Connor, Plummer Crawley, Matthew Cuddy, Karen L. James, Alan S. Murray, Diana Olick, Hampton Pearson, Pat Pugliese, Robert Reynolds, Ashley Stringer, Xuan Thai.
CNC—CAPITOL NEWS CONNECTION—Max Cacas, Heather Dahl, Susan Jackson, Caitlyn Kim, Mark McDonald, Jill Morrison, Chad Pergram, Benjamin H. Shaw, Laura Strickler, Brian Sussman, Joanna Roufa Welch, Melinda Wittstock, Yanmei Xie.
CNN—(202) 898–7670; 820 First Street, NE., Washington,DC 20002:Khalil Abdallah, William Alberter, Kate Albright-Hanna, Kelli Arena, Stephen Bach, Craig Baker, Michael A. Bannigan, James Barnett, Ted Barrett, Caitlin Barry, Elizabeth Belanger, John Bena, Pamela S. Benson, Thomas Bentz, Kathy Benz, Laura Bernardini, Barbara Berti, John Bisney, John Bodnar, Kevin Bohn, David Bohrman, Joshua S. Braun, Claire Brinberg, Ray Britch, Rebecca Brittain, Craig A. Broffman, Ashley Huffman Brulle, Melanie Buck, Jennifer Burch, Matthew Byrne, Juan E. Cabral, Silvio Carrillo, Damian Catanza, David Keith Catrett, Bethany Chamberland, Marina Chase, Trish Chicca, Jocelyn Christensen, Bobby Clemons (America), Megan Clifford, Woodrow Compton, Paul S. Courson, Benjamin Coyte, Carol A. Cratty, Karla Crosswhite-Chigbue,Candy Crowley, John Cunha, Emily A. D'Alberto, Mousumi Das, Michael R.M. David, Derek Davis, Kristin Davis, Patrick A.Davis, David de Sola, Anastasia Diakides, Geoffrey Dietrich, Erika Dimmler, Stephen Dolce, Martin Dougherty, Megan Duke, John Dunaway, Thomas Dunlavey, Lisa Durham, Carlton Downer, Kareen Wynter Dyson, Edie Emery, Adiam Eyasu, Kathryn Farrell, Christy Feig, Sam Feist, Eric JamesFiegel, Craig Fingar, Robley Fletcher, Liz Flynn, Thomas Foreman, Robert Franken, Terry Frieden, Timothy C. Garraty, Mara Gassman, Ben Geldon, Maurice George, Sean Gibbons, Evan Glass, Heather Goldman, Karina Gomes, David Gracey, James Graydon, Thomas Greene, Rex Grigg, Eddie S. Gross, Jr., Mike Haan, Hunter Hackett, Thomas Hannon, Arthur Hardy, Jeremy Harlan, Lanese Harris, Guerin Hays, Ronald G. Helm, Ed Henry, Joseph Hickey Benjamin F. Hill, Conrad Hirzel, Julie Hofler, Sarah B. Holland, Matthew Hoye, Christian Hudson, Shirley Hung, Charles Hurley, Nicole Jackson, Lesa Jansen, NuNu Japaridze, David Jenkins, Joseph Johns, Kyle Johnsen, Sasha Johnson, Pamela Kelley, Christopher Kenny, Charley Keyes, Worth Kinlaw, George P. Kinney, Adilson Kiyasu, James Knott, Kathleen Koch, Beth Anne Kotatori, Stephanie Kotuby, Robert S. Kovach, Gary Krakower, Ronald Kuczynski, Myron A. Leake, Hilary Lefebvre, Adam Levine, Molly Levinson, Frances L. Lewine, Aaron T. Lewis, Kim Linden, Philip Littleton, Willie A. Lora, Kathryn Lynch, Vito Maggiolo, Michael Maltas, Mark Anthony Marchione, Sandra Martinez, Timothy McCaughan, Kerith McFadden, William McGraw, Denise McIntosh, Michael McManus, Samuel J. McMichael IV, Melissa McNamara, William Mears, John

NETWORKS, STATIONS, AND SERVICES REPRESENTED—Continued

Mercurio, Jeanne Meserve, Edward Metzger, Peter Mohen, Jeremy Moorhead, Peter Morris, Rick Morse, Bruce Morton, Thomas Murphy, Deborah Nelson, Suzanne Nelson, Virginia Nicolaidis, Ernest G. Nocciolo, Kerry Ogata, Andre Parker, Robert Geoffrey Parker, Sital S. Patel, Aaron C. Payne, Nathan Payne, Alysia Pearson, Bryan Pearson, Susan Pettit, Jordan Placie, Stephen Pless, Michael Poley, Elaine Quijano, Elizabeth Ray, Stuart S. Redisch, Justine Redman, Jean R. Renaud, Greg Robertson, David Robinson, Laura Robinson, Janet Rodriguez, Brian Rokus, Alissa Rooney, H. Michael Roselli, Rachel Rosen, Jessica Rosgaard, Lindy Royce, David W. Ruff, Diane Ruggiero, David A. Russell, Emily Rust, Stephen Samaniego, Jose G. Santos, Douglas N. Schantz, Kristine Schantz, David Scherer, Barry C. Schlegel, Reginald G. Selma, Erin Sermeus, Lawrence Shaughnessy, Sarah Shepherd, Shawna Shepherd, Joann Sierra, Jeffery Simms, Kathy Slobogin, Matthew Speiser, Eleanor Spektor, Jim Spellman, Philip Scott Spoerry, Jonathan St. John, Kenneth Stanford, Paul Steinhauser, Julian Styles, Sherrell Swanier, Lisa Sylvester, Abbi Tatton, Erik Tavcar, Pilar Tejerina, David J. Theall, James B. Thomas III, Jerry Thompson, Lisa Thompson, William Tipper, Brian Todd Steve Turnham, Brett Tyler, Kim Uhl, Richard J. Uliano, Kenya S. Ulmer, Anthony R. Umrani, Laurie Ure, Juliette Vallese, Fernando Vega, Tu H. Vu, Darius Walker, Deirdre Walsh, Hunter Waters, Michael Watts, David E. Williams, Judy Woodruff, Brian Yaklyvich, Floyd Yarmuth, Robert Yoon, Saundra Young, Shirley Zilberstein.

CNN RADIO—(202) 515–2229; 820 First Street, NE., Washington, DC 20002.

CNN/TVS—(202) 898–7670; 820 First Street, NW., Washington, DC 20002: John B. Simons, Lisa Manes.

CNSNEWS.COM—(703) 683–9733; 325 South Patrick Street, Alexandria, VA 22314: Scott Hogenson.

CONNECTLIVE—Michael Lessin.

COPE RADIO—Juan Martinez Fierro.

COURT TV (METRO TELEPRODUCTIONS)—(202) 828–0366; 1400 East-West Highway, #628, Silver Spring, MD 20910: Dave Lilling.

COX BROADCASTING—(202) 777–7000; 400 North Capitol Street, NW., #750, Washington, DC 20001: Lindsey Arent, Alison Burns, David Chase, Jamie Dupree, Molette Green, Ryan Jackson, Kevin Johnson, Brigette Langmade, Michael Majchrowitz, Carolyn Presutti, Zelda Wallace, Heidi Wiedenbauer, Jeffrey L. Williams.

C–SPAN—(202) 737–3220; 400 North Capitol Street, NW., #650, Washington, DC 20001: Kenneth Alexander, Thomas Alldredge, Manuel Alvarez, Todd Baham, Michelle Bailor, Brett Betsill, Michael Biddle, Michael Brannock, Paul Brown, Susan J. Bundock, Leslie Burdick, James Burke, Nancy Calo-Christian, Yang Cao, Craig Caplan, Leslie Capstick, Michael Cavaiola, Tanya Chattman, James Clark, Josh Cohen, Eloise Collingwood, Bruce Collins, William Conover, Abigail Conway, James L. Cook, Liam Currier, Alexander Curtis, Greg Czzowitz, Matthew Dauchess, Deborah Davenport, Constance Doebele, Kenneth Dyball, Pedro L. Echevarria, Ronald Eisenbarth, Gary Ellenwood, Seth Engel, Greg Fabic, Mark Farkas, Richard Fleeson, Tom Fortenberry, Carl Foster, William Frazier, Rick Gabala, John Garlock, Garney Gary, Ari Goldberg, Robert Gould, Richard Hall, Eric Hansen, Chris Hanson, Stephen Harkness, Robb Harleston, Maurice Haynes, William Heffley, Jonelle P. Henry, Douglas Heyman, Dallas Hill, Leta Hix, Robert Hoffmaster, Michael Holden, George Howell, Roger Hunter, Jennifer Imdorf, Roberta Jackson, Taryn Jackson, Katherine Jeffries, Afrika Bell Kathuria, Barry Katz, Steven Kehoe, Jonathan Kelley, Robert Kennedy, Roxane Kerr, Lew Ketcham, Kevin King, Felix Laboy, Brian P. Lamb, Darren Larade, Molly Laville, Robert Lazar, Paul Loeschke, David Luck, Mark Lindblom, Charles Logan, David Knighton, Jose Maranho, Valerie Matthews, Michael McCann, Sean McCann, Kate McCarthy, Gerard McGarrity, Bradley McGuire, Seeno Merobshoev, Theresa Michel, Andrew P. Miller, Kate Mills, Thomas Mock, Jennifer Moire, David Monack, Garrette Moore, Linwood Moore, Bridget Morrison, Dan Morton, Kathy Murphy, Terence Murphy, Andrew Murray, Andrew Nason, Donna Norris, Benjamin O'Connell, Maikel O'Hanlon, Paul Orgel, Kyneesha Parham, Michael Patruznick, Vernon Perkins, Andrea Perry, Elizabeth Pfotzer, Paul Pickett, Maura Pierce, Nickolas Pitocco, Almon Porter, Christina Porter, Taylor Porter, Deidre Potter, Anne Preloh, Tony Pronko, Nikhil Raval, John Christophe Ray, Kankali Reddy, James Regan, Robert Reilly, David Ridgeway, Amy Roach, Martine Rodriguez, Tracy Ruby, Frederico Sampaio, Sherry Sanders-Smith, Michele Sandiford, Mary Scanlon, William Scanlan, John Scheuer, Ellen Schweiger, Steven Scully, Sima Shah, James E. Sides, Tiffany Silver, Gary Simpson, Peter Slen, James Slone, Alan Speck, Robert Spence, Eric Stepney, Norman Stewart, Rick Stoddard, Matthew Stoner, David Storper, Jason Surbey, Susan M. Swain, Molly Sanders, Kristi Slafka, Gregory St. James, Kelly Tagliaferri, Brian Taylor, Joseph Teeples, James Thompson, Eric Thoman, Arthur Tiller, Brandon Tilman, Annie Tin, Emmanuel Touhey, Corey Tutt, Keith Warehime, Kevin Washburn, Richard Weinstein, Sherry Wilk, Ruthann Winterhalter, Kathleen Wixted, Christopher Wood, Edward Woodhouse, Robert Latimer Young.

CTI–TV (TAIWAN)—(202) 331–9110; 1825 K Street, NW., #716, Washington, DC 20006: Chia-Lu Hsia, Guohua Zang.

CTV–CANADIAN TELEVISION—(202) 466–3595; 2000 M Street, NW., #330, Washington, DC 20036: Stephane Brisson, Tom Clark, Alan Fryer, Jana Juginovic, Jared Kindestin, Jim MacDonald, Joy Malbon, Kathleen Monk.

NETWORKS, STATIONS, AND SERVICES REPRESENTED—Continued

DANISH BROADCASTING CORPORATION—(202) 785–1597; 2000 M Street, NW., #870,Washington, DC 20036: Kyle Lanningham, Kim Lassen, Hans Stadsing, Grethe Winther.

DEUTSCHE PRESS AGENCY—(202) 662–1220; 969 14th Street, NW., Washington, DC 20045: Christina Eck, Herbert Winkler.

DEUTSCHE WELLE TV—(703) 931–6644; 2000 M Street, NW., #335,Washington, DC 20036: Stephan Bachenheimer, Hillery Gallasch, Ruediger Lentz, Daniel Scheschkewitz.

DEUTSCHLAND RADIO—(703) 917–1561; 7420 Georgetown Court,McLean, VA 22102: Siegrfried Buschschluter.

DISPATCH BROADCAST GROUP—(202) 737–4630; 400 North Capitol Street, NW., #850, Washington, DC 20001: John J. Cardenas, Michael J.Smith, Tom Walker.

DIVERSIFIED COMMUNICATIONS, INC. (DCI)—(202) 775–4300; 2000 M Street, NW., Suite 340, Washington, DC 20036: Jay D. Alvey, James Balsamo, Robert Baumann, Theodore Carroll, Tom Fabian, Robert Fetzer, Masano Hidaka, Yoshiki Hidaka, Matthew Iverson, Chris Maylett, Kerry Meyer, Misa Rossetti-Meyer, Chanlee Saray-Yim, Terry L. Straub, Robert T. Zajko.

EAST COAST TELEVISION—(202) 775–0894; 1919 M Street, NW.,Washington, DC 20036: Brian M. Ahearn, John Michael Bruchas, Brenda Cecil, Chris Cowman, John Craig, Duane Empey, Adam R. Golau, Kathleen Gural, Cheryl Hammons, Yvonne P. Hawkins, Barry O'Donnell, James M. Sproesser.

EGYPTIAN TV—(202) 293–9371; c/o EBU Washington 2000 M Street, NW., #300, Washington, DC 20036: Hanan H. Elbadry, Tharwat Mekky.

ETTV—Yi Qiu Chen.

EUROVISION AMERICAS, INC.—(202) 293–9371; 2030 M Street, NW., #300, Washington, DC 20036: James Banks, Emilie de Schaetzen, William Dunlop, Sarah Gibbons, Marc Granena, Simon Mahoney, Adam Mandelson, Nathalie Minard, Priya Narahari, Didier Piette, Jean Pierre Roberts, Jeroen Schuiten, Matthew J. Silverstein, Peggy Soucy.

FDCH E–MEDIA, INC.—(301) 731–1728; 4100 Forbes Boulevard,Lanham, MD 20706: Ronald H. Claxton, Jeffrey Cooper, Michael Eldridge, Michael Everist, Elizabeth H. Hofstad, Gail Martin, Kimberly Ann Meyerdirk.

FEATURE STORY NEWS—(202) 296–9012; 1730 Rhode Island Avenue, NW.,Washington, DC 20036: Malcolm Brown, Julie Donnelly, Priscilla Huff, Laura Iiyama, Simon Marks, Keith Porter, Huff Priscilla.

FEDERAL NEWS SERVICE—Cheryl Reagan.

FEDNET—(202) 393–7300; 50 F Street, NW., Suite #1C, Washington,DC 20001: Keith Carney, Thomas L. Clark, Alvin Jones, Grant Kevin Lane, Rodney Lee Minor, Stephen A. Raffaelli, Jr.

FINNISH BROADCASTING COMPANY (YLE)—(202) 795–2087; 2000 M Street, NW., #890, Washington, DC 20036: Hans-Peter Dhuy, Benita Enqvist, Petri Sarvamaa, Olli-PekkaSulasma.

FORMOSA TV—(202) 775–8112; 1825 K Street, NW., #6F, Washington, DC 20006: Dr. Stephen Chang, Chen-Fang Tina Chung.

FOX NEWS CHANNEL—(202) 824–6369; 400 North Capitol Street, NW., Washington, DC 20001: Gregory E. Ahlquist, Abigail K. Alcott, James L. Angle, Robert Armfield, Julie Asher, Bret Baier, Les Baker, Katy Ballenger, Dennis Baltimore, Christopher Barnes, Stuart Basinger, Bruce Becker, Varuna Bhatia, Sarah Blumberg, Bryan Boughton, Didier Bourgeois, Megan Bovim, John Brandt, Fletcher Bransford, Edgar Brown, Jr., Aaron Bruns, Carl Cameron, Steve Carlson, Michael Carpel, Mone Sha Carter, Walter Carter, Jr., Steve Centanni, Kelly Chernenkoff, Richard A. Cockerham, Bryan Cole, Eric Colimore, Eric Conner, Mitch Davis, Wendy Dawson, Debra DeFrank, Mary Pat Dennert, Andrea DeVito, Richard DiBella, Brian Doherty, Megan Dumpe, Jerry Echols, Danaj Edmond, James W. Eldridge, Mike Emanuel, Mark Finch, Alexander Y. Finland, Justin Fishel, Kurt Foster, George J. Fridrich, David Futrowsky, Dan Gallo, Major Garrett, Jake Gibson, Wendell Goler, Gregg L. Gursky, Gavin Gibbons, Fred Haberstick, Brian Haefeli, Greg Headen, Mary Janne Henneberg, Sarah Herndon, Catherine Herridge, Stacy Hickman, Stephen Hirsh, Molly Hooper, Adrienne Moira Hopkins, Cory R. Howard, Richard Howell, Brit Hume, Kim Hume, Rhonda J. Jenkins, William G. Jenkins, Richard Johnson, Torrance Jones, Daniela Kelley, Megyn Kendall, Philip Kersey, Grigory Khananayev, Mary Kreinbihl, Stephanie Kwisnek, Donna Lacey, Philip LeCroy, Michael Levine, Edward Lewis, Sharon Kehnemui Liss, Catherine Loper, Wayne Lowman, Brigitte Lyles, Michael Lyon, Laurie Luhn, Tracey Madorma, Michael Marno, Tina Marie Martinez, Frank McCaffrey, Kevin McClam, George McCloskey, Anne McGinn, Lila Merideth, Michael Miller, Jim Mills, Seleena M. Muhammad, James Nelson, Reena Ninan, Michele Novy, P. Andrew Och, Quillie Odom, Dominique Pastre, Bradford S. Paxton, Shana Pearlman, Anna Persky, Jacqueline Pham, Michele Remillard, David Renken, Elizabeth Rhodes, Anne Marie Riha, Corbett Riner, Michael Robbins, Querry Robinson, Douglas Rohrbeck, James Rosen, Lee Ross, Marty Ryan, Sarah Santer, Craig Savage, Jason Scanlon, James R. Schule, Teri Schultz, Paul Schur, Christina Shand, Steve Shelton, Mandi Shifflet, Caroline Shively, Courtney Wells Shott, David Shott, Anita Siegfriedt, Nick Simeone, Ashley Smith, Heather Smith, Tony Snow, Teresa Spector, Daniel J. Stay, Matthew Stout, Patrick Summers, Greta Van Susteren, Christina Svolopoulos, George Szucs, Mary Ellen Tasillo, Bert Thomas, Ande Torgerson, Robert Torpey, Patricia Turner, Ellen Uchimiya, Bryce Vinson, Todd Visioli, Kelley Beaucar Vlahos, Amit Vyas, Chris Wallace, John L. Wallace, Amy Wehinger, Carla Wendy, Walter Whitley, Colleen Williams, Brian Wilson, Thomas Woodley, Kelly Wright, Mariam Zerehi, Eve Zibel, Maya Zumwalt.

NETWORKS, STATIONS, AND SERVICES REPRESENTED—Continued

FRANCE 2 TELEVISION—(202) 833–1818; 2030 M Street, NW., Washington, DC 20036: Etienne Leenhardt.

FREE SPEECH RADIO NEWS—(212) 209–2811; 1929 MLK Jr. Way, #73,Berkeley, CA 94704: Josh Chaffin, Ingrid Drake, Jennifer L. Johnson, Kata Mester.

FRENCH TELEVISION TF1—(202) 342–0466; 3331 Dent Place, NW., Washington, DC 20007: Bertrand Aguirre, Jean-Pascal Azais, Loick Berrou, Helene Davieaud, Sylvie Deroche, Bruce Frankel, Andree-Lyne Jacques, Remi Cadoret-Manier, Vincent Mortreux.

FUJI TELEVISION—(202) 347–1600; 529 14th Street, NW., #330, Washington, DC 20045: Peter Gold, Shin Kazama, Toshiyuki Matsuyama, Matthew Mosley, Yoshio Ninoseki, Setsu Nishiumi, Nicholas Szecheny.

GERMAN BROADCASTING SYSTEMS–ARD—(202) 944–5290; 1200 Eton Court, NW., #100, Washington, DC 20007: Hans-Peter Reise, Christian Gramsch, Gunnar Schultz-Burkel.

GERMAN PUBLIC RADIO–ARD—(202) 625–6203; 1200 Eton Court, NW., #200, Washington, DC 20007: Hannelore Jones, Arthur Landwehr, Martin Wagner.

GERMAN TELEVISION AGENCY—(202) 393–7571; 529 14th Street, NW., #1199, Washington, DC 20045: Roger Horne, Helmut Keiser.

GERMAN TELEVISION N24/SAT 1—(202) 331–7883; 1620 I Street, NW., Washington, DC 20006.

GERMAN TELEVISION–ARD—(202) 298–6535; 3132 M Street, NW., Washington, DC 20007: Christine Adelhardt, Thorsten Bachmann, Thomas Berbner, Herta Borniger, Tom Buhrow, Edward Castner, Silvia Charpa, Stephan Fiedler, Uwe Geleschun, Roland Hanka, Sonia Mayr, Christiane Meier, Linh Ong, Hans-Peter Reise, Thea Rosenbaum, Stefan Scheuer, Norbert Tinnefeld.

GERMAN TELEVISION–ZDF—(202) 333–3909; 1077 31st Street, NW., Washington, DC 20007: Kirsten Candia, Manuel Ernst, Kristin Foellmer-Suchorski, Ruben Herrera, Georg Juenger, Alice Kelley, Kay Lendzian, Wolfgang Macholz, Ursula Marquardt, Claudia Offermann, Eberhard Piltz, Steffanie Riess, Hildrun Rowe, Claudia Anke Rueggeberg, Elke Tucker, Thomas Walde.

GLOBAL TV CANADA—(202) 842–1254; 1333 H Street, NW., #500, Washington, DC 20005: Kimberly Halkett, Carl Hanlon, William Montague, Troy Reeb, Jeffrey Lynn Saffelle, Tracey Marie Wright.

HAMILTON PRODUCTIONS—(703) 734–5444; 7732 Georgetown Pike, McLean, VA 22102: Anne H. Deger, Jay Hamilton, John Hamilton.

HDA PICTURES, INC./ORBITE—(202) 332–9019; 2231 California Street, NW., #301, Washington, DC 20008: Freelance Org.

HEARST–ARGYLE TELEVISION—(202) 457–0220; 1825 K Street, NW., #720, Washington, DC 20006: William T. Aldridge, Traci Mitchell Austin, Soyini Canton, Meredith Gunning, Jennifer Hitchcock, Steven C. Jacobi, Sally F. Kidd, Laura Kinney, Erin T. McManamon, Rebecca Moser, Douglas Perkins, Jessica Rinne, William B. Smith, Megan West, Wendy Wilk.

HEDRICK SMITH PRODUCTIONS/FRONTLINE—(301) 654–9848; 6935 Wisconsin Avenue, #208, Chevy Chase, MD 20815: Hedrick Smith, Mike Sullivan.

HELLENIC BROADCAST CORPORATION (ERT)—(202) 223–5423; 4201 Massachusetts Avenue, NW., #A249C, Washington, DC 20016: Dimitrios Amperiadis, Dimitrios Apokis.

HISPANIC RADIO NETWORK—(202) 637–8800; 740 National Press Building, Washington, DC 20045: Pablo R. de Oliveira, Julio Gonzalez, Karina Hurley, Jeff Kline, Mercy Padilla-Cirino, Silvana Quiroz, Alison Rodden, Jeff Santos.

INDEPENDENT TELEVISION NEWS (ITN)—(202) 429–9080; 400 North Capitol Street, NW., Suite 899, Washington, DC 20001: Alexander Anstey, Dai Baker, Michaela T. Byrne, Luke Collinson, Ian Glover-James, Robert Moore, Keme Nzerem, Jonathan A. Rugman, David Sampy, Chris Shlemon.

INTERFAITH VOICES—Josephine Reed.

IRISH RADIO AND TELEVISION (RTE)—(202) 223–7989; 2030 M Street, NW., 5th Floor, Washington, DC 20036: Harvey Cofske, Carole Coleman, Heather Dorf-Dolce, Robert Shortt.

ISRAEL ARMY RADIO/GALEI–TZAHAL—(301) 622–1591; 112 Shaw Avenue, Silver Spring, MD 20904: Drora Perl.

ISRAEL TELEVISION AND RADIO—(202) 331–2859; 1620 I Street, NW., Washington, DC 20006: Yaron Deckel, Yaniv Dorenbush.

KGO RADIO—Ivan Scott.

KOMO–TV—(202) 265–3229; 1317 Rhode Island Avenue, NW., #201, Washington, DC 20005: Timothy Hillard, Robert Throndsen.

KOREAN BROADCASTING SYSTEM—Min Kyungwook, Joong Wan Lee, Kwang Chool Lee, Sun Jae Lee, Tae Kyu Yu.

KTUU–TV—(202) 661–0065; 400 North Capitol Street, NW., Washington, DC 20001: Seth Litzenblatt, Rene Lopez, Steve MacDonald.

LEBANESE BROADCASTING CORP—(202) 783–5544; 529 14th Street, NW., #1185, Washington, DC 20045.

LIVING ON EARTH—(617) 868–8810; 8 Story Street, Cambridge, MA 02138–4956: Christopher Ballman, Jeffrey A. Young.

MARKETPLACE RADIO—(202) 223–6699; 1333 H Street, NW., Suite 1200 West, Washington, DC 20005: John Dimsdale, William Kistner, Scott Tong, Hillary Wicai, JJ Yore.

NETWORKS, STATIONS, AND SERVICES REPRESENTED—Continued

MBC–TV (MIDDLE EAST BROADCAST CENTER)—(202) 898–8047; 1510 H Street, NW., #B2, Washington, DC 20005: Lukman Ahmed, Talal Al-Haj, Babu Aryankalayil, Nadia Charters, Aziz Fahmy Farag, Danny Farkas, Christopher B. Hamilton, Balajia Kanawati, Abdel Kareem Khader, Richard Y. Melhem, W. Harrison Moore, Luis Munoz, Sharief Salih, Muna Shikaki, Dima Zalatimo, Elizabeth Zosso.

MBC–TV KOREA (MUNHWA)—(202) 347–4147; 529 14th Street, NW., #1131, Washington, DC 20045: Chang Young Choi, Myung-Ghil Choi, Annabel Kim, Young Hoe Ku, Jai Hong Kwon, Jae Gu Shim, Jae Yong Yoo.

MEDILL NEWS SERVICE—(202) 347–8700; 1325 G Street, NW., Washington, DC 20005: Mary Coffman, Ben Harper, Sharon Kornely.

METRO NETWORKS—(301) 718–4949 5454 Wisconsin Avenue, Chevy Chase, MD 20815: Kelly Clendenon, John Irving, Gene Kuleta, Terrence Moore, Mike Ross, Wendell Williams.

MIDDLE EAST TELEVISION NETWORK (ALHURRA)—(703) 852–9174; 7600 Boston Blvd., Suite 100 Springfield, VA 22153: Rana Abtar, Daoud Abuelhawa, Larissa Aoun, Hisham Bourar, Moufac Harb, Elizabeth MacKay, John Mueller, Mohamed Nassar, James F. Norris, Fausto Ramon, Jr., Vatche Sarkisian.

MOBILE VIDEO SERVICES—(202) 331–8882; 1620 I Street, NW., #1000, Washington, DC 20006: Nic Beery, Howard Collender, William Griffitts, Joseph Holtschneider, Robert H. Milford, Joaquim Neto, Alexander Papadopoulos, Peter Rosenbaum, Todd M. Swain, Lawrence VanderVeen.

MSNBC/NBC NEWS—(202) 884–4210; 4001 Nebraska Avenue, NW., Washington, DC 20001: Brady Daniels, Brock Meeks, Robert Merrill.

MTV3 (FINLAND)—(202) 364–2880; 6144 Utah Avenue, NW., Washington, DC20015: Heikki Piuhola.

N–TV NEWS TELEVISION—Markus Meier, Christian Wilp.

NATIONAL PUBLIC RADIO—(202) 414–2000; 635 Massachusetts Avenue, NW., Washington, DC 20001: Stacey Abbott, Larry Abramson, Reena Advani, Nubar Alexanian, David Argentieri, Brendan Banaszak, Emily Barocas, Elizabeth Blair, Amy N. Blaszyk, Melissa Block, Nell Boyce, Tom Bullock, Ivan Burketh, Barbara Campbell, Lisa Chow, Theodore E. Clark, Felix J. Contreras, Leslie Cook, William C. Craven, Mary (Bebe) Crouse, Michael Cullen, Nerissa Daniels, Rebecca Davis, Brian DeMar, Steven Drummond, Robert Duncan, Hugh M. Eaton, Neal Ellis, Ronald Elving, Susan Feeney, Pamela Fessler, David B. Folkenflik, Langfitt Frank, Jeffrey K. Freymann-Weyr, Gregory Gavin, Benjamin Gilbert, Peggy Girshman, Tom Gjelten, Juan Carlos Gomez, Don Gonyea, Susan Goodwin, Gisele Grayson, David Greene, Barbara Bradley Hagerty, Jonathan Hamilton, Cheryl Hampton, Richard Harris, Anne Hawke, Jordana Hochman, Johney Burke Hunn, Steve Inskeep, Andrea Jackson-Gewirtz, Brian David Jarboe, Helena Johnson-McNeely, Kimberly Jones, Rachel Jones, Christopher Joyce, Sheilah A. Kast, John C. Keator, Michele Kelemen, Mary Louise Kelly, Justine Kenin, David Kestenbaum, Beverly Kirk, Terrence Knight, Martin R. Kurcias, Kevin D. Langley, Arthur Laurent, Russell Lehman, Libby Lewis, David Aram Malakoff, Nancy Marshall, Matthew D. Martinez, Charles Mayer, Petra Mayer, William McQuay, William T. Mebane, Hannah Misol, Parris Morgan, Lowell Muse, Muthoni Muturi, Brian Naylor, Lynn Neary, Joe R. Neel, Christopher Nelson, Michele Norris, Jackie Northam, Victoria O'Hara, Lizzie O'Leary, Quinn O'Toole, Peter Overby, Joe Palca, Marisa Penaloza, Snigdha Prakash, Richard Howell Rarey, Andrew Reynolds, Jeffrey Rosenberg, Ken Rudin, Stuart Rushfield, Claudio Sanchez, Setsuko Sato, Kathleen Schalch, Didrik Schonche, Michael Schweppe, Andrea Seabrook, Joseph Shapiro, Cathy Shaw, Elizabeth Shogren, Daniel Shukhin, Robert C. Siegel, Joanne Silberner, Ari Silverman, Graham Smith, Cal R. Southworth, John C. Speer, Susan L. Stamberg, Simone Steverson, Evie Stone, Laura Sullivan, Virginia L. Sullivan, Jeffrey Sutherland, Jr., David Sweeney, Gerald W. Tennent, Neil David Tevault, Sharahn Thomas, Charles Thompson, Nina Totenberg, Neda Ulzby, Anna Vigran, Tracy Wahl, Kevin Wait, Walter Ray Watson, Andrew M. Watts, David Welna, Linda C. Wertheimer, Eric Westervelt, John Flawn Williams, Juan Williams, Thom J. Woodward, John Ydstie, Daniel Zwerdling.

NATIONAL SCENE NEWS—(202) 898–7670; 1718 M Street, NW., #333 Washington, DC 20036: Askia Muhammad.

NATIVE AMERICAN TELEVISION—(571) 218–8277; 444 North Capitol Street, NW., Washington, DC 20001: Larry Adams, Robert Cohencious, Richard DiMassimo, Michael Dunkley, Randolph Flood, Larry Leeds, Michael Nephew, James R. Prior.

NBC NEWS—(202) 885–4210; 4001 Nebraska Avenue, NW., Washington,DC 20016: Douglas A. Adams, Maria Afsharian, Shujaat Ali, Patrick G.Anastasi, Jeannie Ohm Andress, Nelson Archer, Percy Arrington, Kenneth L. Austin, Rodney Batten, Khepera Batties, Gary Glenn Beall, Michael Benetato, Jacques Benjoar, Regina Blackburn, Jay Blackman, Sarah Blackwill, Victoria Blooston, Jeffrey Blount, Joseph Bohannon, John D. Boyd, Anthony Capra, Ashley J. Cesarano, Major Coleman, Kevin Corke, Thomas Costello, Brady G. Daniels, Sharia Davis, Alyssa Delafield, Richard E. Dodson, Christopher Donovan, Geoffrey C. Doyle, Rich Dubroff, Victoria Duncan, Melissa Dunlop, Barbara Fant, Douglas Farnum, Robert Faw, Matthew Fields, Sheldon Fielman, Elizabeth Fischer, David Forman, Scott Foster, Wilfred Fraser, Jr., Lawrence Gaetano, Jamie Gangel, Gina Garcia, Richard Gardella, William A. Gebhardt, Michelle Germany, Frank L. Gibson, Jr., Edward Gorsky, Erin Green, James M. Greene, David

NETWORKS, STATIONS, AND SERVICES REPRESENTED—Continued

Gregory, Marsha Groome, Andrew F. Gross, Sylvia Haller, Harold Paul Hayley, Jr., Alan Harvey, Emily Herman, Ricardo Higgins, John F. Holland, Jeffrey K. Horne, Matthew A. Hosford, Salim I. Ishaq, Michelle Jaconi, Alicia Jennings, Leroy Johnson, Gwyneth Jones, Rosiland Jordan, Hans P. Juergens, Christopher C. Joyce, Allison Kaminsky, Ryan Kiernan, Marc Koslow, Michael J. Kosnar, Thaddeus Kresse, Lester A. Kretman, Courtney Kube, Tamara Kupperman, Robert E. Kur, Susan A. LaSalla, Margaret Lehrman, Elizabeth Leist, John Libretto, Arthur Lien, Lydia Lively, Joseph W. Loebach, James V. Long, David L. Lurch, Jr., Lessandra MacHamer, Fred Malone, Yolanda McCutchen, Karen McKinley, Carroll Ann Mears, Martinez Mebane, James Miklaszewski, Richard Minner, Andrea Mitchell, Shannon Scott Mizell, Lester Moses, Mark Murray, Lisa M. Myers, Jason W. Neal, Jeffrey Nelson, Elizabeth Nevins, Kelly O'Donnell, Norah O'Donnell, Faith Okpotor, Douglas S. Pasternak, Michelle Perry, William Petras, Debra Pettit, Katharine Pitra, James K. Popkin, Alonzo Ray, Chip Reid, Alan Rice, A. Christine Egy Rose, Raymond Rose, Aram Roston, Johnie F. Roth, Timothy Russert, John H. Rutherford, Howard Sacks, Maia T. Samuel, Jose A. Sanfuentes, Aaron Sasson, Max Schindler, Christopher Scholl, Carmine Scicchitano, Wesley Scruggs, Carl V. Sears, Joel Seidman, Joseph Shalhoup, Kimberly Sneed, Kenneth Strickland, Leigh Sutherland, Ronald Thornton, Renee Turner, Allan Van Horn, Michael J.Viqueira, Susan Vitorovich, David Vukmer, David Weakly, Christopher Whittington, Wendla Wilkinson, Louis A. Williams, Robert T. Williams, Mary Dorman Wilmeth, Elizabeth Wilner, Ronald Winters, Robert Witten, Scott Wygal, Huma Zaidi.

NBC NEWSCHANNEL—(202) 783–2615; 400 North Capitol Street, NW., #850, Washington, DC 20001: Cesar A. Canizales, Cynthia Conatser, Sheila Conlin, H. Estel Dillon, Nancy Ellard, Sheri Lynn Gibson, William Glynn, Andrew Louis Godsick, Adam Greenbaum, Steve Handelsman, James Hurt, Jay Hurt, Julie Jarvis, Virginia Kreindler, Richard McDermott, Nicole McManus, Brian Mooar, Steven Muskat, Tom Newberry, Mike O'Connell, Tracie Potts, Bonnie Rollins, Brooke Hart Salkoff, Cecil John Sills, Todd Sutton, Nick Thompson, Matthew Tureck, Christopher Wiggins, Snorre Wik, Randy Wolfe.

NEED TO KNOW NEWS—Dennis Moore.

NEWSHOUR WITH JIM LEHRER—(703) 998–2170; 2700 S. Quincy Street, #250, Arlington, VA 22206: Anne Davenport Anderson, Lorna Baldwin, Carl Ballard, Emily Birr, Jeffrey Brown, Terence Burlij, David Butterworth, Elizabeth Callan, Lete M. Childs, Sarah Clune, David Coles, Alexis Cox, Lester M. Crystal, Anne Davenport, Antoinette Dean, Susan Dentzer, Bridget DeSimone, Laura Dine, Larisa Epatko, Molly Farrell, Brian Gottlieb, Elizabeth Harper, Monique Hayes, Kwame Holman, Gwen Ifill, Shermaze Ingram, Murrey Jacobson, Georgette Knuckles, Jim Lehrer, Diane Lincoln, Tony Lucas, Jason Manning, Kathleen McCleery, Michael K. Melia, Annette L. Miller, Susan L. Mills, Michael D. Mosettig, Kristina Nwazota, Jennifer Lynn O'Shea, Timothy Perry, Margaret Robinson, Karin Rotchford, Daniel Sagalyn, Michael Saltz, Anne Schleicher, Linda J. Scott, Diane Silver, David C. Sit, Terence Smith, Rafael A. Suarez, Elizabeth Summers, Kenneth Taylor, Samara Thery, Renu Thomas, Morgan Till, James Trengrove, Adrienne Urbina, Margaret Warner, Jason White, Judith Willis.

NHK–JAPAN BROADCASTING—(202) 828–5180; 2030 M Street, NW., #706, Washington, DC 20036: Sylvain Coudoux, Seiki Hara, Kaori Iida, Atsushi Kato, Lisa Lane, Masami Musha, Mari Ono, Yusuke Takahashi, Harue Teshima, Ryuichi Teshima, Hideki Yui.

NIGHTLY BUSINESS REPORT—(202) 682–9029; 1325 G Street, NW., Washington, DC 20045: Stephanie Dhue, Darren Gersh, Dana Greenspon, Christopher Norris, Ervin Washington.

NIPPON TV NETWORK—(202) 638–0890; 529 14th Street, NW., #400, Washington, DC 20045: Takaaki Abe, Mina Ichikawa, Aya Imaida, Fumihiko Kure, Keiichi Sato, Andrew Sawka, Kenji Teranishi, Ai Tilman.

NORWEGIAN BROADCASTING CORPORATION—(202) 785–1460; 2030 M Street, NW., #700, Washington, DC 20036: Jan Espen Kruse, Joar Hoel Larsen, Grethe Winther.

NOS DUTCH PUBLIC BROADCASTING—(202) 466–8793; 2000 M Street, NW., #365, Washington, DC 20036: Yohan Depoortere, Charles Groenhuijsen, Wouter Kurpershoek, Ron Linker, Marjan Moolenaar, Hans van den Nieuwendijk, Tim Overdiek.

N–TV NEWS TELEVISION—(202) 393–7571; 1919 M Street, NW., #258, Washington, DC 20036: Markus Foderl.

ORBITE TELEVISION, INC.—Hugues-Denver Akassy.

PACIFICA RADIO—(202) 588–0999; 2390 Champlain Street, NW., Washington, DC 20001.

PENTAGON CHANNEL—(202) 428–0480; 601 N. Fairfax Street, Suite 370, AlexandriaVA 22314: Paul M Waldrop.

PHOENIX SATELLITE TELEVISION—(703) 920–6558; 400 North Capitol Street, NW., #550, Washington, DC 20001: Nai Chian Katz, Jing Wei, Yan Xiao, Zhou Zhou.

POTOMAC RADIO NEWS—(202) 484–0447; 3130 Wisconsin Avenue, #519, Washington, DC 20016: Josh Carothers, Michael J. Duncan.

POTOMAC TELEVISION—(202) 783–8000; 529 14th Street, NW., #480, Washington, DC 20045: Jim Boothby, Daniel Burton, Paul M. Crosariol, Nicole Garner, Walter T.S. Greenaway, Jamie Norins, Ryan Primmer, Mike Ryan.

NETWORKS, STATIONS, AND SERVICES REPRESENTED—Continued

PRINCE GEORGE'S COMMUNITY TELEVISION—(301) 773–0900; 9475 Lottsford Road, Largo, MD 20774: Maniko Barthelemy, Curtis Crutchfield, Patricia Villone Garcia, David Goldman, Ara Laughlin, Ian McAllister, Jerome Rivers, Torri Silver.
PRO PLUS (SLOVENIA)—Natasa Briski.
PUBLIC AFFAIRS TELEVISION (BILL MOYERS)—(212) 560–8600; 450 West 33rd Street, 7th Floor, New York, NY 10001: Sally Roy.
RADIO–TV—Gail Davis, Olga Ramirez Kornacki.
RADIO BILINGUE—(202) 234–0280; 1420 N Street, NW., #101, Washington, DC 20005: Maria Erana.
RADIO FRANCE—(202) 965–1327; 4512 Q Lane, NW.,Washington, DC 20007: Claude L. Porsella, Laura D. Simon, Ann Toulouse.
RADIO FREE ASIA—(202) 530–4999; 2025 M Street, NW., #300, Washington, DC 20036: Jaehoon Ahn, David Bach, Marsha J. Barnhart, David Beasley, Bhungyal Bhungyal, Huidong Cao, Lobsang Chophel, Thao Dao, Dawa Dolma, Rigdhen Dolma, Karma Dorjee, Richard Finney, Teddy Fung, Dhondup Namgyal Gonsar, King Man Ho, Laura Huang, Hassan Kasem, Yonho Kim, Vivian Kwan, Chun Bon Lai, Hiumei Lau, Daniel N. Lee, Dong Hyuk Lee, Jinhee Lee, Kyu Lee, Yue Li, Xiao Qiang Liao, Ted Liu, Cideng Liushar, Kalden Lodoe, Lucy Lu, Tseten Namgyal, Louise Ng, An Nguyen, Bich-Ha Nguyen, Dien M. Nguyen, Harry Lee Scott, Chakmo Tso, Ngo Toai, Nadia Usaeva, Yau Wang, Sungwon Yang, Mary Ye, Lobsang Yeshi.
RADIO FREE EUROPE—(202) 457–6930; 1201 Connecticut Avenue, NW., 11th Floor, Washington, DC 20036: Frank T. Csongos, Allan Davydov, Robert McMahon, Andrew Tully.
RADIO MARTI—Diana Molineaux.
RADIO ONE—(301) 429–2673; 5900 Princess Garden Parkway, Lanham, MD20706: Mike Abrams, LaFontaine Oliver, Ron Thompson, George Wilson.
RADIO VALERA VENEZUELA—Sonia Schott.
RCN–TV (COLOMBIA)—(202) 572–0389; 1825 K Street, NW., #501, Washington, DC 20006: Rocio Arias.
REGIONAL NEWS NETWORK (RNN)—(202) 347–7631; 400 North Capitol Street, #775, Washington, DC 20001: Richard French, Katelynn R. Metz, Jeff Santos.
RELIGION & ETHICS NEWSWEEKLY—(202) 216–2384; 1333 H Street, NW., 6th Floor, Washington, DC 20005: Arnold Labaton, Kim Lawton, Judy Reynolds, Noelle Serper.
REUTERS TELEVISION—(202) 898–0056; 1333 H Street, NW., 6th Floor, Washington, DC 20045: Keith Allen, Victor Antonie, Peter Bullock, Andrea Clarke, John Clarke, Kevin Fogarty, Peter Fox, Ben Gruber, Kia Johnson, Justin Kenny, Predrag Kojovic, Lisa Lewnes, Deborah Lutterbeck, Ian MacSpadden, Tipp K. McClure, Robert Muir, Gershon Peaks, Steven Phillips, Bryan Rager, Roger Shull, George Tamerlani, Scott Vaughan.
ROMANIAN RADIO—(202) 625–6284; 2519 39th Street, NW., #102, Washington, DC 20007: Dan Santa.
ROMANIAN TELEVISION—(202) 248–7140; 2511 Q Street, NW., #201, Washington, DC 20007: Lucian Sarb.
ROWE NEWS SERVICE—(301) 977–6252; 922 Beacon Sqr. Ct., #324, Gaithersburg, MD 20878.
RTP PORTUGUESE PUBLIC TELEVISION—(202) 775–2969; 1120 G Street, NW., Washington, DC 20005: Pedro Bicudo.
RTV SLOVENIJA—(703) 845–8171; 1462 South Greenmount Drive, #107, Alexandria, VA 22311: Vladimir Kara-Murza, Vladimir Sergueev, Tanja Staric.
RUSSIAN STATE TV AND RADIO (RTR)—(202) 298–5748; 2650 Wisconsin Avenue, NW., Washington, DC 20007: Eugene Poskounov.
RUSTAVI–2 BROADCASTING COMPANY—David Nikuradze.
SAGARMATHA TELEVISION—(703) 926–9530; P.O. Box 12272, Burke, VA 22009: Ram C. Kharel.
SBS RADIO (AUSTRALIA)—(202) 452–5552; 4808 Arburis Avenue, Rockville, MD 20853: Mike Kellerman.
SEOUL BROADCASTING SYSTEM—Young Joo Chang, Hyun Duk Chung, In Koo Huh, Sung Joon Kim.
SINCLAIR BROADCAST GROUP—(202) 293–1092; 1620 I Street, Washington, DC: Christine Bennett,Michael Broleman, Brandi Chavis, Stephanie Davis, Joe DeFeo, Jennifer Gladstone, Alison Kosik Goltzman, Donald Hammond, Morris Jones, Ashley Kellogg-Wheeler, Timothy Knapp, Lyle Wayne Mills, Jody Weldon, Traci Wilson.
SKY NEWS—(202) 864–6583; #550, North Capitol Street, Washington, DC 20001: Ian Woods.
SLOVAK RADIO—(202) 244–4971; 4418 35th Street, NW., Washington, DC20008.
SRN NEWS (SALEM)—(703) 528–6213; 1901 N. Morse Street, #201, Arlington, VA 22209: Garry Beausoleil, George Bonzagni, Jennifer Borrasso, Gregory Clugston, Jeff Crites, William Davis, Phil Fleischman, Linda Kenyon, John Lormand, Andrea Mikus, Janet Parshall, Sam Parshall, Evan Sonderegger, Ronald Stafford, Andrew Stewart, Kyria Timmons.
STATELINE.ORG—(202) 339–6146; 1101 30th Street, NW., #301, Washington, DC 20007: Gene Gibbons, Kathleen Hunter, Eric Kelderman, Kathleen Murphy, Kavan Peterson, Barbara Rosewicz.
SWEDISH TELEVISION—(202) 785–1956; 2030 M Street, NW., Washington,DC 20036: Stefan Asberg, Leif Carlsson, Lisa Carlsson.

NETWORKS, STATIONS, AND SERVICES REPRESENTED—Continued

SWISS BROADCASTING—(202) 293–7477; 2030 M Street, NW., Washington, DC20036: Pierre Bavaud, Michele Galfetti, Rudolf Maeder, Marco Nilsson, Julie Noce, Fritz Reimann, Alessio Veronelli, Francoise Weilhammer.

TAIWAN TELEVISION—(202) 223–6642; 1825 K Street, #717, Washington,DC20006: Shu-Ling Chen, Min Lee.

TALK RADIO NEWS SERVICE—(202) 337–8715; 2514 Mill Road, NW., Washington, DC 20007: Jay Byrne, Cholene Espinoza, Lovisa Frost, Gregory A. Gorman, Elia Herman, Micah Johnson, Victoria Jones, Richard F. Miller, Ellen Ratner, Gareth Schweitzer, Adam Sharon, Myron Sponder, Jay Tamboli, Wendy Wang.

TECH TV—(202) 783–0095; 400 North Capitol Street, NW., #775, Washington, DC 20001: Peter Barnes.

TELEMUNDO NETWORK—(202) 737–7830; 400 North Capitol Street, NW., Washington, DC 20001: Maria Aspiazu, Pedro Correa, Pablo Gato, Lilliam Martinez-Bustos, Lori Montenegro, Wingel G. Pinzon, Max Ramirez, Victor Reyes, Viktor Reyes.

TELEVISA NEWS NETWORK (ECO)—(202) 714–8446; 1825 K Street, NW., #718, Washington, DC 20006: Gregorio Meraz, Hector Montaut.

TELEVISION NACIONAL DE CHILE (TVN)—(202) 483–2392; 2407 15th Street, NW., #410, Washington, DC 20009: Ralf Oberti.

THE WASHINGTON BUREAU—(202) 347–6396; 400 North Capitol Street, NW., #775, Washington, DC 20001: Rhydwyn Davies, Mercedes Eldridge,John Getter, Joseph Loomis, Marshall D. Merritt II, Joseph Nelson, Russell Nohelty, Julia Rockler, Robbie B. Snow, Ira Sockowitz, Melissa A. Thompson, C. Patrick Thorne, Richard Tillery, Michael Whitney.

TO THE CONTRARY (PERSEPHONE PRODUCTIONS)—(202) 973–2066; 1825 K Street, NW., 9th Floor, Washington, DC 20006: Alika Codispoti, Bonnie Erbe, Joy Fowlin, Paul Malkie, Cari Stein.

TRIBUNE BROADCASTING—(202) 824–8444; 1325 G Street, NW., #200, Washington, DC 20005: Cynthia L. Aitken, Gregory Aspery, Cissy Baker, Richard Chamberlain, Caroline J. Comport, Thomas Coughlin, Derek Danilko, Jason M. Dorn, Sabrina Fang Farley, Gregg K. Hamlin, Thomas Kolodziejczak, Matthew Murray, Christopher Novack, R. Grant Rampy, Sonja Deaner Schulken, Ronald Windham, Edward White, Thomas Sileo.

TV ASAHI—(202) 347–2933; 529 14th Street, NW., #670, Washington,DC 20045: Robert H. Gentry, Hitoshi Inoue, Shingo Ishida, Kazuhiko Ota, Ena Suto, Tadashi Tabata.

TV AZTECA—(703) 927–4664; 3800 Dade Drive, Annandale, VA 22003: Amada Castanon.

TV TOKYO—(202) 638–0441; 1333 H Street, NW., Washington, DC 20005: Katsumi Hino, Shigenori Kanehira, Kaoru Kokufuda, Atsushi Kyodo, Michael Lavallee, Eric Weiner, Ayako Mie, Yuko Miyake, Masanobu Murai, Mika Otsuka, Andrew Schlosberg, Masaaki Shimada.

TV2–DENMARK—(202) 828–4555; 2030 M Street, NW., #506, Washington, DC 20036: Charlotte Ernst, Scott Rensberger, Allan Silberbrandt.

TV2–NORWAY—(202) 466–7505; 2000 M Street, NW., #380, Washington, DC 20036: Gerhard Helskog, Var Staude.

TVBS—(202) 310–5449; 1333 H Street, NW., 5th Floor, Washington, DC 20007: Che-Wei Shih, Shih Yuan Tuan.

T.V.E.–SPANISH PUBLIC TELEVISION—Anna Bosch, Carmelo Machin, Xavier Roca, Eduardo Rodriguez, Anna Ubeda.

TVN Poland—Katarzyna Slawinska.

UNITED NEWS AND INFORMATION—(410) 778–4148; 754 S. Bayview Drive, Chestertown, MD 20620: Dennis Crowley, Jonathan Decker, Sharon Gotkin.

UNIVISION NEWS—(202) 682–6160; 101 Constitution Ave., NW., #810, East Washington, DC 20001: Jorge Contreras, Deborah Durham, Marco Granda, Maria Rosa Lucchini, Lourdes Meluza, Norma Montenegro, Fernando Pizarro, Edwin Ramirez, Raul Ramos, Pablo Sanchez, Mario Vizcarra.

USA RADIO NETWORK—(972) 484–3900; 2290 Springlake Road, Dallas, TX75234: Jonathan P. Decker.

USA TODAY LIVE—(703) 854–7610; 7950 Jones Branch Drive, McLean, VA 22108: Lauren Ashburn, Victor Blandburg, Kellyanne E. Dignan, William Harding, Ginger Gadsden, Richard Moore.

VENEZUELAN TELEVISION—Esther M. Gentile.

VENTANA PRODUCTIONS—(202) 785–7155; 1825 K Street, NW., 5th Floor, Washington, DC 20006: Richard Feather.

VIDEO NEWS SERVICE—(202) 393–3604; 1825 K Street, NW., #900, Washington, DC 20006: Alejandro Harding, Thanh Hoai, Stephen Tomko, Joe Tomko.

VIEWPOINT COMMUNICATIONS—(301) 565–1650; 8607 Second Avenue, #402, Silver Spring, MD 20910: William Donald, Randy Feldman, Benjamin Finkel, Larry Greenblatt, Steve Hamberg, Robert Shire, Austin Steo.

VOICE OF AMERICA—(202) 619–2412; 330 Independence Avenue, SW., Washington, DC 20547: Niharika Acharya, Adriana Ahmad, M. Anis Ahmed, Darrell Allen, Jaroslaw Anders, Vedran Andonovski, Faraj Ardalan, Mary Arobaga-Reardon, James Bertelmann, Deborah Block, Jane Bojadzievski, Jonathan D. Brandkamp, Mike Bromberger, Jerome Brown, Meredith S. Buel, Ronald Cesar, Enoch Chan, Robert Cole, Michael J. Collins, Jeffery Daugherty, Avi Davidi, Penny Dixon-Gumm, Jerry R. Earnest,

NETWORKS, STATIONS, AND SERVICES REPRESENTED—Continued

Ali B. Farhoodi, Parichehr Farzam, Hector Federico, Leta Hong Fincher, Craig Fitzpatrick, Joseph Gallagher, Valer Gergely, William Henry Greenback, Esther Githui, Abdul Wahar Hadi, Stephanie J. Ho, Joseph L.R. Hopkins, Gary M. Jaffe, Syed Jafri, Douglas Johnson, Amy D. Katz, Lilica Kitanovska, Ivana Kuhar, Rohit N. Kulkarni, Libo Liu, Vincent Makori, James Malone, Jeffrey Wendell Means, Abdul Rauf Mehrpore, Russell James Mitchell, Irawan Nugroho, Zulima Palacio, Serena Ravenel Parker, Suzanne Presto, John D. Quinn, Robert Raffaele, Syed Ziaur Rahman, Jim Randle, Daniel Robinson, Sayed S. Shah, Chris Simkins, Paul Sisco, June Soh, Sandra Bechan Stavisky, James Stevenson, Deborah Tate, Jeffrey T. Tofani, Mohammad R. Vakili, Julija Velkovska, Yuni Wilcox, Candace A. Williams, Paula Wolfson, Raymond Yam.

VOYAGE PRODUCTIONS—(202) 276–2848; 1825 K Street, NW., #501, Washington, DC 20006: Susan Baumel.

WAMU–FM—(202) 885–1200; 4000 Brandywine Street, NW., Washington, DC 20016: Kevin Beesley, Susan Goodman, Sarah Hughes, Danielle Karson, Samuel Litzinger, Lisa Nurnberger, Sidsel Overgaard, Jennifer Strong.

WASHINGTON BUREAU NEWS SERVICE—(202) 544–4800; 230 Princess Garden Parkway, #230, Lanham, MD 20706: Mike Eldridge, Mike Whitney.

WASHINGTON CHINESE TELEVISION—Bing Li, Wei-Ming Liu.

WASHINGTON NEWS NETWORK—(202) 628–4000; 400 North Capitol Street, NW., #650, Washington, DC 20001: Neil Alpert, Alan Cohn, Micah Johnson, Nan Hee McMinn, David Oziel, Icarus N. (Ike) Pappas, Adrianna Roome, Michael Seium.

WASHINGTON RADIO & PRESS SERVICE—(301) 229–2576; 6702 Pawtucket Road, Bethesda, MD 20817: Hanna Gutmann.

WBAL–TV—(410) 467–3000; 3800 Hooper Avenue, Baltimore, MD 21211: Margaret Cronan, Timothy Matkosky.

WEST VIRGINIA PUBLIC BROADCASTING—(304) 876–9313; P.O. Box 3210, Shepherdstown, WV 25443: Cecelia Mason.

WETA–TV—(703) 998–1800; 3620 S. 27th Street, Arlington, VA 22206: Lynn Quarles Allison, William Barber, Timothy Bowen, Donald Brawner, Joseph Buckingham, Joseph Camp, John Christophe Cardon, Martin Carr, Julius Dumarr Fauntleroy, Frank Fitzmaurice, David Gillette, Eileen Griffin, Stephen Howard, John Hyater, Charles Ide, Gregory King, Christopher Lane, Mary Lawrence, Edward Lee, Jerry S. Lewis, Robert Ludwig, Michael Mayes, Donald McClurkin, Nancy Gerstman Morgan, John C. Nash, Chuck Nixon, Alan Perlmeter, Jeffrey Rathner, Mark Robbins, Willliam Seabrook, Darwin Silver, Randal Stanley, Sampath Vasa, Charles Voth.

WGN RADIO/U.S. FARM REPORT—(301) 942–1996; 9915 Hillridge Drive, Kensington, MD 20895: Patrick B. Haggerty, Orion Samuelson.

WJLA–TV/NEWSCHANNEL 8—(703) 236–9480; 1100 Wilson Boulevard, Arlington, VA 22209: Jason Bacon, Frank K. Becker, Bradley Bell, Alan Matthew Brock, Karen E. Brown, Melissa Brown, Maureen Bunyan, Zeke Changuris, James Church, Rebecca J. Cooper, Walter Crawford, Gordon Davis, Bruce DePuyt, Martin C. Doane, Lauren Dunn, Andre Dunston, Jamie L. Foster, Michael Forcucci, Sam Ford, Kathy Fowler, Elliott Francis, Eric Freeland, Pege Gilgannon, John Gonzalez, Miles Grant, Richard Guastadisegni, Stephen Hackett, Michael E. Hagerty, Peter Hakel, Sabrina Hall, John Hamilton, Leon Harris, John R. Harter, Horace Holmes, Brian Hopkins, Thomas Hormuth, LaTanya E. Horne, Winston Hylton, Katherine Jackson, Irene Johnson, Suzanne Kennedy, Nikole Killion, Christianne Klein, Vanessa M. Koolhof, Jay Korff, Greta Kreuz, Gabriel LeMay, H. Ming Leong, John B. Lewis, Alexander Likowski, John D. Lisle, Bill Lord, Dave Lucas, Jonathon Mann, Kathleen Matthews, Andrea McCarren, Rebecca McDevitt, Kathryn McGriff, Douglas McKelway, Buchanan Michael, Jay Mishkin, Melissa Mollet, Andrew Nyland, Kyle Osborne, Aru Pande, Alisa Parenti, Sarah Lee Park, Julie Parker, Daniel Patrick, Gail Pennybacker, Gordon Peterson, Christopher Plater, Stephen Pozniak, Richard Reeve, Brian M. Reid, Malissa Reyes, Leslie Cook Rhode, Nathan Roberts, Jeff Rose, Joseph Rose, Michael Rudd, Ian Rushing, Angela Russell, Kathleen R. Rynn, F. Kevin Schultze, Holly Shannon, Shelley A. Simpson, Scott D. Smith, Rebecca Miller Spicer, Angela B. Starke, Alison Starling, Abraham Stubblefield, Michael R. Vaughn, Vincent Vaughan, James William Walker, Tarik Warner, David Allen Webb, Dave Willingham, G. Edwin Wilson, Melanie Hastings Wotring, Dale Wright, Stephen Tschida, Andrew Zmidzinski.

WMAL RADIO—(202) 686–3020; 4400 Jenifer Street, NW., Washington, DC 20015: Pat Brogan.

WORLDNET TELEVISION—(202) 401–8272; 330 Independence Avenue, SW., Washington, DC 20547.

WPFW–FM—(202) 797–1482; 2390 Champlain Street, NW., Washington,DC 20009: Gloria Minott, Tony Regusters.

WPWC–AM (RADIO FIESTA)—(703) 494–0100; 14416 Jefferson Davis Hwy., #20, Woodbridge, VA 22191: Carlos Aragon.

WRC–TV/NBC–4—(202) 885–4111; 400 Nebraska Avenue, NW., Washington, DC 20016: James M. Adams, Jay Alvey, Katherine Banks, Jackie Bensen, Charles Bragale, Shannon D. Bream, Larry Bullard, Arch Campbell, Julie Carey, Sean Casey, Pat Collins, Elizabeth Crenshaw, Tony Dorsey, Edward Durkin, Elizabeth Feldman, Michael Francis Flynn, James M. Forrest, Doreen Gentzler, Matt Glassman,

NETWORKS, STATIONS, AND SERVICES REPRESENTED—Continued

Charles A. Goodknight, Chris Herbert Gordon, John K. Greenwood, James Handly, Ira John Hudson, Philip H. Jacobs, Ede R. Jermin, Susan M. Kidd, James S. Kizer, Joe Krebs, Ronald Leidelmeyer, Robert Long, Anthony S. Lopez-Isa, Megan McGrath, Patrick T. McKenna, Michelle M. Michael, Pat Lawson Muse, Jeff Napshin, James J. Neustadt, Michael O'Regan, Chester Panzer, Wendy Rieger, Murray H. Schweitzer, Tom Sherwood, Milton T. Shockley, Bill Starks, Jamie Stone, Donald Stumpo, Michael Swann, Robert Sweeney, Luis Urbina, Erin Van der Bellen, Jim Vance, Jane Watrel, Tracee Wilkins.

WTOP RADIO—(202) 895–5060; 3400 Idaho Avenue, NW., Washington,DC 20016: Shawn Anderson, Neal Augenstein, Paul Brandus, Melvin Chase, I-Fang Chen, Sara D'Angelo, Richard Day, Barton Eckert, Gary Froseth, Jessie J. Green, Nathaniel Hager, Jack Hicks, Colleen Kelleher, Maria Leaf, Kristi King Lilleston, Dave McConnell, Mike McMearty, Ira Mellman, Adrienne Metil, Mitchell Miller, Amy Morris, Brian Oliger, Sharon Rae Pettigrew, Mark Plotkin, Robert Publicover, Art Rose, Mark Segraves, Jeffrey Seldin, Hank Silverberg, Patrick Spence, Adam Tuss, Michael Wesson, Derek Williams, Lisa Wolfe, Julia Ziegler.

WTOP2 (FEDERAL NEWS RADIO)—(202) 895–5086; 3400 Idaho Avenue, NW., Washington, DC 20016: Marlis Majerus, Lisa Wolfe.

WTTG–FOX TELEVISION—(202) 895–3000; 5151 Wisconsin Avenue, NW., Washington, DC 20016: Melanie Alnwick, Jeffrey Andrew, Jeffrey Ballou, Bob Barnard, Denley Barnette, Gary Bender, Elisa Berkowitz, Michael P. Berry, Brian Bolter, Daryl Brown, Paul Buehler, Charles Carson, Carlos Castro, Roby Chavez, Steve Chenevey, Holley Coil, Anthony Colella, Patricia Corcoran, Stephen Davies-Williams, Patricia DiCarlo, Michell Doell, Carolyn Dolcimascolo, Laura Evans, Joseph Feeney, Michael Fischoff, Tom Fitzgerald, B.J. Forte, John Foundas, John Frame, Matt Gaffney, Michael Gargiulo, Max Giammetta, Jeff Gilman, Carlos Alberto Gonzalez, Peter P. Greer, Michael Hafer, Craig J. Harrington, John Henrehan, Carlos E. Hernandez, Jill Sorenson Hooven, Michael Horan, Karen Gray Houston, Lance Ing, Virg Jacques, Sheila Jaskot, Lyrone Steven Jones, Nelson Jones, Nathalie Joost, Donald Kearly, Ira Lazernik, Elisabeth Leamy, Craig Little, Sherri Ly, Elizabeth Mancini, Michael Marantz, Wisdom Martin, Lark McCarthy, Sean McGarvy, Patrick McGrath, Lorna McGuire, Holly Morris, Karen Meyers, Richard D. Murphy, Beth Parker, Gurvir Dhindsa Phillips, Roz Plater, Rena Popp, Shannon Powell, Michael Rickard, F. David Rysak, Mark Sargent, Allison Seymour, Robert Shon, Misty Showalter, Jason H. Smith, Joe Spevak, Donald E. Stanke, Louis Stevenson, Will Thomas, Terri Tolliver, Maureen Umeh, Paul Wagner, Duane Watkins, Don Watrud, Wendy Wilk, Douglas H. Wilkes, Steven Williams, Joel Witte, Scott Wolfson, Shawn Yancy

WUSA–TV—(202) 895–5700; 4100 Wisconsin Avenue, NW., Washington, DC 20016: Phyllis Armstrong, Audrey Barnes, James P. Beahn, Dennis Bly, Mark Bost, Bruce Bookhultz, Kurt Brooks, Aubrey Bryant, Douglas Buchanan, Anthony M. Castrilli, David Chaytor, William Clemann, Stacey Cohan, Jeffrey Cridland, Emily Cyr, Mark Dougherty, Thomas Dukehart, Samara Martin Ewing, Danielle Flanagan, Michael W. Flynn, Lesli Foster, Janet Fox, Peggy Fox, Brian Franco, Gregory Guise, Michelle Handleman, James Hash, Jacqueline Hayward, Chris Houston, Ryan Hunter, Chester Bruce Johnson, James Joslyn, Kevin G. King, William Lawlor, Bruce Leshan, Frank McDermott, Todd McDermott, Derek G. McGinty, William McKnight, Paul Monte-Bovi, Victor Murphy, James R. Nichols, Celinda Pena, Ron Peters, Karen Peterson, James Pratt, Kari Pugh, Gary Reals, Amy Repke, Janet Terry, Raul Jorge Rivero, Andrea Roane-Skehan, David Roberts, Sean L. Root, David Roycraft, Jennifer Ryan, Alija Sakota, David Satchell, Emily Schmidt-Massey, Gregory Seaby, Holly B. Sheppard, Jimmie Silman, Michael Stafford-Walter, Louis David Statter, Michael Trammell, Lauren Vance, Mike Walter, Keith Williams, Stephanie Wilson, Nancy M. Yamada.

FREELANCERS: Matt Ackland, Stuart Ammerman, Charles Anderson, John Anglim, Bruno Arena, Adrian Conrad Armwood, Martin Babington-Heina, Lantz Barbour, Eric Barreda, Stephen Bartlett, Megan Oliver Basinger, David Bentley, Erin Beverly, Tim Raymond Bintrim, Adam Blickstein, Charles Borniger Amanda Boskent-Norris, Wayne Boyd, Richard E. Breed, William Brennan, Annette Brieger, Brett Carlson, Jill Chappell, Travis Renee Chrisinger, David Cilberti, Juanita Clogston, Camille Connolly, David M. Cooke, John Cooper, Robert J. Corbey, Bob Constantini, Thomas Craca, Anthony W. Crook, Patrick J. Curran, Anna Davalos, Jennifer Davis, Michael DeMark, Gary DeMoss, Dominic DeSantis, Colin Dobbins, Maggie Dore, Jonathan Ebinger, Alicia Edwards, Alfred Scott Eisenhuth, Steve Epstein, Thomas Everly, Glenn Faigen, Al Faison, Mary Elizabeth Fay, Anne-Marie Fendrick, Bruce Ferder, Andrew Field, Michael Finnigan, Daniel Fiorito, Cesar Flores, Tom Foster, Tom Foty, Hida Fouladvand, F. Patrick French, David Friedman, Dennis Gaffney, Randall Gafner, Christian Galdabini, Michael Travis Galindo, Joshua Gallu, Martina Gauss, Philip Geyelin, Edward Giebel, John Glennon, Augusto G. Gomez, Liliana Gonzalez, Jeffrey Goodman, Lindsay Graves, Nicholas Greiner, Sean Hall, Claus Harding, Steven Harper, Roy J. Harris, John Hartge, Thomas Hass, Barry Haywood, Jens Heik, Troy Allen Hermes, Ione Hess, Hugh Hinds, Paul Hollenbeck, John Holubar, Toni Hoover, David Hopper, Ryan Huebler, James Hughes, Trudy Marie Hutcherson, Adia Jacobs, Martin Jimenez, Darryl B. Johnson, Jennifer Johnson, Rolanda Johnson, Derek Johnston, Pascal Jouffriault, Abdelhakim Kabbaj, William Kaplan, Nazira Karimi, Terence Kelly, Jonathan Kessler, Michael Kinney, Elliot Klayman, Robert Klein, Martin A. Kos, Wolfgang Kotke, David Krupin, Peter Kulsziski, Carmen Kupper, Marianna

NETWORKS, STATIONS, AND SERVICES REPRESENTED—Continued

LaFollette, Laurence Langton, Gregory Larson, Katherine Leiken, David Lent, Dexter Leong, Solomon Levine, Kevin Loftus, Malik Lomax, Jayne Lukas, Julio Luzquinos, J. Thomas Marchitto, Antonio Marques, Mai Marriott, Marc Marriott, Jeffrey Martino, Claude L. Matthews, Patrice McCannon, Dennis McCarty, Jay McCarty, Douglas McCash, Angela McCrae, Natashka Patricia McDonald, Johnny McEachin, Patty McFarland, Bob McHenry, Daniel J. McLellan, Kevin A. McManus, Michael McMullan, Alexander Milenic, Gil Miller-Muro, Steven E. Mitnick, Bryan Mong, Virginia A. Moubray, Tiffany Msonthi, Tateki Muratani, Frederick R. Murphy, Alexander Mursa, Michael Neapolitan, Anh Nguyen, Eric Niiler, Richard Norling, Gary Nurenberg, David O'Brien, Thomas W. O'Connor, Patrick O'Donnell, Daniel J. O'Shea, Krystyna Osinski, Hartmut Pauls, Scott Payne, Grant Peacock, James P. Peterson, Robert Peterson, Murray Pinczuk, Keith Plummer, Shelby Poduch, William Prasad, Richard Puckett, John J. Quinnette, Omar Quinonez, Ali Rad, R. Brian Rainey, Richard J.Reaux, Sharon Reich, Ed Reinsel, Daniel Riesser, Tyrone W. Riggs, Diane Roberts, Earle Robinson, Carl Rochelle, Peter Roof, Floyd T. Rose, Robert J. Sasek, Kathie Scarrah, Fred Schall, Terese Schlachter, Hans-Peter Schloemer, Donald Schoenmann, Ivan Scott, Sarah Scott, Leslie Sewell, Susan Shand, Harry Shoffner, David Silver, Robert Silverthorne, Ronald Simeone, Y. Sean Simmons, Paul Sisco, Paul Skomal, Charles Slie, Hedrick Smith, Gilbert Solorzano, Randall Sorenson, Darcy Spencer, Thomas Staton, Rick Suddeth, Mark E. Teboe, Editha Tendencia, Andrew Thomas, Shari Thomas, Joseph Thompson, Jr., Deborah J. Todd, George Toman, Brad Ulery, Christopher D. Vassil, Charles Walter, Gary Waxler, Aaron S. Webster, Arlene Weisskopf, George Weller, John P. Whiteside, Stefan Wiesen, John A. Williams, Tony Winthrop, Paul Young, Rick Young, Stratis Zervos.

PERIODICAL PRESS GALLERIES*

HOUSE PERIODICAL PRESS GALLERY

The Capitol, H–304, 225–2941

Director.—Robert M. Zatkowski.
Assistant Directors: Laura L. Eckart, Robert L. Stallings.

SENATE PERIODICAL PRESS GALLERY

The Capitol, S–320, 224–0265

Director.—Edward V. Pesce.
Assistant Directors: Kristyn K. Socknat, Justin Wilson.

EXECUTIVE COMMITTEE OF CORRESPONDENTS

Lorraine Woellert, Business Week, Chairman
Heidi Glenn, Tax Notes, Secretary-Treasurer
Richard E. Cohen, National Journal
Tim Curran, Roll Call
Douglas Waller, Time Magazine
Terence Samuel, U.S. News & World Report
Fawn Johnson, BNA News

RULES GOVERNING PERIODICAL PRESS GALLERIES

1. Persons eligible for admission to the Periodical Press Galleries must be bona fide resident correspondents of reputable standing, giving their chief attention to the gathering and reporting of news. They shall state in writing the names of their employers and their additional sources of earned income; and they shall declare that, while a member of the Galleries, they will not act as an agent in the prosecution of claims, and will not become engaged or assist, directly or indirectly, in any lobbying, promotion, advertising, or publicity activity intended to influence legislation or any other action of the Congress, nor any matter before any independent agency, or any department or other instrumentality of the Executive branch; and that they will not act as an agent for, or be employed by the Federal, or any State, local or foreign government or representatives thereof; and that they will not, directly or indirectly, furnish special or "insider" information intended to influence prices or for the purpose of trading on any commodity or stock exchange; and that they will not become employed, directly or indirectly, by any stock exchange, board of trade or other organization or member thereof, or brokerage house or broker engaged in the buying and selling of any security or commodity. Applications shall be submitted to the Executive Committee of the Periodical Correspondents' Association and shall be authenticated in a manner satisfactory to the Executive Committee.

2. Applicants must be employed by periodicals that regularly publish a substantial volume of news material of either general, economic, industrial, technical, cultural, or trade character. The periodical must require such Washington coverage on a continuing basis and must be owned and operated independently of any government, industry, institution, association, or lobbying organization. Applicants must also be employed by a periodical that is published for profit and is supported chiefly by advertising or by subscription, or by a periodical meeting the conditions in this paragraph but published by a nonprofit organization that, first, operates independently of any government, industry, or institution and, second, does not engage, directly or indirectly, in any lobbying or other activity intended to influence any matter before Congress or before any independent agency or any department or other instrumentality of the Executive branch. House organs are not eligible.

---

*Information is based on data furnished and edited by each respective gallery.

1010

3. Members of the families of correspondents are not entitled to the privileges of the galleries.

4. The Executive Committee may issue temporary credentials permitting the privileges of the galleries to individuals who meet the rules of eligibility but who may be on short-term assignment or temporarily residing in Washington.

5. Under the authority of rule 6 of the House of Representatives and of rule 33 of the Senate, the Periodical Galleries shall be under the control of the Executive Committee, subject to the approval and supervision of the Speaker of the House of Representatives and the Senate Committee on Rules and Administration. It shall be the duty of the Executive Committee, at its discretion, to report violations of the privileges of the galleries to the Speaker or the Senate Committee on Rules and Administration, and pending action thereon, the offending correspondent may be suspended. The committee shall be elected at the start of each Congress by members of the Periodical Correspondents' Association and shall consist of seven members with no more than one member from any one publishing organization. The committee shall elect its own officers and a majority of the committee may fill vacancies on the committee. The list in the Congressional Directory shall be a list only of members of the Periodical Correspondents' Association.

J. DENNIS HASTERT,
Speaker, House of Representatives.

TRENT LOTT,
Chairman, Senate Committee on Rules and Administration.

MEMBERS ENTITLED TO ADMISSION

PERIODICAL PRESS GALLERIES

Abramson, Julie L.: National Journal
Ackerman, Spencer: New Republic
Ackley, Kate: Roll Call
Acord, David: Food Chemical News
Adde, Nicholas L.: Army Times Publishing Co.
Addison, Eric: Career Communications Group
Adhicary, Dave: Tax Notes
Akers, Mary Ann: Roll Call
Albright, Nicole Gaudiano: Army Times Publishing Co.
Aldrich, Nancy: Business Publishers
Alexis, Alexei: BNA News
Allen, LaQuesha: Tax Notes
Allen, Tonya: CD Publications
Allizon, Marie B.: Internewsletter
Almeras, Jon S.: Tax Notes
Aluise, Beth: National News Syndicate
Aluise, Susan J.: National News Syndicate
Amber, Michelle: BNA News
Ament, Lucy: Food Chemical News
Analore, Andrew: Inside Mortgage Finance
Anand, Vineeta: Crain Communications
Anselmo, Joseph: Aviation Week
Antonides, David Scott: Tax Notes
Aplin, Donald G.: BNA News
Archer, Jeffrey Robert: Education Week
Arnold, Andrew: Business Publishers
Arnone, Michael: Federal Computer Week
Arnoult, Sandra: Penton Media Inc.
Arora, Vasantha K.: News India Times
Ashworth, Jerry: Thompson Publishing Group
Asker, James R.: Aviation Week
Assam, Cecelia: BNA News
Atkins, Pamela S.: BNA News
Atwood, John Filar: CCH Inc.
August, Lissa: Time Magazine
Ayayo, Herman P.: Tax Notes
Ayers, Carl Albert: UCG
Ayoub, Nina Cary: Chronicle of Higher Education
Bacon, Lance M.: Army Times Publishing Co.
Bacon, Jr., Perry: Time Magazine
Baghdadi, Ramsey: FDC Reports
Bailey, Holly: Newsweek
Bailey, Laura: Army Times Publishing Co.
Ballard, Tanya N.: Government Executive
Bancroft, John: Inside Mortgage Finance
Banervee, Bidisha: Slate
Barak, Sarah: Thompson Publishing Group
Barber, Jeffrey: McGraw-Hill Co.
Barnes, Fred: Weekly Standard
Barnes, James A.: National Journal

Barnes, Julian E.: U.S. News & World Report
Barnett, Megan L.: U.S. News & World Report
Barnett, Pamela: Business Publishers
Barone, Michael: U.S. News & World Report
Barreto, Eric: Washington Business Information
Barry, John A.: Newsweek
Bartlett, Thomas: Chronicle of Higher Education
Barton, Robert: Washington Business Information
Bashaw, Savannah: Thompson Publishing Group
Basu, Sandra: U.S. Medicine
Baughman, Natalie: Inside Washington Publishers
Baumann, David: National Journal
Baumann, Jeannie: BNA News
Beaman, William P.: Reader's Digest
Beaven, Lara W.: Inside Washington Publishers
Bedard, Paul: U.S. News & World Report
Behling, Bridget: FDC Reports
Beinart, Peter: New Republic
Beizer, Douglas: Washington Technology
Bell, Kevin A.: Tax Notes
Bell, Peter: National Journal
Belton, Beth: Business Week
Bender, Lisa J.: Tax Notes
Bennett, Alison: BNA News
Bennett, Brian: Time Magazine
Bennett, Heather: Tax Notes
Bennett, John T.: Inside Washington Publishers
Benjamin, Mark: Salon
Benjamin, Matthew: U.S. News & World Report
Benton, Nicholas F.: Falls Church News Press
Berger, Brian: Space News
Berger, James R.: Washington Trade Daily
Berger, Mary: Washington Trade Daily
Berkowitz, Lois: Title I Report
Berlin, Joshua L.: FDC Reports
Berman, Dan: Environment & Energy Publishing
Bernstein, Aaron: Business Week
Besser, James David: New York Jewish Week
Best, Frank M.: U.S. Medicine
Beswick, Ellen: Natural Gas Intelligence
Bhambhani, Dipka: McGraw-Hill Co.
Bigman-Galimore, Cabral: FDC Reports
Billings, Deborah: BNA News
Billings, Erin P.: Roll Call
Blake, Elizabeth: Thompson Publishing Group
Blalock, Cecelia: Periodicals News Service
Blank, Peter L.: Kiplinger Washington Editors
Bluey, Robert B.: Human Events
Blum, Vanessa: American Lawyer Media
Blumenstyk, Goldie: Chronicle of Higher Education

1011

MEMBERS ENTITLED TO ADMISSION, PERIODICAL PRESS GALLERIES—Continued

Bolen, Cheryl: BNA News
Boles, Margaret: Telecommunications Reports
Bollag, Burton: Chronicle of Higher Education
Bolton, Alexander: The Hill
Bolton, Elizabeth: Thompson Publishing Group
Bond, David: Aviation Week
Booker, Simeon S.: Jet/Ebony
Borchersen-Keto, Sarah A.: CCH Inc.
Borger, Gloria: U.S. News & World Report
Borja, Rhea R.: Education Week
Borrus, Amy: Business Week
Bowling, C. Jane: BNA News
Bowman, Darcia Harris: Education Week
Boyle, Christina: UCG
Boyles, Katharine K.: Health Market Survey
Boyles, William R.: Health Market Survey
Bracken, Leonard: BNA News
Bradley, Ann B.: Education Week
Brady, Jessica: National Journal
Brady, Matthew: National Underwriter
Brainard, Jeffrey H.: Chronicle of Higher Education
Brandolph, David Barry: BNA News
Brandon, George E.: Kiplinger Washington Editors
Brandon, Priscilla Thayer: Kiplinger Washington
    Editors
Brant, Martha: Newsweek
Braun, Kevin D.: Environment & Energy Publishing
Bresnahan, John: Roll Call
Brevetti, Rossella: BNA News
Brion, Theresa Markley: Research Institute of
    America Group
Briscoe, Daren: Newsweek
Bristow, Melissa Star: Kiplinger Washington Editors
Britt, Angela L.: BNA News
Broderick, Brian J.: BNA News
Broida, Bethany: American Lawyer Media
Bronson, Richard James: BNA News
Brooks, George A.: Inside Mortgage Finance
Brooks, Kelly: IMAS Publishing
Brostoff, Steven: Liability & Insurance Week
Brown, David: Army Times Publishing Co.
Brown, David L.: American Lawyer Media
Brown, Janet M.: Press Associates
Brown, Jill: Atlantic Information Services
Brownstein, Andrew: Thompson Publishing Group
Bruce, R. Christian: BNA News
Brumfiel, Geoff: Nature
Bruninga, Susan: BNA News
Bruno, Debra: American Lawyer Media
Bruno, Michael: Aviation Week
Brunori, David E.: Tax Notes
Bryant, Sue: BNA News
Buchta, Cheryl: McGraw-Hill Co.
Buntin, John: Governing
Burd, Stephen: Chronicle of Higher Education
Burger, Timothy: Time Magazine
Burkhart, Lori: Public Utilities Fortnightly

Burnham, Michael P.: Environment & Energy
    Publishing
Buschman, Thomas: Thompson Publishing Group
Bushell, Brian Andrew: Rolling Stone
Bushweller, Kevin: Education Week
Butchock, Steve: Medical Devices Report
Butler, Amy: Aviation Week
Butts, Thomas: IMAS Publishing
Byerrum, Ellen: BNA News
Byrne, James: CD Publications
Cabrera, Raul: BNA News
Cahlink, George: Government Executive
Cain, Derrick: BNA News
Calabresi, Massimo: Time Magazine
Caldwell, Christopher: Weekly Standard
Cannon, Carl M.: National Journal
Cano, Craig: McGraw-Hill Co.
Canonica, Rocco: Natural Gas Intelligence
Carey, John A.: Business Week
Carhart, Susan: BNA News
Carlile, Amy: Roll Call
Carlson, Caron: Eweek
Carlson, Jeffrey E.: CCH Inc.
Carnahan, Ira: Forbes
Carnevale, Dan: Chronicle of Higher Education
Carney, Eliza Newlin: National Journal
Carney, James F.: Time Magazine
Carpenter, Alison: BNA News
Carr, Jennifer: Tax Notes
Carter, Cynthia: Washington Business Infromation
Caruso, Lisa: National Journal
Cash, Catherine: McGraw-Hill Co.
Cassidy, William B.: Traffic World
Castelli, Chistopher: Inside Washington Publishers
Cauthen, Carey: Thompson Publishing Group
Cavallaro, Gina: Army Times Publishing Co.
Cavanagh, Sean: Education Week
Cavas, Christopher: Army Times Publishing Co.
Cecala, Guy David: Inside Mortgage Finance
Chadwick, Melissa: UCG
Chait, Jonathan: New Republic
Chappell, Kevin: Jet/Ebony
Check, Erika: Nature
Chen, Shawn: Nationaljournal.com
Cherkasky, Mara: Thompson Publishing Group
Cherry, Sheila: BNA News
Chibbaro Jr., Louis M.: Washington Blade
Childress, Rasheeda Crayton: Business Publishers
Chineson, Joel: American Lawyer Media
Chronister, Gregory: Education Week
Ciampoli, Paul: Natural Gas Intelligence
Cillizza, Chris: Roll Call
Clapp, Stephen: Food Chemical News
Clark, Colin: Space News
Clark, Kim: U.S. News & World Report
Clark, Paul Coe: Telecommunications Reports
Clark, Timothy: Government Executive
Clarke, David Paul: Inside Washington Publishers

MEMBERS ENTITLED TO ADMISSION, PERIODICAL PRESS GALLERIES—Continued

Clarke-Gomez, Irene: BNA News
Clemmitt, Marcia: CQ Researcher
Click, Jennifer S.: BNA News
Clift, Eleanor: Newsweek
Cline, Regina P.: BNA News
Cloakley, Emily: CD Publications
Coffin, James B.: Public Lands News
Cohen, Richard E.: National Journal
Cohn, Elizabeth: Chronicle of Higher Education
Colarusso, Laura: Army Times Publishing Co.
Coleman, Janet: FDC Reports
Colenso, Robert: Army Times Publishing Co.
Collins, Brian: National Mortgage News
Collins, Eve: Atlantic Information Services
Collins Jr., Donald: Time Magazine
Collogan, David L.: Aviation Week
Combemale, Martine: Milan Presse
Combs, Jennifer: BNA News
Comer, Matt: Environment & Energy Publishing
Compart, Andrew: Travel Weekly
Conant, Eve: Newsweek
Conconi, Charles N.: Washingtonian
Connors, Kathleen: FDC Reports
Conroy, Declan: Setanta Publishing
Continetti, Matthew: Weekly Standard
Cook, Steven: BNA News
Cook, Jr., Charles E.: Cook Political Report
Cooper, Matthew: Time Magazine
Cooper, Stephen K.: CCH Inc.
Corbett, Warren: Set-Aside Alert
Cordes, Craig: Inside Washington Publishers
Corley, Matilda Monroe: BNA News
Corn, David: Nation
Costa, Keith J.: Inside Washington Publishers
Cottle, Michelle: New Republic
Coughlin, Brett: UCG
Couillard, Lauren: BNA News
Cowden, Richard H.: BNA News
Cox, Matthew: Army Times Publishing Co.
Coyle, Marcia: National Law Journal
Coyne, Martin: McGraw-Hill Co.
Craig, David Brian: Army Times Publishing Co.
Crain, Chris: Washington Blade
Craver, Martha L.: Kiplinger Washington Editors
Crawley, Vince: Army Times Publishing Co.
Crea, Joseph Ross: Washington Blade
Crider, Richard: Thompson Publishing Group
Crock, Stan: Business Week
Crowley, Michael: New Republic
Cruickshank, Paula L.: CCH Inc.
Curran, John: Telecommunications Reports
Curran, Timothy: Roll Call
Currie, Duncan: Weekly Standard
Curry, Leonard: Washington Crime News Services
Curthoys, Kathleen A.: Army Times Publishing Co.
Cusack, Robert: The Hill
Cusick, Daniel: Environment & Energy Publishing

Dagostino, Emily: Tax Notes
Dalecki, Kenneth B: Kiplinger Washington Editors
Darcey, Sue: BNA News
Davenport, Melissa: Governing
Davidson, Daniel: Army Times Publishing Co.
Davidson, Mark: McGraw-Hill Co.
Davies, Stephen: Endangered Species & Wetlands Report
Davis, Brett: Aviation Week
Davis, Emily: Tax Notes
Davis, Lauren: IMAS Publishing
Davis, Michelle R: Education Week
Davis, Paris D.: Metro Herald Newspaper
Davis, Shannon: Inside Washington Publishers
Davis, Steve: Atlantic Information Services
Day, Jeff: BNA News
Degen, Colin: Business Publishers
Deigh, Gloria: BNA News
Delamaide, Darrell: UCG
DeLeon, Carrie: Telecommunications Reports
Dembicki, Matthew: Kiplinger Washington Editors
DeMott, Kathryn: International Medical News Group
Diamond, Phyllis: BNA News
DiCarlo, Rachel: Weekly Standard
Dickerson, John F.: Time Magazine
Dickey, Beth: Government Executive
Diegmueller, Karen: Education Week
DiMascio, Jennifer: Inside Washington Publishers
Dinnage, Russell: Food Chemical News
DiPasquale, Cynthia: Inside Washington Publishers
DiSciullo, Joseph: Tax Notes
Dizard, Wilson: Government Computer News
Doan, Michael F.: Kiplinger Washington Editors
Dobson, Jon: FDC Reports
Doi, Ayako: Japan Digest
Dolley, Steven: McGraw-Hill Co.
Doman, Kimberlee Smith: BNA News
Donefer, Charles: Environment & Energy Publishing
Donlan, Thomas G.: Barron's
Donnelly, Sally: Time Magazine
Donoghue, James A.: Penton Media Inc.
Doolan, Kelley: McGraw-Hill Co.
Dorobek, Christopher: Federal Computer Week
Dorrian, Patrick: BNA News
Dove, Andrew: FDC Reports
Doyle, John M.: Aviation Week
Doyle, Kenneth P.: BNA News
Drew, Elizabeth: New York Review of Books
Duffy, Jennifer: Cook Political Report
Duffy, Michael: Time Magazine
Duffy, Thomas Patrick: Inside Washington Publishers
Dufour, Jeff: The Hill
duMond, Marge: National Journal
Dunham, Richard S.: Business Week
Dunn, William: Research Institute of America Group

Dupont, Daniel G.: Inside Washington Publishers
Duran, Nicole: Roll Call
Earle, Geoff: The Hill
Easterbrook, Gregg: New Republic
Eastland, Terry: Weekly Standard
Eby, Deborah: Business Publishers
Edmondson, Thomas: BNA News
Edmonson, Robert G.: Traffic World
Edney, Hazel Trice: Afro American Newspapers
Edwards, Charles J.: Thompson Publishing Group
Edwards, Thomas J.: CD Publications
Ege, Konrad: Blatter
Eggerton, John S.: Broadcasting & Cable
Egna, Martin: CCH Inc.
Ehrenhalt, Alan: Governing
Eichenseher, Tasha: Environment & Energy
  Publishing
Eisele, Albert: The Hill
Eiserer, Leonard A. C.: Business Publishers
Eisler, Kim: Washingtonian
Eldridge II, Scott A.: Inside Washington Publishers
Elfin, Dana: BNA News
Ellis, Isobel: National Journal
Elmore, Wesley: Tax Notes
Emeigh Jr., Geoffrey: BNA News
Engdahl, Elizabeth: American Lawyer Media
Ericksen, Charles: Hispanic Link News Service
Esquivel, J. Jesus: Proceso
Evangelauf, Jean: Chronicle of Higher Education
Evans, Jeffrey: International Medical News Group
Evelyn, Jamilah: Chronicle of Higher Education
Ezzard, Catherine Sullivan: BNA News
Fallows, James: Atlantic Monthly
Falvella-Garraty, Susan: Irish Echo
Fang, Bay: U.S. News & World Report
Fanshel, Fran: UCG
Faram, Mark: Army Times Publishing Co.
Farrar, Loren S.: Penton Media Inc.
Farrell, Elizabeth: Chronicle of Higher Education
Fehrs, Peter: FDC Reports
Feltman, Peter E.: CCH Inc.
Ferguson, Andrew: Weekly Standard
Ferguson, Brett: BNA News
Fernandez, Lourdes: Inside Washington Publishers
Ferraro: National Journal
Ferullo, Michael: BNA News
Field, Christopher: Human Events
Field, David: Airline Business
Field, Kelly: Chronicle of Higher Education
Filmore, David: FDC Reports
Finan, Colin: Inside Washington Publishers
Fineman, Howard: Newsweek
Finkling, Amy: McGraw–Hill Co.
Fiorino, Frances: Aviation Week
Fischer, Craig: Letter Publications
Fischer, Karin: Chronicle of Higher Education
Fisher, Elizabeth: National Review
Fitzpatrick, Erika: Capitol City Publishers

Flanagan, John David: CCH Inc.
Fleet, Leslie G.: BNA News
Fleming, Christopher T.: Healthcare Information
Flint, Perry: Penton Media Inc.
Flynn, Joan Marie: Thompson Publishing Group
Flynn, Lauren: Atlantic Information Services
Foer, Franklin: New Republic
Fogg, E. Piper: Chronicle of Higher Education
Fong, Tony: Crain Communications
Foster, Andrea: Chronicle of Higher Education
Foster, Cassandra P.: Roll Call
Foster, Lawrence D.: McGraw-Hill Co.
Fourney, Susan: Government Executive
Francis, David: Inside Washington Publishers
Francis, Eileen: FDC Reports
Francis, Laura: BNA News
Franklin, Mary Beth: Kiplinger Washington Editors
Fraser, Katharine: McGraw-Hill Co.
Fredo, Diane: BNA News
Freddoso, David: Evans-Novak Political Report
Frederick, Melissa: CD Publications
Freedberg, Jr., Sydney J.: National Journal
Freedman, Andrew: Environment & Energy
  Publishing
Freeman, Allison: Environment & Energy
  Publishing
Freeman III, William A.: Penton Media Inc.
Frieden, Joyce: International Medical News Group
Friel, Brian: National Journal
Fulghum, David: Aviation Week
Fullerton, Jane: Farm Journal
Funk, Deborah M.: Army Times Publishing Co.
Funk, Kathryn: Pace Publications
Gable, Eryn: Environment & Energy Publishing
Gallagher, John: Traffic World
Gannon, John: BNA News
Garamfalui, Alexia: Inside Washington Publishers
Garcia, Rodney D.: Thompson Publishing Group
Garfield, Bob: Crain Communications
Garner, Lynn: BNA News
Gasparello, Linda A.: King Publishing Group
Gatty, Mary Ann: Periodicals News Service
Gehring, John: Education Week
Geisel, Jerome M.: Crain Communications
Geman, Ben: Environment & Energy Publishing
Gerecht, Michael: CD Publications
Gerin, Roseanne: Washington Technology
Gersemann, Olaf: Wirtschaftswoche
Getter, Lisa: UCG
Gettinger, Steve: National Journal
Gettlin, Robert: National Journal
Gewertz, Catherine: Education Week
Gibb, Steven K.: Inside Washington Publishers
Gilbert, Lorraine S.: BNA News
Gilgoff, Daniel: U.S. News & World Report
Gillies, Andrew: Forbes
Gillis, Christopher: American Shipper
Gizzi, John: Human Events

Glass, Andrew J.: The Hill
Glazer, Gwen: Nationaljournal.com
Gleckman, Howard: Business Week
Glenn, David G.: Chronicle of Higher Education
Glenn, Heidi: Tax Notes
Glenzer, Michael: Exchange Monitor Publications
Gloger, Katja: Stern
Gnaedinger, Chuck: Tax Notes
Goindi, Geeta: Express India
Goldberg, Kirsten: Cancer Letter
Goldberg, Paul: Cancer Letter
Goldman, Ted: American Lawyer Media
Goldstein, Peter: Kiplinger Washington Editors
Goldstein, Sid: Pace Publications
Goldwasser, Joan: Kiplinger Washington Editors
Goldwyn, Brant: CCH Inc.
Goodman, Glenn W.: Army Times Publishing Co.
Goodwine, Velma: Research Institute of America Group
Gordon, Kelly J.: Thompson Publishing Group
Gordon, Meryl: Elle
Gorman, S. Siobhan: National Journal
Gotsch, Ted: Telecommunications Reports
Gould, Dawn: Washington Information Source
Goulder, Robert: Tax Notes
Goyal, Raghubir: Asia Today
Grabow, Colin: Defense Focus
Graham, Neil: BNA News
Grass, Michael: Roll Call
Green, Charles A.: National Journal
Green, Joshua: Atlantic Monthly
Greenblatt, Alan: Governing
Greenhalgh, Keiron: McGraw-Hill Co.
Gregg, Diana I.: BNA News
Gregorits, Angela: BNA News
Griffith, Cara: Tax Notes
Grimes, Bradley: Government Computer News
Gross, Grant: IDG News Service
Grossman, Elaine M.: Inside Washington Publishers
Gruber, Amelia: Government Executive
Gruber, Peter: Focus
Gruenberg, Mark J.: Press Associates
Gruss, Jean: Kiplinger Washington Editors
Gsell, James: Federal Employees News Digest
Guay, Thomas: Progressive Business Publications
Guerra, John: Billing World Magazine
Gunter, Chris: Nature
Gurdon, Hugo: The Hill
Guterman, Lila: Chronicle of Higher Education
Haas, Joseph: CD Publications
Hadley, Richard D.: UCG
Hagstrom, Jerry: National Journal
Hall, Holly: Chronicle of Higher Education
Halonen, Douglas J.: Crain Communications
Halloran, Elizabeth: U.S. News & World Report
Hamaker, Christian: Public Utilities Fortnightly
Hammond, Brian: Telecommunications Reports
Hammond, Sarah Spencer: Business Publishers

Haniffa, Aziz: India Abroad
Hansard, Sara: Crain Communications
Hansen, Brian: McGraw-Hill Co.
Hansen, David: CCH Inc.
Hanson, Melinda: BNA News
Harbert, Tam: Electronic Business
Harbrecht, Douglas: Business Week
Hardin, Angela Y.: McGraw-Hill Co.
Hardy, Michael: Federal Computer Week
Harkness, Peter A.: Governing
Harman, Thomas: Inside Washington Publishers
Harris, Donna L.: Crain Communications
Harris, Joann Christine: Tax Notes
Harris, Lona C.: Time Magazine
Harris, Louise: Business Publishers
Harris, Shane: Government Executive
Harrison, David: BNA News
Harrison, Tom: McGraw-Hill Co.
Hasson, Judith B.: Federal Computer Week
Hawkins, Andrew: FDC Reports
Hayes, Lisa L.: Thompson Publishing Group
Hayes, Peter S.: BNA News
Hayes, Stephen: Weekly Standard
Healey, Daniel: FDC Reports
Hearn, Edward T.: Multichannel News
Hearn, Josephine: The Hill
Hebel, Sara: Chronicle of Higher Education
Heckathorn, Mark: McGraw-Hill Co.
Hedges, Joyce: BNA News
Heflin, Jay: UCG
Hegland, Corine: National Journal
Henary, Laura Beth: Weekly Standard
Henderson, Kristina: Inside Washington Publishers
Hendrie, Caroline: Education Week
Henneberger, Melinda: Newsweek
Hennig, Jutta: Inside Washington Publishers
Henning, Jonathan: Defense Focus
Henning, Lily: American Lawyer Media
Hernandez, Luis: Thompson Publishing Group
Hess, Glenn H.: Chemical Market Reporter
Hess, Ryan E.: MII Publications
Hettinger, Christian: Thompson Publishing Group
Heyd, Cindy Ann: Tax Notes
Hicks, Travis: Thompson Publishing Group
Higgins, John: Business Publishers
Hilburn, Matthew: Army Times Publishing Co.
Hill, Keith M.: BNA News
Hill, Richard: BNA News
Hill, Tichakorn: Army Times Publishing Co.
Hirsh, Michael: Newsweek
Hiruo, Elaine: McGraw-Hill Co.
Hobbs, M. Nielsen: FDC Reports
Hobbs, Susan: BNA News
Hocking, Bryanna: Roll Call
Hodierne, Robert: Army Times Publishing Co.
Hoff, David: Education Week
Hoffman, Donald B.: Thompson Publishing Group

Hoffman, Rebecca: BNA News
Hoffman, William: Traffic World
Hofmann, Mark A.: Crain Communications
Holahan, Elizabeth: Government Contractor
Holder, Christina: Evans-Novak Political Report
Holland, Bill: Billboard Magazine
Holland, William: McGraw-Hill Co.
Hollingsworth, Catherine: BNA News
Holmes, Gwendolyn: BNA News
Holmes, Natalie C.: Capitol City Publishers
Honawar, Vaishali: Education Week
Hoover, Eric: Chronicle of Higher Education
Hoover, Kent: Washington Business Journal
Horner, Daniel: McGraw-Hill Co.
Horowitz, Jay: BNA News
Horwood, Rachel Jane: Economist
Hosenball, Mark: Newsweek
Hosten, Allissa: Food Chemical News
Houghton, Mary: FDC Reports
Hoversten, Paul: Aviation Week
Howard, Joe: Radio & Records
Hsu, Susan: Business Publishers
Hubbard, Catherine A.: CCH Inc.
Hughes, Jr., John D.: Aviation Week
Hurst, Marianne Delinda: Education Week
Hutnyan, Joseph D.: McGraw-Hill Co.
Hyland, Terence: BNA News
Ichniowski, Thomas F.: McGraw-Hill Co.
Idaszak, Jerome: Kiplinger Washington Editors
Iekel, John F.: Thompson Publishing Group
Irvin, Helen: BNA News
Isikoff, Michael: Newsweek
Iyengar, Sunil: FDC Reports
Jackman, Frank: McGraw-Hill Co.
Jackson, Anthony: Time Magazine
Jackson, Joab: Government Computer News
Jackson, Rochelle D.: BNA News
Jackson, Valarie: McGraw-Hill Co.
Jackson, William K.: Government Computer News
Jacobson, Jennifer: Chronicle of Higher Education
Jacobson, Ken: Manufacturing & Technology News
Jacobson, Louis: Roll Call
Jadadeesan, Gomati: Inside Washington Publishers
James, Betty: Interpreter Releases
Javers, Eamon: Business Week
Jeffrey, Terence P.: Human Events
Jenkins, Scott: FDC Reports
Jensen, Brennen: Chronicle of Higher Education
Jeong, Hye: Environment & Energy Publishing
Johnson, Alisa: BNA News
Johnson, Angela: CCH Inc.
Johnson, Fawn: BNA News
Johnson, Greg: Inside Mortgage Finance
Johnson, Kimberly E.: Aviation Week
Johnson, Lyrica: Government Contractor
Johnson, Regina: McGraw-Hill Co.
Johnson, Wendy: UCG

Johnston, Robert C.: Education Week
Jones, George: CCH Inc.
Jones, Helen: BNA News
Jones, Joyce: Black Enterprise
Jones, Mary Lynn: The Hill
Jonson, Nick: McGraw-Hill Co.
Jordan, Anne: Governing
Jordan, Brian D.: McGraw-Hill Co.
Jordan, Bryant: Army Times Publishing Co.
Joslyn, Heather: Chronicle of Higher Education
Jost, Kenneth W.: CQ Researcher
Jowers, Karen Grigg: Army Times Publishing Co.
Joyce, Stephen: BNA News
Judis, John B.: New Republic
June, Audrey Williams: Chronicle of Higher Education
Kahn, Jeremy: New Republic
Kalb, Deborah: The Hill
Kalowski, Lee: FDC Reports
Kane, Paul: Roll Call
Kaplan, Hugh B.: BNA News
Kaplan, Jonathan: The Hill
Kaplun, Alex: Environment & Energy Publishing
Karp, Aaron: Traffic World
Kash, William: Government Computer News
Kasper, Andrew: FDC Reports
Kasperowicz, Peter: Inside Washington Publishers
Kass, Marcia: BNA News
Kassabian, Gloria B.: Business Week
Katel, Peter: CQ Researcher
Katz, Marissa: New Republic
Kauffman, Tim: Army Times Publishing Co.
Kaufman, Bruce S.: BNA News
Kavanagh, Susan: Washington Service Bureau
Kavruck, Deborah A.: Washington Counseletter
Kavruck, Samuel: Washington Counseletter
Keane, Angela Greiling: Traffic World
Keller, Amy M.: Roll Call
Keller, Bess: Education Week
Keller, Gail S.: BNA News
Kelley, Jaimie: FDC Reports
Kelly, Cathy: FDC Reports
Kelly, Patrice Wingert: Newsweek
Kelly, Spencer: UCG
Kennedy, Hugh: UCG
Kenney, Allen: Tax Notes
Kersten, Denise: Government Executive
Khan, Altaf U.: BNA News
Kiernan, Vincent: Chronicle of Higher Education
Kim, Angela: Aviation Week
Kime, Patricia: Army Times Publishing Co.
King, Maureen: Telecommunications Reports
Kinnard, Meg: Nationaljournal.com
Kirby, Paul: Telecommunications Reports
Kirkland, Joel: McGraw-Hill Co.
Kirkland, John Robert: BNA News
Kitfield, James: National Journal
Kittross, David: CD Publications

MEMBERS ENTITLED TO ADMISSION, PERIODICAL PRESS GALLERIES—Continued

Klaidman, Daniel: Newsweek
Kleine-Brockhoff, Thomas: Die Zeit
Kleiner, Henry E.: Business Publishers
Klimko, Frank: CD Publications
Kline, Jerry Lee: Thompson Publishing Group
Klumpp, Helena: Tax Notes
Knapik, Michael: McGraw-Hill Co.
Knight, Danielle: U.S. News & World Report
Koch, Kathy: CQ Researcher
Kondracke, Morton M.: Roll Call
Koons, Jennifer: Nationaljournal.com
Kornacki, John: The Hill
Kosova, Weston: Newsweek
Koss, Geoffrey: Inside Washington Publishers
Kosterlitz, Julie A.: National Journal
Kraft, Scott: UCG
Kramer, David: Science & Government Report
Kramer, Linda: People Magazine
Kraus, Mary Jo: BNA News
Kraushaar, Josh: National Journal
Kriz, Margaret E.: National Journal
Krughoff, Alexander: Federal Employees News
  Digest
Kubetin, W. Randy: BNA News
Kucher, Liane: McGraw-Hill Co.
Kucinich, Jacqueline: The Hill
Kuckro, Rod: McGraw-Hill Co.
Kuhn, Mark: CD Publications
Kukis, Mark: National Journal
Kuli, Alexander: Inside Washington Publishers
Kulman, Linda: U.S. News & World Report
Kurtz, Josh: Roll Call
Kushner, Adam: New Republic
Laas, Molly: FDC Reports
Labash, Matt: Weekly Standard
LaBrecque, Louis C.: BNA News
Lacey, Anthony: Inside Washington Publishers
Laffler, Mary Jo: FDC Reports
Lake, Jessica: FDC Reports
Lally, Rosemarie: Thompson Publishing Group
Lamoreaux, Denise: Thompson Publishing Group
Landrigan, Dan: Atlantic Information Services
Langel, Stephen: Inside Washington Publishers
Lankford, Kimberly: Kiplinger Washington Editors
Larsen, Kathy Caroline: McGraw-Hill Co.
Lash, Jennifer: Roll Call
Lassman, Teresa: International Medical News Group
Last, Jonathan: Weekly Standard
Laurent, Anne: Government Executive
Lavelle, Marianne: U.S. News & World Report
Lawrence, Richard: Traffic World
Learner, Neal: Washington Business Information
Leavitt, David I.: Environment & Energy Publishing
Lee, Robin: BNA News
Leeuwenburgh, Todd: UCG
Legard, Lauren: Washington Business Information
Leheny, Claire: UCG
Leibowitz, Wendy: BNA News

Lekus, Eric: BNA News
Lemov, Penelope: Governing
Leopold, George: CMP Media Inc.
Leshnoff, Jessica: Research USA
Leske, Gisela: Der Spiegel
LeSueur, Steve: Washington Technology
Levin, Joshua: Slate
Levin-Epstein, Marcy: Business Publishers
Levin-Epstein, Michael: Business Publishers
Lewis, Nicole: Chronicle of Higher Education
Liang, John: Inside Washington Publishers
Limpert, Charles: Washingtonian
Lindeman, Ralph: BNA News
Lindsay, Drew: Washingtonian
Linger, Kristyn: BNA News
Linnehan, Janet: Kiplinger Washington Editors
Lipka, Sara: Chronicle of Higher Education
Lipman, Harvy: Chronicle of Higher Education
Lipowicz, Alice: Washington Technology
Lipper, Tamara: Newsweek
Lithwick, Dahlia Hannah: Slate
Lizza, Ryan: New Republic
Lockett, Brian A.: BNA News
Logue, Wayne: Research Institute of America Group
Loos, David: Environment & Energy Publishing
Loos, Ralph: Crain Communications
Lopes, Gregory: Inside Washington Publishers
Lorenzetti, Maureen Shields: Oil & Gas Journal
Losey, Stephen: Army Times Publishing Co.
Lott, Steven: Aviation Week
Loveless, William E.: McGraw-Hill Co.
Lowe, Christian: Army Times Publishing Co.
Lowe, Paul: Aviation International News
Lowther, William: Mail on Sunday
Lubold, Gordon: Army Times Publishing Co.
Lumb, Jacquelyn: Washington Service Bureau
Lundgren, Kari: The Hill
Lunney, Kellie: National Journal
Lustig, Joe: Thompson Publishing Group
Lynch, Kerry: Aviation Week
Ma, Jason: Inside Washington Publishers
MacDonald, Neil: Technology Commercialization
Macilwain, Colin: Nature
MacKeil, Brain: Army Times Publishing Co.
Madigan, Erin: Nationaljournal.com
Maffei, Glenn: Inside Washington Publishers
Maggs, John J.: National Journal
Magill, Barbara: Thompson Publishing Group
Magnusson, Paul: Business Week
Mahoney, Fabia H.: BNA News
Mahtesian, Charles: National Journal
Maine, Amanda: CCH Inc.
Maixner, Edward: Kiplinger Washington Editors
Mangu-Ward, Katherine: Weekly Standard
Manley, Mary Ann G.: BNA News
Manzo, Kathleen K.: Education Week
Marcoux, Michel: FDC Reports

Marcucci, Carl: Radio Business Report
Marois, Denise: Aviation Week
Marre, Klaus: The Hill
Marron, Jessica: McGraw-Hill Co.
Marson, Brian: FDC Reports
Maschas, Andrew Jason: CCH Inc.
Mascolo, Georg Ranier: Der Spiegel
Matishak, Martin: Inside Washington Publishers
Matthews, Martha A.: BNA News
Matthews, Sidney William: Army Times Publishing Co.
Mauro, Antony: American Lawyer Media
Maze, Richard: Army Times Publishing Co.
Mazumdar, Anandashankar: BNA News
McAdams, Deborah: IMAS Publishing
McAllister, William: Linn's Stamp News
McArdle, John: Roll Call
McBeth Laping, Karen: McGraw-Hill Co.
McCaffery, Gregory: BNA News
McCaney, Kevin: Government Computer News
McCaughan, Michael: FDC Reports
McClements, Amanda: Roll Call
McClenahen, John: Penton Media Inc.
McConnell, William: Broadcasting & Cable
McCormack, Richard: Manufacturing & Technology News
McCormally, Kevin: Kiplinger Washington Editors
McCracken, Rebecca P.: BNA News
McDermott, Kevin: Research Institute of America Group
McGeehon, Dale: Thompson Publishing Group
McGlinchey, David: Government Executive
McGoffin, Michael J.: Research Institute of America Group
McGolrick, Susan J.: BNA News
McHugh, Jane Claire: Army Times Publishing Co.
McIntosh, Toby: BNA News
McKenna, Edward: Traffic World
McKenna, Edward: Washington Business Information
McLane, Paul J.: IMAS Publishing
McLaughlin, Matthew J.: Government Computer News
McLure, Jason: American Lawyer Media
McMurtrie, Beth: Chronicle of Higher Education
McNamee, Michael D.: Business Week
McTague, James: Barron's
McTague, Rachel: BNA News
McVicker, William: Recall
Mechcatie, Elizabeth: International Medical News Group
Meehan, Chris: Atlantic Information Services
Melendez, Sonia: Hispanic Link News Service
Melillo, Wendy: Adweek Magazine
Melzer, Eartha: Washington Blade
Menon, Veena: Inside Washington Publishers
Merrion, Paul Robert: Crain Communications
Metzger, Andrew: American Lawyer Media

Meyers, David B.: Roll Call
Micco, Linda: BNA News
Miller, Jason: Government Computer News
Miller, John J.: National Review
Miller, Julie A.: Title I Report
Miller, Karla L.: Tax Notes
Miller, Reed J.: FDC Reports
Miller, Richard: Business Week
Miller, W. Kent: Army Times Publishing Co.
Miller, William H.: Penton Media Inc.
Milligan, Michael: Travel Weekly
Minikon, Patricia: Interpreter Releases
Minton-Beddoes, Zanny: Economist
Mitchell, John: Reader's Digest
Mitchell, Robert W.: Thompson Publishing Group
Miyashita, Shigeki: Hispanic Link News Service
Mokhiber, Russell: Corporate Crime Reporter
Mola, Roger Andrew: Aviation International News
Monastersky, Richard: Chronicle of Higher Education
Monroe, John: Federal Computer Week
Montgomery, Erin: Weekly Standard
Montwieler, Nancy H.: BNA News
Moore, James Gerry: Kiplinger Washington Editors
Moore, Jennifer Lynn: Chronicle of Higher Education
Moore, Michael: BNA News
Moore, Miles David: Crain Communications
Moore, Nancy J.: BNA News
Moore, Pamela Susan: Capitol Publications
Moragne, Lenora: Black Congressional Monitor
Morales, Cecilio: MII Publications
Morehouse, Macon: People Magazine
Morello, Lauren: Environment & Energy Publishing
Morin, Christopher Scott: Thompson Publishing Group
Morring, Jr., Frank: Aviation Week
Morris, Emma: Nature
Morris, Jefferson F.: Aviation Week
Morris, Jodie: National Journal
Morris, Joe: Inside Washington Publishers
Morrison, David Carlisle: Credit Union Times
Morrissey, James A.: Textile World
Morton, Peter: Financial Post
Mosquera, Mary: Government Computer News
Mullen, Thomas: Healthcare Information
Mullen II, Theophite: McGraw-Hill Co.
Mulrine, Anna: U.S. News & World Report
Munoz, German: News Bites
Munro, Neil P.: National Journal
Munsey, Christopher: Army Times Publishing Co.
Muolo, Paul: National Mortgage News
Muradian, Vago: Army Times Publishing Co.
Murdoch, Joyce M.: National Journal
Mutcherson-Ridley, Joyce: CCH Inc.
Najor, Pamela: BNA News
Nartker, Michael: Exchange Monitor Publications
Nash, James L.: Penton Media Inc.

MEMBERS ENTITLED TO ADMISSION, PERIODICAL PRESS GALLERIES—Continued

Nations, Deborah L. Acomb: National Journal
Naylor, Sean D.: Army Times Publishing Co.
Neill, Alex: Army Times Publishing Co.
Nelson, Ryan: FDC Reports
Nelson, Suzanne: Roll Call
Netram, Christopher M.: Tax Notes
Newkumet, Christopher J.: McGraw-Hill Co.
Newman, Richard J.: U.S. News & World Report
Newmyer, Arthur: Roll Call
Nichols, Hans: The Hill
Nicholson, Jonathan: BNA News
Nir, Ori: The Forward
Noah, Timothy Robert: Slate
Novack, Janet: Forbes
Novak, Viveca: Time Magazine
Nutt, Audrey: Tax Notes
O'Beirne, Kate Walsh: National Review
Oberdorfer, Carol: BNA News
Oberle, Sean F.: Oberle Communications
Obey, Douglas: Inside Washington Publishers
O'Brien, Erin: Thompson Publishing Group
O'Connor, Patrick: The Hill
O'Driscoll, Mary: Environment & Energy
  Publishing
Ognanovich, Nancy: BNA News
Olaya, Phillip: BNA News
Oliphant, James: American Lawyer Media
Olsen, Florence: Federal Computer Week
Olson, Lynn: Education Week
Omestad, Thomas E.: U.S. News & World Report
O'Neill, Sean F.: Kiplinger Washington Editors
Onley, Dawn S.: Government Computer News
Onley, Gloria R.: BNA News
Oram, Mark Alexander: McGraw-Hill Co.
Orleans, Anne: Washington News Observer
Orrick, Sarah: Congressional Digest
Orth, Maureen: Vanity Fair
Ostroff, Jim: Kiplinger Washington Editors
O'Toole, Thomas: BNA News
Page, Paul: Traffic World
Pak, Janne Kum Cha: USA Journal
Palmer, Anna: American Lawyer Media
Palmer, Avery: Inside Washington Publishers
Palmer, Kimberly: Government Executive
Pannell, Susan J.: BNA News
Pappalardo, Denise: IDG Communications
Parisi, Gretchen: FDC Reports
Parker, Andrew: Professional Pilot Magazine
Parker, John: Economist
Parker, Susan T.: Natural Gas Intelligence
Parrish, Molly R.: Pace Publications
Paschal, Mack Arthur: BNA News
Patrick, Steven: BNA News
Patton, Oliver B.: Heavy Duty Trucking
Patton, Zachary L.: Governing
Paulson, William Clifford: FDC Reports
Pazanowski, Bernard J.: BNA News
Peed, Michael F.: National Journal

Pekow, Charles: LP/Gas
Peniston, Brad: Army Times Publishing Co.
Perera, David: Federal Computer Week
Perlman, Ellen: Governing
Perry, Joellen: U.S. News & World Report
Pershing, Benjamin: Roll Call
Peters, Katherine M.: Government Executive
Petersen, Tina: McGraw-Hill Co.
Pexton, Patrick: National Journal
Pfeiffer, Eric: National Review
Phibbs, Pat: BNA News
Phillips, Cathleen M.: Tax Notes
Phillips, Lyda: BNA News
Phinney, David: Army Times Publishing Co.
Piemonte, Philip M.: Federal Employees News
  Digest
Pierce, Emily: Roll Call
Pimley, Ward: BNA News
Plank, Kendra Casey: BNA News
Plotz, David: Slate
Podesta, Jane: People Magazine
Poe, Sheryll: Inside Washington Publishers
Polster, Nathaniel: Adolescent Medicine
Ponnuru, Ramesh: National Review
Postal, Arthur D.: National Underwriter
Powers, Martha C.: Mid-Atlantic Research
Powers, William: National Journal
Prah, Pamela: CQ Researcher
Precht, Paul: Inside Washington Publishers
Preston, Mark: Roll Call
Preston, Meredith: BNA News
Pringle, Rodney: Aviation Week
Prochoroff, Alan: UCG
Pryde, Joan: Kiplinger Washington Editors
Pueschel, Matt: U.S. Medicine
Pulley, John L.: Chronicle of Higher Education
Pulliam, Daniel: Government Executive
Quay, Christopher: Tax Notes
Quenqua, Douglas: PR Week
Radford, Bruce W.: Public Utilities Fortnightly
Ragavan, Chitra: U.S. News & World Report
Raju, Manu: Inside Washington Publishers
Rancourt, Jr., John: FDC Reports
Rankin, Ken: Lebhar-Friedman Publications
Ranson, Lori: Aviation Week
Ratnam, Gopal: Army Times Publishing Co.
Rawson, Kathleen: FDC Reports
Rees, Elizabeth: Inside Washington Publishers
Rees, John: Mid-Atlantic Research
Reeves, Dawn: Inside Washington Publishers
Rehring, Emily: Traffic World
Reid, Karla S.: Education Week
Reistrup, John: CD Publications
Rhein, Jr., Reginald W.: Scrip World Pharmaceutical
  News
Richard, Alan: Education Week
Richardson, Jenn: Army Times Publishing Co.
Richardson, Nathaline: BNA News

MEMBERS ENTITLED TO ADMISSION, PERIODICAL PRESS GALLERIES—Continued

Richert, Catharine: Inside Washington Publishers
Rickman, Johnathan: Tax Notes
Ridgeway, James: Village Voice
Riley, Karen: Clinica
Ripley, Amanda: Time Magazine
Ritterpusch, Kurt: BNA News
Robelen, Erik: Education Week
Roberts, Edward S.: Credit Union Journal
Roberts, Sharon: Time Magazine
Roberts, Vanessa Jo: Government Computer News
Roberts, Victoria: BNA News
Robertson, Jack W.: CMP Media Inc.
Robinson, Linda: U.S. News & World Report
Robinson, Thomas Steven: Mass Transit Lawyer
Rockwell, L. Mark: Wireless Week
Rodeffer, Mark H.: The Hill
Rodriguez, Eva: American Lawyer Media
Roeder, Linda: BNA News
Rogers, Amy: CMP Media Inc.
Rogers, Robert: American Lawyer Media
Rogers, Warren: Associated Features
Roha, Ronaleen: Kiplinger Washington Editors
Rohde, Peter: Inside Washington Publishers
Rohrer, S. Scott: National Journal
Rojas, Warren A.: Tax Notes
Rolfsen, Bruce: Army Times Publishing Co.
Rollow, Jake: Hispanic Link News Service
Roos, John: Army Times Publishing Co.
Roque, Ashley: Inside Washington Publishers
Rose, Lois: BNA News
Rose, Phil: Professional Pilot Magazine
Rosen, Anne: Construction Contracts Law Report
Rosen, Jeffrey: New Republic
Rosenberg, Debra: Newsweek
Rosenkranz, Rolf: Inside Washington Publishers
Roston, Eric: Time Magazine
Roth, Nancy: Business Publishers
Rothenberg, Stuart: Rothenberg Political Report
Rothman, Heather M.: BNA News
Rothstein, Betsy: The Hill
Rowings, Kathy: Kiplinger Washington Editors
Roy, Daniel J.: BNA News
Rudd, Terence: International Medical News Group
Rugaber, Chris: BNA News
Rummell, Nicholas: UCG
Rushford, Greg: Rushford Report
Ryan, Margaret: McGraw-Hill Co.
Sack, Joetta: Education Week
Sain Jr., Kenneth: Washington Blade
Sala, Susan: BNA News
Saletan, William: Slate
Saloom, Elizabeth: Federal Employees News Digest
Salt, Matthew: Washington Business Information
Salzano, Carlo J.: Waterways Journal
Sammon, Richard: Kiplinger Washington Editors
Samuel, Terence: U.S. News & World Report
Samuels, Christina: Education Week

Samuelsohn, Darren: Environment & Energy Publishing
Samuelson, Robert: Newsweek
Sanders, Anthony T.: Billboard Magazine
Sangillo, Gregg Thomas: National Journal
Santiago, Annette R.: Aviation Week
Sarkar, Dibya: Federal Computer Week
Sartipzadeh, Saied Ali: BNA News
Savodnik, Peter: The Hill
Savoie, Andy: Aviation Week
Scales, Sirena J.: Tax Notes
Scarlett, Thomas: Inside Mortgage Finance
Scheiber, Noam: New Republic
Scherman, Bob: Satellite Business News
Schieken, William: Government Contractor
Schmidt, Peter: Chronicle of Higher Education
Schmidt, Mike: McGraw-Hill Co.
Schmitt, Shawn: UCG
Schneider, Andrew C.: Kiplinger Washington Editors
Schneider, Martin A.: Exchange Monitor Publications
Schneider, Mary Ellen: International Medical News Group
Schoenberg, Tom: American Lawyer Media
Schofield, Adrian: Aviation Week
Schofield, Lorraine: Inside Washington Publishers
Schomisch, Jeffrey: Thompson Publishing Group
Schorr, Burt: UCG
Schoultz, Cathleen O.: BNA News
Schuff, Sally: Farm Progress News
Schwartz, Emma: American Lawyer Media
Schwartz, Lauren: FDC Reports
Scoblic, J. Peter: New Republic
Scorza, John Forrest: CCH Inc.
Scott, Cordia: Tax Notes
Scott, Dean T.: BNA News
Scott, Judith: BNA News
Scully, Megan: The Hill
Scutro, Andrew: Army Times Publishing Co.
Sedlak, Teresa: People Magazine
Selinger, Marc: Aviation Week
Selingo, Jeffrey: Chronicle of Higher Education
Serafini, Marilyn Werber: National Journal
Setze, Karen Jeanne: Tax Notes
Seyler, David P.: Radio Business Report
Sfiligoj, Mark L.: Kiplinger Washington Editors
Shafer, Jack: Slate
Shah, Aarti A.: Inside Washington Publishers
Shannon, Elaine: Time Magazine
Sharpe, Kieran: Thompson Publishing Group
Sharpe, Stephanie: McGraw-Hill Co.
Shartel, J. Stratton: BNA News
Shea, Richard L.: Construction Contracts Law Report
Sheets, Andy: Tax Notes
Shelton, Andrew: FDC Reports
Sheppard, Doug: Tax Notes

MEMBERS ENTITLED TO ADMISSION, PERIODICAL PRESS GALLERIES—Continued

Sherman, Jason: Inside Washington Publishers
Sherman, Mark W.: Business Publishers
Sherrod, Lawrence: CD Publications
Shields, Todd: Adweek Magazine
Shipman, William Matthew: Inside Washington Publishers
Shoop, Thomas J.: Government Executive
Shute, Nancy: U.S. News & World Report
Sidey, Hugh S.: Time Magazine
Silva, Chris: Washington Business Information
Silva, Jeffrey S.: Crain Communications
Silverman, Jennifer: International Medical News Group
Simendinger, Alexis A.: National Journal
Simmonds, Susan Jeane: Tax Notes
Simmons, Jessica: BNA News
Simmons, Nancy: BNA News
Simon, Roger: U.S. News & World Report
Singer, Jeremy: Space News
Singer, Paul: National Journal
Singleton, Joe: Inside Washington Publishers
Sinnex, Cecil: CD Publications
Skinner, David: Weekly Standard
Skovron, James W.: BNA News
Slaughter, David A.: Thompson Publishing Group
Smaglik, Paul: Nature
Small, John R.: BNA News
Smallen, Jill: National Journal
Smallwood, Scott: Chronicle of Higher Education
Smith, Anne Kates: Kiplinger Washington Editors
Smith, Douglas: Tax Notes
Smith, John Allen: Thompson Publishing Group
Smith, Joseph: CD Publications
Smith, Marcus: UCG
Smith, Michael: Kiplinger Washington Editors
Smith, Noah J.: BNA News
Smith, Rhonda M.: Washington Blade
Snider, Adam: BNA News
Snyder, Jim: The Hill
Sobieraj, Sandra: People Magazine
Socha, Evamarie: Washington Technology
Solheim, Mark: Kiplinger Washington Editors
Solomon, Goody L.: News Bites
Southern, E. Richard: Government Contractor
Spangler, DianaLouise: U.S. Medicine
Spangler, Donna Kemp: Exchange Monitor Publications
Spangler, Matthew: McGraw-Hill Co.
Spence, Charles F.: General Aviation News
Spencer, Duncan: The Hill
Spencer, Patricia: BNA News
Splete, Heidi: International Medical News Group
Spotswood, Stephen: U.S. Medicine
Sprague, John: Budget & Program
Sprenger, Sebastian: Inside Washington Publishers
Stam, John: BNA News
Stamper, Dustin: Tax Notes
Stanton, Lynn: Telecommunications Reports

Starobin, Paul: National Journal
Starr, Beth: BNA News
Stavros, Richard: Public Utilities Fortnightly
Steele, Zaira: Steele Communications
Stein, Keith: King Publishing Group
Stein, Lisa: U.S. News & World Report
Steinberg, Julie A.: BNA News
Steinke, Scott A.: FDC Reports
Steis, Alexander Beswick: Natural Gas Intelligence
Stempeck, Brian: Environment & Energy Publishing
Sternstein, Aliya: Federal Computer Week
Stewart, William H.: Thompson Publishing Group
Stimson, Leslie: IMAS Publishing
Stoffer, Harry: Crain Communications
Stokeld, Frederick W.: Tax Notes
Stokes, Bruce: National Journal
Stoler, Judith: Time Magazine
Stone, Peter H.: National Journal
Stratton, Sheryl: Tax Notes
Strohm, Chris: Government Executive
Strout, Erin: Chronicle of Higher Education
Sturges, Peyton Mackay: BNA News
Sugarman, Carole: Food Chemical News
Suggs, Welch: Chronicle of Higher Education
Sullivan, Colin: Environment & Energy Publishing
Sullivan, Eileen: Army Times Publishing Co.
Sullivan, John H.: BNA News
Sullivan, Monica C.: National Journal
Sultan, Michael: Natural Gas Week
Sutter, Susan M.: FDC Reports
Swanson, Ian: Inside Washington Publishers
Sweeney, Jeanne: Title I Report
Sweeting, Paul: Reed Business Information
Swibel, Matthew: Forbes
Swisher, Larry: BNA News
Swope, Christopher: Governing
Tacconelli, Gail: Newsweek
Tandon, Crystal: Tax Notes
Tatum, Melanie: McGraw-Hill Co.
Taube, Herman: Jewish Forward—Yiddish
Taulbee, Pamela D.: Atlantic Information Services
Taylor, Ronald: BNA News
Taylor, Vincent: UCG
Taylor II, B.J.: Atlantic Information Services
Taylor Jr., Stuart: National Journal
Teinowitz, Ira: Crain Communications
Tell, David: Weekly Standard
Temin, Thomas R.: Government Computer News
Templin, Kate: CQ Researcher
Teske, Steven: BNA News
Thibodeau, Patrick: IDG Communications
Thomas, Katherine: FDC Reports
Thomas, R. Griffith: Congressional Digest
Thomas, Richard K.: Newsweek
Thomas, Steele: FDC Reports
Thompson, Jason: Nationaljournal.com
Thompson, Mark J.: Time Magazine

Thormeyer, Robert J.: McGraw-Hill Co.
Thorn, Judith: BNA News
Thorndike, Joseph: Tax Notes
Thurneysen-Lukow, Rachel: Newsweek
Tiboni, Frank: Federal Computer Week
Tice, James S.: Army Times Publishing Co.
Tiernan, Tom: McGraw-Hill Co.
Tinkelman, Joseph: BNA News
Todaro, Jane: Business Week
Toloken, Steve: Crain Communications
Tonn, Jessica: Education Week
Tosh, Dennis A.: Thompson Publishing Group
Triplett, Michael R.: BNA News
Trompeter, Erin: Research Institute of America
  Group
Troshinsky, Lisa: Aviation Week
Trotter, Andrew: Education Week
Trowbridge, Gordon: Army Times Publishing Co.
Tsui, Amy: BNA News
Tucker, Miriam E.: International Medical News
  Group
Tumulty, Karen: Time Magazine
Tuttle, Steve: Newsweek
Tyson, Daniel: Business Publishers
Uhlendorf, Karl: FDC Reports
Urdan, Rachel: Inside Washington Publishers
Vaida, Bara: National Journal
Vample, Gwendolyn: Thompson Publishing Group
Vandegrift, Beth: Thompson Publishing Group
Verton, Daniel: IDG Communications
Viadero, Debra: Education Week
Victor, Kirk: National Journal
Villemez, Jennifer T.: Washington Business
  Information
Vinch, Charles: Army Times Publishing Co.
Vissiere, Helene: Le Point
Von Zeppelin, Cristina L.: Forbes
Wachter, Kerri: International Medical News Group
Wait, Patience: Government Computer News
Wakeman, Nick: Washington Technology
Walczak, Lee: Business Week
Walker, Christopher: FDC Reports
Walker, Elizabeth: FDC Reports
Walker, Karen: Army Times Publishing Co.
Walker, Richard: Government Computer News
Wallace, Nicole: Chronicle of Higher Education
Waller, Douglas C.: Time Magazine
Wallison, Ethan: Roll Call
Walsh, Gertrude: Government Computer News
Walsh, Kenneth T.: U.S. News & World Report
Walsh, Mark: Education Week
Walter, Amy: Cook Political Report
Ware, Patricia: BNA News
Warnecke, Michael: BNA News
Warner, Veronica Lynn: Tax Notes
Watkins, Steve: Army Times Publishing Co.
Weaver, Heather Forsgren: Crain Communications
Webster, James C.: Webster Communications

Webster, Susan: BNA News
Wechsler, Jill: Pharmaceutical Executive
Weil, Jenny: McGraw-Hill Co.
Weinstein, Gary A.: BNA News
Weisskopf, Michael: Time Magazine
Welch, Jake: National Journal
Wells, Robert J.: Tax Notes
Welsh, William E.: Washington Technology
Werner, Karen Leigh: BNA News
Westbrook, Roberto: American Lawyer Media
Whalen, John M.: BNA News
Whalley-Hill, Jayne: UCG
Wheeler, David L.: Chronicle of Higher Education
Whieldon, Esther: McGraw-Hill Co.
White, Elizabeth A.: BNA News
White, Rodney A.: McGraw-Hill Co.
Whitelaw, Kevin: U.S. News & World Report
Whitten, Daniel: McGraw-Hill Co.
Whittington, Lauren: Roll Call
Wieser, Eric: McGraw-Hill Co.
Wilczek, Michael J.: McGraw-Hill Co.
Wilczek, Yin: BNA News
Wildavsky, Ben: U.S. News & World Report
Wildstrom, Stephen H.: Business Week
Wilhelm, Ian: Chronicle of Higher Education
Wilkerson, John: Inside Washington Publishers
Willen, Mark: Kiplinger Washington Editors
Willenson, Kim: Japan Digest
Williams, Eileen J.: BNA News
Williams, Grant: Chronicle of Higher Education
Williams, Jeffrey: Satellite Business News
Williams, Risa: Tax Notes
Wilson, Stanley E.: Institutional Investor
Winebrenner, Jane A.: BNA News
Winston, Sherie: McGraw-Hill Co.
Winter, Thomas S.: Human Events
Wisniowski, Charles: CD Publications
Witkin, Gordon: U.S. News & World Report
Witt, Elder: Governing
Wittman, Amy: Army Times Publishing Co.
Woellert, Lorraine: Business Week
Wolffe, Richard: Newsweek
Wolverton, Bradley: Chronicle of Higher Education
Woo, Steve: CD Publications
Wooldridge, Adrian: Economist
Wright, Charlotte: McGraw-Hill Co.
Wyand, Michael W.: BNA News
Yachnin, Jennifer: Roll Call
Yaksick Jr., George L.: CCH Inc.
Yamazaki, Kazutami: Washington Watch
Yang, Catherine T.: Business Week
Yarborough, Mary Helen: Thompson Publishing
  Group
Yasin, Rutrell: Federal Computer Week
Yerkey, Gary G.: BNA News
Yingling, Jennifer: The Hill
Yochelson, Mindy: BNA News
Yohannan, Suzanne: Inside Washington Publishers

MEMBERS ENTITLED TO ADMISSION, PERIODICAL PRESS GALLERIES—Continued

York, Byron: National Review
Young, Jeffrey: The Hill
Young, Jeffrey R.: Chronicle of Higher Education
Yuill, Barbara: BNA News
Zagorin, Adam: Time Magazine
Zaneski, Cyril (Cy): Environment & Energy Publishing
Zehr, Mary Ann: Education Week

Zeller, Shawn: Government Executive
Zengerle, Jason: New Republic
Zhu, Jing: Inside Washington Publishers
Ziegler, Mollie: Army Times Publishing Co.
Zimmerman, Sacha: Reader's Digest
Zung, Robert Te-Kang: BNA News
Zurcher, Anthony W.: Congressional Digest

PERIODICALS REPRESENTED IN PRESS GALLERIES

House Gallery 225–2941, Senate Gallery 224–0265

ADOLESCENT MEDICINE—(301) 770–1884; 5901 Montrose Road Suite 408 North, Rockville, MD 20852: Nathaniel Polster.

ADWEEK MAGAZINE—(202) 833–2551, 910 17th Street NW., Suite 215, Washington, DC 20005, Wendy Melillo, Todd Shields.

AFRO AMERICAN NEWSPAPERS—(202) 319–1292; 3200 13th Street NW., Washington, DC 20010: Hazel Trice Edney.

AIRLINE BUSINESS—(703) 836–7442; 333 N. Fairfax Street, Suite 301, Alexandria, VA 22314: David Field.

AMERICAN LAWYER MEDIA—(202) 457–0686; 1730 M Street NW., Suite 800, Washington, DC 20036: Vanessa Blum, Bethany Broida, David L. Brown, Debra Bruno, Joel Chineson, Elizabeth Engdahl, Ted Goldman, Lily Henning, Antony Mauro, Jason McLure, Andrew Metzger, James Oliphant, Anna Palmer, Eva Rodriguez, Robert Rogers, Tom Schoenberg, Emma Schwartz, Roberto Westbrook.

AMERICAN SHIPPER—(202) 347–1678; National Press Building, Room 1269, Washington, DC 20045: Christopher Gillis.

ARMY TIMES PUBLISHING CO.—(703) 750–9000; 6883 Commercial Drive, Springfield, VA 22159: Nicholas L. Adde, Nicole Gaudiano Albright, Lance M. Bacon, Laura Bailey, David Brown, Gina Cavallaro, Christopher Cavas, Laura Colarusso, Robert Colenso, Matthew Cox, David Brian Craig, Vince Crawley, Kathleen A. Curthoys, Daniel Davidson, Mark Faram, Deborah M. Funk, Glenn W. Goodman, Matthew Hilburn, Tichakorn Hill, Robert Hodierne, Bryant Jordan, Karen Grigg Jowers, Tim Kauffman, Patricia Kime, Stephen Losey, Christian Lowe, Gordon Lubold, Brain MacKeil, Sidney William Matthews, Richard Maze, Jane Claire McHugh, W. Kent Miller, Christopher Munsey, Vago Muradian, Sean D. Naylor, Alex Neill, Brad Peniston, David Phinney, Gopal Ratnam, Jenn Richardson, Bruce Rolfsen, John Roos, Andrew Scutro, Eileen Sullivan, James S. Tice, Gordon Trowbridge, Charles Vinch, Karen Walker, Steve Watkins, Amy Wittman, Mollie Ziegler.

ASIA TODAY—(202) 271–1100; 27025 McPhearson Square, Washington, DC 20038: Raghubir Goyal.

ASSOCIATED FEATURES—(202) 965–0802; 1622 30th Street NW., Washington, DC 20007: Warren Rogers.

ATLANTIC INFORMATION SERVICES—(202) 775–9008; 1100 17th Street NW., Suite 300, Washington, DC 20036: Jill Brown, Eve Collins, Steve Davis, Lauren Flynn, Dan Landrigan, Chris Meehan, Pamela D. Taulbee, B.J. Taylor II.

ATLANTIC MONTHLY—(202) 739–8400; 600 New Hampshire Avenue NW., Washington, DC 20037: James Fallows, Joshua Green.

AVIATION INTERNATIONAL NEWS—(203) 798–2400; 8020 Needwood Road, Suite 101, Derwood, MD 20855: Paul Lowe, Roger Andrew Mola.

AVIATION WEEK—(202) 383–2350; 1200 G Street NW., Suite 900, Washington, DC 20005: Joseph Anselmo, James R. Asker, David Bond, Michael Bruno, Amy Butler, David L. Collogan, Brett Davis, John M. Doyle, Frances Fiorino, David Fulghum, Paul Hoversten, John D. Hughes, Jr., Kimberly E. Johnson, Angela Kim, Steven Lott, Kerry Lynch, Denise Marois, Frank Morring, Jr., Jefferson F. Morris, Rodney Pringle, Lori Ranson, Annette R. Santiago, Andy Savoie, Adrian Schofield, Marc Selinger, Lisa Troshinsky,

BNA NEWS—(202) 452–4200; 1231 25th Street NW., Washington, DC 20037: Alexei Alexis, Michelle Amber, Donald G. Aplin, Cecelia Assam, Pamela S. Atkins, Jeannie Baumann, Alison Bennett, Deborah Billings, Cheryl Bolen, C. Jane Bowling, Leonard Bracken, David Barry Brandolph, Rossella Brevetti, Angela L. Britt, Brian J. Broderick, Richard James Bronson, R. Christian Bruce, Susan Bruninga, Sue Bryant, Ellen Byerrum, Raul Cabrera, Derrick Cain, Susan Carhart, Alison Carpenter, Sheila Cherry, Irene Clarke-Gomez, Jennifer S. Click, Regina P. Cline, Jennifer Combs, Steven Cook, Matilda Monroe Corley, Lauren Couillard, Richard H. Cowden, Sue Darcey, Jeff Day, Gloria Deigh, Phyllis Diamond, Kimberlee Smith Doman, Patrick Dorrian, Kenneth P. Doyle, Thomas Edmondson, Dana Elfin, Geoffrey Emeigh Jr., Catherine Sullivan Ezzard, Brett Ferguson, Michael Ferullo, Leslie G. Fleet, Laura Francis, Diane Freda, John Gannon, Lynn Garner, Lorraine S. Gilbert, Neil Graham, Diana I. Gregg, Angela Gregorits, Melinda Hanson, David Harrison, Peter S. Hayes, Joyce Hedges, Keith M. Hill, Richard Hill, Susan Hobbs, Rebecca Hoffman, Catherine Hollingsworth, Gwendolyn Holmes, Jay Horowitz, Terence Hyland, Helen Irvin, Rochelle D. Jackson, Alisa Johnson, Fawn Johnson, Helen Jones, Stephen Joyce, Hugh B. Kaplan, Marcia Kass, Bruce S. Kaufman, Gail S. Keller, Altaf U. Khan, John Robert Kirkland, Mary Jo Kraus, W. Randy Kubetin, Louis C. LaBrecque, Robin Lee, Wendy Leibowitz, Eric Lekus, Ralph Lindeman, Kristyn Linger, Brian A. Lockett, Fabia H. Mahoney, Mary Ann G. Manley, Martha A. Matthews, Anandashankar Mazumdar, Gregory McCaffery, Rebecca P. McCracken, Susan J. McGolrick, Toby McIntosh, Rachel McTague, Linda Micco, Nancy H. Montwieler, Michael Moore, Nancy J. Moore, Pamela Najor, Jonathan Nicholson, Carol Oberdorfer, Nancy Ognanovich, Phillip Olaya, Gloria R. Onley, Thomas O'Toole, Susan J. Pannell, Mack Arthur Paschal, Steven Patrick, Bernard J. Pazanowski, Pat Phibbs, Lyda Phillips, Ward Pimley, Kendra Casey Plank, Meredith Preston, Nathaline Richardson, Kurt Ritterpusch, Victoria Roberts, Linda Roeder, Lois Rose, Heather M. Rothman, Daniel J. Roy, Chris Rugaber, Susan Sala, Saied Ali Sartipzadeh,

PERIODICALS REPRESENTED IN PRESS GALLERIES—Continued

Cathleen O. Schoultz, Dean T. Scott, Judith Scott, J. Stratton Shartel, Jessica Simmons, Nancy Simmons, James W. Skovron, John R. Small, Noah J. Smith, Adam Snider, Patricia Spencer, John Stam, Beth Starr, Julie A. Steinberg, Peyton Mackay Sturges, John H. Sullivan, Larry Swisher, Ronald Taylor, Steven Teske, Judith Thorn, Joseph Tinkelman, Michael R. Triplett, Amy Tsui, Patricia Ware, Michael Warnecke, Susan Webster, Gary A. Weinstein, Karen Leigh Werner, John M. Whalen, Elizabeth A. White, Yin Wilczek, Eileen J. Williams, Jane A. Winebrenner, Michael W. Wyand, Gary G. Yerkey, Mindy Yochelson, Barbara Yuill, Robert Te-Kang Zung.

BARRON'S—(202) 862–6605; 1025 Connecticut Avenue NW., Suite 800, Washington, DC 20036: Thomas G. Donlan, James McTague.

BILLBOARD MAGAZINE—(646) 654–4610; 4704 40th Avenue, Hyattsville, MD 20781: Bill Holland.

BILLING WORLD MAGAZINE—(301) 855–5112; 743 Walnut Avenue, North Beach, MD 20714: John Guerra.

BLACK CONGRESSIONAL MONITOR—(202) 488–8879; P.O. Box 75035, Washington, DC 20013: Lenora Moragne.

BLACK ENTERPRISE—(212) 242–8000; 1507 Massachusetts Avenue SE., Washington, DC 20003: Joyce Jones, David Ruffin.

BLATTER—4506 32nd Street, Mount Rainier, MD 20712: Konrad Ege.

BROADCASTING & CABLE—(202) 659–3835; 1701 K Street NW., Suite 510, Washington, DC 20006: John S. Eggerton, William McConnell.

BUDGET & PROGRAM—(202) 628–3860; P.O. Box 6269, Washington, DC 20015: John Sprague.

BUSINESS PUBLISHERS—(301) 587–6300; 8737 Colesville Road, 10th Floor, Silver Spring, MD 20910: Nancy Aldrich, Andrew Arnold, Pamela Barnett, Rasheeda Crayton Childress, Colin Degen, Deborah Eby, Leonard A.C. Eiserer, Sarah Spencer Hammond, Louise Harris, John Higgins, Susan Hsu, Henry E. Kleiner, Marcy Levin-Epstein, Michael Levin-Epstein, Nancy Roth, Mark W. Sherman, Daniel Tyson.

BUSINESS WEEK—(202) 383–2100; 1200 G Street NW., Suite 1100, Washington, DC 20005: Beth Belton, Aaron Bernstein, Amy Borrus, John A. Carey, Stan Crock, Richard S. Dunham, Howard Gleckman, Douglas Harbrecht, Eamon Javers, Gloria B. Kassabian, Paul Magnusson, Michael D. McNamee, Richard Miller, Jane Todaro, Lee Walczak, Stephen H. Wildstrom, Lorraine Woellert, Catherine T. Yang.

CCH INC.—(847) 267–7000; 1015 15th Street NW., Suite 1000, Washington DC 20005: John Filar Atwood, Sarah A. Borchersen-Keto, Jeffrey E. Carlson, Stephen K. Cooper, Paula L. Cruickshank, Martin Egna, Peter E. Feltman, John David Flanagan, Brant Goldwyn, David Hansen, Catherine A. Hubbard, Angela Johnson, George Jones, Amanda Maine, Andrew Jason Maschas, Joyce Mutcherson-Ridley, John Forrest Scorza, George L. Yaksick, Jr.

CD PUBLICATIONS—(301) 588–6380; 8204 Fenton Street, Silver Spring, MD 20910: Tonya Allen, James Byrne, Emily Cloakley, Thomas J. Edwards, Melissa Frederick, Michael Gerecht, Joseph Haas, David Kittross, Frank Klimko, Mark Kuhn, John Reistrup, Lawrence Sherrod, Cecil Sinnex, Joseph Smith, Charles Wisniowski, Steve Woo.

CMP MEDIA INC.—(703) 243–1123; 601 13th Street NW., Suite 560 South, Washington, DC 20005: George Leopold, Jack W. Robertson, Amy Rogers.

CQ RESEARCHER—(202) 729–1800; 1255 22nd Street NW., Washington, DC 20037: Marcia Clemmitt, Kenneth W. Jost, Pater Katel, Kathy Koch, Pamela Prah, Kate Templin.

CANCER LETTER—(202) 362–1809; 3821 Woodley Road NW., Washington, DC 20016: Kirsten Goldberg, Paul Goldberg.

CAPITOL CITY PUBLISHERS—(202) 543–4368; 605 10th Street NE., Washington DC 20002: Natalie C. Holmes, Erika Fitzpatrick.

CAPITOL PUBLICATIONS—(202) 312–6072; 1333 H Street NW., Washington, DC 20005: Pamela Susan Moore.

CAREER COMMUNICATIONS GROUP—(410) 244–7101; 729 East Pratt Street, 5th Floor, Baltimore, MD, 21202: Eric Addison.

CHEMICAL MARKET REPORTER—(212) 791–4200; 900 N. Randolph Street, Suite 303, Arlington, VA 22203: Glenn H. Hess.

CHRONICLE OF HIGHER EDUCATION—(202) 466–1000; 1255 23rd Street NW., Suite 700, Washington, DC 20037: Nina Cary Ayoub, Thomas Bartlett, Goldie Blumenstyk, Burton Bollag, Jeffrey H. Brainard, Stephen Burd, Dan Carnevale, Elizabeth Cohn, Jean Evangelauf, Jamilah Evelyn, Elizabeth Farrell, Kelly Field, Karin Fischer, E. Piper Fogg, Andrea Foster, David G. Glenn, Lila Guterman, Holly Hall, Sara Hebel, Eric Hoover, Jennifer Jacobson, Brennen Jensen, Heather Joslyn, Audrey Williams June, Vincent Kiernan, Nicole Lewis, Sara Lipka, Harvy Lipman, Beth McMurtrie, Richard Monastersky, Jennifer Lynn Moore, John L. Pulley, Peter Schmidt, Jeffrey Selingo, Scott Smallwood, Erin Strout, Welch Suggs, Nicole Wallace, David L. Wheeler, Ian Wilhelm, Grant Williams, Bradley Wolverton, Jeffrey R. Young.

CLINICA—(301) 927–1485; 4004 Jeferson Street, Hyattsville, MD 20781: Karen Riley.

CONGRESSIONAL DIGEST—(202) 333–7332; 1525B 29th Street NW., Washington, DC, 20007: Sarah Orrick, R. Griffith Thomas, Anthony W. Zurcher.

PERIODICALS REPRESENTED IN PRESS GALLERIES—Continued

CONSTRUCTION CONTRACTS LAW REPORT—(800) 328–9378; 901 15th Street NW., Suite 1010, Washington, DC 20005: Anne Rosen, Richard L. Shea.

COOK POLITICAL REPORT—(202) 739–8400; 600 New Hamsphire Avenue NW., Washington, DC 20037: Charles E. Cook, Jr., Jennifer Duffy, Amy Walter.

CORPORATE CRIME REPORTER—(202) 737–1680; 1209 National Press Building, Washington, DC 20045: Russell Mokhiber.

CRAIN COMMUNICATIONS—(202) 662–7200; 814 National Press Building, Washington, DC 20045: Vineeta Anand, Tony Fong, Bob Garfield, Jerome M. Geisel, Douglas J. Halonen, Sara Hansard, Donna L. Harris, Mark A. Hofmann, Ralph Loos, Paul Robert Merrion, Miles David Moore, Jeffrey S. Silva, Harry Stoffer, Ira Teinowitz, Steve Toloken, Heather Forsgren Weaver.

CREDIT UNION JOURNAL—(888) 832–2929; 1325 G Street NW., Suite 910, Washington, DC 20005: Edward S. Roberts.

CREDIT UNION TIMES—(800) 345–9936; 4600 South Four Mile Run, Suite 930, Arlington, VA 22201: David Carlisle Morrison.

DEFENSE FOCUS—(703) 528–3770; 1300 North 17th Street, 11th Floor, Arlington, VA 22209: Colin Grabow, Jonathan Henning.

DER SPIEGEL—(202) 347–5222; 1202 National Press Building, Washington, DC 20045: Gisela Leske, Ranier Mascolo.

DIE ZEIT—(202) 223–0165; 1730 Rhode Island Avenue NW., Suite 502, Washington, DC 20036: Thomas Kleine-Brockhoff.

ECONOMIST—(202) 783–5753; 1331 Pennsylvania Avenue NW., Suite 510, Washington, DC 20004: Rachel Jane Horwood, Zanny Minton-Beddoes, John Parker, Adrian Wooldridge.

EDUCATION WEEK—(301) 280–3100; 6935 Arlington Road, Suite 100, Bethesda, MD 20814: Jeffrey Robert Archer, Rhea R. Borja, Darcia Harris Bowman, Ann B. Bradley, Kevin Bushweller, Sean Cavanagh, Gregory Chronister, Michelle R. Davis, Karen Diegmueller, John Gehring, Catherine Gewertz, Caroline Hendrie, David Hoff, Vaishali Honawar, Marianne Delinda Hurst, Robert C. Johnston, Bess Keller, Kathleen K. Manzo, Lynn Olson, Karla S. Reid, Alan Richard, Erik Robelen, Joetta Sack, Christina Samuels, Jessica Tonn, Andrew Trotter, Debra Viadero, Mark Walsh, Mary Ann Zehr.

ELECTRONIC BUSINESS—(301) 738–0071; P.O. Box 4190, Rockville, MD 20849: Tam Harbert.

ELLE—(202) 462–2951; 3133 Connecticut Avenue NW., Suite 315, Washington, DC 20008: Meryl Gordon.

ENDANGERED SPECIES & WETLANDS REPORT—(301) 891–3791; 6717 Poplar Avenue, Takoma Park, MD 20912: Stephen Davies.

ENVIRONMENT & ENERGY PUBLISHING—(202) 628–6500; 122 C Street NW., Suite 722, Washington, DC 20001: Dan Berman, Kevin D. Braun, Michael P. Burnham, Matt Comer, Marty Coyne, Daniel Cusick, Charles Donefer, Tasha Eichenseher, Andrew Freedman, Allison Freeman, Eryn Gable, Ben Geman, Hye Jeong, Alex Kaplun, David I. Leavitt, David Loos, Lauren Morello, Mary O'Driscoll, Darren Samuelsohn, Brian Stempeck, Colin Sullivan, Cyril (Cy) Zaneski.

EVANS–NOVAK POLITICAL REPORT—(202) 393–4340; 1750 Pennsylvania Avenue NW., Suite 1203, Washington, DC 20006: David Freddoso, Christina Holder.

EWEEK—(202) 365–3281; 14345 Long Green Drive, Silver Spring, MD 20906: Caron Carlson.

EXCHANGE MONITOR PUBLICATIONS—(202) 296–2814; 1725 K Street NW., Suite 1203, Washington, DC 20006: Michael Glenzer, Michael Nartker, Martin A. Schneider, Donna Kemp Spangler.

EXPRESS INDIA—(703) 893–5565; 1541 Wellingham Court, Vienna, VA 22182: Geeta Goindi.

FALLS CHURCH NEWS PRESS—(703) 532–3267; 929 West Board Street, Suite 200, Falls Church, VA 22046: Nicholas F. Benton.

FARM JOURNAL—(703) 331–3073; 12161 Cheshire Court, Bristow, VA 20136: Jane Fullerton.

FARM PROGRESS NEWS—(952) 930–4346; 520 N Street SW, Suite S–514, Washington, DC 20024: Sally Schuff.

FDC REPORTS—(301) 657–9830; 5550 Friendship Boulevard, Suite One, Chevy Chase, MD 20815: Ramsey Baghdadi, Bridget Behling, Joshua L. Berlin, Cabral Bigman-Galimore, Janet Coleman, Kathleen Connors, Jon Dobson, Andrew Dove, Peter Fehrs, David Filmore, Eileen Francis, Andrew Hawkins, Daniel Healey, M. Nielsen Hobbs, Mary Houghton, Sunil Iyengar, Scott Jenkins, Lee Kalowski, Andrew Kasper, Jaimie Kelley, Cathy Kelly, Molly Laas, Mary Jo Laffler, Jessica Lake, Michel Marcoux, Brian Marson, Michael McCaughan, Reed J. Miller, Ryan Nelson, Gretchen Parisi, William Clifford Paulson, John, Rancourt, Jr., Kathleen Rawson, Lauren Schwartz, Andrew Shelton, Scott A. Steinke, Susan M. Sutter, Katherine Thomas, Steele Thomas, Karl Uhlendorf, Christopher Walker, Elizabeth Walker.

FEDERAL COMPUTER WEEK—(703) 876–5100; 3141 Fairview Park Drive, Suite 777, Falls Church, VA 22042: Michael Arnone, Christopher Dorobek, Michael Hardy, Judith B. Hasson, John Monroe, Florence Olsen, David Perera, Dibya Sarkar, Aliya Sternstein, Frank Tiboni, Rutrell Yasin.

FEDERAL EMPLOYEES NEWS DIGEST—(703) 707–8434; 619 Herndon Parkway, Suite 400, Herndon, VA 20170: James Gsell, Alexander Krughoff, Philip M. Piemonte, Elizabeth Saloom.

FINANCIAL POST—(202) 842–1190; National Press Club, Suite 1206, Washington, DC 20045: Peter Morton.

PERIODICALS REPRESENTED IN PRESS GALLERIES—Continued

FOCUS—(301) 581–0999; 8515 Rosewood Drive, Bethesda, MD 20814: Peter Gruber.
FOOD CHEMICAL NEWS—(202) 887–6320; 1725 K Street NW., Suite 506, Washington, DC 20006: David Acord, Lucy Ament, Stephen Clapp, Russell Dinnage, Allissa Hosten, Carole Sugarman.
FORBES—(202) 785–1480; 1101 17th Street NW., Suite 409, Washington, DC 20036: Ira Carnahan, Andrew Gillies, Janet Novack, Matthew Swibel, Cristina L. Von Zeppelin.
GENERAL AVIATION NEWS—(301) 330–2715; 1915 Windjammer Way, Gaithersburg, MD 20879: Charles F. Spence.
GOVERNING—(202) 862–8802; 1100 Connecticut Avenue NW., Suite 1300, Washington, DC 20036: John Buntin, Melissa Davenport, Alan Ehrenhalt, Alan Greenblatt, Peter A. Harkness, Anne Jordan, Penelope Lemov, Zachary L. Patton, Ellen Perlman, Christopher Swope, Elder Witt.
GOVERNMENT COMPUTER NEWS—(202) 772–2500; 10 G Street NE., Suite 500, Washington, DC 20002: Wilson Dizard, Bradley Grimes, Joab Jackson, William K. Jackson, William Kash, Kevin McCaney, Matthew J. McLaughlin, Jason Miller, Mary Mosquera, Dawn S. Onley, Vanessa Jo Roberts, Thomas R. Temin, Patience Wait, Richard Walker, Gertrude Walsh.
GOVERNMENT CONTRACTOR—(800) 328–9378; 901 15th Street NW., Suite 230, Washington, DC 20005: Elizabeth Holahan, Lyrica Johnson, William Schieken, Richard Southern.
GOVERNMENT EXECUTIVE—(202) 739–8400; 600 New Hampshire Avenue NW., Washington, DC 20037: Tanya N. Ballard, George Cahlink, Timothy Clark, Beth Dickey, Susan Fourney, Amelia Gruber, Shane Harris, Denise Kersten, Anne Laurent, David McGlinchey, Kimberly Palmer, Katherine M. Peters, Daniel Pulliam, Thomas J. Shoop, Chris Strohm, Shawn Zeller.
HEALTH MARKET SURVEY—(202) 362–5408; P.O. Box 9902, Friendship Heights Office, Washington, DC 20016: Katharine K. Boyles, William R. Boyles.
HEALTHCARE INFORMATION—(202) 233–0013; 450 National Press Building, Washington, DC 20045: Christopher T. Fleming, Thomas Mullen.
HEAVY DUTY TRUCKING—(703) 683–9935; 802 South Overlook Drive, Alexandria, VA 22305: Oliver B. Patton.
HISPANIC LINK NEWS SERVICE—(202) 234–0280; 1420 N Street NW., Suite 101, Washington, DC 20005: Charles Ericksen, Sonia Melendez, Shigeki Miyashita, Jake Rollow.
HUMAN EVENTS—(202) 216–0600; One Massachusetts Avenue NW., Washington, DC 20001: Robert B. Bluey, Christopher Field, John Gizzi, Terence P. Jeffrey, Thomas S. Winter.
IDG COMMUNICATIONS—(202) 333–2448; 922 24th Street NW., Suite 804, Washington, DC 20037: Denise Pappalardo, Patrick Thibodeau, Daniel Verton.
IDG NEWS SERVICE—(301) 604–6250; 906 Phillip Powers Drive, Laurel, MD 20707: Grant Gross.
IMAS PUBLISHING—(703) 998–7600; 5827 Columbia Pike, 3rd Floor, Falls Church, VA 22041: Kelly Brooks, Thomas Butts, Lauren Davis, Deborah McAdams, Paul J. McLane, Leslie Stimson.
INDIA ABROAD—(703) 218–0790; 5026 Huntwood Manor Drive, Fairfax, VA 22030: Aziz Haniffa.
INSIDE MORTGAGE FINANCE—(301) 951–1240; 7910 Woodmont Avenue, Suite 1010, Bethesda, MD 20814: Andrew Analore, John Bancroft, George A. Brooks, Guy David Cecala, Greg Johnson, Thomas Scarlett.
INSIDE WASHINGTON PUBLISHERS—(703) 416–8500; 1225 South Clark Street, Suite 1400, Arlington, VA 22202: Natalie Baughman, Lara W. Beaven, John T. Bennett, Christopher Castelli, David Paul Clarke, Craig Cordes, Keith J. Costa, Shannon Davis, Jennifer DiMascio, Cynthia DiPasquale, Thomas Patrick Duffy, Daniel G. Dupont, Scott A. Eldridge II, Lourdes Fernandez, Colin Finan, David Francis, Alexia Garamfalui, Steven K. Gibb, Dawn Reeves, Elaine M. Grossman, Thomas Harman, Kristina Henderson, Jutta Hennig, Gomati Jadadeesan, Peter Kasperowicz, Geoffrey Koss, Alexander Kuli, Anthony Lacey, Stephen Langel, John Liang, Gregory Lopes, Jason Ma, Glenn Maffei, Martin Matishak, Veena Menon, Joe Morris, Douglas Obey, Avery Palmer, Sheryll Poe, Paul Precht, Manu Raju, Elizabeth Rees, Catharine Richert, Peter Rohde, Ashley Roque, Rolf Rosenkranz, Lorraine Schofield, Aarti A. Shah, Jason Sherman, William Matthew Shipman, Joe Singleton, Sebastian Sprenger, Ian Swanson, Rachel Urdan, John Wilkerson, Suzanne Yohannan, Jing Zhu.
INSTITUTIONAL INVESTOR—(202) 393–0728; 1319 F Street NW., Suite 805, Washington, DC 20004: Stanley E. Wilson.
INTERNATIONAL MEDICAL NEWS GROUP—(301) 816–8700; 12230 Wilkins Avenue, Rockville, MD 20852: Kathryn DeMott, Jeffrey Evans, Joyce Frieden, Teresa Lassman, Elizabeth Mechcatie, Terence Rudd, Mary Ellen Schneider, Jennifer Silverman, Heidi Splete, Miriam E. Tucker, Kerri Wachter.
INTERNEWSLETTER—1063 National Press Building, Washington, DC 20045: Marie B. Allizon.
INTERPRETER RELEASES—(800) 328–9378, 901 15th Street NW., Suite 230, Washington, DC 20005: Betty James, Patricia Minikon.
IRISH ECHO—(301) 404–9773; 9534 Fernwood Road, Bethesda, MD 20817: Susan Falvella-Garraty.
JAPAN DIGEST—(703) 931–2500; 3424 Barger Drive, Falls Church, VA 22044: Ayako Doi, Kim Willenson.
JET/EBONY—(202) 393–5860; 1750 Pennsylvania Avenue NW., Suite 1201, Washington, DC, 20006: Simeon S. Booker, Kevin Chappell.
JEWISH FORWARD—YIDDISH—(301) 530–8109; 10500 Rockville Pike, Suite 604, Rockville, MD 20852: Herman Taube.

PERIODICALS REPRESENTED IN PRESS GALLERIES—Continued

KING PUBLISHING GROUP—(202) 638–4260; 1325 G Street NW., Suite 1003, Washington, DC 20005: Linda A. Gasparello, Keith Stein.
KIPLINGER WASHINGTON EDITORS—(202) 887–6400; 1729 H Street NW., Washington, DC 20006: Peter L. Blank, George E. Brandon, Priscilla Thayer Brandon, Melissa Star Bristow, Martha L. Craver, Kenneth B. Dalecki, Matthew Dembicki, Michael F. Doan, Mary Beth Franklin, Peter Goldstein, Joan Goldwasser, Jean Gruss, Jerome Idaszak, Kimberly Lankford, Janet Linnehan, Edward Maixner, Kevin McCormally, James Gerry Moore, Sean F. O'Neill, Jim Ostroff, Joan Pryde, Ronaleen Roha, Kathy Rowings, Richard Sammon, Andrew C. Schneider, Mark L. Sfiligoj, Anne Kates Smith, Michael Smith, Mark Solheim, Mark Willen.
LE POINT—(202) 244–6656; 3234 McKinley Street NW., Washington, DC 20015: Helene Vissiere.
LEBHAR–FRIEDMAN PUBLICATIONS—5025 Durham Road West, Columbia, MD 21044: Ken Rankin.
LIABILITY & INSURANCE WEEK—(703) 536–6172; 5822 Washington Boulevard, Arlington, VA 22205: Steven Brostoff.
LINN'S STAMP NEWS—(937) 498–0801; 10121 Ratcliffe Manor Drive, Fairfax, VA 22030: William McAllister.
LP/GAS—(440) 891–2616; 5225 Pooks Hill Road #1118N, Bethesda, MD 20814: Charles Pekow.
MAIL ON SUNDAY—(202) 547–7980; 510 Constitution Avenue NE., Washington, DC 20002: William Lowther.
MANUFACTURING & TECHNOLOGY NEWS—(703) 750–2664; P.O. Box 36, Annandale, VA 22003: Ken Jacobson, Richard McCormack.
MASS TRANSIT LAWYER—(703) 548–5177; 1216 Michigan Court, Alexandria, VA 22314: Thomas Steven Robinson.
McGRAW–HILL CO.—(212) 512–2000; 1200 G Street NW., Suite 1000, Washington, DC 20005: Jeffrey Barber, Dipka Bhambhani, Cheryl Buchta, Craig Cano, Catherine Cash, Martin Coyne, Mark Davidson, Steven Dolley, Kelley Doolan, Amy Finkling, Lawrence D. Foster, Katharine Fraser, Keiron Greenhalgh, Brian Hansen, Angela Y. Hardin, Tom Harrison, Mark Heckathorn, Elaine Hiruo, William Holland, Daniel Horner, Joseph D. Hutnyan, Thomas F. Ichniowski, Frank Jackman, Valarie Jackson, Regina Johnson, Nick Jonson, Brian D. Jordan, Joel Kirkland, Michael Knapik, Liane Kucher, Rod Kuckro, Kathy Carolin Larsen, William E. Loveless, Jessica Marron, Karen McBeth Laping, Theophite Mullen II, Christopher J. Newkumet, Mark Alexander Oram, Tina Petersen, Margaret Ryan, Mike Schmidt, Stephanie Sharpe, Matthew Spangler, Melanie Tatum, Robert J. Thormeyer, Tom Tiernan, Jenny Weil, Esther Whieldon, Rodney A. White, Daniel Whitten, Eric Wieser, Michael J. Wilczek, Sherie Winston, Charlotte Wright.
MEDICAL DEVICES REPORT—(703) 361–6472; 7643 Bland Drive, Manassas, VA 20109: Steve Butchock.
METRO HERALD NEWSPAPER—(703) 548–8891; 901 North Washington Street, Suite 603, Alexandria, VA 22314: Paris D. Davis.
MID–ATLANTIC RESEARCH—(800) 227–7140; 2805 St. Paul Street, Baltimore, MD 21218: Martha C. Powers, John Rees.
MII PUBLICATIONS—(202) 347–4822, 733 15th Street NW., Suite 900, Washington, DC 20005: Ryan E. Hess, Cecilio Morales.
MILAN PRESSE—7711 Tilbury Street, Bethesda, MD 20814: Martine Combemale.
MULTICHANNEL NEWS—(202) 463–3737; 1627 K Street NW., 10th Floor, Washington, DC 20006: Edward T. Hearn.
NATION—(212) 203–5400; 110 Maryland Avenue NE., Suite 308, Washington, DC 20002: David Corn.
NATIONAL JOURNAL—(202) 739–8400; 600 New Hampshire Avenue NW., Washington, DC 20037: Julie L. Abramson, James A. Barnes, David Baumann, Peter Bell, Jessica Brady, Carl M. Cannon, Eliza Newlin Carney, Lisa Caruso, Richard E. Cohen, Marge duMond, Isobel Ellis, Ferraro, Sydney J. Freedberg, Jr., Brian Friel, Steve Gettinger, Robert Gettlin, S. Siobhan Gorman, Charles A. Green, Jerry Hagstrom, Corine Hegland, James Kitfield, Julie A. Kosterlitz, Josh Kraushaar, Margaret E. Kriz, Mark Kukis, Kellie Lunney, John J. Maggs, Charles Mahtesian, Jodie Morris, Neil P. Munro, Joyce M. Murdoch, Deborah L. Acomb Nations, Michael F. Peed, Patrick Pexton, William Powers, S. Scott Rohrer, Gregg Thomas Sangillo, Marilyn Werber Serafini, Alexis A. Simendinger, Paul Singer, Jill Smallen, Paul Starobin, Bruce Stokes, Peter H. Stone, Monica C. Sullivan, Stuart Taylor, Jr., Bara Vaida, Kirk Victor, Jake Welch.
NATIONAL LAW JOURNAL—(212) 313–9083; 1730 M Street NW., Suite 802, Washington, DC 20036: Marcia Coyle.
NATIONAL MORTGAGE NEWS—(202) 434–0323, 1325 G Street NW., Suite 900, Washington, DC 20005: Brian Collins, Paul Muolo.
NATIONAL NEWS SYNDICATE—(703) 356–6599; 1350 Beverly Road, Suite 115–229, McLean, VA 22101: Beth Aluise, Susan J. Aluise.
NATIONAL REVIEW—(212) 679–7330; 219 Pennsylvania Avenue SE., 3rd Floor, Washington, DC 20003: Elizabeth Fisher, John J. Miller, Kate Walsh O'Beirne, Eric Pfeiffer, Ramesh Ponnuru, Byron York.
NATIONAL UNDERWRITER—(202) 777–1102; National Press Building, Suite 941, Washington, DC 20045: Matthew Brady, Arthur D. Postal.

PERIODICALS REPRESENTED IN PRESS GALLERIES—Continued

NATIONALJOURNAL.COM—(202) 739–8400; 600 New Hampshire Avenue NW., Washington, DC 20037: Shawn Chen, Gwen Glazer, Meg Kinnard, Jennifer Koons, Erin Madigan, Jason Thompson.

NATURAL GAS INTELLIGENCE—(703) 318–8848; 22648 Glenn Drive, Suite 305, Sterling, VA 20164: Ellen Beswick, Rocco Canonica, Paul Ciampoli, Susan T. Parker, Alexander Beswick Steis.

NATURAL GAS WEEK—(202) 662–0700; 1401 New York Avenue NW., Suite 500, Washington, DC 20005: Michael Sultan.

NATURE—(212) 726–9200; 968 National Press Building, Washington, DC 20045: Geoff Brumfiel, Erika Check, Chris Gunter, Colin Macilwain, Emma Morris, Paul Smaglik.

NEW REPUBLIC—(202) 508–4444; 1331 H Street NW., Suite 700, Washington, DC 20005: Spencer Ackerman, Peter Beinart, Jonathan Chait, Michelle Cottle, Michael Crowley, Gregg Easterbrook, Franklin Foer, John B. Judis, Jeremy Kahn, Marissa Katz, Adam Kushner, Ryan Lizza, Jeffrey Rosen, Noam Scheiber, J. Peter Scoblic, Jason Zengerle.

NEW YORK JEWISH WEEK—(212) 921–7822; 8713 Braeburn Drive, Annandale, VA 22203: James David Besser.

NEW YORK REVIEW OF BOOKS—(212) 757–8070; 3000 Woodland Drive, Washington, DC 20008: Elizabeth Drew.

NEWS BITES—(202) 723–2477; 1712 Taylor Street NW., Washington, DC 20011: German Munoz, Goody L. Solomon.

NEWS INDIA TIMES—(212) 675–7515; 7911 Edinburgh Drive, Springfield, VA 22153: Vasantha K. Arora.

NEWSWEEK—(202) 626–2000; 1750 Pennsylvania Avenue NW., Suite 1220, Washington, DC 20006: Holly Bailey, John A. Barry, Martha Brant, Daren Briscoe, Eleanor Clift, Eve Conant, Howard Fineman, Melinda Henneberger, Michael Hirsh, Mark Hosenball, Michael Isikoff, Patrice Wingert Kelly, Daniel Klaidman, Weston Kosova, Tamara Lipper, Debra Rosenberg, Robert Samuelson, Gail Tacconelli, Richard K. Thomas, Rachel Thurneysen-Lukow, Steve Tuttle, Richard Wolffe.

OBERLE COMMUNICATIONS—(703) 289–9432; 2573 Holly Manor Drive, Suite 110, Falls Church, VA 22043: Sean F. Oberle.

OIL & GAS JOURNAL—(301) 365–5510; 9704 Corkran Lane, Bethesda, MD 20817: Maureen Shields Lorenzetti.

PACE PUBLICATIONS—(202) 835–1770; 1900 L Street NW., Suite 312, Washington, DC 20036: Craig Fischer, Kathryn Funk, Sid Goldstein, Molly R. Parrish.

PENTON MEDIA INC.—(202) 659–8500; 1350 Connecticut Avenue NW., Suite 902, Washington, DC 20036: Sandra Arnoult, James A. Donoghue, Loren S. Farrar, Perry Flint, William A. Freeman III, John McClenahen, William H. Miller, James L. Nash.

PEOPLE MAGAZINE—(202) 861–4000; 555 12th Street NW., Suite 600, Washington, DC 20004: Linda Kramer, Macon Morehouse, Jane Podesta, Teresa Sedlak, Sandra Sobieraj.

PERIODICALS NEWS SERVICE—(301) 725–2756; 9206 Vollmerhausen Road, Jessup, MD 20794: Cecelia Blalock, Mary Ann Gatty.

PESTICIDE REPORT—(301) 864–3088; 3918 Oglethorpe Street, Hyattsville, MD 20782.

PHARMACEUTICAL EXECUTIVE—(301) 656–4634; 7715 Rocton Avenue, Chevy Chase, MD 20815: Jill Wechsler.

PR WEEK—731 6th Street SE., Washington, DC 20003: Douglas Quenqua.

PRESS ASSOCIATES—(202) 898–4825; 1000 Vermont Avenue NW., Suite 101, Washington, DC 20005: Janet M. Brown, Mark J. Gruenberg.

PROCESO—(202) 737–1538; 480 National Press Building, Washington, DC 20045: J. Jesus Esquivel.

PROFESSIONAL PILOT MAGAZINE—(703) 370–0606; 30 South Quaker Street, Alexandria, VA 22314: Andrew Parker, Phil Rose.

PROGRESSIVE BUSINESS PUBLICATIONS—(410) 349–8200; 1528 Circle Drive, Annapolis, MD 21401: Thomas Guay.

PUBLIC LANDS NEWS—(703) 533–0552; P.O. Box 41320, Arlington, VA 20005: James B. Coffin.

PUBLIC UTILITIES FORTNIGHTLY—(703) 847–7720; 8229 Boone Boulevard, Suite 400, Vienna, VA 22182: Lori Burkhart, Christian Hamaker, Bruce W. Radford, Richard Stavros.

RADIO & RECORDS—(301) 951–9050; 7900 Wisconsin Avenue, Suite 400, Bethesda, MD 20814: Joe Howard.

RADIO BUSINESS REPORT—(703) 492–8191; 2050 Old Bridge Road B–01, Lake Ridge, VA 22192: Carl Marcucci, David P. Seyler.

READER'S DIGEST—(914) 238–1000; 1730 Rhode Island Avenue NW., Suite 212, Washington, DC 20036: William P. Beaman, John Mitchell, Sacha Zimmerman.

RECALL—(301) 460–1439; 14208 Oakvale Street, Rockville, MD 20853: William McVicker.

REED BUSINESS INFORMATION—(202) 659–3825; 1701 K Street NW., Suite 510, Washington, DC 20006: Paul Sweeting.

RESEARCH INSTITUTE OF AMERICA GROUP—(703) 706–8260; 1340 Braddock Place, Suite 205, Alexandria, VA 22314: Theresa Markley Brion, William Dunn, Velma Goodwine, Wayne Logue, Kevin McDermott, Michael J. McGoffin, Erin Trompeter.

PERIODICALS REPRESENTED IN PRESS GALLERIES—Continued

RESEARCH USA—529 14th Street NW., Suite 499, Washington, DC 20045: Jessica Leshnoff.
ROLL CALL—(202) 824–6800; 50 F Street NW., Suite 700, Washington DC 20001: Kate Ackley, Mary
    Ann Akers, Erin P. Billings, John Bresnahan, Amy Carlile, Chris Cillizza, Timothy Curran, Nicole
    Duran, Cassandra P. Foster, Michael Grass, Bryanna Hocking, Louis Jacobson, Paul Kane, Amy
    M. Keller, Morton M. Kondracke, Josh Kurtz, Jennifer Lash, John McArdle, Amanda McClements,
    David B. Meyers, Suzanne Nelson, Arthur Newmyer, Benjamin Pershing, Emily Pierce, Mark Preston,
    Ethan Wallison, Lauren Whittington, Jennifer Yachnin.
ROLLING STONE—(212) 484–1616; 6129 North 35th Street, Arlington, VA 22213: Brian Andrew Bushell.
ROTHENBERG POLITICAL REPORT—(301) 738–6816; 50 F Street NW., Suite 700, Washington, DC
    20001: Stuart Rothenberg.
RUSHFORD REPORT—(703) 938–9420; 261 Commons Drive, Vienna, VA 22180: Greg Rushford.
SALON—(202) 333–5695; 3409½ M Street NW., Washington, DC 20007: Mark Benjamin.
SATELLITE BUSINESS NEWS—(202) 785–0505; 1990 M Street NW., Suite 510, Washington, DC 20036:
    Bob Scherman, Jeffrey Williams.
SCIENCE & GOVERNMENT REPORT—(210) 348–1000; P.O. Box 190, Churchton, MD 20733: David
    Kramer.
SCRIP WORLD PHARMACEUTICAL NEWS—(301) 229–7910; 6102 Princeton Avenue, Glen Echo, MD
    20812: Reginald W. Rhein, Jr.
SETANTA PUBLISHING—(703) 548–3146; 109 North Henry Street, Alexandria, VA 22314: Declan Conroy.
SET–ASIDE ALERT—(301) 229–5561; 4701 Sangamore Road, #S–155, Bethesda, MD 20814: Warren
    Corbett.
SLATE—(202) 261–1310; 1800 M Street NW., Suite 330, Washington, DC 20036: Bidisha Banervee,
    Joshua Levin, Dahlia Hannah Lithwick, Timothy Robert Noah, David Plotz, William Saletan, Jack
    Shafer.
SPACE NEWS—(703) 658–8400; 6883 Commerce Drive, Springfield, VA 22159: Brian Berger, Colin
    Clark, Jeremy Singer.
STEELE COMMUNICATIONS—(301) 916–7132; 11109 Yellow Leaf Way, Germantown, MD 20876:
    Zaira Steele.
STERN—(301) 229–4108; 4829 Fort Sumner Drive, Bethesda, MD 20814: Katja Gloger.
TAX NOTES—(703) 533–4400; 6830 North Fairfax Drive, Arlington, VA 22213: Dave Adhicary, LaQuesha
    Allen, Jon S. Almeras, David Scott Antonides, Herman P. Ayayo, Kevin A. Bell, Lisa J. Bender,
    Heather Bennett, David E. Brunori, Jennifer Carr, Emily Dagostino, Emily Davis, Joseph DiSciullo,
    Wesley Elmore, Heidi Glenn, Chuck Gnaedinger, Robert Goulder, Cara Griffith, Joann Christine Harris,
    Cindy Ann Heyd, Allen Kenney, Helena Klumpp, Karla L. Miller, Christopher M. Netram, Audrey
    Nutt, Cathleen M. Phillips, Christopher Quay, Johnathan Rickman, Warren A. Rojas, Sirena J. Scales,
    Cordia Scott, Karen Jeanne Setze, Andy Sheets, Doug Sheppard, Susan Jeane Simmonds, Douglas
    Smith, Dustin Stamper, Frederick W. Stokeld, Sheryl Stratton, Crystal Tandon, Joseph Thorndike,
    Veronica Lynn Warner, Robert J. Wells, Risa Williams.
TECHNOLOGY COMMERCIALIZATION—(703) 522–6648; P.O. Box 100595, Arlington, VA 22210:
    Neil MacDonald.
TELECOMMUNICATIONS REPORTS—(202) 312–6060; 1333 H Street NW., Suite 100 East, Washington,
    DC 20005: Margaret Boles, Paul Coe Clark, John Curran, Carrie DeLeon, Ted Gotsch, Brian Hammond,
    Maureen King, Paul Kirby, Lynn Stanton.
TEXTILE WORLD—(703) 421–5283; 20911 Royal Villa Terrace, Potomac Falls, VA 20165: James A.
    Morrissey.
THE FORWARD—(212) 889–8200; 5412 North 26th Street, Arlington, VA 22207: Ori Nir.
THE HILL—(202) 628–8500; 733 15th Street NW., Suite 1140, Washington, DC 20005: Alexander Bolton,
    Robert Cusack, Jeff Dufour, Geoff Earle, Albert Eisele, Andrew J. Glass, Hugo Gurdon, Josephine
    Hearn, Mary Lynn Jones, Deborah Kalb, Jonathan Kaplan, John Kornacki, Jacqueline Kucinich, Kari
    Lundgren, Klaus Marre, Hans Nichols, Patrick O'Connor, Mark H. Rodeffer, Betsy Rothstein, Peter
    Savodnik, Megan Scully, Jim Snyder, Duncan Spencer, Jennifer Yingling, Jeffrey Young.
THOMPSON PUBLISHING GROUP—(202) 872–4000; 1725 K Street NW., Suite 700, Washington, DC
    20006: Jerry Ashworth, Sarah Barak, Savannah Bashaw, Elizabeth Blake, Elizabeth Bolton, Andrew
    Brownstein, Thomas Buschman, Carey Cauthen, Mara Cherkasky, Richard Crider, Charles J. Edwards,
    Joan Marie Flynn, Rodney D. Garcia, Kelly J. Gordon, Lisa L. Hayes, Luis Hernandez, Christian
    Hettinger, Travis Hicks, Donald B. Hoffman, John F. Iekel, Jerry Lee Kline, Rosemarie Lally, Denise
    Lamoreaux, Joe Lustig, Barbara Magill, Dale McGeehon, Robert W. Mitchell, Christopher Scott Morin,
    Erin O'Brien, Jeffrey Schomisch, Kieran Sharpe, David A. Slaughter, John Allen Smith, William
    H. Stewart, Dennis A. Tosh, Gwendolyn Vample, Beth Vandegrift, Mary Helen Yarborough.
TIME MAGAZINE—(202) 861–4000; 555 12th Street NW., Suite 600, Washington, DC 20004: Lissa
    August, Perry Bacon, Jr., Brian Bennett, Timothy Burger, Massimo Calabresi, James F. Carney, Donald
    Collins, Jr., Matthew Cooper, John F. Dickerson, Sally Donnelly, Michael Duffy, Lona C. Harris,
    Anthony Jackson, Viveca Novak, Amanda Ripley, Sharon Roberts, Eric Roston, Elaine Shannon,
    Hugh S. Sidey, Judith Stoler, Mark J. Thompson, Karen Tumulty, Douglas C. Waller, Michael Weisskopf,
    Adam Zagorin.

PERIODICALS REPRESENTED IN PRESS GALLERIES—Continued

TITLE I REPORT—(202) 636–5534; 9211 Setter Place, Springfield, VA 22153: Lois Berkowitz, Julie A. Miller, Jeanne Sweeney.

TRAFFIC WORLD—(202) 355–1150; 1270 National Press Building, Washington, DC 20045: William B. Cassidy, Robert G. Edmonson, John Gallagher, William Hoffman, Aaron Karp, Angela Greiling Keane, Richard Lawrence, Edward McKenna, Paul Page, Emily Rehring.

TRAVEL WEEKLY—(201) 902–2000; 1627 K Street NW., 10th Floor, Washington, DC 20006: Andrew Compart, Michael Milligan.

UCG—(301) 287–2700; 11300 Rockville Pike, Suite 1100, Rockville, MD 20852: Carl Albert Ayers, Christina Boyle, Melissa Chadwick, Brett Coughlin, Darrell Delamaide, Fran Fanshel, Lisa Getter, Richard D. Hadley, Jay Heflin, Wendy Johnson, Spencer Kelly, Hugh Kennedy, Scott Kraft, Todd Leeuwenburgh, Claire Leheny, Alan Prochoroff, Nicholas Rummell, Shawn Schmitt, Burt Schorr, Marcus Smith, Vincent Taylor, Jayne Whalley-Hill.

U.S. MEDICINE—(202) 463–6000; 2021 L Street NW., Suite 400, Washington, DC 20036: Sandra Basu, Frank M. Best, Matt Pueschel, DianaLouise Spangler, Stephen Spotswood.

U.S. NEWS & WORLD REPORT—(202) 955–2000; 1050 Thomas Jefferson Street NW., Washington, DC 20007: Julian E. Barnes, Megan L. Barnett, Michael Barone, Paul Bedard, Matthew Benjamin, Gloria Borger, Kim Clark, Bay Fang, Daniel Gilgoff, Elizabeth Halloran, Danielle Knight, Linda Kulman, Marianne Lavelle, Anna Mulrine, Richard J. Newman, Thomas E. Omestad, Joellen Perry, Chitra Ragavan, Linda Robinson, Terence Samuel, Nancy Shute, Roger Simon, Lisa Stein, Kenneth T. Walsh, Kevin Whitelaw, Ben Wildavsky, Gordon Witkin.

USA JOURNAL—(703) 379–2520; P.O. Box 714, Washington, DC 20044: Janne Kum Cha Pak.

VANITY FAIR—(202) 363–5557; 4907 Rockwood Parkway NW., Washington, DC 20016: Maureen Orth.

VILLAGE VOICE—(202) 331–7718; 1312 18th Street NW., Washington, DC 20036: James Ridgeway.

WASHINGTON BLADE—(202) 797–7000; 1408 U Street NW., Second Floor, Washington, DC 20009: Louis M. Chibbaro, Jr., Chris Crain, Joseph Ross Crea, Eartha Melzer, Kenneth Sain, Jr., Rhonda M. Smith.

WASHINGTON BUSINESS INFORMATION—(703) 538–7600; 300 North Washington Street, Suite 200, Falls Church, VA 22046: Eric Barreto, Robert Barton, Cynthia Carter, Neal Learner, Lauren Legard, Edward McKenna, Matthew Salt, Chris Silva, Jennifer T. Villemez.

WASHINGTON BUSINESS JOURNAL—(703) 816–0330; 1555 Wilson Boulevard, Suite 400, Arlington, VA 22209: Kent Hoover.

WASHINGTON COUNSELETTER—(800) 622–7284; 5712 26th Street NW., Washington, DC 20015: Deborah A. Kavruck, Samuel Kavruck.

WASHINGTON CRIME NEWS SERVICES—(202) 662–7035; National Press Building, Suite 901, Washington, DC 20045: Leonard Curry.

WASHINGTON INFORMATION SOURCE—(703) 779–8777; 208 South King Street, Suite 303, Leesburg, VA 20175: Dawn Gould.

WASHINGTON NEWS OBSERVER—(301) 657–1966; 5101 River Road, Suite 1204, Bethesda, MD 20816: Anne Orleans.

WASHINGTON SERVICE BUREAU—(847) 267–7000; 1015 15th Street NW., Suite 1000, Washington, DC 20005: Susan Kavanagh, Jacquelyn Lumb.

WASHINGTON TECHNOLOGY—(202) 772–2500; 10 G Street NE., Suite 500, Washington, DC 20002: Douglas Beizer, Roseanne Gerin, Steve LeSueur, Alice Lipowicz, Evamarie Socha, Nick Wakeman, William E. Welsh.

WASHINGTON TRADE DAILY—(301) 946–0817; P.O. Box 1802, Wheaton, MD 20915: James R. Berger, Mary Berger.

WASHINGTON WATCH—(301) 461–9688; 5923 Onondaga Road, Bethesda, MD 20816: Kazutami Yamazaki.

WASHINGTONIAN—(202) 296–3600; 1828 L Street NW., Suite 200, Washington, DC 20036: Charles N. Conconi, Kim Eisler, Charles Limpert, Drew Lindsay.

WATERWAYS JOURNAL—(314) 241–7354; 5220 North Carlin Springs Road, Arlington, VA 22203: Carlo J. Salzano.

WEBSTER COMMUNICATIONS—(314) 241–7354; 3835 North 9th Street, Suite 401W, Arlington, VA 22203: James C. Webster.

WEEKLY STANDARD—(202) 293–4900; 1150 17th Street NW., Suite 505, Washington, DC 20036: Fred Barnes, Christopher Caldwell, Matthew Continetti, Duncan Currie, Rachel DiCarlo, Terry Eastland, Andrew Ferguson, Stephen Hayes, Laura Beth Henary, Matt Labash, Jonathan Last, Katherine Mangu-Ward, Erin Montgomery, David Skinner, David Tell.

WIRELESS WEEK—(202) 659–3809; 1701 K Street NW., 10th Floor, Washington, DC 20006: L. Mark Rockwell.

WIRTSCHAFTSWOCHE—(202) 238–0130; 1779 Church Street NW., Washington, DC 20036: Olaf Gersemann.

CONGRESSIONAL DISTRICT MAPS

ALABAMA—Congressional Districts—(7 Districts)

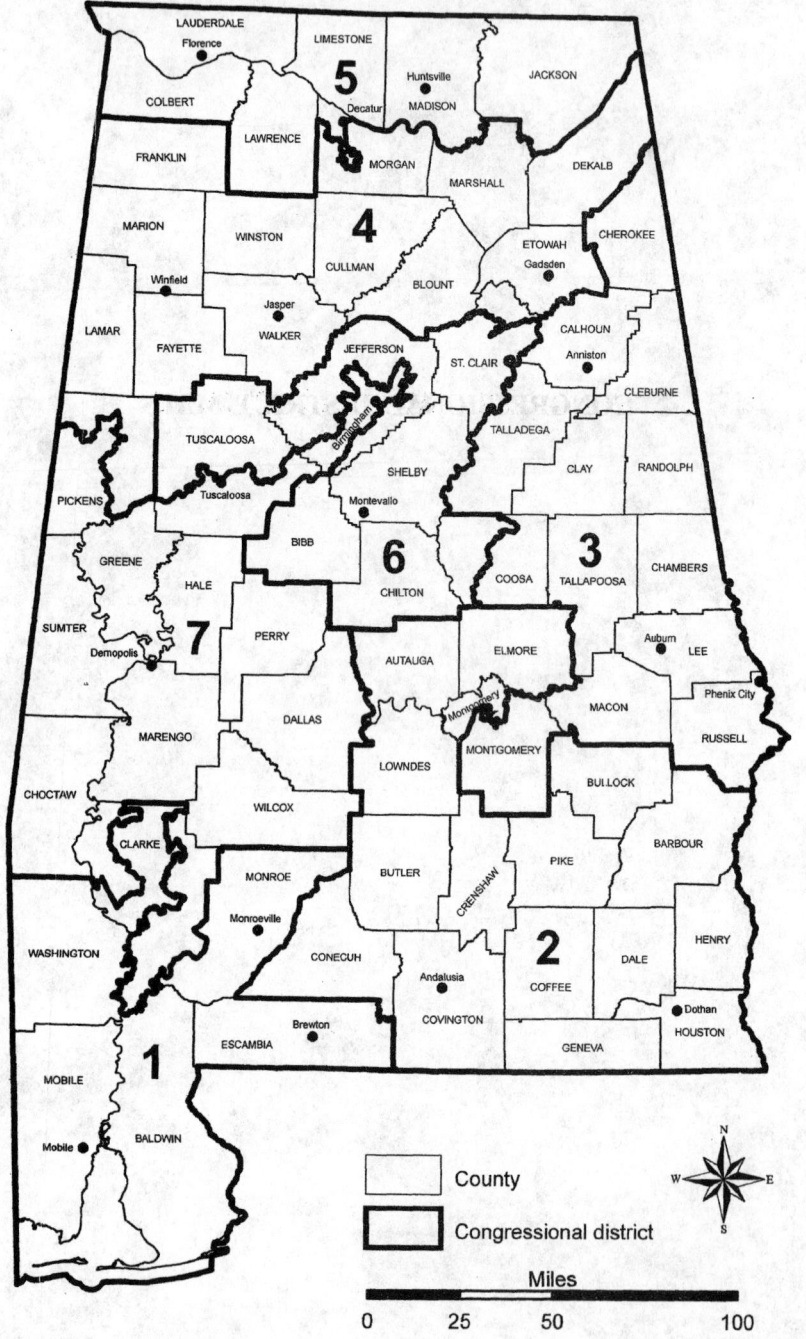

ALASKA—Congressional District—(1 District At Large)

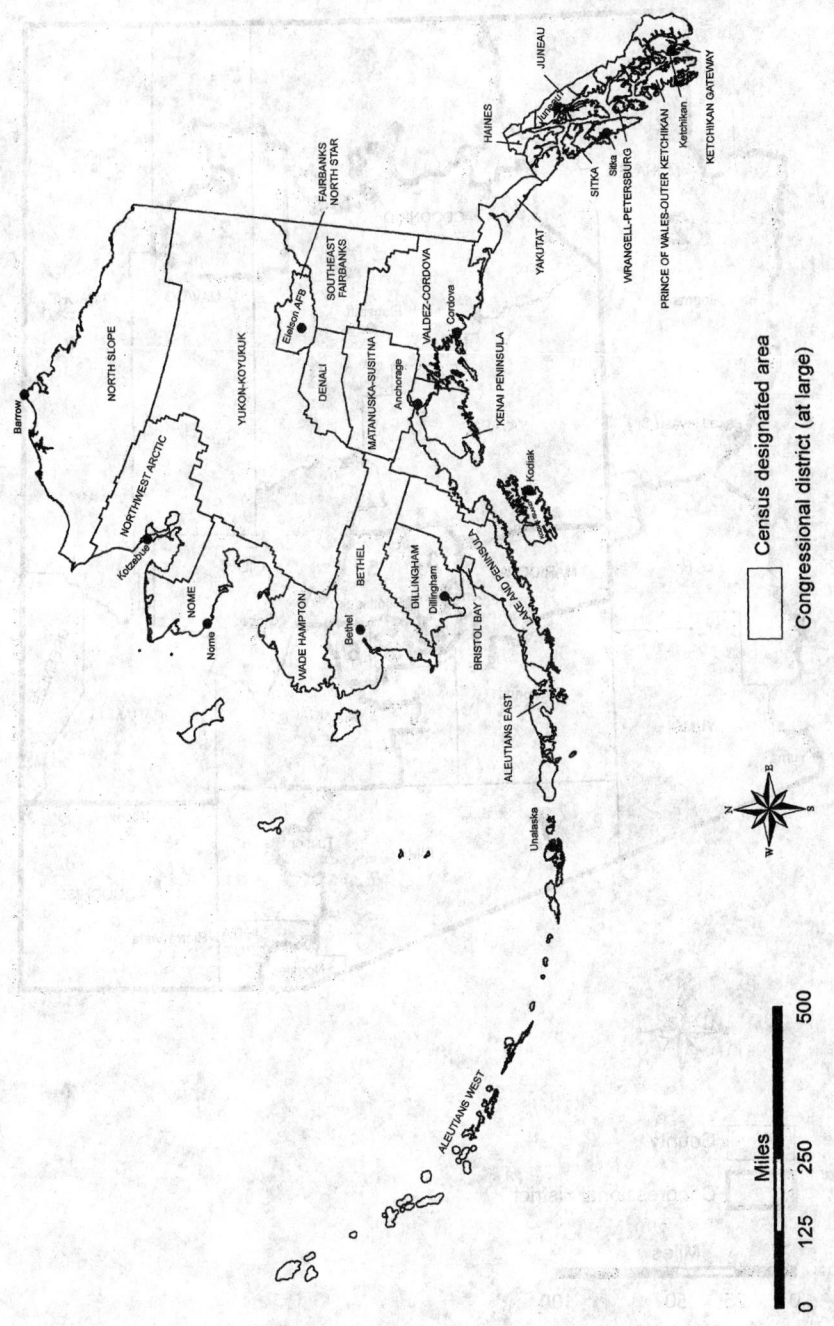

ARIZONA—Congressional Districts—(8 Districts)

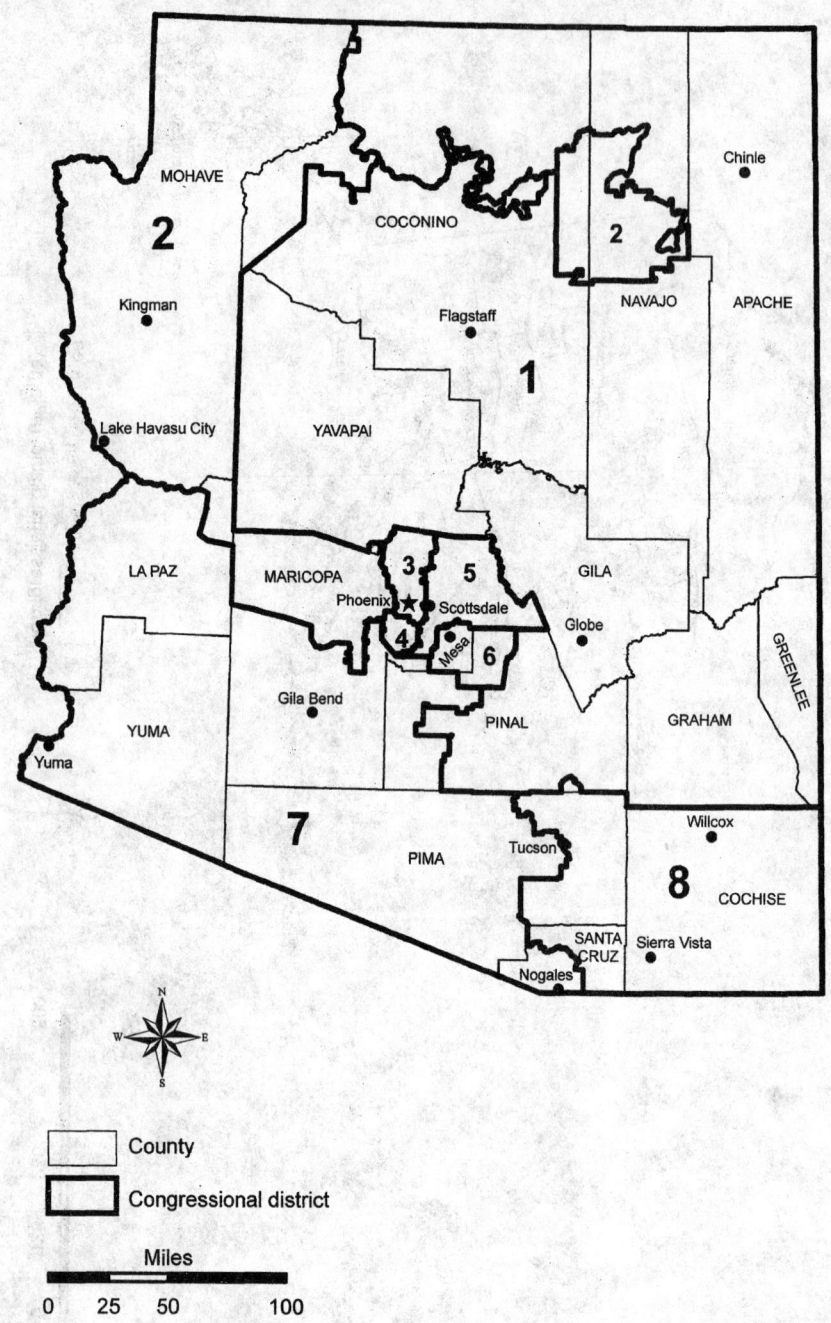

County

Congressional district

Miles

0   25   50   100

ARKANSAS—Congressional Districts—(4 Districts)

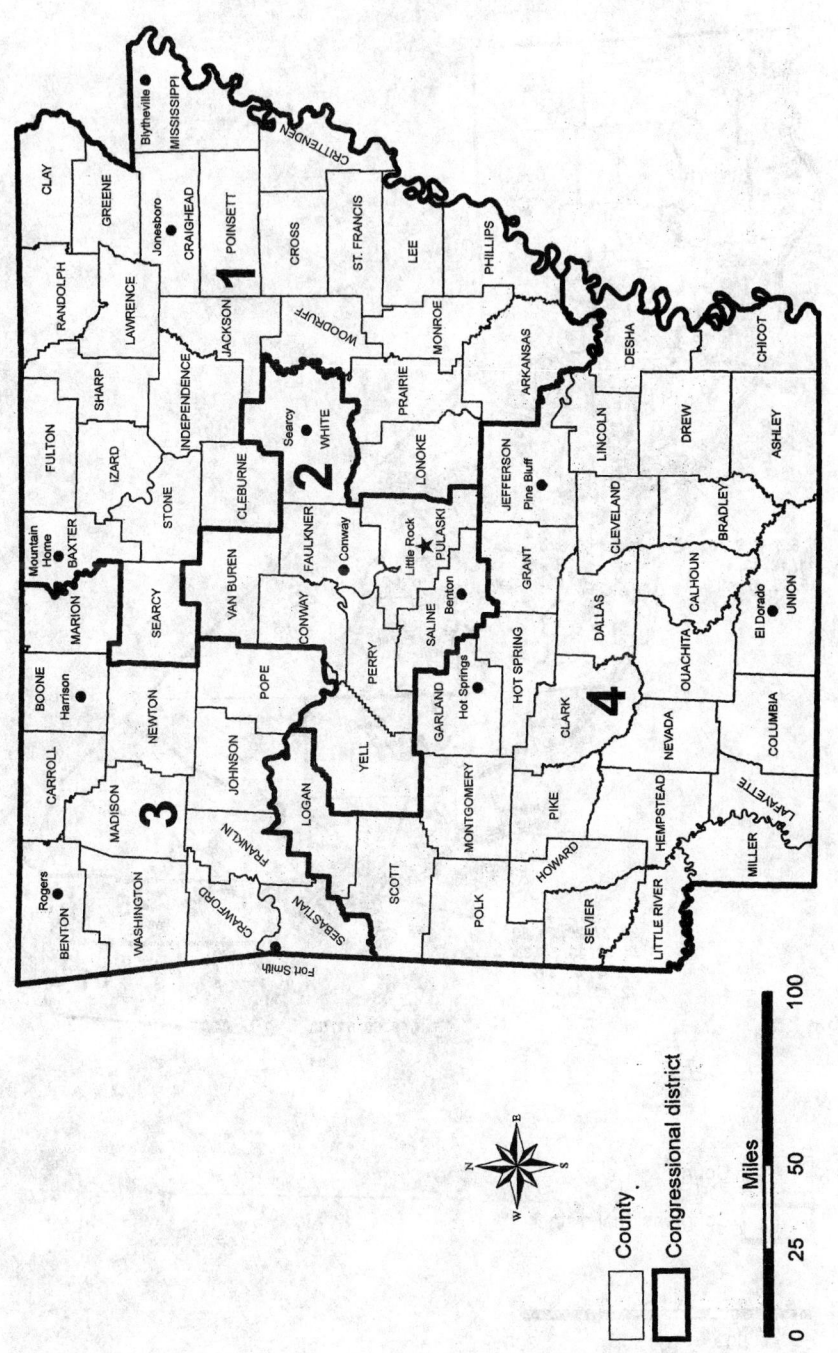

CALIFORNIA—Congressional Districts—(53 Districts)

COLORADO —Congressional Districts—(7 Districts)

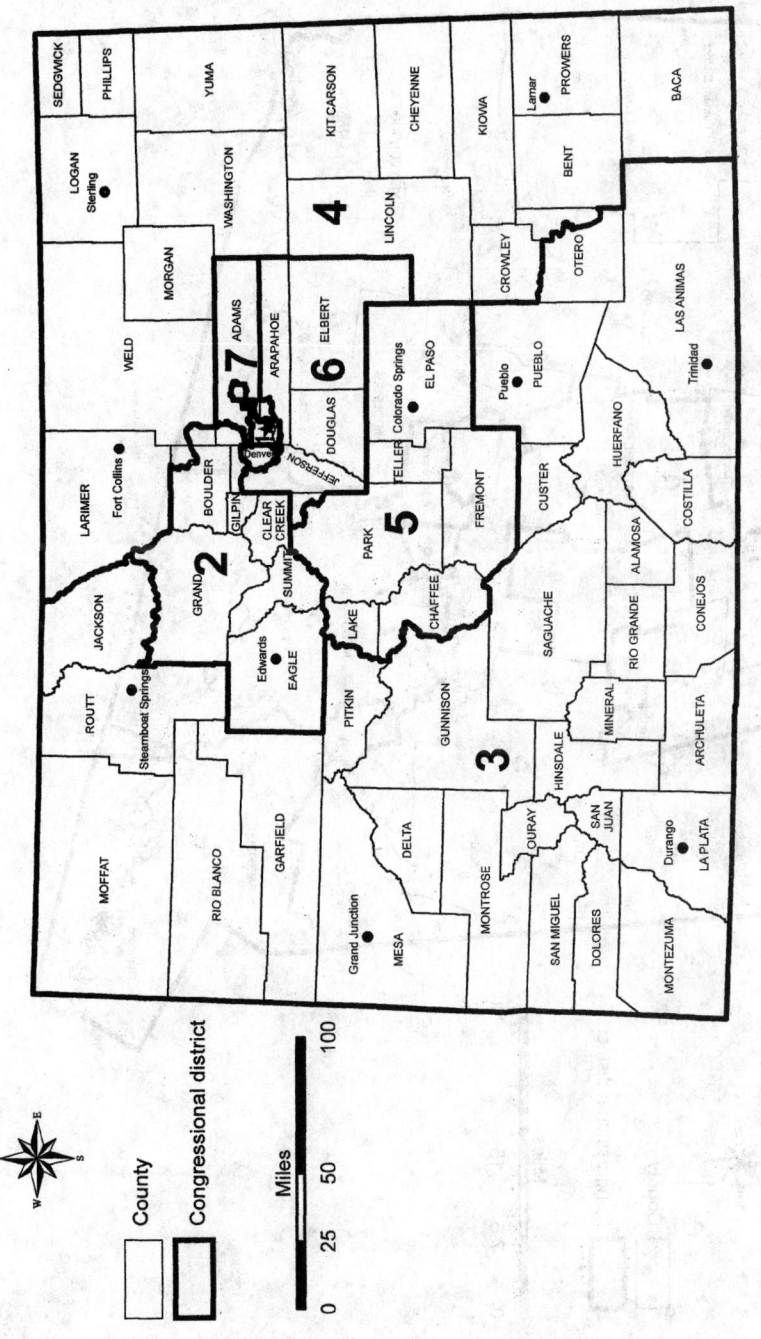

CONNECTICUT—Congressional Districts—(5 Districts)

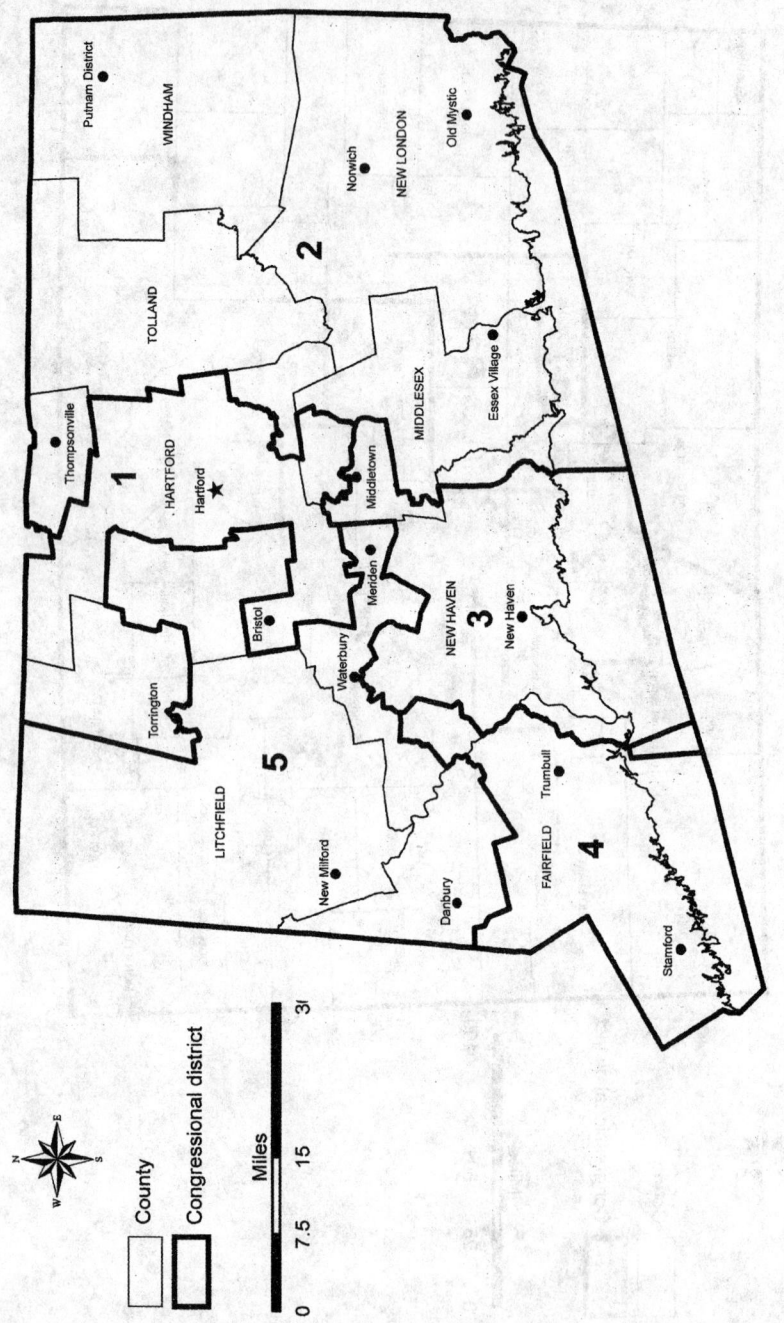

DELAWARE—Congressional District—(1 District At Large)

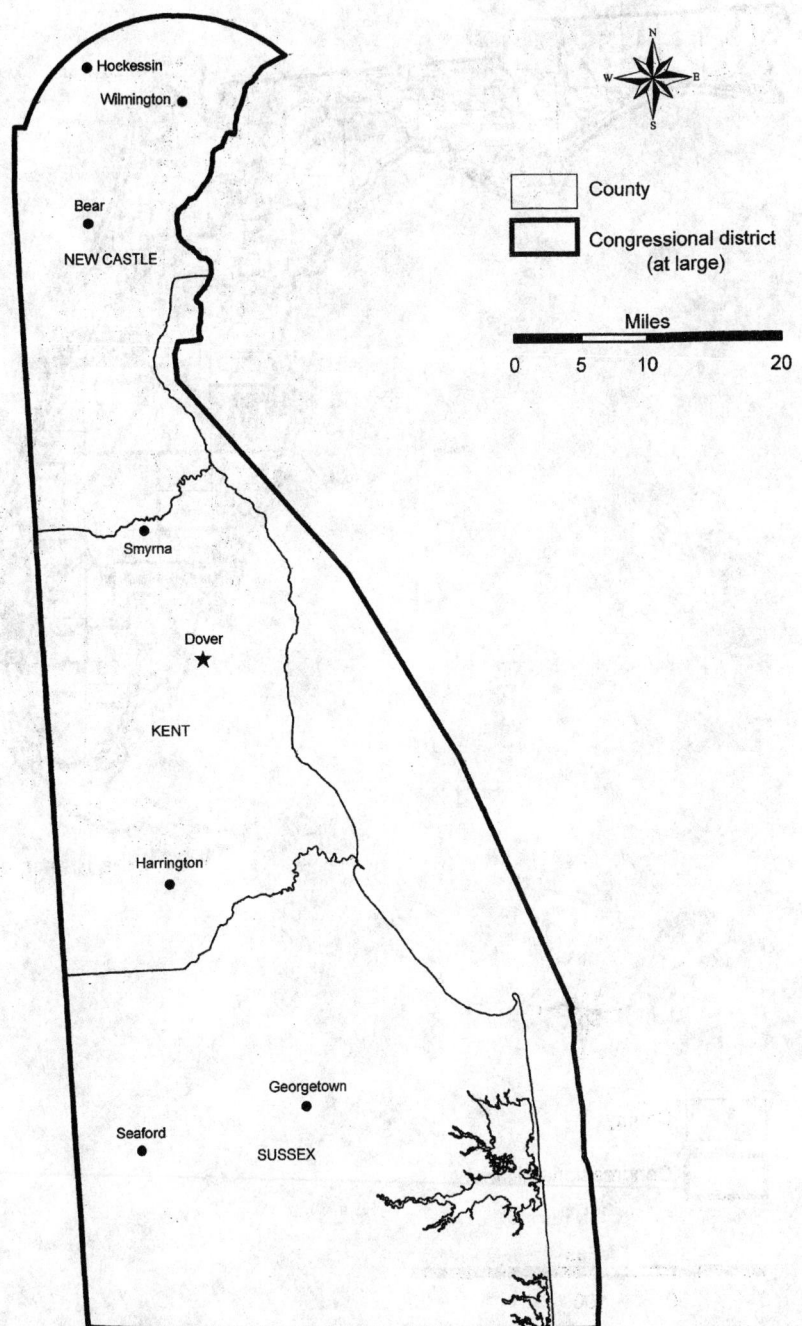

FLORIDA—Congressional Districts—(25 Districts)

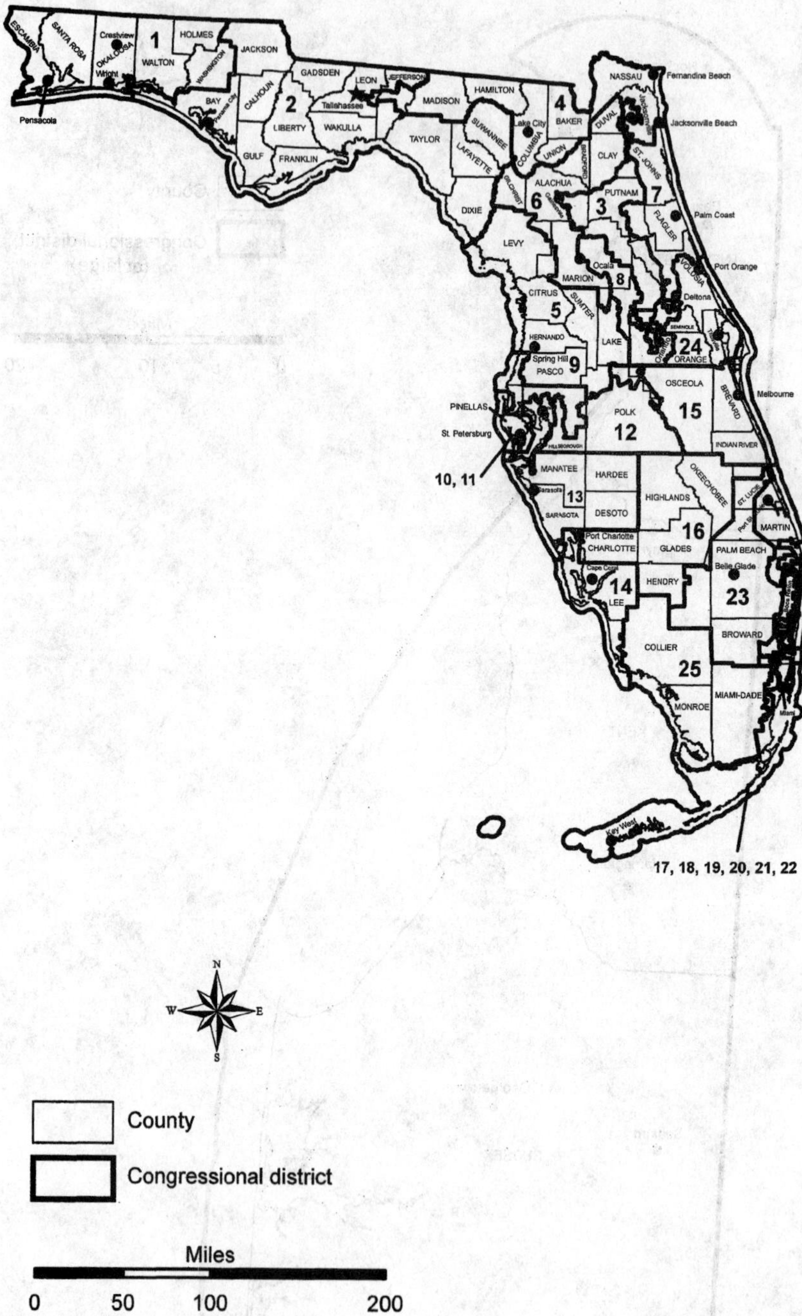

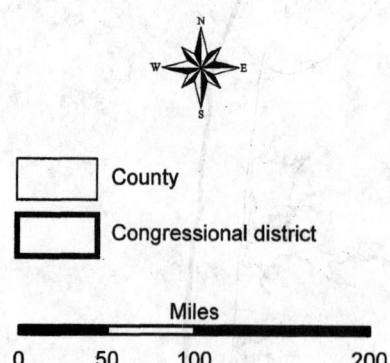

GEORGIA—Congressional Districts—(13 Districts)

County

Congressional district

Miles

0   25   50   100

HAWAII—Congressional Districts—(2 Districts)

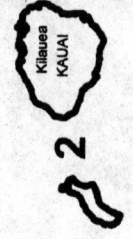

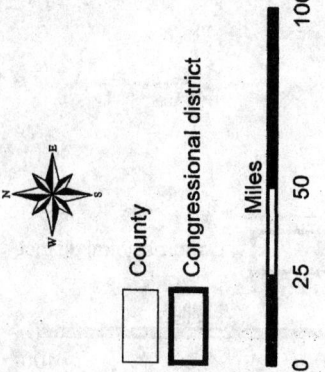

IDAHO—Congressional Districts—(2 Districts)

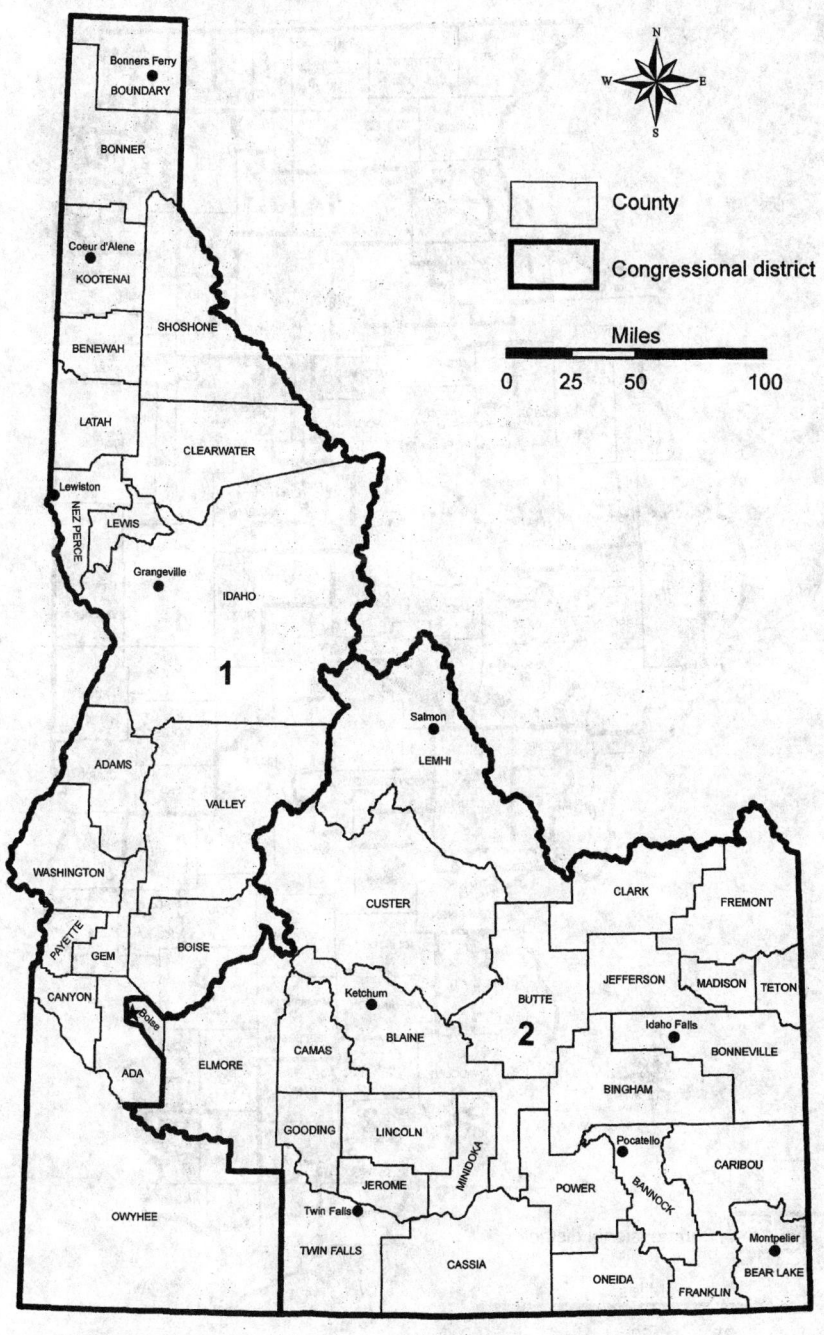

ILLINOIS—Congressional Districts—(19 Districts)

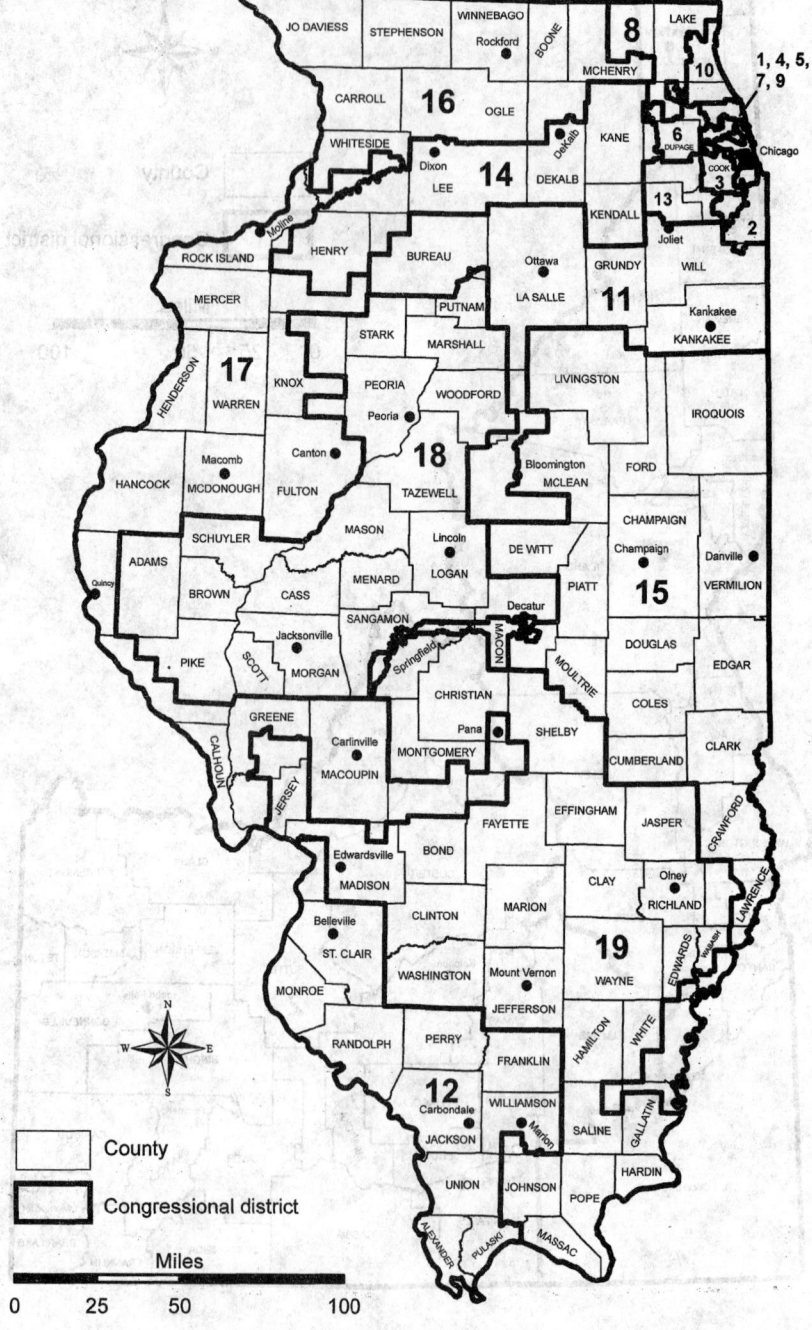

INDIANA—Congressional Districts—(9 Districts)

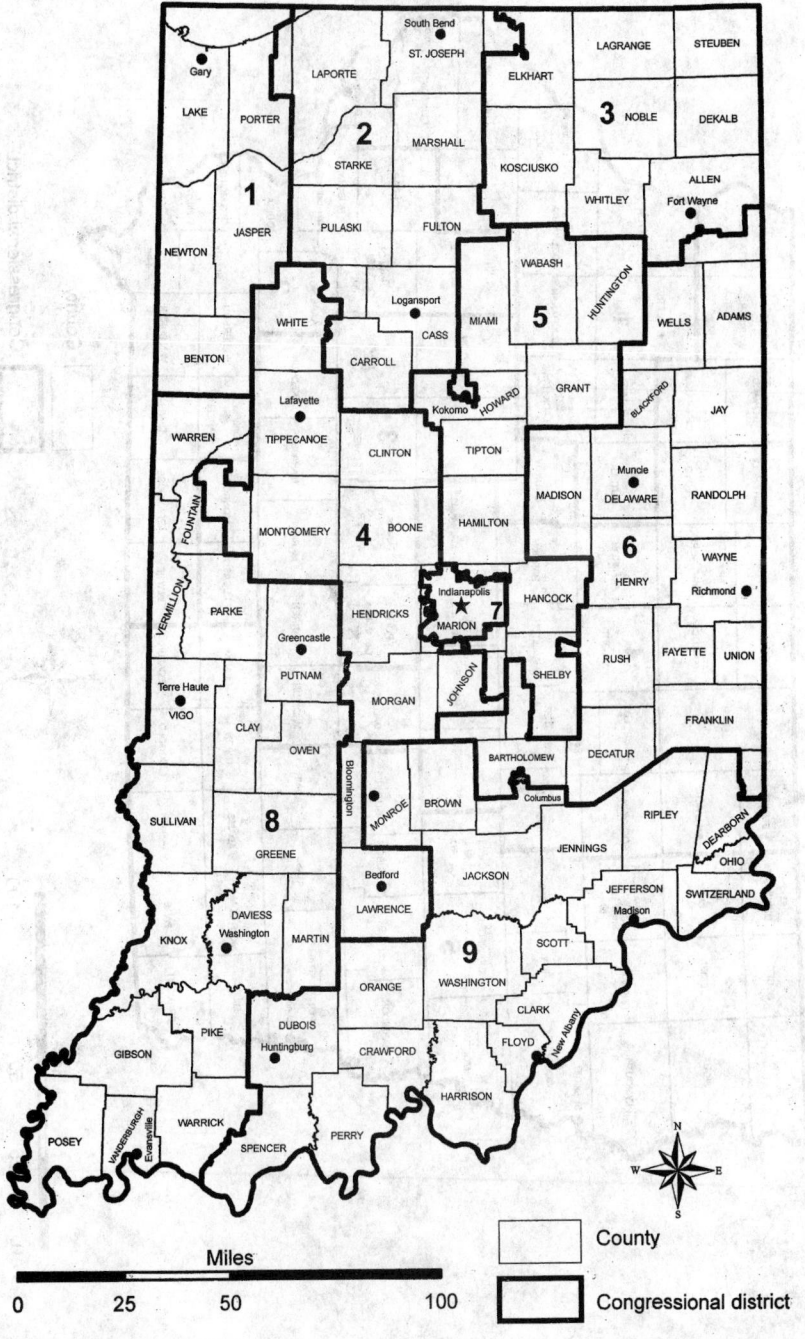

IOWA—Congressional Districts—(5 Districts)

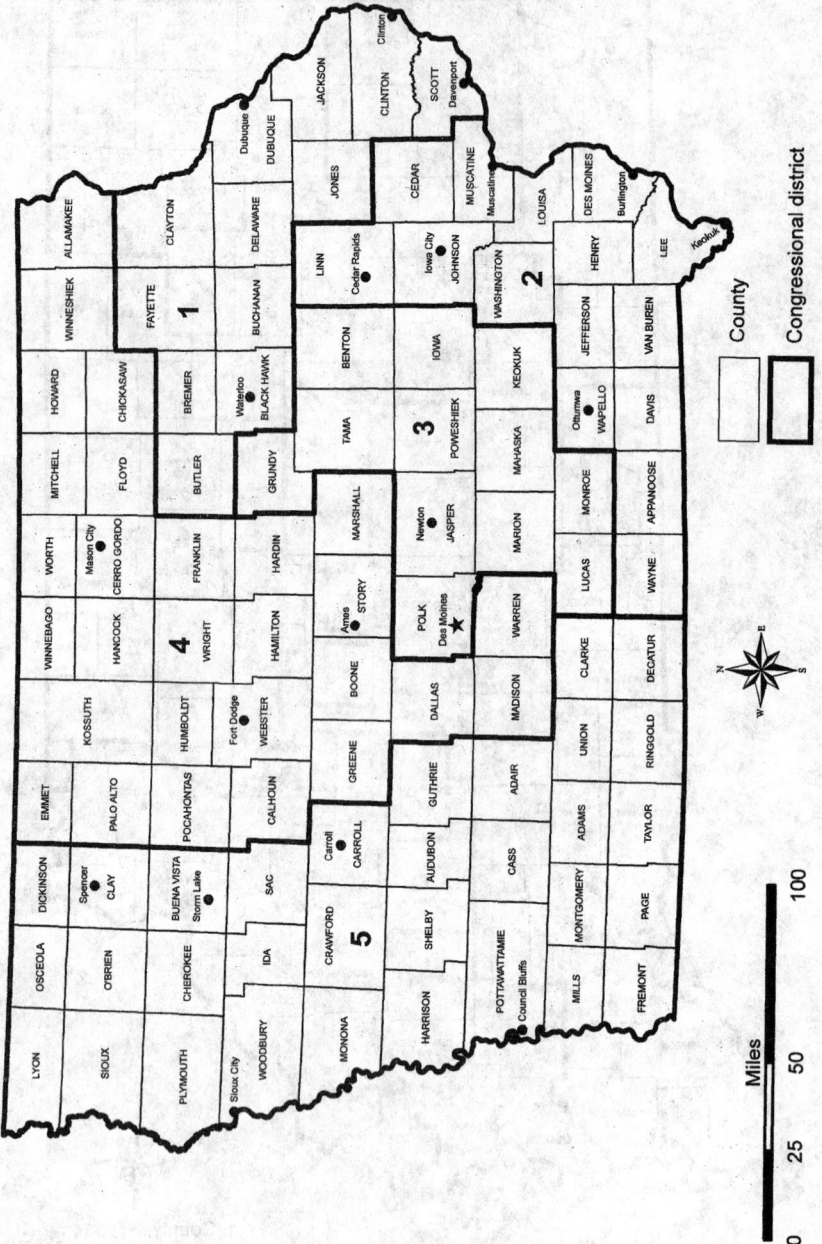

County

Congressional district

KANSAS—Congressional Districts—(4 Districts)

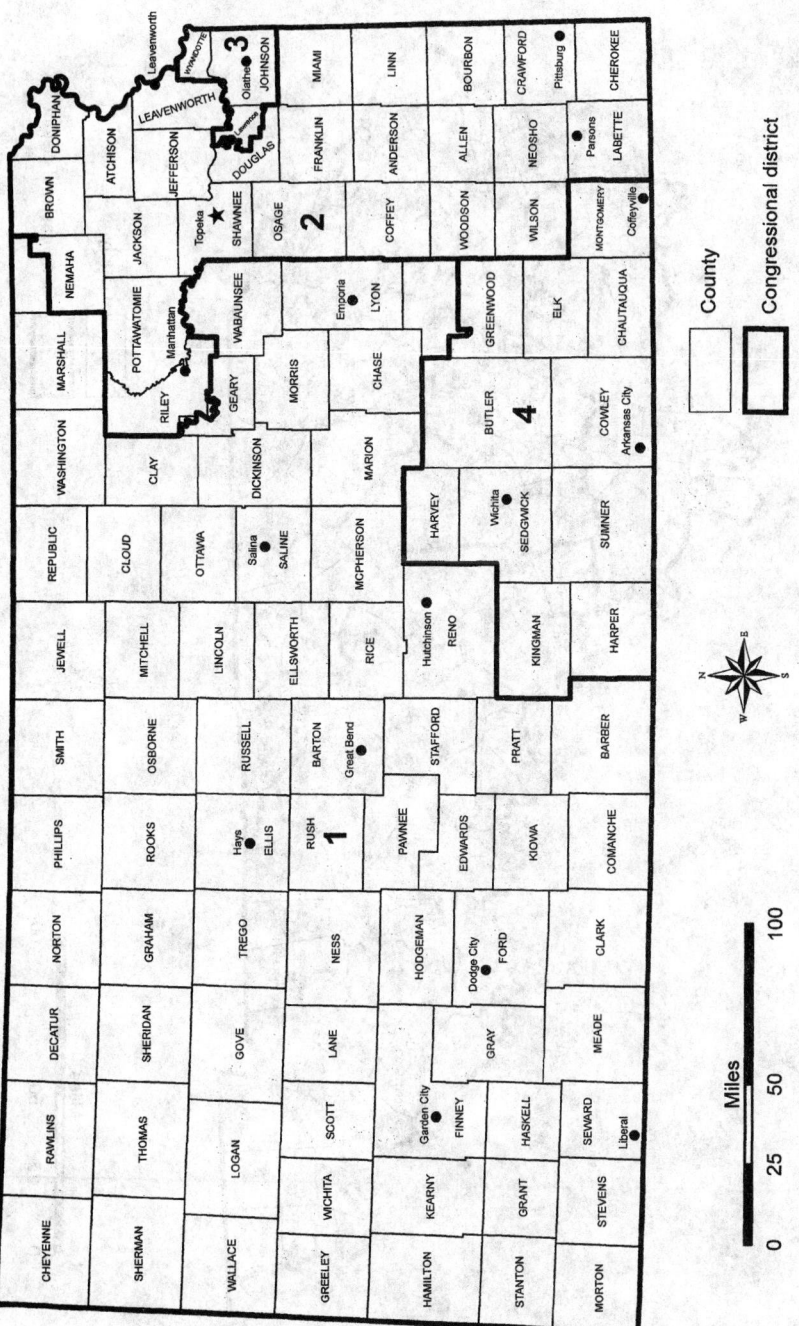

County

Congressional district

Miles

0   25   50   100

KENTUCKY—Congressional Districts—(6 Districts)

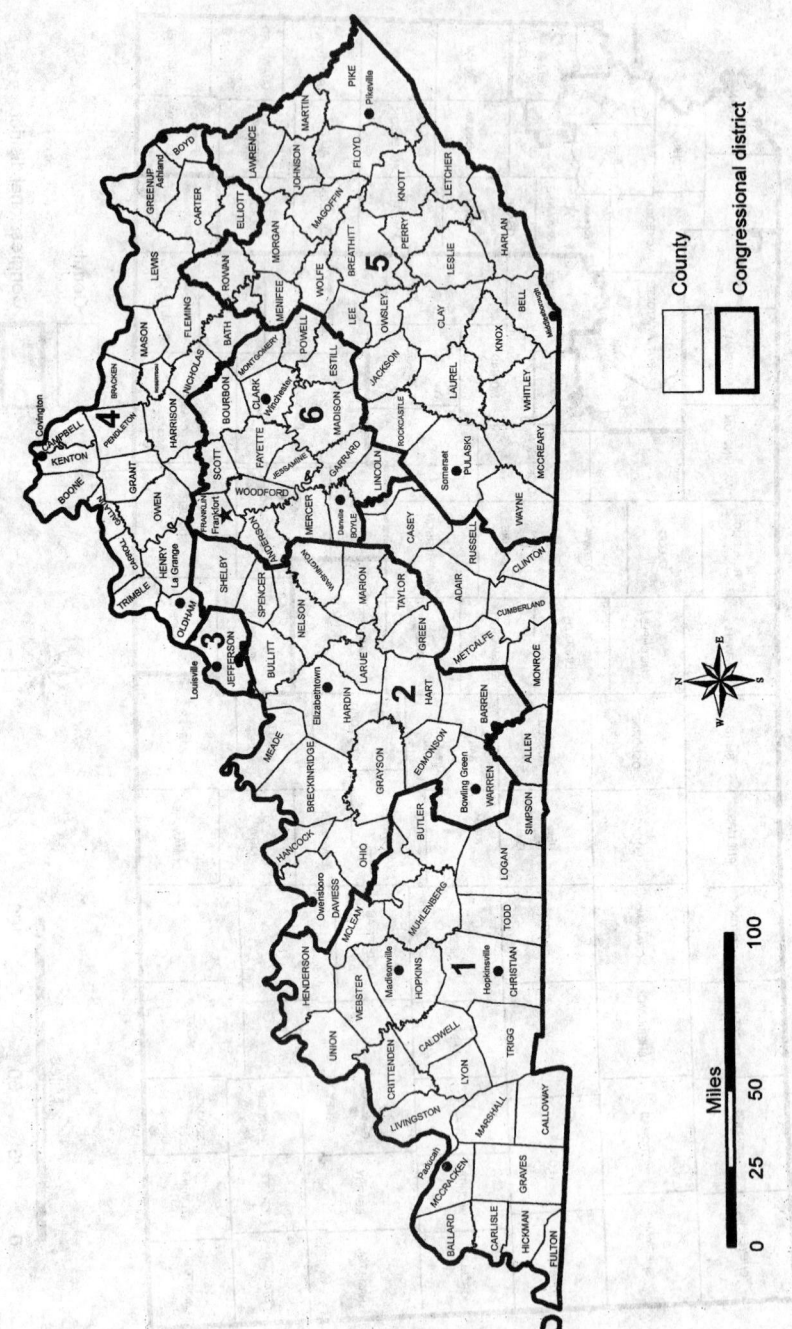

County

Congressional district

Miles

0   25   50   100

LOUISIANA—Congressional Districts—(7 Districts)

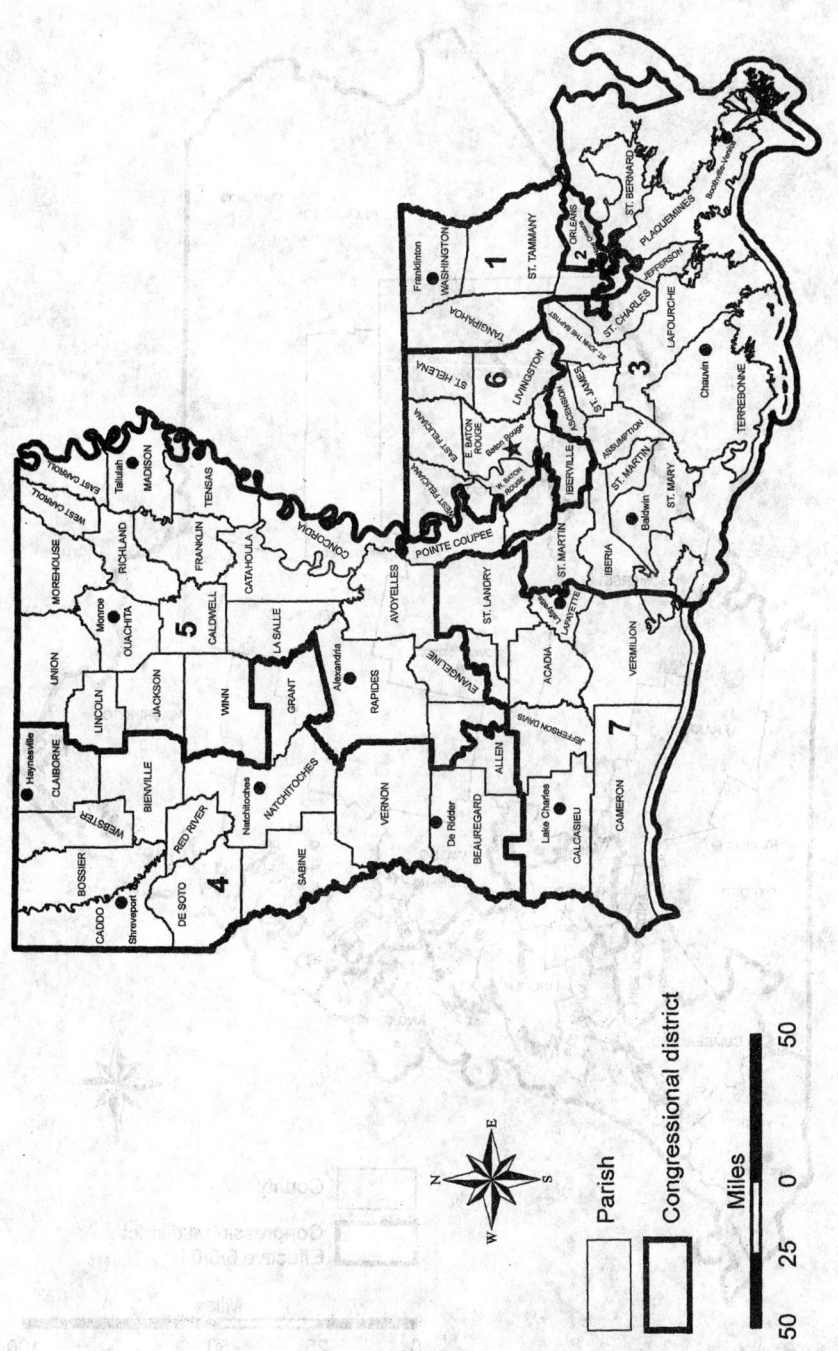

MAINE—Congressional Districts—(2 Districts)

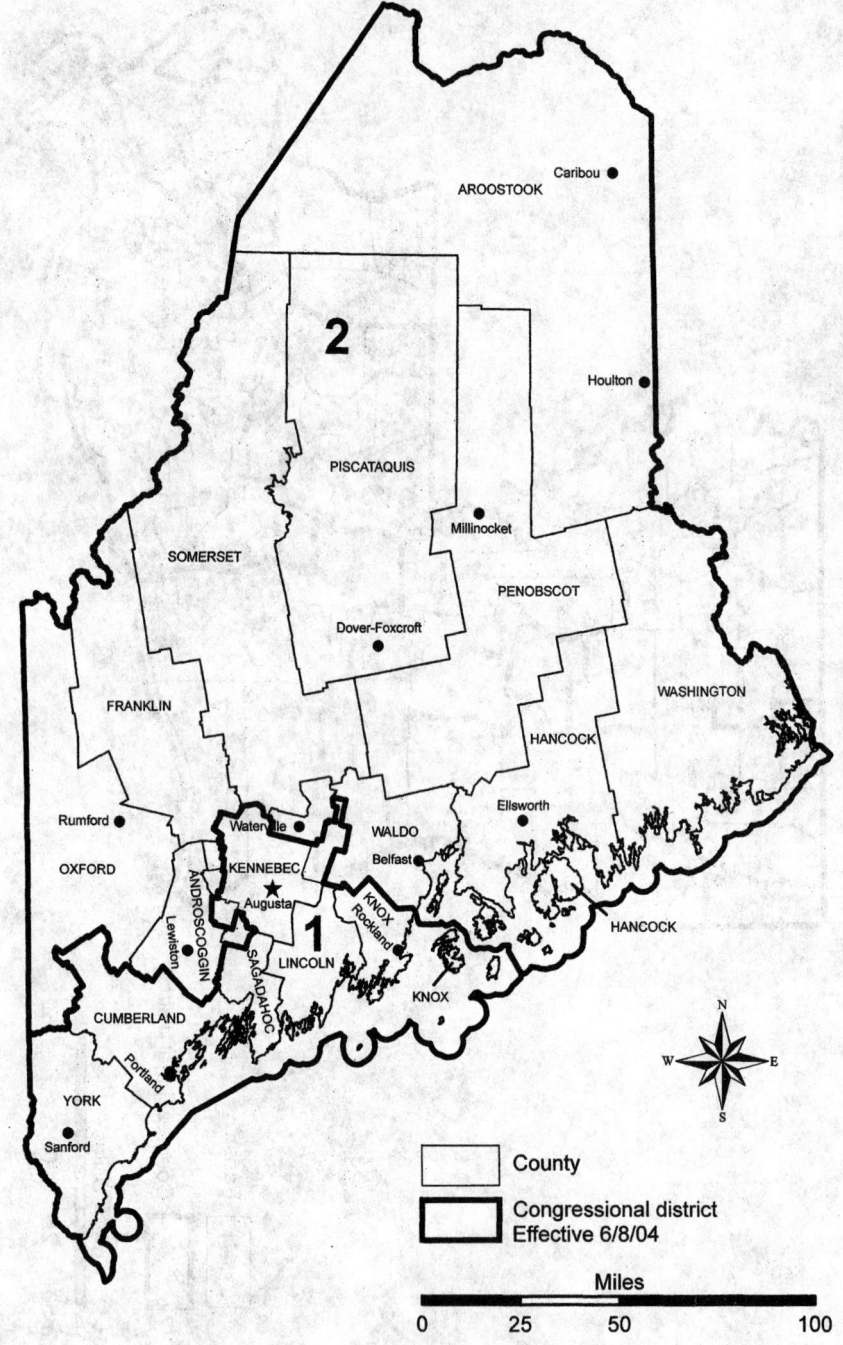

MARYLAND—Congressional Districts—(8 Districts)

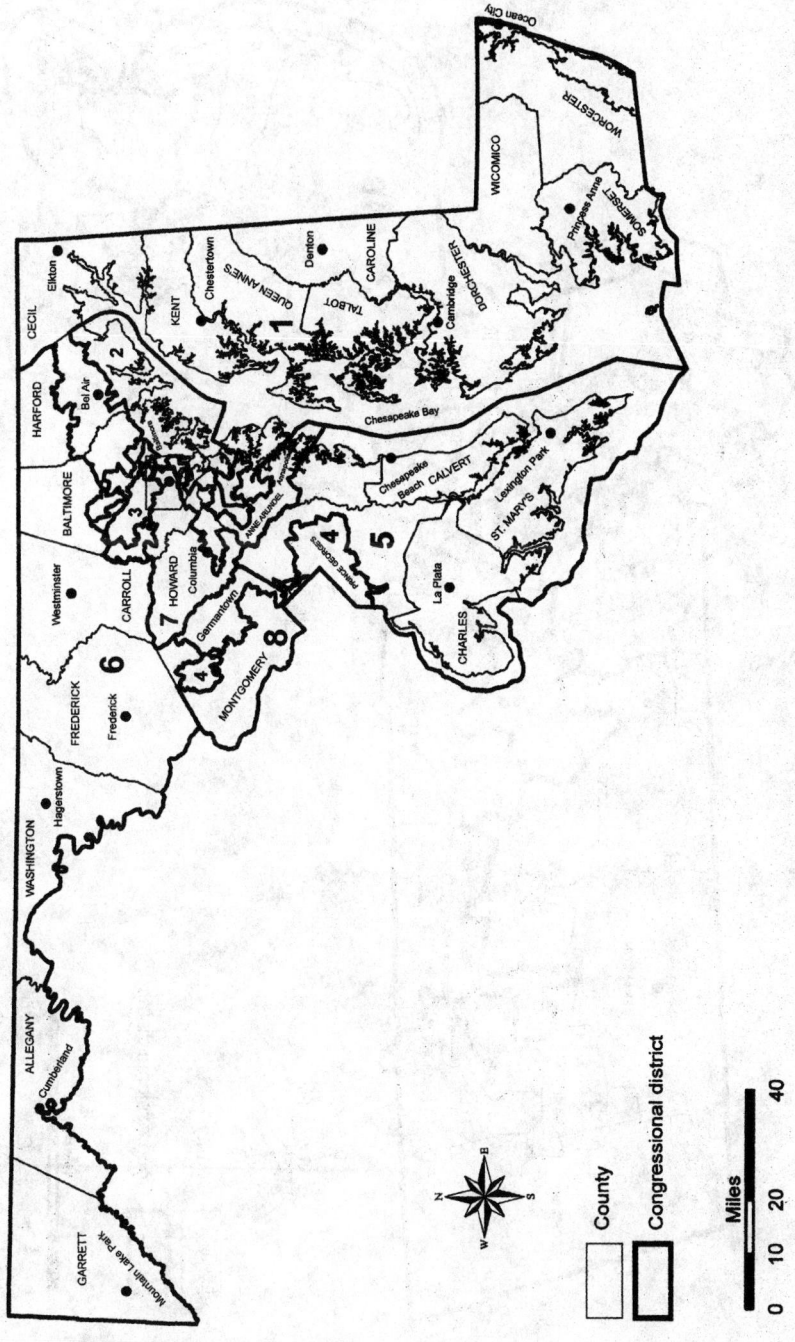

MASSACHUSETTS—Congressional Districts—(10 Districts)

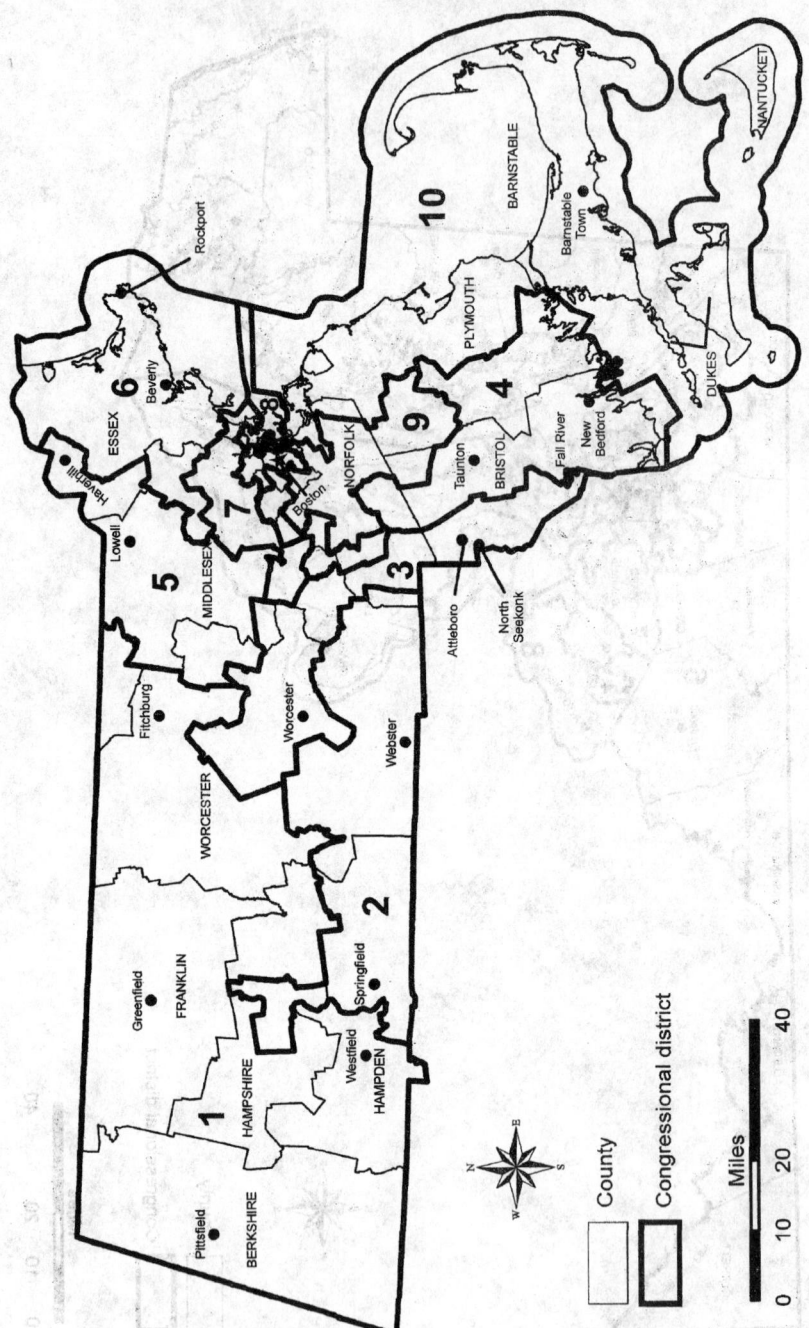

MICHIGAN—Congressional Districts—(15 Districts)

County

Congressional district

Miles

0   25   50   100

MINNESOTA—Congressional Districts—(8 Districts)

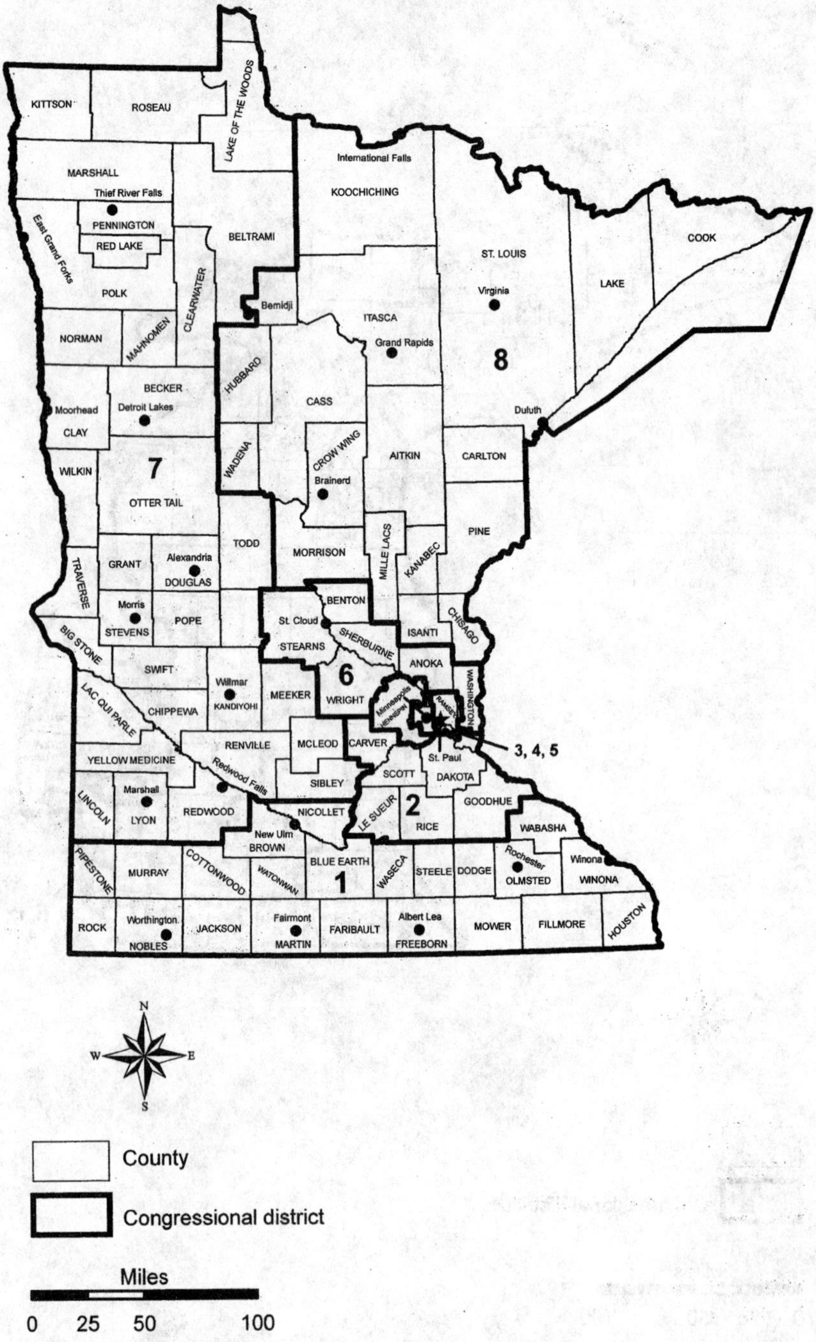

MISSISSIPPI—Congressional Districts—(4 Districts)

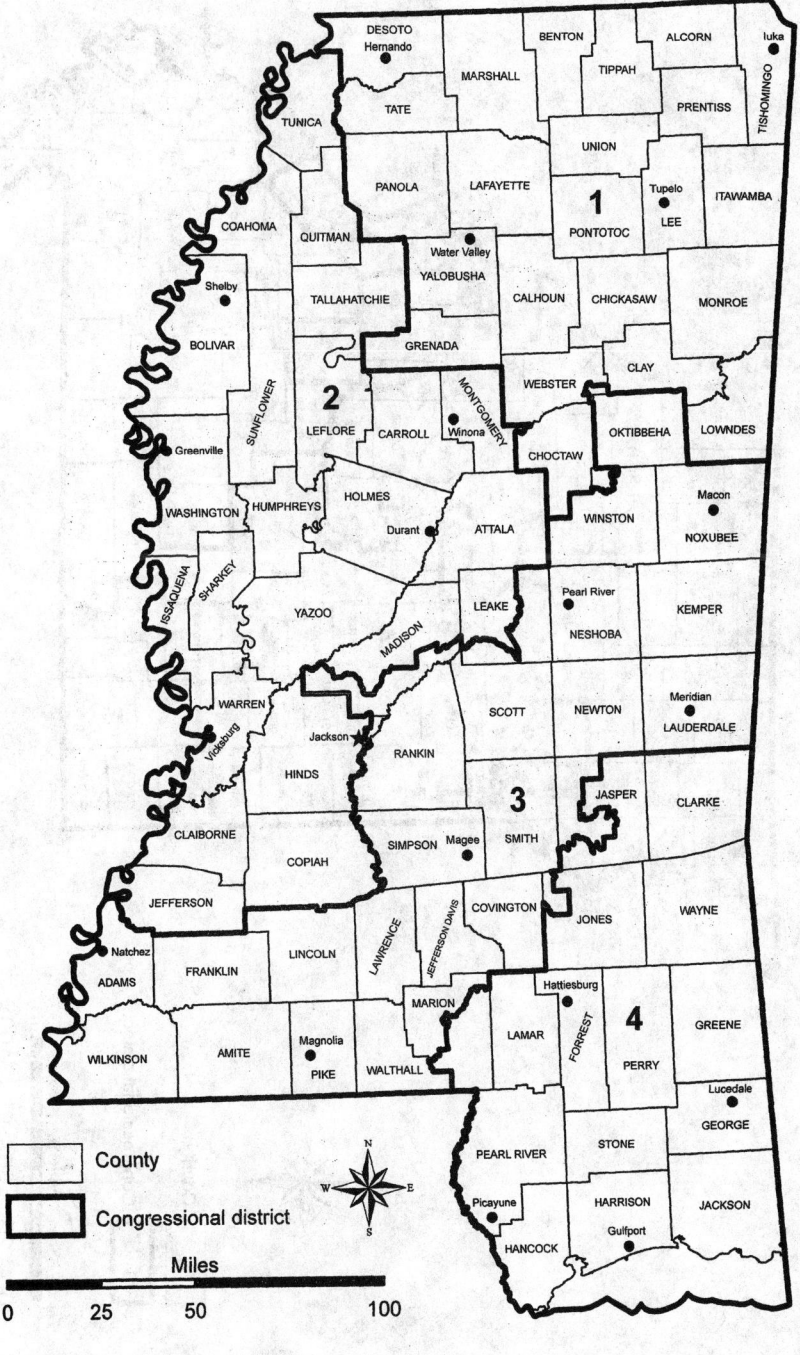

MISSOURI—Congressional Districts—(9 Districts)

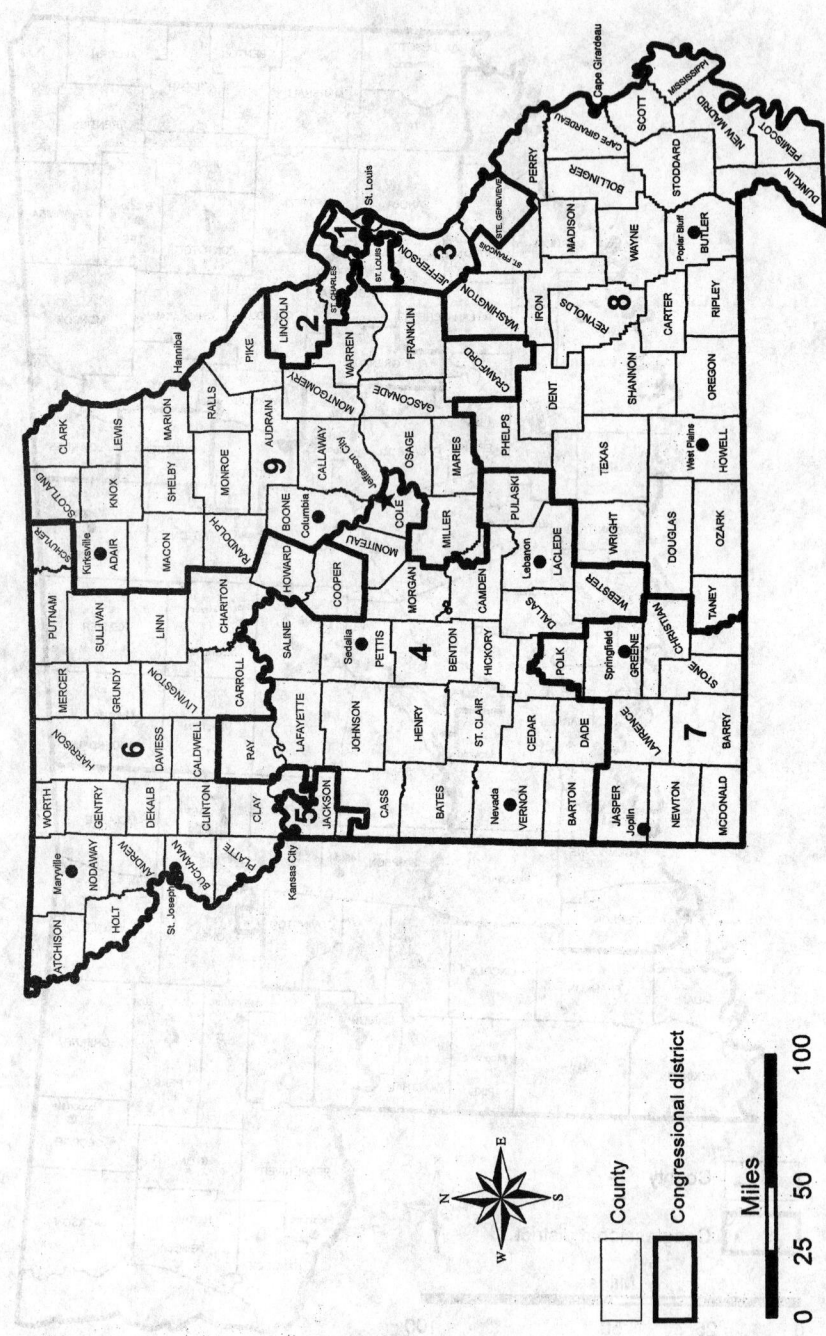

MONTANA—Congressional District—(1 District At Large)

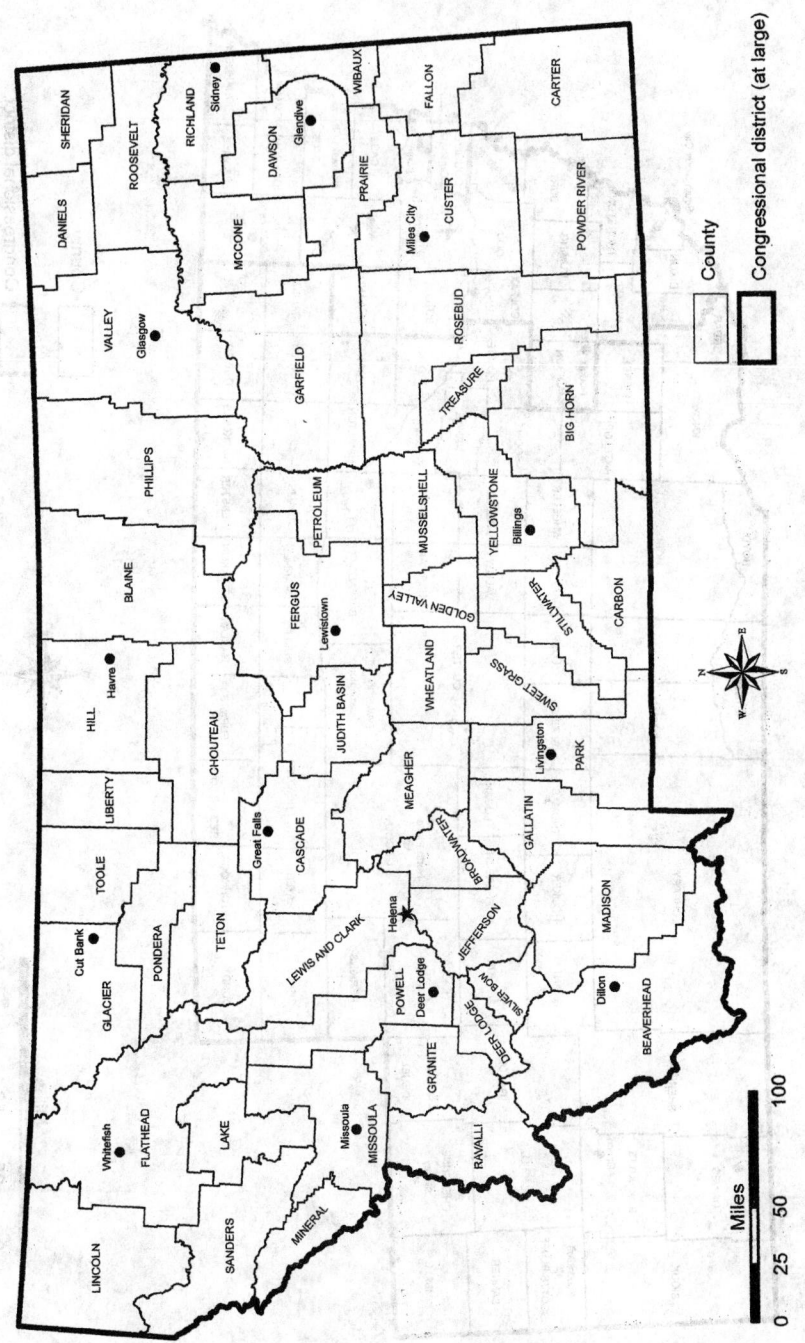

NEBRASKA—Congressional Districts—(3 Districts)

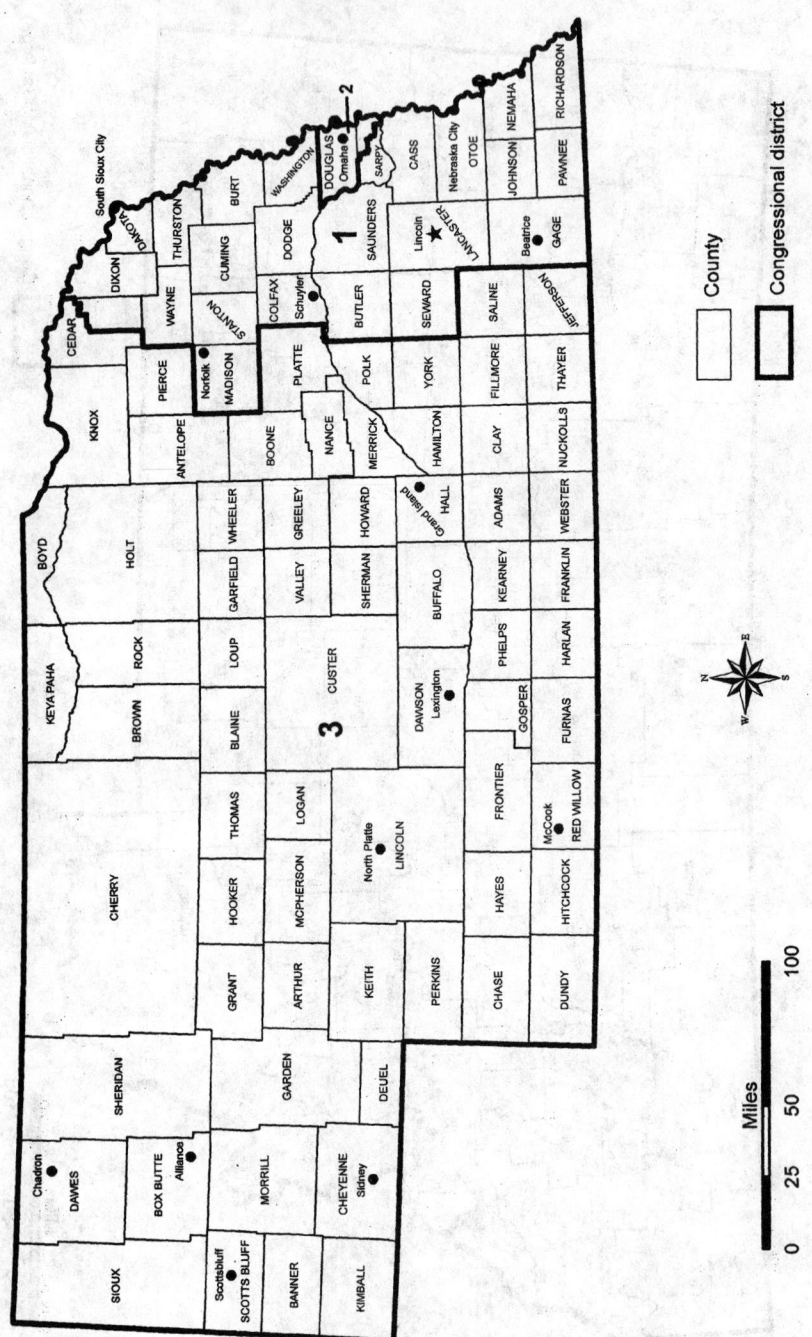

County

Congressional district

Miles

0   25   50   100

NEVADA—Congressional Districts—(3 Districts)

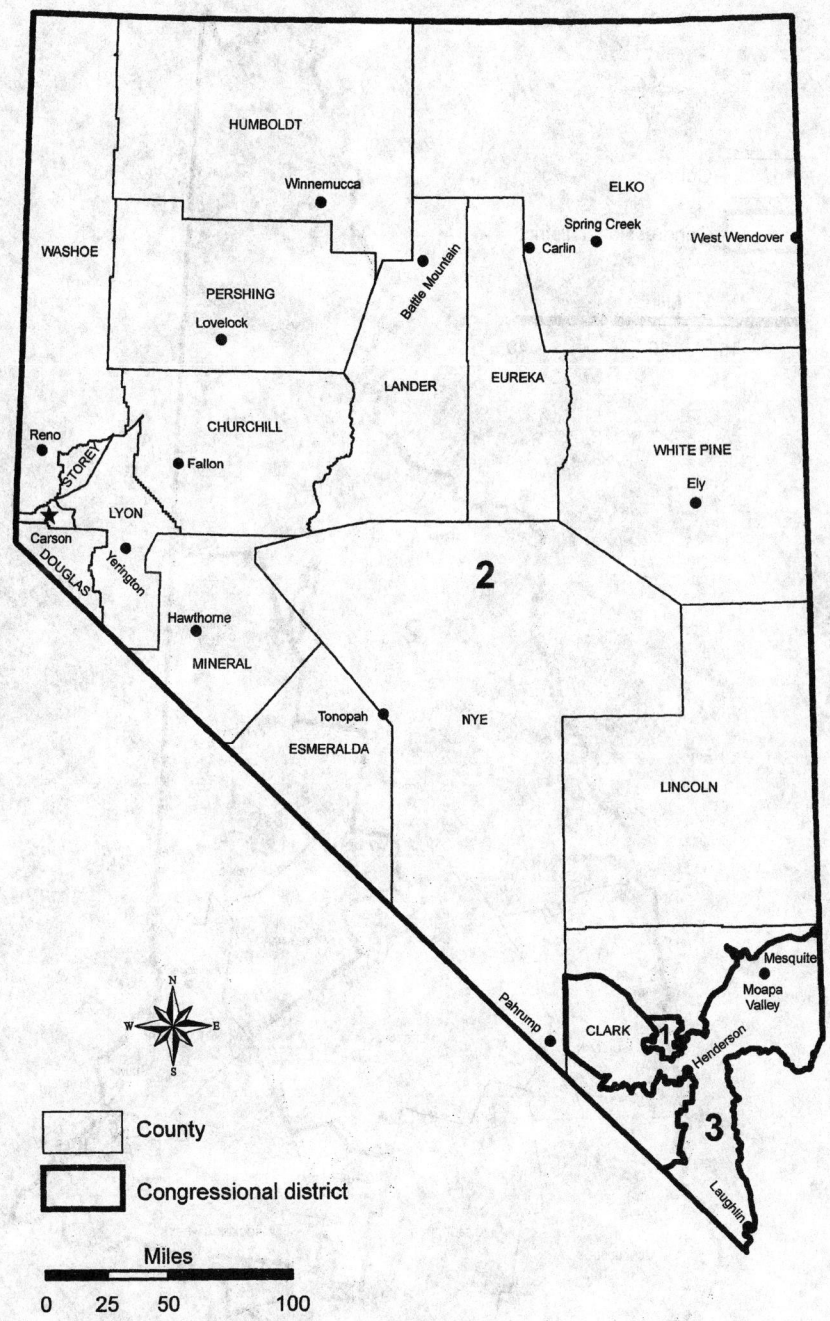

NEW HAMPSHIRE—Congressional Districts—(2 Districts)

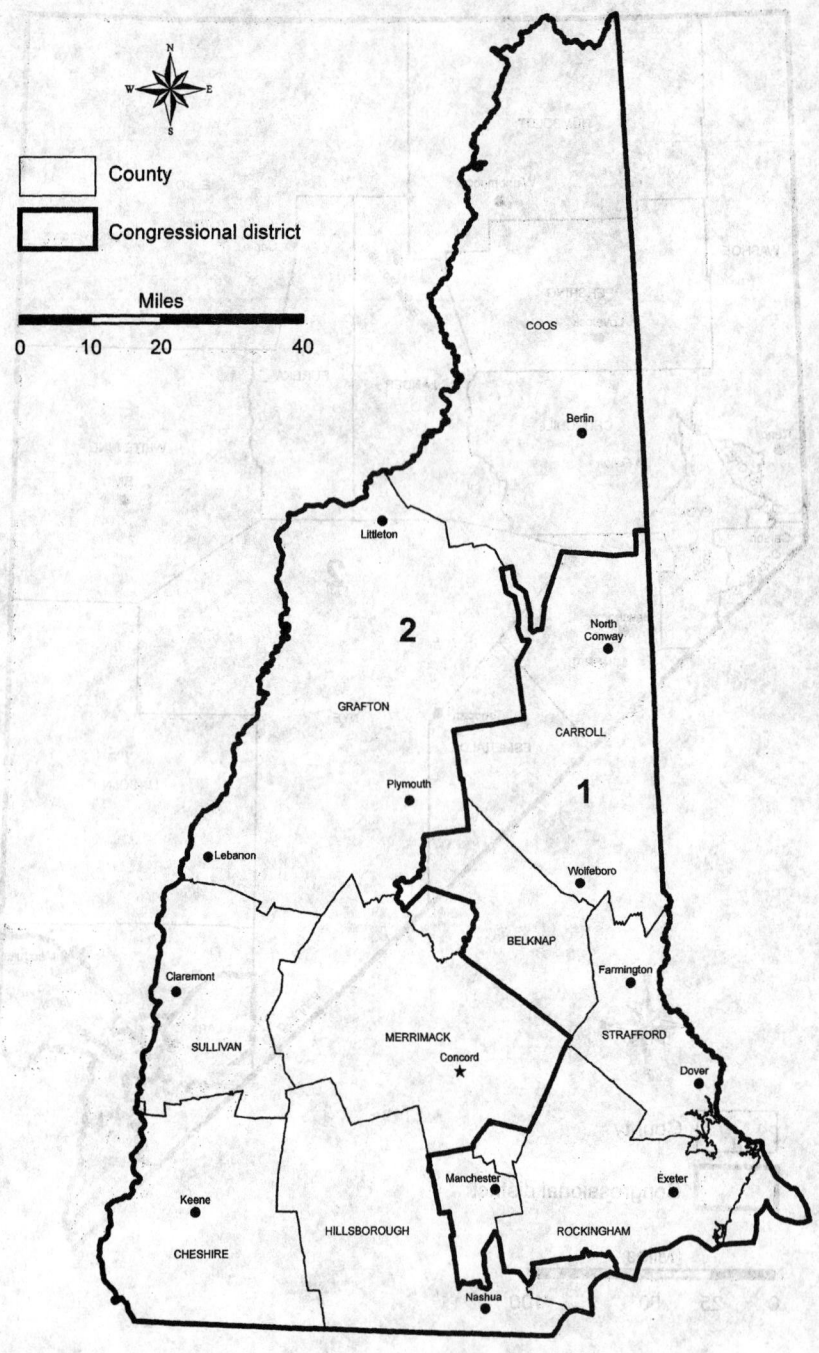

NEW JERSEY—Congressional Districts—(13 Districts)

NEW MEXICO—Congressional Districts—(3 Districts)

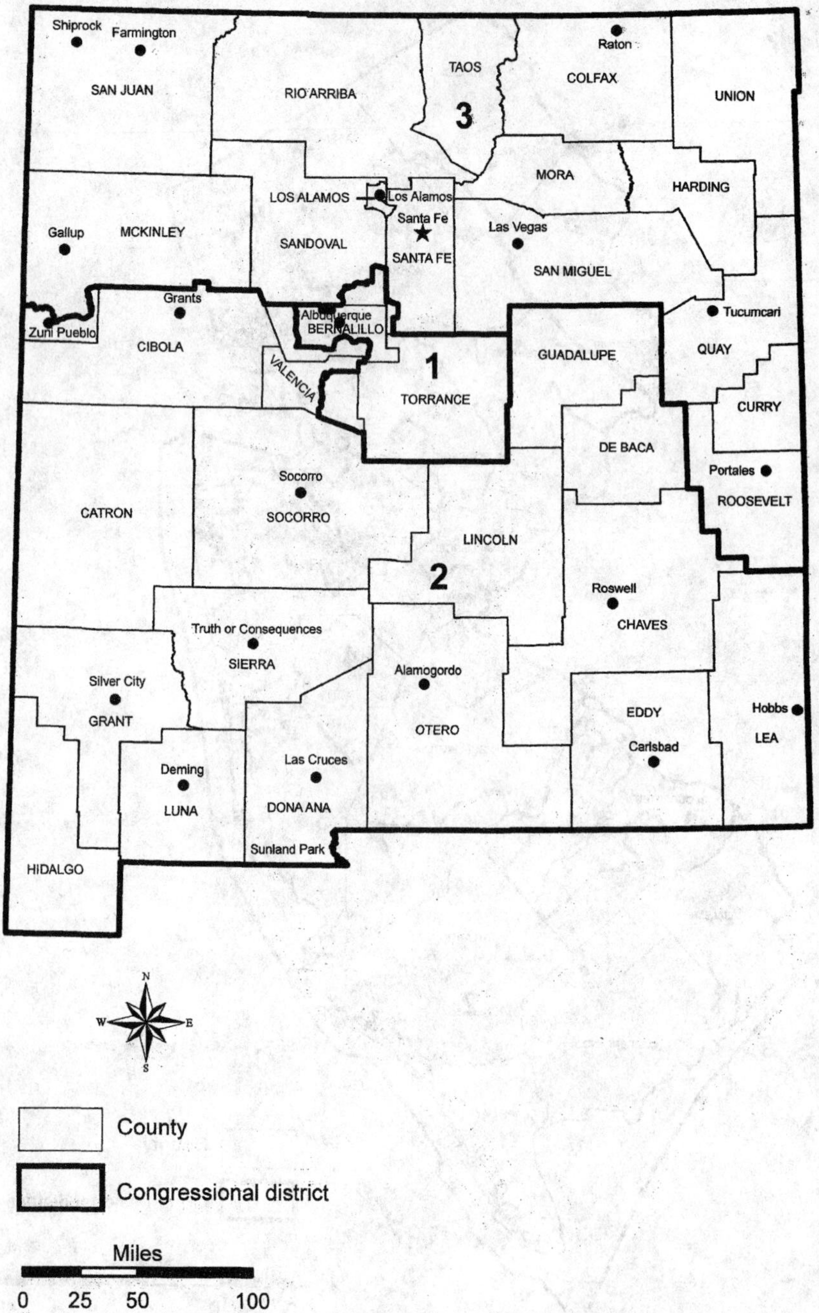

County

Congressional district

Miles

0   25   50   100

NEW YORK—Congressional Districts—(29 Districts)

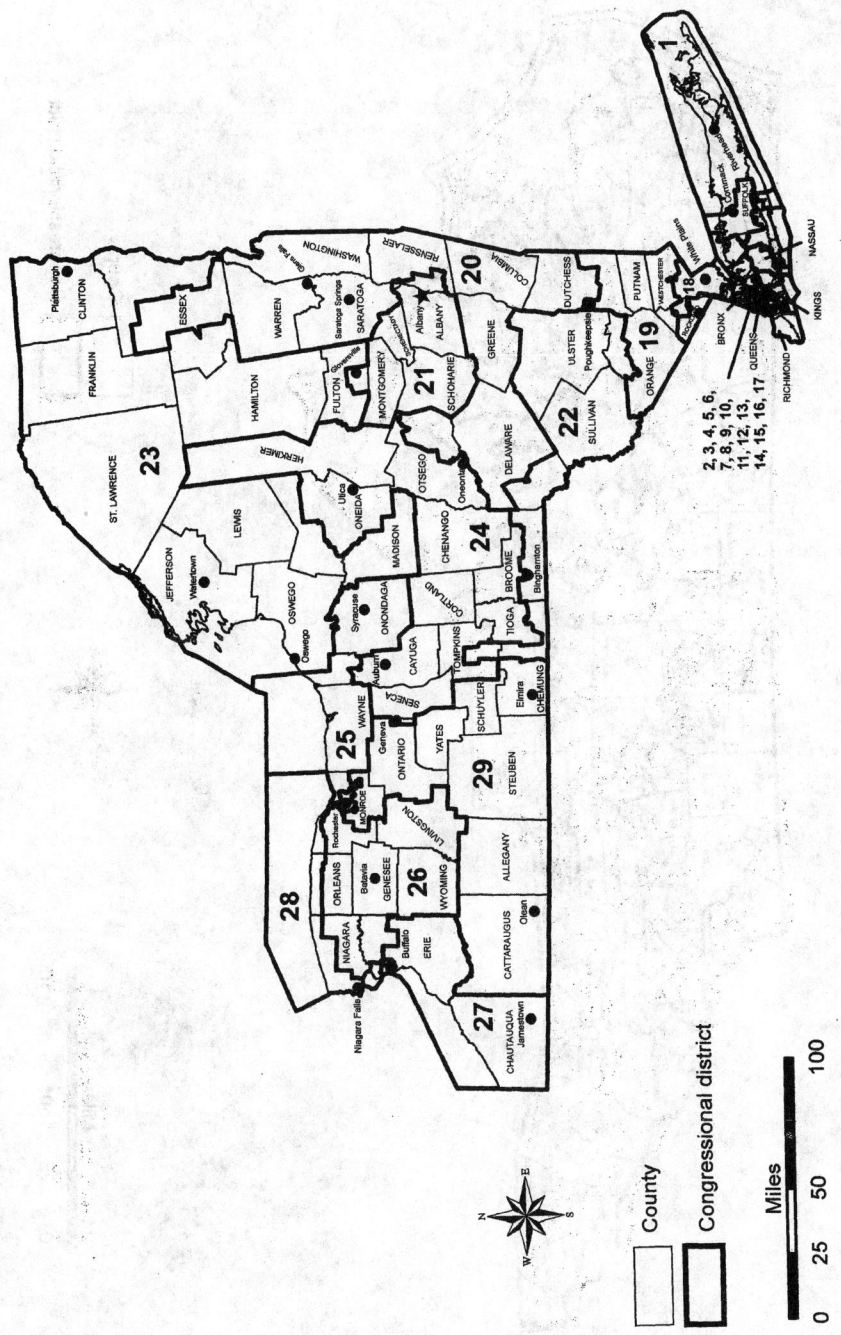

NORTH CAROLINA—Congressional Districts—(13 Districts)

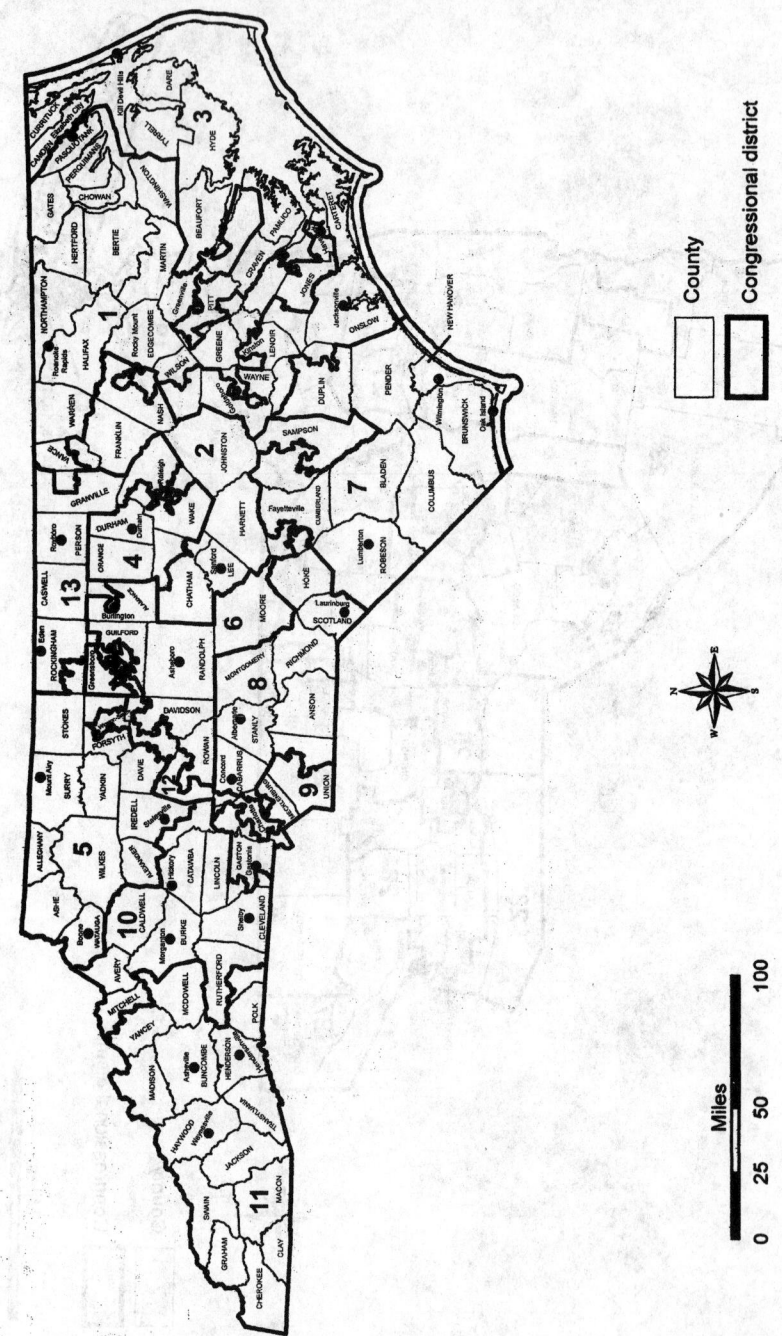

NORTH DAKOTA—Congressional District—(1 District At Large)

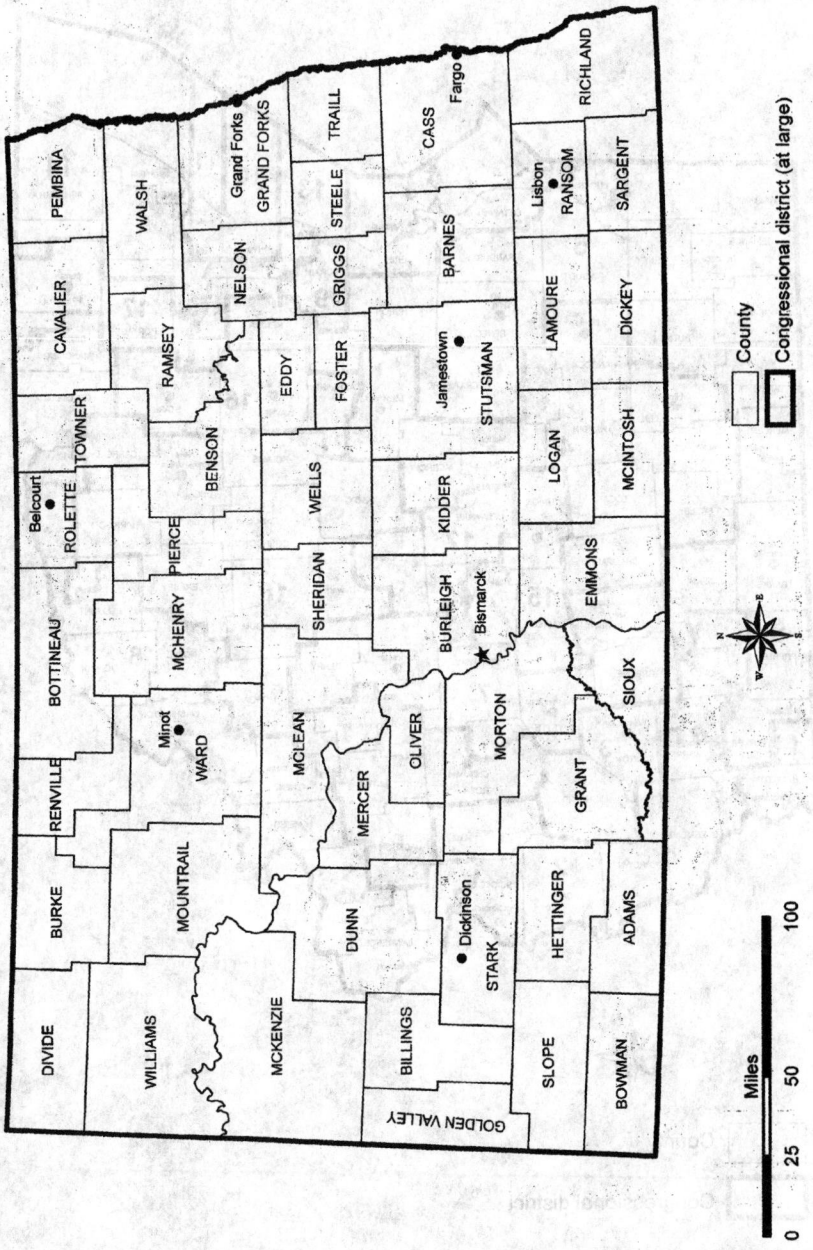

OHIO—Congressional Districts—(18 Districts)

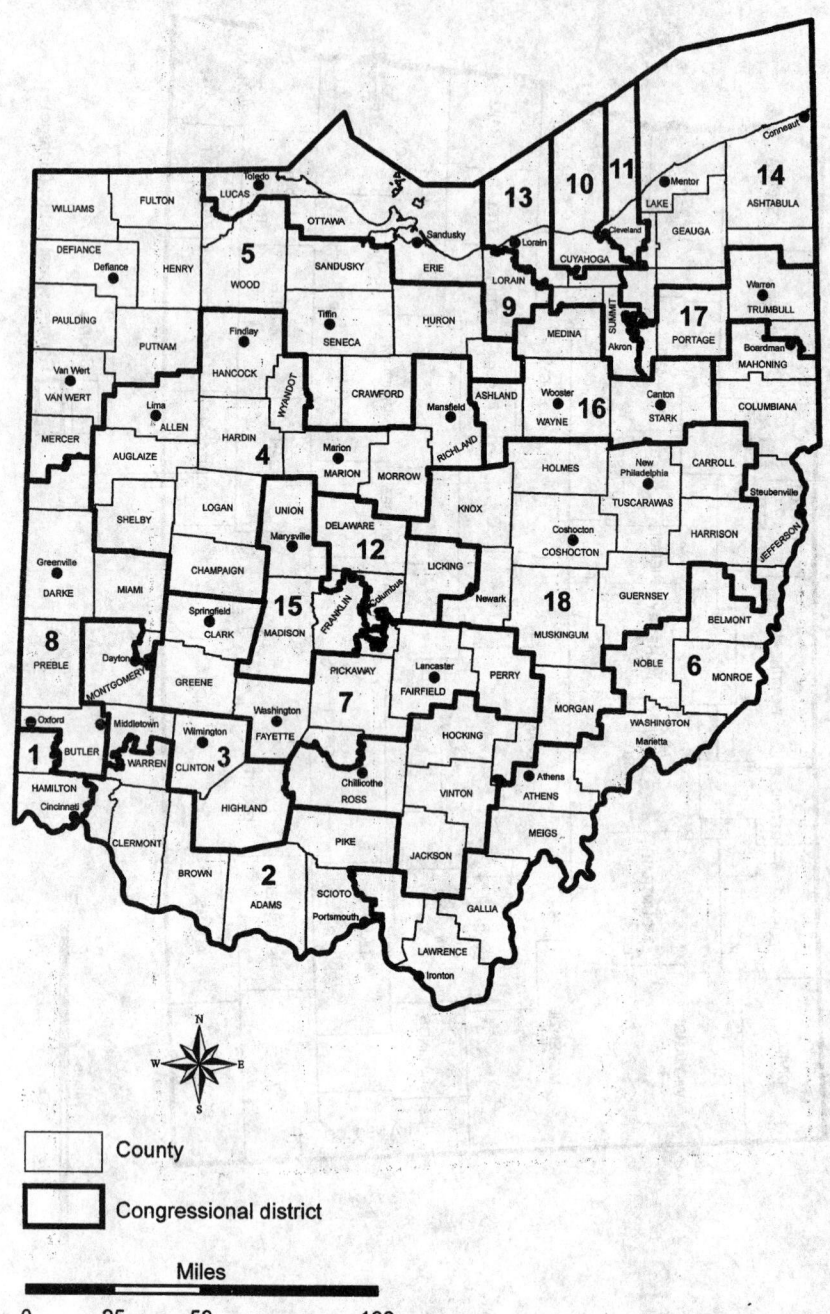

OKLAHOMA—Congressional Districts—(5 Districts)

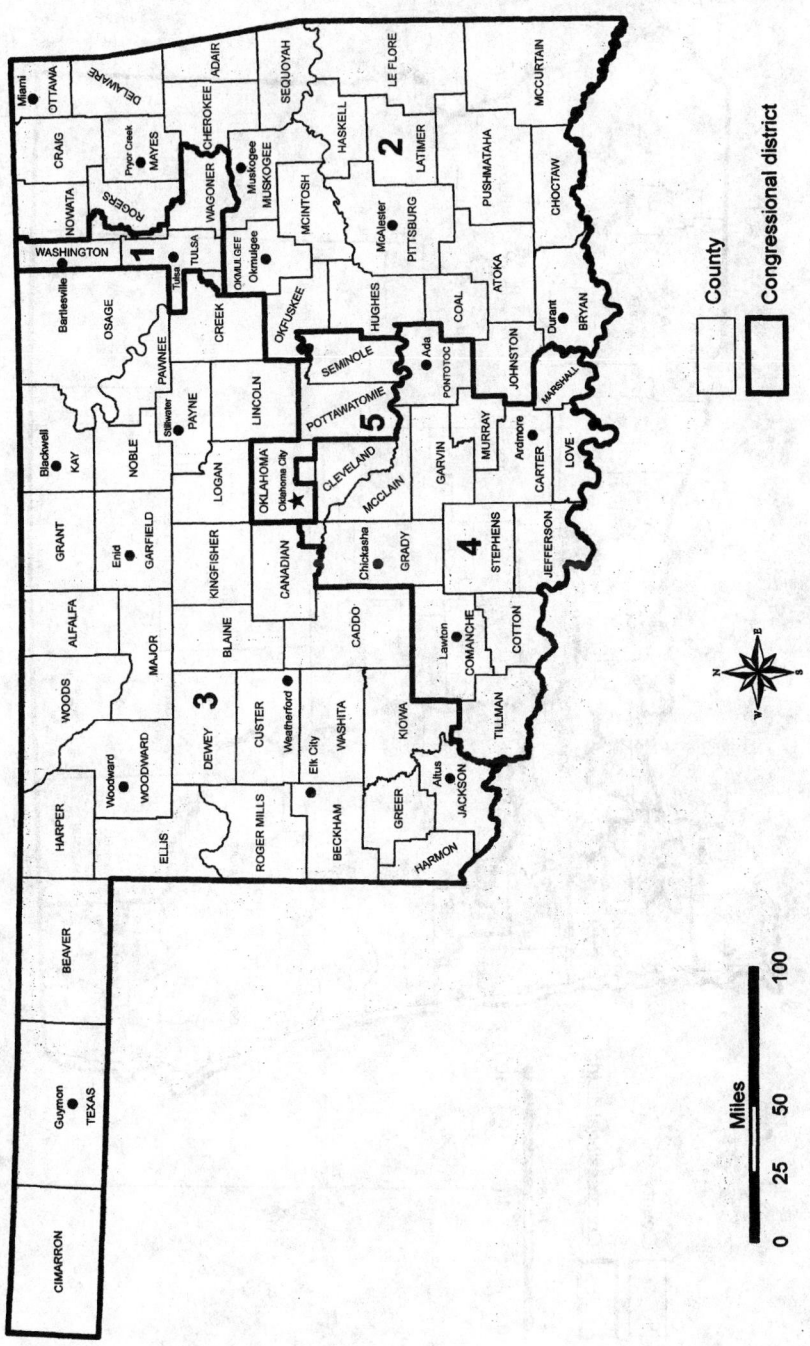

OREGON—Congressional Districts—(5 Districts)

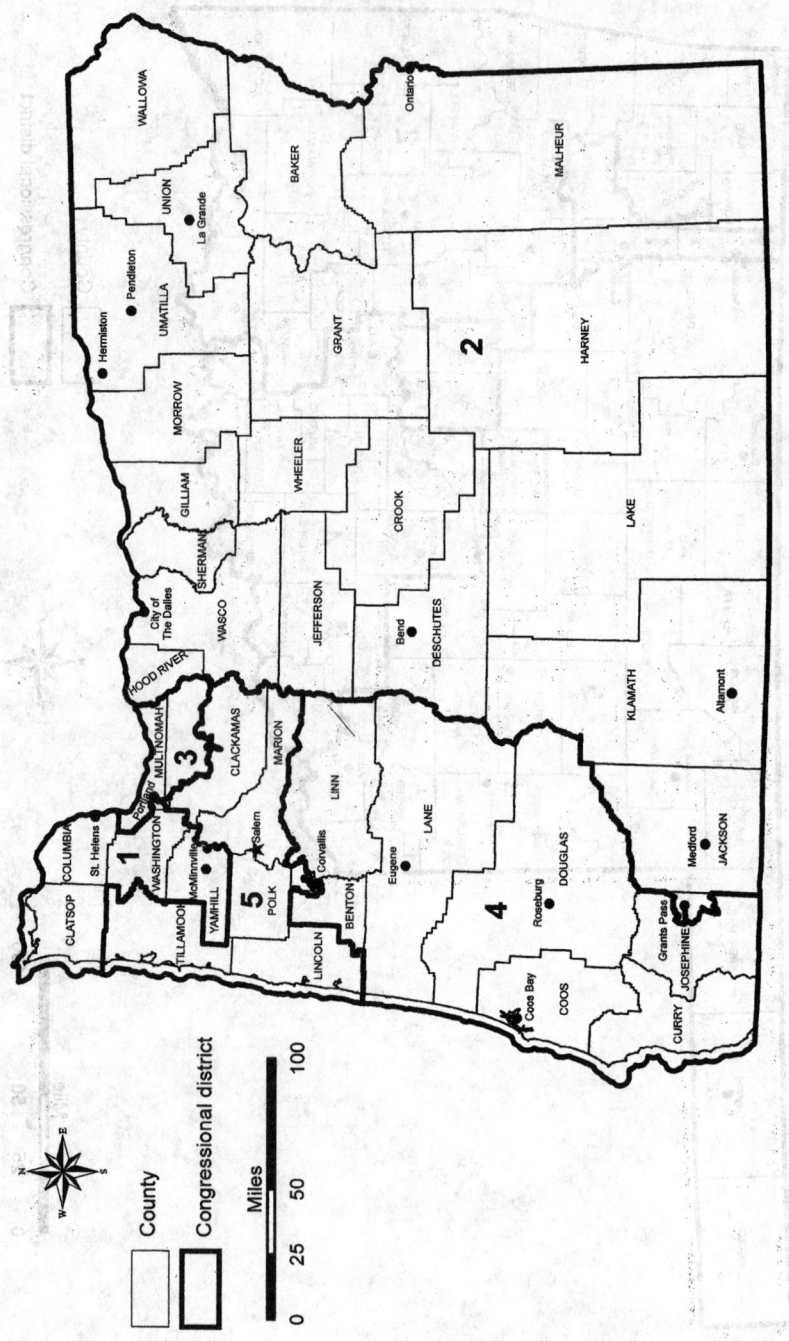

PENNSYLVANIA—Congressional Districts—(19 Districts)

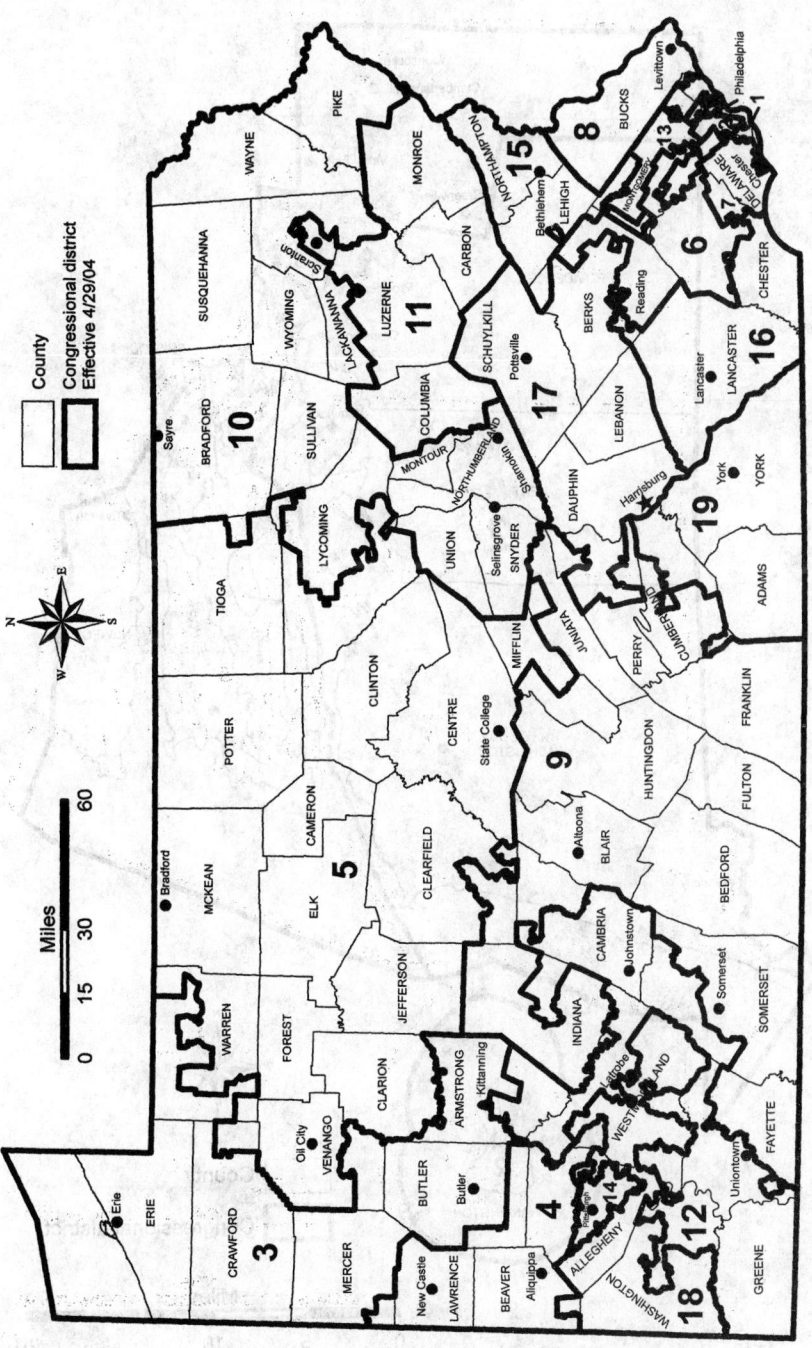

RHODE ISLAND—Congressional Districts—(2 Districts)

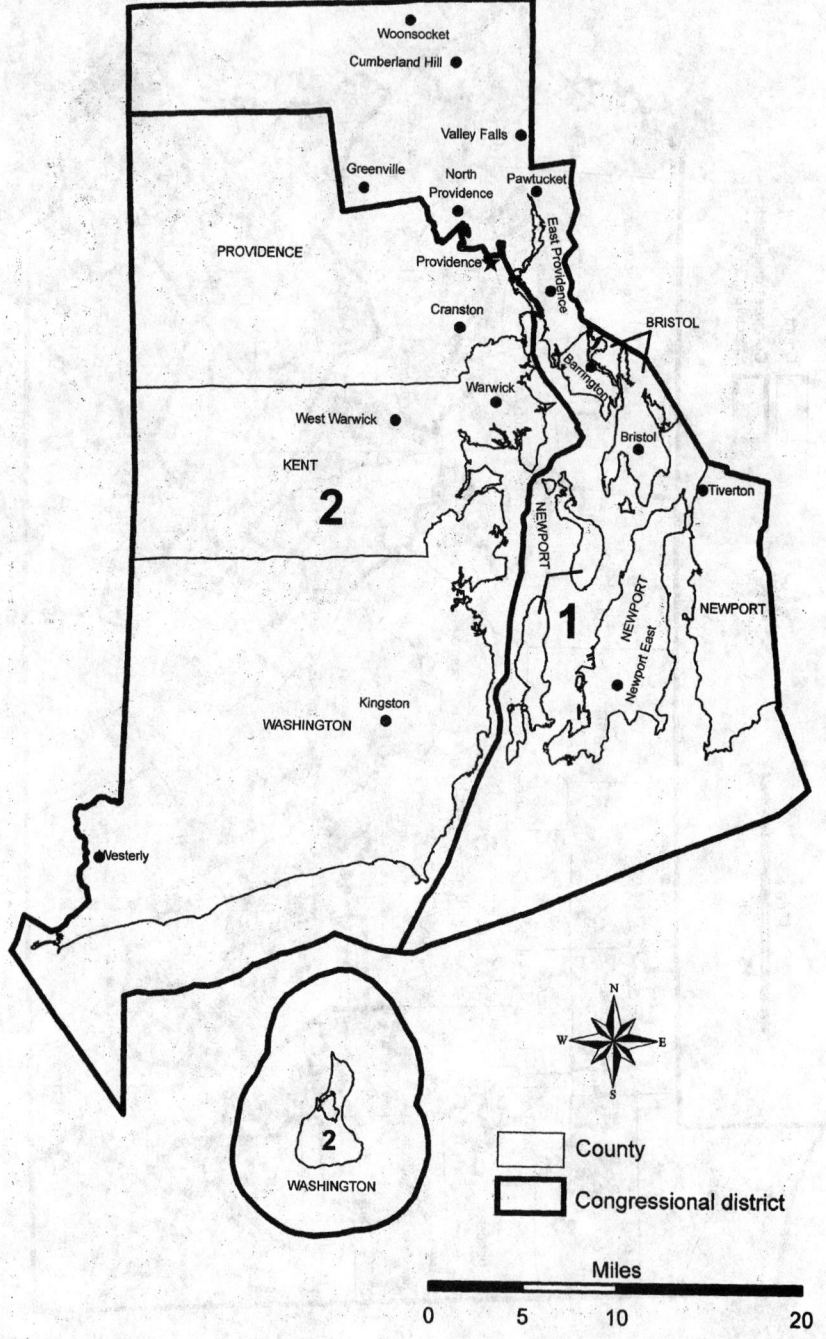

SOUTH CAROLINA—Congressional Districts—(6 Districts)

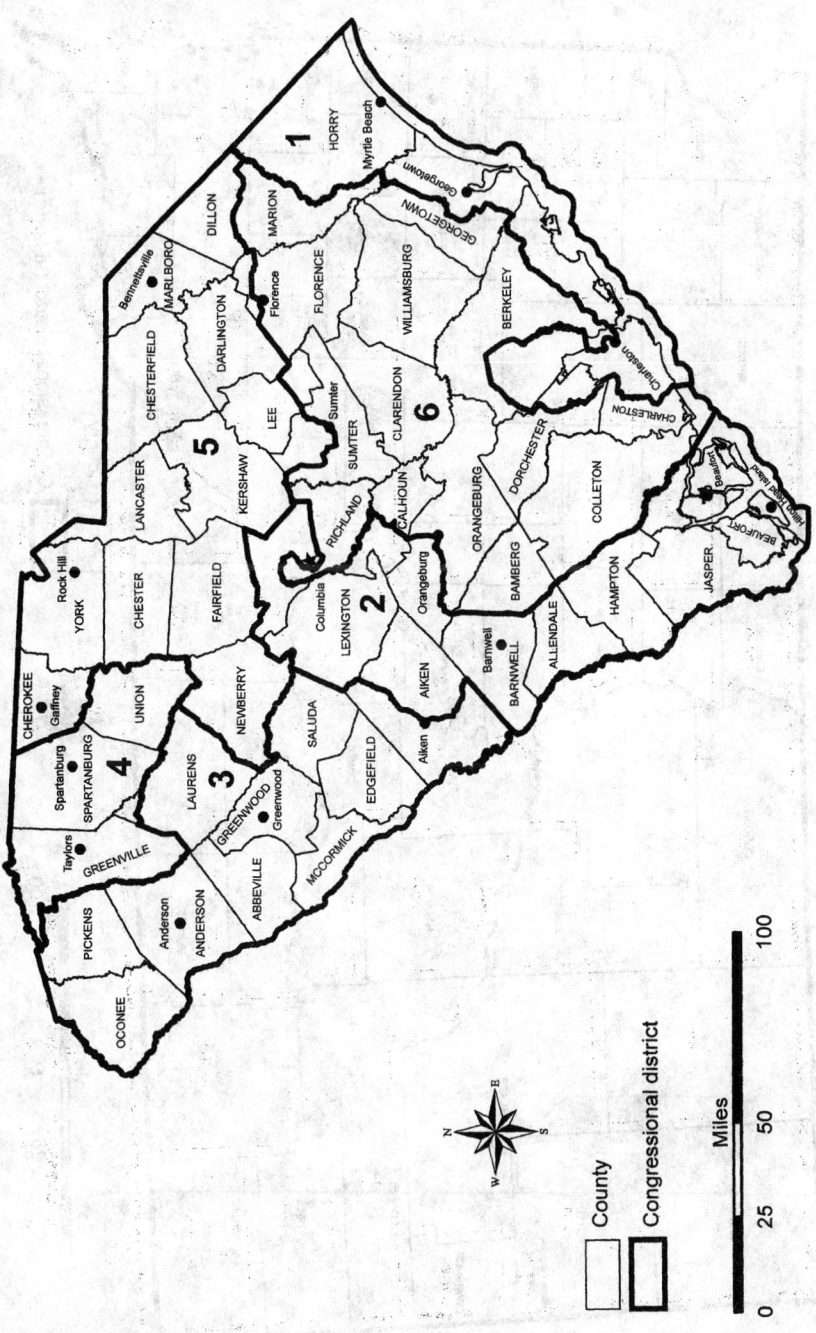

SOUTH DAKOTA—Congressional District—(1 District At Large)

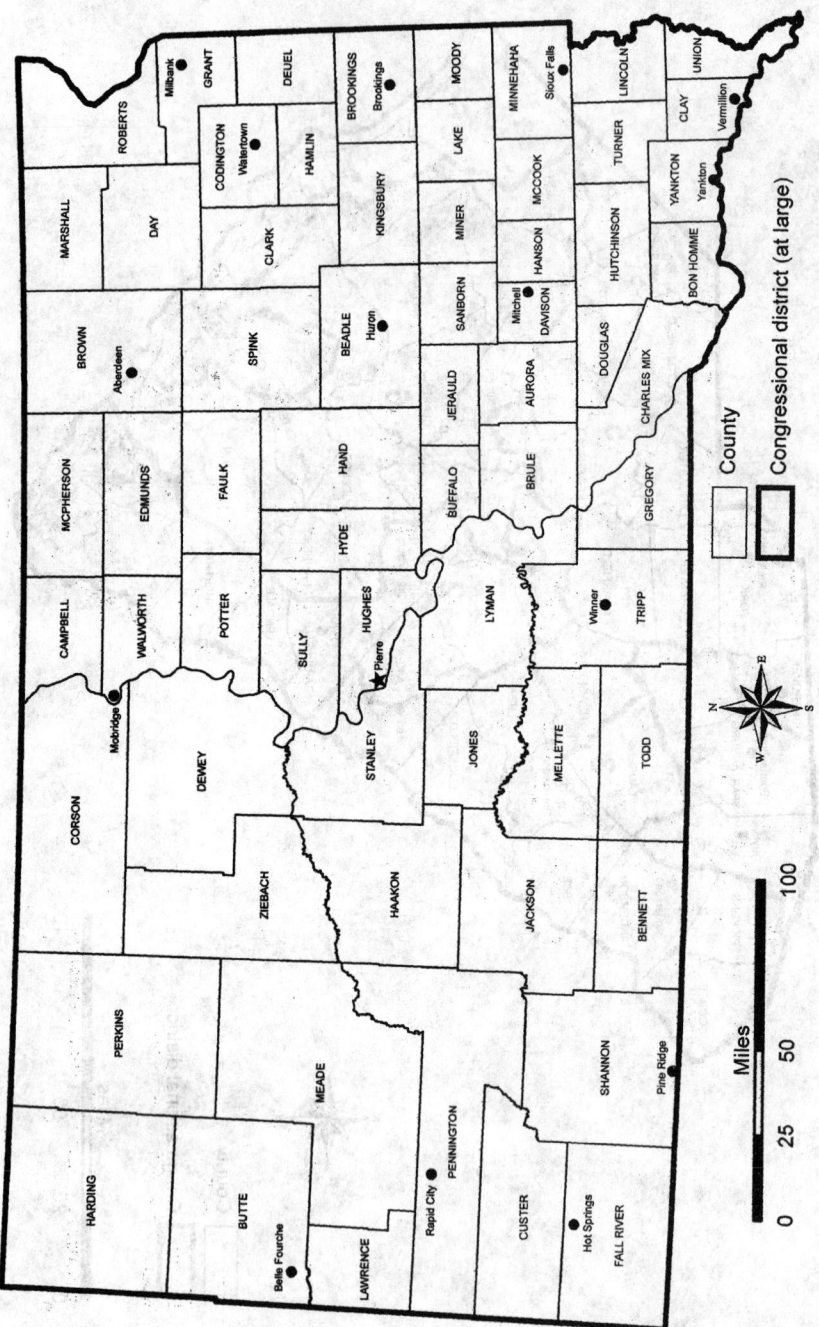

TENNESSEE—Congressional Districts—(9 Districts)

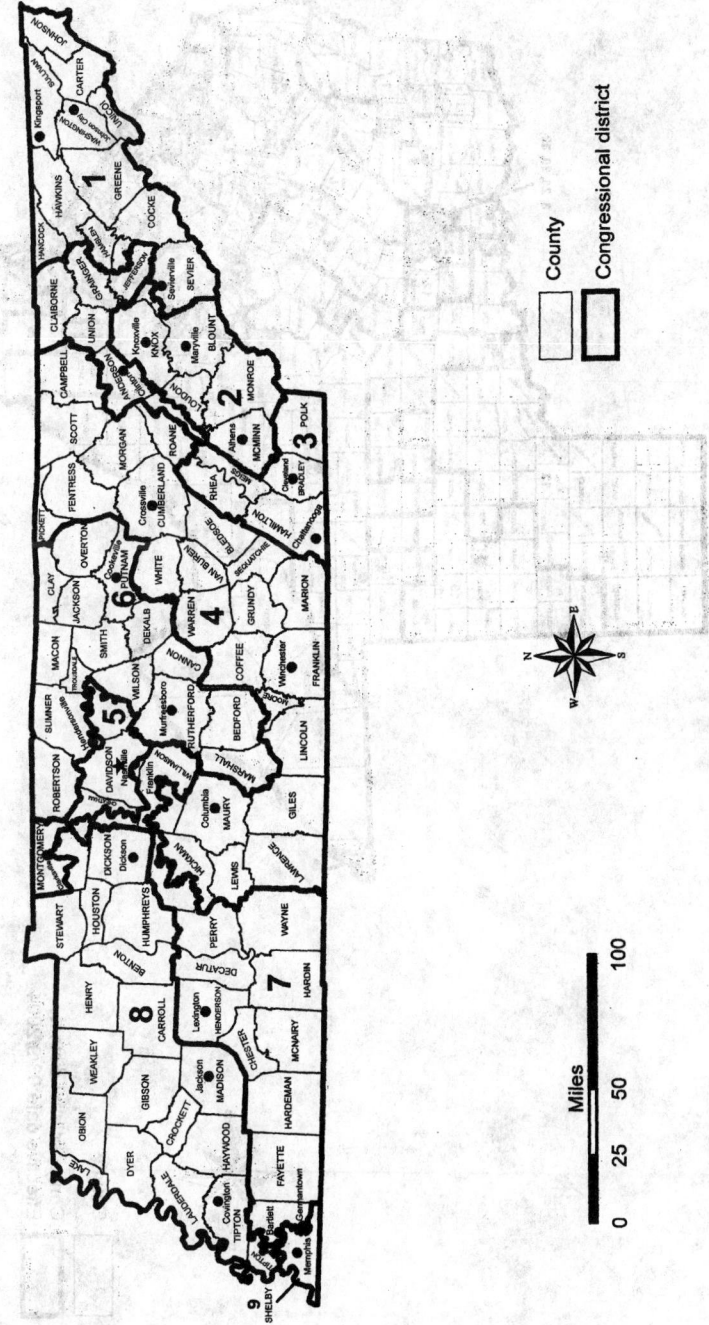

County

Congressional district

Miles

0   25   50   100

TEXAS—Congressional Districts—(32 Districts)

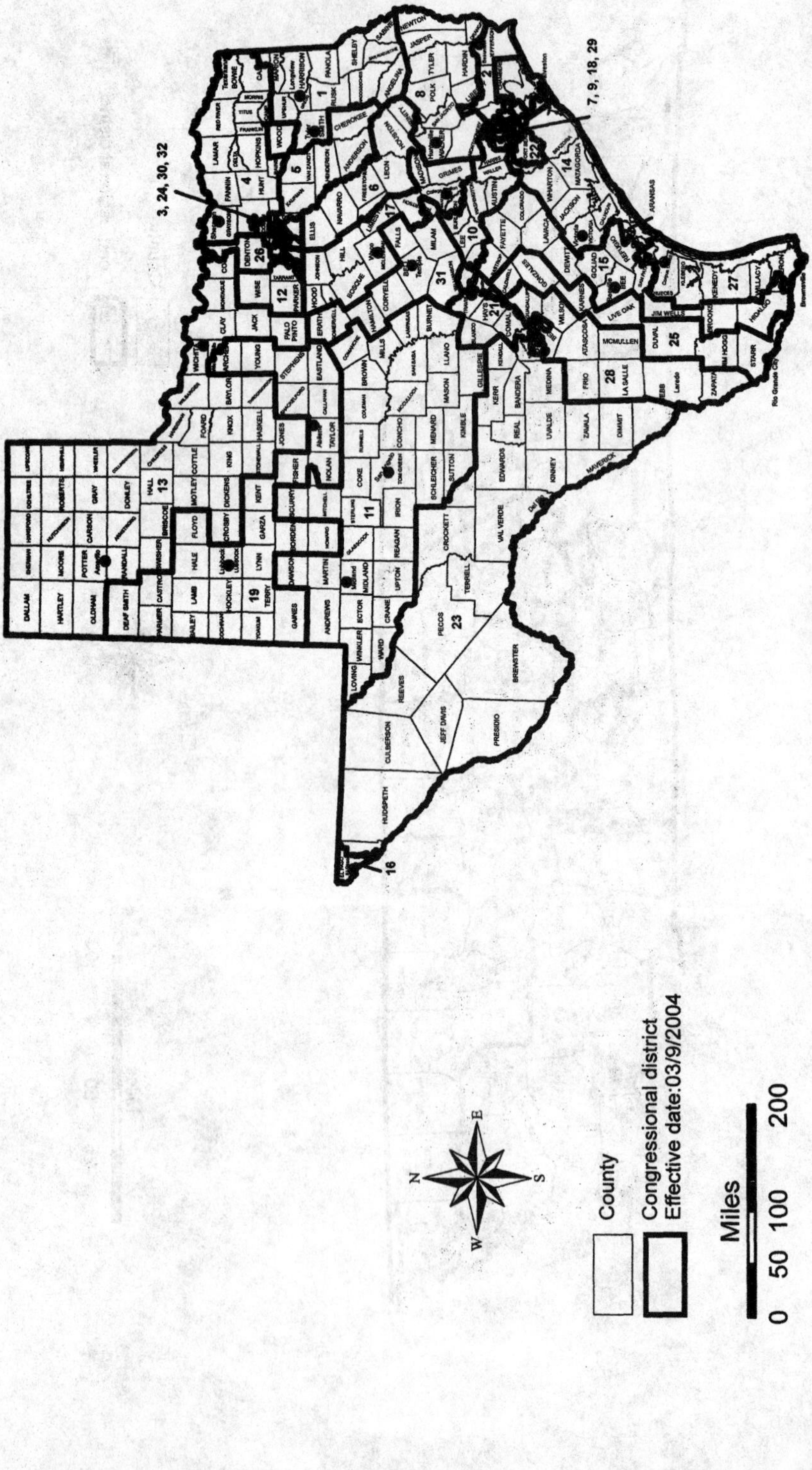

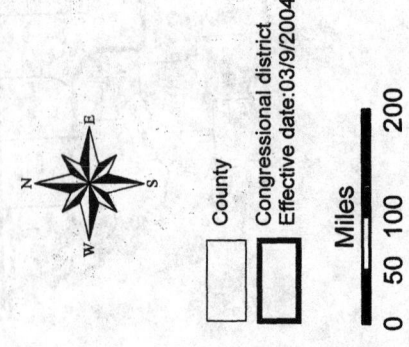

County

Congressional district
Effective date:03/9/2004

Miles

0   50   100   200

UTAH—Congressional Districts—(3 Districts)

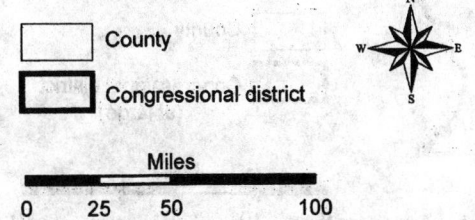

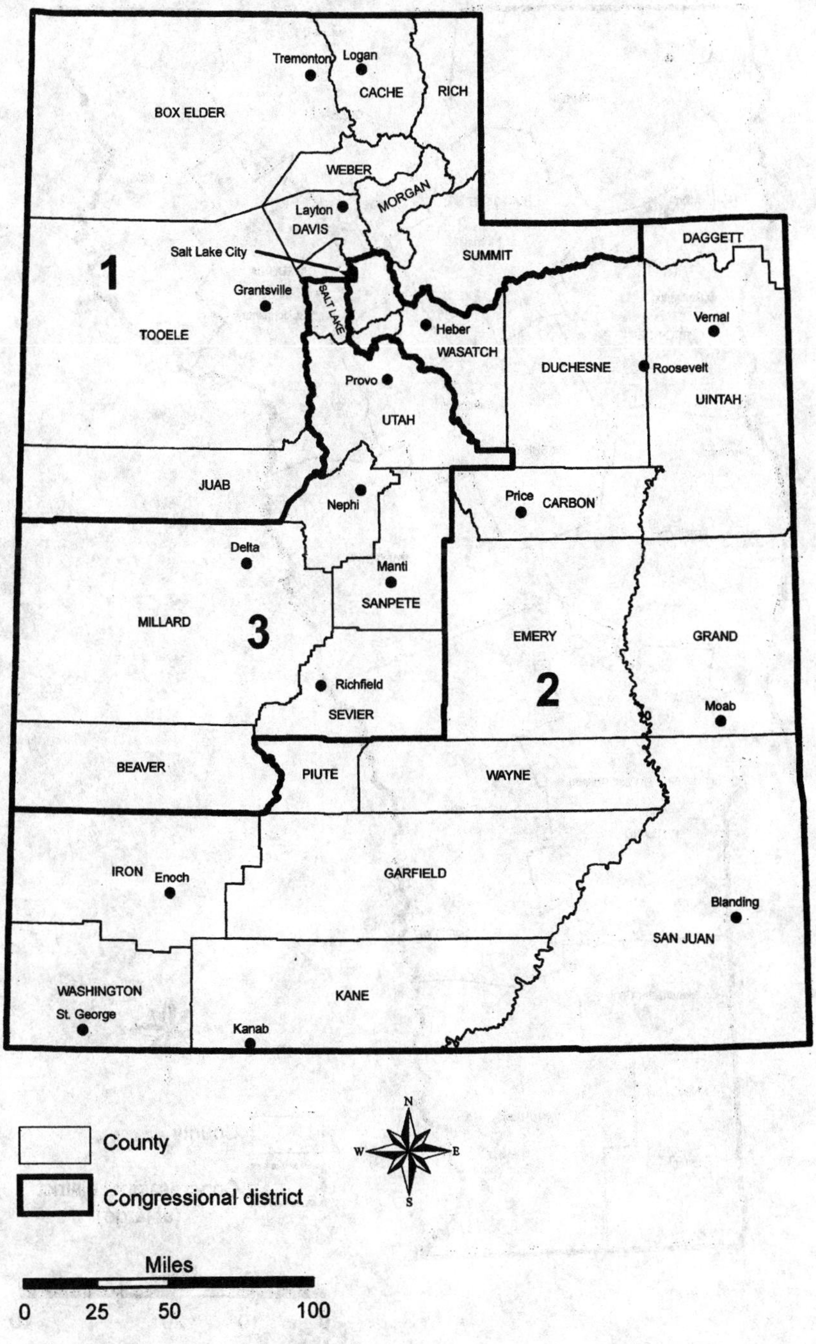

County

Congressional district

Miles

0   25   50   100

VERMONT—Congressional District—(1 District At Large)

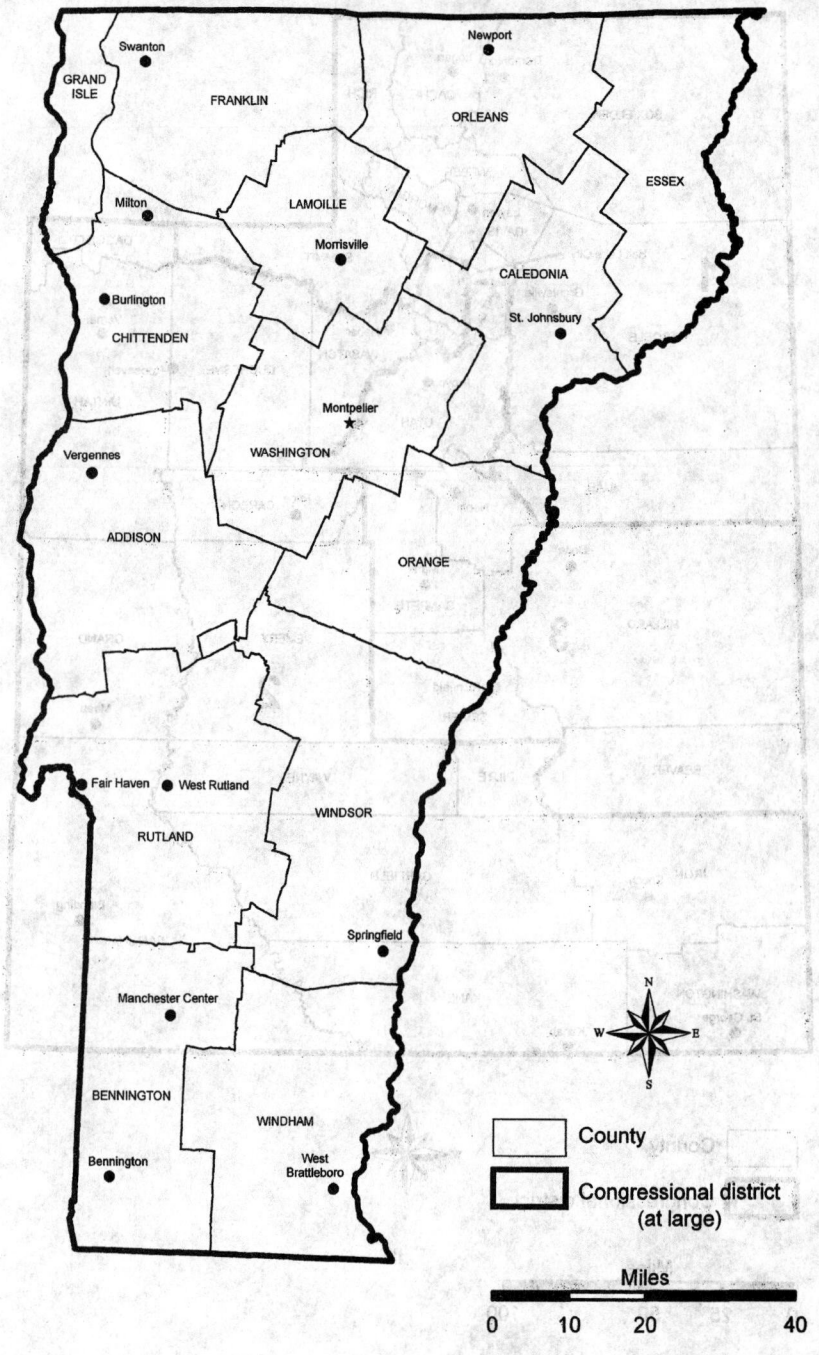

VIRGINIA—Congressional Districts—(11 Districts)

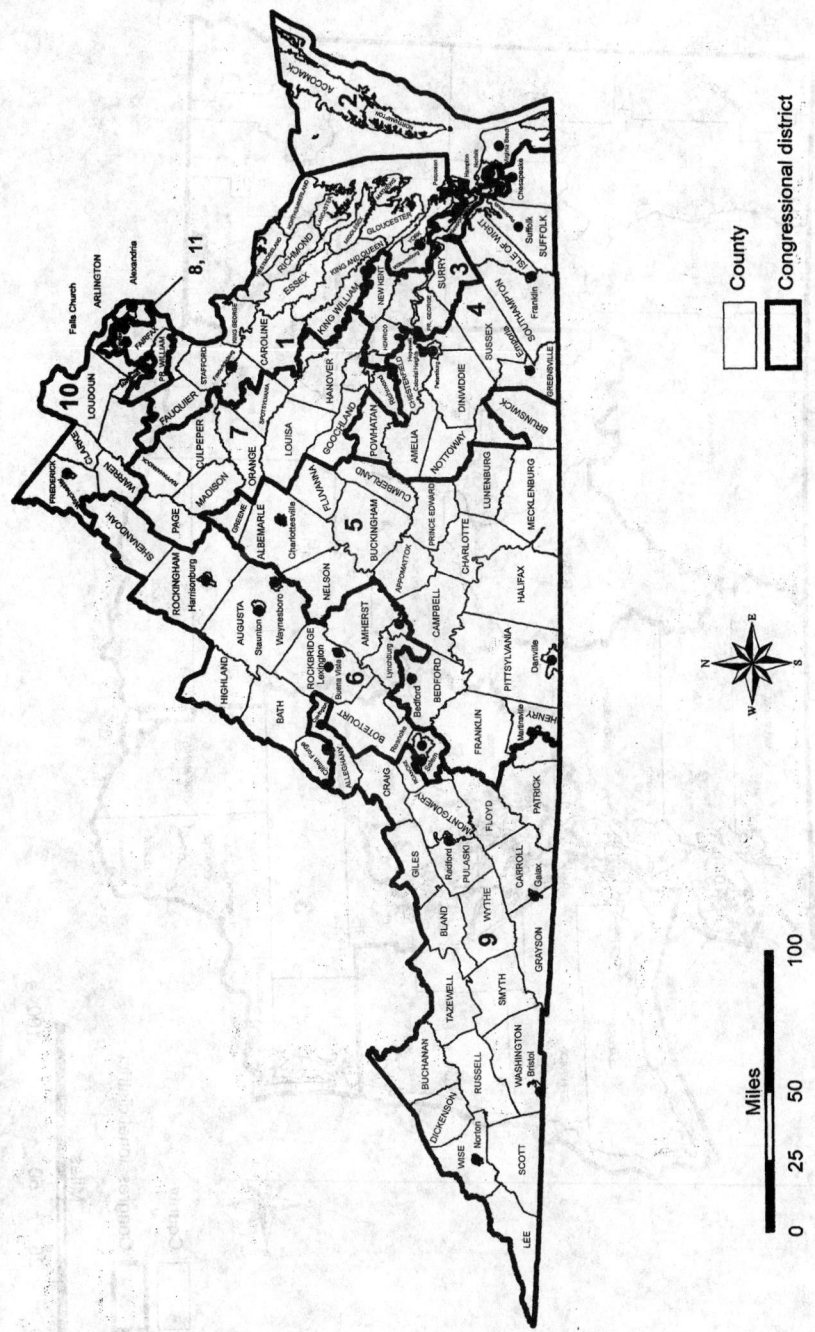

WASHINGTON—Congressional Districts—(9 Districts)

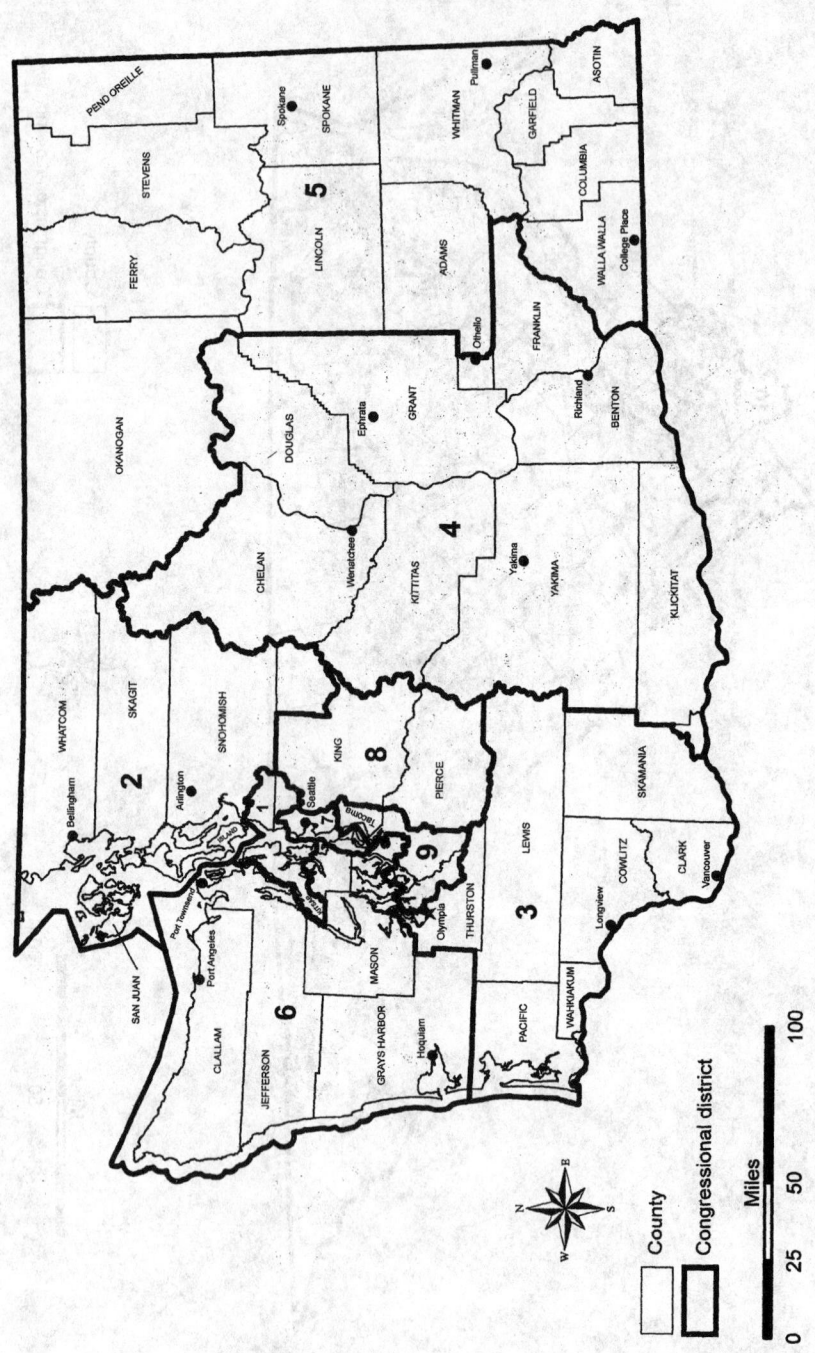

WEST VIRGINIA—Congressional Districts—(3 Districts)

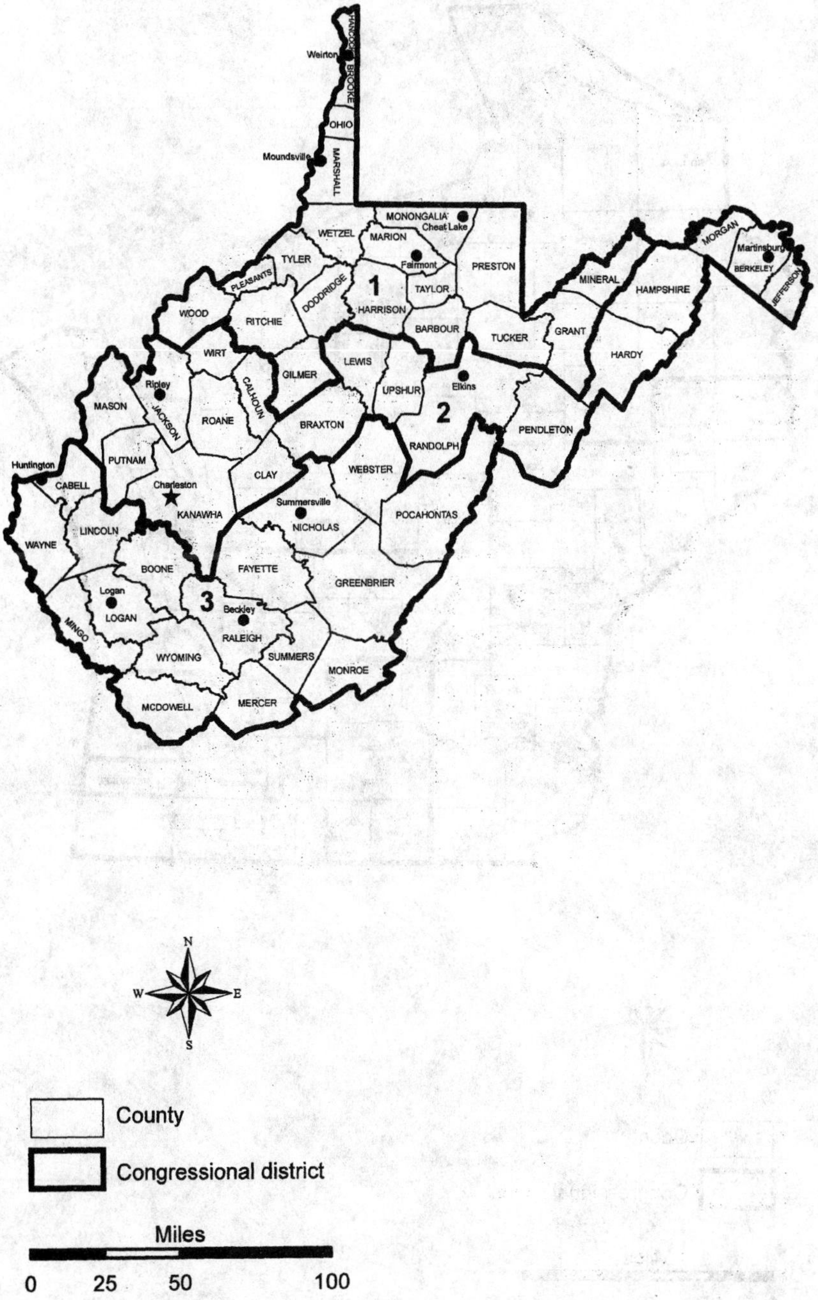

County

Congressional district

Miles

0   25   50   100

WISCONSIN—Congressional Districts—(8 Districts)

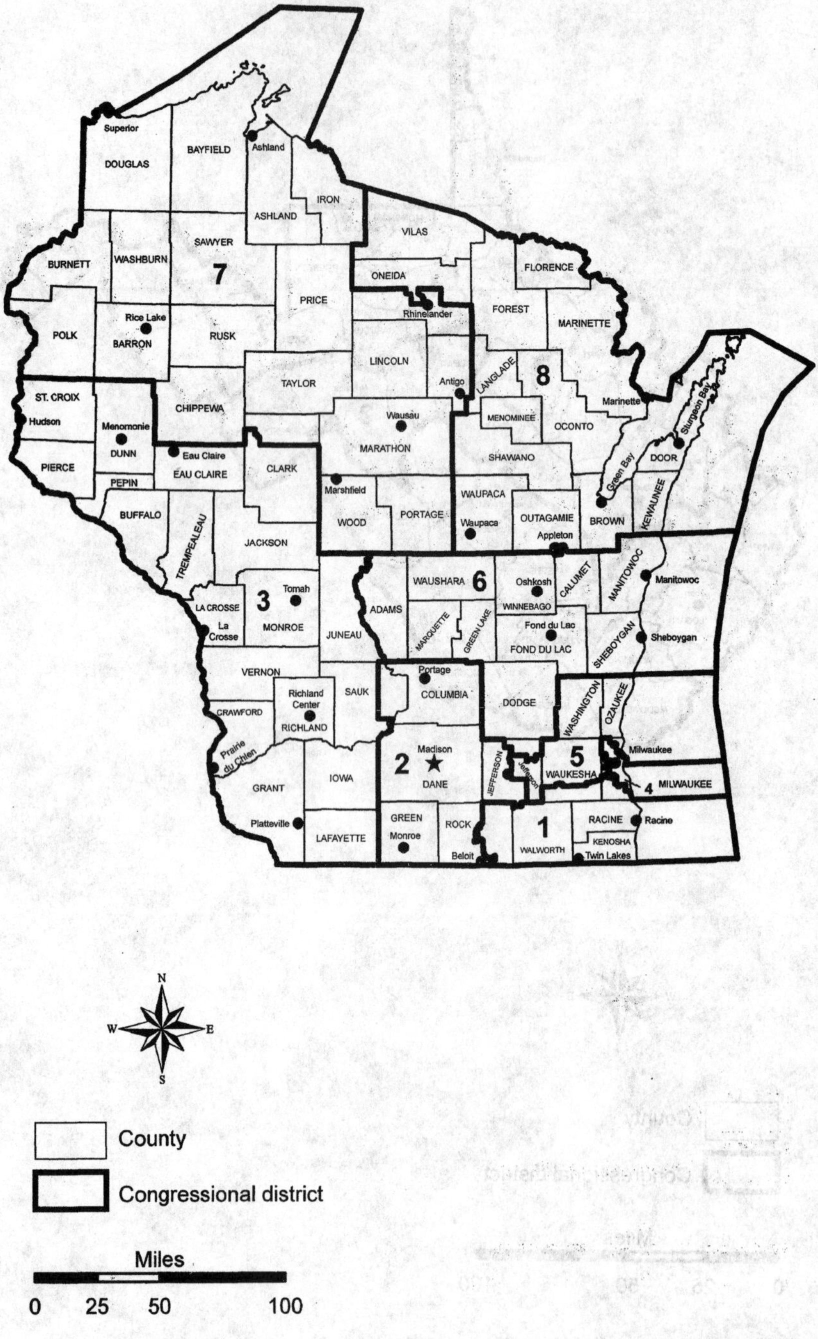

County

Congressional district

Miles

0   25   50   100

WYOMING—Congressional District—(1 District At Large)

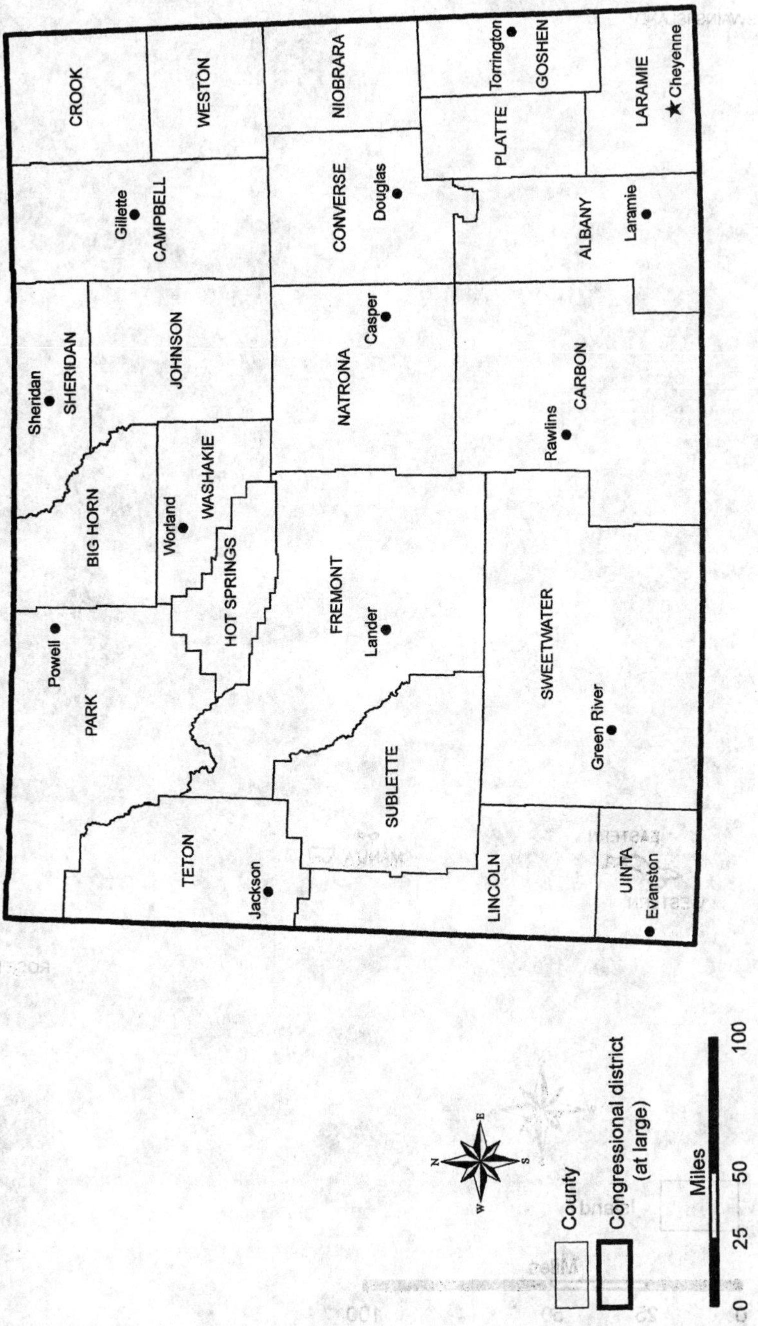

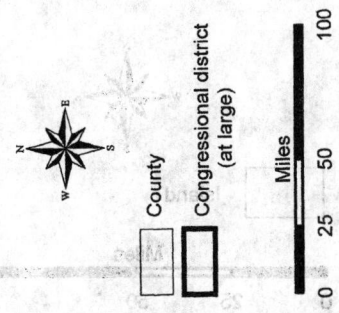

AMERICAN SAMOA—(1 Delegate At Large)

SWAINS ISLAND

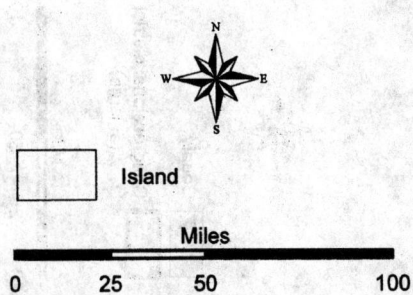

EASTERN

WESTERN

MANU'A

ROSE ISLAND

Island

Miles

0   25   50   100

DISTRICT OF COLUMBIA—(1 Delegate At Large)

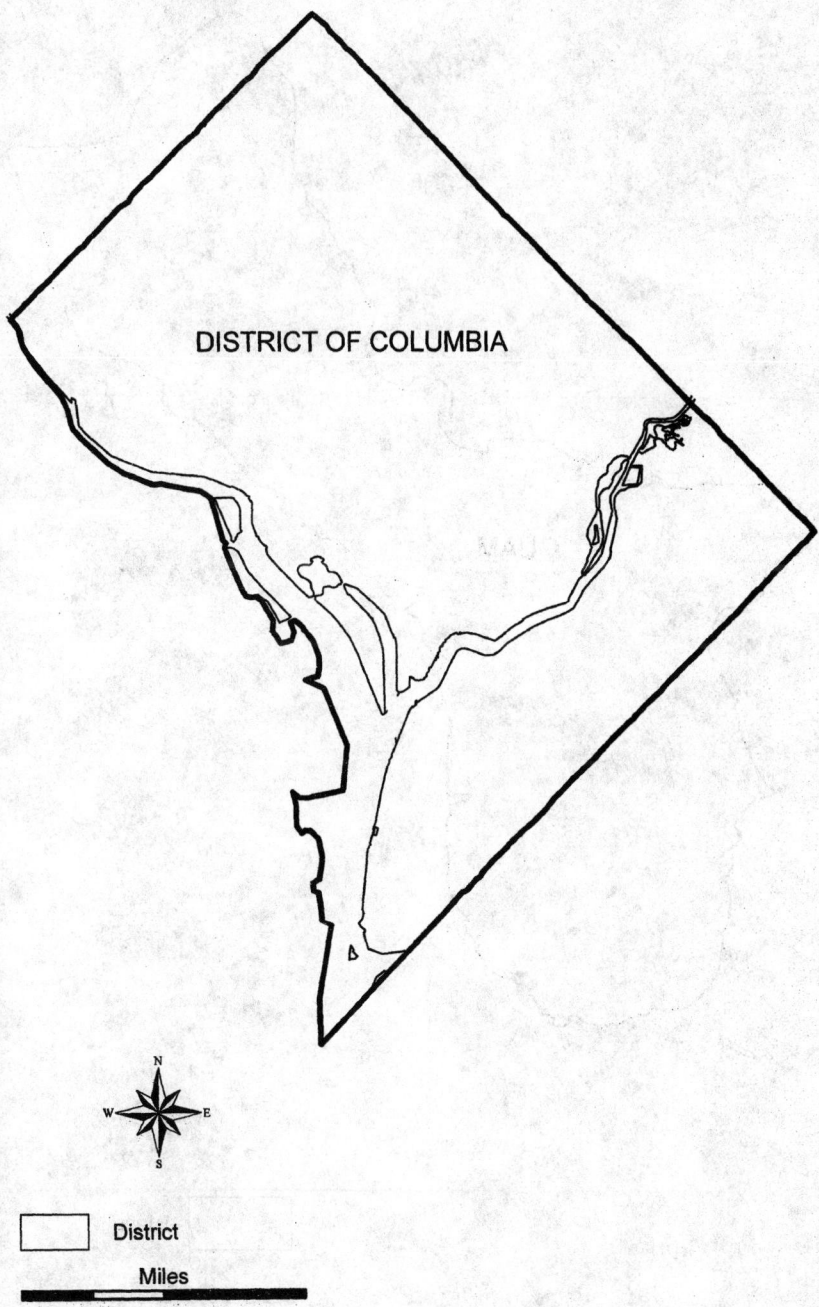

GUAM—(1 Delegate At Large)

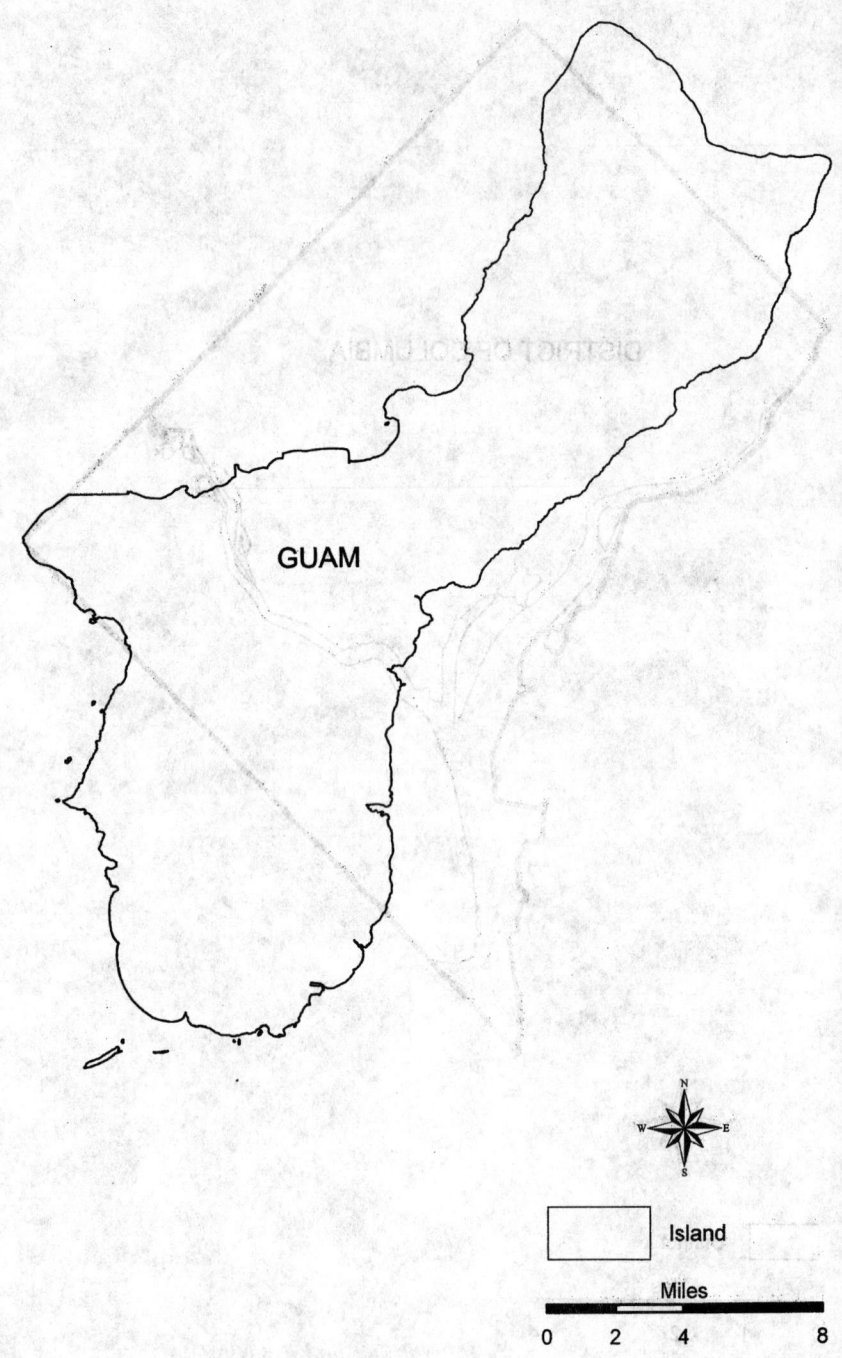

GUAM

Island

Miles

0   2   4   8

PUERTO RICO—(1 Resident Commissioner At Large)

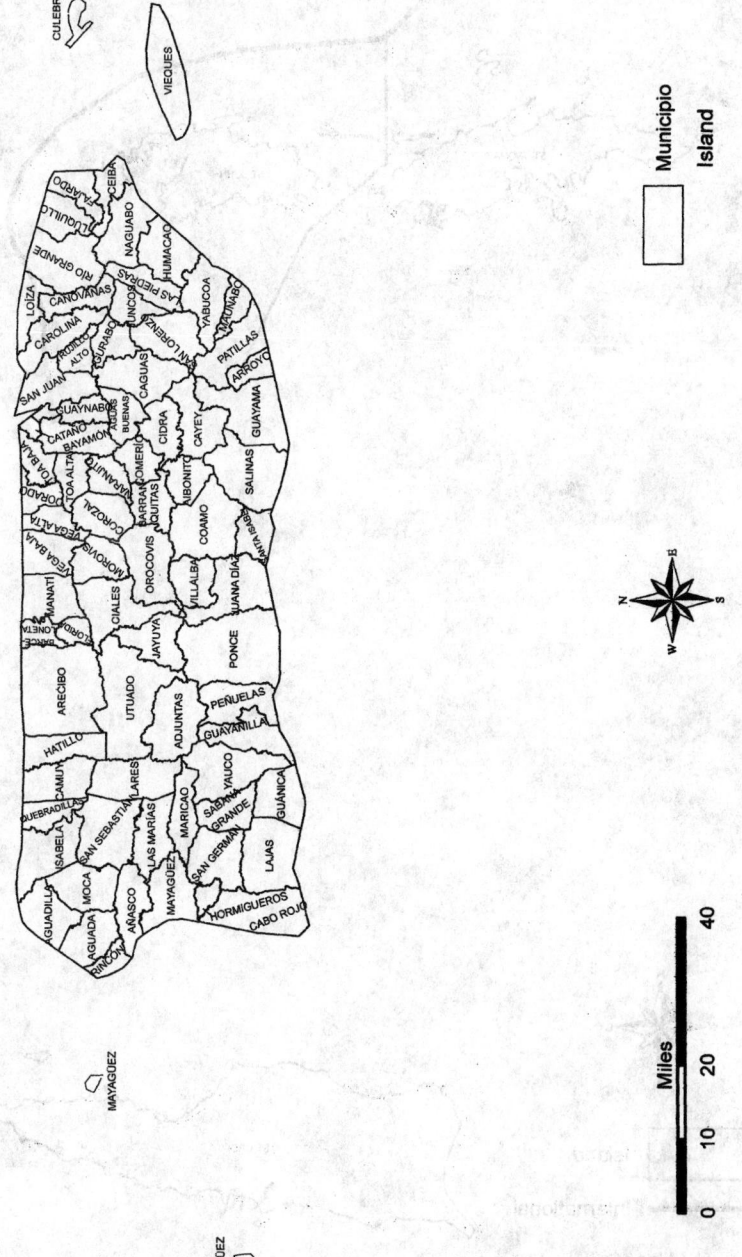

THE VIRGIN ISLANDS OF THE UNITED STATES—(1 Delegate At Large)

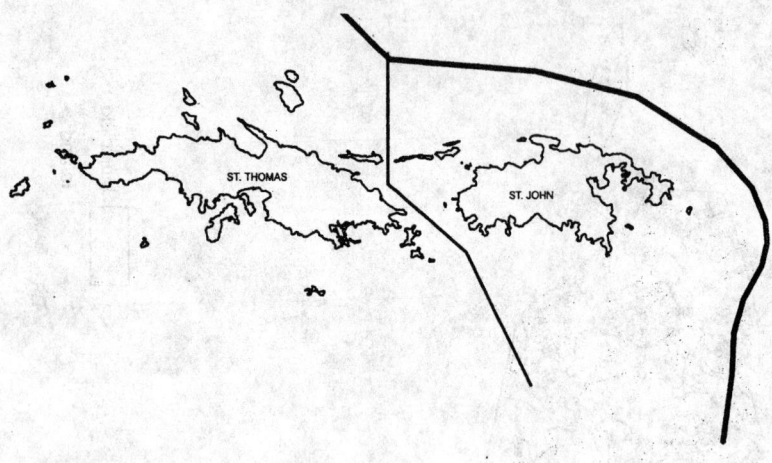

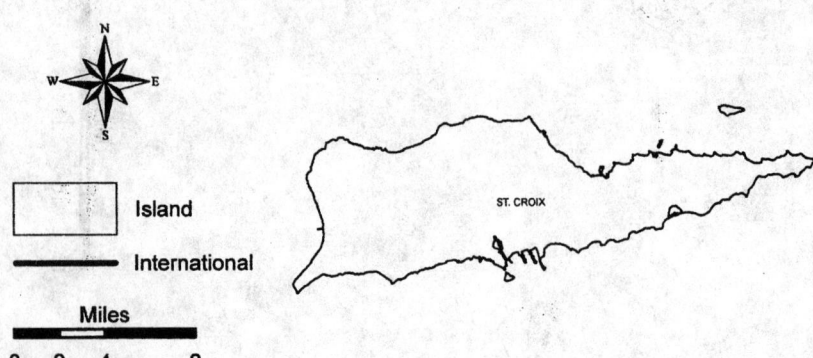

Island

——— International

Miles

0   2   4   8

NAME INDEX

Name Index

Margin Index:
To use, bend book and align index marker with black-edged page mark in text.